CALL AND RESPONSE
≈ *Key Debates in African American Studies*

HENRY LOUIS GATES, JR.
Harvard University

JENNIFER BURTON
University of California, San Diego

W. W. NORTON AND COMPANY
NEW YORK · LONDON

To Maggie Gates: May our profession give you the
pleasure and satisfaction that it has given me.

For Evelyn Brooks Higginbotham:
For being there for me, first, foremost, and always.
HLG

———————

For the Burton family and Aniruddh,
Roger, and Lilia: my past, present, and future.
JB

W. W. Norton & Company has been independent since its founding in 1923, when William Warder Norton and Mary D. Herter Norton first published lectures delivered at the People's Institute, the adult education division of New York City's Cooper Union. The Nortons soon expanded their program beyond the Institute, publishing books by celebrated academics from America and abroad. By mid-century, the two major pillars of Norton's publishing program—trade books and college texts—were firmly established. In the 1950s, the Norton family transferred control of the company to its employees, and today—with a staff of four hundred and a comparable number of trade, college, and professional titles published each year— W. W. Norton & Company stands as the largest and oldest publishing house owned wholly by its employees.

Editor: Julia Reidhead
Editor: Carly Fraser
Managing Editor, College: Marian Johnson
Project Editor: Melissa Atkin
Copyeditors: Erin Granville and Abigail Winograd
Production Manager: Eric Pier-Hocking
Design Director: Rubina Yeh
Marketer: Tamara McNeill
Book Designer: Martin Lubin Graphic Design
Photo Editor: Stephanie Romeo
Composition by Westchester Book Group
Manufacturing by QuadGraphics

Library of Congress Cataloging-in-Publication Data

Call and response : key debates in African American studies / edited by Henry Louis Gates, Jr., Jennifer Burton.—1st ed.
    p.   cm.
    Includes bibliographical references and index.

ISBN 978-0-393-97578-9 (pbk.)

    1. African Americans—History—Sources.   2. African Americans—History—Study and teaching.   3. United States—Race relations—Sources.   4. United States—Race relations—Study and teaching.   I. Gates, Henry Louis. II. Burton, Jennifer, 1964–

    E184.6.C35   2011
    973'.0496073—dc22

2010037258

W.W. Norton & Company, Inc., 500 Fifth Avenue, New York, NY 10110
www.wwnorton.com
W.W. Norton & Company, Ltd., Castle House, 75/76 Wells Street, London W1T3QT

1 2 3 4 5 6 7 8 9 0

≈ Contents

KEY DEBATE: *Migration and Emigration*

* = image

KEY DEBATE: *Strategies for Change*

KEY DEBATE: *Education*

KEY DEBATE: *Religion*

KEY DEBATE: *The Government: Civic Rights and Civic Duties*

PART TWO ~ *Reconstruction and the Nadir (1865–1909)*   173

* = image

PART THREE ~ *The Great Migration and the Harlem Renaissance*
                    (1910–1929)   249

* = image

KEY DEBATE: *Separatism versus Integration*

KEY DEBATE: *The Government: Civic Rights and Civic Duties*

* = image

KEY DEBATE: *Separatism versus Integration*

KEY DEBATE: *Education*

KEY DEBATE: *Religion*

KEY DEBATE: *The Government: Civic Rights and Civic Duties*

KEY DEBATE: *Race and Class*

* = image

* = image

PART FIVE ∼ The Civil Rights Movement and Black Feminism (1954–1979)   511

KEY DEBATE: *Separatism versus Integration*

* = image

PART SIX ～ *The Contemporary Era (1980 to the Present)*   837

* = image

KEY DEBATE: *Religion*

KEY DEBATE: *The Government: Civic Rights and Civic Duties*

* = image

KEY DEBATE: *Gender*

* = image

≈ *Thematic Contents*

KEY DEBATE ⁓ *Migration and Emigration*

* = image

* = image

KEY DEBATE ~ *Separatism versus Integration*

≈ Black-Jewish Relations

≈ The Million Man March

KEY DEBATE ≈ *Strategies for Change*

≈ Violence, Moral Suasion, and Change

≈ Protest and Accommodation

KEY DEBATE ⁓ *Education*

KEY DEBATE ⁓ *Religion*

⁓ *Christianity and Church Leaders*

⁓ *On Father Divine's Peace Mission*

⁓ *Christianity, Islam, and Black Theology*

* = image

KEY DEBATE ≈ *Race and Class*

* = image

* = image

≈ Acknowledgments

We are grateful to our colleagues and friends who contributed their insights and advice to this project. To Evelyn Brooks Higginbotham, for her partnership in constructing the debates class at Harvard. Special thanks go to Mary Anne Boelcskevy (BU), whose contributions during the initial stage of this book were invaluable. For their critiques and support, our gratitude to Richard Newman (Harvard), Joanne Kendall (Harvard), Donald Yacovone (Harvard), Kwame Spearman (Harvard), Amy Gosdanian (Harvard), Vera Grant (Harvard), Kathleen Cloutier (Harvard), William Julius Wilson (Harvard), Lawrence Bobo (Harvard), Marcyliena Morgan (Harvard), Vincent Brown (Harvard), Glenda Carpio (Harvard), Werner Sollors (Harvard), John Stauffer (Harvard), Emmanuel K. Akyeampong (Harvard), Ali S. Asani (Harvard), Robert H. Bates (Harvard), Homi K. Bhabba (Harvard), Suzanne P. Blier (Harvard), Caroline Elkins (Harvard), Maria F. Frederick (Harvard), Duana Fullwiley (Harvard), Claudine Gay (Harvard), Evelynn M. Hammonds (Harvard), Jennifer L. Hochschild (Harvard), Biodun Jeyifo (Harvard), Walter Johnson (Harvard), Michael R. Kremer (Harvard), Michèle Lamont (Harvard), Ingrid Monson (Harvard), John M. Mugane (Harvard), Jacob Olupona (Harvard), Tommie Shelby (Harvard), Kay Kaufman Shelemay (Harvard), James Sidanius (Harvard), Doris Sommer (Harvard), David R. Williams (Harvard), Pat Kimball (Harvard), Alvin F. Poussaint (Harvard), David Brion Davis (Yale), Farah Jasmine Griffin (Columbia), Donna Harden (University of Chicago), Tricia Rose (NYU), Karla FC Holloway (Duke), Kim Benston (Haveford), Nellie Y. McKay (late of UW-Madison), Michael Dawson (U. of Chicago), Molefi Kete Asante (Temple), Glenn C. Loury (Brown), Ernest J. Wilson III (USC), David W. Blight (Yale), Jeffrey B. Ferguson (Amherst), R. Baxter Miller (UGA), Melba J. Boyd (Wayne State), Alice A. Deck (UIUC), Hazel Carby (Yale), William L. Andrews (UNC-Chapel Hill), Robert A. Hill (UCLA), Arnold Rampersad (Standford), Mary F. Berry (UPenn), Robert L. Harris (Cornell), Ali A. Mazrui (SUNI-Binghamton), Charles V. Willie (Harvard), Barbara J. Fields (Columbia), Ernest Wilson III (USC, Annenberg), Bennett Singer, Walter Naegle, Karen Halil, Terri Oliver, Frances Smith Foster (Emory), Richard Hull

(TAAA), Fred Miller Robinson (USD), Ann duCille (Wesleyan), Jackie Giordano (UCSD), Christine Norris (UCSD), Michael Davidson (UCSD), Don Wayne (UCSD), Julia Fulton (UCSD) and Allan Havis (UCSD). For their help with organizing the extensive collection of manuscript pages, our thanks to Darcie Plunkett, Breanna Holm, Rose Hoffman, and Adriana Benitez.

Our gratitude for institutional support from Harvard University's Department of African and African American Studies, Department of English, and W. E. B. Du Bois Institute, the University of San Diego's English Department, and the University of California, San Diego's Department of Literature, and Thurgood Marshall College.

We are indebted to our astute and meticulous team at Norton, particularly our editors Julia Reidhead, Carly Fraser, and Erin Granville, as well as Christina Grenawalt and Brian Baker, our Managing Editor Marian Johnson, our Project Editor Melissa Atkin, our permission group, including Nancy Rodwan and Megan Jackson, Photo Editor Stephanie Romeo, Marketer Tamara McNeill, Production Manager Eric Pier-Hocking, Design Director Rubina Yeh and our copyeditor Abby Winograd.

We are grateful to the friends and family who read drafts, discussed ideas, and provided encouragement throughout: Roger Burton, Gabrielle Burton, Maria Burton, Ursula Burton, Darin Henry, Gabrielle C. Burton, Graeme Boone, Charity Burton, Steve Duron, Jean Kluver, Larry Rosenstock, Rebekah Sager, Jamie Sheldon-Villalobos, and Marsanne Brammer. Aniruddh Patel's intellectual engagement, skillful editing, and steady support were vital to both process and project. And finally, to the next generation—Roger, Lilia, Dashiell, Athena, Annabella, Philip, and James—who remind us how quickly change, however dramatic, can become the norm.

⁓ Forty Million Ways to Be Black

"It seems to me," said Booker T.,
That all you folks have missed the boat
Who shout about the right to vote,
And spend vain days and sleepless nights
In uproar over civil rights.
Just keep your mouths shut, do not grouse,
But work, and save, and buy a house."

"I don't agree," said W. E. B.
"For what can property avail
If dignity and justice fail?
Unless you help to make the laws,
They'll steal your house with trumped-up clause.
A rope's as tight, a fire as hot,
No matter how much cash you've got.
Speak soft, and try your little plan,
But as for me, I'll be a man."

"It seems to me," said Booker T. —
"I don't agree," said W. E. B.

—"Booker T. and W. E. B.," by Dudley Randall

"It's very important to understand the other side of the argument. If you are a litigator, a critical skill is trying to anticipate and dissect the best argument your opponent is going to make, so you drill down and understand his [or her] argument as well as your own. That gives you a certain humility, because it forces you to face the weaknesses in your own position and to appreciate that any difficult problem has, by definition, good arguments on both sides."

—Christopher Edley Jr., Dean of Berkeley Law

This book is a chronicle of an extended chapter in the history of ideas, a record of the most salient debates over what it means to be black in America. It is also an experiment in pedagogy, a blueprint for a fresh, catholic, embracing, cosmopolitan approach to the teaching of African American Studies—an approach that enables a plethora of voices and viewpoints, methodologies and ideologies, disciplines and fields, to be introduced to the classroom in the most open manner possible, without bias or judgment in favor of one position or another. Left, right, and center; separatist and nationalist; nativist and emigrationist; gay and straight; capitalist and socialist; feminist and chauvinist: representatives of all of these positions have weighed in on debates about the Black Experience, and their positions and opinions are found here.

The fundamental premise upon which this book rests is that African American culture has long been characterized by diversity, that the African American people are multiple in their roots and multiple in their branches, and that this multiplicity has been evident in virtually every aspect of their culture and in the social institutions they have constructed since arriving in this country in the seventeenth century. And they have amply given voice to this range of viewpoints and ideologies, whether about matters in the secular realm or the sacred; in slavery or freedom; in politics, religion, culture, or the arts; in matters concerning class, gender, race; and just about anything else. Indeed, one could fairly say that one of the hallmarks of the black tradition is the passionately expressive way in which African Americans have defined unity through division, and used divisions of opinion and approach to forge and maintain a sense of solidarity as a people, even when their powerlessness to effect their destiny made the notion of a "community" far more virtual than actual.

One thing is for sure, however: either because of affinity or adversity or a bit of both, the descendants of the African slaves in this country very early on found the idea of being members of a group a sometimes troubling, sometimes comforting concept. But, ultimately, they found it a most efficacious concept, even if they seemed to take an enormous amount of pleasure expending a great deal of energy arguing with each other about the nature and destiny of that group. And the record of these engaged exchanges is as old as the Republic itself.

In his 1817 letter to Paul Cuffe, the black colonizationist and extraordinarily successful sea captain (and the first black man to meet with a president at the White House), the black abolitionist James Forten, himself a wealthy sail maker, made one of the first attempts to define what, if anything, bound the descendants of African slaves in the United States together as a people, whether slave or free, whether born here or back in Africa: "they [the still enslaved] are our brothers [Forten and Cuffe were free] by the ties of consanguinity, of suffering, and of wrongs. . . ." Four decades later, Forten's deeply felt but rather vague idea of consanguinity, suffering, and wrongs had evolved into the notion that black people occupied something akin to an invisible nationhood, that they were millions of people joined together not only by color and condition and a shared history of suffering and wrongs, but by a shared consciousness not only about those wrongs, but about all sorts of things, like life and love, meaning and belief, culture and society; a people within a people, as it were. Martin R. Delany boldly noted as early as 1854 that black people living in the United States were not merely an assortment of victims of an economic order of racialized slavery. Delany was referring, of course, to his black countrymen in the middle of the nineteenth century, who would number 4.4 million on the eve of the Civil War, the descendants of the original 450,000 Africans randomly and brutally gathered from about fifty ethnic groups and shipped from the west and central coasts of Africa to the United States largely between 1619 and 1820, by which time 99% had arrived. Rather, Delany asserted, these people, whose antecedents were the victims of a brutally harsh and enforced immigration, constituted a "community" of shared interests, concerns, vulnerabilities, and structures of feeling within the United States. While these people had descended from admittedly various inhabitants of sub-Saharan Africa, they now spoke a common vernacular version of American English, and shared a common culture—especially forms of music and dance and religious practices—that was at once American and "black."

Accordingly, Delany argued, these Africans living in America were now a "nation," a subnation of their own, "a nation within a nation," as he so aptly put it: "We are a nation within a nation—as the Poles in Russia, the Hungarians in Austria, the Welsh, Irish, and Scotch in the British dominions." Even then, Delany—sometimes called "the father of black nationalism" and a staunch abolitionist and "Pan-Africanist" who visited and wrote about sub-Saharan Africa—understood the definition of a "nation" to include "a body of people who share a real or imagined common history, culture, language, or ethnic origin," which is a standard dictionary definition today. If we reflect upon Benedict Anderson's highly influential definition of an "imagined community" as a construct "whose members . . . will never know most of their fellow members, meet them or even hear of them, yet in the minds of each lives the image of their communion," then we can begin to understand the remarkable feat of shared and willed imagination that lay behind Delany's claim.

Over the two hundred and thirty years between the first slave ship's landing in 1619 and the date of Delany's writing, the horrific institution of American slavery became the crucible in which African slaves speaking disparate languages and embracing distinct belief systems forged in this country a shared identity, "a historically constituted, stable community of people, formed on the basis of a common language, territory, economic life, and psychological make-up manifested in a common culture," as Joseph Stalin, of all people, put it in 1913. But while most definitions of nationhood or peoplehood stress commonality, very few focus upon the shared ways in which people within a common culture disagree, the patterns of argument and debate over key questions affecting their fate that unite them in a shared discourse, even sometimes in heated, vitriolic terms. Patterns of disagreement, like patterns of commonality, are cultural; they can express shared culture through a shared discourse just as directly and tellingly as patterns of agreement can. While this may seem obvious outside of the classroom, it is sometimes quite shocking to students and even to some scholars how deeply contentious and argumentative the African American intellectual tradition has been, from its birth in the late eighteenth century to the present. (While Africans began arriving as slaves on this continent in 1619, it took a long time, understandably, for intellectual expression to find a way into print. It wasn't until 1761 that a slave published a poem, and not until a decade later when they began to publish books.)

I have for a long time been fascinated by the contours of this sometimes fractious, always lively, self-referential intellectual tradition. It is not a phenomenon limited to black writers in America, but one that lays at the heart of what the sociologist Paul Gilroy has aptly named the "Black Atlantic" tradition, which traces the curious fascination that writers of African descent on both sides of the Atlantic in England and the United States manifested for each other's writings, even to the point of rewriting or signifying upon key tropes found in each other's works. This curious practice, which began in the eighteenth century signals the start of the Anglo-African intellectual tradition. The furious and creative rewritings of what I call the trope of the talking book paradoxically connect five of the first slave narratives published between 1770 and 1811 (by James Gronniosaw, John Marrant, Ottobah Cugoano, Olaudah Equiano, and John Jea) and echo and resonate in the works of Jupiter Hammon, Phillis Wheatley, and Ignatius Sancho.

Even as late as 1845, when Frederick Douglass was reinventing the genre of the slave narrative in Boston, he turned to Equiano's slave narrative of 1789, published in London, to ground his own text. Nineteenth-century writers such as Alexander Crummel and Edward Wilmot Blyden, among others, worked both sides of the Atlantic, writing about the Black Experience in the United States and in Africa. And the relation between the Harlem Renaissance of the 1920s and the birth of the Negritude Movement in Paris in 1935 (including translations of works from one movement to the other by the Renaissance poet par excellence, Langston Hughes) has been well-documented. But the idea of a shared "culture" or "tradition" based on the race of the authors and shared, self-reflexive content in their work—of a Negro or Pan-African intellectual tradition, in which "nation" could be defined broadly through "race," and "race" could be the basis of transnational tradition or discourse—would become one of the most contentious debates among African American writers in the twentieth century, one of many given voice in this volume.

Ideas about traditions in African American arts, discourse, and history are further complicated by the rich contributions of non-African Americans. While this anthology focuses on debates that have African Americans on different sides of each issue (with the notable exception of the opening debate on "the nature of the Negro" that established the cultural framework for subsequent debates), it also reflects the participation in these debates of artists and writers from diverse backgrounds—from Harriet Beecher Stowe to Melville Herskovits. The authors and subjects represented here also embrace issues related to Africa, Europe, the Caribbean, and Latin America, while maintaining a primary focus on questions debated among African Americans. The multiplicity of voices and viewpoints in these debates reveals the complexity of our history, moving us beyond pro-con dichotomies, including the oversimplified idea of African American history as the story of cohesive racial groups in conflict with each other.

In 1998, I decided to edit this book to provide a model for a new approach to teaching an introduction to an African American Studies course. I approached Julia Reidhead, my editor at W. W. Norton, which had just published *The Norton Anthology of African American Literature*. Julia embraced this idea most enthusiastically, as did my Harvard colleague, Jennifer Burton, who agreed to edit this volume with me. A decade of research later, after consulting with dozens of scholars, collecting essays, and then, with enormous agony, eliminating many selections because of limitations of space, we publish our first edition here. While there are many valid approaches to a course that is a staple of African American Studies curricula, including thematic, sociological, historical, political, economic, and cultural schema, it seemed to me then that a productive if unusual approach would be to enable students to cover the whole of the African American Experience through documents—essays, speeches, petitions, editorials, newspaper and journal articles, manifestos, political cartoons, plays, advertisements, and photographs—representing a range of thought about a particular problem or event from 1750 to the present. In this way, the key debates in the tradition could serve as the structuring principle of the course. I decided to experiment with this idea at Harvard by actually introducing it to the classroom.

Five years ago, I approached my friend and colleague, Evelyn Brooks Higginbotham, now the chair of the department, and floated my idea. Not only did she find the idea intriguing, but, with a bit of coaxing and some skepticism, agreed to teach it with me. We made lists of critical debates in the tradition, restricted the number to match the number of classes in a semester, and divided the readings between us. Each year we refine the list, adding new debates as they evolve, whether the subject is some new development in hip-hop, a debate over a film such as *Good Hair*, or the election of the nation's first black president. The course has turned out to be very popular with Harvard undergraduates, and I believe I know one reason for our students' quite positive reception to the approach. I think it affords our students a large measure of relief to learn that there is not, nor ever has been, one way to think about a social or political issue affecting the black community. I think it is a profound relief for students—particularly African American students—to learn that there is not, nor ever has been, one way to be black, and that individuality is a value that the tradition itself has valorized and protected, at least since the middle of the eighteenth century.

To the contrary, a signal aspect of being black in America has been the insistence upon a stubborn intellectual integrity and rigorous independence of thought. Somewhere within the great debates of the black tradition, our students can find their own beliefs reflected, without fear of being labeled one of the bywords for "not black enough" or some sort of ideological traitor to the race. Decent, honest, thoughtful people, even—or especially—in the same culture, can honorably disagree. That is the lesson of our class at Harvard; that is the lesson of this book; and it is a lesson we would do well to broadcast widely.

The idea that forty million people could ever speak with one voice or think with one mind is frankly ridiculous, an exercise in ahistorical thinking, or romantic black nationalism, or wishful thinking at best and ideological censorship at worst. Similarly, the idea that African Americans or any people could ever have been unanimous in their beliefs or ideas or political approaches is equally ridiculous. I tell our students that if there are forty million African Americans, then there are forty million ways to be black. And the debates represented in this book dramatize my belief in the inherent diversity of opinion historically among African Americans in the most vivid and lively fashion imaginable. From the panoply of voices here, indeed it would seem that black people have been disagreeing with each other almost since the day the slaves emerged from the hauls of the ships of the Middle Passage, trying to figure out how best to negotiate this New World system if, indeed, they could not return home.

In other words, there never was a time in the whole sweep of black history when black people didn't disagree passionately with each other about the most basic aspects of their experience in this country, whether we are talking about how to end slavery, which political party represents our people's interests more effectively, whether black people should return to Africa or remain here and fight the good fight for civil rights, whether hip-hop is a positive or negative force within contemporary black culture, whether the church remains an important and vital cultural force, and whether or not Barack Obama has the best interests of the black community at heart in his presidential policies. If there is a subject that can be debated, black people have debated, and will debate, that subject, and they will do so vehemently. Just go to a black barbershop or beauty parlor, and listen.

The African American community is comprised of a multiplicity of intellectual and ideological complexions, and has been since slavery. Why should African Americans be different from other people? After all, there are more African Americans living in the United States than there are people living in Algeria, Canada, Uganda, Morocco, Peru, Iraq, Saudi Arabia, Nepal, or Afghanistan, among many other countries. And no one would ever attempt to argue for some putative unanimity of national opinion among Canadians or Moroccans! Why should African Americans be any different? Well, it turns out that African Americans are just like everyone else on the planet, especially in terms of our people's intellectual diversity, a grand and noble tradition within the Black American Experience.

When black studies began as an academic discipline in the late sixties, a debate-centered approach to courses was quite common; however, through the pressures of camps within the field and the larger culture, the various shades of thinking and feeling of black writers were subsumed, by and large, under two large rubrics, that of "Separation" versus that of "Integration" or "Accommodation," in terms similar to Dudley Randall's humorous and telling poem that I use as an epigraph to this essay. In those ideologically fraught intra-cultural wars within the black community during the era of Black Power and the Black Arts Movement, "integration" was generally bad, while "separation" was generally a good thing. But those two extremely broad categories elided much of the nuance in arguments classified within either one or the other.

My own education in the range of debates began in courses on the Harlem Renaissance that I took as an undergraduate at Yale between 1969 and 1973, where I encountered the deep and subtle arguments among black thinkers such as W. E. B. Du Bois and Booker T. Washington (Du Bois's political positions evolved so much over the course of a very long life that one could pit Du Bois's opinions at any given point in his career against his own positions articulated later in his career!), Du Bois and Marcus Garvey, Langston Hughes and George Schuyler, or Zora Neale Hurston and Richard Wright. At the same time, I was party to the ideological wars of words my generation was witnessing first-hand in the debates between Martin Luther King Jr. and Malcolm X, or the Black Panthers and cultural nationalists such as Maulana Karenga and Amiri Baraka. All of these debates, it turned out, had a long and deep history in the tradition, originating in the late eighteenth and early nineteenth centuries. Even the debate over what we should call ourselves—whether "Africans" or "Negroes" or "Blacks" or "Afro-Americans"—I would later learn, had raged just as vigorously in the 1830s and 1840s, and, quite frankly, in every era since! In my own career, essays that I have written have generated considerable debate, from pieces on rap music (particularly the censorship of 2 Live Crew), anti-Semitism within the black community, and the role of Africans selling other Africans in the Trans-Atlantic Slave Trade. And this is as it should be. Debate is a sign of health and life in any intellectual tradition. In our selections, we have tried to include as wide an array of positions and arguments as space would allow, without concern for reflecting our own deeply held opinions about these matters. That, too, is how it should be. For even a cursory familiarity with the black tradition reveals that diversity and multiplicity and the passion for debate are cardinal values of the tradition, virtues we as teachers and scholars should encourage among our students, just as our professors did when we were students. After all, isn't this what education is about, rather than the vain attempt to suppress dissent or encourage monolithic thinking or enlist members in a political party? One thing for sure: what is "radical" today, all too readily is seen as "conservative" in another era, even within the discourse of an individual thinker. And that, too, is a necessary part of intellectual health and growth.

These principles of pluralism, of a certain intellectual cosmopolitanism first voiced by the philosopher Alain Locke and most recently by Kwame Anthony Appiah, are at the heart our approach to introducing students to African American Studies through the selections included in this book. And I hope that it proves to be as useful a tool of pedagogy in the classroom as it has been for us at Harvard.

Henry Louis Gates, Jr.
Cambridge, Massachusetts
September 16, 2010

≈ *Thematic Introduction: The Politics of Difference*

A century and a half after the first Africans arrived in the English colony of Jamestown, African Americans began to participate publicly, in print and in speeches, in the debate about their own enslavement. After Briton Hammon published his slave narrative in 1760, Africans in the United States employed a variety of forums—letters, pamphlets, sermons, letters to the editors of newspapers, petitions, court documents, and especially autobiographies—to express opinions about issues affecting their status as would-be equal citizens in the new republic. Their quest to be heard, to participate in debates about their liberation, was pursued against great obstacles: participation in public discussion had long been governed by privilege of access—whether due to literacy, education, wealth, race, gender, and especially the willingness of a printer or publisher to make opinions public. In the eighteenth century, even the most accomplished black writers, such as Phillis Wheatley or Benjamin Banneker in the United States, or Ignatius Sancho or Olaudah Equiano in England, were to a great extent at the mercy of sympathetic religious or political allies to vouch for their "authenticity" (the fact that they had, indeed, written their own words published under their name) and for patronage that enabled those words to appear in print.

Because early black writers and activists recognized that unfettered access to public discourse was key to participation, they soon joined together to create their own newspapers and magazines, starting in 1827, and at about the same time, launched their own convention movements that led to annual publications of the thoughts voiced by their members. Black and abolitionist newspapers, perhaps more than any other media, democratized access for African Americans to the public discourse of slavery and race in America, and simultaneously encouraged the airing of contrary opinions within the race, in particular leveling gender barriers so that the voices of remarkable individuals such as Maria Stewart, Harriet Tubman, and Sojourner Truth joined the public conversation. Anyone with access to a pen could aspire to have her or his opinions published in a newspaper, and numerous African Americans did.

Two and a half centuries after Benjamin Banneker's groundbreaking letters, anyone with access to a wired device can participate in public debate. This astonishing democratization of debate, for better and for worse, has reduced the role of traditional gate-keepers, such as newspaper editors and publishers. And this openness of access has weakened the influence of traditional privileged elites, demystifying the publication process and opening public discourse to a multiplicity of voices unimaginable to any previous generation. But with the proliferation of voices on the Internet, the coverage of current events in traditional print, television, and radio media (whether driven by ratings or politics or an attempt to appear neutral) is frequently presented as a duel, pitting one commentator against another. This "pro-con" format tends to reduce complex arguments to sound bites, and to obscure the fact that there are often many more than two opinions about a particular topic. In this anthology, we have resisted the simplifications of pro-con debate by presenting multiple positions that show the complexity of thinking about an issue. Multiple views help readers become alert to false debates, in which an opinion held only by a few is given equal weight with a widely held view, a tactic favored by television news. Indeed, since President Barack Obama's election, demonstrating that one's opinions are shared by at least one African American has become such a common strategy of pundits and politicians that Stephen Colbert made the practice a word of the day: "blackwashing."

While open public debate exposes manufactured controversies for what they are, the democratization of debate has its dangers. Though traditional media gatekeepers have historically limited diversity of opinion, they have also helped to filter information for accuracy and reliability, and to promote informed opinions. The proliferation of voices on the Web threatens to overwhelm us with information, some of which is inaccurate, drawing upon "data" based on shoddy research or no research at all. And the tendency to narrow our conversations to include only those who already share our opinions—debating with the choir, as it were—not only limits our own intellectual development and understanding, it fosters the polarization of society at large. The detrimental effect of the widening gulf between different people with radically different, but equally entrenched, opinions is evident in the lack of respect and real exchange in public discourse—with town halls sometimes reduced to shouting matches and opponents demonized as enemies of the people.

The debates in this anthology offer a lens on how different voices and viewpoints have shaped public opinion in African American history. It is our hope that this book will help students understand that many of the questions they are grappling with today—ranging from what is the best type of education to what names African Americans should call themselves—have been asked and considered by our progenitors before, with grace and rigor and the same passion with which we contemplate these issues today. To encounter the voices of ancestors ruminating and fulminating on issues that we naively think that we are creating or confronting for the first time can be an exhilarating and surprising experience, and also a profoundly humbling one.

The Themes

As we made the selections for this anthology, we have tried to include statements that represent multiple perspectives on most of the important questions about which African Americans have felt compelled to debate with each other. We have drawn on diverse forums to expand the range of voices in key debates, by setting letters, petitions, manifestos, cartoons, advertisements, and photographs alongside speeches, editorials, auto-biographical excerpts, and essays. After collecting thousands of potential texts and consulting with other scholars, we decided to focus on controversies with the greatest historical significance (such as separatism versus integration), and on those that repeat over time (such as debates over the best terms of self-identification). Focusing on debates with African Americans on different sides of a question (while not excluding contributions by non-African Americans) provides a more textured picture of African American history, broadening it beyond the simple binary paradigm of conflict between black people and white people, and deconstructing the notion that, somehow, some golden age of unanimity once existed in the misty African American past to which the present generation should ideally aspire to return. Black people have almost never voiced unanimity on any topic, and have been arguing with each other, it would seem, since the first twenty "negars" landed in Jamestown in 1619, and probably almost a century before that, when the black conquistador, Juan Garrido, arrived in Florida along with Ponce de Leon in 1513.

In organizing this anthology for convenient use in courses in African American Studies, we have tried to be mindful of the benefits of both chronological and thematic approaches to teaching. The primary table of contents is organized chronologically, with the debates clustered into six historical periods, each with a period introduction. Using a historical approach allows students to understand the contexts of these debates, it seemed to us, more readily than does a thematic organization. It also reveals how African American intellectual history has unfolded over time.

But we also provide a second, alternative, table of contents, for those teachers who prefer a thematic approach to African American intellectual history. This approach invites readers to trace a single theme or concern through different historical periods, to ascertain how a specific question is posed and how different generations have answered it. A thematic approach can show how answers to recurring questions change over time. This approach reveals the deep history of many issues that are still debated in our society today, a phenomenon that the poet Amiri Baraka has aptly termed "the changing same."

Call and Response explores eleven broad themes that have driven key debates in African American history: nature, culture, and slavery; migration and emigration; separatism versus integration; strategies for change; education; religion; the government: civic rights and civic duties; race and class; the politics of art; society and individual choice; and gender. These thematic groupings are designed as a starting point for discussion, not as strict conceptual boundaries, because many of the texts simultaneously engage in multiple debates. For example, pieces on the Million Man March touch on religion, black national-ism, homosexuality, and gender, in addition to questions of political strategy.

For pedagogical convenience, we have identified one central theme in each text, even if the selection could have fallen into two or more categories. For instance, placing Claudia Jones's "An End to the Neglect of the Problems of the Negro Woman!" (1949) alongside other discussions of communism deepens that debate. It also avoids the pitfall of relegating all feminist perspectives to "Gender," which would obscure how women's voices have contributed to many debates. What follows is a short introduction to each of the key themes, with a focus on questions addressed and on how these themes have evolved through the different periods of African American history.

Nature, Culture, and Slavery

While many key debates in the African American tradition began in the time of slavery, the texts in this section explore two areas of debate specifically about the enslavement of Africans in the New World. First are the pre-emancipation discussions about the "nature of the Negro," arguments about whether Europeans and Africans are equally or simi-larly human, if indeed they are both "human" at all. Second are the academic debates that emerged in the twentieth century about the nature of the slave experience, on top-ics such as the effect of the trauma of the Middle Passage and the horrors of the slave experience on the retention of African belief systems and cultural practices among the newly forming African American people.

Debate about the "nature of the Negro" laid the foundation for both the justification of slavery in the eighteenth century and its abolition in the nineteenth. In the mid-1700s, the rise of the Enlightenment theories of "the rights of man," the burgeoning science of anthropology, and the growth of the anti-slavery movement in England and the United States fueled interest in the idea of race and in the question of whether people of Afri-can descent were naturally inferior or equal to those of other "races." The idea of the "Negro race" as uniquely distinct and inferior, developed by European philosophers such as David Hume and Immanuel Kant, were drawn upon to justify the African slave trade. During the same period, other philosophers such as James Beattie and Johann Gottfried von Herder advocated the equality of the human species, and these arguments were drawn upon to fuel resistance to the slave trade and to slavery in general. In the newly forming United States, Enlightenment ideas about the innate inferiority of differ-ent races existed uneasily beside the democratic principle that "all men are created equal," a conflict exemplified by the life and work of Thomas Jefferson.

Enslaved and free blacks in early America challenged imported ideas about the innate inferiority of black people, but they had few opportunities to participate in direct, public debates on the topic. Until publication of the New York *Freedom's Journal*—the first African American newspaper, founded in 1827,—black involvement in the debate about the "nature of the Negro" was mainly expressed through petitions, letters, or indi-vidual artistic and scientific accomplishments, such as Phillis Wheatley's poetry or Ben-jamin Banneker's annual almanacs, published in the 1790s, which anti-slavery advocates used to challenge ideas about innate racial limitations. African Americans used slave narratives to great effect to enter into the public discourse over racial difference and the evils of slavery, although the publication and distribution of these writings were still largely dependent on support from white patrons. In 1829, David Walker's *Appeal* heralded a dramatic shift not only in the debate about the "nature of the Negro," but also in the history of African American debate itself. By addressing and widely distributing his *Appeal* to black people, Walker moved outside traditional restrictive roles of black-white discourse, and spurred the development of direct, public debates among African Americans and others who supported emancipation.

But definitions of who was whom among the human species and the difference that those ostensible physical distinctions in nature made to a people's political and social status continued to haunt the discourse of race and rights into the nineteenth century, and well beyond. By the middle of the century, a group of prominent white scientists and scholars (collectively known as the "American School of Ethnology") dedicated themselves to quantifying and qualifying so-called "racial" differences. Some of these people consciously sought to rank and classify non-white peoples into permanent inferiority vis-à-vis Europeans under the aura and mystification of "science." Some even posited a theory of "polygenesis," the idea that human beings had diverse or separate origins, and hence were of different and distinct species, not directly descended from a common progenitor. This idea represented a radical departure from the commonly accepted theory of "monogenesis" (the unity of human origins), which was ostensibly supported by the Judeo-Christian conviction that all humans evolved from Adam and Eve (and later by Charles Darwin's theory of evolution).

In the years leading up to the Civil War, polygenesist beliefs were called upon to justify the continuation and expansion of slavery and the restriction of the rights of African Americans, including the 1857 Dred Scott Supreme Court decision, which stated that African Americans could not be citizens of the United States; as Chief Justice Roger B. Taney put it, "Negroes" were "beings of an inferior order, and altogether unfit to associate with the white race . . . and so far inferior that they had no rights which the white man was bound to respect." As outrageous as such statements strike us today, ideas about the genetic construction of "race," of supposedly race-based characteristics, and innate, biological differences between races have continued to shape debates about the rights and lives of African Americans from the post-emancipation era to the present day, which some have called a "new age of biology." The debate over the genetic component of intelligence has, frankly, never abated, and will be renewed as full genome sequencing becomes more common.

With the growth of the study of African American history in the latter part of the twentieth century, debates over slavery took on a new dimension, based on competing historiographical interpretations of the past. Efforts to understand slavery more fully have been complicated by the unevenness of the historical record and by the questionable reliability of sources. Many of the people who directly experienced slavery could not or did not document their lives in writing, since slaves did not have the benefits of freedom of speech or ready access to literacy. (It is estimated that only about 5 percent of the 3.9 million slaves in 1860 could read.) This fragmented historical record has fueled dramatic disagreement over the nature of slavery and over its effects on African American psychology, culture, and social institutions.

One recurring academic debate concerns whether African cultures played a significant role in shaping African American culture. This issue, which continues to be discussed today, is known as the Herskovits/Frazier debate, because the anthropologist Melville J. Herskovits and the sociologist E. Franklin Frazier established the key terms of the debate and marked out two poles of thinking on what Herskovits defined as "Africanisms," the retention of cultural practices, belief systems, or ways of being that the slaves carried with them through the Middle Passage. On one end of the spectrum are those who, like Herskovits, argue that African cultures have had a demonstrable, palpable influence on African Americans, especially in music, the dance, the arts, and religion. On the other end are those who, like Frazier, contend that the dreaded Middle Passage and the horrors of slavery effectively erased the African cultural heritage, creating a new being something akin to a human tabula rasa. Over half a century after staking out their positions, Frazier and Herskovits continue to be touchstones for contemporary disputes about the same set of questions concerning the relation between persons of African descent in the New World and persons of African descent on the African continent.

Migration and Emigration

African American history has its roots in the involuntary forced migration of approximately 450,000 slaves. The first slaves in the New World arrived in the Spanish colony of Santo Domingo in 1502, and slavery began in what is now the United States in 1526, when Spaniards brought African slaves to the colony of San Miguel de Guandape, on the coast of what is now South Carolina or Georgia. (The tradition of voluntary migration to what is now the United States dates back to 1513, when the Spanish conquistador Juan Garrido, born in West Africa, landed in Florida.) The first twenty slaves famously arrived in the English colonies, specifically in Virginia, in 1619, and African slaves would continue to arrive into the nineteenth century. Though the slave trade ended officially in 1808, a few slaves continued to arrive in this country after that; but by 1820, 99 percent of our African ancestors had arrived here. That first extended, forced migration laid the foundation for the later waves of migrations (movements within the country) and emigrations or colonization (movements of black people from the United States to other countries, such as Liberia and Haiti) that punctuate African American history.

The experiences of descendents of slaves stand in marked contrast to the experiences of other immigrant groups in America. Other immigrants typically chose to leave their native lands in favor of the religious or economic opportunities offered by the United States, and often they maintained strong ties to the culture and people of their homeland. For African Americans, the involuntary break from their African cultural roots complicated their relationships both with America and with Africa. While the impact of slavery and discrimination discouraged full assimilation, the forced immersion in various versions of American culture and the loss of direct ties with native African cultures provided numerous challenges to identifying Africa as "home." (The recent migration of Africans to the United States provides an interesting counterpoint: between 1990 and 2000, more Africans willingly migrated here than came in the entire history of the slave trade.)

Throughout American history, African Americans have often chosen to migrate or emigrate as part of larger, collective movements, so community debate over these matters has played a large role in the process. As for most immigrants, these large migrations follow periods of political or economic challenges in one region and opportunities in another. A positive change somewhere acts as a pull factor toward a more promising life, while a negative change is a push factor prompting an exodus. For example, the push factors of racism and lack of economic opportunities stimulated movement out of the rural South to urban centers in the South and North in the early part of the twentieth century. Then, the demand for labor in the North and the decrease in foreign immigration—both results of World War I—combined to make northern cities such as Chicago, Detroit, and Baltimore magnetic destinations for African Americans from the South, leading to a dramatic transformation of the regional and cultural identity of African Americans. (By 1930, just under half of all black people lived in urban areas; in 1910, only about a quarter did. And whereas only 794,916 black people lived in the North in 1910, by 1930 that number had changed to 2,409,219.) A more abstract "pull" factor in other migration and emigration movements is the lure of the possibility of becoming a part of a black majority. The recurring arguments for going "back to Africa," arguments for settling in black-majority countries such as Haiti, and arguments for black settlements within America, such as the "Black Belt Republic" plan of the 1930s, all show the "pull" of black nationalism.

Yet the active debates over emigration and migration included in this book underscore the fact that these various migration and emigration movements were much more than a series of seemingly irresistible push/pull factors acting on a relatively passive population. As historian Joe William Trotter, Jr. has argued, "[Migrants] were not merely reflectors of larger forces, . . . but were shapers of such forces as well." These imagined or hypothetical migrations and actual migrations were grassroots social movements, part of a continuing conversation about self-transformation and the meaning of home.

Separatism versus Integration

The tension between black separatism (the belief that black people should form their own separate communities) and integration (the belief that they should incorporate into the larger American community) began decades before most black people in America could imagine gaining their freedom. In 1829, David Walker—whom historian Sterling Stuckey considers to be "the father of black nationalist theory in America"—summoned "the Coloured Citizens of the World" to accept and rally around a new racially based unity. Since Walker published his stirring manifesto, other African American leaders have also taken anti-black racialism in the United States and transformed it into a nationalist philosophy of community based on color, culture or "race," and used it as a unifying force for collective action. As a counterpoint, other leaders have developed the position that adopting a separate national identity—rather than a primary identity as Americans—undercuts the demand of African Americans for full and equal rights as citizens under the Constitution of the United States and amounts to capitulating to racism. Like debates over colonization—over whether to stay or whether to leave—these debates have been quite contentious ones.

Variations of this pre-emancipation debate recur throughout African American history, primarily in times of mounting discrimination. Running through the particular controversies are three main areas of concern: personal and group identity (seen, for instance, in the debates on naming and Pan-Africanism), the benefits and drawbacks of separate cultural and economic institutions (seen in the debates over black newspapers, black social, educational, and cultural institutions, and voluntary or self-segregation), and the choice of political allies (seen in the debates over black/Jewish relations and coalition politics).

The longest running of these debates is the "Namestakes" (a term coined by historian and writer Dorothy Sterling), and this debate concerns by what proper names should black people in America be called; what are the respective costs and benefits of a given name for the group? This debate was already quite heated by the 1830s, much to the surprise of those of us debating it in the sixties, who thought that our own contentious arguments about whether we were "Negroes" or "Black" or "Afro-American" were novel moments in the history of our people. Names carry with them ethnic, cultural, and/or national markers. Choosing any term specifically for Americans of African descent (i.e., black, African American) is an act of linguistic self-definition. The counterpart is the choice of a general, inclusive term, such as "American." The different choices of terms reflect changing conditions in the United States and also expose the history of tension between the forces of separatism and integration. Curiously enough, the history of this particular debate reveals that a word such as "Colored" or "Negro" can be radical in one generation and conservative in another generation. In this anthology, we have mostly alternated between "African American" and "black," with "white American" as the main reference for Americans of European descent.

Like naming, Pan-Africanism (which first emerged in the writing of Martin R. Delany in the 1850s, and then again with the Pan-African Congresses and Marcus Garvey's "Back to Africa" movement in the opening decades of the twentieth century) explores the idea of group identity. Focusing on the worldwide scope of modern (that is, post Columbus) racial origins and identification, Pan-Africanism recasts group identity in global terms. Such separatist thought takes David Walker's black nationalist position to its logical conclusion, imagining a racial identity and community that supersede national boundaries.

The strategy of self-segregation or group identification represents an inward route toward group affirmation and preservation that contrasts with assimilation. It is related to, but distinct from, the global perspective of Pan-Africanism, both of which draw upon race or color as the primary element in group identification, but to different ends. Self-segregation was first promoted after Reconstruction (as "Jim Crow" laws formalized repressive policies of segregation) and was reintroduced during the harsh economic times of the Great Depression and again during the civil rights movement of the 1950s and 1960s. Passionate debates during these periods exposed the difficulties of reconciling anti-segregationist ideals with the realities of limited economic or social opportunities. Some African Americans sought to develop both their communities and racial pride by turning away from the possibility of total integration—not by accepting forced segregation, but by choosing a form of self-sufficiency or voluntary separation. Organized self-segregation offered an alternative to pure separatism and full integration— one that carved out a power base within a still racist society.

The modern civil rights movement also spurred debate about interracial coalition politics where groups with distinct ideologies and identities join together to work on common goals (as with the "liberal-labor-civil rights coalition" promoted by Bayard Rustin). Coalition politics addresses the problem of choosing allies, a debate that began before emancipation, when black abolitionists argued about the contributions and roles of white abolitionists such as William Lloyd Garrison and Harriet Beecher Stowe, and this question continues to this day in discussions such as those on black/Jewish relations. Like naming and self-segregation, these debates hinge on ideas about integration and separatism. For example, some leaders in the 1960s pushed for extending the use of coalition politics (since these allegiances had led to significant legislative gains for African Americans) with full integration as the end goal. Others argued that new methods were needed to confront the inequalities and injustice that remained entrenched in the United States. The rise of the Black Power movement marked a turning away from interracial coalition politics. Black Power developed strategies of solidarity and separatism in order to establish a power bloc and consolidate leadership of African Americans in ways that echoed arguments made in the opening decades of the twentieth century. This time, however, such exclusionary politics matched worldwide power shifts as a stronger advocacy of Pan-Africanism emerged alongside revolutionary politics.

The emergence of the black feminist movement in the 1970s turned the spotlight onto the power dynamics *within* civil rights groups, particularly black nationalist movements. Critics argued that civil rights groups of the past and present perpetuated repressive ideas about gender and sexuality even as they mounted fights against racial repression. Black feminist critics also put under harsh light the class and race assumptions of the women's liberation movement of the 1960s and 1970s, which was heavily influenced by white middle-class women.

The tension between separatism and integration continues today. The self-segregation that W. E. B. Du Bois championed in the 1930s (which led to his forced resignation from the NAACP) has found new life in contemporary arguments for girls-only science classes and for single gender or race-restricted schools. And the "Namestakes" debate has been complicated by the rapid growth in recent years of interracialism (historically called "miscegenation"), which has underscored how identity formation involves both external and internal forces. Interracialism forces us to reexamine how culture, lineage, and physical features contribute to identification as African American. For example, what does it mean to identify President Obama as our first black president, when he was raised mainly by his white mother?

Strategies for Change

From the earliest responses to slavery in the New World to the most recent uprisings in urban centers, the struggle for racial justice has been marked by recurring debates over the most effective strategies for change. Some methods focus on changing the behavior of others (for instance, protest, rebellion, politics, and moral suasion use writing and speeches to convince others that, say, slavery or Jim Crow segregation, are morally wrong), while others focus on internal community behavioral change (for instance, economic development, education, and migration). Tactics for implementing these strategies generally fall into one of three categories: force, nonviolent action (i.e., moving to a new state or participating in a sit-in), or rhetoric (ranging from speeches to legislation). Some positions defy strict classification, however, as they advocate a variety of strategies or combine various tactics. For example, the Black Panther Party endorsed a range of methods from bloc politics to socialist economic development. Likewise, the 1946 "Journey of Reconciliation," in which volunteers challenged segregation in interstate travel, was a physical, nonviolent protest action (a multileveled category termed "nonviolent direct action").

One of the most divisive areas of debate has been the role of violence in effecting change. Some early abolitionists (black and white) viewed violent revolution as an emancipation strategy fully justified by the violence of slavery. In his 1843 speech to the National Convention of Colored Citizens, Henry Highland Garnet supported the use of "every destructive agent and element" to combat slavery, foreshadowing Malcolm X's position over a hundred years later that civil rights should be obtained "by any means necessary." Other leaders, from William Lloyd Garrison to Martin Luther King Jr., have countered calls for armed self-defense or rebellion with arguments for nonviolent methods ranging from moral suasion to direct action.

Personal viewpoints and historical context shape how people view different strategies, including their judgments about effectiveness, efficiency, and potential unintended consequences. Thus, patience can be seen as accommodationism (that is, compromising or adapting to an opposing position), while demands for direct and immediate action may seem to ignore the fact that change takes time. Violent protest and rebellion have at times been particularly potent strategies in American society, which historically has prided itself on fighting for what is right and that recognizes certain forms of violence as acceptable for self-defense or self-definition, as in the American Revolution. But use of violence by African Americans has always prompted accusations that they lack moral stature or civic responsibility. The strategy of deliberate nonviolence was introduced in the 1940s and became a primary tactic of the civil rights movement during the 1950s and early 1960s. Strategic nonviolence claimed a moral high ground and sought to avoid the extremes of accommodation or violence, but some, such as the Black Power advocates and the Black Panthers, rejected it as merely a new kind of submissiveness and, faced with entrenched racism that resisted nonviolent methods, began to accept Malcolm X's argument that "the day of turning the other cheek to those brute beasts is over."

Issues of leadership also complicate debates over strategies. While dissatisfaction with the results of older approaches used by established leaders can give rise to new leadership, those same established leaders often avoid new or controversial strategies in order to maintain their power bases. For example, Booker T. Washington, known for his rejection of protest methods in favor of self-help and accommodation, did in fact support some protest actions by other leaders, but primarily in private. While established leaders tend to steer away from potentially controversial strategies, more marginal figures sometimes choose to advocate extreme positions as a way of getting heard. This voicing of radical ideas in turn often bolsters leaders viewed as less extreme, by making their positions appear moderate in comparison. Some leaders use this fact as part of their own strategies, as Martin Luther King Jr. did in "Letter from Birmingham Jail" when he presented the primary choice for Americans as one between nonviolence and violence (as advocated by Malcolm X), rather than as one between the status quo and his call for full civil rights.

Education

"[W]hat kind of [educational] Institution would best befit *us*?" delegates asked during the 1853 National Negro Convention. "[O]ne that would develop *power*," was the response. This connection between education and power propels the educational debates that have played such a prominent role in African American history. The National Negro Conventions, which began in 1831 and were the earliest organized political gatherings of African Americans outside of the church, also introduced two fundamental questions: "What is the best type of education to promote?" and its underlying corollary, "What is the role of education?" These basic questions underlie educational debates throughout African American history. For example, arguments in favor of vocational programs, such as those espoused by Booker T. Washington, are grounded in the idea that the role of education is to provide training for employment. On the other hand, arguments for a liberal arts education, espoused by W. E. B. Du Bois, with goals ranging from promoting an expanded world vision to fostering leadership skills, are grounded in the idea that education should play a more general role in human development.

Beneath the wide range of opinions about the best type of education for black people is a general agreement that the history of African Americans demands a special approach to education. This history is one in which belief in the promise of education has been in constant tension with society's failure to fulfill that promise. This societal failure began with the systematic withholding of educational opportunities during the years of slavery. Later, after the Civil War, the economic deprivation inherited from slavery meant that black schools had to find funding sources outside black communities. Much of the funding for the establishment of post-Civil War black schools came from a combination of missionary and (largely white) philanthropic sources, whose often-conservative agendas shaped the curriculum of these schools. Later societal obstacles for black education include the historic discrepancy between public funds spent on black children and those spent on white children, a Eurocentric traditional curriculum that ignores African American experiences, and the limitation of post-graduate economic opportunities for poorer black people compared to poorer white people with comparable or less education.

The educational debates present a wide range of pragmatic solutions to these obstacles. Responses to a lack of educational opportunities range from establishing separate institutions to fighting for access to traditionally white institutions. For funding, some leaders courted white philanthropists, while others helped establish the public school system in America. Different remedies for biased curricula include the development of separate black studies programs and demands that courses in traditional disciplines include material about African Americans. The so-called "canon wars" in the 1990s are a good example of the latter.

Throughout African American history, educational gains have paved the way for the attainment of other civil rights. In the modern era, the legal battles over education, culminating in *Brown v. Board of Education* (1954), provided the foundation for dismantling official segregation. Subsequent gains in educational access through affirmative action programs have been instrumental in the rise of the black middle and upper class. However, contemporary debates such as the Ebonics controversy explore whether special attention still needs to be paid to the education of some black children. Challenges to black education also continue to emerge in different forms, such as the elimination of literacy programs for the (disproportionately black) prison population. In addition, there is the controversial idea that the current achievement gap between black and white students is tied to a connection among black students between school achievement and "acting white." Thus, the long history of societal obstacles to black education continues to create an ever more complex layering of questions, moving from how best to provide access to education to questioning the content of that education to questioning whether there is breakdown in the very belief in education itself.

Religion

Until the 1960s, debates in black religious history could be roughly divided into two groups: activist discussions about religion that had an eye toward the future and scholarly works that looked back to the past. In the first group, political and religious leaders explored the intersection of religion and politics and worked to shape the future of the church and religion in the lives of African Americans. In the second group, scholars strove to understand the historic and sociological roles of church institutions and religion in the formation of African American culture. But the 1960s saw the emergence of a new kind of debate that combined the direct political engagement of the first group with the scholarly grounding and academic techniques of the second. In these debates, church leaders and theologians committed to developing new directions in theology (including black and womanist theologies) combined the future-oriented activism of the black church leaders with the past-oriented historical consciousness of the foundational religious scholars.

A number of core issues recur throughout African American religious history from different perspectives, whether activist, academic, or a combination of the two. These issues include the definition of the "black church" and "black religion;" religious separatism versus integration; leadership roles for women in churches; identification of and working with allies; the effect of religion as accommodationist or political; and specific elements of church doctrine and religious practice (such as positions on gender roles and homosexuality, and whether the focus is on heavenly or earthly justice). Leaders and scholars have also discussed the role of debates themselves, exploring how the choice of which debate to focus on not only influences the direction of suggested courses of action, but also determines the definitions of allies and antagonists.

The participants in future-oriented activist debates about religion include religious and political leaders from Richard Allen and Jarena Lee down through Martin Luther King Jr. and Malcolm X. These debates explore what role religion and churches should play in the lives of African Americans and society. Questions include: What are the benefits and drawbacks of separatist black churches versus multiracial denominations? Who will lead the church? Who are one's allies (from workers to Jews to white Christians)? How can one balance criticism of allies with the fostering of mutual interests?

In 1903, W. E. B. Du Bois's "On the Faith of Our Fathers," published in *Souls of Black Folk*, heralded the beginning of the academic study of African American religion. The rise of scholarly work on African American religion introduced the second group of debates: those focused on religion and the church in the present or past. Academic scholars, including E. Franklin Frazier, Melville J. Herskovits, and Evelyn Brooks Higginbotham, explored questions such as what influence African traditions have had on the religious practices of African Americans; what roles church leaders and congregants (especially women) have had in the running and organization of the church; and whether black churches have been predominantly accommodationist or political, or a combination of the two.

In the 1960s, the rise of Black Power brought theological and political challenges for religious leaders committed to advancing civil rights. Religious leaders strove to reconcile the calls for dramatic social change with theological tenets. The role of denominational churches was also called into question, particularly since there was a growing recognition of and outrage over the historical roles played by white Christians and orthodox denominations in the perpetuation of *de jure* and *de facto* segregation.

A number of Christian church leaders and theologians began to develop an alternative "black theology." A touchstone moment came in 1966 when a group of politically engaged church leaders came together to form the National Conference of Negro Churchmen. They produced "The Black Power Statement," published as a full-page advertisement in *The New York Times* on July 31, 1966. The statement responded to both white and black church leaders who saw the rising Black Power Movement as a radical challenge to Christian traditions. By proposing that power and love were complementary, instead of inherently in conflict, the statement pointed the way toward the development of new theologies grounded in African American experiences, including black theology (a form of liberation theology dedicated to eliminating the oppression of black people) and womanist theology (a form of liberation theology addressing the intertwined experiences of gender, class, and race).

Fueled by their engagement with the past, present, and future, contemporary theologians have revisited many of the historic debates. In addition, expanding forums for diverse perspectives on religion, particularly in recent decades, have contributed to rigorous examinations of far-ranging topics, from what constitutes a sacred text to how to define fundamental concepts, including the meaning of the "black church." Other new areas of inquiry include exploring the relationship between political activism and religiosity and examining the history and impact of contemporary African American theological movements themselves.

An interesting feature of the new "activist academy" in theology is the blurring of the lines between academic debate and community action. For scholars engaged in developing communities of faith, there is the challenge of developing a "believing scholarship," to use theologian Gayraud Wilmore's interesting term. This challenge of doing scholarship grounded in religious faith brings with it the difficulty of developing arguments that are convincing to those who do not share the same religious convictions, as well as the challenge of extending the impact of the theological work beyond the academy into African American communities. Furthermore, African American theologians, like other African American scholars, often serve as "public intellectuals," called on to publicly voice their opinions about issues ranging from the Million Man March to President Obama's relationship with the Reverend Jeremiah Wright.

Like most debates, those about African American religion do not support simple "either-or" answers. Whether reviewing the impact of past religious movements, analyzing the operation of particular religious organizations, or theorizing about emerging theological frameworks, the different historical, sociological, and political perspectives represented in these debates offer multifaceted insights into "black religion." Moreover, by examining how issues such as race, gender, class, and sexual orientation have shaped religion in the past and present, contemporary theologians and church leaders have been opening up the possibility for imagining alternatives for the future.

The Government: Civic Rights and Civic Duties

What are the mutual obligations between African Americans and the federal government? There are two main categories in this debate. The first explores existing and prospective laws, specifically, asking whether existing laws protect the rights of African Americans or if new laws are needed. The second examines the enforcement of current laws, including whether laws are being enforced fairly and, if not, whether African Americans have a moral obligation to abide by the laws of a government that does not protect their rights.

The first discussions about existing laws began before emancipation. The Slavery Grievance, which explicitly argued against allowing slavery in America, was omitted from the Declaration of Independence when it became clear that if it were included, the Declaration would not have enough support from the thirteen colonies. But the question of whether the Constitution, the nation's founding document, supported slavery fueled debates between leading abolitionists until the Fourteenth Amendment to the Constitution was passed in 1865, granting citizenship and civil rights to African Americans.

Most of the subsequent debates about laws explored what new laws were needed to protect the rights of African Americans and what were the best strategies for passing these laws. At the end of the Civil War, suffrage became a key area of focus, since it was a privilege reserved for white males in most of the United States. People who had fought together for emancipation now clashed over whether to give priority to fighting for suffrage rights for (white) women, for African American men, or for everyone. The issue was settled when the Fifteenth Amendment extended suffrage to all male U.S. citizens. (American women would not be granted suffrage until the Nineteenth Amendment was passed in 1920.)

A more recent area of contention about new laws involves the series of legislation known as "affirmative action." Two passages by Martin Luther King Jr. point to the different poles in the debate. In his "I Have A Dream" speech, King looks forward to the day when children will "not be judged by the color of their skin but by the content of their character." Later, in his 1963 book *Why We Can't Wait*, King writes:

> Whenever this issue of compensatory or preferential treatment for the Negro is raised, some of our friends recoil in horror. The Negro should be granted equality, they agree; but he should ask for nothing more. On the surface, this appears reasonable, but it is not realistic. For it is obvious that if a man is entering the starting line in a race three hundred years after another man, the first would have to perform some impossible feat in order to catch up with his fellow runner.

The tension between the goal of a "color-blind" equality and the use of "preferential treatment" as a means to gain equality has driven the contentious debate behind affirmative action to the present day. Since its inception, affirmative action has been a lightning rod for debate and continues to face challenges in the courts.

The debates about new laws at the close of the twentieth century returned full circle to the role that slavery has played in the United States. The laws of the land have defined African Americans as property, as partial human beings, as people with limited rights, and finally as full citizens. They may ultimately determine whether or not the United States is obligated to pay monetary reparations to the descendants of the African American slaves whose unpaid labor helped to build the country.

Once foundational civil rights laws had been passed—particularly the Fourteenth and Fifteenth Amendments, which granted African Americans citizenship, equal protection under the law, and the right to vote—debate expanded to address the enforcement of those laws. Failure by the government to protect the rights of African Americans fueled conflict over the responsibility of African Americans to support the government, particularly in times of war. On an even deeper level, indifference to or overt hostility toward the rights of African Americans raised this question: If the government does not protect the rights of a group of people, do members of that group even need to abide by the rules of that government?

Times of war have repeatedly brought debates about mutual responsibilities between black citizens and their government to a head. Since the Revolutionary War, when the British offered freedom to slaves who fought against the American forces, black people in America have had to struggle with questions of whether to give allegiance to a country that did not recognize or protect their rights as full citizens. When the United States entered World War I in 1917, the country was mired in a period marked by Jim Crow legal segregation, lynchings, and racially motivated riots. A widely discussed question was whether black citizens had an obligation to defend their country abroad when their country did not defend them or their rights at home. Also, due to military practice and regulations, many African Americans would quite literally "serve," as most were restricted to menial, noncombat positions in the service branches (including the quartermaster and transportation corps). The enforcement of such racial restrictions contributed to a great deal of controversy about military service.

The memories of the racial discrimination and unkept promises of World War I were still fresh when World War II broke out in Europe in September 1939. Despite the progress represented by Executive Order 8802, known as the "Fair Employment Act," which banned discrimination based on "race, creed, color, or national origin" in the defense industries, discrimination and segregation in the armed forces continued. The treatment of African American soldiers by white civilians was often abysmal, and at home tensions escalated between whites and African Americans drawn to the North for employment in war industries, just as they had during World War I and the Great Migration. These conditions renewed the debates about military service that raged during World War I.

The courts have also come under scrutiny in debates about the enforcement of laws. The disproportionately high number of African American inmates in U.S. prisons has prompted many to look at racial discrimination in the justice system, from the police and juries to the discretion in sentencing allowed to judges. On the broadest level is the question of whether African American citizens can ever receive fair and equal justice under the law. The 1995 criminal murder trial of O. J. Simpson brought national awareness to the problematic relationship between African Americans and the justice system, but agreement over solutions remains elusive.

Since pre-emancipation times, debates about government have alternated between discussions about laws themselves and about the enforcement of laws. At times the choice of focus itself has been pivotal—as in 1938 when leaders were unable to gain support for a new antilynching law and the head NAACP council Charles Hamilton Houston argued that key laws were already in place but required enforcement, a strategy that ultimately led to the dismantling of segregation. And, in this new millennium, controversy about racial profiling is bringing both these areas of debate about government together, with calls for a new law to end unequal enforcement of existing laws.

The Politics of Art

In her 1895 speech to the First Congress of Colored Women of the United States, Virginia Earle Matthews argued that African American artists and critics have a fundamental role in combating race prejudice. She proclaimed the necessity "of thoughtful, well-defined and intelligently placed efforts . . . to serve as counter irritants against all such writing that shall stand, having as an aim the supplying of influential and accurate information, on all subjects relating to the Negro and his environments . . ." In making her case, Matthews addressed questions about the relationship between art and politics that became key areas of debate during subsequent artistic movements, from the Harlem Renaissance to the Black Arts Movement to the hip-hop era. First, what is the relationship of art to protest and propaganda? Second, how does the representation of African Americans in art affect political and social advancement? Finally, what elements, if any, define a "black aesthetic" in the arts?

Debates about the relationship between art and propaganda question whether art is by definition political, and, if it is, whether overt propaganda or more nuanced artistic expression is more effective as a political tool. These debates first became prominent among leading artists and critics during the Harlem Renaissance, a period of intense artistic activity by African Americans that flourished in the 1920s. Questions raised include whether the word *propaganda* should be rejected or embraced; whether artistic freedom is desirable or even possible; and what type of art best fosters the advancement of civil rights. Divergent answers to these questions shaped the development of two branches of African American art: the protest and the modernist traditions. Protest art—including Richard Wright's naturalistic novel *Native Son*—directly explores political conflict between different groups, often using characters as representatives of a larger group. Art in the modernist tradition—including Zora Neale Hurston's *Their Eyes Were Watching God* or Ralph Ellison's *Invisible Man*—focuses on the complexity of individual will and individual choices lived within a society. The political impact of different types of art, and the larger question of propaganda's role in the production and consumption of art, remain areas of contention among contemporary artists and critics alike.

Debates about the role of "representation" in art are based on the assumption that the arts have a political role in society. If art has the power to shape public perception, questions arise as to how certain images or characters shape perceptions of African Americans, and what, accordingly, this relation demands, morally, of the artist. Should artists only use exemplary black characters to counteract negative stereotypes in mainstream culture? What is the effect of creating flawed or three-dimensional black characters? Positions on these issues reveal an underlying set of questions concerning the consumer of a work of art. Are certain works of art directed to particular groups of consumers (e.g., black or white people, females or males, a mass audience or select elites)? If so, how does this focus affect their power either as art or as effective propaganda, and the responsibilities of the artist?

The debates about aesthetics generally center around the question, "is there such a thing as a black aesthetic?" Efforts to identify and develop African American artistic traditions have long grappled with the issue of how to define black art. Many early notions of a black aesthetic were grounded in biological ideas of race, but even when artists rejected essentialism in favor of cultural or experiential definitions of "blackness," complicated questions arose when defining black art. Does black art have identifiable aesthetic elements, or does anything by an African American artist qualify as black art? For example, are performances of Shakespeare by African American actors black art? What about a black pianist's performance of Chopin? Is art that reflects elements of a distinctive black culture more authentic than art that does not (even if it is created or performed by African Americans)? Is a novel written by a black author about white characters still black literature? If blackness is culturally constructed, can non-African Americans learn a black aesthetic, or does such an aesthetic only result from the experience of being black in America? Is one born with that aesthetic? How does the involvement of white artists (from white jazz musicians to Eminem) complicate the idea of black art forms? In sum, what, if anything—the race of the artist, the subject matter, or the artistic form—distinguishes a work of art as black?

These three areas of debate are basically about three fundamental elements of artistic structure: the choice of theme (which is the focus of debate on propaganda and art); the choice of character (the focus of discussions about representation); and the choice of form (the focus of debate on the black aesthetic). Some of the debates examine the production of these elements (that is, the role of the artist), while others look at consumption (that is, the effects on people who experience the art). Questions about production include the following: Do artists have a responsibility to consider the political implications of their art, or should they be free to create without constraint? Questions about consumption center on the political impact of the art, ranging from what types of art would be most effective in advancing civil rights, to whether the use of dialect in art has a detrimental or beneficial impact on the lives of African Americans. Many of these debates also explore the relationship of consumption to production, raising questions about what could or should be done to influence the direction of art (e.g., censorship, boycotting, or political pressure). Running through the different debates and perspectives is an area of general agreement: namely, that the arts are important modes of communication with the potential to powerfully affect people's lives.

Race and Class

The earliest public discussions about the effects of class on the lives of African Americans took place shortly after the 1917 Russian Revolution created the world's first communist state. The controversy over whether race or class was a greater source of discrimination was a particularly fraught one in a nation that envisioned itself as affording opportunity to all; and the fluidity of American class lines, compared to those in Europe, suggested to many that the United States was fundamentally a classless society. The rise of communism in the United States in the early twentieth century, however, forced people to reconsider not only classlessness but sources of discrimination as well. The Communist Party actively recruited African Americans. By redefining political struggle as one of class—of proletariat against bourgeoisie—rather than one of race, the Party tapped into growing black frustration with newly formed labor unions, which viewed African Americans as potential strikebreakers rather than as fellow laborers. Subsequent debates suggested that the "problem of the color line" be reformulated to incorporate the idea of class, a process that gained momentum with the rise of the African American middle class because of affirmative action and the subsequent class divide within the African American community itself in the latter half of the twentieth century.

A fundamental question drives the nearly century-long history of debate on class and race: is it better to focus on race issues or class issues when working to improve the economic lives of African Americans? Underlying the divergent responses are related questions about allegiances, leadership, and the role of theory in guiding action.

Discussions about allegiances explore ideas such as whether whites can be allies in the struggle for civil rights. In the 1920s and 1930s, leaders debated whether white unionists or Communists were truly interested in helping black people, or whether any professed allegiance was mainly a political strategy to advance their own interests. These responses often reveal distrust not only of white Communists but also of black working-class leaders. E. Franklin Frazier's controversial work on the "black bourgeoisie" in the 1950s, drawing on Du Bois's canonical essay of 1903 called "The Talented Tenth" and the Martinican philosopher Franz Fanon's "Black Skins, White Masks," pushed this discussion in a new direction, suggesting that middle-class African Americans contributed to the problems of racism and classism by trying to foster cross-racial class allegiances based on privilege in order to escape perceived bonds of race.

Discussions about allegiances often also explore ideas about leadership. A key area of debate about leadership is whether the educated elite or members of the working class should spearhead the struggle for economic advancement. This question of leadership extends beyond class to issues of gender, with some insisting on female leaders to address the particular experiences of black working-class or middle-class women.

Finally, there is long-running debate about the role of theory versus practice. Even when people agree about principles of class theory, they may disagree about how that abstract theory may be applied to practical problems and what historical experience can reveal about the relationship between theory and practice.

The effects of the civil rights movement brought a dramatic shift in debates about race and class. Since that time, some African Americans made dramatic individual economic gains, which has spurred debate about whether race remains primary in determining or limiting choices, or if class is now of primary importance. Discussions over whether America has progressed into a "post-race" or "post-black" society became widespread following the election of President Barack Obama in 2008. But fraught discussions about race and class (such as those following the 2010 firing and rehiring of USDA worker Shirley Sherrod because of a dishonestly edited version of a speech she gave at the NAACP on race and class) continue to emerge, suggesting how powerful and intertwined race and class remain.

Society and Individual Choice

What role does society have in directing choices made by individuals? Discussions on a number of diverse topics—including interracial relationships, homosexuality, birth control, and the politics of hair—address this key area of debate. At their core, these discussions question whether no limits should be placed on an individual's right to control her or his body, or if there are certain socially or culturally undesirable choices that need to be controlled. (Many contemporary laws in the United States assume this second tenet, from restrictions of personal drug use to the prohibition of suicide.) Who determines what is socially or culturally undesirable? Should these unsanctioned choices be discouraged by legal or cultural pressure, or should they be classified as purely personal decisions? Finally, is it possible to define certain choices as "personal" when they are shaped by societal and cultural biases?

Interracial relationships provide a useful starting point for exploring how these issues have been addressed throughout African American history, since legal sanctions against black-white intermarriage lasted over 300 years—from the first anti-interracial marriage statute passed in Maryland in 1664 to the 1967 Supreme Court decision in *Virginia v. Loving* declaring all such laws unconstitutional—and cultural pressures discouraging these unions still exist today. Since "miscegenation" first became a topic of public debate before the Civil War, African Americans have voiced conflicted opinions. This ambivalence is clear in the ways people historically have answered two fundamental questions: Should interracial marriage be legal; and, if so, should African Americans choose to exercise that legal right? Few African Americans disagreed about the injustice of legal restrictions against interracial relationships, but eliminating such restrictions was rarely a priority within black political movements. For one thing, such laws affected a relatively tiny proportion of black Americans, especially compared with the number affected by restrictions against economic and educational advancement. For another, many felt uncomfortable with the idea of people choosing to exercise such a right and "abandoning the race."

Debates about interracialism erupted in the 1920s and again in the 1960s, as decreases in segregation and in legal restrictions propelled greater opportunities for interracial relations. Those on different sides of the issue often agreed that marriage was ultimately a personal decision. However, those opposed to interracial unions argued that that decision should take into account the cost of such a union to the community, separate individuals, their spouses, and their children. Another typical spur for debate has been the common phenomenon of famous African Americans marrying non-African

Americans. These discussions are often driven by the idea that famous black people have a particular responsibility to "the black community," because they function as societal representatives of the race.

Gender issues further complicate debates on interracialism. Since pre-emancipation, there has been a distinction between unions involving white men and black women and those involving black men and white women. The starkest example is the tacit acceptance among white slave owners of white men having sexual relations with female slaves; in contrast, the justification given for the lynching of a black man has characteristically been that he violated, or threatened to violate, a white woman. During the twentieth century, a huge discrepancy existed between the relatively large number of black male and white female couples and the relatively few black female and white male couples. Furthermore, black women became increasingly vocal about their concerns over mixed marriage as the number of available, similarly positioned black men decreased (propelled by such societal factors as gender differentials in education level and earning power, and a sharp increase in the percentage of black men who were incarcerated).

Debates about homosexuality hinge on many of the same issues as those about interracialism. The basic underlying question is whether each individual should be able to make her or his own sexual choices, or whether others may apply legal or cultural pressures to influence choices viewed as more socially beneficial. Discussions about homosexuality among African Americans suggest that there is a similar level of homophobia in African American communities as in other communities, often reinforced by strong religious convictions, but these discussions also reveal key differences in African American attitudes toward homosexuality and homophobia. First of all, some are surprised and disappointed by homophobia among African Americans, because they expect people who have experienced discrimination to be more tolerant of difference. In contrast, critics such as Cheryl Clarke suggest that homophobia may actually be promoted by experiences of racism, since claiming heterosexual privilege is one of the only routes to hegemonic power open to African Americans. (Anti-Semitism may also be promoted by this impulse to ally with a socially dominant group.) Secondly, there are a number of race-specific discussions about homosexuality that range in focus from whether homosexuality threatens the black family (raising the issue of so-called "race suicide") to whether black homosexuality has origins in African cultures or arose after contact with European cultures. Thirdly, artistic portrayals of black homosexuality not only prompt debates about homosexuality, they raise issues of representation. For example, the controversy surrounding the homosexual relation between Celie and her husband's lover in Alice Walker's *The Color Purple* evoked the position that a fictional black character functions as a "representative of the race."

"Race suicide" has also been a common charge leveled against birth control use by black people. The other common charge against birth control is that it is "genocide," an argument stressing the role of external, societal forces as opposed to the internal choice implied by "race suicide." Indeed, this tension between involuntary (societal) and voluntary (personal) control of the body underscores the entire range of positions on birth control throughout African American history.

Birth control began to be an active topic of public discussion among African Americans in the 1920s. During this period, birth control became increasingly available in black communities with the establishment of local clinics sponsored by the national movement for birth control led by the nurse Margaret Sanger. The birth control movement in the United States was encouraged by the rise of the eugenics movement, with its ostensive goal of improving the human race through selective breeding. Those drawn to social engineering (who were often of a well-educated and privileged class) typically favored increased birth control programs (or even sterilization) for poorer and less educated classes, disproportionately including African Americans. Much of the controversy about birth control in black communities has stemmed from concern over the underlying elitism or inherent racism in eugenic theories that define certain types of human beings as genetically "desirable."

Opinions about birth control have typically divided along class lines. Educated and privileged African Americans have had a long history of both supporting and practicing birth control, while poorer and less educated African Americans have been more likely to oppose the use of birth control. Scholars, including W. E. B. Du Bois, have traced this trend back to emancipation, when the "intelligent class" supported their economic advancement by marrying later and having fewer children, while others, constrained from using birth control by religious views or lack of education, remained mired in poverty. This class division is further complicated by the historical links between support for birth control and eugenics. If some birth control programs are motivated by goals of social engineering, it makes birth control less voluntary for some women than for others. The feminist argument for "a woman's right to choose" is thus complicated in African American communities where the ability to choose freely has been compromised by efforts to control information or economic resources in order to promote (or discourage) birth control or sterilization. Ideas related to eugenics have also influenced debates about "quality versus quantity," involving questions such as whether the high birth rate among African Americans caused the high infant mortality rate (and higher death rate for black mothers and black people in general) or vice versa.

Arguments drawing on biology or on religious convictions have historically played a dominant role in debates about birth control in African American communities. Starting in the 1950s, the civil rights movement and the subsequent women's liberation movement brought a shift, as debates increasingly addressed social and cultural factors. Some advocates for high birth rates over birth control began to place the blame for high black mortality on racism rather than biological factors. Birth control advocates also stressed social factors over biological ones (such as the disproportionate effects of illegal abortions on minority women), but used them to support increased access to birth control.

As with birth control and other issues involving the body, attitudes toward image and desire raise questions about the social context of individual decisions. Black styles of dress or fashion are often viewed as having political connotations, whether intentional or not. Discussions about hair highlight how societal and cultural factors complicate personal choices about self-presentation and the desired physical traits in one's potential mate.

America's history of associating Caucasian features with power and beauty has had a complex influence on black self-image and desire. Attitudes toward hair have been shaped by this history of racist aesthetics. The development of the concept of "bad" hair (tightly curled or "kinky" hair) is parallel to the devaluation of darker skin color, and cultural shifts tend to highlight the links between the two. For example, during the Black Power movement of the 1960s, darker skin and "natural" hair both gained value as reflections of a more "authentic" black aesthetic. While this dramatic reversal of racialized aesthetics was relatively short-lived, or at least not as completely effective as many hoped at the time, it contributed enormously to the remarkable diversity of contemporary black aesthetic choices and values, and a much broader acceptance of a range of black phenotypes was considered "beautiful," aesthetically pleasing or sexually desirable in the marketplace, in the media, in fashion, and in personal choices for partners.

Hair and color also share a common history of gender disparity, with greater importance attached to these issues for women than for men—reflecting the general pattern in the United States of linking women's power to their appearance and men's power to their economic or social success. The tradition of short hair for men has contributed to a difference between black men and women in terms of both the energy dedicated to and the meaning attributed to hair. However, hair still has clear political connotations for men as well, as evident in Malcolm X's decision to change from a "conk" style to a "natural" style as a self-conscious reflection of his political awakening and the widespread adoption of Afros during the Black Power era.

These controversies make clear that the politics of hair go beyond a simplistic dichotomy between assimilationist desires (or between self-hatred)—expressed through preferences for lighter skin or naturally "white" or straightened hair—and black nationalist sentiments that elevate the aesthetics of "natural" black hair, expressed in the sixties slogan "Black is beautiful." Self-image and desire are influenced by all sorts of forces, including external or internalized racism, but they cannot be reduced to simple reflections of these forces. The debates over personal aesthetics reveal a complex history in which attitudes and behavior have been shaped by seemingly contradictory impulses (pride/assimilation, imitation/creativity) operating simultaneously to produce rich and diverse aesthetic options.

The debates about interracialism, homosexuality, birth control, and the politics of hair underscore the extent to which the personal is political in issues of the black body. Some critics clearly favor the individual's right to choose, while others argue for curbs on choices deemed harmful to black culture and society. The objections to these positions make clear the near impossibility of separating the personal from a social context. Discussions about these topics may thus play a political role themselves, helping to raise the consciousness of individuals about how their attitudes and choices about the body are influenced by cultural and societal pressures. Greater awareness about how personal attitudes and choices affect the community, and vice versa, may create a greater openness and acceptance of certain choices, or even influence which particular choices are made.

Gender

From African colonization to religion to birth control to communism, black women have been engaged in all key debates, at times specifically addressing the ways gender influences the issues under discussion. But the 1970s brought a dramatic change. With the rise of the contemporary black feminist movement, gender issues moved to center stage, becoming a central focus of inquiry and debate in and of themselves.

The catalyst for the rise of the black feminist movement was the combination of empowerment and marginalization that black women experienced in the civil rights movement, in the Black Power movement, and in the women's movement in the 1960s and 1970s. Key questions addressed in the gender debates reflect this historical beginning. First and foremost was this question: can oppressions be ranked or separated? Specifically, are black people more oppressed than women or vice versa, or is it impossible to isolate the effects of various components of one's identity? Positions on this fundamental issue influence answers to a related question: who are one's primary political allies? Some argue that gender issues need to be addressed first, making women of all races primary allies. Others view racial issues as dominant and give racial allegiances primacy. A third position, which became widespread as black feminist theory developed, is that oppressions are intertwined and cannot be ranked or separated (leading some black feminists to focus on alliances with other black women). The black feminist movement grew to condemn all oppressions, including that of class and sexual orientation, maintaining that only the freedom of the most oppressed would bring freedom for all.

In addition to these issues about gender versus race, other recurring questions in the gender debates include whether black women are better off than black men. Controversial aspects of this question are the idea that black women are going to surpass black men economically (largely due to educational advantages and the black male incarceration rate), and whether black women have allied with white men to the detriment of black male interests. Other questions arise from the examination of the personal arena of male/female relationships. For example, how do interracial relationships relate to gender and race issues? Does a traditional domestic family model represent "natural" gender roles, or does it reflect a problematic adoption of a white middle-class model? Are these issues a matter of personal choice, or is the personal also political?

Recent historical events, including Clarence Thomas's Senate confirmation hearings, the Million Man March, and the presidential primary race between Barack Obama and Hillary Clinton, have re-ignited heated debate about gender and race. They show the rise of new allegiances based on shared political or personal interests, rather than along race or gender lines, and demonstrate that gender issues are not "women's issues" exclusively, but affect all. These recent debates also explore how those in power manipulate gender and race issues to try to limit political change or to reinforce other oppressions (including homophobia), raising some doubts about whether instruments of institutional power (the government, police, or the media) can be used to promote social justice. Finally, questions recur surrounding the issue of silence. Can divisive issues with potential negative implications for some African Americans (e.g., black male sexual harassment) be discussed publicly? Is the breaking of silences in itself a political act or does solidarity require muting or modifying some positions?

Hearing Others and Finding Ourselves

As a counterpoint to the primary historical structure of this anthology, these eleven key themes offer other ways of looking at the debates that have shaped African American history. The flexibility of multiple approaches builds on the other elements of the anthology (from diverse types of texts to multiperspective debates) to widen conversations and foster interaction with new perspectives. Martin Luther King Jr. encouraged engaging with diverse thinkers "from a dialectical point of view, combining a partial 'yes' and a partial 'no.'" Poet June Jordan went even further, suggesting that even texts that seem at odds with each other may both be approached with a "yes." "We need everybody and all that we are," Jordan writes. "We need to know and make known the complete, constantly unfolding, complicated heritage that is our Black experience." By opening ourselves up to the range of different views represented in this anthology, we may discover different ways of seeing that enrich our understanding of history and of each other.

Jennifer Burton and Henry Louis Gates, Jr.

Works Cited

Bell, Howard Holman, ed. *Minutes of the Proceedings of the National Negro Conventions, 1830–1864.* Volume 1. New York: Arno Press and the *New York Times*, 1969.

Colbert, Stephen. "The Word—Blackwashing." *The Colbert Report.* 9/24/09.

Du Bois, W. E. B. "Black Folk and Birth Control." *Birth Control Review* 16 (June 1932): pp. 166–167.

Garnet, Henry Highland. "An Address to the Slaves of the United States of America." *David Walker's Appeal, with a Brief Sketch of His Life by Henry Highland Garnet, and also Garnet's Address to the Slaves of the United States of America.* New York: J. H. Tobitt, 1948.

Jordan, June. "On Richard Wright and Zora Neale Hurston: Notes Toward a Balancing of Love and Hatred." *Black World* (August 1974): pp. 4–8.

King, Martin Luther Jr. "I Have A Dream." *I Have A Dream: Writings and Speeches That Changed the World.* Ed. James Melvin Washington. New York: HarperCollins, 1992.

King, Martin Luther Jr. "My Pilgrimage to Nonviolence." *Fellowship* (September 1958): pp. 4–9.

King, Martin Luther Jr. *Why We Can't Wait.* New York: Harper and Row, 1963.

Malcolm X. *By Any Means Necessary: Speeches, Interviews, and a Letter.* Ed. George Breitman. New York: Pathfinder Press, 1970.

Malcolm X. Telegram to Martin Luther King Jr. June 30, 1964. http://brothermalcolm.net/mxwords/letters/telegramtomartin.gif.

Matthews, Victoria Earle. "The Value of Race Literature: An Address, Delivered at the First Congress of Colored Women of the United States, at Boston, Mass., July 30th, 1895." *The Massachusetts Review*, XXVII, No. 2 (Summer 1986): 169–185.

Painter, Nell Irvin. *The History of White People.* New York: W. W. Norton, 2010.

Stuckey, Sterling. *Slave Culture: Nationalist Theory and the Foundations of Black America.* New York: Oxford University Press, 1987.

Trotter, Joe William, Jr. *The Great Migration in Historical Perspective: New Dimensions of Race, Class, and Gender.* Bloomington: Indiana UP, 1991.

Walker, David. *Walker's Appeal, in Four Articles; Together, with a Preamble, to the Coloured Citizens of the World, but in Particular, and Very Expressly, to Those of the United States of America, Written in Boston, State of Massachusetts, September 28, 1829,* rev. ed. (Boston: David Walker, 1830).

Wilmore, Gayraud S., ed. *African American Religious Studies.* Durham, N.C.: Duke University Press, 1989.

≈ Timeline

Bold-face titles indicate works included or excerpted in the anthology.

1740	In response to Stono Rebellion, South Carolina outlaws teaching slaves to write	1746	Lucy Terry, "Bars Fight," (the first extant work of creative writing written by an African American; not published until 1855)
		1748	David Hume, *Of National Characters*
1756–1763	African Americans fight in French and Indian War		
1757	Phillis Wheatley purchased in Boston		
1758	First black Baptist church in the colonies is erected on a plantation in Virginia	1760	Jupiter Hammon, *An Evening Thought: Salvation by Christ with Penitential Cries* (printed as a broadside, the first poetry published by an African American)
		1764	Immanuel Kant, *Observations on the Feeling of the Beautiful and Sublime*
		1770	James Beattie, *A Essay on the Nature and Immutability of Truth*
1773	Slaves in Massachusetts petition legislature for freedom for first time	1773	Peter Bestes, Sambo Freeman, Felix Holbrook, and Chester Joie, *Petition* • Phillis Wheatley, *Poems on Various Subjects, Religious and Moral* (published in London, first book published by an African American and second book published by an American woman)
1774	Continental Congress prohibits importation of slaves after December 1, 1774	1774	Phillis Wheatley, *Letter to the Reverend Samson Occum*
1775–1783	American Revolutionary War; battles fought by African Americans include Bunker Hill, Lexington, and Concord	1784	Thomas Jefferson, *Notes on the State of Virginia*
1775	First antislavery society organized by Philadelphia Quakers • Royal governor of Virginia offers freedom to any slave joining the British army; 800 respond to form "Ethiopian Regiment" • Second Continental Congress resolves against the importation of slaves		
1776	Declaration of Independence adopted without antislavery statement proposed by Thomas Jefferson		
1777	Vermont is one of the first states to abolish slavery in state constitution • New York is the first state to extend vote to black males, but limits voting in 1815 and 1821 with permit, property, and residency requirements		

1780 Pennsylvania becomes the first state to allow interracial marriage • Group of free black people in Massachusetts protest "taxation without representation" and petition for exemption from taxes

1783 Massachusetts Supreme Court grants black taxpayers suffrage

1784–1791 Johann Gottfried von Herder, *Ideas on the Philosophy of the History of Mankind*

1785 Immanuel Kant, **Review of Herder's Ideas on the Philosophy of the History of Mankind**

1786 Free African Americans join in Shays's Rebellion.

1787 Constitution ratified, classifying one slave as three-fifths of one person for congressional apportionment, postponing prohibition of slave importation until 1808, and requiring the return of fugitive slaves to owners • Congress passes Northwest Ordinance, banning slavery in Northwest Territories and all land north of Ohio River • Absalom Jones and Richard Allen organize Philadelphia Free African Society • Group of free black people in Rhode Island establish African Union Society to promote repatriation to Africa.

1789 Olaudah Equiano, *The Interesting Narrative of the Life of Olaudah Equiano*

1790 Pennsylvanian abolitionists submit the first anti-slavery petitions to U.S. Congress

1791 Benjamin Banneker, *Letter to Thomas Jefferson* • Thomas Jefferson, *Reply to Benjamin Banneker*

1793 U.S. Congress passes the first Fugitive Slave Law • Invention of the cotton gin increases demand for slaves in South

1794 U.S. Congress prohibits slave trade with foreign countries • French National Convention abolishes slavery in French territories (ban will be repealed by Napoleon in 1802) • Richard Allen founds the first African Methodist Episcopal church (AME), in Philadelphia

1796 "Bars Fight" poet Lucy Terry Prince becomes the first woman to argue before Supreme Court, successfully defending against a white man trying to steal her family's land • Joshua Johnson, the first black portrait painter to gain recognition in the United States, opens studio in Baltimore

1798 Georgia is last state to abolish slave trade

1800	U.S. citizens are prohibited from exporting slaves • Group of free black people in Pennsylvania petition U.S. Congress to outlaw slavery • Gabriel Prosser and Jack Bowler organize 1,000 fellow slaves to seize Richmond, but plan is quelled by militia and leaders are executed along with many others
1802	Haitians force French government to end slavery in Haiti; Francois-Dominique Toussaint-Louverture is made governor
1803	Louisiana Purchase doubles size of the United States
1804	York, a slave, serves as guide for Lewis and Clark expedition to Pacific • Ohio sets precedent with passage of the first "Black Laws" restricting rights and movements of free African Americans in North
1807	Britain abolishes slave trade
1808	Congress bans the importation of slaves from Africa on January 1, the earliest date allowed by the Constitution
1811	Slave revolt in Louisiana led by Charles Deslondes ends with over 100 slaves killed or executed by U.S. troops
1812	Slaves and free African Americans fight in War of 1812
1815	Quaker Levi Coffin establishes Underground Railroad to help slaves escape to Canada
1816–1818	First Seminole War, involving runaway slaves and Native Americans fighting U.S. federal government in Florida
1816	American Colonization Society formed in Washington, D.C., to promote African repatriation of freed slaves; the society is supported by leading white members of Congress
1817	Over 3,000 free African Americans in Philadelphia meet to protest American Colonization Society
1818	President given power to use armed vessels in Africa to halt illegal slave trade • U.S. Congress allots $100,000 to transport illegally imported slaves back to Africa

1809   Thomas Jefferson, *Letter to Joel Barlow*

1817   James Forten, *Letter to Paul Cuffe*

1818   James Forten and Russell Parrott, *Address to the Humane and Benevolent Inhabitants of the City and County of Philadelphia*

1820	Missouri Compromise reached, allowing Maine into Union as free state, Missouri as slave state in 1821, and outlawing slavery in all new northern plains states • American Colonization Society sends expedition to begin establishment of Liberia, a black republic in West Africa; the first repatriation ship *Mayflower of Liberia*, leaves from New York City with 86 African Americans		

| 1821 | African Grove Theatre, the first all-black U.S. acting troupe, begins performances in New York City |

| 1822 | Denmark Vesey organizes slave revolt to take over Charleston, South Carolina, but is betrayed by servant • Liberia formally founded by African American colonizers |

| 1823 | Alexander L. Twilight graduates from Middlebury College, Vermont, becoming the first African American college graduate |

| 1826 | The first U.S. colony for free African Americans, Nashoba, is established near Memphis, Tennessee |

| | | 1828 | Thomas L. Jennings, *Letter in* **Freedom's Journal** |

| 1829 | Three-day race riot breaks out in Cincinnati; more than 1,000 African Americans flee to Canada after white mobs attack them and burn their homes | | 1829 | David Walker, *Walker's* **Appeal** |

| 1830 | The first National Negro Convention convenes in Philadelphia |

| 1831 | Nat Turner leads slave uprising in Southampton County, Virginia; at least fifty seven white people are killed; 3,000 soldiers and Virginia militia react by killing black people indiscriminately; Turner is captured and hanged • William Lloyd Garrison begins publishing *The Liberator*, a weekly paper committed to the complete abolition of slavery | | 1831 | Ella, *Letter in* **The Liberator** • "A Subscriber," *Letter in* **The Liberator** • "A Subscriber and a Citizen of the United States," *Letter in* **The Liberator** • William Lloyd Garrison, *Editorial on Walker's* **Appeal** |

| 1832 | Maria W. Stewart, the first American woman to engage in public political debates, begins speaking tour in Boston | | 1832 | Anonymous, *Minutes of the Second Annual Convention for the Improvement of the Free People of Color* • Anonymous, *Address to the Female Literary Association of Philadelphia* • "A Colored Female of Philadelphia," *Emigration to Mexico* • [Ralph Randolph Gurley] and "A South Carolinian," *Opinions of a Freeman of Colour in Charleston* |

1833	Oberlin College is founded as the first coeducational U.S. college and is racially integrated from its inception	1833	Maria W. Stewart, *An Address Delivered at the African Masonic Hall* • Richard Allen, *The Life, Experience, and Gospel Labors of the Rt. Rev. Richard Allen*
1834	Henry Blair, inventor of corn planter, is the first recorded African American to receive patent • Antiabolitionist riots in Philadelphia and New York • British Parliament abolishes slavery in British Empire	1835	William Whipper, *Minutes of the Fifth Annual Convention for the Improvement of The Free People of Color In the United States*
1835–1842	Second Seminole War		
1836	U.S. House of Representatives passes the first "gag rule," preventing any anti-slavery petition or bill from being introduced, read, or discussed	1836	Jarena Lee, *The Life and Religious Experience of Jarena Lee*
		1837	Samuel E. Cornish and Philip A. Bell, *Editorial in* **The Colored American**
1838	Frederick Douglass escapes from slavery • Joshua Giddings of Ohio is the first abolitionist elected to U.S. Congress		
1839	Cinque leads successful slave revolt on Spanish ship *Amistad* • U.S. State Department rejects passport application by Philadelphia black man on basis that African Americans are not citizens		
1840	Pope Gregory XVI states opposition to slave trade and slavery		
1841	Quintuple Treaty signed by England, France, Russia, Austria, and Prussia, allowing mutual search of vessels on high seas to halt slave trade	1841	Sidney, *Letters in* **The Colored American** • William Whipper, *Letter to the Editor* • Sidney, *Letter to the Editor*
1842	Frederick Douglass makes his first anti-slavery speech, in Nantucket, Massachusetts		
1843	Vermont and Massachusetts defy 1793 Fugitive Slave Act	1843	Henry Highland Garnet, *An Address to the Slaves of the United States of America* • Anonymous, *Report on Debate between Frederick Douglass and Henry Highland Garnet at the National Convention of Colored Citizens*
		1844	Ralph Waldo Emerson, *Address Delivered on the Anniversary of the Emancipation of the Negroes in the British West Indies*
1846	Frederick Douglass launches his abolitionist newspaper		
1847	Liberia declares independence and becomes the first African republic		

1848	Frederick Douglass speaks at the first Women's Rights Convention, in Seneca Falls, New York · Ohio reverses "Black Laws"

1848   Henry Highland Garnet, **The Past and the Present Condition and the Destiny of the Colored Race**

1849   Harriet Tubman escapes from slavery and begins work as a leader of the Underground Railroad · Massachusetts Supreme Court upholds "separate but equal" ruling in the first U.S. integration suit

1849   Frederick Douglass, **Too Much Religion, Too Little Humanity** · C. H. Chase, **Letter to Frederick Douglass** · Frederick Douglass, **Reply to C. H. Chase** · Frederick Douglass and Samuel Ringgold Ward, **Resolved, That the Constitution of the United States, in Letter, Spirit, and Design, Is Essentially Anti-Slavery** · Frederick Douglass, **The Colonizationist Revival**

1850   Clay Compromise strengthens 1793 Fugitive Slave Act, outlaws slave trade in Washington, D.C., admits California as free state, and admits Utah and New Mexico as either slave or free · Lucy Sessions becomes the first recorded African American woman college graduate, receiving her degree from Oberlin College in Ohio

1851   Sojourner Truth delivers "Ar'n't I A Woman?" at Women's Rights Conference in Acron, Ohio

1852   Harriet Beecher Stowe, *Uncle Tom's Cabin*

1853   Frederick Douglass, **Letter to Harriet Beecher Stowe** · Harriet Beecher Stowe, **Letter to William Lloyd Garrison** · Martin Delany, **Letter to Frederick Douglass** · Frederick Douglass, **Remarks** · Martin Delany, **Letter to Frederick Douglass** · Frederick Douglass, **Reply to Martin Delany** · William Wells Brown, *Clotel; or, The President's Daughter* (published in London, considered the first novel published by an African American)

1854   Kansas-Nebraska Act repeals Missouri Compromise of 1820 · Republican Party founded to oppose extension of slavery

1854   Josiah Clark Nott and George R. Gliddon, **Types of Mankind** · Frederick Douglass, **The Claims of the Negro Ethnologically Considered** · Martin R. Delany, **The Political Destiny of the Colored Race on the American Continent**

1855   "Bleeding Kansas" fighting begins as anti-slavery and pro-slavery settlers hold separate state conventions · John Mercer Langston is elected clerk of Brownhelm Township, Ohio, becoming the first African American elected to political office

1855   Anonymous, **Minutes of the Colored National Convention** · Frederick Douglass, *My Bondage and My Freedom*

1857	In *Dred Scott* decision, U.S. Supreme Court declares African Americans are not citizens and rules that the Missouri Compromise of 1820 is unconstitutional, thereby allowing slavery in all territories
1859	John Brown leads abolitionist raid in Harpers Ferry, West Virginia • Last U.S. slave ship lands in Alabama
1860	South Carolina is the first state to secede from Union
1861–1865	American Civil War
1862	Congress bans slavery in District of Columbia and U.S. territories • President Lincoln issues Emancipation Proclamation, effective January 1, 1863, freeing slaves in the rebel states • United States recognizes Liberia as free nation
1863	Slavery abolished in all Dutch colonies
1864	Fugitive Slave Laws repealed
1865	General Sherman orders up to 40 acres given to each African American family, a policy later reversed by President Andrew Johnson • Slavery outlawed by Thirteenth Amendment • Freedmen's Bureau established • "Black Codes" issued in former Confederate states, severely limited rights of freed women and men • President Lincoln assassinated • Ku Klux Klan founded in Tennessee
1866	Congress passes the first Civil Rights Act declaring freed black people U.S. citizens and nullifying Black Codes • Edward G. Walker and Charles L. Mitchell are the first African Americans elected to state legislature
1867	Congress passes First Reconstruction Act granting suffrage to black males in rebel states, among other rights • Last slave ship arrives in Cuba, marking the end of the Trans-Atlantic Slave Trade

1857	Frederick Douglass, ***Speech on the* Dred Scott *Decision***
1859	Frederick Douglass, ***African Civilization Society*** • Henry Highland Garnet, ***Speech at an Enthusiastic Meeting of the Colored Citizens of Boston*** • James McCune Smith, ***On the Fourteenth Query of Thomas Jefferson's* Notes on Virginia** • Harriet Adams Wilson, *Our Nig* (the first novel by an African American published in America)
1861	Harriet Jacobs, *Incidents in the Life of a Slave Girl* • Frances Harper, *The Two Offers* (the first short story published by an African American)
1867	Sojourner Truth, ***Address to the First Annual Meeting of the American Equal Rights Association***

1868	Congress passes Fourteenth Amendment, granting African Americans equal citizenship and civil rights	1868	***Debate on Compulsory Free Public Education*** • Frederick Douglass, ***Letter to Josephine Sophia White Griffing***
1869	National Women's Suffrage Association formed • Wyoming Territory is the first to grant women suffrage in the United States • Howard University's law school is established, the first black law school in the United States	1869	Frederick Douglass and Frances E. W. Harper, ***Proceedings of the American Equal Rights Association Convention***
1870	Congress passes Fifteenth Amendment, guaranteeing suffrage to all male U.S. citizens • Congress passes Enforcement Acts to control Ku Klux Klan and to federally guarantee civil and political rights • Hiram R. Revels of Mississippi is elected the first African American U.S. senator • Joseph H. Hainey is seated as the first African American U.S. representative; five other African American men are also elected to U.S. House of Representatives • Richard T. Greener is the first African American graduate of Harvard College		
1871	Congress passes second Ku Klux Klan Act to enforce Fourteenth Amendment		
1874	Women's Christian Temperance Union founded in Ohio		
1875	Congress passes Civil Rights Act of 1875, giving equal treatment in public places and access to jury duty		
1877	Federal troops withdraw from South, officially ending Reconstruction	1878	Benjamin "Pap" Singleton, ***Ho for Kansas!***
1879	Tens of thousands of African Americans, later known as "Exodusters," migrate from southern states to Kansas	1879	***Proceedings of the National Conference of Colored Men of the United States***
1881	Booker T. Washington founds Tuskegee Institute • Spelman College founded as first college for black women in the United States	1882	Ida B. Wells, ***Southern Horrors: Lynch Law in All Its Phases***
1883	Supreme Court overturns Civil Rights Act of 1875		
1884	Moses Fleetwood Walker plays baseball for Toledo Blue Stockings as one of the first black major leaguers	1887	Ida B. Wells, ***"Iola" On Discrimination***
		1889	Josephine Turpin Washington, ***Needs of Our Newspapers***

1890	Oklahoma admitted as the first state with women's suffrage • Mississippi limits black suffrage through "understanding" test, setting precedent for other southern states
1894	*The Women's Era*, later to become the official organ of the National Association of Colored Women, begins publication
1896	Supreme Court approves segregation with "separate but equal" ruling in *Plessy v. Ferguson* • National League of Colored Women and National Federation of Afro-American Women merge to form National Association of Colored Women with Mary Church Terrell as president
1898	Spanish-American War
1904	*AME Church Review* calls for "New Negro Renaissance"
1905	Niagara Movement, dedicated to "aggressive action" for equal rights, is founded by Du Bois and others
1906	Madam C. J. Walker opens hair-care business, eventually becoming one of the first female American millionaires
1907	Alain Locke becomes first African American Rhodes scholar
1908	Jack Johnson becomes first African American heavyweight champion of the world
1909	National Association for the Advancement of Colored People (NAACP) founded by Du Bois and others
1910–1930	Great Migration of over one million southern African Americans to northern cities
1910	*The Crisis*, the official journal of the NAACP, is launched with Du Bois as editor

1892	Frances E. W. Harper, *Iola Leroy*
1895	Booker T. Washington, **The Atlanta Exposition Address** • Henry McNeal Turner, **Response to the Atlanta Exposition Address** • James Crawford Embry, **Afro-American vs. Negro** • Ida B. Wells-Barnett, *A Red Record: Tabulated Statistics and Alleged Causes of Lynching in the United States: 1892, 1893, and 1894*
1900	W. E. B. DuBois, **To the Nations of the World** • Booker T. Washington, *Up From Slavery*
1903	Booker T. Washington, **Industrial Education for the Negro** • W. E. B. Du Bois, **The Talented Tenth** • W. E. B. Du Bois, *The Souls of Black Folk* • W. E. B. Du Bois, **Of Mr. Booker T. Washington and Others**
1912	James Weldon Johnson, *The Autobiography of an Ex-Colored Man*

1914–1918 World War 1

1914 Marcus Garvey organizes The Universal Negro Improvement Association (UNIA) in Jamaica

1915 Booker T. Washington dies

1915 Kelly Miller, *The Risk of Woman Suffrage* • W. E. B. Du Bois, **Woman Suffrage**

1916 Marcus Garvey emigrates to New York from Jamaica and begins Back to Africa movement, establishing the first UNIA branch in the U.S. the following year • Margaret Sanger opens first birth control clinic in United States

1916 Angela Weld Grimké, *Rachel* (performed in Washington, D.C., the first full-length play written, performed, and produced by African Americans in the twentieth century)

1917 United States enters World War I • Thousands of African Americans in a "silent protest parade" down Fifth Avenue in New York City to protest lynching and Jim Crow

1917 *Letters from Southern African Americans to the Chicago Defender* • E. W. Cooke, *Letter to The Montgomery Advertiser* • R. Taylor, *Letter to Professor T. Atwater* • The Reverend I. N. Fritzpatrick, *Letter to The Atlanta Constitution*

1918 Marcus Garvey establishes the newspaper *Negro World*

1918 George Edmund Hayes, *These Are They with Hope in Their Heart* • W. E. B. Du Bois, *Close Ranks* • Hubert Harrison, *The Descent of Du Bois*

1919 Du Bois organizes the first Pan-African Congress in Paris • Eighty three lynchings recorded during Red Summer • American Communist Party organized

1919 Chicago Commission on Race Relations, *A Negro Family Just Arrived from the Rural South* • Wilfred Adolphus Domingo, *What Are We, Negroes or Colored People?* • W. E. B. Du Bois, *Returning Soldiers* • The Messenger, *Following the Advice of the "Old Crowd" Negro and The "New Crowd Negro" Making America Safe for Himself* • W. E. B. Du Bois, *I. W. W.* • A. Philip Randolph and Chandler Owen, *The Crisis of The Crisis* • W. E. B. Du Bois, *Labor Omnia Vincit*

1920 Ratification of Nineteenth Amendment, granting suffrage to women

1920 *The Messenger, Negroes, Leave the South!* • Angelina Weld Grimké, *Rachel: The Play of the Month; The Reason and Synopsis by the Author*

1921 W. E. B. Du Bois, *What Du Bois Thinks of Garvey* • Marcus Garvey, *What Garvey Thinks of Du Bois* • Marcus Garvey, *Address to the Second UNIA Convention* • W. E. B. Du Bois, *Manifesto of the Second Pan-African Congress* • W. E. B. Du Bois, *The Negro and Radical Thought*

1922–1933 Harlem Renaissance

1922	Dyer Anti-Lynching Bill passes U.S. House of Representatives but fails in Senate	**1922**	James Weldon Johnson, **Preface to The Book of American Negro Poetry**
1923	Oklahoma declares martial law to curb KKK	**1923**	Marcus Garvey, *W. E. B. Du Bois as a Hater of Dark People* • A. Philip Randolph, *The Only Way to Redeem Africa* Jean Toomer, *Cane*
		1924	W. E. B. Du Bois, *Marcus Garvey: A Lunatic or a Traitor?* • A. Philip Randolph, *Battling Du Bois vs. Kid Garvey*
1925–1927	Annual literary contests sponsored by *The Crisis* and *Opportunity* magazines		
1925	40,000 KKK members parade in Washington, D.C. • Josephine Baker becomes sensation in Paris through *La Revue Negre*	**1925**	Zora Neale Hurston, *The Emperor Effaces Himself* • Elise Johnson McDougald, *The Double Task: The Struggle of Women for Sex and Race Emancipation* • [W.E.B. Du Bois], Nell Battle Lewis, William S. Turner, and W.A. Robinson, *Race Drama* • Caroline Bond Day, *What Shall We Play?* • W. E. B. Du Bois, *Inter-marriage* • Joel Augustus Rogers, *The Critic: Dean Miller Takes Fright at the Emancipation of the Negro Woman* • Alain Locke, *The New Negro*
		1926	W. E. B. Du Bois, *Criteria of Negro Art* • W. E. B. Du Bois, *"Krigwa Players Little Negro Theatre"* • W. E. B. Du Bois et al., *The Negro in Art* • George S. Schuyler, *The Negro-Art Hokum* • Langston Hughes, *The Negro Artist and the Racial Mountain* • George S. Schuyler, *Letter to the Editor* • Langston Hughes, *Letter to the Editor* • Langston Hughes, *The Weary Blues*
1927	*The Jazz Singer* is the first "talkie" motion picture, with white actor Al Jolson as black-faced minstrel singer	**1927**	George S. Schuyler, *Pan-Africanism: A Waste of Time* • Samuel A. Haynes, *Pan-Africanism: A Mighty Force* • George S. Schuyler, *Pan-Africanism: A Wild Scheme* • Samuel A. Haynes, *Pan-Africanism: The One and Only Way*
		1928	Alain Locke, *Art or Propaganda?* • Zora Neale Hurston, *How it Feels to Be Colored Me* • Nella Larsen, *Quicksand* and *Passing* • Claude McKay, *Home To Harlem* • Marita Bonner, *The Purple Flower*
1929	Stock market crash ushers in Great Depression	**1929**	Augusta Savage, *Gamin* • William Henry Johnson, *Self-Portrait* • Jesse Fauset, *Plum Bun*

1930	W. D. Fard founds Nation of Islam	**1930**	Clarence Mitchell, ***Amos 'n' Andy*** · Roy Wilkins, ***More Amos 'n' Andy*** · *The Crisis*, ***Inter-Marriage: A Symposium*** · A Reader of *The Crisis* and W. E. B. Du Bois, ***About Marrying***
1931	"Scottsboro boys" unjustly convicted of raping two white women in Alabama, prompting nationwide protest	**1932**	Robert Lee Vann, ***Back to the Farm?*** · William Nesbit Jones, ***Self-Determination: The Black Belt Republic Plan*** · Carl Murphy et al., ***Negro Editors on Communism*** · W. E. B. Du Bois, ***Black Folk and Birth Control*** · George S. Schuyler, ***Quantity or Quality*** · Constance Fisher, ***The Negro Social Worker Evaluates Birth Control***
1933	President Roosevelt pushes "New Deal" through Congress	**1933**	Carter G. Woodson, ***The Mis-Education of the Negro*** · W. E. B. Du Bois, ***Marxism and the Negro Problem***
		1934	W. E. B. Du Bois, ***On Segregation*** · W. E. B. Du Bois, ***The N.A.A.C.P. and Race Segregation*** · Walter F. White, ***Reply to W. E. B. Du Bois*** · W. E. B. Du Bois, ***Segregation in the North*** · W. E. B. Du Bois, ***Counsels of Despair*** · Aaron Douglas, ***An Idyll of the Deep South*** · Daily Gleaner, ***Marcus Garvey on Birth Control***
1935	National Council of Negro Women founded	**1935**	Sargent Johnson, ***Head of a Negro Woman*** · Zora Neale Hurston, *Mules and Men*
1936	Jesse Owens wins four gold medals at "Nazi Olympics" in Berlin	**1936**	Father Divine, ***As a Man Thinketh in His Heart So Is He*** · Marcus Garvey, ***Big Conference of UNIA in Canada*** · Palmer Hayden, ***Midsummer Night in Harlem***
1937	Joe Lewis becomes boxing's world heavyweight champion	**1937**	Richard Wright, ***Blueprint for Negro Writing*** · Zora Neale Hurston, *Their Eyes Were Watching God* · Richard Wright, ***Between Laughter and Tears: A Review of Hurston's*** Their Eyes Were Watching God
1938	Chrystal Bird Fauset is the first female African American state legislator	**1938**	Richard Wright, ***Uncle Tom's Children*** · Zora Neale Hurston, ***Stories of Conflict: A Review of Wright's*** Uncle Tom's Children
1939–1945	World War II		
1939	Contralto Marian Anderson sings at Lincoln Memorial for 75,000 after her concert at Constitution Hall was prevented by Daughters of American Revolution		

1940	Hattie McDaniel becomes the first African American to win Academy Award for her role in *Gone With the Wind* (1939)		**1940**	Richard Wright, *Native Son*
1941	United States enters war after Japanese attack on Pearl Harbor · A. Philip Randolph of the Brotherhood of Sleeping Car Porters organizes march on Washington to protest segregation in military and employment discrimination; President Roosevelt issues executive order forbidding racial and religious discrimination in government training programs and defense industries; Randolph calls off march		**1941**	Melville J. Herskovits, **On West African Influences**
			1942	A. Philip Randolph, **Why Should We March?** · Alain Locke, **Who and What Is "Negro"?**
1943	The first successful "sit-in" demonstration staged by Congress of Racial Equality (CORE) · Over 40 killed in race riots in Detroit and Harlem		**1943**	Ralph Ellison, **Editorial Comment** · A. Philip Randolph, **March on Washington Movement Flyer**
			1944	Horace R. Cayton Jr., Frederick Douglass Patterson, and George S. Schuyler, **Round Table: Should Negroes in the South Migrate North?** · William L. Patterson and George S. Schuyler, **Round Table: Have Communists Quit Fighting for Negro Rights?**
			1945	Lelia B. Strayhorn et al., **Round Table: Should Negroes Attend Mixed or Negro Colleges?** · George S. Schuyler and Josephine Schuyler, **Does Interracial Marriage Succeed?** · Julian Lewis, **Can the Negro Afford Birth Control?** · E. Franklin Frazier, **Birth Control for More Negro Babies**
1947	Jackie Robinson signs with the Brooklyn Dodgers, integrating Major League Baseball		**1946**	Ann Petry, *The Street*
1948	President Truman approves desegregation of the military and creates Fair Employment Board		**1948**	Dorothy West, *The Living Is Easy*
			1949	E. Franklin Frazier, **The Negro Family in America** · Claudia Jones, **An End to the Neglect of the Problems of the Negro Woman!** · James Baldwin, **Everybody's Protest Novel** · *Ebony*, **Opposing Views of Newspapers on Walter White's Marriage** · Gwendolyn Brooks, *Annie Allen* (wins Pulitzer Prize in 1950, the first African American to win Pulitzer Prize, in any category)
1950–1953	Korean War			
1950	Ralph J. Bunche is awarded the Nobel Peace Prize for negotiating the 1949 Armistice Agreements that ended the			

1948 Arab-Israeli War, becoming the first
African American to receive the prize

1952   Malcolm X joins Nation of Islam after
release from prison

1954   In *Brown v. Board of Education*, Supreme
Court declares segregated schools unconstitutional, overturning *Plessy v. Ferguson*
(1896) • Malcolm X promoted to Minister of Nation of Islam's New York Temple

1955   Fourteen-year-old Emmett Till lynched
in Mississippi • Rosa Parks arrested for
refusing to give seat on bus to white man,
setting off Montgomery bus boycott led
by Dr. Martin Luther King Jr. • Supreme
Court orders speedy integration of schools
• Interstate Commerce Commission
orders integration of buses, trains, and
waiting rooms for interstate travel

1956   The U.S. Supreme Court rules that
segregation of the Montgomery, Alabama, buses is unconstitutional • One
hundred and one southern congressmen
sign Southern Manifesto against school
desegregation

1957   King and others found the Southern
Christian Leadership Conference (SCLC)
to fight for equal rights • Congress approves Civil Rights Act of 1957 • Federal
troops sent to Alabama to enforce school
desegregation • Ghana is the first African
nation to gain independence from colonial
rule • Althea Gibson is the first African
American woman to win a major title at
Wimbledon

1960   Sit-in staged by four African American
students at Woolworth's lunch counter
in North Carolina; six months later the
same students are served lunch at the
same Woolworth's counter • Student
Nonviolent Coordinating Committee
(SNCC) founded • Congress passes
Civil Rights Act of 1960

1961   Thirteen Freedom Riders sponsored by
CORE take bus trip across South to force

1952   Ralph Ellison, *Invisible Man*

1953   James Baldwin, *Go Tell It on the Mountain*

1955   James Baldwin, *Notes of a Native Son*

1956   Richard Wright, ***Tradition and Industrialization: The Plight of the Tragic Elite
in Africa*** • Esther Popel Shaw, ***Review of
Frazier's* Bourgeoisie Noire**

1957   E. Franklin Frazier, ***Black Bourgeoisie***

1958   Martin Luther King Jr., ***My Pilgrimage to
Nonviolence***

1959   Lorraine Hansberry, *A Raisin in the Sun*
(first Broadway play by an African American woman)

1960   Malcolm X and Bayard Rustin, ***A Choice
of Two Roads***

integration of terminals • Hoyt Fuller
revives *Negro Digest*

1962 Riots break out after Supreme Court
orders University of Mississippi to accept James H. Meredith as the first black
student; nearly 30,000 federal troops are
employed to restore order and ensure
Meredith's admission

1963 National support for civil rights roused
after police attacked Alabama demonstration led by King; King arrested • Civil
rights March on Washington attracts
over 200,000 demonstrators; King delivers
"I Have a Dream" speech • Vivian Malone and James Hood register for classes
at University of Alabama, even though
Governor George Wallace tries to physically block them • President Kennedy
assassinated • Bombing of the Sixteenth
Street Baptist Church in Birmingham,
Alabama, kills four African American girls

1964 Congress passes Civil Rights Act of
1964 and Economic Opportunity Act
• Malcolm X founds Organization of
Afro-American Unity, officially splitting
with Elijah Muhammad and the Black
Muslims • Civil rights groups including
SNCC, CORE, and the NAACP launch
Mississippi "Freedom Summer," a massive voter registration drive; three CORE
workers murdered in Mississippi by white
segregationists • King wins Nobel Peace
Prize • Twenty-fourth Amendment
ratified, outlawing poll tax used to limit
black suffrage • Sidney Poitier becomes
the first black actor to win an Academy
Award for Best Actor for *Lilies of the
Field* (1963) • Cassius Clay wins world
heavyweight boxing championship, subsequently converts to Islam and changes
name to Muhammad Ali

1965–73 Vietnam War

1965 Malcolm X assassinated in New York
City • King leads march from Selma to
Montgomery, Alabama • Voting Rights
Act outlaws efforts to disenfranchise
voters • Watts riot is most serious single

1962 James Farmer and Malcolm X, *A Debate
at Cornell University* • E. Franklin
Frazier, *Preface to* **Black Bourgeoisie**
• Adrienne Kennedy, *Funnyhouse of a
Negro* (wins Obie award in 1964)

1963 Malcolm X, *Message to the Grassroots*
• Martin Luther King Jr., *Letter from
Birmingham Jail* • Irving Howe, *Black
Boys and Native Sons* • LeRoi Jones,
Enter the Middle Class • Ralph Ellison,
The World and the Jug

1964 Howard Zinn, *The Limits of Nonviolence*
• Malcolm X, *Letter from Saudi Arabia*
• Ralph Ellison, *Review of Jones's* **Blues
People** • Amiri Baraka, *Dutchman*
(wins Obie award)

1965 Bayard Rustin, *Protest to Politics*
• Staughton Lynd, *Coalition Politics or
Nonviolent Revolution?* • James Farmer,
Freedom—When? • Elijah Muhammad,
Program and Position: What Do the

racial disturbance in U.S. history · Black Arts Movement started by Amiri Baraka in Harlem

Muslims Want? · Daniel Patrick Moynihan, *The Negro Family: The Case For National Action* · William Ryan, *The New Genteel Racism* · Alex Haley, *The Autobiography of Malcolm X*

1966 Black Panther Party founded · National Organization for Women (NOW) founded · SNCC leader Stokely Carmichael coins the phrase Black Power in a speech in Seattle · Black Power concept is adopted by CORE and SNCC · Kwanzaa is created by Maulana Ron Karenga

1966 Martin Luther King Jr., **Nonviolence: The Only Road to Freedom** · Huey Newton and Bobby Seale, **October 1966 Black Panther Platform and Program** · Phyl Garland, **The Natural Look: Many Negro Women Reject White Standards of Beauty** · Readers of *Ebony*, **Letters on "The Natural Look"** · Long Aid Brands, **Long Aid K7** · Supreme Beauty Products, **Duke Greaseless Hair Pomade**

1967 King announces his opposition to Vietnam War · Worst race riot in U.S. history in Detroit kills fourty three; major riots in Newark and Chicago · Senator Edward W. Brooke (R-MA) becomes the first African American senator since Reconstruction · Thurgood Marshall becomes the first African American U.S. Supreme Court justice · Supreme Court overturns law against interracial marriage in *Virginia v. Loving*

1968 King assassinated in Memphis · Senator Robert F. Kennedy assassinated in Los Angeles · President Johnson signs Civil Rights Act of 1968 outlawing discrimination in housing · Shirley Chisholm becomes the first African American woman elected to U.S. Congress · Arthur Ashe is the first African American to win the U.S. Open

1968 Larry Neal, **The Black Arts Movement** · Huey Newton, **Huey Newton Talks to The Movement** · Elsie C. Rollock, **A Negro Speaks to Jews** · Rayner W. Mann, **A Negro Discusses Anti-Semitism**

1969 Major antiwar demonstrations in Washington, D.C.

1969 Eugene D. Genovese, **Black Studies: Trouble Ahead** · June Jordan, **Black Studies: Bringing Back the Person** · James H. Cone, **Black Theology and Black Power** · Nikki Giovanni, **Black Poems, Poseurs, and Power** · Morrie Turner, **Humor in Hue** · Charles Gordon, *No Place to Be Somebody* (wins Pulitzer Prize in 1970)

1970 Toni Cade Bambara edits *The Black Woman* · The business magazine *Black Enterprise* established

1970 Shirley Chisholm, **Facing the Abortion Question** · Frances M. Beal, **Double Jeopardy: To Be Black and Female** · Linda La Rue, **The Black Movement and Women's Liberation** · Darwin T. Turner, **The Teaching of Afro-American Literature**

• Albert Murray, **James Baldwin, Protest Fiction, and the Blues Tradition** • Toni Morrison, *The Bluest Eye*

1971 Supreme Court approves busing as method of desegregation • Supreme Court rules closing of Mississippi swimming pools to avoid desegregation is constitutional • Jessie Jackson founds Operation PUSH (People United to Serve Humanity) • Congressional Black Caucus formed by fifteen African American members of Congress

1971 Addison Gayle Jr., **Introduction to The Black Aesthetic** • Joan Downs, **Black/White Dating** • Readers of *Life*, **Letters on "Black/White Dating"** • Dick Gregory, **My Answer to Genocide** • Readers of *Ebony*, **Letters on "My Answer to Genocide"**

1972 Congress passes Equal Rights Amendment, which goes to states for ratification • Congress passes Equal Employment Opportunity Act that extends enforcement and punishment for job discrimination • Chisholm is the first African American woman to run for U.S. president • Barbara Jordan of Houston and Andrew Young of Atlanta become the first African Americans elected to Congress from the South since Reconstruction

1973 Supreme Court prohibits state restrictions on abortions in *Roe v. Wade* • Tom Bradley elected mayor of Los Angeles • Maynard Jackson elected mayor of Atlanta

1973 Barbara Sizemore, **Sexism and the Black Male** • William R. Jones, **Divine Racism: The Unacknowledged Threshold Issue for Black Theology**

1974 Henry Louis "Hank" Aaron breaks Babe Ruth's record by hitting his 715th home run • Clive "Hercules" Campbell, aka "Kool Herc," initiates rap music in the Bronx

1974 June Jordan, **On Richard Wright and Zora Neale Hurston: Notes toward a Balancing of Love and Hatred**

1975 Arthur Ashe is the first African American man to win the single's championship at Wimbledon

1975 Ntozake Shange, **for colored girls who have considered suicide when the rainbow is enuf** (the second play by an African American woman to reach Broadway)

1976 Alex Haley, *Roots* (awarded special Pulitzer Prize in 1977)

1977 TV miniseries based on Alex Haley's *Roots* attracts more viewers than any television program in history

1977 Barbara Smith, **Toward a Black Feminist Criticism** • Combahee River Collective, **A Black Feminist Statement** • James Allen McPherson, *Elbow Room* (wins Pulitzer Prize in 1978)

1978 In *Regents of the University of California v. Bakke*, Supreme Court disallows quotas for college admissions but gives limited approval to affirmative action programs

1978 Thurgood Marshall, **Opinion on Regents of the University of California v. Bakke** • William Julius Wilson, **The Declining**

Significance of Race • Charles Vert Willie, *The Inclining Significance of Race* • William Julius Wilson, **The Declining Significance of Race: Revisited but Not Revised**

1979 Jacquelyn Grant, **Black Theology and the Black Woman** • Michele Wallace, **Black Macho and the Myth of the Superwoman** • Robert Staples, **The Myth of Black Macho: A Response to Angry Black Feminists** • Alice Walker, *I Love Myself When I Am Laughing . . . And Then Again When I Am Looking Mean and Impressive: A Zora Neale Hurston Reader* (brings Hurston's work back into print)

1980 Liberian president William Tolbert ousted by Staff Sergeant Samuel K. Doe, ending over 130 years of Americo-Liberian rule over indigenous Africans • Robert L. Johnson founds Black Entertainment Television (BET), later selling it to Viacom for some $3 billion

1981 Charles Fuller, *A Soldier's Play* (wins Pulitzer Prize in 1982)

1982 Michael Jackson's *Thriller* sells $110 million, becoming the best-selling recording of all time • Equal Rights Amendment fails after ten years, three states short of ratification

1982 Alice Walker, *The Color Purple* (wins Pulitzer Prize and the National Book Award in 1983)

1983 Louis Gossett, Jr., wins Academy Award for Best Actor in a Supporting Role for *An Officer and a Gentleman* (1982) • Vanessa Williams crowned the first black Miss America

1983 Cheryl Clarke, **The Failure to Transform: Homophobia in the Black Community**

1984 August Wilson's *Ma Rainey's Black Bottom* opens on Broadway • Jesse Jackson wins 17 percent of the popular vote in the Democratic primary in the first serious bid by an African American man for the U. S. presidency • *The Cosby Show*, about a professional African American family in Brooklyn, New York, premieres and becomes the biggest hit on television during the 1980s, running for eight seasons

1985 Oprah Winfrey's talk show *The Oprah Winfrey Show* is syndicated in more than 120 cities, eventually becoming the highest rated talk show in television history

1985 Glenn C. Loury, **Beyond Civil Rights** • Beth E. Richie, **Battered Black Women: A Challenge for the Black Community**

1986 Martin Luther King Jr's birthday officially celebrated as federal holiday • Wole

1986 Clarence Thomas, **Views on Affirmative Action** • Randall Kennedy, **Persuasion**

Soyinka of Nigeria is the first person of African descent to win Nobel Prize for Literature

and Distrust • August Wilson, *Fences* (wins Pulitzer Prize in 1987) • Rita Dove, *Thomas and Beulah* (wins Pulitzer Prize in 1987)

1987 Henry Louis Gates, Jr. et al., ***The Black Person in Art: How Should S/He Be Portrayed?*** • Delores S. Williams, ***Womanist Theology: Black Women's Voices*** • Toni Morrison, *Beloved* (wins Pulitzer Prize in 1988)

1988 Jesse Jackson receives 24 percent of the popular vote in the democratic presidential primary, coming in second to Michael Dukakis

1989 Frederick Drew Gregory becomes the first African American to command a space shuttle • L. Douglas Wilder of Virginia is the first elected black governor since Reconstruction • General Colin Powell becomes the first black Chief of Staff for U.S. Armed Forces • 500,000 march in Washington for pro-choice rally • Supreme Court approves state limits on abortion

1990 Nelson Mandela is freed after twenty seven years in prison in South Africa • August Wilson wins Pulitzer Prize for Broadway play *The Piano Lesson* (1989) • Charles Johnson's *Middle Passage* wins National Book Award • Denzel Washington wins Best Supporting Actor Academy Award for his role in *Glory* (1989), about the all-black 54th Massachusetts regiment in the Civil War

1990 William Julius Wilson, ***Race-Neutral Programs and the Democratic Coalition*** • Laura B. Randolph, ***What Can We Do about the Most Explosive Problem in Black America: The Widening Gap between Women Who Are Making It and Men Who Aren't*** • Portia K. Maultsby, ***Africanisms in African American Music***

1991 Clarence Thomas confirmed as Supreme Court Justice following contentious confirmation hearings that included sexual harassment testimony from Anita Hill • Civil Rights Act of 1991 strengthens laws against job discrimination and provides damages for intentional employment discrimination

1991 Clarence Thomas, ***First Statement to the Senate Judiciary Committee*** • Anita F. Hill, ***Statement to the Senate Judiciary Committee*** • Clarence Thomas, ***Second Statement to the Senate Judiciary Committee*** • Orlando Patterson, ***Race, Gender and Liberal Fallacies*** • Elsa Barkley Brown, Deborah King, Barbara Ransby, et al., ***African American Women in Defense of Themselves***

1992 Police acquitted of beating Rodney King, setting off riots in Los Angeles • Mae Jemison becomes the first black female astronaut • Carol Moseley Braun of Illinois becomes the first African American woman elected to the U.S. Senate

1992 Deborah K. King, ***Unraveling Fabric, Missing the Beat: Class and Gender in Afro-American Social Issues*** • Kathy Russell, Midge Wilson, and Ronald Hall, ***Hair: The Straight and Nappy of It All*** • Angela Y. Davis and Ice Cube, ***Nappy Happy:***

• Supreme Court rules against state bans of "hate speech"

A Conversation with Ice Cube • Henry Louis Gates, Jr., **Black Demagogues and Pseudo-Scholars**

1993 Toni Morrison is the first African American to win Nobel Prize for Literature • Rita Dove becomes the first African American U.S. Poet Laureate • Maya Angelou reads "On the Pulse of Morning" at Clinton inauguration, becoming the first black poet to participate in a U.S. presidential inauguration • Supreme Court disallows congressional districts drawn to increase black representation

1993 Evelyn Brooks Higginbotham, **The Black Church: A Gender Perspective** • Barbara Ransby and Tracye Matthews, **Black Popular Culture and the Transcendence of Patriarchal Illusions** • Barbara Smith, **Blacks and Gays: Healing the Great Divide** • Vince Nobile, **White Professors, Black History: Forays into the Multicultural Classroom** • Cynthia Fleming, **Race beyond Reason** • Molefi Kete Asante, **Where Is the White Professor Located?** • Yosef Komunyahkaa, *Neon Vernacular* (wins Pulitzer Prize) • David Levering Lewis, *W. E. B. DuBois: Biography of a Race, 1868–1919* (wins Pulitzer Prize in 1994)

1994 O. J. Simpson accused of murdering ex-wife and her friend; ensuing trial grips nation

1995 O. J. Simpson acquitted of murder charges in criminal trial • Million Man March in Washington organized by Nation of Islam minister Louis Farrakhan • Colin Powell is the first African American seriously considered as a presidential candidate of a major party

1995 Cornel West, **Why I'm Marching in Washington** • A. Leon Higginbotham, Jr., **Why I Didn't March** • Johnnie Cochran, **Closing Argument of the Defense in The People v. Orenthal James Simpson** • Christopher Darden, **Closing Argument of the Prosecution in The People v. Orenthal James Simpson** • Henry Louis Gates, Jr., **Thirteen Ways of Looking at a Black Man** • August Wilson, *Seven Guitars* (opens on Broadway in 1996)

1996 Texaco settles $176-million class action racial discrimination suit by African American employees denied promotions and pay increases

1996 Cornel West, **Affirmative Action in Context** • Michael Eric Dyson, **Gangsta Rap and American Culture** • Afro.com Website Commentators, **Reactions to the Million Man March** • Roy L. Brooks, **The Case for a Policy of Limited Separation** • Board of Education of the Oakland, California, Unified School District, **Resolution Adopting the Report and Recommendations of the African American Task Force** (rev. 1997)

1997 California voters pass Proposition 209 banning all state affirmative action; initiative sponsored by Ward Connerly • Tiger Woods becomes the youngest and the first African American golfer to win the Master's tournament

1997 Dorothy Roberts, **The Dark Side of Birth Control** • Louis Farrakhan and Tim Russert, **Interview on Meet the Press** • Bill Cosby, **Elements of Igno-Ebonics Style** • Ellis Cose, **Why Ebonics Is Irrelevant** • John R. Rickford, **Letter to the**

Editor on Cose's *"Why Ebonics Is Irrelevant"* · Brent Staples, *The Last Train
from Oakland: Will the Middle Class Flee
the Ebonics Fad?* · John Baugh, *Ebonics
Isn't 'Street English' but a Heritage*

1998   Voters in Washington state pass Initiative
        200 outlawing all state affirmative action,
        also sponsored by Ward Connerly · O. J.
        Simpson found guilty of wrongful death
        in civil trial

1998   Brent Staples, *The Quota Bashers Come
        In from the Cold*

1999   African American farmers win class ac-
        tion suit against U.S. Department of Ag-
        riculture for discrimination in granting
        of loans and subsidies · Amadou Diallo
        is mistakenly shot and killed by police
        officers in New York, raising public outcry

1999   John Baugh, *Interview with an Unidenti-
        fied Woman* · Margo Jefferson, *Labels
        Change, Carrying Different Emotional
        Baggage* · John Baugh, *Changing Terms
        of Self-Reference among American Slave
        Descendants* · Kara Walker, *Out of
        Africa* · Ralph Ellison, *Juneteenth*
        (published posthumously)

2000   Coca-Cola Company settles largest
        racial discrimination suit in U.S. history,
        agreeing to pay 192.5 million to African
        American employees · Venus Williams
        wins singles title in tennis at Wimbledon,
        the first black woman to win since Althea
        Gibson in 1958 · President Bush ap-
        points General Colin L. Powell secretary
        of state and Condoleezza Rice national
        security advisor

2000   John R. Rickford, *Linguistics, Education,
        and the Ebonics Firestorm* · Aaron Mc-
        Gruder, *The Boondocks: Because I Know
        You Don't Read the Newspaper* · Jack
        Hitt et al., *Making the Case for Racial
        Reparations* · Adolph L. Reed Jr., *The
        Case against Reparations* · Randall
        Robinson, *The Debt: What America
        Owes to Blacks*

2001   Lewis wins second Pulitzer Prize in
        Biography for *W. E. B. Du Bois: The Fight
        for Equality and the American Century,
        1919–1963* · On September 11, terrorists
        hijack four commercial jetliners; two crash
        into World Trade Center in New York,
        one into Pentagon, and one into a field in
        Pennsylvania

2001   Us Helping Us, *On the Down Low*

2002   Halle Berry becomes the first African
        American woman to win Academy
        Award for Best Actress, for *Monster's Ball*
        (2001) · Denzel Washington is the first
        black actor since Poitier to win an Oscar
        for Best Actor, for *Training Day* (2001)
        · Honorary Lifetime Achievement
        Academy Award given to Sidney Poitier
        · Suzan-Lori Parks wins Pulitzer Prize in
        Drama for *Topdog/Underdog*

2002   Hannah Craft, *The Bondwoman's Nar-
        rative* (written c. 1850s, the only known
        novel written by a female fugitive slave)

2003 Illinois governor George Ryan grants clemency to all 160 death-row inmates after his 2002 blue-ribbon Commission on Capital Punishment finds systematic failures • In *Grutter v. Bollinger,* Supreme Court rules that University of Michigan Law School's affirmative action policy is constitutional

2005 Condoleezza Rice becomes the first black female secretary of state • Hurricane Katrina hits Mississippi and Louisiana, devastating New Orleans

2006 Michael Eric Dyson, ***Is Bill Cosby Right?***

2006 Barack Obama (D-IL) elected to the U.S. Senate, becoming the third African American elected to the Senate since Reconstruction

2007 Tony Cox and Bishop Harry Jackson, ***Homosexuality in the Black Church*** • Noma LeMoine, ***Contrastive Analysis: A Linguistic Strategy for Advancing Language Acquisition in Standard English Learners (SELs)*** • K. T. Bradford, ***Why "Black" and Not "African-American"?***

2008 Obama becomes the first African American nominated for president by a major party, defeating Senator Hilary Clinton • Obama elected President of the United States, defeating Senator John McCain

2008 Barack Obama, ***A More Perfect Union*** • Gloria Steinem, ***Women are Never Front-Runners*** • DeNeen L. Brown, ***A Vote of Allegiance***

2009 Obama sworn in as 44th president of the United States • Eric H. Holder, Jr. becomes first African American Attorney General of the United States

The Time of Slavery (to 1865)

A fricans were among the earliest explorers of the New World. Thirty black explorers, including Nuflo de Olano, were with Balboa when the Spaniard documented the discovery of the Pacific Ocean in 1513, and a Moroccan-born man named Estéban was part of Pánfilo de Narváez's expedition to Florida in 1528. It was the European colonization of the New World and the introduction of chattel slavery, however, that brought the overwhelming majority of Africans to the Americas. Between 1501 and 1867, 12.5 million Africans embarked for the Americas as forced labor, the vast majority to South America and the Caribbean Islands, in one of the largest and most oppressive migrations in human history. Although only about 450,000 Africans arrived in the United States, their forced enslavement fundamentally informed the subsequent unprecedented economic development of the country.

African slavery existed on a small scale in Europe at least since the Middle Ages and throughout the Renaissance, but these enslaved men and women mostly labored as servants for wealthy white Europeans. Europeans justified the enslavement of Africans by claiming that they were civilizing them, introducing them to the wonders of "reason" and saving their souls by converting them to Christianity. European colonization of the New World, beginning in the late 1400s, dramatically increased the need for inexpensive labor to exploit the New World's extensive natural resources. At first, the colonists used Native Americans as slaves, but the diseases brought by the Europeans devastated the native population. The Spanish began using African slave labor in the early 1500s in their colonies, first in the Caribbean and then in the Americas.

The first record of black slave labor in the territory that would become the United States—as well as the first black slave rebellion and escape—dates to 1526. Black slaves with a Spanish expedition led by Lucas Vásquez de Ayllón helped found the colony of San Miguel de Gualdape, on the coast of what is now South Carolina or Georgia. When the colony foundered following Ayllón's death from fever the same year, the slaves rebelled; some escaped to live with Native Americans.

When the British began colonizing the New World, starting with Jamestown, Virginia, in 1607, they did not use slavery. Instead, they mostly relied on white indentured servants, who were bound to work for a specific period of time—usually between four and seven years—in exchange for their passage to the colony. It took decades for a system of racial slavery to develop in the British colonies. But once it did arrive, its effects were devastating for the African population back on the continent. Yet, it was such a fundamental component of economic prosperity in America that only a dreadfully costly civil war could bring an end to this brutal institution.

In 1619, the first African slaves arrived in Jamestown. "Twenty and odd" slaves, captured in what is today Angola by Portuguese slavers, were traded to Jamestown settlers in exchange for food. Since the Africans had been baptized, they couldn't be enslaved under English law and instead became like indentured servants, supplementing the labor of European indentured servants in the colony.

The system of indentured servitude had its problems: as poor Europeans learned of the harsh conditions in the colonies, fewer volunteered for indenture, and servants who had completed their terms of service became part of an increasingly large and disorderly population of poor free people, a situation that threatened the prosperous settlers. African slavery was proving to be highly profitable in the Caribbean, and the British colonists began to see slavery as a way to supplement and eventually replace indentured servitude. Less than fifty years after the first Africans arrived in Jamestown, the British colonies in the New World began slowly and systematically passing laws to limit the rights of black people while increasingly relying on African labor.

The first evidence of an African being declared a slave in America comes from 1640. John Punch was one of three indentured servants who were sentenced by a Virginia court for running away. The two other servants, a Scotsman and a Dutchman, were each sentenced to four years of service beyond their indenture. In contrast, the court ordered the African to "serve his said master or his assigns for the time of his natural life here or elsewhere." The court's justification for the discrepancy in sentencing was that the African was the only non-Christian. The colonial leaders could not use religion as the basis for a stable system of slavery, however, since non-Christians could readily convert. In response, they began passing explicitly race-based laws to narrow or eliminate the rights of all people of African descent.

In 1641, Massachusetts became the first colony to recognize slavery as a legal institution, and the other colonies soon followed suit. By 1705, Virginia and other colonies had established a system of racial slavery that was both a life sentence and hereditary— slaves not only were slaves for the course of their own lives but also passed along the condition of servitude in perpetuity, through the mother, with children of an enslaved mother enslaved as well, forever. Other than for a brief period in Maryland, children of a white mother and a black father were free, once they had served a period of indenture mandated in some colonies.

The rights of free black people were simultaneously eroded. In 1691, it was declared illegal to free a black slave in Virginia unless the freed person left the colony. Moreover, free black people were sometimes captured and sold illegally back into slavery. Beginning with North Carolina in 1715, colonies began eliminating the voting rights of all black residents. The emergence of Enlightenment natural philosophy in the middle of the eighteenth century provided a "scientific" basis for this systematic racial discrimination. European philosophers and the forerunners of today's anthropologists developed pseu-

doscientific theories about a supposedly causal relation among apparent biological differences, group characteristics, and the cultures of different ethnic groups. Ideologically
driven ideas about the intellectual inferiority of people of African descent were drawn
on to reinforce an economic system based on the exploitation of free African slave labor.

African slavery provided enormous economic benefits to colonists in both the
North and the South. Slave labor fueled agriculture in the South, and southern crops in
turn provided the raw materials for the industrial economy of the North. The slave trade
itself was also extremely profitable. The Royal African Company, chartered in 1672,
established a triangle of trade that began and ended in England. Ships took goods from
English ports to Africa to trade in exchange for slaves. The wretched second leg—
known as the Middle Passage—took the enslaved Africans to the New World, where
they were traded for raw materials. To maximize profits, slave traders typically packed
more than 300 Africans into the hold of a ship, and over 12 percent of them died during
the journey from disease, dehydration, shipwrecks, or, sometimes, suicide. The third leg
of the slave trade took raw materials and finished products from the New World back to
England, where they were sold.

Between 1700 and 1770, the number of black slaves in the North grew from about
5,000 to nearly 50,000. In the South, the enslaved population increased sixteen-fold,
from under 25,000 to over 400,000, with black people outnumbering white people in
some communities. A turning point in the relations between the white colonists and the
enslaved Africans came in 1739. A group of enslaved Angolans in South Carolina staged
an uprising that grew to roughly 100 marching toward freedom in Florida, killing white
colonists along the way. The uprising, known as the Stono Rebellion, terrified white
enslavers and convinced them that black slaves had to be controlled absolutely. South Carolina passed the restrictive Negro Act of 1740, and black slaves lost what few limited rights
they had been allowed. They were prohibited from learning to read, gathering in large
groups, earning money, playing the drum, or traveling without a pass. Owners were permitted to maim or kill slaves who tried to escape. The Negro Act of 1740 served as a model
for restrictive slave codes in other southern states, such as the Georgia slave code of 1755.

The abolitionist movement developed coterminously with the introduction and
expansion of racial slavery. Rhode Island passed the first law abolishing slavery in 1652
(which was reversed in 1715), and in 1712 Pennsylvania became the first colony to pass a
law to prevent slave trading, although it was disallowed by Great Britain the following
year. In the era of the Revolutionary War, the language of liberty and freedom used by
the colonists resonated with enslaved and free alike. Even though the Declaration of
Independence pointedly did not address slavery, its central principle, that "all men are
created equal," became a rallying cry for abolitionists. But under George Washington's
command, black men were denied a place in the Continental army until 1777, two years
into the war, and when the British promised to free any slaves who fought for the Crown,
tens of thousands joined the Loyalist army against the Patriots—only to be reenslaved
when the British were defeated in 1783. (Scholars estimate that 5,000 black men served

in the Continental army.) After the Revolutionary War, slavery declined in the North but grew even more deeply entrenched in the South, especially after the invention of Eli Whitney's cotton gin.

In 1777, Vermont became the first territory to outlaw slavery in its constitution, and New York extended suffrage to qualified black males the same year, with other northern states soon following. This division between North and South shaped the writing of the U.S. Constitution. Wary of the growing political power of the North, southerners at the Constitutional Convention of 1787 insisted that slaves be counted as part of the population when determining how many representatives a state would send to Congress. Northern and southern representatives reached a compromise by agreeing to count each slave as three fifths of a person. The Constitution also included the Fugitive Slave Clause, which mandated that runaway slaves be returned to their owners, and a guarantee that the international slave trade could continue for another twenty years. Even though the word *slavery* never appears in the Constitution, it was deeply ingrained in this founding document of the republic of the United States.

Although slavery had been waning in many regions of the United States since the Revolutionary War, it received a powerful boost in 1794, when the northern inventor Eli Whitney patented the cotton gin. By mechanizing the removal of seeds from raw cotton, the invention made harvesting cotton much less labor intensive—and therefore much more profitable. Plantation owners in the South began planting more cotton and employing more slave labor to grow and pick it, thereby increasing the demand for slaves. Northerners also benefited from the cotton boom, as they established factories to mill the cotton and supplied the ships and the crews to transport cotton, which grew to account for over one half of all U.S. exports. After the Louisiana Purchase of 1803 (which doubled the size of the United States), the cotton boom propelled westward expansion and extended slavery into new territories. The cotton boom would also lead to the passage in 1830 of the Indian Removal Act, which led to the expulsion of the Five Civilized Tribes—the Choctaw, Chickasaw, Creek, Cherokee, and Seminole peoples—from Mississippi, Alabama, Georgia, and Florida. The Cherokee took their black slaves along with them to Indian Territory, today's state of Oklahoma, on the arduous 1838 march known as the Trail of Tears.

While states in the Deep South planted more and more cotton, states in the Upper South were shifting to crops that required less labor, like wheat. After the United States outlawed the importation of slaves on January 1, 1808 (the first day allowed by the Constitution), the value of slaves escalated, fueled by demand in newly opened territories, including Alabama, Mississippi, Louisiana, and Texas. The ban on importing new slaves from Africa (spottily enforced) stimulated the internal slave trade, and the states of the Upper South became the main suppliers, leading to one of the largest migrations in American history, as more than one million slaves were transported from the Upper South to the Deep South. Families and communities that had been relatively stable were torn apart as slave owners sold more and more people into the Deep South. A much smaller number of African Americans managed to run away to the North to avoid being sold into the harsh working and living environment of what, after 1830, would become known as the Cotton Kingdom.

One of the main threats to slavery at the turn of the century was the rapidly growing free black population. Between 1790 and 1810, the free black population in the North and the South grew from 60,000 to 186,000, propelled by a variety of factors. These included states passing manumission laws and individuals, particularly Quakers after 1782, freeing their own slaves and sometimes even purchasing slaves in order to free them. Not only did the economic, literary, and political success of free African Americans challenge the theory that they were inferior—the primary rationale for their enslavement—but many free African Americans also became leading figures in the expanding abolitionist movement. Southern states responded by further restricting the rights of free black people, with some states even requiring them to leave the state if they gained their freedom, just as Virginia had mandated in the colonial era. Nevertheless, by 1860 more free African Americans were living in the states that would form the Confederacy and the border states than were living in the North. And a significant percentage of the free Negro heads of households in those states owned slaves themselves, often family members whom they couldn't free due to restrictive state laws. In 1816, a group of influential white men established the American Colonization Society, dedicated to sending free black Americans to colonies in Africa. Although some embraced the idea of emigration—perhaps 15,000 free black Americans moved to Africa, founding the country of Liberia and settling in Sierra Leone through the support of the American Colonization Society—the vast majority of African Americans adamantly rejected proposals to send them to Africa. Indeed, widespread resistance to the American Colonization Society helped to galvanize the black abolitionist movement.

The evangelical religious movement known as the Second Great Awakening, which started in the 1790s and continued to the 1840s, also gave life to a nascent anti-slavery movement. The Second Great Awakening stressed individual morality and motivated both black and white converts to fight the "sin" of slavery. Although the Second Great Awakening dramatically increased the scale of religion-based abolitionist fervor throughout the North, religion had long played a large role in the abolitionist movement. Quakers established the first anti-slavery society in the world in 1775, and Quakers like Paul Cuffe (the wealthiest black man in America and a staunch African colonizationist) and, much later, Susan B. Anthony were leaders in the abolitionist movement. Moreover, some of the rebellions against slavery were inspired by the religious convictions of their leaders, such as Nat Turner's slave rebellion in 1831 and John Brown's ill-fated attempt to take over the federal arsenal in Harpers Ferry, Virginia (now West Virginia), in 1859.

While the abolitionist movement expanded in the North, the federal government attempted to manage the widening gulf between the interests of the slaveholding and free states, which would eventually culminate in the Civil War. The Missouri Compromise of 1820 regulated the growth of slavery in the new western territories, allowing slavery in Missouri and the Arkansas Territory but prohibiting it in the unorganized territory of the Great Plains. While Missouri joined the Union as a slave state, Maine entered the Union as a free state, thereby maintaining an even number of slaveholding and free states. A series of subsequent legislative compromises attempted to balance the interests of slaveholding states and free states. Among them was the Compromise of 1850, which involved the much-hated Fugitive Slave Act, according to which runaway slaves had to be returned to their owners and anyone aiding a slave who had escaped to the North would be punished. The Kansas-Nebraska Act of 1854 overturned the Missouri Compromise by allowing territories in the Great Plains to determine their own status as free or slave states even though they were formerly designated as free. Violence erupted between free-staters and pro-slavery settlers in a proxy war that became known as Bleeding Kansas and lasted until Kansas entered the Union as a free state in 1861. In the decades leading up to the Civil War, the North outpaced the South in both population growth and economic development, and the escalating abolitionist movement further fractured the fragile balance of power between the regions.

The conflict between pro- and anti-slavery sentiments was further inflamed by the 1857 *Dred Scott* decision and John Brown's 1859 raid on Harpers Ferry. In the *Dred Scott* decision, the Supreme Court ruled that no black person, free or slave, could be a citizen of the United States. It also declared that the Missouri Compromise of 1820 was unconstitutional because prohibiting slavery in new states violated citizens' property rights. While southerners supported the ruling for upholding state sovereignty, northerners saw it as a signal that slaveholding interests were determined to extend slavery throughout the nation. The raid on Harpers Ferry—in which Brown and twenty-one followers raided a federal arsenal with the hope of distributing arms to rebelling slaves and sparking a broad contagious insurrection—had the opposite effect. Many northerners were swayed by Brown's passionate anti-slavery testimony during his trial and hailed him as a martyr. Southern slaveholders, however, saw the event as evidence that northerners were going to stop at nothing to overturn slavery.

Abraham Lincoln's election as president in 1860 was the final straw for the South. Afraid that Lincoln would outlaw slavery, South Carolina seceded from the Union and was quickly followed by other states in the Deep South. Lincoln attempted to prevent the border states from seceding by distancing himself from the abolitionist cause and instead framed the conflict as a fight to preserve the Union. After the Civil War began, following an attack on Fort Sumter by South Carolina troops, Lincoln refused to accept African Americans into the military, believing that doing so would further ignite southern rebellion. Only after the North appeared to be losing the war did Lincoln, like George Washington in the Revolutionary War, reverse his decision and allow African Americans to fight in the Union army. Indeed, Lincoln included this provision as part of the Emancipation Proclamation itself.

On January 1, 1863, Lincoln issued the Emancipation Proclamation, freeing all slaves owned by rebels in the South. The proclamation did not free slaves in states under the control of the Union, including the border states—Delaware, Maryland, Missouri, Kentucky, and West Virginia. The proclamation was aimed at destroying the rebel war effort and its economy, not ending slavery per se. In the minds of the free and the enslaved alike, however, the proclamation officially transformed the conflict into a war to end slavery. Two hundred thousand free black Americans and former slaves joined the Union forces, and some 500,000 slaves—of the 3.9 million registered in the 1860 census—escaped across Union lines to gain their freedom. On December 6, 1865, eight months after the end of the Civil War, the Thirteenth Amendment—passionately supported by Abraham Lincoln in the last months of his presidency—was ratified, permanently outlawing the institution of slavery in the United States.

KEY DEBATE ⁓ *Nature, Culture, and Slavery*

DAVID HUME

from *Of National Characters* [1748, revision published 1777]

David Hume (Scottish; 1711–1776), the first modern philosopher to develop a secular moral philosophy, played a central role in the development of Western ideas about racial classification. In "Of National Characters," originally published in 1748, Hume develops the idea that different "species" of humans have different types of moral characters and that these differences are innate, not a result of environment. The short excerpt reprinted here contains one of Hume's only specific statments about Africans, yet despite its brevity, it was hugely influential. At the time that Hume was writing "Of National Characters," the field of racial classification was in its infancy, and Hume's prominence as a philosopher lent credence to theories about the innate superiority and inferiority of different races.

In *Race and the Enlightenment* (1997), Emmanuel Chukwudi Eze notes that Hume revised his essay between 1753 and 1754 and again before his death, in 1776, to characterize Africans explicitly as racially inferior. In 1754, Hume added a footnote to state, "I am apt to suspect the negroes and in general all other species of men (for there are four or five different kinds) to be naturally inferior to the whites. There never was a civilized nation of any other complexion than white." In the version that was published posthumously in 1777, however, Hume changed the claim to "I am apt to suspect the negroes to be naturally inferior to the whites. There scarcely ever was a civilized nation of that complexion, nor even any individual eminent either in action or speculation." Instead of distinguishing "whites" as unique among all "species" (in superiority), the revision tellingly asserts that "negroes" are the unique "species" (in inferiority). The later version also expands the idea of inferiority from a general claim for a "species" to one that extends to each individual.

From David Hume, *Essays: Moral, Political, and Literary*, ed. Eugene F. Miller (Indianapolis: Liberty Classics, 1987), pp. 207–08.

If the characters of men depended on the air and climate, the degrees of heat and cold should naturally be expected to have a mighty influence; since nothing has a greater effect on all plants and irrational animals. And indeed there is some reason to think, that all the nations, which live beyond the polar circles or between the tropics, are inferior to the rest of the species, and are incapable of all the higher attainments of the human mind. The poverty and misery of the northern inhabitants of the globe, and the indolence of the southern, from their few necessities, may, perhaps, account for this remarkable difference, without our having recourse to *physical* causes. This however is certain, that the characters of nations are very promiscuous in the temperate climates, and that almost all the general observations, which have been formed of the more southern or more northern people in these climates, are found to be uncertain and fallacious.[1]

1. I am apt to suspect the negroes to be naturally inferior to the whites. There scarcely ever was a civilized nation of that complexion, nor even any individual eminent either in action or speculation. No ingenious manufactures amongst them, no arts, no sciences. On the other hand, the most rude and barbarous of the whites, such as the ancient GERMANS, the present TARTARS, have still something eminent about them, in their valour, form of government, or some other particular. Such a uniform and constant difference could not happen, in so many countries and ages, if nature had not made an original distinction between these breeds of men. Not to mention our colonies, there are NEGROE slaves dispersed all over EUROPE, of whom none ever discovered any symptoms of ingenuity; though low people, without education, will start up amongst us, and distinguish themselves in every profession. In JAMAICA, indeed, they talk of one negro as a man of parts and learning; but it is likely he is admired for slender accomplishments, like a parrot, who speaks a few words plainly. [Hume's note]

JAMES BEATTIE

from *An Essay on the Nature and Immutability of Truth* [1770, revised 1771]

Opposition to David Hume's ideas about racial traits (p. 8) came from his fellow Scottish philosopher James Beattie (1735–1803). Beattie was part of the Scottish "common-sense" school of philosophers, which challenged the skepticism associated with Hume. He was best known for *An Essay on the Nature and Immutability of Truth* (1770), which, he claimed in the essay, "avenged insulted Christianity" and disputed the racial generalizations proposed in Hume's "Of National Characters." Beattie's work was propelled by abolitionist values and met with wide attention, especially in England, in part because Beattie neglected to treat Hume with the deference routinely accorded him by other contemporary critics. As a result of the success of *An Essay on the Nature and Immutability of Truth*, Beattie received an honorary degree from Oxford University and a yearly pension from King George III. As for Hume, he dismissed Beattie's essay, declaring it "a horrible large lie" and calling Beattie "a bigoted silly Fellow."

Beattie published revisions of this essay in 1771 (the version reprinted here) and again in 1776.

From James Beattie, *An Essay on the Nature and Immutability of Truth* (Edinburgh: Printed for W. and J. Deas, 1807), pp. 330–34.

That I may not be thought a blind admirer of antiquity, I would here crave the reader's indulgence for one short digression more, in order to put him in mind of an important error in morals, inferred from partial and inaccurate experience, by no less a person than Aristotle himself. He argues, "That men of little genius, and great bodily strength, are by nature destined to serve, and those of better capacity, to command; that the natives of Greece, and of some of other countries, being naturally superior in genius, have a natural right to empire; and that the rest of mankind, being naturally stupid, are destined to labour and slavery."[1] This reasoning is now, alas! of little advantage to Aristotle's countrymen, who have for many ages been doomed to that slavery, which, in his judgment, nature had destined them to impose on others; and many nations whom he would have consigned to everlasting stupidity, have shown themselves equal in genius to the most exalted of humankind. It would have been more worthy of Aristotle, to have inferred man's natural and universal right to liberty, from that natural and universal passion with which man desires it, and from the salutary consequences to learning, to virtue, and to every human improvement, of which it never fails to be productive. He wanted, perhaps, to devise some excuse for servitude; a practice which to their eternal reproach, both Greeks and Romans tolerated even in the days of their glory.

Mr HUME argues nearly in the same manner in regard to the superiority of white man over black. "I am apt to suspect," says he, "the negroes, and in general, all the other species of men, (for there are four or five different kinds), to be naturally inferior to the whites. There *never* was a civilized nation of any other complexion than white, *nor even any individual* eminent either in action or speculation. *No* ingenious manufactures among them, *no* arts, *no* sciences. —There are negroe-slaves dispersed all over Europe, of whom *none* ever discovered any symptoms of ingenuity."[2] These assertions are strong; but I know not whether they have any thing else to recommend them. —For, first, tho' true, they would not prove the point in question, except were it also proved, that the Africans and Americans, even though arts and sciences were introduced among them, would still remain unsusceptible to cultivation. The inhabitants of Great Britain and France were as savage 2,000 years ago, as those of Africa and America are to this day. To civilize a nation is a work which requires long time to accomplish. And one may as well say of an infant, that he can never become a man,

1. De Republ. lib. 1. cap. 5. 6. [Beattie's note]
2. Hume's essay, "Of National Characters." [Beattie's note]

as of a nation, now barbarous, that it never can be civilized. —Secondly, of the facts here asserted, no man could have sufficient evidence, except from a personal acquaintance with all the negroes that now are, or ever were, on the face of the earth. These people write no histories; and all of the travellers that ever visited them, will not amount to any thing like a proof of what is here affirmed. But, thirdly, we know that these assertions are not true. The empires of Peru and Mexico could not have been governed, nor the metropolis of the latter built after so singular a manner, in the middle of a lake, without men eminent, both for action and speculation. Every body has heard of the magnificence, good government, and ingenuity of the ancient Peruvians. The Africans and Americans are known to have many ingenious manufactures and arts among them, which even Europeans would find it no easy matter to imitate. Sciences indeed they have none, because they have no letters; but in oratory, some of them, particularly the Indians *of the Five Nations*, are said to be greatly our superiors. It will be readily allowed that the condition of a slave is not favourable to genius of any kind; and yet, the negro-slaves dispersed over Europe, have often discovered symptoms of ingenuity, notwithstanding their unhappy circumstances. They become excellent handicraftsmen, and practical musicians, and indeed learn everything their masters are at pains to teach them, perfidy and debauchery not excepted. That a negro-slave, who can neither read, nor write, nor speak any European language, who is not permitted to do anything but what his master commands, and who has not a single friend on earth, but is universally considered and treated as if he were of a species inferior to the human;—that such a creature should so distinguish himself among Europeans, as to be talked of through the world for a man of genius, is surely no reasonable expectation. To suppose him of an inferior species, because he does not thus distinguish himself, is just as rational as to suppose any private European of an inferior species, because he has not raised himself to the condition of royalty.

Had the Europeans been destitute of the arts of writing and working in iron, they might have remained to this day as barbarous as the natives of Africa and America. Nor is the invention of these arts to be ascribed to our superior capacity. The genius of the inventor is not always to be estimated according to the importance of the invention. Gun-powder and the mariner's compass have produced wonderful revolutions in human affairs, and yet were accidental discoveries. Such, probably, were the first essays in writing and working iron. Suppose them the effects of contrivance; they were at least contrived; by a few individuals; and if they required a superiority of understanding, or of species, in the inventors, those inventors, and their descendants, are the only persons who can lay claim to the honour of that superiority.

That every practice and sentiment is barbarous which is not according to the usages of modern Europe, seems to be a fundamental maxim with many of our critics and philosophers. Their remarks often put us in mind of the fable of the man and the lion. If Negroes and Indians were disposed to recriminate; if a Lucian or a Voltaire from the coast of Guinea, or from the five nations, were to pay us a visit, what a picture of European manners might he present to his countrymen at his return! Nor would caricatura, or exaggeration, be necessary to render it hideous. A plain historical account of some of our most fashionable duelists, gamblers, and adulterers, (to name no more), would exhibit specimens of brutish barbarity, and sottish infatuation, such as might vie with any that ever appeared in Kamschatka, California, or the land of the Hottentots.[3]

It is easy to see with what views some modern authors throw out these hints to prove the natural inferiority of negroes. But let every friend to humanity pray, that they may be disappointed. Britons are famous for generosity; a virtue in which it is easy for them to excel both the Romans and Greeks. Let it never be said, that slavery is countenanced by the bravest, and most generous people on earth, by a people who are animated with that heroic passion, the love of liberty, beyond all nations ancient or modern; and the fame of whose toilsome, but unwearied perseverance, in vindicating, at the expense of life and fortune, the sacred rights of mankind, will strike terror into the hearts of sycophants and tyrants, and excite the admiration and gratitude of all good men to the latest posterity.

---

3. The Khoikhoi, native people of southern Africa who practiced pastoral agriculture.

IMMANUEL KANT

from *Observations on the Feeling of the Beautiful and Sublime* [1764]

Immanuel Kant (1724–1804), perhaps the most influential of Europe's metaphysical philosophers, built his ideas about race on the foundation laid by David Hume (p. 8). His *Observations on the Feeling of the Beautiful and Sublime* contains a section titled "Of National Characteristics," signaling the connection to Hume's work, and in his discussion of "Negroes," Kant directly refers to Hume's essay.

Following Hume's model, Kant divides humanity into different groups, classifying them not only according to their looks but also according to their development of aesthetic and moral feeling. For Kant, the pinnacles of aesthetic experience are the sublime (inspiring awe) and the beautiful (inspiring happiness). Only those who are most aesthetically and morally developed can achieve those pinnacles. In opposition to those elevated sentiments, he places "coarse pleasures," which all humans, regardless of intellectual or moral development, are capable of experiencing. "Negroes," Kant states, "[* * *] have by nature no feeling that rises above the trifling." In a collection of notes on his lectures on physical geography, published in 1802, he developed his ideas further, concluding, "Humanity is at its greatest perfection in the race of the whites. The yellow Indians do have a meager talent. The Negroes are far below them and at the lowest point are a part of the American peoples."

From Emmanuel Chukwudi Eze, ed., *Race and the Enlightenment: A Reader* (Cambridge, Mass.: Blackwell, 1997), pp. 55–57.

The Negroes of Africa have by nature no feeling that rises above the trifling. Mr Hume challenges anyone to cite a single example in which a Negro has shown talents, and asserts that among the hundreds of thousands of blacks who are transported elsewhere from their countries, although many of them have even been set free, still not a single one was ever found who presented anything great in art or science or any other praiseworthy quality, even though among the whites some continually rise aloft from the lowest rabble, and through superior gifts earn respect in the world. So fundamental is the difference between these two races of man, and it appears to be as great in regard to mental capacities as in color. The religion of fetishes so widespread among them is perhaps a sort of idolatry that sinks as deeply into the trifling as appears to be possible to human nature. A bird feather, a cow's horn, a conch shell, or any other common object, as soon as it becomes consecrated by a few words, is an object of veneration and of invocation in swearing oaths. The blacks are very vain but in the Negro's way, and so talkative that they must be driven apart from each other with thrashings.

Among all savages there is no nation that displays so sublime a mental character as those of North America. They have a strong feeling for honor, and as in quest of it they seek wild adventures hundreds of miles abroad, they are still extremely careful to avert the least injury to it when their equally harsh enemy, upon capturing them, seeks by cruel pain to extort cowardly groans from them. The Canadian savage, moreover, is truthful and honest. The friendship he establishes is just as adventurous and enthusiastic as anything of that kind reported from the most ancient and fabled times. He is extremely proud, feels the whole worth of freedom, and even in his education suffers no encounter that would let him feel a low subservience. Lycurgus probably gave statutes to just such savages; and if a lawgiver arose among the Six Nations, one would see a Spartan republic rise in the New World; for the undertaking of the Argonauts is little different from the war parties of these Indians, and Jason excels Attakakullakulla in nothing but the honor of a Greek name. All these savages have little feeling for the beautiful in moral understanding, and the generous forgiveness of an injury, which is at once noble and beautiful, is completely unknown as a virtue among the savages, but rather is disdained as a miserable cowardice. Valor is the greatest merit of the savage and revenge his sweetest bliss. The remaining natives of this part of the world show few traces of a mental character disposed to the finer feelings, and an extraordinary apathy constitutes the mark of this type of race.

If we examine the relation of the sexes in these parts of the world, we find that the European alone has found the secret of decorating with so many flowers the sensual charm of a mighty inclination and of interlacing it with so much morality that he has not only extremely elevated its agreeableness but has also made it very decorous.

* * *

In the lands of the black, what better can one expect than what is found prevailing, namely the feminine sex in the deepest slavery? A despairing man is always a strict master over anyone weaker, just as with us that man is always a tyrant in the kitchen who outside his own house hardly dares to look anyone in the face. Of course, Father Labat reports that a Negro carpenter, whom he reproached for haughty treatment toward his wives, answered: "You whites are indeed fools, for first you make great concessions to your wives, and afterward you complain when they drive you mad." And it might be that there were something in this which perhaps deserved to be considered; but in short, this fellow was quite black from head to foot, a clear proof that what he said was stupid.

PHILLIS WHEATLEY

Letter to the Reverend Samson Occum [1774]

As the first person of African descent to publish a book of poetry in English, Phillis Wheatley (ca. 1753–1784) was an originator of the African American literary tradition. Through her poetry, letters, and other accomplishments, Wheatley also played an instrumental role in the first years of the American debate over "the nature of the Negro." Wheatley's poetry subtly stressed the existence of one human race created by God, rather than multiple races: humans were "all lovely copies of the Maker's plan," as she wrote in "Thoughts on the Works of Providence" (1773). Her most direct indictment of racial justifications for slavery appeared in her February 11, 1774, letter to the Reverend Samson Occum, a Mohegan poet and ordained Presbyterian minister; the letter was published a month later in *The Connecticut Gazette; and the Universal Intelligencer*. Wheatley's assertion that "in every human Breast, God has implanted a Principle, which we call Love of Freedom" linked her belief in a common humanity to her faith in God's plan for civil and religious liberty for all. Wheatley's friendship with Occum had begun nearly a decade earlier, in 1765, when Wheatley, then about twelve years old, wrote a letter to the forty-two-year-old Occum. Her letter of 1774, the only surviving piece of their correspondence, was in response to a letter from Occum condemning slavery. Occum also corresponded with Phillis's owner, Susanna Wheatley, and a letter to her that survives, from March 5, 1771, discusses Phillis and indicates his respect for her. After requesting that Susanna "remember me to Phillis and the rest of your Servants," Occum asks her to consider sending Phillis to Africa as a missionary. "Pray Madam," he wrote, "what harm woud it be to Send Phillis to her Native Country as a Female Preacher to her kindred, you know Quaker Women are alow'd to preach, and why not others in an Extraordinary Case."

Wheatley wrote only one poem referring to her childhood in Africa, and little is known about her early years. Likely kidnapped in the Senegal-Gambia region of West Africa when she was around seven years old, Wheatley was bought by Susanna Wheatley and her husband, John, a Boston tailor. Tutored by their teenage daughter, Mary, Phillis learned to read and write English in sixteen months. By twelve, she was studying Latin as well as English poets, including Alexander Pope, who became one of her primary poetic influences. She published her first poem, "On Messrs. Hussey and Coffin," in 1767 in *The Newport Mercury*. A broadside published in 1770, *An Elegiac Poem, on the Death of that Celebrated Divine, and eminent Servant of Jesus Christ, the late Reverend, and pious George Whitefield, Chaplain to the Right Honourable the Countess of Huntingdon*, helped launch her into international renown. At about age twenty, she was sent to London, where she published *Poems on Various Subjects, Religious and Moral* (1773), becoming the first American of African descent to publish a book of imaginative writing. The volume includes a letter signed by eighteen prominent Boston men and a statement by John Wheatley to authenticate Phillis Wheatley's authorship of the poems. Phillis Wheatley gained her freedom around the time of Susanna Wheatley's death in 1774 (and possibly as late as 1778, the year John Wheatley died and she married John Peters, a newly freed Bostonian). With the onset of the Revolutionary War, Phillis Wheatley lost financial patronage for her poetry, although she continued to write. She lived in poverty, supporting herself in later years by working as a domestic, an experi-ence echoed by a significant number of African American women writers who followed her, including Maria W. Stewart (p. 60), Jarena Lee (p. 152), and in the twentieth century, Zora Neale Hurston (p. 267). Wheatley died shortly after her third childbirth, at about age thirty-one. None of her children survived past early childhood. The unpublished manuscript of her second book of poetry disappeared after her death and has never been recovered.

From *The Connecticut Gazette; and the Universal Intelligencer,* March 11, 1774; reprinted in Phillis Wheatley, *Complete Writings,* ed. Vincent Cardetta (New York: Penguin Books, 2001), pp. 152–53.

The following is an extract of a Letter from Phillis, a Negro Girl of Mr. Wheatley's, in Boston, to the Rev. Samson Occum, which we are desired to insert as a Specimen of her Ingenuity.—It is dated 11th Feb., 1774.

Rev'd and honor'd Sir,

I have this Day received your obliging kind Epistle, and am greatly satisfied with your Reasons respecting the Negroes, and think highly reasonable what you offer in Vindication of their natural Rights: Those that invade them cannot be insensible that the divine Light is chasing away the thick Darkness which broods over the Land of Africa; and the Chaos which has reign'd so long, is converting into beautiful Order, and [r]eveals more and more clearly, the glorious Dispensation of civil and religious Liberty, which are so inseparably united, that there is little or no Enjoyment of one Without the other: Otherwise, perhaps, the Israelites had been less solicitous for their Freedom from Egyptian slavery; I do not say they would have been contented without it, by no means, for in every human Breast, God has implanted a Principle, which we call Love of Freedom; it is impatient of Oppression, and pants for Deliverance; and by the Leave of our modern Egyptians I will assert, that the same Principle lives in us. God grant Deliverance in his own Way and Time, and get him honour upon all those whose Avarice impels them to countenance and help forward the Calamities of their Fellow Creatures. This I desire not for their Hurt, but to convince them of the strange Absurdity of their Conduct whose Words and Actions are so diametrically, opposite. How well the Cry for Liberty, and the reverse Disposition for the exercise of oppressive Power over others agree,—I humbly think it does not require the Penetration of a Philosopher to determine.

JOHANN GOTTFRIED VON HERDER
from *Ideas on the Philosophy of the History of Mankind* [1784–1791]

Opposition to Kant's ideas about race (p. 11) came from one of his former students, Johann Gottfried von Herder (1744–1803), a cleric and leading advocate of German romanticism. Unlike Kant, Herder rejects the idea of using skin color to classify people in different races and, significantly, proposes that every culture possesses its own intrinsic value. Herder's multicultural viewpoint repudiates Kant's belief that cultures can be ranked according to their development from the "primitive" to the "civilized." Herder's pluralistic views were unusual for his time, but his theories about the interaction between natural forces and the physical and mental traits of specific groups reflect the ethnocentric beliefs typical of the period.

From Emmanuel Chukwudi Eze, ed., *Race and the Enlightenment: A Reader* (Cambridge, Mass.: Blackwell, 1997), pp. 71, 74–78.

It is but just, when we proceed to the country of the blacks, that we lay aside our proud prejudices, and consider the organization of this quarter of the globe with as much impartiality, as if there were no other. Since whiteness is a mark of degeneracy in many animals near the pole, the negro has as much right to term his savage robbers albinoes and white devils, degenerated through the weakness of nature, as we have to deem him the emblem of evil, and a descendant of Ham,[1] branded by his father's curse. I, might he say, I, the black, am the original man. I have taken the deepest draughts from the source of life, the Sun: on me, and on every thing around me, it has acted with the greatest energy and vivacity. Behold my country: how fertile in fruits, how rich in gold! Behold the height of my trees! the strength of my animals! Here each element swarms with life, and I am the centre of this vital action. Thus might the negro say; let us then enter the country appropriate to him with modesty.

* * *

But how deficient are we in authentic information respecting this country! We barely know its coasts; and are in many parts acquainted with these no further than our cannons reach. No modern European has traversed the interior of Africa, which the Arabian caravans frequently do (Schott's *Account of Senegal*, pp. 49, 50); and what we know of it is either from tales of the blacks, or pretty ancient accounts of lucky or unfortunate adventures (Zimmermann's comparison of the known and unknown parts, an essay replete with learning and sound judgement, in the *Geographical History of Man*, book III, p. 104, and following). Even the nations, that we might know as things are, the eye of the European seems to behold with too tyrannical indifference, to attempt to investigate the variation of national form in wretched black slaves. Men handle them like cattle, and when they buy them, distinguish them by the marks of their teeth. A single Moravian missionary (Oldendorp's *Missionsgeschichte auf St Thomas*, p. 270 and following) has transmitted us from another quarter of the globe more accurate discriminations of the negroes, than all the voyagers

that have infested the African shores. How fortunate would it have been for the knowledge of nature, and of man, had a company of travellers, endued with the penetration of Forster, the patience of Sparmann, and the science of both, visited this undiscovered country!

* * *

But I forget, that I had to speak of the form of the negroes, as of an organization of the human species; and it would be well, if natural philosophy had applied its attention to all the varieties of our species, as much as to this. The following are some of the results of its observations.

1 The black colour of the negro has nothing in it more wonderful than the white, brown, yellow, or reddish, of other nations. Neither the blood, the brain, nor the seminal fluid of the negro is black, but the reticular membrane beneath the cuticle, which is common to all, and even in us, at least in some parts, and under certain circumstances, is more or less coloured. Camper has demonstrated this (See Camper's *Kleine Schriften*, "Tracts", vol. I, p. 24 and following); and according to him we all have the capacity of becoming negroes. Even amid the frosts of Samoieda we have noticed the sable mark in the female breast: the germ of the negro blackness could not be farther extended in that climate.

2 All depends therefore on the causes, that were capable of unfolding it here; and analogy instructs us, that sun and air must have had great share in it. For what makes us brown? What makes the difference between the two sexes in almost every country? What has rendered the descendants of the Portuguese after residing some centuries in Africa, so similar in colour to the negroes? Nay, what so forcibly discriminates the negro races in Africa itself? The climate, considered in the most extensive signification of the word, so as to include the manner of life, and kind of food. The blackest negroes live precisely in that region where the east wind, blowing wholly over the land, brings the most intense heat; where the heat is diminished, or cooled

---

1. A person of black African ancestry; the biblical story of the curse of Noah's son Ham (Genesis 9:20–27) provided justification for racism and the enslavement of black people, who were believed to be descendants of Ham.

by the sea breeze, the black is softened into yellow. The cool heights are inhabited by white, or whitish people; while in the close lower regions the oil, that occasions the black appearance beneath the cuticle, is rendered more a dust by the heat of the sun. Now if we reflect, that these blacks have resided for ages in this quarter of the world, and completely naturalized themselves to it by their mode of life; if we consider the several causes, that now operate more feebly, but which in earlier periods, when all the elements were in their primitive rude force, must have acted with greater power; and if we take into the account, that so many thousands of years must have brought about a complete revolution as it were of the wheel of contingencies, which at one period or another turns up every thing that can take place upon this earth; we shall not wonder at the trifling circumstance, that the skin of some nations is black. Nature, in her progressive secret operations, has produced much greater changes than this.

3 And how did she effect this small change? To me the thing seems to speak for itself. It is an oil, that colours the reticular membrane. The sweat of the negroes, and even of Europeans, in this country frequently has a yellow colour. The skin of the blacks is a thick, soft velvet, not so tense and dry as that of the whites; the heat of the sun having drawn from their inner parts an oil, which, ascending as near as it could to the surface, has softened their cuticle, and coloured the membrane beneath it. Most of the diseases of this country are bilious; and if we read the descriptions of them (See Schott's *Treatise on the Synochus atrabiliofa*), we shall not wonder at the yellow or black complexions of the inhabitans.

4 The woolly hair of the negro may be accounted for on similar principles. As the hair is nourished only by the finer juices of the skin, and is generated as it were unnaturally in the fat, it becomes curled in proportion to the abundance of nutriment it receives, and dies where this is deficient. Thus in the coarser organization of brutes, we find their wool converted into rough hair, in countries uncongenial to their nature, where the juices, that flow into it, are incapable of elaboration. The finer organization of man on the contrary, intended for all climates, is capable of converting the

hair into wool, when the oil, that moistens the skin, is superabundant.

5 But the peculiar formation of the members of the human body says more than all these; and this appears to me explicable in the African organization. According to various physiological observations, the lips, breasts, and private parts, are proportionate to each other; and as Nature, agreeably to the simple principle of her plastic art, must have conferred on these people, to whom she was obliged to deny nobler gifts, an ampler measure of sensual enjoyment, this could not but have appeared to the physiologist. According to the rules of physiognomy thick lips are held to indicate a sensual disposition; as thin lips, displaying a slender rosy line, are deemed symptoms of a chaste and delicate taste; not to mention other circumstances. What wonder then, that in a nation, for whom the sensual appetite is the height of happiness, external marks of it should appear? A negro child is born white; the skin around the nails, the nipples, and the private parts, first become coloured; and the same consent of parts in the disposition to colour is observable in other nations. A hundred children are a trifle to a negro; and an old man, who had not above seventy, lamented his fate with tears.

6 With this oleaginous organization to sensual pleasure, the profile, and the whole frame of the body, must alter. The projection of the mouth would render the nose short and small, the forehead would incline backwards, and the face would have at a distance the resemblance of that of an ape. Conformably to this would be the position of the neck, the transition to the occiput, and the elastic structure of the whole body, which is formed, even to the nose and skin, for sensual animal enjoyment (Camper has shown in the *Haarlem Transactions*, that the negro has the centres of motion nearer together than the European, and in consequence possesses greater elasticity of body). Since in this quarter of the globe, as the native land of the solar heat, the loftiest and most succulent trees arise, herds of the largest, strongest, and most active animals are generated, and vast multitudes of apes in particular sport, so that air and water, the sea and the lands, swarm with life and fertility; organizing human nature could not fail to follow, with respect to its animal part, this general

simple principle of the plastic powers. That finer intellect, which the creature, whose breast swells with boiling passions beneath this burning sun, must necessarily be refused, was countervailed by a structure altogether incompatible with it. Since then a nobler boon could not be conferred on the negro in such a climate, let us pity, but not despise him; and honour that parent, who knows how to compensate, while she deprives. He spends his life void of care in a country which yields him food with unbounded liberality. His limber body moves in the water, as if it had been formed for that element; he runs and climbs, as if each were his sport; and not less strong and healthy than light and active, his different constitution supports all the accidents and diseases of his climate, under which so many Europeans sink. What to him are the tormenting sensations of superior joys, for which he was not formed? The materials were not wanting; but Nature took him in hand, and formed of him what was most fit for his country, and the happiness of his life. Either no Africa should have been created, or it was requisite, that negroes should be made to inhabit Africa.

Immanuel Kant

from *Review of Herder's* Ideas on the Philosophy of the History of Mankind [1785]

Kant's review of Herder's *Ideas on the Philosophy of the History of Mankind* (p. 13) prompted one of the major intellectual debates of the period. Kant (p. 11) maintains that all civilizations are in the process of progressing toward a universal and civilized human nature, propelled by an innate human capacity for reason. Grounding his theory in logic and science rather than religious belief, Kant sought to define universal principles to explain human society and history. Kant's views conflict with his student's principles of cultural relativism, in which each society develops organically toward its own unique future. As Herder writes in the first chapter of his *Ideas on the Philosophy of the History of Mankind*, "Nations modify themselves, according to time, place, and their internal character; each bears in itself the standard of its perfection, totally independent of all comparison with that of others." For Herder, God is the source of this diversity, making human judgments of different cultures impossible. In his introduction to *Kant: Political Writings*, Hans Reiss suggests that Kant was so harsh in his critique of his former student because "he apparently sensed that here was not only the issue that separated his approach to knowledge from Herder's, but it was also the watershed between those who wish to understand the world principally in terms of science and logic and those who do not."

From Emmanuel Chukwudi Eze, ed., *Race and the Enlightenment: A Reader* (Cambridge, Mass.: Blackwell, 1997), pp. 67–69.

There is one precondition which the reviewer would have liked to see realized, both for our author and for any other philosopher who should embark on a general natural history of mankind—namely that a historical and critical mind had done all the preparatory work for them, selecting from the boundless mass of ethnographical descriptions or travelogues, and from all the reports in these which can be presumed to shed light on human nature, those in particular which are mutually contradictory, placing them side by side and supplementing them with comments on the credibility of their respective authors; for if this had been done, no one would so boldly rely on one-sided accounts without first having carefully assessed the reports of others. But as it is, one may prove if one wishes, from numerous descriptions of various countries, that Americans, Tibetans, and other genuine Mongolian peoples are beardless—but also, if one prefers, that they are all naturally bearded and merely pluck their hair out. Or one may prove that Americans and Negroes are races which have sunk below the level of other members of the species in terms of intellectual abilities—or alternatively, on the evidence of no less plausible accounts, that they should be regarded as equal in natural ability to all the other inhabitants of the world. Thus, the philosopher is at liberty to choose whether he wishes to assume natural differences or to judge everything by the principle *tout comme chez nous*,[1] with the result that all the systems he constructs on such unstable foundations must take on the appearance of ramshackle hypotheses. Our author disapproves of the division of mankind into races especially on the basis of inherited colour, presumably because he believes that the concept of race is not yet clearly defined. In the third numbered section of Book VII, he calls the cause of the climatic differences between human beings genetic force. As the reviewer understands it, the sense in which the author uses this expression is as follows. He wishes to reject the system of evolution on the one hand, but also the purely mechanical influence of external causes on the other, as worthless explanations. He assumes that the cause of such differences is a vital principle which modifies *itself* from within in accordance with variations in external circumstances, and in a manner appropriate to these. The reviewer is fully in agreement with him here, but with this reservation: if the cause which organizes *from within* were limited by its nature to only a certain number and degree of differences in the development of the creature which it organizes (so that, once these differences were exhausted, it would no longer be free to work from another archetype under altered circumstances), one could well describe this natural determinant of formative nature in terms of germs or predispositions, without thereby regarding the differences in question as originally implanted and

only occasionally activated mechanisms or buds (as in the system of evolution); on the contrary, such differences should be regarded simply as limitations imposed on a self-determining power, limitations which are as inexplicable as the power itself is incapable of being explained or rendered comprehensible.

A new train of thought begins with Book VIII and continues to the end of this portion of the work. It deals with the origin of man's education as a rational and moral creature, and hence with the beginning of all culture. This, in the author's opinion, is to be sought not in an inherent capacity of the human species, but completely outside it in the instruction and guidance provided by other natures. From this beginning, as he sees it, all cultural advances are simply the further transmission and casual exploitation of an original tradition; and it is this, rather than his own efforts, that man has to thank for all his progress towards wisdom. Since the reviewer becomes completely lost as soon as he strays from the path of nature and rational knowledge—for he is not conversant with learned philology nor familiar with ancient documents and able to assess them, and therefore has no idea how to make philosophic use of the facts they relate and attest—he readily accepts that he cannot pass judgement on such matters. Nevertheless, the author's wide reading and his particular aptitude for bringing scattered data into focus probably allow us to expect that we shall at least read many valuable observations on the course of human affairs, in so far as this can afford greater insight into the character of the species, and even perhaps into certain classical differences within it—observations which could be instructive even for someone who held different views on the ultimate origin of all human culture.

THOMAS JEFFERSON

from *Notes on the State of Virginia* [1784, reprinted 1787]

The writings and actions of Thomas Jefferson (1743–1826) reveal a complex relationship to slavery. Jefferson was a prime architect of American democracy and

the idea of individual liberty, and the author of the Declaration of Independence, yet he was also a slave owner. Unlike his fellow slave owner George Washington,

1. Just as with us [French].

Jefferson neglected to free his slaves in his will. There were more than 200 enslaved men, women, and children on his Monticello plantation, of whom Jefferson freed only 5 in his will, all of them relatives of Sally Hemings, an enslaved woman at the plantation with whom he had had a long-term relationship. The rest were sold to repay his debts. (Two of those freed in the will were Hemings's children, likely fathered by Jefferson. During his lifetime, Jefferson freed only two other people, also children of Hemings's. Two of Hemings's other children ran away and were not pursued by Jefferson.) At the same time, in his letters and speeches Jefferson repeatedly condemned slavery as an evil that must end. As Jefferson wrote in a 1788 letter to the French revolutionary Jacques-Pierre Brissot de Warville, "Nobody wishes more ardently to see an abolition, not only of the trade, but of the condition of slavery; and certainly, nobody will be more willing to encounter every sacrifice for that object." Jefferson could envision the eventual emancipation of all slaves but not a country where free black people lived side by side with their former owners. He believed that the solution was sending former slaves to the west coast of Africa.

Jefferson's *Notes on the State of Virginia* reveals deep-seated beliefs about the inferior natural abilities and attributes of black people. Subsequent writings (including an 1809 letter to Henri Grégoire) qualify these beliefs as "doubts" honed by his experiences with slaves, but his stated wish that his doubts might be proved wrong only underlines his sustained belief in black inferiority. Yet he continued to argue for the rights of African Americans, "whatever their degree of talent."

Jefferson's own life has been a point of controversy because of his relationship with Sally Hemings, which began in 1788 and ended with his death. Although neither Hemings nor Jefferson left behind writings about their relationship, in 2000, DNA data and mounting historical evidence led the Thomas Jefferson Memorial Foundation to conclude that Jefferson "most likely was the father of all six of Sally Hemings's children appearing in Jefferson's records." At the same time, the report includes dissenting arguments, recognizing "that honorable people can disagree on this subject, as indeed they have for over two hundred years."

Originally written in 1781 and updated and expanded in 1782–83, *Notes* was first published privately in Paris in 1784 in a limited edition of several hundred copies. The first public English-language printing was in London in 1787, the source for the 1807 edition excerpted here.

Thomas Jefferson, *Notes on the State of Virginia* (Boston: Lilly and Walt; 1832), pp. 144–151, 170–171.

I t will probably be asked, Why not retain and incorporate the blacks into the state, and thus save the expense of supplying by importation of white settlers, the vacancies they will leave? Deep–rooted prejudices entertained by the whites; ten thousand recollections, by the blacks, of the injuries they have sustained; new provocations; the real distinctions which nature has made; and many other circumstances, will divide us into parties, and produce convulsions, which will probably never end but in the extermination of the one or the other race.—To these objections, which are political, may be added others, which are physical and moral. The first difference which strikes us is that of colour.— Whether the black of the negro resides in the reticular membrane between the skin and scarf-skin,[1] or in the scarf-skin itself; whether it proceeds from the colour of the blood, the colour of the bile, or from that of some other secretion, the difference is fixed in nature, and is as real as if its seat and cause were better known to us. And is this difference of no importance? Is it not the foundation of a greater or less share of beauty in the two races? Are not the fine mixtures of red and white, the expressions of every passion by greater or less suffusions of colour in the one, preferable to that eternal monotony, which reigns in the countenances, that immovable veil of black which covers all the emotions of the other race? Add to these, flowing hair, a more elegant symmetry of form, their own judgment in favour of the whites, declared by their preference of them, as uniformly as is the preference of the Ora-

---

1. Topmost layer of the skin.

nootan[2] for the black women over those of his own species. The circumstance of superior beauty, is thought worthy attention in the propagation of our horses, dogs, and other domestic animals; why not in that of man? Besides those of colour, figure, and hair, there are other physical distinctions proving a difference of race. They have less hair on the face and body. They secrete less by the kidneys, and more by the glands of the skin, which gives them a very strong and disagreeable odour. This greater degree of transpiration renders them more tolerant of heat, and less so of cold than the whites. Perhaps too a difference of structure in the pulmonary apparatus, which a late ingenious[3] experimentalist has discovered to be the principal regulator of animal heat, may have disabled them from extricating, in the act of inspiration, so much of that fluid from the outer air, or obliged them in expiration, to part with more of it. They seem to require less sleep. A black after hard labour through the day, will be induced by the slightest amusements to sit up till midnight, or later, though knowing he must be out with the first dawn of the morning. They are at least as brave, and more adventuresome. But this may perhaps proceed from a want of forethought, which prevents their seeing a danger till it be present.—When present, they do not go through it with more coolness or steadiness than the whites. They are more ardent after their female: but love seems with them to be more an eager desire, than a tender delicate mixture of sentiment and sensation. Their griefs are transient. Those numberless afflictions, which render it doubtful whether heaven has given life to us in mercy or in wrath, are less felt, and sooner forgotten with them. In general, their existence appears to participate more of sensation than reflection. To this must be ascribed their disposition to sleep when abstracted from their diversions, and unemployed in labour. An animal whose body is at rest, and who does not reflect, must be disposed to sleep of course. Comparing them by their faculties of memory, reason, and imagination, it appears to me that in memory they are equal to the whites; in reason much inferior, as I think one could

scarcely be found capable of tracing and comprehending the investigations of Euclid; and that in imagination they are dull, tasteless, and anomalous. It would be unfair to follow them to Africa for this investigation. We will consider them here, on the same stage with the whites, and where the facts are not apocryphal on which a judgment is to be formed. It will be right to make great allowances for the difference of condition, of education, of conversation, of the sphere in which they move. Many millions of them have been brought to, and born in America. Most of them indeed have been confined to tillage, to their own homes, and their own society: yet many have been so situated, that they might have availed themselves of the conversation of their masters; many have been brought up to the handicraft arts, and from that circumstance have always been associated with the whites. Some have been liberally educated, and all have lived in countries where the arts and sciences are cultivated to a considerable degree, and have had before their eyes samples of the best works from abroad. The Indians, with no advantages of this kind, will often carve figures on their pipes not destitute of design and merit. They will crayon out an animal, a plant, or a country, so as to prove the existence of a germ in their minds which only wants cultivation. They astonish you with strokes of the most sublime oratory; such as prove their reason and sentiment strong, their imagination glowing and elevated. But never yet could I find that a black had uttered a thought above the level of plain narration; never saw even an elementary trait of painting or sculpture. In music they are more generally gifted than the whites with accurate ears for tune and time, and they have been found capable of imagining a small catch.[4] Whether they will be equal to the composition of a more extensive run of melody, or of complicated harmony, is yet to be proved. Misery is often the parent of the most affecting touches in poetry. Among the blacks is misery enough, God knows, but no poetry. Love is the peculiar oestrum of the poet. Their love is ardent, but it kindles the senses only, not the imagina-

2. Orangutan, a type of great ape found in Southeast Asia.
3. Crawford. [Jefferson's note]
4. The instrument proper to them is the Banjar, which they brought hither from Africa, and which is the original of the guitar, its chords being precisely the four lower chords of the guitar. [Jefferson's note] Catch: A type of round, in singing, often comic or ribald.

tion. Religion indeed has produced a Phyllis Whately[5]; but it could not produce a poet. The compositions published under her name are below the dignity of criticism. The heroes of the Dunciad are to her, as Hercules to the author of that poem. Ignatius Sancho has approached nearer to merit in composition; yet his letters do more honour to the heart than the head. They breathe the purest effusions of friendship and general philanthropy, and show how great a degree of the latter may be compounded with strong religious zeal. He is often happy in the turn of his compliments, and his style is easy and familiar, except when he affects a Shandean fabrication of words. But his imagination is wild and extravagant, escapes incessantly from every restraint of reason and taste, and, in the course of its vagaries, leaves a tract of thought as incoherent and eccentric, as is the course of a meteor through the sky. His subjects should often have led him to a process of sober reasoning: yet we find him always substituting sentiment for demonstration. Upon the whole, though we admit him to the first place among those of his own colour who have presented themselves to the public judgment, yet when we compare him with the writers of the race among whom he lived, and particularly with the epistolary class, in which he has taken his own stand, we are compelled to enrol him at the bottom of the column. This criticism supposes the letters published under his name to be genuine, and to have received amendment from no other hand; points which would not be of easy investigation. The improvement of the blacks in body and mind, in the first instance of their mixture with the whites, has been observed by every one, and proves that their inferiority is not the effect merely of their condition of life. We know that among the Romans, about the Augustan age especially, the condition of their slaves was much more deplorable than that of the blacks on the continent of America.

* * *

Yet notwithstanding these and other discouraging circumstances among the Romans, their slaves were often their rarest artists. They excelled too in science, insomuch as to be usually employed as tutors to their masters' children. Epictetus, Terence, and Phaedrus, were slaves. But they were of the race of whites. It is not their condition then, but nature, which has produced the distinction.

* * *

To our reproach it must be said, that though for a century and a half we have had under our eyes the races of black and of red men, they have never yet been viewed by us as subjects of natural history. I advance it therefore as a suspicion only, that the blacks, whether originally a distinct race, or made distinct by time and circumstances, are inferior to the whites in the endowments both of body and mind. It is not against experience to suppose, that different Species of the same genus, or varieties of the same species, may possess different qualifications. Will not a lover of natural history then, one who views the gradations in all the races of animals with the eye of philosophy, excuse an effort to keep those in the department of man as distinct as nature has formed them? This unfortunate difference of colour, and perhaps of faculty, is a powerful obstacle to the emancipation of these people. Many of their advocates, while they wish to vindicate the liberty of human nature are anxious also to preserve its dignity and beauty. Some of these, embarrassed by the question 'What further is to be done with them?' join themselves in opposition with those who are actuated by sordid avarice only. Among the Romans emancipation required but one effort. The slave, when made free, might mix with, without staining the blood of his master. But with us a second is necessary, unknown to history. When freed, he is to be removed beyond the reach of mixture.

* * *

And can the liberties of a nation be thought secure when we have removed their only firm basis, a conviction in the minds of the people that these liberties are of the gift of God? That they are not to be violated but with his wrath? Indeed I tremble for my country when I reflect that God is just: that his justice cannot sleep forever: that considering numbers, nature and natural means only, a revolution of the wheel of fortune, an

5. Phillis Wheatley (ca. 1753–84), the first African American to publish a book of poetry, see p. 12.

exchange of situation is among possible events: that it may become probable by supernatural interference! The almighty has no attribute which can take side with us in such a contest.—But it is impossible to be temperate and to pursue this subject through the various considerations of policy, of morals, of history natural and civil. We must be contented to hope they will force their way into every one's mind. I think a change already perceptible, since the origin of the present revolution. The spirit of the master is abating, that of the slave rising from the dust, his condition mollifying, the way I hope preparing, under the auspices of heaven, for a total emancipation, and that this is disposed, in the order of events, to be with the consent of the masters, rather than by their extirpation.

On the Secrets of Nature

BENJAMIN BANNEKER: *Letter to Thomas Jefferson* [1791]
THOMAS JEFFERSON: *Reply to Benjamin Banneker* [1791]
THOMAS JEFFERSON: from *Letter to Joel Barlow* [1809]

On August 19, 1791, the prominent mathematician Benjamin Banneker (1731–1806) sent a manuscript copy of *Benjamin Banneker's Almanac* to Secretary of State Thomas Jefferson. With the manuscript, Banneker included a letter in which he used religious and political arguments to challenge common beliefs about the inferior abilities of African Americans. Banneker had had previous contact with Jefferson. In 1791, Banneker's neighbor George Ellicott, a Quaker, had recommended Banneker for the post of assistant surveyor for the new federal District of Columbia, and Jefferson had approved the appointment.

The freeborn child of a mother who was freeborn and a father who had bought his way out of slavery, Banneker worked on his parents' farm in Maryland for much of his life. Gifted in math, he taught himself the physical sciences and became an astronomer and surveyor. Banneker published his almanac annually from 1791 until 1797, and it was widely used in the United States and England. Historians recognize Banneker as the first African American scientist.

Jefferson's polite response to Banneker on August 30 is strikingly devoid of any comments about Banneker's almanac or the challenges raised in his letter. In a letter to the white American poet and diplomat Joel Barlow in 1809, three years after Banneker's death, Jefferson reveals that he did not consider Banneker's work or ideas worthy of serious engagement. For people in power, simply refusing to recognize or engage with alternative voices can be a strategy of debate, since it restricts the direction of the public conversation.

BENJAMIN BANNEKER

Letter to Thomas Jefferson [1791]

SIR,

I AM fully sensible of the greatness of that freedom, which I take with you on the present occasion; a liberty which seemed to me scarcely allowable, when I reflected on that distinguished and dignified station in which you stand, and the almost general prejudice and prepossession, which is so prevalent in the world against those of my complexion.

I suppose it is a truth too well attested to you, to need a proof here, that we are a race of beings, who have long labored under the abuse and censure of the world; that we have long been looked upon with an eye of contempt; and that we have long been considered rather as brutish than human, and scarcely capable of mental endowments.

Sir, I hope I may safely admit, in consequence of that report which hath reached me, that you are a man far less inflexible in sentiments of this nature, than many others; that you are measurably friendly, and well disposed towards us; and that you are willing and ready to lend your aid and assistance to our relief, from those many distresses, and numerous calamities, to which we are reduced. Now Sir, if this is founded in truth, I apprehend you will embrace every opportunity, to eradicate that train of absurd and false ideas and opinions, which so generally prevails with respect to us; and that your sentiments are concurrent with mine, which are, that one universal Father hath given being to us all; and that he hath not only made us all of one flesh, but that he hath also, without partiality, afforded us all the same sensations and endowed us all with the same faculties; and that however variable we may be in society or religion, however diversified in situation or color, we are all of the same family, and stand in the same relation to him.

Sir, if these are sentiments of which you are fully persuaded, I hope you cannot but acknowledge, that it is the indispensible duty of those, who maintain for themselves the rights of human nature, and who possess the obligations of Christianity, to extend their power and influence to the relief of every part of the human race, from whatever burden or oppression they may unjustly labor under; and this, I apprehend, a full conviction of the truth and obligation of these principles should lead all to. Sir, I have long been convinced, that if your love for yourselves, and for those inestimable laws, which preserved to you the rights of human nature, was founded on sincerity, you could not but be solicitous, that every individual, of whatever rank or distinction, might with you equally enjoy the blessings thereof; neither could you rest satisfied short of the most active effusion of your exertions, in order to their promotion from any state of degradation, to which the unjustifiable cruelty and barbarism of men may have reduced them.

Sir, I freely and cheerfully acknowledge, that I am of the African race, and in that color which is natural to them of the deepest dye; and it is under a sense of the most profound gratitude to the Supreme Ruler of the Universe, that I now confess to you, that I am not under that state of tyrannical thraldom, and inhuman captivity, to which too many of my brethren are doomed, but that I have abundantly tasted of the fruition of those blessings, which proceed from that free and unequalled liberty with which you are favored; and which, I hope, you will willingly allow you have mercifully received, from the immediate hand of that Being, from whom proceedeth every good and perfect Gift.

Sir, suffer me to recal to your mind that time, in which the arms and tyranny of the British crown were exerted, with every powerful effort, in order to reduce you to a state of servitude: look back, I entreat you, on the variety of dangers to which you were exposed; reflect on that time, in which every human aid appeared unavailable, and in which even hope and fortitude wore the aspect of inability to the conflict, and you cannot but be led to a serious and grateful sense of your miraculous and providential preservation; you cannot but acknowledge, that the present freedom and tranquility which you enjoy you have mercifully received, and that it is the peculiar blessing of Heaven.

This, Sir, was a time when you cleary saw into the injustice of a state of slavery, and in which you had just apprehensions of the horrors of its condition. It was now that your abhorrence thereof was so excited, that you publicly held forth this true and invaluable doctrine, which is worthy to be recorded and remembered in all succeeding ages: "We hold these truths to be self-evident, that all men are created equal; that they are endowed by their Creator with certain unalienable rights, and that among these are, life, liberty, and the pursuit of happiness." Here was a time, in which your tender feelings for yourselves had engaged you thus to declare, you were then impressed with proper ideas of the great violation of liberty, and the free possession of those blessings, to which you were entitled by nature; but, Sir, how pitiable is it to reflect, that although you were so fully convinced of the benevolence of the Father of Mankind, and of his equal and impartial distribution of these rights and privileges, which he hath conferred upon them, that you should at the same time counteract his mercies, in detaining by fraud and violence so numerous a part of my brethren, under groaning captivity and cruel oppression, that you should at the same time be found guilty of that most criminal act, which you professedly detested in others, with respect to yourselves.

I suppose that your knowledge of the situation of my brethren, is too extensive to need a recital here; neither shall I presume to prescribe methods by which they may be relieved, otherwise than by recommending to you and all others, to wean yourselves from those narrow prejudices which you have imbibed with respect to them, and as Job proposed to his friends, "Put your soul in their souls' stead;" thus shall your hearts be enlarged with kindness and benevolence towards them; and thus shall you need neither the direction of myself or others, in what manner to proceed herein. And now, Sir, although my sympathy and affection for my brethren hath caused my enlargement thus far, I ardently hope, that your candor and generosity will plead with you in my behalf, when I make known to you, that it was not originally my design; but having taken up my pen in order to direct to you, as a present, a copy of an Almanac, which I have calculated for the succeeding year, I was unexpectedly and unavoidably led thereto.

This calculation is the production of my arduous study, in this my advanced stage of life; for having long had unbounded desires to become acquainted with the secrets of nature, I have had to gratify my curiosity herein, through my own assiduous application to Astronomical Study, in which I need not recount to you the many difficulties and disadvantages, which I have had to encounter.

And although I had almost declined to make my calculation for the ensuing year, in consequence of that time which I had allotted therefor, being taken up at the Federal Territory, by the request of Mr. Andrew Ellicott,[1] yet finding myself under several engagements to Printers of this state, to whom I had communicated my design, on my return to my place of residence, I industriously applied myself thereto, which I hope I have accomplished with correctness and accuracy; a copy of which I have taken the liberty to direct to you, and which I humbly request you will favor-

ably receive; and although you may have the opportunity of perusing it after its publication, yet I choose to send it to you in manuscript previous thereto, that thereby you might not only have an earlier inspection; but that you might also view it in my own hand writing.

And now, Sir, I shall conclude, and subscribe myself, with the most profound respect,

Your most obedient humble servant,

BENJAMIN BANNEKER.

Printed by Daniel Lawrence, Philadelphia, 1792; also, Scholars' Lab (formerly, the EText Center), University of Virginia Library.

THOMAS JEFFERSON

Reply to Benjamin Banneker [1791]

To MR. BENJAMIN BANNEKER.
Philadelphia, August 30, 1791.

SIR,

I THANK you, sincerely, for your letter of the 19th instant,[2] and for the Almanac it contained. No body wishes more than I do, to see such proofs as you exhibit, that nature has given to our black brethren talents equal to those of the other colors of men; and that the appearance of the want of them, is owing merely to the degraded condition of their existence, both in Africa and America. I can add with truth, that no body wishes more ardently to see a good system commenced, for raising the condition, both of their body and mind, to what it ought to be, as far as the imbecility of their present existence, and other circumstances, which cannot be neglected, will admit.

I have taken the liberty of sending your Almanac to Monsieur de Condozett,[3] Secretary of the Academy of Sciences at Paris, and Member of the Philanthropic

---

1. Surveyor from a prominent Quaker family (1754–1820), founder of Ellicott Mills (now Ellicott City), Maryland, and the uncle of Banneker's friend George Ellicott.
2. Of the present month.
3. Marie-Jean-Antoine-Nicholas de Caritat, Marquis de Condorcet (1743–94), French mathematician and philosopher.

Society, because I considered it as a document, to which your whole color had a right for their justification, against the doubts which have been entertained of them.

I am with great esteem, Sir, Your most obedient Humble Servant,

THOMAS JEFFERSON.

Banneker's letter to Jefferson, with Jefferson's reply: Printed by Daniel Lawrence, Philadelphia, 1792; also, Scholars' Lab (formerly, the EText Center), University of Virginia Library.

THOMAS JEFFERSON
From *Letter to Joel Barlow* [1809]

Monticello, October 8, 1809.

DEAR SIR, It is long since I ought to have acknowledged the receipt of your most excellent oration on the 4th of July. I was doubting what you could say, equal to your own reputation on so hackneyed a subject; but you have really risen out of it with lustre, and pointed to others a field of great expansion. A day or two after I received your letter to Bishop Grégoire, a copy of his diatribe to you came to hand from France. I had not before heard of it. He must have been eagle-eyed in quest of offence, to have discovered ground for it among the rubbish massed together in the print he animadverts on. You have done right in giving him a sugary answer. But he did not deserve it. For, notwithstanding a compliment to you now and then, he constantly returns to the identification of your sentiments with the extravagances of the Revolutionary zealots. I believe him a very good man, with imagination enough to declaim eloquently, but without judgment to decide. He wrote to me also on the doubts I had expressed five or six and twenty years ago, in the *Notes of Virginia,* as to the grade of understanding of the negroes, and he sent me his book on the literature of the negroes. His credulity has made him gather up every story he could find of men of color, (without distinguishing whether black, or of what degree of mixture) however slight the mention, or light the authority on which they are quoted. The whole do not amount, in point of evidence, to what we know ourselves of Banneker. We know he had spherical trigonometry enough to make almanacs, but not without the suspicion of aid from Ellicot, who was his neighbor and friend, and never missed an opportunity of puffing him. I have a long letter from Banneker, which shows him to have had a mind of very common stature indeed. As to Bishop Gregoire, I wrote him, as you have done, a very soft answer. It was impossible for doubt to have been more tenderly or hesitatingly expressed than that was in the *Notes of Virginia,* and nothing was or is farther from my intentions, than to enlist myself as the champion of a fixed opinion, where I have only expressed a doubt. St. Domingo will, in time, throw light on the question.

From *The Works of Thomas Jefferson,* vol. 2, ed. Paul Leicester Ford (New York: G. P. Putnam's Sons, 1905), 120–21.

OLAUDAH EQUIANO
from *The Interesting Narrative of the Life of Olaudah Equiano* [1789]

In his 1789 autobiography, *The Interesting Narrative of the Life of Olaudah Equiano, or Gustavus Vassa, the African, Written by Himself,* Olaudah Equiano (ca. 1745–1797) engages in the contemporary debate about the nature of Africans and people of African descent. By contrasting the supportive and artistic African community of his youth with the brutality epitomized by white people involved with slavery, he challenges those who elevated European cultures above others and ranked African societies among the least "civilized" on earth. Even his description of African complicity in the slave trade reinforces his characterization of the essential goodness of

Africans. In his account, African slaves are traditionally treated almost as if they were members of the owner's family; the savage treatment of African slaves by other Africans he attributes to the influence of white culture.

Equiano's autobiography provides a unique first-person account of the Middle Passage and of eighteenth-century village life in Africa. Recently, however, Equiano's narrative itself has become a center of debate. While editing a new edition, Vincent Carretta, a white American professor of English at the University of Maryland, College Park, uncovered evidence suggesting that Equiano was born in South Carolina rather than Africa: a 1759 baptismal record and a 1773 ship's muster roll listing Equiano's place of birth as South Carolina. As for why Equiano might have fictionalized the early portion of his narrative, Carretta argues that Equiano's leading role in the British abolitionist movement gave him a strong motivation. As Carretta said in a September 2005 interview in *The Chronicle of Higher Education*, "Whether [* * *] [Equiano] invented his African birth or not, he knew that what that movement needed was a first-person account. And because they were going after the slave trade, it had to be an account of someone who had been born in Africa and was brought across the Middle Passage. An African-American voice wouldn't have done it." Equiano's autobiography, for which he owned the copyright, was an instant best seller in England, went through nine editions during his lifetime, and made him a wealthy man.

While some scholars are persuaded by Carretta's argument, others, such as Paul E. Lovejoy, professor of history and director of the Harriet Tubman Resource Centre on the African Diaspora at York University in Toronto, remain convinced of Equiano's African origins. Carretta himself has expressed concern that the controversy over Equiano's birthplace might eclipse the literary and historical importance of the text, as well as new directions of inquiry. "Are we wasting time and energy arguing about the authenticity of Africanness instead of what he may have meant by African?" Carretta asks in the *Chronicle* interview. He suggests that a more interesting question is, "In what way is he 'the African,' as he calls himself—the representative of millions of others who have been enslaved?"

From *The Interesting Life of Olaudah Equiano, or Gustavus Vassa, the African, Written by Himself* (London: T. Wilkins, [1789]): 20–27, 42–44; also, Documenting the American South, University Libraries, University of North Carolina, Chapel Hill.

O ur land is uncommonly rich and fruitful, and produces all kinds of vegetables in great abundance. We have plenty of Indian corn, and vast quantities of cotton and tobacco. Our pine apples grow without culture; they are about the size of the largest sugar-loaf, and finely flavoured. We have also spices of different kinds, particularly pepper; and a variety of delicious fruits which I have never seen in Europe; together with gums of various kinds, and honey in abundance. All our industry is exerted to improve those blessings of nature. Agriculture is our chief employment; and every one, even the children and women, are engaged in it. Thus we are all habituated to labour from our earliest years. Every one contributes something to the common stock; and as we are unacquainted with idleness, we have no beggars. The benefits of such a mode of living are obvious. The West-India

planters prefer the slaves of Benin or Eboe[1] to those of any other part of Guinea, for their hardiness, intelligence, integrity, and zeal. Those benefits are felt by us in the general healthiness of the people, and in their vigour and activity; I might have added too in their comeliness. Deformity is indeed unknown amongst us; I mean that of shape. Numbers of the natives of Eboe now in London might be brought in support of this assertion: for, in regard to complexion, ideas of beauty are wholly relative. I remember while in Africa to have seen three negro children, who were tawny, and another quite white, who were universally regarded by myself, and the natives in general, as far as related to their complexions, deformed. Our women too were in my eyes at least uncommonly graceful, alert, and modest to a degree of bashfulness; nor do I remember to have ever heard of an instance of incon-

1. Southern Nigeria, home of the Igbo people, a large and influential ethnic group.

tinence amongst them before marriage. They are also remarkably cheerful. Indeed cheerfulness and affability are two of the leading characteristics of our nation.

Our tillage is exercised in a large plain or common, some hours walk from our dwellings, and all the neighbours resort thither in a body. They use no beasts of husbandry; and their only instruments are hoes, axes, shovels, and beaks, or pointed iron to dig with. Sometimes we are visited by locusts, which come in large clouds, so as to darken the air, and destroy our harvest. This however happens rarely, but when it does, a famine is produced by it. I remember an instance or two wherein this happened. This common is often the theatre of war; and therefore when our people go out to till their land, they not only go in a body, but generally take their arms with them for fear of a surprise; and when they apprehend an invasion they guard the avenues to their dwellings, by driving sticks into the ground, which are so sharp at one end as to pierce the foot, and are generally dipt in poison. From what I can recollect of these battles, they appear to have been irruptions of one little state or district on the other, to obtain prisoners or booty. Perhaps they were incited to this by those traders who brought the European goods I mentioned amongst us. Such a mode of obtaining slaves in Africa is common; and I believe more are procured this way, and by kidnaping, than any other. When a trader wants slaves, he applies to a chief for them, and tempts him with his wares. It is not extraordinary, if on this occasion he yields to the temptation with as little firmness, and accepts the price of his fellow creatures liberty with as little reluctance as the enlightened merchant. Accordingly he falls on his neighbours, and a desperate battle ensues. If he prevails and takes prisoners, he gratifies his avarice by selling them; but, if his party be vanquished, and he falls into the hands of the enemy, he is put to death: for, as he has been known to foment their quarrels, it is thought dangerous to let him survive, and no ransom can save him, though all other prisoners may be redeemed. We have fire-arms, bows and arrows, broad two-edged swords and javelins: we have shields also which cover a man from head to foot. All are taught the use of these weapons; even our women are warriors, and march boldly out to fight along with the men. Our whole district is a kind of militia: on a certain signal given, such as the firing of a gun at night, they all rise in arms and rush upon their enemy. It is perhaps something remarkable, that when our people march to the field a red flag or banner is borne before them. I was once a witness to a battle in our common. We had been all at work in it one day as usual, when our people were suddenly attacked. I climbed a tree at some distance, from which I beheld the fight. There were many women as well as men on both sides; among others my mother was there, and armed with a broad sword. After fighting for a considerable time with great fury, and after many had been killed our people obtained the victory, and took their enemy's Chief prisoner. He was carried off in great triumph, and, though he offered a large ransom for his life, he was put to death. A virgin of note among our enemies had been slain in the battle, and her arm was exposed in our market-place, where our trophies were always exhibited. The spoils were divided according to the merit of the warriors. Those prisoners which were not sold or redeemed we kept as slaves: but how different was their condition from that of the slaves in the West Indies! With us they do no more work than other members of the community, even their masters; their food, clothing and lodging were nearly the same as theirs, (except that they were not permitted to eat with those who were free-born); and there was scarce any other difference between them, than a superior degree of importance which the head of a family possesses in our state, and that authority which, as such, he exercises over every part of his household. Some of these slaves have even slaves under them as their own property, and for their own use.

* * *

These instances, and a great many more which might be adduced, while they shew how the complexions of the same persons vary in different climates, it is hoped may tend also to remove the prejudice that some conceive against the natives of Africa on account of their colour. Surely the minds of the Spaniards did not change with their complexions! Are there not causes enough to which the apparent inferiority of an African may be ascribed, without limiting the goodness of God, and supposing he forbore to stamp understanding on certainly his own image, because "carved in ebony." Might it not naturally be ascribed to their situation? When they come among Europeans, they are ignorant of their language, religion, manners, and customs. Are any pains taken to teach them these? Are they treated as men? Does not slavery itself depress the mind, and extinguish all its fire and every noble sentiment? But, above all, what advantages do not a refined people possess over those who are rude and uncultivated. Let the polished and haughty European recollect that his ancestors were once, like the Africans, uncivilized, and even barbarous. Did Nature make *them* inferior to their sons? and should *they too* have been made slaves? Every rational mind answers, No. Let such reflections as these melt the pride of their superiority into sympathy for the wants and miseries of their sable brethren, and compel them to acknowledge, that understanding is not confined to feature or colour. If, when they look round the world, they feel exultation, let it be tempered with benevolence to others, and gratitude to God, "who hath made of one blood all nations of men for to dwell on all the face of the earth and whose wisdom is not our wisdom, neither are our ways his ways."[2]

DAVID WALKER

Article I, Our Wretchedness in Consequence of Slavery, from *Walker's Appeal* [1829, revision published 1830]

With the publication of his fiery *Appeal* in 1829, and its revision the following year, the abolitionist David Walker radically changed the terms of debate over the nature of African Americans. In contrast to Benjamin Banneker (p. 21), who pursued a private exchange with Thomas Jefferson, Walker issued a public challenge, calling on others to continue his attack on Jefferson's ideas (p. 17). Moreover, he directed his challenge not to white leaders, but to other black people, with an emphasis on those enslaved in the United States.

The *Appeal* galvanized the abolitionist movement, increased black racial pride and resistance to slavery, and compelled many white Americans to rethink their assumptions about race. Confronted by Walker's revolutionary position and prompted by fears of uprisings, southern apologists were forced to abandon their long-held argument that slavery was mutually beneficial and that enslaved people were content with their circumstances. As a result, the *Appeal* promoted the split between the North and the South that eventually led to the Civil War.

The *Appeal*'s dramatic impact was due to both its galvanizing ideas and the effectiveness of its distribution. Directed to the enslaved people of the South, the *Appeal* was distributed not only through the mail but also via unorthodox channels—for instance, it was sewn into the lining of the clothes of sailors heading to the South. Southern states responded by enacting laws that severely restricted teaching slaves to read. Rumors percolated of a $3,000 reward for Walker's death and a $10,000 reward for anyone who brought him alive to the South. When his friends urged him to flee to Canada for his safety, Walker responded with characteristic fortitude: "I will stand my ground. Somebody must die in this cause. I may be doomed to the stake and to the fire, or to the scaffold tree, but it is not in me to falter if I can promote the work of emancipation."

Biographical details of Walker's life are sketchy. He was born on September 28, 1785, the son of an enslaved man and a free woman in Wilmington, North Carolina. Although free (the status of children was determined by that of the mother), Walker witnessed firsthand many atrocities of the southern slave system. In 1825, he established himself in Boston, where he operated a used-clothing business, became a leader of the Massachusetts General Colored Association and of the Prince Hall Freemasons—organizations dedicated to abolition and equal rights—and served as an agent for *Freedom's Journal*, promoting and selling

2. Acts, c. xvii, v. 26.

subscriptions to the nation's first black newspaper. A year after the publication of his *Appeal*, Walker died suddenly, on June 28, 1830. Although many of his contemporaries believed him to have been poisoned, modern research points to tuberculosis as the cause of death.

From David Walker, *Walker's Appeal, in Four Articles; Together, with a Preamble, to the Coloured Citizens of the World, but in Particular, and Very Expressly, to Those of the United States of America, Written in Boston, State of Massachusetts, September 28, 1829*, rev. ed. (Boston: David Walker, 1830), 9–21.

My beloved brethren:—The Indians of North and of South America—the Greeks—the Irish, subjected under the king of Great Britain—the Jews, that ancient people of the Lord—the inhabitants of the islands of the sea—in fine, all the inhabitants of the earth, (except however, the sons of Africa) are called *men,* and of course are, and ought to be free. But we, (coloured people) and our children are *brutes!!* and of course are, and *ought to be* SLAVES to the American people and their children forever!! to dig their mines and work their farms; and thus go on enriching them, from one generation to another with our *blood* and our *tears!!!!*

I promised in a preceding page to demonstrate to the satisfaction of the most incredulous, that we, (coloured people of these United States of America) are the *most wretched, degraded* and *abject* set of beings that *ever lived* since the world began, and that the white Americans having reduced us to the wretched state of *slavery,* treat us in that condition *more cruel* (they being an enlightened[1] and Christian people), than any heathen nation did any people whom it had reduced to our condition. These affirmations are so well confirmed in the minds of all unprejudiced men, who have taken the trouble to read histories, that they need no elucidation from me. But to put them beyond all doubt, I refer you in the first place to the children of Jacob, or of Israel in Egypt, under Pharaoh and his people. Some of my brethren do not know who Pharaoh and the Egyptians were—I know it to be a fact, that some of them take the Egyptians to have been a gang of *devils,* not knowing any better, and that they (Egyptians) having got possession of the Lord's people, treated them *nearly* as cruel as *Christian Americans* do us, at the present day. For the information of such, I would only mention that the Egyptians, were Africans or coloured people, such as we are—some of them yellow and others dark—a mixture of Ethiopians and the natives of Egypt—about the same as you see the coloured people of the United States at the present day.—I say, I call your attention then, to the children of Jacob, while I point out particularly to you his son Joseph, among the rest, in Egypt.

"And Pharaoh, said unto Joseph, thou shalt be over my house, and according unto thy word shall all my people be ruled: only in the throne will I be greater than thou."[2]

"And Pharaoh said unto Joseph, see, I have set thee over all the land of Egypt."[3]

"And Pharaoh said unto Joseph, I am Pharaoh, and without thee shall no man lift up his hand or foot in all the land of Egypt."[4]

Now I appeal to heaven and to earth, and particularly to the American people themselves, who cease not to declare that our condition is not *hard,* and that we are comparatively satisfied to rest in wretchedness and misery, under them and their children. Not, indeed, to show me a coloured President, a Governor, a Legislator, a Senator, a Mayor, or an Attorney at the Bar.—But to show me a man of colour, who holds the low office of a Constable, or one who sits in a Juror Box, even on a case of one of his wretched brethren, throughout this great Republic!!—But let us pass Joseph the son of Israel a little farther in review, as he existed with that heathen nation.

---

1. Several typographical errors from the 1830 printing are corrected here, including enlightened (enlighted), observed (o berved) and consciences (consciencies). [Editor's note]

2. See Genesis, chap. xli. [Unless otherwise indicated, all footnotes are those of the author.] [Genesis 41: 39–40, Editor's note]

3. xli. 44 [Correct passage is 41: 41, Editor's note]

4. xli. 44.

"And Pharaoh called Joseph's name Zaphnath-paaneah; and he gave him to wife Asenath the daughter of Potipherah priest of On. And Joseph went out over all the land of Egypt."[5]

Compare the above, with the American institutions. Do they not institute laws to prohibit us from marrying among the whites? I would wish, candidly, however, before the Lord, to be understood, that I would not give a *pinch* of *snuff* to be married to any white person I ever saw in all the days of my life. And I do say it, that the black man, or man of colour, who will leave his own colour (provided he can get one, who is good for any thing) and marry a white woman, to be a double slave to her, just because she is *white,* ought to be treated by her as he surely will be, viz: as a NIGER!!!! It is not, indeed, what I care about inter-marriages with the whites, which induced me to pass this subject in review; for the Lord knows, that there is a day coming when they will be glad enough to get into the company of the blacks, notwithstanding, we are, in this generation, levelled by them, almost on a level with the brute creation: and some of us they treat even worse than they do the brutes that perish. I only made this extract to show how much lower we are held, and how much more cruel we are treated by the Americans, than were the children of Jacob, by the Egyptians.—We will notice the sufferings of Israel some further, under *heathen Pharaoh,* compared with ours under the *enlightened Christians of America.*

"And Pharaoh spake unto Joseph, saying, thy father and thy brethren are come unto thee":

"The land of Egypt is before thee: in the best of the land make thy father and brethren to dwell; in the land of Goshen let them dwell: and if thou knowest any men of activity among them, then make them rulers over my cattle."[6]

I ask those people who treat us so *well,* Oh! I ask them, where is the most barren spot of land which they have given unto us? Israel had the most fertile land in all Egypt. Need I mention the very notorious fact, that I have known a poor man of colour, who laboured night and day, to acquire a little money, and having acquired it, he vested it in a small piece of land, and got

him a house erected thereon, and having paid for the whole, he moved his family into it, where he was suffered to remain but nine months, when he was cheated out of his property by a white man, and driven out of door! And is not this the case generally? Can a man of colour buy a piece of land and keep it peaceably? Will not some white man try to get it from him, even if it is in a *mud hole?* I need not comment any farther on a subject, which all, both black and white, will readily admit. But I must, really, observe that in this very city, when a man of colour dies, if he owned any real estate it most generally falls into the hands of some white person. The wife and children of the deceased may weep and lament if they please, but the estate will be kept snug enough by its white possessor.

But to prove farther that the condition of the Israelites was better under the Egyptians than ours is under the whites. I call upon the professing Christians, I call upon the philanthropist, I call upon the very tyrant himself, to show me a page of history, either sacred or profane, on which a verse can be found, which maintains, that the Egyptians heaped the *insupportable insult* upon the children of Israel, by telling them that they were not of the *human family.* Can the whites deny this charge? Have they not, after having reduced us to the deplorable condition of slaves under their feet, held us up as descending originally from the tribes of *Monkeys* or *Orang-Outangs?* O! my God! I appeal to every man of feeling—is not this insupportable? Is it not heaping the most gross insult upon our miseries, because they have got us under their feet and we cannot help ourselves? Oh! pity us we pray thee, Lord Jesus, Master.—Has Mr. Jefferson declared to the world, that we are inferior to the whites, both in the endowments of our bodies and of minds? It is indeed surprising, that a man of such great learning, combined with such excellent natural parts, should speak so of a set of men in chains. I do not know what to compare it to, unless, like putting one wild deer in an iron cage, where it will be secured, and hold another by the side of the same, then let it go, and expect the one in the cage to run as fast as the one at liberty. So far, my brethren, were the Egyptians from heaping these insults upon their slaves,

5. xli. 45.
6. Genesis, chap. xlvii. 5, 6.

that Pharoah's daughter took Moses, a son of Israel for her own, as will appear by the following.

"And Pharoah's daughter said unto her, [Moses' mother] take this child away, and nurse it for me, and I will pay thee thy wages. And the woman took the child [Moses] and nursed it."

"And the child grew, and she brought him unto Pharoah's daughter and he became her son. And she called his name Moses: and she said because I drew him out of the water." [7]

In all probability, Moses would have become Prince Regent to the throne, and no doubt, in process of time but he would have been seated on the throne of Egypt. But he had rather suffer shame, with the people of God, than to enjoy pleasures with that wicked people for a season. O! that the coloured people were long since of Moses' excellent disposition, instead of courting favour with, and telling news and lies to our *natural enemies,* against each other—aiding them to keep their hellish chains of slavery upon us. Would we not long before this time, have been respectable men, instead of such wretched victims of oppression as we are? Would they be able to drag our mothers, our fathers, our wives, our children and ourselves, around the world in chains and hand-cuffs as they do, to dig up gold and silver for them and theirs? This question, my brethren, I leave for you to digest; and may God Almighty force it home to your hearts. Remember that unless you are united, keeping your tongues within your teeth, you will be afraid to trust your secrets to each other, and thus perpetuate our miseries under the *Christians* ! ! ! ! ! ADDITION.—Remember, also to lay humble at the feet of our Lord and Master Jesus Christ, with prayers and fastings. Let our enemies go on with their butcheries, and at once fill up their cup. Never make an attempt to gain our freedom of *natural right,* from under our cruel oppressors and murderers, until you see your way clear[8]—when that hour arrives and you move, be not afraid or dismayed; for be you

assured that Jesus Christ the King of heaven and of earth who is the God of justice and of armies, will surely go before you. And those enemies who have for hundreds of years stolen our *rights,* and kept us ignorant of Him and His divine worship, he will remove. Millions of whom, are this day, so ignorant and avaricious, that they cannot conceive how God can have an attribute of justice, and show mercy to us because it pleased Him to make us black—which colour, Mr. Jefferson calls unfortunate ! ! ! ! ! ! As though we are not as thankful to our God, for having made us as it pleased himself, as they, (the whites,) are for having made them white. They think because they hold us in their infernal chains of slavery, that we wish to be white, or of their color—but they are dreadfully deceived—we wish to be just as it pleased our Creator to have made us, and no avaricious and unmerciful wretches, have any business to make slaves of, or hold us in slavery. How would they like for us to make slaves of, and hold them in cruel slavery, and murder them as they do us?—But is Mr. Jefferson's assertions true? viz. "that it is unfortunate for us that our Creator has been pleased to make us *black.*" We will not take his say so, for the fact. The world will have an opportunity to see whether it is unfortunate for us, that our Creator *has made us* darker than the *whites.*

Fear not the number and education of our *enemies,* against whom we shall have to contend for our lawful right; guaranteed to us by our Maker; for why should we be afraid, when God is, and will continue, (if we continue humble) to be on our side?

The man who would not fight under our Lord and Master Jesus Christ, in the glorious and heavenly cause of freedom and of God—to be delivered from the most wretched, abject and servile slavery, that ever a people was afflicted with since the foundation of the world, to the present day—ought to be kept with all of his children or family, in slavery, or in chains, to be butchered by his *cruel enemies.*

---

7. See Exodus, chap. ii. 9, 10.

8. It is not to be understood here, that I mean for us to wait until God shall take us by the hair of our heads and drag us out of abject wretchedness and slavery, nor do I mean to convey the idea for us to wait until our enemies shall make preparations, and call us to seize those preparations, take it away from them, and put every thing before us to death, in order to gain our freedom which God has given us. For you must remember that we are men as well as they. God has been pleased to give us two eyes, two hands, two feet, and some sense in our heads as well as they. They have no more right to hold us in slavery than we have to hold them, we have just as much right, in the sight of God, to hold them and their children in slavery and wretchedness, as they have to hold us, and no more.

I saw a paragraph, a few years since, in a South Carolina paper, which, speaking of the barbarity of the Turks, it said: "The Turks are the most barbarous people in the world—they treat the Greeks more like *brutes* than human beings." And in the same paper was an advertisement, which said: "Eight well built Virginia and Maryland Negro *fellows* and four *wenches* will positively be *sold* this day, to the highest *bidder!*" And what astonished me still more was, to see in this same *humane* paper!! the cuts of three men, with clubs and budgets on their backs, and an advertisement offering a considerable sum of money for their apprehension and delivery. I declare, it is really so amusing to hear the Southerners and Westerners of this country talk about *barbarity,* that it is positively, enough to make a man *smile.*

The sufferings of the Helots among the Spartans, were somewhat severe, it is true, but to say that theirs, were as severe as ours among the Americans, I do most strenuously deny—for instance, can any man show me an article on a page of ancient history which specifies, that, the Spartans chained, and hand-cuffed the Helots, and dragged them from their wives and children, children from their parents, mothers from their suckling babes, wives from their husbands, driving them from one end of the country to the other? Notice the Spartans were heathens, who lived long before our Divine Master made his appearance in the flesh. Can Christian Americans deny these barbarous cruelties? Have you not, Americans, having subjected us under you, added to these miseries, by insulting us in telling us to our face, because we are helpless, that we are not of the human family? I ask you, O! Americans, I ask you, in the name of the Lord, can you deny these charges? Some perhaps may deny, by saying, that they never thought or said that we were not men. But do not actions speak louder than words?—have they not made provisions for the Greeks, and Irish? Nations who have never done the least thing for them, while *we,* who have enriched their country with our blood and tears—have dug up gold and silver for them and their children, from generation to generation, and are in more miseries than any other people under heaven, are not seen, but by comparatively, a handful of the American people? There are indeed, more ways to kill a dog, besides choking it to death with butter. Further—The Spartans or Lacedaemonians, had some frivolous pretext, for enslaving the Helots, for they (Helots) while being free inhabitants of Sparta, stirred up an intestine commotion, and were, by the Spartans subdued, and made prisoners of war. Consequently they and their children were condemned to perpetual slavery.[9]

I have been for years troubling the pages of historians, to find out what our fathers have done to the white *Christians of America,* to merit such condign punishment as they have inflicted on them, and do continue to inflict on us their children. But I must aver, that my researches have hitherto been to no effect. I have therefore, come to the immoveable conclusion, that they (Americans) have, and do continue to punish us for nothing else, but for enriching them and their country. For I cannot conceive of any thing else. Nor will I ever believe otherwise, until the Lord shall convince me.

The world knows, that slavery as it existed among the Romans, (which was the primary cause of their destruction) was, comparatively speaking, no more than a *cypher,* when compared with ours under the Americans. Indeed I should not have noticed the Roman slaves, had not the very learned and penetrating Mr. Jefferson said, "when a master was murdered, all his slaves in the same house, or within hearing, were condemned to death."[1]—Here let me ask Mr. Jefferson, (but he is gone to answer at the bar of God, for the deeds done in his body while living,) I therefore ask the whole American people, had I not rather die, or be put to death, than to be a slave to any tyrant, who takes not only my own, but my wife and children's lives by the inches? Yea, would I meet death with avidity far! far!! in preference to such *servile submission* to the murderous hands of tyrants. Mr. Jefferson's very severe remarks on us have been so extensively argued upon by men whose attainments in literature, I shall never be able to reach, that I would not have meddled with it, were it not to solicit each of my brethren, who

9. See Dr. Goldsmith's History of Greece—page 9. See also, Plutarch's Lives. The Helots subdued by Agis, king of *Sparta.*
1. See his Notes on Virginia, page 210.

has the spirit of a man, to buy a copy of Mr. Jefferson's "Notes on Virginia," and put it in the hand of his son. For let no one of us suppose that the refutations which have been written by our white friends are enough—they are *whites*—we are *blacks*. We, and the world wish to see the charges of Mr. Jefferson refuted by the blacks *themselves,* according to their chance; for we must remember that what the whites have written respecting this subject, is other men's labours, and did not emanate from the blacks. I know well, that there are some talents and learning among the coloured people of this country, which we have not a chance to develope, in consequence of oppression; but our oppression ought not to hinder us from acquiring all we can. For we will have a chance to develope them by and by. God will not suffer us, always to be oppressed. Our sufferings will come to an *end,* in spite of all the Americans this side of *eternity.* Then we will want all the learning and talents among ourselves, and perhaps more, to govern ourselves.—"Every dog must have its day," the American's is coming to an end.

But let us review Mr. Jefferson's remarks respecting us some further. Comparing our miserable fathers, with the learned philosophers of Greece, he says: "Yet notwithstanding these and other discouraging circumstances among the Romans, their slaves were often their rarest artists. They excelled too, in science, insomuch as to be usually employed as tutors to their master's children; Epictetus, Terence and Phædrus, were slaves,—but they were of the race of whites. It is not their *condition* then, but *nature,* which has produced the distinction."[2] See this, my brethren!! Do you believe that this assertion is swallowed by millions of the whites? Do you know that Mr. Jefferson was one of as great characters as ever lived among the whites? See his writings for the world, and public labours for the United States of America. Do you believe that the assertions of such a man, will pass away into oblivion unobserved by this people and the world? If you do you are much mistaken—See how the American people treat us—have we souls in our bodies? Are we men who have any spirits at all? I know that there are many *swell-bellied* fellows among us, whose greatest object is to fill their stomachs. Such I do not

mean—I am after those who know and feel, that we are MEN, as well as other people; to them, I say, that unless we try to refute Mr. Jefferson's arguments respecting us, we will only establish them.

But the slaves among the Romans. Every body who has read history, knows, that as soon as a slave among the Romans obtained his freedom, he could rise to the greatest eminence in the State, and there was no law instituted to hinder a slave from buying his freedom. Have not the Americans instituted laws to hinder us from obtaining our freedom? Do any deny this charge? Read the laws of Virginia, North Carolina, &c. Further: have not the Americans instituted laws to prohibit a man of colour from obtaining and holding any office whatever, under the government of the United States of America? Now, Mr. Jefferson tells us, that our condition is not so hard, as the slaves were under the Romans!!!!!!

It is time for me to bring this article to a close. But before I close it, I must observe to my brethren that at the close of the first Revolution in this country, with Great Britain, there were but thirteen States in the Union, now there are twenty-four, most of which are slave-holding States, and the whites are dragging us around in chains and in handcuffs, to their new States and Territories to work their mines and farms, to enrich them and their children—and millions of them believing firmly that we being a little darker than they, were made by our Creator to be an inheritance to them and their children for ever—the same as a parcel of brutes.

Are we MEN!!—I ask you, O my brethren! are we MEN? Did our Creator make us to be slaves to dust and ashes like ourselves? Are they not dying worms as well as we? Have they not to make their appearance before the tribunal of Heaven, to answer for the deeds done in the body, as well as we? Have we any other Master but Jesus Christ alone? Is he not their Master as well as ours?—What right then, have we to obey and call any other Master, but Himself? How we could be so *submissive* to a gang of men, whom we cannot tell whether they are as *good* as ourselves or not, I never could conceive. However, this is shut up with the Lord, and we cannot precisely tell—but I declare, we judge men by their works.

2. See his *Notes on Virginia,* p. 211.

The whites have always been an unjust, jealous, unmerciful, avaricious and blood-thirsty set of beings, always seeking after power and authority.—We view them all over the confederacy of Greece, where they were first known to be any thing, (in consequence of education) we see them there, cutting each other's throats—trying to subject each other to wretchedness and misery—to effect which, they used all kinds of deceitful, unfair, and unmerciful means. We view them next in Rome, where the spirit of tyranny and deceit raged still higher. We view them in Gaul, Spain, and in Britain.—In fine, we view them all over Europe, together with what were scattered about in Asia and Africa, as heathens, and we see them acting more like devils than accountable men. But some may ask, did not the blacks of Africa, and the mulattoes of Asia, go on in the same way as did the whites of Europe. I answer, no—they never were half so avaricious, deceitful and unmerciful as the whites, according to their knowledge.

But we will leave the whites or Europeans as heathens, and take a view of them as Christians, in which capacity we see them as cruel, if not more so than ever. In fact, take them as a body, they are ten times more cruel, avaricious and unmerciful than ever they were; for while they were heathens, they were bad enough it is true, but it is positively a fact that they were not quite so audacious as to go and take vessel loads of men, women and children, and in cold blood, and through devilishness, throw them into the sea, and murder them in all kind of ways. While they were heathens, they were too ignorant for such barbarity. But being Christians, enlightened and sensible, they are completely prepared for such hellish cruelties. Now suppose God were to give them more sense, what would they do? If it were possible, would they not *dethrone* Jehovah and seat themselves upon his throne? I therefore, in the name and fear of the Lord God of Heaven and of earth, divested of prejudice either on the side of my colour or that of the whites, advance my suspicion of them, whether they are as good *by nature* as we are or not. Their actions, since they were known as a people, have been the reverse, I do indeed suspect them, but this, as I before observed, is shut up with the Lord, we cannot exactly tell, it will be proved in succeeding generations.—The whites have had the essence of the gospel as it was preached by my master and his apostles—the Ethiopians have not, who are to have it in its meridian splendor—the Lord will give it to them to their satisfaction. I hope and pray my God, that they will make good use of it, that it may be well with them.[3]

RALPH WALDO EMERSON

from *Address Delivered on the Anniversary of the Emancipation of the Negroes in the British West Indies* [1844]

The American poet and philosopher Ralph Waldo Emerson (1803–1882) was a prominent figure in the anti-slavery movement from the 1840s until the Civil War. Before he could align himself with the abolitionist move-ment, Emerson had to overcome his wariness of single-issue causes and group organizations in general, as well as his underlying doubts about the natural attributes of "the negro." By 1844, however, when he delivered the

---

3. It is my solemn belief, that if ever the world becomes Christianized, (which must certainly take place before long) it will be through the means, under God of the Blacks, who are now held in wretchedness, and degradation, by the white Christians of the world, who before they learn to do justice to us before our Maker—and be reconciled to us, and reconcile us to them, and by that means have clear consciences before God and man.—Send out Missionaries to convert the Heathens, many of whom after they cease to worship gods, which neither see nor hear, become ten times more the children of Hell, than ever they were, why what is the reason? Why the reason is obvious, they must learn to do justice at home, before they go into distant lands, to display their charity, Christianity, and benevolence; when they learn to do justice, God will accept their offering, (no man may think that I am against Missionaries for I am not, my object is to see justice done at home, before we go to convert the Heathens.)

speech reprinted here, he had come to categorically reject "this old indecent nonsense over the nature of the negro."

Emerson was a leading figure of the philosophical movement of American transcendentalism. Central to transcendental thought was a belief in self-reliance, as developed in Emerson's 1837 speech, "The American Scholar": "We will walk on our own feet; we will work with our own hands; we will speak our own minds ... A nation of men will for the first time exist, because each believes himself inspired by the Divine Soul which also inspires all men." This idea of individual moral development as the key to progress made Emerson sympathetic to abolitionists such as William Lloyd Garrison (p. 111), who advocated moral suasion (the use of moral argument rather than political or physical force to bring about change). However, Emerson was hesitant to embrace the larger abolitionist movement, which also used social and political strategies to bring about change. In addition, until the 1840s, Emerson saw little evidence of achievement by black people that might contradict his assumptions about their natural inferiority. As he wrote in his journal, "Strange history this of *abolition*. The negro must be very old & belongs, one would say, to the fossil formations. What right has he to be intruding into the late & civil daylight of this dynasty of the Caucasians & Saxons? It is plain that so inferior a race must perish shortly like the poor Indians."

By 1844, however, Emerson's growing outrage over the expansion of slavery in the United States had contributed to his passionate rejection of American slavery, as had his recognition of outstanding black individuals and the dramatic progress made by the newly freed black slaves in the West Indies. Emerson's wife, Lydia (known as Lidian), was active in the anti-slavery movement, and when the Women's Anti-Slavery Society requested that he address its members, Emerson, at Lidian's urging, accepted the invitation. On August 1, 1844, Emerson publicly signaled his conversion to the anti-slavery cause in his speech to the group, delivered at the courthouse in Concord, Massachusetts, on the occasion of the tenth anniversary of the end of slavery in the West Indies. In a letter to the Catholic priest Isaac Hecker written on August 4, 1844, three days after Emerson delivered his speech in Concord, George Curtis, a member of the utopian experiment at Brook Farm and an admirer of Emerson's, noted that the speech represented a dramatic departure for Emerson: "It was not of that cold, clear, intellectual character that chills so many people, but full of ardent Life. His recent study of Anti Slavery history has infused a fine enthusiasm into his spirit & the address was very eloquent." The address brought Emerson recognition as an active member of the abolitionist movement, and he was asked to give encore readings of it at a number of subsequent abolitionist meetings.

From *The Complete Works of Ralph Waldo Emerson, Vol. 11, Miscellanies* (Boston: Houghton Mifflin, 1884); also, IV: Emancipation in the British West Indies, Works of Ralph Waldo Emerson, Ralph Waldo Emerson Institute, www.rwe.org.

The First of August marks the entrance of a new element into modern politics, namely, the civilization of the negro. A man is added to the human family. Not the least affecting part of this history of abolition is the annihilation of the old indecent nonsense about the nature of the negro. In the case of the ship Zong, in 1781, whose master had thrown one hundred and thirty-two slaves alive into the sea, to cheat the underwriters, the first jury gave a verdict in favor of the master and owners: they had a right to do what they had done. Lord Mansfield is reported to have said on the bench, "The matter left to the jury is,—Was it from necessity? For they had no doubt—though it shocks one very much—

that the case of slaves was the same as if horses had been thrown overboard. It is a very shocking case." But a more enlightened and humane opinion began to prevail. Mr. Clarkson, early in his career, made a collection of African productions and manufactures, as specimens of the arts and culture of the negro; comprising cloths and loom, weapons, polished stones and woods, leather, glass, dyes, ornaments, soap, pipe-bowls and trinkets. These he showed to Mr. Pitt, who saw and handled them with extreme interest. "On sight of these," says Clarkson, "many sublime thoughts seemed to rush at once into his mind, some of which he expressed;" and hence appeared to arise a project which was always dear to him, of the civilization of Africa,—a dream which forever elevates his fame. In 1791, Mr. Wilberforce announced to the House of Commons, "We have already gained one victory: we have obtained for these poor creatures the recognition of their human nature, which for a time was most shamefully denied them." It was the sarcasm of Montesquieu, "it would not do to suppose that negroes were men, lest it should turn out that whites were not;" for the white has, for ages, done what he could to keep the negro in that hoggish state. His laws have been furies. It now appears that the negro race is, more than any other, susceptible of rapid civilization. The emancipation is observed, in the islands, to have wrought for the negro a benefit as sudden as when a thermometer is brought out of the shade into the sun. It has given him eyes and ears. If, before, he was taxed with such stupidity, or such defective vision, that he could not set a table square to the walls of an apartment, he is now the principal if not the only mechanic in the West Indies; and is, besides, an architect, a physician, a lawyer, a magistrate, an editor, and a valued and increasing political power. The recent testimonies of Sturge, of Thome and Kimball, of Gurney, of Philippo, are very explicit on this point, the capacity and the success of the colored and the black population in employments of skill, of profit and of trust; and best of all is the testimony to their moderation. They receive hints and advances from the whites that they will be gladly received as subscribers to the Exchange,[1] as members of this or that committee of trust. They hold back, and say to each other that "social position is not to be gained by pushing."

I have said that this event interests us because it came mainly from the concession of the whites; I add, that in part it is the earning of the blacks. They won the pity and respect which they have received, by their powers and native endowments. I think this a circumstance of the highest import. Their whole future is in it. Our planet, before the age of written history, had its races of savages, like the generations of sour paste, or the animalcules that wiggle and bite in a drop of putrid water. Who cares for these or for their wars? We do not wish

a world of bugs or of birds; neither afterward of Scythians, Caraibs or Feejees. The grand style of Nature, her great periods, is all we observe in them. Who cares for oppressing whites, or oppressed blacks, twenty centuries ago, more than for bad dreams? Eaters and food are in the harmony of Nature; and there too is the germ forever protected, unfolding gigantic leaf after leaf, a newer flower, a richer fruit, in every period, yet its next product is never to be guessed. It will only save what is worth saving; and it saves not by compassion, but by power. It appoints no police to guard the lion but his teeth and claws; no fort or city for the bird but his wings; no rescue for flies and mites but their spawning numbers, which no ravages can overcome. It deals with men after the same manner. If they are rude and foolish, down they must go. When at last in a race a new principle appears, an idea,—that conserves it; ideas only save races. If the black man is feeble and not important to the existing races, not on a parity with the best race, the black man must serve, and be exterminated. But if the black man carries in his bosom an indispensable element of a new and coming civilization; for the sake of that element, no wrong nor strength nor circumstance can hurt him: he will survive and play his part. So now, the arrival in the world of such men as Toussaint,[2] and the Haytian heroes, or of the leaders of their race in Barbadoes and Jamaica, outweighs in good omen all the English and American humanity. The anti-slavery of the whole world is dust in the balance before this,—is a poor squeamishness and nervousness: the might and the right are here: here is the anti-slave: here is man: and if you have man, black or white is an insignificance. The intellect,—that is miraculous! Who has it, has the talisman: his skin and bones, though they were of the color of night, are transparent, and the everlasting stars shine through, with attractive beams. But a compassion for that which is not and cannot be useful or lovely, is degrading and futile. All the songs and newspapers and money subscriptions and vituperation of such as do not think with us, will avail nothing against a fact. I say to you, you must save yourself, black or white, man or woman; other help is none. I esteem the occasion of

1. Investors in the stock market.
2. Toussaint-Louverture (ca. 1743–1803), originally François-Dominique Toussaint, a former slave who rose to lead the Haitian Revolution that brought about the abolition of slavery and independence from France in 1804.

this jubilee to be the proud discovery that the black race can contend with the white: that in the great anthem which we call history, a piece of many parts and vast compass, after playing a long time a very low and subdued accompaniment, they perceive the time arrived when they can strike in with effect and take a master's part in the music. The civility of the world has reached that pitch that their more moral genius is becoming indispensable, and the quality of this race is to be honored for itself. For this, they have been preserved in sandy deserts, in rice-swamps, in kitchens and shoe-shops, so long: now let them emerge, clothed and in their own form.

There remains the very elevated consideration which the subject opens, but which belongs to more abstract views than we are now taking, this, namely, that the civility of no race can be perfect whilst another race is degraded. It is a doctrine alike of the oldest and of the newest philosophy, that man is one, and that you can-not injure any member, without a sympathetic injury to all the members. America is not civil, whilst Africa is barbarous.

These considerations seem to leave no choice for the action of the intellect and the conscience of the country. There have been moments in this, as well as in every piece of moral history, when there seemed room for the infusions of a skeptical philosophy, when it seemed doubtful whether brute force would not triumph in the eternal struggle. I doubt not that, sometimes, a despairing negro, when jumping over the ship's sides to escape from the white devils who surrounded him, has believed there was no vindication of right; it is horrible to think of, but it seemed so. I doubt not that sometimes the negro's friend, in the face of scornful and

brutal hundreds of traders and drivers, has felt his heart sink. Especially, it seems to me, some degree of despondency is pardonable, when he observes the men of conscience and of intellect, his own natural allies and champions,—those whose attention should be nailed to the grand objects of this cause, so hotly offended by whatever incidental petulances or infirmities of indiscreet defenders of the negro, as to permit themselves to be ranged with the enemies of the human race; and names which should be the alarums of liberty and the watchwords of truth, are mixed up with all the rotten rabble of selfishness and tyranny. I assure myself that this coldness and blindness will pass away. A single noble wind of sentiment will scatter them forever. I am sure that the good and wise elders, the ardent and generous youth, will not permit what is incidental and exceptional to with-draw their devotion from the essential and permanent characters of the question. There have been moments, I said, when men might be forgiven who doubted. Those moments are past. Seen in masses, it cannot be disputed, there is progress in human society. There is a blessed necessity by which the interest of men is always driving them to the right; and, again, making all crime mean and ugly. The genius of the Saxon race, friendly to liberty; the enterprise, the very muscular vigor of this nation, are inconsistent with slavery. The Intellect, with blazing eye, looking through history from the beginning onward, gazes on this blot and it disappears. The sentiment of Right, once very low and indistinct, but ever more articulate, because it is the voice of the universe, pronounces Freedom. The Power that built this fabric of things affirms it in the heart; and in the history of the First of August, has made a sign to the ages, of his will.

Josiah Clark Nott and George R. Gliddon
from *Types of Mankind* [1854]

Polygenism, the theory that different races have different ancient origins, gained widespread recognition with the 1854 publication of Josiah Nott and George Gliddon's *Types of Mankind*. So popular was this book of over 800

pages that it was reprinted nine times before the turn of the century. Nott (1804–1873) and Gliddon (1809–1857) built on the work of fellow members of the "American school of ethnology" (also known as the American school of anthropology), a loose-knit group of white American historians and scientists that included Louis Agassiz and Samuel Morton. Using "scientific methods," such as measuring the cranial capacity of skulls of people of different ethnicities, members of the school of ethnology strove to quantify the existence of innate racial differences and locate those differences in diverse ancestries.

In this illustration from *Types of Mankind*, Nott and Gliddon represent the "ideal" type of human with a drawing of a famous statue of the Greek god Apollo. In contrast, they point to similarities between their depictions of the "Negro" and the "Young Chimpanzee," citing them as proof of both the theory of polygenism and the innate intellectual inferiority of "Negroes."

From Josiah Clark Nott, George Robins Gliddon, Samuel George Morton, Louis Agassiz, William Usher, Henry Stuart Patterson, *Types of Mankind* (Philadelphia: Lippincott, Grambo & co., 1854), p. 459.

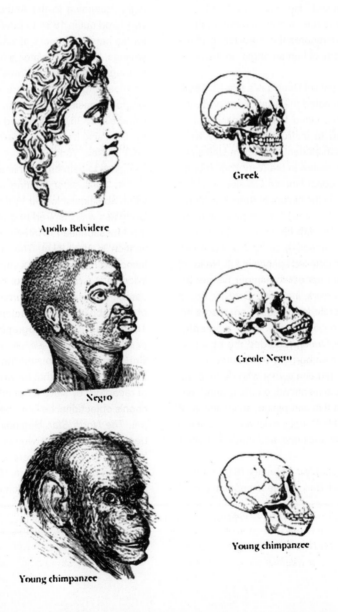

Apollo Belvidere

Greek

Negro

Creole Negro

Young chimpanzee

Young chimpanzee

FREDERICK DOUGLASS

from *The Claims of the Negro Ethnologically Considered* [1854]

The year the famed abolitionist Frederick Douglass (ca. 1818–1895) delivered this historic commencement address at Western Reserve College was a high point of the polygenism movement in America, propelled by the publication of Josiah Clark Nott and George R. Gliddon's ethnological tome *Types of Mankind* (p. 36). In his speech, Douglass directly attacks *Types of Mankind* as both "unsound" and "wicked." He also refutes polygenist claims by stressing the role of environment in shaping human traits and underscores the importance of the debate about the "diversity of human origin" in the overall debate about slavery.

Contemporary accounts of Douglass's July 12, 1854, commencement address noted the symbolic importance of the occasion, with one citing the significance of "a black man [* * *] invited to instruct the already well-instructed Anglo-American student in his own University halls." The July 31, 1854, review in the *New York Tribune* by the white newspaper editor Horace Greeley heralded the event as "an anomaly in the history of American literature" and "a triumph for humanity." In keeping with the occasion, Douglass broke with his habitual custom of speaking either extemporaneously or from a few notes and instead wrote out his detailed speech in full. Reading from a manuscript did not appear to hamper his performance, and several observers, including Greeley, noted how Douglass used his oratorical skills to underscore his argument. James M. Gregory, in his 1893 biography, *Frederick Douglass, the Orator*, recorded the observations of one audience member: "In the course of his address, Mr. Douglass cited one author who decried the claim of the negro to equal manhood, on the ground that 'the voice of the negro is thin and piping, an evidence of inferiority.' This passage Mr. Douglass delivered in a voice of thunder, convulsing the audience, and rendering other reply needless."

Born into slavery, probably in February 1818, Frederick Douglass (né Frederick Bailey) rose to become one of the most influential leaders of his time. Douglass lived with his grandparents on a plantation in Maryland until he was six. He and his mother belonged to Aaron Anthony, a white man who was the plantation supervisor and possibly Douglass's father, but he rarely saw his mother, as she was hired out to a neighboring plantation. He began to learn to read after being sent to live in Baltimore at age eight. Returning to the Anthony farm as a teenager, he was hired out in 1834 to Edward Covey, who was known for his harsh treatment of slaves. In his autobiographical writings, Douglass relates a turning point in his life when he fought back against Covey's abuse, renewing his spirit and learning that "men are whipped oftenist who are whipped easiest." After an unsuccessful attempt to escape in 1836, he managed to gain his freedom in 1838 by disguising himself as a sailor and traveling by train and boat to New York City. That year, he took the name of Douglass to help protect himself from slave catchers.

In 1841, after hearing a speech delivered by the white abolitionist leader William Lloyd Garrison (p. 111), Douglass was inspired to give his first public speech, at the Massachusetts Anti-Slavery Society's annual convention in Nantucket. The success of his appearance launched his career as a public speaker, and Garrison became Douglass's mentor during the first years of that career. Douglass gained international fame as a leader of the abolitionist movement with the publication in 1845 of his first autobiography, *The Narrative of the Life of Frederick Douglass, an American Slave*. In 1846, British supporters raised the money to buy Douglass's freedom legally so that he would no longer be in danger of recapture by slave catchers. The next year, over Garrison's objections, he launched his own weekly newspaper, *The North Star*. Beginning in 1848, Douglass also became active in the women's rights movement. In his later years, he held numerous government posts. Douglass died of heart failure in 1895, following a speech at the National Council of Women.

From Fredrick Douglass, *The Claims of the Negro, Ethnologically Considered* (Rochester, N.Y.: Press of Lee, Mann & Co., 1854).

Perhaps, of all the attempts ever made to disprove the unity of the human family, and to brand the negro with natural inferiority, the most compendious and barefaced is the book, entitled *"Types of Mankind,"* by Nott and Glidden.[1] One would be well employed, in a series of Lectures, directed to an exposure of the unsoundness, if not the wickedness of this work.

THE AFRICAN RACE BUT ONE PEOPLE.

But I must hasten. Having shown that the people of Africa are, probably, one people; that each tribe bears an intimate relation to other tribes and nations in that quarter of the globe, and that the Egyptians may have flung off the different tribes seen there at different times, as implied by the evident relations of their language, and by other similarities; it can hardly be deemed unreasonable to suppose, that the African branch of the human species—from the once highly civilized Egyptian to the barbarians on the banks of the Niger—may claim brotherhood with the great family of Noah, spreading over the more Northern and Eastern parts of the globe. I will now proceed to consider those physical peculiarities of form, features, hair and color, which are supposed by some men to mark the African, not only as an inferior race, but as a distinct species, naturally and originally different from the rest of mankind, and as really to place him nearer to the brute than to man.

THE EFFECT OF CIRCUMSTANCES UPON THE PHYSICAL MAN.

I may remark, just here, that it is impossible, even were it desirable, in a discourse like this, to attend to the anatomical and physiological argument connected with this part of the subject. I am not equal to that, and if I were, the occasion does not require it. The form of the *negro*—[I use the term *negro,* precisely in the sense that you use the term Anglo Saxon; and I believe, too, that the former will one day be as illustrious as the latter]—has often been the subject of remark. His flat feet, long arms, high cheek bones and retreating forehead, are especially dwelt upon, to his disparagement,

and just as if there were no white people with precisely the same peculiarities. I think it will ever be found, that the *well* or *ill* condition of any part of mankind, will leave its mark on the physical as well as on the intellectual part of man. A hundred instances might be cited, of whole families who have degenerated, and others who have improved in personal appearance, by a change of circumstances. A man is worked upon by what *he* works on. He may carve out his circumstances, but his circumstances will carve him out as well. I told a boot maker in New Castle upon Tyne, that I had been a plantation slave. He said I must pardon him; but he could not believe it; no plantation laborer ever had a high instep. He said he had noticed, that the coal heavers and work people in low condition, had, for the most part, flat feet, and that he could tell, by the shape of the feet, whether a man's parents were in high or low condition. The thing was worth a thought, and I have thought of it, and have looked around me for facts. There is some truth in it; though there are exceptions, in individual cases.

The day I landed in Ireland, nine years ago, I addressed, (in company with Father SPRATT, and that good man who has been recently made the subject of bitter attack; I allude to the philanthropic JAMES HAUGHTON, of Dublin,) a large meeting of the common people of Ireland, on temperance. Never did human faces tell a sadder tale. More than five thousand were assembled; and I say, with no wish to wound the feelings of any Irishman, that these people lacked only a black skin and woolly hair, to complete their likeness to the plantation negro. The open, uneducated mouth—the long, gaunt arm—the badly formed foot and ankle—the shuffling gait—the retreating forehead and vacant expression—and, their petty quarrels and fights—all reminded me of the plantation, and my own cruelly abused people. Yet, *that* is the land of GRATTAN, of CURRAN, of O'CONNELL, and of SHERIDAN. Now, while what I have said is true of the common people, the fact is, there are no more really handsome people in the world, than the educated Irish people. The Irishman educated, is a model gentleman; the Irishman ignorant and degraded, compares in form and feature, with the negro!

I am stating facts. If you go into Southern Indiana, you will see what climate and habit can do, even in one generation. The man may have come from New England,

1. Gliddon: Referred to as Glidden by Frederick Douglass and others.

but his hard features, sallow complexion, have left little of New England on his brow. The right arm of the blacksmith is said to be larger and stronger than his left. The ship carpenter is at forty round shouldered. The shoemaker carries the marks of his trade. One locality becomes famous for one thing, another for another. Manchester and Lowell, in America, Manchester and Sheffield, in England, attest this. But what does it all prove? Why, nothing positively, as to the main point; still, it raises the inquiry—May not the condition of men explain their various appearances? Need we go behind the vicissitudes of barbarism for an explanation of the gaunt, wiry, apelike appearance of some of the genuine negroes? Need we look higher than a vertical sun, or lower than the damp, black soil of the Niger, the Gambia, the Senegal, with their heavy and enervating miasma, rising ever from the rank growing and decaying vegetation, for an explanation of the negro's color? If a cause, full and adequate, can be found here, *why seek further?*

The eminent Dr. LATHAM [* * *] says that nine tenths of the white population of the globe are found between 30 and 65 degrees North latitude. Only about one fifth of all the inhabitants of the globe are white; and they are as far from the Adamic complexion as is the negro. The remainder are—*what?* Ranging all the way from the brunette to jet black. There are the red, the reddish copper color, the yellowish, the dark brown, the chocolate color, and so on, to the jet black. On the mountains on the North of Africa, where water freezes in winter at times, branches of the same people who are *black* in the valley are *white* on the mountains. The Nubian, with his beautiful curly hair, finds it becoming frizzled, crisped, and even woolly, as he approaches the great Sahara. The Portuguese, white in Europe, is brown in Asia. The Jews, who are to be found in all countries, never intermarrying, are white in Europe, brown in Asia, and black in Africa. Again, what does it all prove? Nothing, absolutely; nothing which places the question beyond dispute; but it *does* justify the conjecture before referred to, that Outward circumstances *may* have something to do with modifying the various phases of humanity; and that color itself is at the control of the world's climate and its various concomitants. It is the sun that paints the peach—and may it not be, that

he paints the *man* as well? My reading, on this point, however, as well as my own observation, have convinced me, that from the beginning the Almighty, within certain limits, endowed mankind with organizations capable of countless variations in form, feature and color, without having it necessary to begin a new creation for every new variety.

A powerful argument in favor of the oneness of the human family, is afforded in the fact that nations, however dissimilar, may be united in one social state, not only without detriment to each other, but, most clearly, to the advancement of human welfare, happiness and perfection. While it is clearly proved, on the other hand, that those nations freest from foreign elements, present the most evident marks of deterioration. Dr. JAMES MCCUNE SMITH,[2] himself a colored man, a gentleman and scholar, alledges—and not without excellent reason—that this, our own great nation, so distinguished for industry and enterprise, is largely indebted to its composite character. We all know, at any rate, that now, what constitutes the very heart of the civilized world—(I allude to England)—has only risen from barbarism to its present lofty eminence, through successive invasions and alliances with her people. The Medes and Persians constituted one of the mightiest empires that ever rocked the globe. The most terrible nation which now threatens the peace of the world to make its will the law of Europe, is a grand piece of Mosaic work, in which almost every nation has its characteristic feature, from the wild Tartar to the refined Pole.

But, gentlemen, the time fails me, and I must bring these remarks to a close. My argument has swelled beyond its appointed measure. What I intended to make special, has become, in its progress, somewhat general. I meant to speak here to-day, for the lonely and the despised ones, with whom I was cradled, and with whom I have suffered; and now, gentlemen, in conclusion, what if all this reasoning be unsound? What if the negro may not be able to prove his relationship to Nubians, Abyssinians and Egyptians? What if ingenious men are able to find plausible objections to all arguments maintaining the oneness of the human race? What, after all, if they are able to show very good rea-

2. See p. 42.

sons for believing the negro to have been created precisely as we find him on the Gold Coast—along the Senegal and the Niger—I say, what of all this?—*"A man's a man for a' that."*[3] I sincerely believe, that the weight of the argument is in favor of the unity of origin of the human race, or species—that the arguments on the other side are partial, superficial, utterly subversive of the happiness of man, and insulting to the wisdom of God. Yet, what if we grant they are not so? What, if we grant that the case, on our part, is not made out? Does it follow, that the negro should be held in contempt? Does it follow, that to enslave and imbrute him is either *just* or *wise*? I think not. Human rights stand upon a common basis; and by all the reason that they are supported, maintained and defended, for one variety of the human family, they are supported, maintained and defended for *all* the human family; because all mankind have the same wants, arising out of a common nature. A diverse origin does not disprove a common nature, nor does it disprove a united destiny. The essential characteristics of humanity are everywhere the same. In the language of the eloquent CURRAN, "No matter what complexion, whether an Indian or an African sun has burnt upon him," his title deed to freedom, his claim to life and to liberty, to knowledge and to civilization, to society and to Christianity, are just and perfect. It is registered in the Courts of Heaven, and is enforced by the eloquence of the God of all the earth.

I have said that the negro and white man are likely ever to remain the principal inhabitants of this country. I repeat the statement now, to submit the reasons that support it. The blacks can disappear from the face of the country by three ways. They may be colonized,—they may be exterminated,—or, they may die out. Colonization is out of the question; for I know not what hardships the laws of the land can impose, which can induce the colored citizen to leave his native soil. He was here in its infancy; he is here in its age. Two hundred years have passed over him, his tears and blood have been mixed with the soil, and his attachment to the place of his birth is stronger than iron. It is not probable that he will be exterminated; two considerations must prevent a crime so stupendous as that—the influence of Chris-

tianity on the one hand, and the power of self interest on the other; and, in regard to their dying out, the statistics of the country afford no encouragement for such a conjecture. The history of the negro race proves them to be wonderfully adapted to all countries, all climates, and all conditions. Their tenacity of life, their powers of endurance, their maleable toughness, would almost imply especial interposition on their behalf. The ten thousand horrors of slavery, striking hard upon the sensitive soul, have bruised, and battered, and stung, but have not killed. The poor bondman lifts a smiling face above the surface of a sea of agonies, *hoping on, hoping ever.* His tawny brother, the Indian, dies, under the flashing glance of the Anglo-Saxon. *Not* so the negro; civilization cannot kill him. He accepts it—becomes a part of it. In the Church, he is an Uncle Tom; in the State, he is the most abused and least offensive. All the facts in his history mark out for him a destiny, united to America and Americans. Now, whether this population shall, by FREEDOM, INDUSTRY, VIRTUE and INTELLIGENCE, be made a blessing to the country and the world, or whether their multiplied wrongs shall kindle the vengeance of an offended God, will depend upon the conduct of no class of men so much as upon the Scholars of the country. The future public opinion of the land, whether anti-slavery or pro slavery, whether just or unjust, whether magnanimous or mean, must redound to the honor of the Scholars of the country or cover them with shame. There is but one safe road for nations or for individuals. The fate of a wicked man and of a wicked nation is the same. The flaming sword of offended justice falls as certainly upon the nation as upon the man. God has no children whose rights may be safely trampled upon. The sparrow may not fall to the ground without the notice of his eye, and men are more than sparrows.

Now, gentlemen, I have done. The subject is before you. I shall not undertake to make the application. I speak as unto wise men. I stand in the presence of Scholars. We have met here to-day from vastly different points in the world's condition. I have reached here—if you will pardon the egotism—by little short of a miracle; at any rate, by dint of some application and perseverance. Born, as I was, in obscurity, a stranger to the

---

3. Common name for "Is There for Honest Poverty," a song written by the Scottish poet Robert Burns in 1795; Burns is famous for expressing egalitarian ideals.

halls of learning, environed by ignorance, degradation, and their concomitants, from birth to manhood, I do not feel at liberty to mark out, with any degree of confidence, or dogmatism, what is the precise vocation of the Scholar. Yet, this I *can* say, as a denizen of the world, and as a citizen of a country rolling in the sin and shame of Slavery, the most flagrant and scandalous that ever saw the sun, "Whatsoever things are true, whatsoever things are honest, whatsoever things are just, whatsoever things are pure, whatsoever things are lovely, whatsoever things are of good report, if there be any virtue, and if there be any praise, think on these things."[4]

JAMES MCCUNE SMITH

from *On the Fourteenth Query of Thomas Jefferson's Notes on Virginia* [1859]

Thomas Jefferson's 1784 *Notes on the State of Virginia* (p. 17) is divided into twenty-three chapters, or "queries." Query 14, "Laws," includes a discussion of the political, physical, and moral problems that would arise if freed slaves were to remain in the United States after emancipation. In "On the Fourteenth Query of Thomas Jefferson's *Notes on Virginia*," James McCune Smith (1813–1865), the first African American to receive a medical degree, argues that understanding "the nature of the people" is key to answering the fundamental question posed by Jefferson: "Can the black and the white live together in harmony under American institutions?" For McCune Smith, "nature" includes physical, mental, and moral characteristics, and he devotes his article to a systematic examination of the claims Jefferson and his followers make about "the physical differences between the races." At the end of his essay, McCune Smith promises a subsequent essay discussing claims about mental and moral differences. However, as the editor James Stauffer notes in *The Works of James McCune Smith* (2006), no later article on this topic has been found.

Like Frederick Douglass in "The Claims of the Negro Ethnologically Considered" (p. 38), McCune Smith ultimately links physical differences to external conditions such as climate and soil. In addition, he proposes that nearly all races are mixtures; only the albino—"a deformed variety of the human species"—is pure white. Interestingly, McCune Smith alludes to evidence of Thomas Jefferson's relationship with Sally Hemings, who was of mixed race, in his argument that there is a natural attraction between peoples of different races—a response to Jefferson's assertion that white people are naturally more beautiful.

In his writing, McCune Smith frequently drew on science to challenge what he termed "a constructive negro," an abstract image of African Americans so distorted by ignorance and prejudice that it inhibited reason, justice, and mercy. As he wrote in an 1852 essay published in *Frederick Douglass' Paper* (as *The North Star* was later called), "The *negro* 'with us' is not an actual physical being of flesh and bones and blood, but a hideous monster of the mind." As an alternative to racial characterizations, McCune Smith fought for viewing people as individuals and even used statistical data to show that there was more variation between people of the same "race" than between people of different "races," a radical theory at the time.

From *Anglo-American Magazine,* August 1859.

4. From Saint Paul's letter to the Philippians (Philippians 4:8).

What further is to be done with them?" enquired Thomas Jefferson in 1787.[1] "What, then, *is* to be done" is demanded of Dr. Dewey fifty-seven years afterwards.[2] These questions relate to the colored population of these United States. "What further is to be done with them?" "What is to be done with them?" Can they be elevated to the same rank with the white citizens of this great Republic? This question involves another: Is the standard occupied by the whites really elevated above that occupied by the black population? What is the standard of mind—of excellence? Is it ingenuity in constructing machinery? Is it in morals? Is it in physical courage? Or is it to be measured by the tone of a "shop-keeping gentility?" The standard of excellence is not fixed. The question of elevation must therefore be an undeterminate question. It is hard to say who is more elevated: the master, learned, acute, ingenious, the constructer of splendid machinery, the framer of laws, the successful financier, the acute philosopher—the one master of all this, with a slave-whip in his hand—or the poor Christian slave, his breast heaving, his eyes raining tears, his flesh rooted up, quivering beneath the lash, whilst he prays to God to soften the heart [of] the accomplished torturer. Who is the more elevated?

It is better to lay aside, then, this word *"elevation,"* because it is uncertain in its meaning. Let us put the same question in another form: Can the black and the white live together in harmony under American institutions, each contributing to the peace and prosperity of the country, and to the development of the problem of self-government involved in American institutions?

If there be any reason why they can not live together and contribute to the general advancement, this reason must be found either in the institutions of the country, or in the nature of the people.

There is no such reason to be found in the institutions of the country, when those institutions are in accordance with the principles of democracy. In Maine, Massachusetts, and Rhode Island, where the laws are made equal for all men, we find all men, including black and white, living in peace and harmony. And these States are bright examples of progress. It is only where the institutions of the State make invidious distinctions, as in South Carolina, Mississippi, and Georgia, that we find the whites and blacks living together, in peace indeed, but retrograding rather than advancing in civil and religious liberty and in general prosperity.

There is nothing, therefore, in institutions, purely and equally democratic, which bars the mutual harmony and general progress of these races.

If there be no reason, founded upon democratic institutions, which prevents the harmonious dwelling together of these two races, is there anything in the races themselves which constitutes such a prohibition?

Mr. Jefferson contends that there are physical and mental distinctions between the negro and the white man—distinctions which must ever prevent them from an equal and harmonious participation in the blessings of democratic freedom.

This constitutes the main proposition in his fourteenth query. In support of this proposition he produces certain views, speculations, and reasonings, which many writers since his day, including de Tocqueville[3] and Dr. Dewey, have admitted without questioning, and have urged as quite unanswerable.

* * *

On the 268th page of his Notes on Virginia, Mr. Jefferson asks: "Why not retain and incorporate the blacks into the State," &c. He answers, on the next page, "Deep-rooted prejudices entertained by the whites; ten thousand recollections by the blacks of the injuries they have sustained; new provocation; the real distinctions which nature has made; and many other circumstances, will divide us into parties, and produce convulsions which will probably never end but in the extermination of the one or the other race. To these

---

1. Jefferson's Notes, Fourteenth Query, p. 202. Edit. 1801. Philad. [McCune Smith's note] The first public edition in English was published in 1787 (see p. 17).
2. A Discourse on Slavery and the Annexation of Texas, by Orville Dewey. New York: C. S. Francis, 1844. [McCune Smith's note] Dewey (1794–1882), a Unitarian minister and highly regarded preacher, was not an abolitionist but opposed slavery.
3. Alexis de Tocqueville (1805–59), French writer and politician who wrote the two-volume *Democracy in America* (1835, 1840), an influential study of early America.

objections, which are political, may be added others which are physical and moral," &c.

Mr. Jefferson then states the physical and mental differences which exist, and which, in his opinion, will forever prevent the incorporation of the blacks into the State. His arrangement of these views is so mixed and confused, that we must depart from it, and consider, *first* the physical, *secondly* the mental differences between the races.

First, In regard to the physical differences between the races.

In discussing this portion of the subject, we will not confine ourselves to the views announced by Thomas Jefferson, but will examine all the views and statements which have been urged since his work appeared, and which support his views.

The physical differences which are urged as existing between whites and blacks are: *first,* those which relate to the bones of the body; *secondly,* those which relate to the muscles; *thirdly,* those which relate to the texture of the hair; and *fourthly,* the color of the skin.

THE OSTEOLOGICAL DIFFERENCES,

Or those which are said to exist in the bones, do not relate to the number of the bones, for in this both races are alike; nor do they relate to the form of the bones, because as much difference is found to exist between the forms of the bones of different individuals, who are undoubtedly white, as are laid to exist between the blacks and the whites. And these very differences, so far from being characteristic, simply prove this: that whilst there are the same individual varieties in each race, there are also the same general resemblances. The fallacy in the argument has consisted in this: the variations in the black race have been arranged together and have been called the type of the race, and as such have been compared with, not the varieties, but the general type of the whites, and from this unfair comparison the illogical conclusion has been adduced that there is a permanent difference between these two

races. This argument is about as conclusive as if we were to select all the white men in this city who have grey eyes, and to argue that because the color of their eyes differs from that of the remainder, therefore the two classes belong to different races.

In illustration of this view, let us take up one of the osteological differences alleged to exist between the white and black races. It has been said by many writers, and among the rest by Dr. John Augustine Smith, that there is a permanent difference in the form of the skull exhibited by these two races. This view will be found in the abstract of a lecture on the different races of men, by Dr. J. A. Smith, in an appendix to Lyell's *Lectures on Geology,* printed at the office of the "Tribune."

It is said by the learned lecturer, Dr. Smith, that the skull of the negro approaches very nearly to the form of the skull of the ape, and recedes very much from the form of the skull of the white or Caucasian race.

In proof of this, he states that the facial angle in the Caucasian is eighty degrees, in the ape sixty-four degrees, in the black seventy degrees.

The skulls selected from the white race for this admensuration were rather above than below the usual admeasurement; whilst the skulls selected from the blacks were extreme cases of acuteness of this angle or flatness of the forehead. They constituted the exceptions. That there are cases amongst the whites in whom the facial angle is equally acute will be evident to anyone who will take the trouble to look at a profile of Henry Clay, General Lafayette,[4] or at most of the heads found on French and Spanish coins of the latter part of the last century.

This is sufficient to destroy the general conclusion that there is less difference between the facial angle of the ape and the black than between the angle of the latter and the white.

There is further proof that this conclusion is not a true one. The skulls of the apes used by Professor Camper, who was the author of this mode of mensuration, were the skulls of young apes; in the skull of the young of this animal there is a greater approximation

---

4. Marie-Joseph-Paul-Yves-Roch-Gilbert du Motier de Lafayette (1757–1834), French general in the Continental Army during the American Revolution. Henry Clay (1777–1852), prominent politician from Kentucky and co-founder of the American Colonization Society, was dedicated to sending former slaves to Africa.

to the facial angle of man, than in the adult ape. Mr. Owen, the most distinguished of British naturalists, has shown that the facial angle of the adult troglodyte is only thirty-five degrees, and that of the ourang, or satyr thirty degrees.[5]

Hence, if we grant that the facial angle of the negro measured only seventy degrees, it is between thirty-five and forty degrees larger than the facial angle of the ape, while it is only ten degrees less than the most obtuse angle of the European head. And this is only one of the many wide chasms, if they may be so called, which divide the human species from all other species of animals.

It is unnecessary to cite the statements of travelers in Africa to prove that the flat, retreating forehead is not the type but the variety in the heads of the native blacks. Any who are curious in this matter may visit any of our colored churches, and will find the low, retreating forehead to be the exception, and not the rule.

But this facial angle itself has been assumed to be the measurer of intellect; and this assumption is based upon two things not yet proven: *First,* that intelligence bears some proportion to the development of the brain; *Second,* that the facial angle is a measure of the quantity of brain. It would require more time than we have at present to expose the fallacy of the first assumption; but its relation to this subject is destroyed if we can overthrow the second. The facial angle is not a measure of the quantity of brain in man. So far from this, it is neither a measure of the solid contents of the skull, nor of the relative position of the different parts of the brain contained in the skull.

It simply measures the position of the upper jaw in regard to the orifice of the ear and edge of the orbit: these last two being points fixed upon the skull, and the latter moving in the skull. Hence if two skulls of precisely the same shape have the upper jaw placed differently upon them, they will measure facial angles differing ten degrees, or even twenty degrees.

Other admeasurements of the skull have been taken, with a view to prove that there is a wide difference between the skulls of blacks and whites, and a close resemblance between the crania of blacks and monkeys. But these comparisons fail in like manner with the above.

Mr. Owen has recently set this question at rest by showing "that strongly marked and most important characters distinguish the quadrumanous type from that of the human skull."

* * *

From these and similar facts, it is evident that far from there being any great and uniformly marked differences in the elementary shape, form, or size of the skulls of the African and the white, there exists in reality a uniform resemblance, proving that from the bony structure of the human frame, there can be deduced the sublime argument of the unity of the human race.

Before leaving this part of the subject, it may be well to state that the researches of the best anatomists have not been able, on a careful comparison, to discover in the brains of the white and the black any differences in size, weight, consistence, or color of the two.

* * *

Much stress has been laid upon the fact that the bones of the leg in the black are somewhat more bent than in the white races. This is not universally true. On the coast of Africa, where we are to look for the type of this race, we find this bending of the tibia to be the exception, and not the rule. And these exceptions are traced to the geological, or rather the topographical aspect of the country inhabited by a small portion of the native tribes.

That climate, or, more properly speaking, geological position, has a powerful influence upon the bony structure of man, is a proposition which numerous facts in our own sphere of observation tend to support. The colored race now living in Maryland and Virginia have a depth of chest and symmetry of form so very remarkable that we have been able to tell the birthplace of very many men of those States by a simple examination of their chests.

Only two hundred years have elapsed since their ancestors, made up of every of the many diversities of

5. Zool[ogical] Transact[ion], vol. 1 [1835], pp. 372, 373. [McCune Smith's note] Sir Richard Owen (1804–92), a British paleontologist who was one of the foremost specialists in comparative anatomy; Ourang or satyr: orangutan.

the African tribes, first landed at Jamestown. Yet two centuries have made a marked uniformity in the frames of men who would otherwise have retained their original varieties. This could only be the result of geological influences.

By an inspection of the busts of Daniel Webster, Henry Clay, and Thos. H. Benton,[6] as a distinguished sculptor informed me, any one may trace the perceptible developments of the Indian form of skull, and this is equally true of all the descendants of families that have resided during several generations on this continent. Here is other proof of the influence of geology on the bony frame of mankind, for these results cannot be traced to the "admixture" of Indian blood.

Thus much on the topic of osteology. There is no reason to infer, from the structure of the skeleton, that there are distinctions and permanent differences between the framework of the white and black races.

We shall say little about the *muscular system*. One poor, persecuted muscle—that which constitutes, principally, the calf of the leg—has been the cause of earnest speculation by those who have sought differences where the Almighty has stamped uniformity. These earnest seekers after not the truth, but the differences, cannot deny the fact that this muscle *does* exist in both races, but they rejoice in finding it smaller and higher up in the leg of the black than in that limb in the white.

The head and front of this offending is that the black race have less *calf* than their brethren of the fairer hue. Even this "soft-impeachment" is not universally true. It is only the exception; and it is to be found, as Mr. Walsh states in his Notes on Brazil, among those miserable slaves who are made to bear very heavy burdens on their heads from an early age. By this means the arch of the foot is flattened down, this muscle is scarcely brought into use, and hence dwindles away, whilst the bones of the leg, necessarily thrown forward, acquire a curve. The same thing is brought about by the low, miserable diet on which some of this class are forced to subsist.

This low diet produces rachitis, or rickets, in which disease the bones assume the peculiar form above named. And this fact is true of all men of every race. "Bandy legs," as they are termed, may be found as frequently among the masters as among the slaves of the South. And if this peculiar bend should be sufficient to rule the blacks out from the circle of mandom, it would, if rigidly applied, rule out many who have a white complexion. It is a curious confirmation of this view that the inhabitants of a portion of the western coast of Ireland, a people who submit to the same low diet, and other privations analogous to those endured by a portion of the natives of the African coast, have very nearly the same osteological and muscular deformities with those above named.

HAIR.

The hair is named by Mr. Jefferson as affording one of those physical differences between the whites and blacks, which must ever prevent the blacks from being incorporated into the State. The short, curly, or crisp hair of the negro is compared with the long, flowing locks of the whites, and from this comparison it is inferred that the two races cannot live in the same land. Nay, other writers—Dr. Nott, of Mobile, for example—enumerates this among the reasons which led him to believe that the two races are of a distinct species—as much so as the "swan and the goose."

In regard to these points, we cannot do better than quote the opinion of the late Dr. Samuel Forry, who says on the 165th page of the first volume of the *"New York Journal of Medicine"*: "As much stress has always been laid upon the national differences of the human hair, by those who hold that the negro is a distinct species from our own, a few general observations will not be deemed out of place. While the head of the Caucasian race is adorned with an ample growth of fine locks, and his face with a copious beard, the negro's head presents short, woolly knots, and that of the American or Mongolian coarse and straight hair, all having nearly beardless faces; and with this diminution of the beard is combined a general smoothness of the whole body. That the coloring principle in the

6. Three prominent white senators—Webster (1782–1852) from Massachusetts, Clay from Kentucky (see note 4), and Benton (1782–1858) from Missouri—during the 1830s and 1840s who labored to avert the Civil War by crafting compromises on slavery.

skin and hair is of a common nature is evident from the fact that among the white races, every gradation, from the fair to the dark, is accompanied by a corresponding alteration in the tint of the hair. This remark applies equally to the colored varieties of men, for all these men have black hair." To this particular assertion of Dr. Forry, there are some apparent, but not real exceptions: we mean the cases of nearly black men having red hair. A close examination of the color of such will detect the fact that, instead of pure jet black, there is a reddish black tint which pervades the hue of the skin. Dr. Forry continues: "But among the spotted Africans, according to Blumenbach," (by spotted Africans are meant the class who are partially Albinos), "the hairs growing out of a white patch of the head are white. These facts, with others observed among inferior animals, as the dog, sheep, and goat, prove sufficiently that a distinction of *species* cannot be established on the mere difference in the hair. Upon this point Dr. Prichard very happily remarks that 'if this cuticular excresence of the negro were really not hair, but a fine wool—if it were precisely analogous to the finest wool—still this would by no means prove the negro to be of a peculiar and separate stock, since we know that some tribes of animals bear wool, while others of the same species are covered with hair.'

"But," continues Dr. Forry, "the so-called *woolly* hair of the negro is not wool in fact, but merely a curled and twisted hair. This has been proved by microscopic observation, upon the well-known law that the character which distinguishes wool from hair consists in the serrated nature of its external surface, giving to wool its felting property."

The cause of the extreme crispness of the hair of the black may be sought, not merely in the heat of the torrid zone, but in addition of the low, marshy locations on the coasts of Africa and other tropical localities, in which this close tight hair is found indigenous. [* * *] We all know that heat and pressure will curl the straightest hair.

There is another fact which may be added, to wit: that this wooly hair of the negro may, by proper care, be made nearly straight. This must be consolatory to those who have gazed upon this, to them, insurmountable difficulty in the way of incorporating the blacks into the State. Any one whose observation extends twenty years back, must observe that the hair of the colored population in the Southern and Northern States is growing more and more straight. This is partly the result of extreme culture on their part, and partly the result of the climatic or geological influences under which they live. That these influences—climate and culture—will ultimately produce a uniform character to the hair of the different races upon this portion of the American continent, is a question even now capable of solution. On the eastern coast of Africa are, living on a marshy sea coast, a race of negroes who speak a language which identifies them with another race who live somewhat farther back, but on land elevated above the level of the sea. These last have hair that is nearly straight, doubtless in consequence of the difference of the climate under which they have, during several centuries, lived.[7]

7. The most recent writer on this subject is Peter A. Browne, L.L.D., of Philadelphia, whose work, "Trichologia Mammalium," at the 51st page, professes to set forth the discovery that the difference of *species* in man may be determined by the difference in the shapes of the hair, or rather hair disc. Dr. Browne does not "split," but slices hair into infinitely small discs, cut off as epicures do Bologna sausages. He claims that in the Indian the hair disc is round, in the white man oval, and in the negro a flattened ellipse, or "eccentrically elliptical." Of course, in accordance with the principles of inductive logic, all individuals of the several species must present the identical phenomenon of "round," "oval," or "eccentrically elliptical" hair discs. Blacks, for example, with wooly hair, if that hair be "eccentrically elliptical" are negroes, and of a separate species; but if their hair be not "eccentrically elliptical," then they are not negroes, not a separate species. Unfortunately for the Doctor's discovery, he says, (p. 65) "It might easily be supposed that, in a city like Philadelphia, abounding in black faces, no difficulty would be encountered in procuring pure negro hair. It is quite the contrary; with great exertions, we have been able to obtain the following only." He enumerates fifteen specimens, *not one of which was procured from Philadelphia*, and only *four* of negroes born in the United States. Hence, either the twenty-five thousand blacks in Philadelphia are not negroes, or the Doctor's test fails to prove them such. The Doctor is very learned, however, on "crosses" between whites and blacks, which he enumerates as follows: *Simple Hybrids,* white to black—1. Hepta Mulattin; 2. Hexa Mulattin; 3. Penta Mullatin; 4. Tetra Mulattin; 5. Tria Mulattin; 6. Di Mulattin; 7. Mono Mulattin; 8. Black; *Compound Hybrids*—1. White; 2. Hepta-hypo-mono-mullatin; 3. Hexa-mono-mulattin; 4. Penta-hyper-mono-mulattin; 5. Tetra-di-mulattin; 6. Tria-hypo-tria-mulattin; 7. Di-tria-mullatin; 8. Mono-hyper-tria-mulattin; 9. Tetra-mullatin. Which is truly the most formidable attack on "our people" we have yet seen in print! [McCune Smith's note] Browne's *Trichologia Mammalium* was published in Philadelphia in 1853.

The Color of Their Skin

is, in the opinion of Thomas Jefferson and his follow-ers, another objection to incorporating the blacks into the American Republic. This may be called the "physical distinction" upon which the question is made to rest by the opponents of the black man in this Republic.

Mr. Jefferson asks, with an air of triumph, "Is this difference of no importance? Is it not the foundation of a greater or less share of beauty in the two races? Are not the fine mixtures of red and white, the expressions of every passion by greater or less suffusions of color in the one, preferable to that eternal monotony which reigns in the countenances, that immovable veil of black which covers all the emotions of the other race?" We regret that a sense of propriety prohibits us from finishing this quotation, for the argument against the part which must be omitted is full and conclusive.

In reply to what has been quoted from Mr. Jeffer-son, it would be sufficient to give the testimony of Mr. Waddington in regard to a race of black men whom he saw on the eastern coast of Africa. He says, "The gen-eral complexion of the Shegya is jet black—clear, glossy, jet black—which appeared to my then unprejudiced eyes to be the finest color that could be selected for a human being." Mr. Jefferson himself, if we may credit the statement of Dr. Bacon in his account of the colored Virginians, who are now living in Liberia—Mr. Jeffer-son himself has left living testimony against his own expressions above quoted—testimony whose close resemblance to himself, and partial inheritance of his talents, should forever close the mouths of men who refer to Jefferson's *Notes on Virginia* as proof of the impossibility of incorporating the colored race into the State. "That testimony," says Dr. Bacon, "is a colored grand-daughter of Thomas Jefferson." Those who are anxious to examine this matter will find the statements alluded to in the "Wanderings on the Seas and Shores of Africa," by Dr. F. R. Bacon.

Another witness against this view of Mr. Jefferson is Bishop Heber. On his first entrance into the Hoogly river he described the crew of a vessel as *"extremely black,* but well made, with good counte-nances and fine features—certainly a handsome race."[8]

There is higher testimony than Mr. Wadding-ton, or Thomas Jefferson, or Bishop Heber, on this subject—testimony which we can hold in regard, if the apostle of democracy did not—"I am black but comely, oh ye daughters of Jerusalem, as the tents of Kedar, as the curtains of Solomon. Look not upon me because I am black, because the sun hath looked upon me: my mother's children were angry with me; they made me the keeper of the vineyards"[9]—"I am black but comely"—"for we are all His workman-ship."—*Esphes. 2:10*

Such testimony is enough to show that there is nothing essentially hideous or distinctly deformed in a black complexion.

Let us take a more general view of this matter, the complexion of the human skin. The fact is that the term white is an arbitrary one, when used in contradis-tinction to black, the latter meaning the colored mixed race now enslaved in this Republic.

A more accurate investigation of the subject has shown that there are but three great varieties to the human complexion, varieties under which all man-kind may be classed. The Leucos or white variety, the Xanthic or yellow variety, and the Melanic or black variety.

1st. In regard to the leucos or white complexion. The word white in physics means a combination of all colors—a reflection from the white object, of all the rays of color—hence the object itself is perfectly color-less. In the leucos or white skinned variety of man-kind, therefore, there is an entire absence of coloring matter in the skin, which is milk white—in the hair, which is also white, and in the iris, which suffers the red blood to gleam through its colorless parietes. There is an absence of the dark pigment in the colored coat. This color, or rather colorless skin, is not con-fined to mankind. It occurs frequently among domes-ticated animals, in rabbits, cats and dogs, sheep, hogs, goats, &c. It has been found in many wild species, as in

8. Prichard, Phys. Hist. vol. 4, p. 236. [McCune Smith's note] The third edition of Prichard's *Physical History of Mankind* was pub-lished in London in 1844; Hoogly, also Hooghly or Hugli: a river in northeastern India.
9. Song of Songs 1:5–6. [McCune Smith's note]

monkeys, squirrels, rats, and mice; several species of birds, as crows, blackbirds, canary birds, partridges, &c., exhibit similar phenomena, having their feathers of a pure white color and their eyes red.

White has often been termed, from Lord Bacon's time, the color of *defect*. The whiteness of the hair is owing to a defect of a peculiar secretion. It is in age, when the frame has lost its vigor and the life has extended beyond its prime, that the hair of men—not albinos—turns white. A similar delicacy, or deficiency in strength of constitution, appears to accompany the leucos or albino variety of mankind from birth. It is congenital deficiency. Hence the pure white is a deformed variety of the human species. The leucos, or white class of men are very few. But the most curious fact is that they may be children of either the negro or the European, the Indian or the Asiatic. All have seen, in the museums, white children with black parents. These are leucos or albino children. Cases are recorded of albinos born of white parents. We saw one a few months ago. The complexion was the same milk-white with the albinos of African origin. The features were European, and the hair, also white, was straight. Horace Greeley is nearly an albino. Far from being the rule or distinctive type of any race, then, the albino, or white, is a variety, an exception, occurring in all races, whether African, or Caucasian, Indian or Mongolian.

2nd. The xanthous variety of complexion is marked by yellow hair and light eyes. The color of the skin is fair but not white, and is agreeably relieved by that ruddy tint which characterizes the sanguine temperament. The xanthous variety of mankind appears to have a degree of the same delicacy which marks the leucoses. Medical writers, from the time of Galen, have remarked a certain degree of irritability and delicacy of constitution in what they term the sanguine temperament. Persons of very fair complexion are often less robust than those of more swarthy hue. The xanthous variety composes a much larger proportion of mankind than the leucos variety. The north of Europe, including the Danes, the Belgians, a portion of the Germans, and the northeastern part of Asia—to wit, Eastern Siberia—and even some of the Highlands of Africa, are principally inhabited by the xanthous variety of mankind.

3d. The melanocomous, or dark-haired variety of mankind, is distinguished by black hair, dark eyes, and a complexion varying from a bright brunette of the Italian to jet black of the negro. Men of the melanic variety are of the choleric or melancholic temperament and have generally sounder and more vigorous constitutions, and are less susceptible of morbific impressions from external causes than the sanguine. This variety composes the greatest proportion of the human race. The south of Europe, nearly all Asia, all Africa and Australia, with a large portion of the American Continent, are occupied by the melanic or dark variety of mankind. To this variety of mankind, says Dr. Prichard, the *negro* belongs.

Hence it appears that the black comprises no special variety of the human race, no distinctive species of mankind, but is part and parcel of the great original stock of humanity—of the rule, and not of the exception. He also belongs to that variety which is endowed with the most powerful constitutions.

This black complexion does not constitute him a special or distinctive variety in the melanic race. Far from it. In America and in India are found men of the melanic race quite as black as the African negro.

* * *

From these facts, it is evident that the black complexion is not confined to the negroes of Africa and their descendants in this country.

There *is* proof on another point—namely, that the black complexion of the negro is not peculiar to him as a variety of the melanic race, but arises from a climatic influence which produces the same color on men who are not negroes. These climatic agencies are a low, flat soil, in a very hot climate. It is a popular opinion that all the natives of Negroland, or the slave region of Africa, are black. This is not true.

* * *

From these facts it is plain that the black complexion of the negro race is not a distinctive mark separating them from the rest of mankind, but is, on the contrary, a result of the combined influence of the hot climate and low, marshy soil, on which they or their ancestors resided in Africa.

From these facts it would appear, that under climatic influences of a peculiar kind, the complexion of the dark races, even of the black, can be changed to lighter, even a white hue. The Ethiopian can change his skin.

It is a familiar fact that the hue of a white man can be greatly changed by a residence in a torrid climate.

Hence it would seem that the color of the skin, be that color what it may, does not mark a distinct species in man.

* * *

We have now arrived at a resting place in this tedious array of facts. We have carefully examined into the principal physical differences, which are alleged to constitute a bar in the way of incorporating the black men into the American State.

Do these differences in reality constitute such a bar? "Words," said Mirabeau, "are things." The history of words would be one of the most interesting of all histories. You may have observed that we use the word black, as distinguishing the class whom we have under consideration. This word "black," and the other word "negro," were the common, the usual, term used for this class at the time Mr. Jefferson wrote. That is more than fifty years ago. The newspapers, sure indices of public opinion, NOW call this same class *"colored people."* The class is the same, the name is changed; they are no longer blacks, bordering on beastiality; they are "colored," and they are a "people." I will not stop to enquire whether the word "colored" be used as a euphony for black, nor whether it marks the fact of an already perceptible change in the hue of the skin of this class. It answers our argument if it show, and it does show, a lessening of the distance—a step towards harmony and reciprocal kindness between man and his fellow man—between the black and the white man in this Republic.

The question is already partly answered; the physical differences do not constitute a permanent bar, because the public voice has already softened the terms which denote those differences.

Then there is that other word, "people." What does it mean? Tell us, poor, cringing sycophant, thou who art fearful that the two races can only live together as master and slave, what does this word "people" mean? In Thomas Jefferson's time, "we, the people" meant men endowed with certain inalienable rights; men exercising those rights, the noblest of which was the great, the God-like right of governing themselves! There was, then, in that word "people," a profound, a sublime import. It meant men who were part and parcel of—were the great sires and the great inheritors of this

"Fair broad Empire, State with State,"[1]

which their prowess in war had snatched from tyrannical hands—which their wisdom in peace had erected into a magnificent fabric, capable of holding within its ample dome the majestic presence of Liberty!

Hic currus fuit! hic illius arma![2]

Here were her arms, and here reposed her chariot. The same import which the word "people" had then, the same import it has now. Place before it what epithet you may, let the American public but call men "people," and those men, residing in this Republic, are already raised by the public voice into the dignity and privileges of citizenship. I care not if the fact be delayed a few years; the principle is already established; the physical distinctions of the black class in this country are not any longer a bar against their being incorporated with the people of the State.

The question asked by Mr. Jefferson in his fourteenth query, would never have been propounded had he been acquainted with the philosophy of human progress. Instead of asking, How shall we get rid of them?—instead of affirming that they could never be safely incorporated in the State—had he possessed the insight or sagacity for which he is so celebrated, he would have welcomed their presence as one of the positive elements of natural progress. Why this is so we have endeavored to show in the first number of this

---

1. From line 4 of William Cullen Bryant's "Ode, Written for the Fiftieth Anniversary of the Inauguration of Washington," April 30, 1839.
2. Here was the chariot! here was her armor! [Latin], transposition of lines from Virgil's *Aeneid* (book 1, lines 16–17).

magazine, in the article on "Civilization," &c. That essay, written in 1844, was slightly amended when published in 1859. Its views are mainly the same with those of Mr. Buckle, in his work on "Civilization in England," and receive support from the higher authority of Mr. Mill, in his remarkable work on "Liberty," published recently in London. Mr. Mill says, (p. 129): "The modern *regime* of public opinion is, in an unorganized form, what the Chinese educational and political systems are in an organized; and unless individuality shall be able successfully to assert itself against this yoke, Europe, notwithstanding its noble antecedents and its professed Christianity, will tend to become another China. What is it that has hitherto preserved Europe from this lot? What has made the European family of nations an improving instead of a stationary portion of mankind? Not any superior excellence in them, which, when it exists, exists as an effect, not as a cause; but their remarkable diversity of character and culture. Individuals, classes, and nations have been extremely unlike one another; they have struck out a great variety of paths, each leading to something valuable; and although at every period those who traveled in different paths have been intolerant of one another, [* * *] each has in time endured to receive the good which the others have offered. [* * *] Wilhelm Von Humboldt points out two things as necessary conditions of human development, because necessary to *render people unlike one another*—namely: freedom and variety of situations."

Whilst Jefferson, Dewey, and last of all Doolittle, raise their impotent voices to exclude the blacks from the United States, Henry Ward Beecher exclaims from his pulpit, with higher instincts and keener insight, "What! drive out the colored people from among us? I would as soon, with these two hands, undertake to uproot and cast out every shrub, bush, and tree that grows between this and the Rocky Mountains!"

Having briefly discussed the physical differences between the whites and blacks, a future article will be devoted to the mental and moral differences in these classes.

Peter Bestes, Sambo Freeman, Felix Holbrook, and Chester Joie
Petition [1773]

Perhaps the earliest written argument for African colonization is contained in this petition composed by Peter Bestes, Sambo Freeman, Felix Holbrook, and Chester Joie and given to select members of the Massachusetts legislature. All four men were enslaved in the Boston area and were seeking to gain their freedom by emigrating to Africa. This document, written three years before the Declaration of Independence, presents a plan for gradual emancipation using the same rhetoric of freedom and liberty that colonials used in their fight against the Crown, in this case with African colonization as the goal.

Transcript of freedom petition submitted by four slaves in Boston to the provincial [British] legislature (1773), collection of The New York Historical Society, negative 51012.

BOSTON, April 20th, 1773.

Sir,

The efforts made by the legislative of this province in their last sessions to free themselves from slavery, gave us, who are in that deplorable state, a high degree of satisfaction. We expect great things from men who have made such a noble stand against the designs of their *fellow-men* to enslave them. We cannot but wish and hope Sir, that you will have the same grand object, we mean civil and religious liberty, in view in your next session. The divine spirit of *freedom*, seems to fire every humane breast on this continent, except such as are bribed to assist in executing the execrable plan.

We are very sensible that it would be highly detrimental to our present masters, if we were allowed to demand all that of *right* belongs to us for past services; this we disclaim. Even the *Spaniards*, who have not those sublime ideas of freedom that English men have, are conscious that they have no right to all the services of their fellowmen, we mean the *Africans*, whom they have purchased with their money; therefore they allow them one day in a week to work for themselves, to enable them to earn money to purchase the residue of their time, which they have a right to demand in such portions as they are able to pay for (a due appraizment of their services being first made, which always stands at the purchase money.) We do not pretend to dictate to you Sir, or to the honorable Assembly, of which you are a member: We acknowledge our obligations to you for what you have already done, but as the people of this province seem to be actuated by the principles of equity and justice, we cannot but expect your house will again take our deplorable case into serious consideration, and give us that ample relief which, *as men*, we have a natural right to.

But since the wise and righteous governor of the universe has permitted our fellow men to make us slaves, we bow in submission to him, and determine to behave in such a manner, as that we may have reason to expect the divine approbation of, and assistance in, our peaceable and lawful attempts to gain our freedom.

We are willing to submit to such regulations and laws, as may be made relative to us, until we leave the province, which we determine to do as soon as we can from our joynt labours procure money to transport ourselves to some part of the coast of *Africa*, where we propose a settlement. We are very desirous that you should have instructions relative to us, from your town, therefore we pray you to communicate this letter to them, and ask this favor for us.

In behalf of our fellow slaves in this province,
And by order of their Committee.

PETER BESTES,
SAMBO FREEMAN,
FELIX HOLBROOK,
CHESTER JOIE.

For the REPRESENTATIVE of the town of [Thompson].[1]

JAMES FORTEN
Letter to Paul Cuffe [1817]

Paul Cuffe (1759–1817), a wealthy merchant from Massachusetts, began the first substantial African colonization effort. Believing that the best opportunities for free black Americans like himself were back in Africa, in 1815 he personally financed and accompanied a boatload of thirty-eight immigrants to Freetown, Sierra Leone. The subsequent controversy over African colonization is evident in the January 25, 1817, letter to Cuffe from James Forten (1766–1842), a wealthy sailmaker in Philadelphia. Although clearly in favor of the emigration effort, Forten was affected by mounting opposition to African colonization. This opposition was spurred by widespread distrust of the motives of the American Colonization Society (ACS). The ACS, established in December 1816 by a group of influential white men, avowed to have the interest of free black people at heart, but was largely supported by slave owners who would have benefited from their removal from American society.

A turning point for Forten was the 1817 meeting at the African Methodist Episcopal (AME) church in Philadelphia, established by the Reverend Richard Allen (p. 144), described in his letter to Cuffe. Over 3,000 attended the meeting, the vast majority of the free black male population of Philadelphia. Afterward, the attendees unanimously passed a resolution rejecting African colonization and underscoring their connection to those still in bondage, proclaiming: "Whereas our ancestors (not of choice) were the first successful cultivators of the wilds of America, we their descendents feel ourselves entitled to participate in the blessings of her luxuriant soil. [* * *] Resolved, That we never will separate ourselves voluntarily from the slave population in this country; they are our brethren by the ties of consanguinity, of suffering, and of wrong." These strong arguments influenced Forten's views, and before the year was over he had shifted his position, becoming a vocal opponent of the American Colonization Society.

From the Paul Cuffe Papers, New Bedford Free Public Library, New Bedford, Mass.; reprinted in William Loren Katz, ed., *Eyewitness: The Negro in American History* (New York: Pitman, 1967), pp. 146–47.

ESTEEMED FRIEND [* * *]

The African Institution met at the Rev. R. Allens the very night your letter came to hand. I red that part to them that wished them a happy New Year, for which they desired me to return you many thanks. I must now mention to you that the whole continent seems to be agitated concerning Colonising the People of Colour.

[* * *] Indeed the People of Colour, here was very much fritened at first. They were afrade that all the free people would be Compelled to go, particularly in the southern States. We had a large meeting of Males at the Rev. R. Allens Church the other evening Three thousand at least attended, and there was not one sole that was in favour of going to Africa. They think that the slave holders want to get rid of them so as to make

1. The petition copy held at the New York Historical Society has the town name "Thompson" written in by hand; copies for other representatives would have been personalized with the names of their towns.

their property more secure. However it appears to me that if the Father of all mercies, is in this interesting subject [* * *] the way will be made strate and clear. We however have agreed to remain silent, as the people here both the white & colour are decided against the measure. My opinion is that they will never become a people until they com out from amongst the white people, but as the majority is decidedly against me I am determined to remain silent, accept as to my opinion which I freely give when asked. [* * *]

I remain very affectionately
Yours unalterably,
JAMES FORTEN

JAMES FORTEN AND RUSSELL PARROTT

Address to the Humane and Benevolent Inhabitants of the City and County of Philadelphia [1818]

James Forten, a wealthy sailmaker and a former supporter of colonization efforts (p. 53), and Russell Parrott (1791–1824), a prominent leader of Philadelphia's black community and head of the African Literary Society, rallied Philadelphia's black community against the American Colonization Society. The ACS presented itself as a benevolent friend of black Americans and offered colonization as a way to reduce the impact of slavery, assist African Americans, and bring Christianity to Africa. However, as Forten and Parrott make clear in their address, delivered on December 10, 1818, they see no such benefits in colonization. Instead, they assert that colonization would make life worse for all black Americans, whether free or enslaved.

Forten went on to become a leader in the abolitionist movement and convinced many—including the abolitionist leader William Lloyd Garrison (p. 111)—that freed slaves must be given full rights as U.S. citizens instead of being taken from their homeland through African colonization.

From *Minutes of the Proceedings of a Special Meeting of the Fifteenth American Convention for Promoting the Abolition of Slavery, and Improving the Condition of the African Race* (Philadelphia: Hall and Atkinson, 1818).

T he free people of color, assembled together, under circumstances of deep interest to their happiness and welfare, humbly and respectfully lay before you this expression of their feelings and apprehensions.

Relieved from the miseries of slavery, many of us by your aid, possessing the benefits which industry and integrity in this prosperous country assure to all its inhabitants, enjoying the rich blessings of religion, by opportunities of worshipping the only true God, under the light of Christianity, each of us according to his understanding; and having afforded to us and to our children the means of education and improvement; we have no wish to separate from our present homes, for any purpose whatever. Contented with our present situation and condition, we are not desirous of increasing their prosperity but by honest efforts, and by the use of those opportunities for their improvement, which the constitution and laws allow to all. It is therefore with painful solicitude, and sorrowing regret, we have seen a plan for colonizing the free people of color of the United States on the coast of Africa, brought forward under the auspices and sanction of gentlemen whose names give value to all they recommend, and who certainly are among the wisest, the best, and the most benevolent of men, in this great nation.

If the plan of colonizing is intended for our benefit, and those who now promote it will never seek our injury, we humbly and respectfully urge, that it is not asked for by us: nor will it be required by any circumstances, in our present or future condition, as long as we shall be permitted to share the protection of the excellent laws and just government which we now enjoy, in common with every individual of the community.

We, therefore, a portion of those who are the objects of this plan, and among those whose happiness, with that of others of our color, it is intended to promote, with humble and grateful acknowledgments to those who have devised it, renounce and disclaim every connexion with it; and respectfully but firmly declare our determination not to participate in any part of it.

If this plan of colonization now proposed, is intended to provide a refuge and a dwelling for a portion of our brethren who are now held in slavery in the south, we have other and stronger objections to it, and we entreat your consideration of them.

The ultimate and final abolition of slavery in the United States, by the operation of various causes, is, under the guidance and protection of a just God, progressing. Every year witnesses the release of numbers of the victims of oppression, and affords new and safe assurances that the freedom of all will be in the end accomplished. As they are thus by degrees relieved from bondage, our brothers have opportunities for instruction and improvement; and thus they become in some measure fitted for their liberty. Every year, many of us have restored to us by the gradual, but certain march of the cause of abolition—parents, from whom we have been long separated—wives and children whom we had left in servitude—and brothers, in blood as well as in early sufferings, from whom we had been long parted.

But if the emancipation of our kindred shall, when the plan of colonization shall go into effect, be attended with transportation to a distant land, and shall be granted on no other condition; the consolation for our past sufferings and of those of our color who are in slavery, which have hitherto been, and under the present situation of things would continue to be, afforded to us and to them, will cease for ever. The cords, which now connect them with us, will be stretched by the distance to which their ends will be carried, until they break; and all the sources of happiness, which affection and connexion and blood bestow, will be ours and theirs no more.

Nor do we view the colonization of those who may become emancipated by its operation among our southern brethren, as capable of producing their happiness. Unprepared by education and a knowledge of the truths of our blessed religion for their new situation, those who will thus become colonists will themselves be surrounded by every suffering which can afflict the members of the human family.

Without arts, without habits of industry, and unaccustomed to provide by their own exertions and foresight for their wants, the colony will soon become the abode of every vice, and the home of every misery. Soon will the light of Christianity, which now dawns among that portion of our species, be shut out by the clouds of ignorance, and their day of life be closed, without the illuminations of the gospel.

To those of our brothers who shall be left behind, there will be assured perpetual slavery and augmented sufferings. Diminished in numbers, the slave population of the southern states, which by its magnitude alarms its proprietors, will be easily secured. Those among their bondmen who feel that they should be free, by rights which all mankind have from God and from nature, and who thus may become dangerous to the quiet of their masters, will be sent to the colony; and the tame and submissive will be retained, and subjected to increased rigor. Year after year will witness these means to assure safety and submission among their slaves, and the southern masters will colonize only those whom it may be dangerous to keep among them. The bondage of a large portion of our brothers will thus be rendered perpetual.

Should the anticipations of misery and want among the colonists, which with great deference we have submitted to your better judgment, be realized, to emancipate and transport to Africa will be held forth by slaveholders as the worst and heaviest of punishments; and they will be threatened and successfully used to enforce increased submission to their wishes, and subjection to their commands.

Nor ought the sufferings and sorrows which must be produced by an exercise of the right to transport and colonize such only of their slaves as may be selected by the slaveholders, escape the attention and consideration of those whom with all humility we now address. Parents will be torn from their children—husbands from their wives—brothers from brothers—and all the heart-rending agonies which were endured by our forefathers when they were dragged into bondage from Africa will be again renewed, and with increased anguish. The shores of America will, like the sands of Africa, be watered by the tears of those who will be left behind. Those who shall be carried away will roam childless, widowed, and alone, over the burning plains of Guinea.

Disclaiming, as we emphatically do, a wish or desire to interpose our opinions and feelings between all plans of colonization, and the judgment of those whose wisdom as far exceeds ours as their situations are exalted above ours; we humbly, respectfully, and fervently intreat and beseech your disapprobation of the plan of colonization now offered by "the American Society for colonizing the free people of color of the United States,"—Here, in the city of Philadelphia, where the voice of the suffering sons of Africa was first heard; where was first commenced the work of abolition, on which heaven has smiled, for it could have had success only from the Great Maker; let not a

purpose be assisted which will stay the cause of the entire abolition of slavery in the United States, and which may defeat it altogether; which proffers to those who do not ask for them what it calls benefits, but which they consider injuries; and which must insure to the multitudes whose prayers can only reach you through us, misery, sufferings, and perpetual slavery.

JAMES FORTEN, Chairman.

RUSSELL PARROTT, Secretary.

"A COLORED FEMALE OF PHILADELPHIA"
Emigration to Mexico [1832]

The conflict over African colonization encouraged many to consider alternative destinations for emigration. In this January 2, 1832, letter to *The Liberator*, the nation's leading anti-slavery newspaper, "A Colored Female of Philadelphia" suggests that African Americans would find in Mexico the economic and educational opportunities denied to them in the United States. She is drawn to the idea of becoming part of a society of color, and her position is pointedly assimilationist, with the notable exception of her views on Mexican Catholicism. Her ultimate resolution to the problem of moving to a place with a non-Protestant culture reflects a sense of religious mission common to many emigration proposals.

From *The Liberator*, January 28, 1832, p. 14.

Mr. Editor—I am happy to learn that the sentiments of some of my Trenton brethren are in accordance with my own, in regard to our locating in Mexico and Upper Canada; for, in my humble opinion, one thing is needful for us as a people, even emigration; but not to Africa, nor to place ourselves as a distinct people anywhere, but to attach ourselves to a nation already established. The government of these United States is not the only one in this hemisphere that offers equal rights to men; but there are others under whose protection we may safely reside, where it is no disgrace to wear a sable complexion, and where our rights will not be continually trampled upon, on that account. We profess to be republicans, and such I hope we are; but wherein do we show our republican spirit, by sitting still and sighing for that liberty our white brethren tell us we never shall obtain, or in hoping that in some fifty

or a hundred years hence, our children's children will be made free? I think we do not evince republicanism by this conduct, but verily believe that the time has arrived when we, too, ought to manifest that spirit of independence which shines so conspicuously in the character of Europeans, by leaving the land of oppression and emigrating where we may be received and treated as brothers; where our worth will be felt and acknowledged, and where we may acquire education, wealth and respectability, together with a knowledge of the arts and sciences; all of which may be in our power—of the enjoyment of which the government of the separate states in the union is adopting means to deprive us.

The author of this article is aware, that the subject is not popular, and perhaps will not be kindly received; but it is one that I hope will be deeply pondered in the mind of every colored citizen of this country before he passes sentence against it.

Some of your readers may inquire, where is that country to which we may remove, and thus become free and equal? I believe that country to be Mexico. There is an independent nation, where indeed "all men are born free and equal," possessing those inalienable rights which our constitution guarantees. The climate is healthy and warm, and of course adapted to our nature; the soil is rich and fertile, which will contribute to our wealth; and there we may become a people of worth and respectability; whereas in this country we are kept poor, and of course, cannot aspire to anything more than what we always have been. I have been waiting to hear of some way being pointed out that will tend to better the present generation; but, as yet, have heard of nothing that appears to be permanent. I would not wish to be thought pleading the cause of colonization, for no one detests it more than I do. I would not be taken to Africa, were the Society to make me queen of the country; and were I to move to Canada, I would not settle in the colony, but take up my abode in some of the cities where a distinction is not known; for I do not approve of our drawing off into a separate body anywhere. But, I confess, I can see no just reason why we should not cultivate the spirit of enterprise as well as the whites. They are found in every quarter of the globe, in search of situations to better their condition; and why may we not "go and do likewise?"

I am informed that the population of Mexico is eight millions of colored, and one million of whites; and by the rapid growth of amalgamation amongst them, there is every probability that it will ere long become one entire colored nation. I am of opinion that Mexico would afford us a large field for speculation, were we to remove thither; and who can say that the day will not soon arrive when the flag of our colored American merchants' ships from the Mexican ports shall be seen proudly waving in the breeze of the American harbors? And shall not our sons feel proud to enlist under the Mexican banner, and support her government? Surely they will.

There is one objection, however, that may arise in the minds of some; that is, the religion of that nation being Papist; but we can take with us the Holy Bible, which is able to make us wise unto salvation; and perhaps we may be made the honored instruments, in the hands of an all-wise God, in establishing the holy religion of the Protestant Church in that country; and that alone might be a sufficient inducement for the truly pious.

A COLORED FEMALE OF PHILADELPHIA.
Philadelphia, January 2, 1832.

[RALPH RANDOLPH GURLEY] and "A SOUTH CAROLINIAN"
Opinions of a Freeman of Colour in Charleston [1832]

The African Repository, a quarterly established in March 1825 and edited by Ralph Randolph Gurley (1797–1872), was the official publication of the American Colonization Society. Not surprisingly, it published testimonials by African Americans who, like "the respectable free coloured man of Charleston," espoused arguments promoted by the American Colonization Society: that African American emigration is inevitable, Liberia is the most promising destination for African Americans, and emigration will lead to economic and social advancement. Although the writer of the opinions reprinted here expresses frustration with American racial inequality, he accepts such prejudice as unchangeable and argues that emigration is the only solution for ambitious African Americans. His letter conveys an imperialist zeal, which undercuts the idea of emigration as a religious mission. It also reveals a lack of connection to African culture, as the writer elevates white missionaries and assures would-be African American colonists who object to the native Africans that "locating in Liberia does not necessarily compel you to form private alliance in families that you dislike."

From *The African Repository, and Colonial Journal* 8 (October 1832), pp. 239–43.

We have received a communication from a respectable free coloured man of Charleston, which contains some thoughts which merit the serious consideration of all his brethren. May the noble spirit of devotedness which he manifests to the good of mankind, soon animate ten thousand of his coloured brethren, that they may go forth, not merely to improve their own condition, but to relieve and bless the long afflicted and degraded children of Africa. We have omitted some sentences in this article, and made some slight corrections; not affecting materially the sense of the writer. His remarks have reference to the three following heads.

I. *A Brief Inquiry into the propriety of the Free People of Colour migrating to Liberia or elsewhere.*
II. *The objections urged by many of the Coloured People against emigration.*
III. *The good likely to result to those who may determine to emigrate.*

1st. When we reflect upon the laws of Ohio, that expel from her territory our brethren—when we look to Virginia, to Maryland, to Alabama and to Tennessee, we must candidly confess that we have much fearful apprehension in regard to the laws that may be enacted bearing heavily upon us, even in our own dear Carolina, which generously cherishes all her inhabitants and gives them support and employment in all of the various and useful branches of mechanism, without regard to colour or condition. There are many callings in which the coloured people in Carolina have a decided preference; in some cases they have no competitors; how long this favorable state of things will remain, we are not prepared to say—time alone can correctly decide in this matter. This is an era, however, in our affairs, that we cannot shut our eyes to, and it must appear to the philosopher, the Christian, and the sagacious politician, a period of deep and anxious solicitude as regards the future prospects, hopes, and interests of a people little known but as a nuisance—mere laborers in the most menial capacity; at best a people who seldom deserve

notice, or the exercise of charitable acts bestowed on them. Their friends and their foes both desire the removal of the free people of colour; although it is a fact not denied but by a very few, that the descendants of Africa, when transplanted in a country favorable to their improvement, and when their advantages are equal to others, seldom fail to answer all of the ends suited to their capacity, and in some instances rise to many of the virtues, to the learning and piety of the most favored nation. Yet, alas! the prevalence of popular prejudice against our colour (which is the more surprising, as it is well known that God alone creates different classes of men, that he may be adored and worshipped by all in the spirit of truth, without regard to complexion) has almost invariably stood as a barrier to our advancement in knowledge. Hence some of us appear to be useless,[1] and when it is considered that we are a large body of people, growing rapidly every day, without that improvement which the present age seems to require, in moral virtue and intellectual attainments; indeed, when we examine our own conduct and that of our brethren, and compare the advantages we do actually possess, with so many bright examples before us of christianizing and improving the condition of mankind, both far and immediately under our eyes, we cannot but enquire "how can these things be?" My friends, if we will venture to look around us, we will behold the most encouraging proofs of happiness in the emigrants from Europe to this country. You have no call to look farther than our city (Charleston) to witness the most lively encouragements given to emigrants.[2] Many who arrive here very poor, are soon made rich (and so it will be with us in Liberia): enterprising, industrious individuals, also families incorporating themselves in the community, enjoying all the blessings peace can confer on society, and soon successfully advancing on the high road to wealth and respectability, whilst we sink daily in the estimation of all.

Our apparently inactive habits may, in a great measure, be attributed to this reason—"That we have no opportunity for the cultivation of our minds by education." As a matter of course, generally speak-

1. Except it may be when we are employed as laborers. [Author's note]
2. Without any tax whatever, whilst we pay a heavy one. [Author's note]

ing, we lose all regard for any, but our individual self [* * *]—satisfied with every moral privation, with this certain conviction in our hearts: that our children are likely to be much worse situated than we are, as we ourselves are not as well situated in many respects as our parents were. The next enquiry is, what are we to do? I answer honestly and without hesitation, migrate to Liberia, in preference to any other country, under the protecting hand and influence of the Colonization Society. *Here comes my second proposition*; a consideration of the objections many have to emigrating to a country whose inhabitants are shrouded in deep ignorance—whom long and deep-rooted custom forbids us to have social intercourse with in the various relations of civilized life upon fair and equal terms of husband and wife, and whose complexion is darker than many of ours. But in all this, my friends, there is no reasonable ground of objection to your removal to a country more adapted to promote your interests, because a very plain reason presents itself for such removal—and that is, in Liberia you will enjoy moral and political liberty. Besides, the heralds of the cross who first preached salvation to the benighted sons of Africa, were white men, and numbers of ladies also withdrew themselves from the beauties of highly polished circles in Europe to accompany their husbands in spreading the light in dark places. Those who contribute in money to carry on the splendid work of colonization and religion, who sacrifice their health on the shrine of humanity and deprive themselves of all earthly comforts, even stare death in the face, and prefer to die in the attempt, rather than relinquish the spread of virtue and religion amongst this very people you affect to despise—they are white. Who are they at this very period, rearing up an establishment at Liberia, that bids fair under the protecting smiles of Providence, to crush forever the monster (the slave trade) that has led to captivity, and chains, and perpetual disgrace, our brethren, who, although formed in the image of God, are doomed in most countries, Liberia excepted, to degradation and servitude? They are white men. Surely this is at least one strong reason that should induce you, cheerfully to migrate to a country, where you can possess *all* of the importance of free citizens; in fact, all your objections dwindle into insignificance, in view of this one fact stated above. Besides,

locating in Liberia does not necessarily compel you to form private alliance in families that you dislike; on the contrary, there is no country where you could indulge your own opinions in this respect with more freedom, than in that land of equality.

If you do go, and I hope in my heart all of us may speedily go—will we not go with our families and friends, cementing more strongly the bond of our connections, our customs, and our habits? Look for example to the Jews and other ancient people, scattered all over the world; look at our own situation, wherever we are placed: we see no innovation, nothing likely to break in and change the existing face of society.

III. Much good is likely to result to those who are meek and humble, who can see the advantages of liberty and equality, with the courage to embark in an enterprise, under such favorable circumstances. *This is the truth*, which is useful for all of us to know, and I have endeavored briefly to lay it before you, for your reflection, and if you once bring your minds to serious reflection, your friends will never blush—no—never under any circumstances, on account of dissensions on your part. Surely, my brethren, there are very strong reasons for us to go—yes go—and invoke Jehovah for his favorable protection to you, and to that country which holds out to us, and to our children, forever, protection, in life, liberty, and property—beside every honor of office, within the gift of a free people. He who holds in the hollow of his hand the destiny of nations, will be with you, and will bless you with health and vigor to contribute your personal services of pious example, to improve the country that invites you to possess its soil. Moreover, you will have the great privilege of sharing in your own government, and finally of becoming a perfectly free and independent people. And where would you go (go you must, sooner or later) to look for this noble privilege—the power of electing your officers or removing them when need requires. Yes, my brethren, perhaps much depends on your present zeal and activity for success—and if God be with us, and I have a lively hope that he influences and directs you in this matter, before long the emigrants to Liberia will become a distinguished nation; and who can prophesy and foretell the future destiny of Liberia? The day, however, may not be far distant, when those who now despise the humble, degraded emigrants to Liberia, will make arrangements with them, to improve navigation, to extend commerce, and perhaps we may soon conduct and carry on our trade with foreign nations in our own bottoms[3] without molestation or fear. Such, my brethren, are some of the high expectations to be derived from a well established colony in Liberia, and to you Carolinians, all eyes are directed, all hearts are uplifted to God in prayer, to know what course your good sense will induce you to pursue, under existing circumstances. Your reputation as a body of first-rate mechanics is well known; distinguished for your industry and good behaviour, you have with you, carpenters, millers, wheel-wrights, ship builders, engineers, cabinet mak-

ers, shoe makers, tailors, and a host of others, all calculated at once to make you a great people. In Liberia you can erect a temple to worship God in the beauty of holiness; without fear you can set up and protect your sacred altars, and pour out the orisons of the devout and pious heart before them, in praise and thanksgiving to God. In Liberia, you can establish Academies and Colleges, to instruct youth in Theology, in Physic, and in Law. You will there know no superiors but virtue, and the laws of your country—no religion but the revealed revelation of God—and recollect all of this is for you yourselves.

A SOUTH CAROLINIAN.

MARIA W. STEWART
An Address Delivered at the African Masonic Hall [1833]

While the American Colonization Society promoted colonization as a way to bring Christianity to Africans, the abolitionist Maria W. Stewart (1803–1879) employed religion to attack the society and its colonization of Liberia. Stewart blames history and continued racism for black disadvantage but calls for African Americans to effect change themselves by practicing self-improvement. Traditionally, women championed only those positions that met with little overt resistance, such as the virtues of education and temperance. Stewart draws on those traditional areas of female authority as an entry into the contentious debate about emigration, concluding with the powerful declaration: "They would drive us to a strange land. But before I go, the bayonet shall pierce me through." Her speech also includes a defense of her right to address her audience, which conveys the powerful cultural pressure during the period for women not to participate in public speaking or debate.

The response to Stewart's speech was decidedly mixed, with many writers thinking she had gone beyond the bounds of acceptability in her criticism of black male leadership. As a result of the negative reviews, Stewart relinquished her short career as a public speaker, giving only one more speech, "a farewell address to her friends in the city of Boston" (also 1833), before moving to New York City to become a schoolteacher.

Born in Connecticut to free parents, Stewart (née Maria Miller) was orphaned at age five. She spent the next ten years as an indentured servant for a cleric's family. After working a number of years as a domestic servant, she moved to Boston, where she met and was inspired by the activist David Walker (p. 27). In her subsequent speeches, Stewart, like Walker, addressed her words to fellow black Americans rather than white abolitionists. In 1829, after her husband of three years had died, Stewart was cheated out of her inheritance by white businessmen and had to go back to work as a domestic to support herself. Following her husband's death, she had a religious experience that convinced her to become a "warrior" for her people. She responded to an 1831 call from white American abolitionist William Lloyd Garrison (p. 111) for contributions from black women. *The Liberator's* publication of her essay "Religion and the Pure Principles of Morality, the Sure Foundation on Which We Must Build" made her the first black female political writer in America. The next year, she gave her first speech, for the African-American Female Intelligence Society of America. With her speech on September 21, 1832, for a meeting of the New England Anti-Slavery Society, Stewart became the first American-born woman to give a public political speech. She was also the first

3. Ships.

American-born woman to lecture in support of women's rights. Her publications include *Meditations from the Pen* of Mrs. Maria W. Stewart (1832, 1879) and *Productions of Mrs. Maria W. Stewart* (1835).

From *Maria W. Stewart, America's First Black Woman Political Writer: Essays and Speeches,* ed. Marilyn Richardson (Bloomington: Indiana University Press, 1987), pp. 56–64.

African rights and liberty is a subject that ought to fire the breast of every free man of color in these United States, and excite in his bosom a lively, deep, decided and heart-felt interest. When I cast my eyes on the long list of illustrious names that are enrolled on the bright annals of fame among the whites, I turn my eyes within, and ask my thoughts, "Where are the names of our illustrious ones?" It must certainly have been for the want of energy on the part of the free people of color, that they have been long willing to bear the yoke of oppression. It must have been the want of ambition and force that has given the whites occasion to say that our natural abilities are not as good, and our capacities by nature inferior to theirs. They boldly assert that did we possess a natural independence of soul, and feel a love for liberty within our breasts, some one of our sable race, long before this, would have testified it, notwithstanding the disadvantages under which we labor. We have made ourselves appear altogether unqualified to speak in our own defence, and are therefore looked upon as objects of pity and commiseration. We have been imposed upon, insulted and derided on every side, and now, if we complain, it is considered as the height of impertinence. We have suffered ourselves to be considered as dastards, cowards, mean, faint-hearted wretches, and on this account (not because of our complexion) many despise us, and would gladly spurn us from their presence.

These things have fired my soul with a holy indignation, and compelled me thus to come forward, and endeavor to turn their attention to knowledge and improvement, for knowledge is power. I would ask, is it blindness of mind, or stupidity of soul, or the want of education that has caused our men who are 60 or 70 years of age, never to let their voices be heard, nor their hands be raised in behalf of their color? Or has it been for the fear of offending the whites? If it has, O ye fearful ones, throw off your fearfulness, and come forth in the name of the Lord, and in the strength of the God of Justice, and make yourselves useful and active members in society, for they admire a noble and patriotic spirit in others; and should they not admire it in us? If you are men, convince them that you possess the spirit of men; and as your day, so shall your strength be. Have the sons of Africa no souls? Feel they no ambitious desires? Shall the chains of ignorance forever confine them? Shall the insipid appellation of "clever negroes," or "good creatures," any longer content them? Where can we find among ourselves the man of science, or a philosopher, or an able statesman, or a counsellor at law? Show me our fearless and brave, our noble and gallant ones. Where are our lecturers in natural history, and our critics in useful knowledge? There may be a few such men among us, but they are rare. It is true our fathers bled and died in the revolutionary war, and others fought bravely under the command of Jackson, in defence of liberty. But where is the man that has distinguished himself in these modern days by acting wholly in the defence of African rights and liberty? There was one, although he sleeps, his memory lives.[1]

I am sensible that there are many highly intelligent men of color in these United States, in the force of whose arguments, doubtless, I should discover my inferiority; but if they are blessed with wit and talent, friends and fortune, why have they not made themselves men of eminence, by striving to take all the reproach that is cast upon the people of color, and in endeavoring to alleviate the woes of their brethren in bondage? Talk, without effort, is nothing; you are abundantly capable, gentlemen, of making yourselves men of distinction; and this gross neglect, on your part, causes my blood to boil within me. Here is the grand cause which hinders the rise and progress of people of color. It is their want of laudable ambition and requisite courage.

---

1. Reference to David Walker, the abolitionist, who died in 1830; see pp. 27, 86, and 103.

Individuals have been distinguished according to their genius and talents, ever since the first formation of man, and will continue to be while the world stands. The different grades rise to honor and respectability as their merits may deserve. History informs us that we sprung from one of the most learned nations of the whole earth; from the seat, if not the parent, of science. Yes, poor despised Africa was once the resort of sages and legislators of other nations, was esteemed the school for learning, and the most illustrious men in Greece flocked thither for instruction. But it was our gross sins and abominations that provoked the Almighty to frown thus heavily upon us, and give our glory unto others. Sin and prodigality have caused the downfall of nations, kings and emperors; and were it not that God in wrath remembers mercy, we might indeed despair; but a promise is left us; "Ethiopia shall again stretch forth her hands unto God."[2]

But it is of no use for us to boast that we sprung from this learned and enlightened nation, for this day a thick mist of moral gloom hangs over millions of our race. Our condition as a people has been low for hundreds of years, and it will continue to be so, unless by true piety and virtue, we strive to regain that which we have lost. White Americans, by their prudence, economy, and exertions, have sprung up and become one of the most flourishing nations in the world, distinguished for their knowledge of the arts and sciences, for their polite literature. While our minds are vacant and starve for want of knowledge, theirs are filled to overflowing. Most of our color have been taught to stand in fear of the white man from their earliest infancy, to work as soon as they could walk, and to call "master" before they could scarce lisp the name of mother. Continual fear and laborious servitude have in some degree lessened in us that natural force and energy which belong to man; or else, in defiance of opposition, our men, before this, would have nobly and boldly contended for their rights. But give the man of color an equal opportunity with the white from the cradle to manhood, and from manhood to the grave, and you would discover the dignified statesman, the man of science, and the philosopher. But there is no such opportunity for the sons of Africa, and I fear that our powerful ones are fully determined that there never shall be. Forbid, ye Powers on high, that it should any longer be said that our men possess no force. O ye sons of Africa, when will your voices be heard in our legislative halls, in defiance of your enemies, contending for equal rights and liberty? How can you, when you reflect from what you have fallen, refrain from crying mightily unto God, to turn away from us the fierceness of his anger, and remember our transgressions against us no more forever? But a god of infinite purity will not regard the prayers of those who hold religion in one hand, and prejudice, sin and pollution in the other; he will not regard the prayers of self-righteousness and hypocrisy. Is it possible, I exclaim, that for the want of knowledge we have labored for hundreds of years to support others, and been content to receive what they chose to give us in return? Cast your eyes about, look as far as you can see; all, all is owned by the lordly white, exept here and there a lowly dwelling which the man of color, midst deprivations, fraud, and opposition has been scarce able to procure. Like King Solomon, who put neither nail nor hammer to the temple, yet received the praise, so also have the white Americans gained themselves a name, like the names of the great men that are in the earth, while in reality we have been their principal foundation and support. We have pursued the shadow, they have obtained the substance; we have performed the labor, they have received the profits; we have planted the vines, they have eaten the fruits of them.

I would implore our men, and especially our rising youth, to flee from the gambling board and the dance-hall; for we are poor, and have no money to throw away. I do not consider dancing as criminal in itself, but it is astonishing to me that our fine young men are so blind to their own interest and the future welfare of their children as to spend their hard earnings for this frivolous amusement, for it has been carried on among us to such an unbecoming extent that it has become absolutely disgusting. "Faithful are the wounds of a friend, but the kisses of an enemy are deceitful."[3] Had those men among us who had an

2. Paraphrase of a line from Psalm 68:31, "Ethiopia shall soon stretch out her hands unto God."
3. Proverbs 27:6.

opportunity, turned their attention as assiduously to mental and moral improvement as they have to gambling and dancing, I might have remained quietly at home and they stood contending in my place. These polite accomplishments will never enroll your names on the bright annals of fame who admire the belle void of intellectual knowledge, or applaud the dandy that talks largely on politics without striving to assist his fellow in the revolution, when the nerves and muscles of every other man forced him into the field of action. You have a right to rejoice, and to let your hearts cheer you in the days of your youth; yet remember that for all these things God will bring you into judgment. Then, O ye sons of Africa, turn your mind from these perishable objects, and contend for the cause of God and the rights of man. Form yourselves into temperance societies. There are temperate men among you; then why will you any longer neglect to strive, by your example, to suppress vice in all its abhorrent forms? You have been told repeatedly of the glorious results arising from temperance, and can you bear to see the whites arising in honor and respectability without endeavoring to grasp after that honor and respectability also?

But I forbear. Let our money, instead of being thrown away as heretofore, be appropriated for schools and seminaries of learning for our children and youth. We ought to follow the example of the whites in this respect. Nothing would raise our respectability, add to our peace and happiness, and reflect so much honor upon us, as to be ourselves the promoters of temperance, and the supporters, as far as we are able, of useful and scientific knowledge. The rays of light and knowledge have been hid from our view; we have been taught to consider ourselves as scarce superior to the brute creation, and have performed the most laborious part of American drudgery. Had we as a people received one-half the early advantages the whites have received, I would defy the government of these United States to deprive us any longer of our rights.

I am informed that the agent of the Colonization Society has recently formed an association of young men for the purpose of influencing those of us to go to Liberia who may feel disposed. The colonizationists are blind to their own interest, for should the nations of

the earth make war with America, they would find their forces much weakened by our absence; or should we remain here, can our "brave soldiers" and "fellow citizens," as they were termed in time of calamity, condescend to defend the rights of whites and be again deprived of their own, or sent to Liberia in return? Or, if the colonizationists are the real friends to Africa, let them expend the money which they collect in erecting a college to educate her injured sons in this land of gospel, light, and liberty; for it would be most thankfully received on our part, and convince us of the truth of their professions, and save time, expense, and anxiety. Let them place before us noble objects worthy of pursuit, and see if we prove ourselves to be those unambitious negroes they term us. But, ah, methinks their hearts are so frozen toward us they had rather their money should be sunk in the ocean than to administer it to our relic: and I fear, if they dared, like Pharaoh, king of Egypt, they would order every male child among us to be drowned. But the most high God is still as able to subdue the lofty pride of these white Americans as He was the heart of that ancient rebel. They say, though we are looked upon as things, yet we sprang from a scientific people. Had our men the requisite force and energy they would soon convince them by their efforts, both in public and private, that they were men, or things in the shape of men. Well may the colonizationists laugh us to scorn for our negligence; well may they cry: "Shame to the sons of Africa." As the burden of the Israelites was too great for Moses to bear, so also is our burden too great for our noble advocate to bear. You must feel interested, my brethren, in what he undertakes, and hold up his hands by your good works, or in spite of himself his soul will become discouraged and his heart will die within him; for he has, as it were, the strong bulls of Bashan[4] to contend with.

It is of no use for us to wait any longer for a generation of well educated men to arise. We have slumbered and slept too long already; the day is far spent; the night of death approaches; and you have sound sense and good judgment sufficient to begin with, if you feel disposed to make a right use of it. Let every man of color throughout the United States, who possesses the spirit and principles of a man, sign a petition to

---

4. Psalm 22:12.

Congress to abolish slavery in the District of Columbia, and grant you the rights and privileges of common free citizens; for if you had had faith as a grain of mustard seed,[5] long before this the mountain of prejudice might have been removed. We are all sensible that the Anti-Slavery Society has taken hold of the arm of our whole population, in order to raise them out of the mire. Now all we have to do is, by a spirit of virtuous ambition, to strive to raise ourselves; and I am happy to have it in my power thus publicly to say that the colored inhabitants of this city, in some respects, are beginning to improve. Had the free people of color in these United States nobly and freely contended for their rights, and showed a natural genius and talent, although not so brilliant as some; had they held up, encouraged and patronized each other, nothing could have hindered us from being a thriving and flourishing people. There has been a fault among us. The reason why our distinguished men have not made themselves more influential, is because they fear that the strong current of opposition through which they must pass would cause their downfall and prove their overthrow. And what gives rise to this opposition? Envy. And what has it amounted to? Nothing. And who are the cause of it? Our whited sepulchres,[6] who want to be great, and don't know how; who love to be called of men "Rabbi, Rabbi;" who put on false sanctity, and humble themselves to their brethren for the sake of acquiring the highest place in the synagogue and the uppermost seat at the feast. You, dearly beloved, who are the genuine followers of our Lord Jesus Christ—the salt of the earth, and the light of the world—are not so culpable. As I told you in the very first of my writing, I will tell you again, I am but as a drop in the bucket—as one particle of the small dust of the earth.[7] God will surely raise up those among us who will plead the cause of virtue and the pure principles of morality more eloquently than I am able to do.

It appears to me that America has become like the great city of Babylon, for she has boasted in her heart: "I sit a queen and am no widow, and shall see no sorrow."[8] She is, indeed, a seller of slaves and the souls of men; she has made the Africans drunk with the wine of her fornication; she has put them completely beneath her feet, and she means to keep them there; her right hand supports the reins of government and her left hand the wheel of power, and she is determined not to let go her grasp. But many powerful sons and daughters of Africa will shortly arise, who will put down vice and immorality among us, and declare by Him that sitteth upon the throne that they will have their rights; and if refused, I am afraid they will spread horror and devastation around. I believe that the oppression of injured Africa has come up before the majesty of Heaven; and when our cries shall have reached the ears of the Most High, it will be a tremendous day for the people of this land: for strong is the hand of the Lord God Almighty.

Life has almost lost its charms for me; death has lost its sting, and the grave its terrors;[9] and at times I have a strong desire to depart and dwell with Christ, which is far better. Let me entreat my white brethren to awake and save our sons from dissipation and our daughters from ruin. Lend the hand of assistance to feeble merit; plead the cause of virtue among our sable race: so shall our curses upon you be turned into blessings; and though you should endeavor to drive us from these shores, still we will cling to you the more firmly; nor will we attempt to rise above you: we will presume to be called your equals only.

The unfriendly whites first drove the native American from his much loved home. Then they stole our fathers from their peaceful and quiet dwellings, and brought them hither, and made bond-men and bond-women of them and their little ones. They have obliged our brethren to labor; kept them in utter ignorance; nourished them in vice, and raised them in degrada-

---

5. Matthew 13:31–32: "The Kingdom of heaven is like to a grain of mustard seed, which a man took, and sowed in his field: Which indeed is the least of all seeds: but when it is grown, it is the greatest among herbs, and becometh a tree, so that the birds of the air come and lodge in the branches thereof."

6. Matthew 23:27: "Woe unto you, scribes and Pharisees, hypocrites! for ye are like unto whited sepulchres, which indeed appear beautiful outward, but are within full of dead men's bones, and of all uncleanness."

7. Isaiah 40:15: "Behold, the nations are as a drop of a bucket, and are counted as the small dust of the balance."

8. Revelation 18:7: "How much she hath glorified herself, and lived deliciously, so much torment and sorrow give her: for she saith in her heart, I sit a queen, and am no widow, and shall see no sorrow."

9. 1 Corinthians 15:55: "O death, where is thy sting? O grave, where is thy victory?"

tion; and now that we have enriched their soil and filled their coffers, they say that we are not capable of becoming like white men, and that we can never rise to respectability in this country. They would drive us to a strange land. But before I go, the bayonet shall pierce me through. African rights and liberty is a subject that ought to lire the breast of every free man of color in these United States, and excite in his bosom a lively, deep, decided, and heartfelt interest.

FREDERICK DOUGLASS

from *The Colonizationist Revival* [1849]

In February 1849, Henry Clay—U.S. senator from Kentucky, president of the American Colonization Society from 1836 to 1849, and a slaveholder—proposed using African colonization as part of a plan to eliminate slavery in Kentucky. Frederick Douglass (p. 38), one of the most vocal opponents of colonization, offered a scathing indictment of the plan at a convention of the New England Anti-Slavery Society in Boston on May 31, 1849. Although Clay linked his ideas to emancipation, Douglass asserts that the scheme would only allow Kentucky slaveholders to maximize their profits while identifying themselves as residents of a "free" state. The mention of both "hisses" and "applause" in accounts of the meeting demonstrate the contentiousness of the colonization issue, even among those who shared anti-slavery values.

From *The Liberator*, June 8, 1849.

Mr. Chairman, Ladies and Gentlemen—I never rise to speak in Faneuil Hall, without a deep sense of my want of ability to do justice to the subject upon which I undertake to speak. I can do a pretty good business, some have said, in the country school houses in Western New York and elsewhere; but when I come before the people of Boston in Faneuil Hall, I feel my exceeding weakness. I am all the more embarrassed this evening, because I have to speak to you in respect to a subject concerning which an apology seems to be demanded. I allude to the subject of the American Colonization Society—a subject which has had a large measure of anti-slavery attention, and been long since disposed of at the hands of Wm. Lloyd Garrison. The only apology that I can make for calling attention to it this evening, is, that it has had a sort of "revival," of late, through the agency of a man whom I presume a large portion of this audience esteem and admire. I allude to the Honorable Henry Clay of Kentucky. (Applause.) Though not a Yankee, you see I guessed correctly. I have presumed rightly that you esteem and admire that gentleman. Now, if you admire Mr. Clay, of course you would like to know all about him. You would like, of course, to hear whatever can be said of him, and said fairly, although a black man may presume to say it.

Mr. Clay has recently given to the world a letter, purporting to advocate the emancipation of the slaves of Kentucky. That letter has been extensively published in New England as well as [in] other parts of the United States; and in almost every instance where a Whig paper has spoken of the letter, it has done so in terms of high approval. The plan which Mr. Clay proposes is one which seems to meet almost the universal assent of the Whig party at the North; and many religious papers have copied the article, and spoken in terms of high commendation of the humanity, of the clear-sightedness and philanthropy of Henry Clay. Now, my friends, I am going to speak to you in a manner that, unless you allow your reason and not your prejudices to prevail, will provoke from you demonstrations of disapprobation. I beg of you, then, to hear me calmly—without prejudice or opposition. You, it must be remembered, have in your hands all power in this land. I stand here not only in a minority, but identified with a class whom every body can insult with impunity. Surely, the ambition for superiority must be great indeed in honorable men to induce them to insult a poor black man, whom the basest fellow in the street can insult with impunity. Keep this in mind, and hear what I have to say with regard to Mr. Clay's letter, and his position as a slaveholder.

The letter of Mr. Clay commences in a manner that gives promise to the reader that he shall find it a consistent, straight-forward anti-slavery document. It commences by refuting, with one or two strokes of the pen, the vast cart-loads of sophistry piled up by Mr. Calhoun and others, in favor of perpetual slavery. He shows clearly, that Mr. Calhoun's theory of slavery, if admitted to be sound, would enslave the whites as readily as it enslaves the blacks;—this would follow necessarily. Glancing at the question of the natural inferiority of the colored man, [he says:—admitting a question he does not raise—admitting the whites of this country are superior to the blacks,] the fact devolves upon the former the duty of enlightening, instructing and improving the condition of the latter." These are noble sentiments, worthy of the heart and head of a great and good man. But how does Mr. Clay propose to carry out this plan? He goes on to state that, in carrying out his proposed plan of gradual emancipation, great care should be taken that the rights and interests of the slaveholder should not be jeoparded. He proceeds to state that the utmost caution and prudence should guide the hand that strikes down slavery in Kentucky. With reference to emancipation, he affirms that it should not commence until the year 1885. The plan is, that all children born of slave parents in Kentucky after the year 1860, shall be free after arriving at the age of twenty-five. He sets therefore the day of emancipation beyond the average length of the slave's life; for a generation of slaves in the far South dies out in seven years. But how would he have these children of slave parents free? Not free to work for themselves—not free to live on the soil that they have cultivated with their own hard hands—that they have nourished with their best blood and toiled over and beautified and adorned—but that then they shall be let out under an agent of the State, for three long years, to raise one hundred and fifty dollars, with

which to pay the price of their own expatriation from their family and friends. (Voices—"Shame!")

MR. DOUGLASS.—I hear the cry of shame—yes, it is a deep and damning shame. He declares in that letter, that not only shall these emancipated slaves work three years, but that he, Mr. Clay, will oppose any measure for emancipation without the expatriation of the emancipated slaves. Just look at the peculiar operation of this plan. Let us suppose that it is adopted, and that in the year 1860 it commences. All children born of slave parents are to be free in the year 1888. It is well known that all persons in the South have contracted marriages long before this period, and have become parents, some having children from one to four years of age. Henry Clay's plan is, that when these persons arrive at the age of twenty-eight, these parents shall be torn away from their tender children, and hurried off to Liberia or somewhere else; and that the children taken from these parents, before they have become acquainted with the paternal relation, shall remain another twenty-eight years; and when they have remained that period, and have contracted matrimonial alliances, and become fathers and mothers, they too shall be taken from their children, the slaveholders having kept them at work for twenty-eight years, and hurried off to Liberia.

But a darker, baser feature than all these appears in this letter of Mr. Clay. It is this:—He speaks of the loss which the slaveholder will be called on to experience by the emancipation of his slaves. But he says that even this trifling expenditure may be prevented by leaving the slaveholder the right to sell—to mortgage—to transfer his slave property any time during the twenty-five years. Only look at Henry Clay's generosity to the slaveholders of Kentucky. He has twenty-five long years during which to watch the slave markets of New Orleans, of Memphis, of Vicksburg and other Southern cities, and to watch the prices of cotton and rice and tobacco on the other side of the Atlantic, and as the prices rise there in these articles, he may expect a corresponding rise in the price of flesh in the slave market, and then he can sell his slaves to the best advantage. Thus it is that the glorious State of Kentucky shall be made free, and yet her purse be made the heavier in consequence of it. This is not a proposition for emancipation, but a proposition to

Kentucky to sell off the slaves she holds in her possession, and throw them off into the far Southern States—and then hypocritically boast of being a free State, while almost every slave born upon her soil remains a slave. And this is the plan of the good Henry Clay, whom you esteem and admire so much. (Applause and hisses.) You that like to hiss, if you had the chain on your own limbs, and were pent up in Henry Clay's own quarter, and had free access to Henry Clay's own meal-tub, I think would soon change your tune. (Laughter.)

I want to say a word about the Colonization Society, of which Henry Clay is President. He is President of nothing else. (Laughter.) That Society is an old enemy of the colored people in this country. Almost every *respectable* man belongs to it, either by direct membership or by affinity. I meet with colonizationists everywhere; I met with a number of them the other day, on board the steamer *Alida,* going from Albany to New York. I wish to state my experience on board of that steamer, and as it is becoming a subject of newspaper remark, it may not be out of place to give my version of the story:—On Thursday last, I took my passage on board the steamer *Alida,* as I have stated, to go from Albany to New York. I happened to have, very contrary to American taste and American prejudices and customs, in my company, a couple of friends from England—persons who had not been ashamed—nor had they cause to be ashamed from any feeling that exists in that country against the colored man—of being found on equal social terms with him in the city of London. They happen now to be sojourning in this country; and as if unaware of the prejudice existing in this country, or, if aware, perfectly regardless of it, they accompanied me on the steamer, and shared, of course, my society, or permitted me to share theirs on the passage to New York. About noon, I went into the cabin, and inquired of one of the waiters if we could have dinner. The answer was, we could. They had on a sign on each side of the captain's office, words to this effect: "Meals can be received in the cabin at any hour during the day, by application to the steward." I made the application, and expected, of course, that dinner would be forthcoming at the time appointed. The bell rung—and though I do not know as it was altogether wise and prudent, I took a lady on each arm—for my friends

were white ladies, you must know—and moved forward to the cabin. The fact of their being white ladies will enable you more readily to understand the cause of the intensity of hate displayed towards me. I went below, forgetting all about my complexion, the curl of my hair, or the flatness of my nose, only remembering I had two elbows and a stomach, and was exceedingly hungry. (Laughter.) I walked below, as I have said, and took my seat at the table, supposing that the table was the place where a man should eat.

I had been there but a very few moments, before I observed a large number of American gentlemen rising up gradually—for we are *gradualists* in this country—and moving off to another table, on the other side. But feeling I was there on my own responsibility, and that those gentlemen could not eat dinner for me, and I must do it for myself, I preferred to sit still, unmoved by what was passing around me. I had been there but a few moments, when a white man—after the order of American white men—for I would say, for your consolation, that you are growing darker and darker every year—the steward came up to me in a very curious manner, and said, "Yer must get up from that table." (Laughter.) I demanded by what authority he ordered me from the table. "Well," said he, "yer know the rule." "Sir," said I, "I know nothing of your rules. I know that *the* rule is, that the passengers can receive their meals at any hour of the day on applying to the steward." Says he, "Now, it is no use for yer to talk, yer must leave." (Laughter.) "But where is the rule?" "Well," said he, "yer cannot get dinner on any boat on this river." I told him I went up the river in the *Confidence,* and took dinner, and no remark had been made. "Well," said he, "what yer can do on the *Confidence,* yer can't do on the *Alida.*" (Laughter.) ["Are yer a going to get up?" "No, sir," said I. "Well," says he, "I will have you up."] So off he goes to the upper deck, and brings down the captain, mate, clerk, and two or three hands. I sat still during the time of his absence; but finding they were mustering pretty strong, and remembering I had but one coat, and not caring to have it torn, and feeling I had borne a sufficient testimony against their unrighteous treatment, I arose from the table, and walked to the other end of the cabin, in company with my friends. A scene then occurred which I shall never forget; not because of its impudence, but because of its malignity. A large number of American ladies and gentlemen, seated around the table on the other side of the cabin, the very moment we walked away, gave three cheers for the captain, and applauded in the most uproarious manner the steward, for having driven two ladies and one gentleman from the table, and deprived them of dinner.

MR. GARRISON.—That is a fact for Europe.

MR. DOUGLASS.—They drove us from the table, and gave three cheers for the captain for driving us away. I looked around on the audience there assembled, to see if I could detect one line of generous magnanimity on any face—any indignation manifested against the outrage that had been perpetrated upon me and my friends. But not a look, not a word, not the slightest expression of disapprobation in any part of the vessel. Now, I have travelled in England, Ireland and Scotland—I mention this, not by way of boast, but because I want to contrast the freedom of our glorious country—and it is a glorious one, after all—with that of other countries through which I have travelled—by railroads, in highways and byways, steamboats, stage coaches, and every imaginable kind of vehicle—I have stayed at some of the first hotels in London, Liverpool, Edinburgh, Glasgow, Dublin, and elsewhere—and I must say to you, good Americans, that I never, in any of those cities or towns, received the first mark, or heard the first word of disapprobation on account of the color of my skin. I may tell you, that one of the ladies with me on the steamboat, though not a believer in the right of women to speak in public, was so excited and so indignant at the outrage perpetrated, that she went to the *American* captain, and told him that she had heard much of the country, much of the gallantry of American gentlemen—that they would be willing to rise from their seats to allow a lady to be seated—and she was very happy in having the opportunity of witnessing a manifestation of American gallantry and American courtesy. I do think I saw one neck hang when this rebuke was administered. (Applause.)

Most of the passengers were of the baser sort, very much like some Western men—dark-complexioned, lean, lank, pinched up, about the ugliest set of men I ever saw in my life. (Laughter.) I went to the steward about two hours after they had cleared off the dinner table for those hungry, wolfish-looking people. (Laughter.) My dear friends, if you had seen them, you would have agreed with me. I then inquired of the steward if now, after this hungry multitude had been fed, we could have a cup of coffee and a biscuit. Said he—"Who are you? If you are the servant of those ladies, you shall have what you want." I thought that was kind, any how. "Yes," said I, "I am their most humble servant." (Great laughter.) "Well," said he, "what are you walking about on deck with them for, if you are their servant?" I told him they were very courteous to me—putting him off in that way. He then told me if I did not get out of the cabin, he would split my head open. He was rather a diminutive being, and would not have been a mouthful for any thing like a Tom Hyer[1] man. (Applause.) However, seeing his Anglo-Saxon blood was up, I thought I would move off; but tapping him on the shoulder, I told him I wanted to give him a piece of advice: "I am a passenger, you are a servant; and therefore you should always consult the wants of the passengers." (Laughter.) He finally told me he was ready to give me my dinner in the capacity of a servant, but not otherwise. This acknowledgment told the whole story of American prejudice. There were two or three slaveholders on board. One was a lady from New Orleans; rather a dark-looking person—for individuals from that quarter are dark, except the blacks, and they are getting lighter. (Laughter.) This woman was perfectly horrified with my appearance, and she said to gentlemen standing by, that she was really afraid to be near me, and that I would draw a bowie-knife. Indeed, she had liked to have fainted. This woman, I learned from good authority, owned three hundred slaves in Louisiana; and yet she was afraid of a black man, and expected every moment I would attempt to commit violence on her. At the time she was affecting this horror of a negro, she was being waited on at the table by colored men. It was, "Waiter, come here!" and "waiter, go there!" and there they were actually cutting up the meat, standing right over it, quite near those white persons who really shouted when I was driven out.

---

1. White American heavyweight champion (1819–64).

This tells the whole story. You have no prejudice against blacks—no more than against any other color—but it is against the black man appearing as the colored gentleman. He is then a contradiction of your theory of natural inferiority in the colored race. It was not in consequence of my complexion that I was driven out of the cabin, for I could have remained there as a servant; but being there as a gentleman, having paid my own passage, and being in company with intelligent, refined persons, was what awakened the hatred, and brought down upon me the insulting manifestations I have alluded to.

It is because the American Colonization Society cherishes and fosters this feeling of hatred against the black man, that I am opposed to it. And I am especially disposed to speak out my opposition to this colonization scheme to-night, because not only of the renewed interest excited in the colonization scheme by the efforts of Henry Clay and others, but because there is a lecturer in the shape of the Rev. Mr. Miller, of New Jersey, now in England, soliciting funds for our expatriation from this country, and going about trying to organize a society, and to create an impression in favor of removing us from this country. I would ask you, my friends, if this is not mean and impudent in the extreme, for one class of Americans to ask for the removal of another class? I feel, sir, I have as much right in this country as any other man. I feel that the black man in this land has as much right to stay in this land as the white man. Consider the matter in the light of possession in this country. Our connection with this country is contemporaneous with your own. From the beginning of the existence of this people, as a people, the colored man has had a place upon the American soil. To be sure, he was not driven from his home in pursuit of a greater liberty than he enjoyed at home, like the Pilgrim fathers; but in the same year that the Pilgrims were landing in this State, slaves were landing on the James River, in Virginia.[2] We feel on this score, then, that we have as much right here as any other class of people.

We have other claims to being regarded and treated as American citizens. Some of our number have fought and bled for this country, and we only ask to be treated as well as those who have fought against it. We are lovers of this country, and we only ask to be treated as well as the haters of it. We are not only told by Americans to go out of our native land to Africa, and there enjoy our freedom—for we must go there in order to enjoy it—but Irishmen newly landed on our soil, who know nothing of our institutions, nor of the history of our country, whose toil has not been mixed with the soil of the country as ours—have the audacity to propose our removal from this, the land of our birth. For my part, I mean, for one, to stay in this country; I have made up my mind to live among you. I had a kind offer, when I was in England, of a little house and lot, and the free use of it, on the banks of the river Eden. I could easily have staid there, if I had sought for ease, undisturbed, unannoyed by American *skin-aristocracy;* for it is an aristocracy of skin (applause),—those passengers on board the *Alida* only got their dinner that day in virtue of color; if their skins had been of my color, they would have had to fast all day. Whatever denunciations England may be entitled to on account of her treatment of Ireland and her own poor, one thing can be said of her, that no man in that country, or in any of her dominions, is treated as less than a man on account of his complexion. I could have lived there; but when I remembered this prejudice against color, as it is called, and slavery, and saw the many wrongs inflicted on my people at the North that ought to be combatted and put down, I felt a disposition to lay aside ease, to turn my back on the kind offer of my friends, and to return among you—deeming it more noble to suffer along with my colored brethren, and meet these prejudices, than to live at ease, undisturbed, on the other side of the Atlantic. (Applause.) I had rather be here now, encountering this feeling, bearing my testimony against it, setting it at defiance, than to remain in England undisturbed. I have made up my mind wherever I go, I shall go as a man, and not as a slave. When I go on board of your steamboats, I shall always aim to be courteous and mild in my deportment towards all with whom I come in contact, at the same time firmly and constantly endeavoring to assert my equal right as a man and a brother.

---

2. The Pilgrims actually arrived in 1620, one year after a Dutch ship traded "twenty and odd" African slaves to the British colonists at Jamestown, Virginia; see pp. 1–4 for more on the development of slavery in colonial America.

But the Colonization Society says this prejudice can never be overcome—that it is natural,—God has implanted it. Some say so; others declare that it can only be removed by removing the cause, that is, by removing us to Liberia. I know this is false, from my own experience in this country. I remember that, but a few years ago, upon the railroads from New Bedford and Salem and in all parts of Massachusetts, a most unrighteous and proscriptive rule prevailed, by which colored men and women were subjected to all manner of indignity in the use of those conveyances. Anti-Slavery men, however, lifted up their testimony against this principle from year to year; and from year to year, he whose name cannot be mentioned without receiving a round of applause, WENDELL PHILLIPS (applause), went abroad, exposing this proscription in the light of justice. What is the result? Not a single railroad can be found in any part of Massachusetts, where a colored man is treated and esteemed in any other light than that of a man and a traveller. Prejudice has given way, and must give way. The fact that it is giving way, proves that this prejudice is not invincible. The time was, when it was expected that a colored man, when he entered a church in Boston, would go into the Jim Crow pew—and I believe such is the case now, to a large extent; but then there were those who would defend the custom. But you can scarcely get a defender of this proscription in New England now.

The history of the repeal of the intermarriage law shows that the prejudice against color is not invinci-ble. The general manner in which white persons sit with colored persons, shows plainly that the prejudice against color is not invincible. When I first came here, I felt the greatest possible diffidence to sitting with whites. I used to come up from the ship-yard where I worked, with my hands hardened with toil, rough and uncomely, and my movements awkward, (for I was unacquainted with the rules of politeness), I would shrink back, and would not have taken my meals with the whites, had they not pressed me to do so. Our president,[3] in his earlier intercourse with me, taught me, by example, his abhorrence of this prejudice. He has, in my presence, stated to those who visited him, that if they did not like to sit at the table with me, they could have a separate one for themselves.

The time was, when I walked through the streets of Boston, I was liable to insult, if in company with a white person. To-day I have passed in company with my white friends, leaning on their arm and they on mine, and yet the first word from any quarter on account of the color of my skin, I have not heard. It is all false, this talk about the invincibility of prejudice against color. If any of you have it, and no doubt some of you have, I will tell you how to get rid of it. Commence to do something to elevate, and improve and enlighten the colored man, and your prejudice will begin to vanish. The more you try to make a man of the black man, the more you will begin to think him a man.

MARTIN R. DELANY

from *Political Destiny of the Colored Race, on the American Continent* [1854]

In the 1850s, a number of prominent black abolitionists attempted to reclaim the emigration movement by promoting emigration plans that they emphatically dissociated from the reviled American Colonization Society. In 1852, Martin R. Delany (1812–1885), a physician, early black nationalist, and leading abolitionist, became a leading advocate of emigration with the publication of his groundbreaking book, *The Condition, Elevation, Emigration, and Destiny of the Colored People of the* *United States.* The body of the book advocates emigration to Central America, South America, and the West Indies, while the widely read appendix, "A Project for an Expedition of Adventure to the Eastern Coast of Africa," introduces Africa as a promising destination for black Americans. As the varied destinations suggest, Delany's nationalism arose less from a sense of attraction to any one particular destination than from his belief that African Americans, no matter how much they loved their

3. Wendell Phillips (1811–84).

country, would never obtain full civil rights as long as they remained in America. Delany's powerful argument— that "we are a nation within a nation—as the Poles in Russia, the Hungarians in Austria, the Welsh, Irish, and Scotch in the British dominions"—established him as a founding figure of black nationalism.

In 1854, Delany and other leading emigrationists held a National Emigration Convention of Colored People in Cleveland. The convention directly responded to the contentious division between emigrationists and anti-emigrationists that occurred at the 1853 Colored National Convention, where a group of anti-emigrationists, led by Frederick Douglass, persuaded its members to go on record as opposing emigration. At the Cleveland conference, Delany delivered the keynote address, "Political Destiny of the Colored Race, on the American Continent," which was adopted as the convention's official report. Delany's speech sets forth the emigrationists' case for relocation to Central America, South America, and the West Indies. It also proposes buying land in Canada, as "places of temporary relief." Only those in favor of emigration to selected destinations (not including Africa, Asia, or Europe) were invited to attend this National Emigration Convention. Frederick Douglass criticized the predetermined consensus, writing in *The North Star,* "A convention to consider the subject of emigration when every delegate must declare himself in favor of it before hand, as a condition of taking his seat, is like the handle of the jug, all on one side."

The report is underscored by a subtle militancy, which acknowledges the failure of attempts at peaceful change within the United States while proposing a plan of action to give black Americans control of their political destiny. It largely avoids the undercurrent of imperialism common to many emigration plans. Instead, it introduces a rare expression of solidarity with the indigenous colored populations of the proposed destinations.

Martin Robinson Delany was born free in Charles Town, Virginia (now West Virginia). Although his mother, Pati, was free, his father, Samuel, was enslaved at a nearby plantation. After receiving a spelling primer from a traveling peddler, Delany and his siblings taught themselves to read and write. In Virginia, it was illegal to teach

African Americans to read. When Delany and his siblings were discovered studying by a white man in 1822, their mother and grandmother decided to move them for safety to Pennsylvania, a free state, even though it meant leaving behind their father (who was able to buy his freedom the following year and join the family in Pennsylvania).

Delany continued his studies, eventually being accepted by Harvard University to study medicine. A month into his studies, a group of white students protested, and Delany, along with the two other black students, was dismissed. The experience fueled Delany's growing conviction that only outside the United States would black people be able to fulfill their potential. He grew to be a leader in the emigration movement, publishing *The Condition* in 1852, organizing the National Emigration Convention in Cleveland in 1854, leaving the United States himself for Canada in 1856 (though he returned in the 1860s to raise black recruits for the Civil War), and traveling to Liberia in 1859 to scout the region. In 1877, with the retrenchment of discrimination against African Americans in the South at the end of Reconstruction, Delany recommitted himself to emigration efforts, leading the finance committee of the Liberian Exodus Joint Stock Steamship Company; he withdrew in 1880, returning to the practice of medicine in order to meet the financial needs of his family. In addition to practicing medicine throughout his life, Delany was active in politics (attending a National Negro Convention for the first time in 1835), journalism (starting his own paper, *The Mystery,* in 1843 and co-editing Frederick Douglass's *North Star* from its launch in 1847 until 1849), literature (having his novel *Blake, or The Huts of America* serialized in *The Weekly Anglo-African* from 1861 to 1862, made him one of the first African Americans to publish a novel). He also served in the military (being appointed a major in the army by President Abraham Lincoln during the Civil War, which made him the first black field officer in the U.S. Army), and government (serving in the Freedmen's Bureau and as a judge during Reconstruction). He was the father of eleven children, seven of whom survived past childhood. Delany is remembered as a leading promoter of black pride and one of the first black nationalists. He died of tuberculosis at the age of seventy-two.

From *Proceedings of the National Emigration Convention of Colored People, Held at Cleveland, Ohio, on Thursday, Friday and Saturday, the 24th, 25th and 26th of August, 1854* (Pittsburgh: A. A. Anderson, 1854).

TO THE COLORED INHABITANTS OF THE UNITED STATES.

FELLOW-COUNTRYMEN!—The duty assigned us is an important one. comprehending all that pertains to our destiny and that of our posterity—present and prospectively. And while it must be admitted, that the subject is one of the greatest magnitude, requiring all that talents, prudence and wisdom might adduce, and while it would be fully to pretend to give you the combined result of these three agencies, we shall satisfy ourselves with doing our duty to the best of our ability, and that in the plainest, most simple and comprehensive manner.

Our object, then, shall be to place before you our true position in this country—the United States,—the improbability of realizing our desires, and the sure, practicable and infallible remedy for the evils we now endure.

We have not addressed you as *citizens*—a term desired and ever cherished by us—because such you have never been. We have not addressed you as *freemen*,—because such privileges have never been enjoyed by any colored man in the United States. Why then should we flatter your credulity, by inducing you to believe that which neither has now, nor never before had an existence. Our oppressors are ever gratified at our manifest satisfaction, especially when that satisfaction is founded upon false premises; an assumption on our part, of the enjoyment of rights and privileges which never have been conceded, and which, according to the present system of the United States policy, we never can enjoy.

* * *

There has, of late years, been a false impression obtained, that the privilege of *voting* constitutes, or necessarily embodies, the *rights of citizenship*. A more radical error never obtained favor among an oppressed people. Suffrage is an ambiguous term, which admits of several definitions. But according to strict political construction, means simply "a vote, voice, approbation." Here, then, you have the whole import of the term suffrage. To have the "right of suffrage," as we rather proudly term it, is simply to have the *privilege*—there is no *right* about it—of giving our *approbation* to

that which our *rulers may do,* without the privilege, on our part, of doing the same thing. Where such privileges are granted—privileges which are now exercised in but few of the States by colored men—we have but the privilege granted of saying, in common with others, who shall, for the time being, exercise *right,* which, in him, are conceded to be *inherent* and *inviolable:* Like the indented apprentice, who is summoned to give his approbation to an act which would be fully binding without his concurrence. Where there is no *acknowledged sovereignty,* there can be no binding power; hence, the suffrage of the black man, independently of the white, would be in this country unavailable.

Much might be adduced on this point to prove the insignificance of the black man, politically considered in this country, but we deem it wholly unnecessary at present, and consequently proceed at once to consider another feature of this important subject.

Let it then be understood, as a great principle of political economy, that no people can be free who themselves do not constitute an essential part of the *ruling element* of the country in which they live. Whether this element be founded upon a true or false, a just or an unjust basis; this position in community is necessary to personal safety. The liberty of no man is secure, who controls not his own political destiny. What is true of an individual, is true of a family; and that which is true of a family, is also true concerning a whole people. To suppose otherwise, is that delusion which at once induces its victim, through a period of long suffering, patiently to submit to every species of wrong; trusting against probability, and hoping against all reasonable grounds of expectation, for the granting of privileges and enjoyment of rights, which never will be attained. This delusion reveals the true secret of the power which holds in peaceable subjection, all the oppressed in every part of the world.

A people, to be free, must necessarily be *their own rulers:* that is, *each individual* must, in himself, embody the *essential ingredient*—so to speak—of the *sovereign principle* which composes the *true basis* of his liberty.

* * *

In other periods and parts of the world—as in Europe and Asia—the people being of one common, direct origin of race, though established on the presumption of difference by birth, or what was termed *blood,* yet the distinction between the superior classes and common people, could only be marked by the difference in the dress and education of the two classes. To effect this, the interposition of government was necessary; consequently, the costume and education of the people became a subject of legal restriction; guarding carefully against the privileges of the common people.

In Rome, the Patrician and Plebeian were orders in the ranks of her people—all of whom were termed citizens (*cives*)—recognized by the laws of the country; their dress and education being determined by law, the better to fix the distinction. In different parts of Europe, at the present day, if not the same, the distinction among the people is similar, only on a modified—and in some kingdoms—probably more tolerant or deceptive policy.

In the United States, our degradation being once—as it has in a hundred instances been done—legally determined, our color is sufficient, independently of costume, education, or other distinguishing marks, to keep up that distinction.

In Europe, when an inferior is elevated to the rank of equality with the superior class, the law first comes to his aid, which, in its decrees, entirely destroys his identity as an inferior, leaving no trace of his former condition visible.

In the United States, among the whites, their color is made, by law and custom, the mark of distinction and superiority; while the color of the blacks is a badge of degradation, acknowledged by statute, organic law, and the common consent of the people.

With this view of the case—which we hold to be correct—to elevate to equality the degraded subject of law and custom, it can only be done, as in Europe, by an entire destruction of the identify of the former condition of the applicant. Even were this desirable—which we by no means admit—with the deep seated prejudices engendered by oppression, with which we have to contend, ages incalculable might reasonably be expected to roll around, before this could honorably be accomplished; otherwise, we should encourage and at once commence an indiscriminate concubinage and immoral commerce, of our mothers, sisters, wives and daughters, revolting to think of, and a physical curse to humanity.

* * *

But we have fully discovered and comprehended the great political disease with which we are affected, the cause of its origin and continuance; and what is now left for us to do, is to discover and apply a sovereign remedy—a healing balm to a sorely diseased body—a wrecked but not entirely shattered system. We propose for this disease a remedy. That remedy is Emigration. This Emigration should be well advised, and like remedies applied to remove the disease from the physical system of man, skillfully and carefully applied, within the proper time, directed to operate on that part of the system, whose greatest tendency shall be, to benefit the whole.

Several geographical localities have been named, among which rank the Canadas. These we do not object to as places of temporary relief, especially to the fleeing fugitive—which, like a palliative, soothes for the time being the misery—but cannot commend them as permanent places upon which to fix our destiny, and that of our children, who shall come after us. But in this connexion, we would most earnestly recommend to the colored people of the United States generally, to secure by purchase all of the land they possibly can, while selling at low rates, under the British people and government. As that time may come, when, like the lands in the United States territories generally, if not as in Oregon and some other territories and States, they may be prevented entirely from settling or purchasing them; the preference being given to the white applicant.

And here, we would not decieve you by disguising the facts, that according to political tendency, the Canadas—as all British America—at no very distant day, are destined to come into the United States.

And were this not the case, the odds are against us, because the ruling element there, as in the United States, is, and ever must be, white—the population now standing, in all British America, two and a half millions of whites, to but forty thousand of the black race; or sixty-one and a fraction, whites, to one black!—the difference being eleven times greater than in the United States—so that colored people might never hope for anything more than to exist politically by mere suffrance—occupying a secondary position to the whites of the Canadas. The Yankees from this side of the lakes, are fast settling in the Canadas, infusing, with industrious success, all the malignity and negro-hate, inseparable from their very being, as Christian Democrats and American advocates of equality.

Then, to be successful, our attention must be turned in a direction towards those places where the black and colored man comprise, by population, and constitute by necessity of numbers, the *ruling element* of the body politic. And where, when occasion shall require it, the issue can be made and maintained on this basis. Where our political enclosure and national edifice can be reared, established, walled, and proudly defended on this great elementary principle of original identity. Upon this solid foundation rests the fabric of every substantial political structure in the world, which cannot exist without it; and so soon as a people or nation lose their original identity, just so soon must that nation or people become extinct.—Powerful though they may have been, they must fall. Because the nucleus which heretofore held them together, becoming extinct, there being no longer a centre of attraction, or basis for a union of the parts, a dissolution must as naturally ensue, as the result of the neutrality of the basis of adhesion among the particles of matter.

This is the secret of the eventful downfall of Egypt, Carthage, Rome, and the former Grecian States, once so powerful—a loss of original identity; and with it, a loss of interest in maintaining their fundamental principles of nationality.

This, also, is the great secret of the present strength of Great Britain, Russia, the United States, and Turkey; and the endurance of the French nation, whatever its strength and power, is attributable only to their identity as Frenchmen.

* * *

Nor is this the only important consideration. Were we content to remain as we are, sparsely interspersed among our white fellow-countrymen, we never might be expected to equal them in any honorable or respectable competition for a livelihood. For the reason that,

according to the customs and policy of the country, we for ages would be kept in a secondary position, every situation of respectability, honor, profit or trust, either as mechanics, clerks, teachers, jurors, councilmen, or legislators, being filled by white men, consequently, our energies must become paralysed or enervated for the want of proper encouragement.

This example upon our children, and the colored people generally, is pernicious and degrading in the extreme. And how could it otherwise be, when they see every place of respectability filled and occupied by the whites, they pandering to their vanity, and existing among them merely as a thing of conveniency.

Our friends in this and other countries, anxious for our elevation, have for years been erroneously urging us to lose our identity as a distinct race, declaring that we were the same as other people; while at the very same time their own representative was traversing the world and propagating the doctrine in favor of a *universal Anglo-Saxon predominence*. The "Universal Brotherhood," so ably and eloquently advocated by that Polyglot Christian Apostle[1] of this doctrine, had established as its basis, a universal acknowledgment of the Anglo-Saxon rule.

The truth is, we are not identical with the Anglo-Saxon or any other race of the Caucasian or pure white type of the human family, and the sooner we know and acknowledge this truth, the better for ourselves and posterity.

The English, French, Irish, German, Italian, Turk, Persian, Greek, Jew, and all other races, have their native or inherent peculiarities, and why not our race? We are not willing, therefore, at all times and under all circumstances to be moulded into various shapes of eccentricity, to suit the caprices and conveniences of every kind of people. We are not more suitable to everybody than everybody is suitable to us; therefore, no more like other people than others are like us.

We have then inherent traits, attributes—so to speak—and native characteristics, peculiar to our race—whether pure or mixed blood—and all that is required of us is to cultivate these and develope them in their purity, to make them desirable and emulated by the rest of the world.

1. Elihu Burritt. [Delany's note]

That the colored races have the highest traits of civilization, will not be disputed. They are civil, peaceable and religious to a fault. In mathematics, sculpture and architecture, as arts and sciences, commerce and internal improvements as enterprises, the white race may probably excel; but in languages, oratory, poetry, music and painting as arts and sciences, and in ethics, metaphysics, theology and legal jurisprudence; in plain language—in the true principles of morals, correctness of thought, religion, and law or civil government, there is no doubt but the black race will yet instruct the world.

It would be duplicity longer to disguise the fact, that the great issue, sooner or later, upon which must be disputed the world's destiny, will be a question of black and white; and every individual will be called upon for his identity with one or the other. The blacks and colored races are four-sixths of all the population of the world; and these people are fast tending to a common cause with each other. The white races are but one-third of the population of the globe—or one of them to two of us—and it cannot much longer continue, that two-thirds will passively submit to the universal domination of this one-third. And it is notorious that the only progress made in territorial domain, in the last three centuries, by the whites, has been a usurpation and encroachment on the rights and native soil of some of the colored races.

The East Indies, Java, Sumatria, the Azores, Madeira, Canary, and Cape Verde Islands; Socotra, Guardifui and the Isle of France; Algiers, Tunis, Tripoli, Barca and Egypt in the North, Sierra Leon in the West, and Cape Colony in the South of Africa; besides many other Islands and possessions not herein named. Australia, the Ladrone Islands, together with many others of Oceanica; the seizure and appropriation of a great portion of the Western Continent, with all its Islands, were so many encroachments of the whites upon the rights of the colored races. Nor are they yet content, but, intoxicated with the success of their career, the Sandwich Islands are now marked out as the next booty to be seized, in the ravages of their exterminating crusade.

We regret the necessity of stating the fact—but duty compels us to the task—that for more than two thousand years, the determined aim of the whites has been to crush the colored races wherever found. With a determined will, they have sought and pursued them in every quarter of the globe. The Anglo-Saxon has taken the lead in this work of universal subjugation. But the Anglo-American stands pre-eminent for deeds of injustice and acts of oppression, unparalleled perhaps in the annals of modern history.

We admit the existence of great and good people in America, England, France, and the rest of Europe, who desire a unity of interests among the whole human family, of whatever origin or race.

But it is neither the moralist, Christian, nor philanthropist whom we now have to meet and combat, but the politician—the civil engineer and skillful economist, who direct and control the machinery which moves forward with mighty impulse, the nations and powers of the earth. We must, therefore, if possible, meet them on vantage ground, or, at least, with adequate means for the conflict.

Should we encounter an enemy with artillery, a prayer will not stay the cannon shot; neither will the kind words nor smiles of philanthropy shield his spear from piercing us through the heart. We must meet mankind, then, as they meet us—prepared for the worst, though we may hope for the best. Our submission does not gain for us an increase of friends nor respectability—as the white race will only respect those who oppose their usurpation, and acknowledge as equals those who will not submit to their rule. This may be no new discovery in political economy, but it certainly is a subject worthy the consideration of the black race.

After a due consideration of these facts, as herein recounted, shall we stand still and continue inactive—the passive observers of the great events of the times and age in which we live; submitting indifferently to the usurpation, by the white race, of every right belonging to the blacks? Shall the last vestage of an opportunity, outside of the continent of Africa, for the national development of our race, be permitted, in consequence of our slothfulness, to elude our grasp and fall into the possession of the whites? This, may Heaven forbid. May the sturdy, intelligent Africo-American sons of the Western Continent forbid.

Longer to remain inactive, it should be borne in mind, maybe to give an opportunity to despoil us of every right and possession sacred to our existence, with which God has endowed us as a heritage on the earth.

For let it not be forgotten, that the white race—who numbers but *one* of them to *two* of us—originally located in Europe, besides possessing all of that continent, have now got hold of a large portion of Asia, Africa, all North America, a portion of South America, and all of the great Islands of both Hemispheres, except Paupau, or New Guinea, inhabited by negroes and Malays, in Oceanica; the Japanese Islands, peopled and ruled by the Japanese; Madigascar, peopled by negroes, near the coast of Africa; and the Island of Haiti, in the West Indies, peopled by as brave and noble descendants of Africa, as they who laid the foundation of Thebias, or constructed the everlasting pyramids and catecombs of Egypt.—A people who have freed themselves by the might of their own will, the force of their own power, the unfailing strength of their own right arms, and their unflinching determination to be free.

Let us, then, not survive the disgrace and ordeal of Almighty displeasure, of two to one, witnessing the universal possession and control by the whites, of every habitable portion of the earth. For such must inevitably be the case, and that, too, at no distant day, if black men do not take advantage of the opportunity, by grasping hold of those places where chance is in their favor, and establishing the rights and power of the colored race.

We must make an issue, create an event, and establish for ourselves a position. This is essentially necessary for our effective elevation as a people, in shaping our national developement, directing our destiny, and redeeming ourselves as a race.

If we but determine it shall be so, it *will* be so; and there is nothing under the sun can prevent it. We shall then be but in pursuit of our legitimate claims to inherent rights, bequeathed to us by the will of Heaven—the endowment of God, our common parent. A distinguished economist has truly said, "God has implanted in man an infinite progression in the career of improvement. A soul capacitated for improvement ought not to be bounded by a tyrant's landmarks." This sentiment is just and true, the application of which to our case, is adapted with singular fitness.

Having glanced hastily at our present political position in the world generally, and the United States in particular—the fundamental disadvantages under which we exist, and the improbability of ever attaining citizenship and equality of rights in this country—we call your attention next, to the places of destination to which we shall direct Emigration.

The West Indies, Central and South America, are the countries of our choice, the advantages of which shall be made apparent to your entire satisfaction.

Though we have designated them as countries, they are in fact but one country—relatively considered—a part of this, the Western Continent.

Frederick Douglass

African Civilization Society [1859]

Henry Highland Garnet, an abolitionist and Presbyterian minister (p. 80), established the African Civilization Society in 1858 to fulfill his long-held goal of African resettlement. Frederick Douglass (p. 38) and other anti-emigrationists immediately attacked the new society, stressing similarities to the hated American Colonization Society. The criticism gained some credibility because some members of Garnet's organization had been associated with the ACS, including the white Quaker merchant Benjamin Coates, and because Garnet's organization shared a building with the New York branch of the American Colonization Society.

Garnet challenged Douglass to defend his attacks on the African Civilization Society, asking, "What objection have you to an organization that shall endeavor to check and destroy the African slave trade, and that desires to co-operate with anti-slavery men and women of every grade in our own land, and to toil with them for the overthrow of American slavery?" In his reply, reprinted here, which he published in his paper *Douglass' Monthly*, Douglass praises vigorous debate among

African Americans but dismisses Garnet's attack on his own commitment to abolition and states his view that migration is a question of individual choice. "*You* go there, *we* stay here," he instructs Garnet, implying that he speaks for the majority of African Americans when he rejects the "narrow, bitter and persecuting idea, that Africa, not America, is the Negro's true home."

From *Douglass' Monthly,* February 1859.

"But I entreated you to tell your readers what your objections are to the civilization and christianization of Africa. What objection have you to colored men in this country engaging in agriculture, lawful trade, and commerce in the land of my forefathers? What objection have you to an organization that shall endeavor to check and destroy the African slave-trade, and that desires to co-operate with anti-slavery men and women of every grade in our own land, and to toil with them for the overthrow of American slavery?— Tell us, I pray you, tell us in your clear and manly style. 'Gird up thy loins,[1] and answer thou me, if thou canst.'"—Letter from Henry Highland Garnet.

Hitherto we have allowed ourselves but little space for discussing the claims of this new scheme for the civilization of Africa, doing little more than indicating our dissent from the new movement, yet leaving our columns as free to its friends as to its opponents. We shall not depart from this course, while the various writers bring good temper and ability to the discussion, and shall keep themselves within reasonable limits. We hope the same impartiality will be shown in the management of the *Provincial Freeman,* the adopted organ of the African Civilization Society. We need discussion among ourselves, discussion to rouse our souls to intenser life and activity.—"Communipaw" did capital service when he gave the subtle brain of Wm. Whipper[2] a little work to do, and our readers the pleasure of seeing it done. Anything to promote earnest thinking among our people may be held as a good thing in itself, whether we assent to or dissent from the proposition which calls it forth.

We say this much before entering upon a compliance with the request of our friend Garnet, lest any should infer that the discussion now going on is distasteful to us, or that we desire to avoid it. The letter in question from Mr. Garnet is well calculated to make that impression. He evidently enjoys a wholesome confidence, not only in the goodness of his own cause, but in his own ability to defend it.—Sallying out before us, as if in "complete steel," he entreats us to appear "in manly style," to *"gird up our loins,"* as if the contest were one requiring all our strength and activity. "Answer thou me if thou canst?"—As if an answer were impossible. Not content with this, he reminds us of his former similar entreaties, thus making it our duty to reply to him, if for no better reason than respect and courtesy towards himself.

The first question put to us by Mr. Garnet is a strange and almost preposterous one. He asks for our "objections to the civilization and christianization of Africa." The answer we have to make here is very easy and very ready, and can be given without even taking the trouble to observe the generous advice to "gird up our loins." We have not, dear brother, the least possible objection either to the civilization or to the christianization of Africa, and the question is just about as absurd and ridiculous as if you had asked us to "gird up our loins," and tell the world what objection Frederick Douglass has to the abolition of slavery, or the elevation of the free people of color in the United States! We not only have no objection to the civilization and christianization of Africa, but rejoice to know that through the instrumentality of commerce, and the labors of faithful missionaries, those very desirable blessings are already being realized in the land of my fathers Africa.

Brother Garnet is a prudent man, and we admire his tact and address in presenting the issue before us,

1. Allusion to Job 40:7: "Gird up thy loins now like a man: I will demand of thee, and declare thou unto me."
2. Communipaw, an Indian name, was used as a pseudonym by James McCune Smith (p. 42) to express a connection to Native Americans as symbols of resistance; Whipper (p. 90) was an abolitionist and properous businessperson.

while we cannot assent entirely to its fairness. *"I did not ask you for a statement of your preference of America to Africa."* That is very aptly said, but is it impartially said? Does brother Garnet think such a preference, in view of all the circumstances, a wise and proper one? Or is he wholly indifferent as to the one preference or the other? He seems to think that our preferences have nothing to do with the question between us and the African Civilization Society, while we think that this preference touches the very bone of contention. The African Civilization Society says to us, go to Africa, raise cotton, civilize the natives, become planters, merchants, compete with the slave States in the Liverpool cotton market, and thus break down American slavery. To which we simply and briefly reply, "we prefer to remain in America"; and we do insist upon it, in the very face of our respected friend, that that is both a direct and candid answer. There is no dodging, no equivocation, but so far as we are concerned, the whole matter is ended. *You* go there, *we* stay here, is just the difference between us and the African Civilization Society, and the true issue upon which co-operation with it or opposition to it must turn.

Brother Garnet will pardon us for thinking it somewhat cool in him to ask us to give our objections to this new scheme. Our objections to it have been stated in substance, repeatedly. It has been no fault of ours if he has not read them.

As long ago as last September, we gave our views at large on this subject, in answer to an eloquent letter from Benjamin Coates, Esq., the real, but not the ostensible head of the African Civilization movement.

Meanwhile we will state briefly, for the benefit of friend Garnet, seven considerations, which prevent our co-operation with the African Civilization Society.

1.   No one idea has given rise to more oppression and persecution toward the colored people of this country, than that which makes Africa, not America, their home. It is that wolfish idea that elbows us off the side walk, and denies us the rights of citizenship. The life and soul of this abominable idea would have been thrashed out of it long ago, but for the jesuitical and persistent teaching of the American Colonization Society. The natural and unfailing tendency of the African Civilization Society, by sending *"around the*

hat" in all our towns and cities for money to send colored men to Africa, will be to keep life and power in this narrow, bitter and persecuting idea, that Africa, not America, is the Negro's true home.

2.   The abolition of American slavery, and the moral, mental and social improvement of our people, are objects of immediate, pressing and transcendent importance, involving a direct and positive issue with the pride and selfishness of the American people. The prosecution of this grand issue against all the principalities and powers of church and state, furnishes ample occupation for all our time and talents; and we instinctively shrink from any movement which involves a substitution of a doubtful and indirect issue, for one which is direct and certain, for we believe that the demand for the abolition of slavery now made in the name of humanity, and according to the law of the Living God, though long delayed, will, if faithfully pressed, certainly triumph.—The African Civilization Society proposes to plant its guns too far from the battlements of slavery for us. Its doctrines and measures are those of doubt and retreat, and it must land just where the American Colonization movement landed, upon the lying assumption, that white and black people can never live in the same land on terms of equality. Detesting this heresy as we do, and believing it to be full of all "deceivableness" of unrighteousness, we shun the paths that lead to it, no matter what taking names they bear, or how excellent the men who bid us to walk in them.

3.   Among all the obstacles to the progress of civilization and of christianity in Africa, there is not one so difficult to overcome as the African slave trade. No argument is needed to make this position evident. The African Civilization Society will doubtless assent to its truth. Now, so regarding the slave trade, and believing that the existence of slavery in this country is one of the strongest props of the African slave trade, we hold that the best way to put down the slave trade, and to build up civilization in Africa, is to stand our ground and labor for the abolition of slavery in the U.S. But for slavery here, the slave trade would have been long since swept from the ocean by the united navies of Great Britain, France and the United States. The work, therefore, to which we are naturally and logically conducted, as the one of primary importance, is to abolish slavery. We thus get the example of a great nation on the right side, and break up, so far as America is concerned, a demand for the slave trade. More will have been done. The enlightened conscience of our nation, through its church and government, and its press, will be let loose against slavery and the slave trade wherever practiced.

4.   One of the chief considerations upon which the African Civilization Society is recommended to our favorable regard, is its tendency to break up the slave trade. We have looked at this recommendation, and find no reason to believe that any one man in Africa can do more for the abolition of that trade, while living in Africa, than while living in America. If we cannot make Virginia, with all her enlightenment and christianity, believe that there are better uses for her energies than employing them in breeding slaves for the market, we see not how we can expect to make Guinea, with its ignorance and savage selfishness, adopt our notions of political economy. Depend upon it, the savage chiefs on the western coast of Africa, who for ages have been accustomed to selling their captives into bondage, and pocketing the ready cash for them, will not more readily see and accept our moral and economical ideas, than the slave-traders of Maryland and Virginia. We are, therefore, less inclined to go to Africa to work against the slave-trade, than to stay here to work against it. Especially as the means for accomplishing our object are quite as promising here as there, and more especially since we are here already, with constitutions and habits suited to the country and its climate, and to its better institutions.

5.   There are slaves in the United States to the number of four millions. They are stigmatized as an inferior race, fit only for slavery, incapable of improvement, and unable to take care of themselves. Now, it seems plain that here is the place, and we are the people to meet and put down these conclusions concerning our race. Certainly there is no place on the globe where the colored man can speak to a larger audience, either by precept or by example, than in the United States.

6.   If slavery depended for its existence upon the cultivation of cotton, and were shut up to that single production, it might even then be fairly questioned whether any amount of cotton culture in Africa would materially affect the price of that article in this country, since demand and supply would go on together. But the case is very different. Slave labor can be employed in raising anything which human labor and the earth can produce. If one does not pay, another will. Christy says "Cotton is King," and our friends of the African Civilization movement are singing the same tune; but clearly enough it must appear to common sense, that "King Cotton" in America has nothing to fear from King Cotton in Africa.

7.   We object to enrolling ourselves among the friends of that new Colonization scheme, because we believe that our people should be let alone, and given a fair chance to work out their own destiny where they are. We are perpetually kept, with wandering eyes and open mouths, looking out for some mighty revolution in our affairs here, which is to remove us from this country. The consequence is, that we do not take a firm hold upon the advantages and opportunities about us. Permanent location is a mighty element of civilization. In a savage state men roam about, having no continued abiding place. They are *"going, going, going."* Towns and cities, houses and homes, are only built up by men who halt long enough to build them. There is a powerful motive for the cultivation of an honorable character, in the fact that we have a country, a neighborhood, a home. The full effect of this motive has not hitherto been experienced by our people. When in slavery, we were liable to perpetual sales, transfers and removals; and now that we are free, we are doomed to be constantly harassed with schemes to get us out of the country. We are quite tired of all this, and wish no more of it.

To all this it will be said that Douglass is opposed to our following the example of white men. They are pushing East, West, North and South. They are going to Oregon, Central America, Australia, South Africa and all over the world. Why should we not have the same right to better our condition that other men have and exercise? Any man who says that we deny this right, or even object to its exercise, only deceives the ignorant by such representations.

If colored men are convinced that they can better their condition by going to Africa, or anywhere else, we shall respect them if they will go, just as we respect others who have gone to California, Fraser Island, Oregon and the West Indies. They are self-moved, self-sustained, and their success or failure is their own individual concern. But widely different is the case, when men combine, in societies, under taking titles, send out agents to collect money, and call upon us to help them travel from continent to continent to promote some selfish or benevolent end. In the one case, it is none of our business where our people go.—They are of age, and can act for themselves.—But when they ask the public to go, or for money, sympathy, aid, or co-operation, or attempt to make it appear anybody's duty to go, the case ceases to be a private individual affair

and becomes a public question, and he who believes that he can make a better use of his time, talents, and influence, than such a movement proposes for him, may very properly say so, without in any measure calling in question the equal right of our people to migrate.

Again it may be said that we are opposed to sending the Gospel to benighted Africa; but this is not the case. The *American Missionary Society*,[3] in its rooms at 48 Beekman Street, has never had occasion to complain of any such opposition, nor will it have such cause. But we will not anticipate the objections which may be brought to the foregoing views. They seem to us sober, rational, and true; but if otherwise, we shall be glad to have them honestly criticised.

HENRY HIGHLAND GARNET
Speech at an Enthusiastic Meeting of the Colored Citizens of Boston [1859]

The remarks of Henry Highland Garnet (1815–1882) that were delivered on August 29, 1859, at Boston's Joy Street Church (and published on September 10 in *The Weekly Anglo-African*, the leading black paper of the era) serve as a reply to Frederick Douglass's criticism of the African Civilization Society (p. 76). Garnet echoes Douglass's argument in favor of debate among African Americans, but suggests that anti-emigrationists have been trying to hinder open discussion about emigration. He agrees with Douglass that emigration is a matter of personal choice, but continues to assert that Africa holds more promise for black Americans than America does. He mocks those who would choose not to go to a better place simply because whites say they should go. "I believe

some people wouldn't go to Heaven if a white man should say they must go," he tells the laughing crowd. Garnet's speech was repeatedly interrupted and challenged by members of the audience, testifying to the contentiousness surrounding the issue of emigration to Africa.

Born into slavery in Maryland in 1815, Garnet escaped to freedom with his entire family when he was nine. He went on to become a Presbyterian minister, and upon delivering a sermon in the House of Representatives in 1865, in response to a request by President Lincoln, he became the first African American to speak in the U.S. Capitol. His own emigration to Liberia just months before his death underscored his lifelong dedication to direct action and black self-determination.

From *The Weekly Anglo-African*, September 10, 1859.

T uesday evening, 29th ult.,[1] the citizens of Boston assembled in the Joy Street Baptist Church to hear a lecture by Rev. Henry Highland Garnet,

on African Civilization. He was introduced to the audience by Rev. J. Sella Martin, who remarked as follows:

3. American Missionary Association, an integrated group established in 1846 to promote abolition, black education, racial equality, and Christianity.
1. Ultimo: in the month preceding the present one.

Ladies and gentlemen: In introducing our staunch friend and able advocate, I feel that it would be superfluous for me to utter one word of eulogy upon his character, or one sentence in commendation of his course (*Applause*). I am confident that the generosity and wisdom of this audience will accord to him all that he wishes or needs, both in respect and courtesy and justice. But, while this is true, I feel it incumbent upon me to remove some unfavorable impressions which others (and I know not but he) may entertain in regard to the conduct of some of the leading men of the Twelfth (colored) Baptist Church of this city. When Mr. Garnet's personal friends applied for that church for him to speak in, the reason assigned for the refusal to open it to him was that the citizens of Boston did not wish to hear him, because they were tired of the discussion of the African civilization question. Now, without stopping to refute these reasons, admitting that they were true, it may not be out of place for me to state that I did all that I could, in one of the preliminary meetings which were taking measures for the success of the Convention, to dissuade the originators of the Convention from introducing that subject as a matter of discussion; but all to no purpose. Not that I feared discussion, but because I did not wish to interrupt more important objects of the Convention by the introduction of a topic which I know would not benefit our people generally, as the Convention would not have time to examine the merits of the question.

Now, my friends, no matter what the self-elected guardians of the colored people of Boston may say, I feel that I am prepared to deny the charge that the colored people of Boston are so unjust and uncourteous as to refuse to hear any man in his defense and efforts to remove imputations cast upon his character in his absence by those who disagree with him (*Applause*). I know too much about the generosity of the colored people of this city to allow our *dear friend,* Mr. Garnet, to go away with the impression that you are enemies to free discussion. During my labors in Tremont Temple, where the largest white congregation in New England assembles, I have been cheered by the presence of our most intelligent and respectable colored friends, and when, during the week I have been out among you, you have given me words of sympathy and encouragement (*Applause*). And if you have acted thus kindly towards me in my humbleness and obscurity, I know you will not depart from this course when the character of H. H. Garnet is at stake and submitted to your just judgment (*Applause*). A man who is celebrated for his charity towards both his friends and his enemies, as he is admired for the ability with which he defends the one and overthrows the other when they dare to meet him (*Applause*). Could it be possible for Boston, with all its talent and respectability, with courtesy and love of freedom, to act worse than the slave-holder does toward his slave? When a slave is tried in the South they will at least allow him the privilege of pleading guilty or not guilty. I repeat, it has not been done by the colored people of Boston (*Applause*). A few men, whose minds and hearts melted into one would find room to rattle in the shell of a mustard seed (*Laughter*), whose perceptions are as dull as their conscience are elastic, and whose highest sense of right is to go with what may for the time appear popular, and the utmost of whose usefulness is measured by the power of their lungs (*Laughter*); these men are the only persons to be blamed in Boston, and upon these the blame shall fall (*Applause*). Mr. Grimes knew, when he refused to open his church, and his satellites, when they refused to hire the church (notwithstanding it has been hired to every and any man who could command five dollars to pay for it), they knew that the people, had they known of it at the time, as they have done since, would have given expression to their just indignation at this ostracism and unmanliness. I, for one, am not sorry for the state of shame and confusion into which his contemptible unkindness has precipitated him (*Applause*). A man who would violate the courtesy which he owed to a brother minister, with so little compunction of conscience as to go to every colored church to get them to act as he had done in refusing his church—a man who would outrage every claim of hospitality in the person of a man from whom he had enjoyed hospitable entertainment, by refusing his church and his house to one who took him for a friend up to the moment of refusal, simply because that man differed with him in opinion—a man who would strike down freedom of speech in the person of a great leader among colored people, while he affects to condemn the same thing among pro-slavery white people, is at once too contemptible for condemnation and too hypocritical to secure confidence (*Applause and laughter*). Had I a dog who should treat another dog in this manner, I don't know but what I should swap him off for a snake, and then kill the snake (*Applause and laughter*). The time is coming, my friends, when the deeds of our people in regard to the great cause of human liberty, are to be committed to the historian's page, and upon the exercise of justice, which we owe to our leading men, depends the beauty of the portrait which shall be drawn of the people in Boston. Respecting the African Civilization Society, and my connection with it, I have this to say: The cloud of revolution is ascending, and the great spirit of Liberty enthroned upon it is hurling his thunderbolts thick and hot against the garrisons of slavery and of wrong; and if that society is wrong it will not escape, and if it is right God will do with it what we cannot do without it—make it a mighty instrument of the overthrow of slavery. Another among the many reasons why I support it is, that here I see a man who has made twenty-five years of sacrifice to the cause of colored people in this country, who stands today as much respected and as dearly beloved as any man among us, who is as calm in his judgment, as zealous in his advocacy, and as eloquent and efficient in his efforts as he has been unchanging and unchanged in his fidelity, who advocates the movement, who has given his time and talent to it without reward, and who now comes to remove the aspersions cast upon him in the late New England Convention, and to vindicate, by his own statements, the position he occupies with regard to this movement. Allow me, then, to introduce to you the Rev. Henry Highland Garnet. (*Prolonged applause*)

MR. GARNET SPOKE AS FOLLOWS,

I am happy that one impression, unfavorable to the liberality of the sentiment of the people of Boston, which, for a little while, had rested on my mind; has been altogether removed.

On the first day of August, when the Convention was held here, I was engaged in the State of Pennsylvania, away down almost on the borders of Maryland. I was lifting up my feeble voice in behalf of my oppressed and down-trodden brethren. I had been engaged to labor there at that time, eighteen months previous. Had my engagement been of such a character that I could easily have broken it, I should have foregone the pleasure of being at that meeting, and should have hastened to Boston to attend the Convention of colored men that was to be held here on that day.

DR. KNOX—And of white men also.

MR. GARNET—Well, and of white men also—put a pin there! (*Laughter*). I emphasized the words "colored men" to show that we are in an age of progression. I remember when, a few years ago, to talk in New England of holding a Colored Men's Convention was to have the idea scouted. We had got so far ahead as to suppose we need not make any effort in the cause of liberty, especially as people of color. I knew they were wrong. I told them so. That spirit ran all over the free States; and bye and bye we swelled up to such dimensions that we despised to take the name of color; and then we said we must talk only about universal rights and universal liberty. I knew that the day would come when you would think that we, as colored people, had peculiar interests—feelings and interests that no other people had—and that we understood the cause better than any others, and that if we wanted the work done at all we must do it ourselves; and that when we had accomplished the object, we should lay aside all distinctive labors, and come together as men and women, members of the great American family. I looked, therefore, upon this fact as a matter of importance, that *colored men,* as it was stated in the call for the Convention, were to meet here. I wished the time might have been altered; that we of New York might have been here also. I thought it was to be a Convention to consider the interests of the colored people of this country, and do something to advance the great cause of human freedom.

I found, when the Convention was over, and I read the minutes, that there seemed to be two objects which that Convention had in view, and to which they most strictly and faithfully attended. The first was to attack the African Civilization Society generally, and its President in particular, to misrepresent my views on that subject, and on the great subject of humanity. That seemed to be the first object, and, mind you, it was a concerted plan to carry out this same measure in other parts of the country. In Poughkeepsie, Mr. Myers, of Albany, introduced a resolution, not among the regular resolutions brought forward by the Business Committee, but introduced by him on his own responsibility, and when the Secretary read it, a friend of mine and old co-worker in the cause of freedom, though not altogether agreeing with me, said:

"This is not the time and place for such action; you have sprung this on the Convention."

Mr. Myers said: *"O, yes, you must do it for it is to be done in Boston, and at all the other celebrations to-day."* So you see, while we knew nothing about it, it was a plan concerted, well arranged, among those ready to take that course.

MR. NELL—Will you give way for a correction?

MR. GARNET—Certainly.

MR. NELL—I regret that you made that statement. I am authorized to deny it. It was not a part, at all, of the plan.

MR. GARNET—I expect the gentleman will get up many times before I am done. I intend to make some of your seats warm, to-night (*Laughter*). If it was not a concerted plan then what mean the resolutions brought forward on that subject by the Business Committee? I think my friend Nell was the Chairman. How do you get up resolutions unless by a concerted plan? Do you get up, and by instinct or intuition, frame and propose your resolutions? Were they not arranged in private before you came to that meeting? Yes, perhaps weeks before; and the officers knew exactly what kind of resolutions were to be passed, and come up armed to the teeth to battle them through; and you bagged them altogether, good and evil, so that the good could not be accepted without endorsing the bad, nor the bad rejected without rejecting the good.

The next object, which was far the best, and one of which I highly approve, was to give my old friend, George Downing, a bunch of flowers (*Great laughter*). Now, I approve of this courtesy on the part of Boston ladies, and I am sure it must have made my friend feel comfortable when he received those elegant flowers from the beauty and fashion of this Athens of America.

Now, then, as to my object in coming here to-night: Don't think I am come for the purpose of stirring up

strife, of dealing in vituperation and misrepresentation, as some gentlemen did at that Convention. Let it be known that I come here simply to present my views on the subject in question, not to define my position. If twenty-five years of labor in the anti-slavery cause has not defined my position, certainly I shall not do it to-night. But I came to speak as a man to men, to tell what I believe on the subject, and to deny some things said by others.

I wrote to my friend, Rev. L. A. Grimes, of this city, a gentleman whom I respected for his amiable Christian character. I knew he was not with me and therefore I selected him and his church. I wanted the world to know I did nothing in a corner, but was willing to speak upon the house-tops. Brother Grimes wrote back, saying: "I am sorry to say that you cannot have my church for the purpose and at the time you request, and I must be excused from having anything whatever to do with the meeting." While I feel the wound, let me say to him come to New York, and, while I am the minister of Shiloh Church, if he wants to advocate any cause relating to humanity, to justice and truth, let him but ask the use of that church, and if it is in my power to give the pulpit to him, it shall be his, and if I cannot give it to him, I will pay for its use (*Applause*).

I wrote to my friend, Mr. Nell. In his usual manner, always courteous and kind, he told me very reasonably, that many of the people were out of town, and it was very difficult to get a meeting at this time of the year. He thought it was doubtful if there would be any to-night. I thought there would be, and my opinion seems to be sustained. I asked him to advertise the meeting in the "Liberator." Brother Nell did not do it—it was not done, though I wished the advertisement only to give publicity to the announcement. You are here, nevertheless.

I there referred to my friends on the platform [Messrs. Martin, Smith, and Pitts], and asked them if they would not see to it that a house should be open for me to speak upon this subject. They provided this house, and I extend to you my hearty and sincere thanks for your kindness on this occasion. But let me tell those brethren that, had there not been a church open for me in the city of Boston, I would have stood on the corners of your streets, or on Boston Common, and lifted up my voice (*Applause*). One word more. It is high time black men should stop imitating white men in deviltry (*Laughter*). They talk about humanity, and say, "Let justice be done though the heavens fall!"[2] And if the heavens did fall, they would fall right upon them (*Renewed laughter*). We talk about white men closing the door upon us, and shutting out humanity—about ministers being afraid of their people, and allowing padlocks to be put upon their mouths. But may not white men say, "Physicians, heal yourselves"[3]—"Go and take out the beam that is in your own eyes, and then shall ye see clearly to take out the mote that is in your brothers' eyes!"[4] We have got to learn to tolerate free discussion. That is the first thing we want as colored people. Don't you know there are some colored men in Boston who, if they should, by circumstances, become slave-holders in the South, with their whips in their hands, would make the blood fly from their slaves till the very ground would be slippery with the crimson gore? (*"Yes!" "Yes!"*) They declaim against white men, and imitate them in their meanest and most devilish practices (*Applause*), to hold back the progress of the age, stifle free discussion, and lock the lips of those who would utter any sentiments not to their liking.

Ladies and gentlemen, the first matter I wished to speak of this evening is the charge that I am a Colonizationist. To my friend Mr. Downing—for I shall call him such still; nothing shall separate him from my heart, no matter how he esteems me—I still say to him, Go on; so far as you are right, God bless you! I sent a letter to him informing him that I should be here, and I asked him to be here also, and said I did not wish to say a word behind his back, as he has so freely talked behind mine, misrepresenting my feelings and views. Probably he is in the house tonight, and I shall be glad to see him and greet him. I am going to speak plainly and deliberately, so that it may be distinctly known what are my sentiments. It has been said that I am a Colonizationist. I am *not* a Colonizationist. Any man that says I am behind my back is an assassin and a coward; any man that says it to my face is a liar, and I stamp the infamous charge upon his forehead! I have

hated the sentiments of the American Colonization Society from my childhood. I have learned to hold the same opinion in regard to the sentiments advocated by its slave-holding leaders up to the present time. I expect to do so until that Society shall change its sentiments, and let that change be known to the world. The American Colonization Society says this is not the home of the colored man. I say it *is* the home of the colored man, and it is my home (*Applause*). The American Colonization Society says the colored man cannot be elevated in this country. I believe nothing of the kind. There is no people in this world advancing faster in the cause of equal rights than the colored people. I believe the sky is brightening, and though I may not live to see it, the day is not distant when, from the Atlantic to the Pacific, from Maine to California, the shouts of redeemed millions shall be heard—when truth and peace shall fill the land, and songs of rejoicing shall go up to Heaven. The American Colonization Society says that nobody but black men are bound to evangelize and civilize Africa. I believe nothing of the kind. I believe that black men in general are bound by the laws of love and humanity, and the principles of the Gospel to do all they can for the land of our forefathers, and that the white people are bound in particular to do it, since they have robbed us of our lives, and become rich by our blood, and it is therefore for them to make sacrifices that Africa may be redeemed, and that they may bless it as they have so long cursed it.

These are my views in general. I will read them as I have written them down. These are my sentiments, and no others on the subject:

THE OBJECTS OF THE AFRICAN CIVILIZATION SOCIETY

1st.   The immediate and unconditional abolition of slavery in the United States and in Africa, and the destruction of the African slave-trade both in this and that country.

If there is anyone who objects to that, please to rise and show me where the objection is. Silence

2. Translation of Latin phrase *fiat justitia ruat caelum,* a maxim cited in English law and literature since 1601.
3. Reference to Luke 4:23: "Physician, heal thyself."
4. Reference to Matthew 7:5: "Thou hypocrite, first cast out the beam out of thine own eye; and then shalt thou see clearly to cast out the mote out of thy brother's eye."

gives consent. I knew there was common sense in Boston (*Applause*).

2. The destruction of prejudice against colored people in the United States, especially in the nominal free States of the North; and we propose to do this by urging upon the Abolitionists and the friends of humanity of every grade "the necessity of giving trades and employment to ourselves and to our children."

Do you object to that? If so, rise and speak.

A GENTLEMAN—Mr. Garnet, is that the Constitution of the Society you are reading there?

MR. GARNET—I am speaking my own sentiments, and those cherished by the men and women who act with me.

DR. KNOX—I would inquire if you are representing the Civilization Society in these sentiments?

MR. GARNET—I am representing what I proposed to represent—my own views and the objects of the African Civilization Society—nothing more or less.

3. To assist in giving the Gospel to Africa, and thus render obedience unto the unrepealed command of our Lord Jesus Christ, to go into all the world and preach the Gospel to every creature.

4. The civilization of Africa, by the introduction into that country of lawful trade and commerce; by the cultivation of cotton to supply the British and other cotton consuming markets, and delivering the civilized world from dependence on the cotton raised in the Southern States by slave labor, and by this means to strike the death-blow to American slavery.

Is this contrary to the laws of God, Christian love, or common sense? (*No! No!*)

Dr. Knox expressed his dissent, and offered to argue the question.

Mr. Garnet declined to discuss the subject, he having sufficient in the object which brought him to Boston to occupy the evening. Some people, he thought, would object to God Almighty sitting on His throne. (*Yes! Yes!*)

5. To establish a grand centre of negro nationality, from which shall flow the streams of commercial, intellectual, and political power which shall make colored people respected everywhere.

Is there any objection to that?

DR. KNOX—Is this to be in the United States or Africa?

MR. GARNET—I hope in the United States, especially if they reopen the African slave trade. Then, if we do not establish a nationality in the South, I am mistaken in the spirit of my people. Let them bring in a hundred thousand a year! We do not say it is not a great crime, but we know that from the wickedness of man God brings forth good; and if they do it, before half a century shall pass over us we shall have a negro nationality in the United States. In Jamaica there are forty colored men to one white; Hayti is ours; Cuba will be ours soon, and we shall have every island in the Caribbean Sea (*Applause*).

I wish your attention to the next point, for it is something we do not understand—the proper management of money. We know how to make it, but not to keep it. We have gone to white men to borrow a dollar when we wanted one. If we are to stand on the right footing, we must act so that we can lend money instead of borrow.

6. By the power of money and union of action in this country, to encourage our professional men of every occupation in arts and sciences of every grade, and thus keep the colored people here from the disrespect and contumely shown by others, and the despondency and despair felt by themselves under too many circumstances.

7. All this to be done by the voluntary cooperation of the friends of universal freedom, irrespective of color, either by working with the Society here or assisting its objects in Africa.

Does anybody object to either of those sentiments?

These are our views. I have nothing more or less to say. Any man that has represented me as having other views, has made representations false and unkind. These are my views in public and in private.

KEY DEBATE ∽ *Separatism versus Integration*

The Question of Naming

THOMAS L. JENNINGS: *Letter in* Freedom's Journal [1828]
DAVID WALKER: from *Walker's Appeal* [1829, revision printed 1830]
ELLA: *Letter in* The Liberator [1831]
"A SUBSCRIBER": *Letter in* The Liberator [1831]
"A SUBSCRIBER AND CITIZEN OF THE UNITED STATES": *Letter in* The Liberator [1831]
SAMUEL E. CORNISH AND PHILIP A. BELL: *Editorial in* The Colored American [1837]
WILLIAM WHIPPER: from *Minutes of the Fifth Annual Convention for the Improvement of the Free People of Color in the United States* [1835]
SIDNEY: from *Letter in* The Colored American [1841]
HENRY HIGHLAND GARNET: from *The Past and the Present Condition, and Destiny, of the Colored Race* [1848]

Until the late 1820s, *African* (along with its variations, such as *Afric*) was the common term for Americans of African descent. In his description of an 1827 celebration of the abolition of slavery in the state of New York, the doctor and activist James McCune Smith (p. 42) commented on the use of *African* in self-references by black Americans at that time. Writing in 1865 in his introduction to *A Memorial Discourse* by Henry Highland Garnet (p. 80), McCune Smith observed with a sense of loss that "the people of those days rejoiced in their nationality and hesitated not to call each other 'Africans' or 'descendants of Africa;' it was in after years, when they set up their just protest against the American Colonization Society and its principles that the term 'African' fell into disuse and finally discredit."

Unlike the Caribbean, where slavery was maintained by a constant influx of new people brought from Africa, the United States early on developed a self-sustaining system of slavery, which depended on the growth of slave families and the enslaving of the children of female slaves. Still, in 1750, nearly one half of the slaves in the United States had been born in Africa. Only after 1808, when the international slave trade was outlawed in the United States, did the percentage of African Americans who had been transported from Africa fall below 20 percent. The first formal organizations of black Americans reflected that connection to Africa by adopting names that typically included the word *African;* the earliest such organization was the African Union Society

of Newport, Rhode Island, a mutual-aid society established in 1780. Subsequent mutual-aid societies, dedicated to supporting members of their communities in times of sickness and death, included the Free African Society of Philadelphia, established in 1787 by Richard Allen (p. 144) and others who would later establish the African Methodist Episcopal Church; the African Society of Boston, founded in 1796; and the New York African Society for Mutual Relief, founded in 1808.

In the late 1820s, however, the question of the best name for Americans of African descent became a matter of intense debate. Several factors motivated the rise of "the Namestakes," as the historian Dorothy Sterling labeled this controversy. First, except for a few older people, most black people in the U.S. by that time were American born, with relatively loose connections to Africa compared with their ties to their native land. Second, the American Colonization Society, established in 1816 by white leaders alarmed by the increasing free black population, was pushing to send that group to Africa. Many black people began avoiding the term *African* (in favor of *colored*, also spelled *coloured*) to emphasize their rejection of the goals of the ACS and their commitment to staying in the United States. Third, beginning in 1830, African Americans held "Conventions of Colored Men," which were instrumental in fostering a sense of national identity among black people that superseded prior identities as residents of individual states. However, the simultaneous emergence of interracial allegiances as black abolitionists began working alongside white abolitionists in such groups as the American Anti-Slavery Society, formed in 1833, led some African Americans to question the need for separate organizations based on race.

"The Namestakes" of the 1820s and 1830s launched a debate on racial nomenclature that continues to the present day. The various terms of self-definition favored during different periods may be divided into those stressing racial identity (*Negro, colored, black, Black*), those emphasizing national identity (*American*), and some combination of those (*Afro-American, African American, black American*). The dominant term or terms of a particular era serve as a window onto prevailing attitudes toward integration and separatism.

Arguments in favor of nonracial terms include the biological (for example, skin color is only a surface physical attribute and thus should not be a core factor of identity) and the strategic (for example, using terms such as *American* helps to diminish the focus on racial differences and thus contributes to integrationist goals). On the other hand, choosing to use a distinct name is an act of linguistic nationalism, underscoring a separate group identity based on race.

After the initial flurry of debate in the 1820s and 1830s, "the Namestakes" reemerged at key moments in American history. As Sterling Stuckey argues in *Slave Culture: Nationalist Theory and the Foundations of Black America* (1987), "The final resolution of the names controversy is not likely to come until African peoples as a whole have won freedom, a development inevitably linked to their status in America." For more on this controversy, see pp. 867–69, pp. 869–73, and pp. 873–74.

THOMAS L. JENNINGS

Letter in Freedom's Journal [1828]

Our claims are on America; it is the land that gave us birth. We know no other country. It is a land in which our fathers have suffered and toiled. They have watered it with their tears and fanned it with their sighs.

Our relation with Africa is the same as the white man's is with Europe. We have passed through several generations in this country and consequently we have become naturalized. Our habits, our manners, our passions, our dispositions have become the same. The same mother's milk has nourished us both in infancy; the white child and the colored have both hung on the same breast. I might as well tell the white man about England, France or Spain, the country from whence his forefathers emigrated, and call him a European, as for him to call us Africans. Africa is as foreign to us as Europe is to them.

From *Freedom's Journal*, April 4, 1828.

DAVID WALKER

from *Walker's Appeal* [1829, revision reprinted 1830]

"Niger," is a word [* * *] used by the old Romans, to designate inanimate beings, which were black: such as soot, pot, wood, house, &c. Also, animals which they considered inferior to the human species, as a black horse, cow, hog, bird, dog, &c. The white Americans have applied this term to Africans, by way of reproach for our colour, to aggravate and heighten our miseries, because they have their feet on our throats.

From David Walker, *Walker's Appeal, in Four Articles; Together with a Preamble, to the Coloured Citizens of the World, but in Particular, and Very Expressly, to Those of the United States of America, Written in Boston, State of Massachusetts*, September 28, 1829, rev. ed. (Boston: David Walker, 1830), p. 61.

ELLA
Letter in The Liberator [1831]

Philadelphia, May 25, 1831

TO THE EDITOR:

Why do our friends as well as our enemies call us "Negroes?" We feel it to be a term of reproach, and could wish our friends would call us by some other name. If you, Sir, or one of your correspondents would condescend to answer this question, we would esteem it a favor.

ELLA

From *The Liberator,* June 4, 1831.

"A SUBSCRIBER"
Letter in The Liberator [1831]

TO THE EDITOR:

The term "colored" is not a good one. Whenever used, it recalls to mind the offensive distinctions of color. The name "African" is more objectionable yet, and is no more correct than "Englishman" would be to a native-born citizen of the United States.

The colored citizen is an American of African descent. Cannot a name be found that will explain these two facts? I suggest one, and I beg your readers to reflect on it before you reject it as unsuitable. It is "Afric-American" or, written in one word, "Africamerican." It asserts that most important truth, that the colored citizen is as truly a citizen of the United States as the white.

A SUBSCRIBER

From *The Liberator,* September 24, 1831.

"A SUBSCRIBER AND CITIZEN
OF THE UNITED STATES"
Letter in The Liberator [1831]

Philadelphia, September 1, 1831

MR. EDITOR:

"A Subscriber" has suggested the appropriateness of the term "Afric-American." The suggestion is as absurd as the sound of the name is inharmonious. It is true that we should have a distinct appellation—we being the only people in America who feel all the accumulated injury which pride and prejudice can suggest. But sir, since we have been so long distinguished by the title "men of color," why make this change, so uncouth and jargon-like? A change we do want and a change we will have. When it comes, we shall be called *citizens of the United States and Americans.*

A SUBSCRIBER AND CITIZEN
OF THE UNITED STATES

From *The Liberator,* September 24, 1831.

SAMUEL E. CORNISH AND PHILIP A. BELL
Editorial in The Colored American [1837]

The editor, aware of the diversity of opinion in reference to the title of this "Paper" thinks it not amiss to state some reasons for selecting this name. Many would gladly rob us of the endeared name "AMERICAN," a distinction more emphatically belonging to us than five-sixths of this nation and one that we will never yield.

But why colored? Because our circumstances require special action. We have in view objects peculiar to ourselves and in contradistinction from the mass. How, then, shall we be known and our interests presented but by some distinct, specific name—and what appellation is so inoffensive, so acceptable as COLORED PEOPLE—COLORED AMERICANS?

From *The Colored American,* March 4, 1837.

WILLIAM WHIPPER

From *Minutes of the Fifth Annual Convention for the Improvement of the Free People of Color in the United States* [1835]

T hat we recommend as far as possible to our people to abandon the use of the word "colored" when either speaking or writing concerning themselves; and especially to remove the title of African from their institutions, the marbles of churches, &c.

William Whipper's resolution in relation to using the words "colored" and "Africans" was called up, and after an animated and interesting discussion, it was unanimously adopted.

From *Minutes of the Fifth Annual Convention for the Improvement of the Free People of Color in the United States* (Philadelphia, 1835).

SIDNEY

From *Letters in* The Colored American [1841]

W e do not think that by watering and preserving the plant that perfumes our room that *therefore* we dislike all other plants in the world. We do not believe that in loving our own mother's sons, our brothers, that therefore we exclude mankind. In fine we have no sympathy with that cosmopoliting disposition which tramples upon all nationality.

And pray, for what are we to turn around and bay the whole human family? Why are we to act different from all others in this important matter? Why, because we *happen* to be—COLORED.

That we are colored is a fact, an undeniable fact. That we are descendants of Africans is true. We affirm there is nothing in it that we need to be ashamed of, yea, rather much that we may be proud of.

For ourselves we are quite well satisfied. And we intend, in all our public efforts, to go to the power-holding body and tell them, "Colored as we are, *black*

though we may be, yet we demand our rights, the same rights other citizens have."

From *The Colored American*, March 6 and 13, 1841.

HENRY HIGHLAND GARNET

From *The Past and the Present Condition, and the Destiny, of the Colored Race* [1848]

I n regard to the enslavement of our race, this Country presents as mournful a picture as any other beneath the sun; but still it is not hopelessly enshrouded in darkness. The good institutions of the land are well adapted to the developement of the mind. So far as the oppressed shall make their own way towards them, and shall escape the influence of those that are evil, so far shall they succeed in throwing off their bitter thraldom, and in wrenching the scourge from the hands of tyranny.

Slavery has done much to ruin us, and we ourselves have done some things which effect the same. Perhaps the evils of which I am about to speak arise from slavery, and are the things without which the system cannot exist. But nevertheless we must contribute largely towards their overthrow. If it is in our power to destroy these evils, and we do not, then much of our own blood will be found on us.

We are divided by party feuds, and are torn in pieces by dissensions. Some men have prostituted good talents, for the base purpose of kindling the fires of discord. Some who officiated in the temples said to be dedicated to God, are idolaters to sectarianism. And some too would draw a line of blood distinction, and would form factions upon the shallow basis of complexion. But I am glad to know that the number of this class is small, and small as it is, I pray that we may soon be able to write a cypher in its place. Let there be no strife between us, for we are brethren, and we must rise or fall together. How unprofitable it is for us to spend our golden moments in long and solemn debate upon the questions whether we shall be called *"Africans" "Colored Americans,"* or *"Africo Americans,"* or *"Blacks."*

The question should be, my friends, *shall we arise and act like men, and cast off this terrible yoke?* Many are too apt to follow after shams, and to neglect that which is solid. Thousands are often expended for an hours' display of utter emptiness, which ought to be laid aside to increase our wealth, and for the acquirement of knowledge, and for the promotion of education. Societies, called benevolent, frequently squander more money for the purchase of banners and badges, and in feasting, than they use in acts of charity. What are regalia and other trappings worth, if they signify nothing but sham and parade? In 1846, $5000 were paid by the oppressed Colored people at the Temperance Celebration held in Poughkeepsie, N. Y., and yet we do not adequately support a single Newspaper in the United States.

From Henry Highland Garnet, *The Past and Present Condition, and the Destiny, of the Colored Race: A Discourse Delivered at the Fifteenth Anniversary of the Female Benevolent Society of Troy, N.Y.* (Troy, N.Y.: Steam Press of J. C. Kneeland, 1848), pp. 18–19.

WILLIAM WHIPPER
Letter to the Editor [1841]

Black state conventions played an important role in the pre-emancipation struggle for civil rights, but some leaders questioned the strategy of organizing such meetings along racial lines. The New York State Convention of Negroes, held in Albany in 1840—which focused on the New York law that required African Americans (unlike white Americans) to own property in order to vote—prompted an epistolary debate between William Whipper (1804–1876) and a man who called himself Sidney (p. 92). Their exchange was published in *The Colored American* from January through March of 1841.

In three letters to the editor, Whipper argues that separatist politics contradict the universalist premise underlying black claims to full and equal civil rights. His first letter, written on January 3, 1841, and published on January 30, addressed the first resolution of the 1840 meeting (often called the Albany Convention), which attacked racial distinctions in "all laws established for human government, and all systems, of *whatever* kind." In his second letter reprinted here, written on January 12 and published on February 6, Whipper focuses on the convention's second resolution, which criticized the state constitution and its "toleration of complexional distinctions in the State of New York." He concluded his argument with a third letter, written on January 17 and published on February 20, in which he extends his criticisms to the official call for the convention, which sought to bring together "Colored Inhabitants of the State of New York." Through his critique of the modes of organization of black social and political groups, Whipper asks his fellow reformers, "Can we hope to be successful in reforming others before we procure a reformation among ourselves?"

William Whipper was born in Lancaster, Pennsylvania, on February 22, 1804, and became one of the wealthiest African Americans of his time. His black mother was a servant to his white father, who provided his son with a tutor to teach him to read and write. While pursuing various business ventures, including a lumberyard and a shipping concern, Whipper began lecturing on moral reform. When he was twenty-four, he published his "Address on Non-resistance to Offensive Aggression," which foreshadows key aspects of the nonviolence movement of the 1950s and 1960s associated with Martin Luther King Jr. (p. 559). Throughout the 1830s, Whipper remained dedicated to an integrationist vision (a position he changed in later years). As an alternative to separatist political groups, Whipper co-founded the short-lived American Moral Reform Society in 1835 and became the editor of its journal, *The National Reformer*, which stressed self-help, nonviolence, political and social integration, and the rights of women. Whipper died in 1876, at the age of seventy-two.

From *The Colored American*, February 6, 1841.

DEAR SIR:—I regard the action of the "Albany Convention" as calculated to produce a new era in our cause. It matters but little whether we contemplate the object which called the delegates together, or the distinctive feature of their organization, the effect of their proceedings must produce important results. I am therefore constrained by a sense of duty to solicit for them the consideration their importance demands. In the execution of this task I crave your indulgence.

In my letter of the 3d inst.,[1] I endeavored to notice the operation of the general principles involved in the first resolution, as well as its practical bearing on the whole people in their various forms of government.

I must now proceed to the 2d resolution which is marked by a boundary line, but is equally strong in principle over the space it is intended to operate. It reads as follows:

"Resolved, That the toleration of complexional difference in the State of New York is a stain upon its constitution, and attaches it to the great system of oppression in the land, so vital to our national character, since it is upheld, not only in direct opposition to the common rights of humanity, but also runs counter to those very political principles asserted by the framers of our republican government." Now, sir, it is to be expected, that state action by the colored people of New York as a means of attaining their rights as Americans, will be followed by a state action, among the same class in other states. I do therefore appeal to them in behalf of their down-trodden situation—their love of republican principles—of civil and religious liberty to strictly examine the principles on which the "Albany Convention" was based, in order that they may discover whether its *model* claims their admiration, as the most righteous and successful method for the government of their future operations. Now I aver that the above resolution is either true or false. If it be true that the "toleration of complexional distinction in the state of New York, is a stain upon its constitution, and attaches it to the great system of oppression in the land, and in direct opposition to the rights of humanity," it is equally true of every other state constitution where that distinction exists, as well as the constitution of the

United States. But the principle of the resolution does not stop here. It protests against the "toleration of complexional distinction in the State of New York." I cannot but regard this protest as an implicit appeal to the Legislature of New York to repeal all the "complexionally" distinctive charters within the state, in order that such institutions and associations may not only be regarded as odious, but unlawful. If this be the true meaning of the resolution, it meets my cordial approbation. It is peculiarly appropriate for any people that have long been trodden under foot by the "iron heel" of any peculiar despotism that when they appeal to the rectitude of just principles in behalf of their deliverance, that they should first exhibit to the world, that they were not only prepared to act upon those principles themselves, but that they had hurled that principle of despotism from their own borders. It speaks well for the purity of principle that must have existed in the convention to have passed such a resolution, yet it appears passing strange that such a body convened under a complexionally distinct call should so far transgress the principle of their own organization as virtually to declare it in direct opposition to the "rights of humanity." Now, sir, I respectfully ask if the amended constitution of the State of New York is "in opposition to the rights of humanity" on account of complexional difference, are not the "Colored Churches," schools, benevolent and beneficial societies, formed and sustained in equal violation of the great fundamental principles of human rights? What evidence will the colored people as a body be able to exhibit to the legislators, of your great commonwealth, that you are in principle opposed to that obnoxious feature in your State Constitution, while you use no endeavors to abolish it from those institutions within your control? They will very naturally conclude that interest alone animates you in your arduous labors to obtain a full and complete enfranchisement. I do not however anticipate that any thing that I have written will have a tendency to change the position of our brethren in your state, but I hope they may pursue such a course of action, as will render them consistent in the eyes of those on whom they wish to operate, by commencing a warfare against

1. "Instant," of the present month.

the complexionally distinctive feature in every institution whether formed by white or colored people.

The spirit of the resolution truly contemplates such a method of action.

What I have said respecting the Albany Convention and what I regard as their very inconsistent course as equally applicable to our people in this state. We too protested against the insertion of the term "white" in our State Constitution while we were nurturing and sustaining in our midst near one hundred institutions with "colored and African" charters, and the result was as might have been expected, I might *almost* say as we deserved.

There is no people on earth justly entitled to the commiseration of mankind on account of their peculiar situation until they are equally ready and willing to render the same justice to others.

As a people we are deeply afflicted with "colorophobia" (and notwithstanding there may have been causes sufficient to implant it into our minds), it is arrayed against the spirit of Christianity, republican freedom, and our common happiness, and ought once now and forever to be abolished. It is an evil that must

be met, and we *must meet it now*. The holy cause of human freedom, the success and happiness of future generations depend upon it. We must throw off the distinctive features in the charters of our churches, and other institutions. We have refused to hear ministers preach from the pulpit, because they would not preach against slavery. We must pursue the same course respecting prejudice against complexion. I verily believe that no man ought to be employed as a pastor of any Christian Church, that would consent to preach to a congregation where the "negro pew" exists; and I also believe it to be a violation of Christian principles for any man to accept the pastoral charge of a Church under a charter based on complexional distinction. You now see my friend, that I am willing to accept the resolution in its catholic spirit. I trust that it will not be asking too much of you, and those that voted for it, to aid in promoting its faithful application to all existing institutions within your control.

I remain yours in the cause of liberty and equality.

WM. WHIPPER
Columbia, January 12, 1841

SIDNEY

Letter to the Editor [1841]

In his response to William Whipper (p. 90), a man identifying himself as Sidney, "a member of the Albany Convention committee," explores the competing strategies of separatism and interracial political organization. The identity of Sidney remains a focus of critical debate; many scholars consider the most likely candidates to be Henry Highland Garnet (p. 80), who was one of the secretaries of the convention, and Alexander Crummell, who gave an address at the convention. In four letters to the editor of *The Colored American* (published on February 13 and 20 and March 6 and 13, 1841), Sidney warns against the danger of becoming divided over relatively small differences of opinion. He seeks to shift the attention of black leaders from "color" to a shared experience of oppression as an organizing principle for political action.

He makes a key distinction between segregation (based on discrimination) and separate black social and political groups (based on concentrated power and group strength).

Sidney's ideas foreshadow key political positions of the twentieth and twenty-first centuries. His championing of black social and cultural groups heralds the black pride movement of the 1960s. His belief that those who do not personally experience oppression can be allies but cannot be part of the core political group evokes subsequent black nationalist political ideas, such as the Black Panthers' position concerning white revolutionaries (see p. 548). Finally, Sidney's rejection of integration as "monomania" anticipates the celebration of difference that grounds contemporary ideas of multiculturalism.

From *The Colored American*, March 13, 1841.

It has been our purpose, in our last two preceding articles, to answer, in a summary manner the questions and objections proposed by Mr. Whipper in his letters, to show the duty and necessity of special exertions on the part of the oppressed, as a principle—that it is identical with the testimony of history, and that, inasmuch as it comported with the peculiar relations of the oppressed, it was in accordance with common sense.

It is a remarkable fact, that obstreperous as have been the friends of this new theory, in their advocacy of it, yet they have never attempted to show its feasibility in the light of history. Now, we always suspect any theory that cannot be supported by facts. The world is old enough, the human family have had sufficient experience to give some few illustrations of any principle of importance, that may be proposed for the benefit of man. And although new combinations of known truth may be made, and thus originality be produced, yet, save in this way, there is nothing new under the sun. How unreasonable, then, in such a matter as this—a matter so practical in its nature, so begirt by the teachings and supports of common sense, and in the light of history, so luminous—a matter upon which the human family have been schooled for centuries; how unreasonable it is, we say, for gentlemen to come forward and require us to leave a well known and long tried course, for which we have the authority of the wisest and best of all ages, to enter upon a vain and untried expedient, merely on account of the marvellous, hidden virtues of a new theory.

It has been our object in our former communications, to defend the measures of our fathers, in past time, of our brethren of the present day in their laudable self-exertion to elevate themselves, and especially the "Albany Convention," in its "call" and its after measures. It will be seen that we have argued the matter thus far, without any reference to *color.* The relative position and the relative duties and responsibilities of the oppressed and the oppressors; being, in our opinion, the only grounds upon which any argument was predictable. This endless clamoring about "color," is alike devoid of reason, as it is disreputable to us as a people. The people are perishing by oppression, and our leaders, one opposing the other, upon a *word;*

they are metaphysicising upon *things,* when they should be using the resistless energy of principle, to vindicate their wronged and deeply injured brethren; and instead of giving living, productive action—proposing idle theories! We would discontinue the matter here, were it not that there are some minor points in Mr. W.'s letters, which demand some notice.

We come now to the term "colored."

We would premise here, that we are not frightened at the portentous phrase—"Complexionally distinctive organizations"—not in the least. But we regard it as a "nise deguerre."[1] Is it a want of kindness, or a want of clear vision, that leads our brethren to charge us with preferring our mode of operation, to devotion to color? Our argument is this:—Whenever a people are oppressed, peculiarly (not complexionally), distinctive organization or action, is required on the part of the oppressed, to destroy that oppression. The colored people of this country are oppressed; therefore the colored people are required to act in accordance with this fundamental principle.

If Mr. W. can, for a few minutes, get clear of the idea of color, perhaps he will then be able to understand us.

But to the term "colored." That we are colored, is a fact, an undeniable fact. That we are descendants of Africans—colored people—negroes if you will, is true. We affirm there is nothing in it that we need be ashamed of, yea, rather much that we may be proud of. There is, then, on our part, as identified with the negro race, no reason why the term should be repudiated.

The bearing of this fact (of color), on the whites, does *it* present any sufficient and adequate cause why we should desire the use of the term to be discontinued? Let us see. Prejudice is a moral phenomenon, a wrong exercise of the sentiments and sympathies, a disease of the will. Now, Mr. W. should know enough of human nature to be aware, that repugnances of such a character, are to be met and cured by something entirely diverse from a—term. "As the diseases of the mind are invisible, invisible must the remedies likewise be. Those who have been entrapped by false opinions, are to be liberated by convincing truths."—*Tertullian.*

1. Misspelling of *ruse de guerre* [French], war stratagem or trick.

Discontinue the use of the term—does prejudice die? Oh no, Leviathan is not so tamed. But Mr. W. may say, prejudice is the result of color, and *therefore* we should not use the term "colored." But look again at the matter. If it is the result of *color*, then it does *not* proceed from the word; and if *that* (color) is the cause, and Mr. W. desires to act upon the cause, then let him commence his operations upon the color. For ourselves, we are quite well satisfied. And we intend, in all our public effort, to go [to] the power-holding body, and tell them, "Colored as we are, *black* though we may be, yet we demand our rights, the same rights other citizens have"; and to Christians, "We demand it of you in the name of Christ our common master, to give us as large a share in your affections and sympathies as you give to the rest of the Saviour's fold."

We say our people should not give way the least to the stout-heartedness of our oppressors in this matter. If they have prejudices, they must get over them. As for our color, as God has given it to us, thus we are pleased with it—and so must they get to be. Surely the term colored is not disgusting to Mr. W. and his friends? They cannot be ashamed of their identity with the negro race!

But in the different relations, the two people sustain to each other, some terms are to be used by which each may be known. A definition is correct and proper, when it distinguishes its object or class from all others. The term "colored," then, is a very good one. It has this very commendable qualification, and that there is nothing objectionable in it, is evident from the fact that from time immemorial, different races of men have been distinguished according to their color, and thus not from bad and bitter feelings, as white men, black men, red men, olive, &c., &c. When the English, French, Spanish, and others use these terms, do the *terms* create prejudice, or are they employed from prejudice? Neither one. There is, then, no such marvellous power in the *word* as to make it so repugnant to the tender sensibilities of Mr. W.

To Mr. Whipper's vision, there is but one thing visible—COLOR. For a long period this, apparently, has been his Alpha and Omega. It has been a ghost, haunting him in the day time, and in the night season— a ghost that would not down at his bidding; or rather, we are inclined to think, he is not so displeased with the

ghostly presence, from the deep thought and intense feelings with which he regards it.

So potent and peculiar has its influence been upon him, that it has deprived him of much of that clear thought and peculiar discrimination that generally characterises Mr. Whipper. Objects appear before *him*, confused and disarranged, which to others, and the general mind, are clear and distinct. See, for instance, his second letter (*Colored American*, Feb. 20th),[2] wherein he warns you not to advocate our call and measures on the ground of *necessity*. Why, they can be defended on that ground, and ably and triumphantly. If he will consult but the primer of philosophy, he will discover that much that is fair, and beautiful, and beneficial—some of the brightest features of law, and of the entire frame work of civil polity—are the product of necessity. Observe again how blurred is Mr. Whipper's vision. In the same letter, speaking of the similar "broad platform principle" of the Anti Slavery Society, and the American Moral Reform Society, he remarks: "I maintain whatever is morally right for a white man to do, is morally right for a colored man to do, and vice versa. If this position be correct, and I presume you will not gainsay it," &c., &c. Gainsay it! Most certainly we do, if we understand Mr. W. to say that the moral duties of men are equally and universally alike and the same. On the contrary, we maintain that what is morally right for one man to do, may be morally wrong for another; and thus of entire classes of a whole people. Duties arise from relations. Our responsibilities and obligations receive their hue and coloring from the situation we may maintain, and the connections we may have. Moral right is manifested in innumerable forms. The sun is fixed in the solar system, and the light he imparts is one in nature; yet how diverse in their hues and tints are the rays that come streaming down upon us! And thus is it in the manifestations of duty.

No. We sustain relations to our own people, so peculiar that white men cannot assume them, and according to these relations are our attending duties.

Finally, Mr. Whipper says, "As a people we are deeply afflicted with 'colorphobia.'" True, true! we are deeply afflicted with colorphobia, at least *some of us*. It *is* a "phobia," and it (color) has so perturbed some of

---

2. Sidney is actually referring to Whipper's third letter.

our brethren, that they have devoted a paper to do away with the nuisance; and have written long articles to banish the designating term into oblivion.

For ourselves, we plead *"not guilty"* to the charge. Whatever other phobia we may have, "colorphobia" has not yet afflicted us with its sore and rabid influences. The color God has given us, we are satisfied with; and it is a matter of but little moment to us, who may be displeased with it.

We *are* afflicted with colorphobia, and it is going to work wonders with us—wonders like those Moses wrought in Egypt—of fearful nature, and destructive tendency; unless the right means are used to effect a radical cure, so that henceforth, neither the fact, nor the term indicative of it, shall excite convulsions, nor create a MONOMANIA.

Sidney

IN THE HEADLINES
On Harriet Beecher Stowe and White Allies

Martin Delany: *Letter to Frederick Douglass* [1853]
Frederick Douglass: *Remarks* [1853]
Martin Delany: *Letter to Frederick Douglass* [1853]
Frederick Douglass: *Reply to Martin Delany* [1853]

In February 1853, Frederick Douglass met with Harriet Beecher Stowe (p. 118), the white author of *Uncle Tom's Cabin,* to "consult [* * *] as to some method which should contribute successfully, and permanently, to the improvement and elevation of the free people of color in the United States—a work in which the benevolent lady designs to take a practical part." In his account of the meeting, published as "A Day and a Night in 'Uncle Tom's Cabin'" in *Frederick Douglass' Paper* on March 4, 1853, Douglass extolls both Stowe's "heart for the work" and her "ability to command and combine the means for carrying it forward in a manner likely to be most efficient." Although the account included no specifics (stating that "Mrs. Stowe's plan [* * *] will be made known in due season"), Douglass concludes, "For the present, it is sufficient to know that her attention is now most earnestly turned to this subject; and we have no question that it will result in lasting benefit to our class."

Douglass's alliance with Stowe spurred an epistolary debate with the activist Martin Delany (p. 96) about the role of white Americans as leaders in the civil rights movement of the day. In his March 22, 1853, letter to Douglass, published in *Frederick Douglass' Paper* on April 1, 1853, and reprinted here, Delany calls into question the ability of Stowe, or any white person, to serve as a consul-

tant for the needs of free black people. Echoing his argument in *The Condition . . . of the Colored People of the United States* that "our elevation must be the result of *self-efforts,* and work of our *own hands,*" Delany here calls for a national council of "*intelligent colored* freeman."

In his response, published in the same issue of *Frederick Douglass' Paper* and also reprinted here, Douglass agrees with the goal of unity but pointedly includes white allies as part of that unity. (In his writings and speeches, Douglass also frequently calls for "self-help"; unlike Delany, however, he qualifies that call with an openness to alliances with white Americans.) Douglass rejects Delany's claim that Stowe "*knows nothing about us,*" as well as Delany's underlying premise that African Americans have obtained enough "independence and self-sustaining power" to "reject all aid from our white friends." Douglass also includes a criticism of Delany's 1852 book, *The Condition . . . of the Colored People of the United States,* calling it merely a description of current conditions without concrete suggestions for change; until this point, Douglass had virtually ignored Delany's book in his influential newspaper.

Two weeks later, in the April 15, 1853, issue of *Frederick Douglass' Paper,* Douglass reported on Stowe's trip to England and unveiled the outline for their joint project. "The chief good which we anticipate from Mrs. Stowe's mission," Douglass writes, "is the founding of an INSTITU-TION, in which our oppressed and proscribed youth, MALE and FEMALE, may obtain a plain English education, and a practical knowledge of various useful TRADES." While asserting the need for an industrial college, Douglass also obliquely addresses the controversy over whether *Uncle Tom's Cabin* supported the idea of African colonization, arguing that education and training in the trades would bring about the end of both slavery and the colonization movement. In his proposal for the college—contained in his letter to Stowe of March 8, 1853, which he did not publish until December 2—Douglass pointedly avoids discussing concrete plans, handing over to Stowe the power to determine the organization and administration of the institution because of the "superior wisdom" of Stowe and her friends.

In a lighthearted note referring to their ongoing debate (written the day Douglass's report on Stowe's trip appeared in print and published in *Frederick Douglass' Paper* on April 29, 1853), Delany questions Stowe's originality, suggesting that she modeled her characters and form on the lives and works of African Americans. He ironically suggests that Stowe's publishers give some of the royalties from *Uncle Tom's Cabin* to "the real *Uncle Tom*," the Reverend Josiah Henson, who served as a model for the character in the book. Delany further challenges the book's originality (and Stowe's knowledge about the lives of African Americans) by arguing that her writing drew "largely on all of the best fugitive slave narratives," including Douglass's. Three days later, on April 18, Delany responded directly to Douglass's report in another letter reprinted here, which was published in *Frederick Douglass' Paper* on May 6. In addition to confronting the issue

of Stowe's connection to African colonization, Delany alludes to certain plans for the industrial college that had not been included in Douglass's published letters and reports on the topic, such as the exclusive use of white teachers. Delany modifies his prior statements about the knowledge and position of white Americans, noting that he meant that white people like Stowe know nothing about African Americans "*comparatively* [∗ ∗ ∗] to the intelligent, reflecting, general observers among the Free Colored People of the North" [italics added]. He also points out several exceptional white abolitionists who (in contrast to his vision of Stowe) truly have the best interests of black people at heart.

Douglass's response, the final reading included here, dismisses Delany's letter as premature (since plans for the industrial college remained undefined). Douglass minimizes Stowe's support of the colonization movement. He also suggests that her ideas were evolving as she deepened her association with others in the abolitionist movement.

A brief coda to the debate came in Douglass's January 1854 article about the planned industrial college, in which he curtly reports: "Mrs. Stowe, for reasons which she deems quite satisfactory, does not, at present, see fit to stand forth as the patron of the proposed institution." In his 1881 autobiography, *Life and Times of Frederick Douglass,* Douglass elaborates on his reaction to Stowe's decision: "I have never been able to see any force in the reasons for this change. It is enough, however, to say that they were sufficient for her, and that she no doubt acted conscientiously, though her change of purpose [∗ ∗ ∗] placed me in an awkward position before the colored people of this country, as well as to friends abroad."

MARTIN DELANY
Letter to Frederick Douglass [1853]

PITTSBURGH, March 22, 1853.

FREDERICK DOUGLASS, ESQ.: DEAR SIR:—I notice in your paper of March 4 an article in which you speak of having paid a visit to Mrs. H. E. B. Stowe, for the purpose, as you say, of consulting her, "as to some method which should contribute successfully and permanently, in the improvement and elevation of the free

people of color in the United States." Also, in the number of March 18th, in an article by a writer over the initials of "P. C. S.," in reference to the same subject, he concludes by saying, "I await with much interest the suggestions of Mrs. Stowe in this matter."

Now, I simply wish to say, that we have always fallen into great errors in efforts of this kind, going to others than the *intelligent* and *experienced* among *ourselves;* and in all due respect and deference to Mrs. Stowe, I beg leave to say, that she *knows nothing about us,* "the Free Colored people of the United States," neither does any other white person—and, consequently, can contrive no successful scheme for our elevation; it must be done by ourselves. I am aware, that I differ with many in thus expressing myself, but I cannot help it; though I stand alone, and offend my best friends, so help me God! in a matter of such moment and importance, I will express my opinion. Why, in God's name, don't the leaders among our people make suggestions, and *consult* the most competent among *their own* brethren concerning our elevation? This they do not do; and I have not known one, whose province it was to do so, to go ten miles for such a purpose. We shall never effect anything until this is done.

I accord with the suggestions of H. O Wagoner for a National Council or Consultation of our people, provided *intelligence, maturity,* and *experience* in matters among them, could be so gathered together; other than this, would be a mere mockery—like the Convention of 1848, a coming together of rivals, to test their success for the "biggest offices." As God lives, I will never, knowingly, lend my aid to any such work, while our brethren groan in vassalage and bondage, and I and mine under oppression and degradation, such as we now suffer.

I would not give the counsel of one dozen *intelligent colored* freeman of the *right stamp,* for that of all the white and unsuitable colored persons in the land. But something must be done, and that speedily.

The so called free states, by their acts, are now virtually saying to the South, "you *shall not* emancipate; your blacks *must be slaves;* and should they come North, there is no refuge for them." I shall not be surprised to see, at no distant day, a solemn Convention called by the whites in the North, to deliberate on the propriety of changing the whole policy to that of slave states. This will be the remedy to prevent dissolution; *and it will come, mark that!* anything on the part of the American people to *save* their *Union.* Mark me—the non-slaveholding states *will become slave states.*

Yours for God and Humanity,

M. R. DELANY.

From *Frederick Douglass' Paper,* April 1, 1853. This and the three following readings in this section also appear in *Frederick Douglass' Paper,* at Stephen Railton and the University of Virginia, *Uncle Tom's Cabin* and American Culture: A Multimedia Archive, http://utc.iath.virginia.edu/africam/fdphp.html.

FREDERICK DOUGLASS
Remarks [1853]

REMARKS—That colored men would agree among themselves to do something for the efficient and permanent aid of themselves and their race, "is a consummation devoutly to be wished;" but until they do, it is neither wise nor graceful for them, or for any one of them to throw cold water upon plans and efforts made for that purpose by others. To scornfully reject all aid from our white friends, and to denounce them as unworthy of our confidence, looks high and mighty enough on paper; but unless the back ground is filled up with facts demonstrating our independence and self-sustaining power, of what use is such display of self-consequence? Brother DELANY has worked long and hard, he has written vigorously, and spoken eloquently to colored people—beseeching them, in the name of liberty, and all the dearest interests of humanity, to unite their energies, and to increase their activities in the work of their own elevation; yet where has his voice been heeded? and where is the practical result? Echo answers, where? Is not the field open? Why, then, should any man object to the efforts of Mrs. Stowe, or any one else, who is moved to do anything on our behalf? The assertion that Mrs. Stowe "knows nothing about us," shows that bro. DELANY knows nothing about Mrs. Stowe; for he certainly would not so violate his moral, or common sense if he did. When Brother DELANY will submit any plan for benefitting the colored people, or will candidly criticize any plan already submitted, he will be heard with pleasure. But we expect no plan from him. He has written a book—and we may say that it is, in many respects, an excellent book—on the condition, character and destiny of the colored people; but it leaves us just where it finds us, without chart or compass, and in more doubt and perplexity than before we read it.

Brother Delany is one of our strong men; and we are therefore all the more grieved, that at a moment when all our energies should be united in giving effect to the benevolent designs of our friends, his voice should be uplifted to strike a jarring note, or to awaken a feeling of distrust.

In respect to a national convention, we are for it—and will not only go "ten miles" but a thousand, if need be, to attend it. Away, therefore, with all unworthy flings on that score.—ED.

PITTSBURGH, April 15th, 1853.

From *Frederick Douglass' Paper,* April 1, 1853.

MARTIN DELANY
Letter to Frederick Douglass [1853]

MRS. STOWE'S POSITION.

FREDERICK DOUGLASS, ESQ: DEAR SIR:—I send you, according to promise, the second of my series of letters. In saying, in my letter of the 22nd of March, that "Mrs. Stowe knows nothing about us—'the *Free* Colored People of the United States'—neither does any white person," I admit the expression to be ironical, and not intended to be taken in its literal sense; but I meant to be understood in so saying, that they know nothing, comparatively, about us, to the intelligent, reflecting, general observers among the Free Colored People of the North. And while I readily admit, that I "know nothing about Mrs. Stowe," I desire very much, to *learn* something of her; and as I could not expect it of Mrs. Stowe, to do so, were she in the country at present, I may at least ask it of brother Douglass, and hope that he will neither consider it derogatory to Mrs. Stowe's position nor attainments, to give me the required information concerning her. I go beyond the mere point of asking it as a favor; I demand it as a right—from you I mean—as I am an interested party, and however humble, may put such reasonable questions to the other party—looking upon you, in this case, as the attorney of said party—as may be necessary to the pending proceedings.

First, then, *assertion*; is not Mrs. Stowe a *Colonizationalist?* having so avowed, or at least subscribed to, and recommended their principles in her great work of Uncle Tom.

Secondly; although Mrs. Stowe has ably, eloquently, and pathetically portrayed some of the sufferings of the slave, is it any evidence that she has any sympathy for his thrice-morally crucified, semi-free brethren any

where, or of the *African* race at all; when in the same world-renowned and widely circulated work, she sneers at Hayti—the only truly free and independent civilized black nation as such, or colored if you please, on the face of the earth—at the same time holding up the little dependent colonization settlement of Liberia in high estimation? I must be permitted to draw my own conclusions, when I say that I can see no other cause for this singular discrepancy in Mrs. Stowe's interest in the colored race, than that one is independent of, and the other subservient to, white men's power.

You will certainly not consider this idea *farfetched,* because it is true American policy; and I do not think strange, even of Mrs. Stowe, for following in a path so conspicuous, as almost to become the principal public highway. At least, no one will dispute its being a *well-trodden path.*

Thirdly, says brother Douglass, "Why, then, should any man object to the efforts of Mrs. Stowe, or any one else, who is moved to do anything in our behalf?" Bro. Douglass does not mean, and I will not so torture his language, as to make it imply that he means, that we should permit *any body* to undertake *measures* for our elevation. If so, those of Gurley, Pinney, and other colonizationalists, should be acknowledged by us as *acceptable measures.* But are we to accept of colonization measures for our elevation?—Certainly not, you will readily reply. Then, if that be true, and Mrs. Stowe be what I have predicated—which I hope her friends may prove, satisfactorily, to the contrary—we should reject the proffers of Mrs. Stowe, as readily as those of any other colonizationalist. What! Have our children tutored under colonization measures? God Forbid! But why question Mrs. Stowe's measures? I will tell you. In May last, a colored man,—humble and common placed, to be sure—chanced to meet Mrs. Stowe at the house of Mr. B——, in the city of N——, State of N——, where he had called with some articles for sale. He informs me that Mrs. Stowe was very indifferent towards him—more so, he thought, than nay of the several persons present; and hearing him speak of his elevation in the United States, she asked, very seriously, what he expected to gain by any efforts that could be made here; and when he referred to the West Indies, and South America, &c., as an alternative, she at once asked him, "why he did not go to Liberia"—that moral and political bane of the colored people of this country—manifesting no sympathy whatever with the tortured feelings, crushed spirits and outraged homes of the Free Colored people, even the poor wretch who then stood before her. All this may have been, you may say, and still Mrs. Stowe be all that we could desire. It may be; but he who can believe such things, has stronger faith and confidence than I, in our American people. I must admit, that in them my confidence is terribly shattered. But, I will suppose a case as parallel with this one.

Mrs. Christian, of Vienna, in Austria, a highly intellectual, pious lady, writes a book—an excellent work—which is beginning to attract general public attention, for [its] portrayal of Hungarian wrongs. The deeply-moved sympathies of the lady's soul seems to teem through every chapter and page, exposing Austrian oppression, and, impliedly, advocating Hungarian *rights*—as would be reasonably supposed—the right to live freemen in Austria, or, at least, Hungary, their native part of the Empire. While the public attention is thus aroused, and that lady's book is almost the only topic of conversation among the people, from Paris to St. Petersburgh, what would be thought of *that* lady if a poor Hungarian chanced to meet her, and she manifested no sympathy for him, the *present* representative in poverty and obscurity of the very people whose cause she professed to espouse; and when he claimed the right to live in Austria, she would unconcernedly ask him why he did not go to Siberia, the inhospitable criminal colony of Russia—answering very well to the Liberia of the American colonizationalists, only not so cruel—since Russia sends only her criminals, mostly deserting soldiers and political offenders, while the United States Colonization Society forces innocent men, women and children to go, who never did harm to any one? Surely, according to the supposition predicated above, the Hungarians would have great cause for fearing, if not suspecting Mrs. Christian's fidelity to their cause.

Lastly; the Industrial Institution in contemplation by Mrs. Stowe, for the tuition of colored youth, proposes, as I understand it, the entire employment of white instructors. This, I strongly object to, as having a tendency to engender in our youth a higher degree of respect and confidence for white persons than for those of their own color; and creates the impression that colored persons are incapable of teaching, and only suited to *subordinate* positions. I have observed carefully, in all of my travels in our country—in all the schools that I visited—colored schools I mean—that in those taught in whole or part by colored persons, the pupils were always the most respectful towards me, and the less menial in their general bearing. I do not object to white teachers in part; but I do say, that wherever competent colored teachers could be obtained for any of the departments, they should be employed. Self-respect begets *due* obedience to others; and obedience is the first step to *self-government* among any people. Certainly, this should be an essential part of the training of our people, separated in interests as we have been, in this country. All the rude and abominable ideas that exist among us, in *preferences for color*, have been engendered *from the whites*; and in God's name, I ask them to do nothing more to increase this absurdity.

Another consideration, is, that all of the pecuniary advantages arising from this position go into the pockets of white men and women, thereby depriving colored persons, so far, of this livelihood. This is the same old song sung over again,

"Dimes and dollars—dollars and dimes,"

and I will say, without the fear of offence, that nothing that has as yet been gotten up by our friends, for the assistance of the colored people of the United States, has ever been of any pecuniary benefit to them. Our white friends take care of *that* part. There are, to my knowledge, two exceptions to this allegation—Douglass' printing establishment, and the "Alleghany Institute;" the one having a colored man at the head, and in the other, the assistant being a colored man.

There is an old American story about an Indian and a white man, hunting game together; when they shoot wild turkeys and buzzards, agreeing to divide, taking bird about; the white huntsman being the *teller.* In counting, the white man would say, alternately taking up either bird, "turkey for *me,* and buzzard for *you*—buzzard for *you,* and turkey for *me.*" He growing tired of that method of counting the game, soon accosted his friend: "Uh! How's dis? All *buzzard* for me; but you never say, *turkey* for me, once." I feel somewhat as this Indian did; I am growing weary of receiving the *buzzard* as *our* share, while our tellers get all the *turkeys.* That "is not the way to 'tell' it" to me.

But I have not yet read the "Key to Uncle Tom's Cabin," and it may be that, in that, Mrs. S.—and I sincerely hope she has—has changed her policy, and renounced Colonization as she had made a public avowal of it; and *a priori,* just so far as her work received favor, her opinions on that subject will also be received.

I am aware that I am saying much more than is allowable, as I do not know of any of our professed anti-slavery friends who have taken public positions, who will permit any of their measures to be questioned by a colored person, except in the fullness of those great and good hearts—W. L. Garrison, Gerritt Smith, and that more than excellent woman, *Mrs. Hester Moore,* of Philadelphia, whose name you now scarcely ever hear of. She is an *abolitionist* of the Garrison and Smith sort; she loves the cause of Hungary for the *sake* of the *Hungarians.*

Let me say another thing, brother Douglass; that is, that no enterprise, institution, or anything else, should be commenced *for us,* or our general benefit, without *first consulting us.* By this, I mean, consulting the various communities of the colored people in the United States, by such a correspondence as should make public the measure, and solicit their general interests and coincidence. In this way, the intelligence and desires of the whole people would be elicited, and an intelligent understanding of their real desires obtained. Other than this, is treating us as slaves, and presupposing us all to be ignorant, and incapable of knowing our own *wants.* Many of the measures of our friends have failed from this very cause; and I am fearful that many more will fail.

In conclusion, brother Douglass, let me say, that I am the last person among us who would wilfully "strike a jarring note, or awaken a feeling of distrust," uncalled for; and although you may pronounce it "unwise, ungraceful, and sounding high and mighty on paper;" as much high respect as an humble simple-minded person should have for them, and as much honored as I should feel in having such names enrolled as our benefactors—associated with our degraded position in society; believe me when I tell you, that I speak it as a son, a brother, a husband and a father; I speak it from the consciousness of oppressed human-

ity, outraged manhood, of a degraded husband and disabled father; I speak it from the recesses of a wounded bleeding heart—in the name of my wife and children, who look to me for protection, as the joint partner of our humble fireside; I say, if this great fund and aid are to be sent here to foster and aid the schemes of the American Colonization Society, as I say to you—I say with reverence, and an humbleness of feeling, becoming my position, with a bowed-down head, that the benevolent, great and good, the Duchess of Sutherland, Mr. Gurney, their graces the Earl of Shaftesbury and the Earl of Carlisle; had far better retain their money in the Charity Fund of Stafford House, or any other place, than to send it to the United States for any such unhallowed purposes!— No person will be more gratified, nor will more readily join in commendation, than I, of any good measure attempted to be carried out by Mrs. Stowe, if the contrary of her colonization principles be disproved. I will not accept *chains* from a king, any sooner than from a peasant; and never shall, willingly, submit to any measures for my own degradation. I am in hopes, brother Douglass, as every one else will understand my true position.

Yours for God and down-trodden Humanity,

M. R. DELANY.
Pittsburgh, April 18th, 1853.

From *Frederick Douglass' Paper,* May 6, 1853.

FREDERICK DOUGLASS
Reply to Martin Delany [1853]

THE LETTER OF M. R. DELANY.

This letter is premature, unfair, uncalled for, and, withal, needlessly long; but, happily, it needs not a long reply.

Can brother Delany be the writer of it?—It lacks his generous spirit. The letter is premature, because it attacks a plan, the details of which are yet undefined. It is unfair, because [it] imputes designs (and replies to them) which have never been declared. It is uncalled for, because there is nothing in the position of Mrs. Stowe which should awaken against her a single suspicion of unfriendliness towards the free colored people of the United States; but, on the contrary, there is much in it to inspire confidence in her friendship.

The information for which brother Delany asks, concerning Mrs. Stowe, he has given himself. He says she is a colonizationist; and we ask, what if she is?—names do not frighten us. A little while ago, brother Delany was a colonizationist. If we do not misremember, in his book he declared in favor of colonizing the eastern coast of Africa. Yet, we never suspected his friendliness to the colored people; nor should we feel called upon to oppose any plan he might submit, for the benefit of the colored people, on that account. We recognize friends wherever we find them.

Whoever will bring a straw's weight of influence to break the chains of our brother bondmen, or whisper one word of encouragement and sympathy to our proscribed race in the North, shall be welcomed by us to that philanthropic field of labor. We shall not, therefore, allow the sentiments put in the brief letter of GEORGE HARRIS, at the close of Uncle Tom's Cabin, to vitiate forever Mrs. Stowe's power to do us good. Who doubts that Mrs. Stowe is more of an abolitionist now than when she wrote that chapter?—We believe that lady to be but at the beginning of her labors for the colored people of this country.

Brother Delany says, nothing should be done for us, or commenced for us, without "consulting us." Where will he find "us" to consult with? Through what organization, or what channel could such consulting be carried on? Does he mean by consulting "us" that nothing is do be done for the improvement of the colored people in general, without consulting each colored man in the country whether it shall be done? *How many*, in this case, constitute "*us*"? Evidently brother Delany is a little unreasonable here.

Four years ago, a proposition was made, through the columns of *The North Star,* for the formation of a "*National League,*" and a constitution for said League was drawn up, fully setting forth a plan for united, intelligent and effective co-operation on the part of the free colored people of the United States—a body capable of being "*consulted.*" The colored people, in their wisdom, or in their indifference, gave the scheme little or no

encouragement—and it failed. Now, we happen to know that such an organization as was then proposed, was enquired for, and sought for by Mrs. Harriet Beecher Stowe; she wished, most of all, to hear from such a body *what could* be done for the *free colored people* of the United States? But there was no such body to answer.

The fact is, brother Delany, we are a disunited and scattered people, and very much of the responsibility of this disunion must fall upon such colored men as yourself and the writer of this. We want more confidence in each other, as a race—more self-forgetfulness, and less disposition to find fault with well-meant efforts for our benefit. Mr. Delany knows that, at this moment, he could call a respectable Convention of the free colored people of the Northern States. Why don't he issue his call? and he knows, too, that, were we to issue such a call, it would instantly be regarded as an effort to promote the interests of our paper. This consideration, and a willingness on our part to occupy an obscure position in such a movement, has led us to refrain from issuing a call. *The Voice of the Fugitive,* we observe, has suggested the holding, in New York, of a "World's Convention" during the "World's Fair." A better proposition, we think, would be to hold in that city a "National Convention" of the colored people. Will not friend Delany draw up a call for such a Convention, and send it to us to publication?

But to return. Brother Delany asks, if we should allow "*any body*" to undertake measures for our elevation? YES, we answer—any body, even a slaveholder. Why not? Then says brother Delany, why not accept the measures of "Gurley and Pinney"? We answer, simply because *their measures* do not commend themselves to our judgment. That is all. If "Gurley and Pinney" would establish an industrial college, where colored young men could learn useful trades, with a view to their becoming useful men and respectable citizens of the United States, we should applaud them and co-operate with them.

We don't object to Colonizations because they express a lively interest in the civilization and Christianization of Africa; nor because they desire the prosperity of Liberia; but it is because, like brother Delany, they have not sufficient faith in the people of the United States to believe that the black man can ever get justice at their hands on American soil. It is because they have systematically, and almost universally, sought to spread their hopelessness among the free colored people themselves; and thereby rendered them, if not contented with, at least resigned to the degradation which they have been taught to believe must be perpetual and immutable, while they remain where they are. It is because, having denied the possibility of our elevation here, they have sought to make good this denial, by encouraging the enactment of laws subjecting us to the most flagrant outrages, and stripping us of all the safeguards necessary to the security of our liberty, persons and property.—We say all this of the American Colonization Society; but we are *far* from saying this of many who speak and wish well to Liberia. As to the imputation that all the pecuniary profit arising out of the industrial scheme will probably pass into the pockets of the whites, it will be quite time enough to denounce such a purpose when such a purpose is avowed. But we have already dwelt too long on a letter which perhaps carried its own answer with it.

From *Frederick Douglass' Paper*, May 6, 1853.

KEY DEBATE ~ *Strategies for Change*

DAVID WALKER

Article II, Our Wretchedness in Consequence of Ignorance, from Walker's Appeal [1829, revision published 1830]

David Walker (p. 27), a free African American from North Carolina, settled in Boston in 1825 and quickly emerged as a major leader in the abolitionist movement. In 1828, he spoke before the Massachusetts General Colored Association, challenging its members to act: "Shall we keep slumbering on, with our arms completely folded up, exclaiming every now and then, against our miseries, yet never do the least thing to ameliorate our condition, or that of posterity?" This same call to action distinguished Walker's highly controversial anti-slavery pamphlet, *David Walker's Appeal, in Four Articles*, published the next year. In sharp contrast to prevailing abolitionist plans for gradual abolition or African colonization, Walker champions the immediate emancipation of all enslaved African Americans. Moreover, he advocates violent rebellion as an appropriate and justifiable response to the violence of slavery, repudiating the strategy of "moral suasion" (favored by William Lloyd Garrison [p. 111] and other leading black and white abolitionists), by which moral argument, rather than political or physical force, was to be used to influence others.

From David Walker, *Walker's Appeal, in Four Articles; Together with a Preamble, to the Coloured Citizens of the World, but in Particular, and Very Expressly, to Those of the United States of America, Written in Boston, State of Massachusetts, September 28, 1829*, rev. ed. (Boston: David Walker, 1830), pp. 22–39.

Ignorance, my brethren, is a mist, low down into the very dark and almost impenetrable abyss in which, our fathers for many centuries have been plunged. The Christians, and enlightened of Europe, and some of Asia, seeing the ignorance and consequent degradation of our fathers, instead of trying to enlighten them, by teaching them that religion and light with which God had blessed them, they have plunged them into wretchedness ten thousand times more intolerable, than if they had left them entirely to the Lord, and to add to their miseries, deep down into which they have plunged them tell them, that they are an *inferior* and *distinct race* of beings, which they will be glad enough to recal and swallow by and by. Fortune and misfortune, two inseparable companions, lay rolled up in the wheel of events, which have from the creation of the world, and will continue to take place among men until God shall dash worlds together.

When we take a retrospective view of the arts and sciences—the wise legislators—the Pyramids, and other magnificent buildings—the turning of the channel of the river Nile, by the sons of Africa or of Ham, among whom learning originated, and was carried thence into Greece, where it was improved upon and refined. Thence among the Romans, and all over the then enlightened parts of the world, and it has been enlightening the dark and benighted minds of men from then, down to this day. I say, when I view retrospectively, the renown of that once mighty people, the children of our great progenitor I am indeed cheered. Yea further, when I view that mighty son of Africa, HANNIBAL, one of the greatest generals of antiquity, who defeated and cut off so many thousands of the white Romans or murderers, and who carried his victorious arms, to the very gate of Rome, and I give it as my candid opinion, that had Carthage been well united and had given him good support, he would

103

have carried that cruel and barbarous city by storm. But they were dis-united, as the coloured people are now, in the United States of America, the reason our natural enemies are enabled to keep their feet on our throats.

Beloved brethren—here let me tell you, and believe it, that the Lord our God, as true as he sits on his throne in heaven, and as true as our Saviour died to redeem the world, will give you a Hannibal, and when the Lord shall have raised him up, and given him to you for your possession, O my suffering brethren! remember the divisions and consequent sufferings of *Carthage* and of *Hayti*. Read the history particularly of Hayti, and see how they were butchered by the whites, and do you take warning. The person whom God shall give you, give him your support and let him go his length, and behold in him the salvation of your God. God will indeed, deliver you through him from your deplorable and wretched condition under the Christians of America. I charge you this day before my God to lay no obstacle in his way, but let him go.

The whites want slaves, and want us for their slaves, but some of them will curse the day they ever saw us. As true as the sun ever shone in its meridian splendor, my colour will root some of them out of the very face of the earth. They shall have enough of making slaves of, and butchering, and murdering us in the manner which they have. No doubt some may say that I write with a bad spirit, and that I being a black, wish these things to occur. Whether I write with a bad or a good spirit, I say if these things do not occur in their proper time, it is because the world in which we live does not exist, and we are deceived with regard to its existence.—It is immaterial however to me, who believe, or who refuse—though I should like to see the whites repent peradventure God may have mercy on them, some however, have gone so far that their cup must be filled.

But what need have I to refer to antiquity, when Hayti, the glory of the blacks and terror of tyrants, is enough to convince the most avaricious and stupid of wretches—which is at this time, and I am sorry to say it, plagued with that scourge of nations, the Catholic religion; but I hope and pray God that she may yet rid herself of it, and adopt in its stead the Protestant faith; also, I hope that she may keep peace within her bor-

ders and be united, keeping a strict look out for tyrants, for if they get the least chance to injure her, they will avail themselves of it, as true as the Lord lives in heaven. But one thing which gives me joy is, that they are men who would be cut off to a man, before they would yield to the combined forces of the whole world—in fact, if the whole world was combined against them, it could not do any thing with them, unless the Lord delivers them up.

Ignorance and treachery one against the other—a grovelling servile and abject submission to the lash of tyrants, we see plainly, my brethren, are not the natural elements of the blacks, as the Americans try to make us believe; but these are misfortunes which God has suffered our fathers to be enveloped in for many ages, no doubt in consequence of their disobedience to their Maker, and which do, indeed, reign at this time among us, almost to the destruction of all other principles: for I must truly say, that ignorance, the mother of treachery and deceit, gnaws into our very vitals. Ignorance, as it now exists among us, produces a state of things, Oh my Lord! too horrible to present to the world. Any man who is curious to see the full force of ignorance developed among the coloured people of the United States of America, has only to go into the southern and western states of this confederacy, where, if he is not a tyrant, but has the feelings of a human being, who can feel for a fellow creature, he may see enough to make his very heart bleed! He may see there, a son take his mother, who bore almost the pains of death to give him birth, and by the command of a tyrant, strip her as naked as she came into the world, and apply the cowhide to her, until she falls a victim to death in the road! He may see a husband take his dear wife, not unfrequently in a pregnant state, and perhaps far advanced, and beat her for an unmerciful wretch, until his infant falls a lifeless lump at her feet! Can the Americans escape God Almighty? If they do, can he be to us a God of Justice? God is just, and I know it—for he has convinced me to my satisfaction—I cannot doubt him. My observer may see fathers beating their sons, mothers their daughters, and children their parents, all to pacify the passions of unrelenting tyrants. He may also, see them telling news and lies, making mischief one upon another. These are some of the productions of ignorance, which he will see practised among my dear brethren, who are held in unjust slavery and wretchedness, by avaricious and unmerciful tyrants, to whom, and their hellish deeds, I would suffer my life to be taken before I would submit. And when my curious observer comes to take notice of those who are said to be free, (which assertion I deny) and who are making some frivolous pretentions to common sense, he will see that branch of ignorance among the slaves assuming a more cunning and deceitful course of procedure.—He may see some of my brethren in league with tyrants, selling their own brethren into *hell upon earth,* not dissimilar to the exhibitions in Africa, but in a more secret, servile and abject manner. Oh Heaven! I am full!!! I can hardly move my pen!!! and as I expect some will try to put me to death, to strike terror into others, and to obliterate from their minds the notion of freedom, so as to keep my brethren the more secure in wretchedness, where they will be permitted to stay but a short time (whether tyrants believe it or not)—I shall give the world a development of facts, which are already witnessed in the courts of heaven. My observer may see some of those ignorant and treacherous creatures (coloured people) sneaking about in the large cities, endeavouring to find out all strange coloured people, where they work and where they reside, asking them questions, and trying to ascertain whether they are runaways or not, telling them, at the same time, that they always have been, are, and always will be, friends to their brethren; and, perhaps, that they themselves are absconders, and a thousand such treacherous lies to get the better information of the more ignorant!!! There have been and are at this day in Boston, New-York, Philadelphia, and Baltimore, coloured men, who are in league with tyrants, and who receive a great portion of their daily bread, of the moneys which they acquire from the blood and tears of their more miserable brethren, whom they scandalously delivered into the hands of our *natural enemies!!!!!!*

To show the force of degraded ignorance[1] and deceit among us some farther, I will give here an extract from a paragraph, which may be found in the Columbian Centinel of this city, for September 9, 1829, on the first page of which, the curious may find an article, headed

"AFFRAY AND MURDER."

"Portsmouth, (Ohio) Aug." 22, 1829.

"A most shocking outrage was committed in Kentucky, about eight miles from this place, on 14th inst. A negro driver, by the name of Gordon, who had purchased in Mayland about sixty negroes, was taking them, assisted by an associate named Allen, and the wagoner who conveyed the baggage, to the Mississippi. The men were hand-cuffed and chained together, in the usual manner for driving those poor wretches, while the women and children were suffered to proceed without incumbrance. It appears that, by means of a file the negroes, unobserved, had succeeded in separating the iron which bound their hands, in such a way as to be able to throw them off at any moment. About 8 o'clock in the morning, while proceeding on the state road leading from Greenup to Vanceburg, two of them dropped their shackles and commenced a fight, when the wagoner (Petit) rushed in with his whip to compel them to desist. At this moment, every negro was found to be perfectly at liberty; and one of them seizing a club, gave Petit a violent blow on the head, and laid him dead at his feet; and Allen, who came to his assistance, met a similar fate, from the contents of a pistol fired by another of the gang. Gordon was then attacked, seized and held by one of the negroes, whilst another fired twice at him with a pistol, the ball of which each time grazed his head, but not proving effectual, he was beaten with clubs, and left for dead. They then commenced pillaging the wagon, and with an axe split open the trunk of Gordon, and rifled it of the money, about $2,400. Sixteen of the negroes then took to the woods; Gordon, in the mean time, not being materially injured, was enabled, by the assistance of one of the women, to mount his horse and flee; pursued, however, by one of the gang on another horse, with a drawn pistol; fortunately he escaped with his life barely, arriving at a plantation, as the negro came in sight; who then turned about and retreated."

"The neighbourhood was immediately rallied, and a hot pursuit given—which, we understand, has resulted in the capture of the whole gang and the

---

1. Several typographical errors from the 1830 printing are corrected here, including ignorance (ignorace) and conversation (conversatson). [Editor's note]

recovery of the greatest part of the money. Seven of the negro men and one woman, it is said were engaged in the murders, and will be brought to trial at the next court in Greenupsburg."

Here my brethren, I want you to notice particularly in the above article, the *ignorant* and *deceitful actions* of this coloured woman. I beg you to view it candidly, as for ETERNITY!!!! Here a *notorious wretch*, with two other confederates had SIXTY of them in a gang, driving them like *brutes*—the men all in chains and hand-cuffs, and by the help of God they got their chains and hand-cuffs thrown off, and caught two of the wretches and put them to death, and beat the other until they thought he was dead, and left him for dead; however, he deceived them, and rising from the ground, this *servile woman* helped him upon his horse, and he made his escape. Brethren, what do you think of this? Was it the natural *fine feelings* of this woman, to save such a wretch alive? I know that the blacks, take them half enlightened and ignorant, are more humane and merciful than the most enlightened and refined European that can be found in all the earth. Let no one say that I assert this because I am prejudiced on the side of my colour, and against the whites or Europeans. For what I write, I do it candidly, for my God and the good of both parties: Natural observations have taught me these things; there is a solemn awe in the hearts of the blacks, as it respects *murdering* men:[2] whereas the whites, (though they are great cowards) where they have the advantage, or think that there are any prospects of getting it, they murder all before them, in order to subject men to wretchedness and degradation under them. This is the natural result of pride and avarice. But I declare, the actions of this black woman are really insupportable. For my own part, I cannot think it was any thing but servile deceit, combined with the most gross ignorance: for we must remember that *humanity, kindness* and the *fear of the Lord,* does not consist in protecting *devils.* Here is a set of wretches, who had SIXTY of them in a gang, driving them around the country like brutes, to dig up

gold and silver for them, (which they will get enough of yet.) Should the lives of such creatures be spared? Are God and Mammon in league? What has the Lord to do with a gang of desperate wretches, who go *sneaking about the country like robbers*—light upon his people wherever they can get a chance, binding them with chains and hand-cuffs, beat and murder them as they would rattle-snakes? Are they not the Lord's enemies? Ought they not to be destroyed? Any person who will save such wretches from destruction, is fighting against the Lord, and will receive his just recompense. The black men acted like *blockheads.* Why did they not make sure of the wretch? He would have made sure of them, if he could. It is just the way with black men—eight white men can frighten fifty of them; whereas, if you can only get courage into the blacks, I do declare it, that one good black man can put to death six white men; and I give it as a fact, let twelve black men get well armed for battle, and they will kill and put to flight fifty whites.—The reason is, the blacks, once you get them started, they glory in death. The whites have had us under them for more than three centuries, murdering, and treating us like brutes; and, as Mr. Jefferson wisely said, they have never *found us out*[3]—they do not know, indeed, that there is an unconquerable disposition in the breasts of the blacks, which, when it is fully awakened and put in motion, will be subdued, only with the destruction of the animal existence. Get the blacks started, and if you do not have a gang of tigers and lions to deal with, I am a deceiver of the blacks and of the whites. How sixty of them could let that wretch escape unkilled, I cannot conceive—they will have to suffer as much for the two whom, they secured, as if they had put one hundred to death: if you commence, make sure work—do not trifle, for they will not trifle with you—they want us for their slaves, and think nothing of murdering us in order to subject us to that wretched condition—therefore, if there is an *attempt* made by us, kill or be killed. Now, I ask you, had you not rather be killed than to be a slave to a tyrant, who takes the life of your mother, wife, and dear little children? Look upon your mother, wife and

---

2. Which is the reason the whites take the advantage of us. [Unless otherwise indicated, all footnotes are those of the author.]
3. In *Notes on the State of Virginia,* Jefferson writes, "To our reproach it must be said, that though for a century and a half we have had under our eyes the races of black and of red men, they have never yet been viewed by us as subjects of natural history"; see p. 20. [Editor's note].

children, and answer God Almighty; and believe this, that it is no more harm for you to kill a man, who is trying to kill you, than it is for you to take a drink of water when thirsty; in fact, the man who will stand still and let another murder him, is worse than an infidel, and, if he has common sense, ought not to be pitied. The actions of this deceitful and ignorant coloured woman, in saving the life of a desperate wretch, whose avaricious and cruel object was to drive her, and her companions in miseries, through the country like cattle, to make his fortune on their carcasses, are but too much like that of thousands of our brethren in these states: if any thing is whispered by one, which has any allusion to the melioration of their dreadful condition, they run and tell tyrants, that they may be enabled to keep them the longer in wretchedness and miseries. Oh! coloured people of these United States, I ask you, in the name of that God who made us, have we, in consequence of oppression, nearly lost the spirit of man, and, in no very trifling degree, adopted that of brutes? Do you answer, no?—I ask you, then, what set of men can you point me to, in all the world, who are so abjectly employed by their oppressors, as we are by our *natural enemies?* How can, Oh! how can those enemies but say that we and our children are not of the HUMAN FAMILY, but were made by our Creator to be an inheritance to them and theirs for ever? How can the slaveholders but say that they can bribe the best coloured person in the country, to sell his brethren for a trifling sum of money, and take that atrocity to confirm them in their avaricious opinion, that we were made to be slaves to them and their children? How could Mr. Jefferson but say,[4] "I advance it therefore as a suspicion only, that the blacks, whether originally a distinct race, or made distinct by time and circumstances, are *inferior* to the whites in the endowments both of body and mind"—"It," says he, "is not against experience to suppose, that different species of the same genius, or varieties of the same species, may possess different qualifications." [Here, my brethren, listen to him.] "Will not a lover of natural history, then, one who views the gradations in all the races of *animals* with the eye of philosophy, excuse an effort to keep those in the department of MAN as *distinct* as

nature has formed them?"—I hope you will try to find out the meaning of this verse—its widest sense and all its bearings: whether you do or not, remember the whites do. This very verse, brethren, having emanated from Mr. Jefferson, a much greater philosopher the world never afforded, has in truth injured us more, and has been as great a barrier to our emancipation as any thing that has ever been advanced against us. I hope you will not let it pass unnoticed. He goes on further, and says: "This *unfortunate* difference of colour, and *perhaps* of *faculty,* is a powerful obstacle to the emancipation of these people. Many of their advocates, while they wish to vindicate the liberty of human nature are anxious also to preserve its *dignity* and *beauty.* Some of these, embarrassed by the question, 'What further is to be done with them?' join themselves in opposition with those who are actuated by sordid avarice only." Now I ask you candidly, my suffering brethren in time, who are candidates for the eternal worlds, how could Mr. Jefferson but have given the world these remarks respecting us, when we are so submissive to them, and so much servile deceit prevail among ourselves—when we so *meanly* submit to their murderous lashes, to which neither the Indians nor any other people under Heaven would submit? No, they would die to a man, before they would suffer such things from men who are no better than themselves, and *perhaps not so good.* Yes, how can our friends but be embarrassed, as Mr. Jefferson says, by the question, "What further is to be done with these people?" For while they are working for our emancipation, we are, by our treachery, wickedness and deceit, working against ourselves and our children—helping ours, and the enemies of God, to keep us and our dear little children in their infernal chains of slavery!!! Indeed, our friends cannot but relapse and join themselves "with those who are actuated by *sordid avarice* only!!!" For my own part, I am glad Mr. Jefferson has advanced his positions for your sake; for you will either have to contradict or confirm him by your own actions, and not by what our friends have said or done for us; for those things are other men's labours, and do not satisfy the Americans, who are waiting for us to prove to them ourselves, that we are MEN, before they will be willing to admit the fact;

4. See his Notes on Virginia, page 213.

for I pledge you my sacred word of honour, that Mr. Jefferson's remarks respecting us, have sunk deep into the hearts of millions of the whites, and never will be removed this side of eternity.—For how can they, when we are confirming him every day, by our *groveling submissions* and *treachery*? I aver, that when I look over these United States of America, and the world, and see the ignorant deceptions and consequent wretchedness of my brethren, I am brought oftimes solemnly to a stand, and in the midst of my reflections I exclaim to my God, "Lord didst thou make us to be slaves to our brethren, the whites?" But when I reflect that God is just, and that millions of my wretched brethren would meet death with glory—yea, more, would plunge into the very mouths of cannons and be torn into particles as minute as the atoms which compose the elements of the earth, in preference to a mean submission to the lash of tyrants, I am with streaming eyes, compelled to shrink back into nothingness before my Maker, and exclaim again, thy will be done, O Lord God Almighty.

Men of colour, who are also of sense, for you particularly is my APPEAL designed. Our more ignorant brethren are not able to penetrate its value. I call upon you therefore to cast your eyes upon the wretchedness of your brethren, and to do your utmost to enlighten them—*go to work and enlighten your brethren!*—Let the Lord see you doing what you can to rescue them and yourselves from degradation. Do any of you say that you and your family are free and happy, and what have you to do with the wretched slaves and other people? So can I say, for I enjoy as much freedom as any of you, if I am not quite as well off as the best of you. Look into our freedom and happiness, and see of what kind they are composed!! They are of the very lowest kind— they are the very *dregs!*—they are the most servile and abject kind, that ever a people was in possession of! If any of you wish to know how FREE you are, let one of you start and go through the southern and western States of this country, and unless you travel as a slave to a white man (a servant is a *slave* to the man whom he serves) or have your free papers, (which if you are not careful they will get from you) if they do not take you up and put you in jail, and if you cannot give good evidence of your freedom, sell you into eternal slavery, I am not a living man: or any man of colour, immaterial

who he is, or where he came from, if he is not *the fourth from the negro race!!* (as we are called) the white Christians of America will serve him the same, they will sink him into wretchedness and degradation for ever while he lives. And yet some of you have the hardihood to say that you are free and happy! May God have mercy on your freedom and happiness!! I met a coloured man in the street a short time since, with a string of boots on his shoulders; we fell into conversation, and in course of which, I said to him, what a miserable set of people we are! He asked, why?—Said I, we are so subjected under the whites, that we cannot obtain the comforts of life, but by cleaning their boots and shoes, old clothes, waiting on them, shaving them &c. Said he, (with the boots on his shoulders) "I am completely happy!!! I never want to live any better or happier than when I can get a plenty of boots and shoes to clean!!!" Oh! how can those who are actuated by avarice only, but think, that our Creator made us to be an inheritance to them for ever, when they see that our greatest glory is centered in such mean and low objects? Understand me, brethren, I do not mean to speak against the occupations by which we acquire enough and sometimes scarcely that, to render ourselves and families comfortable through life. I am subjected to the same inconvenience, as you all.—My objections are, to our *glorying* and being *happy* in such low employments; for if we are men, we ought to be thankful to the Lord for the past, and for the future. Be looking forward with thankful hearts to higher attainments than *wielding the razor* and *cleaning boots and shoes.* The man whose aspirations are not *above,* and even *below* these, is indeed, ignorant and wretched enough. I advance it therefore to you, not as a *problematical,* but as an unshaken and for ever immoveable *fact,* that your full glory and happiness, as well as all other coloured people under Heaven, shall never be fully consummated, but with the *entire emancipation of your enslaved brethren all over the world.* You may therefore, go to work and do what you can to rescue, or join in with tyrants to oppress them and yourselves, until the Lord shall come upon you all like a thief in the night. For I believe it is the will of the Lord that our greatest happiness shall consist in working for the salvation of our whole body. When this is accomplished a burst of glory will shine upon you, which will indeed astonish you and the world. Do any of you say this never will be done? I assure you that God will accomplish it—if nothing else will answer, he will hurl tyrants and devils into *atoms* and make way for his people. But O my brethren! I say unto you again, you must go to work and prepare the way of the Lord.

There is a great work for you to do, as trifling as some of you may think of it. You have to prove to the Americans and the world, that we are MEN, and not *brutes*, as we have been represented, and by millions treated. Remember, to let the aim of your labours among your brethren, and particularly the youths, be the dissemination of education and religion.[5] It is lamentable, that many of our children go to school, from four until they are eight or ten, and sometimes fifteen years of age, and leave school knowing but a little more about the grammar of their language than a horse does about handling a musket—and not a few of them are really so ignorant, that they are unable to answer a person correctly, general questions in geography, and to hear them read, would only be to disgust a man who has a taste for reading; which, to do well, as trifling as it may appear to some, (to the ignorant in particular) is a great part of learning. Some few of them, may make out to scribble tolerably well, over a half sheet of paper, which I believe has hitherto been a powerful obstacle in our way, to keep us from acquiring knowledge. An ignorant father, who knows no more than what nature has taught him, together with what little he acquires by the senses of hearing and seeing, finding his son able to write a neat hand, sets it down for granted that he has as good learning as any body; the young, ignorant gump, hearing his father or mother, who perhaps may be ten times more ignorant, in point of literature, than himself, extolling his learning, struts about, in the full assurance, that his attainments in literature are sufficient to take him through the world, when, in fact, he has scarcely any learning at all!!!!

I promiscuously fell in conversation once, with an elderly coloured man on the topics of education, and of the great prevalency of ignorance among us: Said he, "I know that our people are very ignorant but my son has a good education: I spent a great deal of money on his education: he can write as well as any white man, and I assure you that no one can fool him," &c. Said I, what else can your son do, besides writing a good hand? Can he post a set of books in a mercantile manner? Can he write a neat piece of composition in prose or in verse? To these interogations he answered in the negative. Said I, did your son learn, while he was at school, the width and depth of English Grammar? To which he also replied in the negative, telling me his son did not learn those things. Your son, said I, then, has hardly any learning at all—he is almost as ignorant, and more so, than many of those who never went to school one day in all their lives. My friend got a little put out, and so walking off, said that his son could write as well as any white man. Most of the coloured people, when they speak of the education of one among us who can write a neat hand, and who perhaps knows nothing but to scribble and puff pretty fair on a small scrap of paper, immaterial whether his words are grammatical, or spelt correctly, or not; if it only looks beautiful, they say he has as good an education as any white man—he can write as well as any white man, &c. The poor, ignorant creature, hearing this, he is ashamed, forever after, to let any person see him humbling himself to another for knowledge but going about trying to deceive those who are more ignorant than himself, he at last falls an ignorant victim to death in wretchedness. I pray that the Lord may undeceive my ignorant brethren, and permit them to throw away pretensions, and seek after the substance of learning. I would crawl on my hands and knees through mud and mire, to the feet of a learned man, where I would sit and humbly supplicate him to instil into me, that which neither devils nor tyrants could remove, only with my life—for colored people to acquire learning in this country, makes tyrants quake and tremble on their sandy foundation. Why, what is the matter? Why, they know that their infernal deeds of cruelty will be made known to the world. Do you suppose one man of good sense and

---

5. Never mind what the ignorant ones among us may say, many of whom when you speak to them for their good, and try to enlighten their minds, laugh at you, and perhaps tell you plump to your face, that they want no instruction from you or any other Niger, and all such aggravating language. Now if you are a man of understanding and sound sense, I conjure you in the name of the Lord, and of all that is good, to impute their actions to ignorance, and wink at their follies, and do your very best to get around them some way or other, for remember they are your brethren; and I declare to you that it is for your interests to teach and enlighten them.

learning would submit himself, his father, mother, wife and children, to be slaves to a wretched man like himself, who, instead of compensating him for his labours, chains, hand-cuffs and beats him and family almost to death, leaving life enough in them, however, to work for, and call him master? No! no! he would cut his devilish throat from ear to ear, and well do slave-holders know it. The bare name of educating the coloured people, scares our cruel oppressors almost to death. But if they do not have enough to be frightened for yet, it will be, because they can always keep us ignorant, and because God approbates their cruelties, with which they have been for centuries murdering us. The whites shall have enough of the blacks, yet, as true as God sits on his throne in Heaven.

Some of our brethren are so very full of learning, that you cannot mention any thing to them which they do not know better than yourself!!—nothing is strange to them!!—they knew every thing years ago!—if any thing should be mentioned in company where they are, immaterial how important it is respecting us or the world, if they had not divulged it; they make light of it, and affect to have known it long before it was mentioned and try to make all in the room, or wherever you may be, believe that your conversation is nothing!!—not worth hearing! All this is the result of ignorance and ill-breeding; for a man of good-breeding, sense and penetration, if he had heard a subject told twenty times over, and should happen to be in company where one should commence telling it again, he would wait with patience on its narrator, and see if he would tell it as it was told in his presence before—paying the most strict attention to what is said, to see if any more light will be thrown on the subject: for all men are not gifted alike in telling, or even hearing the most simple narration. These ignorant, vicious, and wretched men, contribute almost as much injury to our body as tyrants themselves, by doing so much for the promotion of ignorance amongst us; for they, making such pretensions to knowledge, such of our youth as are seeking after knowledge, and can get access to them, take them as criterions to go by, who will lead them into a channel,

where, unless the Lord blesses them with the privilege of seeing their folly, they will be irretrievably lost forever, while in time!!!

I must close this article by relating the very heart-rending fact, that I have examined school-boys and young men of colour in different parts of the country, in the most simple parts of Murray's English Grammar, and not more than one in thirty was able to give a correct answer to my interrogations. If any one contradicts me, let him step out of his door into the streets of Boston, New-York, Philadelphia, or Baltimore, (no use to mention any other, for the Christians are too charitable further south or west!)—I say, let him who disputes me, step out of his door into the streets of either of those four cities, and promiscuously collect one hundred school-boys, or young men of colour, *who have been to school*, and who are considered by the coloured people to have received an excellent education, because, perhaps, some of them can write a good hand, but who, notwithstanding their neat writing, may be almost as ignorant, in comparison, as a horse.—And, I say it, he will hardly find (in this enlightened day, and in the midst of this *charitable* people) five in one hundred, who, are able to correct the false grammar of their language.—The cause of this almost universal ignorance among us, I appeal to our school-masters to declare. Here is a fact, which I this very minute take from the mouth of a young coloured man, who has been to school in this state (Massachusetts) nearly nine years, and who knows grammar this day, *nearly* as well as he did the day he first entered the school-house, under a white master. This young man says: "My master would never allow me to study grammar." I asked him, why? "The school committee," said he "forbid the coloured children learning grammar"—they would not allow any but the white children "to study grammar." It is a notorious fact, that the major part of the white Americans, have, ever since we have been among them, tried to keep us ignorant, and make us believe that God made us and our children to be slaves to them and theirs. *Oh! my God, have mercy on Christian Americans!!!*

WILLIAM LLOYD GARRISON
Editorial on Walker's Appeal [1831]

On January 1, 1831, the white abolitionist William Lloyd Garrison (1805–1879) launched *The Liberator,* an anti-slavery newspaper dedicated to the immediate emancipation and enfranchisement of all African Americans. In his inaugural editorial, Garrison proclaimed his split from moderate abolitionists who favored gradual emancipation. His unyielding rhetoric set the stage for more than thirty years of agitation against slavery. "I am aware, that many object to the severity of my language; but is there not cause for severity?" Garrison exclaimed in his inaugural editorial.

> I *will be* as harsh as truth, and as uncompromising as justice. On this subject, I do not wish to think, or speak, or write, with moderation. No! no! Tell a man whose house is on fire, to give a moderate alarm; tell him to moderately rescue his wife from the hand of the ravisher; tell the mother to gradually extricate her babe from the fire into which it has fallen;—but urge me not to use moderation in a cause like the present. I am in earnest—I will not equivocate—I will not excuse—I will not retreat a single inch—AND I WILL BE HEARD.

Despite these passionate words, Garrison could not support the armed rebellion David Walker advocated in his *Appeal* (pp. 27, 86, and 103). A deeply religious man and a devoted pacifist, Garrison remained committed to the policy of moral suasion, relying on published and spoken arguments to convince others that slavery was a sin and therefore must be immediately abolished. He recognized the power of the *Appeal,* however, and even published excerpts from it in *The Liberator.*

Born in Newburyport, Massachusetts, Garrison was a printer and a journalist before he joined the Quaker abolitionist Benjamin Lundy in 1829 to publish the anti-slavery newspaper *The Genius of Universal Emancipation.* The following year, Garrison was jailed for libel after writing an editorial condemning a slave trader. He emerged from prison with renewed determination to fight for emancipation and equal rights. With the support of the free black population in the North—in 1834, three quarters of the subscribers to *The Liberator* were African American—Garrison became a leader of the invigorated abolitionist movement of the 1830s. He was instrumental in founding the New England Anti-Slavery Society in 1832 and the American Anti-Slavery Society in 1833, the first organizations dedicated to immediate emancipation. He became a vocal supporter of women's rights and an equally fierce opponent of political engagement, since he believed that fundamental elements of American government, such as the U.S. Constitution, were pro-slavery.

In the 1840s and 1850s, Garrison's influence waned as abolitionist leaders such as Frederick Douglass (p. 38) and Henry Highland Garnet (p. 80) began to argue for the need for political and physical resistance to slavery. Splinter groups established alternative anti-slavery societies, including the American and Foreign Anti-Slavery Society (an all-male group opposed to female participation in the movement) and the Liberty Party (a political organization). Garrison continued as head of the American Anti-Slavery Society and as publisher of *The Liberator* until 1865, when he declared victory with the ratification of the Thirteenth Amendment, which abolished slavery in the United States and its territories. Until his death, Garrison continued his work for women's rights, temperance, and pacifism.

From *The Liberator,* January 1, 1831; also, *The Liberator:* "To the Public," at PBS, Africans in America, part 4, Judgment Day, 1831–1865, www.pbs.org.

Believing, as we do, that men should never do evil that good may come; that a good end does not justify wicked means in the accomplishment of it; and that we ought to suffer, as did our Lord and his apostles, unresistingly—knowing that vengeance belongs to God, and he will certainly repay it where it is due;—believing all this, and that the Almighty will deliver the oppressed in a way which they know not, we deprecate the spirit and tendency of this Appeal. Nevertheless, it is not for the American people, as a nation, to denounce it as bloody or monstrous. Mr. Walker but pays them in their own coin, but follows their own creed, but adopts their own language. *We* do not preach rebellion—no, but submission and peace. Our enemies may accuse us of striving to stir up the slaves to revenge but their accusations are false, and made only to excite the prejudices of the whites, and to destroy our influence. We say, that the possibility of a bloody insurrection at the south fills us with dismay; and we avow, too, as plainly, that if any people were ever justified in throwing off the yoke of their tyrants, the slaves are that people. It is not we, but our guilty countrymen, who put arguments into the mouths, and swords into the hands of the slaves. Every sentence that they write—every word that they speak—

every resistance that they make, against foreign oppression, is a call upon their slaves to destroy them. Every Fourth of July celebration must embitter and inflame the minds of the slaves. And the late dinners, and illuminations, and orations, and shoutings, at the south, over the downfall of the French tyrant, Charles the Tenth, furnish so many reasons to the slaves why they should obtain their own rights by violence.

Some editors have affected to doubt where the deceased Walker wrote this pamphlet.—On this point, skepticism need not stumble: the *Appeal* bears the strongest internal evidence of having emanated from his own mind. No white man could have written in language so natural and enthusiastic.

HENRY HIGHLAND GARNET

An Address to the Slaves of the United States of America [1843]

Henry Highland Garnet's 1843 speech to the National Convention of Colored Citizens in Buffalo brought him to national attention with its call for a rebellion against slavery. Garnet (p. 80) had grown impatient with the gradualist strategy of moral reform favored by abolitionist leaders such as William Lloyd Garrison (p. 111) and, at the time, Frederick Douglass (p. 38). By 1843, Garnet had concluded that African Americans had to take action and assume responsibility for their own destiny. His call to direct action echoes that found in David Walker's *Appeal* (pp. 27, 86, and 103), a connection Garnet himself underscored in 1848, when he published his address alongside Walker's articles in a pamphlet to raise money for the Free-Soil party, a political party committed to restricting the extension of slavery into the western territories.

Garnet's conviction that change could be won only through direct resistance was based on his personal experience. Garnet escaped from slavery with his extended family when he was a child, settling in New Hope, Pennsylvania, with his sister and parents. He and his family maintained their freedom by splitting up after a

narrow escape from slave catchers in 1829, and Garnet later obtained a higher education despite such obstacles as being driven from one school by a segregationist mob. His conviction that African Americans needed to control their own destiny by whatever means necessary led him to found the African Civilization Society in 1858, which advocated emigration to Africa.

The minutes of the 1843 National Convention of Colored Citizens report that Garnet defended his speech, asserting that he was advocating only that enslaved people should confront their enslavers and demand to be free, not that they should rise up in violent rebellion. However, he did suggest the possibility of violent consequences if slaveholders refused to free their slaves, and he honored those who led uprisings. Garnet's proposal of resistance foreshadowed the strategy of "armed self-defense" advocated by groups such as the Black Panthers during the civil rights movement of the 1960s and 1970s (p. 583). In both cases, rebellion was presented as a defensive response to the violence of others, not as an offensive act of violence.

From David Walker, *Walker's Appeal, with a Brief Sketch of His Life by Henry Highland Garnet, and also Garnet's Address to the Slaves of the United States of America* (New York: J. H. Tobitt, 1848).

PREFACE.

The following Address was first read at the National Convention held at Buffalo, N.Y., in 1843. Since that time it has been slightly modified, retaining, however, all of its original doctrine. The document elicited more discussion than any other paper that was ever brought before that, or any other deliberative body of colored persons, and their friends. Gentlemen who opposed the Address, based their objections on these grounds. 1. That the document was war-like, and encouraged insurrection; and 2. That if the Convention should adopt it, that those delegates who lived near the borders of the slave states, would not dare to return to their homes. The Address was rejected by a small majority; and now in compliance with the earnest request of many who heard it, and in conformity to the wishes of numerous friends who are anxious to see it, the author now gives it to the public, praying God that this little book may be borne on the four winds of heaven, until the principles it contains shall be understood and adopted by every slave in the Union.

H. H. G.

Troy, N.Y., April 15, 1848.

ADDRESS TO THE SLAVES OF THE U.S.

BRETHREN AND FELLOW CITIZENS:

Your brethren of the north, east, and west have been accustomed to meet together in National Conventions, to sympathize with each other, and to weep over your unhappy condition. In these meetings we have addressed all classes of the free, but we have never until this time, sent a word of consolation and advice to you. We have been contented in sitting still and mourning over your sorrows, earnestly hoping that before this day, your sacred liberties would have been restored. But, we have hoped in vain. Years have rolled on, and tens of thousands have been borne on streams of blood, and tears, to the shores of eternity. While you have been oppressed, we have also been partakers with you; nor can we be free while you are enslaved. We therefore write to you as being bound with you.

Many of you are bound to us, not only by the ties of a common humanity, but we are connected by the more tender relations of parents, wives, husbands, children, brothers, and sisters, and friends. As such we most affectionately address you.

Slavery has fixed a deep gulf between you and us, and while it shuts out from you the relief and consolation which your friends would willingly render, it afflicts and persecutes you with a fierceness which we might not expect to see in the fiends of hell. But still the Almighty Father of Mercies has left to us a glimmering ray of hope, which shines out like a lone star in a cloudy sky. Mankind are becoming wiser, and better—the oppressor's power is fading, and you, every day, are becoming better informed, and more numerous. Your grievances, brethren, are many. We shall not attempt, in this short address, to present to the world, all the dark catalogue of this nation's sins, which have been committed upon an innocent people. Nor is it indeed, necessary, for you feel them from day to day, and all the civilized world look upon them with amazement.

Two hundred and twenty-seven years ago, the first of our injured race were brought to the shores of America. They came not with glad spirits to select their homes, in the New World. They came not with their own consent, to find an unmolested enjoyment of the blessings of this fruitful soil. The first dealings which they had with those calling themselves Christians, exhibited to them the worst features of corrupt and sordid hearts; and convinced them that no cruelty is too great, no villainy, and no robbery too abhorrent for even enlightened men to perform, when influenced by avarice, and lust. Neither did they come flying upon the wings of Liberty, to a land of freedom. But, they came with broken hearts, from their beloved native land, and were doomed to unrequited toil, and deep degradation. Nor did the evil of their bondage end at their emancipation by death. Succeeding generations inherited their chains, and millions have come from eternity into time, and have returned again to the world of spirits, cursed, and ruined by American Slavery.

The propagators of the system, or their immediate ancestors very soon discovered its growing evil, and its tremendous wickedness, and secret promises were made to destroy it. The gross inconsistency of a people holding slaves, who had themselves "ferried o'er the wave,"[1] for freedom's sake, was too apparent to be entirely overlooked. The voice of Freedom cried, "emancipate your Slaves." Humanity supplicated with tears, for the deliverance of the children of Africa. Wisdom urged her solemn plea. The bleeding captive plead his innocence, and pointed to Christianity who stood weeping at the cross. Jehovah frowned upon the nefarious institution, and thunderbolts, red with vengeance, struggled to leap forth to blast the guilty wretches who maintained it. But all was vain. Slavery had stretched its dark wings of death over the land, the Church stood silently by—the priests prophesied falsely, and the people loved to have it so. Its throne is established, and now it reigns triumphantly.

Nearly three millions of your fellow citizens, are prohibited by law, and public opinion, (which in this country is stronger than law), from reading the Book of Life. Your intellect has been destroyed as much as possible, and every ray of light they have attempted to shut out from your minds. The oppressors themselves have become involved in the ruin. They have become weak, sensual, and rapacious. They have cursed you— they have cursed themselves—they have cursed the earth which they have trod. In the language of a Southern statesman, we can truly say, "even the wolf, driven back long since by the approach of man, now returns after the lapse of a hundred years, and howls amid the desolations of slavery."[2]

The colonists threw the blame upon England. They said that the mother country entailed the evil upon them, and that they would rid themselves of it if they could. The world thought they were sincere, and the philanthropic pitied them. But time soon tested their sincerity. In a few years, the colonists grew strong and severed themselves from the British Government. Their Independence was declared, and they took their station among the sovereign powers of the earth. The declaration was a glorious document. Sages admired it, and the patriotic of every nation reverenced the God-like sentiments which it contained. When the power of Government returned to their hands, did they emancipate the slaves? No; they rather added new links to our chains. Were they ignorant of the principles of Liberty?

Certainly they were not. The sentiments of their revolutionary orators fell in burning eloquence upon their hearts, and with one voice they cried, LIBERTY OR DEATH. O, what a sentence was that! It ran from soul to soul like electric fire, and nerved the arm of thousands to fight in the holy cause of Freedom. Among the diversity of opinions that are entertained in regard to physical resistance, there are but a few found to gainsay that stern declaration. We are among those who do not.

SLAVERY! How much misery is comprehended in that single word. What mind is there that does not shrink from its direful effects? Unless the image of God is obliterated from the soul, all men cherish the love of Liberty. The nice discerning political economist does not regard the sacred right, more than the untutored African who roams in the wilds of Congo. Nor has the one more right to the full enjoyment of his freedom than the other. In every man's mind the good seeds of liberty are planted, and he who brings his fellow down so low, as to make him contented with a condition of slavery, commits the highest crime against God and man. Brethren, your oppressors aim to do this. They endeavor to make you as much like brutes as possible. When they have blinded the eyes of your mind—when they have embittered the sweet waters of life—when they have shut out the light which shines from the word of God—then, and not till then has American slavery done its perfect work.

TO SUCH DEGRADATION IT IS SINFUL IN THE EXTREME FOR YOU TO MAKE VOLUNTARY SUBMISSION. The divine commandments, you are in duty bound to reverence, and obey. If you do not obey them you will surely meet with the displeasure of the Almighty. He requires you to love him supremely, and your neighbor as yourself—to keep the Sabbath day holy—to search the Scriptures—and bring up your children with respect for his laws, and to worship no other God but him. But slavery sets all these at naught and hurls defiance in the face of Jehovah. The forlorn condition in which you are placed does not destroy your moral obligation to God. You are not certain of Heaven, because you suffer yourselves to remain in a state of slavery, where you cannot obey the commandments of

---

1. From William Cowper's poem *The Task*, book 2 (1785).
2. From an 1832 speech to the Virginia legislature by George Washington Parke Custis (1781–1857), a white American writer and army colonel who was the grandson of Martha Washington and the father-in-law of Robert E. Lee.

the Sovereign of the universe. If the ignorance of slavery is a passport to heaven, then it is a blessing, and no curse, and you should rather desire its perpetuity than its abolition. God will not receive slavery, nor ignorance, nor any other state of mind, for love, and obedience to him. Your condition does not absolve you from your moral obligation. The diabolical injustice by which your liberties are cloven down, NEITHER GOD, NOR ANGELS, OR JUST MEN, COMMAND YOU TO SUFFER FOR A SINGLE MOMENT. THEREFORE IT IS YOUR SOLEMN AND IMPERATIVE DUTY TO USE EVERY MEANS, BOTH MORAL, INTELLECTUAL, AND PHYSICAL, THAT PROMISE SUCCESS. If a band of heathen men should attempt to enslave a race of Christians, and to place their children under the influence of some false religion, surely, heaven would frown upon the men who would not resist such aggression, even to death. If, on the other hand, a band of Christians should attempt to enslave a race of heathen men and to entail slavery upon them, and to keep them in heathenism in the midst of Christianity, the God of heaven would smile upon every effort which the injured might make to disenthral themselves.

Brethren, it is as wrong for your lordly oppressors to keep you in slavery, as it was for the man thief to steal our ancestors from the coast of Africa. You should therefore now use the same manner of resistance, as would have been just in our ancestors, when the bloody foot prints of the first remorseless soul thief was placed upon the shores of our fatherland. The humblest peasant is as free in the sight of God, as the proudest monarch that ever swayed a sceptre. Liberty is a spirit sent out from God, and like its great Author, is no respecter of persons.

Brethren, the time has come when you must act for yourselves. It is an old and true saying, that "if hereditary bondmen would be free, they must themselves strike the blow."[3] You can plead your own cause, and do the work of emancipation better than any others. The nations of the old world are moving in the great cause of universal freedom, and some of them at least, will ere long, do you justice. The combined powers of Europe have placed their broad seal of disapprobation upon the African slave trade. But in the slave holding parts of the United States, the trade is as brisk as ever.

They buy and sell you as though you were brute beasts. The North has done much—her opinion of slavery in the abstract is known. But in regard to the South, we adopt the opinion of the New York Evangelist—"We have advanced so far, that the cause apparently waits for a more effectual door to be thrown open than has been yet." We are about to point you to that more effectual door. Look around you, and behold the bosoms of your loving wives, heaving with untold agonies! Hear the cries of your poor children! Remember the stripes your fathers bore. Think of the torture and disgrace of your noble mothers. Think of your wretched sisters, loving virtue and purity, as they are driven into concubinage, and are exposed to the unbridled lusts of incarnate devils. Think of the undying glory that hangs around the ancient name of Africa:—and forget not that you are native-born American citizens, and as such, you are justly entitled to all the rights that are granted to the freest. Think how many tears you have poured out upon the soil which you have cultivated with unrequited toil, and enriched with your blood; and then go to your lordly enslavers, and tell them plainly, that YOU ARE DETERMINED TO BE FREE. Appeal to their sense of justice, and tell them that they have no more right to oppress you, than you have to enslave them. Entreat them to remove the grievous burdens which they have imposed upon you, and to remunerate you for your labor. Promise them renewed diligence in the cultivation of the soil, if they will render to you an equivalent for your services. Point them to the increase of happiness and prosperity in the British West Indies, since the act of Emancipation. Tell them in language which they cannot misunderstand, of the exceeding sinfulness of slavery, and of a future judgment, and of the righteous retributions of an indignant God. Inform them that all you desire, is FREEDOM, and that nothing else will suffice. Do this, and for ever after cease to toil for the heartless tyrants, who give you no other reward but stripes and abuse. If they then commence the work of death, they, and not you, will be responsible for the consequences. You had far better all die—*die immediately,* than live slaves, and entail your wretchedness upon your posterity. If you would be free in this generation, here is your only hope.

3. Paraphrase of lines from *Childe Harold's Pilgrimage*, canto 2, stanza 76, by George Gordon Lord Byron, published between 1812 and 1818.

However much you and all of us may desire it, there is not much hope of Redemption without the shedding of blood. If you must bleed, let it all come at once—rather, *die freemen, than live to be slaves.* It is impossible, like the children of Israel, to make a grand Exodus from the land of bondage. THE PHARAOHS ARE ON BOTH SIDES OF THE BLOOD-RED WATERS! You cannot remove en masse, to the dominions of the British Queen—nor can you pass through Florida, and overrun Texas, and at last find peace in Mexico. The propagators of American slavery are spending their blood and treasure, that they may plant the black flag in the heart of Mexico, and riot in the halls of the Montezumas. In the language of the Rev. Robert Hall, when addressing the volunteers of Bristol, who were rushing forth to repel the invasion of Napoleon, who threatened to lay waste the fair homes of England, "Religion is too much interested in your behalf, not to shed over you her most gracious influences."

You will not be compelled to spend much time in order to become inured to hardships. From the first moment that you breathed the air of heaven, you have been accustomed to nothing else but hardships. The heroes of the American Revolution were never put upon harder fare, than a peck of corn, and a few herrings per week. You have not become enervated by the luxuries of life. Your sternest energies have been beaten out upon the anvil of severe trial. Slavery has done this, to make you subservient to its own purposes; but it has done more than this, it has prepared you for any emergency. If you receive good treatment, it is what you could hardly expect; if you meet with pain, sorrow, and even death, these are the common lot of the slaves.

Fellow-men! patient sufferers! behold your dearest rights crushed to the earth! See your sons murdered, and your wives, mothers, and sisters, doomed to prostitution! In the name of the merciful God! and by all that life is worth, let it no longer be a debateable question, whether it is better to choose LIBERTY or DEATH!

In 1822, Denmark Veazie,[4] of South Carolina, formed a plan for the liberation of his fellow men. In the whole history of human efforts to overthrow slavery, a more complicated and tremendous plan was never formed. He was betrayed by the treachery of his own people, and died a martyr to freedom. Many a brave hero fell, but History, faithful to her high trust, will transcribe his name on the same monument with Moses, Hampden, Tell, Bruce, and Wallace, Touissaint L'Overteur, Lafayette and Washington. That tremendous movement shook the whole empire of slavery. The guilty soul thieves were overwhelmed with fear. It is a matter of fact, that at that time, and in consequence of the threatened revolution, the slave states talked strongly of emancipation. But they blew but one blast of the trumpet of freedom, and then laid it aside. As these men became quiet, the slaveholders ceased to talk about emancipation: and now, behold your condition to-day! Angels sigh over it, and humanity has long since exhausted her tears in weeping on your account!

The patriotic Nathaniel Turner followed Denmark Veazie. He was goaded to desperation by wrong and injustice. By Despotism, his name has been recorded on the list of infamy, but future generations will number him among the noble and brave.

Next arose the immortal Joseph Cinque, the hero of the Amistad. He was a native African, and by the help of God he emancipated a whole ship-load of his fellow men on the high seas. And he now sings of liberty on the sunny hills of Africa, and beneath his native palm trees, where he hears the lion roar, and feels himself as free as that king of the forest. Next arose Madison Washington, that bright star of freedom, and took his station in the constellation of freedom. He was a slave on board the brig Creole, of Richmond, bound to New Orleans, that great slave mart, with a hundred and four others. Nineteen struck for liberty or death. But one life was taken, and the whole were emancipated, and the vessel was carried into Nassau, New Providence. Noble men! Those who have fallen in freedom's conflict, their memories will be cherished by the true hearted, and the God-fearing, in all future generations; those who are living, their names are surrounded by a halo of glory.

We do not advise you to attempt a revolution with the sword, because it would be INEXPEDIENT. Your numbers are too small, and moreover the rising spirit of the age, and the spirit of the gospel, are opposed to war

---

4. Denmark Vesey (ca. 1767–1822) organized what would have been the largest slave rebellion in American history and was executed, along with around thirty-five others, when the plan was discovered.

and bloodshed. But from this moment cease to labor for tyrants who will not remunerate you. Let every slave throughout the land do this, and the days of slavery are numbered. You cannot be more oppressed than you have been—you cannot suffer greater cruelties than you have already. RATHER DIE FREEMEN, THAN LIVE TO BE SLAVES. Remember that you are THREE MILLIONS.

It is in your power so to torment the God-cursed slaveholders, that they will be glad to let you go free. If the scale was turned, and black men were the masters, and white men the slaves, every destructive agent and element would be employed to lay the oppressor low. Danger and death would hang over their heads day and night. Yes, the tyrants would meet with plagues more terrible than those of Pharaoh. But you are a patient people. You act as though you were made for the special use of these devils. You act as though your

daughters were born to pamper the lusts of your masters and overseers. And worse than all, you tamely submit, while your lords tear your wives from your embraces, and defile them before your eyes. In the name of God we ask, are you men? Where is the blood of your fathers? Has it all run out of your veins? Awake, awake; millions of voices are calling you! Your dead fathers speak to you from their graves. Heaven, as with a voice of thunder, calls on you to arise from the dust.

Let your motto be RESISTANCE! RESISTANCE! RESISTANCE!—No oppressed people have ever secured their liberty without resistance. What kind of resistance you had better make, you must decide by the circumstances that surround you, and according to the suggestion of expediency. Brethren, adieu. Trust in the living God. Labor for the peace of the human race, and remember that you are three millions.

ANONYMOUS
Report on Debate between Frederick Douglass and Henry Highland Garnet at the National Convention of Colored Citizens [1843]

After escaping bondage in 1838, Frederick Douglass (p. 38) quickly emerged as a charismatic and influential lecturer for the burgeoning anti-slavery movement. Influenced by William Lloyd Garrison (p. 111), Douglass initially advocated the strategy of "moral suasion," which employed writings and speeches to persuade others that slavery was morally wrong and should be abolished. In the late 1840s, however, Douglass moved away from Garrisonian tactics in favor of political and social action—even physical resistance to slave catchers—that he came to consider more effective in bringing about change. When he gave the speech described here,

however, Douglass was still allied with Garrisonian abolitionism and he led the 1843 National Convention of Colored Citizens' opposition to Henry Highland Garnet's (p. 80) address to the convention, which called for rebellion. The summary of the debate in the convention's minutes reveals that Douglass critiqued Garnet's remarks in an hour-long speech, which was followed by Garnet's hour-and-a-half defense (the actual texts of these speeches have been lost). Douglass's position narrowly prevailed. Garnet's speech was sent to the business committee for modification but failed by one vote to be adopted by the convention.

From Howard Hollman Bell, *Minutes of the Proceedings of the National Negro Conventions, 1830–1864* (New York: Arno Press, 1964), n.p.

T he business committee reported, by their chairman, H. H. Garnit,[1] an address to the slaves of this land, prepared for the occasion, which was read and accepted.

C. B. Ray moved its reference to a select committee of five, of which he hoped Mr. Garnit, whose production the address was, would be the chairman. Mr. Ray remarked, that his object in moving its reference

1. Variant spellings appear throughout the proceedings, including this one for Henry Highland Garnet and, below, Frederic (for Frederick) Douglass.

to a committee was, that it might pass through a close and critical examination, and perceiving some points in it that might in print appear objectionable, to have it somewhat modified, and also that it might proceed forth from a special committee, of which the author should be the chairman, and thus receive the usual credit due to chairman of committees presenting documents to public bodies.

H. H. Garnit arose to oppose the motion of reference, and anticipating more than was contemplated by the mover, and fearing the fate of the address, if the motion prevailed, proceeded to give his reasons why the motion should not prevail, and why the address should be adopted by the Convention, and sent out with its sanction; in doing which Mr. Garnit went into the whole merits of the case. He reviewed the abominable system of slavery, showed its mighty workings, its deeds of darkness and of death—how it robbed parents of children, and children of parents, husbands of wives; how it prostituted the daughters of the slaves; how it murdered the colored man. He referred to the fate of Denmark Vesey and his accomplices—of Nat Turner; to the burning of McIntosh, to the case of Madison Washington, as well as to many other cases—to what had been done to move the slaveholders to let go their grasp, and asked what more could be done—if we have not waited long enough—if it were not time to speak louder and longer—to take higher ground and other steps. Mr. Garnit, in this speech, occupied nearly one hour and a half, the rule having been suspended to allow him to proceed. It was a masterly effort, and the whole Convention, full as it was, was literally infused with tears. Mr. Garnit concluded amidst great applause.

Frederic Douglass, not concurring with certain points in the address, nor with the sentiments advanced by Mr. Garnit, arose to advocate its reference to the committee, and also to reply to Mr. Garnit. Mr. Douglass remarked, that there was too much physical force, both in the address and the remarks of the speaker last up. He was for trying the moral means a little longer; that the address, could it reach the slaves, and the advice, either of the address or the gentleman, be followed, while it might not lead the slaves to rise in insurrection for liberty, would, nevertheless, and necessarily be the occasion of an insurrection; and that was what he wished in no way to have any agency in bringing about, and what we were called upon to avoid; and therefore, he hoped the motion to refer would prevail.

Mr. Garnit arose to reply, and said that the most the address said in sentiment, with what the gentleman excepted to, was, that it advised the slaves to go to their masters and tell them they wanted their liberty, and had come to ask for it; and if the master refused it, to tell them, then we shall take it, let the consequence be what it may.

Mr. Douglass said, that would lead to an insurrection, and we were called upon to avoid such a catastrophy. He wanted emancipation in a better way, as he expected to have it.

The question of reference was further discussed by James N. Gloucester, taking the same view of the case with Mr. Douglass; and by Wm. C. Munro, who opposed its reference, concurring fully in the views expressed by Mr. Garnit.

Harriet Beecher Stowe
Letter to William Lloyd Garrison [1853]

In 1847, after returning to the United States from an eighteen-month speaking tour of Britain and Ireland, Frederick Douglass (p. 38) began moving away from the positions held by the abolitionist leader William Lloyd Garrison (p. 111), who had been a friend and mentor to him. An initial difference centered on Garrison's argument that the northern states should secede from the Union; Douglass came to believe secession would only lead to the abandonment of enslaved African Americans in the South. Douglass also launched his own newspaper, *The North Star*, in 1847, over the objections of Garrison, who advised him to focus his career on oratory.

Douglass's views moved further from Garrison's later that year, after Douglass met John Brown and was impressed by his passionate argument for using direct action to end slavery.

Throughout the late 1840s and the 1850s, the division between Douglass and Garrison grew as Douglass came to believe more firmly that abolitionists should participate in the political system, violence could have a legitimate use in the fight against slavery, and the U.S. Constitution was not inherently pro-slavery. The rift was propelled not just by growing differences of opinion but also by personal issues, including Douglass's desire to be free of Garrison's attempts to shape his opinions and the direction of his career. The bitterness between the two camps was apparent in 1852 at the annual meeting of the American Anti-Slavery Society (which Garrison had co-founded), when Douglass engaged in heated debate with his former Garrisonian allies.

Concerned for her two friends and for the anti-slavery cause, Harriet Beecher Stowe (1811–1896), the author of *Uncle Tom's Cabin* (published as a serial in 1851–1852 and in book form in 1852), attempted to mend the rift between the two leaders. However, her meeting with Douglass and her subsequent letter to Garrison, dated December 19, 1853, failed to bring about a reconciliation. Not until 1861, after the outbreak of the Civil War, did Douglass and Garrison renew their friendship.

Stowe's enormously popular novel galvanized many in the North to oppose slavery and helped fuel the Civil War. Despite that influence, many black leaders criticized its apparent support for African colonization. *Uncle Tom's Cabin* also became controversial for its characterizations of African Americans, particularly the genial Uncle Tom. The combination of genuine anti-slavery conviction and a lack of direct connection to African American experience that pervades *Uncle Tom's Cabin* also marks Stowe's analysis of Douglass in her letter to Garrison. (For more on the various responses to *Uncle Tom's Cabin*, see pp. 95–102.)

From *Life and Letters of Harriet Beecher Stowe*, ed. Annie Fields (Cambridge, Mass.: Riverside Press, 1897), pp. 214–15.

CABIN, December 19, 1853.

MR. GARRISON.

Dear Sir,—After seeing you, I enjoyed the pleasure of a personal interview with Mr. Douglass, and I feel bound in justice to say that the impression was far more satisfactory than I had anticipated.

There did not appear to be any deep underlying stratum of bitterness; he did not seem to me malignant or revengeful. I think it was only a temporary excitement and one which he will outgrow.

I was much gratified with the growth and development both of his mind and heart. I am satisfied that his change of sentiment was not a mere political one but a genuine growth of his own conviction. A vigorous reflective mind like his cast among those who nourish these new sentiments is naturally led to modified views.

At all events, he holds no opinion which he cannot defend, with a variety of richness of thought and expression and an aptness of illustration which shows it to be a growth from the soil of his own mind with a living root, and not a twig broken off other men's thoughts and stock down to subserve a temporary purpose.

His plans for the elevation of his own race are manly, sensible, comprehensive; he has evidently observed closely and thought deeply and will, I trust, act efficiently.

Yon speak of him as an apostate. I cannot but regard this language as unjustly severe. Why is he any more to be called an apostate for having spoken ill-tempered things of former friends than they for having spoken severely and cruelly as they have of him! Where is this work of excommunication to end! Is there but one true anti-slavery church and all others infidels! Who shall declare which it is! I feel bound to remonstrate with this—for the same reason that I do with slavery—because I think it an injustice. I must say still farther, that if the first allusion to his family concerns was unfortunate this last one is more unjustifiable still. I am utterly surprised at it. As a friend to you and to him, I view it with the deepest concern and regret.

What Douglass *is* really, time will show. I trust that he will make no farther additions to the already unfortunate controversial literature of the cause. *Silence* in this case will be eminently—*golden.*

I must indulge the hope you will see reason at some future time to alter your opinion and that what you now cast aside as worthless shall yet appear to be a treasure. There is abundant room in the anti-slavery field for him to perform a work without crossing the track or impeding the movements of his old friends, and perhaps in some future time, meeting each other from opposite quarters of a victorious field, you may yet shake hands together.

I write this note, because in the conversation I had with you, and also with Miss Weston, I admitted so much that was unfavorable to Mr. Douglass that I felt bound in justice to state the more favorable views which had arisen to my mind.

Very sincerely your friend,

H. B. STOWNE.

FREDERICK DOUGLASS

Speech on the Dred Scott Decision [1857]

"Power concedes nothing without a demand," Frederick Douglass declared in an August 1857 speech on West Indian emancipation. "Find out just what any people will quietly submit to and you have found out the exact amount of injustice and wrong which will be imposed upon them; and these will continue till they are resisted with either words or blows, or with both." Douglass's stress on the need for resistance, whether verbal or physical, highlights his shift away from the Garrisonian strategy of moral suasion. In a speech earlier that year, following the U.S. Supreme Court's decision in *Dred Scott v. Sandford*, Douglass underscores his break with Garrison (p. 111) not only over the issue of political and physical resistance, but also over the question of whether the Constitution and the Union itself were worthy of preservation.

Douglass's faith in the governing principals of the United States, which he underscores with his support of the Constitution and the Union, is striking in light of the specifics of the *Dred Scott* decision. Dred Scott, who was enslaved in St. Louis, first filed suit for his freedom in 1846, but over ten years passed before his case reached the Supreme Court. The Court ruled not only that Scott did not have the right to sue for his freedom in a federal court because he was not a U.S. citizen, but that no one of African descent, whether enslaved or free, could become a U.S. citizen. In his majority decision, Chief Justice Roger B. Taney declared, "The Negro has no rights that a white man is bound to respect." Moreover, the Court decided that Congress could not outlaw slavery in the territories, thereby overturning key parts of the Missouri Compromise of 1820. In supporting the Constitution in spite of this landmark decision, Douglass makes a clear distinction between the administration of the Constitution and the document itself.

Frederick Douglass Papers, Library of Congress.

While four millions of our fellow countrymen are in chains—while men, women, and children are bought and sold on the auction-block with horses, sheep, and swine—while the remorseless slave-whip draws the warm blood of our common humanity—it is meet that we assemble as we have done to-day, and lift up our hearts and voices in earnest denunciation of the vile and shocking abomination. It is not for us to be governed by our hopes or our fears in this great work; yet it is natural on occasions like this, to survey the position of the great struggle which is going on between slavery and freedom, and to dwell upon such signs of encouragement as may have been lately developed, and the state of feeling these signs or events have occasioned in us and among the people generally. It is a fitting time to take an observation to ascertain where we are, and what our prospects are.

To many, the prospects of the struggle against slavery seem far from cheering. Eminent men, North and South, in Church and State, tell us that the omens are all against us. Emancipation, they tell us, is a wild, delusive idea; the price of human flesh was never higher than now; slavery was never more closely entwined about the hearts and affections of the southern people than now; that whatever of conscientious scruple, religious conviction, or public policy, which opposed the system of slavery forty or fifty years ago, has subsided; and that slavery never reposed upon a firmer basis than now. Completing this picture of the happy and prosperous condition of this system of wickedness, they tell us that this state of things is to be set to our account. Abolition agitation has done it all. How deep is the misfortune of my poor, bleeding people, if this be so! How lost their condition, if even the efforts of their friends but sink them deeper in ruin!

Without assenting to this strong representation of the increasing strength and stability of slavery, without denouncing what of untruth pervades it, I own myself not insensible to the many difficulties and discouragement, that beset us on every hand. They fling their broad and gloomy shadows across the pathway of every thoughtful colored man in this country. For one, I see them clearly, and feel them sadly. With an earnest, aching heart, I have long looked for the realization of the hope of my people. Standing, as it were, barefoot, and treading upon the sharp and flinty rocks of the present, and looking out upon the boundless sea of the future, I have sought, in my humble way, to penetrate the intervening mists and clouds, and, perchance, to descry, in the dim and shadowy distance, the white flag of freedom, the precise speck of time at which the cruel bondage of my people should end, and the long entombed millions rise from the foul grave of slavery and death. But of that time I can know nothing, and you can know nothing. All is uncertain at that point. One thing, however, is certain; slaveholders are in earnest, and mean to cling to their slaves as long as they can, and to the bitter end. They show no sign of a wish to quit their iron grasp upon the sable throats of their victims. Their motto is, "a firmer hold and a tighter grip" for every new effort that is made to break their cruel power. The case is one of life or death with them, and they will give up only when they must do that or do worse.

In one view the slaveholders have a decided advantage over all opposition. It is well to notice this advantage—the advantage of complete organization. They are organized; and yet were not at the pains of creating their organizations. The State governments, where the system of slavery exists, are complete slavery organizations. The church organizations in those States are equally at the service of slavery; while the Federal Government, with its army and navy, from the chief magistracy in Washington, to the Supreme Court, and thence to the chief marshalship at New York, is pledged to support, defend, and propagate the crying curse of human bondage. The pen, the purse, and the sword, are united against the simple truth, preached by humble men in obscure places.

This is one view. It is, thank God, only one view; there is another, and a brighter view. David, you know, looked small and insignificant when going to meet Goliath, but looked larger when he had slain his foe. The Malakoff was, to the eye of the world, impregnable, till the hour it fell before the shot and shell of the allied army. Thus hath it ever been. Oppression, organized as ours is, will appear invincible up to the very hour of its fall. Sir, let us look at the other side, and see if there are not some things to cheer our heart and nerve us up anew in the good work of emancipation.

Take this fact—for it is a fact—the anti-slavery movement has, from first to last, suffered no abatement. It has gone forth in all directions, and is now felt in the remotest extremities of the Republic.

It started small, and was without capital either in men or money. The odds were all against it. It literally had nothing to lose, and everything to gain. There was ignorance to be enlightened, error to be combatted, conscience to be awakened, prejudice to be overcome, apathy to be aroused, the right of speech to be secured, mob violence to be subdued, and a deep, radical change to be inwrought in the mind and heart of the whole nation. This great work, under God, has gone on, and gone on gloriously.

Amid all changes, fluctuations, assaults, and adverses of every kind, it has remained firm in its purpose, steady in its aim, onward and upward, defying all opposition, and never losing a single battle. Our strength is in the growth of anti-slavery conviction, and this has never halted.

There is a significant vitality about this abolition movement. It has taken a deeper, broader, and more lasting hold upon the national heart than ordinary reform movements. Other subjects of much interest come and go, expand and contract, blaze and vanish, but the huge question of American Slavery, comprehending, as it does, not merely the weal or the woe of four millions, and their countless posterity, but the weal or the woe of this entire nation, must increase in magnitude and in majesty with every hour of its history. From a cloud not bigger than a man's hand, it has overspread the heavens. It has risen from a grain not bigger than a mustard seed. Yet see the fowls of the air, how they crowd its branches.

Politicians who cursed it, now defend it; ministers, once dumb, now speak in its praise; and presses, which once flamed with hot denunciations against it, now surround the sacred cause as by a wall of living fire. Politicians go with it as a pillar of cloud by day, and the press as a pillar of fire by night.[1] With these ancient tokens of success, I, for one, will not despair of our cause.

Those who have undertaken to suppress and crush out this agitation for Liberty and humanity, have been most woefully disappointed. Many who have engaged to put it down, have found themselves put down. The agitation has pursued them in all their meanderings, broken in upon their seclusion, and, at the very moment of fancied security, it has settled down upon them like a mantle of unquenchable fire. Clay, Calhoun, and Webster each tried his hand at suppressing the agitation; and they went to their graves disappointed and defeated.

Loud and exultingly have we been told that the slavery question is settled, and settled forever. You remember it was settled thirty-seven years ago, when Missouri was admitted into the Union with a slaveholding constitution, and slavery prohibited in all territory north of thirty-six degrees of north latitude. Just fifteen years afterwards, it was settled again by voting down the right of petition, and gagging down free discussion in Congress.[2] Ten years after this it was settled again by the annexation of Texas, and with it the war with Mexico. In 1850 it was again settled. This was called a final settlement. By it slavery was virtually declared to be the equal of Liberty, and should come into the Union on the same terms. By it the right and the power to hunt down men, women, and children, in every part of this country, was conceded to our southern brethren, in order to keep them in the Union. Four years after this settlement, the whole question was once more settled, and settled by a settlement which unsettled all the former settlements.

The fact is, the more the question has been settled, the more it has needed settling. The space between the different settlements has been strikingly on the decrease. The first stood longer than any of its successors.

There is a lesson in these decreasing spaces. The first stood fifteen years—the second, ten years—the third, five years—the fourth stood four years—and the fifth has stood the brief space of two years.

This last settlement must be called the Taney settlement. We are now told, in tones of lofty exultation, that the day is lost—all lost—and that we might as well give up the struggle. The highest authority has spoken. The voice of the Supreme Court has gone out over the troubled waves of the National Conscience, saying peace, be still.

This infamous decision of the Slaveholding wing of the Supreme Court maintains that slaves are within the contemplation of the Constitution of the United States, property; that slaves are property in the same sense that horses, sheep, and swine are property; that the old doctrine that slavery is a creature of local law is false; that the right of the slaveholder to his slave does not depend upon the local law, but is secured wherever the Constitution of the United States extends; that Congress has no right to prohibit slavery anywhere; that slavery may go in safety anywhere under the star-spangled banner; that colored persons of African

1. Reference to Exodus 13:21, "And the LORD went before them by day in a pillar of a cloud, to lead them the way; and by night in a pillar of fire, to give them light; to go by day and night."
2. Between 1836 and 1844, Congress passed a series of "gag rules," resolutions banning the reading or discussion of petitions against slavery.

descent have no rights that white men are bound to respect; that colored men of African descent are not and cannot be citizens of the United States.

You will readily ask me how I am affected by this devilish decision—this judicial incarnation of wolfishness? My answer is, and no thanks to the slaveholding wing of the Supreme Court, my hopes were never brighter than now.

I have no fear that the National Conscience will be put to sleep by such an open, glaring, and scandalous tissue of lies as that decision is, and has been, over and over, shown to be.

The Supreme Court of the United States is not the only power in this world. It is very great, but the Supreme Court of the Almighty is greater. Judge Taney can do many things, but he cannot perform impossibilities. He cannot bale out the ocean, annihilate the firm old earth, or pluck the silvery star of liberty from our Northern sky. He may decide, and decide again; but he cannot reverse the decision of the Most High. He cannot change the essential nature of things—making evil good, and good evil.

Happily for the whole human family, their rights have been defined, declared, and decided in a court higher than the Supreme Court. "There is a law," says Brougham, "above all the enactments of human codes, and by that law, unchangeable and eternal, man cannot hold property in man."

Your fathers have said that man's right to liberty is self-evident. There is no need of argument to make it clear. The voices of nature, of conscience, of reason, and of revelation, proclaim it as the right of all rights, the foundation of all trust, and of all responsibility. Man was born with it. It was his before he comprehended it. The *deed* conveying it to him is written in the centre of his soul, and is recorded in Heaven. The sun in the sky is not more palpable to the sight than man's right to liberty is to the moral vision. To decide against this right in the person of Dred Scott, or the humblest and most whip-scarred bondman in the land, is to decide against God. It is an open rebellion against God's government. It is an attempt to undo what God has done, to blot out the broad distinction instituted by the *Allwise* between men and things, and to change the image and superscription of the everliving God into a speechless piece of merchandise.

Such a decision cannot stand. God will be true though every man be a liar. We can appeal from this hell-black judgment of the Supreme Court, to the court of common sense and common humanity. We can appeal from man to God. If there is no justice on earth, there is yet justice in heaven. You may close your Supreme Court against the black man's cry for justice, but you cannot, thank God, close against him the ear of a sympathising world, nor shut up the Court of Heaven. All that is merciful and just, on earth and in Heaven, will execrate and despise this edict of Taney.

If it were at all likely that the people of these free States would tamely submit to this demonical judgment, I might feel gloomy and sad over it, and possibly it might be necessary for my people to look for a home in some other country. But as the case stands, we have nothing to fear.

In one point of view, we, the abolitionists and colored people, should meet this decision, unlooked for and monstrous as it appears, in a cheerful spirit. This very attempt to blot out forever the hopes of an enslaved people may be one necessary link in the chain of events preparatory to the downfall and complete overthrow of the whole slave system.

The whole history of the anti-slavery movement is studded with proof that all measures devised and executed with a view to ally and diminish the anti-slavery agitation, have only served to increase, intensify, and embolden that agitation. This wisdom of the crafty has been confounded, and the counsels of the ungodly brought to nought. It was so with the Fugitive Slave Bill. It was so with the Kansas-Nebraska Bill; and it will be so with this last and most shocking of all pro-slavery devices, this Taney decision.

When great transactions are involved, where the fate of millions is concerned, where a long enslaved and suffering people are to be delivered, I am superstitious enough to believe that the finger of the Almighty may be seen bringing good out of evil, and making the wrath of man redound to his honor, hastening the triumph of righteousness.

The American people have been called upon, in a most striking manner, to abolish and put away forever the system of slavery. The subject has been pressed upon their attention in all earnestness and sincerity. The cries of the slave have gone forth to the world, and up to the throne of God. This decision, in my view, is a means of keeping the nation awake on the subject. It is another proof that God does not mean that we shall go to sleep, and forget that we are a slaveholding nation.

Step by step we have seen the slave power advancing; poisoning, corrupting, and perverting the institutions of the country; growing more and more haughty, imperious, and exacting. The white man's liberty has been marked out for the same grave with the black man's.

The ballot box is desecrated, God's law set at nought, armed legislators stalk the halls of Congress, freedom of speech is beaten down in the Senate. The rivers and highways are infested by border ruffians, and white men are made to feel the iron heel of slavery. This ought to arouse us to kill off the hateful thing. They are solemn warnings to which the white people, as well as the black people, should take heed.

If these shall fail, judgment, more fierce or terrible, may come. The lightning, whirlwind, and earthquake may come. Jefferson said that he trembled for his country when he reflected that God is just, and his justice cannot sleep forever. The time may come when even the crushed worm may turn under the tyrant's feet. Goaded by cruelty, stung by a burning sense of wrong, in an awful moment of depression and desperation, the bondman and bondwoman at the south may rush to one wild and deadly struggle for freedom. Already slaveholders go to bed with bowie knives, and apprehend death at their dinners. Those who enslave, rob, and torment their cooks, may well expect to find death in their dinner-pots.

The world is full of violence and fraud, and it would be strange if the slave, the constant victim of both fraud and violence, should escape the contagion. He, too, may learn to fight the devil with fire, and for one, I am in no frame of mind to pray that this may be long deferred.

Two remarkable occurrences have followed the presidential election; one was the unaccountable sickness traced to the National Hotel at Washington, and the other was the discovery of a plan among the slaves, in different localities, to slay their oppressors. Twenty or thirty of the suspected were put to death. Some were shot, some hanged, some burned, and some died under the lash. One brave man owned himself well acquainted with the conspiracy, but said he would rather die than

disclose the facts. He received seven hundred and fifty lashes, and his noble spirit went away to the God who gave it. The name of this hero has been by the meanness of tyrants suppressed. Such a man redeems his race. He is worthy to be mentioned with the Hoffers and Tells, the noblest heroes of history. These insurrectionary movements have been put down, but they may break out at any time, under the guidance of higher intelligence, and with a more invincible spirit.

> The fire thus kindled, may be revived again;
> The flames are extinguished, but the embers remain;
> One terrible blast may produce an ignition,
> Which shall wrap the whole South in wild conflagration.

> The pathway of tyrants lies over volcanoes
> The very air they breathe is heavy with sorrows;
> Agonizing heart-throbs convulse them while sleeping,
> And the wind whispers Death as over them sweeping.

By all the laws of nature, civilization, and of progress, slavery is a doomed system. Not all the skill of politicians, North and South, not all the sophistries of Judges, not all the fulminations of a corrupt press, not all the hypocritical prayers, or the hypocritical refusals to pray of a hollow-hearted priesthood, not all the devices of sin and Satan, can save the vile thing from extermination.

Already a gleam of hope breaks upon us from the south-west. One Southern city has grieved and astonished the whole South by a preference for freedom. The wedge has entered. Dred Scott, of Missouri, goes into slavery, but St. Louis declares for freedom. The judgment of Taney is not the judgment of St Louis.

It may be said that this demonstration in St. Louis is not to be taken as an evidence of sympathy with the slave; that it is purely a white man's victory. I admit it. Yet I am glad that white men, bad as they generally are, should gain a victory over slavery. I am willing to accept a judgment against slavery, whether supported by white or black reasons—though I would much rather have it supported by both. He that is not against us, is on our part.

Come what will, I hold it to be morally certain that, sooner or later, by fair means or foul means, in quiet or in tumult, in peace or in blood, in judgment or in mercy, slavery is doomed to cease out of this otherwise goodly land, and liberty is destined to become the settled law of this Republic.

I base my sense of the certain overthrow of slavery, in part, upon the nature of the American Government, the Constitution, the tendencies of the age, and the character of the American people; and this, notwithstanding the important decision of Judge Taney.

I know of no soil better adapted to the growth of reform than American soil. I know of no country where the conditions for affecting great changes in the settled order of things, for the development of right ideas of liberty and humanity, are more favorable than here in these United States.

The very groundwork of this government is a good repository of Christian civilization. The Constitution, as well as the Declaration of Independence, and the sentiments of the founders of the Republic, give us a platform broad enough, and strong enough, to support the most comprehensive plans for the freedom and elevation of all the people of this country, without regard to color, class, or clime.

There is nothing in the present aspect of the anti-slavery question which should drive us into the extravagance and nonsense of advocating a dissolution of the American Union as a means of overthrowing slavery, or freeing the North from the malign influence of slavery upon the morals of the Northern people. While the press is at liberty, and speech is free, and the ballot-box is open to the people of the sixteen free States; while the slaveholders are but four hundred thousand in number, and we are fourteen millions; while the mental and moral power of the nation is with us; while we are really the strong and they are the weak, it would look worse than cowardly to retreat from the Union.

If the people of the North have not the power to cope with these four hundred thousand slaveholders inside the Union, I see not how they could get out of the Union. The strength necessary to move the Union must ever be less than is required to break it up. If we have got to conquer the slave power to get out of the Union, I for one would much rather conquer, and stay in the Union. The latter, it strikes me, is the far more rational mode of action.

I make these remarks in no servile spirit, nor in any superstitious reverence for a mere human arrangement. If I felt the Union to be a curse, I should not be far behind the very chiefest of the disunion Abolitionists in denouncing it. But the evil to be met and abolished is not in the Union. The power arrayed against us is not a parchment.

It is not in changing the dead form of the Union, that slavery is to be abolished in this country. We have to do not with the dead, but the living; not with the past, but the living present.

Those who seek slavery in the Union, and who are everlastingly dealing blows upon the Union, in the belief that they are killing slavery, are most woefully mistaken. They are fighting a dead form instead of a living and powerful reality. It is clearly not because of the peculiar character of our Constitution that we have slavery, but the wicked pride, love of power, and selfish perverseness of the American people. Slavery lives in this country not because of any paper Constitution, but in the moral blindness of the American people, who persuade themselves that they are safe, though the rights of others may be struck down.

Besides, I think it would be difficult to hit upon any plan less likely to abolish slavery than the dissolution of the Union. The most devoted advocates of slavery, those who make the interests of slavery their constant study, seek a dissolution of the Union as their final plan for preserving slavery from Abolition, and their ground is well taken. Slavery lives and flourishes best in the absence of civilization; a dissolution of the Union would shut up the system in its own congenial barbarism.

The dissolution of the Union would not give the North one single additional advantage over slavery to the people of the North, but would manifestly take from them many which they now certainly possess.

Within the Union we have a firm basis of anti-slavery operation. National welfare, national prosperity, national reputation and honor, and national scrutiny; common rights, common duties, and common country, are so many bridges over which we can march to the destruction of slavery. To fling away these advantages because James Buchanan is President, or Judge Taney gives a lying decision in favor of slavery, does not enter into my notion of common sense.

Mr. Garrison and his friends have been telling us that, while in the Union, we are responsible for slavery; and in so telling us, he and they have told us the truth. But in telling us that we shall cease to be responsible for slavery by dissolving the Union, he and they have not told us the truth.

There now, clearly, is no freedom from responsibility for slavery, but in the Abolition of slavery. We have gone too far in this business now to sum up our whole duty in the cant phrase of "no Union with slaveholders."

To desert the family hearth may place the recreant husband out of the sight of his hungry children, but it cannot free him from responsibility. Though he should roll the waters of three oceans between him and them, he could not roll from his soul the burden of his responsibility to them; and, as with the private family, so in this instance with the national family. To leave the slave in his chains, in the hands of cruel masters who are too strong for him, is not to free ourselves from responsibility. Again: If I were on board of a pirate ship, with a company of men and women whose lives and liberties I had put in jeopardy, I would not clear my soul of their blood by jumping in the long boat, and singing out no union with pirates. My business would be to remain on board, and while I never would perform a single act of piracy again, I should exhaust every means given me by my position, to save the lives and liberties of those against whom I had committed piracy. In like manner, I hold it is our duty to remain inside this Union, and use all the power to restore to enslaved millions their precious and God-given rights. The more we have done by our voice and our votes, in times past, to rivet their galling fetters, the more clearly and solemnly comes the sense of duty to remain, to undo what we have done. Where, I ask, could the slave look for release from slavery if the Union were dissolved? I have an abiding conviction founded upon long and careful study of the certain effects of slavery upon the moral sense of slaveholding communities, that if the slaves are ever delivered from bondage, the power will emanate from the free States. All hope that the slaveholders will be self-moved to this great act of justice, is groundless and delusive. Now, as of old, the Redeemer

must come from above, not from beneath. To dissolve the Union would be to withdraw the emancipating power from the field.

But I am told this is the argument of expediency. I admit it, and am prepared to show that what is expedient in this instance is right. "Do justice, though the heavens fall." Yes, that is a good motto, but I deny that it would be doing justice to the slave to dissolve the Union and leave the slave in his chains to get out by the clemency of his master, or the strength of his arms. Justice to the slave is to break his chains, and going out of the union is to leave him in his chains, and without any probable chance of getting out of them.

But I come now to the great question as to the constitutionality of slavery. The recent slaveholding decision, as well as the teachings of anti-slavery men, make this a fit time to discuss the constitutional pretensions of slavery.

The people of the North are a law abiding people. They love order and respect the means to that end. This sentiment has sometimes led them to the folly and wickedness of trampling upon the very life of law, to uphold its dead form. This was so in the execution of that thrice accursed Fugitive Slave Bill. Burns and Simms were sent back to the hell of slavery after they had looked upon Bunker Hill, and heard liberty thunder in Faneuil Hall. The people permitted this outrage in obedience to the popular sentiment of reverence for law. While men thus respect law, it becomes a serious matter so to interpret the law as to make it operate against liberty. I have a quarrel with those who fling the Supreme Law of this land between the slave and freedom. It is a serious matter to fling the weight of the Constitution against the cause of human liberty, and those who do it, take upon them a heavy responsibility. Nothing but absolute necessity, shall, or ought to drive me to such a concession to slavery.

When I admit that slavery is constitutional, I must see slavery recognized in the Constitution. I must see that it is there plainly stated that one man of a certain description has a right of property in the body and soul of another man of a certain description. There must be no room for a doubt. In a matter so important as the loss of liberty, everything must be proved beyond all reasonable doubt.

The well known rules of legal interpretation bear me out in this stubborn refusal to see slavery where slavery is not, and only to see slavery where it is.

The Supreme Court has, in its day, done something better than make slaveholding decisions. It has laid down rules of interpretation which are in harmony with the true idea and object of law and liberty.

It has told us that the intention of legal instruments must prevail; and that this must be collected from its words. It has told us that language must be construed strictly in favor of liberty and justice.

It has told us where rights are infringed, where fundamental principles are overthrown, where the general system of the law is departed from, the Legislative intention must be expressed with irresistible clearness, to induce a court of justice to suppose a design to effect such objects.

These rules are as old as law. They rise out of the very elements of law. It is to protect human rights, and promote human welfare. Law is in its nature opposed to wrong, and must everywhere be presumed to be in favor of the right. The pound of flesh, but not one drop of blood,[3] is a sound rule of legal interpretation.

Besides there is another rule of law as well of common sense, which requires us to look to the ends for which a law is made, and to construe its details in harmony with the ends sought.

Now let us approach the Constitution from the standpoint thus indicated, and instead of finding in it a warrant for the stupendous system of robbery, comprehended in the term slavery, we shall find it strongly against that system.

"We, the people of the United States, in order to form a more perfect Union, establish justice, insure domestic tranquility, provide for the common defence, promote the general welfare, and secure the blessings of liberty to ourselves and our posterity, do ordain and establish this constitution for the United States of America."

Such are the objects announced by the instrument itself, and they are in harmony with the Declaration of Independence, and the principles of human well-being.

Six objects are here declared, "Union," "defence," "welfare," "tranquility," and "justice," and "liberty."

Neither in the preamble nor in the body of the Constitution is there a single mention of the term *slave* or *slave holder, slave master* or *slave state,* neither is there any reference to the color, or the physical peculiarities of any part of the people of the United States. Neither is there anything in the Constitution standing alone, which would imply the existence of slavery in this country.

"We, the people"—not we, the white people—not we, the citizens, or the legal voters—not we, the privileged class, and excluding all other classes but we, the people; not we, the horses and cattle, but we the people—the men and women, the human inhabitants of the United States, do ordain and establish this Constitution, &c.

I ask, then, any man to read the Constitution, and tell me where, if he can, in what particular that instrument affords the slightest sanction of slavery?

Where will he find a guarantee for slavery? Will he find it in the declaration that no person shall be deprived of life, liberty, or property, without due process of law? Will he find it in the declaration that the Constitution was established to secure the blessing of liberty? Will he find it in the right of the people to be secure in their persons and papers, and houses, and effects? Will he find it in the clause prohibiting the enactment by any State of a bill of attainder?

These all strike at the root of slavery, and any one of them, but faithfully carried out, would put an end to slavery in every State in the American Union.

Take, for example, the prohibition of a bill of attainder. That is a law entailing on the child the misfortunes of the parent. This principle would destroy slavery in every State of the Union.

---

3. Allusion to Portia's ruling in Shakespeare's *The Merchant of Venice,* Act IV, Scene I, which prevents a death as settlement of a debt:

> Then take thy bond, take thou thy pound of flesh;
> But, in the cutting it, if thou dost shed
> One drop of Christian blood, thy lands and goods
> Are, by the laws of Venice, confiscate
> Unto the state of Venice.

The law of slavery is a law of attainder. The child is property because its parent was property, and suffers as a slave because its parent suffered as a slave.

Thus the very essence of the whole slave code is in open violation of a fundamental provision of the Constitution, and is in open and flagrant violation of all the objects set forth in the Constitution.

While this and much more can be said, and has been said, and much better said, by Lysander Spooner, William Goodell, Beriah Green, and Gerrit Smith, in favor of the entire unconstitutionality of slavery, what have we on the other side?

How is the constitutionality of slavery made out, or attempted to be made out?

First, by discrediting and casting away as worthless the most beneficent rules of legal interpretation; by disregarding the plain and common sense reading of the instrument itself; by showing that the Constitution does not mean what it says, and says what it does not mean, by assuming that the WRITTEN Constitution is to be interpreted in the light of a SECRET and UNWRITTEN understanding of its framers, which understanding is declared to be in favor of slavery. It is in this mean, contemptible, under-hand method that the Constitution is pressed into the service of slavery.

They do not point us to the Constitution itself, for the reason that there is nothing sufficiently explicit for their purpose; but they delight in supposed intentions—intentions no where expressed in the Constitution, and every where contradicted in the Constitution.

Judge Taney lays down this system of interpreting in this wise:

"The general words above quoted would seem to embrace the whole human family, and, if they were used in a similar instrument at this day, would be so understood. But it is too clear for dispute that the enslaved African race were not intended to be included, and formed no part of the people who framed and adopted this declaration; for if the language, as understood in that day, would embrace them, the conduct of the distinguished men who framed the Declaration of Independence would have been utterly and flagrantly inconsistent with the principles they asserted; and instead of the sympathy of mankind, to which they appealed, they would have deserved and received universal rebuke and reprobation.

"It is difficult, at this day, to realize the state of public opinion respecting that unfortunate class with the civilized and enlightened portion of the world at the time of the Declaration of Independence and the adoption of the Constitution; but history shows they had, for more than a century, been regarded as beings of an inferior order, and unfit associates for the white race, either socially or politically, and had no rights which white men are bound to respect; and the black man might be reduced to slavery, bought and sold, and treated as an ordinary article of merchandise. This opinion, at that time, was fixed and universal with the civilized portion of the white race. It was regarded as an axiom of morals, which no one thought of disputing, and everyone habitually acted upon it, without doubting, for a moment, the correctness of the opinion. And in no nation was this opinion more fixed, and generally acted upon, than in England; the subjects of which government not only seized them on the coast of Africa, but took them, as ordinary merchandise, to where they could make a profit on them. The opinion, thus entertained, was universally maintained on the colonies this side of the Atlantic; accordingly, negroes of the African race were regarded by them as property, and held and bought and sold as such in every one of the thirteen colonies, which united in the Declaration of Independence, and afterwards formed the Constitution."

The argument here is, that the Constitution comes down to us from a slaveholding period and a slaveholding people; and that, therefore, we are bound to suppose that the Constitution recognizes colored persons of African descent, the victims of slavery at that time, as debarred forever from all participation in the benefit of the Constitution and the Declaration of Independence, although the plain reading of both includes them in their beneficent range.

As a man, an American, a citizen, a colored man of both Anglo-Saxon and African descent, I denounce this representation as a most scandalous and devilish perversion of the Constitution, and a brazen misstatement of the facts of history.

But I will not content myself with mere denunciation; I invite attention to the facts.

It is a fact, a great historic fact, that at the time of the adoption of the Constitution, the leading religious denominations in this land were anti-slavery, and were laboring for the emancipation of the colored people of African descent.

The church of a country is often a better index of the state of opinion and feeling than is even the government itself.

The Methodists, Baptists, Presbyterians, and the denomination of Friends, were actively opposing slavery, denouncing the system of bondage, with language as burning and sweeping as we employ at this day.

Take the Methodists. In 1780, that denomination said: "The Conference acknowledges that slavery is contrary to the laws of God, man, and nature, and hurtful to society—contrary to the dictates of conscience and true religion, and doing to others that we would not do unto us." In 1784, the same church declared, "that those who buy, sell, or give slaves away, except for the purpose to free them, shall be expelled immediately." In 1785, it spoke even more stringently on the subject. It then said: "We hold in the deepest abhorrence the practice of slavery, and shall not cease to seek its destruction by all wise and proper means."

So much for the position of the Methodist Church in the early history of the Republic, in those days of darkness to which Judge Taney refers.

Let us now see how slavery was regarded by the Presbyterian Church at that early date.

In 1794, the General Assembly of that body pronounced the following judgment in respect to slavery, slaveholders, and slaveholding.

"1st Timothy, 1st chapter, 10th verse: 'The law was made for man-stealers.' 'This crime among the Jews exposed the perpetrators of it to capital punishment,' Exodus, xxi, 15.[4]—And the apostle here classes them with sinners of the first rank. The word he uses in its original import, comprehends all who are concerned in bringing any of the human race into slavery, or in retaining them in it. Stealers of men are all those who bring off slaves or freemen, and keep, sell, or buy them. 'To steal a freeman,' says Grotius, 'is the highest kind of theft.' In other instances, we only steal human property, but when we steal or retain men in slavery, we seize those who, in common with ourselves, are constituted, by the original grant, lords of the earth."

I might quote, at length, from the sayings of the Baptist Church and the sayings of eminent divines at this early period, showing that Judge Taney has grossly falsified history, but will not detain you with these quotations.

The testimony of the church, and the testimony of the founders of this Republic, from the declaration downward, prove Judge Taney false; as false to history as he is to law.

Washington and Jefferson, and Adams, and Jay, and Franklin, and Rush, and Hamilton, and a host of others, held no such degrading views on the subject of slavery as are imputed by Judge Taney to the Fathers of the Republic.

All, at that time, looked for the gradual but certain abolition of slavery, and shaped the constitution with a view to this grand result.

George Washington can never be claimed as a fanatic, or as the representative of fanatics. The slaveholders impudently use his name for the base purpose of giving respectability to slavery. Yet, in a letter to Robert Morris, Washington uses this language—language which, at this day, would make him a terror of the slaveholders, and the natural representative of the Republican party.

"There is not a man living, who wishes more sincerely than I do, to see some plan adopted for the abolition of slavery; but there is only one proper and effectual mode by which it can be accomplished, and that is by Legislative authority; and this, as far as my suffrage will go, shall not be wanting."

Washington only spoke the sentiment of his times. There were, at that time, Abolition societies in the slave States—Abolition societies in Virginia, in North Carolina, in Maryland, in Pennsylvania, and in Georgia—all slaveholding States. Slavery was so weak, and liberty so strong, that free speech could attack the monster to its teeth. Men were not mobbed and driven out of the presence of slavery, merely because they condemned the slave system. The system was then on its knees

---

4. The correct citations are 1 Timothy 1:9 and Exodus 21:16.

imploring to be spared, until it could get itself decently out of the world.

In the light of these facts, the Constitution was framed, and framed in conformity to it.

It may, however, be asked, if the Constitution were so framed that the rights of all the people were naturally protected by it, how happens it that a large part of the people have been held in slavery ever since its adoption? Have the people mistaken the requirements of their own Constitution?

The answer is ready. The Constitution is one thing, its administration is another, and, in this instance, a very different and opposite thing. I am here to vindicate the law, not the administration of the law. It is the written Constitution, not the unwritten Constitution, that is now before us. If, in the whole range of the Constitution, you can find no warrant for slavery, then we may properly claim it for liberty.

Good and wholesome laws are often found dead on the statute book. We may condemn the practice under them and against them, but never the law itself. To condemn the good law with the wicked practice, is to weaken, not to strengthen our testimony.

It is no evidence that the Bible is a bad book, because those who profess to believe the Bible are bad. The slaveholders of the South, and many of their wicked allies at the North, claim the Bible for slavery; shall we, therefore, fling the Bible away as a pro-slavery book? It would be as reasonable to do so as it would be to fling away the Constitution.

We are not the only people who have illustrated the truth, that a people may have excellent law, and detestable practices. Our Savior denounces the Jews, because they made void the law by their traditions. We have been guilty of the same sin.

The American people have made void our Constitution by just such traditions as Judge Taney and Mr. Garrison have been giving to the world of late, as the true light in which to view the Constitution of the United States. I shall follow neither. It is not what Moses allowed for the hardness of heart, but what God requires, ought to be the rule.

It may be said that it is quite true that the Constitution was designed to secure the blessings of liberty and justice to the people who made it, and to the posterity of the people who made it, but was never designed to do any such thing for the colored people of African descent.

This is Judge Taney's argument, and it is Mr. Garrison's argument, but it is not the argument of the Constitution. The Constitution imposes no such mean and satanic limitations upon its own beneficent operation. And, if the Constitution makes none, I beg to know what right has anybody, outside of the Constitution, for the special accommodation of slaveholding villainy, to impose such a construction upon the Constitution?

The Constitution knows all the human inhabitants of this country as "the people." It makes, as I have said before, no discrimination in favor of, or against, any class of the people, but is fitted to protect and preserve the rights of all, without reference to color, size, or any physical peculiarities. Besides, it has been shown by William Goodell and others, that in eleven out of the old thirteen States, colored men were legal voters at the time of the adoption of the Constitution.

In conclusion, let me say, all I ask of the American people is, that they live up to the Constitution, adopt its principles, imbibe its spirit, and enforce its provisions.

When this is done, the wounds of my bleeding people will be healed, the chain will no longer rust on their ankles, their backs will no longer be torn by the bloody lash, and liberty, the glorious birthright of our common humanity, will become the inheritance of all the inhabitants of this highly favored country.

ANONYMOUS

from *Minutes of the Second Annual Convention for the Improvement of the Free People of Color* [1832]

In April 1830, a young man from Baltimore, Hezekiah Grice, circulated a flyer proposing a national convention of African American leaders to discuss the idea of emigration. The time was ripe for the novel idea of a national convention, and Grice's efforts resulted in a small meeting in Philadelphia in September of that year. In addition to discussing emigration (they decided on the province of Upper Canada as the most suitable destination), the delegates wrote a constitution and arranged for subsequent national conventions. These conventions met on average every three years through 1864, the concluding year of the Civil War. Collectively, the meetings were known as the National Negro Conventions or the National Colored Conventions. (The specific names of the meetings varied from year to year.)

Beginning with the First Annual Colored Convention of the People of Color in 1831, education was a primary area of discussion. At the 1831 convention, the delegates identified the areas of "Education, Temperance and Economy" as "best calculated to promote the elevation of mankind to a proper rank and standing among men." The delegates ("after an interesting discussion") also unanimously adopted a report proposing the establishment of a black college in New Haven, Connecticut, that would provide students with both "a scientific education" and training in "a useful Mechanical or Agricultural profession." The project met with a number of obstacles, including difficulty raising $20,000 to establish the school and resistance from white citizens in New Haven who did not wish the college to be located there. Despite those obstacles, convention delegates in the following year gave renewed support to the effort. The proceedings of the second annual convention, held in Philadelphia from June 4 to 13, 1832, assert that high schools and colleges on the manual-labor model are the key to enlightened education and refute the idea that primary schools alone can provide an education sufficient to foster moral and productive citizens.

Howard Holman Bell, ed., *Minutes of the Proceedings of the National Negro Conventions, 1830–1864* (New York: Arno Press, 1964), n.p.

It will be seen by a reference to our proceedings, that we have again recommended the further prosecution of the contemplated college, proposed by the last Convention, to be established at New Haven, under the rules and regulations then established. A place for its location will be selected in a climate and neighborhood, where its inhabitants are less prejudiced to our rights and privileges. The proceedings of the citizens of New Haven, with regard to the erection of the college, were a disgrace to themselves, and cast a stigma on the reputed fame of New England and the country. We are unwilling that the character of the whole country shall sink by the proceedings of a few. We are determined to present to another portion of the country not far distant, and at no very remote period, the opportunity of gaining for them the character of a truly philanthropic spirit, and of retrieving the character of the country, by the disreputable proceedings of New Haven. We must have Colleges and high Schools on the Manual Labor system, where our youth may be instructed in all the arts of civilized life. If we ever expect to see the influence of prejudice decrease, and ourselves respected, it must be by the blessings of an enlightened education. It must be by being in possession of that classical knowledge which promotes genius, and causes man to soar up to those high intellectual enjoyments and acquirements, which places him in a situation, to shed upon a country and a people, that scientific grandeur which is imperishable by time, and drowns in oblivions cup their moral degradation. Those who think that our primary schools are capable of effecting this, are a century behind the age, when to have proved a question in the rule of three, was considered a higher attainment, than solving the most difficult problem in Euclid is now. They might have at that time performed, what some people expect of them now, in the then barren state of science, but they are now no longer capable of reflecting brilliancy on our national character, which will elevate us from our present situation.

Anonymous

Address to the Female Literary Association of Philadelphia [1832]

Opportunities for women to participate in the national conventions were few, particularly in the early years. (Notable exceptions were the National Convention of Colored Freemen that met in Cleveland in 1848, in which Martin Delany encouraged the participation of women, and the National Convention of Colored Men that met in Syracuse, New York, in 1864, where the invited speakers included Frances E. W. Harper [p. 244] and Edmonia Highgate.) Although women were actively discouraged from speaking in public, let alone debating, they created outlets, such as female literary societies, for the expression of their opinions. (Maria W. Stewart and Jarena Lee, who have speeches on pp. 60 and 152 of this anthology, were notable for their insistence on public speaking roles for women.) Women also published their ideas in newspapers and journals, although they often disguised their identity by using only initials or submitting their pieces anonymously.

The anonymous Address to the Female Literary Association of Philadelphia was published on June 9, 1832, in *The Liberator*, the famed Boston anti-slavery newspaper established by white abolitionist leader William Lloyd Garrison (p. 111). The writer promotes "a liberal, a classical education," making the case that women in particular need a broad educational foundation because they are largely responsible for the moral upbringing of children. Specifically addressing other black women, the speaker acknowledges the difficulties of pursuing an education and offers remedies. For instance, she suggests reading as a way of educating oneself and fostering relationships with role models as a way of fostering confidence.

In their debates about black education, black men rarely discussed female education. The few exceptions focused on teaching gender-specific skills, as opposed to the anonymous female speaker's call for a broad academic education for women. For example, the manual labor report at the 1853 National Negro Convention briefly sketched a program of industrial education geared toward women, with weaving, straw-hat making, and paper-box making taking the place of carpentry, smithing, and other skills proposed for males. Seventy years after the female speaker addressed the Philadelphia Literary Society, Booker T. Washington (p. 206) would disparage women who were versed in academic disciplines but lacked domestic skills.

From *The Liberator*, June 9, 1832.

Am I Not a Woman and a Sister?

My Friends—I expect you generally understand the reason why you are called together at this time. I shall be as brief as possible. I have long and ardently desired your intellectual advancement, upon which the progress of morality must mainly depend. It is nothing better than affectation to deny the influence that females possess; it is their part to train up the young mind, to instill therein principles that may govern in maturer years; principles that influence the actions of the private citizen, the patriot, philanthropist, lawgivers, yea, presidents and kings. Then what subject can more properly claim, what one more justly and loudly demands solid consideration, deep attention—and yet what one is more carelessly dismissed from the mind, what one more neglected than the proper education of females? I say the proper education, because I do not consider that usually bestowed on them efficient; on the contrary, it tends to debase the moral powers, to enervate the understanding; and renders them incapable of filling the stations allotted them with becoming dignity, or profitably discharging the duties arising from those stations. I am aware that the education of females has become a fashionable theme, that a great deal has been said and written concerning it, that many speculations have been set afloat respecting their capacity of receiving a liberal, a classical education; and I am also aware that an opinion too generally prevails that superficial learning is all that is requisite, and to this cause, may in a great measure be attributed the pravity, the embasement of society. It is not my design to descant at length upon the subject at this time; suffice it to say, I hold that the present system of education abounds with corruption and error, and I fondly anticipate the time when a complete reformation may be wrought therein. I look through the surrounding clouds and mists of prejudice for the shining forth of a light, whose rays shall dispel these vapors; then may the female character be raised to a just stand. At some future period I may explain more particularly my reasons for thinking as I do, although it should elicit the exclamation of "thou art beside thyself, thy great zeal hath made thee mad."[1] My object at present is to call your attention to the necessity of improving the mental faculties, of exalting the moral powers, and of elevating yourselves to the station of rational, intelligent beings, accountable for the use made of the talents committed to your care. The benefits resulting from combinations similar to the one proposed I need not iterate, you are no strangers to them; but allow me, my sisters, to entreat you to banish prejudice from your hearts. If any one imagines that her talents are less brilliant than others, let her not disdain to contrast their superior attainments with her own; suffer not a feeling (shall I say of envy?) to enter that sanctuary, but rather strive to imitate their virtues; seek their society, and whenever they are disposed to aid you, extend to them the right hand of fellowship. And lastly, I would remind you that an attention to your best interests will induce you to encourage those periodicals devoted to your cause. The *Genius of Universal Emancipation* and the *Liberator*, I allude to in particular. Their editors are devoting their time and talents to your service, they have subjected themselves to many privations, and despise the reproach, the calumny, so liberally bestowed upon them by interested, calculating, designing men; they merit your patronage.

Philadelphia, May, 1832

FREDERICK DOUGLASS
Letter to Harriet Beecher Stowe [1853]

As at prior black national conventions, education was a prime subject of debate at the 1853 Colored National Convention in Rochester, New York. At that convention, Frederick Douglass (p. 38) presented a letter he had written to Harriet Beecher Stowe (p. 118) in March 1853, while she was in England, emphasizing the need to promote mechanical training ahead of academic education.

Douglass's letter was written in response to Stowe's question, "What can be done to improve the condition of the free colored people in the United States?"

In his letter, Douglass first presents arguments against common proposals, such as establishing new academic high schools and colleges, instituting farm programs, and promoting emigration. He suggests instead

---

1. Paraphrase of a line from Acts 26:24: "thou art beside thyself; much learning doth make thee mad."

that Stowe could best contribute to black advancement by helping to establish an industrial college "where colored youth can be instructed to use their hands, as well as their heads."

Douglass's stress on mechanical training differs from the proposals for a combination of manual and academic education that were made in the "Report of the Committee on Manual Labor School," also presented at the 1853 convention. In response to the question of "what kind of Institution would best befit *us*?" the committee members proposed this answer: "one that would develop *power.*" They determined that the best route to power was through institutions that stress a combination of manual and academic training rather than one or the other: "In the past the misfortune has been that our knowledge has been much distributed. We have had educated *heads* in one large division among us, and educated *hands* in another." They recommended adding vocational-training programs to existing academic institutions and erecting a new college dedicated to the development of both the intellect and manual skills. In this way, the 1853 delegates moved away from the idea of different types of schools, the idea favored at the 1847 convention, and returned to the broader type of school advocated by earlier conventions.

By 1853, after more than two decades of work on various plans, the delegates were keenly aware of the challenges involved in trying to establish new educational institutions. While they continued to consider plans for new schools, in 1853 the convention delegates also made resolutions that could be implemented immediately in order to improve the training of and educational opportunities for African Americans. Their resolutions to promote apprenticeships and existing educational opportunities demonstrate how the conventions of the 1840s and 1850s increasingly adopted pragmatic solutions in addition to making more activist proposals. Douglass and the other 1853 delegates were continuing a debate that had been introduced during the first National Negro Convention in 1831. The 1831 delegates proposed opening a college based on the manual-labor system, but from the beginning the project faced funding and logistical difficulties. By the National Negro Convention in 1835, there was a nearly even split between delegates on the question of support for the planned college. Delegates appointed a committee to determine how many existing high schools in the United States admitted African American students, thereby opening up a related debate, which also continued for decades, regarding the efficacy of establishing new institutions rather than maximizing access to existing institutions and training opportunities. It would take over a century and the mandated desegregation of public schools to shift the primary argument for promoting black educational institutions from their ability to provide access to education to the ability to control the curriculum and the hiring of faculty.

From Howard Holman Bell, ed., *Minutes of the Proceedings of the National Negro Conventions, 1830–1864* (New York: Arno Press, 1964), n.p.

Pending the motion to adopt, Mr. Douglass read a letter addressed by himself to Mrs. Stowe. This letter was read to inform the Convention what representation the writer had made to Mrs. Stowe, respecting the condition and wants of the free colored people.

ROCHESTER, March 8th, 1853.

DEAR MRS. STOWE:

You kindly informed me, when at your house, a fortnight ago, that you designed to do something which should permanently contribute to the improvement and elevation of the free colored people in the United States. You especially expressed an interest in such of this class as had become free by their own exertions, and desired most of all to be of service to them. In what manner, and by what means, you can assist this class most successfully, is the subject upon which you have done me the honor to ask my opinion.

Begging you to excuse the unavoidable delay, I will now most gladly comply with your request, but before doing so, I desire to express, dear Madam, my deep sense of the value of the services which you have already rendered my afflicted and persecuted people, by the publication of your inimitable book on the subject of slavery. That contribution to our bleeding cause, alone, involves us in a debt of gratitude which cannot be measured; and your resolution to make other exertions on our behalf excites in me emotions and sentiments, which I scarcely need try to give forth in words. Suffice it to say, that I believe you to have the blessings of your enslaved countrymen and country-women; and the still higher reward which comes to the soul in the smiles of our merciful Heavenly father, whose ear is ever open to the cries of the oppressed.

With such sentiments, dear Madam, I will at once proceed to lay before you, in as few words as the nature of the case will allow, my humble views in the premises. First of all, let me briefly state the nature of the disease, before I undertake to prescribe the remedy. Three things are notoriously true of us, as a people. These are POVERTY, IGNORANCE and DEGRADATION. Of course there are exceptions to this general statement; but these are so few as only to prove its essential truthfulness. I shall not stop here to inquire minutely into the causes which have produced our present condition; nor to denounce those whom I believe to be responsible for those causes. It is enough that we shall agree upon the character of the evil, whose existence we deplore, and upon some plan for its removal.

I assert then, that *poverty, ignorance* and *degradation* are the combined evils; or, in other words, these constitute the social disease of the Free Colored people in the United States.

To deliver them from this triple malady, is to improve and elevate them, by which I mean simply to put them on an equal footing with their white fellow-countrymen in the sacred right to "*Life, Liberty* and the pursuit of happiness." I am for no fancied or artificial elevation, but only ask fair play. How shall this be obtained? I answer, first, not by establishing for our use high schools and colleges. Such institutions are, in my judgment, beyond our immediate occasions, and are not adapted to our present most pressing wants. High schools and colleges are excellent institutions, and will, in due season, be greatly subservient to our progress; but they are the result, as well as they are the demand of a point of progress, which we, as a people, have not yet attained. Accustomed, as we have been, to the rougher and harder modes of living, and of gaining a livelihood, we cannot, and we ought not to hope that, in a single leap from our low condition, we can reach that of *Ministers, Lawyers, Doctors, Editors, Merchants, &c.* These will, doubtless, be attained by us; but this will only be, when we have patiently and laboriously,

and I may add successfully, mastered and passed through the intermediate gradations of agriculture and the mechanic arts. Besides, there are (and perhaps this is a better reason for my view of the case) numerous institutions of learning in this country, already thrown open to colored youth. To my thinking, there are quite as many facilities now afforded to the colored people, as they can spare the time, from the sterner duties of life, to avail themselves of. In their present condition of poverty, they cannot spare their sons and daughters two or three years at boarding schools or colleges, to say nothing of finding the means to sustain them while at such institutions. I take it, therefore, that we are well provided for in this respect; and that it may be fairly inferred from the past that the facilities for our education, so far as schools and colleges in the Free States are concerned, will increase quite in proportion with our future wants. Colleges have been open to colored youth in this country during the last dozen years. Yet few, comparatively, have acquired a classical education; and even this few have found themselves educated far above a living condition, there being no methods by which they could turn their learning to account. Several of this latter class have entered the ministry; but you need not be told that an educated people is needed to sustain an educated ministry. There must be a certain amount of cultivation among the people to sustain such a ministry. At present, we have not that cultivation amongst us; and therefore, we value, in the preacher, strong lungs, rather than high learning. I do not say that educated ministers are not needed amongst us.—Far from it! I wish there were more of them; but to increase their number is *not* the largest benefit you can bestow upon us.

You, dear Madam, can help the masses. You can do something for the thousands; and by lifting these from the depths of poverty and ignorance, you can make an educated ministry and an educated class possible. In the present circumstances, prejudice is a bar to the educated black minister among the whites; and ignorance is a bar to him among the blacks.

We have now two or three colored lawyers in this country; and I rejoice in the fact; for it affords very gratifying evidence of our progress. Yet it must be confessed that, in point of success, our lawyers are as great failures as are our ministers. White people will not employ them to the obvious embarrassment of their causes, and the blacks, taking their *cue* from the whites, have not sufficient confidence in their abilities to employ them. Hence, educated colored men, among the colored people, are at a very great discount. It would seem that education and emigration go together with us; for as soon as a man rises amongst us, capable, by his genius and learning, to do us great service, just so soon he finds that he can serve himself better by going elsewhere. In proof of this, I might instance the Russwurms—the Garnetts—the Wards—the Crummells[1] and others—all men of superior ability and attainments, and capable of removing mountains of prejudice against their race, by their simple presence in the country; but these gentlemen, finding themselves embarrassed here by the peculiar disadvantages to which I have referred—disadvantages in part growing out of their education—being repelled by ignorance on the one hand, and prejudice on the other, and having no taste to continue a contest against such odds, they have sought more congenial climes, where they can live more peaceable and quiet lives. I regret their election—but I cannot blame them; for, with an equal amount of education, and the hard lot which was theirs, I might follow their example.

But, again, it has been said that the colored people must become farmers—that they must go on the land, in order to their elevation. Hence, many benevolent people are contributing the necessary funds to purchase land in Canada, and elsewhere, for them. That prince of good men, Gerrit Smith, has given away thousands of acres to colored men in this State, thinking, doubtless, that in so doing he was conferring a blessing upon them. Now, while I do not undervalue the efforts which have been made, and are still being made in this direction, yet I must say that I have far less confidence in such efforts, than I have in the benevolence which prompts them. Agricultural pursuits are not, as I think, suited to our condition. The reason of this is not to be found so much in the occupation, (for it is a noble and

ennobling one,) as in the people themselves. That is only a remedy, which can be applied to the case; and the difficulty in agricultural pursuits, as a remedy for the evils of poverty and ignorance amongst us, is that it cannot, for various reasons, be applied.

We cannot apply it, because it is almost impossible to get colored men to go on the land. From some cause or other, (perhaps the adage that misery loves company will explain,) colored people will congregate in the large towns and cities; and they will endure any amount of hardship and privation, rather than separate, and go into the country. Again, very few have the means so set up for themselves, or to get where they could do so.

Another consideration against expending energy in this direction is our want of self-reliance. Slavery, more than all things else, robs its victims of self-reliance. To go into the western wilderness, and there to lay the foundation of future society, requires more of that important quality than a life of slavery has left us. This may sound strange to you, coming, as it does, from a colored man; but I am dealing with facts; and these never accommodate themselves to the feelings or wishes of any. They don't *ask*, but *take* leave *to be*. It is a fact then, and not less so because I wish it were otherwise, that the colored people are wanting in self-reliance—too fond of society—too eager for immediate results—and too little skilled in mechanics or husbandry to attempt to overcome the wilderness; at least, until they have overcome obstacles less formidable. Therefore, I look to other means than agricultural pursuits for the elevation and improvement of colored people. Of course, I allege this of the many. There are exceptions. Individuals among us, with commendable zeal, industry, perseverance and self-reliance, have found, and are finding, in agricultural pursuits, the means of supporting, improving and educating their families.

The plan which I contemplate will, (if carried into effect,) greatly increase the number of this class—

1. Abolitionist families who favored emigration: John Brown Russwurm (1799–1851), who co-founded the first African American newspaper in the United States, *Freedom's Journal,* emigrated to Liberia in 1829. Henry Highland Garnet (p. 80) worked as a missionary in Jamaica in the early 1850s before returning to the United States; he finally emigrated to Liberia in 1881, near the end of his life. Samuel Ringgold Ward (p. 170) hastily emigrated to Canada in 1851 after participating in Jerry's Rescue (the freeing of a fugitive slave by several thousands of abolitionists in Syracuse, New York) and in 1855 settled in Jamaica. Alexander Crummell (1819–98) moved to England in 1848 and to Liberia in 1853 but returned to the United States in 1873.

since it will prepare others to meet the rugged duties which a pioneer agricultural condition must impose upon all who take it upon them. What I propose is intended simply to prepare men for the work of getting an honest living—not out of dishonest men—but out of an honest earth.

Again, there is little reason to hope that any considerable number of the free colored people will ever be induced to leave this country, even if such a thing were desirable. The black man, (*un*-like the Indian,) loves civilization. He does not make very great progress in civilization himself, but he likes to be in the midst of it, and prefers to share its most galling evils, to encountering barbarism. Then the love of country— the dread of isolation—the lack of adventurous spirit— and the thought of seeming to desert their "brethren in bonds," are a powerful and perpetual check upon all schemes of colonization, which look to the removal of the colored people, without the slaves.—The truth is, dear Madam, we are *here*, and here we are likely to remain. Individuals emigrate—nations never. We have grown up with this Republic; and I see nothing in our character, or even in the character of the American people, as yet, which compels the belief that we must leave the United States. If, then, we are to remain here, the question for the wise and good is precisely that you have submitted to me—and that which I fear I have been, perhaps, too slow in answering—namely, What can be done to improve the condition of the free colored people in the United States? The plan which I humbly submit in answer to this inquiry, (and in the hope that it may find favor with you, dear Madam, and with the many friends of humanity who honor, love, and co-operate with you,) is the establishment in Rochester, N. Y.—or in some other part of the United States, equally favorable to such an enterprise—of an INDUSTRIAL COLLEGE, in which shall be taught several important branches of the mechanic arts. This college to be open to colored youth. I will pass over, for the present, the details of such an institution as that I propose. It is not worth while that I should dwell upon these at all. Once convinced that something of the sort is needed, and the organizing power will be forthcoming. It is the peculiarity of your favored race that they can always do what they think necessary to be done. I can safely trust all details to yourself, and to the wise

and good people whom you represent in the interest you take in my oppressed fellow-countrymen.

Never having myself had a day's schooling in all my life, I may not be expected to be able to map out the details of a plan so comprehensive as that involved in the idea of a college. I repeat then, I leave the organization and administration to the superior wisdom of yourself and the friends that second your noble efforts. The argument in favor of an Industrial College, (a College to be conducted by the best men, and the best workmen, which the mechanic arts can afford—a College where colored youth can be instructed to use their hands, as well as their heads—where they can be put in possession of the means of getting a living— whether their lot in after life may be cast among civilized or uncivilized men—whether they choose to stay here, or prefer to return to the land of their fathers,) is briefly this—prejudice against the free colored people in the United States has shown itself nowhere so invincible as among mechanics. The farmer and the professional man cherish no feeling so bitter as that cherished by these. The latter would starve us out of the country entirely. At this moment, I can more easily get my son into a lawyer's office, to study law, than I can into a blacksmith's shop, to blow the bellows, and to wield the sledge-hammer. Denied the means of learning useful trades, we are pressed into the narrowest limits to obtain a livelihood. In times past we have been the hewers of wood and the drawers of water for American society, and we once enjoyed a monopoly in menial employments, but this is so no longer—even these employments are rapidly passing away out of our hands. The fact is, (every day begins with the lesson, and ends with the lesson,) that colored men must learn trades—must find new employments, new modes of usefulness to society—or that they must decay under the pressing wants to which their condition is rapidly bringing them. We must become mechanics—we must build, as well as live in houses—we must make, as well as use furniture—we must construct bridges, as well as pass over them—before we can properly live, or be respected by our fellow men. We need mechanics, as well as ministers. We need workers in iron, wood, clay, and in leather. We have orators, authors, and other professional men; but these reach only a certain class, and get respect for our race in certain select circles. To live here as we ought, we must fasten ourselves to our countrymen through their every day and cardinal wants. We must not only be able to *black* boots, but to *make* them. At present, we are unknown in the Northern States, as mechanics. We give no proof of genius or skill at the County, the State, or the National Fairs. We are unknown at any of the great exhibitions of the industry of our fellow-citizens—and being unknown, we are unconsidered.

The fact that we make no show of our ability, is held conclusive of our inability to make any. Hence, all the indifference and contempt, with which incapacity is regarded, fall upon us, and that too, when we have had no means of disproving the injurious opinion of our natural inferiority. I have, during the last dozen years, denied, before the Americans, that we are an inferior race. But this has been done by arguments, based upon admitted principles, rather than by the presentation of facts. Now, firmly believing, as I do, that there are skill, invention, power, industry, and real mechanical genius among the colored people, which will bear favorable testimony for them, and which only need the means to develop them, I am decidedly in favor of the establishment of such a college as I have mentioned. The benefits of such an institution would not be confined to the Northern States, nor to the free colored people: they would extend over the whole Union. The slave, not less than the freeman, would be benefitted by such an institution. It must be confessed that the most powerful argument, now used by the Southern slave-holder—and the one most soothing to his conscience—is, that derived from the low condition of the free colored people at the North. I have long felt that too little attention has been given, by our truest friends, in this country, to removing this stumbling block out of the way of the slave's liberation.

The most telling, the most killing refutation of slavery, is the presentation of an industrious, enter-prising, upright, thrifty, and intelligent free black population. Such a population, I believe, would rise in the Northern States, under the fostering care of such a College as that supposed.

To show that we are capable of becoming mechanics, I might adduce any amount of testimony; but dear Madam, I need not ring the changes on such a proposition. There is no question in the mind of any unprejudiced person, that the negro is capable of making a good mechanic. Indeed, even those who cherish the bitterest feelings towards us have admitted that the apprehension that negroes might be employed in their stead, dictated the policy of excluding them from trades altogether; but I will not dwell upon this point, as I fear I have already trespassed too long upon your precious time, and written more than I ought to expect you to read. Allow me to say, in conclusion, that I believe every intelligent colored man in America will approve and rejoice at the establishment of some such institution as that now suggested. There are many respectable colored men, fathers of large families, having boys nearly grown up, whose minds are tossed by day and by night, with the anxious enquiry, what shall I do with my boys? Such an institution would meet the wants of such persons. Then, too, the establishment of such an institution would be in character with the eminently practical philanthropy of your transatlantic friends. America could scarcely object to it, as an attempt to agitate the public mind on the subject of slavery, or to *"dissolve the Union."* It could not be tortured into a cause for hard words by the American people; but the noble and good of all classes would see in the effort an excellent motive, a benevolent object, temperately, wisely, and practically manifested.

Wishing you, dear Madam, renewed health, a pleasant passage and safe return to your native land,

I am, most truly, your grateful friend,

FREDERICK DOUGLASS.

ANONYMOUS

from *Minutes of the Colored National Convention* [1855]

The plan presented at the 1853 convention for establishing an industrial school did not move beyond the committee stage. The committee appointed to review the idea presented its report during the 1855 national convention, held in Philadelphia from October 16 to 18. In addition to outlining numerous problems with the specific plan, the committee members directly rejected the overall goal of combining academic and mechanical studies (a goal championed by delegates during the 1831 and 1853 conventions) as well as Frederick Douglass's 1853 plan for a school stressing mechanical training (p. 133). Instead, they argued that the role of schools should be academic training, since highly educated African Americans advance civil rights by serving as examples of racial equality. To serve the needs of the majority of young people, they proposed a "Mechanical Bureau" that would promote apprenticeships, which might have the same benefits as a new industrial school but without creating the political and practical problems involved in establishing a new institution. The minutes of the national conventions typically include only a summary of the delegates' reactions to reports, with few details of the actual debates. Even with the sketchy record, however, it is clear that the plan for a mechanical bureau was met with resistance from delegates, including James McCune Smith (p. 42). Although delegates did not agree on specific plans to remedy the scarcity of apprenticeships, they did agree that the issue needed further exploration, and they voted unanimously to adopt the "Report of the Committee on Mechanical Branches among the Colored People of the Free States," presented at the convention.

Howard Holman Bell, ed., *Minutes of the Proceedings of the National Negro Conventions, 1830–1864* (New York: Arno Press, 1964), n.p.

The Business Committee, through their Chairman, Professor Charles L. Reason, then made a report of some papers received through the New York and Philadelphia delegations.

The following is from the Philadelphia delegation:

Your committee appointed to report views relative to the Industrial School, respectfully submit as a report, that having carefully considered the subject in the varied aspects which it presents, have arrived at these conclusions:—

In a report like this, it will not be expected that this subject will be handled in the detailed manner which its great weight would seem to demand. We will therefore briefly give some of the reasons for discouraging the enterprise now under consideration.

The first difficulty to be met, is the capital required to carry out instruction to a successful issue. On this point your Committee are of the opinion, that to teach even a few of the trades, much more will be required than will be easily within our reach, and for which a fair return will be received. Besides it will be conceded, that unless a youth acquire a profession congenial to his mental and physical abilities, and to his tastes, the trade thus acquired will avail him but little. For says an author of some note, "The proper choice of a profession is one of the most important steps in life." If but few trades can be taught, owing to limited capital or other causes, this institution can be of use but to few; for if within the circle of professions taught in the institution, a pupil can find none suited to his peculiar demands, it would be worse than useless, and a loss of time and means, to endeavor to acquire one in which his nature forbids he should excel.

Thus we believe that our demand for a variety of employments, is only limited by the trades themselves.

Again, the plan of an industrial school combines the mental culture with mechanical training, which we conceive to be in part going over the ground already occupied. We have institutions of learning of the first stamp open to us, where the rising generation can draw from the fountains of knowledge side by side with the most favored of the land, and at the same time by their contact and influence help materially to do away with that deep-rooted prejudice of which we so bitterly complain. The Industrial School being necessarily (if not in theory, yet in fact) a complexional institution, must foster distinctions, and help to draw more definitely (so far as educational privileges are involved) those lines of demarkation which we have labored and still are endeavoring to eradicate.

The question will also arise, is it possible in the period allotted for a collegiate course, to afford time sufficient for the acquirement of a trade in such a thorough manner as to enable the learner to compete successfully with those who have been trained by the usual method? The time generally considered necessary to learn a mechanic art, is from three to five years, working ten hours per day, and even after this there are many who have still wide room for improvement.

Considering, then, the necessity under which we labor of being at least equal, if not superior as workmen, in order to overcome the prejudice existing against us, we cannot believe that the disconnected hours applied to attaining the said trades will suffice, in the limited period, to give that proficiency of execution and workmanlike ability which we believe to be indispensably necessary to success in business, and the ultimate triumph of our enterprise.

An institution such as is now under consideration, will not be able to accomplish much for the masses. Our people are wide-spread as are the free states of this Confederacy, their wants are varied as their localities, and all demand that their requirements should be equally cared for. The great number of our people are poor, and in consequence would be unable to avail themselves of such advantages as the institution might afford, even if it was their wish so to do.

What then is to be done? What new means must we devise? From all sides we hear the demand for occupations that shall keep pace with the rising intelligence of our people. This then is the subject which is daily forced upon us, and it must be met with a determination to adopt such plans as will be most certain of success within our reach, and likely to do the greatest good to the largest number. Having objected to the plan proposed for the accomplishment of the desired object, it will of course be expected that we will suggest some substitute. This we will endeavor to do, and will present the skeleton of a plan, believing that the concentrated wisdom of the convention now about to assemble will

be able to fashion it into such a "harmonious whole" as will meet the end we have so much desired.

Let the National Council, when duly organized, establish as a part of their operations a Mechanical Bureau, accumulating a fund to be employed in the promotion of the Mechanic Arts amongst colored men. They shall organize in the several States, or any locality, Boards of Control, who, when they shall find a responsible person or persons having a knowledge of any desirable occupation, and willing for a fair remuneration as Agent or Foreman to impart the art to colored youth, shall report the same to the Bureau, giving all necessary information as to the amount of capital &c. required for carrying out the said object. The Bureau, after making such provision as may be necessary, and instituting such supervisorship as may be desirable, shall advance the amount deemed necessary, requiring such reports from time to time as will be consistent with the prudent management of financial affairs, and all profits from such enterprise shall go into the general fund.

By following out such a plan, we may hope for success; and in a few years, we doubt not, the benefits would be plainly perceived. We could then employ our capital and direct our efforts in each and every place where a favorable opening may present; and ere many years shall have rolled away, we may be gladdened with the sight of our people employed in walks of life ennobling in their tendency, and calculated to lead still higher and higher, until we have achieved such a character as will sweep away the dark clouds of prejudice and oppression which would now o'erwhelm us.

Mr. J. C. Wears moved that so much of the report as referred to the mechanical bureaus be adopted. The motion was defended by Mr. Wears, and opposed by Dr. J. McCune Smith and Rev. T. P. Hunt. The Convention adjourned to meet on the following morning at 9½ o'clock in Franklin Hall.

SECOND DAY—MORNING SESSION.

The Convention met pursuant to adjournment. Prayer was offered by Rev. E. J. Adams, Pa. The roll was called, and 109 delegates answered their names. The minutes of Tuesday's proceedings were read by the Secretary, and after being corrected were adopted.

Professor Charles L. Reason then read the following report:

Report. Of the Committee on Mechanical Branches among the Colored People of the Free States.

The development of the physical energies of man, and their control for the weal of society, is one of the prime subjects of political economy. That which God once made in his own image is among the last in the order of creation. The formation of physical proportions come first, then the removal of the darkness which surrounds the practical workings of our physical creations, until there is light, and into that which is formed as the result of first beginnings, shall be breathed the life of superior intelligence. It is the nature of man to follow the order of creation. The physical world in its beautifully enchanting proportions are first spread out before him—he looks, admires, and then tries to imitate. This practice brings the power of thinking into active exercise, and impresses a steady but sure conviction of the necessity of mental culture. The rude tenements brought into existence by physical necessity, are rebuilt and improved upon as time, thought, and culture suggest.

The learning of the world has never been able to keep pace with the development and enlargment of physical power. The mass in the early ages of the world saw the most beautiful arches, dwellings and temples, while the knowledge of letters even was confined to the few.

The wealth of nations commences not in learning, but in physical energies. Learning comes as a necessity of growth. The thinking minds and the energetic wills have been the rulers of the earth; the masses have toiled under the servitude of their control and direction. The spirit of freedom, however, has overcome enslavement by the few, freedom has led to more general education, and hence there is more general intelligence as the result of freedom among the masses. A knowledge of the requirements of freedom, then, in developing the physical powers, must be a part of the foundation of modern civilized society. No people may expect to escape the performance of the duties thus imposed with impunity. It is a law which must be obeyed, or the penalties of its violations suffered. There need be no cavil as to where society is to begin. The Builder of the Universe has settled that by the necessity which he has thrown around the superstructure of human progress. There must be a basis; Learning is a part of society—it must enter into the composition of society; but the masses cannot be deeply learned, in fact only partially developed. Common School education is all that even the most enlightened countries afford the masses. These are foundation facts with all peoples, so must it be with the colored people of these United States. We must begin with the tillage of the earth and the practice of the mechanical branches, with whatever learning we may have, or the best we can now get. The observations above presented are a natural result growing out of the investigations of your Committee on Mechanical Branches among the colored people. An examination of the meagre facts which your Committee have gathered shows that while some have realized the true nature of the necessities of our position, others have wholly neglected the means first to be used, or have been driven by public prejudice and the force of circumstances, into modes of living entirely inconsistent with the principles of human progression, viz: nonproductive labor.

Your Committee beg leave further to state, that having been appointed by the National Council which assembled in the City of New York, May last, to report to the National Convention to assemble in the City of Philadelphia, October 16, 1855, and accepting the appointment, availed itself of the facility of addressing circular letters to such gentlemen, as we thought would aid us in collecting such information as might be used to advantage by the Convention, and to some extent reliable for reference as to the actual state of Mechanical existence of our people; believing in the idea of producing facts rather than sophistical coloring.

The circular was responded to in a satisfactory manner by many to whom it was addressed, and your Committee feel under many obligations for assistance and suggestions from Mr. Nell, of Boston; Mr. Johnson, of New Bedford, Mass.; Peck, of Pittsburgh, Pa.; Bowers, of Philadelphia; Woodson, of Pittsburgh, Pa.

And we thank the "Herald of Freedom," edited by Mr. Peter H. Clark, of Cincinnati, Ohio, for the very liberal course pursued in endeavoring to give us facts.

Living in the midst of progressive civilization as we do, the statistics show that we are not mixing sufficiently in the elements of that progress. Your Committee take pleasure in presenting the views of some gentlemen agreeing in the views of your Committee, and of others differing widely from it, your Committee deem it in keeping with the purpose of its appointment to give them.

Mr. Johnson, of New Bedford, says, "There does not appear any great desire on the part of parents to secure trades for their children. I think the chances for them to obtain situations as apprentices, very few and difficult. There is little or no disposition to encourage colored men in business, who have means to carry it on.

"We have several colored men who possess their thousands, accumulated in California, and are anxious to start in some business, but from well-grounded fear of success, either do nothing here or return to California. Our colored mechanics are principally from the south."

Mr. Nell, of Boston, says, "There is a growing disposition among parents to secure trades for their children, and the avenues are daily being opened to them. The same is true in regard to colored men in business. The past five years a spirit has been very active for real estate investments, both by individuals and land companies.

"The Equal School Rights Reform having triumphed, a brighter day will soon dawn upon the prospects of colored citizens and their children."

Mr. Woodson thinks that white tradesmen think more of a black tradesman than they do of a mere black man, and they will do more for him as a tradesman than they will as a mere man. Where colored mechanics work and live among white ones, they are more regular in their habits, and economical in their expenditures, than where they work and live alone.

Mr. J. Bonner, of Chicago, Ill., says, "Although the best class of our people in this State, are farmers, they constitute much of the wealth and respectability of Illinois. Many of them, however, I am credibly informed, are desirous of giving their sons mechanical trades. The parents in our city are generally in favor of giving their sons and daughters trades; and I am informed that the same disposition is manifested throughout our cities

and towns; but we have no facilities for thus procuring these trades, and hence the few mechanics among us."

Mr. Clark says, "A very large proportion of our population were mechanics before emigrating from the Southern States, but have ceased to follow their trades for want of encouragement."

These gentlemen being in different sections of the country, hold in some degree views differing from each other; but all showing a want of some great desideratum to advancement in this great element of national growth—and wealth and happiness. While in this connection, your Committee is willing to charge on the bulk of this nation all that guilt and wickedness entailed upon us, we would also invite your attention to the many evils among ourselves that do more to retard our movements, "crush out" our aspirations, and place higher and stronger hindrances in our way to obtaining trades, than can all the *whites* put together, notwithstanding their willingness, for circumstances of interest control them, whilst a narrow prejudice emanating from a low estate to a large extent controls us, in the general sense.

The whites taking their cue as they do from the government, we must expect it to be a kind of domestic article purely native in its proclivities, to discourage us. Even this can be removed as circumstances shall show it to he their interest to do so. All prejudice connected with the Yankee spirit is subject to moderation by the influences that might be brought to bear by a vigorous application of the trades within our reach.

We are a part of this great nation, and our interests cannot be entirely separated. We are now one inseparably by the decrees of God.

As a people we must not be dictated to by discouragement;—if discouraged by the whites, we must learn to avail ourselves of every legitimate means to encourage our own mechanics and professional men.

This would enable us to overcome the spirit, that we have inherited from the dark prison house of slavery, casting its pall around our very vitals, and we found to dwell on the inability of our professional men and mechanics or their extravagant rates, or some other pretence too hollow and frivolous to mention.

To remedy some of the evils practiced by us, your Committee recommend that Committees of practical business men, in the large cities, say Boston, New York, Philadelphia, Buffalo, Pittsburg, Cincinnati, hold a series of conversational meetings, and endeavor to cultivate a proper and correct estimate of interest to govern purchase and sale, and inculcate the idea that to encourage our own mechanics, we create means to learn our boys trades and render them more independent of the prejudices around them.

Your Committee would recommend private residences as the most suitable places to conduct these conversations as thereby we should get better access to the minds of our females. They could enter freely into the conversations, and correct ideas would finally be inculcated in the sentiments of wives and mothers as to the important part of the great duties which they are to perform in moulding the future character of our youth for improvement, and also by association and community of ideas the wives will be prepared to introduce more of the element of the German and French character in social existence carried into our "business relations," of mutual assistance by council, clerkship, and physical labor.

As a people, we must understand that all that is not *white* is black, and all that is not *black* is white, we would recommend our clergy, our teachers, and leading men, and above all our women on whom we must depend for our future leaders to inculcate a disposition for trades, agriculture and such of the higher branches of business as are necessary and requisite to develope persistance—our requirement to do something for the advancement of Society from the cradle to the grave! that each may leave his or her foot-prints upon the earth for good—tangible evidence that each has done somewhat to destroy caste—and to destroy the opinion that we raise our children to that sweet stage of life which prepares them for business (16 years) with no other aspirations than to be a waiter, we cannot hope for much until we shall advance the premium— and hypothecate coupons, on the qualifications of our youth.

Your Committee would further suggest the necessity of raising funds in the different cities, towns, &c., to be funded to the best advantage;—not upon the plan of the Franklin fund, but that if A or B learns his trade and continues sufficiently long at work to accumulate something, that the fund, or such part of it as the Trustees thereof shall deem fit, be loaned for a series of years sufficient to guarantee a hopeful success, provided the

applicants can present the legitimate discharge of agreement of apprenticeship, and devotion to business, &c. It would have the effect to build up so many practical mechanics, that young men would not be compelled to turn in disgust from the trades they love and seek the employment of steamships.

This republic is yet in its infancy, and we must grow with it—let us follow in the footsteps of the whites in this respect, as the only tangible ground— we must use similar means to reach similar ends, notwithstanding disabilities. If we can live in this country, bidding defiance to its wicked laws, we can do anything that prosperity requires at our hands.

As a further means of advancement, this Convention might recommend to the different cities, and towns, Trades Unions on a small scale, or as your Committee would call them, Co-partnerships, say from three to five in each business as the parties might prefer to engage; on the principle of division of labor and division of profits according to capability—looking to it that their financial man and book-keeper be looked up to as an index of security—and let all the partners in the Union work to make the Capital pay if possible 25 per cent.—and keep on until the investment becomes a paying one: and thus show the fallaciousness of the 6 per cent. idea of Savings Bank investments. A Thousand Dollars might in a judicious outlay in a lucrative business pay from 25 to 75 per cent.

Your Committee have seen sufficient, by clear evidence, to guarantee the opinion, that our people in Ohio, Illinois, and Michigan, in active business, (aside from Agriculture,) have $1,500,000; in Massachusetts, Maine, Rhode Island, and Connecticut, $2,000,000; in New York and Pennsylvania, $3,000,000; and California, $200,000; saying nothing of the Six Hundred Thousand Dollars invested in Savings Banks in and around New York, and its vicinity, and also similar amounts around other cities.

The youth who has the spirit of accumulation, and is intelligent with figures and the Pen, having saved something as a beginning in life, ought like the whites buy goods and venture his turn in the stream of trade and business. They would find by perseverence that in time they would receive the reward they merit, and the true principle of personal elevation brought to the common stock to destroy the barriers around our feet.

KEY DEBATE ～ *Religion*

RICHARD ALLEN

from *The Life, Experience, and Gospel Labors of the Rt. Rev. Richard Allen* [1833]

"The name of this very man (Richard Allen)," wrote David Walker (pp. 27, 86, and 103) in Article IV of his *Appeal*, "will [* * *] stand on the pages of history among the greatest divines who have lived since the apostolic age." Richard Allen (1760–1831), a founder and the first bishop of the African Methodist Episcopal (AME) church, was born into slavery. At age seventeen, he converted to Methodism and soon bought his freedom. Allen's autobiography, discovered in an old chest after his death, underscores the tension in African American religious history between a commitment to an established church and adherence to one's own beliefs and practices. As his account demonstrates, Allen viewed the establishment of a separate church as an act of resistance against institutionalized racism.

Allen's Bethel Church in Philadelphia was dedicated in 1794, and in 1816 he founded a new Methodist denomination for African American worshippers: the AME church. Other denominations followed. Black Baptists in particular contributed to the rapid expansion in the number of new black churches. By the 1830s, the growth of separate black churches had become so dramatic that a number of African American leaders began to voice concerns openly. In 1837, *The Colored American,* the dominant black paper of the late 1830s, insisted, "We regret that there ever was a separate church or any kind of separate institution built for colored people." In 1848, in his newspaper *The North Star,* Frederick Douglass (p. 38) went so far as to call black churches "negro pews, on a higher and larger scale." "If there be any good reason for a colored church," Douglass argued, "the same will hold good in regard to a colored school, and indeed to every other institution founded on complexion."

From *The Life Experience and Gospel Labors of the Rt. Rev. Richard Allen* (Philadelphia, PA: F. Ford and M. A. Riply, 1880), pp. 5–24.

I was born in the year of our Lord 1760, on February 14th, a slave to Benjamin Chew, of Philadelphia. My mother and father and four children of us were sold into Delaware state, near Dover; and I was a child and lived with him until I was upwards of twenty years of age, during which time I was awakened and brought to see myself, poor, wretched and undone, and without the mercy of God must be lost. Shortly after, I obtained mercy through the blood of Christ, and was constrained to exhort my old companions to seek the Lord. I went rejoicing for several days and was happy in the Lord, in conversing with many old, experienced Christians. I was brought under doubts, and was tempted to believe I was deceived, and was con-

strained to seek the Lord afresh. I went with my head bowed down for many days. My sins were a heavy burden. I was tempted to believe there was no mercy for me. I cried to the Lord both night and day. One night I thought hell would be my portion. I cried unto Him who delighteth to hear the prayers of a poor sinner, and all of a sudden my dungeon shook, my chains flew off, and, glory to God, I cried. My soul was filled. I cried, enough for me—the Saviour died. Now my confidence was strengthened that the Lord, for Christ's sake, had heard my prayers and pardoned all my sins. I was constrained to go from house to house, exhorting my old companions, and telling to all around what a dear Saviour I had found. I joined the Methodist Society and met in class at Benjamin Wells's, in the forest, Delaware state. John Gray was the class-leader. I met in his class for several years.

My master was an unconverted man, and all the family, but he was what the world called a good master. He was more like a father to his slaves than anything else. He was a very tender, humane man. My mother and father lived with him for many years. He was brought into difficulty, not being able to pay for us, and mother having several children after he had bought us, he sold my mother and three children. My mother sought the Lord and found favor with him, and became a very pious woman. There were three children of us remained with our old master. My oldest brother embraced religion and my sister. Our neighbors, seeing that our master indulged us with the privilege of attending meeting once in two weeks, said that Stokeley's Negroes would soon ruin him; and so my brother and myself held a council together, that we would attend more faithfully to our master's business, so that it should not be said that religion made us worse servants; we would work night and day to get our crops forward, so that they should be disappointed. We frequently went to meeting on every other Thursday; but if we were likely to be backward with our crops we would refrain from going to meeting. When our master found we were making no provision to go to meeting, he would frequently ask us if it was not our meeting day, and if we were not going. We would frequently tell him; "No sir, we would rather stay at home and get our work done." He would tell us: "Boys, I would rather you would go to your meeting; if I am not good myself, I like to see you striving yourselves to be good." Our reply would be: "Thank you, sir, but we would rather stay and get our crops forward." So we always continued to keep our crops more forward than our neighbors, and we would attend public preaching once in two weeks, and class meeting once a week. At length, our master said he was convinced that religion made slaves better and not worse, and often boasted of his slaves for their honesty and industry. Some time after, I asked him if I might ask the preachers to come and preach at his house. He being old and infirm, my master and mistress cheerfully agreed for me to ask

some of the Methodist preachers to come and preach at his house. I asked him for a note. He replied, if my word was not sufficient, he should send no note. I accordingly asked the preacher. He seemed somewhat backward at first, as my master did not send a written request; but the class leader (John Gray) observed that my word was sufficient; so he preached at my old master's house on the next Wednesday. Preaching continued for some months; at length, Freeborn Garrettson preached from these words, "Thou art weighed in the balance, and art found wanting."[1] In pointing out and weighing the different characters, and among the rest weighed the slaveholders, my master believed himself to be one of that number, and after that he could not be satisfied to hold slaves, believing it to be wrong. And after that he proposed to me and my brother buying our times, to pay him 60£. gold and silver, or $2000, Continental money, which we complied with in the year 17——.

We left our master's house, and I may truly say it was like leaving our father's house; for he was a kind, affectionate and tender-hearted master, and told us to make his house our home when we were out of a place or sick. While living with him we had family prayer in the kitchen, to which he frequently would come out himself at time of prayer, and my mistress with him. At length he invited us from the kitchen to the parlor to hold family prayer, which we attended to. We had our stated times to hold our prayer meetings and give exhortations at in the neighborhood.

I had it often impressed upon my mind that I should one day enjoy my freedom; for slavery is a bitter pill, notwithstanding we had a good master. But when we would think that our day's work was never done, we often thought that after our master's death we were liable to be sold to the highest bidder, as he was much in debt; and thus my troubles were increased, and I was often brought to weep between the porch and the altar. But I have had reason to bless my dear Lord that a door was opened unexpectedly for me to buy my time and enjoy my liberty. When I left my master's house I knew not what to do, not being used to hard work, what business I should follow to pay my master and get my living. I went to cutting of cord wood. The

1. Daniel 5:27.

first day my hands were so blistered and sore, that it was with difficulty I could open or shut them. I kneeled down upon my knees and prayed that the Lord would open some way for me to get my living. In a few days, my hands recovered and became accustomed to cutting of wood & other hardships; so I soon became able to cut my cord and a half and two cords a day. After I was done cutting I was employed in a brickyard by one Robert Register, at $50 a month, Continental money. After I was done with the brickyard I went to days' work, but did not forget to serve my dear Lord. I used ofttimes to pray, sitting, standing or lying; and while my hands were employed to earn my bread, my heart was devoted to my dear Redeemer. Sometimes I would awake from my sleep, preaching and praying. I was after this employed in driving of wagon in time of the Continental war, in drawing salt from Rehobar,[2] Sussex County, in Delaware. I had my regular stops and preaching places on the road. I enjoyed many happy seasons in meditation and prayer while in this employment.

After peace was proclaimed, I then travelled extensively, striving to preach the Gospel. My lot was cast in Wilmington. Shortly after, I was taken sick with the fall fever and then the pleurisy. September the 3d 1783, I left my native place. After leaving Wilmington, I went into New Jersey, and there traveled and strove to preach the Gospel until the spring of 1784. I then became acquainted with Benjamin Abbott, that great and good apostle. He was one of the greatest men that ever I was acquainted with. He seldom preached but what there were souls added to his labor. He was a man of as great faith as any that ever I saw. The Lord was with him, and blessed his labors abundantly. He was as a friend and father to me. I was sorry when I had to leave West Jersey, knowing I had to leave a father. I was employed in cutting of wood for Captain Cruenkleton, although I preached the Gospel at nights and on Sundays. My dear Lord was with me, and blessed my labors—Glory to God—and gave me souls for my hire. [* * *] In the year 1784, I left East Jersey and labored in Pennsylvania. I walked until my feet became so sore and blistered the first day, that I scarcely could bear them to the ground. I found the people very

humane and kind in Pennsylvania. I having but little money, I stopped at Caesar Waters's, at Radnor township, twelve miles from Philadelphia. I found him and his wife very kind and affectionate to me. In the evening they asked me if I would come and take tea with them; but after sitting awhile, my feet became so sore and painful that I could scarcely be able to put them to the floor. I told them that I would accept of their kind invitation, but my feet pained me so that I could not come to the table. They brought the table to me. Never was I more kindly received by strangers that I had never before seen, than by them. She bathed my feet with warm water and bran; the next morning my feet were better and free from pain. They asked me if I would preach for them. I preached for them the next evening. We had a glorious meeting. They invited me to stay till Sabbath day, and preach for them. I agreed to do so, and preached on Sabbath day to a large congregation of different persuasions, and my dear Lord was with me, and I believe there were many souls cut to the heart, and were added to the ministry. They insisted on me to stay longer with them. I stayed and labored in Radnor several weeks. Many souls were awakened and cried aloud to the Lord to have mercy upon them. I was frequently called upon by many inquiring what they should do to be saved. I appointed them to prayer and supplication at the throne of grace, and to make use of all manner of prayer, and pointed them to the invitation of our Lord and Saviour, Jesus Christ, who has said: "Come unto me, all ye that are weary and heavy laden, and I will give you rest."[3] Glory be to God! and now I know he was a God at hand and not afar off. I preached my farewell sermon, and left these dear people. It was a time of visitation from above, many were the slain of the Lord. Seldom did I ever experience such a time of mourning and lamentation among a people. There were but few colored people in the neighborhood—the most of my congregation was white. Some said, "this man must be a man of God; I never heard such preaching before." We spent a greater part of the night in singing and prayer with the mourners. I expected I should have had to walk, as I had done before; but Mr. Davis had a creature that he made a present to me; but I intended to pay him

2. Rehoboth
3. Slight variation on Matthew 11:28.

for his horse if ever I got able. My dear Lord was kind and gracious to me. [∗ ∗ ∗]

December 1784, General Conference sat in Baltimore, the first General Conference ever held in America. The English preachers just arrived from Europe, Rev. Dr. Coke, Richard Watcoat and Thomas Vasses. This was the beginning of the Episcopal Church amongst the Methodists. Many of the ministers were set apart in holy orders at this conference, and were said to be entitled to the gown; and I have thought religion has been declining in the church ever since. There was a pamphlet published by some person, which stated, that when the Methodists were no people, then they were a people; and now they have become a people they were no people; which had often serious weight upon my mind.

In 1785 the Rev. Richard Watcoat was appointed on Baltimore circuit. He was, I believe, a man of God. I found great strength in travelling with him—a father in Israel. In his advice he was fatherly and friendly. He was of a mild and serene disposition. My lot was cast in Baltimore, in a small meeting-house called Methodist Alley. I stopped at Richard Mould's, and was sent to my lodgings, and lodged at Mr. McCannon's. I had some happy meetings in Baltimore. I was introduced to Richard Russell, who was very kind and affectionate to me, and attended several meetings. Rev. Bishop Asbury sent for me to meet him at Henry Gaff's. I did so. He told me he wished me to travel with him. He told me that in the slave countries, Carolina and other places, I must not intermix with the slaves, and I would frequently have to sleep in his carriage, and he would allow me my victuals and clothes. I told him I would not travel with him on these conditions. He asked me my reason. I told him if I was taken sick, who was to support me? and that I thought people ought to lay up something while they were able, to support themselves in time of sickness or old age. He said that was as much as he got, his victuals and clothes. I told him he would be taken care of, let his afflictions be as they were, or let him be taken sick where he would, he would be taken care of; but I doubted whether it would be the case with myself. He smiled, and told me he would give me from then until he returned from the eastward to make up my mind, which would be about three months. But I made up my mind that I would not

accept of his proposals. Shortly after I left Hartford circuit, and came to Pennsylvania, on Lancaster circuit. I travelled several months on Lancaster circuit with the Rev. Peter Morratte and Irie Ellis. They were very kind and affectionate to me in building me up; for I had many trials to pass through, and I received nothing from the Methodist connection. My usual method was, when I would get bare of clothes, to stop travelling and go to work, so that no man could say I was chargeable to the connection. My hands administered to my necessities. The autumn of 1785 I returned again to Radnor. I stopped at George Giger's, a man of God, and went to work. His family were all kind and affectionate to me. I killed seven beeves, and supplied the neighbors with meat; got myself pretty well clad through my own industry—thank God—and preached occasionally. The elder in charge in Philadelphia frequently sent for me to come to the city. February, 1786, I came to Philadelphia. Preaching was given out for me at five o'clock in the morning at St. George's church. I strove to preach as well as I could, but it was a great cross to me; but the Lord was with me. We had a good time, and several souls were awakened, and were earnestly seeking redemption in the blood of Christ. I thought I would stop in Philadelphia a week or two. I preached at different places in the city. My labor was much blessed. I soon saw a large field open in seeking and instructing my African brethren, who had been a long forgotten people and few of them attended public worship. I preached in the commons, in Southwark, Northern Liberties, and wherever I could find an opening. I frequently preached twice a day, at 5 o'clock in the morning and in the evening, and it was not uncommon for me to preach from four to five times a day. I established prayer meetings; I raised a society in 1786 for forty-two members. I saw the necessity of erecting a place of worship for the colored people. I proposed it to the most respectable people of color in this city; but here I met with opposition. I had but three colored brethren that united with me in erecting a place of worship—the Rev. Absalom Jones, William White and Dorus Ginnings. These united with me as soon as it became public and known by the elder who was stationed in the city. The Rev. C—— B—— opposed the plan, and would not submit to any argument we could raise; but he was shortly removed from the charge. The Rev. Mr. W—— took the charge, and the Rev. L—— G——. Mr. W—— was much opposed to an African church, and used very degrading and insulting language to us, to try and prevent us from going on. We all belonged to St. George's church—Rev. Absalom Jones, William White and Dorus Ginnings. We felt ourselves much cramped; but my dear Lord was with us, and we believed, if it was his will, the work would go on, and that we would be able to succeed in building the house of the Lord. We established prayer meetings and meetings of exhortation, and the Lord blessed our endeavors, and many souls were awakened; but the elder soon forbid us holding any such meetings; but we viewed the forlorn state of our colored brethren, and that they were destitute of a place of worship. They were considered as a nuisance.

A number of us usually attended St. George's church in Fourth street; and when the colored people began to get numerous in attending the church, they moved us from the seats we usually sat on, and placed us around the wall, and on Sabbath morning we went to church and the sexton stood at the door, and told us to go in the gallery. He told us to go, and we would see where to sit. We expected to take the seats over the ones we formerly occupied below, not knowing any better. We took those seats. Meeting had begun, and they were nearly done singing, and just as we got to the seats, the elder said, "Let us pray." We had not been long upon our knees before I heard considerable scuffling and low talking. I raised my head up and saw one of the trustees, H—— M——, having hold of the Rev. Absalom Jones, pulling him up off of his knees, and saying, "You must get up—you must not kneel here." Mr. Jones replied, "Wait until prayer is over." Mr. H—— M—— said "No, you must get up now, or I will call for aid and force you away." Mr. Jones said, "Wait until prayer is over, and I will get up and trouble you no more." With that he beckoned to one of the other trustees, Mr. L—— S—— to come to his assistance. He came, and went to William White to pull him up. By this time prayer was over, and we all went out of the church in a body, and they were no more plagued with us in the church. This raised a great excitement and inquiry among the citizens, in so much that I believe they were ashamed of their con-

duct. But my dear Lord was with us, and we were filled with fresh vigor to get a house erected to worship God in. Seeing our forlorn and distressed situation, many of the hearts of our citizens were moved to urge us forward; notwithstanding we had subscribed largely towards finishing St. George's church, in building the gallery and laying new floors, and just as the house was made comfortable, we were turned out from enjoying the comforts of worshipping therein. We then hired a store-room, and held worship by ourselves. Here we were pursued with threats of being disowned, and read publicly out of meeting if we did continue worship in the place we had hired; but we believed the Lord would be our friend. We got subscription papers out to raise money to build the house of the Lord. By this time we had waited on Dr. Rush and Mr. Robert Ralston, and told them of our distressing situation. We considered it a blessing that the Lord had put it into our hearts to wait upon those gentlemen. They pitied our situation, and subscribed largely towards the church, and were very friendly towards us, and advised us how to go on. We appointed Mr. Ralston our treasurer. Dr. Rush did much for us in public by his influence. I hope the name of Dr. Benjamin Rush and Robert Ralston will never be forgotten among us. They were the first two gentlemen who espoused the cause of the oppressed, and aided us in building the house of the Lord for the poor Africans to worship in. Here was the beginning and rise of the first African church in America. [* * *]

We bore much persecution from many of the Methodist connection; but we have reason to be thankful to Almighty God, who was our deliverer. The day was appointed to go and dig the cellar. I arose early in the morning and addressed the throne of grace, praying that the Lord would bless our endeavors. Having by this time two or three teams of my own—as I was the first proposer of the African church, I put the first spade in the ground to dig a cellar for the same. This was the first African Church or meeting-house that was erected in the United States of America. We intended it for the African preaching-house or church; but finding that the elder stationed in this city was such an opposer to our proceedings of erecting a place of worship, though the principal part of the directors of this church belonged to the Methodist connection, the elder stationed here would neither preach for us, nor have anything to do with us. We then held an election, to know what religious denomination we should unite with. At the election it was determined— there were two in favor of the Methodist, the Rev. Absalom Jones and myself, and a large majority in favor of the Church of England. The majority carried. Notwithstanding we had been so violently persecuted by the elder, we were in favor of being attached to the Methodist connection; for I was confident that there was no religious sect or denomination would suit the capacity of the colored people as well as the Methodist; for the plain and simple gospel suits best for any people; for the unlearned can understand, and the learned are sure to understand; and the reason that the Methodist is so successful in the awakening and conversion of the colored people, the plain doctrine and having a good discipline. But in many cases the preachers would act to please their own fancy, without discipline, till some of them became such tyrants, and more especially to the colored people. They would turn them out of society, giving them no trial, for the smallest offense, perhaps only hearsay. They would frequently, in meeting the class, impeach some of the members of whom they had heard an ill report, and turn them out, saying, "I have heard thus and thus of you, and you are no more a member of society"— without witnesses on either side. This has been frequently done, notwithstanding in the first rise and progress in Delaware state, and elsewhere, the colored people were their greatest support; for there were but few of us free; but the slaves would toll in their little patches many a night until midnight to raise their little truck and sell to get something to support them more than what their masters gave them, but we used often to divide our little support among the white preachers of the Gospel. This was once a quarter. It was in the time of the old revolutionary war between Great Britain and the United States. The Methodists were the first people that brought glad tidings to the colored people. I feel thankful that ever I heard a Methodist preach. We are beholden to the Methodists, under

God, for the light of the Gospel we enjoy; for all other denominations preached so high-flown that we were not able to comprehend their doctrine. Sure am I that reading sermons will never prove so beneficial to the colored people as spiritual or extempore preaching. I am well convinced that the Methodist has proved beneficial to thousands and ten times thousands. It is to be awfully feared that the simplicity of the Gospel that was among them fifty years ago, and that they conform more to the world and the fashions thereof, they would fare very little better than the people of the world. The discipline is altered considerably from what it was. We would ask for the good old way, and desire to walk therein.

In 1793 a committee was appointed from the African Church to solicit me to be their minister, for there was no colored preacher in Philadelphia but myself. I told them I could not accept of their offer, as I was a Methodist. I was indebted to the Methodists, under God, for what little religion I had; being convinced that they were the people of God, I informed them that I could not be anything else but a Methodist, as I was born and awakened under them, and I could go no further with them, for I was a Methodist, and would leave you in peace and love. I would do nothing to retard them in building a church as it was an extensive building, neither would I go out with a subscription paper until they were done going out with their subscription. I bought an old frame that had been formerly occupied as a blacksmith shop, from Mr. Sims, and hauled it on the lot in Sixth near Lombard street, that had formerly been taken for the Church of England. I employed carpenters to repair the old frame, and fit it for a place of worship. In July 1794, Bishop Asbury being in town I solicited him to open the church[4] for us which he accepted. The Rev. John Dickins sung and prayed, and Bishop Asbury preached. The house was called Bethel, agreeable to the prayer that was made. Mr. Dickins prayed that it might be a bethel[5] to the gathering in of thousands of souls. My dear Lord was with us, so that there were many hearty "amen's" echoed through the house. This house of

---

4. This church will at present [c. 1830] accommodate between 3,000 and 4,000 persons. [Allen's note]
5. See Genesis chapter 28. [Allen's note] Verse 19.

worship has been favored with the awakening of many souls, and I trust they are in the Kingdom, both white and colored. Our warfare and troubles now began afresh. Mr. C. proposed that we should make over the church to the Conference. This we objected to, he asserted that we could not be Methodists unless we did; we told him he might deny us their name, but they could not deny us a seat in Heaven. Finding that he could not prevail with us so to do, he observed that we had better be incorporated, then we could get any legacies that were left for us, if not, we could not. We agreed to be incorporated. He offered to draw the incorporation himself, that it would save us the trouble of paying for to get it drawn. We cheerfully submitted to his proposed plan. He drew the incorporation, but incorporated our church under the Conference, our property was then all consigned to the Conference for the present bishops, elders, ministers, etc., that belonged to the white Conference, and our property was gone. Being ignorant of incorporations we cheerfully agreed thereto. We labored about ten years under this incorporation, until J[ames] S[mith] was appointed to take the charge in Philadelphia; he soon waked us up by demanding the keys and books of the church, and forbid us holding any meetings except by orders from him; these propositions we told him we could not agree to. He observed he was elder, appointed to the charge, and unless we submitted to him, he would read us all out of meeting. We told him the house was ours, we had bought it, and paid for it. He said he would let us know it was not ours, it belonged to the Conference; we took counsel on it; counsel informed us we had been taken in; according to the incorporation it belonged to the white connection. We asked him if it couldn't be altered; he told us if two-thirds of the society agreed to have it altered, it could be altered. He gave me a transcript to lay before them; I called the society together and laid it before them. My dear Lord was with us. It was unanimously agreed to, by both male and female. We had another incorporation drawn that took the church from Conference, and got it passed, before the elder knew anything about it. This raised a considerable rumpus, for the elder contended that it would not be good unless he had signed it. The elder, with the trustees of St. George's, called us together, and said we must pay six hundred dollars a year for their services, or they could not serve us. We told them we were not able so to do. The trustees of St. George's insisted that we should or should not be supplied by their preachers. At last they made a move that they would take four hundred; we told them that our house was considerably in debt, and we poor people, and we could not agree to pay four hundred, but we agreed to give them two hundred. It was moved by one of the trustees of St. George's that the money should be paid into their treasury; we refused paying it into their treasury, but we would pay it to the preacher that served; they made a move that the preacher should not receive the money from us. The Bethel trustees made a move that their funds should be shut and they would pay none; this caused a considerable contention. At length they withdrew their motion. The elder supplied us preaching five times in a year for two hundred dollars. Finding that they supplied us so seldom, the trustees of Bethel church passed a resolution that they would pay but one hundred dollars a year, as the elder only preached five times in a year for us; they called for the money, we paid him twenty-five dollars a quarter, but he being dissatisfied, returned the money back again, and would not have it unless we paid him fifty dollars. The trustees concluded it was enough for five sermons, and said they would pay no more; the elder of St. George's was determined to preach for us no more, unless we gave him two hundred dollars, and we were left alone for upwards of one year.

Mr. S[amuel] R[oyal] being appointed to the charge of Philadelphia, declared unless we should repeal the Supplement, neither he nor any white preacher, travelling or local, should preach any more for us; so we were left to ourselves. At length the preachers and stewards belonging to the Academy, proposed serving us on the same terms that we had offered to the St. George's preachers, and they preached for us better than a twelve month, and then demanded $150 per year; this not being complied with, they declined preaching for us, and we were once more left to ourselves, as an edict was passed by the elder, that if any local preacher should serve us, he should be expelled from the connection. John Emory, then elder of the Academy, published a circular letter, in which we were disowned by the Methodists. A house was also hired and fitted up for worship, not far from Bethel, and an invitation given to all who desired to be Methodists to resort thither. But being disappointed in this plan, Robert R. Roberts, the resident elder, came to Bethel, insisted on preaching to us and taking the spiritual charge of the congregation, for we were Methodists. He was told he should come on some terms with the trustees; his answer was, that "He did not come to consult with Richard Allen or other trustees, but to inform the congregation, that on next Sunday afternoon, he would come and take the spiritual charge." We told him he could not preach for us under existing circumstances. However, at the appointed time he came, but having taken previous advice we had our preacher in the pulpit when he came, and the house was so fixed that he could not get but more than half way to the pulpit. Finding himself disappointed he appealed to those who came with him as witnesses, that "That man (meaning the preacher), had taken his appointment." Several respectable white citizens, who knew the colored people had been ill-used, were present, and told us not to fear, for they would see us righted, and not suffer Roberts to preach in a forcible manner, after which Roberts went away.

The next elder stationed in Philadelphia was Robert Birch, who, following the example of his predecessor, came and published a meeting for himself. But the method just mentioned was adopted and he had to go away disappointed. In consequence of this, he applied to the Supreme Court for a writ of mandamus, to know why the pulpit was denied him. Being elder, this brought on a lawsuit, which ended in our favor. Thus by the Providence of God we were delivered from a long, distressing and expensive suit, which could not be resumed, being determined by the Supreme Court.[6] For this mercy we desire to be unfeignedly thankful.

About this time, our colored friends in Baltimore were treated in a similar manner by the white preachers and trustees, and many of them driven away who were disposed to seek a place of worship, rather than go to law.

Many of the colored people in other places were in a situation nearly like those of Philadelphia and Baltimore, which induced us, in April 1816, to call a general meeting, by way of Conference. Delegates from Baltimore and other places which met those of Philadelphia, and taking into consideration their grievances, and in order to secure the privileges, promote union and harmony among themselves, it was resolved: "That the people of Philadelphia, Baltimore, etc., etc., should become one body, under the name of the African Methodist Episcopal Church." We deemed it expedient to have a form of discipline, whereby we may guide our people in the fear of God, in the unity of the Spirit, and in the bonds of peace, and preserve us from that spiritual despotism which we have so recently experienced—remembering that we are not to lord it over God's heritage, as greedy dogs that can never have enough. But with long suffering and bowels of compassion, to bear each other's burdens, and so fulfill the Law of Christ, praying that our mutual striving together for the promulgation of the Gospel may be crowned with abundant success.

> The God of Bethel heard her cries,
> He let his power be seen;
> He stopp'd the proud oppressor's frown,
> And proved himself a King.
>
> Thou sav'd them in the trying hour,
> Ministers and councils joined,
> And all stood ready to retain
> That helpless church of Thine.
>
> Bethel surrounded by her foes,
> But not yet in despair,
> Christ heard her supplicating cries;
> The God of Bethel heard.[7]

---

6. Birch brought the suit in 1816 to the Supreme Court of Pennsylvania, the highest court in the state.

7. In 1801, Allen published a hymnal for his congregation at Bethel Church, which included "The God of Bethel heard her cries" and other songs he had written about the rise of black churches.

JARENA LEE

from *The Life and Religious Experience of Jarena Lee* [1836]

When twenty-one year-old Jarena Lee (1783–ca. 1849) attended the AME church in Philadelphia and heard the Reverend Richard Allen preach (p. 144), she found "the people to which my heart unites." Yet it was Allen who, years later, in 1811, discouraged Lee from answering her call to preach. The Methodist discipline, Allen pointed out, "did not call for women preachers." Instead of establishing a separate church that would allow her full rights to fulfill her religious convictions, as Allen had done for himself, Lee strove to create a place for herself within the strictures of her church, and to do so without sacrificing her sense that she was responding to a divine calling. She went on to write her autobiography, in which she employs theological reasoning to back her case for female preachers, asserting that "as unseemly as it may appear now-a-days for a woman to preach, it should be remembered that nothing is impossible with God." It was not theological reasoning, however, but evidence of her powerful faith that eventually convinced Allen of Lee's calling, eight years after she had first approached him. By that time, the AME church had become an independent denomination, with Allen as its first bishop. Allen not only officially sanctioned Lee's preaching but also became a prime supporter of her work, arranging speaking engagements for her and even taking care of her son for two years while she traveled beyond Philadelphia to preach.

Lee was born free in Cape May, New Jersey. Her parents were poor, and she left home to work as a live-in servant when she was seven, an early childhood experience similar to that of the activist Maria W. Stewart (p. 60). Inspired by Richard Allen, Lee converted to Christianity as a young adult. Married in 1811, Lee—again like Stewart—was widowed at a young age. She then dedicated herself to her religious calling, while also caring for her two small children. Her sole publication is her autobiography, first published in 1836 as *The Life and Religious Experience of Jarena Lee, a Coloured Lady, Giving an Account of Her Call to Preach the Gospel*, and revised and expanded in 1849 as *Religious Experience and Journal of Mrs. Jarena Lee, Giving an Account of Her Call to Preach the Gospel*. The year of her death is unknown, as the documentary record of her life ends in 1849 with the reissue of her autobiography. Lee is recognized as the first authorized female preacher in the AME church.

From Jarena Lee, *Religious Experience and Journal of Mrs. Jarena Lee, Giving an Account of Her Call to Preach the Gospel* (Philadelphia: Jarena Lee, 1849), pp. 10–21, 97–98.

MY CALL TO PREACH THE GOSPEL.

Between four and five years after my sanctification, on a certain time, an impressive silence fell upon me, and I stood as if some one was about to speak to me, yet I had no such thought in my heart.—But to my utter surprise there seemed to sound a voice which I thought I distinctly heard, and most certainly understand, which said to me, "Go preach the Gospel!" I immediately replied aloud, "No one will believe me." Again I listened, and again the same voice seemed to say— "Preach the Gospel; I will put words in your mouth, and will turn your enemies to become your friends."

At first I supposed that Satan had spoken to me, for I had read that he could transform himself into an angel of light for the purpose of deception. Immedi- ately I went into a secret place, and called upon the Lord to know if he had called me to preach, and whether I was deceived or not; when there appeared to my view the form and figure of a pulpit, with a Bible lying thereon, the back of which was presented to me as plainly as if it had been a literal fact.

In consequence of this, my mind became so exer- cised, that during the night following, I took a text and preached in my sleep. I thought those stood before me a great multitude, while I expounded to them the things of religion. So violent were my exertions and so loud were my exclamations, that I awoke from the sound of my own voice, which also awoke the family of the house where I resided. Two days after I went to see the preacher in charge of the African Society, who was the Rev. Richard Allen, the same before named in these pages, to tell him that I felt it my duty to preach the gospel. But as I drew near the street in which his house was, which was in the city of Philadelphia, my courage began to fail me; so terrible did the cross appear, it seemed that I should not be able to bear it. Previous to my setting out to go to see him, so agitated was my mind, that my appetite for my daily food failed me entirely. Several times on my way there, I turned back again; but as often I felt my strength again renewed, and I soon found that the nearer I approached to the house of the minister, the less was my fear. Accordingly, as soon as I came to the door, my fears subsided, the cross was removed, all things appeared pleasant—I was tranquil.

I now told him, that the Lord had revealed it to me, that must preach the gospel. He replied, by asking, in what sphere I wished to move in? I said, among the Methodists. He then replied, that a Mrs. Cook, a Methodist lady, had also some time before requested the same privilege; who, it was believed, had done much good in the way of exhortation, and holding prayer meetings; and who had been permitted to do so by the verbal license of the preacher in charge at the time. But as to women preaching, he said that our Discipline knew nothing at all about it—that it did not call for women preachers. This I was glad to hear, because it removed the fear of the cross—but no sooner did this feeling cross my mind, than I found that a love of souls had in a measure departed from me; that holy energy which burned within me, as a fire, began to be smothered. This I soon perceived.

O how careful ought we to be, last through our by-laws of church government and discipline, we bring into disrepute even the word of life. For as unseemly as it may appear now-a-days for a woman to preach, it should be remembered that nothing is impossible with God. And why should it be thought impossible, heterodox, or improper for a woman to preach? seeing the Saviour died for the woman as well as for the man.

If the man may preach, because the Saviour died for him, why not the woman? seeing he died for her also. Is he not a whole Saviour, instead of a half one? as those who hold it wrong for a woman to preach, would seem to make it appear.

Did not Mary *first* preach the risen Saviour, and is not the doctrine of the resurrection the very climax of

Christianity—hangs not all our hope on this, as argued by St. Paul? Then did not Mary, a woman, preach the gospel? for she preached the resurrection of the crucified Son of God.

But some will say that Mary did not expound the Scripture, therefore, she did not preach, in the proper sense of the term. To this I reply, it may be that the term *preach* in those primitive times, did not mean exactly what it is now *made* to mean; perhaps it was a great deal more simple then, than it is now—if it were not, the unlearned fishermen could not have preached the gospel at all, as they had no learning.

To this it may be replied, by these who are determined not to believe that it is right for a woman to preach, that the disciples, though they were fishermen and ignorant of letters too, were inspired so to do. To which I would reply, that though they were inspired, yet that inspiration did not save them from showing their ignorance of letters, and of man's wisdom; this the multitude soon found out, by listening to the remarks of the envious Jewish priests. If then, to preach the gospel, by the gift of heaven, comes by inspiration solely, is God straitened: must he take the man exclusively? May he not, did he not, and can he not inspire a female to preach the simple story of the birth, life, death, and resurrection of our Lord, and accompany it too with power to the sinner's heart. As for me, I am fully persuaded that the Lord called me to labor according to what I have received, in his vineyard. If he has not, how could he consistently bear testimony in favor of my poor labors, in awakening and converting sinners?

In my wanderings up and down among men, preaching according to my ability, I have frequently found families who told me that they had not for several years been to a meeting, and yet, while listening to hear what God would say by his poor female instrument, have believed with trembling—tears rolling down their cheeks, the signs of contrition and repentance towards God. I firmly believe that I have sown seed, in the name of the Lord, which shall appear with its increase at the great day of accounts, when Christ shall come to make up his jewels.

At a certain time, I was beset with the idea, that seen or late I should fall from grace and lose my soul at last. I was frequently called to the throne of grace about this matter, but found no relief; the temptation pursued me still. Being more and more afflicted with it, till at a certain time, when the spirit strongly impressed it on my mind to enter into my closet and carry my case once more to the Lord; the Lord enabled me to draw nigh to him, and to his mercy soot, at this time, in an extraordinary manner; for while I wrestled with him for the victory over this disposition to doubt whether I should persevere, there appeared a form of fire, about the size of a man's hand, as I was on my knees; at the same moment there appeared to the eye of faith a man robed in a white garment, from the shoulders down to the feet; from him a voice proceeded, saying: "Thou shalt never return from the cross." Since that time I have never doubted, but believe that God will keep me until the day of redemption. Now I could adopt the very language of St. Paul, and my, that nothing could have separated me from the love of God, which is in Christ Jesus. Since that time, 1807, until the present, 1833, I have not even doubted the power and goodness of God to keep me from falling, through the sanctification of the spirit and belief of the truth.

MY MARRIAGE.

In the year 1811, I changed my situation in life, having married Mr. Joseph Lee, pastor of a Society at Snow Hill, about six miles from the city of Philadelphia. It became necessary therefore for me to remove. This was a great trial at first, as I knew no person at Snow Hill, except my husband, and to leave my associates in the society, and especially those who composed the *band* of which I was one. None but those who have been in sweet fellowship with such as really love God, and have together drank bliss and happiness from the same fountain, can tell how dear such company is, and how hard it is to part from them.

At Snow Hill, as was feared, I never found that agreement and closeness in communion and fellowship, that I had in Philadelphia, among my young companions, nor ought I to have expected it. The manners and customs at this place were somewhat different, on

which account I became discontented in the course of a year, and began to importune my husband to remove to the city. But this plan did not suit him, as he was the Pastor of the Society, he could not bring his mind to leave them. This afflicted me a little. But the Lord showed me in a dream what his will was concerning this matter.

I dreamed that as I was walking on the summit of a beautiful hill, that I saw near me a fleck of sheep, fair and white, as if but newly washed; when there came walking toward me a man of a grave and dignified countenance, dressed entirely in white, as it were in a robe, and looking at me, said emphatically, "Joseph Lee must take care of these sheep, or the wolf will come and devour them." When I awoke I was convinced of my error, and immediately, with a glad heart, yielded to the right spirit in the Lord. This also greatly strengthened my faith in his care over them, for fear the wolf should by some means take any of them away. The following verse was beautifully suited to our condition, as well as to all the little flocks of God scattered up and down this land:

> "Us into Thy production take,
>   And gather with Thine arm;
> Unless the fold we first forsake,
>   The wolf can never harm."[1]

After this, I fell into a state of general debility, and in an ill state of health, so much so, that I could not sit up; but a desire to warn sinners to flee the wrath to come, burned vehemently in my heart, when the Lord would send sinners into the house to see me. Such opportunities I embraced to press home on their consciences the things of eternity, and so effectual was the word of exhortation made through the Spirit, that I have seen them fall to the floor crying aloud for mercy.

From this sickness I did not expect to recover, and there was but one thing which bound me to earth, and this was, that I had not as yet preached the gospel to the fallen sons and daughters of Adam's race, to the satisfaction of my mind. I wished to go from one end of the earth to the other, crying, Behold, behold the

---

1. From "Jesus Great Shepherd of the Sheep," a hymn by Charles Wesley (1707–88), British leader of the Methodist movement and writer of over 6,000 hymns.

lamb! To this end I earnestly prayed the Lord to raise me up, if consistent with his will. He condescended to hear my prayer, and to give me a token in a dream, that in due time I should recover my health. The dream was as follows: I thought I saw the sun rise in the morning, and ascend to an altitude of about half an hour high, and then become obscured by a dense black cloud, which continued to hide its rays for about one-third part of the day, and then it burst forth again with renewed splendor.

This dream I interpreted to signify my early life, my conversion to God, and this sickness, which was a great affliction, as it hindered me, and I feared would forever hinder me from preaching the gospel, was signified by the cloud; and the bursting forth of the sun, again, was the recovery of my health, and being permitted to preach.

I went to the throne of grace on this subject, where the Lord made this impressive reply in my heart, while on my knees: "Ye shall be restored to thy health again, and worship God in full purpose of heart."

This manifestation was so impressive, that I could but hide my face as if some one was gazing upon me, to think of the great goodness of the Almighty God to my poor soul and body. From that very time I began to gain strength of body and mind, glory to God in the highest, until my health was fully recovered.

For six years from this time I continued to receive from above, such baptisms of the Spirit as mortality could scarcely bear. About that time I was called to suffer in my family, by death—five, in the course of about six years, fell by his hand; my husband being one of the number, which was the greatest affliction of all.

I was now left alone in the world, with two infant children, one of the age of about two years, the other six months, with no other dependence than the promise of Him who hath said—I will be the widow's God, and a father to the fatherless.[2] Accordingly, he raised me up friends, whose liberality comforted and solaced me in my state of widowhood and sorrows, I could sing with the greatest propriety the words of the poet.

> "He helps the stranger in distress,
> The widow and the fatherless,
> And grants the prisoner sweet release."[3]

I can say even now, with the Psalmist, "Once I was young, but now I am old, yet I have never soon the righteous forsaken, nor his seed begging bread."[4] I have ever been fed by his bounty, clothed by his mercy, comforted and healed when sick, succored when tempted, and every where uphold by his hand.

THE SUBJECT OF MY CALL TO PREACH RENEWED.

It was now eight years since I had made application to be permitted to preach the gospel, during which time I had only been allowed to exhort, and even this privilege but seldom. This subject now was renewed afresh in my mind; it was as a fire shut up in my bones. About thirteen months passed on, while under this renewed impression. During this time, I had solicited of the Rev. Bishop, Richard Allen, who at this time had become Bishop of the African Episcopal Methodists in America, to be permitted the liberty of holding prayer meetings in my own hired house, and of exhorting as I found liberty, which was granted me. By this means, my mind was relieved, as the house soon filled when the hour appointed for prayer had arrived.

I cannot but relate in this place, before I proceed further with the above subject, the singular conversion of a very wicked young man. He was a colored man, who had generally attended our meetings, but not for any good purpose; but rather to disturb and to ridicule our denomination. He openly and uniformly declared that he neither believed in religion, nor wanted any thing to do with it. He was of a Gallio disposition,[5] and took the lead among the young people

---

2. Paraphrase of Psalms 68:5: "A father of the fatherless, and a judge of the widows, is God in his holy habitation."
3. From "I'll Praise My Maker While I've Breath" (1714), a hymn based on Psalm 146 by British hymnwriter Isaac Watts (1674–1748), known as the Father of English Hymnody.
4. Paraphrase of Psalms 37:25.
5. Junius Annaeus Gallio (ca. 5 B.C.–A.D. 65), older brother of the philosopher Seneca and Roman deputy of Achaea (Acts 18:12–17), had a reputation for being amiable and charming.

of color. But after a while he fell sick, and lay about three months in a state of ill health; his disease was a consumption. Toward the close of his days, his sister who was a member of the society, came and desired me to go and see her brother, as she had no hopes of his recovery, perhaps the Lord might break into his mind. I went alone, and found him very low. I soon commenced to inquire respecting his state of feeling, and how he found his mind. His answer was, "O tolerable well," with an air of great indifference. I asked him if I should pray for him. He answered in a sluggish and careless manner, "O yes, if you have time." I then sung a hymn, kneeled down and prayed for him, and then went my way.

Three days after this, I went again to visit the young man. At this time there went with me two of the sisters in Christ. We found the Rev. Mr. Cornish, of our denomination, laboring with him. But he said he received but little satisfaction from him. Pretty soon, however, brother Cornish took his leave; when myself, with the other two sisters, one of which was an elderly woman named Jane Hutt, the other was younger, both colored, commenced conversing with him, respecting his eternal interest; and of his hopes of a happy eternity, if any he had. He said but little; we then kneeled down together and besought the Lord in his behalf, praying that if mercy were not clear gone for ever, to shed a rag of softening grace upon the hardness of his heart. He appeared now to be somewhat more tender, and we thought we could perceive some tokens of conviction, as he wished us to visit him again, in a tone of voice not quite as indifferent as he had hitherto manifested.

But two days had elapsed after this visit, when his sister came to me in haste, saying, that she believed her brother was then dying, and that he had *sent* for me. I immediately called on Jane Hutt, who was still among us as a mother in Israel, to go with me. When we arrived there, we found him sitting up in bed, very restless and uneasy, but he soon laid down again. He now wished me to come to him, by the side of his bed. I asked him how he was. He said, Very ill; and added, "Pray for me, quick!" We now perceived his time in this world to be short. I took up the hymn-book, and opened to a hymn suitable to his case, and commenced to sing, but there seemed to be a *horror* in the room—a darkness of a mental kind, which was felt by us all; there being five persons, except the sick young man and his nurse. We had sung but one verse, when they all gave over singing, on account of this unearthly sensation, but myself. I continued to sing on alone, but in a dull and heavy manner, though looking up to God all the while for help. Suddenly I felt a spring of energy awake in my heart, when darkness gave way in some degree. It was but a glimmer from above. When the hymn was finished, we all, kneeled down to pray for him. While calling on the name of the Lord, to have mercy on his soul, and to grant him repentance unto life, it came suddenly into my mind never to rise from my knees until God should hear prayer in his behalf, until he should convert and save his soul.

Now, while I thus continued importuning heaven, as I felt I was led, a ray of light, more abundant, broke forth among us. There appeared to my view, though my eyes were closed, the Saviour in full stature, nailed to the cross, just over the head of the young man, against the ceiling of the room. I cried out, brother look up, the Saviour is come, he will pardon you, your sins he will forgive. My sorrow for the soul of the young man was gone; I could no longer pray—joy and rapture made it impossible. We rose up from our knees, when lo, his eyes were gazing with ecstacy upwards; over his face there was an expression of joy; his lips were clothed in a sweet and holy smile; but no sound came from his tongue; it was heard in its stillness of bliss; full of hope and immortality. Thus, as I held him by the hand, his happy and purified soul soared away, without a sigh or a groan, to its eternal rest.

I now closed his eyes, straightened out his limbs, and left him to be dressed for the grave. But as for me, I was filled with the power of the Holy Ghost—the very room seemed filled with glory. His sister and all that were in the room rejoiced, nothing doubting but he had entered into Paradise; and I believe I shall see him at the last and great day, safe on the shores of salvation.

But to return to the subject of my call to preach. Soon after this, as above related, the Rev. Richard Williams was to preach at Bethel Church, where I with others were assembled. He entered the pulpit, gave out the hymn, which was sang, and then addressed the throne of grace; took his text, passed through the exordium, and commenced to expound it. The text he took is in Jonah, 2d chap. 9th verse,—"Salvation is of the Lord." But as he proceeded to explain, he seemed to have lost the spirit; when in the same instant, I sprang, as by altogether supernatural impulse, to my feet, when I was aided from above to give an exhortation on the very text which my brother Williams had taken.

I told them I was like Jonah; for it had been then nearly eight years since the Lord had called me to preach his gospel to the fallen sons and daughters of Adam's race, but that I had lingered like him, and delayed to go at the bidding of the Lord, and warn those who are as deeply guilty as were the people of Ninevah.

During the exhortation, God made manifest his power in a manner sufficient to show the world that I was called to labor according to my ability, and the grace given unto me, in the vineyard of the good husbandman.

I now sat down, scarcely knowing what I had done, being frightened. I imagined, that for this indecorum, as I feared it might be called, I should be expelled from the church. But instead of this, the Bishop rose up in the assembly, and related that I had called upon him eight years before, asking to be permitted to preach, and that he had put me off; but that he now as much believed that I was called to that work, as any of the preachers present. These remarks greatly strengthened me, so that my fears of having given an offence, and made myself liable as an offender, subsided, giving place to a sweet serenity, a holy joy of a peculiar kind, untested in my bosom until then.

The next Sabbath day, while sitting under the word of the gospel, I felt moved to attempt to speak to the people in a public manner, but I could not bring my mind to attempt it in the church. I said, Lord, anywhere but here. Accordingly, there was a house not far off which was pointed out to me; to this I went. It was the house of a sister belonging to the same society with myself. Her name was Anderson. I told her I had come to hold a meeting in her house, if she would call in her neighbors. With this request she immediately complied. My congregation consisted of but five persons. I commenced by reading and singing a hymn; when I arose I found my hand resting on the Bible, which I had not noticed till that moment. It now

occurred to me to take a text. I opened the Scripture, as it happened, at the 141st Psalm, fixing my eye on the third verse, which reads: "Set a watch, O Lord, before my mouth, keep the door of my lips." My sermon, such as it was, applied wholly to myself, and added an exhortation. Two of my congregation wept much, as the fruit of my labor this time. In closing, I said to the few, that if any one would open a door, I would hold a meeting the next sixth-day evening: when one answered that her house was at my service. Accordingly I went, and God made manifest his power among the people. Some wept, while others shouted for joy. One whole seat of females, by the power of God, as the rushing of a wind, were all bowed to the floor, at once, and screamed out. Also a sick man and woman in one house, the Lord convicted them both; one lived, and the other died. God wrought a judgment—some were well at night, and died in the morning. At this place I continued to hold meetings about six months. During that time I kept house with my little son, who was very sickly. About this time I had a call to preach at a place about thirty miles distant, among the Methodists, with whom I remained one week, and during the whole time, not a thought of my little son came into my mind; it was hid from me, lost I should have been diverted from the work I had to do, to look after my son. Here by the instrumentality of a poor coloured woman, the Lord poured forth his spirit among the people. Though, as I was told, there were lawyers, doctors, and magistrates present, to hear me speak, yet there was mourning and crying among sinners, for the Lord scattered fire among them of his own kindling. The Lord gave his hand-maiden power to speak for his great name, for he arrested the hearts of the people, and caused a shaking amongst the multitude, for God was in the midst.

I now returned home, found all well; no harm had come to my child, although I left it very sick. Friends had taken care of it which was of the Lord. I now began to think seriously of breaking up housekeeping, and forsaking all to preach the everlasting Gospel. I felt a strong desire to return to the place of my nativity, at Cape May, after an absence of about fourteen years. To this place, where the heaviest cross was to be met with, the Lord sent me, as Saul of Tarsus was sent to

Jerusalem, to preach the same gospel which he had neglected and despised before his conversion.[6] I went by water, and on my passage was much distressed by sea sickness, so much so that I expected to have died, but such was not the will of the Lord respecting me. After I had disembarked, I proceeded on as opportunities offered, toward where my mother lived. When within ten miles of that place, I appointed an evening meeting. There were a goodly number came out to hear. The Lord was pleased to give me light and liberty among the people. After meeting, there came an elderly lady to me and said, she believed the Lord had sent me among them; she then appointed me another meeting there two weeks from that night. The next day I hastened forward to the place of my mother, who was happy to see me, and the happiness was mutual between us. With her I left my poor sickly boy, while I departed to do my Master's will. In this neighborhood I had an uncle, who was a Methodist, and who gladly threw open his door for meetings to be held there. At the first meeting which I held at my uncle's house, there was, with others who had come from curiosity to hear the woman preacher, an old man, who was a Deist, and who said he did not believe the coloured people had any souls—he was sure they had none. He took a seat very near where I was standing, and boldly tried to look me out of countenance. But as I labored on in the best manner I was able, looking to God all the while, though it seemed to me I had but little liberty, yet there went an arrow from the bent bow of the gospel, and fastened in his till them obdurate heart. After I had done speaking, he went out, and called the people around him, said that my preaching might seem a small thing, yet he believed I had the worth of souls at heart. This language was different from what it was a little time before, as he now seemed to admit that coloured people had souls, as it was to these I was chiefly speaking; and unless they had souls, whose good I had in view, his remark must have been without meaning. He now came into the house, and in the most friendly manner shook hands with me, saying, he hoped God had spared him to some good purpose. This man was a great slave holder, and had been very cruel; thinking nothing of knocking down a slave with

a fence stake, or whatever might come to hand. From this time it was said of him that he became greatly altered in his ways for the better. At that time he was about seventy years old, his head as white as snow; but whether he became a converted man or not, I never heard.

The week following, I had an invitation to hold a meeting at the Court House of the County, when I spoke from the 53d chap. of Isaiah, 3d verse. It was a solemn time, and the Lord attended the word; I had life and liberty, though there were people there of various denominations. Here again I saw the aged slaveholder, who notwithstanding his age, walked about three miles to hear me. This day I spoke twice, and walked six miles to the place appointed. There was a magistrate present, who showed his friendship, by saying in a friendly manner, that he had heard of me: he handed me a hymn-book, pointing to a hymn which he had selected. When the meeting was over, he invited me to preach in a schoolhouse in his neighborhood, about three miles distant from where I then was. During this meeting one backslider was reclaimed. This day I walked six miles, and preached twice to large congregations, both in the morning and evening. The Lord was with me, glory be to his holy name. I next went six miles and held a meeting in a coloured friend's house, at eleven o'clock in the morning, and preached to a well behaved congregation of both coloured and white. After service I again walked back, which was in all twelve miles in the same day. This was on Sabbath, or as I sometimes call it, seventh day; for after my conversion I preferred the plain language of the Friends. On the fourth day, after this, in compliance with an invitation received by note, from the same magistrate who had heard me at the above place I preached to a large congregation, where we had a precious time: much weeping was heard among the people. The same gentleman, now at the close of the meeting, gave out another appointment at the same place, that day week. Here again I had liberty, there was a move among the people. Ten years from that time, in the neighborhood of Cape May, I held a prayer meeting in a school house, which was then the regular place of preaching for the Episcopal Methodists, after service,

6. Book of Acts 9: 1–19; 22: 6–16; 26: 12–18.

there came a white lady, of great distinction, a member of the Methodist Society, and told me that at the same school house ten years before, under my preaching, the Lord first awakened her. She rejoiced much to see me, and invited me home with her, where I staid till the next day. This was bread cast upon the water, seen after many days.

From this place I next went to Dennis Creek meeting house, where at the invitation of an elder, I spoke to a large congregation of various and conflicting sentiments, when a wonderful shock of God's power was felt, shown everywhere by groans, by sighs, and loud and happy amens. I felt as if aided from above. My tongue was cut loose, the stammerer spoke freely; the love of God, and of his service, burned with a vehement flame within me—his name was glorified among the people.

I had my little son with me, and was very much straitened for money—and not having means to procure my passage home, I opened a School, and taught eleven scholars, for the purpose of raising a small sum. For many weeks I knew not what to do about returning home, when the Lord came to my assistance as I was rambling in the fields meditating upon his goodness, and made known to me that I might go to the city of Philadelphia, for which place I soon embarked with a very kind captain. We had a perilous passage—a dreadful storm arose, and before leaving the Delaware bay, we had a narrow escape from being run down by a large ship. But the good Lord held us in the hollow of his hand, and in the afternoon of Nov. 12, 1821, we arrived at the city.

Here I held meetings in the dwelling house of sister Lydia Anderson, and for about three months had as many appointments as I could attend. We had many precious seasons together, and the Lord was with his little praying band, convincing and converting sinners to the truth. I continued in the city until spring, when I felt it impressed upon my mind to travel, and walked fourteen miles in company with a sister to meet with some ministers, there to assemble, from Philadelphia. Satan tempted me while on the way, telling me that I was a fool for walking so far, as I would not be permitted to preach. But I pursued my journey, with the determination to set down and worship with them. When I arrived, a goodly number of people had assembled, and no preacher. They waited the time to commence the exercises, and then called upon me. I took the 3d chapter John, 14th verse for my text. I had life and liberty, and the Lord was in the camp with a shout. Another meeting was appointed three miles from there, when I spoke from Psalms cxxxvii, 1, 2, 3, 4. My master was with me, and made manifest his power.

* * *

But here I feel constrained to give over, as from the smallness of this pamphlet I cannot go through with the whole of my journal, as it would probably make a volume of two hundred pages; which, if the Lord be willing, may at some future day be published. But for the satisfaction of such as may follow after me, when I am no more, I have recorded how the Lord called me to his work, and how he has kept me from falling from grace, as I feared I should. In all things he has proved himself a God of truth to me; and in his service I am now as much determined to spend and be spent, as at the very first. My ardour for the progress of his cause abates not a whit, so far as I am able to judge, though I am now something more than fifty years of age.

As to the nature of uncommon impressions, which the reader cannot but have noticed, and possibly sneered at in the course of these pages, they may be accounted for in this way: It is known that the blind have the sense of hearing in a manner much more acute than those who can see: also their sense of feeling is exceedingly fine, and is found to detect any roughness on the smoothest surface, where those who can see find none. So it may be with such as I am, who has never had more than three months schooling; and wishing to know much of the way and law of God, have therefore watched the more closely, the operations of the Spirit, and have in consequence been led thereby. But let it be remarked that I have never found that Spirit lead me contrary to the Scriptures of truth, as I understand them. "For as many as are led by the *Spirit* of God are the sons of God."—Rom. viii. 14.

I have now only to say, May the blessing of the Father, and of the Son, and of the Holy Ghost, accompany the reading of this poor effort to speak well of his name, wherever it may be read. AMEN.

P. S. Please to pardon errors, and excuse all imperfections, as I have been deprived of the advantages of education (which I hope all will appreciate) as I am measurably a self-taught person. I hope the contents of this work may be instrumental in leaving a lasting impression upon the minds of the impenitent; may it prove to be encouraging to the justified soul, and a comfort to the sanctified.

Though much opposed, it is certainly essential in life, as Mr. Wesley wisely observes. Thus ends the Narrative of JARENA LEE, the first female preacher of the First African Methodist Episcopal Church.

BETHEL AT PHILADELPHIA. Penn., UNITED STATES OF AMERICA.

FINIS.

FREDERICK DOUGLASS

Too Much Religion, Too Little Humanity [1849]

Although avowedly religious himself, Frederick Douglass (p. 38) frequently criticized religious practices he viewed as hypocritical or as distractions from the cause of abolition, whether promoted by abolitionists, slaveholders, or church leaders. As evident in the speech reprinted here, delivered on May 9, 1849, at a meeting of the American Anti-Slavery Society in New York City, Douglass disagreed with the indirect abolitionist strategy of expending resources to spread religion. Interjected into his speech is a debate with James S. Warner (mistakenly called James S. Warren in the reported speech), a member of the executive committee of the rival organization, the American and Foreign Anti-Slavery Society, over the practice of distributing Bibles to slaves. The debate serves as a platform for Douglass to discuss what he views as a fundamental distinction between abstract faith and concrete works that "are of God." The lively debate also bolstered Douglass's characterization of the American Anti-Slavery Society, co-founded by his mentor William Lloyd Garrison (p. 111) in 1833, as a group fostering "free-discussion," in contrast to the American and Foreign Anti-Slavery Society, which split off from the former group in 1840 over such issues as Garrison's rejection of politics, his call to include women delegates at anti-slavery conventions, and his criticism of organized religion.

In this speech, as in other speeches and writings, Douglass attacks the hypocrisy of slaveholders who use the Bible to justify slavery. This argument can be traced to one of Douglass's first recorded speeches, given on November 4, 1841, in which he describes the beating a cousin received at the hands of his master, who was "all the time quoting scripture, for his authority, and appealing to that passage of the Holy Bible which says, 'He that knoweth his master's will, and doeth it not, shall be beaten with many stripes!'" (Luke 12:47). Douglass is also harshly critical of church leaders. While he forcefully condemned white church leaders for their history of acting on behalf of slavery, as in this speech, he did not spare others, including black church leaders, who passively ignored the abolitionist cause by focusing primarily on spiritual needs rather than social or political concerns. In the July 14, 1848, issue of *The North Star*, Douglass expressed regret that "those who have the ear of our people on Sundays, have little sympathy with the anti-slavery cause, or the cause of progress in any of its phases. [* * *] The most they aim at is to get to heaven when they die."

The speech and debate reprinted here were transcribed at the meeting by W. Henry Burr and published in the *National Anti-Slavery Standard*, which had been established in 1840 as the official newspaper of the American Anti-Slavery Society. As reported in the *Standard*, Douglass's speech followed one by William Lloyd Garrison (p. 111), who was the chair of the meeting and who also spoke about the division between churches that did not support abolition and true Christianity. The meeting's resolutions reflected these ideas voiced by Douglass and Garrison, but there was some dissent. A white New Yorker named Mr. Atwill rose after Douglass to speak about his experiences teaching slaves to read the Bible in Georgia, and to express concern that prior speeches reflected what "might better be termed an Anti-Church Society" rather than an anti-slavery society. The prominent white abolitionist Wendell Phillips followed Atwill, giving the last speech of the day in support of Douglass's position over that of Atwill's:

"Now the white man who has passed along the highways of the South, and gone from the table of the slaveholder to such quarters as he may chose to let him, gets up and would place his facts, his traveller's acquaintance, against the knowledge which has been gained by a slave-born man through years of suffering," Phillips declared. "This is testimony, it is fact, and you ought not to place anything beside it, for there is nothing of equal character to place."

From the *National Anti-Slavery Standard,* May 24, 1849.

FREDERICK DOUGLASS.[1]—Mr. Chairman—I think we, as Abolitionists, are apt to overrate the intelligence of our audiences with respect to their knowledge of Slavery, and also with respect to their knowledge of the guilt of the churches. I think there are few people out of the ranks of the Abolitionists, who really know anything of the real position of the American Church in regard to Slavery. We meet in this city from year to year and denounce the pro-slavery position of the American Church and Clergy, but we seldom have time to lay before our meetings any facts connected with the proceedings of the Churches in regard to Slavery. I propose in the few remarks that I shall make this evening to say a word with respect to this sort of evidence, and to give a few facts which are familiar enough to the Abolitionist, but which are quite unknown, I have reason to believe, even to the very church members themselves. The ministers know what action they have taken on the subject of Slavery, but the people know very little about it.

Take for instance, the Methodist Episcopal Church. That Church probably wields an influence in this country second to no other in the land. In the year 1836, when the question of Slavery was rocking this country from centre to circumference and when the lives of Abolitionists were scarcely safe at times from the fury of the mobs that were howling round their persons and their houses, this subject came up before the General Conference of the Methodist Episcopal Church. It seems that two ministers of that denomination ventured to lecture upon, and in favour of emancipation in the city of Cincinnati. The very next day after these lectures were given, the Rev. Stephen G. Roszell, a distinguished minister in that Church, brought forward two or three distinct resolutions setting forth the views of the General Conference with respect to Slavery. What were these views? They declared in their first resolution, in Annual Conference assembled, "that they were wholly opposed to modern Abolitionism, and that they wholly disapproved of the conduct of the two ministers who were reported to have lectured upon and in favour of this agitated topic." They went further; and in another resolution declared, "that they were not only wholly opposed to modern Abolitionists, but *they had no right, no wish, no intention to interfere with the relations existing between masters and slaves in the Southern States of our Union.*" These resolutions were adopted by that large conference, with only eleven voting against them. An overwhelming concourse of divines professing to be called of God to preach the Gospel, to proclaim deliverance to the captive and the opening of the prison doors to those that were bound, declared before the world that they had "no right, no wish, no intention to interfere with the relations of masters and slaves." The slaveholders rejoiced in that action. They could smoke their pipes in comfort when they got a knowledge of the proceedings of that body of divines. They could hear of revivals of religion going on in the Church with the utmost complacency. They felt in no wise alarmed but rather strengthened by the members that were added to that Church, for that Church so far from being an abolition Church, had "no right, no wish, no intention to interfere with the relation of master and slave." That is the religion for me,

1. Additional reports on Douglass's speech and the May 9, 1849 meeting of the American Anti-Slavery Society are in the May 18 and May 25 issues of *The North Star* and the May 17 issue of the *National Anti-Slavery Standard;* Douglass reprinted both his and Garrison's speeches in the June 1, 1849 issue of his influential abolitionist newspaper *The North Star* (which he edited from 1847 until 1851, when he merged it with the *Liberty Party Paper* and renamed it *Frederick Douglass' Paper*).

said the slaveholder. There sat the bondman before that body of Methodist divines in his chains calling upon them in the name of God and of humanity to give him his freedom and deliver him from his bonds. Deliver me from my chains! was the cry that came up from the lips of three millions of bondmen, and yet these Methodist clergymen responded, "We have no right, no wish, no intention to give you freedom."

How is it with the Presbyterian Christian? You know that a few years ago, through the agency of the Abolitionists in New England, a large number of petitions and memorials were sent to the General Assembly of the Presbyterian Church, calling upon that body to pass resolutions declaring Slavery to be only a *moral evil*. They stated that that body had already denounced dancing, declaring it to be incompatible with church membership to move the feet at the sound of music, and they believed that their consciences were now becoming alive at least to something more than the sin of dancing. They were encouraged therefore to send petitions asking these divines merely to consider Slavery to be a moral evil. So the General Assembly passed this resolution in answer to their memorials:

"Resolved, that it is inexpedient and not for the edification of the Church to pass any judgment in respect to Slavery."

It is the boast of the Protestant Episcopal Church of this country that it never has anything to do with such sins as Slavery. It is their boast that their Church has not been distracted or disturbed by this agitating topic. To be sure it has had some other topics that have agitated the public mind to some extent, which I need not mention here. If I were in a Moral Reform meeting I might speak of them. (Laughter.) But as to the question of American Slavery, it is their boast that they are not disturbed by it. The groans of heart-broken millions come up on every breeze, but they do not hear them, they are indifferent about them: "We are worshipping the Lord," say they, "we are engaged in giving honours to God; that is our business."

Now I have taken these three Christian Churches and they are for samples of the rest. The Baptists are no better than the Methodists and Presbyterians, and the Episcopalians are as bad as either. They are all as proslavery as they well can be. It is because these churches

have passed resolutions favouring Slavery, and have in other cases resolved to have nothing to do with the matter, that we are compelled to attack them if we would be faithful to [Anti-]Slavery. And if there is one thing that leads me to identify myself with the American Anti-Slavery Society, more than another, it is their readiness at all times and in all circumstances to apply the highest and the most radical Anti-Slavery tests to all parties, all institutions, and all organizations of the land. [I have been into various] Anti-Slavery meetings since I came to this city, and I have heard speeches on various branches of the Anti-Slavery topic; but the most earnest, the most sincere, the most radical tone of sentiment from any quarter has been from the platform of the old fashioned Garrisonian Abolitionists. (Applause.) I mention this for the benefit of some I see before me who attended these other meetings, and who think that because everything went on orderly at them it indicates great progress.

Why, the other day I went into the meeting of the American and Foreign Anti-Slavery Society, and after a long abstract of the report was read and my soul was fired up with the expectation of hearing Slavery denounced and its supporters held up to the detestation of all those who loved the slave, while I was waiting to get my spiritual strength renewed, a grave gentleman arose and said "The next thing in order will be music." (Laughter.) Now Anti-Slavery meetings, according to my notion, should not be very orderly. I like the wild disorder of our free-discussion meetings. I like to hear the earnest voice of Anti-Slavery, so far forgetting the character of its speech, and manner of its delivery, that almost any person may be able to take exceptions to the remarks made. I always feel glad when I have a thousand explanations to make after I go away from Anti-Slavery meetings. When I have spoken in such a way as to lead the people to think that I am a despiser of religion, or that I hate the very name of a clergyman, or that I am myself an Infidel, then I feel that I have done something towards leading the people to think of their responsibility in regard to Slavery.

I believe the grand reason why we have Slavery in this land at the present moment is that we are too religious as a nation, in other words, that we have substituted religion for humanity—we have substituted a form of Godliness, an outside show for the real thing itself. We have houses built for the worship of God, which are regarded as too sacred to plead the cause of the down-trodden millions in them. They will tell you in these churches that they are willing to receive you to talk to them about the sins of the Scribes and Pharisees, or on the subject of the heathenism of the South Sea Islands, or on any of the subjects connected with missions, the Tract Society, the Bible Society, and other Societies connected with the Church, but the very moment you ask them to open their mouths for the liberation of the Southern slaves, they tell you, that is a subject with which they have nothing to do, and which they do not wish to have introduced into the Church; it is foreign to the object for which churches in this country were formed, and houses built.

The American and Foreign Anti-Slavery Society seems to have fallen into the error of supposing that the distribution of the Bible among the slaves will be the means of their ultimate liberation. I should not wonder, if the slaves could be allowed to make known to that Society [their] view of [its] efforts to give them liberty, if they should say "First give us ourselves and then we will get Bibles." What the slave begs for is his freedom and the American and Foreign Anti-Slavery Society comes forward and says "Here is a Bible." To be sure, they say they would be glad to have the slave free, but I ask any of you who were present in their meeting yesterday and heard the speech made by Mr. Henry Bibb if the chief design of that Society did not seem to be, to give the slave the Bible, which when it is given him he cannot read. For my part I am not for giving the slave the Bible or anything else this side of his freedom. Give him that first and then you need not give him anything else. He can get what he needs. (Applause.) I know that the inference was left in the minds of some who attended that meeting that the Old Organization were not in favour of giving the Bible to the slaves, for the [American and Foreign Anti-Slavery] Society arrogated to itself a great amount of piety in that it was in favour of giving the Bible to the slave, and it was said by their speaker, I believe, that if the Old Abolitionists had gone to work and tried to distribute the Bible among the slaves, ere this, Slavery

would have been abolished. Now what we want is first to give the slave himself. It is but another attempt to mend old garments with new cloth—to put new wine into old bottles, to think of giving the slave the Bible without first giving him himself. God did not say to Moses "Tell my people to serve me that they may go free," but "Go and tell Pharoah to *let my people go* that they may serve me."[2] (Great applause.) The first thing is freedom. It is the all important thing. There can be no virtue without freedom—there can be no obedience to the Bible without freedom. When the slave is free he can own a Bible; but suppose we carry it to him now, what is the law of Slavery? It is that the slave shall be taken, deemed, reputed, and judged in law to be property to all intents and purposes whatsoever. Now how can property own property—how can property own the Bible? It takes persons to own property, but the personality of the slave is annihilated. He is not looked upon or treated in any way as a person except when he is to be punished.

I throw out these remarks because I think there is danger of confounding our Anti-Slavery duties with what are not our Anti-Slavery duties. There is an attempt on the part of some professedly Anti-Slavery advocates to make themselves out as *the religious advocates* of Anti-Slavery and all others as irreligious advocates of the cause.

MR. FOSTER[3] (interposing).—I should like to know if Henry Bibb and the rest of the men concerned in that movement, professedly to give the Bible to the slave, are not, all of them without exception, fully aware of the fact that they cannot give the Bible to the slave and that no matter how much money they may collect for that purpose they dare not and do not mean to do so? I ask therefore if it is not a deceptive mo[ve]ment, intended to misguide and beguile the people of the North who are beginning to be aroused to a sense of their duty of doing something for the slave?

MR. DOUGLASS.—I am inclined to think that a good many who are connected with the movement have been really blinded into the belief that in one or two slave States they can give the Bible.

2. Paraphrase of a passage from Exodus (7:16, 8:1, 8:20, 9:1, 9:13, or 10:3).
3. Stephen Symonds Foster (1809–81), a radical abolitionist.

Mr. Foster.—Are they the slaveholders?

Mr. Douglass.—Mr. Bibb thinks it can be done in Kentucky.

Mr. Foster.—Does he not know that they are not allowed to do it?

Mr. Douglass.—There is a class of men who seem to believe if a man should fall overboard into the sea with a Bible in his pocket it would be hardly possible for him to drown. Mr. Bibb told me in conversation, that he believed if the slave had the Bible, the Lord would help him to read it. (Laughter,) Well, if he has worked himself up into that belief, let us give him the credit for his sincerity, and battle with the belief itself.

A Stranger—(from the back part of the house). Mr. Bibb stated that there were no legal impediments in several of the States.

Mr. Douglass.—And what is more remarkable, he stated that on every plantation at the South where there were any considerable number of slaves, there were always one or more among them who could read. I do not know how he could make such a statement. I am from the State of Maryland, where slaves are as highly favoured as in any State in the Union, and I believe more so, because it is one of the more northerly States, and peopled by persons from the North, and yet I must tell you that in a neighbourhood where there were no fewer than 5,000 slaves in a distance of twelve miles around from where I lived, I never met more than two out of the whole number who could read. And yet Mr. Bibb states to his audience as a sort of plaster to their consciences—as a sort of moral chloroform, as Mr. Pillsbury[4] would say, to the consciences of those who are just opening their eyes and who are alarmed by our rebukes, that there are one or more on every plantation who can read. I do not believe in the statement. I know from my own experience that not more than perhaps one in five thousand can read in the State of Maryland.

Mr. Foster.—Now to test the honesty and integrity of those men, I will state here publicly, and any gentleman present may carry the intelligence to the leaders of that party, that to save them the trouble of raising funds, *I will furnish them with* one thousand Bibles, *if Mr. Bibb or any other prominent man among them will go, openly and in person, and carry them to the slaves.* I will have nothing to do with any underhanded movement to *steal* Bibles into the South. Thieving is bad enough when connected with getting property, but when it is connected with the glory of God it is utterly detestable, and I will have nothing to do with it. And I think I can do more; I think I can pledge that individual one thousand more after he has distributed the first thousand; but I will keep within my means [***] Let them spare themselves the trouble to go through this city to collect funds for that purpose, for I am ready to fulfil my pledge. (Applause.)

Stranger.—There is a missionary in Kentucky distributing Bibles, and if you will present your account tomorrow, the Bibles will be taken. (Applause.)

Mr. Foster.—Will the gentleman repeat this statement? I did not hear it, but from the manner in which it was received, I think it must be interesting.

Stranger.—Call at 61 John street,[5] and your proposition will be faithfully received.

Mr. Foster.—I did not agree to call anywhere. I am here to be called upon. (Applause.) [I will be in] this city to-morrow, and after that I shall be at my residence in Worcester, Mass. I shall be happy to be called upon by any of those gentlemen who are ready to go forward and distribute the Bibles. I do not want to be referred to some impossible shadow at 61 John street, merely for the sake of doing away with the effect of my proposition. Does the gentleman say that he is the man who will take the Bibles to the South?

Stranger.—If you will give me your address, you will be called upon to-morrow.

Mr. Foster.—My address is the Anti-Slavery meeting to-morrow, and after that Stephen S. Foster, Worcester, Mass. (Applause.) Since the gentleman has taken the liberty to ask me my address, of course he will return the favour by giving me and this audience his own address. I want this audience to know who it is

---

4. Parker Pillsbury (1809–98), an abolitionist orator and writer.
5. Address of offices shared by the American and Foreign Anti-Slavery Society and its offshoot, the American Missionary Association.

that backs out of their position, the Old Organization or the New.

STRANGER.—My name is James S. Warren, 9 University Place.

MR. FOSTER.—Mr. James S. Warren may call for his Bibles to-morrow.

MR. DOUGLASS.—I shall be pleased to ask the gentleman a question. Can the gentleman inform me whether it is the intention of the American and Foreign Anti-Slavery Society to get the consent of the slaveholders before giving the slaves the Bible?

MR. WARREN.—The object of the Society is to distribute the Bible among the slaves whether with or without the consent of the slaveholder.

MR. DOUGLASS.—They do not avow their public declarations that they are going to give the Bible *with or without* the consent of the slaveholders.

MR. FOSTER.—I wish, Mr. Chairman, to call the attention of the reporters to that statement of one of the friends of the American and Foreign Anti-Slavery Society, for I want it to go to the world that that Society, avows it through one of its leading members (for I take it that the gentleman would not have pledged the Society if he were not one of its leading members), that the Society avows it as its intention to put the Bible into the hands of the slaves *with or without the consent of the masters.* If the master does not consent, of course, the design is to go there with force and arms to do it. I wish this declaration of one of the prominent members of that Society who feels himself authorized to speak in its behalf, to go forth to the world.

MR. DOUGLASS.—I wish to make a single remark further about giving the Bible to the slaves. Here are three or four facts connected with the matter which make the thing impossible. In the first place the slaveholder's consent must be obtained before any Bibles can be given to the slaves, and the slaveholder will never give his consent to let the slave have anything which may open his mind to the wrong of holding him as his property. If his consent is had at all, it is purchased at the expense of the silence of the person giving the

Bible to his slave, as to its being presented for the purpose of opening his mind to the sin of Slavery.

In the next place, if the Bible is given to the slave he cannot read it. So it is absolutely not giving it at all; for you might as well give him a block with no letters upon it as the Bible with letters in it; because he cannot read it. Now if this Society would only ask for money to educate the slaves whether the masters would or not, and some good volunteer like my friend in the distance should go there professing that his object is to educate the slave whether with or without the consent of the slaveholders, I should think the movement, however impracticable, was in the hands of honest and sincere men at any rate. (Applause.) The fact is they cannot give the Bible to the slave. It is idle to make the Bible and Slavery go hand in hand; they are at war with each other, and the slaveholder knows it as well as any man. The moment they begin to read, that moment they begin to be restless in their chains. There are only three or four passages of Scripture that the slaveholder wants them to learn to read, and these he can read to them. They are the passages which relate to servants being obedient &c., which they torture into a sort of sanction of Slavery. These they like to have the slaves know, but as to knowing anything about the Golden Rule, "All things whatsoever ye would that others should do unto you do ye also to them,"[6] or anything of the doctrine of love to man, they do not want them to know anything about it. The more ignorant he is, the better slave he makes, and hence the most stringent laws are enacted throughout the South to prevent the slaves from learning to read.

The cry of infidelity has long been raised against those who stand on the old platform and adhere to the Old Anti-Slavery Organization. While I was a member of the Methodist Episcopal Church, I had heard Garrison denounced as an infidel and I wanted to hear what his infidelity consisted in; and the moment I heard him pour out his soul in behalf of the downtrodden bondsman and utter his voice against the oppressor as if his own wife and children were in chains, I wanted to know nothing further of his religious views; I felt that in his heart was the love of Christ, and that was the Christianity for me. I did not want

6. Paraphrase of Matthew 7:12.

to know anything of his abstract faith, for I felt very much as I suppose John the Baptist felt when he received the tidings from Christ, saying: "Go tell John that the deaf hear, the blind see, the poor have the Gospel preached unto them."[7] Those works testified as to what manner of man he was, as to whence he came, and what his objects were. When we see men binding up the wounds of those who fall among thieves, administering to the necessities of the down-trodden, and breaking off the chains of the bondsmen, it is evidence enough that their works are of God, and, whatever may be their abstract notions, Christ himself lives within them; for this was his spirit. He went about doing good to the souls and bodies of men. Whenever the cry of sorrow saluted his ear, there he was to soothe and console the afflicted heart. Among the cries of joy and triumph that surrounded him as he marched amid the multitudes, he heard the single voice of the blind man, and when the multitude bid him hold his peace, Christ rebuked them and turning to the poor man, said: "What will thou have me do unto thee?"[8] I believe if he had been on his way to create a world, he would have stopped to attend to the wants of that poor blind man. "I will have mercy and not sacrifice"[9] is the great doctrine which distinguishes the Christian religion from the Jewish ceremonial ritual and the current religion of our times. The Christian religion is one of mercy, lifting up the bowed down and disconsolate. O for a revival of this religion!

The great difficulty about our Christianity is, we have got certain notions about religion that turn off our attention from humanity altogether. We think that religion is the entertainment of a hope. I know there is a hope in religion. I know there is faith and I know there is prayer about religion and necessary to it, but God is most glorified when there is peace on earth and good will towards men. It is said that when our Saviour came into the world, the angels sang "Glory to God in the highest, on earth peace and good will to men."[1] It

may be rendered with no violation to the original text, I am told, "The highest glory to God is peace on earth and good will towards men." (Applause.) This is the religion which Christ came to establish; it was to promote peace on earth and good will towards men. The religion of our country seems to have very little of peace on earth and good will towards men in it. Instead of bestowing blessings on the peacemakers, we as a nation confer blessings on war-makers. Instead of blessing those who feed the hungry and clothe the naked,[2] we confer honour upon men who bury the lash in the quivering flesh of the bondmen, and exalt to the highest office in the gift of the nation the men who have been most skillful in teaching the nations war, and blowing out the brains of our enemies. (Applause and hisses.)

Now I suppose that those who hiss think that I have stated what is not true, but what is the fact? There is Zachary Taylor in the Presidential Chair. You knew nothing about Taylor, until you heard of his blowing out the brains of the Mexicans. (Applause and hisses.) No minister of the Gospel ever came out and endorsed the Christian character of General Taylor before he suc[ceeded in taking Monterrey].[3] No minister of the Gospel ever made him a member of the Home Missionary Society until he heard that he had fought his battles in Mexico. No one thought of saying aught in favour of that man for the Presidency until the Christianity of this country learned that he had favoured the importation of blood-hounds from Cuba to hunt down the Florida Indians. (Hisses and applause.)

MR. GARRISON here repeated the reasons why the applause should be controlled, and stated as a further reason, that he had been informed that there was a sick person near. He hoped the Anti-Slavery friends would control their feelings, and invited those who disapproved of what had been said to come and take the platform when Mr. Douglass had concluded.

7. Paraphrase of Matthew 11:4–5 or Luke 7:22.
8. Reference to the story of Jesus restoring a blind man's sight, in Mark 10:49–51 and Luke 18:40–41.
9. Matthew 9:13 or Matthew 12:7.
1. Luke 2:14.
2. Reference to Isaiah 58:7 and Matthew 25:35–36.
3. These words are taken from the report on the speech in the *North Star* on June 1, 1849, since they are obliterated in the May 24, 1849 report in *The National Anti-Slavery Standard*, an edit suggested by *The Frederick Douglass Papers* (1982), edited by John Blassingame.

MR. DOUGLASS.—I mentioned yesterday in another place, that the great men of the nation might always be taken as fair examples of the moral sentiment of the people. I have taken Zachary Taylor who I believe is just as good as those who voted for him; I do not think he is in any degree worse at heart than those who had no objections to him as their candidate on moral grounds. I am not at all lowering him that you need come to his defence. In him I see yourselves reflected who have no moral objections to Slavery. You only need a geographical change. You need only to be transported from New York to New Orleans to become as much a slaveholder as General Taylor at Baton Rouge. Sir, if the American pulpit had been what it ought to have been, and what I trust it will yet be, no party in this country could have been found base enough to have brought forward the name of such a candidate for the suffrages of the American people. No! had the American pulpit uttered its voice in righteous denunciation against Slavery and War and kindred crimes, we should never have heard of such a being as a legalized cut-throat presiding over the destinies of this nation. (Hisses.)

But I will touch no longer your idol, friends. I will leave him and pass to another who is perhaps less an idol now, because he has not the reins of Government in his hand, and no office to give to those who may be disposed to hiss in his favour. (Laughter.) I allude to Henry Clay. I never was more forcibly struck with the truth of Garrison's remarks, that he never looked upon the slave but as upon a member of his own family, than when I heard the various eulogies showered down upon this man by the North on account of his letter on Emancipation, or rather Expatriation. You are aware of the character of that letter. It sets out with a sort of argument against Slavery, declares that the arguments that are put forth by Calhoun and that class of politicians at the South in favour of eternizing Slavery are erroneous, and then goes on to say, granting that the whites are superior to the blacks, that it is the duty of the whites to instruct, improve, and enlighten the blacks. For so much I thank him, but take this out, and the remainder is full of all manner of sin and injustice. With the exception of these few sentiments, it is one of the most skillfully-contrived schemes for oppressing the slave and perpetuating Slavery that I ever read. Mr.

Clay, after having laid down his platform of principles, that the slaves should be enlightened and instructed by the superior classes, goes on to fix a day when the slaves should be emancipated, and that day is set in this wise: All children born of slave parents after the year 1860, shall be free at twenty-five. And how free? Free to stay where they are, and work for a living? No. Free to be expelled, free to be driven away from Kentucky and transported to Africa, on the ground that it is their native land. But they are not free even then, for he has another proviso, and it is this: That after having arrived at the age of twenty-five, they shall be hired out under an officer of the State for three years, in order to raise $150 to pay for their own exportation from their homes and their families. Yet the people read this letter and say, O! how just, how merciful, how humane, how philanthropic is Henry Clay!

There is another point about this letter to which I object strongly; it is this: You are aware that at the age of twenty-eight almost all the slaves have families. Mr. Clay proposes that the slaves having families and children of three, four, and five years of age shall be snatched from those children and hurried off to Africa, leaving those children parentless, guardianless, with no one to care for them. Those children are to live twenty-five years longer in Slavery, and then to be hired out until they are twenty-eight years of age, and afterward to be hurried out of the country. And yet young men and young women, old men and old women, mothers, sisters, and daughters read the cold-blooded proposition, from which, if it were to be applied to white persons, they would shrink in horror, and they say, how good, how kind, how philanthropic is Mr. Clay. Such is the man in whose pathway they will strew flowers when he comes to the North—a man who boldly proposes to sunder parents from their children, and compel them to leave the country on pain of being again reduced to Slavery.

In another part of that letter he says that the trifling loss that would result from Emancipation may [be] prevented by leaving the rights of the owners undisturbed during the next twenty-five years. What is the meaning of this? It is just this: That Henry Clay would leave the slaveholder, after the year 1860 until the year 1885, in full possession of the right to sell slaves from Kentucky into Louisiana or any of the more southern States. The proposition is not, after all, that they shall emancipate their slaves at the end of twenty-five years, but it allows them twenty-five years in which to watch the New Orleans and Mobile markets, and if they do not see fit to sell them during the course of ten, fifteen or twenty years, just in the last of the twenty-fifth year, when the slave is about to grasp hold of Freedom, their masters can put them upon the block and sell them to the highest bidder; thus Kentucky will only be getting rid of Slavery to send their slaves to clank their chains on Southern plantations.

Oh, the blinded moral sense of the American people! how lost to all principle! how lost to all sense of justice! We can eulogize the man who with iron heart would revive the horrors of the Slave Trade, under the delusive idea of advancing the cause of Freedom.

Friends, I have not used the name of General Taylor or Henry Clay because I have any personal pique towards them, or any difference of political opinion with them, or political ends to serve. You have denied me the right of citizenship, you have trampled on my rights as a man. I have no voice in your politics, I only speak as one of the three millions of slaves in your land. I speak as one of the injured party. I speak in the name of four sisters and one brother who now live, if indeed they live at all, under the burning sun and the biting lash of the slavedriver. I speak in behalf of those whom I have left behind me. How would you speak if you yourselves had relatives and friends in the condition of Slavery? Would you speak soft words of the Church and clergy who could live indifferent to the condition of your sisters and brothers? Think not because I am black that I love not my kindred and friends.

> "Fleecy locks and black complexion
>   Do not alter nature's claims.
> Skins may differ, but affection
>   Dwells in white and black the same"[4]

My sisters are as dear to me as yours can be to you. My brother lies as near my heart as your brother can lie to yours. My mother, my family, my friends are all as dear to me as yours can possibly be to you. O! if you could put yourselves in the place of the slave the question would soon be carried; there would be no differences at all; you would feel that we were your brothers and sisters and Slavery would soon be at an end.

---

4. Paraphrase of British poet William Cowper's "The Negro's Complaint," written in 1788 and first published in 1793; Cowper's second line is: "Cannot forfeit nature's claim;".

On the Constitution as a Pro- or Anti-Slavery Document

C. H. CHASE: *Letter to Frederick Douglass* [1849]

FREDERICK DOUGLASS: *Reply to C. H. Chase* [1849]

FREDERICK DOUGLASS AND SAMUEL RINGGOLD WARD: *Resolved, That the Constitution of the United States, in Letter, Spirit, and Design, Is Essentially Antislavery* [1849]

A 2002 survey conducted by Public Agenda, a nonpartisan organization that conducts public opinion research, asked the following question: "Some people say that when the Constitution was originally written over 200 years ago it had virtually no regard for the rights of African Americans or women. In your opinion, does this mean: that the Constitution is a fundamentally flawed or racist document [or] that the Constitution is a great document that had some blind spots"? A majority of all races focused on the greatness of the document, but 28 percent of black respondents (versus only 8 percent of white respondents) viewed the Constitution as "fundamentally flawed or racist."

Since its creation, in 1787, the Constitution has fueled debates about the relationship between the U.S. government and African Americans. Antebellum debates explored the extent to which the three-fifths clause—which added three-fifths of the slave population to the population of free people when apportioning representation in Congress and direct taxes—undercut claims that the Constitution affirmed equality of all men. Early in 1849, C. H. Chase invited the abolitionist leader Frederick Douglass (p. 38) to debate the merits of the Constitution as a pro-slavery document. Douglass declined the invitation, hinting at his conflicted thoughts about the Constitution's position on slavery. Later that year, however, Douglass did agree to debate the issue in New York with the Reverend Samuel Ringgold Ward (1817–ca. 1866), a former slave and leading abolitionist. Ward emphasized the meaning of the words of the Constitution, while Douglass focused on the intent of the writers. At stake was whether the Constitution could be "wield[ed] [* * *] for the abolition of American slavery," to use the words of the white abolitionist Gerrit Smith. Douglass later wrote that this exchange with Ward, on May 11, 1849, was his first formal debate.

C. H. CHASE

Letter to Frederick Douglass [1849]

Rochester, January 23, 1849

FREDERICK DOUGLASS—DEAR SIR:

I have called twice at the *Star* office, for the purpose of conferring with you about our discussion on American slavery, but did not find you. I am very anxious, in view of the good which I think may be done, to have the discussion immediately, and will cheerfully meet you at any time and place in this city, which you may propose, provided it shall be soon, as business will call me from the city in a few days. The resolution to be discussed, as you doubtless recollect, is the one which I presented at the Anti-Slavery Convention recently held in this city, at which time you challenged me to debate it and I accepted the challenge.

> "Resolved, That the Constitution of the United States, if strictly construed according to its reading, is anti-slavery in all of its provisions."

The word ALL was accepted from your suggestion. An immediate answer is especially requested.

Respectfully and truly yours,

C. H. Chase

From *The Life and Writings of Frederick Douglass,* ed. Philip S. Foner, vol. 1, *Early Years, 1817–1849* (New York: International Publishers, 1950), pp. 352–53.

FREDERICK DOUGLASS
Reply to C. H. Chase [1849]

MY DEAR SIR:

I owe you an apology for not sooner publishing and replying to the above letter. On a close examination of the Constitution, I am satisfied that if strictly "construed according to its reading," it is not a pro-slavery instrument; and while I disagree with you as to the inference to be drawn from this admission, you will see that in the resolution, between us there is no question for debate.

Very respectfully,

FREDERICK DOUGLASS

From the *New York Daily Tribune,* May 14, 1849.

FREDERICK DOUGLASS AND SAMUEL RINGGOLD WARD
Resolved, That the Constitution of the United States, in Letter, Spirit, and Design, Is Essentially Antislavery [1849]

Mr. Ward, in support of his position that the spirit, letter and design of the Constitution was opposed to Slavery, cited Sec. 9, Art. I, prohibiting bills of attainder; Sec. 10 making a like prohibition; Sec. 2, Art. IV, giving to the citizens of each State the privileges of the several States; and the 1st, 4th, 5th, and 8th Amendments, as being Anti-Slavery. These, he contended, were directly opposed to Slavery and Slavery must be unconstitutional. The Slave is not a thing, he is a person, and as such comes under the provisions of the Constitution which says, "nor shall any person be deprived of life, liberty or property without due process of law."[1] Now this was clear in its meaning, and could not be susceptible of misapprehension; it insured to every man his right to Liberty, and agreed with the Declaration of Independence, which declares that "all men are created equal; that they are endowed with certain inalienable rights; that among these are life, liberty, and the pursuit of happiness." It was no matter what were the sentiments of these men when writing that document, we are to go by what is written. The Courts of law will not hold a parole agreement binding upon the parties concerned; it must be written and interpreted according to its sense. The right to hold property in persons did not exist, nor was it acknowledged in any part of the Constitution, for it would be a direct violation of the principles for which the fathers of the Republic struggled. He asserted that when a fugitive slave had been returned to his master, he was not returned in compliance with any law calling him a person, and that as a human being, entitled to rights under the Constitution, he could not be seized upon as a chattel; the Constitution allowed representation to persons only, and here was a direct admission of the slave being a person. Mr. Ward, in support of the validity of a written agreement, and the invalidity of a parole agreement made a very happy illustration. He said that if Mr. Dandher (Mr. W.) had entered into a mere verbal agreement for the sake of convenience to call a horse a cow, and that Mr. D. had signed a written agreement, promising to pay $150 for cow, the parole agreement was null and void in the eyes of the law, and would not be binding on him (Mr. W.). If I, said Mr. W. in accordance with the strict letter of our written agreement, having been paid the money for the cow, should in reality give him a cow for the money so paid, he, Mr. D. would have no redress from a Court of law. Just so it is, said Mr. W. with regard to Slavery. No matter what were the intentions and sentiments of the framers of the Constitution, or what was the

1. From the Fifth Amendment.

understanding the slave-holding and non-slaveholding States had upon the matter, that Constitution in no portion of it acknowledges the rights of property in human beings. I admit, said Mr. Ward, that there are some difficulties in the way of a perfect understanding of that clause of the Constitution, which relates to representation and taxation, but it cannot be proved to clear understanding of it that it sanctions Slavery.

MR. DOUGLASS rose and said:

I am, glad that my friend confesses that there are some difficulties in that clause of the Constitution relating to representation and taxation; that clause of the Constitution has already been read, and I shall not read it again. It declares that representatives and direct taxes shall be apportioned to the several States which may be included within this Union, according to their numbers, which shall be determined by adding to the number of free persons, including Indians not taxed, three-fifths of all other persons. Mr. Ward says that some other persons beside slaves may be included in these three-fifths; he does not deny that the slaves were intended, by any means; he tells you that the term free, in this clause, is not necessarily the correlative of slave. I affirm that slaves are included, were meant to be included; and in proof, I will read a few remarks made in the Convention that framed the Constitution. On Monday, June 11, 1787, this very point which we are now discussing was under discussion in the Convention. I read from the *Madison Papers:* "It was then moved by Mr. Rutledge to add the words 'equitable ratio of representation' at the end of the motion just made," which was, "the proportion of direct taxation shall be regulated by the whole number of inhabitants of every description in proportion to the number of whites," &c., &c. It is evident that this same clause of the Constitution refers to the slaves; on the face of it there is a direct reference to the slaves.

It is said that the clause relating to the three-fifths [ratio] does not support Slavery, in as far as that it takes from the Slaveholder two-fifths of his representative power in the nation, instead of conferring upon him the whole five-fifths. Now this would be taking from him the three-fifths he already enjoys; it was a bonus offered to Slavery. Every slaveholder was virtually told by that Constitution, virtually instructed by it, to add as many to his stock as possible, for the more slaves he possessed he would not only have more wealth but more political power. For every five slaves he might be said to have three votes. I think this case is made out. I cannot flourish trumpets much about it, but it is plain and obvious. I am not sure but that the South—indeed I am certain that it would have an increase of representation in the Legislature, were Slavery and the Slaves permitted to vote. But it would not be an increase of the slave power. You must remember that it was the slave power that demanded a three-fifths representation of their slaves. Some of the good people of the North said, "We had as well ask for a representation for our cows, our sheep and our horses, as you to ask for it in your slaves." The answer was, that although the slave is property, he is a person, and his service is not worth more than three-fifths of the service of freemen, and therefore it was argued that the South had a right to that representation. The North bowed to the mandates of Slavery.

Mr. Douglass concluded with an eloquent denunciation of Slavery, and resumed his seat amid the cheers of the audience. After the discussion the house adjourned, according to previous agreement, without taking a vote on the question.

From the *New York Daily Tribune,* May 14, 1849.

PART ONE ~ *Works Cited*

Quotations and statistics in this section's headnotes and notes were drawn from the following sources:

Bell, Howard Holman, ed. *Proceedings of the National Negro Conventions 1830–1864.* New York: Arno Press, 1969.

Brekas, Catherine. "Catherine Brekas on Jarena Lee." *Africans in America.* http://www.pbs.org/wgbh/aia/part3/3i3127.html.

Carretta, Vincent. *Equiano, the African: Biography of a Self-Made Man.* Athens: University of Georgia Press, 2005.

——. "Introduction." *The Interesting Narrative and Other Writings.* Edited with an introduction and notes by Vincent Carretta. London and New York: Penguin, 2003, x–xi.

——. "Olaudah Equiano or Gustavus Vassa? New Light on an Eighteenth-century Question of Identity." *Slavery and Abolition,* 20, 3 (December 1999), 96–105.

Dain, Bruce. *A Hideous Monster of the Mind: American Race Theory in the Early Republic.* Cambridge: Harvard University Press, 2002.

Delany, Martin. *The Condition, Elation, Emigration and Destiny of the Colored People of the United States, 1852.* New York: Arno Press, 1968.

Douglass, Frederick. "A Day and a Night in 'Uncle Tom's Cabin.'" *Frederick Douglass' Paper,* 4 March, 1853, 2.

——. "The Industrial College." *Frederick Douglass's Paper,* 20 January 1854, 3.

Eze, Emmanuel Chukwudi, ed. *Race and the Enlightenment: A Reader.* Cambridge, Mass.: Blackwell, 1997.

Gilman, William et al., eds. *The Journals and Miscellaneous Notebooks of Ralph Waldo Emerson.* 16 vols. Cambridge: Harvard University Press, 1960–82.

Gougeon, Len. "Emerson and Abolition: The Silent Years 1837–1844." *American Literature* 54, (Dec. 1982), 560–75.

Greeley, Horace, [D. H. G.]. "Frederick Douglass' Speech at Western Reserve College." *New York Tribune,* July 31, 1854.

Gregory, James M. *Frederick Douglass The Orator. Containing an Account of His Life; His Eminent Public Services; His Brilliant Career as Orator; Selections from His Speeches and Writings.* Springfield, Mass.: Willey & Co, 1893.

Herder, J. G. *Reflections on the Philosophy of the History of Mankind.* Ed., Frank E. Manuel. Chicago: University of Chicago Press, 1970.

Howard, Jennifer. "Unraveling the Narrative." *Chronicle of Higher Education.* September 9, 2005.

Levine, Robert S. "*Uncle Tom's Cabin* in Frederick Douglass' Paper: An Analysis of Reception." *American Literature,* 64, 1, (Mar., 1992), 71–93.

Mehlinger, Louis. "The Search For A Homeland." Reprinted in Okon Edet Uya, ed. *Black Brotherhood.* Lexington, Mass.: Heath, 1970.

Public Agenda. "Most Blacks Reject the View That the Constitution is a Fundamentally Flawed or Racist Document." http://www.publicagenda.org/charts/most-blacks-reject-view-constitution-fundamentally-flawed-or-racist-document.

Stauffer, James, ed. *The Works of James McCune Smith.* New York: Oxford University Press: 2006.

Sterling, Dorothy, ed. *Speak Out in Thunder Tones: Letters and Other Writings By Black Northerners, 1787–1865.* New York: Da Capo Press, 1973.

Stuckey, Sterling. *Slave Culture: Nationalist Theory and the Foundations of Black America.* New York: Oxford University Press, 1987.

PART TWO

Reconstruction and the Nadir (1865–1909)

With the end of the Civil War in the spring of 1865, the northern and southern states faced the daunting task of reuniting to form a cohesive, slavery-free nation. After General Robert E. Lee's surrender, President Abraham Lincoln immediately attempted to turn the nation's attention to Reconstruction, which he viewed as no less than "the re-inauguration of the national authority." Lincoln's moderate plans for reunifying the nation met with resistance from both Radical Republicans, a strongly abolitionist faction of the Republican Party whose members wanted the Confederate states to fulfill harsh requirements in order to be readmitted to the Union, and white southerners and other Democrats, who believed that the South had suffered enough from the war.

Even before the war ended, Congress had taken two actions to grant rights to newly freed African Americans and to help enforce those rights: on January 31, 1865, Congress proposed the Thirteenth Amendment, which outlawed slavery (and was approved by President Lincoln on February 1 and ratified on December 6, 1865), and on March 3, 1865, it established the Freedmen's Bureau to aid newly freed black Americans. On April 14, 1865, Lincoln was assassinated, and his vice president, Andrew Johnson—the only southern senator who had not given up his seat in Congress when his state seceded from the Union and who favored policies that were lenient to the South—became president.

The decade that followed was a struggle between those who wanted to ensure equal rights for black southerners and those who wanted to reestablish a system of white supremacy—neo-slavery, as it were. Immediately after the war, newly freed African Americans, along with black and white northerners who went south (or remained in the South) after the war, began working to transform the South's economic and political systems. African Americans were elected in large numbers to local and state offices. Along the southern coast, African Americans successfully established a few communities and began to work the land granted to them by Major General William T. Sherman's Special Field Orders 15, issued in January 1865, before President Johnson abruptly reversed it in September of that year, returning the land to the plantation owners from whom it had been confiscated. Many black people throughout the South ended up as sharecroppers, working the land for their former enslavers, who typically had no interest in their economic advancement or welfare.

By late 1865, southern states had begun enacting black codes to broadly curtail the rights of former slaves. The following April, Congress passed the Civil Rights Act of 1866 over President Johnson's veto, granting citizenship to African Americans and guaranteeing them equal rights. Ironically, as if in parallel fashion, the Ku Klux Klan was established that same year to combat with fear and violence African Americans' still-nascent but growing economic and political power, and deadly riots targeting African Americans erupted in Tennessee and Louisiana. In the 1866 elections, Radical Republicans gained control of Congress and quickly enacted a series of laws designed to protect the rights of African Americans and direct the Reconstruction of the South. Among those laws were the Reconstruction Acts of 1867, which stationed federal troops in the South and instituted black male suffrage in the "rebel States." The Fourteenth Amendment, which guarantees due process and equal protection under the law to all persons born or naturalized in the United States and in effect made former slaves citizens of the United States, was ratified on July 9, 1868, and the ratification of the Fifteenth Amendment, in 1870, officially eliminated race as a barrier to voting, thereby giving all black males legal access to the vote for the first time. The last major advance in civil rights legislation during Reconstruction was the Civil Rights Act of 1875, which guaranteed equal rights to African Americans in jury service and public accommodations.

Despite these legal advances, however, southern states were steadily reestablishing systems of power based on white supremacy. Using intimidation and violence against black voters, white southerners began replacing the biracial state governments established after the Civil War with all-white governments. The Freedmen's Bureau was abolished in 1872, and in 1877 President Rutherford B. Hayes—fulfilling the promise he had made to southern Democrats in order to resolve the bitterly disputed 1876 election, in which both he and the Democratic candidate, Samuel J. Tilden, had claimed victory—withdrew federal troops from the South, effectively ending Reconstruction.

The great black historian Rayford W. Logan (1897–1982) named the period that followed Reconstruction "the nadir"—the lowest point in American history for overt and violent violations of the rights of African Americans. In 1883, the Supreme Court ruled that the Civil Rights Act of 1875 was unconstitutional, signaling a dramatic end to the post–Civil War period of legislative reform. Southern states legalized segregation by establishing Jim Crow laws, which the Supreme Court upheld with the 1896 *Plessy v. Ferguson* decision, ruling that "separate but equal" was the law of the land. States prevented African Americans from voting by establishing poll taxes, property requirements, and literacy tests, and by other seemingly race-neutral means. To prevent white Americans from being disenfranchised as well, some states passed "grandfather clauses," which eliminated the property and literacy requirements for those who could vote, or whose fathers or grandfathers could vote, prior to 1867, thereby excluding all African Americans. In addition to those official restrictions of civil rights, African Americans encountered mounting terrorism and violence. Those who gained economic power or demanded equal rights were often vilified and attacked by vigilante groups such as the Ku Klux Klan. The most extreme form of terrorism was lynching. In 1898 alone, more than 100 African Americans were lynched in the South.

The failure of Reconstruction to bring about permanent structural improvements in the lives of former slaves would eventually lead to mass migrations of black people from the South, beginning with the "Ho for Kansas" movement. By the early 1880s, tens of thousands of black Americans had left the South to settle in Kansas. While the migrants received support from some local people and governments, as well as from sympathizers in the East, they also met with resistance from westerners who were overwhelmed by the number of new settlers and fearful of the economic competition that migrants would create. At the same time, southerners tried to stem the migration of their primary supply of low-wage labor, employing a variety of methods—for example, outlawing the public congregation of more than three people (to inhibit group migration planning) and blaming the exodus on white Republican agitators rather than on the systematic physical, political, and economic persecution of African Americans in the region.

During this tumultuous post-Reconstruction period, Booker T. Washington rose to prominence as a leader. His famous "Atlanta Compromise" speech in September 1895 catapulted him into a position of unrivaled power as a national African American leader. Throughout his long career, he publically encouraged black people to stay in the South and focus on industrial (that is, vocational) education, menial labor, farming, and the skilled crafts in order to improve their economic position and to demonstrate their value in a post-slavery society. However, the period was marred by escalating violence against African Americans who managed to work their way into the middle class—from the massacre of African Americans in Wilmington, North Carolina, in 1898 to the brutal Atlanta riot of 1906. These attacks presented a daunting challenge to Washington's ideas about eventual racial uplift through patience, self-help, industry, and also to his studied avoidance of overt political activity and protest. In the first decade of the 1900s, W. E. B. Du Bois and other emerging black leaders began to challenge Washington's leadership openly, rejecting accommodationist politics in favor of political protest and demands for equal rights. Du Bois spearheaded this attack in his searching critique of Washington's ideology in *The Souls of Black Folk*, published in 1903. Two years later, he and several colleagues, including J. R. Clifford, founded the Niagara Movement, which metamorphosed into the National Association for the Advancement of Colored People in 1909. This landmark event marked the end of "the nadir" and set the stage for the period of dramatic social and cultural change that followed.

In his own symbolic correlative of the Great Migration, Du Bois left the South (where he had taught since 1879), for New York City in 1910. In the years leading up to World War I, a southern rural, agrarian people slowly became a northern urban, industrial people—and the black people who remained in the South migrated internally, seeking economic opportunity in southern cities. A new black culture was born, manifesting itself in the form of jazz and the cultural movement known as the New Negro or Harlem Renaissance. Simultaneously, the NAACP, through the force of W. E. B. Du Bois's editorship of *The Crisis* between 1910 and 1934, would become the leading social and political force within the African American community, working to pull up from "the nadir" through systematic agitation for civil rights.

BENJAMIN "PAP" SINGLETON
Ho for Kansas! [1878]

In the 1860s and 1870s, a small number of African Americans were among the first Americans to migrate to the new state of Kansas, drawn there by the Homestead Act, a federal law signed by President Abraham Lincoln in 1862 that granted settlers 160-acre plots of undeveloped land in the West. The end of Reconstruction in the late 1870s prompted a much larger surge of migration from the southern states, however, with between 20,000 and 40,000 African Americans leaving for Kansas between 1877 and 1881, many during the "Exodus of 1879." The migrants of this movement, known as the "Exodusters," were typically poorer than earlier migrants and not as well equipped to withstand the rigors of the new territory.

A key promoter of the 1879 migration was Benjamin "Pap" Singleton (1809–1892). Singleton, who had escaped slavery in Tennessee, returned to Nashville after the Civil War, and soon began preaching to ex-slaves about opportunities to claim homesteads in the West. In the 1870s, he co-founded the Edgefield Real Estate and Homestead Association, a business dedicated to promoting migration to Kansas. Coining the phrase "Ho for Kansas," Singleton printed up broadsides like the one reprinted here, to encourage migration. In response to leaders such as Frederick Douglass who were urging African Americans to stay and fight for their rights in the South, Singleton proclaimed, "Such men as this should not be leaders of our race any longer."

In addition to marketing the Exodus, Singleton personally led settlers to colonies that he established in Kansas. In the last decade of his life, however, Singleton lost faith in his belief that black people would be able to succeed in America. Shifting his focus to emigration, he established the United Trans-Atlantic Society in 1885 to encourage all African Americans to relocate in Africa.

Photograph of March 18, 1878, broadside courtesy of the Prints and Photographs Division, Library of Congress, Washington, D.C.

from *Proceedings of the National Conference of Colored Men of the United States* [1879]

The participants at the 1879 National Conference of Colored Men convened to discuss numerous important civil rights issues facing black southerners with the end of Reconstruction. However, the mass movement of African Americans from the South to Kansas and other western territories in the Exodus of 1879 had become such a momentous historical force that it overshadowed all other topics under discussion. After the Civil War, as these proceedings illustrate, the destinations proposed in debates about relocation largely shifted from Africa, Central America, and other foreign lands to potential destinations within the United States.

During the often-raucous proceedings, the delegates agreed on the key point that the exodus to the West was a response by southern African Americans to the "wrongs and oppression which have debased their labor, crushed their manhood, and denied them their inalienable and constitutional rights." In particular, delegates protested the denial of educational opportunities, the right to vote, and the right to a fair trial. The delegates disagreed, however, on the appropriate response to those injustices.

From Howard Holman Bell, ed., *Minutes of the Proceedings of the National Negro Conventions, 1830–1864* (New York: Arno Press, 1964), n.p.

When this movement was inaugurated the present migration of colored people from the Southern States had not at that time begun, and it was not seriously apprehended that anything of the kind would be done, certainly not apprehended it would be done to the extent we find it has assumed. This, therefore, was not one of the chief objects for which we were convened or requested to convene, for that question did not present itself but has since assumed important proportions. Now it is to be hoped we will calmly deliberate on that question. It is a question that demands our attention, attracts the attention of the country.

I will take the opportunity to make this suggestion, that in considering this matter you should bear in mind the fact that the South being the home of the colored people, they being adapted to its climate, its soil—having been born and raised there—we should not advise them to leave there unless they have very good reason to do so. On the other hand, we should not advise them to remain where they are not well treated. [Applause.] But we should endeavor to inculcate in their minds a sufficient amount of independence to say to the country and to the people with whom they are surrounded, that "if our labor is valuable, then it should command respect." [Applause.] That if we receive this respect, if our rights and privileges are accorded to us here, doing all we can to improve our condition, to that question I feel that we should live together. Further than that, at least, we should not go. If the colored man can receive that treatment, attention, consideration and respect he is entitled to under the law in the South, the South is the place for him. If not, they are justified in receiving it where they can. [Applause.] Then let us go calmly, dispassionately, and when all classes begin to see their mistakes, perhaps all will come together, seal up all past differences, conceding the rights of all, and continued peace and harmony and good will and friendship will prevail, and the South will prosper.

* * *

J. A. Braboy, of Indiana, offered the following resolutions:

Resolved, That it is the duty of this Conference to hear the grievances of our Southern brethren concerning their impaired rights, concerning education, and all their rights as American citizens, politics excepted.

Resolved, That unless the white friends take immediate steps to guarantee such rights, there will be an immediate emergency exist for all entire exodus of the race from the States in order to ameliorate their condition.

Resolved, That it is the duty of this Conference to appoint an executive committee at the capital of each State of the several States to aid, if deemed necessary, in locating these colonies in the various States, in order that they may make a good living and educate their children.

Resolved, That this Conference should take steps by appointing one man from each State, whose duty it shall be to call a national convention of the Republicans, the convention to meet in Cincinnati, to take under consideration their political rights, and any other business they may deem proper.

The resolutions were referred.

W. A. Pledger offered a resolution providing that all resolutions relating to migration be first referred to the Southern delegates. Referred.

* * *

Second Day.

* * *

By J. Henri Burch, of Louisiana:

Resolved, That the printed report of the recent Labor Convention held at Vicksburg, Miss., on May 3 to 6, be referred to the Committee on Migration, when appointed, with a request that they report back to this Convention whether, in their opinion, the real causes and remedies for the present exodus appear in any part of said report.

Referred.
By R. R. Wright:

Resolved, That each delegation of the several States submit to this Conference, by written report, prior to the discussion of the topic of migration, a succinct statement of the true condition of the masses, or country inhabitants, of their respective States with regard to labor and education; and be it further

Resolved, That such statement govern the action of this Conference with respect to the subject of migration.

Referred.
By W. H. Council, of Alabama:

Resolved, That whereas the principal business men and farmers have entered into contracts for the present year, we deem this an untimely season to agitate the question of migration, believing that it would prove detrimental to the interests of all concerned.

2.   That we are opposed to a general and sudden exodus of our people for any part of the country, but recommend a careful consideration of the matter for all who desire to migrate, and after such mature consideration and calm reflection, if they are satisfied that their condition can be improved by emigration, we advise gradual migration.

3.   That the emigration question should be considered apart from politics, and should be based upon business calculation.

Referred.
By J. H. Burrus, of Nashville:

Whereas by the history of the beginning, progress and final triumph of the idea of the right of the people in contradistinction of the Divine right of kings in the Old World, and by the inception and glorious termination of the "irrepressible conflict" between freedom and slavery in this country, as well as by the beginning, progress and successful ending of all progressive and liberal thought, new ideas in the world, we are admonished of the great need of the continual agitation of the question of familiar wrong to be supplanted by unfamiliar right; be it therefore

Resolved by this Conference, That we recommend to our people everywhere not to cease to protest before the civilized world and their fellow-citizens against the unjust, invidious and unchristian discrimination against their civil rights as American citizens now practiced in these United States, especially the Southern States.

Referred.

By F. D. Morton, of Indiana:

Whereas there are many subjects of the greatest import to the colored citizens of this country, both as a part and a whole; and

Whereas there are many of the ablest and most talented members of this Conference who have spent some time in preparing to make a special effort upon the subject of migration and others of equal import ; therefore

Resolved, That a committee of three be appointed to receive the names of such persons who have especially prepared themselves upon any of the important questions which have been collected for the consideration of this Conference.

Resolved, That a special time be designated and announced, together with the name of the person or persons who desire to present the result of their investigation to this Conference.

Referred.

Samuel Lowery, of Alabama, asked to present the following:

Whereas the Democratic party of the South have proclaimed to the world that this is a white man's Government, made expressly for them, and that they will not suffer, at the peril of their lives, the choice of colored men to positions of honor and emoluments where they are in the majority; and that they will resort to the disruption of this Government rather than suffer or permit the civil and political equality of our race in the South ; and

Whereas we have trusted in vain the hope to enjoy perfect and complete liberty in this land of our ancestry, from whose unpaid labors its wealth and prosperity have sprung, and the pledge given us by the true Republicans of the North for freedom and human rights have been stealthily snatched from us and our posterity in encroachments, without any prospective redress. We are denied the right of a trial by a jury of our countrymen, in the administration of the judicial laws of Alabama, and as a consequence misdemeanors are executed as felonies, and the courts, as now administered, are crowding the prisons, coal mines and penitentiary, where our race are sold into slavery as in the days of yore, under the pretense and forms of law. They deny to us school privileges to improve the minds of our youths equally. We toil by day and night to make more cotton for the landlord than we did in slavery, and we enjoy no more than one peck of meal[1] and two and a half pounds of pork with the labor of our women and children.

Therefore, believing the Lord has provided a land of freedom where we can enjoy all the rights of humanity, and has opened the hearts of the Christian men and women of the American people of the North to aid us in our struggle to settle on them, and as a convention of the most prominent men of our race will shortly assemble at Nashville to perfect and complete such a settlement, on such a basis or plan which will promote our success and the pride and glory of the American people; therefore, be it

Resolved, That this meeting send to the Nashville convention——delegates, and pledge our efforts to aid this cause for our freedom, and we appoint an executive committee of fifteen colored men to organize this work.   Referred.

George M. Perkins,[2] of Arkansas, moved that no more resolutions be offered for the present. Carried.

* * *

The secretary was requested to read several communications or letters from persons unable to attend the convention, among which was the following:

---

1. Eight cups of a coarse powder made of ground grain, seeds, or nuts; during American slavery, the weekly ration per slave on many plantations.

2. Former slave George Napier Perkins (1841–1914) was a prominent lawyer and founder of Campbell, Arkansas; he later moved to the Oklahoma Territories, where he owned and edited *The Oklahoma Guide,* a newspaper that was influential in promoting migration to Oklahoma; the *Proceedings* contain a number of typographical errors, including several incorrect middle initials, as here and on p. 194, where W. H. Bentley should read M. H. Bentley.

CHARLESTON COLORED WESTERN
EMIGRATION SOCIETY,

CHARLESTON, S. C., *April* 30, 1870.

At a meeting of the said society, held at the residence of the chairman on the 30th day of April, 1879, to take into consideration the question of what this society shall do in response to the call issued by our fellow-sufferers, the friends and promoters of the movement for the emigration of the colored people from the former Southern slave States of the Union to the free States and Territories of the country, for a convention to be held at Nashville, Tenn., on the 6th day of May proximo,[3] the officers of this society and many other persons interested being present, and an informal discussion and free interchange of views upon the subject being had, it is on motion voted—

1. That it is with regret that this society finds it impossible to have personal representation at the said convention, and

2. That this society, now counting many adherents and coadjutors in South Carolina, herewith sends its hearty greetings to the convention at Nashville, and pledges co-operation by every lawful means in our power in carrying out the plans and purposes which said convention in its wisdom may devise and promulgate for the accomplishment of the common object of removing our people from the scenes of their great tribulations.

The colored population of the United States throughout the entire land, when the Government by the perfidy of the very people who now oppress us, had to maintain a gigantic struggle at arms to preserve its existence, was faithful among the faithless found.

In slavery itself, when smitten on the one cheek, we turned also the other ; we bided our time. But it hath pleased God to weaken the galling chains of slavery, so far as that consummation could be effected by law. But what is mere freedom to man without civil and political rights? Literally, we have no rights here which a white man is bound to respect.

We are as lambs among wolves. If, at the risk of our lives, we approach the polls to vote at an election, our vote when deposited is rendered inoperative and ineffectual by the deposit by a political opponent of a pack of fifty tissue ballots, or otherwise our vote is wholly suppressed outright and never counted for the candidate of our choice. In the courts the colored man obtains no justice ; partiality is the order there. The boast is proudly made that this is a white government.

Let us appeal to the good people of the country to aid us in changing the place of our abode to the free States and Territories. We have willing hands as ever; we have strong arms still. We are sneeringly told that we are poor and have not the means of defraying our expenses in removing from here to the free States and Territories. We have no apology to make for our poverty. It comes illy from those who have enjoyed our unrequited labor for hundreds of years the taunt that we are poor.

Voted that the foregoing, signed by the officers of this society, be transmitted to the Nashville convention, with the request that the officers of said convention furnish this society with a certified copy of the proceedings of the said convention, and with such other papers as they may be in possession of, of interest.   M. G. CHAMPLIN, *Chairman.*

JAMES N. HAYNE, *Secretary.*

Having read the above communication, J. H. Burrus, of Tennessee, moved the reference of it and other letters to the Executive Committee, which motion was adopted and the papers so referred, after motions to lay on the table, a call for the previous question, and a reference to a special committee had been voted down.

* * *

By Rev. P. C. Murphy, of Alabama:

Whereas the various courts of the Southern States have denied the colored man the right of sitting on juries where civil and political acts are involved; therefore

3. Of or in the next month.

Resolved, That we, in National Conference assembled, do feel aggrieved as citizens of the United States of America, and ask that something be done.

Referred.
By M. H. Bentley,[4] of Georgia:

Resolved, That before taking final steps towards emigration, we ask for and demand our political rights in the South.

Resolved further, That in States where there are eight or nine Congressmen, we claim a representative of two of them; where there are three or four districts, we claim one, and in that proportion throughout the Southern States.

Resolved, That the various districts now represented by white members take in rotation, each in turn, for colored representation.

Referred.
By John J. Bird, of Illinois:

Whereas the late Labor Convention, held in Vicksburg, did, among other things, set forth the following, to wit : "The apprehension on the part of many colored people, produced by insidious reports circulated among them, that their civil and political rights are endangered, or likely to be; and

Whereas said declaration does, as is common among the class of men largely represented in said convention, seek to avoid the real issues underlying the widespread and deep-seated dissatisfaction existing among our people in several of the Southern States; and

Whereas it is the sense of this Conference that the object of calling said convention one day in advance of this Conference, was intended to forestall its action on the subject of emigration; therefore

Resolved, That we, the representatives of the colored people of the United States, in National Conference assembled, do hereby deprecate such action, and denounce this wanton refusal to admit facts as they exist in regard to the political proscription, murderous and unjustifiable assaults upon innocent citizens in their midst, whose only offense is that they seek to exercise the rights accorded to them under the laws of our land and country.

Resolved, That we will not, shall not, receive these specious promises as a sufficient guarantee for future protection, but accept them as cunningly devised schemes to stay the present exodus of the colored people, who are seeking in a legitimate and praiseworthy manner to relieve themselves from the wrongs and oppression which have debased their labor, crushed their manhood, and denied them their inalienable and constitutional rights.

Referred.

* * *

Third Day.

The National Colored Conference reassembled at 9 o'clock, President J. R. Lynch in the chair.

C. O. H. Thomas said he had remarked on the evening previous that he desired the following morning to answer pertinently the reflections cast upon him by

---

4. Nine years earlier, in a markedly less civil debate, Moses H. Bentley, messenger of the Georgia House of Representatives, shot and killed fellow black representative Malcolm Claiborne over a dispute about Bentley's firing of a black page; the July 30, 1870, edition of *The Atlanta Constitution* reported the event as follows:

Moses Bentley was some years ago a well behaved, well bred Savannah mulatto. Shortly after the war in which he served as a drummer, he fell into the hands of the carpet-baggers and scalawag politicians who used him for their selfish and corrupt purposes. Thus demoralized and corrupted he became a politician and by the negro vote was made a member of the black and tan convention, which framed the new State constitution. Since then he has considered himself a public character, and a worthy associate of the herd of carpet-baggers and scalawags with which the State is cursed. He owes his present unfortunate position to his evil associations. He is now a felon and having murdered one of the favored race instead of a white man, he has no right to hope for executive clemency. *Savannah News*

Governor Pinchback,[5] but as the Governor was not present he would postpone his remarks.

The following resolutions were offered and referred:

By B. A. J. Nixon:

To the honorable and august body of Colored Men in
Conference assembled:

We, the people of Giles county, Tennessee, send greeting to your honorable body, and earnestly ask that you, after having carefully considered the various subjects announced by the Executive Committee, to present to us and the colored people all over these United States some remedy for the untold injustices which our people have endured and are enduring. We of Giles county can very easily enumerate the evils under which we have been laboring for more than a decade of years, but our best judgment and most extended research have been baffled when attempting to devise a remedy. It has been said, and wisely, we think, that in counsel there is much wisdom. Therefore, we ask your body to promulgate to the colored people of the United States some remedy for the innumerable injuries we are suffering.

Whereas the colored people of the Southern States are being stirred up on the subject of emigration; therefore

Resolved, That a committee be appointed by this Conference, to be known as the National Emigration Committee, consisting of one gentleman from each State, whose duty it shall be to organize similar committees in each of the Southern States.

By J. Henri Burch, of Louisiana:

Whereas there is now going on, and has been for some time past, an exodus of the colored people of certain Southern States to the State of Kansas and other Northern States; and

Whereas, while said exodus has on the one side attracted the attention, sympathies, and efforts of all lovers of universal equality before the law, it has on the other given rise to various harsh criticisms on the part of those opposed to emigration, who are using the silence of the Negro as a race to declare that it is put into operation solely for political purposes; that the Negro is happy and contented in the South, and that he has no real cause for emigrating, and other specious arguments calculated to place the emigrationists in a false position; and

Whereas the purpose of dealing with this question as colored men and from a national standpoint;

Resolved, That the Committee on Emigration, when appointed, be requested to take under consideration, and report back to this Convention, the following subjects pertaining to said exodus:

1. What are the causes that have given rise to the exodus movement among the colored people?

2. If there is any truth in the report that the scheme was gotten up to irate the North against the South?

3. What are the remedies to be pursued to stop the movement? Would the colored people accept concessions if made to them; and, if so, of what nature?

4. Are the colored people pursuing the wisest course of migration?

5. How is this movement likely to affect the two political parties in their respective States and nationally?

6. Any other observations that may occur to the committee.

By T. W. Lott:

Whereas there is an unsettled state of affairs in the Southern States, resulting in the exodus of a large number of colored people from that section of the country; and

---

5. Pinckney Benton Stewart (P.B.S.) Pinchback (1837–1921) was the first African American governor of a U.S. state, serving for 35 days in 1872–73 after the impeachment of Louisiana's elected governor, Henry Clay Warmoth; the son of a former slave and her former owner (who were living together as husband and wife when he was born), Pinchback was later elected to the U.S. House of Representatives and the U.S. Senate (although both elections were contested), and helped establish the historically black college Southern University.

Whereas this state of unrest is pervading the entire colored community, creating almost uncontrollable anxiety on their part as to the final result; and

Whereas it is not the desire of the people, nor the sense of this Conference that the migration of said people continue without an adequate cause to the evident and irreparable loss to both the colored and the white; and

Whereas it is expected that this Conference take into serious consideration this matter in all its various aspects; be it therefore

Resolved, That it is due to the colored race, especially to those of our suffering brethren of the South, that this body do give a dispassionate, searching, and positive expression as to the existing causes, whether political or otherwise, with a view to the incitement of a more earnest endeavor looking to their removal and immediate restoration to confidence and prosperity in said States, and that, should said causes be traced to the unjust discrimination toward the colored man on account of race, color, or previous condition of servitude as to the real, proper, and unmistakable source, that we, in the name of the oppressed race of which this body is a part, deprecate in unmeasured terms, as shocking to the highest sensibilities of an enlightened civilization, such discrimination, being an unmerited return for the noble achievements of the Negro, the blessings of which the white race are the favored recipients.

Resolved, That in the discussion of this momentous and all-absorbing question we indulge in no language which justly and impartially interpreted will cast any reflection upon the white man or reflect discredit upon this body.

By C. O. H. Thomas:

Resolved, That this Conference of representative colored men of the United States of America are pledged by the sacred bond of kindred blood and of a common humanity, to devote their best efforts for the establishment of civil and political rights ;

Resolved, That the rights of the freedmen are inseparable from the condition of freedom. There-

fore, being free and invested with that potent talisman of liberty, the ballot, which will enable us to maintain our rights, we here declare that we wish to possess and exercise, as prudent, law-abiding citizens, all the rights possessed in common by other citizens of the United States. We furthermore avow our earnest hope that the noble men and women of our country who are seeking to lift up their sisters to a higher plane of womanhood by giving them a larger scope in the activities and responsibilities of life by means of the ballot, may succeed in consummating their great purpose, for it would be a wretched commentary upon our liberty-loving profession if we proved not our faith by our works in refusing to aid in the complete freedom and exaltation of women.

Resolved, That the right to labor and to receive wages commensurate with the labor performed are sacred principles underlying the primal foundation of human society. It is, therefore, as much treason against God and humanity to close up an avenue of labor by which people gain a living as to steal the sweat of their brows by paying them wages inadequate to the work performed. The party in power, if it would continue to be the shepherd of the people, must not waver from the steadfast adherence to the principles which gave it its present glory.

Resolved, That the vast body of the working men of this country, white or colored, require a policy which shall elevate labor, giving them higher wages and better homes in the South, and throw open to them the avenues of industry and emolument to race.

Resolved, That we behold with feelings of deep mortification and regret the widespread demoralization of the almost utter advancement of earnest efforts for self-culture and intellectual development by our young men and women. We call upon our ministers and others to whose care is committed the moral and mental training of the young to strive with all their might to reclaim those who are walking down the broad road that leads to moral and physical death.

Resolved, We also deplore the existence of a fact equally bad. Among our so-called leading men there is no general spirit of public enterprise nor of laudable ambition to place within the hands of their race the means of their self-elevation; no building associations; no industrial avenues through which a knowledge of the various mechanical arts can be obtained. The work-shops, the counting-rooms, clerkships in stores, and employment in the busy commercial marts of our cities and towns are closed to us as a rule, and we have yet to learn the sad lesson that the spirit of caste and of prejudice will continue to prevail just so long as we are poor and needy.

Resolved, That on the subject of migration we will give it our special unbiased and unprejudiced consideration, and will so act as to redound to the good and benefit of all concerned—to both rulers and the ruled.

By L. A. Roberts, of Grand Junction, Tenn.:

Whereas there is at the present time a spirit of emigration existing among the colored people of the South, especially in the valley of the Mississippi, caused by oppression and otherwise, and non-protection in their rights as American citizens in the several Southern States, with no prospect existing of a change for the better; therefore

Resolved, By this, the National Convention of colored citizens: First, that it is expedient and wise for all who can to emigrate to some parts of the United States where they can enjoy all the rights and immunities granted them under the Constitution and laws of the United States, without fear or molestation; second, that in order to carry out the project of emigration systematically and advantageously, an emigration society be organized, whose duty shall be to assist those who desire to leave their homes in the South in so doing, and to reach their destination in any of the Northwestern States or Territories, to establish bureaus and agencies at one or more points on the Mississippi, Tennessee, Cumberland, Ohio and Missouri rivers, connected with the principal railroads leading West and Northwest, to look after the welfare and interest of the emigrants at the several places of embarking, and change of cars and disembarking; third, that as the boats on the Mississippi river have refused to carry colored emigrants, steps be taken to charter one or more boats for that purpose, and if possible bring suit against those who have refused; fourth, this society shall be known as the "North American Colored Emigration Society," and shall in all respects be officered and managed as other societies of the same character which are best adapted to the wants and interests of those whom it seeks to benefit.

Referred to the Committee on Migration.
By James D. Kennedy, of Louisiana:

Resolved, That the Committee on Permanent Organization be instructed to inquire into the practicability of holding a conference every year, and report the result of labor at the earliest moment.

Referred.
By W. F. Yardley:

Resolved, That it is the sense of this Conference that colored people should migrate to those States and Territories where they can enjoy all the rights which are guaranteed by the laws and Constitution of the United States, and enforced by the Executive departments of such States and Territories, and we ask of Congress of the United States an appropriation of $500,000 to aid in the removal of our people from the South.

T. W. Henderson, from Kansas, made a speech in which he stated that there was "smooth sailing" for the colored people in his State, and said he had come to the Conference at the suggestion of Gov. St. John, of Kansas.

R. Allen, of Texas, moved to postpone further consideration of the subject until 3 p. m. Carried.

By D. Jones, of Oregon: Resolution advising migration to the States and Territories of the far West.

By Rev. John A. Clay: Resolution authorizing the appointment of an executive committee, with power to appoint auxiliary committees.

By J. H. Walker: Resolution authorizing the Conference to appoint a conference committee of five from each State, to confer from time to time on the condition of the colored people, and if possible to render aid to the same.

By G. W. Darden, of Kentucky:

Whereas the colored people of the South are so cruelly treated in the South, being slain by rifle clubs and lynch law; and

Whereas in the South slavery is not dead, but sleeping; and

Whereas in the South election day is a day of terror with the colored man; and

Whereas the Southern Negro is not as well treated as the Southern dog by the white man, who rightly claims that this is a white man's Government; and

Whereas the colored man is not recognized here as human, but, as Tom Paine asserted, as a species of the monkey; and

Whereas the ex-Confederate President seems to indorse Tom Paine by saying that the idea of educating the Negro is a piece of nonsense; therefore be it

Resolved, That the colored man of the South save his dollars and cents in order to emigrate.

Resolved, That we pay no heed to such men as Fred. Douglass and his accomplices, for the simple reason that they are well-to-do Northern men who will not travel out of their way to benefit the suffering Southern Negro, and who care not for the interests of their race.

By G. W. Gentry: Resolution to make the subject of migration paramount in the discussion immediately upon the report of the committee.

Wm. R. Lawton, of Missouri, in lieu of a resolution, wished to present an appeal from the colored citizens asking for aid for the destitute emigrants in that State.

Objection was made, and the paper was read as a resolution.

By C. O. H. Thomas: Resolution expressing indignation at an order prohibiting colored citizens in New Orleans from holding their meetings after 10 p. m.

By Rev. G. H. Shaffer: Resolution demanding the employment of colored teachers in colored schools.

By W. F. Anderson: Resolution requesting the railroads to pass all delegates home free who paid full fare to the convention.

By J. H. Kelley: Resolution urging the adoption of a system of emigration.

By T. W. Lott: To appoint a committee of three on the colored press.

By J. W. Grant: Asking Congress to appropriate an amount for 259 years for the assistance of those needing aid to emigrate to Kansas.

By B. A. J. Nixon: That the Conference insist on the authorities in impaneling juries to give the colored a portion of the jury, and especially when the prisoners at the bar are colored; that when candidates are electioneering they be asked whether they are willing to grant that right.

By J. M. Smith, of Tennessee:

Whereas there is great excitement among our race of people that is causing great suffering: We therefore ask of this Conference to use their best influence in pacifying the minds of their countrymen. We ignore the practice that is played upon the colored man in this country. We therefore ask this honorable Conference to give some aid, if possible, to their countrymen. The real cause is the reduction of wages and the shameful manner in which we are treated in traveling over the great thoroughfares of the country. We also clamor for our rights as free citizens in the country, which are denied us. This excitement is causing an exodus which is causing much suffering. They are leaving the homes of their childhood, trusting their fortune to an experiment. It is an experiment which, if it fails, will ruin us forever. We therefore ask that this matter be carefully considered and the minds of the people pacified. Thousands have left their homes penniless, not knowing when nor where it will end. We therefore demand all of our rights as citizens, and, unless we do receive our just rights, we resolve in emigrate to the North or Northwest. We pledge ourselves to come together in all parts of the country as free citizens and demand our rights. We know the color line has been struck, and unless it be withdrawn, we will immediately seek for our suffrage, which, if it cannot be obtained here, we will remove from among them where we can enjoy our free privileges. We therefore ask this honorable

Conference to use their best influence in our behalf.

Referred.
By Rev. Allan Allensworth:

Whereas there is now an exodus of colored people from some of the Southern States; and

Whereas there are certain parties trying to mould a public opinion in the North to the effect that said exodus is a political trick, originated by and is being carried out for the Republican party, and that the Republican party is responsible for the suffering and losses occasioned by said exodus; therefore be it

Resolved, That we enjoin the public that the assertion is not true, but that said dissatisfaction and exodus is caused by the unrighteous, unlawful, unpatriotic and uncivilized treatment we receive from our "best friends" in the South, who exact exorbitant prices and rents for lands; who discriminate in free school facilities, who discriminate upon railroads, steamboats and at railroad stations and hotel accommodations, while at the same time they charge the same fare; who compel our ladies to ride in smoking-cars, among the roughest of travelers; who deny us representation upon juries, and who fail to protect us in our contracts for labor, and who hold up to the world through their papers our ignorance, our superstition, and our crude efforts to live, and at the same time disparage our leading educated men. It is, therefore, at the door of our best friends we lay the source of all these evils.

Be it further resolved, That it is the belief of this conference that the Republican party is not responsible for the Freedman's Saving and Trust Company failure as a party.

By Randall Brown, of Nashville: To appoint a committee of twenty-two to name a place for emigration; that the Conference defray the expenses of this committee.

By L. A. Roberts: To tax each member of the Conference $1 or more to aid emigration.

Mr. J. D. Kennedy, of Louisiana, submitted the following estimate of the value of the colored laborer in the South for 1877 and 1878: Total value of cotton, sugar, molasses, rice and tobacco raised, $177,298,980; of manual and other labor, $158,000.

By J. C. Napier:

Whereas the civil and political rights of the Negro, from the Ohio river to the Gulf of Mexico, are abridged and curtailed in every conceivable manner, he being denied almost every privilege that is calculated to elevate him in his moral, intellectual and political status; as compared with the public school privileges of the white man, his are a mere mockery; in the courts, as compared to that justice which is meted out to white men, his is entirely farcical, he seldom or never enjoying that right which the Constitution of our country guarantees to every citizen, namely, the right to be tried by a jury of his peers; and

Whereas it appears there is no disposition on the part of a great majority of the Southern people to grant to the Negro those rights which the word citizenship should carry with it, or to relinquish any of their old customs and prejudices; therefore,

Resolved, That it is the sense of this conference that the great current of migration which has, within the past few weeks, taken thousands of our people from our midst, and which is daily carrying hundreds from the extreme Southern States, should be encouraged and kept in motion until those who are left are awarded every right and privilege to which the Constitution and laws of our country entitle us; or, until we are all in a land where our rights are in no respect questioned.

* * *

By David Wilson, of Huntsville:

Resolved, That this convention appoint a committee of one from each State a delegation to memorialize Congress and the Executive of the United States to locate in the West the "new Canaan" of the hope to the colored American, and from which he can found a State on Republican principles, to be governed by them, from governor down to the humblest officer, without fear or intimidation, being settlers and owning of the soil.

By Judge M. W. Gibbs: Resolution advising colored men to become land owners.

It was adopted by the Committee on Education, and will be found at the close of that report.

The author of the resolution made a short address, saying that the greatest drawback to the Negro, whether he lived North or South, was his poverty. He advised greater economy and the accumulation of wealth as one of the greatest levers of advancement and power. The colored men were going out of the South and Germans and Northern and Northwestern people were coming into it.

By H. W. Ward, of Arkansas:

Resolved, That a board of commissioners be appointed from the various States to select States and Territories whereto the colored people of the South may migrate.

By M. G. Turner:

Resolved, That the delegates from the different States elect one commissioner on migration from the delegation now in the National Conference, to which all questions of migration may be referred.

By George N. Perkins, of Arkansas:

Resolution 1. Favoring wholesale emigration on account of oppression and intimidation.

2. That from each State one or more emigration commissioners be appointed to select homes for the oppressed.

3. Providing for the appointment of auxiliary emigration commissioners.

4. Indorsing Senator Windom's resolution.

5. Proclaiming that the Negro is not naturally inferior to the white man, and is capable of self-government.

6. To memorialize Congress for a redress of grievances.

* * *

J. P. Jones, of Arkansas, offered the following, which were adopted:

Whereas we learn from well-founded rumor that Hon. Benjamin F. Butler has tendered and donated 20,000 acres of land in Wisconsin, and Hon. Zach Chandler offered homes to one hundred families of color who are fleeing from their homes in various sections of the South; therefore

Resolved, That we extend to the honorable gentlemen our grateful thanks in the name of suffering humanity for their manifestation in recognizing the claims of a people whose condition appeals so strongly to the sympathy of the charitable.

Resolved, That a copy of these resolutions be forwarded to the honorable gentlemen herein indicated.

The resolution of W. F. Yardley, introduced at the morning session, was then taken up.

James D. Kennedy, of Louisiana, moved to suspend the rules and proceed to the resolution memorializing Congress for the appropriation of $350,000 to aid the suffering freedmen in the West. The motion was carried. He offered an amendment that the Vice-President be requested to lay the same before the Senate for such action as they might deem necessary.

Colonel Robert Harlan said:

Mr. President, as to the present migration movement of the colored people, let it be understood that we have the lawful right to stay or to go wherever we please. The southern country is ours. Our ancestors settled it, and from the wilderness formed the cultivated plantation and they and we have cleared, improved, and beautified the land.

Whatever there is of wealth, of plenty, of greatness, and of glory in the South, the colored man has been, and is, the most important factor. The sweat of his brow, his laborer's toil, his patient endurance under the heat of the semi-tropical sun and the chilling blasts of winter, never deterred the laborer from his work.

The blood of the colored man has fertilized the land and has cemented the Union. Aware of these facts, we should be baser than the willing slaves did we consent to the dictation of any men or body of men as to where we may go, when we shall go, or how long we shall stay.

The Republic owes to every citizen protection for his home and security for his rights. Let this security be given, and until that be done, let us cry aloud against those who refuse it, whether in the North or in the South. Let us remember all such in our prayers to the God of Liberty and of Justice, that He may punish them as they deserve. Let us remember them at the ballot-box, and fail not to inflict the retribution which they so justly deserve, and if we be obstructed in casting our votes, we can go where there will be no hindrance, and where we can vote as we please.

He who submits in silence to an injury may be avenged by a righteous heaven, but has little hope from man. Let us, therefore, keep the wrongs under which we labor before the public until an awakened sense of right and justice on both sides of Mason and Dixon's line shall work out a remedy. They need not tell us that there is no way to right our wrongs. The trouble is not in the want of a way; it is the want of a will. Let us exert the will and the way will be found. But this may take time, and while time runs many of us may perish. If the Government should fail to give protection to our people, it can do no less than aid those who wish to change their habitations to safer and better homes.

With these views before us, and believing in an all-wise Providence, we would be recreant to our principles, to our creed, to our race, and to our God should we neglect to use all the means in our power to bring about the desired results.

Such a measure would have a double effect; it would arouse the attention and self-interest of the North that the laws should be sternly enforced that regulate the purity of the ballot and security for the persons of the colored race, and it would strongly appeal to the interest and humanity of the Southern people to see that they should not lose an industrious and worthy population by reason of lawlessness and inhumanity. Let us, therefore, insist on some such measure as an alternative right.

Let us demand that the principles we assert be declared essential, in resolutions of legislatures and conventions, and made a part of our party platform.

Let us agitate, even as other classes agitate when their rights and wishes are disregarded.

We are Americans, and let us act as Americans have ever done when denied their rights. Cry aloud and spare not until our injuries are known and our wrongs are redressed and our demands are granted.

Let us frame an address and make an appeal to Congress for relief. Although the Democrats are in a majority, no matter. Some Democrats have a sense of justice, and others assume the virtue if they have it not; let us put them to the test. Let our motto be "Protection to our homes or homes elsewhere," and until the Government can be brought to aid migration, let private kindliness and enterprise be brought into action. Let us appeal to the people of the North, to corporations and to common carriers for aid, so that all who are oppressed in the land of their birth may find freedom in the land of their adoption. If the leading men of the South will make another Egypt of these bright and sunny valleys, then must the oppressed go forth into the promised land of liberty, into the Western States and Territories, where the people are at peace and the soil is free, and where every man can secure a home for himself and family with none to molest him or make him afraid.

Already many have seen the beacon light of hope and are making their way toward it, and if the oppression is continued more and more will burst their chains and take the road to liberty.

There are some signs of objection to this on the part of the land-owners. They want the colored man to stay and till the soil. Very well; then let them treat him justly and fairly and protect him from criminal lawlessness. If they cannot or will not do this, they have no more right to ask him to stay, as they have no legal right to forbid him to go, and any attempt to restrain this movement will be vain and futile.

It is not a flight of fugitive slaves, but a voluntary movement of freemen, seeking liberty and security. It is the exercise of the right of any American to better his condition by going from one part of the country to another, just as interest or fancy may lead him. If we cannot do this, we are not free, no more than are the serfs of Russia, who, until lately, were a part of the estate and sold as such, but, if *we* are to be re-enslaved we may as well die on the road to liberty as at the feet of tyrants. We may as well expire contending for liberty, aye, and far better, than in base submission to degrading slavery.

At present there seems to be no alternative.

The reaction has robbed Southern Republicans, both white and colored, of their votes and of their voices, and this has thrown the nation into the hands of our opponents, who are determined to strip us of the last measure of protection.

Our political rights in these States are wholly suspended or abrogated. We have nothing but the mockery of legal proceedings, and Attorney-General Devens, the constitutional adviser of the President, informs us that there is no prospect of justice from Southern tribunals for the colored man. Possibly he did not intend to convey that impression, but if not, what does he mean? You may study his long and carefully prepared paragraphs without coming to any other conclusion than this, that at present there is no hope for justice to the colored man from Southern courts.

If, then, all stay, all must submit. If some go they will be free, and possibly, by their going, they will awake the ruling minds of the South to a sense of the necessity of what is right.

For these reasons, therefore, I am an advocate for migration as the only present practicable remedy for our wrongs, and I am for the exercise of that remedy in a large measure and at all hazards.

H. V. Robinson, of Arkansas, said he came here from the convention at Vicksburg. What they did at Vicksburg would have a tranquilizing influence. But what good have you done here today? While you may have done some good, you have done a great deal of harm. One says that the colored people are self-supporting, and can go when and where they please. Another says, they are able to take care of and protect themselves. The next thing is a resolution asking Congress to donate $500,000 for the purpose of sending people to Kansas from this country. When the time comes that we cannot live in this country I am as much in favor of going to Kansas as anybody else. But let us be men; let us be like white men and see the impossibility of taking 4,000,000 of people away and setting them suddenly down in a strange country.

A YOUNG DELEGATE.—Who paid you to come here?

MR. ROBINSON.—I suppose the young man is just out of school, and don't suppose he ever hoed cotton in his life. [Applause.]

THE PRESIDENT.—The gentleman's time has expired.

Hon. J. H. Rainey[6] rose to a point of order, saying:

There is so much noise in this hall that we cannot hear what is being said. I want to add, that I think we ought to permit a difference of opinion to be expressed on so important and vital a question, in which we are so deeply interested. Any cause that cannot be discussed in both phases is no cause worthy of deliberation. I favor migration, but I want to proceed intelligently.

When the President had, by continued efforts, finally secured order, a delegate said, "I ask fair play for the gentleman."

Mr. Robinson:

Fair play need not be asked for me; I will see that I have fair play. How can you expect white men to be tolerant to you when you show that you have no tolerance for each other? If you are right your views will bear the light, and if wrong they will not; if wrong they will not stand the test argument. I never went to school in my life. There are graduates of universities who ought to be able to respond to me, provided they have the facts on their side. I say that this resolution is calculated to deceive every ignorant man in Mississippi. You memorialize Congress to give $500,000 to assist the freedmen who have gone or can go to Kansas. You ask of men whom you have been all day abusing to extend charity to you, and you humble and debase yourselves in doing it. When you talk about poor starving black people, I am with them all the time. With what he earns, gets by law, begs or steals, he gets

6. Former Representative Joseph Hayne Rainey of South Carolina (1832–87); the first African American to be elected to the U. S. House of Representatives, Rainey served in Congress from December 1870 to March 1879.

plenty; and I don't say this with any disrespect to colored men. The country is full of this cry of starvation. I have got five hundred acres in Mississippi; I mingle with them all the time, and they don't starve.

A DELEGATE.—Well, why do they want to migrate?

MR. ROBINSON.—Because it is on account of the oppression of the white people, but I am opposed to encouraging wholesale migration, and having the poor colored man strewn along the banks of the Mississippi, there to die.

Further remarks were made by W. H. Council, of Alabama; D. Wilson and J. Gillem, Arkansas.

John D. Lewis, of Philadelphia, moved the previous question; which was carried, and the resolution was then adopted.

H. V. Cashin, of Alabama, moved that the rules be suspended in order to allow Mrs. Dr. Wylie, of Philadelphia, to read the paper of Rev. Dr. B. T. Tanner, on the "Theory and Practice of American Christianity." [See Appendix G.][7] This motion prevailed, and the paper was accordingly read. A vote of thanks was tendered the author of the paper and also the reader.

The Conference then adjourned.

* * *

FOURTH DAY.

The National Colored Conference reassembled at 9 o'clock, President Lynch in the chair.

Prayer by Rev. T. W. Henderson, of Kansas.

T. Richardson, of Mississippi, offered the following resolutions:

Recognizing the fact that the South is the natural home of the colored man, being adapted to the climate and familiar with the mode of producing that staple that forms a source of profit to the whole country, and with the assurance of his civil liberty and political rights, may in the future become a source of great profit to himself—

Resolved, That the question of the removal of our people from these districts or sections when their civil and political rights are abridged or ignored, be given that careful consideration and due deliberation that its importance demands.

Resolved, That this Conference encourage the removal of our people from those sections of the South alone where race, prejudice, or other consideration, render it apparently impossible for the two elements to live together in peace and harmony.

The resolutions were not entertained.

J. W. Cromwell, of Virginia, read a paper on the "Necessity of Industrial and Technical Education." [See Appendix H.]

J. T. Jenifer, of Arkansas, moved that a vote of thanks be tendered the author of the paper.

Carried.

F. L. Barnett, of Illinois, read a paper on "Race Unity," and on motion of J. P. Jones, of Arkansas, a vote of thanks was tendered the author. [See Appendix I.]

Theodore H. Green, of Mississippi, read a paper on the "Elements of Prosperity," and received the thanks of the Conference. [See Appendix J.]

John J. Bird, of Illinois, said that he rose to a question of privilege. He desired to commend the reports which had been given in the *American,* but in that paper of that morning had appeared an editorial stating that "John J. Bird, of Illinois, rose up in the Conference, Thursday, to denounce by resolution, from the lofty standpoint of a man who knows nothing of the subject, the resolutions of the Vicksburg convention. Illinois is not, perhaps, the place where a man would be most likely to acquire information concerning affairs of the South, except strained through the patent back-action filter of John A. Logan, which reverses the principle of the filter and soils that which runs through it. The resolution of Bird is a substantial reiteration of Logan's cheap political claptrap," &c. Mr. Bird said that, upon reading the editorial through to the close, the very admission of the editor was sufficient justification of the resolutions introduced by

---

7. The 107-page *Proceedings* include fifteen appendices that begin on page 42 and consist of referenced remarks, articles, and committee reports.

him. He did not get his information from Logan, but from the following editorial of the New Orleans *Times* of April 22:

> Again, let us be perfectly frank. As we have said, the Negroes are leaving the State because there exists among them a sense of insecurity—an apprehension that their civil and political rights are in danger—a belief that they cannot have justice. The truth compels us to admit that these apprehensions are not altogether unreasonable; that they are the natural results of the conduct of a class of irresponsible young men—young politicians they think themselves—who have no interest in peace and order, since they have no ambition but to get office. That the acts of these people have been exaggerated by politicians of the other side; that Radical politicians, white and black, have been guilty of equal, if not greater, offenses, is all true. But the fact remains that the threatened emigration of the Negroes is to be traced to the conduct of this class, who scent to emulate the name of bull-dozers.

James D. Kennedy, of Louisiana, made a personal explanation in reference to the resolution offered by C. O. H. Thomas, of Tennessee, expressing indignation at an order prohibiting colored citizens of New Orleans from holding church service after the hour of 10 p. m. He stated that the order issued by the chief of police had been subsequently modified so as to apply to white and black churches alike, and that officers of the peace could not make arrests without the necessary information filed according to law. He made this explanation in justice to the municipal officers in New Orleans and the very general desire on the part of members of the Conference to know the facts of the case.

C. O. H. Thomas, of Tennessee, said the order was made to prevent the colored people from holding emigration meetings.

J. P. Jones, of Arkansas, offered the following resolution:

> *Resolved,* That the several State organizations as perfected under the Committee on Permanent Organization be, and they are hereby, empowered to draft addresses in their several States, appealing to all boards of trade, cotton exchanges, and mercantile influences thereof to lend their aid in restoring that equity in principles that regulate the laws of supply and demand, to the end that the pledges made at the last session holden at Vicksburg by the representative heads of these several arms of industry to the Negroes of the country may meet a happy fruition.

J. W. Cromwell said that the resolution did not go far enough. An appeal to the boards of trade would be ineffectual. The colored people planted too much cotton. They should raise their own meat.

The author of the resolution said he was willing to insert an amendment including an appeal to the planting interests. This amendment was agreed to and the resolution adopted.

Several delegates rose to a question of privilege, but the Chairman stated that they could proceed only by unanimous consent. Objection was made.

Ex-Governor P. B. S. Pinchback, of Louisiana, chairman of the Committee on Address, presented a report, which was read by Rev. Allan Allensworth. [See Appendix K.]

After the reading of the report the Conference took a recess until 2 p. m.

* * *

Mr. Rainey commenced by saying that he hoped the Conference would not be disappointed in what he would say. We may never hold another conference. The same faces will never be mirrored against these walls. It behooves us, then, to do what we can with a purpose; that we send down to history our action, and, when it is read by the world, that we may not be ashamed of our action. We are a proscribed people, not because we crucified a Saviour, but because we have a different colored skin from others of this country. We have stood a great deal. We never rose and struck for freedom, as in San Domingo. The white people boasted of this, but it is well that we did not. Would they have had us strike down defenseless people, defenseless women and children? We showed our nobleness by not taking advantage of the situation. We want to say to the white people the time has come for us to give warning that we have stood all we can, and in more than one way we will show this soon. We have been enriching the white man, and the time has come when forbearance has ceased to be a virtue. We have come to that point when we doubt the protestations of those who say they are our best friends. Those in this Conference are here for a purpose. It is to be hoped that the proceedings will be read everywhere. It is to be deprecated that there was a necessity for emigration. We have stood too much now, and I would not blame any colored man who would advise his people to flee from the oppressors to the land of freedom. Pledges were made at Vicksburg. They have been made before, and they have always been broken.

A VOICE.—Yes, and they will always be broken.

The speaker then read a letter from a young friend in South Carolina, giving a melancholy view of the condition of the Negroes in the "Sunny Southland." He concluded by saying: "The people of South Carolina are with you in this movement, and we but await the time when we can join in a general emigration to a land of freedom."

J. J. Bird, of Illinois, made a lengthy speech similar in substance to the one made during the morning session. He devoted his remarks to a denial of any political significance in the resolutions introduced by the Northern delegates. While he was speaking Governor Marks[8] entered the hall and was escorted to a seat near the reporters' table by Governor Pinchback.

G. S. W. LEWIS, (addressing J. J. Bird).—Is this protracted discussion on this report designed to prevent the report on emigration from being presented?

J. J. BIRD.—It is not my purpose.

W. F. Yardley said the proscription placed on the Negro should be removed. If there were places in the South where he could not vote his sentiments, that was a reason for migration. The shops were closed against him, clerkships could not be obtained, there was no opening for him. If he was a favorite he might get a place as street-scavenger, or in a hotel to polish bones. [Laughter.] He did not believe in the popular delusion of forty acres and a mule.[9] He knew that in any new country hard work would be necessary, but they would be free. It was not so bad in Tennessee as it was in other States, but there was oppression here. He wanted his children to stand higher than he did, to be skilled mechanics or professional men, but where was the opening in Tennessee? [A Voice, "Ain't got none," and laughter.] But they must learn to respect each other. He then moved the previous question, when a tremendous confusion ensued, and a general demand forced the withdrawal of the motion.

Richard Allen, of Texas, rose, but yielded to ex-Congressman J. T. Rapier, of Alabama, who moved the previous question on the adoption of the report.

After a good deal of random disputing, the motion for the previous question was carried.

J. D. Kennedy, of Louisiana, said that migration was not caused by low wages or the high price of land. If the people could be allowed to remain unmolested there would be no cry of migration to Kansas. There were many millions of acres uncultivated land in the South. He had hoped great things from the Vicksburg Conference, but it had adopted only a series of glittering generalities—the same old story. He did not believe that going to Kansas would better the colored race. He did not believe in any hasty exodus. He believed in migration, but he did not believe they should go without means to pay their passage and to buy homes. But to those who had gone, he would say, never return. Better perish in Kansas than come back, for a return would make things ten times worse than it was before. He did not think this was the last Conference. They could find the money to come. It was this uneasiness among the Negroes that would make the white men of the South know that something was the matter.

The only fault in the report was the gingerly use of words where the General Government was concerned.

---

8. Albert Smith Marks of Tennessee (1836–91), white American lawyer who served as Governor of Tennessee from 1878–80.

9. General William T. Sherman's Special Field Orders, No. 15 from January 1865 set aside abandoned lands in Georgia and South Carolina to be redistributed to freed slaves, and the Freedmen's Bureau was put in charge of allocating plots "not to exceed 40 acres"; Sherman's order was quickly overturned by President Andrew Johnson in the summer of 1865, and the land was taken from black settlers and returned to white plantation owners.

He thought the thanks of the Conference were due to the people of Nashville for their courteous treatment of the delegates. They had been uniformly kind. They should also thank the *American* for its able and correct reports of the proceedings.

W. H. Bentley, of Georgia, did not think the report full enough.

J. W. James, of Indiana, said that he once thought that ex-Governor Pinchback had deserted the Negro, but he was glad to find that he was mistaken. He indorsed every word that Pinchback had said. He denounced the statement in the *American* that the Northern Negroes came to encourage migration. He had left Tennessee for the far West because he could not get his rights. He was for migration unless the Negro could get his rights where he was.

Rev. Allan Allensworth, of Kentucky, said he wanted to call attention to an editorial in the *American*, but was interrupted by a delegate, who insisted that the gentleman confine himself to the question.

The report was then adopted.

J. T. Rapier, of Alabama, said that the Committee on Migration had had hundreds of resolutions referred to it, and had done the best they could. He moved an adjournment until 8 o'clock, at which time they would take up the report on migration, and take the vote after three hours' discussion, and call the previous question.

This was carried, and the Conference adjourned to 8 p. m.

* * *

The Committee on Migration submitted its report. [See Appendix N.]

It was read by J. H. Burch, of Louisiana.

Rev. J. C. Embry, who was to have opened with a discussion on migration, sent a letter, which will be found in Appendix O.

A debate of three hours on the report followed. Twenty-three speeches indorsing it were made, and at 12:15 a. m. the report was unanimously adopted.

Resolutions of thanks to the Chairman, Secretaries, Governor of Tennessee, the *American,* and the citizens of Nashville were adopted, and the following offered by T. Green, of Mississippi.

> Whereas invitations to visit several institutions of this city have been tendered this Conference; and
>
> Whereas, a press of business prevented us from complying with said invitations; therefore
>
> *Resolved,* That it is a source of deep regret that we could not find it practicable to visit said universities.
>
> *Resolved,* That these institutions have our hearty support and undivided sympathy and co-operation in their great work of uplifting our people from the thraldom of ignorance to the light of education and refinement.

The Chairman, in a few words of good advice to his brother delegates, then pronounced the conference adjourned *sine die.*[1]

J. W. CROMWELL, *Secretary.*

F. L. BARNETT, *Recording Secretary.*

---

1. Without setting a day for a future meeting or action [Latin], notes the final adjournment of a legislative session.

IDA B. WELLS
"Iola" on Discrimination [1887]

In "'Iola' on Discrimination," first published in the *American Baptist* and reprinted in *The New York Freeman* on January 15, 1887, Ida B. Wells links self-segregation to forced segregation. Although self-segregation would become identified with radical militancy in the civil rights movement of the 1950s and 1960s, during the post-Reconstruction era it was full integration that was the politically radical stance.

Born into slavery in Holly Springs, Mississippi, in 1862, Ida B. Wells (also known as Wells-Barnett after her marriage) committed her life to education, writing, and activism. After her parents and a sibling died in a yellow fever epidemic when she was sixteen, Wells, pretending to be eighteen, secured a teaching post to support her five younger siblings. At twenty-two, she refused to give up her first-class seat in a train and move to the "Jim Crow" car. After two of the train's crewmen forcibly ejected her from her seat (to the cheers of white passengers), Wells successfully sued the railroad, although the Tennessee Supreme Court overturned the ruling on appeal. Equally fearless in her journalism, Wells wrote about the inequalities between black schools and white schools that she witnessed as a teacher, adopting the pen name Iola soon after she began publishing articles in 1884. As a result of her activism, she was dismissed from her teaching post; she then became a full-time journalist. Wells launched her lifelong campaign against lynching after three friends were lynched in 1892. In 1895, Wells married a Chicago lawyer, Ferdinand L. Barnett, and they had four children. Until her death in 1931 from kidney disease, she continued to write and agitate for equal rights for African Americans and women, and she was instrumental in founding numerous organizations, including the NAACP.

In her political and social activities, Wells advocated for integration. At times, however, propelled by both practical considerations and her commitment to racial uplift, she championed alternatives. In 1886, for example, Wells organized a kindergarten to serve the children in a black neighborhood in Chicago. That venture brought her under fire from activists who believed her actions reinforced school segregation (an argument she later concurred with in "'Iola' on Discrimination"). Later, she and her husband became supporters of Marcus Garvey, viewing his black nationalism as a positive force for race unity. Still, from her earliest political actions protesting Jim Crow practices to her belief in the political benefits of black/white social interaction, Wells demonstrated an underlying commitment to integration as an ultimate goal.

From *The New York Freeman*, January 15, 1887; reprinted in Ida B. Wells, *The Memphis Diary of Ida B. Wells: An Intimate Portrait of the Activist as a Young Woman*, ed. Miriam DeCosta–Willis (Boston; Beacon Press) 1995, pp. 186–87.

We howl about the discrimination exercised by other races, unmindful that we are guilty of the same thing. The spirit that keeps Negroes out of the colleges and places him by himself, is the same that drives him in the smoking car; the spirit that makes colored men run excursions with "a separate car for our white friends," etc., provides separate seats for them when they visit our concerts, exhibitions, etc., is the same that sends the Negro to theatres and church galleries and second class waiting rooms; the feeling that prompts colored barbers, hotel keepers and the like to refuse accommodation to their own color is the momentum that sends a Negro right about when he presents himself at any similar first-class establishment run by white men; the shortsightedness that insists on separate Knights of Labor Assemblies for colored men,[1] is the same power that forces them into separate Masonic and Odd Fellow lodges. Consciously and unconsciously we do as much to widen the breach already existing and to keep prejudice alive as the other race. There was not a separate school in the State of California until the colored people asked for it. To say we wish to be to ourselves is a tacit acknowledgement of the inferiority that they take for granted anyway. The ignorant man who is so short-sighted has some excuse, but the man or men who deliberately yield or barter the birthright of the race for money, position, self-aggrandizement in any form, deserve and will receive the contumely of a race made wise by experience.

IOLA.

Memphis, Tenn., Dec. 28, 1886.

JOSEPHINE TURPIN WASHINGTON
Needs of Our Newspapers [1889]

In her article on the black press, Josephine Turpin Washington uses pragmatic arguments to support self-segregation in cultural institutions. She points out that the role of the black press differed from that of the white papers, which did not focus on "race doings" and rarely gave voice to African American opinion or provided opportunities for black Americans to develop journalistic skills and "prove ourselves worthy of equality." Washington argues that separate institutions do not reinforce segregation. Instead, they are a strategic response to "the color-line" (which "is drawn and most persistently by the whites") and contribute to breaking it down.

Josephine Turpin Washington (1861–1949) taught mathematics from 1894 to 1896 at Booker T. Washington's Tuskegee Institute, where her husband, Samuel Somerville Hawkins Washington, was the school's physician. The couple then moved to Montgomery, Alabama. In addition to her contributions to black newspapers, Washington wrote introductions to important early works on black women's history, including Hallie Q. Brown's *Homespun Heroines and Other Women of Distinction*, published in 1926. "Needs of Our Newspapers" appeared in *The New York Age*, one of the leading African American newspapers of its day.

From *The New York Age*, October 19, 1889.

That the Negro requires a press of his own, few will be found to deny. Were it simply that he desires news in general, this requirement would be much less urgent; for the long established and wealthy journals of other races are much better fitted to meet this demand than we can hope for a long time to be. But he wants besides general news, which any reliable and well-conducted organ can furnish, news of a special type, of such a kind as publications owned and controlled by white men will not give. He needs information of race doings; he needs to know how events appear seen through the eyes of leading colored men.

He needs to conduct journalistic enterprises, that he may show to the world his ability in this direction.

You may say that this is drawing the color-line. Why not merge our interests in those of the community, subscribe for the best newspapers only and refuse support to those poor and struggling, irrespective of race or nationality? But why speak of our drawing the color-line? It is drawn and most persistently by the whites. For us to attempt to ignore the fact, would be like trying to walk through a stone wall by simply making up your mind it is not there. The wall stands and you have only a broken head for your pains. The

---

1. The Knights of Labor, one of the most important labor organizations of the period, began accepting African Americans and women after 1878 (but continued to actively exclude Asians); even though they publicly advocated integrating local assemblies, they did nothing to stop the segregation of assemblies in the South.

best way to obliterate this color-line, which is contrary to both reason and Christianity, is not foolishly to ignore it, but to act in accordance with the existing facts, while at the same time protesting against the injustice of the situation, and to develope to the uttermost the powers within us, to prove ourselves worthy of equality of every sort, to "make by force our merit known."

Studying the Negro newspapers of the country, as any member of the race interested in its welfare must do, I have been struck with certain needs, both intrinsic and extrinsic, in drawing attention to which I hope I shall be understood. I had almost said "pardoned," but that would imply a fault in making criticism, which I do not admit.

In the first place the journalistic field is often entered with the wrong motive. Where motive is low and altogether lacking, there can be no high standard for the paper. Some become editors merely for the sake of notoriety, for the delight of being in print; some are simply political tools, hired to profess the principles they avow; others hope to make a fortune, a hope I hardly need add which has never been realized by a colored editor. Every paper should have an aim, and a high and lofty one, should devote itself to principles of right, and should be brave and outspoken in their advocacy.

A good motive is, however, not all sufficient. Journalistic ability is essential. It is true that not every one who can write a good magazine article or even a book, has the peculiar gift necessary to successfully conduct a newspaper. There are Negro editors, however, who cannot write a decent article of any kind, who cannot even speak good English. Such men have no business in the editorial chair. I have sometimes thought that were some of them to read an essay entitled "Writing for the Press," in Matthews' "Hours with Men and Books,"[1] they might lose some of that audacity which, after all, is but in accordance with the familiar quotation, "Fools rush in, where angels fear to tread."[2]

The colored newspaper is too indifferent to the quality of its material. Editors seem to accept contributions through fear of losing subscribers or making enemies. Now, if people think that because they take a certain paper that paper ought to print any and all of their senseless effusions, the sooner they are disabused of this idea, the better for them individually and for the race collectively. Those who have control of newspaper columns should put forth efforts to secure the best writers and when able to do so should pay them for their services.

Many of our papers give too much space and prominence to letters containing the local and personal news of insignificant towns, which cannot be of any interest to the public at large.

We ought to have more original and less patent matter. There are few colored papers without a page or two of patent material. It would be better to have a smaller sheet and that original than one larger mostly patent. It would exact more time and money and brains, but it would accomplish more for the race: and being more acceptable to the public would in the end be more profitable to its proprietors.

The original matter need not, however, as is often the case, be personal abuse of a journalistic brother or some other disputant. If an opponent's reasoning cannot be confuted, it does not help the argument to impugn his motives or seek to destroy his reputation. Nor should the opposite error of giving fulsome and extravagant praise and bestowing titles where they do not belong, be indulged. Our newspaper encomiums are so generally in the superlative degree that one wonders if the authors of such meaningless panegyrics do not experience acute chagrin when something really great is achieved and they can find for its description no language more exalted than that in daily use. Every public man of any ability is a leader, every scribbler of verses a poet, every teacher a professor, every minister a doctor of divinity. All is splendid, grand, magnificent; by criticism praise is understood; and nothing which we do can be surpassed.

Another need is the improvement of the mechanical make-up of the paper. Many of our most talented writers are shy of the Negro press, because of the way in which they are unwittingly misrepresented. Articles appear with misspelt words, mistakes in grammar, sentences and parts of sentences omitted or inserted in

1. White American professor and journalist William Mathews (1818–1909), published *Hours with Men and Books* in 1877.
2. From "Essay on Criticism" (1709) by the English poet Alexander Pope (1688–1744).

the wrong place. Greater care in the selection and superintendence of workmen would remedy this evil.

The editors and managers of our newspapers should also manifest more interest in obtaining subscriptions and advertisements, and in securing active agents throughout the country. Mr. I. Garland Penn, in an able letter published in a recent issue of The Age, gives some pertinent suggestions on this point.

Among what I term the extrinsic needs of the Negro newspaper, one very conspicuous is need of support. This is why they "come to stay" and yet disappear after a fitful existence of a few weeks or months. Of course one reason why many lack support is because they are unworthy of support. The law of the "survival of the fittest" may be usually depended upon, yet there are reasons outside of the press itself why so many of our papers languish and die. Many colored people have a way of sneering at race enterprises. They are not colored men, they say; they are simply men. If the Negro newspaper ranks below white journals which can be bought for the same or a price even lower, they query why should they subscribe for the former. If they subscribe, they openly deride, and do the paper more harm with their tongue than they do good with their purse.

Those who are able ought to help the race by contributions to its literature; but the being able should mean not merely time and taste for writing, but also something to say and a knowledge of how to say it. Too much sameness of subject is a fault to be deplored in our publications. Being Negroes does not prevent us from being also men and women, endowed with powers and inclinations similar to those of others. The race question is a very important question, but it is not the only one for us; nor are church affairs all that concern even church organs. There are political, social, moral, scientific, educational and economic problems which affect us as individuals and as a people. Why not show ourselves capable of aiding in their solution?

This is but one phase of an important subject, and our silence at this time as to the other is no indication that we are either blind or unappreciative. "The Achievements of Negro Newspapers" is a theme worthy of discussion and prolific of material. My preference for this topic which I have chosen is due to the fact that we are already the recipients of too much praise from our friends and too little honest criticism. That vile vituperation of which the race is every day the victim, comes from enemies and, in no sense, can be considered criticism.

The path of the editor, and especially the Negro editor, is thorny and far from being a path of pleasantness and peace.[3] The ideal newspaper can never be realized, but he who works in steady contemplation and pursuit thereof, works more worthily and achieves greater results than those without an ideal. It is encouraging to note that we have newspapers that are striving for dignity and elevation of tone and general excellence of character. Prominent among these are The Age, Detroit *Plaindealer* and the Cleveland *Gazette*, while several others might be mentioned. Let the Negro editor who feels himself in his proper sphere grow not discouraged because of imperfections, but persevere in his efforts to work out the salvation of his people.

James Crawford Embry
Afro-American vs. Negro [1895]

From the late 1800s through the beginning of the 1900s, the common term *Negro* began to be replaced by *Afro-American*, particularly in the names of organizations and publications. The Reverend James Crawford Embry of Philadelphia (1834–1897), later a bishop of the AME church, is representative of his period in his preference for *Afro-American* over the "intended stigma" attached from the time of slavery to the term *Negro*.

From James T. Haley, ed., *Afro-American Encyclopaedia, or The Thoughts, Doings, and Sayings of the Race* (Nashville: Haley and Florida, 1895), pp. 369–70.

3. Paraphrase of Proverbs 3:17: "Her ways are ways of pleasantness, and all her paths are peace."

We prefer this title to all others for the reason that it is euphonious, beautiful, true. It is a correct as well as euphonious description of the class of men to whom it should be applied. We believe that the scholarly descendants of our African forefathers should neither adopt nor recognize the intended stigma which European and American slave holders invented for us. We have the highest and most affectionate regard for "the brother in black" as we ought to have for all the children of our Father's household. The boy in black is as sure to be heard from in the years just before us as the government of God is sure and just. But the point we make is that the title "Negro" is too narrow and exclusive to comprehend the race. It is certain that all Africans are not Negroes, nor are all who are Negroes Africans. But why should the race name of the millions in Africa, and the millions of African descent in America, be derived from *color only?* No such rule is applied to any other of the great races of men. The Caucasian, the Indian, the Mongolian, the Arabian tell us only of the people's origin to which these names apply. We hold that if geographical divisions are sufficient to give title and description to all others, it ought to be sufficient for us. This title "Negro" is an intruder—an outlaw in our literature—it is not the language of science, nor the voice of religion and fraternity. No scholar among us, and especially no Christian scholar, ought to tolerate it, in book, pamphlet or paper. It deserves banishment from our literature. Standing here to-day, we denounce it in the name of Christian scholarship as a device of our enemies, designed to make us contemptible in the eyes of the world. To our cultured fellow citizen, the Hon. John M. Langston, is due the honor of giving us the title most nearly correct. He was the first, so we are informed, to speak and write of the "colored American," with reference to the people of African descent. But there, as in the other case, objection lies against a color title for the race. It is comprehensive enough, to be sure. For as distinguishing its subjects from the people called white, it embraces all blacks, all Indians, Mongolians, Mexicans, Malayans and all others who may choose to come among us. Hence the adjective epithet is too large, and we must reject it. To Mrs. M. I. Lee, an honored foster-child of Wilberforce University,[1] we owe the honor of introducing into our literature the only accurate, beautiful and classic title ever applied to our race. In a thoughtful, rippling poem, first delivered on these grounds and afterward published in the *A. M. E. Church Review,* she gave us the title, "Af-Merican," by contraction from Afer, Afra, Afrum, the pure classic phrase of Horace and Ovid. We say let this just name stand. Tested by any rule, historic, literary or scientific it is gold, containing as it does, all the elements of color, weight and ring. In correcting proof, when you have written and come to this honored title, say to your printer *"stet!"* and if any man ask you why so, tell him she (Africa) is the land of our origin; and since she is, by the facts of history and archaeology, mother of the oldest civilization, the oldest science, the oldest art, she is by eminent fitness placed first in the compound title, "Afro-American." Let it stand!

W. E. B. Du Bois
To the Nations of the World [1900]

Diaspora Pan-Africanism is the idea that people of African descent throughout the world share a bond due to common experiences and interests. It has its roots in the African slave trade, which between 1501 and 1867 forced 12.5 million people from their homeland on the African continent to serve as forced labor in the New World. Ideas associated with diaspora Pan-Africanism—including a return to Africa, cultural Africanisms, black pride, and alliances among people of African descent around the world—have been actively discussed in the Americas since the 1600s. At the end of the nineteenth century, these ideas began coalescing into a cohesive

1. Historically black university established in 1856 in Wilberforce, Ohio; named for the British abolitionist William Wilberforce (1759–1833) and dedicated to providing a classical education and training teachers.

movement, which became known as Pan-Africanism. ("Continental Pan-Africanism," which is dedicated to developing connections among the African nations, is a relatively recent form of Pan-Africanism, becoming prominent only in the mid-twentieth century.)

The Nigerian scholar P. Olisanwuche Esedebe traces the beginning of the modern diaspora Pan-African movement to the 1893 Chicago Conference on Africa. Delegates to that conference included such notable figures as Alexander Crummell, Bishop Henry McNeal Turner, and Bishop Alexander Walters, who would serve as president of the groundbreaking Pan-African Conference in London's Westminster Hall in 1900. W. E. B. Du Bois linked the common use of the term *Pan-African* to the 1900 London conference, at which he served as a secretary. (The coinage of the term is often credited to Edward Wilmot Blyden, an early theorist of Pan-Africanism.)

It was at the 1900 Pan-African Conference that Du Bois first offered his famous assessment that "the problem of the twentieth century is the problem of the colour line" (an idea he revisited in the "Forethought" of his 1903 treatise, *The Souls of Black Folk*). The thirty-two-year-old Du Bois delivered the address reprinted here on July 25, 1900, the closing night of the conference. Revealing a commitment to Pan-Africanism that would last until his death in Ghana in 1963, Du Bois uses a global list of appeals to draw connections between the interests of all people of African descent, whether still in Africa or living around the world.

In the second volume of his Pulitzer Prize–winning biography of Du Bois, David Levering Lewis wrote, "In the course of his long, turbulent career, W. E. B. Du Bois attempted virtually every possible solution to the problem of twentieth-century racism—scholarship, propaganda, integration, cultural and economic separatism, politics, international communism, expatriation, third world solidarity." The foremost scholar-activist of his time, Du Bois was born in Great Barrington, Massachusetts, in 1868, three years after the end of the Civil War. His father left the family shortly after his son's birth, and the young Du Bois was raised by his mother in the small New England town. He first experienced the life and culture of the South when he went to Nashville, Tennessee, in 1885 to study at Fisk University. At Fisk, he met many children of former slaves and experienced first-hand the retrenchment of racial barriers in the South that followed Reconstruction. During two summers

spent teaching school in East Tennessee, Du Bois learned about the culture and the struggles of African Americans in the rural South, and he determined to dedicate his life to fighting economic and racial oppression. After graduating from Fisk in 1888, he attended Harvard College, from which he graduated cum laude in 1890 and earned a master's degree in history in 1891. He then did two years of graduate work in Germany, at the University of Berlin, where he learned the rigorous scientific method that he would employ in his groundbreaking scholarship on African American culture and history. In 1895, he became the first African American to receive a Ph.D. from Harvard University. In 1897, Du Bois joined the faculty at Atlanta University in Georgia, where he established one of the first sociology departments in the United States. For the next thirteen years, he committed himself to sociological studies of black life that could counter the ignorance fueling racism. His first major publication was *The Philadelphia Negro* (1899), and he went on to publish seventeen books in his lifetime, including five novels, and helped found four journals.

At the beginning of the twentieth century, Du Bois became increasingly engaged in political agitation, as can be seen in his critiques of Booker T. Washington, who was then the most powerful black leader in America. Pursuing an alternative to Washington's accomodationism, Du Bois published his monumental work, *The Souls of Black Folk,* in 1903 and in 1905 helped found the Niagara Movement, an organization dedicated to achieving full racial equality. Determining that people "must not only know, they must act," Du Bois moved to New York in 1910 to focus his efforts on direct protest, working as editor of a newly formed magazine, *The Crisis,* the official publication of the NAACP (which Du Bois had helped found in 1909). During his twenty-four years as editor of *The Crisis,* Du Bois fundamentally shaped the key debates of the era. In his editorials, he regularly reexamined his own positions in light of contemporary conditions. His later support of segregation as a pragmatic strategy fueled a conflict with other board members of the NAACP and led to his resignation from *The Crisis* and the NAACP in 1934. Du Bois, then sixty-six years old, returned to Atlanta University. Over the next ten years, he produced several of his monumental works, including *Black Reconstruction* (1935) and *Dusk of Dawn* (1940).

A return to the NAACP from 1944 to 1948 as director of special research ended in a bitter conflict with the organization's longtime executive secretary, Walter White, and thereafter Du Bois's politics turned increasingly toward the left. In 1951, two weeks before his eighty-third birthday, his lifelong openness to socialism and communism led to a federal indictment charging him with being an unregistered agent of a foreign power. Although he was acquitted (in a highly publicized trial), Du Bois continued to face harassment by the federal government during the McCarthy era. He was denied a passport from 1952 until 1958, and then his passport was temporary revoked in 1959. In 1961, he was able to travel to the newly independent African nation of Ghana at the invitation of President Kwame Nkrumah to work on a project he had envisioned decades before, the *Encyclopedia Africana*. He became a citizen of Ghana in 1963 and died that year, on the eve of the historic March on Washington, at which Martin Luther King, Jr., would deliver his "I Have a Dream" speech.

In a 1968 tribute, "Honoring Dr. Du Bois," King recognized how Du Bois had paved the way for the modern civil rights movement. "History cannot ignore W. E. B. Du Bois because history has to reflect truth and Dr. Du Bois was a tireless explorer and a gifted discoverer of social truths," King wrote. "His singular greatness lay in his quest for truth about his own people. There were very few scholars who concerned themselves with honest study of the black man and he sought to fill this immense void. The degree to which he succeeded disclosed the great dimensions of the man."

From Alexander Walters, *My Life and Work* (New York; Chicago [etc.]: Fleming H. Revell Company, c. 1917), pp. 257–60.

In the metropolis of the modern world, in this the closing year of the nineteenth century, there has been assembled a congress of men and women of African blood, to deliberate solemnly upon the present situation and outlook of the darker races of mankind. The problem of the twentieth century is the problem of the colour line, the question as to how far differences of race, which show themselves chiefly in the colour of the skin and the texture of the hair, are going to be made, hereafter, the basis of denying to over half the world the right of sharing to their utmost ability the opportunities and privileges of modern civilisation.

To be sure, the darker races are to-day the least advanced in culture according to European standards. This has not, however, always been the case in the past, and certainly the world's history, both ancient and modern, has given many instances of no despicable ability and capacity among the blackest races of men.

In any case, the modern world must needs remember that in this age, when the ends of the world are being brought so near together, the millions of black men in Africa, America, and the Islands of the Sea, not to speak of the brown and yellow myriads elsewhere, are bound to have great influence upon the world in the future, by reason of sheer numbers and physical contact. If now the world of culture bends itself towards giving Negroes and other dark men the largest and broadest opportunity for education and self-development, then this contact and influence is bound to have a beneficial effect upon the world and hasten human progress. But if, by reason of carelessness, prejudice, greed and injustice, the black world is to be exploited and ravished and degraded, the results must be deplorable, if not fatal, not simply to them, but to the high ideals of justice, freedom, and culture which a thousand years of Christian civilisation have held before Europe.

And now, therefore, to these ideals of civilisation, to the broader humanity of the followers of the Prince of Peace, we, the men and women of Africa in world congress assembled, do now solemnly appeal:

Let the world take no backward step in that slow but sure progress which has successively refused to let the spirit of class, of caste, of privilege, or of birth, debar from like liberty and the pursuit of happiness a striving human soul.

Let not mere colour or race be a feature of distinction drawn between white and black men, regardless of worth or ability.

Let not the natives of Africa be sacrificed to the greed of gold, their liberties taken away, their family life debauched, their just aspirations repressed, and avenues of advancement and culture taken from them.

Let not the cloak of Christian missionary enterprise be allowed in the future, as so often in the past, to hide the ruthless economic exploitation and political downfall of less developed nations, whose chief fault has been reliance on the plighted faith of the Christian church.

Let the British nation, the first modern champion of Negro freedom, hasten to crown the work of Wilberforce, and Clarkson, and Buxton, and Sharpe, Bishop Colenso, and Livingstone, and give, as soon as practicable, the rights of responsible government to the black colonies of Africa and the West Indies.

Let not the spirit of Garrison, Phillips, and Douglass wholly die out in America; may the conscience of a great Nation rise and rebuke all dishonesty and unrighteous oppression toward the American Negro, and grant to him the right of franchise, security of person and property, and generous recognition of the great work he has accomplished in a generation toward raising nine millions of human beings from slavery to manhood.

Let the German Empire and the French Republic, true to their great past, remember that the true worth of Colonies lies in their prosperity and progress, and that justice, impartial alike to black and white, is the first element of prosperity.

Let the Congo Free State become a great central Negro State of the world, and let its prosperity be counted not simply in cash and commerce, but in the happiness and true advancement of its black people.

Let the Nations of the World respect the integrity and independence of the free Negro States of Abyssinia, Liberia, Hayti, etc., and let the inhabitants of these States, the independent tribes of Africa, the Negroes of the West Indies and America, and the black subjects of all Nations take courage, strive ceaselessly, and fight bravely, that they may prove to the World their incontestable right to be counted among the great brotherhood of mankind.

Thus we appeal with boldness and confidence to the Great Powers of the civilized world, trusting in the wide spirit of humanity, and the deep sense of justice of our age, for a generous recognition of the righteousness of our cause.

IDA B. WELLS

from *Southern Horrors: Lynch Law in All Its Phases* [1892]

In her preface to the 1892 pamphlet from which the following text is taken, Ida B. Wells declares her commitment to the crusade against racial injustice, which would occupy the rest of her life. "Somebody must show that the Afro-American race is more sinned against than sinning," she wrote, "and it seems to have fallen upon me to do so." Wells began her career as a teacher and later worked as a journalist, but she did not limit her activity to consciousness raising or to what an earlier generation called moral suasion. Instead, she advocated the use of a full range of strategies, from political agitation to physical (even armed) self-defense.

Wells launched her campaign against lynching when three friends of hers were lynched in 1892. After an earlier version of *Southern Horrors* appeared in *The Memphis Free Speech and Headlight*, replete with details of the lynchings, outraged white townspeople destroyed Wells's printing press, prompting her to move north, first to New York and then to Chicago. Campaigning in the United States and Britain in the early 1890s, Wells became one of the most discussed African American leaders in the black press.

In *To Keep the Waters Troubled: The Life of Ida B. Wells* (1998), Linda O. McMurry argues that in 1895, with the death of Frederick Douglass, Wells was "his logical heir apparent": "She was better known than W. E. B. Du Bois and more ideologically compatible with Douglass than Booker T. Washington—the two men who eventually became the main contenders to fill Douglass's shoes. However, Wells had a major problem: She was a woman." Yet the difficulties of being a female leader at the turn of the century did not stop Wells from raising her voice in the debates of the period. Frederick Douglass himself recognized the importance of her work in a testimonial letter he wrote for *Southern Horrors*. About her "faithful paper on the lynch abomination," he wrote, "There has been no word equal to it in convincing power. I have spoken, but my word is feeble in comparison."

See p. 195 for a synopsis of Wells's life.

From Ida B. Wells, *Southern Horrors: Lynch Law in All Its Phases* (New York: New York Age Print, 1892).

SELF-HELP

In the creation of this healthier public sentiment, the Afro-American can do for himself what no one else can do for him. The world looks on with wonder that we have conceded so much and remain law-abiding under such great outrage and provocation.

To Northern capital and Afro-American labor the South owes its rehabilitation. If labor is withdrawn capital will not remain. The Afro-American is thus the backbone of the South. A thorough knowledge and judicious exercise of this power in lynching localities could many times effect a bloodless revolution. The white man's dollar is his god, and to stop this will be to stop outrages in many localities.

The Afro-Americans of Memphis denounced the lynching of three of their best citizens, and urged and waited for the authorities to act in the matter and bring the lynchers to justice. No attempt was made to do so, and the black men left the city by thousands, bringing about great stagnation in every branch of business. Those who remained so injured the business of the street car company by staying off the cars, that the superintendent, manager and treasurer called personally on the editor of the *Free Speech,* asked them to urge our people to give them their patronage again.

Other business men became alarmed over the situation and the *Free Speech* was run away that the colored people might be more easily controlled. A meeting of white citizens in June, three months after the lynching, passed resolutions for the first time, condemning it. *But they did not punish the lynchers.* Every one of them was known by name, because they had been selected to do the dirty work, by some of the very citizens who passed these resolutions. Memphis is fast losing her black population, who proclaim as they go that there is no protection for the life and property of any Afro-American citizen in Memphis who is not a slave.

The Afro-American citizens of Kentucky, whose intellectual and financial improvement has been phenomenal, have never had a separate car law until now. Delegations and petitions poured into the Legislature against it; yet the bill passed and the Jim Crow Car of Kentucky is a legalized institution. Will the great mass of Negroes continue to patronize the railroad? A special from Covington, Ky., says:

> Covington, June 13.—The railroads of the State are beginning to feel very markedly, the effects of the separate coach bill recently passed by the Legislature. No class of people in the State have so many and so largely attended excursions as the blacks. All these have been abandoned, and regular travel is reduced to a minimum. A competent authority says the loss to the various roads will reach $1,000,000 this year.

A call to a State Conference in Lexington, Ky., last June had delegates from every county in the State. Those delegates, the ministers, teachers, heads of secret and others orders, and the head of every family should pass the word around for every member of the race in Kentucky to stay off railroads unless obliged to ride. If they did so, and their advice was followed persistently the convention would not need to petition the Legislature to repeal the law or raise money to file a suit. The railroad corporations would be so effected they would in self-defense lobby to have the separate car law repealed. On the other hand, as long as the railroads can get Afro-American excursions they will always have plenty of money to fight all the suits

brought against them. They will be aided in so doing by the same partisan public sentiment which passed the law. White men passed the law, and white judges and juries would pass upon the suits against the law, and render judgment in line with their prejudices and in deference to the greater financial power.

The appeal to the white man's pocket has ever been more effectual than all the appeals ever made to his conscience. Nothing, absolutely nothing, is to be gained by a further sacrifice of manhood and self-respect. By the right exercise of his power as the industrial factor of the South, the Afro-American can demand and secure his rights, the punishment of lynchers, and a fair trial for accused rapists.

Of the many inhuman outrages of this present year, the only case where the proposed lynching did *not* occur, was where the men armed themselves in Jacksonville, Fla., and Paducah, Ky, and prevented it. The only times an Afro-American who was assaulted got away has been when he had a gun and used it in self-defense.

The lesson this teaches and which every Afro-American should ponder well, is that a Winchester rifle should have a place of honor in every black home, and it should be used for that protection which the law refuses to give. When the white man who is always the aggressor knows he runs as great risk of biting the dust every time his Afro-American victim does, he will have greater respect for Afro-American life. The more the Afro-American yields and cringes and begs, the more he has to do so, the more he is insulted, outraged and lynched.

The assertion has been substantiated throughout these pages that the press contains unreliable and doctored reports of lynchings, and one of the most necessary things for the race to do is to get these facts before the public. The people must know before they can act, and there is no educator to compare with the press.

The Afro-American papers are the only ones which will print the truth, and they lack means to employ agents and detectives to get at the facts. The race must rally a mighty host to the support of their journals, and thus enable them to do much in the way of investigation.

A lynching occurred at Port Jarvis, N.Y., the first week in June. A white and colored man were implicated in the assault upon a white girl. It was charged that the white man paid the colored boy to make the assault, which he did on the public highway in broad day time, and was lynched. This, too was done by "parties unknown." The white man in the case still lives. He was imprisoned and promises to fight the case on trial. At the preliminary examination, it developed that he had been a suitor of the girl's. She had repulsed and refused him, yet had given him money, and he had sent threatening letters demanding more.

The day before this examination she was so wrought up, she left home and wandered miles away. When found she said she did so because she was afraid of the man's testimony. Why should she be afraid of the prisoner! Why should she yield to his demands for money if not to prevent him exposing something he knew! It seems explainable only on the hypothesis that a *liaison* existed between the colored boy and the girl, and the white man knew of it. The press is singularly silent. Has it a motive? We owe it to ourselves to find out.

The story comes from Larned, Kansas, Oct. 1, that a young white lady held at bay until daylight, without alarming any one in the house, "a burly Negro" who entered her room and bed. The "burly Negro" was promptly lynched without investigation or examination of inconsistant stories.

A house was found burned down near Montgomery, Ala., in Monroe County, Oct. 13, a few weeks ago; also the burned bodies of the owners and melted piles of gold and silver.

These discoveries led to the conclusion that the awful crime was not prompted by motives of robbery. The suggestion of the whites was that "brutal lust was the incentive, and as there are nearly 200 Negroes living within a radius of five miles of the place the conclusion was inevitable that some of them were the perpetrators."

Upon this "suggestion" probably made by the real criminal, the mob acted upon the "conclusion" and arrested ten Afro-Americans, four of whom, they tell the world, confessed to the deed of murdering Richard L. Johnson and outraging his daughter, Jeanette. These

four men, Berrell Jones, Moses Johnson, Jim and John Packer, none of them twenty-five years of age, upon this conclusion, were taken from jail, hanged, shot, and burned while yet alive the night of Oct. 12. The same report says Mr. Johnson was on the best of terms with his Negro tenants.

The race thus outraged must find out the facts of this awful hurling of men into eternity on supposition, and give them to the indifferent and apathetic country. We feel this to be a garbled report, but how can we prove it?

Near Vicksburg, Miss., a murder was committed by a gang of burglars. Of course it must have been done by Negroes, and Negroes were arrested for it. It is believed that two men, Smith Tooley and John Adams belonged to a gang controlled by white men and, fearing exposure, on the night of July 4, they were hanged in the Court House yard by those interested in silencing them. Robberies since committed in the same vicinity have been known to be by white men who had their faces blackened. We strongly believe in the innocence of these murdered men, but we have no proof. No other news goes out to the world save that which stamps us as a race of cutthroats, robbers and lustful wild beasts. So great is Southern hate and prejudice, they legally(?) hung poor little thirteen-year-old Mildrey Brown at Columbia, S.C., Oct. 7, on the circumstantial evidence that she poisoned a white infant. If her guilt had been proven unmistakably, had she been white, Mildrey Brown would never have been hung.

The country would have been aroused and South Carolina disgraced forever for such a crime. The Afro-American himself did not know as he should have known as his journals should be in a position to have him know and act.

Nothing is more definitely settled than he must act for himself. I have shown how he may employ the boycott, emigration and the press, and I feel that by a combination of all these agencies can be effectually stamped out lynch law, that last relic of barbarism and slavery. "The gods help those who help themselves."[1]

1. From Aesop's fable "Hercules and the Wagoner."

BOOKER T. WASHINGTON
The Atlanta Exposition Address [1895]

On September 18, 1895, Booker T. Washington gave his famed "Atlanta Compromise" speech at the Cotton States and International Exposition in Atlanta. "My Dear Mr Washington," W. E. B. Du Bois wrote in a note to Washington following the speech, "Let me heartily congratulate you upon your phenomenal success at Atlanta—it was a word fitly spoken." Moderate white Americans as well as moderate African Americans saw potential in Washington's tactful rhetoric, which stresses the inescapable interdependence of black and white southerners and emphasizes that mutual goals (such as economic development) are obtainable through strategic compromise. Others were less enthusiastic, such as AME bishop Henry McNeal Turner (p. 209), who expressed concern over Washington's concessions on segregation and equal rights. Despite those dissenting voices, the speech launched Washington into the role of a national leader and "spokesperson" for African Americans, a role that Frederick Douglass had played until his death earlier that year. Dubbed both the Great Educator and the Wizard of Tuskegee, Washington served as the most powerful black leader in America for over a decade. With the backing of politicians, northern philanthropists, and southern business leaders, he created a powerful system of patronage, serving as the gatekeeper of resources for black organizations. He used his economic and political clout to advance his vision of economic development (supported by thrift and industrial education) as the best route to racial advancement.

Washington was born into slavery in 1856. While studying at Virginia's Hampton Institute after the Civil War, he became a protégé of the white American educator Samuel Chapman Armstrong, the founder and head of the school and a strong advocate of agricultural and industrial education. Drawing on the Hampton model of vocational schooling, Washington founded the Tuskegee Institute in 1881. His autobiography, *Up from Slavery* (1901), in which he included the complete text of his 1895 Atlanta Exposition address, uses his own rise from poverty as a prime example of the efficacy of self-help, economic development, industrial education, and the importance of remaining in the South.

From Booker T. Washington, *Up From Slavery: An Autobiography* (New York: Doubleday, Page & Co., 1907), pp. 217–25.

The Atlanta Exposition, at which I had been asked to make an address as a representative of the Negro race [. . .] was opened with a short address from Governor Bullock. After other interesting exercises, including an invocation from Bishop Nelson, of Georgia, a dedicatory ode by Albert Howell, Jr., and addresses by the President of the Exposition and Mrs. Joseph Thompson, the President of the Woman's Board, Governor Bullock introduced me with the words, "We have with us to-day a representative of Negro enterprise and Negro civilization."

When I arose to speak, there was considerable cheering, especially from the coloured people. As I remember it now, the thing that was uppermost in my mind was the desire to say something that would cement the friendship of the races and bring about hearty cooperation between them. So far as my outward surroundings were concerned, the only thing that I recall distinctly now is that when I got up, I saw thousands of eyes looking intently into my face. The following is the address which I delivered:—

Mr. President and Gentlemen of the Board of Directors and Citizens

One-third of the population of the South is of the Negro race. No enterprise seeking the material, civil, or moral welfare of this section can disregard this element of our population and reach the highest success. I but convey to you, Mr. President and Directors, the sentiment of the masses of my race when I say that in no way have the value and manhood of the American Negro been more fittingly and generously recognized than by the managers of this magnificent

Exposition at every stage of its progress. It is a recognition that will do more to cement the friendship of the two races than any occurrence since the dawn of our freedom.

Not only this, but the opportunity here afforded will awaken among us a new era of industrial progress. Ignorant and inexperienced, it is not strange that in the first years of our new life we began at the top instead of at the bottom; that a seat in Congress or the state legislature was more sought than real estate or industrial skill; that the political convention or stump speaking had more attractions than starting a dairy farm or truck garden.

A ship lost at sea for many days suddenly sighted a friendly vessel. From the mast of the unfortunate vessel was seen a signal, "Water, water; we die of thirst!" The answer from the friendly vessel at once came back, "Cast down your bucket where you are." A second time the signal, "Water, water; send us water!" ran up from the distressed vessel, and was answered, "Cast down your bucket where you are." And a third and fourth signal for water was answered, "Cast down your bucket where you are." The captain of the distressed vessel, at last heeding the injunction, cast down his bucket, and it came up full of fresh, sparkling water from the mouth of the Amazon River. To those of my race who depend on bettering their condition in a foreign land or who underestimate the importance of cultivating friendly relations with the Southern white man, who is their next-door neighbour, I would say: "Cast down your bucket where you are"—cast it down in making friends in every manly way of the people of all races by whom we are surrounded.

Cast it down in agriculture, mechanics, in commerce, in domestic service, and in the professions. And in this connection it is well to bear in mind that whatever other sins the South may be called to bear, when it comes to business, pure and simple, it is in the South that the Negro is given a man's chance in the commercial world, and in nothing is this Exposition more eloquent than in emphasizing this chance. Our greatest danger is that in the great leap from slavery to freedom we may overlook the fact that the masses of us are to live by the productions of our hands, and fail to keep in mind that we shall prosper in proportion as we learn to dignify and glorify common labour and

put brains and skill into the common occupations of life; shall prosper in proportion as we learn to draw the line between the superficial and the substantial, the ornamental gewgaws of life and the useful. No race can prosper till it learns that there is as much dignity in tilling a field as in writing a poem. It is at the bottom of life we must begin, and not at the top. Nor should we permit our grievances to overshadow our opportunities.

To those of the white race who look to the incoming of those of foreign birth and strange tongue and habits for the prosperity of the South, were I permitted I would repeat what I say to my own race, "Cast down your bucket where you are." Cast it down among the eight millions of Negroes whose habits you know, whose fidelity and love you have tested in days when to have proved treacherous meant the ruin of your firesides. Cast down your bucket among these people who have, without strikes and labour wars, tilled your fields, cleared your forests, builded your railroads and cities, and brought forth treasures from the bowels of the earth, and helped make possible this magnificent representation of the progress of the South. Casting down your bucket among my people, helping and encouraging them as you are doing on these grounds, and to education of head, hand, and heart, you will find that they will buy your surplus land, make blossom the waste places in your fields, and run your factories. While doing this, you can be sure in the future, as in the past, that you and your families will be surrounded by the most patient, faithful, law-abiding, and unresentful people that the world has seen. As we have proved our loyalty to you in the past, in nursing your children, watching by the sick-bed of your mothers and fathers, and often following them with tear-dimmed eyes to their graves, so in the future, in our humble way, we shall stand by you with a devotion that no foreigner can approach, ready to lay down our lives, if need be, in defence of yours, interlacing our industrial, commercial, civil, and religious life with yours in a way that shall make the interests of both races one. In all things that are purely social we can be as separate as the fingers, yet one as the hand in all things essential to mutual progress.

There is no defence or security for any of us except in the highest intelligence and development of all. If anywhere there are efforts tending to curtail the fullest growth of the Negro, let these efforts be turned into stimulating, encouraging, and making him the most useful and intelligent citizen. Effort or means so invested will pay a thousand per cent interest. These efforts will be twice blessed—"blessing him that gives and him that takes."[1]

There is no escape through law of man or God from the inevitable:—

The laws of changeless justice bind
Oppressor with oppressed;
And close as sin and suffering joined
We march to fate abreast.[2]

Nearly sixteen millions of hands will aid you in pulling the load upward, or they will pull against you the load downward. We shall constitute one-third and more of the ignorance and crime of the South, or one-third its intelligence and progress; we shall contribute one-third to the business and industrial prosperity of the South, or we shall prove a veritable body of death, stagnating, depressing, retarding every effort to advance the body politic.

Gentlemen of the Exposition, as we present to you our humble effort at an exhibition of our progress, you must not expect overmuch. Starting thirty years ago with ownership here and there in a few quilts and pumpkins and chickens (gathered from miscellaneous sources), remember the path that has led from these to the inventions and production of agricultural implements, buggies, steam-engines, newspapers, books, statuary, carving, paintings, the management of drug-stores and banks has not been trodden without contact with thorns and thistles. While we take pride in what we exhibit as a result of our independent efforts, we do not for a moment forget that our part in this exhibition would fall far short of your expectations but for the constant help that has come to our educational life, not only from the Southern states, but especially from Northern philanthropists, who have made their gifts a constant stream of blessing and encouragement.

The wisest among my race understand that the agitation of questions of social equality is the extremest folly, and that progress in the enjoyment of all the privileges that will come to us must be the result of severe and constant struggle rather than of artificial forcing. No race that has anything to contribute to the markets of the world is long in any degree ostracized. It is important and right that all privileges of the law be ours, but it is vastly more important that we be prepared for the exercises of these privileges. The opportunity to earn a dollar in a factory just now is worth infinitely more than the opportunity to spend a dollar in an opera-house.

In conclusion, may I repeat that nothing in thirty years has given us more hope and encouragement, and drawn us so near to you of the white race, as this opportunity offered by the Exposition; and here bending, as it were, over the altar that represents the results of the struggles of your race and mine, both starting practically empty-handed three decades ago, I pledge that in your effort to work out the great and intricate problem which God has laid at the doors of the South, you shall have at all times the patient, sympathetic help of my race; only let this be constantly in mind, that, while from representations in these buildings of the product of field, of forest, of mine, of factory, letters, and art, much good will come, yet far above and beyond material benefits will be that higher good, that, let us pray God, will come, in a blotting out of sectional differences and racial animosities and suspicions, in a determination to administer absolute justice, in a willing obedience among all classes to the mandates of law. This, this, coupled with our material prosperity, will bring into our beloved South a new heaven and a new earth.

1. Reference to Portia's ruling in Shakespeare's *The Merchant of Venice* [4.1.184–87]:

The quality of mercy is not strain'd,
It droppeth as the gentle rain from heaven
Upon the place beneath: it is twice blest;
It blesseth him that gives and him that takes:

2. From John Greenleaf Whittier's "At Port Royal" (1862).

HENRY MCNEAL TURNER
Response to the Atlanta Exposition Address [1895]

While moderate black and white Americans praised Washington's address at the 1895 Atlanta Exposition, later known as the "Atlanta Compromise" speech, other leaders and writers harshly criticized it. Bishop Henry McNeal Turner, in his 1895 response to the Atlanta Exposition address, published in the newspaper he founded, *The Voice of Missions,* expressed his conviction that Washington "will have to live a long time to undo the harm he has done our race." Turner reveals the strong reservations some black leaders had about both the speech and Washington's subsequent propulsion into a position of national leadership.

Like Booker T. Washington and Ida B. Wells, Turner was positioned for potential national leadership following the death of Frederick Douglass in 1895 (the year of Washington's address and Turner's response). Like Wells, however, Turner failed to achieve that level of national recognition, in part because he promoted ideas that were out of sync with prevailing opinion. In particular, Turner committed himself to the unpopular position that African colonization was the best route by which to obtain dignity and "manhood." His theological beliefs and actions also made him controversial as a church leader. Not only did he ordain Sarah Ann Hughes as the first woman deacon of the AME church (a move he later felt pressured to rescind), but he also became known for preaching that "we have as much right biblically and otherwise to believe that God is a Negroe, as you buckra or white people have to believe that God is a fine looking, symmetrical and ornamented white man."

Turner was born free in 1834 near Abbeville, South Carolina. His father died when he was a child, and the young boy worked in the cotton fields alongside black slaves to help support his family. When he was in his teens, Turner found work as a janitor in a law firm. Some of the lawyers there recognized his ability and helped him obtain a basic education, even though it was then illegal in South Carolina to teach African Americans to read and write. As a young man, Turner moved to Baltimore, where he continued his education, pursuing his interests in grammar, Latin, Greek, Hebrew, German, and theology. He went on to hold a range of leadership positions, becoming the first African American army chaplain (appointed by President Lincoln to the First Regiment of U.S. Colored Troops), a representative in the Georgia state legislature during Reconstruction, the twelfth bishop of the AME church, and chancellor of Morris Brown College in Atlanta. Turner's obituary in the July 1915 issue of *The Crisis* recognized the difficulties he faced as a southerner struggling to overcome the deprivations of poverty and working to rise to a position of national prominence: "Turner was the last of his clan: mighty men, physically and mentally, men who started at the bottom and hammered their way to the top by sheer brute strength, they were the spiritual progeny of African chieftains."

From *The Voice of Missions*, October 1895.

P rof. Booker T. Washington, president of the State Normal College at Tuskegee, Ala., whose clear, forcible, eloquent, and terse speech before an immense throng of white and colored people at the opening of the great exposition will be found in another column of this issue. Few men could have been more happy in the points raised, and in the manner of their disposition. The circumstances surrounding the occasion required the brightest aspects in the sphere of possibility, and thus no reference was made to the lynchings and enactments of cruel and revolting laws against our race in this country. And as the great professor adjudged it prudent and discreet to pass by those phases of our barbarous civilization, as well as the efforts being made to disfranchise the Negro in some of the states, we only wish he had deemed it impolitic to say: "The wisest among my race understand that the agitation of questions of social equality is the extremest folly." For if the professor means by the term "my race," the colored race of this country, some of them are certainly wise enough and understand the philosophy and genius of national sociology enough to know that social equality carries with it civil equality, political equality, financial equality, judicial equality, business equality, and wherever social equality is denied by legislative enactments and judicial decrees, the sequel must be discrimination, proscription, injustice, and degradation. If the enactment of laws in favor of equal rights is "artificial forcing" when they are in favor of the colored race, as the professor indicates, would not that artificiality be as just and honorable to the black man as laws forbidding them are just and honorable to the white man? But the professor goes further and practically [denies that Negroes are pre]pared for the exercise of all the privileges enjoyed by the whites. If his position is correct, then, as I understand him, we are not prepared for freedom, certainly we are not prepared for citizenship. But let our patrons read his speech and draw their own conclusions.

However, Prof. Washington is a great man, he is doing a great work, and it was a great occasion; and public speaking not being his profession, and the circumstances attending the occasion being so unprecedented in many respects, it was no time to be offensive. We conclude by saying "well done, good and faithful servant." But the next time, please do not raise such an issue. For as long as the whites enforce equality in the price of railroad tickets, and in every other particular, where we are required to pay and do, and be punished, some of us will believe that equality should be carried to a finish. With all due respect to Prof. Washington personally, for we do respect him personally, he will have to live a long time to undo the harm he has done our race. His remarks on social equality, which is nothing more than civil equality, will be quoted by newspapers, magazines, periodicals, legislatures, congressmen, lawyers, judges and all grades of whites to prove that the Negro race is satisfied with being degraded, not that the Professor meant it, but such will be the construction given it by our civil and political enemies. How fortunate it would have been had he said nothing at all about social equality, as the other part of his speech would have immortalized him.

W. E. B. DU BOIS
Of Mr. Booker T. Washington and Others [1903]

"Among the Negroes, Mr. Washington is still far from a popular leader," W. E. B. Du Bois proclaimed in a 1901 review of Booker T. Washington's autobiography, *Up from Slavery*. Although Du Bois had allied himself with Washington early on, by 1901 he had begun to challenge the continued relevance of Washington's leadership and vision. In his review, Du Bois implied that Washington's vision was outmoded, suggesting that "he represents in Negro thought the old attitude of adjustment to environment, emphasizing the economic phase." As alternative strategies, Du Bois offered black nationalism and political protest. Despite his critique of Washington's tactics and focus, however, Du Bois acknowledged Washington's "tact and power" by praising his ability to "steer [* * *] as he must amid so many diverse interests and opinions" and "command [* * *] not simply the applause of those who believe in his theories, but also the respect of those who do not."

"Of Mr. Booker T. Washington and Others," originally published in 1903 as the third chapter of *The Souls of Black Folk* (1903), escalated Du Bois's challenge to Washington's leadership. In the essay, Du Bois subtly rejects the use of violence as a strategy for change, stressing the use of "all civilized methods," but he insists on the need for radical change. By 1904, Du Bois was promoting the broad areas of difference between his and Washington's positions, which included, as he stated in an April 1904 editorial in *The World Today*, "First, the scope of education; second, the necessity of the right of suffrage; third, the importance of civil rights; fourth, the conciliation of the South; fifth, the future of the race in this country." Du Bois highlighted his differences with Washington when he organized the Niagara Movement in 1905, a group of black intellectuals who called for full social, economic, and political power for African Americans. By the end of the decade, Du Bois had become the recognized alternative to Washington as a leader of the African American community, representing the promotion of liberal over industrial education, political power over economic gradualism, and protest over tactful compromise.

From W. E. B. Du Bois, *The Souls of Black Folk* (Chicago: A. C. McClurg & Co., 1903), pp. 41–59.

Easily the most striking thing in the history of the American Negro since 1876 is the ascendancy of Mr. Booker T. Washington. It began at the time when war memories and ideals were rapidly passing; a day of astonishing commercial development was dawning; a sense of doubt and hesitation overtook the freedmen's sons,—then it was that his leading began. Mr. Washington came, with a single definite programme, at the psychological moment when the nation was a little ashamed of having bestowed so much sentiment on Negroes, and was concentrating its energies on Dollars. His programme of industrial education, conciliation of the South, and submission and silence as to civil and political rights, was not wholly original: the Free Negroes from 1830 up to war-time had striven to build industrial schools, and the American Missionary Association had from the first taught various trades; and Price[1] and others had sought a way of honorable alliance with the best of the Southerners. But Mr. Washington first indissolubly linked these things; he put enthusiasm, unlimited energy, and perfect faith into this programme, and changed it from a by-path into a veritable Way of Life. And the tale of the methods by which he did this is a fascinating study of human life.

It startled the nation to hear a Negro advocating such a programme after many decades of bitter complaint; it startled and won the applause of the South, it interested and won the admiration of the North; and after a confused murmur of protest, it silenced if it did not convert the Negroes themselves.

To gain the sympathy and coöperation of the various elements comprising the white South was Mr. Washington's first task; and this, at the time Tuskegee was founded, seemed, for a black man well-nigh impossible. And yet ten years later it was done in the word spoken at Atlanta: "In all things purely social we can be as separate as the five fingers,[2] and yet one as the hand in all things essential to mutual progress." This "Atlanta Compromise" is by all odds the most notable thing in Mr. Washington's career. The South interpreted it in different ways: the radicals received it as a complete surrender of the demand for civil and political equality; the conservatives, as a generously conceived working basis for mutual understanding. So both approved it, and to-day its author is certainly the most distinguished Southerner since Jefferson Davis, and the one with the largest personal following.

Next to this achievement comes Mr. Washington's work in gaining place and consideration in the North. Others less shrewd and tactful had formerly essayed to sit on these two stools and had fallen between them; but as Mr. Washington knew the heart of the South from birth and training, so by singular insight he intuitively grasped the spirit of the age which was dominating the North. And so thoroughly did he learn the speech and thought of triumphant commercialism, and the ideals of material prosperity, that the

---

1. Joseph C. Price; throughout this chapter, Du Bois tends to refer to prominent black figures by only their first or last names; subsequent references include Phillis Wheatley, Crispus Attucks, Peter Salem, Salem Poor, Benjamin Banneker, James C. Derham, Paul Cuffe, John Cuffe, Davis Walker, Robert Purvis, Abraham Shadd, Alexander Du Bois, James G. Barbados, Charles Lenox Remond, William Cooper Nell, William Wells Brown, Robert Brown Elliot, Blanche K. Bruce, John Mercer Langston, Toussaint l'Ouverture, Denmark Vesey, Nat Turner, Archibald H. Grimké, Francis J. Grimké, Charles Brantley Aycock (of North Carolina), and John Tyler Morgan (of Alabama).
2. Paraphrase of Washington's statement, "In all things that are purely social we can be as separate as the fingers, yet one as the hand in all things essential to mutual progress."

picture of a lone black boy poring over a French gram-mar amid the weeds and dirt of a neglected home soon seemed to him the acme of absurdities. One wonders what Socrates and St. Francis of Assisi would say to this.

And yet this very singleness of vision and thor-ough oneness with his age is a mark of the successful man. It is as though Nature must needs make men nar-row in order to give them force. So Mr. Washington's cult has gained unquestioning followers, his work has wonderfully prospered, his friends are legion, and his enemies are confounded. To-day he stands as the one recognized spokesman of his ten million fellows, and one of the most notable figures in a nation of seventy millions. One hesitates, therefore, to criticise a life which, beginning with so little, has done so much. And yet the time is come when one may speak in all sincerity and utter courtesy of the mistakes and short-comings of Mr. Washington's career, as well as of his triumphs, without being thought captious or envious, and without forgetting that it is easier to do ill than well in the world.

The criticism that has hitherto met Mr. Washing-ton has not always been of this broad character. In the South especially has he had to walk warily to avoid the harshest judgments,—and naturally so, for he is deal-ing with the one subject of deepest sensitiveness to that section. Twice—once when at the Chicago cele-bration of the Spanish-American War he alluded to the color-prejudice that is "eating away the vitals of the South," and once when he dined with President Roosevelt—has the resulting Southern criticism been violent enough to threaten seriously his popularity. In the North the feeling has several times forced itself into words, that Mr. Washington's counsels of submis-sion overlooked certain elements of true manhood, and that his educational programme was unnecessar-ily narrow. Usually, however, such criticism has not found open expression, although, too, the spiritual sons of the Abolitionists have not been prepared to acknowledge that the schools founded before Tuske-gee, by men of broad ideals and self-sacrificing spirit, were wholly failures or worthy of ridicule. While, then, criticism has not failed to follow Mr. Washing-ton, yet the prevailing public opinion of the land has been but too willing to deliver the solution of a weari-some problem into his hands, and say, "If that is all you and your race ask, take it."

Among his own people, however, Mr. Washing-ton has encountered the strongest and most lasting opposition, amounting at times to bitterness, and even to-day continuing strong and insistent even though largely silenced in outward expression by the public opinion of the nation. Some of this opposition is, of course, mere envy; the disappointment of displaced demagogues and the spite of narrow minds. But aside from this, there is among educated and thoughtful colored men in all parts of the land a feeling of deep regret, sorrow, and apprehension at the wide cur-rency and ascendancy which some of Mr. Washing-ton's theories have gained. These same men admire his sincerity of purpose, and are willing to forgive much to honest endeavor which is doing something worth the doing. They coöperate with Mr. Washing-ton as far as they conscientiously can, and, indeed, it is no ordinary tribute to this man's tact and power that, steering as he must between so many diverse interests and opinions, he so largely retains the respect of all.

But the hushing of the criticism of honest oppo-nents is a dangerous thing. It leads some of the best of the critics to unfortunate silence and paralysis of effort, and others to burst into speech so passionately and intemperately as to lose listeners. Honest and ear-nest criticism from those whose interests are most nearly touched,—criticism of writers by readers, of government by those governed, of leaders by those led,—this is the soul of democracy and the safeguard of modern society. If the best of the American Negroes receive by outer pressure a leader whom they had not recognized before, manifestly there is here a certain palpable gain. Yet there is also irreparable loss,—a loss of that peculiarly valuable education which a group receives when by search and criticism it finds and commissions its own leaders. The way in which this is done is at once the most elementary and the nicest problem of social growth. History is but the record of such group-leadership; and yet how infinitely change-ful is its type and character! And of all types and kinds, what can be more instructive than the leadership of a group within a group?—that curious double movement where real progress may be negative and actual advance be relative retrogression. All this is the social student's inspiration and despair.

Now in the past the American Negro has had instructive experience in the choosing of group leaders, founding thus a peculiar dynasty which in the light of present conditions is worth while studying. When sticks and stones and beasts form the sole environment of a people, their attitude is largely one of determined opposition to and conquest of natural forces. But when to earth and brute is added an environment of men and ideas, then the attitude of the imprisoned group may take three main forms,—a feeling of revolt and revenge; an attempt to adjust all thought and action to the will of the greater group; or, finally, a determined effort at self-realization and self-development despite environing opinion. The influence of all of these attitudes at various times can be traced in the history of the American Negro, and in the evolution of his successive leaders.

Before 1750, while the fire of American freedom still burned in the veins of the slaves, there was in all leadership or attempted leadership but the one motive of revolt and revenge,—typified in the terrible Maroons, the Danish blacks, and Cato of Stono,[3] and veiling all the Americas in fear of insurrection. The liberalizing tendencies of the latter half of the eighteenth century brought, along with kindlier relations between black and white, thoughts of ultimate adjustment and assimilation. Such aspiration was especially voiced in the earnest songs of Phyllis, in the martyrdom of Attucks, the fighting of Salem and Poor, the intellectual accomplishments of Banneker and Derham, and the political demands of the Cuffes.[4]

Stern financial and social stress after the war cooled much of the previous humanitarian ardor. The disappointment and impatience of the Negroes at the persistence of slavery and serfdom voiced itself in two movements. The slaves in the South, aroused undoubtedly by vague rumors of the Haytian revolt, made three fierce attempts at insurrection,—in 1800 under Gabriel in Virginia,[5] in 1822 under Vesey in Carolina, and in 1831 again in Virginia under the terrible Nat Turner. In the Free States, on the other hand, a new and curious attempt at self-development was made. In Philadelphia and New York color-prescription led to a withdrawal of Negro communicants from white churches and the formation of a peculiar socio-religious institution among the Negroes known as the African Church,—an organization still living and controlling in its various branches over a million of men.

Walker's wild appeal against the trend of the times showed how the world was changing after the coming of the cotton-gin. By 1830 slavery seemed hopelessly fastened on the South, and the slaves thoroughly cowed into submission. The free Negroes of the North, inspired by the mulatto immigrants from the West Indies, began to change the basis of their demands; they recognized the slavery of slaves, but insisted that they themselves were freemen, and sought assimilation and amalgamation with the nation on the same terms with other men. Thus, Forten and Purvis of Philadelphia, Shad of Wilmington, Du Bois of New Haven, Barbadoes of Boston, and others, strove singly and together as men, they said, not as slaves; as "people of color," not as "Negroes." The trend of the times, however, refused them recognition save in individual and exceptional cases, considered them as one with all the despised blacks, and they soon found themselves striving to keep even the rights they formerly had of voting and working and moving as freemen. Schemes of migration and colonization arose among them; but these they refused to entertain, and they eventually turned to the Abolition movement as a final refuge.

---

3. The leader of a major slave rebellion that took place in 1739 near the Stono River in South Carolina; The Danish blacks: thousands of slaves, first led by Kofi (or Cuffy), who rebelled against plantation owners in the Dutch colony of Berbice, now part of Guyana, in 1863–64; Maroons: an eighteenth-century term for escaped slaves who formed independent settlements and established guerrilla bands.

4. Known as "the first to defy, the first to die," Crispus Attucks (c. 1723–70), the son of an African man and a Native American woman, had escaped from slavery as a young man; he was shot in 1770 in the Boston Massacre, becoming the first person to die in the American Revolution.

5. Gabriel (sometimes incorrectly called Gabriel Prosser) was the leader of a slave rebellion that took place near Richmond, Virginia, in 1800.

Here, led by Remond, Nell, Wells-Brown, and Douglass, a new period of self-assertion and self-development dawned. To be sure, ultimate freedom and assimilation was the ideal before the leaders, but the assertion of the manhood rights of the Negro by himself was the main reliance, and John Brown's raid was the extreme of its logic. After the war and emancipation, the great form of Frederick Douglass, the greatest of American Negro leaders, still led the host. Self-assertion, especially in political lines, was the main programme, and behind Douglass came Elliot, Bruce, and Langston, and the Reconstruction politicians, and, less conspicuous but of greater social significance Alexander Crummell and Bishop Daniel Payne.

Then came the Revolution of 1876, the suppression of the Negro votes, the changing and shifting of ideals, and the seeking of new lights in the great right. Douglass, in his old age, still bravely stood for the ideals of his early manhood,—ultimate assimilation *through* self-assertion, and on no other terms. For a time Price arose as a new leader, destined, it seemed, not to give up, but to re-state the old ideals in a form less repugnant to the white South. But he passed away in his prime. Then came the new leader. Nearly all the former ones had become leaders by the silent suffrage of their fellows, had sought to lead their own people alone, and were usually, save Douglass, little known outside their race. But Booker T. Washington arose as essentially the leader not of one race but of two,—a compromiser between the South, the North, and the Negro. Naturally the Negroes resented, at first bitterly, signs of compromise which surrendered their civil and political rights, even though this was to be exchanged for larger chances of economic development. The rich and dominating North, however, was not only weary of the race problem, but was investing largely in Southern enterprises, and welcomed any method of peaceful coöperation. Thus, by national opinion, the Negroes began to recognize Mr. Washington's leadership; and the voice of criticism was hushed.

Mr. Washington represents in Negro thought the old attitude of adjustment and submission: but adjustment at such a peculiar time as to make his programme unique. This is an age of unusual economic development, and Mr. Washington's programme naturally takes an economic cast, becoming a gospel of Work and Money to such an extent as apparently almost completely to overshadow the higher aims of life. Moreover, this is an age when the more advanced races are coming in closer contact with the less developed races, and the race-feeling is therefore intensified; and Mr. Washington's programme practically accepts the alleged inferiority of the Negro races. Again, in our own land, the reaction from the sentiment of war time has given impetus to race-prejudice against Negroes, and Mr. Washington withdraws many of the high demands of Negroes as men and American citizens. In other periods of intensified prejudice all the Negro's tendency to self-assertion has been called forth; at this period a policy of submission is advocated. In the history of nearly all other races and peoples the doctrine preached at such crises has been that manly self-respect is worth more than lands and houses, and that a people who voluntarily surrender such respect, or cease striving for it, are not worth civilizing.

In answer to this, it has been claimed that the Negro can survive only through submission. Mr. Washington distinctly asks that black people give up, at least for the present, three things,—

> First, political power,
> Second, insistence on civil rights,
> Third, higher education of Negro youth,—

and concentrate all their energies on industrial education, the accumulation of wealth, and the conciliation of the South. This policy has been courageously and insistently advocated for over fifteen years, and has been triumphant for perhaps ten years. As a result of this tender of the palm-branch, what has been the return? In these years there have occurred:

1. The disfranchisement of the Negro.

2. The legal creation of a distinct status of civil inferiority for the Negro.

3. The steady withdrawal of aid from institutions for the higher training of the Negro.

These movements are not, to be sure, direct results of Mr. Washington's teachings; but his propaganda has, without a shadow of doubt, helped their speedier accomplishment. The question then comes:

Is it possible, and probable, that nine millions of men can make effective progress in economic lines if they are deprived of political rights, made a servile caste, and allowed only the most meagre chance for developing their exceptional men? If history and reason give any distinct answer to these questions, it is an emphatic *No.* And Mr. Washington thus faces the triple paradox of his career:

1. He is striving nobly to make Negro artisans business men and property-owners; but it is utterly impossible, under modern competitive methods, for workingmen and property-owners to defend their rights and exist without the right of suffrage.

2. He insists on thrift and self-respect, but at the same time counsels a silent submission to civic inferiority such as is bound to sap the manhood of any race in the long run.

3. He advocates common-school and industrial training, and depreciates institutions of higher learning; but neither the Negro common-schools, nor Tuskegee itself, could remain open a day were it not for teachers trained in Negro colleges, or trained by their graduates.

This triple paradox in Mr. Washington's position is the object of criticism by two classes of colored Americans. One class is spiritually descended from Toussaint the Savior, through Gabriel, Vesey, and Turner, and they represent the attitude of revolt and revenge; they hate the white South blindly and distrust the white race generally, and so far as they agree on definite action, think that the Negro's only hope lies in emigration beyond the borders of the United States. And yet, by the irony of fate, nothing has more effectually made this programme seem hopeless than the recent course of the United States toward weaker and darker peoples in the West Indies, Hawaii, and the Philippines,—for where in the world may we go and be safe from lying and brute force?

The other class of Negroes who cannot agree with Mr. Washington has hitherto said little aloud. They deprecate the sight of scattered counsels, of internal disagreement; and especially they dislike making their just criticism of a useful and earnest man an excuse for a general discharge of venom from small-minded opponents. Nevertheless, the questions involved are so fundamental and serious that it is difficult to see how men like the Grimkes, Kelly Miller, J. W. E. Bowen, and other representatives of this group, can much longer be silent. Such men feel in conscience bound to ask of this nation three things:

1. The right to vote.

2. Civic equality.

3. The education of youth according to ability.

They acknowledge Mr. Washington's invaluable service in counselling patience and courtesy in such demands; they do not ask that ignorant black men vote when ignorant whites are debarred, or that any reasonable restrictions in the suffrage should not be applied; they know that the low social level of the mass of the race is responsible for much discrimination against it, but they also know, and the nation knows, that relentless color-prejudice is more often a cause than a result of the Negro's degradation; they seek the abatement of this relic of barbarism, and not its systematic encouragement and pampering by all agencies of social power from the Associated Press to the Church of Christ. They advocate, with Mr. Washington, a broad system of Negro common schools supplemented by thorough industrial training; but they are surprised that a man of Mr. Washington's insight cannot see that no such educational system ever has rested or can rest on any other basis than that of the well-equipped college and university, and they insist that there is a demand for a few such institutions throughout the South to train the best of the Negro youth as teachers, professional men, and leaders.

This group of men honor Mr. Washington for his attitude of conciliation toward the white South; they accept the "Atlanta Compromise" in its broadest interpretation; they recognize, with him, many signs of promise, many men of high purpose and fair judgment, in this section; they know that no easy task has been laid upon a region already tottering under heavy burdens. But, nevertheless, they insist that the way to truth and right lies in straightforward honesty, not in indiscriminate flattery; in praising those of the South who do well and criticising uncompromisingly those who do ill; in taking advantage of the opportunities at hand and urging their fellows to do the same, but at the same time in remembering that only a firm adherence to their higher ideals and aspirations will ever keep those ideals within the realm of possibility. They do not expect that the free right to vote, to enjoy civic rights, and to be educated, will come in a moment; they do not expect to see the bias and prejudices of years disappear at the blast of a trumpet; but they are absolutely certain that the way for a people to gain their reasonable rights is not by voluntarily throwing them away and insisting that they do not want them; that the way for a people to gain respect is not by continually belittling and ridiculing themselves; that, on the contrary, Negroes must insist continually, in season and out of season, that voting is necessary to modern manhood, that color discrimination is barbarism, and that black boys need education as well as white boys.

In failing thus to state plainly and unequivocally the legitimate demands of their people, even at the cost of opposing an honored leader, the thinking classes of American Negroes would shirk a heavy responsibility,—a responsibility to themselves, a responsibility to the struggling masses, a responsibility to the darker races of men whose future depends so largely on this American experiment, but especially a responsibility to this nation,—this common Fatherland. It is wrong to encourage a man or a people in evil-doing; it is wrong to aid and abet a national crime simply because it is unpopular not to do so. The growing spirit of kindliness and reconciliation between the North and South after the frightful difference of a generation ago ought to be a source of deep congratulation to all, and especially to those whose mistreatment caused the war; but if that reconciliation is to be marked by the industrial slavery and civic death of those same black men, with permanent legislation into a position of inferiority, then those black men, if they are really men, are called upon by every consideration of patriotism and loyalty to oppose such a course by all civilized methods, even though such opposition involves disagreement with Mr. Booker T. Washington. We have no right to sit silently by while the inevitable seeds are sown for a harvest of disaster to our children, black and white.

First, it is the duty of black men to judge the South discriminatingly. The present generation of Southern-

ers are not responsible for the past, and they should not be blindly hated or blamed for it. Furthermore, to no class is the indiscriminate endorsement of the recent course of the South toward Negroes more nauseating than to the best thought of the South. The South is not "solid"; it is a land in the ferment of social change, wherein forces of all kinds are fighting for supremacy; and to praise the ill the South is to-day perpetrating is just as wrong as to condemn the good. Discriminating and broad-minded criticism is what the South needs,—needs it for the sake of her own white sons and daughters, and for the insurance of robust, healthy mental and moral development.

To-day even the attitude of the Southern whites toward the blacks is not, as so many assume, in all cases the same; the ignorant Southerner hates the Negro, the workingmen fear his competition, the money-makers wish to use him as a laborer, some of the educated see a menace in his upward development, while others—usually the sons of the masters—wish to help him to rise. National opinion has enabled this last class to maintain the Negro common schools, and to protect the Negro partially in property, life, and limb. Through the pressure of the money-makers, the Negro is in danger of being reduced to semi-slavery, especially in the country districts; the workingmen, and those of the educated who fear the Negro, have united to disfranchise him, and some have urged his deportation; while the passions of the ignorant are easily aroused to lynch and abuse any black man. To praise this intricate whirl of thought and prejudice is nonsense; to inveigh indiscriminately against "the South" is unjust; but to use the same breath in praising Governor Aycock, exposing Senator Morgan, arguing with Mr. Thomas Nelson Page, and denouncing Senator Ben Tillman, is not only sane, but the imperative duty of thinking black men.

It would be unjust to Mr. Washington not to acknowledge that in several instances he has opposed movements in the South which were unjust to the Negro; he sent memorials to the Louisiana and Alabama constitutional conventions, he has spoken against lynching, and in other ways has openly or silently set his influence against sinister schemes and unfortunate happenings. Notwithstanding this, it is equally true to assert that on the whole the distinct impression left by Mr. Washington's propaganda is, first, that the South is justified in its present attitude toward the Negro because of the Negro's degradation; secondly, that the prime cause of the Negro's failure to rise more quickly is his wrong education in the past; and, thirdly, that his future rise depends primarily on his own efforts. Each of these propositions is a dangerous halftruth. The supplementary truths must never be lost sight of: first, slavery and race-prejudice are potent if not sufficient causes of the Negro's position; second, industrial and common-school training were necessarily slow in planting because they had to await the black teachers trained by higher institutions,—it being extremely doubtful if any essentially different development was possible, and certainly a Tuskegee was unthinkable before 1880; and, third, while it is a great truth to say that the Negro must strive and strive mightily to help himself, it is equally true that unless his striving be not simply seconded, but rather aroused and encouraged, by the initiative of the richer and wiser environing group, he cannot hope for great success.

In his failure to realize and impress this last point, Mr. Washington is especially to be criticised. His doctrine has tended to make the whites, North and South, shift the burden of the Negro problem to the Negro's shoulders and stand aside as critical and rather pessimistic spectators; when in fact the burden belongs to the nation, and the hands of none of us are clean if we bend not our energies to righting these great wrongs.

The South ought to be led, by candid and honest criticism, to assert her better self and do her full duty to the race she has cruelly wronged and is still wronging. The North—her co-partner in guilt—cannot salve her conscience by plastering it with gold. We cannot settle this problem by diplomacy and suaveness, by "policy" alone. If worse come to worst, can the moral fibre of this country survive the slow throttling and murder of nine millions of men?

The black men of America have a duty to perform, a duty stern and delicate,—a forward movement to oppose a part of the work of their greatest leader. So far as Mr. Washington preaches Thrift, Patience, and Industrial Training for the masses, we must hold up his hands and strive with him, rejoicing in his honors and glorying in the strength of this Joshua called of God and of man to lead the headless host. But so far as Mr. Washington apologizes for injustice, North or South, does not rightly value the privilege and duty of voting, belittles the emasculating effects of caste distinctions, and opposes the higher training and ambition of our brighter minds,—so far as he, the South, or the Nation, does this,—we must unceasingly and firmly oppose them. By every civilized and peaceful method we must strive for the rights which the world accords to men, clinging unwaveringly to those great words which the sons of the Fathers would fain forget: "We hold these truths to be self-evident: That all men are created equal; that they are endowed by their Creator with certain unalienable rights; that among these are life, liberty, and the pursuit of happiness."

from *Debate on Compulsory Free Public Education* [1868]

In the brief period of Reconstruction following the Civil War, African Americans had the opportunity to shape new legal frameworks to promote the ideals of a post-slavery society. In former slave states, black Americans went from having virtually no voice in the creation of laws to being the dominant voices, even in the creation of new state constitutions. The following debate, on compulsory free public education, is from South Carolina's 1868 constitutional convention, at which the majority of the delegates were African American men. (According to historian Thomas R. Frazier, of the seventy-four black delegates, only fourteen came from the North; of the sixty from the South, thirty-eight were former slaves. All the participants in the debate on compulsory free education were black, except Leslie, Duncan, and Holmes.)

As it was at the pre–Civil War national Negro conventions, education was a primary topic of conversation at the Constitutional Convention of South Carolina. The pre-war conventions, however, had no direct means to implement their resolutions, and so delegates made relatively limited plans to establish schools for black students, whereas the debate at the 1868 South Carolina convention, with African Americans in charge of the government, focused on the then-radical idea that education should be free and available to all, glossing over the question of segregated schools. That the central discussion focuses on the use of the word *compulsory* reveals contemporary ideas about such issues as the rights of parents and suggests that some delegates, such as those seeing the potential for abuse in the punishment of noncomplying parents, were aware that their ability to control the implementation of laws might be limited or short-lived. The final statement reprinted here, by Francis L. Cardozo (1836–1903), the president of Charleston's Avery Institute, summarizes and rejects all objections to compulsory education, conceding only that the state did not yet have enough schools to see the law fully implemented. His proposed amendment provides time in which to overcome practical problems before the law becomes fully effective. The delegates ultimately mandated a system of free, non-segregated schools. The law was never fully implemented, however, as reformers lost power soon after, and white southerners reestablished their control with Jim Crow laws and the end of Reconstruction in 1877.

From *Proceeding of the Constitutional Convention of South Carolina* (Charleston, 1868), pp. 686–94, 705–09.

MR. R. C. DE LARGE—Although laboring under great inconvenience, I shall attempt to defend the amendment proposing to strike out the word "compulsory." In the first place, we have a report which is to become a portion of the Constitution, and that Constitution emphatically declares, in terms that cannot be misunderstood, that "no distinction shall be made on account of race, color, or previous condition." It has been remarked this morning that in the Constitution of Massachusetts, and other Northern States, the same proviso exists. But any one who reflects for a moment upon the condition of the people of Massachusetts, and those of South Carolina, will fully appreciate the great difference between them. As already stated, I object to the word "compulsory," because it is contrary to the spirit and principles of republicanism. Where is the necessity for placing in the Constitution a proviso that can never be enforced. It is just as impossible to put such a section in practical operation, as it would be for a man to fly to the moon. No one will deny that an attempt to enforce it would entail the greatest trouble and expense. Who, I ask, do we propose to set up as a censor of learning? Perhaps the opponents of the measure will say the School Commissioner. I deny that he can do it. He may be the father of half a dozen children. I, too, am the father of children; but will any body tell me that, as a free citizen of South Carolina, I have not the right to choose whether I shall send those children to school or not. Will any one say I shall not teach my child myself? It may be said, such a right is not denied me. Whether it be so or not, I plant myself upon the broad principle of the equality of all men as the basis of true republicanism; and to compel any man to do what this section provides is contrary to this principle.

Again, this clause will lead to difficulties of a serious character, to which neither you nor myself can blind our eyes. In Massachusetts there is a population cradled in the arms of freedom and liberty, free of all prejudice and devoid of passion, to a great extent. In South Carolina we have an entirely different set of people. We are about to inaugurate great changes, which it is our desire shall be successful.

Mr. C. P. Leslie—Do I understand you to say that the people of Massachusetts have no prejudices of race?

Mr. F. L. Cardozo—I would also like to ask the gentleman where he gets his authority for saying that the people of Massachusetts are cradled in the principles of freedom and liberty. Is it so provided in the Constitution of Massachusetts?

Mr. R. C. De Large—I am not well acquainted with all the clauses in the Constitution of Massachusetts, and speak only from my historic knowledge of that people. This section proposes to open these schools to all persons, irrespective of color, to open every seminary of learning to all. Heartily do I endorse the object, but the manner in which it is to be enforced meets my most earnest disapproval. I do not propose to enact in this report a section that may be used by our enemies to appeal to the worst passions of a class of people in this State. The schools may be opened to all, under proper provisions in the Constitution, but to declare that parents "shall" send their children to them whether they are willing or not is, in my judgment, going a step beyond the bounds of prudence. Is there any logic or reason in inserting in the Constitution a provision which cannot be enforced? What do we intend to give the Legislature power to do? In one breath you propose to protect minor children, and in the next to punish their parents by fine and imprisonment if they do not send their children to school. For these reasons I am opposed to the section, and urge that the word "compulsory" shall be stricken out.

Mr. A. J. Ransier—I am sorry to differ with my colleague from Charleston on this question. I contend that in proportion to the education of the people so is their progress in civilization. Believing this, I believe that the Committee have properly provided for the compulsory education of all the children in this State between the ages named in the section.

I recognize the importance of this measure. There is a seeming objection to the word "compulsory," but I do not think it of grave importance. My friend does not like it, because he says it is contrary to the spirit of republicanism. To be free, however, is not to enjoy unlimited license, or my friend himself might desire to enslave again his fellow men.

Now I propose to support this section fully, and believe that the more it is considered in all its bearings upon the welfare of our people, the greater will be the desire that every parent shall, by some means, be compelled to educate his children and fit them for the responsibilities of life. As to the particular mode of enforcing attendance at school, we leave that an open question. At present we are only asserting the general principle, and the Legislature will provide for its application.

Upon the success of republicanism depends the progress which our people are destined to make. If parents are disposed to clog this progress by neglecting the education of their children, for one, I will not aid and abet them. Hence, this, in my opinion, is an exceedingly wise provision, and I am content to trust to the Legislature to carry out the measures to which it necessarily leads.

Vice and degradation go hand in hand with ignorance. Civilization and enlightenment follow fast upon the footsteps of the schoolmaster; and if education must be enforced to secure these grand results, I say let the compulsory process go on.

Mr. R. C. De Large—Can the gentleman demonstrate how the Legislature is to enforce the education of children without punishment of their parents by fine or imprisonment.

Mr. A. J. Ransier—When that question arises in the Legislature, I hope we shall have the benefit of my friend's counsel, and he himself may possibly answer that question. If there is any one thing to which we may attribute the sufferings endured by this people, it is the gross ignorance of the masses. While we propose to avoid all difficulties which may be fraught with evil to the community, we shall, nevertheless, insist upon our right to provide for the exercise of the great moral agencies which education always brings to bear upon public opinion. Had there been such a provision as this in the Constitution of South Carolina heretofore, there is no doubt that many of the evils which at present exist would have been avoided, and the people would have been advanced to a higher stage of civilization and morals, and we would not have been called upon to mourn the loss of the flower of the youth of our country. In conclusion, I favor this section as it stands. I do not think it will militate against the cause of republicanism, but, on the contrary, be of benefit both to it and to the people whom we represent. Feeling that everything depends on the education of the rising generation, I shall give this measure my vote, and use all my exertions to secure its adoption into this Constitution.

MR. B. F. RANDOLPH—In favoring, as I do, compulsory attendance at school, I cannot for the life of me see in what manner republicanism is at stake. It seems to have been the fashion on this floor to question a man's republicanism because he chooses to differ with others on general principles. Now this is a question which does not concern republicanism at all. It is simply a matter of justice which is due to a people, and it might be just as consistently urged that it is contrary to republican principles to organize the militia, to force every man to enroll his name, and to arm and equip them, as to urge that this provision is anti-republican because it compels parents to see to the education of their children.

MR. B. O. DUNCAN—Does the gentleman propose to educate children at the point of the bayonet, through the militia?

MR. B. F. RANDOLPH—If necessary we may call out the militia to enforce the law. Now, the gentlemen on the other side have given no reasons why the word "compulsory" should be stricken out.

MR. R. C. DE LARGE—Can you name any State where the provision exists in its Constitution?

MR. B. F. RANDOLPH—It exists in Massachusetts.

MR. R. C. DE LARGE—That is not so.

MR. F. L. CARDOZO—This system has been tested in Germany, and I defy the gentleman from Charleston to deny the fact. It has also been tested in several States of the Union, and I defy the gentleman to show that it has not been a success. It becomes the duty of the opposition if they want this section stricken from the report, to show that where it has been applied it has failed to produce the result desired.

MR. J. J. WRIGHT—Will you inform us what State in the Union compels parents to send their children to school?

MR. B. F. RANDOLPH—The State of New Hampshire is one. It may be asked what is the object of law? It is not only for the purpose of restraining men from doing wrong, but for the protection of all the citizens of a State, and the promotion of the general welfare. Blackstone lays it down as one of the objects, the furthering, as far as it can consistently be done, of the general welfare of the people. It is one of the objects of law, as far as practicable, not to restrain wrong by punishing man for violating the right, but also one of its grand objects to build up civilization, and this is the grand object of this provision in the report of the Committee on Education. It proposes to further civilization, and I look upon it as one of the most important results which will follow the defeat of the rebel armies, the establishment among the people who have long been deprived of the privilege of education, a law which will compel parents to send their children to school.

MR. R. B. ELLIOTT—Is it not regulated by general statutes in the State of Massachusetts, that parents shall be compelled to send their children to school?

MR. B. F. RANDOLPH—We propose to do that here. I consider this one of the most important measures which has yet come before this body. I think I can read it in the eyes of the members of this Convention to favor this measure. I feel that every one here believes it to be his duty to the people he represents. I believe every one here is zealous in doing all he can to further civilization, in building up educational institutions in the State, and doing all that is calculated to diffuse intelligence among the people generally. I had the honor of being principal of a free school two years; and, in the midst of one of the most intelligent systems of schools, the most trying thing which teachers had to contend with was the want of regular attendance on the part of the children. The most intelligent parents would sometimes neglect to send their children to school. The teachers had to adopt rules closing their doors to those who were irregular in their attendance. This law will assist the teachers and assist our school system. It will prove beneficial to the State not only for the reasons I have given, but for various other reasons. I hope you will all vote for it. I shall vote for it with all my heart, because I believe it to be something beneficial to the welfare of the people of the State.

Mr. A. C. Richmond—I desire to say but a few words on this subject. I shall speak principally in reference to our common schools and public funds. We expect to have a public school fund, although it may not be very large. We expect our parishes to be divided into school districts of convenient size. We can erect only a limited number of school houses each year, and it may be five or ten years before school houses are erected in all the districts, and the fund becomes large enough to assist in the education of all the people. If the word "compulsory" remains, it will be impossible to enforce the law for sometime to come. We say the public schools shall be opened to all. Every school district will have its school houses and its teachers. There is to be a particular school fund, school districts, and school houses. It is supposed by legislators and others that it is an excellent thing to have the children to go to school. It opens up a vast field for discussion, and affords a beautiful opportunity for making buncombe speeches. It is admitted by all legislators in every State of the Union, that cheap education is the best defense of the State. There must be schools to which colored children can go; but we wish to look into the propriety of compelling parents to send their children to school. I believe the efforts of the teachers, preachers, and all those interested in the welfare of the State, and the efforts of all those interested in the welfare of the colored people, will bring out nearly all the colored children. I believe nearly all the colored children of the State will go to school. We have societies that will help to furnish the books; we have preachers who are much interested; we have missionaries, all of whom are interested in this class of our people, and who will see to it that the colored children are educated, so that settles that point. The next point is, how are the white children going to

school? By means of moral suasion nearly all the colored children will be brought to school; and by means of white schools, nearly all white children will go to school and be educated. It will regulate itself. The word "compulsory" is used to compel the attendance of children in one or the other class of schools.

Mr. R. C. De Large—What does the tenth section of that report say?

Mr. A. C. Richmond—I believe it is the meaning, that if families of white people are not able to send their children to private schools, they shall be obliged to send their children to the public schools, in which all white and colored shall be educated.

Mr. F. L. Cardozo—We only compel parents to send their children to some school, not that they shall send them with the colored children; we simply give those colored children who desire to go to white schools, the privilege to do so.

Mr. A. C. Richmond—By means of moral suasion, I believe nearly all the colored people, as well as a large number of the children of white parents will go to school; such schools as their parents may select. If parents are too proud to take advantage of the means of education afforded, why then I say let their children grow up in ignorance.

Mr. J. A. Chestnut—So far as I have been able to see and judge, this report of the Committee is a sensible one, and ought to be adopted as it stands. How it can affect the rights of the people, or interfere with the spirit of republicanism, I am at a loss to discover. On the contrary, from all the experience I have had among the people, I unhesitatingly declare that no measure adopted by this Convention will be more in consonance with their wishes than this, or more productive of material blessings to all classes. Sir, you cannot by any persuasive and reasonable means establish civilization among an ignorant and degraded community, such as we have in our country. Force is necessary, and, for one, I say let force be used. Republicanism has given us freedom, equal rights, and equal laws. Republicanism must also give us education and wisdom.

It seems that the great difficulty in this section is in the fact that difficulty may arise between the two races in the same school, or that the whites will not send their children to the same schools with the colored children. What of that? Has not this Convention a right to establish a free school system for the benefit of the poorer classes? Undoubtedly. Then if there be a hostile disposition among the whites, an unwillingness to send their children to school, the fault is their own, not ours. Look at the idle youths around us. Is the sight not enough to invigorate every man with a desire to do something to remove this vast weight of ignorance that presses the masses down? I have no desire to curtail the privileges of freemen, but when we look at the opportunities neglected, even by the whites of South Carolina, I must confess that I am more than ever disposed to compel parents, especially of my own race, to send their children to school. If the whites object to it, let it be so. The consequences will rest with themselves.

I hope, therefore, that the motion to strike out the word "compulsory" will be laid upon the table.

MR. R. H. CAIN—It seems to me that we are spending a great deal of unnecessary time in the discussion of this subject. It is true, the question is one of great interest, and there are few who are not anxious that provisions shall be made by this Convention for the education of all classes in the State. But I am confident that it will not be necessary to use compulsion to effect this object. Hence, I am opposed to the insertion of the obnoxious word. I see no necessity for it. You cannot compel parents to send their children to school; and if you could, it would be unwise, impolitic, and injudicious. Massachusetts is fifty years ahead of South Carolina, and, under the circumstances which exist in that State, I might, if a resident, insist upon a compulsory education; but in South Carolina the case is different. There is a class of persons here whose situation, interests and necessities are varied, and controlled by surroundings which do not exist at the North. And justice is demanded for them. To do justice in this matter of education, compulsion is not required. I am willing to trust the people. They have good sense, and experience itself will be better than all the force you can employ to instill the idea of duty to their children.

Now, as a compromise with the other side, I propose the following amendment, namely that "the General Assembly may require the attendance at either public or private schools," &c.

This is a question that should be left to the Legislature. If the circumstances demand it, compulsion may be used to secure the attendance of pupils; but I do not believe such a contingency ever will occur.

As to the idea that both classes of children will be compelled to go to school together, I do not think it is comprehended in the subject at all. I remember that in my younger days I stumped the State of Iowa for the purpose of having stricken from the Constitution a clause which created distinction of color in the public schools. This was prior to the assembling of the Constitutional Convention. All we claimed was that they should make provision for the education of all the youth. We succeeded, and such a clause was engrafted in the Constitution, and that instrument was ratified by a majority of ten thousand. We said nothing about color. We simply said "youth."

I say to you, therefore, leave this question open. Leave it to the Legislature. I have great faith in humanity. We are in a stage of progress, such as our country never has seen, and while the wheels are rolling on, depend upon it, there are few persons in this country who will not seek to enjoy it by sending their children to school. White or black, all will desire to have their children educated. Let us then make this platform broad enough for all to stand upon without prejudice or objection. The matter will regulate itself, and to the Legislature may safely be confided the task of providing for any emergency which may arise.

MR. R. G. HOLMES—If there is anything we want in this State, it is some measure to compel the attendance of children between the ages of six and sixteen at some school. If it is left to parents, I believe the great majority will lock up their children at home. I hope, therefore, we shall have a law compelling the attendance of all children at school. It is the statute law in Massachusetts, and I hope we will have the provision inserted in our Constitution. The idea that it is not republican to educate children is supremely ridiculous. Republicanism, as has been well said, is not license. No man has the right, as a republican, to put his hand in my pocket, or steal money from it, because he wishes to do it. I can conceive of a way in which my child may be robbed by that system of republicanism which some members have undertaken to defend. My child may be left an orphan, poor and dependent on the kindness of neighbors or friends. They may think it to the best interest of that child to bind it out as an apprentice to some person. My child may be robbed of an education, because the person to whom it was bound does not think it advisable to send that child to school, as there may happen to be some objectionable children in the school. I have seen white children sitting by the side of colored children in school, and observed that there could not have been better friends. I do not want this privilege of attending schools confined to any exclusive class. We want no laws made here to prevent children from attending school. If any one chooses to educate their children in a private school, this law does not debar them that privilege.

But there are some who oppose all education. I remember the case of an individual who refused to have his children educated because, as he said, he himself had got along well enough without it, and he guessed his children could do the same. There is too much of that spirit in our State, and we want to contrive something to counteract it. In the case to which I have alluded, that individual some fifteen years afterwards, when his children had grown up, regretted his action, and was very much mortified because his children had no education. I hope we will engraft something into the Constitution, making it obligatory upon parents to send their children to school, and with that view, I hope the section will pass as it is.

* * *

MR. F. L. CARDOZO—Before I resume my remarks this morning, I would ask the favor of the Convention, and especially the opposition, to give me their close attention, and I think I can settle this matter perfectly satisfactory to every one in the house.

It was argued by some yesterday, with some considerable weight, that we should do everything in our power to incorporate into the Constitution all possible measures that will conciliate those opposed to us.

No one would go farther in conciliating others than I would. But those whom we desire to conciliate consist of three different classes, and we should be careful, therefore, what we do to conciliate.

In the first place there is an element which is opposed to us, no matter what we do will never be conciliated. It is not that they are opposed so much to the

Constitution we may frame, but they are opposed to us sitting in Convention. Their objection is of such a fundamental and radical nature, that any attempt to frame a Constitution to please them would be utterly abortive.

In the next place, there are those who are doubtful, and gentlemen here say if we frame a Constitution to suit these parties they will come over with us. They are only waiting, and I will say these parties do not particularly care what kind of a Constitution you frame, they only want to see whether it is going to be successful, and if it is, they will come any way.

Then there is a third class who honestly question our capacity to frame a Constitution. I respect that class, and believe if we do justice to them, laying our corner stone on the sure foundation of republican government and liberal principles, the intelligence of that class will be conciliated, and they are worthy of conciliation.

Before I proceed to discuss the question, I want to divest it of all false issues, of the imaginary consequences that some gentlemen have illogically thought will result from the adoption of this section with the word compulsory. They affirm that it compels the attendance of both white and colored children in the same schools. There is nothing of the kind in the section. It means nothing of the kind, and no such construction can be legitimately placed upon it. It simply says all the children shall be educated; but how is left with the parents to decide. It is left to the parent to say whether the child shall be sent to a public or private school. The eleventh section has been referred to as bearing upon this section. I will ask attention to this fact. The eleventh section does not say, nor does the report in any part say there shall not be separate schools. There can be separate schools for white and colored. It is simply left so that if any colored child wishes to go to a white school, it shall have the privilege to do so. I have no doubt, in most localities, colored people would prefer separate schools, particularly until some of the present prejudice against their race is removed.

We have not provided that there shall be separate schools; but I do not consider these issues as properly belonging to the question. I shall, therefore, confine myself to the more important matter connected with this subject.

My friend yesterday referred to Prussia and Massachusetts as examples that we should imitate, and I was much surprised to hear some of the members who have spoken, ridicule that argument. It was equivalent to saying we do not want the teachings of history, or the examples of any of those countries foremost in civilization.

It was said that the condition of affairs in Prussia and Massachusetts was entirely different. But they are highly civilized countries, with liberty-loving, industrious citizens, and the highest social order exists there. I want South Carolina to imitate those countries, which require the compulsory attendance of all children of certain ages for fixed periods, at some school. If you deem a certain end worthy of being attained, it must be accompanied by precisely the same means those countries have attained it.

Prussia, in her late victories over Austria, reaped the fruits of the superiority of her school system and the intelligence of her people, and in every conflict with the powers of darkness and error we should imitate just such a country as Prussia. To ignore the example of a country because far from us, would be to ignore all philosophy and history.

It was also remarked that there was no other State that compelled the attendance of their children at schools. Arkansas does it in her Constitution, and notwithstanding assertions to the contrary, I would say that Massachusetts does it in her statutes.

Another argument was that this matter had better be left to the Legislature. I have been charged with appealing to the prejudices and feelings of the colored delegates to this Convention. It is true to a certain extent. I do direct their attention to matters concerning their peculiar interests but if it is meant to charge me with appealing to their passions or against the white people, I respectfully deny the charge, and stamp the assertion as gratuitous. But I do desire we shall use the opportunities we now have to our best advantage, as we may not ever have a more propitious time. We know when the old aristocracy and ruling power of this State get into power, as they undoubtedly will, because intelligence and wealth will win in the long run, they will never pass such a law as this. Why? Because their power is built on and sustained by ignorance. They will take precious good care that the colored people shall never be enlightened.

Again, it has been argued that it was anti-republican, and an infringement of individual rights to pass such a law. Men living in a savage, uncivilized state are perfectly free, and should be untrammeled. But the first thing, when a man goes into society, is to concede certain individual rights necessary for the protection and preservation of society. If you deny this great principle, there can be no law, for every law you propose is an infringement of my individual right. If you tax me for the education of the poor people of the State, I simply say that it shall not be exclusively for the rich to build up their power, but that it is for all the people, the poor as well as the rich.

I hope every gentleman will see that the argument against it is anti-republican and utterly groundless. Some may think that we go too far, and take away too many individual rights. I maintain that in this instance it is only for the benefit of the State, as well as for the benefit of society.

The question is, will you pay the poll tax to educate your children in schools, or support them in penitentiaries? No intelligent person will prefer to support them as criminals.

Some ask how it is to be enforced, and say it is impossible. I will simply say what has been done elsewhere can be done here. Our Legislature will at first, of course, make the penalties very light, will consider all the circumstances by which we are surrounded, and will not make the law onerous. Every law should be considered in a two-fold aspect—in its moral effect and its penalties. The moral power of a law almost always compels obedience. Ninety-nine out of one hundred men who may be indifferent to their children, when they know there is a law compelling them to send their children to school, will make sacrifices in order not to violate that law.

I have had several years experience as a teacher, and I know exactly its effects. I can best satisfy the house by simply describing one out of the one hundred cases that have come under my own observation.

In my school I have the highest class of boys who were kept under my own special care and tuition. Among these boys was one highly gifted, universally loved, and talented. He was not only superior in regard to intellectual qualities, but also in regard to moral qualities. He was a noble boy, truly loveable and talented. I had watched the development of that boy's mind, and took the highest pleasure in assisting that development. I spent much time in assisting the development of that boy's mind, and watched his career with much interest and jealousy. At the commencement of our last session, he came to me with tears in his eyes, and bid me good bye. I asked him, "are you really going to leave school?" "Yes," he answered, "I must go; my parents are going to take me away." "Tell them," I said, "that I will consult with them." The mother, with tears, said she did not want the child to leave, but the father insisted upon it. I talked with him, but with no effect. He was a low, degraded, besotted drunkard. I endeavored by every argument in my power, by praising his boy as he deserved, and by offering to adopt him and take him North to one of the best institutions in the country, to effect my object in giving that boy a thorough education. What do you think was the reply? "No," he said, "I cannot spare him. In the morning he chops wood, gets the water, and I want him to run on errands." Those errands, I learned, were running to the corner to buy beer and brandy for his father. If by a law of the State we could

have taken that boy from his drunken father, and educated him, he would have been an ornament to us and an honor to the State. As I meet him in the street now, he slinks away from me to go, perhaps, to the corner to get liquor for his father. He told me from the time his father takes a glass in the morning till night he is never sober, and he wished his father was dead.

I am anxious to reconcile all differences on this question, and I move a reconsideration of the previous question, in order to offer an amendment, to the following effect:

> *Provided,* That no law to that effect shall be passed until a system of public schools has been thoroughly and completely organized, and facilities afforded to all the inhabitants of the State for the free education of their children.

The motion to reconsider was agreed to, and the question being taken on the adoption of this amendment, it was agreed to, and the fourth section passed to its third reading.

BOOKER T. WASHINGTON
Industrial Education for the Negro [1903]

Although the relative advantages of industrial and academic education were actively discussed decades before the Civil War, the classic debate on the topic took place between Booker T. Washington and W. E. B. Du Bois at the beginning of the twentieth century. The essays laying out their respective positions, Washington's "Industrial Education" (reprinted here) and Du Bois's "The Talented Tenth" (p. 230), were originally published in *The Negro Problem: A Series of Articles by Representative American Negroes of Today* (1903). The volume privileges Washington's position, placing it first in the volume (followed immediately by Du Bois's) and including his photograph in the front matter. By 1903, Washington was a national spokesperson on issues important to African Americans, having risen to national prominence with his 1895 address at the Atlanta Exposition (p. 206).

Contrary to popular perception, Washington did not believe in exclusive industrial training for African Americans, but rather supported a combination of mental, moral, and industrial education. He contrasts his ideal with models that stress one aspect of education over others, from the industrial training sometimes received in slavery to the emphasis on academic training during Reconstruction. Washington advocates working within the confines of the contemporary situation rather than insisting on immediate social change. In the future, after African Americans are able to satisfy their own material needs and those of their community, Washington contends, opportunities will develop for "professional education" and "positions of public responsibility" as well as for "leisure and the opportunity for the enjoyment of literature and the fine arts."

From Booker T. Washington, W. E. Burghardt Du Bois, Charles W. Chesnutt, Wilford H. Smith, H. T. Kealing, Paul Laurence Dunbar, and T. Thomas Fortune, *The Negro Problem: A Series of Articles by Representative American Negroes of Today* (New York: J. Pott, 1903), pp. 9–29.

One of the most fundamental and far-reaching deeds that has been accomplished during the last quarter of a century has been that by which the Negro has been helped to find himself and to learn the secrets of civilization—to learn that there are a few simple, cardinal principles upon which a race must start its upward course, unless it would fail, and its last estate be worse than its first.

It has been necessary for the Negro to learn the difference between being worked and working—to learn that being worked meant degradation, while working means civilization; that all forms of labor are honorable, and all forms of idleness disgraceful. It has been necessary for him to learn that all races that have got upon their feet have done so largely by laying an economic foundation, and, in general, by beginning in a proper cultivation and ownership of the soil.

Forty years ago my race emerged from slavery into freedom. If, in too many cases, the Negro race began development at the wrong end, it was largely because neither white nor black properly understood the case. Nor is it any wonder that this was so, for never before in the history of the world had just such a problem been presented as that of the two races at the coming of freedom in this country.

For two hundred and fifty years, I believe the way for the redemption of the Negro was being prepared through industrial development. Through all those years the Southern white man did business with the Negro in a way that no one else has done business with him. In most cases if a Southern white man wanted a house built he consulted a Negro mechanic about the plan and about the actual building of the structure. If he wanted a suit of clothes made he went to a Negro tailor, and for shoes he went to a shoemaker of the same race. In a certain way every slave plantation in the South was an industrial school. On these plantations young colored men and women were constantly being trained not only as farmers but as carpenters, blacksmiths, wheelwrights, brick masons, engineers, cooks, laundresses, sewing women and housekeepers.

I do not mean in any way to apologize for the curse of slavery, which was a curse to both races, but in what I say about industrial training in slavery I am simply stating facts. This training was crude, and was given for selfish purposes. It did not answer the high-est ends, because there was an absence of mental training in connection with the training of the hand. To a large degree, though, this business contact with the Southern white man, and the industrial training on the plantations, left the Negro at the close of the war in possession of nearly all the common and skilled labor in the South. The industries that gave the South its power, prominence and wealth prior to the Civil War were mainly the raising of cotton, sugar cane, rice and tobacco. Before the way could be prepared for the proper growing and marketing of these crops forests had to be cleared, houses to be built, public roads and railroads constructed. In all these works the Negro did most of the heavy work. In the planting, cultivating and marketing of the crops not only was the Negro the chief dependence, but in the manufacture of tobacco he became a skilled and proficient workman, and in this, up to the present time, in the South, holds the lead in the large tobacco manufactories.

In most of the industries, though, what happened? For nearly twenty years after the war, except in a few instances, the value of the industrial training given by the plantations was overlooked. Negro men and women were educated in literature, in mathematics and in the sciences, with little thought of what had been taking place during the preceding two hundred and fifty years, except, perhaps, as something to be escaped, to be got as far away from as possible. As a generation began to pass, those who had been trained as mechanics in slavery began to disappear by death, and gradually it began to be realized that there were few to take their places. There were young men educated in foreign tongues, but few in carpentry or in mechanical or architectural drawing. Many were trained in Latin, but few as engineers and blacksmiths. Too many were taken from the farm and educated, but educated in everything but farming. For this reason they had no interest in farming and did not return to it. And yet eighty-five per cent. of the Negro population of the Southern states lives and for a considerable time will continue to live in the country districts. The charge is often brought against the members of my race—and too often justly, I confess—that they are found leaving the country districts and flocking into the great cities where temptations are more frequent and harder to resist, and where the Negro people too often become demoralized. Think, though, how frequently it is the case that from the first day that a pupil begins to go to school his books teach him much about the cities of the world and city life, and almost nothing about the country. How natural it is, then, that when he has the ordering of his life he wants to live it in the city.

Only a short time before his death the late Mr. C. P. Huntington, to whose memory a magnificent library has just been given by his widow to the Hampton Institute for Negroes, in Virginia, said in a public address some words which seem to me so wise that I want to quote them here:

"Our schools teach everybody a little of almost everything, but, in my opinion, they teach very few children just what they ought to know in order to make their way successfully in life. They do not put into their hands the tools they are best fitted to use, and hence so many failures. Many a mother and sister have worked and slaved, living upon scanty food, in order to give a son and brother a "liberal education," and in doing this have built up a barrier between the boy and the work he was fitted to do. Let me say to you that all honest work is honorable work. If the labor is manual, and seems common, you will have all the more chance to be thinking of other things, or of work that is higher and brings better pay, and to work out in your minds better and higher duties and responsibilities for yourselves, and for thinking of ways by which you can help others as well as yourselves, and bring them up to your own higher level."

Some years ago, when we decided to make tailoring a part of our training at the Tuskegee Institute, I was amazed to find that it was almost impossible to find in the whole country an educated colored man who could teach the making of clothing. We could find numbers of them who could teach astronomy, theology, Latin or grammar, but almost none who could instruct in the making of clothing, something that has to be used by every one of us every day in the year. How often have I been discouraged as I have gone through the South, and into the homes of the people of my race, and have found women who could converse intelligently upon abstruse subjects, and yet could not tell how to improve the condition of the poorly cooked and still more poorly served bread and meat which they and their families were eating three times a day. It is discouraging to find a girl who can tell you the geographical location of any country on the globe and who does not know where to place the dishes upon a common dinner table. It is discouraging to find a woman who knows much about theoretical chemistry, and who cannot properly wash and iron a shirt.

In what I say here I would not by any means have it understood that I would limit or circumscribe the mental development of the Negro student. No race can be lifted until its mind is awakened and strengthened. By the side of industrial training should always go mental and moral training, but the pushing of mere abstract knowledge into the head means little. We want more than the mere performance of mental gymnastics. Our knowledge must be harnessed to the things of real life. I would encourage the Negro to secure all the mental strength, all the mental culture—whether gleaned from science, mathematics, history, language or literature that his circumstances will allow, but I believe most earnestly that for years to come the education of the people of my race should be so directed that the greatest proportion of the mental strength of the masses will be brought to bear upon the every-day practical things of life, upon something that is needed to be done, and something which they will be permitted to do in the community in which they reside. And just the same with the professional class which the race needs and must have, I would say give the men and women of that class, too, the training which will best fit them to perform in the most successful manner the service which the race demands.

I would not confine the race to industrial life, not even to agriculture, for example, although I believe that by far the greater part of the Negro race is best off in the country districts and must and should continue to live there, but I would teach the race that in industry the foundation must be laid—that the very best service which any one can render to what is called the higher education is to teach the present generation to provide a material or industrial foundation. On such a foundation as this will grow habits of thrift, a love of work, economy, ownership of property, bank accounts. Out of it in the future will grow practical education, professional education, positions of public responsibility. Out of it will grow moral and religious strength. Out of it will grow wealth from which alone can come leisure and the opportunity for the enjoyment of literature and the fine arts.

In the words of the late beloved Frederick Douglass: "Every blow of the sledge hammer wielded by a sable arm is a powerful blow in support of our cause. Every colored mechanic is by virtue of circumstances an elevator of his race. Every house built by a black man is a strong tower against the allied hosts of prejudice. It is impossible for us to attach too much importance to this aspect of the subject."[1] Without industrial development there can be no wealth; without wealth there can be no leisure; without leisure no opportunity for thoughtful reflection and the cultivation of the higher arts.

I would set no limits to the attainments of the Negro in arts, in letters or statesmanship, but I believe the surest way to reach those ends is by laying the foundation in the little things of life that lie immediately about one's door. I plead for industrial education and development for the Negro not because I want to cramp him, but because I want to free him. I want to see him enter the all-powerful business and commercial world.

It was such combined mental, moral, and industrial education which the late General Armstrong set out to give at the Hampton Institute when he established that school thirty years ago. The Hampton Institute has continued along the lines laid down by its great founder, and now each year an increasing number of similar schools are being established in the South, for the people of both races.

Early in the history of the Tuskegee Institute we began to combine industrial training with mental and moral culture. Our first efforts were in the direction of agriculture, and we began teaching this with no appliances except one hoe and a blind mule. From this small beginning we have grown until now the Institute owns two thousand acres of land, eight hundred of which are cultivated each year by the young men of the school. We began teaching wheelwrighting and blacksmithing in a small way to the men, and laundry work, cooking and sewing and housekeeping to the young women. The fourteen hundred and over young men and women who attended the school during the last school year received instruction—in addition to academic and religious training—in thirty-three trades and industries, including carpentry, blacksmithing, printing, wheelwrighting, harnessmaking, painting, machinery, founding, shoemaking, brickmasonry and brickmaking, plastering, sawmilling, tinsmithing, tailoring, mechanical and architectural drawing, electrical and steam engineering, canning, sewing, dressmaking, millinery, cooking, laundering, housekeeping, mattress making, basketry, nursing, agriculture, dairying and stock raising, horticulture.

Not only do the students receive instruction in these trades, but they do actual work, by means of which more than half of them pay some part or all of their expenses while remaining at the school. Of the sixty buildings belonging to the school all but four were almost wholly erected by the students as a part of their industrial education. Even the bricks which go into the walls are made by students in the school's brick yard, in which, last year, they manufactured two million bricks.

When we first began this work at Tuskegee, and the idea got spread among the people of my race that the students who came to the Tuskegee school were to be taught industries in connection with their academic studies, were, in other words, to be taught to work, I received a great many verbal messages and letters from parents informing me that they wanted their children taught books, but not how to work. This protest went on for three or four years, but I am glad to be able to say now that our people have very generally been educated to a point where they see their own needs and conditions so clearly that it has been several years since we have had a single protest from parents against the teaching of industries, and there is now a positive enthusiasm for it. In fact, public sentiment among the students at Tuskegee is now so strong for industrial training that it would hardly permit a student to remain on the grounds who was unwilling to labor.

It seems to me that too often mere book education leaves the Negro young man or woman in a weak position. For example, I have seen a Negro girl taught by

---

1. From Douglass's "Address to the Colored People of the United States" (1948); the remainder of the quotation, after "aspect of the subject," is not from Douglass's speech, but rather from a 1900 Michigan State University commencement address by Washington.

her mother to help her in doing laundry work at home. Later, when this same girl was graduated from the public schools or a high school and returned home she finds herself educated out of sympathy with laundry work, and yet not able to find anything to do which seems in keeping with the cost and character of her education. Under these circumstances we cannot be surprised if she does not fulfill the expectations made for her. What should have been done for her, it seems to me, was to give her along with her academic education thorough training in the latest and best methods of laundry work, so that she could have put so much skill and intelligence into it that the work would have been lifted out from the plane of drudgery. The home which she would then have been able to found by the results of her work would have enabled her to help her children to take a still more responsible position in life.

Almost from the first Tuskegee has kept in mind—and this I think should be the policy of all industrial schools—fitting students for occupations which would be open to them in their home communities. Some years ago we noted the fact that there was beginning to be a demand in the South for men to operate dairies in a skillful, modern manner. We opened a dairy department in connection with the school, where a number of young men could have instruction in the latest and most scientific methods of dairy work. At present we have calls—mainly from Southern white men—for twice as many dairymen as we are able to supply. What is equally satisfactory, the reports which come to us indicate that our young men are giving the highest satisfaction and are fast changing and improving the dairy product in the communities into which they go. I use the dairy here as an example. What I have said of this is equally true of many of the other industries which we teach. Aside from the economic value of this work I cannot but believe, and my observation confirms me in my belief, that as we continue to place Negro men and women of intelligence, religion, modesty, conscience and skill in every community in the South, who will prove by actual results their value to the community, I cannot but believe, I say, that this will constitute a solution to many of the present political and social difficulties.

Many seem to think that industrial education is meant to make the Negro work as he worked in the days of slavery. This is far from my conception of industrial education. If this training is worth anything to the Negro, it consists in teaching him how not to work, but how to make the forces of nature—air, steam, water, horse-power and electricity—work for him. If it has any value it is in lifting labor up out of toil and drudgery into the plane of the dignified and the beautiful. The Negro in the South works and works hard; but too often his ignorance and lack of skill causes him to do his work in the most costly and shiftless manner, and this keeps him near the bottom of the ladder in the economic world.

I have not emphasized particularly in these pages the great need of training the Negro in agriculture, but I believe that this branch of industrial education does need very great emphasis. In this connection I want to quote some words which Mr. Edgar Gardner Murphy, of Montgomery, Alabama, has recently written upon this subject:

"We must incorporate into our public school system a larger recognition of the practical and industrial elements in educational training. Ours is an agricultural population. The school must be brought more closely to the soil. The teaching of history, for example, is all very well, but nobody can really know anything of history unless he has been taught to see things grow—has so seen things not only with the outward eye, but with the eyes of his intelligence and conscience. The actual things of the present are more important, however, than the institutions of the past. Even to young children can be shown the simpler conditions and processes of growth—how corn is put into the ground—how cotton and potatoes should be planted—how to choose the soil best adapted to a particular plant, how to improve that soil, how to care for the plant while it grows, how to get the most value out of it, how to use the elements of waste for the fertilization of other crops; how, through the alternation of crops, the land may be made to increase the annual value of its products—these things, upon their elementary side are absolutely vital to the worth and success of hundreds of thousands of these people of the Negro race, and yet our whole educational system has practically ignored them. . . .

"Such work will mean not only an education in agriculture, but an education through agriculture and education, through natural symbols and practical forms, which will educate as deeply, as broadly and as truly as any other system which the world has known. Such changes will bring far larger results than the mere improvement of our Negroes. They will give us an agricultural class, a class of tenants or small land owners, trained not away from the soil, but in relation to the soil and in intelligent dependence upon its resources."

I close, then, as I began, by saying that as a slave the Negro was worked, and that as a freeman he must learn to work. There is still doubt in many quarters as to the ability of the Negro unguided, unsupported, to hew his own path and put into visible, tangible, indisputable form, products and signs of civilization. This doubt cannot be much affected by abstract arguments, no matter how delicately and convincingly woven

together. Patiently, quietly, doggedly, persistently, through summer and winter, sunshine and shadow, by self-sacrifice, by foresight, by honesty and industry, we must re-enforce argument with results. One farm bought, one house built, one home sweetly and intelligently kept, one man who is the largest tax payer or has the largest bank account, one school or church maintained, one factory running successfully, one truck garden profitably cultivated, one patient cured by a Negro doctor, one sermon well preached, one office well filled, one life cleanly lived—these will tell more in our favor than all the abstract eloquence that can be summoned to plead our cause. Our pathway must be up through the soil, up through swamps, up through forests, up through the streams, the rocks, up through commerce, education and religion!

W. E. B. DU BOIS

The Talented Tenth [1903]

Like Washington (p. 225), Du Bois argues for a combination of mental, moral, and industrial education. The educational models of the two leaders reveal radically different priorities, however. While Washington contends that industrial education will act as a foundation leading to opportunities for moral and mental development, Du Bois views academic education as the very foundation of "manhood," on which will be built "bread winning, skill of hand and quickness of brain." Washington's program is directly geared toward training "the masses." Du Bois argues that the first educational priority must be to provide the privileged few, which he calls the "Talented Tenth," with access to higher education. Out of this pool of educated African Americans will come the teachers, political leaders, and other role models who can propel a true advancement of the masses.

Washington's argument for practical training incorporates a critique of the societal value of specific disciplines such as Latin and higher mathematics. For Du Bois, it is not the particular subject of study that is of

paramount importance but the critical role that academic discipline and knowledge play in the creation of leaders, particularly teachers. Du Bois stresses the broader cultural framework that training in academic disciplines provides: "Men we shall have only as we make manhood the object of the work of the schools— intelligence, broad sympathy, knowledge of the world that was and is, and of the relation of men to it—this is the curriculum of that Higher Education which must underlie true life."

Du Bois displays his own academic background by citing sociological and historical data to refute vague claims made by Washington. He also personalizes his challenge of Washington by pointing out that the teachers at Washington's Tuskegee Institute (as well as Washington's own wife) were products of the very type of institution of higher education that Washington did not publicly support, thereby giving greater weight to his "top-down" theory of education, as opposed to Washington's "bottom-up" philosophy.

From Booker T. Washington, W. E. Burghardt Du Bois, Charles W. Chesnutt, Wilford H. Smith, H. T. Kealing, Paul Laurence Dunbar, and T. Thomas Fortune, *The Negro Problem* (New York: J. Pott, 1903), pp. 33–75.

The Negro race, like all races, is going to be saved by its exceptional men. The problem of education, then, among Negroes must first of all deal with the Talented Tenth; it is the problem of developing the Best of this race that they may guide the Mass away from the contamination and death of the Worst, in their own and other races. Now the training of men is a difficult and intricate task. Its technique is a matter for educational experts, but its object is for the vision of seers. If we make money the object of man-training, we shall develop money-makers but not necessarily men; if we make technical skill the object of education, we may possess artisans but not, in nature, men. Men we shall have only as we make manhood the object of the work of the schools—intelligence, broad sympathy, knowledge of the world that was and is, and of the relation of men to it—this is the curriculum of that Higher Education which must underlie true life. On this foundation we may build bread winning, skill of hand and quickness of brain, with never a fear lest the child and man mistake the means of living for the object of life.

If this be true—and who can deny it—three tasks lay before me; first to show from the past that the Talented Tenth as they have risen among American Negroes have been worthy of leadership; secondly, to show how these men may be educated and developed; and thirdly, to show their relation to the Negro problem.

You misjudge us because you do not know us. From the very first it has been the educated and intelligent of the Negro people that have led and elevated the mass, and the sole obstacles that nullified and retarded their efforts were slavery and race prejudice; for what is slavery but the legalized survival of the unfit and the nullification of the work of natural internal leadership? Negro leadership, therefore, sought from the first to rid the race of this awful incubus that it might make way for natural selection and the survival of the fittest. In colonial days came Phillis Wheatley and Paul Cuffe striving against the bars of prejudice; and Benjamin Banneker, the almanac maker, voiced their longings when he said to Thomas Jefferson, "I freely and cheerfully acknowledge that I am of the African race, and in colour which is natural to them, of the deepest dye; and it is under a sense of the most profound gratitude to the Supreme Ruler of the Universe, that I now confess to you that I am not under that state of tyrannical thraldom and inhuman captivity to which too many of my brethren are doomed, but that I have abundantly tasted of the fruition of those blessings which proceed from that free and unequalled liberty with which you are favored, and which I hope you will willingly allow, you have mercifully received from the immediate hand of that Being from whom proceedeth every good and perfect gift.

"Suffer me to recall to your mind that time in which the arms of the British crown were exerted with every powerful effort, in order to reduce you to a state of servitude; look back, I entreat you, on the variety of dangers to which you were exposed; reflect on that period in which every human aid appeared unavailable, and in which even hope and fortitude wore the aspect of inability to the conflict, and you cannot but be led to a serious and grateful sense of your miraculous and providential preservation, you cannot but acknowledge, that the present freedom and tranquility which you enjoy, you have mercifully received, and that a peculiar blessing of heaven.

"This, sir, was a time when you clearly saw into the injustice of a state of Slavery, and in which you had just apprehensions of the horrors of its condition. It was then that your abhorrence thereof was so excited, that you publicly held forth this true and invaluable doctrine, which is worthy to be recorded and remembered in all succeeding ages: 'We hold these truths to be self evident, that all men are created equal; that they are endowed with certain inalienable rights, and that among these are life, liberty and the pursuit of happiness.'"

Then came Dr. James Derham, who could tell even the learned Dr. Rush[1] something of medicine, and

---

1. Du Bois often refers to prominent black leaders by only their first or last names; in addition to Dr. Benjamin Rush mentioned here, references in the text reprinted here include Robert Purvis, Charles L. Remond, James E. C. Pennington, Henry Highland Garnet, James McCune Smith, John Brown Russwurm, Elias Neau, Anthony Benezet, John M. Langston, Blanche K. Bruce, Robert Brown Elliot, Jacob Greener, George Washington Williams, Daniel A. Payne, Edmund Asa Ware, Erastus Milo Cravath, Thomas N. Chase, Horace Bumstead, and Adam Knight Spence.

Lemuel Haynes, to whom Middlebury College gave an honorary A. M. in 1804. These and others we may call the Revolutionary group of distinguished Negroes—they were persons of marked ability, leaders of a Talented Tenth, standing conspicuously among the best of their time. They strove by word and deed to save the color line from becoming the line between the bond and free, but all they could do was nullified by Eli Whitney and the Curse of Gold. So they passed into forgetfulness.

But their spirit did not wholly die; here and there in the early part of the century came other exceptional men. Some were natural sons of unnatural fathers and were given often a liberal training and thus a race of educated mulattoes sprang up to plead for black men's rights. There was Ira Aldridge,[2] whom all Europe loved to honor; there was that Voice crying in the Wilderness, David Walker, and saying:

"I declare it does appear to me as though some nations think God is asleep, or that he made the Africans for nothing else but to dig their mines and work their farms, or they cannot believe history, sacred or profane. I ask every man who has a heart, and is blessed with the privilege of believing—Is not God a God of justice to all his creatures? Do you say he is? Then if he gives peace and tranquility to tyrants and permits them to keep our fathers, our mothers, ourselves and our children in eternal ignorance and wretchedness to support them and their families, would he be to us a God of Justice? I ask, O, ye Christians, who hold us and our children in the most abject ignorance and degradation that ever a people were afflicted with since the world began—I say if God gives you peace and tranquility, and suffers you thus to go on afflicting us, and our children, who have never given you the least provocation—would He be to us a God of Justice? If you will allow that we are men, who feel for each other, does not the blood of our fathers and of us, their children, cry aloud to the Lord of Sabaoth against you for the cruelties and murders with which you have and do continue to afflict us?"

This was the wild voice that first aroused Southern legislators in 1829 to the terrors of abolitionism.

In 1831 there met that first Negro convention in Philadelphia, at which the world gaped curiously but which bravely attacked the problems of race and slavery, crying out against persecution and declaring that "Laws as cruel in themselves as they were unconstitutional and unjust, have in many places been enacted against our poor, unfriended and unoffending brethren (without a shadow of provocation on our part), at whose bare recital the very savage draws himself up for fear of contagion—looks noble and prides himself because he bears not the name of Christian." Side by side this free Negro movement, and the movement for abolition, strove until they merged into one strong stream. Too little notice has been taken of the work which the Talented Tenth among Negroes took in the great abolition crusade. From the very day that a Philadelphia colored man became the first subscriber to Garrison's "Liberator," to the day when Negro soldiers made the Emancipation Proclamation possible, black leaders worked shoulder to shoulder with white men in a movement, the success of which would have been impossible without them. There was Purvis and Remond, Pennington and Highland Garnett,[3] Sojourner Truth and Alexander Crummel, and above all, Frederick Douglass—what would the abolition movement have been without them? They stood as living examples of the possibilities of the Negro race, their own hard experiences and well wrought culture said silently more than all the drawn periods of orators—they were the men who made American slavery impossible. As Maria Weston Chapman once said, from the school of anti-slavery agitation "a throng of authors, editors, lawyers, orators and accomplished gentlemen of color have taken their degree! It has equally implanted hopes and aspirations, noble thoughts, and sublime purposes, in the hearts of both races. It has prepared the white man for the freedom of the black man, and it has made the black man scorn the thought of enslavement, as does a white man, as far as its influence has extended. Strengthen that

---

2. Aldridge (1807–67) was raised in Maryland and New York; he moved to Europe and became a star of the theater, specializing in Othello and other Shakespearean roles.

3. Du Bois spells names unconventionally multiple times in this essay, e.g. "Highland Garnett" for Henry Highland Garnet, "Alexander Crummel" for Alexander Crummell, and "Russworm" for John Brown Russwurm.

noble influence! Before its organization, the country only saw here and there in slavery some faithful Cudjoe or Dinah, whose strong natures blossomed even in bondage, like a fine plant beneath a heavy stone. Now, under the elevating and cherishing influence of the American Anti-slavery Society, the colored race, like the white, furnishes Corinthian capitals for the noblest temples."[4]

Where were these black abolitionists trained? Some, like Frederick Douglass, were self-trained, but yet trained liberally; others, like Alexander Crummell and McCune Smith, graduated from famous foreign universities. Most of them rose up through the colored schools of New York and Philadelphia and Boston, taught by college-bred men like Russworm, of Dartmouth, and college-bred white men like Neau and Benezet.

After emancipation came a new group of educated and gifted leaders: Langston, Bruce and Elliot, Greener, Williams and Payne. Through political organization, historical and polemic writing and moral regeneration, these men strove to uplift their people. It is the fashion of to-day to sneer at them and to say that with freedom Negro leadership should have begun at the plow and not in the Senate—a foolish and mischievous lie; two hundred and fifty years that black serf toiled at the plow and yet that toiling was in vain till the Senate passed the war amendments; and two hundred and fifty years more the half-free serf of to-day may toil at his plow, but unless he have political rights and righteously guarded civic status, he will still remain the poverty-stricken and ignorant plaything of rascals, that he now is. This all sane men know even if they dare not say it.

And so we come to the present—a day of cowardice and vacillation, of strident wide-voiced wrong and faint hearted compromise; of double-faced dallying with Truth and Right. Who are to-day guiding the work of the Negro people? The "exceptions" of course. And yet so sure as this Talented Tenth is pointed out, the blind worshippers of the Average cry out in alarm: "These are exceptions, look here at death, disease and crime—these are the happy rule." Of course they are the rule, because a silly nation made them the rule: Because for three long centuries this people lynched Negroes who dared to be brave, raped black women who dared to be virtuous, crushed dark-hued youth who dared to be ambitious, and encouraged and made to flourish servility and lewdness and apathy. But not even this was able to crush all manhood and chastity and aspiration from black folk. A saving remnant continually survives and persists, continually aspires, continually shows itself in thrift and ability and character. Exceptional it is to be sure, but this is its chiefest promise; it shows the capability of Negro blood, the promise of black men. Do Americans ever stop to reflect that there are in this land a million men of Negro blood, well-educated, owners of homes, against the honor of whose womanhood no breath was ever raised, whose men occupy positions of trust and usefulness, and who, judged by any standard, have reached the full measure of the best type of modern European culture? Is it fair, is it decent, is it Christian to ignore these facts of the Negro problem, to belittle such aspiration, to nullify such leadership and seek to crush these people back into the mass out of which by toil and travail, they and their fathers have raised themselves?

Can the masses of the Negro people be in any possible way more quickly raised than by the effort and example of this aristocracy of talent and character? Was there ever a nation on God's fair earth civilized from the bottom upward? Never; it is, ever was and ever will be from the top downward that culture filters. The Talented Tenth rises and pulls all that are worth the saving up to their vantage ground. This is the history of human progress; and the two historic mistakes which have hindered that progress were the thinking first that no more could ever rise save the few already risen; or second, that it would better the unrisen to pull the risen down.

How then shall the leaders of a struggling people be trained and the hands of the risen few strengthened? There can be but one answer: The best and most capable of their youth must be schooled in the colleges and universities of the land. We will not quarrel as to

4. From "'How Can I Help To Abolish Slavery?' or, Counsels To The Newly Converted" published by the Office of the American Anti-Slavery Society; a "mainspring" of the abolitionist movement, Chapman (1806–85) was described by fellow white female activist Lydia Marie Child as "one of the most remarkable women of the age."

just what the university of the Negro should teach or how it should teach it—I willingly admit that each soul and each race-soul needs its own peculiar curriculum. But this is true: A university is a human invention for the transmission of knowledge and culture from generation to generation, through the training of quick minds and pure hearts, and for this work no other human invention will suffice, not even trade and industrial schools.

All men cannot go to college but some men must: every isolated group or nation must have its yeast, must have for the talented few centers of training where men are not so mystified and befuddled by the hard and necessary toil of earning a living, as to have no aims higher than their bellies, and no God greater than Gold. This is true training, and thus in the beginning were the favored sons of the freedmen trained. Out of the colleges of the North came, after the blood of war, Ware, Cravath, Chase, Andrews, Bumstead and Spence to build the foundations of knowledge and civilization in the black South. Where ought they to have begun to build? At the bottom, of course, quibbles the mole with his eyes in the earth. Aye! truly at the bottom, at the very bottom; at the bottom of knowledge, down in the very depths of knowledge there where the roots of justice strike into the lowest soil of Truth. And so they did begin; they founded colleges, and up from the colleges shot normal schools, and out from the normal schools went teachers, and around the normal teachers clustered other teachers to teach the public schools; the college trained in Greek and Latin and mathematics, 2,000 men; and these men trained full 50,000 others in morals and manners, and they in turn taught thrift and the alphabet to nine millions of men, who to-day hold $300,000,000 of property. It was a miracle—the most wonderful peace-battle of the 19th century, and yet to-day men smile at it, and in fine superiority tell us that it was all a strange mistake; that a proper way to found a system of education is first to gather the children and buy them spelling books and hoes; afterward men may look about for teachers, if haply they may find them; or again they would teach men Work, but as for Life— why, what has Work to do with Life, they ask vacantly.

Was the work of these college founders successful; did it stand the test of time? Did the college graduates, with all their fine theories of life, really live? Are they useful men helping to civilize and elevate their less fortunate fellows? Let us see. Omitting all institutions which have not actually graduated students from a college course, there are to-day in the United States thirty-four institutions giving something above high school training to Negroes and designed especially for this race.

Three of these were established in border States before the War; thirteen were planted by the Freedmen's Bureau in the years 1864–1869; nine were established between 1870 and 1880 by various church bodies; five were established after 1881 by Negro churches, and four are state institutions supported by United States' agricultural funds. In most cases the college departments are small adjuncts to high and common school work. As a matter of fact six institutions—Atlanta, Fisk, Howard, Shaw, Wilberforce and Leland—are the important Negro colleges so far as actual work and number of students are concerned. In all these institutions, seven hundred and fifty Negro college students are enrolled. In grade the best of these colleges are about a year behind the smaller New England colleges and a typical curriculum is that of Atlanta University. Here students from the grammar grades, after a three years' high school course, take a college course of 136 weeks. One-fourth of this time is given to Latin and Greek; one-fifth, to English and modern languages; one-sixth, to history and social science; one-seventh, to natural science; one-eighth to mathematics, and one-eighth to philosophy and pedagogy.

In addition to these students in the South, Negroes have attended Northern colleges for many years. As early as 1826 one was graduated from Bowdoin College, and from that time till to-day nearly every year has seen elsewhere, other such graduates. They have, of course, met much color prejudice. Fifty years ago very few colleges would admit them at all. Even to-day no Negro has ever been admitted to Princeton, and at some other leading institutions they are rather endured than encouraged. Oberlin was the great pioneer in the work of blotting out the color line in colleges, and has more Negro graduates by far than any other Northern college.

The total number of Negro college graduates up to 1899, (several of the graduates of that year not being reported), was as follows:

	NEGRO COLLEGES.	WHITE COLLEGES.
Before '76	137	75
'75–80	143	22
'80–85	250	31
'85–90	413	43
'90–95	465	66
'95–99	475	88
Class Unknown	57	64
Total[5]	1,914	390

Of these graduates 2,079 were men and 252 were women; 50 per cent. of Northern-born college men come South to work among the masses of their people, at a sacrifice which few people realize; nearly 90 per cent. of the Southern-born graduates instead of seeking that personal freedom and broader intellectual atmosphere which their training has led them, in some degree, to conceive, stay and labor and wait in the midst of their black neighbors and relatives.

The most interesting question, and in many respects the crucial question, to be asked concerning college-bred Negroes, is: Do they earn a living? It has been intimated more than once that the higher training of Negroes has resulted in sending into the world of work, men who could find nothing to do suitable to their talents. Now and then there comes a rumor of a colored college man working at menial service, etc.

Fortunately, returns as to occupations of college-bred Negroes, gathered by the Atlanta conference, are quite full—nearly sixty per cent. of the total number of graduates.

This enables us to reach fairly certain conclusions as to the occupations of all college-bred Negroes. Of 1,312 persons reported, there were:

	PER CENT.
Teachers,	53.4
Clergymen,	16.8
Physicians, etc.,	6.3
Students,	5.6
Lawyers,	4.7
In Govt. Service,	4.0
In Business,	3.6
Farmers and Artisans,	2.7
Editors, Secretaries and Clerks,	2.4
Miscellaneous	.5

Over half are teachers, a sixth are preachers, another sixth are students and professional men; over 6 per cent. are farmers, artisans and merchants, and 4 per cent. are in government service. In detail the occupations are as follows:

Occupations of College-Bred Men.

Teachers:
    Presidents and Deans, ... 19
    Teacher of Music, ... 7
    Professors, Principals and Teachers, ... 675   Total 701
Clergymen:
    Bishop, ... 1
    Chaplains U. S. Army, ... 2
    Missionaries, ... 9
    Presiding Elders, ... 12
    Preachers, ... 197   Total 221

5. The first column adds up to 1940 (not 1914) and the second column adds up to 389 (not 390), making a total of 2,329 African American college graduates; Du Bois subsequently notes that 2,079 of the graduates were men and 252 were women, which makes a total of 2,331.

Physicians,
  Doctors of Medicine, ... 76
  Druggists, ... 4
  Dentists, ... 3   Total 83
Students, ...   74
Lawyers, ...   62
Civil Service: ....
  U. S. Minister Plenipotentiary, ... 1
  U. S. Consul, ... 1
  U. S. Deputy Collector, ... 1
  U. S. Gauger, ... 1
  U. S. Postmasters, ... 2
  U. S. Clerks, ... 44
  State civil service 2
  City civil service, ... 1   Total 53
Business Men: ....
  Merchants, etc., ... 30
  Managers, ... 13
  Real Estate Dealers, ... 4   Total 47
Farmers, ...   26
Clerks and Secretaries: ....
  Secretary of National Societies, ... 7
  Clerks, etc., ... 15   Total 22
Artisans, ...   9
Editors, ...   9
Miscellaneous, ...   5

These figures illustrate vividly the function of the college-bred Negro. He is, as he ought to be, the group leader, the man who sets the ideals of the community where he lives, directs its thoughts and heads its social movements. It need hardly be argued that the Negro people need social leadership more than most groups: that they have no traditions to fall back upon, no long established customs, no strong family ties, no well defined social classes. All these things must be slowly and painfully evolved. The preacher was, even before the war, the group leader of the Negroes, and the church their greatest social institution. Naturally this preacher was ignorant and often immoral, and the problem of replacing the older type by better educated men has been a difficult one. Both by direct work and by direct influence on other preachers, and on congregations, the college-bred preacher has an opportunity for reformatory work and moral inspiration, the value of which cannot be overestimated.

It has, however, been in the furnishing of teachers that the Negro college has found its peculiar function. Few persons realize how vast a work, how mighty a revolution has been thus accomplished. To furnish five millions and more of ignorant people with teachers of their own race and blood, in one generation, was not only a very difficult undertaking, but a very important one, in that, it placed before the eyes of almost every Negro child an attainable ideal. It brought the masses of the blacks in contact with modern civilization, made black men the leaders of their communities and trainers of the new generation. In this work college-bred Negroes were first teachers, and then teachers of teachers. And here it is that the broad culture of college work has been of peculiar value.

Knowledge of life and its wider meaning, has been the point of the Negro's deepest ignorance, and the sending out of teachers whose training has not been simply for bread winning, but also for human culture, has been of inestimable value in the training of these men.

In earlier years the two occupations of preacher and teacher were practically the only ones open to the black college graduate. Of later years a larger diversity of life among his people, has opened new avenues of employment. Nor have these college men been paupers and spendthrifts; 557 college-bred Negroes owned in 1899, $1,342,862.50 worth of real estate, (assessed value) or $2,411 per family. The real value of the total accumulations of the whole group is perhaps about $10,000,000, or $5,000 a piece. Pitiful, is it not, beside the fortunes of oil kings and steel trusts, but after all is the fortune of the millionaire the only stamp of true and successful living? Alas! it is, with many, and there's the rub.

The problem of training the Negro is to-day immensely complicated by the fact that the whole question of the efficiency and appropriateness of our present systems of education, for any kind of child, is a matter of active debate, in which final settlement seems still afar off. Consequently it often happens that persons arguing for or against certain systems of education for Negroes, have these controversies in mind and miss the real question at issue. The main question, so far as the Southern Negro is concerned, is: What under the present circumstance, must a system of education do in order to raise the Negro as quickly as possible in the scale of civilization? The answer to this question seems to me clear: It must strengthen the Negro's character, increase his knowledge and teach him to earn a living. Now it goes without saying, that it is hard to do all these things simultaneously or suddenly, and that at the same time it will not do to give all the attention to one and neglect the others; we could give black boys trades, but that alone will not civilize a race of ex-slaves; we might simply increase their knowledge of the world, but this would not necessarily make them wish to use this knowledge honestly; we might seek to strengthen character and purpose, but to what end if this people have nothing to eat or to wear? A system of education is not one thing, nor does it have a single definite object, nor is it a mere matter of schools. Education is that whole system of human training within and without the school house walls, which molds and develops men. If then we start out to train an ignorant and unskilled people with a heritage of bad habits, our system of training must set before itself two great aims—the one dealing with knowledge and character, the other part seeking to give the child the technical knowledge necessary for him to earn a living under the present circumstances. These objects are accomplished in part by the opening of the common schools on the one, and of the industrial schools on the other. But only in part, for there must also be trained those who are to teach these schools—men and women of knowledge and culture and technical skill who understand modern civilization, and have the training and aptitude to impart it to the children under them. There must be teachers, and teachers of teachers, and to attempt to establish any sort of a system of common and industrial school training, without *first* (and I say *first* advisedly) without *first* providing for the higher training of the very best teachers, is simply throwing your money to the winds. School houses do not teach themselves—piles of brick and mortar and machinery do not send out *men*. It is the trained, living human soul, cultivated and strengthened by long study and thought, that breathes the real breath of life into boys and girls and makes them human, whether they be black or white, Greek, Russian or American. Nothing, in these latter days, has so dampened the faith of thinking Negroes in recent educational movements, as the fact that such movements have been accompanied by ridicule and denouncement and decrying of those very institutions of higher training which made the Negro public school possible, and make Negro industrial schools thinkable. It was Fisk, Atlanta, Howard and Straight, those colleges born of the faith and sacrifice of the abolitionists, that placed in the black schools of the South the 30,000 teachers and more, which some, who depreciate the work of these higher schools, are using to teach their own new experiments. If Hampton, Tuskegee and the hundred other industrial schools prove in the future to be as successful as they deserve to be, then their success in training black artisans for the South, will be due primarily to the white colleges of the North and the black colleges of the South, which trained the teachers who to-day conduct these institutions. There was a time when the American people believed pretty devoutly that a log of wood with a boy at one end and Mark Hopkins at the other, represented the highest ideal of human training. But in these eager days it would seem that we have changed all that and think it necessary to add a couple of saw-mills and a hammer to this outfit, and, at a pinch, to dispense with the services of Mark Hopkins.

I would not deny, or for a moment seem to deny, the paramount necessity of teaching the Negro to work, and to work steadily and skillfully; or seem to depreciate in the slightest degree the important part industrial schools must play in the accomplishment of these ends, but I *do* say, and insist upon it, that it is industrialism drunk with its vision of success, to imagine that its own work can be accomplished without providing for the training of broadly cultured men and women to teach its own teachers, and to teach the teachers of the public schools.

But I have already said that human education is not simply a matter of schools; it is much more a matter of family and group life—the training of one's home, of one's daily companions, of one's social class. Now the black boy of the South moves in a black world—a world with its own leaders, its own thoughts, its own ideals. In this world he gets by far the larger part of his life training, and through the eyes of this dark world he peers into the veiled world beyond. Who guides and determines the education which he receives in his world? His teachers here are the group-leaders of the Negro people—the physicians and clergymen, the trained fathers and mothers, the influential and forceful men about him of all kinds; here it is, if at all, that the culture of the surrounding world trickles through and is handed on by the graduates of the higher schools. Can such culture training of group leaders be neglected? Can we afford to ignore it? Do you think that if the leaders of thought among Negroes are not trained and educated thinkers, that they will have no leaders? On the contrary a hundred half-trained demagogues will still hold the places they so largely occupy now, and hundreds of vociferous busy-bodies will multiply. You have no choice; either you must help furnish this race from within its own ranks with thoughtful men of trained leadership, or you must suffer the evil consequences of a headless misguided rabble.

I am an earnest advocate of manual training and trade teaching for black boys, and for white boys, too. I believe that next to the founding of Negro colleges the most valuable addition to Negro education since the war, has been industrial training for black boys. Nevertheless, I insist that the object of all true education is not to make men carpenters, it is to make carpenters men; there are two means of making the carpenter a man, each equally important: the first is to give the group and community in which he works, liberally trained teachers and leaders to teach him and his family what life means; the second is to give him sufficient intelligence and technical skill to make him an efficient workman; the first object demands the Negro college and college-bred men—not a quantity of such colleges, but a few of excellent quality; not too many college-bred men, but enough to leaven the lump, to inspire the masses, to raise the Talented Tenth to leadership; the second object demands a good system of common schools, well-taught, conveniently located and properly equipped.

The Sixth Atlanta Conference truly said in 1901:

"We call the attention of the Nation to the fact that less than one million of the three million Negro children of school age, are at present regularly attending school, and these attend a session which lasts only a few months.

"We are to-day deliberately rearing millions of our citizens in ignorance, and at the same time limiting the rights of citizenship by educational qualifications. This is unjust. Half the black youth of the land have no opportunities open to them for learning to read, write and cipher. In the discussion as to the proper training of Negro children after they leave the public schools, we have forgotten that they are not yet decently provided with public schools.

"Propositions are beginning to be made in the South to reduce the already meagre school facilities of Negroes. We congratulate the South on resisting, as much as it has, this pressure, and on the many millions it has spent on Negro education. But it is only fair to point out that Negro taxes and the Negroes' share of the income from indirect taxes and endowments have fully repaid this expenditure, so that the Negro public school system has not in all probability cost the white taxpayers a single cent since the war.

"This is not fair. Negro schools should be a public burden, since they are a public benefit. The Negro has a right to demand good common school training at the hands of the States and the Nation since by their fault he is not in position to pay for this himself."

What is the chief need for the building up of the Negro public school in the South? The Negro race in the South needs teachers to-day above all else. This is the concurrent testimony of all who know the situation. For the supply of this great demand two things are needed—institutions of higher education and money for school houses and salaries. It is usually assumed that a hundred or more institutions for Negro training are to-day turning out so many teachers and college-bred men that the race is threatened with an over-supply. This is sheer nonsense. There are to-day less than 3,000 living Negro college graduates in the United States, and less than 1,000 Negroes in college. Moreover, in the 164 schools for Negroes, 95 per cent. of their students are doing elementary and secondary work, work which should be done in the public schools. Over half the remaining 2,157 students are taking high school studies. The mass of so-called "normal" schools for the Negro, are simply doing elementary common school work, or, at most, high school work, with a little instruction in methods. The Negro colleges and the post-graduate courses at other institutions are the only agencies for the broader and more careful training of teachers. The work of these institutions is hampered for lack of funds. It is getting increasingly difficult to get funds for training teachers in the best modern methods, and yet all over the South, from State Superintendents, county officials, city boards and school principals comes the wail, "We need TEACHERS!" and teachers must be trained. As the fairest minded of all white Southerners, Atticus G. Haygood, once said: "The defects of colored teachers are so great as to create an urgent necessity for training better ones. Their excellencies and their successes are sufficient to justify the best hopes of success in the effort, and to vindicate the judgment of those who make large investments of money and service, to give to colored students opportunity for thoroughly preparing themselves for the work of teaching children of their people."

The truth of this has been strikingly shown in the marked improvement of white teachers in the South.

Twenty years ago the rank and file of white public school teachers were not as good as the Negro teachers. But they, by scholarships and good salaries, have been encouraged to thorough normal and collegiate preparation, while the Negro teachers have been discouraged by starvation wages and the idea that any training will do for a black teacher. If carpenters are needed it is well and good to train men as carpenters. But to train men as carpenters, and then set them to teaching is wasteful and criminal; and to train men as teachers and then refuse them living wages, unless they become carpenters, is rank nonsense.

The United States Commissioner of Education says in his report for 1900: "For comparison between the white and colored enrollment in secondary and higher education, I have added together the enrollment in high schools and secondary schools, with the attendance on colleges and universities, not being sure of the actual grade of work done in the colleges and universities. The work done in the secondary schools is reported in such detail in this office, that there can be no doubt of its grade."

He then makes the following comparisons of persons in every million enrolled in secondary and higher education:

	WHOLE COUNTRY.	NEGROES.
1880	4,362	1,289
1900	10,743	2,061

And he concludes: "While the number in colored high schools and colleges had increased somewhat faster than the population, it had not kept pace with the average of the whole country, for it had fallen from 30 per cent. to 24 per cent. of the average quota. Of all colored pupils, one (1) in one hundred was engaged in secondary and higher work, and that ratio has continued substantially for the past twenty years. If the ratio of colored population in secondary and higher education is to be equal to the average for the whole country, it must be increased to five times its present average." And if this be true of the secondary and higher education, it is safe to say that the Negro has not one-tenth his quota in college studies. How baseless, therefore, is the charge of too much training! We need Negro teachers for the Negro common schools, and we need first-class normal schools and colleges to train them. This is the work of higher Negro education and it must be done.

Further than this, after being provided with group leaders of civilization, and a foundation of intelligence in the public schools, the carpenter, in order to be a man, needs technical skill. This calls for trade schools. Now trade schools are not nearly such simple things as people once thought. The original idea was that the "Industrial" school was to furnish education, practically free, to those willing to work for it; it was to "do" things—i. e.: become a center of productive industry, it was to be partially, if not wholly, self-supporting, and it was to teach trades. Admirable as were some of the ideas underlying this scheme, the whole thing simply would not work in practice; it was found that if you were to use time and material to teach trades thoroughly, you could not at the same time keep the industries on a commercial basis and make them pay. Many schools started out to do this on a large scale and went into virtual bankruptcy. Moreover, it was found also that it was possible to teach a boy a trade mechanically, without giving him the full educative benefit of the process, and, vice versa, that there was a distinctive educative value in teaching a boy to use his hands and eyes in carrying out certain physical processes, even though he did not actually learn a trade. It has happened, therefore, in the last decade, that a noticeable change has come over the industrial schools. In the first place the idea of commercially remunerative industry in a school is being pushed rapidly to the background. There are still schools with shops and farms that bring an income, and schools that use student labor partially for the erection of their buildings and the furnishing of equipment. It is coming to be seen, however, in the education of the Negro, as clearly as it has been seen in the education of the youths the world over, that it is the *boy* and not the material product, that is the true object of education. Consequently the object of the industrial school came to be the thorough training of boys regardless of the cost of the training, so long as it was thoroughly well done.

Even at this point, however, the difficulties were not surmounted. In the first place modern industry has taken great strides since the war, and the teaching of trades is no longer a simple matter. Machinery and long processes of work have greatly changed the work of the carpenter, the ironworker and the shoemaker. A really efficient workman must be to-day an intelligent man who has had good technical training in addition to thorough common school, and perhaps even higher training. To meet this situation the industrial schools began a further development; they established distinct Trade Schools for the thorough training of better class artisans, and at the same time they sought to preserve for the purposes of general education, such of the simpler processes of elementary trade learning as were best suited therefor. In this differentiation of the Trade School and manual training, the best of the industrial schools simply followed the plain trend of the present educational epoch. A prominent educator tells us that, in Sweden, "In the beginning the economic conception was generally adopted, and everywhere manual training was looked upon as a means of preparing the children of the common people to earn their living. But gradually it came to be recognized that manual training has a more elevated purpose, and one, indeed, more useful in the deeper meaning of the term. It came to be considered as an educative process for the complete moral, physical and intellectual development of the child."

Thus, again, in the manning of trade schools and manual training schools we are thrown back upon the higher training as its source and chief support. There was a time when any aged and wornout carpenter could teach in a trade school. But not so to-day. Indeed the demand for college-bred men by a school like Tuskegee, ought to make Mr. Booker T. Washington the firmest friend of higher training. Here he has as helpers the son of a Negro senator, trained in Greek and the humanities, and graduated at Harvard; the son of a Negro congressman and lawyer, trained in Latin and mathematics, and graduated at Oberlin; he has as his wife, a woman who read Virgil and Homer in the same class room with me; he has as college chaplain, a classical graduate of Atlanta University; as teacher of science, a graduate of Fisk; as teacher of history, a graduate of Smith,—indeed some thirty of his chief teachers are college graduates, and instead of studying French grammars in the midst of weeds, or buying pianos for dirty cabins, they are at Mr. Washington's right hand helping him in a noble work. And yet one of the effects of Mr. Washington's propaganda has been to throw doubt upon the expediency of such training for Negroes, as these persons have had.

Men of America, the problem is plain before you. Here is a race transplanted through the criminal foolishness of your fathers. Whether you like it or not the millions are here, and here they will remain. If you do not lift them up, they will pull you down. Education and work are the levers to uplift a people. Work alone will not do it unless inspired by the right ideals and guided by intelligence. Education must not simply teach work—it must teach Life. The Talented Tenth of the Negro race must be made leaders of thought and missionaries of culture among their people. No others can do this work and Negro colleges must train men for it. The Negro race, like all other races, is going to be saved by its exceptional men.

SOJOURNER TRUTH

Address to the First Annual Meeting of the American Equal Rights Association [1867]

In 1867, overriding a veto by President Andrew Johnson, Congress granted the right to vote to African American men in the District of Columbia. This victory for black male suffrage sparked a speech by Sojourner Truth (1797?–1883), delivered on May 6, 1867, in which she explores the dangers that inequality of power holds for black women. Truth's warning not to wait until things settle down to demand women's suffrage proved to be prescient. It did "take a great while" (until 1920) for women to secure the right to vote throughout the United States.

Abolitionist and women's rights activist Sojourner Truth (originally Isabella Bomefree, or Baumfree) grew up in slavery in Ulster County, New York. Shortly before July 4, 1827 (the date New York State emancipated people born into slavery before July 4, 1799). Truth escaped with the youngest of her five children, finding refuge with a nearby couple, Isaac and Maria Van Wagenen (or Wagener). The Van Wagenens paid Isabella's former enslaver $20 to prevent her recapture, and she became known as Isabella Van Wagenen. In 1843, after settling in New York City, she renamed herself Sojourner Truth, meaning "itinerant preacher." Truth eventually became a prominent speaker on women's rights, civil rights, and religion. In an April 1863 article for *The Atlantic Monthly*, the novelist Harriet Beecher Stowe (p. 118) described Truth's power as a speaker: "I do not recollect ever to have been conversant with any one who had more of that silent and subtle power which we call personal presence. [. . .] She seemed perfectly self-possessed and at her ease. [. . .] An audience was what she wanted—it mattered not whether high or low, learned or ignorant. She had things to say, and was ready to say them at all times, and to any one."

Not only was Truth an active participant in debates during her lifetime, but recently the historical account of her words has also fueled debates about how her persona was shaped by others. Because she was unable to write, her words survived only through the filter of transcriptions and reports. (The speech reprinted here was transcribed and published the following day in the *New York Tribune*.) Even her "autobiography," *The Narrative of Sojourner Truth* (1850), was filtered in that it was transcribed by the white abolitionist Olive Gilbert from Truth's dictation—Gilbert is credited by some publishers as the editor or the writer of the work, reflecting her role as a "collaborator" on or a "mediator" in the creation of the text. One key source of controversy is Truth's famous 1851 speech for women's rights, popularized as "Ain't I a Woman" in the 1863 transcription by the white American abolitionist and feminist Frances Dana Barker Gage (1808–1884). The heavy dialect of Gage's version contrasts sharply with other versions, such as the 1851 report of the speech the white American abolitionist Marius Robinson, in which the phrase "ain't I a woman" does not even appear.

From the *New York Tribune*, May 10, 1867.

M y Friends, I am rejoiced that you are glad, but I don't know how you will feel when I get through. I come from another field—the country of the slave. They have got their rights—so much good luck. Now what is to be done about it? I feel that I have got as much responsibility as anybody else. I have as good rights as anybody. There is a great stir about colored men getting their rights, but not a word about the colored women;

and if colored men get their rights, and not colored women get theirs, there will be a bad time about it. So I am for keeping the thing going while things are stirring; because if we wait still it is still, it will take a great while to get it going again. White women are a great deal smarter and know more than colored women, while colored women do not know scarcely anything. They go out washing, which is about as high as a colored woman gets, and their men go about idle, strutting up and down; and when the women come home, they ask for their money and take it all, and then scold because there is no food. I want you to consider on that, chil'n. I want women to have their rights. In the courts women have no right, no voice; nobody speaks for them. I wish woman to have her voice there among the pettifoggers. If it is not a fit place for women, it is unfit for men to be there. I am above eighty years old; it is about time for me to be going. But I suppose I am kept here because something remains for me to do; I suppose I am yet to help break the chain. I have done a great deal of work—as much as a man, but did not get so much pay. I used to work in the field and bind grain, keeping up with the cradler; but men never doing no more, got twice as much pay. So with the German women. They work in the field and do as much work, but do not get the pay. We do as much, we eat as much, we want as much. I suppose I am about the only colored woman that goes about to speak for the rights of the colored woman, I want to keep the thing stirring, now that the ice is broken. What we want is a little money. You men know that you get as much again as women when you write, or for what you do. When we get our rights, we shall not have to come to you for money, for then we shall have money enough of our own. It is a good consolation to know that when we have got this we shall not be coming to you any more. You have been having our right so long, that you

think, like a slaveholder, that you own us. I know that it is hard for one who has held the reins for so long to give up; it cuts like a knife. It will feel all better when it closes up again. I have been in Washington about three years, seeing about those colored people. Now colored men have a right to vote; and what I want is to have colored women have the right to vote. There ought to be equal rights more than ever, since colored people have got their freedom.

I know that it is hard for men to give up entirely. They must run in the old track. I was amused how men speak up for one another. They cannot bear that a woman should say anything about the man, but they will stand here and take up the time in man's cause. But we are going, tremble or no tremble. Men are trying to help us. I know that all—the spirit they have got; and they cannot help us much until some of the spirit is taken out of them that belongs among the women. Men have got their rights, and women has not got their rights. That is the trouble. When woman gets her rights man will be right. How beautiful that will be. Then it will be peace on earth and good will to men. But it cannot be until it be right. [***] It will come. [***] Yes, it will come quickly. It must come. And now when the waters is troubled, and now is the time to step into the pool. There is a great deal now with the minds, and now is the time to start forth. [***] The great fight was to keep the rights of the poor colored people. That made a great battle. And now I hope that this will be the last battle that will be in the world. Let us finish up so that there be no more fighting. I have faith in God and there is truth in humanity. Be strong women! Blush not! Tremble not! I want you to keep a good faith and good courage. And I am going round after I get my business settled and get more equality. People in the North, I am going round to lecture on human rights. I will shake every place I go to.

FREDERICK DOUGLASS
Letter to Josephine Sophia White Griffing [1868]

The abolitionist movement brought together black and white Americans in the fight against slavery. Once slavery had been abolished, the movement's leaders redirected the skills honed on abolitionist platforms to the fight for suf-frage. That shift strained earlier alliances between prominent white female reformers and black reformers (male and female), who often disagreed on which fight should take precedence: women's suffrage or black suffrage.

Frederick Douglass, who called himself "a woman's-rights-man," had long stressed a connection between civil rights and women's rights. He had spoken at the historic 1848 Woman's Rights Convention in Seneca Falls, New York, giving an "excellent and appropriate speech, [which] ably supported the cause of woman," according to the convention proceedings. In an editorial on the convention, published on July 28, 1848, Douglass underscored his support of women's suffrage, arguing: "All that distinguishes man as an intelligent and accountable being, is equally true of woman, and if that government only is just which governs by the free consent of the governed, there can be no reason in the world for denying to woman the exercise of the elective franchise, or a hand in making and administering the laws of the land."

The question of whether black (male) or (white) women's suffrage should be given precedence caused a division between Douglass and a number of women's rights leaders, including Elizabeth Cady Stanton and Susan B. Anthony. Douglass's 1868 letter to Josephine Sophia White Griffing (1814–1872), a white American reformer active in both the anti-slavery and the women's rights movements, alludes to the growing division between leaders in the black and women's suffrage movements. Griffing had previously demonstrated her sustained commitment to civil rights by moving to Washington after the Civil War to help newly freed African Americans obtain jobs and homes. Her lobbying efforts resulted in the creation of the federal Freemen's Bureau in 1865 to aid the 4 million former slaves in the United States.

From Joseph Borome, "Two Letters of Frederick Douglass," *The Journal of Negro History* 33, no. 4 (October 1948): 469–71.

Rochester, Sept. 27, 1868

My dear Friend:

I am impelled by no lack of generosity in refusing to come to Washington to speak in behalf of woman's suffrage. The right of woman to vote is as sacred in my judgment as that of man, and I am quite willing at any time to hold up both my hands in favor of this right. It does not however follow that I can come to Washington or go elsewhere to deliver lectures upon this special subject. I am now devoting myself to a cause not more sacred, certainly more urgent, because it is one of life and death to the long-enslaved people of this country; and this is: Negro suffrage. While the negro is mobbed, beaten, shot, stabbed, hanged, burnt, and is the target of all that is malignant in the North and all that is murderous in the South, his claims may be pre-

ferred by me without exposing in any wise myself to the imputation of narrowness or meanness towards the cause of woman. As you very well know, woman has a thousand ways to attach herself to the governing power of the land and already exerts an honorable influence on the course of legislation. She is the victim of abuses, to be sure, but it cannot be pretended I think that her cause is as urgent as that of ours. I never suspected you of sympathizing with Miss Anthony and Mrs. Stanton in their course. Their principle is: that no negro shall be enfranchised while woman is not. Now, considering that white men have been enfranchised always and colored men have not, the conduct of these white women, whose husbands, fathers and brothers are voters, does not seem generous.

Very truly yours,
Fred Douglass

Frederick Douglass and Frances Ellen Watkins Harper
from *Proceedings of the American Equal Rights Association Convention* [1869]

The debate over the primacy of black male versus women's suffrage did not break down neatly along gender lines, and there were prominent black female leaders on

both sides. At the 1869 convention of the American Equal Rights Association in New York City, the writer and activist Frances Ellen Watkins Harper joined Frederick

Douglass (p. 38) in asserting that black male suffrage should be given preference "if the nation could only handle one question." Nevertheless, Harper remained a strong proponent of women's suffrage.

The American Equal Rights Association was founded in 1866 by Douglass, Elizabeth Cady Stanton, and Susan B. Anthony in order to bring together the women's rights and racial-equality movements to fight for universal suffrage. Disagreements about race and gender were primary factors in the disintegration of the association in 1869, which led to the establishment of two rival suffrage groups: the American Woman Suffrage Association, which remained committed to equal rights for African Americans, and the National Woman Suffrage Association, established by Stanton and Anthony to focus on white women's rights. After the American Equal Rights Association was disbanded, Harper became a member of the American Woman Suffrage Association and often spoke for women's suffrage at public meetings. Unlike others in the women's suffrage movement, Harper supported the Fourteenth and Fifteenth Amendments, which granted voting rights to black men but not to black (or white) women. Her support for those amendments was based on her belief that black Americans needed an immediate political voice to protect them from lynching and other severe manifestations of discrimination. (The Fourteenth Amendment, which introduced the word *male* into the Constitution for the first time, was proposed by Congress in 1866 and ratified in 1868; the Fifteenth Amendment was proposed by Congress in 1869, the year of the American Equal Rights Association Convention, and ratified in 1870.)

Frances Ellen Watkins was born to free parents in 1825 in Baltimore. When she was three years old, her mother died, and she was raised by an aunt and uncle. Her uncle, William Watkins, was a leading abolitionist, and Frances was educated at his school, the Academy for Negro Youth. Her uncle's activism helped shape her later work as a leading campaigner for abolition, civil rights, women's rights, and temperance. In 1854, after four years as a teacher, she became a lecturer in her role as a representative of the State Anti-Slavery Society of Maine. She curtailed her busy lecturing schedule after marrying Fenton Harper in 1860 and giving birth to a daughter, Mary, in 1862. Like her predecessors Jarena Lee and Maria W. Stewart, Harper was widowed early in her marriage, and she resumed public lecturing after her husband's death in 1864. After the Civil War, Harper toured the South, helping with Reconstruction efforts and campaigning for education for former slaves. In 1896, she joined other prominent black female activists— including Ida B. Wells, Harriet Tubman, and Mary Church Terrell—to found the National Association of Colored Women, and she served as its vice president until her death, in 1911.

In addition to her work as an activist, Harper was a prominent writer. When she was fourteen, she began working as a domestic for a Quaker couple, who gave her access to their library and encouraged her literary efforts. She published her first volume of poetry, *Forest Leaves*, in 1845, and went on to publish numerous collections of poetry and works of fiction, including the novel *Iola Leroy* (1892). Harper's 1859 story "The Two Offers" was the first short story published by an African American.

From "Proceedings of the American Equal Rights Association Convention, Steinway Hall, New York City, May 12, 1869," in *Frederick Douglass on Women's Rights,* edited by Philip S. Foner (Westport, Conn.: Greenwood Press, 1976), pp. 86–90.

MR. DOUGLASS:—I come here more as a listener than to speak and I have listened with a great deal of pleasure to the eloquent address of the Rev. Mr. Frothingham and the splendid address of the President. There is no name greater than that of Elizabeth Cady Stanton in the matter of woman's rights and equal rights, but my sentiments are tinged a little against *The Revolution.*[1] There was in the address to which I allude the employment of certain names, such as "Sambo," and the gardener, and the bootblack, and the daughters of Jefferson and Washington and other daughters. (Laughter.) I must say that I asked what difference there is between the daughters of Jefferson and Washington and other daughters. (Laughter.) I must say that I do not see how any one can pretend that there is the same urgency in giving the ballot to woman as to the negro.

---

1. Newspaper focused on women's rights, edited and published from 1868 to 1870 by the prominent white American feminists Elizabeth Cady Stanton (1815–1902) and Susan B. Anthony (1820–1906).

With us, the matter is a question of life and death, at least, in fifteen States of the Union. When women, because they are women, are hunted down through the cities of New York and New Orleans; when they are dragged from their houses and hung upon lamp-posts; when their children are torn from their arms, and their brains dashed out upon the pavement; when they are objects of insult and outrage at every turn; when they are in danger of having their homes burnt down over their heads; when their children are not allowed to enter schools; then they will have an urgency to obtain the ballot equal to our own. (Great applause.)

A Voice.—Is that not all true about black women?

Mr. Douglass.—Yes, yes, yes; it is true of the black woman, but not because she is a woman, but because she is black. (Applause.) Julia Ward Howe,[2] at the conclusion of her great speech delivered at the convention in Boston last year said: "I am willing that the negro shall get the ballot before me. (Applause.) Woman! why, she has 10,000 modes of grappling with her difficulties. I believe that all the virtue of the world can take care of all the evil. I believe that all the intelligence can take care of all the ignorance. (Applause.) I am in favor of woman's suffrage in order that we shall have all the virtue and vice confronted. Let me tell you that when there were few houses in which the black man could have put his head, this wooly head of mine found a refuge in the house of Mrs. Elizabeth Cady Stanton, and if I had been blacker than sixteen midnights, without a single star, it would have been the same. (Applause.)

Miss Anthony:—The old anti-slavery school says women must stand back and wait until the negroes shall be recognized. But we say, if you will not give the whole loaf of suffrage to the entire people, give it to the most intelligent first. (Applause.) If intelligence, justice, and morality are to have precedence in the Government, let the question of woman be brought up first and that of the negro last. (Applause.) While I was canvassing the State with petitions and had them filled with names for our cause to the Legislature, a man dared to say to me that the freedom of women was all a theory and not a practical thing. (Applause.) When Mr. Douglass mentioned the black man first and the woman last, if he had noticed he would have seen that it was the men that clapped and not the women. There is not the woman born who desires to eat the bread of dependence, no matter whether it be from the hand of father, husband, or brother; for any one who does so eat her bread places herself in the power of the person from whom she takes it. (Applause.) Mr. Douglass talks about the wrongs of the negro; but with all the outrages that he to-day suffers, he would not exchange his sex and take the place of Elizabeth Cady Stanton. (Laughter and applause.)

Mr. Douglass:—I want to know if granting you the right of suffrage will change the nature of our sexes? (Great laughter.)

Miss Anthony:—It will change the pecuniary position of woman; it will place her where she can earn her own bread. (Loud applause.) She will not then be driven to such employments only as man chooses for her.

Mrs. Norton said that Mr. Douglass' remarks left her to defend the Government from the inferred inability to grapple with the two questions at once. It legislates upon many questions at one and the same time, and it has the power to decide the woman question and the negro question at one and the same time. (Applause.)

Mrs. Lucy Stone:—Mrs. Stanton will, of course, advocate the precedence for her sex, and Mr. Douglass will strive for the first position for his, and both are perhaps right. If it be true that the government derives its authority from the consent of the governed, we are safe in trusting that principle to the uttermost. If one has a right to say that you can not read and therefore can not vote, then it may be said that you are a woman and therefore cannot vote. We are lost if we turn away from the middle principle and argue for one class. [***] Zz The gentleman who addressed you claimed that the negroes had the first right to the suffrage, and drew a picture which only his great word-power can do. He again in

---

2. Julia Ward Howe (1819–1910), prominent white American abolitionist and writer of "The Battle Hymn of the Republic," said these words at a meeting in Boston in 1868 to form the New England Women's Suffrage Association; unlike the National Women's Suffrage Association, led by Elizabeth Cady Stanton and Susan B. Anthony, Howe's group supported the passage of the Fifteenth Amendment giving black men the right to vote, with women's suffrage to follow.

Massachusetts, when it had cast a majority in favor of Grant and negro suffrage, stood upon the platform and said that woman had better wait for the negro; that is, that both could not be carried, and that the negro had better be the one. But I freely forgave him because he felt as he spoke. But woman suffrage is more imperative than his own; and I want to remind the audience that when he says what the Ku-Kluxes did all over the South, the Ku-Kluxes here in the North in the shape of men, take away the children from the mother, and separate them as completely as if done on the block of the auctioneer. Over in New Jersey they have a law which says that *any* father—he might be the most brutal man that ever existed—*any* father, it says, whether he be under age or not, may by his last will and testament dispose of the custody of his child, born or to be born, and that such disposition shall be good against all persons, and that the mother may not recover her child; and that law modified in form exists over every State in the Union except in Kansas. Woman has an ocean of wrongs too deep for any plummet, and the negro, too, has an ocean of wrongs that can not be fathomed. There are two great oceans; in the one is the black man, and in the other is the woman. But I thank God for that XV. Amendment, and hope it will be adopted in every State. I will be thankful in my soul if *any* body can get out of the terrible pit. But I believe that the safety of the government would be more promoted by the admission of woman as an element of restoration and harmony than the negro. I believe that the influence of woman will save the country before every other power. (Applause.) I see the signs of times pointing to this consummation, and I believe that in some parts of the country women will vote for the President of the United States in 1872. . . .

* * *

MRS. PAULINA W. DAVIS said she would not be altogether satisfied to have the XVth Amendment passed without the XVIth, for woman would have a race of tyrants raised above her in the South, and the black women of that country would also receive worse treatment than if the Amendment was not passed. Take any class that have been slaves, and you will find that they are the worst when free, and become the hardest masters. The colored women of the South say they do not want to get married to the negro, as their husbands can take their children away from them, and also appropriate their earnings. The black women are more intelligent than the men, because they have learned something from their mistresses. She then related incidents showing how black men whip and abuse their wives in the South. One of her sister's servants whipped his wife every Sunday regularly. (Laughter.) She thought that sort of men should not have the making of the laws for the government of the women throughout the land. (Applause.)

MR. DOUGLASS said that all disinterested spectators would concede that this Equal Rights meeting had been pre-eminently a Woman's Rights meeting. (Applause.) They had just heard an argument with which he could not agree—that the suffrage to the black men should be postponed to that of the women. [* * *] "I do not believe the story that the slaves who are enfranchised become the worst of tyrants. (A voice—"Neither do I." Applause.) I know how this theory came about. When a slave was made a driver, he made himself more officious than the white driver so that his master might not suspect that he was favoring those under him. But we do not intend to have any master over us. (Applause.)"

THE PRESIDENT (MRS. STANTON) argued that not another man should be enfranchised until enough women are admitted to the polls to outweigh those already there. (Applause.) She did not believe in allowing ignorant negroes and foreigners to make laws for her to obey. (Applause.)

MRS. HARPER (colored) said that when it was a question of race, she let the lesser question of sex go. But the white women all go for sex, letting race occupy a minor position. She liked the idea of work-women, but she would like to know if it was broad enough to take colored women.

MISS ANTHONY and several others: Yes, yes.

MRS. HARPER said that when she was at Boston there were sixty women who left work because one colored woman went to gain a livelihood in their midst. (Applause.) If the nation could only handle one question, she would not have the black woman put a single straw in the way, if only the men of the race could obtain what they wanted. (Great applause.) . . .

PART TWO ~ *Works Cited*

Quotations and statistics in this section's headnotes and notes were drawn from the following sources:

Brown, Hallie Q. *Homespun Heroines and Other Women of Distinction*. Xenia, Ohio: Aldine Pub. Co., 1926.

Douglass, Frederick. "Honor To Whom Honor" ("Why I Became a 'Woman's Rights Man'" speech). *Life and Times of Frederick Douglass: His Early Life as a Slave, His Escape from Bondage, and His Complete History to the Present Time*. Hartford, CT: Park Publishing Co, 1881, 473–82.

Douglass, Frederick. "The Rights of Women." *The North Star*. July 28, 1848.

Du Bois, W. E. B. "The Evolution of Negro Leadership." *Dial*, XXXI (July 16, 1901), 53–55.

Du Bois, W. E. B. "The Parting of the Ways." *World Today* 6 (April 1904), 521–32.

Du Bois, W. E. B. Telegram to Booker T. Washington, August 24, 1895. Reprinted in Harlan, Louis R., ed. *Booker T. Washington Papers*, vol. 4 (Illinois: University of Illinois Press, 1975), 26.

Du Bois, W. E. B. "Three Senior Bishops." *The Crisis*. July 1915, 129–132.

Esedebe, P. Olisanwuche. *Pan-Africanism: The Idea and Movement, 1776–1991*. Washington, D.C.: Howard University Press, 1994.

Gage, Frances D. "Sojourner Truth." *National Anti-Slavery Standard*. May 2, 1863, 4.

Gilbert, Olive, ed. *Narrative of Sojourner Truth: A Northern Slave*. 1850. Reprinted as *Narrative of Sojourner Truth: A Bondwoman of Olden Time*. Margaret Washington, ed. New York: Vintage, 1993.

King, Martin Luther, Jr. "Honoring Dr. Du Bois, Address delivered on February 23, 1968 at the Freedomways Magazine International Cultural Evening, New York, N.Y." *Freedomways* 8 (1968): 104–11.

Lewis, David Levering. *W. E. B. Du Bois: The Fight for Equality and the American Century 1919–1963*. New York: Henry Holt and Company, 2000.

Lincoln, Abraham. "Speech on Reconstruction." Washington, D.C. April 11, 1865.

Logan, Rayford W. *The Negro in American Life and Thought: The Nadir, 1877–1901*. New York: The Dial Press, 1954.

McMurry, Linda O. *To Keep the Waters Troubled: The Life of Ida B. Wells*. New York: Oxford University Press, 1998.

"Proceedings of the Woman's Rights Conventions, Held at Seneca Falls and Rochester, New York, July and August, 1848." New York: R. J. Johnson, printer, 1870.

Redkey, Edwin S., ed. *Respect Black: The Writings and Speeches of Henry McNeal Turner*. New York: Arno Press, 1971.

Robinson, Marius. "Women's Rights Convention: Sojourner Truth," *The Anti-Slavery Bugle* (Salem, Ohio), 6, 41 (June 21, 1851): 160. Reprinted in Painter, Nell Irvin. *Sojourner Truth: A Life, A Symbol*. New York: W. W. Norton, 1996, 125–26.

Singleton, Benjamin "Pap". Singleton Scrapbook, unpaginated fliers. Cited in Painter, Nell Irvin. *Exodusters: Black Migration to Kansas after Reconstruction*. New York: W. W. Norton, 1992, 115.

Stowe, Harriet Beecher. "Sojourner Truth, The Libyan Sibyl." *The Atlantic Monthly* 11 (April 1863): 473–81.

PART THREE

The Great Migration and the Harlem Renaissance (1910–1929)

In 1910, only 1 million of America's 9.8 million black citizens lived outside the South. Between 1910 and 1930, the black population outside the South more than doubled as over 1 million more African Americans fled the South. This mass movement was the first wave of the twentieth century's Great Migration, which began about 1910, gained strength during World War I, and continued through the 1920s. A second wave began in the 1940s, during World War II. Both waves of the Great Migration were spurred by a number of factors. In the South, African Americans continued to face economic hardship and political disenfranchisement. Given the precariousness of their finances, southern black sharecroppers were especially vulnerable to the severe flooding and boll weevil invasions that plagued the region. (Boll weevils are beetles that destroy cotton plants, thus damaging crops.) Many rural African Americans were prompted to flee to southern cities, but the lack of economic opportunities there, along with an increase in anti-black terrorism, drove the migration to northern cities.

Even as those negative forces generated the massive exodus of African Americans from the South, various positive aspects of life in the North attracted the migrants. Most important, industrial development in the North created employment opportunities for black workers in factories and, particularly, in the service industries abandoned by white workers who were moving into higher-paying factory jobs. With the advent of World War I in Europe in 1914, the demand for war goods meant even more jobs in the North just as the supply of new immigrant workers diminished as a result of disruptions caused by the war.

The effects of World War I on the lives of African Americans went far beyond the immediate economic opportunities the war fostered. Over 200,000 black Americans served in the military in Europe, an experience that afforded them a glimpse of people and cultures whose ideas about race were less rigid and less discriminatory than those of many whites back home. That experience, along with a dramatic increase in terrorism against African Americans in the South after the war (aimed in particular at returning soldiers emboldened by their service abroad) further fueled the Great Migration.

With the increase in the black population in the North came an explosion in the size and influence of the black press, a phenomenon that helped northern cities develop into centers of black arts and politics. Black publications in turn helped to drive further migration by reaching readers in the South as well as the North. In the North, journalists could report on civil rights abuses without the fear of reprisal faced by their southern counterparts. The Pan-African activist Marcus Garvey and his Universal Negro Improvement Association (UNIA), the NAACP, and the National Urban League all used their official publications to promote their causes. The popular magazines of the last two organizations—*The Crisis* and *Opportunity,* respectively—helped create a "renaissance" in African American culture that flourished in the 1920s, an era of unprecedented creative development in African American literature, theater, and art. This explosion— commonly known as the Harlem Renaissance because so many of its most influential artists and writers lived in New York City's Harlem neighborhood—launched the careers of many foundational artists, including the jazz musicians Duke Ellington and Louis Armstrong, the classic blues singers Mamie Smith and Bessie Smith, and the writers Langston Hughes and Zora Neale Hurston, and led to worldwide recognition of African American culture and arts.

Not all of the changes spurred by The Great Migration were positive, however. The exodus of black laborers from the South and the sudden influx of black migrants in the North increased racial tension in both regions. During the Red Summer of 1919, named for the blood that was shed, over twenty race riots broke out across the country, all of them initiated by white Americans. In response, black Americans joined political organizations such as the NAACP in unprecedented numbers. In a fundamental shift in both attitude and actions that was heralded as the New Negro movement, a growing number of assertive, self-confident African Americans began using political protest and the arts to fight for cultural, social, and political change. On the political level, organizations committed themselves to both fighting prejudice and raising awareness of racial violence, with the NAACP making the passage of a federal anti-lynching law its top priority. (The law was never passed.)

In October 1929, the stock market crashed. As the nation slid into the Great Depression, the sense of hope and the economic opportunities that had fueled the Great Migration, the New Negro movement, and the Harlem Renaissance dimmed. By then, however, those political and cultural movements had begun to transform the very fabric of American life, setting the stage for the profound political and cultural transformations that would come during and after the 1960s. As the novelist Nella Larsen told an interviewer in 1929, "Even if the fad for our writings passes presently, as it is bound to do I suppose, we will in the meantime have laid the foundation for our permanent contribution to American culture." Yet even prescient artists and activists of the period, such as Larsen, could scarcely have imagined the profoundly transforming legacy of their cultural and political achievements. That legacy would take decades to realize.

KEY DEBATE ⁓ *Migration and Emigration*

Letters from Southern African Americans to the *Chicago Defender* [1917]

In the early part of the twentieth century, the black press played a critical role in mobilizing prospective migrants in the South. The *Chicago Defender,* one of the leading black-owned papers in the North, led a campaign to urge African Americans to leave the South. On January 6, 1917, the *Defender* announced "the Great Northern Drive," setting May 15 of that year as the day for "Millions to Leave the South." Robert Abbott, the editor of the *Defender,* correctly hypothesized that for the tens of thousands of black Americans who had been considering migration, naming a particular day for the move would provide the motivation they needed to make the commitment, even though the reports of reduced railroad fares and other special arrangements for that day proved to be false. The *Defender* also advanced the cause of migration by publishing job advertisements that helped would-be migrants make concrete plans, and it fielded numerous letters from prospective migrants, heightening public awareness of and enthusiasm for migration to the North. The three letters from the *Defender* that follow, all from May 1917, demonstrate the range in age, experience, and preparedness among southern African Americans seeking better opportunities in the North.

From the *Chicago Defender,* May 11, 19, and 21, 1917.

Selma, Ala., May 19, 1917.

DEAR SIR: I am a reader of the Chicago Defender I think it is one of the Most Wonderful Papers of our race printed. Sirs I am writeing to see if You all will please get me a job. And Sir I can wash dishes, wash iron nursing work in groceries and dry good stores. Just any of these I can do. Sir, who so ever you get the job from please tell them to send me a ticket and I will pay them. When I get their as I have not got enough money to pay my way. I am a girl of 17 years old and in the 8 grade at Knox Academy School. But on account of not having money enough I had to stop school. Sir I will thank you all with all my heart. May God Bless you all. Please answer in return mail.

Mobile, Ala., May 11, 1917.

DEAR SIR AND BROTHER: on last Sunday I addressed you a letter asking you for information and I have received no answer. but we would like to know could 300 or 500 men and women get employment? and will the company or thoes that needs help send them a ticket or a pass and let them pay it back in weekly payments? We have men and women here in all lines of work we have organized a association to help them through you.

We are anxiously awaiting your reply.

New Orleans, La., May 21, 1917.

DEAR SIR: As it is my desire to leave the south for some portion of the north to make my future home I desided to write to you as one who is able to furnish proper information for such a move. I am a cook of plain meals and I have knowledge of industrial training. I received such training at Tuskegee Inst. some years ago and I have a letter from Mrs. Booker T. Washington bearing out such statement and letters from other responsible corporations and individuals and since I know that I can come up to such recommendations, I want to come north where it is said such individuals are wanted. Therefore will you please furnish me with names and addresses of railroad officials to whom I might write for such employment as it is my desire to work only for railroads, of possible. I have reference to officials who are over extra gangs, bridge gangs, paint gangs and pile drivers over any boarding department which takes in plain meals. I have 25 years experience in this line of work and understand the method of saving the company money.

You will please dig into this in every way that is necessary and whatever charges you want for your trouble make your bill to me, and I will mail same to you.

Wishing you much success in your papers throughout the country, especially in the south as it is the greatest help to the southern negro that has ever been read.

Letters from African Americans Printed in Southern Papers

E. W. COOKE: Letter to *The Montgomery Advertiser* [1917]

R. TAYLOR: Letter to Professor T. Atwater [1917]

THE REVEREND I. N. FRITZPATRICK: *from* Letter to *The Atlanta Constitution* [1917]

In contrast to the encouraging letters and editorials printed by the northern press (p. 251), letters from African Americans that were printed in southern papers often ranged from cautiously to strongly anti-migration. E. W. Cooke's letter to *The Montgomery Advertiser* suggests that some migration is good but warns that most migrants are not prepared for what they find in the North. Echoing the famous phrase of the accommodationist Booker T. Washington, Cooke argues that many southern black Americans would fare better if they "cast down their buckets where they are."

R. Taylor's letter, on the other hand, offers a positive assessment of the fate of southerners who have migrated to the urban North. He warns new migrants, however, of the high cost of housing and urges them either to secure employment before making the move or to bring enough money to support themselves during a job search. The Reverend I. N. Fritzpatrick offers a third take on migration, rejecting it wholesale and asserting that southern African Americans would be better off remaining in the South because "the southern people (white) know the indiosyncracies of the uncultured Negro and, with such sympathy, will make allowances for his shortcomings and defects." Fritzpatrick, an elderly pastor of the African Methodist Episcopal (AME) church and president of the Law and Order League, goes so far as to assert that the lynchings plaguing the South are extreme—but understandable—reactions to criminal lawbreaking.

E. W. COOKE

Letter to *The Montgomery Advertiser* [1917]

Editor: Please, may I have the space to say a few New Year words on this unsettled question of Negro exodus? Since my letter of November 1st, I have been made to know some things that I had not up to that, been published; such as the box car crowding, death on the roads and in the mines of the places where our people are engaged to work. On receiving a letter from Mr. W. A. Wadsworth of Prattville, Ala., in a friendly and fairminded way, he expressed the real deplorable condition under which most of our people had to live and work after leaving here. Since then I have met with some who have come back. I heartily agree with him that it is not the going that we so much oppose, but the manner of going and the mode of living after going, are the facts that make the inner man revolt. Then, too, the coming back to take less jobs than some of them had before leaving and therefore receiving less pay and consideration than if they had not gone. As Mr. Wadsworth has further said: "If those who go will stay, then it will be better for those who remain." Races, like crops, need thinning out and so that the others that are left can thrive more vigorously and be more productive. I still contend that our people in masses are not prepared to leave this part of the country, from the fact that they do not know conditions and will have to do much suffering before learning the same. There are three things the unlearned and uneducated Negro has not learned and which very much handicap us in working with the class of people that look upon these as being very essential to success. They are accuracy of work, quickness of work and continuation of work. The average unlearned Negro works down here about eight months in the year and uses the other four for what he calls a good time, and then at the end of the year holds that the white man has changed his account. He did change it, but the Negro was the cause, for he was feeding the Negro his mule as well as his family, sometimes families when the Negro was frolicking or stepping off to see somebody. When he is at work he loses three days in the week at his best. He takes Saturday to get ready for Sunday, Sunday is his all day, Monday he gets in late and has as his excuse his wife was sick last night or he had such a cramp in the stomach that he thought he was going to die, so it takes him that day to get right for the next. Lots of times he hasn't been home more than one hour before reporting to work. Thus his account got changed. I think we have a dance they call the "slow drag." This fittingly expresses the kind of work that class of Negro has been doing. Not "slow drag" dancing, but "slow drag" farming. Left without intelligent guidance he exhibits no interest in neither stock or tools, and is thus a constant worry and expense to the employer. This kind of service will bankrupt a nation, to say nothing of the South. One only has to look around the fields and the homes of this class to observe that no accuracy is displayed.

I am glad to see that the churches are taking a prominent part in helping to intelligently direct our people as to what is best to do, but I feel that the church should also impress the fact and insist upon it being one of the fundamental principles of religion, that "an honest man is the noblest workman of God,"[1] and should place more emphasis on economy and living at home. Gathering up the fragments is a great part of Scriptural teaching. I believe that it is the schools' duty to co-operate with the State to make its citizens through the boys and girls, by making them industrious and self-supporting. It is all right to teach a man to know how to increase his desires, but to leave off teaching him how to supply these desires, we have only a half man. In other words, we have been too largely consumers and not producers of our many needs. I am glad to say, however, that the young men who have come out from these institutions of learning are not those who are crowding themselves off to other places to get jobs. For the most part they are finding a way or helping to make one. Therefore, the Negro should be encouraged educationally, so that whatever he does will be done intelligently.

Now since the springtime is near at hand, I feel that the white people should bestir themselves and have as many acres of land cultivated as possible; for every acre of land that is idle is fifty dollars or more taken from their bank account. Land that is not cultivated is like machinery lying idle and is a constant expense. Since this change has come, the white man should help to pick the best and most desirable colored citizens and make provisions for them to stay where they are. I say desirable, because there are many desirable ones and all of us will be delighted to see these remain. The white people can do this by having meetings and devising plans and means by which the colored man can see his way clear, and he will be too glad to enter into the race of partnership with the spirit of work and its return. I do not believe in the mob idea of keeping the Negroes away from the trains, for that is but little better than the box car method of taking them North; but to talk to him as man to man such as no one knows like the white man, how to reach the Negro's heart for after all you can do more with him through his heart than any other way. It is a fact that the white man is most easily reached through his pocket book, but if you want to use a Negro, it must be done through his feelings.

When we have chosen this better class of people, the manly thing then to do is to stand squarely by our choice and see that justice and fair play be given in proportion as they measure up to the responsibility and requirements; hence we will have a better land, more thrifty people, and safer homes. Mr. Wadsworth is thoroughly right when he says that the Negro is not looking for social equality. There is no respectable Negro that would have his social life changed by external force, for he delights to have the other man stay out of his functions. In many cases, his leaving this section is purely for the want of encouragement and the want of needed advice. Let some of our best white farmers be made president and officers of the Farm Bank Association and use this money in ways that will save the farms. Then, they can both advise and do. Now is the time for the "Solid South" to act.

Some are constantly writing to us and others are coming to ask what is the best thing to do. We have, in nearly every case, made them see that they should "cast down their buckets where they are."[2] If the white people will get together in money matters and devise plans to lead us, we are no less disobedient than heretofore, and will be sure to follow. It is useless to discuss

---

1. Paraphrase of "an honest Man's the noblest work of God" from Alexander Pope's "An Essay on Man" [Epistle IV, line 248].
2. Reference to Booker T. Washington's advice to African Americans in the South to "cast down your bucket where you are"; from Washington's 1895 Atlanta Compromise Speech [p. 206].

the evils of either race, for "there is so much good in the worst of us, and so much bad in the best of us, that it hardly behooves any of us to talk about the rest of us." We all must allow the great Shepherd of the Universe to lead us into green pastures, besides the still waters in the valleys of the Sunny South.[3]

From *The Montgomery Advertiser,* January 11, 1917.

R. TAYLOR
Letter to Professor T. Atwater [1917]

DEAR SIR: Please publish this letter. Those who came from the South to this city are making good.

This city has a population of 500,000, for which 40,000 are colored and they find employment in shops, mills and foundries. The colored people are not Jim Crowed here, but are admitted to the public parks and other places of interest. Color don't cut any ice here. We have not had any summer weather yet, there is a continual cool breeze which makes it pleasant during the day; the nights are real cool.

The greatest trouble that the newcomer is having is to find somewhere to live. So many have come until one cannot find a house very easily. Houses rent from $20.00 to $30.00 per month. I would not advise anyone to think of coming North unless you are prepared to take care of yourself until a job is secured.

Mr. Editor, I thank you very much for publishing my former letter. Please continue to send me the Enterprise as I am lonesome without it. I hope you a continued succes in all of your plans.

From the *Rome (Ga.) Enterprise,* July 21, 1917.

THE REVEREND I. N. FRITZPATRICK
from Letter to *The Atlanta Constitution* [1917]

EDITOR CONSTITUTION: I delivered the annual sermon of the Atlanta district conference of the A.M.E. Church in the city of Atlanta a few days ago. When the minutes were read the following morning, on motion to adopt, one of the preachers of the Conference rose up and asked me why, in my sermon of the day before, I advised the colored people to remain in the South. I told him I would answer this question through the columns of the *Constitution.*

I now re-iterate my statements with emphasis, without fear of successful contradiction. Having traveled extensively through portions of Great Britain, Europe and Africa, and throughout the states, and having come in contact with different nations and races, I feel competent to advise my people for their best interest. I know that the South is the Negro's best home, because he is better known and better understood by the southern white people, who have grown up with him and by many considered as one family. The northern people do not know these intrinsic ties. The southern people (white) know the indiosyncracies of the uncultured Negro and, with such sympathy, will make allowances for his shortcomings and defects.

I know that many of my race have been lynched, but let the Negro strive to remove the cause leading up to this infraction of the law, as well as to condemn the act of lynching. Let the good, law-abiding Negro separate himself from the criminal classes and seek to expose and apprehend such villains and turn them over to. [* * *][1]

From *The Atlanta Constitution,* August 30, 1917.

---

3. Paraphrase of Psalm 23: 1–2, "The LORD is my shepherd; I shall not want. He maketh me to lie down in green pastures: he leadeth me beside the still waters."
1. The remainder of the letter is missing. [Editor's note]

Representing the Great Migration

CHICAGO COMMISSION ON RACE RELATIONS: *A Negro Family Just Arrived in Chicago from the Rural South* [1919]
GEORGE EDMUND HAYNES: *These Are They with Hope in Their Hearts* [1918]

Photographs of migrants from the Great Migration are rare. The few that do exist create radically different impressions of how migrants looked. Among the most-often reproduced photographs is the one shown here, originally published in 1922 by the Chicago Commission on Race Relations, of a stylishly dressed family complete with hats. Their dress, however, would have been highly unusual for a rural southern family newly arrived in Chicago. The second photograph, from a 1918 article by sociologist George Edmund Haynes (1880–1960), co-founder of the National Urban League, shows a family from rural Florida in ill-fitting clothes, outfits that would have been more common for most migrants, who were largely escaping poverty.

A Negro Family Just Arrived in Chicago from the Rural South [1919]

From Chicago Commission on Race Relations, *The Negro in Chicago: A Study of Race Relations and a Race Riot* (Chicago: University of Chicago Press, 1922), p. 92.

These Are They with Hope in Their Hearts [1918]
The boll weevil caused this southern colored family to lose their cotton crop in Florida and they came North chiefly, they say, to give their children better schooling. The picture was taken shortly after their arrival in Newark, N.J.

From George Edmund Haynes, "Negroes Move North," *The Survey* May 4, 1918, vol. 40, No. 5 (New York), p. 117.

THE MESSENGER

Negroes, Leave the South! [1920]

Although the end of World War I was marked by friction between southern African Americans who had migrated to the North and returning white soldiers, the Great Migration persisted through the 1920s, until the Great Depression curtailed job opportunities. Black publications continued to encourage migration after World War I, as is evident in this 1920 editorial from *The Messenger*, which links migration to better opportunities for both migrants and those who stay in the South. It also hints at hardships in the North. Such hardships may have been responsible for the resurrection of emigration movements in the 1920s—most famously, Marcus Garvey's Back to Africa campaign—as new migrants discovered that the South did not hold a monopoly on racism and economic hardship.

From *The Messenger*, March 1920.

Fellow Negroes of the South, leave there. Go North, East, and West—anywhere—to get out of that hell hole. There are better schools here for your children, higher wages for yourselves, votes if you are twenty-one, better housing and more liberty. All is not rosy here, by any means, but it is Paradise compared with Georgia, Arkansas, Texas, Mississippi and Alabama. Besides, you make it better for those you leave behind. Labor becomes scarce, so that the Bourbons of Dixie[1] are compelled to pay your brothers back home more wages. They will give them more schools and privileges, too, to try to get them to come back and, secondly, to try to keep you from leaving.

Stop buying property in the South, to be burned down and run away from over night. Sell out your stuff quietly, saying nothing to the Negro lackeys, and leave! Come into the land of at least incipient civilization!

---

1. Reference to Bourbon Democrats who sought to reestablish white supremacy in the South after the Civil War.

IN THE HEADLINES:
Marcus Garvey's Back to Africa Movement

W. E. B. Du Bois: *from* What Du Bois Thinks of Garvey [1921]
Marcus Garvey: What Garvey Thinks of Du Bois [1921]
Marcus Garvey: *from* W. E. B. Du Bois as a Hater of Dark People [1923]
W. E. B. Du Bois: Marcus Garvey: A Lunatic or a Traitor? [1924]
Zora Neale Hurston: *from* The Emperor Effaces Himself [1925]
A. Philip Randolph: The Only Way to Redeem Africa [1923]
A. Philip Randolph: *from* Battling Du Bois vs. Kid Garvey [1924]

From 1916 through the early 1920s, Marcus Garvey (1887–1940) was the crusading leader of a grassroots black nationalist movement in the United States and the head of the Back to Africa colonization movement. Before coming to the United States in 1916 from his native Jamaica, Garvey had established the Universal Negro Improvement and Conservation Association and African Communities League (known by the initials UNIA), which, according to the edition of its constitution written in 1929, is dedicated to "the general uplift of the people of African ancestry of the world." In the United States, a number of factors propelled the growth of the UNIA, making it the largest black mass movement to date, involving millions of people around the world: the racial unrest following World War I, the persistence of institutionalized racial prejudice, and in the North the large population of uprooted African Americans who had left the South during the Great Migration.

The UNIA pursued a variety of ventures to promote the economic and political independence of black people (funded by the sale of stock to members and nonmembers alike), including a chain of grocery stores and other small businesses. Although many of Garvey's more grandiose plans remained mere visions, the businesses he did establish helped foster his Back to Africa emigration movement. These included *The Negro World,* the official journal of the UNIA, which published Garvey's editorials, and the Black Star Line, a steamship company designed to transport emigrants to Africa. Unfortunately for the UNIA and Garvey, his business acumen did not match his ability to harness the power of black disaffection. The failure of the Black Star Line, incorporated in 1919 and nearly bankrupt within two years, helped bring down Garvey's entire organization. In 1922, Garvey was arrested for mail fraud, and he was imprisoned three years later. In 1927, his sentence was commuted, and he was deported to Jamaica.

Garvey's dedication to black separatism, his rejection of other black leaders and organizations, his financial problems, and his penchant for pomp made him the subject of criticism by prominent African American leaders such as W. E. B. Du Bois, James Weldon Johnson, Zora Neale Hurston, and A. Philip Randolph. Debates between Garvey and other leaders tended to disintegrate into personal attacks, as in the heated exchanges between Garvey and Du Bois reprinted here. The author and Columbia University–trained anthropologist Zora Neale Hurston wrote a satirical review of a Garvey procession, "The Emperor Effaces Himself," which skewers Garvey's pomp and pretense. The unpublished manuscript was discovered posthumously among her papers, and the final pages are missing, most likely lost when many of her papers were burned immediately after her death. A. Philip Randolph's 1923 editorial "The Only Way to Redeem Africa" condemns Garvey's Back to Africa movement, his Black Star Line, and his other enterprises. Although Randolph dismisses most of Garvey's plans, his detailed assessment demonstrates how seriously leaders took Garvey's mass appeal. By 1924, Garvey's waning power had invited Randolph's mock sports commentary, "Battling Du Bois vs. Kid Garvey," which humorously summarizes the match between the two black leaders, tellingly awarding the bout to Du Bois.

W. E. B. DU BOIS

from *What Du Bois Thinks of Garvey* [1921]

When it comes to Mr. Garvey's industrial and commercial enterprises there is more ground for doubt and misgiving than in the matter of his character. First of all his enterprises are incorporated in Delaware, where the incorporation laws are loose and where no financial statements are required. So far as I can find, and I have searched with care, Mr. Garvey has never published a complete statement of the income and expenditures of the Negro Improvement Association or of the Black Star Line or any of his enterprises, which really revealed his financial situation. A courteous letter of inquiry sent to him July 22, 1920, asking for such financial data as he was willing for the public to know, remains to this day unacknowledged and unanswered.

* * *

This is a serious situation, and even this does not tell the whole story: the real estate, furniture, etc., listed above[1] are probably valued correctly. But how about the boats? The Yarmouth is a wooden steamer of 1,452 tons, built in 1887. It is old and unseaworthy; it came near sinking a year ago and it has cost a great deal for repairs. It is said that it is now laid up for repairs with a large bill due. Without doubt the inexperienced purchasers of this vessel paid far more than it is worth, and it will soon be utterly worthless unless rebuilt at a very high cost.

The cases of the Kanawha (or Antonio Maceo) and the Shadyside are puzzling. Neither of these boats is registered as belonging to the Black Star Line at all. The former is recorded as belonging to C. L. Dimon, and the latter to the North and East River Steamboat Company. Does the Black Star Line really own these boats, or is it buying them by installments, or only leasing them? We do not know the facts and have been unable to find out. Under the circumstance they look like dubious "assets."

* * *

Garvey himself tells of one woman who had saved about four hundred dollars in gold: "She brought out all the gold and bought shares in the Black Star Line." Another man writes this touching letter from the Canal Zone: "I was sent twice to buy shares amounting to $125 (numbers of certificates 3742 and 9617). Now I am sending $35 for seven more shares. You might think I have money but the truth, as I stated before, is that I have no money now. But if I'm to die of hunger it will be all right because I'm determined to do all that's in my power to better the conditions of my race."

* * *

On the other hand, full credit must be given Garvey for a bold effort and some success. He has at least put vessels manned and owned by black men on the seas and they have carried passengers and cargoes. The difficulty is that he does not know the shipping business, he does not understand the investment of capital, and he has few trained and staunch assistants.

The present financial plight of an inexperienced and headstrong promoter may therefore decide the fate of the whole movement. This would be a calamity. Garvey is the beloved leader of tens of thousands of poor and bewildered people who have been cheated all their lives. His failure would mean a blow to their faith and a loss of their little savings, which it would take generations to undo.

* * *

Then too, Garvey increases his difficulties in other directions. He is a British subject. He wants to trade in British territory. Why then does he needlessly antagonize and even insult Britain? He wants to unite all Negroes. Why then does he sneer at the work of the powerful group of his race in the United States where he finds asylum and sympathy? Particularly, why does he decry the excellent and rising business enterprises of Harlem—intimating that his schemes alone are honest and sound when the facts flatly contradict him?

---

1. In the longer version of this editorial originally published in *The Crisis*, which was entitled "Marcus Garvey," Du Bois lists the assets and liabilities from the one available balance sheet for the Black Star Line; this balance sheet, originally published July 26, 1920, includes $12,975.01 in furniture and equipment, $26,000 in real estate, and $288,515.37 in boats.

* * *

And, finally, without arms, money, effective organization or base of operations, Mr. Garvey openly and wildly talks of "Conquest" and of telling white Europeans in Africa to "get out!" and of becoming himself a black Napoleon!

* * *

To sum up: Garvey is a sincere, hard-working idealist; he is also a stubborn, domineering leader of the mass; he has worthy industrial and commercial schemes but he is an inexperienced business man. His dreams of Negro industry, commerce and the ultimate freedom of Africa are feasible; but his methods are bombastic, wasteful, illogical and ineffective and almost illegal. If he learns by experience, attracts strong and capable friends and helpers instead of making needless enemies; if he gives up secrecy and suspicion and substitutes open and frank reports as to his income and expenses, and above all if he is willing to be a co-worker and not a czar, he may yet [succeed] in [at least starting some of][2] in his schemes toward accomplishment. But unless he does these things and does them quickly he cannot escape failure.

From *The Crisis*, January 1921; reprinted in the *Baltimore Afro-American*, January 7, 1921.

MARCUS GARVEY
What Garvey Thinks of Du Bois [1921]

The January number of the Crisis magazine contained a four page article on Marcus Garvey. The first half of the article is devoted to a survey of the Black Star Line, the second half is devoted to Mr. Garvey's industrial enterprises and the feasibility of his general plans. The article follows the general line of DuBois[3] articles when treating the products of a Negro's brain, pen or hand. It is 75 percent criticism and 25 percent appreciation.

A brilliant student of sociology, a literary genius, a man of letters, Dr. DuBois could grace a chair in any university in the world, but when it comes to mingling with men and dealing with practical affairs, he sometimes strikes the wrong note. When he taught in Wilberforce University[4] and Atlanta University, and when he gathered facts in Philadelphia for sociological study he could rarely get close to the heart of colored people. His literary ventures, the "Moon" and the "Horizon," did not pan out well. His Niagara movement died a natural death. It was not until a few Boston and New York philanthropists took Dr. DuBois under their aegis and threw around him the prestige of their wealth and fame that he was able to make the Crisis and the NAACP go. And if these men should withdraw their support and prestige the Crisis might go the way of the "Moon" and the "Horizon," and the NAACP might go the way of the Niagara movement.

As we study the personality of Dr. DuBois, we find that he only appreciates one type of men, and that is the cultured, refined type which lingers around universities and attends pink tea affairs. The men of dynamic force of the Negro race, the men with ability to sway and move the masses, Dr. DuBois cannot appraise at their face value, and that is why the author of the "Souls of Black Folk," while the idol of the drawing room aristocrats, could not thus far become the popular leader of the masses of his own race.

To read Dr. DuBois' statement about the Black Star Line, one would imagine that no business concern ever made mistakes and that everything was always smooth sailing.

It took the Crisis, backed by millionaires, by big Negroes and edited by a distinguished scholar over five years to become self supporting. Suppose some over-inquisitive critic, before the NAACP was two years old, should demand an accounting and ask how much the philanthropists and Negro public were

---

2. These words were missing in this condensed version of Du Bois's editorial as it was reprinted in the *Baltimore Afro-American*.
3. During this period, Du Bois was often printed as one word.
4. See footnote 1 on p. 199.

forced to contribute annually to keep the NAACP or the Crisis going, what would DuBois have said?

As a matter of fact, history is not made by the hypersensitive critics of the type of Walter Pater, Mark Pattison, Coventry Patmore, Prof. George Santayana and Dr. W.E.B. DuBois. But the men like Garvey, men of faith and vision, men of one idea, who have thrown their whole personality towards the realization of that idea, have been the makers of history and will be as long as men are men, created in the divine image and breathing the breath of a spiritual life. It was not the doubting Thomas but the crusading Peter and Paul who launched Christianity upon its world career.

Dr. DuBois is undoubtedly right when he says that there is no necessary antagonism between Garvey and other Negro leaders, between the UNIA and other movements for racial uplift. DuBois appeals to the "Talented Tenth," while Garvey appeals to the "Oi Polloi."[5] The NAACP appeals to the Beau Brummell, Lord Chesterfield, kid gloved, silk stocking, creased trousers, patent leather shoe, Bird of Paradise hat and Hudson seal coat with beaver or skunk collar element, while the UNIA appeals to the sober, sane, serious, earnest, hard-working man, who earns his living by the sweat of his brow. The NAACP appeals to the cavalier element in the Negro race, while the UNIA appeals to the self reliant yeomanry. Hence, in no sense are Dr. DuBois and Mr. James Weldon Johnson rivals of Marcus Garvey. DuBois and Johnson as writers and speakers and Garvey as prophet, propagandist and organizer and inspirer of the masses are doing good work and all should be free and unimpeded in perfecting their plans.

The only objection that we have had to some of the Caucasian philanthropists behind Hampton, Tuskegee and NAACP selecting leaders for the Negro race was not because they elevated those Negro leaders who they thought were safe, sane and conservative and whom they could manipulate, but because they attempted to suppress those radical Negroes who manifested initiative, individuality and independence of character, regardless of their intellectual attainments and achievements and their worth as men.

From *The Negro World*, January 1, 1921; reprinted in the *Baltimore Afro-American*, January 7, 1921.

MARCUS GARVEY

from *W. E. B. Du Bois as a Hater of Dark People* [1923]

Calls His Own Race "Black and Ugly," Judging From the White Man's Standard of Beauty
Trick of National Association for the Advancement of Colored People to Solve Problem by Assimilation and Color Distinction

W. E. Burghardt DuBois, the Negro "misleader," who is editor of the "Crisis," the official organ of the National Association for the Advancement of "certain" Colored People, situated at 70 Fifth Avenue, New York City, has again appeared in print. This time he appears as author of an article in the February issue of the "Century" Magazine under the caption, "Back to Africa," in which he makes the effort to criticize Marcus Garvey, the Universal Negro Improvement Association and the Black Star Line. [∗∗∗]

"FAT, BLACK, UGLY MAN"

In describing Marcus Garvey in the article before mentioned, he referred to him as a "little, fat, black man; ugly, but with intelligent eyes and a big head." Now, what does DuBois mean by ugly? This so-called professor of Harvard and Berlin ought to know by now that the standard of beauty within a race is not arrived at by comparison with another race; as, for instance, if we were to desire to find out the standard of beauty among the Japanese people we would not judge them from the Anglo-Saxon viewpoint, but from the Japanese. How he arrives at his conclusion that Marcus Garvey is ugly, being a Negro, is impossible to determine, in that if there is any ugliness in the Negro race it would be reflected more through DuBois than Marcus Garvey, in that he himself tells us that he is a little Dutch, a little French, and a little Negro. Why, in fact, the man is a monstrosity. So, if there is any ugliness it is on the part of DuBois and not on the part of the "little fat, black man with a big head," because all this description is typical of the African. But this only goes to show how much hate DuBois has for the black blood in his veins. Anything that is black, to him, is ugly, is hideous, is monstrous, and this is why in 1917 he had but the lightest of colored people in his office, when one could hardly tell whether it was a white show or a colored vaudeville he was running at Fifth avenue. It was only after the Universal Negro Improvement Association started to pounce upon him and his National Association for the Advancement of Colored People that they admitted that colored element into the association that could be distinguished as Negro, and it was during that period of time that Weldon Johnson and Pickens[1] got a look-in. [* * *]

DuBois and White Company

It is no wonder that DuBois seeks the company of white people, because he hates black as being ugly. That is why he likes to dance with white people, and dine with them, and sometimes sleep with them, because from his way of seeing things all that is black is ugly, and all that is white is beautiful. Yet this professor, who sees ugliness in being black, essays to be a leader of the Negro people and has been trying for over fourteen years to deceive them through his connection with the National Association for the Advancement of Colored People. Now what does he mean by advancing colored people if he hates black so much? In what direction must we expect his advancement? We can conclude in no other way than that it is in the direction of losing our black identity and

becoming, as nearly as possible, the lowest whites by assimilation and miscegenation.

This probably is accountable for the bleaching processes and the hair straightening escapades of some of the people who are identified with the National Association for the Advancement of Colored People in their mad desire of approach to the white race, in which they see beauty as advocated by the professor from Harvard and Berlin. It is no wonder some of these individuals use the lip stick, and it is no wonder that the erudite Doctor keeps a French Beard. Surely that is not typical of Africa, it is typical of that blood which he loves so well and which he bewails in not having more in his veins—French.

Lazy and Dependent

In referring to the effort of Marcus Garvey and the Universal Negro Improvement Association to establish a building in Harlem, he says in the article: "There was a long, low, unfinished church basement roofed over. It was designed as the beginning of a church long ago, but abandoned. Marcus Garvey roofed it over, and out of this squat and dirty old Liberty Hall he screams his propaganda. As compared with the homes, the business and church, Garvey's basement represents nothing in accomplishment and only waste in attempt."

Here we have this "lazy dependent mulatto" condemning the honest effort of his race to create out of nothing something which could be attributed to their ownership, in that the "dirty old Liberty Hall" he speaks of is the property of Negroes, while in another section of his article he praises the "beautiful and luxurious buildings" he claims to be occupied by other black folk, making it appear that these buildings were really the property of these people referred to, such as, according to his own description, "a brick block on Seventh Avenue stretching low and beautiful from the Y.W.C.A. with a moving picture house of the better class and a colored 5 and 10 cent store, built and owned by black folks." DuBois knows he lies when he says that the premises herein referred to were built and are

---

1. William Pickens (1881–1954), educator, author, and activist; as NAACP field secretary, Pickens was one of eight leaders who sent a letter entitled "Garvey Must Go" to the U.S. Attorney General, helping to propel Garvey's arrest; James Weldon Johnson (1871–1938), author, critic, and activist; for brief biography, see p. 311.

owned by black folks. They are the property of industrious Jews who have sought an outlet for their surplus cash in the colored district. [* * *]

INDEPENDENT NEGRO EFFORT

Liberty Hall represents the only independent Negro structure referred to in the classification of DuBois about buildings up in Harlem, but he calls this independent effort "dirty and old," but that which has been contributed by white people he refers to in the highest terms. This shows the character of the man—he has absolutely no respect and regard for independent Negro effort but that which is supported by white charity and philanthropy, and why so? Because he himself was educated by charity and kept by philanthropy. He got his education by charity, and now he is occupying a position in the National Association for the Advancement of Colored People, and it is felt that his salary is also paid by the funds that are gathered in from the charity and philanthropy of white people. This "soft carpet" idea is going to be the undoing of W. E. B. DuBois. He likes too much the luxurious home and soft carpets, and that is why he is naturally attracted to white folks, because they have a lot of this; but if he were in Georgia or Alabama he would now be stepping on the carpets of Paradise; but that is not all of the man, as far as this is concerned. He ridicules the idea that the Universal Negro Improvement Association should hold a social function in Liberty Hall on the 10th of August, 1922, at which certain social honors were bestowed upon a number of colored gentlemen, such as Knighthood and the creation of the Peerage.

SOCIAL HONORS FOR NEGROES

In referring to the matter, he says in the article: "Many American Negroes and some others were scandalized by something which they could but regard as a simple child's play. It seemed to them sinister. This enthronement of a demagogue, a blatant boaster, who with monkey-shines was deluding the people, and taking their hard-earned dollars; and in high Harlem there arose an insistent cry, 'Garvey Must Go!'" Indeed

DuBois was scandalized by the creation of a Peerage and Knighthood by Negroes, and in truth the person who is responsible for such a thing should go, because DuBois and those who think like him can see and regard honor conferred only by their white masters. If DuBois was created a Knight Commander of the Bath by the British King, or awarded a similar honor by some white Potentate, he would have advertised it from cover to cover of the "Crisis," and he would have written a book and told us how he was recognized above his fellows by such a Potentate, but it was not done that way. This was an enthronement of Negroes, in which DuBois could see nothing worth while.

[* * *]

COMPARISON BETWEEN TWO MEN

Marcus Garvey was born in 1887; DuBois was born in 1868; that shows that DuBois is old enough to be Marcus Garvey's father. But what has happened? Within the fifty-five years of DuBois' life we find him still living on the patronage of good white people, and with the thirty-six years of Marcus Garvey (who was born poor and whose father, according to DuBois, died in a poor house) he was able to at least pass over the charity of white people and develop an independent program originally financed by himself to the extent of thousands of dollars, now taken up by the Negro peoples themselves. Now which of the two is poorer in character and in manhood? The older man, who had all these opportunities and still elects to be a parasite, living off the good will of another race, or the younger man, who had sufficient self-respect to make an effort to do for himself, even though in his effort he constructs a "dirty brick building" from which he can send out his propaganda on race self-reliance and self-respect.

MOTIVE OF DUBOIS

To go back to the motive of DuBois in the advocacy of the National Association for the Advancement of Colored People is to expose him for what he is. The National Association for the Advancement of Colored People executives have not been honest enough to explain to the people of the Negro race their real solution for the Negro problem, because they are afraid that they would be turned down in their intention. They would make it appear that they are interested in the advancement of the Negro people of America, when, in truth, they are but interested in the subjugation of certain types of the Negro race and the assimilation of as many [* * *] as possible into the white race.

[* * *]

GARVEY CHALLENGES DUBOIS

DuBois says that "Garvey had no thorough education and a very hazy idea of the technique of civilization." DuBois forgets that Garvey has challenged him over a dozen times to intellectual combat, and he has for as many times failed to appear. Garvey will back his education against that of DuBois at any time in the day from early morning to midnight, and whether it be in the classroom or on the public platform, will make him look like a dead duck on a frozen lake.

IS DUBOIS EDUCATED

DuBois seems to believe that the monopoly of education is acquired by being a graduate of Fisk, Harvard and Berlin. Education is not so much the school that one has passed through, but the use one makes of that which he has learned.

If DuBois' education fits him for no better service than being a lackey for good white people, then it were better that Negroes were not educated. DuBois forgets that the reason so much noise was made over him and his education was because he was among the first "experiments" made by white people on colored men along the lines of higher education. No one experimented with Marcus Garvey, so no one has to look upon him with surprise that he was able to master the classics and graduate from a university.

DuBois is a surprise and wonder to the good white people who experimented with him, but to us moderns

he is just an ordinarily intelligent Negro, one of those who does not know what he wants.

THE MAN WHO LIES

DuBois is such a liar when it comes to anything relating to the Universal Negro Improvement Association, the Black Star Line and Marcus Garvey that we will not consider his attacks on the Black Star Line seriously. He lied before in reference to this corporation and had to swallow his vomit. He has lied again, and we think a statement is quite enough to dispose of him in this matter.

This envious, narrow-minded man has tried in every way to surround the Universal Negro Improvement Association and Marcus Garvey with suspicion. He has been for a long time harping on the membership of the Universal Negro Improvement Association as to whether we have millions of members or thousands. He is interested because he wants to know whether these members are all paying dues or not, in that he will become very interested in the financial end of it, as there would be a lot of money available. DuBois does not know that whether the Universal Negro Improvement Association had money or not he wouldn't have the chance of laying his hands on it, in that there are very few "leaders" that we can trust with a dollar and get the proper change. This is the kind of leadership that the Universal Negro Improvement Association is about to destroy for the building up of that which is self-sacrificing; the kind of leadership that will not hate poor people because they are poor, as DuBois himself tells us he does, but a kind of leadership that will make itself poor and keep itself poor so as to be better able to interpret the poor in their desire for general uplift. He hates the poor. Now, what kind of leader is he? Negroes are all poor black folk. They are not rich. They are not white; hence they are despised by the great professor. What do you think about this logic, this reasoning, professor? You have been to Berlin, Harvard and Fisk; you are educated and you have the "technique of civilization."

From *The Negro World*, February 13, 1923.

W. E. B. DU BOIS

Marcus Garvey: A Lunatic or a Traitor?
[1924]

In its endeavor to avoid any injustice toward Marcus Garvey and his followers, THE CRISIS has almost leaned backward. Notwithstanding his wanton squandering of hundreds of thousands of dollars we have refused to assume that he was a common thief. In spite of his monumental and persistent lying we have discussed only the larger and truer aspects of his propaganda. We have refrained from all comment on his trial and conviction for fraud. We have done this too in spite of his personal vituperation of the editor of THE CRISIS and persistent and unremitting repetition of falsehood after falsehood as to the editor's beliefs and acts and as to the program of the N.A.A.C.P.

In the face, however, of the unbelievable depths of debasement and humiliation to which this demagog has descended in order to keep himself out of jail, it is our duty to say openly and clearly:

Marcus Garvey is, without doubt, the most dangerous enemy of the Negro race in America and in the world. He is either a lunatic or a traitor. He is sending all over this country tons of letters and pamphlets appealing to Congressmen, business men, philanthropists and educators to join him on a platform whose half concealed planks may be interpreted as follows:

That no person of Negro descent can ever hope to become an American citizen.

That forcible separation of the races and the banishment of Negroes to Africa is the only solution of the Negro problem.

That race war is sure to follow any attempt to realize the program of the N.A.A.C.P.

We would have refused to believe that any man of Negro descent could have fathered such a propaganda if the evidence did not lie before us in black and white signed by this man. Here is a letter and part of a symposium sent to one of the most prominent business men of America and turned over to us; we select but a few phrases; the italics are ours:

"Do you believe the Negro to be a *human being*?

"Do you believe the Negro *entitled to all the rights of humanity*?

"Do you believe that the Negro should be taught *not to aspire to the highest political positions in Governments of the white race,* but to such positions among his own race in a Government of his own?

"Would you help morally *or otherwise* to bring about such a possibility? Do you believe that the Negro should be *encouraged to aspire* to the highest industrial and commercial positions in the countries of the white man in competition with him and to his exclusion?

"Do you believe that the Negro should be encouraged to regard and *respect the rights of all other races* in the same manner as the other races would respect the rights of the Negro?"

The pamphlets include one of the worst articles recently written *by a Southern white man* advocating the deportation of American Negroes to Liberia and several articles by Garvey and his friends. From one of Garvey's articles we abstract one phrase:

"THE WHITE RACE CAN BEST HELP THE NEGRO BY TELLING HIM THE TRUTH, AND NOT BY FLATTERING HIM INTO BELIEVING THAT HE IS AS GOOD AS ANY WHITE MAN."

Not even Tom Dixon or Ben Tillman[1] or the hatefulest enemies of the Negro have ever stooped to a more vicious campaign than Marcus Garvey, sane or insane, is carrying on. He is not attacking white prejudice, he is grovelling before it and applauding it; his only attack is on men of his own race who are striving for freedom; his only contempt is for Negroes; his only threats are for black blood. And this leads us to a few plain words:

1. No Negro in America ever had a fairer and more patient trial than Marcus Garvey. He convicted himself by his own admissions, his swaggering monkey-shines in the court room with monocle and long tailed coat and his insults to the judge and prosecuting attorney.

---

1. White American politician, governor of South Carolina from 1890 to 1894, and U.S. Senator from 1895 to 1918, Benjamin Ryan Tillman promoted the disenfranchisement of African Americans and the establishment of Jim Crow laws, designed to reinstate white supremacy in the South; Thomas Dixon (1864–1946), writer of *The Clansman*, the play celebrating white supremacy and the Ku Klux Klan and the inspiration for D. W. Griffith's film, *The Birth of a Nation* (1915).

2. Marcus Garvey was long refused bail, not because of his color, but because of the repeated threats and cold blooded assaults charged against his organizations. He himself openly threatened to "get" the District Attorney. His followers had repeatedly to be warned from intimidating witnesses and one was sent to jail therefor. One of his former trusted officials after being put out of the Garvey organization brought the long concealed cash account of the organization to this office and we published it. Within two weeks the man was shot in the back in New Orleans and killed. We know nothing of Garvey's personal connection with these cases but we do know that today his former representative lies in jail in Liberia sentenced to death for murder. The District Attorney believed that Garvey's "army" had arms and ammunition and was prepared to "shoot up" colored Harlem if he was released. For these and no other reasons Garvey was held in the Tombs[2] so long without bail and until he had made abject promises, apologizing to the judge and withdrawing his threats against the District Attorney. Since his release he has not dared to print a single word against white folk. All his vituperation has been heaped on his own race.

Everybody, including the writer, who has dared to make the slightest criticism of Garvey has been intimidated by threats and threatened with libel suits. Over fifty court cases have been brought by Garvey in ten years. After my first unfavorable article on Garvey, I was not only threatened with death by men declaring themselves his followers, but received letters of such unbelievable filth that they were absolutely unprintable. When I landed in this country from my trip to Africa I learned with disgust that my friends stirred by Garvey's threats had actually felt compelled to have secret police protection for me on the dock!

Friends have even begged me not to publish this editorial lest I be assassinated. To such depths have we dropped in free black America! I have been exposing white traitors for a quarter century. If the day has come when I cannot tell the truth about black traitors it is high time that I died.

The American Negroes have endured this wretch all too long with fine restraint and every effort at cooperation and understanding. But the end has come. Every man who apologizes for or defends Marcus Garvey from this day forth writes himself down as unworthy of the countenance of decent Americans. As for Garvey himself, this open ally of the Ku Klux Klan should be locked up or sent home.

From *The Crisis*, May 1924.

ZORA NEALE HURSTON

from *The Emperor Effaces Himself* [1925]

Eight modest, unassuming brass bands blared away down Lenox Avenue.[1] It was August 1, 1924, and the Emperor Marcus Garvey was sneaking down the Avenue in terrible dread lest he attract attention to himself. He succeeded nobly, for scarcely fifty thousand persons saw his parade file past trying to hide itself behind numerous banners of red, green, and black.

This self-effacement was typical of Mr. Garvey and his organization. He would have no fuss nor bluster—a few thousand pennants strung across the street overhead, eight or nine bands, a regiment or two, a few floats, a dozen or so of titled officials and he was ready for his annual parade. It was pointed out that the pennants were used solely to indicate the route as the "Royal African Guards" were mounted and the horses had to [be][2] shown which way to go.

2. Nickname for the Manhattan Detention Complex; the original building for the detention center and jail, built between 1835 and 1840, was modeled after an illustration of an Egyptian tomb.
1. Originally part of Sixth Avenue, this primary north-south route through Harlem runs from 110th Street to 147th Street; in 1987, co-named Malcolm X Boulevard.
2. In addition to several missing words, Hurston's typed manuscript contains numerous missing spaces, doubled spaces, and doubled letters, which are corrected in this reprint; Hurston's original spelling is maintained; although Hurston supported herself by working at one point as a personal assistant, her secretarial skills were notoriously poor, and she told a friend: "My idea of Hell is that I would all through eternity be typing a book."

The uniforms worn by the paraders were so colorless that they gave strength to the rumor that Mr. Garvey's visit to Col. Simmons of the K. K. K.[3] had been successful and that he and all of his followers had become members of the "Invisible Empire".

Mr. Garvey himself wore an Admiral's hat hidden under a mass of red and green plumes. Not to appear too partial to the navy, he wore a General's uniform set off by a few fat ropes of gold braid a sash and a sabre. His men wore black suits with stripes of red braid running hither and yon. Perhaps under anyone else they would have been dressed entirely in scarlet, but Mr. Garvey said "no". He was very firm in the matter.

Back in 1920 for his parade Garvey had worn a purple robe with a black hood lined with red and green silk. But he revolted against such gaudiness—hence the plumes.

II

As a military genius he had no faith in himself at all. Tho he was Admiralissimo of the "African Navy", Generalissimo of the "African Legions", he frequently expressed a fearful lack of confidence. But these expressions placed side by side with his mighty accomplishments are proof positive of the man's overwhelming modesty.

"When I get to Africa with my invincible Black Army, I shall not ask Great Britian what she is doing there, I shall tell her to 'get out!. I shall not ask France what she is doing there, I shall tell her to 'get out!' I shall not ask Belgium what she is doing there, I shall tell her to 'get out! and so on until I have kicked every white man out of Africa!"

Perhaps he felt this charming reserve because he had never had a day of military experience in his life.

On the walls of his living room in 129th Street, there hung a large picture of Napoleon. On the opposite wall hung one, still larger, of himself. It is evident he wished no comparisons drawn. If he had, he would have caused them to be hung side by side.

"You already have the governors of Europe trembling" He announced a little further on. "Lloyd George[4] has warned the other statesmen to look out for Marcus Garvey, and you can rest assured that Marcus Garvey is looking out for Lloyd George".

III

With his Negro contemporaries, whom lesser souls might have considered rivals and consequently felt the pangs of jealousy, he was never too busy to pause and pay them compliments. Of W. E. Burghardt Dubois he said: "Fifty years from now, Dubois will still be sending petitions to Congress. Marcus will be coming up the Hudson Bay (river) with a flotilla of battleships, dreadnaughts, cruisers, submarines and aeroplanes to land the first African ambassador in the United States. The next day he will dine at the White House."

The indolence of some of his race bretheren stirred his great spirit. He himself was willing to serve, was eager to save. They not only refrained from saving themselves, but actively objected to his saving so much. Tearfully he read them out—expelled them bodaciously from the race. Bleached and faded, they go mewing about the limbo of nothingness that borders the land of races. Thus passed DuBois, James Weldon Johnson and William Pickens from among the Negro living, and are seen no more.

But with his officers and others who shared his zeal, he was most generous. Of his wealth of titles, he gave and gave till it hurt them to carry all that he gave them. Behold his "Duke of Uganda!" His "Knight Commander of the Sublime Order of the Nile!" "Supreme Deputy Potentates," "High Chancellor," "High Auditor" and "Lords" and "Ladies" aplenty.

For himself he kept almost nothing. He was merely Managing Editor of the Negro World, Pres. of the Black Star Steamship and Navigation Line, Pres.-General of the Universal Negro Imprivement Association, Supreme Ruler of the Sublime Order of the Nile,

---

3. William Joseph Simmons (1880–1945), founder of the second Ku Klux Klan in 1915.
4. David Lloyd George (1863–1945), liberal British statesman from Wales; prime minister of Great Britain during World War I, from 1916–22.

Provisional Pres. of Africa and Commander-in-Chief of the "African Legions".

IV

With rare foresight, he saw that the redeeming of the entire continent of Africa would take time. It would be no easy task to make it safe for the black folk of the world. They must not be too optimistic he told them.

"Ninety days from now (Aug. 1920) we will have an ambassador at the court of France; ninety days from now we will have an ambassador at the court of St. James; ninety days from now we will have an ambassador at the court of St. Petersburg; ninety days from now we will have an ambassador at the court of Moscow; ninety days from now we will have a Black House side by side with the White House in Washington."

He might have demanded the entire site on which the White House stands, but you see, he generously offers to share it. He will permit even the conquered whites to have an executive mansion side by side with his.

V

Democratic soul that he was, he frequently humored the whims of his subordinates. If the military men wished to call themselves the "Royal Afrivan Guards" and trick themselves out in the uniform of the Jamaica Police, he could not find it in his heart to deny them so simple a pleasure. They probably derived great happiness from the parades in which they figured. He yeilded also to the women who wished to call themselves "The Ladies of the Royal Court of Ethiopia."

Modest and reserved himself, he loved those qualities in others. He was most severe with those who endeavored in one way or another to thrust themselves into prominence unduly.

For instance, a stockholder, coming to Garvey's office one day while the guard was absent, actually entered the place unannounced! The President promptly

threw him out again. Such methods of advancing one's self in the world cannot be too vigorously squelched.

A. L. Gaines, Capt. of the African Legions, to whom the organization owed a few hundred dollars, went to the office and brazenly demanded his pay. This flagrant example of selfish greed was put down ruthlessly. The Capt. was thrown out also. How else could Mr. Garvey preach to the world the high spiritual aims of the organization if his officers' minds clung to thoughts of pay? Why, he himself would not accept more than five hundred or more dollars per month— scarcely enough to keep a millionaire alive!

Even Sir William H. Ferris, K. C. S. O. N. (Knight Commander of the Sublime Order of the Nile), Vice Pres. of the U. N. I. A., Treasurr of the Negro Factory Corporation, Literary Ed. of the Negro World was so lacking in taste as to lead a group of factory workers seeking pay into the Imperial suite. He was severely rebuked.

"How dare you bring anyone into my office without my consent"? Mr. Garvey asked him. Any amount of abuse heaped upon such vulgar social climbing would not be too much.

One is not surprised to learn that he hated praise. One of his followers who continually shouted "God and Garvey" at every meeting, was silenced by being made Speaker of the Convention.

VI

Mr. Garvey hired several lawyers to advise him at various times. They were evidently men of small calibres. They purported to be lawyers, but invariably he knew more about legal processes than they. Furthermore, a more sensitive, touchy lot never lived. If Mr. Garvey playfully hinted that [they] were useless and need not clutter up the place any longer, they resigned. He was forced more than once to take cases out of their hands and go into court and conduct them himself. He knew no law, but 'his not to reason why, his but to go and try'.[5]

5. Paraphrase of two lines from Alfred, Lord Tennyson's "The Charge of the Light Brigade": "Theirs not to reason why, / Theirs but to do and die."

Once he was forced to be both lawyer and witness, to ask and answer his own questions.

Garvey, Lawyer: Do you know Capt. Gaines?

Garvey, Witness: Yes.

Garvey, Lawyer: How long have you known him?

Garvey, Witness: Four years.

Garvey, Lawyer: Was he ever employed by you?

Garvey, Witness: Yes

Garvey, Lawyer: In what capacity?

Garvey, Witness: I appointed him Captain of the "African Legions".

Later on, he was forced to conduct his own defense before the U.S. Supreme Court. The Govt. either out of fear of Mr. Garvey, or envy of his great conquests, arrested him on the flimsy charge of using the mails to defraud. Fraud? Ridiculous! Of course, he had sold a few trifling thousand dollars worth of Black Star Line stock before he had a ship, he had sold a few passages to Africa on a ship that did not exist, but what's a few little ships among emperors! But why the cry of fraud? He had taken the people's money and he was keeping it. That was how he had become the greatest man of his race. Booker T. Washington had achieved some local notice for collecting monies and spending it on a Negro school. It had never occurred to him to keep it. Marcus Garvey was much in advance of the old school of thinkers. Hence he stood in places never dreamed of by Booker T. Washington. There have been some whisperings concerning W. E. B. DuBois on account of his efforts to lower the violent mortality rate among his people, and advance their interests generally, but he never learned how to keep the people's money, and so missed true greatness.

Mr. Garvey sat up one night and learned law. The next day he bravely took the burden of the case upon himself. Even tho he realized he had not a chance in the world against the District Attorney, he assumed the responsibility.

"When I get thru with that little Jew Dist. Atty., he will be so small you will have to hunt for him with a candle".

These are some of the telling points he drove home for the defense in spite of the prosecution.

1. Capt. Gaines, prosecution witness on the stand. (The same who had been dismissed without pay by Mr. Garvey, and thrown out of the office)

> **Garvey:** What is your personal opinion of Marcus Garvey—is he honest and sincere?
>
> **Capt. Gaines:** No. He spent the money you got by fraud on race horses and women.

2. Sidney De Bourg: Prosecution witness.

> **Garvey:** Did you ever have a conversation with "Lady" Doctor concerning Marcus Garvey?
>
> **De Bourg:** Yes.
>
> **Garvey:** What was said during this conversation about Marcus Garvey?
>
> **De Bourg:** She said you were impossible and the only thing to do was to let you fall over a precipice and break your neck.

Judge Julien Mack, before whom the case was being tried, asked both sides to rush because a Zionist convention was to be held soon in Chicago, and he wished to be present. With rare self effacement Garvey asked, "Would you rush this case to attend a convention when the liberty of Marcus Garvey is at stake.

His unselfish desire to help is shown by a remark he made to one of his officers out of court.

"I have preached and shown those preachers how to preach, and now I'll show these lawyers how to practice law".

Very Touching! With only one night of law to his name, he was willing to share it with the benighted legal profession.

The he had no college training, he was a thirster after knowledge. After his address to the jury, he decided to study law, and asked a law student about entrance requirements.

Garvey: Do you have to have a college degree?

Student: Yes.

Garvey: How about a man as famous as me—don't they have any special provisions?

The jury endangered his college career by finding him guilty, but Judge Mack was more sympathetic. He urged Mr. Garvey to take a five-year course in Practical Geology as being more helpful than the practice of law.

That instance is not absence of affection for the higher learning. He wanted to be a patron of Letters so he founded or rather created Booker T. Washington University out of a twenty-foot board and nailed it up where all might see. Of course, the alumnae of this university might be only splinters, but even so, it shows the lofty ambition of the man.

VII

He was a fearless seeker after truth. By scientific investigation, he discovered that The Virgin Mary was a black woman, and that Jesus Christ a mulatto who has been "passing" these two thousand years. So, what could be fairer than showing them in their true colors? Or what could be darker? Nothing, according to the 1924 edition of his modest little parade.

VIII

In five years he will be free. Already he has forgiven us our sins and is willing to stay and help us. But the Government says, 'no'. The Black [end of manuscript. Last page missing.]

From the Zora Neale Hurston Collection, Beinecke Rare Book and Manuscript Library, Yale University.

A. Philip Randolph
The Only Way to Redeem Africa [1923]

Of course, there is nothing more normal and logical than that the idea of building up a Negro empire should flow from the "Back to Africa" movement. A word about the difficulties to be overcome. First, with the opposition of the white powers, it would not be possible for the Garvey crowd to even land in Africa. Second, granting that they were allowed to land, they would have nothing to conquer Africa with, for it is not conceivable that Great Britain, France, Italy or America would supply their foe with the means for overthrowing their own dominion anywhere; and there is no spot in Africa where a landing can be effected which is not controlled by a great white power. In Africa, three obstacles would have to be overcome by the Garvey group, namely, the great white powers, the natives who are opposed to alien rule, and nature in Africa, such as the intensely hot tropical climate, the uncultivated soil, the wild beasts and deadly reptiles, together with a forbidding forest. *Neither one of these three obstacles could a group of uneducated, unarmed and unorganized Negroes—such as the Garvey crew—overcome.*

ESTABLISHING A NATION IN JAMAICA

In view of the foregoing difficulties, it ought to be clear to the most Africoid-Negro Garveyite that it would require unlimited technical, scientific skill and knowledge, together with billions of dollars of capital to subdue, harness up and develop the nature aspect of Africa alone, to say nothing of driving out the entrenched white powers and subjecting the intractable natives. *Conquering Africa is not any less difficult than conquering Europe.*

Thus, I think that we are justified in asking the question, that if Mr. Garvey is seriously interested in establishing a Negro nation why doesn't he begin with Jamaica, West Indies (*not Jamaica, Long Island*). Jamaica is but a small island with a population of 850,000—the white population consisting of less than 20,000. Obviously, on a small island where the ratio of black and white inhabitants is 42 to 1 the Negroes ought to be able to overcome the whites and establish control. Then, too, Jamaica is Mr. Garvey's home. He ought to know the geography of the island, the language and customs of the people. In other words, he is far better qualified to establish a Negro nation in Jamaica than he is in Africa—a land which he has never visited, of the customs and languages of whose inhabitants he is entirely ignorant. Besides, I submit that it is much easier to overthrow one white power such as controls Jamaica, than it is to overthrow six white powers equipped with the greatest armies and navies the world has ever known, such as control Africa. And, too, it requires much less capital, less brains, less power. Don't you think that Jamaica is the logical place for Mr. Garvey to begin his plans for establishing a Negro nation?

There is also Liberia who tried to sell her independence to the investment bankers of America for a loan of $5,000,000. If Mr. Garvey is so interested in a Negro nation, why didn't he come to the rescue of Liberia, by raising five millions, to save her from being gobbled up by the American Imperialist Eagle. *No, he didn't do that, but responsible persons say that he raised money presumably as a loan for a redemption fund for Liberia and that only an insignificant part of it was ever used in the interest of Liberia. As an evidence of the thought which Liberia gives the Garvey movement, when President King of Liberia was in the United States seeking a loan of five million dollars, he never had the slightest association in any way with the Garvey outfit.* Besides, Haiti is a struggling black nation which needs help. *Why doesn't Mr. Garvey expel the United States from Haiti?* Here is a black people who won their liberty over a hundred years ago. Now they are under the imperial heel of the United States. Why doesn't Brother Marcus help keep a Negro nation independent instead of trying to build up a new one? For if a Negro nation is all he wants, then he has two: Liberia and Haiti.

PASSING OF EMPIRE BUILDING

But granting that it were possible to establish a black empire in Africa, it would not be desirable. *Black despotism is as objectionable as white despotism.* A black landlord is no more sympathetic with black tenants than white landlords are. A Negro is no more interested in having his pocketbook stolen by a black thief than he is in having it stolen by a white thief. Death is no sweeter at the hands of a black murderer than it is at the hands of a white murderer.

Again, empires are passing. Witness Russia, Germany and Austria-Hungary. Garvey has begun Empire building too late. Even Germany started in the empire business too late. She wanted to build a "mittel europa" from Berlin to Bagdad, but she was thwarted. Great Britain, France, Italy, and Russia of the Czar were not interested in having any more competitors in the empire business. Hence they crushed her. Such would be the fate of an African empire, granting that one could be established. It is also of special moment to note that no people love empires save the ruling class who live by the exploitation of the subject or working class. Such was the reason for the revolt of the Russian people against the Russian empire. *The ruling and subject classes were both white, but that fact did not keep back the revolution.* Note also the revolutions in Germany and Austria-Hungary, and the revolt in Ireland, India and Korea against empire-rule. Then there is Mexico under Diaz. Oppression produced revolutions whether in white or black empires. *Thus, an African empire would last no longer than the African workers became conscious of oppression and their power to remove it, and then, they would overthrow and decapitate a black king as quickly as they would overthrow and decapitate a white king.*

THE BLACK STAR LINE

In harmony with the "Back to Africa," "anti-white man" and "Negro First" doctrines, the Black Star Line is the maritime appositive of the White Star Line, the Red Star Line, etc. Mr. Garvey never took any thought of the existing monopoly in the shipping business, the need of hundreds of millions in capital, banking houses to manipulate international exchange, as well as the necessity of having experts in the shipping game to handle the business. The absence of either one of these indispensables would spell failure to any shipping project, and needless to say that Mr. Marcus neither had nor has either. Think of the Black Star Line competing in maritime affairs when the United States Government is compelled to subsidize the United States Marine. It is difficult to make the shipping business pay when operated by the best brains with unlimited capital. *What will the Black Star Line do without brains or capital?* Negroes can no more expect to succeed in the shipping business than they can hope to succeed in the subway or telephone or gas business in New York City, or in the railroad business between New York and Chicago or New York and Washington, D.C. *These are monopolies that cannot thrive where duplication or competition exists. It is sheer folly to talk of building a ship line to transport Negroes only.* Not enough Negroes travel to Africa, the West Indies—*or to anywhere for that matter*—to support such an enterprise.

It would appear, then, that Mr. Garvey is not so much concerned about the soundness, feasibility or value of a project as he is about getting together something that will duplicate the efforts and works of the whites. As fortune or misfortune would have it, he always selects the most impossible things among the whites to imitate. His policy is to run the entire gamut of slavish imitation from empire building, ship lines, a Black House in Washington, D.C., a Black Cross Nurse, a Provisional President with a Royal Court. (Little different this, eh?) *Presidents don't have courts; it's the pastime of kings; but what's that ridiculous contradiction to the "Most Dishonorable," etc.*

GARVEY'S IMITATION DOCTRINE

The Garveyites are so strong on imitation that they attempt to justify the Black Star Line disgrace by pointing to the millions of dollars that the United States Shipping Board lost. *In other words, if a white man takes arsenic, a Negro ought to take it too.* A sort of getting even policy, with the Negroes always the victim. *Think of Negroes competing in losing money with the United States Government, which has the power to tax both white and black to raise revenue.*

If Mr. Garvey was competing for the first prize for producing the largest number of failures among Negroes, he would win with hands down. All his efforts are of a piece with the Black Star Line in practicality. As fast as one little, dirty, mismanaged, junk grocery shop fails, he starts another one in his senseless efforts to compete with James Butler, Andrew Davey, The Atlantic & Pacific Tea Co. and Daniel Reeves, the largest chain store systems in the world, operating with hundreds of millions of capital, and the greatest business experts in their line.

In order to inveigle the enthusiastic but uncritical, the Brother proceeds from one pipe-dream to another, calling for each and every Negro of the 400 millions in the world, (*remember it's not one more and not one less*) to slip from one to one hundred beans into his various schemes, and new ones are always in the making. Note the Booker T. Washington University, if you please, the Negro Daily *Times,* The Phyllis Wheatley Hotel, the Universal Publishing House. These gestures are intended to impress the Garvey fanatics with the idea that they are owned by the U.N.I.A., that they represent great business strides of the organization, so

that they will not be unwilling to dig down into their jeans again for more cash to drop into the Garvey bottomless money pits. *It is too evident that the running of the Negro Daily Times will rival the Black Star Line in not running.* It is well that the Negro is not fated to depend upon this *Times* to find out the *time* of the happening of anything. They will not be able to even buy the paper, to say nothing about printing it. And, of course, the Booker T. Washington University is mere moonshine. It will neither have students nor teachers. *Students will not trust it to give out knowledge; nor will teachers trust it to give out pay.*

BOGUS MEMBERSHIP

But if there were any ground of reality to his rabid, sensational, theatrical, kaleidoscopic blandishments, then Brother Garvey ought to be able to operate some of the *smaller* things, at least.

For instance, if he actually had 4,500,000 members in his organization paying dues of 40 cents a month, he would have a revenue of $1,800,000 per month or $21,600,000 a year. But it is obvious that if he were getting that revenue, it would not be necessary for the "Yarmouth," a ship for which the U.N.I.A. paid the handsome sum of $145,000, and upon which, according to Mr. Garvey, testifying in the Seventh Municipal District Court, they had lost $300,000 on its first voyage, to be sold at auction, by the United States Marshal on December 2, 1921, for the pitiful sum of $1,625. Nor would it be necessary for the organization to be constantly sued for wages by its employees.

From *The Messenger,* January 1923.

A. PHILIP RANDOLPH

from *Battling Du Bois vs. Kid Garvey*[1]
[1924]

[* * *] Battling DuBois and Kid Garvey face each other with sneers, refuse to shake hands. Gong sounds—fighters are off.

1. The original title in *The Messenger* was "Heavyweight Championship Bout for Afro-American-West Indian Belt, Between Battling DuBois and Kid Garvey . . . Referee—Everybody and Nobody."

First round: Garvey leads, raining blows in DuBois' head: "DuBois goes to Peace Conference to betray Negro peoples of the world."[2] DuBois parries, rushes Garvey to ropes.

Second round: Garvey lands staggering blow to jaw: "DuBois is the agent of the National Association for the Advancement of *Certain* People." DuBois looks dazed and with a lofty Mephistophelian sneer, grunts that "The answer is written in the stars," and flees of Europe; stages Pan-African Pow Wow. . . .

[* * *]

Fourth round: DuBois leads again with light tap: "Believes Garvey is honest and Black Star Line feasible, but—" Garvey, furious, rushes DuBois. They clinch. Garvey does vicious in-fighting: "DuBois is bought and paid for by the white people. The N.A.A.C.P. cannot lead Negroes because it is headed and controlled by white people." Scrappy Weldon Johnson rushes to ringside and threatens to join bout to defend N.A.A.C.P. DuBois, pale and groggy, gropes blindly to corner. . . .

[* * *]

Seven round: DuBois returns from Africa and wades into Garvey with a smashing wicked haymaker to the mid-section: "Garvey is either a lunatic or a traitor"—editorial, May *Crisis*. Garvey crumples up and hits the mat with a deafening thud. Is almost counted out; rises and staggers to corner. DuBois, in a fierce rage, dancing like a wild Indian for Garvey's scalp, lands stiff right to solar plexus, but Garvey is too weak and badly beaten to return to fray. . . .

[* * *]

Decision reserved on account of charge by Kid Garvey that Battling DuBois struck foul blow below the belt, and that gloves were loaded.

From *The Messenger*, June 1924, pp. 179, 184, 193.

---

2. See p. 283 for more on Du Bois's participation in the 1919 Paris Peace Conference.

KEY DEBATE ∼ *Separatism versus Integration*

WILFRED ADOLPHUS DOMINGO

What Are We, Negroes or Colored People? [1919]

By 1919, in the aftermath of the First World War, the word *Negro* regained popularity, fueled by the development of the trope of the "New Negro." (*The New Negro* was an assertive and confident African American—in contrast to the *Old Negro* or *Uncle Tom* type, associated with accommodation and subservience.) In the editorial reprinted here, Wilfred Adolphus Domingo argues that the revived debate over nomenclature— already decades old—should be resolved by settling on the generic term *Negro*, which he prefers to *colored*.

Born in Jamaica in 1889, Domingo was an activist in a Jamaican nationalist group with Marcus Garvey, before immigrating to the United States in 1910. After moving to New York City in 1912, Domingo worked with

socialist and black nationalist groups, associating with leading activists including Chandler Owen and A. Philip Randolph (p. 259). When Garvey immigrated to New York in 1916, Domingo helped him get established, and Garvey appointed Domingo as the first editor of *The Negro World* (the official magazine of Garvey's UNIA) in 1918. Garvey fired him a year later for publishing socialist views, and Domingo became a contributing editor of *The Messenger*, until splitting with Chandler and Owen in 1923. Following a thirteen-year break from politics to develop a Caribbean food importing business, Domingo spent his last decades fighting for Jamaican independence. He died in 1968.

From *The Messenger*, May–June 1919, pp. 23–25.

The discussion as to what should be the racial cognomen of the composite people of Negroid descent living in the Western world is not a new one, but has been a moot question for nearly fifty years. This discussion, strangely enough, has always been waged among the people in question themselves, and while arguing the, to them, momentous matter, the white race, which controls the literature of the world, has gone its way placidly, fixing the term according to local usage or the particular language.

But among the disputants considerable bitterness and acerbity of feelings have been engendered, which in the long run have only helped to make a breach in the ranks of a people who, despite their foibles and intra-racial distinctions, are destined by the dominant white man for a position of social inferiority.

In other words, while we are fighting among ourselves over inconsequentials, the Caucasian keeps his determination fastened to the more important matter of a fixed relationship between himself and us. However,

as the question seems to disturb Negro minds so much and having a definite opinion on the matter, we are treating it editorially without importing either personality or petty antagonisms into the subject.

According to modern ethnologists, the human family is capable of two main divisions, viz., the colorless race and the colored races. This division is arrived at from a purely scientific standpoint. White, as any scientific book or any dictionary proves, is not a color, but is the negation of all colors, and since there is no pigmentation in white people, science correctly regards them as being the colorless race. On the other hand pigment is to be found in the skins of all the colored races whether it be yellow, Mongolian; black, Negro; red, Indian, or brown, Malay. From these major divisions, subdivisions are made, as for instance among the Caucasians, who are classified as Latins, Teutons, Slavs, etc.

It is, therefore, easily seen that the term colored can with equal exactness be applied to a Chinese, a Nubian, an Apache or a Hindu. But the term colored has a special as well as a general usage. When the Kaiser is trying to unite the white people of the world, he refers to the bogey of the colored races uniting; when a person refers to a man of Negroid extraction in the United States, he speaks of a colored man, but that conveys to the hearer's mind no idea as to the man's actual color; but in the West Indies when the word colored is used in statistics or in describing a person, the understanding is that it refers to a person of visible white and black ancestry. Hence the term has three meanings:

The first meaning is scientific, the American meaning is vague and interchangeable with Negro, while the West Indian meaning is definite, if inappropriate. What the West Indian use of the word really implies is that a colored person is a person of white origin but who has been "colored" because of an infiltration of non-white blood, and, but for this coloration, such a person would be white. In other words, the original use of the word came from the white man's reluctance to admit into his racial group anyone who is not altogether white. But this terminology is weak, for by the same process of reasoning, a person of Hindu-Caucasian parentage is a "colored" person, because such a person has an infusion of some kind of pigment into his otherwise colorless self. But out in India such persons have a distinct group name, one that connotes both their social status and their origin—Eurasian. The same thing is also true of the hybrid of Indian and white in Brazil; they are called Mestizo, and not colored.

There is this that can be said, though, of the West Indian usage. It is possible of continued acceptance and currency despite its obvious weakness, because the people so classified have become a more or less exclusive or distinct group with definite color and group interests, which fact makes the term colored one of value to them. The average West Indian of visible white admixture would be insulted to be called a Negro, because he realizes that that word connotes, in that country, a status lower than that connoted by the word colored. Hence, the clinging to an ethnologically vague and philologically inexact terminology. In the United States the situation is different, as there is no material or social gain in the use of either term. Whether a person is called colored or Negro, the dominant white man has a fixed status for that person.

If a man applies for a position and refers to himself as colored, it does not insure him greater possibility of success over the other applicant who refers to himself as a Negro. The two terms are used interchangeably, as both connote to Negroes and Caucasians in America, the same social, civic and industrial destiny. When either colored or Negro is used, it means any person in America who is not a Mongolian, an Indian or a Causian. And, if he hasn't on his native robes, it may even include a Hindu!

Both the words Negro and colored are terminological inexactitudes in so far as they refer to the composite millions of America; for a person one-eighth black is more a "colored" man than is the person who is one-eighth white a Negro. The so-called colored or Negro race, so far as the Western world is concerned, is neither black, yellow nor brown but a composite people carrying in their veins the blood of many different types of the human family. What holds them together is the pressure exerted from the outside upon them by a dominant and domineering stronger race. This pressure has produced oneness of destiny and for that reason the "race" is developing a sentiment and consciousness of unity. Working from the inside is a centrifugal force that tends to disrupt, but stronger than that is the centripetal force exerted by the white man.

The Caucasian has said that if a man has one-sixteenth black blood, such a person is black. While this is an absurdity in logic, still it is a fact in practice, hence such a person has no choice but to accept the name given to the black race, a little of whose blood flows in his veins. To do otherwise would be to proclaim a longing to be included in a race that despises him.

Of the two terms "colored" and "Negro" the former is the weaker, as it is too loose, too inexact and means nothing specific in America; while the latter is generic and is reinforced by a history that is worthy of pride. The word colored, as apart from the people called "colored," connotes shame and implies an insult. Besides, with what kind of logic could anyone insist that such an indefinite adjective as colored should be capitalized? On the other hand, the generic term Negro is gradually being capitalized because the word designates a racial group and not a particular color, and it would be absurd in speaking English to designate color by saying "a Negro hat," but it would be eminently correct to refer to "a colored hat," meaning a hat that is not white.

The word Negro is never used to describe skin color, but rather to fix racial affiliation; while a majority of Negroes are black, nevertheless, even in Africa itself, there are yellow Hottentot, brown Zulu and ebon-black Nubian, all of whom are generally grouped as Negroes.

Whenever color descriptions are being made, the race name is used as a noun and is preceded by a distinguishing adjective thus—a brown-skinned Negro, a yellow Negro or a black Negro. Nor is it correct to think that all black people are Negroes, as the supporters of the word colored unconsciously imply, for there are black Hindus with aquiline features, black Arabs and black Jews. And conversely all so called Negroes of Africa, even if black, have not the other alleged Negro characteristics; for there are aquiline featured Mandingoes with curly hair on the West coast, and straight haired black Somali on the East Coast, while as already pointed out, there are yellow and brown Kaffirs with kinky hair in South Africa. These facts make the conclusion unavoidable that the word Negro covers, as applied to Africa, a people of varying external physical characteristics.

Even as the word Mongolian includes Tartars and Chinese, and Japanese who are of various degrees of mixture of Chinese, Malays and the aboriginal hairy Ainus of their island kingdom, and the word Caucasian includes blonde and "black" Germans, pigmented Spaniards and South Italians and red-headed Celts the word "Negro" can include all the people of African blood in this country who are, because of that blood, given the same ethnological classification. It might be permissible to use the indefinite word colored as a more or less general term, or as a colloquialism, but as a specific racial designation it is fatally weak, as it is not on a par with Malay, Caucasian, Mongolian or Indian; nor is it as terminologically precise as Eurasian or Metizo; nor is it specific in fixing mixture or racial types as muiatto, quadroon, zambo or octoroon! Et[h]nologically, anthropologically and terminologically the word colored cannot stand the test of even a casual examination.

Many persons object to the Negro because they hate its corrupted form "nigger." But have they ever

stopped to think that any word in any language is susceptible of being debased into a corrupted term of contempt? What word would they suggest that is ethnologically exact and yet would be free from being corrupted? The term "nigger" lives largely because of the careful nurture given to it by Negroes themselves. White people can hardly be blamed for using the objectionable corruption when Negroes are the principal peddlers of the term. And what does "nigger" mean? According to the dictionary it is "a term of contempt applied to Negroes," just as the terms "cracker" and "greaser" are terms of contempt applied to certain other peoples. Will white people stop calling Negroes "niggers" because Negroes refer to themselves as colored? That is too childish for belief.

No one has ever heard of any agitation on the part of the natives of Japan to change their national name of Japanese to something else because of the use of the, to them, offensive abbreviated corruption "Jap" by the English speaking world. Instead, they have by their achievements made the words "Jap" and "Japanese" synonyms of prowess, daring, energy and progress— synonyms that are respected and feared by all races of mankind.

Another objection advanced is that the word Negro connotes slavery, but since colored and Negro are synonyms in America, how can one word connote something which the other does not connote? This objection is puerile.

Every one of the other races has a generic race name and since the composite gets its present status from one branch of its origin, it seems but sensible to accept the generic term that specifically designates that branch. Unless they can control American literature, it will be utterly impossible for Negroes to obliterate the word Negro. And the word is more worthy of living than the vague substitute offered. Instead of fighting a windmill and doing the futile. energy-dissipating thing, Negroes should concentrate upon demanding that the word Negro be capitalized in the literature of the English language even as its fellow generic terms Malay, Mongolian, Caucasian and Indian are capitalized. No amount of exclusion from racial newspapers will kill the word, for although no Negro newspaper is so shameless as to use the word "nigger" still that word has great currency among Negroes and is still to be found, in the dictionary. Negroes can do better than fritter away their energy on non-essentials, and start in right now to give prestige to the word Negro, first, by capitalizing it and next by deeds that any race would be proud to have connected with its name.

To sum up: the word "colored" is objectionable because, first, it is philologically weak; second, it is ethnologically inexact; third, its origin is not pleasant; fourth, it tends towards division inside the "race"; fifth, it has comparatively no history; sixth, it cannot be capitalized; seventh, it is a makeshift.

The word Negro, on the other hand, has all the qualities lacking in colored, and is the word, more or less, in one or other of its forms, incorporated into all modern languages.

In the absence of a nomenclature that is satisfactory to all types of so-called Negroes or colored people in America, the word Negro should stand, and it is for the people so designated to use all their influence to see that their race name is lifted from the same literary status as pig, monkey and dog, to the level of other race names, and be spelt with a capital "N."

MARCUS GARVEY

Address to the Second UNIA Convention [1921]

The global changes brought about by the end of World War I renewed momentum for a Pan-African movement. A major promoter of the movement was W. E. B. Du Bois, who organized the First Pan-African Congress—with 57 delegates representing fifteen nations—in Paris in 1919. The Second Pan-African Congress, in 1921, met in London, Brussels, and Paris and drew more than 100 delegates. The Third Pan-African Congress, however, in 1923, was less well attended, due to poor organization, and the Fourth Pan-African Congress, held four years later in New York—after organizers were denied venues in Europe and the West Indies—essentially echoed the resolutions issued at prior congresses. Some difficulties that Du Bois faced in generating momentum for his vision of Pan-Africanism were due to the rising popularity of an alternative Pan-African vision offered by the Jamaican leader Marcus Garvey.

"Garveyism" offered a compelling mix of economic development and race pride. Garvey's idea of an international Buy-Black campaign—led by the black-owned Black Star Line, which was established to transport goods as well as Back to Africa emigrants—captured the imagination of many working-class African Americans. Garveyism began to falter, however, after Garvey's 1923 conviction and 1925 imprisonment for mail fraud in connection with the bankruptcy of the Black Star Line. Garvey's sentence was commuted in 1927, and he was deported. Although he established new headquarters

in Jamaica and Europe, the Pan-African movement he founded became increasingly fragmented in the late 1920s because of financial pressures and internal power struggles.

In 1921, however, when Garvey organized the second UNIA convention in New York City, his influence as a leader in the United States was still rising. In a challenge to Du Bois, Garvey scheduled the convention to take place just prior to the Second Pan-African Congress (to which Garvey had not been invited, an omission Du Bois justified by declaring Garvey's movement "dangerous, ill-considered [and] impracticable"). *The Negro World* harshly criticized Du Bois's conference, with a June 1921 editorial claiming that Du Bois was running it like "an exclusive college function." To underscore differences between the movements, Garvey made a point of publicly inviting Du Bois to his UNIA convention, publishing the invitation in the pages of *The Negro World*. Garvey also attacked Du Bois's decision to include white representatives "from the colonial offices of Europe," writing in *The Negro World* on August 13, 1921: "Just imagine that! It reminds me of the conference of rats endeavoring to legislate against the cats and the secretary of the rats convention invites the cat to preside over the convention." At the UNIA conference, held August 1 to 31, delegates unanimously passed a resolution rejecting Du Bois's Pan-African "movement," which was then cabled to European journalists.

In his closing-night speech at the convention, reprinted here, Garvey positions himself as the alternative to Du Bois, demonstrating how he, with the support of the "400,000,000 Negroes of the world," was prepared to lead the way to a separate and powerful future.

From *The Negro World*, September 10, 1921.

MARCUS GARVEY SPEAKS

Immediately the President-General arose, smiling and bowing to the right and then to the left like a black Napoleon, whereupon the audience again broke into great cheering and hurrahing, followed by the association yell of the Junior Motor Corps girls. When the audience, after a period of about five minutes, had spent itself, and quiet was restored, the President-General spoke as follows:—

May it please your Highness the Potentate, Right Honorable Members of the Executive Council, Deputies and Delegates to the Second International Convention of Negroes of the World, Ladies and Gentlemen:— We are assembled here tonight to bring to a close our great convention of thirty-one days and thirty-one nights. Before we separate ourselves and take our departure to the different parts of the world from which we came, I desire to give you a message; one that you will, I hope, take home and propagate among the scattered millions of Africa's sons and daughters.

We have been here, sent here by the good will of the 400,000,000 Negroes of the world to legislate in their interests, and in the time allotted to us we did our best to enact laws and to frame laws that in our judgment, we hope, will help solve the great problem that confronts us universally. The Universal Negro Improvement Association seeks to emancipate the Negro everywhere, industrially, educationally, politically and religiously. It also seeks a free and redeemed Africa. It has a great struggle ahead; it has a gigantic task to face. Nevertheless, as representatives of the Negro people of the world we have undertaken the task of freeing the 400,000,000 of our race, and of freeing our bleeding Motherland, Africa. We counselled with each other during the thirty-one days; we debated with each other during the thirty-one days, and out of all we did, and out of all we said, we have come to the one conclusion—

that speedily Africa must be redeemed! (Applause.) We have come to the conclusion that speedily there must be an emancipated Negro race everywhere (applause); and on going back to our respective homes we go with our determination to lay down, if needs be, the last drop of our blood for the defense of Africa and for the emancipation of our race.

The handwriting is on the wall. You see it as plain as daylight; you see it coming out of India, the tribes of India rising in rebellion against their overlords. You see it coming out of Africa, our dear motherland, Africa; the Moors rising in rebellion against their overlords, and defeating them at every turn. (Applause.) According to the last report flashed to this country from Morocco by the Associated Press, the Moors have again conquered and subdued the Spanish hordes. The same Associated Press flashes to us the news that there is a serious uprising in India, and the English people are marshaling their troops to subdue the spirit of liberty, of freedom, which is now permeating India. The news has come to us, and I have a cable in my pocket that comes from Ireland that the Irish are determined to have liberty and nothing less than liberty. (Applause.)

THE LEAGUE OF NATIONS

The handwriting is on the wall, and as we go back to our respective homes we shall serve notice upon the world that we also are coming; coming with a united effort; coming with a united determination, a determination that Africa shall be free from coast to coast. (Applause.) I have before me the decision of the League of Nations. Immediately after the war a Council of the League of Nations was called, and at that Council they decided that the territories wrested from Germany in West Africa, taken from her during the conflict, should be divided between France and England—608,000 square miles—without even asking the civilized Negroes of the world what disposition shall be made of their own homeland, of their own country. An insult was hurled at the civilized Negroes of the world when they thus took upon themselves the right to parcel out and apportion as they pleased 608,000 square miles of our own land; for we never gave it up; we never sold it. It is still our[s]. (Cries of "Yes!") They parceled it out between these two nations—England and France—gave away our property without consulting us, and we are aggrieved, and we desire to serve notice on civilization and on the world that 400,000,000 Negroes are aggrieved. (Cries of "Yes!" and applause.)

And we are the more aggrieved because of the lynch rope, because of segregation, because of the Jim Crowism that is used, practised and exercised here in this country and in other parts of the world by the white nations of the earth, wherever Negroes happen accidentally or otherwise to find themselves. If there is no safety for Negroes in the white world, I cannot see what right they have to parcel out the homeland, the country of Negroes, without consulting Negroes and asking their permission so to do. Therefore, we are aggrieved. This question of prejudice will be the downfall of civilization (applause), and I warn the white race of this, and of their doom. I hope they will take heed, because the handwriting is on the wall. (Applause.) No portion of humanity, no group of humanity, has an abiding right, an everlasting right, an eternal right to oppress other sections or portions of humanity. God never gave them the right, and if there is such a right, man arrogated it to himself, and God in all ages has been displeased with the arrogance of man. I warn those nations which believe themselves above the law of God, above the commandments of God. I warn those nations that believe themselves above human justice. You cannot long ignore the laws of God; you cannot long ignore the commandments of God; you cannot long ignore human justice, and exist. Your arrogance will destroy you, and I warn the races and the nations that have arrogated to themselves the right to oppress, the right to circumscribe, the right to keep down other races. I warn them that the hour is coming when the oppressed will rise in their might, in their majesty, and throw off the yoke of ages.

The world ought to understand that the Negro has come to life, possessed with a new conscience and a new soul. The old Negro is buried, and it is well the world knew it. It is not my purpose to deceive the world. I believe in righteousness; I believe in truth; I belie[ve] in honesty. That is why I warn a selfish world of the outcome of their actions towards the oppressed. There will come a day, Josephus Daniels wrote about it, a white statesman, and the world has talked about it, and I warn the world of it, that the day will come when the races of the world will marshal themselves in great conflict for the survival of the fittest. Men of the Universal Negro Improvement Association, I am asking you to prepare yourselves, and prepare your race the world over, because the conflict is coming, not because you will it, not because you desire it, but because you will be forced into it. The conflict between the races is drawing nearer and nearer. You see it; I see it; I see it in the handwriting on the wall, as expressed in the uprising in India. You see the handwriting on the wall of Africa; you see it, the handwriting on the wall of Europe. It is coming; it is drawing nearer and nearer. Four hundred million Negroes of the world, I am asking you to prepare yourselves, so that you will not be found wanting when that day comes. Ah! what a sorry day it will be. I hope it will never come. But my hope, my wish, will not prevent its coming. All that I can do is to warn humanity everywhere, so that humanity may change its tactics, and warn them of the danger. I repeat: I warn the white world against the prejudice they are practising against Negroes; I warn them against the segregation and injustice they mete out to us, for the perpetuation of these things will mean the ultimate destruction of the present civilization, and the building up of a new civilization founded upon mercy, justice and equality.

I know that we have good men in all races living at the present time. We have good men of the black race, we have good men of the white race, good men of the yellow race, who are endeavoring to do the best they can to ward off this coming conflict. White men who have the vision, go ye back and warn your people of this coming conflict! Black men of vision, go ye to the four corners of the earth, and warn your people of this coming conflict. Yellow men, go ye out and warn your people of this coming conflict, because it is drawing nearer and nearer; nearer and nearer. Oh! if the world will only listen to the heart-throbs, to the soul-beats of those who have the vision, those who have God's love, in their hearts.

I see before me white men, black men and yellow men working assiduously for the peace of the world; for the bringing together of this thing called human brotherhood; I see them working through their organizations. They have been working during the last fifty years. Some worked to bring about the emancipation, because they saw the danger of perpetual slavery. They brought about the liberation of 4,000,000 black people. They passed away, and others started to work, but the opposition against them is too strong; the opposition against them is weighing them down. The world has gone mad; the world has become too material; the world has lost its spirit of kinship with God, and man can see nothing else but prejudice, avarice and greed. Avarice and greed will destroy the world and I am appealing to white, black and yellow whose hearts, whose souls are touched with the true spirit of humanity, with the true feeling of human brotherhood, to preach the doctrine of human love, more, to preach it louder, to preach it longer, because there is great need for it in the world at this time. Ah! if they could but see the danger—the conflict between the races—races fighting against each other. What a destruction, what a holocaust it will be! Can you imagine it?

Just take your idea from the last bloody war, wherein a race was pitted against itself (for the whole white races united as one from a common origin), the members of which, on both sides, fought so tenaciously that they killed off each other in frightful, staggering numbers. If a race pitted against itself could fight so tenaciously to kill itself without mercy, can you imagine the fury, can you imagine the mercilessness, the terribleness of the war that will come when all the races of the world will be on the battlefield, engaged in deadly combat for the destruction or overthrow of the one or the other, when beneath it and as a cause of it lies prejudice and hatred? Truly, it will be an ocean of blood; that is all it will be. So that if I can sound a note of warning now that will echo and reverberate around the world and thus prevent

such a conflict, God help me to do it; for Africa, like Europe, like Asia, is preparing for that day. (Great applause.)

AFRICA'S POSSIBILITIES

You may ask yourselves if you believe Africa is still asleep. Africa has been slumbering; but she was slumbering for a purpose. Africa still possesses her hidden mysteries; Africa has unused talents, and we are unearthening them now for the coming conflict. (Applause.) Oh, I hope it will never come; therefore, I hope the white world will change its attitude towards the weaker races of the world, for we shall not be weak everlastingly. Ah, history teaches us of the rise and fall of nations, races and empires. Rome fell in her majesty; Greece fell in her triumph; Babylon, Assyria, Carthage, Prussia, the German Empire—all fell in their pomp and power; the French Empire fell from the sway of the great Napoleon, from the dominion of the indomitable Corsican soldier. As they fell in the past, so will nations fall in the present age, and so will they fall in the future ages to come, the result of their unrighteousness.

I repeat, I warn the world, and I trust you will receive this warning as you go into the four corners of the earth. The white race should teach humanity. Out there is selfishness in the world. Let the white race teach humanity first, because we have been following the cause of humanity for three hundred years, and we have suffered much. If a change must come, it must not come from Negroes; it must come from the white race, for they are the ones who have brought about this estrangement between the races. The Negro never hated; at no time within the last five hundred years can they point to one single instance of Negro hatred. The Negro has loved eve[n] under the severest punishment. In slavery the Negro loved his master; he protected his master; he saf[e]guarded his master's home. "Greater love hath no man than that he should lay down his life for another."[1] We gave not only our services, our unrequited labor; we gave also our souls, we gave our hearts, we gave our all, to our oppressors.

---

1. Paraphrase of John 15:13, "Greater love hath no man than this, that a man lay down his life for his friends."

But, after all, we are living in a material world, even though it is partly spiritual, and since we have been very spiritual in the past, we are going to take a part of the material now, and will give others the opportunity to practice the spiritual side of life. Therefore, I am not telling you to lead in humanity; I am not telling you to lead in the bringing about of the turning of humanity, because you have been doing that for three hundred years, and you have lost. But the compromise must come from the domina[n]t races. We are warning them. We are not preaching a doctrine of hatred, and I trust you will not go back to your respective homes and preach such a doctrine. We are preaching, rather, a doctrine of humanity, a doctrine of human love. But we say love begins at home; "charity begins at home."[2]

We are aggrieved because of this partitioning of Africa, because it seeks to deprive Negroes of the chance of higher national development; no chance, no opportunity, is given us to prove our fitness to govern, to dominate in our own behalf. They impute so many bad things against Haiti and against Liberia, that they themselves circumvented Liberia so as to make it impossible for us to demonstrate our ability for self-government. Why not be honest? Why not be straightforward[?] Having desired the highest development, as they avowed and professed, of the Negro, why not give him a fair chance, an opportunity to prove his capacity for governing? What better opportunity ever presented itself than the present, when the territories of Germany in Africa were wrested from her control by the Allies in the last war—what better chance ever offered itself for trying out the higher ability of Negroes to govern themselves than to have given those territories to the civilized Negroes, and thus give them a trial to exercise themselves in a proper system of government? Because of their desire to keep us down, because of their desire to keep us apart, they refuse us a chance. The chance that they did give us is the chance that we are going to take. (Great applause.) Hence tonight, before I take my

seat, I will move a resolution, and I think it is befitting at this time to pass such a resolution as I will move, so that the League of Nations and the Supreme Council of the Nations[3] will understand that Negroes are not asleep; that Negroes are not false to themselves; that Negroes are wide awake, and that Negroes intend to take a serious part in the future government of this world; that God Almighty created him and placed him in it. This world owes us a place, and we are going to occupy that place.

We have a right to a large part in the political horizon, and I say to you that we are preparing to occupy that spot.

Go back to your respective corners of the earth and preach the real doctrine of the Universal Negro Improvement Association—the doctrine of universal emancipation for Negroes, the doctrine of a free and a redeemed Africa!

RESOLUTION

Be It Resolved, That we, the duly elected representatives of the Negro peoples of the world, assembled in this Second Annual Convention, do protest against the distribution of the land of Africa by the Supreme Council and the League of Nations among the white nations of the world. Africa, by right of heritage, is the property of the African races, and those at home and those abroad are now sufficiently civilized to conduct the affairs of their own homeland. This convention believes in the right of Europe for the Europeans; Asia for the Asiatics, and Africa for the Africans, those at home and those abroad. We believe, further, that only a close and unselfish application of this principle will prevent threatening race wars that may cast another gloom over civilization and humanity. At this time humanity everywhere is determined to reach a common standard of nationhood. Hence 400,000,000 Negroes demand a place in the political sun of the world.

---

2. Translation of *Proximus sum egomet mihi* [Latin] from *Andria* Act IV, Scene 1, 12, by Terence (185 B.C.E.–159 B.C.E.), Roman playwright.

3. Known commonly as the Supreme Council or the Supreme Council of the Allies, this group was made up of representatives from the Allied Nations of World War I; established in 1917 by British Prime Minister Lloyd George to coordinate allied forces, the group negotiated peace agreements and treaties after the war.

W. E. B. DU BOIS
Manifesto of the Second Pan-African Congress [1921]

Following the end of World War I, Du Bois renewed his commitment to the development of Pan-Africanism. In conjunction with his trip to Paris in 1919 as an observer at the Paris Peace Conference for the National Association for the Advancement of Colored People, he organized the First Pan-African Congress, an international conference aimed at increasing the attention paid to problems faced by black people in Africa and around the world. In his historic 1945 report, "The Pan-African Movement," Du Bois recalled: "I went [to Paris] with the idea of calling a 'Pan-African Congress' and trying to impress upon the members of the Peace Congress meeting at Versailles the importance of Africa in the future world. I was without credentials or influence, but the idea took on." Building on his success, Du Bois organized several more congresses, in 1921, 1923, and 1927. He also served as honorary chair of the Fifth Pan-African Congress, in 1945, which was propelled by the burgeoning African independence movement.

Du Bois's "Manifesto of the Second Pan-African Congress" illustrates the differences between Du Bois's vision of Pan-Africanism and that offered by Marcus Garvey. Key areas of debate centered on who should lead the movement ("the thinking intelligentsia," as Du Bois proposes, or a representative of the black masses, as Garvey argued), the relationship between Pan-Africanism and international groups such as the League of Nations, and especially a vision for the future. A fundamental issue was whether Pan-Africanism should work toward an egalitarian diaspora or a world of autonomous race-based states. At the time, Du Bois rejected the race-based separatism of Garvey's Back to Africa movement, viewing Pan-Africanism as a strategy for securing civil rights around the world. However, Du Bois's conclusions about the future of Africa—that it might end up divided among and assimilated with several world states or as an autonomous "great black African state"—reveal that his own ideas about the relationship of Pan-Africanism to separatism and integration were evolving.

The Crisis, November 1921, pp. 5–8, 10.

The absolute equality of races,—physical, political and social—is the founding stone of world peace and human advancement. No one denies great differences of gift, capacity and attainment among individuals of all races, but the voice of science, religion and practical politics is one in denying the God-appointed existence of super-races, or of races naturally and inevitably and eternally inferior.

That in the vast range of time, one group should in its industrial technique, or social organization, or spiritual vision, lag a few hundred years behind another, or forge fitfully ahead, or come to differ decidedly in thought, deed and ideal, is proof of the essential richness and variety of human nature, rather than proof of thé co-existence of demigods and apes in human forms. The doctrine of racial equality does not interfere with individual liberty, rather, it fulfills it. And of all the various criteria by which masses of men have in the past been prejudged and classified, that of the color of the skin and texture of the hair, is surely the most adventitious and idiotic.

It is the duty of the world to assist in every way the advance of the backward and suppressed groups of mankind. The rise of all men is a menace to no one and is the highest human ideal; it is not an altruistic benevolence, but the one road to world salvation.

For the purpose of raising such peoples to intelligence, self-knowledge and self-control, their intelligentsia of right ought to be recognized as the natural leaders of their groups.

The insidious and dishonorable propaganda, which, for selfish ends, so distorts and denies facts as to represent the advancement and development of certain races of men as impossible and undesirable, should be met with widespread dissemination of the truth. The experiment of making the Negro slave a free citizen in the

United States is not a failure; the attempts at autonomous government in Haiti and Liberia are not proofs of the impossibility of self-government among black men; the experience of Spanish America does not prove that mulatto democracy will not eventually succeed there; the aspirations of Egypt and India are not successfully to be met by sneers at the capacity of darker races.

We who resent the attempt to treat civilized men as uncivilized, and who bring in our hearts grievance upon grievance against those who lynch the untried, disfranchise the intelligent, deny self-government to educated men, and insult the helpless, we complain; but not simply or primarily for ourselves—more especially for the millions of our fellows, blood of our blood, and flesh of our flesh, who have not even what we have—the power to complain against monstrous wrong, the power to see and to know the source of our oppression.

How far the future advance of mankind will depend upon the social contact and physical intermixture of the various strains of human blood is unknown, but the demand for the interpenetration of countries and intermingling of blood has come in modern days, from the white race alone, and has been imposed upon brown and black folks mainly by brute force and fraud. On top of this, the resulting people of mixed race have had to endure innuendo, persecution, and insult, and the penetrated countries have been forced into semi-slavery.

If it be proven that absolute world segregation by group, color or historic affinity is best for the future, let the white race leave the dark world and the darker races will gladly leave the white. But the proposition is absurd. This is a world of men, of men whose likenesses far outweigh their differences; who mutually need each other in labor and thought and dream, but who can successfully have each other only on terms of equality, justice and mutual respect. They are the real and only peace-makers who work sincerely and peacefully to this end.

The beginning of wisdom in interracial contact is the establishment of political institutions among suppressed peoples. The habit of democracy must be made to encircle the earth. Despite the attempt to prove that

its practice is the secret and divine gift of the few, no habit is more natural or more widely spread among primitive people, or more easily capable of development among masses. Local self-government with a minimum of help and oversight can be established tomorrow in Asia, in Africa, in America and in the Isles of the Sea.[1] It will in many instances need general control and guidance, but it will fail only when that guidance seeks ignorantly and consciously its own selfish ends and not the people's liberty and good.

Surely in the 20th century of the Prince of Peace, in the millennium of Buddha and Mahmoud,[2] and in the mightiest Age of Human Reason, there can be found in the civilized world enough of altruism, learning and benevolence to develop native institutions for the native's good, rather than continue to allow the majority of mankind to be brutalized and enslaved by ignorant and selfish agents of commercial institutions, whose one aim is profit and power for the few.

And this brings us to the crux of the matter: It is the shame of the world that today the relation between the main groups of mankind and their mutual estimate and respect is determined chiefly by the degree in which one can subject the other to its service, enslaving labor, making ignorance compulsory, uprooting ruthlessly religion and customs, and destroying government, so that the favored Few may luxuriate in the toil of the tortured Many. Science, Religion and Philanthropy have thus been made the slaves of world commerce and industry, and bodies, minds, souls of Fiji and Congo, are judged almost solely by the quotations on the Bourse.[3]

The day of such world organization is past and whatever excuse be made for it in other ages, the 20th century must come to judge men as men and not as material and labor.

The great industrial problem which has hitherto been regarded as the domestic problem of culture lands, must be viewed far more broadly, if it is ever to reach just settlement. Labor and capital in England, France, and America can never solve their problem as long as a similar and vastly greater problem of poverty

1. Pacific Islands.
2. Muhammad, prophet of Islam; Prince of Peace: Jesus Christ.
3. A stock exchange, from the name of the French stock exchange in Paris.

and injustice marks the relations of the whiter and darker peoples. It is shameful, unreligious, unscientific and undemocratic that the estimate, which half the peoples of earth put on the other half, depends mainly on their ability to squeeze profit out of them.

If we are coming to recognize that the great modern problem is to correct maladjustment in the distribution of wealth, it must be remembered that the basic maladjustment is in the outrageously unjust distribution of world income between the dominant and suppressed peoples; in the rape of land and raw material, and monopoly of technique and culture. And in this crime white labor is *particeps criminis*[4] with white capital. Unconsciously and consciously, carelessly and deliberately, the vast power of the white labor vote in modern democracies has been cajoled and flattered into imperialistic schemes to enslave and debauch black, brown and yellow labor, until with fatal retribution, they are themselves today bound and gagged and rendered impotent by the resulting monopoly of the world's raw material in the hands of a dominant, cruel and irresponsible few.

And, too, just as curiously, the educated and cultured of the world, the well-born and well-bred, and even the deeply pious and philanthropic, receive their training and comfort and luxury, the ministrations of delicate beauty and sensibility, on condition that they neither inquire into the real source of their income and the methods of distribution or interfere with the legal props which rest on a pitiful human foundation of writhing white and yellow and brown and black bodies.

We claim no perfectness of our own nor do we seek to escape the blame which of right falls on the backward for failure to advance, but *noblesse oblige,* and we arraign civilization and more especially the colonial powers for deliberate transgressions of our just demands and their own better conscience.

England, with her Pax Britannica,[5] her courts of justice, established commerce and a certain apparent recognition of native law and customs, has nevertheless systematically fostered ignorance among the natives, has enslaved them and is still enslaving some of them, has usually declined even to try to train black and brown men in real self-government, to recognize civilized black folks as civilized, or to grant to colored colonies those rights of self-government which it freely gives to white men.

Belgium is a nation which has but recently assumed responsibility for her colonies, and has taken some steps to lift them from the worst abuses of the autocratic regime; but she has not confirmed to the people the possession of their land and labor, and she shows no disposition to allow the natives any voice in their own government, or to provide for their political future. Her colonial policy is still mainly dominated by the banks and great corporations. But we are glad to learn that the present government is considering a liberal program of reform for the future.

Portugal and Spain have never drawn a legal caste line against persons of culture who happen to be of Negro descent. Portugal has a humane code for the natives and has begun their education in some regions. But, unfortunately, the industrial concessions of Portuguese Africa are almost wholly in the hands of foreigners whom Portugal cannot or will not control, and who are exploiting land and reestablishing the African slave trade.

The United States of America after brutally enslaving millions of black folks suddenly emancipated them and began their education; but it acted without system or forethought, throwing the freed men upon the world penniless and landless, educating them without thoroughness and system, and subjecting them the while to lynching, lawlessness, discrimination, insult and slander, such as human beings have seldom endured and survived. To save their own government, they enfranchised the Negro and then when danger passed, allowed hundreds of thousands of educated and civilized black folk to be lawlessly disfranchised and subjected to a caste system; and, at the same time, in 1776, 1812, 1861, 1897,[6] and 1917, they asked and allowed thousands of black men to offer up

---

4. An accessory to the crime [Latin].
5. "British Peace" [Latin], term coined for the half-century period starting in 1815 when the British empire was a dominant power in Europe and around the world.
6. Reference to the Spanish-American War; should be 1898.

their lives as a sacrifice to the country which despised and despises them.

France alone of the great colonial powers has sought to place her cultured black citizens on a plane of absolute legal and social equality with her white and given them representation in her highest legislature. In her colonies she has a widespread but still imperfect system of state education. This splendid beginning must be completed by widening the political basis of her native government, by restoring to the indigenes the ownership of the soil, by protecting native labor against the aggression of established capital and by asking no man, black or white, to be a soldier unless the country gives him a voice in his own government.

The independence of Abyssinia, Liberia, Haiti and San Domingo, is absolutely necessary to any sustained belief of the black folk in the sincerity and honesty of the white. These nations have earned the right to be free, they deserve the recognition of the world: notwithstanding all their faults and mistakes, and the fact that they are behind the most advanced civilization of the day, nevertheless they compare favorably with the past, and even more recent, history of most European nations, and it shames civilization that the treaty of London practically invited Italy to aggression in Abyssinia, and that free America has unjustly and cruelly seized Haiti, murdered and for a time enslaved her workmen, overthrown her free institutions by force and has so far failed in return to give her a single bit of help, aid or sympathy.[7]

What do those wish who see these evils of the color line and racial discrimination and who believe in the divine right of suppressed and backward peoples to learn and aspire and be free?

The Negro race through its thinking intelligentsia is demanding:

I—The recognition of civilized men as civilized despite their race or color

II—Local self government for backward groups, deliberately rising as experience and knowledge grow to complete self government under the limitations of a self-governed world

III—Education in self knowledge, in scientific truth and in industrial technique, undivorced from the art of beauty

IV—Freedom in their own religion and social customs, and with the right to be different and nonconformist

V—Co-operation with the rest of the world in government, industry and art on the basis of Justice, Freedom and Peace

VI—The ancient common ownership of the land and its natural fruits and defence against the unrestrained greed of invested capital

VII—The establishment under the League of Nations[8] of an international institution for the study of Negro problems

VIII—The establishment of an international section in the Labor Bureau of the League of Nations, charged with the protection of native labor.

The world must face two eventualities: either the complete assimilation of Africa with two or three of the great world states, with political, civil and social power and privileges absolutely equal for its black and white citizens, or the rise of a great black African state founded in Peace and Good Will, based on popular education, natural art and industry and freedom of trade; autonomous and sovereign in its internal policy, but from its beginning a part of a great society of peoples in which it takes its place with others as co-rulers of the world.

In some such words and thoughts as these we seek to express our will and ideal, and the end of our untiring effort. To our aid we call all men of the Earth who love Justice and Mercy. Out of the depths we have cried unto the deaf and dumb masters of the world. Out of the depths we cry to our own sleeping souls.

The answer is written in the stars.

---

7. The United States' occupation of Haiti lasted from 1915 until 1934.
8. By 1921, the U.S. Congress had rejected the Treaty of Versailles and U.S. participation in the League of Nations.

On Pan-Africanism

George S. Schuyler: *from* Pan-Africanism: A Waste of Time [1927]
Samuel A. Haynes: *from* Pan-Africanism: A Mighty Force [1927]
George S. Schuyler: *from* Pan-Africanism: A Wild Scheme [1927]
Samuel A. Haynes: *from* Pan-Africanism: The One and Only Way [1927]

The late 1920s brought new challenges to the Pan-African movement in the United States. While various Pan-African groups were still battling over leadership and philosophy, critics such as George S. Schuyler began questioning the value of Pan-Africanism itself. In contrast to earlier debates that explored the best type of Pan-African movement, the 1927 editorial exchange between Schuyler, an editor of the *Pittsburgh Courier,* and Samuel Alfred Haynes, a soldier, journalist, and activist from Belize, explores the importance of Pan-Africanism itself. Schuyler does not distinguish between the visions offered by Du Bois's Pan-African Congress and Marcus Garvey's UNIA movement. His rejection of all Pan-Africanism, reminiscent of William Whipper's earlier stand (p. 90), is tied to his belief that there are no substantial differences between African Americans and European Americans, except for skin color. In his July 23, 1927, editorial (reprinted here) he charges that black nationalists are "nothing more than lampblacked Ku Klux Klansmen," echoing the language of his famous 1926 article, "The Negro-Art Hokum" (p. 362), in which he argues that "the Aframerican is merely a lampblacked Anglo-Saxon."

Schuyler regularly published his opinions in his column "Views and Reviews," which was considered a centerpiece of the *Pittsburgh Courier,* a popular black weekly known for championing black capitalism. Schuyler was an iconoclastic thinker whose outspoken opinions often challenged the positions of both black and white leaders. Throughout his life, Schuyler "constantly fashioned himself an enemy of convention and established power," as Jeffrey Ferguson writes in *The King of Sugar Hill: George S. Schuyler and the Harlem Renaissance.* Born in 1895, he grew up in Providence, Rhode Island. While serving in W.W.I., he began writing the type of satirical pieces for which he became well known. In 1923, he started writing for *The Messenger,* a socialist newspaper, but he later became a critic of socialism as well as a staunch anti-Communist. In 1928, he married

Josephine Cogdell, a white Texan; their daughter, Philippa, was a child prodigy and celebrated pianist.

In addition to serving as a columnist for the *Pittsburgh Courier,* Schuyler wrote numerous short stories and novels, including *Black No More* (1931), a satire about American race relations, and *Black Empire* (1937–1938), which lampoons Garvey's Back to Africa movement. Starting in the McCarthy era, his politics turned sharply to the right. In 1965, he joined the John Birch Society, an ultra-conservative political organization, and began contributing pieces to their magazine *American Opinion.* His autobiography, *Black and Conservative,* was published in 1966; Schuyler died eleven years later. His acerbic satire, evident in the Pan-African editorials, earned him the nickname the "Black Mencken", a reference to the famous white American writer H. L. Mencken, who was also his friend and mentor.

Samuel Alfred Haynes's impassioned responses to Schuyler's editorials reveal how the idea of Pan-Africanism remained of central importance to some in the late 1920s, despite the legal woes of Marcus Garvey and the inability of leaders like W. E. B. Du Bois to gain wide support for the movement. Haynes (1899–1971) regularly wrote for *The Negro World,* the official journal of Garvey's UNIA, which had a worldwide distribution and printed sections in French and Spanish. Haynes first gained prominence as an activist in his native Belize, where he was a leader of the 1919 uprising by World War I veterans who, having fought for Britain, were no longer willing to accept racial discrimination. In the 1920s, Haynes became a leading voice for Garveyism in the United States, sustaining his support even after the movement splintered following Garvey's deportation to Jamaica. At the 1929 UNIA convention in Jamaica, Garvey's public vilification of high-level UNIA leaders in the United States and his reorganization of his movement as a rival organization with a new name—"the UNIA, August 1929, of the World"—fueled the further disintegration of the American wing of Garveyism. During the 1930s, when many of Garvey's followers in the United States either established their own groups or began following other charismatic leaders, such as Father Divine (p. 423), Haynes stayed loyal to Garvey. His faithfulness was rewarded in January 1934, when Garvey made Haynes his personal representative in the United States. In 1963, Haynes wrote the lyrics to "Land of the Gods," which became the Belizean national anthem, "Land of the Free," in 1981, ten years after Haynes's death.

GEORGE S. SCHUYLER

Pan-Africanism: A Waste Of Time [1927]

The Pan-African Congress is a sheer waste of money, time and energy [* * *] insofar as the Negro peoples of the world are concerned it might as well not be held. In that respect it is as useless as the U.N.I.A. In the first place no other Negroes except a handful in the United States are interested in the idea of Pan-Africa. [* * *]

It might just as well be understood that this talk of organizing the Negroes of the world and getting them to understand one another and work in unison is about as nonsensical as talk of hewing down Mt. Everest with a toothpick. To the majority of Negroes of the world the words "Negro" and "African" mean nothing whatever. They call themselves French, British, Yorubas, Vais, Fantis, Basutos, Zulus and so forth. Only the blacks in the United States and the West Indies refer to themselves by that uncertain term.[* * *]

The fact is that the dark peoples everywhere, like the light peoples everywhere, are nationalists. There is no unanimity of opinion on anything among the light or "white" peoples of the world, not even on the race question. It is just as [difficult] to get American, British, French, Belgian, Spanish and Italian Negroes to agree on any one thing as it is to get the white peoples of various countries to agree on any one thing.

From the *Pittsburgh Courier,* July 9, 1927.

SAMUEL A. HAYNES

Pan-Africanism: A Mighty Force [1927]

This is one of the most crushing indictments against the Race and its intelligence that has ever emanated from the pen of a prominent writer. It is sensational because of the apparent incompetency of the writer to deal scholarly with the subject matter under review. It does not in any way enhance Mr. Schuyler's reputation as a journalist and would-be advisor on racial matters. The criticism is foolish. It comes at a time when Africa and Asia are about to join hands in combat against western imperialism, at a time when the peoples of both countries are reaching out for sympathy and understanding from these shores of light and learning. It will be received with much surprise in England, home of the West African Students' Union, in Africa, home of the African National Congress, and in the West Indies and Central America, where the idea of "Africa for the Africans" is a mighty spiritual force.[* * *]

If Mr. Schuyler's statement that no other Negroes except a handful in the United States are interested in the idea of Pan-Africa is true, then why is it that hundreds of others in Europe, Africa, Asia, Canada, the West Indies, South and Central America [* * *] are supporting the U.N.I.A., the West African Students' Union of Great Britain, and the African National Congress? Why is it that the Negro World is barred in South Africa, more especially in the [* * *] diamond fields of Kimberley and the Rand? [* * *] Why do the British and French governments take such pains to admit only a certain class of Africans from abroad to their territories in Africa, and ignore the right of the African at home to communicate freely with his brethren abroad? What have these powerful governments to fear from a handful of Negroes in the United States?

That internationalism is foreign matter to Mr. Schuyler is evident when he states there is no unanimity of opinion on anything among the light peoples of the world, not even on the race question. What is more unanimous than the agreement between white peoples of the world to so shape the destiny of society that they will always remain strong and other races weak? They the masters, we the slaves?

From *The Negro World,* July 16, 1927.

GEORGE S. SCHUYLER

Pan-Africanism: A Wild Scheme [1927]

A couple of weeks ago in commenting on the coming Pan-African Congress, I stated that no other Negroes except a handful in the United States were interested in the idea of Pan-Africa. Mr. S. A. Haynes, a columnist on the staff of the Negro World, hastens to take me to task. After claiming that what I wrote is "one of the most crushing indictments against the race," "sensational because of the apparent incompetency of the writer," and much more to the same effect. As would be expected by me from an adherent of Garvey and his moonshine schemes, the writer claims that "Africa and Asia are about to join hands in combat against western imperialism," and waxes wroth because I am unable to see it. My friend, Mr. Haynes, with the characteristic insight of a Garveyite, assumes that because a few psychopaths here and there in Europe, Africa and America are screaming about "the race" and "Africa the Homeland" that means that the Negroes of the world are awakening and about to join hands. One might as well say that the world is going Bolshevik because there is a Communist Party in every country in the world. Agitation doesn't mean organization.

[***] Fellows like Mr. Haynes upbraid me because I do not "see the world through black spectacles." Well, I am content to see the world as it is, and not through black, red or yellow spectacles. No more wild and insane scheme than that of NEGRO NATIONALISM has even been promulgated. The idea of anyone talking of founding a nation on the basis merely of skin coloration! As well talk about getting all the long-eared people like Mr. Haynes together in one nation. These fellows are nothing more than lampblacked Ku Klux Klansmen, leading their followers astray with absurd doctrines of fanatical racialism destined to cause infinitely more pain than pleasure.

Mr. Haynes' logic is amusing. He takes me to task for telling the American Negro to attend to his own business and put his own house in order, saying heatedly, "What house? Any Negro who calls these United States or Europe or Asia, his house is impertinent and unreasonable. Ownership denotes rights of possession, and rights of possession denote authority. The Negro has but one house that is divinely and legally his own. This is the house of Africa. It needs to be put in order very badly. That's why we need the U.N.I.A." Passing over the obvious comment that the U.N.I.A. just had to get rid of its own house on 135th street at the earnest solicitation of creditors and sheriffs because it wasn't in order, let us examine this fellow's logic. If ownership denotes rights of possession, and rights of possession denote authority, then Africa properly belongs to Great Britain, France, Italy, Spain, Belgium and Portugal. Aside from Abyssinia and Liberia, the Negroes are only inhabiting the land of sufferance, toiling to make the owners rich. I may not, as this gentleman says, know anything about internationalism, but I know that Negroes in Africa have no rights of possession and almost no authority, except in a couple of native states, such as Basutoland and Zululand.[1]

Mr. Haynes is also wrong when he states that there is unanimity of opinion among whites as to their treatment of Negroes. That is to argue that the attitude of Elihu Root is the same as that of "Pat" Harrison; that the Governor of Arkansas thinks the same about Negroes as Branting, the Swedish Socialist; that the views of the late E. D. Morel and Roger Casement were identical to those held by Imperial Wizard Evans and Bibb Graves of Alabama; that Mary White Ovington thinks the same of the Negro as Premier Hertzog of South Africa; that Frank Harris looks upon his darker brother with the prejudiced eye of Thomas Dixon; that J. E. Spingarn and the Governor of Mississippi are equally bitten by the bug of colorphobia. [***]

---

1. The Zulu Kingdom was a monarchy in southern Africa that lasted from 1818 to 1894, when it was defeated by the British and became part of the Natal Colony, now the KwaZulu-Natal province of South Africa; Basutoland: the Territory of Basutoland was a British colony in southern Africa from 1884 until 1966, when it gained independence and become the Kingdom of Lesotho.

If there had been no difference of opinion among white people, the Belgian atrocities would never have been investigated, slavery in this country would never have been abolished, most of our Negro schools and colleges would never have been founded and would not now be supported, there would be much more persecution of the black man than there is; there would be no black men voting at the polls and Mr. Haynes wouldn't be able to preach unreasoning hatred against white folks.

From the *Pittsburgh Courier*, July 23, 1927.

SAMUEL A. HAYNES

Pan-Africanism: The One and Only Way [1927]

In one of his reviews some weeks ago Mr. George S. Schuyler referred to me as a black klansman and a preacher of hatred against white people. Writing in the Pittsburgh Courier he informed the public that Negro Nationalism is a wild and insane scheme. He called the writer a "lampblacked klansman," leading his followers astray with absurd doctrines of fanatical racialism destined to cause infinitely more pain than pleasure. This brilliant young man, ignorant of what is going on behind the scenes in Africa, says: "But I know that Negroes in Africa have no rights of possession and almost no authority, except in a couple of native states, such as Basutoland and Zululand." He does not agree that "there is a unanimity of opinion among whites as to their treatment of Negroes," and calls me a "shallow-pated propagandist" for broadcasting the contention that Elihu Root and "Pat" Harrison, the Governor of Arkansas, and Branting of Sweden, E. D. Morel and Roger Casement, Imperial Wizard Evans and Bibb Graves of Alabama, Mary White Ovington and Premier Hertzog of South Africa, Frank Harris and Thomas Dixon, J. E. Spingarn and the Governor of Mississippi are equally bitten by the bug of colorphobia. That there is a difference of opinion among white people in the treatment of Negroes, Mr. Schuyler cites the investigation of the Belgian atrocities, the abolition of slav-

ery in this country, the birth and support of our Negro schools and colleges, the right of Negroes to vote at the polls, and closes his argument by saying that "Mr. Haynes wouldn't be able to preach unreasoning hatred against white folks."

WHEN BLACK SEES WHITE

Such contentions as these are the logical conclusions of a white mind encased in a black body. Like millions of others, alien education and environment have not made Mr. Schuyler "see the world as it is," but as it should be seen from the white man's point of view. No white journalist speaks of a "United States of Europe" as a wild and insane scheme, nor does a Scotchman refer likewise to the program for "Scottish independence," "Chinese Nationalism," "Egyptian independence," "India for the Indians." These are slogans accepted by those who shape the destiny of mankind as within the bounds of justice and reason. And an awkward public conscience looks upon "Negro Nationalism" as a valid demand, though belated. It is only wild and insane in the opinion of white men who fear its success, and Negroes like Mr. Schuyler who are like "dumb driven cattle." Years of travel and experience coupled with a persistent study of those problems which make for jealousy, hatred and war, have convinced me that peace on earth may be realized only when the families of the human race recognize the rights and privileges of each other, remain within the bounds of their habitation, and dwell together in brotherly love. Two families with the same ambitions cannot live peacefully under the same roof. [* * *] Let the white man rule in America and Europe, let the yellow man rule in Asia, and let the black man live at peace with the world in Africa, the land of his fathers. If this is Ku Klux Klanism, then make the best of it.

COURAGE, MAN, COURAGE!

Mr. Schuyler says that such absurd doctrines of fanatical racialism are destined to cause infinitely more pain than pleasure. [* * *] Who ever heard of pleasure in the quest for freedom? The thought of pain and suffering frightens Mr. Schuyler. There is no pleasure in the struggle for freedom and independence, save the knowledge that truth and justice always triumph. [* * *]

The One and Only Way

Because the thoughts and actions of certain white men and women in the higher walks of life, as they affect the treatment of Negroes, appear more civilized than that of their brethren, this cannot be used as a criterion of the whole. Ethical standards demand that responsible leaders of the white race eloquently deny and upbraid the actions of their fellowmen in mistreating Negroes; this is but a means to an end and no definite proof that they are really in earnest. [* * *]

How Hatred Is Engendered

The Belgian atrocities were investigated not because of a difference in heart on the part of Belgian citizens, but because of the pricking of a guilty conscience and fear of open rebellion in the Belgian Congo, and probably all Africa. It is well established by now by responsible historians that Lincoln did not free the slaves because of humanitarian impulses. The safety of the Union and the force of peculiar circumstances which then existed made the Emancipation Proclamation expedient. Negro schools and colleges are not given us because of any special desire to make us equals, but the white man knows from his experience that it is far easier to subdue a group educated through his tutelage than one dependent only on its primitive faculties. To boast of Negroes voting at the polls is like a doctor without patients boasting of his skill. If telling the Negroes the truth about certain phases of life as I see and understand it, if inviting Negroes to redeem Africa from the hands of those who exploit and ravish her is preaching hatred against white folks, then I have no apology to offer. In July 1919, I saved a number of white men—British, Scot, Irish, German and American—from probably wholesale massacre at the hands of an infuriated contingent of returned soldiers in a British colony, receiving the commendation of the Secretary of State for the Colonies in a special dispatch to the Governor of the Colony for my restraining influence. I volunteered for service in 1915 and served four years in Egypt and Mesopotamia, earning two medals and an honorable discharge. Hatred finds no haven in my youthful life. I am for peace and good will between men and races. I don't believe in hypocrisy, in deceit between races. Herein lies the incentive to race hatred which the U.N.I.A., to which I am proud to belong, is endeavoring to wipe out. No one need waste his time preaching to Negroes to hate white folks. Only white folks can make Negroes hate them. [* * *] I understand well Mr. Schuyler's position and sympathize with him, but when men of his type go so far as to incite hatred against Negroes who are earnestly seeking the truth about black and white relationship, they court the disrespect of their fellowmen.

From The Negro World, August 13, 1927.

KEY DEBATE ∼ *The Government: Civic Rights and Civic Duties*

KELLY MILLER

from The Risk of Woman Suffrage [1915]

The post Civil War friction between civil rights leaders and the women's suffrage movement (pp. 242–47) continued after the ratification of the Fifteenth Amendment in 1870, which granted qualified black men the right to vote. While some abolitionists, such as Frederick Douglass, had emphasized a connection between African Americans and women fighting for the vote, some later black leaders saw the two struggles as distinctly different. In this *Crisis* article from November 1915, Kelly Miller uses both biological and cultural arguments to assert that there is "scarcely any common ground between" black suffrage and women's suffrage. Miller wrote his article in response to the August 1915 symposium in *The Crisis* on "Votes for Women," in which twenty-six "leading thinkers of Colored America" (ranging from the Reverend Francis J. Grimké to Mary Church Terrell) argued in favor of women's suffrage.

Miller (1863–1939) was a highly respected educator and writer. He was born in South Carolina, the child of a free black father and an enslaved mother. After receiving his bachelor's degree in mathematics from Howard University, he entered graduate school at Johns Hopkins University, becoming the first African American to study

there. He went on to become a professor and dean of the College of Arts and Sciences at Howard, as well as a prolific author, writing five books and numerous articles, including the syndicated column "Kelly Miller Speaks," which appeared in more than 100 newspapers over a span of more than twenty years.

In addition to opposition from black male leaders such as Miller, black women faced resistance to their demand for the vote from national women's suffrage organizations. Seeking the support of white southerners, some white women distanced themselves from the black women who were actively campaigning for women's suffrage. In 1913, at a parade in Washington, D.C., for a women's suffrage amendment to the Constitution, the activists Ida B. Wells and Mary Church Terrell were asked to march in the back in order to minimize the connection between women's suffrage and black suffrage. Terrell agreed to walk with other members of the Alpha Suffrage Club behind the white demonstrators. Wells refused to march at all but emerged from the crowd during the event to march between two white supporters in the parade's Illinois contingent.

From *The Crisis*, November 1915.

I am wholly unable to see wherein the experiment of woman suffrage promises any genuine advantage to social well-being.

* * *

Woman is physically weaker than man and is incapable of competing with him in the stern and strenuous activities of public and practical life. In the final analysis, politics is a game of force, in which no weakling may expect to be assigned a conspicuous role.

As part of her equipment for motherhood, woman has been endowed with finer feelings and a more highly emotional nature than man. She shows tender devotion and self sacrifice for those close to her by ties of blood or bonds of endearment. But by the universal law of compensation, she loses in extension what is gained in intensity. She lacks the sharp sense of public justice and the common good, if they seem to run counter to her personal feeling and interest. She is far superior to man in purely personal and private virtue, but is his inferior in public qualities and character. Suffrage is not a natural right, like life and liberty.

* * *

It is alleged that Negro suffrage and woman suffrage rest on the same basis. But on close analysis it is found that there is scarcely any common ground between them. The female sex does not form a class separate and distinct from the male sex in the sense that the Negro forms a class separate and distinct from

the whites. Experience and reason both alike show that no race is good enough to govern another without that other's consent. On the other hand both experience and reason demonstrate that the male seeks the welfare and happiness of the female even above his own interest. The Negro can not get justice or fair treatment without the suffrage. Woman can make no such claim, for man accords her not only every privilege which he himself enjoys but the additional privilege of protection.

W. E. B. Du Bois
from Woman Suffrage [1915]

In this November 1915 editorial, Du Bois cites the publication of Kelly Miller's "The Risk of Women's Suffrage," (p. 292), in the same issue of *The Crisis,* as a demonstration of his belief in the need for debate. On the other hand, Du Bois minimizes the relevance of anti-suffrage opinions by referring readers to the symposium he published in August of that year, in which twenty-six black leaders, men and women, unanimously supported women's suffrage. In his own editorial, Du Bois draws connections between the women's suffrage movement and both class struggle and the struggle for civil rights. He

rejects the biological and cultural bases for discrimination, including the idea of women as the "weaker sex" and the exclusionary role of motherhood. By emphasizing how ideas about marriage have already shifted through history, Du Bois points to the possibility of further change in contemporary gender roles. The distinction Du Bois makes between "different" and "inferior" foreshadows principles of the multicultural movement of the 1970s, which promoted the recognition and celebration of difference.

From *The Crisis,* November 1915.

If we turn to easily available statistics we find that instead of the women of this country or of any other country being confined chiefly to childbearing they are as a matter of fact engaged and engaged successfully in practically every pursuit in which men are engaged. The actual work of the world today depends more largely upon women than upon men. Consequently this man-ruled world faces an astonishing dilemma: either Woman the Worker is doing the world's work successfully or not. If she is not doing it well why do we not take from her the necessity of working? If she is doing it well why not treat her as a worker with a voice in the direction of work?

The statement that woman is weaker than man is sheer rot: It is the same sort of thing that we hear about "darker races" and "lower classes." Difference, either physical or spiritual, does not argue weakness or inferiority. [* * *]

To say that men protect women with their votes is to overlook the flat testimony of the facts. [* * *]

There was a day in the world when it was considered that by marriage a woman lost all her individuality as a human soul and simply became a machine for making men. We have outgrown that idea. A woman is just as much a thinking, feeling, acting person after marriage as before.

W. E. B. DU BOIS

Close Ranks [1918]

America's entry into World War I, in 1917, compelled African Americans to consider what obligations they owed a nation that did not fully recognize their citizenship. Jim Crow culture and the nation's rigidly segregated armed forces influenced the views of African American about a war that President Woodrow Wilson characterized as a war to make the world "safe for democracy."

The controversy over military duty made Du Bois's "Close Ranks" one of the most controversial editorials of his career. Appealing to readers to put aside their "special grievances," he departed from the uncompromising tone of protest that had marked his previous *Cri-*

sis writings. At the time, the federal government was pressuring African American editors like Du Bois to avoid criticism that might appear unpatriotic or even seditious. In his posthumously published *Autobiography of W. E. B. Du Bois: A Soliloquy on Viewing My Life from the Last Decade of Its First Century* (1968), Du Bois reflects on his frame of mind when he published "Close Ranks": "I felt for a moment as the war progressed that I could be without reservation a patriotic American. The government was making sincere efforts to meet our demands. [* * *] I am not sure that I was right, but certainly my intentions were."

From *The Crisis*, July 1918.

T his is the crisis of the world. For all the long years to come men will point to the year 1918 as the great Day of Decision, the day when the world decided whether it would submit to military despotism and an endless armed peace—if peace it could be called—or whether they would put down the menace of German militarism and inaugurate the United States of the World.

We of the colored race have no ordinary interest in the outcome. That which the German power represents today spells death to the aspirations of Negroes and all darker races for equality, freedom and democracy. Let us not hesitate. Let us, while this war lasts, forget our special grievances and close our ranks shoulder to shoulder with our own white fellow citizens and the allied nations that are fighting for democracy. We make no ordinary sacrifice, but we make it gladly and willingly with our eyes lifted to the hills.

HUBERT HARRISON

The Descent of Du Bois [1918]

Among those who challenged Du Bois's call to "close ranks" was the prominent writer, editor, and activist Hubert Harrison. In "The Descent of Du Bois," Harrison focuses on *The Crisis's* editor's use of the term "special grievances" as evidence that Du Bois had surrendered his principles. Harrison allied himself with leaders such as A. Philip Randolph (p. 297), who criticized the war as an imperialist adventure and believed that fighting abroad to make the world "safe for democracy" (to use Presi-

dent Wilson's phrase) would not improve conditions for African Americans back home.

Harrison (1883–1927), known as the "father of Harlem radicalism" and the "black Socrates," was born in St. Croix, in the Danish West Indies (now the U.S. Virgin Islands), and moved to New York City when he was seventeen. He became an active member of the Socialist party, wrote for *The Masses,* and influenced the views of rising leaders such as A. Philip Randolph and Chandler

Owen. In 1917, Harrison broke with socialism in favor of a "race-first" ideology. He formed the Liberty League of Negro Americans and edited the organization's journal, *The Voice*. His ideas were an inspiration to the young Marcus Garvey, and Harrison later became the editor of Garvey's newspaper, *The Negro World,* a position he held for four years.

From *The Voice*, July 25, 1918.

In a recent bulletin of the War Department it was declared that "justifiable grievances" were producing and had produced "not disloyalty, but an amount of unrest and bitterness which even the best efforts of their leaders may not be able always to guide." This is the simple truth. The essence of the present situation lies in the fact that the people whom our white masters have "recognized" as our leaders (without taking the trouble to consult us) and those who, by our own selection, had actually attained to leadership among us are being revaluated and, in most cases, rejected.

The most striking instance from the latter class is Dr. W. E. Du Bois, the editor of the *Crisis*. Du Bois's case is the more significant because his former services to his race have been undoubtedly of a high and courageous sort. Moreover, the act by which he has brought upon himself the stormy outburst of disapproval from his race is one which of itself, would seem to merit no such stern condemnation. To properly gauge the value and merit of this disapproval one must view it in the light of its attendant circumstances and of the situation in which it arose.

Dr. Du Bois first palpably sinned in his editorial "Close Ranks" in the July number of the *Crisis*. But this offense (apart from the trend and general tenor of the brief editorial) lies in a single sentence: "Let us, while this war lasts, *forget our special grievances* and close our ranks, shoulder to shoulder with our white fellow citizens and the allied nations that are fighting for democracy." From the latter part of the sentence there is no dissent, so far as we know. The offense lies in that part of the sentence which ends with the italicized words. It is felt by all his critics, that Du Bois, of all Negroes, knows best that our "special grievances"

which the War Department Bulletin describes as "justifiable" consist of lynching, segregation and disfranchisement, and that the Negroes of America can not preserve either their lives, their manhood or their vote (which is their political life and liberties) with these things in existence. The doctor's critics feel that America can not use the Negro people to any good effect unless they have life, liberty and manhood assured and guaranteed to them. Therefore, instead of the war for democracy making these things less necessary, it makes them more so.

"But," it may be asked, "why should not these few words be taken merely as a slip of the pen or a venal error in logic? Why all this hubbub?" Is it because the so-called leaders of the first-mentioned class have already established an unsavory reputation by advocating this same surrender of life, liberty and manhood, masking their cowardice behind the pillars of war-time sacrifice? Du Bois's statement, then, is believed to mark his entrance into that class, and is accepted as a "surrender" of the principles which brought him into prominence—and which alone kept him there.

Later, when it was learned that Du Bois was being preened for a berth in the War Department as a captain-assistant (adjutant) to Major Spingarn, the words used by him in the editorial acquired a darker and more sinister significance. The two things fitted too well together as motive and self-interest.

For these reasons Du Bois is regarded much in the same way as a knight in the middle ages who had had his armor stripped from him, his arms reversed and his spurs hacked off. This ruins him as an influential person among Negroes at this time, alike whether he becomes a captain or remains an editor.

W. E. B. Du Bois
Returning Soldiers [1919]

After World War I, W. E. B. Du Bois reasserted his commitment to protest with the editorial "Returning Soldiers." While maintaining that it was "right" for African Americans to participate in the fight to defeat "German race arrogance," Du Bois condemns the United States for failing to live up to the ideals of democracy. His call for soldiers to "return fighting" presaged the Red Summer of 1919, a period marked by over twenty bloody racial conflicts across the United States, many involving recently returned soldiers.

With his post-war writings in *The Crisis*, Du Bois became a vocal critic of the U.S. military. In his auto-biography, he wrote that he "was convinced and said that American white officers fought more valiantly against Negroes within our ranks than they did against the Germans," a belief supported by "astonishing documents of systematic slander and attack upon Negroes," which Du Bois collected with plans to publish as "A History of the Negro Race in the World War and After." (He published the first chapter in *The Crisis* in January 1924, along with calls for a subscription for the book, which was never completed.) The U.S. government responded to Du Bois's critiques with a short-lived censorship attempt, refusing to permit distribution of *The Crisis* through the mail.

From *The Crisis*, May 1919, pp. 13–14.

W e are returning from war! THE CRISIS and tens of thousands of black men were drafted into a great struggle. For bleeding France and what she means and has meant and will mean to us and humanity and against the threat of German race arrogance, we fought gladly and to the last drop of blood; for America and her highest ideals, we fought in far-off hope; for the dominant southern oligarchy entrenched in Washington, we fought in bitter resignation. For the America that represents and gloats in lynching, disfranchisement, caste, brutality and devilish insult—for this, in the hateful upturning and mixing of things, we were forced by vindictive fate to fight, also.

But today we return! We return from the slavery of uniform which the world's madness demanded us to don to the freedom of civil garb. We stand again to look America squarely in the face and call a spade a spade. We sing: This country of ours, despite all its better souls have done and dreamed, is yet a shameful land.

It *lynches*.

And lynching is barbarism of a degree of contemptible nastiness unparalleled in human history. Yet for fifty years we have lynched two Negroes a week, and we have kept this up right through the war.

It *disfranchises* its own citizens.

Disfranchisement is the deliberate theft and robbery of the only protection of poor against rich and black against white. The land that disfranchises its citizens and calls itself a democracy lies and knows it lies.

It encourages *ignorance*.

It has never really tried to educate the Negro. A dominant minority does not want Negroes educated. It wants servants, dogs, whores and monkeys. And when this land allows a reactionary group by its stolen political power to force as many black folk into these categories as it possibly can, it cries in contemptible hypocrisy: "They threaten us with degeneracy; they cannot be educated."

It *steals* from us.

It organizes industry to cheat us. It cheats us out of our land; it cheats us out of our labor. It confiscates our savings. It reduces our wages. It raises our rent. It steals our profit. It taxes us without representation. It keeps us consistently and universally poor, and then feeds us on charity and derides our poverty.

It *insults* us.

It has organized a nation-wide and latterly a world-wide propaganda of deliberate and continuous insult and defamation of black blood wherever found. It decrees that it shall not be possible in travel nor residence, work nor play, education nor instruction for a black man to exist without tacit or open acknowledgment of his inferiority to the dirtiest white dog. And it looks upon any attempt to question or even discuss this dogma as arrogance, unwarranted assumption and treason.

This is the country to which we Soldiers of Democracy return. This is the fatherland for which we fought! But it is *our* fatherland. It was right for us to fight. The faults of *our* country are *our* faults. Under similar circumstances, we would fight again. But by the God of Heaven, we are cowards and jackasses if now that that war is over, we do not marshal every ounce of our brain and brawn to fight a sterner, longer, more unbending battle against the forces of hell in our own land.

We *return*.

We *return from fighting*.

We *return fighting*.

Make way for Democracy! We saved it in France, and by the Great Jehovah, we will save it in the United States of America, or know the reason why.

THE MESSENGER
Following the Advice of the "Old Crowd" Negro *and* The "New Crowd Negro" Making America Safe for Himself [1919]

Many African Americans became radicalized by their experiences during and immediately after World War I. A fresh sense of possibility fueled by wartime job opportunities and encounters with foreign cultures combined with frustration over the perpetuation of racial discrimination to help spark the growth of the New Negro movement. The "New Negro" symbolized the self-confident and assertive African American who sought political, cultural, and social change through political protest and the arts. The term first appeared in *The Ohio Democrat* on May 20, 1893, but gained widespread popularity as a movement after World War I.

During the war, *The Messenger,* an African American–owned socialist newspaper, argued that black soldiers had no business fighting abroad to make the world "safe for democracy" when at home the U.S. government did nothing to ensure civil rights or to stop the waves of violence directed at African Americans. For its persistent condemnation of America's involvement in World War I, the newspaper suffered censorship and harassment, with government agents raiding *The Messenger*'s Chicago office, revoking its mailing privileges, and arresting its editors, A. Philip Randolph and Chandler Owen—although a judge later threw out the charges against them. After the war, the newspaper built on its radical reputation to stake a claim as the voice of the New Negro, a position evident in the second panel of a Sep-

tember 1919 cartoon, "The 'New Crowd Negro' Making America Safe for Himself." In the first panel of the cartoon, "Following the Advice of the 'Old Crowd' Negro," *The Messenger* portrayed W. E. B. Du Bois, Kelly Miller, and Tuskegee President Robert Russa Moton with the old, ineffectual leadership that was willing to compromise and accommodate.

The black soldier's flag in the second panel refers to three of the violent race riots of 1919: in Longview, Texas, from July 10 to 13; in Washington, D.C., from July 19 to 23; and in Chicago from July 27 to August 3. By 1919, two decades of large-scale black migration from the South had more than doubled the black population in cities such as Chicago. Post-war shortages of housing and jobs fueled rising racial tensions, which exploded in riots across the country. During the Red Summer of 1919, over twenty violent clashes took place across the country, all of them initiated by white Americans. In contrast to pre-war clashes, however, African Americans mobilized and fought back in groups. In a letter to *The Crisis* following the clashes in Washington, a "Southern black woman" rejoiced at the rise in resistance: "The Washington riot gave me a thrill that comes once in a lifetime [* * *] at last our men had stood up like men. [* * *] I stood up alone in my room [* * *] and exclaimed aloud, 'Oh I thank God, thank God.' The pent up horror, grief and humiliation of a life time—half a century—was being stripped from me."

From *The Messenger,* September 1919.

W. E. B. Du Bois
I.W.W. [1919]

Beginning in 1918, W. E. B. Du Bois became involved in a series of debates about labor unions and class politics, publishing his own opinions as well as dissenting ones in the pages of *The Crisis,* thereby sparking further discussion in *The Crisis* and other publications. While openly supporting socialism and, later, communism, Du Bois became a vocal critic of the labor movement in the United States, particularly the discriminatory racial policies of the American Federation of Labor (AFL). A turning point for Du Bois was the 1917 East St. Louis race riot, which he wrote about in a March 1918 editorial called "The Black Man and the Unions." Before that, Du Bois had chosen to focus on the labor movement's potential to gain rights for all workers, and he had stayed largely silent about the movement's widespread racial discrimination. However, when white trade unionists participated in the killing of more than 100 African Americans in the East St. Louis riot, Du Bois began speaking out against the systematic race discrimination by labor unions. He also explored the way in which employers played black workers against white workers as a union busting tactic. Subsequent editorials in *The Crisis* by Du Bois and others continued to recognize the importance of class issues in the lives of African Americans but also began to emphasize the ways in which class politics were being negotiated at the expense of racial politics.

The Crisis's critiques of labor unions and class politics were highly controversial. The debate explored in Du Bois's 1919 "I.W.W." editorial, reprinted here, began in April 1919 with an anonymous editorial, "Easter 1919," which appeared in *The Crisis* while Du Bois was on leave from his editorial duties. After asserting that the wartime efforts of Africans and African Americans had not only "helped save the world" but had also "saved ourselves," the editorialist harshly criticized the Industrial Workers of the World (IWW), a radical labor union, by linking it to "pro-Germans" who had also opposed the war. This "Easter" editorial also aroused vigorous debate because of its opposition to Pan-African patriotism.

Freeman Henry Morris Murray, a clerk in the War Department and former associate of Du Bois's, wrote to Du Bois regarding the "Easter" editorial's implications that there were no black workers in the IWW and that the cause of the labor organization was not in the interest of African Americans. In response, Du Bois wrote the "I.W.W." editorial (which includes Murray's letter) to defend and clarify *The Crisis*'s position.

From *The Crisis,* June 1919.

An editorial in the Easter CRISIS (written during the Editor's absence) has been misunderstood and was perhaps, itself partially misleading.

Mr. F. H. M. Murray of Washington, D.C., writes us:

> In a recent editorial in your magazine the statement is made that there are no Negroes among the Industrial Workers of the World. While I am certain that the statement is erroneous, I am not at this moment able to lay my hands on anything in print to confirm my denial, except the following from an article in last Sunday's New York *Call* magazine, by David Karsner, who reported the trial of the big batch of members of the I. W. W. in Chicago last summer and later the trial of the five Socialists at the same place. He is writing about Judge Kenesaw M. Landis, who presided at both trials and who imposed upon the hundred or so I. W. W., who were convicted, and the five Socialists, sentences aggregating over nine

hundred years in prison and fines aggregating over two millions of dollars. Mr. Karsner says:

"There was only one defendant among the I. W. W., to my knowledge, who refused to believe in Judge Landis [during the trial.] He was Ben Fletcher, the sole Negro defendant. One day in the corridor I asked Ben what he thought of Judge Landis. Ben smiled broadly, 'He's a fakir. Wait until he gets a chance; then he'll plaster it on thick.' Ben was a sure-thing prophet, for the Judge plastered him with ten years, and his counsel said with not enough evidence to invite a reprimand."

So it turns out that not only are there Negroes who are members of this militant workingmen's organization, but some—or at least one—prominent enough to be regarded as worth putting behind the bars with the leaders—Haywood, Fanning and others.

I think that in the interest of the truth of history and for the honor of the black workers, you should correct the statement to which I refer.

I say "honor," for even if we regard the I. W. W. as visionaries (John Brown, you know, was a "visionary") however mistaken are their methods, if their methods are as generally set forth (which I do not believe) the success of the cause for which they are struggling and sacrificing and suffering should be particularly dear to our people, since in no other race or element of our population is there a larger percentage of workers; albeit, too many—what a pity!—are obliged to work in a menial, that is, a parasitic capacity.

THE CRISIS did not say or intend to say that no Negroes belonged to the Industrial Workers of the World, nor did it intend to condemn that organization. On the contrary, we respect it as one of the social and political movements in modern times that draws no color line. We sought to say that we do not believe that the *methods* of the I. W. W. are today feasible or advisable. And too we believe the Socialist Party wrong in its attitude toward the war, but we raise our hats silently to men like Eugene Debs[1] who let not even the shadow of public shame close their lips when they think themselves right.

We believe that the crushing of the monstrous pretentions of the military caste of Germany was a duty so pressing and tremendous that it called for the efforts of every thoughtful American. But we recognize that some people did not agree with us and these folk we honor for their honesty, even though we question their reasoning.

It is no credit to American Negroes if they had NO "Conscientious Objectors." It is tremendously to their credit that the vast majority of them thought straight and fought true in a mighty world crisis.

A. Philip Randolph and Chandler Owen
from The Crisis of *The Crisis* [1919]

The Messenger, the socialist journal founded by A. Philip Randolph and Chandler Owen, swiftly responded to *The Crisis*'s "Easter 1919" and "I.W.W." editorials. The editorial titled "The Crisis of *The Crisis*" demonstrates a common strategy used by Randolph and Owen, in which they took a *Crisis* editorial on a specific issue and used it to challenge broadly the *Crisis*'s relevance and Du Bois's abilities as a leader.

"The Crisis of *The Crisis*" jointly critiques the "Easter 1919" editorial and Du Bois's subsequent clarifica-

tion in "I.W.W.," attributing both editorials to Du Bois despite Du Bois's claim that "Easter 1919" had been written during his absence. This conflation allows for statements that sound like sweeping rebuttals of Du Bois's ideas but are actually in line with what Du Bois expressed in "I.W.W." For example, *The Messenger* proclaims: "The I.W.W. is the only national organization of labor unions which does not discriminate against Negroes. A Negro, therefore, should be the last person to try to cast aspersion upon the I.W.W." This is not a

1. Prominent white American socialist (1855–1926); founding member of the Industrial Workers of the World (IWW), who made historic bids as the Socialist party candidate for president of the United States in the five elections from 1900 to 1920.

rebuttal but an echo of Du Bois's statement that "THE CRISIS did not [* * *] intend to condemn that organization. On the contrary, we respect it as one of the social and political movements in modern times that draws no color line."

Although the tone of *The Messenger* editorial implies otherwise, the editors and Du Bois were not in disagreement over whether there was a need to fight *"the institutions of Jim-Crowism, lynching, race discrimination, segregation, [and] disfranchisement"* in the United States.

Where they differed was on the question of whether the U.S. government itself was one of those institutions. Unlike Du Bois, Randolph and Owen had opposed the participation of African Americans in World War I. Their editorial's stand in favor of people being "traitorous to their tyrants and oppressors" and its support for black conscientious objectors implies not only that other problems were more pressing than fighting Germany but also that the U.S. government itself was part of the problem.

From *The Messenger*, July 1919.

The MESSENGER has frequently pointed out that the editor of the Crisis, Dr. W. E. B. Du Bois, while possessing more intelligence than most Negro editors, is nevertheless comparatively ignorant of the world problems of sociological and economic significance.

In the June Crisis he enters an apology for the leading editorial in the April Crisis. The June issue's editorial, entitled "I. W. W." reads:

"An editorial in the Easter Crisis (written during the editor's absence) has been misunderstood and was, perhaps, itself partially misleading."

Note this argument, if it may be dignified by that name. The editor of the Crisis attempts to excuse his errors and misstatements on the ground that he was absent from his office. But obviously the editor had no business writing if conditions were such that he did not and could not know the facts.

In the April Crisis, Dr. Du Bois says: "Suppose we had yielded to German propaganda, suppose we had refused to shoulder arms, or had wrought mischief and confusion, patterning ourselves after the I. W. W. and the pro-Germans of this country. How should we hold up our heads?"

We take Du Bois to task here for two reasons: first, the statement of fact, and, second, his erroneous interpretation. A Negro alleged professor of sociology and economics doesn't understand the difference between the I. W. W. and pro-Germans. The I. W. W. is the only national organization of labor unions which does not discriminate against Negroes. A Negro, therefore, should be the last person to try to cast aspersion upon the I. W. W.

Again, the Negro has gotten absolutely nothing from his *shouldering arms and failing to produce mischief and confusion. He has been most loyal, but in turn, as his deserts, he is most lynched, most Jim-Crowed, most segregated, most discriminated against, most disfranchised.* The Germans were alleged to be the enemy. But Germans are not lynched, while Negroes are. Germans can ride in any part of the car in any state in the Union. The Negro is confined to the Jim-Crow car in the South. Negroes are disfranchised. Germans are not. Negroes cannot enter most places of public accommodation and amusement free and unhindered. Germans can enter any place of public accommodation and amusement in any part of the United States. (Lest we should be misunderstood, we wish to state that we do not think that any bar should be set up against the Germans. We only call attention to this discrepancy to expose the hypocrisy of the United States government on the one hand and the venality and ignorance of Negro leaders on the other.)

In the April Crisis the editorial continues, "We are not by nature traitors." This statement does not sound like the Du Bois of old. It partakes more of the old, me-too-Boss, hat-in-hand Negro generally represented by Robert Russa Moton of Tuskegee. Of all the fool-hardy claims made by the Negro, not one is so silly and asinine as "we are not by nature traitors." The vice of being traitorous depends entirely upon what one is traitorous to. *Treason of the slave to his master is a virtue. Loyalty of a slave to his master is a vice.* Liberty and justice have advanced in the world in proportion as people have been traitorous to their tyrants and oppressors. George Washington was a traitor—to British tyranny. Wendell Philips, William Lloyd Garrison, Lovejoy and Lincoln were traitors—to the slave autocracy of the United States. John Brown, upon whom the same Du Bois writes a worthless rhetorical book—was a traitor to old slave holding Virginia. The 200,000 Negroes who fought on the Union side to free themselves and their brothers from chattel slavery—were traitors to the slave-holders. It was treason beyond doubt for any slave to attempt his emancipation. But the actual character and type of the treason and the traitor depends entirely upon what that treason is to. The Russian people were largely traitors—traitors to the Czar, the proper kind of traitors. *The Negro will never gain his just rights until the great masses, 12 million strong, become thoroughly permeated, saturated and shot through with treason to the institutions of Jim-Crowism, lynching, race discrimination, segregation, disfranchisement, and to every instrument which maintains, perpetuates and fosters these pernicious institutions.*

The Crisis continues; "The Crisis did not say or intend to say that no Negroes belong to the Industrial Workers of the World, nor did it intend to condemn that organization. On the contrary, we respect it as one of the social and political movements in modern times that draws no color line. We sought to say that we do not believe that the methods of the I. W. W. are today feasible or advisable, and too, we believe the Socialist Party, wrong in its attitude toward the war, but we raise our hats silently to men like Eugene Debs, who let not even the shadow of public shame close their lips when they think themselves right."

The MESSENGER takes sharp issue with the Crisis on every one of its fundamental propositions both with respect to the questions of fact and the questions of opinion. The Crisis clearly implied that Negroes did not belong to the I. W. W. and spoke disparagingly of it as a Pro-German machine. Not only that. The Crisis representatives, like William Pickens, constantly speak of I. W. W.'s and Pro-Germans in their speeches as did William Pickens in the recent conference on "Lynching" held in New York. As to the methods of I. W. W., we state advisedly, and with sufficient reservation, that Dr. Du Bois, like most Negro professors, has no more knowledge of them than he has of the Bolsheviki. For his edification, and that of our readers who desire real information, we wish to say that the chief methods of the I. W. W. are industrial unionism. They oppose the principles of pure and simple unionism. They organize by the industry rather than by the trade. To illustrate, in a printing plant where the pressmen are on strike, by the American Federation of Labor pure and simple unionism methods, scab pressmen could be employed side by side with the union linotypers, compositors and others employed in the establishment. The principles of industrial unionism, adopted by the I. W. W. would demand that when the pressmen strike, the compositors, linotypers and all others employed in the shop should lay down their tools and cease from work until the strike is won. This method is both simple and feasible. It is advisable in every respect. Its efficiency and feasibility are shown by the fact that organized labor of the most advanced countries of Europe, Australia, Canada, and South America are rapidly adopting the One-Big-Union principle for their labor organizations. This no doubt is as new to the editor of the Crisis as it is to the average clay eating cracker of Georgia.

W. E. B. Du Bois
Labor Omnia Vincit [1919]

In "Labor Omnia Vincit" ("Labor Conquers All"), Du Bois engages in the ongoing debate about the relative impact of class, gender, and race in society. While Du Bois acknowledges the importance of combating class, gender, and racial oppression, he formulates the issue so that the problem of racial equality is primary. He opens by proclaiming his support for the labor movement but then places black Americans in the center of the labor struggle. In the second half of the editorial, he continues to shift the emphasis from labor issues to racial issues, expanding on the subtle criticism of white laborers contained in the charge that black laborers are still only "half-recognized" in unions. Du Bois also touches on the problem of women's rights. Unlike early feminists such as Elise Johnson McDougald (p. 307), however, he privileges racial discrimination over that of gender as well as class, presenting the fight "against white domination of black and brown and yellow 'serfs'" as a global issue of paramount importance.

From *The Crisis*, September 1919.

L abor conquers all things—but slowly, O, so slowly. Ever the weary worldlings seek some easier, quicker way—the Way of Wealth, of Privilege, of Chance, of Power; but in the end all that they get— Food, Raiment, Palace and Pleasure—is the result of Toil, but not always of their own toil. The great cry of world Justice today is that the fruit of toil go to the Laborer who produces it. In this labor of Production we recognize effort of all sorts—lifting, digging, carrying, measuring, thinking, foreseeing; but we are refusing to recognize Chance, Birth or Monopoly as just grounds for compelling men to serve men.

In this fight for Justice to Labor the Negro looms large. In Africa and the South Seas, in all the Americas and dimly in Asia he is a mighty worker and potentially, perhaps, the mightiest. But of all laborers cheated of their just wage from the world's dawn to today, he is the poorest and bloodiest.

In the United States he has taken his fastest forward step, rising from owned slave to tied serf, from servant to day laborer, from scab to half-recognized union man in less than a century. Armies, mobs, lynchers, laws and customs have opposed him, yet he lurches forward. His very so-called indolence is his dimly-conceived independence; his singing soul is his far-flaming ideal; and nothing but organized and persistent murder and violence can prevent him from becoming in time the most efficient laboring force in the modern world.

Meantime, in the world round him, the battle of Industrial Democracy is being fought and the white laborers who are fighting it are not sure whether they want their black fellow-laborer as ally or slave. If they could make him a slave, they probably would; but since he can underbid their wage, they slowly and reluctantly invite him into the union. But can they bring themselves inside the Union to regard him as a man—a fellow-voter, a brother?

No—not yet. And there lies the most stupendous labor problem of the twentieth century—transcending the problem of Labor and Capital, of Democracy, of the Equality of Women—for it is the problem of the Equality of Humanity in the world as against white domination of black and brown and yellow serfs.

W. E. B. Du Bois
The Negro and Radical Thought [1921]

The debate explored in W. E. B. Du Bois's editorial "The Negro and Radical Thought" began with his May 1921 editorial "The Drive." In "The Drive," Du Bois argued that the best way to advance civil rights for African Americans was by protesting unjust conditions in the United States (including lynching and Jim Crow segregation)— the strategy of the NAACP. Although Du Bois did not name those who were promoting alternative strategies, that editorial criticized African colonization movements (with descriptions suggesting Marcus Garvey's Back-to-Africa Movement) and revolutionary labor movements. He presented a variety of activist positions as either misguided or dishonest, dismissing the "scoundrels and bubble-blowers ready to conquer Africa, join the Russian revolution, and vote in the Kingdom of God tomorrow."

The poet Claude McKay (1890–1948) responded to "The Drive" with a letter to the editor, parts of which are reprinted in Du Bois's editorial. McKay condemns Du Bois for "sneer[ing] at the Russian Revolution," which

McKay views as "the greatest event in the history of humanity" and a model for African Americans in their struggle for social and political rights. He also challenges Du Bois's hierarchy of race and class—unlike Du Bois, McKay sees racial conflict as a subset of the labor conflict. The rights of black Americans are protected only when that protection suits business interests, he maintains, and "the ruling classes will not grant Negroes those rights which, on a lesser scale and more plausibly, are withheld from the white proletariat."

In his response to McKay's letter, Du Bois assures readers that "Mr. McKay is wrong in thinking that we have ever intentionally sneered at [the Russian Revolution]." Du Bois was concerned with two fundamental questions, which he raises in this editorial: "What is today the right program of socialism?" and "How far can the colored people of the world, and particularly the Negroes of the United States, trust the working classes?" Du Bois was an avowed socialist, but he nevertheless remained cautious about adopting the party line of Marx or Lenin without knowing how those philosophies might translate in practice. Furthermore, unlike McKay, Du Bois did not trust that African Americans "have only to embrace the working class program to have the working class embrace ours." Ultimately, Du Bois espoused a pragmatic politics based on the day-to-day experience of how labor and racial issues influenced the lives of African Americans.

Du Bois continued to explore the relationship between the civil rights and class movements in subsequent editorials in *The Crisis*, including one in October 1921, "Socialism and the Negro," which includes excerpts from a letter from pioneer black communist, John H. Owens, in response to "The Negro and Radical Thought." Underlying Du Bois's writings on class is his belief that the "talented tenth" of the world will provide the best solutions for the problems of the uneducated masses. While Du Bois supported movements that would improve life for the working class, he was wary of the ignorance and inexperience of the members of the working class themselves. This idea grounded his support for an "evolutionary" transformation of the current industrial system rather than a revolution propelled by the working class.

From *The Crisis*, July 1921.

Mr. Claude Mckay, one of the editors of *The Liberator* and a Negro poet of distinction, writes us as follows:

"I am surprised and sorry that in your editorial, 'The Drive', published in THE CRISIS for May, you should leap out of your sphere to sneer at the Russian Revolution, the greatest event in the history of humanity; much greater than the French Revolution, which is held up as a wonderful achievement to Negro children and students in white and black schools. For American Negroes the indisputable and outstanding fact of the Russian Revolution is that a mere handful of Jews, much less in ratio to the number of Negroes in the American population, have attained, through the Revolution, all the political and social rights that were denied to them under the regime of the Czar.

"Although no thinking Negro can deny the great work that the N. A. A. C. P. is doing, it must yet be admitted that from its platform and personnel the Association cannot function as a revolutionary working class organization. And the overwhelming majority of American Negroes belong by birth, condition and repression to the working class. Your aim is to get for the American Negro the political and social rights that are his by virtue of the Constitution, the rights which are denied him by the Southern oligarchy with the active co-operation of the state governments and the tacit support of northern business interests. And your aim is a noble one, which deserves the support of all progressive Negroes.

"But the Negro in politics and social life is ostracized only technically by the distinction of color; in reality the Negro is discriminated against because he is of the lowest type of worker. . . .

"Obviously, this economic difference between the white and black workers manifests itself in various forms, in color prejudice, race hatred, political and social boycotting and lynching of Negroes. And all the entrenched institutions of white

America,—law courts, churches, schools, the fighting forces and the Press,—condone these iniquities perpetrated upon black men; iniquities that are dismissed indifferently as the inevitable result of the social system. Still, whenever it suits the business interests controlling these institutions to mitigate the persecutions against Negroes, they do so with impunity. When organized white workers quit their jobs, Negroes, who are discouraged by the whites to organize, are sought to take their places. And these strike-breaking Negroes work under the protection of the military and the police. But as ordinary citizens and workers, Negroes are not protected by the military and the police from the mob. The ruling classes will not grant Negroes those rights which, on a lesser scale and more plausibly, are withheld from the white proletariat. The concession of these rights would immediately cause a Revolution in the economic life of this country."

We are aware that some of our friends have been disappointed with THE CRISIS during and since the war. Some have assumed that we aimed chiefly at mounting the band wagon with our cause during the madness of war; others thought that we were playing safe so as to avoid the Department of Justice; and still a third class found us curiously stupid in our attitude toward the broader matters of human reform. Such critics, and Mr. McKay is among them, must give us credit for standing to our guns in the past at no little cost in many influential quarters, and they must also remember that we have one chief cause,—the emancipation of the Negro, and to this all else must be subordinated—not because other questions are not important but because to our mind the most important social question today is recognition of the darker races.

Turning now to that marvelous set of phenomena known as the Russian Revolution, Mr. McKay is wrong in thinking that we have ever intentionally sneered at it. On the contrary, time may prove, as he believes, that the Russian Revolution is the greatest event of the nineteenth and twentieth centuries, and

its leaders the most unselfish prophets. At the same time THE CRISIS does not know this to be true. Russia is incredibly vast, and the happenings there in the last five years have been intricate to a degree that must make any student pause. We sit, therefore, with waiting hands and listening ears, seeing some splendid results from Russia, like the cartoons for public education recently exhibited in America, and hearing of other things which frighten us.

We are moved neither by the superficial omniscience of Wells nor the reports in the New York *Times*; but this alone we do know: that the immediate work for the American Negro lies in America and not in Russia, and this, too, in spite of the fact that the Third Internationale has made a pronouncement which cannot but have our entire sympathy:

> "The Communist Internationale once forever breaks with the traditions of the Second Internationale which in reality only recognized the white race. The Communist Internationale makes it its task to emancipate the workers of the entire world. The ranks of the Communist Internationale fraternally unite men of all colors: white, yellow and black—the toilers of the entire world."[1]

Despite this there come to us black men two insistent questions: What is today the right program of socialism? The editor of THE CRISIS considers himself a Socialist but he does not believe that German State Socialism or the dictatorship of the proletariat are perfect panaceas. He believes with most thinking men that the present method of creating, controlling and distributing wealth is desperately wrong; that there must come and is coming a social control of wealth; but he does not know just what form that control is going to take, and he is not prepared to dogmatize with Marx or Lenin. Further than that, and more fundamental to the duty and outlook of THE CRISIS, is this question: How far can the colored people of the world, and particularly the Negroes of the United States, trust the working classes?

---

1. The Communist Internationale, also known as the Third Internationale or Comintern, was formed by the Soviets in Moscow in 1919 to coordinate communist activities abroad; the Second Internationale, formed in Paris in 1889 and dissolved in 1916 over disagreements about military involvement in World War I, was made up of representatives from international labor parties and socialist groups.

Many honest thinking Negroes assume, and Mr. McKay seems to be one of these, that we have only to embrace the working class program to have the working class embrace ours; that we have only to join trade Unionism and Socialism or even Communism, as they are today expounded, to have Union Labor and Socialists and Communists believe and act on the equality of mankind and the abolition of the color line. THE CRISIS wishes that this were true, but it is forced to the conclusion that it is not.

The American Federation of Labor, as representing the trade unions in America, has been grossly unfair and discriminatory toward Negroes and still is. American Socialism has discriminated against black folk and before the war was prepared to go further with this discrimination. European Socialism has openly discriminated against Asiatics. Nor is this surprising. Why should we assume on the part of unlettered and suppressed masses of white workers, a clearness of thought, a sense of human brotherhood, that is sadly lacking in the most educated classes?

Our task, therefore, as it seems to THE CRISIS, is clear: We have to convince the working classes of the world that black men, brown men, and yellow men are human beings and suffer the same discrimination that white workers suffer. We have in addition to this to espouse the cause of the white workers, only being careful that we do not in this way allow them to jeopardize our cause. We must, for instance, have bread. If our white fellow workers drive us out of decent jobs, we are compelled to accept indecent wages even at the price of "scabbing". It is a hard choice, but whose is the blame? Finally despite public prejudice and clamour, we should examine with open mind in literature, debate and in real life the great programs of social reform that are day by day being put forward.

This was the true thought and meaning back of our May editorial. We have an immediate program for Negro emancipation laid down and thought out by the N. A. A. C. P. It is foolish for us to give up this practical program for mirage in Africa or by seeking to join a revolution which we do not at present understand. On the other hand, as Mr. McKay says, it would be just as foolish for us to sneer or even seem to sneer at the blood-entwined writhing of hundreds of millions of our whiter human brothers.

ELISE JOHNSON MCDOUGALD

from The Double Task: The Struggle of Women for Sex and Race Emancipation [1925]

With "The Double Task," the educator and activist Elise Johnson McDougald (1884–1971) wrote one of the earliest explorations of how gender influences the experiences of both race and class. She opens with one of the most common topics for black female leaders of the day, a defense of the moral character of black women, and goes on to assert that "sex irregularities are not a matter of race but of socio-economic conditions." McDougald also explores the influence of class on relations between black men and women, citing a "growing economic independence of Negro working women [that] is causing her to rebel against the domineering family attitude of the cruder working-class Negro man." At the same time, McDougald attributes domestic domination by working-class black men to frustration at their inability to "determine their economic life."

According to McDougald, few black female activists at the time focused on gender equality because they were concentrating on the fight for racial equality. Nevertheless, she concludes, "The wind of the race's destiny stirs more briskly because of [* * *] [the black woman's] striving." Her emphasis on the interaction of race, class, and gender makes her 1925 essay a critical precursor to the writings of the black feminist movement of the 1970s.

Born Gertrude Elise Johnson to a successful family in New York City, McDougald studied at Hunter College, Columbia University, City College of New York, and New York University. In 1911, she married the lawyer Cornelius W. McDougald, who in 1923 defended Marcus Garvey against charges of mail fraud. In 1935, she became the first black principal in the history of the New York City public school system. (By this time, she had taken her second husband's name and was known as Gertrude Ayer.) Among her students was the young James Baldwin, who later told his biographer David Leeming: "I loved and feared the lady—for she really was a lady, and a great one—with that trembling passion only twelve year olds can feel." Throughout her life, McDougald was an activist for progressive causes, working with a range of organizations, from the National Urban League to the Negro Labor Committee. After nearly twenty years as a principal of schools in New York City, she retired in 1954 and died some years later, at the age of eighty-six.

Survey Graphic, which originally published McDougald's essay, was established in 1921 as a mainstream illustrated magazine to complement *Survey*, a journal of social work. The March 1925 issue of *Survey Graphic*, subtitled "Harlem: Mecca of the New Negro," was edited by the critic Alain Locke (p. 333) and focused on black arts and culture in Harlem. It contains contributions by key figures of the Harlem Renaissance, including W. E. B. Du Bois, Charles S. Johnson, James Weldon Johnson, Angelina Weld Grimké, Langston Hughes, Claude McKay, Jean Toomer, and Walter White. Expanded and republished by Locke as a book about the Harlem Renaissance in the United States, the special issue of *Survey Graphic* became the core of his groundbreaking anthology *The New Negro* (1925).

From *Survey Graphic*, March 1925, pp. 689–91.

Throughout the long years of history, woman has been the weather-vane, the indicator, showing in which direction the wind of destiny blows. Her status and development have augured now calm and stability, now swift currents of progress. What then is to be said of the Negro woman today?

In Harlem, more than anywhere else, the Negro woman is free from the cruder handicaps of primitive household hardships and the grosser forms of sex and race subjugation. Here she has considerable opportunity to measure her powers in the intellectual and industrial fields of the great city. Here the questions naturally arise: "What are her problems?" and "How is she solving them?"

To answer these questions, one must have in mind not any one Negro woman, but rather a colorful pageant of individuals, each differently endowed. Like the red and yellow of the tiger-lily, the skin of one is brilliant against the star-lit darkness of a racial sister. From grace to strength, they vary in infinite degree, with traces of the race's history left in physical and mental outline on each. With a discerning mind, one catches the multiform charm, beauty, and character of Negro women; and grasps the fact that their problem cannot be thought of in mass.

Because only a few have caught this vision, the attitude of mind of most New Yorkers causes the Negro woman serious difficulty. She is conscious that what is left of chivalry is not directed toward her. She realizes that the ideals of beauty, built up in the fine arts, exclude her almost entirely. Instead, the grotesque Aunt Jemimas of the street-car advertisements proclaim only an ability to serve, without grace or loveliness. Nor does the drama catch her finest spirit. She is most often used to provoke the mirthless laugh of ridicule; or to portray feminine viciousness or vulgarity not peculiar to Negroes. This is the shadow over her. To a race naturally sunny comes the twilight of self-doubt and a sense of personal inferiority. It cannot be denied that these are potent and detrimental influences, though not generally recognized because they are in the realm of the mental and spiritual. More apparent are the economic handicaps which follow her recent entrance into industry. It is conceded that she has special difficulties because of the poor working conditions and low wages of her men. It is not surprising that only the determined women forge ahead to results other than mere survival. The few who do prove their mettle stimulate one to a closer study of how this achievement is won in Harlem.

Better to visualize the Negro woman at her job, our vision of a host of individuals must once more resolve itself into groups on the basis of activity. First, comes a very small leisure group—the wives and daughters of men who are in business, in the professions and a few well-paid personal service occupations. Second, a most active and progressive group, the women in business and the professions. Third, the many women in the trades and industry. Fourth, a group weighty in numbers struggling on in domestic service, with an even less fortunate fringe of casual workers, fluctuating with the economic temper of the times.

* * *

Negro women are of a race which is free neither economically, socially, nor spiritually. Like women in general, but more particularly like those of other oppressed minorities, the Negro woman has been forced to submit to over-powering conditions. Pressure has been exerted upon her, both from without and within her group. Her emotional and sex life is a reflex of her economic station. The women of the working class will react, emotionally and sexually, similarly to the working-class women of other races. The Negro woman does not maintain any moral standard which may be assigned chiefly to qualities of race, any more than a white woman does. Yet she has been singled out and advertised as having lower sex standards. Superficial critics who have had contact only with the lower grades of Negro women, claim that they are more immoral than other groups of women. This I deny. This is the sort of criticism which predicates of one race, to its detriment, that which is common to all races. Sex irregularities are not a matter of race, but of socio-economic conditions. Research shows that most of the African tribes from which the Negro sprang have strict codes for sex relations. There is no proof of inherent weakness in the ethnic group.

Gradually overcoming the habitual limits imposed upon her by slave masters, she increasingly seeks legal sanction for the consummation and dissolution of sex contracts. Contrary to popular belief, illegitimacy among Negroes is cause for shame and grief. When economic, social, and biological forces combined bring about unwed motherhood, the reaction is much the same as in families of other racial groups. Secrecy is maintained if possible. Generally the married aunt, or even the mother, claims that the illegitimate child is her own. The foundling asylum is seldom sought. Schooled in this kind of suffering in the days of slavery, Negro women often temper scorn with sympathy for weakness. Stigma does fall upon the unmarried mother, but perhaps in this matter the Negroes' attitude is nearer the modern enlightened ideal for the social treatment of the unfortunate. May this not be considered another contribution to America?

With all these forces at work, true sex equality has not been approximated. The ratio of opportunity in the sex, social, economic, and political spheres is about that which exists between white men and women. In the large, I would say that the Negro woman is the cultural equal of her man because she is generally kept in school longer. Negro boys, like white boys, are usually put to work to subsidize the family income. The growing economic independence of Negro working women is causing her to rebel against the domineering family attitude of the cruder working-class Negro man. The masses of Negro men are engaged in menial occupations throughout the working day. Their baffled and suppressed desires to determine their economic life are manifested in over-bearing domination at home. Working mothers are unable to instill different ideals in their sons. Conditions change slowly. Nevertheless, education and opportunity are modifying the spirit of the younger Negro men. Trained in modern schools of thought, they begin to show a wholesome attitude of fellowship and freedom for their women. The challenge to young Negro womanhood is to see clearly this trend and grasp the preferred comradeship with sincerity. In this matter of sex equality, Negro women have contributed few outstanding militants. Their feminist efforts are directed chiefly toward the realization of the equality of the races, the sex struggle assuming a subordinate place.

Obsessed with difficulties that might well compel individualism, the Negro woman has engaged in a considerable amount of organized action to meet group needs. She has evolved a federation of her clubs, embracing between eight and ten thousand women throughout the state of New York. Its chief function is to crystallize programs, prevent duplication of effort, and to sustain a member organization whose cause might otherwise fail. It is now firmly established, and is about to strive for conspicuous goals. In New York City, one association makes child welfare its name and special concern. Others, like the Utility Club, Utopia Neighborhood, Debutante's League, Sempre Fidelius, etc., raise money for old folks' homes, a shelter for delinquent girls, and fresh air camps for children. The Colored Branch of the Y.W.C.A. and the womens' organizations in the many churches, as well as in the beneficial lodges and associations, care for the needs of their members.

On the other hand, the educational welfare of the coming generation has become the chief concern of the national sororities of Negro college women. The first to be organized in the country, Alpha Kappa Alpha, has a systematized and continuous program of educational and vocational guidance for students of the high schools and colleges. The work of Lambda Chapter, which covers New York City and its suburbs, is outstanding. Its recent campaign gathered together nearly one hundred and fifty such students at a meeting to gain inspiration from the life-stories of successful Negro women in eight fields of endeavor. From the trained nurse, who began in the same schools as they, these girls drank in the tale of her rise to the executive position in the Harlem Health Information Bureau. A commercial artist showed how real talent had overcome the color line. The graduate physician was a living example of the modern opportunities in the newer fields of medicine open to women. The vocations as outlets for the creative instinct became attractive under the persuasion of the musician, the dress-maker, and the decorator. Similarly, Alpha Beta Chapter of the national Delta Sigma Theta Sorority recently devoted a week to work along similar lines. In such ways as these are the progressive and privileged groups of Negro women expressing their community and race consciousness.

We find the Negro woman, figuratively, struck in the face daily by contempt from the world about her. Within her soul, she knows little of peace and happiness. Through it all, she is courageously standing erect, developing within herself the moral strength to rise above and conquer false attitudes. She is maintaining her natural beauty and charm and improving her mind and opportunity. She is measuring up to the needs and demands of her family, community, and race, and radiating from Harlem a hope that is cherished by her sisters in less propitious circumstances throughout the land. The wind of the race's destiny stirs more briskly because of her striving.

JAMES WELDON JOHNSON
Preface to *The Book of American Negro Poetry* [1922]

In his preface to *The Book of American Negro Poetry*, written in 1921 and published in 1922, James Weldon Johnson proclaims the need for a "new and distinctive form of expression" for African American poets. This is not merely an aesthetic concern: he views the development and recognition of black art as critical to the fight for political and social equality for African Americans. He places folk art and popular culture at the center of his concept of an emerging black aesthetic and goes on to define that aesthetic with reference to other black artists. For example, he points to Phillis Wheatley in order to explore how artistic influences, education, and environment shape the development of art by African Americans; he traces Paul Laurence Dunbar's artistic experience in order to examine how dialect might both contribute to and detract from the establishment of a black aesthetic.

Johnson touches on a number of contested topics: Is black dialect a key raw material for black art, or is it too confined by conventions to be of use to an artist striving to make original and universal art? When does an aesthetic become the trap of an artistic niche? Are different aesthetic devices necessary to capture different aspects of African American experience, such as rural and urban experience? Johnson's evocation of white authors' use of dialect and white musicians' appropriation of black folk music brings into question how the popularization of black culture affects the idea of a black aesthetic. On a larger level, Johnson's preface explores how an artist might achieve universality in art. Is a more promising route through artistic assimilation or through a conscious development of difference?

Although he is known today primarily as a writer, Johnson attained success in a wide variety of endeavors during his lifetime, as a school principal, for example, and as a writer of Broadway show tunes, a U.S. consul in Latin America, and secretary of the NAACP. He was born in 1871 in Jacksonville, Florida, the son of a head-waiter at a resort hotel and of the first black female public school teacher in Florida. After studying at his mother's school and at a local high school, Johnson attended Atlanta University. Like W. E. B. Du Bois, he spent two summers teaching in the rural South, an experience that shaped the style and subject matter of his later writing. After graduating from college in 1894, Johnson returned to his hometown to serve as principal of the school where his mother had taught, a position he held for eight years. In 1895, he co-founded the first black daily newsletter, the *Daily American,* which shut down after eight months on account of financial difficulties. He then began studying law, becoming the first African American to be admitted to the Florida bar since Reconstruction. It was around this time that he began working with his brother John Rosamond, a composer, on song lyrics, completing in 1900 "Lift Ev'ry Voice and Sing," later known as the Negro national anthem. In 1902, Johnson moved to New York with his brother to work in the theater, where they achieved considerable success. In 1906, he was appointed U.S. consul in Venezuela and in 1909 was transferred to Nicaragua. While serving in Latin America, he began publishing poetry and in 1912 anonymously published a novel, *The Autobiography of an Ex-Colored Man* (Johnson claimed authorship fifteen years later, in 1927). Returning to the United States in 1913 and to New York in 1914 to become editor of *The New York Age,* Johnson became one of the central figures of the Harlem Renaissance. In addition to writing influential critical and creative works—including his first collection of poetry, *Fifty Years, and Other Poems* (1917), and *God's Trombones: Seven Negro Sermons in Verse* (1927)—Johnson fostered the careers of other writers. Among his anthologies are the groundbreaking *The Book of American Negro Poetry,* which helped launch the careers of Claude McKay and Anne Spencer (1892–1975), and *The Book of American Negro Spirituals* (1925). Johnson was also a dedicated activist, working for the NAACP from 1916 to 1930, first as a field organizer and then as executive secretary, the first African American to serve in that capacity. In 1930, he became a professor of creative literature and writing at Fisk University, where he wrote a number of books, including his autobiography, *Along This Way* (1933). In 1934, he became the first African American professor at New York University (NYU). He died in 1938, at the age of sixty-seven, in an automobile accident. Over 2,000 mourners attended his funeral in Harlem.

From James Weldon Johnson, *The Book of American Negro Poetry* (New York: Harcourt, 1931), pp. vii–xlviii.

There is, perhaps, a better excuse for giving an Anthology of American Negro Poetry to the public than can be offered for many of the anthologies that have recently been issued. The public, generally speaking, does not know that there are American Negro poets—to supply this lack of information is, alone, a work worthy of somebody's effort.

Moreover, the matter of Negro poets and the production of literature by the colored people in this country involves more than supplying information that is lacking. It is a matter which has a direct bearing on the most vital of American problems.

A people may become great through many means, but there is only one measure by which its greatness is recognized and acknowledged. The final measure of the greatness of all peoples is the amount and standard of the literature and art they have produced. The world does not know that a people is great until that people produces great literature and art. No people that has produced great literature and art has ever been looked upon by the world as distinctly inferior.

The status of the Negro in the United States is more a question of national mental attitude toward the race than of actual conditions. And nothing will do more to change that mental attitude and raise his status than a demonstration of intellectual parity by the Negro through the production of literature and art.

Is there likelihood that the American Negro will be able to do this? There is, for the good reason that he possesses the innate powers. He has the emotional endowment, the originality and artistic conception, and, what is more important, the power of creating that which has universal appeal and influence.

I make here what may appear to be a more startling statement by saying that the Negro has already proved the possession of these powers by being the creator of the only things artistic that have yet sprung from American soil and been universally acknowledged as distinctive American products.[1]

These creations by the American Negro may be summed up under four heads. The first two are the Uncle Remus stories, which were collected by Joel Chandler Harris, and the "spirituals"[2] or slave songs, to which the Fisk Jubilee Singers made the public and the musicians of both the United States and Europe listen. The Uncle Remus stories constitute the greatest body of folk lore that America has produced, and the "spirituals" the greatest body of folk song. I shall speak of the "spirituals" later because they are more than folk songs, for in them the Negro sounded the depths, if he did not scale the heights, of music.

The other two creations are the cakewalk and ragtime.[3] We do not need to go very far back to remember when cakewalking was the rage in the United States, Europe and South America. Society in this country and royalty abroad spent time in practicing the intricate steps. Paris pronounced it the "poetry of motion." The popularity of the cakewalk passed away but its influence remained. The influence can be seen today on any American stage where there is dancing.

The influence which the Negro has exercised on the art of dancing in this country has been almost absolute. For generations the "buck and wing" and the "stop-time" dances, which are strictly Negro, have been familiar to American theater audiences. A few years ago the public discovered the "turkey trot," the

1. This statement should probably be modified by the inclusion of American Skyscraper architecture [Johnson's note, added in the 1931 revised edition].
2. A touring vocal group of male students from Fisk University founded in 1871 to raise money for the school; in 1881, the white American writer Harris (1848–1908) published *Uncle Remus: His Song and His Savings*, a compilation of African American folktales written in dialect.
3. Musical style originated by black musicians in the 1890, characterized by a syncopated melody over a steady accompaniment; cakewalk: African American dance style that grew out of a contest where a cake was awarded for the most stylish walk.

"eagle rock," "ballin' the jack," and several other varieties that started the modern dance craze. These dances were quickly followed by the "tango," a dance originated by the Negroes of Cuba and later transplanted to South America. (This fact is attested by no less authority than Vicente Blasco Ibañez in his *Four Horsemen of the Apocalypse*.) Half the floor space in the country was then turned over to dancing, and highly paid exponents sprang up everywhere. The most noted, Mr. Vernon Castle, and, by the way, an Englishman, never danced except to the music of a colored band, and he never failed to state to his audiences that most of his dances had long been done by "your colored people," as he put it.

Any one who witnesses a musical production in which there is dancing cannot fail to notice the Negro stamp on all the movements; a stamp which even the great vogue of Russian dances that swept the country about the time of the popular dance craze could not affect. That peculiar swaying of the shoulders which you see done everywhere by the blond girls of the chorus is nothing more than a movement from the Negro dance referred to above, the "eagle rock." Occasionally the movement takes on a suggestion of the now outlawed "shimmy."

As for Ragtime, I go straight to the statement that it is the one artistic production by which America is known the world over. It has been all-conquering. Everywhere it is hailed as "American music."

For a dozen years or so there has been a steady tendency to divorce Ragtime from the Negro; in fact, to take from him the credit of having originated it. Probably the younger people of the present generation do not know that Ragtime is of Negro origin. The change wrought in Ragtime and the way in which it is accepted by the country have been brought about chiefly through the change which has gradually been made in the words and stories accompanying the music. Once the text of all Ragtime songs was written in Negro dialect, and was about Negroes in the cabin or in the cotton field or on the levee or at a jubilee or on Sixth Avenue or at a ball, and about their love affairs. Today, only a small proportion of Ragtime songs relate

at all to the Negro. The truth is, Ragtime is now national rather than racial. But that does not abolish in any way the claim of the American Negro as its originator.

Ragtime music was originated by colored piano players in the questionable resorts of St. Louis, Memphis, and other Mississippi River towns. These men did not know any more about the theory of music than they did about the theory of the universe. They were guided by their natural musical instinct and talent, but above all by the Negro's extraordinary sense of rhythm. Any one who is familiar with Ragtime may note that its chief charm is not in melody, but in rhythms. These players often improvised crude and, at times, vulgar words to fit the music. This was the beginning of the Ragtime song.

Ragtime music got its first popular hearing at Chicago during the World's Fair in that city. From Chicago it made its way to New York, and then started on its universal triumph.

The earliest Ragtime songs, like Topsy, "jes' grew."[4] Some of these earliest songs were taken down by white men, the words slightly altered or changed, and published under the names of the arrangers. They sprang into immediate popularity and earned small fortunes. The first to become widely known was "The Bully," a levee song which had been long used by roustabouts along the Mississippi. It was introduced in New York by Miss May Irvin, and gained instant popularity. Another one of these "jes' grew" songs was one which for a while disputed for place with Yankee Doodle; perhaps, disputes it even today. That song was "A Hot Time in the Old Town Tonight"; introduced and made popular by the colored regimental bands during the Spanish-American War.

Later there came along a number of colored men who were able to transcribe the old songs and write original ones. I was, about that time, writing words to music for the music show stage in New York. I was collaborating with my brother, J. Rosamond Johnson, and the late Bob Cole. I remember that we appropriated about the last one of the old "jes' grew" songs. It was a song which had been sung for years all through the South. The words were unprintable, but the tune was

4. Harriet Beecher Stowe's enslaved orphan character from *Uncle Tom's Cabin*, who says only that she "jes' grew" when telling about her past.

irresistible, and belonged to nobody. We took it, re-wrote the verses, telling an entirely different story from the original, left the chorus as it was, and published the song, at first under the name of "Will Handy." It became very popular with college boys, especially at football games, and perhaps still is. The song was "Oh, Didn't He Ramble!"

In the beginning, and for quite a while, almost all of the Ragtime songs that were deliberately composed were the work of colored writers. Now, the colored composers, even in this particular field, are greatly outnumbered by the white.

The reader might be curious to know if the "jes' grew" songs have ceased to grow. No, they have not; they are growing all the time. The country has lately been flooded with several varieties of "The Blues." These "Blues," too, had their origin in Memphis, and the towns along the Mississippi. They are a sort of lament of a lover who is feeling "blue" over the loss of his sweetheart. The "Blues" of Memphis have been adul-terated so much on Broadway that they have lost their pristine hue. But whenever you hear a piece of music which has a strain like this in it:

[see bottom of page]

you will know you are listening to something which belonged originally to Beale Avenue, Mem-phis, Tennessee. The original "Memphis Blues," so far as it can be credited to a composer, must be cred-ited to Mr. W. C. Handy, a colored musician of Mem-phis.

As illustrations of the genuine Ragtime song in the making, I quote the words of two that were popu-lar with the Southern colored soldiers in France. Here is the first:

Mah mammy's lyin' in her grave,
    Mah daddy done run away,
Mah sister's married a gamblin' man,
    An' I've done gone astray.
Yes, I've done gone astray, po' boy,
    An' I've done gone astray,
Mah sister's married a gamblin' man,
    An' I've done gone astray, po' boy.

These lines are crude, but they contain something of real poetry, of that elusive thing which nobody can define and that you can only tell is there when you feel it. You cannot read these lines without becoming reflective and feeling sorry for "Po' Boy."

Now, take in this word picture of utter dejection:

I'm jes' as misabul as I can be,
I'm unhappy even if I am free,
I'm feelin' down, I'm feelin' blue;
I wander 'round, don't know what to do.
I'm go'n lay mah haid on de railroad line,
Let de B. & O.[5] come and pacify mah min'.

These lines are, no doubt, one of the many ver-sions of the famous "Blues." They are also crude, but they go straight to the mark. The last two lines move with the swiftness of all great tragedy.

In spite of the bans which musicians and music teachers have placed on it, the people still demand and enjoy Ragtime. In fact, there is not a corner of the civi-lized world in which it is not known and liked. And this proves its originality, for if it were an imitation, the people of Europe, at least, would not have found it a novelty. And it is proof of a more important thing, it is proof that Ragtime possesses the vital spark, the power to appeal universally, without which any artis-

5. Baltimore and Ohio Railroad.

tic production, no matter how approved its form may be, is dead.

Of course, there are those who will deny that Ragtime is an artistic production. American musicians, especially, instead of investigating Ragtime, dismiss it with a contemptuous word. But this has been the course of scholasticism in every branch of art. Whatever new thing the people like is pooh-poohed; whatever is popular is regarded as not worth while. The fact is, nothing great or enduring in music has ever sprung full-fledged from the brain of any master; the best he gives the world he gathers from the hearts of the people, and runs it through the alembic of his genius.

Ragtime deserves serious attention. There is a lot of colorless and vicious imitation, but there is enough that is genuine. In one composition alone, "The Memphis Blues," the musician will find not only great melodic beauty, but a polyphonic structure that is amazing.

It is obvious that Ragtime has influenced and, in a large measure, become our popular music; but not many would know that it has influenced even our religious music. Those who are familiar with gospel hymns can at once see this influence if they will compare the songs of thirty years ago, such as "In the Sweet Bye and Bye," "The Ninety and Nine," etc., with the up-to-date, syncopated tunes that are sung in Sunday Schools, Christian Endeavor Societies, Y.M.C.A.'s and like gatherings today.

Ragtime has not only influenced American music, it has influenced American life; indeed, it has saturated American life. It has become the popular medium for our national expression musically. And who can say that it does not express the blare and jangle and the surge, too, of our national spirit?

Any one who doubts that there is a peculiar heel-tickling, smile-provoking, joy-awakening, response-compelling charm in Ragtime needs only to hear a skillful performer play the genuine article, needs only to listen to its bizarre harmonies, its audacious resolutions often consisting of an abrupt jump from one key to another, its intricate rhythms in which the accents fall in the most unexpected places but in which the fundamental beat is never lost, in order to be convinced. I believe it has its place as well as the music which draws from us sighs and tears.

Now, these dances which I have referred to and Ragtime music may be lower forms of art, but they are evidence of a power that will some day be applied to the higher forms. And even now we need not stop at the Negro's accomplishment through these lower forms. In the "spirituals," or slave songs, the Negro has given America not only its only folk songs, but a mass of noble music. I never think of this music but that I am struck by the wonder, the miracle of its production. How did the men who originated these songs manage to do it? The sentiments are easily accounted for; they are, for the most part, taken from the Bible. But the melodies, where did they come from? Some of them so weirdly sweet, and others so wonderfully strong. Take, for instance. "Go Down, Moses"; I doubt that there is a stronger theme in the whole musical literature of the world.

[see bottom of page]

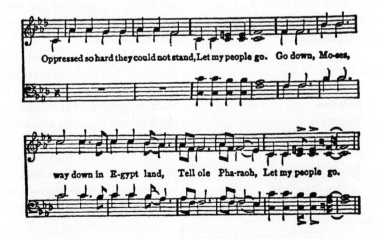

It is to be noted that whereas the chief characteristic of Ragtime is rhythm, the chief characteristic of the "spirituals" is melody. The melodies of "Steal Away to Jesus," "Swing Low Sweet Chariot," "Nobody Knows de Trouble I See," "I Couldn't Hear Nobody Pray," "Deep River," "O, Freedom Over Me," and many others of these songs possess a beauty that is—what shall I say? poignant. In the riotous rhythms of Ragtime the Negro expressed his irrepressible buoyancy, his keen response to the sheer joy of living; in the "spirituals" he voiced his sense of beauty and his deep religious feeling.

Naturally, not as much can be said for the words of these songs as for the music. Most of the songs are religious. Some of them are songs expressing faith and endurance and a longing for freedom. In the religious songs, the sentiments and often the entire lines are taken bodily from the Bible. However, there is no doubt that some of these religious songs have a meaning apart from the Biblical text. It is evident that the opening lines of "Go Down, Moses,"

> Go down, Moses,
> > 'Way down in Egypt land;
> Tell old Pharaoh,
> > Let my people go.

have a significance beyond the bondage of Israel in Egypt.

The bulk of the lines to these songs, as is the case in all communal music, is made up of choral iteration and incremental repetition of the leader's lines. If the words are read, this constant iteration and repetition are found to be tiresome; and it must be admitted that the lines themselves are often very trite. And, yet, there is frequently revealed a flash of real primitive poetry. I give the following examples;

> Sometimes I feel like an eagle in de air.

> You may bury me in de East,
> You may bury me in de West,
> But I'll hear de trumpet sound
> > In-a dat mornin'.

> I know de moonlight, I know de starlight;
> > I lay dis body down.

> I walk in de moonlight, I walk in de starlight;
> > I lay dis body down.
> I know de graveyard, I know de graveyard.
> > When I lay dis body down.
> I walk in de graveyard, I walk troo de graveyard
> > To lay dis body down.

> I lay in de grave an stretch out my arms;
> > I lay dis body down.
> I go to de judgment in de evenin' of de day
> > When I lay dis body down.
> An' my soul an' yo soul will meet in de day
> > When I lay dis body down.

Regarding the line, "I lay in de grave an' stretch out my arms," Col. Thomas Wentworth Higginson of Boston, one of the first to give these slave songs serious study, said: "Never, it seems to me, since man first lived and suffered, was his infinite longing for peace uttered more plaintively than in that line."

These Negro folk songs constitute a vast mine of material that has been neglected almost absolutely. The only white writers who have in recent years given adequate attention and study to this music, that I know of, are Mr. H. E. Krehbiel and Mrs. Natalie Curtis Burlin. We have our native composers denying the worth and importance of this music, and trying to manufacture grand opera out of so-called Indian themes.

But there is a great hope for the development of this music, and that hope is the Negro himself. A worthy beginning has already been made by Burleigh, Cook, Johnson, and Dett. And there will yet come great Negro composers who will take this music and voice through it not only the soul of their race, but the soul of America.

And does it not seem odd that this greatest gift of the Negro has been the most neglected of all he possesses? Money and effort have been expended upon his development in every direction except this. This gift has been regarded as a kind of side show, something for occasional exhibition; wherein it is the touchstone, it is the magic thing, it is that by which the Negro can bridge all chasms. No persons, however hostile, can listen to Negroes singing this wonderful music without having their hostility melted down.

This power of the Negro to suck up the national spirit from the soil and create something artistic and original, which, at the same time, possesses the note of universal appeal, is due to a remarkable racial gift of adaptability; it is more than adaptability, it is a transfusive quality. And the Negro has exercised this transfusive quality not only here in America, where the race lives in large numbers, but in European countries, where the number has been almost infinitesimal.

Is it not curious to know that the greatest poet of Russia is Alexander Pushkin, a man of African descent; that the greatest romancer of France is Alexandre Dumas, a man of African descent; and that one of the greatest musicians of England is Coleridge-Taylor, a man of African descent?

The fact is fairly well known that the father of Dumas was a Negro of the French West Indies, and that the father of Coleridge-Taylor was a native-born African; but the facts concerning Pushkin's African ancestry are not so familiar.

When Peter the Great was Czar of Russia, some potentate presented him with a full-blooded Negro of gigantic size. Peter, the most eccentric ruler of modern times, dressed this Negro up in soldier clothes, christened him Hannibal, and made him a special bodyguard.

But Hannibal had more than size, he had brain and ability. He not only looked picturesque and imposing in soldier clothes, he showed that he had in him the making of a real soldier. Peter recognized this, and eventually made him a general. He afterwards ennobled him, and Hannibal, later, married one of the ladies of the Russian court. This same Hannibal was great-grandfather of Pushkin, the national poet of Russia, the man who bears the same relation to Russian literature that Shakespeare bears to English literature.

I know the question naturally arises: If out of the few Negroes who have lived in France there came a Dumas; and out of the few Negroes who have lived in England there came a Coleridge-Taylor; and if from the man who was at the time, probably, the only Negro in Russia there sprang that country's national poet, why have not the millions of Negroes in the United States with all the emotional and artistic endowment claimed for them produced a Dumas, or a Coleridge-Taylor, or a Pushkin?

The question seems difficult, but there is an answer. The Negro in the United States is consuming all of his intellectual energy in this grueling race-struggle. And the same statement may be made in a general way about the white South. Why does not the white South produce literature and art? The white South, too, is consuming all of its intellectual energy in this lamentable conflict. Nearly all of the mental efforts of the white South run through one narrow channel. The life of every Southern white man and all of his activities are impassably limited by the ever present Negro problem. And that is why, as Mr. H. L. Mencken puts it, in all that vast region, with its thirty or forty million people and its territory as large as a half dozen Frances or Germanys, there is not a single poet, not a serious historian, not a creditable composer, not a critic good or bad, not a dramatist dead or alive.[6]

But, even so, the American Negro has accomplished something in pure literature. The list of those who have done so would be surprising both by its length and the excellence of the achievements. One of the great books written in this country since the Civil War is the work of a colored man, *The Souls of Black Folk,* by W. E. B. Du Bois.

Such a list begins with Phillis Wheatley. In 1761 a slave ship landed a cargo of slaves in Boston. Among them was a little girl seven or eight years of age. She attracted the attention of John Wheatley, a wealthy gentleman of Boston, who purchased her as a servant for his wife. Mrs. Wheatley was a benevolent woman. She noticed the girl's quick mind and determined to give her opportunity for its development. Twelve years later Phillis published a volume of poems. The book was brought out in London, where Phillis was for several months an object of great curiosity and attention.

Phillis Wheatley has never been given her rightful place in American literature. By some sort of conspiracy she is kept out of most of the books, especially the text-books on literature used in the schools. Of course,

---

6. This statement was quoted in 1921. The reader may consider for himself the changes wrought in the decade [Johnson's note, added in the 1931 revised edition].

she is not a *great* American poet—and in her day there were no great American poets—but she is an important American poet. Her importance, if for no other reason, rests on the fact that, save one,[7] she is the first in order of time of all the women poets of America. And she is among the first of all American poets to issue a volume.

It seems strange that the books generally give space to a mention of Urian Oakes, President of Harvard College, and to quotations from the crude and lengthy elegy which he published in 1667; and print examples from the execrable versified version of the Psalms made by the New England divines, and yet deny a place to Phillis Wheatley.

Here are the opening lines from the elegy by Oakes, which is quoted from in most of the books on American literature:

> Reader, I am no poet, but I grieve.
> Behold here what that passion can do,
> That forced a verse without Apollo's leave,
> And whether the learned sisters would or no.

There was no need for Urian to admit what his handiwork declared. But this from the versified Psalms is still worse, yet it is found in the books:

> The Lord's song sing can we? being
> in stranger's land, then let
> lose her skill my right hand if I
> Jerusalem forget.

Anne Bradstreet preceded Phillis Wheatley by a little over one hundred and twenty years. She published her volume of poems, *The Tenth Muse*, in 1650. Let us strike a comparison between the two. Anne Bradstreet was a wealthy, cultivated Puritan girl, the daughter of Thomas Dudley, Governor of Bay Colony. Phillis, as we know, was a Negro slave girl born in Africa. Let us take them both at their best and in the same vein. The following stanza is from Anne's poem entitled "Contemplation":[8]

> While musing thus with contemplation fed,
> And thousand fancies buzzing in my brain,
> The sweet tongued Philomel percht o'er my head,
> And chanted forth a most melodious strain,
> Which rapt me so with wonder and delight,
> I judged my hearing better than my sight,
> And wisht me wings with her awhile to take my
>   flight.

And the following is from Phillis' poem entitled "Imagination":

> Imagination! who can sing thy force?
> Or who describe the swiftness of thy course?
> Soaring through air to find the bright abode,
> Th' empyreal palace of the thundering God,
> We on thy pinions can surpass the wind,
> And leave the rolling universe behind.
> From star to star the mental optics rove,
> Measure the skies, and range the realms above;
> There in one view we grasp the mighty whole,
> Or with new worlds amaze th' unbounded soul.

We do not think the black woman suffers much by comparison with the white. Thomas Jefferson said of Phillis: "Religion has produced a Phillis Wheatley, but it could not produce a poet; her poems are beneath contempt." It is quite likely that Jefferson's criticism was directed more against religion than against Phillis' poetry. On the other hand, General George Washington wrote her with his own hand a letter in which he thanked her for a poem which she had dedicated to him. He later received her with marked courtesy at his camp at Cambridge.

It appears certain that Phillis was the first person to apply to George Washington the phrase, "First in peace." The phrase occurs in her poem addressed to "His Excellency, General George Washington," written in 1775. The encomium, "First in war, first in peace, first in the hearts of his countrymen," was originally used in the resolutions presented to Congress on the death of Washington, December, 1799.

7. White American poet Anne Bradstreet (1612–72), the first published poet in North America.
8. "Contemplations"; Johnson uses a number of unconventional spellings of names and titles for poems in this essay; subsequent examples include Phillis Wheatley's poem "On Imagination," Jupiter Hammon's poem "An Evening Thought, Salvation by Christ, with Penitential Cries (1778)," and Albery A. Whitman.

Phillis Wheatley's poetry is the poetry of the Eighteenth Century. She wrote when Pope and Gray were supreme; it is easy to see that Pope was her model. Had she come under the influence of Wordsworth, Byron or Keats or Shelley, she would have done greater work. As it is, her work must not be judged by the work and standards of a later day, but by the work and standards of her own day and her own contemporaries. By this method of criticism she stands out as one of the important characters in the making of American literature, without any allowances for her sex or her antecedents.

According to *A Bibliographical Checklist of American Negro Poetry*, compiled by Mr. Arthur A. Schomburg, more than one hundred Negroes in the United States have published volumes of poetry ranging in size from pamphlets to books of from one hundred to three hundred pages. About thirty of these writers fill in the gap between Phillis Wheatley and Paul Laurence Dunbar. Just here it is of interest to note that a Negro wrote and published a poem before Phillis Wheatley arrived in this country from Africa. He was Jupiter Hammon, a slave belonging to a Mr. Lloyd of Queens Village, Long Island. In 1760 Hammon published a poem, eighty-eight lines in length, entitled "An Evening Thought, Salvation by Christ, with Penettential Cries." In 1788 he published "An Address to Miss Phillis Wheatley, Ethiopian Poetess in Boston, who came from Africa at eight years of age, and soon became acquainted with the Gospel of Jesus Christ." These two poems do not include all that Hammon wrote.

The poets between Phillis Wheatley and Dunbar must be considered more in the light of what they attempted than of what they accomplished. Many of them showed marked talent, but barely a half dozen of them demonstrated even mediocre mastery of technique in the use of poetic material and forms. And yet there are several names that deserve mention. George M. Horton, Frances E. Harper, James M. Bell and Alberry A. Whitman, all merit consideration when due allowances are made for their limitations in education, training and general culture. The limitations of Horton were greater than those of either of the others; he was born a slave in North Carolina in 1797, and as a young man began to compose poetry without being able to write it down. Later he received some instruction from professors of the University of North Carolina, at which institution he was employed as a janitor. He published a volume of poems, *The Hope of Liberty*, in 1829.

Mrs. Harper, Bell, and Whitman would stand out if only for the reason that each of them attempted sustained work. Mrs. Harper published her first volume of poems in 1854, but later she published "Moses, a Story of the Nile," a poem which ran to 52 closely printed pages. Bell in 1864 published a poem of 28 pages in celebration of President Lincoln's Emancipation Proclamation. In 1870 he published a poem of 32 pages in celebration of the ratification of the Fifteenth Amendment to the Constitution. Whitman published his first volume of poems, a book of 253 pages, in 1877; but in 1884 he published "The Rape of Florida," an epic poem written in four cantos and done in the Spenserian stanza, and which ran to 97 closely printed pages. The poetry of both Mrs. Harper and of Whitman had a large degree of popularity; one of Mrs. Harper's books went through more than twenty editions.

Of these four poets, it is Whitman who reveals not only the greatest imagination but also the more skillful workmanship. His lyric power at its best may be judged from the following stanza from the "Rape of Florida":

"Come now, my love, the moon is on the lake;
Upon the waters is my light canoe;
Come with me, love, and gladsome oars shall make
A music on the parting wave for you.
Come o'er the waters deep and dark and blue;
Come where the lilies in the marge have sprung,
Come with me, love, for Oh, my love is true!"
This is the song that on the lake was sung,
The boatman sang it when his heart was young.

Some idea of Whitman's capacity for dramatic narration may be gained from the following lines taken from "Not a Man, and Yet a Man," a poem of even greater length than "The Rape of Florida."

A flash of steely lightning from his hand,
Strikes down the groaning leader of the band;
Divides his startled comrades, and again
Descending, leaves fair Dora's captors slain.
Her, seizing then within a strong embrace,
Out in the dark he wheels his flying pace;

He speaks not, but with stalwart tenderness
Her swelling bosom firm to his doth press;
Springs like a stag that flees the eager hound,
And like a whirlwind rustles o'er the ground.
Her locks swim in disheveled wildness o'er
His shoulders, streaming to his waist and more;
While on and on, strong as a rolling flood,
His sweeping footsteps part the silent wood.

It is curious and interesting to trace the growth of individuality and race consciousness in this group of poets. Jupiter Hammon's verses were almost entirely religious exhortations. Only very seldom does Phillis Wheatley sound a native note. Four times in single lines she refers to herself as "Afric's muse." In a poem of admonition addressed to the students at the "University of Cambridge in New England" she refers to herself as follows:

Ye blooming plants of human race divine,
An Ethiop tells you 'tis your greatest foe.

But one looks in vain for some outburst or even complaint against the bondage of her people, for some agonizing cry about her native land. In two poems she refers definitely to Africa as her home, but in each instance there seems to be under the sentiment of the lines a feeling of almost smug contentment at her own escape therefrom. In the poem, "On Being Brought from Africa to America," she says:

'Twas mercy brought me from my pagan land,
Taught my benighted soul to understand
That there's a God and there's a Saviour too;
Once I redemption neither sought nor knew.
Some view our sable race with scornful eye—
"Their color is a diabolic dye."
Remember, Christians, Negroes black as Cain,
May be refined, and join th' angelic train.

In the poem addressed to the Earl of Dartmouth, she speaks of freedom and makes a reference to the parents from whom she was taken as a child, a reference which cannot but strike the reader as rather unimpassioned:

Should you, my lord, while you peruse my song,
Wonder from whence my love of Freedom sprung,

Whence flow these wishes for the common good,
By feeling hearts alone best understood;
I, young in life, by seeming cruel fate
Was snatch'd from Afric's fancy'd happy seat;
What pangs excruciating must molest,
What sorrows labor in my parents' breast?
Steel'd was that soul and by no misery mov'd
That from a father seiz'd his babe belov'd;
Such, such my case. And can I then but pray
Others may never feel tyrannic sway?

The bulk of Phillis Wheatley's work consists of poems addressed to people of prominence. Her book was dedicated to the Countess of Huntingdon, at whose house she spent the greater part of her time while in England. On his repeal of the Stamp Act, she wrote a poem to King George III, whom she saw later; another poem she wrote to the Earl of Dartmouth, whom she knew. A number of her verses were addressed to other persons of distinction. Indeed, it is apparent that Phillis was far from being a democrat. She was far from being a democrat not only in her social ideas but also in her political ideas; unless a religious meaning is given to the closing lines of her ode to General Washington, she was a decided royalist:

A crown, a mansion, and a throne that shine
With gold unfading, Washington! be thine.

Nevertheless, she was an ardent patriot. Her ode to General Washington; (1775), her spirited poem, "On Major General Lee" (1776), and her poem, "Liberty and Peace," written in celebration of the close of the war, reveal not only strong patriotic feeling but an understanding of the issues at stake. In her poem, "On Major General Lee," she makes her hero reply thus to the taunts of the British commander into whose hands he has been delivered through treachery:

O arrogance of tongue!
And wild ambition, ever prone to wrong!
Believ'st thou, chief, that armies such as thine
Can stretch in dust that heaven-defended line?
In vain allies may swarm from distant lands,
And demons aid in formidable bands.
Great as thou art, thou shun'st the field of fame,

Disgrace to Britain and the British name!
When offer'd combat by the noble foe
(Foe to misrule) why did the sword forego
The easy conquest of the rebel-land?
Perhaps TOO easy for thy martial hand.

What various causes to the field invite!
For plunder YOU, and we for freedom fight;
Her cause divine with generous ardor fires,
And every bosom glows as she inspires!
Already thousands of your troops have fled
To the drear mansions of the silent dead:
Columbia, too, beholds with streaming eyes
Her heroes fall—'tis freedom's sacrifice!
So wills the power who with convulsive storms
Shakes impious realms, and nature's face deforms;
Yet those brave troops, innum'rous as the sands,
One soul inspires, one General Chief commands;
Find in your train of boasted heroes, one
To match the praise of Godlike Washington.
Thrice happy Chief in whom the virtues join,
And heaven taught prudence speaks the man divine.

What Phillis Wheatley failed to achieve is due in no small degree to her education and environment. Her mind was steeped in the classics; her verses are filled with classical and mythological allusions. She knew Ovid thoroughly and was familiar with other Latin authors. She must have known Alexander Pope by heart. And, too, she was reared and sheltered in a wealthy and cultured family,—a wealthy and cultured Boston family; she never had the opportunity to learn life; she never found out her own true relation to life and to her surroundings. And it should not be forgotten that she was only about thirty years old when she died. The impulsion or the compulsion that might have driven her genius off the worn paths, out on a journey of exploration, Phillis Wheatley never received. But, whatever her limitations, she merits more than America has accorded her.

Horton, who was born three years after Phillis Wheatley's death,[9] expressed in all of his poetry strong complaint at his condition of slavery and a deep longing for freedom. The following verses are typical of his style and his ability:

Alas! and am I born for this,
  To wear this slavish chain?
Deprived of all created bliss,
  Through hardship, toil, and pain?

Come, Liberty! thou cheerful sound,
  Roll through my ravished ears;
Come, let my grief in joys be drowned,
  And drive away my fears.

In Mrs. Harper we find something more than the complaint and the longing of Horton. We find an expression of a sense of wrong and injustice. The following stanzas are from a poem addressed to the white women of America:

You can sigh o'er the sad-eyed Armenian
  Who weeps in her desolate home.
You can mourn o'er the exile of Russia
  From kindred and friends doomed to roam.

But hark! from our Southland are floating
  Sobs of anguish, murmurs of pain;
And women heart-stricken are weeping
  O'er their tortured and slain.

Have ye not, oh, my favored sisters,
  Just a plea, a prayer or a tear
For mothers who dwell 'neath the shadows
  Of agony, hatred and fear?

Weep not, oh, my well sheltered sisters,
  Weep not for the Negro alone,
But weep for your sons who must gather
  The crops which their fathers have sown.

Whitman, in the midst of "The Rape of Florida," a poem in which he related the taking of the State of Florida from the Seminoles,[1] stops and discusses the

---

9. George Moses Horton was born c. 1797, around 13 years after Wheatley's death in 1784.
1. Group of Native American people (mostly from the Creek Confederation of tribes) and escaped African American slaves who came to Florida to escape persecution ("Seminoles" translates as "run-a-ways"); following the 1830 Indian Removal Act, most Seminoles were forced to Oklahoma, but some stayed in Florida and fought the U.S. Army in the second Seminole War (1835–42).

race question. He discusses it in many other poems; and he discusses it from many different angles. In Whitman we find not only an expression of a sense of wrong and injustice, but we hear a note of faith and a note also of defiance. For example, in the opening to Canto II of "The Rape of Florida":

Greatness by nature cannot be entailed;
It is an office ending with the man,—
Sage, hero, Saviour, tho' the Sire be nailed,
The son may reach obscurity in the van:
Sublime achievements know no patent plan,
Man's immortality's a book with seals,
And none but God shall open—none else can—
But opened, it the mystery reveals,—
Manhood's conquest of man to heaven's respect
    appeals.

Is manhood less because man's face is black?
Let thunders of the loosened seals reply!
Who shall the rider's restive steed turn back?
Or who withstand the arrows he lets fly
Between the mountains of eternity?
Genius ride forth! Thou gift and torch of heav'n!
The mastery is kindled in thine eye;
To conquest ride! thy bow of strength is giv'n—
The trampled hordes of caste before thee shall be
    driv'n!

'Tis hard to judge if hatred of one's race,
By those who deem themselves superior-born,
Be worse than that quiescence in disgrace,
Which only merits—and should only—scorn.
Oh, let me see the Negro night and morn,
Pressing and fighting in, for place and power!
All earth is place—all time th' auspicious hour,
While heaven leans forth to look, oh, will he quail or
    cower?

Ah! I abhor his protest and complaint!
His pious looks and patience I despise!
He can't evade the test, disguised as saint;
The manly voice of freedom bids him rise,
And shake himself before Philistine eyes!
And, like a lion roused, no sooner than
A foe dare come, play all his energies,

And court the fray with fury if he can;
For hell itself respects a fearless, manly man.

It may be said that none of these poets strike a deep native strain or sound a distinctly original note, either in matter or form. That is true; but the same thing may be said of all the American poets down to the writers of the present generation, with the exception of Poe and Walt Whitman. The thing in which these black poets are mostly excelled by their contemporaries is mere technique.

Paul Laurence Dunbar stands out as the first poet from the Negro race in the United States to show a combined mastery over poetic material and poetic technique, to reveal innate literary distinction in what he wrote, and to maintain a high level of performance. He was the first to rise to a height from which he could take a perspective view of his own race. He was the first to see objectively its humor, its superstitions, its shortcomings; the first to feel sympathetically its heart-wounds, its yearnings, its aspirations, and to voice them all in a purely literary form.

Dunbar's fame rests chiefly on his poems in Negro dialect. This appraisal of him is, no doubt, fair; for in these dialect poems he not only carried his art to the highest point of perfection, but he made a contribution to American literature unlike what any one else had made, a contribution which, perhaps, no one else could have made. Of course, Negro dialect poetry was written before Dunbar wrote, most of it by white writers; but the fact stands out that Dunbar was the first to use it as a medium for the true interpretation of Negro character and psychology. And yet, dialect poetry does not constitute the whole or even the bulk of Dunbar's work. In addition to a large number of poems of a very high order done in literary English, he was the author of four novels and several volumes of short stories.

Indeed, Dunbar did not begin his career as a writer of dialect. I may be pardoned for introducing here a bit of reminiscence. My personal friendship with Paul Dunbar began before he had achieved recognition, and continued to be close until his death. When I first met him he had published a thin volume, *Oak and*

Ivy,[2] which was being sold chiefly through his own efforts. *Oak and Ivy* showed no distinctive Negro influence, but rather the influence of James Whitcomb Riley.[3] At this time Paul and I were together every day for several months. He talked to me a great deal about his hopes and ambitions. In these talks he revealed that he had reached a realization of the possibilities of poetry in the dialect, together with a recognition of the fact that it offered the surest way by which he could get a hearing. Often he said to me: "I've got to write dialect poetry; it's the only way I can get them to listen to me." I was with Dunbar at the beginning of what proved to be his last illness. He said to me then: "I have not grown. I am writing the same things I wrote ten years ago, and am writing them no better." His self-accusation was not fully true; he had grown, and he had gained a surer control of his art, but he had not accomplished the greater things of which he was constantly dreaming; the public had held him to the things for which it had accorded him recognition. If Dunbar had lived he would have achieved some of those dreams, but even while he talked so dejectedly to me he seemed to feel that he was not to live. He died when he was only thirty-three.

It has a bearing on this entire subject to note that Dunbar was of unmixed Negro blood; so, as the greatest figure in literature which the colored race in the United States has produced, he stands as an example at once refuting and confounding those who wish to believe that whatever extraordinary ability an Aframerican shows is due to an admixture of white blood.

As a man, Dunbar was kind and tender. In conversation he was brilliant and polished. His voice was his chief charm, and was a great element in his success as a reader of his own works. In his actions he was impulsive as a child, sometimes even erratic; indeed, his intimate friends almost looked upon him as a spoiled boy. He was always delicate in health. Temperamentally, he belonged to that class of poets who Taine says are vessels too weak to contain the spirit of poetry, the poets whom poetry kills, the Byrons, the Burnses, the De Mussets, the Poes.

To whom may he be compared, this boy who scribbled his early verses while he ran an elevator, whose youth was a battle against poverty, and who, in spite of almost insurmountable obstacles, rose to success? A comparison between him and Burns is not unfitting. The similarity between many phases of their lives is remarkable, and their works are not incommensurable. Burns took the strong dialect of his people and made it classic: Dunbar took the humble speech of his people and in it wrought music.

Mention of Dunbar brings up for consideration the fact that, although he is the most outstanding figure in literature among the Aframericans of the United States, he does not stand alone among the Aframericans of the whole Western world. There are Plácido and Manzano in Cuba; Vieux and Durand in Haiti; Machado de Assis in Brazil, and others still that might be mentioned, who stand on a plane with or even above Dunbar; Plácido and Machado de Assis rank as great in the literatures of their respective countries without any qualifications whatever. They are world figures in the literature of the Latin languages. Machado de Assis is somewhat handicapped in this respect by having as his tongue and medium the lesser known Portuguese, but Plácido, writing in the language of Spain, Mexico, Cuba and of almost the whole of South America, is universally known. His works have been republished in the original in Spain, Mexico and in most of the Latin-American countries; several editions have been published in the United States; translations of his works have been made into French and German.

Plácido is in some respects the greatest of all the Cuban poets. In sheer genius and the fire of inspiration he surpasses his famous compatriot, Heredia. Then, too, his birth, his life and his death ideally contained the tragic elements that go into the making of a halo about a poet's head. Plácido was born in Habana in 1809. The first months of his life were passed in a foundling asylum; indeed, his real name, Gabriel de la Concepción Valdés, was in honor of its founder. His father took him out of the asylum, but shortly afterwards went to Mexico and died there. His early life was

---

2. Dunbar's first collection of poetry, published in 1893.
3. White American poet (1849–1916) known as "the Hooser poet" for his use of Indiana dialect and regional characters.

a struggle against poverty; his youth and manhood was a struggle for Cuban independence. His death placed him in the list of Cuban martyrs. On the twenty-seventh of June, 1844, he was lined up against a wall with ten others and shot by order of the Spanish authorities on a charge of conspiracy. In his short but eventful life he turned out work which bulks more than six hundred pages. During the few hours preceding his execution he wrote three of his best-known poems, among them his famous sonnet, "Mother, Farewell!"

Plácido's sonnet to his mother has been translated into every important language; William Cullen Bryant did it in English; but in spite of its wide popularity, it is, perhaps, outside of Cuba the least understood of all Plácido's poems. It is curious to note how Bryant's translation totally misses the intimate sense of the delicate subtility of the poem. The American poet makes it a tender and loving farewell of a son who is about to die to a heart-broken mother; but that is not the kind of a farewell that Plácido intended to write or did write.

The key to the poem is in the first word, and the first word is the Spanish conjunction *Si* (if). The central idea, then, of the sonnet is, "If the sad fate which now overwhelms me should bring a pang to your heart, do not weep, for I die a glorious death and sound the last note of my lyre to you." Bryant either failed to understand or ignored the opening word, "If," because he was not familiar with the poet's history.

While Plácido's father was a Negro, his mother was a Spanish white woman, a dancer in one of the Habana theaters. At his birth she abandoned him to a foundling asylum, and perhaps never saw him again, although it is known that she outlived her son. When the poet came down to his last hours he remembered that somewhere there lived a woman who was his mother; that although she had heartlessly abandoned him; that although he owed her no filial duty, still she might, perhaps, on hearing of his sad end feel some pang of grief or sadness; so he tells her in his last words that he dies happy and bids her not to weep. This he does with nobility and dignity, but absolutely without affection. Taking into account these facts, and especially their humiliating and embittering effect upon a soul so sensitive as Plácido's, this sonnet, in spite of the obvious weakness of the sestet as compared with the octave, is a remarkable piece of work.

In considering the Aframerican poets of the Latin languages I am impelled to think that, as up to this time the colored poets of greater universality have come out of the Latin-American countries rather than out of the United States, they will continue to do so for a good many years. The reason for this I hinted at in the first part of this preface. The colored poet in the United States labors within limitations which he cannot easily pass over. He is always on the defensive or the offensive. The pressure upon him to be propagandic is well nigh irresistible. These conditions are suffocating to breadth and to real art in poetry. In addition he labors under the handicap of finding culture not entirely colorless in the United States. On the other hand, the colored poet of Latin America can voice the national spirit without any reservations. And he will be rewarded without any reservations, whether it be to place him among the great or declare him the greatest.

So I think it probable that the first world-acknowledged Aframerican poet will come out of Latin America. Over against this probability, of course, is the great advantage possessed by the colored poet in the United States of writing in the world-conquering English language.

This preface has gone far beyond what I had in mind when I started. It was my intention to gather together the best verses I could find by Negro poets and present them with a bare word of introduction. It was not my plan to make this collection inclusive nor to make the book in any sense a book of criticism. I planned to present only verses by contemporary writers; but, perhaps, because this is the first collection of its kind, I realized the absence of a starting-point and was led to provide one and to fill in with historical data what I felt to be a gap.

It may be surprising to many to see how little of the poetry being written by Negro poets today is being written in Negro dialect. The newer Negro poets show a tendency to discard dialect; much of the subject-matter which went into the making of traditional dialect poetry, 'possums, watermelons, etc., they have discarded altogether, at least, as poetic material. This tendency will, no doubt, be regretted by the majority of white readers; and; indeed, it would be a distinct loss if the American Negro poets threw away this quaint and musical folk speech as a medium of expression. And yet, after all, these poets are working through a problem not realized by the reader, and, perhaps, by many of these poets themselves not realized consciously. They are trying to break away from, not Negro dialect itself, but the limitations on Negro dialect imposed by the fixing effects of long convention.

The Negro in the United States has achieved or been placed in a certain artistic niche. When he is thought of artistically, it is as a happy-go-lucky, singing, shuffling, banjo-picking being or as a more or less pathetic figure. The picture of him is in a log cabin amid fields of cotton or along the levees. Negro dialect is naturally and by long association the exact instrument for voicing this phase of Negro life; and by that very exactness it is an instrument with but two full stops, humor and pathos. So even when he confines himself to purely racial themes, the Aframerican poet realizes that there are phases of Negro life in the United States which cannot be treated in the dialect either adequately or artistically. Take, for example, the phases rising out of life in Harlem, that most wonderful Negro city in the world. I do not deny that a Negro in a log cabin is more picturesque than a Negro in a Harlem flat, but the Negro in the Harlem flat is here, and he is but part of a group growing everywhere in the country, a group whose ideals are becoming increasingly more vital than those of the traditionally artistic group, even if its members are less picturesque.

What the colored poet in the United States needs to do is something like what Synge[4] did for the Irish; he needs to find a form that will express the racial spirit by symbols from within rather than by symbols from without, such as the mere mutilation of English spelling and pronunciation. He needs a form that is freer and larger than dialect, but which will still hold the racial flavor; a form expressing the imagery, the idioms, the peculiar turns of thought, and the distinctive humor and pathos, too, of the Negro, but which will also be capable of voicing the deepest and highest emotions and aspirations, and allow of the widest range of subjects and the widest scope of treatment.

Negro dialect is at present a medium that is not capable of giving expression to the varied conditions of Negro life in America, and much less is it capable of giving the fullest interpretation of Negro character and psychology. This is no indictment against the dialect as dialect, but against the mold of convention in which Negro dialect in the United States has been set. In time these conventions may become lost, and the colored poet in the United States may sit down to write in dialect without feeling that his first line will put the general reader in a frame of mind which demands that the poem be humorous or pathetic. In the meantime, there is no reason why these poets should not continue to do the beautiful things that can be done, and done best, in the dialect.

In stating the need for Aframerican poets in the United States to work out a new and distinctive form of expression I do not wish to be understood to hold any theory that they should limit themselves to Negro poetry, to racial themes; the sooner they are able to write *American* poetry spontaneously, the better. Nevertheless, I believe that the richest contribution the Negro poet can make to the American literature of the future will be the fusion into it of his own individual artistic gifts.

Not many of the writers here included, except Dunbar, are known at all the general reading public; and there is only one of these who has a widely recognized position in the American literary world, William Stanley Braithwaite. Mr. Braithwaite is not only unique in this respect, but he stands unique among all the Aframerican writers the United States has yet produced. He has gained his place, taking as the standard and measure for his work the identical standard and measure applied to American writers and American literature. He has asked for no allowances or rewards, either directly or indirectly, on account of his race.

Mr. Braithwaite is the author of two volumes of verses, lyrics of delicate and tenuous beauty. In his more recent and uncollected poems he shows himself more and more decidedly the mystic. But his place in American literature is due more to his work as a critic

4. John Millington Synge (1871–1909), Irish playwright and folklorist, who helped found the Irish National Theater Society and was dedicated to the development of Irish drama.

and anthologist than to his work as a poet. There is still another rôle he has played, that of friend of poetry and poets. It is a recognized fact that in the work which preceded the present revival of poetry in the United States, no one rendered more unremitting and valuable service than Mr. Braithwaite. And it can be said that no future study of American poetry of this age can be made without reference to Braithwaite.

Two authors included in the book are better known for their work in prose than in poetry: W. E. B. Du Bois whose well-known prose at its best is, however, impassioned and rhythmical; and Benjamin Brawley[5] who is the author, among other works, of one of the best handbooks on the English drama that has yet appeared in America.

But the group of the new Negro poets, whose work makes up the bulk of this anthology, contains names destined to be known. Claude McKay, although still quite a young man, has already demonstrated his power, breadth and skill as a poet. Mr. McKay's breadth is as essential a part of his equipment as his power and skill. He demonstrates mastery of the three when as a Negro poet he pours out the bitterness and rebellion in his heart in those two sonnet-tragedies, "If We Must Die" and "To the White Fiends," in a manner that strikes terror; and when as a cosmic poet he creates the atmosphere and mood of poetic beauty in the absolute, as he does in "Spring in New Hampshire" and "The Harlem Dancer." Mr. McKay gives evidence that he has passed beyond the danger which threatens many of the new Negro poets—the danger of allowing the purely polemical phases of the race problem to choke their sense of artistry.

Mr. McKay's earliest work is unknown in this country. It consists of poems written and published in his native Jamaica. I was fortunate enough to run across this first volume, and I could not refrain from reproducing here one of the poems written in the West Indian Negro dialect. I have done this not only to illustrate the widest range of the poet's talent and to offer a comparison between the American and the West Indian dialects, but on account of the intrinsic worth of the poem itself. I was much tempted to introduce several more, in spite of the fact that they might require a glossary, because however greater work Mr. McKay may do he can never do anything more touching and charming than these poems in the Jamaica dialect.

Fenton Johnson is a young poet of the ultra-modern school who gives promise of greater work than he has yet done. Jessie Fauset shows that she possesses the lyric gift, and she works with care and finish. Miss Fauset is especially adept in her translations from the French. Georgia Douglas Johnson[6] is a poet neither afraid nor ashamed of her emotions. She limits herself to the purely conventional forms, rhythms and rhymes, but through them she achieves striking effects. The principal theme of Mrs. Johnson's poems is the secret dread down in every woman's heart, the dread of the passing of youth and beauty, and with them love. An old theme, one which poets themselves have often wearied of, but which, like death, remains one of the imperishable themes on which is made the poetry that has moved men's hearts through all ages. In her ingenuously wrought verses, through sheer simplicity and spontaneousness, Mrs. Johnson often sounds a note of pathos or passion that will not fail to waken a response, except in those too sophisticated or cynical to respond to natural impulses. Of the half dozen or so colored women writing creditable verse, Anne Spencer is the most modern and least obvious in her methods. Her lines are at times involved and turgid and almost cryptic, but she shows an originality which does not depend upon eccentricities. In her "Before the Feast of Shushan" she displays an opulence, the love of which has long been charged against the Negro as one of his naïve and childish traits, but which in art may infuse a much needed color, warmth and spirit of abandon into American poetry.

John W. Holloway, more than any Negro poet writing in the dialect today, summons to his work the lilt, the spontaneity and charm of which Dunbar was the supreme master whenever he employed that

---

5. Benjamin Griffith Brawley (1882–1939), historian, literary critic, poet, and educator, who wrote *A Short History of English Drama* (1921) as well as numerous books on African American literature and culture.
6. Poet and playwright (1880?–1966) who was recognized for fostering the talents of her fellow artists of the Harlem Renaissance; Fenton Johnson: poet, playwright, and short story writer (1888–1958); Jessie Fauset: poet, novelist (1882–1961), who wrote *Plum Bun* (1928) and three other novels and was literary editor of *The Crisis* from 1919–1926.

medium. It is well to say a word here about the dialect poems of James Edwin Campbell. In dialect, Campbell was a precursor of Dunbar. A comparison of his idioms and phonetics with those of Dunbar reveals great differences. Dunbar is a shade or two more sophisticated and his phonetics approach nearer to a mean standard of the dialects spoken in the different sections. Campbell is more primitive and his phonetics are those of the dialect as spoken by the Negroes of the sea islands off the coasts of South Carolina and Georgia, which to this day remains comparatively close to its African roots, and is strikingly similar to the speech of the uneducated Negroes of the West Indies. An error that confuses many persons in reading or understanding Negro dialect is the idea that it is uniform. An ignorant Negro of the uplands of Georgia would have almost as much difficulty in understanding an ignorant sea island Negro as an Englishman would have. Not even in the dialect of any particular section is a given word always pronounced in precisely the same way. Its pronunciation depends upon the preceding and following sounds. Sometimes the combination permits of a liaison so close that to the uninitiated the sound of the word is almost completely lost.

The constant effort in Negro dialect is to elide all troublesome consonants and sounds. This negative effort may be after all only positive laziness of the vocal organs, but the result is a softening and smoothing which makes Negro dialect so delightfully easy for singers.

Daniel Webster Davis wrote dialect poetry at the time when Dunbar was writing. He gained great popularity, but it did not spread beyond his own race. Davis had unctuous humor, but he was crude. For illustration, note the vast stretch between his "Hog Meat" and Dunbar's "When de Co'n Pone's Hot," both of them poems on the traditional ecstasy of the Negro in contemplation of "good things" to eat.

It is regrettable that two of the most gifted writers included were cut off so early in life. R. C. Jamison and Joseph S. Cotter, Jr.,[7] died several years ago, both of them in their youth. Jamison was barely thirty at the time of his death, but among his poems there is one, at least, which stamps him as a poet of superior talent and lofty inspiration. "The Negro Soldiers" is a poem with the race problem as its theme, yet it transcends the limits of race and rises to a spiritual height that makes it one of the noblest poems of the Great War. Cotter died a mere boy of twenty, and the latter part of that brief period he passed in an invalid state. Some months before his death he published a thin volume of verses which were for the most part written on a sick bed. In this little volume Cotter showed fine poetic sense and a free and bold mastery over his material. A reading of Cotter's poems is certain to induce that mood in which one will regretfully speculate on what the young poet might have accomplished had he not been cut off so soon.

As intimated above, my original idea for this book underwent a change in the writing of the introduction. I first planned to select twenty-five to thirty poems which I judged to be up to a certain standard, and offer them with a few words of introduction and without comment. In the collection, as it grew to be, that "certain standard" has been broadened if not lowered; but I believe that this is offset by the advantage of the wider range given the reader and the student of the subject.

I offer this collection without making apology or asking allowance. I feel confident that the reader will find not only an earnest for the future, but actual achievement. The reader cannot but be impressed by the distance already covered. It is a long way from the plaints of George Horton to the invectives of Claude McKay, from the obviousness of Frances Harper to the complexness of Anne Spencer. Much ground has been covered, but more will yet be covered. It is this side of prophecy to declare that the undeniable creative genius of the Negro is destined to make a distinctive and valuable contribution to American poetry.

[* * *]

New York City, 1921

---

7. Poet (1895–1919) whose books include *The Band of Gideon and Other Lyrics* (1918) and *Poems* (1925); poet Rosco C. Jamison (1886–1918) wrote *Negro Soldiers and Other Poems* (1918).

W. E. B. DU BOIS

Criteria of Negro Art [1926]

In this speech, W. E. B. Du Bois explores key questions about the relationship between propaganda and art, discussing what the roles are of art and artists and what types of art are most politically effective. Highlighting the centrality of art to civil rights, Du Bois argues not only that art is critical to political advancement but also that *all* art is propaganda. Though he does not ask it directly, his essay raises the question of whether it is naïve for young black artists to strive for artistic freedom when the predominantly white cultural establishment persistently produces and promotes works that misrepresent black people. Do black artists have a duty to counteract negative propaganda with their own propaganda? Du Bois originally gave this address at the Chicago conference of the National Association for the Advancement of Colored People in June, 1926, publishing it in *The Crisis* the following October.

From *The Crisis*, October 1926.

I do not doubt but there are some in this audience who are a little disturbed at the subject of this meeting, and particularly at the subject I have chosen. Such people are thinking something like this: "How is it that an organization like this, a group of radicals trying to bring new things into the world, a fighting organization which has come up out of the blood and dust of battle, struggling for the right of black men to be ordinary human beings—how is it that an organization of this kind can turn aside to talk about Art? After all, what have we who are slaves and black to do with Art?"

Or perhaps there are others who feel a certain relief and are saying, "After all it is rather satisfactory after all this talk about rights and fighting to sit and dream of something which leaves a nice taste in the mouth."

Let me tell you that neither of these groups is right. The thing we are talking about tonight is part of the great fight we are carrying on and it represents a forward and an upward look—a pushing onward. You and I have been breasting hills; we have been climbing upward; there has been progress and we can see it day by day looking back along blood-filled paths! But as you go through the valleys and over the foothills, so long as you are climbing, the direction,—north, south, east or west,—is of less importance. But when gradually the vista widens and you begin to see the world at your feet and the far horizon, then it is time to know more precisely whither you are going and what you really want.

What do we want? What is the thing we are after? As it was phrased last night it had a certain truth: We want to be Americans, full-fledged Americans, with all the rights of other American citizens. But is that all? Do we want simply to be Americans? Once in a while through all of us there flashes some clairvoyance, some clear idea, of what America really is. We who are dark can see America in a way that white Americans can not. And seeing our country thus, are we satisfied with its present goals and ideals?

In the high school where I studied we learned most of Scott's "Lady of the Lake" by heart.[1] In after life once it was my privilege to see the lake. It was Sunday. It was quiet. You could glimpse the deer wandering in unbroken forests; you could hear the soft ripple of romance on the waters. Around me fell the cadence of that poetry of my youth. I fell asleep full of the enchantment of the Scottish border. A new day broke and with it came a sudden rush of excursionists. They were mostly Americans and they were loud and strident. They poured upon the little pleasure boat,—men with their hats a little on one side and drooping cigars in the wet corners of their mouths; women who shared their conversation with the world. They all tried to get everywhere first. They pushed other people out of the way. They made all sorts of incoherent noises and gestures so that the quiet home folk and the visitors from other lands silently and half-wonderingly gave way before them. They struck a note not evil but wrong. They carried, perhaps, a sense of strength and accomplishment, but their hearts had no conception of the beauty which pervaded this holy place.

If you tonight suddenly should become full-fledged Americans; if your color faded, or the color line here in Chicago was miraculously forgotten; suppose, too, you became at the same time rich and powerful;—what is it that you would want? What would you immediately seek? Would you buy the most powerful of motor cars and outrace Cook County? Would you buy the most elaborate estate on the North Shore? Would you be a Rotarian or a Lion[2] or a What-not of the very last degree? Would you wear the most striking clothes, give the richest dinners and buy the longest press notices?

Even as you visualize such ideals you know in your hearts that these are not the things you really want. You realize this sooner than the average white American because, pushed aside as we have been in America, there has come to us not only a certain distaste for the tawdry and flamboyant but a vision of what the world could be if it were really a beautiful world; if we had the true spirit; if we had the Seeing Eye, the Cunning Hand, the Feeling Heart; if we had, to be sure, not perfect happiness, but plenty of good hard work, the inevitable suffering that always comes with life; sacrifice and waiting, all that—but, nevertheless, lived in a world where men know, where men create, where they realize themselves and where they enjoy life. It is that sort of a world we want to create for ourselves and for all America.

After all, who shall describe Beauty? What is it? I remember tonight four beautiful things: The Cathedral at Cologne, a forest in stone, set in light and changing shadow, echoing with sunlight and solemn song; a village of the Veys in West Africa, a little thing of mauve and purple, quiet, lying content and shining in the sun; a black and velvet room where on a throne rests, in old and yellowing marble, the broken curves of the Venus of Milo; a single phrase of music in the

Southern South—utter melody, haunting and appealing, suddenly arising out of night and eternity, beneath the moon.

Such is Beauty. Its variety is infinite, its possibility is endless. In normal life all may have it and have it yet again. The world is full of it; and yet today the mass of human beings are choked away from it, and their lives distorted and made ugly. This is not only wrong, it is silly. Who shall right this well-nigh universal failing? Who shall let this world be beautiful? Who shall restore to men the glory of sunsets and the peace of quiet sleep?

We black folk may help for we have within us as a race new stirrings, stirrings of the beginning of a new appreciation of joy, of a new desire to create, of a new will to be; as though in this morning of group life we had awakened from some sleep that at once dimly mourns the past and dreams a splendid future; and there has come the conviction that the Youth that is here today, the Negro Youth, is a different kind of Youth, because in some new way it bears this mighty prophecy on its breast, with a new realization of itself, with new determination for all mankind.

What has this Beauty to do with the world? What has Beauty to do with Truth and Goodness—with the facts of the world and the right actions of men? "Nothing", the artists rush to answer. They may be right. I am but an humble disciple of art and cannot presume to say. I am one who tells the truth and exposes evil and seeks with Beauty and for Beauty to set the world right. That somehow, somewhere eternal and perfect Beauty sits above Truth and Right I can conceive, but here and now and in the world in which I work they are for me unseparated and inseparable.

This is brought to us peculiarly when as artists we face our own past as a people. There has come to us— and it has come especially through the man we are going to honor tonight[3]—a realization of that past, of which for long years we have been ashamed, for which we have apologized. We thought nothing could come out of that past which we wanted to remember; which

1. Poem published in 1810 by the Scottish writer Sir Walter Scott (1771–1882).
2. A member of the Rotary Club or the Lions Club, service club organizations.
3. Carter Godwin Woodson, 12th Spingarn Medalist [Du Bois's note]; Du Bois's speech was during the dinner awarding the NAACP medal to historian and author Woodson (1875–1950); for a brief biographical sketch of Woodson, see p. 412.

we wanted to hand down to our children. Suddenly, this same past is taking on form, color and reality, and in a half shamefaced way we are beginning to be proud of it. We are remembering that the romance of the world did not die and lie forgotten in the Middle Age; that if you want romance to deal with you must have it here and now and in your own hands.

I once knew a man and woman. They had two children, a daughter who was white and a daughter who was brown; the daughter who was white married a white man; and when her wedding was preparing the daughter who was brown prepared to go and celebrate. But the mother said, "No!" and the brown daughter went into her room and turned on the gas and died. Do you want Greek tragedy swifter than that?

Or again, here is a little Southern town and you are in the public square. On one side of the square is the office of a colored lawyer and on all the other sides are men who do not like colored lawyers. A white woman goes into the black man's office and points to the white-filled square and says, "I want five hundred dollars now and if I do not get it I am going to scream."

Have you heard the story of the conquest of German East Africa?[4] Listen to the untold tale: There were 40,000 black men and 4,000 white men who talked German. There were 20,000 black men and 12,000 white men who talked English. There were 10,000 black men and 400 white men who talked French. In Africa then where the Mountains of the Moon raised their white and snow-capped heads into the mouth of the tropic sun, where Nile and Congo rise and the Great Lakes swim, these men fought; they struggled on mountain, hill and valley, in river, lake and swamp, until in masses they sickened, crawled and died; until the 4,000 white Germans had become mostly bleached bones; until nearly all the 12,000 white Englishmen had returned to South Africa, and the 400 Frenchmen to Belgium and Heaven; all except a mere handful of the white men died; but thousands of black men from East, West and South Africa, from Nigeria and the Valley of the Nile, and from the West Indies still struggled, fought and died. For four years they fought and

won and lost German East Africa; and all you hear about it is that England and Belgium conquered German Africa for the allies!

Such is the true and stirring stuff of which Romance is born and from this stuff come the stirrings of men who are beginning to remember that this kind of material is theirs; and this vital life of their own kind is beckoning them on.

The question comes next as to the interpretation of these new stirrings, of this new spirit: Of what is the colored artist capable? We have had on the part of both colored and white people singular unanimity of judgment in the past. Colored people have said: "This work must be inferior because it comes from colored people." White people have said: "It is inferior because it is done by colored people." But today there is coming to both the realization that the work of the black man is not always inferior. Interesting stories come to us. A professor in the University of Chicago read to a class that had studied literature a passage of poetry and asked them to guess the author. They guessed a goodly company from Shelley and Robert Browning down to Tennyson and Masefield. The author was Countée Cullen. Or again the English critic John Drinkwater went down to a Southern seminary, one of the sort which "finishes" young white women of the South. The students sat with their wooden faces while he tried to get some response out of them. Finally he said, "Name me some of your Southern poets". They hesitated. He said finally, "I'll start out with your best: Paul Laurence Dunbar"!

With the growing recognition of Negro artists in spite of the severe handicaps, one comforting thing is occurring to both white and black. They are whispering, "Here is a way out. Here is the real solution of the color problem. The recognition accorded Cullen, Hughes,[5] Fauset, White and others shows there is no real color line. Keep quiet! Don't complain! Work! All will be well!"

I will not say that already this chorus amounts to a conspiracy. Perhaps I am naturally too suspicious. But I will say that there are today a surprising number of white people who are getting great satisfaction out of

4. Now Tanzania.
5. For a brief biographical sketch of Langston Hughes, see p. 362.

these younger Negro writers because they think it is going to stop agitation of the Negro question. They say, "What is the use of your fighting and complaining; do the great thing and the reward is there". And many colored people are all too eager to follow this advice; especially those who are weary of the eternal struggle along the color line, who are afraid to fight and to whom the money of philanthropists and the alluring publicity are subtle and deadly bribes. They say, "What is the use of fighting? Why not show simply what we deserve and let the reward come to us?"

And it is right here that the National Association for the Advancement of Colored People comes upon the field, comes with its great call to a new battle, a new fight and new things to fight before the old things are wholly won; and to say that the Beauty of Truth and Freedom which shall some day be our heritage and the heritage of all civilized men is not in our hands yet and that we ourselves must not fail to realize.

There is in New York tonight a black woman molding clay by herself in a little bare room, because there is not a single school of sculpture in New York where she is welcome. Surely there are doors she might burst through, but when God makes a sculptor He does not always make the pushing sort of person who beats his way through doors thrust in his face. This girl is working her hands off to get out of this country so that she can get some sort of training.

There was Richard Brown.[6] If he had been white he would have been alive today instead of dead of neglect. Many helped him when he asked but he was not the kind of boy that always asks. He was simply one who made colors sing.

There is a colored woman in Chicago who is a great musician. She thought she would like to study at Fontainebleau this summer where Walter Damrosch and a score of leaders of Art have an American school of music. But the application blank of this school says: "I am a white American and I apply for admission to the school."

We can go on the stage; we can be just as funny as white Americans wish us to be; we can play all the sor-

did parts that America likes to assign to Negroes; but for any thing else there is still small place for us.

And so I might go on. But let me sum up with this: Suppose the only Negro who survived some centuries hence was the Negro painted by white Americans in the novels and essays they have written. What would people in a hundred years say of black Americans? Now turn it around. Suppose you were to write a story and put in it the kind of people you know and like and imagine. You might get it published and you might not. And the "might not" is still far bigger than the "might". The white publishers catering to white folk would say, "It is not interesting"—to white folk, naturally not. They want Uncle Toms, Topsies,[7] good "darkies" and clowns. I have in my office a story with all the earmarks of truth. A young man says that he started out to write and had his stories accepted. Then he began to write about the things he knew best about, that is, about his own people. He submitted a story to a magazine which said, "We are sorry, but we cannot take it". "I sat down and revised my story, changing the color of the characters and the locale and sent it under an assumed name with a change of address and it was accepted by the same magazine that had refused it, the editor promising to take anything else I might send in providing it was good enough."

We have, to be sure, a few recognized and successful Negro artists; but they are not all those fit to survive or even a good minority. They are but the remnants of that ability and genius among us whom the accidents of education and opportunity have raised on the tidal waves of chance. We black folk are not altogether peculiar in this. After all, in the world at large, it is only the accident, the remnant, that gets the chance to make the most of itself; but if this is true of the white world it is infinitely more true of the colored world. It is not simply the great clear tenor of Roland Hayes that opened the ears of America. We have had many voices of all kinds as fine as his and America was and is as deaf as she was for years to him. Then a foreign land heard Hayes and put its imprint on him and immediately America with all its imitative snobbery

---

6. Richard L. Brown (1893–1917), artist described by James Porter in *Modern Negro Art* (1943) as one of "two of the most talented men of this epoch [who] died in mid-career before fulfilling early promises."
7. Topsy and Uncle Tom are black characters in Harriet Beecher Stowe's *Uncle Tom's Cabin* (1852).

woke up. We approved Hayes because London, Paris and Berlin approved him and not simply because he was a great singer.

Thus it is the bounden duty of black America to begin this great work of the creation of Beauty, of the preservation of Beauty, of the realization of Beauty, and we must use in this work all the methods that men have used before. And what have been the tools of the artist in times gone by? First of all, he has used the Truth—not for the sake of truth, not as a scientist seeking truth, but as one upon whom Truth eternally thrusts itself as the highest handmaid of imagination, as the one great vehicle of universal understanding. Again artists have used Goodness—goodness in all its aspects of justice, honor and right—not for sake of an ethical sanction but as the one true method of gaining sympathy and human interest.

The apostle of Beauty thus becomes the apostle of Truth and Right not by choice but by inner and outer compulsion. Free he is but his freedom is ever bounded by Truth and Justice; and slavery only dogs him when he is denied the right to tell the Truth or recognize an ideal of Justice.

Thus all Art is propaganda and ever must be, despite the wailing of the purists. I stand in utter shamelessness and say that whatever art I have for writing has been used always for propaganda for gaining the right of black folk to love and enjoy. I do not care a damn for any art that is not used for propaganda. But I do care when propaganda is confined to one side while the other is stripped and silent.

In New York we have two plays: "White Cargo" and "Congo."[8] In "White Cargo" there is a fallen woman. She is black. In "Congo" the fallen woman is white. In "White Cargo" the black woman goes down further and further and in "Congo" the white woman begins with degradation but in the end is one of the angels of the Lord.

You know the current magazine story: A young white man goes down to Central America and the most beautiful colored woman there falls in love with him. She crawls across the whole isthmus to get to him. The white man says nobly, "No". He goes back to his white sweetheart in New York.

In such cases, it is not the positive propaganda of people who believe white blood divine, infallible and holy to which I object. It is the denial of a similar right of propaganda to those who believe black blood human, lovable and inspired with new ideals for the world. White artists themselves suffer from this narrowing of their field. They cry for freedom in dealing with Negroes because they have so little freedom in dealing with whites. DuBose Heywood writes "Porgy"[9] and writes beautifully of the black Charleston underworld. But why does he do this? Because he cannot do a similar thing for the white people of Charleston, or they would drum him out of town. The only chance he had to tell the truth of pitiful human degradation was to tell it of colored people. I should not be surprised if Octavius Roy Cohen[1] had approached the *Saturday Evening Post* and asked permission to write about a different kind of colored folk than the monstrosities he has created; but if he has, the *Post* has replied, "No. You are getting paid to write about the kind of colored people you are writing about."

In other words, the white public today demands from its artists, literary and pictorial, racial prejudgment which deliberately distorts Truth and Justice, as far as colored races are concerned, and it will pay for no other.

On the other hand, the young and slowly growing black public still wants its prophets almost equally unfree. We are bound by all sorts of customs that have come down as second-hand soul clothes of white patrons. We are ashamed of sex and we lower our eyes when people will talk of it. Our religion holds us in superstition. Our worst side has been so shamelessly emphasized that we are denying we have or ever had a worst side. In all sorts of ways we are hemmed in and our new young artists have got to fight their way to freedom.

---

8. *Kongo* (1926) by the white American playwrights Kilbourn Gordon and Chester DeVonde; *White Cargo: A Play of the Primitive* (1925) by the English-born white actor and playwright Leon Gordon (1895–1960).

9. The 1924 novel *Porgy* by the white American writer DuBose Heyward (1885–1940) was the basis for George Gershwin's 1935 opera, *Porgy and Bess*.

1. The white American writer Octavus Roy Cohen (1891–1959) became famous for writing stories with exaggerated characterizations of African Americans from the South.

The ultimate judge has got to be you and you have got to build yourselves up into that wide judgment, that catholicity of temper which is going to enable the artist to have his widest chance for freedom. We can afford the Truth. White folk today cannot. As it is now we are handing everything over to a white jury. If a colored man wants to publish a book, he has got to get a white publisher and a white newspaper to say it is great; and then you and I say so. We must come to the place where the work of art when it appears is reviewed and acclaimed by our own free and unfettered judgment. And we are going to have a real and valuable and eternal judgment only as we make ourselves free of mind, proud of body and just of soul to all men.

And then do you know what will be said? It is already saying. Just as soon as true Art emerges; just as soon as the black artist appears, someone touches the race on the shoulder and says, "He did that because he was an American, not because he was a Negro; he was born here; he was trained here; he is not a Negro—what is a Negro anyhow? He is just human; it is the kind of thing you ought to expect".

I do not doubt that the ultimate art coming from black folk is going to be just as beautiful, and beautiful largely in the same ways, as the art that comes from white folk, or yellow, or red; but the point today is that until the art of the black folk compels recognition they will not be rated as human. And when through art they compel recognition then let the world discover if it will that their art is as new as it is old and as old as new.

I had a classmate once who did three beautiful things and died. One of them was a story of a folk who found fire and then went wandering in the gloom of night seeking again the stars they had once known and lost; suddenly out of blackness they looked up and there loomed the heavens; and what was it that they said? They raised a mighty cry: "It is the stars, it is the ancient stars, it is the young and everlasting stars!"[2]

ALAIN LOCKE

Art or Propaganda? [1928]

In this introduction to the inaugural issue of the literary journal *Harlem: A Forum of Negro Life,* Alain Locke addresses the shift in perspective of the "younger generation" (for which he coined the term the "New Negro" in his formative 1925 book of the same name). Like Du Bois, Locke believed that art could lead the way in improving the lives of African Americans. Unlike Du Bois, Locke vocally supported young artists' desire for creative freedom. He also considered the shift away from overt political engagement in art as a positive step toward greater political and artistic development, arguing that propaganda "perpetuates the position of group inferiority even in crying out against it."

The November 1928 issue of *Harlem* featured a combination of art and criticism by key figures of the Harlem Renaissance. In addition to Locke's essay, it contained creative writing by Langston Hughes, Alice Dunbar-Nelson, and George S. Schuyler, theater criticism by Theophilus Lewis, and illustrations by Aaron Douglas and Richard Bruce Nugent. *Harlem* was edited by Wallace Thurman (1902–1934), who also edited the influential 1926 literary magazine *Fire!!* Like *Fire!! Harlem* did not survive beyond its inaugural issue.

Born into a prominent Philadelphia family in 1886, Locke grew up to become one of the foremost intellectuals of his time and a key promoter of the Harlem Renaissance. After receiving his undergraduate degree from Harvard College in 1907, Locke became the first African American to be awarded a Rhodes scholarship to study at Oxford University in England. He earned another bachelor's degree at Oxford, did graduate work at the University of Berlin, and in 1918 received a doctorate in philosophy from Harvard. His spent the core of his long academic career at Howard University in Washington,

2. From William Vaughn Moody's play *The Fire-Bringer* (1904).

D.C., where he began teaching in 1912. In the mid-1920s, Locke clashed with the university administration over his efforts to add African American studies to the curriculum and was dismissed in 1925. Although protests by students and faculty resulted in his reinstatement as a faculty member, Locke stayed away from Howard until 1928, by which time Mordecai Wyatt Johnson, who shared Locke's commitment to promoting African and African American studies, had been hired as the university's first black president. During the years away from Howard, Locke committed himself to the development of the Harlem Renaissance, writing theory and criticism and promoting the work of African and African American artists, including Zora Neale Hurston and Langston Hughes. As he wrote in his foreword to *The New Negro,* "Negro life is not only establishing new contacts and founding new centers, it is finding a new soul." When Locke returned to Howard's Philosophy Department in 1928, he continued to develop his theory of "cultural pluralism," which recognized the distinctiveness of different traditions, placing them within the context of an inclusive, democratic society. In 1953, the year before he died, Locke succeeded in establishing a chapter of the scholarly society Phi Beta Kappa at Howard.

From *Harlem: A Forum of Negro Life,* November 1928.

Artistically it is the one fundamental question for us today,—Art or Propaganda. Which? Is this more the generation of the prophet or that of the poet; shall our intellectual and cultural leadership preach and exhort or sing? I believe we are at that interesting moment when the prophet becomes the poet and when prophecy becomes the expressive song, the chant of fulfillment. We have had too many Jeremiahs,[1] major and minor;—and too much of the drab wilderness. My chief objection to propaganda, apart from its besetting sin of monotony and disproportion, is that it perpetuates the position of group inferiority even in crying out against it. For it leaves and speaks under the shadow of a dominant majority whom it harangues, cajoles, threatens or supplicates. It is too extroverted for balance or poise or inner dignity and self-respect. Art in the best sense is rooted in self-expression and whether naive or sophisticated is self-contained. In our spiritual growth genius and talent must more and more choose the role of group expression, or even at times the role of free individualistic expression,—in a word must choose art and put aside propaganda.

The literature and art of the younger generation already reflects this shift of psychology, this regeneration of spirit. David should be its patron saint: it should confront the Phillistines with its five smooth pebbles fearlessly.[2] There is more strength in a confident camp than in a threatened enemy. The sense of inferiority must be innerly compensated, self-conviction must supplant self-justification and in the dignity of this attitude a convinced minority must confront a condescending majority. Art cannot completely accomplish this, but I believe it can lead the way.

Our espousal of art thus becomes no mere idle acceptance of "art for art's sake,"[3] or cultivation of the last decadences of the over-civilized, but rather a deep realization of the fundamental purpose of art and of its function as a tap root of vigorous, flourishing living. Not all of our younger writers are deep enough in the sub-soil of their native materials,—too many are pot-plants seeking a forced growth according to the exotic tastes of a pampered and decadent public. It is the art of the people that needs to be cultivated, not the art of the coteries. Propaganda itself is preferable to shallow, truckling imitation. Negro things may reasonably be a fad for others; for us they must be a religion. Beauty, however, is its best priest and psalms will be more effective than sermons.

1. The writings of the prophet Jeremiah are collected in the Book of Jeremiah, considered part of the Jewish canon.
2. David conquered the Philistine giant Goliath with a slingshot and some stones [1 Samuel, chapter 17].
3. Translation of "l'art pour l'art," French term coined by Theophile Gautier (1811–72) meaning that art does not need to serve any useful purpose beyond being art.

To date we have had little sustained art unsubsidized by propaganda; we must admit this debt to these foster agencies. The three journals which have been vehicles of most of our artistic expressions have been the avowed organs of social movements and organized social programs. All our purely artistic publications have been sporadic. There is all the greater need then for a sustained vehicle of free and purely artistic expression. If HARLEM should happily fill this need, it will perform an honorable and constructive service. I hope it may, but should it not, the need remains and the path toward it will at least be advanced a little.

We need, I suppose in addition to art some substitute for propaganda. What shall that be? Surely we must take some cognizance of the fact that we live at the centre of a social problem. Propaganda at least nurtured some form of serious social discussion, and social discussion was necessary, is still necessary. On this side; the difficulty and shortcoming of propaganda is its partisanship. It is one-sided and often prejudging. Should we not then have a journal of free discussion, open to all sides of the problem and to all camps of belief? Difficult, that,—but intriguing. Even if it has to begin on the note of dissent and criticism and assume Menckenian[4] scepticism to escape the common-places of conformity. Yet, I hope we shall not remain at this negative pole. Can we not cultivate truly free and tolerant discussion, almost Socratically[5] minded for the sake of truth? After Beauty, let Truth come into the Renaissance picture,—a later cue, but a welcome one. This may be premature, but one hopes not,—for eventually it must come and if we can accomplish that, instead of having to hang our prophets, we can silence them or change their lamentations to song with a Great Fulfillment.

ANGELINA WELD GRIMKÉ

Rachel: The Play of the Month; The Reason and Synopsis by the Author [1920]

Angelina Weld Grimké's play *Rachel* was critical in the development of African American theater. Produced by the NAACP's Drama Committee in 1916, *Rachel* was the first dramatic play by an African American to be professionally produced and performed by African Americans in the twentieth century, and it heralded the establishment of a black theatrical tradition. Grimké's subsequent attempts to interest professional producers in the play were unsuccessful, and in 1920 she published the play as a way of reaching the largest possible audience. Grimké (1880–1958) was the niece of the Reverend Francis J. Grimké and the grandniece of Angelina Grimké Weld, a white abolitionist, for whom she was named.

Later playwrights built on Grimké's strategies, including her focus on motherhood and her mode of racial despair. Perhaps more important, controversial elements of the play stimulated discussions about the function of theater and the proper role of black drama. In fact, the alternative folk-theater movement arose from the active repudiation of Grimké's strategies, particularly her focus on racial victimization. Two leaders of the folk-theater movement, Alain Locke and Montgomery Gregory, were among the dissenting members of the NAACP Drama Committee who viewed *Rachel* as a "propagandist platform." Around 1919, when Gregory was appointed chairman of Howard University's Speech Department, the school's drama club became known as the Howard Players. The Players, Locke and Gregory recalled, "promot[ed] the purely artistic approach and the folk-drama idea."

In the article reprinted here—first published in the short-lived (1920–1921) Pittsburgh journal *Competitor*,

---

4. The white American writer and critic Henry Louis (H. L.) Mencken (1880–1956) was well-known for his acerbic satire, often tinged with scorn.
5. Drawing on the teaching method developed by the Greek philosopher Socrates of asking questions as a way of helping students come to an understanding of a truth.

which was aimed at the black middle class and high-lighted black achievements—Grimké defends *Rachel* against its critics. She argues that her characters are direct challenges to false stereotypes of African Americans and contends that racism is caused by distorted representations of black people. Her position raises a number of questions about how art influences its audience. Does presenting a contrasting image (for instance, an educated African American) counter racist stereotypes? How does this strategy compare with that of exposing stereotypes by directly representing them as ridiculous images?

Grimké also addresses the idea of art as propaganda. She promotes her play as a political tool to combat the racism of white women. This argument raises the question of how the target audience for a work of art might affect how audiences and critics judge it. Also, can artists gear their work toward one type of audience, or must they also consider the effects of their work on others outside their intended audience?

From *The Competitor*, January 1920.

Since it has been understood that "Rachel" preaches race suicide, I would emphasize that that was not my intention. To the contrary, the appeal is not primarily to the colored people, but to the whites.

Because of environment and certain inherent qualities each of us reacts correspondingly and logically to the various forces about us. For example, if these forces be of love we react with love, and if of hate with hate. Very naturally all of us will not react as strongly or in the same manner—that is impossible.

Now the colored people in this country form what may be called the "submerged tenth." From morning until night, week in week out, year in year out, until death ends all, they never know what it means to draw one clean, deep breath free from the contamination of the poison of that enveloping force which we call race prejudice. Of necessity they react to it. Some are embittered, made resentful, belligerent, even dangerous; some are made hopeless, indifferent, submissive, lacking in initiative; some again go to any extreme in a search for temporary pleasures to drown their memory, thought, etc.

Now the purpose was to show how a refined, sensitive, highly-strung girl, a dreamer and an idealist, the strongest instinct in whose nature is a love for children and a desire some day to be a mother herself—how this girl would react to this force.

The majority of women, everywhere, although they are beginning to awaken, form one of the most conservative elements of society. They are, therefore, opposed to changes. For this reason and for sex reasons the white women of this country are about the worst enemies with which the colored race has to contend. My belief was, then, that if a vulnerable point in their armor could be found, if their hearts could be active or passive enemies, they might become, at least, less inimical and possibly friendly.

Did they have a vulnerable point and, if so, what was it? I believed it to be motherhood. Certainly all the noblest, finest, most sacred things in their lives converge about this. If anything can make all women sisters underneath their skins it is motherhood. If, then, the white women of this country could see, feel, understand just what effect their prejudice and the prejudice of their fathers, brothers, husbands, sons were having on the souls of the colored mothers everywhere, and upon the mothers that are to be, a great power to affect public opinion would be set free and the battle would be half won.

This was the main purpose. There is a subsidiary one as well. Whenever you say "colored person" to a white man he immediately, either through an ignorance that is deliberate or stupid, conjures up in his mind the picture of what he calls "the darkey." In other words, he believes, or says he does, that all colored people are a grinning, white-toothed, shiftless, carefree set, given to chicken-stealing, watermelon-eating, always, under all circumstances, properly obsequious to a white skin and always amusing. Now, it is possible that this type is to be found among the colored people; but if the white man is honest and observant he will have to acknowledge that the same type can be duplicated in his own race. Human nature, after all, is the same. And if the white man only cared to find out he would know that, type for type, he could find the same in both races. Certainly colored people are living in homes that are clean, well-kept with many evidences of taste and refinement about them. They are many of them well educated, cultivated and cultured; they are well-mannered and, in many instance, more moral than the whites; they love beauty; they have ideals and ambitions, and they do not talk—this educated type—in the Negro dialect. All the joys and sorrows and emotions the white people feel they feel; their feelings are as sensitive; they can be hurt as easily; they are as proud. I drew my characters, then, from the best type of colored people.

Now as to the play itself. In the first act Rachel, loving, young, joyous and vital, caring more to be a mother than anything else in the world, comes suddenly and terribly face to face with what motherhood means to the colored woman in the South. Four years elapse between the first and second acts. Rachel has learned much. She is saddened, disillusioned and embittered. She knows now that organized society in the North has decreed that if a colored man or woman is to be an economic factor, then he or she must, with comparatively few exceptions, remain in the menial class. This has been taught her by her own experience, by the experience of her brother, Tom, and by the experience of John Strong, the man she loves. She has learned that she may not go to a theater for an evening's entertainment without having it spoiled for her since, because of her color she must sit as an outcast, a pariah in a segregated section. And yet in spite of all this youth in her dies hard and hope and the desire for motherhood. She loves children, if anything, more than ever. It is in this act that she feels certain, for the first time, that John Strong loves her. She is made very happy by this knowledge, but in the midst of her joy

there comes a knocking at the door. And very terribly and swiftly again it is brought home to her what motherhood means, this time to the colored woman in the North. The lesson comes to her through a little black girl and her own little adopted son, Jimmy. Not content with maiming and marring the lives of colored men and women she learns this baneful thing, race prejudice, strikes at the souls of little colored children. In her anguish and despair at the knowledge she turns against God, believing that He has been mocking at her by implanting in her breast this desire for motherhood, and she swears by the most solemn oath of which she can think never to bring a child here to have its life blighted and ruined.

A week elapses between Acts II, and III. During the time Rachel has been very ill, not in body, but in mind and soul. She is up and about again, but is in a highly overwrought, nervous state. John Strong, whom she has not seen since she has been sick, comes to see her. She knows what his coming means and tries unsuccessfully to ward off his proposal. He pleads so well that, although she feels she is doing a wicked thing she finally yields. Just at the moment of her surrender, however, the sound of little Jimmy's heartbreaking weeping comes to her ears. She changes immediately and leaves him to go to Jimmy. Every night since Jimmy has undergone that searing experience in the previous act he has dreamed of it and awakens weeping. With that sound in her ears and soul she finds that she cannot break her oath. She returns and tells John Strong she cannot marry him. He is inclined, at first, not to take her seriously; but she shows him that this time her answer is final. Although her heart is breaking she sends him away. The play ends in blackness and with the inconsolable sounds of little Jimmy weeping.

[W. E. B. DU BOIS], NELL BATTLE LEWIS, WILLIAM S. TURNER, AND W. A. ROBINSON

from Race Drama [1925]

The 1925 exchange presented in "Race Drama" extends the discussion of representation beyond Angelina Weld Grimké's consideration of the type of black characters that should be portrayed on stage (p. 335) to the question of whether black actors should move beyond playing only black characters. The questions raised by the white American critic Nell Battle Lewis (1893–1956) and by the African Americans who responded to her fall into two groups. The first group concerns black actors playing non-black characters: Should casting be determined by the origin of the playwright or the play? How should character descriptions affect casting? Does the actor's makeup or skill or the audience's suspension of disbelief increase casting options?

The second set of questions pertains to the production of plays by non-black playwrights and the effect of such plays on the development of black drama—questions that were of particular interest to critics and artists in the 1920s: Does exposure to Shakespeare's plays contribute to or distract from the creation of "genuine" African American drama? Do African or non-English-language plays have a place in the development of African American drama?

From *The Crisis*, June 1925.

N ell Battle Lewis who writes a column in the Raleigh, North Carolina, *News* saw Negroes at Shaw University play "Twelfth Night":

> They did it on the whole creditably, and they were letter-perfect. Yet the play seemed to weigh heavily upon the cast, and the general effect of the performance was strikingly artificial. I say this without the slightest desire to belittle the effort which was admirable. I am very much interested in the advancement of the Negroes along any artistic line. I should greatly like to see them develop a genuine drama of their own.
>
> But Shakespeare, I think, is not their vehicle except, perhaps, in the case of extraordinarily talented actors of their race. Ira Aldridge,[1] for instance, played Othello with great success.
>
> Though Shakespeare wrote in what is now the Negroes' language, he does not express their spirit, nor do I think that, in general, they can ever adequately express his. This means nothing more than that the spirit of races differs. English actors would probably be very unsuccessful in giving a play of the Chinese.
>
> Racial consciousness and racial pride can be very easily carried to excess. We have a wicked example of it in this country now. But I am a great believer in trying to be what you are, in "taking yourself for better or worse as your portion".[2] Just as I think individuals are never so surely at their best as when they are simply themselves, I think this principle applies to races, too. It is unfortunate that the advancement of the Negroes has been largely imitative. But perhaps this has been inevitable because of their close proximity and association with the whites in this country. But for their own sake I am very much in favor of their emphasizing as much as possible in their art their own distinct racial character.

Negroes immediately answered Miss Lewis and she gamely published what they said. The Dean of Shaw[3] writes:

---

1. Actor (1807–67) who was raised in Maryland and New York and then moved to Europe and became a star of the theater, specializing in Othello and other Shakespearean roles.
2. Paraphrase from Emerson's "Self-Reliance": "There is a time in every man's education when he arrives at the conviction that envy is ignorance; that imitation is suicide; that he must take himself for better, for worse, as his portion."
3. William S. Turner, from 1921–1930, was dean of Shaw University, the oldest historically black college in the South.

"I wish, however, not as one competent to pass criticism upon the merits of dramatic art, but as a student of social psychology with due appreciation for the results of modern biological investigation, to call attention to a question discussed by you with respect to race capacities and art. You assert by implication that Shakespeare cannot be properly the vehicle of *Negro* dramatic expression because the language of Shakespeare is for Negroes only an adopted language. English is an adopted language not for Negroes only, but for all who speak it. Psychologists and sociologists are now quite generally agreed that language, whether it be English, French or German or what not, is a part of man's social heritage, and as such it is a thing to be adopted or appropriated in fundamentally the same way by every individual, regardless of race or nationality. The recent researches of John B. Watson[4] further confirm this view. Science is now reasonably certain that we bring nothing into the world in the form of language, nor any racial predilection for any particular language. The child born of any race will accept with equal facility the language of any group in which it may, be born. No language is native to anyone except in relation to the social environment of birth. White babies learn language through the same process that black babies learn. The former may learn to talk more correctly owing to superior environment, but not on account of differences in biological heredity.

"What you and others deplore as excessive imitation on the part of Negroes is, after all, but the natural attempt of black folk to appropriate their only social heritage. The transition of the Negro from Africa to America involved a sharper break with the past than that experienced by any other race group on this continent. The efficiency of the slave system necessitated as completely as possible the destruction of the Negro's African culture, his fam-

ily and tribal organization. Africa is as blank to American Negroes as China. Anyone who is waiting for the Negroes in this country to produce something distinctly African has a long time to wait. I, too, think that it would be an excellent thing for Negroes to produce plays portraying their own life.

[I]t is probably true that Americans generally and Negroes particularly have not the cultural background to interpret Shakespeare adequately. But it is not a matter of blood. Our social heritage does not pass through the blood."

W. A. Robinson of the State Division of Negro Education[5] adds:

"We cannot agree with you that English is our 'adopted language' any more than it is yours. We were born and nurtured in it and have known no other language, nor have we inherited the body of traditions of any other land than this. To act in terms of this inheritance in which we live and move and have our being we do not call imitation.

"We surely must agree that Shakespeare is 'for all the world and for all time',[6] but we think that Hamlet was a Dane, Shylock a Jew, Olivia an Illyrian, and Cleopatra an Egyptian. Is not all drama 'artificial', a dream world where Fay Bainter makes a most acceptable Chinese, though most miraculously transformed, features and all, into an Occidental for a happy ending; where also Jane Cowl[7] is a wonderful Egyptian even without iodine? Even girls may be boys!

"We hesitate to analyze your feeling in the matter but seeing the play from our own angle we feel sure that, far from 'heavy', those young people at Shaw rollicked through those parts even of dukes and countesses with as much abandon as the occasion would allow. Now the 'heaviness' of traditional

---

4. American psychologist, known as the "father of behaviorism."
5. Educator and high school principal; at the time worked for the Division of Negro Education in North Carolina.
6. Paraphrase of lines from Ben Jonson's poem, "To the Memory of My Beloved Master William Shakespeare, and What He Hath Left Us": "To whom all Scenes of Europe homage owe. / He was not of an age, but for all time!"
7. White American actress (1884–1950), whose famous parts included the title role in Shakespeare's *Antony and Cleopatra*; Fay Bainter (1891–1968), white American actress who played Ming Toy in *East Is West* (1919), a character who, when it is discovered that she is adopted and of Spanish origin rather than Chinese as originally thought, is able to marry her white American sweetheart.

thought may make it difficult for some to associate those parts with Negroes.

"True, we want the sorrows and humors of certain phases of Negro life of this and past periods of our acceptance in America preserved in dramatic values, but the 'Be Yourselves' idea surely would not limit us to those vehicles in dramatic expression.

For where would we get the technique even for producing such things if we do not first study the universal standard drama? Really, Shakespeare emancipates, as some would put it, while others might feel that nothing, even Shakespeare, is safe from these grasping Negroes."

CAROLINE BOND DAY
What Shall We Play? [1925]

In the essay reprinted here, Caroline Bond Day (1889–1948), a Radcliffe College graduate and teacher who did pioneering studies of biracial families, provides a practical response to questions about casting raised by "Race Drama" (p. 338). However, her focus on locating "suitable plays" for black actors (as well as her argument that the range of looks in "this 'bouquet race' of ours" can provide physical types for all parts) raises new questions: First, is physical suitability of paramount importance to casting? Second, does the importance of physical suitability vary depending on the particular set-ting of the play or ethnicity of the characters? For example, Day suggests that in Shakespearean plays, looks are paramount. For Day, a light-skinned black actor would be a more convincing Italian than a (presumably fair) white actor, and casting the plays would be difficult for some amateur groups. Yet her list of "appropriate" plays suggests that identifiably black actors can convincingly play Asian or Native American characters, in which case the physical restrictions for black actors are looser in plays with non-white characters.

From *The Crisis*, September 1925.

Twenty years ago at one of our Southern universities I witnessed the production of a Greek tragedy. The first scene represented the interior of a Greek temple. The stage was small, and when the curtains were drawn we beheld in the strong glare of the footlights a bust of Booker T. Washington pedestaled on the one side, and on the other, one of Beethoven. The tragedy became a comedy. The rest of the play was in keeping with the stage-setting. Most of us have had similar experiences which we knew to be the result of ill-chosen plays.

Since that day we have gone a far way in school dramatics. Yet, until we have enough indigenous playwrights to anticipate our needs we shall continue to have problems in play-selection.

As a result of the recent discussion in the columns of "The Looking Glass"[1] concerning the ability of Negro students to produce Shakespearean plays, the question has arisen—"What may be substituted in their stead?" Not, however, that we have agreed for a moment that they should be eliminated from our schools, or that they may not be done acceptably. We simply grant that these and certain others of the English Classics are produced with difficulty by our students and by amateur groups in general.

Obviously the most outstanding difficulty in this situation is one of physical suitability for the parts. Nevertheless for seven consecutive years I witnessed Shakespearean performances at Atlanta University which were thoroughly enjoyable and for which somehow suit-

---

1. Reference to "Race Drama" (p. 338), published in "The Looking Glass" section of *The Crisis*; "The Looking Glass" consisted of a series of short editorials, many of which discussed news coverage of African Americans in other media outlets.

able persons were secured, for this "bouquet race" of ours can supply types for all parts. I recall a blue-eyed, flaxen-haired Miranda, and her equally fair Ferdinand, a pale and thoroughly patrician Olivia, a Katharine[2] who was a prototype of England's Virgin Queen[3] in looks as well as disposition, and dukes and gentlemen a plenty, handsome and swaggering enough for all that some of them were more like the Italians and other Latins whom they represented than like white men made up.

Yet to secure artistic production such as these were, a certain elimination of material is necessary for uniformity in the caste. Now in a club or group where all wish a turn at acting this means an added tax on a director already beset with the difficulties of amateur production.

It is for such groups as these then that we offer the following short list of plays. They are for the most part free from royalties, not necessarily expensive, entirely within the grasp of amateurs, and all of them allow some parts for persons of mixed blood and of purely Negroid types.

These I have divided arbitrarily into three groups and will offer a word of suggestion about one or two from each.[4]

1. *Allegories, Moralities and adapted Fairy Tales.*
   Every Man (old Morality Play)
   Every Youth
   Every Woman
   *The Slave with Two Faces—Mary Davis[5]
   At the sign of the Greedy Pig—Charles S. Brooks
   The Dragon—Lady Gregory
   *Six who Pass while the Lentils Boil—Stuart Walker
   Sir David Wears a Crown—Stuart Walker.

2. *Plays of Different Nationalities*
   (a) *Oriental*
      Chitra—Rabindranath Tagore
      The Post office—Rabindranath Tagore
      The Tents of the Arabs—Lord Dunsany
      *King Aregimenes and the Unknown Warrior— Lord Dunsany
      A Night at an Inn—Lord Dunsany
      *Gods of the Mountains—Lord Dunsany
      *The Golden Doom—Lord Dunsany
      *The Judgment of Indra—Dhan Gopal Mukey
   Egyptian
      Caesar and Cleopatra—G. B. Shaw
   (b) *Chinese*
      The Yellow Jacket—Hazelton and Bemino
      The Chinese Lantern—Lawrence Housman
      *The Turtle Dove—Margaret S. Oliver
   (c) *American Indian*
      *The Glory of the Morning—Leanord
      *The Arrow Maker—Mary Austin
      *The Last of the Lowries—Paul Greene Pokey— Moeller
      Hiawatha (adapted version)—Longfellow
   (e) *Negro*
      *Three Plays for a Negro Theatre—Ridgely Torrence.
      Emperor Jones—Eugene O'Neill
      The Octoroon or Life in Louisiana—Dion Boucicault
      The No 'Count Boy—Paul Green (Theatre-Arts Magazine Nov., 1924)
   (f) *Spanish*
      *A Sunny Morning—Ouintero, Sarafin, and Joaquinn Alverez

---

2. Katherine from Shakespeare's *The Taming of the Shrew*; Miranda and Ferdinand from Shakespeare's *The Tempest*; Olivia from Shakespeare's *Twelfth Night*.

3. Queen Elizabeth I of England (1533–1603).

4. Asterisks indicate one-act plays.

5. Day's list contains unconventional or incorrect spellings for a number of the plays and playwrights, including this author, Mary Carolyn Davies; other examples include "The Gods of the Mountain" by Edward J. M. D. Plunkett, Lord Dunsany; "The Judgment of Indra" by Dhan Gopal Mukerji; "The Yellow Jacket" by George C. Hazelton and [Joseph Henry] Benrimo; "The Chinese Lantern" by Laurence Housman; "The Glory of the Mountain" by William Ellery Leonard; "The Arrow-Maker" by Mary Hunter Austin; "The Last of the Lowries" by Paul Green; "The Song of Hiawatha" by Henry Wadsworth Longfellow; "Sunny Morning" by Serafin and Joaquín Álvarez Quintero; "Miss Civilization" by Richard Harding Davis; "Dinner at Seven Sharp" by Amabel and Tudor Jenks; "The Maker of Dreams" by Oliphant Down; "A Scrap of Paper" by Victorien Sardou; "The Neighbors" by Zona Gale; "The Constant Lover" by St. John E. C. Hankin; and "The Cherry Orchard" by Anton Chekhov.

3. *Modern*

  *Miss Civilization—R. H. Davies
  *Dinner at Seven Sharp—Tudor Jenks
  *Maker of Dreams—Oliphant Downs
  A Scrap of Paper—Sardou
  *Neighbors—Zona Gale
  *The Constant Lover—St. John C. Hankin
  *The Lost Silk Hat—Lord Dunsany
  *Will O' the Wisp—Doris Holman
  *Spreading the News—Lady Gregory
  The Cherry Orchard—Tchekhov

In the first we have allegories, moralities and adapted fairy-tales which are usually written without reference to a definite time or place. This leaves a wide latitude for the imagination. In "The Slave with Two Faces", a charming little sketch in one act, the characters are simply, First-Girl, Second-Girl, and Life.[6] The girls are supposed to represent peasants of any nationality and Life may be so represented that like "Death" in "Everyman" one forgets all else save that he is a great elemental Power.

In a recent production of "Six Who Pass While the Lentils Boil", my "Ballad-Singer", so swarthy and handsome was he, might have come from Portugal, or the "Mimi",[7] if any one had questioned her origin, from Japan. The interior of a French peasant kitchen was easily arranged and altogether we had a naive and refreshing entertainment for very little trouble and expense.

In the second group, "King Argimenes and the Unknown Warrior" is a typical Dunsany satire, and again is easily staged and costumed. An easy arrangement for scenery for this play is a simple back-drop or cyclorama on which is represented one or more of the pyramids in the distance. A cluster of large palm trees (rented if that is easier than to paint them) grouped at one side. The whole thing is merely suggestive of the desert. The caste includes a number of slaves who wear inconspicuous garments of brown burlap, or some other coarse material but it also boasts four Egyptian queens and one King who may be attired as gorgeously as desired. Another simple and beautiful play for amateurs is Tagore's "Chitra". It is a sort of East Indian Romeo and Juliet, with an opportunity for colorful costumes and out-of-door scenes.

In several other of the Dunsany plays as well as those of Tagore there are opportunities for Mohammedan[8] costumes which are invariably becoming. The white and colored turbans and flowing robes add dignity and grace. These may be made of unbleached domestic cheese cloth or any suitable inexpensive cotton material and dyed in cold water dyes to the required shades.

Among the modern sketches there are few more appealing both to actors and audience than those of the Pierrot and Pierette type. One of the most graceful and attractive Pierrots whom I have seen was a young West Indian lad of seventeen. He sang and danced his way into the hearts both of his hearers and of the maiden in Oliphant Dawn's "The Maker of Dreams". The scenes were laid in a room so scantily furnished as to be almost bare and the costumes were the conventional ones for plays of the "Prunella" type.[9]

Two of the best reference books for amateur directors are "Dramatics for School and Community" by C. M. Wise and "Producing in Little Theatres" by Clarence Stratton. In the former may be found a complete list of plays for school-production with all necessary information as to the number of male and female characters in each, titles of volumes in which shorter plays are included, and names of publishers.

It is to be hoped that with their latent histrionic ability our younger group is going to develop a splendid technic by producing the better type of plays. The time is not far off when there will be a great demand for good Negro actors and actresses.

---

6. There are seven main characters in this one-act play, as well as "Others" who appear as voices; the main characters are Life (The Slave), First Girl, Second Girl, A Woman, A Man, A Young Man, and A Workman.
7. This play has the character of a "Mime," typically played by a man, which this production may have changed to a female "Mimi."
8. Arab.
9. Character who falls in love with Pierrot in Harley Granville-Barker and Laurence Housman's "Prunella; or, Love in a Dutch Garden," first performed in 1904 and published in 1906.

W. E. B. Du Bois

"Krigwa Players Little Negro Theatre": The Story of a Little Theatre Movement [1926]

In a 1972 interview, the playwright May Miller (1899–1995) recalled how the birth of the Little Theater Movement in the 1920s was a key moment in the development of the African American theatrical tradition: "The great Krigwa Movement was sponsored by the *Crisis* magazine, and it established all over the country little one-act play groups that performed in churches and schools, and all this was a forerunner to what we're doing now. We would have no Lorraine Hansberry if there had not been behind her those people who were slowly leading up to her great productions."

W. E. B. Du Bois was a motivating force behind this new dramatic movement. In September 1925, he launched a literary contest in *The Crisis,* which offered awards of $75, $40, and $10 for plays "deal[ing] with some phase of Negro history or experience and [* * *] occupy[ing] from five to seven pages of THE CRISIS in length." With articles such as "Playwrighting" in February 1925, which outlines the basic principles of crafting a play, he encouraged aspiring playwrights to participate in the contest. He established Krigwa (Crisis Guild of Writers and Artists, or CriGWA, with the initial letter later changed to a *K*) and helped launch the Krigwa Players in Harlem to perform the new plays.

In the July 1926 editorial in *The Crisis* reprinted here, Du Bois outlines the theory driving his investment in the Little Theater Movement, offering four principles for a "real Negro theater": plays must be "about us," "by us," "for us," and "near us." Du Bois's article responds to key questions in the contemporary debate about the development of African American drama. First, should theater be used as a political tool to influence a white audience (as suggested by Angelina Weld Grimké in her essay on *Rachel,* p. 335), or should plays be geared toward African American audiences and performed in black neighborhoods? Second, are some plays by non-black playwrights good choices for black actors (as proposed by Caroline Bond Day in "What Shall We Play?," p. 340), or should black actors focus on plays by African Americans? Finally, can and should black actors act in Shakespearean and other classical plays (as argued by Day and the two respondents in the "Race Drama" discussion, p. 338), or are such productions "miss[ing] the real path"? Not only does Du Bois explore questions about what constitutes "black theater," but his adamant commitment to a "new birth" of black theater also provides an answer to the larger question of whether the development of black drama is important from a social and political perspective.

From *The Crisis,* July 1926.

I t is customary to regard Negroes as an essentially dramatic race; and it is probably true that tropical and sub-tropical peoples have more vivid imagination, are accustomed to expressing themselves with greater physical and spiritual abandon than most folk. And certainly, life as black and brown and yellow folk have known it is big with tragedy and comedy. The home life of Africans shows this natural dramatic tendency; the strides of the native African, the ceremony of home and assembly, the intense interest in music and play, all attest this.

In America, on the other hand, the road to freedom for the Negro lay through religious organization long before physical emancipation came. The Negro church gave the slave almost his only freedom of spirit and of the churches that came to proselyte among the slaves, only those were permanently successful which were strongly tinged with Puritanism, namely: the Baptist and the Methodist. These churches frowned upon drama and the play, upon the theatre and the dance; and for this reason the American Negro has been hindered in his natural dramatic impulses.

Today as the renaissance of art comes among American Negroes, the theatre calls for new birth. But most people do not realize just where the novelty must come in. The Negro is already in the theatre and has been there for a long time; but his presence there is not yet thoroughly normal. His audience is mainly a white audience, and the Negro actor has, for a long time, been asked to entertain this more or less alien group. The demands and ideals of the white group and their conception of Negroes have set the norm for the black actor. He has been a minstrel, comedian, singer and lay figure of all sorts. Only recently has he begun tentatively to emerge as an ordinary human being with everyday reactions. And here he is still handicapped and put forth with much hesitation, as in the case of "The Nigger", "Lulu Belle" and "The Emperor Jones".[1]

In all this development naturally then the best of the Negro actor and the most poignant Negro drama have not been called for. This could be evoked only by a Negro audience desiring to see its own life depicted by its own writers and actors.

For this reason, a new Negro theatre is demanded and it is slowly coming. It needs, however, guiding lights. For instance, some excellent groups of colored amateurs are entertaining colored audiences in Cleveland, in Philadelphia and elsewhere. Almost invariably, however, they miss the real path. They play Shakespeare or Synge or reset a successful Broadway play with colored principals.

The movement which has begun this year in Harlem, New York City, lays down four fundamental principles. The plays of a real Negro theatre must be: 1. *About us.* That is, they must have plots which reveal Negro life as it is. 2. *By us.* That is, they must be written by Negro authors who understand from birth and continual association just what it means to be a Negro today. 3. *For us.* That is, the theatre must cater primarily to Negro audiences and be supported and sustained by their entertainment and approval. 4. *Near us.* The theatre must be in a Negro neighborhood near the mass of ordinary Negro people.

Only in this way can a real folk-play movement of American Negroes be built up. Even this building encounters certain difficulties. First, there is the problem of the plays. Five years ago there were practically no plays that filled the specifications noted. Already, however, this situation has begun to change on account of the prizes offered by THE CRISIS magazine and other agencies and for other reasons. There are available today a dozen or more plays of Negro life worth staging and the quantity and quality will increase very rapidly as the demand grows. The problem of actors is the least of the difficulties presented. In any group of colored people it is possible to get an unusual number of persons gifted with histrionic ability. The only trouble comes when effort is made to select the actors from limited groups or exclusively from among social acquaintances or friends. The third difficulty, that of a suitable playhouse, is real and must be worked out as circumstances permit. There are usually halls that can be used temporarily. Now and then a church is liberal enough to house a play.

In the New York movement, advantage is being taken of the fact that in the center of Harlem there is a branch of the New York Public Library which has in its basement a lecture room. The administration of this library has in the last few years changed from an attitude of aloofness from its Negro surroundings, and even resentment, to an attitude which recognizes that this library is serving a hundred thousand Negroes or more. It specializes on books which Negroes want to read; it subscribes to their periodicals and has lectures and art exhibits which attract them.

Some time ago Miss Ernestine Rose, the Librarian, suggested that a Little Theatre movement be started in connection with this library; but other activities interfered. This year the library authorities expressed their willingness to help equip a small and inexpensive stage in the lecture room and a group of 30 persons interested in such a theatre has been organized.

Foremost among these is Charles Burroughs. Charles Burroughs was trained in the college depart-

---

1. Three popular plays by white playwrights that featured black lead characters; Eugene O'Neill's "The Emperor Jones" is a tragic psychological drama about Brutus Jones, an African American convict who escapes to a Caribbean island and sets himself up as a monarch who exploits his people until they overthrow him; Edward Sheldon's "The Nigger" follows a young Southerner, Phillip Morrow, who finds out that he is part African American after he has been elected governor, and loses almost everything, including the white woman he loves; "Lulu Belle" (1926) by Charles MacArthur and Edward Shelton, is a melodrama about an African American prostitute, Lulu Belle (originated by white actress Lenore Ulric in blackface), who seduces and leaves a variety of white men until she is murdered in Paris by a spurned lover.

ment of Wilberforce and at the School of Expression in Boston and has been a dramatic reader for many years for the Board of Education in New York City. He has been unusually successful in training actors as was shown by his training the groups which gave the pageant, "The Star of Ethiopia",[2] in New York, Washington, Philadelphia and Los Angeles.

In the Harlem Little Negro Theatre the library authorities built the stage and dressing rooms and furnished the lighting equipment. The players group furnished the curtain, the scenery, gave the plays and secured the audiences. Three one-act plays were selected, for the initial experiment. Two were tragedies by Willis Richardson: "Compromise", which was published in *The New Negro*, and "The Broken Banjo", which took the first prize in The Crisis Contest of 1925. The third, "The Church Fight", by Mrs. R. A. Gaines-Shelton, is a comedy which took the second prize in The Crisis

Contest of 1925. A cast of 20 persons was required and they rehearsed faithfully. Louise Latimer, assisted by Aaron Douglas, painted the scenery and on May 3, 10 and 17 the plays were given before full houses averaging 200 persons at each performance.

The success of the experiment is unquestioned. The audiences were enthusiastic and wanted more. The price of admission to membership in the group which gave the right to see the performances was only 50 cents and the total expense of staging the plays, not counting expenditures by the Library, was about $165 while the returns were something over $240. The players not only perform plays but they welcome other groups under easy conditions to come and use their playhouse under their patronage.

A second K. P. L. N. T.[3] is being organized in Washington, D. C., and it is hoped the movement will spread widely.

W. E. B. Du Bois et al.
The Negro in Art: How Shall He Be Portrayed? [1926]

Many of the most prominent artists and critics of the 1920s, both black and white, as well as several *Crisis* readers, participated in *The Crisis*'s 1926 symposium on "The Negro in Art: How Shall He Be Portrayed?" Over seven issues, between March and November, *The Crisis* published reactions to the diverse questions posed by W. E. B. Du Bois in the February issue, which included whether "any author can be criticized for painting the worst or the best characters of a group" and what African Americans should do "when they are continually painted at their worst and judged by the public as they are painted." The responses included here capture the wide range of opinion about the representation of black people in visual art and literature.

The responses raise additional questions, particularly about how an artist's or critic's own experiences of race and class shape his or her opinions about the representation of black characters. For example, four of the white participants in the symposium (Carl Van Vechten, H. L. Mencken, John Farrar, and Sherwood Ander-

son) do not differentiate between stereotyped portrayals of black characters and exaggerated representations of white characters; they see extreme types of any race as rich material for artists. A number of the African American participants, including Walter White and Langston Hughes, also emphasize the importance of different artists' being free to gravitate toward material that resonates with them. Some make the case, however, that the way in which representations of race shape the lives of black Americans differs from the way in which those representations shape the lives of white Americans, making questions about how to represent black characters not only legitimate but also of cultural and political importance. This belief of African American participants in the interaction between art and politics also serves as a basis for calls by Jesse Fauset and Walter White for the African American public to support black artists.

Du Bois's phrasing of the questions and his introduction to the questionnaire reveal his own opinions about the roles of artists, authors, and publishers in

2. Historical pageant about black history by W. E. B. Du Bois, first produced on October 22, 1913.
3. Krigwa Players Little Negro Theatre.

fostering representations of black people in the arts. Two years later, Du Bois's harsh critique of Claude McKay's *Home to Harlem* (1928) would convey his continued conviction that the negative impact of representing African Americans as part of the criminal underworld superseded the ideal of unfettered freedom for artists. (Du Bois famously wrote that McKay's novel "for the most part nauseates me, and after the dirtier parts of its filth I feel distinctly like taking a bath.")

The 1926 symposium participants, with the exception of Georgia Douglas Johnson, largely reject the specific class elements of Du Bois's argument, especially the idea that artists should balance the typical portrayal of African Americans as "prostitutes, thieves and fools" with educated and cultured characters. On the other hand, many of the black symposium participants do recognize a special responsibility of black artists to fully develop their black characters, regardless of class. With the exception of Charles W. Chesnutt (who rejects distinctions between white and black writers), the black participants lean toward Countee Cullen's argument that white writers are "not under the same obligations" to create "types that are truly representative." Cullen goes even further, arguing that white writers cannot truly understand how African Americans feel about the issue of "racial defamation, even for art's sake."

From *The Crisis*, February–November 1926.

A QUESTIONNAIRE

There has long been controversy within and without the Negro race as to just how the Negro should be treated in art—how he should be pictured by writers and portrayed by artists. Most writers have said naturally that any portrayal of any kind of Negro was permissible so long as the work was pleasing and the artist sincere. But the Negro has objected vehemently—first in general to the conventional Negro in American literature; then in specific cases: to the Negro portrayed in the "Birth of a Nation"; in MacFall's "Wooings of Jezebel Pettyfer" and in Stribling's "Birthright"; in Octavius Roy Cohen's monstrosities.[1] In general they have contended that while the individual portrait may be true and artistic, the net result to American literature to date is to picture twelve million Americans as prostitutes, thieves and fools and that such "freedom" in art is miserably unfair.

This attitude is natural but as Carl Van Vechten writes us: "It is the kind of thing, indeed, which might be effective in preventing many excellent Negro writers from speaking any truth which might be considered unpleasant. There are plenty of unpleasant truths to be spoken about any race. The true artist speaks out fearlessly. The critic judges the artistic result; nor should he be concerned with anything else".

In order to place this matter clearly before the thinking element of Negro Americans and especially before young authors, THE CRISIS is asking several authors to write their opinions on the following matters:

1. When the artist, black or white, portrays Negro characters is he under any obligations or limitations as to the sort of character he will portray?

2. Can any author be criticized for painting the worst or the best characters of a group?

3. Can publishers be criticized for refusing to handle novels that portray Negroes of education and accomplishment, on the ground that these characters are no different from white folk and therefore not interesting?

4. What are Negroes to do when they are continually painted at their worst and judged by the public as they are painted?

5. Does the situation of the educated Negro in America with its pathos, humiliation and tragedy call for

1. Reference to stereotyped African American characters in stories by white American writer Octavus Roy Cohen; *Birth of a Nation*: 1915 silent movie directed by D. W. Griffith celebrating the Ku Klux Klan; *Wooings: The Wooings of Jezebel Pettyfer: Being the Personal History of Jehu Sennacherib Dyle; Together with an Account of Certain Things That Chanced in the House of the Sorcerer; Here Set Down*, a 1926 novel about a West Indian black man by the white British writer Haldane MacFall (1860–1928); *Birthright*: 1922 novel about a multiracial man by the white southern writer Thomas Sigismund Stribling (1881–1965).

artistic treatment at least as sincere and sympathetic as "Porgy" received?

6. Is not the continual portrayal of the sordid, foolish and criminal among Negroes convincing the world that this and this alone is really and essentially Negroid, and preventing white artists from knowing any other types and preventing black artists from daring to paint them?

7. Is there not a real danger that young colored writers will be tempted to follow the popular trend in portraying Negro character in the underworld rather than

W e have asked the artists of the world these questions:

1. When the artist, black or white, portrays Negro characters is he under any obligations or limitations as to the sort of character he will portray?

2. Can any author be criticized for painting the worst or the best characters of a group?

3. Can publishers be criticized for refusing to handle novels that portray Negroes of education and accomplishment, on the ground that these characters are no different from white folk and therefore not interesting?

4. What are Negroes to do when they are continually painted at their worst and judged by the public as they are painted?

5. Does the situation of the educated Negro in America with its pathos, humiliation and tragedy call for artistic treatment at least as sincere and sympathetic as "Porgy" received?

6. Is not the continual portrayal of the sordid, foolish and criminal among Negroes convincing the world that this and this alone is really and essentially Negroid, and preventing white artists from knowing any other types and preventing black artists from daring to paint them?

7. Is there not a real danger that young colored writers will be tempted to follow the popular trend in portray-

seeking to paint the truth about themselves and their own social class?

We have already received comments on these questions from Sinclair Lewis, Carl Van Vechten, Major Haldane MacFall and others. We shall publish these and other letters in a series of articles. *Meantime let our readers remember our contest for $600 in prizes and send in their manuscripts no matter what attitude they take in regard to this controversy. Manuscripts, etc., will be received until May 1, 1926.*

ing Negro character in the underworld, rather than seeking to paint the truth about themselves and their own social class?

Here are some answers. More will follow:

I am fully aware of the reasons why Negroes are sensitive in regard to fiction which attempts to picture the lower strata of the race. The point is that this is an attitude completely inimical to art. It has caused, sometimes quite unconsciously, more than one Negro of my acquaintance to refrain from using valuable material. Thank God, it has not yet harmed Rudolph Fisher![2] But the other point I raise is just as important. Plenty of colored folk deplore the fact that Fisher has written stories like "Ringtail" and "High Yaller". If a white man had written them he would be called a Negro hater. Now these stories would be just as good if a white man had written them, but the sensitive Negro—and heaven knows he has reason enough to feel sensitive— would see propaganda therein.

You speak of "this side of the Negro's life having been overdone". That is quite true and will doubtless continue to be true for some time, for a very excellent reason. The squalor of Negro life, the vice of Negro life, offer a wealth of novel, exotic, picturesque material to the artist. On the other hand, there is very little difference if any between the life of a wealthy or

---

2. Short-story writer, novelist, and physician (1897–1934) who wrote about life in Harlem, especially about black migrants from the South; his two novels are *The Walls of Jericho* (1928) and *The Conjure-Man Dies* (1932), one of the earliest black detective novels; in his review of *The Walls of Jericho* in *The Crisis*, Du Bois critiqued Fisher's character choices: "Why does Mr. Fisher fear to use his genius to paint his own kind . . . the glimpses of the better classes of Negroes which he gives us are poor, ineffective make-believes."

cultured Negro and that of a white man of the same class. The question is: Are Negro writers going to write about this exotic material while it is still fresh or will they continue to make a free gift of it to white authors who will exploit it until not a drop of vitality remains?

CARL VAN VECHTEN.

(See also Mr. Van Vechten's article in *Vanity Fair*, *Feb.*, 1926.)[3]

1. The artist is under no obligations or limitations whatsoever. He should be free to depict things exactly as he sees them.

2. No, so long as his portrait is reasonably accurate.

3. I know of no publisher who sets up any such doctrine. The objection is to Negro characters who are really only white men, *i.e.*, Negro characters who are false.

4. The remedy of a Negro novelist is to depict the white man at his worst. Walter White[4] has already done it, and very effectively.

5. This question is simply rhetorical. Who denies the fact?

6. The sound artist pays no attention to bad art. Why should he?

7. If they are bad artists, yes. If they are good, no.

It seems to me that in objecting to such things as the stories of Mr. Cohen[5] the Negro shows a dreadful lack of humor. They are really very amusing. Are they exaggerations? Of course they are. Nevertheless they always keep some sort of contact with the truth. Is it argued that a white man, looking at Negroes, must always see them as Negroes see themselves? Then what is argued is nonsense. If he departs too far from plausibility and probability his own people will cease to read him. They dislike palpable falsifications. Everyone does. But they enjoy caricatures, recognizing them as such.

The remedy of the Negro is not to bellow for justice—that is, not to try to apply scientific criteria to works of art. His remedy is to make works of art that pay off the white man in his own coin. The white man, it seems to me, is extremely ridiculous. He looks ridiculous even to me, a white man myself. To a Negro he must be an hilarious spectacle, indeed. Why isn't that spectacle better described? Let the Negro sculptors spit on their hands! What a chance!

H. L. MENCKEN.[6]

No. 1. If the author's object is the creation of a piece of art I feel that he should not be limited as to the sort of character he portrays. He should attempt that which moves him most deeply.

No. 2. If he is a sincere artist, no.

No. 3. Yes. On the grounds of bad business judgment, if nothing else. I feel that there is a growing public everywhere in America for literature dealing sincerely with any aspect of Negro life. The educated and artistic Negro, if presented with skill and insight, will find his public waiting for him when the publishers are willing to take the chance.

No. 4. Educated Negroes are rapidly arriving at a point where they are their own best refutation of this type of portrayal. They should, and doubtless will, soon be producing their own authentic literature.

No. 5. Emphatically yes. The point is that it must be treated *artistically*. It destroys itself as soon as it is made a vehicle for propaganda. If it carries a moral or a lesson they should be subordinated to the *artistic* aim.

6, 7. I cannot say. I think the young colored writer in America need not be afraid to portray any aspect of his racial life. And I may say further that I feel convinced that he alone will produce the ultimate and authentic record of his own people. What I have done in "Porgy" owes what social value it has to its revelation of *my*

---

3. The article was called "Negro Blues Singers" and demonstrated Vechten's interest in African American culture; Vechten, a white American writer and photographer (1880–1964), wrote the controversial novel *Nigger Heaven* (1926), a book about life in Harlem.
4. White is mentioned by a number of participants, and his own response to the questionnaire is on p. 350.
5. The stories featuring exaggerated black characters by the white American writer Octavus Roy Cohen are also critiqued by W. E. B. Du Bois on pp. 332 and 346 and by George Schuyler on p. 363, and are praised by John Farrar on p. 352.
6. The white American critic and writer Henry Louis Mencken (1880–1956).

feeling *toward* my subject. A real subjective literature must spring from the race itself.

DuBose Heyward.[7]

In a recent number of Harper's, J. B. Priestley[8] discusses the American novel and describes a snag that has caught many an American writer. Our country contains so much variety in its background that our writers forget that this background is of comparatively little importance and think over-much of local color. They thus create fixed types. But the important thing, Priestley emphasizes, is to note "the immense difference between your neighbors".

With this in mind I can quickly answer a number of your questions. A novel isn't made up of all good or all bad, of all buffoons or all wise men. When a book over-emphasizes one type, whether it be the buffoon, the villain or the heroically good young man, it isn't a true book and will soon be forgotten. What publishers, at least the best, want today is art, not propaganda. They don't want to know what the writer thinks on the Negro question, they want to know about Negroes.

Publishers will take books dealing with the educated Negro if he can be written of without our continually seeing his diploma sticking out of his pocket. Just as soon as the writer can believe that his reader knows there are educated Negroes, and doesn't have to be told that they live in pleasant homes and don't eat with their knives, he can begin seriously to write about them. Surely it is unimportant whether a book deals with the rich or the poor. Porgy and Crown and Bess[9] are great figures in a powerful love story. John is a

strong figure in Waldo Frank's "Holiday". So is Bob in Walter White's "Fire in the Flint".

Question six speaks of the "continual portrayal of the sordid, foolish, and criminal among Negroes". This has not been true within the past few years. White artists are beginning to see the true Negro and colored writers are beginning to drop their propaganda and are painting reality.

Question seven, the danger of the Negro writer's following the popular trend, is a question every writer has to face. It has nothing to do with color. Are you so poor that you yield to the temptation to copy the trivial success? If you do you'll have plenty of company in this world of cheap popular magazines.

Mary W. Ovington.[1]

I think like this: What's the use of saying anything—the true literary artist is going to write about what he chooses anyway regardless of outside opinions. You write about the intelligent Negroes; Fisher about the unintelligent. Both of you are right. Walpool pictures the better class Englishman;[2] Thomas Burke the sailors in Limehouse. And both are worth reading. It's the way people look at things, not what they look at, that needs to be changed.

Langston Hughes.[3]

Are white publishers justified in rejecting novels dealing with the lives of cultivated colored people? If they publish mediocre white novels and reject mediocre colored novels, it is hard on a few colored writers, but should not the rest of us thank our stars that we are

7. DuBose Heyward (1885–1940), a member of the white aristocracy of Charleston, South Carolina, was working as an insurance agent when he wrote his successful 1924 novel *Porgy*, about poor African Americans from the tightly knit Gullah community; the play *Porgy*, written by Heyward and his wife Dorothy Heyward, debuted on Broadway in 1927.
8. John Boynton Priestley (1894–1984), British writer and critic who published more than 100 novels; *Harper's*: monthly magazine established in 1850.
9. Bob is the brother of the lead character, Dr. Kenneth Parker, in White's 1924 novel about entrenched racism in the South; see p. 350 for White's own comments on his novel; *Holiday*: 1923 novel about a lynching written by white American writer Waldo Frank (1889–1967), based on Frank's experiences traveling through the South disguised as a black man with his friend and fellow novelist Jean Toomer; Porgy and Crown and Bess: characters in DuBose Heyward's novel, *Porgy*.
1. Mary White Ovington (1865–1951) was a white American activist who founded the NAACP in 1909 and was a leader in the organization for thirty-eight years; her books include *Half a Man* (1911), about African Americans in New York City, *Status of the Negro in the United States* (1913), *Socialism and the Feminist Movement* (1914), *Portraits in Color* (1927), her autobiography *Reminiscences* (1932), and *The Walls Come Tumbling Down* (1947), a history of the NAACP.
2. Sir Hugh Seymour Walpole (1884–1941) was a best-selling white writer who was born in New Zealand and grew up in England; he published over fifty books and plays, including thirty-six novels.
3. For a brief biographical sketch of Hughes, see p. 362.

spared at least some of the poor books of the world? For surely, whatever the subject of the novel, it should be rejected if it is a mediocre book, and will not be rejected if it is really a powerful one; we may be sure that in the end a work of genius will find some form of publication.

This is the obvious answer to the crucial question in the questionnaire of THE CRISIS—indeed, an answer too obvious to be satisfactory. Complex problems cannot be solved in this airy way. For a novel, and in fact every other kind of book, is two things: It may be considered a contribution to the *literature* of the world or as a contribution to the *culture* of a race. The problems are so different that THE CRISIS questionnaire would demand a totally different set of answers in each case. From the standpoint of the critic, there is only one answer to the question as to what should be done with a mediocre book; but from the standpoint of Negro culture it may be important that some writers should get a hearing, even if their books are comparatively poor. The culture of a race must have a beginning, however simple; and imperfect books are infinitely better than a long era of silence. If the white publisher hesitates, on the ground that it is his business to be a publisher and not a champion of Negro culture, colored brains should create colored periodicals. The world will not close its ears to the voice of a great writer merely because of the imprint on the title-page.

The tendency today is to overestimate rather than underestimate colored books because of their subject, their delightfully exotic material. Their writers are valued by some people, as Dr. Johnson[4] said of the first women preachers, not because they preached well but because of the surprise that they could preach at all. This will soon pass away; nothing disappears so quickly as a fashion in the subject of books. Great books may be made out of any subject under the sun; and colored writers will more and more have to depend not on their

subjects but on their own excellence. In the meanwhile they should realize that all of the complex problems of literature cannot be magically solved by a childish formula like that of "art versus propaganda". They must understand that a book may be of high value to a race's culture without being of high rank in the world's literature, just as a man may be a very useful citizen yet a rather mediocre dentist. The Negro race should not sniff at the *Uncle Tom's Cabins* and the *Jungles*[5] of its own writers, which are instruments of progress as real as the ballot-box, the school-house or a stick of dynamite.

J. E. SPINGARN.[6]

It is unfortunate, it seems to me, that at the very time when Negro writers are beginning to be heard there should arise a division of opinion as to what or what not he should write about. Such a conflict, however, is, I suppose, to be expected. There are those who say that the only interesting material in Negro lives is in the lives of the lower or lowest classes—that upper class Negro life is in no wise different from white life and is therefore uninteresting.

I venture to question the truth of this statement. Like all other people who have struggled against odds, upper class Negroes have through that very struggle sharpened their sensitiveness to the intense drama of race life in the United States. They never come into contact with the outside world but there is potential drama, whether of comedy or tragedy, in each of those contacts. By this I do not mean simply unpleasant aspects of the lives of these people. This sensitiveness to pain and insult and tragedy has its compensation in a keener awareness and appreciation of the rhythmic beauty and color and joyousness which is so valuable a part of Negro life.

The lives of so-called upper class Negroes have advantages as literary material, judged even by the most arbitrary standards. "Babbitt" or "Jean Chris-

---

4. Samuel Johnson (1709–84), British writer, critic, and lexicographer.

5. 1906 novel by white American writer Upton Sinclair exploring poverty and working conditions in the meatpacking industry; designed to be, in Sinclair's own words, "the *Uncle Tom's Cabin* of the labor movement."

6. Joel Elias Spingarn (1875–1939), white American literary critic and publisher; second president of the NAACP and chair of the NAACP board from 1913 until his death; established the Spingarn Medal in 1913 to honor outstanding achievement by an African American.

7. Ten-volume novel (1904–1912) telling the story of a German musician from birth to death, by French writer Romain Rolland (1866–1944) who received the Nobel Prize for Literature in 1915; *Babbitt*: 1922 novel satirizing white middle-class American culture by the white American writer Sinclair Lewis (1885–1951), the first American awarded the Nobel Prize for Literature (in 1930); see Lewis's answers to the questionnaire on p. 353.

tophe"[7] or any other novel is interesting in direct proportion to the ability of the writer to depict impingement of events and experiences, trivial or great, on the more or less sensitive photographic plates which are the minds of the characters. Life for any Negro in America has so many different aspects that there is unlimited material for the novelist or short story writer. For the reasons I have already given, there is no lack of this material among upper class Negroes if one only has the eye to see it.

Suppose we carry this objection to the utilization of experiences of educated Negroes to its logical conclusion. Would not the result be this: Negro writers should not write, the young Negro is told, of educated Negroes because their lives paralleling white lives are uninteresting. If this be true, then it seems just as reasonable to say that all writers, white or colored, should abandon all sources of material save that of lower class Negro life. Manifestly this is absurd. It makes no difference, it seems to me, what field a writer chooses if he has the gift of perception, of dramatic and human material and the ability to write about it.

Those who would limit Negro writers to depiction of lower class Negro life justify their contention by saying, "The artist must have the right to choose his material where he will; and the critic can judge him only by the artistic result." These same persons often nullify or negative their contention for freedom by following this assertion immediately with insistence that the Negro writer confine himself to one field. The Negro writer, just like any other writer, should be allowed to write of whatever interests him whether it be of lower, or middle, or upper class Negro life in America; or of white—or Malay—or Chinese—or Hottentot characters and should be judged not by the color of the writer's skin but solely by the story he produces.

I, myself, have not as yet written extensively of prostitutes or gamblers or cabaret habitues. Fortunately, or unfortunately, my life thus far has not given me as intimate a knowledge of these classes as I feel would be necessary for me to write about them. I am not boasting of this innocence, if one chooses to call it that. I am merely stating it as a fact. An honest craftsman, in my opinion, can only pour his knowledge and experience, real or imagined, through the alembic of his own mind and let the creations of his subjective or objective self stand or fall by whatever literary standards are current at the time. I do not mean that Zola or Flaubert had to live as "Nana" or "Emma Bovary" did to achieve subjective treatment of these characters—such obviously being a physical impossibility. But Zola *did* find himself drawn to write of the experiences of his character "Nana", as did Flaubert to the luckless "Emma". Certainly we could not have condemned either Zola or Flaubert if they had chosen instead to depict women less carnal minded.

To summarize specifically, it seems to me that:

1. The artist should be allowed full freedom in the choice of his characters and material.

2. An artist can rightly be criticized if he portrays only the worst or only the best characters of any group. (I, myself, was lambasted most enthusiastically by the South because Kenneth Harper in "The Fire in the Flint" seemed to me much more intelligent and decent than any of his white fellow townsmen.)

3. Publishers can and should be criticized for refusing to handle manuscripts, *provided they have merit,* that portray Negroes of superior talent because the lives of these Negroes do not vary from white people's.

4. When Negroes are painted only at their worst and judged accordingly by the public, Negroes must write stories revealing the other side and make these stories of such excellence that they command attention. (This is not an advertisement but in this same connection more Negroes must buy books by Negro writers for then sales will cause publishers actively to seek Negro writers of ability.)

5. The situation of the Negro in America is pregnant enough in drama and color and beauty to make of him a subject for artistic treatment.

6. Continual portrayal of any type to the exclusion of all others is not only harmful but bad art.

7. If young Negro writers can be saved or, better, save themselves from too hostile or too friendly critics, editors, publishers or public, from spending all their time and energy in restricted areas, they can have the freedom to explore whatever fields to which their fancy or inclination draws them.

In brief, sycophants and weaklings will follow whatever trend is mapped out for them; genuine artists will write or paint or sing or sculpt whatever they please.

WALTER WHITE.[8]

I have yours of January 22 and will try to answer your questions promptly and briefly.

1. No.

2. No.

3. This question seems to me to be senseless.

4. To write books—fiction and non-fiction—to supply the deficiency.

5. Yes.

6. I doubt it.

7. I doubt it.

ALFRED A. KNOPF.[9]

I feel that the Negro should be treated by himself and by others who write about him with just as little self-consciousness as possible. Realizing how untrue Octavius Roy Cohen's stories may be, they have amused me immensely, nor do they mean to me any very great libel on the Negro—any more than an amusing story about the Yankee would seem to me a libel on myself.

On the other hand, I have always thought that Walter White's novel was a trifle one sided, although I realize that I speak as one who does not truly know conditions in the South.

It therefore seems to me that although I realize it is inevitable under the circumstances that this discussion should arise, you will have Negroes writing about the Negro as the Jews have written about the Jews in "Potash and Perlmutter"[1] and other such things, and

that racial characteristics are bound to be presented in burlesque as well as real drama; and that, as Mr. Van Vechten has pointed out, the creative spirit, even though it may not be classed as art, will always disregard moral issues such as these.

JOHN FARRAR.[2]

1. The only obligation or limitation that an artist should recognize is the truth.

2. He cannot be criticized unless he takes the worst as typical.

3. If a publisher takes the ground mentioned in this question, it would be absurd.

4. The Negroes must protest in print and must hope that by setting a good example in their lives they can correct the false impression.

5. Of course it calls for artistic treatment, sincere and sympathetic, but I have not read "Porgy".

6. There is a certain danger of this.

7. I think there might be a danger also here.

WILLIAM LYON PHELPS.[3]

1. Neither the black nor the white artist should be under obligations or limitations as to the sort of character he will portray. His own experience and his inmost perception of truth and beauty, in its severest interpretation, should be his only criteria.

2. An author can be criticized for painting the worst or best characters of a group if his portrayal thereby becomes artistically false; he should be free to choose his characters according to his desire and purpose.

3. Publishers assuredly may be criticized for refusing to handle novels portraying Negroes of education and accomplishment, on the ground that these characters

8. Author and civil rights leader (1893–1955); chief secretary of the NAACP from 1929 to 1955.
9. White American publisher and writer (1892–1984); founder in 1915 of Alfred A. Knopf, Inc., a major New York publishing house.
1. Play (1913) by white American writer Montague Glass (1877–1934) about Jewish Americans working in the garment industry; based on Glass's 1910 story of the same name published in the *Saturday Evening Post*; the play was co-written with an uncredited Charles Klein (1867–1915), a British playwright.
2. White American writer and publisher (1896–1974); in 1926, Farrar was editor of the book review *The Bookman*; the next year he began working in publishing, and later founded two publishing houses, Farrar and Rinehart in 1929 and Farrar, Straus and Giroux in 1946.
3. White American author and critic (1865–1943); professor in the English department at Yale University for forty-one years from 1892 to 1933.

are no different from white folk and therefore not interesting. The Negro of this type has an artistic as well as a social right to speak for himself; and what he has to say is all too interesting, as a rule.

4. The work of such magazines as The Crisis and *Opportunity* suggests a possible way out. Through his songs, through drama, poetry and fiction, the Negro should make every effort to put before the public a true picture of the race, in totality; and white folk of sufficient intelligence and courage to recognize the issue as it stands should be enlisted as an auxiliary force to the same end.

5. The situation of the educated Negro in America surely merits all possible sincere and artistic treatment. If such enterprises seem doomed to failure in this country, they should be taken to Canada or England, or to the continental countries, and so finally reach the United States public with their prestige already established.

6. The portrayal of sordid, foolish and criminal types among Negroes is not convincing the world that such groups alone comprise the essentially Negroid, but it surely is doing a great deal to foster that opinion in the United States, where there are many anxious to believe it. The portrayal of such types by no means damns a race; look at the long line of English, French, Spanish and Russian novels and plays dealing with such characters; nor does one need to confine the list to those countries exclusively. Such portrayals have their place and deep significance artistically; but they at once become false and evil if used for propagandist purposes, or with ulterior racial motives.

7. Such a danger can scarcely be stated as a general phenomenon. The average young colored writer, if he be honest as an artist, will write the thing that is in his heart to write regardless of so-called "popular trends". Any artist who speaks the truth as he sees it and refuses to compromise with Mammon[4] has none too easy a time; it is not a question of color, it is

a question of courage. One has no reason to believe that the sincere black artist will be more easily daunted than a sincere white or brown or yellow artist. The one difficulty that does seem to exist, in the light of a thoughtful reading of recent Negro novels and poems, is that many times an ingrained bitterness tinges work otherwise clearly and beautifully carried out. For that the Negro is not to blame, nor can one state the solution of the problem back of it. The only way out is up; and that seems to be the way which the younger Negro artists, singers and writers have chosen for themselves and for their people. More power to them.

Vachel Lindsay.[5]

After reading your letter it suddenly occurred to me that just possibly *all* of the astounding and extraordinarily interesting Negro fiction which is now appearing may be entirely off on the wrong foot. All of you, or very nearly all, are primarily absorbed in the economic and social problems of the colored race. Complicated though these problems are in detail, yet inevitably they fall into a few general themes; so that there is the greatest danger that all of your novels will be fundamentally alike.

For example, this problem of going over and passing for white must be one which will appeal to all of you. It must needs be much the same in your book or in Walter White's.

Ordinarily I hate committees, conferences and organizations like the very devil. But I wonder if there isn't a problem here which demands a real and serious conference? Should American Negroes write as Americans or Negroes? Should they follow the pattern of the Jewish authors who are quite as likely to write about Nordics as about fellow Jews or that of Zangwill,[6] who is of importance only when he is writing about Jews? Should there be a Negro publishing house so that the Negro author can tell all of the ordinary publishing houses to go to the devil? Should there be a club—a comfortable small hotel in Paris to

---

4. False god of greed and riches in the New Testament.
5. White American poet (1889–1931) who wrote about the American Midwest and developed "singing poetry," poems meant to be sung or chanted.
6. Israel Zangwill (1864–1926), British writer whose parents had immigrated to England from Russia; active first in the Zionist movement and later in Territorialism; wrote play *The Melting Pot* celebrating assimilation in the United States.

which the American Negroes can go and be more than welcome?

These and a thousand like topics suggest themselves to me as they have, of course, suggested themselves to Dr. DuBois and yourself. Their very complexity makes me feel that it is impossible to give any definite answer to them. Of this alone I am sure—you cannot, all of you, go on repeating the same novel (however important, however poignant, however magnificently dramatic) about the well-bred, literate and delightful Negro intellectual finding himself or herself blocked by the groundless and infuriating manner of superiority assumed by white men frequently less white than people technically known as Negroes.

SINCLAIR LEWIS.[7]

Naturally I think it a great mistake for Negroes to become too sensitive. If, as a race, you were the ideal people sentimentalists sometimes try to make you how uninteresting you would be.

Why not quit thinking of Negro art? If the individual creating the art happens to be a Negro and some one wants to call it Negro Art let them.

As to Negroes always being painted at their worst I think it isn't true. Suppose I were to grow indignant every time a white man or woman were badly or cheaply done in the theatre or in books. I might spend my life being indignant.

I have lived a good deal in my youth among common Negro laborers. I have found them about the sweetest people I know. I have said so sometimes in my books.

I do not believe the Negroes have much more to complain of than the whites in this matter of their treatment in the arts.

SHERWOOD ANDERSON.[8]

1. No.

2. No. Unless in a long series of articles he invariably chooses the worst types and paints them, even though truthfully, with evident malice.

3. I should think so. And what is more, it seems to me that white people should be the first to voice this criticism. Aren't *they* supposed to be interesting?

4. They must protest strongly and get their protestations before the public. But more than that they must learn to write with a humor, a pathos, a sincerity so evident and a delineation so fine and distinctive that their portraits, even of the "best Negroes", those presumably most like "white folks", will be acceptable to publisher and reader alike.

But above all colored people must be the buyers of these books for which they clamor. When they buy 50,000 copies of a good novel about colored people by a colored author, publishers will produce books, even those that depict the Negro as an angel on earth—and the public in general will buy 50,000 copies more to find out what it's all about. Most best sellers are not born,—they're made.

5. I should say so.

6. I think this is true. And here I blame the publisher for not being a "better sport". Most of them seem to have an *idee fixe*. They, even more than the public, I do believe, persist in considering only certain types of Negroes interesting and if an author presents a variant they fear that the public either won't believe in it or won't "stand for it". Whereas I have learned from an interesting and rather broad experience gleaned from speaking before white groups that many, many of these people are keenly interested in learning about the better class of colored people. They are quite willing to be shown.

7. Emphatically. This is a grave danger making for a literary insincerity both insidious and abominable.

JESSIE FAUSET.[9]

1. An artist must be free; he can not be bound by any artificial restrictions. At the same time we heartily wish that so many artists would not prefer today to portray only what is vulgar. There is beauty in the world as well as ugliness, idealism as well as realism.

7. White American writer (1885–1951); in 1930 became first American to win the Nobel Prize for literature.
8. White American novelist and short story writer (1876–1941); wrote about small town American life in *Winesberg Ohio* (1919) and other books.
9. Poet and novelist (1882–1961); literary editor of *The Crisis* from 1919 to 1926.

2. This is really covered by 1. It may be added, however, that anyone, even an artist, becomes liable to criticism when his work gives a distorted idea of truth.

3. This question seems to me involved. However, aside from their other reasons for accepting or rejecting books, publishers can hardly be criticised for refusing to bring out books that do not promise a reasonable return on the investment. They are engaged in a business and not in a missionary enterprise.

4. When Negroes feel that they are imperfectly or improperly portrayed, they should find the way to truthful portrayal through any possible channel. Any plant that is struggling in the darkness must find its way to the light as well as it can.

5. Certainly.

6. Yes.

7. Yes.

General answer: Several of the questions seem to me to suggest that the Negro wants patronage. On the whole I think American publishers will be found to be hospitable; they have certainly been hospitable to the Negro in recent years. What we need to do first of all is to produce the really finished work of art. Sooner or later recognition will come.

Benjamin Brawley.[1]

1. No. The artist, black or white, must be in sympathy with his creations, or creatures, be they what they may be ethically and ethnically. If he is in sympathy with them, he has nothing to fear regarding the effect of his work. His art will justify itself.

2. No, not if he observes the laws of proportion, relation and emphasis. It is the artist's business to portray not merely the typical, the average, but the ultimate.

3. Publishers can be censured only for commercial stupidity.

4. Produce first-rate artistic works with which to kill travesties, as they are beginning to do.

5. Why not? No theme, absolutely none, offers greater opportunities to the novelist and the poet, whatever their race. It is a human situation. If white artists do not discern the potencies of this material in Negro life, the supreme artists in the near future will be black.

6. Yes, to all three questions: (1) But avowed fiction has not done such dastardly damage here as the daily press; (2) the white "artist" who thus takes his material second hand must be flayed; (3) the duty of the black artist is to be a true artist and if he is such he will show the "sordid", the "foolish", and the "criminal" Negro in the environment and the conditions—of white creation, of course—which have made him what he is. Let the black artist not hesitate to show what white "civilization" is doing to both races.

7. No. The cultivated Negro is up against a world hostile to him, ignorant of him, perplexed, uncomfortable, nonplussed by the contradictions arising. No one knows this better than the cultured Negro. It affords him laughter and tears—and out of these, lit by flames of anger, love, pride, aspiration, comes art, in which both the individual and the race are somehow expressed. The Negro artist is going to continue to be mainly concerned with himself, not with any grotesque caricature of himself—though he will not despise the broken image.

Robert T. Kerlin.[2]

Your critic, Mr. Emmett J. Scott, Junior, has every right to pour contempt on my literary gifts; but he has none to attribute to me "sustained contempt, almost hatred, for Negroes". He is again within his rights to find my novel feeble in wit and humour—though his own writing reveals scant glint of either, which I must suppose he is holding in reserve in order to show up my "sustained contempt, almost hatred, for Negroes". At the same time he admits "flashes of ability". But then

1. Historian, literary critic, poet, and educator (1882–1939); his books include *The Negro Literature and Art* (1918), *A Social History of the American Negro* (1919), and *Early Negro American Writers* (1935).
2. Robert Thomas Kerlin (1866–1950), white Southern poet, literary critic, educator, and civil rights activist; his books include *The Voice of the Negro* (1920) and *Negro Poets and Their Poems* (1923).

he attacks Kemble![3] Surely as kindly an artist as the Negro ever had to utter the exquisite humour of a greatly humorous race! . . .

When I was a youngster, I was left in command of a company of Zouaves[4] at Port Royal in Jamaica. I was a mere boy. There was brought before me as prisoner a magnificent bronze god of a man whom they called "Long" Burke—he flits through my novel. I stood six feet high; this big fellow stood head and shoulders taller. Well—it appeared that he had knocked the stuffing out of a little black corporal, which is bad for discipline, and, being no hanging judge, I was grieved and worried when, to my relief, the corporal said he wished to add that Burke had always been a good soldier and he, the corporal, may have been over-impatient with him. I took it as a case of attempted murder with a recommendation to mercy. I talked to Burke like a father, and then told him that after what the corporal had said I would only give him a nominal punishment—changed his charge on the crime-sheet to a paltry offence—and, God forgive me, only confined him to barracks for three days. . . . . When I got back to my quarters I found an orderly waiting for me to tell me that Long Burke had "gone fantee"[5] into the cocoa-nut grove with a rifle and ten rounds of ball cartridge to shoot me, and begging me not to go near the grove until Burke had been caught. Anyway, if I hate Negroes, the Negroes did not hate *me*, since they were prepared to risk their lives to save mine from harm. To cut a long story short, they waited until sunset, when Burke fell asleep, and they got him—took him to the guard room—and reported to me. I buckled on the sword of authority and made across the square in the twilight to the guard room. There the Sergeant-major and the Sergeant of the Guard begged me not to go near Burke who was in the cells foaming at the mouth—he had torn his uniform to tatters, and was sitting on the plank bed bare as Venus, scowling and vowing vengeance. Now I knew that this great mad devil of a man could crack me like a nut if he put his mind to it; but I knew equally well that if I did not close with him

there and then I should live a life of misery as long as that man lived. And a brain-wave came to me. I called to the Sergeant of the Guard that I wanted to see Burke—what was he a prisoner for?—told him to throw open the door of the "clink", which he did most reluctantly,—and taking off my sword with a melodramatic air I handed it—in a majestic bluff and a gorgeous funk—to the Sergeant—walked boldly up to Burke who sat as naked as when born, a huge bronze god of sullen wrath on the plank bed—sat down beside him, laying my hand on his shoulder, and said: "Burke, they tell me that you wanted to shoot me—It's a shabby lie." I noticed that the Sergeant of the guard was "taking a bead" through the small window in the twilight on poor Burke—and he was a deadly sure shot!

The fellow said never a word; and the thought of that giant taking me by the throat made me feel about as small as I have ever felt. I turned to the open door:

"Sergeant," I called, "it's all too dam-silly about Burke. Send for his kit and let him go back to his barrack-room, and tell the men it was only Burke's joke. Good Lord! if it gets to the ears of the General that I only gave him three days confined to barracks for hitting my corporal, I shall have to leave the army." . . .

"Burke," said I,—"you would not see me punished for letting you off penal servitude, would you? Come, old man, get into your trousers, and be a man and a soldier! Damme, I've got you down for lance-corporal! Don't make me look a fool!"

I strolled out of the place, hoping to God he would not jump on my back. . . .

Long Burke became the most devoted friend to me for the rest of my service—and he maintained a discipline in my company such as I have never seen bettered. And it was not because of my contempt and hatred for Negroes. . . .

HALDANE MACFALL.[6]

When it is fully realized that "a man's a man",—the problems of this sort will cease. Peoples long subjected

---

3. Frances [Fanny] Anne Kemble (1809–93); white British actress and author; wrote a diary, later published as *Journal of Residence on a Georgian Plantation* (1862), which was popular among abolitionists.
4. Regiments of the French Army.
5. Gone native; from Fanti, ethnic group in southwestern Ghana.
6. White British writer, critic, and soldier (1860–1928) who wrote about his experiences serving in Jamaica, West Africa, and the West Indies.

to travail, depressing and repressing environment, and the long list of handicaps common to men of color, naturally find it difficult to reach the high levels *en masse*. It would be strange, miraculous if they did. The few who do break thru the hell-crust of prevalent conditions to high ground should be crowned, extolled and emulated.

This is the work of the artist. Paint, write, let the submerged man and the world see those who have proven stronger than the iron grip of circumstance.

Let the artist cease to capitalize the frailties of the struggling or apathetic mass—and portray the best that offers. This is naturally unpopular, and why? The thinker knows! To the ignorant it does not matter—yet. Depict the best, with or without approbation and renown.

GEORGIA DOUGLAS JOHNSON.[7]

This question of what material the Negro writer should draw upon, and how he should use it, is no simon pure problem with a sure, mathematical conclusion; it has innumerable ramifications, and almost all arguments can be met with a dissenting *but* equally as strong. Opinions will probably be as various as the writers' several constitutions; moreover, it is a question of whether the work is the *thing,* or its moral, social and educational effect.

I should be the last person to vote for any infringement of the author's right to tell a story, to delineate a character, or to transcribe an emotion in his own way, and in the light of truth as he sees it. That is the one inalienable right into which the Negro author ought to be admitted with all other authors, as a slight compensation for other rights so described in which he does not share. I do believe, however, that the Negro has not yet built up a large enough body of sound, healthy race literature to permit him to speculate in abortions and aberrations which other people are all too prone to accept as truly legitimate. There can be no doubt that there is a fictional type of Negro, an ignorant, burly, bestial person, changing somewhat today, though not for the better, to the sensual habitue of dives and loose living, who represents to the mass of white readers the be—all and end—all of what constitutes a Negro. What

would be taken as a type in other literatures is, where it touches us, seized upon as representative so long as it adheres to this old pattern. For Negroes to raise a great hue and cry against such misrepresentations without attempting, through their artists, to reconstruct the situation seems futile as well as foolish. Negro artists have a definite duty to perform in this matter, one which should supersede their individual prerogatives, without denying those rights. We must create types that are truly representative of us as a people, nor do I feel that such a move is necessarily a genuflexion away from true art.

As far as I am concerned the white writer is totally out of the scene. He will write as he pleases, though it offend; and when he does offend, he can always plead the extenuation of a particular incident and of particular characters that appeal to him because of their novelty. He is not under the same obligations to us that we are to ourselves. Nor can he, as a member of a group with a vast heritage of sound literature behind it, quite rise to an understanding of what seems to him an oversensitiveness on our part; he cannot quite understand our disinclination as a people toward our racial defamation, even for art's sake.

I do not feel that we can so severely criticize publishers who reject our work on the score that it will not appeal to their readers. Publishers, in general, are caterers, not martyrs and philanthropists. But if they reject a treatment of educated and accomplished Negroes for the avowed reason that these do not differ from white folk of the same sort, they should reject those about lower class Negroes for the reason that they do not differ essentially from white folk of the same sort; unless they feel that, difference or no difference, the only time a Negro is interesting is when he is at his worst. This does not mean that the Negro writer has either to capitulate or turn away from his calling. Even among publishers there are those rare eccentrics who will judge a work on its merits.

The danger to the young Negro writer is not that he will find his aspiration in the Negro slums; I dare say there are as fine characters and as bright dream material there as in the best strata of Negro society, and that is as

---

7. Poet and playwright (1880?–1966); books of poetry include *The Heart of a Woman* (1918), *Bronze* (1922), and *An Autumn Love Cycle* (1928); active in the Little Theater Movement, and her play *Blue Blood* was performed by the KRIGWA players in 1926; also known for fostering the talents of other writers and artists of the Harlem Renaissance.

it should be. Let the young Negro writer, like any artist, find his treasure where his heart lies. If the unfortunate and less favored find an affinity in him, let him surrender himself; only let him not pander to the popular trend of seeing no cleanliness in their squalor, no nobleness in their meanness and no commonsense in their ignorance. A white man and a southerner gave us *Porgy*, the merits of which few will deny, nor wish away because the story deals with illiterate Negroes. Mr. Heyward gave us a group of men and women; the Negro writer can in strict justice to himself attempt no less than this, whether he writes of Negroes or of a larger world.

COUNTEE CULLEN.[8]

I am a bit excited about your magazine. There is in it stimulation for the darker races as well as a prod, a fetching good dig in the ribs, for the pale of face. There is perhaps one thing that needs stress and that is the proposition to forget race. Lay that old bogey man. And now may I give to you just an ordinary, average man's opinion in answer to your questionnaire? I know that my opinion is unsolicited but I wish to let you know that even an ordinary man may think upon the things you ask and to good advantage.

1. The inarticulate artist in me cries out that no man can be judged an artist by his race or creed. Paul Robeson is an artist first and a Negro next. When I have heard him sing I never think "What a wonderful Negro voice". I forget the qualification of race. The obligation of the artist is not to his race but to his talent.

2. An author can be criticized only when he deliberately falsifies with malice aforethought.

3. Such a publisher is missing his main chance. An absorbing tale can surely be written about Negroes of good education and refinement. A publisher who cannot see that is not on to his onions.

4. Bring out the supreme spectacle of the Nordic's obverse side. That ought to be a good tonic for all races.

5. No one but a numskull could treat him otherwise.

6. No. Wiley and Cohen are hardly artists. They are authors. Perhaps the latter is becoming one. He will I think some day write a real story of the Negro and do it with understanding. There is a false notion among a great number of peoples that the sordid-foolish-criminal side is all there is to the Negro. The Negro will have to fight that down as the Jew has had to fight down the same impression by proving the contrary.

7. The young author may have a tendency to pick-up easy money by writing only of the underworld but the compelling urge of a real artist, be he Negro or some other tint, will not allow mere facetiousness to mar his canvas. Things as he sees them—he paints.

Luck to your mission.

J. HERBERT ENGBECK.[9]
Salt Lake City, Utah.

Please excuse my delay in answering your letter of Feb. 24th and the Questionnaire which you submitted to me. Many incidental circumstances have intervened and these, along with the exigencies of my own work and the need for careful reflection regarding your inquiries, have prevented an earlier reply.

Let me say at the outset that I am not a propagandist for or against the Negro; that for the most part I have small sympathy with propagandists of any kind or color. In my opinion, the minute any one becomes an advocate he ceases to be an artist. Propagandists may be able and admirable persons and, on occasion, be actuated by most worthy purposes; but, broadly speaking, it seems to me that special pleading is not conducive to the development of a judicial view-point.

I believe that the crying need among Negroes is a development in them of racial pride; and a cessation on their own part as well as on the part of other races, who attempt to portray their character, to estimate their worth according to their success in imitating their white brethren.

---

8. Poet, novelist, and educator (1903–46); books include poetry collections *Color* (1925) and *Copper Sun* (1927), and a novel *One Way To Heaven* (1932); assistant literary editor and columnist for *Opportunity*.
9. *The Crisis* solicited responses to its questionnaire from "the artists of the world," but also printed some of the unsolicited responses received from readers, including Engbeck (a white American who was a hatter by trade, had fought in World War I in Germany, and had won honorable mention in a 1925 *Life* Magazine short essay contest) and Otto F. Mack (a white German from Struttgart).

The Negro is racially different in many essential particulars from his fellow mortals of another color. But this certainly does not prove that he has not racial qualifications of inestimable value without the free and full development of which a perfected humanity will never be achieved.

Racial antagonisms are not necessarily a matter of color. Religion has produced and still perpetuates them in a most accentuated form. But pride of race has enabled the Hebrew to maintain himself against an age-old proscription; and it establishes him today as a recognized leader among the peoples of the earth.

So far as your complaint at the variety of derogatory portrayals of Negro life, character and self-expression, does it occur to an Irishman or a Jew to imagine for a moment that the cultural standing or development of their races are or could be seriously affected by the grotesqueries of "Mr. Jiggs" or "Mr. Potash"? The illiterate may feel irritated, but the Irishman or Jew who knows that his people have racially so lived and wrought and achieved that the world would be impoverished by the loss of their contribution to its civilization, laughs and is not remotely disturbed by these portrayals of Mr. McManus and Mr. Glass.

If America has produced a type more worthy of admiration and honor than the "Black Negro Mammy" I fail to have heard of it. The race that produced them has to its credit an achievement which may well be envied by any people. Without imitating anybody, often sinned against and seldom sinning, they wrote a page in human history that is not only an honor to themselves but to the Creator of life. Yet when a proposal was made in Congress that the nation erect a monument to commemorate the splendid virtues of these devoted black women, a number of Negroes protested against it, saying that their race wished to forget the days of its bondage.

It seems to me that a man who is not proud that he belongs to a race that produced the Negro Mammy of the South is not and can never be either an educated man or a gentleman.

My answer to all your queries may be summed up in my belief that the Negro must develop in himself and in his race such things as that race distinctly possesses and without which humanity and the civilization which represents it cannot permanently do.

Of course it is better for Mr. DuBose Heyward to write of him with pitying, pathetic sympathy than for Mr. Cohen (who may himself have felt the sting of racial antipathy and ridicule) to picture him as a perpetual exponent of primitive buffoonery. And it would be better for Negro authors to demonstrate that their race has things the white race has not in equal degree and that cannot be duplicated; to magnify these things instead of minimizing them.

A true artist, black or white, will search for these tokens of racial worth and weave around them his contribution to literature.

Yet it seems futile to cavil because one man writes this way and another, that, as varying abilities and inclinations may dictate.

I write about Negroes because they represent human nature obscured by so little veneer; human nature groping among its instinctive impulses and in an environment which is tragically primitive and often unutterably pathetic. But I am no propagandist for or against any race. I devoutly hope I shall never be one. I am interested in humanity *per se* without regard to color or conditions.

Julia Peterkin.[1]

I am neither an artist nor a writer, yet I have traveled much, am a graduate of the school of hard knocks and have thought a great deal. So I would like to say something.

1. No.

2. No.

3. Yes, because these editors show their ignorance in the race question. Every race has its own peculiar talents and abilities. The danger in the United States is not that you have too many original minds and people, but the opposite is the case. No nation or people in the world are being moulded into such a sameness as the

---

1. Southern white American writer (1880–1961) who spoke Gullah and often wrote about African Americans from the Gullah community in South Carolina; won the Pulitzer Prize for literature in 1929 for *Scarlet Sister Mary* (1928); in the 1930s, worked for the WPA collecting folklore from African American and white communities in the South.

people of the United States. And if the Negro writes about the cultured of his race I am sure that these writings will be different from those of white writers and therefore should be welcome. Although the American Negro is, I am sorry to say, being Americanized, I think there will always be a difference between the coloured and white race, even in America. Therefore I think the portrayal of educated coloured folks and their lives will be as interesting if not more so than of the whites.

4. Be true to themselves. The Negro is no worse than the white man, given equal chances. Just here is where the Negro artist and writer must try to counteract the bad influence and as I have said before show up the cultured and good people of his race. If he cannot find white publishers then he must go into the publishing business himself. If the books are well written and the painter is a real artist, painting true to nature, he need not fear for the result.

5. Yes, and more so. The world, especially the European world, should be made acquainted with the condition of the educated Negro in the United States and wherever the Anglo Saxons rule. He has got to learn to be a fighter and to fight so hard till the conscience of the world is awakened and justice is done the coloured people.

6. I do not think so. Thinking people are beginning to see that a great, almost unspeakable injustice has been and is still being done to the coloured races, and scientists are pointing out that there are no inferior races. That those which appear backward are only so not in kind but in degree.

7. There may be some danger in that the Negro artist must not be afraid and must show up the coloured races true to nature, the good and the bad sides. Here is where the Negro must show himself master of the situation and must be willing to make the sacrifice for the benefit of his race. Even if for a time his work may be unpopular the time will come, if he is a true artist, when he will win out.

OTTO F. MACK,
Stuttgart, Germany.

1. The realm of art is almost the only territory in which the mind is free, and of all the arts that of creative fiction is the freest. Painting, sculpture, music, poetry, the stage, are all more or less hampered by convention—even jazz has been tamed and harnessed, and there are rules for writing free verse. The man with the pen in the field of fiction is the only free lance, with the whole world to tilt at. Within the very wide limits of the present day conception of decency, he can write what he pleases. I see no possible reason why a colored writer should not have the same freedom. We want no color line in literature.

2. It depends on how and what he writes about them. A true picture of life would include the good, the bad and the indifferent. Most people, of whatever group, belong to the third class, and are therefore not interesting subjects of fiction. A writer who made all Negroes bad and all white people good, or *vice versa*, would not be a true artist, and could justly be criticised.

3. To the publisher, the one indispensable requisite for a novel is that it should sell, and to sell, it must be interesting. No publisher wants to bring out and no reader cares to read a dull book. To be interesting, a character in a novel must have personality. It is perhaps unfortunate that so few of the many Negro or Negroid characters in current novels are admirable types; but they are interesting, and it is the privilege and the opportunity of the colored writer to make characters of a different sort equally interesting. Education and accomplishment do not of themselves necessarily make people interesting—we all know dull people who are highly cultured. The difficulty of finding a publisher for books by Negro authors has largely disappeared—publishers are seeking such books. Whether the demand for them shall prove to be more than a mere passing fad will depend upon the quality of the product.

4. Well, what can they do except to protest, and to paint a better type of Negro?

5. The Negro race and its mixtures are scattered over most of the earth's surface, and come in contact with men of other races in countless ways. All these contacts, with their resultant reactions, are potential themes of fiction, and the writer of genius ought to be able, with this wealth of material, to find or to create interesting types. If there are no super-Negroes, make some, as Mr. Cable did in his *Bras Coupé*. Some of the men and women who have had the greatest influence on

civilization have been purely creatures of the imagination. It might not be a bad idea to create a few white men who not only think they are, but who really are entirely unprejudiced in their dealings with colored folk—it is the highest privilege of art to depict the ideal. There are plenty of Negro and Negroid types which a real artist could make interesting to the general reader without making all the men archangels, or scoundrels, or weaklings, or all the women unchaste. The writer, of whatever color, with the eye to see, the heart to feel and the pen to record the real romance, the worthy ambition, the broad humanity, which exist among colored people of every class, in spite of their handicaps, will find a hearing and reap his reward.

6. I do not think so. People who read books read the newspapers, and cannot possibly conceive that crime is peculiarly Negroid. In fact, in the matter of serious crime the Negro is a mere piker compared with the white man. In South Carolina, where the Negroes out number the whites, the penitentiary has more white than colored inmates. Of course the propagandist, of whatever integumentary pigment, will, of purpose or unconsciously, distort the facts. My most popular novel was distorted and mangled by a colored moving picture producer to make it appeal to Negro race prejudice.

7. I think there is little danger of young colored writers writing too much about Negro characters in the underworld, so long as they do it well. Some successful authors have specialized in crook stories, and some crooks are mighty interesting people. The colored writer of fiction should study life in all its aspects. He should not worry about his social class. Indeed, it is doubtful whether the general reading public can be interested today in a long serious novel based upon the social struggles of colored people. Good work has been done along this line with the short story, but colored society is still too inchoate to have developed the fine shades and nuances of the more sophisticated society with which the ordinary novel of manner

deals. Pride of caste is hardly convincing in a people where the same family, in the same generation, may produce a bishop and a butler, a lawyer and a lackey, not as an accident or a rarity but almost as a matter of course. On the other hand it can be argued that at the hand of a master these sharp contrasts could be made highly dramatic. But there is no formula for these things, and the discerning writer will make his own rules.

The prevailing weakness of Negro writings, from the viewpoint of art, is that they are too subjective. The colored writer, generally speaking, has not yet passed the point of thinking of himself first as a Negro, burdened with the responsibility of defending and uplifting his race. Such a frame of mind, however praiseworthy from a moral standpoint, is bad for art. Tell your story, and if it is on a vital subject, well told, with an outcome that commends itself to right-thinking people, it will, if interesting, be an effective brief for whatever cause it incidentally may postulate.

Why let Octavus Roy Cohen or Hugh Wiley have a monopoly of the humorous side of Negro life? White artists caricatured the Negro on the stage until Ernest Hogan and Bert Williams discovered that colored men could bring out the Negro's more amusing characteristics in a better and more interesting way.

Why does not some colored writer build a story around a Negro oil millionaire, and the difficulty he or she has in keeping any of his or her money? A Pullman porter who performs wonderful feats in the detection of crime has great possibilities. The Negro visionary who would change the world over night and bridge the gap between races in a decade would make an effective character in fiction. But the really epical race novel, in which love and hatred, high endeavor, success and failure, sheer comedy and stark tragedy are mingled, is yet to be written, and let us hope that a man of Negro blood may write it.

Charles W. Chesnutt.[2]

---

2. Writer, legal stenographer, and activist (1858–1932); had a mixed race background and appearance, but self-identified as African American; common themes in his writing include lynching, interracialism, and racial passing; books include *The Conjure Woman* (1899), *The Wife of His Youth and Other Stories of the Color-Line* (1899), *Frederick Douglass* (1899), and *The House Behind the Cedars* (1900).

On "Negro Art"

GEORGE S. SCHUYLER: *The Negro-Art Hokum* [1926]
LANGSTON HUGHES: *The Negro Artist and the Racial Mountain* [1926]
GEORGE S. SCHUYLER: *Negroes and Artists* [1926]
LANGSTON HUGHES: *American Art or Negro Art?* [1926]

This exchange between the journalist George S. Schuyler (p. 287) and the poet Langston Hughes in *The Nation* (a progressive journal founded in New York in 1865) illustrates a controversy over the idea of black culture that flared during the Harlem Renaissance and continues today. The central question is, What, if anything, is "Negro art"? Does "Negro art" mean all art by African Americans, or are certain types of expression more authentically African American?

In "The Negro-Art Hokum," published in *The Nation* on June 16, 1926, Schuyler identifies the same distinctive art forms developed by African Americans that James Weldon Johnson mentions in his preface to *The Book of American Negro Poetry* (p. 311)—jazz, ragtime, and so on. Schuyler, however, pointedly rejects the idea that the artists' race is instrumental—or even relevant—to their innovations. Moreover, he suggests that championing the idea of a black aesthetic reinforces restrictive myths about permanent, fundamental differences between white and black Americans.

In "The Negro Artist and the Racial Mountain," published in *The Nation* the following week, Langston Hughes presents racial identity not as a limitation but as a key asset for artists. Class is also central to his ideas. For Hughes, the "common people" hold the key for black artists "because they still hold their own individuality in the face of American standardizations." The "better-class Negro," on the other hand, must overcome the pressure to try to live "like white folks." This pressure is detrimental to the development of artists, but it does not prevent the upper class from contributing to the wealth of material available to black artists.

Schuyler's and Hughes's subsequent letters to *The Nation* underscore the differences in their ideas about the relationship of race to artistic development. Both men stress the importance of environment, but they differ in their assessments of how race and class influence environment. Hughes's letter also introduces the idea that an African American artist's relationship to assimilation might be different from that of other African Americans, who are more concerned with maximizing possibilities for economic and social advancement than with capturing examples of difference.

Born James Langston Hughes in 1902 in Missouri, Hughes had a somewhat turbulent childhood, moving frequently around the Midwest between the homes of his grandmother, family friends, and his mother and stepfather. It was in those childhood cities in Kansas, Illinois, and Ohio that he first encountered jazz and the blues, which came to be dominant influences on the style and content of his poetry and other writing. He began composing poetry as a young teenager and was named Class Poet in the eighth grade. In 1920, after graduation from high school, he lived with his father for a year in Mexico, an experience that profoundly shaped his concepts of race and class. His most famous poem, "The Negro Speaks of Rivers," which he wrote while traveling to Mexico, was published in 1921 in *The Crisis*.

In order to secure the financial support of his father (who did not approve of his desire to be a writer), Hughes began studying engineering at Columbia University but withdrew in 1922. The following year, he spent six months as a sailor on the S.S. *Malone*, traveling to Africa and leaving the ship in France. In Paris, Hughes continued to publish poems and short stories, many of which drew on his experiences abroad. Returning to the United States in 1924, Hughes held various jobs, from assistant to the historian Carter G. Woodson to busboy. His first book of poetry, *The Weary Blues*, was published in 1926, and the following year he enrolled in Lincoln University, America's first historically black university, graduating in 1929. Over the next thirty-eight years, he lived mainly in Harlem and published more than thirty-five books—poetry, anthologies, novels, children's books, and plays—as well as two autobiographies and countless works of journalism. His writing celebrated black folk culture as a way of instilling in African Americans racial consciousness and pride. In his words, he was seeking "to explain and illuminate the Negro condition in America and obliquely that of all human kind."

Recognized at the time as a central figure of the Harlem Renaissance, Hughes was also a subject of controversy among critics because of his use of dialect and his frequent portrayals of lower-class black characters. He avoided some conflict during his life by keeping his homosexuality private and publishing poems and stories with only veiled references to gay experience. Late in his life, during the McCarthy era, he again spurred controversy by disavowing his earlier Communist sympathies.

Hughes died from complications from prostate cancer in 1967, at the age of sixty-five. New York City honored his contribution to American culture by renaming the block where he lived, on East 127th Street, Langston Hughes Place.

GEORGE S. SCHUYLER
The Negro-Art Hokum [1926]

Negro art "made in America" is as non-existent as the widely advertised profundity of Cal Coolidge, the "seven years of progress" of Mayor Hylan, or the reported sophistication of New Yorkers. Negro art there has been, is, and will be among the numerous black nations of Africa, but to suggest the possibility of any such development among the ten million colored people in this republic is self-evident foolishness. Eager apostles from Greenwich Village, Harlem, and environs proclaimed a great renaissance of Negro art just around the corner waiting to be ushered on the scene by those whose hobby is taking races, nations, peoples, and movements under their wing. New art forms expressing the "peculiar" psychology of the Negro were about to flood the market. In short, the art of Homo Africanus was about to electrify the waiting world. Skeptics patiently waited. They still wait.

True, from dark-skinned sources have come those slave songs based on Protestant hymns and Biblical texts known as the spirituals, work songs and secular songs of sorrow and tough luck known as the blues, that outgrowth of rag-time known as jazz (in the development of which whites have assisted), and the Charleston, an eccentric dance invented by the gamins around the public market-place in Charleston, S. C. No one can or does deny this. But these are contributions of a caste in a certain section of the country. They are foreign to Northern Negroes, West Indian Negroes, and African Negroes. They are no more expressive or characteristic of the Negro race than the music and dancing of the Appalachian highlanders or the Dalmatian peasantry[1] are expressive or characteristic of the Caucasian race. If one wishes to speak of the musical contributions of the peasantry of the South, very well. Any group under similar circumstances would have produced something similar. It is merely a coincidence that this peasant class happens to be of a darker hue than the other inhabitants of the land. One recalls the remarkable likeness of the minor strains of the Russian mujiks to those of the Southern Negro.

As for the literature, painting, and sculpture of Aframericans—such as there is—it is identical in kind with the literature, painting, and sculpture of white Americans: that is, it shows more or less evidence of European influence. In the field of drama little of any merit has been written by and about Negroes that could not have been written by whites. The dean of the Aframerican literati is W. E. B. DuBois, a product of Harvard and German universities; the foremost Aframerican sculptor is Meta Warwick Fuller,[2] a graduate of leading American art schools and former student of Rodin; while the most noted Aframerican painter, Henry Ossawa Turner, is dean of American painters in Paris and has been decorated by the French Government. Now the work of these artists is no more "expressive of the Negro soul"—as the gushers put it—than are the scribblings of Octavus Cohen or Hugh Wiley.

This, of course, is easily understood if one stops to realize that the Aframerican is merely a lampblackened Anglo-Saxon. If the European immigrant after two or three generations of exposure to our schools, politics, advertising, moral crusades, and restaurants becomes indistinguishable from the mass of Americans of the

1. Sharecroppers and laborers on farms in Dalmatia, a region on the East coast of the Adriatic Sea and inland, in current day Croatia.
2. Meta Vaux Warrick Fuller (1877–1968), poet and artist who celebrated African American themes, foreshadowing the art of the Harlem Renaissance.

older stock (despite the influence of the foreign-language press), how much truer must it be of the sons of Ham who have been subjected to what the uplifters call Americanism for the last three hundred years. Aside from his color, which ranges from very dark brown to pink, your American Negro is just plain American. Negroes and whites from the same localities in this country talk, think, and act about the same. Because a few writers with a paucity of themes have seized upon imbecilities of the Negro rustics and clowns and palmed them off as authentic and characteristic Aframerican behavior, the common notion that the black American is so "different" from his white neighbor has gained wide currency. The mere mention of the word "Negro" conjures up in the average white American's mind a composite stereotype of Bert Williams, Aunt Jemima, Uncle Tom, Jack Johnson, Florian Slappey,[3] and the various monstrosities scrawled by the cartoonists. Your average Aframerican no more resembles this stereotype than the average American resembles a composite of Andy Gump, Jim Jeffries, and a cartoon by Rube Goldberg.[4]

Again, the Aframerican is subject to the same economic and social forces that mold the actions and thoughts of the white Americans. He is not living in a different world as some whites and a few Negroes would have us believe. When the jangling of his Connecticut alarm clock gets him out of his Grand Rapids bed to a breakfast similar to that eaten by his white brother across the street; when he toils at the same or similar work in mills, mines, factories, and commerce alongside the descendants of Spartacus, Robin Hood, and Erik the Red;[5] when he wears similar clothing and speaks the same language with the same degree of perfection; when he reads the same Bible and belongs to the Baptist, Methodist, Episcopal, or Catholic church; when his fraternal affiliations also include the Elks, Masons, and Knights of Pythias; when he gets the same or similar schooling, lives in the same kind of houses, owns the

same makes of cars (or rides in them), and nightly sees the same Hollywood version of life on the screen; when he smokes the same brands of tobacco and avidly peruses the same puerile periodicals; in short, when he responds to the same political, social, moral, and economic stimuli in precisely the same manner as his white neighbor, it is sheer nonsense to talk about "racial differences" as between the American black man and the American white man. Glance over a Negro newspaper (it is printed in good Americanese) and you will find the usual quota of crime news, scandal, personals, and uplift to be found in the average white newspaper—which, by the way, is more widely read by the Negroes than is the Negro press. In order to satisfy the cravings of an inferiority complex engendered by the colorphobia of the mob, the readers of the Negro newspaper are given a slight dash of racialistic seasoning. In the homes of the black and white Americans of the same cultural and economic level one finds similar furniture, literature, and conversation. How, then, can the black American be expected to produce art and literature dissimilar to that of the white American?

Consider Coleridge-Taylor, Edward Wilmot Blyden, and Claude McKay, the Englishmen; Pushkin, the Russian; Bridgewater, the Pole; Antar, the Arabian; Latino, the Spaniard; Dumas, *père* and *fils*, the Frenchmen; and Paul Laurence Dunbar, Charles W. Chesnutt, and James Weldon Johnson, the Americans. All Negroes; yet their work shows the impress of nationality rather than race. They all reveal the psychology and culture of their environment—their color is incidental. Why should Negro artists of America vary from the national artistic norm when Negro artists in other countries have not done so? If we can foresee what kind of white citizens will inhabit this neck of the woods in the next generation by studying the sort of education and environment the children are exposed to now, it should not be difficult to reason that the adults of today are what they are because of the education and environment they were

3. Detective character who spoke in exaggerated black dialect, created by the white American writer Octavus Roy Cohen, whose short-story collection *Come Seven* was advertised as "for one who likes Nigger stuff"; John Arthur "Jack" Johnson (1878–1946), first black world heavyweight boxing champion.

4. Some cartoon series created by Rube Goldberg include "Mike and Ike" and "Boob McNutt," and his most famous cartoons depict elaborate devices for doing simple things, commonly known as "Rube Goldberg devices"; Jim Jeffries: white American boxer who became the world heavyweight champion in 1899; Andy Gump: father in popular comic strip "The Gumps," by the white American cartoonist Sidney Smith, about the domestic lives of a middle-class family, designed to appeal to the masses.

5. Greeks, English, and Scandinavians.

exposed to a generation ago. And that education and environment were about the same for blacks and whites. One contemplates the popularity of the Negro-art hokum and murmurs, "How come?"

This nonsense is probably the last stand of the old myth palmed off by Negrophobists for all these many years, and recently rehashed by the sainted Harding, that there are "fundamental, eternal, and inescapable differences"[6] between white and black Americans. That there are Negroes who will lend this myth a helping hand need occasion no surprise. It has been broadcast all over the world by the vociferous scions of slaveholders, "scientists" like Madison Grant and Lothrop Stoddard, and the patriots who flood the treasury of the Ku Klux Klan; and it is believed, even today, by the majority of free, white citizens. On this baseless premise, so flattering to the white mob, that the blackamoor[7] is inferior and fundamentally different, is erected the postulate that he must needs be peculiar; and when he attempts to portray life through the medium of art, it must of necessity be a peculiar art. While such reasoning may seem conclusive to the majority of Americans, it must be rejected with a loud guffaw by intelligent people.

From *The Nation*, June 16, 1926.

LANGSTON HUGHES

The Negro Artist and the Racial Mountain
[1926]

One of the most promising of the young Negro poets said to me once, "I want to be a poet—not a Negro poet," meaning, I believe, "I want to write like a white poet"; meaning subconsciously, "I would like to be a white poet"; meaning behind that, "I would like to be white." And I was sorry the young man said that, for no great poet has ever been afraid of being himself. And I doubted then that, with his desire to run away spiritually from his race, this boy would ever be a great poet. But this is the mountain standing in the way of any true Negro art in America—this urge within the race toward whiteness, the desire to pour racial individuality into the mold of American standardization, and to be as little Negro and as much American as possible.

But let us look at the immediate background of this young poet. His family is of what I suppose one would call the Negro middle class: people who are by no means rich yet never uncomfortable nor hungry—smug, contented, respectable folk, members of the Baptist church. The father goes to work every morning. He is a chief steward at a large white club. The mother sometimes does fancy sewing or supervises parties for the rich families of the town. The children go to a mixed school. In the home they read white papers and magazines. And the mother often says "Don't be like niggers" when the children are bad. A frequent phrase from the father is, "Look how well a white man does things." And so the word white comes to be unconsciously a symbol of all the virtues. It holds for the children beauty, morality, and money. The whisper of "I want to be white" runs silently through their minds. This young poet's home is, I believe, a fairly typical home of the colored middle class. One sees immediately how difficult it would be for an artist born in such a home to interest himself in interpreting the beauty of his own people. He is never taught to see that beauty. He is taught rather not to see it, or if he does, to be ashamed of it when it is not according to Caucasian patterns.

For racial culture the home of a self-styled "high-class" Negro has nothing better to offer. Instead there will perhaps be more aping of things white than in a less cultured or less wealthy home. The father is perhaps a doctor, lawyer, landowner, or politician. The mother may be a social worker, or a teacher, or she may do nothing and have a maid. Father is often dark but he has usually married the lightest woman he could find. The family attend a fashionable church where few really colored faces are to be found. And they themselves draw a color line. In the North they go to white theatres and white movies. And in the South they have

6. President Warren G. Harding's words in a 1921 speech in Birmingham, Alabama.
7. A term for a dark-skinned person, now considered derogatory, from "black moor," a reference to northern Africans.

at least two cars and a house "like white folks." Nordic[8] manners, Nordic faces, Nordic hair, Nordic art (if any), and an Episcopal heaven. A very high mountain indeed for the would-be racial artist to climb in order to discover himself and his people.

But then there are the low-down folks, the so-called common element, and they are the majority—may the Lord be praised! The people who have their nip of gin on Saturday nights and are not too important to themselves or the community, or too well fed, or too learned to watch the lazy world go round. They live on Seventh Street in Washington or State Street in Chicago and they do not particularly care whether they are like white folks or anybody else. Their joy runs, bang! into ecstasy. Their religion soars to a shout. Work maybe a little today, rest a little tomorrow. Play awhile. Sing awhile. O, let's dance! These common people are not afraid of spirituals, as for a long time their more intellectual brethren were, and jazz is their child. They furnish a wealth of colorful, distinctive material for any artist because they still hold their own individuality in the face of American standardizations. And perhaps these common people will give to the world its truly great Negro artist, the one who is not afraid to be himself. Whereas the better-class Negro would tell the artist what to do, the people at least let him alone when he does appear. And they are not ashamed of him—if they know he exists at all. And they accept what beauty is their own without question.

Certainly there is, for the American Negro artist who can escape the restrictions the more advanced among his own group would put upon him, a great field of unused material ready for his art. Without going outside his race, and even among the better classes with their "white" culture and conscious American manners, but still Negro enough to be different, there is sufficient matter to furnish a black artist with a lifetime of creative work. And when he chooses to touch on the relations between Negroes and whites in this country with their innumerable overtones and undertones, surely, and especially for literature and the drama, there is an inexhaustible supply of themes at hand. To these the Negro artist can give his racial individuality, his heritage of rhythm and warmth, and his incongruous humor that so often, as in the Blues, becomes ironic laughter mixed with tears. But let us look again at the mountain.

A prominent Negro clubwoman in Philadelphia paid eleven dollars to hear Raquel Meller sing Andalusian popular songs. But she told me a few weeks before she would not think of going to hear "that woman," Clara Smith, a great black artist, sing Negro folksongs. And many an upper-class Negro church, even now, would not dream of employing a spiritual in its services. The drab melodies in white folks' hymnbooks are much to be preferred. "We want to worship the Lord correctly and quietly. We don't believe in 'shouting.' Let's be dull like the Nordics," they say, in effect.

The road for the serious black artist, then, who would produce a racial art is most certainly rocky and the mountain is high. Until recently he received almost no encouragement for his work from either white or colored people. The fine novels of Chesnutt go out of print with neither race noticing their passing. The quaint charm and humor of Dunbar's dialect verse brought to him, in his day, largely the same kind of encouragement one would give a side-show freak (A colored man writing poetry! How odd!) or a clown (How amusing!).

The present vogue in things Negro, although it may do as much harm as good for the budding colored artist, has at least done this: it has brought him forcibly to the attention of his own people among whom for so long, unless the other race had noticed him beforehand, he was a prophet with little honor. I understand that Charles Gilpin[9] acted for years in Negro theaters without any special acclaim from his own, but when Broadway gave him eight curtain calls, Negroes, too, began to beat a tin pan in his honor. I know a young colored writer, a manual worker by day, who had been writing

---

8. Associated with white people; literally "of the Northern Lands," a reference to the Scandinavian people from Northern Europe and the North Atlantic (including Norway, Sweden, and Denmark); this term gained popularity in the mid-1920s and was frequently used in place of previously popular terms, Caucasian and Anglo-Saxon.

9. Actor (1878–1930); in 1920, originated the title role in Eugene O'Neill's *The Emperor Jones*, the first drama in a white-run theater to star an African American; for his Broadway performance, he was honored at the White House by President Warren G. Harding and awarded the NAACP's Spingarn Medal, but later (spurred by his heavy drinking and by his problems with the play, especially the frequent use of "nigger"), fell out with O'Neill and the role for the 1924 London revival was given to Paul Robeson (1898–1976) instead.

well for the colored magazines for some years, but it was not until he recently broke into the white publications and his first book was accepted by a prominent New York publisher that the "best" Negroes in his city took the trouble to discover that he lived there. Then almost immediately they decided to give a grand dinner for him. But the society ladies were careful to whisper to his mother that perhaps she'd better not come. They were not sure she would have an evening gown.

The Negro artist works against an undertow of sharp criticism and misunderstanding from his own group and unintentional bribes from the whites. "O, be respectable, write about nice people, show how good we are," say the Negroes. "Be stereotyped, don't go too far, don't shatter our illusions about you, don't amuse us too seriously. We will pay you," say the whites. Both would have told Jean Toomer not to write "Cane." The colored people did not praise it. The white people did not buy it. Most of the colored people who did read "Cane" hate it. They are afraid of it. Although the critics gave it good reviews the public remained indifferent. Yet (excepting the work of DuBois) "Cane" contains the finest prose written by a Negro in America. And like the singing of Robeson,[1] it is truly racial.

But in spite of the Nordicized Negro intelligentsia and the desires of some white editors we have an honest American Negro literature already with us. Now I await the rise of the Negro theater. Our folk music, having achieved world-wide fame, offers itself to the genius of the great individual American Negro composer who is to come. And within the next decade I expect to see the work of a growing school of colored artists who paint and model the beauty of dark faces and create with new technique the expressions of their own soul-world. And the Negro dancers who will dance like flame and the singers who will continue to carry our songs to all who listen—they will be with us in even greater numbers tomorrow.

Most of my own poems are racial in theme and treatment, derived from the life I know. In many of them I try to grasp and hold some of the meanings and rhythms of jazz. I am sincere as I know how to be in these poems and yet after every reading I answer questions like these from my own people: Do you think Negroes should always write about Negroes? I wish you wouldn't read some of your poems to white folks. How do you find anything interesting in a place like a cabaret? Why do you write about black people? You aren't black. What makes you do so many jazz poems?

But jazz to me is one of the inherent expressions of Negro life in America: the eternal tom-tom beating in the Negro soul—the tom-tom of revolt against weariness in a white world, a world of subway trains, and work, work, work; the tom-tom of joy and laughter, and pain swallowed in a smile. Yet the Philadelphia clubwoman is ashamed to say that her race created it and she does not like me to write about it. The old subconscious "white is best" runs through her mind. Years of study under white teachers, a lifetime of white books, pictures, and papers, and white manners, morals, and Puritan standards made her dislike the spirituals. And now she turns up her nose at jazz and all its manifestations—likewise almost everything else distinctly racial. She doesn't care for the Winold Reiss portraits of Negroes because they are "too Negro." She does not want a true picture of herself from anybody. She wants the artist to flatter her, to make the white world believe that all Negroes are as smug and as near white in soul as she wants to be. But, to my mind, it is the duty of the younger Negro artist, if he accepts any duties at all from outsiders, to change through the force of his art that old whispering "I want to be white," hidden in the aspirations of his people, to "Why should I want to be white? I am a Negro—and beautiful!"

So I am ashamed for the black poet who says, "I want to be a poet, not a Negro poet," as though his own racial world were not as interesting as any other world. I am ashamed, too, for the colored artist who runs from the painting of Negro faces to the painting of sunsets after the manner of the academicians because he fears the strange un-whiteness of his own features. An artist must be free to choose what he does, certainly, but he must also never be afraid to do what he might choose.

---

1. Paul Robeson singer and actor, who popularized African American spirituals and played Othello in the longest-running Shakespeare production ever on Broadway; starting in the 1940s, he began to focus his work on social activism and became a political target during the McCarthy era.

Let the blare of Negro jazz bands and the bellowing voice of Bessie Smith singing Blues penetrate the closed ears of the colored near-intellectuals until they listen and perhaps understand. Let Paul Robeson singing Water Boy, and Rudolph Fisher writing about the streets of Harlem, and Jean Toomer holding the heart of Georgia in his hands, and Aaron Douglas drawing strange black fantasies cause the smug Negro middle class to turn from their white, respectable, ordinary books and papers to catch a glimmer of their own beauty. We younger Negro artists who create now intend to express our individual dark-skinned selves without fear or shame. If white people are pleased we are glad. If they are not, it doesn't matter. We know we are beautiful. And ugly too. The tom-tom cries and the tom-tom laughs. If colored people are pleased we are glad. If they are not, their displeasure doesn't matter either. We build our temples for tomorrow, strong as we know how, and we stand on top of the mountain, free within ourselves.

From *The Nation*, June 23, 1926.

George Schuyler
Negroes and Artists [1926]

To the Editor of the Nation:

Sir: Langston Hughes, defending racial art in America, forgets that the Negro masses he describes are no different from the white masses we are all familiar with. Both "watch the lazy world go round" and "have their nip of gin on Saturday nights" (love of strong liquors is supposed to be a Nordic characteristic). If there is anything "racial" about the spirituals and the blues, then there should be immediate ability to catch the intricate rhythm on the part of Negroes from Jamaica, Zanzibar, and Sierra Leone. Such is not the case, and we must conclude that they are the products of a certain American environment: the South. They are American folk-songs, built around Anglo-Saxon religious concepts.

An artist, it seems to me, is one who, able to see life about him, and, struck by its quick interchange of comedy, drama, and tragedy, attempts to portray it or interpret it in music, poetry, or prose, on canvas or in stone. He can only use the equipment furnished him by education and environment. Consequently his creation will be French, British, German, Russian, Zulu, or Chinese, depending on where he lives. The work of the artist raised and educated in this country must necessarily be American.

It is the Aframerican masses who consume several millions' worth of hair-straightener and skin-whitener per annum in an effort to reach the American standard in pigmentation and hair-texture. This does not look as if they did not care whether they were like white folks or not. Negro propaganda-art, even when glorifying the "primitiveness" of the American Negro masses, is hardly more than a protest against a feeling of inferiority, and such a psychology seldom produces art.

Atlanta, Georgia, June 21

George S. Schuyler

From *The Nation*, July 14, 1926.

Langston Hughes
American Art or Negro Art [1926]

To the Editor of the Nation:

Sir: For Mr. Schuyler to say that "the Negro masses . . . are no different from the white masses" in America seems to me obviously absurd. Fundamentally, perhaps, all people are the same. But as long as the Negro remains a segregated group in this country he must reflect certain racial and environmental differences which are his own. The very fact that Negroes do straighten their hair and try to forget their racial background makes them different from white people. If they were exactly like the dominant class they would not have to try so hard to imitate them. Again it seems quite as absurd to say that spirituals and blues are not Negro as it is to say that cowboy songs are not cowboy songs or that the folk-ballads of Scotland do not belong to Scotland. The spirituals and blues are American, certainly, but they are also very much American Negro. And if one can say that some of my poems have no racial distinctiveness about them or that "Cane" is not Negro, one can say with equal truth that "Nize Baby" is purely American.[2]

From an economic and sociological viewpoint it may be entirely desirable that the Negro become as much like his white American brother as possible. Surely colored people want all the opportunities and advantages that anybody else possesses here in our country. But until America has completely absorbed the Negro and until segregation and racial self-consciousness have entirely disappeared, the true work of art from the Negro artist is bound, if it have any color and distinctiveness at all, to reflect his racial background and his racial environment.

New York, June 14

LANGSTON HUGHES

From *The Nation,* August 18, 1926.

2. 1926 comic strip and book about Jewish immigrants by the white American writer Milt Gross, written in heavy dialect; *Cane:* Jean Toomer's 1923 novel is a combination of poems, sketches, and short stories about black urban and rural life, which is widely regarded as a masterpiece of the Harlem Renaissance.

KEY DEBATE ~ *Society and Individual Choice*

W. E. B. DU BOIS
Inter-marriage [1925]

In this *Crisis* column, W. E. B. Du Bois outlines arguments against legal restrictions on interracial relations, associating the laws with the Ku Klux Klan and denouncing them as "indefensible and disgraceful." Citing the high number of "mulattoes" in states with anti-intermarriage laws, Du Bois asserts that such laws do not prevent interracial relations but merely eliminate the legal protections provided by marriage for the partners and their children. Du Bois's column sparked no opposition, nor did he seem to expect any, which argues for a general agreement among African Americans regarding the injustice of legal restrictions to interracial relationships.

From *The Crisis*, April 1925.

The Ku Klux Klan has secured the introduction of bills into certain legislatures, including Ohio, Iowa and Michigan, which should be called proposals "to encourage prostitution and degrade women of Negro descent". These bills have secured the backing of Christian ministers, women's clubs and some prominent citizens, because they prevent legal marriage between persons of different "races".

It is astonishing that muddled thinking will lead to such indefensible and disgraceful proposals. There is nothing to prevent today a white man from refusing to marry a colored woman. There is no law compelling a white woman to take a Negro mate. Decent custom in all civilized communities compels the scoundrel who seduces a girl to marry her no matter what race she belongs to. Does decency ask change in such custom? There are laws which say that if white people wish to consort with colored people they must marry. Can civilization demand less?

Must Nordic culture admit that the only way to prevent intermarriage is to make it illegal and if they admit this can they prove it? Mississippi makes interracial marriage illegal and Mississippi has 122,000 acknowledged mulattoes. The whole South refuses to black girls any adequate protection against white brutes or gentlemen and yet the South admits to a million and half mulattoes.

If reason and science, social pressure and parental advice cannot keep white and colored folk from inter-marriage, will law do it? Shame on a race and a people that must stoop to such measures in order to maintain their vaunted superiority.

JOEL AUGUSTUS ROGERS
The Critic: Dean Miller Takes Fright at the Emancipation of the Negro Woman [1925]

White birth control advocates of the 1920s and 1930s frequently employed the theory of eugenics to support their arguments, decrying the high birth rates of the poor and poorly educated compared to the low birth rates of the professional class. In "The Critic," the journalist and historian Joel Augustus Rogers (1883–1966) criticizes Kelly Miller, dean of Howard University, for using that comparison to urge professional women not to use birth control.

Miller grounded his case in biology, asserting that "the biological function of the female is to bear and rear children, which, if effectively performed, will necessarily engage the chief energies of the producing sex." Rogers, on the other hand, calls for "more cultivation of the species and less propagation of it. He links Miller's use of biological arguments ("boundaries fixed in nature") to ideas about "the nature of the Negro" historically used to limit the overall advancement of African Americans ("the assertion of the Nordics that intellectual development is bad for the Negro"). *The Messenger's* socialist bent is evident in Rogers's buoyant response to Miller's concern about the rise of "the lower stratum": "Is not the scum frequently the highest stratum of the pot?" This argument underscores the distance between Rogers's position and that of birth control proponents of the period who drew on eugenics to argue that the poor were "undesirables" whose birth rate should be reduced.

Born in Jamaica, where he became acquainted with the black nationalist leader Marcus Garvey, Rogers immigrated to the United States in 1906. He traveled around the country as a Pullman porter, gaining an education through his experiences with diverse people and places, as well as through the books he borrowed from libraries along his route. In his subsequent career as a journalist, Rogers wrote for a wide variety of publications, including the *Pittsburgh Courier, The Crisis,* and *The Messenger,* and was a copy editor of Marcus Garvey's *Daily Negro Times.* In his numerous books, many of which he self-published, he specialized in highlighting the contributions of Africans and African culture and in exploring the impact of interracialism on world history.

From *The Messenger,* April 1925.

Kelly Miller,[1] of Howard University, thinks that the Negro woman is venturing too far from Kaiser Wilhelm's four K's—Kinder, Kuche, Kleider, Kurche (Children, Kitchen, Clothes, Church)[2]—and rises to warn her.

En passant[3]—one might say that that is what Prof. Miller says the Kaiser's aggregation of K's are. Unless I am much mistaken, they read: Kaiser, Kurche, Kinder, Kuche (Kaiser, Church, Children, Kitchen). It wasn't the late "Almighty's" habit to omit himself from the head of any list. One suspects that the dean introduced those four K's into his article rather because of their alliterative, spectacular effect. Women neglecting clothes? Ye gods!

For the first of his four, Dean Miller bases his belief upon "studies in eugenics, based upon the 55 colored members of the Howard University faculty. He found that in the families from which these teachers came there was a total of 363 children, or an average of 6.5 for each family. On the other hand, the 55 offspring have a total of 37, or only seven-tenths of a child, for each potential family."

Armed with these figures, the dean goes on to say:

"From a wide acquaintance with the upper section of the Negro race under a variety of circumstances and conditions, I am fully persuaded that the Howard University group is typical of the like element throughout the race, so far as fecundity is concerned. A study of the teachers in the public schools of Washington, the physicians, lawyers and other educated groups would tell the same sterile story."

Dean Miller concludes with:

"I take little stock in the derogation of these degenerate days. I do not believe that the cut of hair or the style of dress is coefficient of character, nor that girlish liveliness is inconsistent with womanly loveliness and worth. But I do believe, with an unshakable conviction, that our women are venturing too far from the four K's—Kinder, Kuche, Kleider and Kirche."

1. For a brief biographical sketch of Miller, see p. 292.
2. William II of Germany (1859–1941), the last emperor of Germany and king of Prussia from 1888 to 1918, who was forced to abdicate during World War I, defined a woman's role as centered on the three K's, Kirche, Kinder, and Küche (Church, Children, and Kitchen), an idea later adopted by the Nazis.
3. By the way, literally "in passing" [French].

IS PROF. MILLER'S PESSIMISM JUSTIFIED?

Far from sharing the dean's fright, I think his article a piece of optimism so unwarranted that it moves one to laughter. Dean Schuyler ought to be able to whittle any number of shafts from it.

The intellectual gap between the Negro man and the Negro woman is a very wide one. "Who's Who In America," is by no means a criterion of worth and accomplishment, still it is a fairly reliable gauge. Of sixty-four Negroes named in "Who's Who," only one was a woman. The white women, on the other hand, were one in sixteen of the white men. Four times as many as the colored women!

Of the half a dozen or so principal groups composing this nation, the Negro woman is by far the most backward, if we except the Indian. She has been far too devoted to a fifth K (kinks).[4] Now, however, some of the members of this very backward group are beginning to step out into the intellectual field and, God bless you, the timid dean arises to warn them that they are "venturing too far!"

Speaking of kitchens, does the dean think, for instance, that the Negro woman is venturing too far from the white woman's kitchen? Would he have the lady professors and doctors back there?

"RACE SUICIDE"

The cautious dean also deplores so-called race suicide, saying:

"The biological function of the female is to bear and rear children, which, if effectively performed, will necessarily engage the chief energies of the producing sex. No scheme of philosophy or social reform can alter this basic responsibility imposed by nature from the foundation of the world of living things.

"The liberalization of woman must always be kept within the boundary fixed by nature. Tampering with the decrees of nature jeopardizes the very continuance of the human race."

The biological function of woman *is* to bear and rear children. But has she no other functions? Again, far from agreeing with Prof. Miller, I give the Negro woman credit if she endeavors to be something other than a mere breeding machine.

Having children is by no means the sole reason for being. Birth and death are as inevitable and immutable forces as the winds, the tides, and the motions of the planet, hence we needn't worry our heads so much there. Mankind grows as spontaneously as the weeds in a clearing. Root them up as fast as you will, but they appear nevertheless.

Moreover, the world has probably millions of years more to last—time for countless generations to be born in. Why not, then, more cultivation of the species and less propagation of it? In proportion as you have more of the latter you have less of the former.

What if the race is being recruited from "the lower stratum," as the dean complains: it has ever been thus.

And, speaking of the lower stratum, is not the scum frequently the highest stratum of the pot?

Yes, there are other things quite as worthy as bearing children, and that is the cultivation and pruning of society by these "sage femmes" decried by Dean Miller.

"The liberalization of woman must always be kept within the boundary fixed by nature," says the dean.

What is that boundary? How reminiscent is this argument of one the dean has always inveighed against: the assertion of the Nordics that intellectual development is bad for the Negro and that he should be kept within the boundaries set by the Almighty?

In an attempt to tone down his reactionary views, Prof. Miller makes a gesture at liberality by stating:

"I believe that the superior women, equally with the superior men, should have the fullest opportunity to develop and exert their higher capacities." But this is more reactionary yet, for here again is the Nordic doctrine of superior race, pure and simple. Why not opportunity for everybody, for so-called inferior as well as superior?

4. Tight curls; for debates about hair, see pp. 769–77, 1084, 1096.

Part Three ∼ Works Cited

Quotations and statistics in this section's headnotes and notes were drawn from the following sources:

Burton, Jennifer. "Introduction." Zora Neale Hurston, Eulalie Spence, Marita Bonner, and Others. *The Prize Plays and Other One-Acts Published in Periodicals.* Eds. Henry Louis Gates, Jr. and Jennifer Burton. New York: G. K. Hall, 1996, pp. xx–xlvii.

The Crisis [unsigned editorial]. "Easter, 1919." *The Crisis* 17 (April 1919): 267–68.

Du Bois, W. E. B. "The Amy Spingarn Prizes in Literature and Art." *The Crisis* 29, No. 1 (November 1924): 24.

——. *The Autobiography of W. E. B. Du Bois: A Soliloquy on Viewing My Life from the Last Decade of Its First Century.* New York: International Publishers Co., Inc., 1968.

——. "The Black Man and the Unions." *The Crisis* 15 (March 1918): 216–17.

——. "A History of the Negro Race in the World War and After." *The Crisis* (January 1924): 110–114.

——. "Letter to the Editor, *New York Age.*" June 20, 1921. Reprinted in *Negro World* (July 2, 1921).

——, ed. "The Negro in Art: How Shall He Be Portrayed: A Symposium." *The Crisis* 31–33 (March–June, August, September, and November 1926).

——. "The Pan-African Movement." *History of the Pan-African Congress: Colonial and Coloured Unity, a Programme of Action.* Ed. George Padmore. Manchester: Pan-African Federation, 1945, pp. 13–26.

——. "Review of Nella Larsen's *Quicksand*, Claude McKay's *Home to Harlem*, and Melville Herskovits' *The American Negro*." *The Crisis* 35, No. 6 (June 1928): 202.

—— and John H. Owens. "Socialism and the Negro." *The Crisis* (October 1919), pp. 245–247.

Ferguson, Jeffrey, B. *The Sage of Sugar Hill: George S. Schuyler and the Harlem Renaissance.* New Haven: Yale University, 2005.

[Ferris, William H.] Editorial. *Negro World.* July 2, 1921.

Garvey, Marcus. "*Negro World Report—The Pan African Congress.*" Liberty Hall, New York: August 2, 1921. www.marcusgarvey.com.

"General Clarkson's Address." *The Ohio Democrat.* Logan, Ohio (May 20, 1893): 1.

Grimké, Angelina Weld. *Rachel: A Play in Three Acts.* Boston: The Cornhill Company, 1920.

Hill, Robert, ed. *Garvey and Universal Negro Improvement Association Papers.* Berkeley and Los Angeles: University of California Press, 1983.

Hurston, Zora Neale. Papers. Beinecke Rare Book and Manuscript Library. New Haven: Yale University, 1925.

Leeming, David Adams. *James Baldwin: A Biography.* New York: Knopf, 1994.

The New Negro: An Interpretation. New York: Albert and Charles Boni, 1925.

——. "Propaganda—Or Poetry" (1936).

——. "Steps Towards the Negro Theatre." *Crisis* 25 (December 1922), pp. 66–68.

——, ed. *Survey Graphic: Harlem: Mecca of the New Negro.* Vol. 6, No. 6 (1 March 1925). Reprinted Baltimore: Black Classic Press, 1980.

——. and Montgomery Gregory, eds. *Plays of Negro life: A Source-book of Native American Drama.* New York: Harper and Brothers, 1927.

Miller, May. Interview with Cassandra Willis. Cited in Winifred 1. Stoelting, "May Miller," *Directory of Literary Biography 41*, 243.

Rampersad, Arnold. *The Life of Langston Hughes, Volume 2: 1941–1967: I Dream a World.* New York: Oxford University Press, 2002.

A Southern Colored Woman, "A Letter," *The Crisis* 19 (November 1919): 339.

Thurman, Wallace, ed. *FIRE!!* November 1926.

——, ed. *Harlem: A Forum of Negro Life.* November 1928.

United Negro Improvement Association and African Communities League. "Constitution and By-Laws," 1929. www.unia-acl.com (accessed 5/19/10).

Wilson, Woodrow. Address, April 2, 1917. Sixty-Fifth Congress, 1 Session, Senate Document No. 5.

PART FOUR

Interregnum: From the Great Depression to the Civil Rights Movement (1929–1953)

"The Depression brought everybody down a peg or two," the poet Langston Hughes recalled in his 1940 autobiography, *The Big Sea*. "And the Negroes had but few pegs to fall." The Great Depression—which was ushered in by the stock market crash of 1929 and lasted until the onset of World War II in Europe, in September 1939—devastated economies around the world. At its height, 25 percent of the U.S. population was unemployed, and those Americans who held on to their jobs saw their wages decrease dramatically. As bad as it was for all Americans, the percentage of African Americans who were unemployed during the Depression was twice the national average: no less than 50 percent by 1932.

In the North, the manufacturing industry was hit particularly hard by the economic devastation, and many of the African Americans who had migrated north during the 1920s found themselves out of work or facing mounting aggression from white Americans demanding that black workers be fired to alleviate white unemployment. As the economy contracted, racial tensions mounted in the South, where, despite the steady movement of African Americans to the North in the Great Migration, nearly 80 percent of the African American community still lived. Lynchings, the ultimate barometer of anti-black racism and Negrophobia, surged from six in 1932 to twenty-four in 1933. The Depression further dampened the southern farm economy, which had been in turmoil since the collapse of the price of cotton in the 1920s. Both black and white sharecroppers, who worked the land at subsistence wages in exchange for a share of the yield, suffered most dramatically from the devastating economic collapse.

In 1930, the Communist Party entered this tumultuous southern landscape, helping to organize the Sharecroppers' Union in 1931. Although wealthy white landowners attempted to maintain control of their workers through violence and the constant threat of violence, mass arrests, and the enforcement of both *de jure* (by law) and *de facto* (by custom) segregation, the union attracted several thousand members. Communists also assumed a leadership role in defending the Scottsboro Boys, nine young black men who had been falsely convicted of raping two white women in Alabama in 1931. The convictions ignited nationwide protests, and as the Communist Party spearheaded the

Scottsboro Boys' defense through appeals and retrials, its high-profile activism helped promote communism as a potentially viable option for the economic and political liberation of the black masses in those desperate times.

The crisis of the Great Depression encouraged African Americans to consider a wide array of extreme solutions in addition to communism, including self-segregation, reverse migration to the South, and charismatic religious movements, such as that of Father Divine. The Depression also brought about an enormous transformation in Americans' relationship to their government as it ushered in social policies—from Social Security to unemployment insurance—that might have been rejected in other, less traumatic times. The transformation of the federal government began with the 1932 election of Franklin Delano Roosevelt, who served as president from 1933 until his death, in 1945, the only president to serve more than two terms. (A constitutional amendment, ratified in 1951, limited the presidential tenure to two terms.) To combat the Depression, Roosevelt instituted a broad platform of reform legislation, known collectively as the New Deal. The New Deal included national relief and employment programs, as well as broad regulation of banking and trade.

First Lady Eleanor Roosevelt was a major supporter of African American rights, and she worked hard to ensure that African Americans received 10 percent of the payments from the new federal relief programs, corresponding to their proportion of the population. Through New Deal programs, African Americans helped build new roads, bridges, and buildings. African Americans comprised over 15% of the work force of the Works Progress Administration (WPA), the largest New Deal agency, created in 1935 to provide jobs. The New Deal also enabled some continued development of the Harlem Renaissance, the artistic movement that had thrived in the 1920s but abruptly faltered with the onset of the Depression in 1929, dependent as it was on patronage. With federal support, particularly from the Federal Arts Project (FAP, established in 1935), artists created murals, sculptures, and works of public art, produced plays, and wrote fiction. The WPA also preserved over 2,300 first-person accounts of slavery by sending out writers to interview former slaves.

The New Deal programs were not without their faults, including the perpetuation of segregation through separate work groups. Still, the role of the federal government as employer opened up opportunities for black Americans, particularly in formerly closed white-collar occupations, and Roosevelt's attention to their concerns inspired many African Americans to change their allegiance from the Republican Party, the party of Abraham Lincoln, to Roosevelt's Democratic Party. By 1936, a majority of black voters had cast their lot with Roosevelt and the Democrats. Roosevelt's politically motivated refusal to champion a federal anti-lynching law therefore came as a blow to black supporters. However, the NAACP's brilliant legal counsel, Charles Hamilton Houston, was already at work on an alternative strategy for achieving civil rights. According to Houston—a Harvard-trained lawyer, the dean of the School of Law at Howard, and the architect of the modern civil rights movement—the critical civil rights laws were already in place; they just needed to be enforced.

From 1935 until his death, in 1950, Houston, along with his stellar student and co-counsel, Thurgood Marshall, worked to craft the judicial strategy that would eventually overturn *Plessy v. Ferguson,* the 1896 Supreme Court decision that legalized segregated facilities if they were "separate but equal." Instead of challenging segregation directly, Houston's shrewd strategy involved documenting structural inequalities between black and white schools, mounting systematic legal challenges based on those inequalities, and demonstrating that providing truly separate and equal facilities would be impossibly expensive.

Late in 1941, the United States entered World War II, declaring war against the Axis powers after the Japanese bombed Pearl Harbor, in Hawaii, on December 7. World War II brought a definitive end to the Great Depression. The federal government injected a massive amount of money into the economy through military spending, dwarfing the amount spent on New Deal programs. The manufacturing industry grew dramatically in order to produce military supplies, thereby fueling the second wave of the Great Migration. During this wave, which lasted from about 1940 until about 1970, over 5 million African Americans left the South to seek new opportunities elsewhere in the nation.

Over 1 million African Americans served in the military during World War II. Remembering their experiences of discrimination during and after World War I, many committed themselves to the Double Victory (or Double V) campaign, which insisted that racism at home and in the U.S. military be fought simultaneously with the war for freedom abroad. Among the civil rights leaders who challenged discrimination in the military, none was more vocal than A. Philip Randolph, founder of the powerful Brotherhood of Sleeping Car Porters. In 1941, Randolph, along with Bayard Rustin and other leaders, planned a massive march on Washington to protest discrimination in the military and defense industries. The march was called off only after President Roosevelt signed Executive Order 8802, also known as the Fair Employment Act, outlawing employment discrimination by federal agencies, businesses, and unions involved in war-related work.

The end of the war, in 1945, brought escalating demands for civil rights at the local and national level. African Americans in the North and the South reinvigorated or established branches of the NAACP, often propelled by the work of local female leaders, and began agitating for voting rights and equality in pay. In addition to fostering local community activities, advocacy groups such as the NAACP and the Congress (originally Committee) of Racial Equality (CORE) coordinated national legal and political strategies and organized high-profile protests. In 1947, CORE helped organize the Journey of Reconciliation, in which eight white men and eight black men traveled together on public buses throughout the South to protest segregation. A major civil rights victory came in 1948, when President Harry Truman issued Executive Orders 9980 and 9981, eliminating segregation in the civil service and the military. Then, in 1954, Charles Hamilton Houston's visionary legal campaign realized its most telling victory: the landmark unanimous Supreme Court decision in *Brown v. Board of Education,* which mandated the desegregation of public schools. *Brown* would spark the dramatic transformation in American race relations that would evolve with the Montgomery, Alabama, bus boycott in 1955 (under the leadership of a young minister named Martin Luther King Jr.), the 1961 Freedom Ride, the March on Washington in 1963, and the passage of the Civil Rights Act of 1964 and the Voting Rights Act of 1965. However, it was the strategies developed by civil rights leaders during the 1940s and early 1950s—including incremental legal challenges, well-organized nonviolent protest marches and sit-ins, and the Journey of Reconciliation—that lay the foundation for the civil rights movement that followed.

KEY DEBATE ~ *Nature, Culture, and Slavery*

MELVILLE J. HERSKOVITS

from On West African Influences [1941]

The mid-twentieth century brought rapid growth in the academic study of African American history. One important early debate that emerged concerned the question of whether African culture played a significant role in shaping African American culture. That issue, which continues to be discussed today, is known as the Herskovits–Frazier debate, because the scholars Melville J. Herskovits and E. Franklin Frazier established the key questions and marked out two poles of thinking on "Africanisms," linguistic or cultural aspects of African culture that are evident in African American and other cultures of the African diaspora. At one end of the spectrum are those who, like Herskovits, argue that African culture has had a penetrating influence on African American culture. At the other end are those who, like Frazier, contend that slavery effectively erased the African cultural heritage.

Starting with his early publications, including a 1925 article in Alain Locke's *The New Negro* and his first book, *The American Negro: A Study in Racial Crossing* (1928), the white American anthropologist Melville J. Herskovits (1895–1963) distinguished himself by applying anthopological methods to the study of African Americans. With the publication in 1941 of *The Myth of the Negro Past,* from which this piece is taken, Herskovits became established as a key proponent of the idea that important aspects of African American culture are traceable to African customs and traditions (a reversal of his position from his early publications, in which he stressed acculturation of African Americans). Like Zora Neale Hurston shortly after him, Herskovits studied anthropology with Franz Boas at Columbia University and began applying anthropological methods to the study of American ethnic cultures. He received his doctorate in 1923, taught at Howard University from 1925 to 1927, and in 1927 moved to Northwestern University, where he was instrumental in developing the field of African studies.

From Melville J. Herskovits, *The Myth of the Negro Past* (New York: Harper and Brothers, 1941), pp. 167–86.

W hat are the causes which, in the United States, have brought into being a type of family organization that is so distinctive when compared with the common family pattern? The preceding discussion makes it clear that no single reason will account for its establishment and persistence. Explanations based on assumptions of a theoretical nature concerning the origin of the human family may be dismissed out of hand, since the validity of such propositions has been successfully challenged many times both on methodological and on historical grounds. Thus when Puckett points out that,

> It is also rather noticeable that in the Negro folk-songs, mother and child are frequently sung of, but seldom father—possibly pointing back to the African love for the mother and the uncertainty and slight consideration of fatherhood ... [1]

the only possible comment is that his conception of African attitudes and the facts of African family life is false in the light of known facts. Similarly, when Frazier speaks of the "maternal family" as representing "in its purest and most primitive manifestation a natural family group similar to what Briffault has described as the original or earliest form of the human family,"[2] he is merely repeating poor anthropology.

One of the most popular explanations of the aberrant forms taken by the Negro family is by reference to

1. *Folk Beliefs of the Southern Negro*, p. 23. [Unless otherwise noted, all notes are those of the author.]
2. "Tradition and Patterns of Negro Family Life in the United States," p. 198.

the experience of slavery. A less extreme example of this position, conventionally phrased, is to be found in Johnson's work. Noting that the role of the mother is of "much greater importance than that in the more familiar American group," he goes on to state:

> This has some explanation in the slave origins of these families. Children usually remained with the mother; the father was incidental and could very easily be sold away. The role of mother could be extended to that of "mammy" for the children of white families.[3]

Frazier has presented this point of view at greater length. One statement reads:

> We have spoken of the mother as the mistress of the cabin and as the head of the family. . . . Not only did she have a more fundamental interest in her children than the father, but as a worker and a free agent, except where the master's will was concerned, she developed a spirit of independence and a keen sense of her personal rights.[4]

"In spite of the numerous separations," it is stated, "the slave mother and her children, especially those under ten, were treated as a group,"[5] while, "because of the dependence of the children upon the mother it appears that the mother and smaller children were sold together."[6] To make the point, slave advertisements such as the following are cited:

> A Wench, complete cook, washer, and ironer, and her four children—a Boy 12, another 9, a Girl 5 that sews, and a Girl about 4 years old. Another family— a Wench, complete washer and ironer, and her Daughter, 14 years old, accustomed to the house.[7]

These citations are not made to suggest that due attention has not been paid to the place of the father in the slave family, though it is undoubtedly true that he has received less study than has the mother in research into the derivation of present-day family types among the Negroes. The fact of the matter, however, is that the roles of both parents were individually determined, varying not only from region to region and plantation to plantation but also being affected by the reactions of individual personalities on one another. Not only was the father a significant factor during slaving, but a reading of the documents will reveal how the selling of children—even very young children— away from their mothers is stressed again and again as one of the most anguishing aspects of the slave trade. Whether in the case of newly arrived Negroes sold from the slave ships or of slaves born in this country and sold from the plantations, there was not the slightest guarantee than a mother would not be separated from her children. The impression obtained from the contemporary accounts, indeed, is that the chances were perhaps more than even that separation would occur. This means, therefore, that, though the mechanism ordinarily envisaged in establishing this "maternal" family was operative to some degree, the role of slavery cannot be considered as having been quite as important as has been assumed.

The total economic situation of the Negro was another active force in establishing and maintaining the "maternal" family type. No considerable amount of data are available as to the inner economic organization of Negro families, but the forms of Negro family life themselves suggest that the female members of such families, and especially the elderly women, exercise appreciable control over economic resources. That the economic role of the women not only makes of them managers but also contributors whose earnings are important assets is likewise apparent. This economic aspect of their position is described by Johnson in the following terms:

> The situation of economic dependence of women in cities is reversed in this community and is reflected rather strikingly in the economic independence on

---

3. *Shadow of the Plantation*, p. 29.
4. *The Negro Family in the United States*, pp. 57f.
5. *Ibid.*, p. 55.
6. "The Negro Slave Family," p. 234.
7. *Ibid.*

the part of the Negro women in the country. Their earning power is not very much less than that of the men, and for those who do not plan independent work there is greater security in their own family organization, where many hands contribute to the raising of cotton and of food, than there is for them alone with a young and inexperienced husband.[8]

In Mississippi the following obtains in plantation families:

> In many cases the woman is the sole breadwinner. Often there is no man in the household at all. In a number of instances, elderly women in their seventies and their middle-aged daughters with or without children and often without husbands form one household with the old woman as head.[9]

It is to be expected that such a situation will be reflected in property ownership:

> In this town of a little more than three thousand inhabitants, ... 202 colored people own property. The assessed value for the majority of these holdings ranges from $300 to $600. Of the 202 owners, 100 are men, owning property valued at $61,250, and 93 are women, with holdings valued at $57,460. Nine men and women own jointly property totaling $3280 in value. Among the Whites also, about half the owners are women. When White women are owners, it usually means that a man has put his property in his wife's name so that it cannot be touched if he gets into difficulty. Among the Negroes, many women bought the property themselves, with their own earnings.[1]

Of the high proportion of holdings by men in the more favored socio-economic group of Negroes, it is stated, "if more property were owned by Negroes in the lower strata, there would probably be a higher percentage of female ownership." Yet as it is, the percentage would seem to be sufficiently high in terms of current American economic patterns, especially since, as stated,

Negro women actually bought and hold their property for themselves rather than for their husbands, as is the common case among the whites.

The absence of any reference to African background in the citations concerning Negro families headed by women is merely another instance of the tendency to overlook the fact that the Negro was the carrier of a pre-slavery tradition. It is in the writings dealing with this aspect of Negro life that we find truncated history in its most positive expression, since in this field the existence of an African past has been recognized only in terms of such denials of its vitality as were cited in the opening pages of this work. Yet the aspects of Negro family which diverge most strikingly from patterns of the white majority are seen to deviate in the direction of resemblances to West African family life.

It cannot be regarded only as coincidence that such specialized features of Negro family life in the United States as the role of women in focusing the sentiment that gives the family unit its psychological coherence, or their place in maintaining the economic stability essential to survival, correspond closely to similar facets of West African social structure. And this becomes the more apparent when we investigate the inner aspects of the family structure of Negroes in the New World outside the United States. Though everywhere the father has his place, the tradition of paternal control and the function of the father as sole or principal provider essential to the European pattern is deviated from. In the coastal region of the Guianas, for example, the mother and grandmother are essentially the mainstays of the primary relationship group. A man obtains his soul from his father, but his affections and his place in society are derived from his mother; a person's home is his mother's, and though matings often endure, a man's primary affiliation is to the maternal line. In Trinidad, Jamaica, the Virgin Islands, or elsewhere in the Caribbean, should parents separate, the children characteristically remain with their mother, visiting their father from time to time if they stay on good terms with him.

The woman here is likewise an important factor in the economic scene. The open-air market is the

8. *Shadow of the Plantation*, pp. 48f.
9. Powdermaker, *After Freedom*, p. 146.
1. *Ibid.*, p. 127.

effective agent in the retail distributive process, and business, as in West Africa, is principally in the hands of women. It is customary for them to handle the family resources, and their economic independence as traders makes for their personal independence, something which, within the family, gives them power such as is denied to women who, in accordance with the prevalent European custom, are dependent upon their husbands for support. In both West Africa and the West Indies the women, holding their economic destinies in their own hands, are fully capable of going their own ways if their husbands displease them; not being hampered by any conception of marriage as an ultimate commitment, separation is easily effected, and a consequent fluidity in family personnel such as has been noted in the preceding pages of this section results. Now if to this complex is added the tradition of a sentimental attachment to the mother, derived from the situation within the polygynous households of West Africa, ample justification appears for holding that the derivations given for Negro family life by most students of the Negro family in the United States present serious gaps.

As in the case of most other aspects of Negro life, the problem becomes one of evaluating multiple forces rather than placing reliance on simpler explanations. From the point of view of the search for Africanisms, the status of the Negro family at present is thus to be regarded as the result of the play of various forces in the New World experience of the Negro projected against a background of aboriginal tradition. Slavery did not cause the "maternal" family; but it tended to continue certain elements in the cultural endowment brought to the New World by the Negroes. The feeling between mother and children was reinforced when the father was sold away from the rest of the family; where he was not, he continued life in a way that tended to consolidate the obligations assumed by him in the integrated societies of Africa as these obligations were reshaped to fit the monogamic, paternalistic pattern of the white masters. That the plantation system did not differentiate between the sexes in exploiting slave labor tended, again, to reinforce the tradition of the part played by women in the tribal economics.

Furthermore, these African sanctions have been encouraged by the position of the Negro since freedom. As underprivileged members of society, it has been necessary for Negroes to continue calling on all the labor resources in their families if the group was to survive; and this strengthened woman's economic independence. In a society fashioned like that of the United States, economic independence for women means sexual independence, as is evidenced by the personal lives of white women from the upper socioeconomic levels of society. This convention thus fed back into the tradition of the family organized about and headed by women, continuing and reinforcing it as time went on. And it is for these reasons that those aspects of Negro family life that depart from majority patterns are to be regarded as residues of African custom. Families of this kind are not African, it is true; they are, however, important as comprehending certain African survivals. For they not only illustrate the tenacity of the traditions of Africa under the changed conditions of New World life but also in larger perspective indicate how, in the acculturative situation, elements new to aboriginal custom can reinforce old traditions, while at the same time helping to accommodate a people to a setting far different from that of their original milieu.

It will be recalled that at the outset of this section it was stated that other survivals than those to which attention has been given thus far are betokened by certain facts mentioned more or less in passing in the literature. One of these concerns the size of the relationship group. The African immediate family, consisting of a father, his wives, and their children, is but a part of a larger unit. This immediate family is generally recognized by Africanists as belonging to a local relationship group termed the "extended family," while a series of these extended families, in turn, comprise the the matrilineal or patrilineal sibs, often totemic in sanction, which are the effective agents in administering the controls of the ancestral cult.

That such larger relationship groupings might actually exist in the United States was indicated during the course of a study of the physical anthropology of Mississippi Negroes, where, because of the emphasis placed on the genetic aspects of the problem being studied, entire families were measured wherever possible.[2] In the town of Amory (Monroe County) and its surrounding country, 639 persons representing 171 families were studied, the word "family" in this context signifying those standing in primary biological relationship—parents, children, and grandchildren but not collateral relatives. How large the kinship units of wider scope are found to be in this area, however, is indicated by one group of related immediate families which comprised 141 individuals actually measured. Such matters as how many more persons this particular unit includes and its sociological implications cannot be stated, since no opportunity to probe its cultural significance has presented itself. The mere fact that a feeling of kinship as widespread as this exists among a group whose ancestors were carriers of a tradition wherein the larger relationship units are as important as in Africa does, however, give this case importance as a lead for future investigation.

Instances of similarly extensive relationship groupings are occasionally encountered in the literature. A description of one of these corresponds in almost every detail to the pattern of the extended family in West African patrilineal tribes:

> The other community, composed of black families who boast of pure African ancestry, grew out of a family of five brothers, former slaves, and is known as "Blacktown," after the name of the family. Although the traditions of this community do not go back as far as those of Whitetown, the group has exhibited considerable pride in its heritage and has developed as an exclusive community under the discipline of the oldest male in the family. The founder of the community, the father of our informant, was reared in the house of his master. . . . The boundaries of the present community are practically the same as those of the old plantation, a part of which is rented. . . . But most of the land is owned by this Negro family. The oldest of the five brothers was, until his death fifteen years ago, the acknowledged

head of the settlement. At present the next oldest brother is recognized as the head of the community. His two sons, one of whom was our informant, have never divided their 138 acres. He and his three brothers, with their children numbering between forty and fifty and their numerous grandchildren, are living in the settlement. Twelve of their children have left the county, and three are living in a near-by town. Our informant left the community thirty-four years ago and worked at a hotel in Boston and as a longshoreman in Philadelphia but returned after five years away because he was needed by the old folks and longed for the association of his people. One of the sons of the five brothers who founded the settlement is both the teacher of the school and pastor of the church which serve the needs of the settlement.[3]

This passage is to be compared with the account of the formation and later constitution of the Dahomean "collectivity" and extended family.[4] In such matters as the inheritance of headship from the eldest sibling to his next in line, in the retained identity of the family land as a part of the mechanism making for retention of identity by the relationship group itself, and in the relatively small proportion of members who leave their group, immediate correspondences will be discerned.

Like the neighboring "Whitetown"—both these terms are fictitious, but the communities are presumably located in Virginia—sanctions and controls are to be seen such as mark off the African extended family group, succession from elder brother to younger being especially striking in this regard. This kind of "extended" family is also found among the racially mixed stock who, descended from freed Negroes, comprise the population of Whitetown:

> At present there are in the settlement ten children and thirty grandchildren of our informant. His brother, who also lives in the settlement, has six

2. M. J. Herskovits, V. K. Cameron, and Harriet Smith, "The Physical Form of Mississippi Negroes," *American Journal of Physical Anthropology*, 17:193–201, 1931.

3. Frazier, *The Negro Family in the United States*, pp. 258 f.

4. Herskovits, *Dahomey*, Vol. I, pp. 139 ff.

children and one grandchild. Working under the control and direction of the head of the settlement, the children and grandchildren raise cotton, corn, peanuts, peas, and tobacco. In this isolated community with its own school this family has lived for over a century.... These closely knit families have been kept under the rigorous discipline of the older members and still have scarcely any intercourse with the black people in the county.[5]

Botume writes of the strangeness to her, a white northerner, of this tradition of extended familial affiliation in the Sea Islands during the Civil War:

> It was months before I learned their family relations. The terms "bubber" for brother and "titty" for sister, with "nanna" for mother and "mother" for grandmother and father for all leaders in church and society were so generally used I was forced to believe that they all belonged to one immense family.[6]

It is not unreasonable to suppose that this passage is indicative of survival on the islands of the classificatory terminology so widely employed in West Africa, though this, as well as the entire problem of the wider ramifications of kinship among Negroes in the United States, remains for future research. On the basis of such data as have been cited, however, African tradition must in the meantime be held as prominent among those forces which made for the existence of a sense of kinship among Negroes that is active over a far wider range of relationship than among whites.

What vestiges of totemic belief have persisted in the United States cannot be said. Certainly no relationship groups among Negroes claiming descent from some animal, plant, or natural phenomenon, in the classic manner of this institution, have been noted in the literature. But what may be termed the "feel" given by certain attitudes toward food may perhaps be indicative of a certain degree of retention of this African concept. Firsthand inquiry among Negroes has brought to light a surprising number of cases where a certain kind of meat—veal, pork, and lamb among others—is not eaten by a given person. Inquiry usually elicits the response "It doesn't agree with me," and only in one or two instances did the inhibition seem to extend to relatives. Yet this fact that violation of a personal food taboo derived from the totemic animal in West Africa and in Dutch Guiana is held to bring on illness, especially skin eruptions, strikes one immediately as at least an interesting coincidence and perhaps as a hint toward a survival deriving from this element in African social organization, since it is so completely foreign to European patterns. Puckett records a statement published by Bergen in 1899 that "some Negroes will not eat lamb because the lamb represents Christ";[7] and this may be an instance of that syncretism which is so fundamental a mechanism in the acculturative process undergone by New World Negroes. Systematic inquiry concerning kinds of foods not eaten by given persons, the reasons or rationalizations which explain these avoidances, and particularly whether or not such taboos are held by entire families and if so, how they are transmitted are badly needed. Such data, when available, should provide information which will tell whether or not this one aspect of an important African belief has had the strength to survive, in no matter how distorted a form, even where contact with European custom has been greatest and retention of aboriginal custom made most difficult.

Before considering other survivals of African culture, a point which touches upon certain practical implications of the materials dealt with in this section may be mentioned. At the outset of this discussion, it was noted that stress on values peculiar to Euro-American tradition has tended seriously to derogate the customary usages of Negroes which depart from the modes of life accepted by the majority. It was also pointed out that when the logical conclusions to be drawn from the position taken are accepted by Negroes themselves, this tends to destroy such sanctions as the Negroes may have developed and injects certain

5. Frazier, *op. cit.*, pp. 257 f.
6. *First Days amongst the Contrabands*, p. 48.
7. *Folk Beliefs of the Southern Negro*, p. 559; the reference made is to Fanny D. Bergen, "Animal and Plant Lore," *Mem. Amer. Folk-Lore Society*, Vol. VII, 1899, p. 84.

added psychological difficulties into a situation that is at best difficult enough. Comment along these lines becomes especially pertinent when one encounters a passage such as the following, where the disavowal of a cultural heritage is emphasized by the assumptions mirrored in its phrases:

> These settlements ... of ... higher economic status ... and ... deeply rooted patriarchal family traditions ... represent the highest development of a moral order and a sacred society among the rural Negro population. This development has been possible because economic conditions have permitted ... germs of culture, which have been picked up by Negro families, to take root and grow.[8]

The community referred to does not matter; it is the use of a figure which envisages a people "picking up" "germs of culture," to name but one such to be found in these lines, that gives us pause. To accept as "moral" only those values held moral by the whites, to regard as "culture" only those practices that have the sanctions of a European past is a contributory factor in the process of devaluation, if only because to draw continually such conclusions has so cumulative an effect. A people without a past are a people who lack an anchor in the present. And recognition of this is essential if the psychological foundations of the interracial situation in this country are to be probed for their fullest significance, and proper and effective correctives for its stresses are to be achieved.

E. FRANKLIN FRAZIER

from The Negro Family in America [1949]

The wide-ranging work of the sociologist E. Franklin Frazier (1894–1962) was extremely influential as well as controversial in the fields of sociology and African American studies. After receiving his undergraduate degree from Howard University in 1916, Frazier completed his master's in sociology at Clark University, in Worcester, Massachusetts, in 1920 and taught at Morehouse College, in Atlanta. During his doctoral studies, at the University of Chicago from 1927 to 1931, Frazier became steeped in the thought of the developing Chicago school of sociology, which focused on urban environments and their effects on culture. Frazier's writing on the development of the African American family reveals a concept of culture as an external force that serves to curb the desires and impulses of the individual. According to Frazier, culture is a civilizing force that requires an intact society in order to function, making it vulnerable to destructive forces such as slavery and racism. Without the restraining mores of a healthy culture, the individual tends to make decisions that are destructive to others and to society. (In contrast, the work of Melville J. Herskovits

(p. 379) suggests a fundamentally different idea of culture: a group of beliefs, customs, and behaviors that individuals transmit from generation to generation.) For Frazier, the debate about Africanisms was not merely of academic interest but had direct political implications. He argued that if African American culture is viewed as arising from an African past (as Herskovits claimed it should be) rather than as having been created out of the devastation of slavery, then better-off Americans would have no responsibility for the economic and social problems facing African Americans.

More than fifty years after the Herskovits-Frazier debate began, Frazier and Herskovits continue to be touchstones for contemporary disputes. Arguments that focus on the legacy of slavery tend to underscore Frazier's ideas, as Randall Robinson does when he argues in favor of reparations in *The Debt* (p. 980). Others have expanded on Herskovits's ideas to develop the concept of a rich, distinctive African American culture. For example, Portia K. Maultsby in "Africanisms in African American Music" (p. 840) argues that Africanisms go beyond

8. Frazier, *op. cit.*, p. 259.

direct "survivalisms" (Herskovits's term for specific African cultural traditions retained in diaspora cultures) and Kara Walker in her cut-paper silhouette *Out of Africa* (p. 857) depicts the far-reaching influence of Africa on "white" culture.

From Ruth Nanda Anshen, ed., *The Family: Its Function and Destiny*, rev. ed., Science of Culture Series, vol. 5 (New York: Harper and Brothers, 1949), pp. 65–84.

THE evolution of the Negro family in the United States has a special significance for the science of culture. Within the short space of 150 years, the Negro family has telescoped the age-long evolution of the human family.[1] On the basis of concrete factual materials it is possible to trace the evolution of the Negro family from its roots in human nature to a highly institutionalized form of human association. During the course of its evolution, the Negro family has been forced to adjust itself to different forms of social organization and to the stresses and strains of modern civilization. In studying the adjustments which the Negro family has made to these changes, it is possible to gain a clearer understanding of the relation of human motivations to culture. Moreover, the evolution of Negro family life not only has provided additional evidence of the primary importance of the family in the transmission of culture but also has shown the role of the family in the building of new cultures.

Under the Institution of Slavery

As a result of the manner in which the Negro was enslaved, the Negro's African cultural heritage has had practically no effect on the evolution of his family life in the United States. The slave traders along the coast of Africa, who were primarily interested in healthy young Negroes—generally males—had no regard for family relationships. In fact, the human cargo which they collected were the remnants of various tribes and clan organizations. The manner in which men and women were packed indiscriminately in slave ships during the Middle Passage tended to destroy social bonds and tribal distinctions. Then the process of "breaking" the Negroes into the slave system in the West Indies, where they often landed before shipment

to the colonies and the United States, tended to efface the memories of their traditional culture. In the colonies and later in the southern United States, the slaves were widely scattered on comparatively small plantations, where there was little opportunity to reknit social bonds or regenerate the African culture.

Doubtless, memories of African culture regarding mating survived, but these memories became meaningless in the New World. The mating or sexual associations which Negroes formed on American soil were largely in response to their natural impulses and the conditions of the new environment. There was, first, a lack of females in the slave population until the 1830s, and this caused the slaves in some sections to seek satisfaction of their sexual hunger among Indian women. Then there was the discipline of the plantation or the arbitrary will of the masters which regulated sexual association and the selection of mates among the slaves. Thus it came about that sexual selection and mating were no longer culturally defined or regulated by African mores.

Nevertheless, there was selection of mates on the basis of spontaneous impulses and mutual attraction. There was the wooing of females by males who attempted to win their favor by gifts and expressions of affection. The stability of these matings was dependent largely upon the temperaments of the mates and the strength of the mutual attraction and affection. Where the mates were inclined or were permitted to live together as husband and wife, mutual sympathies and understanding developed as the result of habitual association. Pregnancy and offspring sometimes resulted in the breaking of bonds, but they often provided a new bond of sympathy and common interest. A common interest in the relationship was more likely to develop where there were mutual services and the

---

1. See the writer's *The Negro Family in the United States,* Chicago, University of Chicago Press, 1939. [Frazier's note]

sharing of benefits, as for example in the cultivation of a garden. Under such conditions the Negro family acquired the character of a natural organization in that it was based primarily upon human impulses and individual wishes rather than upon law and the mores.

Under favorable conditions the family as a natural organization developed considerable stability during slavery. The first requirement for stable family life among the slaves was, of course, that the family groups should not be broken up through sale or arbitrary action on the part of the masters. Where the plantation became a settled way of life and a social as well as an economic institution, the integrity of the slave family was generally respected by the masters. Moreover, the social relations which grew up facilitated the process by which the Negro took over the culture of the whites. The close association between whites and Negroes, often from childhood, enabled the slaves to take over the language, manners, and ideas of the masters. These close contacts were enjoyed by the slaves who worked in and about the master's house. On many plantations the masters provided religious and moral instruction for the slaves. The moral supervision included, in some cases at least, the chaperonage of the female slaves. It was through those channels that the white man's ideas and sentiments in regard to sex and family relations were communicated to the slaves. These cultural advantages, which were restricted mainly to the house servant, became the basis of social distinctions among the slaves. The house servants enjoyed a certain prestige in the slave society which grew up about the Negro quarters.

In the division of labor on the plantation there was some opportunity for the expression of talents and intelligence. This was especially true in regard to the black mechanics who were so necessary to the maintenance of self-sufficiency on the plantation. Often it was the son of a favored house servant who was apprenticed to a craftsman to learn a trade. In becoming a skilled craftsman or mechanic, the intellectual powers as well as the manual dexterity of the slave were improved. In addition, because of his skill he was accorded recognition by the master and acquired a higher status among the slaves. The recognition which was accorded the personality of the skilled craftsman was reflected in his pride in his workmanship. What was more important was that it was a moralizing influence, which was reflected in the family life of the skilled artisans. The skilled mechanic often assumed the conventional role of husband and father and was recognized as the head of his family. The fruits of his skill, so far as a premium was placed upon good performance, were often shared with his family. Consequently, these family groups, which were without the support of law, often achieved the solidarity and stability of a legally sanctioned family.

The development of family life described above represents the development of the slave family under the most favorable conditions. Among the vast majority of slaves, the Negro mother remained the most stable and dependable element during the entire period of slavery. Despite a benevolent master, the slave family was often dispersed when the plantation was sold or an estate was settled. With indifferent or cruel masters the slave family was constantly being broken up and its members scattered. But in either case some regard had to be shown for the bond between the Negro mother and her children. The masters' economic interest in the survival of the children caused them to recognize the dependence of the young children upon the mother. Then, too, the master, whether out of humanity or self-interest, was compelled to respect the mother's often fierce attachment to her children. Wherever the charge that slave mothers were indifferent to their offspring has any factual support, it can be explained by the forced pregnancies and harsh experiences attending motherhood. Most of the evidence indicates that the slave mother was devoted to her children and made tremendous sacrifices for their welfare. She was generally the recognized head of the family group. She was the mistress of the cabin, to which the "husband" or father often made only weekly visits. Under such circumstances a maternal family group took form and the tradition of the Negro woman's responsibility for her family took root.

The development of the maternal family among the slaves was further encouraged by the sexual association between blacks and whites. In the cities, where slaves moved about freely and there were many free Negroes, the sexual relations between Negro women and white men were casual and often of a debased character. But it was not only in the cities that the races mixed. Although there is no way of measuring the extent of the sexual association between slaveholders and slaves, there is abundant evidence of concubinage and polygamy on the part of the masters. The character of the sexual associations between the two races ran the gamut of human relationships. At one extreme the slave woman or Negro woman was used to satisfy a fleeting impulse. At the other extreme the sexual association was supported by personal attachment and deep sentiment. In the latter case, the white father in rare instances might assume the role of a father which lacked only a legal sanction. Nevertheless, because of the ideas and sentiments embodied in the institution of slavery, the Negro or mulatto mother remained the responsible and stable head of the family group. On the other hand, it was from such associations that the free Negro population continued to increase until the Civil War.

THE FAMILY AMONG THE FREE NEGROES

The free Negro population increased steadily from the time when Negroes were first introduced into the Virginia colony in 1619. For three or four decades the servitude of the Negroes was limited to seven years, as in the case of white servants. Even after the status of the Negro servants became one of perpetual servitude, or slavery, the free Negro population continued to increase. The increase in the free Negro population came from five sources: (1) children born of free colored parents; (2) mulatto children born of free colored mothers; (3) mulatto children born of white servants and of free white women; (4) children of free Negro and Indian parentage; and (5) manumitted slaves.[2] Although it is not possible to know the increase in the free Negro population through each of these sources, it appears that the manumission of slaves was relatively the most important source. Slaves achieved freedom through manumission both because of the action of their owners and because of their own efforts. A large number of the white fathers emancipated their mulatto offspring; as a result about three-eighths of the free Negroes were mulattoes, as compared with only one-twelfth of the slave population. In numerous cases the white fathers provided for the economic welfare and education of their colored offspring. Slaves were able to become free through their own efforts especially in Maryland, Virginia, and North Carolina, where the economic basis of slavery was being undermined. In these areas skilled artisans were permitted to hire out their time and save enough money to buy their freedom. Whether they were freed because of their relation to their white masters or because of their own efforts, the free Negroes possessed certain cultural advantages which were reflected in their family life.

It was among the free Negroes that the family first acquired an institutional character. This was possible primarily because the free Negroes were able to establish family life on a secure economic foundation. In the southern cities the free Negroes had a secure position in the economic organization. Partly on the basis of wealth and occupation, a class system emerged among the free Negroes. Among the wealthier free colored families in Louisiana and in Charleston, some of whom were themselves slaveholders, the family was similar to that of the white slaveholders. It was patriarchal in organization, and the status of women was similar to that of the women among the white slaveholding class. Moreover, these families were founded upon traditions which had been built up over several generations. Those traditions were a measure, in a sense, of the extent to which the Negro had assimilated the American cultural heritage.

It has already been pointed out how the house servants and the slave artisans had been able, because of their favored position, to take over American culture. Here it should be pointed out how the free Negroes, who had come largely from these groups, incorporated the American culture and transmitted it through their families to succeeding generations. Because of their relationship to the white race the mulattoes generally had a conception of themselves different from that of the pure-blooded Negro. Where they were favored by their white fathers, the close association with their fathers or their position in the household enabled them to take over the attitudes and sentiments as well

2. John H. Russell, *The Free Negro in Virginia*, Baltimore, Johns Hopkins University Press, 1913, pp. 40–41. [Frazier's note]

as the overt behavior of the father. As freedmen with some economic competence or with a mechanical skill which afforded a good income, they were able to maintain a way of life that accorded with their conception of themselves and with the patterns of behavior taken over from the whites. This led to the beginning of an institutional life within the free colored communities similar to that in the white communities. The free Negroes established schools, churches, literary societies, and organizations for mutual aid. The families with traditions formed the core of the organized social life in the free Negro communities. Not only did these families give support to the institutional life, but they were supported in turn by the institutions of the community. Although it is true that because of social isolation the culture of the free Negroes became provincial and ingrown, it nevertheless provided a heritage for their children.

CIVIL WAR AND EMANCIPATION

The Civil War and emancipation created a crisis in the family life of the Negro. This crisis affected the free Negro family as well as the slave family. It tended to destroy whatever stability the slave family had achieved under the slave regime. It tore the free Negro family from its moorings in a society where it occupied a privileged position. The distinction between slave and free was wiped out. How did the Negro family meet this crisis? How was its organization and stability influenced by its new relation to American culture? How, specifically, was its role or function in mediating American culture to the Negro affected by the Negro's new relation to American life? These are some of the questions which we shall attempt to answer in the present chapter.

As the Union armies penetrated the South, the plantation regime was disrupted and the slaves were uprooted from their customary way of life. Thousands of Negroes flocked to army camps and to the cities; thousands joined the march of Sherman to the sea.[3]

The disorder and confusion were a test of the strength and character of family ties. In many cases the family ties, which were supported only by habit and custom were broken. Negro men deserted their families, and even some Negro mothers deserted their children. On the other hand, many fathers took their families with them when they went in search of freedom. Many Negroes went in search of relatives from whom they had been separated through sale while they were slaves. Throughout this chaotic situation, the Negro mother held the family group together and supported her children. This devotion was based partly upon her traditional role and partly upon the deep emotional attachment to her young that was evoked in the face of danger.

The northern missionaries who went south to establish schools and hospitals and to assist the Negro during his first steps in freedom were faced with the problems of the Negro family. They encouraged the Negro to get a legal sanction for his marital relations and to settle down to orderly monogamous marriage. They had to contend with the confusion which slavery had caused by the selling away of "husbands" who returned to claim "wives" who had "married" other men. Then there was the problem of giving the Negro husband and father a status in family relations which he had not enjoyed during slavery. The missionaries depended chiefly upon exhortation and moralizing to establish conventional marital and familial relations among the freedmen. These methods had some effect, but they did not determine the future development of the Negro family. The course of that development was determined by the dominant economic and social forces in the South as well as by the social heritage of the freedmen.

When conditions became settled in the South, the landless and illiterate freedman had to secure a living on a modified form of the plantation system. Concessions had to be made to the freedman in view of his new status. One of the concessions affected the family organization. The slave quarters were broken up, and the Negroes were no longer forced to work in gangs.

---

3. The Savannah Plan, called the March to the Sea as it began in the captured city of Atlanta and moved southeast for 300 miles until the port of Savannah was captured, was led by Union Army Major General William Tecumseh Sherman in November and December 1864.

Each family group moved off by itself to a place where it could lead a separate existence. In the contracts which the Negroes made with their landlords, the Negro father and husband found a substantial support for his new status in family relations. Sometimes the wife, as well as the husband, made her cross for her signature to the contract, but more often it was the husband who assumed responsibility for the new economic relation with the white landlord. Masculine authority in the family was even more firmly established when the Negro undertook to buy a farm. Moreover, his new economic relationship to the land created a material interest in his family. As the head of the family he directed the labor of his wife and children and became concerned with the discipline of his children, who were to succeed him as owners of the land.

As the result of emancipation the Negro was thrown into competition with the poor whites. At the same time he became estranged from the former slaveholding class, and the sympathetic relations which had been built up during slavery were destroyed. Since the nature of the contacts between whites and blacks was changed, the character of the process of acculturation was changed. The estrangement between the whites and blacks was inevitable when the color caste was established in the South. If the democratic aims set up during the Reconstruction Period had been achieved, this estrangement would not have occurred. But where race was made the basis of status, the Negroes in defense withdrew from the whites and suspected even their attempts to help the freedmen. Consequently, there came into existence two separate social worlds and, as far as spatial separation permitted, two separate communities. Since the Negro's personal life was oriented toward the separate Negro world, he derived his values from that world. The patterns of behavior and ideals which he took over from the white man were acquired generally through formal imitation of people outside his social world. In their social isolation the majority of Negroes were forced to draw upon the meager social heritage which they had acquired during slavery.

In the world of the Negro folk in the rural areas of the South, there grew up a family system that met the needs of the environment. Many of the ideas concerning sex relations and mating were carried over from slavery. Consequently, the family lacked an institutional character, since legal marriage and family traditions did not exist among a large section of the population. The family groups originated in the mating of young people, who regarded sex relations outside of marriage as normal behavior. When pregnancy resulted, the child was taken into the mother's family group. Generally the family group to which the mother belonged had originated in a similar fashion. During the disorder following slavery, a woman, after becoming pregnant, would assume the responsibility of motherhood. From time to time other children were added to the family group through more or less permanent "marriage" with one or more men. Sometimes the man might bring his child or children to the family group, or some orphaned child or the child of a relative might be included. Thus the family among a large section of the Negro population became a sort of amorphous group held together by the feelings and common interests that might develop in the same household during the struggle for existence.

From the standpoint of marriage statistics the rural Negro population has shown a large percentage of illegitimacy. But these statistics have little meaning if they are not related to the folkways regarding sex and marriage relations which have grown up in those isolated rural areas. The type of sex and marital relations which have been described does not indicate that sex relations have been promiscuous and free from controls. There has been, in the first place, the general recognition of the obligation of the mother to her children. In fact, pregnancy has been regarded as a phase of the maturing or fulfillment of the function of a woman. On the other hand, marriage meant subordination to a man or the formation of a new type of relationship. Often, therefore, when a girl became pregnant and the man wanted to marry her, the girl's mother objected. Later the girl might marry the father of her child or some other man. But this meant forming a partnership in working a farm together and assuming other obligations. In a society of this type the mother continued to occupy a dominant position in the family. The grandmother enjoyed an even more important position and has always been a leading figure in the Negro family.

Statistics have always shown a large number of Negro families with women as heads. These statistics have reflected the conditions described above. It appears that about 10 percent of the Negro families in the rural areas, as compared with about 30 percent in urban areas, have had women as heads. This difference is doubtless due to the fact that in the rural areas of the South the Negro man and the woman with her children need each other more in the struggle for existence than do those in the city. In fact, the stability of these family groups in the rural areas has depended largely upon the coöperation of man and woman in the struggle for a livelihood. As the result of this coöperation, deep sentiments and attachments have developed not only between spouses but also between the fathers and their children. This has caused these family groups to have on the whole the stability of conventional family groups.

* * *

The survival of the Negro in American civilization is a measure, in a sense, of his success in adopting the culture of the whites or an indication of the fact that the Negro has found within the white man's culture a satisfying life and a faith in his future. His future survival in a highly mobile and urbanized society will be on a different basis. In the large metropolitan communities of the North, Negroes are increasingly intermarrying with whites. Thus the Negro family is incorporating new traditions, and the children of mixed marriages have a new view on American life. As the result of these developments the Negro will have to face greater stresses in his personal life, and the segregated groups and institutions will no longer provide an adequate refuge in the white man's world. During all these changes and crises the family will continue to play an important role in transmitting the new conception which the Negro will acquire of himself and of his place in American society.

KEY DEBATE ≈ *Migration and Emigration*

ROBERT LEE VANN

from Back to the Farm? [1932]

Although black migrants in the United States have typically moved from southern rural areas to southern cities and then to northern cities, American history has been punctuated by periodic reverse migrations. As with other migrations, these tend to occur during periods of political or economic change. It is not surprising, therefore, that the hardships of the Great Depression prompted debates in the black press about the so-called Black Belt Republic plan, which encouraged struggling African Americans to leave the urban North for the rural South. (The Black Belt, a region running through the Southeastern United States with an African American majority population, offered the possibility of political autonomy for African Americans.) More recent reverse migrations have been spurred largely by positive forces: from 1970 to 1975, following the civil rights movement's success in breaking down institutionalized southern segregation, over 300,000 African Americans migrated to the South, and over 400,000 more migrated between 1975 and 1980.

"Back to the Farm?," written during one of the worst years of the Depression, offered return to the South as a potential solution to the economic hardships faced by migrant African Americans living in the North. Robert Lee Vann (1879–1940), a lawyer who served in President Franklin Roosevelt's administration and was the publisher and editor of the *Pittsburgh Courier* for three decades, looks to cooperative agricultural ventures in Europe as a possible model for African Americans.

From *Pittsburgh Courier*, September 24, 1932.

During these dark days of depression there is much talk among thoughtful persons in Aframerica over the feasibility of the Negro returning to the farm, from whence he trekked hopefully to the Southern and Northern urban centers during and after the World War.

There should be more discussion of this proposition, especially in those cities where there is a considerable unemployed Negro population subsisting precariously on the dole. Certainly the chances of a Negro obtaining food, clothing, shelter and wholesome recreation are not growing any better in our cities with the passage of time. Even more than the impoverished white worker he is becoming an authentic proletarian,[1] without economic security or hope for anything better.

If by these conferences we can formulate some plan by which scores of thousands of these black paupers and dependents may become self-supporting and useful citizens on their own farms, we shall have gone a long way on the road to solving our economic problems as a group. Any plan, however, must reckon with the fact that thousands of farms are being abandoned in all parts of the country because of high taxes and low prices for crops. How can the Negro returning to the farm defeat these inexorable economic forces that are driving millions away from rural areas and into the gilded vortex of the city?

We might with great profit study the history and development of agriculture in Denmark, Holland, Scandinavia and Ireland, where through producer's co-operative associations under intelligent, informed

1. A person without property who must rely on income from labor for support; a member of the working class.

leadership, so much has been done to elevate the farmer to a position of security and independence realized by very few followers of agriculture and stock raising in the United States.

But in urging Negroes—or whites for that matter—to return to the soil, we must take care that only farmers are included. . . . Useless people on a farm are as bad as useless people in the city.

WILLIAM NESBIT JONES

from Self-Determination: The Black Belt Republic Plan [1932]

William Nesbit Jones (1882–1940), columnist and managing editor of the *Baltimore Afro-American*, framed reverse migration to the South in terms of black nationalism. By migrating to just one area, African Americans could concentrate their political strength and perhaps even dominate the politics of an entire state. Before it could be put into action, however, the Black Belt Republic plan was struck a blow by the Agricultural Adjustment Act (AAA) of 1933, which was part of President Franklin

Roosevelt's New Deal program aimed at helping the country recover from the Great Depression. The AAA, by paying landowners to grow fewer crops as a way of raising prices, had the unintended consequence of curtailing the need for sharecroppers. In addition, technological advances in farming further reduced the need for unskilled agricultural labor. With even fewer opportunities for work in the rural South, another wave of black migrants set off for the urban North.

From *Baltimore Afro-American*, September 24, 1932.

"Young white men and women here [White Plains, New York] working in shops and factories in New York City, discuss self determination for the Negro in what is known as the black belt of the South. By self determination these young Communists explain that wherever there is a majority of colored voters in any community city or state, that they should not only elect their own officers, but decide upon what kind government they should have.

"In their argument they point out that one of the things colored people in this country need is the administrative practice which will obliterate the inferiority complex and make them know they can construct governments as well as follow the white man's idea of government."

While this specific preachment won't be calculated to attract many voters for the Communist ticket, it is something young men and women might think about.

In this country we have been, in the main, just followers. Perhaps we have not had time to be anything else. We started out following the Republican Party

and to some extent we still trail the will-o-the-wisp. . . .

Perhaps a wise and studied concentration of political strength would be a good thing. Perhaps the making of a unified political program, comprising the entire voting group in this country, would be a good thing. Set off to ourselves as a voting group, we could make alignments as dozens of minority groups do in European governments.

It might also be argued that such a concentrated voting population, dominating completely some state, could insure representation in both branches of the law-making bodies in Washington, become a powerful lever in close elections, and, most of all, become a practical training ground for future American citizenship.

For the working masses, however, there would be no reason to conclude that in a colored state they would fare any better than the white working class fares in white controlled states. But there would be no reason not to feel that a group of young colored radicals would not rise up to smash Negro capitalism just as white workers are trying throughout the world to smash white capitalism. Even this might be good training.

The idea of separatism, however, is not a popular one among colored people. Much that they suffer in this country has come through segregation. Marcus Garvey got kicked out of the country, not so much because he did the American act of misappropriating or squandering huge amounts of money, but because he threatened to build up a powerful Negro government somewhere in the world.

European powers have kept a choking grip on Liberia and Haiti, not merely because of the bad governments in those countries but because they feared there would really be at some time efficient and strong governments in these republics. There might come a crisis in international affairs when a few airplanes sent out from either Liberia or Haiti, might decide the outcome of a war. More than this, the white capitalistic world does not want the millions of dark-skinned people in Africa to wake up. One or two successful republics might give these exploited millions a hunch.

HORACE R. CAYTON JR., FREDERICK DOUGLASS PATTERSON, AND GEORGE S. SCHUYLER

from Round Table: Should Negroes in the South Migrate North? [1944]

For its June 1944 issue, *Negro Digest* asked black and white Americans in a nationwide poll: "Should Negroes in the South migrate North?" According to the poll director, Wallace Lee, replies were "heated and vehement" on both sides. The results showed that attitudes toward migration were influenced by region as much as by race. Black northerners overwhelmingly supported migration to the North, with 86 percent in favor of it, often citing their own positive experiences. A smaller majority of white northerners, 60 percent, also supported migration. At the time, western states were experiencing a surge of black migration, which was creating tension among black and white Americans already established in the West. The poll reflected those tensions: only a slim majority, 51 percent, of western African Americans favored migration, while white Americans in the West decidedly rejected it, with 60 percent in opposition and 21 percent undecided. Only in the South did a majority of black Americans disapprove of migration—perhaps unsurprisingly, since those African Americans still in the South had chosen not to migrate—with 39 percent in favor, 51 percent opposed, and the rest undecided. White Americans in the South overwhelmingly rejected migration, with 75 percent opposed, only 13 percent in favor, and 12 percent undecided.

The same issue of *Negro Digest* included several short opinion pieces on the question of northern migration. Those diverse opinions, reprinted here, reflect the

same regional divisions as the poll results. Of the three respondents, the lone southerner, Frederick Douglass Patterson (1901–1988), president of the Tuskegee Institute in Alabama, is the only one to oppose migration. Patterson, who became head of Tuskegee in 1935 and founded the United Negro College Fund in 1943, argues that African Americans should stay in the South to await the benefits of its future development. He echoes the ideas of Booker T. Washington (p. 206), the founder of the Tuskegee Institute, who famously proclaimed in his 1895 address at the Cotton States and International Exposition in Atlanta, "Cast down your bucket where you are."

Like the western respondents to the poll, Horace R. Cayton, Jr. (1903–1976), a Seattle native who moved to Chicago in 1929 to study sociology and later became a leading sociologist, supports migration with some hesitation. Recognizing that migration was causing racial tension to escalate in the West, he nevertheless predicts that higher concentrations of African Americans in cities will lead to economic, political, and cultural advances.

New York City resident George S. Schuyler (p. 287) agrees that "the southern Negro should move North," but unlike Cayton, he argues for "spreading out evenly" around the United States. Schuyler regularly published his opinions in his "Views and Reviews" column in the *Pittsburgh Courier*, a black weekly with a national readership of almost 200,000.

From *Negro Digest*, June 1944, pp. 39–45.

YES: BY HORACE R. CAYTON

There is no need of talking about whether the Negro should migrate North. He has been doing it for the past two hundred years, and will continue. Perhaps the question might be phrased, "Is Negro migration to the North a good thing?" I think it is.

A Negro leaving Mississippi becomes enfranchised as soon as he crosses the Mason-Dixon line.[1] He has a right to send his children to a school which approximates, if it does not equal, the type of school white children attend. He has the theoretical right to use the public services of the community and seldom encounters gross inequalities from social service agencies.

He has, on paper at least, equal civil rights and protection from the law. Certainly he can shake off many of the fears and insecurities which attend everyday life in the South. If he happens to talk back to a white man, he will not be lynched. He does not have to live in constant fear that white men will insult or molest his daughter while he is helpless to protect her.

Until recently 90 per cent of the Negro population lived in the South. The Negro problem was considered as sectional. But since the time of the old Underground Railroad, there has been a constant stream of migration. During and after the first World War, the great migration took place, when probably a million and a half Negroes moved from southern cities, towns, and rural areas to the great industrial centers of the middle West and East.

Although the migration slowed down after 1924, there was a constant trickle which gradually increased in size as the depression set in. Negroes could obtain more on relief in Chicago, Philadelphia, or New York than they could as sharecroppers in Georgia. With the advent of the second World War, the migration of Negroes to all sections of the North has further increased as well as to the cities of the Far West.

The migration to the West, although it does not involve such large numbers of people as that to the eastern and middle-western cities, is probably the most dramatic.

This section of the country is experiencing the same problems in adjusting southern Negroes to an industrial environment that middle-western and eastern cities experienced during World War I. Seattle has increased its Negro population from 3,500 to nearly 15,000; San Francisco's has grown from around 4,000 to nearly 20,000.

Los Angeles, with a Negro population of 60,000 in 1940, had approximately 125,000 by the end of 1943. The West Coast, then, provides a microcosm in which to examine the relative merits and demerits of Negro migration of the present era.

The rapid expansion of the Negro community of these western cities has created tension and friction. The old Negro settlers in these cities—relatively privileged in comparison with other sections of the country—have suffered certain losses of civil and social rights because of the influx of the uncouth, crude, and uneducated southern plantation Negroes, who have had none of their advantages.

The old pattern of a tolerant race relations situation is being strained to the breaking point, and a new pattern, incorporating many more aspects of segregation and discrimination, is evolving. All this is of great concern to the old Negro residents of Seattle, of San Francisco, and of Los Angeles.

If we can use Chicago and New York as examples, however, we can predict that this is just a transitory stage and there are many advantages which these old residents will gain from the migration if their prejudices and fears do not keep them from exploiting the situation. In a few years, the same people who have bemoaned the coming of the crude southern Negroes will be the businessmen who serve the migrants.

As professional people—doctors, lawyers, ministers, social workers—they will have an economic base on which to exist as a functional upper class. As professional politicians they will begin to have a voice in the municipality by virtue of an organized Negro vote. Cultural activities denied them to a large extent will be possible within a larger and expanded Negro community.

All this will more than compensate for the rather spurious civil and social rights that they enjoyed as an isolated and small minority in cities which did not show a great deal of acute prejudice toward them but

---

1. Symbolic boundary between the North and the South.

extended them few economic, political, or cultural opportunities. Northern Negroes should not only welcome the migration but encourage it in every way possible. This would be the best possible contribution they could make to the advancement of the entire Negro population.

The protection of Negroes in the South, as well as their advancement in the North, is dependent on the concerted political action of Negroes who migrated to the North during the first World War.

Much more important than their political strength, however, is the fact that by this migration the Negro problem is becoming a national problem. Many northern whites—including northern liberals—could weep crocodile tears about lynchings and other forms of maltreatment of Negroes in the South without feeling that the question in any way involved them.

At the present time, there is hardly a city in the country which does not have its share of Negroes and does not feel the pressure of this problem in some form. Their presence has done more than almost anything else to force upon the consciousness of the nation as a whole the moral necessity for dealing with the Negro problem.

If the northern migrations have made the Negro a national problem, then the war has made the American Negro an international problem. The interaction of these two facts has called the plight of the Negro to the attention not only of the nation but of the world—a gain which is immeasurable.

There is no need denying that there will be friction, perhaps violence. Riots are the characteristic manner in which Americans react to social problems they do not care to approach rationally. But this is of relatively slight importance when we consider that the Negro has gained tools with which to fight locally and nationally, has a higher standard of living, and has focussed the attention of the nation and of the world on his problem and the necessity for its immediate solution.

No: By F. D. Patterson

It is pretty obvious that there is much to be said on both sides of this question. My taking the negative side in this instance is not intended to imply that I feel normal migration of Negroes from the South to other sections of the country in response to specific opportunity, or because of manpower demands created by war necessity, is bad.

Nor do I feel that some migration in the spirit of the pioneer is unwise. There are undeniably certain advantages, not economic, available to Negroes who live outside of the South which are not available in the same degree at least to those living in the South.

I am definitely of the opinion that a wholesale exodus of southern Negroes is not a wise procedure for several reasons. Among these are the following: If Negroes enter areas in large numbers without invitation, an attitude of hostility is at once created which will require years to overcome.

An unwanted immigration is one which a city is frequently not physically prepared to receive and frequently does little to make the unwelcome migrant comfortable. This attitude is reported to have taken the form of an agreement to refuse employment as a means of discouraging certain groups.

Those who join a mass migration are usually destitute. They, therefore, seek inevitably the slum areas, and here they make overcrowded and foul conditions worse. Such migrants are those among whom birth rates are highest, which means they carry with them many children to be exposed at the most impressionable age to disease and crime. Such children are denied any reasonable chance to develop normally.

Perhaps a more important reason why there should be no migration that would deplete the Negro population of the South relates to an increasing opportunity which is available in this section. Evidence of this is to be found in the increased expenditures of public funds for the education of Negro youth, the development of hospital facilities, and opportunities for wholesome recreation.

The South is the nation's largest remaining frontier with the greatest resources in its human and material wealth. It must develop all of its human wealth to the point of a positive contribution as it attempts to stop the prodigal waste of its natural resources and acquire the technological skill needed to create the abundant artificial wealth which it and the rest of the Nation needs.

To realize this potential development from the South, billions in money from other sections must be invested. This will come, as is already the case, from both private and federal sources. Any effort to offset a post war slump will include a large public works program involving reforestation, flood control, water power development, and the erection of all conceivable structures in the interest of public welfare.

The South, both from the standpoint of its large numbers in the low income group as compared with other sections and its need for the kinds of projects mentioned, will inevitably receive a disproportionately large share of public spending. Add to this the planned decentralization of industry under private management, and the nation's number one problem becomes its number one hope.

This new day in the South is not awaiting the post war. The program is underway in wartime activity. The large cantonments[2] and the development of munitions and other war industry is developing, according to Donald Nelson,[3] the "know how" which will have its definite carryover in the post war.

The Negro is sharing in this southern prosperity. He is being upgraded in industry as a skilled craftsman and is being employed at a number of places in highly technical fields. His right to these opportunities is increasingly conceded.

The recent Supreme Court decision granting the right of the ballot as one of the inalienable rights of every citizen brings in another important and fundamental privilege of citizenship which gives great encouragement to Negroes in the South.[4]

Obviously there is a gap between the privilege of the ballot and the exercise of that privilege. Opposition must be overcome and time shall be required for the growth needed to enable its effective use or its use at all. Nevertheless, it is a democratic privilege even when it is not exercised.

No section is more indebted to the Negro than is the South for what his labor and loyalty have contributed in the past. Why then should Negroes abandon the section of the nation where they have an established claim to share in the tremendous investment the nation is destined in the future to make in the South and its people?

YES: BY GEORGE S. SCHUYLER

Colored Americans have been answering affirmatively for many generations the question, "Should Negroes in the South Migrate North?" Even before Emancipation they made their way openly or surreptitiously from the South to the North, often in the face of great danger and the ever-present uncertainty of making a living, but they nevertheless made the trip, thus revealing their native intelligence.

People, regardless of color, always go from a worse to a better place. Europeans have migrated from their continent to the Americas and Australia, but Americans and Australians do not migrate to Europe, except as tourists or as plutocrats hunting for play.

American whites have migrated from the East to the West and from the South to the North, but seldom in the opposite directions. Southern Negroes go North, but rarely do northern Negroes go South, except as teachers.

Southern Negro ruralites flock to the southern cities, but only very rarely do southern urbanites migrate to the farm districts. Their next move is usually to Washington, Philadelphia, St. Louis, Los Angeles, Chicago, Detroit, or New York. Why? Because they want to improve themselves socially, educationally, and economically.

Take voting, for instance. Negroes pay taxes, directly or indirectly, like everyone else. If they have no say in the spending of those taxes or the selection of the officials who will spend them, they suffer a severe handicap, having no means whatever of wielding influence or expressing their opinion about the government.

With few exceptions the southern Negroes have no vote and consequently no voice in government and must depend upon the efforts of their brethren in the

2. Temporary quarters for troops.
3. Chair of the War Production Board.
4. *Smith v. Allwright* (1944).

North, East, and West. But once they have moved out of the South, they can vote freely, with all of the advantages that privilege affords.

In the North his vote is solicited; in the South it is rejected, often violently. In the North officeholders are influenced by what he says, thinks and does, but not so in the South. Obviously for political purposes the southern Negro should move North.

Regardless of what the economic situation once may have been in the South for the Negro, the gradual vanishing of "Negro jobs" down there has made the North a better place. There the Negro has a wider variety of jobs and is paid the same wage rate as the white American. Throughout the North, East, and West there are thousands of Negroes in municipal, county, and state jobs. In the South there are few so fortunate.

Where in the South will you find colored motormen and conductors, police officials, firemen, clerks, and such tax-paid workers? Wherever they are, they are extremely few in number. Outside the South Negroes have become a power in organized labor, battering down barriers to employment and opening doors to promotion. There are Negro unionists in the South— tens of thousands of them—but they lack the power of their Northern brethren. So from an economic viewpoint the Negro is better off in the North.

Statistics will show that proportionately the Northern Negroes have more business per capita, a wider variety of businesses, and do more business per retail unit. Their real estate is more valuable. They have superior recreational facilities, better schools and libraries, more parks and playgrounds, less illiteracy, better diet, and better clinics and hospitals.

Bad as some of the slum areas may be in some Northern Negro districts, the housing and sanitation are far superior to that available to Negroes of similar socio-economic status in the South. Culturally there is simply no comparison between the South and the North. Living in a constant state of uncertainty or terror, hemmed in on all sides by color restrictions, exposed to the vicious propaganda of Negro inferiority from infancy, continued residence in the South conditions the native to acceptance of a slavish status from which there is no escape except flight.

In brief, the South is a vast insane asylum, and only the money-grubbing opportunist or the subhuman intellect would prefer it to the far freer North.

It is true that there is widespread discrimination and segregation in the North, East, and West. But it is equally true that Negroes there have economic, political, and educational means of fighting it. In the North we have civil rights laws; in the South, Jim Crow laws. That is the measure of the difference between the two regions.

Negroes should leave the South and go North not only because of the concrete advantages of living in a civilized region but because such migration actually helps Southern Negroes. It was the vast migration of Negroes from the South during and after the First World War that shocked the South into building more and better schools. Such migration lessens the proportion of Negroes in the Southern population and consequently reduces white fears of Negro domination.

The mistake Negroes have made in moving North has been their concentration in just a few places instead of spreading out evenly. It is unfortunate that Northern Negroes have been so busy organizing fraternities and churches that they have never got around to setting up a strong agricultural society for the purpose of putting Negroes on the land, where they could be more the masters of their fate if efficiently directed.

Spread the Negro people more evenly over the nation, and the lot of all Negroes everywhere will be greatly improved in every way, even in the lower South.

KEY DEBATE ⁓ *Separatism versus Integration*

W. E. B. Du Bois
On Segregation [1934]

The Great Depression brought an end to the optimism that fueled the Harlem Renaissance. By 1935, economic and social conditions had deteriorated to such an extent that a riot swept through Harlem, spurred by resentment over disproportionately high unemployment among African Americans, employment discrimination by white business owners, and police brutality. Even before the riot signaled a shift from the Renaissance period, however, leaders such as W. E. B. Du Bois were exploring alternatives to the Renaissance focus on the arts as a route to racial equality.

In a series of *Crisis* editorials on segregation, beginning with this one from January 1934, Du Bois revealed a fundamental change in his stance on integration. Distinguishing between segregation imposed from without and voluntary self-segregation, Du Bois argued for voluntary separation. His position instigated a heated debate with the NAACP's board of directors, which eventually led to his resignation from the board and from his position as editor of *The Crisis*. At odds with the official NAACP position rejecting segregation in any form, Du Bois viewed self-segregation as a means to an end—a marked contrast to Garveyism (and the subsequent "black pride" nationalism of the 1960s), which viewed the creation of a "black nation" as a positive end in itself.

The controversy proved all the more divisive because Du Bois had founded *The Crisis* and served as its editor for over twenty years, blurring the line between the journal as the official organ of the NAACP and as a personal platform for his own opinions. In *The Autobiography of W. E. B. Du Bois: A Soliloquy on Viewing My Life from the Last Decade of Its First Century* (published posthumously in 1968), Du Bois extolled the advantages of the arrangement while recognizing its inherent tension and fragility:

> It was perhaps rather unusual that for two decades the two lines of thinking ran so largely together. If on the other hand *The Crisis* had not been in a sense a personal organ and the expression of myself, it could not possibly have attained its popularity and effectiveness. It would have been the dry kind of organ that so many societies support for purposes of reference and not for reading. It took on the part of the organization, a great deal of patience and faith to allow me the latitude that they did for so many years; and on the other hand I was enabled to lay down for the NAACP a clear, strong and distinct body of doctrine that could not have been stated by majority vote. It was probably inevitable that in the end a distinct and clear-cut difference of opinion on majority policies should lead to the dissolution of this interesting partnership.

From *The Crisis*, January 1934.

The thinking colored people of the United States must stop being stampeded by the word segregation. The opposition to racial segregation is not or should not be any distaste or unwillingness of colored people to work with each other, to cooperate with each other, to live with each other. The opposition to segregation is an opposition to discrimination. The experience in the United States has been that usually when there is racial segregation, there is also racial discrimination.

But the two things do not necessarily go together, and there should never be an opposition to segregation pure and simple unless that segregation does involve discrimination. Not only is there no objection to colored people living beside colored people if the surroundings and treatment involve no discrimination, if streets are well lighted, if there is water, sewerage and police protection, and if anybody of any color who wishes, can live in that neighborhood. The same way in schools, there is no objection to schools attended by colored pupils and taught by colored teachers. On the contrary, colored pupils can by our own contention be as fine human beings as any other sort of children, and we certainly know that there are no teachers better than trained colored teachers. But if the existence of such a school is made reason and cause for giving it worse housing, poorer facilities, poorer equipment and poorer teachers, then we do object, and the objection is not against the color of the pupils' or teachers' skins but against the discrimination.

In the recent endeavor of the United States government to redistribute capital so that some of the disadvantaged groups may get a chance for development, the American Negro should voluntarily and insistently demand his share. Groups of communities and farms inhabited by colored folk should be voluntarily formed. In no case should there be any discrimination against white and blacks. But, at the same time, colored people should come forward, should organize and conduct enterprises, and their only insistence should be that the same provisions be made for the success of their enterprise that is being made for the success of any other enterprise. It must be remembered that in the last quarter of a century, the advance of the colored people has been mainly in the lines where they themselves, working by and for themselves, have accomplished the greatest advance.

There is no doubt that numbers of white people, perhaps the majority of Americans, stand ready to take the most distinct advantage of voluntary segregation and cooperation among colored people. Just as soon as they get a group of black folk segregated, they use it as a point of attack and discrimination. Our counter attack should be, therefore, against this discrimination; against the refusal of the South to spend the same amount of money on the black child as on the white child for its education; against the inability of black groups to use public capital; against the monopoly of credit by white groups. But never in the world should our fight be against association with ourselves because by that very token we give up the whole argument that we are worth associating with.

Doubtless, and in the long run, the greatest human development is going to take place under experiences of widest individual contact. Nevertheless, today such individual contact is made difficult and almost impossible by petty prejudice, deliberate and almost criminal propaganda and various survivals from prehistoric heathenism. It is impossible, therefore, to wait for the millennium of free and normal intercourse before we unite, to cooperate among themselves in groups of likeminded people and in groups of people suffering from the same disadvantages and the same hatreds.

It is the class-conscious working man uniting together who will eventually emancipate labor throughout the world. It is the race-conscious black man cooperating together in his own institutions and movements who will eventually emancipate the colored race, and the great step ahead today is for the American Negro to accomplish his economic emancipation through voluntary determined cooperative effort.

W. E. B. Du Bois
The N.A.A.C.P. and Race Segregation [1934]

The cover of *The Crisis* in February 1934 contained this lead headline: "Du Bois: N.A.A.C.P. and Segregation." At three and a half columns, the editorial it heralded was more than twice as long as the January "On Segregation" editorial that touched off Du Bois's fierce debate with the NAACP board over the organization's official stand on segregation (p. 399).

By tracing the NAACP's statements on the subject over time, Du Bois makes the case that his new support of self-segregation is actually in line with the organization's historical position. Du Bois harshly criticizes those who hold rigidly to an "anti-segregation" stance regardless of changes in circumstances. At the same time, his conclusion, in which he welcomes a wide-ranging discussion involving "ample and fair representation to all shades of opinion" indicates that at this point, Du Bois believed that the debate would play itself out through articles in the pages of *The Crisis*, as had happened with other contentious issues in the past.

From *The Crisis*, February 1934, p. 52.

There is a good deal of misapprehension as to the historic attitude of the National Association for the Advancement of Colored People and race segregation. As a matter of fact, the Association, while it has from time to time discussed the larger aspects of this matter, has taken no general stand and adopted no general philosophy. Of course its action, and often very effective action, has been in specific cases of segregation where the call for a definite stand was clear and decided. For instance, in the preliminary National Negro Convention which met in New York May 31st and June 1st, 1909, segregation was only mentioned in a protest against Jim-Crow car laws, and that because of an amendment by William M. Trotter. In the First Annual Report, January 1, 1911, the Association evolved a statement of its purpose, which said that "it seeks to uplift the colored men and women of this country by securing to them the full enjoyment of their rights as citizens, justice in all courts, and equality of opportunity everywhere." Later, this general statement was epitomized in the well-known declaration: "It conceives its mission to be the completion of the work which the great Emancipator began. It proposes to make a group of ten million Americans free from the lingering shackles of past slavery, physically free from peonage, mentally free from ignorance, politically free from disfranchisement, and socially free from insult." This phrase which I first wrote myself for the Annual Report of 1915 still expresses pregnantly the object of the N. A. A. C. P. and it has my own entire adherence.

It will be noted, however, that here again segregation comes in only by implication. Specifically, it was first spoken of in the Second Report of the Association, January 1, 1912, when the attempt to destroy the property of Negroes in Kansas City because they had moved into a white section was taken up. This began our fight on a specific phase of segregation, namely, the attempt to establish a Negro ghetto by force of law. This phase of segregation we fought vigorously for years and often achieved notable victories in the highest courts of the land.

But it will be noted here that the N. A. A. C. P. expressed no opinion as to whether it might not be a feasible and advisable thing for colored people to establish their own residential sections, or their own towns; and certainly there was nothing expressed or implied that Negroes should not organize for promoting their own interests in industry, literature or art. Manifestly, here was opportunity for considerable difference of opinion, but the matter never was thoroughly threshed out.

The Association moved on to other matters of color discrimination: the "Full Crew" bills[1] which led to dismissal of so many Negro railway employees; the "Jim-Crow" car laws on railway trains and street cars; the segregation in government departments. In all these matters, the stand of the Association was clear and unequivocal: it held that it was a gross injustice to make special rules which discriminated against the color of employees or patrons.

In the Sixth Annual Report, issued in March, 1916, the seven lines of endeavor of the Association included change of unfair laws, better administration of present laws, justice in the courts, stoppage of public slander, the investigation of facts, the encouragement of distinguished work by Negroes, and organizations.

Very soon, however, there came up a more complex question, and that was the matter of Negro schools. The Association had avoided from the beginning any thoroughgoing pronouncement on this matter. In the resolutions of 1909, the conference asked: "Equal educational opportunities for all and in all the

1. Bill requiring employment on each train of a minimum number of brakemen and other union workers, effectively eliminating the jobs of black porter brakemen, who also acted as brakemen but were not officially recognized as brakemen because they were excluded from the all-white unions.

states and that public school expenditure be the same for the Negro and white child." This of course did not touch the real problem of separate schools. Very soon, however, definite problems were presented to the Association: the exclusion of colored girls from the Oberlin dormitories in 1919: the discrimination in the School of Education at the University of Pennsylvania, and the Cincinnati fight against establishing a separate school for colored children brought the matter squarely to the front. Later, further cases came: the Brooklyn Girls' High School, the matter of a colored High School in Indianapolis, and the celebrated Gary case.[2]

Gradually, in these cases the attitude of the Association crystalized. It declared that further extension of segregated schools for particular races and especially for Negroes was unwise and dangerous, and the Association undertook in all possible cases to oppose such further segregation. It did not, however, for a moment feel called upon to attack the separate schools where most colored children are educated throughout the United States and it refrained from this not because it approved of separate schools, but because it was faced by a fact and not a theory. It saw no sense in tilting against windmills.[3]

The case at Cheyney was a variation; here was an old and separate private school which became in effect though not in law a separate public normal school; and in the city of Philadelphia a partial system of elementary Negro schools was developed with no definite action on the part of the N. A. A. C. P.

It will be seen that in all these cases the Association was attacking specific instances and not attempting to lay down any general rule as to how far the advancement of the colored race in the United States was going to involve separate racial action and segregated organization of Negroes for certain ends.

To be sure, the overwhelming and underlying thought of the N. A. A. C. P. has always been that any discrimination based simply on race is fundamentally wrong, and that consequently purely racial organizations must have strong justification to be admissable. On the other hand, they faced certain unfortunate but undeniable facts. For instance, War came. The Negro was being drafted. No Negro officers were being commissioned. The N. A. A. C. P. asked for the admission of Negroes to the officers schools. This was denied. There was only one further thing to do and that was to ask for a school for Negro officers. There arose a bitter protest among many Negroes against this movement. Nevertheless, the argument for it was absolutely unanswerable, and Joel E. Spingarn, Chairman of the Board, supported by the students of Howard University, launched a movement which resulted in the commissioning of seven hundred Negro officers in the A. E. F.[4] In all the British Dominions, with their hundreds of millions of colored folk, there was not a single officer of known Negro blood. The American Negro scored a tremendous triumph against the Color Line by their admitted and open policy of segregation. This did not mean that Mr. Spingarn or any of the members of the N. A. A. C. P. thought it right that there should be a separate Negro camp, but they thought a separate Negro camp and Negro officers was infinitely better than no camp and no Negro officers and that was the only practical choice that lay before them.

Similarly, in the question of the Negro vote, the N. A. A. C. P. began in 1920 an attempt to organize the Negro vote and cast it in opposition to open enemies of the Negro race who were running for office. This was without doubt a species of segregation. It was appealing to voters on the grounds of race, and it brought for that reason considerable opposition. Nevertheless, it could be defended on the ground that the election of enemies of the Negro race was not only a blow to that race but to the white race and to all civilization. And while our attitude even in the Parker case,[5] has been criticized, it has on the whole found abundant justification.

---

2. In response to the influx of African American migrants during the Great Migration, Gary, Indiana, established its first segregated high school, Roosevelt High School, in 1927, and African Americans there were no longer allowed to attend other high schools until the Indiana General Assembly passed an anti-segregation law in 1949.

3. Reference to Miguel de Cervantes's novel *Don Quixote*, meaning to fight an impossible or imaginary battle.

4. American Expeditionary Forces.

5. 1930 protest against Supreme Court nominee John Parker, a white American judge who supported laws that discriminated against African Americans.

The final problem in segregation presented to us was that of the Harlem Hospital. Here was a hospital in the center of a great Negro population which for years did not have and would not admit a single Negro physician to its staff. Finally, by agitation and by political power, Negroes obtained representation on the staff in considerable numbers and membership on the Board of Control. It was a great triumph. But it was accompanied by reaction on the part of whites and some Negroes who had opposed this movement, and an attempt to change the status of the hospital so that it would become a segregated Negro hospital, and so that presumably the other hospitals of the city would continue to exclude Negroes from their staffs. With this arose a movement to establish Negro hospitals throughout the United States.

Here was an exceedingly difficult problem. On the one hand, there is no doubt of the need of the Negro population for wider and better hospitalization and of the demand on the part of Negro physicians for opportunities of hospital practice. This was illustrated by the celebrated Tuskegee hospital where nearly all the Negro veterans are segregated but where an efficient Negro staff has been installed. Perhaps nothing illustrates better than this the contradiction and paradox of the problem of race segregation in the United States and the problem which the N. A. A. C. P. faced and still faces.

The N. A. A. C. P. opposed the initial establishment of the hospital at Tuskegee although it is doubtful if it would have opposed such a hospital in the North. On the other hand, once established, we fought to defend the Tuskegee hospital and give it widest opportunity.

In other words, the N. A. A. C. P. has never officially opposed separate Negro organizations—such as churches, schools and business; and cultural organizations. It has never denied the recurrent necessity of united separate action on the part of Negroes for self-defense and self-development; but it has insistently and continually pointed out that such action is in any case a necessary evil involving often a recognition from within of the very color line which we are fighting without. That race pride and race loyalty, Negro ideals and Negro unity, have a place and function today, the N. A. A. C. P. never has denied and never can deny.

But all this simply touches the whole question of racial organization and initiative. No matter what we may wish or say, the vast majority of the Negroes in the United States are born in colored homes, educated in separate colored schools, attend separate colored churches, marry colored mates, and find their amusement in colored Y. M. C. A.'s and Y. W. C. A.'s. Even in their economic life, they are gradually being forced out of the place in industry which they occupied in the white world and are being compelled to seek their living among themselves. Here is segregation with a vengeance, and its problems must be met and its course guided. It would be idiotic simply to sit on the side lines and yell: "No segregation" in an increasingly segregated world.

On the other hand, the danger of easily and eagerly yielding to suggested racial segregation without reason or pressure stares us ever in the face. We segregate ourselves. We herd together. We do things such as this clipping from the *Atlanta Constitution* indicates:

> "A lecture on the raising of Lazarus from the dead will be delivered at the city auditorium on Friday night. The Big Bethel choir will sing and the Graham Jackson band will give additional music. Space has been set aside for white people."

The "Jim Crow" galleries of Southern moving picture houses are filled with some of the best Negro citizens. Separate schools and other institutions have been asked by Negroes in the north when the whites had made no real demand.

Such are the flat and undeniable facts. What are we going to do about them? We can neither yell them down nor make them disappear by resolutions. We must think and act. It is this problem which THE CRISIS desires to discuss during the present year in all its phases and with ample and fair representation to all shades of opinion.

Walter F. White

Reply to W. E. B. Du Bois [1934]

On February 18, 1934, Walter White wrote a confidential memo to James Weldon Johnson, White's predecessor as executive secretary of the NAACP, concerning the conflict between that organization and W. E. B. Du Bois: "It is somewhat disheartening when we have cut our force and salaries, gone practically without literature, which has hurt the Association, to pay over to *The Crisis* during the last four years more than thirty thousand dollars from the funds of the Association and then on top of this to be accused of trying to 'oust' him." White's more measured, public response to the conflict with Du Bois, reprinted here, appeared as part of "Segregation—A Symposium" in the March 1934 issue of *The Crisis*. In addition to the symposium, the issue included another article on segregation by Du Bois, "History of Segregation Philosophy," in which he bolsters his arguments for self-segregation by retracing responses of African Americans to entrenched racism, with a particular focus on the establishment of the AME church.

White's reply accentuates the "distinct and clear-cut difference of opinion" between the NAACP's board of directors and Du Bois (p. 399). Although he professes to be merely expressing his "personal opinion," White's byline reads "Secretary, N. A. A. C. P.," giving his response the weight of official sanction. He emphasizes his position of authority by stating, "It is fitting and proper that the statement of the Secretary's position should first appear in *The Crisis,* the official organ of the Association." (As executive secretary, he held the highest position in the organization.) White glosses over the issue of social self-segregation, defining it as a private

affair. He then indicates his firm commitment to integration as the ultimate goal for African Americans and his adamant rejection of segregation as a political strategy.

Born in Atlanta in 1893, Walter White was deeply affected by his childhood experience of the 1906 Atlanta riots. After graduating from Atlanta University, he went to work for a black-owned insurance company. In 1916, he established the Atlanta branch of the NAACP and organized a successful protest against the Atlanta Board of Education, which had proposed eliminating the seventh grade for black students in order to build a new high school for white students. In 1918, he became the assistant secretary of the national branch of the NAACP under James Weldon Johnson. Taking advantage of his extremely light skin and blue eyes, White went undercover as a white man in the South to investigate the brutal practice of lynching. Although his efforts to promote anti-lynching legislation were ultimately unsuccessful, his long-term commitment to the cause helped increase national awareness of lynching and decrease instances of lynching murders.

White led the NAACP from 1931 until 1955, the year of his death. During his tenure, the organization became a leading legal advocacy group, propelled in 1940 by the establishment of the NAACP Legal Defense and Educational Fund, headed by Thurgood Marshall. Major victories in areas advanced by the NAACP during White's years included President Harry Truman's 1948 executive order integrating the military and culminated with *Brown v. Board of Education* in 1954, the Supreme Court decision outlawing segregation in public schools.

From *The Crisis,* April 1934.

Numerous requests have been made of the National Association for the Advancement of Colored People for a statement of the position of the Association on editorials by Dr. Du Bois on "Segregation" in the January and February issues of *The Crisis*. It is fitting and proper that the statement of the Secretary's position should first appear in *The Crisis,* the official organ of the Association.

Various interpretations have been placed upon Dr. Du Bois's editorial, a number of them erroneous and especially the one which interprets the editorial as a statement of the position of the N.A.A.C.P. The historic position of the N.A.A.C.P. has from the date of its foundation been opposed to segregation. Dr. Du Bois's editorial is merely a personal expression on his part that the whole question of segregation should be examined and discussed anew. There can be no objection to frank and free discussion on any subject, and *The Crisis* is the last place where censorship or restriction of freedom of speech should be attempted. I wish to call attention to the fact that the N.A.A.C.P. has never officially budged in its general opposition to segregation. Since Dr. Du Bois has expressed his personal opinion why this attitude might possibly have to be altered I should like to give my personal opinion why I believe we should continue to maintain the same attitude we have for nearly a quarter of a century, but I repeat that what I am about to say is merely my personal opinion just as Dr. Du Bois's editorial expressed his personal opinion.

Let us put aside for the moment the ethical and moral principles involved. It is my firm conviction, based upon observation and experience, that the truest statement in the January editorial is:

> ... there is no doubt that numbers of white people, perhaps the majority of Americans, stand ready to take the most distinct advantage of voluntary segregation and cooperation among colored people. Just as soon as they get a group of black folk segregated, they use it as a point of attack and discrimination.

It is for this very reason that thoughtful colored people will be opposed to following the advice that "groups of communities and farms inhabited by colored folk should be voluntarily formed" where they involve government-financed and -approved arrangements like the Homestead Subsistence projects.

It is unfortunate that Dr. Du Bois's editorial has been used, we learn, by certain government officials at Washington to hold up admission of Negroes to one of the government-financed relief projects. Protests have been made to Mrs. Roosevelt and others by the N.A.A.C.P. against such exclusion. Plans to admit Negroes as a result of the protest are being delayed, with the editorial in question used as an excuse for such delay.

To accept the status of separateness, which almost invariably in the case of submerged, exploited and mar-

ginal groups means inferior accommodations and a distinctly inferior position in the national and communal life, means spiritual atrophy for the group segregated. When Negroes, Jews, Catholics or Nordic white Americans voluntarily choose to live or attend church or engage in social activity together, that is their affair and no one else's. But Negroes and all other groups must without compromise and without cessation oppose in every possible fashion any attempt to impose from without the establishment of pales[1] and ghettoes. Arbitrary segregation of this sort means almost without exception that less money will be expended for adequate sewerage, water, police and fire protection and for the building of a healthful community. It is because of this that the N.A.A.C.P. has resolutely fought such segregation, as in the case of city ordinances and state laws in the Louisville, New Orleans and Richmond segregation cases, has opposed restrictive covenants written into deeds of property, and all other forms, legal and illegal, to restrict the areas in which Negroes may buy or rent and occupy property.

This principle is especially vital where attempts are made to establish separate areas which are financed by moneys from the Federal or state governments for which black people are taxed at the same rate as white. No self-respecting Negro can afford to accept without vigorous protest any such attempt to put the stamp of Federal approval upon discrimination of this character. Though separate schools do exist in the South and though for the time being little can be done toward ending the expensive and wasteful dual educational system based upon caste and color prejudice, yet no Negro who respects himself and his race can accept these segregated systems without at least inward protest.

I cannot agree with the statement made by Dr. Du Bois in the February *Crisis* that the N.A.A.C.P. opposed the establishment of the veterans' hospital at Tuskegee "although it is doubtful if it would have opposed such a hospital in the North." The N.A.A.C.P. did oppose, and successfully, the recent attempt to establish a segregated veterans' hospital at Chester, Pennsylvania. It was the feeling of many of us then and is now that the fight should be made for the acceptance of

---

1. Areas separated from others with imposed boundaries.

Negro physicians, specialists and nurses on the basis of ability to the staffs of *all* veterans' hospitals rather than to ask for Jim Crow hospitals.

Nor can I agree that the failure of the citizens of Philadelphia to resist more persistently, intelligently and militantly the establishment of a partial system of elementary Negro schools is necessarily approval of the segregation which has been established. This opening wedge will undoubtedly result in *more* segregation in schools and other public institutions unless aggressively fought. Like cancer, segregation grows and must be, in my opinion, resisted wherever it shows its head.

It is admittedly a longer and more difficult road to full and unrestricted admission to schools, hospitals and other public institutions, but the mere difficulty of the road should not and will not serve as a deterrent to either Negro or white people who are mindful not only of present conditions but of those to which we aspire. In a world where time and space are being demolished by science it is no longer possible to create or imagine separate racial, national or other compartments of human thought and endeavor. The Negro must, without yielding, continue the grim struggle *for* integration and *against* segregation for his own physical, moral, and spiritual well-being and for that of white America and of the world at large.

W. E. B. Du Bois
Segregation in the North [1934]

With this editorial from the April 1934 issue of *The Crisis*, Du Bois attempted to respond to his critics by elaborating on his stand on self-segregation as a strategy of self-defense, but his dismissal of Walter White as white only intensified the growing acrimony between the two men. Du Bois's conflict with White had begun three years earlier, when Du Bois led a group of NAACP executive officers in protesting White's "attitude and actions" after he became the executive secretary of the NAACP. In his autobiography, Du Bois repeatedly noted that he "did not like Mr. White's methods" and never trusted him. However, when Du Bois dismissed White's viewpoint on the basis of his skin color, writers representing a variety of ideologies rallied to White's defense. In the *Pittsburgh Courier*, George Schuyler disparagingly compared Du Bois to Marcus Garvey and proclaimed, "Imagine the Top Sergeant of the Talented Tenth fouling like a punch drunk pugilist despairing of victory by fair means!" A number of black newspapers called for Du Bois's resignation, with the *Philadelphia Tribune* declaring, "Because of his former efforts in a glorious cause he should be permitted to resign. But if he refuses, he should be fired because all of the honor and glory which are his turn to bitter gall."

From *The Crisis*, April 1934.

I have read with interest the various criticisms on my recent discussions of segregation. Those like that of Mr. Pierce of Cleveland[1] do not impress me. I am not worried about being inconsistent. What worries me is the Truth. I am talking about conditions in 1934 and not in 1910. I do not care what I said in 1910 or 1810 or in B.C. 700.

The arguments of Walter White, George Schuyler, and Kelly Miller have logic, but they seem to me quite beside the point. In the first place, Walter White is white. He has more white companions and friends than colored. He goes where he will in New York City and naturally meets no color line for the simple and sufficient reason that he isn't "colored"; he feels his

---

1. David H. Pierce, president of the Cleveland NAACP and participant in "Segregation: A Symposium," published in *The Crisis*, March 1934.

new freedom in bitter contrast to what he was born to in Georgia. This is perfectly natural, and he does what anyone else of his complexion would do.

But it is fantastic to assume that this has anything to do with the color problem in the United States. It naturally makes Mr. White an extreme opponent of any segregation based on a myth of race. But this argument does not apply to Schuyler or Miller or me. Moreover, Mr. White knows this. He moved once into a white apartment house and it went black on him. He now lives in a colored apartment house with attendant limitations. He once took a friend to dine with him at the celebrated café of the Lafayette Hotel, where he had often been welcomed. The management humiliated him by refusing to serve Roland Hayes.

The attitudes of Schuyler and Kelly Miller are historically based on the amiable assumption that there is little or no segregation in the North and that agitation and a firm stand is making this disappear, that obvious desert and accomplishment by Negroes can break down prejudice. This is a fable. I once believed it passionately. It may become true in two hundred and fifty or a thousand years. Now it is not true. No black man, whatever his culture or ability, is today in America regarded as a man by any considerable number of white Americans. The difference between North and South in the matter of segregation is largely a difference of degree; a wide degree certainly, but still of degree.

In the North, neither Schuyler nor Kelly Miller nor anyone with a visible admixture of Negro blood can frequent hotels or restaurants. They have difficulty in finding dwelling places in better-class neighborhoods. They occupy "Lower 13" on Pullmans,[2] and if they are wise they do not go into dining cars when any large number of white people is there. Their children go either to colored schools or to schools nominally for both races but actually attended almost exclusively by colored children. In other words, they are confined by unyielding public opinion to a Negro world. They earn a living on colored newspapers or in colored colleges or other racial institutions. They treat colored

patients and preach to colored pews. Not one of the twelve colored Ph.D.'s of last year, trained by highest American and European standards, is going to get a job in any white university. Even when Negroes in the North work side by side with whites, they are segregated, like the postal clerks, or refused by white unions, or denied merited promotion.

No matter how much we may fulminate about "No segregation," there stand the flat facts. Moreover, this situation has in the last quarter century been steadily growing worse. Mr. Spingarn may ask judicially as to whether or not the N.A.A.C.P. should change its attitude toward segregation. The point that he does not realize is that segregation has changed its attitude toward the N.A.A.C.P. The higher the Negro climbs or tries to climb, the more pitiless and unyielding the color ban. Segregation may be just as evil today as it was in 1910, but it is more insistent, more prevalent, and more unassailable by appeal or argument. The pressing problem is: What are we going to do about it?

In 1910, colored men could be entertained in the best hotels in Cleveland, Detroit, and Chicago. Today, there is not a single Northern city, except New York, where a Negro can be a guest at a first-class hotel. Not even in Boston is he welcome; and in New York the number of hotels where he can go is very small. Roland Hayes was unable to get regular hotel accommodations, and Dr. Moton[3] succeeds only by powerful white influence and by refraining from use of the public dining room or the public lobbies.

If, as Spingarn asserts, the N.A.A.C.P. has conducted a quarter-century campaign against segregation, the net result has been a little less than nothing. We have by legal action steadied the foundation so that, in the future, segregation must be by wish and will and not law, but beyond that we have not made the slightest impress on the determination of the overwhelming mass of white Americans not to treat Negroes as men.

These are unpleasant facts. We do not like to voice them. The theory is that by maintaining certain fictions

---

2. Private drawing rooms; after the outlawing of Jim Crow laws, Langston Hughes (p. 362) wrote of the irony that rail companies began upgrading African Americans to these private rooms for no extra charge, so that they "might suffer segregation by being given its finest accommodations rather than permitted the democracy of the open coaches."

3. Robert Russa Moton (1867–1940) became the second president of Tuskegee Institute after the death of its founder Booker T. Washington in 1915.

of law and administration, by whistling and keeping our courage up, we can stand on the "principle" of no segregation and wait until public opinion meets our position. But can we do this? When we were living in times of prosperity, when we were making postwar incomes, when our labor was in demand, we perhaps could afford to wait. But today, faced by starvation and economic upheaval and by the question of being able to survive at all in this land in the reconstruction that is upon us, it is ridiculous not to see, and criminal not to tell, the colored people that they cannot base their salvation upon the empty reiteration of a slogan.

What, then, can we do? The only thing that we not only can but must do is voluntarily and insistently to organize our economic and social power, no matter how much segregation it involves. Learn to associate with ourselves and to train ourselves for effective association. Organize our strength as consumers; learn to cooperate and use machines and power as producers; train ourselves in methods of democratic control within our own group. Run and support our own institutions.

We are doing this partially now, only we are doing it under a peculiar attitude of protest and with only transient and distracted interest. A number of excellent young gentlemen in Washington, having formed a Negro Alliance,[4] proceed to read me out of the congregation of the righteous because I dare even discuss segregation. But who are these young men? The products of a segregated school system, the talent selected by Negro teachers, the persons who can today, in nine cases out of ten, earn a living only through segregated Negro social institutions. These are the men who are yelling against segregation. If most of them had been educated in the mixed schools in New York instead of the segregated schools of Washington, they never would have seen college, because Washington picks out and sends ten times as many Negroes to college as New York does.

It would, of course, be full easy to deny that this voluntary association for great social and economic ends is segregation; and if I had done this in the beginning of this debate, many people would have been eas-

ily deceived and would have yelled "No segregation" with one side of their mouths and "Race pride and race initiative" with the other side. No such distinction can possibly be drawn. Segregation may be compulsory by law, or it may be compulsory by economic or social condition, or it may be a matter of free choice. At any rate, it is the separation of human beings and separation despite the will to humanity. Such separation is evil; it leads to jealousy, greed, nationalism, and war; and yet it is today and in this world inevitable; inevitable to Jews because of Hitler, inevitable to Japanese because of white Europe, inevitable to Russia because of organized greed over all the white world, inevitable to Ethiopia because of white armies and navies, inevitable because without it the American Negro will suffer evils greater than any possible evil of separation: we would suffer the loss of self-respect, the lack of faith in ourselves, the lack of knowledge about ourselves, the lack of ability to make a decent living by our own efforts and not by philanthropy.

This situation has been plunged into crisis and precipitated to an open demand for thought and action by the depression and the New Deal. The government, national and state, is helping and guiding the individual. It has entered and entered for good into the social and economic organization of life. We could wish, we could pray, that this entrance could absolutely ignore lines of race and color, but we know perfectly well it does not and will not, and with the present American opinion it cannot. The question is, then, are we going to stand out and refuse the inevitable and inescapable government aid because we first wish to abolish the color line? This is not simply tilting at windmills; it is, if we are not careful, committing race suicide.

Back of all slogans lies the difficulty that the meanings may change without changing the words. For instance, "No segregation" may mean two very different things:

1. A chance for the Negro to advance without the hindrances which arise when he is segregated from the main group and the main social institutions upon which society depends. He becomes, thus, an outsider,

4. The New Negro Alliance, formed in 1933 by Belford V. Lawson, Jr., John Aubrey Davis, and M. Franklin Thorne, initiated "Don't Buy Where You Can't Work" campaigns to protest businesses in black neighborhoods with no black employees.

a hanger-on, with no chance to function properly as a man.

2. It may mean utter lack of faith of Negroes in Negroes and the desire to escape into another group, shirking, on the other hand, all responsibility for ignorance, degradation, and lack of experience among Negroes while asking admission into the other group on terms of full equality and with full chance for individual development.

It is in the first sense that I have always believed and used the slogan "No segregation." On the other hand, in the second sense, I have no desire or right to hinder or estop those persons who do not want to be Negroes. But I am compelled to ask the very plain and pertinent question: Assuming for the moment that the group into which you demand admission does not want you, what are you going to do about it? Can you demand that they want you? Can you make them by law or public opinion admit you when they are supreme over this same public opinion and make these laws? Manifestly, you cannot. Manifestly, your admission to the other group on the basis of your individual desert and wish can be accomplished only if they too join in the wish to have you. If they do so join, all problems based mostly on race and color disappear, and there remain only the human problems of social uplift and intelligence and group action. But there is in the United States today no sign that this objection to the social and even civic recognition of persons of Negro blood is going to occur during the life of persons now living. In which case there can be only one meaning to the slogan "No segregation," and that is, no hindrance to my effort to be a man. If you do not wish to associate with me, I am more than willing to associate with myself. Indeed, I deem it a privilege to work with and for Negroes, asking only that my hands be not tied nor my feet hobbled.

What is the object of those persons who insist by law, custom, and propaganda to keep the American Negro separate in rights and privileges from other citizens of the United States? The real object, confessed or semiconscious, is to so isolate the Negro that he will be spiritually bankrupt, physically degenerate, and economically dependent.

Against this it is the bounden duty of every Negro and every enlightened American to protest, to oppose

the policy so far as it is manifest by laws, to agitate against customs by revealing facts, and to appeal to the sense of decency and justice in all American citizens.

I have never known an American Negro who did not agree that this was a proper program. Some have disagreed as to the emphasis to be put on this and that method of protest, on the efficacy of any appeal against American prejudice; but all Negroes have agreed that segregation is bad and should be opposed.

Suppose, however, that this appeal is ineffective or nearly so. What is the Negro going to do? There is one thing that he can and must do, and that is to see to it that segregation does *not* undermine his health, does *not* leave him spiritually bankrupt, and does *not* make him an economic slave; and he must do this at any cost.

If he cannot live in sanitary and decent sections of a city, he must build his own residential quarters and raise and keep them on a plane fit for living. If he cannot educate his children in decent schools with other children, he must, nevertheless, educate his children in decent Negro schools and arrange and conduct and oversee such schools. If he cannot enter American industry at a living wage or find work suited to his education and talent, or receive promotion and advancement according to his deserts, he must organize his own economic life so that just as far as possible these discriminations will not reduce him to abject exploitation.

Every one of these movements on the part of colored people is not only necessary but inevitable. And at the same time they involve more or less active segregation and acquiescence in segregation.

Here again, if there be any number of American Negroes who have not in practical life made this fight of self-segregation and self-association against the compulsory segregation forced upon them, I am unacquainted with such persons. They may, of course, explain their compulsory retreat from a great ideal by calling segregation by some other name. They may affirm with fierce insistency that they will never, no, never, under any circumstances acquiesce in segregation. But if they live in the United States in the year of our Lord 1934 or in any previous year since the foundation of the government, they are segregated; they accept segregation, and they segregate themselves because they must. From this dilemma I see no issue.

Extreme opponents of segregation act as though there was but one solution of the race problem and that, complete integration of the black race with the white race in America, with no distinction of color in political, civil, or social life. There is no doubt but what this is the great end toward which humanity is tending and that so long as there are artificially emphasized differences of nationality, race, and color, not to mention the fundamental discriminations of economic class, there will be no real Humanity.

On the other hand, it is just as clear that not for a century, and more probably not for ten centuries, will any such consummation be reached. No person born will ever live to see national and racial distinctions altogether abolished, and economic distinctions will last many a day.

Since this is true, the practical problem that faces us is not a choice between segregation and no segregation, between compulsory interferences with human intercourse and complete liberty of contact; the thing that faces us is, given varying degrees of segregation, how shall we conduct ourselves so that in the end human differences will not be emphasized at the expense of human advance.

It is perfectly certain that not only shall we be compelled to submit to much segregation, but sometimes it will be necessary to our survival and a step toward the ultimate breaking down of barriers to increase by voluntary action our separation from our fellow men.

When my roommate gets too noisy and dirty, I leave him; when my neighbors get too annoying and insulting, I seek another home; when white Americans refuse to treat me as a man, I will cut my intercourse with white Americans to the minimum demanded by decent living.

It may be and often has been true that oppression and insult have become so intense and so unremitting that there is no alternative left to self-respecting men but to herd by themselves in self-defense until the attitude of the world changes. It happens that today is peculiarly a day when such voluntary union for self-expression and self-defense is forced upon large numbers of people. We may rail against this. We may say that it is not our fault, and it certainly is not. Nevertheless, to do nothing in the face of it, to accept opposition without united counteropposition, is the program of fools.

Moreover, if association and contact with Negroes is distasteful to you, what is it to white people? Remember that the white people of America will certainly never want us until we want ourselves. We excuse ourselves in this case and say we do not hate Negroes but we do hate their condition, and immediately the answer is thrown back on us in the very words. Whose job is it to change that condition—the job of the white people or the job of the black people themselves, and especially of their uplifted classes?

W. E. B. Du Bois
Counsels of Despair [1934]

The NAACP board tried to distance the organization from W. E. B. Du Bois's support of self-segregation. The chair of the board, Joel Spingarn, and the secretary, Walter White (p. 404), both wrote critical commentaries in "Segregation, A Symposium," published in the March 1934 issue of *The Crisis*. The board also revised a position paper on segregation that Du Bois himself had written. Du Bois responded by opening the internal conflict to the public. For the May issue of *The Crisis*, he wrote an editorial called "The Board of Directors on Segrega-

tion," and included three drafts of the NAACP's official position: his original draft, Joel Spingarn's slightly modified version, and Walter White's substantial revision, which was approved by the board. Du Bois concluded with a biting indictment of the board of directors and proclaimed to readers that their final resolution implied disapproval of any separate organization or category, such as the black church and black history. The board responded by passing a resolution on May 21, 1934, according to which *The Crisis* was to be the association's official organ, and "no salaried officer of the Association shall criticize the policy, work, or officers of the Association" in its pages. For Du Bois, this move by the board confirmed his conviction that the controversy was really over the issue of censorship, not segregation.

In the June issue of *The Crisis*, Du Bois briefly attempted to clarify his position on self-segregation. The editorial reprinted here emphasizes the opportunity to use self-segregation for the "uplift and development of the Negro race" and points to the long history of self-help as embodied in such organizations as the National Association of Colored Women's Clubs (with its motto "Lifting As We Climb").

The following month, Du Bois submitted his resignation as editor of *The Crisis*. It was initially rejected by the board, but Du Bois resubmitted it in August and terminated not only his editorship of *The Crisis* but also his association with the organization. He moved back to Atlanta and rejoined the faculty of Atlanta University.

Du Bois continued to expand on his ideas about self-segregation after leaving the NAACP. By June of the next year, in an article in *Current History*, he was calling for a combination of "voluntary and increased segregation" and black economic self-sufficiency. In his autobiography, written more than thirty years after his initial conflict with the NAACP, Du Bois indicated a sense of vindication over the way in which history was playing itself out with regard to black self-segregation: "What was true in 1910 was still true in 1940 and will be true in 1970. But with this vast difference: that the segregated Negro institutions are better organized, more intelligently planned and more efficiently conducted, and today form in themselves the best and most compelling argument for the ultimate abolition of the color line."

From *The Crisis,* June 1934.

Many persons have interpreted my reassertion of our current attitude toward segregation as a counsel of despair: We can't win; therefore, give up and accept the inevitable. Never, and nonsense. Our business in this world is to fight and fight again and never to yield. But, after all, one must fight with his brains, if he has any. He gathers strength to fight. He gathers knowledge, and he raises children who are proud to fight and who know what they are fighting about. And, above all, they learn that what they are fighting for is the opportunity and the chance to know and associate with black folk. They are not fighting to escape themselves. They are fighting to say to the world: The opportunity of knowing Negroes is worth so much to us and is so appreciated that we want you to know them too.

Negroes are not extraordinary human beings. They are just like other human beings, with all their foibles and ignorance and mistakes. But they are human beings, and human nature is always worth knowing and, withal, splendid in its manifestations. Therefore, we are fighting to keep open the avenues of human contact; but in the meantime, we are taking every advantage of what opportunities of contact are already open to us, and among those opportunities which are open, and which are splendid and inspiring, is the opportunity of Negroes to work together in the twentieth century for the uplift and development of the Negro race. It is no counsel of despair to emphasize and hail the opportunity for such work.

KEY DEBATE ∼ *Education*

CARTER G. WOODSON
from The Mis-Education of the Negro [1933]

"Only by careful study of the Negro himself and the life which he is forced to lead can we arrive at the proper procedure in this crisis," Carter G. Woodson writes in the preface to *The Mis-Education of the Negro* (excerpts from which are reprinted below). "The only question which concerns us here is whether these 'educated' persons are actually equipped to face the ordeal before them or unconsciously contribute to their own undoing by perpetuating the regime of the oppressor." Woodson's preface underscores his lifelong commitment not only to the rigorous study and promotion of African American history and culture but also to African Americans' application of that knowledge to programs that improve economic and social conditions. He rejected "nominal equality"—black people's using the same educational and other programs that white people used even when those programs were flawed—in favor of fostering originality and allowing the needs of black people to determine the programs they used. This stance would resonate over the following decades in such debates as the 1985 controversy over the use of "Ebonics" as a method of teaching standard English (p. 895).

Known as the "Father of Black History," Carter G. Woodson (1875–1950) was born in Virginia ten years after the end of the Civil War. The son of former slaves who could not read or write, Woodson's formal schooling was sparse through his teenage years, as he had to work on the family farm and later as a miner to help support his parents and siblings. Largely self-taught, he finally entered high school at the age of twenty. He received his master's degree in history from the University of Chicago in 1907 and in 1912 became the second African American to receive a Ph.D. from Harvard, after W. E. B. Du Bois's receipt of the degree in 1895. He went on to become one of the most prominent historians and publishers of his era. He wrote numerous books on African American history and culture, focusing on migration, family life, and education. He established the Association for the Study of Negro Life and History in 1915; founded *The Journal of Negro History* in 1916; organized Associated Publishers in 1921, an enterprise dedicated to publishing scholarly books on black life; and began publishing the *Negro History Bulletin* in 1937. In 1926, Woodson launched Negro History Week (which in 1976 evolved into Black History Month), arguing that it would both build self-esteem among black people and help eliminate prejudice among white people.

For Woodson, a key to improving the lives of African Americans lay in broadening access to African and African American studies, including "the history of the Negro race, its economic progress, its social problems, African art, African Anthropology, and African Philosophy," as he wrote in a 1927 letter promoting correspondence classes on these topics. "The fact is that the so-called history teaching in our schools and colleges is downright propaganda, an effort to praise one race and to decry the other to justify social repression and exploitation," Woodson argued. Through his work as a publisher and scholar, he sought "to bring before the world the whole truth that the truth may make men free."

From *The Mis-Education of the Negro* (Washington, D.C.: Associated Publishers, 1933).

"Highly educated" Negroes denounce persons who advocate for the Negro a sort of education different in some respects from that now given the white man. Negroes who have been so long inconvenienced and denied opportunities for development are naturally afraid of anything that sounds like discrimination. They are anxious to have everything the white man has even if it is harmful. The possibility of originality in the Negro, therefore, is discounted one hundred per cent to maintain a nominal equality. If the whites decide to take up Mormonism, the Negroes must follow their lead. If the whites neglect such a study, then the Negroes must do likewise.

The author, however, does not have such an attitude. He considers the educational system as it has developed both in Europe and America an antiquated process which does not hit the mark even in the case of the needs of the white man himself. If the white man wants to hold on to it, let him do so; but the Negro, so far as he is able, should develop and carry out a program of his own.

The so-called modern education, with all its defects, however, does others so much more good than it does the Negro, because it has been worked out in conformity to the needs of those who have enslaved and oppressed weaker peoples. For example, the philosophy and ethics resulting from our educational system have justified slavery, peonage, segregation, and lynching. The oppressor has the right to exploit, to handicap, and to kill the oppressed. Negroes daily educated in the tenets of such a religion of the strong have accepted the status of the weak as divinely ordained, and during the last three generations of their nominal freedom they have done practically nothing to change it. Their pouting and resolutions indulged in by a few of the race have been of little avail.

No systematic effort toward change has been possible, for, taught the same economics, history, philosophy, literature, and religion which have established the present code of morals, the Negro's mind has been brought under the control of his oppressor. The problem of holding the Negro down, therefore, is easily solved. When you control a man's thinking you do not have to worry about his actions. You do not have to tell him not to stand here or go yonder. He will find his "proper place" and will stay in it. You do not need to send him to the back door. He will go without being told. In fact, if there is no back door, he will cut one for his special benefit. His education makes it necessary.

The same educational process which inspires and stimulates the oppressor with the thought that he is everything and has accomplished everything worth while depresses and crushes at the same time the spark of genius in the Negro by making him feel that his race does not amount to much and never will measure up to the standards of other peoples. The Negro thus educated is a hopeless liability of the race.

The difficulty is that the "educated Negro" is compelled to live and move among his own people, whom he has been taught to despise. As a rule, therefore, the "educated Negro" prefers to buy his food from a white grocer because he has been taught that the Negro is not clean. It does not matter how often a Negro washes his hands, then; he cannot clean them; and it does not matter how often a white man uses his hands he cannot soil them. The educated Negro, moreover, is disinclined to take part in Negro business, because he has been taught in economics that Negroes cannot operate in this particular sphere. The "educated Negro" gets less and less pleasure out of the Negro church, not on account of its primitiveness and increasing corruption, but because of his preference for the seats of "righteousness" controlled by his oppressor. This has been his education, and nothing else can be expected of him.

If the "educated Negro" could go off and be white he might be happy, but only a mulatto now and then can do this. The large majority of this class, then, must go through life denouncing white people because they are trying to run away from the blacks and decrying the blacks because they are not white.

CHAPTER I. THE SEAT OF THE TROUBLE

* * *

As another has well said, to handicap a student by teaching him that his black face is a curse and that his struggle to change his condition is hopeless is the worst sort of lynching. It kills one's aspirations and dooms him to vagabondage and crime. It is strange, then, that the friends of truth and the promoters of freedom have not risen up against the present propaganda in the schools and crushed it. This crusade is much more important than the anti-lynching movement, because there would be no lynching if it did not start in the schoolroom. Why not exploit, enslave, or exterminate a class that everybody is taught to regard as inferior?

To be more explicit, we may go to the seat of the trouble. Our most widely known scholars have been trained in universities outside of the South. Northern and Western institutions, however, have had no time to deal with matters which concern the Negro especially. They must direct their attention to the problems of the majority of their constituents, and too often they have stimulated their prejudices by referring to the Negro as unworthy of consideration. Most of what these universities have offered as language, mathematics, and science may have served a good purpose, but much of what they have taught as economics, history, literature, religion and philosophy is propaganda and cant that involved a waste of time and misdirected the Negroes thus trained.

And even in the certitude of science or mathematics it has been unfortunate that the approach to the Negro has been borrowed from a "foreign" method.

* * *

When a Negro has finished his education in our schools, then, he has been equipped to begin the life of an Americanized or Europeanized white man, but before he steps from the threshold of his alma mater he is told by his teachers that he must go back to his own people from whom he has been estranged by a vision of ideals which in his disillusionment he will realize that he cannot attain. He goes forth to play his part in life, but he must be both social and bisocial at the same time. While he is a part of the body politic, he is in addition to this a member of a particular race to which he must restrict himself in all matters social. While serving his country he must serve within a special group. While being a good American, he must above all things be a "good Negro"; and to perform this definite function, he must learn to stay in a "Negro's place."

For the arduous task of serving a race thus handicapped, however, the Negro graduate has had little or no training at all. The people whom he has been ordered to serve have been belittled by his teachers to the extent that he can hardly find delight in undertaking what his education has led him to think is impossible. Considering his race as blank in achievement, then, he sets out to stimulate their imitation of others. The performance is kept up a while; but, like any other effort at meaningless imitation, it results in failure.

Facing this undesirable result, the highly educated Negro often grows sour. He becomes too pessimistic to be a constructive force and usually develops into a chronic fault-finder or a complainant at the bar of public opinion. Often when he sees that the fault lies at the door of the white oppressor whom he is afraid to attack, he turns upon the pioneering Negro who is at work doing the best he can to extricate himself from an uncomfortable predicament.

In this effort to imitate, however, these "educated people" are sincere. They hope to make the Negro conform quickly to the standard of the whites and thus remove the pretext for the barriers between the races. They do not realize, however, that even if the Negroes do successfully imitate the whites, nothing new has thereby been accomplished. You simply have a larger number of persons doing what others have been doing. The unusual gifts of the race have not thereby been developed, and an unwilling world, therefore, continues to wonder what the Negro is good for.

These "educated" people, however, decry any such thing as race consciousness; and in some respects they are right. They do not like to hear such expressions as "Negro literature," Negro poetry," "African art," or "thinking black"; and roughly speaking, we must concede that such things do not exist. These things did not figure in the courses which they pursued in school, and why should they? "Aren't we all Americans? Then, whatever is American is as much the heritage of the Negro as of any other group in this country."

The "highly educated" contend, moreover, that when the Negro emphasizes these things he invites racial discrimination by recognizing such differentness of the races. The thought that the Negro is one thing and the white man another is the stock-in-trade argument of the Caucasian to justify segregation. Why, then, should the Negro blame the white man for doing what he himself does?

These "highly educated" Negroes, however, fail to see that it is not the Negro who takes this position. The white man forces him to it, and to extricate himself therefrom the Negro leader must so deal with the situation as to develop in the segregated group the power with which they can elevate themselves. The differentness of races, moreover, is no evidence of superiority or of inferiority. This merely indicates that each race has certain gifts which the others do not possess. It is by the development of these gifts that every race must justify its right to exist.

* * *

CHAPTER X. THE LOSS OF VISION

* * *

[* * *] In our so-called democracy we are accustomed to give the majority what they want rather than educate them to understand what is best for them. We do not show the Negro how to overcome segregation, but we teach him how to accept it as final and just.

Numerous results from this policy may be cited. the white laboring man refuses to work with Negroes because of the false tradition that the Negro is an inferior, and at the same time the Negro for the same reason becomes content with menial service and drudgery. The politician excludes the Negro from the councils of his party and from the government because he has been taught that such is necessary to maintain the supremacy of his race; the Negro, trained in the same school of thought, accepts this as final and contends for such meager consideration as the bosses may begrudgingly grant him. An irate resident in an exclusive district protests against an invasion by Negroes because he has learned that these poverty-stricken people are carriers of disease and agents of crime; the Negroes, believing that such is the truth, remain content in the ghetto. The irrational parent forces the separation of the races in some schools because his child must occupy a seat next to a pupil of "tainted" African blood; the educated Negro accepts this as inevitable and welcomes the makeshift for his people. Children of Negroes are excluded from the playgrounds because of the assertion that they will contaminate those of the whites; the Negroes yielding, settle down to a policy of having their children grow up in neglected fashion in the most undesirable part of the city. The Negro is forced to ride in a Jim Crow car to stamp upon him more easily the badge of his "inferiority"; the "educated Negro" accepts it as settled and abandons the fight against this social proscription.

And thus goes segregation, which is the most far-reaching development in the history of the Negro since the enslavement of the race. In fact, it is a sequel of slavery. It has been made possible by our system of mis-educating innocent people who did not know what was happening. It is so subtle that men have participated in promoting it without knowing what they were doing.

There are a few defenders of segregation who are doubtless sincere. Although nominally free they have never been sufficiently enlightened to see the matter other than as slaves. One can cite cases of Negroes who opposed emancipation and denounced the abolitionists. A few who became free re-enslaved themselves. A still larger number made no effort to become free because they did not want to disconnect themselves from their masters, and their kind still object to full freedom.

Ever since the Civil War when Negroes were first given a chance to participate in the management of their affairs they have been inconsistent and compromising. They have tried to gain one thing on one day by insisting on equality for all, while at the same time endeavoring to gain another point the next day by segregation. At one moment Negroes fight for the principle of democracy, and at the very next moment they barter it away for some temporary advantage. You cannot have a thing and dispose of it at the same time.

For example, the Negro political leaders of the Reconstruction period clamored for suffrage and the right of holding office, serving in the militia, and sitting on the jury; but few of them wanted white and colored children to attend the same school. When expressing themselves on education most of them took the position of segregationists; and Charles Sumner[1] in his fight for the civil rights of the Negro had to eliminate mixed schools from his program not only because many whites objected but also because the Negroes themselves did not seem to want them. All of these leaders might not have been looking for jobs in those days; but as nominal freemen, who were still slaves, they did not feel comfortable in the presence of their former masters.

These timorous men were very much like home Negroes who were employed near the author's home in Virginia by a Northern farmer, who had moved into the State after the Civil War. When breakfast time came the first morning he called them in to eat at the table with his family. These actual slaves, however, immediately lost their appetite. One finally called the employer aside and settled the matter in another way. He said:

---

1. White American antislavery leader and member of the Radical Republicans in the U.S. Senate (1811–74).

"Now boss, you ain't used to de rules ob dis country. We just can't sit at de table wid wite folks. We been use ter eating a cake er bread out yonder 'tween de plow handles. Les us go out dar."

The system, therefore, has extended from one thing to another until the Negroes today find themselves hedged in by the color bar almost every way they turn; and, set off by themselves, the Negroes cannot learn from the example of others with whom they might come into contact. In the ghetto, too, they are not permitted to construct and carry out a program of their own. These segregating institutions interfere with the development of self-help among Negroes, for often Negroes fail to raise money to establish institutions which they might control, but they readily contribute large sums for institutions which segregate persons of African blood.

Denied participation in the higher things of life, the "educated" Negro himself joins, too, with ill-designing persons to handicap his people by systematized exploitation. Feeling that the case of the Negro is hopeless, the "educated" Negro decides upon the course of personally profiting by whatever he can do in using these people as a means to an end. He grins in their faces while "extracting money" from them, but his heart shows no fond attachment to their despised cause. With a little larger income than they receive, he can make himself somewhat comfortable in the ghetto; and he forgets those who have no way of escape.

Some of this "educated" class join with unprincipled real estate men in keeping Negroes out of desirable parts of the city and confining them to unsanitary sections. Such persons help the profiteer to collect from Negroes thus cornered a larger rental than that exacted from whites for the same property. In similar fashion a Negro minister sometimes goes into a community where the races are moving along amicably together in their churches and rents a shack or an old empty store to start a separate church for "our people," not to supply any practical need but to exploit those who have never learned to think. Professional men, too, walking in their footsteps, impose also upon the poor innocent Negroes, who do not know when they are being treated properly and when they are not, but

high fees may be obtained from them inasmuch as they cannot always go to others for service.

Settling in a community with mixed schools, the educated Negro often advocates their separation that his daughter may secure a position in the system. The Negro politician is accustomed to corner the Negro vote, by opening a separate office from which he may bargain with the chieftains of the machine for the highest price available. When paid off by some position, which is not very lofty, this office-holder accepts such employment with the understanding that he will be set off by himself as if he were destructive of the rest of mankind.

In the present crisis, however, the "highly educated" Negroes find very little to exploit, and in their untoward condition they have no program of finding a way out. They see numerous instances of Negroes losing their jobs in white establishments. In fact, these things occur daily. Janitors who have been giving satisfaction are abruptly told that they will no longer be needed. Negro waiters in hotels are being informed that their places will go to white workers. Negro truck drivers are ordered to step down and let the needy of the other race go up. We hear so much of this that we wonder what the outcome will be.

In this readjustment, of course, when there are fewer opportunities left for those who cannot or do not have the opportunity to operate machines the Negroes will naturally be turned out of their positions by their employer who think first of their own race. In the ultimate passing of the depression, however, Negroes will not be much better off when some of the whites now displacing them will rise to higher levels. In the economic order of tomorrow there will be little use for the factotum or scullion. Man will not need such personal attention when he can buy a machine to serve him more efficiently. The menial Negroes, the aggregate of parasites whom the "highly educated" Negro has exploited, will not be needed on tomorrow. What, then, will become of "our highly educated" Negroes who have no initiative?

We have appealed to the talented tenth for a remedy,[2] but they have nothing to offer. Their minds

---

2. African Americans with the potential to be leaders; see 1903 article by W. E. B. Du Bois (p. 230) urging higher education to develop the "Talented Tenth."

have never functioned in this all-important sphere. The "educated" Negro shows no evidence of vision. He should see a new picture. The Negroes are facing the alternative of rising in the sphere of production to supply their proportion of the manufacturers and merchants or of going down to the graves of paupers. The Negro must now do for himself or die out as the world undergoes readjustment. If the whites are to continue for some time in doing drudgery to the exclusion of Negroes, the latter must find another way out. Nothing forces this upon one more dramatically than when he learns that white women in Montgomery, Alabama, are coming to the back door of Negro homes asking for their washing. If the whites have reached this extremity, and they must be taken care of first, what will be left for the Negroes?

At this moment, then, the Negroes must begin to do the very thing which they have been taught that they cannot do. They still have some money, and they have needs to supply. They must begin immediately to pool their earnings and organize industries to participate in supplying social and economic demands. If the Negroes are to remain forever removed from the producing atmosphere, and the present discrimination continues, there will be nothing left for them to do.

There is no reason for lack of confidence because of the recent failure of Negro enterprises, although the "highly educated" Negroes assert the contrary. This lack of confidence is the cause of the failure of these enterprises. If the Negroes had manifested enough confidence in them and had properly supported them, they would have been strong enough to stand the test in the crisis. Negro banks, as a rule, have failed because the people, taught that their own pioneers in business cannot function in this sphere, withdrew their deposits. An individual cannot live after you extract the blood from his veins. The strongest bank in the United States will last only so long as the people will have sufficient confidence in it to keep their money there. In fact, the confidence of the people is worth more than money.

The lack of confidence of the Negro in himself and in his possibilities is what has kept him down. His mis-education has been a perfect success in this respect. Yet it is not necessary for the Negro to have more confidence in his own workers than in others. If the Negro would be as fair to his own as he has been to others, this would be all that is necessary to give him a new lease on life and start the trend upward.

Here we find that the Negro has failed to recover from his slavish habit of berating his own and worshipping others as perfect beings. No progress has been made in this respect because the more "education" the Negro gets the worse off he is. He has just had so much longer to learn to decry and despise himself. The race looking to this educated class for a solution of its problems does not find any remedy; and, on the contrary, sees itself further and further away from those things to which it has aspired. By forgetting the schoolroom for the time being and relying upon an awakening of the masses through adult education we can do much to give the Negro a new point of view with respect to economic enterprise and group cooperation. The average Negro has not been sufficiently mis-educated to become hopeless.

Our minds must become sufficiently developed to use segregation to kill segregation, and thus bring to pass that ancient and yet modern prophecy, "The wrath of man shall praise thee."[3] If the Negro in the ghetto must eternally be fed by the hand that pushes him into the ghetto, he will never become strong enough to get out of the ghetto. This assumption of Negro leadership in the ghetto, then, must not be confined to matters of religion, education, and social uplift; it must deal with such fundamental forces in life as make these things possible. If the Negro area, however, is to continue as a district supported wholly from without, the inept dwellers therein will merit and will receive only the contempt of those who may occasionally catch glimpses of them in their plight.

As Frederick Douglass said in 1852, "It is vain that we talk of being men, if we do not the work of men. We must become valuable to society in other departments of industry than those servile ones from which we are rapidly being excluded. We must show that we can do as well as they. When we can build as well as live in houses; when we can make as well as wear shoes; when

---

3. Psalms 76:10.

we can produce as well as consume wheat, corn and rye—then we shall become valuable to society.

"Society," continued Douglass, "is a hard hearted affair. With it the helpless may expect no higher dig-

nity than that of paupers. The individual must lay society under obligation to him or society will honor him only as a stranger and sojourner."[4]

Lelia B. Strayhorn, Vivian Freeman, Kay Cremin, and Mildred E. Delaney

from Round Table: Should Negroes Attend Mixed or Negro Colleges? [1945]

In 1945, *Negro Digest* held an essay contest for college students on the topic "Should Negroes Attend Mixed or Negro Colleges?" Winning entries appeared in the July 1945 issue, along with a national poll on the question, which showed responses divided most dramatically along regional lines, with more subtle differences along racial lines. The majority of northern and western African Americans favored black colleges over mixed institutions, with less than a third declaring themselves undecided. Northern and western white Americans also favored mixed colleges over black colleges, but the margin was much narrower, with the largest category of responses listed as undecided. In the South, the response was just the reverse, with both black and white Americans favoring black institutions over mixed ones, and a greater proportion of southern respondents had opinions on the subject than did respondents in the other regions. Southern black Americans chose black schools two to one, with only 19 percent undecided. Southern white Americans proved strikingly united on the issue, with 94 percent favoring black schools, 1 per-

cent preferring mixed schools, and only 5 percent undecided.

The winning essay supporting mixed institutions, by a midwesterner, Lelia B. Strayhorn, links black institutions to segregation and focuses on the need to educate white people about black people. An essay that was accorded honorable mention, by northerner Kay Cremin (the only white student among the contest winners), also focuses on the power of mixed institutions to break down white stereotypes about black people. The winning essay supporting separate black colleges focuses not on what black students can teach their white contemporaries but, rather, on the college experience for black students. While Strayhorn and Cremin view integrated campuses as providing an opportunity—even as having an obligation—to diminish white prejudice, the Fisk University student, Vivian Freeman, perceives battles about race as distractions from academic study. The honorable mention essay by Mildred E. Delaney, a northern black student, also focuses on the positive influence that separate colleges have on black students.

From *Negro Digest,* July 1945, pp. 71–77.

Mixed: By Lelia B. Strayhorn

I believe that Negroes should accept democracy whenever and wherever it is offered. I believe that Negro students should attend mixed colleges even if it were possible to obtain an equal education in a Negro college. Free colleges, open to all irrespective of race or color, are no more than what is to be expected in a democracy. In semi-democratic America, the free col-

lege can be a powerful instrument for the attaining of real democracy in other aspects of American life.

Today the word "democracy" is used too glibly. Negroes especially are forever prating about it; yet by our very actions we prove that we do not in reality want democracy at all. Complete consolidation of the school systems in America is essential if we mean to practice democracy; yet some of us prefer to attend Negro colleges.

4. From "Learn Trades or Starve" published in *Frederick Douglass' Paper* March 4, 1853.

This means, of course, that if Negroes do not attend in large numbers the existing mixed colleges, the contribution that higher education can make to the integration of the Negro into American society will be pushed farther and farther into the future. As long as Negro students make demands upon the various states for "separate but equal" education, Negro colleges will be enlarged. As Negro institutions grow, Jim Crow education becomes more firmly rooted.

Negroes can get equal educational opportunities only by attending mixed schools because there is no such thing as "separate but equal" education. The very undemocratic spirit which segregates us also provides us inferior makeshift schools operated on limited budgets.

In most mixed schools, Negroes are free to use all equipment and facilities, and are taught by the same professors as are the whites. Therefore, they have equal educational opportunities. There can be no double standard. An "A" earned in a mixed college by a Negro student will be accepted at face value by any college. Students transferring from Negro to mixed colleges sometimes find that some of their credits are not acceptable and they are therefore admitted on condition.

In mixed colleges where little or no attention is given to the Negro problem, the Negro student can render a service to democracy by urging that courses in the social sciences pay adequate attention to the role of the Negro in the development of the nation. Only thus can white students gain sufficient knowledge of the Negro's background, and only by such a knowledge can he realize the common destiny of all American citizens. God speed the day when the realization of that common destiny will make it unnecessary for colleges to teach anything but American history.

Another reason for attending a mixed college is that Negro students strive to excel in mixed colleges because they realize that they are competing with the best. They also realize that they are representing a racial group to white students who have never known any Negroes on their intellectual plane.

Negro students know that if the white student has had any personal contact with Negroes at all, usually he has met only the domestic worker with whom he has very little in common. If the attendance of Negroes at mixed colleges did nothing more than to show white students that all Negroes are not domestic workers, it would have served a useful purpose. Such acquaintances will give white students an opportunity to know, at first hand, that the stereotype presented to him in the movies, on the radio, and in a certain type of fiction are entirely false.

However, all the enemies of democracy are not white people. Negroes themselves need to be educated in race tolerance. There are many Negroes who, whether with good cause or not, actually hate all white people. The mixed college can help the Negro rid himself of the bitterness with which he regards the white race.

Negroes are a mystery to white people. Hardly a Negro can say that he has not at any time been approached by a white person who, with the utmost sincerity wants to ask such questions as these: (1) Are Negro babies born white and turn dark very soon after birth? (2) Why are Negroes so many different colors? (3) How do Negro girls fix their hair? (4) Do Negroes want to marry white people? (5) What kind of life does a Negro expect to live after death? (6) Are Negro men and women sexually better, but with less mentality than white men and women?

The mixed college provides an excellent opportunity to help educate white people respecting 13 million unknown American citizens who want to believe that democracy is intended for ALL of the people in America.

NEGRO: BY VIVIAN FREEMAN

Although Negro students have been faced with the question as to whether they should attend mixed or Negro colleges since 1856 when Wilberforce[1] was started, a solution is of great concern today. With the increased flow of money, more Negro students have found themselves in position financially to consider attending mixed colleges. The fact that more mixed colleges have opened their doors to Negro students in the last decade adds further complexity to the problem.

1. Historically black university established in 1856 in Wilberforce, Ohio.

In order to arrive at a wise solution it is necessary to examine some of the outstanding factors involved. The place of Negro students on the college campus and the effects produced must be considered.

Negro students can adjust themselves more readily at Negro colleges.

They are not subjected to a strained environment dominated by race prejudice. From past actions it is quite obvious that Negro students are not wanted in the best white colleges. By 1936 Vassar had graduated but one Negro and was ignorant of it at the time. Princeton has never admitted a Negro to its undergraduate school; Johns Hopkins admitted Negro students but refused to let them participate in field trials for the Olympic meet.

Such examples of discrimination show that in the mixed college the Negro student has to spend time breaking down barriers often in preference to his studies without assurance of favorable results. A college education is too serious to take such chances. In the Negro college the students have greater opportunities for social and extracurricular activities. Their sex associations are natural, and they may become members of Greek letter organizations if they desire. When Negroes on mixed campuses do establish fraternities, they have no representation on the Inter-Fraternal Council.

Since the Negro student belongs to a minority group, his social and economic background demands special attention. This the personnel departments of Negro colleges can do better, for they can secure the information with which to work. The student does not feel that someone is prying into his private affairs when questions are asked by his own group. Negroes have a natural tendency to give illusive information when approached by a white. Once a friend of mine filling out a questionnaire described his race as "human race" and his color as "high brown."

In attending Negro colleges the Negro student comes in contact with the best of his race. Some of the nationally recognized Negroes have been or are now instructors in Negro colleges—Dr. W. E. B. DuBois at Atlanta University; Dr. George Edmund Haynes, Dr. St. Elmo Brady, Dr. Charles S. Johnson, and Dr. James Weldon Johnson at Fisk; Dr. Charles Wesley and Dr. Alain Locke at Howard. Not only is there contact with prominent faculty members, but there are usually exceptional young people in the student body. Negro colleges are interested in the development of the race; therefore the student learns to understand his race and to appreciate the contributions Negroes have made to culture. These he would not be likely to learn in mixed colleges.

In his *Dusk of Dawn,* Dr. DuBois says:

"At Fisk, the problem of race was faced openly and essential racial equality asserted and natural inferiority strenuously denied . . . At Harvard, on the other hand, I began to face scientific race dogma . . . It was continually stressed in the community and in classes that there was a vast difference in the development of the whites and the 'lower' races; that this could be seen in the physical development of the Negro."

It is often argued that the Negro college does not prepare the student for life—first because his training is inferior and second because he cannot adjust himself to a mixed society. However, Negro education cannot be much inferior, for statistics show that graduates of Negro colleges have met the requirements for higher degrees of the leading universities. Between 1876 and 1936 one hundred forty Negro college graduates received Ph.D. degrees. Even granting the fact that mixed colleges have better organized curricula does not mean that Negro education is inferior. Education is not a mere matter of high scholarship; it is also developing a well-rounded personality that will best fit a student to meet the problems of living. As far as society is concerned, the Negro is only a segregated part of the mixed culture, so there is little adjusting to be done. All his close friends and associates will belong to his small world within.

Since Negro colleges were established for Negro students, and since they afford greater opportunities for character building, leadership, and service than do mixed colleges, Negro students should attend Negro colleges.

MIXED: BY KAY CREMIN

This is our hope: that our children will scoff at the dimensions of our problems; that "Which colleges for which color Americans?" will seem silly in 1970; that our children will not be able to say "All kids in my school are white."

They will note, as we did not, the parallel between entrance requirements to the Master Race and to some of our Better Colleges. They will be angry that their parents bled overseas to kill an idea flourishing at home. In a racial sense, they will be better brought up than we. If white and colored students struggle with the same theses from the same books on the same campuses and under the same dormitory roofs, our hope will be fulfilled.

Of course, the picture of black and white colleges is too extreme; many colleges admit men and women of all races. Racial qualifications are seldom printed in any catalogues, though it is a rare college which does not ask the race of the applicant. Statistics are few; we can only look around black-and-white campuses and see how few Negroes are enrolled. Are there racial quotas? Do colleges admit only enough Negroes to give the campus "a liberal air?" Have Negroes neither the money nor the proper secondary education? Do these sum it up, or are most colored students streaming into Negro colleges? Although mixed colleges may have bigger endowments and more famous professors, Negroes might understandably forego material advantages for four years of comparative respite from racial tension.

However, none of us can afford to prepare for living in a black or a white world; our world is international, interracial. To isolate ourselves racially in colleges is to scorn the tragic lesson of the pre–Pearl Harbor decade.

The buck has been passed from generation to generation on a million graduation platforms for half a century of Junes. Speakers have told each high-school class that it was "The Hope of America." If the class of 1945 is actually to produce a world of which they may be proud, colored and white students must end isolationism and work together, as their parents failed to do. We must have all races in our college classrooms, among our exchange students, and on our faculties. That done, we must so absorb ourselves in the real problems of our tremendous time that we will forget race entirely.

Were I the high-school graduation speaker for 1945's Negroes, I would ask how many consider themselves citizens first of the world, then of America, and lastly, if at all, of their race. I would say to them:

"America needs help from the strongest, wisest, and wittiest of Negro youth. These qualities are necessary; in mixed colleges Negroes move in a four-year spotlight and, inevitably, are judged as typical of thirteen million others. Not to feel martyred or superior or resentful of your contemporaries, even though you are living exhibits in visual education for them, will be most difficult of all. College-material Negroes have been unsubstantiated myths to many white students. Real estate restrictions, employment barriers, newspapers, radios, and movies present Negroes to them only as servants, entertainers, criminals, and bums. And where positive knowledge does not exist, misconceptions and generalizations thrive; glimpses of Robeson, Simms,[2] or DuBois are too rare to counteract such stereotypes. Many of the whites with whom you will live have been isolated and therefore are ignorant about you. Understanding this, you will help them.

"But race is a tertiary consideration; you are Americans, caring deeply about winning this war and a real peace. We all have heard windborne mutterings from Negro servicemen resentful of the possibility of losing a leg for democracy only to be jimcrowed in peace time. It is for you, in the colleges, to dissolve prejudice until returning colored veterans can see the walls sufficiently crumbled to quell their indignation.

"But the great reply transcends issues temporal as racial discrimination, dwarfs areas small as America. This war is unique books were burned, scholars saw twilight through barbed wire. This is a war against free minds. Early fascism worked effectively; for ten years, intellectual isolationism in America permitted near-strangulation of that freedom. To resurrect it and to guard it against apathy and isolationism is the task of democratic scholars.

"Ours is a job so big it mocks at separate camps. The battle must be waged by all who recognize in the attitude toward the Mind's freedom the primary bond or barrier between men, whatever their color."

2. Hilda Simms (1918–94), lead actress in 1944 Broadway production of *Anna Lucasta*, the first black-cast production on Broadway without a specifically racial theme; Paul Robeson, singer, actor, and activist.

NEGRO: BY MILDRED E. DELANEY

Too few Negroes know enough of the important role that the economic factor plays in the race problem; too many Negroes still believe in the fallacy of the "superior white race;" too few Negroes realize that not only whites but also Negroes would exploit them for their own selfish ends.

In the Negro college, one receives more abundant knowledge of the Negro and his problems. Sociology courses stress the social conditions of the Negro. These courses reveal how the customs and mores of the Negro people are not the outgrowth of an inferior race, but the result of social and economic oppression. They show the correlation between the Negro's living conditions and his tendencies toward crime.

There are Negro history courses which acquaint the student with the struggles and achievements of the Negro for several generations. Direct contact with his people is available to the student of the Negro college; he learns their attitudes; he better understands their actions; he realizes their shortcomings.

Most Negro colleges are located in Negro communities which afford the student a greater opportunity for direct contact with members of his race. In the community he meets in reality the social and economic conditions of the Negro. He may learn more about their manner of living, and the social factors which are involved.

The student of a Negro college gains self-confidence which is conducive to leadership. He may ask questions which baffle him regarding his unfair status in society without fear of being rebuffed. He is given the opportunity to participate in all campus activities. He need not fear unfair recognition in his classes because of color. He may attend the social functions without having to take a back seat. With these liberties a realization grows within him that he is capable of accomplishing feats as great as those accomplished by other individuals.

Without ample knowledge of the problems which prevail among the Negro people, it is impossible for one to direct his actions profitably in diminishing them. Without the ability of leadership, one would be unable to execute his knowledge regardless of its potential value. Adequate knowledge and the ability of leadership are indispensable in diminishing the excessive ignorance of the Negro, and the pathway which leads to the attainment of these two qualities is the Negro college.

On Father Divine's Peace Mission

FATHER DIVINE: from *As a Man Thinketh in His Heart So Is He* [1936]
MARCUS GARVEY: *Big Conference of UNIA in Canada* [1936]

After emerging in Brooklyn around 1919, Father Divine's Peace Mission reached the zenith of its popularity during the Great Depression. Father Major Jealous Divine (born George Baker around 1880) founded Peace Missions across the country, presenting himself as the "Second Coming of Christ" and offering a ministry of racial and gender equality. Some of Divine's followers were former members of Marcus Garvey's Universal Negro Improvement Association (UNIA), which lost momentum after Garvey's conviction on mail-fraud charges and his deportation in 1927 (see p. 278). The two movements had much in common. Both featured a charismatic leader, promoted a program of economic enterprise and political engagement, offered their members concrete benefits, such as jobs, and proved especially appealing to lower-income African Americans. Such similarities helped smooth the transition to the Peace Mission movement for some former Garveyites in the late 1920s and early 1930s, even though Garvey was becoming an increasingly vocal critic of Father Divine during that period.

Garvey focused his criticism on Divine's claim to be God and his movement's principle of celibacy, which Garvey linked to race suicide. Those criticisms were fueled by the increasing popularity of Divine's movement, which offered alternative views on race, gender, and national affiliation. While Garvey stressed race-based politics, Divine emphasized a race-neutral outlook, referring to himself and his followers simply as "American." Divine further defied social convention by establishing interracial communal housing and by marrying (despite the movement's celibacy requirement) a twenty-one-year-old white Canadian, a woman more than forty years his junior, after the death of his first wife. While the UNIA attracted more men than women, Father Divine's movement consisted mostly of women, who were drawn in part by its rejection of gender categorizations. Finally, in contrast to Garvey's African-centered black nationalism, Divine promoted a version of American patriotism that characterized the U.S. Constitution and Declaration of Independence as divinely inspired.

FATHER DIVINE

from *As a Man Thinketh in His Heart So Is He* [1936]

GOD WILL TAKE CARE OF YOU

When GOD's Body, in which I AM now living, went through thirty-two lynch mobs without a thought of prevention and without a thought of prohibition, refusing to allow MYSELF to place MYSELF in a way where there would be a visible prohibition and possible prevention, but that the prevention would come from within ME, as the Master of Omnipotency and the Controller of your destiny—when you can stand before bayonets and guns, when you can stand before everything that may come, and praise GOD wholeheartedly and refuse to fret or murmur, refuse to tremble, but stand in the liberty upon the promises I have given, you can relax your conscious mentality then and there, and know GOD will take care of you.

When you sang the song, "GOD will take care of you," this is not a supposition, this is not an imagination, this is not merely to be sung for to be reiterated, and to be repeated and spoken as a melody, but it is a song sung. When it is reiterated spontaneously by the true and the faithful, if you say it sincerely and mean it sincerely, the very reaction of your conscious conviction according to your sincerity will respond within you. Oh it is something to consider! That is why the vibrations are so high here; it is because the believers are sincere. It is because they will not say it unless they mean it! If they happen to start to say it and do not mean it, I will change the version instantaneously and cause the reincarnation of sincerity, and quicken the Spirit of the meaning and cause them to mean it and sing it sincerely. Oh it is indeed Wonderful!

When you live in this recognition and dial in on it continually, in other words, keep your dials on this number, you will not have to dial in on it continually, for the dials being on this number, when the Message is broadcast, the Message will come forth through the station, therefore you will receive it.

REALNESS OF GOD

There are many things I could say, but I feel if I refrain from speaking Personally you may relax yourselves individually a little more that MY Spirit might tell you. If you relax your conscious thinking and allow MY Spirit to tell you, then and there the Scripture is fulfilled within you, "It is better revealed than told." GOD in the midst of you, I say, is mighty to save—to bring about the conditions you have been seeking, and to adjust matters satisfactorily. When you realize it, you can be still; you can still yourselves personally and know GOD is real.

I heard you say, "FATHER is real." As real as you see ME to be, even so real will I be to thee. The realness is created between you and the object you visualize to be real or unreal, but especially of GOD. As you visualize HIM to be, so will it be with thee. Now isn't that Wonderful! There are those who have not seen ME Personally, but merely thought on ME vividly. Through vividly thinking on ME harmoniously, harmonious conditions resulted in the place of inharmony, sickness, diseases, and corruption. That is the mystery! With harmonious thoughts in the positive direction, by concentrating on the Perfect Person, the reaction of your concentration was the result. That result was the desirable condition. By the desirable you had visualized vividly the reaction of the nature and the characteristics of such an expres-

sion was reincarnated in you through transmission, by concentrating on ME as an Individual.

TRY ME NOW

I believe I have said enough to stir up your pure minds, but I desire to see others in this land of Perfection, even as those of you MY Followers concentrated on this light of understanding and concentrating on it harmoniously, the reaction of your concentration will bring an harmonious and a desirable result, and you will be abundantly blessed. Oh, it is something to consider! I stress it vividly, because if you will only try ME without coming near ME Personally—TRY ME NOW! I heard one say by composition, "I tried everything but it failed." Now TRY ME! It is indeed Wonderful! You need not come near ME Personally to concentrate on the Impersonal Presence, and yet PERSONIFIED as I AM expressing it. The contact through your concentration will bring harmonious conditions immediately. Tell all of your friends, whether they be in trouble through sickness, afflictions, diseases, or disappointments and failures, whatsoever may be the cause, if you concentrate on ME harmoniously I will answer your heart's faintest cry. . . .

"WE SHALL HAVE A RIGHTEOUS GOVERNMENT"

> RIGHTEOUSNESS, JUSTICE AND TRUTH
> Shall have access in the land;
> These together with MERCY shall govern every
>   man;
> EQUITY and FAIR DEALING exercised on every hand,
> For GOD is REIGNING now!

Chorus

> Now we have a righteous Government,
> Now we have a righteous Government,
> Now we have a righteous Government,
> For GOD is reigning now.

Verses

(2)

> Crime, vice, and corruption shall never more have
>   sway,

In these transformed Temples from which sin is washed
   away;
GOD is dwelling in them and forever HE shall stay,
For GOD is reigning now.

(3)

Every unjust official shall be moved off of the bench;
No more political corruption, no more judicial stench,
No more fraud and gambling shall be practiced in our
   defense,
For GOD is reigning now.

(4)

The Kingdom it has come and the Will is being done;
All men have been brought together and unified in ONE:
No more separation, for GOD HIMSELF has come,
And HE is reigning now!

(5)

No races, creeds nor colors shall be known here in this land;
We all shall be UNITED in just one big Holy Band.
GOD HIMSELF is ruling, for the time is out for man,
Since GOD is reigning now.

(6)

GOD's condescension to us to bring Heaven to the earth,
Was to bring about Salvation of mankind's mortal birth,
And thus fulfil the Scriptures that "the last shall be the
   first,"[1]
For GOD is reigning now.

(7)

This happy day has dawned for all since FATHER DIVINE is
   here,
For in HIS precious BODY HE has made HIS meaning clear:
That the Righteous, Just and True Ones now have nothing
   more to fear,
For GOD is reigning now.

(Presented—January 10, 11, 12, 1936 A.D.F.D.)[2]

From *The New Day,* July 9, 1936.

MARCUS GARVEY
Big Conference of UNIA in Canada
[1936]

BIG CONFERENCE OF U.N.I.A. IN CANADA

Several of the Divisions of the Universal Negro
Improvement Association and Garvey Clubs of the
United States of America and Canada were called
together at a Conference in Toronto from the 20th to
the 25th August, by the President-General,[1] who jour-
neyed from the Headquarters of the Association in
London to preside over the gathering. A large number
of representatives came from the United States and
Canada and the Conference was indeed a magnificent
success. The spirit that was shown was something most
unique, and a positive demonstration of the present
serious mind and attitude of those who are identified
with the Universal Negro Improvement Association.
The Conference was held in Community Hall, 355, College Street, local Headquarters and Liberty Hall of the
Toronto Division of the Universal Negro Improvement
Association, of which Barrister J. Spencer Pitt is President. Matters of vital importance were discussed and
the President-General took the opportunity of addressing the representatives on many occasions, further educating them in the new policy of the Universal Negro
Improvement Association. The Sessions could be considered as a College Course to leaders of the movement,
and from all appearances the hundreds of representatives benefited greatly and showed a wonderful spirit of
reception. The details of the Conference are not for publication, as they are of an executive nature affecting the
good and welfare of the Organization in the United
States and Canada. Before the adjournment of the Conference several important resolutions were drafted, discussed, and passed, among them the following:—

Father Divine Exposed

WHEREAS the activities in the United States of America of one J. M. Divine,[2] commonly referred to as

---

1. Matthew 20:16.
2. Anno Domini Father Divine, *in the year of our Lord Father Divine* [Medieval Latin].
1. Marcus Garvey.
2. Father Divine used the initials M. J. for Major Jealous.

"Father Divine," tend religiously and morally to upset the mental and spiritual equilibrium of a certain number and type of heretofore normal minded persons, and;

WHEREAS the said J. M. Divine impresses himself upon the said people as God Almighty and refers to himself as God, and attempts to behave as if he were such, thereby having his followers to refer to him as God Almighty, the one and only God of heaven and earth, and;

WHEREAS this doctrine and profession of being God Almighty, which makes him absolute in himself as a creator and dispenser of all spirit and life, is vile, and;

WHEREAS this constitutes blasphemy of the worst kind;

BE IT RESOLVED: that this conference of representative delegates of the Universal Negro Improvement Association of the United States of America and Canada, assembled at Community Hall, 355, College Street, Toronto, Canada, do hereby declare the said J. M. Divine blasphemous in his doctrine and do advise all sane, intelligent, and self-respecting Negroes throughout the United States of America and Canada not to accept and follow the blasphemous doctrine, as by so doing it constitutes a spiritual condemnation of the soul of the believer and separates the said soul from the spirit of the One True and Living God, and;

That the said doctrine is wors[e] than paganism and heathenism and idolatry in all shape and form and is surprising as a product of 20th century civilization

And that the belief in and practice of such a faith constitute the stigma of the grossest ignorance and backwardness on the part of any people in the civilization of the 20th century, and;

WHEREAS the said J. M. Divine is causing his followers and particularly of the Negro race to surrender their properties to him in his so-called kingdoms (real, personal and otherwise), including their immediate savings of money, before they may become members of his kingdom (and that is actually being done), that such persons be advised that in the expression of modern American terminology this constitutes a "colossal racket," the result of which will lead to the complete pauperization of each and every such person who surrenders his property or his values, in that, the Great God of heaven and the Creator of the universe needs no material properties or values because He is the Creator of all, and;

WHEREAS the said J. M. Divine is surrounded by a coterie of white men and women whose motives are questionable, it is to be suspected that this "colossal racket" has been originated for the purpose of destroying religiously, morally, socially, politically, and financially, the character and standing of the Negro race in the United States of America, thereby exposing the progressive and intelligent Negroes in the North of the United States to the same reaction of their white fellow citizens as happened to the Negroes in the South of the United States during the period of Reconstruction when the carpet-bagger[3] exercised a similar and unholy influence over the Negro, causing him to lose his franchise as an American citizen, which up to the present he has not recovered, and;

WHEREAS the said J. M. Divine make[s] it a condition that all members of his kingdoms must separate themselves sexually from the bond of matrimony and not to reproduce the species of the race by having children,

BE IT RESOLVED: That this constitutes a gross attempt at race suicide, leading to the complete extermination of the Negro race in the United States in one generation, and that this unholy practice should be condemned, and;

WHEREAS it appears that the said J. M. Divine is bestowing charity upon those who enter his kingdoms and that it is a great incentive and attraction to become members thereof, that it be known that the supposed charity dispensed by the said J. M. Divine comes from no other source than that contributed by the people themselves, who surrender their property, real, personal and financial, to this supposed god, who cashes in on the said properties and appropriate[s] for this supposed charity as much as he and his confederates deem necessary for the purpose of attracting other subjects who, in turn, will also surrender their properties and values,

---

3. Disparaging term used by southerners to describe northerners who came to the South after the Civil War, drawn by political and economic opportunities.

and that it is anticipated that when the said J. M. Divine and his collaborators have accumulated all that is possible from the people they'll cease to function charitably and will disappear with the accumulated assets of their unfortunate subjects, when it will appear that the said Father Divine, as god, has gone to his spiritual kingdom, at which time his subjects and followers will be left at the mercy of circumstances and become a charge upon the society of their environment, and;

WHEREAS it is not the intention of this conference to do any injury or harm to anyone.

BE IT RESOLVED: That any attempt to expose the activities of the said J. M. Divine be not interpreted to mean an effort to destroy him by any process of persecution, but that he be severely let alone to suffer for his own sins as expressed in his blasphemy of being Almighty God.

The resolution bearing on the conduct of Fr. Divine brought out testimonies of the most grave nature, showing how this man has been corrupting the religious and ethical morals of the people of the United States and actually playing into the hands of those Negro haters who are endeavouring to exterminate the race in every way possible. It was suggested that Fr. Divine is being subsidized by such persons and Organizations who desire the complete corruption and ultimate extermination of the race and that his cult practice is most offensive and detrimental to the interest of the group. As proof of the state of mind of the followers of Fr. Divine who claims to be God Almighty, and who is being followed by the adherents as such, the following communication is reproduced for general information:

Brooklyn, New York, N.Y.
March 13th, 1936, A.D.F.D.

"PEACE"

Marcus Garvey,
2, Beaumont Crescent, West Kensington,
London, W.14, England

MY DEAR MR. GARVEY,

Because of that brotherly love in my heart for you (not racial love), I am prompted to write you these few loving lines, hoping sincerely that you may receive them in the spirit they are given.

CONNECTION. You will be able to recognize the name, when you were in Atlanta prison I sent you a little money by Mrs. Garvey; when you were in England, 1929, I did the same. From Jamaica, when you sent out the tickets for the International Drawing, you sent me one. I sold the tickets, sent you the money, two days, later, the postal officials notified me to come and get the money back, so I did and I told them a piece of my mind. Your mail was censured, so I refunded the money. I mention this to prove my close affiliation, connection and activity in the U.N.I.A. at that time, and from that standpoint and in the Spirit of Brotherly Love, I am prompted to write you. In all seriousness, in all earnestness, using that limited expression "Garveyism" was the highest grace this so-called race had, according to the division among the sons of earth. But to-day a greater than Garvey is here. Shiloh[4] has truly come unto whom shall the gathering of the Nations be. When the Spirit of Truth is come, we need no man to teach us, and HE has come in reality. Knowing my past loyalty and devotion to the U.N.I.A., a present member called my attention to the "Black Man,"[5] of which I bought a copy, and upon reading I discovered that you had forgotten what you told us on more than one occasion, that GOD is supposed to be looking like us. Did you not—in your article under the heading "Father Divine as God"—it is not "as GOD" but it is "IS GOD." You said there are people around HIM in HIS Presence who really think that HE is GOD, and some of them are not what we call the ordinary ignorant people, and you are right. Because government officials, from all over the civilized world, including Washington, D.C., are recognizing HIM as the very same CHRIST of 1900 years ago. Professors from Universities, Ministers in groups, Politicians in groups weekly, Metaphysicians, Psychologists, Principals of schools, Teachers, Scientists, men of all walks

4. Reference to Joshua 18:1, "And the whole congregation of the children of Israel assembled together at Shiloh, and set up the tabernacle of the congregation there. And the land was subdued before them."
5. Garvey published *The Black Man: A Monthly Magazine of Negro Thought and Opinion* from 1933 to 1939.

of life, are seeking HIM. Why—because HE heals the sick; HE raises the dead; He gives sight to the blind, causes the deaf to hear, looses the tongue of the dumb, feeds the hungry, shelters the homeless, clothes the naked and preaches the Gospel to the poor. That is the reason people from every walk of life and from all parts of the world are flocking to HIM, because HE gives far exceeding abundant more than you or any other "man" could ever offer. You end up by calling attention to the news of the fictitious baby and you say it is a disgrace, before man and God, sure enough you would have heard of that; but we here in New York who know the sister, know that there was nothing said in that light. The source from which you draw such information is the very source which helps to undermine, mis-direct and mis-lead and mis-interpret that powerful movement to which you gave birth, that helped this so-called race so much until FATHER DIVINE, GOD ALMIGHTY manifested HIMSELF; you were regarded as the world's most fearless leader in this present civilization before the coming of FATHER DIVINE.

You know how you were humiliated in every way imaginable by the forces directed against RIGHTEOUSNESS, JUSTICE and TRUTH and that should be a landmark in your memory. I am not surprised, however, because you are no exception; you know no more who FATHER DIVINE is than any of us did, few of us who did not condemn or criticise HIM until we were convinced who HE really is. Then in shame we called on HIS NAME and were healed of all our diseases and afflictions. Now I am wondering how one of your calibre would so grossly criticise and be criticising without considering, but those of us who have followed under your leadership are acquainted with the fact that you are asthmatic and can assure you that if you in all sincerity call on the Name of FATHER DIVINE you will be instantly healed. Please try HIM out as 23,000,000 of us did; you need HIM as all the World does. In this so-called depression and crisis FATHER DIVINE, GOD in Reality, has taken thousands from the City charge and from off relief and still more thousands out of the breadlines. I am a living witness of what I am talking about. When I was a member of the U.N.I.A. and you appealed for funds I would be very grieved to know I could not help in proportion to my love for the cause, but now FATHER DIVINE has lifted me out of all lacks and wants. This you could not do, or any other man, although your intentions and desires are good and your ideals are still high.

You see, Mr. Garvey, in you and I lies nothing but matter, which fades away like a flower, but in FATHER DIVINE dwelleth all the fullness of the GODHEAD BODILY, HE neither fades nor wanes, but of HIS Increase and Power, and of HIS KINGDOM, there shall be no end. This TRUTH is so dynamic, so convincing and far-reaching, that it is sweeping aside every barrier, overcoming all seeming opposition and drawing all humanity unto itself, melting us down in the melting pot of LOVE and rising together as "one man at Jerusalem" out of races, creeds, colours, denominations, nationalism, theories, and doctrines, recognizing only that sacred duty, "THE BROTHERHOOD OF MAN—and the FATHERHOOD OF GOD."

We no doubt have done our best, but our best is only filthy rags in the sight of GOD ALMIGHTY, FATHER DIVINE. In fact our best was mere talk and confusion, nothing practical in deeds nor actions; but since FATHER DIVINE came, HE has put HIS SPIRIT in us and causes us to be walking in HIS STATUTES and we are now expressing HIM in deeds and in actions. I am calling your attention for a moment to the great miraculous transformation of Harlem, not "reformation" but Transformation!

1. FATHER DIVINE has overflowed the evening schools, in New York City, Brooklyn, and Newark, New Jersey especially, with thousands of HIS followers;

2. HE is causing us to become American Citizens;

3. HE is teaching us the value of the Ballot, and how to use them and not the bullets;

4. In fact we have entered into the "Political Arena."

5. And tens of thousands have received Evangelical names and discarded those cursed slave names, and many of them have lost their identity since living Evangelical Lives. You could not identify many of them whom you once knew. In short FATHER DIVINE has transformed the degenerates of Harlem into Angels of Light and—the underworld into HEAVEN! HE has materialized the Spiritual expression of things and Spiritualized the expression of material things.

This is quite difficult, I know, for you to understand, but if we could understand GOD in every move, then HIS ways would not be past finding out. HE could not move in a mysterious way HIS Wonders to perform, as we are told. We could easily measure HIM with the measure of a man. But to the extreme opposite who can find out GOD by Wisdom.

Everything you told us has come true, whatsoever is done in secret shall be known on the housetops. FATHER DIVINE has told the Political and Religious World's especially, since HE came, they have no more cloak for sins, and if you read the daily papers, you no doubt will see HIS Spirit is cleaning up this Nation. Hundreds of Official offices are being investigated and a great number are indicted, 27 Judges in Pennsylvania were also indicted. The source of corruption of New York's vice and crime maintained its strong-hold for years, only four blocks away from the Police Headquarters, in Manhattan, and did not come to light, until FATHER DIVINE turned on the Search-Light. You see, Mr. Garvey, HE is that stone that is hewed out of the mountain and is grinding to powder everything it falls on, so that the Kingdoms of this World might become to be the Kingdom of our GOD and HIS CHRIST, which HE is establishing in RIGHTEOUSNESS, JUSTICE, and TRUTH.

I have sent you a copy of the RIGHTEOUS GOVERNMENT PLATFORM OF FATHER DIVINE'S PEACE MISSION MOVEMENT, a copy of the Constitution of the UNITED STATES and a Subscription to the "SPOKEN WORD" for three months, all of which will inform you better than any feeble tongue of mine in it's highest intellectual form, about FATHER DIVINE. Human tongue cannot explain FATHER DIVINE satisfactorily. You no doubt, Mr. Garvey, will discover that I made no attempt to attack, ridicule, criticise nor condemn, but to inform you of this TRUTH which has set more than 23,000,000 of us free of every race, and nation, creed and colour.

Now if you care to get first-hand information let me hear from you, if you wish to. I hope you will contact even as HE IS, for HE IS HEALTHY, JOYFUL, PEACEFUL, LIVELY, LOVING, SUCCESSFUL, PROSPEROUS, and HAPPY, in HIS SPIRIT, BODY and MIND and in every organ, muscle, sinew, vein, and bone and even in every atom, fibre, and cell of HIS BODILY FORM! Past member of U.N.I.A. Sincerely, I thank you, FATHER!

C. D. AUSTIN

From *The Black Man*, September–October 1936.

KEY DEBATE ～ *The Government: Civic Rights and Civic Duties*

RALPH ELLISON
Editorial Comment [1943]

Ralph Ellison's unsigned editorial comment, published in the Winter–Spring 1943 issue of *The Negro Quarterly,* offers an overview of different African American perspectives on World War II. Rather than accepting existing conditions wholesale or rejecting the conflict outright as yet another "white man's war," Ellison offers a middle ground of "critical participation," which allows for active engagement in the war effort while protesting racism in the military and at home. Ellison was the managing editor of *The Negro Quarterly,* published in 1942 and 1943. Although short-lived, the Communist-backed publication helped publicize the contributions of African Americans to the war effort and American society. In addition, the poems, essays, and articles it published—including works by Ellison, Langston Hughes (p. 362), and the novelist Richard Wright (p. 471)—explored the problems faced by black Americans at the time: Jim Crow segregation in the South and discrimination throughout the United States.

The middle ground of "critical participation"—to use Ellison's term—was widely supported by other African American publications. The *Chicago Defender,* for instance, promoted the popular Double V campaign, which advocated simultaneous resistance to fascism abroad and racial discrimination at home. In contrast, few published pieces expressed direct opposition to the war, as wartime prosecution of sedition stifled the publication of overt criticism of the government and its policies. Even those who simply voiced their dissent ran the risk of arrest. For example, Elijah Muhammad (p. 612), the head of the Nation of Islam, was prosecuted on the basis of evidence that he had given a pro-Japanese speech in August 1942 at his Chicago temple, in which he declared: "You shouldn't fear the devil when he tells you that you must go and fight in this war. You should refuse to fight. The newspapers are lying when they say the Japanese are losing. We are going to win." Muhammad was convicted of draft evasion and served four years in a federal prison.

Ralph Ellison was born in 1914 in Oklahoma City, only seven years after Oklahoma became a state. Growing up in a frontier state without a legacy of African slavery helped shape Ellison's views on the open-ended possibilities of America. His father died when he was three, and his mother supported Ellison and his younger brother with work as a maid. Ellison received a scholarship to the Tuskegee Institute, where he studied music from 1933 to 1936 and also discovered a love of modernist literature. He left Tuskegee after his third year and moved to New York City, where he studied sculpture and photography. There he met Richard Wright, who encouraged him to pursue a career in writing. Until World War II (when he joined the Merchant Marines), Ellison worked on writing book reviews, short stories, and articles, and also worked as an editor for *The Negro Quarterly.* After the war, Ellison concentrated on writing *Invisible Man* (1952), which won the National Book Award in 1953. Ellison moved to Rome, Italy, for several years, and then returned to the U.S. in 1958 to teach at Bard College. He began writing his second novel, *Juneteenth,* which he continued to work on for nearly four decades but never finished. Ellison published his first collection of essays, *Shadow and Act,* in 1964, and his second collection, *Going to the Territory,* in 1985. He taught extensively and received numerous literary awards before dying in 1994 of pancreatic cancer.

In his work, Ellison grappled with capturing the complexity of American experience, as he discussed in a 1960's interview:

> Power for the writer, it seems to me, lies in his ability to reveal—only a little bit more about the

complexity of humanity. And in this country, I think it's very, very important for the writer to, no matter what the agony of his experience, he should stick to what he's doing, because the slightest thing that is new or the slightest thing which has been overlooked, which would tell us about the unity of American experience, beyond all considerations of class, of race or religion are very, very important.

At his death, Ellison left behind numerous unpublished manuscripts. The stories were collected and published as *Flying Home: And Other Stories* in 1996. His novel *Juneteenth* was published posthumously in 1999, edited to 368 pages from over 2,000 pages of manuscript by his literary executor, the white American editor, writer, and professor John F. Callahan. In 2010, the *Juneteenth* manuscripts were published together as *Three Days Before the Shooting*.

From *The Negro Quarterly: A Review of Negro Life and Culture*, Winter–Spring 1943, 295–301.

By way of group self-examination it might be profitable to list a few of the general attitudes held by Negroes toward their war-time experiences.

First might be listed the attitude of unqualified acceptance of the limited opportunity for Negro participation in the conflict, whether in the war industries or in the armed forces. Along with this is found an acceptance of the violence and discrimination which so contradicts a war for the Four Freedoms.[1] This attitude is justified by the theory that for Negroes to speak out in their own interests would be to follow a "narrow Negro approach" and to disrupt war-unity. This attitude (sometimes honestly held) arises, on one hand, out of a lack of group self-consciousness which precluded any confidence in the Negro people's own judgment, or in its potentialities for realizing its own will. Others who voice this attitude, however, are simply expressing what they are paid to express. Still others suffer from what might be termed a "disintegration of the sense of group personality." For these the struggle has been too difficult; in order to survive they feel that Negroes must resort to the most vicious forms of uncle-tomism. Its most extreme expression, to date, has been Warren Brown's plaint—in the face of the United States' glaring jim crow system—that most of the Negro press desires to be "Negro first and American second." While another striking instance of it is seen among those Negro actors who continue to accept Hollywood's anti-Negro roles.

Back of this attitude lies a fear and uncertainty that is almost psychopathic. It results in the most disgusting forms of self-abasement. The decadent Negro counterpart of American rugged individualism, it would willingly have the Negro people accept the depths of degradation rather than risk offending white men by lifting a hand in its own defense. Men who hold this attitude are comfortable only when taking orders; they are happy only when being kicked. It is this basic attitude that produces the spy, the stool pigeon, and the agent provocateur—all of which types are found today among those who call themselves Negro leaders.

A second attitude encountered is that of *unqualified rejection*: of the war, of the Allies statement of their war aims, and of the role which Negroes have been elected to play in any of its phases. Arising out of a type of Negro nationalism which, in a sense, is admirable, it would settle all problems on the simple principle that Negroes deserve equal treatment with all other free human beings. It is this which motivates those Negroes who go to jail rather than endure the Jim Crow conditions in the Armed forces. It is the basis of Negro cynicism and it views every situation which requires Negroes to struggle against fascist forces within our own country as evidence that the United States is fighting a "white man's" war.

But this is the attitude of one who, driven into a corner, sees no way of asserting his manhood except to

---

1. Goals for all people articulated in a January 6, 1941, speech by President Franklin D. Roosevelt: freedom of speech, freedom of religion, freedom from want, and freedom from fear.

choose his own manner of dying. And during the folk period, before the Negro masses became politically conscious, such an attitude created folk heroes and gave birth to legend and folksong. For Negroes admire men who die rather than compromise their principles. But on the day John Henry's great heart burst in his struggle against the machine, this attitude became impractical. Today we live in a political world and such an attitude is inadequate to deal with its complex problems. Not that courageous display of manhood no longer has a place in our lives, but that when asserted blindly it results only in empty, individualistic action—or worse, admiration for the ruthless and violent *action* of fascism. Feeling that so much experience by Negroes in the U.S. is tinged with fascism, some Negroes went so far as to join the pro-Japanese Pacific Movement.

Superficially, this attitude seems the direct opposite of the first; and in basic human terms it is. Yet, when expressed in action in the present political situation it is revealed as a mere *inversion* of the first. For in its blind rejection it falls over backwards into an even blinder acceptance. Unconsciously it regards all acts of aggression against Negroes as inevitable, the forces behind these acts as invincible. Being blind it does not recognize that Negroes *have their own stake in the defeat of fascism*—which would be true even if white Americans were still practicing isolationism. It conceives of positive action for the Negro people only in terms of death—or passivity, which is another form of death. Individuals who hold this attitude become conscious of themselves as *Negroes* only in terms of dying; they visualize themselves only as followers, never as leaders. Deep down they see no possibility of an allied victory being a victory for Negroes as well as for others. Refusing to see the *peoples'* aspect of the war, they conceive of victory as the triumph of "good white men" over "bad white men"; never as the triumph of the common peoples of the world over those who foster decayed political forms and systems. Should "good white men" triumph they will, perhaps, *give* Negroes a few more opportunities. Should "bad white men" win, then things will continue as before, perhaps a little worse. And since during the course of the war the sincerity of even good white men frequently appears doubtful, the Negro can expect but little in any case.

This is a political form of self-pity, and an attitude of political children. Actually it holds no desire for Negroes to assume an adult role in government. And perhaps its most naive expression is found among those who, frustrated and impotent before the complex problems of the Negro situation, would resort to a primitive form of magic and solve the whole problem by simply abolishing the word *Negro* from the American language. It never occurs to them that no matter what name they give themselves that name will mean no more than they can *make* it mean. Nor do they understand that in the process of fighting for a free America and a free world, Negro Americans (insofar as they approach it consciously) are also creating themselves as a free people and as a nation.

Fortunately there is a third attitude. Also a manifestation of Negro nationalism, it is neither an attitude of blind acceptance, nor one of unqualified rejection. It is broader and more human than the first two attitudes; and it is scientific enough to make use of both by transforming them into strategies of struggle. It is committed to life and it holds that the main task of the Negro people is to work unceasingly toward creating those democratic conditions in which it can live and recreate itself. It believes the historical role of Negroes to be that of integrating the larger American nation and compelling it untiringly toward true freedom. And while it will have none of the slavishness of the first attitude, it is imaginative and flexible enough, to die if dying is forced upon it.

This is an attitude of critical participation, based upon a sharp sense of the Negro people's group personality. Which is the basis of its self-confidence and morale in this period of confusion. Thus, while affirming the justice of the Allies' cause, it never loses sight of the Negro peoples' stake in the struggle. This for them is the point of departure, a basic guide to theory and action which allows for objectivity and guards against both the fearful acceptance of the first and the sullen rejection of the second. It regards men unsentimentally; their virtues are evaluated and cherished, their weaknesses anticipated and guarded against. This attitude holds that any action which is advantageous to the United Nations must also be advantageous for the Negro and colonial peoples. Programs which would sacrifice the Negro or any other people are considered dangerous for the United Nations; and the only honorable course for Negroes to take is first to protest and then to fight against them. And while willing to give and take in the interest of national unity, it rejects that old pattern of American thought that regards any Negro demand for justice as an assault against the state. It believes that to fail to protest the wrongs done Negroes as we fight this war is to participate in a crime, not only against Negroes, but against all true anti-Fascists. To fight against defects in our prosecution of the war is regarded as a responsibility. To remain silent simply because friends commit these wrongs is no less dangerous than if Negroes should actively aid the enemy.

Recently this attitude has led Negroes to employ the contradictory tactic of withdrawal for the purpose of closer unity. It motivated Judge William H. Hastie's resignation from the War Department, where it was expected of him to remain silent while the window-dressing air school at Tuskegee was palmed off on the American people as the real thing. For Hastie this might have been an act of courage which lost him prestige among Fascist-minded whites, but it has made his name meaningful among thousands of Negroes, bringing eligibility for that support which is the basis of true leadership. One wonders when the other members of the so-called "Black Cabinet"[2] will learn this basic truth? As yet, however, this attitude is found implied in the sentiments of the Negro masses, rather than in the articulated programs of those who would lead them. Hastie's action is the first by a public figure.

The existence of the attitude, however, emphasizes more than ever before the need for representative Negroes to come to terms with their own group through a consideration of the major problems of our revolutionary times. First in terms of the problem of the centralization of political power. They must (1) see the Negro people realistically as a political and economic force which has, since the Civil War, figured vitally in the great contest for power between the two large economic groups within the country; that (2) despite the very real class divisions within the Negro group itself during periods of crisis—especially during periods of war—these divisions are partially suspended by outside pressures, making for a kind of group unity in which great potential political power becomes centralized—even though Negro leadership ignores its existence, or are too timid to seize and give it form and direction; that (3) although logically and historically the Negro's interests are one with those of Labor, this power is an objective force which might be channelized for Fascist ends as well as for democratic ones; and (4) that they as leaders have a responsibility in seeing to it that this vital force does not work for Fascism—either native or foreign. To the extent that Negro leadership ignores the power potential of the group, to that extent will the Negro people be exploited by others: either for the good ends of democratic groups or for the bad ends of Fascist groups. And they have the Civil War to teach them that no revolutionary situation in the United States will be carried any farther toward fulfilling the needs of Negroes than Negroes themselves are able, through a strategic application of their own power to make it go. As long as Negroes fail to centralize their power they will always play the role of a sacrificial goat; they will always be "expendable." Freedom, after all, cannot be imported or acquired through an act of philanthropy; it must be won.

In order to plan the direction of power, Negro leaders must obey the impetus toward Negro self-evaluation which the war has made a necessity. They must integrate themselves with the Negro masses; they must be constantly alert to new concepts, new techniques and new trends among other peoples and nations with an eye toward appropriating those which are valid when tested against the reality of Negro life. By the same test they must be just as alert to reject the faulty programs of their friends. When needed concepts, techniques or theories do not exist they must create them. Many new concepts will evolve when the people are closely studied in action. And it will be out of this process that true leadership will come; fortunately, the era of subsidized Negro leadership is fast pressing. Even the mild protest of a William Pickens[3]

2. An informal advisory group of African American community leaders, organized by President Franklin D. Roosevelt and First Lady Eleanor Roosevelt in the 1930s to help develop government policy, especially New Deal programs.
3. Educator, author and activist (1881–1954).

has become too radical for those who for years have pulled the strings of Negro middle class leadership.

A second problem for Negro leadership to master is that of accurately defining the relation between the increasing innovations in technology and the Negro people's political and economic survival and advancement. During the war the mastery of hitherto unavailable techniques by Negroes is equivalent to the winning of a major military objective: after the war they will be able to give leadership to the working class and that leadership always rests with those workers who are most skilled.

A third major problem, and one that is indispensible to the centralization and direction of power, is that of learning the meaning of the myths and symbols which abound among the Negro masses. For without this knowledge, leadership, no matter how correct its program, will fail. Much in Negro life remains a mystery; perhaps the zoot suit conceals profound political meaning; perhaps the symmetrical frenzy of the Lindy-hop[4] conceals clues to great potential power—if only Negro leaders would solve this riddle. On this knowledge depends the effectiveness of any slogan or tactic. For instance, it is obvious that Negro resentment over their treatment at the hands of their allies is justified. This naturally makes for resistance to our stated war aims, even though these aims are essentially correct; and they will be accepted by the Negro masses only to the extent that they are helped to see the bright star of their own hopes through the fog of their daily experiences. The problem is psychological; it will be solved only by a Negro leadership that is aware of the psychological attitudes and incipient forms of action which the black masses reveal in their emotion-charged myths, symbols and war-time folklore. Only through a skillful and wise manipulation of these centers of repressed social energy will Negro resentment, self-pity and indignation be channelized to cut through temporary issues and become transformed into positive action. This is not to make the problem simply one of words, but to recognize (as does the O.W.I.[5] with its fumbling *Negroes and the War* pamphlet) that words have their own vital importance.

Negro participation in other groups is valuable only to the extent that it is objectively aggressive and aware of this problem of self-knowledge. For no matter how sincere their intentions, misunderstandings between Negroes and whites are inevitable at this period of our history. And unless these leaders are objective and aggressive they have absolutely no possibility of leading the black masses—who are thoroughly experienced with leaders who, in all crucial situations, capitulate to whites—in any direction. Thus instead of participating along with labor and other progressive groups as equals with the adult responsibility of seeing to it that all policies are formulated and coordinated with full consideration of the complexities of the Negro situation, they will have in effect, chosen simply to be subsidized by Labor rather than by Capital.

Finally, the attitudes list above must be watched, whether displayed by individuals or organizations. They take many forms the first two being exploited by those who like the Negro best when he is unthinking or passive. The second will help only Fascism. The third contains the hope of the Negro people and is spreading; but these hopes can be used by the charlatan and agent provocateur as well as by the true leader. In this time of confusion many wild and aggressive-sounding programs will be expounded by Negroes who, seeking personal power, would lead the people along paths away from any creative action. Thus all programs must be measured coldly against reality. Both leaders and organizations must be measured not by their words, but by their actions.

---

4. Popular dance style developed during the 1920s and 1930s; zoot suit: style of suit from the 1930s and 1940s, featuring padded shoulders, wide lapels, and wide-legged pegged trousers.
5. Office of War Information.

The March on Washington Movement

A. PHILIP RANDOLPH: *Why Should We March?* [1942]

A. PHILIP RANDOLPH: *March on Washington Movement Flyer* [c. 1943]

In the first years of World War II, U.S. federal defense contracts were almost exclusively awarded to companies that only employed white workers. In 1940, for example, out of 100,000 aircraft workers, only 240 were black. In 1941, A. Philip Randolph (1889–1979), head of the powerful Brotherhood of Sleeping Car Porters, organized a mass march on Washington, D.C., to protest this systematic discrimination in wartime employment. Just days before 100,000 protesters were set to march, President Franklin Roosevelt signed Executive Order 8802, banning discrimination in government hiring.

In the 1942 article in *Survey Graphic* that is reprinted here, Randolph declares that the 1941 march on Washington was merely postponed. He situates the march not as an event that ended with Executive Order 8802 but as the beginning of a movement: the March on Washington Movement (MOWM). Declaring the movement "All-Negro and Pro-Negro" (partly as a way to avoid potential control by the Communist Party), Randolph organized a series of mass protests around the country using flyers such as the one reprinted here. Even though the MOWM stopped meeting in 1946, the movement paved the way for the effective use of civil disobedience during the civil rights movement, most notably the landmark 1963 March on Washington for Jobs and Freedom, initiated by Randolph and featuring Martin Luther King's "I Have a Dream" speech.

A. PHILIP RANDOLPH

Why Should We March? [1942]

Though I have found no Negroes who want to see the United Nations lose this war, I have found many who, before the war ends, want to see the stuffing knocked out of white supremacy and of empire over subject peoples. American Negroes, involved as we are in the general issues of the conflict, are confronted not with a choice but with the challenge both to win democracy for ourselves at home and to help win the war for democracy the world over.

There is no escape from the horns of this dilemma. There ought not to be escape. For if the war for democracy is not won abroad, the fight for democracy cannot be won at home. If this war cannot be won for the white peoples, it will not be won for the darker races.

Conversely, if freedom and equality are not vouchsafed the peoples of color, the war for democracy will not be won. Unless this double-barreled thesis is accepted and applied, the darker races will never wholeheartedly fight for the victory of the United Nations. That is why those familiar with the thinking of the American Negro have sensed his lack of enthusiasm, whether among the educated or uneducated, rich or poor, professional or nonprofessional, religious or secular, rural or urban, north, south, east, or west.

That is why questions are being raised by Negroes in church, labor union, and fraternal society; in poolroom, barbershop, schoolroom, hospital, hair-dressing parlor; on college campus, railroad, and bus. One can hear such questions asked as these: What have Negroes to fight for? What's the difference between Hitler and that "cracker" Talmadge of Georgia[1]? Why has a man got to be Jim Crowed to die for democracy? If you haven't got democracy yourself, how can you carry it to somebody else?

What are the reasons for this state of mind? The answer is: discrimination, segregation, Jim Crow.

1. Eugene Talmadge (1884–1946) white southern Democrat elected four times as governor of Georgia.

Witness the navy, the army, the air corps and also government services at Washington. In many parts of the South, Negroes in Uncle Sam's uniform are being put upon, mobbed, sometimes even shot down by civilian and military police, and on occasion lynched. Vested political interests in race prejudice are so deeply entrenched that to them winning the war against Hitler is secondary to preventing Negroes from winning democracy for themselves. This is worth many divisions to Hitler and Hirohito.[2] While labor, business, and farm are subjected to ceilings and doors and not allowed to carry on as usual, these interests trade in the dangerous business of race hate as usual.

When the defense program began and billions of the taxpayers' money were appropriated for guns, ships, tanks and bombs, Negroes presented themselves for work only to be given the cold shoulder. North as well as South, and despite their qualifications, Negroes were denied skilled employment. Not until their wrath and indignation took the form of a proposed protest march on Washington, scheduled for July 1, 1941, did things begin to move in the form of defense jobs for Negroes. The march was postponed by the timely issuance (June 25, 1941) of the famous Executive Order No. 8802 by President Roosevelt. But this order and the President's Committee on Fair Employment Practice, established thereunder, have as yet only scratched the surface by way of eliminating discriminations on account of race or color in war industry. Both management and labor unions in too many places and in too many ways are still drawing the color line.

It is to meet this situation squarely with direct action that the March on Washington Movement launched its present program of protest mass meetings. Twenty thousand were in attendance at Madison Square Garden, June 16; sixteen thousand in the Coliseum in Chicago, June 26; nine thousand in the City Auditorium of St. Louis, August 14. Meetings of such magnitude were unprecedented among Negroes. The vast throngs were drawn from all walks and levels of Negro life—businessmen, teachers, laundry workers, Pullman porters, waiters, and red caps;[3] preachers, crapshooters, and social workers; jitterbugs[4] and Ph.D.'s. They came and sat in silence, thinking, applauding only when they considered the truth was told, when they felt strongly that something was going to be done about it.

The March on Washington Movement is essentially a movement of the people. It is all Negro and pro-Negro, but not for that reason anti-white or anti-Semitic, or anti-Catholic, or anti-foreign, or anti-labor. Its major weapon is the non-violent demonstration of Negro mass power. Negro leadership has united back of its drive for jobs and justice. "Whether Negroes should march on Washington, and if so, when?" will be the focus of a forthcoming national conference. For the plan of a protest march has not been abandoned. Its purpose would be to demonstrate that American Negroes are in deadly earnest and all out for their full rights. No power on earth can cause them today to abandon their fight to wipe out every vestige of second class citizenship and the dual standards that plague them.

A community is democratic only when the humblest and weakest person can enjoy the highest civil, economic, and social rights that the biggest and most powerful possess. To trample on these rights of both Negroes and poor whites is such a commonplace in the South that it takes readily to anti-social, anti-labor, anti-Semitic and anti-Catholic propaganda. It was because of laxness in enforcing the Weimar constitution[5] in republican Germany that Nazism made headway. Oppression of the Negroes in the United States, like suppression of the Jews in Germany, may open the way for a fascist dictatorship.

By fighting for their rights now, American Negroes are helping to make America a moral and spiritual arsenal of democracy. Their fight against the poll tax, against lynch law, segregation, and Jim Crow, their fight for economic, political, and social equality, thus becomes part of the global war for freedom.

From *Survey Graphic*, November 1942, pp. 488–89.

---

2. Emperor of Japan from 1926 to 1989, also known as Emperor Showa (1901–89).
3. Baggage handlers in train stations, organized in 1937 as the International Brotherhood of Red Caps.
4. Dancers of the jitterbug, a jazzy and acrobatic swing style.
5. German constitution written in 1919 after World War I, making Germany a republic with an elected parliament and universal suffrage.

A. PHILIP RANDOLPH
March on Washington Movement Flyer [c. 1943]

What Are Our Immediate Goals?

1. To mobilize five million Negroes into one militant mass for pressure.

2. To assemble in Chicago the last week in May, 1943, for the celebration of

"WE ARE AMERICANS – TOO" WEEK

And to ponder the question of Non-Violent Civil Disobedience and Non-Cooperation, and a Mass March On Washington.

WHY SHOULD WE MARCH?

15,000 Negroes Assembled at St. Louis, Missouri
20,000 Negroes Assembled at Chicago, Illinois
23,500 Negroes Assembled at New York City
Millions of Negro Americans all Over This Great Land Claim the Right to be Free!

FREE FROM WANT!
FREE FROM FEAR!
FREE FROM JIM CROW!

"Winning Democracy for the Negro is Winning the War for Democracy!" — A. Philip Randolph

A. Philip Randolph Papers, Manuscript Division (8–8), Library of Congress.

KEY DEBATE ≈ *Race and Class*

CARL MURPHY, P. B. YOUNG, WILLIAM M. KELLEY, E. WASHINGTON RHODES,

J. ALSTON ATKINS, FRANK M. DAVIS, AND C. F. RICHARDSON

from Negro Editors on Communism [1932]

In April and May 1932, *The Crisis* offered a venue for fourteen African American newspaper and magazine editors to consider the importance of communism to the black community. Carl Murphy of the *Baltimore Afro-American* praises Communist support for social, political, and economic equality, but the other thirteen editors express ambivalence toward, if not outright rejection of,

communism. Yet despite their reservations, running through most of the editorials is a warning: if white Americans do not respect the rights of African Americans within the democratic system, they will have only themselves to blame for a Communist uprising supported by African Americans who are weary of injustice. Of the fourteen comments, seven, including Murphy's, are reprinted here.

From *The Crisis*, April and May 1932, pp. 117–19.

CARL MURPHY, *THE AFRO-AMERICAN*, MARYLAND

The Communist appear to be the only party going our way. They are as radical as the N.A.A.C.P. were twenty years ago.

Since the abolitionists passed off the scene, no white group of national prominence has openly advocated the economic, political and social equality of black folks.

Mr. Clarence Darrow[1] speaking in Washington recently declared that we should not care what political candidates think of prohibition, the League of Nations, the tariff or any other general issue. What we should demand, Mr. Darrow said, is candidates who are right on all questions affecting the colored people. I agree with him.

Communism would appeal to Mr. Darrow if he were in my place.

Communists in Maryland saved Orphan Jones[2] from a legal lynching. They secured a change of venue from the mob-ridden Eastern Shore.

They fought the exclusion of colored men from the jury, and on that ground financed an appeal of the case to Maryland's highest court. They compelled estimable Judge Duncan of Towson, Maryland, to testify that he had never considered colored people in picking jurors in his court for twenty-six years.

The Communists are going our way, for which Allah be praised.

P. B. YOUNG, *NORFOLK JOURNAL AND GUIDE*, VIRGINIA

Because we recognize that throughout all ages new voices and new movements for the creation of a better social order have always been anathema to the "old

---

1. White American lawyer (1857–1938) who was a leader in the American Civil Liberties Union and defended John T. Scopes in the 1925 Scopes Trial about the teaching of evolution.
2. Nickname for Euel Lee Jones, a Maryland farm worker who was tried and found guilty of the 1931 murder of his white employer and family; the defense by his young white Communist lawyer, Bernard Ades, hinged partly on testimony of racial bias by Judge Frank Duncan.

guards" and the "stand-patters" of the period, it has been the policy of *The Journal and Guide* not to view Communism as a thoroughgoing, death-dealing evil but to regard it as just one of the factors in a growing world-wide ideal to improve the conditions of the under-privileged, to make government more the servant of all the people, to give the rank and file of those who labor a larger share in the fruits of production, and to afford to all men equality before the law, and equal opportunity to work and live.

The Communists in America have commendably contended for and have practiced equality of all races, and in their many activities, have accepted Negroes into their ranks in both high and lowly positions; more, they have dramatized the disadvantages of the Negro by walking in a body out of a jim-crow Pittsburgh hospital, by aiding ejected tenement dwellers, and in industrial strikes directed by them fighting against the practice of excluding Negroes from labor unions. All these accomplishments go to the credit side for the Communists.

To the debit side must go, however, the fact that they in their efforts to "sell" Communism, have not taken into full consideration the economic dependence of the Negro race, its minority position, and the traditional aversion of the rank and file of Americans to the "blood and thunder" appeals of "revolution" and "mass action." Forgetful, they have aroused such charged feelings in many sections which make it difficult for the best of both races to get together and study and correct problems in an orderly way. Besides, because the Negro is marked racially, he becomes a ready target for anti-Communist venom whenever that develops as at Camp Hill[3] and in Chicago.

The Negro is patriotic and loyal, if he is anything, and Communism has gained adherents, and will continue to do so, only because traditional American conditions with their race prejudice, economic semi-enslavement, lack of equal opportunity, and discrimination of all sorts have made the Negro susceptible to any doctrine which promises a brighter future, where race and color will not be a penalty.

These barriers to the more abundant growth of the Negro must be removed, but despite the theories behind Communism, we do not think it offers the way out for the Negro which shall be most beneficial and lasting in the long run.

If the Negro masses are to be made Communism-proof, the disadvantages which have been raised against them by the white majority in power, must be voided by the union of the whites and Negroes of vision working together—fighting by all legal and sane means the proscriptions which are neither Christian, humane, or in the spirit of the fundamental laws of the land.

WILLIAM M. KELLEY, *AMSTERDAM NEWS*, NEW YORK

"Neither was there any among them that lacked: for as many as were possessors of lands or houses, sold them, and brought the prices of the things that were sold,

"And laid them down at the apostles' feet: and distribution was made unto every man according as he had need."—Acts IV; 34, 35.

This Communistic pronouncement, written about two thousand years before Karl Marx and Frederick Engels issued their famous Communistic Manifesto,[4] proves conclusively that the idea back of the middle-class Socialistic movement and the working-class Communistic movement is by no means a new one. However, it is only in comparatively recent years that the Negro in America has given any thought whatever to the subject.

Since America's twelve million Negro population is so largely identified with the working class, the wonder is not that the Negro is beginning, at least, to think along Communistic lines, but that he did not embrace that doctrine enmasse long ago. Oppressed on every hand, denied equal educational facilities, discriminated against in public places and in employment, Jim-Crowed on street cars and railroad trains, imprisoned for long terms without due process of law and even lynched, it would seem that any program—Communistic or

---

3. Attempts to organize sharecroppers in Camp Hill, Alabama, erupted into violence and the murder of one organizer; the International Labor Defense, associated with the Communist Party, successfully defended sharecroppers tried for the murder.
4. German philosophers Karl Marx (1818–83) and Friedrich Engels (1820–85) published *The Communist Manifesto* on February 21, 1848.

Socialistic, inaugurated by force or brought about by pacifistic means—should readily find converts among American Negroes.

The one question for the Negro to decide is whether it is better to continue to remain loyal to a republican form of government under a Federal Constitution that is being grossly violated where he is concerned, or, to throw his support to a communistic form of government and help bring about a dictatorship under a propertyless white proletariat.[5]

We have no quarrel with Communism in theory for, like Christianity, its doctrine is applicable to any race or nationality; but similarly like the latter, which was cited to justify human slavery, and which at the present time exerts but little influence against racial prejudice, Communism in America can also be made to function in a manner contrary to its principles and detrimental to the Negro.

The treatment given the few thousand Negroes in Russia under the Soviet form of government is not, necessarily, the same treatment that would be accorded the twelve million Negroes in America should this propertyless white proletariat come into power; for it is this same ignorant white class in the North and South which now fails to respond to just and intelligent appeals for racial and religious tolerance—the same ignorant white working class which forms the backbone of every lynching mob.

Communism in Russia has brought about revolutionary reforms affecting the welfare of that nation's hitherto subjugated masses; but these are for the most part white. And, white members of the party here have, almost without exception, revealed themselves as being without bias as to race or creed—we need have no fear so long as they are in control—but it is such a far cry from Ku Klux Klanism to Communism, and from the narrow-minded, unwieldy white working-class in America to the unlettered, but wieldy, masses in Russia, the Negro can well afford to wait until he has more definite information as to how Communism in America would be practiced by those poor whites upon whose shoulders would ultimately fall the responsibilities of government.

E. Washington Rhodes, *Philadelphia Tribune*, Pennsylvania

Whether for better or for worse, thousands of Negroes are playing with the Communists. They approach Communism, the glittering symbol of absolute equality, carefully and almost fearfully—as a child takes up a strange toy. But the evidence shows that Negroes *are* flirting with Communism. Many of them, perhaps, without understanding the deeper significance of its principles, are preaching the gospel of the "Reds."[6]

Thousands of converts have sought solace and comfort within the folds of the deep-pink banner of the party of Lenin and Stalin. Is it not paradoxical that Negroes must seek protection under some flag other than the Stars and Stripes, the flag for which they have fought to keep flying in the cause of justice and human liberty?

The ideals of the Soviet Union of Russia have a fascinating appeal to American Negroes because they hold out a ray of hope for equality of opportunity which the present American system denies to them.

Thoughtful Negroes may reason that the philosophy and economic theories of Communism are unsound and will not obtain for them a more equitable distribution of the products of their labor, or a larger degree of justice—but a drowning man will grab at a straw.

When it is considered that equality is the theory of Communism, and that inequality is the result of the present system, it is amazing that millions of Negroes have not joined the followers of the Red flag, instead of a few thousands.

The Communists have been conducting a special drive for Negro adherents. They believe that racial prejudice makes the Negro a fertile field for the sowing of revolutionary propaganda. It will be difficult for the seeds to sprout and bring forth much fruit because of the peculiar love which Negroes have for America and American institutions—a love which transcends all human understanding.

---

5. Working class.
6. Communists, from the red revolutionary banner symbolizing the blood of the people.

I am told that there are more dark-skinned than white Communists in Philadelphia. If numbers mean success, then the drive for Negro members succeeded. In fact, the leaders of the movement are anxious now to prevent it from becoming a black party. This is undesirable because it is the purpose of the organizers to make the Communist party inter-racial. It is difficult to ascertain just how seriously Negroes are considering the Red movement. I doubt that many of those who are members of the "party" would participate in a revolution requiring physical violence. However, the Reds are masters of propaganda. They are painting vivid pictures of justice and equality for all men under a Communistic form of government. They went into Scottsboro and Salisbury[7] with banners flying, condemning the persecution of Negroes. That these expressions of goodwill have had their effect in swaying Negroes is indisputable. Were not Negroes affected thereby, they would not be human.

Whether it is better for the Negro to endure his present ills or fly to others he knows not of, I am unable to say. But this one thing I know—Negroes are flirting with Communism; and if it develops into something more serious, the white American must blame himself.

J. ALSTON ATKINS, *HOUSTON INFORMER* AND *TEXAS FREEMAN*, TEXAS

I believe that any people who put their trust in a name will sooner or later be disappointed. A mere shibboleth[8] has never been adequate for the solution of personal or group problems. The more complex and intricate the problem, the less adequate mere words become. It is my understanding that in Soviet Russia, Communism represents the "Plan" by which the Communist Party is undertaking to construct a new social order. In the life of the American Negro, Communism does not represent any plan for the solution of his problems: it is but a name. So far as I can discover it represents a planless urge to rebel against the oppressions and injustices from which Negroes suffer. It gives me the impression of an emotional, desperate effort to break away, rather than a scientific and experimental program, evolved out of a careful and objective study of the facts and forces which make the problems of American Negroes as a minority peculiarly different from the problems of the homogeneous majority in Soviet Russia, or even the oppressed of the majority in the United States.

Furthermore, in Russia, Communism is planned, continually improved upon, and assiduously worked by the Russians themselves from within. In the life of the American Negro every expression which is labeled "Communism" is for the most part both planned and worked from without. In my opinion we can not solve the problems which Negroes face in America except as we develop our own plan suited to our own needs, and as we ourselves continually improve upon and sacrificially and unselfishly work that plan from within. It can not be done by having some person from the outside pin a badge upon our lapels.

On the other hand, American Negroes have no program of their own for the solution of their peculiar problems; and they have as yet no Lenin who is wise enough and unselfish enough to formulate such a plan, and who is in a position to start a tendency toward its realization. When such a new leader arises, he will no doubt learn something from Communism, something from the philosophy and program of Booker Washington, something from the continually developing ideas of Du Bois, something from Moton and the rest, but more from his own creative genius, working upon the facts and forces in operation in his own day and generation.

Until that time arrives, Negroes may be expected, like other drowning people grabbing at straws, to be lured by Communism and every other name that holds out to them bright hopes for relief from their burdens. The influence of so-called Communistic propaganda in the Scottsboro incident is the most natural thing in the world for a people who must always wait for typical emergencies to arise, before they decide what to do about them. Nor will Negro leaders who themselves have no plan,—nothing but a hue and cry

---

7. In 1931, Matthew Williams was lynched in Salisbury, Maryland; Scottsboro: see pp. 375–76 for details on the Communist Party's involvement in the defense of the nine "Scottsboro Boys" accused of rape in 1931 in Alabama.

8. A word or pronunciation used by a particular group.

against the dark dangers of Communism—be able to stem this tide.

FRANK M. DAVIS, *THE ATLANTA WORLD*, GEORGIA

If, when the United States awoke some morning, it were suddenly discovered that everybody classed as a Negro had gone Red, it would cause an immediate change in race relations. There might be trouble for a day or so, but it would not long last. Whites, thoroughly aroused and afraid, would attempt to remove those injustices heaped upon Afro-America which cradled black Communists; for 12,000,000 souls, backed by the U.S.S.R. and possibly other jealous nations wishing secretly to wreck the United States, would be too big a group to deal with by force.

This is too remote and improbable, however, to merit serious consideration.

It is a fact that the Negro, getting the dirty end of the economic, social and political stick, finds in Communistic ideals those panaceas he seeks. Yet I believe that were our government adjusted according to Red standards, few members of this kaleidoscopic race would have sense enough to take advantage of it.

Actually, the Negro as a whole fears Communism—probably because white America has not accepted it. Some frankly believe Red promises would be forgotten were they in power, for aren't they white men too? Further: would the average, every-day white man be willing to forget his prejudices even if ruled by and imbued with Communistic ideals?

Small groups of Negroes in the South going Red have harmed themselves and others in the community. Violence and bloodshed have resulted. The defense that black Reds "started it" has been an A-1 excuse for police officials killing and wounding Negroes. Camp Hill bears this out and last year's sentiment in Alabama is proof of the damage done to race relations.

I have known personally of some racial brethren going Red purely because of the chance to mingle freely with white women in the movement. Then they need no longer ogle secretly or with their personal safety threatened. Talks with a few Atlanta relatives of

the Scottsboro boys showed me that Communistic friendliness, pronouncements of social equality, the use of "Mr." and "Mrs." and their treatment in Dixie as men and women instead of Negroes was what got 'em.

But I have no fear of the rainbow brotherhood going Red in wholesale numbers—at least not until white America takes long steps in that direction. This race is slow to change. It would prefer keeping its present status, no matter how low, than fly to a system, no matter what its worth, that is constantly lambasted by press and radio. Too, the Negro considers himself too dependent upon white America to take any chance at losing the crusts now thrown him. Nor is the Communistic policy of crude and noisy militancy liked by this race, for every Negro knows that what he has obtained from white men has been through diplomacy or basically intellectual campaigning.

The past two years has been a mating season for Reds with blacks, yet few of the 12,000,000 have wed. If the Communists cannot make headway amid the disgust of Negroes with our economic order by which they lose their jobs in times of industrial illness, there is hardly any chance of success when the nation rides high.

If enough of us would go Red, Okeh[9]; when we get that way in little bunches it breathes nothing but new trouble for an already over-burdened race.

C. F. RICHARDSON, *HOUSTON DEFENDER*, TEXAS

FOR several decades following his liberation from the thralldom of human bondage, the American Negro was rather reluctant to pay much attention to strange and peculiar political panaceas and governmental doctrines. However, after observing that the existing political parties, governmental agencies and public officials had either left or counted him out of the equation, many modern-day Negroes, both literate and illiterate, educated and uneducated, are at least willing to lend a listening ear to any school of political thought and economy which promises to improve the race's political, economic, industrial and civic status in this country.

9. Alternate spelling of OK.

Most new cults and "isms" seek to appeal to the weaknesses and prejudices of the desired converts and prospective adherents, just as the klan movement did in its sweep of the country immediately after the World War. Today the majority of its duped followers are sadder but wiser men.

Communism is trying to capitalize the injustices and inequalities meted out to American Negroes and is making a bold bid for racial support and members through the assurance that their organization will change these unsavory and unwholesome conditions and make the Negro a free and full-grown American citizen, exercising and enjoying the same constitutional rights and warranties as other racial groups in our polyglot population.

While the end is certainly worthy of attainment, the means employed are destined to defeat the Communistic program and objective. Negroes are being impressed, however, by the doctrines and activities of the Communists, since the black race has been held literally between the Republican Scylla and Democratic Charybdis,[1] with the capitalistic and ruling class holding the masses in virtual serfdom in several sections of the country.

Communism is a form of socialistic government which advocates the doctrine of having or possessing all property in common, or popular ownership and control of all property. Fundamentally, Communism is opposed to violence and does not seek nor advocate revolutionary methods to change existing conditions and governments, but essays to accomplish political reformation and economic equality through orderly and evolutionary processes.

Being an exploited, maltreated and disadvantaged minority group, there is grave danger that Negroes will embrace any doctrine which offers them relief from certain oppressive, repressive and depressive conditions under which they live and eke out an existence in various parts of the United States.

If Communism is a menace to American ideals and institutions, the only panacea or solution appears to be *real democracy*—"government of *the people*, for *the people*, and by *the people*," rather than government of *a people*, for *a people*, and by *a people*.

W. E. B. Du Bois
Marxism and the Negro Problem [1933]

Du Bois admired the writings of Karl Marx, but his May 1933 *Crisis* editorial, reprinted here, outlines the difficulties of applying Marxist philosophy to social conditions in the United States. Although Du Bois was committed to progressive labor politics, he maintains in this editorial that the problems of black laborers are fundamentally a matter of race, not class. Du Bois argues that black workers are the only ones invested in progress toward a truly just economy, since white workers are hindered by racism and self-interest from bonding with all their fellow workers. It would take nearly thirty years for Du Bois to shift his allegiance officially from socialism to communism, as he did by joining the Communist Party in 1961, at the age of ninety-three. Still, this 1933 editorial conveys his longtime appreciation of Communist efforts to fight racism and of Communist principles of economics.

From *The Crisis*, May 1933, pp. 103–04.

Karl Marx was a Jew born at Treves, Germany, in March, 1818.[1] He came of an educated family and studied at the Universities of Bonn and Berlin, planning first to become a lawyer and then to teach philosophy. But his ideas were too radical for the government. He turned to journalism, and finally gave his life to economic reform, dying in London in 1883, after having lived in Germany, Belgium, France, and, for the last

1. Two sea monsters from Greek mythology that lived on opposite sides of a narrow channel, preventing safe passage.
1. Marx was born in May 1818 in Treves, known today as Trier.

thirty-five years of his life, in England. He published in 1867 the first volume of his monumental work, "Capital."

There are certain books in the world which every searcher for truth must know: the Bible, the Critique of Pure Reason, the Origin of Species,[2] and Karl Marx' "Capital."

Yet until the Russian Revolution,[3] Karl Marx was little known in America. He was treated condescendingly in the universities, and regarded even by the intelligent public as a radical agitator whose curious and inconvenient theories it was easy to refute. Today, at last, we all know better, and we see in Karl Marx a colossal genius of infinite sacrifice and monumental industry and with a mind of extraordinary logical keenness and grasp. We may disagree with many of the great books of truth that I have named, and with "Capital," but they can never be ignored.

At a recent dinner to Einstein,[4] another great Jew, the story was told of a professor who was criticized as having "no sense of humor" because he tried to explain the Theory of Relativity in a few simple words. Something of the same criticism must be attached to anyone who attempts similarly to indicate the relation of Marxian philosophy and the American Negro problem. And yet, with all modesty, I am essaying the task knowing that it will be but tentative and subject to much criticism, both on my own part and that of other abler students.

The task which Karl Marx set himself was to study and interpret the organization of industry in the modern world. One of Marx's earlier works, "The Communist Manifesto," issued in 1848, on the eve of the series of democratic revolutions in Europe,[5] laid down this fundamental proposition.

"That in every historical epoch the prevailing mode of economic production and exchange, and the social organization necessarily following from it, form the basis upon which is built up, and from which alone can be explained, the political and intellectual history of that epoch; that consequently the whole history of mankind. . . . has been a history of class struggles, contest between exploiting and exploited, ruling and oppressed classes; that the history of these class strug-

gles forms a series of evolution in which, now-a-days, a stage has been reached where the exploited and oppressed class (the proletariat) cannot attain its emancipation from the sway of the exploiting and ruling class (the bourgeoisie) without, at the same time, and once and for all, emancipating society at large from all exploitation, oppression, class-distinction, and class-struggles."

All will notice in this manifesto phrases which have been used so much lately and so carelessly that they have almost lost their meaning. But behind them still is living and insistent truth. The *class struggle* of exploiter and exploited is a reality. The capitalist still today owns machines, materials, and wages with which to buy labor. The laborer even in America owns little more than his ability to work. A wage contract takes place between these two and the resultant manufactured commodity or service is the property of the capitalist.

Here Marx begins his scientific analysis based on a mastery of practically all economic theory before his time and on an extraordinary, thoroughgoing personal knowledge of industrial conditions over all Europe and many other parts of the world.

His final conclusions were never all properly published. He lived only to finish the first volume of his "Capital," and the other two volumes were completed from his papers and notes by his friend Engels. The result is an unfinished work, extraordinarily difficult to read and understand and one which the master himself would have been first to criticize as not properly representing his mature and finished thought.

Nevertheless, that first volume, together with the fairly evident meaning of the others, lay down a logical line of thought. The gist of that philosophy is that the value of products regularly exchanged in the open market depends upon the labor necessary to produce them; that capital consists of machines, materials, and wages paid for labor; that out of the finished product, when materials have been paid for and the wear and tear and machinery replaced and wages paid, there remains a surplus value. This surplus value arises from labor and is the difference between what is actually paid laborers for their wages and the market value of

2. Charles Darwin's *On the Origin of Species* (1859); Immanuel Kant's *Critique of Pure Reason* (1881).
3. 1917 overthrow of the Tsarist autocracy that led to the creation of the Soviet Union.
4. German physicist Albert Einstein (1879–1955).
5. Uprisings throughout Europe sparked by the 1848 French Revolution.

the commodities which the laborers produce. It represents, therefore, exploitation of the laborer, and this exploitation, inherent in the capitalistic system of production, is the cause of poverty, of industrial crises, and eventually of social revolution.

This social revolution, whether we regard it as voluntary revolt or the inevitable working of a vast cosmic law of social evolution, will be the last manifestation of the class struggle and will come by inevitable change induced by the very nature of the conditions under which present production is carried on. It will come by the action of the great majority of men who compose the wage-earning proletariat, and it will result in common ownership of all capital, the disappearance of capitalistic exploitation, and the division of the products and services of industry according to human needs and not according to the will of the owners of capital.

It goes without saying that every step of this reasoning and every presentation of supporting facts have been bitterly assailed. The labor theory of value has been denied, the theory of surplus value refuted, and inevitability of revolution scoffed at, while industrial crises—at least until this present one—have been defended as unusual exceptions proving the rule of modern industrial efficiency.

But with the Russian experiment and the World Depression most thoughtful men today are beginning to admit:

That the continued recurrence of industrial crises and wars based largely on economic rivalry, with persistent poverty, unemployment, disease, and crime, are forcing the world to contemplate the possibilities of fundamental change in our economic methods, and that means thorough-going change, whether it be violent, as in France or Russia, or peaceful, as seems just as possible, and just as true to the Marxian formula, if it is fundamental change; in any case, Revolution seems bound to come.

Perhaps nothing illustrates this better than recent actions in the United States: our re-examination of the whole concept of Property, our banking moratorium, the extraordinary new agriculture bill, the plans to attack unemployment, and similar measures.[6] Labor,

rather than gambling, is the sure foundation of value, and whatever we call it—exploitation, theft or, business acumen—there is something radically wrong with an industrial system that turns out simultaneously paupers and millionaires and sets a world starving because it has too much food.

What now has all this to do with the Negro problem? First of all, it is manifest that the mass of Negroes in the United States belong distinctly to the working proletariat. Of every thousand working Negroes less than a hundred and fifty belong to any class that could possibly be considered bourgeois.[7] And even this more educated and prosperous class has but small connection with the exploiters of wage and labor. Nevertheless, this black proletariat is not a part of the white proletariat. Black and white work together in many cases and influence each other's rates of wages. They have similar complaints against capitalists, save that the grievances of the Negro worker are more fundamental and indefensible, ranging as they do, since the day of Karl Marx, from chattel slavery to the worst paid, sweated, mobbed, and cheated labor in any civilized land.

And while Negro labor in America suffers because of the fundamental inequities of the whole capitalistic system, the lowest and most fatal degree of its suffering comes not from the capitalists but from fellow white laborers. It is white labor that deprives the Negro of his right to vote, denies him education, denies him affiliation with trade unions, expels him from decent houses and neighborhoods, and heaps upon him the public insults of open color discrimination.

It is no sufficient answer to say that capital encourages this oppression and uses it for its own ends. This may have excused the ignorant and superstitious Russian peasants in the past and some of the poor whites of the South today. But the bulk of American white labor is neither ignorant nor fanatical. It knows exactly what it is doing and it means to do it. William Green and Mathew Woll of the A.F. of L. have no excuse of illiteracy or religion to veil their deliberate intention to keep Negroes and Mexicans and other elements of common labor, in a lower proletariat as subservient to their interests as theirs are to the interests of capital.

---

6. New Deal programs initiated by President Franklin D. Roosevelt immediately following his inauguration in March 1933.
7. Related to the social middle classes, who are considered to be overly concerned with material goods and the semblance of respectability.

This large development of a petty bourgeoisie within the American laboring class is a post-Marxian phenomenon and the result of the tremendous and world wide development of capitalism in the 20th Century. The market of capitalistic production has gained an effective world-wide organization. Industrial technique and mass production have brought possibilities in the production of goods and services which out-run even this wide market. A new class of technical engineers and managers has arisen, forming a working class aristocracy between the older proletariat and the absentee owners of capital. The real owners of capital are small as well as large investors—workers who have deposits in savings banks and small holdings in stocks and bonds, families buying homes and purchasing commodities on installment, as well as the large and rich investors.

Of course, the individual laborer gets but an infinitesimal part of his income from such investments. On the other hand, such investments, in the aggregate, largely increase available capital for the exploiters, and they give investing laborers the capitalistic ideology. Between workers and owners of capital stand today the bankers and financiers, who distribute capital and direct the engineers.

Thus the engineers and the saving better-paid workers form a new petty bourgeois class, whose interests are bound up with those of the capitalists and antagonistic to those of common labor. On the other hand, common labor in America and white Europe, far from being motivated by any vision of revolt against capitalism, has been blinded by the American vision of the possibility of layer after layer of the workers escaping into the wealthy class and becoming managers and employers of labor.

Thus in America we have seen a wild and ruthless scramble of labor groups over each other in order to climb to wealth on the backs of black labor and foreign immigrants. The Irish climbed on the Negroes. The Germans scrambled over the Negroes and emulated the Irish. The Scandinavians fought forward next to the Germans and the Italians and "Bohunks"[8] are crowding up, leaving Negroes still at the bottom chained to helplessness, first by slavery, then by disfranchisement and always by the Color Bar.

The second influence on white labor both in America and Europe has been the fact that the extension of the world market by imperial expanding industry has established a world-wide new proletariat of colored workers, toiling under the worst conditions of 19th century capitalism, herded as slaves and serfs and furnishing by the lowest paid wage in modern history a mass of raw material for industry. With this largess the capitalists have consolidated their economic power, nullified universal suffrage and bribed the white workers by high wages, visions of wealth and the opportunity to drive "niggers." Soldiers and sailors from the white workers are used to keep "darkies" in their "places" and white foremen and engineers have been established as irresponsible satraps[9] in China and India, Africa and the West Indies, backed by the organized and centralized ownership of machines, raw materials, finished commodities and land monopoly over the whole world.

How now does the philosophy of Karl Marx apply today to colored labor? First of all colored labor has no common ground with white labor. No soviet[1] of technocrats would do more than exploit colored labor in order to raise the status of whites. No revolt of a white proletariat could be started if its object was to make black workers their economic, political and social equals. It is for this reason that American socialism for fifty years has been dumb[2] on the Negro problem, and the communists cannot even get a respectful hearing in America unless they begin by expelling Negroes.

On the other hand, within the Negro groups, in the United States, in West Africa, in South America, and in the West Indies, petty bourgeois groups are being evolved. In South America and the West Indies such groups drain off skill and intelligence into the white group and leave the black labor poor, ignorant and leaderless save for an occasional demagog.

8. Disparaging term for Central Europeans.
9. An official or a bureaucrat.
1. Council [Russian].
2. Silent.

In West Africa, a Negro bourgeoisie is developing with invested capital and employment of natives and is only kept from the conventional capitalistic development by the opposition and enmity of white capital and the white managers and engineers who represent it locally and who display bitter prejudice and tyranny, and by white European labor which furnishes armies and navies and Empire "preference." African black labor and black capital are therefore driven to seek alliance and common ground.

In the United States also a petty bourgeoisie is being developed, consisting of clergymen, teachers, farm owners, professional men, and retail business men. The position of this class, however, is peculiar: they are not the chief or even large investors in Negro labor and therefore exploit it only here and there; and they bear the brunt of color prejudice because they express in word and work the aspirations of all black folk for emancipation. The revolt of any black proletariat could not, therefore, be logically directed against this class, nor could this class join either white capital, white engineers, or white workers to strengthen the color bar.

Under these circumstances, what shall we say of the Marxian philosophy and of its relation to the American Negro? We can only say, as it seems to me, that the Marxian philosophy is a true diagnosis of the situation in Europe in the middle of the 19th Century despite some of its logical difficulties. But it must be modified in the United States of America and especially so far as the Negro group is concerned. The Negro is exploited to a degree that means poverty, crime, delinquency, and indigence. And that exploitation comes not from a black capitalistic class but from the white capitalists and equally from the white proletariat. His only defense is such internal organization as will protect him from both parties, and such practical economic insight as will prevent inside the race group any large development of capitalistic exploitation.

Meantime, comes the Great Depression. It levels all in mighty catastrophe. The fantastic industrial structure of America is threatened with ruin. The trade unions of skilled labor are double-tongued and helpless. Unskilled and common white labor is too frightened at Negro competition to attempt united action. It only begs a dole. The reformist program of Socialism meets no response from the white proletariat because it offers no escape to wealth and no effective bar to black labor, and a mud-sill[3] of black labor is essential to white labor's standard of living. The shrill cry of a few communists is not even listened to, because, and solely because, it seeks to break down barriers between black and white. There is not at present the slightest indication that a Marxian revolution based on a united class-conscious proletariat is anywhere on the American far horizon. Rather race antagonism and labor group rivalry is still undisturbed by world catastrophe. In the hearts of black laborers alone, therefore, lie those ideals of democracy in politics and industry which may in time make the workers of the world effective dictators of civilization.

WILLIAM L. PATTERSON AND GEORGE S. SCHUYLER

from Round Table: Have Communists Quit Fighting for Negro Rights? [1944]

In December 1944, near the close of World War II, *Negro Digest* published a roundtable exploring the question "Have Communists Quit Fighting for Negro Rights?" The five participants fell into three camps: lawyer William L. Patterson, activist Benjamin A. Davis, and organizer James W. Ford argued that the Communists had fought for civil rights in the past and were continuing to do so; journalist and politician Horace R. Cayton argued that the Communists had fought for civil rights in the past but were no longer doing so in the present; and

---

3. Allusion to the "Mudsill Theory" proposed by the white American politician James Henry Hammond in a 1858 pro-slavery speech to the U.S. Senate; from the building construction term for the lowest sill of a structure that supports the frame.

journalist and editor George S. Schuyler (p. 287) held that the Communists had never fought for civil rights. Patterson's and Schuyler's responses are reprinted here.

Accompanying the roundtable discussion was a poll conducted by Wallace Lee on the same question. The questioning "of a representative group of the Negro population" resulted in a nearly 2–1 margin of negative responses to positive ones in the North and the South, and nearly 3–1 margin in the West. With nearly 22 percent of all respondents undecided, the actual proportion of those who believed that Communists were continuing "to put up a militant fight for Negro rights" represented about half of all respondents. Those who thought that the Communists had retreated from their former support attributed the shift for the most part to the Communist commitment to the war effort, which resulted in a "sacrifice" of the interests of African Americans in order to avoid "embarrassing the administration." On the other hand, the majority of respondents saw the Communist commitment to the war as complementary to their commitment to racial justice, since racial equality represented one of the Allied forces' war aims. Furthermore, many valued the Communists' vocal opposition to the Jim Crow policies of the U.S. military and their strong support of President Roosevelt's Fair Employment Practice Committee.

From *Negro Digest*, December 1944, pp. 57–70.

NO: BY WILLIAM L. PATTERSON

America is indeed passing through a great crisis. If the grave issues of the war and the postwar period[1] were not sufficient evidence, proof of the critical character of the moment is definitely shown by the revival of the now badly tarnished question—have the Communists betrayed the aspirations and struggles of the Negro people?

This question has been placed in circulation in every crisis our country has confronted since the formation of the Communist Party of the United States. What provokes it?

First, fear of the growing political consciousness of Negro America.

Second, fear that Negroes may play a leading part in the ranks of the progressive forces, since they are the balance of power in some places.

Third, fear of the increasing influence of the Communists among the Negro people.

That is why reaction raises a question of Communist desertion.

Normally few, however, would be fooled by this question. Like a phony coin the question ordinarily would have little circulation. Something sensational had to be done. Faith in the Communists must be broken.

It's that simple.

And so this time we have the "knockout" question raised by a well-known Negro writer who says: "I Tried to Be a Communist!!!"[2] To give the question the widest possible reception and discussion, it is circulated in the most elite of America's elite magazines. We thank both the writer and the Atlantic Monthly, even though we gravely doubt the sincerity of their purpose. We thank them because this slanderous attack will enable us to speak to thousands we would not otherwise reach.

Think for a moment. Is it not true that to pose this question is to admit the great vitality of the Communist movement among Negroes? Is there not implied in the very asking of it the idea that the Communists have a solution for the Negro problem? They have a solution. Negro America is becoming ever more conscious of the tremendous impetus the Communists have given to its battle for democracy.

Even a casual examination of the great body of Communist literature will put one into possession of facts completely refuting the slander of desertion.

From its inception the Communist Party has regarded what is called the Negro problem as one of the most urgent of issues confronting American democracy. So aggressively and zealously, persistently and systematically has it fought for an equal status for Negroes

1. The period following the end of World War I in 1918.
2. Essay by Richard Wright published in the August/September 1944 issue of *The Atlantic Monthly*.

that the poll taxers and white supremists of the South and their Northern friends—the Tafts, Deweys, Hoovers and company[3]—have commonly referred to the Communist Party as "the n – – – – r party."

American Communists study every written word of Communists elsewhere who were or ever had been confronted with the liberation problems of colonial peoples, national minorities or oppressed nations. Their understanding of the Negro question has deepened and matured with their experiences, and they for the first time in the history of the United States gave the question exact definition.

Perhaps the most famous and certainly one of the most effective of Communist-led campaigns is the Scottsboro case. Out of it the right of Negroes to sit on juries in the South was won again. Never before had there been so vigorous a defense of Negro victims of lynch terror. The case was made a cause celebre, because it was made symbolic of Negro persecution. The world began to talk about the treatment of black men in the greatest of the Western democracies.

The Scottsboro case was but one of many methods of struggle. There was need to change tactics in the fight to aid the sharecroppers, to secure relief during the Hoover hunger. The Communists reacted to the new conditions, but always drew closer to the Negro people. A wealth of forms, shades and methods of struggle for Negro rights resulted. Always the Communists were seeking allies for the Negro people.

It was not alone the manner in which the Communists dramatized and politicized the famous Scottsboro case that aroused democracy's enemies against it. Nor was it the desperate struggle led by the Communists to organize the sharecroppers of Georgia, Alabama, and Mississippi. It was the unchallengeable manner that the Communists had of revealing the inseparable relation of the Negro problem to every other question of democracy that provoked its enemies to rant and rage and seek to destroy that party.

Follow the course of the Communists further. They stood back of the nation-wide agitation to organize the basic industries on the basis of industrial unionism. They sought tirelessly to integrate the Negro

worker into the labor movement. The Negro could learn greater organization and discipline, struggling side by side with white labor. In the common fight the narrow nationalistic prejudices, which white labor had accepted from the hands of the monopolists who seek only to divide and conquer, would be broken down.

On the economic front of struggle the Negro would learn through experience the true answer to the question: Who are the friends of the Negro people? In all of this, the judgment of the Communists was correct. The experiences have been of inestimable value to Negro labor and the whole Negro people.

Nothing has contributed more to the political development of the Negro than the work of Communists within the labor movement to secure for him a place of equal opportunity. No one denies this. Some fear it. Others condemn it. Others recognize its essential democracy.

Communists are the greatest champions of national unity because they see in it not only a guarantee to solve war and peace problems but because it gives to every progressive force a voice of power. The Communists have defended with the greatest zeal the right of the Negro to a firm and secure position in the ranks of national unity.

Earl Browder, the leader of the Communist Political Association, said recently on the Negro question as it relates to the war:

"It would be disastrously destructive of national unity to try to make peace with the status quo, which is a status of a shameful heritage from chattel slavery based on Hitler-like racial conceptions. . . . We must as a war necessity, proceed to the systematic and relentless wiping out of every law, custom and habit of thought which in flagrant violation of our Constitution, enforces an unequal status between Negro and white citizens of the United States."

The war has changed America. It has changed the world. The Negro now need not, indeed he can not, fight alone. He is a part of a great democratic coalition. His problems are merged with the problems of the colonial peoples, the nations enslaved by Nazism, those who at home are menaced by unemployment in

---

3. Prominent white Republicans such as Ohio Senator Robert A. Taft (1889–1953), New York Governor Thomas E. Dewey (1902–71), and President Herbert Hoover (1874–1964).

the postwar period. All of the issues of social security bear directly on him because of the weakness of his economic position.

The solution of all these issues rests in the realization of the momentous Moscow, Cairo, and Teheran declarations by Messrs. Churchill, Roosevelt, and Stalin and the Economic Bill of Rights of the Roosevelt government.[4]

Negro boys died in the jungles of India that lynching be ended in the jungles of Mississippi. Fascism in all its forms must be rooted out everywhere, or nowhere is democracy safe. Democracy is indivisible. The first task before mankind seeking freedom from tyranny and want is the destruction of the base of fascism.

Millions who yesterday ignored or were indifferent to the issue of Negro rights are today in the forefront of the battle to secure them for the black man. Behind this change in attitude lies the whole background of struggle led by Communists. Once the Communists stood almost alone in the struggle for the Negro. Today the difference is amazing.

Today although Communists no longer constitute a political party, their outlook toward the extension of our democracy has not weakened. It is richer and deeper.

The Communists everywhere are fighting for a world of free men. In the eyes of the Negro, they have given new content and meaning to the dignity of manhood. To raise the question of whether they have deserted the struggles of the Negro is to show abysmal ignorance of Communist philosophy or to consciously seek to deceive people, or both.

YES: BY GEORGE S. SCHUYTER

Communists have not quit fighting for Negro rights because they never began.

Ever since the military collapse of Czarist Russia in 1917 and the furnishing of transportation to Lenin and his conspirators by the shrewd German General Staff, which enabled them to get into Russia and undermine the democratic Kerensky government, the Communists have fought for nobody's rights except their own.

They have pretended to fight for the Negro and other groups but always with the object of creating internal dissension, undermining existing institutions, good and bad, and snatching power in the ensuing disorder.

This has been their policy in every country where they have been permitted to work: in China, in Hungary, in the Baltic States, in Germany, the United States, and elsewhere. If it had not been for their collaboration with the Nazis against the Social Democrats in Germany, Hitler never would have come to power.

Their policy has been one of complete expediency unburdened by principle or scruple, and in their drive for power they have used anybody, served anybody, double-crossed anybody, and destroyed everybody they could, including their own leading party members.

Whereas at first in this country they advocated the violent overthrow of the government and the substitution of a dictatorship of the proletariat; i.e., of their gang, they are now praising "free enterprise," "postponing Socialism and the class struggle," and supporting reactionary politicians like Mayor Hague of Jersey City, Mayor Kelly of Chicago, and Senator Truman of the Pendergast machine.

Initially they were a group of warring cliques all swearing allegiance to Karl Marx but bitterly fighting each other.

They made little or no effort to use American Negroes until local Communist leaders went to Moscow in 1928,[5] and received new orders from dictator Stalin who had slaughtered or exiled his opposition and launched the drive for "Socialism in one country,"

---

4. Roosevelt's January 11, 1944, State of the Union Address presented a list of rights geared to establish both security and well-being, including the rights to earn a living wage, to have a decent home, and to have health care; Moscow: The 1943 Moscow Declaration, written by British Prime Minister Winston Churchill (1874–1965) and signed by the U.S., Britain, the Soviet Union and China in 1943, focused on Germany and included the Statement on Atrocities setting up the prosecution of war crimes under Hitler; Cairo: the 1943 Cairo Declaration, signed by the U.S., Britain, the Soviet Union and China, focused on Japan; it also set up independence for Korea and the return to China of Taiwan and other territories conquered by Japan; Teheran: the 1943 Tehran Declaration, which pledged mutual support during and after the war, was signed by Churchill, Roosevelt, and Stalin.
5. The Sixth World Congress of the Communist International (a group also known as the Third Internationale).

an abandonment of Lenin's and Trotsky's program of world revolution.

The orders were to make an all-out drive to corral American Negroes as the weakest link in the capitalist chain and to do likewise in all the colonies of the great imperialist powers.

The primary object was not to win what they derisively called "bourgeois rights" for Negroes or colonials but to blackmail the imperialist powers into granting diplomatic recognition to Russia in exchange for ceasing underground conspiratorial activities aimed at civil war.

Upon the return of Foster, Browder and other American Communist leaders from the Bolshevist Valhalla, they began picking up and sending to Russia for training such Negroes as William Patterson, Eugene Gordon and James Ford.[6]

There was really nothing legitimate for them to do to win the approval of Negroes except to pretend to fight for "bourgeois rights" such as defending Negroes grabbed by the police and to stage fruitless demonstrations, because everything that could be done for Negroes was being done by such organizations as the National Association for the Advancement of Colored People, the National Urban League, the Negro Labor Committee and others. They sought to undermine confidence in these movements by paralleling their work and attacking them as "reactionary."

Thus the National Negro Congress and the Negro Labor Victory Committee were launched to undermine respectively the NAACP and the Negro Labor Committee. Neither accomplished its aim. For the past few years we have been burdened with the People's Voice, whose executive editor, Doxey Wilkerson, is a Communist organizer and whose financial backing is suspect. All of these faithfully follow the party lines and if either has helped increase the fight for rights, it has not been discernible.

The Scottsboro case was an example. By a piece of trickery of which Ben Davis has boasted, they stole the defense of the boys from the NAACP. Then, although Leibowitz was defending the case free of charge, they collected nearly a half million dollars from ignorant humanitarians "for legal defense," using a couple of dozen "Scottsboro Mothers" to lure coin into the collection cans.

They were not interested in getting the boys out of jail; they only wanted to use the case for revolutionary propaganda. Their reckless and callous tactics made it impossible for the boys to get free, and when there was no more money to be milked out of the public to save the lads they were willing to turn over the case to a group of Negro and white liberals.

At this time they were plugging the fantastic program of "Self-Determination for the Black Belt," which envisaged the formation of a Jim Crow area including all of the predominantly Negro counties of the South[7] in imitation of Soviet Russia's nationalist "republics."

This got no rise out of Negroes who are overwhelmingly opposed to any more segregation, even a segregated state.

Another scheme was to win over allegiance of certain key Negroes with the bait of white women, and it had a considerable measure of success. Nevertheless the Negro masses stayed away in droves and the black Communist contingent remained an insignificant handful of the colored Americans.

Moscow then hit upon the device of threatening to produce a film *Black and White* exposing the horrors of the Anglo-American slave traffic. The intention was really to blackmail United States into recognition of the Red regime.

Negro actors (?) such as Langston Hughes, Louise Thompson, Henry Moon, and Ted Poston went to Moscow to participate in the production of the film.

Nothing came of this venture of value to Negroes, but in exchange for "postponing" it, recognition was won from Roosevelt.

A similar double-cross was perpetrated on the colonial comrades who had been carrying on revolutionary agitation in their homelands under the direction of Soviet agents with a head office in Amsterdam, Hamburg, and later in Copenhagen.

---

6. James W. Ford (1893–1957) ran for Vice President on the Communist Party ticket in 1932, 1936, and 1940, with white presidential candidate Earl Russell Browder (1891–1973); white labor organizer William Z. Foster (1881–1961); lawyer William Patterson (1891–1980) was the head of the International Labor Defense, a legal group supported by the Communist Party; journalist and editor Eugene Gordon (b. 1890?) was married to early black feminist writer and scholar Edythe Mae Gordon (b. 1896?).

7. For debate on the Black Belt Republic Plan, see pp. 392–98.

As soon as Stalin made his diplomatic deal with France and England, Otto Huiswoud, an American Communist hailing originally from Surinam, was sent down from Moscow by Zinoviev to oust George Padmore from the office which was ultimately closed. The Reds had double-crossed the colored folks again.

Having failed to successfully "bore from within," the American labor movement, the Communists now came forward with a program for a "United Front" to succeed the slogan "No Collaboration with the Bourgeoisie," which had been shouted internationally during the depths of the depression but had got nowhere.

Those were the days of the League Against War and Fascism (except the Stalinist brand) when money was being collected wholesale to "save" the Spanish Revolution.[8] About twenty-five cents out of every dollar collected actually purchased supplies for Spain while the rest went to pay overhead expenses such as Pullman trips for favored Negro and white Communists and fellow travelers.

Those were the days when the Communists were wooing the Negro churches (which had the masses they could not get) and the comrades were parading solemnly with Father Divine's highly vocal cohorts[9] echoing the chorus "Peace. It's Wonderful!"

When the war came it was promptly dubbed a capitalist war since Russia was then allied with Hitler and busily engaged in grabbing half of Poland, all of the Baltic states and waging war against the Finnish "aggressors." The Communists were then against any American preparation for war and denouncing Roosevelt as a betrayer and warmonger. If Negroes had listened to the Communists they would have truly been in the doghouse, but few paid any attention.

Already some of the old Communists among Negroes had begun to doubt the counsel of Moscow. Many were relieved as leaders, some were ousted, and others quit in disgust over double-dealing and opportunism.

The record shows that where and when the Communists seemed to be fighting for Negro rights, their object was simply to strengthen the hand of Russia. When this was accomplished, they abandoned the fight and turned to something else.

Whereas at one time they were all for stopping production because of Jim Crow employment policies, low pay or bad working conditions, they are now all-out for the Government's policy of no wartime strikes and have actually endorsed labor conscription: i.e., human slavery. Everything must be done to save Russia even if Negro rights have to go by the board.

Some Negro comrades and fellow travelers who should have been wise to the racket long ago have suddenly become disillusioned because of the devious Bolshevist tactics and are saying that the Communists have ceased fighting for Negro rights.

Since the Reds are a foreign-controlled conspiratorial organization, and if it is assumed that at any time they were really fighting for Negro rights, colored Americans can thank their lucky stars that the Communist "aid" has been lost amid "larger" issues, because the embrace of this conscienceless gang is truly the kiss of death.

Claudia Jones

from An End to the Neglect of the Problems of the Negro Woman! [1949]

In "Marxism and the Negro Problem" (p. 443), W. E. B. Du Bois concluded that the double burden of race and class made "black laborers" central to the quest for democratic justice. In her 1949 essay "An End to the Neglect of the Problems of the Negro Woman!," reprinted here, Claudia Jones adds gender to that analysis and concludes that black women are "the vital link to this heightened political consciousness" necessary not only for the emancipation of women but also for the liberation of "the entire American working class." Jones explores the interplay of class, race, and gender. She recognizes that the large percentage of working-class

8. The Spanish Civil War lasted from 1936 to 1939.
9. For debate on Father Divine's Peace Movement, see pp. [423–25].

black women and men makes the class issue critical to the lives of African Americans, and she foregrounds the experiences of black working women, who "—as workers, as Negroes and as women—are the most oppressed stratum of the whole population." This focus on black working women underscores her argument that all progressives must actively combat the forces that exploit black women, since they are the same forces that oppress all black people, women, and workers.

In forming alliances, Jones finds common cause with white feminists, but she does not absolve white people from blame for the exploitation of black women. Moreover, while she asserts that black men "have a special responsibility particularly in relation to rooting out attitudes of male superiority as regards women in general," Jones warns black people against becoming distracted by gender issues and losing sight of "their common oppressors, the white ruling class." In this way, she highlights the gendered experiences of black women while subtly privileging the impact of racial oppression over that of gender oppression.

Jones (1915–1964) was an early leader of the Communist movement in the United States. Born in Trinidad, she moved with her family to Harlem when she was seven years old. At twenty-one, she joined the Young Communist League, and two years later she became chair of New York State's Young Communist League and a member of its national council. In the 1940s, she was elected to the National Committee of the Communist Party United States and became editor of the "Negro Affairs" column of the Communist Party's newspaper, the *Daily Worker.* In 1951, two years after writing "An End to the Neglect of the Problems of Negro Woman!," Jones was indicted under the Smith Act (the Alien and Registration Act of 1940), which was used to outlaw the teaching of Marxism. After being jailed repeatedly, she was deported to England in 1955, where she continued to play a leading role as an advocate for racial equality. Having been in fragile health for much of her life, she died—in poverty—at the age of forty-nine.

From *Political Affairs,* June 1949.

An outstanding feature of the present stage of the Negro liberation movement is the growth in the militant participation of Negro women in all aspects of the struggle for peace, civil rights, and economic security. Symptomatic of this new militancy is the fact that Negro women have become symbols of many present-day struggles of the Negro people. This growth of militancy among Negro women has profound meaning, both for the Negro liberation movement and for the emerging anti-fascist, anti-imperialist coalition.

To understand this militancy correctly, to deepen and extend the role of Negro women in the struggle for peace and for all interests of the working class and the Negro people, means primarily to overcome the gross neglect of the special problems of Negro women. This neglect has too long permeated the ranks of the labor movement generally, of Left-progressives, and also of the Communist Party. The most serious assessment of these shortcomings by progressives, especially by Marxist-Leninists, is vitally necessary if we are to help accelerate this development and integrate Negro women in the progressive and labor movement and in our own Party.

The bougeoisie is fearful of the militancy of the Negro woman, and for good reason. The capitalists know, far better than many progressives seem to know, that once Negro women undertake action, the militancy of the whole Negro people, and thus of the anti-imperialist coalition, is greatly enhanced.

Historically, the Negro woman has been the guardian, the protector, of the Negro family. From the days of the slave traders down to the present, the Negro woman has had the responsibility of caring for the needs of the family, of militantly shielding it from the blows of Jim-Crow insults, of rearing children in an atmosphere of lynch terror, segregation, and police brutality, and of fighting for an education for the children. The intensified oppression of the Negro people, which has been the hallmark of the postwar reactionary offensive, cannot therefore but lead to an acceleration of the militancy of the Negro woman. As mother, as Negro, and as worker, the Negro woman fights against the wiping out of the Negro family, against the Jim-Crow ghetto existence which destroys the health, morale, and very life of millions of her sisters, brothers, and children.

Viewed in this light, it is not accidental that the American bourgeoisie has intensified its oppression, not only of the Negro people in general, but of Negro women in particular. Nothing so exposes the drive to fascization in the nation as the callous attitude which the bourgeoisie displays and cultivates toward Negro women. The vaunted boast of the ideologist of Big Business that American women possess "the greatest equality" in the world is exposed in all its hypocrisy when one sees that in many parts of the world, particularly in the Soviet Union, the New Democracies, and the formerly oppressed land of China, women are attaining new heights of equality. But above all else, Wall Street's boast stops at the water's edge where Negro and working class women are concerned. Not equality, but degradation and super exploitation: this is the actual lot of Negro women!

Consider the hypocrisy of the Truman Administration, which boasts about "exporting democracy throughout the world" while the state of Georgia keeps a widowed Negro mother of twelve children under lock and key. Her crime? She defended her life and dignity—aided by her two sons—from the attacks of a "white supremacist." Or ponder the mute silence with which the Department of Justice has greeted Mrs. Amy Mallard, widowed Negro school teacher, since her husband was lynched in Georgia because he had bought a new Cadillac and become, in the opinion of the "white supremacists," "too uppity." Contrast this with the crocodile tears shed by the U.S. delegation to the United Nations for Cardinal Mindszenty, who collaborated with the enemies of the Hungarian People's Republic and sought to hinder the forward march to fuller democracy by the formerly oppressed workers and peasants of Hungary. Only recently, President Truman spoke solicitously in a Mother's Day Proclamation about the manifestation of "our love and reverence" for all mothers of the land. The so-called "love and reverence" for the mothers of the land by no means includes Negro mothers who, like Rosa Lee Ingram, Amy Mallard, the wives and mothers of the Trenton Six,[1] or the other countless victims, dare to fight back against lynch law and "white supremacy" violence.

ECONOMIC HARDSHIPS

Very much to the contrary, Negro women—as workers, as Negroes, and as women—are the most oppressed stratum of the whole population.

In 1940, two out of every five Negro women, in contrast to two out of every eight white women, worked for a living. By virtue of their majority status among the Negro people, Negro women not only constitute the largest percentage of women heads of families, but are the main breadwinners of the Negro family. The large proportion of Negro women in the labor market is primarily a result of the low-scale earnings of Negro men. This disproportion also has its roots in the treatment and position of Negro women over the centuries.

Following emancipation, and persisting to the present day, a large percentage of Negro women—married as well as single—were forced to work for a living. But despite the shift in employment of Negro women from rural to urban areas, Negro women are still generally confined to the lowest-paying jobs. The Women's Bureau, U.S. Department of Labor, *Handbook of Facts for Women Workers* (1948, Bulletin 225), shows white women workers as having median earnings more than twice as high as those of non-white women, and non-white women workers (mainly Negro women) as earning less than $500 a year! In the rural South, the earnings of women are even less. In three large Northern industrial communities, the median income of white families ($1,720) is almost sixty percent higher than that of Negro families ($1,095). The super-exploitation of the Negro woman worker is thus revealed not only in that she receives, as woman, less than equal pay for equal work with men, but in that the majority of Negro women get less than half the pay of white women. Little wonder, then, that in Negro communities the conditions of ghetto-living—low salaries, high rents, high prices, etc.—virtually become an iron curtain hemming in the lives of Negro children and undermining their health and spirit! Little wonder that the maternity death rate for Negro women is triple that of white women! Little wonder that one out

---

1. Young African American men convicted in New Jersey by an all-white jury of the murder of a shopkeeper; the legal defense unit of the Communist Party and the NAACP led successful appeals for four of the accused.

of every ten Negro children born in the United States does not grow to manhood or womanhood!

The low scale of earnings of the Negro woman is directly related to her almost complete exclusion from virtually all fields of work except the most menial and underpaid, namely, domestic service. Revealing are the following data given in the report of 1945, *Negro Women War Workers* (Women's Bureau, U.S. Department of Labor, Bulletin 205): Of a total seven and a half million Negro women, over a million are in domestic and personal service. The overwhelming bulk— about 918,000—of these women workers are employed in private families, and some 98,000 are employed as cooks, waitresses, and in like services in other than private homes. The remaining 60,000 workers in service trades are in miscellaneous personal service occupations (beauticians, boarding house and lodging-house keepers, charwomen, janitors, practical nurses, housekeepers, hostesses, and elevator operators).

The next largest number of Negro women workers are engaged in agricultural work. In 1940, about 245,000 were agricultural workers. Of them, some 128,000 were unpaid family workers.

Industrial and other workers numbered more than 96,000 of the Negro women reported. Thirty-six thousand of these women were in manufacturing, the chief groups being 11,300 in apparel and other fabricated textile products, 11,000 in tobacco manufactures, and 5,600 in food and related products.

Clerical and kindred workers in general numbered only 13,000. There were only 8,300 Negro women workers in civil service.

The rest of the Negro women who work for a living were distributed along the following lines: teachers, 50,000; nurses and student nurses, 6,700; social and welfare workers, 1,700; dentists, pharmacists, and veterinarians, 120; physicians and surgeons, 129; actresses, 200; authors, editors, and reporters, 100; lawyers and judges, 39; librarians, 400; and other categories likewise illustrating the large-scale exclusion of Negro women from the professions.

During the anti-Axis war,[2] Negro women for the first time in history had an opportunity to utilize their skills and talents in occupations other than domestic and personal service. They became trail blazers in many fields. Since the end of the war, however, this has given way to growing unemployment, to the wholesale firing of Negro women, particularly in basic industry.

This process has been intensified with the development of the economic crisis. Today, Negro women are being forced back into domestic work in great numbers. In New York State, for example, this trend was officially confirmed recently when Edward Corsi, Commissioner of the State Labor Department, revealed that for the first time since the war, domestic help is readily obtainable. Corsi in effect admitted that Negro women are not voluntarily giving up jobs, but rather are being systematically pushed out of industry. Unemployment, which has always hit the Negro woman first and hardest, plus the high cost of living, is what compels Negro women to re-enter domestic service today. Accompanying this trend is an ideological campaign to make domestic work palatable. Daily newspaper advertisements which base their arguments on the claim that most domestic workers who apply for jobs through U.S.E.S.[3] "prefer this type of work to work in industry," are propagandizing the "virtues" of domestic work, especially of "sleep-in positions."

Inherently connected with the question of job opportunities where the Negro woman is concerned, is the special oppression she faces as Negro, as woman, and as worker. She is the victim of the white chauvinist stereotype as to where her place should be. In the film, radio, and press, the Negro woman is not pictured in her real role as breadwinner, mother, and protector of the family, but as a traditional "mammy" who puts the care of children and families of others above her own. This traditional stereotype of the Negro slave mother, which to this day appears in commercial advertisements, must be combatted and rejected as a device of the imperialists to perpetuate the white chauvinist ideology that Negro women are "backward," "inferior," and the "natural slaves" of others.

* * *

2. World War II.
3. United States Employment Service.

THE NEGRO WOMAN WORKER

The negligible participation of Negro women in progressive and trade-union circles is [* * *] startling. In union after union, even in those unions where a large concentration of workers are Negro women, few Negro women are to be found as leaders or active workers. The outstanding exceptions to this are the Food and Tobacco Workers' Union and the United Office and Professional Workers' Union.

But why should these be exceptions? Negro women are among the most militant trade unionists. The sharecroppers' strikes of the '30s were sparkplugged by Negro women. Subject to the terror of the landlord and white supremacist, they waged magnificent battles together with Negro men and white progressives in that struggle of great tradition led by the Communist Party. Negro women played a magnificent part in the pre-C.I.O.[4] days in strikes and other struggles, both as workers and as wives of workers, to win recognition of the principle of industrial unionism, in such industries as auto, packing, steel, etc. More recently, the militancy of Negro women unionists is shown in the strike of the packinghouse workers, and even more so, in the tobacco workers' strike—in which such leaders as Moranda Smith and Velma Hopkins[5] emerged as outstanding trade unionists. The struggle of the tobacco workers led by Negro women later merged with the political action of Negro and white which led to the election of the first Negro in the South (in Winston-Salem, N.C.) since Reconstruction days.[6]

It is incumbent on progressive unionists to realize that in the fight for equal rights for Negro workers, it is necessary to have a special approach to Negro women workers, who, far out of proportion to other women workers, are the main breadwinners in their families. The fight to retain the Negro woman in industry and to upgrade her on the job, is a major way of struggling for the basic and special interests of the Negro woman worker. Not to recognize this feature is to miss the special aspects of the effects of the growing economic crisis, which is penalizing Negro workers, particularly Negro women workers, with special severity.

THE DOMESTIC WORKER

One of the crassest manifestations of trade union neglect of the problems of the Negro woman worker has been the failure not only to fight against relegation of the Negro woman to domestic and similar menial work but to *organize* the domestic worker. It is merely lip-service for progressive unionists to speak of organizing the unorganized without turning their eyes to the serious plight of the domestic worker, who, unprotected by union standards, is also the victim of exclusion from all social and labor legislation. Only about one in ten of all Negro women workers is covered by present minimum-wage legislation, although about one-fourth of all such workers are to be found in states having minimum-wage laws. All of the arguments heretofore projected with regard to the real difficulties of organizing the domestic workers—such as the "casual" nature of their employment, the difficulties of organizing day workers, the problem of organizing people who work in individual households, etc.—must be overcome forthwith. There is a danger that Social-Democratic forces may enter this field to do their work of spreading disunity and demagogy, unless progressives act quickly.

* * *

It is incumbent on the trade unions to assist the Domestic Workers' Union in every possible way to accomplish the task of organizing the exploited domestic workers, the majority of whom are Negro women. Simultaneously, a legislative fight for the inclusion of domestic workers under the benefits of the Social Security Law is vitally urgent and necessary. Here, too, recurrent questions regarding "administrative problems" of applying the law to domestic workers should be challenged and solutions found.

---

4. Congress of Industrial Organizations; union organized for industrial workers.

5. Smith (1915–50) and Hopkins were North Carolina tobacco workers whose union activism for the Food and Tobacco Workers Union and the C.I.O. combined labor organization and civil rights.

6. Support from Local 22 in 1947 helped elect the Reverend Kenneth R. Williams, the first African American alderman in the South since 1900.

The continued relegation of Negro women to domestic work has helped to perpetuate and intensify chauvinism directed against all Negro women. Despite the fact that Negro women may be grandmothers or mothers, the use of the chauvinist term "girl" for adult Negro women is a common expression. The very economic relationship of Negro women to white women, which perpetuates "madam-maid" relationships, feeds chauvinist attitudes and makes it incumbent on white women progressives, and particularly Communists, to fight consciously against all manifestations of white chauvinism, open and subtle.

Chauvinism on the part of progressive white women is often expressed in their failure to have close ties of friendship with Negro women and to realize that this fight for equality of Negro women is in their own self-interest, inasmuch as the super-exploitation and oppression of Negro women tends to depress the standards of all women. Too many progressives, and even some Communists, are still guilty of exploiting Negro domestic workers, of refusing to hire them through the Domestic Workers' Union (or of refusing to help in its expansion into those areas where it does not yet exist), and generally of participating in the vilification of "maids" when speaking to their bourgeois neighbors and their own families. Then, there is the expressed "concern" that the exploited Negro domestic worker does not "talk" to, or is not "friendly" with, her employer, or the habit of assuming that the duty of the white progressive employer is to "inform" the Negro woman of her exploitation and her oppression which she undoubtedly knows quite intimately. Persistent challenge to every chauvinist remark as concerns the Negro woman is vitally necessary, if we are to break down the understandable distrust on the part of Negro women who are repelled by the white chauvinism they often find expressed in progressive circles.

MANIFESTATIONS OF WHITE CHAUVINISM

Some of the crassest expressions of chauvinism are to be found at social affairs, where, all too often, white men and women and Negro men participate in dancing, but Negro women are neglected. The acceptance of white ruling-class standards of "desirability" for women (such as light skin), the failure to extend courtesy to Negro women and to integrate Negro women into organizational leadership, are other forms of chauvinism.

Another rabid aspect of the Jim-Crow oppression of the Negro woman is expressed in the numerous laws which are directed against her as regards property rights, inter-marriage (originally designed to prevent white men in the South from marrying Negro women)—and laws which hinder and deny the right of choice, not only to Negro women, but Negro and white men and women.

For white progressive women and men, and especially for Communists, the question of social relations with Negro men and women is above all a question of strictly adhering to social equality. This means ridding ourselves of the position which sometimes finds certain progressives and Communists fighting on the economic and political issues facing the Negro people, but "drawing the line" when it comes to social intercourse or inter-marriage. To place the question as a "personal" and not a political matter, when such questions arise, is to be guilty of the worst kind of Social-Democratic, bourgeois-liberal thinking as regards the Negro question in American life; it is to be guilty of imbibing the poisonous white-chauvinist "theories" of a Bilbo or a Rankin.[7] Similarly, too, with regard to guaranteeing the "security" of children. This security will be enhanced only through the struggle for the liberation and equality of all nations and peoples, and not by shielding children from the knowledge of this struggle. This means ridding ourselves of the bourgeois-liberal attitudes which "permit" Negro and white children of progressives to play together at camps when young but draw the line when the children reach teen-age and establish boy-girl relationships.

* * *

The responsibility for overcoming these special forms of white chauvinism rests not with the

---

7. John Elliott Rankin (1882–1960), white member of the U.S. House of Representatives from Mississippi who supported segregation; Theodore Gilmore Bilbo (1877–1947), white Mississippi governor and later U.S. senator who vocally promoted white supremacy.

"subjectivity" of Negro women, as it is often put, but squarely on the shoulders of white men and white women. Negro men have a special responsibility particularly in relation to rooting out attitudes of male superiority as regards women in general. There is need to root out all "humanitarian" and patronizing attitudes toward Negro women. In one community, a leading Negro trade unionist, the treasurer of her Party section, would be told by a white progressive woman after every social function: "Let me have the money; something may happen to you." In another instance, a Negro domestic worker who wanted to join the Party was told by her employer, a Communist, that she was "too backward" and "wasn't ready" to join the Party. In yet another community, which since the war has been populated in the proportion of sixty percent Negro to forty percent white, white progressive mothers maneuvered to get their children out of the school in this community. To the credit of the initiative of the Party section organizer, a Negro woman, a struggle was begun which forced a change in arrangements which the school principal, yielding to the mothers' and to his own prejudices, had established. These arrangements involved a special class in which a few white children were isolated with "selected Negro kids" in what was termed an "experimental class in race relations."

These chauvinist attitudes, particularly as expressed toward the Negro woman, are undoubtedly an important reason for the grossly insufficient participation of Negro women in progressive organizations and in our Party as members and leaders.

The American bourgeoisie, we must remember, is aware of the present and even greater potential role of the masses of Negro women and is therefore not loathe to throw plums to Negroes who betray their people and do the bidding of imperialism.

Faced with the exposure of their callous attitude to Negro women, faced with the growing protests against unpunished lynching and the legal lynchings "Northern style," Wall Street is giving a few token positions to Negro women. Thus, Anna Arnold Hedge-man,[8] who played a key role in the Democratic National Negro Committee to Elect Truman, was rewarded with the appointment as Assistant to Federal Security Administrator Ewing. Thus, too, Governor Dewey appointed Irene Diggs[9] to a high post in the New York State Administration.

Another straw in the wind showing attempts to whittle down the militancy of Negro women was the State Department's invitation to a representative of the National Council of Negro Women—the only Negro organization so designated—to witness the signing of the Atlantic Pact.

KEY ISSUES OF STRUGGLE

There are many key issues facing Negro women around which struggles can and must be waged.

But none so dramatizes the oppressed status of Negro womanhood as does the case of Rosa Lee Ingram, widowed Negro mother of fourteen children—two of them dead—who faces life imprisonment in a Georgia jail for the "crime" of defending herself from the indecent advances of a "white supremacist." The Ingram case illustrates the landless, Jim-Crow, oppressed status of the Negro family in America. It illumines particularly the degradation of Negro women today under American bourgeois democracy moving to fascism and war. It reflects the daily insults to which Negro women are subjected in public places, no matter what their class, status, or position. It exposes the hypocritical alibi of the lynchers of Negro manhood who have historically hidden behind the skirts of white women when they try to cover up their foul crimes with the "chivalry" of "protecting white womanhood." But white women, today, no less than their sisters in the abolitionist and suffrage movements, must rise to challenge this lie and the whole system of Negro oppression.

American history is rich in examples of the cost—to the democratic rights of both women and men—of failure to wage this fight. The suffragists,

8. Educator, politician, and writer (1899–1990).
9. Anthropologist and activist (1906–98) who specialized in the study of people of African descent outside the United States, particularly those living in Cuba.

during their first jailings, were purposely placed on cots next to Negro prostitutes to "humiliate" them. They had the wisdom to understand that the intent was to make it so painful that no woman would dare to fight for her rights if she had to face such consequences. But it was the historic shortcoming of the women's suffrage leaders, predominantly drawn as they were from the bourgeoisie and the petty-bourgeoisie, that they failed to link their own struggles to the struggles for the full democratic rights of the Negro people following emancipation.

A developing consciousness on the woman question today, therefore, must not fail to recognize that the Negro question in the United States is *prior* to, and not equal to, the woman question; that only to the extent that we fight all chauvinist expressions and actions as regards the Negro people and fight for the full equality of the Negro people, can women as a whole advance their struggle for equal rights. For the progressive women's movement, the Negro woman, who combines in her status the worker, the Negro, and the woman, is the vital link to this heightened political consciousness. To the extent, further, that the cause of the Negro woman worker is promoted, she will be enabled to take her rightful place in the Negro proletarian leadership of the national liberation movement and by her active participation contribute to the entire American working class, whose historic mission is the achievement of a Socialist America—the final and full guarantee of woman's emancipation.

* * *

The struggle for jobs for Negro women is a prime issue. The growing economic crisis, with its mounting unemployment and wage-cuts and increasing evictions, is making its impact felt most heavily on the Negro masses. In one Negro community after another, Negro women, the last to be hired and the first to be fired, are the greatest sufferers from unemployment. Struggles must be developed to win jobs for Negro women in basic industry, in the white-collar occupations, in the communities, and in private utilities.

The successful campaign of the Communist Party in New York's East Side to win jobs for Negro women

in the five-and-dime stores has led to the hiring of Negro women throughout the city, even in predominantly white communities. This campaign has extended to New England and must be waged elsewhere.

Close to fifteen government agencies do not hire Negroes at all. This policy gives official sanction to, and at the same time further encourages, the pervasive Jim-Crow policies of the capitalist exploiters. A campaign to win jobs for Negro women here would thus greatly advance the whole struggle for jobs for Negro men and women. In addition, it would have a telling effect in exposing the hypocrisy of the Truman Administration's "Civil Rights" program.

A strong fight will also have to be made against the growing practice of the United States Employment Service to shunt Negro women, despite their qualifications for other jobs, only into domestic and personal service work.

Where consciousness of the special role of Negro women exists, successful struggle can be initiated which will win the support of white workers. A recent example was the initiative taken by white Communist garment workers in a shop employing twenty-five Negro women where three machanics were idle. The issue of upgrading Negro women workers became a vital one. A boycott movement has been initiated and the machines stand unused as of this writing, the white workers refusing to adhere to strict seniority at the expense of Negro workers. Meanwhile, negotiations are continuing on this issue. Similarly, in a Packard U.A.W. local[1] in Detroit, a fight for the maintenance of women in industry and for the upgrading of 750 women, the large majority of whom were Negro, was recently won.

THE STRUGGLE FOR PEACE

* * *

Our Party, based on its Marxist-Leninist principles, stands foursquare on a program of full economic, political, and social equality for the Negro people and of equal rights for women. Who, more than the Negro woman, the most exploited and oppressed,

---

1. Branch of the United Auto Workers union for Packard, an American luxury automobile brand established in 1899.

belongs in our Party? Negro women can and must make an enormous contribution to the daily life and work of the Party. Concretely, this means prime responsibility lies with white men and women comrades. Negro men comrades, however, must participate in this task. Negro Communist women must everywhere now take their rightful place in Party leadership on all levels.

The strong capacities, militancy, and organizational talents of Negro women, can, if well utilized by our Party, be a powerful lever for bringing forward Negro workers—men and women—as the leading forces of the Negro people's liberation movement, for cementing Negro and white unity in the struggle against Wall Street imperialism, and for rooting the Party among the most exploited and oppressed sections of the working class and its allies.

In our Party clubs, we must conduct an intensive discussion of the role of the Negro women, so as to equip our Party membership with clear understanding for undertaking the necessary struggles in the shops and communities. We must end the practice, in which many Negro women who join our Party, and who, in their churches, communities, and fraternal groups, are leaders of masses, with an invaluable mass experience to give to our Party, suddenly find themselves viewed in our clubs, not as leaders, but as people who have "to get their feet wet" organizationally. We

must end this failure to create an atmosphere in our clubs in which new recruits—in this case Negro women—are confronted with the "silent treatment" or with attempts to "blueprint" them into a pattern. In addition to the white chauvinist implications in such approaches, these practices confuse the basic need for Marxist-Leninist understanding which our Party gives to all workers and which enhances their political understanding, with chauvinist disdain for the organizational talents of new Negro members, or for the necessity to promote them into leadership.

To win the Negro women for full participation in the anti-fascist, anti-imperialist coalition, to bring her militancy and participation to even greater heights in the current and future struggles against Wall Street imperialism, progressives must acquire political consciousness as regards her special oppressed status.

It is this consciousness, accelerated by struggles, that will convince increasing thousands that only the Communist Party, as the vanguard of the working class, with its ultimate perspective of Socialism, can achieve for the Negro women—for the entire Negro people—the full equality and dignity of their stature in a Socialist society in which contributions to society are measured, not by national origin, or by color, but a society in which men and women contribute according to ability, and ultimately under Communism receive according to their needs.

On Amos 'n' Andy, and Representation

CLARENCE MITCHELL: *Amos 'n' Andy* [1930]
ROY WILKINS: *More Amos 'n' Andy* [1930]

In January 1926, two white American actors in Chicago, Freeman Gosden (1899–1982) and Charles Correll (1890–1972), launched the radio program, *Sam 'n' Henry*. The show followed the lives of recent African American migrants to Chicago from the South, which Gosden and Correll played using exaggerated black dialect. They had both begun their career performing in amateur minstrel shows, and Gosden later explained, "We chose black characters because blackface comics could tell funnier stories than whiteface comics." In March 1928, they moved the show to another Chicago station, renaming it *Amos 'n' Andy*, and became the first radio show to be syndicated across the country. By 1930, *Amos 'n' Andy* had grown to become the most popular radio program in the United States, with 30 million listeners. Spin-offs that year included a book about the show and a movie, *Check and Double Check* (starring Gosden and Correll in blackface). *Amos 'n' Andy* went on to become radio's biggest, longest-running hit, with Gosden and Correll producing new shows in various formats until 1960. Controversy trailed *Amos 'n' Andy* from its beginning to its end in 1966, when CBS finally pulled the television show from syndication due to the NAACP and other protests from civil rights groups. The two letters written in 1930 to the *Baltimore Afro-American* reprinted here lay out key points of the debate. Clarence LeRoy Mitchell, then a student at Howard University, focuses on the effects of the show on white listeners. He argues that white Americans are largely unfamiliar with "our better selves," and that shows like *Amos 'n' Andy* reinforce a stereotyped image of African Americans as ignorant. Roy Wilkins (1901–1981), then the editor of the *Kansas City Call*, argues that suppressing shows like *Amos 'n' Andy* does nothing to expand awareness among white Americans about the "finer qualities" of African Americans. In fact, he sees *Amos 'n' Andy* not as a negative force, but as "clean fun" with "universal appeal." His suggestion that

African American artists should themselves develop the material about lower-class African American life mined by such shows echoes ideas voiced by some Harlem Renaissance writers, such as Charles Chestnutt (p. 360). (Two decades later, Wilkins shifted his position when, as executive secretary of the NAACP in the 1950s and 60s, he helped spearhead the protest against the radio and television show that concluded with their cancellations.)

1930 saw other letters protesting the show (including one by Theresa Smith Kennedy in *The Post-Dispatch* and one by Bishop W. J. Walls in *Abbot's Monthly*.) The following year, the *Pittsburgh Courier*, the second largest African American newspaper in the U.S. at the time, expanded the debate. The paper launched a six-month campaign to gather a million signatures on a petition calling for the removal of the show from the air. Although the *Courier* claimed to have gathered over 600,000 signatures by the end of the campaign, the protest of these civil rights activists of the 1930s had little effect on plans to continue the popular show.

By the 1950s, however, when *Amos 'n' Andy* was being re-configured into a television show, the political climate in the United States had changed. Controversy began with the casting. Gosden and Correll decided not to play the lead characters in blackface (after shooting a pilot episode) and instead cast black actors (making it the first all black TV series). One of the actors, Nick Stewart, originally turned down the part of the lawyer Algonquin J. Calhoun because he did not want to play such an overtly stereotyped role. He later accepted the part of Lightnin', however, so that he could use the income to start a black cast theater in Los Angeles (the Ebony Showcase Theatre) where actors could play a wide variety of roles besides butlers and maids. Protests by the NAACP and other groups began as soon as the television show went on the air in June 1951, contributing to its demise after only two seasons. At the time, there were no other television shows with African Americans in serious roles.

Negative feelings by some about the show persisted after its cancellation. As comic Bill Cosby (p. 895) stated in a 1969 interview, "That show still gets to me, man. Now, audiences weren't supposed to laugh with these people; they were supposed to laugh at them, because they were so dumb." By the 1980s, however, many had begun to recall *Amos 'n' Andy* with fond nostalgia. As documented in the 1983 film *Amos and Andy: Anatomy of a Controversy*, many African Americans remembered faithfully watching the television show, appreciating the exaggerated humor and the fact that it was about black characters, most of whom were professionals. Alvin Childress who played Amos on the television series expressed appreciation for the show from a performer's perspective: "Negroes had got better parts in *Amos 'n' Andy* than they ever got in their lives—doctors, lawyers, school teachers, and all that kind of stuff." Finally, interviews in the documentary with comedian Redd Foxx, comedian George Kirby, and activist Jessie Jackson suggest that *Amos 'n' Andy* was groundbreaking, pioneering the way for African American stories and performers to come. "I think the record must show that they paid the dues that made it possible for those who now play roles of much more dignity," Jackson stated. "There was a tradition of our community of funny people, who played even in these minstrel shows. But then there was another tradition (with Martin Luther King, Malcolm X, . . .). It did not dominate black life to the extent that it has been projected to be. Even to this day . . . our struggle is for a struggle of balance—to show the breadth and depth of the black experience."

CLARENCE MITCHELL

Amos 'n' Andy [1930]

TO THE EDITOR:

William S. Hedges, white, writing in the Washington Post, Sunday, February 2, had much to say in a complimentary way of Mr. Gosden and Mr. Correll, who play the role of Amos 'n Andy over the N.B.C. hock-up.

We are not surprised at what Mr. Hedges thinks of the average Negro, for we know that there are thousands of white persons who would go into the office of any Negro enterprise and expect to find Amos 'n Andy; to any Negro church and see and hear "Hallelujah"; to any section of a city inhabited by colored people and expect to find the "Two Black Crows"; in every enterprise or to any Negro home and see Roy Cohen's short stories in action.

Speaking of Amos 'n Andy, "So fair,' says Mr. Hedges, "have they been in their depicting of a pair of Southren Negroes in Northern cities that, not only have they brought amusement to millions of whites, but they have brought amusement

and are especial favorites among colored people in the radio audience. In fact, there has never been a protest from a Negro regarding the broadcast."

I wonder do we really care? Mr. Gosden, Mr. Correll, and others have a come-back when they remind us of our own people who carry such acts upon the stages and even a litle bit of free clowning by bell boys, porters and waiters, for their white spectators.

Not so very long ago, I said to an old white man, who had used the word "nigger" too frequently for my comfort. "I beg your paroon, sir—I must correct you. "Why," he said, "I didn't think you would object to that when I hear the word so much among your own people."

As a matter of fact, when we are thrilled at seeing "Hallelujah"; when we buy all the records of the "Two Black Crows," because "they are so funny," and are particularly impressed with Roy Cohen's short stories in the Saturday Evening Post, and enjoy hearing Amos 'n Andy tell us how ignorant we are, we are not only as "patient as a jackass," but just about as sensible.

It is quite noticeable now that the Jews, Irish and even the Chinese have almost put an end to belittling jokes about the less fortunate in their groups.

If one really finds amusement in ignorance, he could go to any Southern town, or Northern one for that matter, and find among the unfortunate whites plenty of "funny" ignorance just as realistic as Amos 'n Andy. But what thinking person would dare poke fun at the darker side of life of his people?

There is one big reason why we should protest Amos 'n Andy, and all other ridiculous portrayals of Negro life. The average white person does not know as much about our finer qualities as we think he does, and the logical conclusion is that he is more likely to judge the whole group by what comes to him in the way of amusement, which he is forced to believe because of his lack of knowledge of our achievements.

> For instance, a leading business man of Washington did not know that Dr. Emmett J. Scott was colored: another did not know that Howard University had a colored president: a leading Philadelphia physician had never heard of Howard at all. He thought that Lincoln was the only Negro university in the country.

A white girl engaged in social work in a small western town, had never heard of a colored physician; in fact, she admitted she had never thought about it. A member of the staff of the Cook County (Illinois) Hospital had never heard of an exclusively Negro medical school. These are a few of many examples that illustrate the white man's lack of knowledge of our better selves.

If we care, there will be no more Amos 'n Andy

CLARENCE LeROY MITCHELL,

HOWARD UNIVERSITY.

From the *Baltimore Afro-American*, February 15, 1930, A6.

ROY WILKINS
More Amos 'n' Andy [1930]

TO THE EDITOR:

In your issue of February 15 I see a letter signed Clarence Leroy Mitchell, who is evidently a student at Howard University, which bemoans Amos 'n Andy, Octavius Roy Cohen, and the "Two Black Crows." This young writer is afflicted with the same kind of reasoning which has held the race up to more ridicule and prevented more rapid progress than anything a black-faced comedy team, or a burlesque writer could ever broadcast. I submit that if we grant that Amos 'n Andy and the rest are giving an inaccurate picture of Negro life, is it not the duty of the "better element" (of which Mr. Mitchell obviously considers himself a part) to present, "publicize" and propagandize what he calls "our better selves"?

* * *

I ask you if the suppression of Amos 'n Andy will make Emmett Scott known to any greater number of people in Washington, D.C., or Peoria, Illinois? If, in all the years of its existence, Howard University has not been able to attract the attention of a lone physician in Philadelphia, or Walla Walla, will the stopping of the sale of records of "the Two Black Crows" help the situation any?

> If Negroes turn their dials, boycott the Black Crow records and read the New Republic instead of the Saturday Evening Post, would the "better selves" be any more prominent or of any more use than they are now?

* * *

Obviously not. Nor, in turn, would white people be more informed regarding them.

It seems to me that Mr. Mitchell has fastened on the development of appearances as an objective rather than on the development of intrinsic worth. If Amos 'n Andy, the Two Black Crows and Roy Cohen's stories are true and typical, then no amount of glossing over, rarin' and pitching, by Mr. Mitchell or anyone else will be able to suppress them; if they are not true and typical, but only burlesques and humor, then they do no harm.

Amos 'n Andy, now, if the feature be carefully analyzed, will be found to contain absolutely no offensive matter at all—no offensive words or titles, not a single "coon," "nigger," "darky," "spade," "inky," or "blackie."

> In this respect, I'll wager it is far cleaner than any campus group which may be got together at Howard University or any other College. The feature is clean fun from beginning to end. It has all the pathos, humor, vanity, glory, problems and solutions that beset ordinary mortals and therein lies its universal appeal.

* * *

How would Mr. Mitchell like to have Amos 'n Andy? In plug hats, with morning coats, striped trousers, glassined hair, spats, patent leather shoes and an Oxford accent? Instead of having them struggling with the immediate and universal problem of how to get and keep a decent and usable spare tire for the taxicab, would he have them prating of mergers, mortgages, international loans and foreign trade balances?

All this, if you please, for the purpose of demonstrating that Negroes are not like Amos 'n Andy, but like Owen D. Young or W. E. B. DuBois?

* * *

Absurd, of course. What Mr. Mitchell and all the so-called "better element" need to do is stop straining after the appearance of what they are not, and give some attention to being a whole-some, genuine edition of what they really are, Rest assured that if Howard University does its work well, its products will make it known to the far corners of the land, let alone the neighboring city of Philadelphia: that if Emmett Scott be known as a useful citizen, it does not matter what his racial identity may be: and if Negro doctors give up congregating in large centers for social purposes and devote themselves to medicine where they are needed, any moderately informed social worker in any town big enough to boast a social agency will know about them.

> Remember also that while we have been sniffing about with our heads in the clouds, Mr. Gosden and Mr. Correll have a $100,000 a year contract: Mr. Cohen sojourns in Palm Beach; and Mr. Moran and Mr. Mack travel about the country in a specially-built Packard with (of all the irony) a Negro chauffeur. . . . all off material which we, if we had more wit and less false pride, might have set down in much better fashion.

No, we do not need a can for the innocent fun and harmless burlesques, but we do need one for the articulate, but non-performing pretenders in the so-called "better element."

ROY WILKINS,

KANSAS CITY, MO.

From the *Baltimore Afro-American*, March 22, 1930, A6.

AARON DOUGLAS
An Idyll of the Deep South [1934]

Through their paintings and sculptures, particularly those depicting the human form, visual artists engage in debates about representation. In their art from the 1920s and 1930s, Aaron Douglas and his contemporaries (Sargent Johnson [p. 465], Augusta Savage [p. 466], William Henry Johnson [p. 467], and Palmer Hayden [p. 469]) explored cultural and historical identity. In 1934, during the Depression, the federal Public Works of Art Project (PWAP) commissioned Aaron Douglas to paint a multipart mural for the 135th Street branch of the New York Public Library, to be titled *Aspects of Negro Life.* For the form of these murals, Douglas drew inspiration from the African design tradition. At the same time, his subject matter was firmly

rooted in African American history and culture. In *An Idyll of the Deep South,* reproduced here, Douglas's two-dimensional shadow figures engage in a range of activities, with mourning for a lynching victim pictured alongside daily activities such as working, playing, and praying. By using simple stylized figures to represent people, Douglas emphasizes the power of social and historical context rather than the role of the individual.

Aaron Douglas (1899–1979) was a leading figure of the Harlem Renaissance. Championed by both W. E. B. Du Bois and Alain Locke (who called him a "pioneering Africanist"), Douglas often had his work published in *The Crisis,* and he illustrated landmark books of the period, including Locke's *The New Negro* (1925) and James Weldon Johnson's *God's Trombones* (1927). In 1937, he joined Fisk University where he established the Fine Arts Department, serving as its chair until his retirement in 1966.

Schomburg Center for Research in Black Culture, The New York Public Library.

SARGENT JOHNSON
Head of a Negro Woman [1935]

Like Aaron Douglas's mural, *An Idyll of the Deep South* (p. 464), Sargent Johnson's ca. 1935 sculpture *Head of a Negro Woman* shows the influence of African artistic traditions. While Douglas drew on African design, Johnson found inspiration in African statues and masks. Johnson's sculpture presents the woman as a type—rather than a specific individual—and celebrates black beauty through a romanticized vision that strongly echoes idealized African images.

Sargent Johnson (1888–1967) was born in Boston to a father of Swedish ancestry and a mother of Cherokee and African American ancestry. Orphaned as a

child, he lived with an uncle and aunt. The aunt was May Howard Jackson, a well-known sculptor who encouraged and inspired her nephew's early artistic works. Johnson moved to San Francisco in 1915 and attended the Best Art School and the California School of Fine Arts. In 1925, the Harmon Foundation, an influential arts organization, began promoting his work, catapulting him to national recognition. Although based on the West Coast, he became closely associated with the artistic outpouring of the Harlem Renaissance. Like Aaron Douglas, he benefited from federal arts projects during the Depression.

San Francisco Museum of Modern Art, Albert M. Bender Collection.

Augusta Savage
Gamin [1929]

Like Sargent Johnson, Augusta Savage employed sculpture to represent the image of a single human figure. But while Johnson focused on abstract or idealized forms (p. 465), Savage explored the representation of realistic African American figures. Her promotion of the beauty found within the African American community makes *Gamin* (meaning street urchin) a visual foreshadowing of the rallying cry of the 1960s "black pride" movement: "Black is beautiful."

Born in Florida, Augusta Fells (1892–1962) defied her father, a Methodist minister, to pursue a career in art. In 1921, she moved to New York City and enrolled in an art program at the Cooper Union, a prestigious college of arts and science that charges its students no tuition. Supporting herself by taking in laundry, Savage (as she became known after a marriage that proved short-lived) gained prominence as a sculptor, and in 1929 she was awarded a Julius Rosenwald Fellowship to study in Europe. Dedicated to teaching as well as creating, she founded the Savage Studio of Arts and Crafts in 1932 to train adult artists. In 1937, she became director of the Harlem Community Art Center, which was sponsored by the Works Progress Administration and the Federal Arts Project, and helped organize the Harlem Arts Guild. About

her decision to spend most of her later years teaching art to children rather than doing her own sculpture, she proclaimed, "if I can inspire one of these youngsters to develop the talent I know they possess, then my monument will be in their work."

Smithsonian American Art Museum, Gift of Benjamin and Olya Margolin.

WILLIAM HENRY JOHNSON
Self-Portrait [1929]

The strong brushstrokes of William Henry Johnson's paintings, including those in his 1929 *Self-Portrait,* powerfully evoke European art traditions, particularly the work of Vincent van Gogh, thereby raising questions about how an artist's style shapes issues of identity and artistic tradition. The style and self-reflective subject matter of *Self-Portrait* present Johnson as part of the international art world rather than as an artist shaped by identifiably African or African American subject matter or styles.

Born into poverty in Florence, South Carolina, Johnson (1901–1970) did fieldwork as a child to help support his family. He moved to New York City around 1919 with the

intention of studying art but had to work for several years in order to raise enough money. Eventually he studied at the National Academy of Design. From 1926 to 1929, he lived in Paris, then returned to New York, where he won a Gold Award from the Harmon Foundation in 1930. After being unjustly arrested for loitering while working on a painting of a hotel in his hometown, Johnson returned to Europe, where he stayed until the rise of the Nazis in the late 1930s prompted his repa-

triation. He was hospitalized for mental illness in 1947 and remained institutionalized for the last twenty-three years of his life. He struggled financially throughout his life, never achieving prominence as an artist during his lifetime. In the mid-1950s, learning that over 1,300 paintings and other works were in storage and slated for destruction, directors of the Harmon Foundation saved them, donating them to the Smithsonian American Art Museum in 1967.

National Museum of American Art, Smithsonian Institution.

PALMER HAYDEN
Midsummer Night in Harlem [1936]

Like Sargent Johnson's sculpture (p. 465) Palmer Hayden's 1936 painting *Midsummer Night in Harlem* explores the idea of people as visual types. However, Hayden's types are rooted in an African American social context, conveying a tone of satiric amusement rather than abstract beauty. Hayden's painting demonstrates how the level of individual detail of figures, the cultural context, and the source of artistic inspiration interact to shape the way a piece of art engages with cultural and political issues of the day.

Palmer Hayden (1890–1973) was born Peyton Cole Hedgeman in Virginia. In 1919, after serving in World War I, he moved to New York City, becoming part of the burgeoning Harlem Renaissance and studying at the Cooper Union School of Art. In 1925, he traveled to Boothbay Harbor, Maine, to study at an artists' colony,

and the following year he won a Harmon Foundation award for *The Schooner.* From 1927 to 1932, he lived in Paris, where he studied privately with an instructor at the Ecole des Beaux-Arts. After returning to the United States in 1932, he benefited from commissions from the WPA, as did his contemporaries Aaron Douglas and Sargent Johnson (pp. 464 and 465). Despite his academic training and immersion in European artistic traditions,

Hayden intentionally adopted a "naive" folk style. He drew on folk themes and included African images in some of his work, such as *Fétiche et Fleurs*, a still life featuring Gambonese mask and Zairean textile, for which he won a second Harmon Foundation award in 1933. Hayden's work from the 1930s, including *Midsummer Night in Harlem,* made him a controversial figure due to his use of forms and themes that evoke black racial stereotypes.

Harmon Collection, National Archives.

IN THE HEADLINES:

Reconciling the Protest School of Richard Wright and the Modernist Individual of Zora Neale Hurston

Zora Neale Hurston: How It Feels to Be Colored Me [1928]
Richard Wright: Blueprint for Negro Writing [1937]
Richard Wright: Between Laughter and Tears: A Review of Hurston's *Their Eyes Were Watching God* [1937]
Zora Neale Hurston: Stories of Conflict: A Review of Wright's *Uncle Tom's Children* [1938]

Do African American artists have an obligation to contribute to a collective political vision—or is the pursuit of an individual vision an equally valid undertaking? Are some styles or themes more appropriate than others for black artists? During the late 1930s, the work of two groundbreaking writers, Richard Wright and Zora Neale Hurston, became identified with divergent answers to these questions about the relationship of artistic expression to politics.

Contemporary critics recognize Wright and Hurston as foundational figures in the African American literary tradition. Assessing their work as complementary rather than antithetical to each other is a relatively recent phenomenon, however, fueled by such work as June Jordan's 1974 essay "On Richard Wright and Zora Neale Hurston: Notes toward a Balancing of Love and Hatred" (p. 720). The prior tendency to regard the two writers as oppositional has its roots not only in the choices they made in their fiction but also in the ways they presented themselves and their ideas on African American writing.

Certainly, fundamental differences divide their work, particularly as reflected in their best-known novels, Wrights's *Native Son* (1940) and Hurston's *Their Eyes Were Watching God* (1937). On the broadest level of

function, *Native Son* is a prototypical novel of protest, while *Their Eyes Were Watching God* is a quintessential work of affirmation. The difference is underscored by the hostile, interracial, urban world of *Native Son* and the relatively nurturing southern, black, rural environment of *Their Eyes Were Watching God.* Wright's novel also explores the concept of synecdoche, where, in this case, a person is used to represent a group, while Hurston's novel portrays characters as distinctive individuals.

Wright's and Hurston's critical writing contributed to the idea that their artistic and political choices required choosing one artistic vision over the other. "Blueprint for Negro Writing," Wright's sets of rules to guide the development of political writers, contrasts markedly with Hurston's self-presentation as an independent writer in her 1928 essay "How It Feels to Be Colored Me." Interestingly, even though Wright champions art grounded in Marxism, he rejects the idea of propaganda, arguing for a balance between art and politics.

When *Their Eyes Were Watching God* was published, in 1937, Wright gave it a highly critical review. To Wright, Hurston's focus on relationships among black people was an avoidance of the primary political imperative of the day, which called for representations of conflicts between black people and the dominant white world. Hurston repaid Wright when she reviewed his *Uncle Tom's Children* in April 1938. Her dismissal of the work as "a book about hatreds" contributed to the growing perception of their work as dichotomous.

Wright's and Hurston's positions on art, racism, and the role of the audience raise a number of questions about different types of artistic production—for example: Are experiences of discrimination aberrations or the norm? (Incidents of racism "astonish" Hurston, while Wright sees them as dominant factors in shaping black lives.) Is art a route to wholeness, or is wholeness a given for an artist? (Wright presents art as a way for African Americans, having been "torn" from Africa, to become whole again, while Hurston begins with the premise that she is already whole.) Finally, what is the dominant force in shaping the type of art that is produced and consumed? Is it the artist, as Hurston believed, or the audience, as Wright believed? Is there a target audience, and is that audience white or black? If black, is it "the black bourgeoisie" or "the black masses"?

Exploring the contrasts between Hurston's and Wright's works illuminates key aspects of their writing and political frameworks. At the same time, later critics such as June Jordan (p. 720) offer an alternative to the traditional focus on the differences between their artistic visions.

Zora Neale Hurston claimed different birth dates throughout her life, ranging from 1898 to 1910, but scholars have recently determined that she was born on January 15, 1891 in Notasulga, Alabama. The next year, her family moved to Eatonville, Florida, the first incorporated black community in America, where her father, a Baptist minister and politician, later served as mayor. As a young woman, Hurston worked as a domestic. She didn't attend high school until she was 26, but then went on to study at Howard University, where she began publishing short stories, including "Spunk," published in *Opportunity*. Transferring to Barnard in New York City, she became a key figure in the Harlem Renaissance movement. Her study of anthropology with Frank Boas took her to the American South (and later Jamaica and Haiti) where she collected black folklore, a rich body of material that informed both her non-fiction and fiction writing. Her publications include *Mules and Men* (1935, on voodoo practice and black rural culture), an autobiography, *Dust Tracks on a Road* (1942) and four novels, the second being *Their Eyes Were Watching God* (1937). During her later years, out of step with the poli-

tics of the emerging civil rights movement, Hurston descended into obscurity and poverty, supporting herself as a domestic while working on a final novel, *Herod the Great*. She died penniless in a Florida welfare home on January 28, 1960. Her belongings were ordered burned following her death, but a sheriff who knew her intervened and extinguished the fire, saving many of her manuscripts and photographs.

Richard Wright was born in 1908 in Roxie, Mississippi. His early schooling was repeatedly interrupted by family upheaval (his father left the family when he was a child), by frequent moves (among different households in different towns and even an orphanage), and by the need for him to earn money to help support his brother and mother. Still, when he was fifteen, he managed to write and publish his first short story ("The Voodoo of Hell's Half-Acre"), and the next year he graduated as valedictorian of his ninth grade class. Moving to Chicago in 1927, he found work as a postal clerk among other jobs, and continued to study writing on his own by reading extensively. He became involved with the John Reed Club, a Marxist group of artists and intellectuals, and eventually joined the Communist Party in 1933. He published poems in *New Masses* and other periodicals while working on his first novel, *Cesspool* (published in 1963 as *Lawd Today*). After conflicts with Communist leaders in Chicago over racial and artistic issues, Wright moved to New York in 1937, where he worked on the WPA Writers' Project and also wrote for the *Daily Worker*. He gained national attention as a writer when he won first prize in *Story* magazine's literary contest for his first collection of short stories, *Uncle Tom's Children*, published in 1938. In 1939, he won a Guggenheim Fellowship and the next year, he published his first novel *Native Son*, which became the first book by an African American author to be selected by the Book of the Month Club. After a short-lived marriage to the Russian ballet dancer Dhimah Rose Meadman in 1938 (with writer Ralph Ellison as the best man), Wright married the white American communist activist Ellen Poplar in 1941, with whom he later had two children. Wright was awarded the Spingarn Medal from the NAACP in 1941. He left the Communist Party in 1942, then publicly critiqued his experiences within the party in the 1944 article "I Tried to Be a Communist." The following year, he published *Black Boy*, the first part of his autobiography (the second part was published posthumously as *American Hunger* in 1977). In 1946, Wright immigrated to Paris, France, where he became involved with leading existentialist writers, including Jean-Paul Sartre. He continued to publish books (though none met with the success of his earlier works), to travel and to engage with political causes until his death from a heart attack in 1960 at the age of 52.

ZORA NEALE HURSTON

How It Feels to Be Colored Me [1928]

I am colored but I offer nothing in the way of extenuating circumstances except the fact that I am the only Negro in the United States whose grandfather on the mother's side was *not* an Indian chief.

I remember the very day that I became colored. Up to my thirteenth year. I lived in the little Negro town of Eatonville, Florida. It is exclusively a colored town. The only white people I knew passed through the town going to or coming from Orlando. The native whites rode dusty horses, the Northern tourists chugged down the sandy village road in automobiles. The town knew the Southerners and never stopped cane chewing when they passed. But the Northerners were something else again. They were peered at cautiously from behind curtains by the timid. The more venturesome would come out on the porch to watch them go past and got just as much pleasure out of the tourists as the tourists got out of the village.

The front porch might seem a daring place for the rest of the town, but it was a gallery seat for me. My favorite place was atop the gate-post. Proscenium box[1] for a born first-nighter. Not only did I enjoy the show, but I didn't mind the actors knowing that I liked it. I usually spoke to them in passing. I'd wave at them and when they returned my salute, I would say something like this: "Howdy-do-well-I-thank-you-where-you-goin?" Usually automobile or the horse paused at this, and after a queer exchange of compliments, I would probably "go a piece of the way" with them, as we say in farthest Florida. If one of my family happened to come to the front in time to help me, of course negotiations would be rudely broken off. But even so, it is clear that I was the first "welcome-to-our-state" Floridian, and I hope the Miam Chamber of Commerce will please take notice.

During this period, white people differed from colored to me only in that they rode through town and never lived there. They liked to hear me "speak pieces" and sing and wanted to see me dance the parse-me-la and gave me generously of their small silver for doing these things, which seemed strange to me for I wanted to do them so much that I needed bribing to stop. Only they didn't know it. The colored people gave no dimes. They deplored any joyful tendencies in me, but I was their Zora nevertheless. I belonged to them, to the nearby hotels, to the county—everybody's Zora.

But changes came in the family when I was thirteen, and I was sent to school in Jacksonville. I left Eatonville, the town of the oleanders, as Zora. When I disembarked from the river-boat at Jacksonville, she was no more. It seemed that I had suffered a sea change. I was not Zora of Orange County any more, I was now a little colored girl. I found it out in certain ways. In my heart as well as in the mirror, I became a fast[2] brown—warranted not to rub nor run.

But I am not tragically colored. There is no great sorrow dammed up in my soul, nor lurking behind my eyes. I do not mind at all. I do not belong to the sobbing school of Negrohood who hold that nature somehow has given them a lowdown dirty deal and whose feelings are all hurt about it. Even in the helter-skelter skirmish that is my life, I have seen that the world is to the strong regardless of a little pigmentation more or less. No, I do not weep at the world—I am too busy sharpening my oyster knife.[3]

Someone is always at my elbow reminding me that I am the granddaughter of slaves. It fails to register depression with me. Slavery is sixty years in the past.

1. Theater box seats on each side of and closest to the stage.
2. Colorfast.
3. Reference to Shakespeare's *The Merry Wives of Windsor* 2.2.3–4: "Why, then the world's mine oyster,/Which I with sword will open."

The operation was successful and the patient is doing well, thank you. The terrible struggle that made me an American out of a potential slave said "On the line!" The Reconstruction said "Get set!": and the generation before said "Go!" I am off to a flying start and I must not halt in the stretch to look behind and weep. Slavery is the price I paid for civilization, and the choice was not with me. It is a bully adventure and worth all that I have paid through my ancestors for it. No one on earth ever had a greater chance for glory. The world to be won and nothing to be lost. It is thrilling to think—to know that for any act of mine, I shall get twice as much praise or twice as much blame. It is quite exciting to hold the center of the national stage, with the spectators not knowing whether to laugh or to weep.

The position of my white neighbor is much more difficult. No brown specter pulls up a chair beside me when I sit down to eat. No dark ghost thrusts its leg against mine in bed. The game of keeping what one has is never so exciting as the game of getting.

I do not always feel colored. Even now I often achieve the unconscious Zora of Eatonville before the Hegira.[4] I feel most colored when I am thrown against a sharp white background.

For instance at Barnard. "Beside the waters of the Hudson" I feel my race. Among the thousand white persons, I am a dark rock surged upon, and overswept, but through it all, I remain myself. When covered by the waters, I am; and the ebb but reveals me again.

Sometimes it is the other way around. A white person is set down in our midst, but the contrast is just as sharp for me. For instance, when I sit in the drafty basement that is The New World Cabaret with a white person, my color comes. We enter chatting about any little nothing that we have in common and are seated by the jazz waiters. In the abrupt way that jazz orchestras have, this one plunges into a number. It loses no time in cricumlocutions, but gets right down to business. It constricts the thorax and splits the heart with its tempo and narcotic harmonies. This orchestra grows rambunctious, rears on its hind legs and attacks the tonal veil with primitive fury, rending it, clawing it

until it breaks through to the jungle beyond. I follow those heathen—follow them exultingly. I dance wildly inside myself; I yell within, I whoop; I shake my assegai[5] above my head, I hurl it true to the mark *yeeeeooww!* I am in the jungle and living in the jungle way. My face is painted red and yellow and my body is painted blue. My pulse is throbbing like a war drum. I want to slaughter something—give pain, give death to what, I do not know. But the piece ends. The men of the orchestra wipe their lips and rest their fingers. I creep back slowly to the veneer we call civilization with the last tone and find the white friend sitting motionless in his seat, smoking calmly.

"Good music they have here," he remarks, drumming the table with his fingertips.

Music. The great blobs of purple and red emotion have not touched him. He has only heard what I felt. He is far away and I see him but dimly across the ocean and the continent that have fallen between us. He is so pale with his whiteness then and I am *so* colored.

At certain times I have no race, I am *me*. When I set my hat at a certain angle and saunter down Seventh Avenue, Harlem City, feeling as snooty as the lions in front of the Forty-Second Street Library,[6] for instance. So far as my feelings are concerned, Peggy Hopkins Joyce on the Boule Mich[7] with her gorgeous raiment, stately carriage, knees knocking together in a most aristocratic manner, has nothing on me. The cosmic Zora emerges. I belong to no race nor time. I am the eternal feminine with its string of beads.

I have no separate feeling about being an American citizen and colored. I am merely a fragment of the Great Soul that surges within the boundaries. My country, right or wrong.

Sometimes, I feel discriminated against, but it does not make me angry. It merely astonishes me. How *can* any deny themselves the pleasure of my company? It's beyond me.

But in the main, I feel like a brown bag of miscellany propped against a wall. Against a wall in company with other bags, white, red and yellow. Pour out the

4. Allusion to Muhammad's emigration to Medina from Mecca, referring here to Hurston's move from Eatonville to Jacksonville.
5. Spear.
6. The main branch of the New York Public Library.
7. Boulevard Saint-Michel, a major street in the Latin Quarter of Paris; Joyce: white American actress and celebrity (1893–1957).

contents, and there is discovered a jumble of small things priceless and worthless. A first-water diamond,[8] an empty spool, bits of broken glass, lengths of string, a key to a door long since crumbled away, a rusty knifeblade, old shoes saved for a road that never was and never will be, a nail bent under the weight of things too heavy for any nail, a dried flower or two still a little fragrant. In your hand is the brown bag. On the ground before you in the jumble it held—so much like the jumble in the bags, could they be emptied, that all might be dumped in a single heap and the bags refilled without altering the content of any greatly. A bit of colored glass more or less would not matter. Perhaps that is how the Great Stuffer of Bags filled them in the first place—who knows?

From *The World Tomorrow, May 1928,* p. 215.

RICHARD WRIGHT
Blueprint for Negro Writing [1937]

1. THE ROLE OF NEGRO WRITING: TWO DEFINITIONS

Generally speaking, Negro writing in the past has been confined to humble novels, poems, and plays, prim and decorous ambassadors who went a-begging to white America. They entered the Court of American Public Opinion dressed in the knee-pants of servility, curtsying to show that the Negro was not inferior, that he was human, and that he had a life comparable to that of other people. For the most part these artistic ambassadors were received as though they were French poodles who do clever tricks.

White America never offered these Negro writers any serious criticism. The mere fact that a Negro could write was astonishing. Nor was there any deep concern on the part of white America with the role Negro writing should play in American culture; and the role it did play grew out of accident rather than intent or design. Either it crept in through the kitchen

in the form of jokes or it was the fruits of that foul soil which was the result of a liaison between inferiority-complexed Negro "geniuses" and burnt-out white Bohemians with money.

On the other hand, these often technically brilliant performances by Negro writers were looked upon by the majority of literate Negroes as something to be proud of. At best, Negro writing has been something external to the lives of educated Negroes themselves. That the productions of their writers should have been something of a guide in their daily living is a matter which seems never to have been raised seriously.

Under these conditions Negro writing assumed two general aspects: (1) It became a sort of conspicuous ornamentation, the hallmark of "achievement." (2) It became the voice of the educated Negro pleading with white America for justice.

Rarely was the best of this writing addressed to the Negro himself, his needs, his sufferings, his aspirations. Through misdirection, Negro writers have been far better to others than they have been to themselves. And the mere recognition of this places the whole question of Negro writing in a new light and raises a doubt as to the validity of its present direction.

2. THE MINORITY OUTLOOK

Somewhere in his writings Lenin makes the observation that oppressed minorities often reflect the techniques of the bourgeoisie more brilliantly than some sections of the bourgeoisie themselves. The psychological importance of this becomes meaningful when it is recalled that oppressed minorities, and especially the petty bourgeois sections of oppressed minorities, strive to assimilate the virtues of the bourgeoisie in the assumption that by doing so they can lift themselves into a higher social sphere. But not only among the oppressed petty bourgeoisie does this occur. The workers of a minority people, chafing under exploitation, forge organizational forms of struggle to better their lot. Lacking the handicaps of false ambition and property, they have access to a wide social vision and a

8. A diamond of the highest quality.

deep social consciousness. They display a greater freedom and initiative in pushing their claims upon civilization than even do the petty bourgeoisie. Their organizations show greater strength, adaptability, and efficiency than any other group or class in society.

That Negro workers, propelled by the harsh conditions of their lives, have demonstrated this consciousness and mobility for economic and political action there can be no doubt. But has this consciousness been reflected in the work of Negro writers to the same degree as it has in the Negro workers' struggle to free Herndon[1] and the Scottsboro Boys, in the drive toward unionism, in the fight against lynching? Have they as creative writers taken advantage of their unique minority position?

The answer decidedly is *no*. Negro writers have lagged sadly, and as time passes the gap widens between them and their people.

How can this hiatus be bridged? How can the enervating effects of this longstanding split be eliminated?

In presenting questions of this sort an attitude of self-consciousness and self-criticism is far more likely to be a fruitful point of departure than a mere recounting of past achievements. An emphasis upon tendency and experiment, a view of society as something becoming rather than as something fixrd and admired is the one which points the way for Negro writers to stand shoulder to shoulder with Negro workers in mood and outlook.

3. A WHOLE CULTURE

There is, however, a culture of the Negro which is his and has been addressed to him a culture which has, for good or ill, helped to clarify his consciousness and create emotional attitudes which are conducive to action. This culture has stemmed mainly from two sources: (1) the Negro church and (2) the folklore of the Negro people.

It was through the portals of the church that the American Negro first entered the shrine of western culture. Living under slave conditions of life, bereft of his African heritage, the Negroes' struggle for religion on the plantations between 1820–60 assumed the form of a struggle for human rights. It remained a relatively revo-

lutionary struggle until religion began to serve as an antidote for suffering and denial. But even today there are millions of American Negroes whose only sense of a whole universe, whose only relation to society and man, and whose only guide to personal dignity comes through the archaic morphology of Christian salvation.

It was, however, in a folklore moulded out of rigorous and inhuman conditions of life that the Negro achieved his most indigenous and complete expression. Blues, spirituals, and folk tales recounted from mouth to mouth; the whispered words of a black mother to her black daughter on the ways of men, to confidential wisdom of a black father to his black son; the swapping of sex experiences on street corners from boy to boy in the deepest vernacular; work songs sung under blazing suns—all these formed the channels through which the racial wisdom flowed.

One would have thought that Negro writers in the last century of striving at expression would have continued and deepened this folk tradition, would have tried to create a more intimate and yet a more profoundly social system of artistic communication between them and their people. But the illusion that they could escape through individual achievement the harsh lot of their race swung Negro writers away from any such path. Two separate cultures sprang up: one for the Negro masses, unwritten and unrecognized and the other for the sons and daughters of a rising Negro bourgeoisie, parasitic and mannered.

Today the question is: Shall Negro writing be for the Negro masses, moulding the lives and consciousness of those masses toward new goals, or shall it continue begging the question of the Negroes' humanity?

4. THE PROBLEM OF NATIONALISM IN NEGRO WRITING

In stressing the difference between the role Negro writing failed to play in the lives of the Negro people, and the role it should play in the future if it is to serve its historic functions in pointing out the fact that Negro writing has been addressed in the main to a small white audience rather than to a Negro one, it should be stated that no attempt is being made here to

---

1. Angelo Herndon (1913–97), union organizer convicted in 1932 in Georgia for insurrection.

propagate a specious and blatant nationalism. Yet the nationalist character of the Negro people is unmistakable. Psychologically this nationalism is reflected in the whole of Negro culture, and especially in folklore.

In the absence of fixed and nourishing forms of culture, the Negro has a folklore which embodies the memories and hopes of his struggle for freedom. Not yet caught in paint or stone, and as yet but feebly depicted in the poem and novel, the Negroes' most powerful images of hope and despair still remain in the fluid state of daily speech. How many John Henrys have lived and died on the lips of these black people? How many mythical heroes in embryo have been allowed to perish for lack of husbanding by alert intelligence?

Negro folklore contains, in a measure that puts to shame more deliberate forms of Negro expression, the collective sense of Negro life in America. Let those who shy at the nationalist implications of Negro life look at this body of folklore, living and powerful, which rose out of a unified sense of a common life and a common fate. Here are those vital beginnings of a recognition of value in life as it is *lived,* a recognition that marks the emergence of a new culture in the shell of the old. And at the moment this process starts, at the moment when a people begin to realize a *meaning* in their suffering, the civilization that engenders that suffering is doomed.

The nationalist aspects of Negro life are as sharply manifest in the social institutions of Negro people as in folklore. There is a Negro church, a Negro press, a Negro social world, a Negro sporting world, a Negro business world, a Negro school system, Negro professions; in short, a Negro way of life in America. The Negro people did not ask for this, and deep down, though they express themselves through their institutions and adhere to this special way of life, they do not want it now. This special existence was forced upon them from without by lynch rope, bayonet and mob rule. They accepted these negative conditions with the inevitability of a tree which must live or perish in whatever soil it finds itself.

The few crumbs of American civilization which the Negro has got from the tables of capitalism have been through these segregated channels. Many Negro institutions are cowardly and incompetent; but they are all that the Negro has. And, in the main, any move, whether for progress or reaction, must come through these insti-

tutions for the simple reason that all other channels are closed. Negro writers who seek to mould or influence the consciousness of the Negro people must address their messages to them through the ideologies and attitudes fostered in this warping way of life.

5. The Basis and Meaning of Nationalism in Negro Writing

The social institutions of the Negro are imprisoned in the Jim Crow political system of the South, and this Jim Crow political system is in turn built upon a plantation-feudal economy. Hence, it can be seen that the emotional expression of group-feeling which puzzles so many whites and leads them to deplore what they call "black chauvinism" is not a morbidly inherent trait of the Negro, but rather the reflex expression of a life whose roots are imbedded deeply in Southern soil.

Negro writers must accept the nationalist implications of their lives, not in order to encourage them, but in order to change and transcend them. They must accept the concept of nationalism because, in order to transcend it, they must *possess* and *understand* it. And a nationalist spirit in Negro writing means a nationalism carrying the highest possible pitch of social consciousness. It means a nationalism that knows its origins, its limitations that is aware of the dangers of its position that knows its ultimate aims are unrealizable within the framework of capitalist America a nationalism whose reason for being lies in the simple fact of self-possession and in the consciousness of the interdependence of people in modern society.

For purposes of creative expression it means that the Negro writer must realize within the area of his own personal experience those impulses which, when prefigured in terms of broad social movements, constitute the stuff of nationalism.

For Negro writers even more so than for Negro politicians, nationalism is a bewildering and vexing question, the full ramifications of which cannot be dealt with here. But among Negro workers and the Negro middle class the spirit of nationalism is rife in a hundred devious forms; and a simple literary realism which seeks to depict the lives of these people devoid of wider social connotations, devoid of the revolutionary significance of these nationalist tendencies, must of necessity do a rank injustice to the Negro people and alienate their possible allies in the struggle for freedom.

6. SOCIAL CONSCIOUSNESS AND RESPONSIBILITY

The Negro writer who seeks to function within his race as a purposeful agent has a serious responsibility. In order to do justice to his subject matter, in order to depict Negro life in all of its manifold and intricate relationships, a deep, informed, and complex consciousness is necessary a consciousness which draws for its strength upon the fluid lore of a great people, and moulds this lore with the concepts that move and direct the forces of history today.

With the gradual decline of the moral authority of the Negro church, and with the increasing irresolution which is paralyzing Negro middle class leadership, a new role is devolving upon the Negro writer. He is being called upon to do no less than create values by which his race is to struggle, live and die.

By his ability to fuse and make articulate the experiences of men, because his writing possesses the potential cunning to steal into the inmost recesses of the human heart, because he can create the myths and symbols that inspire a faith in life, he may expect either to be consigned to oblivion, or to be recognized for the valued agent he is.

This raises the question of the personality of the writer. It means that in the lives of Negro writers must be found those materials and experiences which will create a meaningful picture of the world today. Many young writers have grown to believe that a Marxist analysis of society presents such a picture. It creates a picture which, when placed before the eyes of the writer, should unify his personality, organize his emotions, buttress him with a tense and obdurate will to change the world.

And, in turn, this changed world will dialectically change the writer. Hence, it is through a Marxist conception of reality and society that the maximum degree of freedom in thought and feeling can be gained for the Negro writer. Further, this dramatic Marxist vision, when consciously grasped, endows the writer with a sense of dignity which no other vision can give. Ultimately, it restores to the writer his lost heritage, that is, his role as a creator of the world in which he lives, and as a creator of himself.

Yet, for the Negro writer, Marxism is but the starting point. No theory of life can take the place of life. After Marxism has laid bare the skeleton of society, there remains the task of the writer to plant flesh upon those bones out of his will to live. He may, with disgust and revulsion, say *no* and depict the horrors of capitalism encroaching upon the human being. Or he may, with hope and passion, say *yes* and depict the faint stirrings of a new and emerging life. But in whatever social voice he chooses to speak, whether positive or negative, there should always be heard or *over*-heard his faith, his necessity, his judgement.

His vision need not be simple or rendered in primer-like terms; for the life of the Negro people is not simple. The presentation of their lives should be simple, yes; but all the complexity, the strangeness, the magic wonder of life that plays like a bright sheen over the most sordid existence, should be there. To borrow a phrase from the Russians, it should have a *complex simplicity*. Eliot, Stein, Joyce, Proust, Hemingway, and Anderson, Gorky, Barbusse, Nexø, and Jack London[2] no less than the folklore of the Negro himself should form the heritage of the Negro writer. Every iota of gain in human thought and sensibility should be ready grist for his mill, no matter how far-fetched they may seem in their immediate implications.

7. THE PROBLEM OF PERSPECTIVE

What vision must Negro writers have before their eyes in order to feel the impelling necessity for an about face? What angle of vision can show them all the forces of modern society in process, all the lines of economic development converging toward a distant point of hope? Must they believe in some "ism"?

2. White American and European writers T. S. Eliot (1888–1965), Gertrude Stein (1874–1946), Marcel Proust (1871–1922), Ernest Hemingway (1899–1961), Sherwood Anderson (1876–1941), Maxim Gorky (1868–1936), Henri Barbusse (1873–1935), Martin Anderson Nexø (1869–1954), and Jack London (1876–1916).

They may feel that only dupes believe in "isms"; they feel with some measure of justification that another commitment means only another disillusionment. But anyone destitute of a theory about the meaning, structure and direction of modern society is a lost victim in a world he cannot understand or control.

But even if Negro writers found themselves through some "ism," how would that influence their writing? Are they being called upon to "preach"? To be "salesmen"? To "prostitute" their writing? Must they "sully" themselves? Must they write "propaganda"?

No; it is a question of awareness, of consciousness; it is, above all, a question of perspective.

Perspective is that part of a poem, novel, or play which a writer never puts directly upon paper. It is that fixed point in intellectual space where a writer stands to view the struggles, hopes, and sufferings of his people. There are times when he may stand too close and the result is a blurred vision. Or he may stand too far away and the result is a neglect of important things.

Of all the problems faced by writers who as a whole have never allied themselves with world movements, perspective is the most difficult of achievement. At its best, perspective is a pre-conscious assumption, something which a writer takes for granted, something which he wins through his living.

A Spanish writer recently spoke of living in the heights of one's time. Surely, perspective means just *that*.

It means that a Negro writer must learn to view the life of a Negro living in New York's Harlem or Chicago's South Side with the consciousness that one-sixth of the earth surface belongs to the working class. It means that a Negro writer must create in his readers' minds a relationship between a Negro woman hoeing cotton in the South and the men who loll in swivel chairs in Wall Street and take the fruits of her toil.

Perspective for Negro writers will come when they have looked and brooded so hard and long upon the harsh lot of their race and compared it with the hopes and struggles of minority peoples everywhere that the cold facts have begun to tell them something.

8. The Problem of Theme

This does not mean that a Negro writer's sole concern must be with rendering the social scene; but if his con-

ception of the life of his people is broad and deep enough, if the sense of the *whole* life he is seeking is vivid and strong in him, then his writing will embrace all those social, political, and economic forms under which the life of his people is manifest.

In speaking of theme one must necessarily be general and abstract; the temperament of each writer moulds and colors the world he sees. Negro life may be approached from a thousand angles, with no limit to technical and stylistic freedom.

Negro writers spring from a family, a clan, a class, and a nation; and the social units in which they are bound have a story, a record. Sense of theme will emerge in Negro writing when Negro writers try to fix this story about some pole of meaning, remembering as they do so that in the creative process meaning proceeds *equally* as much from the contemplation of the subject matter as from the hopes and apprehensions that rage in the heart of the writer.

Reduced to its simplest and most general terms, theme for Negro writers will rise from understanding the meaning of their being transplanted from a "savage" to a "civilized" culture in all of its social, political, economic, and emotional implications. It means that Negro writers must have in their consciousness the foreshortened picture of the *whole*, nourishing culture from which they were torn in Africa, and of the long, complex (and for the most part, unconscious) struggle to regain in some form and under alien conditions of life a *whole* culture again.

It is not only this picture they must have, but also a knowledge of the social and emotional milieu that gives it tone and solidity of detail. Theme for Negro writers will emerge when they have begun to feel the meaning of the history of their race as though they in one life time had lived it themselves throughout all the long centuries.

9. Autonomy of Craft

For the Negro writer to depict this new reality requires a greater discipline and consciousness than was necessary for the so-called Harlem school of expression. Not only is the subject matter dealt with far more meaningful and complex, but the new role of the writer is qualitatively different. The Negro writers' new position demands a sharper definition of the status of his craft, and a sharper emphasis upon its functional autonomy.

Negro writers should seek through the medium of their craft to play as meaningful a role in the affairs of men as do other professionals. But if their writing is demanded to perform the social office of other professions, then the autonomy of craft is lost and writing detrimentally fused with other interests. The limitations of the craft constitute some of its greatest virtues. If the sensory vehicle of imaginative writing is required to carry too great a load of didactic material, the artistic sense is submerged.

The relationship between reality and the artistic image is not always direct and simple. The imaginative conception of a historical period will not be a carbon copy of reality. Image and emotion possess a logic of their own. A vulgarized simplicity constitutes the greatest danger in tracing the reciprocal interplay between the writer and his environment.

Writing has its professional autonomy; it should complement other professions, but it should not supplant them or be swamped by them.

10. THE NECESSITY FOR COLLECTIVE WORK

It goes without saying that these things cannot be gained by Negro writers if their present mode of isolated writing and living continues. This isolation exists *among* Negro writers as well as *between* Negro and white writers. The Negro writers' lack of thorough integration with the American scene, their lack of a clear realization among themselves of their possible role, have bred generation after generation of embittered and defeated literati.

Barred for decades from the theater and publishing houses, Negro writers have been *made* to feel a sense of difference. So deep has this white-hot iron of exclusion been burnt into their hearts that thousands have all but lost the desire to become identified with American civilization. The Negro writers' acceptance of this enforced isolation and their attempt to justify it is but a defense-reflex of the whole special way of life which has been rammed down their throats.

This problem, by its very nature, is one which must be approached contemporaneously from *two* points of view. The ideological unity of Negro writers and the alliance of that unity with all the progressive ideas of our day is the primary prerequisite for collective work. On the shoulders of white writers and Negro writers alike rest the responsibility of ending this mistrust and isolation.

By placing cultural health above narrow sectional prejudices, liberal writers of all races can help to break the stony soil of aggrandizement out of which the stunted plants of Negro nationalism grow. And, simultaneously, Negro writers can help to weed out these choking growths of reactionary nationalism and replace them with hardier and sturdier types.

These tasks are imperative in light of the fact that we live in a time when the majority of the most basic assumptions of life can no longer be taken for granted. Tradition is no longer a guide. The world has grown huge and cold. Surely this is the moment to ask questions, to theorize, to speculate, to wonder out of what materials can a human world be built.

Each step along this unknown path should be taken with thought, care, self-consciousness, and deliberation. When Negro writers think they have arrived at something which smacks of truth, humanity, they should want to test it with others, feel it with a degree of passion and strength that will enable them to communicate it to millions who are groping like themselves.

Writers faced with such tasks can have no possible time for malice or jealousy. The conditions for the growth of each writer depend too much upon the good work of other writers. Every first rate novel, poem, or play lifts the level of consciousness higher.

From *New Challenge*, Fall 1937, pp. 53–65.

RICHARD WRIGHT
Between Laughter and Tears: A Review of Hurston's Their Eyes Were Watching God [1937]

It is difficult to evaluate Waters Turpin's *These Low Grounds* and Zora Neale Hurston's *Their Eyes Were Watching God*. This is not because there is an esoteric meaning hidden or implied in either of the two novels;

but rather because neither of the two novels has a basic idea or theme that lends itself to significant interpretation. Miss Hurston seems to have no desire whatever to move in the direction of serious fiction. With Mr. Turpin the case is different; the desire and motive are present, but his "saga" of four generations of Negro life seems to have been swamped by the subject matter.

These Low Grounds represents, I believe, the first attempt of a Negro writer to encompass in fiction the rise of the Negro from slavery to the present. The greater part of the novel is laid on the eastern shore of Maryland where Carrie, upon the death of her slave mother, is left to grow up in a whorehouse. After several fitful efforts to escape her lot, Carrie finally marries a visiting farmer, Prince, with whom she leads a life of household drudgery. Having helped Prince become the leading Negro farmer in the country, Carrie rebels against his infidelities and domination and, taking her two young daughters, runs away. Years later Prince discovers her and persuades her to return home. As she is about to make the journey, she is murdered by Grundy, her drunken and jealous lover. The two daughters return to the farm; Blanche remains with her father, but Martha flees North to escape the shame of pregnancy when her lover is killed in an accident. Martha's subsequent career on the stage enables her to send her son, Jimmy-Lew, to college to become a teacher. The novel closes with a disillusioned Jimmy-Lew comforted by his wife because of his bitterness over the harsh and unfair conditions of southern life.

The first half of the book is interesting, for Turpin deals with a subject which he knows intimately. Those sections depicting post-war Negro life in the North do not ring true or full; in fact, toward the conclusion the book grows embarrassingly sketchy, resolving nothing.

Oddly enough, Turpin seems to have viewed those parts of his novel which deal with the modern Negro through the eyes and consciousness of one emotionally alien to the scene. Many of the characters—Carrie, Prince, Martha—are splendid social types, but rarely do they become human beings. It seems that Turpin

drew these types from intellectual conviction, but lacked the artistic strength to make us feel the living quality of their experiences. It seems to me, he should strive to avoid the bane of sheer competency. He deals with great characters and a great subject matter; what is lacking is a great theme and a great passion.

Their Eyes Were Watching God is the story of Zora Neale Hurston's Janie who, at sixteen, married a grubbing farmer at the anxious instigation of her slave-born grandmother. The romantic Janie, in the highly-charged language of Miss Hurston, longed to be a pear tree in blossom and have a "dust-bearing bee sink into the sanctum of a bloom, the thousand sister-calyxes arch to meet the love embrace." Restless, she fled from her farmer husband and married Jody, an up-and-coming Negro business man who, in the end, proved to be no better than her first husband. After twenty years of clerking for her self-made Jody, Janie found herself a frustrated widow of forty with a small fortune on her hands. Tea Cake, "from in and through Georgia," drifted along and, despite his youth, Janie took him. For more than two years they lived happily; but Tea Cake was bitten by a mad dog and was infected with rabies. One night in a canine rage Tea Cake tried to murder Janie, thereby forcing her to shoot the only man she had ever loved.

Miss Hurston can write; but her prose is cloaked in that facile sensuality that has dogged Negro expression since the days of Phillis Wheatley.[1] Her dialogue manages to catch the psychological movements of the Negro folk-mind in their pure simplicity, but that's as far as it goes.

Miss Hurston *voluntarily* continues in her novel the tradition which was *forced* upon the Negro in the theater, that is, the minstrel technique that makes the "white folks" laugh. Her characters eat and laugh and cry and work and kill; they swing like a pendulum eternally in that safe and narrow orbit in which America likes to see the Negro live: between laughter and tears.

Turpin's faults as a writer are those of an honest man trying desperately to say something; but Zora Neale Hurston lacks even that excuse. The sensory sweep of her novel carries no theme, no message, no

---

1. The first African American to publish a book of poems; for more information on Wheatley, see p. 12.

thought. In the main, her novel is not addressed to the Negro, but to a white audience whose chauvinistic tastes she knows how to satisfy. She exploits the phase of Negro life which is "quaint," the phase which evokes a piteous smile on the lips of the "superior" race.

From *New Masses,* October 5, 1937, pp. 22–25.

ZORA NEALE HURSTON

Stories of Conflict: A Review of Wright's Uncle Tom's Children [1938]

This is a book about hatreds. Mr. Wright serves notice by his title that he speaks of people in revolt, and his stories are so grim that the Dismal Swamp of race hatred must be where they live. Not one act of understanding and sympathy comes to pass in the entire work.

But some bright new lines to remember come flashing from the author's pen. Some of his sentences have the shocking-power of a forty-four.[1] That means that he knows his way around among words. With his facility, one wonders what he would have done had he dealt with plots that touched the broader and more fundamental phases of Negro life instead of confining himself to the spectacular. For, though he has handled himself well, numerous Negro writers, published and unpublished, have written of this same kind of incident. It is the favorite Negro theme just as how the stenographer or some other poor girl won the boss or the boss's son is the favorite white theme. What is new in the four novelettes included in Mr. Wright's book is the wish-fullfilment theme. In each story the hero suffers but he gets his man.

In the first story, "Big Boy Leaves Home," the hero, Big Boy, takes the gun away from a white soldier after he has shot two of his chums and kills the white man. His chum is lynched, but Big Boy gets away. In the second story there is a flood on the Mississippi and in a fracas over a stolen rowboat, the hero gets the white owner of the boat and is later shot to death himself. He is a stupid, blundering character, but full of pathos. But then all the characters in this book are elemental and brutish. In the third story, the hero gets the white man most Negro men rail against—the white man who possesses a Negro woman. He gets several of them while he is about the business of choosing to die in a hurricane of bullets and fire because his woman has had a white man. There is lavish killing here, perhaps enough to satisfy all male black readers. In the fourth story neither the hero nor his adversary is killed, but the white foe bites the dust just the same. And in this story is summed up the conclusions that the other three stories have been moving towards.

In the other three stories the reader sees the picture of the South that the communists have been passing around of late. A dismal, hopeless section ruled by brutish hatred and nothing else. Mr. Wright's author's solution, is the solution of the PARTY—state responsibility for everything and individual responsibility for nothing, not even feeding one's self. And march!

Since the author himself is a Negro, his dialect is a puzzling thing. One wonders how he arrived at it. Certainly he does not write by ear unless he is tone-deaf. But aside from the broken speech of his characters, the book contains some beautiful writing. One hopes that Mr. Wright will find in Negro life a vehicle for his talents.

From *The Saturday Review of Literature,* April 2, 1938, p. 32.

1. A type of handgun bullet.

ALAIN LOCKE

from Who and What Is "Negro"? [1942]

Alaine Locke's "Who and What Is 'Negro'?" examines the question of "whether the racial concept has any legitimate business in our account of art." Locke acknowledges that classification of art as "Negro" may have an effect on the way artists, consumers, and critics create and perceive art. Even if racial classification has an effect, though, the question that interests Locke is whether taking race into account is justified on a theoretical level. First, he examines the idea of racial "type" and asks whether it is possible to be both diverse and racial. Second, he examines different elements that contribute to racial classification, posing the question, "What makes a work of art Negro, if indeed any such nomenclature is proper—its authorship, its theme or its idiom?" By suggesting that diversity and inclusiveness need not be incompatible with racial categorizations, Locke presents a pluralist position that foreshadows late-twentieth-century calls for a hyphenated concept of identity.

From *Opportunity*, February–March 1942, pp. 36–41, 83–87.

A Janus-faced[1] question—"who and what is Negro"—sits like a perennial sphinx[2] at the door of every critic who considers the literature or the art of the Negro. One may appease it, as many do, with literary honey-cakes and poppy-seed, but hackneyed clichés and non-committal concepts only postpone the challenge. Sooner or later the critic must face the basic issues involved in his use of risky and perhaps untenable terms like "Negro art" and "Negro literature," and answer the much-evaded question unequivocally,—who and what is Negro?

This year our sphinx, so to speak, sits in the very vestibule with almost no passing space; for several of the most important books of 1941 pose this issue unavoidably. It is useless to throw the question back at the sociologist or the anthropologist, for they scarcely know themselves, having twin sphinxes in their own bailiwicks. Indeed it is a pertinent question in its own right whether the racial concept has any legitimate business in our account of art. Granted even that folks are interested in "Negro art" and "Negro literature," and that some creative artists consciously accept such a platform of artistic expression, it is warrantable to ask whether they should and whether it should be so. After all, mayn't we be just the victims of an ancient curse of prejudice in these matters and so, unwittingly blind partisans of culture politics and its traditional factionalisms?

Let us take first the question "Who is Negro," provocatively posed by the challenging foreword of Richard Wright's *12 Million Black Voices*. "This text," he says, "while purporting to render a broad picture of the processes of Negro life in the United States, intentionally does not include in its considerations those areas of Negro life which comprise the so-called 'Talented Tenth,'[3] or the isolated islands of mulatto leadership which are still to be found in many parts of the South, or the growing middle-class professional and business men of the North who have, in the past thirty years or more, formed a certain liaison corps between the whites and the blacks. Their exclusion from these pages does not imply any invidious judgment, nor does it stem from any desire to underestimate their progress and contributions; they are omitted in an effort to simplify a depiction of a complex movement of debased feudal folk toward a twentieth-century urbanization.

---

1. Having two faces; from Janus, the Roman god of gates, doors, beginnings, and endings.
2. Greek name for Egyptian mythical creature with a human head on a lion's body; in the myth of Oedipus, a sphinx guarded the entrance to Thebes, killing travelers unable to answer her riddle.
3. African Americans with the potential to be leaders; see 1903 article by W. E. B. Du Bois (p. 230) urging higher education to develop the "Talented Tenth."

ALAIN LOCKE   *Who and What Is "Negro"?* ≈ **483**

This text assumes that those few Negroes who have lifted themselves, through personal strength, talent or luck, above the lives of their fellow-blacks—like single fishes that leap and flash for a split second above the surface of the sea—are but fleeting exceptions to that vast tragic school that swims below in the depths, against the current, silently and heavily, struggling against the waves of vicissitudes that spell a common fate. It is not, however, to celebrate or exalt the plight of the humble folk who swim in the depths that I select the conditions of their lives as examples of normality, but rather to seize upon that which is qualitatively and abiding in Negro experience, to place within full and constant view the collective humanity whose triumphs and defeats are shared by the majority, whose gains in security mark an advance in the level of consciousness attained by the broad masses in their costly and tortuous upstream journey."

Here is a clear and bravely worded challenge. Who is the real Negro? Well, not only the mass Negro as over against both the culturally "representative" elite or "talented tenth" and the "exceptional" or "untypical" few of the bourgeoisie, but that "mass Negro" who in spite of the phrase about what is "qualitative and abiding in Negro experience," is common denominator proletarian rather than racially distinctive. For all its local and racial color, then, this approach practically scraps the racial factor as inconsequential and liquidates that element culturally as well as sociologically.

As I shall say later, this is an important book, a valuable social analysis, dramatically exposed and simplified, more than that—a sound working hypothesis for the proletarian artist who has a right to his artistic *Weltanschauung*.[4] But a school of thought or art or social theory that lays claim to totalitarian rectitude must, I think, be challenged. The fallacy of the "new" as of the "older" thinking is that there is a type Negro who, either qualitatively or quantitatively, is the type symbol of the entire group. To break arbitrary stereotypes it is necessary perhaps to bring forward counter-stereotypes, but none are adequate substitutes for the whole truth. There is, in brief, no *"The Negro."* More and more, even as we stress the right of the mass Negro to his important place in the picture, artistically and sociologically, we must become aware of the class structure of the Negro population, and expect to see, hear and understand the intellectual elite, the black bourgeoisie as well as the black masses. To this common stratification is added in the Negro's case internal splits resulting from differential response to particular racial stresses and strains, divergent loyalties which, in my judgment, constitute racial distinctiveness, not by some magic of inheritance but through some very obvious environmental conditionings. For just as we have, for comparative example, the orthodox and the assimilate, the Zionist[5] and anti-Zionist Jew, so in Negro life we have on practically all of these levels the conformist and the non-conformist strains,— the conformist elite and the racialist elite, the lily-white and the race-patriotic bourgeois, the folk and the ghetto peasant and the emerging Negro proletarian. Each is a significant segment of Negro life, and as they severally come to articulate expression, it will be increasingly apparent that each is a representative facet of Negro life and experience. For a given decade one or the other may seem more significant or "representative," chiefly as it may succeed to the historical spotlight or assume a protagonist role in group expression or group movement. However, as our historical perspective lengthens and our social insight deepens, we should no longer be victims of the still all-too-prevalent formula psychology. Common denominator regional and national traits are there to be taken into account, as are also, more and more as overtones, the factors of group and racial distinctiveness. In cultural and creative expression, the flavor of idiom seems to count especially, which to me seems a valid reason for not scraping the racialist emphasis, provided of course, it does not proceed to the isolationist extreme of ghetto compartmentalization. But more important even than this emphasis is the necessity of an objective but corrective insistence on the variety of Negro types and their social and cultural milieu.

Turning to the other basic question,—what is Negro, we may ask ourselves what makes a work of art

---

4. Worldview [German].
5. One who supports the re-establishment of a Jewish homeland in the land of Israel.

Negro, if indeed any such nomenclature is proper,—its authorship, its theme or its idiom? Different schools of criticism are obviously divided on these criteria. Each has had its inning, and probably no one regrets the comparative obsolescence of the artificial separatist criterion of Negro authorship. Only in the hectic early striving for credit and recognition could it be forgotten that the logical goal of such a viewpoint is an artistic Ghetto of "Negro art" and "Negro literature," isolated from the common cultural heritage and the vital and necessary fraternalisms of school and generation tendencies. The editors of the brilliantly panoramic anthology, *The Negro Caravan*, pose the issue this way: "In spite of such unifying bonds as a common rejection of the popular stereotypes and a common racial cause, writings by Negroes do not seem to the editors to fall into a unique cultural pattern. Negro writers have adopted the literary traditions that seemed useful for their purposes. They have therefore been influenced by Puritan didacticism, sentimental humanitarianism, local color, regionalism, realism, naturalism, and experimentalism." . . . The editors do not believe that the expression "Negro literature" is an accurate one, and in spite of its convenient brevity, they have avoided using it. "Negro literature" has no application if it means structural peculiarity, or a Negro school of writing. The Negro writes in the forms evolved in English and American literature. A "Negro novel," "a Negro play" are ambiguous terms. If they mean a novel or play by Negroes, then such works as *Porgy* and *The Green Pastures*[6] are left out. If they mean works about Negro life, they include more works by white authors than by Negro, and these works have been most influential upon the American mind. The editors consider Negro writers to be American writers, and literature by American Negroes to be a segment of American literature." . . . "The chief cause for objection to the term is that Negro literature is too easily placed by certain critics, white and Negro, in an alcove apart. The next step is a double standard of judgment, which is dangerous for the future of Negro writers."

Again, these are brave and necessary words. But there is a trace in them of corrective counter-emphasis, and the objective truth lies probably somewhere between, as indeed the dual significance of the anthology itself evidences. Simultaneously, a segment of American literature and a special chapter of racial expression and reaction, most of the materials in this same anthology have a double character as well as a double significance. The logical predicament is in not seeing the complete compatibility between nationally and racially distinctive elements, arising from our oversimplified and chauvinistic conception of culture. Neither national nor racial cultural elements are so distinctive as to be mutually exclusive. It is the general composite character of culture which is disregarded by such over-simplifications. By that logic, a typical American character could never have been expected as a modification of English artistic and institutional culture, but there it is, after some generations of divergence, characteristically Anglo-Saxon and American at the same time. Strictly speaking, we should consistently cite this composite character in our culture with hyphenate descriptions, but more practically, we stress the dominant flavor of the blend. It is only in this same limited sense that anything is legitimately styled "Negro"; actually it is Afro- or Negro-American, a hybrid product of Negro reaction to American cultural forms and patterns. And when, as with many of our Negro cultural products, it is shared in the common cultural life,—our jazz music, as a conspicuous example,—it becomes progressively even more composite and hybridized, sometimes for the better, sometimes not. For we must abandon the idea of cultural purism as a criterion under the circumstances just as we have abandoned the idea of a pure race under the more scientific and objective scrutiny of the facts of history.

Thus the interpenetration of national and racial characteristics, once properly understood, resolves the traditional dilemma of the racialists and on the cultural level puts an essential parity on racial, national and regional idioms. As the point of view matures, per-

---

6. 1930 Pulitzer Prize–winning play by the white American writer Marc Connelly, adapted from the 1928 short story collection *Ol' Man Adam an' His Chillun* by the white American writer Roark Bradford; *Porgy*: 1924 novel by the white writer DuBose Heyward.

haps we shall regard all three as different dimensions of cultural variation, interchangeably blended in specific art forms and combinations. Such reciprocity actually exists, and would have been recognized but for our politically minded notions of culture, which flatter majority strains in our culture and minimize minority culture elements. As a matter of fact, the racial evolves by special emphasis from the general cultural heritage and in turn flows back into the common culture. With neither claiming more than its proper due, no such invidious and peculiar character accrues to the racial, and, on such a basis, it should not be necessary to play down the racial contribution in order to prove the essential cultural solidarity of Negro creative effort with American art and letters. The position leads, if soundly developed, not to cul-

tural separatism but to cultural pluralism. To be "Negro" in the cultural sense, then, is not to be radically different, but only to be distinctively composite and idiomatic, though basically American, as is to be expected, in the first instance.

According to such criteria, the critic has, like the chemist, the analytical job of breaking down compounds into their constituent culture elements. So far as characterization goes, this involves the task of assessing the accent of representativeness among the varying regional, racial and national elements. Theme and idiom would bulk more significantly than source of authorship, and important expressions of Negro material and idiom by white authors would belong as legitimately in a Negro as in a general anthology.

JAMES BALDWIN
Everybody's Protest Novel [1949]

In this controversial essay, James Baldwin (1924–1987) links the classic anti-slavery novel, *Uncle Tom's Cabin*, by Harriet Beecher Stowe (p. 118), with Richard Wright's prototypical novel of naturalistic protest, *Native Son*, ultimately rejecting the protest novel itself. In championing the complexity, ambiguity, and paradox of "truth" and human experience, Baldwin reopens the 1930s debate between Wright and Zora Neale Hurston over the relationship between politics and artistic expression (see p. 470).

As a young writer living in New York City's Greenwich Village, Baldwin sought out Wright's friendship and guidance and enlisted his help in securing a fellowship that allowed him to complete his first novel. Wright

saw "Everybody's Protest Novel" as a betrayal, though Baldwin insisted that his intention was not to betray. In a 1984 interview in *The New York Times Book Review*, Baldwin stated that his essay was not a personal attack but instead represented a critical part of his development as a writer. "I knew Richard and I loved him," Baldwin said. "I was not attacking him; I was trying to clarify something for myself." Six years after writing "Everybody's Protest Novel," Baldwin published his first collection of essays. Although the collection opens with "Everybody's Protest Novel," Baldwin's choice of a title for the book—*Notes of a Native Son*—underscored his complex literary and personal connection to his former mentor.

From *Partisan Review,* June 16, 1949; reprinted in James Baldwin, *Notes of a Native Son* (Boston: Beacon Press, 1955), pp. 13–23.

In *Uncle Tom's Cabin*, that cornerstone of American social protest fiction, St. Clare, the kindly master, remarks to his coldly disapproving Yankee cousin, Miss Ophelia, that, so far as he is able to tell, the blacks have been turned over to the devil for the benefit of the

whites in this world—however, he adds thoughtfully, it may turn out in the next. Miss Ophelia's reaction is, at least, vehemently right-minded: "This is perfectly horrible!" she exclaims. "You ought to be ashamed of yourselves!"

Miss Ophelia, as we may suppose, was speaking for the author; her exclamation is the moral, neatly framed, and incontestable like those improving mottoes sometimes found hanging on the walls of furnished rooms. And, like these mottoes, before which one invariably flinches, recognizing an insupportable, almost an indecent glibness, she and St. Clare are terribly in earnest. Neither of them questions the medieval morality from which their dialogue springs: black, white, the devil, the next world—posing its alternatives between heaven and the flames—were realities for them as, of course, they were for their creator. They spurned and were terrified of the darkness, striving mightily for the light; and considered from this aspect, Miss Ophelia's exclamation, like Mrs. Stowe's novel, achieves a bright, almost a lurid significance, like the light from a fire which consumes a witch. This is the more striking as one considers the novels of Negro oppression written in our own, more enlightened day, all of which say only: "This is perfectly horrible! You ought to be ashamed of yourselves!" (Let us ignore, for the moment, those novels of oppression written by Negroes, which add only a raging, near-paranoiac postscript to this statement and actually reinforce, as I hope to make clear later, the principles which activate the oppression they decry.)

Uncle Tom's Cabin is a very bad novel, having, in its self-righteous, virtuous sentimentality, much in common with *Little Women*.[1] Sentimentality, the ostentatious parading of excessive and spurious emotion, is the mark of dishonesty, the inability to feel; the wet eyes of the sentimentalist betray his aversion to experience, his fear of life, his arid heart; and it is always, therefore, the signal of secret and violent inhumanity, the mask of cruelty. *Uncle Tom's Cabin*—like its multitudinous, hard-boiled descendants—is a catalogue of violence. This is explained by the nature of Mrs. Stowe's subject matter, her laudable determination to flinch from nothing in presenting the complete picture; an explanation which falters only if we pause to ask whether or not her picture is indeed complete; and what constriction or failure of perception forced her to so depend on the description of brutality—unmotivated, senseless—and to leave unanswered and unnoticed the only important question: what it was, after all, that moved her people to such deeds.

But this, let us say, was beyond Mrs. Stowe's powers; she was not so much a novelist as an impassioned pamphleteer; her book was not intended to do anything more than prove that slavery was wrong; was, in fact, perfectly horrible. This makes material for a pamphlet but it is hardly enough for a novel; and the only question left to ask is why we are bound still within the same constriction. How is it that we are so loath to make a further journey than that made by Mrs. Stowe, to discover and reveal something a little closer to the truth?

But that battered word, truth, having made its appearance here, confronts one immediately with a series of riddles and has, moreover, since so many gospels are preached, the unfortunate tendency to make one belligerent. Let us say, then, that truth, as used here, is meant to imply a devotion to the human being, his freedom and fulfillment; freedom which cannot be legislated, fulfillment which cannot be charted. This is the prime concern, the frame of reference; it is not to be confused with a devotion to Humanity which is too easily equated with a devotion to a Cause; and Causes, as we know, are notoriously bloodthirsty. We have, as it seems to me, in this most mechanical and interlocking of civilizations, attempted to lop this creature down to the status of a time-saving invention. He is not, after all, merely a member of a Society or a Group or a deplorable conundrum to be explained by Science. He is—and how old-fashioned the words sound!—something more than that, something resolutely indefinable, unpredictable. In overlooking, denying, evading his complexity—which is nothing more than the disquieting complexity of ourselves—we are diminished and we perish; only within this web of ambiguity, paradox, this hunger, danger, darkness, can we find at once ourselves and the power that will free us from ourselves. It is this power of revelation which is the business of the novelist, this journey toward a more vast reality which must take precedence over all other claims. What is today parroted as his Responsibility—which seems to mean that he must make formal declaration that he is involved in, and affected by, the lives of other people

---

1. Best-selling novel published in two parts in 1868 and 1869 by the white American author Louisa May Alcott.

and to say something improving about this somewhat self-evident fact—is, when he believes it, his corruption and our loss; moreover, it is rooted in, interlocked with and intensifies this same mechanization. Both *Gentleman's Agreement* and *The Postman Always Rings Twice*[2] exemplify this terror of the human being, the determination to cut him down to size. And in *Uncle Tom's Cabin* we may find foreshadowing of both: the formula created by the necessity to find a lie more palatable than the truth has been handed down and memorized and persists yet with a terrible power.

It is interesting to consider one more aspect of Mrs. Stowe's novel, the method she used to solve the problem of writing about a black man at all. Apart from her lively procession of field hands, house niggers, Chloe, Topsy, etc.—who are the stock, lovable figures presenting no problem—she has only three other Negroes in the book. These are the important ones and two of them may be dismissed immediately, since we have only the author's word that they are Negro and they are, in all other respects, as white as she can make them. The two are George and Eliza, a married couple with a wholly adorable child—whose quaintness, incidentally, and whose charm, rather put one in mind of a darky bootblack doing a buck and wing to the clatter of condescending coins. Eliza is a beautiful, pious hybrid, light enough to pass—the heroine of *Quality* might, indeed, be her reincarnation—differing from the genteel mistress who has overseered her education only in the respect that she is a servant. George is darker, but makes up for it by being a mechanical genius, and is, moreover, sufficiently un-Negroid to pass through town, a fugitive from his master, disguised as a Spanish gentleman, attracting no attention whatever beyond admiration. They are a race apart from Topsy. It transpires by the end of the novel, through one of those energetic, last-minute convolutions of the plot, that Eliza has some connection with French gentility. The figure from whom the novel takes its name, Uncle Tom, who is a figure of controversy yet, is jet-black, wooly-haired, illiterate; and he is

phenomenally forbearing. He has to be; he is black; only through this forbearance can he survive or triumph. (*Cf.* Faulkner's preface to *The Sound and the Fury:*[3] These others were not Compsons. They were black:—They endured.) His triumph is metaphysical, unearthly; since he is black, born without the light, it is only through humility, the incessant mortification of the flesh, that he can enter into communion with God or man. The virtuous rage of Mrs. Stowe is motivated by nothing so temporal as a concern for the relationship of men to one another—or, even, as she would have claimed, by a concern for their relationship to God—but merely by a panic of being hurled into the flames, of being caught in traffic with the devil. She embraced this merciless doctrine with all her heart, bargaining shamelessly before the throne of grace: God and salvation becoming her personal property, purchased with the coin of her virtue. Here, black equates with evil and white with grace; if, being mindful of the necessity of good works, she could not cast out the blacks—a wretched, huddled mass, apparently, claiming, like an obsession, her inner eye—she could not embrace them either without purifying them of sin. She must cover their intimidating nakedness, robe them in white, the garments of salvation; only thus could she herself be delivered from ever-present sin, only thus could she bury, as St. Paul demanded, "the carnal man, the man of the flesh."[4] Tom, therefore, her only black man, has been robbed of his humanity and divested of his sex. It is the price for that darkness with which he has been branded.

Uncle Tom's Cabin, then, is activated by what might be called a theological terror, the terror of damnation; and the spirit that breathes in this book, hot, self-righteous, fearful, is not different from that spirit of medieval times which sought to exorcize evil by burning witches; and is not different from that terror which activates a lynch mob. One need not, indeed, search for examples so historic or so gaudy; this is a warfare waged daily in the heart, a warfare so vast, so relentless and so powerful that the interracial

2. 1934 crime novel by the white American writer James M. Cain; *Gentleman's Agreement:* 1947 novel about anti-Semitism by the white American author Laura Z. Hobson, made into a movie the same year directed by Elia Kazan.
3. 1929 novel by the white American author William Faulkner (1897–1962); *Cf:* confer [Latin], meaning compare.
4. Saint Paul lists the varieties of carnal sin in Galatians 5:16–26.

handshake or the interracial marriage can be as cruci-fying as the public hanging or the secret rape. This panic motivates our cruelty, this fear of the dark makes it impossible that our lives shall be other than superficial; this, interlocked with and feeding our glittering, mechanical, inescapable civilization which has put to death our freedom.

This, notwithstanding that the avowed aim of the American protest novel is to bring greater freedom to the oppressed. They are forgiven, on the strength of these good intentions, whatever violence they do to language, whatever excessive demands they make of credibility. It is, indeed, considered the sign of a frivolity so intense as to approach decadence to suggest that these books are both badly written and wildly improbable. One is told to put first things first, the good of society coming before niceties of style or characterization. Even if this were incontestable—for what exactly is the "good" of society?—it argues an insuperable confusion, since literature and sociology are not one and the same; it is impossible to discuss them as if they were. Our passion for categorization, life neatly fitted into pegs, has led to an unforeseen, paradoxical distress; confusion, a breakdown of meaning. Those categories which were meant to define and control the world for us have boomeranged us into chaos; in which limbo we whirl, clutching the straws of our definitions. The "protest" novel, so far from being disturbing, is an accepted and comforting aspect of the American scene, ramifying that framework we believe to be so necessary. Whatever unsettling questions are raised are evanescent, titillating; remote, for this has nothing to do with us, it is safely ensconced in the social arena, where, indeed, it has nothing to do with anyone, so that finally we receive a very definite thrill of virtue from the fact that we are reading such a book at all. This report from the pit reassures us of its reality and its darkness and of our own salvation; and "As long as such books are being published," an American liberal once said to me, "everything will be all right."

But unless one's ideal of society is a race of neatly analyzed, hard-working ciphers, one can hardly claim for the protest novels the lofty purpose they claim for themselves or share the present optimism concerning them. They emerge for what they are: a mirror of our confusion, dishonesty, panic, trapped and immobilized in the sunlit prison of the American dream. They are fantasies, connecting nowhere with reality, sentimental; in exactly the same sense that such movies as *The Best Years of Our Lives*[5] or the works of Mr. James M. Cain are fantasies. Beneath the dazzling pyrotechnics of these current operas one may still discern, as the controlling force, the intense theological preoccupations of Mrs. Stowe, the sick vacuities of *The Rover Boys*.[6] Finally, the aim of the protest novel becomes something very closely resembling the zeal of those alabaster missionaries to Africa to cover the nakedness of the natives, to hurry them into the pallid arms of Jesus and thence into slavery. The aim has now become to reduce all Americans to the compulsive, bloodless dimensions of a guy named Joe.

It is the peculiar triumph of society—and its loss—that it is able to convince those people to whom it has given inferior status of the reality of this decree; it has the force and the weapons to translate its dictum into fact, so that the allegedly inferior are actually made so, insofar as the societal realities are concerned. This is a more hidden phenomenon now than it was in the days of serfdom, but it is no less implacable. Now, as then, we find ourselves bound, first without, then within, by the nature of our categorization. And escape is not effected through a bitter railing against this trap; it is as though this very striving were the only motion needed to spring the trap upon us. We take our shape, it is true, within and against that cage of reality bequeathed us at our birth; and yet it is precisely through our dependence on this reality that we are most endlessly betrayed. Society is held together by our need; we bind it together with legend, myth, coercion, fearing that without it we will be hurled into that void, within which, like the earth before the Word[7]

5. 1947 American movie about returning World War II veterans that won seven Academy Awards.
6. Children's book series by "Arthur M. Winfield" (a pen name used by the white American writer and publisher Edward Strate-meyer, 1862–1930), originally published between 1899 and 1926.
7. John 1.1: "In the beginning was the Word, and the Word was with God, and the Word was God."

was spoken, the foundations of society are hidden. From this void—ourselves—it is the function of society to protect us; but it is only this void, our unknown selves, demanding, forever, a new act of creation, which can save us—"from the evil that is in the world." With the same motion, at the same time, it is this toward which we endlessly struggle and from which, endlessly, we struggle to escape.

It must be remembered that the oppressed and the oppressor are bound together within the same society; they accept the same criteria, they share the same beliefs, they both alike depend on the same reality. Within this cage it is romantic, more, meaningless, to speak of a "new" society as the desire of the oppressed, for that shivering dependence on the props of reality which he shares with the *Herrenvolk*[8] makes a truly "new" society impossible to conceive. What is meant by a new society is one in which inequalities will disappear, in which vengeance will be exacted; either there will be no oppressed at all, or the oppressed and the oppressor will change places. But, finally, as it seems to me, what the rejected desire is, is an elevation of status, acceptance within the present community. Thus, the African, exile, pagan, hurried off the auction block and into the fields, fell on his knees before that God in Whom he must now believe; who had made him, but not in His image. This tableau, this impossibility, is the heritage of the Negro in America: *Wash me,* cried the slave to his Maker, *and I shall be whiter, whiter than snow!*[9] For black is the color of evil; only the robes of the saved are white. It is this cry, implacable on the air and in the skull, that he must live with. Beneath the widely published catalogue of brutality—bringing to mind, somehow, an image, a memory of church-bells burdening the air—is this reality which, in the same nightmare notion, he both flees and rushes to embrace. In America, now, this country devoted to the death of the paradox—which may, therefore, be put to death by one—his lot is as ambiguous as a tableau by Kafka.[1] To flee or not, to move or not, it is all the same; his doom is written on his forehead, it is carried in his heart. In *Native Son,* Bigger Thomas stands on a Chicago street corner watching airplanes flown by white men racing against the sun and "Goddamn" he says, the bitterness bubbling up like blood, remembering a million indignities, the terrible, rat-infested house, the humiliation of home-relief, the intense, aimless, ugly bickering, hating it; hatred smoulders through these pages like sulphur fire. All of Bigger's life is controlled, defined by his hatred and his fear. And later, his fear drives him to murder and his hatred to rape; he dies, having come, through this violence, we are told, for the first time, to a kind of life, having for the first time redeemed his manhood. Below the surface of this novel there lies, as it seems to me, a continuation, a complement of that monstrous legend it was written to destroy. Bigger is Uncle Tom's descendant, flesh of his flesh, so exactly opposite a portrait that, when the books are placed together, it seems that the contemporary Negro novelist and the dead New England woman are locked together in a deadly, timeless battle; the one uttering merciless exhortations, the other shouting curses. And, indeed, within this web of lust and fury, black and white can only thrust and counter-thrust, long for each other's slow, exquisite death; death by torture, acid, knives and burning; the thrust, the counter-thrust, the longing making the heavier that cloud which blinds and suffocates them both, so that they go down into the pit together. Thus has the cage betrayed us all, this moment, our life, turned to nothing through our terrible attempts to insure it. For Bigger's tragedy is not that he is cold or black or hungry, not even that he is American, black; but that he has accepted a theology that denies him life, that he admits the possibility of his being subhuman and feels constrained, therefore, to battle for his humanity according to those brutal criteria bequeathed him at his birth. But our humanity is our burden, our life; we need not battle for it; we need only to do what is infinitely more difficult—that is, accept it. The failure of the protest novel lies in its rejection of life, the human being, the denial of his beauty, dread, power, in its insistence that it is his categorization alone which is real and which cannot be transcended.

8. Master race [German].
9. Allusion to Psalms 51:7: "Purge me with hyssop, and I shall be clean: wash me, and I shall be whiter than snow."
1. Franz Kafka (1883–1924), writer of fiction from Prague, Austria-Hungary.

KEY DEBATE ～ *Society and Individual Choice*

On Intermarriage

A Reader of *The Crisis* and W. E. B. Du Bois: *About Marrying* [1930]
The Crisis: *Inter-Marriage: A Symposium* [1930]

Du Bois's January 1930 *Crisis* column on marriage and the subsequent anonymous letters on the subject reveal general agreement on the social and economic struggles faced by interracial couples but disagreement on whether a particular couple should get married despite those struggles. Responding to a letter from a young white man who wants to marry a black woman, Du Bois recognizes the prejudice of the general white and black populations against interracial couples but advises the letter writer: "If you wish to marry the girl and she wishes to marry you, then get married." Among the responses published the following month in *The Crisis,* only one (the sole white respondent) offers unequivocal support for the marriage. Others advise against it, citing the interests of the individual woman or man or the interest of society, which are seen as superseding individual interests.

A READER OF *THE CRISIS* AND W. E. B. DU BOIS
About Marrying [1930]

DEAR MR. DU BOIS:

I imagine in all appeals for your advice you rarely are called upon to aid Cupid, and certainly still more rarely for such a case as mine. Briefly, I am a white young man and am in love with a colored girl.

Now to give some details so you can better understand the situation. I graduated from —— in 1924 and she from —— in 1923. Since then she has taught in various colored schools and I have been here most of the time teaching music, taking some college work and occasionally doing music study in —— . I now am 25 and she is 27.

My parents are friendly to Negroes and in —— we associated with them to quite an extent. Because I inherited no racial prejudice I presume is one main factor in my "falling in love" with a colored girl. The first time I remember seeing her was in her high school Latin class when she was a Senior. I had a passing impression that she was the most beautiful girl I had ever seen. She comes from one of the better colored families, of course, and is a light mulatto—too dark though to pass as white and I am of German-English descent with sandy red hair and could never pass for colored. So The next time I remember her especially was at high school commencement when she took a $20 gold piece prize in English and was one of the honor students. I did not meet her until three years later when she was a junior in college—she 19 and I, 17. It was at her brother-in-law's home, with whom I was chumming at the time. Then the deed was done and I passed two or three of the happiest weeks of my life. This was around Christmas time and when I went home for the holidays the wrath fell in earnest—they had warnings of it before. With all my parents' broad-mindedness they, of course, drew the line at this not only because of race but religious reasons. I was brought up with conservative ideas on religion and to honor and obey my parents. Then began the struggle between obedience to my parents and my own desires. This struggle still continues. Of course, all our friends, colored and white, had their say—even the college and conservatory deans. They had no objections usually to her as a person but only because of racial difference.

Our interests are common—music and French. It is now six years since I have seen her but we have corresponded most of the time. I still love her as intensely as at first. I am sure she was in love with me too *but,* you probably know and feel more keenly than I just what the but means. Some people think from some gossip passed on to me that our relations were immoral. That is not so. As I said, I am conservative and my ideas of love, marriage and divorce and religion by the modern flaming youth would be considered hopelessly mid-Victorian, Puritanical, old fogey and all the other scornful terms applied to such. I do not smoke, drink, dance, play cards, rarely go to a movie and my relations with her were just as "narrow". Of course, since I do none of the above I *never* have a good time! Singing Beethoven's ninth symphony under Dr. —— at ——, playing a Chopin and Mendelssohn concerto with orchestra, listening to the club give the "Messiah", playing the "Messiah" and "Elijah" for the chorus here, listening to Roland Hayes,[1] speaking French, and studying with the most noted Composition teacher in —— does not come under the category of "good time"!

But that is all beside the point. The point is I still am madly in love with her and want her to be with me to share all these good things, yes, and be the mother of my children.

I do not advocate racial inter-marriage in general. But, Mr. Du Bois, since she is more white than Negro, why should she not marry white? It's just as logical that way as the other. I think the standard of husband-wife relationship should be made principally on a spiritual and intellectual basis. We have had intellectual fellowship as I have said. She is more liberal in her social and religious views, but I think we agree on *the* fundamental—the God-Christ as atonement for sin. She is neat and attractive in her personal habits as I am. It is only the *but* that hinders.

I want your view on inter-marriage and advice as to whether you think I should persuade her to marry me. I feel we could manage somehow. Our friends and relatives would have to accept us willy-nilly. And anyhow we would not be marrying principally each other's relatives. A great majority of mother's folks I have not seen for twenty years and they mean nothing special to me. It's her I want.

We would have our own social contacts to make as any newly married couple does with its own peculiar problems.

I have nearly written you several times for three or four years but never could get to the point of doing so. I presume I will act like a dear friend of father and mother's whom I have heard them speak of very often when she asked for advice would say: "Now I want to know what you all think, but I will go ahead and do as I please afterwards."

—— – ——

P.S. Can you recommend any book on the subject that will be helpful?

MY DEAR MR. ——:

I have your letter of September 23rd. My advice is that if you wish to marry the girl and she wishes to marry you, then get married.

I assume that both of you know exactly the kind of difficulties you are going to meet. I need hardly to rehearse them. You are going to have restricted social intercourse, naturally so far as the whites are concerned; but also, so far as the colored people are concerned. In this matter, they are just as prejudiced as the whites. You are going to meet more or less insult and embarrassment in public places, if your wife is dark enough to have her color noticeable; and finally, (perhaps this is the most serious), you are going to have difficulty in finding work or in keeping it if people know that you have married a colored woman. It will be practically impossible for you to find work in any college, white or colored.

These are all facts which you have got to face frankly. If, before you had fallen in love you had consulted me as to the possibility, I should have pointed out these facts and emphasized them and advised you to go no further. But now the question simply is, are both of you ready, in the face of this situation, to face a world "well lost for love"?[2]

I know of no book which treats this matter sanely to any extent. Haldeman-Julius has just published

---

1. Concert tenor (1887–1977); the son of former slaves, Hayes toured with the Fisk University Singers in college and went on to become the first African American concert singer to achieve international fame.
2. Allusion to John Dryden's 1677 play about Anthony and Cleopatra, *All for Love, or The World Well Lost.*

a little Blue Book by Schuyler[3] which takes up the subject. I have also treated it briefly in my book "Darkwater"[4]

W. E. B. Du Bois.

And now, Reader—white, black, green or yellow, what do you say in answer to this letter? Answer and we will publish a few of the letters.

From *The Crisis*, January 1930.

The Crisis
Inter-Marriage: A Symposium [1930]

GENERAL discussions on inter-marriage usually get no where because there is no agreement as to fundamental facts. In the January CRISIS, we publishd a genuine specific case and after giving our own opinion, asked the opinions of our readers. Here are a few:

In regard to the letter "About Marrying" recently printed in your esteemed paper, it seems to me that the young people should be advised to follow their inclinations as to marriage.

The question of racial intermarriage is a vital one, and one upon which conservatives and progressives differ. If we believe in economic and social equality of the races, we must perforce believe in racial inter-marriage. Racial inter-marriage and amalgamation of the races, however hateful to the reactionary, is favored by all those who have the feeling that all men are created equal, irrespective of color.

In the case of love between the races, questions of expediency vanish. The question is, is love worth while? If so, we must approve of the marriage of the young couple.

A White Woman of Connecticut.

In the Postscript of the January number of THE CRISIS, the letter of the young white man in love with a mulatto girl has drawn my sympathy and I respond to your invitation to give him advice.

Since he states they have been separated for six years, I think he should continue it.

Marriage such as he contemplates would involve all that you have suggested, ostracism, insult, and embarrassment in public places—possible loss of work and difficulty in getting other work—and while he and, perhaps, she may be willing to endure it all for each other's sake—if he loves her as he claims he does, he will not want her to suffer martyrdom in seeing her children boycotted by both his race and her race and perhaps endure the reproaches they may fling upon their parents.

Other men in love have considered the loved one's best interest on happiness before their own desires, and in my opinion, they have chosen the better part.

A Colored Woman of Texas.

My advice to you is, "Don't". Not that the cause which occasions your letter does not need a champion nor that the issue is not simply just spoiling for a franker demonstration of its possibilities for good and ill, but after reading your letter I am convinced beyond even the shadow of a doubt that you are not the one to start a crusade which doubtless requires unusual qualities of a pioneer soul in the realm of things social.

That you have thus through the past five years wavered on the brink of decision and that you now seek advice from without to aid you, or confirm you in a decision already made in a momentous and necessarily personal matter, reveal most significantly your attitudes which would hardly stand the supreme testing which the union you propose might involve. The cause, like all controversial issues of historical record, stands in need of the services of potential martyrs willing to offer themselves in the clinic of social investigation and research, but I fear (and on this statement I risk whatever reputation I may have as a psychologist as well as prophet) you do not possess the abdominal

3. George S. Schuyler, *Racial Inter-Marriage in the United States*, Little Blue Book, no. 1387 (Girard, Kans.: Haldeman-Julius, 1929).
4. *Darkwater: Voices from the Veil* (New York: Harcourt, Brace and Howe, 1920) is a collection of new and previously published short fiction and essays by Du Bois.

ingredients which constitute the visceral investiture of traditional witnesses unto death.

Then let me, at the risk of appearing unkind, suggest that you turn your attentions and deliver your affections to another where *only* the ordinary (and God only knows what they be) risks attend. Assuming again the analytic role for which I have already rendered an implied apology, let me predict that you will find the solace which your nature seems to require and to the ultimate utter exclusion of the former attachment.

O yes, the libraries are full of books which treat of the matter which seems to trouble you. We have in tenthousand volume lots the stories of men who have dared convention and offered a willing sacrifice for the demonstration of the worthwhileness of principles which they deemed eternal. Read again, with this in mind, the story of the young Galilean carpenter[5] whose philosophy was so new and strange and simple that he had to be summarily dealt with before he had time to turn right-side up the topsy turvy world to which he came. Read of Joan of Arc,—Saint Joan now, who saw light through the mists of doubt and fear which hovered so darkly over her beloved land. Read of Savonarola Martin Luther, John Brown, Wm. Lloyd Garrison, Moorfield Storey, and the Rev. Mr. Adelbert J. Helm, late of Detroit.——Yes, the library of your home town is full of books—but I fear they won't do you any good in your present predicament nor help you in the solution of the personal problem which you raise.

A COLORED MAN OF COLORADO.

The young man seems to know the difficulties he and his loved one will have to go through and the social ostracism they will have to face from both white and colored, and it's for him to decide if his love is strong enough to stand up under those things. If he thinks "the world well lost for love" then let him hop to it. Of course, she has to make the same decision, although he doesn't mention what she thinks about their union. He seems to think, man-like, that all he has to do is propose and with a little "persuasion" she'll fly to his

arms. He doesn't seem to realize that such a marriage would mean as much sacrifice on her part as on his.

Personally, I wouldn't have him. If he had a love to offer her that was great enough to compensate her for the loss of so much, he would have taken her long ago.

A COLORED WOMAN OF NEW YORK.

And now for the young Nordic who wants to marry a Negress. I do not think that the sage advice of *Punch*[6] was ever so witty, so pithy, and so full of worldly wisdom as when applied to the Great Question now confronting this young man. *Your* answer, Dear Dr. Du Bois, leaves nothing to say on the subject providing one inclines to your angle of opinion. So that there is nothing to say unless one has a different perspective. I have. I say to the young man *"You cannot!"* The institution of Marriage from the most impartial standpoint must be regarded as a covenant between the individual and the Social Order. The Social Order endows its highest privileges, dignities, and protection, upon the individual in return for *conformity with its laws and customs*. In short, the utmost any man can do for any woman, is to marry her; the utmost any woman can do for any man is to marry him. Of all human institutions that of marriage has unique significance. The term, "A respectable married woman—or man" loses not one particle of value when applied to prince or pauper, Negro or Nordic. One marries to confer upon the partner the highest of all human distinctions. Then how can one think of marriage if this high distinction be not forthcoming? How *dare* this young man expose this young woman (and the reverse holds true) to a position so horribly invidious, and exclaim "I love you" at the same time? This young man and woman propose to ignore Society and live for themselves. Impossible. As eternal as the hills is the dictum, Man cannot live alone. Yet they deserve great credit for daring to face discussion. In the millennium there will be no obstacle to their marriage before Man: before God there never has been: but this is not the millennium. You must, each of you find within your own race or group (call it whatever you will) one who can place

5. Jesus.
6. Satirical British magazine published from 1841–1992 and from 1996–2002.

you in the light of Society's benign approval—and keep you there, secure in the most exalted earthly happiness. Finally, it is only fair to say that while it is true the above opinions are merely those of one man, yet they should be regarded with deep sincerity, as they are expressed, because they were formed under experiences just a trifle out of the ordinary, extending over my lifetime.

A COLORED MAN OF NEW YORK.

From *The Crisis*, February 1930, pp. 50, 67.

GEORGE S. SCHUYLER AND JOSEPHINE SCHUYLER

Does Interracial Marriage Succeed? [1945]

In the mid-1940s, while the United States was embroiled in World War II, the *Negro Digest* ran a periodic column called "Does Interracial Marriage Succeed?," guest-written by people in interracial marriages, including the heavyweight boxing champion Jack Johnson (whose three wives were all white) and the social worker, teacher, and activist Thyra Edwards Gitlin and her white husband, the writer Murray Gitlin. This June 1945 article by the well-known journalist George Schuyler (p. 287) and his white wife, the artist and writer Josephine Schuyler, demonstrates the perseverance of prejudice against interracialism. Many of the facts and arguments echo those in debates on intermarriage from the 1920s and 1930s (pp. 370 and 490). However, the column also reveals a shift in focus away from the strength of societal pressures toward the strength of the individual couple who resist the pressures of racism and misunderstanding. The Schuylers also stress the benefits of interracial marriage, mentioning unexpectedly a lack of social isolation. They conclude that such unions are difficult in some ways but in other ways are "far more interesting and stimulating."

From *Negro Digest*, June 1945, pp. 15–17.

Obviously racial intermarriage does succeed, since many couples like us seem to be getting on quite well.

However, individuals who cross the marital color line must be people of superior courage. Or at least they should have a healthy disdain for the opinions of the crowd.

Both white and colored groups in America theoretically fear and oppose interracial marriage. Just as they fear, and therefore condemn, anything very different, unusual, exciting or exotic.

Most people are so timorous about nearly every step they take that a slight difference in pigmentation would seem like an insurmountable barrier. These human mice should always mate with someone not only of their own color but of their own class, religion, and occupation.

For this reason, were the legal barriers against interracial marriage lowered tomorrow, it is probable there would not be the great rush to the altar that most Southerners visualize. There would scarcely be much more mixed marriages than now. Abolition of such laws would legalize more unions, of course, and therefore protect the offspring and thus improve the general moral tone of society. That is all.

The very thing which frightens the little people away from unorthodox unions, attracts the robust individuals. They prefer that which is different and enjoy the risk of the situation.

It has been our experience that there is no such thing as fundamental racial differences. It is all very much on the surface, like the color of flowers.

Only among human beings with their miseducated opinions and complicated fears do you find the strange idea of the significance of color and feature. Animals, which are far more intelligent and courageous, if less skillful, do not concern themselves with absurdities like hair texture and the cephalic index.[1]

These are man-made prejudices created by the necessity to justify the exploitation of one group by another. Everything the exploiter had or did must be "right." Since all the books were written by and for those in power, they naturally made the most out of the accidental differences between the exploited and the exploiter. So minor details have been blown up into vast differences.

Unless you believe in this myth, the difference in skin and hair is just as important or as unimportant as the color and material of the clothes you wear.

Since these bugaboos have been erected to scare the meek and middling and maintain the status quo, the only thing really intelligent people can do is to ignore the whole business as much as possible. Sometimes, it is like walking through a madhouse, one must walk quietly lest one frighten the inmates into gestures of violence.

Sometimes, it is a bore to do this, often it is amusing. Certainly, one must not be insane oneself on this point, or any point, if one crosses the color line. There should be no fixations of any kind, or the relationship will not last. Like an army on a battlefield, mobility is the greatest asset.

Although we have not been able to find any real differences between us due to what is called "race," we have found that we have certain unlike methods of doing things due to the fact that Mr. Schuyler was born in the North and Mrs. Schuyler was born in the South.

Mrs. Schuyler had many of those ways known as "colored" but which are really just Southern. She had little sense of time or order. She was voluble, communicative, genial and reckless.

Mr. Schuyler, on the other hand, was a typical Yankee with all those disagreeable qualities of caution, punctuality, taciturnity and exactitude.

As often happens in marriage, there has been an exchange of characteristics and a modification on both sides. After seventeen years, Mrs. Schuyler laments her now uncomfortable habit of being punctual and careful. While Mr. Schuyler admits that due to the association, he is far more aesthetic in his appreciations, more amiable and talkative. We believe we have both gained considerably by our marriage.

Mrs. Schuyler believes that because she is an artist, Mr. Schuyler's darker skin probably attracted her in the first place while he thinks that her fairness and vivacity drew him in the beginning. But it was personality (which has nothing to do with race or color) which determined the success of the match. Their opinions, although developed in widely separated parts of the country, were practically identical and remain so.

Having children complicates any union, especially interracial ones. Although we have never had any trouble at all about schools or associations, the necessity of explaining the unjustness of American society, of the hypocrisy of this democracy, of the need to be just when others are not, of taking less than one deserves, of being proud without becoming bitter, of being brave without seeming bold—these fine shades of conduct cannot be taught anywhere except in the home.

There is, too, the even bigger problem of keeping the child from favoring either racial group. Young people, always prone to over-simplify on one hand and exaggerate on the other, are apt to idealize whichever party they see the least of—or have the least disagreeable experiences with.

Because most couples in our position rear their families in colored sections where the slum is always just around the corner, the children may grow too critical of the slum.

Divorced white mothers of colored children, on the contrary, keep their offspring almost entirely separated from the Negro, often in high priced progressive schools. These youngsters only hearing of the injustices done the Negro and not having to endure any of the results in the form of dirt, disease and ignorance, over-idealize the Negro. Both attitudes are dangerous and must be corrected.

The chief objection to interracial marriage, however, is supposed to be that of isolation. The myth is that the couple will be ostracized by both groups and so be forced into a life of great loneliness. The truth is that either from curiosity or admiration or both, they are sought out by both "races" so they have twice the company they would normally attract . . .

We have found much sympathy for our marriage in the least likely places. Childhood friends of Mrs. Schuyler have taken the trouble to look her up and express their interest. She has traveled extensively in Afriamerica and has been warmly received there, too.

---

1. Ratio of head width multiplied by 100 and divided by head length, used by anthropologists in the 19th and early 20th centuries to categorize people of different races.

The most hopeful thing about the whole situation seems to be that humanity is inconsistent and unpredictable. Even those who condemn mixed marriages in public, may turn right around and do something nice for it in private.

We think that if you really love each other and are people of superior courage, you will find interracial marriage more difficult in some ways, but in others, far more interesting and stimulating.

Ebony

Opposing Views of Newspapers on Walter White's Marriage [1949]

As part of a feature titled "Famous Negroes Who Married Whites," the December 1949 issue of *Ebony* republished editorials from two black newspapers—the *Norfolk Journal and Guide* and *The Black Dispatch,* an Oklahoma publication—discussing the marriage of Walter White (p. 404), the executive secretary of the NAACP, to the South African-born writer Poppy Cannon (1905–1975), who was white. While emphasizing that White has the legal right to marry whomever he chooses and that marriage is "a purely personal proposition," the *Norfolk Journal and Guide* comes out strongly against the marriage. The paper claims that White, as a representative of the NAACP, should have realized the damage to the orga-

nization caused by his "personal" decision. The *Journal's* position suggests that the behavior of leaders should be shaped by the allegations of their opponents, in this case the detractors of the NAACP, who charge that the group's anti-segregation efforts are motivated by the desire of black people to marry white people. *The Black Dispatch,* on the other hand, condemns both white people and black people who oppose interracial marriage. The *Dispatch* draws on religion and American history to challenge White's detractors, ultimately linking both black and white resistance to intermarriage to the racist idea that white women are fundamentally different from other women.

From *Ebony*, December 1949.

CON: *Norfolk Journal and Guide*

Serious embarrassment, if not something worse, is likely to befall the National Association for the Advancement of Colored People as a result of the recent marriage of its executive secretary, Walter White, to a white divorcee.

Within three weeks after being presented a consent divorce from his wife of 27 years, Mr. White, now on leave of absence from his position for a year, became the fourth husband of the thrice-wed lady of the Caucasian race.

Of course, as an individual of maturity, the gentleman possessed the legal right to marry the woman of his choice, subject to her consent.

Marriage is, after all, a purely personal proposition, one in which persons are supposed to be free to enter in accordance with their own will.

But in view of the nature, character, professed aims, and objectives of the NAACP, Mr. White, in his capacity as its most publicized officer, official spokesman, and supposed personification of its ideals, might have, for the sake of the organization, used better judgment.

The detractors of the association have made much of the charge that its anti-segregation program is in reality a disguise of the Negro's yearnings to marry whites.

This is a fallacy, of course, which is vigorously denied by friends of the organization, but the denial is subjected to a deflating slap when it is recalled that the association's most vocal official hopped across the race line in matrimony.

His was a case in which discretion and genuine interest in the association on which he has been able to fatten and grow influential for a number of years, demanded that he above all others, make no move that might be construed effectively to misrepresent the objectives of the NAACP.

Mr. White acted upon a personal right; he exercised a lawful right. But, to paraphrase a famous quotation, what is lawful may not always be expedient.

It is not likely, however, that this gentleman, prone as he is to serve his selfish interests, will feel overly concerned about what happens to the NAACP, now that he has attained his latest ambition, but a prompt and official announcement that he will not return to his post at the expiration of his leave is in order.

PRO: Oklahoma *Black Dispatch*

We suspect the usefulness of Walter White, now on leave as NAACP secretary, is at an end because of the distorted, twisted and prejudicial concept people have respecting the rights of a man to select his mate. There will be propaganda units of the Nordic group who will seek to jam a wedge in between Negroes because of this latest decision of Mr. White respecting his domestic affairs, and we are equally sure there will be a lot of Uncle Tom blacks who will offer aid and comfort to the enemy by denouncing interracial marriages, forgetting entirely that they are in fact criticizing God Himself in doing so, for it was God who endorsed the marriage of Moses to an Ethiopian woman.[1]

Walter White has shown far greater respect for white womanhood than several of our honored Presidents have shown for black mothers. If one will take time to peruse available documents in the Congressional Library he will discover that George Washington had a colored sweetheart, Mary Gibbon; that Thomas Jefferson was the father of a child by a black mother, while Andrew Jackson had three of them. How can we condemn Walter White who has become joined in marriage with a white woman and at the same time honor Washington, Jefferson and Jackson for their depraved relationship with slave women?

Walter White's usefulness with the NAACP is perhaps ended because of the deep-seated feeling millions of Negroes have on this subject. Thousands of blacks honestly and sincerely forget all the realities of life and actually feel it is a crime for black people to marry out of their race. In the marital relationship the average black man and woman, if they will search diligently for the cause of their dissent, will discover it rests wholly in the fact they seek to do the same thing to the white man they feel the Nordics have done to them.

Proof of this rests in the fact that Negroes in Oklahoma for years intermarried with Indians with no such reaction. When we set the white woman out aside from the Oriental, the Indian and the Asiatic, we are agreeing in the concept the white man offers that his mate is something different from other women in the world. That is where unreason leads us. When we can think in terms of women and men and not in terms of colors we will have reached the abstract ground we should stand upon in human relationships and marriage.

W. E. B. Du Bois
Black Folk and Birth Control [1932]

In July 1932, the *Birth Control Review*, a monthly magazine established in 1917 by the white birth control activist Margaret Sanger (1879–1966), published a special issue titled the "Negro Number," which included twelve articles by black and white leaders and professionals supporting the use of birth control by African Americans. In his essay, reprinted here, W. E. B. Du Bois traces the origins of the high birth rate among African Americans to the interests of slaveholders and calls for a reassessment of birth control practices from a black perspective while deflating the black nationalist call for African Americans to "increase and multiply." Du Bois links the dramatic increase in class stratification in the black population after emancipation to variations in birth control practices. Although he argues that changing the laws regulating birth control

---

1. Numbers 12: "And Miriam and Aaron spake against Moses because of the Ethiopian woman whom he had married . . . And the anger of the LORD was kindled against them; . . . and, behold, Miriam became leprous, white as snow."

is of primary importance, he stresses the role of black churches, which could act either as impediments to or as promoters of the advancement of birth control in black communities.

From *Birth Control Review*, June 1932.

The American Negro has been going through a great period of stress, not only in this present depression, but long before it. His income is reduced by ignorance and prejudice and his former tradition of early marriage and large families has put grave strain on a budget on which he was seeking, not merely to maintain, but to improve his standard of living.

As slaves, every incentive was furnished to raise the largest number of children possible. The chief surplus crop of Virginia and other border States consisted of this natural increase of slaves and it was realized in the consequent slave trade to feed the plantations of the lower South and Southwest. Frederick Bancroft has recently shown us that this trade, in the decade 1850–60, involved average annual sales of nearly 80,000 human beings, representing $100,000,000 of capital.

Even then birth control was secretly exercised by the more intelligent slaves, as we know from many reminiscences.

After emancipation, there arose the inevitable clash of ideals between those Negroes who were striving to improve their economic position and those whose religious faith made the limitation of children a sin. The result, among the more intelligent class, was a postponement of marriage which greatly decreased the number of children. Today, among this class of Negroes, few men marry before thirty, and numbers of them after forty. The marriage of women of this class has similarly been postponed.

In addition to this, the low income which Negroes receive, make bachelorhood and spinsterhood widespread, with the naturally resultant lowering, in some cases, of sex standards. On the other hand, the mass of ignorant Negroes still breed carelessly and disastrously, so that the increase among Negroes, even more than the increase among whites, is from that part of the population least intelligent and fit, and least able to rear their children properly.

There comes, therefore, the difficult and insistent problem of spreading among Negroes an intelligent and clearly recognized concept of proper birth control, so that the young people can marry, have companionship and natural health, and yet not have children until they are able to take care of them. This, of course, requires in the first place a revision of the general laws, and in the second place, it calls for a more liberal attitude among Negro churches. The churches are open for the most part to intelligent propaganda of any sort, and the American Birth Control League and other agencies ought to get their speakers before church congregations and their arguments in the Negro newspapers. As it is, the mass of Negroes know almost nothing about the birth control movement, and even intelligent colored people have a good many misapprehensions and a good deal of fear at openly learning about it. Like most people with middle-class standards of morality, they think that birth control is inherently immoral.

Moreover, they are quite led away by the fallacy of numbers. They want the black race to survive. They are cheered by a census return of increasing numbers and a high rate of increase. They must learn that among human races and groups, as among vegetables, quality and not mere quantity really counts.

GEORGE S. SCHUYLER

Quantity or Quality [1932]

The journalist George Schuyler (p. 362) opens this article from the *Birth Control Review* by declaring, "There is no great opposition to birth control among the twelve million brown Americans." He immediately modifies this claim, however, by adding, "Certainly none has been expressed in writing." While few people published their views opposing the use of birth control by African Americans, Schuyler's article, as well as many others in the special issue of *Birth Control Review* titled the "Negro Number," includes responses to common arguments against birth control that were voiced in black communities. For instance, Schuyler cites the black nationalist argument for propagation of the race (an argument that was resurrected in the 1960s).

Questions such as "Shall they produce children who are going to be an asset to the group and to American society[?]" suggest a link between Schuyler's position and the eugenics movement. Schuyler bases his conclusions not on an elitist devaluation of the poor, however, but on an assessment of the needs and desires of the poor themselves. He notes the widespread use of folk methods of birth control and the prevalence of dangerous abortions. Underscoring his attempt to address the interests of others, he concludes, "Most Negroes, especially the women, would go in for quality production if they only knew how."

From *Birth Control Review,* June 1932.

There is no great opposition to birth control among the twelve million brown Americans. Certainly none has been expressed in writing. On the contrary one encounters everywhere a profound interest in and desire for information on contraceptive methods among them.

The reason for this interest is readily apparent. The Negro death rate is twice as high as that of the white people; the death rate from tuberculosis is three times as high. There are 100 per cent more stillbirths among Negroes than among Caucasians, and the same is true of the ratio of deaths in childbirth. In Tennessee the death rate among Negro elementary school children is ten times as great as among white children of the same age period. In many cities and states in the North, the Negro birth rate is less than the death rate. This includes cities like Louisville and the states of Illinois, Wisconsin, Kansas, Minnesota, Iowa, Indiana and Michigan. In New Orleans the Negro death rate equals the deplorably high rates of Bombay and Calcutta. The Negro expectancy of life is only 45 years as compared with the Caucasian expectancy of 55 years. In other words, Negro health is just about where white health was 40 years ago.

This tremendous burden rests heaviest upon the shoulders of the Negro women, who in all urban centers exceed the men in number. Due to discrimination which relegates the black man to the position of perpetual menial—the first to be fired and the last to be hired—and practically bars him from advancement or promotion, the Negro woman has always had to bear a large part of the burden of maintaining the home and raising the family. This double load takes a heavy financial and physical toll, and contributes not a little to the tragic number of still births and deaths of mothers during childbirth. The only gainers by this state of affairs are the undertakers and the physicians.

Jim Crowism having doomed the brown woman to work along with her man and sometimes to become the sole support of the family, it has been necessary, because of the paucity of day nurseries and recreation centers, to allow the Negro children to grow up in the streets without proper parental supervision. The result has been an inordinate amount of juvenile delinquency, illegitimacy and crime, aggravated by lax policing and the quaint American custom in most cities of permitting vice to flourish unrestrained in the various Black Belts alongside private residences, churches and schools. The more children there are, the greater is the burden on the Negro woman and on Negro society, which must bear the odium of a condition forced upon it by a white civilization.

Again, because of the disparity between the Negro urban female population and the number of urban males, coupled with the lamentable lack of proper recreational facilities, the percentage of illegitimacy among Negroes has grown in the past decade or so from 110 to 136 per 1000. It is hardly unfair to say that the great majority of these children were and are unwanted. Most of them probably died at birth or within the first year.

Only women can thoroughly appreciate the dreadful toll in sickness and death the Negro woman must pay for her lack of knowledge of contraceptive methods. Every child takes a great deal of vitality from even those mothers who are in the best of health and enjoy the benefit of security and leisure during the pre-natal and post-natal periods. For the mother who must work daily and is generally undernourished, poorly clothed and miserably housed, childbearing in far too many cases proves fatal or leaves in its train a score of ailments. Since most Negro mothers are emphatically in this category, their general physical condition can be easily appreciated. What little money they do earn is eaten up in insurance payments and the unending levy to physicians, abortionists and undertakers.

Why should the Negroes who are conducting a desperate struggle against the social and economic forces aimed at their destruction continue to enrich the morticians and choke the jails with unwanted children? It were far better to have less children and improve the social and physical well-being of those they have.

Negroes are perhaps more receptive to this information than white folk. Despite their vaunted superiority, the white brethren have a full quota of illusions and, one might say, hypocrisies, especially about anything dealing with sex. Brown Americans are somewhat different because they have been forced to face more frankly the hard facts of life. More of them take a realistic rather than a romantic attitude toward marriage and children. Life at best is for them a grim battle; when children come, it is frequently a losing one. No wonder one sometimes hears a colored woman say "it's a sin to bring a black child into the world."

After all, a woman is biologically a child factory, as a cow is a milk factory and a hen an egg factory. Certain ingredients of a certain quality are necessary to produce a healthy child under proper conditions of rest and security. If these are absent, the child will usu-ally be an inferior product. Unfortunately, the off-spring of the lower economic classes fill the morgues, jails and hospitals largely for this very reason.

There are some Negroes, mostly men (who do not, of course, bear children) who have a feeling that in some way the increase in the Negro population due to unrestricted reproduction will aid the group in its struggle to survive in an unfriendly society. This is fallacious reasoning, based on the assumption that an increase of births necessarily means an increase in the Negro population, which it does not. If twenty-five per cent of the brown children born die at birth or in infancy because of the unhealthful and poverty-stricken condition of the mothers, and twenty-five per cent more die in youth or vegetate in jails and asylums, there is instead of a gain a distinct loss.

If anyone should doubt the desire on the part of Negro women and men to limit their families, it is only necessary to note the large sale of "preventive devices" sold in every drug store in the various Black Belts and the great number of abortions performed by medical men and quacks. Scientific birth control is what is needed.

The question for Negroes is this: Shall they go in for quantity or quality in children? Shall they bring children into the world to enrich the undertakers, the physicians and furnish work for social workers and jailers, or shall they produce children who are going to be an asset to the group and to American society. Most Negroes, especially the women, would go in for quality production if they only knew how.

Constance Fisher
The Negro Social Worker Evaluates Birth Control [1932]

Constance Clemintine Fisher (1902–1979) was the only woman among the twelve contributors to the "Negro Number," published by the *Birth Control Review* in July 1932. Her perspective, honed by her experiences working with the poor as a district supervisor for the Associated Charities in Cleveland, complements the theoretical and historical perspectives of George S. Schuyler (p. 498) and W. E. B. Du Bois (p. 497).

Fisher associates the absence of birth control among poor African Americans with the gamut of social ailments confronting her impoverished clients, including alcoholism, infidelity, and desertion. Fisher, like Schuyler, notes a difference between female and male perspectives on birth control. And like both Schuyler and Du Bois, Fisher invokes debates about birth control in black communities. While Schuyler mentions the mostly male black nationalist sentiment and Du Bois focuses on the disapproval of the church, Fisher focuses on the hesitation of individuals who have internalized cultural disapproval. Nevertheless, Fisher identifies "a new trend" involved increasing numbers of African Americans seeking advice on birth control because they understand the economic and emotional toll of unchecked reproduction.

From *Birth Control Review,* June 1932.

With the general tendency today of more tolerance of birth control clinics and information, and with the increasing freedom in asking for direction in matters concerning birth control, attention is drawn to cross sections of people as well as to the general group. We are naturally interested to know what this new trend means in terms of social conditions or solutions of problems.

The Negro has been emerging from an agricultural to an industrial state of existence in the past fifteen years, more or less. Just before and after the World War the transition seemed to take place speedily. In earlier years, in the more predominantly agricultural state, each child born to a family became an economic asset; all life was a struggle with nature and the more children there were to fight, the easier and better it was. Moreover, the large family was supposed to be the happy family and the more children a man had the more he won the respect and regard of his community. Then, too, there was the sense of security in old age, which parents felt because of the children who would always take them in and care for them. But when the pendulum began to swing in the direction of an industrial existence, it seemed that a wage Utopia had come and it was no longer necessary to have such large families to insure the bare necessities of life; still every additional person was of value in bringing in extra money and security to the home.

With the present period of economic depression the story has begun to change. When a plant closes down for lack of work or when Negro labor or help is being replaced by others, the larger family does not help matters. When landlords refuse to accept a family because of too many children, and force it to go from house to house hunting a place to stay, the children become liabilities rather than assets. Despite the fact that many say "the Lord will provide," each new baby seems, inevitably, more of a burden than the last. Negroes are usually the first to feel any cuts in jobs or wages or any general lay-off. What their future in industry is no one knows. Suffice to say that in the present situation the smaller family is an asset.

Family case workers frequently hear what might be called the song of regret from their clients who are finding their other problems intensified because of the narrow economic margin on which they are forced to exist; they want no more children now and they ask often where they may obtain *bona fide* and scientific information concerning this. Not only is the question coming from those concerned chiefly over their economic situation, but also from those homes in which the social worker finds domestic incompatibility, alcoholism, and many other social ailments. In many instances the case worker sees the need for birth control where and when the couple involved do not. Where there is low mentality, a serious health impairment, or other very obvious complications, it is very easy to see the need for information of this sort.

In making a study of desertion a few years ago, the writer was impressed with the fact that in even the small sample studied at the time, the factor at the bottom of the difficulties in well over half the situations was sex maladjustment. This frequently bred feelings of inadequacy, insecurities of every sort, alcoholism, infidelity, desertion, and generally broken homes. And in most of the families the objections to constant pregnancy came from the mother, though the father was often greatly discouraged over the situation too.

THE SOCIAL WORKER'S RESPONSIBILITY

Obviously the family case worker must play some role in this new trend in public opinion, whether it is active or passive. When her clients come to her with their questions and problems, she must make some effort to help them find solutions, and when she goes into their homes she needs to be alert for causative factors as well as symptoms of difficulties. Her job is not to proselytize, but to administer her treatment of the case on as sound and thoughtful a basis as possible. If the family recognizes the need for birth control as either one of or the chief factor in working out its problems, and asks the worker for advice on the matter, she must meet her responsibility adequately. In instances where she sees a definite need for advice of this sort, the writer feels that she owes it to the community, as well as to the family, to use the birth control clinic as a tool for preventive social therapy as well as remedial or palliative treatment.

The trend toward greater use of birth control clinics is one which must be recognized and reckoned with. Not every worker is qualified to suggest or advise procedures to families on this level of treatment, any more than every medical doctor is capable of diagnosing a psychosis or neurosis, but in the hands of an alert and capable worker, there is little danger. The Negro

client is feeling less and less guilty about asking for and receiving information on birth control and is expressing himself freely as having wanted such guidance for a long time without knowing where to get it. There are still a great many who have not lost their sense of sinning in seeking such help, or who have superstitions concerning it, or who fear that it will only breed greater difficulties in the home. Yet, there are increasing numbers who seek birth control information because they feel that if they go on resenting themselves and their mates for physical, economic, and emotional reasons, greater problems are certain to arise, and the existing tensions in their family life are bound to be stretched to their logical ends—the breaking point.

DAILY GLEANER

Marcus Garvey on Birth Control [1934]

During the 1920s and 1930s, Marcus Garvey became a leading force against the use of birth control by black people. His staunch opposition is evident in the resolution passed during the August 1934 meeting of the International Convention of the Negro Peoples of the World in Kingston, Jamaica, which was sponsored by a branch of the Universal Negro Improvement Association. (Garvey continued to lead that branch of the UNIA after his deportation from the United States in 1927.) As reported in the article from a local Jamaican newspaper reprinted here, "It was chiefly through his

strong and pronounced views that the resolution obtained a sweeping majority for adoption."

Garvey's Roman Catholic upbringing provided the basis for his belief that contraception represents an "attempt . . . to interfere with the course of Nature and with the purpose of the God in whom we believe." But even with Garvey's powerful support, the resolution created a heated debate among the convention's delegates. The two American delegates remained opposed to Garvey—and to each other—through the final vote, with one voting against the resolution and the other abstaining.

From the Kingston *Daily Gleaner*, August 31, 1934.

T he Assembly Hall at Edelweiss Park in Lower St. Andrew, was packed all day yesterday, from 10 in the forenoon to 4.30 in the afternoon, at the two Sessions of the International Convention of the Negro Peoples of the World, being held at the park, under the auspices of the Parent Body of the Universal Negro Improvement Association, of which Mr. Marcus Garvey is President-General. The unusual attendance, both

of delegates and visitors, seems to have been brought about by the fact that the Convention is drawing to its official close, and that it was announced that at the Sessions yesterday, the five-year plan[1] of the Organization, which is to be a scheme of financing the many legislations enacted by the Convention during the month, affecting the social, economic, political, religious, educational, scientific, artistic, literary and com-

---

1. Garvey's plan evokes the 5-year development plans developed by Joseph Stalin for the Soviet Union in 1928 and 1934 (and later in 1937).

mercial development of the race, was to be discussed. The morning Session opened with further legislation on Education, and among the many resolutions adopted, which subsequently became the law of the Convention, was the following:

That in consideration of the fact that humanity is not its own creator, and that Nature regulates her own course under the obedience of her own Source, that this Convention considers it criminal and irreligious to advocate or to spread information among mankind that would tend to limit their physical and spiritual reproduction or productivity in that we accept the theory and the belief of a God and that man is made in the image and likeness of God, physically and spiritually, hence any attempt to interfere with the natural function of life is a rebellion against the conceived purpose of Divinity in making man a part of His Spiritual Self: hence this Convention advises the Negro peoples of the world not to accept or practice the THEORY OF BIRTH CONTROL SUCH as is being advocated by irresponsible speculators who are attempting to interfere with the course of Nature and with the purpose of the God in whom we believe.

The above resolution drew out a heated debate which caused a division, and when the vote was finally taken it showed that Delegate [A. L.] King of New York, declined to vote and Delegate [Charles] James of Gary stood out as the only Delegate against. The resolution was moved by Delegate [Elinor Robinson] White of Chicago, and seconded by Delegate [J. A. G.] Edwards of Kingston.[2] The Chairman of the Convention was called upon at many points during the debate to give his scientific and religious views on the subject of the resolution. It was chiefly through his strong and pronounced views that the resolution obtained a sweeping majority for adoption. He pointed out that it was not the prerogative of man to improperly conceive the absolute idea of God in His plan of creation,

and that it was therefore a presumptuous attempt for man to assume the responsibility of limiting life physical or spiritual, when he himself could not create it; and since spirit was of God, the attempt to interfere with the existence of the individual was attempting to limit the spirit of God, which was beyond the province of man. Hence it was not only criminal to practice birth-control in the forms suggested by its advocates, but it was a direct attempt to hinder the spreading of God's spirit which generally is acknowledged to be a part of the embodiment of man. He claimed that if man was made in the likeness and image of God, and the spirit of God dwells within man, any attempt to limit man's existence by man was presumption to limit the spirit of God. He also suggested that God, Who is absolute wisdom, must have had a proper purpose when He made the universe and since man is only a part of the universe, it was not man's prerogative to ultimately decide on his final destiny, but it was the right of the Creator; hence what man may think to be a temporary embarrassment i[n] affecting the convenience of his own life, could really be left to the purpose of God in His final disposition toward all life, and that man should only use his intelligence in conformity with his scope to live but not to stop spiritual life.

After the legislations on Education, the Convention went into discussing the five-year plan. This discussion WAS ALSO HEATED and interesting. The Chairman again took the lead in outlining the subject and the Delegates one by one brought out the convincing points that will make it necessary for the Convention to adopt the plan. The Rev. S. M. Jones, was the last speaker at 4.25. After his speech, the Convention adjourned for its night Session, which was called together at Edelweiss Park, at 7.30 last night. There was a huge gathering of delegates and members of the Universal Negro Improvement Association, and the general public, and a very interesting programme was rendered. To-night the Convention will stage its second biggest demonstration for the month, the first being on the night of the first of August. At to-night's demonstration, Councillor

2. Captain A. L. King (New York Officer), Charles Llynell James of Gary, Indiana (later President General of UNIA), Elinor Robinson White of Robbins, Illinois, and J. A. G. Edwards; White remained a Garvey loyalist through the 1960s and edited editions of Garvey's pamphlets and speeches, including *My People: History-Making Speeches by Marcus Garvey* (Robbins, Ill., 1958) and *Excerpts of the Late Marcus Garvey* (Robbins, Ill., N.D.).

Marcus Garvey, will deliver the official speech of review of the work of the Convention, calculated for information of the Negro peoples of the world in whose interest the Convention is being held. There will be several prominent visitors at to-night's demonstration.

On Sunday night, the Convention will also stage a big programme at which Mr. William Corcoran, the American Consul, will be the chief guest of honour. This meeting should have been staged last Sunday night, but was washed out by the heavy showers of rain.

JULIAN LEWIS
Can the Negro Afford Birth Control? [1945]

The pathologist Julian Lewis (c. 1893–1989), the first African American professor at the University of Chicago, argues passionately against the use of birth control by black Americans in this 1945 *Negro Digest* article. He acknowledges the "good faith" of birth control advocates but offers biological arguments to show that "their zeal is misguided." The high fecundity of African Americans, Lewis asserts, is a biological response to their high death rate, which can be traced to their African origins. He sees the growth of the overall proportion of African Americans in the United States despite their high death rate as a biological victory of adaptation. Until the death rate decreases, in his view, birth control is "race suicide."

Lewis rejects the position taken by W. E. B. Du Bois (p. 497), George Schuyler (p. 498), and Constance Fisher (p. 500), according to which controlling black population growth would improve African Americans' chances for economic and social advancement. Instead, he advocates alleviating economic and social problems directly rather than adjusting to the lack of economic and social resources by reducing the population. Lewis's position privileges the interests of society over those of the individual since he proposes limiting the dissemination of birth control information even though many African Americans wanted access to that information.

From *Negro Digest*, May 1945, pp. 19–22.

U nder the doctrine of equality of races, there are many Negroes who maintain that if birth control is good enough for the white race, it is good enough for the Negro.

It is this doctrine which is the motivating force behind those Negroes, who in good faith are joining in the drive to further the practice of birth control among their race.

Their zeal is misguided, however. They forget that the biologic background of Negroes is entirely different from that of most other races in this country.

Whereas Negro survival in America is dependent upon a high birth rate, growth of the white race is assured by an ever increasing low death rate.

Negroes today are still dying at a much greater rate than any other race in America. In 1940, some 139 died out of every 10,000 Negroes while only 104 died out of every 10,000 non-Negroes.

But despite this higher death rate, the Negro population in the United States in the past eighty years since emancipation has virtually tripled from 4,441,830 in 1860 to 12,865,518 in 1940. This growth without aid of immigration came entirely by natural means.

These figures tell of a biologic victory for the black man. It tells how a race, acclimated for ages to one country, is able within a period of about 300 years to successfully establish itself in a wholly different land, a performance rarely ever duplicated.

The reason that Negroes can absorb this excessive loss and yet show an increase in population is their high birth rate.

There were, in 1940, 217 Negro births for every 10,000 Negroes in the population, while there were only 175 non-Negro births for each 10,000 non-Negroes. There was a gain, therefore, of 78 persons among each

10,000 Negroes at the end of the year as compared to 71 among each 10,000 non-Negroes.

Afro-Americans have long been known for their fecundity. It is a residue of their African struggle to survive. Because Africa is a strenuous country to inhabit, the death rate there is naturally high and necessitates a high birth rate in order to maintain the population.

The precocious fertility of Negroes was exploited to its fullest capacity by avaricious slaveholders. It is said that the highest human reproductivity ever observed was attained by slaves and reached the enormous figure of 550 births per 10,000 as compared with the 1940 rate of 217 per 10,000. There was an average of nine children per mother, with one child born every thirteen months over the whole reproductive period.

An analysis of vital statistics indicates the explanation for the present high birth rate of Afro-Americans.

In the first place, there are more Negro women than Negro men. The opposite is true of the white population.

Second, the reproductive period of Negro women is longer, that is, it begins at earlier ages and terminates at later ages.

And finally, the number of plural births is larger, there being three times as many births of twins and triplets.

It is obvious that the integrity of the present proportion of Negroes in the general population depends on the maintenance of their high birth rate.

If, for some reason, the Negro birth rate was reduced to the level of the non-Negro rate and the prevailing high death rate maintained, there would have been 53,722 less colored babies in 1940. It would mean that the non-Negro population would increase at twice the rate of the Negro population.

If the altered birth rate were maintained from year to year, the rate of increase would still further decrease with the final result that Negroes, instead of forming 9.2 per cent of the general population and constituting its largest minority group, as it did in 1940,[1] would eventually become an inconspicuous group.

For these reasons Negroes must look askance at any proposals that threaten to reduce their birth rate.

Already the race can expect a substantial reduction as the result of the war. The huge migration of Negroes from the rural South to urban areas of the North and West is bound to affect the numerical growth of the race.

The greatest birth rate of Negroes is found in the South. Not only is the largest number of Negro babies born in this part of the country (because it has the largest Negro population) but also the highest birth rate occurs there. In 1940, there were 227 Negro births for each 10,000 Negroes in the South and only 167 for each 10,000 in the North.

The differential between the North and the South is in part explained by the biologic fact that warm climates accelerate reproduction while colder ones retard it. But in addition, the more strenuous economic life of the North, its less stable family relations, the congested and unhygienic conditions of Negro urban communities, the war employment of women and the absence of approximately one million young males who are in military service, certainly adversely affect the Negro birth rate.

But one of the most alarming threats to the birth rate of Negroes comes from another direction. It is a new movement which has been initiated to promote the practice of birth control among Negroes. The campaign is motivated by the conviction that the Negro race has especially much to gain from birth control.

A special committee with a large Negro personnel directs the activity of a Negro field staff that teaches the advantages and techniques of birth control.

The aims of this birth control group, the Planned Parenthood Federation, are as a whole lofty. It attempts to improve the quality of the human race at the cost of numbers. No doubt, the leaders of the birth control movement conscientiously want Negroes to share with other races the benefits they have to offer. It proposes to reduce the evil of unwanted children and to indirectly influence health by its effect on social conditions.

The chief field of activity chosen by the Planned Parenthood movement is the South.

For those who have a broad view of the Negro's future, nothing could be more undesirable since it could

---

1. According to U.S. Census data, African Americans made up 9.8 percent of the general population in 1940 and nearly 10 percent in 1950.

constitute a serious threat to the most potent source of his ability to hold his present rank as an important constituent of the American population. When Southern Negroes get contraceptive knowledge in their new homes and when they find contraceptive clinics readily available, the problem of maintaining the Negro population will be well nigh insurmountable.

The existence in the South of circumstances most undesirable for rearing children cannot be denied. But these conditions are imposed on the race and are beyond its control.

Can one be so naive as to believe that a reduction in the population will improve these conditions, that a halving of attendance in a school will double its efficiency, that community facilities will be bettered if the population is decreased, that hospital treatment will be more adequate if the number of patients is lowered?

Actually, Negroes find that large families are an insurance against many of the adverse conditions of the South. A large number of children in a family is an investment where income from the labor of each increases the possibility of security.

Of course there is a way by which the rate of increase of Negro population can be guaranteed other than by maintaining the present birth rate, namely, by lowering the death rate.

If something could be done to lower the large number of stillbirths, a still further saving of lives could be accomplished. Stillbirths are recorded in vital statistics as neither births nor deaths but represent nevertheless an enormous waste of human lives, amounting in 1940 to 16,236 among the Negro population. This gives a rate of 582 stillbirths per 10,000 live births. Some 5.5 per cent of all Negro pregnancies resulted in dead babies. This rate is over twice that for non-Negroes.

A marked reduction in the Negro death rate and stillbirth rate is possible and feasible. Indeed, this may have been the objective of the birth control people when they decided to increase efforts among Negroes.

By adjusting the size of a family to its economic level there will be a better opportunity for Negroes to escape the baneful circumstances that lead to a high death rate.

But if congestion, low economic level, illiteracy and poor medical facilities are responsible for a high death rate, and they certainly are, then it is much more logical to eliminate these deterents of health than to reduce the level of the population to the point where there are enough houses, jobs, schools, and doctors.

It is, moreover, questionable whether a reduction in the Negro population, in some areas at least, will in the least bit better the conditions under which Negroes live.

Birth control does have a certain place as a method of meeting adverse social conditions. But it would be race suicide for Negroes to adopt its extensive practice for other than medical purposes as determined by the medical profession. Until the present high death rate is lowered to at least that of the general population, and a constant satisfactory rate of increase assured, Negroes cannot afford birth control.

While there is room for improvement of the quality of the Negro race, which is also true of every other race, methods must be sought to accomplish this without involving the risk of tampering with its greatest factor of safety—its high birth rate.

E. Franklin Frazier
Birth Control for More Negro Babies [1945]

Although he does not mention Julian Lewis by name, in this article in the July issue of the *Negro Digest* the sociologist E. Franklin Frazier (p. 385) responds to the issues Lewis raised in his article published two months earlier in the same publication (p. 504). While Lewis held that the birth rate must not be lowered until the death rate was lowered, Frazier contends that the birth rate must be lowered *in order* to lower the death rate. He rejects Lewis's emphasis on biology over culture, economics, and political rights. Frazier was on the board of Planned Parenthood's Division of Negro Service, and he offers that organization's educational program as a model, underscoring its aim "not to limit the number of Negro births in this country but to assure the birth of more healthy babies who will live to grow up." His outline of Planned Parenthood's multifaceted program, which offered infertility treatment as well as help spacing pregnancies, shows a commitment not to limiting births but to giving individuals greater control over reproduction.

From *Negro Digest*, July 1945, pp. 41–44.

Self-appointed guardians of the Negro race have spotted a new danger. "Beware," they say, "of birth control. Our death rate is high—our birth rate must be even higher—we must have more and more children if a sufficient number are to survive!" These prophets are declaring that "our strength lies in numbers, our only salvation!"

The prophets, unfortunately, are only half correct.

It is true that disease, poor living conditions, and lack of medical care take far too great a toll among Negro families. For every white mother who dies in childbirth, there are two Negro mothers who fail to survive. Negro babies die at one and a half times the rate of white infants. Each year there are 40,000 who are either born dead or who die before reaching their first birthday.

But more and more babies, born indiscriminately, without thought of the parent's health or ability to rear them, is not the answer.

The survival and progress of the Negro race depends not upon how many babies are *born,* but on how many *live* to become strong, healthy, useful adults. It depends upon the number of well-trained clear thinking leaders it can develop, not upon masses of cheap, unlettered labor to be exploited and cast aside "because there are plenty more where they came from."

When planned parenthood is decried and a high birth rate is urged regardless of the cost, I am always reminded of a Negro peasant woman I once met in a rural area of North Carolina. She was struggling to make a living as best she could and had as "many children as the Lord saw fit to send." Recognizing that life is a rugged business, she fed them solid food during the first week of life to "toughen their stomachs." She had thirteen children in all, of which ten had died— some stillborn, others in infancy.

No one could quarrel with the birth rate in this instance—it was sufficiently high to satisfy the most demanding, yet the end result was three children. With some knowledge of child spacing, general health and feeding of children, this woman still could have contributed three or perhaps six children to the population without the suffering and waste of human life which her ignorance entailed.

A study made at Fisk University revealed that the teachers' families averaged 1.5 children each. Obviously many of these families practiced birth control and had only such children as they felt they could provide for adequately.

Strangely enough, the rate of survival among Negro relief clients in the same area was also 1.5 children per family. But in their case the figure was arrived at after heavy losses from tuberculosis, miscarriages, abortions, and the high rates of maternal mortality and sterility which obtains among Negro families when syphillis is not discovered and treated at the earliest possible stage.

In other words, by careful planning one group had three healthy, energetic children for every two families and the parents had the opportunity to bring them to their highest level of development. The other group, dragged down by ill health, economic pressure, poor housing and a high infant and maternal death rate, achieved the same goal *in numbers,* but at the sacrifice of those factors of education and achievement which add to the stature of the individual and the race. Under better economic conditions the first group undoubtedly would have planned larger families.

Planned parenthood is no substitute for security and a rising level of income—but planning and forethought are equally important to the family of a sharecropper or the president of a university.

There was a time in our racial development when really large families were an advantage. When life in America was largely rural, when many hands were needed to till the fields and tend the crops, when life was lived out of doors with plenty of room for children to grow and play, large families were the rule for Negroes and whites alike. Then the advent of another baby meant more than "just one more mouth to feed." It meant another pair of hands to help with the work and a large family was an economic asset.

But life in America has changed greatly during the past twenty-five years. Negroes and whites have left the land and moved to the cities. Food is no longer to be had for the harvesting, and children, who could once be turned out to play, must fit themselves into crowded living quarters. Machines have taken over the work that once was done by countless pairs of hands, and the miseries and ills which accompany civilization have taken firm root.

The American Negro has found himself transplanted once more and must learn to adjust to a new social pattern and live by different standards.

Today about half of the Negro population lives under urban conditions. If the Negro is to survive in modern urban civilization he cannot depend upon ignorance, superstition and folklore as he did in the rural south.

The fecundity of the race, prized and encouraged by slave owners who stood to profit by each new, healthy baby, is no longer the "Negro's most valuable attribute." His survival depends not upon some instinctive urge like sex, but upon intelligence and understanding in his family as well as in his integration into industry and the employment of political rights.

One of the most important consequences of city living for the Negro has been the reduction of his birth rate. This is especially true in northern cities where from 40 to 50 per cent of the Negro marriages are childless. They are childless not because of birth control—for there is evidence that comparatively few Negroes are familiar with the most reliable, medically approved methods of family limitation. The infertility of Negro marriages (which is about twice that of the white) is due to venereal infection, to the high proportion of still births and probably to abortions.

The educational program upon which the Planned Parenthood Federation of America is now engaged is aimed at correcting these very conditions. Its design is not to limit the number of Negro births in this country, but to assure the birth of more healthy babies who will live to grow up. It seeks to avoid the needless waste of still births, many of which can be prevented if mothers are given time to recover from one pregnancy before undertaking another and if they are in good physical condition themselves before they attempt to create new life.

Planned parenthood seeks to give parents suffering from tuberculosis, venereal and other infections, which can be contracted by their children, an opportunity to postpone childbirth until they can assure their children of a heritage of health and a wholesome environment.

Through its marriage counselling services planned parenthood is helping young couples establish their marriages on a lasting foundation of mutual understanding and adjustment, so that their babies may be born into homes built to hold together rather than break apart leaving the children as the helpless victims.

And finally, planned parenthood is encouraging the early diagnosis and treatment of infertility to make parenthood possible to many of those who want children but find themselves unable to have them. Science has made important advances in this phase of medicine, and in a number of cases it is possible to overcome a childless marriage if the couples but know where to find competent physicians, trained in this highly specialized field.

If the Negro is to survive, if he is to progress and develop and assume an enduring and respected place in community life, he cannot afford to overlook this basic health and family welfare measure. He cannot afford to hold Negro life so cheap that he will create it heedlessly without thought for its care and training, nor will he continue to sacrifice the lives of Negro mothers, who if given the instruction necessary to plan and space their babies, might be spared to raise the children they already have and add healthy, vigorous, members to the total population.

Planned parenthood is not a panacea for the ills of the Negro. But together with other equally important health and social measures, it can help the Negro to survive and to attain his desired goals. For to live decently and efficiently, whether his relative numbers are greater or smaller, will depend upon knowledge and the intelligent ordering of his life rather than upon ignorance and uncontrolled impulse.

PART FOUR ≈ *Works Cited*

Quotations and statistics in this section's headnotes and notes were drawn from the following sources:

Amos and Andy: Anatomy of a Controversy. Directed by Stanley Sheff. 1983; Burbank, CA: Avery Home Video, 1986.

Du Bois, W. E. B. "A Negro Nation within the Nation." *Current History* 42 (June 1935): 265–70.

———. *The Autobiography of W. E. B. Du Bois: A Soliloquy on Viewing My Life from the Last Decade of Its First Century.* New York: International Publishers Co., Inc., 1968.

———. "The Board of Directors on Segregation." *The Crisis* 41 (May 1934): 149.

———. "History of Segregation Philosophy." *The Crisis* 41 (March 1934): 85.

Ellison, Ralph. Audio clip of 1960's interview. www.pbs.org/newshour/bb/entertainment/jan=june99/ellison6=21.html.

Ely, Melvin Patrick. *The Adventures of Amos 'n' Andy: A Social History of an American Phenomenon.* New York: Free Press, 1991.

FBI HQ file on Elijah Muhammad. Cited in Evanzz, Karl. *The Messenger: The Rise and Fall of Elijah Muhammad.* New York: Pantheon Books, 1999, 144.

Gosden, Freeman. 1981 interview. Quoted in McLeod, Elizabeth. *The original Amos 'n' Andy: Freeman Gosden, Charles Correll, and the 1928–1943 Radio Serial.* London: McFarland, 2005.

Hughes, Langston. "From Rampart Street to Harlem I Follow the Trail of the Blues." *Chicago Defender.* December 6, 1952.

———. *The Big Sea: An Autobiography by Langston Hughes.* New York: Alfred A. Knopf, Inc., 1940.

Kirschke, Amy Helene. *Aaron Douglas: Art, Race, and the Harlem Renaissance.* Jackson, Mississippi: University Press of Mississippi, 1995.

Lee, Wallace. "Negro Digest Poll: Have Communists Quit Fighting for Negro Rights?" *Negro Digest* 2 (Dec. 1944): 56.

———. "Negro Digest Poll: Should Negroes Attend Mixed or Negro Colleges." *Negro Digest* 3 (July 1945): 70.

———. "Negro Digest Poll: Should Negroes in the South Migrate North." *Negro Digest* 2 (June 1944): 146.

Lester, Julius. "James Baldwin—Reflections of a Maverick." *The New York Times Book Review*, 27 May 1984, pp. 1, 22–24.

Lindeman, Lawrence. "Playboy Interview: Bill Cosby—a Candid Conversation with the Kinetic Comedian-Actor-Singer-Entrepreneur." *Playboy*, May 1969.

Philadelphia Tribune, April 12, 1934. Schomburg Library newspaper clippings file. Cited in Rudwick, Elliott, M. "Du Bois's Last Year as *Crisis* Editor." *The Journal of Negro Education* 27, 4 (Autumn, 1958): 529.

Poston, T. R. "Augusta Savage." *Metropolitan Magazine* (Jan. 1935): 28–31, 51, 66–67.

Schuyler, George. *Pittsburgh Courier*, April 7, 1934: Schomburg Library newspaper clippings file. Cited in Rudwick, Elliott, M. "Du Bois's Last Year as *Crisis* Editor." *The Journal of Negro Education* 27, 4 (Autumn, 1958): 529.

Spingarn, Joel E., David H. Pierce, Walter White, Leslie Pinckney Hill, et al. "Segregation—A Symposium." *The Crisis* 41 (March 1934): 79–82.

White, Walter. "Walter White to James Weldon Johnson." February 18, 1934. James Weldon Johnson Memorial Collection, Beinecke Rare Books and Manuscript Library, Yale University.

Woodson, Carter G. "Carter G. Woodson to Thomas H. Barnes." October 1, 1927. Scan of original letter in "Dr. Carter G. Woodson: Founder of Black History Month," The Freeman Institute, http://www.freemaninstitute.com/woodson.htm.

The Civil Rights Movement and Black Feminism (1954–1979)

On May 17, 1954, the Supreme Court, in *Brown v. Board of Education,* unanimously ruled that racial segregation in public schools was unconstitutional, overturning the "separate but equal" doctrine established in 1896 in *Plessy v. Ferguson.* Civil rights activists were astonished and energized by the decision—W. E. B. Du Bois himself declared that he had lived to see the impossible happen. The major civil rights organizations, with the NAACP Legal Defense and Education Fund under the direction of Thurgood Marshall in the forefront, rapidly expanded their attack on *de jure* and *de facto* segregation. In a little over a year, a spontaneous bus boycott in Montgomery, Alabama, helped create a national movement, led by a young minister named Martin Luther King Jr., which culminated in the passage of the Civil Rights Act of 1964 and the Voting Rights Act of 1965. In 1964 King himself would be awarded the Nobel Peace Prize. During the two decades that followed *Brown v. Board of Education,* the legal, social, and cultural changes wrought by the civil rights movement would dramatically transform both the African American community and American culture as a whole.

The single galvanizing event that marked the birth of the modern civil rights movement occurred the year after the *Brown* decision. On December 1, 1955, the civil rights activist Rosa Parks (1913–2005) refused to give up her seat on a Montgomery bus to a white male passenger. Parks's protest sparked the Montgomery bus boycott, which in turn led to the establishment of the Montgomery Improvement Association (MIA) to guide the boycott. A then-unknown Baptist minister, Martin Luther King Jr., was chosen to be chair of the MIA. The boycott ultimately resulted in the Supreme Court's declaration in 1956 that laws requiring segregated buses were unconstitutional, and the success of the nonviolent campaign propelled King to international prominence.

As black and white Americans united across the country to end segregation in public plans and in the voting booth, they faced harsh and often violent resistance from both private citizens and public officials, including police officers, judges, and even elected officeholders. White supremacist groups such as the Ku Klux Klan organized campaigns of terror to intimidate activists. In 1956, 101 members of Congress signed the Southern Manifesto in protest of school integration, and the FBI established

COINTELPRO (counterintelligence program) to monitor and disrupt the work of political dissidents. King was among COINTELPRO's targets in the civil rights movement, as was the Black Panther Party for Self-Defense, which the FBI systematically annihilated.

In the fall of 1957, the governor of Arkansas ordered the state's National Guard to prevent nine black students from entering Central High School in Little Rock. Televised images of angry white students and adults harassing black students and of state troops defying federal law shocked the nation. After three weeks, President Dwight Eisenhower sent federal troops to Little Rock and took over the command of the Arkansas National Guard, ensuring that the "Little Rock Nine" could safely enroll in Central High School.

After Little Rock, slowly mounting public support for the civil rights movement helped usher in a period marked by sweeping legislative changes. First came the Civil Rights Act of 1957, proposed by President Eisenhower to empower the federal government to ensure that all citizens have the right to vote. The first civil rights legislation to be passed by Congress since Reconstruction, it was so diluted during the legislative process that it ended up having little effect. It did, however, pave the way for the Civil Rights Act of 1964, which forbade segregation and discrimination on the basis of race (as well as religion, sex, and national origin), and the Voting Rights Act of 1965, which guaranteed African Americans the right to vote one full century after the passage of the Thirteenth Amendment, which abolished the institution of slavery.

In addition to the passage of these laws protecting civil rights, the 1960s saw the establishment of affirmative action, an effort that propelled rapid and profound economic and social change, particularly for members of the black middle class. In 1961, President John F. Kennedy issued an executive order calling for employers with federal contracts to "take affirmative action to ensure that applicants are employed, and that employees are treated during employment, without regard to their race, creed, color, or national origin." President Lyndon Johnson echoed Kennedy's language in his 1965 executive order requiring equal employment opportunity—which he expanded in 1967 to include women. Johnson subsequently strengthened his executive order by providing direction and justification for effective affirmative action programs, and later administrations introduced quotas and timetables and expanded affirmative action to include higher education.

Opponents of affirmative action soon launched challenges through the courts, drawing largely on the Fourteenth Amendment, which mandates equal protection under the law for all persons. The first substantial victory for opponents came in 1978, in *Regents of the University of California v. Bakke,* when the Supreme Court outlawed racial quotas in university admissions, although it allowed race to be used as one of several factors in the college admissions process.

By the time of the *Bakke* decision, affirmative action had already brought dramatic changes to universities. Beginning in 1968, the number of black students admitted to historically white colleges and universities began a steep rise, accompanied by a vociferous demand for courses in African and African American history and culture. Until that point, courses dealing with the black experience on the African continent and in the United States had been virtually absent from traditionally white institutions, although courses in black history and literature had been taught at black institutions such as Howard University since the 1920s. In response to increased demand for relevant texts, a number of publishers—most notably the Arno Press and Negro Universities Press—began publishing more works by African Americans and reissuing books that had languished out of print for decades.

In addition to effecting legislative change, the civil rights movement slowly helped propel meaningful changes in American social and cultural life. As increasing numbers of black and white Americans attended school and worked together, other social barriers began to break down. For example, interracial relationships (depicted famously in Sidney Poitier's 1967 film *Guess Who's Coming to Dinner*), once the ultimate symbol of anti-black paranoia and negrophobia, gradually became more socially acceptable. Indeed, in 1967, well in advance of public opinion, the Supreme Court, in *Loving v. Virginia,* ruled against state laws prohibiting interracial marriage. And in large part because of affirmative action, the size of the black middle class almost quadrupled between 1968—the year King was murdered—and the beginning of the twenty-first century.

The civil rights era was also a time of artistic development in the African American community. Fueled initially by the Black Arts Movement and then by the black women's literary renaissance, a period of intense artistic activity was born that would culminate with Toni Morrison's receipt of the Nobel Prize in Literature in 1993. A growing sense of critical black consciousness prompted subsequent generations of visual artists, writers, and playwrights to reexamine ideas about identity, representation, and American culture in a variety of styles, ranging from modernism through post-modernism in literature, dance, music, and visual art.

The roots of today's flowering of black culture, as seen especially in the popularity of hip-hop, can be traced to the birth of the Black Arts Movement. About the time that LeRoi Jones renamed himself Amiri Baraka, he coined the term "Black Arts" in his 1965 essay "State/meant," which declares, "Black art / s we make in black labs of the heart." His poem "Black Art" (1965) sums up the zeitgeist of the movement with the famous declaration "We want 'poems that kill.'" The Black Arts Movement flourished over the next decade as the cultural wing of the Black Power movement. It faded for various reasons, among them that Baraka's own political ideology metamorphosed from Black Power into Marxism. Ironically, the very success of the Black Arts Movement contributed to its decline in the mid-1970s as some commercially successful writers left smaller black publishers and black cultural venues for more mainstream outlets. In addition, some artists and critics found the movement to be ideologically restrictive and believed that they could develop their work more freely outside it. Perhaps most important, Black Power and black cultural consciousness, especially through black studies programs in colleges and universities, become a hallmark of the newly expanding black middle classes, which embraced the cultural aspects of black nationalism without its more radical or extreme ideological orthodoxies. Black Power, in other words, moved from the inner city to the suburbs.

Commencing in 1970 with the publication of *I Know Why the Caged Bird Sings* by Maya Angelou, the final years of the civil rights movement fostered the black women's literary renaissance and the establishment of the black women's literary tradition. In the early 1970s, black feminist critics dedicated themselves to finding and teaching works by historic and contemporary women writers—resurrecting Zora Neale Hurston and canonizing Alice Walker and Toni Morrison—even though many works, such as Hurston's classic, *Their Eyes Were Watching God* (1937), were out of print. Their efforts helped fuel the explosion of work in the latter half of the 1970s by other black women writers, including Toni Cade Bambara, Sherley Anne Williams, Ntozake Shange, Michele Wallace, Jamaica Kincaid, Andrea Lee, Rita Dove, Gloria Naylor, June Jordon, and Nikki Giovanni.

While civil rights activists fought against centuries of discriminatory laws and customs, they also faced internal challenges and dissent. Perhaps most famously, Martin Luther King's nonviolent philosophy existed uneasily alongside Malcolm X's black nationalistic belief in gaining rights "by any means necessary." Groups differed on other issues too, such as whether to integrate with white people or attempt to maintain a separate culture and economy. These disagreements, which had manifested themselves by the middle of the nineteenth century, veritably exploded in the mid-1960s as mainstream methods (identified with King) seemed to be having little effect on structurally entrenched problems, particularly black poverty and employment discrimination. Martin Luther King's assassination, on April 4, 1968, just two months before that of Robert Kennedy—and some three years after that of Malcolm X, on February 21, 1965—was a terrible blow to the civil rights movement, which, since the birth of the Black Power movement in 1966, had come under increasing attack for being tame and ineffective. Although various civil rights groups continued to fight against discrimination in a variety of ways, the national movement became fragmented after King's death. Ironically, the success of desegregation contributed to the loss of unity, especially along class lines. Mechanisms for upward social mobility (such as Wall Street, the media, universities, and the government) allowed entry to more and more black people, relatively speaking, thereby creating more avenues for the expression of talent and the realization of ambition than a segregated America ever had.

Similarly, the development of black feminism set the course of the civil rights movement in new directions. Black feminist theory proposed that it was impossible to separate oppression due to race from oppression due to gender or class. Furthermore, it held that all such oppression must be battled simultaneously and that only through the liberation of the most oppressed would freedom be achieved for the larger black community. These ideas not only influenced the black political movement and the white feminist movement but also shaped subsequent progressive political movements, such as that for gay rights.

By the end of the 1970s, civil rights laws and empowerment programs had succeeded in breaking down many traditional race-based economic and social barriers. Partly because of that success, the idea of a racial politics that had grown out of *de jure* segregation—the idea that had driven the civil rights movement since its nineteenth-century origins as the legatee of the abolitionist movement—came increasingly into question by people on both ends of the political spectrum. Some scholars on the left, such as William Julius Wilson, argued that race was no longer the totalizing force that it once had been in the lives of many African Americans; commentators on the right, such as Thomas Sowell and Shelby Steele, suggested that programs designed to alleviate racial discrimination, such as affirmative action, in fact served to reinforce racism and were detriments to individual black progress.

The civil rights movement irrevocably transformed the lives of African Americans. Yet as the nation headed into a period of increasing conservatism, marked by the election of President Ronald Reagan in 1980, it became increasingly apparent that certain structural problems, particularly those affecting the black poor, remained deeply entrenched, even as significant numbers of African Americans had begun to reach the highest levels of achievement in American politics, business, and culture. It was also becoming clear that addressing these problems would require a more nuanced analysis of the complex relationship between economics and race before broader solutions, affecting a larger portion of the black community, could be found.

KEY DEBATE ~ *Separatism versus Integration*

JAMES FARMER AND MALCOLM X
Separation or Integration: A Debate [1962]

"It is not integration that Negroes in America want," Malcolm X once said; "it is human dignity." During his years as a leader of the Nation of Islam, Malcolm X rejected as misguided the goal of integration, which activists had pursued since the emergence of the modern civil rights movement in the 1940s. At Cornell University, in Ithaca, New York, on March 7, 1962, Malcolm X debated the competing strategies of integration and separation with the civil rights activist James Farmer (1920–1999). A transcript of that debate is reprinted here.

Farmer, a founder of the Committee (later, Congress) of Racial Equality (CORE) in 1942, had long combined coalition politics—the forging of alliances in the face of race, gender, or other differences—and nonviolent confrontation to seek rights denied to African Americans. He was instrumental in developing some of the nonviolent techniques used during the civil rights movement. As a leader of CORE, he helped popularize the use of sit-ins, and organized the 1961 Freedom Rides, which used an integrated team of volunteers to challenge Jim Crow segregation on interstate buses. Traveling through southern states, black volunteers used "white" facilities (restrooms, restaurants, waiting rooms), and white volunteers used "colored" facilities, raising awareness of segregation in interstate travel.

In 1966, as CORE became influenced by black nationalism, Farmer left his position as National Director (eventually severing all ties with the organization a decade later). He became directly involved in politics when he ran for Congress in 1968 as a liberal Republican, losing the election to the Democratic candidate, Shirley Chisholm, who became the first black woman to serve in Congress. He served as assistant secretary of Health, Education, and Welfare under President Richard Nixon from 1969 to 1970, resigning in protest over

the slow pace of change fostered by the administration. Farmer dedicated his later years to writing and teaching. In 1998, the year before he died, he was awarded the Presidential Medal of Freedom by President Bill Clinton.

Malcolm X's views on black nationalism shifted over his lifetime, shaped first by his relationship with the Nation of Islam and later by his embrace of orthodox Islam. Born in Omaha in 1925, Malcolm Little first encountered the ideas of the Lost-Found Nation of Islam during visits from his family while he was serving a prison term for grand larceny and firearms possession in the late 1940s. (Four of his siblings had converted to Islam.) After his release, in 1952, he traveled to Chicago to meet the Honorable Elijah Muhammad, the leader of the Nation of Islam, who rechristened him Malcolm X. A charismatic speaker, Malcolm X helped build the Nation of Islam during its period of greatest growth, from the 1950s to the early 1960s. Malcolm X's increasing popularity led to tensions between him and Muhammad, fueled by Malcolm X's disillusionment with Muhammad upon discovering evidence of Muhammad's adultery (considered a grave sin in Islam). In early December 1963, Malcolm X was asked what he thought of the recent assassination of President John F. Kennedy. As a result of his reply—that Kennedy "never foresaw that the chickens would come home to roost so soon"—the Nation of Islam suspended him from representing the organization for ninety days. Shortly afterward, in March 1964, Malcolm X permanently left the Nation of Islam and founded the Muslim Mosque, Inc., in New York City. His pilgrimage to Mecca in April of that year (p. 610) was a turning point in his thinking, particularly regarding black separatism. He was assassinated less than a year later, on February 21, 1965, while speaking at the Audubon Ballroom in upper Manhattan. The three convicted gunmen were members of the Nation of Islam.

From *Dialogue Magazine* 2 (May 1962), 14–18.

JAMES FARMER

When the Freedom Riders left from Montgomery, Alabama, to ride into the conscience of America and into Jackson, Mississippi, there were many persons who said to us, "Don't go into Mississippi, go anyplace you like, go to the Union of South Africa, but stay out of Mississippi." They said, "What you found in Alabama will be nothing compared to what you will meet in Mississippi." I remember being told a story by one minister who urged us not to go. He said, "Once upon a time there was a Negro who had lived in Mississippi, lived for a long time running from county to county. Finally he left the state, and left it pretty fast, as Dick Gregory[1] would put it, not by Greyhound, but by bloodhound, and he went to Illinois to live, in Chicago. And unable to find a job there, after several weeks of walking the street unemployed, he sat down and asked God what he should do. God said, "Go back to Mississippi." He said, "Lord you surely don't mean it, you're jesting. You don't mean for me to go back to Mississippi. There is segregation there!" The Lord said, "Go back to Mississippi." The man looked up and said, "Very well, Lord, if you insist, I will do it, I will go. But will you go with me?" The Lord said "As far as Cincinnati."

The Freedom Riders felt that they should go all the way because there is something wrong with our nation and we wanted to try to set it right. As one of the nation's scholars' wrote at the turn of the century, "The problem of the twentieth century will be the problem of the color-line, of the relations between the lighter and the darker peoples of the earth, Asia and Africa, in America, and in the islands of the sea.[2] What prophetic words, indeed. We have seen the struggle for freedom all over the world. We have seen it in Asia; we have seen it in the island of the sea; we have seen it in Africa, and we are seeing it in America now. I think the racist theories of Count DeGobineau, Lothrop Stoddard and the others have set the pattern for a racism that exists within our country. There are theories that are held today, not only by those men and their followers and successors, but by Ross Barnett, John Patterson[3] devotees and followers of the Klan and the White Citizens Councils, and Lincoln Rockwell of the American Nazi Party.

These vicious racist theories hold that Negroes are inferior and whites are superior innately. Ordained by God, so to speak. No more vicious theory has existed in the history of mankind. I would suggest to you that no theory has provided as much human misery throughout the centuries as the theory of races— The theories that say some people are innately inferior and that others are innately superior. Although we have some of those theories in our country, we also have a creed of freedom and of democracy. As Pearl Buck[4] put it, "Many Americans suffer from a split personality. One side of that personality is believing in democracy and freedom, as much as it is possible for a man so to believe. The other side of this personality is refusing just as doggedly, to practice that democracy and that freedom, in which he believes." That was the split personality. Gunnar Myrdal, in his book, *The American Dilemma*, indicated that this was basically a moral problem, and that we have this credo which Americans hold to, of freedom, and democracy, and equality, but still we refuse to practice it. Gunnar Myrdal[5] indicated that this is sorely troubling the American conscience.

All of us are a part of this system, *all* a part of it. We have all developed certain prejudices, I have mine, you have yours. It seems to me that it is extremely dangerous when any individual claims to be without prejudice, when he really does have it. I'm prejudiced against

1. Comedian and activist (b. 1932), known for social satire (p. 791).
2. Paraphrase of passage from W. E. B. Du Bois's *The Souls of Black Folk* (1903): "THE PROBLEM of the twentieth century is the problem of the color-line,—the relation of the darker to the lighter races of men in Asia and Africa, in America and the islands of the sea."
3. White governor of Alabama from 1959–63 who clashed with the civil rights movement in protests against segregation (b. 1921), Barnett: white southern Democrat who served as Governor of Mississippi from 1960 to 1964 and was known for his support of segregation (1898–1987).
4. Nobel prize-winning white American author (1891–1973), whose writing was shaped by having spent most of her first forty years in China.
5. Nobel prize-winning Swedish economist (1898–1987), whose 1944 study *An American Dilemma: The Negro Problem and Modern Democracy* had a strong influence on the development of anti-segregation and affirmative action policies in the U.S.

women drivers. I think they are a menace to civilization, and the sooner they are removed from the highways, the safer we will all be, but I know that's nothing but a prejudice. I have seen women drivers who are better drivers than I am, but does that destroy my prejudice? No. What I do then, is to separate her from the group of women drivers and say, "Why she is an exception." Or maybe I say she is driving very well because she feels guilty. She knows that other women in the past have had accidents, and so she drives cautiously.

I remember several years ago when I was a youth, attending a church youth conference, and a young fellow from Mississippi and I became very good friends. The last day of the conference as we walked along the road he put his arm on my shoulder and said, "Jim, I have no race prejudice." "No," said I. "Absolutely not," said he. I raised my eyebrows. "As a matter of fact," he went on, "I was thirteen years old before I knew I was any better than a Negro." Well sometimes a supposed absence of racial prejudice runs quite along those lines. Now prejudice is a damaging thing to Negroes. We have suffered under it tremendously. It damages the lives of little children. I remember when I first came into contact with segregation; it was when I was a child in Mississippi when my mother took me downtown, and on the way back this hot July day I wanted to stop and get a coke, and she told me I couldn't get a coke, I had to wait until I got home. "Well why can't I, there's a little boy going in," said I, "I bet he's going to get a coke." He was. "Well, why can't I go?" "Because he's white," she said, "and you're colored." It's not important what happened to me, the fact is that the same thing over and over again happens to every mother's child whose skin happens to be dark.

If the damage that is done to Negroes is obvious, the damage that is done to whites in America is equally obvious, for they're prejudiced. I lived in Texas a large part of my life; remember driving through the state, and after dusk had fallen being followed by cars of whites who forced me off the road and said to me, "Don't you know that your kind is not supposed to be in this town after sundown." I wondered what was happening to these people; how their minds were being twisted, as mine and others like me had had our minds twisted by this double-edged sword of prejudice. It is a disease

indeed. It is an American disease. It is an American dilemma.

The damage to Negroes is psychological, it is also economic. Negroes occupying the bottom of the economic ladder, the poorest jobs, the lowest paying jobs. Last to be hired, and first to be fired, so that today the percentage of unemployed Negroes is twice as high as that of whites. There has been political damage as well. In the south we find that comparatively few Negroes are registered to vote. Many are apathetic even when they could register. The percentage who are registered in the north is almost equally as low. As a result, comparatively few Negroes are elected to political office. Thus, the damage to the Negroes, as a result of the disease of segregation has been psychological, economic, social, and political. I would suggest to you that the same damages have occurred to whites. Psychological damages are obvious. Economic—the nation itself suffers economically, as a result of denying the right of full development to one-tenth of its population. Skills, talents, and abilities, are crushed in their cradle, are not allowed to develop. Snuffed out. Thus, the nation's economy has suffered. People who could be producing are instead walking the streets. People who could be producing in better jobs and producing more are kept in the lower jobs, sweeping the floors and serving other persons. The whole nation has been damaged by segregation. Now, all of us share the guilt too. I myself am guilty. I am guilty because I spent half of my life in the South. During those years I participated in segregation, cooperated with it, and supported it.

We are all intricately involved in the system of segregation. We have not yet extricated ourselves. Negroes are involved, and guilty, and share the blame to the extent they themselves have, by their deeds and their acts, allowed segregation to go on for so long. I do not believe that guilt is a part of my genes or your genes. It hinges upon the deeds that you have done. If you have supported segregation, then you are guilty. If you continue to support it, then your guilt is multiplied. But that is your guilt, that is mine. We share the guilt for the disease of segregation, and its continued existence. All too long, Negro Americans have put up with the system of segregation, North and South. Incidentally, it is not a Southern problem, it is a Northern one as well. Segregation exists in housing and in jobs, and in schools. We have put up with it, have done nothing about it.

The day before the Freedom Riders left Washington, D. C. to ride into the South, I visited my father who was in the hospital on what proved to be his deathbed. I told him I was going on a freedom ride into the South. He wanted to know what it was and I told him. "Where are you going?" he asked, and I told him. He said, "Well, I'm glad that you're going, son, and I hope you survive. I realize you may not return, but," said he, "I'm glad you're going because when I was a child in South Carolina and Georgia, we didn't like segregation either, but we thought that's the way things always had to be and the way they always would be, so we put up with it, took part in it, decided to exist and to stay alive. I am glad," said he, "that there are lots of people today who are no longer willing to put up with the evil of segregation, but want to do something about it and know that something can be done." How right he was indeed.

The masses of Negroes are through putting up with segregation; they are tired of it. They are tired of being pushed around in a democracy which fails to practice what it preaches. The Negro students of the South who have read the Constitution, and studied it, have read the amendments to the Constitution, and know the rights that are supposed to be theirs—they are coming to the point where they themselves want to do something about achieving these rights, not depend on somebody else. The time has passed when we can look for pie in the sky, when we can depend upon someone else on high to solve the problem for us. The Negro students want to solve the problem themselves. Masses of older Negroes want to join them in that. We can't wait for the law. The Supreme Court decision in 1954 banning segregated schools has had almost eight years of existence, yet, less than eight percent of the Negro kids are in integrated schools. That is far too slow. Now the people themselves want to get involved, and they are. I was talking with one of the student leaders of the South only last week; he said, "I myself desegregated a lunch counter, not somebody else, not some big man, some powerful man, but me, little me. I walked

the picket line and I sat in and the walls of segregation toppled. Now all people can eat there." One young prize fighter was a cell-mate of mine in the prisons of Mississippi as a freedom rider; he had won his last fight and had a promising career. I saw him three weeks ago, and asked him, "How are you coming along?" He said, "Not very well, I lost the last fight and I am through with the prize ring, I have no more interest in it. The only fight I want now," said he, "is the freedom fight. Because I, a little man, can become involved in it, and can help to win freedom." So that's what's happening; you see, we are going to do something about freedom now, we are not waiting for other people to do it. The student sit-ins have shown it; we are winning. As a result of one year of the student sit-ins, the lunch counters were desegregated in more than 150 cities. The walls are tumbling down.

Who will say that lunch counters, which are scattered all over the country are not important? Are we not to travel? Picket lines and boycotts brought Woolworth's to its knees. In its annual report of last year, Woolworth's indicated that profits had dropped and one reason for the drop was the nationwide boycott in which many Northern students, including Cornellians participated. The picketing and the nationwide demonstrations are the reason that the walls came down in the south, because people were in motion with their own bodies marching with picket signs, sitting in, boycotting, withholding their patronage. In Savannah, Georgia, there was a boycott, in which ninety-nine percent of the Negroes participated. They stayed out of the stores. They registered to vote. The store owners then got together and said, "We want to sit down and talk; gentlemen, you have proved your point. You have proved that you can control Negroes' purchasing power and that you can control their votes. We need no more proof, we are ready to hire the people that you send." Negroes are hired in those stores now as a result of this community-wide campaign. In Lexington, Kentucky, the theatres were opened up by CORE as a result of picketing and boycotting. Some of the theatres refused to admit Negroes, others would let Negroes sit up in the balcony. They boycotted that one, picketed the others. In a short period of time, the theatre owners sat down to negotiate. All of the theatres there are open now.

Using the same technique, they provided scores of jobs in department stores, grocery stores, and more recently as city bus drivers.

Then came the freedom rides. 325 people were jailed in Jackson, Mississippi, others beaten, fighting for freedom non-violently. They brought down many many barriers. They helped to create desegregation in cities throughout the South. The ICC order was forthcoming as a result of the freedom rides and a more recent Supreme Court ruling.[6] CORE sent test teams throughout the South after the ICC order went into effect. The test teams found that in hundreds of cities throughout the South, where terminals had been previously segregated, they now were desegregated and Negroes were using them. Mississippi is an exception, except for two cities; Louisania is an exception, except for one pocket of the state; but by and large the Rides were successful. And then on Route 40. How many Negroes and interracial groups have driven route 40 to Washington or to New York and carried their sandwiches, knowing that they could not eat between Wilmington and Baltimore. The freedom rides there, and some Cornell students participated in those freedom rides, brought down the barriers in more than half of those restaurants and each weekend, rides are taking place aimed at the others. By Easter we will have our Easter dinner in any place we choose on Route 40. At least 53 out of the 80 are now desegregated. In voter registration projects, we have registered 17,000 Negroes in South Carolina, previously unregistered. The politicians, segregationists, it's true, now call up our leaders and say, "I would like to talk to you because I don't believe in segregation as much as my opponent," or, "We would like to sit down and talk," or, "Can you come by my house and let's talk about this thing." Because they are realizing that now they have to be responsible to the votes of Negroes as well as the handful of whites, these are the things that are being done by people themselves in motion. Not waiting for someone else to do it, not looking forward to pie in the sky at some later date, not expecting a power on high to solve the problem for them; but working to solve it themselves and winning.

What are our objectives; segregation, separation? Absolutely not! The disease and the evils that we have pointed to in our American culture have grown out of segregation and its partner, prejudice. We are for integration, which is the repudiation of the evil of segregation. It is a rejection of the racist theories of DeGobineau, Lothrop Stoddard and all the others. It matters not whether they say that whites are superior to Negroes and Negroes are inferior, or if they reverse the coin and say that Negroes are superior and whites are inferior. The theory is just as wrong, just as much a defiance of history. We reject those theories. We are working for the right of Negroes to enter all fields of activity in American life. To enter business if they choose, to enter the professions, to enter the sciences, to enter the arts, to enter the academic world. To be workers, to be laborers if they choose. Our objective is to have each individual accepted on the basis of his individual merit and not on the basis of his color. On the basis of what he is worth himself.

This has given a new pride to a large number of people. A pride to the people in Mississippi, who themselves saw others, white and Negro, joining them in the fight for freedom; 41 local citizens went into the jails of Mississippi joining the freedom riders. They have come out now and they have started their own nonviolent Jackson movement for Freedom. They are sitting in. They are picketing, they are boycotting, and it is working. In Macomb, Mississippi, local citizens are now seeking to register to vote, some of them registering. In Huntsville, Alabama, as a result of CORE's campaign there (and we are now under injunction), for the past six weeks local Negro citizens have been sitting in every day at lunch counters. One of the white CORE leaders there in Huntsville was taken out of his house at gun point, undressed and sprayed with mustard oil. That's the kind of treatment they have faced, but they will not give up because they know they are right and they see the effects of their efforts; they see it in the crumbling walls in inter-state transportation and in other public facilities.

We are seeking an open society, an open society of freedom where people will be accepted for what

---

6. *Boynton v. Virginia* (1960); ICC order: 1955 ruling by the Interstate Commerce Commission that went into effect in 1961.

they are worth, will be able to contribute fully to the total culture and the total life of the nation.

Now we know the disease, we know what is wrong with America, we know now that the CORE position is in trying to right it. We must do it in interracial groups because we do not think it is possible to fight against caste in a vehicle which in itself is a representative of caste. We know that the students are still sitting in, they are still fighting for freedom. What we want Mr. X, the representative of the Black Muslims and Elijah Muhammad, to tell us today, is what his program is, what he proposes to do about killing this disease. We know the disease, physician, what is your cure? What is your program and how do you hope to bring it into effect? How will you achieve it? It is not enough to tell us that it may be a program of a black state. The Communists had such a program in the thirties and part of the forties, and they dropped it before the fifties as being impractical. So we are not only interested in the terminology. We need to have it spelled out, if we are being asked to follow it, to believe in it, what does it mean? Is it a separate Negro society in each city? As a Harlem, a South Side Chicago? Is it a separate state in one part of the country? Is it a separate nation in Africa, or elsewhere? Then we need to know how is it to be achieved. I assume that before a large part of land could be granted to Negroes or to Jews or to anybody else in the country it would have to be approved by the Senate of the United States.

You must tell us, Mr. X, if you seriously think that the Senate of the United States which has refused or failed for all these years to pass a strong Civil Rights Bill, you must tell us if you really think that this Senate is going to give us, to give you, a black state. I am sure that Senator Eastland[7] would so vote, but the land that he would give us would probably be in the bottom of the sea. After seeing Alabama and Mississippi, if the power were mine, I would give you those states, but the power is not mine, I do not vote in the Senate. Tell us how you expect to achieve this separate black state.

Now it is not enough for us to know that you believe in black businesses, all of us believe that all Americans who wish to go into business, should go into business. We must know, we need to know, if we are to appraise your program, the kind of businesses, how they are to be established; will we have a General Motors, a General Electric? Will I be able to manufacture a Farmer Special? Where I am going to get the capital from? You must tell us if we are going to have a separate interstate bus line to take the place of Greyhound and Trailways. You must tell us how this separate interstate bus line is going to operate throughout the country if all of us are confined within one separate state.

You must tell us these things, Mr. X, spell them out. You must tell us also what the relationship will be between the black businesses which you would develop and the total American economy. Will it be a competition? Will it be a rival economy, a dual economy or will there be cooperation between these two economies?

Our program is clear. We are going to achieve our goals of integration by non-violent direct action on an interracial level with whites and Negroes jointly cooperating to wipe out a disease which has afflicted and crippled all of them, white and black alike. The proof of the pudding is the eating. We have seen barriers fall as the result of using these techniques. We ask you, Mr. X, what is your program?

MALCOLM X

In the name of Allah, the Beneficent, the Merciful, to whom all praise is due whom we forever thank for giving America's 20 million so-called Negroes, the most honorable Elijah Muhammad as our leader and our teacher and our guide.

I would point out at the beginning that I wasn't born Malcolm Little. Little is the name of the slave master who owned one of my grandparents during slavery, a white man, and the name Little was handed down to my grandfather, to my father and on to me. But after

---

7. James Eastland (1904–86), conservative white southern Democratic politician; U.S. Senator from Mississippi in 1941 and from 1943 to 1978; known for his support of segregation and opposition to the civil rights movement.

hearing the teachings of the Honorable Elijah Muhammad and realizing that Little is an English name, and I'm not an Englishman, I gave the Englishman back his name; and since my own had been stripped from me, hidden from me, and I don't know it, I use X; and someday, as we are taught by the Honorable Elijah Muhammad, every black man, woman and child in America will get back the same name, the same language, and the same culture that he had before he was kidnaped and brought to this country and stripped of these things.

I would like to point out in a recent column by James Reston on the editorial page of the New York *Times*, December 15, 1961, writing from London, Mr. Reston, after interviewing several leading European statesmen, pointed out that the people of Europe, or the statesman in Europe, don't feel that America or Europe have anything to worry about in Russia; that the people in Europe foresee the time when Russia, Europe, and America will have to unite together to ward off the threat of China and the non-white world. And if this same statement was made by a Muslim, or by the honorable Elijah Muhammad, it would be classified as racist; but Reston who is one of the leading correspondents in this country and writing for one of the most respected newspapers, points out that the holocaust that the West is facing is not something from Russia, but threats of the combined forces of the dark world against the white world.

Why do I mention this? Primarily because the most crucial problem facing the white world today is the race problem. And the most crucial problem facing white America today is the race problem. Mr. Farmer pointed out beautifully and quoted one writer actually as saying that the holocaust that America is facing is primarily still based upon race. This doesn't mean that when people point these things out that they are racist; this means that they are facing the facts of life that we are confronted with today. And one need only to look at the world troubles in its international context, national context, or local context, and one will always see the race problem right there, a problem that it is almost impossible to duck around.

It so happens that you and I were born at a time of great change, when changes are taking place. And if we can't react intelligently to these changes, then we are going to be destroyed. When you look into the United Nations set-up, the way it is, we see that there is a change of power taking place, a change of position, a change of influence, a change of control. Wherein, in the past, white people used to exercise unlimited control and authority over dark mankind, today they are losing their ability to dictate unilateral terms to dark mankind. Whereas, yesterday dark nations had no voice in their own affairs, today the voice that they exercise in their own affairs is increasing, which means in essence that the voice of the white man or the white world is becoming more quiet every day, and the voice of the non-white world is becoming more loud every day. These are the facts of life and these are the changes that you and I, this generation, have to face up to on an international level, a national level, or a local level before we can get a solution to the problems that confront not only the white man, but problems that confront also the black man, or the non-white man.

When we look at the United Nations and see how these dark nations get their independence—they can out-vote the western block or what is known as the white world—and to the point where up until last year the U.N. was controlled by the white powers, or Western powers, mainly Christian powers, and the secretaryship used to be in the hands of a white European Christian; but now when we look at the general structure of the United Nations we see a man from Asia, from Burma, who is occupying the position of Secretary,[8] who is a Buddhist, by the way, and we find the man who is occupying the seat of President is a Moslem from Africa, namely Tunisia.[9] Just in recent times all of these changes are taking place, and the white man has got to be able to face up to them, and the black man has to be able to face up to them, before we can get our problem solved, on an international level, a national level, as well as on the local level.

In terms of black and white, what this means is that the unlimited power and prestige of the white world is decreasing, while the power and prestige of the

8. U Thant (1909–74).
9. Mongi Slim (1908–69).

non-white world is increasing. And just as our African and Asian brothers wanted to have their own land, wanted to have their own country, wanted to exercise control over themselves and govern themselves—they didn't want to be governed by whites or Europeans or outsiders, they wanted control over something among the black masses here in America. I think it would be mighty naive on the part of the white man to see dark mankind all over the world stretching out to get a country of his own, a land of his own, an industry of his own, a society of his own, even a flag of his own, it would be mighty naive on the part of the white man to think that same feeling that is sweeping through the dark world is not going to leap 9000 miles across the ocean and come into the blank people here in this country, who have been begging you for 400 years for something that they have yet to get.

In the areas of Asia and Africa where the whites gave freedom to the non-whites a transition took place, of friendliness and hospitality. In the areas where the non-whites had to exercise violence, today there is hostility between them and the white man. In this, we learn that the only way to solve a problem that is unjust, if you are wrong, is to take immediate action to correct it. But when the people against whom these actions have been directed have to take matters in their own hands, this creates hostility, and lack of friendliness and good relations between the two.

I emphasize these things to point up the fact that we are living in an era of great change; when dark mankind wants freedom, justice, and equality. It is not a case of wanting integration or separation, it is a case of wanting freedom, justice, and equality.

Now if certain groups think that through integration they are going to get freedom, justice, equality and human dignity, then well and good, we will go along with the integrationists. But if integration is not going to return human dignity to dark mankind, then integration is not the solution to the problem. And oft times we make the mistake of confusing the objective with the means by which the objective is to be obtained. It is not integration that Negroes in America want, it is human dignity. They want to be recognized as human beings. And if integration is going to bring us recognition as human beings, then we will integrate. But if integration is not going to bring us recognition as human

beings, then integration "out the window," and we have to find another means or method and try that to get our objectives reached.

The same hand that has been writing on the wall in Africa and Asia is also writing on the wall right here in America. The same rebellion, the same impatience, the same anger that exists in the hearts of the dark people in Africa and Asia is existing in the hearts and minds of 20 million black people in this country who have been just as thoroughly colonized as the people in Africa and Asia. Only the black man in America has been colonized mentally, his mind has been destroyed. And today, even though he goes to college, he comes out and still doesn't even know he is a black man; he is ashamed of what he is, because his culture has been destroyed, his identity has been destroyed; he has been made to hate his black skin, he has been made to hate the texture of his hair, he has been made to hate the features that God gave him. Because the honorable Elijah Muhammad is coming along today and teaching us the truth about black people to make us love ourselves instead of realizing that it is you who taught us to hate ourselves and our own kind, you accuse the honorable Elijah Muhammad of being a hate teacher and accuse him of being a racist. He is only trying to undo the white supremacy that you have indoctrinated the entire world with.

I might point out that it makes America look ridiculous to stand up in world conferences and refer to herself as the leader of the free world. Here is a country, Uncle Sam, standing up and pointing a finger at the Portuguese, and at the French, and at other colonizers, and there are 20 million black people in this country who are still confined to second-class citizenship, 20 million black people in this country who are still segregated and Jim-Crowed, as my friend, Dr. Farmer has already pointed out. And despite the fact that 20 million black people here yet don't have freedom, justice and equality, Adlai Stevenson has the nerve enough to stand up in the United Nations and point the finger at South Africa, and at Portugal and at some of these other countries. All we say is that South Africa preaches what it practices and practices what it preaches; America preaches one thing and practices another. And we don't want to integrate with hypocrites who preach one thing and practice another.

The good point in all of this is that there is an awakening going on among whites in American today, and this awakening is manifested in this way: two years ago you didn't know that there were black people in this country who didn't want to integrate with you; two years ago the white public had been brainwashed into thinking that every black man in this country wanted to force his way into your community, force his way into your schools, or force his way into your factories; two years ago you thought that all you would have to do is give us a little token integration and the race problem would be solved. Why? Because the people in the black community who didn't want integration were never given a voice, were never given a platform, were never given an opportunity to shout out the fact that integration would never solve the problem. And it has only been during the past year that the white public has begun to realize that the problem will never be solved unless a solution is devised acceptable to the black masses, as well as the black bourgeoisie—the upper class or middle class Negro. And when the whites began to realize that these integration-minded Negroes were in the minority, rather than in the majority, they began to offer an open forum and give those who want separation an opportunity to speak their mind to.

We who are black in the black belt, or black community, or black neighborhood can easily see that our people who settle for integration are usually the middle-class so-called Negroes, who are in the minority. Why? Because they have confidence in the white man; they have absolute confidence that you will change. They believe that they can change you, they believe that there is still hope in the American dream. But what to them is an American dream to us is an American nightmare, and we don't think that it is possible for the American white man in sincerity to take the action necessary to correct the unjust conditions that 20 million black people here are made to suffer morning, noon, and night. And because we don't have any hope or confidence or faith in the American white man's ability to bring about a change in the injustices that exist, instead of asking or seeking to integrate into the American society we want to face the facts of the problem the way they are, and separate ourselves. And in separating ourselves this doesn't mean that we are anti-white or anti-America, or anti-anything. We feel, that if integration all these years hasn't solved the problem yet, then we want to try something new, something different and something that is in accord with the conditions as they actually exist.

The honorable Elijah Muhammad teaches us that there are over 725 million Moslems or Muslims on this earth. I use both words interchangeably. I use the word Moslem for those who can't undergo the change, and I use the word Muslim for those who can. He teaches us that the world of Islam stretches from the China Seas to the shores of West Africa and that the 20 million black people in this country are the lost-found members of the nation of Islam. He teaches us that before we were kidnaped by your grandfathers and brought to this country and put in chains, our religion was Islam, our culture was Islamic, we came from the Muslim world, we were kidnaped and brought here out of the Muslim world. And after being brought here we were stripped of our language, stripped of our ability to speak our mother tongue, and it's a crime today to have to admit that there are 20 million black people in this country who not only can't speak their mother tongue, but don't even know they ever had one. This points up the crime of how thoroughly and completely the black man in America has been robbed by the white man of his culture, of his identity, of his soul, of his self. And because he has been robbed of his self, he is trying to accept your self. Because he doesn't know who he is, now he wants to be who you are. Because he doesn't know what belongs to him, he is trying to lay claim to what belongs to you. You have brain-washed him and made him a monster. He is black on the outside, but you have made him white on the inside. Now he has a white heart and a white brain, and he's breathing down your throat and down your neck because he thinks he's a white man the same as you are. He thinks that he should have your house, that he should have your factory, he thinks that he should even have your school, and most of them even think that they should have your woman, and most of them are after your woman.

The honorable Elijah Muhammad teaches us that the black people in America, the so-called Negroes, are the people who are referred to in the Bible as the lost sheep, who are to be returned to their own in the last days. He says that we are also referred to in the Bible, symbolically, as the lost tribe. He teaches us in our religion, that we are those people whom the Bible refers to who would be lost until the end of time. Lost in a house that is not theirs, lost in a land that is not theirs; lost in a country that is not theirs, and who will be found in the last days by the Messiah who will awaken them and enlighten them, and teach them that which they had been stripped of, and then this would give them the desire to come together among their own kind and go back among their own kind.

And this, basically, is why we who are followers of the honorable Elijah Muhammad don't accept integration: we feel that we are living at the end of time, by this, we feel that we are living at the end of the world. Not the end of the earth, but the end of the world. He teaches us that there are many worlds. The planet is an earth, and there is only one earth, but there are many worlds on this earth, the Eastern World and the Western World. There is a dark world and a white world. There is the world of Christianity, and the world of Islam. All of these are worlds and he teaches us that when the book speaks of the end of time, it doesn't mean the end of the earth, but it means the end of time for certain segments of people, or a certain world that is on this earth. Today, we who are here in America who have awakened to the knowledge of ourselves; we believe that there is no God but Allah, and we believe that the religion of Islam is Allah's religion, and we believe that it is Allah's intention to spread his religion throughout the entire earth. We believe that the earth will become all Muslim, all Islam, and because we are in a Christian country we believe that this Christian country will have to accept Allah as God, accept the religion of Islam as God's religion, or otherwise God will come in and wipe it out. And we don't want to be wiped out with the American white man, we don't want to integrate with him, we want to separate from him.

The method by which the honorable Elijah Muhammad is straightening out our problem is not teaching us to force ourselves into your society, or force ourselves even into your political, economic or any phase of your society, but he teaches us that the best way to solve this problem is for complete separation. He says that since the black man here in America is actually the property that was stolen from the East by the American white man, since you have awakened today and realized that this is what we are, we should be separated from you, and your government should ship us back from where we came from, not at our expense, because we didn't pay to come here. We were brought here in chains. So the honorable Elijah Muhammad and the Muslims who follow him, we want to go back to our own people. We want to be returned to our own people.

But in teaching this among our people and the masses of black people in this country, we discover that the American government is the foremost agency in opposing any move by any large number of black people to leave here and go back among our own kind. The honorable Elijah Muhammad's words and work is harassed daily by the F.B.I. and every other government agency which use various tactics to make the so-called Negroes in every community think that we are all about to be rounded up, and they will be rounded up too if they will listen to Mr. Muhammad; but what the American government has failed to realize, the best way to open up a black man's head today and make him listen to another black man is to speak against that black man. But when you begin to pat a black man on the back, no black man in his right mind will trust that black man any longer. And it is because of this hostility on the part of the government toward our leaving here that the honorable Elijah Muhammad says then, if the American white man or the American government doesn't want us to leave, and the government has proven its inability to bring about integration or give us freedom, justice and equality on a basis, equally mixed up with white people, then what are we going to do? If the government doesn't want us to go back among our own people, or to our own people, and at the same time the government has proven its inability to give us justice, the honorable Elijah Muhammad says if you don't want us to go and we can't stay here and live in peace together, then the best solution is separation. And this is what he means when he says that some of the territory here should be set aside, and let our people go off to ourselves and try and solve our own problem.

Some of you may say, Well, why should you give us part of this country? The honorable Elijah Muhammad says that for 400 years we contributed our slave labor to make the country what it is. If you were to take the individual salary or allowances of each person in this audience it would amount to nothing individually, but when you take it collectively all in one pot you have a heavy load. Just the weekly wage. And if you realize that from anybody who could collect all of the wages from the persons in this audience right here for one month, why they would be so wealthy they couldn't walk. And if you see that, then you can imagine the result of millions of black people working for nothing for 310 years. And that is the contribution that we made to America. Not Jackie Robinson, not Marian Anderson, not George Washington Carver,[1] that's not our contribution; our contribution to American society is 310 years of free slave labor for which we have not been paid one dime. We who are Muslims, followers of the honorable Elijah Muhammad, don't think that an integrated cup of coffee is sufficient payment for 310 years of slave labor.

REBUTTAL: JAMES FARMER

I think that Mr. X's views are utterly impractical and that his so-called "black state" cannot be achieved. There is no chance of getting it unless it is to be given to us by Allah. We have waited for a long time for God to give us other things and we have found that the God in which most of us happen to believe helps those who help themselves. So we would like you to tell us, Mr. X, just what steps you plan to go through to get this black state. Is it one that is going to be gotten by violence, by force? Is it going to be given to us by the Federal government? Once a state is allocated, then are the white people who happen to live there to be moved out forcibly, or Negroes who don't want to go to your black state going to be moved in forcibly? And what does this do to their liberty and freedom?

Now Mr. X suggests that we Negroes or so-called Negroes, as he puts it, ought to go back where we came from. You know, this is a very interesting idea. I think the solution to many of the problems, including the economic problem of our country, would be for all of us to go back where we came from and leave the country to the American Indians. As a matter of fact, maybe the American Indian can go back to Asia, where I understand the anthropologists tell us he came from, and I don't know who preceded him there. But if we search back far enough I am sure that we can find some people to people or populate this nation. Now the overwhelming number of Negroes in this country consider it to be their country; their country more than Africa: I was in Africa three years ago, and while I admire and respect what is being done there, while there is certainly a definite sense of identification, and sympathy with what is going on there, the fact is that the cultures are so very different. Mr. X, I am sure that you have much more in common with me or with several people whom I see sitting here than you do with the Africans, than you do with Tom Mboya.[2] Most of them could not understand you, or you they, because they speak Swahili or some other language and you would have to learn those languages.

I tell you that we are Americans. This is our country as much as it is white American. Negroes came as slaves, most of us did. Many white people came as indentured servants; indentured servants are not free. Don't forget it wasn't all of you who were on that ship, The Mayflower.

Now separation of course has been proposed as the answer to the problem, rather than integration. I am pleased however that Malcolm, oh pardon me, Mr. X, indicated that if integration works, and if it provides dignity, then we are for integration. Apparently he is almost agreeing with us there. He is sort of saying as King Agrippa said to St. Paul, "Almost Thou Persuadest Me."[3] I hope that he will be able to come forth and make the additional step and join me at the integrationist side of this table. In saying that separation really is the answer and the most effective solution to this problem, he draws a distinction between separation and segregation, saying that segregation is forced

---

1. Scientist and inventor (1864–1943); Robinson: first African American Major League Baseball player (1919–72); Anderson: popular contralto singer (1897–1993) who gave a concert on the steps of Lincoln Memorial in 1939 at the request of First Lady Eleanor Roosevelt, after being denied a venue by the Daughters of the American Revolution.
2. Kenyan politician (1930–69).
3. Acts 26:28.

ghettoism while separation is voluntary ghettoism. Well now, I would like to ask Mr. X whether it would be voluntary for Negroes to be segregated as long as we allow discrimination in housing throughout our country to exist. If you live in a black state and cannot get a house elsewhere, then are you voluntarily separated, or are you forcibly segregated?

Now Mr. X suggests that actually the Negroes in this country want the white man's women. Now this is a view, of course, which is quite familiar to you; I've heard it before, there are some Negroes who are married to white people, and I, just before I came up, was looking over a back issue of the paper of the Muslims, and saw in there an indication that I myself have a white wife. And it was suggested that therefore I have betrayed my people in marrying a white woman. Well you know I happen to have a great deal of faith in the virtues and the abilities and capacities of Negroes. Not only Negroes, but all of the people too. In fact, I have so much faith in the virtues of Negroes that I do not even think those virtues are so frail that they will be corrupted by contact with other people.

Mr. X also indicated that Negroes imitate whites. It is true, we do, he is right. We fix our hair and try to straighten it; I don't do mine, I haven't had a conk[4] in my life, I think they call it a process now, etc. But this is a part of the culture of course. After the black culture was taken away from us, we had to adapt the culture that was here, adopt it, and adapt to it. But it is also true that white people try to imitate Negroes, with their jazz, with their hair curlers, you know, and their man-tans. I think, Mr. X, that perhaps the grass is always greener on the other side of the fence. Now when we create integration, perhaps it won't be so necessary for us to resort to these devices.

The black bourgeoisie—is it only the middle class that wants integration. Were the sit-in students black bourgeoisie? They didn't fit into the definition in E. Franklin Frazier's book on the black bourgeoisie.[5] Quite to the contrary, these students were lower class people. Many of them were workers working to stay in school. In the Freedom Rides, were they black bour-

geoisie? No, we didn't have exceptions there, we had some people who were unemployed. These are not the black bourgeoisie who want integration. Quite to the contrary, very frequently, the middle class developed a vested interest in the maintenance of segregation. Because if they have a store, and if segregation is eliminated, then I'll be in open competition with the white stores. And thus it is most often true as Frazier pointed out in his book, that the middle class tends to be opposed to desegregation. Now I would wonder also in the building of black businesses if we are not going to be building another black bourgeoisie? If Negroes may not perhaps be giving up one master for another, a white one for a black one? Are we going to build a new Negro middle class, and say that no matter how tyrannical it may prove to be it is my own and therefore, I like it?

Now we of course know that the Negro is sick, the white man is sick, we know that psychologically we have been twisted by all of these things; but still, Mr. X, you have not told us what the solution is except that it is separation, in your view. You have not spelled it out. Well, now, this sickness, as I tried to indicate in my first presentation, springs from segregation. It is segregation that produces prejudice, as much as prejudice produces segregation. In Detroit, at the time of the race riot, the only rioting, the only fighting, was in the all-Negro and all-white sections of the city, where separation was complete. In those several sections of the city where Negroes and whites lived together, next door to each other, there was no fighting because there the people were neighbors or friends. Now you propose separation as the solution to this problem, as the cure to the disease. Here we have a patient that is suffering from a disease caused by mosquitoes, and the physician proposes as a cure that the man go down and lie in a damp swamp and play with wiggletails.

MALCOLM X

I hadn't thought, or intended anyway, to get personal with Mr. Farmer in mentioning his white wife; I

4. Hairstyle with chemically straightened hair.
5. See p. 734.

thought that perhaps it would probably have been better left unsaid, but it's better for him to say than for me to say it, because then you would think I was picking on him. I think you will find if you were to have gone into Harlem a few years back you would have found on the juke boxes, records by Belafonte, Eartha Kitt, Pearl Bailey, all of these persons were very popular singers in the so-called Negro community a few years back. But since Belafonte divorced Marguerite and married a white woman it doesn't mean that Harlem is anti-white, but you can't find Belafonte's records there; or maybe he just hasn't produced a hit. All of these entertainers who have become involved in inter-marriage, and I mean Lena Horne, Eartha Kitt, Sammy Davis,[6] Belafonte, they have a large white following, but you can't go into any Negro community across the nation and find records by these artists that are hits in the so-called Negro community. Because, sub-consciously, today the so-called Negro withdraws himself from the entertainers who have crossed the line. And if the masses of black people won't let a Negro who is involved in an inter-marriage play music for him, he can't speak for him.

The only way you can solve the race problem as it exists, is to take into consideration the feelings of the masses, not the minority; the majority not the minority. And it is proof that the masses of white people don't want Negroes forcing their way into their neighborhood and the masses of black people don't think it's any solution for us to force ourselves into the white neighborhood, so the only ones who want integration are the Negro minority, as I say, the bourgeoisie and the white minority, the so-called white liberals. And that same white liberal who professes to want integration whenever the Negro moves to his neighborhood, he is the first one to move out. And I was talking with one today who said he was a liberal and I asked him where did he live, and he lived in an all-white neighborhood and probably might for the rest of his life. This is conjecture, but I think it stands true. The Civil War was fought 100 years ago, supposedly to solve this problem. After the Civil War was fought, the problem still existed. Along behind that, the thirteenth and fourteenth Amendments were brought about in the Constitution supposedly to solve the problem;

after the Amendments, the problem was still right here with us.

Most Negroes think that the Civil War was fought to make them citizens; they think that it was fought to free them from slavery because the real purpose of the Civil War are clothed in hypocrisy. The real purpose of the Amendments are clothed in hypocrisy. The real purpose behind the Supreme Court Desegregation decision was clothed in hypocrisy. And any time integrationists, NAACP, CORE, Urban League, or what you have, will stand up and tell me to spell out how we are going to bring about separation, and here they are integrationists, a philosophy which is supposed to have the support of the Senate, Congress, President, and the Supreme Court, and still with all of that support and hypocritical agreeing, eight years after the desegregation decision, you still don't have what the court decided on.

So we think this, that when whites talk integration they are being hypocrites, and we think that the Negroes who accept token integration are also being hypocrites, because they are the only ones who benefit from it, the handful of hand-picked high-class, middle-class Uncle Tom Negroes. They are hand-picked by whites and turned loose in a white community and they're satisfied. But if all of the black people went into the white community, over night you would have a race war. If four or five little black students going to school in New Orleans bring about the riots that we saw down there, what do you think would happen if all the black people tried to go to any school that they want, you would have a race war. So our approach to it, those of us who follow the honorable Elijah Muhammad, we feel that it is more sensible than running around here waiting for the whites to allow us inside their attic or inside their basement.

Every Negro group that we find in the Negro community that is integrated is controlled by the whites who belong to it, or it is led by the whites who belong to it. NAACP has had a white president for 53 years, it has been in existence for 53 years; Roy Wilkins is the Executive Secretary, but Spingarn, a white man has been the president for the past 23 years, and before him, his brother, another white man was president.

6. Popular singers: Sammy Davis Jr. (1925–80), Harry Belafonte (b. 1927), Kitt (1927–2008), Bailey (1918–90), and Horne (1917–2010).

They have never had a black president. Urban League, another so-called Negro organization, doesn't have a black president, it has a white president. Now this doesn't mean that that's racism, it only means that the same organizations that are accusing you of practicing discrimination, when it comes to the leadership they're practicing discrimination themselves.

The honorable Elijah Muhammad says, and points out to us that in this book ("Anti-Slavery") written by a professor from the University of Michigan, Dwight Lowell Dumond, a person who is an authority on the race question or slave question, his findings were used by Thurgood Marshall[7] in winning the Supreme Court Desegregation decision. And in the preface of this book, it says that second-class citizenship is only a modified form of slavery. Now I'll tell you why I'm dwelling on this; everything that you have devised yourself to solve

the race problem has been hypocrisy, because the scientists who delved into it teach us or tell us that second-class citizenship is only a modified form of slavery, which means the Civil War didn't end slavery and the Amendments didn't end slavery. They didn't do it because we still have to wrestle the Supreme Court and the Congress and the Senate to correct the hypocrisy that's been practiced against us by whites for the past umteen years.

And because this was done, the American white man today subconsciously still regards that black man as something below himself. And you will never get the American white man to accept the so-called Negro as an integrated part of his society until the image of the Negro the white man has is changed, and until the image that the Negro has of himself is also changed.

BAYARD RUSTIN
From Protest to Politics [1965]

From the moment of its publication, "From Protest to Politics" was the subject of heated debate. It appeared at a time when many in the civil rights community were beginning to question whether the dominant strategy of nonviolent direct action (sit-ins, marches, boycotts) was the most effective way of confronting the entrenched economic and political problems facing African Americans in both the North and the South. Although the passage of the Civil Rights Act in the preceding year had shown that political engagement could bring about fundamental changes in the law, there was growing doubt whether those changes would directly translate into substantial improvements in the lives of many African Americans.

A primary source of the controversy surrounding Rustin's article was not that it advocated a practical, broad platform of coalition politics (a position advocated by other socialist and black leaders) but that it came from Rustin himself. To the dismay of many, Rustin seemed to be abandoning protest and its rigid moral stands—with which he had been associated throughout his long career as an activist—in favor of the pragmatic compromises necessary in politics.

Rustin was no stranger to controversy. His early advocacy of direct action in the 1947 Journey of Reconciliation—a two-week bus trip through the South to challenge segregation in interstate travel—was opposed by prominent leaders such as Thurgood Marshall, the head of NAACP's legal division, who contended that a "disobedience movement on the part of Negroes and their white allies, if employed in the South, would result in wholesale slaughter with no good achieved." Indeed, Rustin and other leaders of the protest were arrested, and the trip produced few concrete results. The Journey of Reconciliation did, however, become a model for the 1961 Freedom Rides, which succeeded in prompting the passage of legislation banning segregation in interstate transportation.

Rustin's politics and his personal life were also sources of conflict. His early ties to the Communist Party haunted him for decades after he relinquished communism in favor of socialism. His homosexuality, which he was relatively open about given the period, made his leadership in the civil rights movement problematic for some other leaders.

7. See p. 657.

Rustin was born in West Chester, Pennsylvania, in 1912 and was raised by his maternal grandparents. The two main threads that run through his long and influential career—pacifism and activism in the black protest movement—reflect the early influence of his grandmother, who was a Quaker and a charter member of the NAACP. Rustin became a leading figure in many key political organizations of the mid-twentieth century, including A. Philip Randolph's Brotherhood of Sleeping Car Porters, the Fellowship of Reconciliation (FOR), and the Congress of Racial Equality (CORE). He worked closely with Martin Luther King Jr. in organizing the Montgomery bus boycott and in establishing the Southern Christian Leadership Conference (SCLC). He also served as the chief organizer and deputy director of the 1963 March on Washington for Jobs and Freedom, the largest demonstration in U.S. history at the time and the occasion for King's "I Have a Dream" speech. His initial support of President Lyndon Johnson and the Vietnam War, along with his rejection of the identity politics of the Black Power movement, decreased his influence among fellow activists. In the 1980s, however, Rustin became a prominent figure in the gay rights movement, arguing in 1986, the year before he died, that "the barometer of where one is on human rights questions is no longer the black community, it's the gay community, because it is the community which is most easily mistreated."

From *Commentary*, February 1965.

I

The decade spanned by the 1954 Supreme Court decision on school desegregation and the Civil Rights Act of 1964 will undoubtedly be recorded as the period in which the legal foundations of racism in America were destroyed. To be sure, pockets of resistance remain; but it would be hard to quarrel with the assertion that the elaborate legal structure of segregation and discrimination, particularly in relation to public accommodations, has virtually collapsed. On the other hand, without making light of the human sacrifices involved in the direct-action tactics (sit-ins, Freedom Rides, and the rest) that were so instrumental to this achievement, we must recognize that in desegregating public accommodations, we affected institutions which are relatively peripheral both to the American socioeconomic order and to the fundamental conditions of life of the Negro people. In a highly industrialized twentieth-century civilization, we hit Jim Crow precisely where it was most anachronistic, dispensable, and vulnerable—in hotels, lunch counters, terminals, libraries, swimming pools, and the like. For in these forms, Jim Crow does impede the flow of commerce in the broadest sense; it is a nuisance in a society on the move (and on the make). Not surprisingly, therefore, the most mobility-conscious and relatively liberated groups in the Negro community—lower-middle-class college students—launched the attack that brought down this imposing but hollow structure.

The term "classical" appears especially apt for this phase of the civil rights movement. But in the few years that have passed since the first flush of sit-ins, several developments have taken place that have complicated matters enormously. One is the shifting focus of the movement in the South, symbolized by Birmingham; another is the spread of the revolution to the North; and the third, common to the other two, is the expansion of the movement's base in the Negro community. To attempt to disentangle these three strands is to do violence to reality. David Danzig's perceptive article, "The Meaning of Negro Strategy" (*Commentary*, February 1964), correctly saw in the Birmingham events the victory of the concept of collective struggle over individual achievement as the road to Negro freedom. And Birmingham remains the unmatched symbol of grass-roots protest involving all strata of the black community. It was also in this most industrialized of Southern cities that the single-issue demands of the movement's classical stage gave way to the "package deal." No longer were Negroes satisfied with integrating lunch counters. They now sought advances in employment, housing, school integration, police protection, and so forth.

Thus the movement in the South began to attack areas of discrimination which were not so remote from the Northern experience as were Jim Crow lunch counters. At the same time, the interrelationship of these apparently distinct areas became increasingly evident. What is the value of winning access to public accommodations for those who lack money to use them? The minute the movement faced this question, it was compelled to expand its vision beyond race relations to economic relations, including the role of education in modern society. And what also became clear is that all these interrelated problems, by their very nature, are not soluble by private, voluntary efforts but require government action—or politics. Already Southern demonstrators had recognized that the most effective way to strike at the police brutality they suffered from was to get rid of the local sheriff. That meant political action, which in turn meant, and still means, political action within the Democratic party, where the only meaningful primary contests in the South are fought.

And so in Mississippi, thanks largely to the leadership of Bob Moses,[1] a turn toward political action has been taken. More than voter registration is involved here. A conscious bid for *political power* is being made, and in the course of that effort a tactical shift is being effected. Direct-action techniques are being subordinated to a strategy calling for the building of community institutions or power bases. Clearly, the implications of this shift reach far beyond Mississippi. What began as a protest movement is being challenged to translate itself into a political movement. Is this the right course? And if it is, can the transformation be accomplished?

II

The very decade which has witnessed the decline of legal Jim Crow has also seen the rise of *de facto* segregation in our most fundamental socioeconomic institutions. More Negroes are unemployed today than in 1954, and the unemployment gap between the races is wider. The median income of Negroes has dropped from 57 per cent to 54 per cent of that of whites. A higher percentage of Negro workers is now concentrated in jobs vulnerable to automation than was the case ten

years ago. More Negroes attend *de facto* segregated schools today than when the Supreme Court handed down its famous decision; while school integration proceeds at a snail's pace in the South, the number of Northern schools with an excessive proportion of minority youth proliferates. And behind this is the continuing growth of racial slums, spreading over our central cities and trapping Negro youth in a milieu which, whatever its legal definition, sows an unimaginable demoralization. Again, legal niceties aside, a resident of a racial ghetto lives in segregated housing, and more Negroes fall into this category than ever before.

These are the facts of life which generate frustration in the Negro community and challenge the civil rights movement. At issue, after all, is not *civil rights*, strictly speaking, but social and economic conditions. Last summer's riots[2] were not race riots; they were outbursts of class aggression in a society where class and color definitions are converging disastrously. How can the (perhaps misnamed) civil rights movement deal with this problem?

Before trying to answer, let me first insist that the task of the movement is vastly complicated by the failure of many whites of good will to understand the nature of our problem. There is a widespread assumption that the removal of artificial racial barriers should result in the automatic integration of the Negro into all aspects of American life. This myth is fostered by facile analogies with the experience of various ethnic immigrant groups, particularly the Jews. But the analogies with the Jews do not hold for three simple but profound reasons. First, Jews have a long history as a literate people, a resource which has afforded them opportunities to advance in the academic and professional worlds, to achieve intellectual status even in the midst of economic hardship, and to evolve sustaining value systems in the context of ghetto life. Negroes, for the greater part of their presence in this country, were forbidden by law to read or write. Second, Jews have a long history of family stability, the importance of which in terms of aspiration and self-image is obvious. The Negro family structure was totally destroyed by slavery and with it the possibility of cultural transmission (the right of

1. Robert Parris Moses (b. 1935), leading civil rights activist and educator.
2. Uprisings occurred in Harlem and Rochester in July and in Philadelphia in August.

Negroes to marry and rear children is barely a century old). Third, Jews are white and have the *option* of relinquishing their cultural-religious identity, intermarrying, passing, etc. Negroes, or at least the overwhelming majority of them, do not have this option. There is also a fourth, vulgar reason. If the Jewish and Negro communities are not comparable in terms of education, family structure, and color, it is also true that their respective economic roles bear little resemblance.

This matter of economic role brings us to the greater problem—the fact that we are moving into an era in which the natural functioning of the market does not by itself ensure for every man with will and ambition a place in the productive process. The immigrant who came to this country during the late nineteenth and early twentieth centuries entered a society which was expanding territorially and/or economically. It was then possible to start at the bottom, as an unskilled or semi-skilled worker, and move up the ladder, acquiring new skills along the way. Especially was this true when industrial unionism was burgeoning, giving new dignity and higher wages to organized workers. Today the situation has changed. We are not expanding territorially, the western frontier is settled, labor organizing has leveled off, our rate of economic growth has been stagnant for a decade. And we are in the midst of a technological revolution which is altering the fundamental structure of the labor force, destroying unskilled and semi-skilled jobs—jobs in which Negroes are disproportionately concentrated.

Whatever the pace of this technological revolution may be, the *direction* is clear: the lower rungs of the economic ladder are being lopped off. This means that an individual will no longer be able to start at the bottom and work his way up; he will have to start in the middle or on top, and hold on tight. It will not even be enough to have certain specific skills, for many skilled jobs are also vulnerable to automation. A broad educational background, permitting vocational adaptability and flexibility, seems more imperative than ever. We live in a society where, as Secretary of Labor Willard Wirtz puts it, machines have the equivalent of a high school diploma. Yet the average educational attainment of American Negroes is 8.2 years.

Negroes, of course, are not the only people being affected by these developments. It is reported that there are now 50 per cent fewer unskilled and semi-skilled jobs than there are high school dropouts. Almost one-third of the 26 million young people entering the labor market in the 1960's will be dropouts. But the proportion of Negro dropouts nationally is 57 per cent, and in New York City, among Negroes twenty-five years of age or over, it is 68 per cent. They are without a future.

To what extent can the kind of self-help campaign recently prescribed by Eric Hoffer in the *New York Times Magazine*[3] cope with such a situation? I would advise those who think that self-help is the answer to familiarize themselves with the long history of such efforts in the Negro community, and to consider why so many foundered on the shoals of ghetto life. It goes without saying that any effort to combat demoralization and apathy is desirable, but we must understand that demoralization in the Negro community is largely a common-sense response to an objective reality. Negro youths have no need of statistics to perceive, fairly accurately, what their odds are in American society. Indeed, from the point of view of motivation, some of the healthiest Negro youngsters I know are juvenile delinquents. Vigorously pursuing the American dream of material acquisition and status, yet finding the conventional means of attaining it blocked off, they do not yield to defeatism but resort to illegal (and often ingenious) methods. They are not alien to American culture. They are, in Gunnar Myrdal's phrase, "exaggerated Americans." To want a Cadillac is not un-American; to push a cart in the garment center is. If Negroes are to be persuaded that the conventional path (school, work, etc.) is superior, we had better provide evidence which is now sorely lacking. It is a double cruelty to harangue Negro youth about education and training when we do not know what jobs will be available for them. When a Negro youth can reasonably foresee a future free of slums, when the prospect of gainful employment is realistic, we will see motivation and self-help in abundant enough qualities.

Meanwhile, there is an ironic similarity between the self-help advocated by many liberals and the doctrines of the Black Muslims. Professional sociologists,

3. "The Negro Is Prejudiced Against Himself," *The New York Times Magazine* (November 29, 1964), 27–34.

psychiatrists, and social workers have expressed amazement at the Muslims' success in transforming prostitutes and dope addicts into respectable citizens. But every prostitute the Muslims convert to a model of Calvinist virtue the ghetto replaces with two more. The Muslims, dedicated as they are to maintenance of the ghetto, are powerless to affect substantial moral reform. So too with every other group or program which is not aimed at the destruction of slums, their causes and effects. Self-help efforts must be geared, directly or indirectly, to mobilizing people into power units capable of effecting social change. That is, their goal must be genuine self-help, not merely self-improvement. Obviously, where self-improvement activities succeed in imparting to their participants a feeling of some control over their environment, those involved may find their appetites for change whetted; they may move into the political arena.

III

Let me sum up what I have thus far been trying to say. The civil rights movement is evolving from a protest movement into a full-fledged *social movement*—an evolution calling its very name into question. It is now concerned not merely with removing the barriers to full *opportunity* but with achieving the fact of *equality*. From sit-ins and Freedom Rides we have gone into rent strikes, boycotts, community organization, and political action. As a consequence of this natural evolution, the Negro today finds himself stymied by obstacles of far greater magnitude than the legal barriers he was attacking before: automation, urban decay, *de facto* school segregation. These are problems which, while conditioned by Jim Crow, do not vanish upon its demise. They are more deeply rooted in our socioeconomic order; they are the result of the total society's failure to meet not only the Negro's needs but human needs generally.

These propositions have won increasing recognition and acceptance, but with a curious twist. They have formed the common premise of two apparently contradictory lines of thought which simultaneously nourish and antagonize each other. On the one hand, there is the reasoning of the *New York Times* moderate who says that the problems are so enormous and complicated that Negro militancy is a futile irritation, and that the need is for "intelligent moderation." Thus, during the first New York school boycott, the *Times* editorialized that Negro demands, while abstractly just, would necessitate massive reforms, the funds for which could not realistically be anticipated; therefore the just demands were also foolish demands and would only antagonize white people. Moderates of this stripe are often correct in perceiving the difficulty or impossibility of racial progress in the context of present social and economic policies. But they accept the context as fixed. They ignore (or perhaps see all too well) the potentialities inherent in linking Negro demands to broader pressures for radical revision of existing policies. They apparently see nothing strange in the fact that in the last twenty-five years we have spent nearly a trillion dollars fighting or preparing for wars, yet we throw up our hands before the need to overhaul our schools, clear the slums, and really abolish poverty. My quarrel with these moderates is that they do not even envision radical changes; their admonitions of moderation are, for all practical purposes, admonitions to the Negro to adjust to the status quo, and are therefore immoral.

The more effectively the moderates argue their case, the more they convince Negroes that American society will not or cannot be reorganized for full racial equality. Michael Harrington[4] has said that a successful war on poverty might well require the expenditure of a $100 billion. Where, the Negro wonders, are the forces now in motion to compel such a commitment? If the voices of the moderates were raised in an insistence upon a reallocation of national resources at levels that could not be confused with tokenism (that is, if the moderates stopped being moderates), Negroes would have greater grounds for hope. Meanwhile, the Negro movement cannot escape a sense of isolation.

It is precisely this sense of isolation that gives rise to the second line of thought I want to examine—the tendency within the civil rights movement to pursue, despite its militancy, what I call a "no-win" policy.

4. White American socialist leader and educator (1928–89).

Sharing with many moderates a recognition of the magnitude of the obstacles to freedom, spokesmen for this tendency survey the American scene and find no forces prepared to move toward radical solutions. From this they conclude that the only viable strategy is shock; above all, the hypocrisy of white liberals must be exposed. These spokesmen are often described as the radicals of the movement, but they are really its moralists. They seek to change white hearts—by traumatizing them. Frequently abetted by white self-flagellants, they may gleefully applaud (though not really agreeing with) Malcolm X because, while they admit he has no program, they think he can frighten white people into doing the right thing. To believe this, of course, you must be convinced, even if unconsciously, that at the core of the white man's heart lies a buried affection for Negroes—a proposition one may be permitted to doubt. But in any case, hearts are not relevant to the issue; neither racial affinities nor racial hostilities are rooted there. It is institutions—social, political, and economic institutions—which are the ultimate molders of collective sentiments. Let these institutions be reconstructed *today,* and let the ineluctable gradualism of history govern the formation of a new psychology.

My quarrel with the "no-win" tendency in the civil rights movement (and the reason I have so designated it) parallels my quarrel with the moderates outside the movement. As the latter lack the vision or will for fundamental change, the former lack a realistic strategy for achieving it. For such a strategy they substitute militancy. But militancy is a matter of posture and volume and not of effect.

I believe that the Negro's struggle for equality in America is essentially revolutionary. While most Negroes—in their hearts—unquestionably seek only to enjoy the fruits of American society as it now exists, their quest cannot *objectively* be satisfied within the framework of existing political and economic relations. The young Negro who would demonstrate his way into the labor market may be motivated by a thoroughly bourgeois[5]

ambition and thoroughly "capitalist" considerations, but he will end up having to favor a great expansion of the public sector of the economy. At any rate, that is the position the movement will be forced to take as it looks at the number of jobs being generated by the private economy and if it is to remain true to the masses of Negroes.

The revolutionary character of the Negro's struggle is manifest in the fact that this struggle may have done more to democratize life for whites than for Negroes. Clearly, it was the sit-in movement of young Southern Negroes which, as it galvanized white students, banished the ugliest features of McCarthyism[6] from the American campus and resurrected political debate. It was not until Negroes assaulted *de facto* school segregation in the urban centers that the issue of quality education for *all* children stirred into motion. Finally, it seems reasonably clear that the civil rights movement, directly and through the resurgence of social conscience it kindled, did more to initiate the war on poverty[7] than any other single force.

It will be—it has been—argued that these by-products of the Negro struggle are not revolutionary. But the term revolutionary, as I am using it, does not connote violence; it refers to the qualitative transformation of fundamental institutions, more or less rapidly, to the point where the social and economic structure which they comprised can no longer be said to be the same. The Negro struggle has hardly run its course; and it will not stop moving until it has been utterly defeated or won substantial equality. But I fail to see how the movement can be victorious in the absence of radical programs for full employment, the abolition of slums, the reconstruction of our educational system, new definitions of work and leisure. Adding up the cost of such programs, we can only conclude that we are talking about a refashioning of our political economy. It has been estimated, for example, that the price of replacing New York City's slums with public housing would be $17 billion. Again, a multi-billion dollar federal public works program, dwarfing the currently

5. Related to the social middle classes; considered to be overly concerned with material goods and the semblance of respectability.
6. Term arising from the anti-Communist crusade of Senator Joseph McCarthy (1908–57) in the 1940s and 50s, meaning the politically driven practice of making excessive or unsubstantiated attacks on the patriotism or loyalty of others.
7. 1964 initiative announced by President Lyndon B. Johnson (1908–73) that led to the establishment of programs aimed at reducing poverty, including Head Start and Job Corp.

proposed $2 billion program, is required to reabsorb unskilled and semi-skilled workers into the labor market—and this must be done if Negro workers in these categories are to be employed. "Preferential treatment" cannot help them.

I am not trying here to delineate a total program, only to suggest the scope of economic reforms which are most immediately related to the plight of the Negro community. One could speculate on their political implications—whether, for example, they do not indicate the obsolescence of state government and the superiority of regional structures as viable units of planning. Such speculations aside, it is clear that Negro needs cannot be satisfied unless we go beyond what has so far been placed on the agenda. How are these radical objectives to be achieved? The answer is simple, deceptively so: *through political power.*

There is a strong moralistic strain in the civil rights movement which would remind us that power corrupts, forgetting that the absence of power also corrupts. But this is not the view I want to debate here, for it is waning. Our problem is posed by those who accept the need for political power but do not understand the nature of the object and therefore lack sound strategies for achieving it; they tend to confuse political institutions with lunch counters.

A handful of Negroes, acting alone, could integrate a lunch counter by strategically locating their bodies so as *directly* to interrupt the operation of the proprietor's will; their numbers were relatively unimportant. In politics, however, such a confrontation is difficult because the interests involved are merely *represented.* In the execution of a political decision a direct confrontation may ensue (as when federal marshals escorted James Meredith[8] into the University of Mississippi— to turn from an example of nonviolent coercion to one of force backed up with the threat of violence). But in arriving at a political decision, numbers and organizations are crucial, especially for the economically disenfranchised. (Needless to say, I am assuming that the

forms of political democracy exist in America, however imperfectly, that they are valued, and that elitist or putschist[9] conceptions of exercising power are beyond the pale of discussion for the civil rights movement.)

Neither that movement nor the country's twenty million black people can win political power alone. We need allies. The future of the Negro struggle depends on whether the contradictions of this society can be resolved by a coalition of progressive forces which becomes the *effective* political majority in the United States. I speak of the coalition which staged the March on Washington, passed the Civil Rights Act, and laid the basis for the Johnson landslide[1]— Negroes, trade unionists, liberals, and religious groups.

There are those who argue that a coalition strategy would force the Negro to surrender his political independence to white liberals, that he would be neutralized, deprived of his cutting edge, absorbed into the Establishment. Some who take this position urged last year that votes be withheld from the Johnson-Humphrey ticket as a demonstration of the Negro's political power. Curiously enough, these people who sought to demonstrate power through the non-exercise of it also point to the Negro "swing vote" in crucial urban areas as the source of the Negro's independent political power. But here they are closer to being right: the urban Negro vote will grow in importance in the coming years. If there is anything positive in the spread of the ghetto, it is the potential political power base thus created, and to realize this potential is one of the most challenging and urgent tasks before the civil rights movement. If the movement can wrest leadership of the ghetto vote from the machines, it will have acquired an organized constituency such as other major groups in our society now have.

But we must also remember that the effectiveness of a swing vote depends solely on other votes. It derives its power from them. In that sense, it can never be independent, but must opt for one candidate or the other,

8. After twice being denied admission to the University of Mississippi, Meredith (b. 1933) became the plaintiff in a NAACP-backed court battle; the Supreme Court ruled that he should be admitted, but Governor Ross Barnett tried to block him from attending, and violent riots erupted; U.S. Marshals and other federal officials were required to ensure Meredith's safety on campus.
9. Sudden uprising or political revolt [German].
1. Johnson, with Vice President Hubert Humphrey (1911–78), won 61% of the popular vote in the 1964 presidential election, the highest percentage since 1820, and every Republican running for Congress that year lost.

even if by default. Thus coalitions are inescapable, however tentative they may be. And this is the case in all but those few situations in which Negroes running on an independent ticket might conceivably win. Independence, in other words, is not a value in itself. The issue is which coalition to join and how to make it responsive to your programs. Necessarily there will be compromise. But the difference between expediency and morality in politics is the difference between selling out a principle and making smaller concessions to win larger ones. The leader who shrinks from this task reveals not his purity but his lack of political sense.

The task of molding a political movement out of the March on Washington coalition is not simple, but no alternatives have been advanced. We need to choose our allies on the basis of common political objectives. It has become fashionable in some no-win Negro circles to decry the white liberal as the main enemy (his hypocrisy is what sustains racism); by virtue of this reverse recitation of the reactionary's litany (liberalism leads to socialism, which leads to communism), the Negro is left in majestic isolation, except for a tiny band of fervent white initiates. But the objective fact is that *Eastland and Goldwater*[2] are the main enemies— they and the opponents of civil rights, of the war on poverty, of medicare, of social security, of federal aid to education, of unions, and so forth. The labor movement, despite its obvious faults, has been the largest single organized force in this country pushing for progressive social legislation. And where the Negro-labor-liberal axis was weak, as in the farm belt, it was the religious groups that were most influential in rallying support for the Civil Rights Bill.

The durability of the coalition was interestingly tested during the election. I do not believe that the Johnson landslide proved the "while backlash" to be a myth. It proved, rather, that economic interests are more fundamental than prejudice: the backlashers decided that loss of social security was, after all, too high a price to pay for a slap at the Negro. This lesson was a valuable

first step in reeducating such people, and it must be kept alive, for the civil rights movement will be advanced only to the degree that social and economic welfare gets to be inextricably entangled with civil rights.

The 1964 elections marked a turning point in American politics. The Democratic landslide was not merely the result of a negative reaction to Goldwaterism; it was also the expression of a majority liberal consensus. The near unanimity with which Negro voters joined in that expression was, I am convinced, a vindication of the July 25 statement by Negro leaders[3] calling for a strategic turn toward political action and a temporary curtailment of mass demonstrations. Despite the controversy surrounding the statement, the instinctive response it met with in the community is suggested by the fact that demonstrations were down 75 per cent as compared with the same period in 1963. But should so high a percentage of Negro voters have gone to Johnson, or should they have held back to narrow his margin of victory and thus give greater visibility to our swing vote? How has our loyalty changed things? Certainly the Negro vote had higher visibility in 1960, when a switch of only 7 per cent from the Republican column of 1956 elected President Kennedy. But the slimness of Kennedy's victory—of his "mandate"—dictated a go-slow approach on civil rights, at least until the Birmingham upheaval.

Although Johnson's popular majority was so large that he could have won without such overwhelming Negro support, that support was important from several angles. Beyond adding to Johnson's total national margin, it was specifically responsible for his victories in Virginia, Florida, Tennessee, and Arkansas. Goldwater took only those states where fewer than 45 per cent of eligible Negroes were registered. That Johnson would have won those states had Negro voting rights been enforced is a lesson not likely to be lost on a man who would have been happy with a unanimous electoral college. In any case, the 1.6 million Southern Negroes who voted have had a shattering impact on

---

2. White American Republican Senator Barry Goldwater from Arizona (1909–98) campaigned against social security and lost to Johnson in the 1964 presidential election.

3. The statement (written by James Farmer, Basil Patterson, Bayard Rustin, Cleveland Robinson, Percy E. Sutton, Madison S. Jones, and Richard A. Hildebrand) declared that the period of relative calm following uprisings among the urban poor was the right time for a program to combat underlying problems; the main areas of focus were a job creation program and confronting police brutality; see "7 Harlem Leaders Agree Time Is Ripe to Cure Slum Evils," *The New York Times,* July 27, 1964.

the Southern political party structure, as illustrated in the changed composition of the Southern congressional delegations. The "backlash" gave the Republicans five house seats in Alabama, one in Georgia, and one in Mississippi. But on the Democratic side, seven segregationists were defeated while all nine Southerners who voted for the Civil Rights Act were reelected. It may be premature to predict a Southern Democratic party of Negroes and white moderates and a Republican party of refugee racists and economic conservatives, but there certainly is a strong tendency toward such a realignment; and an additional 3.6 million Negroes of voting age in the eleven Southern states are still to be heard from. Even the *tendency* toward disintegration of the Democratic party's racist wing defines a new context for presidential and liberal strategy in the congressional battles ahead. Thus the Negro vote (North as well as South), while not *decisive* in the presidential race, was enormously effective. It was a dramatic element of a historic mandate which contains vast possibilities and dangers that will fundamentally affect the future course of the civil rights movement.

The liberal congressional sweep raises hope for an assault on the seniority system, Rule Twenty-two, and other citadels of Dixiecrat[4]-Republican power. The overwhelming of this conservative coalition should also mean progress on much bottlenecked legislation of profound interest to the movement (e.g., bills by Senators Clark and Nelson on planning, manpower, and employment). Moreover, the irrelevance of the South to Johnson's victory gives the President more freedom to act than his predecessor had and more leverage to the movement to pressure for executive action in Mississippi and other racist strongholds.

None of this *guarantees* vigorous executive or legislative action, for the other side of the Johnson landslide is that it has a Gaullist[5] quality. Goldwater's capture of the Republican party forced into the Democratic camp many disparate elements which do not belong there, big business being the major example. Johnson, who wants to be President "of all the people," may try to keep his new coalition together by sticking close to the political center. But if he decides to do this, it is unlikely that even his political genius will be able to hold together a coalition so inherently unstable and rife with contradictions. It must come apart. Should it do so while Johnson is pursuing a centrist course, then the mandate will have been wastefully dissipated. However, if the mandate is seized upon to set fundamental changes in motion, then the basis can be laid for a new mandate, a new coalition including hitherto inert and dispossessed strata of the population.

Here is where the cutting edge of the civil rights movement can be applied. We must see to it that the reorganization of the "consensus party" proceeds along lines which will make it an effective vehicle for social reconstruction, a role it cannot play so long as it furnishes Southern racism with its national political power. And nowhere has the civil rights movement's political cutting edge been more magnificently demonstrated than at Atlantic City, where the Mississippi Freedom Democratic party[6] not only secured recognition as a bona fide component of the national party, but in the process routed the representatives of the most rabid racists—the white Mississippi and Alabama delegations. While I still believe that the FDP made a tactical error in spurning the compromise, there is no question that they launched a political revolution whose logic is the displacement of Dixiecrat power. They launched that revolution within a major political institution and as part of a coalitional effort.

The role of the civil rights movement in the reorganization of American political life is programmatic as well as strategic. We are challenged now to broaden our social vision, to develop functional programs with

---

4. Faction of southern Democrats formed in 1948 to support segregation and white supremacy; Rule Twenty-two: a.k.a. the "cloture rule," is the only formal procedure for breaking a filibuster in the U.S. Senate and limits additional debate to 30 hours.

5. Resembling the coalition government of Charles de Gaulle (1890–1970), the president of France from 1959 to 1969.

6. Interracial party organized in Mississippi in 1964 to oppose the Democratic Party in Mississippi, which only allowed white people to vote or run for office; 68 delegates elected by the MFDP, including activist Fannie Lou Hamer (1917–77) challenged the legitimacy of the regular Mississippi delegates at the Democratic convention in New Jersey on the grounds of discrimination; fearing a loss of southern democratic support, President Johnson and the democratic leaders ultimately offered a compromise of two at-large seats to the MFDP, which they refused; as Hamer declared: "We didn't come all this way for no two seats, 'cause all of us is tired."

concrete objectives. We need to propose alternatives to technological unemployment, urban decay, and the rest. We need to be calling for public works and training, for national economic planning, for federal aid to education, for attractive public housing—all this on a sufficiently massive scale to make a difference. We need to protest the notion that our integration into American life, so long delayed, must now proceed in an atmosphere of competitive scarcity instead of in the security

of abundance which technology makes possible. We cannot claim to have answers to all the complex problems of modern society. That is too much to ask of a movement still battling barbarism in Mississippi. But we can agitate the right questions by probing at the contradictions which still stand in the way of the Great Society.[7] The questions having been asked, motion must begin in the larger society, for there is a limit to what negroes can do alone.

STAUGHTON LYND

from *Coalition Politics or Nonviolent Revolution?* [1965]

The critical response to Bayard Rustin's "From Protest to Politics" (p. 529) did not break down along racial lines. Both black and white socialist and civil rights leaders rejected Rustin's embrace of mainstream Democratic party and labor groups, viewing it, in the words of Staughton Lynd, as an abandonment of radicalism that would leave the "least organized parts of the population out in the cold." In this 1965 article, Lynd (b. 1929), a white American historian and labor lawyer, summarizes the dis-

may and distress of many socialists over Rustin's apparent shift in his choice of allies. Lynd became prominent as an opponent of the Vietnam War, but his earlier activism had focused on civil rights. He began his academic career as a history professor at Spelman College in Atlanta, where he met the civil rights activist Howard Zinn (p. 573), and in 1964 served as the coordinator of the Mississippi Freedom Schools project, which was organized by the Student Nonviolent Coordinating Committee (SNCC).

From *Liberation*, June–July 1965, pp. 18–21.

Bayard Rustin's "From Protest to Politics: The Future of the Civil Rights Movement" [* * *] has been widely criticized in radical publications Ronald Radosh wrote an effective response in *Freedom North*,[1] and Stanley Aronowitz will comment in a forthcoming issue of *Studies on the Left*. [* * *].

The gist of the radical critique might be summarized as follows:

• 1. Rustin writes that "the objective fact is that Eastland and Goldwater are the main enemies." In so doing he exaggerates the liberalism of the Johnson coalition, even asserting that Big Business, forced into the Democratic Party by Goldwater, "does not belong there."

• 2. Not only does Rustin urge that direct action be abandoned for politics, he argues also that independent political action is only rarely appropriate. The accurate perception that Negroes need white allies leads him to the conclusion that one must choose between existing aggregations of political forces: "The issue is which coalition to join and how to make it responsive to your program."

• 3. Thus, by exaggerating the Johnson coalition's capacity to solve fundamental social problems and by underestimating the need for independent action by Negroes, Rustin arrives at a stance which (in Radosh's words) "leads to a dissolution of the old

7. Set of sweeping programs initiated by Lyndon B. Johnson to eliminate poverty and racial injustice, including the establishment of Head Start, federal funding for schools through the Elementary and Secondary Education Act, Medicare, Medicaid, the National Endowment for the Arts, the National Endowment for the Humanities, the Corporation of Public Broadcasting, and the Department of Transportation.
1. Published by the Northern Student Movment, 514 West 126 Street, New York 27, N. Y. [Lynd's note]; Ronald Radosh (b. 1937), white American historian and writer.

Rights movement, as well as assuring that any new Movement will not develop in a more radical fashion." The effect of his advice would be to assimilate Negro protest to the Establishment just as labor protest was coopted at the end of the 1930s, in each case leaving the poorest, least organized parts of the population out in the cold.

I agree with Radosh's analysis, but I think it is not sufficiently fundamental. Fully to appraise Rustin's *Commentary* article, one must see it as the second in a series of three Rustin actions during the past three years. First was his attempt to get the credentials committee offer of token seating accepted by the Mississippi Freedom Democratic Party delegates at Atlantic City [* * *]. Second was the article [* * *]. Third was the effort to undermine and stop the March on Washington against the war in Vietnam (March–April, 1965). In this perspective, the most basic criticisms of his article should be these: (1) The coalition he advocates turns out to mean implicit acceptance of Administration foreign policy, to be coalition with the marines; (2) The style of politics he advocates turns out to mean a kind of elitism which Bayard has been fighting all his life, in which the rank-and-file persons would cease to act on their own behalf and be (in the words of "From Protest to Politics") "merely represented."

* * *

Coalitionism, then, is pro-Americanism. It is what Sidney Lens[2] has called "two-and-a-half campism." It is a posture which subordinates foreign to domestic politics, which mutes criticism of American imperialism so as to keep open its channels to the White House, which tacitly assumes that no major war will occur. But war is occurring in Vietnam. [* * *]

Coalitionism is also elitism. Its assumption is that major political decisions are made by deals between the representatives of the interests included in the coalition. Negro protest, according to the Rustin formula, should now take on the role of such an interest. And men like Rustin will become the national spokes-

man who sell the line agreed on behind doors to the faithful followers waiting in the street.

This was the meaning of Atlantic City. What was at stake, as it seemed to the SNCC people there, was not so much the question, Should compromise be accepted? as the question, Are plain people from Mississippi competent to decide? Rustin, Martin Luther King, and Roy Wilkins answered the latter question: No. The decision, they insisted, involved "national considerations." [* * *] Hence it should be made wisely, by the leaders, and put over to the delegates from Mississippi.

* * *

[* * *] Direct action is inseparable from the idea that everyone involved in a movement has some ultimate responsibility and initiative. Decentralization was the hallmark of the early *Liberation,* which Bayard helped to found. Participatory democrats, as they move from direct action into politics, insist that direct action must continue along with politics, that there comes into being a new politics which forces the representative back to his people, and politics back to life.

* * *

THE NONVIOLENT ALTERNATIVE

I think the time has come to begin to think of "nonviolent revolution" as the only long-run alternative to coalition with the marines [* * *]. The events of the past year—the creation of the Mississippi Freedom Democratic Party and the protest against the war in Vietnam—suggest [* * *] One can now begin to envision a series of nonviolent protests which would from the beginning question the legitimacy of the Administration's authority where it has gone beyond constitutional and moral limits, and might, if its insane foreign policy continues, culminate in the decision of hundreds of thousands of people to recognize the authority of alternative institutions of their own making.

Robert Parris[3] has sketched out such a scenario as a possibility in Mississippi. What [* * *] if Mississippi

2. White American labor leader and writer (1912–86).
3. Robert ("Bob") Parris Moses, leader of SNCC and of the Council of Federated Organizations (COFO), an umbrella group for the major civil rights organizations operating in Mississippi.

Freedom Democratic Party voters elected not only leg-islators but public officials as well? What if the Negroes of Neshoba County, Mississippi began to obey the instructions of the Freedom Sheriff rather than Sheriff Rainey[4]? What if the Freedom Sheriff impaneled a Freedom Grand Jury which indicted Sheriff Rainey for murder?

* * *

Suppose (I take this idea from Tom Hayden[5]) there were convened in Washington this summer a new continental congress. The congresses of 1774 and 1775 came about on the initiative of committees of cor-respondence of the individual colonies. The continen-tal congress of 1965 might stem from the initiative of the community union in a Northern ghetto, or the Freedom Party of a Southern state. Suppose, at any rate, that such a call goes out, saying in effect: This is a desperate situation; our government no longer repre-sents us; let us come together at Washington to con-sult on what needs to be done.

[* * *] [T]he continental congress of 1965 would seriously and responsibly begin to debate the policies of the United States. The discussions which have failed to take place in the Senate about Vietnam would take place here. [* * *]

* * *

[* * *] Six months ago [* * *] liberals congratulated themselves that America had turned the last corner, integrating the Negro into the happy permanent soci-etal consensus. This was an illusion. America's situa-tion was less secure, Johnson[6] was less rational, the American people were less brainwashed than they seemed [* * *]. Now we know: whom the gods would destroy they first make mad; but also: we can overcome.

JAMES FARMER
from *Freedom—When?* [1965]

In his 1965 book *Freedom—When?*, James Farmer (p. 516) explores the issues of coalition politics and pro-test raised by Bayard Rustin's article "From Protest to Politics" (p. 529). While Staughton Lynd's response (p. 538) focused on the choice of allies, Farmer raises the question of whether coalition politics and direct action are oppositional or complementary strategies.

Farmer was a longtime ally of Rustin's. Both joined the Fellowship of Reconciliation in 1941, and in 1942 they worked together in the influential civil rights group CORE, which was dedicated to protest through nonviolent direct action. Like Rustin, Farmer later shifted his focus from protest to mainstream politics, although, unlike his col-league, Farmer supported the Republican party.

From James Farmer, *Freedom—When?* (New York: Random House, 1965), pp. 25–27, 36, 47–50.

"**B**ut when will the demonstrations end?" The per-petual question. And a serious question. Actually it is several questions, for the meaning of the question differs, depending upon who asks it.

Coming from those whose dominant consider-ation is peace—public peace and peace of mind—the question means: "When are you going to stop tempt-ing violence and rioting?" Some put it more strongly: "When are you going to stop *sponsoring* violence?" Assumed is the necessary connection between dem-onstration and violence.

* * *

4. Lawrence A. Rainey (1923–2002), white elected sheriff in Mississippi connected to the murders of three civil rights activists in 1964; Mississippi Freedom Democratic Party: see p. 537.
5. White American anti-war and civil rights activist (b. 1939).
6. President Lyndon Baines Johnson.

"Isn't the patience of the white majority wearing thin? Why nourish the displeasure of 90 per cent of the population with provocative demonstrations? Remember, you need allies." And the assumption of these Cassandras[1] of the backlash is that freedom and equality are, in the last analysis, wholly gifts in the white man's power to bestow.

And then the question we shall face again and again in this book: "Even granting that there was a time when demonstrations were useful, can we not, now that the Negro civil rights are nearly secure, turn to more familiar techniques of political participation and press for sorely needed economic reforms?" And the assumptions of those questioners, who include some of the most formidable figures in the civil rights movement, are both that Negro rights are secure and that demonstrations will be ineffective in gaining economic reform.

* * *

OF DEMONSTRATIONS AND RIOTS

I must insist that a demonstration is not a riot. On the contrary, rather than leading to riots, demonstrations tend to help prevent them by providing an alternative outlet for frustrations. [* * *]

What the public must realize is that in a demonstration more things are happening, at more levels of human activity, than meets the eye. Demonstrations in the last few years have provided literally millions of Negroes with their first taste of self-determination and political self-expression. We might think of the demonstration as a rite of initiation through which the black man is mustered into the sacred order of freedom. It is also a rite the entire nation must undergo to exorcise the demons of racial hate. If in a spasm of emancipated exuberance these rites should cause inconvenience or violate the canons of cultivated good taste or trouble the dreams of some good-livers—I think it is forgivable. Enlightened people will understand that exuberance and occasional inconvenience are small prices to

pay when a nation is undoing historic wrong. The very least the nation can do is give us room to demonstrate. That is only a small sacrifice, considering the debt.

* * *

HAVE WE NOT MOVED NOW TO A STAGE "BEYOND DEMONSTRATIONS"?

Yes and no. Clearly the rights movement today faces new problems demanding new techniques. [* * *] If segregation and discrimination were eliminated tomorrow, many, many Negroes would still be ill-equipped to do the work demanded of today's worker. For these problems, traditional demonstrations are not as effective. We will need the financial resources and the concentrated effort of all levels of government, and it will take more money and concentrated effort than is dreamed of in the philosophies of the anti-poverty program. And to persuade the government to undertake needed measures, we will need to engage in forms of political activity other than direct action. But demonstrations will be an indispensable adjunct to almost every new effort.

Demonstrations *alone* did not achieve the civil rights bill[2] either. Without a half century of legal preparation and lobbying by the NAACP and others, the Congress and the President would not have known where to begin in formulating and passing a civil rights law. We have never denied the necessity for expertise and politics-as-usual at one level of the movement's activities. But without a decade's demonstration of deep and legitimate grievances, the law today would still be a dream.

* * *

. . . BUT WHEN WILL THE DEMONSTRATIONS END?

I remember the comment of a red-necked young man from St. Augustine, Florida, the leader of a gang of whites who had attacked Negroes trying to swim in

---

1. Reference to Cassandra in Greek mythology who could foresee the future but was believed by no one.
2. The Civil Rights Act of 1964 outlawed racial segregation in the workplace, in schools, and in public accommodations, and also outlawed unequal application of voter registration policies.

the Atlantic Ocean: "If I thought the niggers would be satisfied with just swimming, I'd let them in. But they won't be. First it's this, and then they'll want more, and before you know it they'll be laying hands on our women. We've got to take a stand now, because the more we let them have, the harder it'll be to draw the line."

Sometimes, I think that the racists have deeper insight into things than the moderates. The gentleman is right. Nothing short of full equality will stop us. One cannot simply draw up a list of ten or twenty things whose fulfillment would spell equality. [* * *] The moderate sincerely searches for the concession which will finally satisfy and silence us. He is willing to negotiate and temporarily sacrifice his security to get rid of the problem. The racist knows better how deep the problem is and how long he will need to resist our efforts. But we shall persist, that I promise.

Linda La Rue

from *The Black Movement and Women's Liberation* [1970]

In this 1970 article, Linda La Rue introduces gender issues into the debate over whether coalition politics and Black Power nationalism are complementary or antithetical strategies. For La Rue, gender issues are central in determining the most effective basis for political alliances. Although she privileges racial ties over gender bonds, she criticizes the oversimplified answers offered by racial politics and exposes the way in which assumptions about gender roles were shaping strate- gies and goals of the emerging Black Power movement. At the same time, La Rue dismisses the idea of an interracial feminist coalition based on shared gender discrimination, a strategy pursued at that time by feminists such as Shirley Chisholm (p. 787). Flo Kennedy (1916–2000) and Aileen Hernandez (b. 1926), who were early leaders of the National Organization for Women (NOW), established in 1966.

From *The Black Scholar* 1 (May 1970), pp. 36–42.

L et us first discuss what common literature addresses as the "common oppression" of blacks and women. This is a tasty abstraction designed purposely or inadvertently to draw validity and seriousness to the women's movement through a universality of plight. Every movement worth its "revolutionary salt" makes these headliner generalities about "common oppression" with others—but let us state unequivocally that, with few exceptions, the American white woman has had a better opportunity to live a free and fulfilling life, both mentally and physically, than any other group in the United States, with the exception of her white husband. Thus, any attempt to analogize black oppression with the plight of the American white woman has the validity of comparing the neck of a hanging man with the hands of an amateur mountain climber with rope burns.

"Common oppression" is fine for rhetoric, but it does not reflect the actual distance between the oppression of the black man and woman who are unemployed, and the "oppression" of the American white woman who is "sick and tired" of *Playboy* foldouts, or of Christian Dior lowering hemlines or adding ruffles, or of Miss Clairol telling her that blondes have more fun.[1]

Is there any logical comparison between the oppression of the black woman on welfare who has difficulty feeding her children and the discontent of the suburban mother who has the luxury to protest the washing of the dishes on which her family's full meal was consumed?

The surge of "common oppression" rhetoric and propaganda may lure the unsuspecting into an intellectual alliance with the goals of women's liberation, but it is not a wise alliance. It is not that women ought

1. 1960s ad campaign for Clairol hair coloring.

not to be liberated from the shackles of their present unfulfillment, but the depth, the extent, the intensity, the importance—indeed, the suffering and depravity of the *real* oppression blacks have experienced—can only be minimized in an alliance with women who heretofore have suffered little more than boredom, genteel repression, and dishpan hands.[2]

For all the similarities and analogies drawn between the liberation of women and the liberation of blacks, the point remains that when white women received their voting rights, most blacks, male and female, had been systematically disenfranchised since Reconstruction. And even in 1970, when women's right of franchise is rarely questioned, it is still a less than common occurrence for blacks to vote in some areas of the South.

Tasteless analogies like abortion for oppressed middle-class and poor women idealistically assert that all women have the right to decide if and when they want children and thus fail to catch the flavor of the actual circumstances. Actual circumstances boil down to middle-class women deciding when it is convenient to have children, while poor women decide the prudence of bringing into a world of already scarce resources another mouth to feed. Neither their motives nor their objectives are the same. But current literature leads one to lumping the decisions of these two women under one generalization, when in fact the difference between the plights of these two women is as clear as the difference between being hungry and out of work, and skipping lunch and taking a day off.

If we are realistically candid with ourselves, we will accept the fact that despite our beloved rhetoric of Pan-Africanism, our vision of Third-World liberation, and perhaps our dreams of a world state of multi-racial humanism, most blacks and a good many who generally exempt themselves from categories still want the proverbial "piece of cake." American values are difficult to discard, for, unlike what more militant "brothers" would have us believe, Americanism does not end with the adoption of Afro hairstyles on pregnant women covered in long African robes.

Indeed, the fact that the independent black capitalism demonstrated by the black Muslims and illustrated in Nixon's[3] speeches appeared for many blacks as the way out of the ghetto into the light lends a truthful vengeance to the maxim that perhaps blacks are nothing more than black Anglo-Saxons. Upon the rebirth of the liberation struggle in the sixties, a whole genre of "women's place" advocates immediately relegated black women to home and babies which is almost as ugly an expression of black Anglo-Saxonism as is Nixon's concept of "black capitalism."

The study of many developing areas and countries reflects at least an attempt to allow freedom of education and opportunity to women. Yet black Americans have not adopted developing areas' "new role" paradigm, but rather the Puritan-American status of "home and babies" which is advocated by the capitalist Muslims. This reflects either ingrained Americanism or the lack of the simplest imagination.

Several weeks ago, women's lib advocates demanded that a local women's magazine be "manned" by a woman editor. Other segments of the women's movement have carried on smaller campaigns in industry and business.

If white women have heretofore remained silent while white men maintained the better position and monopolized the opportunities by excluding blacks, can we really expect that white women, when put in direct competition for employment, will be any more openminded than their male counterparts when it comes to the hiring of black males and females in the same positions for which they are competing? From the standpoint of previous American social interaction, it does not seem logical that white females will not be tempted to take advantage of the fact that they are white in an economy that favors whites. It is entirely possible that women's liberation has developed a sudden attachment to the black liberation movement as a ploy to share the attention that it has taken blacks 400 years to generate. In short, it can be argued that women's liberation not only attached itself to the black movement, but did so with only marginal concern for

---

2. For an alternative position on interracial feminist coalitions, see Elizabeth M. Almquist's "Untangling the Effects of Race and Sex: The Disadvantaged Status of Black Women," *Social Science Quarterly* 56 (1975): 129–42.

3. Richard Milhous Nixon (1913–94), 37th president of the United States from 1969–74; faced with probable impeachment over the Watergate scandal, Nixon became the only president to ever resign the office.

black women and black liberation and with functional concern for the rights of white women.

The industrial demands of two world wars temporarily offset the racial limitations to mobility and allowed the possibility of blacks entering industry, as an important labor force, to be actualized. Similarly women have benefited from an expanded science and industrialization. Their biological limitation, successfully curbed by the pill[4] and by automation, which makes stressing physical labor more the exception than the rule, has created an impressively large and available labor force of women.

The black labor force, never fully employed and always representing a substantial percentage of the unemployed in the American economy, will now be driven into greater unemployment as white women converge at every level on an already dwindling job market.

Ideally, we chanced to think of women's liberation as a promising beginning of the "oppressed rising everywhere" in the typically Marxian fashion that many blacks seem drawn to. Instead, the spectre of racism and inadequate education, job discrimination, and even greater unequal opportunity will be, more than ever before, a function of neither maleness nor femaleness, but of blackness.

This discussion has been primarily to ward off any unintelligent alliance of black people with white women in this new liberation movement. Rhetoric and anathema hurled at the right industrial complex, idealism that speaks of a final humanism, and denunciation of the system that makes competition a fact of life, do not mean that women's liberation has as its goal anyone else's liberation except its own.

It is time that definitions be made clear. Blacks are *oppressed,* and that means unreasonably burdened, unjustly, severely, rigorously, cruelly, and harshly fettered by white authority. White women, on the other hand, are only *suppressed,* and that means checked, restrained, excluded from conscious and overt activity. And there is a difference.

For some, the dangers of an unintelligent alliance with women's liberation will suggest female suppression as the only protection against a new economic threat. For others, a greater answer is needed, and required, before women's liberation can be seen in perspective.

To say that black women must be freed before the black movement can attain full revolutionary consciousness is meaningless because of its malleability. To say that black women must be freed from the unsatisfactory male-female role relationship that we adopted from whites as the paradigm of the good family has more meaning because it indicates the incompatibility of white role models with the goal of black liberation. If there is anything to be learned from the current women's lib agitation, it is that roles are not ascribed and inherent, but adopted and interchangeable in every respect except pregnancy, breast feeding, and the system generally employed to bring the two former into existence.

Role integration, which I will elaborate upon as the goal and the strength of the black family, is substantially different from the role "usurpation" of men by women. The fact that the roles of man and woman are deemed in American society as natural and divine leads to false ego attachments to these roles. During slavery and following Reconstruction, black men felt inferior for a great number of reasons, among them that they were unable to work in positions comparable to the ones to which black women were assigned. With these positions often went fringe benefits of extra food, clothes, and perhaps elementary reading and writing skills. Black women were in turn jealous of white women and felt inadequate and inferior, because paraded in front of them constantly was the white woman of luxury who had no need for work, who could, as Sojourner Truth[5] pointed out, "be helped into carriages and lifted over ditches and . . . have the best place everywhere."

The resulting "respect" for women and the acceptance of the dominating role for men encouraged the myth of the immutability of these roles. The term "matriarchy" Frazier employed and Moynihan[6] exploited

---

4. Oral contraceptives for women were first approved by the FDA in June 1960 and quickly became the most popular form of reversible birth control for Americans.
5. Abolitionist and women's rights activist (1797?–1883); see p. 242.
6. Daniel Patrick Moynihan (1927–2003), white American sociologist; for debate on the Moynihan Report, see pp. 638–57; Frazier: E. Franklin Frazier, American sociologist; see pp. 385, 506, and 734–47.

was used to indicate a dastardly, unnatural role alteration, which could be blamed for inequality of opportunity, discrimination in hiring, and sundry other ills. It was as if "matriarchy" were transgression of divine law or natural law and thus would be punished until the proper hierarchy of man over woman was restored.

Black people have an obligation, as do white women, to recognize that the designation of "mother-head" and "father-head" does not imply inferiority of one and the superiority of the other. They are merely arbitrary role distinctions that vary from culture to culture and circumstance to circumstance.

Thus to quip, as has been popularly done, that the only place in the black movement for black women is prone[7] is actually supporting a white role ideal, and it is a compliment neither to men nor to women to advocate sexual capitalism or sexual colonialism.

It seems incongruous that the black movement has sanctioned the involvement of women in the Algerian revolution,[8] even though its revolutionary circumstances modified and often altered the common role models, but they have been duped into hating even their own slave grandmothers, who in not so admirable yet equally frightening and demanding circumstances also modified and altered the common role models of the black family. Fanon wrote in glorious terms about this role change:

> The unveiled Algerian woman, who assumed an increasingly important place in revolutionary action, developed her personality, discovered the exalting realm of responsibility. . . . This woman who, in the avenues of Algiers or of Constantine, would carry the grenades or the submachine gun charges, the woman who tomorrow would be outraged, violated, tortured, could not put herself back into her former state of mind and relive her behavior of the past. . . .[9]

Can it not be said that in slavery black women assumed an increasingly important place in the survival action and thus developed their personalities and

sense of responsibility? And after being outraged, violated, and tortured, could she be expected to put herself back into her former state of mind and relive her behavior of the past?

The crux of this argument is essentially that blacks, since slavery and throughout their entire existence in America, have also been living in revolutionary circumstances and under revolutionary pressures. Simply because the black liberation struggle has taken 400 years to come to fruition does not mean that it is not every bit as dangerous or psychologically exhausting as the Algerian struggle. Any revolution calls upon the best in both its men and its women. This is why Moynihan's statements that "matriarchy" is a root *cause* of black problems is as unfounded as it is inane. He does not recognize the liberation struggle and the demands that it has made on the black family.

How unfortunate that blacks and whites have allowed the most trying and bitter experience in the history of black people to be interpreted as the beginning of an "unashamed plot" to usurp the very manhood of black men. But the myth was perpetuated, and thus what brought the alteration of roles in Algeria was distorted and systematically employed to separate black men and women in America.

> Black women take kindness for weakness. Leave them the least little opening and they will put you on the cross. . . . It would be like trying to pamper a cobra. . . .[1]

Unless we realize how thoroughly the American value of male superiority and female inferiority has permeated our relationships with one another, we can never appreciate the role it plays in perpetuating racism and keeping black people divided.

Most, but not all, American relationships are based on some type of "exclusive competition of the superior and the exclusive competition of the inferior." This means essentially that the poor, the uneducated, the deprived, and the minorities of the aforementioned

---

7. At an SNCC staff retreat in 1964, activist Stokely Carmichael (1941–98) reportedly joked, "What is the position of women in SNCC? The position of women in SNCC is prone," referring to both white and black female activists; outrage over the comment helped spark the second wave of the feminist movement in the 1960s.
8. Algerian War of Independence, resulting in independence from France in 1962.
9. Frantz Fanon, *A Dying Colonialism* (New York: Grove, 1965), 107. [La Rue's note]
1. Eldridge Cleaver, *Soul on Ice* (New York: McGraw-Hill, 1968), 158 [La Rue's note]; Cleaver (1935–98) was a leading member of the Black Panther Party.

groups compete among themselves for the same scarce resources and inferior opportunities, while the privileged, middle-class, educated, and select white minorities compete with one another for rather plentiful resources and superior opportunities for prestige and power. Competition among groups is rare, due to the fact that elements who qualify are almost invariably absorbed to some extent (note the black middle class) by the group to which they seek entry. We may well understand that there is only one equal relationship between man and woman, black and white, in America, and this equality is based on whether or not you can force your way into qualifying for the same resources.

But instead of attempting to modify this competitive definition within the black movement, many black males have affirmed it as a way of maintaining the closure of male monopolization of scarce benefits and making the "dominion of males" impenetrable to black females. This is, of course, very much the American way of exploitation.

The order of logic that makes it possible to pronounce, as did Dr. Robert Staples, that "black women cannot be free qua women until all blacks attain their liberation,"[2] maintains, whether purposely or not, that black women will be able to separate their femaleness from their blackness, and thus they will be able to be free as blacks, if not free as women; or, that male freedom ought to come first; or, finally, that the freedom of black women and men and the freedom of black people as a whole are not one and the same.

Only with the concept of role integration can we hope to rise above the petty demarcations of human freedom that America is noted for and that are unfortunately inherent in Dr. Staples's remark. Role integration is the realization that:

- ego attachments to particular activities or traits must be abolished as a method of determining malehood and femalehood; that instead, ego attachments must be distributed to a wider variety of tasks and traits in order to weaken the power of one activity in determining self-worth, and

- the flexibility of a people in effecting role alternation and role integration has been a historically proven asset to the survival of any people—witness Israel, China, and Algeria.

Thus, the unwitting adoption and the knowing perpetuation of this American value reflects three interrelated situations:

- black people's growing sense of security and well-being and their failure to recognize the expanse of black problems;

- people's over-identification with the dominant group, even though the survival of blacks in America is not assured; and

- black people's belief in the myth of "matriarchy" and their subsequent rejection of role integration as unnatural and unnecessary.

While the rhetoric of black power and the advocates of cultural nationalism laud black people for their ability to struggle under oppressive odds, they simultaneously seek to strip away or incapacitate the phenomenon of role integration—the very means by which blacks were able to survive! They seek to replace it with a weak, intractable role separation which would completely sap the strength of the black movement because it would inhibit the mobilization of both women and men. It was this ability to mobilize black men and black women that guaranteed survival during slavery.

The strength of role integration is sorely overlooked as blacks throw away the hot comb, the bleach cream, the lye, and yet insist on maintaining the worst of American values by placing the strength of black women in the traction of the white female status.

I would think black men would want a better status for their sister black women; indeed, black women would want a better status for themselves, rather than a warmed-over throne of women's inferiority, which white women are beginning to abandon.

Though most white women's lib advocates fail to realize the possibility, their subsequent liberation may spell a strengthening of the status quo values from which they sought liberation. Since more and more women will be participating in the decision-making process, those few women participating in the "struggle" will be outnumbered by the more traditional middle-class women. This means that the traditional women will be in a position to take advantage of new opportunities, which radical women's liberation has

---

2. Robert Staples, "The Myth of the Black Matriarchy," *Black Scholar* (January/February 1970):16. [La Rue's note] See p. 826.

struggled to win. Voting studies now reflect that the traditional women, middle-class and above, tend to vote the same way as their husbands. Because blacks have dealt with these husbands in the effort to secure jobs, housing, and education, it does not seem likely that blacks will gain significantly from the open mobility of less tolerant women whose viewpoints differ little from those of their husbands.

If white radical thought has called upon the strength of all women to take a position of responsibility and power, can blacks afford to relegate black women to "home and babies" while white women reinforce the status quo?

The cry of black women's liberation is a cry against chaining very much needed labor and agitating forces to a role that once belonged to impotent, apolitical white women. Blacks speak lovingly of the vanguard and the importance of women in the struggle and yet fail to recognize that women have been assigned a new place, based on white-ascribed characteristics of women, rather than on their actual potential. The black movement needs its women in a position of struggle, not prone. The struggle blacks face is not taking place between knives and forks, at the washboard, or in the diaper pail. It is taking place on the labor market, at the polls, in government, in the protection of black communities, in local neighborhood power struggles, in housing, and in education.

Can blacks afford to be so unobservant of current events as to send their women to fight a nonexistent battle in a dishpan?

Even now, the black adoption of the white values of women has begun to show its effects on black women in distinctive ways. The black liberation movement has created a politicized, unliberated copy of white womanhood. Black women who participated in the struggle have failed to recognize, for the most part, the unique contradiction between renunciation of capitalistic competition and the acceptance of sexual colonialism. The failure of the black movement to resolve and deal with this dilemma has perpetuated the following attitudes in American politicized black women:

- The belief in the myth of matriarchy. The black woman has been made to feel ashamed of her strength, and so to redeem herself she has adopted from whites the belief that superiority and dominance of the male is the most "natural" and "normal" relationship. She consequently believes that black women ought to be suppressed in order to attain that "natural balance."

- Because the white women's role has been held up as an example to all black women, many black women feel inadequate and so ardently compete in "femininity" with white females for black males' attention. She further competes with black females in an attempt to be the "blackest and the most feminine," thereby superior to her fellow black sisters in appealing to black politicized men. She competes also with the apolitical black female in an attempt to keep black males from "regressing" back to females whom she feels have had more "practice" in the traditional role of white woman than has she.

- Finally, she emphasizes the traditional roles of women, such as housekeeping, children, supportive roles, and self-maintenance, but she politicizes these roles by calling them the roles of black women. She then adopts the attitude that her job and her life is to have more children which can be used in the vanguard of the black struggle.

- Black women, as the song "Black Pearl"[3] relates, have been put up where they belong, but by American standards. Is it so inconceivable that the American value of respect and human relationships is distorted? It has taken the birth of women's liberation to bring the black movement back to its senses.

- The black woman is demanding a new set of female definitions and a recognition of herself as a citizen, companion, and confidante, not a matriarchal villain or a stepstool babymaker. Role integration advocates the complementary recognition of man and woman, not the competitive recognition of same.

The recent unabated controversy over the use of birth control in the black community is of grave importance here. Black people, even the "most liberated of mind," are still infused with ascribed inferiority of

---

3. Song recorded by Sonny Charles and the Checkmates in 1969 and by Horace Faith in 1970.

females and the natural superiority of males. These same values foster the idea of "good blood" in our children. If indeed there can be any black liberation, it must start with the recognition of contradictions like the following.

It gives a great many black males pride to speak, as Dr. Robert Staples does, of "...the role of the black woman in the black liberation struggle [as] an important one [that] cannot be forgotten. From her womb have come the revolutionary warriors of our time."[4]

How many potential revolutionary warriors stand abandoned in orphanages while blacks rhetorize disdain for birth control as a "trick of The Man" to halt the growth of black population? Why are there not more revolutionary couples adopting black children? Could it be that the American concept of "bastard," which is equivalent to inferior in our society, reflects black Anglo-Saxonism? Do blacks, like whites, discriminate against black babies because they do not represent "our own personal" image? Or do blacks, like the most racist of whites, require that a child be of their own blood before they can love that child or feed it? Does the vanguard of which Dr. Staples so reverently speaks recognize the existence of the term "bastard"?

Someone once suggested that the word "bastard" be deleted from the values of black people. Would it not be more revolutionary for blacks to advocate a five-year moratorium on black births until every black baby in an American orphanage was adopted by one or more black parents? Then blacks could really have a valid reason for continuing to give birth. Children would mean more than simply a role for black women to play or fuel for the legendary vanguard. Indeed, blacks would be able to tap the potential of the existing children and could sensibly add more potential to the black struggle for liberation. To do this would be to do something no other civilization, modern of course, has ever done, and blacks would be allowing every black child to have a home and not just a plot in some understaffed children's penal farm.

* * *

[* * *]We can conclude that black women's liberation and black men's liberation is what we mean when we speak of the liberation of black people. I maintain that the true liberation of black people depends on their rejection of the inferiority of women, the rejection of competition as the only viable relationship between men, and their reaffirmation of respect for general human potential in whatever form—man, child, or woman—it is conceived.

HUEY NEWTON

from *Huey Newton Talks to* The Movement [1968]

In the 1968 interview reprinted here, Black Panther member Huey Newton (p. 583) champions revolutionary strategies over moderate reform and revisits issues that had been controversial since the abolitionists' debates of the 1800s, such as the use of violence to achieve liberation. He examines in detail the question of political allegiances, portraying the Black Panther Party as a complex mix of ideologies and racial politics. On the most basic level, the party stressed racial unity, as only black people could be full members. But ideology ultimately trumped race, since the "black bourgeoisie" were categorized as enemies while "white revolutionaries" were allowed a supportive role. In his discussion of the role of "white revolutionaries," Newton explores the idea of collective bloc politics, in which different groups work together periodically. Collective bloc politics contrasts with the broader strategy of coalition politics, embraced by leaders such as Bayard Rustin (p. 529), in which people who share a common interest bond to form a larger political group.

From *The Movement*, August 1968.

4. Ibid. [Staples, "Myth":16] [La Rue's note] See p. 826.

THE MOVEMENT: The question of nationalism is a vital one in the black movement today. Some have made a distinction between cultural nationalism and revolutionary nationalism. Would you comment on the differences and give us your views?

HUEY P. NEWTON: There are two kinds of nationalism, revolutionary nationalism and reactionary nationalism. Revolutionary nationalism is first dependent upon a people's revolution with the end goal being the people in power. Therefore to be a revolutionary nationalist you would by necessity have to be a socialist. If you are a reactionary nationalist you are not a socialist and your end goal is the oppression of the people.

Cultural nationalism, or pork chop nationalism, as I sometimes call it, is basically a problem of having the wrong political perspective. It seems to be a reaction instead of responding to political oppression. The cultural nationalists are concerned with returning to the old African culture and thereby regaining their identity and freedom. In other words, they feel that the African culture will automatically bring political freedom. Many times cultural nationalists fall into line as reactionary nationalists.

Papa Doc[1] in Haiti is an excellent example of reactionary nationalism. He oppresses the people but he does promote the African culture. He's against anything other than black, which on the surface seems very good, but for him it is only to mislead the people. He merely kicked out the racists and replaced them with himself as the oppressor. Many of the nationalists in this country seem to desire the same ends.

The Black Panther Party, which is a revolutionary group of black people, realizes that we have to have an identity. We have to realize our black heritage in order to give us strength to move on and progress. But as far as returning to the old African culture, it's unnecessary and it's not advantageous in many respects. We believe that culture itself will not liberate us. We're going to need some stronger stuff.

REVOLUTIONARY NATIONALISM

A good example of revolutionary nationalism was the revolution in Algeria when Ben Bella[2] took over. The French were kicked out but it was a people's revolution because the people ended up in power. The leaders that took over were not interested in the profit motive where they could exploit the people and keep them in a state of slavery. They nationalized the industry and plowed the would-be profits into the community. That's what socialism is all about in a nutshell. The people's representatives are in office strictly on the leave of the people. The wealth of the country is controlled by the people and they are considered whenever modifications in the industries are made.

The Black Panther Party is a revolutionary Nationalist group and we see a major contradiction between capitalism in this country and our interests. We realize that this country became very rich upon slavery and that slavery is capitalism in the extreme. We have two evils to fight, capitalism and racism. We must destroy both racism and capitalism.

MOVEMENT: Directly related to the question of nationalism is the question of unity within the black community. There has been some question about this since the Black Panther Party has run candidates against other black candidates in recent California elections. What is your position on this matter?

HUEY: Well a very peculiar thing has happened. Historically you got what Malcolm X calls the field nigger and the house nigger. The house nigger had some privileges, a little more. He got the worn-out clothes of the master and he didn't have to work as hard as the field black. He came to respect the master to such an extent until he identified with the master because he got a few of the leftovers that the field blacks did not get. And through this identity with him, he saw the slavemaster's interest as being his interest. Sometimes he would even protect the slavemaster more than the slavemaster would protect himself. Malcolm makes the point

1. Dr. François Duvalier (1907–71) ruled Haiti as President for Life from 1964 until his death; during his repressive and violent regime, Papa Doc followed a noirist strategy, filling positions formerly held by the mulatto elite with black Haitians of his own choosing.
2. Muhammad Ahmed Ben Bella (b. 1918) was a leader of the Algerian War of Independence against France (1954–62) and the first president of the Algerian Republic.

that if the master's house happened to catch on fire the house Negro will work harder than the master to put the fire out and save the master's house, while the field Negro, the field blacks was praying that the house burned down. The house black identified with the master so much that when the master would get sick the house Negro would say, "Master, we's sick!"

BLACK BOURGEOISIE

The Black Panther Party are the field blacks, we're hoping the master dies if he gets sick. The Black bourgeoisie seem to be acting in the role of the house Negro. They are pro-administration. They would like a few concessions made, but as far as the overall setup, they have a little more material goods, a little more advantage, a few more privileges than the black have-nots; the lower class. And so they identify with the power structure and they see their interests as the power structure's interest. In fact, it's against their interest.

The Black Panther Party was forced to draw a line of demarcation. We are for all of those who are for the promotion of the interests of the black have-nots, which represents about 98% of blacks here in America. We're not controlled by the white mother country radicals nor are we controlled by the black bourgeoisie. We have a mind of our own and if the black bourgeoisie cannot align itself with our complete program, then the black bourgeoisie sets itself up as our enemy. And they will be attacked and treated as such.

MOVEMENT: The Black Panther Party has had considerable contact with white radicals since its earliest days. What do you see as the role of these white radicals?

HUEY: The white mother country radical is the offspring of the children of the beast that has plundered the world exploiting all people, concentrating on the people of color. These are children of the beast that seek now to be redeemed because they realize that their former heroes, who were slave masters and murderers, put forth ideas that were only facades to hide the treachery they inflicted upon the world. They are turning their backs on their fathers.

The white mother country radical, in resisting the system, becomes somewhat of an abstract thing because he's not oppressed as much as black people are. As a matter of fact his oppression is somewhat abstract simply because he doesn't have to live in a reality of oppression.

Black people in America and colored people throughout the world suffer not only from exploitation, but they suffer from racism. Black people here in America, in the black colony, are oppressed because we're black and we're exploited. The whites are rebels, many of them from the middle class and as far as any overt oppression this is not the case. So therefore I call their rejection of the system somewhat of an abstract thing. They're looking for new heroes. They're looking to wash away the hypocrisy that their fathers have presented to the world. In doing this they see the people who are really fighting for freedom. They see the people who are really standing for justice and equality and peace, throughout the world. They are the people of Vietnam, the people of Latin America, the people of Asia, the people of Africa, and the black people in the black colony here in America.

WHITE REVOLUTIONARIES

This presents somewhat of a problem in many ways to the black revolutionary especially to the cultural nationalist. The cultural nationalist doesn't understand the white revolutionaries because he can't see why anyone white would turn on the system. So they think that maybe this is some more hypocrisy being planted by white people.

I personally think that there are many young white revolutionaries who are sincere in attempting to realign themselves with mankind, and to make a reality out of the high moral standards that their fathers and forefathers only expressed. In pressing for new heroes the young white revolutionaries found the heroes in the black colony at home and in the colonies throughout the world.

The young white revolutionaries raised the cry for the troops to withdraw from Vietnam, hands off Latin America, withdraw from the Dominican Republic and also to withdraw from the black community or the black colony. So you have a situation in which the young white revolutionaries are attempting to identify with the oppressed people of the colonies and against the exploiter.

The problem arises then in what part they can play. How can they aid the colony? How can they aid the Black Panther Party or any other black revolutionary group? They can aid the black revolutionaries first by simply turning away from the establishment, and secondly by choosing their friends. For instance, they have a choice between whether they will be a friend of Lyndon Baines Johnson or a friend of Fidel Castro. A friend of Robert Kennedy or a friend of Ho Chi Minh.[3] And these are direct opposites. A friend of mine or a friend of Johnson's. After they make this choice then the white revolutionaries have a duty and a responsibility to act.

The imperialistic or capitalistic system occupies areas. It occupies Vietnam now. They occupy them by sending soldiers there, by sending policemen there. The policemen or soldiers are only a gun in the establishment's hand. They make the racist secure in his racism. The gun in the establishment's hand makes the establishment secure in its exploitation. The first problem it seems is to remove the gun from the establishment's hand. Until lately the white radical has seen no reason to come into conflict with the policemen in his own community. The reason I said until recently is because there is friction now in the mother country between the young white revolutionaries and the police. Because now the white revolutionaries are attempting to put some of their ideas into action, and there's the rub. We say that it should be a permanent thing.

Black people are being oppressed in the colony by white policemen, by white racists. We are saying they must withdraw. We realize that it is not only the Oakland police department but rather the security forces in general. On April 6 it wasn't just the Oakland police

department who ambushed the Panthers.[4] It was the Oakland police department, the Emeryville police department and I wouldn't be surprised if there were others. When the white revolutionaries went down to close up the Army terminal in October 1965 it wasn't the Oakland police by themselves who tried to stop them. It was the Oakland police, the Berkeley police, the Highway Patrol, the Sheriff's Department and the national guard was standing by. So we see that they're all part of the security force to protect the status quo; to make sure that the institutions carry out their goals. They're here to protect the system.

As far as I'm concerned the only reasonable conclusion would be to first realize the enemy, realize the plan, and then when something happens in the black colony—when we're attacked and ambushed in the black colony—then the white revolutionary students and intellectuals and all the other whites who support the colony should respond by defending us, by attacking the enemy in their community. Every time that we're attacked in our community there should be a reaction by the white revolutionaries; they should respond by defending us, by attacking part of the security force. Part of that security force that is determined to carry out the racist ends of the American institutions.

As far as our party is concerned, the Black Panther Party is an all black party, because we feel as Malcolm X felt that there can be no black-white unity until there first is black unity. We have a problem in the black colony that is particular to the colony, but we're willing to accept aid from the mother country as long as the mother country radicals realize that we have, as Eldridge Cleaver says in SOUL ON ICE, a mind of our own. We've regained our mind that was taken away from us and we will decide the political as well as the practical stand that we'll take. We'll make the theory and we'll carry out the practice. It's the duty of the white revolutionary to aid us in this.

3. Communist leader of North Vietnam (1890–1969); Johnson: 36th president of the United States from 1963–69; Castro: Communist leader of Cuba since the 1959 Cuban Revolution (b. 1926); Kennedy: (1925–68) Attorney General under his brother President John F. Kennedy (1917–63) and President Johnson and then New York State Senator and front-running presidential candidate until his assassination in 1968.
4. Shoot-out between police and the Black Panthers in 1968 in which 17-year-old Bobby Hutton was shot dead.

So the role of the mother country radical, and he does have a role, is to first choose his friend and his enemy and after doing this, which it seems he's already done, then to not only articulate his desires to regain his moral standard and align himself with humanity, but also to put this into practice by attacking the protectors of the institutions.

MOVEMENT: You have spoken a lot about dealing with the protectors of the system, the armed forces. Would you like to elaborate on why you place so much emphasis on this?

HUEY: The reasons that I feel very strongly about dealing with the protectors of the system is simply because without this protection from the army, the police and the military, the institutions could not go on in their racism and exploitation. For instance, as the Vietnamese are driving the American imperialist troops out of Vietnam, it automatically stops the racist imperialist institutions of America from oppressing that particular country. The country cannot implement its racist program without the guns. And the guns are the military and the police. If the military were disarmed in Vietnam then the Vietnamese would be victorious.

We are in the same situation here in America. Whenever we attack the system the first thing the administrators do is to send out their strongarm men. If it's a rent strike, because of the indecent housing we have, they will send out the police to throw the furniture out the window. They don't come themselves. They send their protectors. So to deal with the corrupt exploiter you are going to have to deal with his protector, which is the police who take orders from him. This is a must.

MOVEMENT: Would you like to be more specific on the conditions which must exist before an alliance or coalition can be formed with predominantly white groups? Would you comment specifically on your alliance with the California Peace and Freedom Party?[5]

HUEY: We have an alliance with the Peace and Freedom Party. The Peace and Freedom Party has supported our program in full and this is the criterion for a coalition with the black revolutionary group. If they had not supported our program in full, then we would not have seen any reason to make an alliance with them, because we are the reality of the oppression. They are not. They are only oppressed in an abstract way; we are oppressed in the real way. We are the real slaves! So it's a problem that we suffer from more than anyone else and it's our problem of liberation. Therefore we should decide what measures and what tools and what programs to use to become liberated. Many of the young white revolutionaries realize this and I see no reason not to have a coalition with them.

MOVEMENT: Other black groups seem to feel that from past experience it is impossible for them to work with whites and impossible for them to form alliances. What do you see as the reasons for this and do you think that the history of the Black Panther Party makes this less of a problem?

SNCC AND LIBERALS

HUEY: There was somewhat of an unhealthy relationship in the past with the white liberals supporting the black people who were trying to gain their freedom. I think that a good example of this would be the relationship that SNCC had with its white liberals. I call them white liberals because they differ strictly from the white radicals. The relationship was that the whites controlled SNCC for a very long time. From the very start of SNCC until here recently whites were the mind of SNCC. They controlled the program of SNCC with money and they controlled the ideology, or the stands SNCC would take. The blacks in SNCC were completely controlled program-wise; they couldn't do any more than these white liberals wanted them to do, which wasn't very much. So the white liberals were not working for self-determination for the black community. They were interested in a few concessions from the power structure. They undermined SNCC's program.

Stokely Carmichael came along and realizing this started to follow Malcolm X's program of Black Power. This frightened many of the white liberals who were supporting SNCC. Whites were afraid when Stokely came along with Black Power and said that black people have a mind of their own and that SNCC would be

---

5. Political party founded in 1967 by social activists against the war in Vietnam and in favor of expanding civil rights.

an all-black organization and that SNCC would seek self-determination for the black community. The white liberals withdrew their support leaving the organization financially bankrupt. The blacks who were in the organization, Stokely and H. Rap Brown,[6] were left very angry with the white liberals who had been aiding them under the disguise of being sincere. They weren't sincere.

The result was that the leadership of SNCC turned away from the white liberal, which was very good. I don't think they distinguished between the white liberal and the white revolutionary, because the white revolutionary is white also and they are very much afraid to have any contact whatsoever with white people. Even to the point of denying that the white revolutionaries could give support, by supporting the programs of SNCC in the mother country. Not by making any programs, not by being a member of the organization, but simply by resisting. Just as the Vietnamese people realize that they are supported whenever other oppressed people throughout the world resist. Because it helps divide the troops. It drains the country militarily and economically. If the mother country radicals are sincere then this will definitely add to the attack that we are making on the power structure. The Black Panther Party's program is a program where we recognize that the revolution in the mother country will definitely aid us in our freedom and has everything to do with our struggle!

HATE THE OPPRESSOR

I think that one of SNCC's great problems is that they were controlled by the traditional administrator: the omnipotent administrator, the white person. He was the mind of SNCC. And so SNCC regained its mind, but I believe that it lost its political perspective. I think that this was a reaction rather than a response. The Black Panther Party has NEVER been controlled by white people. The Black Panther Party has always been a black group. We have always had an integration of mind and body. We have never been controlled by whites and therefore we don't fear the white mother country radicals. Our alliance is one of organized black groups with organized white groups. As soon as the organized white groups do not do the things that would benefit us in our struggle for liberation, that will be our departure point. So we don't suffer in the hangup of a skin color. We don't hate white people; we hate the oppressor. And if the oppressor happens to be white then we hate him. When he stops oppressing us then we no longer hate him. And right now in America you have the slave-master being a white group. We are pushing him out of office through revolution in this country. I think the responsibility of the white revolutionary will be to aid us in this. And when we are attacked by the police or by the military then it will be up to the white mother country radicals to attack the murderers and to respond as we respond, to follow our program.

IN THE HEADLINES:
Black–Jewish Relations

ELISE C. ROLLOCK: *A Negro Speaks to Jews* [1968]
RAYNER W. MANN: *A Negro Discusses Anti-Semitism* [1968]

It is an often-unexamined statement that African Americans and Jewish Americans are natural allies in the struggle for social justice. Certainly, both groups share a history of harsh discrimination. But the historic experiences of black and Jewish people in the United States have been strikingly different, particularly in the realms of economic advancement and cultural assimilation. Moreover, internal and external cultural forces—from the anti-Semitism inherent in some Christian and Islamic traditions to the racism and anti-Semitism in American

---

6. Also known as Jamil Abdullah Al-Amin (b. 1943 as Hubert Gerald Brown), chair of SNCC in the 1960s and later Justice Minister of the Black Panther Party; currently serving a life sentence in prison for killing a black police officer.

culture—have fostered divisions. Overly high expectations for the alliance have also contributed to tensions between the two groups, particularly since the mid-twentieth century.

The assumption that black and Jewish people have common interests has also led to heightened public scrutiny of black anti-Semitism and Jewish racism. Controversial figures such as Louis Farrakhan have acted as lightning rods for conflict. But black and Jewish leaders often question the prudence of spotlighting instances of prejudice within minority groups. Some argue that a zero-tolerance policy is necessary to keep bigotry from proliferating. Others contend that highlighting black anti-Semitism or Jewish racism distracts from the fight for common goals and interests and so perpetuates the status quo. But few suggest that the tensions between black and Jewish people should be completely ignored. Acknowledging the differences in their experiences, as well as the similarities, may be a key step toward a solid alliance in the fight against oppression.

In the first selection reprinted here, from 1968, Elise C. Rollock, a Christian assistant principal in New York City, expresses some of the resentment she feels toward Jewish people who offer advice on how to "make it" in America. Rayner W. Mann, a schoolteacher in Los Angeles, responds to Rollock's remarks, calling black anti-Semitism "irrational." Expressions of resentment like Rollock's, Mann contends, try to make the Jew a "scapegoat for the oppressed Negro." For more on this debate, see p. 861.

Elise C. Rollock

A Negro Speaks to Jews [1968]

To say that Negroes are anti-Semitic is to deny the humanity of both Negroes and Jews. Every human being is by nature ambivalent in his loves and hatreds. On a personal level the individual one loves most, often becomes the object of the most intense hatred. The child loves its parents but also hates them intensely when they must exercise control or deny a trifling privilege that seems important to him. The adult loves other adults who are mentally attuned to the ideals that he considers right and just, and hates others who seem to deny him his rights. To say that Negroes love or hate Jews or that Jews love or hate Negroes is to say that neither group is composed of human beings with the normal human components of virtues and weaknesses.

I, an African-American adult, respect and love many Jews with whom I work and in whom I confide personal and family problems as they confide in me. The longer our association lasts, the closer we become as we realize that our problems are the universal problems of mankind.

As a black American, living in a Negro community, I can empathize with the human problems of the poor Jewish couple eking out a miserable existence in the local candy store. I feel an emotional response to the wife when she tells me of a sick child at home in the care of an older child. She must help her husband in the store because he speaks little English and is easily frustrated by the teasing and the petty pilfering of some of the neighborhood youths.

She also bears the hostility of some prejudiced colored folk who, despite the evidence of their eyes, insist on identifying her with "the rich Jews who take bags of money out of the Negro ghetto every night to deposit their ill-gotten gains in a Chase National Bank, which thereupon uses this money to buy bonds in South Africa to keep apartheid a going concern." As a mother, I know about sick children. As a wife I know about protecting a husband from committing suicide by instinctively lashing out against his tormentors. How could I possibly hate these people who are trapped in the same vicious cycle in which I am caught?

Yet, as a black adult, I too have my "Antis." When my Jewish colleagues tell me that I must struggle for recognition in these United States as they did when they migrated here a generation or two ago, I agree. When they tell me I must be peaceful and affable while conducting the struggle and that I must disassociate myself immediately and vocally from those who talk militantly and those who throw rocks, my "Antis" come rushing forth. I know and I am sure they know that no struggle has ever been won by people sitting down and chanting, "We shall overcome, some day."[1]

When a Jewish colleague of mine goes to South Africa and writes back that life is wonderful there, "no civil rights demonstrations and no riots"; when he is welcomed back among his complacent colleagues and chided gently for this *faux pas,* my "Antis" boil over again.

All life consists of a struggle to reach the ideal. The ideal for each of us is the same, the development of the best qualities of our own humanity and the recognition of these qualities in all other human beings. When any group, whether Negro or Jewish, decides that the acquisition of money and power can substitute for the human ideal of concern for one's brothers, that group is in trouble.

Anti-Semitism among Negroes arises very often from the well-meaning attitude of some Jews which says, in effect: "See where we are. You can become just as rich and just as important if you will only become educated. Stop fighting the Establishment and get into it, as we did."

Any schoolboy, black or white, in New York City, can accept that statement at face value. The Establishment he knows is largely Jewish. Most of his teachers and his school principal are likely to be Jewish. He later learns that these positions of authority were achieved at tremendous cost to generations of Jews who struggled to educate their children to fill them.

The black adult, however, realizes that he now has an additional hurdle to face. Jewish members of the Establishment, ready with good advice as to how they made it, have no intention of jeopardizing their hard-won positions by advocating the right of another group to come in. They would be more than human if they did. Therefore, if the African-American wishes to join the Establishment he faces a struggle not only with the so-called Christians but also with those Jews who keep telling him, "See how we did it."

It should be obvious to all of us that a democracy which permits the murder of a Chaney, a Schwerner, a Goodman[2] to go unpunished has no regard for the rights of its African-American nor its Jewish citizens. Therefore, the stance of the Jewish liberal who tells us, "we have arrived. Do as we did and you too will arrive," is utterly ridiculous. The Jew who fights on the side of human rights is fighting his own battle for survival, whether he is standing beside a Negro or another Jew.

The question of anti-Semitism is irrelevant and meaningless in the context of our struggle for human rights. More important, it puts a handle to something that endangers us all. The pilfering black youth who snatches your wallet or who breaks your store window does not do it because you are Jewish. He would as soon do it to me. The Jew who refuses to rent an apartment to me in his building doesn't do it because I am black. He also refuses to rent to another Jew whose old-world customs would embarrass his middle class tenants.

Unquestionably, there is at least as much anti-Semitism among certain Jews, against the Jew whose manners and customs seem to fit an ancient stereotype, as there is anti-Negroism among certain middle class Negroes who deplore the manners and customs of the unsophisticated, loud-mouthed Negro. It is ironic for one group to ask the members of any other group to accept us and love us as a group when none of us can accept and love our own group in its entirety.

Both as individuals and as groups we are involved in the struggle to reach the full development of our own humanity and the recognition of humanity's best qualities in our fellow man. It is necessary that we cooperate with those who are fighting the same battle. It is also essential that we awaken the complacent in our own groups who think their battle is already won.

Had Andrew Goodman been slain in a foreign land with an American passport in his pocket, his murderers would have been sought out and punished immediately lest the mighty forces of the United States move in to make this an international incident. Has the "self help and mutual responsibility that Jews have practiced from 1880 to 1914" helped to avenge the death of Andrew Goodman? Has it made it safe for a Jew to travel in Mississippi, with or without a beard?

---

1. Based on a gospel protest song published in 1947; became an anthem of the U.S. civil rights movement.
2. Three civil rights activists murdered in 1964 in Mississippi; white Jewish student Andrew Goodman (1943–64) was 20 years old, white Jewish CORE activist Michael Schwerner (1939–64) was 24, and black CORE activist James Cheney (1943–64) was 21.

Or does it mean that Jews are willing to write off their casualties in the struggle because certain Negroes are being "abrasive" in saying to smug Jews the same harsh words they are saying to other complacent whites and blacks who think they can rest on their laurels now that the battle is won.

The battle, my friends, has just begun. If you wish to pick up your toy guns and go home because I call you a harsh name, then by all means go in peace. I can only hope that you will discover, before it is too late, that this struggle for human rights is not just a Negro struggle in which you have the choice of helping us or not. It is also your struggle. You bought it with the blood of Andrew Goodman and Michael Schwerner, just as I bought it with the blood of James Chaney and all those others who have gone in the same way before and since.

You and I, my friends, are in the same leaky boat. Neither you nor I have a choice of leaving or staying. It doesn't really matter what we say to each other at this point. Perhaps we just ought to stop talking and keep rowing together, if we wish to survive.

From *Jewish Currents*, February 1968, pp. 13–15.

RAYNER W. MANN
A Negro Discusses Anti-Semitism [1968]

The recent article published in *JEWISH CURRENTS* in Feb., 1968, written by Mrs. Elise C. Rollock, a Negro assistant principal in the New York schools, leads one to conclude that anti-Semitic sentiments and attitudes are simply normal behavior in human beings. Mrs. Rollock wrote: "To say that Negroes are anti-Semitic is to deny the humanity of both Negroes and Jews." In other words, to be anti-Semitic is to be human. She argues that substantiating evidence for the phenomenon may be observed in the selective and discriminating behavior in all human beings in a variety of social settings.

We do not deny the validity of the concept that all human beings seem to be highly selective and discriminating in social areas. However, we do deny that anti-Semitism is a necessary concomitant of the way human beings see reality.

There is a recent and frightening upsurge of anti-Semitic pronouncements by Negro militants, who are in the vanguard of the civil rights movement in the United States. Anti-Semitism is generalized and universalistic in nature and serves an altogether different function in society. It is not a consequence nor concomitant of man's discriminating powers. One is first anti-Semitic or prejudiced toward Negroes; the results are expressed in the forms of segregation, discrimination and in the extreme phenomenon of genocide.

Generalized attitudes and sentiments of human beings result from the socialization process by which an individual learns to live in a group. One does not make a particular choice as in particularized behavior. Quite the contrary occurs. The process of socialization precludes the opportunity for one to discover the irrationality of anti-Semitism without deliberate and conscious effort. Anti-Semitism is anti-social and is not required for the human being to survive in his environment. Anti-Semitism is a force in society for annihilation of human beings rather than for survival. When a Negro expresses and even justifies anti-Jewish sentiments, he is expressing attitudes acquired during the socialization process in a society in which anti-Semitism has been accepted and given channels of expression.

The following is a recent example of anti-Semitic sentiments pronounced by a Negro militant: The Negro has identified with the colored people of the Arab World and is responding to "Israeli acts of imperialism" against his brothers. Also the Jews in the United States have been attacked and identified as the sole exploiters in the Negro ghettos. The attackers neglect to point out that exploitation is a necessary feature of all business interests regardless of their ethnic identification.

The irrationality of such attacks may be clearly seen in the existing and historical stance of Arab leaders in regard to colonial economic exploiters of both the African and Arab masses. Neither the Arab World nor its leadership took a position against the shipment of African slaves to the United States, the enslavement of Africans in the Sudan nor the exploitation of the Arab masses. The economic reality is that Arab leaders collaborated with colonial exploiters.

Why then attack the Jews? Certainly there are other vulnerable minorities that could serve just as well the function of a scapegoat for the oppressed Negro. The explanation is that the Jews are an easy scapegoat, made so by centuries of persecution and propaganda throughout the Christian world. Economic stereotypes have replaced the old Christian notions and anti-Semitism is perpetuated in Western society. The Negro has acquired the prejudices against Jews and accepted the economic and social myths. Therefore, instead of attacking the Jews in the name of Christianity or Aryan purity, the Negro denounces the Jew as an economic exploiter in the ghetto in the name of social and economic justice.

A look at the structure of the ghetto is important in understanding the phenomenon in the present social context. A most striking feature of the ghetto is the absence of a business class among Negroes. The lack of opportunity and capital along with emerging large chain-markets are factors which militate against the Negro's ability to rise as entrepreneur.

The businesses of immigrant groups remained in the ghettos as their community moved into better living conditions, for they too are a relatively insecure group, sometimes merely subsisting from the returns of the shop. When they retire, their progeny rarely continues the business, for they have become educated for other economic pursuits. Therefore, when the large supermarket is established in the ghetto, the Negro mistakenly assumes that Jewish shopkeepers have become rich and acquired supermarkets by exploiting the Negro community.

Contrary to sociological research findings, Negro-Jew proximity and relationships have not resulted in eliminating the racial prejudice in either group. The Negro masses too are victims of the social disease that exists throughout the Western world. Blatant anti-Semitism exists in the Negro community despite the disproportionate numbers of Jewish youth who have gone into the Southern areas, lending their skills to the Negro organizations, even dying with Negro youth at the hands of white Southern extremists. The Jewish community has also been a great source of funds for the civil rights movement.

Lacking an independent frame of reference and code of ethics, the Negro has been unable critically to assess the values of the society in which he finds himself. It is not necessary here to repeat the history of Negro enslavement and dehumanization in the United States. However, a disastrous consequence of the Negro's historical experience in the United States is that he was stripped of his cultural base for evaluating the norms and values of the oppressor. This cultural condition grossly contributes to the narrow perspective observed in the literary works of Negroes in the United States. This is the disadvantage point from which the Negro begins to assess his condition in the social structure.

Negro militants who call for economic and political power and direct an attack against Jewish economic interests in the Negro ghettos are reflecting this narrow perspective when they fail to perceive the economic system in its relation to the economic oppression of their people. Fundamental to Stokely Carmichael's concept of black power is the "take over" of the economic means in the black community, and since the Negro has been conditioned to believe that the Jews control their economic destiny, it follows that the Jews must be driven from this base of economic and political power in the ghetto. Missing is the ability to see that the interests of the former master and the racist elements in the society are buttressed and served through this conflict.

It is an accepted fact that Negro political representation can be achieved only by forming meaningful alliances with other minorities; the Jews have been both manifestly and latently a dominant political ally. Even in the Black Belt of the United States, where Negroes outnumber whites, minority coalitions are fundamental to the achievement of Negro representation. Financial resources for independent political efforts simply do not exist in the Negro community. All this suggests that anti-Semitism does not serve the interests of the Negro civil rights movement.

Then why has the Jew become the target of attack of the Negro radical? Till the present generation, the Negro in the United States has unreservedly accepted the culture of his white master and thus became infected with the virus of anti-Semitism, which is endemic to the Christian world. In the act of hating Jews, the Negro joins the Christian world in using the Jew as a scapegoat. Like prejudice against Negroes, anti-Semitism is one of the symptoms in the racist syndrome.

When the Negro radical seizes upon anti-Semitism to mobilize the Negro in the ghetto around achieving economic and political goals, and to account for the economic condition of Negroes in the ghetto, he follows the illogic of the lynch mobs in the South as observed by several social scientists: "If the per-acre value of cotton in the southeastern section of the United States is low, the number of lynchings of Negroes in that area is high." Lynch mobs do not relate their actions to the cotton price. However, in both cases, the justification is the same. The scapegoat has been fashioned by the society; there is no sanction against persecuting or destroying a scapegoat.

Mrs. Rollock states that the Negro sees the system as his enemy and sees the Jews as a part of the system. We can add: so is the Negro a part of the system as expressed by his goals, aspirations and expectations. The Negro entrepreneur is also forced in the profit-making system to exploit his own people.

In the Russian pogroms in 1881,[1] the same paradox was observed: complaints of Russian serfs had substance. Through propaganda, attacks of the dispossessed were directed away from the real enemy and toward the also victimized Jews. They were both victims of a system of economic oppression.

There is no doubt that the power structure in the United States will not accept the concept of redistribution of the economic resources in order to create a society in which all people will share in the goods of the society more equitably. It is an imperative that the Negro re-evaluates the methods of achieving his economic share.

The Negro must examine sentiments and attitudes of anti-Semitism in the present social context in terms of its meaning for perpetuating the status quo in this society. Present solutions articulated and outlined by some Negro militants can have only disastrous consequences for both minorities. Negroes and Jews must cooperate to secure necessary equitable means for accomplishing this transition. Negro leadership must take time out to explore the problems and the issue of anti-Semitism in the Negro civil rights movement. Creative means rather than old techniques of the oppressor must be devised for achieving black people's economic goals. Black power cannot be achieved by the Negro's joining the ranks of those who commit crimes against any minority in the name of social progress.

From *Jewish Currents*, June 1968, pp. 14–17.

---

1. The wave of over 200 anti-Jewish attacks in Russia lasted from 1881 to 1884.

KEY DEBATE ∽ *Strategies for Change*

MARTIN LUTHER KING JR.
from *My Pilgrimage to Nonviolence* [1958]

"Violence solves no social problems; it merely creates new and more complicated ones," Martin Luther King Jr. declared in his 1957 essay "Nonviolence and Racial Justice." As his involvement with the burgeoning civil rights movement grew, King became increasingly convinced that nonviolence not only was the most effective strategy for political gain but also should be a "way of life." He defined the struggle for civil rights as one "between justice and injustice, between the forces of light and the forces of darkness," and he saw nonviolence as an active, moral means of creating "the beloved community" and avoiding the "tragic bitterness" that results from violence. These ideas became powerful frames for the discussions about nonviolence that were taking place within and outside the civil rights movement.

"My Pilgrimage to Nonviolence," a condensed version of one chapter of King's first book, *Stride toward Freedom: The Montgomery Story* (1958), appeared in *Fellowship* magazine. In this autobiographical statement, King relates how he developed his philosophical and political ideas by reading the works of a wide range of thinkers, even those with whom he fundamentally disagreed. As King did in his doctoral dissertation and other writings, he utilizes here the ideas and phrases of another writer without giving proper credit. (The discussion of communism is based on an essay by the Reverend Robert McCracken.) But in contrast to that scholastic failure, King's approach to diverse "influential historical thinkers," reading them "from a dialectical point of view, combining a partial 'yes' and a partial 'no,'" provides a model for intellectual engagement that is both open-minded and discriminating.

King was born in Atlanta on January 15, 1929, the son of a Baptist minister and a schoolteacher. In 1948, after his ordination as a Baptist minister and his graduation from Morehouse College, King attended Crozer

Theological Seminary, outside Philadelphia, and in 1955 earned a doctorate in theology from Boston University. He married Coretta Scott in 1953 and moved the following year to Montgomery, Alabama, to become pastor of the Dexter Avenue Baptist Church. In December 1955, after Rosa Parks was arrested in Montgomery for refusing to give up her seat on a bus to a white passenger, community activists formed the Montgomery Improvement Association, and King was elected its president. The organization's citywide bus boycott became a model for nonviolent protest and vaulted King to national prominence. In 1957, King and other black ministers formed the Southern Christian Leadership Conference, which coordinated nonviolent protests around the nation. King's 1963 "I Have a Dream" speech, delivered during the March on Washington, solidified his position as the nation's preeminent spokesperson for the nonviolent civil rights movement.

For his persistent advocacy of nonviolence, King received the Nobel Peace Prize in 1964. Just thirty-five years old, he was the youngest recipient of the prize in history. In his acceptance speech, he described the award as "a profound recognition that nonviolence is the answer to the crucial political and moral question of our time—the need for man to overcome oppression and violence without resorting to violence and oppression." But King faced growing challenges from members of the Nation of Islam and others who championed aggressive tactics. On March 28, 1968, one of King's own protest marches erupted in violence for the first time. A week later, on April 4, King was assassinated while standing on the balcony of the Lorraine Motel in Memphis, Tennessee. James Earl Ray, a white escaped convict, confessed to the murder and was sentenced to ninety-nine years in prison. Ray later changed his story, however, sparking debates about whether King's assassination was part of a conspiracy, possibly involving the U.S. government.

The birthday of Martin Luther King, Jr. observed on the third Monday in January, was established as a federal holiday in 1986 to recognize King as a leader whose words, actions, and philosophy dramatically transformed American culture.

From *Fellowship*, September 1958, pp. 4–9.

I was deeply concerned from my early teen days about the gulf between superfluous wealth and abject poverty, and my reading of Marx made me ever more conscious of this gulf. Although modern American capitalism had greatly reduced the gap through social reforms, there was still need for a better distribution of wealth. Moreover, Marx had revealed the danger of the profit motive as the sole basis of an economic system: capitalism is always in danger of inspiring men to be more concerned about making a living than making a life. We are prone to judge success by the index of our salaries or the size of our automobiles, rather than by the quality of our service and relationship to humanity—thus capitalism can lead to a practical materialism that is as pernicious as the materialism taught by communism.

In short, I read Marx as I read all of the influential historical thinkers—from a dialectical[1] point of view, combining a partial "yes" and a partial "no." In so far as Marx posited a metaphysical materialism, an ethical relativism, and a strangulating totalitarianism, I responded with an unambiguous "no"; but in so far as he pointed to weaknesses of traditional capitalism, contributed to the growth of a definite self-consciousness in the masses, and challenged the social conscience of the Christian churches, I responded with a definite "yes."

My reading of Marx also convinced me that truth is found neither in Marxism nor in traditional capitalism. Each represents a partial truth. Historically capitalism failed to see the truth in collective enterprise, and Marxism failed to see the truth in individual enterprise. Nineteenth century capitalism failed to see that life is social and Marxism failed and still fails to see that life is individual and personal. The Kingdom of God is neither the thesis of individual enterprise nor the antithesis of collective enterprise, but a synthesis which reconciles the truths of both.

MUSTE, NIETZSCHE AND GANDHI

During my stay at Crozer, I was also exposed for the first time to the pacifist position in a lecture by A. J. Muste.[2] I was deeply moved by Mr. Muste's talk, but far from convinced of the practicability of his position. Like most of the students of Crozer, I felt that while war could never be a positive or absolute good, it could serve as a negative good in the sense of preventing the spread and growth of an evil force. War, horrible as it is, might be preferable to surrender to a totalitarian system—Nazi, Fascist, or Communist.

During this period I had about despaired of the power of love in solving social problems. Perhaps my faith in love was temporarily shaken by the philosophy of Nietzsche.[3] I had been reading parts of *The Genealogy of Morals* and the whole of *The Will to Power*. Nietzsche's glorification of power—in his theory all life expressed the will to power—was an outgrowth of his contempt for ordinary morals. He attacked the whole of the Hebraic-Christian morality—with its virtues of piety and humility, its other worldliness and its attitude toward suffering—as the glorification of weakness, as making virtues out of necessity and impotence. He looked to the development of a superman who would surpass man as man surpassed the ape.

1. Philosophical method of examining contrasting ideas on a topic to arrive at a truth, associated with German philosopher Georg Wilhelm Friedrich Hegel (1770–1831).
2. Socialist activist born in the Netherlands who became a leader in the United States in the pacifist, labor, and civil rights movements (1885–1967).
3. Friedrich Nietzsche (1844–1900), philosopher born in Prussia; known for developing the idea that "God is dead," which challenged the unifying basis for meaning of Western philosophy.

Then one Sunday afternoon I traveled to Philadelphia to hear a sermon by Dr. Mordecai Johnson, president of Howard University. He was there to preach for the Fellowship House of Philadelphia. Dr. Johnson had just returned from a trip to India, and, to my great interest, he spoke of the life and teachings of Mahatma Gandhi.[4] His message was so profound and electrifying that I left the meeting and bought a half-dozen books on Gandhi's life and works.

Like most people, I had heard of Gandhi, but I had never studied him seriously. As I read I became deeply fascinated by his campaigns of nonviolent resistance. I was particularly moved by the Salt March to the Sea[5] and his numerous fasts. The whole concept of "Satyagraha" (*Satya* is truth which equals love, and *agraha* is force; "Satyagraha," therefore, means truth-force or love force) was profoundly significant to me. As I delved deeper into the philosophy of Gandhi my skepticism concerning the power of love gradually diminished, and I came to see for the first time its potency in the area of social reform. Prior to reading Gandhi, I had about concluded that the ethics of Jesus were only effective in individual relationship. The "turn the other cheek" philosophy and the "love your enemies" philosophy were only valid, I felt, when individuals were in conflict with other individuals; when racial groups and nations were in conflict a more realistic approach seemed necessary. But after reading Gandhi, I saw how utterly mistaken I was.

Gandhi was probably the first person in history to lift the love ethic of Jesus above mere interaction between individuals to a powerful and effective social force on a large scale. Love, for Gandhi, was a potent instrument for social and collective transformation. It was in this Gandhian emphasis on love and nonviolence that I discovered the method for social reform that I had been seeking for so many months. The intellectual and moral satisfaction that I failed to gain from the utilitarianism of Bentham and Mill, the revolutionary methods of Marx and Lenin, the social-contracts theory of Hobbes, the "back to nature" optimism of Rousseau,[6] the superman philosophy of Nietzsche, I found in the nonviolent resistance philosophy of Gandhi. I came to feel that this was the only morally and practically sound method open to oppressed people in their struggle for freedom.

AN ENCOUNTER WITH NIEBUHR

But my intellectual odyssey to nonviolence did not end here. During my last year in theological school, I began to read the works of Reinhold Niebuhr.[7] The prophetic and realistic elements in Niebuhr's passionate style and profound thought were appealing to me, and I became so enamored of his social ethics that I almost fell into the trap of accepting uncritically everything he wrote.

About this time I read Niebuhr's critique of the pacifist position. Niebuhr had himself once been a member of the pacifist ranks. For several years, he had been national chairman of the Fellowship of Reconciliation.[8] His break with pacifism came in the early thirties, and the first full statement of his criticism of pacifism was in *Moral Man and Immoral Society*. Here he argued that there was no intrinsic moral difference between violent and nonviolent resistance. The social consequences of the two methods were different, he contended, but the differences were in degree rather than kind. Later Niebuhr began emphasizing the irresponsibility of relying on nonviolent resistance when there was no ground for believing that it would be successful in preventing the spread of totalitarian tyranny. It could only be successful, he argued, if the groups against whom the resistance was taking place had some degree of moral conscience, as was the case

4. Mohandas Karamchand Gandhi (1869–1948), leader of the Indian independence movement; developed the technique of nonviolent civil disobedience; *mahatma* means "great soul" in Sanskrit.
5. 1930 march to the sea to make salt; Ghandi led the 241 mile march from Dandi as a protest against a British tax on Indian salt.
6. European political philosophers: Jeremy Bentham (1748–1832), John Stuart Mill (1806–73), Thomas Hobbes (1588–1679), and Jean-Jacques Rousseau (1712–78).
7. Karl Paul Reinhold Niebuhr (1892–1971), white American Christian theologian.
8. In 1931–32, Niebuhr was the national chair of the FOR, an international and interfaith movement established in 1914 and dedicated to justice and peace through compassionate action.

in Gandhi's struggle against the British. Niebuhr's ultimate rejection of pacifism was based primarily on the doctrine of man. He argued that pacifism failed to do justice to the reformation doctrine of justification by faith, substituting for it a sectarian perfectionism which believes "that divine grace actually lifts man out of the sinful contradictions of history and establishes him above the sins of the world."

At first, Niebuhr's critique of pacifism left me in a state of confusion. As I continued to read, however, I came to see more and more the shortcomings of his position. For instance, many of his statements revealed that he interpreted pacifism as a sort of passive nonresistance to evil expressing naive trust in the power of love. But this was a serious distortion. My study of Gandhi convinced me that true pacifism is not nonresistance to evil, but nonviolent resistance to evil. Between the two positions, there is a world of difference. Gandhi resisted evil with as much vigor and power as the violent resister, but he resisted with love instead of hate. True pacifism is not unrealistic submission to evil power, as Niebuhr contends. It is rather a courageous confrontation of evil by the power of love, in the faith that it is better to be the recipient of violence than the inflicter of it, since the latter only multiplies the existence of violence and bitterness in the universe, while the former may develop a sense of shame in the opponent, and thereby bring about a transformation and change of heart.

In spite of the fact that I found many things to be desired in Niebuhr's philosophy, there were several points at which he constructively influenced my thinking. Niebuhr's great contribution to contemporary theology is that he has refuted the false optimism characteristic of a great segment of Protestant liberalism, without falling into the anti-rationalism of the continental theologian Karl Barth, or the semi-fundamentalism of other dialectical theologians. Moreover, Niebuhr has extraordinary insight into human nature, especially the behavior of nations and social groups. He is keenly aware of the complexity of human motives and of the relation between morality and power. His theology is a persistent reminder of the reality of sin on every level of man's existence. These elements in Niebuhr's thinking helped me to recognize the illusions of a superficial optimism concerning human nature and the dangers of a false idealism.

While I still believed in man's potential for good, Niebuhr made me realize his potential for evil as well. Moreover, Niebuhr helped me to recognize the complexity of man's social involvement and the glaring reality of collective evil.

Many pacifists, I felt, failed to see this. All too many had an unwarranted optimism concerning man and leaned unconsciously toward self-righteousness. It was my revolt against these attitudes under the influence of Niebuhr that accounts for the fact that in spite of my strong leaning toward pacifism, I never joined a pacifist organization. After reading Niebuhr, I tried to arrive at a realistic pacifism. In other words, I came to see the pacifist position not as sinless but as the lesser evil in the circumstances. I felt then, and I feel now, that the pacifist would have a greater appeal if he did not claim to be free from the moral dilemmas that the Christian nonpacifist confronts.

The next stage of my intellectual pilgrimage to nonviolence came during my doctoral studies at Boston University. Here I had the opportunity to talk to many exponents of nonviolence, both students and visitors to the campus. Boston University School of Theology, under the influence of Dean Walter Muelder and Professor Allen Knight Chalmers, had a deep sympathy for pacifism. Both Dean Muelder and Dr. Chalmers had a passion for social justice that stemmed, not from a superficial optimism, but from a deep faith in the possibilities of human beings when they allowed themselves to become co-workers with God. It was at Boston University that I came to see that Niebuhr had overemphasized the corruption of human nature. His pessimism concerning human nature was not balanced by an optimism concerning divine nature. He was so involved in diagnosing man's sickness of sin that he overlooked the cure of grace.

I studied philosophy and theology at Boston University under Edgar S. Brightman and L. Harold DeWolf. Both men greatly stimulated my thinking. It was mainly under these teachers that I studied personalistic philosophy—the theory that the clue to the meaning of ultimate reality is found in personality. This personal idealism remains today my basic philosophical position. Personalism's insistence that only personality—finite and infinite—is ultimately real strengthened me in two convictions: it gave me metaphysical and philosophical grounding for the idea of a personal God, and it gave me a metaphysical basis for the dignity and worth of all human personality.

Just before Dr. Brightman's death, I began studying the philosophy of Hegel with him. Although the course was mainly a study of Hegel's monumental work, *Phenomenology of Mind*, I spent my spare time reading his *Philosophy of History* and *Philosophy of Right*. There were points in Hegel's philosophy that I strongly disagreed with. For instance, his absolute idealism was rationally unsound to me because it tended to swallow up the many in the one. But there were other aspects of his thinking that I found stimulating. His contention that "truth is the whole" led me to a philosophical method of rational coherence. His analysis of the dialectical process, in spite of its shortcomings, helped me to see that growth comes through struggle.

In 1954 I ended my formal training with all of these relatively divergent intellectual forces converging into a positive social philosophy. One of the main tenets of this philosophy was the conviction that nonviolent resistance was one of the most potent weapons available to oppressed people in their quest for social justice. At this time, however, I had merely an intellectual understanding and appreciation of the position, with no firm determination to organize it in a socially effective situation.

When I went to Montgomery as a pastor, I had not the slightest idea that I would later become involved in a crisis in which nonviolent resistance would be applicable. I neither started the protest nor suggested it. I simply responded to the call of the people for a spokesman. When the protest began, my mind, consciously or unconsciously, was driven back to the Sermon on the Mount,[9] with its sublime teachings on love, and the Gandhian method of nonviolent resistance. As the days unfolded, I came to see the power of nonviolence more and more. Living through the actual experience of the protest, nonviolence became more than a method to which I gave intellectual assent; it became a commitment to a way of life. Many of the things that I had not cleared up intellectually concerning nonviolence were now solved in the sphere of practical action.

MALCOLM X AND BAYARD RUSTIN
A Choice of Two Roads [1960]

On issues such as separatism and relations with white people, Malcolm X (p. 516) shifted his position over time. On armed self-defense, however, he remained a firm advocate. An early debate with the prominent civil rights leader and pacifist Bayard Rustin (p. 529) displays their differing views on nonviolence. The debate, broadcast on the New York City radio station WBAI, also captures Malcolm X's positive view of separatism, a position that changed radically after he left the Nation of Islam and visited Mecca in 1964. (Malcolm X and Rustin also debated in 1961 at Howard University and twice in 1962 in New York and Chicago.)

Malcolm X's support of self-defense was characterized by some leaders and media outlets as a call for violence. Malcolm X frequently commented on the irony of that perspective. As he pointed out at a public forum in New York on December 12, 1964, "By violence they only mean when a black man protects himself against the attacks of a white man. [* * *] When it comes time for a black man to explode they call it violence. But white people can be exploding against black people all day long, and it's never called violence." At the same time, Malcolm X vigorously criticized civil right leaders' continued reliance on nonviolent strategies, often singling out Martin Luther King Jr. as the leader most closely associated with nonviolent tactics. Because of his vocal support for gaining rights "by any means necessary," Malcolm X and the Nation of Islam were often associated with hate, while King was presented as a proponent of love. Malcolm X countered this notion with the assertion that "the Honorable Elijah Muhammad doesn't teach hate, he teaches black people to love each other," as he said in a 1963 interview, "The Old Negro and the New Negro." For Malcolm X, the need for self-defense

9. Matthew 5–7, detailing the moral teachings of Jesus.

arose from the love for one's community and from self-respect. The transcript reprinted here, published in the January–February 1993 issue of *Freedom Review*, is a streamlined version of the live debate.

WBAI-FM debate hosted by John Donald, New York, November 7, 1960.

MALCOLM X: In the past two years, the Honorable Elijah Muhammad has become the most talked about black man in America because he is having such miraculous success in getting his program over among the so-called Negro masses. *Time* magazine last year wrote that he has eliminated from among his followers alcohol, dope addiction, profanity—all of which stems from disrespect of self. He has successfully eliminated stealing and crime among his followers. *Time* also pointed out that he has eliminated adultery and fornication, and prostitution, making black men respect their women, something that has been characteristically absent among our men. *Time* also pointed out that Muslims, followers of Elijah Muhammad, have eliminated juvenile delinquency.

When you think about it, *Time* was giving Mr. Muhammad credit for being one of the greatest moral reformers that has appeared among the so-called Negroes yet. A few months later, *US News and World Report* pointed out that Mr. Muhammad was successful in stressing the importance of economics. The point behind his program—farms to feed our people, factories to manufacture goods for ourselves, businesses to create jobs for ourselves—is to be economically independent rather than sit around waiting for the white man to give us jobs.

What the Honorable Elijah Muhammad has been teaching is not what we have been accused of: nationalism. Nationalism is the political approach to the problems that are confronting the so-called Negro in America. The aim of the black nationalist is the same as the aim of the Muslim. We are pointing toward the same goal. But the difference is in method. We say the only solution is the religious approach; this is why stress the importance of a moral reformation. I would like to stress that Mr. Muhammad is not a politician. He does not believe politics is the solution to the so-called Negro's problem. It will take God. God will have to have a hand in it, because the problem of the

so-called Negro is different from the problems of any other black people anywhere on this earth since the beginning of time. Every condition of the so-called Negro was pre-ordained and prophesied. And we believe that we are living in the fulfillment of that prophecy today. We believe that our history in America, our experiences at the hands of slave masters, is in line with Biblical prophecy. And we believe that Mr. Muhammad's presence among so-called Negroes here in America is in line with Biblical prophecies.

HOST: Does this involve the creation of a separate state in America?

X: It involves the creation of a black state for the black man if not in America then somewhere on this earth. If not abroad, then here in America. Primarily it involves acquiring some land that the black man can call his own. If the powers that be don't want it here, then they should make it possible for us to do it somewhere else.

HOST: It does involve politics, then?

X: Any religion that does not take into consideration the freedom and the rights of the black man is the wrong religion. But politics as such is not the solution. But the divine solution would have to have that ingredient in it. You can call it politics if you want, but the overall problem of the so-called Negro in America is not a political problem as such, it is an economic problem, a social problem, a mental problem, and a spiritual problem. Only God can solve the whole problem.

BAYARD RUSTIN: I am very happy to be here and I think Malcolm X can clarify some of the questions he has brought up in my mind. I believe the great majority of the Negro people, black people, are not seeking anything from anyone. They are seeking to become full-fledged citizens. Their ancestors have toiled in this country, contributing greatly to it. The United States belongs to no particular people, and in my view the great majority of Negroes and their leaders take integration as their key word—which means that rightly or wrongly they seek to become an integral part of the United States. We have, I believe, much work yet to do, both politically and through the courts, but I believe we have reached the point where most Negroes, from a sense of dignity and pride, have organized themselves to demand to become an integral part of all the institutions of the U.S. We are doing things by direct action which we feel will further this cause. We believe that justice for all people, including Negroes, can be achieved.

This is not a unique position, and while a controversial one it is certainly not as controversial as the one Malcolm X supports. Therefore I would like to ask him this question: The logic of your position is to say to black people in this country: "We have to migrate and set up some state in Africa." It seems to me that this is where you have to come out.

X: Well, Mr. Rustin, let me say this about "full-fledged" or as they say "first-class" citizenship. Most of the so-called Negro leaders have got the Negro masses used to thinking in terms of second-class citizenship, of which there is no such thing. We who follow the Honorable Elijah Muhammad believe that a man is either a citizen or he is not a citizen. He is not a citizen by degree. If the black man in America is not recognized as a first-class citizen, we don't feel that he is a citizen at all. People come here from Hungary and are integrated into the American way of life overnight, they are not put into any fourth class or third class or any kind of class. The only one who is put in this category is the so-called Negro who is forced to beg the white man to accept him. We feel that if 100 years after the so-called Emancipation Proclamation the black man is still not free, then we don't feel that what Lincoln did set them free in the first place.

RUSTIN: This is all well and good but you are not answering my question.

X: I am answering your question. The black man in America, once he gets his so-called freedom, is still 9,000 miles away from that which he can call home. His problem is different from that of others who are striving for freedom. In other countries they are the majority and the oppressor is the minority. But here, the oppressor is the majority. The white man can just let you sit down. He can find someone else to run his factories.

So we don't think the passive approach can work here. And we don't see that anyone other than the so-called Negro was encouraged to seek freedom this way. The liberals tell the so-called Negro to use the passive approach and turn the other cheek, but they have never told whites who were in bondage to use the passive approach. They don't tell the whites in Eastern Europe who are under the Russian yoke to be passive in their resistance. They give them guns and make heroes out of them and call them freedom fighters. But if a black man becomes militant in his striving against oppression then immediately he is classified as a fanatic.

The white man is posing as the leader of the so-called Free World, and the only way he can be accepted as the leader of the so-called Free World is to be accepted by the majority of the people on this earth, the majority of whom are not white people. And they measure him by the way he treats the nonwhite people here in America. This integration talk is hypocrisy, meant to impress our brothers in Africa or Asia.

RUSTIN: Then what you are saying is that you are opposed to integration because it is not meaningful and can't work. If you believe that integration is not possible, then the logic of your position should be that you are seeking to find a piece of territory and go to it. Either you are advocating the continuation of slavery, since you feel we cannot get integration by the methods that I advocate—which is to say the slow, grinding process of integration—or you are proposing separation.

X: We believe integration is hypocrisy. If the government has to pass laws to let us into their education system, if they have to pass laws to get the white man to accept us in better housing in their neighborhoods, that is the equivalent of holding a gun to their head, and that is hypocrisy. If the white man were to accept us, without laws being passed, then we would go for it.

RUSTIN: Do you think that is going to happen?

X: Well, your common sense tells you, sir, that it's not going to happen.

Rustin: But if you cannot do it through the constitutional method, and you cannot do it through brotherhood, then what do you see as the future of black people here and why should they stay?

X: As any intelligent person can see, the white man is not going to share his wealth with his ex-slaves. But God has taught us that the only solution for the ex-slave and the slave master is separation.

Rustin: Then you do believe in separation.

X: We absolutely do believe in separation.

Rustin: Well, are you being logical by saying, "Let's take over a territory, a part of the U.S." or are you saying, "Let's go outside"?

X: I think both are logical. The land could be anywhere. When the Honorable Elijah Muhammad teaches us that we have to have some land of our own, it means just that, that we have to have some land of our own. Now if the master's intention is good, since we have been faithful workers, I should say faithful servants, all these years, then it seems he should give us some of these states.

Rustin: All right, now it is clear that you are advocating separation.

X: Separation not integration.

Rustin: All right, now that is clear we can put that out of the way and move on to other things. Isn't there an inconsistency in your economic position? Where are they going to move to? When Moses took his people into the desert, he had a pretty clear idea of where he was going.

X: Well, mentioning Moses is just right. The people that Moses was leading were probably the closest parallel to the problems confronting the so-called Negro. Moses' people were slaves in a land that was not theirs. Moses' people had a slave mentality, they were worshipping a god that was not their own. The Negro in America is the same way, he worships the white man's god, and he is following the white man's religion. They are in the same fix—socially, mentally, politi-cally, spiritually—as the people whom Moses grew up amongst, 4,000 years ago. Now, if you'll recall, Moses didn't advocate integration. Moses advocated separation. Nowhere in the Bible will you find that Moses told his people to integrate themselves with Pharaoh. His one doctrine was: Let my people go. That meant separate, not seek integration in the house of bondage. It did not mean to seek the acceptance of the slave master. He said: if you follow me, I will lead you to a land flowing with milk and honey. He never told anyone where that land was. He never told the people where he was taking them, or what they would have to go through. And if you go back to that time you will see that some of them believed in him but many were afraid of the slave master. They didn't believe they could get along without Pharaoh. They didn't believe anybody would give them a job if Pharaoh didn't. They didn't believe they could have an economic system free of Pharaoh. Remember, Pharaoh himself never opposed Moses. He always got magicians to oppose Moses. And today the modern slave master gets a lot of so-called Negro politicians to oppose Elijah Muhammad and work a lot of magic to make the so-called Negroes think he is a crazy man, just as Pharaoh had magicians to make the Hebrews think Moses was some kind of crazy man.

But now let me say this: we feel the Honorable Elijah Muhammad is a modern Moses! Some people say Adam Clayton Powell[1] is a modern Moses and some say Martin Luther King is a modern Moses, but no one can claim to be a modern Moses until he finds out what the first Moses did. And Moses never advocated integration. He advocated complete separation. And he didn't advocate passive resistance, he advocated an eye for an eye and a tooth for a tooth. "Love your enemy." As long as you teach a man that kind of philosophy, he'll remain a slave.

Rustin: Well, I am a great advocate of nonviolence, but I think all this talk about whether to integrate or not, and getting involved in the economic life of this country, might be more interesting to me if I knew where you wanted to lead people. But I don't know where you want to go. And I don't think you do, either.

---

1. Baptist pastor and politician (1908–72); in 1944 Powell became the first African American elected from New York State to the U.S. House of Representatives, where he served until 1971.

X: Yes we do. We can take some land right here, sir.

RUSTIN: Yes, but if you do not believe in integration, and they don't love you, do you think they are going to give you ten or twelve states?

Ah, Mr. Rustin: the predicament that a man is in is what makes him reach certain decisions. America is in the worst predicament of any country in the history of the world.

RUSTIN: I agree . . .

X: Now what is causing this predicament? The race problem. America's number one problem is the so-called Negro. What must we do? What must I do about this Negro problem? And whenever America is attacked on the race problem, what can she say?

RUSTIN: She can say a lot.

X: What?

RUSTIN: I'll tell you what. I have spent twenty-five years of my life on the race question, and I have been twenty-two times to jail. America can say that until 1954, Negroes could not go to school with whites. Now they can. Negroes could not join trade unions, but now they can. I do not say any of this is perfect, but it is enough for America to be able to answer Russia and China and the rest on the race question and, more important, it is enough to keep the great majority of Negroes feeling that things can improve here. Until you have some place to go to, they are going to want to stay here.

Now, I want to stop right here and get something clear. In Muhammad's mind, this may be a religious matter, but in the minds of his followers the Muslim movement is a psychological and political concept. They do not read the Koran, they read the Bible. They are essentially, culturally, Christian, not Muslims. Why therefore do they call themselves Muslims? Because they do not want to use the same religious terminology that their masters used.

Most Negroes who were brought to America came from the West coast of Africa, long before the spread of Islam to that part of Africa . . .

X: That is what the white man taught you . . . after stripping you of your original culture. Now consider the Mali empire—this shows the influence of the Muslim religion in West Africa before the discovery of America.

RUSTIN: I am not putting down the culture of West Africa, I am just saying that the Islamic influence came later. All over West Africa you will find wonderful sculptures which were the sources for much twentieth-century European art, notably Picasso and Cubism.[2] Now these figures could not have been made if the influence of Islam had prevailed, because, as you ought to know, Muslims are not allowed to create figures in their art objects.

X: Let me quote from the *Times* last Sunday. It says that Islam is spreading like wildfire in Nigeria and Christianity is only skin-deep.

HOST: Does progress involve a greater sense of racial identity?

RUSTIN: I believe it is very important to have a great sense of racial identity because I believe it is quite impossible for people to struggle creatively if they do not truly believe in themselves. I believe that dignity is first. This for me is doubly important because believing in integration and not being told where we are to go, I can see nothing more logical than staying here and struggling for one's rights. Also because of moral principles—but leave them aside for the moment— I can see no way for the Negro to struggle except through nonviolence and a dedication to a strategic nonviolence as a matter of principle. Now therefore if you are going to struggle with nonviolence, to a certain extent you are going to have a certain affection for the people who are mistreating you.

Now affection for the other fellow is not possible without a great sense of dignity of oneself, and therefore the dignity of the Negro for me is not something that is an aside. It is an essential of the struggle. The people in Montgomery were able to struggle and get integration on their buses for a simple reason: ten years before, they could not have done it because they did not believe in themselves. When they believed in themselves they could be socially affectionate to the opposition while at the same time they could be extremely militant and walking and being prepared to

---

2. Spanish artist Pablo Picasso (1881–1973) was a pioneer of Cubism, a style of art developed between 1906 and 1921 in which objects are broken up and depicted from multiple viewpoints simultaneously.

sacrifice. I think this is most important and I would therefore agree with Malcolm X that doing away with the ugliness resulting from poverty and their position in society is very necessary and important. We can certainly agree here.

But now let me ask you another question because I want to clarify your position on the Jewish question. Where do you and your group come out on this question? I've been given to understand that your position is—particularly in Harlem—that one of the reasons that Negroes are so oppressed is that the Jews are exploiting them and that the Jews are attempting to exploit the Arab world and stir up difficulties in the Middle East. I'd like to know if this is a misunderstanding I have.

X: If you have read what the Honorable Elijah Muhammad has written and he has written much, I don't think you can find an article where he has ever pointed out the Jew as an exploiter of the black man. He speaks of the exploiter. Period. He doesn't break it down in terms of Frenchmen or Englishmen or a Jew or a German. He speaks of the exploiter and sometimes the man who is the most guilty of exploitation

will think you are pointing the finger at him and put out the propaganda that you're anti-this or anti-that. We make no distinction between exploitation and exploiter.

RUSTIN: Now what do you mean that the man who is the most exploited will put out propaganda?

X: I say this, that when a man puts out propaganda against Muslims usually that man feels that the finger is being pointed at him but . . .

RUSTIN: In other words, you feel that many Jews feel that way.

X: I don't know. But I say that you cannot find anything that the Honorable Elijah Muhammad has written or said that at any time will label the Jew as an exploiter. No sir, but he speaks about the exploitation and oppression and the deception that has been used against the black people in America. Now the man that is guilty [let] whoever is guilty wear that shoe. But he has never made that distinction between a Frenchman—and again—or a Jew or a German. An exploiter is an exploiter, I don't care what kind of label you put on him—you can't duck it.

MALCOLM X
from *Message to the Grassroots* [1963]

In 1961 and 1962, Martin Luther King Jr. worked with the Albany movement in Albany, Georgia, to try to desegregate the community using nonviolent protest. After eight months of protests and the jailing of more than 1,000 protesters, King left Albany, viewing the movement there as a failure. For Malcolm X, that failure of nonviolent methods reinforced his belief in the necessity of armed revolution. In August 1963, Malcolm X traveled to Washington, D.C., to observe the March on Washington, at which Martin Luther King Jr. delivered his "I Have a Dream" speech. Labeling the march "the Farce on Washington," Malcolm X underscored the differences between his and King's visions with the proclamation that "while King was having a dream, the rest of us Negroes are having a nightmare."

In "Message to the Grassroots," a speech delivered at the Northern Negro Grass Roots Leadership Conference in Detroit on November 10, 1963, Malcolm X sets up a dichotomy between "house Negroes" (such as Martin Luther King, A. Philip Randolph, and other leaders of the march) and the "field Negroes" (members of the black masses, including himself). He rejects the nonviolence of the false "Negro revolution" in favor of a true "Black revolution" committed to establishing black nationalism through bloodshed. Malcolm X's support of black nationalism also marked his growing independence from Elijah Muhammad, who defined the Nation of Islam as strictly religious and apolitical.

Three weeks after giving his "Message to the Grassroots" address, Malcolm X was silenced by Muhammad and stripped of his ministry for ninety days. In March

1964, he officially broke with the Nation of Islam. In April and May, he traveled to Africa and the Middle East, making the hajj (pilgrimage) to Mecca. From his return until his death nine months later, on February 21, 1965, he moved away from a number of his former positions. While maintaining his belief in armed resistance, Malcolm X increasingly advocated political solutions, rejected black separatism, and moved toward establishing connections with more moderate civil rights groups and leaders, including Martin Luther King. (See p. 516 for additional information about Malcolm X's life.)

Speech delivered November 10, 1963, Detroit, Michigan.

We have a common enemy. We have this in common: We have a common oppressor, a common exploiter, and a common discriminator. But once we all realize that we have this common enemy, then we unite on the basis of what we have in common. And what we have foremost in common is that enemy—the white man. He's an enemy to all of us. I know some of you all think that some of them aren't enemies. Time will tell.

* * *

Instead of us airing our differences in public, we have to realize we're all the same family. And when you have a family squabble, you don't get out on the sidewalk. If you do, everybody calls you uncouth, unrefined, uncivilized, savage. If you don't make it at home, you settle it at home; you get in the closet—argue it out behind closed doors. And then when you come out on the street, you pose a common front, a united front. And this is what we need to do in the community, and in the city, and in the state. We need to *stop* airing our differences in front of the white man. Put the white man out of our meetings, number one, and then sit down and talk shop with each other. All you gotta do.

I would like to make a few comments concerning the difference between the black revolution and the Negro revolution. There's a difference. Are they both the same? And if they're not, what is the difference? What is the difference between a black revolution and a Negro revolution? First, what is a revolution? Sometimes I'm inclined to believe that many of our people are using this word "revolution" loosely, without taking careful consideration what this word actually means, and what its historic characteristics are. When you study the historic nature of revolutions, the motive of a revolution, the objective of a revolution, and the result of a revolution, and the methods used in a revolution, you may change words. You may devise another program. You may change your goal and you may change your mind.

Look at the American Revolution in 1776. That revolution was for what? For land. Why did they want land? Independence. How was it carried out? Bloodshed. Number one, it was based on land, the basis of independence. And the only way they could get it was bloodshed. The French Revolution—what was it based on? The land-less against the landlord. What was it for? Land. How did they get it? Bloodshed. Was no love lost; was no compromise; was no negotiation. I'm telling you, you don't know what a revolution is. 'Cause when you find out what it is, you'll get back in the alley; you'll get out of the way. The Russian Revolution—what was it based on? Land. The land-less against the landlord. How did they bring it about? Bloodshed. You haven't got a revolution that doesn't involve bloodshed. And you're afraid to bleed. I said, you're afraid to bleed.

Long as the white man sent you to Korea,[1] you bled. He sent you to Germany, you bled. He sent you to the South Pacific to fight the Japanese, you bled. You bleed for white people. But when it comes time to seeing your own churches being bombed and little black girls be murdered,[2] you haven't got no blood. You bleed when the white man says bleed; you bite when the white man says bite; and you bark when the white man says bark. I hate to say this about us, but it's true. How are you going to be nonviolent in Mississippi, as violent as you were in Korea? How can you

---

1. During the Korean War (1950–53), the United States and the United Nations fought with the South Koreans against the North Koreans, who were supported by the People's Republic of China and the Soviet Union.
2. Four girls were killed in the September 15, 1963 bombing of the 16th Street Baptist Church in Birmingham, Alabama.

justify being nonviolent in Mississippi and Alabama, when your *churches* are being bombed, and *your* little girls are being murdered, and at the same time you're going to [be] violent with Hitler, and Tojo,[3] and somebody else that you don't even know?

If violence is wrong in America, violence is wrong abroad. If it's wrong to be violent defending black women and black children and black babies and black men, then it's wrong for America to draft us and make us violent abroad in defense of her. And if it is right for America to draft us, and teach us how to be violent in defense of her, then it is right for you and me to do whatever is necessary to defend our own people right here in this country.[4]

* * *

So I cite [* * *] various revolutions, brothers and sisters, to show you—you don't have a peaceful revolution. You don't have a turn-the-other-cheek revolution. There's no such *thing* as a nonviolent revolution. Only kind of revolution that's nonviolent is the Negro revolution. The only revolution based on loving your enemy is the Negro revolution. The only revolution in which the goal is a desegregated lunch counter, a desegregated theater, a desegregated park, and a desegregated public toilet; you can sit down next to white folks on the toilet. That's no revolution. Revolution is based on land. Land is the basis of all independence. Land is the basis of freedom, justice, and equality.

The white man knows what a revolution is. He knows that the black revolution is world-wide in scope and in nature. The black revolution is sweeping Asia, sweeping Africa, is rearing its head in Latin America. The Cuban Revolution[5]—that's a revolution. They overturned the system. Revolution is in Asia. Revolution is in Africa. And the white man is screaming because he sees revolution in Latin America. How do you think he'll react to you when you learn what a real

revolution is? You don't know what a revolution is. If you did, you wouldn't use that word.

A revolution is bloody. Revolution is hostile. Revolution knows no compromise. Revolution overturns and destroys everything that gets in its way. And you, sitting around here like a knot on the wall, saying, "I'm going to love these folks no matter how much they hate me." No, you need a revolution. Whoever heard of a revolution where they lock arms, as Reverend Cleage[6] was pointing out beautifully, singing "We Shall Overcome"? Just tell me. You don't do that in a revolution. You don't do any singing; you're too busy swinging. It's based on land. A revolutionary wants land so he can set up his own nation, an independent nation. These Negroes aren't asking for no nation. They're trying to crawl back on the plantation.

When you want a nation, that's called nationalism. When the white man became involved in a revolution in this country against England, what was it for? He wanted this land so he could set up another white nation. That's white nationalism. The American Revolution was white nationalism. The French Revolution was white nationalism. The Russian Revolution too— yes, it was—white nationalism. You don't think so? Why you think Khrushchev and Mao[7] can't get their heads together? White nationalism. All the revolutions that's going on in Asia and Africa today are based on what? Black nationalism. A revolutionary is a black nationalist. He wants a nation. I was reading some beautiful words by Reverend Cleage, pointing out why he couldn't get together with someone else here in the city because all of them were afraid of being identified with black nationalism. If you're afraid of black nationalism, you're afraid of revolution. And if you love revolution, you love black nationalism.

To understand this, you have to go back to what young brother here referred to as the house Negro and the field Negro—back during slavery. There was two

---

3. Hideki Tojo (1844–1948); as Prime Minister of Japan from 1941 to 1944, led Japan's entry into World War II and authorized the bombing of Pearl Harbor in 1941; executed as a war criminal after the war.
4. In the next two paragraphs, not reprinted here, Malcolm X discusses revolutions and independence movements in China, Kenya, and Algeria.
5. On January 1, 1959, a group of revolutionaries led by Fidel Castro ousted Fulgencio Batista (1901–73), a dictator backed by the U.S. government.
6. Albert Cleage (1911–2000), civil rights leader who developed a black nationalist vision of Christianity; founder of the Black Christian National Movement and author of *The Black Messiah* (1968).
7. Mao Zedong (1893–1976), revolutionary leader of the People's Republic of China from 1949 to 1976; Nikita Sergeyevich Khrushchev (1894–1971), First Secretary of the Communist Party of the Soviet Union from 1953 to 1964.

kinds of slaves. There was the house Negro and the field Negro. [* * *]

* * *

Just as the slavemaster of that day used Tom, the house Negro, to keep the field Negroes in check, the same old slavemaster today has Negroes who are nothing but modern Uncle Toms, 20th century Uncle Toms, to keep you and me in check, keep us under control, keep us passive and peaceful and nonviolent. That's Tom making you nonviolent. [* * *]

* * *

The slavemaster took Tom and dressed him well, and fed him well, and even gave him a little education— a little education; gave him a long coat and a top hat and made all the other slaves look up to him. Then he used Tom to control them. The same strategy that was used in those days is used today, by the same white man. He takes a Negro, a so-called Negro, and make him prominent, build him up, publicize him, make him a celebrity. And then he becomes a spokesman for Negroes—and a Negro leader.

I would like to just mention just one other thing else quickly, and that is the method that the white man uses, how the white man uses these "big guns," or Negro leaders, against the black revolution. They are not a part of the black revolution. They're used against the black revolution.

When Martin Luther King failed to desegregate Albany, Georgia, the civil-rights struggle in America reached its low point. King became bankrupt almost, as a leader. Plus, even financially, the Southern Christian Leadership Conference was in financial trouble; plus it was in trouble, period, with the people when they failed to desegregate Albany, Georgia. Other Negro civil-rights leaders of so-called national stature became fallen idols. As they became fallen idols, began to lose their prestige and influence, local Negro leaders began to stir up the masses. In Cambridge, Maryland, Gloria Richardson[8]; in Danville, Virginia,[9] and other parts of the country, local leaders began to stir up our people at the grassroots level. This was never done by these Negroes, whom you recognize, of national stature. They controlled you, but they never incited you or excited you. They controlled you; they contained you; they kept you on the plantation.

As soon as King failed in Birmingham, Negroes took to the streets. King got out and went out to California to a big rally and raised about—I don't know how many thousands of dollars. Come to Detroit and had a march and raised some more thousands of dollars. And recall, right after that Wilkins attacked King, accused King and the CORE of starting trouble everywhere and then making the NAACP get them out of jail and spend a lot of money; and then they accused King and CORE of raising all the money and not paying it back.[1] This happened; I've got it in documented evidence in the newspaper. Roy started attacking King, and King started attacking Roy, and Farmer started attacking both of them. And as these Negroes of national stature began to attack each other, they began to lose their control of the Negro masses.

And Negroes was out there in the streets. They was talking about we was going to march on Washington. By the way, right at that time Birmingham had exploded, and the Negroes in Birmingham—remember, they also exploded. They began to stab the crackers in the back and bust them up 'side their head—yes, they did. That's when Kennedy sent in the troops, down in Birmingham.[2] So, and right after that, Kennedy got on the television and said "this is a moral issue." That's when he

8. Leader (b. 1922) of the Cambridge Movement, a community-based, grass-roots movement to eliminate segregation and advance civil rights that gained national attention partly due to demonstrations that erupted into violence; one of the founders of the Cambridge Nonviolent Action Committee, the only group affiliated with SNCC that was not led by students.

9. Site of civil rights protests in the summer of 1963 organized by the Danville Christian Progressive Association; came to national attention due to violent responses by the police force, which included the use of fire hoses, clubs, and mass arrests.

1. Although occasionally at odds over strategy, style, or funding, Roy Wilkins (1901–81), James Farmer, and King were allies in the civil rights movement; Wilkins was Executive Secretary of the NAACP from 1955–64 and Executive Director from 1964 to 1977; James Farmer helped found CORE, and left the organization in 1966 when it moved toward black nationalism.

2. During the 1963 Birmingham campaign led by King, the Birmingham police attacked protesters with high-pressure fire hoses, dogs, and clubs; images of the police violence galvanized national support for the civil rights movement; near the end of the campaign, bombs exploded at the hotel where King had been staying and at his brother's house; after local black citizens threw rocks at police who came to investigate, President Kennedy sent 3,000 federal troops to restore order; for more on the Birmingham campaign, see p. 601.

said he was going to put out a civil-rights bill. And when he mentioned civil-rights bill and the Southern crackers started talking about they were going to boy-cott or filibuster it, then the Negroes started talking—about what? We're going to march on Washington, march on the Senate, march on the White House, march on the Congress, and tie it up, bring it to a halt; don't let the government proceed. They even said they was going out to the airport and lay down on the run-way and don't let no airplanes land. I'm telling you what they said. That was revolution. That was revolution. That was the black revolution.

It was the grass roots out there in the street. Scared the white man to death, scared the white power structure in Washington, D.C. to death; I was there. When they found out that this black steamroller was going to come down on the capital, they called in Wilkins; they called in Randolph; they called in these national Negro leaders that you respect and told them, "Call it off." Kennedy said, "Look, you all letting this thing go too far." And Old Tom said, "Boss, I can't stop it, because I didn't start it." I'm telling you what they said. They said, "I'm not even in it, much less at the head of it." They said, "These Negroes are doing things on their own. They're running ahead of us." And that old shrewd fox, he said, "Well if you all aren't in it, I'll put you in it. I'll put you at the head of it. I'll endorse it. I'll welcome it. I'll help it. I'll join it."

A matter of hours went by. They had a meeting at the Carlyle Hotel in New York City. The Carlyle Hotel is owned by the Kennedy family; that's the hotel Kennedy spent the night at, two nights ago; belongs to his family.[3] A philanthropic society headed by a white man named Stephen Currier called all the top civil-rights leaders together at the Carlyle Hotel. And he told them that, "By you all fighting each other, you are destroying the civil-rights movement. And since you're fighting over money from white liberals, let us set up what is known as the Council for United Civil Rights Leadership. Let's form this council, and all the civil-rights organizations will belong to it, and we'll use it for fund-raising purposes." Let me show you how tricky the white man is. And as soon as they got it formed, they elected Whitney Young as the chairman, and who you think became the co-chairman? Stephen Currier, the white man, a millionaire. Powell was talk-ing about it down at the Cobo[4] today. This is what he was talking about. Powell knows it happened. Ran-dolph knows it happened. Wilkins knows it happened. King knows it happened. Everyone of that so-called Big Six[5]—they know what happened.

Once they formed it, with the white man over it, he promised them and gave them $800,000 to split up between the Big Six; and told them that after the march was over they'd give them $700,000 more. A million and a half dollars—split up between leaders that you've been following, going to jail for, crying crocodile tears for. And they're nothing but Frank James and Jesse James and the what-do-you-call-'em brothers.[6]

Soon as they got the setup organized, the white man made available to them top public relations experts; opened the news media across the country at their disposal; and then they begin to project these Big Six as the leaders of the march. Originally, they weren't even in the march. You was talking this march talk on Hastings Street—is Hastings Street still here?—on Hasting Street. You was talking the march talk on Lenox Avenue, and out on—what you call it?—Fillmore Street, and Central Avenue, and 32nd Street and 63rd Street.[7] That's where the march talk was being talked. But the white man put the Big Six [at the] head of it; made them the march. They became the march. They took it over. And the first move they made after they took it over, they invited Walter Reuther, a white

---

3. John F. Kennedy owned an apartment at the Carlyle Hotel, but his family never owned the hotel.
4. Cobo Hall, now Cobo Center, is a convention center in downtown Detroit that was opened in 1960.
5. Along with King, the Big Six (a term first coined by Malcolm X) included Randolph (founder of *The Messenger*, the March on Washington movement, and the Brotherhood of Sleeping Car Porters), Farmer (co-founder of CORE), Wilkins (executive leader of the NAACP), Young (1921–71, executive director of the National Urban League from 1961 until his death), and John Lewis (b. 1940, chair of SNCC during the Birmingham campaign).
6. After the Civil War, four Younger brothers (Thomas Coleman, James Hardin, John Harrison, and Robert Ewing) joined the two James brothers to form the James-Younger gang, one of the most famous outlaw gangs in American history.
7. Various streets in predominately black areas of cities around the country, including Hastings Street in Detroit, Lenox Avenue in Har-lem, Fillmore Street in San Francisco, Central Avenue in Los Angeles, 32nd Street in Philadelphia, and 63rd Street in Chicago.

man[8]; they invited a priest, a rabbi, and an old white preacher. Yes, an old white preacher. The same white element that put Kennedy in power—labor, the Catholics, the Jews, and liberal Protestants; same clique that put Kennedy in power, joined the march on Washington.

It's just like when you've got some coffee that's too black, which means it's too strong. What you do? You integrate it with cream; you make it weak. If you pour too much cream in, you won't even know you ever had coffee. It used to be hot, it becomes cool. It used to be strong, it becomes weak. It used to wake you up, now it'll put you to sleep. This is what they did with the march on Washington. They joined it. They didn't integrate it; they infiltrated it. They joined it, became a part of it, took it over. And as they took it over, it lost its militancy. They ceased to be angry. They ceased to be hot. They ceased to be uncompromising. Why, it even ceased to be a march. It became a picnic, a circus. Nothing but a circus, with clowns and all. You had one right here in Detroit—I saw it on television—with clowns leading it, white clowns and black clowns. I know you don't like what I'm saying, but I'm going to tell you anyway. 'Cause I can prove what I'm saying. If you think I'm

telling you wrong, you bring me Martin Luther King and A. Philip Randolph and James Farmer and those other three, and see if they'll deny it over a microphone.

No, it was a sellout. It was a takeover. When James Baldwin came in from Paris, they wouldn't let him talk, 'cause they couldn't make him go by the script. Burt Lancaster read the speech that Baldwin was supposed to make[9]; they wouldn't let Baldwin get up there, 'cause they know Baldwin's liable to say anything. They controlled it so tight—they told those Negroes what time to hit town, how to come, where to stop, what signs to carry, what song to sing, what speech they could make, and what speech they couldn't make; and then told them to get out town by sundown. And everyone of those Toms was out of town by sundown. Now I know you don't like my saying this. But I can back it up. It was a circus, a performance that beat anything Hollywood could ever do, the performance of the year. Reuther and those other three devils should get a Academy Award for the best actors 'cause they acted like they really loved Negroes and fooled a whole lot of Negroes. And the six Negro leaders should get an award too, for the best supporting cast.

HOWARD ZINN
The Limits of Nonviolence [1964]

In 1964, the white American historian and social activist Howard Zinn (1922–2010) argued for the use of force to protect African American civil rights, particularly in smaller towns in the South. "The Limits of Nonviolence" reflects the civil rights movement's growing disillusionment with the power of nonviolent action, particularly following the failed campaign of mass protests in Albany, Georgia, led by Martin Luther King Jr. and other activists. Zinn's essay raises the question,

Who should enforce the law when local and state authorities either ignore infractions or are themselves the ones breaking the law? Zinn's conclusions demonstrate his continued faith in the federal government as an enforcer of civil rights. Within two years, community action groups such as the Black Panthers would revisit this question but come to a markedly different conclusion, opting for law enforcement by community members instead of government officials.

From *Freedomways* 4, no. 1 (1964), pp. 143–48.

8. American labor union leader (1907–70).
9. The week before the march, Baldwin (p. 485) organized a march on the American Embassy in Paris; at the March on Washington, Bert Lancaster displayed a scroll that he and Baldwin had brought from Europe with signatures of support for the march by 1,500 artists overseas, and Charlton Heston read the statement written by Baldwin expressing the support of a community of artists, including Lena Horne, Sidney Poitier, Harry Belafonte, Diahann Carroll, Ossie Davis, Sammy Davis Jr., Paul Newman, and Marlon Brando.

When I went to Albany, Georgia, during the first wave of demonstrations and mass arrests in December of 1961, I had been in Atlanta for five years and thought I had learned some important things about the South, as observer and minor participant in the the civil rights struggle. I had written an optimistic article for *Harper's Magazine* about the possibility of changing the *behavior* (not immediately his *thinking*) of the white Southerner without violence, by playing upon his self-interest, whether through economic pressure or other means which would forcefully confront him with hard choices. And in Atlanta, I saw such changes come about, through the pressure of lawsuits, sit-ins, boycotts, and sometimes by just the threat of such actions. Nonviolence was not only hugely appealing as a concept. It worked.

And then I took a good look at Albany, and came back troubled. Eight months later, when the second crisis broke out in Albany, in the summer of 1962, I drove down again from Atlanta. The picture was the same. Again, mass demonstrations and mass arrests. Again, the federal government stood by impotent while the chief of police took control of the constitutional rights of citizens.

My optimism was shaken but still alive. To those people around me who said that Albany was a huge defeat, I replied that you could not measure victories and defeats only by tangible results in the desegregation of specific facilities, that a tremendous change had taken place in the thinking of Albany's Negroes, that expectations had been raised which could not be stilled until the city was transformed.

Today, over a year later, after studying events in Birmingham and Gadsden and Danville and Americus,[1] after interviewing staff workers of the Student Nonviolent Coordinating Committee just out of jail in Greenwood, Mississippi, watching state troopers in action in Selma, Alabama, and talking at length to voter registration workers in Greenville, Mississippi,[2] I am rethinking some of my old views. Albany, it seems to me, was the first dramatic evidence of a phenomenon which now has been seen often enough to be believed: that there is a part of the South impermeable by the ordinary activities of nonviolent direct action, a monolithic South completely controlled by politicians, police, dogs, and prod sticks. And for this South, special tactics are required.

One portion of the South has already been removed from the old Confederacy. This part of the South, represented by places like Richmond, Memphis, Nashville, Louisville, and Atlanta, is still fundamentally segregationist—as is the rest of the nation, North and South—but the first cracks have appeared in a formerly solid social structure. In these places, there is fluidity and promise, room for maneuver and pressure and accommodation; there is an economic elite sophisticated enough to know how badly it can be hurt by outright resistance, and political leaders shrewd enough to take cognizance of a growing Negro electorate. There will be much conflict yet in Atlanta and in Memphis. But the tactics of nonviolent direct action can force ever greater gains there.

Then there is the South of Albany and Americus, Georgia; of Gadsden and Selma, Alabama; of Danville, Virginia; of Plaquemines, Louisiana[3]; of Greenwood and Hattiesburg and Yazoo City, Mississippi—and a hundred other towns of the Black Belt. Here, where the smell of slavery still lingers, politicians are implacable, plantation owners relentless, policemen unchecked by the slightest fear of judgment. In these towns of the Black Belt, a solid stone wall separates black from white, and reason from fanaticism; nonviolent demonstrations smash themselves to bits against this wall, leav-

1. Sites of grassroots movements that attracted the support of national civil rights organizations; in the summer of 1960, police attacked nonviolent protesters in Gadsden, Alabama, with cattle prods and other weapons; four organizers of the "Americus Movement" in Georgia in the summer of 1963 were accused of "Seditious Conspiracy," a charge subject to the death penalty, and were kept in jail for months until a federal appeals court overturned the charge.
2. From 1961 to 1963, SNCC organized voter drives across Mississippi starting in McComb; the setbacks faced in McComb shaped subsequent efforts in Greenwood, Greenville, and other Mississippi towns, as well as towns in other southern states, such as Selma, Alabama; in Greenwood, town officials tried to stop voter registration of African Americans by jailing the organizers and instituting a food blockade affecting the majority of the black population, who depended on federal food stamps.
3. The city of Plaquemine is located in the parish of Plaquemines.

ing pain, frustration, bewilderment, even though the basic resolve to win remains alive, and some kind of ingenuous optimism is left untouched by defeat after defeat.

I still believe that the Albany Movement, set back again and again by police power, has done a magnificent service to the Negroes of Albany—and ultimately, to the whites who live in that morally cramped town. I still believe that the three hundred Negroes who waited in line near the county courthouse in Selma, Alabama, from morning to evening in the shadow of clubs and guns to register to vote, without even entering the doors of that courthouse, accomplished something. But I no longer hold that a simple repetition of such nonviolent demonstrative action—which effectively broke through barriers in the other part of the South—will bring victory. I am now convinced that the stone wall which blocks expectant Negroes in every town and village of the hard-core South, a wall stained with the blood of children, as well as others, and with an infinite capacity to absorb the blood of more victims—will have to be crumbled by hammer blows.

This can be done, it seems to me, in one of two ways. The first is a Negro revolt, armed and unswerving, in Mississippi, Alabama and southwest Georgia, which would result in a terrible waste of human life. That may be hard to avoid unless the second alternative comes to pass: the forceful intervention of the national government, to smash, with speed and efficiency, every attempt by local policemen or politicians to deprive Negroes (or others) of the rights supposedly guaranteed by the Constitution.

Unaware of the distinction between the two Souths, not called upon for such action in places like Atlanta and Nashville, and uncommitted emotionally and ideologically to racial equality as a first-level value, the national government has played the role of a hesitant, timorous observer. It will have to move into bold action, or face trouble such as we have not seen yet in the civil rights crisis. This is my thesis here, and the story of Albany, Georgia may help illustrate it.

Federal law was violated again and again in Albany, yet the federal government did not act. In effect, over a thousand Negroes spent time in prison, and thousands more suffered and sacrificed, in ways that cannot be expressed adequately on paper, as a mass substitute for federal action.

Judicial decisions in this century have made it clear that the Fourteenth Amendment, besides barring officials from dispensing unequal treatment on the basis of race, also prohibits them from interfering with the First Amendment rights of free speech, petition, and assembly. Yet in Albany over one thousand Negroes were locked up in some of the most miserable jails in the country for peacefully attempting to petition the local government for a redress of grievances. *And the Justice Department did nothing.*

Section 242 of the U.S. Criminal Code, which comes from the Civil Rights Act of 1866 and the Enforcement Act of 1870, creates a legal basis for prosecution of "Whoever, under color of any law . . . wilfully subjects . . . any inhabitant of any State . . . to the deprivation of any rights, privileges, or immunities secured or protected by the Constitution and laws of the United States. . . ."[4] Three times in succession, in November and December 1961, the police of the city of Albany, by arresting Negroes and whites in connection with their use of the terminal facilities in that city, violated a right which has been made clear beyond a shadow of a doubt. Yet the federal government took no action.

Today, the wheels of the nonviolent movement are churning slowly, in frustration, through the mud of national indifference which surrounds the stone wall of police power in the city of Albany. As if to give a final blow to the Albany Movement, the Department of Justice is now prosecuting nine of its leaders and members, who face jail sentences up to ten years, in connection with the picketing of a white grocer who had served on a federal jury. One of the defendants is Dr. W. G. Anderson, former head of the Albany Movement. Another is Slater King, now heading the Movement. *It is the bitterest of ironies that Slater King, who pleaded in vain for federal action while he himself was jailed, while his*

---

4. From U.S. Code, Title 18, Crimes and Criminal Procedure, Part 1, Crimes, Chapter 13, Civil Rights, Section 242, Deprivation of rights under color of law.

wife was beaten by a deputy sheriff, while his brother was beaten, is now being vigorously prosecuted by the U.S. Department of Justice on a charge which can send him to jail for five years.

The simple and harsh fact, made clear in Albany, and reinforced by events in Americus, Georgia, in Selma and Gadsden, Alabama, in Danville, Virginia, in every town in Mississippi, is that the federal government abdicated its responsibility in the Black Belt. The Negro citizens of that area were left to the local police. The United States Constitution was left in the hands of Neanderthal creatures who cannot read it, and whose only response to it has been to grunt and swing their clubs.

The responsibility is that of the President of the United States, and no one else. It is his job to enforce the law. And the law is clear. Previously the civil rights movement joined in thrusting the responsibility on Congress when the President himself, without any new legislation, had the constitutional power to enforce the Fourteenth Amendment in the Black Belt.

The immediate necessity is for a *permanent* federal presence in the Deep South. I am not talking of occupation by troops, except as an ultimate weapon. I am suggesting the creation of a special force of federal agents, stationed throughout the Deep South, and authorized to make immediate on-the-spot arrests of any local official who violates federal law. The action would be preventive, before a crisis has developed, and would snuff out incipient fires before they got going, by swift, efficient action. Such a force would have taken Colonel Al Lingo into custody as he was preparing to use his electric prod sticks on the Freedom Walkers crossing the border into Alabama. Such a force would have taken Governor Wallace[5] to the nearest federal prison the very first time he blocked the entrance of a Negro student into the University of Alabama, and would have arrested Sheriff Jim Clark as he moved to drag those two SNCC youngsters off the steps of the federal building in Selma.

Many liberals are affronted by such a suggestion; they worry about civil war. My contention is that the white Southerner submits—as do most people—to a clear show of authority; note how Governors Wallace and Barnett gave in at the last moment rather than go to jail. Once Southern police officials realize that the club is in the other hand, that *they* will be behind bars, that *they* will have to go through all the legal folderal of getting bond and filing appeal, etc., which thousands of Negroes have had to endure these past few years— things will be different. The national government needs to drive a wedge, as it began to do in the First Reconstruction, between the officialdom and the ordinary white citizen of the South, who is not a rabid brute but a vacillating conformist.

Burke Marshall, head of the Civil Rights Division of the Department of Justice, has been much disturbed by this suggestion of "a national police force or some other such extreme alternative." If a national police force is extreme, then the United States is already "extremist," because the Federal Bureau of Investigation is just that. It is stationed throughout the country and has the power to arrest anyone who violates federal law. Thus, it arrests those who violate the federal statutes dealing with bank robberies, interstate auto thefts and interstate kidnapping. But it does *not* arrest those who violate the civil rights laws. I am suggesting an organization of special agents, who will arrest violators of civil rights laws the way the F.B.I. arrests bank robbers.

The continued dependence on nonviolence by the civil rights movement is now at stake. Nonviolent direct action can work in social situations where there are enough apertures through which economic and political and moral pressure can be applied. But it is ineffective in a totally closed society, in those Black Belt towns of the Deep South where Negroes are jailed and beaten and the power structure of the community stands intact.

The late President Kennedy's political style was one of working from crisis to crisis rather than under-

---

5. In his inaugural speech in 1963, Alabama governor George Wallace (1919–98) declared, "In the name of the greatest people that have ever trod this earth, I draw the line in the dust and toss the gauntlet before the feet of tyranny, and I say segregation now, segregation tomorrow, segregation forever"; one of Wallace's first acts as governor was to fire Alabama Public Safety Director Floyd Mann, who had stopped the beating of Freedom Riders by the Ku Klux Klan, and replace him with Al Lingo, who was known for his segregationist views.

taking fundamental solutions—like a man who settles one debt by contracting another. This can go on and on, until the day of reckoning. And that day may come, in the civil rights crisis, this summer just before the election.

There is a strong probability that this July and August will constitute another "summer of discontent." The expectations among Negroes in the Black Belt have risen to the point where they cannot be quieted. CORE (Congress of Racial Equality), SCLC (Southern Christian Leadership Conference) and the intrepid youngsters of the Student Nonviolent Coordinating Committee, are determined to move forward.

With the probability high of intensified activity in the Black Belt this summer, the President will have to decide what to do. He can stand by and watch Negro protests smashed by the local police, with mass jailings, beatings, and cruelties of various kinds. Or he can take the kind of firm action suggested above, which would simply establish clearly what the Civil War was fought for a hundred years ago, the supremacy of the U.S. Constitution over the entire nation. If he does not act, the Negro community may be pressed by desperation to move beyond the nonviolence which it has maintained so far with amazing self-discipline.

Thus, in a crucial sense, the future of nonviolence as a means for social change rests in the hands of the President of the United States. And the civil rights movement faces the problem of how to convince him of this, both by words and by action. For, if nonviolent direct action seems to batter itself to death against the police power of the Deep South, perhaps its most effective use is against the national government. The idea is to persuade the executive branch to use its far greater resources of nonviolent pressure to break down the walls of totalitarian rule in the Black Belt.

The latest victim of this terrible age of violence—which crushed the life from four Negro girls in a church basement in Birmingham, and in this century has taken the lives of over fifty million persons in war—is President John F. Kennedy, killed by an assassin's bullet. To President Johnson will fall the unfinished job of ending the violence and fear of violence which has been part of the everyday life of the Negro in the Deep South.

MARTIN LUTHER KING JR.
Nonviolence: The Only Road to Freedom [1966]

In this 1966 article for the popular magazine *Ebony*, Martin Luther King Jr. (p. 559) responds to the advocacy of violence by militant groups such as the Black Panthers by reframing the debate on the use of violence. King's language is strikingly militaristic, but he reverses the traditional association of violence with power: calls for violence are the "posturing of cowards," while nonviolence is linked to action. Throughout the essay, he uses words typically associated with war to describe the nonviolent movement. To King, marches, boycotts, and political and economic organization are weapons, and violent "self-defense" distracts from the main fight. Rejecting the use of violence as a way to end violence, King calls for people to have the courage to accept suffering as the way to end suffering.

Although King and Malcolm X never directly debated each other, critics often place King's views in opposition to those of Malcolm X. Malcolm X's critiques of King reinforce the idea that their platforms were oppositional. For example, when asked to comment on King in a 1963 interview, Malcolm X replied bluntly: "I think that any black man who goes among so-called Negroes today who are being brutalized, spit upon in the worst fashion imaginable, and teaches those Negroes to turn the other cheek, to suffer peacefully, or love their enemy is a traitor to the Negro. [* * *] It is time for the black people in this country to come together and unite and do whatever is necessary to gain the recognition and respect of the world." In 1964, however, after his break with the Nation of Islam, Malcolm X sent a number of telegrams to King offering to work with him, albeit on his terms. His three-sentence telegram of June 30, 1964, sent to King in St. Augustine, Florida, says simply:

> We have been witnessing with great concern the vicious attacks of the white races against our poor

defenseless people there in St. Augustine. If the federal government will not send troops to your aid, just say the word and we will immediately dispatch some of our brothers there to organize self defense units among our people and the Klu Klux Klan [*sic*] will then receive a taste of its own medicine. The day of turning the other cheek to those brute beasts is over.

Malcolm X had also expressed his desire to form a "united front" with King nearly a year earlier. In a July 31, 1963, letter inviting King to express his views at a Black Muslim-led rally in Harlem, Malcolm X proclaimed, "it is a disgrace for Negro leaders not to be able to submerge our 'minor' differences in order to seek a common solution to a common problem posed by a *Common Enemy.*" King did not attend that rally, and consistently declined to debate Malcolm X directly, for, as his secretary, Dora McDonald, wrote in November 1962, King "has always considered his work in a positive action framework rather than engaging in consistent negative debate." Although the two men met face-to-face only once (on March 26, 1964, while King was waiting for a news conference at the U.S. Capitol), they came to represent opposite poles of thought on the use of violence in the civil rights movement, a dichotomy that tends to obscure the complexity of their thought on nonviolence and armed self-defense.

From *Ebony,* October 1966, pp. 27–34.

The year 1966 brought with it the first public challenge to the philosophy and strategy of nonviolence from within the ranks of the civil rights movement. Resolutions of self-defense and Black Power sounded forth from our friends and brothers. At the same time riots erupted in several major cities. Inevitably a link was made between the two phenomena though movement leadership continued to deny any implications of violence in the concept of Black Power.

The nation's press heralded these incidents as an end of the Negro's reliance on nonviolence as a means of achieving freedom. Articles appeared on "The Plot to Get Whitey," and, "Must Negroes Fight Back?" and one had the impression that a serious movement was underway to lead the Negro to freedom through the use of violence.

Indeed, there was much talk of violence. It was the same talk we have heard on the fringes of the nonviolent movement for the past ten years. It was the talk of fearful men, saying that they would not join the nonviolent movement because they would not remain non-violent if attacked. Now the climate had shifted so that it was even more popular to talk of violence, but in spite of the talk of violence there emerged no action in this direction. One reporter pointed out in a recent *New Yorker* article, that the fact that Beckwith, Price, Rainey, and Collie Leroy Wilkins[1] remain alive is living testimony to the fact that the Negro remains nonviolent. And if this is not enough, a mere check of the statistics of casualties in the recent riots shows that the vast majority of persons killed in riots are Negroes. All the reports of sniping in Los Angeles' expressways did not produce a single casualty. The young demented white student at the University of Texas[2] has shown what damage a sniper can do when he is serious. In fact, this one young man killed more people in one day than all the Negroes have killed in all the riots in all the cities since the Harlem riots of 1964. This must raise a serious question about the violent intent of the Negro, for certainly there are many ex-GIs within our ghettos, and no small percentage of those recent migrants from the South have demonstrated some proficiency hunting squirrels and rabbits.

1. White southerners linked to the murders of civil rights workers: Byron De La Beckwith was convicted of killing Medgar Evers; Sheriff Lawrence A. Rainey and his deputy Cecil Price were tied to the murders of Michael Schwerner, James Chaney, and Andrew Goodman, and to the subsequent cover-up; Rainey and Price were both indicted for conspiracy, and Price was convicted; Collie Leroy Wilkins was twice tried for the murder of Viola Liuzzo, and ultimately convicted of conspiracy.
2. On August 1, 1966, after killing his wife and mother, Charles Whitman (1941–66) went to the University of Texas campus where he shot 27 people, 14 of whom died.

I can only conclude that the Negro, even in his bitterest moments, is not intent on killing white men to be free. This does not mean that the Negro is a saint who abhors violence. Unfortunately, a check of the hospitals in any Negro community on any Saturday night will make you painfully aware of the violence within the Negro community. Hundreds of victims of shooting and cutting lie bleeding in the emergency rooms, but there is seldom if ever a white person who is the victim of Negro hostility.

I have talked with many persons in the ghettos of the North who argue eloquently for the use of violence. But I observed none of them in the mobs that rioted in Chicago. I have heard the street corner preachers in Harlem and in Chicago's Washington Park, but in spite of the bitterness preached and the hatred espoused, none of them has ever been able to start a riot. So far, only the police through their fears and prejudice have goaded our people to riot. And once the riot starts, only the police or the National Guard have been able to put an end to them. This demonstrates that these violent eruptions are unplanned, uncontrollable temper tantrums brought on by long neglected poverty, humiliation, oppression and exploitation. Violence as a strategy for social change in America is non-existent. All the sound and fury seems but the posturing of cowards whose bold talk produces no action and signifies nothing.[3]

I am convinced that for practical as well as moral reasons, nonviolence offers the only road to freedom for my people. In violent warfare, one must be prepared to face ruthlessly the fact that there will be casualties by the thousands. In Viet Nam, the United States has evidently decided that it is willing to slaughter millions, sacrifice some 200,000 men and $20 billion a year to secure the freedom of some 14 million Vietnamese. This is to fight a war on Asian soil, where Asians are in the majority. Anyone leading a violent conflict must be willing to make a similar assessment regarding the possible casualties to a minority population confronting a well armed, wealthy majority with a fanatical right wing that is capable of exterminating the entire black population and which would not hesitate such an attempt if the survival of white Western materialism were at stake.

Arguments that the American Negro is a part of a world which is two-thirds colored and that there will come a day when the oppressed people of color will rise together to throw off the yoke of white oppression are at least 50 years away from being relevant. There is no colored nation, including China, which now shows even the potential of leading a revolution of color in any international proportion. Ghana, Zambia, Tanzania and Nigeria are fighting their own battles for survival against poverty, illiteracy, and the subversive influence of neo-colonialism, so that they offer no hope to Angola, Southern Rhodesia, and South Africa, and much less to the American Negro.

The hard cold facts of racial life in the world today indicate that the hope of the people of color in the world may well rest on the American Negro and his ability to reform the structures of racist imperialism from within and thereby turn the technology and wealth of the West to the task of liberating the world from want.

This is no time for romantic illusions about freedom and empty philosophical debate. This is a time for action. What is needed is a strategy for change, a tactical program which will bring the Negro into the main stream of American life as quickly as possible. So far, this has only been offered by the nonviolent movement.

Our record of achievement through nonviolent action is already remarkable. The dramatic social changes which have been made across the South are unmatched in the annals of history. Montgomery, Albany, Birmingham, and Selma have paved the way for untold progress. Even more remarkable is the fact that this progress occurred with a minimum of human sacrifice and loss of life.

Not a single person has been killed in a nonviolent demonstration. The bombings of the 16th Street Baptist Church occurred several months after demonstrations stopped. Rev. James Reeb, Mrs. Viola Liuzzo, and Jimmie Lee Jackson[4] were all murdered at night

---

3. Allusion to *Macbeth* Act 5, Scene 5: "it is a tale/Told by an idiot, full of sound and fury,/Signifying nothing."
4. While trying to protect his mother from being beaten after a march in Marion, Alabama, Jackson (1938–65), a Baptist deacon, was shot by police; Reeb (1927–65), a white American Unitarian minister, died after being beaten by segregationists during the march in Selma on March 9, 1965; Liuzzo, a white civil rights activist from Michigan, was shot by Ku Klux Klan members after the March 25, 1965, march from Selma to Montgomery.

following demonstrations. And fewer people have been killed in ten years of action across the South than were killed in three nights of rioting in Watts.[5] No similar changes have occurred without infinitely more sufferings, whether it be Gandhi's drive for independence in India or any African nation's struggle for independence.

THE QUESTION OF SELF-DEFENSE

There are many people who very honestly raise the question of self-defense. This must be placed in perspective. It goes without saying that people will protect their homes. This is a right guaranteed by the Constitution and respected even in the worst areas of the South. But the mere protection of one's home and person against assault by lawless night riders does not provide any positive approach to the fears and conditions which produce violence. There must be some program for establishing law. Our experience in places like Savannah and Macon, Ga. has been that a drive which registers Negroes to vote can do more to provide protection of the law and respect for Negroes by even racist sheriffs than anything we have seen.

In a nonviolent demonstration, self defense must be approached from quite another perspective. One must remember that the cause of the demonstration is some exploitation or form of oppression that has made it necessary for men of courage and good will to demonstrate against the evil. For example, a demonstration against the evil of *de facto* school segregation is based on the awareness that a child's mind is crippled daily by inadequate educational opportunity. The demonstrator agrees that it is better for him to suffer publicly for a short time to end the crippling evil of school desegregation than to have generation after generation of children suffer in ignorance.

In such a demonstration, the point is made that schools are inadequate. This is the evil to which one seeks to point; anything else detracts from that point and interferes with confrontation of the primary evil against which one demonstrates. Of course, no one wants to suffer and be hurt. But it is more important to get at the cause than to be safe. It is better to shed a little blood from a blow on the head or a rock thrown by an angry mob than to have children by the thousands grow up reading at a fifth or sixth grade level.

It is always amusing to me when a Negro man says that he can't demonstrate with us because if someone hit him he would fight back. Here is a man whose children are being plagued by rats and roaches, whose wife is robbed daily at over-priced ghetto food stores, who himself is working for about two-thirds the pay of a white person doing a similar job and with similar skills, and in spite of all this daily suffering it takes someone spitting on him or calling him a nigger to make him want to fight.

Conditions are such for Negroes in America that all Negroes ought to be fighting aggressively. It is as ridiculous for a Negro to raise the question of self-defense in relation to nonviolence as it is for a soldier on the battlefield to say he is not going to take any risks. He is there because he believes that the freedom of his country is worth the risk of his life. The same is true of the nonviolent demonstrator. He sees the misery of his people so clearly that he volunteers to suffer in their behalf and put an end to their plight.

Furthermore, it is extremely dangerous to organize a movement around self-defense. The line between defensive violence and aggressive or retaliatory violence is a fine line indeed. When violence is tolerated even as a means of self-defense there is grave danger that in the fervor of emotion the main fight will be lost over the question of self-defense.

When my home was bombed in 1955 in Montgomery, many men wanted to retaliate, to place an armed guard on my home. But the issue there was not my life, but whether Negroes would achieve first class treatment on the city's buses. Had we become distracted by the question of my safety we would have lost the moral offensive and sunk to the level of our oppressors.

I must continue by faith or it is too great a burden to bear and violence, even in self-defense, creates more problems than it solves. Only a refusal to hate or kill can put an end to the chain of violence in the world and lead us toward a community where men can live together without fear. Our goal is to create a beloved community and this will require a qualitative change in our souls as well as a quantitative change in our lives.

---

5. During the 6-day uprising in the Watts neighborhood of Los Angeles in August 1965, 34 people were killed and over 1,000 injured.

STRATEGY FOR CHANGE

The American racial revolution has been a revolution to "get in" rather than to overthrow. We want a share in the American economy, the housing market, the educational system and the social opportunities. This goal itself indicates that a social change in America must be nonviolent.

If one is in search of a better job, it does not help to burn down the factory. If one needs more adequate education, shooting the principal will not help, or if housing is the goal, only building and construction will produce that end. To destroy anything, person or property, can't bring us closer to the goal that we seek.

The nonviolent strategy has been to dramatize the evils of our society in such a way that pressure is brought to bear against those evils by the forces of good will in the community and change is produced.

The student sit-ins of 1960 are a classic illustration of this method. Students were denied the right to eat at a lunch counter, so they deliberately sat down to protest their denial. They were arrested, but this made their parents mad and so they began to close their charge accounts. The students continued to sit in; and this further embarrassed the city, scared away many white shoppers and soon produced an economic threat to the business life of the city. Amid this type of pressure, it is not hard to get people to agree to change.

So far, we have had the Constitution backing most of the demands for change, and this has made our work easier, since we could be sure that the federal courts would usually back up our demonstrations legally. Now we are approaching areas where the voice of the Constitution is not clear. We have left the realm of constitutional rights and we are entering the area of human rights.

The Constitution assured the right to vote, but there is no such assurance of the right to adequate housing, or the right to an adequate income. And yet, in a nation which has a gross national product of 750 billion dollars a year, it is morally right to insist that every person has a decent house, an adequate education and enough money to provide basic necessities for one's family. Achievement of these goals will be a lot more difficult and require much more discipline, understanding, organization and sacrifice.

It so happens that Negroes live in the central city of the major cities of the United States. These cities control the electoral votes of the large states of our nation. This means that though we are only ten per cent of the nation's population, we are located in such a key position geographically—the cities of the North and the Black belts of the South—that we are able to lead a political and moral coalition which can direct the course of the nation. Our position depends upon a lot more than political power, however. It depends upon our ability to marshal moral power as well. As soon as we lose the moral offensive, we are left with only our ten per cent of the power of the nation. This is hardly enough to produce any meaningful changes, even within our own communities, for the lines of power control the economy as well and once the flow of money is cut off, progress ceases.

The past three years have demonstrated the power of a committed, morally sound minority to lead the nation. It was the coalition molded through the Birmingham movement which allied the forces of the churches, labor and the academic communities of the nation behind the liberal issues of our time. All of the liberal legislation of the past session of Congress can be credited to this coalition. Even the presence of a vital peace movement and the campus protest against the war in Viet Nam can be traced back to the nonviolent action movement led by the Negro. Prior to Birmingham, our campuses were still in a state of shock over the McCarthy era and Congress was caught in the perennial dead-lock of Southern Democrats and Mid-Western Republicans. Negroes put the country on the move against the enemies of poverty, slums and inadequate education.

TECHNIQUES OF THE FUTURE

When Negroes marched, so did the nation. The power of the nonviolent march is indeed a mystery. It is always surprising that a few hundred Negroes marching can produce such a reaction across the nation. When marches are carefully organized around well defined issues, they represent the power which Victor Hugo[6] phrased as the most powerful force in the world, "an idea

6. French writer (1802–85).

whose time has come." Marching feet announce that time has come for a given idea. When the idea is a sound one, the cause a just one, and the demonstration a righteous one, change will be forthcoming. But if any of these conditions are not present, the power for change is missing also. A thousand people demonstrating for the right to use heroin would have little effect. By the same token, a group of ten thousand marching in anger against a police station and cussing out the chief of police will do very little to bring respect, dignity and unbiased law enforcement. Such a demonstration would only produce fear and bring about an addition of forces to the station and more oppressive methods by the police.

Marches must continue in the future, and they must be the kind of marches that bring about the desired result. But the march is not a "one shot" victory-producing method. One march is seldom successful, and as my good friend Kenneth Clark[7] points out in *Dark Ghetto*, it can serve merely to let off steam and siphon off the energy which is necessary to produce change. However, when marching is seen as a part of a program to dramatize an evil, to mobilize the forces of good will, and to generate pressure and power for change, marches will continue to be effective.

Our experience is that marches must continue over a period of 30 to 45 days to produce any meaningful results. They must also be of sufficient size to produce some inconvenience to the forces in power or they go unnoticed. In other words, they must demand the attention of the press, for it is the press which interprets the issue to the community at large and thereby sets in motion the machinery for change.

Along with the march as a weapon for change in our nonviolent arsenal must be listed the boycott. Basic to the philosophy of nonviolence is the refusal to cooperate with evil. There is nothing quite so effective as a refusal to cooperate economically with the forces and institutions which perpetuate evil in our communities.

In the past six months simply by refusing to purchase products from companies which do not hire Negroes in meaningful numbers and in all job categories, the Ministers of Chicago under SCLC's Operation Breadbasket have increased the income of the Negro community by more than two million dollars annually.

In Atlanta the Negroes' earning power has been increased by more than twenty million dollars annually over the past three years through a carefully disciplined program of selective buying and negotiations by the Negro minister. This is nonviolence at its peak of power, when it cuts into the profit margin of a business in order to bring about a more just distribution of jobs and opportunities for Negro wage earners and consumers.

But again, the boycott must be sustained over a period of several weeks and months to assure results. This means continuous education of the community in order that support can be maintained. People will work together and sacrifice if they understand clearly why and how this sacrifice will bring about change. We can never assume that anyone understands. It is our job to keep people informed and aware.

Our most powerful nonviolent weapon is, as would be expected, also our most demanding, that is organization. To produce change, people must be organized to work together in units of power. These units might be political, as in the case of voters leagues and political parties; they may be economic units such as groups of tenants who join forces to form a tenant union or to organize a rent strike; or they may be laboring units of persons who are seeking employment and wage increases.

More and more, the civil rights movement will become engaged in the task of organizing people into permanent groups to protect their own interests and to produce change in their behalf. This is a tedious task which may take years, but the results are more permanent and meaningful.

In the future we will be called upon to organize the unemployed, to unionize the businesses within the ghetto, to bring tenants together into collective bargaining units and establish cooperatives for purposes of building viable financial institutions within the ghetto that can be controlled by Negroes themselves.

There is no easy way to create a world where men and women can live together, where each has his own job and house and where all children receive as much education as their minds can absorb. But if such a world is created in our lifetime, it will be done in the United States by Negroes and white people of good will. It will be accomplished by persons who have the

---

7. Psychologist (1914–2005); with his wife, psychologist Mamie Phipps Clark (1917–83), conducted influential experiments using dolls to study children's ideas about race.

courage to put an end to suffering by willingly suffering themselves rather than inflict suffering upon others. It will be done by rejecting the racism, materialism

and violence that has characterized Western civilization and especially by working toward a world of brotherhood, cooperation, and peace.

HUEY NEWTON AND BOBBY SEALE

October 1966 Black Panther Platform and Program [1966]

On October 15, 1966, Huey P. Newton (1949–1982), a law student, and Bobby Seale (b. 1936), an employee of the city of Oakland, California, drafted a ten-point program calling for racial equality in employment, housing, education, and civil rights. Their "What We Believe" manifesto became the founding document of a new organization, which they dedicated to enforcing the rights of African Americans "by any means necessary," with the teachings of Malcolm X as its philosophical model. Inspired by the illustration of a panther that served as the emblem of the Lowndes County Freedom Organization (a political party founded earlier in 1966 in Lowndes County, Alabama, by Stokely Carmichael) Newton and Seale called their new organization the Black Panther Party for Self-Defense (later shortened to the Black Panther party). As Seale recalled in an August 1996 interview for the *Cold War* series on CNN:

> And at another point that day, Huey says, "You know, I think the nature of a panther is that if you push that black panther into a corner, he will try to go left to get out of your way. And if you keep him there, then he's going to try to go right to get out of your way. And if you keep oppressing him and pushing him into that corner, sooner or later that panther's going to come out of that corner to try to wipe out whoever's oppressing it in the corner."
>
> I says, "Huey, that's just like us, that's just like black people."

In 1967, when they launched their official newspaper, *The Black Panther Intercommunal News Service*, they included their "What We Believe" platform in each issue. The following year, they added a separate section outlining "What We Want," and gave the new document the title "October 1966 Black Panther Party Platform and Program." The final version, reprinted here, with the "What We Believe" and "What We Want" sections interleafed, was first published in 1969.

The Black Panthers challenged police brutality by monitoring police activity in predominantly black neighborhoods. Members armed themselves for patrols not only with loaded weapons but also with tape recorders and knowledge of the law. Although the Black Panthers later moved toward more revolutionary positions, their philosophy was initially rooted in the idea of armed self-defense as a way of stopping further violence. As Newton is famous for saying, "Sometimes if you want to get rid of the gun, you have to pick the gun up."

During their first year, the Black Panthers became influenced by Marxist ideas and began organizing community programs, such as free breakfast programs for schoolchildren and free medical clinics. As the Panthers gained popularity and started forming coalitions with other groups to further the goal of "all power to all the people" (in contrast to the black nationalist idea of Black Power, which was stressed by other groups), they became a target of the FBI, especially its counterintelligence program, COINTELPRO. J. Edgar Hoover, the longtime director of the FBI, called the Black Panthers "the greatest threat to the internal security of the country" and utilized police harassment, spying, infiltration, and the fostering of internal conflict to destroy the organization.

Further complicating their goal of attaining legitimacy within the black community, some Panther members engaged in illegal activity; Newton, for example, engaged in violent behavior and abused drugs. Seale left the organization in 1974, and Newton went into self-imposed exile in Cuba in 1974 to avoid being tried for the murder of a seventeen-year-old girl. The organization never regained its momentum, even after Newton's return (and acquittal) in 1977. With internal conflicts exacerbating the external attacks by the government, the Black Panthers had faded in political relevance by the end of the 1970s. In a 1997 interview with Henry Louis Gates Jr. for PBS's *Frontline,* former Black Panther Eldridge Cleaver (1935–1998) linked the rise of random urban violence to the government's suppression of organized liberation groups like the

Black Panthers, while also pointing to an unfulfilled shift in Black Panther strategies toward politics:

> And I regret the way that the Party was repressed because it left a lot of unfinished business because we had planned to make a transition to the political arena and we would have been able to transmute that violence and that legacy into legitimate and peaceful channels. As it was they chopped off the head and left the body there armed. That's why all these young bloods out there now, they've got the rhetoric but without the political direction and they've got the guns.

From *The Black Panther* (February 19, 1969).

WHAT WE WANT
WHAT WE BELIEVE

1. <u>We want freedom. We want power to determine the destiny of our Black Community.</u>[1]

<u>We believe</u> that black people will not be free until we are able to determine our destiny.

2. <u>We want full employment of our people.</u>

<u>We believe</u> that the federal government is responsible and obligated to give every man employment or a guaranteed income. We believe that if the white American businessmen will not give full employment, then the means of production should be taken from the businessmen and placed in the community so that the people of the community can organize and employ all of its people and give a high standard of living.

3. <u>We want an end to the robbery by the white man of our Black Community.</u>

<u>We believe</u> that this racist government has robbed us and now we are demanding the overdue debt of forty acres and two mules. Forty acres and two mules was promised 100 years ago as restitution for slave labor and mass murder of black people. We will accept the payment as currency which will be distributed to our many communities. The Germans are now aiding the Jews in Israel for the genocide of the Jewish people. The Germans murdered six million Jews. The American racist has taken part in the slaughter of over twenty million[2] black people; therefore, we feel that this is a modest demand that we make.

4. <u>We want decent housing, fit for shelter of human beings.</u>

<u>We believe</u> that if the white landlords will not give decent housing to our black community, then the housing and the land should be made into cooperatives so that our community, with government aid, can build and make decent housing for its people.

5. <u>We want education for our people that exposes the true nature of this decadent American society. We want education that teaches us our true history and our role in the present-day society.</u>

<u>We believe</u> in an educational system that will give to our people a knowledge of self. If a man does not have knowledge of himself and his position in society and the world, then he has little chance to relate to anything else.

---

1. The Black Panthers revised their platform in March 1972, moving away from exclusive black nationalism to include "our Black and oppressed communities;" the revised paltform was published in *The Black Panther Intercommunal News* on May 13, 1972; both the original and revised platforms are included in Stanford University's "History of the Black Panther Party" at http://www.stanford.edu/group/blackpanthers/history.shtml.
2. In the 1972 revision, this number was changed to "over fifty million."

6. <u>We want all black men to be exempt from military service.</u>

<u>We believe</u> that Black people should not be forced to fight in the military service to defend a racist government that does not protect us. We will not fight and kill other people of color in the world who, like black people, are being victimized by the white racist government of America. We will protect ourselves from the force and violence of the racist police and the racist military, by whatever means necessary.

7. <u>We want an immediate end to POLICE BRUTALITY and MURDER of black people.</u>

<u>We believe</u> we can end police brutality in our black community by organizing black self-defense groups that are dedicated to defending our black community from racist police oppression and brutality. The Second Amendment to the Constitution of the United States gives a right to bear arms. We therefore believe that all black people should arm themselves for self defense.

8. <u>We want freedom for all black men held in federal, state, county and city prisons and jails.</u>

<u>We believe</u> that all black people should be released from the many jails and prisons because they have not received a fair and impartial trial.

9. <u>We want all black people when brought to trial to be tried in court by a jury of their peer group or people from their black communities, as defined by the Constitution of the United States.</u>

<u>We believe</u> that the courts should follow the United States Constitution so that black people will receive fair trials. The 14th Amendment of the U.S. Constitution gives a man a right to be tried by his peer group. A peer is a person from a similar economic, social, religious, geographical, environmental, historical and racial background. To do this the court will be forced to select a jury from the black community from which the black defendant came. We have been, and are being tried by all-white juries that have no understanding of the "average reasoning man" of the black community.

10. <u>We want land, bread, housing, education, clothing, justice and peace. And as our major political objective, a United Nations—supervised plebiscite to be held throughout the black colony in which only black colonial subjects will be allowed to participate for the purpose of determining the will of black people as to their national destiny.</u>

When in the course of human events, it becomes necessary for one people to dissolve the political bands which have connected them with another, and to assume, among the powers of the earth, the separate and equal station to which the laws of nature and nature's God entitle them, a decent respect to the opinions of mankind requires that they should declare the causes which impel them to the separation.

We hold these truths to be self evident, that all men are created equal; that they are endowed by their Creator with certain unalienable rights; that among these are life, liberty, and the pursuit of happiness. <u>That, to secure these rights, governments are instituted among men, deriving their just powers from the consent of the governed; that, whenever any form of government becomes destructive of these ends, it is the right of the people to alter or to abolish it, and to institute a new government, laying its foundation on such principles, and organizing its powers in such form, as to them shall seem most likely to effect their safety and happiness.</u> Prudence, indeed, will dictate that governments long established should not be changed for light and transient causes; and accordingly, all experience hath shown, that mankind are more disposed to suffer, while evils are sufferable, than to right themselves by abolishing the forms to which they are accustomed. <u>But, when a long train of abuses and usurpations, pursuing invariably the same object, evinces a design to reduce them under absolute despotism, it is their right, it is their duty, to throw off such government, and to provide new guards for their future security.</u>[3]

3. These last two paragraphs are the opening of the Declaration of Independence.

KEY DEBATE ~ *Education*

EUGENE D. GENOVESE
Black Studies: Trouble Ahead [1969]

In 1968, San Francisco College established the first black studies department in the United States. Upset by the minimal resources committed to the new department, students and faculty launched a strike that shut down the college for nearly five months. The college ultimately agreed to many demands, including hiring twelve (instead of one) full-time professors and dramatically increasing the number of admitted black students.

Across the country, black students at public and private universities were also having success with demands for new black studies courses and departments, more faculty positions, and increased African American student enrollment. For example, in 1969 the number of black applicants accepted at the eight Ivy League colleges increased by 89 percent over the number admitted in the prior year, and out of 185 colleges and universities in a 1969 survey, 23 pledged to offer new majors in black studies the following year. The rapid establishment of new departments created philosophical, pedagogical, and even legal problems. Administration, faculty, and students clashed over issues such as whether non-black students and faculty should be included in black studies classes, whether students should be involved in the selection of faculty, and whether faculty requirements should be relaxed given the shortage of experienced professors in African American studies.

The white American historian Eugene Genovese (b. 1930) brought a Marxist perspective to his work on the American history of slavery (including *Roll Jordan Roll: The World The Slaves Made* [1974]). In 1969, when he wrote the essay reprinted here, Genovese was teaching in Montreal, Canada at Sir George Williams University. Genovese acknowledges the legitimacy of students' demands for black studies departments.

However, he is critical of a college or university's bowing to the demands of a group of students when those demands run counter to the essential values of the institution. For Genovese, an institution's agreeing to programs that have a narrow political perspective or exclude white faculty or students reflects the institution's underlying racism just as much as its refusal to change at all to accommodate students' desires. He offers a third option: that universities have "a principled but flexible response to legitimate black demands." Furthermore, Genovese suggests that accepting the demands of a small group of black students as indicative of "one black voice" represents racist essentialism (the idea that key traits are innate or universal rather than socially constructed). It also obscures the powerful role of debate in African American history.

From *The Atlantic Monthly,* June 1969, pp. 37–41.

No problem so agitates the campuses today as that posed by the growing pressure for black studies programs and departments. The agitation presents special dangers since it can be, and sometimes is, opportunistically manipulated by the nihilist factions of the radical white student movement. For the most part, black students have shown considerable restraint in dealing with dubious white allies and have given strong indication of being much more interested in reforming the universities than in burning them down. The black student movement, like some parts of the white radical student movement and very much unlike others, represents an authentic effort by young people to take a leading role in the liberation of an oppressed people and, as such, exhibits impressive seriousness and developing sophistication. The political forms that the agitation takes and the deep frustrations from which it stems nonetheless open the way to reckless elements among black, as well as white, student militants.

The universities must now choose among three courses: a principled but flexible response to legitimate black demands; a dogmatic, repressive adherence to traditional, liberal, and essentially racist policies; and a cowardly surrender to all black demands, no matter how destructive to the university as an institution of higher learning or to American and Afro-American society in general. This last option, which has been taken in a notable number of places, ironically reflects as much racism in its assumptions and implications as the second, and it takes little skill in prophecy to realize that its conclusion will be a bloodbath in which blacks are once again the chief victims. Yet, the debate over black studies proceeds without attention to the major features of the alternatives; it proceeds, in fact, in a manner that suggests the very paternalistic white racism against which so many blacks are today protesting.

The demand for black studies and for special black studies departments needs no elaborate explanation or defense. It rests on an awareness of the unique and dual nature of the black experience in the United States. Unlike European immigrants, blacks came here involuntarily, were enslaved and excluded from access to the mainstream of American life, and as a result have had a special history with a profoundly national-cultural dimension. Unlike, say, Italo-Americans, Afro-Americans have within their history the elements of a distinct nationality at the same time that they have participated in and contributed immensely to a common American nationality. Despite the efforts of many black and some white scholars, this paradoxical experience has yet to be explored with the respect and intellectual rigor it deserves.

This essential justification for black studies, incidentally, raises serious questions about the demands by white radicals for "ethnic studies" and for special attention to people from the "third world," especially since the term "third world" is, from a Marxist and revolutionary point of view, a reactionary swindle. These demands, when sincere, have their origin in a proper

concern for the fate of Mexican-Americans, Puerto Ricans, Asians, and other ethnic groups in a white-racist culture, but the study of the attendant problems does not, at least on the face of it, require anything like an approach similar to that of black studies. For the most part, the discrimination against these groups is largely a class question, requiring sober analysis of class structure in America; for the rest, much of the racism directed against these minorities can be traced directly to the by-products of the enslavement of blacks by whites and the ideology derived therefrom. In any case, the issues are clearly different, for the black question is simultaneously one of class and nationality (not merely minority ethnic status), and it is therefore a disservice to the cause of black liberation to construct a politically opportunist equation that can only blur the unique and central quality of the black experience in the United States.

The duality of the black experience haunts the present debate and leads us immediately into a consideration of the ideological and political features of the black studies programs. It is, at best, irrelevant to argue, as DeVere E. Pentony does in the April, 1969, issue of the *Atlantic,* that all professors of history and social science bring a particular ideology and politics to their classroom and that a black ideological bias is no worse than any other. There is no such thing as a black ideology or a black point of view. Rather there are various black-nationalist biases, from left-wing versions such as that of the Panthers to right-wing versions such as that of Ron Karenga[1] and other "cultural nationalists." There are also authentic sections of the black community that retain conservative, liberal, or radical integrationist and antinationalist positions. Both integrationist and separatist tendencies can be militant or moderate, radical or conservative (in the sense generally applied to white politics in relation to social questions). The separatists are riding high today, and the integrationists are beating a retreat; but this has happened before and may be reversed tomorrow.

All these elements have a right to participate in the exploration of black historical and cultural themes. In one sense, the whole point of black studies programs

1. Activist, author, and professor (b. 1941); changed his name from Ronald McKinley Everett to Maulana Karenga; active in the Black Panthers and founded the black nationalist US Organization; created Kwanzaa in 1966.

in a liberal arts college or university ought to be to provide for the widest and most vigorous exchange among all these groups in an atmosphere of free discussion and mutual toleration. The demand for an exclusively black faculty and especially the reactionary demand for student control of autonomous departments must be understood as demands for the introduction of specific ideological and political criteria into the selection of faculty and the composition of programs. Far from being proposals to relate these programs to the black community, they are in fact factionally based proposals to relate them to one or another political tendency within the black community and to exclude others. The bloody, but by no means isolated, feud between black student factions on the UCLA campus[2] ought to make that clear.

One of the new hallmarks of white racism is the notion of one black voice, one black experience, one black political community, one black ideology—of a black community without an authentic inner political life racked by discussion and ideological struggle. In plain truth, what appears on the campuses as "what the blacks want" is almost invariably what the dominant faction in a particular black caucus wants. Like all people who fight for liberation, blacks are learning the value of organizational discipline and subordination to a firm and united line of action. Sometimes, the formulation of particular demands and actions has much less to do with their intrinsic merits or with the institution under fire than with the momentary balance in the struggle for power within the caucus itself. This discipline presents nothing unprincipled or sinister, but it does present difficult and painful problems, which must be evaluated independently by those charged with institutional and political responsibility in the white community.

The pseudo-revolutionary middle-class totalitarians who constitute one temporarily powerful wing of the left-wing student movement understand this dimension, even if few others seem to. Accordingly, they support demands for student control as an entering wedge for a general political purge of faculties, a purge they naïvely hope to dominate. These suburban putschists[3] are most unlikely to succeed in their stated objectives of purging "reactionaries," for they are isolated, incoherent, and without adequate power. But they may very well help to reestablish the principle of the campus purge and thereby provide a moral and legal basis for a new wave of McCarthyism. The disgraceful treatment of Professors Staughton Lynd and Jesse Lemisch,[4] among many who have been recently purged from universities by both liberal and right-wing pressure, has already set a tone of renewed repression, which some fanatical and unreasoning left-wing militants are unwittingly reinforcing. If black studies departments are permitted to become political bases and cadre-training schools for one or another political movement, the door will be open for the conversion of other departments to similar roles; that door is already being forced in some places.

Those blacks who speak in harsh nationalist accents in favor of all-black faculties, departmental autonomy, and student power open themselves to grave suspicions of bad faith. The most obvious objection, raised sharply by several outstanding black educators in the South, concerns the systematic raiding of black colleges by financially stronger white ones. The shortage of competent black specialists in black history, social science, and black culture is a matter of general knowledge and concern. Hence, the successful application of the all-black principle in most universities would spell the end of hopes to build one or more distinguished black universities to serve as a center for the training of a national Afro-American intelligentsia. One need not be partial to black nationalism in any of its varieties to respect the right of black people to self-determination, for this right flows directly from the

2. In 1969, a disagreement between members of the Black Panthers and the US Organization over who should run the new UCLA Afro-American Studies Center escalated until two members of the Black Panthers were shot and killed.
3. People behind a sudden uprising or political revolt [German].
4. White history professor of the New Left (b. 1936), known for writing history "from the bottom up"; in 1968, while he was an activist with Students for a Democratic Society, he was fired as an assistant professor from the University of Chicago's history department; Lynd (p. 538): white civil rights and peace activist [b. 1929]; his teaching position in Yale University's history department ended after a 1966 trip to Hanoi as part of his activism against the Vietnam War.

duality of their unique experience in the United States. Even those who dislike or distrust black nationalism as such should be able to view the development of such centers of higher education as positive and healthy. If there is no place in the general American university for ideological homogeneity and conformity, there is a place in American society for universities based on adherence to a specific ideology, as the Catholic universities, for example, have demonstrated.

Responsible black scholars have been working hard for an end to raiding and to the scattering of the small number of black professors across the country. Among other obstacles, they face the effort of ostensibly nationalist black students who seek to justify their decision to attend predominantly white institutions, often of high prestige, by fighting for a larger black teaching staff. The outcome of these demands is the obscurantist nonsense that black studies can and should be taught by people without intellectual credentials since these credentials are "white" anyway. It is true that many black men are capable of teaching important college-level courses even though they do not have formal credentials. For example, the Afro-American tradition in music, embracing slave songs, spirituals, blues, jazz, and other forms, could probably be taught best by a considerable number of articulate and cultured, if sometimes self-taught, black musicians and free-lance critics who are largely unknown to the white community. But few good universities have ever refused to waive formalities in any field when genuine intellectual credentials of a nonacademic order could be provided. What has to be resisted firmly is the insanity that claims, as in one recent instance, that experience as a SNCC field organizer should be considered more important than a Ph.D. in the hiring of a professor of Afro-American history. This assertion represents a general contempt for all learning and a particular contempt for black studies as a field of study requiring disciplined, serious intellectual effort—an attitude that reflects the influence of white racism, even when brought forth by a black man.

The demand for all-black faculties rests on the insistence that only blacks can understand the black experience. This cant is nothing new: it forms the latest version of the battle cry of every reactionary nationalism and has clear antecedents, for example, in the nineteenth-century German Romantic movement. To be perfectly blunt, it now constitutes an ideologically fascist position and must be understood as such. The general reply to it—if one is necessary—is simply that the history of every people can only be written from within and without. But there is a specific reply too. However much the black presence has produced a unique and distinctly national Afro-American experience, it has also formed part of a broader, integrated national culture. It would be absurd to try to understand the history of, say, the South without carefully studying black history. Any Southern historian worth his salt must also be a historian of black America—and vice versa—and if so, it would be criminal to deny him an opportunity to teach his proper subject. Certainly, these remarks do not add up to an objection to a preference for black departmental directors and a numerical predominance of blacks on the faculty, if possible, for every people must write its own history and play the main role in the formation of its own intelligentsia and national culture. These measures would be justified simply on grounds of the need to establish relations of confidence with black students, for they involve no sacrifice of principle and do not compromise the integrity of the university. But preference and emphasis are one thing; monopoly and ideological exclusion are quite another.

We might mention here the problem of the alleged "psychological need" of black people to do this or that or to be this or that in order to reclaim their manhood, reestablish their ostensibly lost dignity, and God knows what else. There is a place for these questions in certain kinds of intellectual discussions and in certain political forums, but there is no place for these questions in the formation of university policy. In such a context they represent a benevolent paternalism that is neither more nor less than racist. Whites in general and university professors and administrators in particular are not required to show "sympathy," "compassion," "understanding," and other manifestations of liberal guilt feelings; they are required to take black demands seriously—to take them straight, on their merits. That is, they are required to treat political demands politically and to meet their responsibility to fight white racism while also meeting their responsibility to defend the integrity and dignity of the university community as a whole.

The Civil Rights Movement and Black Feminism (1954–1979)

Only if the universities have a clear attitude toward themselves will they be able to fulfill their duty to the black community. Our universities, if they are to survive—and their survival is problematical—must redefine themselves as institutions of higher learning and firmly reject the role of cadre-training schools for government, business, or community organizations of any kind. Blame for the present crisis ought to be placed on those who, especially after World War II, opened the universities to the military, to big-business recruitment, to the "fight against Communism," to the CIA, and to numerous other rightist pressures. If Dow Chemical or ROTC belongs on a college campus, so does the Communist Party, the Black Panthers, the John Birch Society, the Campfire Girls, or the Mafia for that matter. Students have a clear political right to organize on campuses as Democrats, Republicans, Communists, Panthers, or whatever, provided their activities are appropriate to campus life, but the universities have no business making special institutional arrangements with this or that faction off campus and then putting down other factions as illicit. And government and business represent political intrusions quite as much as do political parties. The same is true for the anachronistic and absurd practice of having American universities controlled by boards of trustees instead of by their faculties in consultation with the students. In short, the black studies question, like the black revolt as a whole, has raised all the fundamental problems of class power in American life, and the solutions will have to run deep into the structure of the institutions themselves.

What the universities owe to black America is what they owe to white America: an atmosphere of freedom and dissent for the pursuit of higher learning. Black people have largely been excluded in the past, for the atmosphere has been racist, the history and culture of black people have been ignored or caricatured, and access to the universities themselves has been severely circumscribed. Black studies programs, shaped in a manner consistent with such traditional university values as ideological freedom and diversity, can help to correct this injustice. So can scholarships and financial assistance to black students and special facilities for those blacks who wish to live and work with some degree of ethnic homogeneity. But no university is required to surrender its basic standards of competence in the selection of faculty or the admission of students. If not enough black students are equipped to enter college today, it is because of atrocious conditions in lower education. The universities can take a few steps to correct this injustice, but the real fight must take place elsewhere in society and must be aimed at providing black communities with the financial resources, independence, and autonomy necessary to educate their people properly from the earliest appropriate ages. There are limits to what a particular institution like a university can do, and it dare not try to solve problems that can be solved only by the political institutions of society as a whole. And above all, no university need surrender its historical role and essential content in order to right the wrongs of the whole political and social system; it need only reform itself to contribute to a solution of the broader problems in a manner consistent with its character as a place of higher learning with limited functions, possibilities, and responsibilities.

Black studies programs have two legitimate tasks. First, they can, by their very nature, provide a setting within which black people can forge an intelligentsia equipped to provide leadership on various levels of political and cultural action. Black studies programs themselves can do only part of this job. For that reason many able and sophisticated sections of the Black Student Alliance organizations wisely call on their brothers and sisters to participate in these programs but also to specialize in medicine, engineering, sociology, economic analysis, or in fact any scientific or humanistic field. They know that only the emergence of a fully developed intelligentsia, with training in every field of knowledge, can ultimately meet the deepest needs of the black community. In this respect, notwithstanding strong elements of nihilism in their own organizations, their seriousness, maturity, discipline, and realism stand in striking contrast to the childish anti-intellectualism of those bourgeois whites who currently claim to speak for the radical student movement and who impose upon it their own version of generational revolt.

Second, black studies can help immeasurably to combat the racism of white students. The exclusion of whites from the faculty and student body of the black studies programs would therefore defeat half the purpose of the programs themselves. Undoubtedly, there are problems. To the extent that black students view these courses as places of refuge where they can rap with their brothers, they are certain to resent the white presence, not to mention a possible white numerical predominance among the student body. Black students who want an exclusively black setting are entitled to it—in a black university. They are not entitled to tear any institution apart to suit their present mood. The universities owe black people a chance to get a liberal or technical education, but that debt can only be paid in a way consistent with the proper role of the university in society. Beyond that, no university may safely go. If it tries, the result can only be the end of any worthwhile higher education. The inability of so many radical whites to grasp this obvious point is especially galling. It ought to be obvious that the elite schools will protect themselves from this kind of degradation, even if they continue to accept the degradation that accompanies complicity with the war machine and with big business. It is the others—the ones serving the working-class and lower-middle-class youth—that will perish or be transformed into extensions of low-grade high schools. Uni-

versities must resist the onslaught now being made against them by superficially radical bourgeois students who have exploited the struggles over black studies programs to advance their own tactical objectives. Fortunately, these elements do not speak for the radical student movement as a whole but represent only a tendency within it; the internal diversity of organizations like SDS,[5] for example, far exceeds the level revealed in the press.

No matter how painful some of the battles are or will become, the advent of black studies programs represents a momentous step toward the establishment of relations of equality between white and black intellectuals. But, if these programs are to realize their potential in support of black liberation and in the fostering of genuinely free and critical scholarship, our universities must resolve honestly the questions of limits and legitimacy. Those who blindly ignore or cynically manipulate these questions, and the reforms they imply, corrupt the meaning of black studies and risk the destruction of institutions necessary to the preservation of freedom in American life.

JUNE JORDAN
Black Studies: Bringing Back the Person [1969]

Whereas Eugene Genovese's "Black Studies: Trouble Ahead" (p. 586) expresses a fundamental belief that universities are committed to upholding moral principles, June Jordan's "Black Studies: Bringing Back the Person" conveys a basic distrust of universities as institutions that perpetuate a discriminatory status quo. Jordan (1936–2002), a writer, editor, educator, and activist, questions cherished university precepts such as "reasonable discourse" (as she demonstrates her own academic expertise with literary and historical examples). She sees education as traditionally inhibiting the development of black cultural values. Nevertheless, she views university education as a critical route to power for black people.

Furthermore, Genovese considers segregated programs out of place in integrated institutions while Jordan sees self-segregation in universities as a way for students to discover their own identity. In her support of black studies taught by black teachers, Jordan emerges as a pioneer of embodied scholarship, which recognizes connections between the mind and body. In her discussion, Jordan invokes the idea of a common black community, signaled by her repeated use of the word *we*. Ultimately, she suggests that adding black studies to university curricula could be the beginning of a reform movement that fundamentally transforms the university.

From *Evergreen Review*, October 1969, pp. 39–41, 71–72.

5. Students for a Democratic Society, national activist group that lasted through the 1960s.

All my life I had been looking for something, and everywhere I turned someone tried to tell me what it was. I accepted their answers too, though they were often in contradiction and even self-contradictory. I was naïve. I was looking for myself and asking everyone except myself questions which I, and only I, could answer.

Ralph Ellison, *Invisible Man*[1]

Body and soul, Black America reveals the extreme questions of contemporary life, questions of freedom and identity: *How can I be who I am?*

* * *

We lead the world stubbornly down the road to Damascus[2] knowing, as we do, that this time we must name our god. This time, gods will grow from the graveyard and the groin of our experience. There will be no skyborne imagery, no holy labels slapped around our wrists. Now we arise, alert, determining, and new among ourselves. I am no longer alone. We move into community of moment. We will choose. But not as we were chosen, weighed and measured, pinched, bent backwards, under heel; not as we were named: by forced dispersal of the seed, by burial of history, by crippling individuality that led the rulers into crimes of dollar blood.

We, we know the individuality that isolates the man from other men, the either/or, the lonely-one that leads the flesh to clothing, jewelry, and land, the solitude of sight that separates the people from the people, flesh from flesh, that jams material between the spirit and the spirit. We have suffered witness to these pitiful, and murdering, masquerade extensions of the self.

Instead, we choose a real, a living enlargement of our only life. We choose community: Black America, in white. Here we began like objects chosen by the blind. And it is here that we see fit to continue—as subjects of human community. We will to bring back the person, alive and sacrosanct; we mean to rescue the person from the amorality of time and science.

History prepares the poor, the victims of unnecessary injustice, to spit at tradition, to blow up the lab-oratories, to despise all knowledge recklessly loosened from the celebration of all human life.

And still, it lies there, the university campus, frequently green, and signifying power: power to the people who feed their egos on the grass, inside the gates.

Black American history prepares black students to seize possibilities of power even while they tremble about purpose. *Efficiency, competence:* black students know the deadly, neutral definition of these words. There seldom has been a more efficient system for profiteering, through human debasement, than the plantations of a while ago. Today, the whole world sits, as quietly scared as it can sit, afraid that tomorrow America may direct its efficiency and competence toward another forest for defoliation, or clean-cut laser-beam extermination.

Black American history prepares black people to believe that true history is hidden and destroyed, or that history results from a logical bundling of lies that mutilate and kill. We have been prepared, by our American experience, to believe that civilization festers between opposite poles of plunder and pain. And still the university waits, unavoidable at the end of compulsory education, to assure the undisturbed perpetuity of this civilization.

We have learned to suspect and to beware the culture belied by phrases such as "the two-car family," or "job security," or "the Department of Defense," or "law and order."

We do not deride the fears of prospering white America. A nation of violence and private property has every reason to dread the violated and the deprived. Its history drives the violated into violence, and one of these days violence will literally signal the end of violence as a means. We are among those who have been violated into violence.

Black American experience staggers away from the resurrecting lord of love. In his place, we must examine the life, through death, of Bigger Thomas.[3] We know he was not paranoid. Crazy, yes. Paranoid, no. We know how his sanity died, and who his well-

---

1. Groundbreaking novel published in 1952; the only novel Ellison (p. 430) published during his lifetime.
2. In Acts:9, Saul (who became Saint Paul) is on his way to persecute Christians in Damascus when he has a sudden conversion experience.
3. Twenty-year old protagonist of the 1940 novel *Native Son* by Richard Wright (p. 471).

educated executioners were. And the black student of his life brims hatred for the hateful choice allowed to Bigger Thomas, hatred for an efficiency that cancels, equally, the humanity of the oppressed and the oppressor. Even so, we confront a continuing tyranny that means Bigger Thomas may yet symbolize the method of our liberation into human community.

How will the American university teach otherwise? One favorite university precept is that of reasonable discourse. We ask, when Bigger Thomas stood there, black-male-in-white-girl's-bedroom, what did reasonable discourse offer to him? Who would have listened to his explanation of himself next to the drunken white woman, on her bed?

In America, the traditional routes to black identity have hardly been normal. Suicide (disappearance by imitation, armed revolt), and exemplary moral courage: none of these is normal.

And, if we consider humankind, if we consider the origins of human society, we realize that in America the traditional routes to white identity have not been normal, either. Identity of person has been pursued through the acquisition of material clues admittedly irrelevant to the achievement of happiness. Identity has been secured among watery objects ceaselessly changing value. Worse, the marketplace has vanquished the workable concept of homeground or, as children say in their games: home-safe.

But Black America has striven toward human community even within the original situation that opposed its development, the situation of slavery. Often enough, at the expense of conceivably better working circumstances, those enslaved pleaded not to be sold away from the extended family they had so desperately scraped together, inside the slave quarters of a particular plantation. The intensity of black desiring may be measured when one remembers that legal marriage was forbidden for slaves. Yet the records are bursting with accounts demonstrating human fealty—as when the freedman saved his earnings over seven or eight years in order to purchase the freedom of his "wife."

Prospering white America perverted, and perverts, the fundamental solace and nurture of community even to the point of derogating the extended family discoverable among America's white and black impoverished; as any college graduate can tell you, the extended family is "compensation for failure." According to these norms, success happens when the man and his immediate family may competently provide for greater and greater privacy, i.e., greater and greater isolation from others, independence from others, capability to delimit and egotistically control the compass of social experience. Faced with the humanly universal dilemma of individual limit, prospering white America has turned away from the normal plunging into expanded family and commitment. Instead, the pursuit of exclusive power—the power to exclude and to manipulate—plus the pursuit of insulating layers of material shell, have preempted the pursuit of community and ridiculed happiness as an invalid, asinine goal.

Blocked by white America, in its questing for community, as the appropriate arena for the appearance and shaping of person, Black America has likewise been blocked, in its wayward efforts to emulate the inhumanity of white compensation. Thus, the traditional routes of suicide, violence and exemplary moral courage have emerged. They have emerged despite the spectacular absence of literature and history to document and support black life. Or perhaps, precisely because the usual tools a people employ in the determining of identity were strictly prohibited, these alternative, bizarre, and heroic methods devolved.

But community does not form by marriage between martyr and a movie star. The hero is one, and we remain the many. We have begun like objects belonging to the blind. We have spent our generations in a scream that wasted in the golden ear. Giant, demon, clown, angel, bastard, bitch, and, nevertheless, a family longing, we have made it to the gates: our hearts hungry on the rocks around the countryside, our hopes the same: our hopes, unsatisfied. Now we have the choice, and we must make that choice our own. We are at the gates.

Who are we?

There has been no choosing until now. Until the university, there is no choice. Education is compulsory. Education has paralleled the history of our black lives; it has been characterized by the punishment of nonconformity, abridgement, withered enthusiasm, distortion, and self-denying censorship. Education has paralleled the life of prospering white America; it has been characterized by reverence for efficiency, cultivation of competence unattended by concern for aim, big white lies, and the mainly successful blackout of black life.

Black students arrive at the university from somewhere. Where is that, exactly? Where is Black America, all of it, from the beginning? Why do we ask? How does it happen that we do not know?

What is the university until we arrive? Is it where the teachers of children receive their training? It is where the powerful become more powerful. It is where the norms of this abnormal power, this America, receive the ultimate worship of propagation. It is where the people become usable parts of the whole machine. Machine is not community.

Is the university where the person learns how to become a valuable member of society? Even so, it is not, the university is not, where the person learns how he is always a valuable member of an always valuable society of people. (It probably takes a college graduate to explain the "higher learning" that does not teach the unearned sanctity and value of each person.)

Yet it waits there, at the end of coercion, the citadel of technique and terminology. At the gates, a temporary freedom plays between the student and the school. Choice confronts both sides. It seems. But like the others who have been violated, whose joy has been bled and viciously assaulted even unto birth, the black student can choose to refuse the university only at incredible cost. He needs power if he will spring free from dependency upon those who exploit, isolate, and finally destroy. If he will liberate "homebase" he must, for a time, separate himself from the identity of the powerless. No. He must learn to assume the identity of the powerless, in a powerful way. No. He must understand homebase. But where is that? Who is he, this student the university chooses to accept? Does the university have any idea?

Fortified by the freaks, the heroes, the saints, the rebels in exile, black students reject the necessity of miracle, where identity is concerned. Every saint and every rebel of Black America reinforces the determination of the majority to achieve a normal, ordinary access to person. The majority knows it is, by definition, incapable of the miraculous. And yet it admires the consequences of black miracle in white America: All of us hunt identity.

And so, the black student enters the gates. Choice of entry is delusional. He must go inside, or perish through dependency. But he rejects the university as it panders to his potential for neither/nor anonymity, or for dysfunctional amnesia. He enters the university and, snatching at the shred reality of freedom-at-last, or first choice, he chooses his family.

The black student clutches at family precisely at that moment when he enters the ultimate glorification of a society that has rejected him. Why is anyone amazed?

Before this moment, family has been merely given, or else taken away. Finally freed from the obedience, the slavery of childhood, black students choose a family for the first time: "When I was a child, I spoke like a child, I thought like a child, I reasoned like a child; when I became a man, I gave up childish ways. For now we see in a mirror dimly, but then face to face. Now I know in part; then I shall understand fully, even as I have been fully understood."[4]

From our knees, we have fought tall enough to look into the question of the mirror. More than any other people, we cannot afford to forget the mirror is a questioning. And *face to face* we eat together in the dining rooms, we dorm together, sleep together, talk together, love ourselves, together, face to face; the family mirror clears to person in that chosen clarity. We, Black America, on the prospering white American university campus, we come together as students, black students. How shall we humanly compose the knowledge that troubles the mind into ideas of life? How can we be who we are?

Black studies. The engineer, the chemist, the teacher, the lawyer, the architect, if he is black, cannot honorably engage in a career except as black engineer, black architect. *Of course, he must master the competence:* the perspectives of physics, chemistry, economics, and so forth. But he cannot honorably, or realistically, forsake the origins of his possible person. Or she cannot. Nor can he escape the tyranny of ignorance except as he displaces ignorance with study: study of the impersonal, the amorality of the sciences *anchored by black studies.* The urgency of his heart, his breath, demands the knowing of the truth about himself: the truth of black experience. And so, black students, looking for the

---

4. 1 Corinthians 13: 11–12.

truth, demand teachers least likely to lie, least likely to perpetuate the traditions of lying—lies that deface the father from the memory of the child. We request black teachers of black studies.

It is not that we believe only black people can understand the black experience. It is rather that we acknowledge the difference between criticism and reality as the difference between the Host and the Parasite.

As Fanon[5] has written, the colonized man does not say he knows the truth, he *is* the truth. Likewise, we do not say we know the truth: we are the truth; we are the living black experience and, therefore, We are the primary sources of information.

For us, there is nothing optional about "black experience" and/or "black studies": we must know ourselves. But theories and assertions do not satisfy anymore. Studies are called for. And, regardless how or where these studies lead, the current facts support every effort to create study alliances among nonwhite or nonprospering white Americans who, all of us, endure as victims of materialism versus our lives.

We look for community. We have already suffered the alternatives to community, to human commitment. We have borne the whiplash of "white studies" unmitigated by the stranger ingredient of humane dedication. Therefore, we cannot, in sanity, pass by the potentiality of black studies: studies of the person consecrated to the preservation of that person.

On the contrary, "white studies" should do likewise: At this date when humankind enjoys wild facility to annihilate, no human study can sanely ignore the emergency requirements for efficient, yes, competent affirmation of the values of life, and that most precious burden of identity that depends, beggarly, on love.

The university may choose among a thousand different responses to black demands, but if the decision bespeaks the traditional process of majority overrule, white choice will sputter to no effect. Like the rest of America that is no longer willing to endure hostile control, Black America will not accept any choice affecting their lives unless they control even the terms under consideration. And if it is true that black rejection of majority overrule will lead to a white-predicted

"bloodbath," it is also true that he who makes such a prophecy will bear responsibility for its fulfillment.

Poverty is a bloodbath. Exploitation of human life for material gain is unforgivable-letting-bloodflow for the sake of other currencies. Perforce, the natural element of black children has been the American bloodbath. We know American violence, power, and success. Is the university prepared to teach us something new?

Black studies. White studies: revised. What is the curriculum, what are the standards that only human life threatens to defile and "lower"? Is the curriculum kin to that monstrous metaphor of justice seated, under blindfold, in an attitude and substance of absolute stone? Life appealing to live, and to be, and to know a community that will protect the living simply because we are alive: this is the menace to university curriculum and standards. This is the possibility of survival we must all embrace: the possibility of life, as has been said, by whatever means necessary.

In New York City, the metaphor of Harlem contains the symbol, and the fact, of City College.[6] On that campus, the most recent miracle of Black America has become a manifest reality. There, black and Puerto Rican students have joined to issue what they describe as "the fourth demand." This demand exceeds the scope of lately typical negotiation between school and student. It speaks to community. It reads: "The racial composition of the entering class to reflect the Black and Puerto Rican Population of the New York City Schools."

Obviously, the fourth demand reaches outside the university province and into high school habits of student tragedy. In the predominantly black and Puerto Rican high school nearest City College, the academic diploma rate steadies at 1.2 percent. Since black and Puerto Rican students constitute the majority of public students, and since the majority of them receive no academic diploma, how can the City College reflect their majority status? Either the high schools or the college will have to change almost beyond current planning imagination. To meet the fourth demand, New York City lower schools will have to decide that a 65 per cent dropout rate for students, of any color, is

---

5. Frantz Fanon (1925–61), psychiatrist and philosopher from Martinique; pioneer in the field of postcolonial studies.
6. City College of New York (CUNY) campus in Harlem near 134th Street and Amsterdam Avenue.

intolerable, and that a 1.2 per cent academic diploma rate, at any high school, cannot continue.

In fact, how will City College continue unless it may admit the children of the city? Will the City College of New York resort to importation of students from Iowa and Maine? The children of the city are black and Puerto Rican; they are the children of suffering and impotence; they are the children coerced into lower grade education that alienates upward of 65 per cent of them so that the majority of this majority disappears into varieties of ruin.

If the university will not teach, will not instruct the lower schools by its example, how will they learn? If the university is not the ultimate teaching institution, the ultimate, the most powerful institution to decree the hope of education, *per se*, what is it?

And yet, City College cries "curriculum" and worries about "standards" even while the future of its conceivable justification, the students of the city schools, disappear except for self-destructive trace.

Black and Puerto Rican students at City College, nevertheless, insist upon the fourth demand; they insist upon community. Serving the positive implications of black studies (*life* studies), students everywhere must insist on new college admission policies that will guide and accelerate necessary, radical change, at all levels of education. Universities must admit the inequities of the civilization they boast. These inequities mean that the children of Other America have been vanquished by the consequences of compulsory, hostile instruction and inescapable, destructive experience.

It is appropriate that the university should literally adopt these living consequences as its own humane privilege, for service. Such embrace waits upon the demonstration of majority conscience. Black America waits upon the demonstration of a conscience that will seek justice with utmost, even ruthless, efficiency.

Yet we do not only wait. Black America moves, headstrong, down toward Damascus. Everybody on the ladder, hanging on identity opposed to the hatred of life. And if we do not name the gods according to the worship of our lives, then what will we worship, in deed?

DARWIN T. TURNER
The Teaching of Afro-American Literature [1970]

In this 1970 essay, the professor and literary critic Darwin Turner (1931–1991) develops the case for creating courses in black studies and revising courses in other disciplines to incorporate material by and about African Americans. He discusses how predominantly white universities have treated African American studies differently from other disciplines, a reference to the history of special treatment that would later be cited by Vince Nobile and others as the root of the student distrust that emerged in the 1990s (see p. 887).

In an argument similar to Eugene Genovese's in "Black Studies: Trouble Ahead" (p. 586), Turner stresses the importance of academic rigor and the positive effects that black studies may have on white students. Like June Jordan in "Bringing Back the Person" (p. 591), Turner examines the university's historical role in perpetuating racism and the power of knowledge to combat racist myths. After discussing curriculum and both Eurocentric and Afrocentric perspectives, Turner closes by examining whether white professors can teach African American studies, a question that continued to be contentious for decades, even after African American studies had become an established part of university curricula.

From *College English* 31, no. 7 (April 1970), pp. 666–70.

Although Afro-Americans have been writing literature in English since 1746 and publishing books in English since 1773,[1] literature by Afro-Americans has become significantly visible in colleges only within the past several years. As late as 1967 most of the relevant materials were out of print, including the only anthology adequate for a course in Afro-American literature; few, if any, non-black colleges offered courses in Afro-American literature or even studied Afro-American writers, except possibly Richard Wright, James Baldwin, and Ralph Ellison[2]; and scholarly societies and publishers seemed disinterested in studies about black writers. Today, three major anthologies of Afro-American literature are already in print, and two more are on the way; at least six publishers—Arno, Atheneum, Negro Universities Press, Mnemosyne Press, the U of Michigan and Collier are frantically reprinting books by and about black writers; courses are burgeoning in predominantly white universities, even in Alabama and Mississippi; and almost any meeting of a professional society in literature will include at least one paper related to Afro-American writers. In truth, the frenzy of attention has elevated Afro-American literature (and Afro-American studies) to a pinnacle recently occupied by atomic physics and new mathematics: It is the exciting new concern of the educational world.

I do not propose to discuss here the nature and scope of Afro-American literature itself. Instead, I wish to consider two controversial issues: 1) the place of Afro-American literature in the curriculum, and 2) criteria for teachers and scholars of Afro-American literature.

I will not spend a lot of time endorsing the academic value of Afro-American literature. Already too much time and breath have been wasted on this issue. Those of us who have sat in meetings of curriculum committees know how seldom the members question the academic value of a proposed course. The committee's most frequent worry is, "How much will it cost?" We also know that some institutions entice a professor to them by guaranteeing that he can "work up" any course he wishes to teach—even one narrowly restricted to a study of Washington Irving, Edgar Allan Poe, and James Fenimore Cooper.[3] Few institutions of prestige question the intellectual content of such courses. (Probably they should; but most do not.)

In a discipline which thus continually reaffirms its assumption that any segment of literary heritage is intellectually valid for study in higher education, it is both absurd and hypocritical to raise the question of academic respectability about the study of the literature of an ethnic group composed of people who have been publishing literary works in America for more than 200 years, who have created some of the best-known folktales in America, and who include among their number such distinguished writers as Jean Toomer, Countee Cullen, Richard Wright, Gwendolyn Brooks, Ralph Ellison, James Baldwin, Lorraine Hansberry, and LeRoi Jones.[4] If anyone has doubts about the respectability of this literature, I urge him merely to read Frederick Douglass's *Narrative of a Slave* or Charles W. Chesnutt's *The Conjure Woman* or Jean Toomer's *Cane* or Robert Hayden's *Selected Poems* or Melvin Tolson's *Rendezvous with America* or *Harlem Gallery* or Margaret Walker's *Jubilee*.[5]

A more significant question to ask is whether these writers should be studied in a separate course or as part of the usual surveys and period courses in American literature. My answer is that they should be studied in both ways.

There is no difficulty about including Afro-American writers in any American literature survey based on aesthetic and thematic criteria. Phillis Wheatley is sometimes praised as the best American

1. Lucy Terry (c. 1730–1821) wrote "Bars Fight" in 1746, and *Poems on Various Subjects* by Phillis Wheatley (p. 12) was first published in London in 1773.
2. See p. 471, p. 485, p. 430.
3. Irving (1783–1859), Poe (1809–49), and Cooper (1789–1851) were early popular white American writers.
4. Toomer (1894–1967), Cullen (1903–46), Wright (see p. 471), Brooks (1917–2000), Ellison (see p. 430), Baldwin (see p. 485), Hansberry (1930–65), and Jones (a.k.a. Amiri Baraka, see p. 694).
5. *The Narrative of the Life of Frederick Douglass, an American Slave* was published in 1845 (see p. 38), *Cane* in 1923, *Selected Poems* by Hayden (1913–80) in 1966, *Rendezvous with America* in 1944 and *Harlem Gallery* in 1965, both by Tolson (1898–1966), and *Jubilee* in 1966 by Walker (1915–98).

neo-classical poet of the 18th century. David Walker's *Appeal* (1828) is as exciting a document as any by Tom Paine. The slave narratives offer interesting parallels with the autobiographies of early white Americans. Any course which wades through James Whitcomb Riley, Thomas Page, and other writers of American dialects can scrutinize Paul Laurence Dunbar. The folktales of Charles Chesnutt furnish intriguing counterpoint to the better known tales of Joel Chandler Harris. James Weldon Johnson's *Autobiography of an Ex-Coloured Man* (1912) compares favorably with the realistic novels of William Dean Howells. Claude McKay's *Home to Harlem* (1928) vividly depicts a segment of that jazzy, lost generation which found other biographers in Ernest Hemingway and Scott Fitzgerald. In spirit and style Countee Cullen frequently reminds readers of Edna St. Vincent Millay, and Jean Toomer is a logical inclusion in a discussion of the stylistic experiments of Sherwood Anderson and Gertrude Stein. Zora Neale Hurston's *Moses, Man of the Mountain* resembles and perhaps surpasses John Erskine's satires about Helen of Troy and Galahad.[6] And on and on and on. Certainly, if he wishes to, a knowledgeable teacher has no problem fitting Afro-American writers into an American literature survey; for stylistically, black writers often resemble white American authors more closely than they resemble their black contemporaries.

But, for a different reason, Afro-American authors should also be taught in a separate course—not a black "rap"[7] course for revolutionaries, not a watered-down "sop" designed to give three credits to the disadvantaged, but an academically sound course, which may be even more valuable for white students than for black. The reason for such a course is educational or—

if you wish—political. Before protesting that our concern is artistic literature not politics, let us remind ourselves that college teachers do teach those documents at the beginnings of most anthologies of American literature—the writings of John Smith and Cotton Mather, the Mayflower Compact, etc.[8] Let us remember also the courses in New England Writers and Southern Regional Writers. The documents provide a student with awareness of the intellectual and social history of America; the regional courses help him to understand the styles and attitudes of writers who represent a selected population in America. For similar reasons, courses in literature by Afro-American writers must be taught.

As we all know, in a two-term survey of American literature we cannot include all the writers who deserve to be taught: some worthy writers must be omitted. A concerned teacher consoles himself that a student's intellectual growth is not seriously impaired by lack of knowledge of the writers omitted; for, at some point between the first grade and the sixteenth, a student will probably read most of the writers omitted from the survey. Or if he does not read those specific writers, he reads others who offer comparable styles and attitudes: Bret Harte or Mark Twain rather than Riley, Stephen Crane or Edith Wharton rather than Howells, Ernest Hemingway or Edgar Lee Masters[9] rather than Gertrude Stein. Thus, a student learns that literary excellence can be discovered in all regions of America and in all periods of American history. If no writer is included who can be identified as Hungarian or Italian or Polish, neither the teacher nor the student is alarmed; for, in other courses, the student has already learned that intellectual and artistic masterpieces have been produced in all of the countries of Europe.

6. Writers in the African American tradition include Wheatley (see p. 12), Walker (see p. 27, his *Appeal* was first published in 1829), Dunbar (1872–1906), Chesnutt (1858–1932), Johnson (see p. 470), McKay (1889–1948), Hurston (see p. 259, *Moses, Man of the Mountain* was first published in 1939); writers in the white European tradition include Paine (1737–1809), Riley (1849–1916), Page (1853–1922), Harris (1845–1908), Howells (1837–1920), Hemingway (1899–1961), F. Scott Fitzgerald (1896–1940), Millay (1892–1950), Anderson (1876–1941), Stein (1874–1946), and Erskine (1879–1951).

7. Talk or conversation, often drawn from personal experiences.

8. First governing document of Plymouth Colony signed by English colonists in 1620; English explorer Smith (1580–1631) helped found Jamestown, Virginia, the first permanent English settlement in North America, and encouraged colonization in his writings; Mather (1663–1728), prolific white American Puritan writer who was a key figure in the Salem Witch Trials.

9. Other writers in the white European tradition include: Harte (1836–1902), Twain (né Samuel Clemens, 1835–1910), Crane (1871–1900), Wharton (1862–1937), and Masters (1868–1950).

One cannot, however, regard with such complacency the omission of Afro-American writers from the survey; for in sixteen years of schooling, a student will probably never read these writers in any other course except a course about Afro-American writers. As I have stated, the reason for concern is not merely an aesthetic issue of whether a student may miss an opportunity for pleasure or art that a black writer may provide. Even more important is the fact that the student lives in a society which, for more than three hundred years, has denigrated the intellectual and cultural capability of black Africans and their descendants. The student has been taught this doctrine of inferiority in books and lectures prepared by respectable professors, in newspapers and magazines, in motion pictures and theater, and even in the church and his home. The only way to repudiate this myth of inferiority is to amass as much evidence to the contrary as possible. But the evidence cannot rest upon two or three black writers since 1940 or 1950: Richard Wright, James Baldwin, and Ralph Ellison, for example. Too easily these few are adjudged the exceptions or are used to exemplify a second myth—that Afro-Americans have developed respectable culture only within the past twenty-five years. The requisite education must study *many* black writers from the eighteenth century to the present—not in a chauvinistic glorification of their effort but in a critical examination of their literary and intellectual merits in relation to the standards, customs, interest, and knowledge which characterized the periods during which they wrote.

A second controversial issue concerns the criteria for selecting a teacher. Conventionally, a teacher's competence to offer a course is determined from evidence of his study and publication in the area. But a serious question has been raised about the competence of a white teacher to teach literature by black writers. Few people of academic background deny that white teachers can learn to teach black literature, just as black teachers can teach white literature. And they realize that, if all colleges were to establish courses in Afro-American literature, the number of courses alone would necessitate the use of white teachers. Nevertheless, many black educators continue to worry that some white teachers will teach the course so badly that they will create more harm than good. Frequently, a black teacher who makes such a statement is accused of racist thinking. Perhaps the accusers are remembering with guilt the fact that, until recently, most white administrators and faculties made little effort to hire qualified black scholars to teach courses in English and American literature. But the black who objects to white teachers is not merely prejudiced; he sees weaknesses which the white teacher must overcome if he wishes to teach Afro-American literature well.

First, some white teachers will teach the course badly because, ignorant of the complexity of the subject matter, they will not take the time to prepare themselves adequately. In the English departments of most universities, a teacher is entrusted with the responsibility for an advanced course, such as one in American Romantics or Victorian Prose, only after years of preparation. In several years of college, he studies the works, critical commentaries about the works, the lives of the authors, and the historical culture in which the works were produced. He not only listens to lectures and reads assigned works; he even conducts independent research in the materials. After such preparation, he is finally permitted to teach a traditional course. In contrast, a teacher may be thrust into a course in Afro-American literature after formal preparation of a summer or even less.

Furthermore, the average white teacher is handicapped by the fact that he has not had the informal or extra-disciplinary experiences which might familiarize him with the material. Consider, in contrast, the manner in which the black teacher of American literature, let us say, is provided, outside the English classroom, with awareness of the materials about which white Americans are writing. He has been forced to read many, many books of history about white Americans; he cannot read a newspaper or magazine without reading factual as well as propagandistic articles about their attitudes, desires, virtues, vices, and living habits. He sees them advertised on the motion picture screen, on television, on billboards. In short, wherever he turns— even within the black community—he is learning about white Americans. The average *white* American, however, has probably known few black people intimately, has read few books by black writers, and until recently has read few presentations about black Americans (and those few have concentrated on the "problem" which the black man poses for America or for himself). Putting it simply, the average white teacher is ignorant about black people and does not even know where to turn for reliable information about such basic matters as the meanings of slang used by blacks, the traditional jokes, and the popular stereotypes of heroes and villains. This individual will teach Afro-American literature ineptly until he learns what he needs to know.

A second failing of the well-intentioned teacher is that, subconsciously, he may be a racist. That is, subconsciously, he may believe that black people actually are innately inferior or that historically they have been made inferior by society. This attitude may cause him to bungle the course in either of two different ways. One, believing that a black writer cannot produce literary work of a quality which would be required of a white writer, the teacher may praise trash because he does not expect anything better from a black writer. Such unconscious patronizing insults black writers. Or, two, a well-meaning humanitarian may become paternalistic. Believing himself securely established in American society and, therefore, superior in judgment to those who are not, he may condemn the philosophy of life which the black author proposes for himself. A teacher has the right to assert that any writer—black or white—has failed to clarify his ideas or has failed to develop them effectively, but only a pompous paternalist will insist that he is better qualified than the writer to determine what the writer should have thought about himself, his race, and his relation to other people. I wish that I were exaggerating these failings, but one sees them too frequently in articles currently published about Afro-American literature.

A third well-intentioned teacher who fails is the one who becomes excessively sentimental about the problems which black people experience in a white-oriented society. Such a teacher may wail about the problems in a frenzy which sickens black students who have learned that tears offer escape not solutions.

These three types of teachers—the unprepared, the subconscious racist, the sentimentalist—can be pitied for their failure. A fourth cannot be. He is the individual who views Afro-American literature as a vehicle for rapid promotion. He is the "instant expert," striving solely for grants and publications.

A final problem for the white teacher is not directly of his own making. Even if he *has* prepared conscientiously, black students may distrust him because their years of living in America have taught them to distrust white men's attitudes towards black culture. They will be looking for the teacher who makes the mistake, if he selects autobiography, of choosing *Manchild in the Promised Land* rather than *The Autobiography of Malcolm X*.[1] They will be waiting for the teacher who does not understand the slang of the black community. In short, they will be looking for the racist or the fool hidden behind a mask. And a lot of valuable course time can be lost while the teacher proves himself to his students.

The white teacher of Afro-American literature must recognize and anticipate these problems and potential failings. But do not let my castigation of white teachers promote false assumptions about the ability of blacks. A black or brown face is not in itself sufficient qualification for teaching Afro-American literature. True, a black man is generally more sensitive to the language, attitudes, and nuances of the black writer: he has the informal, extra-disciplinary knowledge of the subject matter of the writers. But he too must study sufficiently to know Afro-American literature in its historical development, and he must be competent to teach literature.

Literature by Afro-Americans is a new, exciting subject matter for curricula. It needs to be taught, but only by teachers—black or white—who do all the homework which is required.

---

1. 1965 nonfiction book written by Alex Haley (1921–92) based on conversations with Malcolm X in 1964 and 1965; *Manchild*: 1965 autobiography by Claude Brown (1937–2002) about growing up in Harlem in the 1940s and 1950s amid drug abuse and gang violence.

Key Debate ≈ *Religion*

Martin Luther King Jr.
Letter from Birmingham Jail [1963]

Martin Luther King's "Letter from Birmingham Jail" engages in two central debates of the era simultaneously. It is, first, a direct response to an open letter to the *Birmingham Post-Herald* from eight white Alabama clergymen who criticized the Birmingham civil rights demonstrations, calling them "unwise," "untimely," and "extreme." King (p. 559) not only rejects their assertions but also characterizes the nonviolent civil rights movement as a model of Christian action. At the same time, King uses this letter to suggest that the more important debate of the era is not one between white and black Americans but one between moderate groups (such as King's Southern Christian Leadership Conference) and radical groups (such as Elijah Muhammad's Nation of Islam). By privileging this second debate, between black political movements, King positions himself as an ally of the white clergymen and others who favor more moderate change over revolutionary change.

Originally published as "The Negro Is Your Brother" in *The Atlantic Monthly*, August 1963; Martin Luther King Jr., *Why We Can't Wait* (New York: Harper and Row, 1964), pp. 77–100.

April 16, 1963

My Dear Fellow Clergymen:[1]

While confined here in the Birmingham city jail, I came across your recent statement calling my present activities "unwise and untimely." Seldom do I pause to answer criticism of my work and ideas. If I sought to answer all the criticisms that cross my desk, my secretaries would have little time for anything other than such correspondence in the course of the day, and I would have no time for constructive work. But since I feel that you are men of genuine good will and that your criticisms are sincerely set forth, I want to try to answer your statement in what I hope will be patient and reasonable terms.

I think I should indicate why I am here in Birmingham, since you have been influenced by the view which argues against "outsiders coming in." I have the honor of serving as president of the Southern Christian Leadership Conference, an organization operating in every southern state, with headquarters in Atlanta, Georgia. We have some eighty-five affiliated organizations across the South, and one of them is the Alabama Christian Movement for Human Rights. Frequently we share staff, educational and financial resources with our affiliates. Several months ago the affiliate here in Birmingham asked us to be on call to engage in a nonviolent direct-action program if such were deemed necessary. We readily consented, and when the hour came we lived up to our promise. So I, along with several members of my staff, am here because I was invited here. I am here because I have organizational ties here.

But more basically, I am in Birmingham because injustice is here. Just as the prophets of the eighth

1. This response to a published statement by eight fellow clergymen from Alabama (Bishop C. C. J. Carpenter, Bishop Joseph A. Durick, Rabbi Hilton L. Grafman, Bishop Paul Hardin, Bishop Holan B. Harmon, the Reverend George M. Murray, the Reverend Edward V. Ramage and the Reverend Earl Stallings) was composed under somewhat constricting circumstances. Begun on the margins of the newspaper in which the statement appeared while I was in jail, the letter was continued on scraps of writing paper supplied by a friendly Negro trusty and concluded on a pad my attorneys were eventually permitted to leave me. Although the text remains in substance unaltered, I have indulged in the author's prerogative of polishing it for publication. [King's note] [Trusty: a prisoner regarded by guards as trustworthy and given special privileges.]

century B.C. left their villages and carried their "thus saith the Lord" far beyond the boundaries of their home towns, and just as the Apostle Paul left his village of Tarsus and carried the gospel of Jesus Christ to the far corners of the Greco-Roman world, so am I compelled to carry the gospel of freedom beyond my own home town. Like Paul, I must constantly respond to the Macedonian call for aid.[2]

Moreover, I am cognizant of the interrelatedness of all communities and states. I cannot sit idly by in Atlanta and not be concerned about what happens in Birmingham. Injustice anywhere is a threat to justice everywhere. We are caught in an inescapable network of mutuality, tied in a single garment of destiny. Whatever affects one directly, affects all indirectly. Never again can we afford to live with the narrow, provincial "outside agitator" idea. Anyone who lives inside the United States can never be considered an outsider anywhere within its bounds.

You deplore the demonstrations taking place in Birmingham. But your statement, I am sorry to say, fails to express a similar concern for the conditions that brought about the demonstrations. I am sure that none of you would want to rest content with the superficial kind of social analysis that deals merely with effects and does not grapple with underlying causes. It is unfortunate that demonstrations are taking place in Birmingham, but it is even more unfortunate that the city's white power structure left the Negro community with no alternative.

In any nonviolent campaign there are four basic steps: collection of the facts to determine whether injustices exist; negotiation; self-purification; and direct action. We have gone through all these steps in Birmingham. There can be no gainsaying the fact that racial injustice engulfs this community. Birmingham is probably the most thoroughly segregated city in the United States. Its ugly record of brutality is widely known. Negroes have experienced grossly unjust treatment in the courts. There have been more unsolved

bombings of Negro homes and churches in Birmingham than in any other city in the nation. These are the hard, brutal facts of the case. On the basis of these conditions, Negro leaders sought to negotiate with the city fathers. But the latter consistently refused to engage in good-faith negotiation.

Then, last September, came the opportunity to talk with leaders of Birmingham's economic community. In the course of the negotiations, certain promises were made by the merchants—for example, to remove the stores' humiliating racial signs. On the basis of these promises, the Reverend Fred Shuttlesworth[3] and the leaders of the Alabama Christian Movement for Human Rights agreed to a moratorium on all demonstrations. As the weeks and months went by, we realized that we were the victims of a broken promise. A few signs, briefly removed, returned; the others remained.

As in so many past experiences, our hopes had been blasted, and the shadow of deep disappointment settled upon us. We had no alternative except to prepare for direct action, whereby we would present our very bodies as a means of laying our case before the conscience of the local and the national community. Mindful of the difficulties involved, we decided to undertake a process of self-purification. We began a series of workshops on nonviolence, and we repeatedly asked ourselves: "Are you able to accept blows without retaliating?" "Are you able to endure the ordeal of jail?" We decided to schedule our direct-action program for the Easter season, realizing that except for Christmas, this is the main shopping period of the year. Knowing that a strong economic withdrawal program would be the by-product of direct action, we felt that this would be the best time to bring pressure to bear on the merchants for the needed change.

Then it occurred to us that Birmingham's mayoral election was coming up in March, and we speedily decided to postpone action until after election day. When we discovered that the Commissioner of Public

---

2. Acts: 16, 8–9: "And a vision appeared to Paul in the night; There stood a man of Macedonia, and prayed him, saying, Come over into Macedonia, and help us. / And after he had seen the vision, immediately we endeavoured to go into Macedonia, assuredly gathering that the Lord had called us for to preach the gospel unto them."
3. Minister and civil rights activist (b. 1922); one of the founders of the Southern Christian Leadership Conference, along with King, Ella Baker, Bayard Rustin, and others.

Safety, Eugene "Bull" Connor,[4] had piled up enough votes to be in the run-off, we decided again to postpone action until the day after the run-off so that the demonstrations could not be used to cloud the issues. Like many others, we waited to see Mr. Connor defeated, and to this end we endured postponement after postponement. Having aided in this community need, we felt that our direct-action program could be delayed no longer.

You may well ask: "Why direct action? Why sit-ins, marches and so forth? Isn't negotiation a better path?" You are quite right in calling for negotiation. Indeed, this is the very purpose of direct action. Non-violent direct action seeks to create such a crisis and foster such a tension that a community which has constantly refused to negotiate is forced to confront the issue. It seeks so to dramatize the issue that it can no longer be ignored. My citing the creation of tension as part of the work of the nonviolent-resister may sound rather shocking. But I must confess that I am not afraid of the word "tension." I have earnestly opposed violent tension, but there is a type of constructive, nonviolent tension which is necessary for growth. Just as Socrates[5] felt that it was necessary to create a tension in the mind so that individuals could rise from the bondage of myths and half-truths to the unfettered realm of creative analysis and objective appraisal, so must we see the need for nonviolent gadflies to create the kind of tension in society that will help men rise from the dark depths of prejudice and racism to the majestic heights of understanding and brotherhood.

The purpose of our direct-action program is to create a situation so crisis-packed that it will inevitably open the door to negotiation. I therefore concur with you in your call for negotiation. Too long has our beloved Southland been bogged down in a tragic effort to live in monologue rather than dialogue.

One of the basic points in your statement is that the action that I and my associates have taken in Birmingham is untimely. Some have asked: "Why didn't you give the new city administration time to act?" The only answer that I can give to this query is that the new Birmingham administration must be prodded about as much as the outgoing one, before it will act. We are sadly mistaken if we feel that the election of Albert Boutwell[6] as mayor will bring the millennium to Birmingham. While Mr. Boutwell is a much more gentle person than Mr. Connor, they are both segregationists, dedicated to maintenance of the status quo. I have hope that Mr. Boutwell will be reasonable enough to see the futility of massive resistance to desegregation. But he will not see this without pressure from devotees of civil rights. My friends, I must say to you that we have not made a single gain in civil rights without determined legal and nonviolent pressure. Lamentably, it is an historical fact that privileged groups seldom give up their privileges voluntarily. Individuals may see the moral light and voluntarily give up their unjust posture; but, as Reinhold Niebuhr has reminded us, groups tend to be more immoral than individuals.

We know through painful experience that freedom is never voluntarily given by the oppressor; it must be demanded by the oppressed. Frankly, I have yet to engage in a direct-action campaign that was "well timed" in the view of those who have not suffered unduly from the disease of segregation. For years now I have heard the word "Wait!" It rings in the ear of every Negro with piercing familiarity. This "Wait" has almost always meant "Never." We must come to see, with one of our distinguished jurists, that "justice too long delayed is justice denied."

We have waited for more than 340 years for our constitutional and God-given rights. The nations of Asia and Africa are moving with jetlike speed toward gaining political independence, but we still creep at horse-and-buggy pace toward gaining a cup of coffee at a lunch counter. Perhaps it is easy for those who have never felt the stinging darts of segregation to say, "Wait." But when you have seen vicious mobs lynch your mothers and fathers at will and drown your sisters and brothers at whim; when you have seen hate-filled

---

4. White southern Democratic politician and official (1897–1973); photographs of Connor fighting civil rights protesters in Birmingham, Alabama, with fire hoses and dogs helped to galvanize the national civil rights movement.
5. Greek philosopher (c. 469–369 BC) who developed the Socratic Method of teaching, first described by his student Plato, in which a teacher asks a series of questions designed to uncover a student's preconceptions and lead to the discovery of new insight.
6. White southern Democratic politician (1904–78) who beat "Bull" Connor to become the mayor of Birmingham in 1963; considered a moderate, Boutwell had served as Lieutenant Governor of Alabama from 1959 to 1963.

policemen curse, kick and even kill your black brothers and sisters; when you see the vast majority of your twenty million Negro brothers smothering in an airtight cage of poverty in the midst of an affluent society; when you suddenly find your tongue twisted and your speech stammering as you seek to explain to your six-year-old daughter why she can't go to the public amusement park that has just been advertised on television, and see tears welling up in her eyes when she is told that Funtown is closed to colored children, and see ominous clouds of inferiority beginning to form in her little mental sky, and see her beginning to distort her personality by developing an unconscious bitterness toward white people; when you have to concoct an answer for a five-year-old son who is asking: "Daddy, why do white people treat colored people so mean?"; when you take a cross-country drive and find it necessary to sleep night after night in the uncomfortable corners of your automobile because no motel will accept you; when you are humiliated day in and day out by nagging signs reading "white" and "colored"; when your first name becomes "nigger," your middle name becomes "boy" (however old you are) and your last name becomes "John," and your wife and mother are never given the respected title "Mrs."; when you are harried by day and haunted by night by the fact that you are a Negro, living constantly at tiptoe stance, never quite knowing what to expect next, and are plagued with inner fears and outer resentments; when you are forever fighting a degenerating sense of "nobodiness"—then you will understand why we find it difficult to wait. There comes a time when the cup of endurance runs over,[7] and men are no longer willing to be plunged into the abyss of despair. I hope, sirs, you can understand our legitimate and unavoidable impatience.

You express a great deal of anxiety over our willingness to break laws. This is certainly a legitimate concern. Since we so diligently urge people to obey the Supreme Court's decision of 1954 outlawing segregation in the public schools,[8] at first glance it may seem rather paradoxical for us consciously to break laws. One may well ask: "How can you advocate breaking some laws and obeying others?" The answer lies in the fact that there are two types of laws: just and unjust. I would be the first to advocate obeying just laws. One has not only a legal but a moral responsibility to obey just laws. Conversely, one has a moral responsibility to disobey unjust laws. I would agree with St. Augustine[9] that "an unjust law is no law at all."

Now, what is the difference between the two? How does one determine whether a law is just or unjust? A just law is a man-made code that squares with the moral law or the law of God. An unjust law is a code that is out of harmony with the moral law. To put it in the terms of St. Thomas Aquinas[1]: An unjust law is a human law that is not rooted in eternal law and natural law. Any law that uplifts human personality is just. Any law that degrades human personality is unjust. All segregation statutes are unjust because segregation distorts the soul and damages the personality. It gives the segregator a false sense of superiority and the segregated a false sense of inferiority. Segregation, to use the terminology of the Jewish philosopher Martin Buber,[2] substitutes an "I–it" relationship for an "I–thou" relationship and ends up relegating persons to the status of things. Hence segregation is not only politically, economically and sociologically unsound, it is morally wrong and sinful. Paul Tillich[3] has said that sin is separation. Is not segregation an existential expression of man's tragic separation, his awful estrangement, his terrible sinfulness? Thus it is that I can urge men to obey the 1954 decision of the Supreme Court, for it is morally right; and I can urge them to disobey segregation ordinances, for they are morally wrong.

Let us consider a more concrete example of just and unjust laws. An unjust law is a code that a numerical or power majority group compels a minority group to obey but does not make binding on itself. This is *difference* made legal. By the same token, a just law is a code that a majority compels a minority to follow and

---

7. Allusion to Psalms 23:5.
8. *Brown v. Board of Education.*
9. Christian theologian and philosopher Augustine of Hippo (354–430).
1. Italian Roman Catholic priest, philosopher, and theologian (1225–74).
2. Austrian-born philosopher (1878–1965) who developed a philosophy of dialogue.
3. German-American Protestant theologian (1886–1965).

that it is willing to follow itself. This is *sameness* made legal.

Let me give another explanation. A law is unjust if it is inflicted on a minority that, as a result of being denied the right to vote, had no part in enacting or devising the law. Who can say that the legislature of Alabama which set up that state's segregation laws was democratically elected? Throughout Alabama all sorts of devious methods are used to prevent Negroes from becoming registered voters, and there are some counties in which, even though Negroes constitute a majority of the population, not a single Negro is registered. Can any law enacted under such circumstances be considered democratically structured?

Sometimes a law is just on its face and unjust in its application. For instance, I have been arrested on a charge of parading without a permit. Now, there is nothing wrong in having an ordinance which requires a permit for a parade. But such an ordinance becomes unjust when it is used to maintain segregation and to deny citizens the First-Amendment privilege of peaceful assembly and protest.

I hope you are able to see the distinction I am trying to point out. In no sense do I advocate evading or defying the law, as would the rabid segregationist. That would lead to anarchy. One who breaks an unjust law must do so openly, lovingly, and with a willingness to accept the penalty. I submit that an individual who breaks a law that conscience tells him is unjust, and who willingly accepts the penalty of imprisonment in order to arouse the conscience of the community over its injustice, is in reality expressing the highest respect for law.

Of course, there is nothing new about this kind of civil disobedience. It was evidenced sublimely in the refusal of Shadrach, Meshach and Abednego to obey the laws of Nebuchadnezzar, on the ground that a higher moral law was at stake. It was practiced superbly by the early Christians, who were willing to face hungry lions and the excruciating pain of chopping blocks rather than submit to certain unjust laws of the Roman Empire. To a degree, academic freedom is a reality today because Socrates practiced civil disobedience. In our own nation, the Boston Tea Party represented a massive act of civil disobedience.

We should never forget that everything Adolf Hitler did in Germany was "legal" and everything the Hungarian freedom fighters did in Hungary was "illegal." It was "illegal" to aid and comfort a Jew in Hitler's Germany. Even so, I am sure that, had I lived in Germany at the time, I would have aided and comforted my Jewish brothers. If today I lived in a Communist country where certain principles dear to the Christian faith are suppressed, I would openly advocate disobeying that country's antireligious laws.

I must make two honest confessions to you, my Christian and Jewish brothers. First, I must confess that over the past few years I have been gravely disappointed with the white moderate. I have almost reached the regrettable conclusion that the Negro's great stumbling block in his stride toward freedom is not the White Citizen's Counciler[4] or the Ku Klux Klanner, but the white moderate, who is more devoted to "order" than to justice; who prefers a negative peace which is the absence of tension to a positive peace which is the presence of justice; who constantly says: "I agree with you in the goal you seek, but I cannot agree with your methods of direct action"; who paternalistically believes he can set the timetable for another man's freedom; who lives by a mythical concept of time and who constantly advises the Negro to wait for a "more convenient season." Shallow understanding from people of good will is more frustrating than absolute misunderstanding from people of ill will. Lukewarm acceptance is much more bewildering than outright rejection.

I had hoped that the white moderate would understand that law and order exist for the purpose of establishing justice and that when they fail in this purpose they become the dangerously structured dams that block the flow of social progress. I had hoped that the white moderate would understand that the present tension in the South is a necessary phase of the transition from an obnoxious negative peace, in which the Negro passively accepted his unjust plight, to a substantive and positive peace, in which all men will respect the dignity and worth of human personality. Actually, we who engage in nonviolent direct action are not the creators of tension. We merely bring to the surface the hidden tension that is already alive. We bring it out in

---

4. Member of the White Citizens Council, a white supremacist group founded in Mississippi in 1954.

the open, where it can be seen and dealt with. Like a boil that can never be cured so long as it is covered up but must be opened with all its ugliness to the natural medicines of air and light, injustice must be exposed, with all the tension its exposure creates, to the light of human conscience and the air of national opinion before it can be cured.

In your statement you assert that our actions, even though peaceful, must be condemned because they precipitate violence. But is this a logical assertion? Isn't this like condemning a robbed man because his possession of money precipitated the evil act of robbery? Isn't this like condemning Socrates because his unswerving commitment to truth and his philosophical inquiries precipitated the act by the misguided populace in which they made him drink hemlock? Isn't this like condemning Jesus because his unique God-consciousness and never-ceasing devotion to God's will precipitated the evil act of crucifixion? We must come to see that, as the federal courts have consistently affirmed, it is wrong to urge an individual to cease his efforts to gain his basic constitutional rights because the quest may precipitate violence. Society must protect the robbed and punish the robber.

I had also hoped that the white moderate would reject the myth concerning time in relation to the struggle for freedom. I have just received a letter from a white brother in Texas. He writes: "All Christians know that the colored people will receive equal rights eventually, but it is possible that you are in too great a religious hurry. It has taken Christianity almost two thousand years to accomplish what it has. The teachings of Christ take time to come to earth." Such an attitude stems from a tragic misconception of time, from the strangely irrational notion that there is something in the very flow of time that will inevitably cure all ills. Actually, time itself is neutral; it can be used either destructively or constructively. More and more I feel that the people of ill will have used time much more effectively than have the people of good will. We will have to repent in this generation not merely for the hateful words and actions of the bad people but for the appalling silence of the good people. Human progress never rolls in on wheels of inevitability; it comes through the tireless efforts of men willing to be co-workers with God, and without this hard work,

time itself becomes an ally of the forces of social stagnation. We must use time creatively, in the knowledge that the time is always ripe to do right. Now is the time to make real the promise of democracy and transform our pending national elegy into a creative psalm of brotherhood. Now is the time to lift our national policy from the quicksand of racial injustice to the solid rock of human dignity.

You speak of our activity in Birmingham as extreme. At first I was rather disappointed that fellow clergymen would see my nonviolent efforts as those of an extremist. I began thinking about the fact that I stand in the middle of two opposing forces in the Negro community. One is a force of complacency, made up in part of Negroes who, as a result of long years of oppression, are so drained of self-respect and a sense of "somebodiness" that they have adjusted to segregation; and in part of a few middle-class Negroes who, because of a degree of academic and economic security and because in some ways they profit by segregation, have become insensitive to the problems of the masses. The other force is one of bitterness and hatred, and it comes perilously close to advocating violence. It is expressed in the various black nationalist groups that are springing up across the nation, the largest and best-known being Elijah Muhammad's Muslim movement. Nourished by the Negro's frustration over the continued existence of racial discrimination, this movement is made up of people who have lost faith in America, who have absolutely repudiated Christianity, and who have concluded that the white man is an incorrigible "devil."

I have tried to stand between these two forces, saying that we need emulate neither the "do-nothingism" of the complacent nor the hatred and despair of the black nationalist. For there is the more excellent way of love and nonviolent protest. I am grateful to God that, through the influence of the Negro church, the way of nonviolence became an integral part of our struggle.

If this philosophy had not emerged, by now many streets of the South would, I am convinced, be flowing with blood. And I am further convinced that if our white brothers dismiss as "rabble-rousers" and "outside agitators" those of us who employ nonviolent direct action, and if they refuse to support our nonviolent efforts, millions of Negroes will, out of frustration and despair, seek solace and security in black-nationalist ideologies—a development that would inevitably lead to a frightening racial nightmare.

Oppressed people cannot remain oppressed forever. The yearning for freedom eventually manifests itself, and that is what has happened to the American Negro. Something within has reminded him of his birthright of freedom, and something without has reminded him that it can be gained. Consciously or unconsciously, he has been caught up by the *Zeitgeist*,[5] and with his black brothers of Africa and his brown and yellow brothers of Asia, South America and the Caribbean, the United States Negro is moving with a sense of great urgency toward the promised land of racial justice. If one recognizes this vital urge that has engulfed the Negro community, one should readily understand why public demonstrations are taking place. The Negro has many pent-up resentments and latent frustrations, and he must release them. So let him march; let him make prayer pilgrimages to the city hall; let him go on freedom rides—and try to understand why he must do so. If his repressed emotions are not released in nonviolent ways, they will seek expression through violence; this is not a threat but a fact of history. So I have not said to my people: "Get rid of your discontent." Rather, I have tried to say that this normal and healthy discontent can be channeled into the creative outlet of nonviolent direct action. And now this approach is being termed extremist.

But though I was initially disappointed at being categorized as an extremist, as I continued to think about the matter I gradually gained a measure of satisfaction from the label. Was not Jesus an extremist for love: "Love your enemies, bless them that curse you, do good to them that hate you, and pray for them which despitefully use you, and persecute you." Was not Amos an extremist for justice: "Let justice roll down like waters and righteousness like an ever-flowing stream." Was not Paul an extremist for the Christian gospel: "I bear in my body the marks of the Lord Jesus."[6] Was not

Martin Luther[7] an extremist: "Here I stand; I cannot do otherwise, so help me God." And John Bunyan[8]: "I will stay in jail to the end of my days before I make a butchery of my conscience." And Abraham Lincoln: "This nation cannot survive half slave and half free."[9] And Thomas Jefferson: "We hold these truths to be self-evident, that all men are created equal . . ."[1] So the question is not whether we will be extremists, but what kind of extremists we will be. Will we be extremists for hate or for love? Will we be extremists for the preservation of injustice or for the extension of justice? In that dramatic scene on Calvary's hill three men were crucified. We must never forget that all three were crucified for the same crime—the crime of extremism. Two were extremists for immorality, and thus fell below their environment. The other, Jesus Christ, was an extremist for love, truth and goodness, and thereby rose above his environment. Perhaps the South, the nation and the world are in dire need of creative extremists.

I had hoped that the white moderate would see this need. Perhaps I was too optimistic; perhaps I expected too much. I suppose I should have realized that few members of the oppressor race can understand the deep groans and passionate yearnings of the oppressed race, and still fewer have the vision to see that injustice must be rooted out by strong, persistent and determined action. I am thankful, however, that some of our white brothers in the South have grasped the meaning of this social revolution and committed themselves to it. They are still all too few in quantity, but they are big in quality. Some—such as Ralph McGill, Lillian Smith, Harry Golden, James McBride Dabbs, Ann Braden and Sarah Patton Boyle—have written about our struggle in eloquent and prophetic terms. Others have marched with us down nameless streets of the South. They have languished in filthy, roach-infested jails, suffering the abuse and brutality of policemen who view them as "dirty nigger-lovers." Unlike so many of their moderate brothers and sisters,

---

5. The mood or spirit of an era [German].
6. Galatians 6:17; "Love your enemies . . .": Matthew 5:44; "Let justice roll down . . .": paraphrase of Amos 5:25, "But let judgment run down as waters, and righteousness as a mighty stream."
7. Priest and theologian (1483–1546) who broke from the Catholic Church and began the Protestant Reformation.
8. English Christian preacher and writer (1628–88) who wrote *The Pilgrim's Progress* published in 1678.
9. Lincoln's "House Divided" speech delivered in 1858.
1. The second sentence of the Declaration of Independence.

they have recognized the urgency of the moment and sensed the need for powerful "action" antidotes to combat the disease of segregation.

Let me take note of my other major disappointment. I have been so greatly disappointed with the white church and its leadership. Of course, there are some notable exceptions. I am not unmindful of the fact that each of you has taken some significant stands on this issue. I commend you, Reverend Stallings, for your Christian stand on this past Sunday, in welcoming Negroes to your worship service on a nonsegregated basis. I commend the Catholic leaders of this state for integrating Spring Hill College several years ago.

But despite these notable exceptions, I must honestly reiterate that I have been disappointed with the church. I do not say this as one of those negative critics who can always find something wrong with the church. I say this as a minister of the gospel, who loves the church; who was nurtured in its bosom; who has been sustained by its spiritual blessings and who will remain true to it as long as the cord of life shall lengthen.

When I was suddenly catapulted into the leadership of the bus protest in Montgomery, Alabama, a few years ago, I felt we would be supported by the white church. I felt that the white ministers, priests and rabbis of the South would be among our strongest allies. Instead, some have been outright opponents, refusing to understand the freedom movement and misrepresenting its leaders; all too many others have been more cautious than courageous and have remained silent behind the anesthetizing security of stained-glass windows.

In spite of my shattered dreams, I came to Birmingham with the hope that the white religious leadership of this community would see the justice of our cause and, with deep moral concern, would serve as the channel through which our just grievances could reach the power structure. I had hoped that each of you would understand. But again I have been disappointed.

I have heard numerous southern religious leaders admonish their worshipers to comply with a desegregation decision because it is the law, but I have longed to hear white ministers declare: "Follow this decree because integration is morally right and because the Negro is your brother." In the midst of blatant injustices

inflicted upon the Negro, I have watched white churchmen stand on the sideline and mouth pious irrelevancies and sanctimonious trivialities. In the midst of a mighty struggle to rid our nation of racial and economic injustice, I have heard many ministers say: "Those are social issues, with which the gospel has no real concern." And I have watched many churches commit themselves to a completely otherworldly religion which makes a strange, un-Biblical distinction between body and soul, between the sacred and the secular.

I have traveled the length and breadth of Alabama, Mississippi and all the other southern states. On sweltering summer days and crisp autumn mornings I have looked at the South's beautiful churches with their lofty spires pointing heavenward. I have beheld the impressive outlines of her massive religious-education buildings. Over and over I have found myself asking: "What kind of people worship here? Who is their God? Where were their voices when the lips of Governor Barnett dripped with words of interposition and nullification? Where were they when Governor Wallace gave a clarion call for defiance and hatred? Where were their voices of support when bruised and weary Negro men and women decided to rise from the dark dungeons of complacency to the bright hills of creative protest?"

Yes, these questions are still in my mind. In deep disappointment I have wept over the laxity of the church. But be assured that my tears have been tears of love. There can be no deep disappointment where there is not deep love. Yes, I love the church. How could I do otherwise? I am in the rather unique position of being the son, the grandson and the great-grandson of preachers. Yes, I see the church as the body of Christ. But, oh! How we have blemished and scarred that body through social neglect and through fear of being nonconformists.

There was a time when the church was very powerful—in the time when the early Christians rejoiced at being deemed worthy to suffer for what they believed. In those days the church was not merely a thermometer that recorded the ideas and principles of popular opinion; it was a thermostat that transformed the mores of society. Whenever the early Christians entered a town, the people in power became disturbed and immediately sought to convict the Christians for being "disturbers of the peace" and "outside agitators."

But the Christians pressed on, in the conviction that they were "a colony of heaven,"[2] called to obey God rather than man. Small in number, they were big in commitment. They were too God-intoxicated to be "astronomically intimidated." By their effort and example they brought an end to such ancient evils as infanticide and gladiatorial contests.

Things are different now. So often the contemporary church is a weak, ineffectual voice with an uncertain sound. So often it is an arch-defender of the status quo. Far from being disturbed by the presence of the church, the power structure of the average community is consoled by the church's silent—and often even vocal—sanction of things as they are.

But the judgment of God is upon the church as never before. If today's church does not recapture the sacrificial spirit of the early church, it will lose its authenticity, forfeit the loyalty of millions, and be dismissed as an irrelevant social club with no meaning for the twentieth century. Every day I meet young people whose disappointment with the church has turned into outright disgust.

Perhaps I have once again been too optimistic. Is organized religion too inextricably bound to the status quo to save our nation and the world? Perhaps I must turn my faith to the inner spiritual church, the church within the church, as the true *ekklesia*[3] and the hope of the world. But again I am thankful to God that some noble souls from the ranks of organized religion have broken loose from the paralyzing chains of conformity and joined us as active partners in the struggle for freedom. They have left their secure congregations and walked the streets of Albany, Georgia, with us. They have gone down the highways of the South on tortuous rides for freedom. Yes, they have gone to jail with us. Some have been dismissed from their churches, have lost the support of their bishops and fellow ministers. But they have acted in the faith that right defeated is stronger than evil triumphant. Their witness has been the spiritual salt that has preserved the true meaning of the gospel in these troubled times. They have carved a tunnel of hope through the dark mountain of disappointment.

I hope the church as a whole will meet the challenge of this decisive hour. But even if the church does not come to the aid of justice, I have no despair about the future. I have no fear about the outcome of our struggle in Birmingham, even if our motives are at present misunderstood. We will reach the goal of freedom in Birmingham and all over the nation, because the goal of America is freedom. Abused and scorned though we may be, our destiny is tied up with America's destiny. Before the pilgrims landed at Plymouth, we were here. Before the pen of Jefferson etched the majestic words of the Declaration of Independence across the pages of history, we were here. For more than two centuries our forebears labored in this country without wages; they made cotton king; they built the homes of their masters while suffering gross injustice and shameful humiliation—and yet out of a bottomless vitality they continued to thrive and develop. If the inexpressible cruelties of slavery could not stop us, the opposition we now face will surely fail. We will win our freedom because the sacred heritage of our nation and the eternal will of God are embodied in our echoing demands.

Before closing I feel impelled to mention one other point in your statement that has troubled me profoundly. You warmly commended the Birmingham police force for keeping "order" and "preventing violence." I doubt that you would have so warmly commended the police force if you had seen its dogs sinking their teeth into unarmed, nonviolent Negroes. I doubt that you would so quickly commend the policemen if you were to observe their ugly and inhumane treatment of Negroes here in the city jail; if you were to watch them push and curse old Negro women and young Negro girls; if you were to see them slap and kick old Negro men and young boys; if you were to observe them, as they did on two occasions, refuse to give us food because we wanted to sing our grace together. I cannot join you in your praise of the Birmingham police department.

It is true that the police have exercised a degree of discipline in handling the demonstrators. In this sense they have conducted themselves rather "nonviolently" in public. But for what purpose? To preserve the evil

2. Reference to Philippians 3:20.
3. Church [Greek].

system of segregation. Over the past few years I have consistently preached that nonviolence demands that the means we use must be as pure as the ends we seek. I have tried to make clear that it is wrong to use immoral means to attain moral ends. But now I must affirm that it is just as wrong, or perhaps even more so, to use moral means to preserve immoral ends. Perhaps Mr. Connor and his policemen have been rather nonviolent in public, as was Chief Pritchett[4] in Albany, Georgia, but they have used the moral means of nonviolence to maintain the immoral end of racial injustice. As T. S. Eliot has said: "The last temptation is the greatest treason: To do the right deed for the wrong reason."[5]

I wish you had commended the Negro sit-inners and demonstrators of Birmingham for their sublime courage, their willingness to suffer and their amazing discipline in the midst of great provocation. One day the South will recognize its real heroes. They will be the James Merediths, with the noble sense of purpose that enables them to face jeering and hostile mobs, and with the agonizing loneliness that characterizes the life of the pioneer. They will be old, oppressed, battered Negro women, symbolized in a seventy-two-year-old woman in Montgomery, Alabama, who rose up with a sense of dignity and with her people decided not to ride segregated buses, and who responded with ungrammatical profundity to one who inquired about her weariness: "My feets is tired, but my soul is at rest." They will be the young high school and college students, the young ministers of the gospel and a host of their elders, courageously and nonviolently sitting in at lunch counters and willingly going to jail for conscience' sake. One day the South will know that when these disinherited children of God sat down at lunch counters, they were in reality standing up for what is best in the American dream and for the most sacred values in our Judaeo-Christian heritage, thereby bringing our nation back to those great wells of democracy which were dug deep by the founding fathers in their formulation of the Constitution and the Declaration of Independence.

Never before have I written so long a letter. I'm afraid it is much too long to take your precious time. I can assure you that it would have been much shorter if I had been writing from a comfortable desk, but what else can one do when he is alone in a narrow jail cell, other than write long letters, think long thoughts and pray long prayers?

If I have said anything in this letter that overstates the truth and indicates an unreasonable impatience, I beg you to forgive me. If I have said anything that understates the truth and indicates my having a patience that allows me to settle for anything less than brotherhood, I beg God to forgive me.

I hope this letter finds you strong in the faith. I also hope that circumstances will soon make it possible for me to meet each of you, not as an integrationist or a civil-rights leader but as a fellow clergyman and a Christian brother. Let us all hope that the dark clouds of racial prejudice will soon pass away and the deep fog of misunderstanding will be lifted from our fear-drenched communities, and in some not too distant tomorrow the radiant stars of love and brotherhood will shine over our great nation with all their scintillating beauty.

Yours for the cause of Peace and Brotherhood,
MARTIN LUTHER KING, JR.

MALCOLM X
Letter from Saudi Arabia [1964]

After his split with the Nation of Islam in March 1964, Malcolm X took a trip through the Middle East and Africa from April 13 to May 21, making a pilgrimage to Mecca in Saudi Arabia on April 19. The journey had a profound effect on his views about race and Islam. He repudiated his former belief in racial separatism (which was promoted by the Nation of Islam) in favor of a multiracial "brotherhood," as heralded by orthodox Islam. In a speech delivered on

---

4. White southern police chief (1926–2000) who used nonviolence and mass arrests to quell the civil rights campaign in Albany, Georgia, in 1961 and 1962, known as the Albany Movement; his quiet methods attracted little media coverage, boosting their effectiveness.
5. From Eliot's verse drama *Murder in the Cathedral* (1935).

May 23, 1964, immediately following his return, Malcolm X proclaimed, "In the past, I have permitted myself to be used to make sweeping indictments of all white people, and these generalizations have caused injuries to some white people who did not deserve them. Because of the spiritual rebirth which I was blessed to undergo as a result of my pilgrimage to the Holy City of Mecca, I no longer subscribe to sweeping indictments of one race."

The letter reprinted here, written in Saudi Arabia on April 20, 1964, conveys the powerful shift in his beliefs from race separatism to traditional Islam as an answer to America's "race problem."

From George Breitman, ed., *Malcolm X Speaks: Selected Speeches and Statements* (New York: Grove Press, 1965), pp. 59–60.

Jedda, Saudi Arabia
April 20, 1964

Never have I witnessed such sincere hospitality and the overwhelming spirit of true brotherhood as is practiced by people *of all colors and races* here in this ancient holy land, the home of Abraham, Muhammad and all the other prophets of the Holy Scriptures. For the past week I have been utterly speechless and spellbound by the graciousness I see displayed all around me by people *of all colors.*

Last night, April 19, I was blessed to visit the Holy City of Mecca, and complete the "Omra" part of my pilgrimage. Allah willing, I shall leave for Mina tomorrow, April 21, and be back in Mecca to say my prayers from Mt. Arafat on Tuesday, April 22. Mina is about twenty miles from Mecca.

Last night I made my seven circuits around the Kaaba, led by a young Mutawif named Muhammad. I drank water from the well of Zem Zem, and then ran back and forth seven times between the hills of Mt. Al-Safa and Al-Marwah.

There were tens of thousands of pilgrims from all over the world. They were *of all colors,* from blue-eyed blonds to black-skinned Africans, but were all participating in the same ritual, displaying a spirit of unity and brotherhood that my experiences in America had led me to believe could never exist between the white and non-white.

America needs to understand Islam, because this is the one religion that erases the race problem from its society. Throughout my travels in the Muslim world, I have met, talked to, and even eaten with, people who would have been considered "white" in America, but the religion of Islam in their hearts has removed the "white" from their minds. They practice sincere and true brotherhood with other people irrespective of their color.

Before America allows herself to be destroyed by the "cancer of racism" she should become better acquainted with the religious philosophy of Islam, a religion that has already molded people of all colors into one vast family, a nation or brotherhood of Islam that leaps over all "obstacles" and stretches itself into almost all the Eastern countries of this earth.

The whites as well as the non-whites who accept true Islam become a changed people. I have eaten from the same plate with people whose eyes were the bluest of blue, whose hair was the blondest of blond, and whose skin was the whitest of white—all the way from Cairo to Jedda and even in the Holy City of Mecca itself—and I felt the same sincerity in the words and deeds of these "white" Muslims that I felt among the African Muslims of Nigeria, Sudan and Ghana.

True Islam removes racism, because people of all colors and races who accept its religious principles and bow down to the one God, Allah, also automatically accept each other as brothers and sisters, regardless of differences in complexion.

You may be shocked by these words coming from me, but I have always been a man who tries to face facts, and to accept the reality of life as new experiences and knowledge unfold it. The experiences of this pilgrimage have taught me much, and each hour here in the Holy Land opens my eyes even more. If Islam can place the spirit of true brotherhood in the hearts of the "whites" whom I have met here in the Land of the Prophets, then surely it can also remove the "cancer of racism" from the heart of the white American, and perhaps in time to save America from imminent racial disaster, the same destruction brought upon Hitler by his racism that eventually destroyed the Germans themselves. [* * *]

ELIJAH MUHAMMAD

Program and Position: What Do the Muslims Want? [1965]

Elijah Robert Poole, born in Georgia in 1897, was an early follower of Wallace D. Fard, the founder of the Nation of Islam. After Fard mysteriously disappeared in 1934, Poole—who had renamed himself Elijah Muhammad—proclaimed that Fard was an incarnation of Allah. Positioning himself as Fard's prophet, Muhammad became the leader of the Nation of Islam, a title he held until his death, in 1975.

The text reprinted here is from Muhammad's 1965 book, *Message to the Blackman in America.* Published

after the Nation of Islam's official break with Malcolm X, the position statement reconfirms the Nation of Islam's commitment to a black nationalist vision, rejecting both multicultural Islam (which Malcolm X had come to embrace) and the idea of an integrated America. Indeed, six of the ten points of the program (and three points in the following position section) promote separatism. The statement also sets out official positions on other contemporary debates, including reparations, intermarriage, and gender relations (a particular source of controversy, p. 614).

From *Message to the Blackman in America* (Chicago: Muhammad Moslem Mosque of Islam, No. 2, 1965).

This is the question asked most frequently by both the whites and the blacks. The answers to this question I shall state as simply as possible.

1. We want freedom. We want a full and complete freedom.

2. We want justice. Equal justice under the law. We want justice applied equally to all regardless of creed, class or color.

3. We want equality of opportunity. We want equal membership in society with the best in civilized society.

4. We want our people in America whose parents or grandparents were descendants from slaves to be allowed, to establish a separate state or territory of their own—either on this continent or elsewhere. We believe that our former slave-masters are obligated to provide such land and that the area must be fertile and minerally rich. We believe that our former slave-masters are obligated to maintain and supply our needs in this separate territory for the next 20 or 25 years until we are able to produce and supply our own needs.

Since we cannot get along with them in peace and equality after giving them 400 years of our sweat and blood and receiving in return some of the worst treatment human beings have ever experienced, we believe our contributions to this land and the suffering forced

upon us by white America justifies our demand for complete separation in a state or territory of our own.

5. We want freedom for all Believers of Islam now held in federal prisons. We want freedom for all black men and women now under death sentence in innumerable prisons in the North as well as the South.

We want every black man and woman to have the freedom to accept or reject being separated from the slave-masters' children and establish a land of their own.

We know that the above plan for the solution of the black and white conflict is the best and only answer to the problem between two people.

6. We want an immediate end to the police brutality and mob attacks against the so-called Negro throughout the United States.

We believe that the Federal government should intercede to see that black men and women tried in white courts receive justice in accordance with the laws of the land, or allow us to build a new nation for ourselves, dedicated to justice, freedom and liberty.

7. As long as we are not allowed to establish a state or territory of our own, we demand not only equal justice under the laws of the United States but equal employment opportunities—NOW!

We do not believe that after 400 years of free or nearly free labor, sweat and blood, which has helped

America become rich and powerful, so many thousands of black people should have to subsist on relief or charity or live in poor houses.

8. We want the government of the United States to exempt our people from ALL taxation as long as we are deprived of equal justice under the laws of the land.

9. We want equal education—but separate schools up to 16 for boys and 18 for girls on the conditions that the girls be sent to women's colleges and universities. We want all black children educated, taught and trained by their own teacher.

Under such school system we believe we will make a better nation of people. The United States government should provide free all necessary text books and equipment, schools and college buildings. The Muslim teachers shall be left free to teach and train their people in the way of righteousness, decency and self respect.

10. We believe that intermarriage or race mixing should be prohibited. We want the religion of Islam taught without hindrance or suppression.

These are some of the things that we, the Muslims, want for our people in North America.

1. We believe in the One God Whose proper name is Allah.

2. We believe in the Holy Qur-an[1] and in the Scriptures of all the Prophets of God.

3. We believe in the truth of the Bible, but we believe that it has been tampered with and must be reinterpreted so that mankind will not be snared by the falsehoods that have been added to it.

4. We believe in Allah's Prophets and the Scriptures they brought to the people.

5. We believe in the resurrection of the dead—not in physical resurrection but mental resurrection. We believe that the so-called Negroes are most in need of mental resurrection; therefore, they will be resurrected first.

Furthermore, we believe we are the people of God's choice as it has been written that God would choose the rejected and the despised. We can find no other persons fitting this description in these last days more than the so-called Negroes in America. We believe in the resurrection of the righteous.

6. We further believe in the judgment.[2] We believe this first judgment will take place, as God revealed, in America.

7. We believe this is the time in history for the separation of the so-called Negroes and the so-called white Americans. We believe the black man should be freed in name as well as in fact. By this we mean that he should be freed from names imposed upon him by his former slave-masters. Names which identified him as being the slave of a slave-master. We believe that if we are free indeed, we should go in our own people's names— the black peoples of the earth.

8. We believe in justice for all whether in God or not. We believe as others that we are due equal justice as human beings. We believe in equality—as a nation—of equals. We do not believe that we are equal with our slave-masters in the status of "Freed slaves."

We recognize and respect American citizens as independent peoples, and we respect their laws which govern this nation.

9. We believe that the offer of integration is hypocritical and is made by those who are trying to deceive the black peoples into believing that their 400-year-old open enemies of freedom, justice and equality are, all of a sudden, their "friends." Furthermore, we believe that such deception is intended to prevent black people from realizing that the time in history has arrived for the separation from the whites of this nation.

If the white people are truthful about their professed friendship toward the so-called Negro, they can prove it by dividing up America with their slaves.

We do not believe that America will ever be able to furnish enough jobs for her own millions of unemployed in addition to jobs for the 20,000,000 black people.

10. We believe that we who declared ourselves to be righteous Muslims should not participate in wars

---

1. The Qur'an, originally written in Arabic, is the central religious text of Islam.
2. Assessment by God on the Day of Resurrection or the Day of Judgment; a major theme in the Qur'an.

which take the lives of humans. We do not believe this nation should force us to take part in such wars, for we have nothing to gain from it unless America agrees to give us the necessary territory wherein we may have something to fight for.

11. We believe our women should be respected and protected as the women of other nationalities are respected and protected.

12. We believe that Allah (God) appeared in the Person of Master W. Fard Muhammad, July, 1930—the long awaited "Messiah" of the Christians and the "Mahdi" of the Muslims.

We believe further and lastly that Allah is God and besides HIM there is no God and He will bring about a universal government of peace wherein we can live in peace together.

Barbara Sizemore

from *Sexism and the Black Male* [1973]

Barbara Sizemore (1927–2004), superintendent of the Washington, D.C., public schools (the first black woman in the country to head a major school system), asserts in "Sexism and the Black Male" that some black male leaders have constructed definitions of freedom at the expense of black women. She examines Elijah Muhammad's *Message to the Blackman in America* (p. 612) and presents Muhammad's call to "protect" black women as part of a program to control them by, for instance, restricting their freedom of movement and choice of sexual partners. Sizemore's critique is representative of the emerging black feminism of the 1970s in that she focuses on uncovering or examining the underlying sexism in key positions and texts. Later black feminists, building on this groundwork, developed alternative theologies and philosophies, such as black women's theology and womanism.

From *The Black Scholar* 4 (March–April 1973), pp. 2–11.

Some black spokesmen show little awareness of the plight of black women in America. Those which have adopted capitalist models have relegated women to the loser group. Capitalism is based on a contriently interdependent[1] competitive model wherein when A wins B loses. A represents the groups with power and B stands for those with no power. Inherent in the model are always losers. If men are A and women are B, when men win women lose. Such a model has been embraced by the Nation of Islam. In his *Message to the Blackman in America* Elijah Muhammad[2] openly states that women are property. He says "The woman is man's field to produce his nation." He speaks of women as things, comparable to crops and children with great needs for protection and control. He says:

Is not your woman more valuable than the crop of corn, that crop of cotton, that crop of cabbage, potatoes, beans, tomatoes? How much more valuable is your woman than these crops, that you should keep the enemies from destroying the crops. Yet you are not careful about your women.

Further along he argues that the first step is the control and protection of women in order to return to the land with a thorough knowledge of "our own" selves. He says:

Our women are allowed to walk or ride the streets all night long, with any strange men they desire. They are allowed to frequent any tavern or dance hall

1. Where the success of one group depends on the failure of another group, as in a competitive sport where one team's win depends on the loss of the other team.
2. Elijah Muhammad, *Message to the Black Man in America,* Chicago: Muhammad Mosque of Islam #2, 1965, p. 58. [Sizemore's note]

they like, wherever they like. They are allowed to fill our homes with children other than our own. Children that are often fathered by the very devil himself.

He orders the men of the Nation to put the women under guard, to keep them imprisoned in order to protect and control them. Inherent in the *Message* is the warning that women are evil and given to sin while men are noble and given to righteousness.

The story of the beginning in *Message* differs little from that of Christianity as far as women are concerned. Mr. Muhammad sees women as the weaker part of man. He perpetrates the untruth that black women make higher salaries than black men and he denigrates the black woman by seeing her as immoral and ignorant.

In the section on "Program and Position," Mr. Muhammad says that the Muslims want freedom, full and complete; justice under the law applied equally to all regardless of creed, class or color and equality of opportunity. None of these are applied to women. Over and over in *Message* women are mentioned only in terms of protection. It is easier to protect women if they are not free. Kept at home in semi-purdah,[3] men do not need to confront the dangerous white man over her safety. To become good Muslims, black women must become chattel once again, with good and loving masters, to be sure, but chattel nevertheless.

JAMES H. CONE
from *Black Theology and Black Power* [1969]

The publication of James H. Cone's *Black Theology and Black Power* in 1969 was a watershed moment in the development of black theology. Driven by his own growing political consciousness and disillusionment with "white denominational churches," Cone (b. 1938) argues that it is necessary to develop a solid theological grounding for a politically engaged Christianity committed to the eradication of racism. As he states in the book's preface, "For me, the burning theological question was, how can I reconcile Christianity and Black Power, Martin Luther King Jr.'s idea of nonviolence and Malcolm X's 'by any means necessary' philosophy?" Cone, a theologian and an African Methodist Episcopal minister, came to the conclusion that Christ's message was one of liberation for all oppressed peoples, with particular relevance for African Americans. For Cone, "Black Power is the spirit of Christ himself in the black-white dialogue which makes possible the emancipation of blacks from self-hatred and frees whites from their racism." Cone extends this argument by labeling the white church "the enemy of Christ," given its long history of perpetuating racism.

Cone's position sparked lively controversy among black and white theologians, and these debates contributed greatly to his own thinking and to the development of black theology as a discipline. Although *Black Theology and Black Power* remains a touchstone for black theology, Cone has continued to push the development of black theology ever since the book's publication, through his own extensive writings and the publication of essential anthologies on black theology.

From *Black Theology and Black Power* (New York: Harper and Row, 1969), pp. 62–90.

3. Muslim tradition of keeping women in seclusion, often using screens or curtains at home and concealing clothing when in public; from the Persian *pardah* meaning *veil*.

Let the Church discover and identify itself with groups of people that suffer because of unjust situations, and who have no way of making themselves heard. The Church should be the voice of those who have no one. The Church must discover these groups and identify herself with them. Here is the modern Way of the Cross, the way of Christian responsibility.

—*Emilio Castro*[1]

The meaning of Black Power and its relationship to Christianity has been the focal point of our discussion thus far. It has been argued that Black Power is the spirit of Christ himself in the black-white dialogue which makes possible the emancipation of blacks from self-hatred and frees whites from their racism. Through Black Power, blacks are becoming men of worth, and whites are forced to confront them as human beings.

There is no other spirit in American life so challenging as the spirit of Black Power. We can see it affecting every major aspect of American life—economic, political, and social. In major white and black universities its spirit is manifested in the demand for more emphasis on "black studies." Black students have literally taken over some administration buildings in an effort to make white authorities recognize the importance of their demands. In politics, Stokely Carmichael and Charles Hamilton have given the political implications of Black Power.[2] For them Black Power in politics means blacks controlling their political destiny by voting for black people and perhaps eventually forming a coalition with poor whites against middle-class whites. For some others it means black nationalism. Economically it may mean boycotting, or building stores for black people. Religiously or philosophically it means an inner sense of freedom from the structures of white society which builds its economy on the labor of poor blacks and whites. It means that the slave now knows that he is a man, and thus resolves to make the enslaver recognize him. I contend that such a spirit is not merely compatible with Christianity; in America in the latter twentieth century it is Christianity.

Some critics of this thesis may ask about the place of the Church in my analysis. It may appear that its role as an agent of God in the world has been overlooked. This leads us to an investigation of the biblical understanding of the Church and its relationship to white denominational churches.

WHAT IS THE CHURCH?

What is the Church and its relationship to Christ and Black Power? The Church is that people called into being by the power and love of God to share in his revolutionary activity for the liberation of man.

Mythically the interrelation of God, man, and the world is presented in the Genesis picture of the man and the woman in the garden. Man was created to share in God's creative (revolutionary) activity in the world (Gen. 1:27–28). But through sin man rejects his proper activity and destiny. He wants to be God, the creator of his destiny. This is the essence of sin, every man's desire to become "like God." But in his passion to become superhuman, man becomes subhuman, estranged from the source of his being, threatening and threatened by his neighbor, transforming a situation destined for intimate human fellowship into a spider web of conspiracy and violence. God, however, will not permit man thus to become less than the divine intention for him. He therefore undertakes a course of not-so-gentle persuasion for the liberation and restoration of his creatures.

The call of Abraham was the beginning of this revolutionary activity on behalf of man's liberation from his own sinful pride. This was followed by the exodus, the most significant revelatory act in the Old Testament, which demonstrated God's purposes for man. God showed thereby that he was the Lord of history, that his will for man is not to be thwarted by other human wills. And when Pharaoh said to Moses and Aaron, "The Lord is righteous, and I and my people are wicked" (Exod. 9:27), he was saying that even he recognized the righteousness of God in contrast to the wickedness of men.

---

1. Methodist parish pastor from Uruguay who later served as the fourth general secretary of the World Council of Churches from 1985 to 1992. [Editor's note]

2. See their *Black Power: The Politics of Liberation in America* (New York: Random House, 1967). [Unless otherwise indicated, all footnotes are those of the author.]

The history of Israel is a history of God's election of a special, oppressed people to share in his creative involvement in the world on behalf of man. The call of this people at Sinai into a covenant relationship for a special task may be said to be the beginning of the Church.[3] In the Old Testament, Israel often refers to herself as the *qahal*, the assembly or people of God.[4] Israel is called into being as a people of the covenant in which Yahweh promises to be their God and they his people. Israel's task is to be a partner in God's revolutionary activity and thus to be an example to the whole world of what God intends for all men. By choosing Israel, the oppressed people among the nations, God reveals that his concern is not for the strong but for the weak, not for the enslaver but for the slave, not for whites but for blacks. To express the goal of her striving, Israel spoke of the Day of the Lord and the Kingdom of God, in which God would vindicate his people from oppression and the rule of his righteousness would be recognized by all. This would be the day when the lion would lie down with the lamb and men would beat their swords into plowshares.[5]

In the New Testament, the coming of God in Christ means that the Kingdom of God expected in the Old Testament is now realized in Jesus of Nazareth. The Day of the Lord has come in the life, death, and resurrection of Jesus. This day is no longer future but present in the man Jesus. In him is embodied God's Kingdom in which men are liberated. He is, as Paul says, the "New Adam," who has done for man what man could not do for himself. His death and resurrection mean that the decisive battle has been fought and won, and man no longer has to be a slave to "principalities and powers."[6]

With him also comes a new people which the New Testament calls the *ekklesia* (church). Like the people of Old Israel, they are called into being by God himself—to be his agent in this world until Christ's second coming. Like Old Israel, they are an oppressed people, created to cooperate in God's liberation of all men. Unlike Old Israel, their membership is not limited by ethnic or political boundaries, but includes all who respond in faith to the redemptive act of God in Christ with a willingness to share in God's creative activity in the world. Unlike Old Israel, they do not look forward to the coming of the Kingdom, but know that, in Christ, God's Kingdom has already come and their very existence is a manifestation of it. The Church merely waits for its full consummation in Christ's second coming. Therefore, its sole purpose for being is to be a visible manifestation of God's work in the affairs of men. The Church, then, consists of people who have been seized by the Holy Spirit and who have the determination to live as if all depends on God. It has no will of its own, only God's will; it has no duty of its own, only God's duty. Its existence is grounded in God.

The Church of Christ is not bounded by standards of race, class, or occupation. It is not a building or an institution. It is not determined by bishops, priests, or ministers as these terms are used in their contemporary sense. Rather, the Church is God's suffering people. It is that grouping of men who take seriously the words of Jesus: "Blessed are you when men revile you and persecute you and utter all kinds of evil against you falsely on my account" (Matt. 5:11). The call of God constitutes the Church, and it is a call to suffering. As Bonhoeffer put it:

> Man is challenged to participate in the sufferings of God at the hands of a godless world.
>
> He must plunge himself into the life of a godless world, without attempting to gloss over its ungodliness with a veneer of religion or trying to transfigure it. . . . To be a Christian does not mean to be religious in a particular way, to cultivate some particular form of asceticism, . . . but to be a man. It is not some religious act which makes a Christian

---

3. Some biblical scholars identify the call of Abraham as the beginning of the Church, but this involves critical-historical problems that are not pertinent here. As far as Israel's awareness of herself as an elect people is concerned, few authorities would fail to place the beginning at the exodus and wilderness experiences.

4. For an analysis of the relationship between *qahal* and *ekklesia* see J. Robert Nelson, *The Realm of Redemption* (New York: Seabury Press, 1951), pp. 3–19.

5. Allusions to Isaiah 11:6 and Isaiah 2:4. [Editor's note]

6. Ephesians 3:10, 6:12. [Editor's note]

what he is, but participation in the suffering of God in the life of the world.[7]

"Where Christ is, there is the Church."[8] Christ is to be found, as always, where men are enslaved and trampled under foot; Christ is found suffering with the suffering; Christ is in the ghetto—there also is his Church.

The Church is not defined by those who faithfully attend and participate in the 11:00 A.M. Sunday worship. As Harvey Cox says: "The insistence by the Reformers that the church was 'where the word is rightly preached and the sacraments rightly administered' will simply not do today."[9] It may have been fine for distinguishing orthodoxy from heresy, but it is worthless as a vehicle against modern racism. We must therefore be reminded that Christ was not crucified on an altar between two candles, but on a cross between two thieves. He is not in our peaceful, quiet, comfortable suburban "churches," but in the ghetto fighting the racism of churchly white people.

In the New Testament perspective, the Church has essentially three functions: preaching (*kerygma*), service (*diakonia*), and fellowship (*koinonia*). Preaching means proclaiming to the world what God has done for man in Jesus Christ. The Church tells the world about Christ's victory over alien hostile forces. If we compare Christ's work on the cross with warfare, as Oscar Cullmann[1] and others do, then it is the task of the Church to tell the world that the decisive battle in the war has been fought and won by Christ. Freedom has come! The old tyrants have been displaced, and there is no need for anyone to obey evil powers. The Church, then, is men and women running through the streets announcing that freedom is a reality. This is easily translated into the context of modern racism. God in Christ has set men free from white power, and this means an end to ghettos and all they imply. The Church

tells black people to shape up and act like free men because the old powers of white racism are writhing in final agony. The Good News[2] of freedom is proclaimed also to the oppressor, but since he mistakes his enslaving power for life and health he does not easily recognize his own mortal illness or hear the healing word. But the revolution is on, and there is no turning back.

Modern kerygmatic preaching has little to do with white ministers admonishing their people to be nice to "Negroes" or "to obey the law of the land." Nor does it involve inviting a "good Negro" preacher to preach about race relations. Preaching in its truest sense tells the world about Christ's victory and thus invites people to act as if God has won the battle over racism. To preach in America today is to shout "Black Power! Black Freedom!"

It is important to remember that the preaching of the Word presents a crisis situation. The hearing of the news of freedom through the preaching of the Word[3] always invites the hearer to take one of two sides: He must either side with the old rulers or the new one. "He that is not for me is against me."[4] There is no neutral position in a war. Even in silence, one is automatically identified as being on the side of the oppressor. There is no place in this war of liberation for nice white people who want to avoid taking sides and remain friends with both the racists and the Negro. To hear the Word is to decide: Are you with us or against us? There is no time for conferences or talk of any sort. If the hearing of the Word and the encounter with the Spirit do not convict you, then talk will be of little avail.

The Church not only preaches the Word of liberation, it joins Christ in his work of liberation. This is *diakonia*, "service." Though the decisive battle has been fought and won over racism, the war is not over. There is still left what G. P. Lewis calls the "mopping-up operations."[5] Just as the war in Europe continued for months

7. [Dietrich] Bonhoeffer, *Prisoner for God,* ed. Eberhard Bethge, trans. R. H. Fuller (New York: Macmillan, 1953), pp. 166–167. Used with permission.
8. Ignatius, Epistle to the Smyrnaeans 8:2. [Editor's note]
9. Cox, *The Secular City* (New York: Macmillan, 1965), p. 145.
1. Cullmann, *Christ and Time,* trans. F. V. Filson (Philadelphia: Westminster Press, 1949).
2. Gospel. [Editor's note]
3. Scripture; the Word of God. [Editor's note]
4. Matthew 12:30. [Editor's note]
5. Lewis, *The Johannine Epistles* (London: Epworth Press, 1961), p. 84.

after it was "won" at Stalingrad and El Alamein, so the war against the principalities and powers continues after the decisive battle on the cross.[6] We still have to fight racism. The evil forces have been defeated but refuse to admit it. "Although defeated," writes William Hordern, "evil still has sufficient strength to fight a stubborn rear-guard action."[7] It is the task of the Church to join Christ in this fight against evil. Thomas Wieser puts it this way:

> The way of the church is related to the fact that the Kyrios Lord himself is on his way in the world, . . . and the church has no choice but to follow him who precedes. Consequently obedience and witness to the Kyrios[8] require the discernment of the opening which he provides and the willingness to step into this opening.[9]

The opening has been made and the Church must follow. To follow means that the Church is more than a talking or a resolution-passing community. Its talk is backed up with relevant involvement in the world as a witness, through action, that what it says is in fact true.

Where is "the opening" that Christ provides? Where does he lead his people? Where indeed, if not in the ghetto. He meets the blacks where they are and becomes one of them. We see him there with his black face and big black hands lounging on a streetcorner. "Oh, but surely Christ is above race." But society is not raceless, any more than when God became a despised Jew. White liberal preference for a raceless Christ serves only to make official and orthodox the centuries-old portrayal of Christ as white. The "raceless" American Christ has a light skin, wavy brown hair, and sometimes—wonder of wonders—blue eyes. For whites to find him with big lips and kinky hair is as offensive as it was for the Pharisees to find him partying with tax-collectors. But whether whites want to hear it or not, *Christ is black, baby*, with all of the features which are so detestable to white society.

To suggest that Christ has taken on a black skin is not theological emotionalism. If the Church is a continuation of the Incarnation, and if the Church and Christ are where the oppressed are, then Christ and his Church must identify totally with the oppressed to the extent that they too suffer for the same reasons persons are enslaved. In America, blacks are oppressed because of their blackness. It would seem, then, that emancipation could only be realized by Christ and his Church becoming black. Thinking of Christ as nonblack in the twentieth century is as theologically impossible as thinking of him as non-Jewish in the first century. God's Word in Christ not only fulfills his purposes for man through his elected people, but also inaugurates a new age in which all oppressed people become his people. In America, that people is a black people. In order to remain faithful to his Word in Christ, his present manifestation must be the very essence of blackness.

It is the job of the Church to become black with him and accept the shame which white society places on blacks. But the Church knows that what is shame to the world is holiness to God. Black is holy, that is, it is a symbol of God's presence in history on behalf of the oppressed man. Where there is black, there is oppression; but blacks can be assured that where there is blackness, there is Christ who has taken on blackness so that what is evil in men's eyes might become good. Therefore Christ is black because he is oppressed, and oppressed because he is black. And if the Church is to join Christ by following his opening, it too must go where suffering is and become black also.

This is what the New Testament means by the service of reconciliation. It is not smoothing things over by ignoring the deep-seated racism in white society. It is freeing the racist of racism by making him confront blacks as men. Reconciliation has nothing to do with the "let's talk about it" attitude, or "it takes time" attitude. It merely says, "Look man, the revolution is on. Whose side are you on?"

The Church is also a fellowship (*koinonia*). This means that the Church must be in its own community what it preaches and what it seeks to accomplish in the world. Through the preaching of the Word, the Church calls the world to be responsible to God's act in Christ, and through its service it seeks to bring it about. But

---

6. Ibid.
7. Hordern, *Christianity, Communism and History* (London: Lutterworth Press, 1957), p. 27.
8. Kyrios: Lord [Greek]. [Editor's note]
9. Quoted in Cox, *Secular City*, p. 126.

the Church's preaching and service are meaningful only insofar as the Church itself is a manifestation of the preached Word. As Harvey Cox puts it, *koinonia* is "that aspect of the church's responsibility . . . which calls for a visible demonstration of what the church is saying in its kerygma and pointing to in its diakonia."[1] Thus the Church, by definition, contains no trace of racism. Christ "has broken down the dividing walls of hostility" (Eph. 2:14). That is why Karl Barth describes the Church as "God's subjective realization of the atonement."[2]

It is this need to be the sign of the Kingdom in the world which impels the Church continually to ask: "Who in the community does not live according to the spirit of Christ?" This is the kind of question which was so important to the sixteenth-century Anabaptists, and it must be vital for the Church of any age. Speaking to this question, Barth says: "The church which is not deeply disturbed by it is not a Christian church."[3] It cannot be "Christ existing as community" or "Christ's presence in history," as Bonhoeffer would put it, without being seriously concerned about the holiness of its members.

It is true that this concern may cause the community to ask the wrong questions. It may focus on irrelevancies (smoking, dancing, drinking, etc.) rather than on the essential (racism). But it is only through the asking of the question, "What makes men Christians?" that the true Church is able to be Christ in the world. The true Church of Christ must define clearly through its members the meaning of God's act in Christ so that all may know what the Church is up to. There can be no doubt in the minds of its members regarding the nature of its community and its purpose in the world. It must be a community that has accepted Christ's acceptance of us, and in this sense, it must be holy. At all times and in all situations holy members of the holy church, and therefore Christians, were and are the men assembled in it who are thereto elected by the Lord, called by His Word, and constituted by His Spirit: just so many, no more and no less, these men and no others.[4]

THE WHITE CHURCH AND BLACK POWER

If the real Church is the people of God, whose primary task is that of being Christ to the world by proclaiming the message of the gospel (*kerygma*), by rendering services of liberation (*diakonia*), and by being itself a manifestation of the nature of the new society (*koinonia*), then the empirical institutionalized white church has failed on all counts. It certainly has not rendered services of reconciliation to the poor. Rather, it illustrates the values of a sick society which oppresses the poor. Some present-day theologians, like Hamilton and Altizer, taking their cue from Nietzsche and the present irrelevancy of the Church to modern man, have announced the death of God. It seems, however, that their chief mistake lies in their apparent identification of God's reality with the signed-up Christians. If we were to identify the work of God with the white church, then, like Altizer, we must "will the death of God with a passion of faith." Or as Camus[5] would say, "If God *did* exist, we should have to abolish him."

The white church has not merely failed to render services to the poor, but has failed miserably in being a visible manifestation to the world of God's intention for humanity and in proclaiming the gospel to the world. It seems that the white church is not God's redemptive agent but, rather, an agent of the old society. It fails to create an atmosphere of radical obedience to Christ. Most church fellowships are more concerned about drinking or new buildings or Sunday closing than about children who die of rat bites or men who are killed because they want to be treated like men. The society is falling apart for want of moral leadership and moral example, but the white church passes innocuously pious resolutions and waits to be congratulated.

It is a sad fact that the white church's involvement in slavery and racism in America simply cannot be overstated. It not only failed to preach the kerygmatic Word but maliciously contributed to the doctrine of white supremacy. Even today all of the Church's

1. Ibid., p. 144.
2. Barth, *Church Dogmatics*, Vol. IV, Part I, trans. G. Bromiley (Edinburgh: T. & T. Clark, 1956), p. 643.
3. Ibid., p. 695.
4. Ibid., p. 696.
5. Albert Camus (1913–60), French Algerian philosopher who was the first African-born writer to win the Nobel Prize for Literature, winning for *L'Étranger* [*The Stranger*] in 1957. [Editor's note]

institutions—including its colleges and universities—reveal its white racist character. Racism has been a part of the life of the Church so long that it is virtually impossible for even the "good" members to recognize the bigotry perpetuated by the Church. Its morals are so immoral that even its most sensitive minds are unable to detect the inhumanity of the Church on the black people of America. This is at least one of the suggestions by Kyle Haselden, who was in most cases a very perceptive white southern churchman:

> We must ask whether our morality is itself immoral, whether our codes of righteousness are, when applied to the Negro, a violation and distortion of the Christian ethic. Do we not judge what is right and what is wrong in racial relationships by a righteousness which is itself unrighteous, by codes and creeds which are themselves immoral?[6]

The question is asked and the answer is obvious to the astute observer. The Church has been guilty of the gravest sin of all—"the enshrining of that which is immoral as the highest morality."[7] Jesus called this the sin against the Holy Spirit. It is unforgivable because it is never recognized.

Pierre Berton puts it mildly:

> In . . . the racial struggle, there is revealed the same pattern of tardiness, apathy, non-commitment, and outright opposition by the church. . . . Indeed, the history of the race struggle in the United States has been to a considerable extent the history of the Protestant rapport with the status quo. From the beginning, it was the church that put its blessing on slavery and sanctioned a caste system that continues to this day.[8]

As much as white churchmen may want to hedge on this issue, it is not possible. The issue is clear: Racism is a complete denial of the Incarnation and thus of Christianity. Therefore, the white denominational churches are unchristian. They are a manifestation of both a willingness to tolerate it and a desire to perpetuate it.

The old philosophical distinction between the primary and secondary qualities of objects provides an analogy here, where only the primary qualities pertain to the essence of the thing. Regarding the Church, are not fellowship and service primary qualities, without which the "church" is not the Church? Can we still speak of a community as being Christian if that body is racist through and through? It is my contention that the racism implies the absence of fellowship and service, which are primary qualities, indispensable marks of the Church. To be racist is to fall outside the definition of the Church. In our time, the issue of racism is analogous to the Arian Controversy of the fourth century. Athanasius perceived quite clearly that if Arius' views were tolerated, Christianity would be lost. But few white churchmen have questioned whether racism was a similar denial of Jesus Christ. Even Haselden, certainly one of the most sensitive of the white churchmen who have written on the subject, can speak of white Christian racists.

[* * *]

If American theology is going to serve the needs of the Church by relating the gospel to the political, economic, and social situation of America, it must cut its adoring dependence upon Europe as the place to tell us what theology ought to be talking about. Some European theologians, like Barth and Bonhoeffer, may serve as examples of how to relate theology to life, but not in defining *our* major issues.

There is a need for a theology of revolution, a theology which radically encounters the problems of the disinherited black people in America in particular and the oppressed people of color throughout the world in general. As Joseph Washington puts it:

> In the twentieth century white Protestantism has concentrated its personnel, time, energy, and finances on issues that it has deemed more significant than the "American Dilemma": pacifism, politics, liberal versus conservative controversies, prohibition, socialism, Marxism, labor and management aspects of economic justice, civil liberties,

6. Haselden, *The Racial Problem in Christian Perspective* (New York: Harper & Row, 1959), p. 48.
7. Ibid.
8. Berton, *The Comfortable Pew* (Philadelphia: J. B. Lippincott Co., 1965), pp. 28–29.

totalitarianism, overseas mission, fascism, war and peace, reorganization of ecclesiastical structures, and ecumenical issues.[9]

It has overlooked the unique problem of the powerless blacks.

In this new era of Black Power, the era in which blacks are sick of white power and are prepared to do anything and give everything for freedom now, theology cannot afford to be silent. Not to speak, not to "do theology" around this critical problem, is to say that the black predicament is not crucial to Christian faith. At a moment when blacks are determined to stand up as human beings even if they are shot down, the Word of the cross certainly is focused upon them. Will no one speak that Word to the dead and dying? Theologians confronted by this question may distinguish three possible responses. Some will, timidly or passionately, continue to appeal (mistakenly) to Paul's dictum about the "powers that be." We will have law-and-order theologians as we have law-and-order pastors and laymen. Others will insist that theology as such is necessarily unrelated to social upheaval. These men will continue as in a vacuum, writing footnotes on the Aramaic substratum of Mark's Gospel or on the authorship of the *Theologia Germanica* or on the "phenomenon" of faith. Could a black man hope that there are still others who, *as theologians*, will join the oppressed in their fight for freedom? These theologians will speak unequivocally of revelation, Scripture, God, Christ, grace, faith, Church, ministry, and hope, so that the message comes through loud and clear: *The black revolution is the work of Christ.*

If theology fails to re-evaluate its task in the light of Black Power, the emphasis on the death of God will not add the needed dimension. This will mean that the white church and white theology are dead, not God. It will mean that God will choose another means of implementing his word of righteousness in the world. It will mean also that the burden of the gospel is placed solely on the shoulders of the oppressed, without any clear word from the "church." This leads us to our last concern, the black church. It is indeed possible that the only redemptive forces left in the denominational churches are to be found in the segregated black churches.

The white response so far, in and out of the Church, is, "Not yet," which in the twisted rhetoric of the land of the free means, "Never!" "Law and order" is the sacred incantation of the priests of the old order; and the faithful respond with votes, higher police budgets, and Gestapo legislation. Private and public arsenals of incredible destructive force testify to the determination of a sick and brutal people to put an end to black revolution and indeed to black people. The black man has violated the conditions under which he is permitted to breathe, and the air is heavy with the potential for genocide. The confrontation of black people as real persons is so strange and out of harmony with the normal pattern of white behavior that most whites cannot even begin to understand the meaning of black humanity.

In this situation of revolution and reaction, the Church must decide where its identity lies. Will it continue its chaplaincy to the forces of oppression, or will it embrace the cause of liberation, proclaiming in word and deed the gospel of Christ?

WILLIAM R. JONES

Divine Racism: The Unacknowledged Threshold Issue for Black Theology [1973]

In the early 1970s, the premises and conclusions of the emerging field of black theology were vigorously debated among scholars. In the selection reprinted here, from William Ronald Jones's 1973 book, *Is God a White Racist?* (*IGWR*), Jones (b. 1933), a professor and activist,

argues that the focus on black suffering and oppression by black theologians such as James Cone (p. 615) poses problems for the development of a black liberation theology. Jones uses his analysis of specific issues such as theodicy (the study of the problem of evil) to present a

9. J. Washington, *Black Religion* [Boston: Beacon Press, 1964], p. 228.

greater methodological issue. What is needed, Jones asserts, is a *de novo* approach, one that starts afresh instead of accepting and building on established ideas of theology. "Each and every category must be painstakingly inspected, and if it is found to be infected with the virus of racism or oppression, it must be cast aside," Jones argues. In his 1979 essay, "Epilogue: An Interpretation of the Debate Among Black Theologians," Cone recognized Jones's contribution to the field: "Jones's analysis remains as a challenge to Black theological proposals and will continue to require the serious attention of Black theologians."

For the 1998 republication of *IGWR*, Jones added a new preface and afterword to put the debate in historical context and "to correct a basic and distorted misinterpretation of what I was trying to do," as he said in a July 2010

telephone conversation. "I was trying to develop a new methodological structure," Jones explained. "It was an internal critique [of black theology's methodology], not an attempt to solve a particular proposition like 'Is God a white racist?' I think you get into trouble by attempting to do something like that." Jones's 1998 "Afterword" also introduces the idea that historical distance often brings out the commonalities between seemingly divergent positions. "As I survey the coming dialogue and debate that republishing *IGWR* will spawn between black humanism and black theism—conscientious antagonists on the battlefield in the search for black freedom—I am confident that when future generations review the clash, they will conclude that the adversaries discovered, all too late, that they were not too distant relatives," Jones predicted.

From *Is God a White Racist? A Preamble to Black Theology* (Garden City, N.Y.: Anchor Press, 1973), pp. 71–78, 98–120.

This chapter purports to show that the issue of divine racism has been illegitimately ignored by the current black theologians. I say "illegitimately" because the question has been avoided only by disregarding concrete and explicit features of their own thought. Since specific conclusions advanced by the black theologians are meaningful and valid only if they provide a convincing refutation of the charge of divine racism, the absence of an analysis and denial of the question "Is God a white racist?" constitutes a curious inconsistency and removes the necessary support the superstructure of their respective systems requires. I will show specifically that the issue of divine racism is implicit in the following propositions affirmed by the black theologians: black theology is a theology of liberation; the politics of God and blacks as God's chosen people are central themes in black theology; and black theology is committed to a total and comprehensive examination of the Christian tradition.

DIVINE RACISM: EXPLICIT AND IMPLICIT

The same argument cannot be used to demonstrate that the issue of divine racism is central for each black

theologian. For most, it is necessary to proceed by way of inference, showing that an explicit concept, conclusion, or methodological position acknowledged by the black theologian presupposes the question of divine racism or its refutation. However, for one theologian, James Cone, the route of logical inference is not required, for the concept is explicitly asserted in a way that reveals its centrality. Cone declares: "Either God is identified with the oppressed to the point that their experience becomes his, or he is a god of racism."[1] And to remove all doubt regarding the meaning of "identification," he claims in a similar vein, "Black theology refuses to accept a God who is not identified totally with the goals of the black community. If God is not for us and against white people, then he is a murderer, and we had better kill him. The task of black theology is to kill Gods who do not belong to the black community."[2]

These statements clearly indicate that Cone is not only aware of the issue of divine racism, but even more important, he regards it as an unavoidable issue for black theology. Note that his analysis establishes two opposing options, which define the arena for black theological discussion and construction. There is the option of "a God of racism," one who is *against* or *indifferent to*

1. James Cone, *A Black Theology of Liberation* (New York: Lippincott, 1970), pp. 120–21. [Unless otherwise noted, all footnotes are those of the author.]
2. [Cone], *Liberation*, pp. 59–60.

black liberation. The second option is the logical and theological opposite: a God *for* black liberation. By defining the task of black theology as destroying Gods who are not for black liberation, Cone is maintaining that the black theologian must effectively refute the position of divine racism. In fact he appears to claim that the black theologian can defend the position that God is for black liberation, only by refuting the charge that He is a god of racism. His words also convey the meaning that this refutation is the crucial part of the black theologian's task. If the analysis of Cone here is correct, then his own definition of the purpose of black theology creates the exact critical apparatus and the rules of the game I will use to criticize his system.

It is not difficult to show that the theodicy issue is also central for the remaining black theologians, and these factors further establish its centrality for Cone. The starting point for this demonstration is the conclusion already established: suffering introduces the theodicy question. Thus the general issue of theodicy and the particular issue of divine racism are central because of the status the black theologians assign to black suffering. Theodicy and divine racism are controlling issues because black oppression and suffering are made the starting point for theological analysis.

It can now be established that black suffering is either explicitly or implicitly central for the contemporary black theologians. Here is an explicit reference from the theology of James Cone: "The point of departure for black theology is the question, How do we dare speak of God in a suffering world . . . in which blacks are humiliated because they are black? This question . . . occupies the central place in our theological perspective."[3]

A similar emphasis is present in J. Deotis Roberts' discussion of "The Black Man's God."

> I am taking the position that the problem of God presents itself to blacks in terms, not of the existence of God, but rather in terms of the moral attributes of God. . . . The Christian understanding of God must develop out of the black presence in a

white racist society, and out of an experience of oppression endured for almost four centuries.[4]

What is not always explicit in the language of black theology may often lie implicit. For example, once "black liberation" is established as the primary goal or the rationale for black theology, black suffering becomes its necessary starting point. "Liberation" as defined by the black theologians means nothing if it does not mean release from the suffering that lies at the heart of oppression. To define liberation as the *summum bonum*, the highest good for blacks, is, at the same time, to make that suffering which is the core of oppression the essential ingredient of the *summum malum*, the ultimate evil.

Each of the black theologians regards his position as a theology of liberation, and this motif is usually proclaimed in the title of the work: *A Black Theology of Liberation, Liberation and Reconciliation: A Black Theology*. Even where "liberation" is absent from the title, it is soon discovered to be the black theologian's principal focus.

What is less obvious is that the issue of divine racism becomes an unavoidable issue in the context of any "black theology of liberation." To undertake the construction of a black theology of liberation requires the prior conclusion that black suffering is oppressive or negative. God disapproves of it; He does not demand that blacks should endure it. But suffering is multievidential;[5] it can express a relation of divine favor or disfavor. Consequently, the possibility of divine disfavor cannot be avoided.

By virtue of his task, the black theologian of liberation is committed to the view that black oppression is not evidence of divine disfavor. Accordingly, he is required to show—if he is to avoid the indictment of begging the question—that the general class of divine disfavor, of which divine racism is a subclass, does not accurately describe the black situation.

Other segments of the black theologian's thought force the issue of divine racism. It has already been established that ethnic suffering raises the question of

---

3. [Cone], *Liberation*, p. 115.

4. J. Deotis Roberts, *Liberation and Reconciliation: A Black Theology* (Philadelphia: Westminster Press, 1971), p. 83.

5. One point will establish that the multievidentiality of suffering is acknowledged by the black theologians, however inadvertently. Once the black theologian allows that deserved punishment is a possible interpretation of human suffering, and also denies that all suffering is deserved punishment, he cannot avoid the conclusion that suffering is multievidential.

divine racism. Accordingly it is necessary only to demonstrate that the black theologians describe black suffering as a variety of ethnic suffering. It will become clear that each affirms that black suffering is maldistributed, enormous, dehumanizing, and transgenerational. At this juncture, however, it is sufficient to note that to define the black situation as *oppressive* is actually to affirm the essentials of ethnic suffering; and the definition of the black situation as oppressive, we have seen, is the consequence of the black theologian's own definition of his task as a theology of liberation.

THE POLITICS OF GOD, AND BLACKS AS GOD'S CHOSEN PEOPLE

There are other determining factors that oblige the black theologian to resolve the issue of divine racism at the outset of his theological construction, and these are factors common to his basic position. Each black theologian affirms the doctrine of the politics of God as an essential plank. Man must decide where God is working for human liberation in our midst and join Him in the struggle. The following statement from Cone is representative of this viewpoint: "Black theology merely tries to discern the activity of the Holy One as he effects his purpose in the liberation of man from the forces of oppression. We must make decisions about where God is at work so we can join him in his fight against evil."[6]

But given ethnic suffering and the multievidentiality of suffering, certain restrictions are placed on the theological employment of the politics of God. Without the prior refutation of the charge of divine racism, the black theologian begs the question if he affirms the politics of God. It goes without saying that Cone and others advocate joining God because they presuppose that He is on the side of blacks. This is to say that where God is active in human affairs He is engaged for the (a) good of (b) blacks—if not all of mankind. But ethnic suffering and the multievidentiality of suffering call both (a) and (b) into question. The excessive amount of black suffering and its enormity, both of which are admitted by calling the black situation oppressive, make it risky if not foolhardy to affirm that God is at work for the liberation of blacks. Must not the black theologian first explain how their plight came about in the first place in the face of God's alleged activity in their behalf? In sum, it is not possible to make the politics of God the second floor of the edifice of black theology without a foundational theodicy that decisively answers the charge of divine racism. The politics of God presupposes that God is not a white racist, without establishing it.

Much the same argument can be made regarding another favorite motif of black theology: blacks as God's "chosen people." To regard blacks as God's elect involves the prior conclusion that God is favorably inclined toward them. But this claim can be made only if the opposite relation, divine disfavor, has been effectively eliminated. And this, again, demands the refutation of divine racism as logically prior to any proposition about divine favor.

DIVINE RACISM AND A *DE NOVO*[7] THEOLOGY

The precondition for constructing a black theology is the conviction that an unacknowledged white theology, a theology of racism and oppression, dominates the field. Black theology, then, by definition is committed to a theological development not only beyond this white theology but in conscious and fundamental opposition to it. My purpose now is to show that this understanding of black theology requires a *de novo* approach to theologizing and that within this context the issue of divine racism cannot be avoided.

The black theologians assign primacy to the black experience as the theological norm. It is argued, for instance, that theological reflection must begin with the questions and issues that are pressing upon the black mind and heart. In this way, the black experience determines the theological agenda; it selects the appropriate theological issues, and ranks them. Moreover, the answers must not only harmonize with the black experience, they must also hasten the actualization of the aspirations incarnate in the black hope.

Again, the black experience passes final judgment upon the functional and dysfunctional quality of the entire theological tradition. A theological concept is functional if and only if it advances black liberation

---

6. [Cone], *Liberation*, pp. 26–27.
7. Beginning again, afresh [Latin]. [Editor's note]

or liberation-reconciliation. As Cone concludes, "The legitimacy of any language, religious or otherwise, is determined by its usability in the struggle for liberation."[8]

On the basis of the foregoing analysis—and here we arrive at the crucial point for the argument—the black theologian is committed to a total examination of the theological tradition. Once it is concluded that Christianity is infected with "Whitianity," once it is granted that a racist doctrine of the tradition has been perpetuated, the tradition must be scrutinized in the most radical and comprehensive manner. Like the rotten apples in the barrel of good apples, nothing prior to the examination can be regarded as sacrosanct for black theology—be it God, Jesus, or the Bible. Each and every category must be painstakingly inspected, and if it is found to be infected with the virus of racism or oppression, it must be cast aside.[9]

The same point can be made from another perspective: Once the black theologian is convinced that a racist variety of Christian faith has continued, he must proceed, as it were, *de novo*, placing the entire tradition under a rigid theological ban. And this ban can be lifted only when each part proves its orthodoxy by showing its racist quotient to be minimal.

I question whether the black theologians have recognized the sweeping consequences of their presuppositions here. I also take the position that their appraisal has not been sufficiently comprehensive and radical. From my vantage point I see a fatal residue of the oppressor's worldview in some of their theistic premises, in particular the intrinsic goodness of God.

One of the compelling reasons for raising the issue of divine racism is to force a discussion of traditional concepts of God as possible props for oppression.

The major point can now be made: From a *de novo* perspective, the rival claims, God is a white racist and God is a soul brother, stand on equal footing. Accordingly, the black theologian cannot avoid the issue of divine racism. In fact it can be argued that he contradicts himself methodologically if he emphasizes black suffering and calls for a comprehensive scrutiny of the tradition but fails to raise the question of divine racism.

The presuppositions of the black theologians, in summary, force the conclusion that the foundation for their systems must be a theodicy that effectively rebuts the charge that God is a white racist. Whether they provide the requisite rebuttal can only be determined by critical inspection of their thought.

I would insist at the outset that the black theologian cannot simply assume the falsity of the charge. His own norm makes this plain. Black suffering must be analyzed from an existential and not an abstract or theoretical perspective. The question of divine racism emerges because of the blood and guts of black suffering. The black theologian, accordingly, must utilize evidential materials drawn from the actual black experience, past, present—and if he dares—the future. What is to be rejected are mere rational and theoretical formulations that are not substantiated by the actual history of blacks. In this connection I will contend that the liberation of non-blacks, e.g. the Jews in the Exodus account, can never count decisively against the charge that God is a white racist.

JACQUELYN GRANT
Black Theology and the Black Woman [1979]

Just as the black feminist movement was fueled by the simultaneously empowering and frustrating experiences of black women in the civil rights and feminist movements of the 1960s and 1970s, black women's theology (later named womanist theology) was driven by engagement with black theology and feminist theology.

8. [Cone], *Liberation*, pp. 113–14.
9. Jones's 1998 "Afterword" to *IGWR* presents his methodological model as a "virus/vaccine" approach, where fully understanding and mapping the virus/problem is a prerequisite to developing a vaccine/solution. "The model I was using in 1974 was a sort of precursor of that particular approach," Jones explained in a 2010 telephone conversion.

Black female theologians were largely excluded from the early development of black theology. For example, the signatories of the historic "Black Power" statement of the National Committee of Negro Churchmen included forty-seven men and only one woman. Moreover, black theology tended to reinforce patriarchal conceptions of church and society. Yet, by championing the oppressed and by radically reconceptualizing theology as a basis for revolutionary change, black theology provided tools for the development of a new theology grounded in the experiences of black women.

Jacquelyn Grant (b. 1948), an African Methodist Episcopal (AME) minister and scholar of African American religion, earned a Ph.D. from Union Theological Seminary in New York City and founded the Women's Studies in Religion Program at the Harvard Divinity School. Her groundbreaking essay, reprinted here, examines patriarchal elements of the emerging black theology movement and highlights the racism and classism of other emerging liberation theologies. By bringing awareness to how issues of gender, race, and class shape theology and religious practices, Grant and other early black female theologians laid the groundwork for the emergence of womanist theology.

From James H. Cone and Gayraud S. Wilmore, eds., *Black Theology: A Documentary History, 1966–1979* (Maryknoll, N.Y.: Orbis Books, 1979), pp. 418–33.

Liberation theologies have arisen out of the contexts of the liberation struggles of black Americans, Latin Americans, American women, black South Africans, and Asians. These theologies represent a departure from traditional Christian theology. As a collective critique, liberation theologies raise serious questions about the normative use of Scripture, tradition and experience in Christian theology. Liberation theologians assert that the reigning theologies of the West have been used to legitimate the established order. Those to whom the church has entrusted the task of interpreting the meaning of God's activity in the world have been too content to represent the ruling classes. For this reason, say the liberation theologians, theology has generally not spoken to those who are opposed by the political establishment.

Ironically, the criticism that liberation theology makes against classical theology has been turned against liberation theology itself. Just as most European and American theologians have acquiesced in the oppression of the West, for which they have been taken to task by liberation theologians, some liberation theologians have acquiesced in one or more oppressive aspects of the liberation struggle itself. Where racism is rejected, sexism has been embraced. Where classism is called into question, racism and sexism have been tolerated. And where sexism is repudiated, racism and classism are often ignored.

Although there is a certain validity to the argument that any one analysis—race, class, or sex—is not sufficiently universal to embrace the needs of all oppressed peoples, these particular analyses, nonetheless, have all been well presented and are crucial for a comprehensive and authentic liberation theology. In order for liberation theology to be faithful to itself, it must hear the critique coming to it from the perspective of the black woman—perhaps the most oppressed of all the oppressed.

I am concerned in this essay with how the experience of the black woman calls into question certain assumptions in liberation theology in general, and black theology in particular. In the Latin American context, this has already been done by women such as Beatriz Melano Couch and Consuelo Urquiza. A few Latin American theologians have begun to respond. Beatriz Couch, for example, accepts the starting point of Latin American theologians, but criticizes them for their exclusivism with respect to race and sex. She says:

> … we in Latin America stress the importance of the starting point, the praxis, and the use of social science to analyze our political, historical situation. In this I am in full agreement with my male colleagues … with one qualitative difference. I stress the need to give importance to the different cultural forms that express oppression; to the ideology that

divides people not only according to class, but to race, to sex. Racism and sexism are oppressive ideologies, which deserve a specific treatment in the theology of liberation.[1]

More recently, Consuelo Urquiza called for the unification of Hispanic American women in struggling against their oppression in the church and society. In commenting on the contradiction in the Pauline Epistles that undergird the oppression of the Hispanic American woman, Urquiza said: "At the present time all Christians will agree with Paul in the first part of [Galatians 3:28] about freedom and slavery that there should not be slaves. . . . However, the next part of this verse . . . has been ignored, and the equality between man and woman is not accepted. They would rather skip that line and go to the epistle to [1] Timothy [2:9–15]."[2] Women theologians of Latin background are beginning to do theology and to sensitize other women to the necessity of participating in decisions that affect their lives and the life of their communities. Latin American theology will gain from these inputs, which women are making to the theological process.

Third World and black women[3] in the United States will soon collaborate in an attack on another aspect of liberation theology—feminist theology. Black and Third World women have begun to articulate their differences and similarities with the feminist movement, which is dominated by white American women who until now have been the chief authors of feminist theology. It is my contention that the theological perspectives of black and Third World women should reflect these differences and similarities with feminist theology. It is my purpose, however, to look critically at black theology as a black woman in an effort to determine how adequate is its conception of liberation for the total black community.

[* * *]

I want to begin with the question: "Where are black women in black theology?" They are, in fact, invisible in black theology, and we need to know why this is the case. Because the black church experience and black experience in general are important sources for doing black theology, we need to look at the black woman in relation to both in order to understand the way black theology has applied its conception of liberation. Finally, in view of the status of the black woman vis-à-vis black theology, the black church and the black experience, a challenge needs to be presented to black theology. This is how I propose to discuss this important question.

The Invisibility of Black Women in Black Theology

In examining black theology, it is necessary to make one of two assumptions: (1) either black women have no place in the enterprise, or (2) black men are capable of speaking for us. Both of these assumptions are false and need to be discarded. They arise out of a male-dominated culture, which restricts women to certain areas of the society. In such a culture, men are given the warrant to speak for women on all matters of significance. It is no accident that all of the recognized black theologians are men. This is what might be expected, given the status and power accorded the discipline of theology. Professional theology is done by those who are highly trained. It requires, moreover, mastery of that power most accepted in the definition of manhood, the power or ability to "reason." This is supposedly what opens the door to participation in logical, philosophical debates and discussions presupposing rigorous intellectual training, for most of history, out-

1. Beatriz Melano Couch, remarks on the feminist panel of Theology in the Americas Conference in Detroit in August 1975, printed in *Theology in the Americas,* ed. Sergio Torres and John Eagleson (Maryknoll, N.Y.: Orbis Books, 1976), 375. [Unless otherwise indicated, all footnotes are those of the author.] [Praxis: practice or practical application of a theory. Editor's note]
2. Consuelo Urquiza, "A Message from a Hispanic American Woman," *The Fifth Commission: A Monitor for Third World Concerns* IV (June–July 1978), insert. The Fifth Commission is a commission of the National Council of the Churches of Christ in the USA (NCC), 475 Riverside Drive, New York, N.Y.
3. I agree with the Fifth Commission that "the Third World is not a geographic entity, but rather the world of oppressed peoples in their struggle for liberation." In this sense, black women are included in the term "Third World." However, in order to accent the peculiar identity, problems, and needs of black women in the First World or the Third World contexts, I choose to make the distinction between black and other Third World women.

side the "woman's sphere." Whereas the nature of men has been defined in terms of reason and the intellect, that of women has to do with intuition and emotionalism. Women were limited to matters related to the home while men carried out the more important work, involving the use of the rational faculties.[4] These distinctions were not as clear in the slave community.[5] Slaves and women were thought to share the characteristics of emotionality and irrationality. As we move further away from the slave culture, however, a dualism between black men and women increasingly emerges. This means that black males have gradually increased their power and participation in the male-dominated society, while black females have continued to endure the stereotypes and oppressions of an earlier period.

When sexual dualism has fully run its course in the black community (and I believe that it has), it will not be difficult to see why black women are invisible in black theology. Just as white women formerly had no place in white theology—except as the receptors of white men's theological interpretations—black women have had no place in the development of black theology. By self-appointment, or by the sinecure of a male-dominated society, black men have deemed it proper to speak for the entire black community, male and female.

In a sense, black men's acceptance of the patriarchal model is logical and to be expected. Black male slaves were unable to reap the benefits of patriarchy. Before emancipation they were not given the opportunity to serve as protector and provider for black women and children, as white men were able to do for their women and children. Much of what was considered "manhood" had to do with how well one could perform these functions. It seems only natural that the post-emancipation black men would view as of primary importance the reclaiming of their property—their women and their children. Moreover, it is natural that black men would claim their "natural" right to the "man's world." But it should be emphasized that this is logical and natural only if one has accepted without question the terms and values of patriarchy—the concept of male control and supremacy.

Black men must ask themselves a difficult question. How can a white society characterized by black enslavement, colonialism, and imperialism provide the normative conception of women for black society? How can the sphere of the woman, as defined by white men, be free from the evils and oppressions that are found in the white society? The important point is that in matters relative to the relationship between the sexes, black men have accepted without question the patriarchal structures of the white society as normative for the black community. How can a black minister preach in a way that advocates St. Paul's dictum concerning women while ignoring or repudiating his dictum concerning slaves? Many black women are enraged as they listen to "liberated" black men speak about the "place of women" in words and phrases similar to those of the very white oppressors they condemn.

Black women have been invisible in theology because theological scholarship has not been a part of the woman's sphere. The first of the above two assumptions results, therefore, from the historical orientation of the dominant culture. The second follows from the first. If women have no place in theology it becomes the natural prerogative of men to monopolize theological concerns, including those relating specifically to women. Inasmuch as black men have accepted the sexual dualisms of the dominant culture, they presume to speak for black women.

Before finally dismissing the two assumptions, a pertinent question should be raised. Does the absence of black women in the circles producing black theology necessarily mean that the resultant theology cannot be in the best interest of black women? The answer is obvious. Feminist theologians during the past few years have shown how theology done by men in male-dominated cultures has served to undergird patriarchal

---

4. For a discussion of sexual dualisms in our society, see Rosemary Ruether, *New Woman/New Earth* (New York: Seabury Press, 1975), chapter 1; and [Reuther], *Liberation Theology* (New York: Paulist Press, 1972), 16 ff. Also for a discussion of sexual (social) dualisms as related to the brain hemispheres, see Sheila Collins, *A Different Heaven and Earth* (Valley Forge, [Penn.]: Judson Press, 1974), 169–70.

5. Angela Davis, "Reflections on the Black Woman's Role in the Community of Slaves," *Black Scholar* 4, no. 3 (December 1971): 3–15. I do take issue with Davis's point, however. The black community may have experienced "equality in inequality," but this was forced on them from the dominant or enslaving community. She does not deal with the inequality within the community itself.

structures in society.[6] If black men have accepted those structures, is there any reason to believe that the theology written by black men would be any more liberating of black women than white theology was for white women? It would seem that in view of the oppression that black people have suffered, black men would be particularly sensitive to the oppression of others.[7]

James Cone has stated that the task of black theology "is to analyze the nature of the gospel of Jesus Christ in the light of oppressed black people so they will see the gospel as inseparable from their humiliated condition, bestowing on them the necessary power to break the chains of oppression. This means that it is a theology of and for the black community, seeking to interpret the religious dimensions of the forces of liberation in that community."[8] What are the forces of liberation in the black community and the black church? Are they to be exclusively defined by the struggle against racism? My answer to that question is No. There are oppressive realities in the black community that are related to, but independent of, the fact of racism. Sexism is one such reality. Black men seek to liberate themselves from racial stereotypes and the conditions of oppression without giving due attention to the stereotypes and oppressions against women, which parallel those against blacks. Blacks fight to be free of the stereotype that all blacks are dirty and ugly, or that black represents evil and darkness.[9] The slogan "Black is Beautiful" was a counterattack on these stereotypes. The parallel for women is the history of women as "unclean," especially during menstruation and after childbirth. Because the model of beauty in the white male-dominated society is the "long-haired blonde," with all that goes along with that mystique, black women have an additional problem with the Western idea of "ugliness," particularly as they encounter black men who have adopted this white model of beauty. Similarly, the Christian

teaching that woman is responsible for the fall of *mankind* and is, therefore, the source of evil has had a detrimental effect in the experience of black women.

Like all oppressed peoples, the self-image of blacks has suffered damage. In addition they have not been in control of their own destiny. It is the goal of the black liberation struggle to change radically the socioeconomic and political conditions of black people by inculcating self-love, self-control, self-reliance, and political power. The concepts of self-love, self-control, self-reliance, and political participation certainly have broad significance for black women, even though they were taught that, by virtue of their sex, they had to be completely dependent on *man*; yet while their historical situation reflected the need for dependence, the powerlessness of black men made it necessary for them to seek those values for themselves.

Racism and sexism are interrelated just as all forms of oppression are interrelated. Sexism, however, has a reality and significance of its own because it represents that peculiar form of oppression suffered by black women at the hands of black men. It is important to examine this reality of sexism as it operated in both the black community and the black church. We will consider first the black church and secondly the black community to determine to what extent black theology has measured up to its defined task with respect to the liberation of black women.[1]

THE BLACK CHURCH AND THE BLACK WOMAN

I can agree with Karl Barth as he describes the peculiar function of theology as the church's "subjecting herself to a self-test." "She [the church] faces herself with the question of truth, i.e., she measures her action,

---

6. See Sheila Collins, *A Different Heaven;* Rosemary Ruether, *New Woman;* Letty Russell, *Human Liberation in a Feminist Perspective* (Philadelphia: Westminster Press, 1974); and Mary Daly, *Beyond God the Father* (Boston: Beacon Press, 1973).

7. Surely the factor of race would be absent, but one would have to do an in-depth analysis to determine the possible effect on the status of black women.

8. James Cone, *A Black Theology of Liberation* (Philadelphia: J. B. Lippincott, 1970), 23.

9. Eulalio Baltazar discusses color symbolism (white is good; black is evil) as a reflection of racism in the white theology that perpetuates it. *The Dark Center: A Process Theology of Blackness* (New York: Paulist Press, 1973).

1. One may want to argue that black theology is not concerned with sexism but with racism. I will argue in this essay that such a theology could speak only half the truth, if truth at all.

her language about God, against her existence as a church."[2]

On the one hand, black theology must continue to criticize classical theology and the white church. But on the other hand, black theology must subject the black church to a "self-test." The task of the church, according to James Cone, is threefold: (1) "It proclaims the reality of divine liberation. . . . It is not possible to receive the good news of freedom and also keep it to ourselves; it must be told to the whole world. . . ." (2) "It actively shares in the liberation struggle." (3) It "is a visible manifestation that the gospel is a reality. . . . If it [the church] lives according to the old order (as it usually has), then no one will believe its message."[3] It is clear that black theology must ask whether or not the black church is faithful to this task. Moreover, the language of the black church about God must be consistent with its action.[4] These requirements of the church's faithfulness in the struggle for liberation have not been met as far as the issue of women is concerned.

If the liberation of women is not proclaimed, the church's proclamation cannot be about divine liberation. If the church does not share in the liberation struggle of black women, its liberation struggle is not authentic. If women are oppressed, the church cannot possibly be "a visible manifestation that the gospel is a reality"—for the gospel cannot be real in that context. One can see the contradictions between the church's language or proclamation of liberation and its action by looking both at the status of black women in the church as laity and black women in the ordained ministry of the church.

It is often said that women are the "backbone" of the church. On the surface this may appear to be a compliment, especially when one considers the function of the backbone in the human anatomy. Theressa Hoover prefers to use the term "glue" to describe the function of women in the black church. In any case,

the telling portion of the word backbone is "back." It has become apparent to me that most of the ministers who use this term have reference to location rather than function. What they really mean is that women are in the "background" and should be kept there. They are merely support workers. This is borne out by my observation that in many churches women are consistently given responsibilities in the kitchen, while men are elected or appointed to the important boards and leadership positions. While decisions and policies may be discussed in the kitchen, they are certainly not made there. Recently I conducted a study in one conference of the African Methodist Episcopal Church, which indicated that women are accorded greater participation on the decision-making boards of smaller rather than larger churches.[5] This political maneuver helps to keep women "in their place" in the denomination as well as in the local congregations. The conspiracy to keep women relegated to the background is also aided by the continuous psychological and political strategizing that keeps women from realizing their own potential power in the church. Not only are they rewarded for performance in "backbone" or supportive positions, but they are penalized for trying to move from the backbone to the head position—the leadership of the church. It is by considering the distinction between prescribed support positions and the policy-making, leadership positions that the oppression of black women in the black church can be seen more clearly.

For the most part, men have monopolized the ministry as a profession. The ministry of women as fully ordained clergypersons has always been controversial. The black church fathers were unable to see the injustices of their own practices, even when they paralleled the injustices in the white church against which they rebelled.

In the early nineteenth century, the Rev. Richard Allen perceived that it was unjust for blacks, free and

---

2. Karl Barth, *Church Dogmatics*, vol. 1, part 1, 2.
3. Cone, *A Black Theology*, 230–32.
4. James Cone and Albert Cleage do make this observation of the contemporary black church and its response to the struggles against racism. See Cleage, *The Black Messiah* (New York: Sheed and Ward, 1969); and Cone, *A Black Theology*.
5. A study that I conducted in the Philadelphia Conference of the African Methodist Episcopal Church, May 1976. It also included sporadic samplings of churches in other conferences in the First Episcopal District. As for example, a church of 1,660 members (500 men and 1,160 women) had a trustee board of 8 men and 1 woman and a steward board of 13 men and 6 women. A church of 100 members (35 men and 65 women) had a trustee board of 5 men and 4 women and a steward board of 5 men and 4 women.

slaves, to be relegated to the balcony and restricted to a special time to pray and kneel at the communion table; for this he should be praised. Yet because of his acceptance of the patriarchal system, Allen was unable to see the injustice in relegating women to one area of the church—the pews—by withholding ordination from women as he did in the case of Mrs. Jarena Lee.[6] Lee recorded Allen's response when she informed him of her call to "go preach the Gospel":

> He replied by asking in what sphere I wished to move in? I said, among the Methodists. He then replied, that a Mrs. Cook, a Methodist lady, had also some time before requested the same privilege; who it was believed, had done much good in the way of *exhortation,* and *holding prayer meetings;* and who had been permitted to do so by the *verbal license* of the preacher in charge at the time. But as to women preaching, he said that our Discipline knew nothing at all about it—that *it did not call* for women preachers.[7]

Because of this response, Jarena Lee's preaching ministry was delayed for eight years. She was not unaware of the sexist injustice in Allen's response. "Oh how careful ought we be, lest through our by-laws of church government and discipline, we bring into disrepute even the word of life. For as unseemly as it may appear nowadays for a woman to preach, it should be remembered that nothing is impossible with God. And why should

it be thought impossible, heterodox, or improper for a woman to preach, seeing the Saviour died for the woman as well as the man?"[8]

Another "colored minister of the gospel," Elizabeth, was greatly troubled over her call to preach, or more accurately, over the response of men to her call to preach. She said: "I often felt that I was unfit to assemble with the congregation with whom I had gathered.... I felt that I was despised on account of this gracious calling, and was looked upon as a speckled bird by the ministers to whom I looked for instruction ... some [of the ministers] would cry out, 'you are an enthusiast,' and others said, 'the Discipline did not allow of any such division of work.'"[9] Sometime later when questioned about her authority to preach against slavery and her ordination status, she responded that she preached "not by the commission of men's hands: if the Lord had ordained me, I needed nothing better."[1] With this commitment to God rather than to a male-dominated church structure, she led a fruitful ministry.

Mrs. Amanda Berry Smith, like Mrs. Jarena Lee, had to conduct her ministry outside the structures of the A.M.E. Church. Smith described herself as a "plain Christian woman" with "no money" and "no prominence."[2] But she was intrigued with the idea of attending the General Conference of 1872 in Nashville, Tennessee. Her inquiry into the cost of going to Nashville brought the following comments from some of the A.M.E. brethren:

---

6. Jarena Lee, *The Life and Religious Experiences of Jarena Lee: A Colored Lady Giving an Account of Her Call to Preach the Gospel* (Philadelphia, 1836), in *Early Negro Writing 1760–1837,* ed. Dorothy Porter (Boston: Beacon Press, 1971), 494–514. [Allen: p. 144; Lee: p. 152; Editor's note]

7. Ibid., 503 (italics added): Carol George in *Segregated Sabbaths* (New York: Oxford University Press, 1973) presents a very positive picture of the relationship between Jarena Lee and Bishop Richard Allen. She feels that by the time Lee approached Allen, he had "modified his views on women's rights" (129). She contends that since Allen was free from the Methodist Church he was able to "determine his own policy" with respect to women under the auspices of the A.M.E. Church. It should be noted that Bishop Allen accepted the Rev. Jarena Lee as a woman preacher and not as an ordained preacher with full rights and privileges thereof. Even Carol George admitted that Lee traveled with Bishop Allen only "as an unofficial member of their delegation to conference sessions in New York and Baltimore," "to attend," not to participate in them. I agree that this does represent progress in Bishop Allen's view as compared to Lee's first approach; on the second approach, he was at least encouraging. Then he began "to promote her interests" (129)—but he did not ordain her.

8. Ibid.

9. "Elizabeth: A Colored Minister of the Gospel," in *Black Women in Nineteenth-Century American Life,* ed. Bert James Loewenberg and Ruth Bogin (University Park, PA: Pennsylvania State University Press, 1976), 132. The denomination of Elizabeth is not known to this writer. Her parents were Methodists, but she was separated from her parents at the age of eleven. However, the master from whom she gained her freedom was Presbyterian. Her autobiography was published by the Philadelphia Quakers.

1. Ibid., 133.

2. Amanda Berry Smith, *An Autobiography: The Story of the Lord's Dealings with Mrs. Amanda Berry Smith, the Colored Evangelist* (Chicago, 1893), in Loewenberg and Bogin, *Black Women,* 157.

"I tell you, Sister, it will cost money to go down there; and if you ain't got plenty of it, it's no use to go"; . . . another said:

"What does she want to go for?"

"Woman preacher; they want to be ordained," was the reply.

"I mean to fight that thing," said the other.

"Yes, indeed, so will I," said another.[3]

The oppression of women in the ministry took many forms. In addition to not being granted ordination, the authenticity of "the call" of women was frequently put to the test. Lee, Elizabeth, and Smith spoke of the many souls they had brought to Christ through their preaching and singing in local black congregations, as well as in white and mixed congregations. It was not until Bishop Richard Allen heard Jarena Lee preach that he was convinced that she was of the Spirit. He, however, still refused to ordain her. The "brethren," including some bishops of the 1872 General Conference of the A.M.E. Church, were convinced that Amanda Berry Smith was blessed with the Spirit of God after hearing her sing at a session held at Fisk University. Smith tells us that ". . . the Spirit of the Lord seemed to fall on all the people. The preachers got happy. . . ." This experience brought invitations for her to preach at several churches, but it did not bring an appointment to a local congregation as pastor or the right of ordination. She summed up the experience in this way: ". . . after

that many of my brethren believed in me, especially as the question of ordination of women never was mooted in the Conference."[4]

Several black denominations have since begun to ordain women.[5] But this matter of women preachers having the extra burden of proving their call to an extent not required of men still prevails in the black church today. A study in which I participated at Union Theological Seminary in New York City bears this out. Interviews with black ministers of different denominations revealed that their prejudices against women, and especially women in the ministry, resulted in unfair expectations and unjust treatment of women ministers whom they encountered.[6]

It is the unfair expectations placed upon women and blatant discrimination that keeps them "in the pew" and "out of the pulpit." This matter of keeping women in the pew has been carried to ridiculous extremes. At the 1971 Annual Convocation of the National Conference of Black Churchmen,[7] held at the Liberty Baptist Church in Chicago, I was slightly amused when, as I approached the pulpit to place my cassette tape recorder near the speaker, Walter Fauntroy, as several brothers had already done, I was stopped by a man who informed me that I could not enter the pulpit area. When I asked why not, he directed me to the pastor who told me that women were not permitted in the pulpit, but that he would have a man place the recorder there for me. Although I could not

3. Ibid.

4. Ibid., 159.

5. The African Methodist Episcopal Church started ordaining women in 1948, according to the Rev. William P. Foley of Bridgestreet A.M.E. Church in Brooklyn, New York. The first ordained woman was Martha J. Keys.

The African Methodist Episcopal Zion Church ordained women as early as 1884. At that time, Mrs. Julia A. Foote was ordained Deacon in the New York Annual Conference. In 1894, Mrs. Mary J. Small was ordained Deacon, and in 1898, she was ordained Elder. See David Henry Bradley, Sr., *A History of the A.M.E. Zion Church*, vol. 2, *1872–1968* (Nashville: Parthenon Press, 1970), 384, 393.

The Christian Methodist Episcopal Church enacted legislation to ordain women in the 1970 General Conference. Since then approximately seventy-five women have been ordained. See the Rev. N. Charles Thomas, general secretary of the C.M.E. Church and director of the Department of Ministry, Memphis, Tennessee.

Many Baptist churches still do not ordain women. Some churches in the Pentecostal tradition do not ordain women. However, in some other Pentecostal churches, women are founders, pastors, elders, and bishops.

In the case of the A.M.E.Z. Church, where women were ordained as early as 1884, the important question would be, what happened to the women who were ordained? In addition, all of these churches (except for those that do give leadership to women) should answer the following questions: Have women been assigned to pastor "class A" churches? Have women been appointed as presiding elders? (There is currently one woman presiding elder in the A.M.E. Church.) Have women been elected to serve as bishop of any of these churches? Have women served as presidents of conventions?

6. Yolande Herron, Jacquelyn Grant, Gwendolyn Johnson, and Samuel Roberts, "Black Women and the Field Education Experience at Union Theological Seminary: Problems and Prospects" (New York: Union Theological Seminary, May 1978).

7. This organization continues to call itself the National Conference of Black Churchmen despite the protests of women members.

believe that explanation a serious one, I agreed to have a man place it on the pulpit for me and returned to my seat in the sanctuary for the continuation of the convocation. The seriousness of the pastor's statement became clear to me later at that meeting when Mary Jane Patterson, a Presbyterian Church executive, was refused the right to speak from the pulpit.[8] This was clearly a case of sex discrimination in a black church—keeping women "in the pew" and "out of the pulpit."

As far as the issue of women is concerned, it is obvious that the black church described by C. Eric Lincoln has not fared much better than the Negro church of E. Franklin Frazier.[9] The failure of the black church and black theology to proclaim explicitly the liberation of black women indicates that they cannot claim to be agents of divine liberation. If the theology, like the church, has no word for black women, its conception of liberation is inauthentic.

THE BLACK EXPERIENCE AND THE BLACK WOMAN

For the most part, black church*men* have not dealt with the oppression of black women in either the black church or the black community. Frederick Douglass was one notable exception in the nineteenth century. His active advocacy for women's rights was a demonstration against the contradiction between preaching "justice for all" and practicing the continued oppression of women. He, therefore, "dared not claim a right [for himself] which he would not concede to women."[1] These words describe the convictions of a man who was active both in the church and in the larger black community. This is significant because there is usually a direct relationship between what goes on in the black church and the black secular community.

The status of black women in the community parallels that of black women in the church. Black theol-

ogy considers the black experience to be the context out of which its questions about God and human existence are formulated. This is assumed to be the context in which God's revelation is received and interpreted. Only from the perspective of the poor and the oppressed can theology be adequately done. Arising out of the Black Power movement of the 1960s, black theology purports to take seriously the experience of the larger community's struggle for liberation. But if this is, indeed, the case, black theology must function in the secular community in the same way as it should function in the church community. It must serve as a "self-test" to see whether the rhetoric or proclamation of the black community's struggle for liberation is consistent with its practices. How does the "self-test" principle operate among the poor and the oppressed? Certainly black theology has spoken to some of the forms of oppression that exist within the community of the oppressed. Many of the injustices it has attacked are the same as those that gave rise to the prophets of the Old Testament. But the fact that black theology does not include sexism specifically as one of those injustices is all too evident. It suggests that the theologians do not understand sexism to be one of the oppressive realities of the black community. Silence on this specific issue can only mean conformity with the status quo. The most prominent black theologian, James Cone, has recently broken this silence. "The black church, like all other churches, is a male-dominated church. The difficulty that black male ministers have in supporting the equality of women in the church and society stems partly from the lack of a clear liberation-criterion rooted in the gospel and in the present struggles of oppressed peoples. . . . It is truly amazing that many black male ministers, young and old, can hear the message of liberation in the gospel when related to racism but remain deaf to a similar message in the context of sexism. . . ."[2] It is difficult to understand how black men manage to exclude the liberation of black women from their inter-

---

8. NCBC has since made the decision to examine the policies of its host institutions (churches) to avoid the recurrence of such incidents.

9. E. Franklin Frazier, *The Negro Church in America*; C. Eric Lincoln, *The Black Church Since Frazier* (New York: Schocken Books, 1974).

1. Printed in Philip S. Foner, ed., *Frederick Douglass on Women's Rights* (Westport, Conn.: Greenwood Press), 51.

2. Cone, "Black Ecumenism and the Liberation Struggle," delivered at Yale University, February 16–17, 1978, and Quinn Chapel A.M.E. Church, May 22, 1978. In two other recent papers he has voiced concern on women's issues, relating them to the larger question of liberation. These papers are: "New Roles in the Ministry: A Theological Appraisal" and "Black Theology and the Black Church: Where Do We Go From Here?"

pretation of the liberating gospel. Any correct analysis of the poor and oppressed would reveal some interesting and inescapable facts about the situation of women within oppressed groups. Without succumbing to the long and fruitless debate of "who is more oppressed than whom?" I want to make some pointed suggestions to black male theologians.

It would not be very difficult to argue that since black women are the poorest of the poor, the most oppressed of the oppressed, their experience provides a most fruitful context for doing black theology. The research of Jacquelyne Jackson attests to the extreme deprivation of black women. Jackson supports her claim with statistical data that "in comparison with black males and white males and females, black women yet constitute the most disadvantaged group in the United States, as evidenced especially by their largely unenviable educational, occupational, employment, and income levels, and availability of marital partners."[3] In other words, in spite of the "quite insignificant" educational advantage that black women have over black men, they have "had the greatest access to the worst jobs at the lowest earnings."[4] It is important to emphasize this fact in order to elevate to its rightful level of concern the condition of black women, not only in the world at large, but in the black community and the black church. It is my contention that if black theology speaks of the black community as if the special problems of black women do not exist, it is no different from the white theology it claims to reject precisely because of its inability to take account of the existence of black people in its theological formulations.

It is instructive to note that the experience of black women working in the Black Power movement further accented the problem of the oppression of women in the black community. Because of their invisibility in the leadership of the movement they, like women of the church, provided the "support" segment of the movement. They filled the streets when numbers were needed for demonstrations. They stuffed the envelopes in the

offices and performed other menial tasks. Kathleen Cleaver,[5] in a *Black Scholar* interview, revealed some of the problems in the movement that caused her to become involved in women's liberation issues. While underscoring the crucial role played by women as Black Power activists, Kathleen Cleaver, nonetheless, acknowledged the presence of sex discrimination.

> I viewed myself as assisting everything that was done.... The form of assistance that women give in political movements to men is just as crucial as the leadership that men give to those movements. And this is something that is never recognized and never dealt with. *Because women are always relegated to assistance,* and this is where I became interested in the liberation of women. Conflicts, constant conflicts came up, conflicts that would rise as a result of the fact that I was married to a member of the Central Committee and I was also an officer in the Party. Things that I would have suggested myself would be implemented. But if I suggested them the suggestion might be rejected. If they were suggested by a man, the suggestion would be implemented.
>
> It seemed throughout the history of my working with the Party, I always had to struggle with this. The suggestion itself was never viewed objectively. *The fact that the suggestion came from a woman gave it some lesser value.* And it seemed that it had something to do with the egos of the men involved. I know that the first demonstration that we had at the courthouse for Huey Newton[6] I was very instrumental in organizing; the first time we went out on the soundtrucks, I was on the soundtrucks; the first leaflet we put out, I wrote; the first demonstration, I made up the pamphlets. And the members of that demonstration for the most part were women. I've noticed that throughout my dealings in the black movement in the United States, that the *most anxious, the most eager, the most active, the most quick to understand the problem and quick to move are women.*[7]

3. Jacquelyne Jackson, "But Where Are the Men?" *Black Scholar,* op. cit., 30.
4. Ibid., 32.
5. Professor of law and communications secretary for the Black Panther Party in the 1960s (b. 1945). [Editor's note]
6. Co-founder and leader of the Black Panther Party; see p. 583. [Editor's note]
7. Kathleen Cleaver was interviewed by Sister Julia Hervé. Ibid., 55–56. [Hervé: Advocate of Pan-African causes and daughter of Richard Wright; Editor's note]

Cleaver exposed the fact that even when leadership was given to women, sexism lurked in the wings. As executive secretary of the Student Nonviolent Coordinating Committee (SNCC), Ruby Doris Robinson was described as the "heartbeat of SNCC." Yet there were "the constant conflicts, the constant struggles that she was subjected to because she was a woman."[8]

Notwithstanding all the evidence to the contrary, some might want to argue that the central problem of black women is related to their race and not their sex. Such an argument then presumes that the problem cannot be resolved apart from the black struggle. I contend that as long as the black struggle refuses to recognize and deal with its sexism, the idea that women will receive justice from that struggle alone will never work. It will not work because black women will no longer allow black men to ignore their unique problems and needs in the name of some distorted view of the "liberation of the total community." I would bring to the minds of the proponents of this argument the words of President Sékou Touré[9] as he wrote about the role of African women in the revolution. He said, "If African women cannot possibly conduct their struggle in isolation from the struggle that our people wage for African liberation, African freedom, conversely, is not effective unless it brings about the liberation of African women."[1] Black men who have an investment in the patriarchal structure of white America and who intend to do Christian theology have yet to realize that if Jesus is liberator of the oppressed, all of the oppressed must be liberated. Perhaps the proponents of the argument that the cause of black women must be subsumed under a larger cause should look to South African theologians Sabelo Ntwasa and Basil Moore. They affirm that "black theology, as it struggles to formulate a theology of liberation relevant to South Africa, cannot afford to perpetuate any form of domination, not even male domination. If its liberation is not human enough to include the liberation of women, it will not be liberation."[2]

A Challenge to Black Theology

My central argument is this: black theology cannot continue to treat black women as if they were invisible creatures who are on the outside looking into the black experience, the black church, and the black theological enterprise. It will have to deal with the community of believers in all aspects as integral parts of the whole community. Black theology, therefore, must speak to the bishops who hide behind the statement, "Women don't want women pastors." It must speak to the pastors who say, "My church isn't ready for women preachers yet." It must teach the seminarians who feel that "women have no place in seminary." It must address the women in the church and community who are content and complacent with their oppression. It must challenge the educators who would reeducate the people on every issue except the issue of the dignity and equality of women.

Black women represent more than fifty percent of the black community and more than seventy percent of the black church. How then can an authentic theology of liberation arise out of these communities without specifically addressing the liberation of the women in both places? Does the fact that certain questions are raised by black women make them any less black concerns? If, as I contend, the liberation of black men and women is inseparable, then a radical split cannot be made between racism and sexism. Black women are oppressed by racism *and* sexism. It is therefore necessary that black men and women be actively involved in combating both evils.

Only as black women in greater numbers make their way from the background to the forefront will the true strength of the black community be fully realized. There is already a heritage of strong black women and men upon which a stronger nation can be built. There is a tradition that declares that God is at work in the experience of the black woman. This tradition, in the context of the total black experience, can provide

---

8. Ibid., 55.

9. Ahmed Sékou Touré (1922–84), president of Ghana from 1958 until his death. [Editor's note]

1. [Ahmed] Sékou Touré, "The Role of Women in the Revolution," *Black Scholar,* vol. 6, no. 6 (March 1975), 32.

2. Sabelo [Ntwasa] and Basil Moore, "The Concept of God in Black Theology," in *The Challenge of Black Theology in South Africa,* ed. Basil Moore (Atlanta, Ga.: John Knox Press, 1974), 25–26.

data for the development of a holistic black theology. Such a theology will repudiate the God of classical theology who is presented as an absolute Patriarch, a deserting father who created black men and women and then "walked out" in the face of responsibility. Such a theology will look at the meaning of the total Jesus Christ Event; it will consider not only how God through Jesus Christ is related to the oppressed men, but to women as well. Such a theology will "allow" God through the Holy Spirit to work through persons without regard to race, sex, or class. This theology will exercise its prophetic function, and serve as a "self-test" in a church characterized by the sins of racism, sexism, and other forms of oppression. Until black women theologians are fully participating in the theological enterprise, it is important to keep black male theologians and black leaders cognizant of their dereliction. They must be made aware of the fact that black women are needed not only as Christian educators, but as theologians and church leaders. It is only when black women and men share jointly the leadership in theology and in the church and community that the black nation will become strong and liberated. Only then will there be the possibility that black theology can become a theology of divine liberation.

One final word for those who argue that the issues of racism and sexism are too complicated and should not be confused. I agree that the issues should not be "confused." But the elimination of both racism and sexism is so crucial for the liberation of black persons that we cannot shrink from facing them together. Sojourner Truth[3] tells us why this is so. In 1867, she spoke out on the issue of suffrage, and what she said at that time is still relevant to us as we deal with the liberation of black women today.

> I feel that if I have to answer for the deeds done in my body just as much as a man, I have a right to have just as much as a man. There is a great stir about colored men getting their rights, but not a word about the colored women; and if colored men get their rights, and not colored women theirs, you see the colored men will be masters over the women, and it will be just as bad as it was before. So I am for keeping the whole thing going while things are stirring: because if we wait till it is still, it will take a great while to get it going again. . . .[4]

Black women have to keep the issue of sexism "going" in the black community, in the black church, and in black theology until it has been eliminated. To do otherwise means that they will be pushed aside until eternity. Therefore, with Sojourner Truth, I'm for "keeping things going while things are stirring. . . ."

3. See p. 242. [Editor's note]
4. Sojourner Truth, "Keeping the Things Going While Things Are Stirring," printed in Miriam Schneir, ed., *Feminism: The Essential Historical Writings* (New York: Random House, 1972), 129–30.

Daniel Patrick Moynihan

"The Negro Family: The Case for National Action" [1965]

In 1965, the white American sociologist, Daniel Patrick Moynihan, then Assistant Secretary of Labor under President Johnson, wrote an internal government report exploring the relationship between African American culture and poverty. "The Negro Family: The Case for National Action" (commonly known as "The Moynihan Report") was "For Official Use Only," and Johnson intended to use it as a philosophic basis for new Great Society programs to foster achievement by African Americans. When the contents of the report leaked to the public, however, its tone and content fueled tremendous controversy. Johnson drew on the report for his 1965 commencement speech at Howard University, calling for "the next and more profound stage of the battle for civil rights." Pressured by the rising outcry by civil rights leaders over the controversial report, however, Johnson's administration shifted away from a focus on the family back to a focus on discrimination, a response that had long-term effects on public policy, social science, and beyond. As William Julius Wilson argued in "The Moynihan Report and Research on the Black Community," (2009), the report turned out to be both "important and prophetic," especially in its attempt to combine structual and cultural explanations of poverty, but the backlash against it was so severe that it dampened research into the role of culture in poverty for four decades. Only recently, Wilson concluded, have researchers begun to address the key challenge raised by the report, namely, how can we best "synthesize structural and cultural analyses to understand the dynamics of poor black families and the plight of low-skilled black males"?

The first part of the Moynihan Report, not included in this excerpt, outlines the widespread opportunities created by the "Negro Revolution," encompassing changes brought about by recent political, governmental, and legal actions. The second part of the report, reprinted here, explores challenges to accessing these opportunities caused by an accelerating breakdown in the stability of the African American family structure. The third part of the report, not included here, traces the historical roots of this breakdown, concluding that historical discrimination has created a cycle of poverty: "Low education levels in turn produce low income levels, which deprive children of many opportunities, and so the cycle repeats itself." The fourth chapter, reprinted here, explores the "tangle of pathology" caused by a family structure warped by discrimination, with a particular focus on "the matriarchal pattern of so many Negro families." The fifth chapter, reprinted here, concludes that understanding the fundamental problem ("family disorganization") is the first step toward developing effective public policy for bringing "the Negro American to full and equal sharing in the responsibilities and rewards of citizenship."

Born in Tulsa, Oklahoma, in 1927, Moynihan grew up in poverty in New York City. After a year of tuition-free education at the City College of New York, he joined the U.S. Navy, where he served until 1947. He earned his Ph.D. in sociology from Tufts University and then served as Assistant Secretary of Labor first under President Kennedy and then under President Johnson (leaving in 1965 shortly after writing his report). He later served on President Nixon's White House Staff, was a U.N. Ambassador under President Ford, and was elected for four terms as a U.S. Senator from New York. He died in 2003.

Office of Policy Planning and Research, U.S. Department of Labor, March 1965.

[* * *]

THE NEGRO AMERICAN FAMILY

At the heart of the deterioration of the fabric of Negro society is the deterioration of the Negro family.

It is the fundamental source of the weakness of the Negro community at the present time.

There is probably no single fact of Negro American life so little understood by whites. The Negro situation is commonly perceived by whites in terms of the visible manifestation of discrimination and poverty, in part because Negro protest is directed against such obstacles, and in part, no doubt, because these are facts which involve the actions and attitudes of the white community as well. It is more difficult, however, for whites to perceive the effect that three centuries of exploitation have had on the fabric of Negro society itself. Here the consequences of the historic injustices done to Negro Americans are silent and hidden from view. But here is where the true injury has occurred: unless this damage is repaired, all the effort to end discrimination and poverty and injustice will come to little.

The role of the family in shaping character and ability is so pervasive as to be easily overlooked. The family is the basic social unit of American life; it is the basic socializing unit. By and large, adult conduct in society is learned as a child.

A fundamental insight of psychoanalytic theory, for example, is that the child learns a way of looking at life in his early years through which all later experience is viewed and which profoundly shapes his adult conduct.

It may be hazarded that the reason family structure does not loom larger in public discussion of social issues is that people tend to assume that the nature of family life is about the same throughout American society. The mass media and the development of suburbia have created an image of the American family as a highly standardized phenomenon. It is therefore easy to assume that whatever it is that makes for differences among individuals or groups of individuals, it is not a different family structure.

There is much truth to this; as with any other nation, Americans are producing a recognizable family system. But that process is not completed by any means. There are still, for example, important differences in family patterns surviving from the age of the great European migration to the United States, and these variations account for notable differences in the progress and assimilation of various ethnic and religious groups. A number of immigrant groups were characterized by unusually strong family bonds; these groups have characteristically progressed more rapidly than others.

But there is one truly great discontinuity in family structure in the United States at the present time: that between the white world in general and that of the Negro American.

The white family has achieved a high degree of stability and is maintaining that stability.

By contrast, the family structure of lower class Negroes is highly unstable, and in many urban centers is approaching complete breakdown.

N.b. There is considerable evidence that the Negro community is in fact dividing between a stable middle class group that is steadily growing stronger and more successful, and an increasingly disorganized and disadvantaged lower class group. There are indications, for example, that the middle class Negro family puts a higher premium on family stability and the conserving of family resources than does the white middle class family. The discussion of this paper is not, obviously, directed to the first group excepting as it is affected by the experiences of the second—an important exception.

There are two points to be noted in this context.

First, the emergence and increasing visibility of a Negro middle class may beguile the nation into supposing that the circumstances of the remainder of the Negro community are equally prosperous, whereas just the opposite is true at present, and is likely to continue so.

Second, the lumping of all Negroes together in one statistical measurement very probably conceals the extent of the disorganization among the lower-class group. If conditions are improving for one and deteriorating for the other, the resultant statistical averages might show no change. Further, the statistics on the Negro family and most other subjects treated in this paper refer only to a specific point in time. They are a vertical measure of the situation at a given movement. They do not measure the experience of individuals over time. Thus the average monthly unemployment rate for Negro males for 1964 is recorded as 9 percent. But *during* 1964, some 29 percent of Negro males were unemployed at one time or another. Similarly, for example, if 36 percent of Negro children are living in broken homes *at any specific moment,* it is likely that a far higher proportion of Negro children find themselves in that situation *at one time or another* in their lives.

Nearly a Quarter of Urban Negro Marriages are Dissolved.

Nearly a quarter of Negro women living in cities who have ever married are divorced, separated, or are living apart from their husbands.

The rates are highest in the urban Northeast where 26 percent of Negro women ever married are either divorced, separated, or have their husbands absent.

On the urban frontier, the proportion of husbands absent is even higher. In New York City in 1960, it was 30.2 percent, *not* including divorces.

Among ever-married nonwhite women in the nation, the proportion with husbands present *declined* in *every* age group over the decade 1950–60 as follows: [chart not reproduced]

Although similar declines occurred among white females, the proportion of white husbands present never dropped below 90 percent except for the first and last age group.

Nearly One-Quarter of Negro Births are now Illegitimate.

Both white and Negro illegitimacy rates have been increasing, although from dramatically different bases. The white rate was 2 percent in 1940; it was 3.07 percent in 1963. In that period, the Negro rate went from 16.8 percent to 23.6 percent.

The number of illegitimate children per 1,000 live births increased by 11 among whites in the period 1940–63, but by 68 among nonwhites. There are, of course, limits to the dependability of these statistics. There are almost certainly a considerable number of Negro children who, although technically illegitimate, are in fact the offspring of stable unions. On the other hand, it may be assumed that many births that are in fact illegitimate are recorded otherwise. Probably the two opposite effects cancel each other out.

On the urban frontier, the nonwhite illegitimacy rates are usually higher than the national average, and the increase of late has been drastic.

In the District of Columbia, the illegitimacy rate for nonwhites grew from 21.8 percent in 1950, to 29.5 percent in 1964.

A similar picture of disintegrating Negro marriages emerges from the divorce statistics. Divorces have increased of late for both whites and nonwhites, but at a much greater rate for the latter. In 1940 both groups had a divorce rate of 2.2 percent. By 1964 the white rate had risen to 3.6 percent, but the nonwhite rate had reached 5.1 percent—40 percent greater than the formerly equal white rate.

Almost One-Fourth of Negro Families are Headed by Females

As a direct result of this high rate of divorce, separation, and desertion, a very large percent of Negro families are headed by females. While the percentage of such families among whites has been dropping since 1940, it has been rising among Negroes.

The percent of nonwhite families headed by a female is more than double the percent for whites. Fatherless nonwhite families increased by a sixth between 1950 and 1960, but held constant for white families.

It has been estimated that only a minority of Negro children reach the age of 18 having lived all their lives with both of their parents.

Once again, this measure of family disorganization is found to be diminishing among white families and increasing among Negro families.

The Breakdown of the Negro Family Has Led to a Startling Increase in Welfare Dependency.

The majority of Negro children receive public assistance under the AFDC program at one point or another in their childhood.

At present, 14 percent of Negro children are receiving AFDC assistance, as against 2 percent of white children. Eight percent of white children receive such assistance at some time, as against 56 percent of nonwhites, according to an extrapolation based on HEW data. (Let it be noted, however, that out of a total of 1.8 million nonwhite illegitimate children in the nation in 1961, 1.3 million were *not* receiving aid under the AFDC program, although a substantial number have, or will, receive aid at some time in their lives.)

Again, the situation may be said to be worsening. The AFDC program, deriving from the long established Mothers' Aid programs, was established in 1935 principally to care for widows and orphans, although the legislation covered all children in homes deprived of parental support because one or both of their parents are absent or incapacitated.

In the beginning, the number of AFDC families in which the father was absent because of desertion was less than a third of the total. Today it is two thirds. HEW estimates "that between two thirds and three fourths of the 50 percent increase from 1948 to 1955 in the number of absent father families receiving ADC may be explained by an increase in broken homes in the population."

A 1960 study of Aid to Dependent Children in Cook County, Ill. stated:

"The 'typical' ADC mother in Cook County was married and had children by her husband, who deserted; his whereabouts are unknown, and he does not contribute to the support of his children. She is not free to remarry and has had an illegitimate child since her husband left. (Almost 90 percent of the ADC families are Negro.)"

The steady expansion of this welfare program, as of public assistance programs in general, can be taken as a measure of the steady disintegration of the Negro family structure over the past generation in the United States.

[* * *]

THE TANGLE OF PATHOLOGY

That the Negro American has survived at all is extraordinary—a lesser people might simply have died out, as indeed others have. That the Negro community has not only survived, but in this political generation has entered national affairs as a moderate, humane, and constructive national force is the highest testa- ment to the healing powers of the democratic ideal and the creative vitality of the Negro people.

But it may not be supposed that the Negro American community has not paid a fearful price for the incredible mistreatment to which it has been subjected over the past three centuries.

In essence, the Negro community has been forced into a matriarchal structure which, because it is to out of line with the rest of the American society, seriously retards the progress of the group as a whole, and imposes a crushing burden on the Negro male and, in consequence, on a great many Negro women as well.

There is, presumably, no special reason why a society in which males are dominant in family relationships is to be preferred to a matriarchal arrangement. However, it is clearly a disadvantage for a minority group to be operating on one principle, while the great majority of the population, and the one with the most advantages to begin with, is operating on another. This is the present situation of the Negro. Ours is a society which presumes male leadership in private and public affairs. The arrangements of society facilitate such leadership and reward it. A subculture, such as that of the Negro American, in which this is not the pattern, is placed at a distinct disadvantage.

Here an earlier word of caution should be repeated. These is much evidence that a considerable number of Negro families have managed to break out of the tangle of pathology and to establish themselves as stable, effective units, living according to patterns of American society in general. E. Franklin Frazier has suggested that the middle-class Negro American family is, if anything, more patriarchal and protective of its children than the general run of such families. Given equal opportunities, the children of these families will perform as well or better than their white peers. They need no help from anyone, and ask none.

While this phenomenon is not easily measured, one index is that middle class Negroes have even fewer children than middle class whites, indicating a desire to conserve the advances they have made and to insure that their children do as well or better. Negro women who marry early to uneducated laborers have more children than white women in the same situation; Negro women who marry at the common age for the middle class to educated men doing technical or professional work have only four fifths as many children as their white counterparts.

It might be estimated that as much as half of the Negro community falls into the middle class. However, the remaining half is in desperate and deteriorating circumstances. Moreover, because of housing segregation it is immensely difficult for the stable half to escape from the cultural influences of the unstable one. The children of middle class Negroes often as not must grow up in, or next to the slums, an experience almost unknown to white middle class children. They are therefore constantly exposed to the pathology of the disturbed group and constantly in danger of being drawn into it. It is for this reason that the propositions put forth in this study may be thought of as having a more or less general application.

In a word, most Negro youth are in *danger* of being caught up in the tangle of pathology that affects their world, and probably a majority are so entrapped. Many of those who escape do so for one generation only: as things now are, their children may have to run the gauntlet all over again. That is not the least vicious aspect of the world that white America has made for the Negro.

Obviously, not every instance of social pathology afflicting the Negro community can be traced to the weakness of family structure. If, for example, organized crime in the Negro community were not largely controlled by whites, there would be more capital accumulation among Negroes, and therefore probably more Negro business enterprises. If it were not for the hostility and fear many whites exhibit toward Negroes, they in turn would be less afflicted by hostility and fear and so on. There is no one Negro community. There is no one Negro problem. There is no one solution. Nonetheless, at the center of the tangle of pathology is the weakness of the family structure. Once or twice removed, it will be found to be the principal source of most of the aberrant, inadequate, or antisocial behavior that did not establish, but now serves to perpetuate the cycle of poverty and deprivation.

It was by destroying the Negro family under slavery that white America broke the will of the Negro people. Although that will has reasserted itself in our time, it is a resurgence doomed to frustration unless the viability of the Negro family is restored.

Matriarchy

A fundamental fact of Negro American family life is the often reversed roles of husband and wife.

Robert O. Blood, Jr. and Donald M. Wolfe, in a study of Detroit families, note that "Negro husbands have unusually low power," and while this is characteristic of all low income families, the pattern pervades the Negro social structure: "the cumulative result of discrimination in jobs . . . , the segregated housing, and the poor schooling of Negro men." In 44 percent of the Negro families studied, the wife was dominant, as against 20 percent of white wives. "Whereas the majority of white families are equalitarian, the largest percentage of Negro families are dominated by the wife."

The matriarchal pattern of so many Negro families reinforces itself over the generations. This process begins with education. Although the gap appears to be closing at the moment, for a long while, Negro females were better educated than Negro males, and this remains true today for the Negro population as a whole.

The difference in educational attainment between nonwhite men and women in the labor force is even greater; men lag 1.1 years behind women.

The disparity in educational attainment of male and female youth 16 to 21 who were out of school in February 1963, is striking. Among the nonwhite males, 66.3 percent were not high school graduates, compared with 55.0 percent of the females. A similar difference existed at the college level, with 4.5 percent of the males having completed 1 to 3 years of college compared with 7.3 percent of the females.

The poorer performance of the male in school exists from the very beginning, and the magnitude of the difference was documented by the 1960 Census in statistics on the number of children who have fallen one or more grades below the typical grade for children of the same age. The boys have more frequently fallen behind at every age level. (White boys also lag behind white girls, but at a differential of 1 to 6 percentage points.)

In 1960, 39 percent of all white persons 25 years of age and over who had completed 4 or more years of college were women. Fifty-three percent of the nonwhites who had attained this level were women.

However, the gap is closing. By October 1963, there were slightly more Negro men in college than women.

Among whites there were almost twice as many men as women enrolled.

There is much evidence that Negro females are better students than their male counterparts.

Daniel Thompson of Dillard University, in a private communication on January 9, 1965, writes:

"As low as is the aspirational level among lower class Negro girls, it is considerably higher than among the boys. For example, I have examined the honor rolls in Negro high schools for about 10 years. As a rule, from 75 to 90 percent of all Negro honor students are girls."

Dr. Thompson reports that 70 percent of all applications for the National Achievement Scholarship Program financed by the Ford Foundation for outstanding Negro high school graduates are girls, despite special efforts by high school principals to submit the names of boys.

The finalists for this new program for outstanding Negro students were recently announced. Based on an inspection of the names, only about 43 percent of all the 639 finalists were male. (However, in the regular National Merit Scholarship program, males received 67 percent of the 1964 scholarship awards.)

Inevitably, these disparities have carried over to the area of employment and income.

In 1 out of 4 Negro families where the husband is present, is an earner, and someone else in the family works, the husband is not the principal earner. The comparable figure for whites is 18 percent.

More important, it is clear that Negro females have established a strong position for themselves in white collar and professional employment, precisely the areas of the economy which are growing most rapidly, and to which the highest prestige is accorded.

The President's Committee on Equal Employment Opportunity, making a preliminary report on employment in 1964 of over 16,000 companies with nearly 5 million employees, revealed this pattern with dramatic emphasis.

"In this work force, Negro males outnumber Negro females by a ratio of 4 to 1. Yet Negro males represent only 1.2 percent of all males in white collar occupations, while Negro females represent 3.1 percent of the total female white collar work force. Negro males represent 1.1 percent of all male professionals, whereas Negro females represent roughly 6 percent of all female profes-

sionals. Again, in technician occupations, Negro males represent 2.1 percent of all male technicians while Negro females represent roughly 10 percent of all female technicians. It would appear therefore that there are proportionately 4 times as many Negro females in significant white collar jobs than Negro males.

"Although it is evident that office and clerical jobs account for approximately 50 percent of all Negro female white collar workers, it is significant that 6 out of every 100 Negro females are in professional jobs. This is substantially similar to the rate of all females in such jobs. Approximately 7 out of every 100 Negro females are in technician jobs. This exceeds the proportion of all females in technician jobs—approximately 5 out of every 100.

"Negro females in skilled jobs are almost the same as that of all females in such jobs. Nine out of every 100 Negro males are in skilled occupations while 21 out of 100 of all males are in such jobs."

This pattern is to be seen in the Federal government, where special efforts have been made recently to insure equal employment opportunity for Negroes. These efforts have been notably successful in Departments such as Labor, where some 19 percent of employees are now Negro. (A not disproportionate percentage, given the composition of the work force in the areas where the main Department offices are located.) However, it may well be that these efforts have redounded mostly to the benefit of Negro women, and may even have accentuated the comparative disadvantage of Negro men. Seventy percent of the Negro employees of the Department of Labor are women, as contrasted with only 42 percent of the white employees.

Among nonprofessional Labor Department employees—where the most employment opportunities exist for all groups—Negro women outnumber Negro men 4 to 1, and average almost one grade higher in classification.

The testimony to the effects of these patterns in Negro family structure is wide spread, and hardly to be doubted.

Whitney Young:

"Historically, in the matriarchal Negro society, mothers made sure that if one of their children had a chance for higher education the daughter was the one to pursue it."

"The effect on family functioning and role performance of this historical experience [economic deprivation] is what you might predict. Both as a husband and as a father the Negro male is made to feel inadequate, not because he is unlovable or unaffectionate, lacks intelligence or even a gray flannel suit. But in a society that measures a man by the size of his pay check, he doesn't stand very tall in a comparison with his white counterpart. To this situation he may react with withdrawal, bitterness toward society, aggression both within the family and racial group, self-hatred, or crime. Or he may escape through a number of avenues that help him to lose himself in fantasy or to compensate for his low status through a variety of exploits."

Thomas Pettigrew:

"The Negro wife in this situation can easily become disgusted with her financially dependent husband, and her rejection of him further alienates the male from family life. Embittered by their experiences with men, many Negro mothers often act to perpetuate the mother centered pattern by taking a greater interest in their daughters than their sons."

Deton Brooks:

"In a matriarchal structure, the women are transmitting the culture."

Dorothy Height:

"If the Negro woman has a major underlying concern, it is the status of the Negro man and his position in the community and his need for feeling himself an important person, free and able to make his contribution in the whole society in order that he may strengthen his home."

Duncan M. MacIntyre:

"The Negro illegitimacy rate always has been high—about eight times the white rate in 1940 and some-

what higher today even though the white illegitimacy rate also is climbing. The Negro statistics are symtomatic [*sic*] of some old socioeconomic problems, not the least of which are under employment among Negro men and compensating higher labor force propensity among Negro women. Both operate to enlarge the mother's role, undercutting the status of the male and making many Negro families essentially matriarchal. The Negro man's uncertain employment prospects, matriarchy, and the high cost of divorces combine to encourage desertion (the poor man's divorce), increases the number of couples not married, and thereby also increases the Negro illegitimacy rate. In the meantime, higher Negro birth rates are increasing the nonwhite population, while migration into cities like Detroit, New York, Philadelphia, and Washington, D.C. is making the public assistance rolls in such cities heavily, even predominantly, Negro."

Robin M. Williams, Jr. in a study of Elmira, New York:

"Only 57 percent of Negro adults reported themselves as married-spouse present, as compared with 78 percent of native white American gentiles, 91 percent of Italian-American, and 96 percent of Jewish informants. Of the 93 unmarried Negro youths interviewed, 22 percent did not have their mother living in the home with them, and 42 percent reported that their father was not living in their home. One third of the youth did not know their father's present occupation, and two-thirds of a sample of 150 Negro adults did not know what the occupation of their father's father had been. Forty percent of the youths said that they had brothers and sisters living in other communities: another 40 percent reported relatives living in their home who were not parents, siblings, or grandparent."

The Failure of Youth

Williams' account of Negro youth growing up with little knowledge of their fathers, less of their fathers' occupations, still less of family occupational traditions, is in sharp contrast to the experience of the white child. The white family, despite many variants, remains a powerful agency not only for transmitting property from one generation to the next, but also for transmitting no less valuable contracts with the world of education and work. In an earlier age, the Carpenters, Wainwrights, Weavers, Mercers, Farmers, Smiths acquired their names as well as their trades from their fathers and grandfathers. Children today still learn the patterns of work from their fathers even though they may no longer go into the same jobs.

White children without fathers at least perceive all about them the pattern of men working.

Negro children without fathers flounder—and fail.

Not always, to be sure. The Negro community produces its share, very possibly more than its share, of young people who have the something extra that carries them over the worst obstacles. But such persons are always a minority. The common run of young people in a group facing serious obstacles to success do not succeed.

A prime index of the disadvantage of Negro youth in the United States is their consistently poor performance on the mental tests that are a standard means of measuring ability and performance in the present generation.

There is absolutely no question of any genetic differential: Intelligence potential is distributed among Negro infants in the same proportion as among Icelanders or Chinese or any other group. American society, however, impairs the Negro potential. The statement of the HARYOU report that "there is no basic disagreement over the fact that central Harlem students are performing poorly in school" may be taken as true of Negro slum children throughout the United States.

Eighth grade children in central Harlem have a median IQ of 87.7, which means that perhaps a third of the children are scoring at levels perilously near to those of retardation. IQ *declines* in the first decade of life, rising only slightly thereafter.

The effect of broken families on the performance of Negro youth has not been extensively measured, but studies that have been made show an unmistakable influence.

Martin Deutch and Bert Brown, investigating intelligence test differences between Negro and white 1st and 5th graders of different social classes, found that there is a direct relationship between social class and

IQ. As the one rises so does the other: but more for whites than Negroes. This is surely a result of housing segregation, referred to earlier, which makes it difficult for middle class Negro families to escape the slums.

The authors explain that "it is much more difficult for the Negro to attain identical middle or upper middle class status with whites, and the social class gradations are less marked for Negroes because Negro life in a caste society is considerably more homogeneous than is life for the majority group."

Therefore, the authors look for background variables other than social class which might explain the difference: "One of the most striking differences between the Negro and white groups is the consistently higher frequency of broken homes and resulting family disorganization in the Negro group."

Further, they found that children from homes where fathers are present have significantly higher scores than children in homes without fathers.

The influence of the father's presence was then tested *within* the social classes and school grades for Negroes alone. They found that "a consistent trend within both grades at the lower SES [social class] level appears, and in no case is there a reversal of this trend: for males, females, and the combined group, the IQ's of children with fathers in the home are always higher than those who have no father in the home."

The authors say that broken homes "may also account for some of the differences between Negro and white intelligence scores."

The scores of fifth graders with fathers absent were lower than the scores of first graders with fathers absent, and while the authors point out that it is cross sectional data and does not reveal the duration of the fathers' absence, "What we might be tapping is the cumulative effect of fatherless years."

This difference in ability to perform has its counterpart in statistics on actual school performance. Nonwhite boys from families with both parents present are more likely to be going to school than boys with only one parent present, and enrollment rates are even lower when neither parent is present.

When the boys from broken homes are in school, they do not do as well as the boys from whole families. Grade retardation is higher when only one parent is present, and highest when neither parent is present.

The loneliness of the Negro youth in making fundamental decisions about education is shown in a 1959 study of Negro and white dropouts in Connecticut high schools.

Only 29 percent of Negro male dropouts discussed their decision to drop out of school with their fathers, compared with 65 percent of the white males (38 percent of the Negro males were from broken homes). In fact, 26 percent of the Negro males did not discuss this major decision in their lives with anyone at all, compared with only 8 percent of white males.

A study of Negro apprenticeship by the New York State Commission Against Discrimination in 1960 concluded:

"Negro youth are seldom exposed to influences which can lead to apprenticeship. Negroes are not apt to have relatives, friends, or neighbors in skilled occupations. Nor are they likely to be in secondary schools where they receive encouragement and direction from alternate role models. Within the minority community, skilled Negro 'models' after whom the Negro youth might pattern himself are rare, while substitute sources which could provide the direction, encouragement, resources, and information needed to achieve skilled craft standing are nonexistent."

Delinquency and Crime

The combined impact of poverty, failure, and isolation among Negro youth has had the predictable outcome in a disastrous delinquency and crime rate.

In a typical pattern of discrimination, Negro children in all public and private orphanages are a smaller proportion of all children than their proportion of the population although their needs are clearly greater.

On the other hand Negroes represent a third of all youth in training schools for juvenile delinquents.

It is probable that at present, a majority of the crimes against the person, such as rape, murder, and aggravated assault are committed by Negroes. There is, of course, no absolute evidence; inference can only be made from arrest and prison population statistics. The data that follow [chart not reproduced] unquestionably are biased against Negroes, who are arraigned much more casually than are whites, but it may be doubted that the bias is great enough to affect the general proportions.

Again on the urban frontier the ratio is worse: 3 out of every 5 arrests for these crimes were of Negroes.

In Chicago in 1963, three-quarters of the persons arrested for such crimes were Negro; in Detroit, the same proportions held.

In 1960, 37 percent of all persons in Federal and State prisons were Negro. In that year, 56 percent of the homicide and 57 percent of the assault offenders committed to State institutions were Negro.

The overwhelming number of offenses committed by Negroes are directed toward other Negroes: the cost of crime to the Negro community is a combination of that to the criminal and to the victim.

Some of the research on the effects of broken homes on delinquent behavior recently surveyed by Thomas F. Pettigrew in *A Profile of the Negro American* is summarized below, along with several other studies of the question.

Mary Diggs found that three-fourths—twice the expected ratio—of Philadelphia's Negro delinquents who came before the law during 1948 did not live with both their natural parents.

In predicting juvenile crime, Eleanor and Sheldon Glueck also found that a higher proportion of delinquent than nondelinquent boys came from broken homes. They identified five critical factors in the home environment that made a difference in whether boys would become delinquents: discipline of boy by father, supervision of boy by mother, affection of father for boy, affection of mother for boy, and cohesiveness of family.

In 1952, when the New York City Youth Board set out to test the validity of these five factors as predictors of delinquency, a problem quickly emerged. The Glueck sample consisted of white boys of mainly Irish, Italian, Lithuanian, and English descent. However, the Youth Board group was 44 percent Negro and 14 percent Puerto Rican, and the frequency of broken homes within these groups was out of proportion to the total number of delinquents in the population.

"In the majority of these cases, the father was usually never in the home at all, absent for the major proportion of the boy's life, or was present only on occasion."

(The final prediction table was reduced to three factors: supervision of boy by mother, discipline of boy by mother, and family cohesiveness within what family, in fact, existed, but was, nonetheless, 85 percent accurate in predicting delinquents and 96 percent accurate in predicting nondelinquents.)

Researchers who have focussed [sic] upon the "good" boy in high delinquency neighborhoods noted that they typically come from exceptionally stable, intact families.

Recent psychological research demonstrates the personality effects of being reared in a disorganized home without a father. One study showed that children from fatherless homes seek immediate gratification of their desires far more than children with fathers present. Others revealed that children who hunger for immediate gratification are more prone to delinquency, along with other less social behavior. Two psychologists, Pettigrew says, maintain that inability to delay gratification is a critical factor in immature, criminal, and neurotic behavior.

Finally, Pettigrew discussed the evidence that a stable home is a crucial factor in counteracting the effects of racism upon Negro personality.

"A warm, supportive home can effectively compensate for many of the restrictions the Negro child faces outside of the ghetto; consequently, the type of home life a Negro enjoys as a child may be far more crucial for governing the influence of segregation upon his personality than the form the segregation takes— legal or informal, Southern or Northern."

A Yale University study of youth in the lowest socioeconomic class in New Haven in 1950 whose behavior was followed through their 18th year revealed that among the delinquents in the group, 38 percent came from broken homes, compared with 24 percent of nondelinquents.

The President's Task Force on Manpower Conservation in 1963 found that of young men rejected for the draft for failure to pass the mental tests, 42 percent of those with a court record came from broken homes, compared with 30 percent of those without a court record. Half of all the nonwhite rejectees in the study with a court record came from broken homes.

An examination of the family background of 44,448 delinquency cases in Philadelphia between 1949 and 1954 documents the frequency of broken homes among delinquents. Sixty two percent of the Negro delinquents and 36 percent of white delinquents were not living with both parents. In 1950, 33 percent of nonwhite children and 7 percent of white children in Philadelphia were living in homes without both parents. Repeaters were even more likely to be from broken homes than first offenders.

The Armed Forces

The ultimate mark of inadequate preparation for life is the failure rate on the Armed Forces mental test. The Armed Forces Qualification Test is not quite a mental test, nor yet an education test. It is a test of ability to perform at an acceptable level of competence. It roughly measures ability that ought to be found in an average 7th or 8th grade student. A grown young man who cannot pass this test is in trouble.

Fifty six percent of Negroes fail it.

This is a rate almost four times that of the whites.

The Army, Navy, Air Force, and Marines conduct by far the largest and most important education and training activities of the Federal Government, as well as provide the largest single source of employment in the nation.

Military service is disruptive in some respects. For those comparatively few who are killed or wounded in combat, or otherwise, the personal sacrifice is inestimable. But on balance service in the Armed Forces over the past quarter-century has worked greatly to the advantage of those involved. The training and experience of military duty itself is unique, the advantages that have generally followed in the form of the G.I. Bill, mortgage guarantees, Federal life insurance, Civil Service preference, veterans hospitals, and veterans pensions are singular, to say the least.

Although service in the Armed Forces is at least nominally a duty of all male citizens coming of age, it is clear that the present system does not enable Negroes to serve in anything like their proportionate numbers. This is not a question of discrimination. Induction into the Armed Forces is based on a variety of objective tests and standards, but these tests nonetheless have the effect of keeping the number of Negroes disproportionately small.

In 1963 the United States Commission on Civil Rights reported that "A decade ago, Negroes constituted 8 percent of the Armed Forces. Today . . . they continue to constitute 8 percent of the Armed Forces."

In 1964 Negroes constituted 11.8 percent of the population, but probably remain at 8 percent of the Armed Forces.

The significance of Negro under representation in the Armed Forces is greater than might at first be supposed. If Negroes were represented in the same proportions in the military as they are in the population, they would number 300,000 plus. This would be over 100,000 more than at present (using 1964 strength figures). If the more than 100,000 unemployed Negro men were to have gone into the military the Negro male unemployment rate would have been 7.0 percent in 1964 instead of 9.1 percent.

In 1963 the Civil Rights Commission commented on the occupational aspect of military service for Negroes. "Negro enlisted men enjoy relatively better opportunities in the Armed Forces than in the civilian economy in every clerical, technical, and skilled field for which the data permit comparison."

There is, however, an even more important issue involved in military service for Negroes. Service in the United States Armed Forces is the *only* experience open to the Negro American in which he is truly treated as an equal: not as a Negro equal to a white, but as one man equal to any other man in a world where the category "Negro" and "white" do not exist. If this is a statement of the ideal rather than reality, it is an ideal that is close to realization. In food, dress, housing, pay, work—the Negro in the Armed Forces *is* equal and is treated that way.

There is another special quality about military service for Negro men: it is an utterly masculine world. Given the strains of the disorganized and matrifocal family life in which so many Negro youth come of age, the Armed Forces are a dramatic and desperately needed change: a world away from women, a world run by strong men of unquestioned authority, where discipline, if harsh, is nonetheless orderly and predictable, and where rewards, if limited, are granted on the basis of performance.

The theme of a current Army recruiting message states it as clearly as can be: "In the U.S. Army you get to know what it means to feel like a man."

At the recent Civil Rights Commission hearings in Mississippi a witness testified that his Army service was in fact "the only time I ever felt like a man."

Yet a majority of Negro youth (and probably three quarters of Mississippi Negroes) fail the Selective Service education test and are rejected. Negro participation in the Armed Forces would be less than it is, were it not for a proportionally larger share of voluntary enlistments and reenlistments. (Thus 16.3 percent of Army sergeants are Negro.)

Alienation

The term alienation may by now have been used in too many ways to retain a clear meaning, but it will serve to sum up the equally numerous ways in which large numbers of Negro youth appear to be withdrawing from American society.

One startling way in which this occurs is that the men are just not there when the Census enumerator comes around.

According to Bureau of Census population estimates for 1963, there are only 87 nonwhite males for every 100 females in the 30-to-34-year age group. The ratio does not exceed 90 to 100 throughout the 25-to-44-year age bracket. In the urban Northeast, there are only 76 males per 100 females 20-to-24-years of age, and males as a percent of females are below 90 percent throughout all ages after 14.

There are not really fewer men than women in the 20-to-40 age bracket. What obviously is involved is an error in counting: the surveyors simply do not find the Negro man. Donald J. Bogue and his associates, who have studied the Federal count of the Negro man, place the error as high as 19.8 percent at age 28; a typical error of around 15 percent is estimated from age 19 through 43. Preliminary research in the Bureau of the Census on the 1960 enumeration has resulted in similar conclusions, although not necessarily the same estimates of the extent of the error. The Negro male *can* be found at age 17 and 18. On the basis of birth records and mortality records, the conclusion must be that he is there at age 19 as well.

When the enumerators do find him, his answers to the standard questions asked in the monthly unemployment survey often result in counting him as "not in the labor force." In other words, Negro male unemployment may in truth be somewhat greater than reported.

The labor force participation rates of nonwhite men have been falling since the beginning of the century and for the past decade have been lower than the rates for white men. In 1964, the participation rates were 78.0 percent for white men and 75.8 percent for nonwhite men. Almost one percentage point of this difference was due to a higher proportion of nonwhite men unable to work because of long-term physical or mental illness; it seems reasonable to assume that the rest of the difference is due to discouragement about finding a job.

If nonwhite male labor force participation rates were as high as the white rates, there would have been 140,000 more nonwhite males in the labor force in 1964. If we further assume that the 140,000 would have been unemployed, the unemployment rate for nonwhite men would have been 11.5 percent instead of the recorded rate of 9 percent, and the ratio between the nonwhite rate and the white rate would have jumped from 2:1 to 2.4:1.

Understated or not, the official unemployment rates for Negroes are almost unbelievable.

The unemployment statistics for Negro teenagers—29 percent in January 1965—reflect lack of training and opportunity in the greatest measure, but it may not be doubted that they also reflect a certain failure of nerve.

"Are you looking for a job?" Secretary of Labor Wirtz asked a young man on a Harlem street corner. "Why?" was the reply.

Richard A. Cloward and Robert Ontell have commented on the withdrawal in a discussion of the Mobilization for Youth project on the lower East Side of New York.

"What contemporary slum and minority youth probably lack that similar children in earlier periods possessed is not motivation but some minimal sense of competence.

"We are plagued, in work with these youth, by what appears to be a low tolerance for frustration. They are not able to absorb setbacks. Minor irritants and rebuffs are magnified out of all proportion to reality. Perhaps they react as they do because they are not equal to the world that confronts them, and they know it. And it is the knowing that is devastating. Had the occupational structure remained intact, or had the education pro-

vided to them kept pace with occupational changes, the situation would be a different one. But it is not, and that is what we and they have to contend with."

Narcotic addiction is a characteristic form of withdrawal. In 1963, Negroes made up 54 percent of the addict population of the United States. Although the Federal Bureau of Narcotics reports a decline in the Negro proportion of new addicts, HARYOU reports the addiction rate in central Harlem rose from 22.1 per 10,000 in 1955 to 40.4 in 1961.

There is a larger fact about the alienation of Negro youth than the tangle of pathology described by these statistics. It is a fact particularly difficult to grasp by white persons who have in recent years shown increasing awareness of Negro problems.

The present generation of Negro youth growing up in the urban ghettos has probably less personal contact with the white world than any generation in the history of the Negro American.

Until World War II it could be said that in general the Negro and white worlds live, if not together, at least side by side. Certainly they did, and do, in the South.

Since World War II, however, the two worlds have drawn physically apart. The symbol of this development was the construction in the 1940's and 1950's of the vast white, middle and lower middle class suburbs around all the Nation's cities. Increasingly the inner cities have been left to Negroes—who now share almost no community life with whites.

In turn, because of this new housing pattern—most of which has been financially assisted by the Federal government—it is probable that the American school system has become *more*, rather than less segregated in the past two decades.

School integration has not occurred in the South, where a decade after *Brown v. Board of Education* only 1 Negro in 9 is attending school with white children.

And in the North, despite strenuous official efforts, neighborhoods and therefore schools are becoming more and more of one class and one color.

In New York City, in the school year 1957–58 there were 64 schools that were 90 percent of [*sic*] more Negro or Puerto Rican. Six years later there were 134 such schools.

Along with the diminution of white middle class contacts for a large percentage of Negroes, observers report that the Negro churches have all but lost contact with men in the Northern cities as well. This may be a normal condition of urban life, but it is probably a changed condition for the Negro American and cannot be a socially desirable development.

The only religious movement that appears to have enlisted a considerable number of lower class Negro males in Northern cities of late is that of the Black Muslims: a movement based on total rejection of white society, even though it emulates whites more.

In a word: the tangle of pathology is tightening.

THE CASE FOR NATIONAL ACTION

The object of this study has been to define a problem, rather than propose solutions to it. We have kept within these confines for three reasons.

First, there are many persons, within and without the Government, who do not feel the problem exists, at least in any serious degree. These persons feel that, with the legal obstacles to assimilation out of the way, matters will take care of themselves in the normal course of events. This is a fundamental issue, and requires a decision within the government.

Second, it is our view that the problem is so interrelated, one thing with another, that any list of program proposals would necessarily be incomplete, and would distract attention from the main point of interrelatedness. We have shown a clear relation between male employment, for example, and the number of welfare dependent children. Employment in turn reflects educational achievement, which depends in large part on family stability, which reflects employment. Where we should break into this cycle, and how, are the most difficult domestic questions facing the United States. We must first reach agreement on what the problem is, then we will know what questions must be answered.

Third, it is necessary to acknowledge the view, held by a number of responsible persons, that this problem may in fact be out of control. This is a view with which we emphatically and totally disagree, but the view must be acknowledged. The persistent rise in Negro educational achievement is probably the main trend that belies this thesis. On the other hand our study has produced some clear indications that the sit-

uation may indeed have begun to feed on itself. It may be noted, for example, that for most of the post-war period male Negro unemployment and the number of new AFDC cases rose and fell together as if connected by a chain from 1948 to 1962. The correlation between the two series of data was an astonishing .91. (This would mean that 83 percent of the rise and fall in AFDC cases can be statistically ascribed to the rise and fall in the unemployment rate.) In 1960, however, for the first time, unemployment declined, but the number of new AFDC cases rose. In 1963 this happened a second time. In 1964 a third. The possible implications of these and other data are serious enough that they, too, should be understood before program proposals are made.

However, the argument of this paper does lead to one central conclusion: Whatever the specific elements of a national effort designed to resolve this problem, those elements must be coordinated in terms of one general strategy.

What then is that problem? We feel the answer is clear enough. Three centuries of injustice have brought about deep-seated structural distortions in the life of the Negro American. At this point, the present tangle of pathology is capable of perpetuating itself without assistance from the white world. The cycle can be broken only if these distortions are set right.

In a word, a national effort towards the problems of Negro Americans must be directed towards the question of family structure. The object should be to strengthen the Negro family so as to enable it to raise and support its members as do other families. After that, how this group of Americans chooses to run its affairs, take advantage of its opportunities, or fail to do so, is none of the nation's business.

The fundamental importance and urgency of restoring the Negro American Family structure has been evident for some time. E. Franklin Frazier put it most succinctly in 1950:

"As the result of family disorganization a large proportion of Negro children and youth have not undergone the socialization which only the family can provide. The disorganized families have failed to provide for their emotional needs and have not provided the discipline and habits which are necessary for personality development. Because the disorganized family has failed in its function as a socializing agency, it has handicapped the children in their relations to the institutions in the community. Moreover, family disorganization has been partially responsible for a large amount of juvenile delinquency and adult crime among Negroes. Since the widespread family disorganization among Negroes has resulted from the failure of the father to play the role in family life required by American society, the mitigation of this problem must await those changes in the Negro and American society which will enable the Negro father to play the role required of him."

Nothing was done in response to Frazier's argument. Matters were left to take care of themselves, and as matters will, grew worse not better. The problem is now more serious, the obstacles greater. There is, however, a profound change for the better in one respect. The President has committed the nation to an all out effort to eliminate poverty wherever it exists, among whites or Negroes, and a militant, organized, and responsible Negro movement exists to join in that effort.

Such a national effort could be stated thus:

The policy of the United States is to bring the Negro American to full and equal sharing in the responsibilities and rewards of citizenship. To this end, the programs of the Federal government bearing on this objective shall be designed to have the effect, directly or indirectly, of enhancing the stability and resources of the Negro American family.

WILLIAM RYAN
The New Genteel Racism [1965]

One of the most influential critiques of the Moynihan Report (p. 638) was by psychologist and CORE activist William Ryan (1923?–2002). He first published "Savage Discovery: The Moynihan Report" in *The Nation* in November 1965, followed by a condensed version of that article that appeared in *The Crisis* and is reprinted here, and finally his 1971 book on the topic, *Blaming the Victim*. In "The New Genteel Racism," Ryan explores two main areas of disagreement with the Moynihan Report. First, he argues that much of the so-called "pathology" within African American family structure is in fact a result of inaccurate measurement. Secondly, he argues that the remaining problems are caused by active discrimination and by unequal access to resources, contrasting his emphasis on current factors with Moynihan's focus on the past. In his rejection of the idea that "the Negro's condition is directly due to his values, the way he lives," etc., Ryan also starts to explore the tendency of "justifying inequality by finding defects in the victims of inequality," the focus of his 1971 book, *Blaming the Victim*.

The Crisis, December 1965, pp. 623–31.

E ven before it was made public, *The Negro Family*, sometimes called "The Moynihan Report" in reference to its presumed chief author, has had an enormous impact on public discussion about the Negro. The report has been the subject of long articles in newspapers and magazines and was the subject of heated discussion in the panel on the family at the planning session, November 17–18, for the President's While House Conference on civil rights now scheduled for the spring of 1966.

In view of its potential influence, it is particularly important that this report be carefully reviewed and seriously considered. In this review and evaluation three major paints will be made:

1. *The report is inadequate and naive. It draws dangerously inexact conclusions from weak and insufficient data.*

2. *The report (no doubt unintentionally) encourages the development of a bargaining form of subtle racism.*

3. *The report can be read in such a way as to imply that the present unequal status of the Negro in America*

results, not from the obvious causes of discrimination and segregation, but rather from the more basic cause, the "instability" of the Negro family. It is further implied that corrective measures should be focused on increasing the stability of the Negro family, rather than merely on eliminating the discriminatory patterns in American life.

I. THE ART OF READING NUMBERS

The most significant shortcomings of this document are methodological. First, it uses material such as census data without any apparent awareness, either of the inadequacies of this material or, more important, of the context of other well-known or reasonably well-estimated data within which the material must be considered. The most outstanding example of this failure is the extraordinarily sophomoric treatment of illegitimacy data. Second, it contains a number of statements (and these are not accompanied by the customary underpinning of tables and charts) that are manifestly untrue. Third, it consistently commits the unpardonable sin that most social scientists have been warned against since their first year in graduate school—the error of interpreting a statistical relationship in cause-and-effect terms, that is, of stating that since A is associated with B, it is also true that A causes B.

Perhaps even more disquieting is the fact that the report is organized is a most ambiguous and irrational manner. The main argument is that the deterioration of the Negro family is the major underlying cause of the Negro's failure to attain equal status in education, employment, and general community life. However, the authors of the report fail to provide any substantial data to support this conclusion. With several minor exceptions *there is little or no data presented that bears on the thesis being presented.* Indeed the bulk of one whole chapter focuses on findings that point to the completely opposite conclusion: that unemployment and poverty cause "family breakdown" rather than vice versa.

It is important to emphasize the extraordinary point that has been made, a point that would ordinarily be sufficient to discredit this work as a scientific document. The method of argumentation used is, first,

to present data about "family breakdown" among Negroes—separations, illegitimacy, broken homes, female household heads, etc.—and then to present data about "the tangle of pathology" among Negroes. With a few minor exceptions, the connections between the two sets of facts are not documented.

Finally, the authors of the report commit another major sin by presenting the basic terms of their argument—"family breakdown," "family instability"—without any real attempt at rational definition. It is clear that they define these terms by the measures used, but they make no effort to justify this use of the terms or to set them in any theoretical context. Further, they implicitly deny—and even reverse—known facts about trends in Americans family life that would weaken, if not demolish, the basic argument.

Illegitimacy looms large in the Moynihan Report, both in the text and in the graphics. It is of interest to note that only 4 per cent of the relatively dull tables, but fully 22 per cent of the large and dramatic charts and graphs, concern illegitimacy. Negro illegitimacy rates shine through the report as the main index of "family breakdown." Put in an oversimplified way, the implicit hypothesis goes something like this: The values of Negro culture (produced by centuries of slavery and mistreatment, to be sure) are such that there is little commitment to the main components of family organization—legitimacy, marital stability, etc. The implicit point is that the Negro values include tolerance of promiscuity and concomitantly high illegitimacy rates, one-parent families, welfare dependency, and everything else that is supposed to follow.

The basic facts are clear: The Census Bureau reports of recorded illegitimacy rates are about 3 per cent for whites, and about 22 per cent for Negroes. The authors of *The Negro Family* accept these facts at face value and proceed to deduce, elaborate, and draw charts to bolster this hypothesis.

A more, careful examination of the illegitimacy rates, *in the context of other known or reasonably well-estimated data,* would reveal not so much a careless acceptance of promiscuity and illegitimacy, but rather a systematic inequality of access to a variety of services and information. The one-parent Negro family with illegitimate children receiving AFDC (Aid to Families of

Dependent Children) support can then be seen, not as a symptom of the breakdown of Negro family life as a cultural phenomenon, but of continuing and blatant discrimination against the Negro on the part of health and welfare interests of the community.

If we are not to attribute the seven-to-one differences between white and Negro illegitimacy rates to family instability as a subcultural trait, what is it that accounts for these differences? Let us consider, very briefly, a few pieces of additional data:

Reporting. It is widely recognized that illegitimate births are significantly underreported, but this is much more the case for whites than for nonwhites. First, the reporting depends on white sources which act in characteristerically discriminatory fashion. Second, white illegitimate births occur much more frequently in private hospitals, are attended by sympathetic private— and white—doctors, and, in the cases of unmarried mothers, involve the cooperation of social agencies, all of whom work consciously and intentionally to help the white unmarried mother to conceal the fact of illegitimacy. Finally, many Negro births that are recorded as illegitimate are functionally no different from white births recorded as legitimate. The children of a white woman, previously divorced and remarried, are legitimate. The children of a Negro woman, separated but not divorced because divorce is expensive, and now living in an illegal common-law marriage, are illegitimate. What is the real difference between these two situations?

Post-pregnancy marriage. A very substantial portion of first-born children—most estimates are in the range of 20 to 25 per cent—are *conceived* "illegitimately," the parents marrying before the birth. Economic factors that render marriage a financially impossible alternative tend to reduce the rate of such marriages among Negroes.

Abortion. There are an enormous number of illegal, and therefore unreported, induced abortions. The exact number is unknown, of course, but estimates range up to two million per year. A more conservative estimate would be about one million abortions each year. All authorities are in agreement about two main points: a) A substantial minority—25 to 40 per cent— of women obtaining abortions are unmarried, and b) the overwhelming majority of women obtaining abortions are white.

Abortions, them, account for a large part of the differences in white-nonwhite illegitimacy rates. If we were to attempt to estimate "illegitimate conception" rates—an awkward but interesting term—we would find that, although there are only about four million live births a year, there are close to six million conceptions. It can be roughly estimated that the "illegitimate conception" rate for whites is 12 to 15 per cent, for nonwhites 25 to 30 per cent. The differences are clearly not so striking and the ratio drops from seven to one, to about two to one.

Contraception. It is also well known that access to contraceptive information and service is unequally distributed in favor of whites. What the differential rates of access to and use of contraceptive information actually are is not known with any certainty. But, if the differential rates were as low as two to one in favor of whites, we would be able to conclude that "illegitimate intercourse"—if we may push the terminology this far—is about the same among whites and Negroes.

Thus we find that it is not necessary to introduce a complex and highly speculative hypothesis about the malformation of the Negro family by the experiences of slavery and post-Reconstruction semi-slavery— that is, the sins of our grandfathers. The situation is much more easily explained as the result of straightforward discrimination—that is, the sins of ourselves and our contemporaries. The Negro girl, very simply, has unequal access to contraceptive information and devices; unequal access to the expensive services of abortionists; and unequal access to means of concealment and protection. In addition, her young man, if he gets her pregnant, is less likely to be in a position to marry her.

AFDC and Adoption. When they wring their hands about Negro family life, the journalists who have seized on the "Moynihan Report" give most attention to the illegitimacy data, but their next favorite is its presumed consequence: the number of Negro mothers receiving AFDC support. In passing, it might be useful to point out that the majority of children receiving AFDC., white and Negro, are legitimate, though the proportion Negro illegitimate children is, as charged, substantially higher.

Let us consider how the mother of a Negro illegitimate child "gets on" AFDC. The first, and major requirement, of course, is that she keep the child. How does shoe decide whether to keep the child or give it up for adoption? The answer is remarkably simple: she is rarely called on to make the choice. For the most part, the services of maternity homes and adoptoin agencies are used by white girls. Although whites are officially supposed to account for fewer than half the illegitimate children produced each year I (actually, of course, they account for more than half): they account for about 90 per cent of the transactions involving agency adoptions of illegitimate children, and probably an even higher proportion of so-called independent adoptions.

To summarize, the reported rates of illegitimacy among Negroes and whites tell us nothing at all about differences in family structure, historical forces, instability, or anything else the authors choose to speculate about. They tell as only that white girls and Negro girls probably engage in premarital intercourse in about the same proportions, but that the white girl more often takes Enovid or uses a diaphragm; if she gets pregnant, she more often obtains an abortion: if she has the baby, first she is more often able to conceal it, and second, she has infinitely greater opportunity to give it up for adoption.

It is not possible to comment on this smug document without pointing out a few of the outrageous errors of fact. One of the most fantastic errors should be quoted, particularly since it is emphasized by the author. "The white family has achieved a high degree of stability and is maintaining that stability. By contrast, the family structure of lower class Negroes . . . is approaching complete breakdown."

If we take some of the authors' indices of "family breakdown,' such as divorce and illegitimacy, we find, not that the white family "has achieved a high degree of stability," but just the opposite. There has been a marked long-term trend in the United States toward *increases* in these measures of instability, *not decreases*. Number of divorces per 1000 marriages, for example, increased 773 per cent between 1860 and 1956. In the last twenty-five years, the rate of increase of white illegitimate births has been over 50 per cent, while

Negro illegitimate births are only about one-third again as great. Many other statistics could be cited, but the most ready evidence is the great concern apparent everywhere, from the sociological journal to the pupil, about the "breakdown of the American family." Inspected in a narrow framework, the Negro family ones look as if it's falling apart when compared to the white family, but, by the same token, the urban family looks as if it's falling apart when compared with the form family, and the modern family looks as if it's falling apart when compared with the family of our grandfathers.

Another stupefying statement to be found in this report is, "It is probable that, at present, a majority of the crimes against the person, such its rope, murder, and aggravated assault, are committed by Negroes."

It should be noted that this statement is backed up by *arrest rates* and *conviction rates*, which are notoriously quite different from rates of crimes *committed*. One would presume that the authors of this report would have been aware of this difference. It is well known that Negroes—guilty and innocent alike—are arrested and convicted with great abandon. To draw from this fact the conclusion that Negroes commit the majority of major crimes is a shockingly inept piece of interpretation.

In summary, it may be fairly stated that this document is filled with errors of methodology and interpretation that reveal its authors as completely unequipped wish the necessary skills to undertake the tasks that they assumed. As a direct result, they have discovered, and trumpeted to the world, a number of things that simply are not so.

This is not to say that the sociology of the Negro family is not an important issue.

However, some two decades ago, we were presented with the classic study of these matters by E. Franklin Frazier. His work has not materially been improved upon by the white social scientists who have recently entered the arena. For one thing, the latter's work is often based on a "review of the literature," rather than on the hard work of observing and pondering upon reality. Their psychoanalytical and social psychological elaborations are often based on crude data or, worse, on inexact analogies. Their sweeping generalizations are frequently drawn from specific, narrow, often tenuous, results of psychological experiments, some of them animal experiments. In general, their work has served more to distort and oversimplify the problem and the data relevant to it.

And this is no matter of mere academic import. We find ourselves about to initiate the process of achieving a national consensus. It is vitally important that this consensus is not based on sociological opinions that are dangerously in exact.

II. SAVAGE DISCOVERY— THE NEW RACISM

No one can deny that there have been vast changes in the area of race relations. The evidence is to be found all the way from lunch-counters in Birmingham, through legislative forums, to television commercials and newspaper editorials. Strangely, however, the change has little impact on the life of the average American Negro. He remains badly housed, badly educated, underemployed, and underpaid.

On closer examination, there is some reason to believe that much of the change has been merely in the terms of the discourse. We have officially proclaimed that the Negro is no longer to be considered an inferior being. We no longer condone the inequality of his status. But we seem to be spending more energy an *explaining* this inequality than in doing something about it. The rush of popularizations flowing through the pages of newspapers and magazines represent a typical example of this new mania for explaining, rather than condoning, the oppressed status of the Negro. And now we are being told that it is the Negro family structure that is the cause for everything from low I.Q.s to high unemployment rates.

In the paragraphs above, a few points were cited to show that the statistical facts about the Negro family reflect current effects of contemporaneous discrimination. They are a result, not a cause. The same point can be made about other areas of concern—school dropout, education level, type and quantity of employment.

But the new ideology, the new racism, accepted now by liberal and conservative alike, would have it differently. Unemployment, the new ideologists tell us, results from the breakdown of Negro family life;

poor education of Negroes results from "cultural deprivation"; the slum conditions endured by so many Negro families is the result of lack of "acculturation" of Southern rural migrants.

In order in sustain this ideology, it is necessary to engage vigorously in the popular new sport of Savage Discovery and therefore savages are being discovered in great profusion in the Northern ghetto—the favorite being the promiscuous AFDC mother with a litter of illegitimate brats. Other triumphs of savage discovery are the child who cannot read because his parents don't talk to him, whose I.Q. reveals borderline mental retardation as a result of "cultural deprivation"; the "untenantable" Negro family (apparently a neologism for "unbearable") that throws garbage out the window and keeps coal in the bathtub; the assaultive delinquent whose crimes of terror are senseless and unpredictable. The crucial point of the new racism is that these "savages" are, first of all, supposed to be typical of the residents of the Negro slum, and, second, that they are said to reflect the basic culture and values of these residents.

It turns out, paradoxically, if we are to believe the proponents of this new racism, that segregation and discrimination are not the main villains after all. Rather, we are told, the Negro's condition is directly due to his values, the way he lives, the kind of family life he has, his lack of "acculturation." The major qualification—the bow to egalitarianism—is that these conditions are supposed to grow out of the Negro's history of being enslaved and oppressed *generations* age.

It is all an ingenious way of "copping a plea." As the murderer pleads guilty to manslaughter to avoid conviction that might lead to his being electrocuted, liberal America today is pleading guilty, with great beatings of breasts, to the savagery and oppression against the Negro that happened 100 years ago, in order to escape trial for the crimes of today.

This new racism, with its emphasis on save discovery, is, like most psychological compromise formations, an attempt to eat one's cake and have it too. The theme song is: "The Negro is not born inferior, he has been made inferior by generations of hatch treatment." Thus we are enabled in continue to assert that the Negro is inferior, while chastely maintaining our true belief that all men are born equal. It is all rather painful, as well as being utter nonsense.

For the fact is, of course, that the Negro is ill-educated, not because his mother doesn't subscribe to the *Reader's Digest* and doesn't give him colored crayons for his third birthday, but because be has been miseducated in segregated slum schools.

The Negro is more often unemployed because he is last hired and first fired, and because his mother prefers a succession of temporary lovers to a permanent husband. As we move toward full employment, the Negro, at a lesser rate to be sure, is employed, usually at the traditional bottom of the status ladder. And when bodies are needed badly enough to fill the jobs to be done, even the supposed lack of skills and inadequate education of the Negro suddenly becomes less important. This was shown during the War, when it was more important to have someone operating the lathe, even if he were Negro, than it was to preserve our myths of Negro inability. It has been shown again many times in recent years when employers, threatened with boycott or other economic reprisal, who had pleaded that they couldn't find "qualified" Negroes, suddenly found that they could somehow make do with "unqualified" Negroes rather than jeopardize their own material well-being.

And the squalor of the Negro family's home in the slums doesn't require any far-fetched explanations about rural background. In the first place, most of them are not rural. In the second place, the condition of their housing is more easily explained by the neglect of slum landlords, and the crowding caused by the deplorable shortages of decent low-income housing.

III. Forgetting about Discrimination

It is important to underline separately the main point that has been implicit in much said above: that we are most in danger of being seduced into deemphasizing discrimination as the overriding cause of the Negro's current status of inequality. It is tempting, when facing a complex problem, to wallow in the very chaos of complexity, rather than beginning the tortuous task of unraveling and analyzing and, ultimately, of acting. It is obviously true that the Negro suffers from a never-ending cycle of oppression, not only from generation to generation, but, in the case of many individuals, from uncared-for birth to premature death. The education-job-housing-education cycle has become a cliché. The double jeopardy of caste and class is well known. Each condition has its labyrinth of causation, so that we ultimately discover that the Negro family of six in a three-room slum apartment has been placed there, not only by the greedy slumlord and the barbarous realtor, but also and equally by the venal housing inspector and even by the noble woman leagued with her sisters in voting for a "progressive" zoning ordinance in her trim suburhan town.

But to move from the recognition of infernal complexity to seek the refuge of damnably inaccurate simplicity is surely hereys. Much has to be done and all of it is difficult, confusing, tangled and anxious-making. Still it must be done; there's no escape in the world of sociological fakery.

Obviously, if we stop discriminating tomorrow, great damage will remain and it will have to be dealt with, damage ranging from miseducation that is clearly reversible, to hatred and bitterness that may be unalterable. Damage to the family life of the Negro is one problem among the others that calls for correction. But we must be clear what we mean by "compensatory programs" and we must face directly that which we are compensating for.

It is *not* true, in the words of Nathan Glazer that are quoted in *The Negro Family*, that the demands of the oppressed group have shifted from equality of opportunity to equality of results. No one is approaching a Superintendent of Schools and saying: "Do whatever you have to do so that the same proportion of Negroes as of whites pass the college board examinations." The demand is still for educational parity. A possible reason for confusion here is that the Negro is too wise to believe that a Supreme Court decision or an Act of Congress produces the educational equality that he is seeking.

Negroes are perfectly willing to lift themselves by their own boostraps if, in the words of Edwin Berry, we will only get off his damned boots. This analogy can be pushed a bit further, in terms of compensatory programs, by adding that, if we stole the boots in the first place, we first have to give them back. What, then, is to be done? The young Negro man who dropped out of school, or, worse, graduated from high school with a seventh grade education, represents a specific example of damage done—in his lifetime, in our lifetime. The damage should be corrected to the extent possible, by reeducation, by training, by special programs. This is not a demand for equality of results; it is a demand that some human meaning he injected into the concept of equality of opportunity. If one result of the demoralizing experience of growing up Negro is that a man does not have the skills to obtain available work, he cannot be written off and relegated to a life of welfare subsistence. We must provide him, first a job, and second a chance to increase his skills and resources.

Compensatory programs, in this sense, are analogous to legal and theological concepts of restitution. We must give back that which we look away. For the millions of grown and half-grown Negro Americans who have already been damaged, we must compensate for the injury that we did to them. This is what we are compensating for, not some supposed inherent or acquired inferiority or weakness or instability of the victim whom we injured.

So compensatory programs are necessary. But the first order of business is still to end discrimination and segregation. These are the major causes both of the "family instability" and the "tangle of pathology."

We must not forget to stop discriminating or all our good works will amount to very little.

THURGOOD MARSHALL

from *Opinion on* Regents of the University of California v. Bakke [1978]

In 1965, President Lyndon B. Johnson's Executive Order 11246 ushered in an era of proactive measures to promote racial (and, later, gender) diversity in education and employment. The establishment of government affirmative action programs marked a major shift from the assumption that eliminating systematic discrimination would result in equality. Under Johnson, the government funded programs and enacted regulations to proactively counter entrenched conditions that had been caused by centuries of discrimination in education and business.

Since their inception, affirmative action programs have been the target of intense and contentious debate and legal action. A key event in their history was the Supreme Court's 1978 decision in *Regents of the University of California v. Bakke*. The medical school at the University of California at Davis had developed two admissions programs. Its general program accounted for 84 percent of the admissions, and a separate policy, designed to promote diversity, applied only to minorities or other applicants considered as disadvantaged. In 1973 and 1974, Allan Bakke, a white male applicant, was rejected under the general admissions program. Since the university accepted students with significantly lower scores in the separate program, Bakke filed suit in a California state court asserting that the university pol-

icy violated the Civil Rights Act of 1964 and the equal protection clause of the Fourteenth Amendment. In its review of the case, the Supreme Court was sharply divided, with four justices supporting the use of race in admissions, four opposing, and one offering a mediating position. The court ultimately ruled that quotas such as the university's special program were unconstitutional but that race could be used as a "plus factor" in determining admissions. *Bakke* was a landmark case, since it both affirmed the constitutionality of affirmative action and restricted how affirmative action can be administered.

In 1954, Thurgood Marshall (1908–1993), then a lawyer with the NAACP, argued *Brown v. Board of Education* before the Supreme Court, helping to win the case that ended legal segregation in public school. In *Bakke*, Marshall worked on the other side of the bench, for by then he had become the first African American Supreme Court justice. In the two decades since *Brown*, Marshall had come to believe that outlawing race-based segregation was not enough to ensure equal access to opportunities. In his dissenting opinion on *Bakke*, excerpted here, Marshall indicates that he agrees only with the part of the majority ruling that allows race to be considered as a factor in school admissions policy.

Source: *Regents of the University of California v. Bakke*, 438 U.S. 265 (1978).

I t is unnecessary in 20th century America to have individual Negroes demonstrate that they have been victims of racial discrimination; the racism of our society has been so pervasive that none, regardless of wealth or position, has managed to escape its impact. The experience of Negroes in America has been different in kind, not just in degree, from that of other ethnic groups. It is not merely the history of slavery alone but also that a whole people were marked as inferior by the law. And that mark has endured. The dream of America as the great melting pot has not been realized for the Negro; because of his skin color he never even made it into the pot.

[* * *]

It is because of a legacy of unequal treatment that we now must permit the institutions of this society to give consideration to race in making decisions about who will hold the positions of influence, affluence and prestige in America. For far too long the doors to those positions have been shut to Negroes. If we are ever to become a fully integrated society, one in which the color of a person's skin will not determine the opportunities available to him or her, we must be willing to take steps to open those doors. I do not believe that anyone can truly look into America's past and still find that a remedy for the effects of that past is impermissible.

IRVING HOWE
Black Boys and Native Sons [1963]

In "Autobiographical Notes," the opening selection in his 1955 essay collection, *Notes of a Native Son,* James Baldwin (p. 485) extols the writing of the novelist Ralph Ellison (p. 430), describing Ellison as "the first Negro novelist I have ever read to utilize in language, and brilliantly, some of the ambiguity and irony of Negro life"— as opposed to the narrow "categorization" of the black characters Baldwin critiques in the work of his former

mentor, Richard Wright (p. 470). In this 1963 essay, Irving Howe (1920–1993), a socialist and a member of the group of white left-leaning thinkers known as the New York Intellectuals, similarly links Baldwin and Ellison and compares them with Wright. Unlike Baldwin, however, Howe rejects the complexity and ambiguity that Baldwin championed in favor of Wright's clear-cut message of social protest.

From *Dissent,* Autumn 1963; reprinted in Irving Howe, *A World More Attractive: A View of Modern Literature and Politics* (New York: Horizon Press, 1963), pp. 98–122.

[I]

James Baldwin first came to the notice of the American literary public not through his own fiction but as author of an impassioned criticism of the conventional Negro novel. In 1949 he published in *Partisan Review* an essay called "Everybody's Protest Novel," attacking the kind of fiction, from *Uncle Tom's Cabin* to *Native Son,* that had been written about the ordeal of the American Negroes; and two years later he printed in the same magazine "Many Thousands Gone," a tougher and more explicit polemic against Richard Wright and the school of naturalistic "protest" fiction that Wright represented. The protest novel, wrote Baldwin, is undertaken out of sympathy for the Negro, but through its need to present him merely as a social victim or a mythic agent of sexual prowess, it hastens to confine the Negro to the very tones of violence he has known all his life. Compulsively re-enacting and magnifying his trauma, the protest novel proves unable to transcend it. So choked with rage has this kind of writing become, it cannot show the Negro as a unique person or locate him as a member of a community with its own traditions and values, its own "unspoken recognition of shared experience which creates a way

of life." The failure of the protest novel "lies in its insistence that it is [man's] categorization alone which is real and which cannot be transcended."

Like all attacks launched by young writers against their famous elders, Baldwin's essays were also a kind of announcement of his own intentions. He wrote admiringly about Wright's courage ("his work was an immense liberation and revelation for me"), but now, precisely because Wright had prepared the way for all the Negro writers to come, he, Baldwin, would go further, transcending the sterile categories of "Negroness," whether those enforced by the white world or those defensively erected by the Negroes themselves. No longer mere victim or rebel, the Negro would stand free in a self-achieved humanity. As Baldwin put it some years later, he hoped "to prevent myself from becoming *merely* a Negro; or even, merely a Negro writer." The world "tends to trap and immobilize you in the role you play," and for the Negro writer, if he is to be a writer at all, it hardly matters whether the trap is sprung from motives of hatred or condescension.

Baldwin's rebellion against the older Negro novelist who had served him as a model and had helped launch his career, was not of course an unprecedented event. The history of literature is full of such painful

659

ruptures, and the issue Baldwin raised is one that keeps recurring, usually as an aftermath to a period of "socially engaged" writing. The novel is an inherently ambiguous genre: it strains toward formal autonomy and can seldom avoid being a public gesture. If it is true, as Baldwin said in "Everybody's Protest Novel," that "literature and sociology are not one and the same," it is equally true that such statements hardly begin to cope with the problem of how a writer's own experience affects his desire to represent human affairs in a work of fiction. Baldwin's formula evades, through rhetorical sweep, the genuinely difficult issue of the relationship between social experience and literature.

Yet in *Notes of a Native Son,* the book in which his remark appears, Baldwin could also say: "One writes out of one thing only—one's own experience." What, then, was the experience of a man with a black skin, what *could* it be in this country? How could a Negro put pen to paper, how could be so much as think or breathe, without some impulsion to protest, be it harsh or mild, political or private, released or buried? The "sociology" of his existence formed a constant pressure on his literary work, and not merely in the way this might be true for any writer, but with a pain and ferocity that nothing could remove.

James Baldwin's early essays are superbly eloquent, displaying virtually in full the gifts that would enable him to become one of the great American rhetoricians. But these essays, like some of the later ones, are marred by rifts in logic, so little noticed when one gets swept away by the brilliance of the language that it takes a special effort to attend their argument.

Later Baldwin would see the problems of the Negro writer with a greater charity and more mature doubt. Reviewing in 1959 a book of poems by Langston Hughes,[1] he wrote: "Hughes is an American Negro poet and has no choice but to be acutely aware of it. He is not the first American Negro to find the war between his social and artistic responsibilities all but irreconcilable." All but irreconcilable: the phrase strikes a note sharply different from Baldwin's attack upon Wright in the early fifties. And it is not hard to surmise the reasons for this change. In the intervening years Baldwin had been living through some of the experiences that had goaded Richard Wright into rage and driven him into exile; he too, like Wright, had been to hell and back, many times over.

II

Gawd, Ah wish all them white folks was dead.[2]

The day *Native Son* appeared, American culture was changed forever. No matter how much qualifying the book might later need, it made impossible a repetition of the old lies. In all its crudeness, melodrama and claustrophobia of vision, Richard Wright's novel brought out into the open, as no one ever had before, the hatred, fear and violence that have crippled and may yet destroy our culture.

A blow at the white man, the novel forced him to recognize himself as an oppressor. A blow at the black man, the novel forced him to recognize the cost of his submission. *Native Son* assaulted the most cherished of American vanities: the hope that the accumulated injustice of the past would bring with it no lasting penalties, the fantasy that in his humiliation the Negro somehow retained a sexual potency—or was it a childlike good-nature?—that made it necessary to envy and still more to suppress him. Speaking from the black wrath of retribution, Wright insisted that history can be a punishment. He told us the one thing even the most liberal whites preferred not to hear: that Negroes were far from patient or forgiving, that they were scarred by fear, that they hated every moment of their suppression even when seeming most acquiescent, and that often enough they hated *us,* the decent and cultivated white men who from complicity or neglect shared in the responsibility for their plight. If such younger novelists as Baldwin and Ralph Ellison were to move beyond Wright's harsh naturalism and toward more supple modes of fiction, that was possible only because Wright had been there first, courageous enough to release the full weight of his anger.

In *Black Boy,* the autobiographical narrative he published several years later, Wright would tell of an

1. See p. 362.
2. From "Long Black Song," published in Wright's collection of short stories *Uncle Tom's Children* (1938).

experience he had while working as a bellboy in the South. Many times he had come into a hotel room carrying luggage or food and seen naked white women lounging about, unmoved by shame at his presence, for "blacks were not considered human beings anyway...I was a non-man...I felt doubly cast out." With the publication of *Native Son,* however, Wright forced his readers to acknowledge his anger, and in that way, if none other, he wrested for himself a sense of dignity as a man. He forced his readers to confront the disease of our culture, and to one of its most terrifying symptoms he gave the name of Bigger Thomas.

Brutal and brutalized, lost forever to his unexpended hatred and his fear of the world, a numbed and illiterate black boy stumbling into a murder and never, not even at the edge of the electric chair, breaking through to an understanding of either his plight or himself, Bigger Thomas was a part of Richard Wright, a part even of the James Baldwin who stared with horror at Wright's Bigger, unable either to absorb him into his consciousness or eject him from it. Enormous courage, a discipline of self-conquest, was required to conceive Bigger Thomas, for this was no eloquent Negro spokesman, no admirable intellectual or formidable proletarian. Bigger was drawn—one would surmise, deliberately—from white fantasy and white contempt. Bigger was the worst of Negro life accepted, then rendered a trifle conscious and thrown back at those who had made him what he was. "No American Negro exists," Baldwin would later write, "who does not have his private Bigger Thomas living in the skull."

Wright drove his narrative to the very core of American phobia: sexual fright, sexual violation. He understood that the fantasy of rape is a consequence of guilt, what the whites suppose themselves to deserve. He understood that the white man's notion of uncontaminated Negro vitality, little as it had to do with the bitter realities of Negro life, reflected some ill-formed and buried feeling that our culture has run down, lost its blood, become febrile. And he grasped the way in which the sexual issue has been intertwined with

social relationships, for even as the white people who hire Bigger as their chauffeur are decent and charitable, even as the girl he accidentally kills is a liberal of sorts, theirs is the power and the privilege. "We black and they white. They got things and we ain't. They do things and we can't."

The novel barely stops to provision a recognizable social world, often contenting itself with cartoon simplicities and yielding almost entirely to the nightmare incomprehension of Bigger Thomas. The mood is apocalyptic, the tone superbly aggressive. Wright was an existentialist[3] long before he heard the name, for he was committed to the literature of extreme situations both through the pressures of his rage and the gasping hope of an ultimate catharsis.

Wright confronts both the violence and the cripping limitations of Bigger Thomas. For Bigger white people are not people at all, but something more, "a sort of great natural force, like a stormy sky looming overhead." And only through violence does he gather a little meaning in life, pitifully little: "he had murdered and created a new life for himself." Beyond that Bigger cannot go.

At first *Native Son* seems still another naturalistic novel: a novel of exposure and accumulation, charting the waste of the undersides of the American city. Behind the book one senses the molding influence of Theodore Dreiser, especially the Dreiser of *An American Tragedy*[4] who knows there are situations so oppressive that only violence can provide their victims with the hope of dignity. Like Dreiser, Wright wished to pummel his readers into awareness; like Dreiser, to overpower them with the sense of society as an enclosing force. Yet the comparison is finally of limited value, and for the disconcerting reason that Dreiser had a white skin and Wright a black one.

The usual naturalistic novel is written with detachment, as if by a scientist surveying a field of operations; it is a novel in which the writer withdraws from a detested world and coldly piles up the evidence for detesting it. *Native Son,* though preserving some of the

---

3. Philosophy focused on the idea that individuals have freedom of choice and responsibility for their actions, which can produce dread or anxiety.
4. 1925 novel by Dreiser (1871–1945), white American pioneer of naturalism, a literary movement stressing the effects of environmental or structural forces over individual agency.

devices of the naturalistic novel, deviates sharply from its characteristic tone: a tone Wright could not possibly have maintained and which, it may be, no Negro novelist can really hold for long. *Native Son* is a work of assault rather than withdrawal; the author yields himself in part to a vision of nightmare. Bigger's cowering perception of the world becomes the most vivid and authentic component of the book. Naturalism pushed to an extreme turns here into something other than itself, a kind of expressionist outburst, no longer a replica of the familiar social world but a self-contained realm of grotesque emblems.

That *Native Son* has grave faults anyone can see. The language is often coarse, flat in rhythm, syntactically overburdened, heavy with journalistic slag. Apart from Bigger, who seems more a brute energy than a particularized figure, the characters have little reality, the Negroes being mere stock accessories and the whites either "agit-prop" villains or heroic Communists whom Wright finds it easier to admire from a distance than establish from the inside. The long speech by Bigger's radical lawyer Max (again a device apparently borrowed from Dreiser) is ill-related to the book itself: Wright had not achieved Dreiser's capacity for absorbing everything, even the most recalcitrant philosophical passages, into a unified vision of things. Between Wright's feelings as a Negro and his beliefs as a Communist there is hardly a genuine fusion, and it is through this gap that a good part of the novel's unreality pours in.

Yet it should be said that the endlessly-repeated criticism that Wright caps his melodrama with a party-line oration tends to oversimplify the novel, for Wright is too honest simply to allow the propagandistic message to constitute the last word. Indeed, the last word is given not to Max but to Bigger. For at the end Bigger remains at the mercy of his hatred and fear, the lawyer retreats helplessly, the projected union between political consciousness and raw revolt has not been achieved—as if Wright were persuaded that, all ideology apart, there is for each Negro an ultimate trial that he can bear only by himself.

Black Boy, which appeared five years after *Native Son,* is a slighter but more skillful piece of writing. Richard Wright came from a broken home, and as he moved from his helpless mother to a grandmother whose religious fanaticism (she was a Seventh-Day Adventist) proved utterly suffocating, he soon picked up a precocious knowledge of vice and a realistic awareness of social power. This autobiographical memoir, a small classic in the literature of self-discovery, is packed with harsh evocations of Negro adolescence in the South. The young Wright learns how wounding it is to wear the mask of a grinning niggerboy in order to keep a job. He examines the life of the Negroes and judges it without charity or idyllic compensation—for he already knows, in his heart and his bones, that to be oppressed means to lose out on human possibilities. By the time he is seventeen, preparing to leave for Chicago, where he will work on a WPA[5] project, become a member of the Communist Party, and publish his first book of stories called *Uncle Tom's Children,* Wright has managed to achieve the beginnings of consciousness, through a slow and painful growth from the very bottom of deprivation to the threshold of artistic achievement and a glimpsed idea of freedom.

III

Baldwin's attack upon Wright had partly been anticipated by the more sophisticated American critics. Alfred Kazin, for examples, had found in Wright a troubling obsession with violence:

> If he chose to write the story of Bigger Thomas as a grotesque crime story, it is because his own indignation and the sickness of the age combined to make him dependent on violence and shock, to astonish the reader by torrential scenes of cruelty, hunger, rape, murder and flight, and then enlighten him by crude Stalinist[6] homilies.

---

5. Works Progress [later Projects] Administration; New Deal jobs program started by President Franklin Delano Roosevelt in 1935, p. 376.

6. Allusion to Joseph Stalin (1879–1954), Communist leader of the Soviet Union from Vladimir Lenin's death in 1924 until his own death.

The last phrase apart, something quite similar could be said about the author of *Crime and Punishment*[7]; it is disconcerting to reflect upon how few novelists, even the very greatest, could pass this kind of moral inspection. For the novel as a genre seems to have an inherent bias toward extreme effects, such as violence, cruelty and the like. More important, Kazin's judgment rests on the assumption that a critic can readily distinguish between the genuine need of a writer to cope with ugly realities and the damaging effect these realities may have upon his moral and psychic life. But in regard to contemporary writers one finds it very hard to distinguish between a valid portrayal of violence and an obsessive involvement with it. A certain amount of obsession may be necessary for the valid portrayal—writers devoted to themes of desperation cannot keep themselves morally intact. And when we come to a writer like Richard Wright, who deals with the most degraded and inarticulate sector of the Negro world, the distinction between objective rendering and subjective immersion becomes still more difficult, perhaps even impossible. For a novelist who has lived through the searing experiences that Wright has there cannot be much possibility of approaching his subject with the "mature" poise recommended by high-minded critics. What is more, the very act of writing his novel, the effort to confront what Bigger Thomas means to him, is for such a writer a way of dredging up and then perhaps shedding the violence that society has pounded into him. Is Bigger an authentic projection of a social reality, or is he a symptom of Wright's "dependence on violence and shock"? Obviously both; and it could not be otherwise.

For the reality pressing upon all of Wright's work was a nightmare of remembrance, everything from which he had pulled himself out, with an effort and at a cost that is almost unimaginable. Without the terror of that nightmare it would have been impossible for Wright to summon the truth of the reality—not the only truth about American Negroes, perhaps not even the deepest one, but a primary and inescapable truth. Both truth and terror rested on a gross fact which Wright alone dared to confront: that violence is a central fact in the life of the American Negro, defining and crippling him with a harshness few other Americans need suffer. "No American Negro exists who does not have his private Bigger Thomas living in the skull."

Now I think it would be well not to judge in the abstract, or with much haste, the violence that gathers in the Negro's heart as a response to the violence he encounters in society. It would be well to see this violence as part of an historical experience that is open to moral scrutiny but ought to be shielded from presumptuous moralizing. Bigger Thomas may be enslaved to a hunger for violence, but anyone reading *Native Son* with mere courtesy must observe the way in which Wright, even while yielding emotionally to Bigger's deprivation, also struggles to transcend it. That he did not fully succeed seems obvious; one may doubt that any Negro writer can.

More subtle and humane than either Kazin's or Baldwin's criticism is a remark made by Isaac Rosenfeld while reviewing *Black Boy*: "As with all Negroes and all men who are born to suffer social injustice, part of [Wright's] humanity found itself only in acquaintance with violence, and in hatred of the oppressor." Surely Rosenfeld was not here inviting an easy acquiescence in violence; he was trying to suggest the historical context, the psychological dynamics, which condition the attitudes all Negro writers take, or must take, toward violence. To say this is not to propose the condescension of exempting Negro writers from moral judgment, but to suggest the terms of understanding, and still more, the terms of hesitation for making a judgment.

There were times when Baldwin grasped this point better than anyone else. If he could speak of the "unrewarding rage" of *Native Son*, he also spoke of the book as "an immense liberation." Is it impudent to suggest that one reason he felt the book to be a liberation was precisely its rage, precisely the relief and pleasure that he, like so many other Negroes, must have felt upon seeing those long-suppressed emotions finally breaking through?

The kind of literary criticism Baldwin wrote was very fashionable in America during the post-war years. Mimicking the Freudian corrosion of motives and bristling with dialectical agility, this criticism approached all ideal claims, especially those made by radical and

---

7. Fyodor Dostoyevsky (1821–81), Russian novelist, published *Crime and Punishment* in 1866.

naturalist writers, with a weary skepticism and proceeded to transfer the values such writers were attacking to the perspective from which they attacked. If Dreiser wrote about the power hunger and dream of success corrupting American society, that was because he was really infatuated with them. If Farrell[8] showed the meanness of life in the Chicago slums, that was because he could not really escape it. If Wright portrayed the violence gripping Negro life, that was because he was really obsessed with it. The word "really" or more sophisticated equivalents could do endless service in behalf of a generation of intellectuals soured on the tradition of protest but suspecting they might be pigmies in comparison to the writers who had protested. In reply, there was no way to "prove" that Dreiser, Farrell and Wright were not contaminated by the false values they attacked; probably, since they were mere mortals living in the present society, they were contaminated; and so one had to keep insisting that such writers were nevertheless presenting actualities of modern experience, not merely phantoms of their neuroses.

If Bigger Thomas, as Baldwin said, "accepted a theology that denies him life," if in his Negro self-hatred he "*wants* to die because he glories in his hatred," this did not constitute a criticism of Wright unless one were prepared to assume what was simply preposterous: that Wright, for all his emotional involvement with Bigger, could not see beyond the limitations of the character he had created. This was a question Baldwin never seriously confronted in his early essays. He would describe accurately the limitations of Bigger Thomas and then, by one of those rhetorical leaps at which he is so gifted, would assume that these were also the limitations of Wright or his book.

Still another ground for Baldwin's attack was his reluctance to accept the clenched militancy of Wright's posture as both novelist and man. In a remarkable sentence appearing in "Everybody's Protest Novel," Baldwin wrote, "our humanity is our burden, our life; we need not battle for it; we need only to do what is infinitely more difficult—that is, accept it." What Baldwin was saying here was part of the outlook so many American intellectuals took over during the years of a post-war liberalism not very different from conservatism. Ralph Ellison expressed this view in terms still more extreme: "Thus to see America with an awareness of its rich diversity and its almost magical fluidity and freedom, I was forced to conceive of a novel unburdened by the narrow naturalism which has led after so many triumphs to the final and unrelieved despair which marks so much of our current fiction." This note of willed affirmation—as if one could *decide* one's deepest and most authentic response to society!—was to be heard in many other works of the early fifties, most notably in Saul Bellow's *Adventures of Augie March*. Today it is likely to strike one as a note whistled in the dark. In response to Baldwin and Ellison, Wright would have said (I virtually quote the words he used in talking to me during the summer of 1958) that only through struggle could men with black skins, and for that matter, all the oppressed of the world, achieve their humanity. It was a lesson, said Wright with a touch of bitterness yet not without kindness, that the younger writers would have to learn in their own way and their own time. All that has happened since, bears him out.

One criticism made by Baldwin in writing about *Native Son*, perhaps because it is the least ideological, remains important. He complained that in Wright's novel "a necessary dimension has been cut away; this dimension being the relationship that Negroes bear to one another, that depth of involvement and unspoken recognition of shared experience which creates a way of life." The climate of the book, "common to most Negro protest novels . . . has led us all to believe that in Negro life there exists no tradition, no field of manners, no possibility of ritual or intercourse, such as may, for example, sustain the Jew even after he has left his father's house." It could be urged, perhaps, that in composing a novel verging on expressionism Wright need not be expected to present the Negro world with fullness, balance or nuance; but there can be little doubt that in this respect Baldwin did score a major point: the posture of militancy, no matter how great the need for it, exacts a heavy price from the writer, as indeed from everyone else. For "Even the hatred of squalor / Makes the brow grow stern / Even anger

---

8. James Farrell (1904–79), Irish-American novelist who wrote about working-class Irish characters.

against injustice / Makes the voice grow harsh ...".[9] All one can ask, by way of reply, is whether the refusal to struggle may not exact a still greater price. It is a question that would soon be tormenting James Baldwin, and almost against his will.

IV

In his own novels Baldwin hoped to show the Negro world in its diversity and richness, not as a mere spectre of protest; he wished to show it as a living culture of men and women who, even when deprived, share in the emotions and desires of common humanity. And he meant also to evoke something of the distinctiveness of Negro life in America, as evidence of its worth, moral tenacity and right to self-acceptance. How can one not sympathize with such a program? And how, precisely as one does sympathize, can one avoid the conclusion that in this effort Baldwin has thus far failed to register a major success?

His first novel, *Go Tell It on the Mountain,* is an enticing but minor work: it traces the growing-up of a Negro boy in the atmosphere of a repressive Calvinism, a Christianity stripped of grace and brutal with fantasies of submission and vengeance. No other work of American fiction reveals so graphically the way in which an oppressed minority aggravates its own oppression through the torments of religious fanaticism. The novel is also striking as a modest *Bildungsroman,*[1] the education of an imaginative Negro boy caught in the heart-struggle between his need to revolt, which would probably lead to his destruction in the jungles of New York, and the miserly consolations of black Calvinism, which would signify that he accepts the denial of his personal needs. But it would be a mistake to claim too much for this first novel, in which a rhetorical flair and a conspicuous sincerity often eat away at the integrity of event and the substance of character. The novel is intense, and the intensity is due to Baldwin's absorption in that religion of denial which leads the boy to become a preacher in his father's church, to scream out God's word from "a merciless resolve to kill my father rather than allow my father to kill me." Religion has of course played a central role in Negro life, yet one may doubt that the special kind of religious experience dominating *Go Tell It on the Mountain* is any more representative of that life, any more advantageous a theme for gathering in the qualities of Negro culture, than the violence and outrage of *Native Son.* Like Wright before him, Baldwin wrote from the intolerable pressures of his own experience; there was no alternative; each had to release his own agony before he could regard Negro life with the beginnings of objectivity.

Baldwin's second novel, *Giovanni's Room,* seems to me a flat failure. It abandons Negro life entirely (not in itself a cause for judgment) and focusses upon the distraught personal relations of several young Americans adrift in Paris. The problem of homosexuality, which is to recur in Baldwin's fiction, is confronted with a notable courage, but also with a disconcerting kind of sentimentalism, a quavering and sophisticated submission to the ideology of love. It is one thing to call for the treatment of character as integral and unique; but quite another for a writer with Baldwin's background and passions to succeed in bringing together his sensibility as a Negro and his sense of personal trouble.

Baldwin has not yet managed—the irony is a stringent one—in composing the kind of novel he counterposed to the work of Richard Wright. He has written three essays, ranging in tone from disturbed affection to disturbing malice, in which he tries to break from his rebellious dependency upon Wright, but he remains tied to the memory of the older man. The Negro writer who has come closest to satisfying Baldwin's program is not Baldwin himself but Ralph Ellison, whose novel *Invisible Man* is a brilliant though flawed achievement, standing with *Native Son* as the major fiction thus far composed by American Negroes.

What astonishes one most about *Invisible Man* is the apparent freedom it displays from the ideological and emotional penalties suffered by Negroes in this country—I say "apparent" because the freedom is not quite so complete as the book's admirers like to suppose. Still, for long stretches *Invisible Man* does escape

---

9. From "To Posterity," a 1939 poem by German poet, playwright, and theater director Bertolt Brecht (1898–1956).
1. A coming-of-age novel; literally "novel of education" [German].

the formulas of protest, local color, genre quaintness and jazz chatter. No white man could have written it, since no white man could know with such intimacy the life of the Negroes from the inside; yet Ellison writes with an ease and humor which are now and again simply miraculous.

Invisible Man is a record of a Negro's journey through contemporary America, from South to North, province to city, naïve faith to disenchantment and perhaps beyond. There are clear allegorical intentions (Ellison is "literary" to a fault) but with a book so rich in talk and drama it would be a shame to neglect the fascinating surface for the mere depths. The beginning is both nightmare and farce. A timid Negro boy comes to a white smoker in a Southern town: he is to be awarded a scholarship. Together with several other Negro boys he is rushed to the front of the ballroom, where a sumptuous blonde tantalizes and frightens them by dancing in the nude. Blindfolded, the Negro boys stage a "battle royal," a free-for-all in which they pummel each other to the drunken shouts of the whites. Practical jokes, humiliations, terror—and then the boy delivers a prepared speech of gratitude to his white benefactors. At the end of this section, the boy dreams that he has opened the briefcase given him together with his scholarship to a Negro college and that he finds an inscription reading: "To Whom It May Concern: Keep This Nigger-Boy Running."

He keeps running. He goes to his college and is expelled for having innocently taken a white donor through a Negro ginmill which also happens to be a brothel. His whole experience is to follow this pattern. Strip down a pretense, whether by choice or accident, and you will suffer penalties, since the rickety structure of Negro respectability rests upon pretense and those who profit from it cannot bear to have the reality exposed (in this case, that the college is dependent upon the Northern white millionaire). The boy then leaves for New York, where he works in a white-paint factory, becomes a soapboxer for the Harlem Communists, the darling of the fellow-travelling[2] bohemia, and a big wheel in the Negro world. At the end, after

witnessing a frenzied race riot in Harlem, he "finds himself" in some not entirely specified way, and his odyssey from submission to antonomy is complete.

Ellison has an abundance of that primary talent without which neither craft nor intelligence can save a novelist: he is richly, wildly inventive; his scenes rise and dip with tension, his people bleed, his language sings. No other writer has captured so much of the hidden gloom and surface gaiety of Negro life.

There is an abundance of superbly-rendered speech: a West Indian woman inciting her men to resist an eviction, a Southern sharecropper calmly describing how he seduced his daughter, a Harlem street-vender spinning jive. The rhythm of Ellison's prose is harsh and nervous, like a beat of harried alertness. The observation is expert: he knows exactly how zootsuiters walk, making stylization their principle of life, and exactly how the antagonism between American and West Indian Negroes works itself out in speech and humor. He can accept his people as they are, in their blindness and hope: —here, finally, the Negro world does exist, seemingly apart from plight or protest. And in the final scene Ellison has created an unforgettable image: "Ras the Destroyer," a Negro nationalist, appears on a horse dressed in the costume of an Abyssinian chieftain, carrying spear and shield, and charging wildly into the police—a black Quixote,[3] mad, absurd, unbearably pathetic.

But even Ellison cannot help being caught up with *the idea* of the Negro. To write simply about "Negro experience" with the esthetic distance urged by the critics of the fifties, is a moral and psychological impossibility, for plight and protest are inseparable from that experience, and even if less political than Wright and less prophetic than Baldwin, Ellison knows this quite as well as they do.

If *Native Son* is marred by the ideological delusions of the 'thirties, *Invisible Man* is marred, less grossly, by those of the 'fifties. The middle section of Ellison's novel, dealing with the Harlem Communists, does not ring quite true, in the way a good portion of the writings on this theme during the post-war years does not

2. Sympathizer; in the U.S. in the 1940s and 1950s, a reference to those who supported communism, but were not official members of the Communist Party.

3. Reference to the character of *Don Quixote* from the two-volume novel (1605/1615) by Spanish writer Miguel de Cervantes (1547–1616).

ring quite true. Ellison makes his Stalinist figures so vicious and stupid that one cannot understand how they could ever have attracted him or any other Negro. That the party leadership manipulated members with deliberate cynicism is beyond doubt, but this cynicism was surely more complex and guarded than Ellison shows it to be. No party leader would ever tell a prominent Negro Communist, as one of them does in *Invisible Man:* "You were not hired [as a functionary] to think"—even if that were what he felt. Such passages are almost as damaging as the propagandist outbursts in *Native Son.*

Still more troublesome, both as it breaks the coherence of the novel and reveals Ellison's dependence on the post-war *Zeitgeist,* is the sudden, unprepared and implausible assertion of unconditioned freedom with which the novel ends. As the hero abandons the Communist Party he wonders, "Could politics ever be an expression of love?" This question, more portentous than profound, cannot easily be reconciled to a character who has been presented mainly as a passive victim of his experience. Nor is one easily persuaded by the hero's discovery that "my world has become one of infinite possibilities," his refusal to be the "invisible man" whose body is manipulated by various social groups. Though the unqualified assertion of self-liberation was a favorite strategy among American literary people in the 'fifties, it is also vapid and insubstantial. It violates the reality of social life, the interplay between external conditions and personal will, quite as much as the determinism of the 'thirties. The unfortunate fact remains that to define one's individuality is to stumble upon social barriers which stand in the way, all too much in the way, of "infinite possibilities." Freedom can be fought for, but it cannot always be willed or asserted into existence. And it seems hardly an accident that even as Ellison's hero asserts the "infinite possibilities" he makes no attempt to specify them.

Throughout the 'fifties Richard Wright was struggling to find his place in a world he knew to be changing but could not grasp with the assurance he had felt in his earlier years. He had resigned with some bitterness from the Communist Party, though he tried to preserve an independent radical outlook, tinged occa-

sionally with black nationalism. He became absorbed in the politics and literature of the rising African nations, but when visiting them he felt hurt at how great was the distance between an American Negro and an African. He found life in America intolerable, and he spent his last fourteen years in Paris, somewhat friendly with the intellectual group around Jean-Paul Sartre but finally a loner, a man who stood by the pride of his rootlessness. And he kept writing, steadily experimenting, partly, it may be, in response to the younger men who had taken his place in the limelight and partly because he was truly a dedicated writer.

These last years were difficult for Wright, since he neither made a true home in Paris nor kept in imaginative touch with the changing life of the United States. In the early 'fifties he published a very poor novel *The Outsider,* full of existentialist jargon applied but not really absorbed to the Negro theme. He was a writer in limbo, and his better fiction, such as the novelette "The Man Who Lived Underground," is a projection of that state.

In the late 'fifties Wright published another novel, *The Long Dream,* which is set in Mississippi and displays a considerable recovery of his powers. This book has been criticized for presenting Negro life in the South through "old-fashioned" images of violence, but one ought to hesitate before denying the relevance of such images or joining in the criticism of their use. For Wright was perhaps justified in not paying attention to the changes that have occurred in the South these past few decades. When Negro liberals write that despite the prevalence of bias there has been an improvement in the life of their people, such statements are reasonable and necessary. But what have these to do with the way Negroes feel, with the power of the memories they must surely retain? About this we know very little and would be well advised not to nourish preconceptions, for their feelings may be much closer to Wright's rasping outbursts than to the more modulated tones of the younger Negro novelists. *Wright remembered,* and what he remembered other Negroes must also have remembered. And in that way he kept faith with the experience of the boy who had fought his way out of the depths, to speak for those who remained there.

His most interesting fiction after *Native Son* is to be found in a posthumous collection of stories, *Eight Men,* written during the last 25 years of his life. Though they fail to yield any clear line of chronological development, these stories give evidence of Wright's literary restlessness, his often clumsy efforts to break out of the naturalism which was his first and, I think, necessary mode of expression. The unevenness of his writing is highly disturbing: one finds it hard to understand how the same man, from paragraph to paragraph, can be so brilliant and inept. Time after time the narrative texture is broken by a passage of sociological or psychological jargon; perhaps the later Wright tried too hard, read too much, failed to remain sufficiently loyal to the limits of his talent.

Some of the stories, such as "Big Black Good Man," are enlivened by Wright's sardonic humor, the humor of a man who has known and released the full measure of his despair but finds that neither knowledge nor release matters in a world of despair. In "The Man Who Lived Underground," Wright shows a sense of narrative rhythm, which is superior to anything in his full-length novels and evidence of the seriousness with which he kept working.

The main literary problem that troubled Wright in recent years was that of rendering his naturalism a more terse and supple instrument. I think he went astray whenever he abandoned naturalism entirely: there are a few embarrassingly bad experiments with stories employing self-consciously Freudian[4] symbolism. Wright needed the accumulated material of circumstance which naturalistic detail provided his fiction; it was as essential to his ultimate effect of shock and bruise as dialogue to Hemingway's ultimate effect of irony and loss. But Wright was correct in thinking that the problem of detail is the most vexing technical problem the naturalist writer must face, since the accumulation that makes for depth and solidity can also create a pall of tedium. In "The Man Who Lived Underground" Wright came close to solving this problem, for here the naturalistic detail is put at the service of a radical projective image—a Negro trapped in a sewer; and despite some flaws, the story is satisfying both for its tense surface and elasticity of suggestion.

Richard Wright died at 52, full of hopes and projects. Like many of us, he had somewhat lost his intellectual way but he kept struggling toward the perfection of his craft and toward a comprehension of the strange world that in his last years was coming into birth. In the most fundamental sense, however, he had done his work: he had told his contemporaries a truth so bitter, they paid him the tribute of trying to forget it.

V

Looking back to the early essays and fiction of James Baldwin, one wishes to see a little further than they at first invite: —to see past their brilliance of gesture, by which older writers could be dismissed, and past their aura of gravity, by which a generation of intellectuals could be enticed. After this hard and dismal decade, what strikes one most of all is the sheer pathos of these early writings, the way they reveal the desire of a greatly talented young man to escape the scars—and why should he not have wished to escape them?—which he had found upon the faces of his elders and knew to be gratuitous and unlovely.

Chekhov[5] once said that what the aristocratic Russian writers assumed as their birthright, the writers who came from the lower orders had to pay for with their youth. James Baldwin did not want to pay with his youth, as Richard Wright had paid so dearly. He wanted to move, as Wright had not been able to, beyond the burden or bravado of his stigma; he wanted to enter the world of freedom, grace, and self-creation. One would need a heart of stone, or be a brutal moralist, to feel anything but sympathy for this desire. But we do not make our circumstances; we can, at best, try to remake them. And all the recent writing of Baldwin indicates that the wishes of his youth could not be realized, not in *this* country. The sentiments of humanity which had made him rebel against Richard Wright have now driven him back to a position close to Wright's rebellion.

Baldwin's most recent novel *Another Country* is a "protest novel" quite as much as *Native Son,* and anyone vindictive enough to make the effort, could score against it the points Baldwin scored against Wright.

---

4. Drawing on the work of Austrian neurologist Sigmund Freud (1856–1939), who pioneered the psychoanalytic school of psychiatry.
5. Russian playwright, short-story writer, and physician Anton Chekhov (1860–1904).

No longer is Baldwin's prose so elegant or suave as it was once; in this book it is harsh, clumsy, heavy-breathing with the pant of suppressed bitterness. In about half of *Another Country*—the best half, I would judge—the material is handled in a manner somewhat reminiscent of Wright's naturalism: a piling on of the details of victimization, as the jazz musician Rufus Scott, a sophisticated distant cousin of Bigger Thomas, goes steadily down the path of self-destruction, worn out in the effort to survive in the white man's jungle and consumed by a rage too extreme to articulate yet too amorphous to act upon. The narrative voice is a voice of anger, rasping and thrusting, not at all "literary" in the somewhat lacquered way the earlier Baldwin was able to achieve. And what that voice says, no longer held back by the proprieties of literature, is that the nightmare of the history we have made allows us no immediate escape. Even if all the visible tokens of injustice were erased, the Negroes would retain their hatred and the whites their fear and guilt. Forgiveness cannot be speedily willed, if willed at all, and before it can even be imagined there will have to be a fuller discharge of those violent feelings that have so long been suppressed. It is not a pretty thought, but neither is it a mere "unrewarding rage"; and it has the sad advantage of being true, first as Baldwin embodies it in the disintegration of Rufus, which he portrays with a ferocity quite new in his fiction, and then as he embodies it in the hard-driving ambition of Rufus' sister Ida, who means to climb up to success even if she has to bloody a good many people, whites preferably, in order to do it.

Another Country has within it another novel: a nagging portrayal of that entanglement of personal relationships—sterile, involuted, grindingly rehearsed, pursued with quasi-religious fervor, and cut off from any dense context of social life—which has come to be a standard element in contemporary fiction. The author of *this* novel is caught up with the problem of communication, the emptiness that seeps through the lives of many cultivated persons and in response to which he can only reiterate the saving value of true and lonely love. These portions of *Another Country* tend to be abstract, without the veined milieu, the filled-out world, a novel needs: as if Baldwin, once he moves away from the Negro theme, finds it quite as hard to lay hold of contemporary experience as do most other novelists. The two pulls upon his attention are difficult to reconcile, and Baldwin's future as a novelist is decidedly uncertain.

During the last few years James Baldwin has emerged as a national figure, the leading intellectual spokesman for the Negroes, whose recent essays, as in *The Fire Next Time,* reach heights of passionate exhortation unmatched in modern American writing. Whatever his ultimate success or failure as a novelist, Baldwin has already secured his place as one of the two or three greatest essayists this country has ever produced. He has brought a new luster to the essay as an art form, a form with possibilities for discursive reflection and concrete drama which make it a serious competitor to the novel, until recently almost unchallenged as the dominant literary genre in our time. Apparently drawing upon Baldwin's youthful experience as the son of a Negro preacher, the style of these essays is a remarkable instance of the way in which a grave and sustained eloquence—the rhythm of oratory, but that rhythm held firm and hard—can be employed in an age deeply suspicious of rhetorical prowess. And in pieces like the reports on Harlem and the account of his first visit South, Baldwin realizes far better than in his novel the goal he had set himself of presenting Negro life through an "unspoken recognition of shared experience." Yet it should also be recognized that these essays gain at least some of their resonance from the tone of unrelenting protest in which they are written, from the very anger, even the violence Baldwin had begun by rejecting.

Like Richard Wright before him, Baldwin has discovered that to assert his humanity he must release his rage. But if rage makes for power it does not always encourage clarity, and the truth is that Baldwin's most recent essays are shot through with intellectual confusions, torn by the conflict between his assumption that the Negro must find an honorable place in the life of American society and his apocalyptic sense, mostly fear but just a little hope, that this society is beyond salvation, doomed with the sickness of the West. And again like Wright, he gives way on occasion to the lure of black nationalism. Its formal creed does not interest him, for he knows it to be shoddy, but he is impressed by its capacity to evoke norms of discipline from followers at a time when the Negro community is threatened by a serious inner demoralization.

In his role as spokesman, Baldwin must pronounce with certainty and struggle with militancy; he has at the moment no other choice; yet whatever may have been the objective inadequacy of his polemic against Wright a decade ago, there can be no question but that the refusal he then made of the role of protest reflected faithfully some of his deepest needs and desires. But we do not make our circumstances; we can, at best, try to remake them; and the arena of choice and action always proves to be a little narrower than we had sup-posed. One generation passes its dilemmas to the next, black boys on to native sons.

"It is in revolt that man goes beyond himself to discover other people, and from this point of view, human solidarity is a philosophical certainty." The words come from Camus: they might easily have been echoed by Richard Wright: and today one can imagine them being repeated, with a kind of rueful passion, by James Baldwin. No more important words could be spoken in our century, but it would be foolish, and impudent, not to recognize that for the men who must live by them the cost is heavy.

RALPH ELLISON

The World and the Jug [1963–1964]

The novelist and essayist Ralph Ellison (p. 430) wrote "The World and the Jug," his response to Irving Howe's essay "Black Boys and Native Sons" (p. 659), for *The New Leader,* a New York socialist and pro-labor intellectual journal. When Howe defended his position in the February 3, 1964, issue of that journal, Ellison raised the stakes with a fiery rebuttal, published in the same issue as "A Rejoinder." The essay reprinted here is a combination of Ellison's two essays, which he published as "The World and the Jug" in his 1964 book of criticism, *Shadow and Act.*

Ellison rejects Howe's idea of a common "Negroness" based on a shared experience of pain and discrimination, and instead reaffirms a trait he identifies with James Baldwin (p. 485): an insistence on a "complexity of Negro experience." In his challenge to the idea that younger black writers should follow "the path laid down by *Native Son*," Ellison focuses on his own experiences. For example, to Howe's assertion that Wright's release of anger in his writing allowed Ellison to explore alternative literary forms, Ellison exclaims, "Can't I be allowed to release my own [anger]?"

Though Ellison harshly criticizes the way Howe compares him to Wright, he notably avoids disparaging Wright's writing. Ellison instead acknowledges Wright's achievements, as he did in his 1945 essay "Richard Wright's Blues" (also included in *Shadow and Act*), where he wrote that Wright "converted the American Negro impulse toward self-annihilation and 'going-under-ground' into a will to confront the world, to evaluate his experience honestly and throw his finding unashamedly into the guilty conscience of America."

In "The World and the Jug," rather than discussing Wright's writing, Ellison opens up the debate to address larger questions about the relationship between politics and art. As Ellison writes, "The real questions seem to be: How does the Negro writer participate *as a writer* in the struggle for human freedom? To whom does he address his work? What values emerging from Negro experience does he try to affirm?" Those questions go beyond any assessment of Wright as "the authentic Negro writer" and the literary ancestor of Ellison and Baldwin. They explore the idea of the "Negro writer's role as actionist," an idea more frightening to Ellison than "the State of Mississippi."

From *The New Leader,* December 9, 1963; "A Rejoinder" from *The New Leader,* February 3, 1964; both reprinted in Ralph Ellison, *Shadow and Act* (New York: Random House, 1964).

What runs counter to the revolutionary convention is,
in revolutionary histories, suppressed more imperiously
than embarrassing episodes in private memoirs, and by
the same obscure forces....

—Malraux[1]

First, three questions: Why is it so often true that when critics confront the American as *Negro* they suddenly drop their advanced critical armament and revert with an air of confident superiority to quite primitive modes of analysis? Why is it that sociology-oriented critics seem to rate literature so far below politics and ideology that they would rather kill a novel than modify their presumptions concerning a given reality which it seeks in its own terms to project? Finally, why is it that so many of those who would tell us the meaning of Negro life never bother to learn how varied it really is?

These questions are aroused by "Black Boys and Native Sons," an essay by Irving Howe, the well-known critic and editor of *Dissent,* in the Autumn 1963 issue of that magazine. It is a lively piece, written with something of the Olympian authority that characterized Hannah Arendt's "Reflections on Little Rock" in the Winter 1959 *Dissent* (a dark foreshadowing of the Eichmann blowup). And in addition to a hero, Richard Wright, it has two villians, James Baldwin and Ralph Ellison, who are seen as "black boys" masquerading as false, self-deceived "native sons." Wright himself is given a diversity of roles (all conceived by Howe): He is not only the archetypal and true-blue black boy—the "honesty" of his famous autobiography established this for Howe—but the spiritual father of Ellison, Baldwin and all other Negroes of literary bent to come. Further, in the platonic sense he is his own father and the culture hero who freed Ellison and Baldwin to write more "modulated" prose.

Howe admires Wright's accomplishments, and is frankly annoyed by the more favorable evaluation currently placed upon the works of the younger men. His claims for *Native Son* are quite broad:

The day [it] appeared, American culture was changed forever . . . it made impossible a repetition of the old lies . . . it brought into the open . . . the fear and violence that have crippled and may yet destroy our culture. . . . A blow at the white man, the novel forced him to recognize himself as an oppressor. A blow at the black man, the novel forced him to recognize the cost of his submission. *Native Son* assaulted the most cherished of American vanities: the hope that the accumulated injustices of the past would bring with it no lasting penalties, the fantasy that in his humiliation the Negro somehow retained a sexual potency . . . that made it necessary to envy and still more to suppress him. Speaking from the black wrath of retribution, Wright insisted that history can be a punishment. He told us the one thing even the most liberal whites preferred not to hear: that Negroes were far from patient or forgiving, that they were scarred by fear, that they hated every moment of their suppression even when seeming most acquiescent, and that often enough they hated *us*, the decent and cultivated white men who from complicity or neglect shared in the responsibility of their plight. . . .

There are also negative criticisms: that the book is "crude," "melodramatic" and marred by "claustrophobia" of vision, that its characters are "cartoons," etc. But these defects Howe forgives because of the book's "clenched militancy." One wishes he had stopped there. For in his zeal to champion Wright, it is as though he felt it necessary to stage a modern version of the Biblical myth of Noah, Ham, Shem and Japheth[2] (based originally, I'm told, on a castration ritual), with first Baldwin and then Ellison acting out the impious role of Ham: Baldwin by calling attention to Noah-Wright's artistic nakedness in his famous essays, "Everybody's Protest Novel" (1949) and "Many Thousands Gone" (1951); Ellison by rejecting "narrow naturalism" as a fictional method, and by alluding to the "diversity, fluidity magical freedom of American life"[3] on that (for him at least)

---

1. From a 1956 essay "Lawrence and the Demon of the Absolute" by the French writer André Malraux (1901–76).
2. Genesis 9:18–27.
3. The phrase in Howe's essay is: "Thus to see America with an awareness of its rich diversity and its almost magical fluidity and freedom"; in this essay, Ellison often uses quotations that are paraphrases of Howe's words.

rather magical occasion when he was awarded the National Book Award. Ellison also offends by having the narrator of *Invisible Man* speak of his life (Howe either missing the irony or assuming that *I* did) as one of "infinite possibilities" while living in a hole in the ground.

Howe begins by attacking Baldwin's rejection in "Everybody's Protest Novel" of the type of literature he labeled "protest fiction" (*Uncle Tom's Cabin* and *Native Son* being prime examples), and which he considered incapable of dealing adequately with the complexity of Negro experience. Howe, noting that this was the beginning of Baldwin's career, sees the essay's underlying motive as a declaration of Baldwin's intention to transcend "the sterile categories of 'Negroness,' whether those enforced by the white world or those defensively erected by the Negroes themselves. No longer mere victim or rebel, the Negro would stand free in a self-achieved humanity. As Baldwin put it some year later, he hoped to 'prevent himself from becoming merely a Negro; or even, merely, a Negro writer.'" Baldwin's elected agency for self-achievement would be the novel—as it turns out, it was the essay *and* the novel—but the novel, states Howe, "is an inherently ambiguous genre: it strains toward formal autonomy and can seldom avoid being public gesture."

I would have said that it is *always* a public gesture, though not necessarily a political one. I would also have pointed out that the American Negro novelist is himself "inherently ambiguous." As he strains toward self-achievement as artist (and here he can only "integrate" and free himself), he moves toward fulfilling his dual potentialities as Negro and American. While Howe agrees with Baldwin that "literature and sociology are not one and the same," he notes nevertheless that, "it is equally true that such statements hardly begin to cope with the problem of how a writer's own experience affects his desire to represent human affairs in a work of fiction." Thus Baldwin's formula evades "through rhetorical sweep, the genuinely difficult issue of the relationship between social experience and literature." And to Baldwin's statement that one writes "out of one thing only—one's own experience" (I would have added, for the novelist, this qualification: one's own experience as understood and ordered through one's knowledge of self, culture and literature), Howe, appearing suddenly in blackface, replies with a rhetorical sweep of his own:

> What, then, was the experience of a man with a black skin, what *could* it be here in this country? How could a Negro put pen to paper, how could he so much as think or breathe without some impulsion to protest, be it harsh or mild, political or private, released or buried? . . . The "sociology" of his existence forms a constant pressure on his literary work, and not merely in the way this might be true of any writer, but with a pain and ferocity that nothing could remove.

I must say that this brought a shock of recognition. Some twelve years ago, a friend argued with me for hours that I could not possibly write a novel because my experience as a Negro had been too excruciating to allow me to achieve that psychological and emotional distance necessary to artistic creation. Since he "knew" Negro experience better than I, I could not convince him that he might be wrong. Evidently Howe feels that unrelieved suffering is the only "real" Negro experience, and that the true Negro writer must be ferocious.

But there is also an American Negro tradition which teaches one to deflect racial provocation and to master and contain pain. It is a tradition which abhors as obscene any trading on one's own anguish for gain or sympathy; which springs not from a desire to deny the harshness of existence but from a will to deal with it as men at their best have always done. It takes fortitude to be a man and no less to be an artist. Perhaps it takes even more if the black man would be an artist. If so, there are no exemptions. It would seem to me, therefore, that the question of how the "sociology of his existence" presses upon a Negro writer's work depends upon how much of his life the individual writer is able to transform into art. What moves a writer to eloquence is less meaningful than what he makes of it. How much, by the way, do we know of Sophocles' wounds?[4]

---

4. The plays *Philoctetes* and *Ajax* by the Greek playwright Sophocles (c. 497/6 BC–407/6 BC) explore the physical and psychological wounds from war.

One familiar with what Howe stands for would get the impression that when he looks at a Negro he sees not a human being but an abstract embodiment of living hell. He seems never to have considered that American Negro life (and here he is encouraged by certain Negro "spokesmen") is, for the Negro who must live it, not only a burden (and not always that) but also a *discipline—just* as any human life which has endured so long is a discipline teaching its own insights into the human condition, its own strategies of survival. There is a fullness, even a richness here; and here *despite* the realities of politics, perhaps, but nevertheless here and real. Because it is *human life*. And Wright, for all of his indictments, was no less its product than that other talented Mississippian, Leontyne Price.[5] To deny in the interest of revolutionary posture that such possibilities of human richness exist for others, even in Mississippi, is not only to deny us our humanity but to betray the critic's commitment to social reality. Critics who do so should abandon literature for politics.

For even as his life toughens the Negro, even as it brutalizes him, sensitizes him, dulls him, goads him to anger, moves him to irony, sometimes fracturing and sometimes affirming his hopes; even as it shapes his attitudes toward family, sex, love, religion; even as it modulates his humor, tempers his joy—it *conditions* him to deal with his life and, with himself. Because it is *his* life and no mere abstraction in someone's head. He must live it and try consciously to grasp its complexity until he can change it; must live it as he changes it. He is no mere product of his socio-political predicament. He is a product of the interaction between his racial predicament, his individual will and the broader American cultural freedom in which he finds his ambiguous existence. Thus he, too, in a limited way, is his own creation.

In his loyalty to Richard Wright, Howe considers Ellison and Baldwin guilty of filial betrayal because, in their own work, they have rejected the path laid down by *Native Son*, phonies because, while actually "black boys," they pretend to be mere American writers trying to react to something of the pluralism of their predicament.

In his myth Howe takes the roles of both Shem and Japheth, trying mightily (his face turned backward so as not to see what it is he's veiling) to cover the old man's bare belly, and then becoming Wright's voice from beyond the grave by uttering the curses which Wright was too ironic or too proud to have uttered himself, at least in print:

> In response to Baldwin and Ellison, Wright would have said (I virtually quote the words he used in talking to me during the summer of 1958) that only through struggle could men with black skins, and for that matter, all the oppressed of the world, achieve their humility. It was a lesson, said Wright, with a touch of bitterness yet not without kindness, that the younger writers would have to learn in their own way and their own time. All that has happened since bears him out.

What, coming eighteen years after *Native Son* and thirteen years after World War II, does this rather limp cliché mean? Nor is it clear what is meant by the last sentence—or is it that today Baldwin has come to out-Wrighting Richard? The real questions seem to be: How does the Negro writer participate *as a writer* in the struggle for human freedom? To whom does he address his work? What values emerging from Negro experience does he try to affirm?

I started with the primary assumption that men with black skins, having retained their humanity before all of the conscious efforts made to dehumanize them, especially following the Reconstruction,[6] are unquestionably human. Thus they have the obligation of freeing themselves—whoever their allies might be—by depending upon the validity of their own experience for an accurate picture of the reality which they seek to change, and for a gauge of the values they would see made manifest. Crucial to this view is the belief that their resistance to provocation, their coolness under pressure, their sense of timing and their tenacious hold on the ideal of their ultimate freedom are indispensable

---

5. Mary Violet Leontyne Price (b. 1927), American opera singer; the first African American leading prima donna at the Metropolitan Opera.
6. Period from the end of the Civil War in 1865 until the withdrawal of Federal troops from southern states in 1877.

values in the struggle, and are at least as characteristic of American Negroes as the hatred, fear and vindictiveness which Wright chose to emphasize.

Wright believed in the much abused idea that novels are "weapons"—the counterpart of the dreary notion, common among most minority groups, that novels are instruments of good public relations. But I believe that true novels, even when most pessimistic and bitter, arise out of an impulse to celebrate human life and therefore are ritualistic and ceremonial at their core. Thus they would preserve as they destroy, affirm as they reject.

In *Native Son*, Wright began with the ideological proposition that what whites think of the Negro's reality is more important than what Negroes themselves know it to be. Hence Bigger Thomas was presented as a near-subhuman indictment of white oppression. He was designed to shock whites out of their apathy and end the circumstances out of which Wright insisted Bigger emerged. Here environment is all—and interestingly enough, environment conceived solely in terms of the physical, the non-conscious. Well, cut off my legs and call me Shorty! Kill my parents and throw me on the mercy of the court as an orphan! Wright could imagine Bigger, but Bigger could not possibly imagine Richard Wright. Wright saw to that.

But without arguing Wright's right to his personal vision, I would say that he was himself a better argument for my approach than Bigger was for his. And so, to be fair and as inclusive as Howe, is James Baldwin. Both are true Negro Americans, and both affirm the broad possibility of personal realization which I see as a saving aspect of American life. Surely, this much can be admitted without denying the injustice which all three of us have protested.

Howe is impressed by Wright's pioneering role and by the "... enormous courage, the discipline of self-conquest required to conceive Bigger Thomas...." And earlier: "If such younger novelists as Baldwin and Ralph Ellison were able to move beyond Wright's harsh naturalism toward more supple modes of fiction, that was only possible because Wright had been there first,

courageous enough to release the full weight of his anger."

It is not for me to judge Wright's courage, but I must ask just why it was possible for me to write as I write "only" because Wright released his anger? Can't I be allowed to release my own? What does Howe know of my acquaintance with violence, or the shape of my courage or the intensity of my anger? I suggest that my credentials are at least as valid as Wright's, even though he began writing long before I did, and it is possible that I have lived through and committed even more violence than he. Howe must wait for an autobiography before he can be responsibly certain. Everybody wants to tell us what a Negro is, yet few wish, even in a joke, to be one. But if you would tell me who I am, at least take the trouble to discover what I have been.

Which brings me to the most distressing aspect of Howe's thinking: his Northern white liberal version of the white Southern myth of absolute separation of the races. He implies that Negroes can only aspire to contest other Negroes (this at a time when Baldwin has been taking on just about everyone, including Hemingway, Faulkner and the United States Attorney General!),[7] and must wait for the appearance of a Black Hope before they have the courage to move. Howe is so committed to a sociological vision of society that he apparently cannot see (perhaps because he is dealing with Negroes—although not because he would suppress us socially or politically, for in fact he is anxious to end such suppression) that whatever the efficiency of segregation as a socio-political arrangement, it has been far from absolute on the level of *culture*. Southern whites cannot walk, talk, sing, conceive of laws or justice, think of sex, love, the family or freedom without responding to the presence of Negroes.

Similarly, no matter how strictly Negroes are segregated socially and politically, on the level of the imagination their ability to achieve freedom is limited only by their individual aspiration, insight, energy and will.

---

7. White American male writers Ernest Hemingway (1899–1961) and William Faulkner (1897–1962); in 1963, Baldwin, along with playwright Loraine Hansberry (1930–65) and other leaders, had a meeting with U. S. Attorney General Robert "Bobby" Kennedy that became a shouting match, with Baldwin angry at Kennedy for not taking a stronger stand on civil rights.

Wright was able to free himself in Mississippi because he had the imagination and the will to do so. He was as much a product of his reading as of his painful experiences, and he made himself a writer by subjecting himself to the writer's discipline—as he understood it. The same is true of James Baldwin, who is not the product of a Negro store-front church but of the library, and the same is true of me.

Howe seems to see segregation as an opaque steel jug with the Negroes inside waiting for some black messiah to come along and blow the cork. Wright is his hero and he sticks with him loyally. But if we are in a jug it is transparent, not opaque, and one is allowed not only to see outside but to read what is going on out there; to make identifications as to values and human quality. So in Macon County, Alabama, I read Marx, Freud, T. S. Eliot, Pound, Gertrude Stein[8] and Hemingway. Books which seldom, if ever, mentioned Negroes were to release me from whatever "segregated" idea I might have had of my human possibilities. I was freed not by propagandists or by the example of Wright—I did not know him at the time and was earnestly trying to learn enough to write a symphony and have it performed by the time I was twenty-six, because Wagner[9] had done so and I admired his music—but by composers, novelists, and poets who spoke to me of more interesting and freer ways of life. These were works which, by fulfilling themselves as works of art, by being satisfied to deal with Me in terms of their own sources of power, were able to give me a broader sense of life and possibility. Indeed, I understand a bit more about myself as Negro because literature has taught me something of my identity as Western man, as political being. It has also taught me something of the cost of being an individual who aspires to conscious eloquence. It requires real poverty of the imagination to think that this can come to a Negro *only* through the example of *other Negroes,* especially after the performance of the slaves in re-creating themselves, in good part, out of the images and myths of the Old Testament Jews.

No, Wright was no spiritual father of mine, certainly in no sense I recognize—nor did he pretend to be, since he felt that I had started writing too late. It was Baldwin's career, not mine, that Wright proudly advanced by helping him attain the Eugene Saxton Fellowship, and it was Baldwin who found Wright a lion in his path. Being older and familiar with quite different lions in quite different paths, I simply stepped around him.

But Wright was a friend for whose magazine I wrote my first book review and short story, and a personal hero in the same way Hot Lips Paige and Jimmy Rushing[1] were friends and heroes. I felt no need to attack what I considered the limitations of his vision because I was quite impressed by what he had achieved. And in this, although I saw with the black vision of Ham, I was, I suppose, as pious as Shem and Japheth. Still I would write my own books and they would be in themselves, implicitly, criticisms of Wright's, just as all novels of a given historical moment form an argument over the nature of reality and are, to an extent, criticisms each of the other.

While I rejected Bigger Thomas as any *final* image of Negro personality, I recognized *Native Son* as an achievement; as one man's essay in defining the human condition as seen from a specific Negro perspective at a given time in a given place. And I was proud to have known Wright and happy for the impact he had made upon our apathy. But Howe's ideas notwithstanding, history is history, cultural contacts ever mysterious, and taste exasperatingly personal. Two days after arriving in New York I was to read Malraux's *Man's Fate* and *The Days of Wrath,* and after these how could I be impressed by Wright as an ideological novelist. Need my skin blind me to all other values? Yet Howe writers:

> When Negro liberals write that despite the prevalence of bias there has been an improvement in the life of their people, such statements are reasonable and necessary. But what have these to do with the

---

8. White American modernist writers Eliot (1888–1965), Ezra Pound (1885–1972), and Stein (1874–1946).
9. German composer Wilhelm Richard Wagner (1913–1883).
1. Jazz trumpeter, singer, and bandleader Oran Thaddeous "Hot Lips" Page (1908–54); jazz singer James Andrew "Jimmy" Rushing (1901–72).

way Negroes feel, with the power of the memories they must surely retain? About this we know very little and would be well advised not to nourish preconceptions, for their feelings may well be closer to Wright's rasping outbursts than to the more modulated tones of the younger Negro novelists. *Wright remembered,* and what he remembered other Negroes must also have remembered. And in that way he kept faith with the experience of the boy who had fought his way out of the depths, to speak for those who remained there.

Wright, for Howe, is the genuine article, the authentic Negro writer, and his tone the only authentic tone. But why strip Wright of his individuality in order to criticize other writers. He had his memories and I have mine, just as I suppose Irving Howe has his—or has Marx spoken the final word for him? Indeed, very early in *Black Boy,* Wright's memory and his contact with literature come together in a way revealing, at least to the eye concerned with Wright the literary man, that his manner of keeping faith with the Negroes who remained in the depths is quite interesting:

> (After I had outlived the shocks of childhood, after the habit of reflection had been born in me, I used to mull over the strange absence of real kindness in Negroes, how unstable was our tenderness, how lacking in genuine passion we were, how void of great hope, how timid our joy, how bare our traditions, how hollow our memories, how lacking we were in those intangible sentiments that bind man to man and how shallow was even our despair. After I had learned other ways of life I used to brood upon the unconscious irony of those who felt that Negroes led so passional an existence! I saw that what had been taken for our emotional strength was our negative confusions, our flights, our fears, our frenzy under pressure.
>
> (Whenever I thought of the essential bleakness of black life in America, I knew that Negroes had never been allowed to catch the full spirit of Western civilization, that they lived somehow in it but not of it. And when I brooded upon the cultural barrenness of black life, I wondered if clean, posi-

tive tenderness, love, honor, loyalty and the capacity to remember were native with man. I asked myself if these human qualities were not fostered, won, struggled and suffered for, preserved in ritual from one generation to another.)

Must I be condemned because my sense of Negro life was quite different? Or because for me keeping faith would never allow me to even raise such a question about any segment of humanity? *Black Boy* is not a sociological case history but an autobiography, and therefore a work of art shaped by a writer bent upon making an ideological point. Doubtlessly, this was the beginning of Wright's exile, the making of a decision which was to shape his Me and writing thereafter. And it is precisely at this point that Wright is being what I would call, in Howe's words, "literary to a fault."

For just as *How Bigger Was Born* is Wright's Jamesian preface to *Native Son,* the passage quoted above is his paraphrase of Henry James' catalogue of those items of a high civilization which were absent from American life during Hawthorne's[2] day, and which seemed so necessary in order for the novelist to function. This, then, was Wright's list of those items of high humanity which he found missing among Negroes. Thank God, I have never been quite that literary.

How awful that Wright found the facile answers of Marxism before he learned to use literature as a means for discovering the forms of American Negro humanity. I could not and cannot question their existence, I can only seek again and again to project that humanity as I see it and feel it. To me Wright as *writer* was less interesting than the enigma he personified: that he could so dissociate himself from the complexity of his background while trying so hard to improve the condition of black men everywhere; that he could be so wonderful an example of human possibility but could not for ideological reasons depict a Negro as intelligent, as creative or as dedicated as himself.

In his effort to resuscitate Wright, Irving Howe would designate the role which Negro writers are to play more rigidly than any Southern politician—and for the best of reasons. We must express "black" anger and "clenched militancy"; most of all we should not become too interested in the problems of the art of

---

2. References to the white American male writers Henry James (1843–1916) and Nathaniel Hawthorne (1804–64).

literature, even though it is through these that we seek our individual identities. And between writing well and being ideologically militant, we must choose militancy.

Well, it all sounds quite familiar and I fear the social order which it forecasts more than I do that of Mississippi. Ironically, during the 1940s it was one of the main sources of Wright's rage and frustration.

A REJOINDER

I am sorry Irving Howe got the impression that I was throwing bean-balls when I only meant to pitch him a hyperbole. It would seem, however, that he approves of angry Negro writers only until one questions his ideas; then he reaches for his honor, cries "misrepresentation" and "distortion," and charges the writer with being both out of control of himself and with fashioning a "strategy calculated to appeal, ready-made, to the preconceptions of the liberal audience." Howe implies that there are differences between us which I disguised in my essay, yet whatever the validity of this attempt at long-distance psychoanalysis, it was not his honor which I questioned but his thinking; not his good faith but his critical method.

And the major differences which these raised between us I tried to describe. They are to be seen by anyone who reads Howe's "Black Boys and Native Sons" not as a collection of thematically related fragments but as the literary exposition of a considered point of view. I tried to interpret this essay in the light of the impact it made upon my sense of life and literature, and I judged it through its total form—just as I would have Howe base his judgments of writers and their circumstances on as much of what we know about the actual complexity of men living in a highly pluralistic society as is possible. I realize that the uncommon sense of a critic, his special genius, is a gift to be thankful for whenever we find it. The very least I expected of Howe, though, was that he would remember his *common* sense, that he would not be carried away by that intellectual abandon, that lack of restraint, which seizes those who regard blackness as an absolute and who see in it a release from the complications of the real world.

Howe is interested in militant confrontation and suffering, yet evidently he recognizes neither when they involve some act of his own. He *really* did not know the subject was loaded. Very well, but I was brought into the booby-trapped field of his assumptions and finding myself in pain, I did not choose to "hold back from the suffering" inflicted upon me there. Out of an old habit I yelled—without seeking Howe's permission, it is true—where it hurt the most. For oddly enough, I found it far less painful to have to move to the back of a Southern bus, or climb to the peanut gallery of a movie house—matters about which I could do nothing except walk, read, hunt, dance, sculpt, cultivate ideas, or seek other uses for my time—than to tolerate concepts which distorted the actual reality of my situation or my reactions to it.

I could escape the reduction imposed by unjust laws and customs, but not that imposed by ideas which defined me as no more than the *sum* of those laws and customs. I learned to outmaneuver those who interpreted my silence as submission, my efforts at self-control as fear, my contempt as awe before superior status, my dreams of faraway places and room at the top of the heap as defeat before the barriers of their stifling, provincial world. And my struggle became a desperate battle which was usually fought, though not always, in silence; a guerrilla action in a larger war in which I found some of the most treacherous assaults against me committed by those who regarded themselves either as neutrals, as sympathizers, or as disinterested military advisers.

I recall this not in complaint, for thus was I disciplined to endure the absurdities of both conscious and unconscious prejudice, to resist racial provocation and, before the ready violence of brutal policemen, railroad "bulls," and casual white citizens, to hold my peace and bide my time. Thus was I forced to evaluate my own self-worth, and the narrow freedom in which it existed, against the power of those who would destroy me. In time I was to leave the South, although it has never left me, and the interests which I discovered there became my life.

But having left the South I did not leave the battle—for how could I leave Howe? He is a man of words and ideas, and since I, too, find my identity in the world of ideas and words, where would I flee? I still endure the nonsense of fools with a certain patience, but when a respected critic distorts my situation in order to feel comfortable in the abstractions he would impose upon American reality, then it is indeed "in accordance with my nature" to protest. Ideas are important in themselves, perhaps, but when they are interposed between me and my sense of reality I feel threatened; they are too elusive, they move with missile speed and are too often fired from altitudes rising high above the cluttered terrain upon which I struggle. And too often those with a facility for ideas find themselves in the councils of power representing me at the double distance of racial alienation and inexperience.

Taking leave of Howe for a moment—for his lapse is merely symptomatic—let me speak generally. Many of those who write of Negro life today seem to assume that as long as their hearts are in the right place they can be as arbitrary as they wish in their formulations. Others seem to feel that they can air with impunity their most private Freudian fantasies as long as they are given the slightest camouflage of intellectuality and projected as "Negro." They have made of the no-man's land created by segregation a territory for infantile self-expression and intellectual anarchy. They write as though Negro life exists only in light of their belated regard, and they publish interpretations of Negro experience which would not hold true for their own or for any other form of human life.

Here the basic unity of human experience that assures us of some possibility of empathic and symbolic identification with those of other backgrounds is blasted in the interest of specious political and philosophical conceits. Prefabricated Negroes are sketched on sheets of paper and superimposed upon the Negro community; then when someone thrusts his head through the page and yells, "Watch out there, Jack, there're people living under here," they are shocked and indignant. I am afraid, however, that we shall hear much more of such protest as these interpositions continue. And I predict this, not out of any easy gesture of militancy (and what an easy con-game for ambitious, publicity-hungry Negroes this stance of "militancy" has become!) but because as Negroes express increasingly their irritation in this critical area, many of those

who make so lightly with our image shall find their own subjected to a most devastating scrutiny.

One of the most insidious crimes occurring in this democracy is that of designating another, politically weaker, less socially acceptable, people as the receptacle for one's own self-disgust, for one's own infantile rebellions, for one's own fears of, and retreats from reality. It is the crime of reducing the humanity of others to that of a mere convenience, a counter in a banal game which involves no apparent risk to ourselves. With us Negroes it started with the appropriation of our freedom and our labor; then it was our music, our speech, our dance and the comic distortion of our image by burnt-corked, cotton-gloved corn-balls yelling, "Mammy!" And while it would be futile, nontragic, and un-Negro American to complain over the processes through which we have become who and what we are, it is perhaps permissible to say that the time for such misappropriations ran out long ago.

For one thing, Negro American consciousness is not a product (as so often seems true of so many American groups) of a will to historical forgetfulness. It is a product of our memory, sustained and constantly reinforced by events, by our watchful waiting, and by our hopeful suspension of final judgment as to the meaning of our grievances. For another, most Negroes recognize themselves as themselves despite what others might believe them to be. Thus, although the sociologists tell us that thousands of light-skinned Negroes become white each year undetected, most Negroes can spot a paper-thin "white Negro" every time simply because those who masquerade missed what others were forced to pick up along the way: discipline—a discipline which these heavy thinkers would not undergo even if guaranteed that combined with their own heritage it would make of them the freest of spirits, the wisest of men and the most sublime of heroes.

The rhetorical strategy of my original reply was not meant, as Howe interprets it, to strike the stance of a "free artist" against the "ideological critic," although I *do* recognize that I can be free only to the extent that I detect error and grasp the complex reality of my circumstances and work to dominate it through the techniques which are my means of confronting the world. Perhaps I am only free enough to recognize those tendencies of thought which, actualized, would render me even less free.

Even so, I did not intend to take the stance of the "knowing Negro writer" against the "presuming white intellectual." While I am without doubt a Negro, and a writer, I am also an *American* writer, and while I am more knowing than Howe where my own Me and its influences are concerned, I took the time to question his presumptions as one responsible for contributing as much as he is capable to the clear perception of American social reality. For to think unclearly about that segment of reality in which I find my existence is to do myself violence. To allow others to go unchallenged when they distort that reality is to participate not only in that distortion but to accept, as in this instance, a violence inflicted upon the art of criticism. And if I am to recognize those aspects of my role as writer which do not depend primarily upon my racial identity, if I am to fulfill the writer's basic responsibilities to his craft, then surely I must insist upon the maintenance of a certain level of precision in language, a maximum correspondence between the form of a piece of writing and its content, and between words and ideas and the things and processes of his world.

Whatever my role as "race man" (and it knocks me out whenever anyone, black or white, tries to tell me—and the white Southerners have no monopoly here—how to become their conception of a "good Negro"), I am as writer no less a custodian of the American language than is Irving Howe. Indeed, to the extent that I am a writer—I lay no claims to being a thinker—the American language, including the Negro idiom, is all that I have. So let me emphasize that my reply to Howe was neither motivated by racial defensiveness nor addressed to his own racial identity.

It is fortunate that it was not, for considering how Howe identifies himself in this instance, I would have missed the target, which would have been embarrassing. Yet it would have been an innocent mistake, because in situations such as this many Negroes, like myself, make a positive distinction between "whites" and "Jews." Not to do so could be either offensive, embarrassing, unjust or even dangerous. If I would know who I am and preserve who I am, then I must see others distinctly whether they see me so or no. Thus I feel uncomfortable whenever I discover Jewish intel-

lectuals writing as though *they* were guilty of enslaving my grandparents, or as though the Jews were responsible for the system of segregation. Not only do they have enough troubles of their own, as the saying goes, but Negroes know this only too well.

The real guilt of such Jewish intellectuals lies in their facile, perhaps unconscious, but certainly unrealistic, identification with what is called the "power structure." Negroes call that "passing for white." Speaking personally, both as writer and as Negro American, I would like to see the more positive distinctions between whites and Jewish Americans maintained. Not only does it make for a necessary bit of historical and social clarity, at least where Negroes are concerned, but I consider the United States freer politically and richer culturally because there are Jewish Americans to bring it the benefit of their special forms of dissent, their humor and their gift for ideas which are based upon the uniqueness of their experience. The diversity of American life is often painful, frequently burdensome and always a source of conflict, but in it lies our fate and our hope.

To Howe's charge that I found his exaggerated claim for Richard Wright's influence upon my own work presumptuous, I plead guilty. Was it necessary to impose a line of succession upon Negro writers simply because Howe identified with Wright's cause? And why, since he grasps so readily the intentional absurdity of my question regarding his relationship to Marx, couldn't he see that the notion of an intellectual or artistic succession based upon color or racial background is no less absurd than one based upon a common religious background? (Of *course, Irving, I know that you haven't believed in final words for twenty years— not even your own—and I know, too, that the line from Marx to Howe is as complex and as dialectical as that from Wright to Ellison. My point was to try to see to it that certain laspes in your thinking did not become final.*) In fact, this whole exchange would never have started had I not been dragged into the discussion. Still, if Howe could take on the role of man with a "black skin," why shouldn't I assume the role of critic-of-critic?

But how surprising are Howe's ideas concerning the ways of controversy. Why, unless of course he holds no respect for his opponent, should a polemicist be expected to make things *hard* for himself? As for the "preconceptions of the liberal audience," I had not considered them, actually, except as they appear in Howe's own thinking. Beyond this I wrote for anyone who might hesitate to question his formulations, especially very young Negro writers who might be bewildered by the incongruity of such ideas coming from such an authority. Howe himself rendered complicated rhetorical strategies unnecessary by lunging into questionable territory with his flanks left so unprotected that any schoolboy sniper could have routed him with a bird gun. Indeed, his reaction to my reply reminds me of an incident which occurred during the 1937 Recession when a companion and I were hunting the country outside Dayton, Ohio.

There had been a heavy snowfall and we had just put up a covey of quail from a thicket which edged a field when, through the rising whirr of the rocketing, snow-shattering birds, we saw, emerging from a clump of trees across the field, a large, red-faced, mackinawed farmer, who came running toward us shouting and brandishing a rifle. I could see strands of moisture tearing from his working mouth as he came on, running like a bear across the whiteness, the brown birds veering and scattering before him; and standing there against the snow, a white hill behind me and with no tree nor foxhole for cover I felt as exposed as a Black Muslim caught at a meeting of the K.K.K.

He had appeared as suddenly as the quail, and although the rifle was not yet to his shoulder, I was transfixed, watching him zooming up to become the largest, loudest, most aggressive-sounding white man I'd seen in my life, and I was, quite frankly, afraid. Then I was measuring his approach to the crunching tempo of his running and praying silently that he'd come within range of my shotgun before he fired; that I would be able to do what seemed necessary for me to do; that, shooting from the hip with an old twelve-gauge shotgun, I could stop him before he could shoot either me or my companion; and that, though stopped effectively, he would be neither killed, nor blinded, nor maimed.

It was a mixed-up prayer in an icy interval which ended in a smoking fury of cursing, when, at a warning from my companion, the farmer suddenly halted. Then we learned that the reckless man had meant only to warn us off of land which was not even his but that of a neighbor—my companion's foster father. He stood

there between the two shotguns pointing short-ranged at his middle, his face quite drained of color now by the realization of how close to death he'd come, sputtering indignantly that we'd interpreted his rifle, which wasn't loaded, in a manner other than he'd intended. He truly did not realize that situations can be more loaded than guns and gestures more eloquent than words.

Fortunately, words are not rifles, but perhaps Howe is just as innocent of the rhetorical eloquence of situations as the farmer. He does not see that the meaning which emerges from his essay is not determined by isolated statements, but by the juxtaposition of those statements in a context which creates a larger statement. Or that contributing to the judgment rendered by that larger statement is the one in which it is uttered. When Howe pits Baldwin and Ellison against Wright and then gives Wright the better of the argument by using such emotionally weighted terms as "remembered" and "kept faith," the implication to me is that Baldwin and Ellison did *not* remember or keep faith with those who remained behind. If this be true, then I think that in this instance "villain" is not too strong a term.

Howe is not the first writer given to sociological categories who has had unconscious value judgments slip into his "analytical" or "scientific" descriptions. Thus I can believe that his approach was meant to be "analytic, not exhortatory; descriptive, not prescriptive." The results, however, are something else again. And are we to believe that he simply does not recognize rhetoric when he practices it? That when he asks, "what *could* [his italics] the experience of a man with a black skin be . . ." etc., he thinks he is describing a situation as viewed by each and every Negro writer rather than expressing, yes, and in the mode of "exhortation," the views of Irving Howe? Doesn't he recognize that just as the anti-Negro stereotype is a command to Negroes to mold themselves in its image, there sounds through his descriptive "thus it is" the command "thus you become"? And doesn't he realize that in this emotion-charged area definitive description is, in effect, prescription? If he does not, how then can we depend upon his "analysis" of politics of his reading of fiction?

Perhaps Howe could relax his views concerning the situation of the writers with a "black skin" if he examined some of the meanings which he gives to the word "Negro." He contends that I "cannot help being caught up with *the idea* of the Negro," but I have never said that I could or wished to do so—only Howe makes a problem for me here. When he used the term "Negro" he speaks of it as a "stigma," and again, he speaks of "Negroness" as a "sterile category." He sees the Negro writer as experiencing a "constant pressure upon his literary work" from the "sociology of his existence . . . not merely in the way this might be true of any writer, but with a *pain* and *ferocity* that nothing could remove."[1]

Note that this is a condition arising from a *collective* experience which leaves no room for the individual writer's unique existence. It leaves no room for that intensity of personal anguish which compels the artist to seek relief by projecting it into the world in conjunction with other things; that anguish which might take the form of an acute sense of inferiority for one, homosexuality for another, an overwhelming sense of the absurdity of human life for still another. Nor does it leave room for the experience that might be caused by humiliation, by a harelip, by a stutter, by epilepsy—indeed, by any and everything in this life which plunges the talented individual into solitude while leaving him the will to transcend his condition through art. The individual Negro writer must create out of his own special needs and through his own sensibilities, and these alone. Otherwise, all those who suffer in anonymity would be creators.

Howe makes of "Negroness" metaphysical condition, one that is a state of irremediable agony which all but engulfs the mind. Happily, the view from inside the skin is not so dark as it appears to be from Howe's remote position, and therefore my view of "Negroness" is neither his nor that of the exponents of *negritude*. It is not skin color which makes a Negro American but cultural heritage as shaped by the American experience, the social and political predicament; a sharing of that "concord of sensibilities" which the group expresses through historical circumstance and through which it has come to constitute a subdivision of the larger American culture. Being a Negro American has to do with the memory of slavery and the hope of emancipa-

tion and the betrayal by allies and the revenge and contempt inflicted by our former masters after the Reconstruction, and the myths, both Northern and Southern, which are propagated in justification of that betrayal. It involves, too, a special attitude toward the waves of immigrants who have come later and passed us by.

It has to do with a special perspective on the national ideals and the national conduct, and with a tragicomic attitude toward the universe. It has to do with special emotions evoked by the details of cities and countrysides, with forms of labor and with forms of pleasure; with sex and with love, with food and with drink, with machines and with animals; with climates and with dwellings, with places of worship and places of entertainment; with garments and dreams and idioms of speech; with manners and customs, with religion and art, with life styles and hoping, and with that special sense of predicament and fate which gives direction and resonance to the Freedom Movement. It involves a rugged initiation into the mysteries and rites of color which makes it possible for Negro Americans to suffer the injustice which race and color are used to excuse without losing sight of either the humanity of those who inflict that injustice or the motives, rational or irrational, out of which they act. It imposes the uneasy burden and occasional joy of a complex double vision, a fluid, ambivalent response to men and events which represents, at its finest, a profoundly civilized adjustment to the cost of being human in this modern world. More important, perhaps, being a Negro American involves a *willed* (who wills to be a Negro? I do!) affirmation of self as against all outside pressures—an identification with the group as extended through the individual self which rejects all possibilities of escape that do not involve a basic resuscitation of the original American ideals of social and political justice. And those white Negroes (and I do not mean Norman Mailer's dream creatures[2]) are Negroes too—if they wish to be.

Howe's defense against my charge that he sees unrelieved suffering as the basic reality of Negro life is to

1. Italics mine. [Ellison's note]
2. Reference to "The White Negro: Superficial Reflections on the Hipster, "a 1957 essay published in *Dissent* by white American male writer Norman Mailer (1923–2007).

quote favorable comments from his review of *Invisible Man*. But this does not cancel out the restricted meaning which he gives to "Negroness," or his statement that "the sociology of [the Negro writer's] existence forms a constant pressure with a *pain* and *ferocity* that nothing could remove."[3] He charges me with unfairness for writing that he believes ideological militancy is more important than writing well, yet he tells us that "there may of course be times when one's obligation as a human being supersedes one's obligation as a writer. . . ." I think that the writer's obligation in a struggle as broad and abiding as the one we are engaged in, which involves not merely Negroes but all Americans, is best carried out through his role as writer. And if he chooses to stop writing and take to the platform, then it should be out of personal choice and not under pressure from would-be managers of society.

Howe plays a game of pitty-pat with Baldwin and Ellison. First he throws them into the pit for lacking Wright's "pain," "ferocity," "memory," "faithfulness" and "clenched militance," then he pats them on the head for the quality of their writing. If he would see evidence of this statement, let him observe how these terms come up in his original essay when he traces Baldwin's move toward Wright's position. Howe's rhetoric is weighted against "more modulated tones" in favor of "rasping outbursts," the Baldwin of *Another Country* becomes "a voice of anger, rasping and thrusting," and he is no longer "held back" by the "proprieties of literature." The character of Rufus in that novel displays a "ferocity" quite new in Baldwin's fiction, and Baldwin's essays gain resonance from "the tone of unrelenting protest . . . from [their] very anger, even the violence," etc. I am afraid that these are "good" terms in Howe's essay and they led to part of my judgment.

In defense of Wright's novel *The Long Dream*, Howe can write:

> . . . This book has been attacked for presenting Negro life in the South through "old-fashioned" images of violence, but [and now we have "prescription"] one ought to hesitate before denying the rel-

evance of such images or joining in the criticism of their use. For *Wright was perhaps justified* in not paying attention to the changes that have occurred in the South these past few decades.[4]

If this isn't a defense, if not of bad writing at least of an irresponsible attitude toward good writing, I simply do not understand the language. I find it astonishing advice, since novels exist, since the fictional spell comes into existence precisely through the care which the novelist gives to selecting the details, the images, the tonalities, the specific social and psychological processes of specific characters in specific milieus at specific points in time. Indeed, it is one of the main tenets of the novelist's morality that he should write of that which he knows, and this is especially crucial for novelists who deal with a society as mobile and rapidly changing as ours. To justify ignoring this basic obligation is to encourage the downgrading of literature in favor of other values, in this instance "anger," "protest" and "clenched militancy." Novelists create not simply out of "memory" but out of memory modified, extended, transformed by social change. For a novelist to heed such advice as Howe's is to commit an act of artistic immorality. Amplify this back through society and the writer's failure could produce not order but chaos.

Yet Howe proceeds on the very next page of his essay to state, with no sense of contradiction, that Wright failed in some of the stories which comprise *Eight Men* ("The Man Who Lived Underground" was first published, by the way, in 1944) because he needed the "accumulated material of circumstance." If a novelist ignores social change, how can he come by the "accumulated material of circumstance"? Perhaps if Howe could grasp the full meaning of that phrase he would understand that Wright did not report in *Black Boy* much of his life in Mississippi, and he would see that Ross Barnett[5] is not the whole state, that there is also a Negro Mississippi which is much more varied than that which Wright depicted.

For the critic there simply exists no substitute for the knowledge of history and literary tradition. Howe

---

3. The italics in this quotation are Ellison's.
4. Italics mine. [Ellison's note]
5. White southern Democratic politician who supported segregation and white supremacy; as governor of Mississippi in 1962, Barnett gained notoriety for trying to block the enrollment of James Merideth to the University of Mississippi.

stresses Wright's comment that when he went into rooms where there were naked white women he felt like a "non-man ... doubly cast out." But had Howe thought about it he might have questioned this reaction, since most young men would have been delighted with the opportunity to study, at first hand, women usually cloaked in an armor of taboos. I wonder how Wright felt when he saw Negro women acting just as shamelessly? Clearly this was an ideological point, not a factual report. And anyone aware of the folk sources of Wright's efforts to create literature would recognize that the situation is identical with that of the countless stories which Negro men tell of the male slave called in to wash the mistress' back in the bath, of the Pullman porter invited in to share the beautiful white passenger's favors in the berth, of the bellhop seduced by the wealthy blond guest.

It is interesting that Howe should interpret my statement about Mississippi as evidence of a loss of self-control. So allow me to repeat it coldly: I fear the implications of Howe's ideas concerning the Negro writer's role as actionist more than I do the State of Mississippi. Which is not to deny the viciousness which exists there but to recognize the degree of freedom which also exists there precisely because the repression is relatively crude, or at least it was during Wright's time, and it left the world of literature alone. William Faulkner lived neither in Jefferson nor Frenchman's Bend but in Oxford. He, too, was a Mississippian, just as the boys who helped Wright leave Jackson were the sons of a Negro college president. Both Faulkner and these boys must be recognized as part of the social reality of Mississippi. I said nothing about Ross Barnett, and I certainly did not say that Howe was a "cultural authoritarian," so he should not spread his honor so thin. Rather, let him look to the implications of his thinking.

Yes, and let him learn more about the South and about Negro Americans if he would speak with authority. When he points out that "the young Ralph Ellison, even while reading these great writers, could not in Macon County attend the white man's school or movie house," he certainly appears to have me cornered. But here again he does not know the facts and he underplays choice and will. I rode freight trains to Macon County, Alabama, during the Scottsboro trial because I desired to study with the Negro conductor-composer William L. Dawson,[6] who was, and probably still is, the greatest classical musician in that part of the country. I had no need to attend a white university when the master I wished to study with was available at Tuskegee. Besides, why should I have wished to attend the white state-controlled university where the works of the great writers might not have been so easily available.

As for the movie-going, it is ironic but nonetheless true that one of the few instances where "separate but equal" was truly separate and equal was in a double movie house in the town of Tuskegee, where Negroes and whites were accommodated in parallel theaters, entering from the same street level through separate entrances and with the Negro side viewing the same pictures shortly after the showing for whites had begun. It was a product of social absurdity and, of course, no real relief from our resentment over the restriction of our freedom, but the movies were just as enjoyable or boring. And yet, is not knowing the facts more interesting, even as an isolated instance, and more stimulating to real thought than making abstract assumptions? I went to the movies to see pictures, not to be with whites. I attended a certain college because what I wanted was there. What is more, I *never* attended a white school from kindergarten through my three years of college, and yet, like Howe, I have taught and lectured for some years now at Northern, predominantly white, colleges and universities.

Perhaps this counts for little, changes little of the general condition of society, but it is factual and it does form a part of my sense of reality because, though it was not a part of Wright's life, it is my own. And if Howe thinks mine is an isolated instance, let him do a bit of research.

I do not really think that Howe can make a case for himself by bringing up the complimentary remarks which he made about *Invisible Man*. I did not quarrel with them in 1952, when they were first published, and I did not quarrel with them in my reply. His is the right of any critic to make judgment of a novel, and I do not see the point of arguing that I achieved an aesthetic

6. Composer and teacher (1899–1990) who brought international prominence to the Tuskegee Institute Choir.

goal if it did not work for him. I can only ask that my fiction be judged as art; if it fails, it fails aesthetically, not because I did or did not fight some ideological battle. I repeat, however, that Howe's strategy of bringing me into the public quarrel between Baldwin and Wright was inept. I simply did not belong in the conflict, since I knew, even then, that protest is *not* the source of the inadequacy characteristic of most novels by Negroes, but the simple failure of craft, bad writing; the desire to have protest perform the difficult tasks of art; the belief that racial suffering, social injustice or ideologies of whatever mammy-made variety, is enough. I know, also, that when the work of Negro writers has been rejected they have all too often protected their egos by blaming racial discrimination, while turning away from the fairly obvious fact that good art—and Negro musicians are ever present to demonstrate this—commands attention of itself, whatever the writer's politics or point of view. And they forget that publishers will publish almost anything which is written with even a minimum of competency, and that skill is developed by hard work, study and a conscious assault upon one's own fear and provincialism.

I agree with Howe that protest is an element of all art, though it does not necessarily take the form of speaking for a political or social program. It might appear in a novel as a technical assault against the styles which have gone before, or as protest against the human condition. If *Invisible Man* is even "apparently" free from "the ideological and emotional penalties suffered by Negroes in this country," it is because I tried to the best of my ability to transform these elements into art. My goal was not to escape, or hold back, but to work through; to transcend, as the blues transcend the painful conditions with which they deal. The protest is there, not because I was helpless before my racial condition, but because I *put* it there. If there is anything "miraculous" about the book it is the result of hard work undertaken in the belief that the work of art is important in itself, that it is a social action in itself.

I cannot hope to persuade Irving Howe to this view, for it seems quite obvious that he believes there are matters more important than artistic scrupulousness. I will point out, though, that the laws of literary form exert their validity upon all those who write, and

that it is his slighting of the formal necessities of his essay which makes for some of our misunderstanding. After reading his reply, I gave in to my ear's suggestion that I had read certain of his phrases somewhere before, and I went to the library, where I discovered that much of his essay was taken verbatim from a review in the *Nation* of May 10, 1952, and that another section was published verbatim in the *New Republic* of February 13, 1962; the latter, by the way, being in its original context a balanced appraisal and warm farewell to Richard Wright.

But when Howe spliced these materials together with phrases from an old speech of mine, swipes at the critics of the *Sewanee* and *Kenyan* reviews (journals in which I have never published), and the Baldwin-Wright quarrel, the effect was something other than he must have intended. A dialectical transformation into a new quality took place and despite the intention of Howe's content, the form made its own statement. If he would find the absurdities he wants me to reduce to a quotation, he will really have to read his essay whole. One gets the impression that he did a paste-and-scissors job and, knowing what he intended, knowing how the separated pieces had operated by themselves, did not bother to read very carefully their combined effect. It could happen to anyone; nevertheless, I'm glad he is not a scientist or a social engineer.

I do not understand why Howe thinks I said anything on the subject of writing about "Negro experience" in a manner which excludes what he calls "plight and protest"; he must have gotten his Negroes mixed. But as to answering his question concerning the "ways a Negro writer can achieve personal realization apart from the common effort of his people to win their full freedom," I suggest that he ask himself in what way shall a Negro writer achieve personal realization (as writer) *after* his people shall have won their full freedom? The answer appears to be the same in both instances: He will have to go it alone! He must suffer alone even as he shares the suffering of his group, and he must write alone and pit his talents against the standards set by the best practitioners of the craft, both past and present, in any case. For the writer's real way of sharing the experience of his group is to convert its mutual suffering into lasting value. Is

Howe suggesting, incidentally, that Heinrich Heine[7] did not exist?

His question is silly, really, for there is no such thing as "full freedom" (Oh, how Howe thirsts and hungers for the absolute for Negroes!), just as the notion of an equality of talent is silly. I am a Negro who once played trumpet with a certain skill, but alas, I am no Louis Armstrong or Clark Terry.[8] Willie Mays[9] has realized himself quite handsomely as an individual despite coming from an impoverished Negro background in oppressive Alabama; and Negro Americans, like most Americans who know the value of baseball, exult in his success. I am, after all, only a minor member, not the whole damned tribe; in fact, most Negroes have never heard of me. I could shake the nation for a while with a crime or with indecent disclosures, but my pride lies in earning the right to call myself quite simply "writer." Perhaps if I write well enough the children of today's Negroes will be proud that I did, and so, perhaps, will Irving Howe's.

Let me end with a personal note: Dear Irving, I have no objections to being placed beside Richard Wright in any estimation which is based not upon the irremediable ground of our common racial identity, but upon the quality of our achievements as writers. I respected Wright's work and I knew him, but this is not to say that he "influenced" me as significantly as you assume. Consult the text! I *sought out* Wright because I had read Eliot, Pound, Gertrude Stein and Hemingway, and as early as 1940 Wright viewed me as a potential rival, partially, it is true, because he feared I would allow myself to be used against him by political manipulators who were not Negro and who envied and hated him. But perhaps you will understand when I say he did not influence me if I point out that while one can do nothing about choosing one's relatives, one can, as artist, choose one's "ancestors." Wright was, in this sense, a "relative"; Hemingway an "ancestor." Langston Hughes, whose work I knew in grade school and whom I knew before I knew Wright, was a "relative"; Eliot, whom I was to meet only many years later, and Malraux and Dostoievsky[1] and Faulkner, were "ancestors"—if you please or don't please!

Do you still ask why Hemingway was more important to me than Wright? Not because he was white, or more "accepted." But because he appreciated the things of this earth which I love and which Wright was too driven or deprived or inexperienced to know: weather, guns, dogs, horses, love *and* hate and impossible circumstances which to the courageous and dedicated could be turned into benefits and victories. Because he wrote with such precision about the processes and techniques of daily living that I could keep myself and my brother alive during the 1937 Recession by following his descriptions of wing-shooting;[2] because he knew the difference between politics and art and something of their true relationship for the writer. Because all that he wrote—and this is very important—was imbued with a spirit beyond the tragic with which I could feel at home, for it was very close to the feeling of the blues, which are, perhaps, as close as Americans can come to expressing the spirit of tragedy. (And if you think Wright knew anything about the blues, listen to a "blues" he composed with Paul Robeson[3] singing, a *most* unfortunate collaboration!; and read his introduction to Paul Oliver's *Blues Fell This Morning*.)[4] But most important, because Hemingway was a greater artist than Wright, who although a Negro like myself, and perhaps a great man, understood little if anything of these, at least to me, important things. Because Hemingway loved the American language and the joy of writing, making the flight of birds, the loping of lions across an African plain, the mysteries of drink and moonlight, the unique styles of diverse peoples and individuals come alive on the page. Because he was in many ways the true father-as-artist of so many of us who came to writing during the late thirties.

7. German romantic poet and critic (1797–1856).
8. Jazz trumpeters Armstrong (1901–71) and Terry (b. 1920).
9. Baseball player (b. 1931) considered by many the greatest all-around player of all time.
1. Russian novelist Fyodor Dostoyevsky.
2. Shooting birds (or clay pigeons) in flight.
3. Singer, actor, and activist (1898–1976).
4. 1960 study of the blues by British writer and architectural historian Oliver (b. 1927).

I will not dwell upon Hemingway's activities in Spain or during the liberation in Paris, for you know all of that. I will remind you, however, that any writer takes what he needs to get his own work done from wherever he finds it. I did not need Wright to tell me how to be a Negro, or how to be angry or to express anger—Joe Louis[5] was doing that very well—or even to teach me about socialism; my mother had canvassed for the socialists, not the communists, the year I was born. No, I had been a Negro for twenty-two or twenty-three years when I met Wright, and in more places and under a greater variety of circumstances than he had then known. He was generously helpful in sharing his ideas and information, but I needed instruction in other values and I found them in the works of other writers—Hemingway was one of them, T. S. Eliot initiated the search.

I like your part about Chekhov arising from his sickbed to visit the penal colony at Sakhalin Island. It was, as you say, a noble act. But shouldn't we remember that it was significant only because Chekhov was *Chekhov*, the great writer? You compliment me truly, but I have not written so much or so well, even though I *have* served a certain apprenticeship in the streets and even touch events in the Freedom Movement in a modest way. But I can also recall the story of a certain writer who succeeded with a great fanfare of publicity in having a talented murderer released from prison. It made for another very short story which ended quite tragically—though not for the writer: A few months after his release the man killed the mother of two young children. I also know of another really quite brilliant writer who, under the advice of certain wise men who were then managing the consciences of artists, aban-

doned the prison of his writing to go to Spain, where he was allowed to throw away his life defending a worthless hill. I have not heard his name in years but I remember it vividly; it was Christopher Cauldwell,[6] *né* Christopher St. John Sprigg. There are many such stories, Irving. It's heads you win, tails you lose, and you are quite right about my not following Baldwin, who is urged on by a nobility—or is it a demon—quite different from my own. It has cost me quite a pretty penny, indeed, but then I was always poor and not (and I know this is a sin in our America) too uncomfortable.

Dear Irving, I am still yakking on and there's many a thousand gone, but I assure you that no Negroes are beating down my door, putting pressure on me to join the Negro Freedom Movement, for the simple reason that they realize that I am enlisted for the duration. Such pressure is coming only from a few disinterested "military advisers," since Negroes want no more fairly articulate would-be Negro leaders cluttering up the airways. For, you see, my Negro friends recognize a certain division of labor among the members of the tribe. Their demands, like that of many whites, are that I publish more novels—and here I am remiss and vulnerable perhaps. You will recall what the Talmud has to say about the trees of the forest and the making of books, etc. But then, Irving, they recognize what you have not allowed yourself to see; namely, that my reply to your essay is in itself a small though necessary action in the Negro struggle for freedom. You should not feel unhappy about this or think that I regard you either as dishonorable or an enemy. I hope, rather, that you will come to view this exchange as an act of, shall we say, "antagonistic co-operation"?

ALBERT MURRAY

from *James Baldwin, Protest Fiction, and the Blues Tradition* [1970]

"It seems that they find it much easier to praise such writers for being angry (which requires no talent, not to mention genius) than for being innovative or insightful," Albert Murray told an interviewer, referring to critics, like

Irving Howe (p. 659), who championed protest literature. Murray rejected that impulse, although the overtly political Black Arts Movement dominated the 1970s, the time when Murray began publishing his criticism. Instead,

---

5. World heavyweight boxing champion from 1937 to 1949 (1914–81).
6. British writer and Marxist theorist (1907–37); killed in 1937 while fighting as a volunteer with the International Brigade in the Spanish Civil War.

like his classmate and friend at the Tuskegee Institute, the novelist Ralph Ellison (p. 430), Murray consistently emphasized the complexity and diversity of African Americans and their arts while stressing their role in the larger American tradition.

In his 1970 book of essays, *The Omni-Americans*, which includes "James Baldwin, Protest Fiction, and the Blues Tradition," Murray develops his vision of a multifaceted American culture. He continues the 1950s debate about protest art, focusing on James Baldwin's ideas in "Everybody's Protest Novel" (p. 485) and their relationship to Baldwin's own fiction. Murray also discusses Baldwin's idea that music represents the only medium in which African Americans have been fully able to express themselves. Like the critics of the Black Arts Movement, among them LeRoi Jones (p. 694), Murray recognizes music as a primary form of expression for African Americans. He rejects a separatist view of black music, however, as well as a narrow vision of it as protest against discrimination. As for the Black Arts Movement itself, Murray characterizes it as misguided and marked by "esthetic nonsense" and "political naiveté."

Born in Alabama in 1916, Murray dedicated himself to music and literary criticism later in life, after retiring, in 1962, from the U.S. Air Force, having achieved the rank of major. After the publication of *The Omni-Americans*, his first book, Murray continued to write criticism. He has also written two novels and helped the jazz musician Count Basie write his autobiography, *Good Morning Blues* (1985). The success of the critic Stanley Crouch—who described Murray in *The All-American Skin Game, or The Decoy of Race* (1995) as "my mentor and far more my father than the fellow whose blood runs in my veins"—fostered a resurgence of interest in Murray's criticism in the 1990s.

From Albert Murray, *The Omni-Americans: New Perspectives on Black Experience and American Culture* (New York: Outerbridge and Dienstfrey, 1970), pp. 160–68.

Ralph Ellison wrote an article about Richard Wright which was published in the *Antioch Review* in the summer of 1945. This was four years before James Baldwin came to write "Everybody's Protest Novel" and some six before he was to do "Many Thousands Gone." Baldwin, as has been seen, was sharply critical of Wright, who incidentally was an old personal friend and onetime benefactor. Ellison, also an old personal friend, was generous almost to a fault.

So much so that when Wright encountered him shortly afterwards all Wright could do was shake his head in pleased bewilderment, somewhat, one imagines, as the tunesmith of *Body and Soul* must have done upon meeting Coleman Hawkins;[1] and all he could say was almost exactly what one imagines the tunesmith would have said: "Man, you went much further than the book. Much further." (He himself was not to go even as far again.)

All Ellison, a former trumpet player and student of music composition, could do was shake his head in turn and smile reassuringly and reply, "Well, what you wrote made it possible for me to say what I said about it. All I was trying to do was use what you put there. All I was trying to do was play a few riffs on your tune. It was your tune. I just hope I didn't embarrass you. I just hope I did it justice." He did it more than justice.

Ellison's article was a commentary on *Black Boy*. This autobiographical record of Wright's childhood and youth employed all the techniques of fiction and was obviously intended to be a literary work of art as well as a personal document. Ellison called it "Richard Wright's Blues," and his remarks did go far beyond the book itself. They included what the book itself stated, and as in all really perceptive literary criticism, they suggested what was also represented, symbolized, ritualized.

Richard Wright, in spite of the shifts in his formal political affiliations, was always essentially a Marxist thinker. It is true that he maintained, and no doubt believed, that Marxism was only a starting point for Negro writers; and he himself was certainly the kind of intellectual who realized that Negro folklore had important literary significance. He also had a very

1. In 1939, jazz saxophonist Coleman Hawkins (1904–69) and his orchestra recorded "Body and Soul," written in 1930 by a group of composers including white American songwriter Johnny Green (1908–89); Coleman's version focuses almost exclusively on improvisation built on the song's chords.

extensive knowledge of world history and cultures, of ideas as such, and of contemporary world literature. But although his wide intellectual interests, so much broader than those of most other U.S. Negro writers, were a very active part of his everyday writing equipment, he remained primarily a Marxist. He read Eliot, Stein, Joyce, Proust, Hemingway, Gorky, Nexo, and most of the others, and he used much of what he learned, but he was almost always restricted by the provincial limitations of dialectical materialism.[2] He used Freud, for example, primarily to score Marxian points; and even his later involvement with existentialism seemed to have political revolution as its basic motive.

Ellison was very much aware of the comprehensive range of Wright's intellectual and literary background, and in passing he suggested parallels between *Black Boy* and Nehru's *Toward Freedom,* Joyce's *Portrait of the Artist as a Young Man,* Dostoevski's *House of the Dead,* Rousseau's *Confessions,* and Yeats' *Autobiography.*[3] But what impressed him most was that, knowingly or not, Wright had written a book that was in essence a literary equivalent to the blues.

> The blues [Ellison wrote] is an impulse to keep the painful details and episodes of a brutal experience alive in one's aching consciousness, to finger its jagged grain, and to transcend it, not by the consolation of philosophy but by squeezing from it a near-tragic, near-comic lyricism. As a form, the blues is an autobiographical chronicle of personal catastrophe expressed lyrically. And certainly Wright's early childhood was crammed with catastrophic incidents. In a few short years his father deserted his mother, he knew intense hunger, he became a drunkard begging drinks from black stevedores in Memphis saloons; he had to flee Arkansas, where an uncle was lynched; he was forced to live with a fanatically religious grandmother in an atmosphere of constant bickering; he was lodged in an orphan asylum; he observed the suffering of his mother, who became a permanent invalid, while fighting off the blows of the poverty-stricken relatives with whom he had to live; he was cheated, beaten and kicked off jobs by white employees who disliked his eagerness to learn a trade; and to these objective circumstances must be added the subjective fact that Wright, with his sensitivity, extreme shyness and intelligence, was a problem child who rejected his family and was by them rejected.

Thus along with the themes, equivalent descriptions of milieu and the perspectives to be found in Joyce, Nehru, Dostoevski, George Moore and Rousseau, *Black Boy* is filled with blues-tempered echoes of railroad trains, the names of Southern towns and cities, estrangements, fights and flights, deaths and disappointments, charged with physical and spiritual hungers and pain. And like a blues sung by such an artist as Bessie Smith,[4] its lyrical prose evokes the paradoxical, almost surreal image of a black boy singing lustily as he probes his own grievous wound.

"Their attraction" he added, referring again to the blues near the end of the article, "lies in this, that they at once express both the agony of life and the possibility of conquering it through sheer toughness of spirit. They fall short of tragedy only in that they provide no solution, offer no scapegoat but the self."

Baldwin, who made no mention of *Black Boy* or of Ellison's commentary when he wrote about the Negro tradition and the Negro sensibility in "Many Thousands Gone," once stated in an address at the New School in New York that as a writer he had modeled himself on none of the white American writers, not even Hemingway or Faulkner, but on black musicians, black dancers, and so on, even on black whores (or did

---

2. Concept developed by German philosopher Karl Marx that all things are constantly changing through contradiction and struggle.

3. *Autobiographies* by Irish poet and playwright William Butler Yeats (1865–1939) was first published in 1926, with subsequent editions adding other autobiographical writings; *Toward Freedom:* autobiography by Jawaharlal Nehru (1889–1964), the first prime minister of India, was published in 1936; *A Portrait of the Artist as a Young Man*: semi-autobiographical novel by Irish writer James Joyce (1882–1941); *House of the Dead:* Dostoyevsky's novel based on his personal experiences in a Siberian prison was published in 1862; *Confessions:* autobiographical writings by Genevois writer Jean-Jacques Rousseau was published posthumously in 1782.

4. Blues singer and songwriter (c. 1894–1937) known as the "Empress of the Blues."

one hear right?), and of all most assuredly on the blues singers. He then spoke lovingly about Billie Holiday and lamented the current personal and legal difficulties of Ray Charles.[5]

But Baldwin's Broadway play, *Blues for Mister Charley* (1964),[6] had very little if anything to do with the blues. It fills the stage with a highly stylized group of energetic and militant self-righteous Negroes hollering and screaming and cussing and accusing and talking out of school and under other folks' clothes, and threatening to raise hell and all that, but generally feeling as sorry for themselves as if they had all just come from reading *An American Dilemma, The Mark of Oppression,*[7] and most of the "liberal" magazines. There is an up tempo beat which *could* go with a classic Kansas City shout, but what comes out sounds more like the reds than the blues.

Baldwin's criticism of *Native Son* was essentially valid. The people, the situations, and the motivation in that quasi-realistic novel were more than oversimplified. They were exaggerated by an overemphasis on protest as such and by a very specific kind of political protest at that. Oversimplification in these terms does lead almost inevitably to false positions based on false assumptions about human nature itself. Every story whatever its immediate purpose is a story about being man on earth. This is the basis of its universality, the fundamental interest and sense of identification it generates in other people.

If you ignore this and reduce man's whole story to a series of sensational but superficial news items and editorial complaints and accusations, blaming all the bad things that happen to your characters on racial bigotry, you imply that people are primarily concerned with only certain political and social absolutes. You imply that these absolutes are the sine qua non[8] of all human fulfillment. And you also imply that there are people who possess these political and social abso-

lutes, and that these people are on better terms with the world as such and are consequently better people. In other words, no matter how noble your mission, when you oversimplify the reasons why a poor or an oppressed man lies, cheats, steals, betrays, hates, murders, or becomes an alcoholic or addict, you imply that well-to-do, rich, and powerful people don't do these things. *But they do.*

Baldwin in his essays on Wright seemed sensitive to this sort of embarrassment. He accused Wright of trying "to redeem a symbolical monster in social terms," and he spoke of the truth as implying "a devotion to the human being, his freedom and fulfillment; freedom which cannot be legislated, fulfillment which cannot be charted." He also seemed firmly convinced that categories were not real and that man "was not, after all, merely a member of a society or a group"—but "something *resolutely indefinable, unpredictable.*" (Italics added.)

These seemed like the assumptions of a writer who is interested in literature. Assumptions like these underlie all of the world's great stories. The unpredictable is the very stuff of storytelling. It is the very stuff of dramatic power, suspense, thrills, escapades, resolutions; the very stuff of fears, hopes, quests, achievements. It is the very stuff of the human condition.

That a sophisticated intellectual like Richard Wright knew all of this goes without question. But he chose to operate within the framework of his basic political commitment. This was an unfortunate choice. But in spite of his arbitrarily circumscribed point of view, he wrote a number of things that were politically useful, and there were also times, especially in certain parts of *Uncle Tom's Children* and *Black Boy,* when the universal literary values of his work automatically went beyond the material objectives of political ideology.

Now, Baldwin in effect began his literary career by rejecting Wright's achievements as being inadequate and also dangerous. The grounds for his rejection

5. Singer, songwriter, and musician (1930–2004), who was a pioneer of soul music; Holiday: jazz singer and songwriter (1915–59), known for her unique vocal style and improvisation that brought out the emotional content of songs.
6. *Blues for Mr. Charlie* was Baldwin's second play and is dedicated to the memory and family of murdered civil rights activist Medgar Evans and to the memory of the four girls who died in the 1963 church bombing in Birmingham.
7. Gunnar Myrdal's *An American Dilemma: The Negro Problem and Modern Democracy* (1944); Abram Karcliner's and Lionel Ovesey's *The Mark of Oppression: A Psychological Study of the American Negro* (1951) uses psychoanalytic ideas from that era to draw general conclusions about personalities and behavior of African Americans.
8. An essential condition or element [Latin].

generally seemed solid enough. And he seemed to promise not only something different but something more.

So far he has not fulfilled that promise. The only thing really different about Baldwin's work to date has been his special interest in themes related to the so-called sexual revolution. And this is different only from Wright; it is not at all different from a lot of other writers these days, all of them white. Otherwise, Richard Wright is the author that James Baldwin the novelist, playwright, and spokesman resembles more than any other, including Harriet Beecher Stowe.[9]

Baldwin once complained about the climate of anarchy and unmotivated and unapprehended disaster in *Native Son*. But in his own recent novel, *Another Country*, he seems to think this sort of climate has some profound, absurd, existentialist significance. It does not. Wright's existentialism, such as it was, had led to the same mistake in *The Outsider*,[1] which Baldwin had already spotted in *Native Son*.

Both Baldwin and Wright seem to have overlooked the rich possibilities available to them in the blues tradition. Both profess great pride in Negroes, but in practice seem to rate the theories and abstract formulations of French existentialism over the infinitely richer wisdom of the blues. Both, like most other intellectuals (and/or most of the social scientists), seem to have missed what should be one of the most obvious implications of the blues tradition: *It is the product of the most complicated culture, and therefore the most complicated sensibility in the modern world.*

The United States has all of the complexities of all the other nations in the world, and also many of its own which most other nations are either not yet advanced enough or powerful enough to have. And in all these areas of U.S. life one finds Negroes. They are always reacting to what is happening and their reactions become elements in the blues tradition. Racial snobbishness and U.S. provincialism and deference to things European keep many Americans from realizing it, but the most old-fashioned elements in the blues tradition are often avant garde by the artistic standards of most other countries in the world. Europeans seem to appreciate this better than most Americans.

Somehow or other James Baldwin and Richard Wright seem to have missed the literary possibilities suggested by this. Ralph Ellison has not. He went beyond Richard Wright in the very process of commenting on *Black Boy*, and he went beyond every other American writer of his generation when he wrote his first novel. The possibilities he had talked about in "Richard Wright's Blues" were demonstrated most convincingly when he published *Invisible Man*, probably the most mature first novel, American or whatever, since *Buddenbrooks*. (It was certainly more mature both in craftsmanship and in vision than *This Side of Paradise*. And, of course, Hemingway's first was not *The Sun Also Rises* but *Torrents of Spring*, and Faulkner's was *Soldiers' Pay*!)[2]

Invisible Man was *par excellence* the literary extension of the blues. It was as if Ellison had taken an everyday twelve bar blues tune (by a man from down South sitting in a manhole up North in New York singing and signifying about how he got there) and scored it for full orchestra. This was indeed something different and something more than run of the mill U.S. fiction. It had new dimensions of rhetorical resonance (based on lying and signifying). It employed a startlingly effective fusion of narrative realism and surrealism; and it achieved a unique but compelling combination of the naturalistic, the ridiculous, and the downright hallucinatory.

It was a first rate novel, a blues odyssey, a tall tale about the fantastic misadventures of one American Negro, and at the same time a prototypical story about being not only a twentieth century American but also a twentieth century man, the Negro's obvious predicament symbolizing everybody's essential predicament. And like the blues, and echoing the irrepressibility of America itself, it ended on a note of promise, ironic and ambiguous perhaps, but a note of promise still.

---

9. See p. 118.

1. Novel by Wright published in 1950.

2. *Buddenbrooks* by German writer Thomas Mann (1875–1955) was published in 1901; F. Scott Fitzgerald's *This Side of Paradise* was published in 1920 while *The Great Gatsby* came out in 1925; Ernest Hermingway's first novel *Torrents of Spring* and his second novel *The Sun Also Rises* were both published in 1926; William Faulkner's *Soldiers' Pay* was published in 1926.

The blues with no aid from existentialism have always known that there were no clear-cut solutions for the human situation.

Invisible Man was mainstream American writing in the same sense that U.S. Negro music is mainstream. In spite of his status as an entertainer, or sometimes perhaps as a direct result of it, the Negro jazz musician, representing the very spirit of American life itself, has, it seems, always been oriented to something different and something more. And there is much that all U.S. writers can learn from him about working with American experience in esthetic forms that are vernacular and sophisticated at the same time, particularly and peculiarly American and universally contemporary at the same time.

In terms of cultural assimilation, the blues idiom at its best is Omni-American precisely because it sounds as if it knows the truth about all the other music in the world and is looking for something better. Perhaps someday one will be able to say the same thing about American fiction. Black writers can do much to bring about that day, and there is every reason why they should. They will not do so as long as they mistake the illusions of social science for actuality.

RICHARD WRIGHT

from *Tradition and Industrialization: The Plight of the Tragic Elite in Africa* [1956]

In 1956, the First International Congress of Black Writers and Artists convened in Paris. Participants included many of the leaders associated with the international Negritude movement (including the poet Aimé Césaire, who had coined the term Negritude in 1939), which promoted a common black identity as a way of resisting European colonial power.

Richard Wright (p. 470), who had been living in Paris since 1948 and had become involved with existentialist philosophy, spoke at the conference. His speech, excerpted here, focuses on the value of freedom and displays a marked self-consciousness about his own subjectivity, both central ideas of existentialism. Wright's experiences at the conference, where he heard remarks attesting to the continued relevance of religion in Africa, contributed to his self-questioning. Spontaneously commenting on his own arguments in the section of his speech just before this excerpt, Wright debates with himself about whether his optimistic assessment of Africa's future is "idealistic or factual." Overall, however, his speech clearly asserts his firm beliefs in the values of secularism and personal freedom rather than religion and tradition.

Although he focuses on the development of science and industrialization, Wright extends his argument to art, which, as he argues in an earlier part of his speech, "has its own autonomy, an independence that extends beyond the spheres of political or priestly powers." Wright's argument about the benefits Africa would enjoy from the destruction of its traditions stands in stark contrast to past and future artistic movements (including the Negritude movement and the 1960s Black Arts Movement) that embraced African cultural traditions.

From "Congrès International des Écrivains et Artistes Noirs," special issue, *Présence Africaine: Revue Culturelle du Monde Noir*, nos. 8–10 (June–November 1956).

How can the spirit of the Enlightenment and the Reformation be extended now to all men? How can this boon be made global in effect? That is the task that history now imposes upon us. Can a way be found to merge the rational areas and rational personnel of Europe with those of Asia and Africa? How can the curtains of race, color, religion, and tradition—all of which hamper man's mastery of his environment—be collectively rolled back by free men of the West and non-West? Is this a Utopian dream? Is this more wishing? No. It is much more drastic than that. The nations of Asia and Africa and Europe contain too much of the forces of the irrational for anyone to think that the future will take care of itself. The islands of the rational in the East are too tenuously held to permit of optimism. And the same is true of Europe. (We have but to recall reading of ideas to « burn up entire continents» to doff our illusions. The truth is that our world—a world for all men, black, brown, yellow, and white—will either be all rational or totally irrational. For better or worse, it will eventually be one world.

[* * *]

How can these rational regions of the world be maintained? How can the pragmatically useful be made triumphant? Does this entail a surrender of the hard-bought national freedoms on the part of non-Western nations? I'm convinced that that will not happen, for these Asian and Africans nations, led by Western educated leaders, love their freedom as much as the West loves its own. They have had to struggle and die for their freedom and they value it passionately. It is unthinkable that they, so recently freed from color and class domination of the West, would voluntarily surrender their sovereignty. Let me state the problem upsidedown. What Western nation would dream of abdicating its sovereignty and collobarating with powers that once so recently ruled them in interests that were not their own,—powers that created a vast literature of hate against them? Such an act would be irrational in the extreme. And the Western educated leaders of non-Western nations are filled with too much distrust of an imperial-minded West to permit of any voluntary relinquishing of their control over their destinies.

Is there no alternative? Must there be a victorious East or a victorious West? If one or the other must win completely, then the fragile values won so blindly and accidentally and at so great a cost and sacrifice will be lost for us all. Where is the crux of this matter? Who is to act first? Who should act first? The burden of action rests with the West, I say. For it was the West that began this vast process. And of what must the action of the West consist? It must aid and, yes, abet the delicate and tragic elite in Asia and Africa to establish rational areas of living. THE WEST, IN ORDER TO KEEP BEING WESTERN, FREE, RATIONAL, MUST BE PREPARED TO GIVE TO THE ELITE OF ASIA AND AFRICA A FREEDOM WHICH IT ITSELF NEVER PERMITTED IN ITS OWN DOMAIN. THE ASIAN AND AFRICAN ELITE MUST BE GIVEN THEIR HEADS! The West must perform an act of faith and do this. Such a mode of action has long been implied in the very nature of the ideas which the West has instilled into that Asian-African elite. The West must trust that part of itself that it has thrust into Asia and Africa. Nehru, Nkrumah, Nasser, Sukarno,[1] and the Western educated chiefs of these newly created national states must be given *carte blanche*[2] right to modernize their lands without overlordship of the West, and we must understand the methods they will feel compelled to use.

Never, you will say. That is impossible, you will say. Oh, I'm asking a hard thing and I know if. I'm Western, remember, and I know how horrible my words sound to Westerners so used to issuing orders and having those orders obeyed at gun point. But what rational recourse does the West possess other than this? None.

If the West cannot do this, it means that the West does not trust itself, does not trust the ideas which it has cast into the world. Yes, Sukarno, Nehru, Nasser and others will use dictatorial methods to hasten the process of social evolution and to establish order in their lands,—lands which were left voids by a long Western occupation and domination. Why pretend to be shocked at this? You would do the same if you were in their place. You have done it in the West over and over again. You do it in every war you fight, in every crisis, political or economic, you have. And don't you feel and know that, as soon as order has been established by your Western educated elite, they will, in order to be powerful, surrender the personal power that they have had to wield?

Let us recognize what our common problem really is. Let us rethink what the issue is. This problem is vast and complicated. Merely to grasp it takes an act

---

1. Jawaharlal Nehru, first Prime Minister of India from 1947–64; Kwame Nkruman (1909–72), first prime minister of Ghana from 1957–60 and first president of Ghana from 1960–66; Gamal Abdel Nasser (1918–70), second president of Egypt from 1954 until his death; Sukarno (1901–70), first president of Indonesia.
2. Unconditional authority; literally "blank check" [French].

of the imagination. This problem, though it has racial overtones, is not racial. Though it has religious aspects, is not religious. Though it has strong economic motives, is not wholly economic. And though political action will, no doubt, constitute the means, the *modus operandi*,[3] the problem is not basically political.

The problem is freedom. How can Asians and Africans be free of their stultifying traditions and customs and become industrialized, and powerful, if you like, like the West [* * *]?

I say that the West cannot ask the elite of Asia and Africa, even though educated in the West, to copy or ape what has happened in the West. Why? Because the West has never really been honest with itself about how it overcame its own traditions and blinding customs.

Let us look at some examples of Western interpretation of its own history. A Civil War was fought in America and the American school children are taught that it was to free black slaves. It was not. It was to establish a republic, to create conditions of economic freedom, to clear the ground for the launching of an industrial society. (Naturally, slavery had to go in such a situation. I'm emphasizing the positive historic aspects, not the negative and inevitable ones!) The French fought a long and bloody Revolution and the French school children are taught that it was for Liberty, Equality, and Fraternity. Yet we know that it was for the right of a middle class to think, to buy and sell, to enable men with talent to rise in their careers, and to push back (which was inevitable and implied) the power of the Church and the nobility. The English, being more unintentionally forthright than others, never made much bones about the fact that the freedom that they fought for was a freedom of trade.

Do these misinterpretations of Western history by the West negate the power and net gains of the Western World? No. It is not what the West said it did but what the results really were that count in the long run.

Why have I raised these points of Western contradictions? Because, when non-Westerners, having the advantage of seeing more clearly—being psychologically outside of the West—what the West did, and

when the non-Westerners seek to travel the same road, the West raises strong objections. I've had a white Westerner tell me: « You know, we must stay in Africa to protect the naked black natives. If we leave, the blacks we have educated will practice fascism against their own people. » So this man was in a position to endorse the shooting down of a black elite because that black elite wanted to impose conditions relating to the control of imports and exports, something which his country practiced every day!

The same objections are leveled against Nkrumah in the Gold Coast, against Sukarno in Indonesia, against Nasser in Egypt, against Nehru in India. Wise Westerners would insist that stern measures be taken by the elite of Asia and Africa in order to overcome irrational forces, such as racism, superstition, etc. But if a selfish West hamstrings the elite of Asia and Africa, distrusts their motives, a spirit of absolutism[4] will rise in Asia and Africa and will provoke a spirit of counterabsolutism in the West. In case that happen[s], all will be lost. We shall all, Asia and Africa as well as Europe, be thrown back into an age of racial and religious wars, and the precious heritage—freedom of speech, a secular state, the autonomy of science—, which is not Western or Eastern, but human, will be snuffed out of the minds of men.

The problem is freedom from a dead past. And freedom to build a rational future. How much are we willing to risk for freedom? I say let us risk everything. Freedom begets freedom. Europe, I say to you before it is too late: Let the Africans and Asians whom you have educated in Europe have their freedom, or you will lose your own in trying to keep freedom from them.

But how can this be done? Have we any recent precedent for such a procedure? Is my suggestion outlandish? Unheard of? No. A ready answer and a vivid example are close at hand. A scant ten years ago we concluded a tragically desperate and costly war in Europe to beat back the engulfing tides of irrational fascism. During those tense and eventful days I recall hearing Winston Churchill[5] appeal to the Americans when Britain was hard-pressed by hordes of German and Italian fascists. Churchill said:

---

3. Method of operating [Latin].
4. The principle or practice of complete, unrestricted power by a ruler or government.
5. British politician and prime minister of the United Kingdom from 1940–45 and 1951–55.

« Give us the tools and we'll finish the job. »

Today I say to the white men of Europe:

« You have, however misguidedly, trained and educated an elite in Africa and Asia. You have implanted in their hearts the hunger for freedom and rationality. Now this elite of yours—your children, one might say—is hard-pressed by hunger, poverty, disease, by stagnant economic conditions, by unbalanced class structures of their societies, by oppressive and irratio-

nal tides of tribal religions. You men of Europe made an abortive beginning to solve that problem. You failed. Now, I say to you: Men of Europe, give that elite the tools and let it finish that job! »

This conference, I feel must proceed to define the tools and the nature of finishing that job, and the strengthening of that elite.

Freedom is indivisible.

LeRoi Jones

from *Enter the Middle Class* [1963]

In 1962, LeRoi Jones (b. 1934) gave an address at a meeting of the American Society of African Culture titled "Myth of a Negro Literature," in which he dismissed black writers of the past, including Phillis Wheatley (p. 12), Charles Chestnutt, and Zora Neale Hurston (p. 470). The following year, in this essay from his book *Blues People,* Jones expanded that argument, laying the scholarly foundation for the development of the Black Arts Movement.

In contrast to writers like James Baldwin (p. 470) and Ralph Ellison (p. 430), who stressed the complexity of American culture and individual voices, Jones champions the "authentic" black voice of the "lower-classed Negroes." He believes that in the arts only music has maintained a connection to this authentic black voice, one that goes back to its roots in African culture. By

rejecting past works of black literature, painting, and drama as middle-class efforts to "whiten the black culture" for "mainstream" society, Jones sets the stage for the emergence of a new type of art in the years to come, one inspired by the idea of a "black aesthetic."

By 1963, Jones was already a successful poet, and in 1964 he won a *Village Voice* Obie Award for his play *Dutchman.* He became a major force behind the Black Arts Movement, a cultural movement dedicated to the development of a "black aesthetic" and the independent distribution of black art, which thrived from 1965 to 1974. In 1974, in a move that contributed to the decline of the movement, Jones, who had by then adopted the name Amiri Baraka, distanced himself from black cultural nationalism and moved toward an international, multi-ethnic position known as Third World Marxist–Leninism.

From LeRoi Jones, *Blues People: Negro Music in White America* (New York: William Morrow, 1963), pp. 130–34.

The white society's need for Negro laborers and the resulting scramble into the great Northern cities "smeared" the caste lines of an older black society and began to form a sprawling bourgeoisie based on the pay check—an almost exact duplication of the way in which the earlier caste system of white America was "debased." But the white society still had some semblance of caste—its "first" families, intact (although frequently as heads or "captains" of industry). Negroes could not become "captains" of industry and could never have belonged to any first families (except, per-

haps, as family retainers), so it was the professional men—doctors, lawyers, ministers—who were the heads of the new black society. And these people wanted more than anything in life to become *citizens.* They were not ever satisfied with being freedmen, or former slaves. They wanted no connection with that "stain on America's past"; and what is more, they wanted the right (which they thought they could earn by moving sufficiently away from the blacker culture) to look on that "stain" as objectively as possible, when they had to, and to refer to it from the safety of the bastions of the white middle class. They did not even want to be "accepted" as *themselves,* they wanted any self which the mainstream dictated, and the mainstream *always* dictated. And this black middle class, in turn, tried always to dictate that self, or this image of a whiter Negro, to the poorer, blacker Negroes.

The effects of these attempts by the black middle class to whiten the black culture of this country are central to my further discussions on the sociological significance of the changes in Negro music, but I think it might be useful here to consider also the effects this "whitening" had in other cultural areas. I think it is not fantastic to say that only in music has there been any significant Negro contribution to a *formal* American culture. For the most part, most of the other contributions made by black Americans in the areas of painting, drama, and literature have been essentially undistinguished. The reasons for this tragic void are easy to understand if one realizes one important idea about the existence of any black culture in this country. The only Negroes who found themselves in a *position* to pursue some art, especially the art of literature, have been members of the Negro middle class. Only Negro music, because, perhaps, it drew its strength and beauty out of the depths of the black man's soul, and because to a large extent its traditions could be carried on by the "lowest classes" of Negroes, has been able to survive the constant and willful dilutions of the black middle class and the persistent calls to oblivion made by the mainstream of the society. Of course, that mainstream wrought very definite and very constant changes upon the *form* of the American Negro's music, but the emotional significance and vitality at its core remain, to this day, unaltered. It was the one vector out of African culture impossible to eradicate. It signified the existence of an Afro-American, and the existence of an Afro-American culture. And in the evolution of form in Negro music it is possible to see not only the evolution of the Negro as a cultural and social element of American culture but also the evolution of that culture itself.

The "coon shout"[1] proposed one version of the American Negro and of America; Bessie Smith proposed another. (Swing and bebop,[2] as I shall attempt to point out, propose still another.) But the point is that both these versions are accurate and informed with a legitimacy of emotional concern nowhere available in, say, what is called "Negro literature." The reason is as terrifying as it is simple. The middle-class black man, whether he wanted to be a writer, or a painter, or a doctor, developed an emotional allegiance to the middle-class (middle-brow) culture of America that obscured, or actually made hideous, any influences or psychological awareness that seemed to come from outside what was generally acceptable to a middle-class white man, especially if those influences were identifiable as coming from the most despised group in the country. The black middle class wanted no subculture, nothing that could connect them with the poor black man or the slave.

Literature, for most Negro writers, for instance, was always an example of "culture," in the narrow sense of "cultivation" or "sophistication" in an individual within their own group. The Negro artist, because of his middle-class background, carried an artificial social burden as the "best and most intelligent" of Negroes, and usually entered into the "serious" arts to exhibit his social graces—as a method, or means, of displaying his participation in the serious aspects of Western culture. To be a writer was to be "cultivated," in the stunted bourgeois sense of the word. It was also to be a "quality" black man, not merely an "ordinary nigger."

Early Negro novelists such as Charles Chesnutt, Otis Shackelford, Sutton Griggs (even though he was more militant), Pauline Hopkins,[3] produced works that were potboilers for the growing Negro middle class. The books were also full of the same prejudices and conceits that could be found in the novels of their models, the white middle class. The contempt for the

1. Derogatory label for style of sing-shouting lyrics; in the early 1900s, the style was imitated and promoted by white American songwriters writing in a minstrel vein.
2. Jazz styles, with swing developed in the 1930s and bebop in the 1940s.
3. Novelist, playwright, journalist, and editor of *The Colored American Magazine* (1859–1930) whose novels include *Contending Forces: A Romance Illustrative of Negro Life North and South* (1900); Shackelford (1871–?) published *Lillian Simmons: Or the Conflict of Sections* in 1915; Griggs: writer, Baptist minister, and activist (1872–1933) whose novels include *Imperium in Imperio* (1899).

"lower-classed Negroes" found in these novels by black novelists is amazing and quite blatant. And, as Robert A. Bone points out: "It must be understood at once that the early [Negro] novelists believed substantially in the myth of Anglo-Saxon superiority. Pauline Hopkins writes: 'Surely the Negro race must be productive of some valuable specimens, if only from the infusion which amalgamation with a superior race must eventually bring.' " Chesnutt's and Griggs's "heroes" were usually "refined Afro-Americans"; as Bone shows further: "In several of the early novels there is a stock situation in which a 'refined Afro-American' is forced to share a Jim Crow car with dirty, boisterous, and drunken Negroes."

The idea of the "separation," the strata, had developed within the group. The thin division of field hand from house servant had widened, and the legacy of the house servant was given voice constantly in the work of the early Negro writers. As Bone says, "When all the sound and fury of these novels has evaporated, what remains is an appeal for an alliance between 'the better class of colored people' and the 'quality white folks.' "[5] And an "amen" could be heard to that sentiment throughout the rising black churches of the North. Of course, the Negro novelist ceased to be so blatantly patronizing and disparaging of "most Negroes" when the social climate in the country itself became more "liberal." No longer would a member of the Negro middle class be idiotic enough to write, as Shackelford once did in his novel *Lillian Simmons:* "She could understand why Jim Crow cars and all other forms of segregation in the South were necessary, but she could not feel that it was fair to treat all colored people alike, because all were not alike."[6]

By the twenties, spurred again by the movement of Negroes to the North and the change that had made of a basically agricultural country an industrial giant, thereby transforming the core of the Negro population from farm workers into a kind of urban proletariat,[7] a great change also took place among Negro artists and intellectuals. Even though they were still fundamentally the products of the Negro middle class and still maintained rather firmly many emotional and intellectual ties with it, the Negro novelists of the twenties at least began to realize that the earlier attitudes of the black middle class were the most agonizing remnants of the "slave mentality." It was now that the middle class demanded, through its spokesmen the novelists and the more intrepid educators, "at least equality." It was the beginning of what was called the "Negro Renaissance," and the emergence of what Alain Locke (p. 000) called the "New Negro." But if now the more cultivated members of the black middle class began to realize that the old stance of "whiter Negroes" could not effect an entrance into the mainstream of American society (these writers, in fact, rebelled against the entire concept of a slavish disparagement of the Negro by Negroes as a prerequisite for such privilege), this "rebellion" still took form within the confines of the American middle-class mind, even if those confines had been somewhat broadened by the internationalism imposed upon the country by World War I. Even the term *New Negro*, for all its optimistic and rebellious sound, still assumes that it is a different kind of Negro who is asking for equality—not old Rastus the slave. There is still, for all the "race pride" and "race consciousness" that these spokesmen for the Negro Renaissance claimed, the smell of the dry rot of the middle-class Negro mind: the idea that, somehow, Negroes must *deserve* equality.

The spirit of this "Renaissance" was divided as an emotional entity into three separate and easily identifiable reactions, corresponding to the cultural stratum of the particular Negroes who had to interpret it. The rising middle-class-spawned intelligentsia invented the term *New Negro* and the idea of the Negro Renaissance to convey *to the white world* that there had been a change of tactics as to how to climb onto the bandwagon of mainstream American life. The point here is that this *was* to be conveyed to white America; it was

4. Bone's *The Negro Novel in America* was first published in 1958.
5. *Op. cit.* [Bone, *The Negro Novel in America* (New Haven, Conn.: Yale University Press, 1958)], p. 19. [Jones's note]
6. *Ibid.*, p. 18. [Jones's note]
7. Working class.

another conscious reaction to that white America and another adaptation of the middle-class Negro's self-conscious performance for his ever appreciative white audience. There was a loud, sudden, but understand-

ably strained, appreciation for things black by this intelligentsia. The "Harlem School" of writers attempted to glorify the lives of the black masses, but only succeeded in making their lives seem *exotic* as literary themes.

RALPH ELLISON

Review of Jones's Blues People [1964]

In his review of LeRoi Jones's 1963 essay collection *Blues People* (p. 694) for *The New York Review of Books*, Ralph Ellison (p. 430) asserts that African Americans represent a vital part of American culture. He dismisses the division between "mainstream" and black culture proposed by Jones, offering instead a vision of "cultural complexity." Ellison argues that black people have shaped so-called mainstream culture from America's

beginning, and that Jones's narrow idea of black culture leaves no room for people with diverse backgrounds, experiences, and influences—echoing here a key point of his disagreement with Irving Howe (p. 659). Throughout this essay, Ellison draws on a wide variety of black and white writers and critics to develop his position that individuals defy narrow characterization and that art itself is larger than political protest.

From *The New York Review of Books,* February 6, 1964; reprinted in Ralph Ellison, *Shadow and Act* (New York: Random House, 1964), pp. 247–58.

In his Introduction to *Blues People* LeRoi Jones advises us to approach the work as

> ... a strictly theoretical endeavor. Theoretical, in that none of the questions it poses can be said to have been answered definitely or for all time (sic!), etc. In fact, the whole book proposes more questions than it will answer. The only questions it will properly move to answer have, I think, been answered already within the patterns of American life. We need only give these patterns serious scrutiny and draw certain permissible conclusions.

It is a useful warning and one hopes that it will be regarded by those jazz publicists who have the quite irresponsible habit of sweeping up any novel pronouncement written about jazz and slapping it upon the first available record liner as the latest insight into the mysteries of American Negro expression.

Jones would take his subject seriously—as the best of jazz critics have always done—and he himself should be so taken. He has attempted to place the blues within the context of a total culture and to see this

native art form through the disciplines of sociology, anthropology and (though he seriously underrates its importance in the creating of a viable theory) history, and he spells out explicitly his assumptions concerning the relation between the blues, the people who created them and the larger American culture. Although I find several of his assumptions questionable, this is valuable in itself. It would be well if all jazz critics did likewise; not only would it expose those who have no business in the field, but it would sharpen the thinking of the few who have something enlightening to contribute. *Blues People,* like much that is written by Negro Americans at the present moment, takes on an inevitable resonance from the Freedom Movement, but it is in itself characterized by a straining for a note of militancy which is, to say the least, distracting. Its introductory mood of scholarly analysis frequently shatters into a dissonance of accusation, and one gets the impression that while Jones wants to perform a crucial task which he feels *someone* should take on—as indeed someone should—he is frustrated by the restraint demanded of the critical pen and would like to pick up a club.

Perhaps this explains why Jones, who is also a poet and editor of a poetry magazine, gives little attention to the blues as lyric, as a form of poetry. He appears to be attracted to the blues for what he believes they tell us of the sociology of Negro American identity and attitude. Thus, after beginning with the circumstances in which he sees their origin, he considers the ultimate values of American society:

> The Negro as slave is one thing. The Negro as American is quite another. But the *path* the slave took to "citizenship" is what I want to look at. And I make my analogy through the slave citizen's music—through the music that is most closely associated with him: blues and a later, but parallel, development, jazz. And it seems to me that if the Negro represents, or is symbolic of, something in and about the nature of American culture, this certainly should be revealed by his characteristic music. . . . I am saying that if the music of the Negro in America, in all its permutations, is subjected to a socio-anthropological as well as musical scrutiny, something about the essential nature of the Negro's existence in this country ought to be revealed, as well as something about the essential nature of this country, i.e., society as a whole. . . .

The tremendous burden of sociology which Jones would place upon this body of music is enough to give even the blues the blues. At one point he tells us that "the one peculiar reference to the drastic change in the Negro from slavery to 'citizenship' is in his music." And later with more precision, he states:

> . . . The point I want to make most evident here is that I cite the beginning of the blues as one beginning of American Negroes. Or, let me say, the reaction and subsequent relation of the Negro's experience in this country in *his* English is one beginning of the Negro's conscious appearance on the American scene.

No one could quarrel with Mr. Jones's stress upon beginnings. In 1833, two hundred and fourteen years after the first Africans were brought to these shores as slaves, a certain Mrs. Lydia Maria Child, a leading member of the American Anti-Slavery Society, published a paper entitled: *An Appeal in Favor of That Class of Americans Called Africans*. I am uncertain to what extent it actually reveals Mrs. Child's ideas concerning the complex relationship between time, place, cultural and/or national identity and race, but her title sounds like a fine bit of contemporary ironic *signifying*— "signifying" here meaning, in the unwritten dictionary of American Negro usage, "rhetorical understatements." It tells us much of the thinking of her opposition, and it reminds us that as late as the 1890s, a time when Negro composers, singers, dancers and comedians dominated the American musical stage, popular Negro songs (including James Weldon Johnson's "Under the Bamboo Tree," now immortalized by T. S. Eliot[1]) were commonly referred to as "Ethiopian Airs."

Perhaps more than any other people, Americans have been locked in a deadly struggle with time, with history. We've fled the past and trained ourselves to suppress, if not forget, troublesome details of the national memory, and a great part of our optimism, like our progress, has been bought at the cost of ignoring the processes through which we've arrived at any given moment in our national existence. We've fought continuously with one another over who and what we are, and, with the exception of the Negro, over who and what is American. Jones is aware of this and, although he embarrasses his own argument, his emphasis is to the point.

For it would seem that while Negroes have been undergoing a process of "Americanization" from a time preceding the birth of this nation—including the fusing of their blood lines with other non-African strains, there has persisted a stubborn confusion as to their American identity. Somehow it was assumed that the Negroes, of all the diverse American peoples, would remain unaffected by the climate, the weather, the political circumstances—from which not even slaves were exempt—the social structures, the national manners, the modes of production and the tides of the market, the national ideals, the conflicts of values, the

---

1. Johnson wrote the lyrics to this 1901 international hit with Bob Cole, with the music composed by his brother J. Rosamond Johnson; T. S. Eliot incorporated the lyrics in his 1932 play/poem *Sweeney Agonistes*.

rising and falling of national morale, or the complex give and take of acculturalization which was undergone by all others who found their existence within the American democracy. This confusion still persists and it is Mr. Jones's concern with it which gives *Blues People* a claim upon our attention.

Mr. Jones sees the American Negro as the product of a series of transformations, starting with the enslaved African, who became Afro-American slave, who became the American slave, who became, in turn, the highly qualified "citizen" whom we know today. The slave began by regarding himself as enslaved African, during the time when he still spoke his native language, or remembered it, practiced such aspects of his native religion as were possible and expressed himself musically in modes which were essentially African. These cultural traits became transmuted as the African lost consciousness of his African background, and his music, his religion, his language and his speech gradually became that of the American Negro. His sacred music became the spirituals, his work songs and dance music became the blues and primitive jazz, and his religion became a form of Afro-American Christianity. With the end of slavery Jones sees the development of jazz and the blues as results of the more varied forms of experience made available to the freedman. By the twentieth century the blues divided and became, on the one hand, a professionalized form of entertainment, while remaining, on the other, a form of folklore.

By which I suppose he means that some Negroes remained in the country and sang a crude form of the blues, while others went to the city, became more sophisticated, and paid to hear Ma Rainey,[2] Bessie, or some of the other Smith girls sing them in night clubs or theatres. Jones gets this mixed up with ideas of social class—middle-class Negroes, whatever that term actually means, and light-skinned Negroes, or those Negroes corrupted by what Jones calls "White" culture, preferring the "classic" blues, and black, uncorrupted, country Negroes preferring "country blues."

For as with his music, so with the Negro. As Negroes became "middle-class" they rejected their tradition and themselves. "...they wanted any self which the mainstream dictated, and the mainstream *always* dictated. And this black middle class, in turn, tried always to dictate that self, or this image of a whiter Negro, to the poorer, blacker Negroes."

One would get the impression that there was a rigid correlation between color, education, income and the Negro's preference in music. But what are we to say of a white-skinned Negro with brown freckles who owns sixteen oil wells sunk in a piece of Texas land once farmed by his ex-slave parents who were a blue-eyed, white-skinned, red-headed (kinky) Negro woman from Virginia and a blue-gummed, black-skinned, curly-haired Negro male from Mississippi, and who not only sang bass in a Holy Roller church, played the market and voted Republican but collected blues recordings and was a walking depository of blues tradition? Jones's theory no more allows for the existence of such a Negro than it allows for himself; but that "concord of sensibilities" which has been defined as the meaning of culture, allows for much more variety than Jones would admit.

Much the same could be said of Jones's treatment of the jazz during the thirties, when he claims its broader acceptance (i.e., its economic "success" as entertainment) led to a dilution, to the loss of much of its "black" character which caused a certain group of rebellious Negro musicians to create the "anti-mainstream" jazz style called bebop.

Jones sees bop as a conscious gesture of separatism, ignoring the fact that the creators of the style were seeking, whatever their musical intentions—and they were the least political of men—a fresh form of entertainment which would allow them their fair share of the entertainment market, which had been dominated by whites during the swing era. And although the boppers were reacting, at least in part, to the high artistic achievement of Armstrong, Hawkins, Basie and Ellington (all Negroes, all masters of the blues-jazz tradition), Jones sees their music as a recognition of his contention "that when you are black in a society where black is an extreme liability [it] is one thing, but to understand that it is the society which is lacking and is

2. Gertrude "Ma" Rainey (1886–1939) was one of the first professional blues singers; known as "The Mother of the Blues," she was among the first blues singers to record.

impossibly deformed because of this lack, and not *yourself*, isolates you even more from that society."

Perhaps. But today nothing succeeds like rebellion (which Jones as a "beat" poet should know) and while a few boppers went to Europe to escape, or became Muslims, others took the usual tours for the State Department. Whether this makes *them* "middle class" in Jones's eyes I can't say, but his assertions—which are fine as personal statement—are not in keeping with the facts; his theory flounders before that complex of human motives which makes human history, and which is so characteristic of the American Negro.

Read as a record of an earnest young man's attempt to come to grips with his predicament as Negro American during a most turbulent period of our history, *Blues People* may be worth the reader's time. Taken as a theory of American Negro culture, it can only contribute more confusion than clarity. For Jones has stumbled over that ironic obstacle which lies in the path of any who would fashion a theory of American Negro culture while ignoring the intricate network of connections which binds Negroes to the larger society. To do so is to attempt a delicate brain surgery with a switch-blade. And it is possible that any viable theory of Negro American culture obligates us to fashion a more adequate theory of American culture as a whole. The heel bone is, after all, connected, through its various linkages, to the head bone.[3] Attempt a serious evaluation of our national morality and up jumps the so-called Negro problem. Attempt to discuss jazz as a hermetic expression of Negro sensibility and immediately we must consider what the "mainstream" of American music really is.

Here political categories are apt to confuse, for while Negro slaves were socially, politically and economically separate (but only in a special sense even here), they were, in a cultural sense, much closer than Jones's theory allows him to admit.

"A slave," writes Jones, "cannot be a man." But what, one might ask, of those moments when he feels his metabolism aroused by the rising of the sap in spring? What of his identity among other slaves? With his wife? And isn't it closer to the truth that far from considering themselves only in terms of that abstraction, "a slave," the enslaved really thought of themselves as *men* who had been unjustly enslaved? And isn't the true answer to Mr. Jones's question, "What are you going to be when you grow up?" not, as he gives it, "a slave" but most probably a coachman, a teamster, a cook, the best damned steward on the Mississippi, the best jockey in Kentucky, a butler, a farmer, a stud, or, hopefully, a free man! Slavery was a most vicious system and those who endured and survived it a tough people, but it was *not* (and this is important for Negroes to remember for the sake of their own sense of who and what their grandparents were) a state of absolute repression.

A slave was, to the extent that he was a *musician*, one who expressed himself in music, a man who realized himself in the world of sound. Thus, while he might stand in awe before the superior technical ability of a white musician, and while he was forced to recognize a superior social status, he would never feel awed before the music which the technique of the white musician made available. His attitude as "musician" would lead him to seek to possess the music expressed through the technique, but until he could do so he would hum, whistle, sing or play the tunes to the best of his ability on any available instrument. And it was, indeed, out of the tension between desire and ability that the techniques of jazz emerged. This was likewise true of American Negro choral singing. For this, no literary explanation, no cultural analyses, no political slogans—indeed, not even a high degree of social or political freedom—was required. For the art—the blues, the spirituals, the jazz, the dance—was what we had in place of freedom.

Technique was then, as today, the key to creative freedom, but before this came a will toward expression. Thus, Jones's theory to the contrary. Negro musicians have never, as a group, felt alienated from any music sounded within their hearing, and it is my theory that it would be impossible to pinpoint the time when they were not shaping what Jones calls the mainstream of American music. Indeed, what group of musicians has made more of the sound of the American experience? Nor am I confining my statement to

---

3. Reference to "Dem Dry Bones," a traditional spiritual inspired by Ezekiel 37: 1–14, with music attributed to James Weldon Johnson and lyrics attributed to J. Rosamond Johnson.

the sound of the slave experience, but am saying that the most authoritative rendering of America in music is that of American Negroes.

For as I see it, from the days of their introduction into the colonies, Negroes have taken, with the ruthlessness of those without articulate investments in cultural styles, whatever they could of European music, making of it that which would, when blended with the cultural tendencies inherited from Africa, express their own sense of life—while rejecting the rest. Perhaps this is only another way of saying that whatever the degree of injustice and inequality sustained by the slaves, American culture was, even before the official founding of the nation, pluralistic; and it was the African's origin in cultures in which art was highly functional which gave him an edge in shaping the music and dance of this nation.

The question of social and cultural snobbery is important here. The effectiveness of Negro music and dance is first recorded in the journals and letters of travelers but it is important to remember that they saw and understood only that which they were prepared to accept. Thus a Negro dancing a courtly dance appeared comic from the outside simply because the dancer was a slave. But to the Negro dancing it—and there is ample evidence that he danced it well—burlesque or satire might have been the point, which might have been difficult for a white observer to even imagine. During the 1870s Lafcadio Hearn[4] reports that the best singers of Irish songs, in Irish dialect, were Negro dock workers in Cincinnati, and advertisements from slavery days described escaped slaves who spoke in Scottish dialect. The master artisans of the South were slaves, and white Americans have been walking Negro walks, talking Negro flavored talk (and prizing it when spoken by Southern belles), dancing Negro dances and singing Negro melodies far too long to talk of a "mainstream" of American culture to which they're alien.

Jones attempts to impose an ideology upon this cultural complexity, and this might be useful if he knew enough of the related subjects to make it interesting. But his version of the blues lacks a sense of the excitement

and surprise of men living in the world—of enslaved and politically weak men successfully imposing their values upon a powerful society through song and dance.

The blues speak to us simultaneously of the tragic and the comic aspects of the human condition and they express a profound sense of life shared by many Negro Americans precisely because their lives have combined these modes. This has been the heritage of a people who for hundreds of years could not celebrate birth or dignify death and whose need to live despite the dehumanizing pressures of slavery developed an endless capacity for laughing at their painful experiences. This is a group experience shared by many Negroes, and any effective study of the blues would treat them first as poetry and as ritual. Jones makes a distinction between classic and country blues, the one being entertainment and the other folklore. But the distinction is false. Classic blues were both entertainment *and* a form of folklore. When they were sung professionally in theatres, they were entertainment; when danced to in the form of recordings or used as a means of transmitting the traditional verses and their wisdom, they were folklore. There are levels of time and function involved here, and the blues which might be used in one place as entertainment (as gospel music is now being used in night clubs and on theatre stages) might be put to a ritual use in another. Bessie Smith might have been a "blues queen" to the society at large, but within the tighter Negro community where the blues were part of a total way of life, and a major expression of an attitude toward life, she was a priestess, a celebrant who affirmed the values of the group and man's ability to deal with chaos.

It is unfortunate that Jones thought it necessary to ignore the aesthetic nature of the blues in order to make his ideological point, for he might have come much closer had he considered the blues not as politics but as art. This would have still required the disciplines of anthropology and sociology—but as practiced by Constance Rourke,[5] who was well aware of how much of American cultural expression is Negro. And he could learn much from the Cambridge School's[6] discoveries

---

4. Patrick Lafcadio Hearn (1850–1904), Greek-Irish writer.
5. White American author and professor (1885–1941) whose books include *American Humor: A Study of the National Character* (1953).
6. Reference to the department of social anthropology developed at Cambridge University in England.

of the connection between poetry, drama and ritual as a means of analyzing how the blues function in their proper environment. Simple taste should have led Jones to Stanley Edgar Hyman's work on the blues[7] instead of Paul Oliver's sadly misdirected effort.

For the blues are not primarily concerned with civil rights or obvious political protest; they are an art form and thus a transcendence of those conditions created within the Negro community by the denial of social justice. As such they are one of the techniques through which Negroes have survived and kept their courage during that long period when many whites assumed, as some still assume, they were afraid.

Much has been made of the fact that *Blues People* is one of the few books by a Negro to treat the subject. Unfortunately for those who expect that Negroes would have a special insight into this mysterious art, this is not enough. Here, too, the critical intelligence must perform the difficult task which only it can perform.

LARRY NEAL

The Black Arts Movement [1968]

In the summer of 1968, *The Drama Review* published a special issue on black theater, which included the following essay by the poet, playwright, and critic Larry Neal (1937–1981). In this essay, Neal systematically outlines the rationale and direction of the emerging Black Arts Movement, which he views as the "aesthetic and spiritual sister of the Black Power concept." Like James Baldwin in "Everybody's Protest Novel" (p. 485), Neal rejects protest literature. Unlike Baldwin, however, who sought an artistic form that was less restrictive than protest literature, Neal argues for a tighter artistic focus. He asserts that the problem with protest writing is that it is geared to a white audience and that black writers should write for a black audience. For Neal, a key component of making art for black people is the development of a "black aesthetic" that is grounded in African American and third world cultures and can destroy "white ways of looking at the world."

After receiving his Masters from the University of Pennsylvania in 1963, Neal moved to New York City and became arts editor of *The Liberator*, a black nationalist magazine founded in 1960 that published many of the early works of the Black Arts Movement. He was co-editor (with the poet and critic LeRoi Jones/Amiri Baraka, p. 694) of *Black Fire* (1968), the central anthology of the Black Arts Movement.

From *The Drama Review,* Summer 1968; reprinted in Addison Gayle Jr., ed., *The Black Aesthetic* (Garden City, N.Y.: Doubleday, 1971), pp. 273–90.

1.

The Black Arts Movement is radically opposed to any concept of the artist that alienates him from his community. Black Art is the aesthetic and spiritual sister of the Black Power concept. As such, it envisions an art that speaks directly to the needs and aspirations of Black America. In order to perform this task, the Black Arts Movement proposes a radical reordering of the western cultural aesthetic. It proposes a separate symbolism, mythology, critique, and iconology. The Black Arts and the Black Power concept both relate broadly to the Afro-American's desire for self-determination and nationhood. Both concepts are nationalistic. One is concerned with the relationship between art and politics; the other with the art of politics.

Recently, these two movements have begun to merge: the political values inherent in the Black Power concept are now finding concrete expression in the aesthetics of Afro-American dramatists, poets, choreographers, musicians, and novelists. A main tenet of Black Power is the necessity for Black people to define

7. Hyman's writings on the blues include his essay "The Blues" (1964).

the world in their own terms. The Black artist has made the same point in the context of aesthetics. The two movements postulate that there are in fact and in spirit two Americas—one black, one white. The Black artist takes this to mean that his primary duty is to speak to the spiritual and cultural needs of Black people. Therefore, the main thrust of this new breed of contemporary writers is to confront the contradictions arising out of the Black man's experience in the racist West. Currently, these writers are re-evaluating western aesthetics, the traditional role of the writer, and the social function of art. Implicit in this re-evaluation is the need to develop a "black aesthetic." It is the opinion of many Black writers, I among them, that the Western aesthetic has run its course: it is impossible to construct anything meaningful within its decaying structure. We advocate a cultural revolution in art and ideas. The cultural values inherent in western history must either be radicalized or destroyed, and we will probably find that even radicalization is impossible. In fact, what is needed is a whole new system of ideas. Poet Don L. Lee[1] expresses it:

> . . . We must destroy Faulkner, dick, jane, and other perpetuators of evil. It's time for DuBois, Nat Turner, and Kwame Nkrumah. As Frantz Fanon points out: destroy the culture and you destroy the people. This must not happen. Black artists are culture stabilizers; bringing back old values, and introducing new ones. Black Art will talk to the people and with the will of the people stop impending "protective custody."

The Black Arts Movement eschews "protest" literature. It speaks directly to Black people. Implicit in the concept of "protest" literature, as Brother Knight[2] has made clear, is an appeal to white morality:

> Now any Black man who masters the technique of his particular art form, who adheres to the white aesthetic, and who directs his work toward a white audience is, in one sense, protesting. And implicit in the act of protest is the belief that a change will

be forthcoming once the masters are aware of the protestor's "grievance" (the very word connotes begging, supplications to the gods). Only when that belief has faded and protestings end, will Black art begin.

Brother Knight also has some interesting statements about the development of a "Black aesthetic":

> Unless the Black artist establishes a "Black aesthetic" he will have no future at all. To accept the white aesthetic is to accept and validate a society that will not allow him to live. The Black artist must create new forms and new values, sing new songs (or purify old ones); and along with other Black authorities, he must create a new history, new symbols, myths and legends (and purify old ones by fire). And the Black artist, in creating his own aesthetic, must be accountable for it only to the Black people. Further, he must hasten his own dissolution as an individual (in the Western sense)—painful though the process may be, having been breast-fed the poison of "individual experience."

When we speak of a "Black aesthetic" several things are meant. First, we assume that there is already in existence the basis for such an aesthetic. Essentially, it consists of an African-American cultural tradition. But this aesthetic is finally, by implication, broader than that tradition. It encompasses most of the useable elements of Third World culture. The motive behind the Black aesthetic is the destruction of the white thing, the destruction of white ideas, and white ways of looking at the world. The new aesthetic is mostly predicated on an Ethics which asks the question: whose vision of the world is finally more meaningful, ours or the white oppressors'? What is truth? Or more precisely, whose truth shall we express, that of the oppressed or of the oppressors? These are basic questions. Black intellectuals of previous decades failed to ask them. Further, national and international affairs demand that we appraise the world in terms of our own interests. It is clear that the question of human survival is at the

---

1. Lee (b. 1942) later changed his name to Haki Madhubuti.
2. Poet Etheridge Knight (1931–91); the following two passages are from his response to a January 1968 survey in *Negro Digest*, "Black Writers' Views on Literary Lions and Values."

core of contemporary experience. The Black artist must address himself to this reality in the strongest terms possible. In a context of world upheaval, ethics and aesthetics must interact positively and be consistent with the demands for a more spiritual world. Consequently, the Black Arts Movement is an ethical movement. Ethical, that is, from the viewpoint of the oppressed. And much of the oppression confronting the Third World and Black America is directly traceable to the Euro-American cultural sensibility. This sensibility, anti-human in nature, has, until recently, dominated the psyches of most Black artists and intellectuals; it must be destroyed before the Black creative artist can have a meaningful role in the transformation of society.

It is this natural reaction to an alien sensibility that informs the cultural attitudes of the Black Arts and the Black Power movement. It is a profound ethical sense that makes a Black artist question a society in which art is one thing and the actions of men another. The Black Arts Movement believes that your ethics and your aesthetics are one. That the contradictions between ethics and aesthetics in western society is symptomatic of a dying culture.

The term "Black Arts" is of ancient origin, but it was first used in a positive sense by LeRoi Jones:

> We are unfair
> And unfair
> We are black magicians
> Black arts we make
> in black labs of the heart
>
> The fair are fair
> and deathly white
>
> The day will not save them
> And we own the night

There is also a section of the poem "Black Dada Nihilismus" that carries the same motif. But a fuller amplification of the nature of the new aesthetics appears in the poem "Black Art":

> Poems are bullshit unless they are
> teeth or trees or lemons piled
> on a step. Or black ladies dying

> of men leaving nickel hearts
> beating them down. Fuck poems
> and they are useful, would they shoot
> come at you, love what you are,
> breathe like wrestlers, or shudder
> strangely after peeing. We want live
> words of the hip world, live flesh &
> coursing blood. Hearts and Brains
> Souls splintering fire. We want poems
> like fists beating niggers out of Jocks
> or dagger poems in the slimy bellies
> of the owner-jews . . .

Poetry is a concrete function, an action. No more abstractions. Poems are physical entities: fists, daggers, airplane poems, and poems that shoot guns. Poems are transformed from physical objects into personal forces:

> . . . Put it on him poem. Strip him naked
> to the world. Another bad poem cracking
> steel knuckles in a jewlady's mouth
> Poem scream poison gas on breasts in green
>   berets . . .

Then the poem affirms the integral relationship between Black Art and Black people:

> . . . Let Black people understand
> that they are the lovers and the sons
> of lovers and warriors and sons
> of warriors Are poems & poets &
> all the loveliness here in the world

It ends with the following lines, a central assertion in both the Black Arts Movement and the philosophy of Black Power:

> We want a black poem. And a
> Black World.
> Let the world be a Black Poem
> And let All Black People Speak This Poem
> Silently
> Or LOUD

The poem comes to stand for the collective conscious and unconscious of Black America—the real impulse in back of the Black Power movement, which is the will toward self-determination and nationhood, a radical reordering of the nature and function of both art and the artist.

2.

In the spring of 1964, LeRoi Jones, Charles Patterson, William Patterson, Clarence Reed, Johnny Moore, and a number of other Black artists opened the Black Arts Repertoire Theatre School. They produced a number of plays including Jones' *Experimental Death Unit # One*, *Black Mass*, *Jello*, and *Dutchman*.[3] They also initiated a series of poetry readings and concerts. These activities represented the most advanced tendencies in the movement and were of excellent artistic quality. The Black Arts School came under immediate attack by the New York power structure. The Establishment, fearing Black creativity, did exactly what it was expected to do—it attacked the theatre and all of its values. In the meantime, the school was granted funds by OEO through HARYOU-ACT.[4] Lacking a cultural program itself, HARYOU turned to the only organization which addressed itself to the needs of the community. In keeping with its "revolutionary" cultural ideas, the Black Arts Theatre took its programs into the streets of Harlem. For three months, the theatre presented plays, concerts, and poetry readings to the people of the community. Plays that shattered the illusions of the American body politic, and awakened Black people to the meaning of their lives.

Then the hawks from the OEO moved in and chopped off the funds. Again, this should have been expected. The Black Arts Theatre stood in radical opposition to the feeble attitudes about culture of the "War On Poverty" bureaucrats. And later, because of internal problems, the theatre was forced to close. But the Black Arts group proved that the community could be served by a valid and dynamic art. It also proved that there was a definite need for a cultural revolution in the Black community.

With the closing of the Black Arts Theatre, the implications of what Brother Jones and his colleagues were trying to do took on even more significance. Black Art groups sprang up on the West Coast and the idea spread to Detroit, Philadelphia, Jersey City, New Orleans, and Washington, D.C. Black Arts movements began on the campuses of San Francisco State College, Fisk University, Lincoln University, Hunter College in the Bronx, Columbia University, and Oberlin College. In Watts, after the rebellion, Maulana Karenga welded the Black Arts Movement into a cohesive cultural ideology which owed much to the work of LeRoi Jones. Karenga sees culture as the most important element in the struggle for self-determination:

> Culture is the basis of all ideas, images and actions. To move is to move culturally, i.e. by a set of values given to you by your culture.
>
> Without a culture Negroes are only a set of reactions to white people.

The seven criteria for culture are:

1. Mythology
2. History
3. Social Organization
4. Political Organization
5. Economic Organization
6. Creative Motif
7. Ethos

In drama, LeRoi Jones represents the most advanced aspects of the movement. He is its prime mover and chief designer. In a poetic essay entitled "The Revolutionary Theatre," he outlines the iconology of the movement:

> The Revolutionary Theatre should force change: it should be change. (All their faces turned into the lights and you work on them black nigger magic,

---

3. The Black Arts Repertory Theatre School, known as BART/S, produced *Experimental Death Unit #1* in 1965, *A Black Mass* in 1966, *J-E-L-L-O* in 1965, and *Dutchman* in 1964.
4. The local Harlem Youth Opportunities Unlimited (HARYOU) Act was funded by the federal Office of Economic Opportunity (OEO).

and cleanse them at having seen the ugliness. And if the beautiful see themselves, they will love themselves.) We are preaching virtue again, but by that to mean NOW, toward what seems the most constructive use of the word.

The theatre that Jones proposes is inextricably linked to the Afro-American political dynamic. And such a link is perfectly consistent with Black America's contemporary demands. For theatre is potentially the most social of all of the arts. It is an integral part of the socializing process. It exists in direct relationship to the audience it claims to serve. The decadence and inanity of the contemporary American theatre is an accurate reflection of the state of American society. Albee's *Who's Afraid of Virginia Woolf?*[5] is very American: sick white lives in a homosexual hell hole. The theatre of white America is escapist, refusing to confront concrete reality. Into this cultural emptiness come the musicals, an up-tempo version of the same stale lives. And the use of Negroes in such plays as *Hello Dolly* and *Hallelujah Baby*[6] does not alter their nature; it compounds the problem. These plays are simply hipper versions of the minstrel show. They present Negroes acting out the hang-ups of middle-class white America. Consequently, the American theatre is a palliative prescribed to bourgeois patients who refuse to see the world as it is. Or, more crucially, as the world sees them. It is no accident, therefore, that the most "important" plays come from Europe—Brecht, Weiss, and Ghelderode.[7] And even these have begun to run dry.

The Black Arts theatre, the theatre of LeRoi Jones, is a radical alternative to the sterility of the American theatre. It is primarily a theatre of the Spirit, confronting the Black man in his interaction with his brothers and with the white thing.

> Our theatre will show victims so that their brothers in the audience will be better able to understand

that they are the brothers of victims, and that they themselves are blood brothers. And what we show must cause the blood to rush, so that pre-revolutionary temperaments will be bathed in this blood, and it will cause their deepest souls to move, and they will find themselves tensed and clenched, even ready to die, at what the soul has been taught. We will scream and cry, murder, run through the streets in agony, if it means some soul will be moved, moved to actual life understanding of what the world is, and what it ought to be. We are preaching virtue and feeling, and a natural sense of the self in the world. All men live in the world, and the world ought to be a place for them to live.

The victims in the world of Jones' early plays are Clay, murdered by the white bitch-goddess in *Dutchman*, and Walker Vessels, the revolutionary in *The Slave*. Both of these plays present Black men in transition. Clay, the middle-class Negro trying to get himself a little action from Lula, digs himself and his own truth only to get murdered after telling her like it really is:

> Just let me bleed you, you loud whore, and one poem vanished. A whole people neurotics, struggling to keep from being sane. And the only thing that would cure the neurosis would be your murder. Simple as that. I mean if I murdered you, then other white people would understand me. You understand? No. I guess not. If Bessie Smith had killed some white people she wouldn't needed that music. She could have talked very straight and plain about the world. Just straight two and two are four. Money. Power. Luxury. Like that. All of them. Crazy niggers turning their back on sanity. When all it needs is that simple act. Just murder. Would make us all sane.

But Lula understands, and she kills Clay first. In a perverse way it is Clay's nascent knowledge of himself

---

5. Edward Albee's play opened on Broadway in 1962 and won the 1963 Tony Award for Best Play and the 1963 Pulitzer Prize for Drama.

6. In 1967, a black cast version of the 1964 Broadway hit *Hello, Dolly* opened on Broadway, starring Pearl Bailey (1918–90) and Cab Calloway (1907–94); *Hallelujah, Baby!* opened on Broadway in 1967 starring Leslie Uggams (b. 1943) and won the Tony Award for Best Musical.

7. German playwright and director Bertolt Brecht (1898–1956); German writer and artist Peter Weiss (1916–82); Belgian playwright Michel de Ghelderode (1898–1962).

that threatens the existence of Lula's idea of the world. Symbolically, and in fact, the relationship between Clay (Black America) and Lula (white America) is rooted in the historical castration of black manhood. And in the twisted psyche of white America, the Black man is both an object of love and hate. Analogous attitudes exist in most Black Americans, but for decidedly different reasons. Clay is doomed when he allows himself to participate in Lula's "fantasy" in the first place. It is the fantasy to which Frantz Fanon alludes in *The Wretched of the Earth* and *Black Skins, White Mask*:[8] the native's belief that he can acquire the oppressor's power by acquiring his symbols, one of which is the white woman. When Clay finally digs himself it is too late.

Walker Vessels, in *The Slave*, is Clay reincarnated as the revolutionary confronting problems inherited from his contact with white culture. He returns to the home of his ex-wife, a white woman, and her husband, a literary critic. The play is essentially about Walker's attempt to destroy his white past. For it is the past, with all of its painful memories, that is really the enemy of the revolutionary. It is impossible to move until history is either recreated or comprehended. Unlike Todd, in Ralph Ellison's *Invisible Man*,[9] Walker cannot fall outside history. Instead, Walker demands a confrontation with history, a final shattering of bullshit illusions. His only salvation lies in confronting the physical and psychological forces that have made him and his people powerless. Therefore, he comes to understand that the world must be restructured along spiritual imperatives. But in the interim it is basically a question of *who* has power:

EASLEY. You're so wrong about everything. So terribly, sickeningly wrong. What can you change? What do you hope to change? Do you think Negroes are better people than whites . . . that they can govern a society *better* than whites? That they'll be more judicious or more tolerant? Do you think they'll make fewer mistakes? I mean really, if the Western white man has proved one thing . . . it's the futility of modern society. So the have-not peoples become the haves. Even so, will that change the essential functions of the world? Will there be more love or beauty in the world . . . more knowledge . . . because of it?

WALKER. Probably. Probably there will be more . . . if more people have a chance to understand what it is. But that's not even the point. It comes down to baser human endeavor than any social-political thinking. What does it matter if there's more love or beauty? Who the fuck cares? Is that what the Western ofay thought while he was ruling . . . that his rule somehow brought more love and beauty into the world? Oh, he might have thought that concomitantly, while sipping a gin rickey and scratching his ass . . . but that was not ever the point. Not even on the Crusades. The point is that you had your chance, darling, now these other folks have theirs. *Quietly.* Now they have theirs.

EASLEY. God, what an ugly idea.

This confrontation between the black radical and the white liberal is symbolic of larger confrontations occurring between the Third World and Western society. It is a confrontation between the colonizer and the colonized, the slavemaster and the slave. Implicit in Easley's remarks is the belief that the white man is culturally and politically superior to the Black Man. Even though Western society has been traditionally violent in its relation with the Third World, it sanctimoniously deplores violence or self assertion on the part of the enslaved. And the Western mind, with clever rationalizations, equates the violence of the oppressed with the violence of the oppressor. So that when the native preaches self-determination, the Western white man cleverly misconstrues it to mean hate of *all* white men. When the Black political radical warns his people not to trust white politicians of the left and the right, but instead to organize separately on the basis of power, the white man cries: "racism in reverse." Or he will say, as many of them do today: "We deplore both white and black racism." As if the two could be equated.

There is a minor element in *The Slave* which assumes great importance in a later play entitled *Jello*. Here I refer to the emblem of Walker's army: a

---

8. Fanon's *Black Skin, White Masks* was originally published in French in 1952.
9. The narrator in Ellison's 1952 novel is unnamed; Todd is the name of the protagonist of Ellison's 1944 short story "Flying Home."

red-mouthed grinning field slave. The revolutionary army has taken one of the most hated symbols of the Afro-American past and radically altered its meaning.[1] This is the supreme act of freedom, available only to those who have liberated themselves psychically. Jones amplifies this inversion of emblem and symbol in *Jello* by making Rochester (Ratfester) of the old Jack Benny (Penny) program[2] into a revolutionary nationalist. Ratfester, ordinarily the supreme embodiment of the Uncle Tom Clown, surprises Jack Penny by turning on the other side of the nature of the Black man. He skillfully, and with an evasive black humor, robs Penny of all of his money. But Ratfester's actions are "moral." That is to say, Ratfester is getting his back pay; payment of a long over-due debt to the Black man. Ratfester's sensibilities are different from Walker's. He is *blues people* smiling and shuffling while trying to figure out how to destroy the white thing. And like the blues man, he is the master of the understatement. Or in the Afro-American folk tradition, he is the signifying Monkey, Shine, and Stagolee[3] all rolled into one. There are no sterotypes any more. History has killed Uncle Tom. Because even Uncle Tom has a breaking point beyond which he will not be pushed. Cut deeply enough into the most docile Negro, and you will find a conscious murderer. Behind the lyrics of the blues and the shuffling porter loom visions of white throats being cut and cities burning.

Jones' particular power as a playwright does not rest solely on his revolutionary vision, but is instead derived from his deep lyricism and spiritual outlook. In many ways, he is fundamentally more a poet than a playwright. And it is his lyricism that gives body to his plays. Two important plays in this regard are *Black Mass* and *Slave Ship*. *Black Mass* is based on the Muslim myth of Yacub.[4] According to this myth, Yacub, a

Black scientist, developed the means of grafting different colors of the Original Black Nation until a White Devil was created. In *Black Mass*, Yacub's experiments produce a raving White Beast who is condemned to the coldest regions of the North. The other magicians implore Yacub to cease his experiments. But he insists on claiming the primacy of scientific knowledge over spiritual knowledge. The sensibility of the White Devil is alien, informed by lust and sensuality. The Beast is the consummate embodiment of evil, the beginning of the historical subjugation of the spiritual world.

Black Mass takes place in some pre-historical time. In fact, the concept of time, we learn, is the creation of an alien sensibility, that of the Beast. This is a deeply weighted play, a colloquy on the nature of man, and the relationship between legitimate spiritual knowledge and scientific knowledge. It is LeRoi Jones' most important play mainly because it is informed by a mythology that is wholly the creation of the Afro-American sensibility.

Further, Yacub's creation is not merely a scientific exercise. More fundamentally, it is the aesthetic impulse gone astray. The Beast is created merely for the sake of creation. Some artists assert a similar claim about the nature of art. They argue that art need not have a function. It is against this decadent attitude toward art— ramified throughout most of Western society—that the play militates. Yacub's real crime, therefore, is the introduction of a meaningless evil into a harmonious universe. The evil of the Beast is pervasive, corrupting everything and everyone it touches. What was beautiful is twisted into an ugly screaming thing. The play ends with destruction of the holy place of the Black Magicians. Now the Beast and his descendants roam the earth. An off-stage voice chants a call for the Jihad to begin. It is then that myth merges into legitimate his-

---

1. In Jones' study of Afro-American music, *Blues People,* we find the following observation: ". . . Even the adjective *funky,* which once meant to many Negroes merely a stink (usually associated with sex), was used to qualify the music as meaningful (the word became fashionable and is now almost useless). The social implication, then, was that even the old stereotype of a distinctive Negro smell that white America subscribed to could be turned against white America. For this smell now, real or not, was made a valuable characteristic of 'Negro-ness.' And 'Negro-ness,' by the fifties, for many Negroes (and whites) was the only strength left to American culture." [Neal's note]

2. A popular weekly radio program that ran from 1932 to 1955 starred Eddie Anderson as Benny's valet-chauffeur, Rochester.

3. The Signifying Monkey and Shine are mythic trickster figures; Stagolee is a mythic outlaw.

4. Jones's story is based on the doctrine of Yacub, which was first proclaimed by Wallace Fard Muhammad, the founder of the Nation of Islam, and developed by his successor, Elijah Muhammad.

tory, and we, the audience, come to understand that all history is merely someone's version of mythology.

Slave Ship presents a more immediate confrontation with history. In a series of expressionistic tableaux it depicts the horrors and the madness of the Middle Passage. It then moves through the period of slavery, early attempts at revolt, tendencies toward Uncle Tom–like reconciliation and betrayal, and the final act of liberation. There is no definite plot (LeRoi calls it a pageant), just a continuous rush of sound, groans, screams, and souls wailing for freedom and relief from suffering. This work has special affinities with the New Music of Sun Ra, John Coltrane, Albert Ayler, and Ornette Coleman.[5] Events are blurred, rising and falling in a stream of sound. Almost cinematically, the images flicker and fade against a heavy back-drop of rhythm. The language is spare, stripped to the essential. It is a play which almost totally eliminates the need for a text. It functions on the basis of movements and energy—the dramatic equivalent of the New Music.

Slave Ship's energy is, at base, ritualistic. As a matter of fact, to see the play any other way is to miss the point. All the New York reviewers, with the possible exception of John Lahr, were completely cut off from this central aspect of the play when it was performed at the Brooklyn Academy under the brilliant direction of Gilbert Moses.[6] One of the prime motivations behind the work is to suck the audience into a unique and very precise universe. The episodes of this "pageant" do not appear as strict interpretations of history. Rather, what we are digging is ritualized history. That is, history that allows emotional and religious participation on the part of the audience. And, like all good ritual, its purpose is to make the audience stronger, more sensitive to the historical realities that have shaped our lives and the lives of our ancestors. The play acts to extend memory. For black people to forget the realities posed by *Slave Ship* is to fall prey to an existential paralysis. History, like the blues, demands that we witness the painful events of our prior lives; and that we either confront these painful events or be destroyed by them.

3.

LeRoi Jones is the best known and the most advanced playwright of the movement, but he is not alone. There are other excellent playwrights who express the general mood of the Black Arts ideology. Among them are Ron Milner, Ed Bullins, Ben Caldwell, Jimmy Stewart, Joe White, Charles Patterson, Charles Fuller, Aisha Hughes, Carol Freeman, and Jimmy Garrett.

Ron Milner's *Who's Got His Own* is of particular importance. It strips bare the clashing attitudes of a contemporary Afro-American family. Milner's concern is with legitimate manhood and morality. The family in *Who's Got His Own* is in search of its conscience, or more precisely its own definition of life. On the day of his father's death, Tim and his family are forced to examine the inner fabric of their lives: the lies, self-deceits, and sense of powerlessness in a white world. The basic conflict, however, is internal. It is rooted in the historical search for black manhood. Tim's mother is representative of a generation of Christian Black women who have implicitly understood the brooding violence lurking in their men. And with this understanding, they have interposed themselves between their men and the object of that violence—the white man. Thus unable to direct his violence against the oppressor, the Black man becomes more frustrated and the sense of powerlessness deepens. Lacking the strength to be a man in the white world, he turns against his family. So the oppressed, as Fanon explains, constantly dreams violence against his oppressor, while killing his brother on fast weekends.

Tim's sister represents the Negro woman's attempt to acquire what Eldridge Cleaver calls "ultrafemininity." That is, the attributes of her white upper-class counterpart. Involved here is a rejection of the body-oriented life of the working class Black man, symbolized by the mother's traditional religion. The sister has an affair with a white upper-class liberal, ending in abortion. There are hints of lesbianism, i.e., a further rejection of the body. The sister's life is a pivotal factor

---

5. Jazz composer, keyboard player, and philosopher Sun Ra (born Herman Poole Blout, 1914–93); jazz composer and saxophonist Coltrane (1926–67); jazz composer, saxophonist, and singer Ayler (1936–70); and jazz composer, saxophonist, violinist, and trumpeter Coleman (b. 1930).
6. Moses (1942–95) won an Obie Award for directing the 1969 production of *Slave Ship* at the Brooklyn Academy of Music (BAM).

in the play. Much of the stripping away of falsehood initiated by Tim is directed at her life, which they have carefully kept hidden from the mother.

Tim is the product of the new Afro-American sensibility, informed by the psychological revolution now operative within Black America. He is a combination ghetto soul brother and militant intellectual, very hip and slightly flawed himself. He would change the world, but without comprehending the particular history that produced his "tyrannical" father. And he cannot be the man his father was—not until he truly understands his father. He must understand why his father allowed himself to be insulted daily by the "honky" types on the job; why he took a demeaning job in the "shit-house"; and why he spent on his family the violence that he should have directed against the white man. In short, Tim must confront the history of his family. And that is exactly what happens. Each character tells his story, exposing his falsehood to the other until a balance is reached.

Who's Got His Own is not the work of an alienated mind. Milner's main thrust is directed toward unifying the family around basic moral principles, toward bridging the "generation gap." Other Black playwrights, Jimmy Garrett for example, see the gap as unbridgeable.

Garrett's *We Own the Night* (see this issue of [*The Drama Review*], pp. 62–69) takes place during an armed insurrection. As the play opens we see the central characters defending a section of the city against attacks by white police. Johnny, the protagonist, is wounded. Some of his Brothers intermittently fire at attacking forces, while others look for medical help. A doctor arrives, forced at gun point. The wounded boy's mother also comes. She is a female Uncle Tom who berates the Brothers and their cause. She tries to get Johnny to leave. She is hysterical. The whole idea of Black people fighting white people is totally outside of her orientation. Johnny begins a vicious attack on his mother, accusing her of emasculating his father—a recurring theme in the sociology of the Black community. In Afro-American literature of previous decades the strong Black mother was the object of awe and respect. But in the new literature her status is ambivalent and laced with tension. Historically, Afro-American women have had to be the economic mainstays of the family. The oppressor allowed them to

have jobs while at the same time limiting the economic mobility of the Black man. Very often, therefore, the woman's aspirations and values are closely tied to those of the white power structure and not to those of her man. Since he cannot provide for his family the way white men do, she despises his weakness, tearing into him at every opportunity until, very often, there is nothing left but a shell.

The only way out of this dilemma is through revolution. It either must be an actual blood revolution, or one that psychically redirects the energy of the oppressed. Milner is fundamentally concerned with the latter and Garrett with the former. Communication between Johnny and his mother breaks down. The revolutionary imperative demands that men step outside the legal framework. It is a question of erecting *another* morality. The old constructs do not hold up, because adhering to them means consigning oneself to the oppressive reality. Johnny's mother is involved in the old constructs. Manliness is equated with white morality. And even though she claims to love her family (her men), the overall design of her ideas are against black manhood. In Garrett's play the mother's morality manifests itself in a deep-seated hatred of Black men; while in Milner's work the mother understands, but holds her men back.

The mothers that Garrett and Milner see represent the Old Spirituality—the Faith of the Fathers of which DuBois spoke. Johnny and Tim represent the New Spirituality. They appear to be a type produced by the upheavals of the colonial world of which Black America is a part. Johnny's assertion that he is a criminal is remarkably similar to the rebel's comments in Aimé Césaire's play, *Les Armes Miraculeuses* (*The Miraculous Weapons*). In that play the rebel, speaking to his mother, proclaims: "My name—an offense; my Christian name—humiliation; my status—a rebel; my age—the stone age." To which the mother replies: "My race—the human race. My religion—brotherhood." The Old Spirituality is generalized. It seeks to recognize Universal Humanity. The New Spirituality is specific. It begins by seeing the world from the concise point-of-view of the colonialized. Where the Old Spirituality would live with oppression while ascribing to the oppressors an innate goodness, the New Spirituality demands a radical shift in point-of-view. The colonialized native, the oppressed must, of necessity, subscribe to a *separate* morality. One that will liberate him and his people.

The assault against the Old Spirituality can sometimes be humorous. In Ben Caldwell's play, *The Militant Preacher,* a burglar is seen slipping into the home of a wealthy minister. The preacher comes in and the burglar ducks behind a large chair. The preacher, acting out the role of the supplicant minister begins to moan, praying to De Lawd for understanding.

In the context of today's politics, the minister is an Uncle Tom, mouthing platitudes against self-defense. The preacher drones in a self-pitying monologue about the folly of protecting oneself against brutal policemen. Then the burglar begins to speak. The preacher is startled, taking the burglar's voice for the voice of God. The burglar begins to play on the preacher's old time religion. He *becomes* the voice of God insulting and goading the preacher on until the preacher's attitudes about protective violence change. The next day the preacher emerges militant, gun in hand, sounding like Reverend Cleage in Detroit. He now preaches a new gospel—the gospel of the gun, an eye for an eye. The gospel is preached in the rhythmic cadences of the old Black church. But the content is radical. Just as Jones inverted the symbols in *Jello,* Caldwell twists the rhythms of the Uncle Tom preacher into the language of the new militancy.

These plays are directed at problems within Black America. They begin with the premise that there is a well defined Afro-American audience. An audience that must see itself and the world in terms of its own interests. These plays, along with many others, constitute the basis for a viable movement in the theatre—a movement which takes as its task a profound re-evaluation of the Black man's presence in America. The Black Arts Movement represents the flowering of a cultural nationalism that has been suppressed since the 1920's. I mean the "Harlem Renaissance"—which was essentially a failure. It did not address itself to the mythology and the life-styles of the Black community. It failed to take roots, to link itself concretely to the struggles of that community, to become its voice and spirit. Implicit in the Black Arts Movement is the idea that Black people, however dispersed, constitute a *nation* within the belly of white America. This is not a new idea. Garvey said it and the Honorable Elijah Muhammad[7] says it now. And it is on this idea that the concept of Black Power is predicated.

Afro-American life and history is full of creative possibilities, and the movement is just beginning to perceive them. Just beginning to understand that the most meaningful statements about the nature of Western society must come from the Third World of which Black America is a part. The thematic material is broad, ranging from folk heroes like Shine and Stagolee to historical figures like Marcus Garvey and Malcolm X.[8] And then there is the struggle for Black survival, the coming confrontation between white America and Black America. If art is the harbinger of future possibilities, what does the future of Black America portend?

NIKKI GIOVANNI

Black Poems, Poseurs *and Power* [1969]

Written by a prominent Black Arts Movement insider, "Black Poems, *Poseurs* and Power" is a powerful critique of the movement in its formative years. Nikki Giovanni calls her fellow artists to task for their narrow vision of black art and culture, specifically opposing the ideas and behavior of some of the movement's leaders, such as LeRoi Jones (p. 694) and Ron Karenga. In addition to rejecting militarism and competition for power among artists, Giovanni maintains that "culturalists" (artists and intellectuals of all stripes) must recognize the importance of popular culture and black women to the development of "the Black community."

Giovanni (b. 1943) describes herself as "a Black American, a daughter, a mother, a professor of English."

7. See p. 612; Garvey: see p. 259.
8. See p. 516.

In 1966, while a history student at Fisk University, she attended the school's First Black Writers' Conference. There she met a number of people central to the emerging Black Arts Movement, including Dudley Randall (who had founded Broadside Press, which published the work of many of the poets of the movement) and LeRoi Jones. In 1968, she published her first two poetry collections, *Black Feeling Black Talk* and *Black Judgement.* Giovanni went on to publish forty books of poetry, children's poetry, and non-fiction and became one of the most successful artists to emerge from the Black Arts Movement.

From *Negro Digest*, June 1969; reprinted in Nikki Giovanni, *Gemini: An Extended Autobiographical Statement on My First Twenty-Five Years of Being a Black Poet* (Indianapolis: Bobbs-Merrill, 1971), pp. 106–12.

I like all the militant poems that tell how we're going to kick the honkie's backside and purge our new system of all honkie things like white women, TV, voting and the rest of the ugly, bad things that have been oppressing us so long. I mean, I wrote a poem asking, "Nigger, can you kill?" because to want to live under President no-Dick Nixon is certainly to become a killer. Yet in listening to Smokey and the Miracles sing their *Greatest Hits* recently, I became aware again of the revolutionary quality of "You Can Depend on Me." And if you ask, "Who's Loving You?" just because I say he's not a honkie you should still want to know if I'm well laid. There is a tendency to look at the Black experience too narrowly.

The Maulana[1] has pointed out rather accurately that "The blues is counterrevolutionary," but Aretha[2] is a voice of the new Black experience. It's rather obvious that while "Think" was primarily directed toward white America, Ted White could have taken a hint from it. We must be aware of speaking on all levels. What we help to create we will not necessarily be able to control.

The rape of Newark in the 1968 election was criminal. If revolutionaries are going to involve themselves in politics, they should be successful. And while I'm sure poems are being written to explain the "success" of the Newark campaign, and essays and future speeches are being ground out on brand-new Scott tissues in living color blaming the Black community for not supporting the United Brothers, I would imagine the first problem the United Brothers encountered that they were unable to overcome is that they were not united.

LeRoi Jones, for whatever reason, had no business appearing on a show with Anthony Imperiale issuing joint statements about anything at all because he (LeRoi) did not have equal power in his half of the joint. Joint statements and meetings with the Governor did not encourage the Black people of Newark to support the United Brothers. Because of the prestige of LeRoi, no Newark voice is being lifted to analyze what went wrong. In the all-Black central ward, of the people who turned out to vote only 50 percent voted for councilmen, period. They did not vote against the United Brothers but they would not vote for them either. In a year when Black people showed little to no interest in national politics the stage was set for massive involvement in Black Power. There was no opposition—the people were not involved in another camp. So what went wrong?

Militarism, for one thing. To enter the main headquarters of the United Brothers one had to sign in. This turned most people off. Then you were asked quite tersely, "What do you want?" And if you couldn't answer concisely and accurately you were dismissed. The extreme of this behavior at headquarters was reached when a man carrying $600 to give to the campaign was requested to sign in and then engaged in conversation by one of the keepers of headquarters. The man turned from the conversation to speak with someone else and was told by a second headquarters keeper, "The brother wasn't finished with you." When the

---

1. Activist, author, and professor Maulana Karenga.
2. Aretha Franklin (b. 1942), known as the Queen of Soul, released "Think" in 1968; the next year, she divorced her husband and manager Ted White, who was white.

man's response wasn't satisfactory they pushed him up against the wall and the brothers "guarding" him were told, "Do anything necessary to keep him in line." The man with the money finally made his way upstairs and complained to Karenga and LeRoi. He was told his treatment was "an honest mistake."

It was a disaster. If that kind of treatment was accorded a man with as much prestige as he had, I shudder to think what happened to those who just drifted in to see. They offered an apology to the offended brother but that missed the point entirely. The people of Newark became more afraid of the Black candidates and their organization than they were of the present scandal-ridden, Black-hating administration. This is too bad—to put it mildly. The contradictions are too great.

Revolutionary politics has nothing to do with voting anyway. But if we enter electoral politics we should follow the simple formula that every Black person is a potential vote and must be welcomed and treated as such, with or without dashiki, with or without natural.[3]

The latent militarism of the artistic community is even more despicable—art and the military have always been traditionally opposed. We saw the epitome of the new alliance at the 1968 Black Power Conference at Philadelphia. Every artist worth his salt had a military wing attached to him. The conference had guards; the artists had guards; the guards had guards even. One of the highlights of the conference to me was Karenga's guards complaining about Stanford's[4] guards. This is foolish because it has already been proved beyond a reasonable doubt—with the murders of Martin Luther King, Jr., and Robert Kennedy— that anybody the honkie wants to take off he not only can but will, whenever and however he wants to stage it. The artist-guard syndrome seems to center around the impression we can make with the various commu-

nities. The artist impresses the white community with his militancy and the guards impress the Black community with their power. It's a sick syndrome with, again, the Black community being the loser. There is no cause for wonder that the Black community is withdrawing from involvement with the Black artist.

On *Soul,* which appears on educational TV in New York, the same simplistic crap has taken place. *Soul* is funded by the Ford Foundation and the Negro Ensemble Company is funded by them also. Yet the people on *Soul,* after giving Barbara Ann Teer[5] credit for founding NEC, put it down as not being Black enough. And the Last Poets, which is probably a truer title than they know, performed *Die Nigga.* It's just not the same concept as "kill." It would seem to me that the most important and valid aspect of cultural nationalism would be the support of other Black cultural ventures, especially since one cultural function is funded by the same white folks who fund the group being put down.

Since Black people are going to look at TV they should look at "Julia." Diahann Carroll is prettier, i.e., more valid, than Doris Day any day of the year. And while the idea of cops is bad to me, period, and extralegal Black cops are even worse, if Black people are going to watch cop shows on TV then "Mod Squad" beats the other white vigilante shows. And if "I Spy" is indeed, as I've been told, the new Lone Ranger, then Bill Cosby, by becoming the new Tonto, should help make us aware that we are the Indians of this decade. The parallel institutions that we hear so much about must certainly have reached their apex with "I Spy."[6] *For Love of Ivy* is as fine a movie as we've had since *Nothing but a Man.* And it's certainly more valid to us than *Planet of the Apes, 2001* and those other white things we are forced to watch. It would sometimes appear some elements of the Black artistic community are against popular success unless it's theirs. Sidney Poitier[7] has

3. For debate on hairstyles, see pp. 769–75; dashiki: colorful African style of shirt adopted by some black nationalists in the 1960s.
4. Max Stanford (later Muhammad Ahmad, b. 1941), black nationalist activist and professor.
5. Director, playwright, founder, and executive director of the National Black Theater in Harlem (1937–2008); her music, dance, and theater troupe did perform on the Public Television show *Soul!* in 1970.
6. These television shows all had African American leads; *Julia,* starring Diahann Carroll, (b. 1935), was the first to star a black woman since *Beulah,* which first starred jazz singer and actress Ethel Waters (1896–1977) and then actress Louise Beavers (1902–62); Bill Cosby: see p. 895.
7. Bahamian-American actor, director, author, and diplomat (b. 1927); the first black actor to win an Academy Award for Best Actor (for *Lilies of the Field,* 1963); the top box office star of the year in 1967, starring in three movies including *Guess Who's Coming to Dinner* about an interracial romance.

moved into the area where we have said we want actors to go—only we didn't mean, and make money, I guess. Everybody knows *Guess Who's Coming to Dinner?* is a bad movie but it is neither the beginning nor the end of Poitier's career, and the righteous indignation we spout is really quite out of place. Black people will soon quit listening to us if we can't get in tune with them. I would imagine it's a question of wigs.

Everybody has done his wig poem and wig play. You know, where we put Black people down for not having taken care of business. But what we so easily forget is our own wig. While we put down commercially successful artists we scramble to the East Side to work, we fight for spots on TV, we move our plays downtown at the first chance we get—we do the very things we say are not to be done. Just because our hair is natural doesn't mean we don't have a wig. We are niggers-in-residence at white universities and talk about voting as a means to take over a city, and then we put James Brown down for supporting Hubert Humphrey. It's all a wig. We obviously have no concept of power because if we did we'd recognize that the power of Black people forced James Brown to go natural. Everybody can't come up through the civil rights movement because it just doesn't exist anymore. When Black boys and girls from Mississippi to Massachusetts write J.B. letters complaining about *This Is My Country Too* (or was that a John A. Williams book?) then we ought to rejoice that Brown changes his position. The people we purport to speak for have spoken for themselves. We should be glad.

And it's not as though—if we just like to complain—there isn't an abundance of issues to complain about. What was John Coltrane doing with music that made some people murder him? Why isn't Otis Redding's plane brought up from the lake? What about the obvious tieups in the murders of John and Robert Kennedy with Martin Luther King's death? What elements in this country conspired to murder both Richard Wright and Ben Bella? What did Malcolm and Nkrumah say to each other that caused one to die and the other to be overthrown? Why have so many Arabs and people of Arab descent been arrested for murder or conspiracy to commit murder? And I'd like to know what the cultural nationalists think about James

Forman, living with a white woman who has borne his children, controlling and directing SNCC while Stokely, married to a Black woman, was kicked out. These are cultural questions—relating to survival. But it sometimes seems that the only thing that culturalists care about is assuring themselves and the various communities that they are the vanguard of the Black Revolution. They have made Black women the new Jews while they remain the same old niggers. We have got to do better than this.

Our enemy is the *New York Times*, not the *Amsterdam News;* it's *Look* and *Life,* not *Ebony;* and we ought to keep our enemy in sight. If we're going to talk about parallel institutions then we have to recognize the parallel institutions we have. It is just not possible to have a crisis in Negro intellectualism unless we recognize that Negro intellectualism exists. Young writers ought to recognize that an old writer can't put down other old writers for our benefit. It's sometimes better for a swimmer flailing around in a turbulent lake to be left to drown than for other swimmers to go under also in trying to save him. This may, however, be a personal decision.

One of the main points I'd like the culturalists to remember is that the Jews had more than 100 art festivals while in the concentration camps. The Warsaw ghetto itself became the cultural place to play until the Germans carted the inhabitants off. And while it pleases me to know that we are making cultural strides, it also worries me that we are failing to make political connections. Poems are nice, but as someone points out, "They don't shoot no bullets." "We must," as Marvin X[8] says, "read our own poems." As a group we appear to be vying with each other for the title Brother or Sister Black. That will not get us our freedom. Poor people have always known they are Black, as Rap Brown pointed out, just as poor honkies have always known they are white. These are facts. We need to know where our community is going and to give voice to that.

The Onyx Conference in 1969 showed just how far from the community we had strayed—we didn't even want people there who weren't artists. We are in grave danger of slipping away from our roots. The new hustle, starting with Claude Brown and brought to its fin-

8. Poet, playwright, and essayist associated with the Black Arts Movement (b. 1944).

est point by Eldridge Cleaver with his hustle of Huey Newton, seems to be who can get the ear of the enemy for enough money and/or prestige to float on a pink damn cloud to the concentration camps. Everyone who is breathing easy now that Wallace wasn't elected ought to check again—that's gas you're smelling, artist—and it will take more than a Black poem or your Black seed in me to rid this country of it.

ADDISON GAYLE JR.
Introduction to The Black Aesthetic [1971]

Addison Gayle's 1971 anthology of essays, *The Black Aesthetic* laid out a theoretical framework for the Black Arts Movement. The book's epigraph quotes the final lines of Margaret Walker's 1937 poem "For My People": "Let the martial song be / written, let the dirges disappear. Let a race of men now / rise and take control." In his introduction to the volume, Gayle (1932–1991), an editor and critic, takes up Walker's themes of war and the need for African Americans to control their art. For Gayle, the tone of the black aesthetic is typically angry, the intended audience is other black people, and a central goal is the "de-Americanization of black people," in which art serves as "a means of helping black people out of the polluted mainstream of Americanism." At the same time, Gayle rejects the idea of a monolithic theory of the black aesthetic, affirming that each individual has his or her own ideas about the role of black artists, the role of criticism, and the definition of the black aesthetic itself. Literary critic Houston A. Baker, a leading expert on the Black Arts Movement, considered Gayle's *The Black Aesthetic* as "arguably, the theoretical bible" of the movement.

From Addison Gayle Jr., ed., *The Black Aesthetic* (Garden City, N.Y.: Doubleday, 1971), pp. xv–xxiv.

A new note, discernible even to the most biased observer, was sounded in the art of black people during the nineteen fifties and sixties. "I will go on judging and elucidating novels and plays and poetry by Negroes according to what general powers I possess," writes Richard Gilman,[1] "but the kind of Negro *writing* I have been talking about, the act of creation of the self in the face of the self's historic denial by our society, seems to me to be at this point beyond my right to intrude."

Some critics, less amenable to conversion than Gilman, would have us believe that only two elements separate the present-day black artist from his forerunner. One such element is anger! ". . . Negro writers are demonstrating the responsibility of the artist to the disciplines and traditions of art and literature . . . ," writes Herbert Hill;[2] "simple protest and anger are not enough and rhetoric will not be useful in masking the inadequacies of literary craftsmanship." The other is black nationalism, which, according to Robert Bone, "for all its militancy is politically Utopian."

The element of black anger is neither new nor, as Herbert Hill would have us believe, passé. The black artist in the American society who creates without interjecting a note of anger is creating not as a black man, but as an American. For anger in black art is as old as the first utterances by black men on American soil:

> "If I had-a my way,
> I'd tear this building down
> Great God, then, if I had-a my way
> If I had-a my way, little children
> If I had-a my way,
> I'd tear this building down. . . ."

As old as Frances Ellen Watkins,[3] who made one demand of her undertaker:

---

1. White American critic and drama teacher (1923–2006).
2. White American scholar and civil rights activist (1924–2004); labor director of the NAACP from 1948–77.
3. Frances Ellen Watkins [Harper], abolitionist and poet; see p. 244.

"I ask no monument, proud and high
To arrest the gaze of the passer-by,
All that my yearning spirit craves
Is bury me not in a land of slaves."

Nowhere does anger reach more intensive expression than in DuBois, who strikes a note that has found accord in the breast of contemporary black artists:

"I hate them, oh!
I hate them well,
I hate them, Christ!
As I hate hell!
If I were God,
I'd sound their knell
This day."

Neither is black nationalism a new element in black life or black art. In 1836, "... some of the delegates [at the National Negro Convention]," writes Philip S. Foner,[4] "were convinced that Canadian colonization was still the most urgent business at hand. Others felt that it was necessary to concentrate upon building a better social order in the United States.... One group doubted the efficacy of associating with any set of white abolitionists, and advocated restricting the convention to Negro membership. Another, convinced of the inability to achieve equality for Negroes in existing institutions, favored continuing the establishment of separate schools and churches for the Negro people." This sentiment reaches dramatic form in the fiction of Martin Delaney,[5] *Blake, or the Huts of America* (1859); Sutton Griggs, *Imperium in Imperio* (1899); and DuBois, *Dark Princess* (1928).

Again, animosity against the inept, sterile critiques of American academicians—so prevalent in black critical writings today—is not new. As early as 1900, Pauline Hopkins realized that art was "... of great value to any people as a preserver of manners and customs—religious, political, and social. It is a record of growth and development from generation to generation. No one will do this for us; we must ourselves develop the

men and women who will faithfully portray the inmost thoughts and feelings of the Negro with all the fire and romance which lie dormant in our history...." Twenty-two years later, William Pickens was more direct: "It is not simply that the white story teller will not do full justice to the humanity of the black race; *he cannot.*" William Stanley Braithwaite, an American critic in every essential, quotes from an article in the *Independent Magazine* (1925): "The white writer seems to stand baffled before the enigma, and so he expends all his energies on dialect and in general on the Negro's minstrel characteristics.... We shall have to look to the Negro himself to go all the way. It is quite likely that no white man can do it. *It is reasonable to suppose that his white psychology will get in the way.*" (Italics mine)

Nevertheless, there is a discernible element in black art today that is new, and Hoyt W. Fuller has come closest to pointing it out: "The Negro revolt is as palpable in letters as it is in the streets." Change revolt to war, and the characteristics that distinguish the old art from the new are readily apparent. The serious black artist of today is at war with the American society as few have been throughout American history. Too often, as Richard Wright noted, the black (artists) "... entered the court of American public opinion dressed in the knee pants of servility, curtsying to show that the Negro was not inferior, that he was human, and that he had a life comparable to other people." They waged war not against the society but against the societal laws and mores that barred *them* from equal membership. They were, in the main, anxious to become Americans, to share in the fruits of the country's economic system and to surrender their history and culture to a universal melting pot. They were men of another era who believed in the American dream more fervently than their white contemporaries. They saw the nation as a land of innocence, young enough to hold out promises of maturing into a nation of freedom, justice, and equality. The days of innocence have passed. The child has become the adult, and instead of improving with age, she has grown increasingly worse. Yesterday America

4. White American historian and author (1910–94) whose books include *Proceedings of the Black State Conventions, 1840–1965* (1979, co-edited by George E. Walker), *Proceedings of the Black State Conventions, 1865–1900* (1986, also with Walker), *The Black Panthers Speak* (1970), as well as the 10-volume *History of the Labor Movement in the United States* (published between 1947 and 1994).
5. For more on abolitionist Martin Delany, see p. 95.

was evil personified in her youth; today she is evil personified in adulthood.

The dimensions of the black artist's war against the society are highly visible. At the core of black art in the past was a vendetta against the South. The black novel, from William Wells Brown[6] to Richard Wright, was concerned primarily with southern tyranny and injustice. Often the North escaped with no more than a rap on the knuckles. "Northern white people," wrote James Weldon Johnson in *The Autobiography of an Ex-Coloured Man* (1912), "love the Negro in a sort of abstract way, as a race; through a sense of justice, charity, and philanthropy, they will liberally assist in his elevation. . . ."

With the exception of writers such as Dunbar and Chesnutt, who viewed the black man's exodus from South to North as an exchange of one hell for another, black writers spoke of the North as the new Canaan, of northern whites as a different breed of man from their southern counterparts. Is it any wonder that black people, falling sway to increasing southern tyranny, began, in 1917, the exodus that swelled the urban areas of America in the sixties and seventies?

"I've seen them come dark/wondering/wide-eyed/dreaming/out of Penn Station . . . ," writes Langston Hughes, "but the trains are late. The gates open/but there're bars/at each gate." The bars were erected by northern, not southern, whites. Black people had run away from white terrorism in Savannah in 1904 and Atlanta in 1906, only to experience white terrorism in Ohio in 1904, Illinois in 1908, and New York in 1935. The evenhanded treatment of blacks North and South made little imprint upon Negro leaders who, then as now, were more willing to combat injustices down south than up north.

The task of pointing out northern duplicity was left to the black artist, and no writer was more effective in this undertaking than Richard Wright. When Wright placed Bigger Thomas and Mr. Dalton in a northern setting and pointed up the fact that Bigger's condition resulted from Dalton's hypocrisy, he opened a Pandora's box of problems for white liberals and Negro leaders, neither of whom could bring themselves to share his vision. Dalton is a white liberal philanthropist who, although donating money to "Negro uplift organizations," owns the slums in which Bigger Thomas is forced to live. His control of the young black man is more despotic than that of the southern plantation owner over blacks in the South: for him, the weapons of control are economic, social, and political.

He is more sagacious and dishonest than his southern counterpart; he has discovered a way to "keep the nigger in his place" without such aids as signs and restrictive covenants. He has constructed a cosmology that allows him to pose as a humanitarian on the one hand, while he sets about defining the black man's limitations on the other. His most cherished symbol of the black man is Uncle Tom; and he remains enamored of Nigger Jim,[7] the black everyboy toward whom he feels paternalistic. Like Theodore Gross, he is able to share with Joel Chandler Harris[8] ". . . the fears, laughter, and anger of the Negro"; and he is equally convinced with Gross that Harris ". . . contributed the most popular Negro characters to American fiction—Uncle Remus, Balaam, Ananias, and Mingo . . ."—characters whom he, too, believes to be representative of the race.

Thomas Nelson Page, Thomas Dixon, and Hinton Helper[9] might create, for Southerners, the image of the black man as ". . . a degenerate, inferior, irresponsible, and bestial creature 'transformed by the exigency of war from a chattel to be bought and sold into a possible beast to be feared and guarded.'" Dalton, however, will not accept this image. Such portraits of black men disturb

6. Abolitionist, novelist, playwright, and historian (1816–84); Brown's *Clotel, or The President's Daughter: A Narrative of Slave Life in the United States* (1853) is the earliest known novel written by an African American.

7. Reference to character of Jim, an escaped slave, in Mark Twain's *Adventures of Huckleberry Finn* (1885); the name "Nigger Jim" does not appear in the novel, but is often used in literary criticism, originating with Albert Bigelow Paine's 1912 biography of the white American writer Samuel Clemens (a.k.a. Twain).

8. White American writer (1845–1908) who published multiple collections of Uncle Remus stories based on African American folktales; these tales were very popular during his time but have since become a source of controversy for their use of dialect and stereotyped characters; Gross: white American author, editor, and university administer (b. 1932) whose books include *Dark Symphony: Negro Literature in America* (1968, co-edited with poet James A. Emanuel (b. 1921)).

9. White American male writers; Dixon's *The Clansman* (1905), celebrating the Ku Klux Klan, was the basis for D. W. Griffith's film *The Birth of a Nation* (1915).

his humanitarian (read sexual) ideal of the black man. "In an effort to make Hell endurable," Robert Bone writes of James Baldwin, "Baldwin attempts to spiritualize his sexual rebellion. Subjectively, I have no doubt, he is convinced that he has found God. Not the white God of his black father, but a darker deity who dwells in the heart of carnal mystery. . . . The stranger the sex partner, the better the orgasm, for it violates a stronger taboo." Bone's inability to come to grips with the sexual aspects of Baldwin's novels, reveals more about Bone than it does about Baldwin.

At the least, it reveals a great deal about the Daltons of the North. In order to protect the Marys of the earth (Dalton's daughter in *Native Son*), they have defined the black man in the most negative terms possible. To the northern mind, Nigger Jim and Uncle Tom are opposite ends of the same pole; the young boy and the old man are both eunuchs, paternalistic wards who, one step removed from the jungle, are capable of limited, prescribed salvation. The inability of the Daltons to see the black man as other than an impotent sexual force accounts for much of the negative criticism by white writers about black literature; it also accounts for the sexually impotent black men who people the novels of William Styron and Norman Mailer.[1]

The liberal ideology—both social and literary—of the northern Daltons has become the primary target of the Afro-American writer and critic. In the novels of John A. Williams, Sam Greenlee, Cecil Brown, and Ishmael Reed, the criticism of Don L. Lee, Ron Wellburn, LeRoi Jones, and Hoyt Fuller,[2] to name but a few, the liberal shibboleths are called into question. The Daltons are brought before the bar of black public opinion and revealed for the modern-day plantation owners they are.

There is another, more important aspect to this war. The black artist of the past worked with the white public in mind. The guidelines by which he measured his production was its acceptance or rejection by white people. To be damned by a white critic and disavowed by a white public was reason enough to damn the artist in the eyes of his own people. The invisible censor, white power, hovered over him in the sanctuary of his private room—whether at the piano or the typewriter—and, like his black brothers, he debated about what he could say to the world without bringing censure upon himself. The mannerisms he had used to survive in the society outside, he now brought to his art; and, to paraphrase Richard Wright, he was forced to figure out how to sound each note and how to write down each word.

The result was usually an artistic creation filled with half-truths. His works were always seasoned with the proper amount of anger—an anger that dared not reach the explosive level of calling for total demolition of the American society—and condescension; condescension that meant he would assure his audience, at some point in the production, that he believed in the principles of Americanism. To return to Richard Wright, he was not ". . . ever expected to speak honestly about the problem. [He had to] wrap it up in myth, legend, morality, folklore, niceties, and plain lies."

Speaking honestly is a fundamental principle of today's black artist. He has given up the futile practice of speaking to whites, and has begun to speak to his brothers. Ofttimes, as in essays in this anthology, he points up the wide disparity between the pronouncements of liberal intellectuals and their actions. Yet his purpose is not to convert the liberals (one does not waste energy on the likes of Selden Rodman, Irving Howe, Theodore Gross, Louis Simpson, Herbert Hill, or Robert Bone[3]), but instead to point out to black people the true extent of the control exercised upon them by the American society, in the hope that a process of de-Americanization will occur in every black community in the nation.

The problem of the de-Americanization of black people lies at the heart of the Black Aesthetic. "After the Egyptian and Indian, the Greek and Roman, the Teuton and Mongolian," wrote DuBois in 1903, "the Negro

---

1. White American male writers; Styron's *The Confessions of Nat Turner* (1967) spurred widespread debate among critics about issues of representation and authenticity, including *William Styron's Nat Turner: Ten Black Writers Respond* (1968).

2. Williams (b. 1925), novelist, journalist, poet, and professor; Greenlee (b. 1930), novelist and poet; Brown (1907–87), journalist, author, and radio war correspondent; Reed (b. 1938), novelist, poet, essayist, and professor (p. 999); Lee (Haki Madhubuti), poet and member of the performance group The Last Poets; Welburn, poet and professor; Jones (Amiri Baraka), poet, playwright, critic, and professor (p. 694); Fuller (1923–81), editor and critic.

3. White American male critics who published writings on black art and culture; Howe, see p. 659.

is a sort of seventh son, born with a veil, and gifted with second sight in this American world—a world which yields him no true self-consciousness, but only lets him see himself through the revelation of the other world. It is a peculiar sensation, this double consciousness, this sense of always looking at one's self through the eyes of others, of measuring one's soul by the tape of a world that looks on in amused contempt and pity. One ever feels his twoness—an American, a Negro; two souls, two thoughts, two unreconciled strivings; two warring ideals in one dark body, whose dogged strength alone keeps it from being torn asunder."

In 1961 the old master resolved the psychic tension in his own breast by leaving the country that had rewarded his endeavors with scorn and oppression. His denunciations of America and his exodus back to the land of his forefathers provide an appropriate symbol of the black man who de-Americanized himself.

His act proclaimed to black men the world over that the price for becoming an American was too high. It meant, at the least, to desert one's heritage and culture; at the most, to become part of all "... that has been instrumental in wanton destruction of life, degradation of dignity, and contempt for the human spirit." To be an American is to be opposed to humankind, against the dignity of the individual, and against the striving in man for compassion and tenderness: to be an American is to lose one's humanity.

What else is one to make of My Lai, Vietnam? A black soldier has been charged with joining his white compatriots in the murder of innocent Vietnamese women and children. How far has the Americanization of black men progressed when a southern black man stands beside white men and shoots down, not the enemies of his people, but the niggers of American construction?

To understand this incident and what must be done to correct it is to understand the Black Aesthetic. A critical methodology has no relevance to the black community unless it aids men in becoming better than they are. Such an element has been sorely lacking in the critical canons handed down from the academies by the Aristotelian Critics, the Practical Critics, the Formalistic Critics, and the New Critics. Each has this in common: it aims to evaluate the work of art in terms

of *its* beauty and not in terms of the transformation from ugliness to beauty that the work of art demands from its audience.

The question for the black critic today is not how beautiful is a melody, a play, a poem, or a novel, but how much more beautiful has the poem, melody, play, or novel made the life of a single black man? How far has the work gone in transforming an American Negro into an African-American or black man? The Black Aesthetic, then, as conceived by this writer, is a corrective—a means of helping black people out of the polluted mainstream of Americanism, and offering logical, reasoned arguments as to why he should not desire to join the ranks of a Norman Mailer or a William Styron. To be an American writer is to be an American, and, for black people, there should no longer be honor attached to either position.

To paraphrase Saunders Redding,[4] I have been enclothed with no authority to speak for others. Therefore, it is not my intention, in this introduction, to speak for the contributors to this anthology. Few of them may share my views; a great many may find them reprehensible. These are independent artists who demand the right to think for themselves and who, rightfully so, will resist the attempt by anyone—black or white—to articulate positions in their names.

Each has his own idea of the Black Aesthetic, of the function of the black artist in the American society and of the necessity for new and different critical approaches to the artistic endeavors of black artists. Few, I believe, would argue with my assertion that the black artist, due to his historical position in America at the present time, is engaged in a war with this nation that will determine the future of black art. Likewise, there are few among them—and here again this is only conjecture—who would disagree with the idea that unique experiences produce unique cultural artifacts, and that art is a product of such cultural experiences. To push this thesis to its logical conclusion, unique art derived from unique cultural experiences mandates unique critical tools for evaluation. Further than this, agreement need not go!

One final note: Less than a decade ago, anthologies on black writing were edited almost exclusively by whites. Today, there is a noticeable difference: the

4. Jay Saunders Redding (1906–68), historian and literary critic.

white academician edits an anthology and calls upon a black man to write the introduction. The editor then declares that his anthology "represents the best of black literature" or that he has chosen those works "which rank with the best in American artistic production."

This editor makes no such farcical and nonsensical claims. Represented in this anthology is not the best critical thought on the subject of the Black Aesthetic, but critical thought that is among the best. This anthology is not definitive and does not claim to be. The first of its kind to treat of this subject, it is meant as an incentive to young black critics to scan the pages of *The Black World* [*Negro Digest*], *Liberator Magazine*, *Soulbook*,

Journal of Negro Poetry, Amistad, Umbra, and countless other black magazines, and anthologize the thousands of essays that no single anthology could possibly cover.

Many writers whose claim to recognition is equal to that of the other contributors and the editor have been left out of this anthology. This could not be helped. Perhaps it can be rectified. Instead of being content to write introduction[s] for white editors, perhaps our serious black artists will edit anthologies themselves. If this is done, the present renaissance in black letters will escape the fate of its predecessor in the nineteen twenties, and endure. Then and only then will the revolution in black letters gain viability and continue right on!

June Jordan

On Richard Wright and Zora Neale Hurston: Notes Toward a Balancing of Love and Hatred [1974]

June Jordan's 1974 essay reprinted here offers an alternative to the idea that the writings of Richard Wright (p. 470) and Zora Neale Hurston (p. 470) are oppositional. For Jordan, not only do both writers represent important aspects of the African American literary tradition, but they also have fundamental elements in common. Both artists are ultimately part of an encompassing political collective, each presenting ways of viewing the same issues of "want, hope, and confrontation" in the lives of African Americans.

Jordan's essay specifically focuses on the work and

reception of Hurston and Wright, but her opening paragraphs show how her approach can serve as a model for examining any debate. She builds on the method espoused by Martin Luther King Jr. (p. 559) who approached diverse texts "from a dialectical point of view, combining a partial 'yes' and a partial 'no.'" Jordan demonstrates that positions historically seen as dichotomous can both be viewed with a yes, and that such an approach can better capture the complexity of human experience than the divisive alternative of choosing only one side in a polarized debate.

From *Black World* (August 1974): 4–8.

We should take care so that we will lose none of the jewels of our soul. We must begin, now, to reject the white, either/or system of dividing the world into unnecessary conflict. For example, it is tragic and ridiculous to choose between Malcolm X and Dr King: each of them hurled himself against a quite different aspect of our predicament, and both of them, literally, gave their lives to our ongoing struggle.

We need everybody and all that we are. We need to know and make known the complete, constantly

unfolding, complicated heritage that is our Black experience. We should absolutely resist the superstar, one-at-a-time mentality that threatens the varied and resilient, flexible wealth of our Black future, even as it shrinks and obliterates incalculable segments of our history.

In Black literature, we have lost many jewels to the glare of white, mass-media manipulation. According to whitepower, Ralph Ellison was the only Black novelist writing, in this country, while whitepower "allowed" his star to shine. Then, the media "gave" us

James Baldwin—evidently all by himself. And then there was *only* Eldridge Cleaver. (Remember him?)

But towering before and above these media-isolated giants, there was always Richard Wright. He has been presented as a solitary figure on the literary landscape of his period. But, right along with him, and six years his senior, there was Zora Neale Hurston. And the fact is that we almost lost Zora to the choose-between games played with Black Art; until recently, no one had ever heard of her; certainly, no one read her books. And yet, anyone who has dipped into her work, even once, will tell you: the long-term obscurity of her joy and wisdom is an appalling matter of record. So we would do well to carefully reconsider these two, Hurston and Wright. Perhaps that will let us understand the cleavage in their public reception, and prevent such inequity and virtual erasure from taking place, again.

Each of them achieved unprecedented, powerful, and extremely important depths of Black vision and commitment, in their lifework; according to the usual criteria, they were both Great Writers. Yet, while Richard Wright spawned many, many followers, and enjoyed the rewards of well-earned fame, Zora Neale Hurston suffered through devastating critical and popular neglect, inspired no imitators, and finally died, penniless, and was buried in an unmarked grave. Why did this happen?

I believe we were misled into the notion that *only one kind* of writing—protest writing—and that *only one kind* of protest writing—deserves our support and study.

A few years back, Hoyt Fuller posed the primary functions of Protest and Affirmation as basic to an appreciation of Black Art. Wright's *Native Son* is widely recognized as the prototypical, Black, protest novel. By comparison, Hurston's novel, *Their Eyes Were Watching God*, seems to suit, perfectly, the obvious connotations of Black affirmation.

But I would add that the functions of protest and affirmation are not, ultimately, distinct: that, for instance, affirmation of Black values and lifestyle within the American context is, indeed, an act of protest. Therefore, Hurston's affirmative work is profoundly defiant, just as Wright's protest unmistakably asserts

our need for an alternative, benign environment. We have been misled to discount the one in order to revere the other. But we have been misled in a number of ways: several factors help to explain the undue contrast between the careers of Wright and Hurston.

Richard Wright was a Black man born on a white, Mississippi plantation, and carried, by fits and starts, from one white, southern town to the next. In short, he was born into the antagonistic context of hostile whites wielding power against him. In this, his background mirrors our majority Black experience. And so, we readily accept the validity of *Native Son*'s Bigger Thomas, who pits himself against overwhelming, white force.

Moreover, *Native Son,* undoubtedly Wright's most influential book, conforms to white standards we have swallowed, regarding literary weight. It is apparently symbolic (rather than realistic) "serious" (unrelievedly grim), socio-political (rather than "personal" in its scale, and not so much "emotional" as impassioned in its deliberate execution.

Given the antagonistic premise of *Native Son*, the personal beginnings of Richard Wright, a Black man on enemy turf, it follows that his novel should pull you forward with its furious imagination, saturate the reader with varieties of hatred, and horror, climax in violence, and ram hard—ram hard—against a destiny of doom.

But suppose the premise is a different one?

Zora Neale Hurston was born and raised in an all-Black Florida town. In other words, she was born into a supportive, nourishing environment. And without exception, her work—as novelist, as anthropologist/diligent collector and preserver of Black folktale and myth—reflects this early and late, all-Black universe which was her actual and her creative world.

You see her immovable, all-Black orientation in *Their Eyes Were Watching God*. Whites do not figure in this story of Black love; white anything or anybody is not important; what matters is the Black woman and the Black man who come together in a believable, contagious, full Black love that makes you want to go and seek and find, likewise, soon as you finish the book.

---

1. Editor and critic (1923–81); a leader in the Black Arts Movement.

Since white America lies outside the Hurston universe, in fact as well as in her fiction, you do not run up on the man/the enemy; protest, narrowly conceived, is therefore beside the point; rhythm or tones of outrage or desperate flight would be wholly inappropriate in her text. Instead you slip into a total, Black reality where Black people do not represent issues; they represent their own, particular selves in a Family/Community setting that permits relaxation from hunted/warrior postures, and that fosters the natural, person postures of courting, jealousy, ambition, dream, sex, work, partying, sorrow, bitterness, celebration, and fellowship.

Unquestionably, *Their Eyes Were Watching God* is the prototypical Black novel of affirmation; it is the most successful, and convincing, and exemplary novel of Black love that we have, period. But the book gives us more: the story unrolls a fabulously written film of Black life freed from the constraints of oppression; here we may learn Black possibilities of ourselves if we could ever escape the hateful and alien context that has so deeply disturbed and mutilated our rightful efflorescence—*as people*. Consequently, this novel centers itself on Black love—even as *Native Son* rivets itself upon white hatred.

But, because Zora Neale Hurston was a woman, and because we have been misled into devaluating the functions of Black affirmation, her work has been derogated as romantic, the natural purview of a woman (i.e., unimportant), "personal" (not serious) in its scope, and assessed as *sui generis*[2] or idiosyncratic accomplishment of no lasting reverberation, or usefulness. All such derogation derives from ignorance and/or callow thinking we cannot afford to continue. Although few of us have known the happiness of an all-Black town/ universe, every single one of us is the torn-away descendant of a completely Black/African world and, today, increasing numbers of us deem an all-Black circum-

stance/nation as our necessary, overriding goal. Accordingly, this Sister has given us the substance of an exceptional, but imperative vision, since her focus is both an historical truth and a contemporary aim. As for the derision of love as less important than war or violence, that is plain craziness, plain *white* craziness we do not need even to discuss.

And, is it true that *Native Son* represents you and me more than Hurston's heroine, Janie Starks? Both of them bespeak our hurt, our wished-for fulfillment, and, at various times, the nature and the level of our adjustment to complete fulfillment or, on the other hand, complete frustration. What's more, I do not accept that Wright and Hurston should be perceived, properly, as antipathetic in the well-springs of their work. Bigger Thomas, the whole living and dying creation of him, teaches as much about the necessity of love, of being able to love without being destroyed, as Hurston's Janie Starks. Their address to this subject, this agonizingly central need, differs, perhaps, as men and women have been taught to cope with human existence differently. And, elsewhere, I submit that *Their Eyes* treats with a want and a hope and a tragic adjustment that is at least as reverberating, as universal—namely, positive (loving) self-fulfillment—as the material of *Native Son*, which emphasizes the negative trajectories of that same want, hope, and confrontation.

But rightly, we should not choose between Bigger Thomas and Janie Starks; our lives are as big and as manifold and as pained and as happy as the two of them put together. We should equally value and equally emulate Black Protest and Black Affirmation, for we require both; one without the other is dangerous, and will leave us vulnerable to extinction of the body or the spirit. We owe thanks to both the struggle and the love: to the native sons among us, and to those whose eyes are watching their own gods.

---

2. Of its own genus [Latin]; unique, so that it cannot be viewed in relation to a larger framework or concept.

BARBARA SMITH

Toward a Black Feminist Criticism [1977]

The Black Arts Movement was not only criticized internally (by participants like the poet Nikki Giovanni, p. 711), but it was also a source of controversy for critics and artists outside the movement. Black lesbian critics in particular questioned the movement's emphasis on traditional concepts of masculinity and heterosexuality. In this groundbreaking essay, Barbara Smith (b. 1946) introduces criteria for judging works by black artists that do not fit easily within the boundaries of either the Black Arts Movement or the feminist literary movement of the period (which emphasized writing by white women). Like members of those movements, Smith links politics and art and promotes literary theory as a prerequisite for increased artistic production. In her reading of Toni Morrison's *Sula,* Smith moves from abstract theory to concrete literary criticism, providing a model for subsequent scholars. Smith's theory and criticism laid the foundation for the emerging black feminist movement of the 1970s. As Smith predicted, that movement did foster "the creation of consciously Black woman-identified art" (or "womanist" art, to use the term coined by Alice Walker, a key figure in the new critical and artistic movement). Moreover, the study of the black female literary tradition that Smith urged was instrumental in rescuing literary figures (including Zora Neale Hurston) from obscurity.

From *Conditions: Two* 1, no. 2 (October 1977); repr., Smith, Barbara, *The Truth That Never Hurts* (Piscataway, N.J.: Rutgers University Press, 1998), pp. 4–21.

I do not know where to begin. Long before I tried to write this I realized that I was attempting something unprecedented, something dangerous, merely by writing about Black women writers from a feminist perspective and about Black lesbian writers from any perspective at all. These things have not been done. Not by white male critics, expectedly. Not by Black male critics. Not by white women critics who think of themselves as feminists. And most crucially not by Black women critics, who, although they pay the most attention to Black women writers as a group, seldom use a consistent feminist analysis or write about Black lesbian literature. All segments of the literary world—whether establishment, progressive, Black, female, or lesbian—do not know, or at least act as if they do not know, that Black women writers and Black lesbian writers exist.

For whites, this specialized lack of knowledge is inextricably connected to their not knowing in any concrete or politically transforming way that Black women of any description dwell in this place. Black women's existence, experience, and culture and the brutally complex systems of oppression which shape these are in the "real world" of white and/or male consciousness beneath consideration, invisible, unknown.

This invisibility, which goes beyond anything that either Black men or white women experience and tell about in their writing, is one reason it is so difficult for me to know where to start. It seems overwhelming to break such a massive silence. Even more numbing, however, is the realization that so many of the women who will read this have not yet noticed us missing either from their reading matter, their politics, or their lives. It is galling that ostensible feminists and acknowledged lesbians have been so blinded to the implications of any womanhood that is not white womanhood and that they have yet to struggle with the deep racism in themselves that is at the source of this blindness.

I think of the thousands and thousands of books, magazines, and articles which have been devoted, by this time, to the subject of women's writing and I am filled with rage at the fraction of those pages that mention Black and other Third World women. I finally do not know how to begin because in 1977 I want to be writing this for a Black feminist publication, for Black women who know and love these writers as I do and who, if they do not yet know their names, have at least profoundly felt the pain of their absence.

The conditions that coalesce into the impossibilities of this essay have as much to do with politics as with the practice of literature. Any discussion of Afro-American writers can rightfully begin with the fact that for most of the time we have been in this country we have been categorically denied not only literacy but the most minimal possibility of a decent human life. In her landmark essay, "In Search of Our Mothers' Gardens," Alice Walker discloses how the political, economic, and social restrictions of slavery and racism have historically stunted the creative lives of Black women.[1]

At the present time I feel that the politics of feminism have a direct relationship to the state of Black women's literature. A viable, autonomous Black feminist movement in this country would open up the space needed for the exploration of Black women's lives and the creation of consciously Black woman-identified art. At the same time a redefinition of the goals and strategies of the white feminist movement would lead to much-needed change in the focus and content of what is now generally accepted as women's culture.

I want to make in this essay some connections between the politics of Black women's lives, what we write about, and our situation as artists. In order to do this I will look at how Black women have been viewed critically by outsiders, demonstrate the necessity for Black feminist criticism, and try to understand what the existence or nonexistence of Black lesbian writing reveals about the state of Black women's culture and the intensity of *all* Black women's oppression.

The role that criticism plays in making a body of literature recognizable and real hardly needs to be explained here. The necessity for nonhostile and perceptive analysis of works written by persons outside the "mainstream" of white/male cultural rule has been proven by the Black cultural resurgence of the 1960s and 1970s and by the even more recent growth of feminist literary scholarship. For books to be real and remembered they have to be talked about. For books to be understood they must be examined in such a way that the basic intentions of the writers are at least considered. Because of racism Black literature has usually been viewed as a discrete subcategory of American literature, and there have been Black critics of Black literature who did much to keep it alive long before it caught the attention of whites. Before the advent of specifically feminist criticism in this decade, books by white women, on the other hand, were not clearly perceived as the cultural manifestation of an oppressed people. It took the surfacing of the second wave of the North American feminist movement to expose the fact that these works contain a stunningly accurate record of the impact of patriarchal values and practice upon the lives of women, and more significantly, that literature by women provides essential insights into female experience.

In speaking about the current situation of Black women writers, it is important to remember that the existence of a feminist movement was an essential precondition to the growth of feminist literature, criticism, and women's studies, which focused at the beginning almost entirely upon investigations of literature. The fact that a parallel Black feminist movement has been much slower in evolving cannot help but have impact upon the situation of Black women writers and artists and explains in part why during this very same period we have been so ignored.

There is no political movement to give power or support to those who want to examine Black women's experience through studying our history, literature, and culture. There is no political presence that demands a minimal level of consciousness and respect from those who write or talk about our lives. Finally, there is not a developed body of Black feminist political theory whose assumptions could be used in the study of Black women's art. When Black women's books are dealt with at all, it is usually in the context of Black literature, which largely ignores the implications of sexual politics. When white women look at Black women's works they are of course ill-equipped to deal with the subtleties of racial politics. A Black feminist approach to literature that embodies the realization that the politics of sex as well as the politics of race and class are crucially interlocking factors in the works of Black women writers is an absolute necessity. Until a Black feminist criticism exists we will not even know what

1. Alice Walker, "In Search of Our Mothers' Gardens," in *Ms.*, May 1974, and in *Southern Exposure* 4, no. 4, Generations: Women in the South 1 (Winter 1977): 60–64. [Unless otherwise indicated, all notes are those of the author.]

these writers mean. The citations from a variety of critics which follow prove that without a Black feminist critical perspective not only are books by Black women misunderstood, they are destroyed in the process.

Jerry H. Bryant, *The Nation*'s white male reviewer of Alice Walker's *In Love and Trouble: Stories of Black Women*, wrote in 1973:

> The subtitle of the collection, "Stories of Black Women," is probably an attempt by the publisher to exploit not only black subjects but feminine ones. There is nothing feminist about these stories, however.[2]

Blackness and feminism are to his mind mutually exclusive and peripheral to the act of writing fiction. Bryant of course does not consider that Walker might have titled the work herself, nor did he apparently read the book, which unequivocally reveals the author's feminist consciousness.

In *The Negro Novel in America*, a book that Black critics recognize as one of the worst examples of white racist pseudoscholarship, Robert Bone cavalierly dismisses Ann Petry's classic, *The Street*.[3] He perceives it to be "a superficial social analysis" of how slums victimize their Black inhabitants. He further objects:

> It is an attempt to interpret slum life in terms of *Negro* experience, when a larger frame of reference is required. As Alain Locke has observed, *"Knock on Any Door* is superior to *The Street* because it designates class and environment, rather than mere race and environment, as its antagonist."[4]

Neither Robert Bone nor Alain Locke, the Black male critic he cites, can recognize that *The Street* is one of the best delineations in literature of how sex, race, *and* class interact to oppress Black women.

In her review of Toni Morrison's *Sula* for the *New York Times Book Review* in 1973, putative feminist Sara Blackburn makes similarly racist comments:

> Toni Morrison is far too talented to remain only a marvelous recorder of the black side of provincial American life. If she is to maintain the large and serious audience she deserves, she is going to have to address a riskier contemporary reality than this beautiful but nevertheless distanced novel. *And if she does this, it seems to me that she might easily transcend that early and unintentionally limiting classification "black woman writer" and take her place among the most serious, important and talented American novelists now working.*[5] [Italics mine]

Recognizing Morrison's exquisite gift, Blackburn unashamedly asserts that Morrison is "too talented" to deal with mere Black folk, particularly those double nonentities, Black women. In order to be accepted as "serious," "important," "talented," and "American," she must obviously focus her efforts upon chronicling the doings of white men.

The mishandling of Black women writers by whites is paralleled more often by their not being handled at all, particularly in feminist criticism. Although Elaine Showalter in her review essay on literary criticism for *Signs* states that "the best work being produced today [in feminist criticism] is exacting and cosmopolitan," her essay is neither. If it were, she would not have failed to mention a single Black or Third World woman writer, whether "major" or "minor," to cite her questionable categories. That she also does not even hint that lesbian writers of any color exist renders her purported overview virtually meaningless. Showalter obviously thinks that the identities of being Black and female are mutually exclusive, as this statement illustrates:

> Furthermore, there are other literary subcultures (black American novelists, for example) whose

---

2. Jerry H. Bryant, "The Outskirts of a New City," *The Nation*, November 12, 1973, p. 502.

3. Naturalistic novel published in 1946 by Petry (1908–97); the first book by an African American woman to sell over a million copies. [Editor's note]

4. Robert Bone, *The Negro Novel in America* (New Haven, Conn.: Yale University Press, 1958), p. 180. *Knock on Any Door* is a novel by Black writer Willard Motley.

5. Sara Blackburn, "You Still Can't Go Home Again," *New York Times Book Review*, December 30, 1973, p. 3.

history offers a precedent for feminist scholarship to use.[6]

The idea of critics like Showalter *using* Black literature is chilling, a case of barely disguised cultural imperialism. The final insult is that she footnotes the preceding remark by pointing readers to works on Black literature by white males Robert Bone and Roger Rosenblatt!

Two recent works by white women, Ellen Moers's *Literary Women: The Great Writers* and Patricia Meyer Spacks's *The Female Imagination,* evidence the same racist flaw.[7] Moers includes the names of four Black and one Puertorriquena writer in her seventy pages of bibliographical notes and does not deal at all with Third World women in the body of her book. Spacks refers to a comparison between Negroes (*sic*) and women in Mary Ellmann's *Thinking About Women* under the index entry "blacks, women and." "*Black Boy* (Wright)" is the preceding, entry. Nothing follows. Again there is absolutely no recognition that Black and female identity ever coexist, specifically in a group of Black women writers. Perhaps one can assume that these women do not know who Black women writers are, that like most Americans they have little opportunity to learn about them. Perhaps. Their ignorance seems suspiciously selective, however, particularly in the light of the dozens of truly obscure white women writers they are able to unearth. Spacks was herself employed at Wellesley College at the same time that Alice Walker was there teaching one of the first courses on Black women writers in the country.

I am not trying to encourage racist criticism of Black women writers like that of Sara Blackburn, to cite only one example. As a beginning I would at least like to see in print white women's acknowledgment of the contradictions of who and what are being left out of their research and writing.[8]

Black male critics can also *act* as if they do not know that Black women writers exist and are, of course, hampered by an inability to comprehend Black women's experience in sexual as well as racial terms. Unfortunately there are also those who are as virulently sexist in their treatment of Black women writers as their white male counterparts. Darwin Turner's[9] discussion of Zora Neale Hurston in his *In a Minor Chord: Three Afro-American Writers and Their Search for Identity* is a frightening example of the near assassination of a great Black woman writer.[1] His descriptions of her and her work as "artful," "coy," "irrational," "superficial," and "shallow" bear no relationship to the actual quality of her achievements. Turner is completely insensitive to the sexual political dynamics of Hurston's life and writing.

In a recent interview the notoriously misogynist writer Ishmael Reed comments in this way upon the low sales of his newest novel:

> . . . but the book only sold 8000 copies. I don't mind giving out the figure: 8000. Maybe if I was one of those young female Afro-American writers that are so hot now, I'd sell more. You know, fill my books with ghetto women who can do no wrong. . . . But come on, I think I could have sold 8000 copies by myself.[2]

The politics of the situation of Black women are glaringly illuminated by this statement. Neither Reed nor his white male interviewer has the slightest compunction about attacking Black women in print. They need not fear widespread public denunciation since Reed's statement is in perfect agreement with the values of a society that hates Black people, women, and Black women. Finally the two of them feel free to base their actions on the premise that Black women are powerless to alter either their political or their cultural oppression.

6. EIaine Showalter, "Literary Criticism," Review Essay, *Signs* 1 (Winter 1975): 460, 445.
7. Ellen Moers, *Literary Women: The Great Writers* (Garden City, N.Y.: Anchor Books, 1977); Patricia Meyer Spacks, *The Female Imagination* (New York: Avon Books, 1976).
8. An article by Nancy Hoffman, "White Women, Black Women: Inventing an Adequate Pedagogy," *Women's Studies Newsletter* 5 (Spring 1977): 21–24, gives valuable insights into how white women can approach the writing of Black women.
9. See p. 596. [Editor's note]
1. Darwin T. Turner, *In a Minor Chord: Three Afro-American Writers and Their Search for Identity* (Carbondale and Edwardsville: Southern Illinois University Press, 1971).
2. John Domini, "Roots and Racism: An Interview with Ishmael Reed," *Boston Phoenix,* April 5, 1977, p. 20.

In her introduction to "A Bibliography of Works Written by American Black Women" Ora Williams quotes some of the reactions of her colleagues toward her efforts to do research on Black women:

> Others have reacted negatively with such statements as, "I really don't think you are going to find very much written," "Have 'they' written anything that is any good?" and, "I wouldn't go overboard with this woman's lib thing." When discussions touched on the possibility of teaching a course in which emphasis would be on the literature by Black women, one response was, "Ha, ha. That will certainly be the most nothing course ever offered!"[3]

A remark by Alice Walker capsulizes what all the preceding examples indicate about the position of Black women writers and the reasons for the damaging criticism about them. She responds to her interviewer's question, "Why do you think that the black woman writer has been so ignored in America? Does she have even more difficulty than the black male writer, who perhaps has just begun to gain recognition?" Walker replies:

> There are two reasons why the black woman writer is not taken as seriously as the black male writer. One is that she's a woman. Critics seem unusually ill-equipped to intelligently discuss and analyze the works of black women. Generally, they do not even make the attempt; they prefer, rather, to talk about the lives of black women writers, not about what they write. And, since black women writers are not—it would seem—very likable—until recently they were the least willing worshippers of male supremacy—comments about them tend to be cruel."[4]

A convincing case for Black feminist criticism can obviously be built solely upon the basis of the negativity of what already exists. It is far more gratifying, however, to demonstrate its necessity by showing how it can serve to reveal for the first time the profound subtleties of this particular body of literature.

Before suggesting how a Black feminist approach might be used to examine a specific work, I will outline some of the principles that I think a Black feminist critic could use. Beginning with a primary commitment to exploring how both sexual and racial politics and Black and female identity are inextricable elements in Black women's writings, she would also work from the assumption that Black women writers constitute an identifiable literary tradition. The breadth of her familiarity with these writers would have shown her that not only is theirs a verifiable historical tradition that parallels in time the tradition of Black men and white women writing in this country, but that thematically, stylistically, aesthetically, and conceptually Black women writers manifest common approaches to the act of creating literature as a direct result of the specific political, social, and economic experience they have been obliged to share. The way, for example, that Zora Neale Hurston, Margaret Walker, Toni Morrison, and Alice Walker incorporate the traditional Black female activities of rootworking, herbal medicine, conjure, and midwifery into the fabric of their stories is not mere coincidence, nor is their use of specifically Black female language to express their own and their characters' thoughts accidental. The use of Black women's language and cultural experience in books *by* Black women *about* Black women results in a miraculously rich coalescing of form and content and also takes their writing far beyond the confines of white/male literary structures. The Black feminist critic would find innumerable commonalities in works by Black women.

Another principle which grows out of the concept of a tradition and which would also help to strengthen this tradition would be for the critic to look first for precedents and insights in interpretation within the works of other Black women. In other words she would think and write out of her own identity and not try to graft the ideas or methodology of white/male literary thought upon the precious materials of Black women's art. Black feminist criticism would by definition be highly innovative, embodying the daring spirit of the works themselves. The Black feminist critic would

3. Ora Williams, "A Bibliography of Works Written by American Black Women," *College Language Association Journal* 15 (March 1972): 355. There is an expanded book-length version of this bibliography: *American Black Women in the Arts and Social Sciences: A Bibliographic Survey* (Metuchen, N.J.: Scarecrow Press, 1973; rev. and expanded ed., 1978).
4. John O'Brien, ed., *Interviews with Black Writers* (New York: Liveright, 1973), p. 201.

be constantly aware of the political implications of her work and would assert the connections between it and the political situation of all Black women. Logically developed, Black feminist criticism would owe its existence to a Black feminist movement while at the same time contributing ideas that women in the movement could use.

Black feminist criticism applied to a particular work can overturn previous assumptions about it and expose for the first time its actual dimensions. At the "Lesbians and Literature" discussion at the 1976 Modern Language Association convention Bertha Harris[5] suggested that if in a woman writer's work a sentence refuses to do what it is supposed to do, if there are strong images of women and if there is a refusal to be linear, the result is innately lesbian literature. As usual, I wanted to see if these ideas might be applied to the Black women writers that I know and quickly realized that many of their works were, in Harris's sense, lesbian. Not because women are "lovers," but because they are the central figures, are positively portrayed and have pivotal relationships with one another. The form and language of these works are also nothing like what white patriarchal culture requires or expects.

I was particularly struck by the way in which Toni Morrison's novels *The Bluest Eye* and *Sula* could be explored from this new perspective.[6] In both works the relationships between girls and women are essential, yet at the same time physical sexuality is overtly expressed only between men and women. Despite the apparent heterosexuality of the female characters, I discovered in rereading *Sula* that it works as a lesbian novel not only because of the passionate friendship between Sula and Nel but because of Morrison's consistently critical stance toward the heterosexual institutions of male-female relationships, marriage, and the family. Consciously or not, Morrison's work poses both lesbian and feminist questions about Black women's autonomy and their impact upon each other's lives.

Sula and Nel find each other in 1922 when each of them is twelve, on the brink of puberty and the discovery of boys. Even as awakening sexuality "clotted their dreams," each girl desires "a someone" obviously female with whom to share her feelings. Morrison writes:

> ... for it was in dreams that the two girls had met. Long before Edna Finch's Mellow House opened, even before they marched through the chocolate halls of Garfield Primary School ... they had already made each other's acquaintance in the delirium of their noon dreams. They were solitary little girls whose loneliness was so profound it intoxicated them and sent them stumbling into Technicolored visions that always included a presence, a someone who, quite like the dreamer, shared the delight of the dream. When Nel, an only child, sat on the steps of her back porch surrounded by the high silence of her mother's incredibly orderly house, feeling the neatness pointing at her back, she studied the poplars and fell easily into a picture of herself lying on a flower bed, tangled in her own hair waiting for some fiery prince. He approached but never quite arrived. But always, watching the dream along with her, were some smiling sympathetic eyes. Someone as interested as she herself in the flow of her imagined hair, the thickness of the mattress of flowers, the voile sleeves that closed below her elbows in gold-threaded cuffs.

> Similarly, Sula, also an only child, but wedged into a household of throbbing disorder constantly awry with things, people, voices and the slamming of doors, spent hours in the attic behind a roll of linoleum galloping through her own mind on a gray-and-white horse tasting sugar and smelling roses in full view of someone who shared both the taste and the speed.

> So when they met, first in those chocolate halls and next through the ropes of the swing, they felt the ease and comfort of old friends. Because each had discovered years before that they were neither white nor male, and that all freedom and triumph was forbidden to them, they had set about creating something else to be. Their meeting was fortunate, for it let them use each other to grow on. Daughters

---

5. White American novelist best known for her 1976 novel *Lover* and for coauthoring *The Joy of Lesbian Sex* (1977). [Editor's note]
6. Toni Morrison, *The Bluest Eye* (1970; reprint ed., New York: Pocket Books, 1972, 1976) and *Sula* (New York: Alfred A. Knopf, 1974). All subsequent references to this work will be designated in the text.

of distant mothers and incomprehensible fathers (Sula's because he was dead; Nel's because he wasn't), they found in each other's eyes the intimacy they were looking for. (pp. 51–52)

As this beautiful passage shows, their relationship, from the very beginning, is suffused with an erotic romanticism. The dreams in which they are initially drawn to each other are actually complementary aspects of the same sensuous fairy tale. Nel imagines a "fiery prince" who never quite arrives while Sula gallops like a prince "on a gray-and-white horse."[7] The "real world" of patriarchy requires, however, that they channel this energy away from each other to the opposite sex. Lorraine Bethel explains this dynamic in her essay "Conversations with Ourselves: Black Female Relationships in Toni Cade Bambara's *Gorilla, My Love* and Toni Morrison's *Sula*."

> I am not suggesting that Sula and Nel are being consciously sexual, or that their relationship has an overt lesbian nature. I am suggesting, however, that there is a certain sensuality in their interactions that is reinforced by the mirror-like nature of their relationship. Sexual exploration and coming of age is a natural part of adolescence. Sula and Nel discover men together, and though their flirtations with males are an important part of their sexual exploration, the sensuality that they experience in each other's company is equally important.[8]

Sula and Nel must also struggle with the constrictions of racism upon their lives. The knowledge that "they were neither white nor male" is the inherent explanation of their need for each other. Morrison depicts in literature the necessary bonding that has always taken place between Black women for the sake of barest survival. Together the two girls can find the courage to create themselves.

Their relationship is severed only when Nel marries Jude, an unexceptional young man who thinks of her as "the hem—the tuck and fold that hid his raveling edges" (p. 83). Sula's inventive wildness cannot overcome social pressure or the influence of Nel's parents who "had succeeded in rubbing down to a dull glow any sparkle or splutter she had" (p. 83). Nel falls prey to convention while Sula escapes it. Yet at the wedding which ends the first phase of their relationship, Nel's final action is to look past her husband toward Sula,

> a slim figure in blue, gliding, with just a hint of a strut, down the path towards the road. . . . Even from the rear Nel could tell that it was Sula and that she was smiling; that something deep down in that litheness was amused. (p. 85)

When Sula returns ten years later, her rebelliousness full-blown, a major source of the town's suspicions stems from the fact that although she is almost thirty, she is still unmarried. Sula's grandmother, Eva, does not hesitate to bring up the matter as soon as she arrives. She asks:

> "When you gone to get married? You need to have some babies. It'll settle you. . . . Ain't no woman got no business floatin' around without no man." (p. 92)

Sula replies: "I don't want to make somebody else. I want to make myself" (p. 92). Self-definition is a dangerous activity for any woman to engage in, especially a Black one, and it expectedly earns Sula pariah status in Medallion.

Morrison clearly points out that it is the fact that Sula has not been tamed or broken by the exigencies of heterosexual family life which most galls the others.

> Among the weighty evidence piling up was the fact that Sula did not look her age. She was near thirty and, unlike them, had lost no teeth, suffered no bruises, developed no ring of fat at the waist or pocket at the back of her neck. (p. 115)

In other words she is not a domestic serf, a woman run down by obligatory childbearing or a victim of battering. Sula also sleeps with the husbands of the town once and then discards them, needing them even less than her own mother did for sexual gratification and

---

7. My sister, Beverly Smith, pointed out this connection to me.

8. Lorraine Bethel, "Conversations with Ourselves: Black Female Relationships in Toni Cade Bambara's *Gorilla, My Love* and Toni Morrison's *Sula*," unpublished paper written at Yale University, 1976, 47 pp. Bethel has worked from a premise similar to mine in a much more developed treatment of the novel.

affection. The town reacts to her disavowal of patriarchal values by becoming fanatically serious about their own family obligations, as if in this way they might counteract Sula's radical criticism of their lives.

Sula's presence in her community functions much like the presence of lesbians everywhere to expose the contradictions of supposedly "normal" life. The opening paragraph of the essay "The Woman-Identified Woman" has amazing relevance as an explanation of Sula's position and character in the novel. It asks:

> What is a lesbian? A lesbian is the rage of all women condensed to the point of explosion. She is the woman who, often beginning at an extremely early age, acts in accordance with her inner compulsion to be a more complete and freer human being than her society—perhaps then, but certainly later—cares to allow her. These needs and actions, over a period of years, bring her into painful conflict with people, situations, the accepted ways of thinking, feeling and behaving, until she is in a state of continual war with everything around her, and usually with herself. She may not be fully conscious of the political implications of what for her began as personal necessity, but on some level she has not been able to accept the limitations and oppression laid on her by the most basic role of her society—the female role.[9]

The limitations of the *Black* female role are even greater in a racist and sexist society, as is the amount of courage it takes to challenge them. It is no wonder that the townspeople see Sula's independence as imminently dangerous.

Morrison is also careful to show the reader that despite their years of separation and their opposing paths, Nel and Sula's relationship retains its primacy for each of them. Nell feels transformed when Sula returns and thinks:

> It was like getting the use of an eye back, having a cataract removed. Her old friend had come home. Sula. Who made her laugh, who made her see old things with new eyes, in whose presence she felt clever, gentle and a little raunchy. (p. 95)

Laughing together in the familiar "rib-scraping" way, Nel feels "new, soft and new" (p. 98). Morrison uses here the visual imagery which symbolizes the women's closeness throughout the novel.

Sula fractures this closeness, however, by sleeping with Nel's husband, an act of little import according to her system of values. Nel, of course, cannot understand. Sula thinks ruefully:

> Nel was the one person who had wanted nothing from her, who had accepted all aspects of her. Now she wanted everything, and all because of *that*. Nel was the first person who had been real to her, whose name she knew, who had seen as she had the slant of life that made it possible to stretch it to its limits. Now, Nel was one of *them*. (pp. 119–20)

Sula also thinks at the realization of losing Nel about how unsatisfactory her relationships with men have been and admits:

> She had been looking all along for a friend, and it took her a while to discover that a lover was not a comrade and could never be—for a woman. (p. 121)

The nearest that Sula comes to actually loving a man is in a brief affair with Ajax and what she values most about him is the intellectual companionship he provides, the brilliance he "allows" her to show.

Sula's feelings about sex with men are also consistent with a lesbian interpretation of the novel. Morrison writes:

> She went to bed with men as frequently as she could. It was the only place where she could find what she was looking for: *misery and the ability to feel deep sorrow.* . . . During the lovemaking she found and needed to find the cutting edge. When she left off cooperating with her body and began to assert herself in the act, particles of strength gathered in her like steel shavings drawn to a spacious magnetic center, forming a tight cluster that nothing, it seemed, could break. *And there was utmost irony and outrage in lying under someone, in a position of surrender, feeling her own abiding strength and limitless power.* . . . When her partner disengaged himself,

9. New York Radicalesbians, "The Woman-Identified Woman," in *Lesbians Speak Out* (Oakland, Calif.: Women's Press Collective, 1974), p. 87.

she looked up at him in wonder trying to recall his name . . . waiting impatiently for him to turn away . . . *leaving her to the postcoital privateness in which she met herself, welcomed herself, and joined herself in matchless harmony.* (pp. 122–23; italics mine)

Sula uses men for sex which results, not in communion with them, but in her further delving into self.

Ultimately the deepest communion and communication in the novel occurs between two women who love each other. After their last painful meeting, which does not bring reconciliation, Sula thinks as Nel leaves her:

> "So she will walk on down that road, her back so straight in that old green coat . . . thinking how much I have cost her and never remember the days when we were two throats and one eye and we had no price." (p. 147)

It is difficult to imagine a more evocative metaphor for what women can be to each other, the "pricelessness" they achieve in refusing to sell themselves for male approval, the total worth that they can only find in each other's eyes.

Decades later the novel concludes with Nel's final comprehension of the source of the grief that has plagued her from the time her husband walked out:

> "All that time, all that time, I thought I was missing Jude." And the loss pressed down on her chest and came up into her throat. "We was girls together," she said as though explaining something. "O Lord, Sula," she cried, "girl, girl, girlgirlgirl."
>
> It was a fine cry—loud and long—but it had no bottom and it had no top, just circles and circles of sorrow. (p. 174)

Again Morrison exquisitely conveys what women, Black women, mean to each other. This final passage verifies the depth of Sula and Nel's relationship and its centrality to an accurate interpretation of the work.

Sula is an exceedingly lesbian novel in the emotions expressed, in the definition of female character,

and in the way that the politics of heterosexuality are portrayed. The very meaning of lesbianism is being expanded in literature, just as it is being redefined through politics. The confusion that many readers have felt about Sula may well have a lesbian explanation. If one sees Sula's inexplicable "evil" and nonconformity as the evil of not being male-identified, many elements in the novel become clear. The work might be clearer still if Morrison had approached her subject with the consciousness that a lesbian relationship was at least a possibility for her characters. Obviously Morrison did not *intend* the reader to perceive Sula and Nel's relationship as inherently lesbian. However, this lack of intention only shows the way in which heterosexist assumptions can veil what may logically be expected to occur in a work. What I have tried to do here is not to prove that Morrison wrote something that she did not, but to point out how a Black feminist critical perspective at least allows consideration of this level of the novel's meaning.

In her interview in *Conditions: One* Adrienne Rich[1] talks about unconsummated relationships and the need to reevaluate the meaning of intense yet supposedly nonerotic connections between women. She asserts:

> We need a lot more documentation about what actually happened: I think we can also imagine it, because we know it happened—we know it out of our own lives.[2]

Black women are still in the position of having to "imagine," discover, and verify Black lesbian literature because so little has been written from an avowedly lesbian perspective. The near nonexistence of Black lesbian literature which other Black lesbians and I so deeply feel has everything to do with the politics of our lives, the total suppression of identity that all Black women, lesbian or not, must face. This literary silence is again intensified by the unavailability of an autonomous Black feminist movement through which we could fight our oppression and also begin to name ourselves.

---

1. White American poet, essayist, and professor (b. 1929); an activist in the civil rights, anti-war, feminist, and gay and lesbian rights movements. [Editor's note]

2. Elly Bulkin, "An Interview with Adrienne Rich: Part I," *Conditions: One* 1 (April 1977): 62.

In a speech, "The Autonomy of Black Lesbian Women," Wilmette Brown comments upon the connection between our political reality and the literature we must invent:

> Because the isolation of Black lesbian women, given that we are superfreaks, given that our lesbianism defies both the sexual identity that capital gives us and the racial identity that capital gives us, the isolation of Black lesbian women from heterosexual Black women is very profound. Very profound. I have searched throughout Black history, Black literature, whatever, looking for some women that I could see were somehow lesbian. Now I know that in a certain sense they were all lesbian. But that was a very painful search.[3]

Heterosexual privilege is usually the only privilege that Black women have. None of us have racial or sexual privilege, almost none of us have class privilege; maintaining "straightness" is our last resort. Being out, particularly out in print, is the final renunciation of any claim to the crumbs of "tolerance" that non-threatening "ladylike" Black women are sometimes fed. I am convinced that it is our lack of privilege and power in every other sphere that allows so few Black women to make the leap that many white women, particularly writers, have been able to make in this decade, not merely because they are white or have economic leverage, but because they have had the strength and support of a movement behind them.

As Black lesbians we must be out not only in white society but in the Black community as well, which is at least as homophobic. That the sanctions against Black lesbians are extremely high is well illustrated in this comment by Black male writer Ishmael Reed. Speaking about the inroads that whites make into Black culture, he asserts:

> In Manhattan you find people actively trying to impede intellectual debate among Afro-Americans. The powerful "liberal/radical/existentialist" influences of the Manhattan literary and drama establishment speak through tokens, like for example that ancient notion of the *one* black ideologue (who's usually a Communist), the *one* black poetess (who's usually a feminist lesbian).[4]

To Reed, "feminist" and "lesbian" are the most pejorative terms he can hurl at a Black woman and totally invalidate anything she might say, regardless of her actual politics or sexual identity. Such accusations are quite effective for keeping in line Black women writers who are writing with integrity and strength from any conceivable perspective, but especially ones who are actually feminist and lesbian. Unfortunately Reed's reactionary attitude is all too typical. A community which has not confronted sexism, because a widespread Black feminist movement has not required it to, has likewise not been challenged to examine its heterosexism. Even at this moment I am not convinced that one can write explicitly as a Black lesbian and live to tell about it.

Yet there are a handful of Black women who have risked everything for truth. Audre Lorde, Pat Parker, and Ann Allen Shockley have at least broken ground in the vast wilderness of works that do not exist.[5] Black feminist criticism will again have an essential role not only in creating a climate in which Black lesbian writers can survive, but in undertaking the total reassessment of Black literature and literary history needed to reveal the Black woman-identified women that Wilmette Brown and so many of us are looking for.

Although I have concentrated here upon what does not exist and what needs to be done, a few Black feminist critics have already begun this work. Gloria T. Hull at the University of Delaware has discovered

---

3. Wilmette Brown, "The Autonomy of Black Lesbian Women," manuscript of speech delivered July 24, 1976, in Toronto, Canada, p. 7.

4. Domini, "Roots and Racism," p. 18.

5. Audre Lorde, *New York Head Shop and Museum* (Detroit: Broadside Press, 1974); *Coal* (New York: W. W. Norton, 1976); *Between Our Selves* (Point Reyes, Calif.: Eidolon Editions, 1976); *The Black Unicorn* (New York: W. W. Norton, 1978). Pat Parker, *Child of Myself* (Oakland, Calif.: Women's Press Collective, 1972 and 1974); *Pit Stop* (Oakland, Calif.: Women's Press Collective, 1973); *Womanslaughter* (Oakland, Calif.: Diana Press, 1978); *Movement in Black* (Oakland, Calif.: Diana Press, 1978). Ann Allen Shockley, *Loving Her* (Indianapolis: Bobbs-Merrill, 1974). There is at least one Black lesbian writers' collective, Jemima, in New York. They do public readings and have available a collection of their poems. They can be contacted c/o Boyce, 41-11 Parsons Boulevard, Flushing, N.Y. 11355.

in her research on Black women poets of the Harlem Renaissance that many of the women who are considered "minor" writers of the period were in constant contact with each other and provided both intellectual stimulation and psychological support for each other's work. At least one of these writers, Angelina Weld Grimké,[6] wrote many unpublished love poems to women. Lorraine Bethel, a recent graduate of Yale College, has done substantial work on Black women writers, particularly in her senior essay, "This Infinity of Conscious Pain: Blues Lyricism and Hurston's Black Female Folk Aesthetic and Cultural Sensibility in *Their Eyes Were Watching God*," in which she brilliantly defines and uses the principles of Black feminist criticism. Elaine Scott at the State University of New York at Old Westbury is also involved in highly creative and politically resonant research on Hurston and other writers.

The fact that these critics are young and, except for Hull, unpublished merely indicates the impediments we face. Undoubtedly there are other women working and writing whom I do not even know, simply because there is no place to read them. As Michele Wallace states in her article "A Black Feminist's Search for Sisterhood":

> We exist as women who are Black who are feminists, each stranded for the moment, working independently because there is not yet an environment in this society remotely congenial to our struggle— [or our thoughts].[7]

I only hope that this essay is one way of breaking our silence and our isolation, of helping us to know each other.

Just as I did not know where to start I am not sure how to end. I feel that I have tried to say too much and at the same time have left too much unsaid. What I want this essay to do is lead everyone who reads it to examine *everything* that they have ever thought and believed about feminist culture and to ask themselves how their thoughts connect to the reality of Black women's writing and lives. I want to encourage in white women, as a first step, a sane accountability to all the women who write and live on this soil. I want most of all for Black women and Black lesbians somehow not to be so alone. This last will require the most expansive of revolutions as well as many new words to tell us how to make this revolution real. I finally want to express how much easier both my waking and my sleeping hours would be if there were one book in existence that would tell me something specific about my life. One book based in Black feminist and Black lesbian experience, fiction or nonfiction, just one work to reflect the reality that I and the Black women whom I love are trying to create. When such a book exists then each of us will not only know better how to live, but how to dream.

---

6. Playwright, teacher, journalist, and poet of the Harlem Renaissance; see p. 335. [Editor's note]
7. Michele Wallace, "A Black Feminist's Search for Sisterhood," *Village Voice,* July 28, 1975, p. 7.

KEY DEBATE ≈ *Race and Class*

E. FRANKLIN FRAZIER

From *Black Bourgeoisie* [1957, rev. 1962]

E. Franklin Frazier's *Black Bourgeoisie* elicited tremendous debate when it was published in the mid-1950s. At the time of its publication (in French in 1955 and in English in 1957), Frazier (p. 385) was already well-known as a sociologist specializing in African American culture and as the author of the groundbreaking *The Negro Family in the United States* (1939). But unlike his prior works, *Black Bourgeoisie* is a sweeping polemic, tracing the development of black middle-class culture from its pre-emancipation roots through the post–World War II era.

Frazier's depiction of middle-class African Americans is starkly unsympathetic; he shows them leading shallow lives based on conspicuous consumption. He maintains that "Negro business" and "Negro 'society'" are myths perpetuated by the black bourgeoisie with the collusion of the black press. According to Frazier, members of the black middle class live beyond their means as they strive to uphold those myths in order to compensate for deep-seated feelings of inferiority and self-hatred. In the book's final chapter, "Behind the Masks," reprinted here, Frazier argues that these myths are behind a variety of problematic cultural traits common among middle-class African Americans, from anti-Semitism to frustrated gender relations to a desire to "pass" as anything other than African American.

Frazier is particularly concerned that the black bourgeoisie's tendency to foreground class affiliation and minimize racial affiliation has negative political consequences. He suggests that attempts by member's of the black middle class to distance themselves from working-class African Americans not only discourage united efforts to fight racial oppression but also contribute to the perpetuation of racial stereotypes and discrimination. Unlike Claudia Jones (p. 452) and Elise Johnson McDougald (p. 307), Frazier does not see the charitable work done by women's clubs and other middle-class organizations as manifestations of grassroots activism and racial solidarity across classes. Instead, he sees even work for the poor as veiled and ultimately doomed attempts by the black bourgeoisie to advance socially.

From E. Franklin Frazier, *The Black Bourgeoisie: The Rise of a New Middle Class in the United States* (New York: Collier Books, 1962), pp. 176–91.

Since the black bourgeoisie live largely in a world of make-believe, the masks which they wear to play their sorry roles conceal the feelings of inferiority and of insecurity and the frustrations that haunt their inner lives. Despite their attempt to escape from real identification with the masses of Negroes, they can not escape the mark of oppression any more than their less favored kinsmen. In attempting to escape identification with the black masses, they have developed a self-hatred that reveals itself in their deprecation of the physical and social characteristics of Negroes. Likewise, their feelings of inferiority and insecurity are revealed in their pathological struggle for status within the isolated Negro world and craving for recognition in the white world. Their escape into a world of make-believe with its sham "society" leaves them with a feeling of emptiness and futility which causes them to constantly seek an escape in new delusions.

1. THE MARK OF OPPRESSION

There is an attempt on the part of the parents in middle-class families to shield their children against racial discrimination and the contempt of whites for colored people. Sometimes the parents go to fantastic extremes, such as prohibiting the use of the words "Negro" or "colored" in the presence of their children.[1] They sometimes try to prevent their children from knowing that they can not enter restaurants or other public places because they are Negroes, or even that the schools they attend are segregated schools for Negroes. Despite such efforts to insulate their children against a hostile white world, the children of the black bourgeoisie can not escape the mark of oppression. This is strikingly revealed in the statement of a seventeen-year-old middle-class Negro youth. When asked if he felt inferior in the presence of white people, he gave the following answer—which was somewhat unusual for its frankness but typical of the attitude of the black bourgeoisie:

> Off-hand, I'd say no, but actually knowing all these things that are thrown up to you about white people being superior—that they look more or less down upon all Negroes—that we have to look to them for everything we get—that they'd rather think of us as mice than men—I don't believe I or any other Negro can help but feel inferior. My father says that it isn't so—that we only feel inferior to those whom we feel are superior. But I don't believe we can feel otherwise. Around white people until I know them a while I feel definitely out of place. Once I played a ping-pong match with a white boy whose play I know wasn't as good as mine, and boys he managed to beat I beat with ease, but I just couldn't get it out of my mind that I was playing a white boy. Sort of an Indian sign on me, you know.[2]

The statement of this youth reveals how deep-seated is the feeling of inferiority, from which even the most favored elements among Negroes can not escape. However much some middle-class Negroes may seek to soothe their feeling of inferiority in an attitude which they often express in the adage, "it is better to reign in hell than serve in heaven," they are still conscious of their inferior status in American society. They may say, as did a bewildered middle-class youth, that they are proud of being a Negro or proud of being

a member of the upper stratum in the Negro community and feel sorry for the Negro masses "stuck in the mud," but they often confess, as did this youth:

> However, knowing that there are difficulties that confront us all as Negroes, if I could be born again and had my choice I'd really want to be a white boy—I mean white or my same color, providing I could occupy the same racial and economic level I now enjoy. I am glad I am this color—I'm frequently taken for a foreigner. I wouldn't care to be lighter or darker and be a Negro. I am the darkest one in the family due to my constant outdoor activities. I realize of course that there are places where I can't go despite my family or money just because I happen to be a Negro. With my present education, family background, and so forth, if I was only white I could go places in life. A white face holds supreme over a black one despite its economic and social status. Frankly, it leaves me bewildered.[3]

Not all middle-class Negroes consciously desire, as this youth, to be white in order to escape from their feelings of inferiority. In fact, the majority of middle-class Negroes would deny having the desire to be white, since this would be an admission of their feeling of inferiority. Within an intimate circle of friends some middle-class Negroes may admit that they desire to be white, but publicly they would deny any such wish. The black bourgeoisie constantly boast of their pride in their identification as Negroes. But when one studies the attitude of this class in regard to the physical traits or the social characteristics of Negroes, it becomes clear that the black bourgeoisie do not really wish to be identified with Negroes.

2. Insecurities and Frustrations

Since the black bourgeoisie can not escape identification with Negroes, they experience certain feelings of insecurity because of their feeling of inferiority. Their feeling of inferiority is revealed in their fear of

---

1. E. Franklin Frazier, *Negro Youth at the Crossways* (Washington, D. C.: American Council on Education, 1940), p. 62. [Unless otherwise indicated, all footnotes are those of the author.]

2. *Ibid.*, p. 67.

3. *Ibid.*, p. 66.

competition with whites. There is first a fear of competition with whites for jobs. Notwithstanding the fact that middle-class Negroes are the most vociferous in demanding the right to compete on equal terms with whites, many of them still fear such competition. They prefer the security afforded by their monopoly of certain occupations within the segregated Negro community. For example, middle-class Negroes demand that the two Negro medical schools be reserved for Negro students and that a quota be set for white students, though Negro students are admitted to "white" medical schools. Since the Supreme Court of the United States has ruled against segregated public schools, many Negro teachers, even those who are well-prepared, fear that they can not compete with whites for teaching positions. Although this fear stems principally from a feeling of inferiority which is experienced generally by Negroes, it has other causes.

The majority of the black bourgeoisie fear competition with whites partly because such competition would mean that whites were taking them seriously, and consequently they would have to assume a more serious and responsible attitude towards their work. Middle-class Negroes, who are notorious for their inefficiency in the management of various Negro institutions, excuse their inefficiency on the grounds that Negroes are a "young race" and, therefore, will require time to attain the efficiency of the white man. The writer has heard a Negro college president, who has constantly demanded that Negroes have equality in American life, declare before white people in extenuation of the shortcomings of his own administration, that Negroes were a "child race" and that they had "to crawl before they could walk." Such declarations, while flattering to the whites, are revealing in that they manifest the black bourgeoisie's contempt for the Negro masses, while excusing its own deficiencies by attributing them to the latter. Yet it is clear that the black workers who must gain a living in a white man's mill or factory and in competition with white workers can not offer any such excuse for his inefficiency.

The fear of competition with whites is probably responsible for the black bourgeoisie's fear of competence and first-rate performance within its own ranks. When a Negro is competent and insists upon first-rate work it appears to this class that he is trying to be a white man, or that he is insisting that Negroes measure up to white standards. This is especially true where the approval of whites is taken as a mark of competence and first-rate performance. In such cases the black bourgeoisie reveal their ambivalent attitudes toward the white world. They slavishly accept the estimate which almost any white man places upon a Negro or his work, but at the same time they fear and reject white standards. For example, when a group of Negro doctors were being shown the modern equipment and techniques of a white clinic, one of them remarked to a Negro professor in a medical school, "This is the white man's medicine. I never bother with it and still I make $30,000 a year." Negroes who adopt the standards of the white world create among the black bourgeoisie a feeling of insecurity and often become the object of both the envy and hatred of this class.

Among the women of the black bourgeoisie there is an intense fear of the competition of white women for Negro men. They often attempt to rationalize their fear by saying that the Negro man always occupies an inferior position in relation to the white woman or that he marries much below his "social" status. They come nearer to the source of their fear when they confess that there are not many eligible Negro men and that these few should marry Negro women. That such rationalizations conceal deep-seated feelings of insecurity is revealed by the fact that generally they have no objection to the marriage of white men to Negro women, especially if the white man is reputed to be wealthy. In fact, they take pride in the fact and attribute these marriages to the "peculiar" charms of Negro women. In fact, the middle-class Negro woman's fear of the competition of white women is based often upon the fact that she senses her own inadequacies and shortcomings. Her position in Negro "society" and in the larger Negro community is often due to some adventitious factor, such as a light complexion or a meager education, which has pushed her to the top of the social pyramid. The middle-class white woman not only has a white skin and straight hair, but she is generally more sophisticated and interesting because she has read more widely and has a larger view of the world. The middle-class Negro woman may make fun of the "plainness" of her white competitor and the latter's lack of "wealth" and interest in "society"; nevertheless she still feels insecure when white women appear as even potential competitors.

Both men and women among the black bourgeoisie have a feeling of insecurity because of their constant fear of the loss of status. Since they have no status in the larger American society, the intense struggle for status among middle-class Negroes is, as we have seen, an attempt to compensate for the contempt and low esteem of the whites. Great value is, therefore, placed upon all kinds of status symbols. Academic degrees, both real and honorary, are sought in order to secure status. Usually the symbols are of a material nature implying wealth and conspicuous consumption. Sometimes Negro doctors do not attend what are supposedly scientific meetings because they do not have a Cadillac or some other expensive automobile. School teachers wear mink coats and maintain homes beyond their income for fear that they may lose status. The extravagance in "social" life generally is due to an effort not to lose status. But in attempting to overcome their fear of loss of status they are often beset by new feelings of insecurity. In spite of their pretended wealth, they are aware that their incomes are insignificant and that they must struggle to maintain their mortgaged homes and the show of "wealth" in lavish "social" affairs. Moreover, they are beset by a feeling of insecurity because of their struggles to maintain a show of wealth through illegal means. From time to time "wealthy" Negro doctors are arrested for selling narcotics and performing abortions. The life of many a "wealthy" Negro doctor is shortened by the struggle to provide diamonds, minks, and an expensive home for his wife.

There is much frustration among the black bourgeoisie despite their privileged position within the segregated Negro world. Their "wealth" and "social" position can not erase the fact that they are generally segregated and rejected by the white world. Their incomes and occupations may enable them to escape the cruder manifestations of racial prejudice, but they can not insulate themselves against the more subtle forms of racial discrimination. These discriminations cause frustrations in Negro men because they are not allowed to play the "masculine role" as defined by American culture. They can not assert themselves or exercise power as white men do. When they protest against racial discrimination there is always the threat that they will be punished by the white world. In spite of the movement toward the wider integration of the Negro into the general stream of American life, middle-class Negroes are still threatened with the loss of positions and earning power if they insist upon their rights.[4] After the Supreme Court of the United States ruled that segregation in public education was illegal, Negro teachers in some parts of the South were dismissed because they would not sign statements supporting racial segregation in education.

As one of the results of not being able to play the "masculine role," middle-class Negro males have tended to cultivate their "personalities"[5] which enable them to exercise considerable influence among whites and achieve distinction in the Negro world. Among Negroes they have been noted for their glamour.[6] In this respect they resemble women who use their "personalities" to compensate for their inferior status in relation to men. This fact would seem to support the observation of an American sociologist that the Negro was "the lady among the races," if he had restricted his observation to middle-class males among American Negroes.[7]

In the South the middle-class Negro male is not only prevented from playing a masculine role, but generally he must let Negro women assume leadership in any show of militancy. This reacts upon his status in the home where the tradition of female dominance, which is widely established among Negroes, has tended to assign a subordinate role to the male. In fact, in middle-class families, especially if the husband has risen in social status through his own efforts and married a member of an "old" family or a "society" woman, the husband is likely to play a pitiful role. The greatest compliment that can be paid such a husband is that he

---

4. See, for example, the article "YMCA Secretary in Virginia Fired for Equality Fight," *Washington Afro-American*, August, 1954, p. 20.
5. One can not determine to what extent homosexuality among Negro males is due to the fact that they can not play a "masculine role."
6. See *Ebony*, July, 1949, where it is claimed that a poll on the most exciting Negro men in the United States reveals that the heyday of the "glamour boy" is gone and achievement rather than a handsome face and husky physique is the chief factor in making Negro men exciting to women.
7. See Robert E. Park and Ernest W. Burgess, *Introduction to the Science of Sociology* (Chicago: University of Chicago Press, 1924), p. 139.

"worships his wife," which means that he is her slave and supports all her extravagances and vanities. But, of course, many husbands in such positions escape from their frustrations by having extra-marital sex relations. Yet the conservative and conventional middle-class husband presents a pathetic picture. He often sits at home alone, impotent physically and socially, and complains that his wife has gone crazy about poker and "society" and constantly demands money for gambling and expenditures which he can not afford. Sometimes he enjoys the sympathy of a son or daughter who has not become a "socialite." Such children often say that they had a happy family life until "mamma took to poker."

Preoccupation with poker on the part of the middle-class woman is often an attempt to escape from a frustrated life. Her frustration may be bound up with her unsatisfactory sexual life. She may be married to a "glamorous" male who neglects her for other women. For among the black bourgeoisie, the glamour of the male is often associated with his sexual activities. The frustration of many Negro women has a sexual origin.[8] Even those who have sought an escape from frustration in sexual promiscuity may, because of satiety or deep psychological reasons, become obsessed with poker in order to escape from their frustrations. One "society" woman, in justification of her obsession with poker remarked that it had taken the place of her former preoccupation with sex. Another said that to win at poker was similar to a sexual orgasm.

The frustration of the majority of the women among the black bourgeoisie is probably due to the idle or ineffectual lives which they lead. Those who do not work devote their time to the frivolities of Negro "society." When they devote their time to "charity" or worth-while causes, it is generally a form of play or striving for "social" recognition. They are constantly forming clubs which ostensibly have a serious purpose, but in reality are formed in order to consolidate their position in "society" or to provide additional occasions for playing poker. The idle, overfed women among the black bourgeoisie are generally, to use their language, "dripping with diamonds." They are forever dieting and reducing only to put on more weight (which is usually the result of the food that they consume at their club meetings). Even the women among the black bourgeoisie who work exhibit the same frustrations. Generally, they have no real interest in their work and only engage in it in order to be able to provide the conspicuous consumption demanded by "society." As we have indicated, the women as well as the men among the black bourgeoisie read very little and have no interest in music, art or the theater. They are constantly restless and do not know how to relax. They are generally dull people and only become animated when "social" matters are discussed, especially poker games. They are afraid to be alone and constantly seek to be surrounded by their friends, who enable them to escape from their boredom.

The frustrated lives of the black bourgeoisie are reflected in the attitudes of parents towards their children. Middle-class Negro families as a whole have few children, while among the families that constitute Negro "society" there are many childless couples.[9] One finds today, as an American observed over forty years ago, that "where the children are few, they are usually spoiled" in middle-class Negro families.[1] There is often not only a deep devotion to their one or two children, but a subservience to them. It is not uncommon for the only son to be called and treated as the "boss" in the family. Parents cater to the transient wishes of their children and often rationalize their behavior towards them on the grounds that children should not be "inhibited." They spend large sums of money on their children for toys and especially for clothes. They provide their children with automobiles when they go to college. All of this is done in order that the children may maintain the status of the parents and be eligible to enter the "social" set in Negro colleges. When they send their children to northern "white" colleges they often spend more time in preparing them for what they imagine will be their "social" life than in preparing them for the academic requirements of these institutions.

8. See Kardiner and Ovesey, *op. cit.,* pp. 312 ff. concerning this point.
9. See Frazier, *The Negro Family in the United States,* pp. 440-43.
1. Robert E. Park, "Negro Home Life and Standards of Living," in *The Negro's Progress in Fifty Years* (Philadelphia: American Academy of Political and Social Science, 1913), p. 163.

In their fierce devotion to their children, which generally results in spoiling them, middle-class Negro parents are seemingly striving at times to establish a human relationship that will compensate for their own frustrations in the realm of human relationships. Devotion to their children often becomes the one human tie that is sincere and free from the competition and artificiality of the make-believe world in which they live. Sometimes they may project upon their children their own frustrated professional ambitions. But usually, even when they send their children to northern "white" universities as a part of their "social" striving within the Negro community, they seem to hope that their children will have an acceptance in the white world which has been denied them.

3. SELF-HATRED AND GUILT FEELINGS

One of the chief frustrations of the middle-class Negro is that he can not escape identification with the Negro race and consequently is subject to the contempt of whites.[2] Despite his "wealth" in which he has placed so much faith as a solvent of racial discrimination, he is still subject to daily insults and is excluded from participation in white American society. Middle-class Negroes do not express their resentment against discrimination and insults in violent outbreaks, as lower-class Negroes often do. They constantly repress their hostility toward whites and seek to soothe their hurt self-esteem in all kinds of rationalizations. They may boast of their wealth and culture as compared with the condition of the poor whites. Most often they will resort to any kind of subterfuge in order to avoid contact with whites. For example, in the South they often pay their bills by mail rather than risk unpleasant contacts with representatives of white firms.[3] The daily repression of resentment and the constant resort to means of avoiding contacts with whites do not relieve them of their hostility toward whites. Even middle-class Negroes who gain a reputation for exhibiting "objectivity" and a "statesmanlike" attitude on racial discrimination harbor deep-seated hostilities toward whites. A Negro college president who has been considered such an interracial "statesman" once confessed to the writer that some day he was going to "break loose" and tell white people what he really thought. However, it is unlikely that a middle-class Negro of his standing will ever "break loose." Middle-class Negroes generally express their aggressions against whites by other means, such as deceiving whites and utilizing them for their own advantage.

Because middle-class Negroes are unable to indulge in aggressions against whites as such, they will sometimes make other minority groups the object of their hostilities. For example, they may show hostility against Italians, who are also subject to discrimination. But more often middle-class Negroes, especially those who are engaged in a mad scramble to accumulate money, will direct their hostilities against Jews. They are constantly expressing their anti-semitism within Negro circles, while pretending publicly to be free from prejudice. They blame the Jew for the poverty of Negroes and for their own failures and inefficiencies in their business undertakings. In expressing their hostility towards Jews, they are attempting at the same time to identify with the white American majority.

The repressed hostilities of middle-class Negroes to whites are not only directed towards other minority

---

2. A Middle-class mulatto woman, a former school teacher, who was fearful of the impact of this book on European readers and southern detractors of "The Race," concluded her review of the original French edition with these words:

"Isn't it about time our sociologists and specialists on the 'race problem' in America, began to discuss and consider middle class Negroes as middle class Americans, or better, *all* U.S. Negroes as *Americans* with three hundred unbroken years of American tradition, way of life, cultural and spiritual contacts behind them—influences which have moulded them as they have moulded all others who are considered, even when not treated completely so, as members of the American community? Isn't it time to stop thinking of and talking about Negroes as a separate and distinct entity in the general scheme of things? And above all, isn't it time to realize that the melting pot has melted truly and fused together all the myriad (albeit conflicting) racial, cultural, educational, spiritual and social elements which have combined in such peculiar fashion to produce the American Negro of our time?" *Journal of Negro Education*, Vol. XXV, p. 141.

3. See Charles S. Johnson, *Patterns of Negro Segregation* (New York: Harper, 1943), Chapters XII, XIII, and XIV which describe the ways in which Negroes in various classes deal with racial discrimination.

groups but inward toward themselves. This results in self-hatred, which may appear from their behavior to be directed towards the Negro masses but which in reality is directed against themselves.[4] While pretending to be proud of being a Negro, they ridicule Negroid physical characteristics and seek to modify or efface them as much as possible. Within their own groups they constantly proclaim that "niggers" make them sick. The very use of the term "nigger," which they claim to resent, indicates that they want to disassociate themselves from the Negro masses. They talk condescendingly of Africans and of African culture, often even objecting to African sculpture in their homes. They are insulted if they are identified with Africans. They refuse to join organizations that are interested in Africa. If they are of mixed ancestry, they may boast of the fact that they have Indian ancestry. When making compliments concerning the beauty of Negroes of mixed ancestry, they generally say, for example, "She is beautiful; she looks like an Indian." On the other hand, if a black woman has European features, they will remark condescendingly, "Although she is black, you must admit that she is good looking." Some middle-class Negroes of mixed ancestry like to wear Hindu costumes—while they laugh at the idea of wearing an African costume. When middle-class Negroes travel, they studiously avoid association with other Negroes, especially if they themselves have received the slightest recognition by whites. Even when they can not "pass" for white they fear that they will lose this recognition if they are identified as Negroes. Therefore, nothing pleases them more than to be mistaken for a Puerto Rican, Philippino, Egyptian or Arab or any ethnic group other than Negro.

The self-hatred of middle-class Negroes is often revealed in the keen competition which exists among them for status and recognition. This keen competition is the result of the frustrations which they experience in attempting to obtain acceptance and recognition by whites. Middle-class Negroes are constantly criticizing and belittling Negroes who achieve some recognition or who acquire a status above them. They prefer to submit to the authority of whites than to be subordinate to other Negroes. For example, Negro scholars generally refuse to seek the advice and criticism of competent Negro scholars and prefer to turn to white scholars for such co-operation. In fact, it is difficult for middle-class Negroes to co-operate in any field of endeavor. This failure in social relations is, as indicated in an important study, because "in every Negro he encounters his own self-contempt."[5] It is as if he said, "You are only a Negro like myself; so why should you be in a position above me?"

This self-hatred often results in guilt feelings on the part of the Negro who succeeds in elevating himself above his fellows.[6] He feels unconsciously that in rising above other Negroes he is committing an act of aggression which will result in hatred and revenge on their part. The act of aggression may be imagined, but very often it is real. This is the case when middle-class Negroes oppose the economic and social welfare of Negroes because of their own interests. In some American cities, it has been the black bourgeoisie and not the whites who have opposed the building of low-cost public housing for Negro workers. In one city two wealthy Negro doctors, who have successfully opposed public housing projects for Negro workers, own some of the worst slums in the United States. While their wives, who wear mink coats, "drip with diamonds" and are written up in the "society" columns of Negro newspapers, ride in Cadillacs, their Negro tenants sleep on the dirt floors of hovels unfit for human habitation. The guilt feelings of the middle-class Negro are not always unconscious. For example, take the case of the Negro leader who proclaimed over the radio in a national broadcast that the Negro did not want social equity. He was conscious of his guilt feelings and his self-hatred in playing such a role, for he sent word privately to the writer that he never hated so much to do anything in his life, but that it was necessary because of his position as head of a state college which was under white supervision. The self-hatred of the middle-class Negro arises, then, not only from the fact that he does not want to be a Negro but also because of his sorry role in American society.

4. See Kardiner and Ovesey, *op. cit.*, pp. 190, 282, 297.
5. *Ibid.*, p. 177.
6. *Ibid.*, p. 203.

4. ESCAPE INTO DELUSIONS

The black bourgeoisie, as we have seen, has created a world of make-believe to shield itself from the harsh economic and social realities of American life. This world of make-believe is created out of the myth of Negro business, the reports of the Negro press on the achievements and wealth of Negroes, the recognition accorded them by whites, and the fabulous life of Negro "society." Some of the middle-class Negro intellectuals are not deceived by the world of make-believe. They will have nothing to do with Negro "society" and refuse to waste their time in frivolities. They take their work seriously and live in relative obscurity so far as the Negro world is concerned. Others seek an escape from their frustrations by developing, for example, a serious interest in Negro music—which the respectable black bourgeoisie often pretend to despise. In this way these intellectuals achieve some identification with the Negro masses and with the traditions of Negro life. But many more middle-class Negroes, who are satisfied to live in the world of make-believe but must find a solution to the real economic and social problems which they face, seek an escape in delusions.

They seek an escape in delusions involving wealth. This is facilitated by the fact that they have had little experience with the real meaning of wealth and that they lack a tradition of saving and accumulation. Wealth to them means spending money without any reference to its source. Hence, their behavior generally reflects the worst qualities of the gentleman and peasant from whom their only vital traditions spring. Therefore, their small accumulations of capital and the income which they receive from professional services within the Negro community make them appear wealthy in comparison with the low economic status of the majority of Negroes. The delusion of wealth is supported by the myth of Negro business. Moreover, the attraction of the delusion of wealth is enhanced by the belief that wealth will gain them acceptance in American life. In seeking an escape in the delusion of wealth, middle-class Negroes make a fetish of material things or physical possessions. They are constantly buying things—houses, automobiles, furniture and all sorts of gadgets, not to mention clothes. Many of the furnishings and gadgets which they acquire are never used; nevertheless they continue to accumulate things. The homes of many middle-class Negroes have the appearance of museums for the exhibition of American manufactures and spurious art objects. The objects which they are constantly buying are always on display. Negro school teachers who devote their lives to "society" like to display twenty to thirty pairs of shoes, the majority of which they never wear. Negro professional men proudly speak of the two automobiles which they have acquired when they need only one. The acquisition of objects which are not used or needed seems to be an attempt to fill some void in their lives.

The delusion of power also appears to provide an escape for middle-class Negroes from the world of reality which pierces through the world of make-believe of the black bourgeoisie. The positions of power which they occupy in the Negro world often enable them to act autocratically towards other Negroes, especially when they have the support of the white community. In such cases the delusion of power may provide an escape from their frustrations. It is generally, however, when middle-class Negroes hold positions enabling them to participate in the white community that they seek in the delusion of power an escape from their frustrations. Although their position may be only a "token" of the integration of the Negro into American life, they will speak and act as if they were a part of the power structure of American society. Negro advisers who are called into council by whites to give advice about Negroes are especially likely to find an escape from their feelings of inferiority in the delusion of power. Negro social workers, who are dependent upon white philanthropy, have often gained the reputation, with the support of the Negro press, of being powerful persons in American communities.

However, the majority of the black bourgeoisie who seek an escape from their frustrations in delusions seemingly have not been able to find it in the delusion of wealth or power. They have found it in magic or chance, and in sex and alcohol. Excessive drinking and sex seem to provide a means for narcotizing the middle-class Negro against a frustrating existence. A "social" function is hardly ever considered a success unless a goodly number of the participants "pass out."

But gambling, especially poker, which has become an obsession among many middle-class Negroes, offers the chief escape into delusion. Among the black bourgeoisie it is not simply a device for winning money. It appears to be a magical device for enhancing their self-esteem through overcoming fate.[7] Although it often involves a waste of money which many middle-class Negroes can not afford, it has an irresistible attraction which they often confess they can not overcome.

Despite the tinsel, glitter and gaiety of the world of make-believe in which middle-class Negroes take refuge, they are still beset by feelings of insecurity, frustration and guilt. As a consequence, the free and easy life which they appear to lead is a mask for their unhappy existence.

ESTHER POPEL SHAW

Review of Frazier's Bourgeoisie Noire [1956]

Esther Popel Shaw (1896–1958), a poet of the Harlem Renaissance and a former Washington, D.C., public school teacher, responded to the 1955 French publication of *Bourgeoisie Noire* (*Black Bourgeoisie*) with a review that conveys many of the common negative responses that black critics voiced about the content, tone, and potential political ramifications of Frazier's book. Shaw bases her judgment of Frazier's ideas on her own experiences as a member of the black middle class.

Although she purposely leaves academic assessment of the book to sociologists, she subtly challenges the book's scientific merit by arguing that denigration of a particular group, exaggeration, and a tone of ridicule are inappropriate to a scholarly work "such as this study purports to be." Ultimately, Shaw rejects the legitimacy of Frazier's project itself, suggesting that his primary focus on social class oversimplifies the complex mixture of historical and cultural influences that shapes individual black lives.

From *The Journal of Negro Education* (Spring 1956), pp. 25, 140–41.

T he fact that Dr. Grayson, a University of Maryland professor, has published a study of the American Middle Class ("The Crisis of the Middle Class," by Henry Grayson, Rinehart and Co., New York, 172 pp.) almost simultaneously with the appearance of this, the most recent publication by Howard University's Dr. Frazier, should give sociologists a field day, where contrasts and comparisons, as well as points of view on middle class life in America are concerned.

In her review of professor Grayson's book in the Sunday, January 15, 1956 Book Review Section of the Washington *Post-Times-Herald,* Malvina Lindsay gives this brief summary of the author's definition of the term "Middle Class": "He sees a member of the middle class as an individualist who may be anywhere in the social scale, but who is determined to move into a preferred position. The middle class is the 'yeast of society'

because its members are constantly trying to change, rearrange, energize the status quo."

She further comments that: "Americans who always are intrigued with looking at themselves will find in this study (Grayson's) a revealing analysis of their middle class society and also some warnings concerning its trends."

In Dr. Frazier's book about the *Negro* middle class the picture he gives of this segment of American society will also "intrigue" those about whom he writes. But *his* "revealing analysis" is more than likely to dismay many of his readers and create a furore of discussion among many members of the "minority middle class" who will be unwilling to accept his findings as completely true, or completely fair to them.

About the book Dr. Frazier's publishers give this descriptive resumé (translated into English by the

7. *Ibid.,* pp. 313 ff.

present reviewer): "In his latest work which he wanted to see appear in Europe, Franklin Frazier treats an unknown aspect of the Negro problem. From the first chapters he establishes, in effect, that about $1/6$ of the Negro population of the U.S. can actually be designated as "middle class" by the professions they follow. But in developing itself this middle class has disavowed its origins and renounced its deliverance. Parallelly it has turned away from all fruitful creation in the artistic and scientific realm and has rejected its own "culture," knowing only how to imitate the whites in the hope of obtaining a status of equality. Living on the fringe of a society which refuses to recognize it, the Negro middle class has failed in its rôle of the élite, and tends henceforth only to become Nobody. The Negro middle class is nobody! The rigorous and clear analysis to which Frazier submits all the aspects of the problem reveals the dramatic defeat of a minority and the complexes from which it suffers."

With Dr. Frazier recognized "incontestably" as, perhaps, the foremost authority on the Negro problem on our side of the Atlantic today, one can readily appreciate, and with some trepidation, the impact of this study on European readers who are not too well-informed about Negro Americans—to say nothing of the unwholesome effect it is bound to have here at home, on the "professional" (and Southern) detractors of "The Race" in these difficult times of integration or attempts in that direction.

The proper evaluation of this book as a sociological document is in the province of, and should be made by, trained sociologists, of course. From the point of view of a lay reader, however, it is possible to venture a non-sociological opinion and (shall we call it?) a "middle class" impression of the study. The opinion is that too many members of the Negro middle class have been unjustly described by Dr. Frazier in the generalizations he has made, particularly in the final chapters of his book. The impression is that ridicule (which has its place in literature but not in an objective, factual presentation), exaggeration and denigration of any group, black or white, are not desirable techniques to employ in a serious, and for the most part, scholarly presentation, such as this study purports to be.

In the impressive bibliography which is included at the end of the book we note that Dr. Frazier has authored more than sixty articles, books, etc., in the thirty-two years he has been a specialist on the subject of the Negro in America. We note too that he has now in process of publication a study bearing the title of "The Black Middle Class Thirty Years After the Negro Renaissance" which will appear, no doubt, in English. Most likely this study will present much if not all of the data now included in "Bourgeoisie Noire." This is greatly to be desired so that "all who run may read" and thereby be prepared to meet, and to answer, some of the comments, criticisms and questions it is bound to bring from our neighbors overseas, for whose benefit Dr. Frazier's book was published, in French!

By way of conclusion, isn't it about time our sociologists and specialists on the "race problem" in America, began to discuss and consider middle class Negroes as middle class Americans, or better, *all* U.S. Negroes as *Americans* with three hundred unbroken years of American tradition, way of life, cultural and spiritual contacts behind them—influences which have moulded them as they have moulded all others who are considered, even when not treated completely so, as members of the American community? Isn't it time to stop thinking of and talking about Negroes as a separate and distinct entity in the general scheme of things? And above all, isn't it time to realize that the melting pot has melted truly and fused together all the myriad (albeit conflicting) racial, cultural, educational, spiritual and social elements which have combined in such peculiar fashion to produce the American Negro of our time? To try to unscramble the egg at this late date is both a Herculean task and an impossible one, when the "egg" is the Negro of today, whether or not he comes from the masses or belongs to the much maligned middle class which Dr. Frazier discusses in his study of the "Bourgeoisie Noire."

E. FRANKLIN FRAZIER

Preface to Black Bourgeoisie [1962]

For the 1962 edition of *Black Bourgeoisie,* Frazier added a preface addressing the controversy the book provoked. In those remarks, reprinted here, he recognizes the outraged reactions of black and white critics, but he finds that they in fact only support his analysis: black leaders feel betrayed by him for airing their secrets in public, and white Americans have a vested interest in maintaining the myth of a powerful black business community. While flatly defending the continued relevance of his critique of the black bourgeoisie, Frazier suggests that a new type of middle-class African American is developing, as can be seen in the students involved in the civil rights movement who have embraced Frazier's ideas. Tellingly, he asserts that such middle-class students have their roots in black folk culture, a claim that supports his conviction that the promise of civil rights lies with the black masses.

From E. Franklin Frazier, *Black Bourgeoisie: The Rise of a New Middle Class in the United States* (New York: Collier Books, 1962), pp. 7–14.

This book first appeared in France as one of the studies in the collection known as *Recherches en Sciences Humaines.*[1] When the French edition was published I expected that like so many social science studies it would become lost on the shelves of university libraries. It came as a pleasant surprise, therefore, to learn that it attracted sufficient attention in the academic world for it to be made the basis of the MacIver Lectureship award by the American Sociological Society in 1956. When the English edition was published in the United States in 1957, I was even more surprised by the controversy which it aroused among Negroes and by the unfavorable reactions of many whites.

The reaction of the Negro community is understandable when one realizes the extent to which the book created the shock of self-revelation. In fact, if one should undertake to conceptualize the reaction of the Negro community, the initial reaction—at least on the part of its more articulate leaders—was one of shock. It appeared that middle class Negroes were able to see themselves for the first time and, as they feared, in the way they appeared to outsiders. They did not challenge the truth of the picture which had been presented so much as they were shocked that a Negro would dare place on display their behavior and innermost thoughts. Their naive attitude towards their behavior and outlook on life was strikingly revealed in the remark of a journalist whose publication had been drawn on for much illustrative material in the book. When I met his criticism of quoting materials by asking him if his publication was not a reliable source of information, he replied that the facts in the book looked and sounded different from what they did where they appeared in his magazine.

Following the initial shock of self-revelation was intense anger on the part of many leaders in the Negro community. This anger was based largely upon their feeling that I had betrayed Negroes by revealing their life to the white world. I was attacked by some Negroes as being bitter because I had not been accepted socially and by others as having been paid to defame the Negro. In one Negro newspaper there was a sly suggestion that Negroes should use violence to punish me for being a traitor to the Negro race. Some of the anger was undoubtedly due to the fact that I had revealed the real economic position of the Negro. They were particularly incensed by a mere statement of fact that the total assets of all Negro banks in the United States were less than those of a single small white bank in a small town in the State of New York.

The anger of the middle class over this statement showed how much they regarded the book as a threat to their economic interests. They had helped to create the myth of the vast purchasing power of Negroes which had become the justification for large corpora-

1. *Bourgeoisie Noire.* Paris: Librairie Plon, 1955. [Unless otherwise indicated, all footnotes are those of the author.]

tions to employ Negro salesmen so as to exploit the Negro market.

It is interesting to note, however, that the anger on the part of the Negro community was not shared by all strata. From rumors and from what had appeared in book reviews in both white and Negro newspapers, some working class Negroes got the impression that I had written a book attacking "upper-class, light-skinned" Negroes. As a consequence I was even stopped on the street by working-class Negroes who shook my hand for having performed this long overdue service.

As the book became more widely read and discussed Negroes began to judge the book more soberly and in many cases not only to applaud my "courage" in writing the book but to say that it was an important contribution to an understanding of the Negro's plight in the United States. Numerous letters were sent directly to me and sometimes to the Negro newspapers defending the book or congratulating me on my courage. One minister wrote that the book should be read by every Negro preacher in the United States. Letters of this type continue to come to me and I am constantly invited to speak to forums and groups on the position and outlook of the new Negro middle class. This reaction of the Negro community presented a sharp contrast to what happened when the reaction of Negroes was characterized by anger. For example, I was invited by a Negro sorority to discuss the book but so much bitterness was aroused by the invitation that it had to be canceled. One leading member of the sorority accused me of having set the Negro race back fifty years. But such reactions are rare today and I am much more likely to receive copies of articles or speeches in which there are favorable references to the book, discussions of the book's implications or even documentation in support of its analysis.

The reaction of the white people outside the United States was different, on the whole, from that of white Americans. European and Latin American scholars praised the book, on the whole, as a contribution to social science and as a lucid analysis of what is happening to the American Negro. A liberal European scholar living in South Africa said that when she read the book her first reaction was, "My God, the American Negro has finally come of age; he is capable of self-analysis and self-criticism." Under the title, "Un Livre Explosif," a leading French newspaper, *Le Monde* (February 13, 1957) carried a perceptive summary review of the book. In fact, it was often European scholars who were most puzzled by the reactions of white Americans. A European told me two years ago that he could understand why middle-class Negroes might be angry about the book but that he could not understand the anger which it aroused among some white Americans. Let us turn to the reactions of some white Americans and undertake to explain them.

The critical reviews which appeared in American scholarly journals were concerned for the most part with questions involving methodology and the validity of my conclusions. In some of the more serious journals of opinion there also appeared critical reviews. But even in some of the scholarly reviews as well as in the serious journals of opinion there was either an implicit or explicit criticism that the book exhibited anger or lack of sympathy in its stark objectivity. A leading political analyst said that the book was cruel because if Negroes were happy in their world of make-believe, why should I feel it was my duty to let them know the truth about their real position in the United States? Although it appeared that many whites shared this opinion, there were others who welcomed the book as an explanation of the behavior of middle-class Negroes— behavior which had long puzzled them. Some of them came to me and stated frankly that they had been puzzled, for example, by the conspicuous consumption on the part of middle-class Negroes but that after reading the book they could understand it.

Perhaps the main reason for the bitter reaction on the part of some white Americans (some book stores refused to carry the book because it was "controversial") was that it destroyed or tended to destroy the image of Negroes which they wanted to present to the world at this time. The picture which white Americans wanted to present to the world was that although Negroes had been enslaved and had suffered many disabilities since Emancipation, on the whole they were well off economically, had gained civil rights, and had improved their social status. Therefore, what had happened to them during slavery, which was after all a mild paternalistic system, should be forgotten along with the other injustices which they have suffered since.

Moreover, their economic position was superior to that of other peoples of the world, especially the colored peoples. One article published by a distinguished statesman even went so far as to state that Negroes were spending annually an amount equal to the annual national income of Canada.

Now, *Black Bourgeoisie* was a refutation of this image. It showed that slavery was a cruel and barbaric system that annihilated the Negro as a person, a fact which has been well-documented and substantiated in a recent book.[2] Moreover, the book also showed how, since Emancipation, Negroes had been outsiders in American society. Finally, it demonstrated on the basis of factual knowledge that Negroes were not only at the bottom of the economic ladder but that all the pretended economic gains which Negroes were supposed to have made had not changed fundamentally their relative economic position in American life. It revealed also that the new Negro middle class was comprised almost entirely of wage earners and salaried professionals and that so-called Negro business enterprises amounted to practically nothing in the American economy. This was not, of course, the image of Negroes that white Americans wanted to present to the world, especially at a time when they were endeavoring to win the confidence and friendship of the colored world.

Very often the question is asked whether there is need for a revision of this book. Has not the economic position of the Negro middle classes changed? Have not middle-class Negroes become accustomed to their new prosperity and given up much of their conspicuous consumption? From the latest figures on the occupations and the incomes of middle-class Negroes there is no reason to revise what was written about the relative size of the middle class and their occupational status nor the source and amount of their incomes. The essential fact is that they still do not own any of the real wealth of America or play an important role in American business. And it is difficult to see how their economic position could change fundamentally within five years. In reply to the second question one would only need to read Negro newspapers and magazines to see to what extent conspicuous consumption is still the dominant pattern of this class. In the cities of the country middle-class Negro communities are expanding but they are characterized by the same conspicuous consumption the book describes. School teachers and college professors who earn less than $10,000 a year are building homes that cost $40,000 and $50,000 and entertaining lavishly. In this connection one is reminded of the article which appeared recently in a white publication on the Negro aristocracy and Negro millionaires.[3] It should be noted that many Negroes resented this article as a misrepresentation of the real economic position of Negro professional men and women. Since this article appeared I have received numerous letters and comments saying the article confirmed what I had said about the world of make-believe in which middle-class Negroes live.

There is, however, an important aspect of the development of the New Negro middle class that might have been included in this book and certainly could not be omitted from a more detailed study. It is strange that the omission was overlooked by American critics but suggested in a foreign review. I am referring to the most recent accessions to the Negro middle classes who are prominent in the sit-ins and in the other protest movements against racial segregation. They do not have the same social background as the black bourgeoisie in my study who represent a fusion of the peasant and the gentleman. Although they have been influenced to some extent by the genteel tradition, on the whole their social background is essentially that of the Negro folk. Very seldom can they or their parents claim ancestors among the mixed-blood aristocracy which was free before the Civil War.

Some attention must be given to two more serious criticisms of the book as it now stands. The first concerns the materials upon which the analyses are based. Here I am not concerned with the question of adequate samplings of middle-class Negroes with respect to attributes that can be treated statistically. I am referring especially to the analyses of the patterns of behavior and values of this class. Let me begin by stating that it would be difficult to secure a more reliable validation of this study in regard to patterns of behavior and style of life and values of the Negro middle class than that which has been provided in the letters and comments

---

2. Stanley M. Elkins, *Slavery, a Problem in American Institutional and Intellectual Life.* Chicago: The University of Chicago Press, 1959.
3. Bill Davidson, "Our Negro Aristocracy," *The Saturday Evening Post,* January 13, 1962.

which have come to me from cities all over the country. These letters have stated first that they did not know that I had carried on researches in their community until they had read the book which provided such an authentic picture of the middle class in their city. In many cases they complained that the picture was so true to life that they could recognize the people by their behavior and verbal statements and their relation to the rest of the community. As a matter of fact, in most cases I had never made a study in their community. An amusing incident connected with this aspect of the study happened in one city where my junior colleagues had made a housing survey. After the English edition appeared, they were accused of having spied on the behavior of the middle classes and were threatened with a thrashing if they ever returned to that city. The majority of the materials upon which this study was based were materials on thousands of Negro families and many Negro communities which I had collected during studies over the years. For the purposes of this study, additional materials were collected from newspapers and magazines and from students from middle-class families. In many cases, as a participant-observer, I collected case materials in the same manner as an anthropologist gathers materials for studies.

Another criticism which deserves attention was that this study did not reveal anything peculiar to Negroes. This was a criticism offered not only by Negroes who are sensitive about being different from other people, but by white people as well. Some of them were the so-called liberal whites who, when any statement is made which might be considered derogatory concerning Negroes, are quick to say that the "same thing is found among whites." Other whites pointed out what is undoubtedly true: that this book dealt with behavior which is characteristic of middle-class people—white, black or brown. Some of my Jewish friends, including some young sociologists, went so far as to say that the book was the best account that they had ever read concerning middle-class Jews. Here I might repeat what I stated in the book: that the behavior of middle-class Negroes was an American phenomenon and that in writing, I was constantly tempted to make comparisons with middle-class whites, but that the book was essentially a case study of the new Negro middle class. It was not my intention to make a comparative study. As a case study of middle-class Negroes, it does show the peculiar conditions under which a middle class emerged among the Negro minority and the peculiar social and cultural heritage of the Negro middle class which was responsible for its outlook on life.

In retrospect when I consider the reaction of the Negro community and the criticisms of both Negroes and whites of all intellectual levels, I am reminded of a review of the French edition which appeared on the front page of a French newspaper published in the United States.[4] The review concluded with the questions: Would this book arouse heated discussions in which each protagonist would hold stubbornly to his particular opinion? Would it contribute to modifying the mentality of this elite which is oblivious of its duties and responsibilities? A partial answer was given to these questions by some of the young leaders of the sit-ins who said they did not aspire to become the middle-class Negroes described in *Black Bourgeoisie*. Finally, in regard to the charge that the presentation was brutal or cruel, I will only quote the words of a Catholic sociological review concerning the book: "A sad truth is better than a merry lie."

WILLIAM JULIUS WILSON

from *The Declining Significance of Race* [1978]

William Julius Wilson (b. 1935) was a professor of sociology at the University of Chicago when he sparked a widespread debate with the publication of *The Declining*

Significance of Race in 1978. In this excerpt from the book, originally published in the journal *Society*, Wilson argues that the growing class differentiation among

4. *Le Travailleur.* Worcester, Massachusetts, April 12, 1956.

African Americans (which has occurred mostly since the 1960s) has led to a shift in the relative importance of race and class in American society. Although he recognizes that race remains a major factor in modern life—particularly in shaping community and home life—Wilson maintains that class has overtaken race as the primary factor in determining the socioeconomic status of African Americans. He links this shift to a change in the government's role in society and to changes in the economy. At the same time, Wilson finds, increased social stratification has led to an entrenchment of the black underclass. Wilson attributes the disproportionate percentage of black Americans in the underclass to the "historical consequences of racial oppression" rather than to "the current effects of race." His position has direct implications for public policy because they suggest that social programs should alter their outdated focus on different ethnic and racial groups and directly confront inequalities reinforced by social class.

From *Society*, January–February 1978.

R ace relations in the United States have undergone fundamental changes in recent years, so much so that now the life chances of individual blacks have more to do with their economic class position than with their day-to-day encounters with whites. In earlier years the systematic efforts of whites to suppress blacks were obvious to even the most insensitive observer. Blacks were denied access to valued and scarce resources through various ingenious schemes of racial exploitation, discrimination, and segregation, schemes that were reinforced by elaborate ideologies of racism.

But the situation has changed. However determinative such practices were in the previous efforts of the black population to achieve racial equality, and however significant they were in the creation of poverty-stricken ghettoes and a vast underclass of black proletarians—that massive population at the very bottom of the social class ladder plagued by poor education and low-paying, unstable jobs—they do not provide a meaningful explanation of the life chances of black Americans today. The traditional patterns of interaction between blacks and whites, particularly in the labor market, have been fundamentally altered.

NEW AND TRADITIONAL BARRIERS

In the pre–Civil War period, and in the latter half of the nineteenth through the first half of the twentieth century, the continuous and explicit efforts of whites to construct racial barriers profoundly affected the lives of black Americans. Racial oppression was designed, overt, and easily documented. As the nation has entered the latter half of the twentieth century, however, many of the traditional barriers have crumbled under the weight of the political, social, and economic changes of the civil rights era. A new set of obstacles has emerged from basic structural shifts in the economy.

These obstacles are therefore impersonal, but may prove to be even more formidable for certain segments of the black population. Specifically, whereas the previous barriers were usually designed to control and restrict the entire black population, the new barriers create hardships essentially for the black underclass; whereas the old barriers were based explicitly on racial motivations derived from intergroup contact, the new barriers have racial significance only in their consequences, not in their origins. In short, whereas the old barriers portrayed the pervasive features of racial oppression, the new barriers indicate an important and emerging form of class subordination.

It would be shortsighted to view the traditional forms of racial segregation and discrimination as having essentially disappeared in contemporary America; the presence of blacks is still firmly resisted in various institutions and social arrangements, for example, residential areas and private social clubs. However, in the economic sphere class has become more important than race in determining black access to privilege and power. It is clearly evident in this connection that many talented and educated blacks are now entering positions of prestige and influence at a rate comparable to or, in some situations, exceeding that of whites with equivalent qualifications. It is equally clear that the black underclass is in a hopeless state of economic stagnation, falling further and further behind the rest of society.

THREE STAGES OF AMERICAN RACE RELATIONS

American society has experienced three major stages of black-white contact, and each stage embodies a different form of racial stratification structured by the particular arrangement of both the economy and the polity. Stage one coincides with antebellum slavery and the early postbellum era and may be designated the period of *plantation economy and racial-caste oppression.* Stage two begins in the last quarter of the nineteenth century and ends at roughly the New Deal era,[1] and may be identified as the period of *industrial expansion, class conflict, and racial oppression.* Finally, stage three is associated with the modern, industrial, post–World War II era which really began to crystallize during the 1960s and 1970s, and may be characterized as the period of *progressive transition from race inequalities to class inequalities.* The different periods can be identified as the preindustrial, industrial, and modern industrial stages of American race relations, respectively.

Although this abbreviated designation of the periods of American race relations seems to relate racial change to fundamental economic changes rather directly, it bears repeating that the different stages of race relations are structured by the unique arrangements and interaction of the economy and the polity. More specifically, although there was an economic basis of structured racial inequality in the preindustrial and industrial periods of race relations, the polity more or less interacted with the economy either to reinforce patterns of racial stratification or to mediate various forms of racial conflict. Moreover, in the modern industrial period race relations have been shaped as much by important economic changes as by important political changes. Indeed, it would not be possible to understand fully the subtle and manifest changes in

race relations in the modern industrial period without recognizing the dual and often reciprocal influence of structural changes in the economy and political changes in the state. Thus different systems of production and/or different arrangements of the polity have imposed different constraints on the way in which racial groups have interacted in the United States, constraints that have structured the relations between racial groups and that have produced dissimilar contexts not only for the manifestation of racial antagonisms, but also for racial group access to rewards and privileges.

In contrast to the modern industrial period in which fundamental economic and political changes have made the economic class position of blacks the determining factor in their prospects for occupational advancement, the preindustrial and industrial periods of black-white relations have one central feature in common: overt efforts of whites to solidify economic racial domination (ranging from the manipulation of black labor to the neutralization or elimination of black economic competition) through various forms of juridical, political, and social discrimination. Since racial problems during these two periods were principally related to group struggles over economic resources, they readily lend themselves to the economic class theories of racial antagonisms that associate racial antipathy with class conflict.

Although racial oppression, when viewed from the broad perspective of historical change in American society, was a salient and important feature during the preindustrial and industrial periods of race relations in the United States, the problems of subordination for certain segments of the black population and the experience of social advancement for others are more directly associated with economic class in the modern industrial period. Economic and political changes have gradually shaped a black class structure, making it increasingly difficult to speak of a single or uniform black experience. Although a small elite population of free, propertied blacks did in fact exist during the pre–Civil War period, the interaction between race and economic class only assumed real importance

---

1. Reference to economic programs established by President Franklin D. Roosevelt starting in 1933 to combat the effects of the Great Depression, many of which were disbanded during World War II.

in the latter phases of the industrial period of race relations; and the significance of this relationship has grown as the nation has entered the modern industrial period.

Each of the major periods of American race relations has been shaped in different measure both by the systems of production and by the laws and policies of the state. However, the relationships between the economy and the state have varied in each period, and therefore the roles of both institutions in shaping race relations have differed over time.

ANTEBELLUM SOUTH

In the preindustrial period the slave-based plantation economy of the South allowed a relatively small, elite group of planters to develop enormous regional power. The hegemony of the southern ruling elite was based on a system of production that required little horizontal or vertical mobility and therefore could be managed very efficiently with a simple division of labor that virtually excluded free white labor. As long as free white workers were not central to the process of reproducing the labor supply in the southern plantation economy, slavery as a mode of production facilitated the slaveholder's concentration and consolidation of economic power. And the slaveholders successfully transferred their control of the economic system to the political and legal systems in order to protect their class interest in slavery. In effect, the polity in the South regulated and reinforced the system of racial caste oppression, depriving both blacks and nonslaveholding whites of any meaningful influence in the way that slavery was used in the economic life of the South.

In short, the economy provided the basis for the development of the system of slavery, and the polity reinforced and perpetuated that system. Furthermore, the economy enabled the slaveholders to develop a regional center of power, and the polity was used to legitimate that power. Since nonslaveholding whites were virtually powerless both economically and politically, they had very little effect on the developing patterns of race relations. The meaningful forms of black-white contact were between slaves and slaveholders, and southern race relations consequently assumed a paternalistic quality involving the elaboration and specification of duties, norms, rights, and obligations as they pertained to the use of slave labor and the system of indefinite servitude.

In short, the pattern of race relations in the antebellum South was shaped first and foremost by the system of production. The very nature of the social relations of production meant that the exclusive control of the planters would be derived from their position in the production process, which ultimately led to the creation of a juridical system that reflected and protected their class interests, including their investment in slavery.

WORKERS' EMERGING POWER

However, in the nineteenth century antebellum North the form of racial oppression was anything but paternalistic. Here a more industrial system of production enabled white workers to become more organized and physically concentrated than their southern counterparts. Following the abolition of slavery in the North, they used their superior resources to generate legal and informal practices of segregation that effectively prevented blacks from becoming serious economic competitors.

As the South gradually moved from a plantation to an industrial economy in the last quarter of the nineteenth century, landless whites were finally able to effect changes in the racial stratification system. Their efforts to eliminate black competition helped to produce an elaborate system of Jim Crow segregation. Poor whites were aided not only by their number but also by the development of political resources which accompanied their greater involvement in the South's economy.

Once again, however, the system of production was the major basis for this change in race relations, and once again the political system was used to reinforce patterns of race emanating from structural shifts in the economy. If the racial laws in the antebellum South protected the class interests of the planters and reflected their overwhelming power, the Jim Crow segregation laws of the late nineteenth century reflected the rising power of white laborers; and if the political power of the planters were grounded in the system of production in a plantation economy, the emerging political power of the workers grew out of the new division of labor that accompanied industrialization.

CLASS AND RACE RELATIONS

Except for the brief period of fluid race relations in the North between 1870 and 1890 and in the South during the Reconstruction era, racial oppression is the single best term to characterize the black experience prior to the twentieth century. In the antebellum South both slaves and free blacks occupied what could be best described as a caste position, in the sense that realistic chances for occupational mobility simply did not exist. In the antebellum North a few free blacks were able to acquire some property and improve their socioeconomic position, and a few were even able to make use of educational opportunities. However, the overwhelming majority of free northern Negroes were trapped in menial positions and were victimized by lower-class white antagonism, including the racial hostilities of European immigrant ethnics (who successfully curbed black economic competition). In the postbellum South the system of Jim Crow segregation wiped out the small gains blacks had achieved during Reconstruction, and blacks were rapidly pushed out of the more skilled jobs they had held since slavery. Accordingly, there was very little black occupational differentiation in the South at the turn of the century.

Just as the shift from a plantation economy to an industrializing economy transformed the class and race relations in the postbellum South, so too did industrialization in the North change the context for race-class interaction and confrontation there. On the one hand, the conflicts associated with the increased black-white contacts in the early twentieth century North resembled the forms of antagonism that soured the relations between the races in the postbellum South. Racial conflicts between blacks and whites in both situations were closely tied to class conflicts among whites. On the other hand, there were some fundamental differences. The collapse of the paternalistic bond between blacks and the southern business elite cleared the path for the almost total subjugation of blacks in the South and resulted in what amounted to a united white racial movement that solidified the system of Jim Crow segregation.

However, a united white movement against blacks never really developed in the North. In the first quarter of the twentieth century, management attempted to undercut white labor by using blacks as strikebreakers and, in some situations, as permanent replacements for white workers who periodically demanded higher wages and more fringe benefits. Indeed, the determination of industrialists to ignore racial norms of exclusion and to hire black workers was one of the main reasons why the industrywide unions reversed their racial policies and actively recruited black workers during the New Deal era. Prior to this period the overwhelming majority of unskilled and semiskilled blacks were nonunionized and were available as lower-paid labor or as strikebreakers. The more management used blacks to undercut white labor, the greater were the racial antagonisms between white and black labor.

Moreover, racial tension in the industrial sector often reinforced and sometimes produced racial tension in the social order. The growth of the black urban population created a housing shortage during the early twentieth century which frequently produced black "invasions" or ghetto "spillovers" into adjacent poor white neighborhoods. The racial tensions emanating from labor strife seemed to heighten the added pressures of racial competition for housing, neighborhoods, and recreational areas. Indeed, it was this combination of racial friction in both the economic sector and the social order that produced the bloody riots in East Saint Louis in 1917 and in Chicago and several other cities in 1919.

In addition to the fact that a united white movement against blacks never really developed in the North during the industrial period, it was also the case that the state's role in shaping race relations was much more autonomous, much less directly related to developments in the economic sector. Thus, in the brief period of fluid race relations in the North from 1870 to 1890, civil rights laws were passed barring discrimination in public places and in public institutions. This legislation did not have any real significance to the white masses at that time because, unlike in the pre–Civil War North and the post–Civil War South, white workers did not perceive blacks as major economic competitors. Blacks constituted only a small percentage of the total population in northern cities; they had not yet been used in any significant numbers as cheap labor in industry or as strikebreakers; and their earlier antebellum competitors in low-status jobs (the Irish and German immigrants) had improved their economic status in the trades and municipal employment.

POLITY AND RACIAL OPPRESSION

For all these reasons liberal whites and black professionals, urged on by the spirit of racial reform that had developed during the Civil War and Reconstruction, could pursue civil rights programs without firm resistance; for all these reasons racial developments on the political front were not directly related to the economic motivations and interests of workers and management. In the early twentieth century the independent effect of the political system was displayed in an entirely different way. The process of industrialization had significantly altered the pattern of racial interaction, giving rise to various manifestations of racial antagonism.

Although discrimination and lack of training prevented blacks from seeking higher-paying jobs, they did compete with lower-class whites for unskilled and semiskilled factory jobs, and they were used by management to undercut the white workers' union movement. Despite the growing importance of race in the dynamics of the labor market, the political system did not intervene either to mediate the racial conflicts or to reinforce the pattern of labor-market racial interaction generated by the system of production. This was the case despite the salience of a racial ideology system that justified and prescribed unequal treatment for Afro-Americans. (Industrialists will more likely challenge societal racial norms in situations where adherence to them results in economic losses.)

If nothing else, the absence of political influence on the labor market probably reflected the power struggles between management and workers. Thus legislation to protect the rights of black workers to compete openly for jobs would have conflicted with the interests of management. To repeat, unlike in the South, a united white movement resulting in the almost total segregation of the work force never really developed in the North.

But the state's lack of influence in the industrial sector of private industries did not mean that it had no significant impact on racial stratification in the early twentieth century North. The urban political machines, controlled in large measure by working-class ethnics who were often in direct competition with blacks in the private industrial sector, systematically gerrymandered black neighborhoods and excluded the urban black masses from meaningful political participation throughout the early twentieth century. Control by the white ethnics of the various urban political machines was so complete that blacks were never really in a position to compete for the more important municipal political rewards, such as patronage jobs or government contracts and services. Thus the lack of racial competition for municipal political rewards did not provide the basis for racial tension and conflict in the urban political system. This political racial oppression had no direct connection with or influence on race relations in the private industrial sector.

In sum, whether one focuses on the way race relations were structured by the system of production or the polity or both, racial oppression (ranging from the exploitation of black labor by the business class to the elimination of black competition for economic, social, and political resources by the white masses) was a characteristic and important phenomenon in both the preindustrial and industrial periods of American race relations. Nonetheless, and despite the prevalence of various forms of racial oppression, the change from a preindustrial to an industrial system of production did enable blacks to increase their political and economic resources. The proliferation of jobs created by industrial expansion helped generate and sustain the continuous mass migration of blacks from the rural South to the cities of the North and West. As the black urban population grew and became more segregated, institutions and organizations in the black community also developed, together with a business and professional class affiliated with these institutions. Still, it was not until after World War II (the modern industrial period) that the black class structure started to take on some of the characteristics of the white class structure.

CLASS AND BLACK LIFE CHANCES

Class has also become more important than race in determining black life chances in the modern industrial period. Moreover, the center of racial conflict has shifted from the industrial sector to the sociopolitical order. Although these changes can be related to the more fundamental changes in the system of production and in the laws and policies of the state, the relations between the economy and the polity in the modern industrial period have differed from those in previous periods. In the preindustrial and industrial periods the basis of structured racial inequality was primarily economic, and in most situations the state was merely an instrument to reinforce patterns of race relations that grew directly out of the social relations of production.

Except for the brief period of fluid race relations in the North from 1870 to 1890, the state was a major instrument of racial oppression. State intervention in the modern industrial period has been designed to promote racial equality, and the relationship between the polity and the economy has been much more reciprocal, so much so that it is difficult to determine which one has been more important in shaping race relations since World War II. It was the expansion of the economy that facilitated black movement from the rural areas to the industrial centers and that created job opportunities leading to greater occupational differentiation in the black community (in the sense that an increasing percentage of blacks moved into white-collar positions); and it was the intervention of the state (responding to the pressures of increased black political resources and to the racial protest movement) that removed many artificial discrimination barriers by municipal, state, and federal civil rights legislation, and that contributed to the more liberal racial policies of the nation's labor unions by protective union legislation. And these combined political and economic changes created a pattern of black occupational upgrading that resulted, for example, in a substantial drop in the percentage of black males in the low-paying service, unskilled laborer, and farm jobs.

However, despite the greater occupational differentiation within the black community, there are now signs that the effect of some aspects of structural economic change has been the closer association between black occupational mobility and class affiliation. Access to the means of production is increasingly based on educational criteria (a situation which distinguishes the modern industrial from the earlier industrial system of production) and thus threatens to solidify the position of the black underclass. In other words, a consequence of the rapid growth of the corporate and government sectors has been the gradual creation of a segmented labor market that currently provides vastly different mobility opportunities for different segments of the black population.

On the one hand, poorly trained and educationally limited blacks of the inner city, including that growing number of black teenagers and young adults, see their job prospects increasingly restricted to the low-wage sector, their unemployment rates soaring to record levels (which remain high despite swings in the business cycle), their labor force participation rates declining, their movement out of poverty slowing, and their welfare roles increasing. On the other hand, talented and educated blacks are experiencing unprecedented job opportunities in the growing government and corporate sectors, opportunities that are at least comparable to those of whites with equivalent qualifications. The improved job situation for the more privileged blacks in the corporate and government sectors is related both to the expansion of salaried white-collar positions and to the pressures of state affirmative action programs.

In view of these developments, it would be difficult to argue that the plight of the black underclass is solely a consequence of racial oppression, that is, the explicit and overt efforts of whites to keep blacks subjugated, in the same way that it would be difficult to explain the rapid economic improvement of the more privileged blacks by arguing that the traditional forms of racial segregation and discrimination still characterize the labor market in American industries. The recent mobility patterns of blacks lend strong support to the view that economic class is clearly more important than race in predetermining job placement and occupational mobility. In the economic realm, then, the black experience has moved historically from economic racial oppression experienced by virtually all blacks to economic subordination for the black underclass. And as we begin the last quarter of the twentieth century, a deepening economic schism seems to be developing in the black community, with the black poor falling further and further behind middle- and upper-income blacks.

SHIFT OF RACIAL CONFLICT

If race is declining in significance in the economic sector, explanations of racial antagonism based on labor-market conflicts, such as those advanced by economic class theories of race, also have less significance in the period of modern industrial race relations. Neither the low-wage sector nor the corporate and government sectors provide the basis for the kind of interracial job competition and conflict that plagued the economic order in previous periods. With the absorption of blacks into industrywide labor unions, protective union legislation, and equal employment legislation, it is no longer feasible for management to undercut white labor by using black workers. The traditional racial struggles for power and privilege have shifted away from the economic sector and are now concentrated in the sociopolitical order. Although poor blacks and poor whites are still the main actors in the present manifestations of racial strife, the immediate source of the tension has more to do with racial competition for public schools, municipal political systems, and residential areas than with the competition for jobs.

To say that race is declining in significance, therefore, is not only to argue that the life chances of blacks have less to do with race than with economic class affiliation, but also to maintain that racial conflict and competition in the economic sector—the most important historical factors in the subjugation of blacks—have been substantially reduced. However, it could be argued that the firm white resistance to public school desegregation, residential integration, and black control of central cities all indicate the unyielding importance of race in the United States. The argument could even be entertained that the impressive occupational gains of the black middle class are only temporary, and that as soon as affirmative action pressures are relieved, or as soon as the economy experiences a prolonged recession, industries will return to their old racial practices.

Both of these arguments are compelling if not altogether persuasive. Taking the latter contention first, there is little available evidence to suggest that the economic gains of privileged blacks will be reversed. Despite the fact that the recession of the early 1970s decreased job prospects for all educated workers, the more educated blacks continued to experience a faster rate of job advancement than their white counterparts. And although it is always possible that an economic disaster could produce racial competition for higher-paying jobs and white efforts to exclude talented blacks, it is difficult to entertain this idea as a real possibility in the face of the powerful political and social movement against job discrimination. At this point there is every reason to believe that talented and educated blacks, like talented and educated whites, will continue to enjoy the advantages and privileges of their class status.

My response to the first argument is not to deny the current racial antagonism in the sociopolitical order, but to suggest that such antagonism has far less effect on individual or group access to those opportunities and resources that are centrally important for life survival than antagonism in the economic sector. The factors that most severely affected black life chances in previous years were the racial oppression and antagonism in the economic sector. As race declined in importance in the economic sector, the Negro class structure became more differentiated and black life chances became increasingly a consequence of class affiliation.

Furthermore, it is even difficult to identify the form of racial contact in the sociopolitical order as the source of the current manifestations of conflict between lower-income blacks and whites, because neither the degree of racial competition between the have-nots, nor their structural relations in urban communities, nor their patterns of interaction constitute the ultimate source of present racial antagonism. The ultimate basis for current racial tension is the deleterious effect of basic structural changes in the modern American economy on black and white lower-income groups, changes that include uneven economic growth, increasing technology and automation, industry relocation, and labor market segmentation.

FIGHTING CLASS SUBORDINATION

The situation of marginality and redundancy created by the modern industrial society deleteriously affects all the poor, regardless of race. Underclass whites, Hispano Americans, and Native Americans all are victims, to a greater or lesser degree, of class subordination under advanced capitalism. It is true that blacks are disproportionately represented in the underclass population and that about one-third of the entire black population is in the underclass. But the significance of these facts has more to do with the historical consequences of racial oppression than with the current effects of race.

Although the percentage of blacks below the low-income level dropped steadily throughout the 1960s, one of the legacies of the racial oppression in previous years is the continued disproportionate black representation in the underclass. And since 1970 both poor whites and nonwhites have evidenced very little progress in their elevation from the ranks of the underclass. In the final analysis, therefore, the challenge of economic dislocation in modern industrial society calls for public policy programs to attack inequality on a broad class front, policy programs—in other words—that go beyond the limits of ethnic and racial discrimination by directly confronting the pervasive and destructive features of class subordination.

CHARLES VERT WILLIE

The Inclining Significance of Race [1978]

One of the most vocal opponents to Wilson's ideas concerning the relative impact of race and class on African Americans was the Harvard sociologist Charles Vert Willie (b. 1927). In addition to debating Wilson in person after the publication of *The Declining Significance of Race,* Willie participated in a written exchange with Wilson that was published in *Society* in 1978 and was further expanded in his books *The Caste and Class Controversy* (1979) and *The Caste and Class Controversy on Race and Poverty: Round Two of the Willie/Wilson Debate* (1989). Willie argues that Wilson promotes a myth of success based on individual merit and that Wilson's proposals to rectify class inequality ignore the interconnection of class and race, as well as pragmatic issues.

Willie presents an array of economic and sociological data to suggest that race continues to be important in the lives of African Americans of all classes. For Willie, "the significance of race is increasing [* * *] especially for middle-class blacks who, because of school desegregation and affirmative action and other integration programs, are coming into direct contact with whites for the first time for extended interaction."

From *Society,* July–August 1978.

It is all a matter of perspective. From the perspective of the dominant people of power, inequality exists because of the personal inadequacies of those who are less fortunate. Varying degrees of fortune is the essence of the social stratification system in this nation. In America, it is the affluent rather than the poor who use social class theory to explain poverty. Moreover, they assert that poverty is not a function of institutional arrangements but a matter of individual capacities. From the perspective of the dominant people of power, the social stratification system in the United States is open and any who has the capacity can rise within it. This orientation toward individual mobility tends to mask the presence of opportunities that are institutionally based such as attending the "right" school, seeking employment with the "right" company or firm, and being of the "right" race. Also this orientation toward individual mobility tends to deny the presence of opposition and oppression that are connected with institutions. According to the perspective of the dominant people of power, opportunity and especially educational and economic opportunity is a function of merit.

William Julius Wilson has used the perspective of the dominant people of power in his article on "The Declining Significance of Race" that appeared in the January/February edition of *Society*. An individual, including a scholar in the social sciences, is free to use any perspective that he or she wishes to use. The tradition of friendly criticism in this field, however, supports the effort which I shall undertake in this commentary. My purpose is to make explicit that which is implicit so that others may assess the conclusions of Professor Wilson on the basis of the premises and the perspective of his analysis.

At the end of his article which asserts that "Class has become more important than race in determining black life chances in the modern industrial period,"[1] Professor Wilson tries to disassociate himself from the individualism of the dominant people of power by calling for "public policy programs to attack inequality on a broad class front—policy programs, in other words, that go beyond the limits of ethnic and racial discrimination by directly confronting the pervasive and destructive features of class subordination." The action which Professor Wilson calls for ignores the interconnection between race and social class as a complex of interrelated characteristics and further does not take cognizance of the fact that there may be a serial pattern to the solution to social problems.

COMPLEX OF CHARACTERISTICS

An historic example is given. One reason that other scholars did not discover the laws of population genetics before Mendel[2] is that "they treated as units the complexes of characteristics of individuals, races and species and attempted to find rules governing inheritance of such complexes," according to Theodosius Dobzhansky.[3] "Mendel was the first to understand that . . . the inheritance of separate traits [and] not [the inheritance of] complexes of traits . . . had to be studied." With reference to the community and processes of social change, Susan Greenblatt and I have pointed out

in an article entitled, "A New Approach to Comparative Community Analysis" that maybe it is the other way around. "It is possible that we may successfully understand school desegregation [or poverty and race relations] by using a method that analyzes complexes of characteristics." Professor Wilson attempts to analyze the relationships between the races in the United States in terms of individual traits rather than as a complex of characteristics. The traits in which he is most interested have to do with the economy. Professor Wilson acknowledges that "in the modern industrial period race relations have been shaped as much by important economic changes as by important political changes," but then he denies the significance of this complex by stating the following: ". . . ingenious schemes of racial exploitation, discrimination, and segregation, . . . however significant they were in the creation of poverty-stricken ghettos and a vast underclass of black proletarians . . . do not provide a meaningful explanation of the life chances of black Americans today." He goes on to say that the significance of the association between "race and economic class only" has grown as the nation has entered the modern industrial period.

While making this assertion, Professor Wilson acknowledges that "the presence of blacks is still firmly resisted in various institutions and social arrangements, for example, residential areas and private social clubs." By attempting to isolate the economic sphere from the other institutions and social arrangements of society, Professor Wilson has committed the error of particularism, an error committed by many social scientists who attempt to model analysis of the social system after the organic system, who attempt to analyze traits rather than the complex of characteristics. Evidence from other studies have demonstrated an association between economic opportunity, educational opportunity, and residential location. This is what the current movement for school desegregation and the resistance to busing are all about. Thus, resistance to the presence of blacks in residential areas, for example, cannot be dismissed as irrelevant to social mobility in the economic sphere.

1. Quotation from Wilson's 1978 book *The Declining Significance of Race*, p. 150.
2. Gregor Johan Mendel (1822–84), Austrian scientist and priest; recognized posthumously as the originator of the new science of genetics for his work on the inheritance of traits in pea plants.
3. Ukranian geneticist and evolutionary biologist (1900–75).

My own study of the "Relative Contribution of Family Status and Economic Status to Juvenile Delinquency" that was published in *Social Problems* in 1967 illuminates the serial approach to the solution of social problems. In summary, I found "In Washington, D.C., 80 percent of the white population lives in economically affluent areas while 67 percent of the nonwhite population lives in neighborhoods of poverty or marginal economic condition. Since poverty was no longer an overwhelming problem for most white people, family instability was a major remaining and outstanding problem contributing to the incidence of juvenile delinquency. Although the percent of nonwhite children growing up in one-parent families was greater than the percent of white children who had this kind of experience, the impoverished economic circumstances of nonwhites was overwhelming. In the light of the data . . . [I] hypothesized that nonwhites may be able to deal with the family instability factor which is associated with juvenile delinquency only after notable improvements have been experienced in their economic circumstances. The hypothesis is advanced on the basis of the findings . . . pertaining to the white population which is largely beyond the pale of poverty."

SERIAL PATTERN

Out of this analysis I extracted the principle that the solutions of some social problems occur in a serial pattern, that the solution to one problem makes possible the solution of another. There is an ordering of social events into a sequential pattern. Most whites have passed beyond the stage of economic insecurity. Thus strengthening their families is the most significant way to further reduce delinquency in the white population. But efforts to strengthen family ties and increase family stability among blacks probably will not be very successful until opportunities for economic upgrading are provided. This assertation was based on the findings that 40 percent of the variance in the family instability factor could be attributed to socioeconomic status at that time in Washington.

Thus, I concluded that "this society may have the possiblity of helping a population achieve greater family stability . . . only after it has assisted a population to achieve greater economic security." Not only are most social problems a complex of characteristics such as that of juvenile delinquency, socioeconomic status, and race, but also their solution must be approached in a sequential way. Clearly the public policy of strengthening the black family as a way of overcoming various forms of pathology that was advocated by Daniel Patrick Moynihan,[4] first, was a projection most appropriate for whites upon blacks, and second, was a violation of the sequential approach to social problemsolving. Neither social scientists nor public policymakers are free to pick and choose points of intervention that they prefer, if they wish to be effective. Professor Wilson, for example, may wish to focus on the economic sphere and social class as a way of dealing with inequality. But racial discrimination and oppression in "various institutions and social arrangements" may require intervention in these areas first.

Professor Wilson suggests that changes in many spheres other than economic, already have occurred in previous stages which he has designated as stage one, the *plantation economy* and *racial-caste oppression;* stage two, *industrial expansion, class conflict* and *racial oppression* and stage three, during the 1960s and 1970s, *progressive transition from race inequalities to class inequality.* My contention is that the transition is far from complete for upper-class, middle-class, working-class, lower-class, and under-class blacks, and that barriers to economic opportunity still are largely a function of discrimination based on race and sex.

The remainder of this discussion will demonstrate this fact with data and point out errors in the analysis of William Julius Wilson that may be a function of the perspective used that probably caused him to miss some essential information.

INCOME

First, let us look at income. As recently as 1975, the median income for white families was $14,268 compared with a median of $9,321 for blacks and other minority races. This means that blacks and other racial minorities received only two-thirds as much income

4. See p. 638.

as did whites. At both ends of the income scale, the ratio of black to white income was about the same. Under $5,000 a year there was only 10.2 percent of the white families and individuals compared with 26.3 percent of the population of black families and individuals. Earning $25,000 a year and over in 1975, was 15.1 percent of the white population compared with 6.4 percent of the black population. The proportion of blacks who were very poor was two and one-half times greater than the proportion of whites who were very poor; and the proportion of whites who were most affluent was two and one-third times greater than the proportion of blacks with high incomes. There is not much of a difference in these income ratios by race for the poor and the affluent. In general, the proportion of high-income blacks is far less than what it would be if there was no racial discrimination. The 1977 report, *All Our Children,* by the Carnegie Council on Children of which Kenneth Keniston was senior author states that "90 percent of the income gap between blacks and whites is the result . . . of lower pay for blacks with comparable levels of education and experience." Despite this and other findings such as those presented by economist Herman Miller in his book *Rich Man, Poor Man,* Professor Wilson states that "many talented and educated blacks are now entering positions of prestige and influence at a rate comparable to or, in some situations, exceeding that of whites with equal qualifications."

In 1974, 15 percent of the white male population was of the professional or technical workers category compared with 9 percent of the male population of blacks and other minority races. This appeared to be a notable change relative to whites but it represented only an increase of 3 percentage points over the 6 percent of black and other minority males who were professionals 10 years earlier. Moreover, only 5 percent of the black and other racial minority males were managers and administrators in 1974 compared with 15 percent of all white employed males. In summary, 42 percent of the white male population was white collar in 1974 compared with 24 percent of the racial minority males in this nation. These data indicate that blacks have a long way to go before they catch up with whites in high-level occupations.

Moreover, a study by the Survey Research Center of the University of Michigan that was published in the *New York Times* February 26, 1978, reported that 61 percent of all blacks in a nationwide poll believed that whites either don't care whether or not blacks "get a break" or were actively trying to keep blacks down. It would appear that neither the sentiment of blacks nor the facts of the situation are in accord with the analysis of Professor Wilson and his claim that "class has become more important than race in determining black life chances."

The University of Michigan study also found that one out of every two white persons believed that "few blacks . . . miss out on jobs and promotions because of racial discrimination." This response is similar to the conclusion of Professor Wilson and is the reason why I stated earlier that his analysis was from the perspective of the dominant people of power.

EDUCATION

Second, let us look at what is happening to poor blacks to determine whether their circumstances are more a function of social class than of race. This analysis, I believe, reveals a fundamental error in the analysis of Professor Wilson—an error no less serious than that committed by Daniel Patrick Moynihan and Christopher Jencks[5] who made observations on whites and projected these upon blacks. Howard Taylor, a sociologist and expert methodologist, has stated that Jencks took "considerable liberties in discussing the effects of integration, segregation, race, etc., upon occupational and income inequality. He clearly infers that education is not related to success for black people; that if blacks want more money, then more education will not get it. But this inference is based upon path analysis done only on native white nonfarm males who took the armed forces IQ test! Who can say that causal models and estimates based on native white nonfarm males are applicable to blacks? Not one single path analysis in the entire report is performed on even one

5. White American social scientist and professor (b. 1936) whose books include *Inequality: A Reassessment of the Effects of Family and Schooling in America* (with seven co-authors, 1972) and *The Black-White Test Score Gap* (with Meredith Phillips, 1998).

black sample." Howard Taylor made these observations in an article entitled "Playing the Dozens with Path Analysis" that was published in *Sociology of Education* in 1973.

It is obvious that Professor Wilson has analyzed the job situation for affluent blacks. The census data that I reported earlier indicated that blacks were catching up with whites, relatively, so far as employment in the professions is concerned. While the proportion of white male professionals a decade ago was twice as great as the proportion of black and other minority male professionals, the proportion as late as 1974 was only two-thirds greater. On the basis of data like these, Professor Wilson states that "talented and educated blacks are experiencing unprecedented job opportunities in the growing government and corporate sectors." After analyzing the "job situation for the more privileged blacks," Professor Wilson projects these findings upon the poor and says "it would be difficult to argue that the plight of the black underclass is solely the consequence of racial oppression, that is, the explicit and overt efforts of whites to keep blacks subjugated. . . ."

While the facts cited earlier cast doubt upon the conclusion that talented blacks are experiencing "unprecedented job opportunities," even if one accepts the modest improvement for "talented blacks" as fact, it is inappropriate to project middle-class experience upon the underclass of blacks. This is precisely what Professor Wilson has done.

His assertion that "the black experience has moved historically from economic racial oppression experienced by virtually all blacks to economic subordination for the black underclass" cancels out racial discrimination as a key cause of poverty among blacks. If one assumes that there are not extraordinary biological differences between blacks and whites in the United States, then it is difficult to explain why the proportion of poor blacks with an annual income under $5,000 is two and one-half times greater than the proportion of poor whites. Among poor white youth and young adults the unemployment rate is higher for high school dropouts than for persons who graduated from higher schools but did not receive more education. Among blacks, however, the unemployment rate is high and is the same for high school dropouts and for those who graduated from high school but did not receive more

education. Staying in high school seems not to make a difference for blacks so far as the risk of unemployment is concerned.

Among whites with only an elementary school education or less, 50 percent are likely to have jobs as service workers or laborers at the bottom of the occupational heap; but 80 percent of black workers with this limited education are likely to find work only in these kinds of jobs. This was what Herman Miller found in his analysis of 1960 census data. These facts indicate that education alone cannot explain the disproportionate number of blacks in low-paying jobs. If the absence of education is the basis for limited upward mobility in the stratification system, why do whites with little education get better jobs than blacks?

Using 1968 data, Millers analyzed the difference in median income for whites and blacks and other nonwhite minorities. He found that the difference for the races ranged from $880 for those who had completed grade school only to $2,469 for those who had attended or graduated from college. Median income by schooling not only differed by race but tended to widen between the racial groups with increase in education. On the bases of these findings, Miller said that "there is some justification for the feeling by Puerto Ricans, Negroes, and other minority groups that education does not do as much for them financially as it does for others." These findings Miller reported in the 1971 edition of his book, *Rich Man, Poor Man*, and they indicated that racial discrimination is a contributing factor to the occupational opportunities and income received by poor as well as affluent blacks.

RESIDENTIAL SEGREGATION

With reference to residential segregation which Professor Wilson wants to ignore as irrelevant, he has received modest support from the findings of Albert Simkus that were reported in the February 1978 edition of the *American Sociological Review* in an article entitled "Residential Segregation by Occupation and Race in Ten Urbanized Areas, 1950–1970." Simkus said that "historically, blacks with high incomes have been as highly or more highly segregated from whites with similar incomes than have low-income blacks." This fact became "slightly less true . . . by 1970." However, Simkus attributes the slight change to political rather than economic factors. Particularly singled out for credit is civil rights and housing legislation of the 1960s.

Simkus points out that the decrease in residential segregation of affluent blacks is beginning to catch up with the integrated residential areas that characterized lower-income blacks and whites in the past. Specifically, he said that "apart from the comparisons involving nonwhite professionals, nonwhites and whites in the lowest occupational categories were still slightly less segregated than those in the higher categories."

Finally, I call attention to the fact that Professor Wilson's data are at variance with the clinical observations of other blacks. The unprecedented job opportunities simply have not been experienced by some talented and educated blacks. During the summer of 1977, *The New York Times* published an interview with Sanford Allen, a black violinist with the New York Philharmonic Orchestra. Allen announced his intention to resign from his position. He said that he was "simply tired of being a symbol." At that time, Allen was the only black who had been a member of the 133-year-old musical organization. He charged the more prestigious symphony orchestras of this nation, such as the Boston Symphony, the Chicago Symphony, and two or three others, with running a closed shop that excluded blacks. Allen joined the New York Philharmonic in 1962. During a decade and a half, no other blacks had been hired. A story like this one, of course, is clinical evidence and does not carry the same weight as research evidence systematically gathered. But such clinical evidence has been accumulated recently and deserves to be looked at carefully.

The response of white professionals to admissions policies by colleges and universities that are designed to reserve spaces for members of previously excluded racial populations in the first-year classes of professional schools is a case in point. The opposition to such practices indicates that talented and educated blacks are not being given access to privilege and power "at a rate comparable to or, in some situations, exceeding that of whites with equivalent qualifications" as Professor Wilson claims. The opposition to special minority admissions programs is led by white professionals, not white hard-hat or blue-collar workers. This is further clinical evidence that race is not irrelevant and

has not declined in significance for talented and educated blacks.

COUNTERHYPOTHESIS

Actually, I would like to introduce a counterhypothesis that the significance of race is increasing and that it is increasing especially for middle-class blacks who, because of school desegregation and affirmative action and other integration programs, are coming into direct contact with whites for the first time for extended interaction.

My case studies of black families who have moved into racially integrated neighborhoods and racially integrated work situations indicate that race for some of these pioneers is a consuming experience. They seldom can get away from it. When special opportunities are created, such as in the admissions programs, the minorities who take advantage of them must constantly prove themselves. When a middle-class black has been accepted as Sanford Allen was in the Philharmonic, the issue then shifts to whether or not one is being used as a symbol. Try as hard as they may, middle-class blacks, especially middle-class blacks in racially integrated situations at this period in American history are almost obsessed with race. Many have experienced this adaptation especially in residential and work situations.

Any obsession, including obsession with race, is painful. Freedom is circumscribed and options are delimited not because of physical segregation but because of the psychological situation. So painful is the experience of racial obsession that two extreme reactions are likely to occur. Middle-class blacks may attempt to deal with the obsession by capitulation— that is, by assuming everything is race-related, that all whites are racists, and that all events and circumstances must be evaluated first in terms of their racial implications. The other adaptation is denial, believing that race is irrelevant and insignificant even when there is clear and present evidence that it is not. This is one of the personal consequences of a racist society for the oppressed as the old separatist system begins to crumble. The people who most severely experience the pain of dislocation due to the changing times are the racial minorities who are talented and educated and integrated, not those who are impoverished and isolated.

WILLIAM JULIUS WILSON

The Declining Significance of Race: Revisited but Not Revised [1978]

William Julius Wilson continued his debate with Charles Vert Willie (pp. 747, 755) in the pages of the journal *Society*. In his response to Willie, reprinted here, he does not address the subjective topic of perspective that Willie raised. Instead, after summarizing the macrohistorical argument of his book *The Declining Significance of Race*, Wilson focuses on Willie's points that can be discussed using objective analysis. He notes that Willie based his criticism on an advance excerpt of his book and suggests that the complete book addresses many of the points Willie raises.

Although Wilson agrees with Willie that race continues to influence sociopolitical opportunities for all African Americans, he maintains that the strong economic position that some black Americans had achieved in the years before the publication of his book shields them, to some extent, from adverse effects. Wilson concludes that since recent shifts in the economy are disproportionately harmful to poor African Americans, public policies need to address the fact that class—not race—has become the primary determinant of economic opportunity.

From *Society*, July–August 1978.

Professor Charles V. Willie says that it is all a matter of perspective. He is wrong, it is also a matter of interpretation. And his interpretation of the excerpts from my book (*Society*, January/February 1978), *The Declining Significance of Race*, erroneously associates what is in fact a macrosociological argument of inequality with a so-called dominant group perspective of individual mobility.

In my response to Willie's contentions I do not plan to devote much attention to perspectives, the reader can easily make that judgment, instead the bulk of this paper will consider the validity of assertions. In the process I hope to demonstrate that, under close scrutiny, not a single one of Willie's "empirical" criticisms can be upheld, and that contrary to his claims, the data he presents and the counterhypotheses he proposes neither demonstrate errors in my analysis nor undermine my arguments on the growing importance of class and the decreasing significance of race in determining blacks' chances in life.

MACROSOCIOLOGICAL ANALYSIS OF RACE AND CLASS

However, before I directly comment on Willie's article, I would like, in a few succinct paragraphs, to put the basic arguments of my book in proper focus. My book is an attempt to explain race and class in the American experience. I feel that in order to understand the changing issues of race and, indeed, the relationship between class and race in America, a framework that would relate changes in intergroup relations with changes in the American social structure is required. Individual mobility is not used as the independent variable in explaining race and class experiences, as Willie's analysis would suggest. Rather I try to show how the economy and state interacted in different historical periods not only to structure the relations between blacks and whites and to produce dissimilar contexts for the manifestation of racial antagonisms, but also to create different situations for racial group access to rewards and privileges. Using this framework, I define three stages of American race relations (the preindustrial, industrial, and modern industrial), stages in which I describe the role of both the system of production and the state in the development of race and class relations.

Although my book devotes considerable attention to the preindustrial and industrial periods of American race relations, it is my description of the modern industrial period that has generated controversy and has provoked Willie to respond. I contend that in the earlier periods, whether one focuses on the way race relations were structured by the economy or by the state or both, racial oppression (ranging from the exploitation of black labor by the economic elite to the elimination of black competition, especially economic competition, by the white masses) was a characteristic and important aspect of life. However, I also maintain that in the modern industrial period the economy and the state have, in relatively independent ways, shifted the basis of racial antagonisms away from black/white economic contact to social, political, and community issues. The net effect is a growing class division among blacks, a situation, in other words, in which economic class has been elevated to a position of greater importance than race in determining individual black opportunities for living conditions and personal life experiences.

Now, it is difficult to recapture in these few paragraphs the distinctions and arguments presented in *The Declining Significance of Race,* but the preceding synopsis will at least provide the necessary background in considering Willie's interpretation and critique of my thesis.

WILLIE'S ANALYSIS

In fairness to Willie, it should be pointed out that he was responding to the excerpts from my book that appeared in *Society* magazine and therefore did not have the benefit of the full array of data and arguments I use to support my contentions. I will therefore discuss some of these data in the ensuing paragraphs, as well as present some additional facts that were not incorporated in *The Declining Significance of Race,* but which serve to demonstrate the inadequacies of Professor Willie's data.

Willie presents three major arguments: (1) that I "commit the error of particularism" in the sense that I try "to isolate the economic sphere from the other institutions and social arrangements of society"; (2) that barriers to economic opportunities for blacks are still mainly a function of race and that the available data support this contention; and (3) that a counterhypothesis should be proposed, namely that "the significance of race is increasing...especially for middle-class blacks who, because of school desegregation, and affirmative action and other integration programs, are coming into direct contact with whites for the first time for extended interactions."

"ERROR OF PARTICULARISM"

In response to Willie's charge that I "isolate the economic sphere from the other institutions and social arrangements of society," let me say, first of all, that I would be the last to deny that there is an empirical "association between economic opportunity, educational opportunity, and residential location." Indeed, contrary to Willie's assertion, this complex relationship is demonstrated repeatedly in several chapters of my book. The problem has to do with the direction of the relationship. What I attempt to show is that in the modern industrial period, as economic opportunity for blacks increasingly depends on class affiliation, we see corresponding differences in black educational opportunity and residential location. Thus as the black middle class experiences greater occupational mobility, they, like more privileged whites, abandon public schools and send their children to private schools. Accordingly, public schools in large urban areas are not only suffering from racial isolation; they are also suffering from class isolation. By the same token, higher-income blacks are not trapped in depressed ghettoes and, although they have greater difficulty than middle-class whites in finding housing, their economic resources provide them with more opportunities to find desirable housing and neighborhoods either in the central city or in the suburbs than both lower-income blacks and lower-income whites. On the other hand, the lack of economic opportunity for under-class blacks means that they are forced to attend inferior ghetto schools and remain in economically depressed ghettoes. Ghetto isolation and inferior educational opportunities reinforce their low position in the labor market. This process is a vicious circle and, to repeat, is demonstrated in my book, even though I give more weight to economic opportunities than to noneconomic opportunities.

Furthermore, I agree with Willie's assertion that "efforts to strengthen family ties and increase family stability among blacks probably will not be very successful until opportunities for economic upgrading are provided." Indeed, this is one of the major arguments of chapter six of *The Declining Significance of Race.* For example, I show that in 1974, only 18 percent of the children in black families with incomes of less than $4,000 lived with both parents, while 90 percent of the children in black families of $15,000 or more lived with both parents. I argue, therefore, that "to suggest categorically that the problem of female-headed households is characteristic of black families is to overlook the powerful influence of economic-class background. The increase in female-headed households among poor blacks is a consequence of the fact that the poorly trained and educated black males have increasingly restricted opportunities for higher-paying jobs and thus find it increasingly difficult to satisfy the expectations of being a male breadwinner." If Willie and I do have a real difference of opinion on this matter, it is that he associates the increasing difficulties of the black poor with racial discrimination whereas I maintain (and will further elaborate below) that class restrictions associated with structural shifts in the economy are the more important factors in accounting for poor blacks' limited occupational mobility today.

But Willie is not always consistent in his arguments about the "sequential approach to social-problem solving." On the one hand he argues, as in fact I do, that efforts to strengthen black families will not succeed until economic opportunities are upgraded; yet, on the other hand, he contradicts this position with the statement that "Professor Wilson, for example, may wish to focus on the economic sphere and social class as a way of dealing with inequality. But racial discrimination and oppression in 'various institutions and social arrangements' may require intervention in these areas first." I stand by my contention that the factors that most severely affected black life chances in previous years were racial oppression and antagonism in the economic sector. As race declined in importance in the economic sector, the black class structure became more differentiated and black life chances increasingly became a consequence of class affiliation. This is not to deny the importance of racial antagonism in the social-political order, or even to suggest that residential, social, and educational discrimination do not form a part of a vicious circle that feeds back to the economic sector. But this circular process is far more relevant for poor blacks than for more privileged blacks. In terms of understanding life changes, the economic mobility of privileged blacks has offset the negative consequences of racial discrimination in the social-political order. Indeed, one will only be able to understand the grow-

ing class divisions in the black community by recognizing that racial antagonisms in the sociopolitical order have far less effect on black individual or group access to those opportunities and resources that are centrally important for life chances, than have racial antagonisms in the economic sector.

But the bulk of Willie's article concentrates on data he presents to "point out errors" in my analysis. I would now like to examine these data and Willie's interpretation of them.

PAST AND PRESENT EFFECTS OF RACE

In an attempt to refute my assertion that class has become more significant than race in determining black life chances, Willie presents data indicating (1) that the median income for black families in 1975 was several thousand dollars less than the median income for white families; (2) that the proportion of black families who were poor (income of less than $5,000 a year) was two and one-half times greater than the proportion of white families who were poor, and the proportion of white families who were affluent (income of $25,000 or more a year) was two and one-third times greater than the proportion of black families who were affluent; (3) that 90 percent of the black-white income gap is the result of lower pay for blacks with comparable experience and education; (4) that in 1968 "median income by schooling not only differed by race but tended to widen between the racial groups with increase in education"; (5) that staying in high school for blacks does not make a difference with respect to the risk of unemployment; and (6) that "42 percent of the white male population was white collar in 1974 compared with 24 percent of racial minority members in the nation."

The problem with these statistics is not that they are inaccurate or even that some are outdated. The problem is that they obscure the very important distinction between the effects of past discrimination and the current effects of race in the economic world. In other words, they allow investigators to either ignore or overlook the importance of a legacy of past discrimination and therefore to interpret the overall black-white gap in income and employment as an indication of present discrimination. The fact that this approach tends to distort the significance of race today is most clearly revealed when we examine the labor market experiences of various subgroups within the black population.

BLACK EDUCATED MALES

There is compelling evidence that young black male college graduates now receive roughly the same salaries as young white men with college degrees. Data from the 1970 Census of Population show that in 1969 black male graduates age 22 to 24 received a slightly higher average income than comparable whites; and more recent findings from the 1973 *Current Population Survey* show that black men with college degrees in the 25 to 29 age category earned close to $1,000 more than their white counterparts. Moreover, the economist Richard B. Freeman found that the starting salaries of male graduates from black colleges in the South in 1968–70 were comparable to the average starting salaries for male college graduates on a national level. These findings, obscured in Willie's gross income comparisons of all college educated blacks and all college educated whites, represent a significant change from the discriminatory pattern of the past whereby black college graduates at all age levels received substantially lower salaries than white college graduates of comparable ages.

But why have young black male college graduates finally reached income parity with young white male college graduates? Because the combination of an increased demand for white-collar salaried employees in the corporate and government sector and the pressures of state antidiscrimination programs, especially affirmative action pressures, have cleared the path for minority college graduates and have allowed them to enter positions of prestige and influence denied to them in the past. We only need to examine the changing racial practices of corporations to see that opportunities for educated blacks have sharply increased. As shown in Freeman's study, the efforts of corporations to recruit college-trained blacks increased sharply between 1965 and 1970. In fact, the average number of recruitment visits of representatives of corporations to predominantly black colleges rose from 4 in 1960 to 50 in 1965 and then climbed to 297 in 1970. And schools such as Clark University, Atlanta University, and Southern University,[1] to which no visits had been made in 1960, received in 1970, 350, 510, and 600 corporate representatives, respectively. Now Willie may not be impressed with these figures, but I must confess that I am. The vigorous recruitment of highly educated blacks by corporations is one of the principle reasons why the proportion of black male workers in white-collar positions increased from 16 to 24 percent from 1964 to 1974 (the proportion of white males in white-collar positions remained slightly over 40 percent during this period) with the greater portion of this increase occurring in the higher level technical, professional, and administrative positions. Indeed, as David Whitman[2] has observed, in the 1960s "the number of blacks in professional and technical positions increased by 131 percent while the number of blacks in managerial and administrative positions increased by 67 percent." Willie, however, chooses to ignore these unprecedented gains for highly trained and educated blacks, preferring instead to emphasize the frustrations of a black violinist in the New York Philharmonic and to belittle my statement that "talented and educated blacks are now entering positions of prestige and influence at a rate comparable to or, in some situations, exceeding that of whites with equivalent qualifications."

However, despite the fact that younger educated black males have finally reached income parity with younger educated white males, and despite the rapid increase in the number of blacks in higher paying white-collar positions, there is still a significant income gap between all college educated whites and all college educated blacks because of the substantially lower income of older educated blacks. But is this mainly a consequence of present-day discrimination as Willie wants to believe? No, the comparatively low incomes of older educated blacks is one of the legacies of past discrimination. Denied the opportunity to move into the higher

---

1. Historically black colleges and universities (HBCU): Clark College, now Clark Atlanta University, in Atlanta; Atlanta University, the oldest of the HBCUs, first founded as a grammar school in 1865; Southern University, originally established in 1880 in New Orleans, Louisiana, and now located in Baton Rouge.
2. White American journalist specializing in social policy.

paying occupations when they graduated from college or discouraged from even pursuing such occupational careers, older black college graduates tended to be concentrated in the lower paying fields such as teaching, social welfare, and segregated services; rarely were they employed as managers and professionals in large corporations upon entering the labor market. They therefore, in the words of Freeman, "lack the relevant training or managerial experience to take advantage of new opportunities and advanced only moderately in the new job market." Nonetheless younger educated blacks are now entering, and indeed are encouraged to enter, previously neglected fields such as finance, management, chemistry, engineering, accounting, and computer science. Clifton R. Wharton, Jr., Chancellor of the State University of New York, points out, for example, that "in 1966, 45 percent of all Black undergraduates were majoring in education; today only 26 percent are. In 1966 only 5 percent of the blacks were studying business, today 18 percent are." For all these reasons and despite modest gains in recent years, the income of older educated black males lags significantly behind the income of older educated white males. For all these reasons younger college educated black males have reached income parity with younger college educated white males.

COLLEGE EDUCATED BLACK WOMEN

Finally, I should say something about college educated women, another important subgroup hidden in Willie's statistics. College-trained black women like college-trained white women have been victimized by sex discrimination over the years. Indeed in the 1970s the major job market problems confronting female black college graduates are associated with sexual and not racial differences. By 1973, for example, although their earnings were significantly below those of both black and white male college graduates, female black college graduates earned nearly $1,000 more than their white counterparts.

BASIC ECONOMIC CHANGES

But I have yet to say anything about less privileged blacks. A comparison of their situation with the unpre-

cedented gains of educated blacks demonstrates, in very sharp relief, the growing class divisions in the black community and the inadequacy of conventional explanations of racial experience. In interpreting my discussion about the improved job situation for more privileged blacks, Willie manages to infer that I "projected these findings upon the poor" because of my statement that "in view of these *developments* [my emphasis] it would be difficult to argue that the plight of the underclass is solely a consequence of racial oppression, that is, the explicit and overt efforts to keep blacks subjugated...." However, the developments to which I refer and which are discussed in several preceding sentences on the same page, are mainly concerned with the creation of a segmented labor market that has grown out of recent structural shifts in our economy—a labor market providing greatly different mobility opportunities for different segments of the black population. This is one of the central arguments of my book, an argument which reflects my concern about the effects of basic economic changes in advanced industrial society, an argument that Willie curiously ignores while he strains to place "the individual mobility" tag on my approach. The consequences of ignoring these structural dimensions in explaining inequality, as far as the black poor are concerned, is one of the subjects to which I now turn.

BLACK UNDERCLASS

When I argue that "the black experience has moved historically from economic racial oppression experienced by virtually all blacks to economic subordination for the black underclass," Willie complains that I cancel "out racial discrimination as a key cause of poverty among blacks" thereby making it difficult to explain the greater proportion of black families in poverty and the higher unemployment rate for younger blacks. Once again Willie overlooks or chooses to ignore one of my key arguments, namely that "one of the legacies of the racial oppression in previous years is the continued disproportionate black representation in the underclass." In other words, patterns of racial subjugation in the past created the vast black underclass as the accumulation of disadvantages were passed on from generation to generation, and the economic and technological revolution of modern industrial society threatens to insure it a permanent status. Accordingly, even if all racial discrimination were eliminated today, the situation of poor blacks will not be substantially improved unless something is done to remove the structural barriers to decent jobs created by changes in our system of production.

Thus, while Willie and some other social scientists continue to stress the problems of race at the expense of emphasizing the problems of economic dislocation under advanced capitalism, class divisions related to greatly different mobility opportunities are growing more rapidly in the black community than in the white community. For example, while young black male college graduates have reached income parity with comparable whites, the income of young black male high school graduates continues to lag behind the income of young white high school graduates. Whereas government antidiscrimination programs, such as affirmative action, have helped to enhance the economic opportunities of trained and educated blacks, such programs have not noticeably improved the economic conditions of poor blacks.

Unlike the life experiences of young privileged blacks, the growing number of black teenagers and young adults who are isolated in ghettoes and are crippled in inferior inner-city schools do not have the same access to higher paying jobs for which they are qualified as do young whites with similar levels of formal education. Because of the lack of job expansion in the manufacturing sector and the fact that desirable jobs in the service industries require education and training, it matters little whether or not poor blacks graduate from ghetto high schools when they face a situation in which the better paid and more desirable jobs which they can obtain without special skills and/or higher education are decreasing in central cities, not only in relative terms but sometimes in absolute numbers.

In short, because of the historical consequences of racial oppression, underclass blacks find themselves in a situation where they are particularly vulnerable to the negative consequences of uneven economic growth, increasing technology and automation, industry relocation, and labor market segmentation. These are difficult problems that are not going to be addressed by programs based simply upon the premise that current racial discrimination is the major cause of poor blacks' present miseries and limited life chances. Rather these are problems that define the conditions of class subordination, problems that grew out of the previous conditions of racial subordination and are now exacerbated by the economic changes of advanced industrial society. But to repeat, not all blacks are experiencing these difficulties. I would like to make just one more but very important point, in this regard—namely, the growing influence of class background on black experiences with both higher and lower education.

Class and Black Education

According to Willie, the opposition from white professionals to minority admission policies in colleges and universities indicates "that talented and educated blacks are not being given access to privilege and power" at a rate comparable to that of whites with equivalent qualifications. Fortunately, this conclusion is not supported by recent data on school enrollment from the U.S. Bureau of the Census. The number of blacks attending colleges and universities in the United States increased from 340,000 in 1966 to 948,000 in 1975. Wharton points out that today the figure has increased to more than a million. Describing the figures on growing black college enrollments as "awesome," he states that "Blacks, who make up 11 percent of America's population, now make up 10 percent of the 10.6 million college students. . . . In one year, 1974, the percentage of Black high school graduates actually exceeded the percentage of White high school graduates going to college." And whereas almost half of all black college students were enrolled in predominantly Negro colleges in 1966, today almost 80 percent are attending predominantly white institutions. "These young people constitute the largest concentration of Black intellectual manpower in the entire world," states Wharton, "there is now a higher percentage of Blacks going to college in America than there is whites going to college in almost every European nation."

It goes without saying that this rapid rise in black college attendance has enormous implications for the further growth of the black middle class. The class stratification that we observed in the black community today may only be a vague outline of what is to come. This is particularly true when we consider that class or family background for blacks, as shown in the research of the economist Richard B. Freeman and the sociologists Robert Hauser and David Featherman, is becoming an increasingly important factor in determining overall educational attainment and who goes to college. In this connection Freeman points out that "despite all the attention given to enrollment of the ghetto poor into college, it was the children of better educated and wealthier parents who went in increasing numbers in the 1960s." More recent data from the U.S. Department of Commerce reinforce Freeman's conclusion. For example, only 17 percent of both black and white families with incomes of less than $5,000 a year had at least one member (age 18–24) attending college in 1974, and the percentage of family members enrolled in college tended to increase for both blacks and whites as family income increased. Families with incomes of $15,000 had the highest proportion of young adults in college (42 percent for blacks and 50 percent for whites).

But we do not have to restrict ourselves to the examination of the facts on higher education to see the significance of class background in black education and the gap between the haves and the have-nots in the black community. An even more revealing picture emerges when we juxtapose the figures on black higher education with those on black lower education. Specifically, while nearly an equal percentage of white and black high school graduates are entering college, the percentage of young blacks graduating from high school lags significantly behind the percentage of white high school graduates. In 1974, 85 percent of young white adults (20 to 24 years old) but only 72 percent of young black adults graduated from high school. Moreover, only 68 percent of young black adult males graduated from high school. And of those young blacks (18 to 24 years old) who were not enrolled in college and whose family income was less than $5,000, a startling 46 percent did not graduate from high school (the comparable white figure was 39 percent).

Thus, as the class divisions of the black community grow, it will become increasingly difficult for Willie and other social scientists to mask these differences either by speaking of a uniform or single black experience or by presenting gross statistics that neither reflect significant variations in the resources of various subgroups within the black population nor the differences in the effects of race in the past and the effects of race in the present. Andrew Brimmer's[3] warning in 1969 that there is a deepening economic schism in the black community is clearly revealed in the black income, occupational, and educational differences discussed above. And they underscore the central argument of *The Declining Significance of Race* that class has become more important than race in determining black life chances.

WILLIE'S COUNTERHYPOTHESIS

Willie concludes his article by proclaiming that the significance of race is increasing, especially for middle-class blacks who are encountering whites for the first time in integrated situations, for example, in racially integrated neighborhoods. He therefore feels that the "people who most experience the pain of dislocation due to the changing times are the racial minorities who are talented and educated and integrated, not those who are impoverished and isolated." After resisting my arguments concerning the growing class differences in the black community, Willie circuitously acknowledges the progress of talented and educated blacks by discussing the psychological discomforts and pains of dislocation that have accompanied their movement into integrated situations.

Let me say, first of all, that when I speak of the declining significance of race, I am referring to the role it now plays in determining black life chances—in other words, the changing impact of race in the economic sector and, in particular, the importance of race in changing mobility opportunities. Thus, as I have tried to show, as the barriers to entering mainstream occupations were removed for educated blacks, they

---

3. Economist, professor, and consultant (b. 1929); the first African American to serve on the Federal Reserve, having been appointed by President Johnson in 1966.

began to move away from the lower paying professions such as teaching and social work and began in significant numbers to prepare themselves for careers in finance, management, chemistry, engineering, accounting, and other professional areas. Nowhere in my book do I argue that race is "irrelevant or insignificant." It is not simply an either-or situation, rather it is a matter of degree. And I strongly emphasized that there is still a strong basis for racial antagonism on the social, community, and political levels.

I do not disagree with the way in which Willie has proposed his counterhypothesis. Many educated blacks do experience psychological discomfort in new integrated situations. Willie and I could probably draw many personal examples of this. We both are black, and we both teach at elite universities. A few years ago almost no blacks were in such positions. But I am sure that neither of us would trade places with a poor black trapped in the ghetto and handcuffed to a menial, dead-end, and poorly paid job. That is the real problem in the black community, and no cries about the psychological discomfort of the integrated black elite should distract our attention from the abominable and deleterious physical conditions of the isolated black poor.

The Natural Look

PHYL GARLAND: *The Natural Look: Many Negro Women Reject White Standards of Beauty* [1966]
READERS OF EBONY: *Letters on "The Natural Look"* [1966]

In June 1966, *Ebony* magazine published a cover article on the new style of "going natural" that was growing in popularity among black Americans as an alternative to the common practice of straightening their hair. This essay by Phyl Garland (1935–2006), a professor of journalism at Columbia University, was accompanied by photographs (not reproduced here) of a wide range of women who chose different "natural" hairstyles to reflect their personality and politics. In interviews, these women underscore how the personal is political. Their choice of hairstyle is more than just fashion—the hairstyle reveals important aspects of their identity, from cultural ties to their African roots and their dedication to civil rights.

Garland's article reveals the stark divisions within black communities over hair and beauty during the 1960s and 1970s. Women who "went natural" faced disapproval, harassment, or discrimination from both black and white people. As for the women with natural hairstyles, some felt that people should be allowed to adopt a natural style if they felt comfortable with it, while others were adamant that one should "go natural" as a reflection of one's commitment to emerging ideas about black pride and power.

Divisions over hair can be seen in the letters *Ebony* received in response to Garland's article on "the natural look" (p. 772). The most vocal critics of natural hair were black female readers. The black male readers were evenly split, and there is one letter from a white man who found the women in the article "among the most beautiful [women he'd] ever seen." (See pp. 778–87 for the 1960s and 1970s debate on interracialism.)

Among the primary reasons given for opposition to the natural look is that none of the hairstyles favored by women of the period were natural, particularly not the elaborate looks popularized by white women. However, the harsh language that the critical readers use to describe the natural look—including the "woolly skull look," the "'bad' type," and "all those kinky heads"—reveals that their responses reflect more than mere differences in style. In contrast, the supportive respondents see the natural look as contributing to a growing sense of black identity, and one even views the article itself as a contribution to racial advancement, writing, "I thank *Ebony* for the article and look forward to other articles which will help us to see the truth and accept ourselves as we are, for then, perhaps, with this new pride in ourselves we will become unified."

PHYL GARLAND

The Natural Look: Many Negro Women Reject White Standards of Beauty [1966]

A Frenchman who had been in this country but a short time was astonished to encounter on the street one day a shapely, brown-skinned woman whose close-cropped, rough-textured hair was in marked contrast to that of Brigit Bardot[1]—or any other woman he'd ever seen. Intrigued by her extraordinarily curly locks, he rushed up to her and blurted in Gallic impulsiveness: "But I thought only Negro *men* had kinky hair!"

---

1. Brigitte Bardot (b. 1934), French movie star and model with long, blond hair.

His prior observation had not been entirely incorrect, for, throughout the ages, American women of color have conspired to conceal the fact that their hair is not quite like any other. This key element in the black female's mystique was, until recently, challenged only by a few bold bohemians, a handful of entertainers and dancing ethnologists like Pearl Primus,[2] whose identification with the exotic placed them beyond the pale of convention. But for the girl in the street—the coed,[3] the career woman, the housewife, the matron and even the maid who had been born with "bad" or kinky hair, the straightening comb and chemical processes seemingly offered the only true paths to social salvation.

Not so today, for an increasing number of Negro women are turning their backs on traditional concepts of style and beauty by wearing their hair in its naturally kinky state. Though they remain a relatively small group, confined primarily to the trend-making cities of New York and Chicago, they are frequently outspoken, and always aware of definite reasons why they decided to "go natural."

"We, as black women, must realize that there is beauty in what we are, without having to make ourselves into something we aren't," contends Suzi Hill, 23-year-old staff field worker with the Southern Christian Leadership Conference. A veteran of the Dixie civil rights fight currently involved in Dr. Martin Luther King's crusade against Chicago slums, she is quick to add, "It's practical. It rids us of those frustrations Negro women know so well, the fears that begin when you're little. So many little Negro girls feel frustrated because their hair won't grow, or because they have what is called 'bad' hair. They aren't made to realize that they have nothing to be ashamed of and go through a lifetime of hiding from themselves— avoiding swimming, being uneasy at dances when they start to perspire, because their hair will 'go back,' running from rain. By the time they're adults, this feeling has become so much a part of them they're even afraid to answer the telephone if their hair hasn't been done. Negro women are still slaves, in a way."

"Economics is a part of it too," notes Diana Smith, 20, another stalwart at King's urban headquarters where natural hair has become a badge of honor. "It's a shame, but many poor Negro housewives take money that should be grocery money and use it to get their hair done. Now that wigs have come along, I see kids whose families are on welfare, wearing them to high school—wigs and raggedy coats. Society has forced the standard of straight hair on them to the extent where they feel it's something for which they should sacrifice."

Though a note of protest underscores the commentary of most in the natural hair coterie, others present varied reasons for having made the big change. Singer Abbey Lincoln, who has been extolling natural styles and "the beauty of the American black woman" for more than five years, asserts, "Mother Nature is always right and we should concentrate on enhancing what has been given to us. Our women have always had a thing about their hair in this country, but that day is on its way out." A young art student who hasn't straightened her hair for two years, remarks, "I never liked elaborate curls. I just feel more black and realistic this way." An interior designer who alternates between periods of naturals and processes says, "I believe in choosing whatever goes best with my features and the feeling I want to express. That long, straight Caucasian look just doesn't go with me." A part-time model states, "It was the natural thing to do. After all, I wasn't born with a straightening comb in my head." And a New York clerical worker simply states, "I just got tired of getting up every morning and trying to touch up those edges before I went to work."

While some are willing to concede that "A woman shouldn't wear a natural if she doesn't feel comfortable with it, but she should have the right to make a choice," others preach the gospel of kinkiness, viewing the trend not as a fad, or style, but more a religious crusade from which no potential convert should escape. One such center for this revolution in fashion is The African Look, a shop nestled in Chicago's Hyde Park, an area noted for its liberal attitude toward dissenters of

---

2. Trinidadian dancer, choreographer, and anthropologist (1919–94) who was a pioneer of African dance in the United States.
3. Slang term for a woman attending a college or university that used to be exclusively male; in the late 1960s, many higher educational institutions, including Yale University, admitted women for the first time, becoming co-educational.

all sorts. There, co-owners Lee McDaniel and Joyce Gere design and make clothing derived from African styles, meanwhile expounding on their attitude that, "I'm protesting against the black Anglo-Saxon and the white man, because I'm unhappy here in this land with these cats!" and "I'm tired of going through all these changes trying to look like Doris Day and Elizabeth Taylor. I'm not going to measure myself by their yardstick any longer!"

Joyce, who claims to have been, at one time, "the only black chick with a natural in Cincinnati, Ohio," refers to the hair as "an experience that begins when you get up in the morning and goes on from day to day. I've had people shed tears over it," she says of her carefully cultivated coiffure, "and once when I was on a bus, a woman sat behind me for eight blocks, then got up and hit me over the head with her umbrella. I even had a minister preach a sermon on me. Once I went to church and when I quietly took a seat, the minister stopped talking about what he'd been talking about and shouted, 'I have spotted something in our midst that is *evil!*' When he went on to talk about a woman's hair being her crowning glory, I got up right there and asked him if that Bible said anything about that crowning glory having to be straight."

For Lee, the implications of wearing natural hair have been less than humorous, due to the experiences of her two young daughters. Both wore naturals until recently, when name-calling by their grammar school peers sent them scurrying tearfully back to the straightening comb. But the occasional unpleasant incidents are balanced by ironic twists. Lee tells of a young Negro girl who wanted to go natural, "but she had too many white genes going for her and her hair just wouldn't nap up right. I felt so sorry for her when she cried."

Though all women who wear naturals are not rabid individualists, revolutionaries or black nationalists. Most who have adopted the style admit that it requires a dash of daring to cross the hair line. This might account for the fact that the ranks are dominated by the young, who have flourished in an era when rebellion is the mode, and those living away from their families in big cities, where anonymity accords them greater personal freedom. In some major cities, like Los Angeles and Washington, D.C., the naturals are few and far between, possibly due to the more conservative

atmosphere. But even in the most permissive of metropolitan areas, the natural girl is likely to be thrust into touchy situations—especially if she works in an office.

Iola Smith had been a municipal employe for some time before she turned up for her job as a records clerk at Chicago's Sachs Tuberculosis Clinic, wearing a natural. "The nurses couldn't understand what had happened to my hair," she relates, "but what really got me was this one doctor who kept staring at me and saying, 'I'm trying to think of what animal it reminds me of.' Then he finally said, 'Oh, it looks like a porcupine.'"

A few who are sensitive to criticism avoid problems by wearing wigs to work (occasionally at the suggestion of their employers), while one cagey natural who has worked at everything from printing to public relations, assiduously straightens her hair during the first two weeks on a new job, then, without warning, shows up with a kinky style. "My bosses are always shocked," she reports, "but they dare not fire me on the spot. I might accuse them of discrimination."

Many claim whites more readily accept natural hair, while Negroes are most apt to become uneasy. "The men seem to like it, and some even say they're proud to see one of their women wearing their hair like that," says one recent natural, "but Negro women often act hostile. It's as though they think we've pulled the covers off of them and told on them in some way."

A housewife who had worn her hair in an unstraightened style long before a noticeable trend developed was appalled when Negro women would come up to her at social gatherings and ask, "But how did you get your hair to look like that?" She quickly silenced them by answering, "You just wash yours and you'll find out."

Like all women, those who wear naturals are concerned about male response and recognize that short hair might detract from their femininity. Thus the earring, usually of the hoop or dangling variety, has become almost a necessity for those with close-cropped crests. "I didn't realize how important it was until I went to the store one day without my earrings or make-up," says a petite accountant. "I was wearing slacks and thought I looked all right until a man came up to me and asked, 'Son, is this where you catch the bus?' You wouldn't catch me dead without my earrings now." Others have been heartened to detect a corresponding movement toward a natural look for Negro men, meaning that the male disdains processes and wears his hair at a previously frowned-upon length—or height. Frequently naturals of opposite sexes have found themselves attracted to each other out of a kindred spirit.

Though hair has become the focal point in this muted rebellion against prevailing beauty standards, it can not be separated from other changes taking place in the psyche of the American Negro. "Black people have been taught to be ashamed of themselves and their blackness for so long that it has been difficult for them to accept each other," comments a New York clothing designer. "Lips are only right if they're thin, and so are noses. You'd be surprised at the number of people who wear only clothing that is black, brown, or of other dark shades—especially if they happen to be dark-skinned. They must be taught to be proud of themselves as belonging to a beautiful people, a proud people."

While American Negroes are throwing away their straightening combs and taking to African-oriented dress, a corresponding trend is developing on the other side of the ocean. A visitor to the First World Festival of Negro Arts in Dakar, Senegal, was amused to discover that unstraightened heads were rare among African women of the elite class. "Most of them had very high-fashion Parisian hair styles," she noted, "and wigs are all the rage, with the bee-hive being the most popular—the higher the better." Noting that a woman from Chicago owns the biggest beauty parlor in Dakar, the American visitor concluded, "Possibly African women didn't straighten their hair before simply because the means weren't available. They're just as style-conscious as anybody else and have a strong desire to be chic and sophisticated."

This reverse trend also is apparent among Africans studying in the United States. Four natural girls of the American variety recently attended a large dance sponsored by African students and were startled to discover they were the only women present with unpressed hair. The African girls regarded them with curiosity and a touch of disdain.

Though the natural look has yet to take roots in smaller Negro communities throughout the coun-try or among the masses, no one is willing to guess just how far things will go. A fashion commentator detected, more than a decade ago, that women tended to reach for the scissors to chop their hair in times of great social chaos. The pattern was set in Revolutionary France where girls of the Directoire period clipped their hair in a style *à la victime*, in imitation of the cut that preceded a trip to the guillotine. This tendency cropped up again in the America of the mid-20s,[4] when the tumult of the era was exceeded only by the shortness of women's hair styles. If the American Negro, in his quest for justice, does not soon resolve the conflict, there might well be an exodus of hair dressers, bound for African shores.

From *Ebony,* June 1966.

READERS OF *EBONY*

Letters on *"The Natural Look"* [1966]

Thank you for having the guts to print an article on "The Natural Look" (June, 1966). However, a few points seem to escape the author. Because I accept the fact that I am black and not white does not mean I am against white beauty standards. White beauty standards are great, if you are a Caucasian. But for Negroes to judge themselves by another race's beauty standard is like trying to make a poodle look like a collie. And it makes almost as little sense.

Also, the fact that some Africans are now straightening their hair and wearing wigs doesn't add any prestige to it. In all due respect for my African sisters and brothers, the American Negro does not have a monopoly on inferiority complexes.

SAMUEL ABBOTT JR.
Bronx, N.Y.

The "natural" look is not only appealing to the eye. It gives us a much needed sense of identification.

SIDNEY A. TROWER
Brooklyn, New York

4. The upheaval of World War I spurred the tremendous social change in the U.S. during the 1920s; see pp. 294–99.

It may not be a secret that our hair is the so-called "bad" type and gives us trouble sometimes, but let's assure this: "We don't have to go around PROVING it!"

CHERYL HOWARD

Jacksonville, Fla.

Your June, 1966 issue of EBONY is to be commended (*sic*) for attempting to set the Negro back 100 years. There are some misguided young ladies who are enchanted by your magazine cover of "The Natural Look." The young ladies who are practicing this look are just plain lazy, nappy-haired females.

What do you mean by "rejecting Caucasian standards?" If Caucasians did not patronize a beauty salon, they would have the same condition as your so-called "new mode for women." I would like for the Negro woman to continue to be beautiful, with the aid of a beautician, if necessary. All races do. I am emphatically against your opinion.

R. EDWARD DORSEY

Philadelphia, Pa.
Editor's Note: EBONY's *"opinion" neither advocates nor opposes the "natural" look, gladly concedes the right of any woman to make her own choice.*

As a white (and male) reader of EBONY, I was delighted to see your article on "The Natural Look" (June, 1966). To me, the women photographed to illustrate it were among the most beautiful I'd ever seen. The "white standards of beauty" they reject are the same standards that choke our cities and suburbs with garish ugliness.

May we all become more natural . . . in every way!

MALCOLM B. WELLS[1]

Cherry Hill, N.J.

After reading the article on the new mode in Negro women's hairstyles ("The Natural Look," June, 1966), I have only one comment to make: Who needs it?

This "woolly skull" look is nothing more than an affectation and the exponents of it are rationalizing their motivations. If they are so anxious to reflect their African heritage, why don't they wear rings through their noses? Their smug implication that they possess the courage to reject white standards is more of a case for gall than guts. It's presumptuous to subject the public to the sight of their dry, nappy looks, replete with knotted-up hair lines!

Why should Negro women be obliged to prove their racial pride by wearing their hair natural? White women don't do this, because their natural state is stringy and straggly, which is why they, too, spend hours in the beauty salons. And why should Negro women have a mission to extol their ancestry by sporting a certain haircut? Do Irish women do this? Do Jewish ones? Do Chinese?

Having one's hair done is not being guilty of emulating "whitey," but rather a case of catering to vanity, as females from all other nationalities in this country do, by choosing popular coiffures which exemplify attractive grooming.

Furthermore, what offers a better testimony to the racial and ethnic identity of a Negro woman than the color of her skin? Why should hair be the focal point?

CONNIE BRADLEY

Maywood, Ill.

When I got my June, 1966 EBONY and saw the picture on the cover, I thought it was a man. When I found out it was a woman and looked inside and saw all those kinky heads, I just tore the cover off my book. I could not look at it.

MRS. C. TROUT

Brooklyn, N.Y.

Ruby[2] and my two daughters told me I ought to write to you and tell you how much we enjoy your wonderful

1. White American ecological architect (1926–2009).
2. Ruby Dee (b. 1924), actress, writer, and civil rights activist; recent projects include starring in and narrating the 2003 television series *Unchained Memories: Stories from the Slave Narratives* (along with her husband Ossie Davis) and playing Mama Lucas in *American Gangster* (2007), for which she was nominated for an Academy Award for Best Supporting Actress.

magazine, especially the "Natural Look," article by Phyl Garland in the June, 1966 issue.

Marvelous! Keep it up.

OSSIE DAVIS[3]
New Rochelle, N.Y.

I was going to send my picture as an "eligible bachelor" for 1966,[4] but with all these *au naturelles* around, I think I can wait.

PHILIP BOATENG
Kingston, Canada

It's about time we Negro American women appreciated our natural attributes. The white man has been trying to mold us into *his* image for centuries and it's about time we said, "No thanks, chum—I'd like you to take a good look at what I already have."

SYLVIA BYRD
Chicago, Ill.

I am perfectly content to let the naturalists follow their own trend and try diligently not to criticize. However, I am neither a "black Anglo-Saxon" nor an inhibited, frantic sheep conforming to so-called Caucasian standards of beauty. I am, happily, a liberal-minded girl of 16, proud to be a Negro and proud to follow the dictates of my own sense of good grooming.

PAULA E. ROBINSON
Washington, D.C.

I never really knew how very brainwashed Americans of color were until I started discussing the article, "The Natural Look," with my associates. Most of the people did not care for the natural look. A few people were quite indignant, and one lady said: "I think it's disgraceful!" Others commented that next we would be wearing cloths tied around us and rings through our noses.

Such attitudes prove that we really have a battle on our hands. It is true that we are not Africans, but we are not "white" either. Rather than fashioning ourselves after our originals, we try to look like "white" people by pressing our hair and bleaching our skins. How long will it take before we open our eyes?

I thank EBONY for the article and look forward to other articles which will help us to see the truth and accept ourselves as we are, for then, perhaps, with this new pride in ourselves we will become unified.

GILDA COKER
Philadelphia, Pa.

I wonder if our women would accept *us* in the "Natural Look"—with no shave or haircuts?

SP/5 LLOYD PETERSON SR.[5]
DeRidder, La.

A tremendous service is being rendered by these pretty and intelligent women who are striving to re-establish a heritage that has been all but lost. I see no reason why all Negro women with kinky hair must wear it that way, but the crucial part is that hair should be recognized as hair—neither intrinsically good nor bad.

Being both a Negro and a sociologist this trend is particularly significant to me.

LUCIEN B. KEYS, PH.D.
Los Angeles, Calif.

---

3. Actor, director, writer, and civil rights activist (1917–2005); projects later in his life include starring roles in Spike Lee films, such as *Do The Right Thing* (1989).
4. An annual feature of *Ebony Magazine*'s June issue were profiles of "eligible bachelors"; in April, "eligible bachelorettes" were featured.
5. During this period, the specialist rank (in this case 5) was awarded for proficiency in a given field in the U.S. military; by convention, military rank precedes name.

A question if you please—where, if anywhere, can one purchase a "natural" wig? Those of us who—ironic twist—had too many white genes would like to know.

MRS. SYLVIA MULDREW

Los Angeles, Calif.
Editor's Note: *You've got us.*

"The Natural Look" (June, 1966) is for soul brothers only! Let's not lead our women back to grass huts! Can you picture the Supremes[6] natural? Yuck!

ROBERT EARL ANNON

San Francisco, Calif.

I've got news for you; the straightening comb, curlers, permanents, false eyelashes, wigs, etc. aren't being manufactured just for Negro women ("The Natural Look," June, 1966). They were first made for Caucasian women. It has been so ever since Cleopatra. We just borrowed the idea from them, so evidently they are "unnatural," also. And speaking of the Doris Day and Elizabeth Taylor look, how do you suppose they look when they wash their hair or swim?

MRS. DAVID E. HOUSTON SR.

St. Paul, Minn.

From *Ebony*, August 1966.

Hair Product Advertisements

LONG AID BRANDS: *Long Aid K7* [1966]
SUPREME BEAUTY PRODUCTS: *Duke Greaseless Hair Pomade* [1966]

The same June 1966 issue of *Ebony* that featured the cover article on the natural look (p. 769) also contained numerous advertisements for hair-straightening products. The first line of the ad for Long Aid K7 equates long with lovely and suggests that a woman's hair is an important part of her personality: "Lovely hair makes any woman more charming." The ad also demonstrates the transmission of values relating to hair through the generations as the mother shares her secret of obtaining a "long, glossy look" with her young daughter. It is this secret that gives the daughter "a fine head on her shoulders."

The ad for Duke Greaseless Hair Pomade reflects the way hair styles and cultural values are linked for men as well as women. According to the advertisement, the "just right" look for "the Best Dressed Men" is one "that trains and holds your hair in perfect place all day long."

---

6. Most successful popular singing group ever, achieving 12 number one singles on the Billboard chart of top 100 songs; later renamed Diana Ross & the Supremes in recognition of the growing fame of Ross (b. 1944).

LONG AID BRANDS
Long Aid K7 [1966]

SUPREME BEAUTY PRODUCTS
Duke Greaseless Hair Pomade [1966]

MORRIE TURNER

from *Humor in Hue* [1969]

Morrie Turner (b. 1923) began his long career as a cartoonist during World War II, when he published his work in an army newspaper. In the cartoon reprinted here, from the comic strip *Humor in Hue,* he pokes fun at the tenacity of both white and black opposition to interracial marriage. The cartoon reflects the 1960s rise to prominence of radical black nationalist organizations, which favored strategies of separatism over integration. (See pp. 516–52 for a discussion of those strategies.) While the white liberal in Turner's comic rejects the separatist schooling and housing policies proposed by the black radical, the two find common ground in their mutual opposition to interracial marriage.

Black/White Dating

JOAN DOWNS: *Black/White Dating* [1971]

READERS OF LIFE: *Letters on "Black/White Dating"* [1971]

Despite widespread disapproval from both black and white Americans, the number of interracial couples increased dramatically during the 1960s and 1970s. As racial segregation broke down in schools, political and social groups, and the military and other professions, expanding opportunities for interaction between black and white people fueled the rise of interracial relationships. With its 1971 coverage of the issue, *Life*, one of the nation's most popular magazines, marked the shift of interracialism from a relatively fringe phenomenon to the mainstream.

The tone and content of this article mark it as an artifact of the turbulent time in which it was written. For example, it both identifies and reinforces race and gender stereotypes, most prominently in its characterizations of the smooth-talking black male seducer and the sharp-tongued black woman. At the same time, the article and the accompanying poll show the inconsistent and biased reasoning behind some of the resistance to interracialism, and the piece even prompted one reader to try to "overcome whatever prejudices society has indoctrinated into me."

JOAN DOWNS

Black/White Dating [1971]

They are almost lost in the noon spill of students emptying onto the Minnesota mall, a lean dark man and a shy pretty girl with soft swinging hair. Ten years ago Faye Becker and Dexter Clarke, a white woman and a black man, would have risked almost certain ostracism for dating each other. Today, with increased exposure between blacks and whites—in the classroom, on the job, in the armed forces—individuals in growing numbers are moving past old racial barriers.

But the change creates a whole new series of personal dilemmas: how, in a time of deeply troubled black/white relations, does one reconcile group loyalty with friendship—even love—across the color line? On both sides, feelings run deep. Two elements emerge with particular force: the initiative in interracial pairing no longer belongs only to whites; and the black who decides to go out with a white must face the censure of his own people.

The current upsurge in interracial contact began in the '60s and gained impetus from the civil rights move-

ment, the Peace Corps and Vista,[1] all of which provided broader opportunity for the races to meet and to mix. It is still not a stampede. Mixed couples may not be so rare a sight in public today, but they are not entirely accepted, either. Where once those who dated and married interracially could be most often found among the intellectuals, the hip, and the fringes of society, racial interaction now occurs in the middle class as well.

In 1965 nearly half of the respondents to a national poll favored making interracial marriage a crime. This spring LIFE commissioned Louis Harris and Associates to conduct a much broader poll investigating public attitudes toward interracial dating and marriage. The returns [* * *] reveal a growing tolerance of racial mixing—and a great many residual doubts.

In examining the pitfalls of social relationships between young blacks and whites, LIFE interviewed 60 interracial couples and many more individuals, as well as sociologists, psychologists and educators at 28 colleges across the country. The photographs [* * *] [not reprinted here] were taken at the University of Minnesota, although the text includes a much wider sampling of opinion.

---

1. The Peace Corps, a volunteer program run by the U.S. government, was established by President John F. Kennedy in 1961; VISTA (Volunteers in Service to America, now called Americorps VISTA), a domestic service program launched in 1965 by President Johnson to combat poverty.

They Walk Easily Together but Endure Stares

Some are crusaders, some are adventurers off on sexual excursions. Most interracial couples, however, consist of a boy and a girl who like each other and incidentally have different colored skin. "He's just like any other guy I've ever dated, only his skin is black. I've never felt self-conscious with him." Faye Becker, 20, grew up in Benson, Minn. She had never met a Negro until she came to Minneapolis and her roommate arranged a date with Dexter Clarke, who is 21. "He's a good conversationalist and we always have fun, going to shows or just listening to records." A white boyfriend thoughtfully warned Faye that some blacks he had known in the army were "rotten." But when she told her parents she was dating a black, they said, "Go ahead but date others too and don't let it get serious." She adhered to this policy, dating Dexter and others too, both black and white.

The calm of the elder Beckers is not typical. At other households similar news often precipitates explosions and tears. After learning her daughter's date was black, a Philadelphia mother appeared at dinner in dark glasses that barely concealed the ravages of a tearful afternoon. Black families, if not enthusiastic, are generally more sympathetic. Some, like Dexter Clarke's parents, are even cordial. "They're used to a racial mix," Dexter says. "Mother runs an integrated day care center and Dad's a musician. Our friends have always been biracial." This works to Dexter's advantage and he realizes it. "I'm more at home in white groups than Faye, whose experience with blacks is limited, is in my world." He continues: There has to be a certain amount of selection when you date the opposite race. A girl must be sensitive and able to handle herself."

The Black Man: Many Economic Benefits, and Few Pangs

At one time a black man with a white woman was looked on with awe by other blacks—a taboo-defier, a player with lightning. Now, against the growth of black awareness, he is often criticized by his own race for making such a social choice. Some black men, like senior Cordell Pastel [* * *], believe that racial interaction helps destroy racism and is therefore justification enough for dating whites. For a good many other black men, interracial dating is a matter of crass, opportunistic economics. Black Pride can be profitable, and some men make a career of dating white girls. "They pay for dates and give you money. I know one guy who even gets an allowance from his old lady." Donnie, a wide-featured heavyset man, prefers women of his own race, but goes with a white girl, explaining: "To her it's a date, to me it's a job. I'd be with a sister but I'm poor. The time I put into her, I'd have to put into any job. If I lose this one I'll find another." He flashes a broad grin.

White parents eye black boyfriends warily for other reasons. Noel, a black man, complains: "Sandra's folks say they understand, but they were taught races shouldn't mix. They're afraid we'll get married."

What Sandra's parents fear almost as much as interracial marriage, of course, is interracial sex—Pill or no Pill. A white sorority girl comments: "Whenever people see a mixed couple, they immediately assume they're sleeping together. Nobody ever considers maybe they're just having a Coke or happen to dig Fellini[2] films." The powerful myth of black sexual prowess continues to be perpetuated. Black men, well aware of the myth—and often embittered by its dehumanizing implications—regard middle-class white women as more permissive than middle-class black girls. On all campuses Life visited, black men are believed to expect their white dates to permit intimacy sooner than girls of their own race. One white freshman recalls telling her roommates that she had accepted a date with a handsome black football player: "They handed me three sex manuals."

Even interracial friendships between men do not escape the sexual factor. A black law student complains he has never had a white friend who inside of two weeks didn't ask if he'd ever had relations with a white girl. In fact there are some psychiatrists who believe a substantial amount of racial disharmony may be disguised sexual insecurity—*on both sides*.

---

2. Federico Fellini (1920–93), Italian film director.

THE BLACK WOMAN FEELS OUTRAGE, PANIC AND HURT

In dingy student grills at scores of colleges across the country there is a familiar scene played with a cast of three: white woman, black man and, off to the side and crackling mad, the black woman. The dialogue sounds like this: "Baby, I've been digging you for a long time. I've been looking at you." He leans closer to the white girl. "And I called last night but there's never any answer." At a corner booth the black girl looks up. "But I was home studying for the Spanish quiz," the white girl says. He shrugs, reaching over to tease a stray wisp at her collar. "Maybe your phone doesn't work. You should have it checked." Ten minutes later they leave, a pale thin-faced blond girl and a haughty black man in neon orange and purple. "A dashiki, an Afro, the clenched fist, but look what's on his arm," glowers the black girl and resumes drinking her coffee, alone.

Although there is little reason to believe that whites have accepted the new black / white relationship, the loudest voices raised in protest are black, especially black women. "What's wrong will me? There aren't enough black men to go around and *he's* messing with Charlie's daughter." Irene, 19, is a college freshman. Like many other black women she is acutely aware that there is a large national surplus of black women over black men. The numbers of white women preempting black men make her feel panicky. "If the white woman was in my position, she'd feel just as threatened. When your field of choice is wiped out, your world is torn apart." Ironically, the black woman is further disadvantaged when her traditionally greater education creates a gap between her and the black man. While she may improve her social and economic status, each year of school beyond the ninth grade actually reduces her chances of finding a suitable black marriage partner. "The educated black woman doesn't have anybody out there." Small wonder she views with rising concern the competition from white women.

On the streets, black girls stare malevolently at white girls clinging to black dates. In some cities they band together in clubs to "Save Our Men." On campus the sight of an interracial couple incites some black women to physical abuse. One white co-ed who dated black reports being shoved against a wall outside the gym by eight black girls, and given a bloody nose. "I thought my life was on the line, even though I tried to explain I had only wanted to learn how to dance." White girls hear stories of marauding bands of black girls stalking white "invaders." The reality of the rumors is usually quite low—but a biannual episode can sustain the legend. For his part, the black man can be equally intimidated. One recalls being surrounded by a group of black girls outside a lunchroom where he had been having coffee with a white girl. "They were like hornets, man."

"Black girls really mean business," observes a white junior. "Their grapevine is incredible. I dated a black guy one night. The next morning a black girl who lives on the floor below in my dorm came up and asked, 'How long have you been messing with David?' I never saw him again, but the day after summer vacation she wanted to know if I was still 'messing with David.'" Black men and women are quick to assert that in many instances it is the white woman who is the aggressor. Molly, a 25-year-old graduate student, complains: "If a black guy walks up to a group of black and white girls in a bar, the white chick makes her move before he can open his mouth. She monopolizes the conversation. What can you do—say, 'Hey, let me talk, too?' So you sit there awkwardly. At the end of the evening he says, 'What're you so quiet about?' Then he's out the door with the honky and you end up going home alone."

The white woman is not always the instigator. Before the end of their freshman year most white girls have heard about and some have been through what is called the Black Rap. Beginning with a ritual sermon on Black Power, the Rap eases into "I'm a human being, too." There is hardly a campus of any size that doesn't have one student hangout where a white girl can sit down and in ten minutes some black man wearing a tan leather trench coat and a real sincere smile will amble over to inquire, "Do you like black men, baby? Hey, have you ever gone out with one?" All she has to be is white and alone.

Especially if she's blond. Despite blistering Black Nationalist rhetoric, there are few black men who have not been influenced by the white aesthetic. To many, "Black Is Beautiful" is no more than a catchy slogan. "There's that whole business of if you're yellow you're mellow," one black woman says sourly. "Any black who says it's dead is lying. You hear it in very subtle ways: 'Oh man, you know I saw a chick I could really dig. She was black, but man she was pretty.' It is there. Two dudes are waiting for a bus. A white girl goes by, the heads snap, the way they light up—it's all there."

White girls singled out by black men are often ultra-feminine in manner and appearance. They are the handful wearing skirts and pastel sweaters when other co-eds slump around in faded jeans. But, says a black woman who teaches Black Personality at a large midwestern university, "I've never heard a black man say about a white woman, 'I love her,' even when she's his wife. Check it out. Sometimes I'll ask a brother who's been seen with a white girl, 'Why're you doing that?' 'Well,' he'll say, 'she's got a car. She's got bread. If ever I need something, there's never a hassle.' The black man is drawn to the white woman for her convenience."

A certain amount of interracial dating can be accounted for on a sheer numerical basis. The increasing number of blacks on most college campuses makes it more likely that social interaction will occur.

Nevertheless, one crucial fact should not be obscured: young black men and women have a serious problem relating to one another, partly because black women are fatally ready to snipe at black men. The Black Personality professor acknowledges the problem: "Wow, our mouth. White girls have learned to capitalize on that. We'll use that tongue on you, cut you to pieces. We really will. At the same time we're digging you and loving you all the while." The new black man has little patience with his woman's scalding tongue. "I wouldn't go out with one of those nigger bitches for all the money in the world. They're mean, they're evil, they're hard to get along with," snarls a black graduate student who dates white women exclusively. Another says, "It's time black women were busted back where they belong." To many black men the dominant black woman is a symbol of a history he would really rather forget. On the brink of winning his manhood, he has no wish to be put down once again. So they stand apart, glaring at one another, the arrogant man and the proud, bristling woman.

Concealing her longing for appreciation in a cloak of independence, the black woman appears cold and unfriendly, although in isolated spots, such as the

University of Minnesota, one black student felt he detected a recent change. "In 1967 when I came here—before Black Power and Black Is Beautiful—black girls were snobs. Then last year some of them underwent a terrific personality change. Now even when I'm with my white girl friend and I see a black girl, she says 'Hi!' It's kind of nice." The mysterious personality transformation may reflect the efforts of Maureen Wilson, a 24-year-old black graduate student and teacher. Last fall she and her friends mounted a quiet but intensive campaign to help black women reopen the lines of communications with black men. "When you see a brother with a white girl, don't ignore him. Speak to him, force him to speak to you," she urged. "You're not trying to catch him. You're just saying, 'Hi, I'm here, I want you to know I'm here!'" Black men are not blameless. According to Maureen Wilson, "The guys here don't even speak to you. I bend over backwards to meet people, but you can walk down the hall, smile and say hello and they look the other way. Especially the ones who date white girls. They feel superior. Black guys outnumber black girls here three to one, but on weekends attractive black girls sit in their rooms with no place to go. Downstairs black guys wait in line to call up their white dates."

One solution proposed by black psychiatrist Kermit Mehlinger is that the women borrow a leaf from the men's book and date white. Although a few would be willing to "date a Caucasian if he sees me as a person," it is highly unlikely this suggestion will meet widespread acceptance. Most black women are solidly opposed to interracial dating, which they view as a contradiction for a true black person. "I don't want to date a white guy, and I have trouble understanding why black men want to date white women. Progress for us is going to have to start with the improvement of the black male-female relationship." Rose, a black college senior, is strikingly handsome. Her low voice dips almost to a whisper: "There's really no such thing as an individual when you're speaking of the black race. Before, I thought of me—what am I going to accomplish. Now I think what are *we* going to accomplish for the black race as a whole. To survive, the black community must remain unified. Only blacks understand what blacks have been through. I've been exposed to the white viewpoint for so long I'm very preoccupied with the way black people feel. We have a beautiful culture and I want it to get blacker. I want whites to stay white."

FOR THIS COUPLE, "NO PROBLEMS"—THEN THEY POUR OUT

The ultimate and feared outcome of interracial dating is intermarriage. "We're just another couple," maintain Germaine and Walter Lide. Germaine Jones, small and fair with a wide grin, met Walter Lide, tall and reedy with an astonishing Bronx accent, three years ago when both were students at Minnesota. She held a liberal arts scholarship and he was majoring in psychology on the GI Bill.[3] Eight months ago they married and are at the stage where many conversations begin, "Oh, Wally, can we please go to the movies?" and end, "Sure, Germ, sure." At first, they insist they have "no special problems." This denial is characteristic of mixed couples. Soon enough the problems pour out. Germaine winces when Walter reminds her of the letter from home after her family learned she was dating a black. "They called me a slut." For Walter, whose mother had told him never to bring home a white girl, things were not much easier. "I couldn't figure out how to tell her about Germaine. Finally one Sunday afternoon I called and asked her to give a friend the recipe for making collard greens. Now any black girl over ten knows how to cook collard greens. Then I put Germaine on the phone. Two days later I got a letter asking what the hell was going on."

Mixed couples must face some hard questions. One of the most difficult concerns the black's need to reconcile his choice of a white partner with his black identity. "At times I feel like a cop-out." Walter Lide admits. "Occasionally I wonder what I'm doing in this situation. Not very often . . . sometimes . . . in the middle of the night. Being married to Germaine will make certain things harder—above all for the children we hope to have. But Germaine understands me, I've never been able to talk as openly to anyone. After a while marriage was the only thing that made any sense. I'll be stuck with her for the rest of my life, but that's okay. I

love her." But as the poll on the following pages indicates, their years ahead will not be made any easier by the attitudes of many of their fellow Americans.

A POLL REVEALS TOLERANCE TEMPERED BY DOUBTS

The national poll conducted for LIFE by Louis Harris and Associates indicates that almost one American in five has had a date with someone outside his or her own race. (In the West and among young people age 21 to 25 across the nation, the figure rises to one in three. In the South it's less than one in ten.) Yet for most Americans, interracial dating remains something that is done by "other people," and in a fairly restricted circle. In fact, a substantial majority (55%) says it doesn't even *know* anyone who has dated interracially.

The responses to the Harris survey reveal an acceptance of the fact that increased black/white dating, like other contacts between the races, is inevitable. And most people—particularly the young, the affluent, the better educated—have no quarrel with the trend, at least in theory. But when the questions begin to touch on the actual problems of interracial pairing, the responses take on an ambivalence that occasionally amounts to outright self-contradiction. Thus the same person could agree with a statement [* * *] that "if all men are created equal it shouldn't make any difference who goes out with whom," and in the next breath admit that "a white girl who dates a black man is going to ruin her reputation as far as I'm concerned." As Harris reports, "One cannot simply say that half the country is tolerant and the other half intolerant. The most overtly bigoted responses were few, but even among those who professed tolerance, doubts emerged."

The doubts grow larger as the questions hit closer to home. Only 3%, for instance, would actively encourage a member of their own family, male or female, to date someone of another race. Only 28% unreservedly approve such dating for their own children, and more than half would actively discourage it. (Among those who have dated interracially themselves, approval is much higher: 60%.) Two-thirds of those interviewed,

---

3. Common name for the Servicemen's Readjustment Act of 1944 and subsequent veterans bills, which provided veterans with college or vocational training, among other benefits.

including a majority of the well-educated, high-income group, believe that parents should impose at least some restrictions on interracial dating "until children are grown up enough to handle things themselves."

The whole question of how effectively parents can impose their will on their offspring is, to put it mildly, debatable. Nevertheless, for 25% of all parents, the desirable "restriction" is simple and draconic: forbid interracial dating altogether. Another 42% would allow the couple to go out in groups but not alone. About half also would have their child seek guidance first from a clergyman or a school official. The most popular response (72%) was characteristically ambivalent: parents should "discuss the dangers and disadvantages of interracial dating with the young people fully, then allow them to make up their own minds." Harris found an overwhelming feeling that a child's age was an important factor. Almost 80% of those interviewed believe that dating in general is okay at age 16 or younger, but only 11% would allow interracial dating at that age, and a majority disapproves of it for anyone under 21.

As to what kinds of people are most likely to date a member of another race, the most common opinion was "students and hippies," with "broad-minded people without prejudices or hang-ups about race" running a reasonably close second. Thoughts on the reasons why people of different races might want to go out together were fairly humdrum: the two enjoy each other's company, they have common interests, there is a physical attraction. Some 15%, however, believe the reason might be curiosity—the desire for a "different" experience. And 10% believe that people date interracially to shock other people and to get attention.

Though four people out of five have never dated interracially themselves, 42% say they have either seen or heard about an interracial couple having difficulties when they appear in public. When that happens:

57% say they feel sympathy for the couple,
20% believe the couple deserves the hostility,
23% feel no particular reaction either way.

But although they may sympathize with a couple under attack, a large number (44%) contend that it is all right for anyone who honestly believes it's "wrong" to date interracially to express his opinions openly—*i.e.*, to give the couple a bad time. Just over half think that those opposed should mind their own business.

Accurately or not, most of those polled perceived a distinct generation gap in the acceptance of interracial dating. Asked "Do you think most *adults* get upset when they see an interracial couple?" 81% answered yes. "Does it upset young people?" No, 54%. In another touchy area—the question of which combination of sexes disturbs adults more—six times as many people said a black man with a white girl than the reverse.

The answers of blacks to the poll were very close to the total response—in which blacks were included as 11% of the population. Only one in four has ever dated interracially, fewer than half know anyone who has, and almost none would actively encourage it in their own families.

But in several areas, the black response was significantly different from the total. Asked whether they would approve of their children dating someone of a different race, 42% said they would—as opposed to only 28% of all respondents. And blacks are more sensitive than the average to interracial couples being subjected to public hostility. While 71% would feel sympathy for the couple, only 10% would think the hard time deserved. Interestingly, a majority of both blacks and whites believes that where resentment of interracial dating exists, it is shared by members of both races. The reasons offered most often for this are that:

1. Both races are equally prejudiced and neither wants intermingling.

2. Neither race wants intermarriage because of the problem of children.

The specter of interracial marriage lies at the root of many attitudes about dating, even though a majority says it is convinced that young people who date interracially are merely "going through a phase" and that most of them eventually will marry within their own race. The same majority senses that mixed marriages are increasing in number. But they are definitely not optimistic about the chances of a mixed marriage succeeding. Compared to a marriage between two people of the same race, a mixed marriage was rated by a two-thirds majority as less likely to succeed.

The reasons for this pessimism range from "lack of social acceptance" to "marriage has enough problems: mixed marriage just adds one more" and "it's hard on the children." More than 70% are convinced that children of a mixed marriage "face a life of prejudice and harassment."

For all their reservations, most Americans believe that interracial dating is inevitable, and they even foresee a day when mixed couples will be routinely accepted. However, two-thirds of the public thinks that that day is still a generation or more away. Another quarter thinks it will arrive in perhaps five or ten years. And two percent believe it is here now.

People Can Accept the Idea, but Not All That It Implies

The Harris poll asked a nationwide cross section how they felt about a series of statements on interracial dating and marriage. The answers reveal not so much a split between the extremists on either end of the spectrum as an honest, even painful confusion over the many nuances of the problem. On the whole, the responses show a rising acceptance of the idea as a moral proposition. But that abstract acceptance conflicts with a residual distaste for the realities as each individual sees them. Black opinion, which often matches and occasionally contrasts with the total opinion, is shown separately.

The percentages indicate agreement with each of the following statements:

- No matter what older people and parents say, young people of different races are going to see each other socially and we'd better get used to it.
  TOTAL 77%   BLACKS 82%

- Whites who go out with blacks are interested in only one thing: sex.
  TOTAL 25%   BLACKS 25%

- Young people of different races who date each other have a lot of courage and integrity.
  TOTAL 54%   BLACKS 63%

- There is a real risk of being hurt emotionally when a person gets involved with someone of a different race.
  TOTAL 77%   BLACKS 61%

- If two mature people really love each other, that will count more toward a successful marriage than any difference in race.
  TOTAL 62%   BLACKS 76%

- Each couple should have the right to decide their own life without laws telling them they can't marry someone of another race.
  TOTAL 70%   BLACKS 81%

- It just seems to violate God's law for people of different races to marry and produce mixed-blood children.
  TOTAL 40%   BLACKS 26%

- Whites and blacks who date each other are probably just as moral as anyone else.
  TOTAL 68%   BLACKS 78%

- Any white girl who goes out with a black man is going to ruin her reputation as far as I'm concerned.
  TOTAL 51%   BLACKS 35%

- There's nothing wrong with interracial dating in itself, but sex and marriage between races really bothers me.
  TOTAL 47%   BLACKS 34%

- If all men are created equal, it shouldn't make any difference who goes out with whom.
  TOTAL 51%   BLACKS 78%

- If black men had any pride, they'd stay with members of their own race. It's degrading for them to go chasing after white women.
  TOTAL 51%   BLACKS 40%

- If parents would keep boys and girls apart at the time they're dating, they could stop interracial marriage at the source and it wouldn't get to be a problem.
  TOTAL 32%   BLACKS 26%

From *Life*, May 28, 1971.

READERS OF *LIFE*

Letters on "Black/White Dating" [1971]

Sirs: In "Black/White Dating" (May 28), Joan Downs asks the question: "How, in a time of deeply troubled black/white relations, does one reconcile group loyalty with friendship—even love—across the color line?" The answer is clear: by recognizing that one's group is, in reality, the whole human race.

CHARLES F. GOLDBERG

Spring Valley, N.Y.

Sirs: I am one black brother who has no sympathy for those dateless black girls on those large white campuses. These black women passed up the predominantly black schools, where the brothers are true to the sisters, to get a so-called better education. I can't understand how these women can say they "want the black male-female relationship to improve, and our culture to get blacker," when in reality they are running from it.

MICHAEL PENDERGRASS

Rock Hill, S.C.

Sirs: Your recent article on black/white dating was an excellent example of just how far America has fallen.

Our moral climate is far more decadent than was ancient Sodom[4] or Rome.

We can only pray that God will bring swift destruction upon America that will bring us to our knees and leave the "strange peoples" and return to God's original law of segregation.

I will not renew my subscription due to this article, and I have destroyed the issue so that others might not see it.

RAILTON D. LOY[5]

Elkhart, Ind.

Sirs: I began to read your article and had a sudden connecting of thoughts. Read Genesis 11:6–7: "The Lord said, Behold the people is one, and they have all one language . . . and now nothing will be restrained from them, which they have imagined to do." Until we are all able to communicate with each other and accept each other as being the same, we will have to go on suffering. When we people become one again, nothing will be restrained from us.

That's so simple to say. Why is it so hard to do? With this realization I hope I can overcome whatever prejudices society has indoctrinated into me.

MRS. RONALD WOODS

Gifford, Ill.

Sirs: Your article is the most biased and damaging piece of reporting I have read, aimed at perpetuating hate and racism in this country. The black man/white woman theme was played to the hilt. Why didn't you picture and report on the black woman/white man mergers? There are many and you know it.

This was a contrived piece of sensationalism aimed at pitting the white man and the black woman against the black man, to further dehumanize him. I shall continue to subscribe to your magazine because I wouldn't dare not stay aware of your racist schemes.

GERALDINE S. MORAN

Cincinnati, Ohio

Sirs: I am black. Recently I took a white girl to a show. Therefore, your article was remarkably timely for me.

The idea that interracial dating and marriage will be accepted more readily in 20 years is a lot of nonsense. It is in keeping with that old American pastime, passing the buck. The people who tell you "in 20 years" are too stubborn or too foolish to bend a little in their narrow-minded views. They are the ones who probably figure on not being alive then—so that anything that happens is simply not their problem. Talk about escapists!

These people bring up their children with the same numskull ideas. So how in hell are things going to be different for the next generation? The change in people's minds about this topic and others is going to have to take place now—not 20 years from now.

DAVID E. FREEMAN

New York, N.Y.

---

4. Biblical city destroyed by God for its sins; Genesis 19:24–25.
5. Indiana-based white American leader of the Ku Klux Klan.

ANGIE MAY-LIN SHELDON

Los Angeles, Calif.

Sirs: It seems that the whole "problem" is brought about by people of all races who hold opinions about things that are none of their business and do not affect their own lives personally. This includes my opinion, too.

M. E. GWYNNE

Alamo, Calif.

From *Life,* June 18, 1971.

SHIRLEY CHISHOLM
Facing the Abortion Question [1970]

Shirley Chisholm reconfigured the debate about birth control and abortion in "Facing the Abortion Question," written three years before the Supreme Court legalized abortion with *Roe v. Wade* (1973). Chisholm argues that the main issue is not whether women will have abortions, since history shows that women will always find a way to end an unwanted pregnancy. If restrictive policies do not prevent abortions, "the question becomes simply that of what kind of abortions society wants women to have—clean, competent ones performed by licensed physicians or septic, dangerous ones done by incompetent practitioners."

Chisholm acknowledges that many black people are suspicious of birth control and abortion, fearing that they are designed "by the white power structure to keep down the numbers of blacks." She finds that it is mostly black men who hold that opinion, however, and unthoughtful ones at that: "To label family planning and legal abortion programs 'genocide' is male rhetoric, for male ears. It falls flat to female listeners, and to thoughtful male ones." What is truly genocide, Chisholm argues, is the dramatically disproportionate number of minority women who die from illegal abortions.

Born in Brooklyn in 1924, Shirley Anita St. Hill lived with her grandmother in Barbados as a girl. After moving back to New York, she studied sociology, earned a master's from Columbia University, and later worked in the field of early-childhood education. In 1960, she co-founded the Unity Democratic Club in order to promote and support black and Hispanic candidates, and in 1964 she was elected to the New York State Assembly, where she served for four years. In 1968, she became the first black woman elected to Congress, and she served as the representative for New York's Twelfth Congressional District until January 1983. An advocate of civil rights, women's rights, and the poor, and an opponent of the Vietnam War, Chisholm helped found the Congressional Black Caucus and the National Organization for Women (NOW). Her 1972 presidential campaign was a milestone. She explained that she ran for the nation's highest office "despite hopeless odds, to demonstrate the sheer will and refusal to accept the status quo." Known as a leader who was "unbought and unbossed" (the title of her 1970 autobiography), Chisholm died in 2005.

From Shirley Chisholm, *Unbought and Unbossed* (Boston: Houghton Mifflin, 1970).

In August of 1969 I started to get phone calls from NARAL, the National Association for the Repeal of Abortion Laws, a new organization based in New York City that was looking for a national president. In the New York State Assembly I had supported abortion reform bills introduced by Assemblyman Albert

Blumenthal, and this had apparently led NARAL to believe I would sympathize with its goal: complete repeal of all laws restricting abortion. As a matter of fact, when I was in the Assembly I had not been in favor of repealing all abortion laws, a step that would leave the question of having or not having the operation entirely up to a woman and her doctor. The bills I had tried to help pass in Albany would only have made it somewhat easier for women to get therapeutic abortions in New York State, by providing additional legal grounds and simplifying the procedure for getting approval. But since that time I had been compelled to do some heavy thinking on the subject, mainly because of the experiences of several young women I knew. All had suffered permanent injuries at the hands of illegal abortionists. Some will never have children as a result. One will have to go to a hospital periodically for treatment for the rest of her life.

It had begun to seem to me that the question was not whether the law should allow abortions. Experience shows that pregnant women who feel they have compelling reasons for not having a baby, or another baby, will break the law and, even worse, risk injury and death if they must to get one. Abortions will not be stopped. It may even be that the number performed is not being greatly reduced by laws making an abortion a "criminal operation." If that is true, the question becomes simply that of what kind of abortions society wants women to have—clean, competent ones performed by licensed physicians or septic, dangerous ones done by incompetent practitioners.

So when NARAL asked me to lead its campaign, I gave it serious thought. For me to take the lead in abortion law repeal would be an even more serious step than for a white politician to do so, because there is a deep and angry suspicion among many blacks that even birth control clinics are a plot by the white power structure to keep down the numbers of blacks, and this opinion is even more strongly held by some in regard to legalizing abortions. But I do not know any black or Puerto Rican *women* who feel that way. To label family planning and legal abortion programs "genocide" is male rhetoric, for male ears. It falls flat to female listeners, and to thoughtful male ones. Women know, and so do many men, that two or three children who are wanted, prepared for, reared amid love and

stability, and educated to the limit of their ability will mean more for the future of the black and brown races from which they come than any number of neglected, hungry, ill-housed, and ill-clothed youngsters. Pride in one's race, as well as simple humanity, supports this view. Poor women of every race feel as I do, I believe. There is objective evidence of it in a study by Dr. Charles F. Westhoff of the Princeton Office of Population Research. He questioned 5,600 married persons and found that twenty-two percent of their children were unwanted. But among persons who earned less than $4,000 a year, forty-two percent of the children were unwanted. The poor are more anxious about family planning than any other group.

Why then do the poor keep on having large families? It is not because they are stupid or immoral. One must understand how many resources their poverty has deprived them of, and that chief among these is medical care and advice. The poor do not go to doctors or clinics except when they absolutely must; their medical ignorance is very great, even when compared to the low level of medical knowledge most persons have. This includes, naturally, information about contraceptives and how to get them. In some of the largest cities, clinics are now attacking this problem; they are nowhere near to solving it. In smaller cities and in most of the countryside, hardly anything is being done.

Another point is this: not only do the poor have large families, but also large families tend to be poor. More than one-fourth of all the families with four children live in poverty, according to the federal government's excessively narrow definition; by humane standards of poverty, the number would be much larger. The figures range from nine percent of one-child families that have incomes below the official poverty line, up to forty-two percent of the families with six children or more. Sinking into poverty, large families tend to stay there because of the educational and social handicaps that being poor imposes. It is the fear of such a future for their children that drives many women, of every color and social stratum, except perhaps the highest, to seek abortions when contraception has failed.

Botched abortions are the largest single cause of death of pregnant women in the United States, particularly among nonwhite women. In 1964, the president of the New York County Medical Society, Dr. Carl Goldmark, estimated that eighty percent of the deaths of gravid[1] women in Manhattan were from this cause.

Another study by Edwin M. Gold, covering 1960 through 1962, gave lower percentages, but supplied evidence that women from minority groups suffer most. Gold said abortion was the cause of death in twenty-five percent of the white cases, forty-nine percent of the black ones, and sixty-five percent of the Puerto Rican ones.

Even when a poor woman needs an abortion for the most impeccable medical reasons, acceptable under most states' laws, she is not likely to succeed in getting one. The public hospitals to which she must go are far more reluctant to approve abortions than are private, voluntary hospitals. It's in the records: private hospitals in New York City perform 3.9 abortions for every 1,000 babies they deliver, public hospitals only 1 per 1,000. Another relevant figure is that ninety percent of the therapeutic abortions in the city are performed on white women. Such statistics convinced me that my instinctive feeling was right: a black woman legislator, far from avoiding the abortion question, was compelled to face it and deal with it.

But my time did not permit me to be an active president of NARAL, so I asked to be made an honorary president. My appearances on television in September 1969, when the association's formation was announced, touched off one of the heaviest flows of mail to my Washington office that I have experienced. What surprised me was that it was overwhelmingly in favor of repeal. Most of the letters that disagreed with me were from Catholics, and most of them were temperate and reasoned. We sent those writers a reply that said in part, "No one should be forced to have an abortion or to use birth control methods which for religious or personal reasons they oppose. But neither should others who have different views be forced to abide by what they do not and cannot believe in." Some of the mail was from desperate women who thought I could help them. "I am forty-five years old," one wrote, "and have raised a family already. Now I

find that I am pregnant and I need help. Please send me all the information." A girl wrote that she was pregnant and did not dare tell her mother and stepfather: "Please send me the name of a doctor or hospital that would help. You said if my doctor wouldn't do it to write to you. Where can I turn?" We sent the writers of these letters a list of the names and addresses of the chapters of the Clergy Consultation Service on Abortion and suggested that they find a local family planning or birth control clinic.

The reaction of a number of my fellow members of Congress seemed to me a little strange. Several said to me, "This abortion business . . . my God, what are you doing? That's not politically wise." It was the same old story; they were not thinking in terms of right or wrong, they were considering only whether taking a side of the issue would help them stay in office—or in this case, whether taking a stand would help me get reelected. They concluded that it would not help me, so it was a bad position for me to take. My advisers were, of course, all men. So I decided to shake them up a little with a feminist line of counterattack. "Who told you I shouldn't do this?" I asked them. "Women are dying every day, did you know that? They're being butchered and maimed. No matter what men think, abortion is a fact of life. Women will have them; they always have and always will. Are they going to have good ones or bad ones? Will the good ones be reserved for the rich while poor women have to go to quacks? Why don't we talk about real problems instead of phony ones?"

One member asked the question that was on the minds of all the others: "How many Catholics do you have in your district?" "Look," I told him, "I can't worry about that. That's not the problem." Persons who do not deal with politicians are often baffled by the peculiarly simple workings of their minds. Scientists and scholars in particular are bewildered by the political approach. When a member of Congress makes a statement, the scholar's first thought is "Is what he said true? Is he right or wrong?" The falseness or validity of an officeholder's statement is almost never discussed in Washington, or anyplace where politics sets the tone of discourse. The question political people ask is seldom

1. Pregnant.

"Is he right?" but "Why did he say that?" Or they ask, "Where does he expect that to get him?" or "Who put him up to that?"

But returning to abortion, the problem that faced me was what action I should take in my role as a legislator, if any; naturally, I intend to be as active as possible as an advocate and publicist for the cause, but was there any chance of getting a meaningful bill through Congress? Some NARAL officials wanted me to introduce an abortion repeal bill as a gesture. This is very common; probably a majority of the bills introduced in all legislative bodies are put in for the sake of effect, to give their sponsor something to talk about on the stump. That was never my style in Albany, and I have not adopted it in Washington. When I introduce legislation, I try to draft it carefully and then look for meaningful support from people who have the power to help move the bill.

So I looked for House members, in both parties and of all shades of conservatism and liberalism, who might get together on abortion repeal regardless of party. I wrote letters to a number of the more influential House members. It would have been easy to get three or four, or even ten or twelve, liberal Democrats to join me in introducing a bill, but nothing would have happened. A majority of House members would have said, "Oh, that bunch again," and dismissed us. But just a few conservative Republican sponsors, or conservative Democratic ones, would change all that. The approach I took was eminently sound, but it didn't work. A few members replied that they would support my bill if it ever got to the floor, but could not come out for it publicly before then or work for it. I did not doubt their sincerity, but it was a safe thing to say because the chances of a bill's reaching the floor seemed slim. Several others answered with longish letters admiring my bold position and expressing sympathy, but not agreement. "I am not ready to assume such a position," one letter said. Another said, in almost these words, "This kind of trouble I don't need." So I put my roughly drafted bill in a drawer and decided to wait. There is no point in introducing it until congressmen can be persuaded to vote for it, and only one thing will persuade them. If a congressman feels he is in danger of losing his job, he will change his mind—and then try to make it look as though he had been leading the way. The

approach to Congress has to be through the arousal and organization of public opinion.

The question will remain "Is abortion *right*?" and it is a question that each of us must answer for himself. My beliefs and my experience have led me to conclude that the wisest public policy is to place the responsibility for that decision on the individual. The rightness or wrongness of an abortion depends on the individual case, and it seems to me clearly wrong to pass laws regulating all cases. But there is more to it than that. First, it is my view, and I think the majority's view, that abortion should always remain a last resort, never a primary method of limiting families. Contraceptive devices are the first choice: *devices,* because of their established safety compared to the controversial oral contraceptives. The weight of responsible medical opinion, by which I mean the opinions of qualified persons who have never been in the pay of the drug industry, seems to be that the question of the Pill's safety is not proven and that there are clear warnings that much more study is needed. So Pill research should continue, and meanwhile the emphasis—particularly in a publicly supported family planning program—should be on proven, safe and effective methods. Beyond that, still from the standpoint of public policy, there must be far more stress on providing a full range of family planning services to persons of all economic levels. At present, the full gamut of services, from expert medical advice to, as a last resort, safe "legal" abortions, is available for the rich. Any woman who has the money and the sophistication about how things are done in our society can get an abortion within the law. If she is from a social stratum where such advice is available, she will be sent to a sympathetic psychiatrist, and he will be well paid to believe her when she says she is ready to kill herself if she doesn't get rid of her pregnancy. But unless a woman has the $700 to $1000 minimum it takes to travel this route, her only safe course in most states is to have the child.

This means that, whether it was so intended, public policy as expressed in American abortion laws (excepting the handful of states where the repeal effort has succeeded) is to maximize illegitimacy. Illegitimate children have always been born and for the foreseeable future they will continue to be. Their handicap is not some legal blot on their ancestry; few intelligent persons give any thought to that today. The trouble is that illegitimate children are usually the most unwanted of the unwanted. Society has forced a woman to have a child in order to punish her. Our laws were based on the puritan reaction of "You've had your pleasure—now pay for it." But who pays? First, it is the helpless woman, who may be a girl in her early teens forced to assume the responsibility of an adult; young, confused, partially educated, she is likely to be condemned to society's trash heap as a result. But the child is often a worse loser. If his mother keeps him, she may marry or not (unmarried mothers are even less likely to marry than widows or divorcées). If she does not, she will have to neglect him and work at undesirable jobs to feed him, more often than not. His home life will almost certainly be abnormal; he may survive it and even thrive, depending on his mother's personal qualities, but the odds have to be against him.

Of course, there should be no unwanted children. Whether they are legitimate or illegitimate is not of the first importance. But we will not even approach the ideal of having every child wanted, planned for, and cherished, until our methods of contraception are fully reliable and completely safe, and readily available to everyone. Until then, unwanted pregnancies will happen, in marriage and out of it. What is our public policy to be toward them? There are very few more important questions for society to face; this question is one that government has always avoided because it did not dare intrude on the sanctity of the home and marriage. But the catastrophic perils that follow in the train of overpopulation were not well known in the past and those perils were not imminent, so the question could be ducked. It cannot be any longer.

For all Americans, and especially for the poor, we must put an end to compulsory pregnancy. The well-off have only one problem when an unwanted pregnancy occurs; they must decide what they want to do and what they believe is right. For the poor, there is no such freedom. They started with too little knowledge about contraception, often with none except street lore and other misinformation. When trapped by pregnancy, they have only two choices, both bad—a cheap abortion or an unwanted child to plunge them deeper into poverty. Remember the statistics that show which choice is often taken: forty-nine percent of the deaths of pregnant black women and sixty-five percent of those of Puerto Rican women . . . due to criminal, amateur abortions.

Which is more like genocide, I have asked some of my black brothers—this, the way things are, or the conditions I am fighting for in which the full range of family planning services is freely available to women of all classes and colors, starting with effective contraception and extending to safe, legal termination of undesired pregnancies, at a price they can afford?

On Birth Control and Genocide

DICK GREGORY: *My Answer to Genocide* [1971]
READERS OF EBONY: *Letters on "My Answer to Genocide"* [1971]

The comedian Dick Gregory (b. 1932) identified himself as one of the "many blacks" referred to in Shirley Chisholm's essay (p. 787) who saw birth control as genocide. In "My Answer to Genocide," Gregory uses quick comic banter to assert that birth control "goes against Nature" and represents an attempt by white people "to limit the black population." For Gregory, rejecting birth control and producing a large family were acts of resistance against this form of genocide.

Ebony received many letters in response to Gregory's article. The twenty published responses, reprinted here, are divided in their reaction to Gregory's argument, but the majority disagree with it. The thirteen respondents who reject Gregory's position frequently mention the same points: that many black families are too poor to raise such a large family, that overpopulation is a problem for all races, that Gregory (who had eight children at the time the article was published, with another on the way) would serve his community better by adopting some of the many black children in the foster care system, and that perhaps he is motivated by a desire to prove his manhood through a display of virility. In addition, a number of women criticize Gregory for presenting his children and wife as elements of his own political strategy, rather than as individuals in their own right.

The seven respondents who support Gregory, mostly women, express gratitude for his strong sense of black pride and his willingness to speak out for his beliefs. Most of the supportive letters also reveal a moral or religious stance against birth control or abortion.

DICK GREGORY
My Answer to Genocide [1971]

My answer to genocide, quite simply, is eight black kids—and another baby on the way. Now I know that statement is going to upset a whole lot of white folks, and even some black folks. More and more white folks these days who are interested in ecology and over-population ask me why I have such a large family. Hell, I had six kids before white folks started getting concerned about ecology. Now planned parenthood groups are saying that a couple should have a maximum of 2½ children. I'm still trying to figure out that half-a-kid. I know my American history well enough to know what "three-fifths"[1] of a man is, but half-a-kid?

I guess I never will understand white folks. Now they're trying to tell us how many babies we should have. But I'm one black cat who's going to have all the kids he wants. White folks can have their birth control. Personally, I've never trusted anything white folks tried to give us with the word "control" in it. Anything good with the word "control" in it, white folks don't want us to have. As soon as we started talking about *community* control, white folks went crazy.

I guess it is just that "slave master" complex white folks have. For years they told us where to sit, where to eat, and where to live. Now they want to dictate our bedroom habits. First the white man tells me to sit in the back of the bus. Now it looks like he wants me to sleep under the bed. Back in the days of slavery, black folks couldn't grow kids fast enough for white folks to harvest. Now that we've got a little taste of power, white folks want us to call a moratorium on having babies.

Of course, I could never participate in birth control, because I'm against doing anything that goes against Nature. That's why I've changed my eating habits so drastically over the years and have become a vegetarian. And birth control is definitely against Nature. Can you believe that human beings are the only creatures who would ever consider developing birth control pills? You mention contraception to a gorilla and he will tear your head off.

Like most black folks, I come from a large family. There were so many of us kids sleeping in one bed that if I got up to go to the bathroom during the night I'd have to leave a book mark so I wouldn't lose my spot. Our family was so large that once a year my father would pack us up and take us all out to dinner and it would cost him $125. And that was at a 10¢ hamburger stand.

And, of course, like all large black families we were poor. I remember one time I was up tight for money so I went to my father and said, "Dad, if you don't give me a nickel I'm going to run away from home." He looked at me and said, "I'm not going to give you one damn penny, and take your brothers with you." Our family was so poor that one time we got garnisheed[2] by the newspaper boy.

Being so poor, we never had enough food. I remember one time this Thanksgiving my Momma came home with a turkey foot. All of us kids gathered around the pot while Momma boiled the foot and we watched it shrink. Then we all sat around the table looking at that turkey foot and waiting to dive into it, and Momma insisted that we pray over it first. I said, "Momma, I don't have anything against prayers or anything like

1. The three-fifths compromise in the United States Constitution stipulated that each enslaved person be counted as 3/5 of one person for the determination of a state's number of representatives and the distribution of taxes; see p. 169.
2. Having one's wages withheld by an employer for the payment of a debt to a third party (in this case, the newspaper carrier).

that. But if anyone should be praying, it should be the turkey that got away from that foot."

When I was a kid, Halloween was about the only holiday we could enjoy. Halloween was the one day we could wear our regular clothes and people thought we were dressed for the occasion. Folks would look at me and say, "Look at Richard wearing that old man's costume. And he's wearing shoes that look just like feet."

So I guess having a large family just comes natural to me. In fact, my wife had so many babies at the same hospital in Chicago that they put a revolving door on her room in the maternity ward. Some of the Southern white folks used to bad-mouth me for having so many kids. Governor Wallace even accused me of trying to grow my own race.

And there are more large black families than most white folks realize. The government keeps trying to tell us that there are 22 million black folks in America, but you know that's a trick. Just stop and think: Who counts us? The census takers, and most of them are white. Being white, they are afraid to come into the black neighborhoods. Can't you just hear two white census takers standing at the edge of the ghetto? One of them says, "Chuck, how many Negroes do you think there are in that old run-down building over yonder?" And Chuck says, "I don't know. Put down five." Hell, there were 52 black folks in the toilet.

When I was a kid, there were more than 22 million black folks in my neighborhood in St. Louis. I'm 38 years old and I've never seen a census taker. That means they missed me and my wife and eight kids. And next year they'll miss one more. So you know what the census bureau does? They count all the white folks in the United States and then they tell us black folks that we're 10 percent of them.

Every chance I get I state publicly that I don't believe the government's population statistics concerning black folks. I was on a television show not long ago and the white cat interviewing me said, "Mr. Gregory, I understand you don't believe the census bureau's figures as to the number of black people in the United States." And I said, "That's right."

"Well," the cat said, "if you don't believe the census count, just how many black people are there?" And I said calmly, "I don't know." Now that upset him. He got all indignant and said, "If you don't know how many black people there are, how can you dare question the census figures?" So I told him, "All right, I'll tell you. There's googobs of black folks in America." Now that *really* upset him. You've got to admit that googobs does sound better than 22 million! Right away people started phoning into the television studio asking, "What's googobs????"

So the girl at the switchboard slipped a note to the interviewer and he asked me, "Please, Mr. Gregory. Before you go, *please* tell us how many is googobs?" So I said, "Have you ever been out in an open field and looked out over the horizon to where the sky meets the ground?" He said, "Yes." "Well," I said, "googobs means there's some black folks on the other side of that."

One thing I can't understand about black folks with large families is how so many seem to be embarrassed about being on relief. I could never be embarrassed about some free money. Even my Momma used to be embarrassed about the welfare check. I used to tell her, "Momma, you're not on welfare, *we* are. That money's Aid to Dependent Children. If you're embarrassed, just give me my little piece of change now."

And now I've got a cousin who's embarrassed about her welfare check. So I told her she ought to move to Canada; then let the government mail her welfare check up there and call it "Foreign Aid."

So, as I said before, my answer to genocide is my large black family. And that is not at all a flippant statement. To understand the seriousness of my answer, you must first understand the word *genocide* and its insidious manifestations in the United States of America today.

The word *genocide* is rather new to the human vocabulary, although it has a long and inglorious history in human practice. Genocide is a word coined in the 1930s by a Polish scholar, Raphael Lemkin, who combined the Greek word *genos*—clan or religious group—with the Latin word *cide*—killing. *Genocide* has come to mean "acts committed with the intent to destroy, in whole or in part, a national, ethnical, racial or religious group as such; by killing members of the group; causing serious bodily or mental harm to members of the group; deliberately inflicting on the group conditions of life calculated to bring about its physical destruction in whole or in part; imposing measures intended to prevent births within the group; or forcibly transferring children of the group to another group."

So when Adolph Hitler[3] sent 6 million Jews to the gas chambers and ovens, it was genocide. When the Turks slaughtered 1.2 million Armenians in 1915, it was genocide. When the ancient Romans fed Christians to the lions in a conscious effort to wipe out Christianity, it was genocide. Such open and deliberate acts of mass killing are easily recognized as genocide. But there are more subtle forms of genocide, as the above definition indicates, and these less-open acts of genocide occur in America every day.

Consider, for example, the police moving in to raid the headquarters of militant black groups. The police know in advance that the group is armed. So the police arm themselves with heavy weaponry and conduct the raid in such a manner as to be sure to provoke the black militants to open fire in self-defense. Then the police, who outnumber and are better armed than the militants, use the gunfire as an excuse to wipe them out. That is an act of conscious genocide just as surely as throwing the Christians to the lions or herding the Jews into the gas chambers. Especially when you consider that the police never use such tactics when conducting raids on non-black groups—the Malia, the Minutemen,[4] the Ku Klux Klan or the American Nazi party. What does the definition of genocide say? " . . . acts committed with the intent to destroy in whole or *in part.*"

Or consider the portion of the genocide definition which speaks of "deliberately inflicting on the group [black folks] conditions of life calculated to bring about its physical destruction in whole or in part." You could hardly find a better definition of the pattern of segregated housing in this country. Black people are herded into small overcrowded areas called ghettos, made to live in sub-standard housing where heat, water and plumbing facilities are lacking and adequate public services such as garbage removal are withheld, making the ghetto areas breeding grounds for rats, disease and death. Add to this the poor food found in ghetto supermarkets, the absence of health services,

and the fires which consume the run-down houses and the little kids who live in them.

What is the result? Black folks die six years earlier than white folks. The infant mortality rate is at least twice as high for black folks. Death for blacks is the result of the segregated housing patterns in the United States, and the Nixon Administration has made it very clear that the pattern is "deliberate."

What is true for black folks is also true for the American Indians.

Whereas the majority of blacks are confined to ghettos, Indians are confined to reservations. Certainly that pattern of "segregated housing" is also quite deliberate, officially backed by the United States government. On some Indian reservations the infant mortality rate reaches a staggering 100 deaths per 1,000 births. That's about twice the infant mortality rate in the worst black ghettos in America and four times the death rate among white babies. Indians on the reservations have a death rate from influenza and pneumonia twice that of the national average. There is more hunger and malnutrition on the Indian reservations than anywhere else in America. There is one doctor for every 900 Indians, and one dentist for every 2,900. The average Indian on the reservation dies twenty-five years before other Americans.

The word *genocide* is new enough in our vocabulary that many people are not fully aware of its true meaning. Some folks, for example, mistakenly say it means "racial suicide." It is an interesting mistake. The difference between *suicide* and *genocide* is in the conscious choice of the victim. A person chooses to commit suicide. The victim of genocide has no choice in the matter. But it is an act of genocide for a government to create the conditions of hopelessness, frustration and despair among a group of people so that they choose suicide as the only available means of escape.

The black suicide rate has always been higher than that of whites. The suicide rate among Indian *teenagers* is ten times the national average. And the terrible reality of suicide as a way out begins at age seven on the Indian reservations. Can the genocidal "conditions of

---

3. Adolf Hitler (1889–1945).
4. Militant anti-Communist group formed in the 1960s.

life" forced upon the American Indians be more tragically illustrated?

Of course, one of the definitions of genocide is "imposing measures intended to prevent births within the group"—that is, forcing birth control measures upon black folks. There is ample evidence that government programs designed for poor black folks emphasize birth control and abortion availability, both measures obviously designed to limit the black population. Such obvious tactics of genocide are easier to deal with than measures designed to inflict "mental harm and destruction." Birth control measures can be combated by black women refusing to "swallow" that line. But *mental* abuse is more subtle and insidious.

Not long ago a series of tests was conducted in the ghettos of the nation in which five-year-old black kids were asked to draw a picture of themselves. In an alarming number of instances the kids would end up drawing a picture of an animal. Such is the mental abuse of a genocidal system that young black minds think of themselves as animals. It is not hard to understand, however, when you realize that the American system keeps some black folks so poor that they are forced to consume dog food. It is a small step from that economic abuse to the mental identification with an animal.

A walk through the ghetto supermarket is a study in such mental abuse. At the baby food counter you will find jars of fruits and vegetables with pictures of white babies on the outside rather than pictures of the food on the inside. What is being sold? White babies or mashed turnips? At that very tender and impressionable age the black baby has to go through the white baby's picture just to get his food.

When black pictures do appear on boxes, the mental abuse continues. The most common black pictures used in advertising products are Aunt Jemima,[5] Beulah[6] and Uncle Ben.[7] Picture them in your mind. Uncle Ben is the best looking of the three. Uncle Ben is clean, he wears a tuxedo, and he is not fat. Do you think it is an accident that advertisers make the black male more attractive than the black female? You have never seen them use a fat, out-of-shape hillbilly white woman to advertise anything.

So the mental abuse of black folks is subtly, insidiously and deeply woven into the fabric of the America system. It is seen in more open manifestations in the condition of ghetto schools and the quality of public education in black communities. It is little wonder, then, that the United States still has not ratified the 1948 United Nations Genocide Convention[8] which made the crime of genocide a part of international law. Russia, China and 73 other countries have done so but not the United States. Critics of the Genocide Convention in the United States cite the "mental harm" part of the definition as being too vague, while at the same time insisting that this nation would never consider participating in acts of genocide.

I say that it is easily proved. All it would take for the United States to ratify the United Nations Genocide Agreement, thereby exposing this nation to the full weight of international opinion on the matter. Even President Nixon has recommended such action. But obviously the Senate has profound reservations, knowing of the other "reservations" this nation perpetuates.

5. Character created in 1889 by two white American men to sell the first ready-made baking mix; the traditional image of her as a Mammy figure was "updated" in 1968, by, in addition to making her thinner, replacing her original bandana with a headband; in 1989, she lost the headband and gained pearl earrings and a lace collar, and in 1992, her head was tilted so that it was more upright; the Quaker Oats Company now presents her as a mother-figure with "qualities you'll find in loving moms from diverse backgrounds who care for and want the very best for their families" (as stated on the official website devoted to her character).
6. Beulah was the title character of a nationally broadcast weekly television series, the first to star an African American; Ethel Waters played the role from 1950 to 1952, and Louise Beavers took over the role for the final year of the show; the character, who works as a domestic for a white family and is known as the "queen of the kitchen," was originally created and performed by a white, male actor, Marlin Hurt (1906–46), for the *Fibber McGee and Molly* radio program; Hurt starred in the spin-off radio program, *Marlin Hurt and Beulah Show*, for the first year of the show until his death in 1946, when the role was taken over by actress Hattie McDaniel (1895–1952).
7. The Uncle Ben character (based on a real farmer from Houston known for growing superior rice) was launched as a marketing label in the late 1940s by Converted Rice, Inc. (owned and operated by two white American men).
8. The Convention on the Prevention and Punishment of Genocide ultimately was ratified, with conditions, by the U.S. Senate in 1988.

In the meantime, my answer to genocide remains eight black kids. And that means eight black minds in preparation. If they are ever asked to draw a picture of themselves and they draw pictures of animals, it will only mean they can't draw!

From *Ebony,* October 1971.

READERS OF *EBONY*

Letters on "My Answer to Genocide" [1971]

Dick Gregory, in "My Answer to Genocide," (EBONY, Oct. 1971), has done a great disservice to us who believe that overpopulation is the greatest threat to America and the world today.

My mother was one of ten children; my father was one of ten children. I have been married ten years. We have our child. I practice what I preach.

We take EBONY and feel it is a very great magazine. Please give consideration to doing a whole issue on the population question, going into this crucial subject in depth and presenting all sides of the argument so that your readers may be fully informed on this vital matter.

GEORGE GOSTAS
Cataloging Librarian
Westmar College
LeMars, Ia.

If Mr. Richard Gregory is really interested in having the black population rise, why oh why, doesn't be adopt black children that are for various reasons parentless? These kids get tossed from foster home to foster home. Some never acclimate and spend their entire lives in institutions.

If Mr. Gregory really feels that genocide is being subtly pushed, he should further the cause of blacks adopting blacks. I believe that if he inquired of the authorities in Chicago alone he would find there are many black children needing strong permanent homes.

Come on, Dick, lead the way. Get the blacks to adopt the black—otherwise, they'll be adopted by white and eventually true integration will take place and then there will be no need for genocide of any sort. We will all really be brothers—both under and outside the skin.

JOSETTE H. MARTINS
Eau Claire, Wisc.

It is really discouraging to hear that Dick Gregory is preaching against one kind of genocide while at the same time he and his wife are practicing another kind. When our population gets bigger than our farmland can support, people will die, and there is no ethnic magic that will keep the same thing from happening to the black brothers and sisters that will happen to the whites.

RUTH B. BALL
Portland, Ore.

Mr. Gregory says he knows what it's like to be poor and to have come from a large family, and it is precisely this statement that makes it incomprehensible that a commentator on social issues such as he could advocate large families for the average black man and woman. I would think that he knows that average black folks simply do not have the money to provide adequate food, clothing and shelter for eight. A recent article in one of New York's leading magazines attests that in 1970 it cost the average family of four approximately $11,000 a year to live comfortably. If we accept these figures as criteria, how many black families could measure up?

Dr. W. E. B. DuBois advised us to continue to have children despite the obstacles but he also insisted that we be concerned about the QUALITY of those children—not just the QUANTITY. Our answer to genocide might then be the swelling of the ranks of black people who by the efforts of their parents were able to acquire the nourishment, achieve the education and thereby alter the environment of their children to our own satisfaction and hence, destroy the cycle of genocide.

JACK WOODS
Springfield Gardens, N.Y.

I read Dick Gregory's October 1971 EBONY article twice. The first reading made me angry, which I suppose was Gregory's intended effect on white readers. The second reading made me feel sorry for his eight beautiful black kids. They are being raised not for their own individual worths but as a protest against imaginary genocide. After Mr. Gregory is dead and gone, they may have to live in a world made unbearably overcrowded by just such uninformed bigotry.

If birth control is a plot by whites to eliminate blacks then why do white women form the majority of pill users? And why have so many young whites decided to forego having children even though they want them? If Dick Gregory wants to raise a mob of children according to his beliefs, why does he and his wife not adopt some of the black babies who are being emotionally crippled in institutions?

He uses the rationale that he does not believe in unnatural practices, but his oldest daughter wears glasses. I believe the reason he hides behind the "natural way" is that he is too selfish to care about his children's future and too unsure of his manhood to give his wife a respite from being a baby machine.

Dick Gregory's children will have to associate with whites eventually, because we are not going to stop having babies either. If Mr. Gregory is as concerned for his race as he claims to be, let him teach his kids to love their fellow man regardless of his color. Having children to spite your neighbors is foolish.

MRS. MARY SHAW
San Antonio, Tex.

Never before have I read an article that stated so many of the things I would like to say myself. The article I'm referring to is "My Answer to Genocide," by Dick Gregory (October 1971). I am from a large family of 12 children—seven girls and five boys—and I am the oldest.

Mr. Gregory is one black man I truly respect because he speaks his mind and shows the world that he is the head of his house and that no one can tell him what must go on in his bedroom.

"The Lord giveth and the Lord taketh away." Don't play around with the babies yet to be born. Let nature take its course. Don't let man take the place of our Master. Only He knows how far to let you go. The Lord looks out for all of us, and there is a justifiable reason for everything He has anything to do with. God never makes a mistake, so why should man try to change things?

During the time of slavery, the blacks could not have babies fast enough for their master. Look at the change now that we have a little power.

MISS CAROLYN A. DONNELLY
Mullins, S.C.

One may agree or differ with Dick Gregory's opinion on genocide, but when he gets off his subject and states what animals do "naturally," he has entered a field where even his opinions cannot change the facts.

You see, some animals practice infanticide to keep their population down. Other species have smaller litters in times when food is scarce. Still others will *not even* mate if they are unable to provide adequate shelter for their offspring.

Even man, namely the African Bushman, practiced birth control 50,000 years before Dick Gregory was born—but then they didn't know it wasn't natural to do it.

HOWARD FIGOWITT
Harrisburg, Pa.

Dick Gregory is right in predicting that his article, "My Answer to Genocide" (Oct. 1971) "is going to upset a whole lot of white folks . . ." I am a white and I am upset with his article. "Disappointed" is a better word. I am active in the civil rights movement but I am also active in the environmental movement. Believe it or not, they are vitally related. One of the causes of poverty is the inability of many lower-class blacks to break the tradition of large families. I am a member of Zero Population Growth (ZPG) which seeks to educate all (white, black, purple and green) people to the dangers of overpopulation. We are not committing genocide—only trying desperately to stop all of mankind from committing suicide by breeding itself out of existence.

DICK SNYDER
San Angelo, Tex.

Dick Gregory in "My Answer to Genocide" wants to set blacks back several decades. The tragedy is the black people who will believe him and multiply like rabbits, therefore perpetuating the poverty and misery of overpopulation. We don't all have your bread, Dick!

MRS. SOPHIE BROWN
Los Angeles, Calif.

I have just completed reading the outstanding article, "My Answer to Genocide," by Dick Gregory. It is refreshing to know there are blacks like Mr. Gregory who are not reticent but "tell it like it is" and express themselves with pride and concern about the welfare of the black race.

CLAIRE L. JONES
Texarkana, Tex.

It is truly tragic that Dick Gregory's answer to "genocide" is suicide. Black and white, rich and poor, we have only one planet with limited resources to live on. Overpopulation is no answer to any problem. I suspect Dick may still be trying to prove his "manhood"!

MRS. BARBARA M. COOK
Albion, Mieli.

As a black, professional woman, and mother of two, I found the article by Mr. Gregory and his insane reasoning appalling and beyond belief.

The fact that this man wants X amount of children is not my point. The fact that he and his wife share a common desire to have a large family is such an intimate, personal matter, that a comment here would be out of order. But to openly admit that he is capitalizing on the fertility of his wife and herself to strike a blow at the white population of this nation is, in my humble but sincere opinion, bordering on lunacy.

He is using the body of his wife as a weapon, reducing her to the level of a cow, and she apparently accepts her lot as inevitable. It is significant to recall that he did not once mention an offspring as an individual unique personality, did not once speak of a child as a child for his or her own sake, but rather as some wild, distorted joke on the plans and schemes of the white man. Herein lies the crux of my confusion.

I would implore Mr. Gregory in fight his war and his bitterness as a man, and thus allow his wife to become a person, his children to become people in their own right, and not tools for his use, as outlets for his frustrations. As brother James Brown might say, "Check yourself."

MRS. SHIRLEY NALLEY
Roosevelt, L.I., N.Y.

Mr. Gregory is not speaking for blacks; he speaks for Dick Gregory. If all of us blacks had the money he has, we would have no excuse for not having larger families. The majority of us be on smaller incomes which limits the things we can and want to do. Birth control is not forced on us. To obtain it, we must ask for it. I believe it is an individual's choice and wholeheartedly agree that the male involved should have some input. But the female who bears children must also think of herself—physically, financially and mentally. Using a contraceptive does not mean a person cannot have kids ever. It's a means of spacing them, allowing time to plan and prepare a future, also improve healthwise. After a family has reached certain goals they can discontinue limiting their family size. Family planning or birth control is a person's choice.

MRS. PEARLIE MARIE HALL
Counselor
Planned Parenthood Of San Diego
San Diego, Calif.

To this white, female, anti-abortion doctor, Dick Gregory's article, "My Answer to Genocide," was a whiff of oxygen. Thank God, our state has thus far succeeded in resisting the anti-life pressures of abortion proponents.

DR. ANN CINELIS
Sheboygan, Wisc.

Dick Gregory states, "All birth control is definitely against nature. Can you believe that human beings are the only creatures who would ever consider developing birth control pills? You mention contraception to a gorilla. . . ."

Indeed a gorilla does not need birth control because he has no power of death control. The present population explosion is a human problem: most animal species are stable or declining. Within the human species, however, the problem exists in varying degrees for all races. The cause is in part due to great improvements in medical knowledge and resultant reduction in death rates. "Natural" is a high infant mortality; "natural" is a high death rate for women in childbirth and "natural" is a short life expectancy!

Maybe Mr. Gregory will feel better if he reads that the annual rate of population growth in Africa is 2.7 per cent compared to a meager 1.1 per cent in the U.S. But, alas, who is going to catch up with Asia with 2.1 billion people . . . ?

MARINA B. BROWN
Loudonville, N.Y.

Congratulations to EBONY for printing Dick Gregory's excellent article, "My Answer To Genocide." I strongly agree with Gregory's intellectual and moral stand on birth control. It is good to hear his voice loud and clear on this vital issue. I believe firmly that artificial contraceptive birth control is against nature. It is beautiful to hear a strong black voice calling our attention to this simple fact of life.

BROTHER DON FLEISCHRACKER, C.S.C.[1]
St. Edward's University
Austin, Texas

You have the dubious honor of being the recipient of my first "letter to the editor."

This is in response to the many letters (EBONY Dec. 1971) opposing Dick Gregory's article, "My Answer To Genocide" (EBONY, Oct. 1971). Hiding beneath all the rationalizations—pro-birth control—there seemed to be a refusal to acknowledge that genocide does, in fact, exist. The possibility is so frightening that only three of the letter writers could even use the word "genocide," and others resorted to personal attacks on the author's manhood, his wife's womanhood and his children's personhood. That frightens me.

I suggest to these people that they stop attacking Brother Gregory and investigate for themselves the possibility that black genocide is not "imaginary."

In Hitler's Germany, the Jews were forewarned about the concentration camps. They refused to believe the camps existed—until it was too late!

MRS. JANET PEGUES
Security, Colo.

Interesting and mollifying indeed were the printed responses of your readership to Dick Gregory's "Answer." But the December "Backstage" article suggests that you missed the message: the Gregorys' answer to what they define as a problem is fine for them although it possibly represents another kind of genocide for the masses to which it was offered. While too many of us struggle for voice and options in the public schooling of our children the Gregory's exercise a privileged option of Montessori and Laboratory schooling[2] for their children. Gregory is right about one thing: there is strength in numbers, but he doesn't acknowledge that those enumerated need first to possess individual, personal strength.

Your summary sentence: "Maybe what black men really need is many angry black women like Lillian Gregory"[3] is strongly reminiscent of the mindless rhetoric of racists that "if more Negroes were like so and so, things might be better." Black women have the qualities you applaud in Mrs. Gregory. What black women REALLY need is more black men with earning power similar to Gregory's. Black women then could—if they wished—be more like Lillian Gregory. She surely is right when saying she needs no sad songs sung for her. She has a good deal of control of her destiny.

In a word, your December "Backstage" amounts to nothing short of journalistic pandering.

HAROLD E. CHEATHAM
Cleveland, Ohio

---

1. The writer is a member of the Congregation of Holy Cross, a Roman Catholic congregation of priests and brothers, who take vows of celibacy.
2. Experiential schools based on John Dewey's educational philosophy of interactive learning; Montessori: schools based on Maria Montessori's educational method of self-directed learning within an enriched environment.
3. The concluding sentence of "Backstage" in the December 1971 issue of *Ebony*, a profile of Lillian Gregory, who was married to Dick Gregory.

Mr. Gregory's ideas on black genocide and how to prevent it deserves critical study by the black community. Anyone who looks at man and nature can see there is safety in number. The Persians were great in numbers, but they were done in by a few talented and well-trained Greeks. In modern times we can look at the domination of India by little England and the rape of China by the Japanese, and to bring it close to home; look at what Whitey did in Africa. In numbers, there is a kind of comfort, but for success and security we must look elsewhere.

Our survival may require a flexible approach from time to time. It may be the case that for the nest generation we need to limit our family size so that the children we do have can be adequately clothed and fed as well as loved and disciplined and educated. These goals are irrefutable necessities in the black man's battle to survive. In a world of declining jobs and decreasing job creation—half of the shoes and half of the TV sets in this country were made abroad—we must produce only those children who will find means to survive.

I admire Mr. Gregory's point of view and he has a fine family. I am all for large families among successful blacks, but I would think twice before asking every black family to follow his example. Studies show that the well loved and disciplined child with both parents on the home has an excellent chance of succeeding. This is impossible in the average large family where both parents have to work to keep the family alive.

GARY DOUGLAS
Washington, D.C.

I cheered a thousand times for Dick Gregory's article, "My Answer to Genocide." And I understand just where he's coming from. I also just read the comments on his article, in the December issue and it really makes me disgusted to know that black people are still allowing themselves to be brainwashed. I put it like this: If I have a lot of children, God will help make a way for them. That is faith, something I have depended on for so long, even in jail, where I have already been over a year waiting for trial. At this time, I only have one child and am 19, but you better believe I will have more, when I am united with my baby's father again.

C. TRIMBLE
St. Paul, Minn.

From *Ebony*, December 1971 and February 1972.

KEY DEBATE ≈ *Gender*

FRANCES M. BEAL
Double Jeopardy: To Be Black and Female [1970]

Frances Beal's germinal essay "Double Jeopardy: To Be Black and Female" was first published as a pamphlet in 1969. A revision, reprinted here, was included in Robin Morgan's anthology *Sisterhood Is Powerful* (1970) and became one of the most reprinted essays of the emerging black feminist movement. By analyzing both racism and sexism as methods of capitalist exploitation, Beal develops the idea that oppression cannot be attacked piecemeal by separate feminist, civil rights, and labor movements. Instead, men and women must work together in grassroots movements to create a "new world." Beal's essay introduces a central tenet of later black feminists, including the members of the Combahee River Collective (p. 807): that black women are central to the revolutionary struggle because the liberation of the most oppressed is the key to freedom for all.

Frances M. Beal (née Frances Yates) was born in 1940 in Binghamton, New York, to a father of African American and Native American background and a mother of Russian Jewish background. From 1959 to 1966, she lived in France with her husband, James Beal, and they had two children. In Paris, she studied at the Sorbonne, where she became involved in the African liberation movement and associated with many female activists. In 1966, when her marriage ended and she returned to the United States, she worked with many activist groups, including the Student Nonviolent Coordinating Committee (SNNC), SNCC Black Women's Liberation Committee (which she co-founded), the Third World Women's Alliance (TWWA, an outgrowth of SNCC Black Woman's Liberation Committee), and the National Council of Negro Women. Beal also published *The Black Woman* (the newsletter of the National Council of Negro Women), served as an associate editor of *The Black Scholar*, wrote for the radical newspapers *Frontline* and *CrossRoads*, and served as National Secretary of the Black Radical Congress. In her decades of writing and organizing, Beal emphasized the idea that "the liberation of women cannot be separated from the liberation of society," as she wrote in her 1975 essay, "Slave of a Slave No More: Black Women in Struggle."

From Robin Morgan, ed., *Sisterhood Is Powerful: An Anthology of Writings from the Women's Liberation Movement* (New York: Random House, 1970).

In attempting to analyze the situation of the black woman in America, one crashes abruptly into a solid wall of grave misconceptions, outright distortions of fact, and defensive attitudes on the part of many. The system of capitalism (and its afterbirth—racism) under which we all live has attempted by many devious ways and means to destroy the humanity of all people, and particularly the humanity of black people. This has meant an outrageous assault on every black man, woman, and child who resides in the United States.

In keeping with its goal of destroying the black race's will to resist its subjugation, capitalism found it necessary to create a situation where the black man found it impossible to find meaningful or productive employment. More often than not, he couldn't find work of any kind. And the black woman likewise was manipulated by the system, economically exploited, and physically assaulted. She could often find work in the white man's kitchen, however, and sometimes became the sole breadwinner of the family. This predicament has led to many psychological problems on the part of both man and woman and has contributed to the turmoil that we find in the black family structure.

Unfortunately, neither the black man nor the black woman understood the true nature of the forces working upon them. Many black women tended to accept the capitalist evaluation of manhood and womanhood and believed, in fact, that black men were shiftless and lazy, otherwise they would get a job and support their families as they ought to. Personal relationships between black men and women were thus torn asunder and one result has been the separation of man from wife, mother from child, etc.

America has defined the roles to which each individual should subscribe. It has defined "manhood" in terms of its own interests and "feminity" likewise. Therefore, an individual who has a good job, makes a lot of money, and drives a Cadillac is a real "man," and conversely, an individual who is lacking in these "qualities" is less of a man. The advertising media in this country continuously inform the American male of his need for indispensable signs of his virility—the brand of cigarettes that cowboys prefer, the whiskey that has a masculine tang, or the label of the jockstrap that athletes wear.

The ideal model that is projected for a woman is to be surrounded by hypocritical homage and estranged from all real work, spending idle hours primping and preening, obsessed with conspicuous consumption, and limiting life's functions to simply a sex role. We unqualitatively reject these respective models. A woman who stays at home caring for children and the house often leads an extremely sterile existence. She must lead her entire life as a satellite to her mate. He goes out into society and brings back a little piece of the world for her. His interests and his understanding of the world become her own and she cannot develop herself as an individual having been reduced to only a biological function. This kind of woman leads a parasitic existence that can aptly be described as legalized prostitution.

Furthermore it is idle dreaming to think of black women simply caring for their homes and children like the middle-class white model. Most black women have to work to help house, feed, and clothe their families. Black women make up a substantial percentage of the black working force, and this is true for the poorest black family as well as the so-called middle-class family.

Black women were never afforded any such phony luxuries. Though we have been browbeaten with this white image, the reality of the degrading and dehu-

manizing jobs that were relegated to us quickly dissipated this mirage of womanhood. The following excerpts from a speech that Sojourner Truth made at a women's rights convention in the nineteenth century show us how misleading and incomplete a life this model represents for us:

> . . . Well, chilern, whar dar is so much racket dar must be something out o' kilter. I tink dat 'twixt de niggers of de Souf and de women at de Norf all a talkin' 'bout rights, de white men will be in a fix pretty soon. But what's all dis here talkin' 'bout? Dat man ober dar say dat women needs to be helped into carriages, and lifted ober ditches, and to have de best place every whar. Nobody ever help me into carriages, or ober mud puddles, or gives me any best places . . . and ar'nt I a woman? Look at me! Look at my arm! . . . I have plowed, and planted, and gathered into barns, and no man could head me—and ar'nt I a woman? I could work as much as a man (when I could get it), and bear de lash as well—and ar'nt I a woman? I have borne thirteen chilern and I seen 'em mos' all sold off into slavery, and when I cried out with a mother's grief, none but Jesus heard—and ar'nt I a woman?[1]

Unfortunately, there seems to be some confusion in the movement today as to who has been oppressing whom. Since the advent of black power, the black male has exerted a more prominent leadership role in our struggle for justice in this country. He sees the system for what it really is for the most part, but where he rejects its values and mores on many issues, when it comes to women, he seems to take his guidelines from the pages of the *Ladies' Home Journal*. Certain black men are maintaining that they have been castrated by society but that black women somehow escaped this persecution and even contributed to this emasculation.

Let me state here and now that the black woman in America can justly be described as a "slave of a slave." By reducing the black man in America to such abject oppression, the black woman had no protector and was used, and is still being used in some cases, as the scapegoat for the evils that this horrendous system has perpetrated on black men. Her physical image has been

---

1. For a discussion of the controversy about this speech, see p. 242.

maliciously maligned; she has been sexually molested and abused by the white colonizer; she has suffered the worse kind of economic exploitation, having been forced to serve as the white woman's maid and wet-nurse for white offspring while her own children were more often than not starving and neglected. It is the depth of degradation to be socially manipulated, physically raped, used to undermine your own household, and to be powerless to reverse this syndrome.

It is true that our husbands, fathers, brothers, and sons have been emasculated, lynched, and brutalized. They have suffered from the cruelest assault on mankind that the world has ever known. However, it is a gross distortion of fact to state that black women have oppressed black men. The capitalist system found it expedient to enslave and oppress them and proceeded to do so without consultation or the signing of any agreements with black women.

It must also be pointed out at this time that black women are not resentful of the rise to power of black men. We welcome it. We see in it the eventual liberation of all black people from this corrupt system of capitalism. Nevertheless, this does not mean that you have to negate one for the other. This kind of thinking is a product of miseducation; that it's either X or it's Y. It is fallacious reasoning that in order for the black man to be strong, the black woman has to be weak.

Those who are exerting their "manhood" by telling black women to step back into a domestic, submissive role are assuming a counterrevolutionary position. Black women likewise have been abused by the system, and we must begin talking about the elimination of all kinds of oppression. If we are talking about building a strong nation, capable of throwing off the yoke of capitalist oppression, then we are talking about the total involvement of every man, woman, and child, each with a highly developed political consciousness. We need our whole army out there dealing with the enemy and not half an army.

There are also some black women who feel that there is no more productive role in life than having and raising children. This attitude often reflects the condi-tioning of the society in which we live and is adopted from a bourgeois white model. Some young sisters who have never had to maintain a household and accept the confining role which this entails tend to romanticize (along with the help of a few brothers) this role of housewife and mother. Black women who have had to endure this kind of function are less apt to have these utopian visions.

Those who project in an intellectual manner how great and rewarding this role will be and who feel that the most important thing that they can contribute to the black nation is children are doing themselves a great injustice. This line of reasoning completely negates the contributions that black women have historically made to our struggle for liberation. These black women include Sojourner Truth, Harriet Tubman, Mary McLeod Bethune, and Fannie Lou Hamer,[2] to name but a few.

We live in a highly industrialized society, and every member of the black nation must be as academically and technologically developed as possible. To wage a revolution, we need competent teachers, doctors, nurses, electronics experts, chemists, biologists, physicists, political scientists, and so on and so forth. Black women sitting at home reading bedtime stories to their children are just not going to make it.

ECONOMIC EXPLOITATION OF BLACK WOMEN

The economic system of capitalism finds it expedient to reduce women to a state of enslavement. They oftentimes serve as a scapegoat for the evils of this system. Much in the same way that the poor white cracker of the South, who is equally victimized, looks down upon blacks and contributes to the oppression of blacks, so, by giving to men a false feeling of superiority (at least in their own home or in their relationships with women), the oppression of women acts as an escape valve for capitalism. Men may be cruelly exploited and subjected to all sorts of dehumanizing tactics on the part

2. For more on Hamer and the Mississippi Freedom Democratic Party, see p. 537; Truth: see p. 242; Bethune: civil rights leader and educator (1875–1955) who established the Bethune Educational and Industrial Training School for Negro Girls in 1904 in Florida (later Bethune-Cookman University) and was an advisor to President Franklin D. Roosevelt.

of the ruling class, but they have someone who is below them—at least they're not women.

Women also represent a surplus labor supply, the control of which is absolutely necessary to the profitable functioning of capitalism. Women are systematically exploited by the system. They are paid less for the same work that men do, and jobs that are specifically relegated to women are low-paying and without the possibility of advancement. Statistics from the Women's Bureau of the United States Department of Labor show that in 1967 the wage scale for white women was even below that of black men; and the wage scale for nonwhite women was the lowest of all:

White Males	$6,704
Nonwhite Males	$4,277
White Females	$3,991
Nonwhite Females	$2,861

Those industries which employ mainly black women are the most exploitive in the country. Domestic and hospital workers are good examples of this oppression; the garment workers in New York City provide us with another view of this economic slavery. The International Ladies Garment Workers Union (ILGWU), whose overwhelming membership consists of Black and Puerto Rican women, has a leadership that is nearly all lily-white and male. This leadership has been working in collusion with the ruling class and has completely sold its soul to the corporate structure.

To add insult to injury, the ILGWU has invested heavily in business enterprises in racist, apartheid South Africa—with union funds. Not only does this bought-off leadership contribute to our continued exploitation in this country by not truly representing the best interests of its membership, but it audaciously uses funds that black and Puerto Rican women have provided to support the economy of a vicious government that is engaged in the economic rape and murder of our black brothers and sisters in our Motherland, Africa.

The entire labor movement in the United States has suffered as a result of the superexploitation of black workers and women. The unions have historically been racist and chauvinistic. They have upheld racism in this country and have failed to fight the white skin privileges of white workers. They have failed to fight or even make an issue against the inequities in the hiring and pay of women workers. There has been virtually no struggle against either the racism of the white worker or the economic exploitation of the working woman, two factors that have consistently impeded the advancement of the real struggle against the ruling class.

This racist, chauvinistic, and manipulative use of black workers and women, especially black women, has been a severe cancer on the American labor scene. It therefore becomes essential for those who understand the workings of capitalism and imperialism to realize that the exploitation of black people and women works to everyone's disadvantage and that the liberation of these two groups is a stepping-stone to the liberation of all oppressed people in this country and around the world.

BEDROOM POLITICS

I have briefly discussed the economic and psychological manipulation of black women, but perhaps the most outlandish act of oppression in modern times is the current campaign to promote sterilization of nonwhite women in an attempt to maintain the population and power imbalance between the white haves and the nonwhite havenots.

These tactics are but another example of the many devious schemes that the ruling-class elite attempt to perpetrate on the black population in order to keep itself in control. It has recently come to our attention that a massive campaign for so-called birth control is presently being promoted not only in the underdeveloped nonwhite areas of the world, but also in black communities here in the United States. However, what the authorities in charge of these programs refer to as "birth control" is in fact nothing but a method of outright surgical genocide.

The United States has been sponsoring sterilization clinics in nonwhite countries, especially in India, where already some three million young men and boys in and around New Delhi have been sterilized in makeshift operating rooms set up by the American Peace Corps workers. Under these circumstances, it is understandable why certain countries view the Peace Corps not as a benevolent project, not as evidence of America's concern for underdeveloped areas, but rather as a threat to their very existence. This program could more aptly be named the Death Corps.

Vasectomy, which is performed on males and takes only six or seven minutes, is a relatively simple operation. The sterilization of a woman, on the other hand, is admittedly major surgery. This operation (salpingectomy) must be performed in a hospital under general anesthesia. This method of "birth control" is a common procedure in Puerto Rico. Puerto Rico has long been used by the colonialist exploiter, the United States, as a huge experimental laboratory for medical research before allowing certain practices to be imported and used here. When the birth control pill was first being perfected, it was tried out on Puerto Rican women and selected black women (poor), using them as human guinea pigs, to evaluate its effect and its efficiency.

Salpingectomy has now become the commonest operation in Puerto Rico, commoner than an appendectomy or a tonsillectomy. It is so widespread that it is referred to simply as *la operacion. On the island, ten percent of the women between the ages of 15 and 45 have already been sterilized.*

And now, as previously occurred with the pill, this method has been imported into the United States. These sterilization clinics are cropping up around the country in the black and Puerto Rican communities. These so-called maternity clinics specifically outfitted to purge black women or men of their reproductive possibilities are appearing more and more in hospitals and clinics across the country.

A number of organizations have been formed to popularize the idea of sterilization, such as the Association for Voluntary Sterilization, and the Human Betterment (!!!?) Association for Voluntary Sterilization, Inc., which has its headquarters in New York City.

Threatened with the cut-off of relief funds, some black welfare women have been forced to accept this sterilization procedure in exchange for a continuation of welfare benefits. Black women are often afraid to permit any kind of necessary surgery because they know from bitter experience that they are more likely than not to come out of the hospital without their insides. (Both salpingectomies and hysterectomies are performed.)

We condemn this use of the black woman as a medical testing ground for the white middle class.

Reports of the ill effects, including deaths, from the use of the birth control pill only started to come to light when the white privileged class began to be affected. These outrageous Nazi-like procedures on the part of medical researchers are but another manifestation of the totally amoral and dehumanizing brutality that the capitalist system perpetrates on black women. The sterilization experiments carried on in concentration camps some twenty-five years ago have been denounced the world over, but no one seems to get upset by the repetition of these same racist tactics today in the United States of America—land of the free and home of the brave. This campaign is as nefarious a program as Germany's gas chambers, and, in a long-term sense, as effective and with the same objective.

The rigid laws concerning abortions in this country are another vicious means of subjugation and, indirectly, of outright murder. Rich white women somehow manage to obtain these operations with little or no difficulty. It is the poor black and Puerto Rican woman who is at the mercy of the local butcher. Statistics show us that the nonwhite death rate at the hands of the unqualified abortionist is substantially higher than for white women. Nearly half of the childbearing deaths in New York City are attributed to abortion alone, and out of these, seventy-nine percent are among nonwhites and Puerto Rican women.

We are not saying that black women should not practice birth control. *Black women have the right and the responsibility to determine when it is in the interest of the struggle to have children or not to have them, and this right must not be relinquished to anyone.* It is also her right and responsibility to determine when it is in her own best interests to have children, how many she will have, and how far apart. The lack of the availability of safe birth control methods, the forced sterilization practices, and the inability to obtain legal abortions are all symptoms of a decadent society that jeopardizes the health of black women (and thereby the entire black race) in its attempts to control the very life processes of human beings. This is a symptom of a society that believes it has the right to bring political factors into the privacy of the bedchamber. The elimination of these horrendous conditions will free black women for full participation in the revolution, and, thereafter in the building of the new society.

RELATIONSHIP TO WHITE MOVEMENT

Much has been written recently about the white women's liberation movement in the United States, and the question arises whether there are any parallels between this struggle and the movement on the part of black women for total emancipation. While there are certain comparisons that one can make, simply because we both live under the same exploitative system, there are certain differences, some of which are quite basic.

The white women's movement is far from being monolithic. Any white group that does not have an anti-imperialist and antiracist ideology has absolutely nothing in common with the black woman's struggle. In fact, some groups come to the incorrect conclusion that their oppression is due simply to male chauvinism. They therefore have an extremely antimale tone to their dissertations. Black people are engaged in a life-and-death struggle and the main emphasis of black women must be to combat the capitalist, racist exploitation of black people. While it is true that male chauvinism has become institutionalized in American society, one must always look for the main enemy—the fundamental cause of the female condition.

Another major differentiation is that the white women's liberation movement is basically middle class. Very few of these women suffer the extreme economic exploitation that most black women are subjected to day by day. This is the factor that is most crucial for us. It is not an intellectual persecution alone; it is not an intellectual outburst for us; it is quite real. We as black women have got to deal with the problems that the black masses deal with, for our problems in reality are one and the same.

If the white groups do not realize that they are in fact fighting capitalism and racism, we do not have common bonds. If they do not realize that the reasons for their condition lie in the system and not simply that men get a vicarious pleasure out of "consuming their bodies for exploitative reasons" (this kind of reasoning seems to be quite prevalent in certain white women's groups), then we cannot unite with them around common grievances or even discuss these groups in a serious manner because they're completely irrelevant to the black struggle.

THE NEW WORLD

The black community and black women especially must begin raising questions about the kind of society we wish to see established. We must note the ways in which capitalism oppresses us and then move to create institutions that will eliminate these destructive influences.

The new world that we are attempting to create must destroy oppression of any type. The value of this new system will be determined by the status of the person who was low man on the totem pole. Unless women in any enslaved nation are completely liberated, the change cannot really be called a revolution. If the black woman has to retreat to the position she occupied before the armed struggle, the whole movement and the whole struggle will have retreated in terms of truly freeing the colonized population.

A people's revolution that engages the participation of every member of the community, including man, woman, and child, brings about a certain transformation in the participants as a result of this participation. Once you have caught a glimpse of freedom or experienced a bit of self-determination, you can't go back to old routines that were established under a racist, capitalist regime. We must begin to understand that a revolution entails not only the willingness to lay our lives on the firing line and get killed. In some ways, this is an easy commitment to make. To die for the revolution is a one-shot deal; to live for the revolution means taking on the more difficult commitment of changing our day-to-day life patterns.

This will mean changing the traditional routines that we have established as a result of living in a totally corrupting society. It means changing how you relate to your wife, your husband, your parents, and your coworkers. If we are going to liberate ourselves as a people, it must be recognized that black women have very specific problems that have to be spoken to. We must be liberated along with the rest of the population. We cannot wait to start working on those problems until that great day in the future when the revolution somehow miraculously is accomplished.

To assign women the role of housekeeper and mother while men go forth into battle is a highly questionable doctrine for a revolutionary to maintain. Each individual must develop a high political consciousness in order to understand how this system enslaves us all and what actions we must take to bring about its total destruction. Those who consider themselves to be revolutionary must begin to deal with other revolutionaries as equals. And so far as I know, revolutionaries are not determined by sex.

Old people, young people, men and women, must take part in the struggle. To relegate women to purely supportive roles or to purely cultural considerations is dangerous doctrine to project. Unless black men who are preparing themselves for armed struggle understand that the society which we are trying to create is one in which the oppression of *all members* of that society is eliminated, then the revolution will have failed in its avowed purpose.

Given the mutual commitment of black men and black women alike to the liberation of our people and other oppressed peoples around the world, the total involvement of each individual is necessary. A revolutionary has the responsibility not only of toppling those that are now in a position of power, but of creating new institutions that will eliminate all forms of oppression. We must begin to rewrite our understanding of traditional personal relationships between man and woman.

All the resources that the black community can muster up must be channeled into the struggle. Black women must take an active part in bringing about the kind of society where our children, our loved ones, and each citizen can grow up and live as decent human beings, free from the pressures of racism and capitalist exploitation.

COMBAHEE RIVER COLLECTIVE
A Black Feminist Statement [1977]

The Combahee River Collective's 1977 mission statement moves away from the frequently debated question of whether the women's movement or the civil rights movement better addressed the needs of black women. Instead, the statement's authors—Barbara Smith, her sister Beverly Smith, and Demita Frazier—outline the development of a separate black feminist movement created to address the unique position of black women, who face both race and gender oppression.

Inspired by the first meeting of the National Black Feminist Organization, held in New York in 1973, the Smiths and Frazier began meeting at various national conferences. In 1977, Barbara Smith met with like-minded women in Massachusetts to establish a new movement dedicated to addressing issues of gender, race, sexuality, and class, as well as the growing violence in American culture. Boston-area black women formed the core of the national Combahee River Collective, which they named after a Union army expedition led by Harriet Tubman (c. 1820–1913), the famed "conductor" on the Underground Railroad. Barbara Smith later recalled that she "wasn't thinking so much about being a feminist. I was just thinking about how could I add lesbian to being a Black woman. It was just like no place for us. That is what Combahee created, a place where we could be ourselves and where we were valued. A place without homophobia, a place without racism, a place without sexism."

The collective's "Black Feminist Statement" traces the origins of the contemporary black feminist movement to the mixture of empowerment and marginalization that black women experienced in both the women's movement and the civil rights movement. In particular, the feminist technique of consciousness-raising broke down black women's sense of isolation and led to their conviction that they needed "to develop a politics that was antiracist, unlike those of white women, and antisexist, unlike those of black and white men." While the authors indicate the need to address heterosexism and class oppression, they focus on the commonality of experience among all black women. This emphasis rejects lesbian or class separatism and presents all black and third world women as primary allies in the black feminist struggle. Whereas they recognize the need to ally with other progressives, they also see black women as central in the fight against oppression, since, as the most oppressed group, their freedom would mean freedom for all.

From Zillah R. Eisenstein, ed., *Capitalist Patriarchy and the Case for Socialist Feminism* (New York: Monthly Review Press, 1979).

We are a collective of black feminists who have been meeting together since 1974.[1] During that time we have been involved in the process of defining and clarifying our politics, while at the same time doing political work within our own group and in coalition with other progressive organizations and movements. The most general statement of our politics at the present time would be that we are actively committed to struggling against racial, sexual, heterosexual, and class oppression and see as our particular task the development of integrated analysis and practice based upon the fact that the major systems of oppression are interlocking. The synthesis of these oppressions creates the conditions of our lives. As black women we see black feminism as the logical political movement to combat the manifold and simultaneous oppressions that all women of color face.

We will discuss four major topics in the paper that follows: (1) The genesis of contemporary black feminism; (2) what we believe, i.e., the specific province of our politics; (3) the problems in organizing black feminists, including a brief herstory of our collective; and (4) black feminist issues and practice.

1. THE GENESIS OF CONTEMPORARY BLACK FEMINISM

Before looking at the recent development of black feminism, we would like to affirm that we find our origins in the historical reality of Afro-American women's continuous life-and-death struggle for survival and liberation. Black women's extremely negative relationship to the American political system (a system of white male rule) has always been determined by our membership in two oppressed racial and sexual castes. As Angela Davis[2] points out in "Reflections on the Black Woman's Role in the Community of Slaves," black women have always embodied, if only in their physical manifestation, an adversary stance to white male rule and have actively resisted its inroads upon them and their communities in both dramatic and subtle ways. There have

always been black women activists—some known, like Sojourner Truth, Harriet Tubman, Frances E. W. Harper, Ida B. Wells-Barnett, and Mary Church Terrell,[3] and thousands upon thousands unknown—who had a shared awareness of how their sexual identity combined with their racial identity to make their whole life situation and the focus of their political struggles unique. Contemporary black feminism is the outgrowth of countless generations of personal sacrifice, militancy, and work by our mothers and sisters.

A black feminist presence has evolved most obviously in connection with the second wave of the American women's movement beginning in the late 1960s. Black, other Third World, and working women have been involved in the feminist movement from its start, but both outside reactionary forces and racism and elitism within the movement itself have served to obscure our participation. In 1973 black feminists, primarily located in New York, felt the necessity of forming a separate black feminist group. This became the National Black Feminist Organization (NBFO).

Black feminist politics also have an obvious connection to movements for black liberation, particularly those of the 1960s and 1970s. Many of us were active in those movements (civil rights, black nationalism, the Black Panthers), and all of our lives were greatly affected and changed by their ideology, their goals, and the tactics used to achieve their goals. It was our experience and disillusionment within these liberation movements, as well as experience on the periphery of the white male left, that led to the need to develop a politics that was antiracist, unlike those of white women, and antisexist, unlike those of black and white men.

There is also undeniably a personal genesis for black feminism, that is, the political realization that comes from the seemingly personal experiences of individual black women's lives. Black feminists and many more black women who do not define themselves as feminists have all experienced sexual oppression as a constant factor in our day-to-day existence.

Black feminists often talk about their feelings of craziness before becoming conscious of the concepts of

---

1. This statement is dated April 1977. [Authors' note]
2. See p. 629.
3. Civil rights and women's suffrage activist, educator, and journalist (1863–1954); Terrell was also a founding member of the NAACP; Truth: see p. 242; Tubman: see p. 245; Harper: see p. 244; Wells-Barnett: see p. 195.

sexual politics, patriarchal rule, and, most importantly, feminism, the political analysis and practice that we women use to struggle against our oppression. The fact that racial politics and indeed racism are pervasive factors in our lives did not allow us, and still does not allow most black women, to look more deeply into our own experiences and define those things that make our lives what they are and our oppression specific to us. In the process of consciousness-raising, actually life-sharing, we began to recognize the commonality of our experiences and, from that sharing and growing consciousness, to build a politics that will change our lives and inevitably end our oppression.

Our development also must be tied to the contemporary economic and political position of black people. The post–World War II generation of black youth was the first to be able to minimally partake of certain educational and employment options, previously closed completely to black people. Although our economic position is still at the very bottom of the American capitalist economy, a handful of us have been able to gain certain tools as a result of tokenism in education and employment that potentially enable us to more effectively fight our oppression.

A combined antiracist and antisexist position drew us together initially, and as we developed politically we addressed ourselves to heterosexism and economic oppression under capitalism.

2. WHAT WE BELIEVE

Above all else, our politics initially sprang from the shared belief that black women are inherently valuable, that our liberation is a necessity not as an adjunct to somebody else's but because of our need as human persons for autonomy. This may seem so obvious as to sound simplistic, but it is apparent that no other ostensibly progressive movement has ever considered our specific oppression a priority or worked seriously for the ending of that oppression. Merely naming the pejorative stereotypes attributed to black women (e.g., mammy, matriarch, Sapphire, whore, bulldagger), let alone cataloguing the cruel, often murderous, treatment we receive, indicates how little value has been placed upon our lives during four centuries of bondage

in the Western Hemisphere. We realize that the only people who care enough about us to work consistently for our liberation is us. Our politics evolve from a healthy love for ourselves, our sisters, and our community, which allows us to continue our struggle and work.

This focusing upon our own oppression is embodied in the concept of identity politics. We believe that the most profound and potentially the most radical politics come directly out of our own identity, as opposed to working to end somebody else's oppression. In the case of black women this is a particularly repugnant, dangerous, threatening, and therefore revolutionary concept because it is obvious from looking at all the political movements that have preceded us that anyone is more worthy of liberation than ourselves. We reject pedestals, queenhood, and walking ten paces behind. To be recognized as human, levelly human, is enough.

We believe that sexual politics under patriarchy is as pervasive in black women's lives as are the politics of class and race. We also often find it difficult to separate race from class from sex oppression because in our lives they are most often experienced simultaneously. We know that there is such a thing as racial-sexual oppression that is neither solely racial nor solely sexual, e.g., the history of rape of black women by white men as a weapon of political repression.

Although we are feminists and lesbians, we feel solidarity with progressive black men and do not advocate the fractionalization that white women who are separatists demand. Our situation as black people necessitates that we have solidarity around the fact of race, which white women of course do not need to have with white men, unless it is their negative solidarity as racial oppressors. We struggle together with black men against racism, while we also struggle with black men about sexism.

We realize that the liberation of all oppressed peoples necessitates the destruction of the political-economic systems of capitalism and imperialism as well as patriarchy. We are socialists because we believe the work must be organized for the collective benefit of those who do the work and create the products and not for the profit of the bosses. Material resources must be equally distributed among those who create these resources. We are not convinced, however, that a socialist revolution that is not also a feminist and antiracist revolution will guarantee our liberation. We have arrived at the necessity for developing an understanding of class relationships that takes into account the specific class position of black women who are generally marginal in the labor force, while at this particular time some of us are temporarily viewed as doubly desirable tokens at white-collar and professional levels. We need to articulate the real class situation of persons who are not merely raceless, sexless workers, but for whom racial and sexual oppression are significant determinants in their working/economic lives. Although we are in essential agreement with Marx's theory as it applied to the very specific economic relationships he analyzed, we know that this analysis must be extended further in order for us to understand our specific economic situation as black women.

A political contribution that we feel we have already made is the expansion of the feminist principle that the personal is political. In our consciousness-raising sessions, for example, we have in many ways gone beyond white women's revelations because we are dealing with the implications of race and class as well as sex. Even our black women's style of talking/testifying in black language about what we have experienced has a resonance that is both cultural and political. We have spent a great deal of energy delving into the cultural and experiential nature of our oppression out of necessity because none of these matters have ever been looked at before. No one before has ever examined the multilayered texture of black women's lives.

As we have already stated, we reject the stance of lesbian separatism because it is not a viable political analysis or strategy for us. It leaves out far too much and far too many people, particularly black men, women, and children. We have a great deal of criticism and loathing for what men have been socialized to be in this society: what they support, how they act, and how they oppress. But we do not have the misguided notion that it is their maleness, per se—i.e., their biological maleness—that makes them what they are. As black women we find any type of biological determinism a particularly dangerous and reactionary basis upon which to build a politic. We must also question whether lesbian separatism is an adequate and progressive political analysis and strategy, even for those who practice it, since it so completely denies any but the sexual sources of women's oppression, negating the facts of class and race.

3. PROBLEMS IN ORGANIZING BLACK FEMINISTS

During our years together as a black feminist collective we have experienced success and defeat, joy and pain, victory and failure. We have found that it is very difficult to organize around black feminist issues, difficult even to announce in certain contexts that we are black feminists. We have tried to think about the reasons for our difficulties, particularly since the white women's movement continues to be strong and to grow in many directions. In this section we will discuss some of the general reasons for the organizing problems we face and also talk specifically about the stages in organizing our own collective.

The major source of difficulty in our political work is that we are not just trying to fight oppression on one front or even two, but instead to address a whole range of oppressions. We do not have racial, sexual, heterosexual, or class privilege to rely upon, nor do we have even the minimal access to resources and power that groups who possess any one of these types of privilege have.

The psychological toll of being a black woman and the difficulties this presents in reaching political consciousness and doing political work can never be underestimated. There is a very low value placed upon black women's psyches in this society, which is both racist and sexist. As an early group member once said, "We are all damaged people merely by virtue of being black women." We are dispossessed psychologically and on every other level, and yet we feel the necessity to struggle to change our condition and the condition of all black women. In "A Black Feminist's Search for Sisterhood," Michele Wallace arrives at this conclusion:

> We exist as women who are black who are feminists, each stranded for the moment, working independently because there is not yet an environment in this society remotely congenial to our struggle—because,

being on the bottom, we would have to do what no one else has done: we would have to fight the world.[4]

Wallace is not pessimistic but realistic in her assessment of black feminists' position, particularly in her allusion to the nearly classic isolation most of us face. We might use our position at the bottom, however, to make a clear leap into revolutionary action. If black women were free, it would mean that everyone else would have to be free since our freedom would necessitate the destruction of all the systems of oppression.

Feminism is, nevertheless, very threatening to the majority of black people because it calls into question some of the most basic assumptions about our existence, i.e., that gender should be a determinant of power relationships. Here is the way male and female roles were defined in a black nationalist pamphlet from the early 1970s.

> We understand that it is and has been traditional that the man is the head of the house. He is the leader of the house/nation because his knowledge of the world is broader, his awareness is greater, his understanding is fuller and his application of this information is wiser.... After all, it is only reasonable that the man be the head of the house because he is able to defend and protect the development of his home.... Women cannot do the same things as men—they are made by nature to function differently. Equality of men and women is something that cannot happen even in the abstract world. Men are not equal to other men, i.e., ability, experience, or even understanding. The value of men and women can be seen as in the value of gold and silver—they are not equal but both have great value. We must realize that men and women are a complement to each other because there is no house/family without a man and his wife. Both are essential to the development of any life.[5]

The material conditions of most black women would hardly lead them to upset both economic and sexual arrangements that seem to represent some stability in their lives. Many black women have a good understanding of both sexism and racism, but because of the everyday constrictions of their lives cannot risk struggling against them both.

The reaction of black men to feminism has been notoriously negative. They are, of course, even more threatened than black women by the possibility that black feminists might organize around our own needs. They realize that they might not only lose valuable and hard-working allies in their struggles, but that they might also be forced to change their habitually sexist ways of interacting with and oppressing black women. Accusations that black feminism divides the black struggle are powerful deterrents to the growth of an autonomous black women's movement.

Still, hundreds of women have been active at different times during the three-year existence of our group. And every black woman who came, came out of a strongly felt need for some level of possibility that did not previously exist in her life.

When we first started meeting early in 1974 after the NBFO first eastern regional conference, we did not have a strategy for organizing, or even a focus. We just wanted to see what we had. After a period of months of not meeting, we began to meet again late in the year and started doing an intense variety of consciousness-raising. The overwhelming feeling that we had is that after years and years we had finally found each other. Although we were not doing political work as a group, individuals continued their involvement in lesbian politics, sterilization abuse, and abortion rights work, Third World Women's International Women's Day activities, and support activity for the trials of Dr. Kenneth Edelin, Joan Little, and Inez Garcia.[6] During our first summer, when membership had dropped off considerably, those of us remaining devoted serious discussion

---

4. Michele Wallace. "A Black Feminist's Search for Sisterhood," *Village Voice*, 28 July 1975, 6–7. [Authors' note]

5. Mumininas of Committee for Unified Newark, *Mwanamke Mwananchi (The Nationalist Woman)*, Newark, NJ, c. 1971, 4–5. [Authors' note]

6. Defendants in three highly publicized and politicized court cases: in 1974, Garcia (b. 1941), a Puerto Rican and Cuban American woman, was convicted of killing a man who had raped her, but was acquitted on appeal after serving two years in jail; Edelin (b. 1939) was convicted and later acquitted of manslaughter for performing an abortion in 1974; Little (b. 1953) killed a white prison guard in 1974 and was acquitted using the defense that she was resisting a sexual assault.

to the possibility of opening a refuge for battered women in a black community. (There was no refuge in Boston at that time.) We also decided around that time to become an independent collective since we had serious disagreements with NBFO's bourgeois-feminist stance and their lack of a clear political focus.

We also were contacted at that time by socialist feminists, with whom we had worked on abortion rights activities, who wanted to encourage us to attend the National Socialist Feminist Conference in Yellow Springs. One of our members did attend and despite the narrowness of the ideology that was promoted at that particular conference, we became more aware of the need for us to understand our own economic situation and to make our own economic analysis.

In the fall, when some members returned, we experienced several months of comparative inactivity and internal disagreements which were first conceptualized as a lesbian-straight split but which were also the result of class and political differences. During the summer those of us who were still meeting had determined the need to do political work and to move beyond consciousness-raising and serving exclusively as an emotional support group. At the beginning of 1976, when some of the women who had not wanted to do political work and who also had voiced disagreements stopped attending of their own accord, we again looked for a focus. We decided at that time, with the addition of new members, to become a study group. We had always shared our reading with each other, and some of us had written papers on black feminism for group discussion a few months before this decision was made. We began functioning as a study group and also began discussing the possibility of starting a black feminist publication. We had a retreat in the late spring, which provided a time for both political discussion and working out interpersonal issues. Currently we are planning to gather together a collection of black feminist writing. We feel that it is absolutely essential to demonstrate the reality of our politics to other black women and believe that we can do this through writing and distributing our work. The fact that individual black feminists are living in isolation all over the country, that our own numbers are small, and that we have some skills in writing, printing, and publishing makes us want to carry out these kinds of projects as a means of organizing black feminists as we continue to do political work in coalition with other groups.

4. BLACK FEMINIST ISSUES AND PRACTICE

During our time together we have identified and worked on many issues of particular relevance to black women. The inclusiveness of our politics makes us concerned with any situation that impinges upon the lives of women, Third World, and working people. We are of course particularly committed to working on those struggles in which race, sex, and class are simultaneous factors in oppression. We might, for example, become involved in workplace organizing at a factory that employs Third World women or picket a hospital that is cutting back on already inadequate health care to a Third World community, or set up a rape crisis center in a black neighborhood. Organizing around welfare or day-care concerns might also be a focus. The work to be done and the countless issues that this work represents merely reflect the pervasiveness of our oppression.

Issues and projects that collective members have actually worked on are sterilization abuse, abortion rights, battered women, rape, and health care. We have also done many workshops and educationals on black feminism on college campuses, at women's conferences, and most recently for high school women.

One issue that is of major concern to us and that we have begun to publicly address is racism in the white women's movement. As black feminists we are made constantly and painfully aware of how little effort white women have made to understand and combat their racism, which requires among other things that they have a more than superficial comprehension of race, color, and black history and culture. Eliminating racism in the white women's movement is by definition work for white women to do, but we will continue to speak to and demand accountability on this issue.

In the practice of our politics we do not believe that the end always justifies the means. Many reactionary and destructive acts have been done in the name of achieving "correct" political goals. As feminists we do not want to mess over people in the name of politics. We believe in collective process and a nonhierarchical distribution of power within our own group and in our vision of a revolutionary society. We are committed to a continual examination of our politics as they develop through criticism and self-criticism as an essential aspect of our practice. As black feminists and lesbians we know that we have a very definite revolutionary task to perform, and we are ready for the lifetime of work and struggle before us.

NTOZAKE SHANGE

from *for colored girls who have considered suicide when the rainbow is enuf* [1975]

For colored girls, a "choreopoem," was developed in 1974 and 1975 by Ntozake Shange (born Paulette Williams in 1948), first in California and then in New York. Workshopping the composition in bars, university women's studies departments, and other nontraditional spaces, Shange and the choreographer-dancer Paula Moss added movement to Shange's spoken poems. In 1976, *for colored girls* entered the theatrical mainstream, opening off-Broadway at the producer Joseph Papp's Public Theater in June and then on Broadway at the Booth Theatre. In her 1975 introduction to the published text, Shange describes the piece, which is composed of more than twenty poems, as "the words of a young black girl's growing up, her triumphs & errors, our struggle to become all that is forbidden by our environment, all that is forfeited by our gender, all that we have forgotten." That statement, with its shift from "her" to "our," links the particular experience of a character to a vision of a common black female experience.

The tendency to read *for colored girls* as a general reflection of "what it is to be of color and female in the twentieth century" (to quote the dust jacket of the 1997 paperback) provoked heated debate among both critics and admirers. In particular, the choreopoem's descriptions of violent, angry men (and the absence of male characters onstage) prompted charges that the play was anti-male. In addition, the "song of joy" at the end of the piece, where the women repeat the lines "i found god in myself / & i loved her," was interpreted by some as a separatist call for women to go it alone. Others, however, praised it as a call to self-love that would foster healing as well as a greater potential for loving others.

From Ntozake Shange, *for colored girls who have considered suicide when the rainbow is enuf* (New York: Collier Books, 1975), pp. 55–64.

 lady in red
there waz no air/ the sheets made ripples under his
body like crumpled paper napkins in a summer park/
 & lil
specks of somethin from tween his toes or the biscuits
from the day before ran in the sweat that tucked the
 sheet
into his limbs like he waz an ol frozen bundle of chicken/
& he'd get up to make coffee, drink wine, drink
 water/ he
wished one of his friends who knew where he waz wd
 come by
with some blow or some shit/ anythin/ there waz no air/
he'd see the spotlights in the alleyways downstairs movin

in the air/ cross his wall over his face/ & get under the
covers & wait for an all clear or til he cd hear traffic
again/

there waznt nothin wrong with him/ there waznt
 nothin wrong
with him/ he kept tellin crystal/
any niggah wanna kill vietnamese children more n
 stay home
& raise his own is sicker than a rabid dog/
that's how their thing had been goin since he got back/
crystal just got inta sayin whatta fool niggah beau waz
& always had been/ didnt he go all over uptown sayin
 the

child waznt his/ waz some no counts bastard/ & any ol
city
police cd come & get him if they wanted/ cuz as soon as
the blood type & shit waz together/ everybody wd
know that
crystal waz a no good lyin whore/ and this after she'd
been
his girl since she waz thirteen/ when he caught her
on the stairway/

he came home crazy as hell/ he tried to get veterans
benefits
to go to school & they kept right on puttin him in
remedial classes/ he cdnt read wortha damn/ so beau
cused the teachers of holdin him back & got himself
a gypsy cab[1] to drive/ but his cab kept breakin
down/ & the cops was always messin wit him/ plus not
gettin much bread/

& crystal went & got pregnant again/ beau most beat
her to death when she tol him/ she still gotta scar
under her right tit where he cut her up/ still crystal
went right on & had the baby/ so now beau willie had
two children/ a little girl/ naomi kenya & a boy/
kwame beau
willie brown/ & there waz no air/

how in the hell did he get in this mess anyway/
somebody
went & tol crystal that beau waz spendin alla his money
on the bartendin bitch down at the merry-go-round
cafe/
beau sat straight up in the bed/ wrapped up in the sheets
lookin like john the baptist or a huge baby wit stubble
& nuts/ now he hadta get alla that shit outta crystal's
mind/ so she wd let him come home/ crystal had
gone &
got a court order saying beau willie brown had no access
to his children/ if he showed his face he waz subject
to arrest/ shit/ she'd been in his ass to marry her
since she waz 14 years old & here when she 22/ she wanna
throw him out cuz he say he'll marry her/ she burst
out laughin/ hollerin whatchu wanna marry me for now/
so i can support yr

ass/ or come sit wit ya when they lock yr behind
up/ cause they gonna come for ya/ ya goddamn
lunatic/
they gonna come/ & i'm not gonna have a thing to do
wit it/ o no i wdnt marry yr pitiful black ass for
nothin & she went on to bed/

the next day beau willie came in blasted & got ta
swingin
chairs at crystal/ who cdnt figure out what the hell
he waz doin/ til he got ta shoutin bout how she waz
gonna
marry him/ & get some more veterans benefits/ & he
cd
stop drivin them crazy spics round/ while they tryin
to kill him for $15/ beau waz sweatin terrible/ beatin
on crystal/ & he cdnt do no more with the table n
chairs/
so he went to get the high chair/ & lil kwame waz in it/
& beau waz beatin crystal with the high chair & her son/
& some notion got inta him to stop/ and he run out/

crystal most died/ that's why the police wdnt low
beau near where she lived/ & she'd been tellin the kids
their daddy tried to kill her & kwame/ & he just wanted
to marry her/ that's what/ he wanted to marry her/ &
have a family/ but the bitch waz crazy/ beau willie
waz sittin in this hotel in his drawers drinkin
coffee & wine in the heat of the day spillin shit all
over hisself/ laughin/ bout how he waz gonna get crystal
to take him back/ & let him be a man in the house/ &
she
wdnt even have to go to work no more/ he got dressed
all up in his ivory shirt & checkered pants to go see
crystal & get this mess all cleared up/
he knocked on the door to crystal's rooms/ & she
didnt answer/ he beat on the door & crystal & naomi
started cryin/ beau gotta shoutin again how he wanted
to marry her/ & waz she always gonna be a whore/ or
did she wanna husband/ & crystal just kept on
screamin for him to leave us alone/ just leave us
alone/ so beau broke the door down/ crystal held
the children in fronta her/ she picked kwame off the
floor/ in her arms/ & she held naomi by her shoulders/

1. Unlicensed taxicab.

& kept on sayin/ beau willie brown/ get outta here/
the police is gonna come for ya/ ya fool/ get outta here/
do you want the children to see you act the fool again/
you want kwame to brain damage from you throwin him
round/ niggah/ get outta here/ get out & dont show yr
ass again or i'll kill ya/ i swear i'll kill ya/
he reached for naomi/ crystal grabbed the lil girl &
stared at beau willie like he waz a leper or somethin/
dont you touch my children/ muthafucker/ or i'll kill
you/

beau willie jumped back all humble & apologetic/ i'm
sorry/ i dont wanna hurt em/ i just wanna hold em &
get on my way/ i dont wanna cuz you no more trouble/
i wanted to marry you & give ya things
what you gonna give/ a broken jaw/ niggah get outta
    here/
he ignored crystal's outburst & sat down motionin for
naomi to come to him/ she smiled back at her daddy/
crystal felt naomi givin in & held her tighter/
naomi/ pushed away & ran to her daddy/ cryin/ daddy,
    daddy
come back daddy/ come back/ but be nice to mommy/
cause mommy loves you/ and ya gotta be nice/
he sat her on his knee/ & played with her ribbons &
they counted fingers & toes/ every so often he
looked over to crystal holdin kwame/ like a statue/
& he'd say/ see crystal/ i can be a good father/
now let me see my son/ & she didnt move/ &
he coaxed her & he coaxed her/ tol her she waz
still a hot lil ol thing & pretty & strong/ didnt
she get right up after that lil ol fight they had
& go back to work/ beau willie oozed kindness &
crystal who had known so lil/ let beau hold kwame/

as soon as crystal let the baby outta her arms/ beau
jumped up a laughin & a gigglin/ a hootin & a hollerin/
awright bitch/ awright bitch/ you gonna marry me/
you gonna marry me . . .
i aint gonna marry ya/ i aint ever gonna marry ya/
for nothin/ you gonna be in the jail/ you gonna be
under the jail for this/ now gimme my kids/ ya give
me back my kids/

he kicked the screen outta the window/ & held the
    kids

offa the sill/ you gonna marry me/ yeh, i'll marry ya/
anything/ but bring the children back in the
    house/
he looked from where the kids were hangin from the
fifth story/ at alla the people screamin at him/ &
he started sweatin again/ say to alla the neighbors/
you gonna marry me/

i stood by beau in the window/ with naomi reachin
for me/ & kwame screamin mommy mommy from
    the fifth
story/ but i cd only whisper/ & he dropped em

   lady in red
i waz missin somethin

   lady in purple
somethin so important

   lady in orange
somethin promised

   lady in blue
a layin on of hands

   lady in green
fingers near my forehead

   lady in yellow
strong

   lady in green
cool

   lady in orange
movin

   lady in purple
makin me whole

   lady in orange
sense

   lady in green
pure

lady in blue
all the gods comin into me
layin me open to myself

lady in red
i waz missin somethin

lady in green
somethin promised

lady in orange
somethin free

lady in purple
a layin on of hands

lady in blue
i know bout/ layin on bodies/ layin outta man
bringin him alla my fleshy self & some of my
    pleasure
bein taken full eager wet like i get sometimes
i waz missin somethin

lady in purple
a layin on of hands

lady in blue
not a man

lady in yellow
layin on

lady in purple
not my mama/ holdin me tight/ sayin
i'm always gonna be her girl
not a layin on of bosom & womb
a layin on of hands
the holiness of myself released

lady in red
i sat up one nite walkin a boardin house
screamin/ cryin/ the ghost of another woman
who waz missin what i waz missin
i wanted to jump up outta my bones
& be done wit myself
leave me alone
& go on in the wind
it waz too much
i fell into a numbness
til the only tree i cd see
took me up in her branches
held me in the breeze
made me dawn dew
that chill at daybreak
the sun wrapped me up swingin rose light everywhere
the sky laid over me like a million men
i waz cold/ i waz burnin up/ a child
& endlessly weavin garments for the moon
wit my tears

i found god in myself
& i loved her/ i loved her fiercely

> *All of the ladies repeat to them-*
> *selves softly the lines 'i found god*
> *in myself & i loved her.' It soon*
> *becomes a song of joy, started by*
> *the lady in blue. The ladies sing*
> *first to each other, then gradually*
> *to the audience. After the song*
> *peaks the ladies enter into a closed*
> *tight circle.*

lady in brown
& this is for colored girls who have considered
suicide/ but are movin to the ends of their own
rainbows

MICHELE WALLACE

from *Black Macho and the Myth of the Superwoman* [1979]

Michele Wallace's 1979 book *Black Macho and the Myth of the Superwoman* ignited debate over the connection between gender issues and civil rights. Wallace (b. 1952) develops many of the themes of Frances Beal's classic essay, "Double Jeopardy" (p. 801). For example, she refutes the ideas that black men are victims of black matriarchs and that black women have been more economically advantaged than black men. Like Beal, Wallace places the responsibility for change on both black men and black women. However, whereas Beal presented both racism and sexism as offshoots of capitalist oppression, Wallace sees them as tools that white people—particularly white men—use to retain control over black people and women.

The tension between black men and black women, Wallace believes, dates only from the 1930s and results from the adoption of white "standards of family life" and white gender roles. Defining the self and the other sex through white American myths and ideals ("Americanization," to Wallace) led to self-hatred, as black men and black women blamed each other for their failure to conform to the idealized white family model. Wallace also suggests that black men sacrificed their collaboration with black women in the fight against racial oppression in order to pursue their own quest for patriarchal power, especially during Shirley Chisholm's 1972 campaign for president (see p. 824). In the end, Wallace asserts, that split was ultimately propelled by white interests, since "by controlling the black man's notion of what a black man was supposed to be, it [America] would successfully control the very goals of his struggle for 'freedom.'"

From Michele Wallace, *Black Macho and the Myth of the Superwoman* (1979; repr., New York: Verso, 1999), pp. 13–33.

I am saying, among other things, that for perhaps the last fifty years there has been a growing distrust, even hatred, between black men and black women. It has been nursed along not only by racism on the part of whites but also by an almost deliberate ignorance on the part of blacks about the sexual politics of their experience in this country.

As the Civil Rights Movement progressed, little attention was devoted to an examination of the historical black male/female relationship, except for those aspects of it that reinforced the notion of the black man as the sexual victim of "matriarchal" tyranny. The result has been calamitous. The black woman has become a social and intellectual suicide; the black man, unintrospective and oppressive.

It is from this perspective that the black man and woman faced the challenge of the Black Revolution—a revolution subsequently dissipated and distorted by their inability to see each other clearly through the fog of sexual myths and fallacies. They have gone on alternately idealizing and vilifying their relationships, very rarely finding out what they are really made of. This has cost them a great deal. It has cost them unity, for one thing.

Though I am a black feminist, and that label rightly suggests that I feel black men could stand substantial improvement, I still find it difficult to blame them alone. Black men have had no greater part than black women in perpetuating the ignorance with which they view one another. The black man, however, particularly since the Black Movement, has been in the position to define the black woman. He is the one who tells her whether or not she is a woman and what it is to be a woman. And therefore, whether he wishes to or not, he determines her destiny as well as his own.

Though originally it was the white man who was responsible for the black woman's grief, a multiplicity of forces act upon her life now and the black man is one of the most important. The white man is downtown. The black man lives with her. He's the head of her church and may be the principal of her local school or even the mayor of the city in which she lives.

She is the workhorse that keeps his house functioning, she is the foundation of his community, she raises his children, and she faithfully votes for him in elections, goes to his movies, reads his books, watches him on television, buys in his stores, solicits his services as doctor, lawyer, accountant.

She has made it quite clear that she has no intention of starting a black woman's liberation movement. One would think she was satisfied, yet she is not. The black man has not really kept his part of the bargain they made when she agreed to keep her mouth shut in the sixties. When she stood by silently as he became a "man," she assumed that he would subsequently grant her her long overdue "womanhood," that he would finally glorify and dignify black womanhood just as the white man had done for the white woman. But he did not. He refused her. His involvement with white women was only the most dramatic form that refusal took. He refused her across the board. He refused her because he could not do anything else. He refused her because the assertion of his manhood required something quite different of him. He refused her because it was too late to carbon-copy the traditional white male/female relationships. And he refused her because he felt justified in his anger. He claimed that she had betrayed him. And she believed that, even as she denied it. She too was angry, but paralyzed by the feeling that she had no right to be.

Therefore her strange numbness, her determination, spoken or unspoken, to remain basically unquestioning of the black man's authority and thereby seemingly supportive of all he has done, even that which has been abusive of her. She is in the grip of Black Macho and it has created within her inestimable emotional devastation.

The black woman's silence is a new silence. She knows that. Not so long ago it would have been quite easy to find any number of black women who would say with certainty, "A nigga man ain't shit." Perhaps more to the point, there has been from slavery until the Civil Rights Movement a thin but continuous line of black women who have prodded their sisters to self-improvement. These women were of the opinion that being a woman did not exempt one from responsibility. Just like a man, a woman had to struggle to deliver the race from bondage and uplift it. In their time a woman's

interest in herself was not automatically interpreted as hostile to men and their progress, at least not by black people. Day to day these women, like most women, devoted their energies to their husbands and children. When they found time, they worked on reforms in education, medicine, housing, and their communities through their organizations and churches. Little did they know that one day their activities would be used as proof that the black woman has never known her place and has mightily battled the black man for his male prerogative as head of the household.

The American black woman is haunted by the mythology that surrounds the American black man. It is a mythology based upon the real persecution of black men: castrated black men hanging by their necks from trees; the carcasses of black men floating face down in the Mississippi; black men with their bleeding genitals jammed between their teeth; black men shining shoes; black men being turned down for jobs time and time again; black men watching helplessly as their women go to work to support the family; black men behind bars, persecuted by prison guards and police; jobless black men on street corners, with needles in their arms, with wine bottles in their hip pockets; black men being pushed out in front to catch the enemy's bullets in every American war since the Revolution of 1776— these ghosts, rendered all the more gruesome by their increasing absence of detail, are crouched in the black woman's brain. Every time she starts to wonder about her own misery, to think about reconstructing her life, to shake off her devotion and feeling of responsibility to everyone but herself, the ghosts pounce. She is stopped cold. The ghosts talk to her. "*You* crippled the black man. *You* worked against him. *You* betrayed him. *You* laughed at him. *You* scorned him. *You* and the white man."

Not only does the black woman continue to see the black man historically as a cripple, she refuses to take seriously the various ways he's been able to assert his manhood and capabilities in recent years. Granted that many of his gains of the past decade have been temporary and illusory; but he is no longer a pathetic, beaten-down slave (if indeed he ever was only that). He's grown, progressed, developed as a man, and if one recognizes him as a man he must begin to carry some measure of responsibility for what happens to him. But none of this matters to the black woman. Whether he is cast as America's latest sex object, king of virility and violence, master of the ghetto art of cool, or a Mickey Mouse copy of a white capitalist, she pities him. She sees only the masses of unemployed black men, junkies, winos, prison inmates. She does not really see the masses of impoverished, unemployed black women, their numerous children pulling at their skirts; or, if she does, she sees these women and children only as a further humiliation and burden to that poor, downtrodden black man.

She sees only the myth. In fact what most people see when they look at the black man is the myth.

American slavery was a dehumanizing experience for everyone involved. Both black men and women were forced to labor without compensation, to live in an environment totally controlled by their owners, and to live with the fact that their children could not expect any better. They were compelled to accept the quasibenevolence of the Anglo-Saxon patriarchy that was the plantation system, and the relentless deculturalization process that eventually rid them of most of the apparent manifestations of their African origin. In addition, many blacks, male and female, were underfed, overworked, and physically abused. Yet somehow the story goes that the black man suffered a very special and particularly debilitating kind of denigration because, as a slave, he was not permitted to fulfill his traditional role as a man, that is as head of his family, sole provider and protector. Here are some versions of this story:

> For the Negro child, in particular, the plantation offered no really satisfactory father-image other than the master. The "real" father was virtually without authority over his child, since discipline, parental responsibility, and control of rewards and punishments all rested in other hands; the slave father could not even protect the mother of his children except by appealing directly to the master. Indeed, the mother's own role loomed far larger for the slave child than did that of the father. She controlled those few activities—household care, preparation of food, and rearing of children—that were left to the slave family. For that matter, the very eti-

quette of plantation life removed even the honorific attributes of fatherhood from the Negro male, who was addressed as "boy"—until, when the vigorous years of his prime were past, he was allowed to assume the title of "uncle." (Stanley Elkins, "Slavery and Personality," *Slavery: A Problem in American Institutional and Intellectual Life,* Chicago: University of Chicago Press, 1959.)

After black women were brought over to the New World, they served as breeders of children who were treated as property, and as the gratifiers of white plantation owners' carnal desires. More importantly, they became the central figure in black family life. The black man's only crucial function within the family was that of siring the children. The mother's role was far more important than the father's. She cleaned the house, prepared the food, made clothes and raised the children. The husband was at most his wife's assistant, her companion and her sex partner. He was often thought of as her possession, as was the cabin in which they lived. It was common for a mother and her children to be considered a family without reference to the father. (Robert Staples, "The Myth of the Impotent Black Male," *Contemporary Black Thought: The Best from The Black Scholar,* ed. Robert Chrisman and Nathan Hare, New York: Bobbs-Merrill, 1973.)

The black man in America has always been expected to function as less than a man; this was taken for granted, and was the ugliest weight of his enslavement. The liberal white man has always promised the de-testicled black some progress to manhood. In other words, "We will let your balls grow back . . . one day! Just be cool." In slavery times, theoretically, the slave master could make it with any black woman he could get to. The black man was powerless to do anything to prevent it; many times he was even powerless to keep his woman with him, or his children. One effect of this largely one-sided "integration" was to create a very deep hatred and suspicion in the black man for any black woman who had dealings with white men. This is a feeling that still exists. (LeRoi Jones, "American Sexual Reference:

Black Male," *Home*, New York: William Morrow, 1966.)

The picture drawn for us over and over again is of a man who is a child, who is the constant victim of an unholy alliance between his woman and the enemy, the white man. It is an emotional interpretation but it has also been used by the contemporary black man to justify his oppression of the black woman, to justify his getting ahead by walking over her prostrate body. "I don't owe you anything, black woman because (1) you sold me out and (2) you've always been ahead anyway." The facts are a good deal more complicated and ambiguous.

The slave family was constantly subject to disruption by sales of children, of father and mother. Black women did have sex with and bear children for their white masters. The slave father did lack traditional authority over his family. He could not control the destinies of either his wife or his children. For the most part he could not provide for them and protect them. But to accept these features of slavery as the entire picture is to accept that the character of life in the black slave community was solely a product of white oppression.

Despite the obstacles, the slave family was often a stable entity. Herbert Gutman points out in *The Black Family in Slavery and Freedom* (New York: Random House, 1977) that most black families were headed by a stable male/female partnership, by a husband and a wife. Slaves were not usually required by their masters to form permanent unions, but they did nevertheless exist in great quantities. That fact suggests that blacks, both males and females, took traditional marriage and all it entailed, including male authority, quite seriously.

Yes, black men were called boys. Black women were also called girls. But the slaves thought of themselves as "mens and womens." That so many slave narratives show evidence of great attachment for fathers would indicate that the father/child relationship was not taken lightly. Both male and female children were frequently named after dead or sold-away male relatives.

Eugene Genovese suggests in *Roll, Jordan, Roll* that despite the persistence with which whites insisted that blacks were not human, blacks continually found ways to exert their own humanity. There were cases of black women who were raped as their husbands looked on, powerless to do anything about it. There were also cases of men who fought to the death to prevent such things. Most of the women who engaged in interracial unions were probably single. And, although many were unwilling, some were not. Some won certain advantages by it. A large percentage of the free class of blacks were products of such unions. It is impossible to say just how often black women and white men had sexual relations during slavery. There can't be any doubt that it was fairly often but not all of it was strictly abusive. There was also some sexual contact between black male slaves and white women. White men did not seem to become obsessed with preventing such relations until much later.

The slaves were bound by a system that denied them the right to perpetuate their sexual relations and family life in the way they might have liked. But there were certain limitations to the abuse, even laws that slaveholders put on the books in order to better state their case that slavery was beneficial to blacks. Blacks frequently expanded upon these "rights" and turned them to their own advantage. Genovese, who is the author of this thesis, is quite convincing on the subject. There were also ways in which blacks were able to exercise a limited authority and to project an image of black accomplishment. These were available to both men and women.

A slave woman really had four ways in which to distinguish herself. The first way was by excelling at physical labor. The reports tell us of women who could pick cotton faster, haul more, and so on, than any man for miles around. The ability to do heavy labor was of paramount importance on the old Southern plantation. Whereas women who were sensitive, delicate, and fragile suffered a great deal in slavery (and there were a great many such women), women who were physically strong and robust were highly valued by the slave community.

Secondly, there were women who rose above the common lot by becoming the sex partners of their masters. Sometimes their white owners lived openly with them as wives. More often they and their children were given their freedom upon the master's death. But this path was also fraught with risk. Such women were sometimes the victims of special abuse, were sold away to avoid scandal in the larger white community and embarrassment to the master's wife.

The third way a black woman slave might achieve some status was as a mammy. The mammy is a hated figure in black history and perhaps with good reason. Legend has it that she often controlled the household, its white members as well, that she was sometimes overly loyal to her master and guarded his wealth and position with great vigor. But she also served a function that was useful to the slave community. She might intercede in behalf of a slave and prevent his being punished, and she often provided much of the information from the big house.

The fourth way for a black woman to be set apart from the ordinary slaves was as a house servant with a special skill. She might be a laundress, a weaver, a spinner, and, as a good worker, she might come to be greatly valued by the master. But here again the record also shows that she was often the victim of special abuse and suffered under the constant eye of her mistress.

The distinctions available to black male slaves were actually somewhat more impressive and more varied. First, men might become artisans, craftsmen, mechanics. These men were among the most respected members of the slave community and were frequently allowed to take some percentage of their wages when they were hired out. Second, black men might become drivers or even de facto overseers. The black driver, another hated figure in black history, had the job of seeing that the slaves performed well in the fields. Sometimes he was vicious. On occasion he might force some of the slave women to have sex with him. But sometimes he was lenient. Clearly he was an important tool of the master class, but he also benefited the slave community in that he was a living example of a black man in a position of authority, and he helped counter the notion of the black man as a boy.

A black male slave might also distinguish himself in ways comparable to those available to women slaves. For example, he might become the body servant, butler, or coachman of his master. As such, he might, over the years, win a great deal of trust and subsequent authority. And of course it was often the black male, not the female, who won prestige through his achievements in field labor. In addition black men won influence in the slave community by fighting in the American Revolution and then in the War of 1812. Many slaves reported proudly that some male ancestor had fought for his country.

Lastly, it was the men, in all cases, who planned and/or led the slave revolts. Although women participated, every known slave plot or actual rebellion was the result of male initiative.

Viewing American slavery with any kind of objectivity is extremely difficult, mostly because the record was unevenly and inconsistently kept. Nevertheless we can surely doubt the assumption that the black man was totally robbed of his manhood and divested of his authority over the black woman. The system of slavery did much to undermine that authority, but there were certain loopholes in the system; these, combined with the black man's strength and the black woman's determination to maintain what she saw as her role as a woman, left the black man with a challenged but very much intact "manhood." To suggest that the black man was emasculated by slavery is to suggest that the black man and the black woman were creatures without will. Slave men and women formed a coherent and, as much as possible, a beneficial code of behavior, values, and mores, a culture, a way of seeing and dealing with life, that was based upon the amalgamation of their African past and the forced realities of their American experience—in other words, an African-American culture.

Yet the myth of the black man's castration in slavery, or at least the joint participation of the white man and the black woman in a ruthless attempt to castrate him, has been nurtured over a century—along with the black man's contempt for the mostly imaginary self-sufficiency of the black woman. But the presumed dominance of the black female during slavery would not be quite enough to explain the full extent of black male anger, especially since it was more untrue than not, and at some point the black man must have known that. Rather his actual gripe must be, at least in part, that the black woman, his woman, was not *his* slave, that his right to expect her complete service and devotion was usurped. She *was*, after all, the white man's slave.

There can be no doubt that the role of patriarch was made virtually impossible for the black man during slavery and extremely inconvenient afterward. Nevertheless, the record shows that black men and black women emerged from slavery in twos, husbands and wives. It was mostly after slavery that the fear white men had of black men began to take some of its more lascivious forms. It was then that the myth of the black man's sexuality, the myth of the black man as sexual monster, as a threat to pure white womanhood, began to gain force. After the ill-fated Reconstruction period came the rise of the Ku Klux Klan, the thousands of lynchings, and the group effort on the part of white men to sever the black man's penis from his body and render him economically unable to provide for his family, despite his legal freedom.

How did the black family respond to this pressure? For the most part it continued its two-by-two stride, husbands and wives, solid families. And they continued the tradition of adaptation that had marked the evolution of the Afro-American family from slavery. There was the pressure of the American white standard but there was also the standard that black Americans had set for themselves; they understood very well that they were not white. Slave rule, as described by Gutman, provided for trial marriage, for pregnancy followed by marriage—for some degree of sexual experimentation prior to settling down. All of which had precedents in African societies, as well as in most precapitalist agrarian societies. After marriage, however, adultery was considered intolerable. If possible the man worked and provided for all. If not the woman also worked. But at no point in American history have more black women been employed than black men.

Only as American blacks began to accept the standards for family life, as well as for manhood and womanhood embraced by American whites, did black men and women begin to resent one another. And as time went on their culture, under constant attack from the enemy, became more impoverished and dependent and left with fewer self-regenerating mechanisms.

The Americanized black man's reaction to his inability to earn enough to support his family, his "impotence," his lack of concrete power, was to vent his resentment on the person in this society who could do least about it—his woman. His problem was that she was not a "woman." She, in turn, looked at the American ideal of manhood and took the only safe course her own fermenting rage and frustration could allow her. Her problem was that he was not a "man." But neither the black man's nor the black woman's view of their own or their mate's inadequacies was uniform, absolute, or suddenly arrived at. Both continued to feel a substantial group identity. For a long time their own unique Afro-American standard served to reinforce their sense of self-worth, but over the years blacks began to lean more and more toward Americanization—in their case, another word for self-hatred.

Slowly, as the black man began to see himself as America had defined him, he began to accept America's interpretation of his experience. Donald Bogle, the author of *Toms, Coons, Mulattoes, Mammies & Bucks: An Interpretive History of Blacks in American Films* (New York: Viking Press, 1973), advances an intriguing theory. According to him, *Uncle Tom's Cabin* and the later *Birth of a Nation*[1] gave us a set of black stereotypes out of which have come all subsequent characterizations of blacks in American film.

The male stereotypes were Toms, Coons, and Bucks. We are all familiar with Uncle Tom. He is devoted to whites, religious, hard working, loyal, trustworthy, patient, and restrained. The Coon is happy-go-lucky, a clown, a buffoon, a child, clever and witty but unable to perform the most simple task without guidance. He's a trickster, cunning and resourceful. The third stereotype, the Buck, made his last appearance prior to the seventies in *The Birth of a Nation*. The Buck is the only black stereotype that is sexual. He is brutal, violent, virile, tough, strong—and finds white women especially appealing. By constitution he is unable to smile and grovel like the Coon and the Uncle Tom. He is the personification of the black threat to white womanhood and, more importantly, to white male authority and dominance. The Buck is the stereotype, the nightmare, that whites could not handle, and thus he disappeared and did not make his appearance again, Bogle tells us, until the black movies of the seventies such as *Shaft, Superfly,* et al. In other words, rebellion as well as compliance had been determined by whites.

A similar thing occurred in the day-to-day life of the black man. As his Americanization became more

---

1. D. W. Griffith's 1915 film celebrating the Ku Klux Klan based on Thomas Dixon's 1905 novel *The Clansman*.

and more total, he was conditioned to define his rebellion in terms of the white nightmare. He accepted as appropriate the white man's emphasis on his sexuality. And he accepted as sincere the white man's reasons for trying to abort his sexuality.

The Ku Klux Klan, the lynch mob, and Jim Crow legislators said their task was to prevent the black man from violating sacred white womanhood. In pursuit of this mission, thousands of black men were lynched, murdered, degraded, their homes destroyed. Sacred white womanhood had been an economically necessary assumption under the slavery system. It had also been necessary to assume that black women were promiscuous and fickle and gave no more thought to their offspring than pigs did to their litters. Therefore whites might sell black children with impunity. But the white woman would be the mother of the little man who would inherit the white man's fortune. One had to be certain of the child's origin. Thus the white woman's purity, like the black female's promiscuity, was based upon her status as property. After slavery, when the lynching began, white men could not with any kind of dignity admit their sexual fears of black men. But there was good economic reason to perpetuate those fears. The less there was for black men, the more for them. There were many fewer penises cut off than there were men who were kept out of jobs and prevented from making a living. But all of this, the black man was to believe, was in order to protect the white woman.

Thirty Years of Lynching in the United States (New York: Arno Press, 1970), compiled by the NAACP, reported that between 1889 and 1918, 3,224 persons had been killed by lynch mobs; 2,838 of the killings were in the South and 78 percent of the victims were black. It also pointed out that "less than one in five of the colored victims have been accused of rape or 'attacks on women.'" Despite this, Susan Brownmiller points out in *Against Our Will*, her study on rape in America, that the effort mounted to stop the lynching of blacks aimed much of its venom at that hysterical, frigid, masochistic Southern white woman.

. . . it took a woman, a Viennese disciple of Freud who had probably ventured no farther south than Boston, to provide the clincher. . . . Once Dr. Helene Deutsch[2] laid down her dictum of the hysterical, masochistic female, it was adopted with astonishing speed by those who wanted, or needed for their own peace of mind, to dilute white male responsibility for the Southern rape complex. . . .

[* * *] The fact that the white men believe so readily the hysterical and masochistic fantasies and lies of the white women, who claim they have been assaulted and raped by Negroes, is related to the fact that they (the men) sense the unconscious wishes of the women, the psychic reality of these declarations, and react emotionally to them as if they were *real*. The social situation permits them to discharge this emotion upon the Negroes.

With this kind of argument the Left fought successfully to eradicate mob lynching and the institutional murder of black men in the South, but there were some undesirable side effects. As Susan Brownmiller pointed out, the fallacy was perpetuated that the charge of rape was almost never justified, because women who charged rape were having masochistic fantasies.

> As Southern white men continued to round up black men, lynch them or try them in a courtroom and give them the maximum sentence for the holy purpose of "protecting their women," Northern liberals looking at the ghastly pattern through an inverted prism saw the picture of a lying white woman crying rape-rape-rape. (Susan Brownmiller, *Against Our Will,* New York: Simon & Schuster, 1975)

But more importantly, the notion of the black man's access to white women as a prerequisite of his freedom was reinforced. These ideas shaped the minds of both those white women who came South as part of the Civil Rights Movement and the black men who met them.

The Till[3] case became a lesson of instruction to an entire generation of appalled Americans. I know

2. Austrian American psychoanalyst (1884–1982).
3. The highly publicized trial of two white men charged with the murder of Emmett Till, a fourteen year old who was lynched during a visit from Chicago to see his relatives in Mississippi, allegedly for whistling or making advances at a white woman; outrage over the acquittal of the two accused men (who then confessed their guilt to a journalist from *Look* magazine) helped fuel the emerging civil rights movement.

how I reacted. At age twenty and for a period of fifteen years after the murder of Emmett Till whenever a black teen-ager whistled at me on a New York City street or uttered in passing one of several variations on an invitation to congress, I smiled my nicest smile of comradely equality—no supersensitive flower of white womanhood, I.... After all, were not women for flirting? Wasn't a whistle or a murmured "May I fuck you?" an innocent compliment? And did not white women in particular have to bear the white man's burden of making amends for Southern racism? (Brownmiller, *Against Our Will*)

I saw in a magazine a picture of the white woman with whom Emmett Till was said to have flirted. While looking at the picture, I felt that little tension in the center of my chest I experience when a woman appeals to me. I was disgusted and angry with myself. Here was a woman who had caused the death of a black, possibly because, when he looked at her, he also felt the same tensions of lust and desire in his chest—and probably for the same general reasons that I felt them.... I looked at the picture again and again, and in spite of everything and against my will and the hate I felt for the woman and all that she represented, she appealed to me. I flew into a rage at myself, at America, at white women, at the history that had placed those tensions of lust and desire in my chest.... (Eldridge Cleaver, *Soul on Ice*, New York: McGraw-Hill, 1965)

So the black man's Americanization meant more for him than just his coming to view the deviation of his woman from the American ideal as an affront to his manhood. Since he had also come to think of himself in largely physical terms, the inaccessibility of the white woman represented a severe limitation of his manhood.

Around the time that Shirley Chisholm[4] was running for President in 1972, Redd Foxx, the black comedian and television star,[5] made a joke about her. He said that

he would prefer Raquel Welch[6] to Shirley Chisholm any day. The joke was widely publicized, particularly in the black community, and thought quite funny. There was something about it that made black men pay attention, repeat it, savor it.

Shirley Chisholm was the first black woman to run for the office of President of the United States. She had shown by her congressional record, her fiery speeches, and her decision to run a spunk that America hadn't seen in a black woman since Fannie Lou Hamer.[7] The black political forces in existence at the time—in other words, the black male political forces—did not support her. In fact, they actively opposed her nomination. The black man in the street seemed either outraged that she dared to run or simply indifferent.

Ever since then it has really baffled me to hear black men say that black women have no time for feminism because being black comes first. For them, when it came to Shirley Chisholm, being black no longer came first at all. It turned out that what they really meant all along was that the black man came before the black woman. And not only did he come before her, he came before her to her own detriment. The proof is that, as soon as Shirley Chisholm announced her intention to run, black men pulled out their big guns and aimed them at her. They made every attempt to humiliate her, not only as a political being but also as a sexual being.

That blacks fought against Chisholm was a setback for all black people, but it was even more of a setback for black men. The reaction of black men to Chisholm's campaign, a reaction they made no attempt at all to conceal, marked the point at which the Black Movement breathed its last as a viable entity. Black male hostility to Chisholm exploded any illusion that blacks might actually be able to sustain a notion of themselves apart from America's racist/sexist influence, a notion essential to their autonomy and inner direction.

Redd Foxx's joke expressed the comparisons black men were making between black women and white women: responsibility, always tiresome, versus the illusion of liberation and freedom. In some sense, every ethnic group of men wishes to be free of its women for

---

4. See p. 824.
5. Foxx starred in the television show *Stanford and Son* from 1972–77.
6. White American actress (b. 1940).
7. See discussion of Hamer and the Mississippi Freedom Democratic Party, p. 537.

similar reasons. However, although Jewish male comedians are famous for making fun of what is, essentially, the "Jewishness" of their wives, it would never have occurred to a Henny Youngman or an Alan King to make a crack about preferring Raquel Welch to Golda Meir,[8] at least not in public. We black men, Redd Foxx's joke seemed to say, are more interested in going to bed with Raquel Welch than we are in having a black president.

Redd Foxx was at the time NBC's shining star as the lead character in *Sanford and Son*. And I am told that he was financially crucial to them then. Week after week he presented his characterization of the black man as wine guzzling, lazy, idiotic, and strongly contemptuous of all black women except his wife, who was conveniently dead. He felt comfortable enough with white racist Americans to laugh with them about the comparative sexual merits of Shirley Chisholm, his leading black woman politician, and Raquel Welch, a white sex symbol. Surely the white man was laughing all the way to the bank.

The black man of the 1960s found himself wondering why it had taken him so long to realize he had an old score to settle. Yes, yes, he wanted freedom, equality, all of that. But what he really wanted was to be a man.

America had made one point painfully clear. As long as the black man did not have access to white women, he was not a man. The lynchings, murders, beatings, the miscegenation laws designed to keep the black man and the white woman apart while the white man helped himself to black women, created in him a tremendous sense of personal urgency on this matter. America had not allowed him to be a man. He wanted to be one. What bothered America most? The black man and the white woman. Therefore if he had a white woman, he would be more of a man. And as it became more and more apparent that white America would regard any serious bid for social, economic, and political equality as a declaration of full-scale war, the white woman/black man version of freedom began to make a great deal of sense.

But there was more to keep him busy. In 1965 the Moynihan Report on the black family said that the problem with blacks was not so much white racism as it was an "abnormal family structure." This abnormal family structure made it nearly impossible for blacks to benefit from and participate in the American power structure. And the primary feature of this abnormality was the "matriarch," the "strong black woman," the woman who had nearly as much or more education than the black man, who worked more frequently than the white woman, who had a greater percentage of professionals among her rank, though they were mostly nurses, teachers, and social workers, not doctors, lawyers, and Indian chiefs. In other words, Moynihan was suggesting that the existence of anything so subversive as a "strong black woman" precluded the existence of a strong black man or, indeed, any black "man" at all.

In books and articles the black man ripped into this argument and tore it apart. But it had brought his resentment to the surface. Moynihan had hit just the right note. Many might argue that the average black person has no idea of what is contained within the Moynihan Report. But just about any black person, when asked who is more oppressed, the black man or the black woman, would respond with some version of "Well, the black woman has always been liberated because she was able to find work when the black man couldn't get any." There were blacks who would have said that before Moynihan's report but they would have been more difficult to find; they would have been uncertain and willing to argue the point with you. Now they were certain, resolute in their conviction, and they presented this opinion with pride because they were saying something for which they knew there was full support in the black community. Moynihan did that. Moynihan bared the black man's awful secret for all to see—that he had never been able to make his woman get down on her knees.

Come 1966, the black man had two pressing tasks before him: a white woman in every bed and a black woman under every heel. Out of his sense of urgency came a struggle called the Black Movement, which was nothing more nor less than the black man's struggle to attain his presumably lost "manhood." And so America had tightened the noose, although it did not know it yet; by controlling the black man's notion of what a black man was supposed to be, it would successfully control the very goals of his struggle for "freedom."

8. Fourth prime minister of the State of Israel (1898–1978).

But how was he to achieve those goals? By passive resistance, by sitting in at the Barbizon Hotel for Women,[9] by laying his body down in front of the buses that carried black domestics to work? Theoretically the Civil Rights struggle was won with the passing of various kinds of civil rights legislation, but it had cost so many black lives. Blacks still couldn't sit down and eat a decent meal in a white restaurant because they couldn't pay for it. Their vote meant nothing because they had no one to vote for. And, as the final kick in the pants, the white man's mind had not changed one iota. The white man still saw the black man as "a nigga with a big dick" who was after his daughter. Rap Brown[1] had not been wrong when he said that "violence is as American as cherry pie." When the black man had tried restraint, compassion, patience, cautiousness, peaceful means—those good old standards of dear Uncle Tom—the white man had responded in violence and hatred, as if to say "Nigga, you can't fool us. We know what you have in your pants. We know what you're really after." Sex. Violence. The two are really inseparable, aren't they? Who had the white man always been afraid of? Uncle Tom? No. Coon? No. It was that brutal buck who would come to get his daughter and his wife. And how would he come to get her? By ringing the front doorbell and inquiring politely?

No. By force. What had that woman always symbolized to the white man? Everything that he owned, his domination. And it was that simple.

Certainly some black men continued to pursue a more decent and humane existence for all black people, and perhaps a majority continued to believe that that was what it was all about. But as far as the leadership was concerned, the struggle for human rights was more or less left behind with the Civil Rights Movement. To some degree this was because the Movement was largely shaped by those flamboyant aspects of it that particularly interested the white media. But black leadership played to the media and so did many black men on the corner. That was the message of Tom Wolfe's "Mau-Mauing the Flak Catchers" (*Radical Chic & Mau-Mauing the Flak Catchers*, New York: Farrar, Straus & Giroux, 1970). There was more to the protest and furor of the sixties and seventies than an attempt to correct the concrete problems of black people. The real key was the carrot the white man had held just beyond the black man's nose for many generations, that imaginary resolution of all the black man's woes and discontent, something called manhood. It was the pursuit of manhood that stirred the collective imagination of the masses of blacks in this country and led them to almost turn America upside down.

ROBERT STAPLES

The Myth of Black Macho: A Response to Angry Black Feminists [1979]

In this essay, the sociologist Robert Staples critiques both Michele Wallace's *Black Macho and the Myth of the Superwoman* (p. 817) and Ntozake Shange's *for colored girls who have considered suicide when the rainbow is enuf* (p. 813). Staples characterizes Wallace's and Shange's writing as personal, middle-class reflections of grievances against black men that neither reflect black opinion in general nor consider the cultural and

political contexts of black male actions. He also suggests that white racist interests are behind the media attention and success of their work.

Staples dismisses Shange's play as narrow and narcissistic, whereas he takes Wallace's positions more seriously, engaging her arguments and even agreeing with a number of her conclusions. In this way, he positions himself as a moderate, allied with other unifying

---

9. Residence hotel for women established in 1927 as a safe place for single women coming to New York City to live and work; until the 1980s, no men were allowed above the ground floor.
1. SNCC and Black Panther Party leader.

black activists such as Angela Davis and Joyce Ladner, in contrast to those whose more extreme positions contribute to the gender divisions between black men and black women, such as the "extreme male chauvinists, Eldridge Cleaver and LeRoi Jones," as well as Shange and Wallace. Like Frances Beal in "Double Jeopardy" (p. 801), Staples argues that capitalist oppression is primary. However, where Beal sees racism and sexism as capitalist tools to be resisted, Staples uses his capitalist critique to explain why sexism exists among black men. Staple's conclusion—in which he echoes Wallace's call to "make history" but adds that black people "should do it together"—underscores his stated position as a reasonable and moderate unifier who recognizes the positions of both black men and black women. His criticism of Wallace and Shange provoked such an outburst of responses, however, that *The Black Scholar* dedicated its May–June 1979 issue to examining what it called the "Black Sexism Debate."

From *The Black Scholar* 10 (March–April 1979), pp. 24–32.

The modern women's movement is barely ten years old. In that decade it was largely populated by middle class white women who focused on symbolic and class bound issues, such as protesting women as sex objects in magazines and attempts to put more women into corporate boardrooms and other male domains. By and large, black women were not present, in large numbers, in the mainstream women's movement, a conspicuous absence since many white women took them as their model of the strong, independent woman. And, black women such as Aileen Hernandez, Flo Kennedy[1] et al. were leading spokeswomen for women's issues. It was said that black women were already liberated, that white women were as racist as white men and the middle class issues on which the movement focused were irrelevant to the largely working class black population.

Moreover, the black male had been spared as a target of feminists. After all, he was certainly in no position to be sexist, whether he wanted to be or not. White feminists generally left him alone in their assault on men. Many were careful to refer to white male domination as their main gripe. In the last few years, however, a few of them have taken off the gloves. Black males can now be attacked, not as the banker denying white women credit, but as the sadistic rapist lurking in the alley to terrorize and sodomize a white woman to whom he has no other access. Never mind that it was mostly black women who were being raped while it was white women screaming rape.[2] It was almost a throwback to the fifties when the worst crime possible was the violation of a white women's body by a big dicked nigger. To rape black women is not nice; to sexually assault a white woman is an abomination and a sign of not knowing one's place, or, so [we] read in the works of Susan Brownmiller[3] and Diana Russell.[4]

In this era of racist retrenchment it would not do for white women to come down too hard on black men. More naive souls might suspect them of racism and collaboration with the white male's attack on minorities a la Alan Bakke.[5] After all white women had meticulously set themselves apart from white men only a few years ago when they were labelled "minorities" and placed into the affirmative action pool with blacks, Asians, Latinos and Native Americans. Some have called this cynical manipulation of the symbols

---

1. Civil rights and feminist activist and lawyer who was a founder of the National Organization for Women (NOW) but left in 1970 to found the Feminist Party and other organizations; Hernandez: union organizer, activist, and government official; she was the second president of NOW in 1970–71, but in 1979 she left the organization she had helped found, writing an open letter to NOW highlighting the "growing alienation of minority women who have joined feminist organizations like NOW" over the lack of concrete action by these organizations to eliminate racism. [Editor's note]

2. Nathan Hare, "Revolution without a Revolution: The Psychology of Sex and Race," *The Black Scholar* 9 (April, 1978), 2–7. [Unless otherwise indicated, all footnotes are those of the author.]

3. Susan Brownmiller, *Against Our Will*. New York: Simon and Schuster, 1975.

4. Diana Russell, *The Politics of Rape*. New York: Stein and Day, 1975.

5. See discussion of the 1978 case of *Regents of the University of California v. Allan Bakke* and its effect on affirmative action policy, p. 657. [Editor's note]

of minority status. At best it served to defuse the movement of other minorities and decrease their chances at upward mobility.

Since white feminists could not marshall an all-out attack on black males, and well-known black female activists such as Joyce Ladner and Angela Davis would not, how could they be put in their place. Enter Ntozake Shange[6] and Michele Wallace.[7] While other black writers have trouble finding a forum to discuss the persistence of racist conditions, Ms. Shange's play, "For Colored Girls Who Have Considered Suicide," is on-Broadway and road shows have drawn sell-out audiences throughout the United States, composed mostly of black women and whites. Reports that a black male is offered as a sacrificial lamb at the end of her play are greatly over-exaggerated. Michele Wallace's new book, *Black Macho and the Myth of the Superwoman,* has been heralded as the most publicized book on blacks since *Roots.*[8] She can be found on the cover of *Ms.* Magazine and in the pages of the *New York Times.*

While the personal background of an author is no defensible basis for judging their work, I find it difficult to overlook in the case of these two women. Both came from very middle-class backgrounds, had some involvement with street brothers, and are now urging black women to go it alone. That may not be all that is important about them; it is all I know. And, I recognize that both women are angry. It is important that we understand why. Is it because all the gains of the black movement have gone to men? Certainly, this does not appear to be the case in the year 1979. Because of their double minority status, black women have made unprecedented educational and economic gains in the last couple of years. There are over eighty-four thousand more black women enrolled in college than black men.[9] In a recent survey of 25,000 black women,

Essence Magazine reported that more than a third of them earn $20,000 or more a year.[1]

Indeed, it is puzzling why this attack on black men is occurring when black women threaten to overtake them, in terms of education, occupation and income by the next century. True, lower-class black women are not faring well. But, lower-class black men are in even worse condition. Remember, too, that Ms. Shange and Ms. Wallace are middle-class and that, undoubtedly, is their frame of reference. Perhaps we can find the answer in another set of statistics: There are 188 college educated black women to every 100 similar black males; the interracial marriage rate increased by one-third in the Seventies and 54 percent of all adult black women are never married, separated, widowed or divorced.[2] Ms. Wallace, for instance, does not attempt to disguise her anger at black men. But, this is a personal quarrel, which I frankly would be reluctant to air in its most naked form. There are, as always, two sides to the story—which is an ugly one at that. Ms. Wallace gives us the female side and I confess to being troubled at what I hear.

Before dealing with Ms. Wallace, let us examine Ms. Shange's play and the reaction to it. It might be necessary to clarify, on the personal level, that I found little in the Shange or Wallace work that related to my personal experience. Most likely, that is due to my Southern origin and present middle-class environment. The two of them write of the urban Northern lower-class black woman and her experiences. Yet, there is nothing they write which indicates that this is not the universal black experiences. Most blacks may know that; their largely white audience does not. In Ms. Shange's play, we witness the abuse of black women by black men; to waiting for men who do not show; to the horror of watching him drop her baby out of a window. At the end of her play, black women are exhorted to love

6. Ntozake Shange, *For Colored Girls Who Have Considered Suicide when the Rainbow is Enuf: A Choreopoem.* New York: Macmillan, 1977.

7. Michele Wallace, *Black Macho and the Myth of the Superwoman.* New York: Dial Press, 1979.

8. *Roots: A Saga of an American Family,* a 1976 novel by Alex Haley (1921–92) was the basis for the 1977 television series *Roots,* one of the most popular series of all time. [Editor's note]

9. "Number of Blacks in College Tripled, *San Francisco Chronicle,* June 12, 1978, p. 2.

1. *Essence Magazine,* 9 (February 1979), p. 51.

2. U.S. Bureau of the Census, *Perspectives on American Husbands and Wives.* Series P-23, No. 77, U.S. Government Printing Office, Washington, D.C., 1979.

themselves because, presumably, nobody else does or will.

The play is drawn from the real life experiences of some black women. How many I do not know. There are a million stories in the black community and one may choose to tell only a few of them. Ms. Shange does not care to tell us the story of why so many black men feel their manhood, more accurately their feeling of self-respect, is threatened by black women. We are never told that many of these men are acting out because, of all groups in this society, they have no basis for any sense of self-actualization, or somebodiness.

There is a curious rage festering inside black men because, like it or not, they have not been allowed to fulfill the roles (i.e. breadwinner, protector) society ascribes to them. While it is considered sexist to say so, the fact remains that many black women do get a sense of fulfillment from bearing and raising children.[3] Some black men have nothing but their penis, an object which they use on as many women as possible. In their middle years they are deprived of even that mastery of the symbols of manhood, as the sex drive wanes and the consuming chase of women becomes debilitating.

What is curious is the reaction of black women to this play. Watching a performance one sees a collective appetite for black male blood. The reaction, however, is not unanimous, as many women are greatly disturbed by the play and its vicious assault on black men. Particularly upset are the happily married women who have no pent-up frustrations which need a release. At the end of the play, what I especially find unsettling, is Shange's invitation to black women to love themselves. This seems, to me, to be no less than an extension of the culture of Narcissism.[4] She does not mention compassion for misguided black men or a love of child, family and community. It all seems so strange, exhorting black women to go it alone. They, many of them, are already alone. That is their main complaint: black men have deserted them.

A black woman who loves only herself is incapable of loving others. What greater way to insure being alone the rest of your life than the self-centered posture so eloquently expressed in Ntozake Shange's play? This is not to deny the existence, or its prevalence, of black male narcissism, only to question how adding the black woman's to it will help our cause any.

What obscures the issue at hand here is the lack of a reasonable and articulate male point of view. Those things that bother black men, feelings of nobodiness, fear of vulnerability, are not often talked about. What is articulated comes out sounding like insensitive male chauvinism, accusing black women of being domineering, sexually hungup and the like.[5] Little wonder that workshops on black male-female relationships degenerate into shouting matches.

On the other hand, black women have learned to link their grievances to the feminist cause. Michele Wallace, for example, seems to be angriest at black men who date and marry white women, and the poverty of black women. Whether one is for or against miscegenation, and I am indifferent, it would appear to be a matter of personal choice. Certainly, it seems a strange choice of subject to link to the feminist cause.[6] As far as the poverty of black women is concerned, there is little that black men have to do with that and even less that they can do to improve her economic condition. Of course, we can agree that men should help to support, even raise, children that they sire— within the extent of their ability to do so. Again, that is a matter between a husband and wife—or the courts as a last resort. It does not seem to be a strong issue among white feminists.

When Ms. Wallace talks about black men denying women meaningful positions in civil rights organizations, she is on sounder ground. She would, also, have been a more objective writer had she placed the issue in historical context. During the Sixties there was a general consensus—among men and women—that

3. William Grier and Price Cobbs, *Black Rage.* New York: Basic Books, 1968.

4. Christopher Lasch, *The Culture of Narcissism.* New York: Norton, 1979.

5. Ms. Wallace, for example, singles out two extreme male chauvinists, Eldridge Cleaver and LeRoi Jones, to illustrate what black men think of black women.

6. It is certainly not an issue ever tackled by white feminists, partly because many of them are the white women involved with black men. This is no small part of the reason why black women shun alliances with white feminists.

black men would hold the leadership positions in the movement. The reasoning behind this philosophy was that black women had held up their men for too long and it was time for the men to take charge. That some black men used the movement to advance the cause of men only can not be denied. Again, the rationale was the trickle down theory: that by enabling black men to advance, the entire black family would be uplifted. Ms. Wallace has a point when she claims that some black men's vision of freedom only included "a white woman in every bed and a black woman under every heel."[7] Would that we had known. Yet, corrupt leadership is not peculiar to blacks, the betrayal of a movement's ideals is replete in the annals of humanity. To her credit, she acknowledges that the majority of black men pursued a more decent and humane existence for all black people.

Understand me, I have no disagreement with much of Ms. Wallace's argument. If we choose to view roles and behavior, linked to gender, that were traditional and normative ten years ago, as sexist, then we all stand guilty of retroactive male chauvinism. The fact that male behavior was normative behavior until recently redefined as sexism poses some theoretical problems for feminists. Unlike other minorities who suffered physically at the hands of their oppressor, women were generally a protected group that was revered by men and children alike. Obviously they were limited in their intellectual and creative expression. But, society operated on a quid pro quo basis: if you want to dance to the music you have to pay the band.

Many men never liked the idea of having to work to support a family either. Yet, society never held out any other option for them, nor any exemption from fighting America's wars or doing its dirty work. Black women, of course, did not share in the privileges of white women and neither did black men partake of the dominant power of white men. The issue here is that what is often defined as sexist behavior is nothing more than men acting in ways which they have been socialized to behave. That they continue to act this

way, in the face of warnings from feminists, signals that life-long socialization is not easily reversed; many women cater to and prefer traditional male behavior and no group gives up its privileges without a prolonged struggle.

Still, the problem of defining what is sexist behavior among black men is a complicated one. On the institutional level, most black men do not have the power to force women into subordinate roles. Most of the institutions in which black people are located are controlled by whites. The most significant exception, the black church, has a male leadership and a largely female constituency. One, however, can find it difficult to make a case for black male sexism in the church, simply because most black men are not in the church—and could care less who is in charge. That only leaves one other black controlled institution in which sexism can manifest itself: the family. There's considerable disagreement over how much power black men have in the family, since they are almost as absent from the family as they are from the church

In intact black families some black men are absolute patriarchs. When I spoke before a group of married black women recently, it was surprising to hear them talk of the firm control of their lives and actions by their husbands. On the other hand, many single black women complain about how passive black men are, how they won't take responsibility for making decisions.

While watching a Detroit television program the other day, I listened to a Dr. Gail Parker[8] talk about how she happened to achieve such a high educational level. All the strong people in her family, she reported, were women. That was her role model and it never occurred to her that she should subordinate her aspirations for the sake of a man. Both these examples suggest there are two types of black families: ones in which women make the major decisions and those in which men make them. That, incidentally, was the finding of sociologists Blood and Wolfe when they compared black and white wives' decision-making powers almost twenty years ago.[9]

---

7. Wallace, op. cit., pp. 31–32.
8. Psychotherapist, media psychologist, and radio talk show host in Detroit. [Editor's note]
9. Robert Blood and Donald Wolfe, "Negro-White Differences in Blue Collar Marriages in a Northern Metropolis." *Social Forces*, 48 (September 1969), 59–63.

As the percentage of female-headed households increases, and they may be the majority of all black families by the year 2000, the women will make all the decisions because the men will simply not be there. That black men are not staying with their families is due to a confluence of certain factors, not the least among them is the fact that some women do make the decisions and desertion is his form of masculine protest. While this may be abhorrent to some of us, sexism is a strange label to impose on his behavior. Desertion, moreover, is the lower-class male's style of exercising his masculine perquisite.

The middle-class black male, with a wider range of choices, screens out the strong black woman beforehand in his choice of mates. Anyone who has met the typical middle-class black wife knows she scores higher on the "femininity" scale then her unmarried counterpart.[1] Some middle-class black men turn to white women who fit even better the model of femininity as set forth in this country. This accounts, in part, for the reason that interracial marriages often involve the best and brightest of black men.

Black women like to dismiss the interracially involved black male as a classic example of the brainwashed idiot who is seduced by whiteness. Yet, we never question how such a large proportion of black men who can lead our organizations, publish our magazines, star in our films, sing our songs, and write our books, can be so gullible as to be seduced by nothing more than white skin pigmentation. The answer to the question of why middle-class black men date and marry white is not a simple or monolithic one. Certainly, since the Sixties, it had something to do with increased opportunities to do so. Beyond that factor, we have only speculation.

It could be that the most successful black men have values and lifestyles most in tune with white society. That is often why they are successful. Among those values will exist the one that women should be supportive and subordinate. Whether true or not, many black men, including those involved with black women, do not believe black women fit that model

very well. As previously stated, I am personally indifferent to the question of whether black men should date or marry white, a position which often the advocates and opponents of said question assume to place me in the enemy camp. For all the screaming and hollering, race mixing still occurs among less than five percent of the black male population. Prison, drugs and homosexuality have done much more to reduce the number of eligible males available to black women.

In this fluid period, women will not find it easy to carve out an independent career and lifestyle and maintain a stable relationship with a man. In one study of the characteristics of divorced and married women, the divorced women turned out to be significantly more aggressive and independent than the women who remained married.[2] Women, to a large extent, are victimized by the fact that the very same characteristics they need to obtain career mobility (aggressive, strong achievement drive) are the ones which make it difficult to attract and hold a man. Thus, they are often placed in the position of a forced choice between career and marriage. And, men place them in this position by their insistence on women playing supportive, not competitive, roles.

Is this sexism? I guess so. It is, also, a matter of personal choice that cannot be denied men. They have the right to choose a woman that meets their perceived needs, even if their exercise of that right limits the life options of women. In much the same way, women have the right to refuse to enter into a marriage or relationship of any kind that will not permit them freedom of expression. Surely, there must be a better way. And, some black men and women have found it, and live it, in a union based on a quasi-equalitarian model. There rarely can be a completely equalitarian relationship between any two human beings. For many reasons that is an impossibility. So, that is not really the issue. The issue is what, and who, determines the various kinds of inequalities that will exist in a male/female relationship.

As many of us know, one source of black male/female inequalities lies in the shortage of black men,

---

1. There is some question as to whether the single black woman is made more hardened and independent by the necessity of earning a living and some of the negative experiences encountered as a result of being single.
2. Jack Horn, "Personality and Divorce," *Psychology Today*, 9 (October 1976), 138.

thus limiting the choices and alternatives of black women as well as exposing them to the abuse of black men keenly aware of that fact. Before we decry the abuse of black women and the advantages black men achieve from this situation, it would behoove us to closely examine just how great an advantage it is.

First, why is there a black male shortage? At birth the ratio of men to women is about equal. The answer lies in the higher morbidity and mortality rate in the marriageable years. In the ages 15–30, black men have a mortality rate twice that of black women. Even sadder is the fact that homicide and suicide are two of the top three causes of death among them.[3]

How happy can these young men be that the remaining brothers are having a field day with the ladies? However, even the remaining black men are not that well off. Almost a half million of them are behind bars; an estimated one-third of black men in the inner city have a drug problem; and 25–50 percent of them are without steady employment.[4]

Hence, that small minority of black men who are living, free, unaddicted, and employed may be living on easy street. However, if he's run into the same women many men have encountered lately, he has found that as a result of prior abuse by those same men, some of these black women are angry, defensive and manipulative. It is small consolation to have an abundance of women from which to choose, when many of those women have been battered into a very negative response to all men.

Ms. Wallace is, oh, so correct when she says that the last 50 years has seen a growing distrust, even hatred, between black men and women. She acknowledges that it was perpetuated by white racism but claims that black ignorance of the sexual politics of their experience in this country played its part.[5] Again, she has a point. What I question, and why I am troubled by her book, is how she comes to the conclusion that

the addicted, imprisoned and unemployed black male is the main culprit in this scenario. I already know why she and Ms. Shange are being heralded as the main pundits of the black condition. In agreement with Pauline Stone I acknowledge that "within Afro-American culture maleness creates certain privileges—that is, certain freedom and rights are attached to being male."[6] However, she correctly attributes this to the societal strategy of manipulating blacks through the maintenance of sexual inequalities in the home and workplace. In both cases the main beneficiaries of the division that ensues are white male capitalists.

Ms. Shange and Wallace hardly mention this group of beneficiaries in their diatribe against black men. Obviously, they could not get on Broadway or in the pages of the *New York Times* with such an observation. But, the divisive effect of sexism is a two way sword. As psychiatrist Alvin Poussaint notes: "At the college level, particularly in black colleges, black-females out-number the males and [outdo them] in terms of achievement. That's going to tell you something about who's going to be achieving and moving into different spots. The white male and white female feel much more threatened by the black male than by the black female, which may set up a condition for easier access."[7] Is this just another warmed over version of the black matriarchy theory? I think not.

There is every reason to believe that, by the turn of the century, black women will exceed black men in terms of occupation and income. They already have more education. As for black men, their future is revealed in the statistic that of 23 million Americans that are functional illiterates, the highest proportion is among black males.[8]

Who is to blame for this situation? According to Ms. Wallace, it is the black man himself. She says: "Yes, forces conspire against him but he allows others to

---

3. James B. Stewart and Joseph W. Scott, "The Institutional Decimation of Black American Males," *Western Journal of Black Studies,* 2 (Summer 1978), 82–92.
4. Ibid.
5. Wallace, op. cit., p. 13.
6. Pauline Terrelonge Stone, "Feminist Consciousness and Black Women" in *A Feminist Perspective,* 2nd Edition (Jo Freeman, Ed.). Palo Alto, California: Mayfield, 1979, pp. 575–588.
7. Alvin Poussaint, quoted in *Jet,* January 4, 1979, p. 32.
8. Robert Staples, "To Be Young, Black and Oppressed," *The Black Scholar,* 6 (December 1975), 2–9.

make decisions for him, he allows life to happen to him, he trusts the white bureaucracy enough to allow them to put him behind bars, to allow them to take care of his wife and children. . . . Finally, it is the black man who had made this undeclared choice. The black woman is simply along for the ride."[9] There it is: The ultimate extension of existentialist philosophy and the American ideology of free will. Such an existentialist philosophy demeans Ms. Wallace and all those who will listen to her. Surely, we need a decrease of black male sexism, whenever we are able to reach an agreement on what it is. But, we also need something that will unify us and make us whole again.

In that regard, what does Ms. Wallace have to offer? The final pages of her book find her starting off with the admonition that black women should never forget how the black man has let them down. Before some words of praise for her feminist counterpart, Ms. Shange, she is critical of black women who choose to pursue an independent course but have children.[1] Obviously, what is left is for black women to go it alone, without children or man as excess baggage, while she writes her own history. Perhaps she will find some followers for this arcane philosophy.

For what it is worth, I just finished a study of middle-class black singles, most of whom were women.[2] Many of them had become de facto practitioners of the Wallace theory: they were alone, upwardly mobile, without man or child. The older they were, the less satisfactory was this condition. And, the reason why is simple enough. The role of male or female cannot stand alone as a sense of identity. It only makes sense, satisfies the soul, when it relates to some other role. To be ontological, humans are not meant to live out their lives alone with no higher purpose than self-satisfaction.

Ultimately, the issue in America is not that of sexism or racism; it is monopoly capitalism and its impact on human potential. In terms of the Maoist concept of major and minor contradictions in a society, sexism and the problems black women face are derivatives of a larger contradiction between capital and labor. Sex-

ism, as is racism, is beneficial to the capitalist order by maintaining differentials in privileges and rewards within the working class.

Ms. Wallace, unfortunately, does not place the issue of black male sexism in any kind of theoretical framework, thus losing sight of the structural context in which sexism manifests itself. Indeed, the most glaring flaw in her book is her acceptance of the status quo in the degree to which she exonerates capitalism of any responsibility for the problems between black men and women. To completely ignore capitalism's systemic features, and its role in black oppression, is to adopt the normative approach of neoconservative social analysis and bias no different than whites, which makes her book an example of the rightward turn in America.

If she had placed her work in a more global, rather than visceral and race-nationalist, perspective, we might understand why black men exhibit these symptoms of sexism. She speaks, for example, of the growing distrust and hatred between black men and women in the last fifty years. Yet, she does not, in her very descriptive book, tell us why. Could it be that the urban industrial transformation from the rural peasant culture sowed the seeds for the alienation of black men from their cultural moorings? In the South black women were respected and men *helped* to provide for their families. As they came to the urban North materialistic values gained ascendancy. The symbols of manhood, sexual conquest, dominance of women, etc., became important to black men because they lacked the real symbols—political and economic power.

A most fatal flaw of the Shange-Wallace thesis is their misreading of the life experience of blacks and a tendency to read into it the problems of the larger society. Because white women are opposed to the sexist behavior of white men in the form of their complete domination of them, some middle-class black women assume the analogous counterpart can be found in black culture. But, the structural underpinnings for sexism are not the same in black society.

9. Wallace, op. cit., pp. 83–85.
1. Ibid., pp. 172–173.
2. Robert Staples, *The World of Black Singles: A Study of Male/Female Relationships.* Forthcoming. [Staples's book was published in 1981 as *The World of Black Singles: Changing Patterns of Male/Female Relations.* Editor's note]

The problem of Shange-Wallace is, that being middle-class, they were raised away from the realities of the black experience and tend to see it all as pathological in the same way that whites view us. Many of these problems of interpersonal relations between black men and women are resolved in very creative and adaptive ways. The Shanges-Wallaces put down working class black culture without really understanding it. The internal machinations of the capitalist order is sufficient reason to keep most black men and women together, if only in a symbiotic relationship.

The Wallace book, for all its flaws, has revealed some very truthful and painful issues, with which we have to deal. But, the politics of confrontation can be counterproductive when practiced in a society of unequals.

When all is said and done, it is not a matter of being male or female. It is, instead, a matter of people understanding that they are products of their culture and cannot free themselves from it for greater individual freedom unless they first understand the constraints that culture imposes. Thus, perspectives, one's own as they are derived from or freed from culture, largely determine what kinds of experiences men and women have with each other.

Stated differently, we are a product of our cumulative experiences and the interpretations we give those experiences. Hence, experience, culture and perspective are essentially one, unless we consciously separate them, and most people do not. Ms. Wallace is correct when she says we must make our own history or remain victims of it. I think we should do it together.

PART FIVE ～ *Works Cited*

Quotations and statistics in this section's headnotes and notes were drawn from the following sources:

Baker, Houston A. "Addison Gayle Jr." *Norton Anthology of African American Literature.* Eds. Henry Louis Gates Jr. and Nellie Y. McKay. New York: Norton, 1997: 1869–1870.

Baldwin, James. "James Baldwin: Reflections of a Maverick." Interview with Julius Lester. *The New York Times.* May 1984: 1.

———. "Many Thousands Gone." *Partisan Review.* November–December 1951: 673–74.

———. *Notes of a Native Son.* Boston: Beacon Press, 1955.

Beal, Frances. Interview by Loretta J. Ross. Oakland, CA, March 18, 2005. Voices of Feminism Oral History Project. Sophia Smith Collection, Smith College, Northhampton, MA. www.smith.edu/library/libs/ssc/vof/transcripts/Beal.pdf.

———. "Slave of a Slave No More: Black Women in Struggle." *The Black Scholar* 6. March 1975: 2–10.

Black Panther Party. "March 1972 platform." *The Black Panther Intercommunal News Service.* May 13, 1972, p. B of the supplement to the newspaper. http://stanford.edu/group/blackpanthers/history.shtml.

"The Black Sexism Debate: Special Issue." *The Black Scholar.* May/June 1979.

Césaire, Aimé. *Cahier d'un retour au pays natal.* Paris: Volontés, 1939.

Chisholm, Shirley. *The Good Fight.* New York: Harper & Row, 1973.

———. *Unbought and Unbossed.* New York: Houghton Mifflin, Co., 1970.

Cleaver, Eldridge. 1997 interview with Henry Louis Gates Jr. "The Two Nations of Black America." *Frontline.* WGBH-TV. February 11, 1998.

Cone, James H. *Black Theology and Black Power.* New York: Seabury Press, 1969.

———. "Epilogue: An Interpretation of the Debate among Black Theologians." *Black Theology: A Documentary History, vol. 1, 1966–1979.* Eds. Gayraud S. Wilmore and James H. Cone. Maryknoll, N.Y.: Orbis Books, 1993, 425–39.

———. "Malcolm X: The Impact of a Cultural Revolutionary." *The Christian Century* 109. December 23–30, 1992: 1189–1195.

Crouch, Stanley. *The All-American Skin Game, or The Decoy of Race.* New York: Pantheon Books, 1995.

Ellison, Ralph. "Richard Wright's Blues." *The Antioch Review* (Summer 1945). Reprinted in Ralph Ellison, *Shadow and Act.* New York: Random House, 1964, 77–94.

Erikson, Erik H. and Huey P. Newton. *In Search of Common Ground, Conversation with Erik H. Erikson and Huey P. Newton.* New York: W. W. Norton, 1973.

Foner, Philip Sheldon, ed. *The Black Panthers Speak.* New York: HarperCollins, 1970.

Giovanni, Nikki. "Biography." http://nikki-giovanni.com/bio.shtml.

Harris, Duchess. " 'All of Who I Am in the Same Place': The Combahee River Collective." *Woman Theory and Research* 3.1 *(1999).* http://www.uga.edu/~womanist/harris3.1.htm.

Johnson, Lyndon Baines. *The Road to Justice: Three Major Statements on Civil Rights.* 1965.

Jones, LeRoi. "Myth of a 'Negro Literature.' " Address at the American Society for African Culture, March 14, 1962. *The Saturday Review* (April 20, 1963). Reprinted in *Home: Social Essays.* New York: William Morrow, 1966.

Jones, William. "Afterword." *Is God a White Racist: A Preamble to Black Theology.* Boston: Beacon Press, 1998, 205–14.

———. *Is God a White Racist?* Boston: Beacon Press, 1973.

———. Telephone conversation with Jennifer Burton. July 20, 2010.

Kates, Nancy and Bennett L. Singer, dirs. *Brother Outsider: The Life of Bayard Rustin.* 2003. www.rustin.org.

King, Martin Luther Jr. "I Have a Dream" and "Nobel Prize Acceptance Speech." *I Have A Dream: Writings and Speeches That Changed the World.* Ed. James Melvin Washington. New York: HarperCollins, 1992.

——. "Nonviolence and Racial Justice." *The Christian Century,* 74: February 6, 1957, 165–67.

——. *Strive Toward Freedom: The Montgomery Story.* New York: Harper & Brothers, 1958.

Lester, Julius. "James Baldwin: Reflections of a Maverick." *The New York Times Book Review.* May 27, 1984, 1.

Lissner, Will. "7 Harlem Leaders Agree Time is Ripe to Cure Slum Evils." *The New York Times.* July 27, 1964, 1.

Malcolm X (with Alex Haley). *The Autobiography of Malcolm X.* New York: Random House, 1965.

——. *By Any Means Necessary (Malcolm X Speeches & Writings).* New York: Pathfinder Press, 1970, 1992.

——. "God's Judgment of White America." *The End of White World Supremacy: Four Speeches.* Ed. Imam Benjamin Karim. New York: Arcade, 1971.

——. Letter to Whitney Young [Martin Luther King et al]. July 31, 1964. http://www.brothermalcolm.net/mxwords/letters/lettertowhitney.html.

——. Speech delivered May 23, 1964. Cited in George Breitman, ed. *Malcolm X Speaks: Selected Speeches and Statements.* New York: Grove Weidenfeld, 1990, 58.

——. Telegram to Martin Luther King. June 30, 1964. http://www.brothermalcolm.net/mxwords/letters/telegramtomartin.gif.

——. "The Old Negro and the New Negro." In *The End of White World Supremacy: Four Speeches.* Ed. Imam Benjamin Karim. New York: Arcade, 1971.

Marshall, Thurgood. "The Next Twenty Years toward Freedom for the Negro in America." New Orleans, November 22, 1946. Cited in Raymond Arsenault. *Freedom Riders: 1961 and the Struggle for Racial Justice.* New York: Oxford University Press, 2006, 36.

McDonald, Dora. Letter to Frank Clark, 26 November 1962. Cited in James H. Cone. *Martin & Malcolm & America: A Dream or a Nightmare.* Maryknoll, New York: Orbis Books, 1992, 101.

Meehan, Thomas. "Moynihan on the Moynihan Report." *The New York Times Magazine.* July 31, 1966, 5, 48–50, 54–55.

Murray, Albert. *The Blue Devils of Nada: A Contemporary American Approach to Aesthetic Statement.* New York: Pantheon Books, 1996.

National Committee of Negro Churchmen. "Black Power Statement." July 31, 1966." *Black Theology: A Documentary History, vol. 1, 1966–1979.* Eds. James H. Cone and Gayraud S. Wilmore. Maryknoll, N.Y.: Orbis Books, 1993, 23–30.

Ryan, William. *Blaming the Victim.* New York: Vintage Books, 1971.

Seale, Bobby. Interview. "Cold War." Episode 13. CNN. August 1996.

Shange, Ntozake. *for colored girls who have considered suicide when the rainbow is enuf.* New York: Bantham Books, 1980.

Sollors, Werner. *Interracialism: Black-White Intermarriage in American History, Literature, and Law.* New York: Oxford University Press, 2000.

Walker, Margaret. *For My People.* New Haven, CT: Yale University Press, 1942.

Wallace, Michele. "How I Saw It Then, How I See It Now." *Black Macho and the Myth of the Superwoman.* New York: Verso, 1990.

Wilson, William Julius. "The Moynihan Report and Research on the Black Community." *The Annals of the American Academy of Political and Social Science,* 621. January 2009, 34–46.

PART SIX

The Contemporary Era (1980 to the Present)

As Barack Obama was winning the race that would culminate in his election as the first African American president of the United States, the subprime mortgage crisis was creating the largest loss of African American wealth in United States history: more than half of all mortgages held by black families were subprime, and twenty percent of those primarily working- and middle-class families were expected to lose their homes. This juxtaposition illustrates an unprecedented development in the post–civil rights era of African American history: the dramatic class divide within the black community.

Before the 1960s, *de jure* and *de facto* racial segregation and discrimination constrained the lives of all African Americans to one degree or another. And while a pronounced class structure has long characterized the black community and was even in place during slavery, the intraracial class structure of black society has assumed dramatic new proportions since the onset in the 1960s of affirmative action, perhaps the principal economic legacy of the long march for civil rights. Legislative and policy changes achieved by the civil rights movement opened up opportunities for African Americans in education, business, and politics, but primarily members of the old black middle class and select segments of the black working class had the social and material resources needed to access these new opportunities and were therefore its prime economic beneficiaries. Hence, while some members of the black community rapidly transcended former economic and social constraints, others—and their descendants—were likely to become increasingly mired in a self-perpetuating cycle of structural poverty.

This stark gap became clearly visible in the 1980s as the first African Americans to benefit from affirmative action and civil rights legislation advanced in their careers. In 1980 alone, milestone achievements in politics, business, and the arts manifested themselves, along with sobering indicators of escalating problems for poor black Americans. Toni Cade Bambara won the American Book Award for *The Salt Eaters;* Robert L. Johnson launched Black Entertainment Television (BET); and Willie Lewis Brown Jr. was elected as the first black speaker of the California State Assembly. But in that same year, an all-white jury's acquittal of police officers charged with the death of an unarmed black man in Miami led to the worst racial violence there since 1967. And these dichotomous types of events were symptomatic of trends throughout the nation.

After 1980, the gap between the lives of professional African Americans and under-employed African Americans widened dramatically. African American artists won the highest honors in the world, including MacArthur fellowships (the so-called genius awards), the National Medal of Arts, the National Humanities Medal, and Pulitzer Prizes—Alice Walker won in 1983 for *The Color Purple* and Toni Morrison won in 1988 for *Beloved*—and Morrison would go on to win the 1993 Nobel Prize in Literature. Reginald Lewis became the first black CEO of a billion-dollar corporation in 1987, and in 2008 Oprah Winfrey was the highest-paid entertainer in Hollywood. In the military and then in government, Colin Powell became the first black chairman of the Joint Chiefs of Staff in 1989 and the first black secretary of state in 2001. In 2001, Condoleezza Rice became the first black national security adviser and, in 2005, the first black female secretary of state. No less than forty-three black women and men were members of Congress in 2008, and in that year America elected its first black commander-in-chief.

Ironically, the highly visible success of some African Americans often functioned to mute the entrenched problems faced by others. Those problems were exacerbated by the growing physical isolation of poor African Americans as educated and successful African Americans moved away from their former neighborhoods when racial barriers to property ownership in upscale real estate markets fell. During the 1990s and the first decade of the new century, it took dramatic events—such as the 1992 Los Angeles uprising following the acquittal of police officers who had been videotaped beating the black motorist Rodney King and the devastation of the gulf coast of Mississippi and Louisiana by Hurricane Katrina in 2005—to focus the nation's attention on the lives of poor African Americans.

Of course, the influence of anti-black racism in contemporary America is not restricted to poor communities. Events in which African Americans play a prominent role are still largely seen through the lens of race, but these events also show how ideas about race continue to evolve. In 1991, the Supreme Court confirmation hearings of Clarence Thomas emphasized the political rise of conservative African Americans: Thomas advocated an end to affirmative action and other initiatives that had been developed since the civil rights movement to combat discrimination. The confirmation hearings also brought to the forefront of public debate issues of race and gender. Following Professor Anita Hill's testimony concerning alleged workplace sexual harassment by Thomas, media outlets flooded the public with images of black men and women disagreeing about fundamental issues, shattering the myth that African Americans—all thirty-three million of them—shared a unilateral identity and a single opinion. The 1995 murder trial of the former football star O. J. Simpson also brought race—and especially the interplay of race, class, and gender—to the forefront of public debate. However, in contrast to the Thomas hearings, the Simpson trial reinvigorated ideas about fundamental racial differences and internal racial unity, since media reports often reduced a very complex debate to a stereotypical one that pitted black Americans against white Americans.

Senator Barack Obama's 2008 presidential campaign understandably brought race to the center of public discussion. Comments by white American Republicans and Democrats were parsed for their racial overtones, from Georgia representative Lynn Westmoreland's use of the word *uppity* to Senator Joe Biden's characterization of Obama as "the first mainstream African American who is articulate and bright and clean and a nice-looking guy." And in response to public reaction to the controversial sermons of Obama's former pastor, the Reverend Jeremiah Wright, Obama gave what is commonly known as his race speech in March 2008. In that speech, which many place in significance with Abraham Lincoln's second inaugural address and Martin Luther King's "I Have a Dream" speech, Obama, using examples from his friends and family, addressed the historic fears of black and white Americans. He asked all Americans to come together to talk about race in freshly candid and honest ways and to move beyond historic, simplified stereotypes and binary oppositions.

At the dawn of Barack Hussein Obama's historic presidency—which, it is safe to say, no black leader could even have imagined before this century—the influence of race in America is not as easy to define as it was historically, before or even during the civil rights movement. Still, it remains a salient, palpable presence in the very fabric of American life. In spite of unprecedented economic and social progress, conditions continue to be stark for far too many African Americans. Black Americans are disproportionately vulnerable to economic downturns: they are nearly three times more likely than white Americans to fall precipitously from the middle class into poverty or near poverty. Black families have the lowest median income of any ethnic group in America, making only 62 percent of the income of the median white family, and almost 25 percent of black Americans live below the poverty line, nearly three times the percentage of white Americans. Although black people constitute nearly 13 percent of the U.S. population, they make up 36 percent of the prison population and half of the country's murder victims.

Compounding these problems is the fact that contemporary racial discrimination can be remarkably difficult to combat because—unlike, say, previous forms of discrimination in voting or school attendance—it is not codified into laws that can be amended. While *de jure* segregation is dead forever in America, *de facto* segregation is not. For example, overt racial hiring policies are no longer legal, but studies show that black job applicants with no criminal record have less of a chance of being hired for a low-wage job than a white applicant with a felony conviction. The sharp contrast between such statistics and the striking success of many African Americans today indicates the complex mix of color and class that has become the essence of race and racism in America. It will be necessary to delve more subtly than any previous generation of Americans yet has into that complexity of race and economics to address the critical legacies of slavery and segregation that continue to plague America in the twenty-first century. With the increased national focus on race and class following the election of Barack Obama as president of the United States, that arduous process has perhaps begun.

KEY DEBATE ⁓ *Nature, Culture, and Slavery*

PORTIA K. MAULTSBY

Africanisms in African American Music [1990, revised 2005]

The idea that important aspects of African American culture have their roots in African cultures of the past, developed by Melville J. Herskovits (p. 379), has inspired the work of academics in a wide range of fields. In "Africanisms in African American Music," the musicologist Portia K. Maultsby (b. 1947) argues against focusing on particular "survivalisms" from Africa as a way of understanding African cultural influence. Instead, she makes the case for changing a basic idea about culture itself. Instead of viewing culture as "specific cultural elements," Maultsby makes a finely detailed case for seeing culture as a set of frameworks that can be adapted to new environmental and social conditions. Her study of the development of African American music demonstrates how a focus on "conceptual approaches" can shed light on how culture perseveres through time and space.

From James E. Holloway, ed., *Africanisms in American Culture*, 2nd ed. (Bloomington: Indiana University Press, 2005), pp. 326–55.

Since the first quarter of the twentieth century scholars have examined African American history and culture in the context of an African past.[1] Their studies support the premise that the institution of slavery did not destroy the cultural legacy of slaves nor erase the memories of an African past. The survival of slaves in the New World depended on their ability to retain the ideals fundamental to African cultures.

Although slaves were exposed to various European-derived traditions, they resisted cultural imprisonment by the larger society. Slaves adapted to life in the Americas by retaining a perspective on the past. They survived an oppressive existence by creating new expressive forms out of African traditions, and they brought relevance to European American customs by reshaping them to conform to African aesthetic ideals.

1. Historical studies include Ira Berlin, *Slaves without Masters: The Free Negro in the Antebellum South* (New York: Vintage, 1974); Eugene D. Genovese, *Roll, Jordan, Roll: The World the Slaves Made* (New York: Pantheon, 1974); John Blassingame, *The Slave Community* (New York: Oxford University Press, rev. ed., 1979); Gerald W. Mullin, *Flight and Rebellion* (New York: Oxford University Press, 1972); and Robert Haynes, *Blacks in White America before 1865* (New York: David McKay, 1972).

For cultural studies, see John W. Work, *Folk Song of the American Negro* (Nashville, Tenn.: Fisk University Press, 1915; reprinted by Negro Universities Press, New York, 1969); James Weldon and J. Rosamond Johnson, *American Negro Spirituals*, 2 vols. (New York: Viking Press, 1925 and 1926; reprinted in one volume by Da Capo Press, New York, 1969); Zora Neale Hurston, "Spirituals and Neo-Spirituals" [1935], in *Voices from the Harlem Renaissance*, Nathan Huggins, ed. (New York: Oxford University Press, 1976), 344–47; Hall Johnson, "Notes on the Negro Spiritual" [1965], in *Readings in Black American Music*, Eileen Southern, ed. (New York: Norton, 2d ed., 1983), 273–80; Henry Krehbiel, *Afro-American Folksongs* (New York: Ungar, 1914); Melville J. Herskovits, *The Myth of the Negro Past* (Boston: Beacon Press, 1958); Lawrence Levine, *Black Culture and Black Consciousness* (New York: Oxford University Press, 1977); Dena Epstein, *Sinful Tunes and Spirituals* (Urbana: University of Illinois Press, 1977); Alan Dundes, ed., *Mother Wit from the Laughing Barrel* (Englewood Cliffs, N.J.: Prentice-Hall, 1973); Norman E. Whitten and John F. Szwed, eds., *Afro-American Anthropology* (New York: Free Press, 1970); Paul Oliver, *Savannah Syncopators: African Retentions in the Blues* (New York: Stein and Day, 1970); Albert J. Raboteau, *Slave Religion* (New York: Oxford University Press, 1978); Fredrick Kaufman and John Guckin, *The African Roots of Jazz* (Sherman Oaks, Calif.: Alfred Publishing Co., 1979); Olly Wilson, "The Significance of the Relationship between Afro-American Music and West African Music," *Black Perspective in Music* (Spring 1974) 2:3–22; and J. H. Kwabena Nketia, "African Roots of Music in the Americas: An African View," 82–88, Olly Wilson, "The Association of Movement and Music as a Manifestation of a Black Conceptual Approach to Music," 98–105, and David Evans, "African Elements in Twentieth-Century United States Black Folk Music," 54–66, in Report of the 12th Congress, London, American Musicological Society, 1981. [Unless otherwise indicated, all footnotes are those of the author.]

The Evolution of African American Music

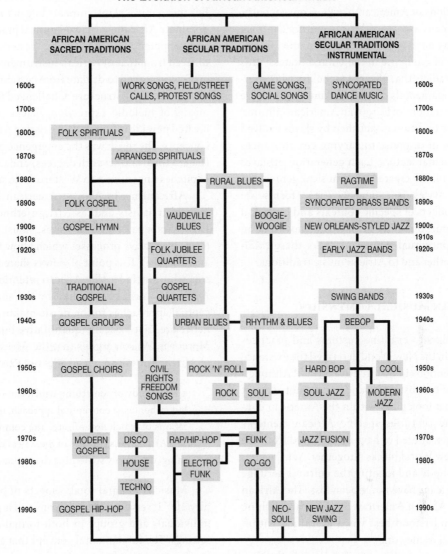

The transformation of African traditions in the New World supports the position of Lawrence Levine that culture is a process rather than a fixed condition. Levine argues that culture is

the product of interaction between the past and present. Its toughness and resiliency are determined not by a culture's ability to withstand change, which indeed may be a sign of stagnation not life, but by its ability to react creatively and responsively to the realities of a new situation.[2]

The continuum of an African consciousness in America manifests itself in the evolution of an African American culture. The music, dance, folklore, religion, language, and other expressive forms associated with

2. Levine, *Black Culture*, 5.

the culture of slaves were transmitted orally to subsequent generations of American blacks. Consequently, Levine adds, many aspects of African culture continue "to exist not as mere vestiges but as dynamic, living, creative parts of group life in the United States." This position contradicts that of earlier scholars who interpreted the fundamentals of African American culture as distorted imitations of European American culture.[3]

The music tradition established by slaves evolved over centuries in response to varying circumstances and environmental factors. Each generation of slaves and freeborn blacks created new musical genres and performance styles (see figure). These forms are unique by-products of specific contexts and historical periods. The purpose of this essay is to show that an identifiable conceptual framework links these traditions to each other and to African music traditions.

THE AFRICAN MUSICAL DIMENSION

The first scholars to examine customs and practices among blacks in the New World described the existence of African retentions in quantitative terms.[4] Although this practice of trait listing is valid, it does not account for changes that took place within the American context. Over the centuries specific African elements either have been altered or have disappeared from the cultures of New World blacks altogether. Yet the concepts that embody and identify the cultural heritage of black Americans have never been lost. The African dimension of African American music is far-reaching and can be understood best when examined within this conceptual framework.

Early accounts of African performance in the New World, for example, document the existence of instruments clearly of African origin.[5] Eventually Western European musical instruments began to infiltrate and dominate African American musical practice. Because the tempered tuning of these Western instruments differed from that of African instruments, black musicians were forced to deviate from certain African principles of melodic structure. Challenged to explore new means of melodic expression, blacks unconsciously created new ideas founded on existing African musical concepts. The result was the emergence of "blue notes" (flatted third and seventh degrees) and the production of pitches uncommon to Western scale structures.

Africanisms in African American music extend beyond trait lists and, as African ethnomusicologist J. H. Kwabena Nketia observes, "must be viewed in terms of creative processes which allow for continuity and change."[6] This point of view is shared by Olly Wilson, who concludes that African retentions in African American music are defined by the sharing of conceptual approaches to the music-making process and hence are "not basically quantitative but qualitative." Moreover, Wilson argues that the African dimension of African American music does not exist as

> a static body of something which can be depleted, but rather [as] a conceptual approach, the manifestations of which are infinite. The common core of this Africanness consists of the way of doing something, not simply something that is done.[7]

Music is integral to all aspects of black community life.[8] It serves many functions and is performed by individuals and groups in both formal and informal settings. The fundamental concept that governs music performance in African and African-derived cultures is that music-making is a participatory group activity

3. For a summary of theories advanced by these writers, see Herskovits, *Myth*, 262–69; Guy B. Johnson, *Folk Culture on St. Helena Island* (Chapel Hill: University of North Carolina Press, 1930); Lawrence Levine, "Slave Songs and Slave Consciousness," in *American Negro Slavery*, Allen Weinstein and Frank Otto Gatell, eds. (New York: Oxford University Press, 2nd ed., 1973), 153–82; and Dena Epstein, "A White Origin for the Black Spiritual? An Invalid Theory and How It Grew," *American Music* (Summer 1983) 1:53–59.
4. Richard Waterman, "African Patterns in Trinidad Negro Music," Ph.D. dissertation, Northwestern University, 1943, 26, 41–42; "Hot Rhythm in Negro Music," *Journal of the American Musicological Society* (1948) 1:24–37; and "On Flogging a Dead Horse: Lessons Learned from the Africanisms Controversy," *Ethnomusicology* (1963) 7:83–87. Alan Lomax, *Folk Song Style and Culture* (Washington, D.C.: American Association for the Advancement of Science, 1968). Herskovits, *Myth*, 261–69. Krehbiel, *Afro-American Folksongs*.
5. For a summary of these accounts, see Epstein, *Sinful Tunes*, 19–99.
6. Nketia, "African Roots," 88.
7. Wilson, "Significance," 20.
8. For a discussion of the way music functions in African societies, see J. H. Kwabena Nketia, *The Music of Africa* (New York: Norton, 1974), 21–50, and Francis Bebey, *African Music: A People's Art*, Josephine Bennett, trans. (New York: Lawrence Hill, 1975), 1–38.

that serves to unite black people into a cohesive group for a common purpose. This use of music in African American communities continues a tradition found in African societies where, as Nketia observes,

> music making is generally organized as a social event. Public performances, therefore, take place on social occasions—that is, on occasions when members of a group or a community come together for the enjoyment of leisure, for recreational activities, or for the performance of a rite, ceremony, festival, or any kind of collective activity.[9]

The conceptualization of music-making as a participatory group activity is evident in the processes by which black Americans prepare for a performance. Since the 1950s, for example, black music promoters have advertised concerts as social gatherings where active audience involvement is expected. Promotional materials encourage potential concertgoers to "Come and be moved by" a gospel music concert or to "Come and jam with," "Come and get down with," or "Come and party with" a secular music concert. As Nketia notes, regardless of context—church, club, dance hall, or concert hall—public performance of black music serves

> a multiple role in relation to the community: it provides at once an opportunity for sharing in creative experience, for participating in music as a form of community experience, and for using music as an avenue for the expression of group sentiments.[1]

This communal approach to music-making is further demonstrated in the way contemporary performers adapt recorded versions of their songs for performance on the concert stage. Many begin their songs with ad lib "rapping" (secular) or "sermonettes" (sacred) to establish rapport with the audience. When the singing actually begins, the style of the performance complements the "we are here to jam" or "we are here to be moved" attitude of the audience/congregation. The

audience/congregation is encouraged to participate in any way, sometimes even to join performers on stage. Soul singer Sam Moore of the duo Sam and Dave recalls how he "would stop the band and get hand-clapping going in the audience [and] make them stand up."[2] Many black performers use this technique to ensure the active participation of audience members in the music event.

Music-making in Africa requires the active involvement of all present at the musical event. This approach to performance generates many of the cultural and aesthetic components that uniquely characterize music-making throughout the African diaspora. In a study of gospel music, ethnomusicologist Mellonee Burnim defines three areas of aesthetic significance in the black music tradition: delivery style, sound quality, and mechanics of delivery.[3] These categories are useful in examining qualities common to both African and African-derived music.

Style of Delivery

Style of delivery refers to the physical mode of presentation—how performers employ body movements, facial expressions, and clothing within the performance context. Burnim accurately asserts that music-making "in Black culture symbolizes vitality, a sense of aliveness."[4] This "aliveness" is expressed through visual, physical, and musical modes, all of which are interrelated in African musical performances. Olly Wilson defines the African musical experience as a

> multi-media one in which many kinds of collective human output are inextricably linked. Hence, a typical traditional [African] ceremony will include music, dance, the plastic arts (in the form of elaborate masks and/or costumes) and perhaps ritualistic drama.[5]

In African American culture, the element of dress in musical performance is as important as the musical

---

9. Nketia, *Music of Africa*, 21.
1. Ibid., 22.
2. Sam Moore, interview with author, Feb. 25, 1983.
3. Mellonee Burnim, "The Black Gospel Music Tradition: A Complex of Ideology, Aesthetic, and Behavior," in *More than Dancing*, Irene V. Jackson, ed. (Westport, Conn.: Greenwood Press, 1985), 154.
4. Ibid., 159.
5. Wilson, "Association of Movement," 99.

sound itself. When performers appear on stage, even before a musical sound is heard, audience members verbally and physically respond if costumes meet their aesthetic expectations. Performers establish an image, communicate a philosophy, and create an atmosphere of "aliveness" through the colorful and flamboyant costumes they wear. In the gospel tradition, Burnim observed that performers dress in "robes of bold, vivid colors and design." She also noted:

> At the 1979 James Cleveland Gospel Music Workshop of America in New Orleans, Louisiana, one evening's activities included a competition to select the best dressed male and female in gospel choir attire. The fashions ranged from brightly colored gowns and tuxedos to matching hooded capes lined in red.[6]

Ethnomusicologist Joyce Jackson, in her study of black gospel quartets, also observed that costumes are judged as part of the overall performance in gospel quartet competitions.[7]

The importance of dress in black music performances is demonstrated further in the popular tradition. In the film *That Rhythm . . . Those Blues,* vocalist Ruth Brown recalled how audiences expected performers to dress in the latest fashions. Responding to this expectation, Brown labeled herself as one of the first female singers

> that became known for the crinoline and multipetticoats and the shoes that matched the dresses. All of the singing groups [of the 1950s and 1960s] were impeccably dressed [in coordinated outfits] when they went on stage. If they wore white shoes . . . they were *white* shoes. Griffin shoe polish made all the money in the world.

The array of colors and fashions seen in concert halls, black churches, and other black performance sites is a vital part of the total visual experience. It is such a fundamental part of black cultural expression that

these same principles of dress are observed by the audience. For example, audiences at Harlem's Apollo theater always wore the latest fashions. During the 1930s, the men "appeared in tight-belted, high-waisted coats" and the women "gracefully glided through the lobby in tight slinky dresses, high heels, and veils."[8]

The visual dimension of performance, according to Burnim's model, extends beyond dress to the physical behavior of musicians and their audiences. In communicating with their audiences, musicians display an intensity of emotion and total physical involvement through use of the entire body. Nketia points out that physical expression is part and parcel of music-making in African cultures:

> The values of African societies do not inhibit this. . . . it is encouraged, for through it, individuals relate to musical events or performing groups, and interact socially with others in a musical situation. Moreover, motor response intensifies one's enjoyment of music through the feelings of increased involvement and the propulsion that articulating the beat by physical movement generates.[9]

Accounts of religious services conducted by slaves illustrate the retention of these cultural values and attitudes in the New World. During the worship, slaves became active participants, freely responding verbally and physically to the sermon, the prayer, the music, and each other. This behavior prompted missionary Charles Colcock Jones to describe a revival meeting of slaves as a "confusion of sights and sounds!"

> Some were standing, others sitting, others moving from one seat to another, several exhorting along the aisles. The whole congregation kept up one loud monotonous strain, interrupted by various sounds: groans and screams and clapping hands. One woman specially under the influence of the excitement went across the church in a quick succession of leaps; now down on her knees with a sharp crack that smote

6. Mellonee Burnim, "Functional Dimensions of Gospel Music Performance," *Western Journal of Black Studies* (Summer 1988) 12:115.
7. Joyce Jackson, "The Performing Black Sacred Quartet: An Expression of Cultural Values and Aesthetics," Ph.D. dissertation, Indiana University, 1988, 161–90.
8. Ted Fox, *Showtime at the Apollo* (New York: Holt, Rinehart and Winston, 1983), 69.
9. Nketia, *Music of Africa*, 206–07.

upon my ear the full length of the church, then up again; now with her arms about some brother or sister, and again tossing them wildly in the air and clapping her hands together and accompanying the whole by a series of short, sharp shrieks.... Considering the mere excitement manifested in these disorderly ways, I could but ask: What religion is there in this?[1]

Observers of other religious gatherings of slaves noted that "there is much melody in their voices; and when they enjoy a hymn, there is a raised expression of the face...." And "they sang so that it was a pleasure to hear, with all their souls and with all their bodies in unison; for their bodies wagged, their heads nodded, their feet stamped, their knees shook, their elbows and their hands beat time to the tunes and the words which they sing...."[2]

The style of delivery that characterized musical performance during the seventeenth, eighteenth, and nineteenth centuries continues to be operative in both sacred and secular spheres of contemporary black America: black people consciously use their entire bodies in musical expression, and music and movement are conceived as a single unit. These concepts clearly are demonstrated in the presentation style of performers of popular music. Soul singer Al Braggs, for example, concluded his shows

> by pulling out all the vocal and choreographic stops...in the general manner of James Brown or Little Richard. He screams; he groans; he crawls rhythmically across the stage on his stomach dragging the microphone behind him; he leaps over, under, and around the microphone behind him; he lies on his back and kicks his feet in the air; he does some syncopated push-ups; he falls halfway over the edge of the stage and grabs the nearest hands; initiating a few unfinished dance steps, he does the limbo; he bumps and grinds; and gradu-

ally maneuvers himself off stage with a flying split or two, still twitching and shouting.[3]

This "unification of song and dance," as Burnim describes it, characterizes contemporary performances of black music. In the gospel tradition, choirs "march" in synchronized movements through the church during the processional and "step," "clap," and "shout" (religious dance) to the music performed during the worship.[4] This intrinsic relationship between music and movement is also seen during performances by popular music groups. Sam Moore commented that he and his partner, Dave Prater, "danced and moved around so much" during their performances that they lost "at least four or five pounds a night in sweat."[5] The accompanying musicians also danced in synchronized steps while playing their instruments, a concept patterned after black marching bands.

Sound Quality

The participatory dimension of music performance is only one aspect of the conceptual approach to music-making. Descriptions of black music performances over several centuries reveal that timbre is a primary feature that distinguishes this tradition from all others. The concept of sound that governs African American music is unmistakably grounded in the African past. As Francis Bebey suggests,

> The objective of African music is not necessarily to produce sounds agreeable to the ear, but to translate everyday experiences into living sound. In a musical environment whose constant purpose is to depict life, nature, or the supernatural, the musician wisely avoids using beauty as his criterion because no criterion could be more arbitrary.
>
> Consequently, African voices adapt themselves to their musical contexts—a mellow tone to welcome a new bride; a husky voice to recount an indiscreet adventure; a satirical inflection for a teasing

1. Letter from Rev. R. Q. Mallard to Mrs. Mary S. Mallard, Chattanooga, May 18, 1859, in *The Children of Pride*, Robert Manson Myers, ed. (New Haven, Conn.: Yale University Press, 1972), 483.
2. Andrew Reed and James Matheson, *A Narrative of the Visit to the American Churches* (London: Jackson and Walford, 1835), 219. Fredrika Bremer, *Homes of the New World*, 1, trans. Mary Howitt (New York: Harper, 1854), 393.
3. Charles Keil, *Urban Blues* (Chicago: University of Chicago Press, 1966), 122.
4. Burnim, "Black Gospel Music Tradition," 160.
5. Sam Moore, interview with author, Feb. 25, 1983.

tone, with laughter bubbling up to compensate for the mockery—they may be soft or harsh as circumstances demand.[6]

In Africa and throughout the diaspora, black musicians produce an array of unique sounds, many of which imitate those of nature, animals, spirits, and speech. They reproduce these sounds using a variety of techniques, including striking the chest and maneuvering the tongue, mouth, cheek, and throat.[7] When arranged in an order and bound together by continuity of time, these sounds form the basis for musical composition.

The unique sound associated with black music results from the manipulation of timbre, texture, and shading in ways uncommon to Western practice. Musicians bring intensity to their performance by alternating lyrical, percussive, and raspy timbres; juxtaposing vocal and instrumental textures; changing pitch and dynamic levels; alternating straight with vibrato tones; and weaving moans, shouts, grunts, hollers, and screams into the melody. The arbitrary notion of beauty has resulted in descriptions of black music as "weird," "strange," "noise," "yelling," "hollering," "hooting," "screaming." The use of these words clearly indicates that the black music tradition does not adhere to European American aesthetic values.

Instrumental sounds in African and African-derived music imitate timbres produced by the voice. Bebey observes that

> Western distinctions between instrumental and vocal music are evidently unthinkable in Africa where the human voice and musical instruments "speak" the same language, express the same feelings, and unanimously recreate the universe each time that thought is transformed into sound.[8]

Black instrumentalists produce a wide range of vocally derived sounds—"hollers," "cries," "grunts,"

"screams," "moans," and "whines," among others—by varying timbre, range, texture, and shading. They create these sounds by altering traditional embouchures, playing techniques, and fingerings and by adding distorting devices.[9] The vocal dimension of instrumental sounds is reflected in such phrases as "make it talk," "talk to me," and "I hear ya talkin' " used by black people to communicate that their aesthetic expectations have been met.

Mechanics of Delivery

The distinct sounds produced by black performers are combined with other aesthetic components to generate a pool of resources for song interpretation. Black audiences demand variety in music performances, and they expect musicians to bring a unique interpretation to each performance and to each song. Black performers meet these expectations in demonstrating their knowledge about technical aspects of performance. Within the African context, Bebey observes that "there is always plenty of scope for improvisation and ornamentation so that individual musicians can reveal their own particular talents and aptitudes. Thus, no two performances of any one piece will be exactly alike."[1] Improvisation is central to the category mechanics of delivery, which forms the third part of Burnim's aesthetic model.

Burnim convincingly argues that time, text, and pitch are the three basic components that form the structural network for song interpretation in black music. The element of time in black music is manipulated in both structural and rhythmic aspects of the performance. Time can be expanded by extending the length of notes at climactic points, by repeating words, phrases, and entire sections of songs, and by adding vocal or instrumental cadenzas. The density of textures can be increased "by gradually adding layers of hand-claps, instrumental accompaniment, and/or solo voices."[2] This latter device, referred to as staggered

6. Bebey, *African Music*, 115.

7. See Ruth M. Stone, "African Music Performed," in *Africa*, Phyllis M. Martin and Patrick O'Meara, eds. (Bloomington: Indiana University Press, 2nd ed., 1986), 236–39, and Bebey, *African Music*, 119–24, for more in-depth discussions of musical sound in African cultures.

8. Bebey, *African Music*, 122.

9. Instrumental playing techniques of black musicians are discussed in Thomas J. Anderson et al., "Black Composers and the Avant-Garde," in *Black Music in Our Culture*, Dominique-René de Lerma, ed. (Kent, Ohio: Kent State University Press, 1970), 66, 68; David Evans, "African Elements," 61; Oliver, *Savannah Syncopators*; and Wilson, "Significance of the Relationship," 15–21.

1. Bebey, *African Music*, 30.

2. Burnim, "Black Gospel," 163.

entrances, characterized the improvised singing of slaves:

> With the first note of the hymn, began a tapping of feet by the whole congregation, gradually increasing to a stamp as the exercises proceeded, until the noise was deafening.... Then in strange contrast to this came the most beautiful melody the negroes have—a chant, carried by full bass voices; the liquid soprano of the melody wandering through and above it, now rising in triumphant swell, now falling in softened cadence.... [3]

The call-response structure is the key mechanism that allows for the manipulation of time, text, and pitch. The response or repetitive chorus provides a stable foundation for the improvised lines of the soloist. The use of call-response structures to generate musical change has been described many times in black music literature.

> These ditties [work songs sung by slaves], though nearly meaningless, have much music in them, and as all join in the perpetually recurring chorus, a rough harmony is produced.... I think the leader improvises the words ... he singing one line alone, and the whole then giving the chorus, which is repeated without change at every line, till the general chorus concludes the stanza.... [4]

The call-response structure also is used by jazz musicians to establish a base for musical change and rhythmic tension.

> [Count] Basie's men played short, fierce riffs. Their riff patterns were not even melodic elements, they were just repetitive rhythmic figures set against each other in the sections of the band. Against this sharp,

pulsing background, Basie set his soloists, and they had free rein. [5]

Perhaps the most noticeable African feature in African American music is its rhythmic complexity. Early descriptions of this tradition reveal that

> Syncopations ... are characteristic of negro music. I have heard negroes change a well-known melody by adroitly syncopating it.... nothing illustrates the negro's natural gifts in the way of keeping a difficult tempo more clearly than his perfect execution of airs thus transformed from simple to complex accentuations. [6]

In both African and African American music, rhythm is organized in multilinear forms. Different patterns, which are repeated with slight, if any, variation, are assigned to various instruments. The combination of these patterns produces polyrhythms. [7] Polyrhythmic structures increase the overall intensity of musical performances because each repetition produces added rhythmic tension. At the same time the repetition of patterns in one part allows for textual and melodic variation in another.

Many accounts of black music have described its repetitious form while noting the creative ways in which performers achieve variety. An example is this 1862 notice:

> Each stanza [of a song sung by slaves] contains but a single thought, set in perhaps two or three bars of music; and yet as they sing it, in alternate recitatives and choruses, with varying inflections and dramatic effect ... [8]

Under the mechanics of delivery category, the element of pitch is manipulated by "juxtaposing voices of

3. [Elizabeth Kilham], "Sketches in Color," *Putnam's,* Mar. 1870, 306.
4. Philip Henry Goose, *Letters from Alabama* (London: Morgan and Chase, 1859), 305.
5. Samuel B. Charters and Leonard Kunstadt, *Jazz: A History of the New York Scene* (New York: Da Capo Press, 1981), 288.
6. Quoted in Epstein, *Sinful Tunes,* 294–95.
7. For discussions of rhythmic structures in black music, see Wilson, "Significance of the Relationship," 3–15; Nketia, *Music of Africa,* 111–38; Evans, "African Elements," 17–18; Portia K. Maultsby, "Contemporary Pop: A Healthy Diversity Evolves from Creative Freedom," *Billboard,* June 9, 1979, BM-22; and Pearl Williams-Jones, "Afro-American Gospel Music," in *Development of Materials for a One Year Course in African Music for the General Undergraduate Student,* Vada Butcher, ed. (Washington, D.C.: Howard University Press, 1970), 211.
8. J[ames Miller] McKim, "Negro Songs," *Dwight's Journal of Music,* Aug. 9, 1862, 148–49.

different ranges or by highlighting the polar extremes of a single voice." Pitch is also varied through the use of "bends, slides, melismas, and passing tones" and other forms of melodic embellishment "in order to achieve the continuous changes, extreme latitude, and personalization"—an identifying trait of black musical expression.[9] "Playing" with pitch—or "worrying the line," as Stephen Henderson calls it[1]—is a technique integral to the solo style of many black performers, including blues singer Bobby Blue Bland.

> All the distinctive features of Bland's vocal style are in evidence, notably the hoarse cry and his use of melisma on key words. Bland's cry usually consists of a twisted vowel at the beginning of a phrase— going from a given note, reaching up to another higher one, and coming back to the starting point.... Almost without exception Bobby uses more than one note per syllable on the concluding word of each phrase.... In slower tempos he will stretch out syllables with even more melisma, using as many as ten or eleven notes over a two-syllable word.[2]

Time, text, and pitch are manipulated by black performers to display their creative abilities and technical skills and to generate an overall intensity within their performance.

When performers create and interpret songs within the aesthetic boundaries framed by black people, audiences respond immediately. Their verbal comments and physical gestures express approval of both the song being performed and the way it is performed. For example, performances by musicians in the popular idiom often are based on principles that govern black worship services. These principles are recognized and valued by black audiences who respond in the same manner as they do to the presentations of black preachers and church choirs. Sam Moore recalled:

> When we performed, we had church. On Sundays the minister would preach and the people in the pews would holler and talk back to him. This is what we started doing. I arranged the parts between Dave and me so that one of us became the preacher and would say "Come on Dave" or "Come on Sam." The audience would automatically shout "Come on Sam" or "Sing Dave" or "Yes Sir." That was our style.[3]

Vocalist Deniece Williams believes that an audience actively participates in her performances because they identify with the gospel roots of her delivery style:

> You hear that [Church of God in Christ] in my music even though it is not the same deliverance of Aretha Franklin. But you feel it. A lot of people say to me "when you sing I feel it." I think that feeling comes from those experiences of church, gospel music and spirituality, which play a big part in my life.[4]

Audiences of Bobby Bland also respond in the character of the Sunday morning service:

> women sprinkled throughout the audience yell back at him, shaking their heads and waving their hands [in response to Bland's melisma].... Suddenly the guitarist doubles the tempo and repeats a particularly funky phrase a few times accompanied by "oohs," "aahs," and "yeahs" from the audience.[5]

When performers demonstrate their knowledge of the black musical aesthetic, the responses of audiences can become so audible that they momentarily drown out the performer. The verbal responses of audiences are accompanied by hand-clapping; foot-stomping; head, shoulder, hand, and arm movement; and spontaneous dance. This type of audience participation is important to performers; it encourages them to explore the full range of aesthetic possibilities, and it is the single criterion by which black artists determine whesther they are meeting the aesthetic expectations of the audience. Songwriter-vocalist Smokey Robinson judges his concerts as unsuccessful if the audience is "not involved in what's happening on the stage."[6]

9. Burnim, "Black Gospel Music Tradition," 165.
1. Stephen Henderson, *Understanding the New Black Poetry* (New York: Morrow, 1973), 41.
2. Keil, *Urban Blues*, 124.
3. Sam Moore, interview with author, Feb. 25, 1983.
4. Deniece Williams, interview with author, Apr. 22, 1983.
5. Keil, *Urban Blues*, 124, 139.
6. Smokey Robinson, radio interview, WBLS, New York City, Jan. 16, 1983.

The concept of "performer-audience" as a single unit is even apparent in the way black people respond to music in nonpublic settings. Twentieth-century technological advances make music accessible twenty-four hours a day, every day. African Americans often use recorded music as a substitute for live performances. While listening to recordings they become involved as active participants, singing along on familiar refrain lines and choruses, snapping their fingers, clapping their hands, moving to the beat, and verbally responding to especially meaningful words or phrases and sounds with "sing it baby," "tell the truth," "play your horn," "tickle them keys," and "get on down." This level of involvement, which replicates interaction at live performances, preserves an African approach to music-making in contemporary society.

Music-making throughout the African diaspora is an expression of life where verbal and physical expression is intrinsic to the process. This conceptual framework links all black music traditions together in the African diaspora while distinguishing these traditions from those of Western and Western-derived cultures. A salient feature of black music is the conceptualization of music-making as a communal/participatory activity. In addition, variation in timbre, song interpretation, and presentation style mirrors the aesthetic priorities of black people.

An African approach to music-making has been translated from one genre to the next throughout African American musical history. Although these genres (see figure) are by-products of specific contexts and time frames, each genre is distinctly African American because it is governed by the conceptual framework already discussed. The remainder of this essay provides a chronology of African American musical forms from slavery to the present.[7] The discussion presents evidence of how this conceptual unity has been transmitted from one African American genre to the next since the first musics were created in the New World.

MUSIC IN THE SLAVE COMMUNITY

For more than 150 years slave traders and slaveholders unwittingly helped preserve an African identity in the African American music tradition. Slave traders brought African instruments on board ships and encouraged slaves to sing and dance for exercise during the long voyage to the New World. These artifacts and creative expressions were among the cultural baggage slaves brought with them to the Americas.[8]

Studies of the institution of slavery point out that slave systems varied throughout the Americas and among colonies in the United States.[9] In situations where slaves had some measure of personal freedom they engaged in leisure activities that clearly reflected their African heritage.[1] In the United States, for example, slaves celebrated holidays for more than two centuries in African style. Two of the most spectacular and festive holidays, 'Lection Day and Pinkster Day celebrations, were observed from the mid-eighteenth through the mid-nineteenth centuries. On 'Lection Day slaves in the New England colonies elected a black governor or king and staged a big parade. Dressed in elaborate outfits, slaves celebrated by playing African games, singing, dancing, and playing African and European instruments in a distinctly African style. Pinkster Day was of Dutch origin, but slaves and free blacks in the North and South transformed it into an African-style festival.[2]

The unique character of the Pinkster Day celebration prompted James Fenimore Cooper[3] to record his impressions:

> Nine tenths of the blacks of the city [New York], and of the whole country within thirty or forty

---

7. My discussion in this limited space necessarily centers on selected genres, but a review of black music literature will show that the principles discussed are applicable to all genres of African American music.

8. See Epstein, *Sinful Tunes,* 8–17.

9. See Laura Foner and Eugene D. Genovese, eds., *Slavery in the New World* (Englewood Cliffs, N.J.: Prentice-Hall, 1969), and Blassingame, *Slave Community.*

1. See Epstein, *Sinful Tunes.*

2. See Eileen Southern, *The Music of Black Americans* (New York: Norton, 2nd ed., 1983), 53–59, and Epstein, *Sinful Tunes,* 66–68.

3. Popular white American writer whose novels include *Last of the Mohicans* (1826). [Editor's note]

miles, indeed, were collected in thousands in those fields, beating banjos [and African drums], singing African songs [accompanied by dancing]. The features that distinguish a Pinkster frolic from the usual scenes at fairs ... however, were of African origin. It is true, there are not now [1845], nor were there then [1757], many blacks among us of African birth; but the traditions and usages of their original country were so far preserved as to produce a marked difference between the festival, and one of European origin.[4]

The diaries of missionaries, travelers, and slaveholders and the accounts of slaves themselves further document that slaves continued to keep African traditions alive in the United States. In 1680 a missionary observed that slaves spent Sundays singing and dancing "as a means to procure Rain." An army general heard his slaves sing a war song in an African language during a visit to his plantation after the Revolutionary War. In another instance, a slave born in 1849 reported that African-born slaves sang their own songs and told stories about African customs during Christmas celebrations. And many observers noted the African flavor of the songs slaves sang while working.[5]

Slaveholders generally did not object to these and other African-derived activities provided they did not interfere with the work routine of slaves. Missionaries, on the other hand, objected to the singing and dancing, which they described as pagan and contrary to the teachings of Christianity. Committed to eliminating these activities, they mounted a campaign to proselytize slaves. Missionaries experienced success in the New England colonies but met resistance among slaveholders in the South, who feared that a change in religious status would alter the social status of slaves as chattel property.[6]

By the nineteenth century southern slaveholders had begun to support the activities of missionaries. Faced with the growing number of slaves who ran away, sabotaged plantation operations, and organized revolts, they believed that tighter control over slaves could be exercised through religion. Many slaveholders allowed their slaves to receive religious instruction, and some even facilitated the process by building "praise houses" on the farms and plantations.[7] Despite these and other efforts, the slaves' acceptance of Christianity was at best superficial. They interpreted Christian concepts and practices through the filter of an African past, transforming the liturgy into an African ritual.

When slaves were allowed to conduct their own religious services, they defied all rules, standards, and structures established by the various denominations and sects. Their services were characterized by an unorthodox sermonizing style, unconventional behavior, and spontaneous musical expressions.[8] Missionaries frequently expressed disapproval of these services:

> The public worship of God should be conducted *with reverence and stillness on the part of the congregation;* nor should the minister—whatever may have been the previous habits and training of the people—encourage demonstrations of approbation or disapprobation, or exclamations, or response, or noises, or outcries of any kind during the progress of divine worship; nor boisterous singing immediately at its close. These practices prevail over large portions of the southern country, and are not confined to one denomination, but appear to some extent in all. I cannot think them beneficial.[9]

Missionaries were especially critical of the music they described as "short scraps of disjointed affirmations ...

---

4. J[ames] Fenimore Cooper, *Satanstoe*, 1 (London: S.&L. Bentley, Wilson, and Fley, 1845), 122–23.

5. Descriptions are found in Morgan Godwyn, *The Negro's and Indians Advocate, Suing for Their Admission to the Church* (London: F. D., 1680), 33; Jeanette Robinson Murphy, "The Survival of African Music in America," *Popular Science* (1899) 55:660–72; Epstein, *Sinful Tunes*, 41, 127–38, 161–83; and Southern, ed., *Readings*, 71–121.

6. See Epstein, *Sinful Tunes*, 63–76, and Charles C[olcock] Jones, *Religious Instruction of the Negroes in the United States* (New York: Negro Universities Press, 1969; reprint of 1842 ed.), 21, for information on the proselytizing activities of missionaries.

7. Praise houses were places designated for the slaves' worship. For detailed information about the conversion of slaves, see Raboteau, *Slave Religion*; Milton Sernett, *Black Religion and American Evangelicalism* (Metuchen, N.J.: Scarecrow Press, 1975); John Lovell, *Black Song: The Forge and the Flame* (New York: Macmillan, 1972), 71–374; and Epstein, *Sinful Tunes*, 100–11, 191–216.

8. See Raboteau, *Slave Religion*; Sernett, *Black Religion*; Epstein, *Sinful Tunes*, 191–237; and Levine, *Black Culture*, 3–80.

9. Quoted in Epstein, *Sinful Tunes*, 201.

lengthened out with long repetitive choruses."[1] The call-response structure and improvisatory style unique to musical performances of slaves did not adhere to European American aesthetic values. These aesthetic differences prompted missionaries to include psalm and hymn singing in the religious instruction of slaves so that they would

> lay aside the extravagant and nonsensical chants, and catches and hallelujah songs of their own composing; and when they sing, which is very often while about their business of an evening in their houses [and in church], they will have something profitable to sing.[2]

In spite of these efforts, slaves continued to sing "songs of their own composing" while adapting psalms and hymns to conform to African aesthetic principles. Henry Russell, an English musician who toured the United States from 1833 to 1841, described this process:

> When the minister gave out his own version of the Psalm, the choir commenced singing so rapidly that the original tune absolutely ceased to exist— in fact, the fine old psalm tune became thoroughly transformed into a kind of negro melody; and so sudden was the transformation, by accelerating the time, that, for a moment, I fancied that not only the choir but the little congregation intended to get up a dance as part of the service.[3]

One observer who witnessed the changing of a hymn into a "Negro song" commented that "Watts and Newton[4] would never recognize their productions through the transformation they have undergone at the hands of their colored admirers."[5]

Other descriptions of religious services conducted by slaves confirm that they frequently fashioned Prot-estant psalms, hymns, and spiritual songs into new compositions by altering the structure, text, melody, and rhythm. They transformed the verse structure of the original song into a call-response or repetitive chorus structure; replaced the original English verse with an improvised text of African and English words and phrases; wove shouts, moans, groans, and cries into the melody of the improvised solo; substituted a faster tempo for the original one; and produced polyrhythmic structures by adding syncopated foot-stomped and hand-clapped patterns.[6] The body of religious music created or adapted by slaves and performed in a distinctly African style became known as "folk spirituals."

The religious tradition of slaves dominated the eighteenth- and nineteenth-century literature on African American music. The scarcity of information on the secular tradition results in part from the reluctance of slaves to sing secular songs in the presence of whites. Missionaries discouraged slaves from singing secular songs, and slaves responded by going underground with these songs. The few accounts of secular music performances nevertheless confirm that this tradition shares the aesthetic qualities characteristic of folk spirituals:

> The negroes [a dozen stout rowers] struck up a song to which they kept time with their oars; and our speed increased as they went on, and become warmed with their singing. . . . A line was sung by a leader, then all joined in a short chorus; then came another [improvised] solo line, and another short chorus, followed by a longer chorus. . . . Little regard was paid to rhyme, and hardly any to the number of syllables in a line; they condensed four or five into one foot, or stretched out one to occupy the space that should have been filled with four or five; yet they never spoiled the tune.[7]

1. Southern, *Readings*, 63.
2. Jones, *Religious Instruction*, 266.
3. Henry Russell, *Cheer! Boys, Cheer!: Memories of Men and Music* (London: John Macqueen, Hastings House, 1895), 85.
4. British hymn writers Isaac Watts and John Newton (1725–1807). [Editor's note]
5. [Kilham], "Sketches," 309.
6. See Portia K. Maultsby, "Afro-American Religious Music 1619–1861," Ph.D. dissertation, University of Wisconsin–Madison, 1974, 182; Epstein, *Sinful Tunes*, 217–358; and Murphy, "Survival of African Music," 660–62. These aesthetic concepts may be heard on recordings: *Been in the Storm So Long*, recorded by Guy Carawan on Johns Island, South Carolina (Folkways Records FS 3842); *Afro-American Spirituals, Work Songs, and Ballads*, ed. Alan Lomax, Library of Congress Music Division (AAPS L3); *Negro Religious Songs and Services*, ed. B. A. Botkin, Library of Congress Music Division (AAFS L10).
7. Epstein, *Sinful Tunes*, 169–70. The secular musical tradition of slaves is discussed in Levine, *Black Culture*, 15; Harold Courlander, *Negro Folk Music U.S.A.* (New York: Columbia University Press, 1963), 80–88, 89–122, 146–61; and Epstein, 161–90.

As in the folk spiritual tradition, the call-response structure allowed for improvised solos and recurring refrain lines.

MUSIC IN THE FREE COMMUNITY

The northern states began to abolish slavery during the first half of the nineteenth century. Yet freed slaves were faced with discriminatory state legislation that once again placed restrictions on their mobility. The small percentage of freed slaves who lived in the South were in precarious positions because their "color suggested servitude, but [their] status secured a portion of freedom." Only a "portion of freedom" was theirs because legislation barred southern free blacks from participating in mainstream society.[8] Determined to create a meaningful life, freed blacks in the North and South established communities and institutions where they defined their own mode of existence and cultural frame of reference.[9] The black church became the center of community life, serving an array of functions—religious, cultural, social, educational, and political. Within this context, many blacks kept alive the cultural traditions and musical practices associated with the praise houses of the South.[1]

The abolition of slavery in the South temporarily disrupted the communal solidarity of the slave community. Individually and in small groups, African Americans attempted to establish new lives within the larger society. Some migrated from rural areas to cities and from South to North in search of social, political, and economic viability. Discriminatory practices, however, restricted their employment possibilities to such menial roles as domestic servants, janitors, chauffeurs, and delivery boys. Many could not find even menial jobs and, as a last resort, worked as sharecroppers on the land they had farmed as slaves. Others attempted to take advantage of educational opportunities to upgrade their social status. Despite these efforts toward "self-improvement," the broader society continued to control the mobility of blacks, forcing the masses to remain economically dependent on whites.[2]

The Fourteenth Amendment to the U.S. Constitution, ratified in 1868, guaranteed citizenship to freed slaves, and the Fifteenth Amendment of 1870 gave black men voting rights. Yet African Americans became victims of discriminatory state legislation.[3] Many blacks survived as free persons in America because they relied on their traditional past for direction. They created a meaningful existence by preserving old values, fashioning new ones when necessary, and reestablishing the group solidarity they had known as slaves.

For many decades following the Civil War, blacks continued to make music from an African frame of reference. White northerners who migrated south to assist blacks in their transition into mainstream society were especially critical of this practice among children at school:

> In the infant schoolroom, the benches were first put aside, and the children ranged along the wall. Then began a wild droning chant in a minor key, marked with clapping of hands and stamping of feet. A dozen or twenty rose, formed a ring in the centre of the room, and began an odd shuffling dance. Keeping time to this weird chant they circled round, one following the other, changing their step to quicker and wilder motion, with louder clapping of the hands as the fervor of the singers reached a climax. The words of their hymns are simple and touching. The verses consist of two lines, the first being repeated twice. . . . As I looked upon the faces of these little barbarians and watched them circling round in this fetish

8. Richard C. Wade, *Slavery in the Cities: The South 1820–1860* (New York: Oxford University Press, 1964), 249.

9. Leon F. Litwack, *North of Slavery* (Chicago: University of Chicago Press, 1961), 14, 64.

1. For descriptions of services associated with independent black churches, see Berlin, *Slaves without Masters,* 284–303; Wade, *Slavery in the Cities,* 160–76; Epstein, *Sinful Tunes,* 197, 223; Portia K. Maultsby, "Music of Northern Independent Black Churches during the Ante-Bellum Period," *Ethnomusicology,* Sept. 1975, 407–18; Avrahm Yarmolinsky, ed., *Picturesque United States of America: 1811, 1812, 1813* (New York: William Edwin Rudge, 1930), 20; and Southern, *Readings,* 52–70.

2. Information about the status of blacks after the Civil War may be found in E. Franklin Frazier, *The Negro in the United States* (New York: Macmillan, 1949), 171–272; Levine, *Black Culture,* 136–70; C. Vann Woodward, *The Strange Career of Jim Crow* (New York: Oxford University Press, 2nd rev. ed., 1966), 11–65; and Jeff Todd Titon, *Early Downhome Blues: A Musical and Cultural Analysis* (Urbana: University of Illinois Press, 1977), 3–15.

3. See Frazier, *Negro in the United States,* 123–68; Woodward, *Strange Career,* 11–65; and Michael Haralambos, *Right On: From Blues to Soul in Black America* (New York: Drake, 1975), 50–51.

dance, doubtless the relic of some African rite, I felt discouraged.... However, the recollection of the mental arithmetic seemed a more cheerful view of the matter.[9]

Another observer concluded that common aesthetic features link the secular and religious traditions:

> Whatever they sing is of a religious character, and in both cases [performances of secular and religious music] they have a leader ... who starts a line, the rest answering antiphonally as a sort of chorus. They always keep exquisite time and tune, and no words seem too hard for them to adapt to their tunes.... Their voices have a peculiar quality, and their intonations and delicate variations cannot be reproduced on paper.[1]

These descriptions confirm that African aesthetic concepts—of music and movement as a single unit, the varying timbres, the shadings, and the use of call-response structures to manipulate time, text, and pitch—remained vital to black musical expression in postbellum African American culture.

Other accounts of postbellum black music reveal that both children and adults continued to sing songs from the past while creating new musical forms out of existing traditions.[2] As I wrote in an earlier essay, "The old form persisted alongside the new and remained a vital form of expression within specific contexts."[3] The new idioms, including blues, jazz, gospel, and popular music, became a unifying and sustaining force in the free black community. These and the older forms reaffirmed the values of an African past and simultaneously expressed a sense of inner strength and optimism about the future.

The secular music tradition became increasingly important. Even though missionaries had attempted to discourage slaves from singing secular songs, many free blacks asserted their independence by responding to the daily events in their lives through secular song. The secular form that became and remains particularly important to African American culture is the blues.

The blues form shares general features and aesthetic qualities with past music traditions. It combines the musical structure and poetic forms of spirituals, work songs, and field cries with new musical and textual ideas. The improvisatory performance style emphasizes call-response (between the voice and accompanying instruments). Integral to the melody are slides, slurs, bends, and dips, and the timbres vary from moans, groans, and shouts to song-speech utterances.[4] The accompanying instruments—guitar, fiddle, piano, harmonica, and sometimes tub basses, washboards, jugs, a wire nailed to the side of a house, and other ad hoc instruments—are played in an African-derived percussive style.[5]

For more than a hundred years the essence of the blues tradition has remained the same. Amplified instruments added in the 1940s, rhythm sections in the 1950s, and horns in the 1960s are perhaps the only significant—yet in a sense only superficial—changes that have taken place in this tradition. In the twentieth century the "blues sound" crossed into the sacred world, giving life to an original body of sacred music called gospel.

Gospel music is a by-product of the late nineteenth- and early-twentieth-century black "folk church." This church, associated with the Holiness and Pentecostal sects, is a contemporary version of plantation praise houses. Its character, as Pearl Williams-Jones has stated, "reflects the traditional cultural values of Black folk life as it has evolved since slave days, and is a cumulative expression of the Black experience."[6] The black folk church is distinguished from black denominational

9. Quoted in Epstein, *Sinful Tunes*, 281–82.
1. J[ames] W[entworth] Leigh, *Other Days* (New York: Macmillan, 1921), 156.
2. Ibid., 274–81, and Levine, *Black Culture*, 191–217, 239–70.
3. Portia K. Maultsby, "The Role of Scholars in Creating Space and Validity for Ongoing Changes in Black American Culture," in *Black American Culture and Scholarship* (Washington, D.C.: Smithsonian Institution, 1985), 11.
4. See Samuel Charters, *The Bluesmen* (New York: Oak Publications, 1967); Haralambos, *Right On*, 76–82; Titon, *Early Downhome Blues*; Levine, *Black Culture*, 217–24; Keil, *Urban Blues*, 50–68; Oliver, *Savannah Syncopators*, 36–66; and Evans, "African Elements," 57–62.
5. See William Ferris, *Blues from the Delta* (New York: Anchor Press, 1978), 37–38; David Evans, "Afro-American One-Stringed Instruments," *Western Folklore* (Oct. 1970) 29:229–45; Oliver, *Savannah Syncopators*, 37–38; and Evans, "African Elements," 59–60.
6. Pearl Williams-Jones, "The Musical Quality of Black Religious Folk Ritual," *Spirit* (1977) 1:21.

churches by the structure and nature of its service, religious practices, and philosophical concepts and the socioeconomic background of its members. The official doctrine of the folk church encourages spontaneous expressions through improvised song, testimonies, prayers, and praises from individuals.[7] Unlike other black churches, the folk church did not evolve from white Protestant denominations. Its musical repertoire, therefore, is distinctly different from that of mainline Protestant churches.

The music of the folk church, known as "church songs," has as its basic repertoire the folk spirituals and modified hymns sung by slaves in plantation praise houses. The new songs that became standards in the folk church were created spontaneously during the service by the preacher and congregation members, and they were performed in the style of folk spirituals. The only substantive change made in this tradition was the addition of musical instruments to the established accompaniment of hand-clapping and foot-stomping.[8] These instruments included tambourines, drums, piano, guitar, various horns and ad hoc instruments, and later the organ. The "bluesy," "jazzy," and "rockin'" sounds from these instruments brought a secular dimension to black religious music. The instrumental accompaniment, which became an integral part of religious music in the folk church, defined new directions for black religious music in the twentieth century.

During the first two decades of this century, the prototype for gospel music was established in the folk church. Horace Boyer noted, however, that members of this church "were not the first to receive recognition as gospel singers. Until the forties, Holiness churches did not allow their members to sing their songs before non-Holiness persons."[9] This policy did not confine the emerging gospel sound to the Holiness church. Members of the black community whose homes surrounded these churches were well aware of their existence.

Gospel music first reached the black masses as a "composed" form through the compositions of ministers and members of black Methodist and Baptist churches. Charles Albert Tindley, a Methodist minister in Philadelphia, created the prototype for a composed body of black religious music between 1900 and 1906. Some of these songs were hymnlike verses set to the melodies and rhythms of folk church songs; others were adaptations of spirituals and revival hymns.[1]

In the 1920s the Baptist songwriter Thomas Dorsey used Tindley's model to compose an identifiable and distinct body of black religious music called gospel. The former blues-jazz pianist organized his compositions around the verse-chorus form in which is embedded the call-response structure. Drawing from his blues background, he fashioned his melodies and harmonies using blues scale structures and developed a "rockin'" piano accompaniment in the boogie-woogie and ragtime traditions.

Unlike other black music genres, gospel songs often are disseminated as printed music. Yet the score provides only a framework from which performers interpret and improvise. Gospel music performances are governed by the same aesthetic concepts associated with the folk spiritual tradition. In interpreting the score, performers must demonstrate their knowledge of the improvisatory devices that characterize black music performances.

For more than eighty years the gospel tradition has preserved and transmitted the aesthetic concepts fundamental to music-making in Africa and African-derived cultures. Since its birth in the Holiness and Pentecostal churches it has found a home in storefront churches of various denominations and in many black middle-class Baptist, Methodist, Episcopal, and Catholic churches. The impact of gospel has been so great that its colorful African-derived kaleidoscope of oratory, poetry, drama, and dance and its musical style

---

7. See ibid., 23, 25, and Melvin D. Williams, *Community in a Black Pentecostal Church* (Pittsburgh: University of Pittsburgh Press, 1974), for religious practices associated with this church.

8. See Pearl Williams-Jones, "Afro-American Gospel Music: A Crystallization of the Black Aesthetic," *Ethnomusicology* (Sept. 1975) 19:374, 381, 383; Levine, *Black Culture*, 179–80; and Mellonee Burnim, "The Black Gospel Music Tradition: A Symbol of Ethnicity," Ph.D. dissertation, Indiana University, 1980. A variety of instruments used to accompany early gospel music may be heard on *An Introduction to Gospel Song*, compiled and edited by Samuel B. Charters (RBF Records RF5).

9. Horace Boyer, "Gospel Music," *Music Education Journal* (May 1978) 64:37.

1. Arna Bontemps, "Rock, Church, Rock!" [*Common*] *Ground* (Autumn 1942) 3:35–39. Bontemps gives the years 1901–06 as the period when Tindley wrote his first songs, whereas Boyer believes the period to be between 1900 and 1905.

established a reservoir of cultural resources that contributed to the development of black popular music.

New secular forms of black musical expression were created in response to changes in society following World War II. The war years stimulated growth in the American economy, which in turn led to changes in the lives of black Americans. As I recounted in an earlier monograph, almost two million southern rural blacks abandoned "their low-paying domestic, sharecropping and tenant-farming jobs for work in factories located throughout the country. In cities, both Blacks and whites earned the highest wages in American history. So Americans, especially Black Americans, had much to celebrate during the postwar years."[2] The music to which they celebrated was termed rhythm and blues—a hybrid form rooted in the blues, gospel, and swing band traditions.

Blacks left the rural South with expectations of improving their economic, social, and political status. They soon discovered that opportunities for advancement in society were limited and that the segregated structure of cities restricted their mobility. Discriminatory housing laws, for example, forced many blacks to live and socialize in designated sections of cities—ghettos. These and other patterns of discrimination led to the reestablishment of familiar institutions, thereby continuing southern traditions and practices in the urban metropolis.

The ambiance of southern jukejoints was transferred to blues bars, lounges, and clubs, which became the center of social gatherings in urban cities. Southern music traditions—blues and jazz—were central to the activity in these establishments. The segregated environment, the faster pace, the factory sounds, the street noises, and the technology of the metropolis gave a different type of luster, cadence, and sophistication to existing black musical forms. In response to new surroundings, the familiar sounds of the past soon were transformed into an urban black music tradition.

Blues, jazz, and gospel performers were among the millions of blacks who moved to the cities. They joined forces to create an urban-sounding dance music, rhythm and blues. This music is characterized by a boogie bass line, "riffing" jazz-derived horn arrangements, blues-gospel piano, "honking" and "screaming" tenor sax, "whining" blues guitar, and syncopated drum patterns. The intensity of this sound was increased by the addition of blues and former gospel singers who "moaned" and "shouted" about life in the city. The rhythmic complexity and the performance style of rhythm and blues music preserved traditional values in the music of the city dwellers.

The spirit that captured the excitement of postwar city living began to fade in the mid-1950s. Conditions deteriorated, and life continued to be harsh for many African Americans, especially the inner-city dwellers. They responded by organizing a series of grass-roots protest activities that quickly gained momentum and attracted national attention. The spread of these political activities throughout the country was the impetus behind the civil rights and black power movements of the 1950s and 1960s. "Soul music" was a byproduct of the 1960s movements.[3]

Leaders of the black power movement encouraged the rejection of standards and values of the broader society and a return to values of an African past. Many soul music performers became ambassadors for this movement. Through song they communicated its philosophy, advocating an awareness of an African heritage, encouraging the practice of African traditions, and promoting the concept of black pride. Their "soul message" was communicated in a style that captured the climate of the times and the spirit of a people. This style embraces all the aesthetic qualities that define the essence of the gospel tradition.[4]

2. Portia K. Maultsby, *Rhythm and Blues (1945–1955): A Survey of Styles* (Washington, D.C.: Smithsonian Institution, 1986), 6.
3. For a history of these movements, see Martin Luther King, Jr., *Why We Can't Wait* (New York: Signet, 1964), and Stokely Carmichael and Charles V. Hamilton, *Black Power: The Politics of Liberation in America* (New York: Vintage, 1967).
4. Portia K. Maultsby, "Soul Music: Its Sociological and Political Significance in American Popular Culture," *Journal of Popular Culture* (Fall 1983) 17: 51–52. Many James Brown recordings released between 1969 and 1974 illustrated the black pride concept in soul music; also see Cliff White, "After 21 Years, Still Refusing to Lose," *Black World,* Apr. 1977, 36. Other performers whose music reflected the social climate of the 1960s and early 1970s include the Impressions, "We're a Winner" and "This Is My Country"; Marvin Gaye, "Inner City Blues"; Staple Singers, "Respect Yourself" and "Be What You Are"; Gladys Knight and the Pips, "Friendship Train"; O'Jays, "Back Stabbers" and "Love Train"; Sly and the Family Stone, "Thank You for Talkin' to Me Africa," "Africa Talks to You," and "The Asphalt Jungle"; Temptations, "Cloud Nine"; and Diana Ross and the Supremes, "Love Child."

The interrelatedness of soul and gospel music is illustrated through the interchangeability of the genres. For example, many gospel songs have been recorded under the label "soul" and vice versa. In some instances the text is the only feature that distinguishes one style from another. In others, genre identification may be determined only by the musical identity of the artist who first recorded the song. Performances of soul and gospel music further illustrate that an aesthetic conceptual framework links the secular and sacred traditions to each other.

The era of soul music reawakened the consciousness of an African past. It sanctioned the new thrust for African exploration and simultaneously gave credence to an obscured heritage. This profound era also established new directions in black popular music that would continue to merge African expressions into new forms. The decade of the 1970s heralded this new music.

The 1960s ended with the anticipation of new opportunities for economic independence and full participation in mainstream life. Affirmative action, school desegregation, and other legislation was passed, and the early 1970s implied future changes in the structure of society. Such legislation cultivated a renewed sense of optimism among blacks, and many began to explore new economic, political, and social opportunities outside the black community.

By the mid-1970s this optimism had begun to fade with increased opposition to affirmative action legislation. The economic recession and the "reverse discrimination" concept of the 1970s led to a retrenchment of civil rights and economic opportunities designed to effect equality for blacks. Whites protested against busing and affirmative action policies. In response, the federal government retreated on earlier commitments to rights for blacks. The "gains"

made in the early 1970s gave way to fiscal and social conservatism in the late 1970s and the 1980s. The general opposition to any social advantages for blacks fostered a return to the status quo where racism shaped the American ethos.[5]

Blacks responded to the realities of the 1970s and 1980s in diverse ways and with mixed feelings. Many assessed progress toward social, economic, and political equality as illusory at best. Some felt conditions had worsened, though a few privileged blacks believed the situation had improved.[6] The ambivalent feelings about social progress for blacks found its expression in new and diverse forms of black popular music—funk, disco, rap music, and personalized or trademark forms.

The song lyrics and music styles of funk, disco, and rap music epitomize the changing and sometimes conflicting viewpoints about progress. Although many performers continued to express optimism about the future, some introduced lyric themes of frustration, disillusionment, and distress. The "soul sound" dominated during the first half of the 1970s, but by the mid-1970s it had been transformed. Whereas soul carries the trademark of "message music," funk, disco, and rap music bore the stamp of "party" music.[7] It injected a new spirit of life into black communities and became a major unifying force for a core of African Americans. This spirit is reflected in the lyric themes: "party," "have a good time," "let yourself go," and "dance, dance, dance." These themes suggest that the music had a therapeutic function. Rather than communicate political or intellectual messages, it encouraged blacks to release tension by simply being themselves. At the same time, the infectious beat of this music created an atmosphere that allowed for self-expression and unrestricted social interactions.

5. See Gerald R. Gill, *Meanness Mania: The Changed Mood* (Washington, D.C.: Howard University Press, 1980); Faustine Childress Jones, *The Changing Mood: Eroding Commitment?* (Washington, D.C.: Howard University Press, 1977); Harry C. Triandis, *Variations in Black and White Perceptions of the Social Environment* (Urbana: University of Illinois Press, 1976); Angus Campbell, *White Attitudes toward Black People* (Ann Arbor: Institute for Social Research, University of Michigan, 1971); Charles Murray, *Losing Ground: American Social Policy, 1950–1980* (New York: Basic Books, 1984); George Davis and Glegg Watson, *Black Life in Corporate America* (New York: Anchor, 1982); William Moore, Jr., and Lonnie H. Wagstaff, *Black Educators in White Colleges* (San Francisco: Jossey-Bass, 1974); Marvin W. Peterson, Robert T. Blackburn, et al., *Black Students on White Campuses: The Impacts of Increased Black Enrollments* (Ann Arbor: Institute for Social Research, University of Michigan, 1978); and Janet Dewart, ed., *The State of Black America* (New York: National Urban League, 1987).
6. See Gill, *Meanness Mania;* Jones, *Changing Mood;* and Dewart, ed., *The State of Black America.*
7. Maultsby, "Role of Scholars," 19–21.

Funk, disco, and rap music are grounded in the same aesthetic concepts that define the soul music tradition. Yet the sound is distinguished from soul because emphasis is given to different musical components. These forms of the late 1970s are conceived primarily as dance music where melody plays a secondary role to rhythm. The African-derived polyrhythmic structures, the call-response patterns, and the quasi-spoken group vocals generate audience participation. The percussive sounds and timbral qualities of synthesizers and other electronic devices add another dimension to the black sound. The musical and cultural features in 1970s and 1980s popular traditions continue to give credence to the vitality of an African past in contemporary forms of black music.

CONCLUSIONS

A study of African American music from the seventeenth through the twentieth centuries reveals that African retentions in African American music can be defined as a core of conceptual approaches. Fundamental to these approaches is the axiom that music-making is conceived as a communal/participatory group activity. Black people create, interpret, and experience music out of an African frame of reference—one that shapes musical sound, interpretation, and behavior and makes black music traditions throughout the world a unified whole.

The New World experiences of black people encouraged them to maintain ties to their African past. This unspoken association enabled them to survive and create a meaningful existence in a world where they were not welcomed. They adapted to environmental changes and social upheavals by relying on familiar traditions and practices. Music played an important role in this process. Although specific African songs and genres eventually disappeared from the culture of African Americans, Nketia points out that new ones were "created in the style of the tradition, using its vocabulary and idiom, or in an alternative style which combined African and non-African resources."[8] In essence, new ideas were recycled through age-old concepts to produce new music styles. The fundamentals of culture established by slaves persist in the twentieth century; they are reinterpreted as social times demand. African retentions in African American culture, therefore, exist as conceptual approaches—as unique ways of doing things and making things happen—rather than as specific cultural elements.

KARA WALKER
Out of Africa [1999]

In the 1990s, the influence of African cultures and of slavery on American culture continued to be explored through the arts. In this work, Kara Walker (b. 1969) juxtaposes starkly racial themes and an old-fashioned, genteel medium (cut-paper silhouettes, whose popularity peaked in the early nineteenth century) to create a striking visual commentary on American history. *Out of Africa* visually captures the idea that African culture is foundational to American culture, but focusing on white figures makes the black influence difficult to see. While the white male figure in *Out of Africa* at first appears dominant, he is actually "being reshaped by an African hand," as Walker said in a *New York Times Magazine* interview. Walker evokes the net of slavery with an image of a web, but she reverses it, trapping the white figure while the black African figures surrounding him are free. In this way, Walker suggests that white culture is trapped by the unacknowledged legacy of slavery and the myth of an uncomplicated colonial heritage.

From *The New York Times Magazine*, September 19, 1999.

8. Nketia, "African Roots," 83–84.

ROY L. BROOKS
from *The Case for a Policy of Limited Separation* [1996]

In 1996, law professor Roy L. Brooks (b. 1950) published *Integration or Separation? A Strategy for Racial Equality*, where the following reading appears. In his systematic argument for a middle ground between integration and separation, Brooks builds on the foundation of civil rights legislation. He underscores that his support for limited separation is a means to an end, not an end in itself, thereby distinguishing himself from black nationalists ranging from Marcus Garvey (p. 259) to Malcolm X (p. 516). Instead, Brooks's conclusions evoke the pragmatic strategies that have been proposed by such leaders as "Sidney" (p. 92), Josephine Turpin Washington (p. 196), and W. E. B. Du Bois (p. 199) and date back to before the Civil War.

From Roy L. Brooks, *Integration or Separation? A Case for Racial Equality* (Cambridge, Mass.: Harvard University Press, 1996), pp. 199–213.

THE ESSENTIAL FEATURES

In proposing limited separation as a legitimate and desirable civil rights policy, I do *not* argue that racial integration should be jettisoned. In a better world I would strongly favor a policy of racial integration over one of limited separation. Even in our imperfect world, I would not personally pursue a course of limited separation, because racial integration has worked well for me and my family. But, as we have seen, it has failed many others. And it just may be that although I have thrived under racial integration thus far, tomorrow may be a different story for me or my children. Hence, notwithstanding my strong personal preference for a policy of racial integration, I think it is necessary to make some form of racial separation available *as an option* for those African Americans or others who need it to legitimately enhance individual opportunity. Limited separation still leaves ample room for many traditional liberal civil rights strategies.

Limited separation, then, promotes racial equality, by which I mean individual dignity and empowerment. It is an aggressive strategy of racial inclusion in mainstream society, providing the best path for many African Americans to achieve worldly success in a racist society without the aid of affirmative action. It leaves African Americans to themselves to create their own "civil rights."

Limited separation can be defined as *any racial or gender classification that promotes individual opportunity but that does not unnecessarily subordinate or trammel the interests of individuals inside or outside the group.* This sort of separation can be established for any racial or gender group. It is not limited to African Americans. To simplify the discussion, my elaboration and application of the concept will, however, focus primarily on African Americans.

Limited separation is allowable only if three conditions are met. The racial classification must have a "good end," a racially compensatory purpose; it must not unnecessarily subordinate individuals within and outside the group; and it may deny an opportunity to a member of another race only if race is established as a bona fide selection qualification (or bfsq). The third condition—the bfsq principle—is obviously an extension of the second condition—the unnecessary subordination principle. I shall elaborate on each condition, or principle, in turn.

Good Ends

A racial classification must have a racially compensatory or worthwhile purpose. This condition is best satisfied when the purpose is to provide a needed supportive environment for individuals within the racial group. In the case of African Americans, this condition is easily met when the purpose of the racial classification is to redress the uneven distribution of poker chips—the socioeconomic and cultural advantages whites have accumulated over African Americans over the years—without attempting a redistribution along racial lines. [***]

Any classification designed to ease racial suffering serves a socially worthwhile and even noble end. But it is important to stress that individual opportunity is key to satisfying the good-ends principle. The helping hand must extend to the individual rather than to the group itself. I would therefore disagree with traditional African American separatists like Marcus Garvey and Malcolm X, inasmuch as they saw one form of racial classification—namely, the African American community—as an end in itself. To my mind the community has instrumental rather than intrinsic value; it exists only for the purpose of facilitating opportunities for African Americans individually. Obviously, the group will benefit from the achievements of many individuals, which is quite desirable, but it must be understood that the community exists primarily to serve the individual.

No form of limited separation should sacrifice the individual to the group. I specifically want to avoid the practices of Black Nationalist groups like the Black Panther Party, whose various expressions of racial separatism in the 1960s (school lunch programs, African American heritage events, and community centers) routinely subordinated women, even party members, in the name of some mystical communal purpose. The minute it ceases to serve the individual, limited separation forfeits its legitimacy.

Unnecessary Subordination

The racial classification must help African Americans without unnecessarily hurting whites. An African American institution such as a public school or employer cannot routinely discriminate against whites by barring them from the institution. Even though such pre-clusion might create opportunities for more African Americans, it would only be acceptable if the admission of whites altered the character and benefits of the institution.

For example, an African American public school established in an African American community must admit white students residing within the school district. There are two conditions for their admission, however. First, they must come with the understanding that this school is set up to deal with the special problems of African American students. Second, they must not tip the school's racial balance from African American to white. This could only happen if the existing white student population is extremely high, which is unlikely. Under these circumstances, race could be considered a bfsq.

Bona Fide Selection Qualification

In civil rights law, some practices otherwise impermissible are deemed permissible under certain circumstances. For example, Title VII of the 1964 Civil Rights Act prohibits employers from making hiring or promotion decisions on the basis of religion, sex, or national origin. An exception is carved out, however, "where religion, sex, or national origin is a bona fide occupational qualification reasonably necessary to the normal operation of that particular business or enterprise."[1] The Supreme Court has interpreted this statement to mean that the employer must have a factual basis for believing that all or substantially all women, for example, would be unable to perform essential job duties safely and efficiently.[2] There is a similar defense for employment decisions based on age under the Age Discrimination in Employment Act,[3] but there is no such defense for race. Congress felt that racial discrimination could never be justified. Of course, this belief has proved to be false, as Congress and the Supreme Court have sustained racial discrimination in the context of affirmative action, at least for now.

I would permit an employer or any other institution to establish a selection qualification in the context of limited separation, to be applied in individual cases

---

1. § 703(e)(1), 42 U.S.C. §2000e-2(e). [Unless otherwise indicated, all footnotes are those of the author.]
2. See *Western Air Lines, Inc. v. Criswell*, 472 U.S. 400 (1985); *International Union, UAW v. Johnson Controls, Inc.*, 111 S.Ct. 1196 (1991).
3. 29 U.S.C § 623(f)(1).

rather than systemically. Thus an African American law firm whose essential purpose is to service the legal and social needs of the African American community and to provide positive role models for young African Americans could use the bfsq defense to deny employment to a qualified white attorney if hiring the attorney would impede the firm's ability to fulfill its essential purpose. There would have to be a factual basis to support this belief. Hiring one or a few white lawyers will not satisfy this burden. Hiring enough to change the firm's character from African American to white would. This, of course, is largely a subjective determination, but so are all difficult questions of law.

White law firms may also be able to use the bfsq defense, but it would be harder for them to do so. A large Wall Street law firm, whose essential purpose is to service the legal problems of large corporations, would have a more difficult time establishing the bfsq defense than a small law firm located in Little Italy, there to service the legal and social needs of the Italian community.

If small enough (fewer than 15 employees) the Italian law firm would be exempted from Title VII's prohibition against discrimination anyway. The same holds true for the African American law firm. So my proposal is not as "radical" as it might seem at first glance.

IN THE HEADLINES
Black–Jewish Relations: Redux

Henry Louis Gates, Jr.: *Black Demagogues and Pseudo-Scholars* [1992]
Louis Farrakhan and Tim Russert: from Interview on *Meet the Press* [1997]

In the 1990s, nearly thirty years after the publication of Rollock's and Mann's articles (p. 554, p. 556), debate about black-Jewish relations reignited. In his 1992 op-ed in *The New York Times*, Henry Louis Gates, Jr. looks at anti-Semitic positions (including the one promoted by Nation of Islam leader Louis Farrakhan) in historical contest and argues that there is a fundamental difference between historic and recent black-Jewish tensions. Black anti-Semitism in the 1930s and 1940s was "bottom-up," Gates asserts, driven by the resentment of poorer African-Americans toward the neighborhood landlord or shopkeeper. In contrast, what has driven black anti-Semitism since the 1960s is not personal resentment toward local business owners but dense treatises promoted by leaders and academics committed to racial separatism—a "top-down" strategy to consolidate power through isolation from former allies.

The 1995 Million Man March, sponsored by Farrakhan (b. 1933), fueled debate about black-Jewish relations and leadership. Farrakhan addresses the controversy in a segment of an interview with Tim Russert on the television program, *Meet the Press*, reprinted here and posted to the NOI's official website. Farrakhan cites Jewish sources to support the idea that much power in America is held by a small group of Jewish leaders. "We cannot allow ourselves to be controlled by any outside group," Farrakhan argues. He is specifically wary of interracial civil rights groups like the NAACP and the Urban Leauge, which were built by a coalition of black and white (including many Jewish) leaders.

Since the 1960s, resentment on both sides, fueled by expanding class divisions, has eroded the historic partnership between black and Jewish Americans. At the same time, particularly from the 1990s on, many educators and scholars have committed to understanding and improving black–Jewish relations. Leaders have established educational organizations such as Blacks and Jews in Conversation (later renamed Not Just Blacks and Jews in Conversation) to foster interaction and discussion. Scholars have written hundreds of volumes exploring the history of black–Jewish relations, including Maurianne Adams and John H. Bracey's *Strangers and Neighbors: Relations between Blacks and Jews in the United States* (1999) and Jack Saltzman's and Cornel West's *Struggles in the Promised Land: Toward a History of Black–Jewish Relations* (1997). The magnitude of scholarship points to the complexity of historic and contemporary relations between black and Jewish Americans, involving a potent mixture of class, race, religion, and politics.

HENRY LOUIS GATES, JR.

Black Demagogues and
Pseudo-Scholars [1992]

CAMBRIDGE, Mass.

During the past decade, the historic relationship between African-Americans and Jewish Americans—a relationship that sponsored so many of the concrete advances of the civil rights era—showed another and less attractive face.

While anti-Semitism is generally on the wane in this country, it has been on the rise among black Americans. A recent survey finds not only that blacks are twice as likely as whites to hold anti-Semitic views but—significantly—that it is among the younger and more educated blacks that anti-Semitism is most pronounced.

The trend has been deeply disquieting for many black intellectuals. But it is something most of us, as if by unstated agreement, simply choose not to talk about. At a time when black America is beleaguered on all sides, there is a strong temptation simply to ignore the phenomenon or treat it as something strictly marginal. And yet to do so would be a serious mistake. As the African-American philosopher Cornel West has insisted, attention to black anti-Semitism is crucial, however discomfiting, in no small part because the moral credibility of our struggle against racism hangs in the balance.

When the Rev. Jesse Jackson, in an impassioned address at a conference of the World Jewish Congress on July 7, condemned the sordid history of anti-Semitism, he not only went some distance toward retrieving the once abandoned mantle of the Rev. Dr. Martin Luther King Jr.'s humane statesmanship, he also delivered a stern rebuke—while not specifically citing black anti-Semitism—to those black leaders who have sought to bolster their own strength through division. Mr. Jackson and others have learned that we must not allow these demagogues to turn the wellspring of memory into a renewable resource of enmity everlasting.

We must begin by recognizing what is new about the new anti-Semitism. Make no mistake: This is anti-Semitism from the top down, engineered and promoted by leaders who affect to be speaking for a larger resentment. This top-down anti-Semitism, in large part the province of the better educated classes, can thus be contrasted with the anti-Semitism from below common among African-American urban communities in the 1930's and 40's, which followed in many ways a familiar pattern of clientelistic hostility toward the neighborhood vendor or landlord.

In our cities, hostility of this sort is now commonly directed toward Korean shop owners. But "minority" traders and shopkeepers elsewhere in the world—such as the Indians of East Africa and the Chinese of Southeast Asia—have experienced similar ethnic antagonism. Anti-Jewish sentiment can also be traced to Christian anti-Semitism, given the historic importance of Christianity in the black community.

Unfortunately, the old paradigms will not serve to explain the new bigotry and its role in black America. For one thing, its preferred currency is not the mumbled epithet or curse but the densely argued treatise; it belongs as much to the repertory of campus lecturers as community activists. And it comes in wildly different packages.

A book popular with some in the "Afro-centric" movement, "The Iceman Inheritance: Prehistoric Sources of Western Man's Racism, Sexism, and Aggression," by Michael Bradley, argues that white people are so vicious because they, unlike the rest of mankind, are descended from the brutish Neanderthals. More to the point, it speculates that the Jews may have been the "'purest' and oldest Neanderthal-Caucasoids," the iciest of the ice people; hence (he explains) the singularly odious character of ancient Jewish culture.

Crackpot as it sounds, the book has lately been reissued with endorsements from two members of the Africana Studies Department of the City College of New York, as well as an introduction by Dr. John Henrik Clarke, professor emeritus of Hunter College and the great paterfamilias of the Afrocentric movement.

Dr. Clarke recently attacked multiculturalism as the product of what he called the "Jewish educational Mafia." And while Dr. Leonard Jeffries's views on supposed Jewish complicity in the subjection of blacks captured headlines, his intellectual cohorts such as Conrad Muhammad and Khallid Muhammad address community gatherings and college students across the country purveying a similar doctrine. College speakers and publications have played a disturbing role in legitimating the new creed. Last year, U.C.L.A.'s black newspaper, Nommo, defended the importance of The Protocols of the Elders of Zion, the notorious Czarist canard that portrays a Jewish conspiracy to rule the world. (Those who took issue were rebuked with an article headlined: "Anti-Semitic? Ridiculous—Chill.") Speaking at Harvard University earlier this year, Conrad Muhammad, the New York representative of the Nation of Islam, neatly annexed environmentalism to anti-Semitism when he blamed the Jews for despoiling the environment and destroying the ozone layer.

But the bible of the new anti-Semitism is "The Secret Relationship Between Blacks and Jews," an official publication of the Nation of Islam that boasts 1,275 footnotes in the course of 234 pages.

Sober and scholarly looking, it may well be one of the most influential books published in the black community in last 12 months. It is available in black-oriented shops in cities across the nation, even those that specialize in Kente cloth and beads rather than books. It can also can be ordered over the phone, by dialing 1-800-48-TRUTH. Meanwhile, the book's conclusions are, in many circles, increasingly treated as damning historical fact. The book, one of the most sophisticated instances of hate literature yet compiled, was prepared by the historical research department of the Nation of Islam. It charges that the Jews were "key operatives" in the historic crime of slavery, playing an "inordinate" and "disproportionate" role and "carv[ing] out for themselves a monumental culpability in slavery—and the black holocaust." Among significant sectors of the black community, this brief has become a credo of a new philosophy of black self-affirmation.

To be sure, the book massively misrepresents the historical record, largely through a process of cunningly selective quotation of often reputable sources. But its authors could be confident that few of its readers would go to the trouble of actually hunting down

the works cited. For if readers actually did so, they might discover a rather different picture.

They might find out—from the book's own vaunted authorities—that, for example, of all the African slaves imported into the New World, American Jewish merchants accounted for less than 2 percent, a finding sharply at odds with the Nation's of Islam's claim of Jewish "predominance" in this traffic.

They might find out that in the domestic trade it appears that all of the Jewish slave traders combined bought and sold fewer slaves than the single gentile firm of Franklin and Armfield. In short, they might learn what the historian Harold Brackman has documented—that the book's repeated insistence that the Jews dominated the slave trade depends on an unscrupulous distortion of the historic record. But the most ominous words in the book are found on the cover: "Volume One." More have been promised, to carry on the saga of Jewish iniquity to the present day.

However shoddy the scholarship of works like "The Secret Relationship," underlying it is something even more troubling: the tacit conviction that culpability is heritable. For it suggests a doctrine of racial continuity, in which the racial evil of a people is merely manifest (rather than constituted) by their historical misdeeds. The reported misdeeds are thus the signs of an essential nature that is evil.

How does this theology of guilt surface in our everyday moral discourse? In New York, earlier this spring, a forum was held at the Church of St. Paul and Andrew to provide an occasion for blacks and Jews to engage in dialogue on such issues as slavery and social injustice. Both Jewish and black panelists found common ground and common causes. But a tone-setting contingent of blacks in the audience took strong issue with the proceedings. Outraged, they demanded to know why the Jews, those historic malefactors, had not apologized to the "descendants of African kings and queens."

And so the organizer of the event, Melanie Kaye Kantrowitz, did. Her voice quavering with emotion, she said: "I think I speak for a lot of people in this room when I say 'I'm sorry.' We're ashamed of it, we hate it, and that's why we organized this event." Should the Melanie Kantrowitzes of the world, whose ancestors survived Czarist pogroms and, latterly, the Nazi Holocaust, be the primary object of our wrath? And what is yielded by this hateful sport of victimology, save the conversion of a tragic past into a game of recrimination? Perhaps that was on the mind of another audience member. "I don't want an apology," a dreadlocked woman told her angrily. "I want reparations. Forty acres and a mule, plus interest."

These are times that try the spirit of liberal outreach. In fact, Louis Farrakhan, leader of the Nation of Islam, himself explained the real agenda behind his campaign, speaking before an audience of 15,000 at the University of Illinois last fall. The purpose of "The Secret Relationship," he said, was to "rearrange a relationship" that "has been detrimental to us."

"Rearrange" is a curiously elliptical term here: If a relation with another group has been detrimental, it only makes sense to sever it as quickly and unequivocally as possible. In short, by "rearrange," he means to convert a relation of friendship, alliance and uplift into one of enmity, distrust and hatred. But why target the Jews? Using the same historical methodology, after all, the researchers of the book could have produced a damning treatise on the involvement of left-handers in the "black holocaust." The answer requires us to go beyond the usual shibboleths about bigotry and view the matter, from the demagogues' perspective, strategically: as the bid of one black elite to supplant another. It requires us, in short, to see anti-Semitism as a weapon in the raging battle of who will speak for black America—those who have sought common cause with others or those who preach a barricaded withdrawal into racial authenticity. The strategy of these apostles of hate, I believe, is best understood as ethnic isolationism—they know that the more isolated black America becomes, the greater their power. And what's the most efficient way to begin to sever black America from its allies? Bash the Jews, these demagogues apparently calculate, and you're halfway there.

I myself think that an aphorist put his finger on something germane when he observed, "We can rarely bring ourselves to forgive those who have helped us." For sometimes it seems that the trajectory of black-Jewish relations is a protracted enactment of this paradox.

Many Jews are puzzled by the recrudescence of black anti-Semitism, in view of the historic alliance. The brutal truth has escaped them: that the new anti-Semitism arises not in spite of the black-Jewish alliance but because of it. For precisely such trans-racial cooperation—epitomized by the historic partnership between blacks and Jews—is what poses the greatest threat to the isolationist movement.

In short, for the tacticians of the new anti-Semitism, the original sin of American Jews was their involvement—truly "inordinate," truly "disproportionate"—not in slavery, but in the front ranks of the civil rights struggle.

For decent and principled reasons, many black intellectuals are loath to criticize "oppositional" black leaders. Yet it has become apparent that to continue to maintain a comradely silence may be, in effect, to capitulate to the isolationist agenda, to betray our charge and trust. And, to be sure, many black writers, intellectuals and religious leaders have taken an unequivocal stand on this issue.

Cornel West aptly describes black anti-Semitism as "the bitter fruit of a profound self-destructive impulse, nurtured on the vines of hopelessness and concealed by empty gestures of black unity."

After 12 years of conservative indifference, those political figures who acquiesced, by malign neglect, to the deepening crisis of black America should not feign surprise that we should prove so vulnerable to the demagogues' rousing messages of hate, their manipulation of the past and present.

Bigotry, as a tragic century has taught us, is an opportunistic infection, attacking most virulently when the body politic is in a weakened state. Yet neither should those who care about black America gloss over what cannot be condoned: That much respect we owe to ourselves. For surely it falls to all of us to recapture the basic insight that Dr. King so insistently expounded. "We are caught in an inescapable network of mutuality," he told us. "Whatever affects one directly affects all indirectly." How easy to forget this—and how vital to remember.

From *The New York Times*, July 20, 1992.

LOUIS FARRAKHAN AND TIM RUSSERT

from *Interview on* Meet the Press [1997]

TIM RUSSERT (TR): Your comments about Jews— and they also are refusing to participate in this meeting—are widely reported, the reference to it as a dirty religion. I went and reviewed what you said and I went back and I watched your speech from 1995. And I'd like to play just a piece of that for you to explain exactly what you meant.

MINISTER LOUIS FARRAKHAN (MLF): Sure.

TR: And let's roll the tape, if we can. (*Videotape from March 19, 1995*)

MLF: German Jews financed Hitler right here in America—Loeb and Kuhn and Jacob Schiff.[1] International bankers financed Hitler, and poor Jews died while big Jews were at the root of what you call the Holocaust. Why don't you tell that one? Little Jews dying while big Jews made money. Little Jews being turned into soap while big Jews washed themselves with it. Jews playing violin. Jews playing music while other Jews (were) marching into the gas chambers. (*End of videotape*)

TR: Now, if you were a Jewish American watching that, your reference to "what you call the Holocaust," suggesting whether there was a Holocaust, and the whole reference to big Jews and little Jews and the emphasis you use, why wouldn't you say that's anti-Semitic?

MLF: The question is: Is it truth? If it is truth, then it is not anti-Semitic, it is truth. My problem with the Jewish community is that most of the Jewish people feel that if you criticize any act of Jews, that is anti-Semitic. If I criticize Arabs, if I criticize the government of the United States, if I criticize white people or my own Black people, I'm not considered anti-Black, anti-Arab. Why should anybody who criticizes Jewish behavior that ill affects Black people and their pursuit

of happiness be considered anti-Semitic? Last week Orthodox Jews made the statement that reform and conservative Jews are off the page of Judaism. I saw it not in the *New York Times*, but I saw it in the Chicago papers, just a little writing. But nobody called them anti-Semitic. But if I said that reformed Jews or conservative Jews are those that do not follow the laws, commandments and statutes given by God to the prophets of Israel are not really Jews, then I'm considered anti-Semitic. I am not anti-Semitic. I do not hate Jewish people. I hate actions of any people, including my own, that are evil and are obstructive to justice, freedom and equity.

TR: Do you believe there was a Holocaust in which six million Jews perished?

MLF: Of course I believe that Jews perished in Germany, and (those) same Jews perished in Germany while the Pope Pius XII looked the other way and the government of America looked the other way. Now there is reconciliation between Jews and Catholics and the government of the United States. What is wrong with reconciliation between those who looked the other way when my fathers were being brought into America as slaves, and to this very moment have not received justice? I think atonement, reconciliation, and responsibility should be the watch word for this time, and I am willing to sit down with any who wish to discuss atonement, reconciliation, and responsibility.

TR: Would you be willing to retract or apologize for some of the things you've said?

MLF: If, in any dialogue, I can be shown to be in error, I would most surely apologize. But you cannot put me off in a corner and not dialogue with me and then say to me, "Farrakhan speaks words that are hateful." If I can defend every word that I speak, and every word that I speak is truth, then I have nothing to apologize for. But if, in a dialogue, you can show me where I am in error, I am not a proud man. I will humble myself and go before the world and apologize. But now the burden is, will you show me where I am wrong?

---

1. Born and raised in Germany, Joseph Schiff (1847–1920) moved to New York in 1865 and went on to run Kuhn, Loeb & Company, one of the largest investment banks on Wall Street; anti-Semitic conspiracy theories, including one in the *The Protocols of the Elders of Zion*, cite as evidence examples of Schiff's power and influence, including that he arranged for $200 million in loans to Japan in 1904 and 1905 that helped the Japanese win the Russo-Japanese War.

TR: I went up on the Internet last night, www.noi—Nation of Islam—.org and found an essay written by one of your followers, and it said the following: "The Jews' awesome control over American society and government, all presidents since Franklin Roosevelt, 1932, are controlled by Jews." Do you believe that?

MLF: I believe that, for the small numbers of Jewish people in the United States, they exercise a tremendous amount of influence on the affairs of government. Right now there is a tremendous problem in the Middle East, a very grave problem. I do not think that President Clinton is handling his role in the most responsible manner. As you know, East Jerusalem was under Palestinian control until the year 1967. After the Six-Day War, it was annexed by Israel. It is part of ongoing negotiations. Now, for Netanyahu[2] to say he wishes to build in East Jerusalem, and the world says he shouldn't do this, and since he said he would build and started moving on that, violence has erupted, and the peace process has been brought to a halt. Mr. Clinton, instead of exercising the strength of a man whose country contributes at least $4 billion every year to the state of Israel, America has influence in Israel, but is not using that influence in a constructive way, but rather pays lip service to the Palestinians while she bows to the dictates of Netanyahu and the strong political Jewish lobby.

TR: Mr. Farrakhan, you seem to be suggesting that what you told Henry Louis Gates in New York . . . or you still believe there's a small Jewish cabal that meets on Park Avenue or Hollywood and tries to shape our culture.

MLF: I don't know why you would put that on me. I was quoting a Jewish movie producer[3] in Jamaica, producing the movie "Lost in the Stars," and it was that Jewish producer who told me this. I didn't ask him. He mentioned this to me.

TR: But this is what you said, sir: "Who controls Black art? Who controls Black sports figures? Who controls Black intellectuals, Black politicians? When I talk to the Jews, I'm talking to a segment of that quorum that holds my people in their grip."

MLF: And that is true. Who controls the movement of the NAACP? The Urban League? Who controls Black politicians?

TR: Who does?

MLF: Why is it that when I go before our brothers in quiet they can say good things about me. But when they fear the Jewish reaction to any kind word . . . look at (*Washington Post* columnist) Mr. Novak.[4] He just said a few kind words about my work, and look at the kind of brickbats he has received. Mayor Rendell invited me to Philadelphia, and look at the brickbats he's receiving from his own people. Yes, they exercise extraordinary control, and Black people will never be free in this country until they are free of that kind of control. And I do intend, by the help of God, to break up that control so that when a new relationship is structured, it is structured on the basis of equity and reciprocity. We cannot allow ourselves to be controlled by any outside group. We must take control of our own destiny. That is what I preach, and that is what I believe, and that is what I'm striving for.

From *Meet the Press*, NBC, April 13, 1997.

---

2. Benjamin Netanyahu (b. 1949), was Prime Minister of Israel from 1996 to 1999, and was reelected Prime Minister in 2009.
3. Ely Landau (1920–93) produced *Lost in the Stars* (1974).
4. Conservative syndicated columnist Robert Novak (1931–2009) was an agnostic of Jewish background who converted to Roman Catholicism in 1998.

The Question of Naming: Redux

MARGO JEFFERSON: *Labels Change, Carrying Different Emotional Baggage* [1999]
JOHN BAUGH: from *Changing Terms of Self-Reference among American Slave Descendants* [1999]
K. T. BRADFORD: *Why "Black" and Not "African American"* [2007]

In the 1960s, *Negro* gave way to *black* (and, to a lesser extent, *Afro-American*), as evident in the speeches of Martin Luther King Jr., which shifted from using *Negro* to *black* as the decade progressed. This era saw the rise of the Black Power movement and the popular slogan "black is beautiful." During the same period, the terms *colored* and *Negro* became increasingly associated with racism, except when retained in titles for historical reasons, as in the United Negro College Fund. In the 1980s, Jesse Jackson championed the use of *African American*, a term that recognizes both ethnicity and nationality in a form parallel to the terms used by other ethnic groups, such as Irish Americans. Although *black* (or *Black*) maintained its popularity, *African American* (with or without a hyphen) also gained widespread use, which continues today, particularly in formal or academic contexts.

In the closing decade of the twentieth century, the linguist John Baugh (b. 1949) and the Pulitzer Prize–winning journalist Margo Jefferson (b. 1947) offered new perspectives on the question of naming. In his systematic examination of the shifting process of naming, Baugh quantified the importance of generational as well as insider and outsider perspectives. In 1999, the debate looped back around as Jefferson suggested that a return to the word *Negro* would embrace a diversity that *African American* cannot include. Finally, the 2005 posting by K. T. Bradford, a.k.a. "the angry black woman," on "Why 'Black' and Not 'African-American'?" touched off a debate on the web, with forty responses divided mainly between preferences for *black* (or *Black*) and *African American*. The numerous debates on the web about naming suggest how controversial the topic remains, while also showing how the web is shaping the form and content of debates themselves, with its open publication leading to quicker, more casual expression by diverse, self-determining communities.

MARGO JEFFERSON

Labels Change, Carrying Different Emotional Baggage [1999]

Warning: What follows neither prescribes nor prohibits. There is too much of that wherever racial facts and fictions are found. It is part confession, part justification, part proposal: a modest proposal to revive the word "Negro," not as an exclusive term but as one that does justice to a group whose histories and bloodlines are too varied and contradictory for any one, all-encompassing definition.

Names matter, especially to those whose status is perpetually subject to debate or attack. It's easy for others to roll their eyes and snicker. ("Queer studies? I remember when gay people didn't want you to use that word." "Am I or am I not supposed to hold the door open for a lady? Oh, pardon me, I mean a woman.") Bad jokes are a sure sign of defensive anxiety. After all, if names didn't matter, the groups with power wouldn't have so many insulting names for the groups without it. The deadly earnest name game can be wearing, I admit, even from the inside. We will get fussy and sanctimonious about our own term of choice, at least until it falls from favor.

Because I came of age in the late 1960's, I still tend to use "black" in everyday conversation. And now that a younger generation has made "African-American" the respectable term of choice, I tend to use it in formal and public settings. And I love to use "Negro" in private, with those (blacks, Hispanics, whites, Asians and "others") who share my appreciation of its tonal variety.

"Black" sprang forth in the mid to late 60's as a war word, assaulting the social and political power of "white." Using it was a psychological exorcism, too, a way to help rid the word of all those shameful, degrading connotations. Its highbrow companion term was Afro-American (a descendant of Aframerican), and together they birthed the current "African-American."

"African-American" is a deliberately formal term, useful in broad historical and political contexts, along with terms like Euro-American, Hispanic-American and Asian-American. And of course as the most recent marker on the long road to respectful nomenclature, it seems to carry the fewest derogatory associations. But it just doesn't suffice. It doesn't capture all the edges and shadings.

At a recent jazz seminar I heard the singer Abbey Lincoln say that she was of African, Cherokee, Irish and English descent and then add (after a short, well-timed pause) that the Africans were the only ones who claimed her. Turn the thing around, and if my great-uncle Lucius were still living, he could say that he was of African, Cherokee, Scottish-Irish and English descent, and then add that the Scottish-Irish and English were the only ancestors he claimed when he grew up and chose to pass for white.

From the moment Negroes appeared in the New World, terms proliferated. By the late 16th century "blacks" (small and capital b), "Negroes" (small and capital), "Moors" and "blackamoors" were in use, along with "Africans" and "Ethiopians."

"Negro" means black or dark in Spanish and Portuguese; an adjective became a noun, a color, a racial classification and as the United States worked to legally confine and categorize the people so named, the word became positively omnivorous. A Negro could be someone with two "African" parents, someone with one white and one black parent (also known as a mulatto) or someone with the tiniest smidgen of what was called, in hushed and stricken tones, "black blood." With her part-African great-grandfather from Martinique, the French novelist Colette would have had to pass for white here in the United States or take her chances as a Negro writer.

As a term, African-American carries more political weight and resonance than it does either anthropological or even biographical exactness. And the same is

true of European-American. Not only are the so-called races more mixed than had been once thought, there are multiple divisions and subdivisions that matter to people in their daily lives. Two centuries ago, when trying to describe the mix of Europeans found in the New World, the French-born writer Crèvecoeur put it this way, "From this promiscuous breed has risen that race now called Americans."

Identity is largely an invention. And black, brown and beige Americans are an invented people, put together, forced together, improvised from the most varied African, American Indian and European elements. "Negro" is a word that can be improvised on almost endlessly. It can be lofty, even mighty, as when the great labor leader A. Philip Randolph[1] said "Negro principles are not for sale." It can be excruciating, as it often was in the 1950s and 60s when politicians and journalists pronounced it with slightly squeamish precision, as if using a pair of verbal tongs to keep the people behind the word at a safe distance.

Black Power radicals demeaned it by pronouncing it "NEE-grow," while for whites growing up in the South it remained a threatening Yankee word. "Colored people" was the genteel term. "Nigger," the nationwide insult of choice has now been renovated. Rappers have turned it into "nigga" with the same defiance that Black Power advocates once bestowed on "black." Rappers' multiracial fans have made it the term they most want to be known by.

But back to "Negro." It can be affectionate or rueful as when one exclaims, "My Negroes!" upon encountering some name, expression or hairdo that runs the gamut from ingenious to entertaining to embarrassing. And I find it old-fashioned and chivalric when we speak of the Negro national anthem ("Lift Ev'ry Voice and Sing") or of Negro life and history.

Scientists have recently reported that children are more likely to have perfect or near-perfect pitch if they speak tonal languages, in which pitch and inflection can shape meaning. The word "Negro" is a tonal word. When intellectuals like W. E. B. DuBois and James Weldon Johnson[2] used it alongside "African" and "colored," their ease and fluidity acknowledged that the lan-

1. See p. 435.
2. See p. 311; Du Bois: see p. 199.

guage of race is a complex tonal one. We all need some ear training. We need to be working for as near-perfect pitch as we can get.

But what about alternative names for whites? Suggestions have ranged from the slangy ("pinkies," not to be confused with lefties) to the politically rigorous ("whites of imperial or refugee descent"). My favorite so far is *Blancos*, the Spanish companion to *Negro*. Please. Make your preferences known.

From *The New York Times*, November 15, 1999.

JOHN BAUGH

From *Changing Terms of Self-Reference among American Slave Descendants* [1999]

> Why don't the blacks make up their minds? The whole subject is becoming tiresome. They chose black because they did not like Negro.
>
> from Valparaiso, Indiana, to Ann Landers,
> April 1989

This chapter examines the evolution of changing terms of self-reference among American slave descendants (ASD).[1] Data for this discussion are derived from fieldwork in black communities in Texas and California, a targeted random telephone survey, political pundits, and other minority scholars. The discussion draws on sociological studies of changing racial attitudes (Bobo 1983; Fairbaugh and Davis 1988; Sears et al. 1979; and Schuman et al. 1985) and variable perceptions of racial and ethnographic boundaries.

As one who began to reintroduce the term *African American* before the Reverend Jesse Jackson formally called for this adoption (Baugh 1988), I didn't anticipate the sudden impact that he would have on this linguistic change in progress. During ceremonies in honor of Dr. Martin Luther King, Jr., Jackson stated, "Just as we were called colored, but were not that, and then Negro, but not that, to be called black is just as baseless. Every ethnic group in this country has reference to some cultural base. African Americans have hit that level of maturity" (1988). Pundits jumped at the bait, and a journalistic frenzy ensued; few dialectologists were consulted during the media blitz, resulting in predictably false prophecies. For example, in an article entitled "The Power of, and behind, a Name," published in the *Washington Post*, 7 February 1989, Charles Paul Freund wrote, "If this label sticks, it will be the first time in U.S. history that an ethnic leader has *single-handedly* changed the name commonly applied to his or her group" (emphasis added).

Readers who are familiar with vernacular African American culture (VAAC) will see the obvious flaw in the preceding assertion, because Reverend Jackson did not initiate this dialogue.[2] Bennett discusses the temporal and ethnographic dimensions of this process: "In periods of reaction and extreme stress, black people usually turn inward. They begin to redefine themselves and they begin to argue seriously about names" (1967, 50).[3] Bennett's remarks are reinforced by Rafky (1970), who observes that some

---

1. I have adopted the term *American slave descendants* (ASD) for two reasons. First, this discussion looks at terms of self-reference, and ASD strives for terminological neutrality in a text that must refer to Americans with African ancestors. The second justification grows from Edmund Morris's self-identification as an "African American." Morris is a naturalized American, and a white native of Kenya. In an article entitled "Just 'Americans'" in the *Washington Post*, 12 February 1989, he labeled himself as an "African American" in order to mock Jesse Jackson's plea. Morris cannot claim to be a descendant of American slavery, and the adopted terminology excludes people like him. [Unless otherwise indicated, all footnotes are those of the author.]

2. Not all American slave descendants are active members of VAAC. By *vernacular African American culture* I refer to the African American cultural traditions that have been developed in racial isolation from the majority culture. Some whites are active in VAAC, including many musicians, dancers, and teachers. Many ASD, on the other hand, have limited contact with VAAC. Thus, as we strive to identify the vernacular African American community, race and active participation in black culture are both taken into account.

3. Geneva Smitherman (1987) continues this tradition among scholars. She recognizes that "standard" English is a political construct, and as such it constitutes a dialect of wider communication. The term *standard* continues to convey a sense of linguistic legitimacy that is not afforded to dialects that are not valued by the majority culture. The type of renaming that she advocates is consistent with similar processes in VAAC.

black activists and black intellectuals were outspoken advocates of the change from "Negro" to "black" and they viewed this process as an attempt to overcome oppression by rejecting the status quo (i.e., self-identification of ASD as "*Negroes*"): "According to this view [advocated by black activists], the goal of Black Americans should be to assert their pride, raise their racial consciousness, and emphasize their separateness by calling themselves 'Blacks' and 'Afro-Americans'" (30).

DuBois's sage observations provide historical depth to the current terminological controversy. In an exchange published in 1928, which debated the merits of ASD self-reference as "Negroes," he offered a young student, Roland Barton, the following advice:

> Do not at the outset of your career make the all too common error of mistaking names for things. Names are only conventional signs for identifying things. Things are the reality that counts. If a thing is despised, either because of ignorance or because it is despicable, you will not alter matters by changing its name. If men despise Negroes, they will not despise them less if Negroes are called "colored" or "Afro-American." (96–97)

DuBois's statement is obvious to anyone capable of viewing the matter objectively, but there is another issue that shouldn't be overlooked: Who is doing the naming, and why?

Jackson's critics were quick to point out that "colored," "Negro," and "black" are all terms that ASD have used to refer to themselves at one time or another, and to imply that these labels were imposed by outsiders is unfair, even racist. However, Jackson's text is ambiguous on this score; he accuses no one of imposing terminology, but because his comments were addressed to all Americans, he failed to make critical social and ethnographic distinctions between those who are familiar with VAAC and others who have little

or no contact with ASD. As Freund observes, in his *Washington Post* article cited above,

> The matter seems to have taken some people, both Black and white, by surprise; "Black" to them was not a problematic term. Columnist William Raspberry, for example, wrote that he "must have been out of the room when the question of racial nomenclature came up." (1989)

This element of "surprise" is a reflection of the "Jackson factor,"[4] which has been evaluated as a questionnaire item in my telephone survey. Did Americans already know of others who advocated the term "African American" before Jackson's speech? Results from the telephone survey show direct correlations between *when* and *where* people first encountered "African American" and their relative personal proximity to VAAC [* * *].[5] Most people first heard the term from Jackson, or more specifically, from news reports about his statement. A majority of this group assumed that he was entirely responsible for this linguistic adoption.

The following anecdote, from a 1987 group interview with young African American men from East Austin, Texas (ages 17–26), confirms Bennett's observation that linguistic conception of this process originates in vernacular community contexts. In contrast with Jackson's argument, the Brother takes umbrage at the label "Afro-American."[6]

> We ain't no abbreviated people. It ain't no "Italo-Americans," or "Japo-(A)mericans," and they ain't no "Mexo-(A)mericans" neither. We the only ones they done abbreviated. That's bullshit! [I hear you.] Black people are Africans in America. Ain't nobody from no place else had to deal with slavery, and that's why they done tried to abbreviate us. But I'll tell you this about that. [What's that?] We all came here in chains, baby, but we all came from Africa. We got just as much right as anybody else to demand

---

4. The "Jackson factor" is employed here for expedience. As the only African American ever to mount a viable presidential campaign, his social influence is unique when compared with any other minority leader in America. This shorthand is discussed in more detail later in the text.

5. Baugh refers readers here to figure 6 in chapter 6, which is "a model of linguistic diversity among African Americans" showing that one's use of African American vernacular English (versus standard American English) is in proportion to one's level of activity within vernacular African American culture. [Editor's note]

6. Black people commonly refer to each other as Brother or Sister as signs of racial solidarity. In this vein, I use the words here as terms of respect for fellow African American men and women.

dignity and self-respect and that's why I say I'm a African-American! [Other men convey verbal and nonverbal approval.]

The Brother makes no reference to "baseless" terms; in fact, he mentions black people during his discussion of "African American" (a practice that I maintain in this text). The preceding illustration is noteworthy, in part, because it presents another point of view, but also because it proves that Jackson did not start this process; debates concerning appropriate terminology among ASD continue to spread by word of mouth, as they have since the inception of slavery. Clearly Jackson sensed the changing linguistic tide of self-reference toward "African American," and he used his media visibility to launch this debate into the broader public forum.

VARIABLE TERMS OF SELF-REFERENCE AMONG AMERICAN SLAVE DESCENDANTS

In order to examine this trend I performed some experiments during fieldwork in ASD/VAAC com-

munities in Texas and California. I simply asked people to provide two lists: one that showed terms of respect for ASD and a second list of insulting terms. The questionnaires were delivered verbally or in writing according to consultant preference. All ASD/VAAC consultants were then asked to identify as many words as they could to complete the following sentences:

1. [Respectful] We should be called _____
2. [Disrespectful] We should not be called ____

Table 2 provides results from 226 ASD/VAAC informants from Texas (primarily Austin) and California (primarily in San Francisco and Oakland).

TEMPORAL DIMENSIONS OF CHANGING SELF-REFERENCE

The results are highly variable, reflecting age-graded differences of opinion regarding terms of (dis)respect. Dialectologists will appreciate that this evidence is also representative of an older trend, from long ago when there were no "white" Americans, but only

TABLE 2

Terms of Self-Identification among American Slave Descendants

AGES OF GROUP	12–17	18–34	35–55	56+
California	16	26	33	12
Texas	28	36	47	28
TOTAL	44	62	80	40
	R/D[a]	R/D	R/D	R/D
African Americans	32/0	51/3	67/5	22/7
Afro-Americans	41/0	59/3	73/2	38/2
Blacks / black people	44/0	62/0	58/18	18/16
Bloods	11/4	4/9	0/0	0/0
Brothers	18/0	28/0	3/0	0/0
Colored (people)	7/23	4/47	23/39	26/9
Homeboys	5/0	14/0	0/3	0/0
Negroes	9/31	6/49	23/50	27/12
Niggers	0/44	0/62	0/80	0/40
Sisters	8/0	32/0	5/0	2/0

[a]R = respectful; D = disrespectful.

"citizens" (Flexner 1976). "Citizens" were, of course, white men with property; women, native Americans, and slaves were not citizens. However, history has witnessed various pieces of legislation designed to overcome past discrimination and include residents of the United States who were once legally disenfranchised; these laws have been partially successful, as illustrated by emancipation and voting-rights laws. Wilson (1987) provides substantial evidence concerning the long-term factors that have thwarted social prospects for America's latent citizens of color. I also agree with Wilson's observation that racism alone does not account for the complexity of forces that have reduced social opportunities for the truly disadvantaged.

What, then, do these economic, attitudinal, and racial trends have to do with black self-reference? The disproportionate social dislocation of slave descendants is no historical accident; perpetual cycles of poverty and discrimination continue to exacerbate the gap between privileged and underprivileged children, regardless of race. These poverty cycles now touch more whites; as the economy of the United States continues to adjust to a growing reliance on global markets, the majority of citizens—regardless of race—face the prospect that the next generation of children will fare less well than the present one, especially children of single female parents. This (admittedly simplistic) historical sketch of the dynamic interplay of racial tensions and the economy is well established and affirms the legacy of economic subordination that has always plagued African Americans (Wilson 1981[7], 1987, 1996; Bobo 1983).

This background also shows the paradox that linguists face as they try to draw coherent conclusions from the rather dramatic social changes that are taking place in black America. African Americans are in limbo between the best and worst of times—"best" in the sense that more blacks than ever have achieved positions of social prominence, including presidential aspirations. The downside is reflected by changing racial attitudes and growing resentment of affirmative action as preferential treatment for minorities. Political rhetoric has become vacuous, as the liberal ethos of the 1960s is replaced by conservative interpretations for the failure of government intervention to eliminate pov-

erty or racial strife. These trends do not bode well for the truly disadvantaged, who, for many long-standing reasons, are less likely to overcome their legacy of poverty as American economic prospects continue to decline.

It is in this changing social climate that slave descendants have sought to sort out their own identity, and debates over the term *African American* are part of this tradition. Table 2 illustrates the transitional nature of the process; terms that were once considered offensive are now acceptable (e.g., *black*) and terms that previously had polite connotations, to whites and blacks alike, are now highly offensive to a majority of ASD/VAAC (e.g., *colored*). One of my black colleagues observed recently that, even though all blacks may not greet the usage of *African American* with enthusiasm, we all know what we don't like: "Blacks are clear on terms they believe are negative—like *nigger*." Positive terms, however, are another matter. These changes are dynamic and usually take time because they originate within the vernacular culture. Jackson accelerated this process when he thrust the issue before the entire nation.

REFERENCES

Baugh, John. (1988). "Language and Race: Some Implications for Linguistic Science." In F. Newmeyer (ed.), *Linguistics: The Cambridge Survey*. Vol. 4, pp. 64–74. Cambridge: Cambridge University.

Bennett, Lerone, Jr. (1967). "What's in a Name?" *Ebony* 23 (Nov. 1967): 46–48, 50–52, 54.

Bobo, Lawrence. (1983). "Whites' Opposition to Busing: Symbolic Racism or Realistic Group Conflict?" *Journal of Personality and Social Psychology* 45: 1196–1210.

Du Bois, W. E. B. (1928). "The Name 'Negro.'" *The Crisis* 35: 96–97.

Fairbaugh, Glenn, and Davis, Kenneth E. (1988). "Trends in Antiblack Prejudice, 1972–1984. Region and Cohort Effects." *American Journal of Sociology* 94: 251–272.

Flexner, Stuart B. (1976). *I Hear America Talking: An Illustrated Treasury of American Words and Phrases*. New York: Van Nostrand.

Rafky, David M. (1970). "The Semantics of Negritude." *American Speech* 45: 30–44.

7. See p. 747.

Sears, David O.; Hensler, Carl P.; and Speer, Leslie K. (1979). "Whites' Opposition to Busing: Self-Interest or Symbolic Politics?" *American Political Science Review* 73: 369–84.

Schuman, Howard; Steeh, Charlotte; and Bobo, Lawrence. (1985). *Racial Attitudes in America: Trends and Interpretations.* Cambridge, Mass.: Harvard University Press.

Smitherman, Geneva. (1987) "Opinion: Toward the Development of a National Language Policy." *College English* 49: 302–317.

Wilson, W. J. (1981). *The Declining Significance of Race.* Chicago: University of Chicago Press.

———. (1987) *The Truly Disadvantaged.* Chicago: University of Chicago Press.

———. (1996) *When Work Disappears: The World of the New Urban Poor.* New York: Knopf.

From John Baugh, *Out of the Mouths of Slaves: African American Language and Educational Malpractice* (Austin: University of Texas Press, 1999), pp. 86–91.

K. T. BRADFORD

Why "Black" and Not "African-American"? [2007]

Last week in the Political Correctness post[1] I mentioned that I have not fought for the use of the term African-American to describe myself or others of my ethnicity. Over the years I've been asked why this is and I've given various answers. Some of them flip, some of them surface, none that really gets into the meat of it. It is, after all, a long conversation.

Good thing I have a blog!

The main reason I prefer the term Black is, I admit, habit. When I was growing up that was the term in use. We'd moved on from the terms Negroes, Colored People, and even Afro-Americans. I also remember "People of Color", though don't know how long that lasted before. For the most part, the people in my family and on TV referred to those of African Descent as Black.

When the term African-American came into vogue I sometimes referred to myself that way, but not all of the time. It felt like a very formal term. One people used in term papers or on the news. Not something I would call myself. Though for a while I struggled to use it whenever I talked about Black people because I thought it was important to do so. African-American highlights the fact that most Black people in America today are the descendants of Africans. It's where we came from, and it shows that we're proud of that fact.

There was, of course, backlash against the term. Some would say, "I'm *American*, and that's all." Others would point out that no one ever called recent African immigrants African-Americans. And still more people would whip out that tired business about "If a white person is born in Africa and then moves here, why aren't they African-American, too?" So much wankery.

I have no problem with the term African-American, per se. I wouldn't object to someone referring to me as one. But I don't use it for myself or (very often) for others. One reason is that I still feel it's an overly formal term. Use it in academic papers or in news reports and even on Census forms. That is appropriate. However, we have to remember that the term African-American contains a key word: American.

A few years ago an editor put out a call for submissions to an anthology of horror stories written by Black authors. However, when he first posted the call, he used the term African-American authors. There was a bit of discussion amongst writers of color about how annoying this was. The editor wanted Black authors, but by using the term African-American without thought, he made it seem like authors from Canada, the Caribbean, Africa, and just about anywhere outside of America were not welcome. That wasn't his intent, of course, but it was just another example in a long string of such behavior.

African-American excludes non-American Blacks. And though American Blacks have a lot in common because of our history in America, we aren't the only people of the Diaspora who were oppressed, enslaved, or are the descendants of those who were. We have a lot in common with Black people all over the globe. Our issues are not always uniquely American.

This is also why I sometimes refer to myself as a Person of Color. It connects me to folks who

---

1. Link to "In Defense of Political Correctness," *The Angry Black Woman: Politics, Race, Gender, Sexuality, Anger,* April 12, 2007, http://theangryblackwoman.com/2007/04/12/in-defense-of-political-correctness/.

may not be Black, but with whom I have a lot in common. Some of the issues I have are definitely Black Issues. Some are Issues Concerning People of Color.

It's all about using language in a more precise way. And as these recent posts illustrate, I'm all about language at the moment. The words we use are powerful.

From K. T. Bradford, *The Angry Black Woman: Race, Politics, Gender, Sexuality, Anger,* April 20, 2007, http://theangryblackwoman .wordpress.com/2007/04/20/why-black-and-not-african-american.

Barack Obama
A More Perfect Union [2008]

In March 2008, during the presidential primaries, ABC News broadcast video clips from several sermons by the Reverend Jeremiah Wright, who had been Barack Obama's pastor at Trinity United Church of Christ in Chicago. Other media outlets, as well as a variety of websites, quickly picked up the excerpts, and Obama's connection to Wright became a major challenge for his campaign, especially after Wright made a series of controversial media appearances in April. Many viewers had little experience with black politics or black churches and were shocked by Wright's bitter indictment of discrimination in America, which seemed both anti-white and anti-American. Instead of simply condemning Wright's statements or disowning him, Obama took the opportunity to address the complexity of race in America. In this historic speech—which evokes speeches by Martin Luther King Jr. (p. 557) and Abraham Lincoln, as well as John F. Kennedy's famous speech on religion in America—Obama stresses the need to recognize the legitimacy of both black anger and white resentment in order to move together as a nation toward "a more perfect union."

Obama's focus is on coalition politics as the best strategy for change, but he also draws on many of the other key themes in African American debate, including slavery and its effects—building on the debate about race and the U.S. Constitution begun by Frederick Douglass, C. H. Chase, and other nineteenth-century abolitionists (pp. 169–171)—as well as education, religion, the role of government, and race and class.

"Transcript: Barack Obama's 'A More Perfect Union,'" March 18, 2008, Philadelphia, PA.

"We the people, in order to form a more perfect union."

Two hundred and twenty-one years ago, in a hall that still stands across the street, a group of men gathered and, with these simple words, launched America's improbable experiment in democracy. Farmers and scholars; statesmen and patriots who had traveled across an ocean to escape tyranny and persecution finally made real their declaration of independence at a Philadelphia convention that lasted through the spring of 1787.

The document they produced was eventually signed but ultimately unfinished. It was stained by this nation's original sin of slavery, a question that divided the colonies and brought the convention to a stalemate until the founders chose to allow the slave trade to continue for at least twenty more years, and to leave any final resolution to future generations.

Of course, the answer to the slavery question was already embedded within our Constitution—a Constitution that had at its very core the ideal of equal citizenship under the law; a Constitution that promised its people liberty, and justice, and a union that could be and should be perfected over time.

And yet words on a parchment would not be enough to deliver slaves from bondage, or provide men and women of every color and creed their full rights and obligations as citizens of the United States. What would be needed were Americans in successive generations who were willing to do their part—through protests and struggle, on the streets and in the courts, through a civil war and civil disobedience and always at great risk—to narrow that gap between the promise of our ideals and the reality of their time.

This was one of the tasks we set forth at the beginning of this campaign—to continue the long march of those who came before us, a march for a more just, more equal, more free, more caring and more prosperous America. I chose to run for the presidency at this moment in history because I believe deeply that we cannot solve the challenges of our time unless we solve them together—unless we perfect our union by understanding that we may have different stories, but we hold common hopes; that we may not look the same and we may not have come from the same place, but we all want to move in the same direction—towards a better future for our children and our grandchildren.

This belief comes from my unyielding faith in the decency and generosity of the American people. But it also comes from my own American story.

I am the son of a black man from Kenya and a white woman from Kansas. I was raised with the help of a white grandfather who survived a Depression to serve in Patton's Army during World War II and a white grandmother who worked on a bomber assembly line at Fort Leavenworth while he was overseas. I've gone to some of the best schools in America and lived in one of the world's poorest nations. I am married to a black American who carries within her the blood of slaves and slaveowners—an inheritance we pass on to our two precious daughters. I have brothers, sisters, nieces, nephews, uncles and cousins, of every race and every hue, scattered across three continents, and for as long as I live, I will never forget that in no other country on Earth is my story even possible.

It's a story that hasn't made me the most conventional candidate. But it is a story that has seared into my genetic makeup the idea that this nation is more than the sum of its parts—that out of many, we are truly one.

Throughout the first year of this campaign, against all predictions to the contrary, we saw how hungry the American people were for this message of unity. Despite the temptation to view my candidacy through a purely racial lens, we won commanding victories in states with some of the whitest populations in the country. In South Carolina, where the Confederate flag still flies, we built a powerful coalition of African Americans and white Americans.

This is not to say that race has not been an issue in the campaign. At various stages in the campaign, some commentators have deemed me either "too black" or "not black enough." We saw racial tensions bubble to the surface during the week before the South Carolina primary. The press has scoured every exit poll for the latest evidence of racial polarization, not just in terms of white and black, but black and brown as well.

And yet, it has only been in the last couple of weeks that the discussion of race in this campaign has taken a particularly divisive turn.

On one end of the spectrum, we've heard the implication that my candidacy is somehow an exercise in affirmative action; that it's based solely on the desire of wide-eyed liberals to purchase racial reconciliation on the cheap. On the other end, we've heard my former pastor, Reverend Jeremiah Wright, use incendiary language to express views that have the potential not only to widen the racial divide, but views that denigrate both the greatness and the goodness of our nation; that rightly offend white and black alike.

I have already condemned, in unequivocal terms, the statements of Reverend Wright that have caused such controversy. For some, nagging questions remain. Did I know him to be an occasionally fierce critic of American domestic and foreign policy? Of course. Did I ever hear him make remarks that could be considered controversial while I sat in church? Yes. Did I strongly disagree with many of his political views? Absolutely—just as I'm sure many of you have heard remarks from your pastors, priests, or rabbis with which you strongly disagreed.

But the remarks that have caused this recent firestorm weren't simply controversial. They weren't simply a religious leader's effort to speak out against perceived injustice. Instead, they expressed a profoundly distorted view of this country—a view that sees white racism as endemic, and that elevates what is wrong with America above all that we know is right with America; a view that sees the conflicts in the Middle East as rooted primarily in the actions of stalwart allies like Israel, instead of emanating from the perverse and hateful ideologies of radical Islam.

As such, Reverend Wright's comments were not only wrong but divisive, divisive at a time when we need unity; racially charged at a time when we need to come together to solve a set of monumental problems—two wars, a terrorist threat, a falling economy, a chronic health care crisis and potentially devastating climate change; problems that are neither black or white or Latino or Asian, but rather problems that confront us all.

Given my background, my politics, and my professed values and ideals, there will no doubt be those for whom my statements of condemnation are not enough. Why associate myself with Reverend Wright in the first place, they may ask? Why not join another church? And I confess that if all that I knew of Reverend Wright were the snippets of those sermons that have run in an endless loop on the television and YouTube, or if Trinity United Church of Christ conformed to the caricatures being peddled by some commentators, there is no doubt that I would react in much the same way.

But the truth is, that isn't all that I know of the man. The man I met more than twenty years ago is a man who helped introduce me to my Christian faith, a man who spoke to me about our obligations to love one another; to care for the sick and lift up the poor. He is a man who served his country as a U.S. Marine; who has studied and lectured at some of the finest universities and seminaries in the country, and who for over thirty years led a church that serves the community by doing God's work here on Earth—by housing the homeless, ministering to the needy, providing day care services and scholarships and prison ministries, and reaching out to those suffering from HIV/AIDS.

In my first book, *Dreams from My Father,* I described the experience of my first service at Trinity:

> People began to shout, to rise from their seats and clap and cry out, a forceful wind carrying the reverend's voice up into the rafters. . . .
>
> And in that single note—hope!—I heard something else; at the foot of that cross, inside the thousands of churches across the city, I imagined the stories of ordinary black people merging with the stories of David and Goliath, Moses and Pharaoh, the Christians in the lion's den, Ezekiel's field of

dry bones. Those stories—of survival, and freedom, and hope—became our story, my story; the blood that had spilled was our blood, the tears our tears; until this black church, on this bright day, seemed once more a vessel carrying the story of a people into future generations and into a larger world. Our trials and triumphs became at once unique and universal, black and more than black; in chronicling our journey, the stories and songs gave us a means to reclaim memories that we didn't need to feel shame about . . . memories that all people might study and cherish—and with which we could start to rebuild.

That has been my experience at Trinity. Like other predominantly black churches across the country, Trinity embodies the black community in its entirety—the doctor and the welfare mom, the model student and the former gang-banger. Like other black churches, Trinity's services are full of raucous laughter and sometimes bawdy humor. They are full of dancing, clapping, screaming and shouting that may seem jarring to the untrained ear. The church contains in full the kindness and cruelty, the fierce intelligence and the shocking ignorance, the struggles and successes, the love and yes, the bitterness and bias that make up the black experience in America.

And this helps explain, perhaps, my relationship with Reverend Wright. As imperfect as he may be, he has been like family to me. He strengthened my faith, officiated my wedding, and baptized my children. Not once in my conversations with him have I heard him talk about any ethnic group in derogatory terms, or treat whites with whom he interacted with anything but courtesy and respect. He contains within him the contradictions—the good and the bad—of the community that he has served diligently for so many years.

I can no more disown him than I can disown the black community. I can no more disown him than I can my white grandmother—a woman who helped raise me, a woman who sacrificed again and again for me, a woman who loves me as much as she loves anything in this world, but a woman who once confessed her fear of black men who passed by her on the street, and who on more than one occasion has uttered racial or ethnic stereotypes that made me cringe.

These people are a part of me. And they are a part of America, this country that I love.

Some will see this as an attempt to justify or excuse comments that are simply inexcusable. I can assure you it is not. I suppose the politically safe thing would be to move on from this episode and just hope that it fades into the woodwork. We can dismiss Reverend Wright as a crank or a demagogue, just as some have dismissed Geraldine Ferraro,[1] in the aftermath of her recent statements, as harboring some deep-seated racial bias.

But race is an issue that I believe this nation cannot afford to ignore right now. We would be making the same mistake that Reverend Wright made in his offending sermons about America—to simplify and stereotype and amplify the negative to the point that it distorts reality.

The fact is that the comments that have been made and the issues that have surfaced over the last few weeks reflect the complexities of race in this country that we've never really worked through—a part of our union that we have yet to perfect. And if we walk away now, if we simply retreat into our respective corners, we will never be able to come together and solve challenges like health care, or education, or the need to find good jobs for every American.

Understanding this reality requires a reminder of how we arrived at this point. As William Faulkner once wrote, "The past isn't dead and buried. In fact, it isn't even past."[2] We do not need to recite here the history of racial injustice in this country. But we do need to remind ourselves that so many of the disparities that exist in the African-American community today can be directly traced to inequalities passed on from an earlier generation that suffered under the brutal legacy of slavery and Jim Crow.

Segregated schools were, and are, inferior schools; we still haven't fixed them, fifty years after *Brown v. Board of Education,* and the inferior education they provided, then and now, helps explain the pervasive achievement gap between today's black and white students.

Legalized discrimination—where blacks were prevented, often through violence, from owning property, or loans were not granted to African-American business owners, or black homeowners could not access FHA mortgages, or blacks were excluded from unions, or the police force, or fire departments—meant that black families could not amass any meaningful wealth to bequeath to future generations. That history helps explain the wealth and income gap between black and white, and the concentrated pockets of poverty that persist in so many of today's urban and rural communities.

A lack of economic opportunity among black men, and the shame and frustration that came from not being able to provide for one's family, contributed to the erosion of black families—a problem that welfare policies for many years may have worsened. And the lack of basic services in so many urban black neighborhoods—parks for kids to play in, police walking the beat, regular garbage pick-up and building code enforcement—all helped create a cycle of violence, blight and neglect that continue to haunt us.

This is the reality in which Reverend Wright and other African Americans of his generation grew up. They came of age in the late fifties and early sixties, a time when segregation was still the law of the land and opportunity was systematically constricted. What's remarkable is not how many failed in the face of discrimination, but rather how many men and women overcame the odds; how many were able to make a way out of no way for those like me who would come after them.

But for all those who scratched and clawed their way to get a piece of the American Dream, there were many who didn't make it—those who were ultimately defeated, in one way or another, by discrimination. That legacy of defeat was passed on to future generations—those young men and increasingly young women who

1. White American politician and attorney (b. 1935) who became the first woman on a major party national ticket when Democratic presidential nominee Walter Mondale selected her as his vice presidential running mate in 1984; in 2008, during the Democratic presidential primaries, Ferraro's controversial comments about Obama's candidacy fueled debate about race and gender: "If Obama was a white man, he would not be in this position. And if he was a woman (of any color) he would not be in this position. He happens to be very lucky to be who he is. And the country is caught up in the concept," she told a reporter.
2. Paraphrase of quote from Faulkner's *Requiem for a Nun* (1951): "The past is never dead. It's not even past."

we see standing on street corners or languishing in our prisons, without hope or prospects for the future. Even for those blacks who did make it, questions of race, and racism, continue to define their worldview in fundamental ways. For the men and women of Reverend Wright's generation, the memories of humiliation and doubt and fear have not gone away; nor has the anger and the bitterness of those years. That anger may not get expressed in public, in front of white co-workers or white friends. But it does find voice in the barbershop or around the kitchen table. At times, that anger is exploited by politicians, to gin up votes along racial lines, or to make up for a politician's own failings.

And occasionally it finds voice in the church on Sunday morning, in the pulpit and in the pews. The fact that so many people are surprised to hear that anger in some of Reverend Wright's sermons simply reminds us of the old truism that the most segregated hour in American life occurs on Sunday morning. That anger is not always productive; indeed, all too often it distracts attention from solving real problems; it keeps us from squarely facing our own complicity in our condition, and prevents the African-American community from forging the alliances it needs to bring about real change. But the anger is real; it is powerful; and to simply wish it away, to condemn it without understanding its roots, only serves to widen the chasm of misunderstanding that exists between the races.

In fact, a similar anger exists within segments of the white community. Most working- and middle-class white Americans don't feel that they have been particularly privileged by their race. Their experience is the immigrant experience—as far as they're concerned, no one's handed them anything, they've built it from scratch. They've worked hard all their lives, many times only to see their jobs shipped overseas or their pension dumped after a lifetime of labor. They are anxious about their futures, and feel their dreams slipping away; in an era of stagnant wages and global competition, opportunity comes to be seen as a zero sum game, in which your dreams come at my expense. So when they are told to bus their children to a school across town; when they hear that an African American is getting an advantage in landing a good job or a spot in a good college because

of an injustice that they themselves never committed; when they're told that their fears about crime in urban neighborhoods are somehow prejudiced, resentment builds over time.

Like the anger within the black community, these resentments aren't always expressed in polite company. But they have helped shape the political landscape for at least a generation. Anger over welfare and affirmative action helped forge the Reagan Coalition. Politicians routinely exploited fears of crime for their own electoral ends. Talk show hosts and conservative commentators built entire careers unmasking bogus claims of racism while dismissing legitimate discussions of racial injustice and inequality as mere political correctness or reverse racism.

Just as black anger often proved counterproductive, so have these white resentments distracted attention from the real culprits of the middle-class squeeze—a corporate culture rife with inside dealing, questionable accounting practices, and short-term greed; a Washington dominated by lobbyists and special interests; economic policies that favor the few over the many. And yet, to wish away the resentments of white Americans, to label them as misguided or even racist, without recognizing they are grounded in legitimate concerns—this too widens the racial divide, and blocks the path to understanding.

This is where we are right now. It's a racial stalemate we've been stuck in for years. Contrary to the claims of some of my critics, black and white, I have never been so naïve as to believe that we can get beyond our racial divisions in a single election cycle, or with a single candidacy—particularly a candidacy as imperfect as my own.

But I have asserted a firm conviction—a conviction rooted in my faith in God and my faith in the American people—that working together we can move beyond some of our old racial wounds, and that in fact we have no choice if we are to continue on the path of a more perfect union.

For the African-American community, that path means embracing the burdens of our past without becoming victims of our past. It means continuing to insist on a full measure of justice in every aspect of American life. But it also means binding our particular grievances—for better health care, and better schools, and better jobs—to the larger aspirations of all Americans—the white woman struggling to break the glass ceiling, the white man who's been laid off, the immigrant trying to feed his family. And it means taking full responsibility for own lives—by demanding more from our fathers, and spending more time with our children, and reading to them, and teaching them that while they may face challenges and discrimination in their own lives, they must never succumb to despair or cynicism; they must always believe that they can write their own destiny.

Ironically, this quintessentially American—and yes, conservative—notion of self-help found frequent expression in Reverend Wright's sermons. But what my former pastor too often failed to understand is that embarking on a program of self-help also requires a belief that society can change.

The profound mistake of Reverend Wright's sermons is not that he spoke about racism in our society. It's that he spoke as if our society was static; as if no progress has been made; as if this country—a country that has made it possible for one of his own members to run for the highest office in the land and build a coalition of white and black; Latino and Asian, rich and poor, young and old—is still irrevocably bound to a tragic past. But what we know—what we have seen—is that America can change. That is the true genius of this nation. What we have already achieved gives us hope—the audacity to hope—for what we can and must achieve tomorrow.

In the white community, the path to a more perfect union means acknowledging that what ails the African-American community does not just exist in the minds of black people; that the legacy of discrimination—and current incidents of discrimination, while less overt than in the past—are real and must be addressed. Not just with words, but with deeds—by investing in our schools and our communities; by enforcing our civil rights laws and ensuring fairness in our criminal justice system; by providing this generation with ladders of opportunity that were unavailable for previous generations. It requires all Americans to realize that your

dreams do not have to come at the expense of my dreams; that investing in the health, welfare, and education of black and brown and white children will ultimately help all of America prosper.

In the end, then, what is called for is nothing more, and nothing less, than what all the world's great religions demand—that we do unto others as we would have them do unto us. Let us be our brother's keeper, Scripture tells us. Let us be our sister's keeper. Let us find that common stake we all have in one another, and let our politics reflect that spirit as well.

For we have a choice in this country. We can accept a politics that breeds division, and conflict, and cynicism. We can tackle race only as spectacle—as we did in the OJ trial[3]—or in the wake of tragedy, as we did in the aftermath of Katrina—or as fodder for the nightly news. We can play Reverend Wright's sermons on every channel, every day and talk about them from now until the election, and make the only question in this campaign whether or not the American people think that I somehow believe or sympathize with his most offensive words. We can pounce on some gaffe by a Hillary supporter as evidence that she's playing the race card, or we can speculate on whether white men will all flock to John McCain in the general election regardless of his policies.

We can do that.

But if we do, I can tell you that in the next election, we'll be talking about some other distraction. And then another one. And then another one. And nothing will change.

That is one option. Or, at this moment, in this election, we can come together and say, "Not this time." This time we want to talk about the crumbling schools that are stealing the future of black children and white children and Asian children and Hispanic children and Native American children. This time we want to reject the cynicism that tells us that these kids can't learn; that those kids who don't look like us are somebody else's problem. The children of America are not those kids, they are our kids, and we will not let them fall behind in a 21st century economy. Not this time.

3. See debate on the Simpson murder trial, pp. 961–80.

This time we want to talk about how the lines in the Emergency Room are filled with whites and blacks and Hispanics who do not have health care; who don't have the power on their own to overcome the special interests in Washington, but who can take them on if we do it together.

This time we want to talk about the shuttered mills that once provided a decent life for men and women of every race, and the homes for sale that once belonged to Americans from every religion, every region, every walk of life. This time we want to talk about the fact that the real problem is not that someone who doesn't look like you might take your job; it's that the corporation you work for will ship it overseas for nothing more than a profit.

This time we want to talk about the men and women of every color and creed who serve together, and fight together, and bleed together under the same proud flag. We want to talk about how to bring them home from a war that never should've been authorized and never should've been waged, and we want to talk about how we'll show our patriotism by caring for them, and their families, and giving them the benefits they have earned.

I would not be running for president if I didn't believe with all my heart that this is what the vast majority of Americans want for this country. This union may never be perfect, but generation after generation has shown that it can always be perfected. And today, whenever I find myself feeling doubtful or cynical about this possibility, what gives me the most hope is the next generation—the young people whose attitudes and beliefs and openness to change have already made history in this election.

There is one story in particular that I'd like to leave you with today—a story I told when I had the great honor of speaking on Dr. King's birthday at his home church, Ebenezer Baptist, in Atlanta.

There is a young, twenty-three-year-old white woman named Ashley Baia who organized for our campaign in Florence, South Carolina. She had been working to organize a mostly African-American community since the beginning of this campaign, and one day she was at a roundtable discussion where everyone went around telling their story and why they were there.

And Ashley said that when she was nine years old, her mother got cancer. And because she had to miss days of work, she was let go and lost her health care. They had to file for bankruptcy, and that's when Ashley decided that she had to do something to help her mom.

She knew that food was one of their most expensive costs, and so Ashley convinced her mother that what she really liked and really wanted to eat more than anything else was mustard and relish sandwiches. Because that was the cheapest way to eat.

She did this for a year until her mom got better, and she told everyone at the roundtable that the reason she joined our campaign was so that she could help the millions of other children in the country who want and need to help their parents too.

Now Ashley might have made a different choice. Perhaps somebody told her along the way that the source of her mother's problems were blacks who were on welfare and too lazy to work, or Hispanics who were coming into the country illegally. But she didn't. She sought out allies in her fight against injustice.

Anyway, Ashley finishes her story and then goes around the room and asks everyone else why they're supporting the campaign. They all have different stories and reasons. Many bring up a specific issue. And finally they come to this elderly black man who's been sitting there quietly the entire time. And Ashley asks him why he's there. And he does not bring up a specific issue. He does not say health care or the economy. He does not say education or the war. He does not say that he was there because of Barack Obama. He simply says to everyone in the room, "I am here because of Ashley."

"I'm here because of Ashley." By itself, that single moment of recognition between that young white girl and that old black man is not enough. It is not enough to give health care to the sick, or jobs to the jobless, or education to our children.

But it is where we start. It is where our union grows stronger. And as so many generations have come to realize over the course of the two hundred and twenty-one years since a band of patriots signed that document in Philadelphia, that is where the perfection begins.

IN THE HEADLINES:
The Million Man March

CORNEL WEST: *Why I'm Marching in Washington* [1995]
A. LEON HIGGINBOTHAM JR.: *Why I Didn't March* [1995]
AFRO.COM WEBSITE COMMENTATORS: *Reactions to the Million Man March* [1996]

"We, as students and followers of the Honourable Elijah Muhammad, are calling on all able-bodied Black men to set aside a day, October 16, 1995, for an historic March on Washington to declare to the Government of America and the world, that we are ready to take our place as the head of our families and our communities and that we, as Black men, are ready to shoulder the responsibility of being the maintainers of our women and children and the builders of our communities," proclaimed a December 14, 1994, article in *The Final Call*, the newspaper of the Nation of Islam. From the time of this first announcement, the Million Man March, promoted as "a Holy Day of Atonement, Reconciliation, and Responsibility," was a source of heated debate, largely due to controversy surrounding its main organizer, Louis Farrakhan (p. 861). Early debates centered on Farrakhan's religious affiliation with the Nation of Islam, his reputation for anti-Semitism and homophobia, his patriarchal ideology, and the organization of the march itself.

Farrakhan's position as head of the Nation of Islam made his spearheading of the march problematic for religious leaders. (The National Baptist Convention, the Progressive National Baptist Convention, and the ministry of Imam W. Deen Mohammed, one of the largest Muslim groups in America, refused to endorse the march.) Black women, gay leaders, and other opponents stressed Farrakhan's history of divisive statements in their critiques of the march. Furthermore, the structure of the march itself appeared to some to enact Farrakhan's beliefs: women were requested to remain at home with the children (albeit with a "study guide" outlining their supporting role) while men marched, and homosexuality was presented as one of the sins requiring atonement.

But for many other African Americans, the march struck a chord. They were inspired by the idea of black men coming together to accept responsibility for their families and communities, to atone for past mistakes,

and to make a commitment to positive change. As more people responded positively and the march grew larger, conversation shifted from Farrakhan's beliefs to the question of whether Farrakhan was still centrally important. In many people's minds, particularly in the months leading up to the march, the march was larger than any individual. The shift was notable in changes of opinion among prominent leaders. For example, Jesse Jackson, who had been criticized both for discussing the march with Jewish leaders early on and for his subsequent decision not to participate, changed his mind and decided to play an active role in the event. Still, some remained concerned that participation might be viewed as tacit support of Farrakhan's views and of his position as a leader of African Americans. The two op-ed pieces reprinted here—"Why I'm Marching on Washington" by the philosophy professor Cornel West (b. 1953) and "Why I Didn't March" by the federal appellate judge and legal scholar A. Leon Higginbotham Jr. (1928–1998)—reveal the complexity of opinions regarding the march and Farrakhan's role as leader.

Commentary after the march—including the comments reprinted here, which were posted on Afro.com, the website of the *Afro-American* newspaper chain—continued to focus on how issues of sexism, homophobia, and anti-Semitism affected the march. There was also an outpouring of tremendously positive statements about the experience from those who marched. A common theme among participants was the feeling of support and inclusion, which inverted the central theme of critics who felt they had not been fully welcomed by the group. The website comments underscore the importance of the march as a cultural event and the diversity of opinions about its meaning and legacy. In addition, the range of voices demonstrates how the Internet has propelled the development of debate in the contemporary era by allowing any computer user to publish his or her views in an open forum.

CORNEL WEST

Why I'm Marching in Washington [1995]

Maybe a million black men will march on Washington. Coming after the O. J. Simpson verdict, the March promises to be a pivotal moment in our nation's life. As the writer Greg Tate has rightly noted, the verdict "may represent the first time in history that a majority black jury has wielded an apparatus of state power against the will of the nation's white citizenry."

Our fragile civic and legal order, with its precious jury system that does not guarantee justice, must now contend with a level of white rage unprecedented in American history. Needless to say, black rage has risen exponentially since bullets ripped through the Reverend Dr. Martin Luther King, Jr., in 1968. Can our deeply divided society wrestle with this challenge without exploding?

For most whites, the Million Man March called by Minister Louis Farrakhan can only worsen race matters. For them, he not only embodies black rage but also black hatred and contempt for whites, Jews, women, gay men, and lesbians. Building on a long and diverse tradition of black nationalism—Marcus Garvey, Elijah Muhammad, Queen Mother Moore, Malcolm X—Minister Farrakhan is white America's worst nightmare.

Why am I supporting the March? After all, I am a radical democrat devoted to a downward redistribution of wealth and a Christian freedom-fighter in the King legacy—which condemns any xenophobia, including patriarchy, homophobia and anti-Semitism.

First, unlike "color-blind" neoliberals and conservatives who cheaply invoke Dr. King's words even as they kill the substance and spirit of his radical message, I take his last efforts seriously. When Dr. King was killed, not only was he working on the multiracial poor people's campaign, he was also meeting with Elijah Muhammad and Amiri Baraka[1]—black nationalists demonized by the white media—to promote black operational unity.

Dr. King sought to use moral and political means to transform the capitalist structure of society while deepening its democratic one. But he realistically assessed the true depth of white supremacy. In short, Dr. King, the integrationist, had no fear of a black united front and no hatred of black nationalists.

The second reason I march: Although Minister Farrakhan—with whom I have deep disagreements—initiated this demonstration, the demonstration is about matters much bigger than him. I have in mind the general invisibility of, and indifference to, black sadness, sorrow, and social misery and the disrespect and disregard in which blacks are held in America and abroad. We agree on highlighting black suffering.

In casting the demonstration as "Farrakhan's march," the mainstream media want to shift the focus from black pain to white anxiety. The media distort and disparage the motivations of most blacks who will march—men who are deeply concerned about black suffering and are outraged at the nation's right-wing turn, yet are neither Nation of Islam members nor Farrakhan followers. No one man is the leader of black America—and most of its best leaders are black women.

Third, I must march because the next major battle in the struggle for black freedom involves moral and political channeling of the overwhelming black rage and despair. To stand on the sidelines and yield the terrain to Minister Farrakhan and other black nationalists would be to forsake not only my King legacy but, more important, my love for black people. Young blacks are hungry for vision, analysis, and action; radical democrats must go to them and be with them.

I believe that if white supremacy can be reduced to a minimum, then patriarchy, homophobia, and anti-Semitism can be lessened in black American.

If I am wrong, America has no desirable future. If I am right, black operational unity need not preclude multiracial democratic movements that target all forms of racism and corporate power. Whether right or wrong, I must fight. So I march.

From *The New York Times*, October 14, 1995.

---

1. See p. 694.

A. Leon Higginbotham Jr.
Why I Didn't March [1995]

Thirty-two years ago, with pride and without hesitation, I participated in the inspiring 1963 March on Washington, holding the hands of my two children, Stephen and Karen, then aged 11 and 8. I was exhilarated by the occasion, proud to be a participant, and admired all of the organizers of that March.

Yet I could not participate in the Million Man March. This was an anguishing decision for me to make. My problem was my inability to separate the message of hope for all African Americans from some of the dialogue of the predominant messenger, Mr. Farrakhan.

The March promoted a protest that dealt with many mutual concerns that he, I, and most African Americans have. Of course there is much to march about. The unemployment rate for African Americans remains twice that of whites. In our inner cities, there are very few jobs for teenagers and young adults. Among teenagers, unemployment ranges from 40 percent to 70 percent. The crime rate is dazzling and accelerating. Drug addiction and drug use are pervasive, and there are hundreds of "Mark Fuhrmans"[1] who, as police officers, harass and abuse innocent citizens.

Newt Gingrich's "Contract With America" will weaken Head Start programs, eliminate some school lunch programs, and destroy many of the safety nets that have made some upward mobility possible. As President Clinton recently noted: "Last year alone, the federal government received more than 90,000 complaints of employment discrimination based on race, ethnicity, or gender."

Because of my own misgivings in not going, and because I have received so many inquiries about my reasons, I write this article.

To the extent that anyone focuses on African American males assuming their full level of responsibility for supporting their children and their families, I join in that rationale and support the concept vigorously. I have attempted to exemplify my concerns about family stability in my personal life and also, for decades, as an active board member in several organizations dedicated to the improvement of the options and leadership of African Americans. I have always supported black male responsibility, and simultaneously, I have insisted that black males must, by our explicit action, demonstrate our continuous respect for the dignity and full sharing of power with women. When I became a federal judge in 1964, my first law clerk was a woman, Eleanor Holmes Norton, who now serves so brilliantly as the congressional delegate for the District of Columbia.

I have always had persistent concerns about the protection, safety, and full development of the potential of all of America's children, and since 1992 I have served as chair or vice chair of the American Bar Association Presidential Working Group on the Unmet Legal Needs of Children and Their Families. From the days when I was the 17-year-old president of my NAACP college chapter to the early 1960s, when I was president of the Philadelphia NAACP (then the national organization's largest branch), I have opposed racial discrimination, and I have spent much of my intellectual energy in writing and discussing these issues as a judge, a professor, and, since my resignation from the court, an activist. I am reluctant to cite this litany of personal experiences, but I do so to make it clear that I, and thousands of persons who did not join in this March, have viable records of effective advocacy for the African American community.

My decision not to participate came about because I believe that in its operational reality, the March was initiated, organized, orchestrated overwhelmingly, and almost exclusively controlled by the agenda established by Mr. Farrakhan and his major aides. This March was far different from the one in which I participated in August 1963. I submit respectfully that Mr. Farrakhan and some of his purported values are not those of the speakers in 1963: Martin Luther King, Jr., Roy Wilkins, Whitney Young, Walter Reuther, Bayard Rustin, John Lewis, and Rabbi Joachim Prinz.

1. Reference to the white American former police detective (b. 1952) who was convicted of perjury for his testimony in the O. J. Simpson murder trial about his use of the word "nigger" and who invoked the Fifth Amendment during the trial to avoid answering whether he had ever falsified police reports or planted evidence in the Simpson case; see pp. 961–80 for debate on the Simpson trial.

I recognize that many of my most thoughtful friends who do not agree with Mr. Farrakhan joined the March. I do not mean to besmirch them or denigrate them in any way. This is a classic case where reasonable people can differ on suitable strategies. But my views have been captured most precisely by Mary Frances Berry, chair of the U.S. Commission on Civil Rights, who said she could not endorse the March because "Mr. Farrakhan expresses the most despicable, anti-Semitic, racist, sexist, and homophobic attitudes imaginable. Mr. Chavis's role in practically destroying the NAACP makes any enterprise in which he engaged suspect."

I had always hoped that Mr. Farrakhan and the Nation of Islam would eliminate any shade of ambiguity and possible deception by publicly announcing that participation in the March was an advocacy of a broader, nonpolarizing agenda and was not intended to be an endorsement of Mr. Farrakhan and the Nation of Islam's political and religious views. If I had reason to question whether I should join the March, the statements of Benjamin F. Chavis, Jr., the national director of the event, and Leonard F. Muhammad, chief of staff of the Nation of Islam, assured me that my hesitation was justified. The Oct. 13 *New York Times* reported that Mr. Chavis said: "The attempt to separate the message from the messenger is not going to work." And Mr. Muhammad said: "People coming to Washington, D.C., are coming because they support Minister Farrakhan. He's become a major, major factor in this country."

If I had gone to Washington, I would have gone because I support all responsible programs that advocate family stability, male and female responsibilities for family and community, economic and social justice for everyone, full equity and parity for all women in both public and private sectors, and, particularly, viable programs for disadvantaged children.

As Jewell Jackson McCabe and others have observed, African American "needs are not served by men declaring themselves the only 'rightful' leaders of our families, our communities, or our ongoing struggle for justice. Justice cannot be achieved with a march that excludes black women and minimizes black women's oppression. Justice cannot be served using a dis-

torted racist view of black manhood with a narrowly sexist vision of men standing 'degrees above women.'"

I did not go because I cannot support those statements of Mr. Farrakhan, and those of some of his key aides, which minimize women and are polarizing, antiwhite, and anti-Semitic. Reasonable people can disagree as to whether one should have joined in the March, and I still have some discomfort for not having been there. But now that the March is over, those who did not march and those who marched, those who criticized the March and those who praised it, must avoid racial and gender polarization and join hands so that as a nation we refocus on our primary task of ensuring equal justice to all citizens, eradicating poverty, and preserving educational opportunities.

From *The Washington Post*, October 17, 1995.

AFRO.COM WEBSITE COMMENTATORS
Reactions to the Million Man March [1996]

FROM: GITTA SUMNER

I'll admit this before I say anything else: I don't know exactly what was said at the MMM and even though I think that the IDEA was good, as a Black African woman I was very disappointed. You don't seem to realise that many things that occur to Black people in America do affect the lives of Black people all over the world.

Yes, Black people in America have been and are still being treated disgustingly, but it didn't happen to the men only, this suppressive[1] behaviour includes women and children in every aspect of life. What exactly is the point of excluding over half of the Black population to restart the process of overcoming oppression? At the end of the day, it simply looks as if you are exchanging one form of oppression for another. I refuse to put up with any kind of negative behaviour from any Black man

1. Although unconventional spelling and punctuation are characteristics of debates on the web, they have been corrected here for clarity.

because he has been subjected to racism because Black women, or any woman who is not white, have been subjected to double the trouble—racism and sexism from white people as well as non-white men.

Another thing I did not like about the MMM was the gentleman who headed it. I do not care what has happened in your life, you do not generalise the negative behaviour of a handful of people to include thousands of others. Any negative comments he said about Jewish people can be construed as prejudiced. I do not see every white person as a racist because I have come across Black people who would rather drag you down than let you succeed in life. People can be evil regardless of their skin colour. Rather than find someone to blame for your problems, why not come together with those willing to help and find solutions to those problems? Instead of giving up when something either goes wrong or seems to be too difficult to complete, take a step back and look for other solutions.

I have come to realise that oppression is not only black and white, but it also happens to come in shades of grey. While some of you try to teach your selves about self-respect, I'll be teaching any daughters or sons I might have that you treat other people the same way you would like to be treated, regardless of their sex or skin colour. I'll be telling them that you do not need to demean another human being to gain self-respect. Loving themselves and believing in themselves are qualities that every child needs to have instilled into them, so that no one can have the power to make them believe anything else.

FROM: JUAN O. RIVERA

It is inspiring to see that somebody (and it does not matter who came up with the idea) is working in creating a sense of community in the african-american community. It is critical for our success as people to create, preserve and mantain meaning through community. Even though this is of utter importance most of our leaders, thinkers and politicians have neglected this. They talk of, either "pumping money" or taking it all away. None of these angles will heal the wound. Do not get me wrong, without help most of us would not be able to attend school, or simply survive.

The issue of female abuse was addressed, the sense of community also, but what happened to the gay and lesbian issues? We need to recognize them as part of the community, and furthermore we need to humanize them. This people, part of our people, are being bashed and abused also.

We also missed part of our people . . . any person that is not white and is fighting white oppression! In white America whatever is not white, is black! It does not matter if you are Oriental, Polynesian or Hispanic, if you are not white, you are trying to clear the same hurdles.

The dream of one, is the dream of all . . . break the shackles.

We are moving in the right direction! ! ! !

FROM: MR NICHOLAS T DE ASIO

Your coverage of the MMM was lacking something. Hmmmn let me think If I can help you to figure out what was Missing . . . .

NOW I KNOW WHAT IT WAS>>>>>

You neglected to capture a Picture of The Black Gay and Lesbian contingent that went to the march to show that we too are part of the heritage of Black America. And Part of it's future. How could you neglect to capture us or even mention our presences there ? The National media Knew we where there, we handed out Press Kits and were on National Television. But, I guess that even among our own Brothers and sisters we are treated like the unwanted step child, We are treated as the one's who don't belong and who don't have a voice in America. Even among our peers we were not important enough for you to acknowledge that we where there lending our voices and our support.

And yet Still We Rise ! ! !

SUBJECT: MILLION MAN MARCH REACTION

Attending the Million Man March was one of the best experiences that I've ever had! It gave me a real sense of pride, and it revitalized my hopes for the black man in America.

Before the march I really didn't know what to expect. I was aware of the march for about one year and didn't hear very many negative things about it, but a couple of weeks before the march I began to hear alot of negative opinions coming from blacks and whites. This disturbed me greatly because I strongly believe in the mission statement of the march.

I was really surprised at some members of the black community and the black church stating that they would not be in attendance because of the involvement of the Nation of Islam. The day before the march and at the march itself Joseph Lowery made a statement that I totally agree with. In essence he said, "The house is on fire and my kids are in the house. I don't care who is carrying the water, somebody has got to put the fire out!"

It makes me wonder what is on the minds of some of these so called community and church leaders. They sit on the fence and throw stones without an agenda of there own to solve any of the problems in the black community. Why aren't they doing anything? Who's got a hand around their throats or who is signing their pay checks?

I can only hope that I will live to feel the brotherhood that I felt at the march again! As I was leaving the event I had tears in my eyes. It was a very great and moving experience. I will continue to keep the spirit of the Million Man March alive! Thank God for the march and the messenger of the march.

Sincerely,

DAVID M. COUNTS

SUBJECT: MY RESPONSE

Hello,

I watched the complete broadcasting of the Million Man March on C-Span. I was particularly impressed with what Allendye Baptist,[2] Maya Angelou, and Min. Louis Farrakhan had to say. I wholeheartedly believe the march was the first step in changing not only what Caucasians think of us, but also in uniting our African-American males. I hope there is a continued success of this mission. We cannot afford to back down now. I only wish I could have been there.

One Nation, One Love, Together, Forever

VELEDA BRIGGS
Student, University of Notre Dame

From "Million Man March: Reactions to the March," at Afro.com the website of the *Afro-American* newspapers, History/Archives, http://www.afro.com/history/million/reaction.html.1996.

---

2. Reference to an eleven-year old boy who spoke at the march.

KEY DEBATE ~ *Education*

VINCE NOBILE

White Professors, Black History: Forays into the Multicultural Classroom [1993]

In 1993, the American Historical Association's newsletter published a personal reflection by Vince Nobile (b. 1946), a white American professor of history at Chaffey College, a community college in California, who explained his decision to stop teaching African American history. Although he believes that white teachers possess the ability to teach black history, he asks if they *should* teach it. Despite his own decision not to, he ultimately answers yes to this question—but with reservations. In contrast to the more welcoming teaching environment of the 1980s, Nobile concludes that the environment of the 1990s made the teaching of black studies by white professors not only difficult and frustrating but perhaps "ill-advised" as well, because of the difficulty of establishing trust among some black students. The American Historical Association used Nobile's essay to launch a forum on the relationship between race and the teaching of black studies, which was published in the same issue of *Perspectives*.

From *Perspectives* 31, no. 6 (September 15, 1993).

A re whites able to teach African American history? I know of no rational argument that proves that they are not. In fact, to make such an argument guts a vital part of our discipline: vicarious knowledge of the past. If whites are unable to teach African American history, they should not be able to teach the history of Latinos or Asian Americans, among others. It would follow, then, that a nonveteran is unable to teach war, an African American is unable to teach African history, a gentile is unable to teach the Holocaust, and so on. To be sure, individuals of a particular race, class, gender, or experiential background might offer special insights—the perspective of the oppressed, perhaps—or have an intuitive feel for the material, but there is very little else that is theoretically beyond the reach of the committed scholar. No, the notion that we must have some certified or symbolic membership card for the fields we teach is itself anti-history and need not detain us.

There is, however, a more delicate question: in this age of multiculturalism, *should* whites teach African American history? Is doing so "politically correct"? (Not only is there no consensus on this matter,

I am not sure it has yet to be raised in a public forum.) As a white who has taught the subject at both the two- and four-year college level over the last ten years, I would answer, yes. However, doing so is also becoming difficult, frustrating, and, depending on the institution, ill-advised. In my personal case, I am taking an indeterminate hiatus, but not before having acquired an appreciation for the demands and dilemmas associated with the subject. This paper is an effort to give voice to these concerns, knowing full well they might apply only to myself, though I doubt it. The intention here, then, is to illuminate problem areas, not to produce fast truths.

African American history seems a logical teaching field for me. My area of specialization was post–World War II U.S. history, the Vietnam War, and the sixties. Among the dominant themes of the period were African American liberation via the Civil Rights and Black Power movements. The latter was no back-of-the-bus American history as I had learned it. Names like Montgomery, Selma, Birmingham, and Watts tolled through my studies with as much authority as Vicksburg, Antietam, and Appomatox. Knowledge of all these momentous events required sojourns back to their antecedents in the African slave trade. When I began teaching in the early 1980s, African American history was in my area and I taught it gladly.

The early years, not surprisingly (especially in retrospect), were different from the last few. From 1982 to 1986 multiculturalism was not yet a household word. Political correctness, though not yet minted, was the subtle and not-so-subtle pressure from the right to teach more "patriotic" U.S. history.

The ensemble of problems associated with teaching African American history in such a climate was unique to that period. First, enrollments were small and students tended to be conservative. More important, students had no discernible world view to be validated or challenged. Instead, they had fragmented ideologies: they were intuitively critical of racism in U.S. society but intellectually conformist and assimilationist.

I conceptualized my role as follows: African Americans taking the class would be taught the history deprived them through the generations. Whites taking the class (about thirty percent then) would be taught a history they too had often been deprived: the history of American freedom, bought by American slavery, as Edmund Morgan so aptly described. I sought to *create* a balanced view of U.S. history, not necessarily to *present* one, since it was obvious these students had scant exposure to the role slavery played in the development of the country. As a result, the classroom environment was subdued, with minimal race tension and a healthy student distrust of my scholar/activist approach. In other words, communication was possible though expanding student horizons was problematic.

Assigned texts during these years ranged from John Hope Franklin's *From Slavery to Freedom: A History of Negro Americans* to Eugene Genovese's *Roll, Jordan, Roll,* Edmund Morgan's *American Slavery, American Freedom,* and Vincent Harding's *There Is a River.* Never were any of the readings challenged for being authored by whites. Never were African American authors like Franklin or Harding criticized as "oreos."

Perhaps I was naive, but the years did not record perplexities that I attributed to my being white. I would confront the race issue during the first meeting. "You are all probably wondering what a white guy is doing teaching African American history?" Then I would pass out John Donne's poem about how "every man is a peece [*sic*] of the Continent, a part of the maine," and how "any man's death diminishes me, because I am involved in Mankinde." With this as an introduction, we would discuss the students' reactions, along with their motivations, as well as mine, for being involved in the class. It was my impression that, once confronted, the issue of my race faded and we got on with learning African American history from the African slave trade to the present (a two-course sequence). The student carryover from course to course was not negligible.

The major frustrations of the early to middle 1980s involved occasional course cancellations due to poor enrollment. The surrounding community from which area campuses drew their students (southwestern San Bernardino County, California) was predominantly white. These demographics were reflected on the campuses and account for the low-interest level in ethnic studies and the less-than-confrontational mood of the students. Although the African American sequence usually drew sufficient numbers, these were anemic years for electives overall. Classes attracted anywhere from seventeen (minimum) to thirty. Students' commitment to the material was minimal, and drop rates were above average.

Student/teacher differences that did surface revolved around my own left-leaning perceptions and the relative conservatism of those enrolled. Still in the throes of the Reagan zeitgeist, black students seemed to want to emphasize gains made, as opposed to conditions still in need of attention. While there was an appreciation for the Nat Turners, David Walkers, and Malcolm Xs as necessary predecessors, my students seemed most interested in taking advantage of the economic opportunities (real and imagined) made possible by previous political action. In a related way, students seemed more interested in individuals who achieved in the face of adversity, and less in collective resistance or rebellion. Activist history, while a curiosity, was secondary to achievement for the majority of my students. As an activist myself, I was frustrated by my students, and they—with a hint of irony that I doubt they appreciated—found me "out of touch."

By the mid-1980s ethnic studies in general began to wane. Class offerings were administratively discouraged for not drawing the magic numbers, so teaching loads shifted to the bread-and-butter survey courses with only occasional electives. I was told, in so many words, that market demand was down, so why offer African American history? As a result, the interim period saw little institutional commitment to minority student needs. Then, in 1990, prompted by the influx of more minority students into the area, the related rise in sensitivity to multiculturalism, and a revival of interest in ethnic studies, I was asked to offer African American history again. My approach was essentially the same; this time, however, the administration committed itself to support the offerings regardless of class size. Moreover, much of the helium had seeped from the party balloons of Reaganomics.

Student enrollments exceeded all expectations, but my reception was wintry, to say the least. The race and ethnic mix was approximately eighty-five percent African American, five percent Hispanic, and ten percent white—much different from that of previous years. The door had not closed on the first day of class when a bright, vocal, African American challenged my race credentials: "Why would this college have a white teaching African American history?" The explanatory sword of John Donne's words was knocked quickly from my hand. I tried the Joan Rivers approach: "Can we talk?" The answer was, not easily.

Another student then criticized one of my texts, *American Slavery, American Freedom* by Edmund Morgan. Other students wanted to know how the book fulfilled their desire to learn about their African roots? How appropriate was the book since it discussed slavery, not from the slaves' point of view, but from that of an evolving Euro-American society? I took all these queries to mean: was Morgan, or I for that matter, "politically correct"?

I defended my choice of *American Slavery, American Freedom* by suggesting that it answered fundamental questions about the origins of slavery in America: why slavery was as much a class consideration as it was racial, and why slavery in America was racial. More important, I argued, Morgan showed how the development of American slavery did not just coincide with the development of American freedom, but was, ironically, an integral part of the process. Finally, since the Morgan reading was accompanied by Vincent Hard-

ing's *There Is a River*, students could observe how the class decisions of certain white American colonists intimately affected the lives of Africans. My defense rested and the students turned to other matters, but I could tell their skepticism remained.

The next class meeting saw an escalation of tensions. I insisted on airing feelings before encountering any material, urging students to mount their best arguments against whites teaching the course. Some fired away: "You're white, you assign white authors who, by definition, can offer only the white point of view." (I'm paraphrasing.) When asked about the Harding book, the response, as I recall, was that he was an integrationist, an "oreo." In addition, I discerned a world view informing student criticisms. It was Afrocentricity, of the variety that claims everyone from Jesus and the Madonna to Beethoven was black. Egypt was the center of all civilizations, according to this ideology; it not only had science and mathematics but had originated them. Jews, according to this perspective, were the masterminds behind the slave trade.

I granted, for the sake of class discussion, all the Afrocentrists' claims and then asked, "Why is this information theoretically unknowable or unteachable for whites?" Most students saw the implications of the question (i.e., there is nothing theoretically unknowable or unteachable about Afrocentricity for whites), but few seemed willing to engage in that level of discourse. Instead, students hinted that whites would inherently try to cover for their race. The discussion reached a chilly impasse, and at that moment I was not sure I understood what lay at the root of these students' acrimonious attitudes.

Certainly these pamphlet Afrocentrists were, as F. Scott Fitzgerald once said in another context, "nibbling at the edges of stale ideas." They reminded me of my undergraduate years when I came to class armed with pamphlet Marxism, gleaned from booklets purchased in radical bookstores for a quarter. The intellectual exchanges of those days helped refine my level of theoretical awareness, so I remained optimistic that I could perform the same service for my students. After all, here were undergraduate students who had read an entire assigned text *before* the first class meeting and had critically assessed it. Here were students who had a world view (albeit in some disarray, by my reckoning) they wished validated or at least tested. Tensions were high but so was energy. True, there were only about five percent who displayed such confrontational behavior; but five percent could carry a class and energize more complacent students. I rolled up my sleeves and hoped a good start had been made.

Unfortunately, there I remained stuck for the next two years, unable to establish the links of communication necessary for effective teaching. Class periods would go by with relative calm, awaiting an incident that would spark another prairie fire. What follows is a typical representation. During a section on U.S. slavery (a subject the black students were none too pleased with, anyway), I examined Eugene Genovese's hypothesis that the master/slave relationship in the United States was characterized by coercion, dependency, and affection. The class read a number of slave narratives and were asked to write a short paper to substantiate or invalidate Genovese's view. During the next class period, the assignment was severely criticized for even insinuating that slaves had affection for masters. Those narratives that spoke of affection (e.g., one by Mary Reynolds) were called fabrications by some of the students, and I was accused of being manipulative. One of the brightest students I've had in the last ten years of teaching was so angered by the assignment that he packed his books and walked out, never to be seen again.

The above scenario repeated itself on numerous occasions during that class and other African American history classes I've taught up to the time of this writing. The incendiary devices might have been different, but the results were the same. I was never even able to convince these students that slavery was a valid subject of inquiry, never able to convince them that there was collective heroism in preserving one's humanity in the face of an inhuman institution.

Not coincidentally, classroom breakdowns affected not only the African American students and me, but the whites and Hispanics as well. Non-blacks complained that the class was too much confrontation over race and too little history. Some threatened to drop the class. If not for the help of my colleagues who encouraged them to stay, they too would have dropped. To my embarrassment, some class encounters would find me simultaneously attacked by Afrocentrists and defended by whites—with the rest of the students looking on in bewilderment. Some black students would leave notes in my box, informing me that my views were rejected primarily because of my race. So, my teaching remained an awkward and unfulfilling foray into classroom multiculturalism.

I did make one attempt to overcome the objections to my race. A black colleague in the English department generously offered to teach her English composition course in conjunction with my African American history class. Students enrolled simultaneously in both classes. Writing assignments were coordinated and graded by my colleague for composition. I graded the historical content. This teaching across the curriculum was the one promising experience I had over the last two years. My colleague's willingness to teach English in conjunction with African American history seemed to give me more credibility. Her experience was, likewise, a pleasant one. At least some of the acrimony in my class subsided. Unfortunately, schedule coordination made the approach untenable on a continuous basis. (If I found myself teaching these courses again, I would try hard to replicate the black/white team approach.) By the next quarter I was on my own and back in the trenches.

I must add here that with all the turmoil and tension, students never once in the last two years sought to have me removed, never organized a boycott of my classes, never pressured the administration other than to informally request that an African American teach the courses, and never baited me in the school newspaper like the "thought police" depicted in Dinesh D'Souza's *Illiberal Education*. These were classroom confrontations between students and professor. While the incidents have made me rethink my decision to teach African American history, I do not see myself as a victim of political correctness or the "thought police" and I do not wish to be seen as such.

Were the Afrocentrist students to blame? A tough question. On the one hand, their version of Afrocentrism struck me as stale and self-referential. They defended Leonard Jeffries' melanin hypothesis,[1] and

---

1. Belief that the higher levels of melanin in dark skin promote intellectual, physical, emotional, and spiritual superiority, promoted by Black Studies professor Jeffries (b. 1937), who became a source of controversy in 1992 when he was dismissed as the chair of the Black Studies department at City College in 1992 following a speech that was criticized as anti-Semitic.

they refused to *consider* that it might be racist. They used the well-worn and highly selective defense that one cannot be racist without the institutional power to impose biases. I found these views objectionable, and momentarily, I blamed students for making my job nearly impossible. Upon further reflection, however, I perceived a more subtle dynamic at play. These were students, mostly freshmen and sophomores, full of energy, seeking answers that might contribute to turning their communities around. Their ideas might be objectionable, but their motivations were genuine. It was my job to educate them, and the others, regardless of the views they carried to class.

Ultimately, however, I could not reach them. But not because their ideology was impenetrable or my grasp of the issues was deficient. I failed largely because I was not trusted, and herein lies the dilemma for whites teaching African American history in this age of multiculturalism: without trust there can be no communication, and without communication there can be no effective teaching.

What created the distrust on my campus? The answer is mere speculation on my part, but I suspect it stems from administrative neglect of ethnic students' needs during the mid- to late 1980s. When budgetary concerns took priority over these needs, and when such students were a small percentage of the student body, relevant class offerings were the first to be cut. When administrative decisions were made after increased ethnic student enrollments, they were made unilaterally and not through consultation with existing student or faculty organizations (on my campus we have a rainbow of ethnic student organizations as well as a faculty of color organization).

Such behavior sends clear messages: the institution's commitment to multicultural education is contingent primarily upon the least important factors. Ethnic students and faculty are not seen as part of the decision-making loop, and in the case of African American history, it's still a back-of-the-bus part of the curriculum. Such messages become embedded into the character of the campus and into the expectations of its students. In such an environment, white teachers, regardless of sincerity and intent, appear as representative of institutional racism. In short, white faculty teaching any ethnic history face a situation where the content of their courses is overwhelmed by the institutional context in which their courses are taught. White professors committed to racial justice in the United States might better serve that cause by pressuring administrators to create an institutional climate of trust. Perhaps then our forays into the multicultural classroom will begin to be met with a level of tolerance conducive to quality history.

Until then, however, our discipline faces a serious internal dilemma. Black students will continue to demand African American professors for African American history. Administrators, interested only in clearing their desks of problems and avoiding charges of racism, will most likely continue to comply with the demand when possible. African American Ph.D.s will continue to fill what will effectively become segregated slots, leaving other fields deprived of their perspectives and talents. Then, will black historians of African American history no longer be thought of as U.S. historians? (Is John Hope Franklin a U.S. Constitutional historian or a historian of African Americans? Professor Franklin has recently raised just this question.) Will the same fate await Latino, Asian, or women historians? Will not our discipline face another, perhaps more serious, dilemma when we realize there are no reserves of black scholars to teach Asian or European history when the need arises? Are we not courting the possibility of creating a compartmentalized, de facto segregated discipline that pigeonholes talent into separate race, gender, and ethnic subject matter? Such a prospect will not be beneficial to any of us.

CYNTHIA FLEMING
Race beyond Reason [1993]

In response to Vince Nobile's essay on the teaching of black studies by white teachers (p. 887), Cynthia Fleming (b. 1949), a professor of history at the University of Tennessee, traces the problems Nobile describes to a history of separatism in the development of African American studies at predominantly white schools. Although she understands students' demands for specialized treatment of black studies classes (as in the hiring of faculty), Fleming warns that such treatment will perpetuate the image of African American history as "a separate and substandard shadow of the real thing" rather than a field of study necessary to a comprehensive and accurate understanding of the American experience.

From *Perspectives* 31, no. 6 (September 15, 1993).

At the very beginning of his discussion Professor Nobile poses the question: "Are whites able to teach African American history?" He logically concludes that "I know of no *rational* argument that proves that they are not" [emphasis added]. Herein lies the very basis of the dilemma confronting Professor Nobile. It goes far beyond pedagogical considerations and curriculum questions: it rests squarely on the single issue of race. And, regardless of the circumstances, race has never been rational in American society.

In the late 1960s scores of young African Americans attending predominantly white colleges and universities all over the nation began demanding courses that were "relevant" to their experience. In response to tenacious black agitation, white college and university administrators added various courses on the African American experience. One of the most popular of those courses among the small numbers of black students attending white schools was African American (black in those days) history. The administrators who approved the addition of this "new" history to their curriculum knew little about these black students on their campuses, and even less about their history. After all, this black student presence on campus was a new experience for many of these schools. The perspectives and experiences of the black students were so different; and they seemed to be so angry all the time. Many white members of the university community found this presence puzzling, and sometimes troubling. So, when these black newcomers had the temerity to demand courses that were relevant to their lives, many white administrators acquiesced with alacrity.

Clearly, white approval of African American history and other related courses was part of the search for ways to cope with this new and troubling black presence on campus. Many hoped black students would see the university's willingness to provide courses in their history as proof of white sincerity and sensitivity. In short, they hoped the inclusion of black history in the curriculum would make black students feel at home. Sadly, such an expectation for African American history took it out of the realm of the scholarly. Many white members of the university community would always see this kind of history as a service for black students rather than as a legitimate field of study. As white students, faculty, and administrators discussed and debated the wisdom of including African American history in their school's curriculum, black students were formulating their own ideas. They saw the addition of their history to the curriculum as a significant victory. After all, many reasoned, it was their agitation that had forced administrators to make this change. Consequently, many believed that African American history was their course. They had a hand in its creation, and it was all about the history of their people. This was one of the few parts of their campus experience that did not make these black students feel isolated and unwanted.

This thicket of black and white expectations and emotions surrounding African American history generated an atmosphere that set it apart from other courses. Now, more than twenty years have passed since these early battles over the inclusion of African American history in the curriculum. Yet, in some ways, little has changed in the intervening years. Many campuses are still plagued by racial unrest; and African American history remains mired in political considerations. In such an atmosphere black student insistence on black professors for African American history courses is understandable. Many of these students still see an African American history class as one of the few places on campus where they feel welcome and included. Consequently, many would see a white professor in such a setting as an unwanted intrusion and a painful reminder of the hostile white campus that surrounds them. At the same time, some white faculty and administrators persist in judging African American history as a course that is valuable because of its political importance—not its intellectual impact. Such an attitude creates the kind of atmosphere that reinforces the growing black student certainty that their history is indeed a separate black enterprise.

Such views of African American history are quite frustrating for those of us who see it as a field worthy of legitimate scholarly inquiry. Along with black historians, there are others who have now begun to recognize the importance of this "other" kind of history to the formation of a comprehensive view that more accurately reflects the American experience. Scholars like Professor Nobile are drawn from the ranks of these people who are attempting to look beyond the ghettoization of African American history. But, regardless of their views, such white scholars are directly affected by the well-established tradition of separate treatment accorded to African American history. Such treatment has sometimes resulted in attempts to ignore or even subvert its scholarly legitimacy. The cumulative effect of such attempts has been the creation of a vision of African American history as a separate and substandard shadow of the real thing. The persistence of this vision of separatism, whether it is in the minds of black students or white administrators, is now coming back to haunt Professor Nobile, and ultimately to haunt us all.

MOLEFI KETE ASANTE
Where Is the White Professor Located? [1993]

Molefi Kete Asante (b. 1942), a professor of African American studies at Temple University, in Philadelphia, and the originator of the theory of Afrocentricity, responded to Vince Nobile's article on the challenges faced by white teachers of black studies (p. 887) by focusing on the individual professor rather than on institutional problems. For Asante, the deciding factor in the question of who should teach black history is not race but the professor's orientation toward the material. Asante asserts that the only proper orientation is an Afrocentric one, which focuses on the influence of African cultures and presents African peoples as subjects rather than objects in world history. In his groundbreaking book *Afrocentricity* (1988), Asante presents Afrocentricity as a "transforming agent" that enables the rediscovery of "the first and only reality for African people." Here, he faults white and black professors alike who employ alternative perspectives in their teaching—including Nobile.

From *Perspectives* 31, no. 6 (September 15, 1993).

As an Afrocentrist my concern is not so much could or should a white person teach African American history but rather what "location" the teacher brings to the subject. I would wish that a teacher who undertook to teach African American history would teach the subject from the standpoint of African Americans as historical agents, not merely as objects or appendages to white American history. The biology of the person neither guarantees nor prohibits centered teaching.

Quite frankly, the real issue for me is whether the professor who teaches African American history is properly oriented to the material. Given the proper orientation, mastery of the facts, basic pedagogical skills, and a willingness to learn from gifted students, any teacher ought to be able to teach any subject.

However, most white teachers and many African American teachers do not have the proper orientation to adequately teach any African American studies. They tend to be off on either orientation, facts, pedagogical skills, or humility, a necessary attitude toward information you do not possess. Some weaknesses in professors are more revealing than others. For example, I am sure the standard facts of African American history are fairly accessible to most scholars, although a few areas may still be debated or debatable. On the other hand, I am just as certain that most whites who teach African American history do so from their own historical perspectives, not from those of African American people. To teach from an African American perspective does not mean one has to be an African American; it means one must attempt to understand the centric position of the African American people.

To turn more precisely to Vince Nobile's intellectual location in asking, "Could a white professor teach African American history?" I would say that it is a narrow, provincial question. But there is something even more disturbing in his second question, "Should whites teach African American history?" Nobile seems not to consider the intellectual location of the professor as a problem, but I believe it to be a fundamental issue in the teaching of African American history because the subject is not simply an extension of Eurocentric history. As a legitimate subject within its own right, the area must be viewed from this perspective. However, this takes a particular type of professor who is committed to understanding the culture he or she teaches as opposed to the professor who does not want to be "detained."

A professor who participates in teaching African American history must do so with a commitment to understand how Africans impacted upon America. This must be done from the standpoint of Africans as agents not merely as sideshows to Europe. Any professor who has a perspective informed by African American agency could teach an Afrocentric history. Of course, Professor Nobile, from the record he presents, should probably not teach African American history.

He fails to integrate African American history into the larger American historiography, thus producing a truncated view of our past. A deeper weakness in Nobile's case is what appears to be his lack of knowledge or sensitivity to the genetic, social, and cultural links between Africa and Europe.

Africalogy, the Afrocentric study of African phenomena, advances when a professor declares a course as a centered study and analysis of African American history. A professor using this approach will announce to the class where he or she stands on African agency, self-consciousness, merely by his or her choices of textbooks, themes, and approaches to the material. Every student will know after the first lecture where the professor is located and will be able to determine if the professor gives agency, subject position, to Africans. In Nobile's case, he argues that students he taught in the early 1980s did not criticize the texts chosen for his class. What he fails to say, however, is that many students had no experience in how to locate a text. Of course, his lament is that those days are gone. Now an African American student will more likely raise questions about the texts and the use of certain terms, such as "African slave trade," "African tribes," "pygmy," and so forth.

Therefore, the problem as I see it is that few white professors have the kind of empathy for the African American history they are teaching to do a good job. Can a German teach the history of the Jewish holocaust? I am sure the answer is "yes" for the same reasons it is possible for a white person to teach African American history. Could a Nazi teach the history of the Jewish holocaust? is another type of question. Such a question is about intellectual location, social orientation, and moral investment.

As I read Nobile, he seems not to understand the preservation of courage, struggle, and valor as icons of resistance in the African American community. He said he did not understand why his students objected to the characterization of Africans as holding affection for the enslavers or why some students walked out of his class when he totalized the psychological adjustments to enslavement by using the literate Mary Reynolds without emphasizing her personal reaction to enslavement. This can only happen when a professor disregards his students and concentrates on "teaching the subject" just as if Africans are objects being manipulated in the European frame of reference.

So, in the end, I would say, yes, whites can teach African American history but a more acute question is: are whites willing to make the necessary commit-ment to teach accurately and Afrocentrically? Only when we are able to answer in the affirmative to the preceding question can we really answer the question of "should" whites teach African American history.

IN THE HEADLINES:

Ebonics

BOARD OF EDUCATION OF THE OAKLAND, CALIFORNIA, UNIFIED SCHOOL DISTRICT: *Resolution Adopting the Report and Recommendations of the African American Task Force* [1996/1997]

BILL COSBY: *Elements of Igno-Ebonics Style* [1997]

ELLIS COSE: *Why Ebonics Is Irrelevant* [1997]

JOHN R. RICKFORD: *Letter to the Editor on Cose's "Why Ebonics Is Irrelevant"* [1997]

BRENT STAPLES: *The Last Train from Oakland: Will the Middle Class Flee the Ebonics Fad?* [1997]

JOHN BAUGH: *Ebonics Isn't "Street English" but a Heritage* [1997]

JOHN BAUGH: *Interview with an Unidentified Woman* [1999]

JOHN R. RICKFORD: *Linguistics, Education, and the Ebonics Firestorm* [2000]

NOMA LeMOINE: *Contrastive Analysis: A Linguistic Strategy for Advancing Language Acquisition in Standard English Learners (SELs)* [2007]

The term *Ebonics* (a combination of *ebony* and *phonics*) was coined by the psychologist Robert Williams in 1973 as an alternative to the label *Black English*. The term did not become popular, however, until the controversial 1996 decision by the Oakland, California, school board to classify Ebonics as the official language of its African American students. The Oakland resolution triggered negative responses from a wide range of black leaders and artists, from Ward Connerly and Shelby Steele to Kweisi Mfume, Maya Angelou, and Bill Cosby. Others, however, countered the initial negative reception with praise for what they viewed as "spoken soul," both outside and inside an educational context.

The resolution provoked two main areas of disagreement, one about what black vernacular is and one about its place in schools. The first area of contention revolved around the question of classifying and naming black vernacular. Is it a language, a dialect, or simply "bad" English? A particular name can celebrate or disparage it: terms such as *African American Vernacular English* (AAVE), *Black English* and *Non-standard English* convey respect for linguistic structure and cultural heritage, whereas such terms as *lazy English, bad grammar,* and *street slang* do not. Likewise, supporters tend to compare black vernacular with *Standard English, mainstream English,* or *corporate English,* while detractors contrast it with *proper English, good English,* or *correct English.* The choice of terms also reflects political positions and worldviews: *Ebonics,* for instance, suggests a black nationalist perspective, as it emphasizes Pan-African linguistic links while avoiding a reference to English. The choice of terminology can also have a direct affect on educational policy. For example, the categorization of black vernacular as either a dialect or a language can determine whether programs to teach Standard English to African Americans qualify for funding reserved for students who do not speak English. (Classifying Ebonics as a language, as the school board did, leaves open the possibility of using federal funds to support classrooms that use it.)

The second and main area of contention in the Oakland controversy wasn't about defining Ebonics or determining its value but was about whether it should be used in a school setting. Much of the uproar resulted from the mistaken belief that educators planned to teach black vernacular as a subject. In response to public reaction, the school board revised its resolution and stressed in press conferences that Ebonics would be used as a method to teach Standard English—and combat the high failure rate among African Americans in the Oakland schools. The revision also modified the claim that Ebonics is a language distinct from English: it kept the classification of Ebonics as a language but said that African Language Systems "are not merely dialects of English," rather than "are not a dialect of English," as in the original. The board proposed that educators build on the "language patterns students bring to schools" in order to teach Standard English while instilling a sense of cultural pride in these language patterns. Supporters of the resolution cited a wide body of scientific data to support this educational application of the vernacular. Historically, however, using black vernacular in schools has evoked negative responses from many black parents, politicians, and the media, who tend to view any use of the vernacular as out of place in schools.

Bill Cosby (b. 1937), the comedian and actor, who holds a doctorate in education, was one of those who reacted negatively to the board's resolution. In "Elements of Igno-Ebonics Style," he presents a satirical vision of the chaos that would ensue if Ebonics were legitimized. Although presented in a comic tone, his examples of the potential breakdown in communication reflect many of the common critiques of Ebonics: that Ebonics has few rules and is really a collection of regional dialects, that legitimizing Ebonics recalls the minstrel tradition of racist characterizations such as those in *The Amos 'n Andy Show* (p. 461), and that teaching with Ebonics will reduce job prospects for students while creating an elite industry for academics and others who specialize in the field.

In "Why Ebonics Is Irrelevant," the author and journalist Ellis Cose (b. 1951) agrees with the Oakland school board about the need for change in the education of black children. However, Cose sees the board's focus on Ebonics as a distraction at best. He examines a number of programs that have improved the academic performance of African Americans, none of which uses "exotic techniques" like Ebonics. Instead, successful programs attribute much of their success to a combination of high expectations and an insistence on positive results. Cose argues that the Ebonics policy at Oakland mistakenly makes the development of self-esteem a goal in itself rather than fostering self-respect rooted in concrete achievement.

In a letter written to but never published in *Newsweek,* where Cose's argument appeared, the Stanford University linguist John R. Rickford (b. 1949) supports Cose's focus on the educational plight of black children and endorses his educational principles. He argues that Cose is wrong to dismiss the educational role of the vernacular, however, and that using the vernacular is critical for fostering language skills. Rickford maintains that making the effort to examine the vernacular, "and contrasting it with the standard variety," is just the type of challenge that Cose espouses.

Whereas the debate between Ellis Cose and John Rickford focuses on the educational applications of black vernacular, the exchange between Brent Staples (b. 1951) and John Baugh (p. 867) explores the linguistic and cultural value of the black vernacular itself. In his harsh criticism of the Oakland resolution, Staples, who has a doctorate in psychology and is a popular author and an editorial writer for *The New York Times,* rejects the idea that Ebonics is a distinct "language system" and instead characterizes it as "broken, inner-city English." He argues that the Oakland policy would legitimate setting low standards for black students in the name of boosting self-esteem.

In his letter to the editor of *The New York Times* about Staples's op-ed piece, the Stanford University linguist John Baugh criticizes Staples's use of derogatory terms such as "broken, inner-city English" and "street English" in reference to "vernacular African-American English" (AAVE). Baugh stresses the importance of recognizing "the unique linguistic heritage of American slave descendents." He built on those ideas in his 1999 book on AAVE, which includes the interview reprinted here with an unidentified African American woman. That woman connects academic achievement and "good English" with white culture. She traces the current achievement gap, as well as her own lack of connection with the educational system, to the history of racism in the U.S. educational system, dating back to the time of slavery. (The idea that school failure in some communities is linked to the connection between school achievement and "acting white" has itself become a source of vigorous debate among social scientists.)

In "Linguistics, Education, and the Ebonics Firestorm," John R. Rickford works to refocus the debate. Arguing that the issue is not about the value of teaching Standard English (a goal everyone can agree on), Rickford discusses the best means of achieving that goal. He approaches the question systematically, providing a summary of the evidence for and against a bidialectical approach to teaching Standard English.

Among the programs Rickford cites is the Los Angeles–based Academic English Mastery Program (AEMP), directed by Noma LeMoine. In "Contrastive Analysis," LeMoine's 2007 paper on the implementation of the AEMP program, she argues that teachers need to understand, appreciate, and build on the home language and culture of "Standard English Learners" (SELs). Empirical data from evaluations done in 2000, 2004–2005, and 2005–2006 support her advocacy of contrastive analysis in the teaching of Standard English.

BOARD OF EDUCATION OF THE OAKLAND, CALIFORNIA, UNIFIED SCHOOL DISTRICT

Resolution Adopting the Report and Recommendations of the African American Task Force [1996, revised 1997]

Whereas, numerous validated scholarly studies demonstrate that African American students as a part of their culture and history as African people possess and utilize a language described in various scholarly approaches as "Ebonics" (literally "Black sounds") or "Pan-African Communication Behaviors" or "African Language Systems"; and

ORIGINAL TEXT OF THE DECEMBER RESOLUTION	REVISED TEXT OF THE JANUARY RESOLUTION
WHEREAS, these studies have also demonstrated that African Language Systems are genetically based and not a dialect of English; and	[WHEREAS, These studies have also demonstrated that African Language Systems _have origins in West and Niger-Congo language and are not merely dialects of English_; and]
WHEREAS, these studies demonstrate that such West and Niger-Congo African languages have been officially recognized and addressed in the mainstream public educational community as worthy of study, understanding or application of its principles,	[WHEREAS, these studies demonstrate that such West and Niger-Congo African languages have been (——) recognized and addressed in the (——) (——) educational community as worthy of study, understanding _and_ application of their principles,

laws and structures for the benefit of African-American students both in terms of positive appreciation of the

language and these students' acquisition and mastery of English language skills; and

WHEREAS, such recognition by scholars has given rise over the past fifteen years to legislation passed by the State of California recognizing the unique language status of descendants of slaves, with such legislation being prejudicially and unconstitutionally vetoed repeatedly by various California state governors; and

WHEREAS, judicial cases in states other than California have recognized the unique language stature of African-American pupils, and such recognition by courts has resulted in court-mandated educational programs which have substantially benefited African American children in the interest of vindicating their equal protection of the law rights under the Fourteenth Amendment to the United States Constitution; and

WHEREAS, the Federal Bilingual Education Act (20 U.S.C. 1402 *et. seq.*) mandates that local educational agencies "build their capacities to establish, implement and sustain programs of instruction for children and youth of limited English proficiency," and

WHEREAS, the interests of the Oakland Unified School District in providing equal opportunities for all of its students dictate limited English proficient educational programs recognizing the English language acquisition and improvement skills of African-American students are as fundamental as is

application of bilingual education principles for others whose primary languages are other than English;	application of bilingual _or second language learner_ principles for others whose primary languages are other than English. _Primary languages are the language patterns children bring to school_; and]

and

WHEREAS, the standardized tests and grade scores of African-American students in reading and language arts skills measuring their application of English skills are substantially below state and national norms and that such deficiencies will be remedied by application of a program featuring African Language Systems principles in instructing African-American children both in their primary language and in English; and

African Language Systems principles to move students from the language patterns they bring to school to English proficiency; and

WHEREAS, standardized tests and grade scores will be remedied by application of a program with teachers and aides who are certified in the methodology of featuring African Language Systems principles in instructing African-American children both in their primary language and in English.

instructional assistants who are certified in the methodology of featuring African Language Systems principles used to transition students from the language patterns they bring to school to English.

The certified teachers of these students will be provided incentives including, but not limited to salary differentials;

NOW, THEREFORE, BE IT RESOLVED that the Board of Education officially recognized the existence, and the cultural and historic bases of West and Niger-Congo African Language Systems, and each language as the predominantly primary language of African-American students; and

many African-American students;

BE IT FURTHER RESOLVED that the Board of Education hereby adopts the report, recommendations and attached policy Statement of the District's African-American Task Force on the language stature of African-American speech; and

BE IT FURTHER RESOLVED that the Superintendent in conjunction with her staff shall immediately devise and implement the best possible academic program for imparting instruction to African-American students in their primary language for the combined purposes of maintaining the legitimacy and richness of such language whether it is known as "Ebonics," "African Language Systems," "Pan-African Communication Behaviors" or other description, and to facilitate their acquisition and mastery of English language skills; and

the best possible academic program for (——) the combined purposes of facilitating the acquisition and mastery of English language skills, while respecting and embracing the legitimacy and richness of the language patterns whether they are known as "Ebonics," "African Language Systems," "Pan-African Communication Behaviors" or other description, and

BE IT FURTHER RESOLVED that the Board of Education hereby commits to earmark District general and special funding as is reasonably necessary and appropriate to enable the Superintendent and her staff to accomplish the foregoing; and

BE IT FURTHER RESOLVED that the Superintendent and her staff shall utilize the input of the entire Oakland educational community as well as state and federal scholarly and educational input in devising such a program; and

BE IT FURTHER RESOLVED that periodic reports on the progress of the creation and implementation of such an education program shall be made to the Board of Education at least once per month commencing at the Board meeting on December 18, 1996.

Reprinted in John Baugh, *Beyond Ebonics: Linguistic Pride and Racial Prejudice* (New York: Oxford University Press, 2000), pp. 43–46.

BILL COSBY
Elements of Igno-Ebonics Style [1997]

I remember one day 15 years ago, a friend of mine told me a racist joke.

QUESTION: Do you know what Toys "R" Us is called in Harlem?

ANSWER: We Be Toys.

So, before the city of Oakland, Calif., starts to teach its teachers Ebonics, or what I call "Igno-Ebonics," I think the school board should study all the ramifications of endorsing an urbanized version of the English language.

After all, Ebonics be a complex issue.

If teachers are going to legitimize Ebonics, then all authority figures who interact with children—such as law-enforcement officers—will have to learn it as well. In fact, the consequences of a grammatical accident could be disastrous during a roadside encounter with a policeman.

The first thing people ask when they are pulled over is: "Why did you stop me, officer?" Imagine an Ebonics-speaking Oakland teenager being stopped on the freeway by a non-Ebonics speaking California Highway Patrol officer. The teenager, posing that same question Ebonically, would begin by saying: "Lemme ax you . . ." The patrolman, fearing he is about to be hacked to death, could charge the kid with threatening a police officer. Thus, to avoid misunderstandings, notices would have to be added to driver's licenses warning: "This driver speaks Ebonics only."

Since people with driver's licenses tend to drive, what happens when an Ebonics-speaking youth drives into another state? Kids who speak Oakland Ebonics would find it difficult to converse with someone fluent in Pennsylvania Ebonics. And Tennessee Ebonics would be impossible to decipher.

Consider the following phrase: "I am getting ready to go." Even before Ebonics, Southern people changed the way they announced their imminent departure by saying: "I am fixing to go." Ebonically schooled Tennessee kids, however, would declare: "Ima fi'n nah go."

Meanwhile, depending on your geograhic locale, that same idea would be expressed in a variety of ways, such as: "Ima go now," or "I be goin' now," or the future imperfect "Ima be goin' now."

If Ebonics is allowed to evolve without any national standard, the only language the next generation would have in common would be body language. At the moment—if there are any current rules to Ebonics—one of them seems to be that any consonant at the end of a word must be dropped, particularly the letter G. This allows certain words to be strung together into one larger word. Ergo, the Ebonically posed question "Where was you workinlas?" translates into English as "Where were you working last?"

Of course, this query is most likely to be found on a job application, which means that Ebonics-speaking youths will not get a job unless they are aware that "working" and "last" are two words instead of one. Therefore, companies interested in recruiting Ebonics-speaking workers would need to hire Ebonics-speaking assistants to provide translations. That would open up employment opportunity by creating the new job of "Ebonics specialist." But even a staff of Ebonics specialists could cause chaos.

Suppose an Ebonics-speaking nurse hands a patient some eye drops and says, "Put 'em in an ear fur near." (Translation: "an hour from now.") A non-Ebonics-speaking patient might fill his ear with Visine.

Then there's the tourist problem. Until now, foreign visitors only had to learn a modicum of English to get by in America. A quick Berlitz course and they could haltingly say: "How are you?" With Ebonics an official language, tourists also would need to learn an Ebonics greeting such as: "Sapnin'?"

Another factor inherent in the widespread acceptance of Ebonics would be its cultural impact. In Hollywood, for instance, film studios would be delighted to have two categories instead of one in which to group African-American actors. While there always would be parts for "non-Ebonics black people," casting agents also would be asking: "Can you act Ebonics?" Naturally there would have to be English subtitles for Ebonics movies. (Maybe Ebonics is actually a conspiracy to resurrect the old "Amos & Andy" show.)

A lot of kids make the argument for Ebonics by insisting: "But this is the way I talk on the street!" In London, I guess Cockney would be the equivalent of Ebonics. And though they may study Cockney at Oxford as part of literature, I doubt they teach it. Granted, if you don't teach Ebonics, the children will find it anyway. But legitimizing the street in the classroom is backwards. We should be working hard to legitimize the classroom—and English—in the street. On the other hand, we could jes letem do wha ever they wanna. Either way, Ima go over heanh an learn some maffa matics an then ge-sum 'n tee an' then I'll be witchya.

From *The Wall Street Journal*, January 10, 1997.

ELLIS COSE

Why Ebonics Is Irrelevant [1997]

If Oakland's school board accomplished nothing else, it gave people (at least those who were not howling in dismay) something to laugh at over the holidays. Yet, all the hooting over "Ebonics" notwithstanding, the board's call for change was justified. America's dereliction of its educational duty to black children is a national tragedy. Unfortunately, in lieu of a solution, Oakland, Calif., came up with stale, silly rhetoric.

The problem is not that the board embraced Ebonics, but that it put Ebonics at the core of its educational strategy. If schoolteachers want to learn black vernacular, or turn themselves into amateur linguists, that is perfectly fine, perhaps even desirable, but it won't necessarily transform them into better teachers. If Oakland educators truly are incapable of communicating with children from the "'hood," they have a problem that a crash course in "black English" won't solve. The key to teaching black children (or any children) is not in convincing them that they speak a foreign language, but that they are capable of mastering any material put in front of them. Numerous teachers are already doing that—and without resorting to jargon about "Niger-Congo" idioms. Sadly, such teachers

don't make up the majority of the educational establishment. And children pay the price.

Last month, the Education Trust, a Washington-based nonprofit organization, released a report documenting educational meltdown on a massive scale. After years of watching the achievement gap between white and minority children narrow, the trust found that the gap has grown over the last six years. Although one third of white eighth graders were judged proficient in mathematics, only one in 33 black students and one in 14 Latinos were performing comparably. The reason is simple, said the report: "we take students who have less to begin with and give them less in school, too."

Yet, even in an ocean of failure, there are islands of success. Waitz Elementary School in Mission, Texas, with a student body that is overwhelmingly poor and Latino, saw well over 90 percent of its fourth graders place at (or above) grade level in the math and English sections of a standardized test. How? By closely monitoring students' work and relentlessly focusing on developing skills, observed the trust's director, Kati Haycock.

Waitz is not alone. Xavier University in New Orleans has worked wonders with black high schoolers through summer enrichment programs that routinely catapult youngsters to new achievement levels. Many of those students end up attending Xavier, which, largely as a result of its single-minded focus on academics, sends more blacks to medical schools than any other institution in the country. Philip Uri Treisman, a mathematician at the University of Texas at Austin, has worked similar educational magic, making math whizzes out of numerous black and Latino students, many of whom, without his help, seemed destined for math mediocrity. Over the last four years, administrators in El Paso, Texas, have reported a stunning turnaround in performance in 15 schools previously rated as disasters. The secret, says Susana Navarro, executive director of the El Paso Collaborative, is a philosophy rooted in the belief that "virtually all students are capable of high achievement." Robert Slavin, codirector of Johns Hopkins University's Center for Research on the Education of Children Placed at Risk, reports equally heartening news from the more than 400 schools in 31 states associated with his center. The typical fifth grader in an affiliated school, he says, is a full academic year ahead of his nonaffiliated peers. "Some bright, enthusiastic, highly motivated kids are washed up by the third grade," beaten down by failure, and expectations of failure, all around them, says Slavin. "We try to break the cycle . . . so that these kids can succeed," he adds.

None of the miracle workers employs exotic techniques. (Delving into Ebonics, notes Slavin, is irrelevant to the enterprise: "It's just not an issue.") They all, however, insist on results, and they develop materials and teaching methods capable of achieving those results. Arthur Whimbey, a psychologist and director of the TRAC Research Institute in Albuquerque, N.M., who helped generate many of the materials used at Xavier and elsewhere, uses "text reconstruction" (which entails having students reconstruct vignettes they are given in scrambled sentence order) to hone grammar and reasoning skills. Although the vignettes may focus on black notables, the purpose is not merely to develop racial pride but to sharpen practical skills.

In my new book, "Color-Blind" (*HarperCollins*), I attempt to distill the principles that make the successful programs work: (1) find a group of young people motivated to learn, or find a way to motivate them; (2) convince them you believe in them; (3) teach them good study skills; (4) challenge them with difficult and practical material; (5) give them adequate support, and (6) demand that they perform. Unfortunately, far too many educators conclude, in effect, that it's easier to teach students to feel good about themselves—and even about their academic failings—than it is to help them raise their level of performance. Self-esteem becomes a goal unto itself.

Certainly, cultivating pride and self-respect is a worthwhile goal, but that self-respect should be rooted in achievement. Students already at an educational disadvantage should not be provided with false pride in the misuse of language. Rather, they should be provided with confidence that they can perform at the highest academic levels, and with the support and tools to do so.

From *Newsweek*, January 13, 1997, p. 80.

JOHN R. RICKFORD

Letter to the Editor on Cose's "Why Ebonics Is Irrelevant" [1997]

DEAR SIR/MADAM:

Ellis Cose's "Lifestyle" column (Jan. 13) on Ebonics was right to focus on "America's dereliction of its educational duty to Black Americans." And the principles which he associates with successful school programs, including greater challenge and motivation, are ones with which we can all agree.

His contention that Ebonics is irrelevant to school success, is, however, simply wrong. On theoretical grounds alone it is unlikely that the mastery of curriculum-central linguistic skills like reading and writing would be unrelated to the language that children bring with them to the classroom. And empirically, studies both in Europe and the United States have shown that with other factors held more or less constant, the ways in which schools respond to the vernacular dialects of their pupils can play a major role in the children's chances of success.

Paradoxically, but quite in line with the principle of increased challenge which Cose espouses, programs in Norway, Sweden, Atlanta, Chicago, Oakland and elsewhere have shown that if teachers and students go through the additional enterprise of recognizing the systematicity of the vernacular and contrasting it with the standard variety, kids learn to read and write more quickly and manage the transition to the standard more successfully than if schools attempt to ignore the vernacular or legislate its demise.

JOHN R. RICKFORD
Stanford, California

Unpublished letter to *Newsweek*, January 17, 1997.

BRENT STAPLES

The Last Train from Oakland: Will the Middle Class Flee the Ebonics Fad? [1997]

The Oakland, Calif., school board deserved the scorn that greeted its December edict declaring broken, inner-city English a distinct, "genetically based" language system that merited a place in the classroom. The policy is intended to build self-esteem for failing students by introducing street language as a teaching tool. In theory, teachers would use street talk as a "bridge" to help children master standard English. But as practiced elsewhere, so-called "ebonics" instruction is based on the premise that street English is as good or better than the standard tongue. This means that students could use urban slang in their schoolwork.

Oakland's attempt to link genes and language was both racist and idiotic. Yesterday's Congressional hearing underscored this point, and brought the city's superintendent under heavy attack. Outraged by the city's proposal, one Congressman suggested restricting Federal aid to the Oakland district.

After the initial barrage of criticism in December, the Oakland board seemed to backtrack, voting last week to drop an explosive passage that spoke of a "genetically based" language. But the board signaled its true intent by saying it would "embrace" broken inner-city English, encouraging children to speak and write it in school. The sanitized resolution is no better than the original. It patronizes inner-city children, holding them to abysmally low standards.

The *Los Angeles Times* reports that while blacks make up slightly more than half the student population in Oakland, they account for 71 percent of the special-education pupils and only 37 percent of those in programs for the gifted. Educators elsewhere might suggest other remedies—early intervention and tutoring programs, a stronger and more coherent curriculum, a forceful effort to persuade parents to support at home what teachers try to accomplish at school. But the Oakland resolution recommends nothing of the sort. It is, rather, a 60's-style rant that condemns politicians while absolving parents and communities of any responsibility for failure. It blames the Federal Government for not providing more money. It blames several former governors for rejecting bills that declared so-called "black English" a distinct language. It blames the teachers for not communicating in urban English—and offers them bonuses if they do. Most catastrophically of all, in the name of promoting "self-esteem" the board has conspired to lower the performance bar, declaring all students to be "equal" regardless of whether they have difficulty speaking, reading, writing, or understanding the English language.

The Oakland strategy is in no way unique. As Jacob Heilbrunn illustrates in the Jan. 20 *New Republic,* so-called "black English"—or "ebonics"—programs have flourished in California schools since the late 1980's, when San Diego began four pilot programs. The programs can be found in San Diego and Los Angeles, where the program is said to reach 31 schools and 25,000 students. "Ebonics" has become a multimillion-dollar affair, with academic theorists, lushly paid consultants and textbook writers all poised to spread the gospel.

Some defenders say "ebonics" functions as a bridge between street and standard English. But in practice, time that should be spent on reading and algebra gets spent giving high fives and chattering away in street language. As a San Diego instructor told *The New Republic,* "If a writing assignment is handed in, written in the home language, the teacher will say 'I like this. This is good. . . .' They will not say 'This is incorrect.'" "Ebonics" theory licenses this approach. As one of its founders wrote 20 years ago in *The Journal of Black Studies,* the theory avoids giving standard English "a higher status than it deserves."

The Oakland policy will further isolate children who are already cut off from mainstream values and ideas. But its most corrosive effect may be to drive out the middle-class families that keep schools and other institutions afloat. Imagine yourself a parent with the Oakland resolution in one hand, an application to private school in the other—and a streetwise teen-ager to educate. What would you do?

From *The New York Times,* January 24, 1997.

JOHN BAUGH

Ebonics Isn't 'Street English' but a Heritage [1997]

To the Editor:

It is regrettable that Brent Staples continues to refer to vernacular African-American English as "broken, inner-city English" and "street English" in his criticisms of the Oakland, Calif., school board for its proposal to treat African-American English as a second language (Editorial Notebook, Jan. 24).

Although Oakland's resolutions are poorly worded, it is wrong to misrepresent the unique and profound linguistic consequences of American slavery.

Whereas typical European immigrants may have come to the United States in poverty, speaking a language other than English, they were not enslaved captives who were isolated from other speakers of their native language, which was a practice employed by slave traders to prevent revolts. Nor were they denied statutory access to schools, literacy or judicial relief in the courts.

The Linguistic Society of America has recently affirmed the unique linguistic heritage of American slave descendants, and Mr. Staples's continued misrepresentation of African-American English only serves to perpetuate uninformed linguistic stereotypes.

JOHN BAUGH
Swarthmore, Pa.
Jan. 24, 1997

From *The New York Times,* January 29, 1997.

JOHN BAUGH

Interview with an Unidentified Woman [1997]

You just can never forget that slavery was a bitch from the get-go. Slaves didn't get no schoolin

and they ain't never really given us [African Americans] equal opportunities, so how we supposed to talk like white folks, and why would we want to? It ain't no white people really care about us, cause if they did they wouldn't try to make you turn into a white person, they'd take you like you is. But they don't do that. All my teachers in school kept tellin me, "If you don't speak proper, you won't get a job." That's bullshit! I know some Brothers that went to college—y'know, they did the "white thing," with good grades and good English, and they still have problems on the job. They done tol me about this Brother who did all the work for a white boy at his job, and then they [the Whites] lied on his ass when the boss found out and he was fired, and nobody tried to help him. How can you trust motherfuckers that do shit like that, and then they say we stupid cause we don't talk proper. Talkin proper don't feel natural to me, but that don't make me stupid—I see what's goin on, and I see what's comin down, and it ain't got nothin to do with how we talk. It's all about money, power, and politics—plain and simple!

From John Baugh, *Out of the Mouths of Slaves: African American Language and Educational Malpractice* (Austin: University of Texas Press, 1999), p. 5.

JOHN R. RICKFORD

Linguistics, Education, and the Ebonics Firestorm [2000]

Introduction. One profession with which linguistics has long been associated—at least through the research and activities of linguists in applied linguistics, sociolinguistics, and other subfields—is education. Applied linguistics has been primarily concerned with the teaching and learning of foreign languages, but it also includes the study of language disorders and mother tongue/bilingual education as well as other topics (Crystal 1991: 22). Key journals in this area, among them *Applied Linguistics* and the *Annual Review of Applied Linguistics,* go back to the early 1980s and the late 1960s, respectively.

In the early 1960s, leading descriptive linguists like Leonard Bloomfield (Bloomfield and Barnhart 1961) and Charles Fries (1962) contributed book-length works on the teaching of reading using a linguistics approach. More recently, Kenneth Goodman (1998) waded in to defend the "whole language" approach to the teaching of reading after the California legislature mandated that reading be taught through phonics and phonemic awareness. And Stephen Krashen (1999) and Kenji Hakuta (www.stanford.edu/~hakuta/) were among the many linguists who rose to the defense of bilingual education, severely restricted in California since 1998 by Proposition 227, a state ballot initiative approved by 61 percent of the voting public.

The closing decade of the twentieth century was an especially vigorous period for public debate about language in the United States and Canada (Heller et al. 1999), and, as the preceding examples suggest, nowhere was this truer than in California. In this paper, I will sketch the outlines of the *other* big language and education controversy that exploded in California in this period—the Ebonics firestorm of 1996 and 1997—and discuss the role of linguistics and linguists in it. At the core of the conflagration were the resolutions approved by the Oakland School Board in December 1996, and I will therefore discuss what those meant, in pedagogical terms, and what the experimental evidence is in favor of and against such pedagogy. But the motivation for the Oakland resolutions was the limited academic progress and success that African-American students experience(d) in elementary, junior, and high schools, particularly in curriculum-central, language arts areas like reading and writing, and it is with the evidence of this that we must properly begin.

[1] How K–12 schools have been failing African-American students. The extent to which African-American students were failing in Oakland schools—or, viewed another way, the extent to which such schools were failing African-American students—was documented by Oakland Superintendent of Schools Carolyn Getridge in the *Montclarion* on December 31, 1996:[1]

The findings on student achievement in Oakland are evidence that the current system is not working for most African-American children. While 53% of the students in the Oakland Unified School District (OUSD) are African-American, only 37% of the students enrolled in Gifted and Talented classes are African-American, and yet 71% of the students enrolled in Special Education are African-American.

The grade point average of African-American students is 1.80 [C–] compared to a district average of 2.40 [C+]. 64% of students who repeat the same grade are African-American; 67% of students classified as truant are African-American; 80% of all suspended students are African-American; and only 81% of the African-American students who make it to the 12th grade actually graduate.

It was statistics like these, which Getridge herself described as "mind-numbing and a cause for moral outrage" (as quoted in Perry and Delpit 1998: 158), that prompted the OUSD to establish a Task Force on the Education of African-American Students in June 1996; the school board's December resolutions were directly based on the task force's findings.

But the statistics that Superintendent Getridge presented, while indeed disturbing, were in one respect too general and in another too specific. They were too general insofar as they did not reveal how African-American students were doing on subjects like reading and writing, justifying a specific response involving language. And they were too specific insofar as they failed to reveal that the situation was similar for African-American students in virtually every urban school district across the country, making it not just Oakland's problem, but America's.

Consider, for instance, reading achievement data for students in several of the largest urban school districts (including Oakland, but also San Francisco, Los Angeles, New York, Atlanta, and fifty others)—districts that are part of a consortium called the Council of the Great City Schools. These statistics were presented by Michael Casserly, Executive Director of

---

1. This article was reprinted in *Rethinking Schools* (an urban education journal), vol. 12, no. 1, fall 1997, 27, and in the book-length version of that issue (Perry and Delpit 1998). [Unless otherwise indicated, all footnotes are those of the author.]

TABLE 1

Students Scoring above the Fiftieth Percentile on 1992–1993 Reading Achievement Tests

ETHNIC GROUP (%)	K–6TH GRADE (%)	7TH–8TH GRADE (%)	9TH–12TH GRADE (%)
Blacks	31.3	26.9	26.6
Whites	60.7	63.4	65.4

TABLE 2

Differences in Average Proficiency of White and Black Students in Reading

YEAR	9-YEAR-OLDS (POINTS)	13-YEAR-OLDS (POINTS)	17-YEAR-OLDS (POINTS)
1994	29	31	37
1984	32	26	31
1971	44	38	53

the Council of the Great City Schools, at a United States Senate Appropriations Subcommittee hearing on Ebonics chaired by Sen. Arlen Specter on January 23, 1997.

Table 1 is a partial representation of Great City School results on standardized, norm-referenced reading achievement tests taken in 1992–93.[2] The achievement tests are normed so that 50 percent of the students who take them should score above the fiftieth percentile. The white students in fifty-five large United States urban school districts surpassed this norm at each school level, the percentage that did so increasing from 60.7 percent at the elementary level to 65.4 percent at the high school level. By contrast, only 31.3 percent of black elementary students scored above the fiftieth percentile, and this proportion declined to 26.6 percent by the high school level.

Reading proficiency data from the National Assessment of Educational Progress (NAEP)—also presented to the 1997 Senate Ebonics hearing by Michael Casserly—were similarly disconcerting. As Table 2 shows, while the gap between black and white reading scores is much less in 1994 than it was in 1971, it is still considerable and shows signs of creeping up from 1984 levels. Moreover, the Table 1 pattern is repeated in Table 2, in the sense that the performance of black students, relative to their white counterparts, steadily declined as they got older. Nine-year-old black students had mean scores 29 points (on a 500-point scale) behind those of their white counterparts; but

thirteen-year-old black students were further behind their white counterparts (31 points), and seventeen-year-old black students further still (37 points behind).

Finally, lest it be imagined that the situation has improved since 1993 and 1994, Table 3 shows 1999 data from the Great City Schools (Michael Casserly, personal communication, December 8, 2000). The data are similar to but not exactly comparable with those of Table 1, since they represent averages for one grade only (fourth, eighth, tenth) at the elementary, middle, and senior high levels, rather than for all the grades at each level. But they are just as devastating, if not more so. The percentage of blacks scoring above the fiftieth percentile norm, which should be 50 percent if the population were reading on target, has sunk even further between 1993 and 1999, from 31 percent to 19 percent at the elementary level and from 27 percent to 10.5 percent at the high school level. The fact that the relative gap between white *and* black students is

TABLE 3

Students Scoring above the Fiftieth Percentile on 1999 Reading Achievement Tests

ETHNIC GROUP	GRADE 4 (%)	GRADE 8 (%)	GRADE 10 (%)
Blacks	19.4	21.5	10.5
Whites	55.5	61.2	36.4

2. Casserly's tables also included results for Hispanic, Asian/Pacific Islander, and Alaskan/Native American/Other students. Of these other groups, the Hispanic students' reading scores were most comparable to those of the African-American students. Thirty-two percent of them scored above the fiftieth percentile at the K–6 grade level, 30.4 percent did so at the middle school level, and 24.2 percent did so at the high school level.

reduced in the tenth grade (they both show a precipitous decline from eighth grade pass rates) is no cause for rejoicing, since the percentage of black students who score above the fiftieth percentile is so abysmally low (10.5 percent).

It is statistics like these—largely ignored by the government, the media, and the general public in their amused and outraged reactions to the Oakland Ebonics resolutions—that prompted Oakland's African-American Task Force and the Oakland School Board to attempt to take corrective action in 1996. In the next section we'll consider the resolutions themselves, bearing in mind that most of Oakland's critics rarely did so.

[2] Oakland's Ebonics Resolutions and testimony before the United States Senate panel. In response to the educational malaise of black students in its district, Oakland's African-American Task Force in 1996 came up with *nine* recommendations, including full implementation of all existing educational programs, with new financial commitments to facilitate this. The Task Force also advocated reviewing the criteria for admitting students to Gifted and Talented Education and Special Education, mobilizing community involvement in partnership with the schools, and developing new procedures for the recruitment of teachers, counselors, and other staff. The number one recommendation, however, had to do with language:

> African American students shall develop English language proficiency as the foundation for their achievements in all core competency areas. (Oakland Unified School District 1996)

In her statement before the United States Senate hearing on Ebonics on January 23, 1997,[3] Oakland School Superintendent Carolyn Getridge explained *why* the Task Force zeroed in on English language proficiency as a key element in improving student achievement:

> The Task Force's research identified the major role language development plays as the primary gate-

keeper for academic success. Without English language proficiency students are unable to access or master advanced level course work in the areas of mathematics and science which have traditionally been viewed as the gatekeepers to enrollment in post-secondary education. (U.S. Senate 1997: 1)

One could of course add that English language proficiency affects not only mathematics and science, but also social studies and every other subject in the curriculum. Going beyond the rationale for the language focus, Superintendent Carolyn Getridge said a little about *how* the OUSD would attempt to achieve increased competency in Standard American English—by building a bridge to it from the African-American students' vernacular:

> Language development for African American students . . . will be enhanced with the recognition and understanding of the language structures unique to many African American students. . . . Our interest is in guaranteeing that conditions exist for high achievement and research indicates that an awareness of these language patterns by educators helps students build a bridge to Standard American English. A variety of strategies will be employed to support language development and achieve our goal of high academic performance for all students. (U.S. Senate 1997: 1–2)

Getridge's testimony added that such bridging would be achieved in part through increased implementation of the Standard English Proficiency program (SEP), a program authorized by state legislation since 1981, which she described briefly as follows:

> S.E.P. is a cultural-linguistic program that empowers African American students with knowledge and understanding of African American culture and languages. Classroom instruction demonstrates the differences in language spoken in the student's home and standard English. The language students bring into the classroom is embraced and a bridge is constructed to standard English. (U.S. Senate 1997: 13)

---

3. More precisely, the hearing was before the United States Senate Subcommittee on Labor, Health and Human Services, and Education, chaired by Sen. Arlen Specter (R-Pa.).

However, Getridge did not provide any experimental evidence in favor of this bridging or Contrastive Analysis (CA) approach. In this respect she failed to respond to the critique of California State Schools Superintendent Delaine Eastin that "We are not aware of any research which indicates that this kind of program will help address the language and achievement problems of African American students."[4] This is an issue that I'll address in the next subsection of this paper. To lay the groundwork, first consider the OUSD's famous (or perhaps infamous) Ebonics Resolutions of December 18, 1996, and their revisions of January 17, 1997, both of which preceded the January 23, 1997, Senate hearing on Ebonics at which Superintendent Getridge testified.[5]

[* * *]

Many comments could be made about the various clauses of this resolution, considering, inter alia, the ones that were the source of public controversy about Ebonics as a separate Niger-Congo and genetically based language (clause 2, in its original wording), and whether the OUSD intended to seek bilingual funding for its Ebonics speakers (clauses 6, 7, and 8). These and related issues are discussed at length in other sources, including McWhorter (1998: 127–260), Baugh (2000: 36–86), Rickford and Rickford (2000: 169–173), Smitherman (2000: 150–162), and Crawford (2001).

What I want to focus on instead is the more fundamental issue of whether the OUSD intended by these resolutions to teach African-American students Ebonics or in Ebonics, as most of the country and the world assumed, or to use Ebonics partly as a springboard for helping them to master Standard English.[6] The quotations from Superintendent Getridge's senate testimony indicate that the latter rather than the former was the main goal. And the preamble (capitalized and unchanged in both versions) to the resolutions does refer explicitly to the goal of improving "the English

language acquisition and application skills of African-American students." It is true that the December 1996 wording of clauses 8, 9, and 12 does refer to instructing African-American children "in their primary language" (as McWhorter 2000: 202–203 and others have pointed out). But, as noted by Rickford and Rickford (2000: 172), these could be legitimately interpreted as referring to technical instruction in the features of the primary or source variety as part of the compare-and-contrast process used to develop mastery in the target variety (in this case, Standard English). And while most Contrastive Analysis approaches are built on a philosophy of respect for the legitimacy of the source variety, which we certainly endorse, it is not necessary to try to develop verbal fluency in Ebonics among inner-city African-American students: "tutoring them on Ebonics would be like giving a veteran angler a lesson on baiting hooks" (Rickford and Rickford 2000: 172).

In any event, the revised resolution wording of January 1997 was clearly intended to remove ambiguities on this score, with clauses like "used to transition students from the language patterns they bring to school to English" replacing the earlier ambiguous wording. And to make the matter maximally explicit, the OUSD issued a press release shortly after the first version of the resolutions came out (and ran into a hornet's nest), emphasizing that:

1. The Oakland Unified School District is not replacing the teaching of Standard American English with any other language.

2. The District is not teaching Ebonics.

3. The District emphasizes teaching Standard American English and has set a high standard of excellence for all its students.

Given that the primary *goal* of the OUSD was to help its African-American students master Standard

---

4. Eastin's comment appeared in the *San Jose Mercury* newspaper, 20 December 1996, 1A, in an article by Frances Dinkelspiel titled, "Black Language Policy in Oakland: Talk of the Town."

5. For the full text of the resolutions, which Rickford included here, see the first text in this discussion of Ebonics (p. 000). [Editor's note]

6. In this paper, as in Rickford (1999c), I will use Ebonics and African-American Vernacular English or Black English as essentially equivalent. Despite claims that they are different (see, e.g., Smith 2001), especially insofar as Ebonics is claimed to be an African variety and NOT a dialect of English, the features cited as representative of these different varieties are virtually identical, as noted in Rickford (1999c).

English (a goal that it ironically shared with its detractors!), the debate can be refocused (as it never was in the media) on the efficacy of the *means* (including CA) that Oakland wanted to use to achieve this end. To the extent that linguists specifically responded to this issue, the answer seemed to be that the approach was efficacious and advisable. But the relevant evidence was not always provided, and the endorsement was not completely unanimous, as we will see.

[3] **Arguments and evidence FOR the Contrastive Analysis approach that Oakland intended to use to implement its resolutions.** The precise methods the OUSD intended to use in teaching its African-American students Standard English were never spelled out in detail, certainly not in its resolutions. The revised (January 17, 1997) resolution's *closing* clause (12) specified, in fact, that "the Superintendent in conjunction with her staff *shall immediately devise and implement* the best possible program for facilitating the acquisition and mastery of English language skills, while embracing the legitimacy and richness of the language patterns . . . known as Ebonics . . ." (emphasis added). The only methodological mandate in this was that the students' vernacular (Ebonics) was to be taken into account in the process. However, as noted above (see quotes at the beginning of section 2), Superintendent Getridge's Senate testimony on January 23, 1997, did indicate that the sixteen-year-old Standard English Proficiency (SEP) program, with its Contrastive Analysis and bridging strategies, was to be an important element in their approach.

The SEP program itself was already in use in some of Oakland's classrooms (the postresolution plan was to implement it more widely), and Oakland was a key SEP site in California, serving as host of its annual statewide conferences for several years. In the SEP handbook, a massive 340-page document,[7] the goal of helping vernacular-speaking African-American students master Standard English is spelled out quite explicitly (SEP handbook n.d.: 5):[8]

> This handbook is designed as a resource for school site administrators and classroom teachers in initiating, implementing and improving Standard English programs. The contributors to this handbook maintain that proficiency in Standard English is essential in providing students with those skills that will afford them the opportunity to experience optimum access to the social and economic mainstream.
>
> The handbook offers a theoretical and functional framework to operate an oral-based language program that is designed to assist speakers of Black Language [Black English or Ebonics] in becoming proficient in Standard English.

Moreover, while emphasizing that a positive attitude towards one's own language is the starting point for the program, the SEP handbook goes on to specify that Contrastive Analysis, with its discrimination, identification, translation, and response drills (see Feigenbaum 1970) is its basic methodology (SEP n.d.: 27):

> The approaches used in this study are drills which are variations of the contrastive analysis and the comparative analysis [techniques] in teaching Black children to use Standard English. . . . By comparing the Standard English structure to be taught and the equivalent or close nonstandard structure, the student can see how they differ. Many students have partial knowledge of standard English; that is, they can recognize and produce it but without accurate control. . . . For many students, this sorting out is the beginning of a series

7. The date of production of the handbook (which is not necessarily followed in all California schools that use the SEP approach) is unclear (in my copy at least), although it appears to be sometime in the 1980s. Its authors/contributors are listed in the acknowledgments (4) as: Sue Boston, Audrey Guess Knight, Yvonne Strozier, Rex Fortune, and Orlando Taylor. Taylor is a Howard University linguist and speech pathologist who has contributed to the study of Ebonics for decades, and who testified before the United States Senate panel on Ebonics in January 1997. He is also one of the coeditors of Adger, Christian, and Taylor (1999).

8. In view of its explicit Standard English orientation, it is especially ironic that California Senate Bill 205 was introduced in 1997 to kill the SEP program, on the argument that it was important for students to master Standard English. Fortunately, the bill died in a state senate committee on April 7, 1997.

of steps from passive recognition to active production.

However, despite its twenty years of implementation and its reported use in over 300 schools, there is no publicly available empirical evidence of the SEP's effectiveness (as noted by Yarborough and Flores 1997). So it is of little use in arguing for the approach the OUSD intended to take in implementing its resolutions or in defending it against its many critics. This is also true of the well-designed "Talkacross" program designed by Crowell and colleagues (1974), featuring Contrastive Analysis between "Black English" and Standard English in a 69-page teacher's manual and a 193-page activity book.

The Linguistic Society of America (LSA), the American Association for Applied Linguistics (AAAL), and Teachers of English to Speakers of Other Languages (TESOL) were among several language-related organizations that approved resolutions of their own in the wake of the Ebonics firestorm.[9] In general, these provided support for the principle of respecting the legitimacy of the linguistic systems students bring to school, recognized the systematic nature of Ebonics, and endorsed the value of taking it into account in teaching Standard English. But even when they made reference to the existence of evidence in favor of the latter approach, they did not specifically cite it. This was also the case with Parker and Christ (1995), who reported that they had used the bidialectal, Contrastive Analysis approach successfully with Ebonics speakers in Tennessee and Illinois, but provided no supporting empirical evidence.

Such evidence does exist, however, in at least three striking cases, and I will turn to them shortly. But it may be useful to enumerate some of the arguments that linguists and others make in favor of Contrastive Analysis specifically, or more generally, in favor of taking Ebonics and other vernacular varieties into account in developing reading, writing, and other language arts skills in Standard English (see Rickford 1999b).

One argument is that this approach proceeds from a position of strength: the students are already competent in a valid, systematic language variety (their vernacular), and this fluency can be used as a springboard for teaching about important qualities of language in general (metaphor and rhyme, logical argument, authentic dialogue, rhetorical strategy) and about differences between the vernacular and the standard or mainstream variety in particular. The general strategy is facilitated by the fact that Ebonics and other vernaculars are often used by award-winning writers (e.g., Langston Hughes, Toni Morrison, Sonia Sanchez, August Wilson—see Rickford and Rickford 2000), several of whose works are already in use in American classrooms,[1] and by the fact that students encounter other fluent and effective vernacular users (e.g., preachers) regularly in their own communities (Rickford and Rickford 2000). Another argument in relation to the specific contrastive strategy is that "this method allows for increased efficiency in the classroom, as teachers can concentrate on the systematic areas of contrast with SE [Standard English] that cause difficulty for vernacular speakers rather than taking on the more daunting task of teaching all of English grammar" (Rickford 1999a: 13).

Moreover, an approach like this, it might be argued, is likely to have positive effects on both teachers and their vernacular-speaking students. Teachers, like many members of the general public, often erroneously perceive students' vernaculars as illogical, unsystematic, and evidence of cognitive deficits or laziness (Labov 1970; Van Keulen, Weddington, and DeBose 1998: 232). These misperceptions irk linguists because they run counter to everything we know about human language. But what's worse, they can lead to lower teacher expectations and poorer student performance in a cycle of self-fulfilling prophecy that's now depressingly well-documented (Tauber 1997). Students in turn are often relieved and delighted to learn that the vernacular they speak naturally is not the source of

---

9. The LSA resolution, approved on January 3, 1997 is reprinted in Perry and Delpit (1998: 160–161), Baugh (2000: 117–118), and Crawford (2001: 358–359). The AAAL resolution was approved on March 11, 1997, and the TESOL resolution on March 10, 1997.
1. I received two requests in the winter of 2000 to speak to Palo Alto high school students studying August Wilson's *Fences* about the pervasive African-American vernacular in his plays.

weakness that teachers often make it out to be, but a source of strength. Not only might their self-identity and motivation be enhanced by this,[2] but the resistance to Standard English that's sometimes reported as an element in black students' limited success in school (cf., Fordham and Ogbu 1986) is likely to be reduced in the process.

A third argument in favor of Contrastive Analysis and taking the vernacular into account is that the prevailing, status quo alternative of ignoring and/or constantly correcting students' vernaculars in an ad hoc and disparaging fashion clearly does NOT seem to work. This is evident, not only from the kinds of statistics reported in section 2, but also from reports in Piestrup (1973) and elsewhere that the corrective, disparaging approach leads students to withdraw from participation, turn to disruptive behavior, and perform more poorly in school.

The fourth and perhaps most effective argument is that there are at least three empirically validated studies of the effectiveness of taking the vernacular into account in teaching Standard English using Contrastive Analysis. The first is an experimental composition program conducted by Hanni Taylor with African-American students at Aurora University, outside Chicago, in the 1980s. The second is a fifth- and sixth-grade program run by Kelli Harris-Wright in DeKalb County, just outside Atlanta, in which home speech and school speech are contrasted. The third is the Academic English Mastery Program (formerly the Language Development Program for African-American Students) in Los Angeles, run by Noma LeMoine. I'll say some more about each of these before considering arguments and evidence against this approach.

In the Aurora University study (Taylor 1989), African-American students from Chicago inner-city areas were divided into two groups. The experimental group was taught the differences between Black English and Standard English through Contrastive Analysis.

The control group was taught composition through conventional techniques, with no specific reference to the vernacular. After eleven weeks, Taylor found that the experimental group showed a dramatic *decrease* (−59 percent) in the use of ten targeted Black English features in their Standard English writing, whereas the control group in fact showed a slight *increase* (+8.5 percent) in their use of such features in their writing.

In the DeKalb County (Georgia) study, described by Harris-Wright (1999), but without the specific results to be presented here, selected fifth and sixth graders in the bidialectal group (primarily African American) have for several years been taught English through a comparative approach that does not involve "devaluing the skills that they learn at home" (Harris-Wright 1999: 55). By contrast, control groups are offered no explicit comparison between their vernacular and Standard English. As the results in Table 4 show (Kelli Harris-Wright, personal communication), between 1995 and 1997, students in the bidialectal group made *bigger relative reading composite gains* every year than students in the control group, who actually showed

TABLE 4

Reading Composite Scores for Bidialectal and Control Groups

Group	1994–95	1995–96	1996–97
Bidialectal Posttest	42.39	41.16	34.26
Bidialectal Pretest	39.71	38.48	30.37
GAIN by			
bidialectal students	+2.68	+2.68	+3.89
Control Posttest	40.65	43.15	49.00
Control Pretest	41.02	41.15	49.05
GAIN by control			
students	−0.37	+2.00	−0.05

Source: *Kelli Harris-Wright, 1999, personal communication.*

2. As Van Keulen, Weddington, and DeBose (1998: 243) note: "when teachers accept Black students' home language and use books, other materials, and activities that incorporate their culture, teachers signal their recognition of Black students' values and concern for their self-esteem. Self-esteem and confidence are very important to academic success because students with high self-esteem will have the confidence to take on new challenges in reading, writing, and other academic tasks."

3. Students in the bidialectal group generally had lower absolute scores (particularly in the 1996–97 year) than students in the control group, although it is striking that the bidialectal group was able to surpass the control group in their posttest performance in 1995.

TABLE 5

Mean Scores and Gains for Experimental and Control Writing Groups, LA Unified School District

GROUP TEST	MEAN PRETEST SCORE	MEAN POSTTEST SCORE	GAIN
Experimental			
Writing	10.80	13.30	2.5
Control			
Writing	9.06	10.74	**1.68**

SOURCE: *Maddahian and Sandamela 2000.*

slight losses in two of the three years.[3] More recent results (1998, 1999) for individual elementary schools in DeKalb County point in the same direction, with the experimental, bidialectal students showing greater gains between pretest and posttest than students in the control group.

Finally, we have results from the Academic English Mastery Program (AEMP) in the Los Angeles Unified School District, shown in Table 5.[4] Once again, students in the experimental group show greater gains (on tests taken in 1998–99) than students in the control group. Similar results obtain for the reading and language components of the SAT-9 test.[5]

[4] **Arguments and evidence AGAINST the Contrastive Analysis, bidialectal approach.** Many, many statements (sometimes diatribes) were broadcast in the media and voiced by the general public AGAINST the Contrastive Analysis vernacular-respecting approach that Oakland proposed to use to implement its resolutions. However, since so many of these were uninformed about the OUSD resolutions and what they might mean in pedagogical terms, and about linguistics and its possible applications, they are of little utility in a reasoned discussion. By contrast, a number of linguists have, over the years, queried various aspects of the Contrastive Analysis, bidialectal approach, and at least one linguist has consistently opposed the Oakland resolutions and their implementation. It is their argumentation and evidence that we'll focus on in this section of the paper.

One of the oldest positions, typified by Sledd (1972), is that the teaching of Standard English under the guise of bidialectalism is both impossible and immoral. The impossibility claim hinged on the argument that "the necessary descriptions of standard and nonstandard dialects are non-existent, and materials and methods of teaching are dubious at best" (372–373). But the situation has changed dramatically in the intervening thirty years, especially in the last five years, which have seen a flood of books and articles about African-American Vernacular English, so this argument is no longer tenable. The immorality argument is that "forcing" students to learn Standard English buys into the prejudices and corruption of the dominant society and ignores the fact that "in job hunting in America pigmentation is more important than pronunciation" (379). We should aim for higher ambitions and deeper values in educating students than kowtowing to the majority, and, if anything, we should work on changing the prejudices and increasing the receptive abilities of whites rather than the productive abilities of blacks. To the extent that this kind of argument takes the linguistic and moral high ground, it is attractive, but not entirely convincing. There does appear to be a relation between the ability to command Standard English (whether or not one retains one's vernacular) and success in school and employment and mobility in a wide range of occupations. In addition, the parents of vernacular speakers are almost unanimous in wanting their children to master some variety of mainstream or Standard English (Hoover 1978).

The preceding argument is not really against Contrastive Analysis but against the explicit teaching of Standard English. However, there does exist a cluster of arguments against Contrastive Analysis and

4. The AEMP involves more than Contrastive Analysis, including language experience approaches, whole language, and an Afrocentric curriculum. But at the heart of it is respect for students' home languages and comparison of African-American language and Standard American English structures. For more information, see LeMoine (2001).

5. For instance, at the 109th Street school, African-American students in the experimental AEMP (n = 12) had mean scores of 21 and 24 on the reading and language components of the SAT-9, whereas a comparison group of African-American students who were not in the AEMP (n = 104) had lower mean scores of 16 and 20, respectively.

bidialectalism as methodologies. One, summarized by Craig (1999: 38), who in turn cites Jagger and Cullinan (1974), is that "such programmes were 'bi' in name only, because there was no structured use or development of cognitive/communicative capacity in the vernacular to match what was being attempted in English." Some programs (including the SEP) involve translation only into Standard English, and never into the vernacular. But, as I have noted in an earlier paper, "if translation is not carried out in both directions, the message . . . conveyed is that the vernacular variety has no integrity or validity" (Rickford 1999a: 14). The boring, stultifying nature of the drills that some contrastive approaches depend on is also problematic. However, as I've observed elsewhere (Rickford 1999a: 15): "these are not intrinsic weaknesses of contrastive analysis," and programs like the AEMP in Los Angeles, which makes extensive use of literature and other techniques, show that "drill and kill" can be minimized or eliminated.

A third methodological argument is that Contrastive Analysis and the interference hypothesis that undergirds it (Lado 1957) no longer hold the theoretical sway they once did in the field of second language acquisition, where it was first developed, since they seem to account for only a limited portion of second language learner's errors (Ellis 1994). However, the interference hypothesis does seem to account for a larger proportion of errors when two dialects of a language are compared and contrasted, and while error analysis and other analytical strategies should also be pursued, we have no substantive evidence that Contrastive Analysis is unhelpful to dialect speakers seeking to add a second variety, and some strong evidence to the contrary (see the end of the section arguing for Contrastive Analysis).

We come now to more specific arguments raised by John McWhorter against the OUSD's "translation approach," as he calls it. I'll use the brief summary from his (1997) paper as my point of reference, but his (1998) book provides further details, especially in chapter 8 (201–261).

McWhorter's first argument is that "Black English is not different enough from standard English to be the cause of the alarming reading scores among black children" (1997: 2). However, the argument made by many linguists is that while there are indeed some major dif-

ferences, it is precisely the many subtle differences between the two varieties that cause students difficulty in reading and especially in writing when they fail to recognize that they are switching between systems (Stewart 1964; Taylor 1989).

McWhorter dubs this latter position "Ebonics II"—especially to the extent that the subtle differences are negatively viewed and stigmatized by teachers—and he calls it a "thoroughly reasonable position." However, he still feels that the concerns could be better addressed by having students learn Standard English via immersion. But "immersion" is already the method in use in most urban school districts; and the results, as noted above, are not encouraging. Moreover, in the homes and communities where the students spend most of their time when not in school, Ebonics is widely heard and spoken, so "immersion" in Standard English on the model of students who go to another country for immersion in the language of that country is quite impractical.

McWhorter's other concerns include the claim that students speaking other dialects (e.g., Brooklyn, Appalachian, or rural Southern white English) "are not taught standard English as a foreign language, even though the latter is extremely similar to Black English. To impose translation exercises on black children implies that they are not as intelligent as white children" (1997: 2). To which I would retort that students from these other dialect areas often do have language arts and other educational problems that may well relate to their language differences. To the extent that this is so, I would rather give them the same benefit of linguistically informed bidialectal methods than deny the latter to everyone. Moreover, I am not convinced by the "intelligence insulting" argument. Nothing is more stultifying than the devastating rates of school failure with existing methods shown in section 2. If Contrastive Analysis and bidialectal education help to alleviate and even reverse the situation, as the evidence suggests, they are worth the effort.

McWhorter also argues that "the reason African American children fail disproportionately in school is due to declining school quality and the pathologies of the inner city" (1997: 2). I would agree that the (primarily) urban schools in which African Americans receive their education are indeed worse off than the ones in which whites do, in general terms (see Rickford 1999a: 5–8), but I would still argue that, other things being equal, an approach that took students' language into account, as the Contrastive Analysis approach does, is still more likely to succeed than one that does not.

McWhorter's biggest argument is that there are at least nine studies, including Melmed (1971), Nolen (1972), Marwit and Neumann (1974), and Simons and Johnson (1974), that show that "dialect readers have no effect whatsoever on African American students' reading scores." (Rickford 1999a: 2). But notwithstanding the fact that these are all nonlongitudinal, one-time studies, and that the only longitudinal dialect reader study involving African-American students (Simpkins and Simpkins 1981) shows very positive results, the crucial point to be noted is that Oakland never proposed using dialect readers in their language arts programs. The SEP program that was to be their primary implementation vehicle used Contrastive Analysis rather than dialect readers as their method of choice. McWhorter does not cite one empirical study that provides evidence against the efficacy of the Contrastive Analysis, bidialectal approach, and we have already seen several arguments and significant experimental evidence in its favor.

Summary and conclusion. My goal in this paper has been to sketch the outlines of a recent major public debate involving language and education—the Oakland school district's resolutions about taking Ebonics into account in teaching Standard English and the language arts—and to summarize the linguistic and pedagogical arguments in favor of and against Contrastive Analysis, the major strategy that they planned to implement. My own preference for the kind of innovative methods the OUSD proposed is probably obvious. I am led to this both because of the obvious failures of existing methods that make no reference to the vernacular, and show no concern for bidialectalism, and by the arguments in favor of Contrastive Analysis approaches, especially the empirical evidence of their success where they have been given time to succeed.

But I am not wedded to this method, and I even tend to feel, with respect to writing at the secondary school level, for instance, that we do have to tackle larger conceptual and organizational problems rather than getting bogged down in grammatical minutiae. Some recent high school writing samples I have seen do indeed have several intrusions from the vernacular into what was supposed/expected to be a Standard English text. But if all those were converted to Standard English immediately, the writing would be no less poor, and we can't fix the minor mechanical issues and ignore the larger conceptual ones. I think the kinds of Contrastive Analysis methods that the OUSD proposed to follow will be most useful and effective at the elementary and middle school levels, and I think that given the myriad problems with existing approaches, the OUSD deserved to be free to experiment with other alternatives.

Regrettably, it must be reported that in early 2001, four years after the OUSD took America and the world by storm with its Ebonics proposals, much of the vigor of that early drive has gone. Key personnel such as Superintendent Carolyn Getridge and School Board Member Toni Cook are no longer in those positions, and the SEP, while still practiced by a valiant few, is no longer a favored districtwide strategy. It is true that personnel from the OUSD partnered with William Labov and others from the University of Pennsylvania in a million-dollar study of "African American Literacy and Culture," but the OUSD component was mostly focused on cultural and general pedagogical strategies rather than specific language-related ones. The SEP itself is very much on the ropes in California, with funding for the annual conference and oversight by personnel in the state superintendent's office no longer available.

At the same time, linguistically aware and committed personnel such as Folasade Oladele remain in the district, and they have been trying, through teacher education sessions, to sensitize teachers to the regularities of African-American vernacular and the value of taking it into account in teaching Standard English. The prospects for larger-scale efforts involving linguists are promising.

REFERENCES

Adger, Carolyn Temple, Donna Christian, and Orlando Taylor (eds.) 1999. *Making the connection: language and* academic achievement among African American students. McHenry, Ill.: Delta Systems, Inc., and Washington, D.C.: Center for Applied Linguistics.

Baugh, John. 2000. *Beyond Ebonics: Linguistic pride and racial prejudice.* New York: Oxford University Press.

Bloomfield, Leonard, and Clarence L. Barnhart. 1961. *Let's read, a linguistic approach.* Detroit: Wayne State University Press.

[Boston, Sue, Audrey Guess Knight, Yvonne Strozier, Rex Fortune, and Orlando Taylor. N.D. *Standard English Proficiency* (Handbook).]

Craig, Dennis R. 1999. *Teaching language and literacy: policies and procedures for vernacular situations.* Georgetown, Guyana: Education and Development Services, Inc.

Crawford, Clinton (ed.). 2001. *Ebonics and language education [of African ancestry students].* New York and London: Sankofa World Publishers.

Crowell, Sheila C., Ellen D. Kolba, William A. Stewart, and Kenneth R. Johnson. 1974. *TALKACROSS: Materials for teaching English as a second dialect.* (Teacher's handbook and student activity book). Montclair, N.J.: Caribou Associated.

Crystal, David. 1991. *A dictionary of linguistics and phonetics.* Oxford: Basil Blackwell. Third edition.

Ellis, Rod. 1994. *The study of second language acquisition.* Oxford: Oxford University Press.

Feigenbaum, Irwin. 1970. "The use of nonstandard English in teaching standard: contrast and comparison." In Ralph W. Fasold and Roger W. Shuy (eds.), *Teaching English in the inner city.* Washington, D.C.: Center for Applied Linguistics. 87–104.

Fordham, Signithia, and John U. Ogbu. 1986. "Black students' school success: Coping with the burden of 'acting white.'" *The Urban Review* 18(3): 176–206.

Fries, Charles C. 1962. *Linguistics and reading.* New York: Holt, Rinehart and Winston.

Goodman, Kenneth (ed.). 1998. *In defense of good teaching: What teachers need to know about the "reading wars."* York, Maine: Stenhouse Publishers.

Harris-Wright, Kelli. 1999. "Enhancing bidialectalism in urban African American students." In Carolyn Temple Adger, Donna Christian, and Orlando Taylor (eds.), *Making the connection: language and academic achievement among African American students.* McHenry, Ill.: Delta Systems, Inc., and Washington, D.C.: Center for Applied Linguistics. 53–60.

Heller, Monica, John R. Rickford, Marty LaForest, and Danielle Cyr. 1999. "Sociolinguistics and public debate." *Journal of Sociolinguistics* 3.2: 260–288.

Hoover, Mary. 1978. "Community attitudes toward Black English." *Language in Society* 7: 65–87.

Jaggar, Angela M., and Bernice E. Cullinan. 1974. "Teaching Standard English to achieve bidialectalism: problems with current practices." Alfred C. Aarons (ed.), *The Florida FL Reporter: Issues in the Teaching of Standard English* (spring/fall): 63–70.

Krashen, Stephen D. 1999. *Condemned without a trial: bogus arguments against bilingual education.* Portsmouth, N.H.: Heinemann.

Labov, William. 1970. "The logic of nonstandard English." In James E. Alatis (ed.), *Twentieth annual round table: Linguistics and the teaching of Standard English to speakers of other languages or dialects 1970.* Washington, D.C.: Georgetown University Press. 1–44.

Lado, Robert. 1957. *Linguistics across cultures: applied linguistics for language teachers.* Ann Arbor: The University of Michigan Press.

LeMoine, Noma. 2001. "Language variation and literacy acquisition in African American students." In Joyce L. Harris, Alan G. Kamhi, [and] Karen E. Pollock (eds.), *Literacy in African American communities.* Mahwah, N.J.: Erlbaum. 169–194.

Maddahian, Ebrahim, and Ambition Padi Sandamela. 2000. *Academic English Mastery Program: 1998 evaluation report.* Publication no. 781, Program Evaluation and Research Branch, Research and Evaluation Unit, LA Unified School District.

Marwit, Samuel J., and Gail Neumann. 1974. "Black and white children's comprehension of standard and nonstandard English passages." *Journal of Educational Psychology* 66.3: 329–332.

McWhorter, John. 1997. "Wasting energy on an illusion: six months later." *The Black Scholar* 27(2): 2–5.

McWhorter, John. 1998. *The word on the street: Fact and fable about American English.* New York and London: Plenum.

McWhorter, John. 2000. *Losing the race: Self-sabotage in Black America.* New York: The Free Press.

Melmed, Paul Jay. 1971. *Black English phonology: The question of reading interference.* (Monographs of the Language Behavior Research Laboratory, No. 1). Berkeley: University of California.

Nolen, Patricia A. 1972. "Reading nonstandard dialect materials: A study at grades two and four." *Child Development* 43: 1092–1097.

Oakland Unified School District. 1996. "Overview of recommendations." In *Synopsis of the adopted policy on Standard English language development.* December. Accessed at www.west.net/~joyland/oakland.htm.

Parker, H. H., and M. I. Christ. 1995. Teaching minorities to play the corporate language game. Columbia: University of South Carolina Resource Center for the Freshman Year Experience and Students in Transition.

Perry, Theresa, and Lisa Delpit [(eds.)] 1998. *The real Ebonics debate: Power, language, and the education of African-American children.* Boston: Beacon Press.

Piestrup, Ann M. 1973. *Black dialect interference and accommodation of reading instruction in the first grade.* (Monographs of the Language Behavior Research Laboratory, No. 4). Berkeley: University of California.

Rickford, John R. 1999a. "Language diversity and academic achievement in the education of African American students—an overview of the issues." In Carolyn Temple Adger, Donna Christian, and Orlando Taylor (eds.), *Making the connection: Language and academic achievement among African American students.* McHenry, Ill.: Delta Systems, Inc., and Washington, D.C.: Center for Applied Linguistics. 1–20.

Rickford, John R. 1999b. "Using the vernacular to teach the standard." In J. David Ramirez, Terrence G. Wiley, Gerda de Klerk, and Enid Lee (eds.), *Ebonics in the urban education debate.* Long Beach: Center for Language Minority Education and Research, California State University. 23–41. Also in J. Rickford [1999c], *African American vernacular English: features, evolution, educational implications.* Oxford, U.K., and Malden, Mass.: Blackwell. 329–347.

Rickford, John R. 1999c. *African American vernacular English: features, evolution, educational implications.* [Oxford, U.K., and Malden, Mass.]: Blackwell.

Rickford, John R., and Russell J. Rickford. 2000. *Spoken soul: The story of Black English.* New York: John Wiley.

Simons, Herbert D., and Kenneth R. Johnson. 1974. "Black English syntax and reading interference." *Research in the Teaching of English* 8: 339–358.

Simpkins, Gary A., and Charlesetta Simpkins. 1981. "Cross cultural approach to curriculum development." Geneva Smitherman (ed.), *Black English and the education of Black children and youth: Proceedings of the national invitational symposium on the King decision.* Detroit: Center for Black Studies, Wayne State University. 221–240.

Sledd, James. 1972. "Doublespeak: Dialectology in the service of big brother." *College English* 33: 439–456.

Smith, Ernie. 2001. "Ebonics and bilingual education of the African American child." In C[linton] Crawford (ed.), *Ebonics and language education [of African ancestry students].* New York and London: Sankofa World Publishers. 123–163.

Smitherman, Geneva. 2000. *Talkin that talk: Language, culture, and education in African America.* London and New York: Routledge.

Stewart, William A. 1964. *Foreign language teaching methods in quasi–foreign language situations. Non-standard speech and the teaching of English.* Washington, D.C.: Center for Applied Linguistics.

Tauber, R. T. 1997. *Self-fulfilling prophecy: a practical guide to its use in education.* Westport, Conn.: Praeger.

Taylor, Hanni U. 1989. *Standard English, Black English, and bidialectalism.* New York: Peter Lang.

U.S. Senate. 1997. Subcommittee on Labor, Health and Human Services, and Education Appropriations. *Ebonics Hearings.* 105th Cong., 2d sess., 23 January.

Van Keulen, Jean E., Gloria Toliver Weddington, and Charles E. DeBose. 1998. *Speech, language, learning, and the African American child.* Boston: Allyn and Bacon.

Yarborough, S., and L. Flores. 1997. "Using Ebonics to teach Standard English." In *Long Beach Press-Telegram,* 30 April 1997: p. A1.

From James E. Alatis, Heidi E. Hamilton, and Ai-Hui Tan, eds. *Georgetown University Round Table on Languages and Linguistics: 2000* (Washington, D.C.: Georgetown University Press, 2002), pp. 25–30, 33–45.

Noma LeMoine

Contrastive Analysis: A Linguistic Strategy for Advancing Language Acquisition in Standard English Learners (SELs) [2007]

Background

Standard English Learners (SELs)—those students for whom Standard English is not native and who represent a high percentage of the public school population in large urban school districts—must become proficient in the use of Standard American and academic English—the base for the development of school language, literacy, and learning. They must become literate in the forms of English that appear in newspapers, magazines, textbooks, voting materials, and consumer contracts. Because students acquire school literacy more easily when their language matches the language of school, African American, Hawaiian American, and Mexican American, Standard English Language Learners (SELs)—students for whom standard English is not native—may not get the same benefits from traditional approaches to literacy acquisition as other students. Reading requires that readers draw upon their personal knowledge in order to make meaning of text. Therefore, school literacy learning environments for SELs must establish linkages between the home and school cultures, languages, and literacies. SELs must be provided opportunities to add school language and literacy to their repertoire of skills using instructional approaches that build on the cultural capital—including the language, learning styles and strengths—they bring to the classroom. Standard English Learners bring to school rich and diverse experiences, "funds of knowledge" and home language and literacy patterns that when embraced can serve as a bridge to the acquisition of school language and literacy. They need instructional support that scaffolds their access to core curricula. They need opportunities to be participants in and see school language and literacy practices modeled. The Los Angeles Unified School District's Academic English Mastery Program (AEMP) is a comprehensive research-based intervention designed to address the acquisition of school language, literacy, and learning in Standard English Learners.

The Academic English Mastery Program Model

The Academic English Mastery Program (AEMP) has been described by linguists as "By far the most concentrated and comprehensive classroom practices embracing a philosophy of multilingualism" for SELs (Smitherman, 1999). Because educators must become familiar with the communication and language patterns of their diverse students and knowledgeable of methodologies that facilitate the acquisition of academic language, and because students must be able to speak, read, and write using the language of school, the AEMP intervention model provides an instructional framework that supports students' mastery of academic language through the infusion of instructional strategies (best practices) drawn from the linguistic research.

On the basis of over thirty years of linguistic research that acknowledges and validates the existence of non-standard language varieties and their impact on learning, and that identifies instructional methodologies that promote literacy and learning in SELs, six research-based Instructional Approaches, efficacious to language and literacy acquisition in Standard English Language Learners, form the base for the AEMP intervention. The six critical approaches that undergird AEMP provide learning opportunities for adding school language and literacy to SELs' already established repertoire of skills by building on the language, learning styles and strengths, prior knowledge, and experiences they bring to the classroom.

The Six Critical Approaches to Instruction include:

  I. Enhancing teacher's knowledge, understanding, and positive attitude toward non-standard language varieties and the students who use them
 II. Integrating linguistically responsive pedagogy and linguistic knowledge about non-standard language varieties into instruction
III. Using second-language acquisition methodologies to support student acquisition of school lan-

guage and literacy, and access to academic content.

IV. Employing a balanced approach to literacy instruction that incorporates Meaning Construction and Phonics and accommodates cultural and linguistic diversity

V. Incorporating culturally relevant and responsive pedagogy into instruction that builds upon the learning styles and strengths of Standard English Learners to facilitate access to standards-based curricula

VI. Infusing the history and culture, including contributions of SELs into the core instructional curriculum.

In this paper we will look at how Instructional Approach II, *Integrating linguistically responsive pedagogy and linguistic knowledge about non-standard language varieties into instruction* is implemented in the Los Angeles Unified School District's Academic English Mastery Program.

INSTRUCTIONAL APPROACH II: INTEGRATING LINGUISTICALLY RESPONSIVE PEDAGOGY AND LINGUISTIC KNOWLEDGE ABOUT NON-STANDARD LANGUAGE VARIETIES INTO INSTRUCTION

William Labov (1972), a distinguished linguist wrote in an article entitled *Academic Ignorance and Black Intelligence* "There is no reason to believe that any nonstandard vernacular is itself an obstacle to learning. The chief problem is ignorance of language on the part of all concerned." (p. 15). That American educational institutions produce so few literate standard English language learners may result in part from the failure of educators to use the available linguistic knowledge to construct learning environments that facilitate literacy acquisition and learning. Many teachers have limited information about non-standard language varieties, the learning profile of the children who use them and their impact on instruction. Teachers' low opinions and misunderstandings about non-standard language varieties have been cited in the research as antecedents of the failure of Standard English Language Learners to acquire lit-

eracy and access content learning (Hoover, 1979). Catherine Snow (1983) maintains that if conversational interactions in children's homes and school do not parallel each other, the academic success of the child may be jeopardized. This view known as the match-mismatch formulation of literacy intimates a need for teachers to have an understanding of the language of their students, and for students to master the language of school. Goodman and Buck (1973) and Drummet (1984) suggest that the rejection of non-standard languages by teachers is the most likely explanation for reading problems experienced by African American and other Standard English Language Learners. Negative teacher attitudes toward non-standard languages interfere with the natural process of learning to read and undermine the confidence of the reader.

How teachers perceive their students and define themselves in relation to them determine, to a large degree, what the educational experiences of students will be. Teachers who have limited knowledge of and who devalue the language, culture, and experiences of SELs convey messages that negatively impact their classroom performance and result in lowered aspirations and achievement levels. The best teachers are themselves learners, and knowledge building becomes an important strategy for combating negative perceptions, often held at a subconscious level, about the ability of Standard English learners. Labov concludes in the above referenced article:

> "Teachers are now being told to ignore the language of black children as unworthy of attention and useless for learning. They are being taught to hear every natural utterance of the child as evidence of his mental inferiority. As linguists we are unanimous in condemning this view as bad observation, bad theory, and bad practice. That educational psychology should be influenced by a theory so false to the facts of language is unfortunate; but that children should be the victims of this ignorance is intolerable." (p. 15).

The language difficulties of SELs may not be recognized until the demands for literacy and learning become greatest, around 3rd or 4th grade. It is imperative that teachers understand that many of the learning problems experienced by Standard English Learners at this time are related to issues of language difference. Children who are learning to read in a language that is different from their own experience more problems than children do whose home language matches the language of school. The problems SELs experience may result from lack of familiarity with the phonological, lexical, semantic, and grammatical constraints of school language, and from their teachers' overt and subtle rejection of the language of their home. Limited familiarity with Standard American English syntax may impair SELs' ability to identify important syntactic relationships in Standard American English, and limited Standard English vocabulary may cause difficulty in using semantic cues for making predictions and comprehending what they read.

There is experimental evidence that mastering the standard language might be made easier if the differences in the student vernacular were made explicit rather than entirely ignored (Rickford, 1999). Standard English Learners (SELs) must come to understand that the language of their home and the language of school differ. Moreover, in order for them to compete successfully in mainstream American language environments, they will need to acquire the ability to use language effectively in cross-cultural situations. The classroom teacher's knowledge of and ability to infuse information about non-standard language forms into instruction is a critical determinant of Standard English Language Learners' success in school (Agee and Smith, 1974, Bowie and Bond, 1994).

Mainstream English Language Development (MELD)—defined in AEMP as the use of standard American and academic English for educational purposes i.e., acquiring listening, speaking, reading and writing skills in Standard American and academic English—is a key strategy for acquiring mastery of school language. Standard or mainstream English language mastery implies competence in Standard English at levels of pragmatics (the social use of language), phonology, grammar, and vocabulary. One MELD instructional strategy that forwards the acquisition of academic language and can be used to address the acquisition of the major dimensions of language is "contrastive analysis". This strategy requires that we construct classroom environments in ways that affirm and accommodate language diversity and by building on the language students bring to the classroom, support language and literacy acquisition.

Contrastive Analysis

In the Academic English Mastery Program we define contrastive analysis as the systemic study of the distinctive elements in a pair of languages with a view to identifying their structural differences and similarities. Through contrastive analysis students are given opportunities to listen to, contrast, and practice patterns of standard American and academic English. As they engage with comparing and contrasting the home and school languages, they increase their metalinguistic and metacognitive awareness and build linguistic competence in the target language. As SELs understand how their home language differs from the language of school, the language of school becomes more comprehensible, and their ability to use the target language—Standard American/Academic English— improves. Recognition of the veiled differences between standard and non-standard language forms helps students to become better able to edit their own work for differences in grammar, syntax, and orthography and to utilize standard form in reading, writing, and speaking.

Taylor (1991) trained teachers in the use of contrastive analysis as a means of improving the writing skills of African American SELs and compared them to teachers using traditional ELA instructional methods. After 11 months of using this approach in the classroom the experimental group showed a 59% reduction in the number of non-standard language features in their writing as compared to the control group which showed an increase in the number of non-standard language features used in their writing. See figure [on p. 919].

The Academic English Mastery Program (AEMP), currently in 81 schools in the Los Angeles Unified School District, seeks to improve academic achievement in Standard English Learners by increasing proficiency in Standard American and academic English in both the oral and written forms. AEMP trains teachers in the use of contrastive analysis as a tool for facilitating the acquisition of school literacy and learning. Teachers in the Academic English Mastery

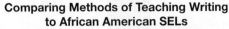

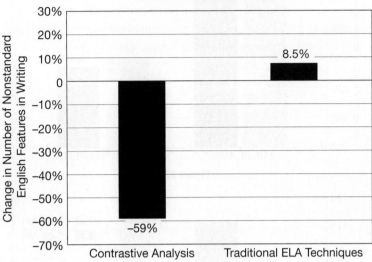

Figure 1
SOURCE: *H. Taylor 1991.*

Program are provided with ongoing opportunities to enhance their knowledge of linguistically responsive pedagogy and their skill at implementing contrastive analysis strategies, through ongoing professional development, collaborative learning communities, and peer coaching.

AEMP teachers are to provide MELD instruction 30–45 minutes daily during which time continuous opportunities are provided for students to interact with each other and the content through instructional conversations and to engage in contrastive analysis.

OUTCOMES

The Los Angeles Unified School District's Program Evaluation and Research Branch (PERB) conducted an evaluation of the Academic English Mastery Program in 2000, to determine the effectiveness of AEMP in increasing students' general and academic use of Mainstream English as measured by the Language Assessment Writing and Speaking Tool. A random sample of 16 out of 31 AEMP schools was contrasted with control schools with similar demographics. Using the Language Assessment Writing and Speaking Tool, Teacher Survey, and Observation Checklists, the study found a statistically significant and educationally meaningful difference between experimental and control groups at the end of the program year as measured by the Language Assessment Writing Test. AEMP program participants outperformed those who did not participate in the program. A conclusion of the study was the Academic English Mastery Program is an effective program in improving academic use of English language for speakers of non-mainstream languages.

2004–05 and 2005–06 comparisons of school Annual Performance Index revealed AEMP schools with greater gains in student performance when compared to schools with similar demographics. See graphs [on p. 920].

Comparing AEMP Schools with Control Schools

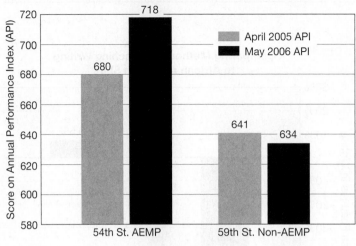

Figure 2a

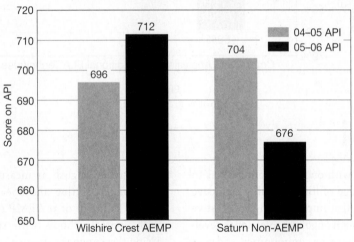

Figure 2b

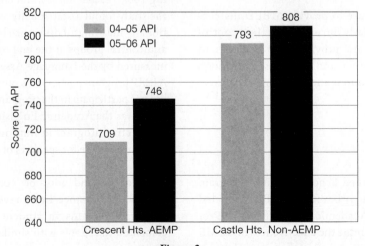

Figure 2c

SUMMARY

In summary, the learning profile of Standard English Language Learners differs in many ways from the profile of students whose home language and culture match the language and culture of the school. In order for culturally and linguistically different SELs to experience greater success in acquiring school literacy and learning teachers will need ongoing, comprehensive professional development to support the construction of learning environments that are authentic, culturally and linguistically responsive, and that build upon the language, experiences, learning styles, and strengths of SELs to promote learning. The AEMP Instructional Framework breaks down barriers to academic success by providing opportunities for teachers to acquire linguistic knowledge that shapes positive attitudes toward SELs and strategies that scaffold learning to increase SELs' access to rigorous standards-based curricula.

For further discussion of these perspectives see:

Lemoine, N., & Hollie, S. (2007). "Developing Academic English for Standard English Learners." In Alim, H. S., Baugh, J. (Eds.), *Talking Black: Language, Education, and Social Change* (pp.43–55). New York: Teachers College Press.

LeMoine, N. (2001). "Language Variation and Literacy Acquisition in African American Students." In Harris, J., Kamhi, A., & Pollock, K. E. (Eds.), *Literacy in African American Communities* (pp. 169–194). Mahwah, N.J.: Lawrence Erlbaum.

LeMoine, N., & Los Angeles Unified School District (1999). *English for Your Success: A Language Development Program for African American Students.* Saddle Brook, N.J.: Peoples Publishing.

LeMoine, N., & Los Angeles Unified School District (1999). *English for Your Success,* Grade Level Curriculum Guides (K–8). Saddle Brook, N.J.: Peoples Publishing.

REFERENCES

Agee, W., & Smith, W. (1974). "Modifying Teachers' Attitudes towards Speakers of Divergent Dialects through Inservice Training." *Journal of Negro Education* 43 (Winter): 82–90.

Bowie, R. L., and C. L. Bond. (1994). "Influencing Teachers' Attitudes Towards Black English: Are We Making A Difference?" *Journal of Teacher Education* 45: 112–118.

Drummett, L. (1984). "The Persistent Failure of Black Children in Learning to Read." *Reading World* 24: 31–37.

Goodman, K., and C. Buck. (1973). "Dialect Barriers to Reading Comprehension Revisited." *Reading Teacher* (October), pp. 6–12.

Goodman, K. (1986). *What's Whole in Whole Language?* Richmond Hill, Ont.: Scholastic.

Hoover, M. (1979). "A Semiforeign Language Approach to Teaching Reading to Bidialectal Children." In Shafer, R. E. (Ed.), *Applied Linguistics and Reading* (pp. 63–71). Newark, Del.: International Reading Association.

Labov, W. (1972). "Academic Ignorance and Black Intelligence." *The Atlantic Monthly* (June), pp. 14–17.

Rickford, J. (1999). *African American Vernacular English: Features, Evolution, Educational Implications.* Oxford: Blackwell.

Smitherman, G. (1999). "Language Policy and Classroom Practice." In Adger, D., Christian, D., & Taylor, O. (Eds.), *Making the Connection: Language and Academic Achievement among African American Students* (pp. 115–124). McHenry, Ill.: Delta Systems; Washington, D.C.: Center for Applied Linguistics.

Snow, C. E. (1983). "Literacy and Language: Relationships during the Preschool Years." *Harvard Educational Review* 53(2): 165–189.

Taylor, H. U. (1991). *Standard English, Black English and bidialectalism: A controversy.* New York: Peter Lang.

Achieving A + Summit: Aquisition of English and Academic Achievement for All, Los Angeles Unified School District, December 14, 2007.

Delores S. Williams

Womanist Theology: Black Women's Voices [1987]

"Womanist reflection is far from monolithic in voice and tone," Emilie M. Townes stated in her foundational anthology on womanism: *A Troubling in My Soul: Womanist Perspectives on Evil and Suffering.* "Perhaps the most common understanding of Womanist," Townes suggested, "is that she is a woman committed to an integrated analysis of race, gender, and class. This arises from a deep concern to address the shortcomings of traditional feminist and Black theological modes of discourse." This broad definition both underscores basic core values of womanist theory and sets up a contrast with alternative liberation theologies.

Delores S. Williams, like Townes, was one of the early prominent figures in womanist theology. In her influential writings, particularly her 1993 book, *Sisters in the Wilderness,* Williams developed womanist thought by exploring experiences of motherhood, color consciousness, and survival strategies in hostile environments (the "wilderness experience"). In this 1987 essay, Williams finds inspiration in a wide variety of sources, a common thread throughout womanist theology. Williams's sources range from the Bible to contemporary writers, including Alice Walker, who is credited with coining the term *womanist* in her book, *In Search of Our Mothers' Gardens* (1983). Williams also lays out principles that continue to propel the development of womanist theology to this day.

From *Christianity and Crisis*, March 2, 1987.

DAUGHTER: *Mama, why are we brown, pink, and yellow, and our cousins are white, beige, and black?*

MOTHER: *Well, you know the colored race is just like a flower garden, with every color flower represented.*

DAUGHTER: *Mama, I'm walking to Canada and I'm taking you and a bunch of slaves with me.*

MOTHER: *It wouldn't be the first time.*

In these two conversational exchanges, Pulitzer Prize–winning novelist Alice Walker begins to show us what she means by the concept "womanist." The concept is presented in Walker's *In Search of Our Mothers' Gardens*, and many women in church and society have appropriated it as a way of affirming themselves as *black* while simultaneously owning their connection with feminism and with the Afro-American community, male and female. The concept of womanist allows women to claim their roots in black history, religion, and culture.

What then is a womanist? Her origins are in the black folk expression "You acting womanish," meaning, according to Walker, "wanting to know more and in greater depth than is good for one . . . outrageous, audacious, courageous and willful behavior." A womanist is also "responsible, in charge, serious." She can walk to Canada and take others with her. She loves, she is committed, she is a universalist by temperament.

Her universality includes loving men and woman, sexually or nonsexually. She loves music, dance, the spirit, food and roundness, struggle, and she loves herself. "Regardless."

Walker insists that a womanist is also "committed to survival and wholeness of entire people, male and female." She is no separatist, "except for health." A womanist is a black feminist or feminist of color. Or as Walker says, "Womanist is to feminist as purple to lavender."

Womanist theology, a vision in its infancy, is emerging among Afro-American Christian women. Ultimately many sources—biblical, theological, ecclesiastical, social, anthropological, economic, and material from other religious traditions—will inform the development of this theology. As a contribution to this process, I will demonstrate how Walker's concept of womanist provides some significant clues for the work of womanist theologians. I will then focus on method and God-content in womanist theology. This contribution belongs to the work of prolegomena—prefatory remarks, introductory observations intended to be suggestive and not conclusive.

CODES AND CONTENTS

In her definition, Walker provides significant clues for the development of womanist theology. Her concept contains what black feminist scholar Bell Hooks in *From Margin to Center* identifies as cultural codes. These are words, beliefs, and behavioral patterns of a people that must be deciphered before meaningful communication can happen cross-culturally. Walker's codes are female-centered and they point beyond themselves to conditions, events, meanings, and values that have crystallized in the Afro-American community *around women's activity* and formed traditions.

A paramount example is mother-daughter advice. Black mothers have passed on wisdom for survival— in the white world, in the black community, and with men—for as long as anyone can remember. Female slave narratives, folk tales, and some contemporary black poetry and prose reflect this tradition. Some of it is collected in "Old Sister's Advice to Her Daughters," in *The Book of Negro Folklore,* edited by Langston Hughes and Arna Bontemps (Dodd Mead 1958).

Walker's allusion to skin color points to an historic tradition of tension between black women over the matter of some black men's preference for light-skinned women. Her reference to black women's love of food and roundness points to customs of female care in the black community (including the church) associated with hospitality and nurture.

These cultural codes and their corresponding traditions are valuable resources for indicating and validating the kind of data upon which womanist theologians can reflect as they bring black women's social, religious, and cultural experience into the discourse of theology, ethics, biblical and religious studies. Female slave narratives, imaginative literature by black women, autobiographies, the work by black women in academic disciplines, and the testimonies of black church women will be authoritative sources for womanist theologians.

Walker situates her understanding of a womanist in the context of nonbourgeois black folk culture. The literature of this culture has traditionally reflected more egalitarian relations between men and women, much less rigidity in male-female roles, and more respect for female intelligence and ingenuity than is found in bourgeois culture.

The black folk are poor. Less individualistic than those who are better off, they have, for generations, practiced various forms of economic sharing. For example, immediately after Emancipation mutual aid societies pooled the resources of black folk to help pay for funerals and other daily expenses. *The Book of Negro Folklore* describes the practice of rent parties which flourished during the Depression. The black folk stressed togetherness and a closer connection with nature. They respect knowledge gained through lived experience monitored by elders who differ profoundly in social class and world view from the teachers and education encountered in American academic institutions. Walker's choice of context suggests that womanist theology can establish its lines of continuity in the black community with nonbourgeois traditions less sexist than the black power and black nationalist traditions.

In this folk context, some of the black female–centered cultural codes in Walker's definition (e.g., "Mama, I'm walking to Canada and I'm taking you and a bunch of slaves with me") point to folk heroines like Harriet Tubman, whose liberation activity earned her the name "Moses" of her people. This allusion to Tubman directs womanist memory to a liberation tradition in black history in which women took the lead, acting as catalysts for the community's revolutionary action and for social change. Retrieving this often hidden or diminished female tradition of catalytic action is an important task for womanist theologians and ethicists. Their research may well reveal that female models of authority have been absolutely essential for every struggle in the black community and for building and maintaining the community's institutions.

FREEDOM FIGHTERS

The womanist theologian must search for the voices, actions, opinions, experience, and faith of women whose names sometimes slip into the male-centered rendering of black history, but whose actual stories remain remote. This search can lead to such little-known freedom fighters as Milla Granson and her courageous work on a Mississippi plantation. Her liberation method broadens our knowledge of the variety of strategies black people have used to obtain freedom. According to scholar Sylvia Dannett, in *Profiles of Negro Womanhood*:

> Milla Granson, a slave, conducted a midnight school for several years. She had been taught to read and write by her former master in Kentucky.... and in her little school hundreds of slaves benefited from her learning.... After laboring all day for their master, the slaves would creep stealthily to Milla's "schoolroom" (a little cabin in a back alley).... The doors and windows ... had to be kept tightly sealed to avoid discovery. Each class was composed of twelve pupils and when Milla had brought them up to the extent of her ability, she "graduated" them and took in a dozen more. Through this means she graduated hundreds of slaves. Many of whom she taught to write a legible hand [forged] their own passes and set out for Canada.

Women like Tubman and Granson used subtle and silent strategies to liberate themselves and large numbers of black people. By uncovering as much as possible about such female liberation, the womanist begins to understand the relation of black history to the contemporary folk expression: "If Rosa Parks had not sat down, Martin King would not have stood up."

While she celebrates and *emphasizes* black women's culture and way of being in the world, Walker simultaneously affirms black women's historic con-

nection with men through love and through a shared struggle for survival and for a productive quality of life (e.g., "wholeness"). This suggests that two of the principal concerns of womanist theology should be survival and community building and maintenance. The goal of this community building is, of course, to establish a positive quality of life—economic, spiritual, educational—for black women, men, and children. Walker's understanding of a womanist as "not a separatist" ("except for health"), however, reminds the Christian womanist theologian that her concern for community building and maintenance must *ultimately* extend to the entire Christian community and beyond that to the larger human community.

Yet womanist consciousness is also informed by women's determination to love themselves. "Regardless." This translates into an admonition to black women to avoid the self-destruction of bearing a disproportionately large burden in the work of community building and maintenance. Walker suggests that women can avoid this trap by connecting with women's communities concerned about women's rights and well-being. Her identification of a womanist as also a feminist joins black women with their feminist heritage extending back into the nineteenth century in the work of black feminists like Sojourner Truth, Frances W. Harper, and Mary Church Terrell.[1]

In making the feminist-womanist connection, however, Walker proceeds with great caution. While affirming an organic relationship between womanists and feminists, she also declares a deep shade of difference between them ("Womanist is to feminist as purple to lavender.") This gives womanist scholars the freedom to explore the particularities of black women's history and culture without being guided by what white feminists have already identified as women's issues.

But womanist consciousness directs black women away from the negative divisions prohibiting community building among women. The womanist loves other women sexually and nonsexually. Therefore, respect for sexual preferences is one of the marks of womanist community. According to Walker, homophobia has no place. Nor does "Colorism" (i.e., "yella" and half-white

1. See pp. 242, 244, and 245.

black people valued more in the black world than black-skinned people), which often separates black women from each other. Rather, Walker's womanist claim is that color variety is the substance of universality. Color, like birth and death, is common to all people. Like the navel, it is a badge of humanity connecting people with people. Two other distinctions are prohibited in Walker's womanist thinking. Class hierarchy does not dwell among women who "... love struggle, love the Folks ... are committed to the survival and wholeness of an entire people." Nor do women compete for male attention when they "... appreciate and prefer female culture ... value ... women's emotional flexibility ... and women's strength."

The intimations about community provided by Walker's definition suggest no genuine community building is possible when men are excluded (except when women's health is at stake). Neither can it occur when black women's self-love, culture, and love for each other are not affirmed and are not considered vital for the community's self-understanding. And it is thwarted if black women are expected to bear "the lion's share" of the work and to sacrifice their well-being for the good of the group.

Yet, for the womanist, mothering and nurturing are vitally important. Walker's womanist reality begins with mothers relating to their children and is characterized by black women (not necessarily bearers of children) nurturing great numbers of black people in the liberation struggle (e.g., Harriet Tubman). Womanist emphasis upon the value of mothering and nurturing is consistent with the testimony of many black women. The poet Carolyn Rogers speaks of her mother as the great black bridge that brought her over. Walker dedicated her novel *The Third Life of Grange Copeland* to her mother "... who made a way out of no way." As a child in the black church, I heard women (and men) give thanks to God for their mothers "... who stayed behind and pulled the wagon over the long haul."

It seems, then, that the clues about community from Walker's definition of a womanist suggest that the mothering and nurturing dimension of Afro-American history can provide resources for shaping criteria to measure the quality of justice in the community. These criteria could be used to assure female-male equity in the presentation of the community's models of author-ity. They could also gauge the community's division of labor with regard to the survival tasks necessary for building and maintaining community.

WOMANIST THEOLOGY AND METHOD

Womanist theology is already beginning to define the categories and methods needed to develop along lines consistent with the sources of that theology. Christian womanist theological methodology needs to be informed by at least four elements: (1) a multidialogical intent, (2) a liturgical intent, (3) a didactic intent, and (4) a commitment both to reason *and* to the validity of female imagery and metaphorical language in the construction of theological statements.

A multidialogical intent will allow Christian womanist theologians to advocate and participate in dialogue and action with *many* diverse social, political, and religious communities concerned about human survival and productive quality of life for the oppressed. The genocide of cultures and peoples (which has often been instigated and accomplished by Western white Christian groups or governments) and the nuclear threat of omnicide mandates womanist participation in such dialogue/action. But in this dialogue/action the womanist also should keep her speech and action focused upon the slow genocide of poor black women, children, and men by exploitative systems denying them productive jobs, education, health care, and living space. Multidialogical activity may, like a jazz symphony, communicate some of its most important messages in what the harmony-driven conventional ear hears as discord, as disruption of the harmony in both the black American and white American social, political, and religious status quo.

If womanist theological method is informed by a liturgical intent, then womanist theology will be relevant to (and will reflect) the thought, worship, and action of the black church. But a liturgical intent will also allow womanist theology to challenge the thought/worship/action of the black church with the discordant and prophetic messages emerging from womanist participation in multidialogics. This means that womanist theology will consciously impact *critically* upon the foundations of liturgy, challenging the church to use justice principles to select the sources that will shape the content of liturgy. The question must be asked: "How does this source portray blackness/darkness, women and economic justice for nonruling-class people?" A negative portrayal will demand omission of the source or its radical reformation by the black church. The Bible, a major source in black church liturgy, must also be subjected to the scrutiny of justice principles.

A didactic intent in womanist theological method assigns a teaching function to theology. Womanist theology should teach Christians new insights about moral life based on ethics supporting justice for women, survival, and a productive quality of life for poor women, children, and men. This means that the womanist theologian must give authoritative status to black folk wisdom (e.g., Brer Rabbit literature) and to black women's moral wisdom (expressed in their literature) when she responds to the question, "How ought the Christian to live in the world?" Certainly tensions may exist between the moral teachings derived from these sources and the moral teachings about obedience, love, and humility that have usually buttressed presuppositions about living the Christian life. Nevertheless, womanist theology, in its didactic intent, must teach the church the different ways God reveals prophetic word and action for Christian living.

These intents, informing theological method, can yield a theological language whose foundation depends as much upon its imagistic content as upon reason. The language can be rich in female imagery, metaphor, and story. For the black church, this kind of theological language may be quite useful, since the language of the black religious experience abounds in images and metaphors. Clifton Johnson's collection of black conversion experiences, *God Struck Me Dead,* illustrates this point.

The appropriateness of womanist theological language will ultimately reside in its ability to bring black women's history, culture, and religious experience into the interpretive circle of Christian theology and into the liturgical life of the church. Womanist theological language must, in this sense be an instrument for social and theological change in church and society.

WHO DO YOU SAY GOD IS?

Regardless of one's hopes about intentionality and womanist theological method, questions must be raised about the God-content of the theology. Walker's mention of the black womanist's love of the spirit is a true reflection of the great respect Afro-American women have always shown for the presence and work of the spirit. In the black church, women (and men) often judge the effectiveness of the worship service not on the scholarly content of the sermon nor on the ritual nor on orderly process. Rather, worship has been effective if "the spirit was high," i.e., if the spirit was actively and obviously present in a balanced blend of prayer, of cadenced word (the sermon), and of syncopated music ministering to the pain of the people.

The importance of this emphasis upon the spirit is that it allows Christian womanist theologians, in their use of the Bible, to identify and reflect upon those biblical stories in which poor oppressed women had a special encounter with divine emissaries of God, like the spirit. In the Hebrew Testament, Hagar's story is most illustrative and relevant to Afro-American women's experience of bondage, of African heritage, of encounter with God/emissary in the midst of fierce survival struggles. Katie Cannon among a number of black female preachers and ethicists urges black Christian women to regard themselves as Hagar's sisters.

In relation to the Christian or New Testament, the Christian womanist theologian can refocus the salvation story so that it emphasizes the beginning of revelation with the spirit mounting Mary, a woman of the poor: ("... the Holy Spirit shall come upon thee, and the power of the Highest shall overshadow thee ..." Luke 1:35). Such an interpretation of revelation has roots in 19th-century black abolitionist and feminist Sojourner Truth. Posing an important question and response, she refuted a white preacher's claim that women could not have rights equal to men's because Christ was not a woman. Truth asked, "Whar did your Christ come from? ... From God and a woman! Man had nothin' to do wid Him!" This suggests that womanist theology could eventually speak of God in a well-developed theology of the spirit. The sources for this theology are many. Harriet Tubman often "went into the spirit" before her liberation missions and claimed her strength for liberation activity came from this way of meeting God. Womanist theology has grounds for shaping a theology of the spirit informed by black women's political action.

Christian womanist responses to the question "who do you say God is?" will be influenced by these many sources. Walker's way of connecting womanists with the spirit is only one clue. The integrity of black church women's faith, their love of Jesus, their commitment to life, love, family, and politics will also yield vital clues. And other theological voices (black liberation, feminist, Islamic, Asian, Hispanic, African, Jewish, and Western white male traditional) will provide insights relevant for the construction of the God-content of womanist theology.

Each womanist theologian will add her own special accent to the understandings of God emerging from womanist theology. But if one needs a final image to describe women coming together to shape the enterprise, Bess B. Johnson in *God's Fierce Whimsy* offers an appropriate one. Describing the difference between the play of male and female children in the black community where she developed, Johnson says:

> the boys in the neighborhood had this game with rope . . . tug-o'-war . . . till finally some side would jerk the rope away from the others, who'd fall down. . . . Girls . . . weren't allowed to play with them in this tug-o'-war; so we figured out how to make our own rope—out of . . . little dandelions. You just keep adding them, one to another, and you can go on and on. . . . Anybody, even the boys, could join us. . . . The whole purpose of our game was to create this dandelion chain—that was it. And we'd keep going, creating till our mamas called us home.

Like Johnson's dandelion chain, womanist theological vision will grow as black women come together and connect piece with piece. Between the process of creating and the sense of calling, womanist theology will one day present itself in full array, reflecting the divine spirit that connects us all.

EVELYN BROOKS HIGGINBOTHAM

from *The Black Church: A Gender Perspective* [1993]

In her groundbreaking study *Righteous Discontent*, from which this reading is excerpted, Evelyn Brooks Higginbotham (b. 1945) argues that the traditional focus on religious leaders in studies of black churches has obscured the powerful roles played by congregants, especially the women, who make up the majority of church membership. While earlier scholars, such as E. Franklin Frazier (p. 385), presented religious leaders as the primary instigators of change in the church, Higginbotham, a professor of history and African and African American studies at Harvard University, focuses on the church as a grassroots organization. For Higginbotham, the church is a place of many missions and voices, a space for debate and dialogue between and among leaders and congregants.

In the polarizing debate about whether churches are primarily accommodationist or centers of resistance, Higginbotham again stakes out a middle ground. She finds that church dialogue contains both conservative and radical elements and that seemingly conservative actions may have subversive implications.

From Evelyn Brooks Higginbotham, *Righteous Discontent: The Women's Movement in the Black Baptist Church 1880–1920* (Cambridge, Mass.: Harvard University Press, 1993), pp. 1–18, 231–37.

As I look about me today in this veiled world of mine,
despite the noisier and more spectacular advance of
my brothers, I instinctively feel and know that it is the
five million women of my race who really count. Black
women (and women whose grandmothers were black)
are . . . the main pillars of those social settlements
which we call churches; and they have with small
doubt raised three-fourths of our church property.

—W. E. B. Du Bois, *Darkwater* (1918)[1]

Much has been written about the importance of the black church in the social and political life of black people. Much less has been written about black women's importance in the life of the church. This book is a study of women in the black church between 1880 and 1920—a period that has come to be known simultaneously as the "woman's era" and the "nadir" in American race relations. I argue that women were crucial to broadening the public arm of the church and making it the most powerful institution of racial self-help in the African American community. During these years, the church served as the most effective vehicle by which men and women alike, pushed down by racism and poverty, regrouped and rallied against emotional and physical defeat.

In some instances, church women contested racist ideology and institutions through demands for anti-lynching legislation and an end to segregation laws. They expressed their discontent with both racial and gender discrimination and demanded equal rights for blacks and women—advocating voting rights or equal employment and educational opportunities. Black women even drew upon the Bible, the most respected source within their community, to fight for women's rights in the church and society at large. During the late nineteenth century they developed a distinct discourse of resistance, a feminist theology. More often, however, their efforts represented not dramatic protest but everyday forms of resistance to oppression and demoralization. Largely through the fund-raising efforts of women, the black church built schools, provided clothes and food to poor people, established old folks' homes and orphanages, and made available a host of needed social welfare services.

This study attempts to rescue women from invisibility as historical actors in the drama of black empowerment. Since women have traditionally constituted the majority of every black denomination, I present the black church not as the exclusive product of a male ministry but as the product and process of male and female interaction. In offering a corrective to the near exclusion of women in most studies of the black church, my book departs from the more recent and positive discussion of exceptional women, the early women preachers.[2] Research on women preachers, while of great value, does not capture the more representative role of the majority of women church members. If taken alone, such discussion continues to render women's role as marginal. Left obscured is the interrelation between the rising black churches in the late nineteenth and early twentieth centuries and the indefatigable efforts of black women's organizations. Left unheard are women's voices within the public discourse of racial and gender self-determination. In short, the focus on the ministry fails to capture adequately the gender dimension of the church's racial mission. Ultimately, my study provides a vantage point for viewing the interplay of race, gender, and class consciousness, for it presents the church, like the black community it mirrors, as a social space of unifying and conflicting discourses.

[* * *]

In the closed society of Jim Crow, the church afforded African Americans an interstitial space in which to critique and contest white America's racial domination. In addition, the church offered black

---

1. *Darkwater* was first published in 1920, but in the opening essay, Du Bois claimed to have finished the book on February 23, 1918, his fiftieth birthday; he made some revisions over the next eighteen months, and the finished manuscript arrived at the publisher in September 1919. [Editor's note]

2. See Jualynne Dodson, "Nineteenth-Century A.M.E. Preaching Women: Cutting Edge of Women's Inclusion in Church Polity," in Hilah F. Thomas and Rosemary Skinner Keller, eds., *Women in New Worlds: Historical Perspectives on the Wesleyan Tradition*, vol. 1 (Nashville: Abingdon Press, 1981), 276–292; Jean McMahon Humez, ed., *Gifts of Power: The Writings of Rebecca Jackson, Black Visionary and Shaker Eldress* (Amherst: University of Massachusetts Press, 1981), 1–50; William L. Andrews, ed., *Sisters of the Spirit: Three Black Women's Autobiographies of the Nineteenth Century* (Bloomington: Indiana University Press, 1986), 25–234. [Unless otherwise indicated, all footnotes are those of the author.]

women a forum through which to articulate a public discourse critical of women's subordination. A gender perspective on the black church facilitates understanding the church's public dimension, since, in emphasizing discursive interaction between men and women, such a perspective more accurately portrays the church's extensive activities and influence at the grassroots level. I describe the black church not as the embodiment of ministerial authority or of any individual's private interests and pronouncements, but as a social space for discussion of public concerns. During the late nineteenth and early twentieth centuries, the church came to represent a deliberative arena, whose character derived from the collective nature of the church itself, namely, as a body of many diverse members, and from race-conscious feelings of nationalism.[3]

[* * *]

The formation of the National Baptist Convention, U.S.A. and its auxiliary women's convention afforded black men and women social space in which to critique openly the United States government, its laws, and its institutions. In fact, the level of public discussion caused one of the leaders of the Woman's Convention to come under government surveillance.[4] There were also subtle, perhaps more far-reaching political implications. The Baptist convention offered black men and women a structure for electing representatives, debating issues, and exercising many rights that white society denied them. Benjamin Mays and Joseph Nicholson, pointing to this surrogate political role, stated that the "local

churches, associations, conventions, and conferences become the Negro's Democratic and Republican Conventions, his Legislature and his Senate and House of Representatives."[5] Through their conventions, African Americans refuted notions of their inability or unreadiness for equal political participation. Among women, this understanding heightened support of women's suffrage. The political rhetoric espoused at black women's annual meetings included the demand not only for voting rights, but for full inclusion in American public life.

The black church constituted a public that stood in opposition to the dominant white public, and yet as the case of women illustrates, it did not form a monolith. Nor did it reveal values completely independent of white America. A gender perspective on the church lends clarity to this matter, since it locates different sites in which black women both embraced and contested the dominant values and norms of northern white Baptists, white women, and even black men. For example, during the 1880s and 1890s southern black and northern white Baptist women worked in a cooperative fashion rare for the times.[6] Their cooperation was not based upon identical motives and interests, but it indicated that divergent motives did not preclude mutual goals. Together, black and white women spread the Gospel, supported one another's organizations, financed black education, and alleviated the plight of the poor. The women's movement in the black Baptist church imagined itself both as part of the black community and as part of an evangelical sisterhood that cut across racial lines.[7] That black women voiced the race-conscious interests and agenda of the

3. Benedict Anderson defines nation as "an imagined political community—and imagined as both inherently limited and sovereign." For black Baptists, the "imagined community" was racially bounded and its sovereignty was perceived as free of white control—hence black denominational hegemony. See Benedict Anderson, *Imagined Communities: Reflections on the Origin and Spread of Nationalism* (London: Verso, 1983), 14–16.

4. In 1917 the Department of War monitored the activities and mail of Nannie Helen Burroughs, corresponding secretary of the Woman's Convention, for remarks in condemnation of Woodrow Wilson. Records of the War Department, General and Special Staffs, Military Intelligence Division, "Black Radicals (Church of God)," from Record Group 165, National Archives.

5. Benjamin E. Mays and Joseph W. Nicholson, *The Negro's Church* (New York, 1933; rpt. New York: Arno Press and the *New York Times,* 1969), 9.

6. The most extensive holdings of northern white Baptist women are the records of the Woman's American Baptist Home Mission Society and the Women's Baptist Home Mission Society, which are located in the American Baptist Archives Center in Valley Forge, Pennsylvania, and the American Baptist–Samuel Colgate Historical Library, Rochester, New York. Materials are also housed at the Franklin Trask Library in Andover-Newton Theological Seminary in Massachusetts.

7. The women's movement in the black Baptist church reflected a trend found in all the denominations in the late nineteenth century. Studies of white women's societies include Lois A. Boyd and R. Douglas Brackenridge, *Presbyterian Women in America: Two Centuries of a Quest for Status* (Westport, Conn.: Greenwood Press, 1983); Virginia Lieson Brereton and Christa Ressmeyer Klein, "American Women in Ministry: A History of Protestant Beginning Points," in Rosemary Ruether and Eleanor McLaughlin, eds., *Women of Spirit: Female Leadership in the Jewish and Christian Traditions* (New York: Simon and Schuster, 1979), chap. 11; Ruether and Rosemary Skinner Keller, *Women and Religion in America: The Nineteenth Century* (San Francisco: Harper and Row, 1981), 243–93.

male-dominated movement precluded neither interracial cooperation with white women nor conflict with black men.

CHURCH WOMEN'S MULTIPLE CONSCIOUSNESS

During the late nineteenth and early twentieth centuries, laws and changing social attitudes were chipping away at barriers to women's right to property, to education, to the professions, and even to suffrage in the western states of Wyoming in 1890 and in 1896 in Utah, Colorado, and Idaho.[8] During the latter decades of the nineteenth century white and black women joined in religious associations and secular clubs to bring about social reform. They fought for temperance, educational opportunity, suffrage, and a variety of gender-related issues. "To be alive at such an epoch is a privilege, to be a woman then is sublime," proclaimed the black educator and feminist Anna J. Cooper during the heady times of the "woman's era."[9] Cooper's exhilaration expressed nothing less than the black Baptist women's rising expectations.

The years between 1890 and 1920 witnessed significant strides for women. The number of all women with professional degrees rose by 226 percent.[1] Hazel Carby notes the increase of black women writers during the decade of the nineties. Anna J. Cooper published her feminist critique *A Voice from the South* (1892); other publications included Ida B. Wells, *On Lynchings* (1892) and Gertrude Mossell, *The Work of the Afro-American Woman* (1894). Black women established their literary presence in novels: Amelia E. Johnson's *Clarence and Corinne* (1890) and *The Hazeley Family* (1894); Emma Dunham Kelley's *Megda* (1891); Frances Ellen Watkins Harper's *Iola Leroy* (1892); and Victoria Earle's *Aunt Lindy* (1893).[2] Moreover, black women's writings drew attention and praise in the burgeoning field of journalism, as was reflected by the chapter devoted to them in I. Garland Penn's *The Afro-American Press and Its Editors* (1890).[3]

The cynical era of Jim Crow and the optimistic woman's era stood entangled one with the other—their imbrication giving shape to the black Baptist women's nationalist, yet feminist appeal. The complexity of the racial and gender meanings of the age suggests both the multiple consciousness and multiple positioning of black women, and also the complexity of the black church itself—an institution overwhelmingly female in membership. The church, like the black community, cannot be viewed solely through the lens of race. A gender perspective on the black church reminds us that the history of African Americans cannot be excluded from the important effort to identify and study social relations between men and women.

The history of black Baptist women discloses not only the gender dimension of the church's racial mission, but its class dimension as well.[4] The leadership of the women's convention movement formed part of an emergent class of school administrators, journalists, businesswomen, and reformers who served an all-black community. This educated female elite, frequently consisting of teachers or wives of ministers associated with educational institutions, promoted middle-class ideals

---

8. Suzanne Lebsock, "Women and American Politics, 1880–1920," in Louise A. Tilly and Patricia Gurin, eds., *Women, Politics, and Change* (New York: Russell Sage Foundation, 1990), 35–59.

9. Anna J. Cooper, *A Voice from the South* (Xenia, Ohio, 1892; rpt. New York: Negro Universities Press, 1969), 143.

1. For black women's educational and social reform activities, see Dorothy Salem, *To Better Our World: Black Women in Organized Reform, 1890–1920*, 7–103; vol. 14 in Darlene Clark Hine, ed., *Black Women in United States History: From Colonial Times to the Present* (Brooklyn: Carlson Press, 1990); Bettina Aptheker, "Black Women's Quest in the Professions," in Aptheker, *Woman's Legacy: Essays on Race, Sex, and Class in American History* (Amherst: University of Massachusetts Press, 1982), 89–110; Cynthia Neverdon-Morton, *Afro-American Women of the South and the Advancement of the Race, 1895–1925* (Knoxville: University of Tennessee Press, 1989), 78–103; Jacqueline Rouse, *Lugenia Burns Hope: Black Southern Reformer* (Athens: University of Georgia Press, 1989), 41–85. Also see for white women, Lynn D. Gordon, *Gender and Higher Education in the Progressive Era* (New Haven: Yale University Press, 1990); Rosalind Rosenberg, *Beyond Separate Spheres: Intellectual Roots of Modern Feminism* (New Haven: Yale University Press, 1982); Robyn Muncy, *Creating a Female Dominion in American Reform, 1890–1935* (New York: Oxford University Press, 1991).

2. For more on Wells, Harper, and Earle, see pp. [000], [000], and [000]. [Editor's note]

3. Hazel V. Carby, *Reconstructing Womanhood: The Emergence of the Afro-American Woman Novelist* (New York: Oxford University Press, 1987), 96–115; I. Garland Penn, *The Afro-American Press and Its Editors* (Springfield, Mass.: Willey, 1891), 366–427.

4. See E. Franklin Frazier's recognition of the middle-class orientation of the National Baptist Convention in Frazier, *Black Bourgeoisie* (New York: Macmillan, 1957), 89. [For an excerpt and debate about *Black Bourgeoisie*, see pp. 734–47. Editor's note]

among the masses of blacks in the belief that such ideals ensured the dual goals of racial self-help and respect from white America. Especially in the roles of missionary and teacher, black church women were conveyers of culture and vital contributors to the fostering of middle-class ideals and aspirations in the black community. Duty-bound to teach the value of religion, education, and hard work, the women of the black Baptist church adhered to a politics of respectability that equated public behavior with individual self-respect and with the advancement of African Americans as a group. They felt certain that "respectable" behavior in public would earn their people a measure of esteem from white America, and hence they strove to win the black lower class's psychological allegiance to temperance, industriousness, thrift, refined manners, and Victorian sexual morals.

On the one hand, the politics of respectability rallied poor working-class blacks to the cause of racial self-help, by inspiring them to save, sacrifice, and pool their scant resources for the support of black-owned institutions. Whether through white-imposed segregation or black-preferred separatism, the black community's support of its middle class surely accounted for the development and growth of black-owned institutions, including those of the Baptist church. On the other hand, the effort to forge a community that would command whites' respect revealed class tensions among blacks themselves. The zealous efforts of black women's religious organizations to transform certain behavioral patterns of their people disavowed and opposed the culture of the "folk"—the expressive culture of many poor, uneducated, and "unassimilated" black men and women dispersed throughout the rural South or newly huddled in urban centers.[5]

The Baptist women's preoccupation with respectability reflected a bourgeois vision that vacillated between an attack on the failure of America to live up

to its liberal ideals of equality and justice and an attack on the values and lifestyle of those blacks who transgressed white middle-class propriety. Thus the women's pronouncements appeared to swing from radical to conservative. They revealed their conservatism when they attributed institutional racism to the "negative" public behavior of their people—as if rejection of "gaudy" colors in dress, snuff dipping, baseball games on Sunday, and other forms of "improper" decorum could eradicate the pervasive racial barriers that surrounded black Americans. The Baptist women never conceded that rejection of white middle-class values by poor blacks afforded survival strategies, in fact spaces of resistance, albeit different from their own. Equally important, while the female leaders of the black Baptist church sought to broaden women's job opportunities and religious responsibilities, they revealed their conservatism in their unquestioning acceptance of man's sole right to the clergy.

LEGACY OF RESISTANCE

Despite the limits of their movement, black Baptist women left an impressive record of protest against the racist and sexist proscriptions of their day. Eugene Genovese[6] has written that "the living history of the Church has been primarily a history of submission to class stratification and the powers that be, but there has remained, despite all attempts at extirpation, a legacy of resistance that could appeal to certain parts of the New Testament and especially to the prophetic parts of the Old."[7] Exposing the black church's public dimension does not invalidate the centrality of its spiritual dimension in the private lives of black people or in the life of the black community. However, my interpretation of the church and black church women stresses the imbrication of the social and the spiritual within a

---

5. Houston Baker, in his discussion of the black vernacular, characterizes the "quotidian sounds of black every day life" as both a defiant and entrancing voice. Similarly, John Langston Gwaltney calls the "folk" culture of today's cities "core black culture," which is "more than ad hoc synchronic adaptive survival." Gwaltney links its values and epistemology to a long peasant tradition. See John Langston Gwaltney, *Drylongso: A Self-Portrait of Black America* (New York: Random House, 1980), xxv–xxvii; also Houston Baker, Jr., *Afro-American Poetics: Revisions of Harlem and the Black Aesthetic* (Madison: University of Wisconsin Press, 1988), 95–107; Baker, *Blues, Ideology, and Afro-American Literature: A Vernacular Theory* (Chicago: University of Chicago Press, 1984), 11–43.

6. See p. 586. [Editor's note]

7. [Eugene D.] Genovese, *Roll, Jordan, Roll* [*:The World The Slaves Made* (New York: Pantheen Books, 1974)], 163.

context akin, but not identical, to what C. Eric Lincoln and Lawrence Mamiya call the "dialectical model of the black church." For Lincoln and Mamiya, this model postulates the black church to be in "dynamic tension" within a series of dialectical polarities: priestly versus prophetic functions; other-worldly versus this-worldly; particularism versus universalism; privatistic versus communal; charismatic versus bureaucratic; and accommodation versus resistance.[8]

I characterize the church as a dialogic model rather than dialectical, recognizing "dynamic tension" in a multiplicity of protean and concurrent meanings and intentions more so than in a series of discrete polarities. Multiple discourses—sometimes conflicting, sometimes unifying—are articulated between men and women, and within each of these two groups as well. The black church constitutes a complex body of shifting cultural, ideological, and political significations. It represents a "heteroglot" conception in the Bakhtinian sense of a multiplicity of meanings and intentions that interact and condition each other.[9] Such multiplicity transcends polarity—thus tending to blur the spiritual and secular, the eschatological and political, and the private and public. The black church represented the realm where individual souls communed intimately with God and where African Americans as a people freely discussed, debated, and devised an agenda for their common good. At the same time that church values and symbols ordered the epistemological and ontological understandings of each individual and gave meaning to the private sphere of family—both as conjugal household and as "household of faith"—church values and symbols helped to spawn the largest number of voluntary associations in the black community. It follows logically, then, that the church would introduce black women to public life. The church connected black women's spirituality integrally with social activism.

Although women's historians tend to focus overwhelmingly on the secular club movement, especially the National Association of Colored Women, as exemplary of black women's activism, clubwomen themselves readily admitted to the precedent of church work in fostering both "woman's consciousness" and a racial understanding of the "common good." Fannie Barrier Williams, a founding member and leader of the National Association of Colored Women, acknowledged in 1900: "The training which first enabled colored women to organize and successfully carry on club work was originally obtained in church work. These churches have been and still are the great preparatory schools in which the primary lessons of social order, mutual trustfulness and united effort have been taught.... The meaning of unity of effort for the common good, the development of social sympathies grew into woman's consciousness through the privileges of church work."[1]

The club movement among black women owed its very existence to the groundwork of organizational skill and leadership training gained through women's church societies. Missionary societies had early on brought together women with little knowledge of each other and created bonds of sisterly cooperation at the city and state levels. Not only Baptists but black Methodists, Presbyterians, and women in other denominations came together in associations that transformed unknown and unconfident women into leaders and agents of social service and racial self-help in their communities. For black Baptist women during the 1880s, the formation of state societies nurtured skills of networking and fund-raising. For more than a decade before the founding of the National Association of Colored Women, church-related societies had introduced mothers' training schools and social service programs, many of which were later adopted into the programs of the secular women's clubs.

---

8. [C. Eric] Lincoln and [Lawrence H. Mamiya], *The Black Church in the African American Experience* [(Durham, N.C.: Duke University Press, 1990)], 10–16.

9. The Russian linguist and critic Mikhail Bakhtin discusses "dialogism" and "heteroglossia" in specific regard to his theory of language: "Everything means, is understood, as part of a greater whole—there is a constant interaction between meanings, all of which have the potential of conditioning others." See M.M. Bakhtin, *The Dialogic Imagination: Four Essays,* ed. Michael Holquist and trans. Caryl Emerson and Michael Holquist (Austin: University of Texas Press, 1981), 293, 352, 426.

1. See Fannie Barrier Williams, "The Club Movement among Colored Women of America," in Booker T. Washington, N. B. Wood, and Fannie Barrier Williams, *A New Negro for a New Century* (Chicago: American Publishing House, 1900), 383.

More than mere precursors to secular reform and women's rights activism,[2] black women's religious organizations undergirded and formed an identifiable part of what is erroneously assumed to be "secular." The black Baptist women's convention thrust itself into the mainstream of Progressive reform, and conversely such clubs as those constituting the secular-oriented National Association of Colored Women included church work as integral and salient to their purpose. This complexity precludes attempts to bifurcate black women's activities neatly into dichotomous categories such as religious versus secular, private versus public, or accommodation versus resistance.

Even such quotidian activities as women's fund raising, teaching in Sabbath schools, ministering to the sick, or conducting mothers' training schools embraced a politically subversive character within southern society. In many respects, the most profound challenge to Jim Crow laws, crop liens, disfranchisement, the dearth of black public schools, and the heinous brutality of lynching rested in the silent, everyday struggle of black people to build stable families, get an education, worship together in their churches, and "work the system," as Eric Hobsbawm terms it, "to their minimum disadvantage."[3] Arguments over the accommodationist versus liberating thrust of the black church miss the range as well as the fluid interaction of political and ideological meanings represented within the church's domain. Equally important, the artificiality of such a dichotomy precludes appreciation of the church's role in the "prosaic and constant struggle" of black people for survival and empowerment.[4] Edward

Wheeler persuasively argues for the paradoxical implications of social uplift and accommodation: "Accommodation, which of course had a submissive tone, also had a subversive quality. On the one hand, uplift meant accommodation and surrender to the concepts, principles, and ideals of the dominant society. On the other, uplift was a denial of what white society meant by accommodation, for it spoke of a possibility to move beyond the limits prescribed by the dominant society."[5]

In the 1909 Atlanta University study of social betterment activities among African Americans, Du Bois[6] attributed the greater part of such activities to the black church and specifically to church women.[7] In the final analysis the women's movement in the black Baptist church may be likened more to Harriet Tubman's repeated, surreptitious efforts to lead slaves step by step away from bondage than to Nat Turner's apocalyptic, revolutionary surge. Women's efforts were valiant attempts to navigate their people through the stifling and dangerous obstacle course of American racism. Committed to the causes of racial self-help and advancement, the convention movement among black Baptist women contributed greatly to the church's tremendous influence in both the spiritual and secular life of black communities. But the women's movement did something more. It gave to black women an individual and group pride that resisted ideologies and institutions upholding gender subordination. The movement gave them the collective strength and determination to continue their struggle for the rights of blacks and the rights of women.

2. For discussion of black and white women's church work as a forerunner to secular reform, see Ann Firor Scott, *The Southern Lady: From Pedestal to Politics, 1830–1930* (Chicago: University of Chicago Press, 1970), 141; Jean Friedman, *The Enclosed Garden: Women and Community in the Evangelical South, 1830–1900* (Chapel Hill: University of North Carolina Press, 1985), 111, 113, 115–126; Jacquelyn Dowd Hall, *Revolt against Chivalry: Jessie Daniel Ames and the Women's Campaign against Lynching* (New York: Columbia University Press, 1979), 70–77; Kathleen C. Berkeley, "'Colored Ladies also Contributed': Black Women's Activities from Benevolence to Social Welfare, 1866–1896," in Walter J. Fraser, Jr., R. Frank Saunders, Jr., and John L. Wakelyn, eds., *The Web of Southern Social Relations: Women, Family, and Education* (Athens: University of Georgia Press, 1985), 181–185.
3. Eric Hobsbawm, "Peasants and Politics," *Journal of Peasant Studies*, 1 (1973): 12, 16.
4. James Scott uses the phrase "prosaic and constant struggle" in his study of everyday forms of resistance in a Malaysian community. See James Scott, *Weapons of the Weak: Everyday Forms of Peasant Resistance* (New Haven: Yale University Press, 1985), 301.
5. Edward L. Wheeler, *Uplifting the Race: The Black Minister in the New South, 1865–1902* (Lanham, Md.: University Press of America, 1986), xvii.
6. For more on Du Bois, see p. 199. [Editor's note]
7. W. E. Burghardt Du Bois, ed., *Efforts for Social Betterment among Negro Americans* (Atlanta: Atlanta University Press, 1909), 16, 22.

Key Debate ≈ *The Government: Civic Rights and Civic Duties*

Clarence Thomas

Views on Affirmative Action [1986]

From 1982 to 1990, Clarence Thomas (b. 1948) served as chairman of the Equal Employment Opportunity Commission (EEOC) under Presidents Ronald Reagan and George H. W. Bush. The EEOC was established by the Civil Rights Act of 1964 to enforce the prohibition of employment discrimination "based on race, sex, color, religion, and national origin." In the 1980s and 1990s, ideas that Thomas conveys in the following interview (conducted ca. 1985), particularly the championing of "color-blindness" and individual merit as alternatives to the "unfairness" of group preferences, became popular among opponents of affirmative action. In this interview, conducted by white American political scientist Jeffrey Elliot (1947–2009), Thomas acknowledges the force of racial prejudice in American life—and in his own family—but argues that "no one should be rewarded or punished because of group characteristics."

In 1991, after contentious confirmation hearings (see pp. 1103–14), Thomas became the only African American justice on the Supreme Court (following Thurgood Marshall's retirement a few weeks earlier). Thomas's 1995 concurring opinion in *Adarand Constructors v. Pena* underscored his opposition to affirmative action programs: "That these programs may have been motivated, in part, by good intentions cannot provide refuge from the principle that under our Constitution, the government may not make distinctions on the basis of race. As far as the Constitution is concerned, it is irrelevant whether a government's racial classifications are drawn by those who wish to oppress a race or by those who have a sincere desire to help those thought to be disadvantaged."

From Jeffrey M. Elliot, ed., *Black Voices in American Politics* (San Diego: Harcourt Brace Jovanorich, 1986), pp. 148–56.

Jeffrey Elliot (JE): In what ways, if any, did your early childhood shape who you are and what you believe about civil rights?

Clarence Thomas (CT): I was raised by my grandparents, who played the single most important role in my life. My grandfather was raised by his grandmother, who, according to him, was freed from slavery at the age of nine. He had a third-grade education and was barely literate. He believed in this country and its values. He believed that this is the land of opportunity—and fought hard for equal opportunity. He knew that discrimination existed and that its existence undermined the values in which he believed and the principles upon which this country was built. It did not

matter that he worked harder than anyone I have ever known. It did not matter that he obeyed the laws. It did not matter that he was religious or that he was a good provider. It did not matter that he exemplified and embodied all that is good about this country. His efforts were all but neutralized by racial discrimination and prejudice. So he turned to fight discrimination. As he fought, I fight today. And like my grandfather, I am firmly committed to preserving and advancing the fundamental values of this country—values rooted in the rights of the individual, but values so often paid only lip service.

JE: How do you view the problems of race and racism?

CT: I adhere to the principle that individuals should be judged on the basis of individual merit and individual contact. No one should be rewarded or punished because of group characteristics. Unfortunately, this principle has not been made a reality. So today we are faced with the challenge of making this country colorblind after it has seen color for so long. And the critical question facing us is how to approach this challenge. Should we push for immediate *parity* or the fairness that has never really existed? Parity tends to show quicker change at least on paper. But is unfairness under the guise of parity any better than just plain unfairness? Should you concede your promotion in the name of parity for those who traditionally have been discriminated against?

On the other hand, it is difficult to tell those who have lost out in the past because of discrimination that we now, as a matter of policy, believe in fair play. This difficulty is exacerbated when we look at the socioeconomic plight of the affected groups and the inextricable relationship of that plight to unlawful discrimination. It is further complicated by the inconsistent but common practice of doling out preferences in this society to various groups for any number of reasons.

I opt for fairness—that is, treating individuals as individuals, neither preferring them nor deterring them on the basis of group characteristics. But I choose this option knowing full well that fairness, though an underpinning of this country, has never been a reality. I choose this option with the painful awareness of the social and economic ravages which have befallen my race and all who suffer discrimination. I choose this option with the enduring hope that this country will live up to the principles enunciated in the Bill of Rights and the Constitution of the United States: that all men are created equal and that they will be treated equally. But more than hope is necessary. These rights must be protected, and the laws protecting them must be vigorously enforced.

It is a sad fact that anti-discrimination laws have *never* been enforced in this country. The current tendency to parcel out rights and preferences on the basis of group characteristics is a poor substitute for protecting an individual's rights.

[* * *]

JE: For many years, the EEOC has been the subject of fierce criticism.

[* * *]

JE: To what extent has the press contributed to the misunderstanding which surrounds the EEOC?

CT: As we become more and more physically removed from the events of the day, we rely more and more on the media to provide us with the facts surrounding those events—to assist us in fully participating in our democratic system. With its constitutional guarantees of freedom, the press has the attendant responsibility of at least being accurate, objective, and fair in reporting the news. The press must live up to this responsibility—reporting the tough issues in the proper context and eschewing the use of shorthand references and loaded signals such as "forced busing" and "reverse discrimination" which inflame rather than inform.

Long ago, I decided not to become defensive about my own press coverage. Suffice it to say, I have been zapped. I sometimes wonder why this bigot is using my name when he talks to the press and why people are surprised to learn upon meeting me that I am not *the* Clarence Thomas they read about.

More important, however, the press must realize that there is not total agreement, even within the black community, on the merits of all civil rights strategies or social programs. We are not a monolith and we certainly are not clones. There are as many shades of black sociopolitical thought as there are in any ethnic group. Just as we don't look alike, we don't think alike. It is critical to balance these varying opinions in our national debate. Moreover, to effectively service our democratic process, we must strive to achieve and maintain a truly democratic press—one with balanced composition as well as views.

[* * *]

JE: To what extent is your strained relationship with the civil rights establishment attributable to the fact that you are both a black Republican and an ardent defender of President Reagan?

CT: My image as a black Republican, working in the Reagan Administration, is not the important factor. I would hope they could see beyond this fact. Rather, the challenge itself is what is crucial. As President

Kennedy said: "I do not shrink from this responsibility, I welcome it." I do not believe that black Americans will accept or reject my ideas on the basis of my party affiliation. They are far too intelligent for that. They know that the great problems facing our country cannot be solved through narrow-minded partisan proposals from either party.

I am a black Republican and proud of it. And I am aware of the image problem I suffer because of my political affiliation and my association with the Reagan Administration. Because of this association, many of us are perceived by our fellow Blacks as being "conservative, opportunistic Uncle Toms." It is presumed that we are not concerned with or sensitive to the problems of Blacks in this country. Consequently, many Blacks have chosen not to work with me and other black Republicans in this administration. That stance has had a paralyzing effect on the progress of Blacks.

While I am aware that we are presented to the American people as uncaring, unfair, and even *unjust*, I refuse to live with such an untrue image—either personally or politically. However, I gladly accept this iconoclasm and abuse to do what I believe is right and necessary. It is a small price to pay.

GLENN C. LOURY
Beyond Civil Rights [1985]

During the 1980s, opponents of affirmative action began to argue not only that the programs were unfair to non-minorities but also that they actually harmed their intended beneficiaries. In this 1985 speech to the National Urban League, the political economist Glenn Loury (b. 1949) asserts that the negative effect of affirmative action policies on the beneficiaries' self-esteem outweighs whatever benefits they receive. He also supports the common argument that preference programs stigmatize minorities. Like Clarence Thomas (p. 934), Loury emphasizes the role and rights of the individual rather than group policies, which he finds ineffective or even harmful. But while Thomas stresses fairness to non-minorities, Loury emphasizes the experiences of minorities, developing the idea of self-respect only "won through the unaided accomplishments of individual persons." In recent years, Loury has shifted from this rejection of affirmative action, with his work now suggesting that social science data support a moderate position on the issue.

From J. D. Williams, ed., *The State of Black America 1986* (New York: National Urban League, 1986), pp. 163–74.

My theme will be the limitations of civil rights strategies for effectively promoting the economic and social progress of minorities. By a "civil rights strategy" I mean two things: first, that the cause of a particular socioeconomic disparity be identified as racial discrimination; and second, that the advocates seek such remedies for the disparity as the courts and administrative agencies provide under the law. It has by now become a common theme in commentary on racial inequality in American society to observe that not all problems of blacks are due to discrimination, nor can they be remedied via civil rights or, more broadly, through racial politics.

More than this, however, I want to suggest that the inappropriate specification of a particular obstacle to minority progress as a civil rights matter can have significant costs. Evoking civil rights remedies for circumstances to which they are not suited can obviate the pursuit of alternative, more direct, and effective approaches to the problem. Such activity uses scarce resources that might otherwise be applied—the time and attention of those engaged directly in the advocacy, but also the goodwill and tolerance of those expected to respond. Finally, I will argue that the broad application of the civil rights method to every instance of differential achievement by blacks can be positively harmful in attaining the long-sought goal of fully equal status in the society, and threatens, if continued successfully, to make it literally impossible for blacks to be genuinely equal in American society.

I continue to believe there is an important role for civil rights law enforcement, and for those organizations that have played such a crucial part in the historic struggle for civil rights in this country. I do not believe racism has disappeared from American life, nor that appeals to conscience, based upon the history of injustice to which blacks have been subject, no longer have a place in our public life. Yet, it is obvious, given the American political and philosophical tradition, that the reach of civil rights law is and will remain insufficient to eliminate all socially and economically relevant discriminatory behavior. In light of this fact (to be elaborated below), it is important for blacks to augment this historically important approach to the problem of racial inequality.

There are enormously important contractual relationships into which people enter, as a result of which their social and economic status is profoundly affected, but among which racial discrimination is routinely practiced. Choice of marital partner is the most obvious. People discriminate here by race with a vengeance. A black woman does not have an opportunity equal to that of a white woman to become the wife of a given white man. Indeed, though this inequality in opportunity cuts both ways, since white men are on the whole better off financially than black men, one could imagine calculating the monetary cost to black women as a class of the fact that white men engage in discrimination of this sort. A class action suit might be filed on their behalf, seeking redress for the "damages" that result. Yet, of course, this is absurd. In large part, its absurdity derives from our acceptance, *in principle* as well as in fact, of an individual's right to engage in discrimination of this sort.

The point is of much more general applicability. Voluntary associations among individuals of all sorts (residential communities, friendship networks, business partnerships) are the result of mutual choices often influenced by racial criteria, but that lie beyond the reach of civil rights laws. A fair-housing law cannot prevent a disgruntled resident from moving away if the racial composition of his neighborhood changes. Bus-

ing for school desegregation cannot prevent unhappy parents from sending their children to private schools. Withdrawal of university support for student clubs with discriminatory selection rules cannot prevent student cliques from forming along racial lines. Application of the nondiscrimination mandate has, in practice, been restricted to the domain of impersonal, public, and economic transactions (employment, credit, housing, voting rights), but has not been allowed to interfere much with personal, private, and intimately social intercourse.

Yet, the fact that such exclusive social "clubs" do form along group lines has important economic consequences. An extensive literature in economics and sociology documents the importance of family and community background as factors influencing a child's latter life success. Studies have shown that access to the right "networks" can beneficially affect the outcome of job search in the labor market. Indeed, it has been theoretically demonstrated that, under plausible assumptions, when social background influences offspring's opportunities to acquire human capital, and when two groups of equal innate capabilities start with unequal economic status, then elimination of racial discrimination in the economic sphere but not in patterns of social attachment is generally insufficient to bring about eventual equalization of economic outcomes. There are, thus, elemental limits on the degree of economic equality between the races that one can hope to achieve through the use of civil rights laws. These limits derive from the fact that the antidiscrimination principle has been, as a matter of historical fact, restricted in its application to a limited domain of personal interactions.

Moreover, it is possible to question the ability of civil rights strategies to reduce group disparities in those areas to which they have been freely applied— education and employment, for example. Elsewhere I have argued that some important part of group economic disparity is due to the nature of social life *within* poor black communities.

With upward of three-fourths of children born out-of-wedlock in some inner-city ghettos, with black high school drop-out rates of better than 40 per cent (measured as the fraction of entering freshmen who do not eventually graduate) in Chicago and Detroit, with 40 per cent of murder victims in the country being blacks killed by other blacks, with fewer black women graduating from college than giving birth while in high school, with black women ages fifteen to nineteen being the most fertile population of that age group in the industrialized world, with better than two in five black children dependent on public assistance, and with these phenomena continuing apace notwithstanding two decades of civil rights efforts—it is reasonably clear that civil rights strategies alone cannot hope to bring about full equality. This is not to deny that, in some basic sense, most of these difficulties are related to our history of racial oppression. I only suggest (as, for example, Eleanor Holmes Norton has argued) that they have by now taken on a life of their own, and cannot be effectively reversed by civil rights policies.

EDUCATION

Further illustration of this point is provided by reference to the field of higher education. In the past (and not-too-distant past at that), there were severely limited opportunities for minorities to participate in higher education, as student or faculty, especially at the elite institutions. Nonetheless, many distinguished black scholars, scientists, inventors, jurists, writers and teachers had overcome the obstacles of racism to contribute to the common intellectual life of their country. Yet, in decades past, these men and women of genius learned and practiced their academic crafts under the most difficult conditions. Even after black scholars studied at the great institutions, their only possibilities for employment were at the historically black colleges, where they faced large teaching loads and burdensome administrative duties. Their accomplishments were often adknowledged by their white peers only grudgingly, if at all.

Today, opportunities for advanced education and academic careers for blacks abound. Major universities throughout the country are constantly searching for qualified black candidates to hire as professors, or admit to study. Most state colleges and universities near black population centers have made a concerted effort to reach those in the inner-city. Almost all institutions of higher learning admit blacks with lower grades or

test scores than white students. There are special programs funded by private foundations to help blacks prepare for advanced study in medicine, economics, engineering, public policy, law, and other fields. Special scholarship and fellowship funds have been set up for black students throughout the country.

Yet, with all these opportunities, and despite some improvement, the number of blacks advancing in the academic world is distressingly low. The percentage of college students who are black, after rising throughout the 1970s, has actually begun to decline. And while the proportion of doctorate degrees granted to blacks has risen slightly over the last decade, it is still the case that the majority of doctorate degrees that blacks earn are in the field of education. Despite constant pressure to hire black professors and strenuous efforts to recruit them, the percentages of blacks on elite university faculties has remained constant or fallen in the past decade.

Meanwhile, other groups traditionally excluded are making impressive gains. Asian Americans, though less than 2 per cent of the population, make up 6.6 per cent of U.S. scientists with doctorate degrees; they constitute 8 per cent of the student body at Harvard, 7.5 per cent at Yale, and 9 per cent at Stanford. Women have also made progress: the fraction of doctorate degrees going to women has risen from less than one-seventh to nearly one-third in the last decade. At Harvard's graduate school less than 3 per cent of the students are black, but more than 30 per cent are women. Less than 2 per cent of Harvard professors at all ranks are black, but more than 25 per cent are women.

No doubt, blacks continue to experience some discrimination at these institutions. But it is not a credible assertion to anyone who has spent time in an elite university community that these institutions are racist in character, and deny opportunities to blacks whose qualifications are outstanding. A case could be made that just the opposite is true—that these institutions are so anxious to raise the numbers of blacks in their ranks that they overlook deficiencies when making admissions or appointment decisions involving blacks. But for my purpose it only need be accepted that this state of affairs, in which black representation languishes at what, for many campus communities are politically unacceptable levels, does not admit a viable civil-rights oriented solution. It would be very difficult to make the case that, upon finding and eliminating the racially discriminatory behavior of faculty and administrators, this circumstance would reverse itself.

One obvious reason for skepticism about the efficacy of a civil rights strategy here would seem to be the relatively poor academic performance of black high school and college students. Black performance on standardized college admissions tests, though improving, still lags far behind whites. In 1982, on the mathematics component of the Scholastic Aptitude Test (SAT), the median white score was 484, while the median black score was 369. There were only 205 blacks in the entire country who scored above 700, though 3,015 Asian Americans achieved this distinction. And, as Robert Klitgaard has shown convincingly, postadmission college performance by black students is less than that of whites, even when controlling for differences in high school grades and SAT scores.

These differences in academic performance are not just limited to poor blacks, or to high school students. On the SAT exam mentioned earlier, blacks from families with income in excess of $50,000 per year still scored 60 to 80 points below comparable whites. On the 1981 Graduate Record Exam, taken by virtually all college seniors seeking to pursue advanced studies in the humanities and sciences, the gap between black and white students' median score on the quantitative mathematics component of this test was 171 points. At Harvard College there is a significant and disturbing difference in the grades earned by black and white students. According to professors at the Harvard Law School there have only been a few black students graduated in the top half of their class in the last five years. Klitgaard found that black law school admittees in the late 1970s had median scores on the Law School Admissions Test at the eighth percentile of the overall distribution of scores among law students.

It is clearly a matter of great concern that such substantial differences in educational results exist. One imagines that social background and limited past opportunities for blacks play an important role in accounting for these test score differences. It is also possible that the psychological effects on blacks of the "rumors of inferiority," which have circulated in American society about the intellectual capabilities of black

people, partly explain this disparity. Arguably, the government should be actively engaged in seeking to attenuate them. But it seems equally clear that this is not a civil rights matter—that it cannot be reversed by seeking out and changing someone's discriminatory behavior. Moreover, it is possible that great harm will be done if the problem is defined and pursued in those terms. This is illustrated by the example of a recent controversy over racial quotas at the Boston Latin School.

The Boston Latin School is the pride and joy of the city's public school system. It was founded before Harvard, in 1635. It has been recognized for centuries as a center of academic excellence. Boston Latin maintains its very high standards through a grueling program of study, including Latin, Greek, calculus, history, science, and the arts. Three hours of homework per night is typical. College admissions personnel acknowledge the excellence of this program. Ninety-five percent of the class of 1985 will go to college: Harvard has accepted twenty-two Latin graduates for next year's freshman class.

The institution admits its students on the basis of their primary school marks, and performance on the Secondary School Admissions Test. In 1974, when Boston's public schools became subject to court-ordered desegregation, Judge Arthur Garrity considered closing Boston Latin, because at that time the student population had been more than 90 per cent white. Upon consideration though, it was ordered that a racial admissions quota be employed requiring 35 per cent of the entering classes to be black and Hispanic. Of the 2245 students [in 1984], over half were female, 57 per cent white, 23 per cent black, 14 per cent Asian, and 6 per cent Hispanic.

Historically the school has maintained standards through a policy of academic "survival of the fittest." Those who were unable to make it through the academic rigors simply transferred to another school. Thus, there has always been a high rate of attrition; it is now in the range of 30–40 per cent. But, unlike the predesegregation era, today most of those who do not succeed at Boston Latin are minority students. Indeed, though approximately 35 per cent of each entering class is black and Hispanic, only 16 per cent of last year's senior class was. That is, for each (non-Asian) minority student who graduates from Latin, there is one who did not. The failure rate for whites is about half as great. Some advocates of minority student interest have, in the face of this racial disparity, complained of discrimination, saying in effect that the school is not doing enough to assist those in academic difficulty. Yet there is reason to doubt the effectiveness of this "civil rights strategy." Surely one reason for the poor performance of the black and Hispanic students is the racial admissions quota ordered by Judge Garrity a decade ago. To be considered for admissions, whites must score at the seventieth percentile or higher on the admission exam, while blacks and Hispanics need only score above the fiftieth percentile. But the problems of minority students at Boston Latin have not prevented some from advocating that the minority admissions quota be increased.

Attorney Thomas Atkins, former general counsel of the NAACP, who has been representing the black plaintiffs in this law suit off and on for ten years, proposed to Judge Garrity in the spring of 1985 that the quota at Boston Latin be raised to roughly 50 per cent black, 20 per cent Hispanic and Asian, and 30 per cent white—a reflection of the racial composition of the rest of Boston's public schools. Absent a significant increase in the size of the school, this could only be accomplished by doubling the number of blacks admitted while cutting white enrollment in half. This in turn, under plausible statistical assumptions, would require an approximate doubling of the now twenty-point gap in threshold test scores of black and white admittees. Since the additional black students admitted would of necessity be less prepared than those admitted under the current quota, one would expect an even higher failure rate among minorities, were this plan to be accepted. The likely consequence would be that more than three-fourths of those leaving Boston Latin without a degree would be blacks and Hispanics. It is also plausible to infer that such an action would profoundly alter, if not destroy, the academic climate in the school.

This is not simply an inappropriate use of civil rights methods, though it is surely that. We have here an almost wanton surrender of the moral high ground by an advocate who would seek remedy from a federal judge for the failure of Boston's black students to excel. By what logic of pedagogy can these students' difficulty be attributed to racism, in view of the fact that the school system has been run by court order for over a decade? By what calculus of fairness do those fighting for justice arrive at the position that outstanding white students, many from poor homes themselves (80 per cent of Latin graduates require financial aid in college) should be denied the opportunity for this special education so that minority students who are not prepared for it may nonetheless enroll? Responding to black student underrepresentation at Boston Latin as if this were a civil rights problem seems patently unwise. Is there so little faith in the aptitude of the minority young people that the highest standards should not be held out for them? Are their advocates so vindictive about the past that they would risk injuring their own children and inflict gross unfairness on the children of others all in the name of numerical racial balance?

Another example from the field of education illustrates how the use of civil rights methods, when not appropriate to the problem at hand, can have significant "opportunity costs." In 1977 the Ann Arbor public school system was sued by representatives of a class of black parents with children in the primary grades. The school system was accused of denying equal educational opportunity to these children. The problem was that the black students were not learning how to read at an acceptable rate, though the white youngsters were. The suit alleged that, by failing to take into account in the teaching of reading to these children the fact that they spoke an identifiable, distinct dialect of the English language—black English—the black students were denied equal educational opportunity. The lawsuit was successful.

As a result, in 1979 the court ordered that reading teachers in Ann Arbor be given special "sensitivity" training so that, while teaching standard English to these children, they might "accommodate" the youngsters' culturally distinct patterns of speech. Ann Arbor's public school system has dutifully complied. A recent discussion of this case with local educators revealed that, as of six years after the initial court order, the disparity in reading achievement between blacks and whites in Ann Arbor persists at a level comparable to that which obtained before the lawsuit was brought. It was their opinion that, though of enormous symbolic importance, the entire process had produced little in the way of positive educational impact on the students.

This is not intended as a condemnation of those who brought the suit, nor do I offer here any opinion on whether promotion of black English is a good idea. What is of interest is the process by which the problem was defined, and out of which a remedy was sought. In effect, the parents of these children were approached by public-interest lawyers and educators active in civil rights, and urged to help their children learn to read by bringing this action. Literally thousands of hours went into conceiving and trying this case. Yet, in the end only a hollow, symbolic victory was won. Apparently, the federal district judge did not have it within his power to eliminate the disparity between black and white children in rates at which reading competency was acquired.

But it is possible that, more than simply ineffective, this line of attack on the problem and the advocative instincts from which it sprang caused other viable strategies not to be pursued. One imagines for example that a direct effort to tutor the first and second graders might have made an impact, giving them special attention and extra hours of study through the voluntary participation of those in Ann Arbor possessed of the relevant skills. With roughly 35,000 students at the University of Michigan's Ann Arbor campus (a fair number of whom are black), it would have required that only a fraction of 1 per cent of them spare an afternoon or evening once a week for there to be sufficient numbers to provide the needed services. There were at most only a few hundred poor black students in the primary grades experiencing reading difficulties. And, more than providing this needed aid for specific kids, such an undertaking would have helped to cultivate a more healthy relationship between the university and its community. It could have contributed to building a tradition of direct service that would be of more general value. But none of this happened, in part because the "civil rights approach" was almost reflexively embraced by the parties concerned.

AFFIRMATIVE ACTION

Indeed, there is a reason to be concerned that the tendency to perceive every instance of differential performance between racial groups as remediable by some affirmative action–like treatment may, if successfully continued, destroy the possibility of attaining "real" equality of status for black Americans.

The simplest version of this argument is by now very familiar—affirmative action creates uncertain perceptions about the qualifications of those minorities who benefit from it. If, in an employment situation say, it is known that differential selection criteria are used for different races, and if it is further known that the quality of performance on the job depends on how one did on the criteria of selection, then in the absence of other information it is a rational statistical inference to impute a lower perceived quality of performance to persons of the race that was preferentially favored in selection. Using race as a criterion of selection in employment, in other words, creates objective incentives for customers, co-workers, etc., to take race into account after the employment decision has been made.

More than this, however, the broad use of race preference to treat all instances of "underrepresentation" introduces uncertainty into the process by which individuals make inferences about their own abilities. A frequently encountered question today from a black man or woman promoted to a position of unusual responsibility in a "mainstream" institution is: "Would I have been offered this position if I had not been a black? Most people in such situations want to be reassured that their achievement has been earned, and is not based simply on the organizational requirement of racial diversity. As a result, the use of racial preference tends to undermine the ability of people to confidently assert, if only to themselves, that they are as good as their achievements would seem to suggest.

It therefore undermines the extent to which the personal success of one black can become the basis of guiding the behavior of other blacks. Fewer individuals in a group subject to such preferences can confidently say to their fellows: "I made it on my own, through hard work, self-application, and native ability, and so can you!" And, disturbingly, the broad use of affirmative action as a vehicle for black achievement puts even the "best and brightest" of the favored group in the position of being the supplicants of benevolent whites.

But this is not the end of the story. Because in order to defend such programs in the political arena—especially at the elite institutions—it becomes necessary to argue that almost no blacks could reach these heights without special favors. This, when examined closely, entails the virtual admission that blacks are unable to perform up to the white standard. Thus, Harvard University president Derek Bok—arguing in defense of black interests, he thinks—has publicly declared that, without the use of quotas in undergraduate admissions, only 1 per cent of the entering class would be black (though roughly eight times as many would be Asian Americans). This practically forces the conclusion that blacks, on the whole, must make up through the use of quotas what they lack in intellectual capabilities.

In New York City, where the last examination for promotion to police sergeant was passed by 10.1 per cent of whites, 4.4 per cent of Hispanics, but only 1.7 per cent of blacks, the city has agreed to scrap the test and promote its quota of blacks. The test, they say, is illegally discriminatory since fewer blacks passed, and since the city's legal department does not think it could be defended as job-related. Yet, the test was explicitly prepared (at a cost of $500,000 and under a court-supervised consent decree), so as only to test job-relevant skills. No one really believes the *test* was unfair to nonwhite officers, only the *results* are questioned. But, after this episode, can anyone be made to believe that blacks are capable of the same results as whites?

The use of racial quotas, deriving from the civil rights approach to problems of racial differences in performance, can have subtle effects on the way in which black people think about themselves. When there is internal disagreement among black intellectuals, for example about the merits of affirmative action, critics of the policy are often attacked as being disingenuous, since they clearly owe their own prominence to the very policy they criticize. The specific circumstances of the individual do not matter in this, for it is presumed that *all* blacks, whether directly or indirectly, are indebted to civil rights activity for their achievements. The consequence of this is a kind of "socialization" of the individual black's accomplishments. The individual's effort to claim achievement for himself, and thus to secure the autonomy and legitimacy needed to lead and shape the groups' views of its condition, is perceived as a kind of betrayal.

This is, in a subtle but nontrivial way, destructive of black self-esteem. There is nothing wrong, of course,

with acknowledging the debt all blacks owe to those who fought and beat the Jim Crow laws. There is everything wrong with a group's most accomplished persons feeling that the celebration of their personal attainments represents betrayal of their fellows.

CONCLUSION

In his recent, highly esteemed comparative history of slavery, *Slavery and Social Death*, Orlando Patterson defines slavery as the "permanent, violent domination of natally alienated and generally dishonored persons." Most discussion of the American slave experience in contemporary policy discourse focuses on the violent character of the institution, its brutalization of the Africans, and its destructive effects on social life among the slaves. There is much debate among historians and philosophers on the precise extent to which this history is related to current-day policy concerns. Less attention is paid nowadays to the *dishonored* condition of the slave, and by extension of the freedman. For Patterson this dishonoring was crucial. He sees as a common feature of slavery wherever it has occurred the parasitic phenomenon whereby masters derive honor and standing from their power over the slaves, and the slaves suffer an extreme marginality by virtue of having no social existence except that mediated by their masters. Patterson rejects the "property in people" definition of slavery, arguing that relations of respect and standing among persons are also crucial. But if this is so, it follows that emancipation—the ending of the master's property claim—is not of itself sufficient to convert a slave (or his descendant) into a genuinely equal citizen. There remains the intractable problem of overcoming the historically generated "lack of honor" of the freedmen.

This problem, in my judgment, remains with us. Its eventual resolution is made less likely by blacks' broad, permanent reliance on racial preferences as remedies for academic or occupational underperformance. A central theme in Afro-American political and intellectual history is the demand for respect—the struggle to gain inclusion within the civic community, to become coequal participants in the national enterprise. This is, of course, a problem that all immigrant groups also faced, and that most have overcome. But here, unlike some other areas of social life, it seems that the black population's slave origins, subsequent racist exclusion, and continued dependence on special favors from the majority uniquely exacerbates the problem.

Blacks continue to seek the respect of our fellow Americans. And yet it becomes increasingly clear that, to win the equal regard of our fellows, black Americans cannot substitute judicial and legislative decree for what is to be won through the outstanding achievements of individual black persons. That is, neither the pity, nor the guilt, nor the coerced acquiescence in one's demands—all of which have been over the last two decades amply available to blacks—is sufficient. For what ultimately is being sought is the freely conveyed respect of one's peers. Assigning prestigious positions so as to secure a proper racial balance—this as a permanent, broadly practiced policy—seems fundamentally inconsistent with the attainment of this goal.

It is a truth worth noting that not everything of value can be redistributed. With respect to personal traits like beauty or intelligence this is readily obvious. But it is no less true for other important nonpecuniary goods like dignity and respect. If, in the psychological calculus by which people determine their satisfaction such status considerations are important, then this observation places basic limits on the extent to which public policy can effect fully egalitarian outcomes. This is especially so with respect to the policy of racially preferential treatment, because its use to "equalize" can actually destroy the good that is being sought on behalf of those initially unequal. It would seem that, where the high regard of others is being sought, there is no substitute for what is to be won through the unaided accomplishments of individual persons.

RANDALL KENNEDY

Persuasion and Distrust [1986]

Randall Kennedy (b. 1954), a professor at Harvard Law School, responds to a wide variety of arguments against affirmative action. In addition to addressing issues ranging from the effects of preference programs to their constitutionality, Kennedy raises questions about the motivations behind the fierce opposition to affirmative action. Having a legal background similar to that of Clarence Thomas (p. 934) and applying his legal knowledge to the controversy of affirmative action, Kennedy reaches the opposite conclusion: that affirmative action is highly beneficial not only to African Americans but to the nation as a whole.

From the *Harvard Law Review* 99 (April 1986): pp. 1327–46.

The controversy over affirmative action[1] constitutes the most salient current battlefront in the ongoing conflict over the status of the Negro in American life. No domestic struggle has been more protracted or more riddled with ironic complication. One frequently noted irony is that the affirmative action

---

1. "Affirmative action," "preferential treatment," and "affirmative discrimination" are used as synonyms. At the level of semantics, "affirmative action" avoids the problem of preference that is inescapable if one uses the term "preferential treatment." It also avoids the problem of discrimination made salient by the term "affirmative discrimination." On all too many occasions, however, proponents of affirmative action have hurt their own cause by evading the difficulties posed and costs incurred by the policy they advance. These difficulties and costs will not disappear behind euphemistic terminology. To properly convince the public that these costs are worth shouldering, proponents of affirmative action will have to grapple straightforwardly with them—a process that involves, at the least, conceding their existence.

[This article] is concerned solely with the debate over affirmative action for American blacks. I recognize that affirmative action programs often include other groups and exclude still others that arguably should be included. And I acknowledge that questions of fairness regarding the criteria by which preference is conferred constitute important issues in the controversy. While practical limitations prevent exploration of this issue, my basic position with respect to it is that the nation should use affirmative action policies to eradicate the oppression and isolation of *any* "specially disadvantaged group." [Unless otherwise indicated, all footnotes are those of the author.]

controversy has contributed significantly to splintering the coalition principally responsible for the civil rights revolution. That coalition was comprised of a broad array of groups—liberal Democrats, moderate Republicans, the national organizations of the black and Jewish communities, organized labor and others—that succeeded in invalidating de jure segregation and passing far-reaching legislation in support of the rights of blacks, including the Civil Rights Act of 1964 and the Voting Rights Act of 1965.

For over a decade this coalition has been riven by bitter disagreement over the means by which American society should attempt to overcome its racist past. Opponents of affirmative action maintain that commitment to a nonracist social environment requires strict color blindness in decisionmaking as both a strategy and a goal. In their view, "one gets beyond racism by getting beyond it now: by a complete, resolute, and credible commitment *never* to tolerate in one's own life—or in the life or practices of one's government—the differential treatment of other human beings by race" (William Van Alstyne). Proponents of affirmative action insist that only *malign* racial distinctions should be prohibited; they favor *benign* distinctions that favor blacks. Their view is that "[i]n order to get beyond racism, we must first take race into account" and that "in order to treat some persons equally, we must treat them differently" (Justice Blackmun).

I conclude that affirmative action should generally be retained as a tool of public policy because, on balance, it is useful in overcoming entrenched racial hierarchy. In addition I argue that division within the civil rights coalition is not the *only* conflict permeating the affirmative action controversy. Also involved is a much older conflict involving sectors of our society that have never authentically repudiated the "old-style religion" of white supremacy. The most important of these sectors is the Reagan administration. I contend that a tenacious and covert resistance to further erosion of racial hierarchy explains much of the Reagan administration's racial policy, especially its attacks on affirmative action.

I focus on both overt and covert discourse, because the affirmative action debate cannot be understood without acknowledging simultaneously the force of the openly stated arguments for and against preferential treatment and the submerged intuitions that disguise themselves with these arguments. To disregard either of these features of the debate is to ignore an essential aspect of the controversy. To appreciate both is to recognize the frustrating complexity of our racial situation.

The Case for Affirmative Action

Affirmative action has strikingly benefited blacks as a group and the nation as a whole. It has enabled blacks to attain occupational and educational advancement in numbers and at a pace that would otherwise have been impossible.[2] These breakthroughs engender self-perpetuating benefits: the accumulation of valuable experience, the expansion of a professional class able to pass its material advantages and elevated aspirations to subsequent generations, the eradication of debilitating stereotypes, and the inclusion of black participants in the making of consequential decisions affecting black interests. Without affirmative action, continued access for black applicants to college and professional education would be drastically narrowed. To insist, for example, upon the total exclusion of racial factors in admission decisions, especially at elite institutions, would mean classes of college, professional, and graduate students that are virtually devoid of Negro representation.

Furthermore, the benefits of affirmative action redound not only to blacks but to the nation as a whole. For example, the virtual absence of black police even in overwhelmingly black areas helped spark the ghetto rebellions of the 1960s. The integration of police forces through strong affirmative action measures has often led to better relations between minority communities and the police, a result that improves public safety for all. Positive externalities have accompanied affirmative action programs in other contexts as well,[3] most

2. To take one famous example, under the "regular" admissions program of the University of California at Davis Medical School, only one black applicant would have qualified for admission between 1970 and 1974; twenty-six were admitted due to affirmative action. In the employment context, affirmative action has played a major role in upgrading the relative position of black workers.
3. Affirmative action in medical school admissions was begun, among other reasons, to ensure the training of persons likely to enter primary care specialties, to practice in underserved areas of the country, and to serve black patient populations. According to a recent study of the career paths of black physicians, these goals are being met.

importantly by teaching whites that blacks, too, are capable of handling responsibility, dispensing knowledge, and applying valued skills.

THE CLAIM THAT AFFIRMATIVE ACTION HARMS BLACKS

In the face of arguments in favor of affirmative action, opponents of the policy frequently reply that it actually harms its ostensible beneficiaries. Various interrelated claims undergird the argument that affirmative action is detrimental to the Negro. The most weighty claim is that preferential treatment exacerbates racial resentments, entrenches racial divisiveness, and thereby undermines the consensus necessary for effective reform. The problem with this view is that intense white resentment has accompanied every effort to undo racial subordination no matter how careful the attempt to anticipate and mollify the reaction. The Supreme Court, for example, tried mightily to preempt white resistance to school desegregation by directing that it be implemented with "all deliberate speed." This attempt, however, to defuse white resistance may well have caused the opposite effect and, in any event, doomed from the outset the constitutional rights of a generation of black school children. Given the apparent inevitability of white resistance and the uncertain efficacy of containment, proponents of racial justice should be wary of allowing fear of white backlash to limit the range of reforms pursued. This admonition is particularly appropriate with respect to affirmative action insofar as it creates vital opportunities the value of which likely outweigh their cost in social friction. A second part of the argument that affirmative action hurts blacks is the claim that it stigmatizes them by implying that they simply cannot compete on an equal basis with whites. Moreover, the pall cast by preferential treatment is feared to be pervasive, hovering over blacks who have attained positions without the aid of affirmative action as well as over those who have been accorded preferential treatment. I do not doubt that affirmative action causes some stigmatizing effect. It is unrealistic to think, however, that affirmative action causes most white disparagement of the abilities of blacks.[4] Such disparagement, buttressed for decades by the rigid exclusion of blacks from educational and employment opportunities, is precisely what engendered the explosive crisis to which affirmative action is a response. Although it is widely assumed that "qualified" blacks are now in great demand, with virtually unlimited possibilities for recognition, blacks continue to encounter prejudice that ignores or minimizes their talent.[5] In the end, the uncertain extent to which affirmative action diminishes the accomplishments of blacks must be balanced against the stigmatization that occurs when blacks are virtually absent from important institutions in the society. The presence of blacks across the broad spectrum of institutional settings upsets conventional stereotypes about the place of the Negro and acculturates the public to the idea that blacks can and must participate in all areas of our national life. This positive result of affirmative action outweighs any stigma that the policy causes.[6]

---

4. The stigma problem, moreover, is mainly an affliction besetting elite occupations. There are a great many jobs, generally those requiring relatively little specialized training, to which the problem of stigma is largely irrelevant. After all, when an occupation requires no more than on-the-job training, there is little reason to suspect that blacks who have undergone such training are any less qualified than their white counterparts.

5. The advancement registered by members of the black middle class is not necessarily evidence that old-fashioned discrimination has been eradicated. Often, this advancement proceeds despite the presence of continuing prejudice and is made possible precisely because of the lift provided by affirmative action.

6. There remains the apprehension that affirmative action will elevate blacks to positions for which they are unqualified and in which they fail, further entrenching the very assumptions that preferential treatment seeks to combat. For example, the lower rates with which black physicians obtain specialty board certification and black attorneys pass state bar examinations lends support to the view that, by and large, even after training, black beneficiaries of affirmative action constitute a class of professionals decidedly less competent to supply vital services than their white counterparts. On the other hand, this fear is probably out of proportion to any real basis in fact. The most comprehensive survey of affirmative action in employment (by Jonathan Leonard) concludes that no significant evidence exists indicating that affirmative action leads to marked efficiency costs. Moreover, there is little support for the frequent allegation that affirmative action necessitates the wholesale abrogation of relevant standards. Any sensible affirmative action program will require the satisfaction of certain minimal requirements appropriate to a given context. Once these minimum standards are met, the minority status of an applicant can then play a legitimate role in hiring or admissions decisions.

A third part of the argument against affirmative action is the claim that it saps the internal morale of blacks. It renders them vulnerable to a dispiriting anxiety that they have not truly earned whatever positions or honors they have attained.[7] Moreover, it causes some blacks to lower their own expectations of themselves. Having grown accustomed to the extra boost provided by preferential treatment, some blacks simply do not try as hard as they otherwise would. There is considerable power to this claim; unaided accomplishment does give rise to a special pride felt by both the individual achiever and her community. But the suggestion that affirmative action plays a major role in undermining the internal morale of the black community is erroneous.

Although I am unaware of any systematic evidence on the self-image of beneficiaries of affirmative action, my own strong impression is that black beneficiaries do not see their attainments as tainted or undeserved—and for good reason.[8] First, they correctly view affirmative action as rather modest compensation for the long period of racial subordination suffered by blacks as a group. Thus they do not feel that they have been merely *given* a preference; rather, they see affirmative discrimination as a form of social justice. Second, and more importantly, many black beneficiaries of affirmative action view claims of meritocracy with skepticism. They recognize that in many instances the objection that affirmative action represents a deviation from meritocratic standards is little more than disappointed nostalgia for a golden age that never really existed. Overt exclusion of blacks from public and private institutions of education and employment was one massive affront to meritocratic pretensions. Moreover, a long-standing and pervasive feature of our society is the importance of a wide range of nonobjective, nonmeritocratic factors influencing the distribution of opportunity. The significance of personal associations and informal networks is what gives durability and resonance to the adage, "It's not *what* you know, it's *who* you know." As Professor Wasserstrom[9] wryly observes, "Would anyone claim that Henry Ford II [was] head of the Ford Motor Company because he [was] the most qualified person for the job?"

Finally, and most importantly, many beneficiaries of affirmative action recognize the thoroughly political—which is to say contestable—nature of "merit"; they realize that it is a malleable concept, determined not by immanent, preexisting standards but rather by the perceived needs of society. Inasmuch as the elevation of blacks addresses pressing social needs, they rightly insist that considering a black's race as part of the bundle of traits that constitute "merit" is entirely appropriate.

A final and related objection to affirmative action is that it frequently aids those blacks who need it least and who can least plausibly claim to suffer the vestiges of past discrimination—the offspring of black middle-class parents seeking preferential treatment in admission to elite universities and black entrepreneurs seeking guaranteed set-asides for minority contractors on projects supported by the federal government. This objection too is unpersuasive. First, it ignores the large extent to which affirmative action has pried open opportunities for blue-collar black workers. Second, it assumes that affirmative action should be provided only to the most deprived strata of the black community or to those who can best document their victimization. In many circumstances, however, affirmative action has developed from the premise that special aid should be given to strategically important sectors of

---

7. Some commentators have stated that beneficiaries of affirmative action feel guilty about their "tainted" achievements. Blacks seem to be the primary targets of such ruminations. Justice Sandra Day O'Connor, the first woman to be appointed to the Supreme Court, was certainly not nominated because of her demonstrated mastery of federal law. Among the principle reasons for her elevation was her status as a competent *woman* jurist. She appears, however, to have escaped the suggestion that she is silently suffering a crisis of conscience or confidence because her sex played an essential role in her appointment.
8. Members of the organized black community, Republicans and Democrats alike, are virtually united in calling for the continuation of affirmative action programs. Black Republican organizations for example have urged President Reagan not to rescind Executive Order 11246, which mandates affirmative hiring goals in all contracts with the government.
9. Richard Alan Wasserstrom (b. 1936), white American lawyer, professor of law and philosophy, and university administrator; worked as a lawyer for the civil rights division of the U.S. Department of Justice during the Kennedy Administration and was a vocal supporter of affirmative action. [Editor's note]

the black community—for example, those with the threshold ability to integrate the professions. Third, although affirmative action has primarily benefitted the black middle class, that is no reason to condemn preferential treatment. All that fact indicates is the necessity for additional social intervention to address unmet needs in those sectors of the black community left untouched by affirmative action. One thing that proponents of affirmative action have neglected to emphasize strongly enough is that affirmative discrimination is but part—indeed a rather small part—of the needed response to the appalling crisis besetting black communities. What is so remarkable—and ominous—about the affirmative action debate is that so modest a reform calls forth such powerful resistance.

DOES AFFIRMATIVE ACTION VIOLATE THE CONSTITUTION?

The constitutional argument against affirmative action proceeds as follows: *All* governmental distinctions based on race are presumed to be illegal and can escape that presumption only by meeting the exacting requirements of "strict scrutiny." Because the typical affirmative action program cannot meet these requirements, most such programs are unconstitutional. Behind this theory lies a conviction that has attained its most passionate and oft-quoted articulation in Alexander Bickel's statement:

> The lesson of the great decisions of the Supreme Court and the lesson of contemporary history have been the same for at least a generation: discrimination on the basis of race is illegal, immoral, unconstitutional, inherently wrong, and destructive of democratic society. Now this is to be unlearned and

we are told that this is not a matter of fundamental principle but only a matter of whose ox is gored.

Among the attractions of this theory are its symmetry and simplicity. It commands that the government be color-blind in its treatment of persons, that it accord benefits and burdens to black and white individuals according to precisely the *same* criteria—no matter whose ox is gored. According to its proponents, this theory dispenses with manipulable sociological investigations and provides a clear *rule* that compels consistent judicial application.

In response, I would first note that the color-blind theory of the Constitution is precisely that—a "theory," one of any number of competing theories that seek to interpret the Fourteenth Amendment's delphic proscription of state action that denies any person "the equal protection of the laws." Implicitly recognizing that neither a theory of original intent nor a theory of textual construction provides suitable guidance, Professor Bickel suggests that a proper resolution of the affirmative action dispute can be derived from "the great decisions of the Supreme Court." Certainly what Bickel had in mind were *Brown v. Board of Education* and its immediate progeny, the cases that established the foundation of our postsegregation Constitution. To opponents of affirmative action, the lesson of these cases is that, except in the narrowest, most exigent circumstances, race can play no legitimate role in governmental decisionmaking.

This view, however, is too abstract and ahistorical. In the forties, fifties, and early sixties, against the backdrop of laws that used racial distinctions to exclude Negroes from opportunities available to white citizens, it seemed that racial subjugation could be overcome by mandating the application of race-blind law.[1] In

---

1. It is quite true that some of the civil rights movement's most illustrious leaders have posited the idea that the constitution mandates strict color blindness in government policy. (See William Bradford Reynolds, "Individualism vs. Group Rights: The Legacy of Brown," *Yale Law Journal*, volume 93, pp. 995, 998–1001 (1984), citing Justice Thurgood Marshall, Jack Greenberg, Roy Wilkins, and Dr. Martin Luther King, Jr.) It is a mistake, however, to view these leaders as a new set of founding fathers whose original intent regarding the post-segregation Constitution must now control contemporary interpretations. First, the meaning of all statements must be derived from the surrounding context. Therefore, little is advanced by merely citing language used by civil rights activists during the initial, crucial victories over the Jim Crow system. After all, insofar as widespread trauma accompanied the demand that blacks simply be treated the same as whites, it made perfect tactical sense not to raise additional issues that could result only in increased resistance. Second, it is clear that initially neither civil rights leaders nor the Supreme Court really knew what racial equality would entail; it was a goal that gained clarity only in the process of actual realization. Racial equality is not a static concept; it is a living idealization that gathers meaning only in the context of changing historical conditions.

retrospect, however, it appears that the concept of race blindness was simply a proxy for the fundamental demand that racial subjugation be eradicated. This demand, which matured over time in the face of myriad sorts of opposition, focused upon the *condition* of racial subjugation; its target was not only procedures that overtly excluded Negroes on the basis of race, but also the self-perpetuating dynamics of subordination that had survived the demise of American apartheid. The opponents of affirmative action have stripped the historical context from the demand for race-blind law. They have fashioned this demand into a new totem and insist on deference to it no matter what its effects upon the very group the Fourteenth Amendment was created to protect. *Brown* and its progeny do not stand for the abstract principle that governmental distinctions based on race are unconstitutional. Rather, those great cases, forged by the gritty particularities of the struggle against white racism, stand for the proposition that the Constitution prohibits any arrangements imposing racial subjugation—whether such arrangements are ostensibly race-neutral or even ostensibly race-blind.

This interpretation, which articulates a principle of antisubjugation rather than antidiscrimination, typically encounters two closely related objections. The first objection is the claim that the constitutional injury done to a white whose chances for obtaining some scarce opportunity are diminished because of race-based allocation schemes is legally indistinguishable from that suffered by a black victim of racial exclusion. Second, others argue that affirmative discrimination based on racial distinctions cannot be satisfactorily differentiated from racial subjugation absent controversial sociological judgments that are inappropriate to the judicial role.

As to the first objection, the injury suffered by white "victims" of affirmative action does not properly give rise to a constitutional claim, because the damage does not derive from a scheme animated by racial prejudice. Whites with certain credentials may be excluded from particular opportunities they would receive if they were black. But this diminished opportunity is simply an incidental consequence of addressing a compelling societal need: undoing the subjugation of the Negro. Whites who would be admitted to professional schools in the absence of affirmative action policies

are not excluded merely because of prejudice, as were countless numbers of Negroes until fairly recently. Rather, whites are excluded "because of a rational calculation about the socially most beneficial use of limited resources for [professional] education" (Ronald Dworkin).

As to the second objection, I concede that distinctions between affirmative and malign discrimination cannot be made in the absence of controversial sociological judgments. I reject the proposition, however, that drawing these distinctions is inappropriate to the judicial role. Such a proposition rests upon the assumption that there exists a judicial method wholly independent of sociological judgment. That assumption is false; to some extent, whether explicitly or implicitly, *every* judicial decision rests upon certain premises regarding the irreducibly controversial nature of social reality. The question, therefore, is not whether a court will make sociological judgments, but the content of the sociological judgments it must inevitably make.

Prior to *Brown,* the Supreme Court's validation of segregation statutes rested upon the premise that they did not unequally burden the Negro. A perceived difficulty in invalidating segregation statutes was that, as written, such laws were race-neutral; they excluded white children from Negro schools just as they excluded Negro children from white schools. The Court finally recognized in *Brown* that racial subjugation constituted the social meaning of segregation laws. To determine that social meaning, the Court had to look past form into substance and judge the legitimacy of segregation laws given their intended and actual effects. Just as the "neutrality" of the segregation laws obfuscated racial subjugation, so too may the formal neutrality of race-blind policies also obfuscate the perpetuation of racial subjugation. That issue can only be explored by an inquiry into the context of the race-blind policy at issue, an inquiry that necessarily entails judicial sociology.

THE NEED FOR ANALYSIS OF MOTIVES

There remains a disturbing lacuna in the scholarly debate. Whether racism is partly responsible for the growing opposition to affirmative action is a question that is virtually absent from many of the leading articles on the subject. These articles typically portray the conflict over affirmative action as occurring in the context of an overriding commitment to racial fairness and equality shared by *all* the important participants in the debate. For example, a recent article by Professors Richard Fallon and Paul Weiler depicts the conflict in terms of "contending models of racial justice"—a depiction suggesting that, despite its bitterness, the affirmative action debate is at least bounded by common abhorrence of explicit racial hierarchy. This portrait, however, of conflict-within-consensus is all too genial. It conjures up the absurd image of Benjamin Hooks and William Bradford Reynolds[2] embracing one another as ideological brethren, differing on the discrete issue of affirmative action but united on the fundamentals of racial fairness.[3] It obscures the emotions that color the affirmative action debate and underestimates the alienation that separates antagonists. It ignores those who believe that much of the campaign against affirmative action is merely the latest in a long series of white reactions against efforts to elevate the status of the Negro in American society. These observers perceive critics of affirmative action not merely as *opponents* but as *enemies*. They perceive ostensibly nonracist objections to affirmative action as rationalizations of white supremacy. They fear that the campaign against affirmative action is simply the opening wedge of a broader effort to recapture territory "lost" in the civil rights revolution of the 1960s.[4] And it is precisely this apprehension that explains the bitterness and desperation with which they wage the affirmative action struggle—emotions that are simply inexplicable in terms of the picture of race relations portrayed by conventional analyses.[5]

The conventional portrait also implicitly excludes from consideration those whose opposition to affirmative action stems from racism. It concedes the presence of prejudice "out there" in the workday world of ordinary citizens. But it assumes that "in here"—in the realm of scholarly discourse and the creation of public policy—prejudice plays no role. In other words, conventional scholarship leaves largely unexamined the possibility that the campaigns against affirmative action now being waged by political, judicial, and intellectual elites reflect racially selective indifference, antipathy born of prejudice, or strategies that seek to capitalize on widespread racial resentments.

Motivation, however, always matters in determining the meaning of a policy, although it is not all that matters. Moreover, attentiveness to motive should be an important aspect of ongoing analysis of the affirmative action controversy for other reasons as well. The simple but basic desire to document accurately the history of our era is justification enough for inquiring into the motives animating political action. That inquiry is essential to answering the most difficult of the questions that beset historians—the question of *why* particular actions are taken, given decisions made. Furthermore baleful consequences attend dependence upon false records of social reality. After all, blindness to contemporary social realities helped spawn the monstrous lie, propagated by the Supreme Court in *Plessy v. Ferguson,* that the segregation of the Negro had nothing to do with racial oppression. Bitter experience should remind us, then, that in matters touching race relations there is an especially pressing need to keep the record straight.

---

2. Conservative Republican white American lawyer (b. 1942) who was the assistant attorney general for civil rights under President Reagan; Hooks: civil rights leader, lawyer, and Baptist minister (1925–2010) who was the executive director of the NAACP from 1977–1992. [Editor's note]

3. Benjamin Hooks, the executive director of the NAACP, recently described Assistant Attorney General Reynolds, who heads the Justice Department's civil rights division, and other leading Reagan administration opponents of affirmative action, as "latter day Bilbos."

4. Representative of the view of many civil rights activists is Vernon Jordan's statement that "the attack on affirmative action is conducted under the cover of concern for individual rights simply because in our enlightened times you need a fig leaf as a cover for a naked defense of racial privilege."

5. The blinders imposed by the conflict-within-consensus perspective may account for Dean Ely's statement that he had "trouble understanding the place of righteous indignation on either side" of the affirmative action debate. If one recognizes, however, that opposition to affirmative action—at least on the part of some—may quite plausibly be viewed as an act of racial aggression, it becomes quite clear why many proponents of preferential treatment wage their struggle with righteous indignation.

The Case of the Reagan Administration

A good way to begin setting the record straight is by assessing the motives of those in high public office. Suspicion characterizes the disposition with which I begin that assessment. My suspicion stems from the recognition that racism in America is an enormously powerful ideological institution, considerably older than the political institutions of our republic, and has often influenced the actions of the executive branch and indeed all levels of government. My preexisting distrust is heightened, however, by the particular background of the Reagan administration and, more specifically, by the political biography of Ronald Reagan himself.

President Reagan now declares himself "heart and soul in favor of the things that have been done in the name of civil rights and desegregation." This commitment, he maintains, accounts for his opposition to affirmative discrimination.[6] What justifies skepticism toward the president's account is his long history of suspect views on racial issues. His active opposition to racial distinctions *benefitting* blacks is not matched by analogous opposition to racial distinctions *harming* Negroes. Indeed, a strikingly consistent feature of President Reagan's long political career is his resistance to practically every major political effort to eradicate racism or to contain its effects. During the height of the civil rights revolution, he opposed the Civil Rights Act of 1964, the Voting Rights Act of 1965 and the Open Housing Act of 1968,[7] legislation that his own assistant attorney general has rightly described as "designed to make equal opportunity a reality."

Of course, although opposition to this landmark legislation is itself tremendously revealing, limits exist to the inferences that one can properly draw from positions adopted over twenty years ago. But President Reagan has provided additional reasons for distrusting his explanation of his racial policies. Repeat-

edly his administration has shown callous disregard for the particular interests of blacks and resisted measures designed to erode racial hierarchy. These actions include the administration's opposition (1) to the amendments that strengthened and extended the Voting Rights Act, (2) to anything more than the most cramped reading of the Civil Rights Act of 1964, (3) to creating a national holiday honoring Dr. Martin Luther King, Jr., (4) to maintaining the integrity of agencies involved in federal enforcement of civil rights, and (5) to imposing sanctions on South Africa for its policy of apartheid.

Perhaps the most instructive episode was the position the Reagan administration took in the now infamous *Bob Jones University* case on the issue of tax exemption for private schools that discriminate against Negroes. The platform of the Republican Party in 1980 promised that its leaders would "halt the unconstitutional regulatory vendetta launched . . . against independent schools." President Reagan fulfilled that pledge by reversing the policy of the Internal Revenue Service (IRS) denying exempt status to discriminatory private schools. The administration stated that it had acted out of a desire to end the IRS's usurpation of powers beyond those authorized by Congress. Subsequent revelations called the honesty of this explanation into doubt. That apparent dishonesty—coupled with the administration's overwhelming defeat in the Supreme Court—turned the tax exemption imbroglio into one of the administration's most politically embarrassing moments. For present purposes, however, the significance of the episode lies in the stark illustration it provides of the underlying impulse behind the administration's racial policy—an impulse to protect the prerogatives of whites at the least hint of encroachment by claims of racial justice.

There are, of course, alternative explanations to the one above. One could disaggregate the record of Ronald Reagan and his administration and rationalize each position on a case-by-case basis, by reference

---

6. Explaining the administration's opposition to affirmative discrimination, President Reagan observed that "we want what I think Martin Luther King asked for. We want a color-blind society."

7. Title VIII of the Civil Rights Act of 1968, known as the Fair Housing Act, originally prohibited discrimination in the sale, rental, or financing of housing based on race, color, national origin, or religion; the act was amended to also prohibit discrimination based on sex (added in 1974), familial status, or disability (added in 1988). [Editor's note]

to concerns having nothing to do with racist sentiments or strategies. Concerns about freedom of association might have prompted Reagan's opposition to
the Civil Rights Act of 1964. Concerns about federal-
ism might account for his opposition to the Voting
Rights Act of 1965. Concerns about the proper allocation of responsibility between the executive and legislative branches might explain the administration's
stance in the tax exemption controversy. And authentic regard for the philosophical premises of individualism might theoretically explain the administration's
opposition to affirmative action.

The problem with this mode of defense is that it
ignores the strong *systematic* tilt of the administration's actions. It disregards as well the political milieu
in which debate over affirmative action and other
racial policies has been waged over the past decade—a
period during which there has been a discernible atten-
uation of public commitment to racial justice and, even
more troubling, a startling reemergence of overt racial
animosity. The Reagan administration's policies reflect,
reinforce, and capitalize on widespread feelings that
blacks have received an undeserved amount of the
nation's attention. Unburdened by the inhibitions
imposed by public office, ordinary white citizens have
expressed quite openly the feelings that color their
analysis of the affirmative action issue. The Reagan
administration has expertly tapped these feelings for
political gain by dint of arguments for race-blindness
that are, in fact, exquisitely attuned to the racial sensitivities of the dominant white majority. Those who have
ignored racism as an important element of the affirmative action controversy should consider SPONGE (The
Society for the Prevention of Niggers Getting Everything), an organization of disaffected whites in the
Canarsie section of Brooklyn, New York, whose arresting title is more revealing of at least part of the opposition to affirmative action than many commentators
seem willing to acknowledge.

CONCLUSION

In the end, perhaps the most striking feature of the
affirmative action debate is the extent to which it highlights the crisis of trust besetting American race relations. Proponents of affirmative action view their
opponents with suspicion for good reason. They know
that not all of their opponents are racist; they also
know that many of them are. Such suspicions corrode
reasoned discourse. Contending claims to truth and
justice are often reduced by opposing camps to disguised grasps for power and privilege. It would be a
mistake, however, to suppose that the antidote to such
corrosion is willful blindness to pretext. The only
thing that will enable affirmative action—or any similarly controversial policy—to be debated in an atmosphere free of suspicion is for the surrounding social
context to be decisively transformed. The essential
element of this transformation is the creation of a sentiment of community strong enough to enable each
group to entrust its fate to the good faith and decency of
the other—the sort of feeling that in the 1960s impelled
groups of black and white mothers to exchange their
children during civil rights marches. Only the presence
of such sentiment can enable the force of persuasion to
supplant the force of distrust.

At this point, *even if* a demonstration of policy and
fact decisively pointed toward eliminating affirmative
action, many of its proponents might well refuse to recognize such a showing and continue to support preferential treatment. Their reaction would stem in large
measure from their fears regarding the ulterior motives
of their opponents. This is another reason why, as a
practical matter, motive is so important. As long as suspect motivation justifiably remains a point of apprehension, inquiry into "the merits" of affirmative action
will play a peripheral, instrumental role in the resolution of the controversy.

WILLIAM JULIUS WILSON

Race-Neutral Programs and the Democratic Coalition [1990]

According to the Harvard University sociologist William Julius Wilson (p. 747) in this 1990 essay, affirmative action policies have outlived their usefulness. Arguing that the disadvantaged are worse off now than they were when affirmative action began, Wilson calls for new strategies to address the needs of the "truly disadvantaged." Although his championing of race-neutral policies appears to echo neoconservative arguments, Wilson is careful to distinguish his position from that of critics who would eliminate affirmative action programs without establishing progressive alternatives in their place.

From *The American Prospect*, March 21, 1990, pp. 74–81.

The election of Ron Brown as the first black chairman of the Democratic National Committee triggered a new round of soul-searching among Democrats. Was the party committing political suicide by becoming too strongly identified with the aspirations of minority voters? Had America become so mired in racism that whites would desert the Democrats because blacks seemed to be running things?

My answer to these questions is an empathic "No." Many white Americans have turned, not against blacks, but against a strategy that emphasizes programs perceived to benefit only racial minorities. In the 1990s the party needs to promote new policies to fight inequality that differ from court-ordered busing, affirmative action programs, and antidiscrimination lawsuits of the recent past. By stressing coalition politics and race-neutral programs such as full employment strategies, job skills training, comprehensive health care, reforms in the public schools, child care legislation, and prevention of crime and drug abuse, the Democrats can significantly strengthen their position. As Chairman Brown himself has emphasized, reinforcing Democratic loyalty among minorities and reaching out to reclaim white support are not mutually exclusive.

Such a change of emphasis is overdue. In the 1960s efforts to raise the public's awareness and conscience about the plight of black Americans helped to enact civil rights legislation and affirmative action programs. However, by the 1980s the civil rights strategy of dramatizing black disadvantage was backfiring. The "myth of black progress" theme, frequently invoked to reinforce arguments for stronger race-specific programs, played easily into the hands of conservative critics of antibias policies. The strategy reinforced the erroneous impression that federal antidiscrimination efforts had largely failed, and it overlooked the significance of complex racial changes since the mid-1960s. It also aroused concern that Democratic politicians' sensitivity to black complaints had come at the expense of the white majority.

The tortuous struggles of the 1960s produced real gains. To deny those achievements only invites demoralization among both black and white advocates of racial justice. Yet the movement for racial equality needs a new political strategy for the 1990s that appeals to a broader coalition and addresses many problems afflicting minorities that originated in racist practices but will not be solved by race-specific remedies.

DIFFERENTIAL RATES OF BLACK PROGRESS

As we entered the 1980s, the accomplishments of the civil rights struggle were clearly registered in the rising number of blacks in professional, technical, managerial, and administrative positions. Progress was evident also in the increasing enrollment of blacks in colleges and universities and the growing number of black homeowners. These increases were proportionately greater than those for whites. On the other hand, among the disadvantaged segments of the black population, especially the ghetto underclass, many dire problems—poverty, joblessness, family breakup, educational retardation in inner-city public schools, increased welfare dependence, and drug addiction—were getting even worse.

The differential rates of progress in the black community persisted through the 1980s. Family incomes among the poorest of the poor reveal the pattern. From 1978 to 1987, the number of blacks with incomes under half the poverty line (below $4,528 for a three-person family in 1987, adjusting for inflation) increased by 69 percent. In 1978 only one of every three poor blacks fell below half the poverty line, but by 1987 the proportion rose to 45 percent. The average poor black family in 1986 and 1987 slipped further below the poverty level than in any year since the Census Bureau started collecting such data in 1967. While the average income of the lowest fifth of black families in the United States was dropping 24 percent, the average income of the highest fifth of black families was climbing by more than $3,000 and that of the top 5 percent by almost $9,000. Upper-income whites are considerably wealther than upper-income blacks, but in 1987 the highest fifth of black families secured a record 47.4 percent of the total black income, compared to the 42.9 percent share of total white family income received by the highest fifth of white families.

So while income inequality widened generally in America during the 1980s, it widened even more dramatically among black Americans. If we are to fashion remedies for black poverty, we need to understand the origins and dynamics of inequality in the black community. Without disavowing the accomplishments of the civil rights movement, black leaders and liberal policy makers now need to focus on remedies that will make a difference to the poor.

PROGRESS AND PROTEST

Before the emergence of activist black protest, the professionals of the National Association for the Advancement of Colored People (NAACP), working mainly through the courts, achieved important victories in the drive for civil rights. Prior to 1960, the NAACP publicly defined the racial problem as legal segregation in the South and set as its major goal the end of all state-enforced segregation—as the civil rights slogan then had it, "free by 1963." In landmark Supreme Court decisions, the NAACP won legal mandates to improve the conditions of black Americans. Most important, of course, was the 1954 Supreme Court ruling against mandatory school segregation, which overturned the "separate but equal" doctrine and authoritatively defined blacks as first-class citizens.

Important and necessary as these victories were, it soon became apparent that they were not sufficient. Jim Crow regimes in the South ingeniously circumvented the new rulings and made it apparent to black leaders that they had defined both the problem and the goal too narrowly. The problem, as they now saw it, was token compliance with the newly created mandates; the goal they now set was the end of both de jure and de facto segregation.

Despite Southern white resistance, black expectations of continued racial progress continued rising. Not only had the Supreme Court ruled in favor of desegregation; the federal government was growing more sensitive to the condition of black America for two reasons.

The first was international. When the new African regimes broke up the old colonial empires, both the West and the Soviet bloc began competing for influence in the new states. Racial violence and animosities in the United States were now more embarrassing to federal officials than in the past. As a result, Southerners, who had enjoyed significant autonomy in handling racial matters prior to World War II, came under closer national scrutiny.

The increased voting power of blacks in national elections was also a factor. Since the elections of the 1920s, civil rights advocates had monitored the voting records of congressmen and policies of presidents. The lure of the black vote sometimes prompted politicians to support racial equality, as did the Democratic and Progressive candidates of 1928. At other times, politicians granted token concessions in the hope of preserving or gaining black support, as did President Franklin D. Roosevelt in 1940 when he increased black participation in the armed forces, though still within segregated units.

As early as the forties, the black vote was substantial enough in pivotal Northern states to decide close national elections. In 1948 President Truman recognized that to defeat his favored Republican opponent,

Thomas E. Dewey, he needed strong black support. For the first time since Reconstruction, the status of blacks emerged as a central presidential campaign issue. Much to the chagrin of its Southern members, the Democratic party adopted a civil rights plank as part of its 1948 platform. That same year, satisfying a demand black leaders introduced eight years earlier, President Truman issued an executive order banning racial segregation in the armed forces. Despite a Dixiecrat walkout from the party, the strategy worked: black voters helped Truman narrowly defeat Dewey. The black vote also provided the margin of victory for Kennedy in 1960, and it almost defeated Nixon again in 1968.

In the 1960s, as blacks increased their political resources, white resistance to complete desegregation intensified and black support for protest action mushroomed. For a brief period, the nonviolent resistance strategy proved highly effective, particularly in forcing local governments and private agencies to integrate facilities in Southern cities and towns. The nonviolent demonstrations also pressed the federal government into passage of civil rights legislation in 1964 and voting rights legislation in 1965.

Nonviolent protest was successful for several reasons. The demands accompanying the protests—for example, "end discrimination in voting"—tended to be fairly specific and hard to oppose in principle. The remedies were also relatively straightforward and did not require immediate sacrifices by most whites, which reduced white political backlash in areas outside the South. Federal officials were receptive not only because they saw the international attention these developments were receiving. They recognized the political resources blacks had developed, including the growing army of Northern whites sympathetic to the civil rights movement and to direct action protests.

The demands of the civil rights movement reflected a general assumption by black leaders in the 1960s that the government could best protect the rights of minority groups not by formally bestowing rewards and punishments based on group membership, but by using antidiscrimination measures to enhance individual freedom. The movement was particularly concerned about access to education, employment, voting, and public accommodations. So from the 1950s to 1970, the emphasis was on freedom of choice; the role of the state was to prevent the formal categorization of people on the basis of race. Antibias legislation was designed to eliminate racial discrimination without considering the proportion of minorities in certain positions. The underlying principle was that individual merit should be the sole determining factor in choosing among candidates for positions. Because civil rights protests clearly upheld this basic American principle, they carried a degree of moral authority that leaders such as Martin Luther King, Jr., repeatedly and effectively invoked.

It would have been ideal if programs based on the principle of freedom of individual opportunity were sufficient to remedy racial inequality. Long periods of racial oppression can result, however, in a system of inequality that lingers even after racial barriers come down. The most disadvantaged minority individuals, crippled by the cumulative effects of both race and class subjugation, disproportionately lack the resources to compete effectively in a free and open market. Conversely, the members of a minority group who stand to benefit most from the removal of racial barriers are the ones who least need extra help.

Eliminating racial barriers creates the greatest opportunities for the better trained, talented, and educated members of minority groups because they possess the most resources to compete. Those resources reflect a variety of advantages—family stability, financial means, peer groups, and schooling—provided or made possible by their parents.

By the late 1960s a number of black leaders began to recognize this dilemma. In November 1967, for example, Kenneth B. Clark said, "The masses of Negroes are now starkly aware of the fact that recent civil rights victories benefited a very small percentage of middle-class Negroes while their predicament remained the same or worsened." Simply eliminating racial barriers was not going to be enough. As the late black economist Vivian Henderson put it in the NAACP journal *The Crisis*, "If all racial prejudice and discrimination and all racism were erased today, all the ills brought by the process of economic class distinction and economic depression of the masses of black people would remain."

Accordingly, black leaders and liberal policy makers began to emphasize the need not only to eliminate active discrimination, but also to counteract the effects of past racial oppression. Instead of seeking remedies only for individual complaints of discrimination, they sought government-mandated affirmative action programs to ensure adequate minority representation in employment, education, and public programs.

However, as the political scientist James Fishkin has argued, if the more advantaged members of minority groups benefit disproportionately from policies that embody the principle of equality of individual opportunity, they also profit disproportionately from policies of preferential treatment based solely on their racial group membership. Why? Again simply because minority individuals from the most advantaged families tend to be disproportionately represented among those of their racial group most qualified for preferred status, such as college admissions, higher-paying jobs, and promotions. Thus policies of preferential treatment are likely to improve further the socioeconomic positions of the more advantaged without adequately remedying the problems of the disadvantaged.

To be sure, affirmative action was not intended solely to benefit the more advantaged minority individuals. As William L. Taylor, the former director of the U.S. Civil Rights Commission, has stated, "The focus of much of the [affirmative action] effort has been not just on white collar jobs, but also on law enforcement, construction work, and craft and production in large companies—all areas in which the extension of new opportunities has provided upward mobility for less advantaged minority workers." Taylor also notes that studies show that many minority students entering medical schools during the 1970s were from families of low income.

Affirmative action policies, however, did not really open up broad avenues of upward mobility for the masses of disadvantaged blacks. Like other forms of "creaming," they provided opportunities for those individuals from low socioeconomic backgrounds with the greatest educational and social resources. Recent data on income, employment opportunities, and educational attainment confirm that relatively few individuals who reside in the inner-city ghettos have benefited from affirmative action.

During the past two decades, as I have argued previously in *The Truly Disadvantaged* (1987), urban minorities have been highly vulnerable to structural changes in the economy, such as the shift from goods-producing to service-producing industries, the increasing polarization of the labor market into low-wage and high-wage sectors, innovations in technology, and the relocation of manufacturing industries out of the central city. These shifts have led to sharp increases in joblessness and the related problems of highly concentrated poverty, welfare dependency, and family breakup, despite the passage of antidiscrimination legislation and the creation of affirmative action programs. In 1974, for example, 47 percent of all employed black males ages twenty to twenty-four held blue-collar, semiskilled operative and skilled-craft positions, which typically earned wages adequate to support a family. By 1986 that figure plummeted to 25 percent. A survey I have directed, randomly sampling residents from poor Chicago neighborhoods, revealed that Puerto Rican men up to age forty-five and black men under age thirty-six have borne the brunt of job losses due to deindustrialization.

However, I do not advance the foregoing arguments to suggest that race-specific programs were inefficacious. They clearly helped to bring about a sharp increase in the number of blacks entering higher education and gaining professional and managerial positions. But neither policies based on the principle of equality of individual opportunity, nor policies that call for preferential group treatment, such as affirmative action, will do much for less advantaged blacks because of the combined effects of past discrimination and current structural changes in the economy. Now more than ever we need broader solutions than those we have employed in the past.

TOWARD A NEW POLITICAL STRATEGY

Full employment policies, job skills training, comprehensive health-care legislation, educational reforms in the public schools, child care legislation, and crime and drug abuse prevention programs—these are the race-neutral policies likely to begin making a difference for the poor, black and white.

When presenting this argument to academic audiences, I am frequently told that such programs would face general opposition not only because of their cost, but also because many whites have become disenchanted with the black movement and its calls for intensified affirmative action.

These programs should be presented, however, not as ways to address the plight of poor minorities (though they would greatly benefit from them), but as strategies to help all groups, regardless of race or economic class. After all, Americans across racial and class lines continue to be concerned about unemployment and job security, declining real wages, escalating medical costs, the sharp decline in the quality of public education, the lack of good child care, and crime and drug trafficking in their neighborhoods.

Public opinion surveys reflect these concerns. For the last several years national opinion polls consistently reveal strong public backing for government labor market strategies, including training efforts to enhance employment. A 1988 Harris poll indicated that almost three quarters of the respondents would support a tax increase to pay for child care. A 1989 Harris poll reports that almost nine out of ten Americans would like to see fundamental change in the U.S. health-care system. And recent surveys conducted by the National Opinion Research Center at the University of Chicago reveal that a substantial majority of Americans want more money spent to improve the nation's schools and to halt rising crime and drug addiction.

Programs that expand employment opportunities and job skills training, improve public education, provide adequate child and health care, and reduce neighborhood crime and drug abuse could alleviate many problems of poor minorities that cannot be successfully attacked by race-specific measures alone. In the 1990s the best political strategy for those committed to racial justice is to promote these programs for all groups in America, not just minorities.

RACE-NEUTRAL PROGRAMS AND COALITION POLITICS

"The economic future of blacks in the United States," Vivian Henderson argued in 1975, "is bound up with that of the rest of the nation. Policies, programs, and politics designed in the future to cope with the problems of the poor and victimized will also yield benefits

to blacks. In contrast, any efforts to treat blacks separately from the rest of the nation are likely to lead to frustration, heightened racial animosities, and a waste of the country's resources and the precious resources of black people."

Henderson's warning seems to be especially appropriate in periods of economic stagnation, when public support of programs targeted for minorities—or associated with real or imagined material sacrifice on the part of whites—seems to wane. The economy was strong when affirmative action programs were introduced during the Johnson administration. When the economy turned down in the 1970s, the public's view of affirmative action turned increasingly sour.

Furthermore, as Joseph A. Califano, Johnson's staff assistant for domestic affairs, observed in 1988, such programs were generally acceptable to whites "only as a temporary expedient to speed blacks' entry into the social and economic mainstream." But as years passed, many whites "saw continuing such preferences as an unjust insistence by Democrats that they do penance for an era of slavery and discrimination they had nothing to do with." They also associated the decline in public schools, not with broader changes in society, but with "forced integration."

The Democrats also came under fire for their support for Great Society programs that increasingly and incorrectly acquired the stigma of being intended for poor blacks alone. Virtually separate medical and legal systems developed in many cities. Public services became identified mainly with blacks, private services mainly with whites. In an era of ostensible racial justice, many public programs ironically seemed to develop into a new and costlier form of segregation. White taxpayers saw themselves as being forced to pay for medical and legal services for minorities that many of them could not afford to purchase for their own families.

From the New Deal to the 1960s, the Democrats were able to link Keynesian economics and middle-class prosperity with programs for integrating racial minorities and the poor into the American mainstream. "In periods of great economic progress when [the incomes of the middle classes] are rising rapidly," argues Lester Thurow, "they are willing to share some of their income and jobs with those less fortunate than themselves, but they are not willing to reduce their real standard of living to help either minorities or the poor."

As the economic situation worsened, Ronald Reagan was able to convince many working- and middle-class Americans that the decline in their living standards was attributable to expensive and wasteful programs for the poor (and implicitly for minorities). When Reagan was elected to office in 1980, the New Deal coalition collapsed; the principal groups supporting the Democratic ticket with wide majorities were blacks, Hispanics, and the poor, who represent only a quarter of the American population.

What are the implications for the Democratic party? After losing three straight presidential elections, the Democrats are reexamining their programs and approaches to voters, partly in the hope of recapturing support from disaffected whites who voted for Reagan and Bush.[1] Those steps ought to involve the development of race-neutral programs. Consider, for example, one issue likely to be at the core of new domestic programs—the future of the American work force.

Social scientists, corporate leaders, and government officials have all expressed concerns about the potential weakening of America's competitive position if we fail to confront the growing shortage of skilled workers. These concerns have led to a heightened awareness of the consequences of poverty, poor education, and joblessness. Many of the new jobs will require higher levels of training and education at the very time when our public schools are graduating too many students who can barely read or write. The 1987 U.S. Department of Labor Study, "Workforce 2000,"[2] pointed out that for demographic reasons members of minority groups will necessarily fill a majority of the new jobs in the next decade.

A major policy initiative to improve the quality of the work force would open up opportunities for the minorities who are heavily represented among the educational have-nots. But such an initiative would also open opportunities for others, and it should draw general support because of concerns over the devastating effects a poorly trained work force will have on the entire economy.

NONRACIAL AFFIRMATIVE ACTION

However, even if minorities would benefit disproportionately from new race-neutral initiatives to combat the problems and consequences of social inequality, are there not severe problems in the inner-city ghetto that can only be effectively addressed by creative programs targeted on the basis of race? For example, Roger Wilkins has argued persuasively that the cumulative effects of racial isolation and subjugation have made the plight of the black poor unique. Many inner-city children have a solo parent and lack educational support and stability in their home; Wilkins contends that they need assistance to enable them to become capable adults who can provide their children with emotional and educational support. Accordingly, he maintains that special social service programs are needed for inner-city (presumably, minority) schools.

No serious initiative to improve the quality of the work force could ignore problems such as poverty, social isolation, and family instability, which impede the formal education of children and ultimately affect their job performance. Service programs to meet these needs could easily fit into an overall race-neutral initiative to improve America's work force. To be sure, this component of the larger initiative would be introduced only in the most disadvantaged neighborhoods, but the neighborhoods would not have to be racially defined. Poor minorities need not be treated separately from the rest of the nation in a national effort to enhance the skill levels of the labor force.

It is particularly important for blacks and other minorities to recognize that they have a stake in the formation of a Democratic coalition that would develop race-neutral initiatives. Only with multiracial support could programs of social and economic reform get approved in Congress. Black voters who are dubious

---

1. George H. W. Bush (b. 1924), 41st president of the United States (from 1989–93), vice president under Ronald Reagan (from 1981–89), and father of George W. Bush (43rd president of the United States from 2001–09).
2. The study was conducted by the Hudson Institute with a grant from the Department of Labor.

about this approach ought to be reminded of the success of the Jesse Jackson presidential campaign. By highlighting problems plaguing all groups in America, the Jackson campaign drew far more support from white working- and middle-class voters than most political observers thought possible.

THE POSITIVE EFFECTS OF RACE-NEUTRAL POLICIES

My emphasis on race-neutral programs should be clearly distinguished from the neoconservative critique of affirmative action that attacks both racial preference and activist social welfare policies. The former is said to be antidemocratic, the latter economically counterproductive to minorities. My approach, in contrast, supports the alliance between activist government and racial justice in three key respects—as guarantor of civil rights, as custodian of coalition politics, and as sponsor of race-neutral strategies that advance the well-being of America's neediest along with that of America as a whole. For those who came of age in the 1970s, it seems paradoxical that this goal is now best achieved via race-neutral approaches. Yet, a society without racial preference has, of course, always been the long-term goal of the civil rights movement.

An emphasis on coalition politics that features progressive, race-neutral policies could have two positive effects. It could help the Democratic party regain lost political support, and it could lead to programs that would especially benefit the more disadvantaged members of minority groups—without being minority policies.

CORNEL WEST

Affirmative Action in Context [1996]

In this essay, the philosopher Cornel West (p. 881) reviews the history of the affirmative action debate in the United States, as William Julius Wilson does in his 1990 essay "Race-Neutral Programs and the Democratic Coalition" (p. 952). West's assessments are in line with many of those in Wilson's essay, including his call for broad social policies to address entrenched poverty and his assertion that neoconservative opponents of affirmative action are motivated by racism. However, West's conclusions about the desirability of continuing affirmative action programs and what their repeal would say about America's moral values are the opposite of Wilson's conclusions.

From George E. Curry, ed., *The Affirmative Action Debate* (Reading, Mass.: Addison-Wesley, 1996), pp. 31–35.

Today's affirmative action policy is not the appropriate starting point for a substantive debate on affirmative action. Instead, we must begin with the larger historical and moral context of the recent controversy. Why was the policy established in the first place? What were the alternatives? Who questioned its operation, and when? How did it come about that a civil rights initiative in the 1960s is viewed by many as a civil rights violation in the 1990s? Whose civil rights are we talking about? Is there a difference between a right and an expectation? What are the limits of affirmative action? What would the consequences be if affirmative action disappeared in America?

THE AIM OF AFFIRMATIVE ACTION

The vicious legacy of white supremacy—institutionalized in housing, education, health care, employment, and social life—served as the historical context for the civil rights movement in the late 1950s and 1960s. Affirmative action was a *weak* response to this legacy. It constituted an imperfect policy conceded by a powerful political, business, and educational establishment in light of the pressures of organized citizens and the disturbances of angry unorganized ones.

The fundamental aim of affirmative action was to put a significant dent in the tightly controlled networks of privileged white male citizens who monopolized the good jobs and influential positions in American society. Just as Catholics and Jews had earlier challenged the white Anglo-Saxon Protestant monopoly of such jobs and positions, in the 1960s blacks and women did also. Yet since the historical gravity of race and gender outweighs that of religion and ethnicity in American society, the federal government had to step in to facilitate black and female entry into the U.S. mainstream and malestream. This national spectacle could not but prove costly under later, more hostile circumstances.

The initial debate focused on the relative lack of fairness, merit, and public interest displayed by the prevailing systems of employment and education, principally owing to arbitrary racist and sexist exclusion. In the 1960s, class-based affirmative action was not seriously considered, primarily because it could easily have been implemented in such a way as to perpetuate exclusion, especially given a labor movement replete with racism and sexism. Both Democratic and Republican administrations supported affirmative action as the painful way of trying to create a multiracial democracy in which women and people of color were not second-class citizens. Initially, affirmative action was opposed by hard-line conservatives, usually the same ones who opposed the civil rights movement led by Dr. Martin Luther King, Jr. Yet the pragmatic liberals and conservatives prevailed.

THE NEOCONSERVATIVE OPPOSITION

The rise of the neoconservatives unsettled this fragile consensus. By affirming the principle of equality of opportunity yet trashing any mechanism that claimed to go beyond merit, neoconservatives drove a wedge between civil rights and affirmative action. By claiming that meritocratic judgments trump egalitarian efforts to produce tangible results, neoconservatives cast affirmative action policies as multiracial reverse racism and the major cause of racial divisiveness and low black self-esteem in the workplace and colleges.

Yet even this major intellectual and ideological assault did not produce a wholesale abandonment of affirmative action on behalf of business, political, and educational elites. The major factor that escalated the drive against affirmative action was the shrinking job possibilities—along with stagnating and declining wages—that were squeezing the white middle class. Unfortunately, conservative leaders seized this moment to begin to more vociferously scapegoat affirmative action, and to seek its weakening or elimination.

Their first move was to define affirmative action as a program for "unqualified" women and, especially, black people. Their second move was to cast affirmative action as "un-American," a quota system for groups rather than a merit system for individuals. The third move was to claim that antidiscrimination laws are enough, given the decline or end of racism among employers. The latest move has been to soothe the agonized consciences of liberals and conservatives by trying to show that black people are genetically behind whites in intelligence; hence, nothing can be done.

The popularity—distinct from the rationality—of these moves has created a climate in which proponents of affirmative action are on the defensive. Even those of us who admit the excesses of some affirmative action programs—and therefore call for correcting, not eliminating, them—give aid and comfort to our adversaries. This reality reveals just how far the debate has moved in the direction of the neoconservative and conservative perceptions in the country. It also discloses that it is far beyond weak policies like affirmative action to confront the legacies of white supremacy and corporate power in the United States—legacies visible in unemployment and underemployment, unaffordable health care and inadequate child care, dilapidated housing and decrepit schools for millions of Americans, disproportionately people of color, women, and children.

The idea that affirmative action violates the rights of fellow citizens confuses a right with an expectation. We all have a right to be seriously and fairly considered for a job or position. But calculations of merit, institutional benefit, and social utility produce the results. In the past, those who were never even considered had their rights violated; in the present, those who are seriously and fairly considered yet still not selected do not have their rights violated but rather had their expectations frustrated.

For example, if Harvard College receives more than ten thousand applications for fourteen hundred slots in the freshman class and roughly four thousand meet the basic qualifications, how does one select the "worthy" ones? Six thousand applicants are already fairly eliminated. Yet twenty-six hundred still will not make it. When considerations of factors other than merit are involved, such as whether candidates are the sons or daughters of alumni, come from diverse regions of the country, or are athletes, no one objects. But when racial diversity is involved, the opponents of affirmative action yell foul play. Yet each class at Harvard remains about 5 to 7% black—far from a black takeover. And affirmative action bears the blame for racial anxiety and division on campus in such an atmosphere. In short, neoconservatives and conservatives fail to see the subtle (and not-so-subtle) white supremacist sensibilities behind their "color-blind" perspectives on affirmative action.

The Limits of Affirmative Action

Yet it would be myopic of progressive to make a fetish of affirmative action. As desirable as those policies are—an insight held fast by much of corporate America except at the almost lily-white senior management levels—they will never ameliorate the plight and predicament of poor people of color. More drastic and redistributive measures are needed in order to address their situations, measures that challenge the maldistribution of wealth and power and that will trigger cultural renewal and personal hope.

If affirmative action disappears from the American scene, many blacks will still excel and succeed. But the larger signal that sends will be lethal for the country. It is a signal that white supremacy now has one less constraint and black people have one more reason to lose trust in the promise of American democracy.

Brent Staples

The Quota Bashers Come In from the Cold [1998]

When judicial challenges in the 1980s and 1990s failed to eliminate affirmative action programs, opponents turned to voters, putting the elimination of affirmative action programs on state ballots. The first to pass was California's Proposition 209, approved by voters in 1996, 54 percent to 46 percent. The wording of the proposition, which opponents decried as misleading, proclaims that "the state shall not discriminate against, or grant preferential treatment to, any individual or group on the basis of race, sex, color, ethnicity, or national origin in the operation of public employment, public education, or public contracting." The effort to pass Proposition 209, labeled the California Civil Rights Initiative, was chaired by California Board of Regents member Ward Connerly and funded by prominent conservative foundations, including the Lynde and Harry Bradley Foundation of Milwaukee.

Implementation of Proposition 209 brought immediate and dramatic results. For example, the admission of black students to the University of California's Berkeley Law School dropped by 80 percent; the admission of Hispanic students dropped 50 percent. In this 1998 *New York Times* editorial, the author and journalist Brent Staples (p. 896) examines how the striking effects of Proposition 209 affected the debate about the future of affirmative action.

From *The New York Times*, April 12, 1998.

California's decision to outlaw the use of race in public college admissions was widely viewed as a death sentence for affirmative action. But Proposition 209 may actually have saved its life. The abruptly diminished black and Latino enrollment in California has raised the specter of "white-outs" not just on campus but in the professions and in the next generation of state leadership. Californians are looking for ways to undo the mess and other states have been frightened into slowing down. A recent survey by The Chronicle of Higher Education finds legislatures from South Carolina to South Dakota back-pedaling furiously from California-style proposals. Texas has ordered its university to accept any student who finishes in the top 10 percent of a public high school.

The emerging consensus is that special admissions measures must remain intact until urban schools do better by black and brown students, who currently have little chance of first-rate preparation for college. This realization has taken root even among the neoconservatives who started the war against affirmative action 20 years ago. The change was on display in the March issue of Commentary, which devoted much of the issue to affirmative action and carried several articles by writers who reluctantly supported measures that increase minority participation.

Some neocons now argue that race should be taken into account in undergraduate admissions, but not beyond. The distinguished hard-liner James Q. Wilson grudgingly accepts affirmative action at public colleges, but proselytizes for it in police and fire departments, arguing that these agencies must be racially representative to work.

The sociologist Nathan Glazer has had a startling change of heart. His 1975 book "Affirmative Discrimination" served as the bible of neoconservative thought on the subject. Twenty years ago, Mr. Glazer argued that taking race into account in hiring and college admissions was morally wrong and socially corrosive. But his most recent book, "We Are All Multiculturalists Now," and subsequent essays in Commentary and The New Republic find this prince of the intellectual right transformed. He now argues that failure to integrate institutions that have become the gateways to wealth and power would "undermine the legitimacy of American Democracy." This was clear enough to

the rest of the country 20 years ago. But Mr. Glazer says he accepted the idea only when the presumption that African-Americans would soon be absorbed by the mainstream—and afforded equal opportunity at school—proved false.

Mr. Glazer has changed his mind on affirmative action, but clings to the rhetorical tics that poisoned the debate in the first place. He insists on speaking of it as a form of discrimination rather than as a measure that enhances minority access and the health of the body politic. Californians killed affirmative action only because it was pitched to them as discrimination. But the whitening of the university has revealed this as a bankrupt formulation.

Mr. Glazer's insistence that Americans on the whole are massively hostile to affirmative action is clearly overstated. Women—who make up a slight majority of the electorate and benefit heavily from Federal set-asides—like it a great deal.

In truth, most Americans prefer multicultural environments, including schools, workplaces, movies and television shows. Elite universities have made diversity a prominent selling point and are unlikely to give it up, no matter what the public colleges do. The same impulse is thriving even at Commentary, whose recent issue featured more black writers than once would have appeared in the course of a dozen issues.

Mr. Glazer's change of heart has created fissures among the neoconservatives. No doubt the most zealous of them will shake their canes at affirmative action even unto the grave. But the most striking feature of the debate is that the impulse toward diversity—and by extension, toward affirmative action—is a mainstream impulse, endorsed in varying degrees even by conservatives who once saw it as the embodiment of evil.

On Race and the Justice System

JOHNNIE COCHRAN: from *Closing Argument of the Defense in* The People v. Orenthal James Simpson [1995]
CHRISTOPHER DARDEN: from *Closing Argument of the Prosecution in* The People v. Orenthal James Simpson [1995]

In the early 1990s, a number of events captured national attention and sparked debate over the role of race in the judicial system. The 1991 confirmation hearings of Clar-

ence Thomas for a seat on the U.S. Supreme Court (see pp. 1103–14) highlighted issues of racial politics in the courts. The 1991 videotaped beating of Rodney King in

Los Angeles, and the riots the next year that followed the acquittal of the police officers who were responsible for the beating, brought the problem of police brutality into the spotlight. But the event that fueled the most varied and prolonged debates about fundamental elements of the U.S. justice system was the 1995 trial of the football star and popular celebrity O. J. Simpson.

In a televised trial that lasted more than a year, Simpson stood trial for the 1994 murder of his ex-wife, Nicole Brown Simpson, and her friend Ronald Goldman, who were both white. After less than four hours of deliberation, the jury acquitted Simpson of all charges. Post-trial media coverage implied that opinions about the verdict were split along racial lines, with a majority of white people disagreeing with the verdict and a majority of black people agreeing. However, debates during and after the trial went far beyond the question of whether Simpson was guilty. The case became a lens through which to examine the interaction of race, gender, and a host of other factors, including celebrity, money, jury selection, trial location, trial strategies, and police corruption.

The closing arguments by the prosecution and the defense offer sharply different visions of the role of racism in the case and of the meaning of a not-guilty or a guilty verdict. In his closing arguments, delivered September 27 and 28, 1995, Johnnie Cochran (1937–2005), Simpson's lead counsel, underscores the idea that the point of the trial had become something much larger than determining who had killed Simpson's ex-

wife and her friend. By focusing on the implications of the racist language that police detective Mark Fuhrman had used in the past and on his actions in the Simpson case, and by casting the jury as the "guardians of the Constitution," Cochran frames an acquittal as a principled vote against police corruption.

Cochran began his legal career as a Los Angeles deputy attorney. After serving as an assistant district attorney in Los Angeles, he established his own law firm. In 1995, he was named America's Trial Lawyer of the Year by the *National Law Journal.* Cochran died at age sixty-seven of an inoperable brain tumor.

Christopher Darden (b. 1956) presented half of the prosecution's closing arguments (the other half was delivered by the lead counsel, Marcia Clark). In the remarks excerpted here, Darden responds to Cochran's closing argument, delivered the previous day. Darden attempts to contain the meaning of Mark Fuhrman's racism and redirects the focus onto the murders themselves, with domestic violence as the larger framework.

Darden began working in the Los Angeles district attorney's office in 1980. Although he had little trial experience, he was brought onto the Simpson case to complement the lead counsel, Clark, who is white. After the Simpson trial ended in 1995, Darden left the district attorney's office, wrote a successful book about the trial, *In Contempt,* and took a faculty position at the Southwestern Law School in Los Angeles. In 1999, he left academia to start his own law firm.

JOHNNIE COCHRAN

from *Closing Argument of the Defense in* The People v. Orenthal James Simpson [1995]

Stop this cover-up. If you don't stop it, then who? Do you think the police department is going to stop it? Do you think the D.A.'s office is going to stop it? Do you think we can stop it by ourselves? It has to be stopped by you. And you know, they talked about Fuhrman, they talked about him in derisive tones now, and that is very fashionable now, isn't it? Everybody wants to beat up on Fuhrman, the favored whipping

boy in America. I told you I don't take any delight in that because you know before this trial started, if you grow up in this country, you know there are Fuhrmans out there. You learn early on in your life that you are not going to be naive, that you love your country, but you know it is not perfect, so you understand that, so it is no surprise to me, but I don't take any pride in it. But for some of you, you are finding out the other side of life. You are finding out—that is why this case is so instructive. You are finding out about the other side of life, but things aren't always as they seem. It is not just rhetoric, it is the actions of people, it is the lack of courage and it is a lack of integrity at high places. That is what we are talking about here. Credibility doesn't attach to a title or position; it attaches to the person, so the person who may have a job where he makes two dollars an hour can have more integrity than the highest person. It is something from within. It is in your heart. It is what the Lord has put there. That is what we are talking about in this case. And so why don't they speak out? Why do they take him to their breast? Compare how our prosecutors treat Fuhrman as opposed to Kato Kaelin.[1] Look at how they treated Mark Partridge[2] as opposed to Kato Kaelin. Look at how they embraced him. And now they want to distance themselves. These same people say, oh, he is not important, but the Rokahr photograph[3] puts the lie to that. He is very important. And what becomes so important when we talk about these two twin demons of evil, Vannatter[4] and Fuhrman, is the jury instruction which you know about now and it says essentially that a witness willfully false—I think Mr. Douglas is going to put that up for us—"A witness willfully false in one material part of his or her testimony is to be distrusted in others. You may reject the whole testimony of a witness who willfully has testified falsely to a material point unless from all the evidence you believe the probability of truth favors his or her testimony in other particulars." Why is this instruction so important? We got the bullet points up there. First of all, both prosecutors have now agreed that we have convinced them beyond a reasonable doubt, by the way, that he is a lying perjuring genocidal racist and he has testified falsely in this case on a number of scores. That is what his big lies tell you. And when you go back in the jury room, some of you may want to say, well, gee, you know, boys will be boys. This is just like police talk. This is the way they talk. That is not acceptable as the consciences of this community if you adopt that attitude. That is why we have this, because nobody has had the courage to say it is

wrong. You are empowered to say we are not going to take that any more. I'm sure you will do the right thing about that. So that what then it says we must do is you have the authority, you may reject the whole testimony, you can then wipe out everything that Fuhrman told you, including the glove and all the things that he recovered with the glove. That is why they are so worried. That is why when people say Fuhrman is not central, they are wearing blinds. They have lost their objectivity. They don't understand what they are talking about. It is embarrassing for learned people to say that, but they are entitled to their opinions, but we are going to speak the truth. In a courtroom you are supposed to speak the truth. A witness who walks through those doors, who raises his or her hand, swears to tell the truth. You've heard lie after lie after lie that has been exposed and when a witness lies in a material part of his testimony, you can wipe out all of his testimony as a judge of the facts. That is your decision again. Nobody can tell you about that. Lest you feel that a greater probability of truth lies in something else, they said wipe it out. This applies not only to Fuhrman, it applies to Vannatter and then you see what trouble their case is in, because they lied to get in there to do these things when Vannatter carries that blood.[5] They can't explain to you why he did that, because they were setting this man up, and that glove, anybody among you think that glove was just sitting there, just placed there, moist and sticky after six and a half hours? The testimony is it will be dried in three or four hours, according to MacDonell. We are not naive. You understand there is no blood on anything else. There is no blood trail. There is no hair and fiber. And you get the ridiculous explanation that Mr. Simpson was running into air conditioners on his own province.

1. White American actor Brian Jerard "Kato" Kaelin (b. 1959) was a witness for the prosecution during the Simpson trial; at the time of the murders, he was staying at Simpson's Rockingham property in the Brentwood neighborhood of Los Angeles.

2. White American trademark attorney (b. 1954) who was a witness for the prosecution during the Simpson trial; he had met and spoken with Simpson on a flight from Chicago to Los Angeles just after Simpson had been officially notified about the murders.

3. Photograph of Mark Fuhrman pointing to the bloody glove allegedly belonging to Simpson, taken by LAPD crime-scene photographer Rolf Rakahr.

4. LAPD Detective Philip Vannatter who was one of the first detectives at the murder scene; he testified that he subsequently went to Simpson's home to notify him; he ended up searching Simpson's property without a proper warrant and was accused of framing Simpson by the defense during the trial.

5. A key point in the defense team's argument Simpson had been framed was the fact that Detective Vannatter had taken the vial of Simpson's blood collected at the police station and delivered it to the police criminologist at the murder scene, raising the possibility that Vannatter could have planted Simpson's blood at the scene.

The Bailiff—Excuse me, your Honor. We need to take a break.

The Court—All right. Anybody else?

(Brief pause.)

The Court—All right. The record will reflect that we now have our complete jury panel.

Mr. Cochran.

(Brief pause.)

Mr. Cochran—Witnesses willfully false in one material part, distrusted in others. These two form basically the cornerstone of the prosecution's case. Now, you know people talk all the time, well, you know, you are being conspiratorial and whatever. Gee, how would all these police officers set up O.J. Simpson? Why would they do that? I will answer that question for you. They believed he was guilty. They wanted to win. They didn't want to lose another big case. That is why. They believed that he was guilty. These actions rose from what their belief was, but they can't make that—the prosecutors can't make that judgment. Nobody but you can make that judgment. So when they take the law into their own hands, they become worse than the people who break the law, because they are the protectors of the law. Who then polices the police? You police the police. You police them by your verdict. You are the ones to send the message. Nobody else is going to do it in this society. They don't have the courage. Nobody has the courage. They have a bunch of people running around with no courage to do what is right, except individual citizens. You are the ones in war, you are the ones who are on the front line. These people set policies, these people talk all this stuff; you implement it. You are the people. You are what makes America so great, and don't you forget it. And so understand how this happened. It is part of a culture of getting away with things. It is part of what looking the other way. We determine the rules as we go along. Nobody is going to question us. We are the LAPD. And so you take these two twins of deception, and if as you can under this law wipe out their testi-

mony, the prosecutors realize their case then is in serious trouble. From Riske to Bushey[6] they came together in this case because they want to win. But it is not about them winning; it is about justice being done. They have other cases. This is this man's one life that is entrusted or will be soon, to you. So when we talked about this evidence being compromised, contaminated and corrupted, some people didn't believe that. Have we proved that? Have we proved that it was compromised, contaminated and corrupted? And yes, even something more sinister—I think you will believe we do, but there is something else about this man Fuhrman that I have to say before I am going to terminate this part of my opening argument and relinquish the floor to my learned colleague Mr. Barry Scheck,[7] is something that Fuhrman said. And I'm going to ask Mr. Douglas and Mr. Harris to put up that Kathleen Bell letter.[8] You know, it is one thing, and I dare say that most of you, when you heard Fuhrman said he hadn't used the "N" word, that you probably thought, well, he is lying, we know that is not true. That is just part of it. That is just what the prosecutors want to do, just talk about that part of it. That is not the part that bothers us on the defense. I live in America. I understand. I know about slights every day of my life. But I want to tell you about what is troubling, what is frightening, what is chilling about that Kathleen Bell letter. Let's see if we can see part of it, and I think you will agree, so I want to put the focus back where it belongs on this letter and its application to this case. You will recall that God is good and he always brings you a way to see light when there is a lot of darkness around, and just through chance this lady had tried to reach Shapiro's office, couldn't reach it, and in July of 1994 she sent this fax to my office, and my good, loyal and wonderful staff got that letter to me early on. And this is one you just couldn't pass up. You get a lot of letters but you couldn't pass this one up because she says some interesting things. And she wasn't a fan of O.J. Simpson. What does she say? "I'm writing to you in regards to a story I saw on the news last night. I thought it ridiculous that the Simpson Defense team would even

---

6. Keith Bushey, police commander in the West Los Angeles District at the time; Robert Riske, an LAPD officer who was in the first police car to arrive at the crime scene.

7. White American lawyer on the defense team.

8. Letter written to Cochran on July 19, 1985, from a white American realtor about a conversation with Furhman in which he describes discriminating when on duty against African Americans, especially black men with white women.

suggest that there might be racial motivation involved in the trial against Mr. Simpson." Yes, there are a lot of people out there who thought that at that time, and you know, you can't fault people for being naive, but once they know, if they continue to be naive, then you can fault them. That is what it is and this is why this case is important. Don't ever say again in this county or in this country that you don't know things like this exist. Don't pretend to be naive any more. Don't turn your heads. Stand up, show some integrity.

"And so I then glanced up at the television. I was quite shocked to see that officer Fuhrman was a man that I had the misfortune of meeting. You may have received the message from your answering service last night that I called to say that Mr. Fuhrman may be more of a racist than you could even imagine." I doubt that, but at any rate, it was something that got my attention. "Between 1985 and 1986 I worked as a real estate agent in Redondo Beach for Century 21 Bob Maher Realty now out of business. At the time my office was located above a marine recruiting center off of Pacific Coast Highway. On occasion I would stop in to say hello to the two marines working there. I saw Mr. Fuhrman there a couple of times. I remember him distinctly because of his height and build, you know, he is tall.

"While speaking to the men I learned that Mr. Fuhrman was a police officer in Westwood." Isn't that interesting? Just exactly the place where Laura McKinny[9] met him. "And I don't know if he was telling the truth but he said that he had been in a special division of the marines. I don't know how this subject was raised but Officer Fuhrman says that when he sees a Nigger, as he called it, driving with a white woman, he would pull them over. I asked what if he didn't have a reason and he said that he would find one. I looked at the two marines to see if they knew he was joking, but it became obvious to me that he was very serious." Now, let me just stop at this point. Let's back it up a minute, Mr. Harris. Pull it back down, please. If he sees an African American with a white woman he would stop them. If he didn't have a reason, he would find one or make up one. This man will lie to set you

up. That is what he is saying there. He would do anything to set you up because of the hatred he has in his heart. A racist is somebody who has power over you, who can do something to you. People could have views but keep them to themselves, but when they have power over you, that is when racism becomes insidious. That is what we are talking about here. He has power. A police officer in the street, a patrol officer, is the single most powerful figure in the criminal justice system. He can take your life. Unlike the Supreme Court, you don't have to go through all these appeals. He can do it right there and justify it. And that is why, that is why this has to be routed out in the LAPD and every place. Make up a reason because he made a judgment. That is what happened in this case. They made a judgment. Everything else after that is going to point toward O.J. Simpson. They didn't want to look at anybody else. Mr. Darden asked who did this crime? That is their job as the police. We have been hampered. They turned down our offers for help. But that is the prosecution's job. The judge says we don't have that job. The law says that. We would love to help do that. Who do you think wants to find these murderers more than Mr. Simpson? But that is not our job; it is their job. And when they don't talk to anybody else, when they rush to judgment in their obsession to win, that is why this became a problem. This man had the power to carry out his racist views and that is what is so troubling. Let's move on. Making up a reason. That is troubling. That is frightening. That is chilling. But if that wasn't enough, if that wasn't enough, the thing that really gets you is she goes on to say: "Officer Fuhrman went on to say that he would like nothing more than to see all niggers gathered together and killed. He said something about burning them or bombing them. I was too shaken to remember the exact words he used. However, I do remember that what he said was probably the most horrible thing I had ever heard someone say. What frightened me even more was that he was a police officer sworn to uphold the law." And now we have it. There was another man, not too long ago in the world, who had those same views who wanted to burn

---

9. Laura Hart McKinny, white American playwright from North Carolina who interviewed Fuhrman in the mid-1980s for a movie project; Furhman's repeatedly used the word "nigger" on the tapes, and that evidence was later used to convict Furhman of perjury for having testified that he had not that word in the past ten years; Furhman claimed that the recorded conversations with McKinney were part of a work of fiction, with imagined dialogue for the fictional screenplay.

people, who had racist views and ultimately had power over people in his country.

People didn't care. People said he was just crazy, he is just a half-baked painter. They didn't do anything about it. This man, this scourge, became one of the worse people in the history of this world, Adolf Hitler, because people didn't care or didn't try to stop him. He had the power over his racism and his anti-religion. Nobody wanted to stop him, and it ended up in World War II, the conduct of this man. And so Fuhrman, Fuhrman wants to take all black people now and burn them or bomb them. That is genocidal racism. Is that ethnic purity? What is that? What is that? We are paying this man's salary to espouse these views? Do you think he only told Kathleen Bell whom he just had met? Do you think he talked to his partners about it? Do you think commanders knew about it? Do you think everybody knew about it and turned their heads? Nobody did anything about it. Things happen for a reason in your life. Maybe this is one of the reasons we are all gathered together this day, one year and two days after we met. Maybe there is a reason for your purpose. Maybe this is why you were selected. There is something in your background, in your character that helps you understand this is wrong. Maybe you are the right people at the right time at the right place to say no more, we are not going to have this. This is wrong. What they've done to our client is wrong. This man, O.J. Simpson, is entitled to an acquittal. You cannot believe these people. You can't trust the message. You can't trust the messengers. It is frightening. It is quite frankly frightening, and it is not enough for the Prosecutors now to stand up and say, oh, well, let's just back off. The point I was trying to make, they didn't understand that it is not just using the "N" word. Forget that. We knew he was lying about that. Forget that. It is about the lengths to which he would go to get somebody black and also white if they are associated with black. That is pretty frightening. It is not just African Americans, it is white people who would associate or deign to go out with a black man or marry one. You are free in America to love whoever you want, so it infects all of us, doesn't it, this one rotten apple, and yet they cover for him. Yet they cover for him.

[∗ ∗ ∗]

And then there was Natalie Singer. Barely knew this man. He was dating her roommate. This man is an indiscriminate racist. He talks so bad that she didn't want him back in the house. What does he say to her in her presence? "The only good Nigger is a dead Nigger."

You probably all heard that expression sometime in your background somewhere or heard somebody say this. And that is tremendously offensive. He just says it in the presence of his partner's girlfriend, like they are going to go on a date. I mean, I hope that in homes throughout this country people aren't acting like this. This happened to come to light, but I would be pretty frightened if I felt that the majority of people in this country acted like this behind closed doors or whatever. Because what you do in the dark is going to come to the light. Remember that. That is what this case is about. It came to the light and just in time to get it to you. So you saw her on the stand. You saw her graphically. We will talk about that. Any doubt in anybody's mind she is telling you the truth? Any one of you think she is not telling you the truth? And then finally we had Roderic Hodge, and this series of witnesses. And Roderic Hodge, intelligent young man, understands something about his rights, too, because when—after this run-in with Fuhrman and his partner when he is in the back of the police car, Fuhrman turns around and says to him words that I want you to remember in this case, "I told you I'd get you, Nigger," that is what he tells Roderic Hodge. Why is that important? Because from 1985, when he went on that one call involving the Mercedes, that was this man's mind-set vis-à-vis O.J. Simpson, I'm going to get that guy. And in '89 when he wrote that report, indelibly impressed on his mind, and in '94 he had his chance, still in West Los Angeles, he had his chance. So Hodge is important because you can espouse all these epithets and talk theoretically about your racism, but when it is directed toward a human being—and I said to him, "Mr. Hodge, tell this jury how that made you feel." He said, "It made me feel angry and upset and frustrated." It was dehumanizing in a free society. But this man, Fuhrman, does it with immunity and his partner sat there and heard it and didn't report it. There is something rotten about this kind of conduct, that it is going on too long, and so that is why he is important.

[∗ ∗ ∗]

Thank you for your attention during this first part of my argument. I hope that during this phase of it I have demonstrated to you that this really is a case about a rush to judgment, an obsession to win, at all costs, a willingness to distort, twist, theorize in any fashion to try to get you to vote guilty in this case where it is not warranted, that these metaphors about an ocean of evidence or a mountain of evidence is little more than a tiny, tiny stream, if at all, that points equally toward innocence, that any mountain has long ago been reduced to little more than a molehill under an avalanche of lies and complexity and conspiracy. This is what we've shown you. And so as great as America is, we have not yet reached the point where there is equality in rights or equality of opportunity. I started off talking to you a little bit about Frederick Douglass and what he said more than a hundred years ago, for there are still the Mark Fuhrmans in this world, in this country, who hate and are yet embraced by people in power. But you and I, fighting for freedom and ideals and for justice for all, must continue to fight to expose hate and genocidal racism and these tendencies. We then become the guardians of the constitution, as I told you yesterday, for if we as the People don't continue to hold a mirror up to the face of America and say this is what you promised, this is what you delivered, if you don't speak out, if you don't stand up, if you don't do what's right, this kind of conduct will continue on forever and we will never have an ideal society, one that lives out the true meaning of the creed of the Constitution or of life, liberty and justice for all.

Closing Argument of the Defense: Superior Court of the State of California for the County of Los Angeles, Department no. 103 Hon. Lance A. Ito, Judge, The People of the State of California, Plaintiff, Vs. No. Ba097211 Orenthal James Simpson, Defendant, Reporter's transcript of proceedings Thursday, September 28, 1995, volume 23.

CHRISTOPHER DARDEN

from *Closing Argument of the Prosecution in* The People v. Orenthal James Simpson [1995]

Y ou've heard a lot of argument over the past couple of days and I know you listened to all of the attorneys in this case intently and I did when I could and I listened yesterday and I had been anticipating yesterday's arguments from the Defense. I knew that those arguments would be passionate, I knew they would be loud and I knew they would be forceful, and I knew that they would be provocative, and I wasn't disappointed. But also I knew that they wouldn't talk much about the evidence. Mr. Scheck did, but that is okay. And I knew they would want to deliver a message to you, and that is, when I spoke to you the other day I said to you, hey, you can't send a message to Fuhrman, you can't send a message to the LAPD, you can't eradicate racism within the LAPD or within the L.A. community or within the nation as a whole by delivering a verdict of not guilty in a case like this where it is clear and you know it is clear, you feel it, you know it in your heart. You know it as you have sat here day after day listening to this testimony, you know it. Everybody knows it. Everybody knows he killed—

MR. COCHRAN—I object to the form of that argument, your Honor.

THE COURT—Overruled. Proceed.

MR. DARDEN—Everybody knows.

MR. COCHRAN—Object to that, your Honor.

THE COURT—Overruled. Proceed.

MR. DARDEN—The evidence is there. You just have to find your way through the smoke. You just have to find your way through the smoke [* * *] Let me ask you this: If you were to acquit him, what explanation would you give the day after that acquittal if someone said why did you acquit him? Would you say racism? Would you say it is because there is racism in the LAPD? That is what they want you to say. That is what they want you to think. You heard all of that—all the speaking and the fiery rhetoric and the quotes from Proverbs and the like. You heard all of that yesterday, all of that fiery rhetoric. Well, let me tell you what Marcia Clark and I are. Let me tell you who we are. We are the voices, the voices of calm and reason in all of this. You just need to calm down, take that common sense God gave you, go back in the jury room. Don't let these people get you all riled up and all fired up because Fuhrman is a racist. Racism blinds you. Those epithets, they blind you. You never heard me use that epithet in this courtroom, did you? I'm not going to put on that kind of show for you know who, for people to watch. That is not where we are coming from. We want you to focus on the evidence. I'm eternally grateful that Mr. Fuhrman was exposed to be what he is, because I think we should know who those people are. I have said it once, I have said it before, we ought to put a big stamp tattooed on their forehead "Racist" so that when we see them we know who they are so that there is no speculation so that we don't have to guess. But what they want you to do and what they have done in this case is they have interjected this racism and now they want you to become impassioned, to be upset, and then they want you to make quantum leaps in logic and in judgment. They want to you say Fuhrman is a racist, he planted the glove. You can't get from point A to point B if you just sit down and use your common sense. If you are logical, if you are reasonable, you can't do that. It is true that Fuhrman is a racist. And it is also true that he [Simpson] killed these two people, and we proved that he killed the two people.

[* * *]

It is time to stand up. The Constitution says that a man has no right to kill and then get away with it just because one of the investigating officers is a racist. Your job as jurors in this case is to get beyond all of that. The fact that Fuhrman is a racist goes to his bias, goes to his credibility and it may go to other things the judge will tell you, and I'm not going to tell you that you should limit your use of that. You should use it in any way you are instructed to use it by the court, but you shouldn't use it for anything else. As I said the other day, the issue of Fuhrman, it may not be an issue for another day, but it certainly is not an issue, that is in terms of sending him a message is not an issue for you in this case. You can't send him a message. You can't send the LAPD a message. You want to send the LAPD a message, I'm sure they will listen to you after this case is over. I am sure that they will.

[* * *]

If you rely on the record and use your common sense, you will find your way through the smoke. And I told you there was going to be some smoke. I told you there had

been some smoke. Yesterday we heard the smoke. It was fiery rhetoric, but that is what we do. We are lawyers.

[* * *]

Some folks would like to get you all riled up and get you so upset that you move suddenly and so that you drown in the minutia, so that you choke on the smoke. Some people want to make you mad and angry and bitter. [Martin Luther] King[1] once wrote that we should never succumb to the temptation of bitterness and that the one thing about bitterness is its blindness. So don't be blinded by all of this; just do your job. I know you know what your job is. I know you know what to do. And I hope you don't mind too much that I—that I keep reminding you of that job, because this is important. This case is important. This is a murder case. There are two people that are dead. I think it is safe to say at this point, after all that I've heard over the last few days, I think it is safe to say that I'm the messenger and I volunteered for that job and I don't mind being the messenger. I told you what the message was. In 1989 the message was that he is going to kill me, he is going to kill me. And Edward[2] said, "Who is going to kill you?" "O.J." "O.J. The football player?" "Yeah, he is going to kill me." That was the message in 1989. The new message today, there is another message. The message in '89 was that he is going to kill me. The message in '95 is he killed me. That is what this has been all about. That is the message we have been trying to send you the past eight months. The message is he killed her. And there is another message. And you might not be able to hear and see it and read it through all the smoke, and through all the shouting and all the rhetoric, but there is another message. And the other message is he killed me, too. He killed me, too. Through all the smoke and over all the rhetoric you have got to be calm and not succumb to bitterness and do the right thing. I heard a lot about courage, and you are fourteen courageous people and everybody in this room knows that. No one could ever call you cowards. No one can ever accuse you people of running away because you have a tough job and you know you have a tough job and you have sat here day after day, even when

1. See p. 559.
2. Police detective John Edwards; in 1989, Simpson pleaded no contest to a charge of spousal battery for allegedly beating Nicole Brown Simpson.

you were sick, even when you were sick, you came here and you listened to us. You listened to Marcia and I and you listened to the Defense. They want you to believe that if you acquit him that that will be the courageous thing to do. I think the courageous thing to do in this case would be to look at all the evidence. I think that takes courage. I think it takes courage not to jump to a snap conclusion. I think it takes courage to recognize within ourselves that what we heard yesterday was appeal to a certain part of us and it was appeal to some of us perhaps and not all of us, but it was an appeal to a certain part of us that only some of us know about. That is what happened yesterday. I think it takes courage to recognize that. If you mistrust the police—I spent seven years prosecuting bad policemen. I understand why you mistrust the police. If you have that basic mistrust—

MR. COCHRAN—Objection, your Honor, improper.

MR. SCHECK—Objection.

THE COURT—Overruled.

MR. DARDEN—I understand that, and perhaps you ought to, but I think that we have to do is we have to take every case on a case by case basis and every cop on a cop by cop basis. Yesterday they took Fuhrman, this racist, and then they put Vannatter with him and pretty soon they were interchanging Vannatter and Fuhrman.

Vannatter has been a detective 27, 28 years. You didn't hear anybody come in here and say he ever used that word. And it is easy to put up a big poster and say "Vannatter's big lies." That is easy to do. They say that he made an off-the-cuff remark eight months ago. That is what some people said. You heard what he said. Do you remember everything you say? Do you know everything that you've said? Does every lawyer in this case know everything that they've said? I heard one of the lawyers say that there was a Caucasian hair on the Rockingham glove[3] and that that hair was—that there was never any attempt to match that hair to anybody and that it could be Fuhrman's. That wasn't true. That is not what is in the record. I'm not going to put up a big poster and say "Defense big lies." Sometimes people

misspeak, sometimes people forget, sometimes people are wrong, sometimes they say things they don't remember saying, sometimes they say things that they do remember saying and we admit to them. We have some of all of that in this case, I suppose. Well, let's talk about some of the things we heard over the last couple of days. Let's talk about some of the evidence.

[* * *]

They talk all this stuff about race and everything. We got one racist cop and on the last time, from what the evidence is—and trust me, I am not an apologist for this man—but the last time, according to the evidence, that anybody heard him use this slur was in 1988. They say since he used it in 1988 he must be a racist. Well, the last time that we know of from the stand that the Defendant beat up was in 1989. If you say it in '88 and you are a racist in '94, well, what are you if you beat her in '89? What are you in '94? But they want you to apply double standards. I will go back to Martin because I feel comfortable with Martin Luther King. Actually I have some Malcolm X,[4] but I'm not going to drop that today. I don't want to get that deep. But Martin Luther King. For Martin Luther King justice was a critical issue in his life here on earth and it was more than a legal issue and it was more than a moral issue; it was a spiritual issue. And let me read to you what he said about justice. And they are just sitting there listening to me instead of staying with me. You got that quote? Are you still looking for that quote?

(Brief pause.)

MR. DARDEN—He never does that when Marcia Clark is up here talking. I think it is a very appropriate quote for this case—and if he lets that happen again—you are lucky today is the last day of the trial. Read along with me what Martin Luther King said about justice. "Justice is the same for all issues. It cannot be categorized. It is not possible to be in favor of justice for some people and not be in favor of justice for all people. Justice cannot be divided. Justice is indivisible." Okay. We can't have a system of law, a system of justice or a concept of justice

---

3. Glove with blood from O. J. Simpson, Nicole Simpson, and Ron Goldman that police reported finding on Simpson's Rockingham estate in Brentwood; police reported finding the matching glove at the murder scene; when Simpson tried on the gloves over latex gloves during the trial, he struggled, saying, "They're too tight."

4. See p. 516.

or a concept of law or a legal standard of burden of proof. We can't have reasonable doubt over here for everybody else and then have another reasonable doubt standard for a particular individual. That ain't justice, okay? That is not justice. That is what he is talking about. That is what he is talking about. He is talking about a double standard of justice. We can't have that.

[* * *]

All I could ever ask from you and all that I ask from you today is that you try and be as objective as you possibly can be, that you not allow any passion or emotion or any bias, any of that human feeling—these human feelings we all have to interfere with the decision you have to make. When I stood before you back in January I said there were many victims in this case. And there are many interests involved in this case. It is an important case to O.J. Simpson and it is an important case to the victims and their families. We

just want you to be fair. I just want you to do the right thing. That means the right thing under the law.

We believe we have proven this case beyond a reasonable doubt. And it is unfortunate, it is unfortunate what jealousy does to you. It is unfortunate that obsession—it is unfortunate that obsession can do these things to you. It is unfortunate that two innocent people are dead because this got in this man's way. That is the message we wanted to deliver and I'm the messenger and I'm proud to have delivered it. I thank you for your verdict in advance, in the event I don't get a chance to talk to you then. All of us owe you a debt gratitude. God bless you.

Closing Argument of the Prosecution: Superior Court of the State of California for the County of Los Angeles, Department no. 103 Hon. Judge Lance A. Ito, Judge, *The People of the State of California, Plaintiff, vs. No. Ba097211 Orenthal James Simpson, Defendant,* Reporter's transcript of proceedings Friday, September 29, 1995, volume 23.

HENRY LOUIS GATES, JR.

Thirteen Ways of Looking at a Black Man [1995]

The vigorous debate that followed O. J. Simpson's acquittal revealed not only stark differences of opinion regarding the trial but also new concerns about the U.S. justice system. In this essay, published three weeks after the verdict, Henry Louis Gates, Jr. (b. 1950) presents numerous perspectives on the trial and its reverberating meanings. He explores the racialization of the trial while refuting the idea that opinions were divided along racial lines (or according to any other clear-cut factor, such as gender or class).

From *The New Yorker*, October 23, 1995; reprinted in Henry Louis Gates, Jr., *Thirteen Ways of Looking at a Black Man* (New York: Random House, 1997), pp. 103–22.

"Every day, in every way, we are getting meta and meta," the philosopher John Wisdom used to say, venturing a cultural counterpart to Émile Coué's famous mantra of self-improvement. So it made sense that in the aftermath of the Simpson trial the focus of attention was swiftly displaced from the verdict to the reaction to the verdict, and then to the reaction to the reaction to the verdict, and, finally, to the reaction to the reaction to the reaction to the verdict—which is to say, black indignation at white anger at black jubilation

at Simpson's acquittal. It was a spiral made possible by the relay circuit of race. Only in America.

An American historian I know registers a widespread sense of bathos when he says, "Who would have imagined that the Simpson trial would be like the Kennedy assassination—that you'd remember where you were when the verdict was announced?" But everyone does, of course. The eminent sociologist William Julius Wilson[1] was in the red-carpet lounge of a United Airlines terminal, the only black in a crowd of white

1. See p. 747.

travelers, and found himself as stunned and disturbed as they were. Wynton Marsalis, on tour with his band in California, recalls that "everybody was acting like they were above watching it, but then when it got to be ten o'clock—zoom, we said, "Put the verdict on!'" Spike Lee was with Jackie Robinson's widow, Rachel, rummaging through a trunk filled with her husband's belongings, in preparation for a bio-pic he's making on the athlete. Jamaica Kincaid was sitting in her car in the parking lot of her local grocery store in Vermont, listening to the proceedings on National Public Radio, and she didn't pull out until after they were over. I was teaching a literature seminar at Harvard from twelve to two, and watched the verdict with the class on a television set in the seminar room. That's where I first saw the sort of racialized response that itself would fill television screens for the next few days: the white students looked aghast, and the black students cheered. "Maybe you should remind the students that this is a case about two people who were brutally slain, and not an occasion to celebrate," my teaching assistant, a white woman, whispered to me.

The two weeks spanning the O. J. Simpson verdict and Louis Farrakhan's Million Man March on Washington[2] were a good time for connoisseurs of racial paranoia. As blacks exulted at Simpson's acquittal, horrified whites had a fleeting sense that this race thing was knottier than they'd ever supposed—that when all the pieties were cleared away, blacks really *were* strangers in their midst. (The unspoken sentiment: *And I thought I knew these people.*) There was the faintest tincture of the Southern slave-owner's disquiet in the aftermath of the bloody slave revolt led by Nat Turner—when the gentleman farmer was left to wonder which of his smiling, servile retainers would have slit *his* throat had the rebellion spread as was intended, like fire on parched thatch. In the day or so following the verdict, young urban professionals took note of a slight *froideur* between themselves and their nannies and babysitters—the awkwardness of an unbroached subject. Rita Dove, who recently completed a term as the United States Poet Laureate, and who believes that Simpson was guilty, found it "appalling that white people were so outraged—more appall-

ing than the decision as to whether he was guilty or not." Of course, it's possible to overstate the tensions. Marsalis invokes the example of team sports, saying, "You want your side to win, whatever the side is going to be. And the thing is, we're still at a point in our national history where we look at each other as sides."

The matter of side-taking cuts deep. An old cartoon depicts a woman who has taken her errant daughter to see a child psychiatrist. "And when we were watching *The Wizard of Oz*," the distraught mother is explaining, "she was rooting for the wicked witch!" What many whites experienced was the bewildering sense that an entire population had been rooting for the wrong side. "This case is a classic example of what I call interstitial spaces," says Judge A. Leon Higginbotham,[3] who recently retired from the federal Court of Appeals, and who last month received the Presidential Medal of Freedom. "The jury system is predicated on the idea that different people can view the same evidence and reach diametrically opposed conclusions." But the observation brings little solace. If we disagree about something so basic, how can we find agreement about far thornier matters? For white observers, what's even scarier than the idea that black Americans were plumping for the villain, which is a misprision of value, is the idea that black Americans didn't recognize him as the villain, which is a misprision of fact. How can conversation begin when we disagree about reality? To put it at its harshest, for many whites a sincere belief in Simpson's innocence looks less like the culture of protest than like the culture of psychosis.

Perhaps you didn't know that Liz Claiborne appeared on *Oprah* not long ago and said that she didn't design her clothes for black women—that their hips were too wide. Perhaps you didn't know that the soft drink Tropical Fantasy is manufactured by the Ku Klux Klan and contains a special ingredient designed to sterilize black men. (A warning flyer distributed in Harlem a few years ago claimed that these findings were vouchsafed on the television program *20/20.*) Perhaps you didn't know that the Ku Klux Klan has a similar arrangement with Church's Fried Chicken—or is it Popeye's?

Perhaps you didn't know these things, but a good many black Americans think they do, and will discuss them with the same intentness they bring to speculations about the "shadowy figure" in a Brentwood driveway. Never mind that Liz Claiborne has never appeared on *Oprah,* that the beleaguered Brooklyn company that makes Tropical Fantasy has gone as far as to make available an F.D.A. assay of its ingredients, and that those fried-chicken franchises pose a threat mainly to black folks' arteries. The folklorist Patricia A. Turner, who has collected dozens of such tales in an invaluable 1993 study of rumor in African-American culture, *I Heard It Through the Grapevine,* points out the patterns to be found here: that these stories encode regnant anxieties, that they take root under particular conditions and play particular social roles, that the currency of rumor flourishes where "official" news has proved untrustworthy.

Certainly the Fuhrman tapes might have been scripted to confirm the old saw that paranoids, too, have enemies. If you wonder why blacks seem particularly susceptible to rumors and conspiracy theories, you might look at a history in which the official story was a poor guide to anything that mattered much, and in which rumor sometimes verged on the truth. Heard the one about the L.A. cop who hated interracial couples, fantasized about making a bonfire of black bodies, and boasted of planting evidence? How about the one about the federal government's forty-year study of how untreated syphilis affects black men? For that matter, have you ever read through some of the F.B.I.'s COINTELPRO files? ("There is but one way out for you," an F.B.I. scribe wrote to Martin Luther King, Jr.,[4] in 1964, thoughtfully urging on him the advantages of suicide. "You better take it before your filthy, abnormal, fraudulent self is bared to the nation.")

People arrive at an understanding of themselves and the world through narratives—narratives purveyed by schoolteachers, newscasters, "authorities," and all the other authors of our common sense. Counternarra-

tives are, in turn, the means by which groups contest that dominant reality and the fretwork of assumptions that supports it. Sometimes delusion lies that way; sometimes not. There's a sense in which much of black history is simply counternarrative that has been documented and legitimized, by slow, hard-won scholarship. The "shadowy figures" of American history have long been our own ancestors, both free and enslaved. In any case, fealty to counternarratives is an index to alienation, not to skin color: witness Representative Helen Chenoweth, of Idaho, and her devoted constituents. With all the appositeness of allegory, the copies of *The Protocols of the Elders of Zion*[5] sold by black venders in New York—who are supplied with them by Lushena Books, a black-nationalist book wholesaler—were published by the white supremacist Angriff Press, in Hollywood. Paranoia knows no color or coast.

Finally, though, it's misleading to view counternarrative as another pathology of disenfranchisement. If the M.I.A. myth[6], say, is rooted among a largely working-class constituency, there are many myths—one of them known as Reaganism[7]—that hold considerable appeal among the privileged classes. "So many white brothers and sisters are living in a state of denial in terms of how deep white supremacy is seated in their culture and society," the scholar and social critic Cornel West[8] says. "Now we recognize that in a fundamental sense we really do live in different worlds." In that respect, the reaction to the Simpson verdict has been something of an education. The novelist Ishmael Reed talks of "wealthy white male commentators who live in a world where the police don't lie, don't plant evidence—and drug dealers give you unlimited credit." He adds, "Nicole, you know, also dated Mafia hit men."

"I think he's innocent, I really do," West says. "I do think it was linked to some drug subculture of violence. It looks as if both O.J. and Nicole had some connection to drug activity. And the killings themselves were clas-

---

4. See p. 559.
5. Anti-Semitic tract first published in the Russian Empire in 1903.
6. "Missing in Action" myth; the widely held idea that Americans who fought in the Vietnam War in the 1960s or their remains are still being held captive by the North Vietnamese; H. Bruce Franklin's 1992 book *M.I.A., or Mythmaking in America* explores the belief in detail.
7. Conservative ideology promoted by President Ronald Reagan that proved to be largely beneficial to the wealthy.
8. See p. 881.

sic examples of that drug culture of violence. It could have to do with money owed—it could have to do with a number of things. And I think that O.J. was quite aware of and fearful of this." On this theory, Simpson may have appeared at the crime scene as a witness. "I think that he had a sense that it was coming down, both on him and on her, and Brother Ron Goldman just happened to be there," West conjectures. "But there's a possibility also that O.J. could have been there, gone over and tried to see what was going on, saw that he couldn't help, split, and just ran away. He might have said, 'I can't stop this thing, and they are coming at me to do the same thing.' He may have actually run for his life."

To believe that Simpson is innocent is to believe that a terrible injustice has been averted, and this is precisely what many black Americans, including many prominent ones, do believe. Thus the soprano Jessye Norman is angry over what she sees as the decision of the media to prejudge Simpson rather than "educate the public as to how we could possibly look at things a bit differently." She says she wishes that the real culprit "would stand up and say, 'I did this and I am sorry I caused so much trouble.'" And while she is sensitive to the issue of spousal abuse, she is skeptical about the way it was enlisted by the prosecution: "You have to stop getting into how they were at home, because there are not a lot of relationships that could be put on television that we would think, O.K., that's a good one. I mean, just stop pretending that this is the case." Then, too, she asks, "Isn't it interesting to you that this Faye Resnick[9] person was staying with Nicole Brown Simpson and that she happened to have left on the eighth of June? Does that tell you that maybe there's some awful coincidence here?" The widespread theory about murderous drug dealers Norman finds "perfectly plausible, knowing what drugs do," and she adds, "People are punished for being bad."

There's a sense in which all such accounts can be considered counternarratives, or fragments of them—subaltern knowledge, if you like. They dispute the tenets of official culture; they do not receive the imprimatur of editorialists or of network broadcasters; they are not seriously entertained on *MacNeil/Lehrer*. And when they do surface they are given consideration primarily for their ethnographic value. An official culture treats their claims as it does those of millenarian cultists in Texas, or Marxist deconstructionists in the academy: as things to be diagnosed, deciphered, given meaning—that is, *another* meaning. Black folk say they believe Simpson is innocent, and then the white gatekeepers of a media culture cajolingly explain what black folk really mean when they say it, offering the explanation from the highest of motives: because the alternative is a population that, by their lights, is not merely counternormative but crazy. Black folk may mean anything at all; just not what they say they mean.

Yet you need nothing so grand as an epistemic rupture to explain why different people weigh the evidence of authority differently. In the words of the cunning Republican campaign slogan, "Who do you trust?" It's a commonplace that white folks trust the police and black folks don't. Whites recognize this in the abstract, but they're continually surprised at the *depth* of black wariness. They shouldn't be. Norman Podhoretz's soul-searching 1963 essay, "My Negro Problem, and Ours"—one of the frankest accounts we have of liberalism and race resentment—tells of a Brooklyn boyhood spent under the shadow of carefree, cruel Negro assailants, and of the author's residual unease when he passes groups of blacks in his Upper West Side neighborhood. And yet, he notes in a crucial passage, "I know now, as I did not know when I was a child, that power is on my side, that the police are working for me and not for them." That ordinary, unremarkable comfort—the feeling that "the police are working for me"—continues to elude blacks, even many successful blacks. Thelma Golden, the curator of the Whitney's "Black Male" show,[1] points out that on the very day the verdict was announced a black man in Harlem was killed by the police under disputed circumstances. As older blacks like to repeat, "When white folks say 'justice,' they mean 'just us.'"

---

9. White American fashion designer and "best friend" of Nicole Simpson at the time of the murders (b. 1957); during the trial, Cochran suggested that drug dealers looking for payment from Resnick committed the murders.
1. 1994 art show at the Whitney Museum of American Art in New York City.

Blacks—in particular, black men—swap their experiences of police encounters like war stories, and there are few who don't have more than one story to tell. "These stories have a ring of cliché about them," Erroll McDonald, Pantheon's executive editor and one of the few prominent blacks in publishing, says, "but, as we all know about clichés, they're almost always true." McDonald tells of renting a Jaguar in New Orleans and being stopped by the police—simply "to show cause why I shouldn't be deemed a problematic Negro in a possibly stolen car." Wynton Marsalis says, "Shit, the police slapped me upside the head when I was in high school. I wasn't Wynton Marsalis then. I was just another nigger standing out somewhere on the street whose head could be slapped and did get slapped." The crime novelist Walter Mosley recalls, "When I was a kid in Los Angeles, they used to stop me all the time, beat on me, follow me around, tell me that I was stealing things." Nor does William Julius Wilson—who has a son-in-law on the Chicago police force ("You couldn't find a nicer, more dedicated guy")—wonder why he was stopped near a small New England town by a policeman who wanted to know what he was doing in those parts. There's a moving violation that many African-Americans know as D.W.B.: Driving While Black.

So we all have our stories. In 1968, when I was eighteen, a man who knew me was elected mayor of my West Virginia county, in an upset victory. A few weeks into his term, he passed on something he thought I should know: the county police had made a list of people to be arrested in the event of a serious civil disturbance, and my name was on it. Years of conditioning will tell. Wynton Marsalis says, "My worst fear is to have to go before the criminal-justice system." Absurdly enough, it's mine, too.

Another barrier to interracial comprehension is talk of the "race card"—a phrase that itself infuriates many blacks. Judge Higginbotham, who pronounces himself "not uncomfortable at all" with the verdict, is uncomfortable indeed with charges that Johnnie Cochran played the race card. "This whole point is one hundred percent inaccurate," Higginbotham says. "If you knew that the most important witness had a history of racism

and hostility against black people, that should have been a relevant factor of inquiry even if the jury had been all white. If the defendant had been Jewish and the police officer had a long history of expressed anti-Semitism and having planted evidence against innocent persons who were Jewish, I can't believe that anyone would have been saying that defense counsel was playing the anti-Semitism card." Angela Davis[2] finds the very metaphor to be a problem. "Race is not a card," she says firmly. "The whole case was pervaded with issues of race."

Those who share her view were especially outraged at Robert Shapiro's famous post-trial rebuke to Cochran—for not only playing the race card but dealing it "from the bottom of the deck." Ishmael Reed, who is writing a book about the case, regards Shapiro's remarks as sheer opportunism: "He wants to keep his Beverly Hills clients—a perfectly commercial reason." In Judge Higginbotham's view, "Johnnie Cochran established that he was as effective as any lawyer in America, and though whites can tolerate black excellence in singing, dancing, and dunking, there's always been a certain level of discomfort among many whites when you have a one-on-one challenge in terms of intellectual competition. If Edward Bennett Williams, who was one of the most able lawyers in the country, had raised the same issues, half of the complaints would not exist."

By the same token, the display of black prowess in the courtroom was heartening for many black viewers. Cornel West says, "I think part of the problem is that Shapiro—and this is true of certain white brothers—has a profound fear of black-male charisma. And this is true not only in the law but across the professional world. You see, you have so many talented white brothers who deserve to be in the limelight. But one of the reasons they are not in the limelight is that they are not charismatic. And here comes a black person who's highly talented but also charismatic and therefore able to command center stage. So you get a very real visceral kind of jealousy that has to do with sexual competition as well as professional competition."

Erroll McDonald touches upon another aspect of sexual tension when he says, "The so-called race card has always been the joker. And the joker is the history of sexual racial politics in this country. People forget the singularity of this issue—people forget that less than a century ago black men were routinely lynched for merely glancing at white women or for having been *thought* to have glanced at a white woman." He adds, with mordant irony, "Now we've come to a point in our history where a black man could, potentially, have murdered a white woman and thrown in a white man to boot—and got off. So the country has become far more complex in its discussion of race." This is, as he appreciates, a less than perfectly consoling thought.

"But he's coming for me," a woman muses in Toni Morrison's 1992 novel, *Jazz,* shortly before she is murdered by a jealous ex-lover. "Maybe tomorrow he'll find me. Maybe tonight." Morrison, it happens, is less interested in the grand passions of love and requital than she is in the curious texture of communal amnesty. In the event, the woman's death goes unavenged; the man who killed her is forgiven even by her friends and relatives. Neighbors feel that the man fell victim to her wiles, that he didn't understand "how she liked to push people, men." Or, as one of them says of her, "live the life; pay the price." Even the woman— who refuses to name the culprit as she bleeds to death—seems to accede to the view that she brought it on herself.

It's an odd and disturbing theme, and one with something of a history in black popular culture. An R. & B. hit from 1960, "There's Something on Your Mind," relates the anguish of a man who is driven to kill by his lover's infidelity. The chorus alternates with spoken narrative, which informs us that his first victim is the friend with whom she was unfaithful. But then:

> Just as you make it up in your mind to forgive her, here come another one of your best friends through the door. This really makes you blow your top, and you go right ahead and shoot her. And realizing what you've done, you say: "Baby, please, speak to me. Forgive me. I'm sorry."

"We are a *forgiving* people," Anita Hill[3] tells me, and she laughs, a little uneasily. We're talking about

the support for O. J. Simpson in the black community; at least, I think we are.

A black woman told the *Times* last week, "He has been punished enough." But forgiveness is not all. There is also an element in this of outlaw culture: the tendency—which unites our lumpenproles with our postmodern ironists—to celebrate transgression for its own sake. Spike Lee, who was surprised but "wasn't happy" at the verdict ("I would have bet money that he was going to the slammer"), reached a similar conclusion: "A lot of black folks said, 'Man, O.J. is *bad,* you know. This is the first brother in the history of the world who got away with the murder of white folks, and a blond, blue-eyed woman at that.'"

But then there is the folk wisdom on the question of why Nicole Brown Simpson had to die—the theodicy of the streets. For nothing could be further from the outlaw ethic than the simple and widely shared certainty that, as Jessye Norman says, people are punished for doing wrong. And compounding the sentiment is Morrison's subject—the culturally vexed status of the so-called crime of passion, or what some took to be one, anyway. You play, you pay: it's an attitude that exists on the streets, but not only on the streets, and one that somehow attaches to Nicole, rather than to her ex-husband. Many counternarratives revolve around her putative misbehavior. The black feminist Bell Hooks notes with dismay that what many people took to be a "narrative of a crime of passion" had as its victim "a woman that many people, white and black, felt was like a whore. Precisely by being a sexually promiscuous woman, by being a woman who used drugs, by being a white woman with a black man, she had already fallen from grace in many people's eyes—there was no way to redeem her." Ishmael Reed, for one, has no interest in redeeming her. "To paint O. J. Simpson as a beast, they had to depict her as a saint," he complains. "Apparently, she had a violent temper. She slapped her Jamaican maid. I'm wondering, the feminists who are giving Simpson such a hard time—do they approve of white women slapping maids?"

Of course, the popular trial of Nicole Brown Simpson— one conducted off camera, in whispers—has further

3. See p. 1103.

occluded anything recognizable as sexual politics. When Anita Hill heard that O. J. Simpson was going to be part of the Million Man March on Washington, she felt it was entirely in keeping with the occasion: a trial in which she believed that matters of gender had been "bracketed" was going to be succeeded by a march from which women were excluded. And while Minister Louis Farrakhan had told black men that October 16 was to serve as a "day of atonement" for their sins, the murder of Nicole Brown Simpson and Ronald Goldman was obviously not among the sins he had in mind. Bell Hooks argues, "Both O.J.'s case and the Million Man March confirm that while white men are trying to be sensitive and pretending they're the new man, black men are saying that patriarchy must be upheld at all costs, even if women must die." She sees the march as a congenial arena for Simpson in symbolic terms: "I think he'd like to strut his stuff, as the patriarch. He is the dick that stayed hard longer." ("The surprising thing is that you won't see Clarence Thomas[4] going on that march," Anita Hill remarks of another icon of patriarchy.) Farrakhan himself prefers metaphors of military mobilization, but the exclusionary politics of the event has clearly distracted from its ostensible message of solidarity. "First of all, I wouldn't go to no war and leave half the army home," says Amiri Baraka,[5] the radical poet and playwright who achieved international renown in the sixties as the leading spokesman for the Black Arts Movement. "Logistically, that doesn't make sense." He notes that Martin Luther King's 1963 March on Washington was "much more inclusive," and sees Farrakhan's regression as "an absolute duplication of what's happening in the country," from Robert Bly[6] on: the sacralization of masculinity.

Something like that dynamic is what many white feminists saw on display in the Simpson verdict; but it's among women that the racial divide is especially salient. The black legal scholar and activist Patricia Williams says she was "stunned by the intensely per-

sonal resentment of some of my white women friends in particular." Stunned but, on reflection, not mystified. "This is Greek drama," she declares. "Two of the most hotly contended aspects of our lives are violence among human beings who happen to be police officers and violence among human beings who happen to be husbands, spouses, lovers." Meanwhile, our attention has been fixated on the rhetorical violence between human beings who happen to disagree about the outcome of the O. J. Simpson trial.

It's a cliché to speak of the Simpson trial as a soap opera—as entertainment, as theater—but it's also true, and in ways that are worth exploring further. For one thing, the trial provides a fitting rejoinder to those who claim that we live in an utterly fragmented culture, bereft of the common narratives that bind a people together. True, Parson Weems[7] has given way to Dan Rather, but public narrative persists. Nor has it escaped notice that the biggest televised legal contests of the last half decade have involved race matters: Anita Hill and Rodney King. So there you have it: the Simpson trial—black entertainment television at its finest. Ralph Ellison's[8] hopeful insistence on the Negro's centrality to American culture finds, at last, a certain tawdry confirmation.

"The media generated in people a feeling of being spectators at a show," the novelist John Edgar Wideman says. "And at the end of a show you applaud. You are happy for the good guy. There is that sense of primal identification and closure." Yet it's a fallacy of "cultural literacy" to equate shared narratives with shared meanings. The fact that American TV shows are rebroadcast across the globe causes many people to wring their hands over the menace of cultural imperialism; seldom do they bother to inquire about the meanings that different people bring to and draw from these shows. When they do make inquiries, the results are often surprising. One researcher talked to Israeli

---

4. See pp. 934 and 1103.
5. See p. 694.
6. White American writer and activist (b. 1926) whose 1990 book *Iron John: A Book About Men* inspired the growth of the "Mythopoetic Men's Movement," which uses self-help and workshops to help men find well-being.
7. White American author (1756–1825) remembered for popularizing apocryphal stories about George Washington, including the story of the cherry tree, in *The Life of Washington* (1800).
8. See p. 430.

Arabs who had just watched an episode of *Dallas*—an episode in which Sue Ellen takes her baby, leaves her husband, J.R., and moves in with her ex-lover and his father. The Arab viewers placed their own construction on the episode: they were all convinced that Sue Ellen had moved in with her *own* father—something that by their mores at least made sense.

A similar thing happened in America this year: the communal experience afforded by a public narrative (and what narrative more public?) was splintered by the politics of interpretation. As far as the writer Maya Angelou is concerned, the Simpson trial was an exercise in minstrelsy. "Minstrel shows caricatured every aspect of the black man's life, beginning with his sexuality," she says. "They portrayed the black man as devoid of all sensibilities and sensitivities. They minimized and diminished the possibility of familial love. And that is what the trial is about. Not just the prosecution but everybody seemed to want to show him as other than a normal human being. Nobody let us just see a man." But there is, of course, little consensus about what genre would best accommodate the material. Walter Mosley says, "The story plays to large themes, so I'm sure somebody will write about it. But I don't think it's a mystery. I think it's much more like a novel by Zola." What a writer might make of the material is one thing; what the audience has made of it is another.

"Simpson is a B-movie star and people were watching this like a B movie," Patricia Williams says. "And this is *not* the American B-movie ending." Or was it? "From my perspective as an attorney, this trial was much more like a movie than a trial," Kathleen Cleaver, who was once the Black Panthers' Minister for Communication and is now a professor of law at Emory, says. "It had the budget of a movie, it had the casting of a movie, it had the tension of a movie, and the happy ending of a movie." Spike Lee, speaking professionally, is dubious about the trial's cinematic possibilities: "I don't care who makes this movie, it is never going to equal what people have seen in their living rooms and houses for eight or nine months." Or is it grand opera? Jessye Norman considers: "Well, it certainly has all the ingredients. I mean, somebody meets somebody and

somebody gets angry with somebody and somebody dies." She laughs. "It sounds like the *Ring* cycle of Wagner—it really does."

"This story has been told any number of times," Angelou says. "The first thing I thought about was Eugene O'Neill's *All God's Chillun*." Then she considers how the event might be retrieved by an African-American literary tradition. "I think a great writer would have to approach it," she tells me pensively. "James Baldwin[9] could have done it. And Toni Morrison could do it."

What about Maya Angelou?

"I don't like that kind of stuff," she replies.

There are some for whom the question of adaptation is not entirely abstract. The performance artist and playwright Anna Deavere Smith has already worked on the 911 tape and F. Lee Bailey's cross-examination of Mark Fuhrman in the drama classes she teaches at Stanford. Now, with a dramaturge's eye, she identifies what she takes to be the climactic moment: "Just after the verdict was read I will always remember two sounds and one image. I heard Johnnie Cochran go '*Ugh*,' and then I heard the weeping of Kim Goldman.[1] And then I saw the image of O.J.'s son, with one hand going upward on one eye and one hand pointed down, shaking and sobbing. I couldn't do the words right now; if I could find a collaborator, I would do something else. I feel that a choreographer ought to do that thing. Part of the tragedy was the fact of that '*Ugh*' and that crying. Because that '*Ugh*' wasn't even a full sound of victory, really." In "Thirteen Ways of Looking at a Blackbird" Wallace Stevens famously said he didn't know whether he preferred "The beauty of inflections / Or the beauty of innuendoes, / The blackbird whistling / Or just after." American culture has spoken as with one voice: we like it just after.

Just after is when our choices and allegiances are made starkly apparent. Just after is when interpretation can be detached from the thing interpreted. Anita Hill, who saw her own presence at the Clarence Thomas hearings endlessly analyzed and allegorized, finds plenty of significance in the trial's reception, but says

---

9. See p. 485.
1. Sister of Ronald Goldman, the man murdered alongside Nicole Simpson.

the trial itself had none. Naturally, the notion that the trial was sui generis is alien to most commentators. Yet it did not arrive in the world already costumed as a racial drama; it had to be racialized. And those critics—angry whites, indignant blacks—who like to couple this verdict with the Rodney King verdict should consider an elementary circumstance: Rodney King was an unknown and undistinguished black man who was brutalized by the police; the only thing exceptional about that episode was the presence of a video camera. But, as Bell Hooks asks, "in what other case have we ever had a wealthy black man being tried for murder?" Rodney King was a black man to his captors before he was anything else; O. J. Simpson was, first and foremost, O. J. Simpson. Kathleen Cleaver observes, "A black superhero millionaire is not someone for whom mistreatment is an issue." And Spike Lee acknowledges that the police "don't really bother black people once they are a personality." On this point, I'm reminded of something that Roland Gift, the lead singer of the pop group Fine Young Cannibals, once told a reporter: "I'm not black, I'm famous."

Simpson, too, was famous rather than black; that is, until the African-American community took its lead from the cover of *Time*[2] and, well, blackened him. Some intellectuals are reluctant to go along with the conceit. Angela Davis, whose early-seventies career as a fugitive and a political prisoner provides one model of how to be famous *and* black, speaks of the need to question the way "O. J. Simpson serves as the generic black man," given that "he did not identify himself as black before then." More bluntly, Baraka says, "To see him get all of this God-damned support from people he has historically and steadfastly eschewed just pissed me off. He eschewed black people all his life and then, like Clarence Thomas, the minute he gets jammed up he comes talking about 'Hey, I'm black.'" And the matter of spousal abuse should remind us of another role-reversal entailed by Simpson's iconic status in a culture of celebrity: Nicole Brown Simpson would have known that her famous-not-black husband commanded a cer-

tain deference from the L.A.P.D. which she, who was white but not yet famous, did not.

"It's just amazing that we in the black community have bought into it," Anita Hill says, with some asperity, and she sees the manufacture of black-male heroes as part of the syndrome. "We continue to create a superclass of individuals who are above the rules." It bewilders her that Simpson "was being honored as someone who was being persecuted for his politics, when he had none," she says. "Not only do we forget about the abuse of his wife but we also forget about the abuse of the community, his walking away from the community." And so Simpson's connection to a smitten black America can be construed as yet another romance, another troubled relationship, another case study in mutual exploitation.

Yet to accept the racial reduction ("WHITES V. BLACKS," as last week's *Newsweek* headline had it) is to miss the fact that the black community itself is riven, and in ways invisible to most whites. I myself was convinced of Simpson's guilt, so convinced that in the middle of the night before the verdict was to be announced I found myself worrying about his prospective sojourn in prison: would he be brutalized, raped, assaulted? Yes, on sober reflection, such worries over a man's condign punishment seemed senseless, a study in misplaced compassion; but there it was. When the verdict was announced, I was stunned—but, then again, wasn't my own outrage mingled with an unaccountable sense of relief? Anna Deavere Smith says, "I am seeing more than that white people are pissed off and black people are ecstatic. I am seeing the difficulty of that; I am seeing people having difficulty talking about it." And many are weary of what Ishmael Reed calls "zebra journalism, where everything is seen in black-and-white." Davis says, "I have the feeling that the media are in part responsible for the creation of this so-called racial divide—putting all the white people on one side and all the black people on the other side."

Many blacks as well as whites saw the trial's outcome as a grim enactment of Richard Pryor's comic rejoinder "Who are you going to believe—me, or your

2. The June 27, 1994, cover of *Time* magazine featured a mugshot of O. J. Simpson that had been digitally manipulated to make Simpson's face darker (as well as blurrier and more unshaven); a spokesperson for *Time* explained later that the magazine's editors had hired an illustrator to alter Simpson's mugshot "to make it more artful, more compelling."

lying eyes?" "I think if he were innocent he wouldn't have behaved that way," Jamaica Kincaid says of Simpson, taking note of his refusal to testify on his own behalf. "If you are innocent," she believes, "you might want to admit you have done every possible thing in the world—had sex with ten donkeys, twenty mules—but did not do this particular thing." William Julius Wilson says mournfully, "There's something wrong with a system where it's better to be guilty and rich and have good lawyers than to be innocent and poor and have bad ones."

The Simpson verdict was "the ultimate in affirmative action," Amiri Baraka says. "I *know* the son of a bitch did it." For his part, Baraka essentially agrees with Shapiro's rebuke of Cochran: "Cochran is belittling folks. What he's saying is 'Well, the niggers can't understand the question of perjury in the first place. The only thing they can understand is 'He called you a nigger.'" He alludes to *Ebony*'s fixation on "black firsts"—the magazine's spotlight coverage of the first black to do this or that—and fantasizes the appropriate *Ebony* accolade. "They can feature him on the cover as 'The first Negro to kill a white woman and get away with it,'" he offers acidly. Baraka has been writing a play called *Othello, Jr.,* so such themes have been on his mind. The play is still in progress, but he *has* just finished a short poem:

> *Free Mumia!*[3]
> *O.J. did it*
> *And you know it.*

"Trials don't establish absolute truth; that's a theological enterprise," Patricia Williams says. So perhaps it is appropriate that a religious leader, Louis Farrakhan, convened a day of atonement; indeed, some worry that it is all too appropriate, coming at a time when the resurgent right has offered us a long list of sins for which black men must atone. But the crisis of race in America is real enough. And with respect to that crisis a mass mobilization is surely a better fit than a criminal trial. These days, the assignment of blame

for black woes increasingly looks like an exercise in scholasticism; and calls for interracial union increasingly look like an exercise in inanity. ("Sorry for the Middle Passage, old chap. I don't know *what* we were thinking." "Hey, man, forget it—and here's your wallet back. No, really, I want you to have it.") The black economist Glenn Loury[4] says, "If I could get a million black men together, I wouldn't march them to Washington, I'd march them into the ghettos."

But because the meanings of the march are so ambiguous, it would become itself a racial Rorschach—a vast ambulatory allegory waiting to happen. The actor and director Sidney Poitier says, "If we go on such a march to say to ourselves and to the rest of America that we want to be counted among America's people, we would like our family structure to be nurtured and strengthened by ourselves and by the society, that's a good point to make." Maya Angelou, who agreed to address the assembled men, views the event not as a display of male self-affirmation but as a ceremony of penitence: "It's a chance for African-American males to say to African-American females, 'I'm sorry. I am sorry for what I did, and I am sorry for what happened to both of us.'" But different observers will have different interpretations. Mass mobilizations launch a thousand narratives—especially among subscribers to what might be called the "great event" school of history. And yet Farrakhan's recurrent calls for individual accountability consort oddly with the absolution, both juridical and populist, accorded O. J. Simpson. Simpson has been seen as a symbol for many things, but he is not yet a symbol for taking responsibility for one's actions.

All the same, the task for black America is not to get its symbols in shape: symbolism is one of the few commodities we have in abundance. Meanwhile, Du Bois's[5] century-old question "How does it feel to be a problem?" grows in trenchancy with every new bulletin about crime and poverty. And the Simpson trial spurs us to question everything except the way that the discourse of crime and punishment has enveloped, and suffocated, the analysis of race and poverty in this

---

3. Mumia Abu-Jamal (b. 1954), journalist and activist on death row in Pennsylvania for the 1981 murder of a police officer; numerous issues with the original trial have prompted a widespread call for a retrial, supported by global leaders and organizations including Nelson Mandela, Archbishop Desmond Tutu, Alice Walker, Maya Angelou, and Amnesty International.

4. See p. 936.
5. See p. 199.

country. For the debate over the rights and wrongs of the Simpson verdict has meshed all too well with the manner in which we have long talked about race and social justice. The defendant may be free, but we remain captive to a binary discourse of accusation and counteraccusation, of grievance and countergrievance, of victims and victimizers. It is a discourse in which O. J. Simpson is a suitable remedy for Rodney King, and reductions in Medicaid are entertained as a suitable remedy for O. J. Simpson: a discourse in which everyone speaks of payback and nobody is paid. The result is that race politics becomes a court of the imagination wherein blacks seek to punish whites for their misdeeds and whites seek to punish blacks for theirs, and an infinite regress of score-settling ensues—yet another way in which we are daily becoming meta and meta. And so an empty vessel like O. J. Simpson becomes filled with meaning, and more meaning—more meaning than any of us can bear. No doubt it is a far easier thing to assign blame than to render justice. But if the imagery of the court continues to confine the conversation about race, it really will be a crime.

IN THE HEADLINES:
Reparations

RANDALL ROBINSON: from *The Debt: What America Owes to Blacks* [2000]

JACK HITT, WILLIE E. GARY, ALEXANDER J. PIRES JR., RICHARD F. SCRUGGS, AND DENNIS C. SWEET III: *Making the Case for Racial Reparations* [2000]

ADOLPH L. REED JR.: *The Case Against Reparations* [2000]

The idea that black Americans are owed reparations for slavery and its aftermath has a long history. In 1865, General William T. Sherman issued Special Field Orders 15, granting freed slaves up to forty acres of tillable land in parts of Georgia, South Carolina, and Florida and a military mule. President Andrew Johnson, upon taking office after the assassination of Abraham Lincoln, swiftly reversed the orders. The idea that there is an unpaid debt owed to African Americans has continued to evolve, gaining popularity during periods of strong black nationalism. Especially noteworthy were Marcus Garvey's (p. 259) demands for reparations in the 1920s and James Forman's 1969 "Black Manifesto," which called for "white Christian churches and Jewish synagogues" to pay African Americans $500 million in damages. The movement for reparations gained an important legal precedent in 1988 when Congress passed the Civil Liberties Act, granting $20,000 to every surviving Japanese American interned during World War II. The next year, Representative John Conyers of Michigan introduced legislation to establish a congressional panel to study reparations proposals and, as Conyers states on his website, "issues such as the lingering negative effects of the institution of slavery, whether an apology is owed, [and] whether compensation is warranted and, if so, in what form and who should [be] eligible." Although the legislation was defeated, Conyers has continued to introduce it every year since then.

At the beginning of the twenty-first century, the movement for reparations regained momentum, largely in response to the publication of *The Debt* in 2000, a book by the lawyer and activist Randall Robinson (b. 1941), and to the success of class actions against the federal government and major corporations. For example, the $368.5 billion settlement against tobacco companies in 1997, and the case in which black farmers won a $1 billion settlement from the U.S. Department of Agriculture in 1999 for having been systematically denied loans provided lawyers with strategies and tactics to use in a reparations class action. Those legal victories also made the goal of securing reparations for 250 years of slavery seem more possible, and once again injected the issue into the national conversation.

Robinson's *The Debt,* which stresses that slavery and its aftermath imposed psychological, cultural, and economic harm on black Americans, set the framework for much of the modern debate on reparations. As is evident in the 2000 roundtable in *Harper's Magazine,* moderated by the white American editor and writer Jack Hitt, and in the 2000 article "The Case against Reparations" by the political science professor Adolph L. Reed (b. 1947), some commentators reject Robinson's arguments, finding that the racialized call for reparations is divisive and a distraction from efforts to build interracial coalitions. Others agree with Robinson about the need for reparations but find that his focus on the emotional and cultural damage done by slavery means that any solution either is politically unfeasible (since it would pit white people against black people) or would have little effect on the lives of African Americans, as in the case of an official apology. While Robinson's position continues to stimulate discussion and provide fodder for the case for reparations, the legal arguments of class action proponents are shifting the discussion away from emotional issues that money cannot solve toward practical questions of how settlements might be used to improve the lives of African Americans today and in the future.

RANDALL ROBINSON

from *The Debt: What America Owes to Blacks* [2000]

Well before the birth of our country, Europe and the eventual United States perpetrated a heinous wrong against the peoples of Africa—and sustained and benefited from the wrong for centuries. Europe followed the grab of Africa's people with the rape, through colonial occupation, of Africa's material resources. America followed slavery with more than a hundred combined years of legal racial segregation and legal racial discrimination of one variety or another. In 1965, after nearly 350 years of legal racial suppression, the United States enacted the *Voting Rights Act* and, virtually simultaneously, began to walk away from the social wreckage that centuries of white hegemony had wrought. The country then began to rub itself with the memory-emptying salve of contemporaneousness. (If the wrong did not *just* occur, it did not occur at all in a way that would render the living responsible.)

But when the black living suffer real and current consequences as a result of wrongs committed by a younger America, then contemporary America must be caused to shoulder responsibility for those wrongs until such wrongs have been adequately compensated and righted. The life and responsibilities of a society or nation are not circumscribed by the life spans of its mortal constituents. Social rights, wrongs, obligations, and responsibilities flow eternal.

There are many ways to begin righting America's massive wrong, some of which you must already have inferred. But let there be no doubt, it will require great resources and decades of national fortitude to resolve economic and social disparities so long in the making.

Habit is the enemy. For whites and blacks have made a habit now, beyond the long era of legal discrimination, of seeing each other (the only way they can remember seeing each other) in a certain relation of economic and social inequality.

American capitalism, which starts each child where its parents left off is not a fair system. This is particularly the case for African Americans, whose general economic starting points have been rearmost in our society because of slavery and its long racialist aftermath. American slaves for two and a half centuries saw taken from them not just their freedom but the inestimable economic value of their labor as well, which, were it a line item in today's gross national product report, would undoubtedly run into the billions of dollars. Whether the monetary obligation is legally enforceable or not, a large debt is owed by America to the descendants of America's slaves.

Here too, habit has become our enemy, for America has made an art form by now of grinding its past deeds, no matter how despicable, into mere ephemera. African Americans, unfortunately, have accommodated this habit of American amnesia all too well. It would behoove African Americans to remember that history forgets, first, those who forget themselves. To do what is necessary to accomplish anything approaching psychic and economic parity in the next half century will not only require a fundamental attitude shift in American thinking but massive amounts of money as well. Before the country in general can be made to understand, African Americans themselves must come to understand that this demand is not for charity. It is simply for what they are *owed* on a debt that is old but compellingly obvious and valid still.

Even the *making* of a well-reasoned case for restitution will do wonders for the spirit of African Americans. It will cause them at long last to understand the genesis of their dilemma by gathering, as have all other groups, all of their history—before, during, and after slavery—into one story of themselves. To hold the story fast to their breast. To make of it, over time, a sacred text. And from it, to explain themselves to themselves and to their heirs. Tall again, as they had been long, long ago.

From Randall Robinson, *The Debt: What America Owes to Blacks* (New York: Dutton, 2000), pp. 230–32.

JACK HITT, WILLIE E. GARY, ALEXANDER J. PIRES JR., RICHARD SCRUGGS, AND DENNIS C. SWEET III

Making the Case for Racial Reparations [2000]

The following forum is based on a discussion held at the Palm restaurant in Washington, D.C. Jack Hitt served as moderator.

JACK HITT *is a contributing editor of* Harper's Magazine.

WILLIE E. GARY *won a $500 million judgment against The Loewen Group Inc., the world's largest funeral-home and cemetery operators, in 1995 and $240 million against The Walt Disney Company last August. He is an attorney with Gary, Williams, Parenti, Finney, Lewis, McManus, Watson & Sperando, in Stuart, Florida.*

ALEXANDER J. PIRES JR. *won a $1 billion settlement for black farmers in their discrimination case against the U.S. Department of Agriculture and is currently working on a multibillion-dollar class-action suit on behalf of Native Americans. He is an attorney with Conlon, Frantz, Phelan & Pires, L.L.P., in Washington, D.C.*

RICHARD F. SCRUGGS *won the historic $368.5 billion settlement for the states in their suit against tobacco companies in 1997 and is currently building a class-action suit against HMOs. He is an attorney with Scruggs, Millette, Bozeman & Dent, P.A., in Pascagoula, Mississippi.*

DENNIS C. SWEET III *won a $400 million settlement in last year's "fen-phen" diet-drug case against American Home Products Corporation and $145 million against the Ford Motor Company. He is an attorney with Langston, Sweet & Freese, in Jackson, Mississippi.*

Hardly a week goes by that we don't read of another gigantic lawsuit with thousands of plaintiffs and billions in damages. Once an esoteric legal device, the class-action lawsuit has become the dominant form of litigation to resolve bitter disputes over collective guilt and innocence that not so long ago played out in Congress. Indeed, our preening national legislature, besotted with special-interest money, seems rivaled by the big budgets and major issues that now thrive in the class-action courtroom.

At the same time, one hears rumblings among historians and philosophers to consider a lawsuit for slave reparations. After all, class-action lawyers have ridden to the rescue of those forced into slave labor in Germany and prostitution in Korea. The academics discuss such a slavery suit in moral, historical, or metaphysical terms. That's nice. But in this, the land of show-me-the-money, the thinking quickly becomes practical: Who gets sued? For how much? What's the legal argument? How do you get a case into court?

To answer these questions, *Harper's Magazine* invited four of the country's most successful class-action lawyers to strategize about how to bring America's most peculiar sorrow into a court of law.

CAUSE OF ACTION

JACK HITT—We're here today to talk about how: how, that is, to repay blacks for what they suffered under slavery and what they've suffered since because of it. But first let's talk about why, because when many people hear the term "slave reparations," they go nuts.

"Oh, that was so long ago," they say. "Can't we just leave this alone? Everybody's got gripes. Blacks should just get over it." To a lot of people, the very idea of a lawsuit seems unreasonable.

DENNIS C. SWEET III—That's because people think slavery ended in 1865. And it did, but the aftermath of slavery is still with us.

ALEXANDER J. PIRES JR.—Every great lawsuit tries to tell a story of injustice in a way that will resonate. There's a lot to work with here. Slavery's the most unacknowledged story in America's history.

HITT—Unacknowledged?

SWEET—This is what Randall Robinson says in his new book, *The Debt.*

HITT—What's unacknowledged?

SWEET—Oh, just about everything. Take our nation's capital. Nearly every brick, every dab of mortar, was put there by slaves. There's not a plaque in all of Washington acknowledging that slaves built the Rome of the New World. This is how it is with slavery. We've heard of it, but we don't really know anything about it.

WILLIE E. GARY—Think about this. In 1865 the federal government of this country freed 4 million blacks. Without a dime, with no property, nearly all illiterate, they were let loose upon the land to wander. That's what begins the aftermath of slavery.

SWEET—How many Americans know that 25 million blacks died in slavery? And how many know that virtual slavery was perpetuated for nearly a century after emancipation? Peonage laws made unpaid workers out of debtors. There were sharecropping schemes. Then Jim Crow laws. And even after that, there were other entrenched policies that have kept African Americans living in ghettos.

HITT—Robinson points out that until 1950 the federal government included in mortgage loans restrictive covenants preventing blacks—and only blacks, no other group—from buying houses in white neighborhoods. So blacks could not make their equity work for them. They couldn't move up.

RICHARD F. SCRUGGS—A house is the largest single investment and asset most people have.

PIRES—And it's how every immigrant first got into the middle class. So that policy effectively delayed the arrival of the black middle class by half a century.

GARY—And banks kept it up—denying loans to blacks, often by redlining, by which they literally would draw lines on a map around a neighborhood and not give loans to even creditworthy people living there. That happened until almost last week.

HITT—These are all compelling examples. And so you wonder: If Koreans can sue the Japanese about heinous acts carried out in the 1930s, and Jews are suing over prewar slave-labor camps, and American POWs imprisoned in Pacific camps are even suing the Japanese for slave-labor wages, why can't blacks also sue for similar recompense?

SWEET—It can be done. In fact, Alex won one of the great reparations lawsuits in the last few decades. He filed on behalf of—how many was it, Alex?

PIRES—Twenty-four thousand black families.

SWEET—Until 1997 the United States Department of Agriculture had an almost zero rate of granting black farmers loans. Until 1997, okay?

PIRES—Ninety-five percent of all farm loans went to white farmers. And until the 1960s, the U.S.D.A. had a special section called Negro Loans, which ensured that black applicants were rejected. It's amazing.

SWEET—It's amazing how young this country is and how close in time, when you come to think about it, all our history is. No part of our history is that far off. The effects of slavery are still with us, we all know that: single parents, black men wandering off from their families, a tradition of not going to school, distrust of the future. This is not black culture. It's slave culture.

GARY—My children and I have talked about your case, Alex. They've never been on a farm, but for them and a lot of black people you changed our whole thinking about what we can be in this country. If you're black, I mean, you're thinking, it's not going to happen, the government isn't going to give you a fair shake. Then all of a sudden you see this happen. I mean, the country stepped up to the plate.

PIRES: In the end, it did.

GARY—Man, it was such a big message. You know, as an African American I felt really good about it.

SWEET—So how do we make a case?

LEGAL STRATEGY I: BREACH OF CONTRACT

GARY—I think this could be a tort, a simple lawsuit where one party sues another.

HITT—So a variation of the classic you-done-me-wrong lawsuit. Just really big.

GARY—Specifically, it could be a breach-of-contract suit, too. After the war, former slaves were promised forty acres and a mule, and we never got it. That was a contract. It was a promise. We just have to stand up and tackle this wrong or try to make it right. So it could be a tort, it could be a breach of contract. You almost have to start a lawsuit to see where it can go. And I don't think that the fact that it's 135 years later should be a hindrance to people waking up, realizing that it was a grave injustice. And until America accounts for its actions, this friction is always going to be there.

SCRUGGS—Breach of contract after 135 years? You *do* have a statute of limitations problem.

GARY—Not if Congress steps in.

HITT—But can you count on that?

PIRES—I don't think the legislature's going to help until the lawsuit goes forward. You have to file that suit, and you have to go forward yourself.

SWEET—Al, it's just like your black farmers' suit. I joined Al on that case. They had studies showing rank discrimination, years and years and years of it, and the courts never did anything about it—

PIRES—This is how these lawsuits go. Everybody said the statute of limitations is against you, as well as other legal problems too. But we just kept marching, marching, marching. Getting more folk, going around the country. And there were motions to dismiss. Then motions against class certification, the process by which you define who is suing. But as the facts started getting out, people started to say, "Hey, this argument makes sense. These people were wronged. Something's not right." The judges began to think, are we

going to let this great injustice go unanswered because of a technicality? I think this situation is like that.

SWEET—We still have to get specific here. We have to get past *Cato*.

HITT—*Cato*?

PIRES—*Cato* v. *United States* was a slave-reparations decision issued in 1995 by the Ninth Circuit Court of Appeals. This case was easily dismissed, because the judges said, "We can't find a theory with which to move the case forward." Since the Ninth Circuit is basically liberal, this decision sort of took the wind out of reparations thinking. You either find a theory under statutes or you're going to have to find it under constitutional law.

SCRUGGS—We have to find a legal theory, then.

PIRES—And people have tried. They considered the Thirteenth Amendment—didn't work. They've considered a tort claims act—didn't work. They've considered the civil rights acts—didn't work. The *Cato* case is useful, because the Ninth Circuit said, "We've looked real hard at it. We can't find a way."

GARY—Let's think about the breach of contract: forty acres and a mule.

PIRES—Well, how can you sue?

HITT—The promise of forty acres and a mule was an executive order sanctioned by Congress.

GARY—It's in writing! Breach of contract.

HITT—Well, that contract was voided by President Andrew Johnson in 1865. Not only did he reverse the very first stab at reparations but the few thousand blacks in Florida and South Carolina who actually *did* get the forty acres and a mule had them taken away.

GARY—Well, that's it right there. The government can take property only under the eminent-domain clause. But they didn't deprive the former slaves of their property for any national purpose. This was theft. If anything, the "takings" clause applies.

HITT—Takings?

GARY—Takings is part of the Fifth Amendment: "nor shall private property be taken for public use without just compensation."

SCRUGGS—But you still have the statute of limitations problem. Look, I've been wrestling with this thing. I mean, I love big stuff. We all do. We love to think of elegant solutions to major national social problems, and this is the biggest one there is.

GARY—I think either way we look at it we're going to need help politically, because we don't have the law squarely on our side. We don't have the statute of limitations on our side. We don't have any of that stuff. So it's going to require more than just a simple, single legal theory.

PIRES—In a federal case you've got six years before the statute of limitations runs out.

SWEET—Unless you can prove fraudulent concealment.

SCRUGGS—But there wasn't any fraudulent concealment here.

PIRES—Wait. In recent cases involving World War II slave-labor victims, the statute of limitations doesn't apply if there is a war crime or if there's a crime upon humanity. So I say: If there ever was a crime upon humanity, what white folks did to black people is the worst that ever happened in this country. We would argue that it's not fair to apply the statute of limitations upon us. But Dickie Scruggs is right. It's the main problem. Well, actually there are two. The second is sovereign immunity—you can't sue the government without its consent.

HITT—But to take Willie's breach of contract argument, no former slave could have sued in, say, 1870 and expected to get a hearing. Is the clock not suspended for the century or so it took us to recognize that the courts should be open to African Americans?

SWEET—If not, you have to ask yourself: Is an injustice no longer an injustice so long as you get away with it for a long period of time?

HITT—Well, that gets us to the next logical question. Who is suing here, who are the plaintiffs?

SWEET—No, no, Jack. That's never the first question.

PIRES—The first question is: Who are the *defendants*?

SWEET—That's better.

HITT—Who are the defendants—i.e., who pays?

GARY—That's it.

THE DEFENDANTS

SWEET—I think you have two defendants here. The government and private individuals.

HITT—Private individuals?

SWEET—I mean private companies.

GARY—*And* private individuals. There are huge, wealthy families in the South today that once owned a lot of slaves. You can trace all their wealth to the free labor of black folks. So when you identify the defendants, there are a vast number of individuals.

HITT—Descendants of former slave owners? You're making me nervous.

GARY—Well, like Dennis said, you've got those families that owned slaves, had the plantations, worked the slaves, and because of the sweat and suffering of the slaves those families are major players now in the United States. I think you just track them down. You have to go into North Carolina, South Carolina—

SWEET—Mississippi, Alabama, all over.

HITT—As the descendant of—I'm not making this up—Martin Van Buren Hitt, slave owner, I think I speak for a lot of people when I ask, "How do you do that?" But you're saying it's possible?

GARY—It's possible. Look, nobody ever said it was going to be easy. You know, if you're not ready to get in the trenches and fight—if you're not ready to get knocked down, kicked out of court, and everything else—then it's not the type of issue you want to pursue, because it will be a struggle.

PIRES—Let's talk about the corporate defendants. You have in America, from the 1830s, 1840s, 1850s, the beginning of the greatest accumulation of our wealth. The early oil industry, for example, predates the Civil War. You've got to look back and find out, because many of those companies still exist, under other names. Standard Oil, a.k.a. Esso, a.k.a. Exxon, is still here. They're all still here.

GARY—Aetna Inc., which has been around since 1853, just apologized to blacks for underwriting slave insurance policies. And the *Hartford Courant*, which is still publishing, also apologized for running ads that assisted in the capture of slaves running away, making a break for freedom.

PIRES—You look at a banker like J. P. Morgan and you look at the other trusts, like the railroads. Fleet bank used to be the Providence Bank, whose original wealth dates back to the family of John Brown,[1] whose descendants underwrote Brown University enough to cover up the embarrassment of where he made his money.

HITT—Embarrassment?

PIRES—The Browns made much of their money as slave traders in the late eighteenth century.

GARY—So we've got the federal government.

PIRES—And we've got the states.

GARY—And we've got the private profiteers.

SWEET—Looking good so far.

THE PLAINTIFFS

PIRES—Since we've agreed that our case would extend beyond the end of slavery, it seems to me that the issue of plaintiffs would be best dealt with if you think of the suit as falling into three time brackets. There's slavery up until 1865. Then you have government-approved segregation for, what, seventy or eighty years? And then we have this kind of fuzzy land we lived in until the 1960s, and I don't even know what you call that.

SWEET—Denial.

PIRES—It's easy to go back to the 1940s, the 1950s, because we have precedent—the Japanese internment, the case of the Jews in Germany, we have lots of cases. So if I say, "We're going to go back to the 1940s, which is sixty years ago, and pick up claims," that's an easy case. But to go back to the second time bracket, which is to the 1860s, is a little tougher, because of sovereign immunity and the statute of limitations.

HITT—Well, that's one of Robinson's points in his book. Why not just sue for the more recent cases, which *stem* from slavery? Their proximity in time gives us two things: living victims and a quantifiable economic case. As was mentioned, the federal government sanctioned mortgage covenants that essentially restricted blacks from entering the middle class. That is an economic damage. We can measure it and put a numerical figure on it—a precise amount of money. And then you can sue. You have a class of African Americans who were struggling to join the middle class—very appealing. Your average jury would support it, easily.

PIRES—And even a case as good as that one leads us to another problem. Willie, let's suppose you are the lead lawyer. We have a plaintiffs' meeting and people say, "How far back are we going? Are we going to go back 250 years, 150 years, or 50 years?" Isn't that the question?

GARY—Obviously as a lawyer you want to make your job as easy as you can and also put yourself in the best position to win. And to do that, you want to put your hands on those damages that you can quantify so that you can develop them. You've got evidence still available, and you've got people. The only problem with it, though, is that this kind of lawsuit is going to appear in the court of public opinion, and you're going to need the support of the people.

PIRES—The white people.

GARY—And black people.

PIRES—Black people you got, right?

GARY—No, not necessarily.

PIRES—Black people aren't going to be happy with such a suit?

GARY—What about those people who, for whatever reason, maybe were excluded because you started in the 1940s? Would we pick up everybody? One third, two thirds, of all living blacks? I don't know. If you leave a substantial number of people outside . . . I mean, it's got to be like we are not leaving anyone behind. Because if we pick the best, most recent case, some people are going to complain. Then we've got to be prepared to meet the fight within the fight. And that could be a major problem.

PIRES—What's more important, to tell the real story of American slavery or to win specific damages from 1940 onward?

---

1. John Brown (1736–1803), a white American slave trader and merchant, was a trustee on the original charter for the college that became Brown University, as were his brothers Nicholas (1729–91), also a slave trader, and Moses (1738–1836), a prominent abolitionist; Brown University was named after Nicholas's son, Nicholas Brown Jr. (1769–1841), who was a major benefactor of the institution.

GARY—It's something we'd have to think about. You would have some people saying—

PIRES—you lawyers didn't do your job.

GARY—No, that we're taking the easiest way out. And that we're leaving people behind. No one should be left behind, and if you're going to do it, you should do it right, and it's not fair just for a few and not for all.

SWEET—Let me say this to you: All black folks are not going to be happy. You can go back 200 years, include every damage in the world, and you still will have blacks who are not happy.

PIRES—Why?

SWEET—I mean, Clarence Thomas'll[2] probably write an opinion saying it stigmatizes black folks to bring any action.

PIRES—Why?

SWEET—You have some self-hating black folks. You'll even have some black folks who feel like they don't want to have the issue brought to the forefront.

SCRUGGS—There are so many different parts here that you have to think about. Let's get to this one. Who are your plaintiffs, first of all?

PIRES—Black people.

SCRUGGS—Well, okay. Does that include Tiger Woods? What are his damages? What are Denzel Washington's damages?

GARY—Well, one thing about a class-action lawsuit, you don't have to try to figure out the damages. You can do that on a grid.

HITT—Do you use some kind of damages formula when you're dealing with a large class like this?

GARY—Yes. But look here, we've got more non–Tiger woodses than we have Tiger Woodses. For every Tiger Woods, we have 100,000 non-Tigers.

PIRES—That's true.

SWEET—Well, the thing about it is, in a class action, you have people with different degrees of damage. In my fen-phen case, some people were hurt. But some weren't. And, hell, some people even lost weight. I mean, they were better off, I guess. Some people died, of course.

GARY—But they were all still members of the class. They each experienced the risk.

SWEET—They were all members of the class, and their damages vary along with the degree of impact.

SCRUGGS—I think you'd need to really define the class pretty well, so you keep the Tiger Woodses and people like that out. You can't have people say, "Well, damn, you're going to give all this money to Tiger Woods or Denzel Washington."

SWEET—When you say "the class," you've got to remember that you're still covering a large majority of the black people in the United States of America. Then you have certain representatives who'll be in court with you.

SCRUGGS—Right, but you've got to come up with an appealing plaintiff, just like you would in an individual personal-injury case.

HITT—Who would you want to be representatives?

SWEET—You go and you pick them.

SCRUGGS—You interview a lot of people to pick somebody who's articulate, who's got an appealing personal case, and who is typical of the class that he's going to represent.

HITT—In the Japanese-American case, they brought forward as class representatives only the Japanese Americans who in the 1940s said, "I acquiesced to this because it was my patriotic duty." They did not bring forward the ones who rioted or resisted the draft.

SCRUGGS—Right. You don't want to trot Mike Tyson out there.

HITT—You want to trot out the black guys who fought in World War II and came back to freedom's home only to be told they couldn't sit at a lunch counter.

SCRUGGS—That's right. You carefully pick them.

PIRES—All our famous plaintiffs are selected. Rosa Parks was selected.

SCRUGGS—Yeah, Rosa Parks. Perfect example.

PIRES—They're all selected. I mean, the history of American plaintiffs, Jack, is that they are all selected. Remember Darrow's famous case, the Scopes trial?

2. See p. 934.

Well, the lawyers found Scopes by taking an ad out in the paper.

Damages

Pires—I have this theory about big lawsuits. Their chance of success is not really a matter of the plaintiff or the defendant, nor of legal theory, nor of arguments of liability. It is a matter of the damages to the plaintiff. People react to damages in a visceral way. Take Dickie's tobacco case. Why did people warm to it? Because the average person knows what medical costs are and how much he or she is spending on them. Poor folks have no medical insurance, and middle-class folks are gagging on paying for it. Then someone like Dickie Scruggs comes along and says, "We're going to sue on behalf of the attorneys general because the tobacco people are responsible for a lot of our medical costs, and they're not paying their fair share!" The average person says, "That's right, yeah. Screw them! It's hundreds of billions of dollars. Good! GET them!" No one cares about the technicalities—

Gary—That case also changed our whole attitude toward tobacco.

Pires—In my black farmers' case, people finally said, "Hey, blacks are farming without access to loans? *I've* had trouble getting loans. Give them a hearing!" People relate to it. They react to those damages, and they say, "We're going to pay these black folks for what we did to them." It wasn't liability-based, it was damages-based. Every decade has its case. In the seventies it was IBM. In the eighties it was AT&T. And in the nineties it was tobacco. People reacted to those damages too. "Break up this big monopoly. Yeah, that's wrong." So how do we make our damages appealing?

Scruggs—First, by making it clear that the damages are not just about money. You know that old saying: If you catch a man a fish, you've fed him for a day; if you teach him how to fish, you've fed him for a lifetime. And that's what I'm talking about here. Regardless of whether the defendant is the federal government or a corporate institution that profited from the inhuman treatment of blacks—like German corporations that used Jewish slave labor to make money and are still reaping the benefits—you've got to describe the damages in such a way that makes sense to the public.

Gary—But a lawsuit is also about the money.

Scruggs—I worked with a tribal corporation established under the Alaska Native Claims Settlement Act. And the way the federal government settled similar claims was that it vested the Indian tribes with large sums of money and land and resources. And I'm afraid that it gave too much wealth too soon to people who were not sophisticated enough to do anything with it, and they were victimized.

Pires—They lost it all.

Scruggs—Many did. In one generation.

Pires—People will worry about that.

Scruggs—I'm not saying that blacks are less sophisticated than whites. If you gave money to a bunch of WASP Harvard graduates, they'd blow through it, too. It's human nature.

Sweet—But Dickie, the better part of the solution would be the victory itself, the benefit that comes when it's recognized by this country that reparations are in order.

Scruggs—That's a different goal.

Gary—But there's got to be money, because it goes a long way toward achieving the very goals you're talking about.

Pires—Let me put my question this way: Say the government finally admitted, "You're right. It's the worst injustice in the history of our country. We're the most successful nation on Earth—ever. You win! What do you want for damages?"

Gary—That's the big issue. You want healing, because you can change the thinking of generations unborn, the future of race relations in America.

Hitt—Let's stick with the law.

Gary—No, this is important. It would say that America stepped up to the plate and acknowledged its wrongdoing and reached out to the people and said there is justice for all. It would change things—the way you and I see each other. It would be nice, you know, sometime to sit down together, and you say "I'm sorry" and I say "I'm sorry," and then we could just break bread together. We can go forward, we can do greater things than we ever anticipated.

HITT—But when I was asking a black woman once about this, I said, "You know, maybe in the end the money should all be directed toward the poorest of African Americans, because they are the real heirs of slavery's worst tragedy, the people in the ghettos. And we'll aim that money at them." And she goes, "No, no. I want some of the money." Wouldn't you want just a little bit of that money, Willie? For the symbolism of it, if nothing else? Just for the satisfaction?

GARY—There *is* the money.

SCRUGGS—Money is not the solution. It's setting in place institutions and programs.

GARY—Education.

SCRUGGS—Exactly. It's the difference between giving them the fish and teaching them how to fish.

SWEET—I think a small part of it is going to be the money and the remedies. But the message that will be sent is so important. By having the whole country come forward and say, "This situation has gone on too long," that's a huge step.

GARY—And for every dollar paid the government would get a $100 return.

HITT—Charles Krauthammer, a conservative columnist, is very much in favor of black reparations.

GARY—Really?

HITT—He says that black reparations make sense. We've done something wrong, we need to pay for it, right? He sees it in pure economic terms, as if it were the nation's biggest tort claim in history. They were done wrong. Let's figure out an adequate sum of compensation and pay. Then he adds: And affirmative action doesn't make sense, because we're unfairly putting one person ahead of another person. So let's eliminate all the minority-preference programs, and then let's move forward with the pay schedule.

GARY—It makes a lot of sense. No doubt about it.

PIRES—Wait a minute. What fundamentally separates black folks from white folks? Not money, but education?

SWEET—I say if you're forced to go through a trial, and you're forced to stand up there and talk about damages, the only thing to do is quantitatively ask for damages, for money.

PIRES—You can't think that money will be enough. What do you really want, Dennis? Huh?

SWEET—I'm saying that's all you can ask for.

PIRES—Suppose the judge says, "What do you want me to give you? You want money? You want education? You want access to housing? You want health care?" Dennis, what do you want?

SWEET—Al, Al, Al, hold on, hold on a second. Let me tell you this: If you're in a situation with a jury, then you can only ask for monetary relief. If you have a judge, you can say, "Judge, I need you to create these programs," or other more nuanced solutions.

SCRUGGS—That's right. All a jury can do is award money.

PIRES—What's that going to fix when the only major difference between black folks and white folks today is education.

SWEET—Oh, no, no, no, no. Noooo.

PIRES—It's the level of education. That's the biggest difference.

SCRUGGS—Well, that attitude's pretty rough.

SWEET—It's not just education. It's like, you know, Chris Rock, the comedian, said it best. He has a bit in his act where he's talking to just a normal white guy and says, "Despite all the changes in society, you wouldn't switch places with me, a black man." Then he pauses. "And I'm rich!" The thing is, there are a lot of benefits to being white. A lot.

HITT—But that's the nice thing about arguing about damages. You get specific. What do we need to fix this? Alex is right to ask, If the judge said, "Okay, you win," then what would you ask for?

SCRUGGS—That was the very toughest thing we faced in our tobacco case. We asked ourselves hypothetically: If the chairmen of the boards of these major tobacco companies walked in here today and said, "Okay, we're ready to do a deal," what did we want? It took us a year to come to some general consensus among the attorneys general and some of the public-health advocates as to what we really wanted if we had these guys by the throat. What we found out later was once we got what everybody had said he or she wanted, that wasn't enough.

PIRES—Not enough money, $368 billion?

SCRUGGS—No, no. It wasn't enough money. There wasn't enough money in the world to satisfy some people. And it wouldn't have mattered. The problem is that there are people invested in the fight, okay? I mean, like, some people in Palestine or Northern Ireland don't want the wars to end.

GARY—That's the other fight within the fight. Some black people are not going to want you to file this case and then win.

SCRUGGS—Exactly. This was the biggest mistake we made in tobacco. We did not anticipate the self-interest of some of the health groups in perpetuating their existence and their fund-raising. Because bashing big tobacco was their fundamental way to raise money.

PIRES—Tobacco-Free Kids?

SCRUGGS—Well, they were on board, strangely enough, but some groups like the American Lung Association saw their fund-raising threatened by a tobacco solution.

PIRES—Because when you take away their core issue, people are not happy. If I said to Dennis, "Is education the problem, is that what we're looking for?" and you say, "Let's educate two generations of black folks," people say, "I'm not happy with that. That doesn't do it."

SWEET—I just want you to realize what Chris Rock is saying. It's more complex than one thing.

HITT—If Congress intervened in this case, Dennis, would you be happy—in return for a generous reparations deal—to eliminate all minority-preference programs?

SWEET—There's so little left. Sure.

SCRUGGS—What I have envisioned would be a super-affirmative-action program, much more than traditional affirmative-action programs.

HITT—So you agree with Krauthammer?

SCRUGGS—I really have not read this gentleman's work, and I may be doing it a disservice. But if he's just

offering money in return for eliminating affirmative action, then no.

HITT—No?

SCRUGGS—I think that's tokenism. Reparations doesn't mean just a bunch of cash payments. The word means "to repair." I'm talking about programs. Straight-out payments will create the excuse for future Congresses to say, "We've done it, and what did they do with the money? They went through it; they blew it like other groups have."

SWEET—I agree with you. But you have to be careful about the remedy. It's like the *Ayers* case, a higher-education case in Mississippi in which the judge said, "The black schools are not being funded properly. The white schools are being funded more properly." The judge says, "Okay, we can show liability. Now let's do the remedy." Hell, the remedy kicked us in the butts. You know what they've started saying? "Okay, we're going to close this black school, and we're going to close that black school because of improper funding." See, the remedy can be worse than the claim. If the outcome of this suit were to give each black person $5,000, that would be a disaster. Then we would have eliminated any moral claim to criticizing the causes that have led to widespread African-American poverty, and in return for what?

PIRES—In this case, the money's necessary but the money's not enough.

LEGAL STRATEGY II: MULTIPLE TORTS

SWEET—I get the feeling that everyone wants to start by suing the United States government. But I'd hate to see the federal government be the only defendant in the case.

PIRES—What about the states? We haven't talked about the states.

SWEET—I'll tell you a claim that's ready to go. It's an idea for a state case that would at least serve as a beginning. In fact, the state of Mississippi is a sitting duck on this. I'm talking about the Sovereignty Commission.

GARY—What was it?

SCRUGGS—It was like a Gestapo organization.

SWEET—Back in the fifties and sixties, white leaders got concerned that black people might gain power, like the right to vote. So elected public officials of the state of Mississippi funded this spy organization whose sole purpose was to keep black people down. They spied on anybody who was supposed to be a leader. They participated in the Byron de la Beckwith trial, the man who killed Medgar Evers, by helping people identify jurors. I mean, there is a library full of material documenting their activities.

GARY—And the state financed that activity?

SWEET—The state financed it. You have a secret state agency that was formed whose only purpose was to keep black folks in place.

GARY—Plus it will be a great place to start if we're going to move forward with the overall issue, including the larger suits dating all the way back.

SCRUGGS—This is a state action. You've got a statute of limitations even under the civil rights acts.

SWEET—Yeah, but you have a fraudulent concealment. So legally, the statute of limitations doesn't kick in until after the fraudulent concealment has been exposed. Well, they said that none of the documents and information conducted in here shall be open to the public; it was fraudulently concealed from the public. And they're *still* concealing some of the Sovereignty Commission's work. So the statute would start from the time those documents were first opened to the public, which is right now.

GARY—So you'd pick up thousands and thousands of people just with that lawsuit. Then you could branch out and pick up families in every state in the union.

PIRES—No problem.

GARY—Just recently American General Life and Accident Insurance Company paid out more than $200 million for overcharging black Americans for standard insurance premiums over the last decades. We could file a couple of those types of lawsuits as well.

HITT—Willie, are you suggesting a strategy of filing, say, a web of lawsuits—the Aetnas, Fleet banks, on the one hand, and then state and federal governments too?

GARY—I think we could get class representatives from each state in the union. If you're going to go after the government, you do all in one.

PIRES—If we filed a pile of lawsuits, you could put a judge in a position where the statute of limitations would be hard to invoke. If there were a national audience watching, then what judge is going to want to be the man who went down a laundry list of several dozen incredibly powerful and legitimate claims and had to dismiss them on a technicality? It might make it difficult.

GARY—If you've got a public outcry, a political movement behind it, while we're in the process of getting ready to file, I think that can affect the way a judge is going to rule. It can make him not want to rule, it can make him hold and then perhaps Congress will step in and you can talk settlement. There are so many things you'd have to do at once. But you definitely need a massive public-relations program. You'd want your Denzel Washingtons and your Danny Glovers on board. You get the black athletes in the NBA to stand with you, you get the NFL to stand with you. And then you might go to someone high in the ministry, because you want top-flight black people—Reverend Jesse Jackson, NAACP president Kweisi Mfume, all these people—to stand with you. Then it's a different ball game.

PIRES—Just prominent black people?

GARY—No, black and white people. And the same with the lawyers. It should not just be black lawyers. Look, right now I'm fighting for a white client down in Orlando, a very conservative area. There aren't going to be any black people on the jury. But I've got an old white fellow who's shuffling around with a walking cane! And I'm helping him in and out of the court. The two of us. Let me tell you, it neutralizes a whole lot of shit.

PIRES—So it would be important to have both black and white lawyers up front?

GARY—That's right. If you need a lawyer today, the best thing you could do is have a black lawyer fight for you. And for this case, black and white lawyers fighting together. Look, it was a long, long time before people came on board with Stevie Wonder when he was fighting all those years to make Dr. Martin Luther King's birthday a holiday. But after a while Barbra Streisand and other people came on board, saying it's the right damn thing to do. And all of a sudden the issue changed.

SCRUGGS—You're right, you can't do this case without a public-relations strategy.

GARY—This is the type of case where if you bring certain pressure to bear, if you have the right kind of public support for it, both black and white, then nobody's going to say, "Okay, here's another example of the blacks just trying to get something for nothing."

HITT—When the Jews suing in the slave-labor case were preparing their strategy, that was one of their concerns—that the suit would also promote an old ugly stereotype of Jews and money.

GARY—Same thing here. Blacks trying to get something for nothing. But not if we have a public-relations strategy in place when we begin.

HITT—But correct me if I'm wrong. Overall, are you saying that you file numerous cases at the same time so that one has a fighting chance to change the way people think about this issue? For example, if you file the slavery-era case and maybe Willie's breach of contract and they are dismissed, then does that make, say, the more recent, more economically quantifiable case about mortgage covenants seem that much more possible to win?

SCRUGGS—Exactly. You can make us look downright reasonable by filing some outrageous case over here.

HITT—Yeah. So some of those filings would be to your best case what historians say Malcolm X was for Martin Luther King.[3] Malcolm made King's once dicey demands look mainstream.

SCRUGGS—That's not a bad strategy. That's something you have to think about. In other words, get Pat Buchanan in your race so that you'll look—no matter how conservative you are—very reasonable.

GARY—If we file a mess of cases against the states, isn't it also likely that the state would implead the federal government?

HITT—What does that mean?

SWEET—A person charged with a crime can implead other defendants, saying, in effect, "Hey, if I did it, this guy did it, too. We should share the punishment."

GARY—The states could bring in the federal government and say, "Hey, wait, we're not going to pick up this tab. We were doing what you all gave us the right to do, all this shit started in Washington, D.C."

3. See p. 516 and p. 559.

SWEET—Neat. The states would try and prove the liability of the federal government for you.

PRO BONO!

PIRES—I have a question for you all, and you should be as honest as you can be. When we put together the black farmers' case, I thought the only way I could get black folks to trust a white lawyer was to give them a retainer agreement that said we would work for free, that they get 100 percent of their recovery. So I got 21,000 retainer agreements with black folks that said they'd get 100 percent of their recovery and we wouldn't get any money from them. And we have to petition the court for legal fees. My thinking was that many black folks, who aren't used to lawyers, would more likely trust us if we didn't take their money. So would you all work for free?

SWEET—What?

SCRUGGS—Um.

GARY—Clients sometimes try to negotiate me down to 10 percent on a case, and I say, "Why would you want me working unhappy for you? I'll get you 100,000 bucks. If you got me happy, I'll get you 2 million."

PIRES—Maybe I'm wrong.

HITT—I guess that issue's resolved.

LEGAL STRATEGY III: DUE PROCESS

SCRUGGS—Before we file a pile of lawsuits, I think there's another way besides a damages lawsuit under traditional theory.

PIRES—Let's hear it.

SCRUGGS—How about a Fourteenth and Fifth Amendment lawsuit against the federal government for either failure to enact sufficient laws to ensure due process or for passing laws that perpetuated the injustice?

SWEET—So a due-process lawsuit?

SCRUGGS—Just like in the sixties when Congress ordered white legislatures in Mississippi and other southern states to appropriate money for black schools or for school integration. They said no state or local government that discriminated could receive federal aid. They forced the state legislatures to appropriate money.

PIRES—So you're suing for a denial of due process to black people.

SCRUGGS—It would be a case under the laws and the Constitution of the United States, to the effect that under the imprimatur of the United States of America and the protection of the government, black men and women were brought to this country as slaves, against their will and were kept in bondage for a hundred or more years. Remember, slavery existed far longer under the Stars and Stripes than under the Stars and Bars. There were certain half-assed measures taken after the Civil War to try to enfranchise and rectify the injustice that had been done. But they were very ineffectual and incomplete. After the Reconstruction era, when whites regained power in the South, where most blacks lived, they went back to an era of repression, keeping blacks uneducated—

PIRES—And segregated.

SCRUGGS—and disenfranchised. There were parallel societies, mostly in the South, less so in most northern cities. Nevertheless, because the federal government failed to enforce the Fifth, Thirteenth, Fourteenth, and Fifteenth Amendments, the state governments were allowed to continue with this disparate treatment of black Americans. And the result is that now blacks are disadvantaged in comparison with whites and most other races in America. The federal government should be compelled to rectify that imbalance by passing legislation that accomplishes certain stated goals. Then there would have to be a federal court order that required the Congress of the United States to accomplish these goals within the satisfaction of the Court—pretty much like what the 1964 Civil Rights Act did to southern legislatures. It required the legislatures in those states to appropriate money for programs that helped rectify the imbalance. If the legislature didn't rectify problems, if it didn't act in good faith, then the states lost federal funding. I think that kind of a lawsuit has a far greater public appeal, and a greater legal foundation, than does simply suing for money for a generation of black people. Because

nobody is going to think that will be effective, other than making a few people rich for a short time—not rich, but getting some money in their pockets for a short time. And then the next generation is going to be in the same spot.

SWEET—You know what's nice about this due-process lawsuit? It does away with a lot of the complaints that "we were also done wrong" from the Irish or other minorities precisely because it recognizes the fundamental difference. African Americans were kept down by the force of law, not custom, and then every effort to lift the burden of the law was met with denial of due process. So under this lawsuit, what you're saying is, We're going to give black folks a fair chance to assimilate, just like we gave that opportunity to assimilate to other groups.

SCRUGGS—That's right, that's right.

HITT—We always come back to the technical hurdles. What's your statute of limitations theory?

SCRUGGS—My statute of limitations theory is: continuing constitutional violation. Happens every day. It's like suing your government the same way you sue your doctor for malpractice for not doing his job. The Constitution tells the three branches of government what they're supposed to be doing, what is supposed to be protected. The case law fills that out, records what is supposed to be done. The government is not doing its duty. So, in essence, it's a malpractice case or a *mandamus* case.

SWEET—Governmental malpractice. Nice.

HITT—A what case? *Mandamus?* "We command," right?

SCRUGGS—Right. In other words, we would argue that what they were supposed to do was not a discretionary function of government. You *must* do it. The Constitution says, "You must." You don't have any discretion, you *must* do it. That's where I think the remedy lies. Because you force the Congress of the United States to pass laws—whether monetary funding for programs or the creation of programs—that pass the courts' scrutiny. Just like southern states were forced to do thirty years ago.

HITT—Very interesting rendition. So do to the feds what the feds did to the South.

SCRUGGS—That's right. In that way, you're not couching it as reparations; there's judicial precedent for it: it's been done to all the southern states that were under the Civil Rights Act, okay? I think that's the approach, and we'll have the greatest result in terms of producing, in a few generations, a better society.

HITT—You know, that argument might even have a lot of appeal among southern whites. It kind of sticks it to the federal government, which, after all, won the war only to set 4 million penniless, propertyless, illiterate black men, women, and children adrift in the South. Slavery was evil, but so were the actions of the victors in Washington, D.C., who set in motion the Black Diaspora of 1865 and then walked away from it.

THE META-STRATEGY

GARY—You know, all these theories have something to them. But I don't think we can sit down and figure out *the* way to legally win this case before we file a lawsuit. I think you've got to put together a concept that can get you there, and it's going to be step-by-step.

HITT—We have to file a lawsuit without knowing where we're going?

GARY—We need to get some star power on the legal side, make a strong opening case, and get it going.

SWEET—To Congress.

HITT—Is that where you're ultimately headed? Is the idea to file a case that gathers enough momentum that Congress will step in and settle it?

SCRUGGS—I think so.

GARY—You want to get to a settlement.

SCRUGGS—That's how a lot of these cases go, to the legislature.

PIRES—That's what happened with the Japanese internment case. Congress was so embarrassed by the claims that it passed a reparations-settlement bill. Each aggrieved Japanese American received $20,000.

HITT—But that case was easier, legally, to get started.

PIRES—Actually, harder. There was a Supreme Court decision in 1944 declaring the Japanese internment "constitutional."

HITT—How did they get around that?

PIRES—They got Congress to open an investigation into the facts that the government supplied the Court in order to make that 1944 decision and found that it was full of deception and lies. So the Court decision suddenly was no longer a roadblock to the case.

SWEET—That's what I was saying at the beginning. There's a way in which educating people about history, through this lawsuit, makes it more possible to file and win such a suit.

PIRES—Congress often gets involved in these cases because there are matters of justice that just can't be litigated fairly within the strictures of our common law and our Constitution.

HITT—What I hear you saying is, ultimately, that many class-action suits are just giant goads to get Congress to deal with politics. You are using the elegance of the law to motivate our legislative branch into doing what, arguably, they should be doing anyway.

SCRUGGS—That's right.

PIRES—It's true. We're getting social change from goddamn lawyers. How the hell did that happen?

SCRUGGS—My view of it is that the guys who wrote the Constitution had just thrown off a dictator, a British king who had exploited them as a colony. They had no rights, no democracy to speak of. They were not about to create a system of government that was going to allow for another dictator. So they created a strong separation of powers so that no one person or one group could gang up on another. More freedom, but at the price of governmental inefficiency. This inefficiency has worsened over time to the point that the political branches of government are capable of solving only the most compelling and broad national problems.

PIRES—Like what?

SCRUGGS—War and peace, things like that. And what's happened is that issues like what we're talking about now, big issues that are very important to people, like abortion, like HMOs, you name it, are—

PIRES—Avoided?

SCRUGGS—No, no. They're exploited, by both political parties. So what's happened is that anything that's going to get solved is punted to the court system.

PIRES—I believe that.

SCRUGGS—The courts have become a safety net. Those in charge of the political branches aren't interested in solutions, only in exploiting the issues for fund-raising purposes.

HITT—Perhaps that explains why the makeup of the Supreme Court is, if you think about, the only thing our two presidential candidates deeply differ on.

GARY—Getting this to Congress also solves the statute of limitations problems.

PIRES—And sovereign immunity.

GARY—Congress can do whatever it wants to do in terms of waiving this and that.

PIRES—It can pass any law it wants.

SCRUGGS—Getting a political solution is the cleanest way to get it done. But today's Congress must be forced to act.

PIRES—Congress won't get there until you get there.

HITT—Very Zen.

SWEET—That's why Congress won't pass the Conyers resolution out of committee.

HITT—What's that?

SWEET—Michigan Representative John Conyers Jr. proposed a bill to apologize for slavery. Congress won't even do that.

HITT—Why not?

SWEET—Probably because it also seeks to authorize a congressional study group to look into slavery.

HITT—A study group?

SWEET—You have to remember: The last congressional study group like this was the one looking into the *Korematsu* decision. It exposed all the injustices underlying the Supreme Court decision permitting the Japanese internment. By the time the study group finished its work, it was clear that a court case was possible. Congress won't apologize or allow the study group, because it's afraid of precisely this law suit—that the lawyers in this *Harper's* forum might reconvene, and not just to chat.

PIRES—And maybe file a complaint before a court. You know, it all gets back to the lack of understanding by the people you mentioned at the beginning, Jack. The people who say, "How could you possibly sue for slavery?" True, you've got all these technical legal problems—the statute of limitations, sovereign immunity, class-certification problems, defining the damages, and the rest. But you have to remember that the judiciary is the only branch of our government that has nothing to do. It sits there, waiting. The legislature writes laws, and the executive carries them out. But our judges sit and wait for us to come with a complaint, which is a kind of prayer. It says, "Judge, I have this story to tell. It's a story of an injustice. It's a new story—a new way of understanding an old injustice. And I ask you today to hear this case, to listen to my story." Sometimes they do. Sometimes, if you play it right, they hear your prayer.

From *Harper's Magazine*, November 2000, pp. 37–51.

ADOLPH L. REED JR.
The Case against Reparations [2000]

The notion that white America, however defined, owes reparations to black Americans for slavery and its legacy has been around for some time. Until recently, its most dramatic eruption into public life was in 1969, when James Forman, the former chairman of the Student Nonviolent Coordinating Committee (SNCC), led a protest at New York's liberal Riverside Church and presented a "Black Manifesto" that demanded, among other things, $500 million in reparations to black Americans from white churches and synagogues. The idea lingered on the periphery of the public agenda for a few years. In 1972, Jesse Jackson's Operation PUSH and the National Economic Association, a black economists' group, attempted to reintroduce it around the Presidential election in conjunction with a demand for a $900 million "freedom budget."

For the next two decades, the idea of organizing to demand reparations circulated mainly within politically marginal, nationalist circles. It did not gain much traction even among black activists.

During the last half-dozen years or so, however, the issue has been threatening to come in from the margins. Partly stimulated by the successful pursuit of compensation for Japanese Americans who were interned by the U.S. government during World War II and for victims of Nazi slave labor, talk of a movement to demand reparations for black Americans has been spreading.

I've watched this with curiosity and bemusement. I imagined that the reparations talk would evaporate because it seemed so clearly a political dead end. No such luck. Publication of *The Debt: What America Owes to Blacks* (E.P. Dutton, 2000) by Randall Robinson, the respected president of TransAfrica, the organization that played a central role in the U.S. movement against apartheid in South Africa, seems to have propelled the reparations issue into the spotlight. Now it seems to be everywhere—in special features on network television, in mainstream publications like *Harper's* and *The New York Times,* and all over the black-oriented media.

How has this happened? And what is its significance? To put it more provocatively, how does a project that seems so obviously a nonstarter in American politics come to capture so much of the public imagination? After all, support for affirmative action has eroded significantly, and reparations raises the ante on compensatory policy exponentially. Why has this idea attained currency now?

Answering these questions requires understanding that the call for reparations blends material, symbolic, and psychological components.

The material component is the most obvious, since the call for reparations responds to the actual harm inflicted on blacks during and after slavery. This component includes direct legacies, such as the federal government's failure to fulfill the promise of Emancipation by adopting the Radical Republican proposals during Reconstruction that would have expropriated the plantations in the South and divided them among the freed people, thus establishing a black yeomanry of independent stakeholders. It also includes the federal government's further capitulation to the former slaveholders by accepting their disenfranchisement of black voters later in the nineteenth and early twentieth centuries. As a result, black citizens were removed from effective participation in public life. What followed was the imposition of the white supremacist regime of official political and economic apartheid that reigned in the South for the first two-thirds of the twentieth century.

The indirect material legacy of slavery includes such explicitly discriminatory practices as the Federal Housing Administration's enforcement of racially exclusionary "restrictive covenants" in its lending policies officially until 1948 and unofficially for some years thereafter. This practice severely disadvantaged black people's pursuit of home ownership, the principal form of capital accumulation for most Americans.

The effects of unequal education, labor market discrimination, and publicly initiated and supported ghettoization are further indirect material legacies of slavery. We could also include the effects of New Deal compromises with Southern Democrats—largely racially inspired—that excluded most black workers from initial coverage under Social Security and agricultural assistance.

That blacks have been systematically disadvantaged as a result of slavery and its aftermath there can be no doubt. That is the strength of the material case for reparations.

The symbolic component of the reparations campaign seems to center on public acknowledgment of the injustices inflicted on black people historically in this country. On the one hand, this could promote public education about the real history of the United States, although that is a project that does not require the rhetoric of reparations. On the other hand, it fits the Clintonoid tenor of sappy public apologies and maudlin psychobabble about collective pain and healing.

Robinson, for his part, seems fixated on pursuing racial parity in monuments and statuary—perhaps a function of his long years in Washington, D.C., and his growing up in Richmond, Virginia, two cities in which the politics of public monuments loom larger than elsewhere. (And how much would you like to bet that that's as far as the restitution would go? Elites will always prefer symbolic gestures to material ones: "Let's see, should we give them college tuition and affordable housing or a heartfelt apology and a few monuments and plaques? Hmmm, which will it be, which will it be?")

The psychological component, though, is most revealing of the dubious politics that undergirds this movement. The demand for reparations is held to be important as a means of raising consciousness among black people, whether or not it can be won. But consciousness of what? Among more populist or radical adherents, this view rests on the premise—a vestige of the nationalist/anti-imperialist radicalism that evolved from Black Power—that mobilizing black people to fight for a better world requires first rectifying their understanding of who they are and where they come from in order to build on the principle of racial solidarity. Of course, cultivation of a general understanding of history is useful, perhaps necessary, for developing and sustaining an insurgent politics, and it's a good thing in its own right. However, it's more than questionable that people must—or even will—mobilize around earlier generations' grievances to pursue current objectives.

The deeper appeal of reparations talk for its proponents is to create or stress a sense of racial peoplehood as the primary basis for political identity. This movement's psychological project is grounded on two beliefs: first, that rank-and-file black people suffer from an improper or defective sense of identity, and second, that an important task of political action is to restore or correct racial consciousness that the legacy of slavery is supposed to have distorted or destroyed.

Among some strains of cultural nationalists, this view unabashedly reproduces the old "damage thesis," which was criticized by historian Daryl Michael Scott in his book *Contempt and Pity: Social Policy and the Image of the Damaged Black Psyche, 1880–1996* (University of North Carolina, 1997). According to this thesis, slavery and its aftermath left black Americans without cultural moorings and therefore especially vulnerable to various social pathologies. This notion has been the foundation of academic and journalistic slanders of black poor and working people. It was famously perpetrated by Daniel Patrick Moynihan in his scurrilous 1965 report, "The Negro Family: A Case for National Action," and it underlies contemporary notions of a self-destructive black urban underclass.

Randall Robinson's argument for pursuit of reparations hinges on this view of the black American population—lucky petit bourgeois people like himself excepted, of course—as defective and in need of moral and psychological repair. The idea resonates with middle class noblesse oblige and a commitment to a racial

politics that ensconces a particular guiding role for upper class blacks. Those are, after all, the people who can conduct the finely calibrated analyses that determine what forms and magnitude just compensation should take; they are the people who would stand to administer whatever compromise palliatives are likely to ensue from this activity.

But the question of compensation opens a plethora of technical problems. Should payments go to individuals or to some presumably representative corporate entity? If the former, who qualifies as a recipient? Would descendants of people who had been enslaved elsewhere (for instance, Brazil or the Caribbean) be eligible? And what of those no longer legally black people with slave ancestors? As a friend of mine has suggested, these issues could produce a lively trade for genealogists, DNA testers, and other such quacks, and already some seem to be rising to the opportunity. These ambiguities, moreover, expose the faultiness of comparisons to payments to victims of Japanese internment and Nazi slave labor camps, who were identifiable individuals whose experience of the ultimate injustice was direct.

If the recipient is to be some corporate entity, as Robinson and others suggest, how can its representativeness and accountability be determined? If the body is a development fund, who would control it and how would the decision be made? Robinson has suggested that philanthropic agencies be the grantees, but which ones and to whom would they be accountable? This talk—as is standard in contemporary black politics—presumes a coherent, knowable black agenda that can be determined outside of democratic, participatory processes among those in whose names decisions are to be made and resources allocated.

What strikes me as most incomprehensible about the reparations movement is its complete disregard for the simplest, most mundanely pragmatic question about any political mobilization: How can we imagine building a political force that would enable us to prevail on this issue?

But the question ultimately does not arise because reparations talk is rooted in a different kind of politics, a politics of elite-brokerage and entreaty to the ruling class and its official conscience, the philanthropic foundations, for racial side-payments. "Until America's white ruling class accepts the fact that the book never closes on massive unredressed social wrongs, America can have no future as one people," Robinson writes. Lest there be any doubt about the limited social vision that makes such an entreaty plausible, he brushes away the deepest foundations of American inequality: "Lamentably, there will always be poverty." His beef is that black Americans are statistically overrepresented at the bottom. This is a protest politics that depends on the good will of those who hold power. By definition, it is not equipped to challenge existing relations of power and distribution other than marginally, with token gestures.

There's a more insidious dynamic at work in this politics as well, which helps us understand why the reparations idea suddenly has spread so widely through mainstream political discourse. We are in one of those rare moments in American history—like the 1880s and 1890s and the Great Depression—when common circumstances of economic and social insecurity have strengthened the potential for building broad solidarity across race, gender, and other identities around shared concerns of daily life. These are concerns that only the minority of comfortable and well-off can dismiss in favor of monuments and apologies and a politics of psychobabble, concerns like access to quality health care, the right to a decent and dignified livelihood, affordable housing, quality education for all. They can be pursued effectively only by struggling to unite a wide section of the American population that is denied those essential social benefits or lives in fear of losing them. Isn't it interesting that at such a moment the corporate-dominated, opinion-shaping media discover and project a demand for racially defined reparations that cuts precisely against building such solidarity?

I know that many activists who have taken up the cause of reparations otherwise hold a politics quite at odds with the limitations that I've described here. To some extent, I suspect their involvement stems from an old reflex of attempting to locate a progressive kernel in the nationalist sensibility. It certainly is an expression of a generally admirable commitment to go where people seem to be moving.

But we must ask: Where can this motion go?

From *The Progressive*, December 2000, pp. 15–17.

KEY DEBATE ⁓ *The Politics of Art*

HENRY LOUIS GATES, JR. ET AL.
The Black Person in Art: How Should S/He Be Portrayed? [1987]

In 1987, Henry Louis Gates, Jr. asked thirteen writers and critics to revisit W. E. B. Du Bois's 1926 questionnaire (p. 345) about the representation of black people in the arts. Seven of the responses are reprinted here. While exploring the idea of artistic freedom, Du Bois's questions highlight issues of class and focus on how white people view black people. A key underlying idea is how the popularity of writings about "sordid, foolish and criminal" black characters can perpetuate stereotypes about African Americans as a group, eclipsing the realities of educated and accomplished African Americans.

The 1926 questionnaire and responses were written in the context of the success of *Porgy,* a 1925 novel by the white American author DuBose Heyward, and the growing market for art featuring "exotic" black characters. The 1926 respondents primarily explored the relationship between artistic freedom and racial characterizations. In contrast, the 1987 debate focuses more on gender characterizations and their relationship to artistic freedom. Many of the 1987 respondents refer to Alice Walker's *The Color Purple* (1982). *The Color Purple* and its 1985 film adaptation spurred widespread debate about the representation of black people, particularly in terms of gender and sexuality. Some people criticized the negative portrayal of male characters, while others, such as the television host Tony Brown, focused their criticism on the lesbian relationship between Shug and Celie. Some critics countered by critiquing the negative representation of women in works by black men, particularly the writing of Ishmael Reed. Central to these criticisms are two ideas: that portraying certain types of African American characters may have a detrimental effect on the way African Americans are viewed and treated by others, and that artists have a responsibility to shape their art to avoid such negative consequences.

Whereas the respondents to Du Bois's 1926 questionnaire stressed the need for artistic freedom and diversity, most of the respondents in 1987 say that artists need only "tell the truth," to quote Barbara Smith. At the same time, many respondents underscore that different people see the truth differently: some see truth in works that others see as incomplete, simplistic, or overly personal. Even when supporting the right of artists to tell their own subjective truth, a number of the 1987 respondents point out that the funding and the promotion of certain works and not others are driven by underlying political, sociological, and financial forces. Some focus on the extent to which the interests of white people shape critical reception of art about black people; Ishmael Reed, for example, characterizes the film *The Color Purple* as propaganda against black men produced and directed by white men. Others ask whether white opinions should even be a factor in discussions of black art. Another question is what effect, if any, representations of black people in literature have on the thoughts and actions of readers. Do artistic representations have virtually no impact on long-held perceptions, as Richard Long claims, or do they have "life-and-death" consequences, as Sandra E. Drake maintains?

The 1987 responses reflect the impact of social change since 1926, but Du Bois's 1926 questions continue to resonate. The fact that these questions remain relevant decades after they were first asked illuminates a key structural characteristic of the history of African American debates. As Drake writes, "The forms and articulations of the Afro-American cultural dilemma vary greatly by epoch, though the basic questions tend to recur." This reexamination of Du Bois's questions after sixty years underscores how the same debates recur throughout African American history, even while the answers shift to reflect their own time and context.

From *Black American Literature Forum* 21, 1–2 (Spring–Summer, 1987), pp. 3–24, and 21, 3 (Autumn, 1987), pp. 324–30.

In a February 1926 *Crisis* "Opinion" column entitled "A Questionnaire," W. E. B. Du Bois posed seven questions in an attempt to explore readers' feelings about the state of black portraiture in American culture:

1. When the artist, black or white, portrays Negro characters is he under any obligations or limitations as to the sort of character he will portray?
2. Can any author be criticized for painting the worst or the best characters of a group?
3. Can publishers be criticized for refusing to handle novels that portray Negroes of education and accomplishment, on the ground that these characters are no different from white folk and therefore not interesting?
4. What are Negroes to do when they are continually painted at their worst and judged by the public as they are painted?
5. Does the situation of the educated Negro in America with its pathos, humiliation, and tragedy call for artistic treatment at least as sincere and sympathetic as "Porgy" received?
6. Is not the continual portrayal of the sordid, foolish, and criminal among Negroes convincing the world that this and this alone is really and essentially Negroid, and preventing white artists from knowing any other types and preventing black artists from daring to paint them?
7. Is there not a real danger that young colored writers will be tempted to follow the popular trend in portraying Negro character in the underworld rather than seeking to paint the truth about themselves and their own social class?

Henry Louis Gates felt that, sixty years later, Du Bois' questions were still timely and that it would be worthwhile to reconsider both the questions and the issues which evolve from them—and, perhaps, to generate some new questions.[1]

[* * *]

BARBARA SMITH[2] RESPONDS

1. The only "obligation" any writer has when portraying characters, developing a plot, and telling a story is the obligation to tell the truth. People's truths differ, however, according to what they have experienced. A writer's social, political, and economic status; her or his sexual, racial, and national identity; and the historical period in which she or he writes all contribute to the writer's specific version of the truth.

2. Authors can be criticized for absolutely anything they write, but that should not stop them from writing. There is a difference between criticism and vicious personal attack, however, and the latter can certainly inhibit the artist's capacity to create.

   The point here is whether these "worst" or "best" characters are realistically drawn. Are they shaped with enough depth and dimension so that they are recognizable and complex, neither all bad nor all good, neither entirely worst nor best? Mr. —— in Alice Walker's *The Color Purple* is an example of a "bad" character who, in the course of the novel, is transformed into a decent person. Although she is the novel's heroine, Celie is not perfect, but grows into a fuller human being as the work progresses, despite the abuse and violence to which she is subjected.

3. Sixty years after Du Bois raised his questions, white publishers, especially the "major" houses that are in fact branches of multinational corporations, can still be criticized for not publishing work by Black authors, period, whatever the subject matter or educational level of the characters. As African Americans we know, of course, that being educated does not make us identical to white people or make us exempt from racism and racial violence. No matter what Black people do that may be similar to what white people do, such as getting an education or raising children, or coping with a serious illness, our political status, historical experience, and cultural practice render our situation in North

---

1. White American editor, university administrator, professor and writer Joe Weixlmann (b. 1946) wrote this introduction to the debate; from 1976 to 2004, Weixlmann served as editor of the quarterly journal *African American Review* (formerly called first *Negro American Literature Forum* and then *Black American Literature and Culture*), receiving the 2005 Distinguished Editor Award from the Conference of Editors and Learned Journals.
2. See p. 723; *BALF* includes the following note with Smith's commentary: "Barbara Smith is a founder of the Kitchen Table: Women of Color Press, the editor of *Home Girls: A Black Feminist Anthology* (1983), and co-editor of *All the Women Are White, All the Blacks Are Men, But Some of Us Are Brave: Black Women's Studies* (1982)."

America different from that of white people and infinitely "interesting."

4. There is a great deal of difference between white racists portraying us negatively and inaccurately and Black women writers accurately portraying the existence of sexual oppression within the Black community. In the first case hostile outsiders are distorting an experience they know little or nothing about. In the second, Black women are courageously revealing the sometimes annihilating and always negative effects of sexual oppression, based upon our direct experiences of it.

5. The situation of educated black people calls for serious artistic treatment, but no more serious than that of Black people from other class backgrounds. Since Du Bois raised his questions some Black authors have created the kinds of characters he felt were missing from Black literature. What concerns me during this era is that being an educated Black person often means being a Black person with little or no racial consciousness whose major preoccupation is with making money and acquiring things. Unless it is a pointed satire, we do not particularly need novels about Buppies.

6. ——

7. I do not see a current trend in Black literature of portraying underworld characters, which I take to mean criminal or unethical types. To portray the *segment* of the Black male population that practices sexual oppression and in some cases sexual violence is not to choose underworld themes but to expose a grievous and all too common situation of inequality and degradation that must be eradicated in order for the entire race to survive. Likewise, to portray Black lesbian and gay male characters positively is not to choose underworld themes but instead to reflect a commitment to portray truthfully a significant component (at least ten percent) of the African American community.

I found it difficult to answer Du Bois' questions in some cases because they are concerned with a situation quite different from the current polarization caused by African American women writers' having the "temerity" to write truthfully about our lives. Du Bois was upset because white racists continued to produce vicious stereotypes about us in the guise of creating literature. He was also disturbed when some younger black writers chose to depict the entire range of Black life and not to focus exclusively upon "the talented tenth."

Some Black men are currently upset because Black women are revealing how we and our mothers, aunts, sisters, and great-great grandmothers have always seen and experienced the world as the objects of both sexual and racial oppression. The ways in which we have experienced our lives may come as news to some of our brothers who have not experienced the same thing. The fact that they have not experienced sexual oppression does not mean, however, that it never happened or that Black women writers are lying about its existence in the Black community and in the society at large. Unlike white racists our motivation in revealing what we have experienced is not to downgrade the image of the race, but simply to tell the truth, and by doing so to bring enlightenment and much needed positive change, especially in relationships between Black women and men.

It is infuriating that some Black women writers are accused of being traitors to the race because we refuse to be silent any longer about the conditions that we have been expected to accept from time out of mind as woman's inevitable lot. It is even more infuriating that superb writers such as Alice Walker and Toni Morrison are accused of exaggeration and distortion when they choose to write about the archetypal female experiences of incest, rape, and battering, among numerous other themes.

I have read absolutely nothing in the creative writing of Black women that even remotely rivals the actual horrors of sexual violence that all kinds of women, whatever their race, are suffering at this very moment all over the globe. Emergency rooms, battered women's shelters, mental hospitals, and graveyards are full of real women, too many of whom are Black, who usually have been brutalized by the men who are closest to them, who are also Black. I would like to organize a tour of these facilities for those Black male literary critics and writers who accuse us of exaggerating and lying. Perhaps after they had traveled to Chicago, and Macon, and Los Angeles, and Long Island, and Harlem, and Kansas City, and Greensboro, and Cleveland, and witnessed the Black three-year-old girl lying in intensive care after being raped and beaten, and the Black twenty-year-old college student stabbed and bludgeoned beyond recognition lying in the morgue, and the Black forty-one-year-old mother blinded in one eye by her battering husband, and the Black seventy-seven-year-old woman raped and murdered in her ghetto apartment on the pretext of robbery, then they might begin to say: "I didn't know. This has got to stop. Somebody has to talk and write about this so it will stop. I will write about it too."

I would like to add five questions to the ones Du Bois asked:

1. Why should Black women writers be expected or forced to lie about our experiences and concerns in order to make certain Black male writers and critics feel comfortable with what we write?

2. Why should Black women writers be expected to have a perspective indistinguishable from that of Black men in their writing?

3. Why should the brief renaissance of Black women's literature during this decade be viewed as a conspiracy against Black male writers, while the centuries-long, male-dominated focus of African American literature has never been viewed as a conspiracy against Black women writers?

4. When will all Black people be as concerned about sexual violence and sexual oppression visited upon more than half of us from inside the race as we are about racial violence and racial oppression visited upon us from outside?

5. When will all Black people, writers and critics included, realize that sexual oppression, class oppression, and homophobia, just like racism, do not serve us or our liberation, but instead serve the dangerous agendas of our enemies?

"Steven[3] Spielberg Plays Howard Beach" by Ishmael Reed[4]

An audience of white and Asian feminists attending a rape awareness workshop held in Berkeley last October said that they imagined the "stereotypical" rapist as Black, until they were informed by Sallie Werson, a women's center counselor, that 75 to 80 percent of rapists are white.

Like the black bear and the North American wolf, the Black male in the United States has been the subject of dangerous myths which often, as in the case of the bear and the wolf, lead people to shoot first and ask questions later. No Black man, whatever his class, is exempt from superstitions about Black men, a situation which causes anxiety and which probably accounts for the fact that Black men suffer disproportionately from cancer, strokes, heart attacks, and other stress-related illnesses, including suicide and murder, which are now being viewed in the same manner as disease epidemics.

My disagreement with some feminists and womanists is that they have, out of ignorance or by design, promoted such myths in the media, a situation which adds to the problems that Black men face in everyday life.

In the film *The Color Purple*, directed and produced by white males, all of the myths that have been directed at Black men since the Europeans entered Africa are joined. In this film, Black men commit heinous crimes against women and children, and though defenders of Walker's book, upon which the movie was based, argue that these creations were merely one woman's story, critics in the media have used both the book and the movie as excuses to indict all Black men. This is not Ms. Walker's fault; however some of her public statements, such as her description of Black men as "evil," gleefully printed in the magazine section of the neoconservative *New York Times*, haven't helped.

Gloria Steinem, media-appointed high priest person of American feminism, set the tone for the current group libel campaign against Black men when she said, in the 2 June 1982 issue of *Ms.*, that the characterizations of Black men in Ms. Walker's book represented "truth-telling." Since then this "truth-telling" line has been picked up by other feminists, womanists, and their male allies: bimps and wimps. Most recently, in an interview with a deferential San Francisco feminist,

3. The names misspelled in Reed's *BALF* article have been corrected here, including "Stephen" Spielberg, "Deidre" English, "Cherrie" Moraga, Gloria "Anzaldus" and "Bernard" Goetz.
4. *BALF* includes the following note with the commentary by Reed (b. 1938): "Ishmael Reed is the author and editor of more than a dozen books, the most recent being his novel *Reckless Eyeballing* (1986). Reed's remarks originally appeared in the New York *Amsterdam News* in January and February of this year and are reprinted, in a slightly amended form...."

Alice Walker said that she was trying to tell the truth (*San Francisco Bay Guardian* 17 Sept. 1986).

Television critics Siskel and Ebert, when reviewing the movie, said that it was about offenses that Black men have committed against Black women. (Would they impute the crime against women by Jason, the hero of the *Friday the 13th* fury, or by Freddy, in the *Nightmare on Elm Street* series, to all white men?) They described Ms. Walker as a feminist, even though Ms. Walker calls herself a womanist so as to separate herself and her followers from white feminists like "feminist scholar" Deirdre English and Gloria Steinem, who publish her articles. Apparently Siskel and Ebert received some irate mail, because the week following their review, they hit Black men again, this time for their inability to take criticism, which, in my opinion, supports charges against the media made by its critics: Once you get hit by the imperial media, whether you're an individual or a group, it's very difficult, if not impossible, to set the record straight.

When an interviewer asked me on *The Today Show* in late March of 1986 about the movie *The Color Purple*, I said that my primary criticism dealt with how "critics in the media were using the behavior of the Black male characters to indict all Black men." I apparently offended some viewers by going on to compare the movie's images of Black men with those of Jewish males as child molesters, muggers, and rapists of Aryan females. This remark was based upon research of German newspapers and films, used in my novel *Reckless Eyeballing*, the publication of which was the ostensible reason for my appearing on *The Today Show*, though the novel was never mentioned.

As soon as the novel *Reckless Eyeballing* was published, it became, as one reviewer said, "a literary tornado." I was invited to appear on *Tony Brown's Journal*. In order to balance the show, Tony Brown's staff invited some prominent Black feminists and womanists, including Michele Wallace,[5] to appear. All of them declined. I suggested Barbara Smith, whose anthologies include *Home Girls* and *All the Women Are White, All the Blacks Are Men, But Some of Us Are Brave*.

Although a few of our exchanges were testy, Ms. Smith, one of the ablest proponents of the Black femi-

nist point of view, and I ended the show on friendly terms and, in April, greeted each other cordially at Storyville, in New Orleans. The famous jazz club had been rented by the Before Columbus Foundation, a multi-cultural organization based in California, for presentation of the American Book Awards. Ms. Smith accepted an award for *This Bridge Called My Back*, edited by Cherríe Moraga and Gloria Anzaldúa,[6] a book that shows my disagreements with feminists to be mild in comparison to those between white feminists and Black feminists.

Some of Ms. Smith's "sisters" were not so friendly as Ms. Smith. A few responded to the exchange between Ms. Smith and me by suggesting that I represented Black male writers who were envious of Black feminist writers. Others dismissed me with feminist rhetoric in which *misogynist* was the frequent buzzword.

A radical Chicago newspaper, which has apparently decided that Black lesbian feminists constitute the revolutionary vanguard, dismissed my criticisms of *The Color Purple* as those of a "bohemian intellectual." One writer, in the *Gay Community News,* said that the issues Ms. Smith and I discussed shouldn't be debated at all, a stance which reinforced an opinion that I formed many years ago in New York's East Village, that, while most Afro-Americans support democratic values, many Black intellectuals yearn for the kind of one-party police states, operating in the rest of the world, where debate is stifled.

When I appeared as a member of a panel on the *Essence* television show in July, a new attack was raised by Max Robinson, the moderator: I was doing the same thing that I was accusing the Black feminists of doing. This line was picked up by Richard Wesley, writing in the August issue of Gloria Steinem's *Ms.* magazine. (As an example of how *Ms.* magazine feminists treat even the Black men who support their arguments, the editors at *Ms.* diminished the thrust of Mr. Wesley's article, which sought to disassociate Ms. Walker from the film *The Color Purple*, by attaching a footnote to the piece which revealed that Ms. Walker was the movie's consultant from the commencement of photography to the final cut.)

5. See p. 817.
6. Chicana writers and critics Moraga (b. 1952) and Anzaldúa (1942–2004).

Though Mr. Wesley, author of the screenplay of Richard Wright's *Native Son,* suggested that there might be a "Literary Tribunal" for my "literary transgressions," neither Mr. Wesley nor Mr. Robinson could point to a single passage in my books in which a Black woman rapes, pimps, or sells her children, nor will they find in my nonfictional writings a passage which says that such behavior is typical of Black women.

The feminists who prompted Mr. Robinson and Mr. Wesley are sore with me because I included a Mammy in my novel *Flight to Canada* (1976). They claim that such a character did not exist, when Mammies appeared wherever colonialists settled. In the South, Black women took care of white children; in Ireland, Irishwomen nurtured Anglo children; in Hawaii, Hawaiian women looked after the invader's children. These feminists, like zealots and ideologues everywhere, desire to rearrange history so that it includes only the parts supporting their feminist arguments, and leave out the parts that don't.

They've been on my case since my 1974 novel *The Last Days of Louisiana Red,* because it includes a feminist radical whose speeches they disapprove of. They complain about Tremonisha Smarts, of *Reckless Eyeballing,* because toward the end of the novel she leaves New York for California to have babies and to "write, write, write," which isn't inconsistent with the announced goal of a new generation of feminists: to have it all, a career and a family.

Some objected to the character's having children at all, because they are soured on reproduction. A group of storm trooper California feminists booed poet Quincy Troupe because he read a poem about his child. One gains the impression that many feminists and womanists would like to do away with men altogether and turn the world into a sort of postgraduate seminar on feminism.

Though the *Essence* panel covered a number of issues over a two-hour period, the program was edited so that it came across as a tribute to Alice Walker, with me as some sort of crank, or cad.

Panelist Amiri Baraka praised Steven Spielberg, whose racism has been cited by Asian-American organizations and most recently by an Irish-American writer, Jack Foley, who, writing in the December 21 issue of *The San Jose Mercury,* complained about the images of Irish-Americans in Spielberg's *An American Tail.* Mr. Baraka[7] said that the right wing was offended by the film because the film exposed racism, which must come as news to Ronald and Nancy Reagan, who told a pre–Academy Awards show in 1986 that they enjoyed the film. Ms. Bush, the Vice-President's wife, attended a New York reception for the film; last I heard, the Reagans and the Bushes belonged to the political right wing.

On October 21, in the course of a hostile review of William Demby's *Love Story Black,* a novel that Steve Cannon and I published in 1978, and sold to E. P. Dutton in 1985, I was subjected to what might be called a drive-by literary shooting, when Greg Tate, writing in the *Village Voice,* remarked that I had "bitchy" attitudes toward "aggressive Black women."

I have noticed that, in recent years, the *Voice* has printed lengthy articles regarding Black male chauvinism, but I have never seen an article about the chauvinism of Italian-American, Irish-American, or Jewish-American males, many of whom, according to the 6 December 1982 *New York Times,* engage in wife beating. Nor have I ever seen an article about women beating and abusing other women, which, according to a book entitled *Naming the Violence: Speaking Out about Lesbian Battering,* edited by Kerry Lobel, is a big problem.

Ms. magazine has also been relentless in its denouncement of Black males, providing Alice Walker with the space to answer her critics in every issue, so it seems.

If the *Voice* and *Ms.* magazine are so concerned with the condition of Black women, then why aren't any employed in the top staff or corporate positions? What are the attitudes of both publications toward "aggressive Black women"? Rather than respond to Mr. Tate by engaging in the kind of blood letting that occurs in the *Village Voice* letters column, on November 1, 1986, I sent out a press release challenging the *Voice* and *Ms.* to express their concerns for "aggressive Black women" by hiring some of them for top positions on both publications. I added that, between

I. Reed Books and *Quilt* anthology, as well as a number of other anthologies I've published since 1972, I've published more Black women than both the *Voice* and *Ms.* combined. (I was the first to publish the fiction of a brilliant young writer named Michele Wallace.) Black women occupy, or have occupied, key positions in the Before Columbus Foundation, which I founded in 1976, and in There City Cinema, a foundation that I launched in 1985 to bring multi-cultural films to Oakland, California, for exhibit at a new cinema being built for the foundation by the City of Oakland.

By contrast the board of directors of the *Voice* are male, as are the publisher and the owner, a man who supports Mayor Koch, whose inflammatory racist rhetoric is partially responsible for the climate of racist terror that is now afflicting New York Blacks. The top executive positions at *Ms.* as well as the important staff positions belong to white feminists.

I also said in the press release that the Black Women writers I publish write about a variety of subjects and are not just used to midwife the ideas of *Village Voice* feminists, who seem to be obsessed with Black chauvinism. Gloria Steinem is not alone. It has been my experience that the most passionate defenders of the images of Black males depicted in books and motion pictures like *The Color Purple,* and their clones, are white feminists.

I responded to a feminist scholar who asked me a belligerent question after I'd read a paper at the English Institute at Harvard last year by asking her why white feminists were so concerned about Black male chauvinism yet seldom criticize the men of their own ethnic groups? She couldn't answer the question. Steven Spielberg said that *The Color Purple,* known in the book trade as a "bodice ripper," attracted a mostly white feminist audience, and with the movie he wanted to expand the audience.

I sent the copy of the press release to Black writers at the *Voice,* whose brilliant prose is the main reason that I buy the newspaper. I also sent a copy to M. Mark, the feminist who edits the *Voice's* book review.

On November 19, Black newspapers, including the *California Sun Reporter,* printed my release. I sent copies of the article to the same *Voice* staff members.

Newsweek, December 1, 1986, carried an article on Blacks in journalism which included a passage that made a similar criticism of the *Village Voice,* which it described as a bastion of New York liberalism, at which only 1 of 16 editors and 1 of 19 staff writers are Black. (*Newsweek* was wrong about there being a Black senior editor at the *Voice*; there is none.)

On December 9, 1986, the head "Ishmael Reed's Female Troubles," introducing a "book review" written by Michele Wallace, appeared on the cover of the *Village Voice.* I think that the article was designed to make me feel bad, because it contained a number of unfriendly remarks, many of them erroneous, about my writings, about my career, and about me. I found it odd that Ms. Wallace, who has expressed her disdain for "patriarchy" in article after article, used the critical tools based upon the ideas of one of the most notorious and misogynistic of patriarchs, Sigmund Freud, to discuss my "perverse misogyny." Here was a man who concealed the fact that his friends were seducing their daughters (certainly a film project for Steven Spielberg). Also, for someone attempting to explain my ideas about "NeoHooDooism" to the *Voice's* readership, Ms. Wallace spends a lot of time "psychoanalyzing" the image of the serpent in my novel *Reckless Eyeballing* without so much as reference to the fact that the serpent is at the heart of Vodun, neo-African religion, upon which "NeoHooDooism" is based.

It seems that womanists who, among them, probably have over 100 years of graduate school, never question the theories pushed by the white male patriarchy. Maybe that's the reason that Ms. Wallace writes that womanists "leave the theorizing to others." I'm hip. This lack of a theory perhaps accounts for the erratic shifts in their concerns.

In a previous article, also printed in the *Village Voice,* during a discussion of Celie and Shug's idealized lesbian relationship, Ms. Wallace wrote that womanism was about achieving clitoral orgasm, yet in the *Voice* article about "Ishmael Reed's Female Troubles," she says that womanism is about poor, single Black women and their children. There is no evidence that Black men are better off than Black women; in fact, one could say that womanists of Ms. Wallace's class are better off than Black males of the same class.

The womanists also lack credibility when they complain about their "double oppression" and "other than otherness," when most of them are college professors or successful intellectuals who are better off than the millions of destitute Americans, male and female, Black and white. (This bickering among the "oppressed" over who is the most "oppressed" reminds me of the conflicts between German Jews and Eastern European Jews; when the Nazis rounded up the Jews, both groups went to the concentration camps.)

Ms. Wallace also errs when she describes such literary forms as the epic as white male inventions. The epic originated in Africa, and the novel form itself was created by Cervantes, a Moor.

The most significant error in the piece, I think, provides evidence for my chief complaint and disagreement with the feminists: their tendency to ascribe criminal sexual offenses committed against women and children by some Black men to the majority of or to all Black men, which is the kind of propaganda spread by the Ku Klux Klan and the American Nazi Party. Citing my remark made on *Tony Brown's Journal* that Justice Department figures, released in July of 1985, attributed 80 percent of the sexual offenses to white males, Ms. Wallace writes that the actual number of sexual offenses committed by white males is 52 percent annually, a figure that not only makes no sense but implies that Black males commit 48 percent of sexual offenses annually. (Another prominent feminist, during a television discussion with me, charged Black men, as a group, with child molestation. Though no one denies that such practices exist, the typical child molester is a white, middle-class male, and his victim is a *boy*, but, when I cited statistics, which were introduced at the 1986 Second National Conference on Social Structure, stating that 52 percent of the victims of female murderers were black men, during a television exchange with two feminists, I was confronted with the emotional outburst and performance art of debating strategies.)

If Ms. Wallace's article was a reply to my press release questioning the *Voice's* and *Ms.* magazine's attitudes toward "aggressive Black women," then it's not sufficient. Until more Black women are hired for the upper-echelon staff and policy-making positions, then one has to view their publications' obsessive concern for Black women to be insincere.

The discussion about the movie *The Color Purple* took a strange turn when it was revealed that Jon Lester, the teenager who led a lynch mob against three Black men at Howard Beach,[8] in Queens, had seen the film *The Color Purple* and was described by a Black girlfriend as being "real emotional" about the film.

Jack Beatty, writing in *The New York Times* on January 7, cited this as evidence that Lester sympathized with the plight of Black people, and that his murderous actions were based upon some "territorial instinct," which is "also part of us." Mr. Beatty, whose magazine *The Atlantic Monthly* spent two issues in 1986 blaming poverty in America on "promiscuous" Black women, described *The Color Purple* as "a story of a Black woman's ordeal in the Jim Crow South," an odd interpretation, since many critics felt that the Jim Crow part was left out in favor of attributing the Black women's ordeal, in the film, to malicious or, as Alice Walker would say, "evil" Black men.

It is possible that Mr. Lester's lawyers might even use a *Color Purple* defense. They could argue, based upon his "emotional" reaction to the film, that the kid really loves Black people, but had drunk so much Southern Comfort that he couldn't think and that his "territorial instinct" took over; or they could plead insanity and say that he went crazy and thought of himself as "Indiana Jones," saving the Celies of this world.

Steven Spielberg said that when he read the book *The Color Purple*, all that he could think of was rescuing Celie. James Yee, one of Spielberg's Chinese-American critics, charged that the movie *Indiana Jones and the Temple of Doom* was about Indiana Jones as "a white savior who rescues hordes of helpless Indian women and children from enslavement at the hands of *evil* Indian men" (my italics). (Ms. Wallace and her womanist clique will have to answer to history regarding the fact that they took a book about Black male misogyny to Steven Spielberg, a man whose misogyny has been cited by a number of feminist critics, including Amy

---

8. In 1986, four black men were driving through Queens, New York, around midnight when their car broke down near Howard Beach, a predominantly Irish and Italian community; as one went to find a pay phone, the three others walked into town where they were attacked by a mob of white teenagers armed with baseball bats, tree limbs, and tire irons; one of the men escaped after drawing a knife, one was hit by a car and killed while trying to escape, and the other man, also severely beaten, was held by police as a suspect for hours without being given medical attention; the incident sparked protests and boycotts, and became a symbol of racial hatred.

Taubin in the *Village Voice*. Does this mean that they'll let any male chauvinist who gives them some cash off the hook? Also, what would be the response if racist Bull Conner produced *The Martin Luther King Story* or Yassar Arafat, an anti-Semite, *Exodus*?)

Gloria Steinem, Steven Spielberg, Siskel and Ebert, and all of the others who've libeled Black men could be called to testify on behalf of Mr. Lester, who no doubt will get his face on the 1980s yuppies, neo-conservative Mount Rushmore, alongside those of Bernhard Goetz,[9] who shot an unarmed Black teenager while he lay wounded on a subway platform, and Colonel Oliver North, who staged the interception of an unarmed Egyptian airliner.[1] Don't you miss John Wayne and Hopalong Cassidy?

I hope that the Howard Beach tragedy will persuade Black feminists and womanists to understand that the criticisms of such films as *The Color Purple* (which made over $100,000,000, more than the annual revenues of many smokestack industries!!!) are not always based upon "envy" or spite but, just maybe, a justifiable paranoia. Film and television, besides being sources of entertainment, are the most powerful instruments of propaganda ever created by man, and the Nazi period has proved that, in sinister hands, they can be used to harm unpopular groups and scapegoats. (On television, Black men are typically shown naked from the waist up, handcuffed, and leaning over a police car.)

A conversation I had with Ed Bullins,[2] standing in a Berkeley bank a few weeks ago, sums it up. We decided that it could have been us, stranded in Howard Beach, with a disabled car.

BLYDEN JACKSON[3] RESPONDS

I remember well that I read Du Bois' "A Questionnaire" when it first appeared in 1926. I was a sophomore in college then at Wilberforce (where Du Bois had taught my father), and I was no less caustic during that long winter (as the Wilberforce basketball team toppled opponent after opponent) in my denunciations of the literary stereotypes and the intolerable attitudes which had driven Du Bois to utter his plea for succor and advice than I often was apropos the Wolseyan[4] behavior I thought I detected in the A.M.E. episcopacy, upon whom I tended to place most of the blame for the anguishing disparities between my Wilberforce and such institutions of higher learning as Harvard and Yale. My views on the A.M.E. episcopacy have grown less unequivocal, I do believe, over the last fifty years. So, I suspect, have my views on virtually all issues involving the conduct, in what they perceive as their own best interests, of the overwhelming majority of ordinary mortals. Would that this impassioned human world were as obedient to absolutes as is the cool, calm world of metaphysics.

Philosophically I take the position that writers should be bound by nothing except their independently conceived creative urges in the selection of the characters they choose to write about. Practically I know that the way Negroes have been portrayed by writers (and composers) in America has left a huge deficit to be overcome in the telling of the truth and the amelioration of injustice. But, also, I know, practically, that things have changed immensely, and for the better, in America

9. In 1984, Goetz (b. 1947), a self-employed white American electronics repairer, shot four black teenagers on a New York City subway train, one of whom (nineteen-year-old Troy Canty) had asked him for money twice; the case became a touchstone for debate about race and crime, self-defense, and vigilantism; at the trial two years later, it was revealed that, although Goetz shot at Canty twice, he only hit him once; from the evidence, it appears Canty was sitting unwounded on the seat of a subway car when he received the gunshot that left him paraplegic, even though it was widely reported that he was wounded when Goetz hit him with the second shot.

1. In 1985, four men representing the Palestinian Liberation Front hijacked the *Achille Lauro* cruise ship; they demanded the release of fifty Palestinians in prison in Israel; after killing a disabled Jewish-American passenger, the hijackers agreed to leave the ship in exchange for safe passage to Egypt aboard an Egyptian airplane; President Reagan ordered U.S. Navy fighter planes to intercept the Egyptian airliner, forcing it to land at a NATO base in Sicily; the hijackers were arrested by the Italians following a diplomatic crisis with the U.S. over the territorial rights of the base; the incident also created conflict between the U.S. and Egypt, which demanded an apology for interfering with their aircraft.

2. Playwright who gained prominence during the Black Arts Movement (b. 1935).

3. *BALF* includes the following note with the commentary by Jackson (1910–2000): "Blyden Jackson is Professor Emeritus at the University of North Carolina at Chapel Hill. His essays are collected in *The Waiting Years* (1976)."

4. Reference to Thomas Wolsey (c. 1471–1530), powerful leader of the Roman Catholic Church and English statesmen under King Henry VIII; commonly criticized for emphasizing his own importance.

insofar as the portraiture of the Negro is concerned. There are many reasons for this change, most of them, quite possibly, outside the realm of literature. *Gone with the Wind* did supply a bulletin from the combat area about America's experiment with democracy, though hardly the one which Margaret Mitchell had intended. It did salute an old order, not so nobly agrarian as Margaret Mitchell pictured it, that was passing and from which an Atlanta with its second black mayor (in immediate succession) and an America where the favorite "sitcom" is *The Cosby Show* are forms of a distinct and distant departure. The migration of Southern black farm laborers into the urban North so symbolic of the very revolution it did much to shape and expedite was well in progress in 1926. It continues until today, even to the point of returning its own black migrants now to a South become essentially as urban as the North, and as respectful of the Negro's civil rights.

Powerful dynamics, then, largely emanating from extensive and enormous social pressures primarily economic or political in their original nature, have accounted more than any other set of determinants for an American Negro in the 1980s who is both not, in a variety of significant characteristics, what his black predecessors were in actual reality and very decidedly an improvement over them in the image projected of him by non-black Americans. Aunt Jemimas no longer reign in entrepreneurial appeals to American consumers. And while the reconstitution of America's collective consciousness to its present state of relative grace (especially in comparison with its sorry past) insofar as racial stereotypes are concerned clearly represents—to repeat in altered terminology a statement just made—a phenomenon primarily attributable to forces having little to do with art, voices in the wilderness such as Du Bois's in his "A Questionnaire," actions such as the dialogue developed at least as early as the 1940s by Negroes like Walter White[5] with Hollywood about its Negro stereotypes, a *Kingsblood Royal* here by a Sinclair Lewis, and *A Raisin in the Sun* there by a Lorraine Hansberry have contributed, however minimally in some individual instances, to a new, much happier day in America's

portraiture of its Negroes. In the rectification of massive, far-reaching and complicated wrong, no item of possible corrective therapy, whatever its size (or lack thereof) and maugre whence it comes, should be disdained.

We all, however, do incline, upon occasion, to be beset by preemptive trains of thought anent subjects that touch us where we are extremely sensitive. For me, in the field of expression about the Negro, it is not what has been said that worries me the most. I have at least the kind of targets I can plainly see in a "Marse Chan"[6] or racistic historiography or the editorial policy of the supposedly liberal *New Republic*. What disturbs me more than any other danger I think I sense to the treatment in literature of Negroes, whether by writers or by critics, as I believe I would wish that treatment to be, is a sort of deliberate neglect, a conspiracy of silence or of balefully tempered approval, which still seems to me to occur too often in America's reception of literary work most forthright in its challenge to American color caste. As powerfully as *Native Son* indicts America for its savaging of Negroes, it yet trains the heaviest of its salvos of discontent upon the American environment, almost as if to depose that, when enough Bigger Thomases live in condominiums along suburban highways, whatever the color of their neighbors, America's race problem will be solved. Ann Petry's *The Street* follows the formula of *Native Son*. Its great villain, too, is America's environment. And neither *Native Son* nor *The Street* has been victimized by a sweeping critical neglect. But Ann Petry's *The Narrows* is another matter. It is a fine novel, written by a woman after she had mastered her craft and risen to the top of her form. It is also, through Lincoln Williams, its superbly realized protagonist, a direct attack on American color caste in its very heart. And it is not a Negro novel about which much is said.

Those who would be considered genteel almost always attempt to dissemble when they feel an attack too potentially threatening to the basic tenets of American racism warrants a tactical move from them to protect the system of arbitrary advantages conferred upon them by caste. Of course, they may sometimes

---

5. See p. 404.

6. "Marse Chan: A Tale of Old Virginia," the short story that brought national prominence to white American southern writer Thomas Nelson Page; published in 1884 in *Century Magazine*, the story features Page's characteristic celebration of pre–Civil war plantation life and use of broad dialect to depict the speech of African American characters.

be the unwitting agents of conditioned reflexes they do not really know they have. Even so, a Lincoln Williams, a Negro as innately, unostentatiously, confidently bourgeois as Catherine Berkley's beloved in *A Farewell to Arms* or as Lambert Strether in *The Ambassadors*, can alarm them. They can esteem, fulsomely, a Tea Cake in *Their Eyes Were Watching God*, whom they define, with relief and gratitude amidst their almost hysterical hosannas, as a member of the black folk. Indeed, black folk do not disturb them. They "go" for Porgy and Bess, whoever fictionalizes them, and it is marvelous how much good art so many of such critics seem to discern in almost anything imaginative they can associate with poor, illiterate Negroes beating their wings in a void. It may well be equally remarkable that these same critics are never charmed by any poetry or prose which eulogizes Negroes as difficult benignly and grandly to patronize as a Charlotte Forten or a Herman Long.

When, long ago, I read Jessie Redmon Fauset, I knew, as would have anyone with half the mind a critic needs, that she was the wrong person for a mission that could very well have been very right. Her portraiture of the American Negro bourgeoisie was too abominably inept for American color caste ever to have anything to fear from it. But novels like John Oliver Killens' *Youngblood* or John A. Williams' *The Man Who Cried I Am* or, although from a somewhat different angle, William Melvin Kelly's *dem* (and, certainly, William Demby's *The Catacombs*) are the width of a cosmos in successful achievement from Jessie Fauset's fiction as works of art even while they are very much in concert with her views in that very mission of representing heroically blacks of her class in literature she failed so signally to accomplish. Nor should it be forgotten that Ida Scott, in Baldwin's *Another Country*, emphasizes values and perspectives linking her, for example, to Robby Youngblood (of *Youngblood*) which Baldwin seems, in *Go Tell It on the Mountain*, to leave thoroughly unexplored. The world of Vivaldo Moore and Ida Scott in *Another Country*—the world of which they are intensely aware in the long, probing, bitter, yet most ambitious and most hopeful, discussion they have with

each other in the scene near the end of *Another Country* that truly brings the novel to its dialectical climax—is anything but a world of simple pastoral, black or white. It is the world of intellectual probity to which problems as abstruse as American color caste ultimately must be brought for their resolution by men and women who would be members of any social order sufficiently sophisticated and astute to survive our twentieth century and to expect to flourish after the year 2000. We need now, as always, not anything like a uniform portraiture of the American Negro in works of art. How could that happen, after all, in any case? And the black folk (and white, as well) deserve our admiration, love, and respect. So let us have *The Color Purple* (which I can take or leave). But let us have, also, more novels like *The Narrows* and *Youngblood,* and let us trust that some day, even some day soon, those critics who are always either stricken dumb or suddenly afflicted with a niagara of crocodile tears for (they invariably bemoan) the sabotage of an enlightened message by execrable art whenever Lincoln Williamses do appear may travel their own road to Damascus and thus grow from Sauls to Pauls.

JACK WHITE[7] RESPONDS

As a journalist, whose currency is facts, not truth, my answers to Du Bois' questions are somewhat different than those of a creative artist, who deals in the opposite. But oddly enough, the issues are perplexingly similar for both journalists and creative artists who are black when they deal with such "negative" subjects as the personal behavior of our "leaders," the growth of the underclass, welfare dependence, black-on-black violence, the breakdown of the black family, and the like. There the facts are always running into somebody's concept of the truth. The danger for a black journalist— particularly one employed by the white press—is to confuse the purveying of facts with the purveying of truths, to set one's self up as an arbiter of what facts about our people are or are not damaging to reveal to the wider public.

---

7. *BALF* includes the following note with the commentary by White: "Jack White is Chief of the Chicago Bureau of *Time* magazine"; after working as a National Correspondent for *Time*, White became a contributor to the daily online magazine *The Root*.

The temptation to counter white propaganda with black propaganda is understandable; I confess that I have succumbed to it myself. But after a great deal of reflection, I've come to the conclusion that I have no right to play that sort of role. I'll leave it to the artists and the politicians and the preachers. But I never forget that someone—granted, usually someone who was not black, until recently—has always tried to dictate to us what (or whether) we should read, what (or whether) we should think, what (or whether) we should write. I'm not more willing to accept censorship imposed by blacks on blacks than I am to accept censorship imposed by whites on blacks. For any reason. I demand from black readers of my stories the same freedom I demand from my white editors: to present the facts as well and as completely as I can. What else can freedom mean?

You will note that I don't say, as many blacks do, journalists and creative artists who "happen" to be black. My color is more a part of me than my arm—if you cut that off, I'm still black. And that changes everything about the way I go about my work and live my life. I simply do not approach my work in the same way a white person who is otherwise much like me approaches his/her work. As a black journalist, my duty, and it is nothing less than that, is to be more complete than my white counterparts might be, particularly when I am writing about black subjects. That obligation to tell all I know arises because, as a black American, I see the world, including the white world, from a different angle than my white counterparts. My duty—as a journalist—is to present the facts as well as I can, particularly those which are most likely to be overlooked. Obviously my color influences the way I unearth them.

Some blacks argue that, because of my race, I should be selective as to which facts are to be presented. It most often comes down to whether we should "wash our dirty laundry in public" or give our enemies ammunition which can be used against blacks. Or, conversely, that, as a black journalist, I should be supportive of black efforts to overcome racism. Should I suppress the fact that a black Presidential candidate uses racial slurs in private conversation? Or that prominent blacks in positions of public trust carry on extramarital affairs or use drugs or otherwise depart from a moralistic public image? Or that they oppress black women or mistreat their families while campaigning for racial equality?

To me, these questions pose no moral dilemma. As a journalist, it is my obligation to share facts with my readers—not enter secret pacts with people I write about. My compact is with those who read my stories, not their subjects. If they cannot believe me when I deal with the unpleasant, how can they trust me when I write about the pleasant? How can they trust any artist—or scholar—who is less than frank? And I try not to confuse individual blacks with the entire race—a confusion that can easily be exploited by those who are written about, not to mention our enemies. There is something patronizing about withholding unpleasant facts from black people on the grounds that it might do damage to us, as a people, for white people to know them. Who am I to judge what facts another black citizen is entitled to? Who decides what it is that black people should or should not know about those, black or white, who profess to lead them or the plight of their fellow citizens? I don't think I'm qualified for that job. Nor do I believe that anyone is qualified to dictate the content of the work of any black artist.

I believe a similar frankness should apply to reportage about black social issues. In the long term, freedom is our only salvation (and that's the truth, journalistic detachment notwithstanding). Why in the world should we abdicate a part in the debate out of fear of embarrassment or a fear that we will be misunderstood? Why should we forego the opportunity—indeed, the obligation—to attempt to shape the outcome? And when our artists—or journalists—bring us face to face with a disturbing truth about ourselves, is it more healthy to confront that truth or to attempt to drown it out in a flood of defensive rhetoric? To steal a phrase from the movie *Cotton Comes to Harlem,* who decides if an idea is black enough for you?

As to the specifics:

1–3. No journalist can accept a limitation on the "sort of character" s/he will report on. Nor do I believe that any creative artist can accede to what amounts to self-censorship. To do so would make a mockery of the idea of free expression. And I believe that black people are best served by freedom, not restraint; by open debate, not self-imposed limitations. Who decides what is "positive" for our people? It used to be the overseer. Put it all out there, and let people, black people, make their own judgments.

Why were so many black women moved by *The Color Purple* and so many black activists/artists/militants revulsed by the film—and the novel? Why did so many black women walk out of *for colored girls...*[8] shouting "Amen," while so many black men denounced the "bitch" who wrote it? Were those works "false," or did they contain too much "truth" for some people to handle? Can all the young black women who found something true in those works be discounted? How? By whom? Is their opinion worth less than that of the blacks who were offended? Is the value of art—or journalism—determined by its popularity alone? Or the lack of it?

None of this means that blacks should not forcefully attack art works—or reportage—that they find offensive, by which I mean incomplete. Stereotyping by definition fails the test of completeness and complexity and therefore fails as either art or journalism. Nor are sociological/political/financial concerns out of bounds. One of the facts about the film and play I mentioned is that they were produced, while many other works with different viewpoints were not. It seems perfectly appropriate to ask why a Hollywood film studio would invest millions in *The Color Purple* or why *She's Gotta Have It* would win critical acclaim while many other works by black artists do not attract either funds or praise. The idea that a story should be rejected because its black characters are "no different from white folk" is laughable. To fail to discern differences, one would have to be blind—an inept journalist or a poor artist. Such a view is racist on its face—and that's a fact.

4. Write their own stories, make their own films, paint their own portraits, produce their own dramas, publish their own books, sing their own songs, broadcast their own television shows, print their own newspapers, and support blacks who do all these things. If it

is true that good ideas can defeat bad ones, we should not fear to compete. The alternative is censorship, which we are not only incapable of imposing but which can easily be turned against us.

5. More than ever. Again, the goal is completeness and complexity. The story of the black middle class that has emerged since the Civil Rights Movement is among the least told stories in America. It is moving and inspiring and fraught with complication. And it is an essential part of our history that we as a people need to come to terms with—before white artists and journalists do.

6. For a black journalist who covers politics and urban affairs, a failure to write of the plight of the black "underclass" would be as criminal as a failure to write about the murder at Howard Beach or the march in Forsyth County, Georgia.[9] There is no question that something pathological, something verging on suicide for a vast number of our people, is happening in America's ghettoes—that's a fact—, and social scientists and journalists can untangle many of the factors that have brought this about. Artists, too, must grapple with the horrific consequences of this social phenomenon. There is beauty there, of course. But it seems irresponsible to me not to recognize the ugliness as well. For the journalist or the artist, however, the relevant facts do not stop with mere description. Writers must also attempt to answer this question: How did this happen? And this one: What will happen if this goes on much longer?

7. Absolutely. There's money in it, and professional rewards.

RICHARD A. LONG[1] RESPONDS

The *Crisis* Questionnaire of 1926 and many of the responses to it had as their underlying premise that depictions in literature and the performing arts have implications for and consequences in social action. That, more particularly, negative depictions of black folk, of "the sordid, foolish, and criminal," served to

8. See p. 813.

9. On January 25, 1987, 20,000 people participated in a "March against Fear and Intimidation," in Cumming, GA; the march was organized to protest the community's historic association with racism after a "walk for brotherhood" was disrupted by the KKK a week earlier; National Guard troops attended to prevent violence.

1. *BALF* includes the following note with the commentary by Long (b. 1927): "Richard A. Long is Professor of English at Atlanta University. With Eugenia Collier, he edited *Afro-American Writing: An Anthology of Prose and Poetry* (1972)."

reinforce the structure of racism in American society under which all blacks suffer. If the premise were, in fact, well taken and if such depictions were indeed consequential, one could say without hesitation that black artists bear a heavy burden of obligation not to make their lives and those of their fellows more onerous, and that white artists should look to their consciences.

The premise is, in fact, a dubious one. At any rate, careful reflection leads one to conclude that very little in literature per se is likely to have inspired the racism confronted by blacks in daily life and that, however visceral the impact of film stereotypes may be, the racism they might effect was well in place before the birth of film.

The *Crisis* Questionnaire poses problems relating to the obligations of artists (1, 2, 7), of brokers (3), and of critics and publics (4, 5). In the 1980s I can conceive of no blanket constraints which it is appropriate to ask artists to observe in their depictions of black characters, any more than in their depictions of characters of any other category. Equally, critics and publics cannot be expected to exercise special constraints in their responses to such depictions. Basically, it is a free market. It is quite likely that admirers of *The Color Purple* are not going to be the most satisfied readers of *Reckless Eyeballing,* and vice versa. That is the way the artistic cookie crumbles.

It is extremely unlikely that any significant change in American society is going to occur based upon depictions of blacks in literature or film; if there is a likelihood of such an event, it will be time for a red alert.

SANDRA E. DRAKE[2] RESPONDS

Du Bois's subject in the *Crisis* essay that constitutes the starting point for my discussion involves a venerable and honorable debate over didactic literature and the powers and responsibilities of those who influence the human imagination. His underlying concern is the role literature plays in interpreting Afro-America to itself and to the white majority of the country, and what the practical, indeed life-and-death, consequences of such portrayal may be. The question as he presents it implies a view of literature that is not narrowly conceived, for it pays literary art the tribute of taking seriously its broad impact on the individual and on society. An adequately comprehensive reply in our society and in our time involves consideration of the professional and social responsibilities of members of four different professions: (a) literary artists; (b) literary and cultural critics, in and out of academia; (c) editors; and (d) publishers.

In my view, no one and no institution should legislate what any imaginative writer writes. Richard Wright[3] and Ralph Ellison,[4] to take two examples, may not reveal anything much about the Afro-American woman's experience, or may grossly misrepresent it in the eyes of some. Alice Walker, to some, may misrepresent relations between Afro-American men and women, or do Afro-American women a disservice by not showing them as fighters. If Grange and Brownfield Copeland's experiences[5] are perhaps complementary to Bigger Thomas's, nevertheless they are no substitute: Neither one is Bigger Thomas. One could argue, perhaps, that each of these authors would have written better novels had they written differently. This is not necessarily so, however, and in any case they didn't; and I would not deprive the world of what each did do on account of what he or she might have done.

Although Du Bois mentions racist white writers, his questions make clear that he is equally concerned with the Afro-American writer's choice of topic: His famous objection to McKay's *Home to Harlem*[6] comes to mind. Such an objection does not seem to me legitimate. Furthermore, I think both Du Bois and many

2. *BALF* includes the following note with the commentary by Drake (b. 1946): "Sandra E. Drake is a member of the English faculty at Stanford University"; Drake's current work focuses on the African Diaspora, especially African American, Caribbean, and West African writings.
3. See p. 470.
4. See p. 430.
5. Alice Walker's 1970 novel, *The Third Life of Grange Copeland,* traces three generations of a black family from Georgia: Grange, his son Brownfield, and his granddaughter Ruth.
6. In his June 1928 review in *The Crisis,* Du Bois wrote: "*Home to Harlem* for the most part nauseates me, and after the dirtier parts of its filth, I feel distinctly like taking a bath"; McKay, see p. 304.

white critics misread that book; Jake, the shrewd analyst of the way the union movement functioned, to take but one example, is hardly the wholly unsophisticated sensualist he has been made out to be. Such misreading or simplification is more likely when one entertains preconceptions not only of what an artist will do but what s/he should do. Preconceptions rigidify perceptions.

The debate about how Afro-Americans should be portrayed is recurrent in Afro-American literary thought, for the peculiar social dilemmas of Afro-American life have remained remarkably constant. Nevertheless, the form they assume varies with place and epoch—hence, the call for this current response in the 1980s, sixty years after Du Bois's article, when similar issues are being raised under circumstances that nevertheless are inevitably somewhat different. Du Bois expresses concern with the portrayals of the black working class or poor, compared to those of middle-class Afro-Americans. The topic is prominent in contemporary Afro-American fiction. To take two examples, Gloria Naylor and Toni Morrison, in *Linden Hills* and *Song of Solomon*, offer critiques of the Afro-American middle class and sympathetic portrayals of the non-middle-class (or, more accurately, non-upwardly-mobile segment) of the Afro-American community. They criticize "their own social class," in Du Bois's words, as materialistic in a way that is out of touch with human values. This criticism, however, does not constitute a romanticization of Afro-American poverty or working-class life. (Consider Morrison's description of a gesture of Hagar's, in *Song of Solomon*, as expressing the deep disorder of the Southside, the poor ghetto; or consider the complexity of Naylor's presentation of Linden Hills as seen by Willie, the poor Afro-American boy, when he compares Lester's life and family in the bourgeois Afro-American community with his own impoverished and brutalized childhood in a poor ghetto neighborhood.) These more recent critiques of bourgeois life and presentations of working-class life differ from McKay's in *Home to Harlem* in ways different from those Du Bois focused on but which are ultimately more significant as indicators of how Afro-America and Anglo-America articulate at two periods sixty years apart. Naylor's and Morrison's critiques are related both historically and by content to the important,

if minority, white critique of mainstream American society which derives from the white counterculture movement of the 1960s. (The question of whether that relationship, and also the relationship of the Black Power and Black Aesthetic movements to parallel white counterculture movements, pandered to white guilt and thrill seeking in a way analogous to that charged of the protégés of "Godmother" and company during the 1920s is beyond the scope of my remarks here. I read the movements of the 1960s, black and white, as more fundamental critiques of the mainstream society than any offered during the Jazz Age or the Harlem Renaissance, and the black movement as less exploited than those during any previous historical period.) Even the glorification in the 1960s of the urban, working-class, macho "revolutionary warrior," while a rejection of middle-class life and aspiration, was not the kind of glorification of the black as a category of being (primarily sensual) considered inferior by white Western culture. The forms and articulations of the Afro-American cultural dilemma vary greatly by epoch, though the basic questions tend to recur.

Any community needs all its art. A full portrayal of all segments of the community—in all their internal variety, in the variety of their interactions with other groups, and in the variety of their individuals and their relations to individuals of other groups—provides enrichment. Making art is the artist's charge; and I am convinced that no artist can produce valuable work to prescriptions or under proscriptions.

If the artist's charge is creating art, its interpretation is the charge of the critic, and the place in the larger literary process at which Du Bois's vital concerns can legitimately be addressed starts with the critic (including the artist when writing as critic). If the literary critic insists that every literary text be given a social context, as well as an intrinsic literary critique, even the most racist work can be confronted and defused—far more effectively than by forbidding, banning, or fleeing it. For that matter, I would argue that identifying the relevant criteria for the intrinsic critique of a work of art *requires* a social and cultural context. The false dichotomy between an intrinsic critique (the "New Critical" approach) and a socially contextualized approach is as much of a mirage as the "nature/nurture" I.Q. controversy from which the

Afro-American community has suffered so much. In both literary and scientific fields, the illusoriness of these dichotomizations is increasingly being recognized. The dichotomy between text-as-literary-artifact alone and extra-textual (and, by implication, illegitimate) considerations must be rejected, both because it does literary scholarship a disservice and because of the deadly social uses to which it has been put, and could be put again. Defending the widest possible dimensions of what is recognized as legitimate literary study is therefore crucial.

The third and fourth professions implicated in the literary portrayal of Afro-America are editing and publishing, and those of us concerned with that portrayal must pay close attention to how these segments of our society articulate with writers and critics in and out of academia. Many people can afford a pad of paper and a ballpoint pen and, thus, produce both literature and literary criticism. But no matter how good one's writing may be, getting it published and distributed, whether commercially or within academia, is a different matter. Ideally, the editor fights for balance and a wide range of perspective, and the publisher accepts the editor's judgments. However, it must be recognized that things do not always work that way. To begin with, editors are generally employees; and, increasingly, they have to select books that sell or lose their jobs. Increasingly, too, publishing companies tend to be subsidiaries of corporations primarily interested in manufacturing dog food or napalm. And now, as always, Afro-Americans represent under fifteen percent of the population and do not, with rare exceptions, own publishing companies. In view of this situation, I see the necessity of continuing to battle as strongly as Du Bois did and, additionally, of trying to take advantage of some of the possibilities that may be inherent in modern technology. To begin with, Afro-Americans should be encouraged to try to occupy positions within the publishing establishment. This will require political activity, in academia and in the society at large, of various sorts:

1. Vigorous support for Civil Rights and Equal Opportunity laws in the society as a whole.

2. Vigorous support for the presence of Afro-American students at institutions of higher learning where they

can qualify for positions that will have to be defended by fighting for Equal Opportunity laws.

3. Vigorous support for the total restructuring of the economy and the public education system from preschool through high school. This is imperative if we wish to see any increase in the pitiful number of Afro-Americans who even get to the point at which they can enter institutions of higher learning and qualify for battles for Equal Opportunity with white publishing companies, not to mention their learning how to read and write well enough to write and read Afro-American literature.

4. For those within the academy, the continuation of the grueling work of retaining faculty who teach Afro-American literature, maintaining admission of Afro-American students and others interested in Afro-American literature, maintaining courses and programs in Afro-American literature, and sustaining discouraged Afro-American students admitted to such programs. This includes fighting with bookstores that "can't find" Afro-American texts and libraries that don't order Afro-American literature and insisting on the validity of ordering textbooks through small, or Afro-American, bookstores that will carry desired items, instead of allowing orders to be channeled through the mainstream corporations, as many university bookstores are doing. Two examples of valuable nontraditional resources that come to mind are Marcus Books, in the San Francisco Bay area, and the Black Scholar Press. In short, those members of the community with resources must distribute them throughout the community.

5. While fighting for admission to established publishing houses, we must support small presses that print alternative literature and a wide-ranging literary criticism. In academia, this can be done both by submitting scholarly work to small presses and (for tenured faculty, because tenure may be difficult to obtain if action is taken before tenure) by insisting on the validity of such presses until appointments and promotions committees concur. The high quality of such presses will be recognized if they publish work written by those who have been certified as bona fide scholars by receiving tenure at bona fide universities. The process is tautological: If enough tenured faculty insist long enough, the committees will recognize them, which is exactly how they have come to recognize Harvard University Press, Oxford University Press, and others of that ilk.

Also essential is the flexible and imaginative use of modern technological resources. Few Afro-Americans can establish Harper and Row, but the possibilities of desktop publishing, laser printing, and so forth are immense and financially within the reach of relatively nonaffluent individuals and groups. The quality of such work is very high; indeed, it is probable that this technology itself represents the wave of the future, even in the mainstream publishing industry.

What follow are direct responses to Du Bois's seven questions:

1. No.

2. Criticized for a choice, no. Critiqued by literary critics in a way that reveals the negative results of a portrayal, yes.

3. Yes.

4. Write literature, write literary criticism, teach young people and older people in and out of the formal educational system, write cultural criticism, vote, picket, march, make movies, go on listener-subscribed radio, talk on soapboxes. In short, be cultural and literary critics and activists in every way possible.

5. Of course. A full portrayal of the whole community is needed, in all its internal variety and the variety of its interactions with other groups.

6. To the extent that this happens, probably yes.

7. As I have discussed above, the formulation is not really applicable at present.

LLOYD RICHARDS[7] RESPONDS

How should any person be portrayed in art? Truthfully as the artist sees him/her "truthfully."

ANGELA Y. DAVIS AND ICE CUBE
Nappy Happy: A Conversation with Ice Cube [1992]

As this exchange between activist, writer, and educator Angela Davis and rapper Ice Cube demonstrates, discussions of hip-hop often extend beyond artistic topics, touching on other key areas of debate in African American history, from separatism to religion. The discussion presented here is from a two-hour conversation between Davis and Ice Cube in which they explore issues specific to rap music, such as the use of profanity in the lyrics, the idea of gangsta rap, and the responsibility of rap artists as teachers. The exchange also opens up into a discussion of abortion, religion (Ice Cube had converted to Islam earlier in 1992), black studies, political strategies, integration, the politics of hair, Afrocentrism, Pan-Africanism, and the biology of race (reversing the debate on "The Nature of the Negro," pp. 8–51, by exploring the nature of the slave owner). Black history is important to both

Ice Cube and Davis. However, Ice Cube advocates education through religion and art rather than traditional academic schooling. His championing of "street culture" and dismissal of college-educated black people reverses W. E. B. Du Bois's idea of "the talented tenth" as a key to racial uplift (see p. 230). In contrast, Davis draws on her academic training in history and philosophy to argue for a larger political community that recognizes the shared interests of women and men and people of different ethnicities and nationalities.

Angela Y. Davis (b. 1944), a professor emeritus at the University of California at Santa Cruz, gained national attention in 1969 when she lost her teaching position at UCLA because of her political activism and membership in the Communist Party. She became involved in prison issues, and in 1970, on the basis of false charges, she

7. *BALF* includes the following note with the commentary by Richards (1919–2006): "Lloyd Richards is a dramatist who has long been involved with the Yale Repertory Theatre"; Richards directed the 1959 Broadway premiere of Lorraine Hansberry's *A Raisin in the Sun* and collaborated on six plays by August Wilson (1945–2005), from *Ma Rainey's Black Bottom* (which opened on Broadway in 1984) to *Seven Guitars* (which had its Broadway premiere in 1996).

was placed on the FBI's Ten Most Wanted List. Imprisoned for sixteen months for allegedly planning and supplying the weapon used in a bloody attempt to free imprisoned Black Panthers, she was acquitted in 1972 following a massive international "Free Angela Davis" campaign. In the 1980s, Davis ran for vice president on the Communist Party ticket.

Born O'Shea Jackson in 1969 in Los Angeles, Ice Cube began writing and recording raps in ninth grade, and gained fame as part of the successful gangsta rap group N.W.A. ("Niggaz with Attitude") formed in 1986. He left the group in 1989 and in 1990 released his debut solo album, *AmeriKKKa's Most Wanted*, which became a commercial success and a lightning rod for criticism of rap music. As a founding member of N.W.A., Ice Cube was also involved in the controversial feud between East Coast and West Coast rappers. The success of N.W.A. helped launch the rivalry between New York–based rappers (associated with "old school" rap and often aligned with the record label Bad Boy Entertainment) and West Coast rappers (who developed such styles as gangsta rap and were often aligned with Death Row Records). The rivalry began in the early 1990s with exchanges of musical insults between artists on opposite coasts. Tensions escalated until they were checked by the (still-unsolved) shooting deaths of Tupac Shakur and Notorious B.I.G. (Christopher Wallace) in 1996 and 1997.

From *Transition* 58 (1992): 174–92.

Y ou may love him or loathe him, but you have to take him seriously. O'Shea Jackson—better known by his *nom de microphone*, Ice Cube—may be the most successful "hardcore" rap artist in the recording industry. And his influence as a trendsetter in black youth culture is unrivaled. According to some academic analysts, Ice Cube qualifies as an "organic intellectual"[1] (in Antonio Gramsci's famous phrase): someone organically connected to the community he would uplift.

He is, at the same time, an American success story. It was as a member of the Compton-based rap group NWA that he first came to prominence in 1988 at the age of 18. Less than two years later, he left the group over a dispute about money, and went solo. *AmeriKKKa's Most Wanted*, his gritty debut album, went platinum— and the rest is recording history.

Ice Cube is also a multimedia phenomenon. Artless, powerful performances in films by John Singleton and Walter Hill have established him as a commanding screen presence. That, combined with his streetwise credibility, has been a boon for St. Ides malt liquor, which has paid generously for his ongoing "celebrity endorsement." Naturally, it's a relationship that has aroused some skepticism. While Public Enemy's Chuck D, for example, has inveighed against an industry that exacts a tragic toll in America's inner cities, even suing a malt liquor company that used one of his cuts to promote its product, Ice Cube defends his role in touting booze in the 'hood—even though, having joined the Nation of Islam, he says he's now a tee-totaller. "I do what I want to do," he says of his malt liquor ads.

Some of his other celebrity endorsements have raised eyebrows as well. For example, at the end of a press conference last year, Ice Cube held up a copy of a book entitled *The Secret Relationship Between Blacks and Jews*, which purports to reveal the "massive" and "inordinate" role of the Jews in a genocidal campaign against blacks. "Try to find this book," he exhorted, *"everybody."*

But then Ice Cube is no stranger to controversy, and his second album, *Death Certificate*, has certainly not been without its critics. The album, which has sold over a million copies, delivers a strong message of uplift and affirmation . . . unless you happen to be female, Asian, Jewish, gay, white, black, whatever.

So, for instance, in the song "No Vaseline," Ice Cube calls for the death of Jerry Heller, his former manager, and imagines torching NWA rapper Eazy-E for having "let a Jew break up your crew." In "Horny Lil' Devil," Cube speaks of castrating white men who go out with black women. ("True Niggers ain't gay," he advises in the course of this cut.) In "Black Korea," he

1. An intellectual from a working-class community who remains engaged with the interests of that community, an idea developed by the Italian Marxist philosopher Gramsci (1891–1937).

warns Korean grocers to "pay respect to the black fist, or we'll burn your store down to a crisp." You get the picture. Not exactly "It's a Small World After All."

Still, Ice Cube's champions—and stalwart defenders—are legion. "I have seen the future of American culture and he's wearing a Raiders hat," proclaimed the music critic James Bernard. "Cube's album isn't about racial hatred," opined Dane L. Webb, then executive editor of Larry Flynt's *Rappages*. "It's about have-nots pointing fingers at those who have. And the reality for most Black people is that the few that *have* in *our* communities are mostly Asian or Jewish. And when a Black man tells the truth about their oppressive brand of democracy in our community, they 'Shut 'Em Down.'"[2] "When Ice Cube says that NWA is controlled by a Jew," Chuck D protested, "how is that anti-Semitism, when Heller *is* a Jew?" The journalist Scott Poulson-Bryant pointedly observed that most of Cube's critics are unconcerned when he advocates hatred and violence toward other blacks. "All the cries of Ice Cube's racism, then, seem dreadfully racist themselves," he argued. "Dismissing the context of *Death Certificate*'s name-calling and venom, critics assume a police-like stance and fire away from behind the smoke screen."

Not all black intellectuals have been as charitable. Thus Manning Marable, the radical scholar and commentator, questions the rap artist's "political maturity and insight" and insists that "people of color must transcend the terrible tendency to blame each other, to emphasize their differences, to trash one another. . . . A truly multicultural democracy which empowers people of color will never be won if we tolerate bigotry with our own ranks, and turn our energies to undermine each other."

And what of the legendary Angela Y. Davis? In some ways, hers, too, was an American success story, but with a twist. Raised in Birmingham, Alabama, Davis went on to graduate magna cum laude from Brandeis University and work on her doctorate under Herbert Marcuse[3] at the University of California, San Diego, and teach philosophy at the University of California, Los Angeles. In a few short years, however, her

political commitments made her a casualty of the government's war against black radicalism: the philosopher was turned into a fugitive from justice. In 1970, by the age of twenty-six, she had made the FBI's Ten Most Wanted List (which described her as "armed and dangerous") and appeared on the cover of *Newsweek*—in chains.

Now a professor in the History of Consciousness program at the University of California, Santa Cruz, Davis has made her mark as a social theorist, elaborating her views on the need for a transracial politics of alliance and transformation in two widely cited collections of essays, *Women, Race, & Class* and *Women, Culture, & Politics*. Cautioning against the narrow-gauged black nationalism of the street, Davis is wont to decry anti-Semitism and homophobia in the same breath as racism. "We do not draw the color line," she writes in her latest book. "The only line we draw is one based on our political principles."

So the encounter between them—a two hour conversation held at Street Knowledge, Cube's company offices—was an encounter between two different perspectives, two different activist traditions, and, of course, two different generations. While Davis's background has disposed her to seek common ground with others, these differences may have been both constraining and productive. Davis notes with misgivings that *Death Certificate* was not released until after the conversation was recorded, so that she did not have the opportunity to listen to more than a few songs. She writes: "Considering the extremely problematic content of 'Black Korea,' I regret that I was then unaware of its inclusion on the album. My current political work involves the negotiation of cross-cultural alliances—especially among people of color—in developing opposition to hate violence. Had I been aware of this song, it would have certainly provided a thematic focus for a number of questions that unfortunately remain unexplored in this conversation."

ANGELA Y. DAVIS: I want to begin by acknowledging our very different positions. We represent different generations and genders: you are a young man and I

2. Reference to Public Enemy's song, "Shut Em Down," from their 1991 album *Apocalypse 91 . . . The Enemy Strikes Back*.
3. German philosopher, social theorist, and political activist (1898–1979).

am a mature woman. But I also want to acknowledge our affinities. We are both African Americans, who share a cultural tradition as well as a passionate concern for our people. So, in exploring our differences in the course of this conversation, I hope we will discover common ground. Now, I am of the same generation as your mother. Hip-hop culture is a product of the younger generation of sisters and brothers in our community. I am curious about your attitude toward the older generation. How do you and your peers see us?

Ice Cube: When I look at older people, I don't think they feel that they can learn from the younger generation. I try and tell my mother things that she just doesn't want to hear sometimes. She is so used to being a certain way: she's from the South and grew up at a time when the South was a very dangerous place. I was born in Los Angeles in 1969. When I started school, it was totally different from when she went to school. What she learned was totally different from what I learned.

AYD: I find that many of the friends I have in my own age group are not very receptive to the culture of the younger generation. Some of them who have looked at my CDs have been surprised to see my collection of rap music. Invariably, they ask, "Do you really listen to *that*?" I remind them that our mothers and fathers probably felt the same way about the music we listened to when we were younger. If we are not willing to attempt to learn about youth culture, communication between generations will be as difficult as it has always been. We need to listen to what you are saying—as hard as it may be to hear it. And believe me, sometimes what I hear in your music thoroughly assaults my ears. It makes me feel as if much of the work we have done over the last decades to change our self-representations as African Americans means little or nothing to so many people in your generation. At the same time, it is exhilarating to hear your appeal to young people to stand up and to be proud of who they are, who we are. But where do you think we are right now, in the 1990s? Do you think that each generation starts where the preceding one left off?

IC: Of course. We're at a point when we can hear people like the L.A. police chief on TV saying we've got

to have a war on gangs. I see a lot of black parents clapping and saying: Oh yes, we have to have a war on gangs. But when young men with baseball caps and T-shirts are considered gangs, what these parents are doing is clapping for a war against their children. When people talk about a war on gangs, they ain't going to North of Pico or Beverly Hills. They are going to come to South Central L.A. They are going to go to Watts, to Long Beach, to Compton. They are going to East Oakland, to Brooklyn. That war against gangs is a war against our kids. So the media, the news, have more influence on our parents than we in the community. The parents might stay in the house all day. They go back and forth to work. They barely know anybody. The gang members know everybody up and down the street.

AYD: During the late sixties, when I lived in Los Angeles, my parents were utterly opposed to my decision to become active in the Black Panther Party and in SNCC [Student Nonviolent Coordinating Committee]. They were angry at me for associating myself with what was called "black militancy" even though they situated themselves in a progressive tradition. In the thirties, my mother was active in the campaign on behalf of the Scottsboro Nine—you know about the nine brothers who were falsely charged with raping three white women in Scottsboro, Alabama. They spent almost all of their lives in prison. My mother was involved in that campaign, confronting racism in a way that makes me feel scared today. But when she saw me doing something similar to what she had done in her youth, she became frightened. Now she understands that what I did was important. But at the time she couldn't see it. I wish that when I was in my twenties, I had taken the initiative to try and communicate with my mother, so that I could have discovered that bridging the great divide between us was a similar passion toward political activism. I wish I had tried to understand that she had shaped my own desire to actively intervene in the politics of racism. It took me many years to realize that in many ways I was just following in her footsteps. Which brings me to some observations about black youth today and the respect that is conveyed in the popular musical culture for those who came before—for Malcolm,[4] for example. What about

4. See p. 516.

the parents of the young people who listen to your music? How do you relate to them?

IC: Well, the parents have to have open minds. The parents have to build a bond, a relationship with their kids, so Ice Cube doesn't have control of their kid. They do. Ice Cube is not raising their kid. They are.

AYD: But you *are* trying to educate them.

IC: Of course. Because the school system won't do it. Rap music is our network. It's the only way we can talk to each other, almost uncensored.

AYD: So what are you talking to each other about?

IC: Everybody has a different way. My first approach was holding up the mirror. Once you hold up a mirror, you see yourself for who you are, and you see the things going on in the black community. Hopefully, it scares them so much that they are going to want to make a change, or it's going to provoke some thought in that direction.

AYD: Am I correct in thinking that when you tell them, through your music, what is happening in the community, you play various roles, you become different characters? The reason I ask this question is because many people assume that when you are rapping, your words reflect your own beliefs and values. For example, when you talk about "bitches" and "hoes," the assumption is that you believe women are bitches and hoes. Are you saying that this is the accepted language in some circles in the community? That this is the vocabulary that young people use and you want them to observe themselves in such a way that may also cause them to think about changing their attitudes?

IC: Of course. People who say Ice Cube thinks all women are bitches and hoes are not listening to the lyrics. They ain't listening to the situations. They really are not. I don't think they really get past the profanity. Parents say, "Uh-oh, I can't hear this," but we learned it from our parents, from the TV. This isn't something new that just popped up.

AYD: What do you think about all the efforts over the years to transform the language we use to refer to ourselves as black people and specifically as black women? I remember when we began to eliminate the word "Negro" from our vocabulary. It felt like a personal victory for me when that word became obsolete. As a child I used to cringe every time someone referred to me as a "Negro," whether it was a white person or another "Negro." I didn't know then why it made me feel so uncomfortable, but later I realized that "Negro" was virtually synonymous with the word "slave." I had been reacting to the fact that everywhere I turned I was being called a slave. White people called me a slave, black people called me a slave, and I called myself a slave. Although the word "Negro" is Spanish for the color black, its usage in English has always implied racial inferiority.

When we began to rehabilitate the word "black" during the mid-sixties, coining the slogan "Black is beautiful," calling ourselves black in a positive and self-affirming way, we also began to criticize the way we had grown accustomed to using the word "nigger." "Negro" was just a proper way of saying "nigger." An important moment in the popular culture of the seventies was when Richard Pryor announced that he was eliminating "nigger" from his vocabulary.

How do you think progressive African Americans of my generation feel when we hear all over again—especially in hip hop culture—"nigger, nigger, nigger"? How do you think black feminists like myself and younger women as well respond to the word "bitch"?

IC: The language of the streets is the only language I can use to communicate with the streets. You have to build people up. You have to get under them and then lift. You know all of this pulling from on top ain't working. So we have to take the language of the streets, tell the kids about the situation, tell them what's really going on. Because some kids are blind to what they are doing, to their own actions. Take a football player—a quarterback. He's on the field, right in the action. But he still can't see what's going on. He's got to call up to somebody that has a larger perspective. It's the same thing I'm doing. It's all an evolution process. It's going to take time. Nothing's going to be done overnight. But once we start waking them up, opening their eyes, then we can start putting something in there. If you start putting something in there while their eyes are closed, that ain't doing no good.

AYD: Your first solo album, *AmeriKKKa's Most Wanted*, went gold in ten days without any assistance from the radio and the normal network, and went platinum in three months. Why do you think young sisters and brothers are so drawn to your voice, your rap, your message?

IC: The truth. We get a lot of brothers who talk to a lot of people. But they ain't saying nothing. Here's a brother who's saying something—who won't sell himself out. Knowing that he won't sell himself out, you know he won't sell you out. We have a brother who ain't looking to get paid. I'm looking to earn, but I'm not looking to get paid. You have a lot of people out there just looking to get paid. We've got a lot of people in the position of doing music, and all they want to talk about is "baby don't go, I love you," "please come back to me," and "don't worry, be happy."

AYD: What's the difference between what you tried to do on *AmeriKKKa's Most Wanted* and on *Death Certificate*?

IC: Well in *AmeriKKKa's Most Wanted*, I was still blind to the facts. I knew a few things, but I didn't know what I know now. I've grown as a person. When I grow as a person, I grow as an artist. I think that this new album, *Death Certificate*, is just a step forward.

AYD: Perhaps you can say how this album is evidence of your own growth and development in comparison to *AmeriKKKa's Most Wanted*.

IC: I think I have more knowledge of self. I am a little wiser than I was. In *AmeriKKKa's Most Wanted*, even though it was a good album—it was one of the best albums of the year—I was going through a lot of pressure personally. With this new album, *Death Certificate*, I can look at everything, without any personal problems getting in the way. It's all about the music.

AYD: I am interested in what you've said about the difference between side A and side B.

IC: *Death Certificate* is side A. Most people liken it to "gangster rap." "Reality rap" is what it is. Side A starts off with a funeral, because black people are mentally dead. It's all about getting that across in the music. A lot of people like the first side. It's got all that you would expect. At the end of the first side, the death side, I explain that people like the first side because we're mentally dead. That's what we want to hear now. We don't love ourselves, so that's the type of music we want to hear. The B side—which is the life side—starts off with

a birth and is about a consciousness of where we need to be, how we need to look at other people, how we need to look at ourselves and reevaluate ourselves.

AYD: Let's talk about "party politics." When kids are partying to your music, they are also being influenced by it, even though they may not be consciously focusing on what they need to change in their lives.

IC: I wouldn't say my music is party music. Some of the music is "danceable." But a lot of it is something that you put on in your Walkman and listen to.

AYD: But what kind of mood does it put you in? Isn't it the rhythm, the beat that captures you, that makes you feel good?

IC: You should feel good when you learn it.

AYD: I have talked to many of my young friends who listen to you and say, "This brother can rap!" They are really impressed by your music, but they sometimes feel embarrassed that they unthinkingly follow the lyrics and sometimes find themselves saying things that challenge their political sensibilities. Like using the word "bitch," for example. Which means that it is the music that is foregrounded and the lyrics become secondary. This makes me wonder whether the message you are conveying sometimes escapes the people that you are trying to reach.

IC: Well, of course it's not going to reach everybody in the same way. Maybe the people that are getting it can tell the brother or the sister that ain't getting it. I think what my man's trying to say here is called *breakdown*. You know what I'm saying? Once you have knowledge, it is just in your nature to give it up.

AYD: I took your video—"Dead Homiez"—to the San Francisco County Jail and screened it for the sisters there who recently had been involved in a series of fights among themselves in the dorm. They had been fighting over who gets to use the telephone, the microwave, and things like that. The guards had constantly intervened—they come in at the slightest pretext, even when somebody raises their voice. Your video, your song about young people killing each other, provided a basis for a wonderful, enlightening conversation among the women in the jail. They began to look at themselves and the antagonisms among them in a way that provoked them to think about changing their attitudes.

IC: Let me tell you something. What we have is kids looking at television, hearing the so-called leaders in this capitalist system saying: It's not all right to be poor—if you're poor you're nothing—get more. And they say to the women: You got to have your hair this way, your eyes got to be this way. You got to have this kind of purse or that kind of shoes. There are the brothers who want the women. And the women have the attitude of "that's what we want." I call it the "white hype." What you have is black people wanting to be like white people, not realizing that white people want to be like black people. So the best thing to do is to eliminate that type of thinking. You need black men who are not looking up to the white man, who are not trying to be like the white man.

AYD: What about the women? You keep talking about black men. I'd like to hear you say: black men and black women.

IC: Black people.

AYD: I think that you often exclude your sisters from your thought process. We're never going to get anywhere if we're not together.

IC: Of course. But the black man is down.

AYD: The black woman's down too.

IC: But the black woman can't look up to the black man until we get up.

AYD: Well why should the black woman look *up* to the black man? Why can't we look at each other as equals?

IC: If we look at each other on an equal level, what you're going to have is a divide.

AYD: As I told you, I teach at the San Francisco County Jail. Many of the women there have been arrested in connection with drugs. But they are invisible to most people. People talk about the drug problem without mentioning the fact that the majority of crack users in our community are women. So when we talk about progress in the community, we have to talk about the sisters as well as the brothers.

IC: The sisters have held up the community.

AYD: When you refer to "the black man," I would like to hear something explicit about black women. That will convince me that you are thinking about your sisters as well as your brothers.

IC: I think about everybody.

AYD: We should be able to speak for each other. The young sister has to be capable of talking about what's happening to black men—the fact that they are dying, they're in prison; they are as endangered as the young female half of our community. As a woman I feel a deep responsibility to stand with my brothers and to do whatever I can to halt that vicious cycle. But I also want the brothers to become conscious of what's happening to the sisters and to stand with them and to speak out for them.

IC: We can't speak up for the sisters until we can speak up for ourselves.

AYD: Suppose I say you can't speak up for yourselves until you can also speak up for the sisters. As a black woman I don't think I can speak up for myself as a woman unless I can speak up for my brothers as well. If we are talking about an entire community rising out of poverty and racism, men will have to learn how to challenge sexism and to fight on behalf of women.

IC: Of course.

AYD: In this context, let's go back to your first album. I know that most women—particularly those who identify with feminism or with women's movements—ask you about "You Can't Faze Me."[5] Having been involved myself with the struggle for women's reproductive rights, my first response to this song was one of deep hurt. It trivializes something that is extremely serious. It grabs people in a really deep place. How many black women died on the desks of back alley abortionists when abortion was illegal before 1973? Isn't it true that the same ultraright forces who attack the rights of people of color today are also calling for the criminalization of abortion? Women should have the right to exercise some control over what happens to our bodies.

AYD: What do you think about the "don't do drugs" message you hear over and over again in rap music? Do you think that it's having any effect on our community?

IC: Maybe, but it's message without action.

AYD: Message without action?

---

5. Reference to "You Can't Fade Me/JD's Gaffilin" from *AmeriKKKa's Most Wanted* (1990).

IC: We've got to start policing and patrolling our own neighborhoods. There's got to be a day when we go into the drug house and kick down the door. Snatch the drug dealer, take his drugs. Destroy his drugs. Take the money and put it into the movement. That's what we gotta do. We can't dial 911, call Sheriff Bill or Deputy Tom who don't care about the community or the drugs.

AYD: But where are the drugs coming from?

IC: Oh, it's coming from them.

AYD: So don't you think that Bill will always be able to find someone who will be able to do their dirty work?

IC: Yes, but there's got to be a time when we say: You can do your dirty work but you're not going to do it here. You are not going to occupy our court.

AYD: Let's get back to your music. Would you say that you're trying to raise people's consciousness?

IC: We get the minds open so we can start feeding into them, break down. The mind revolution has to go on before anything happens.

AYD: So how does the song "Us" help us to achieve this mind revolution?

IC: It makes us look at ourselves again.

AYD: Talk about that.

IC: "Us" is a record saying: Look at who we are. Let's look at ourselves. Because every time you look at the other man you've got to look at yourself, too. See how we reflect him. They fight each other, that's why we fight each other. He's still in our mind. No matter how much we deny it, he's still in our mind. As long as we accept this mentality, we're going to do exactly what the slave did when the master said "I'm sick," and the slave said, "We're sick." The house is burning and he tries to throw water on the house faster than the slave master does. They put us in this trap. Now we're living just like they're living.

AYD: What is the role your music plays in assisting young people to develop an awareness of the self-hatred that they have grown up with? Whether you like it or not, you're out there as a teacher.

IC: My job is to teach what I know and then point to *my* teacher.

AYD: And then there will be the sister or brother who listens to you and who will use your message as the basis for teaching somebody else.

IC: Of course. And then they will point that someone else to their teacher, and then I'll point them to my teacher.

AYD: So what you're talking about is education.

IC: Of course, the revolution.

AYD: So education is the mind revolution.

IC: That's right, education is the mind revolution.

AYD: There's a long tradition of music as education and of situating education at the center of our social struggles. Frederick Douglass,[6] for example, talked about how important it was for enslaved black people to educate themselves. Because once they began to educate themselves they would no longer be slaves.

IC: But we wouldn't educate ourselves: we wanted the slave master to educate us.

AYD: But we created our own schools. Immediately after the abolition of slavery, we began to create our own schools.

IC: But you're still being taught by the slave master. Because whoever's the teacher had to be affected by slavery in one way or another. Reverend Pigfeet ain't giving us what we need to know. He's not telling us what we need to know about who we are. He telling us about the life after this one. Why can't we have heaven right here? Why can't we have heaven here and heaven in the life after?

AYD: What do you think about our African American history, and the contemporary lessons we can learn from our history? I raise this question because we often fail to grasp the complexity of our own culture. The comment you just made about the role religion has played in our history has also been the basis for an unfounded criticism of the spirituals that were created and sung by slaves. When, for example, slaves sang "Swing low, sweet chariot, coming for to carry me home," they may have appeared to be evoking freedom in the afterlife, but wasn't it true that they were also singing about Harriet Tubman—the chariot, Harriet, who rescued so many women and men, helping them

6. See p. 38.

to discover freedom in this life? How do we remember what came before us? How do we maintain a historical memory that helps us to build on the accomplishments and insights that came before us—even if we adopt a critical attitude toward those accomplishments. How do we avoid reinventing the wheel over and over again? As a rap artist, what do you think about the images and icons representing historical personalities that abound in hip-hop culture? Take Malcolm, for example.

IC: Malcolm's a student. You don't know about Malcolm until you go to Malcolm's teacher.

AYD: I know that as a result of rap music young people, especially young African Americans, became interested enough in Malcolm to read his autobiography. This is important, because there is a generation between my generation and yours who didn't know who Malcolm X was—had never heard of him. Now the younger generation at least knows his name, has read the autobiography, and perhaps knows a little of the surrounding history. The question I want to ask you is whether you think it is necessary to probe more deeply into our history, to go beyond the music, as many young people have been stimulated by the music to read Malcolm's autobiography? And especially to look at the women who have still not become a part of our collective historical memory. To look, for example, at Ida B. Wells,[7] the black woman who was the single most important figure in the development of the campaign against lynching. To encourage, for example, an awareness of this woman who traveled all over the country sometimes nursing her baby on stage, organizing throughout the black community, in villages and towns. Ida Wells was responsible for black people realizing that we can stand up and say that we were not going to allow the Ku Klux Klan to deliver tens of thousands of brothers and sisters into the hands of lynch mobs . . .

IC: Like I said, you've got to go to the teacher. Malcolm was a student. You've got to teach all these kids that they can become Malcolm, but you've got to go to

the teacher. Malcolm can teach you what he knows, but he should point you in the direction of the teacher. Same thing with me and my process. I'm just now starting to look at the Nation of Islam. That's how I've learned all that I know, indirectly. So in "Watch Out"[8] at the end of my record, I point to my teacher.

AYD: Continuing the discussion of your latest album, what is "Lord Have Mercy"[9] about?

IC: "Lord Have Mercy" is like a prayer, but it's a rap song. This song evaluates the situation and asks the Lord to help us in our struggle. It's saying, when he sends down the ladder, don't forget us.

AYD: Where do the ideas expressed in this song come from?

IC: They come from my belief in God. Today, they say you've got to go to a church. I think I've been to a church six times in my life. A church should not be like—shhhh quiet, you're in a church—you know what I mean?

AYD: But there are some churches that don't require you to be quiet. In the African tradition, a church is a place where you dance, you move, you sing, where you celebrate in a collective spirit.

IC: Yes.

AYD: Also, in our history, the church is the site where we organized and planned our rebellions.

IC: But we could have done that anywhere.

AYD: What do you mean we could have done it anywhere?

IC: I mean we could have done it anywhere—in the house . . .

AYD: I'm talking about slavery. The religious gathering was the only place we had that was collective and not subject to surveillance. The church had to become a lot of things. That's why ministers became social, political leaders. I know there are a lot of your "Reverend Pigfeet" around. But there is also another tradition . . .

IC: But now, in the 1990s, are they real leaders?

7. See p. 195.
8. Reference to lyric in "Check Yo Self" from *The Predator* (1992).
9. Reference to lyric in "Who Got the Camera" from *The Predator*.

AYD: What do you think about Reverend Jesse Jackson?

IC: I should say this to him in person, though I don't know when I'm going to see him. But I call him "Messy Jesse." I don't believe Jesse Jackson is a leader. I don't look at him as a leader. I look at him as a follower, but he's following the wrong leader. I'm a follower, but I believe I'm following the right leader.

AYD: Well, what do you think about running for political office in more general terms? Jesse Jackson's claim to leadership is based on the fact that he ran twice for president on the Democratic ticket.

IC: That's cool, as long as you don't become a puppet. As long as you don't become a token. I look at him, the relationship between him and Minister Louis Farrakhan. The FOI[1] security was protecting Jesse with their lives and Jesse publicly denounced Farrakhan, at the same time that he was meeting with Farrakhan behind closed doors, in the alley, in the back ways of South Side Chicago. Around the same time, he shook hands with George Wallace. How can you not talk publicly to a man who protected your life, but shake hands on TV with a man who murdered your people?

AYD: Are there any black politicians you respect— who you feel are doing a good job? Take Ron Dellums for example. During the late sixties, he was elected to the Oakland[2] City Council and then to Congress based on the work he did in defense of the Black Panther Party.

IC: I really don't follow politicians. I really can't talk to a politician who would hold up the flag.

AYD: What about the ones who don't?

IC: Who don't hold up the flag? Are they down for the movement? Down to get our people right? Or are they using them as a stepping-stone for themselves?

AYD: I would say that there are a few—like Dellums and Maxine Waters—who are not out for themselves, but for the people. But people shouldn't expect them to accomplish anything progressive without the community demanding it. The election of Maxine Waters to Congress was an important moment in our history. A progressive black woman, solidly backed by her community, whose record as an elected official in California is as strong as it can get. People in South Central Los Angeles can vouch for that. We also need organizers.

IC: Of course, our leaders are organizers.

AYD: Often the leader or the spokesperson can't do everything, and we don't often give credit to those who do the backstage work of organizing. It's unglamorous work, it is not work that people read about. And who usually does that work? Who usually does that housework of the movement?

IC: The people do that work. They need a sense of direction. That's all we need to give our kids—is a sense of direction, a goal that you want them to meet, that you demand them to meet. So then the housework gets done.

AYD: But that work requires you sometimes to learn the skills necessary to do it. You have to learn how to do it.

IC: You have to be taught, you need guidance, direction.

AYD: Take Rosa Parks, for example. People usually think of her only as the woman who refused to sit in the back of the bus in 1955. According to the myth— memorialized in the Neville Brothers song "Sister Rosa"—she was tired. But she had been tired for a long time and was therefore not only motivated by her feelings. She made a conscious political decision, as an organizer. Rosa Parks is a woman who helped pull the community together, who therefore did the work of the backstage organizer. We need to learn how to respect those who do that behind-the-scenes work in the same way that we respect the orators, the theorists, the public representatives of the movement. Often, the people who do the organizing, the people who don't get credit for their work are women. Everybody knows Dr. Martin Luther King[3] as the public representative of the civil rights movement, but not very many people know that it was a group of women who organized the boycott in Montgomery. If it hadn't been for them, nobody would have ever known who Dr. King was. Shouldn't we pay

---

1. Fruit of Islam, the all-male military wing of the Nation of Islam; Farrakhan: see p. 861.
2. Dellums (b. 1935) served on the Berkeley City Council from 1967–70; he subsequently served thirteen terms in the U.S. House of Representatives, from 1971–98, and as mayor of Oakland beginning in 2007.
3. See p. 559.

tribute to those women, whose names are known by only a few of us, and realize that we need organizers in the tradition of the Montgomery women today as well?

IC: You have people who fight for integration, but I'd say we need to fight for equal rights. In the schools, they want equal books, they don't want torn books. That was more important than fighting to sit at the same counter and eat. I think it's healthier if we sit over there, just as long as we have good food.

AYD: Suppose we say we want to sit in the same place or wherever we want to sit, but we also want to eat food of our own choosing. You understand what I'm saying? We want to be respected as equals, but also for our differences. I don't want to be invisible as a black woman. I don't want anyone to tell me I have to eat like white people eat, or have the same thoughts, or do my academic work only in the tradition of Western European philosophy. Which doesn't mean that I am not interested in Western philosophers, but I am also interested in African philosophical traditions and Asian and Native American philosophies . . .

IC: It's all about teaching our kids about the nature of the slave master. Teaching them about his nature, and how he is always going to beat you no matter how many books you push in front of him, no matter how many leaders you send to talk to him, no matter how much you try and educate him. He's always going to be the same way. We've got to understand that everything has natural enemies. There's the chicken, and the chicken hawk. The ant and the anteater. They are enemies by nature. That's what we got to instill in our kids.

AYD: Would you say that there are creatures who are "friends by nature." As human beings, how do we recognize our friends? Shouldn't we be friends with Native Americans?

IC: Oh yes. But that isn't who I'm talking about. You have people trying to love their enemy. That's where the problem is: trying to get them to accept us, trying to get them to "get together" with us. It has never been the intention of the government of the United States to integrate white and black people.

AYD: It may be the government's intention today to integrate a certain kind of black person into the power structure—the Colin Powells and the Clarence Thomases . . .[4]

IC: What everybody thought would work is not working. What you have is people who go to school and go to college, and they are running from their people when their people need them the most.

AYD: Speaking of school, what do you think about the fact that in some schools, rap music is being academically studied. My niece Eisa is a student in Harvard. She wrote her junior thesis on rap music. So what do you have to say about the way hip-hop culture is now being examined and analyzed in the context of university studies?

IC: Rap music is a school system itself, and one of the best school systems that we have. It's entertainment, but it's also a school system. Right now we are more unified on the surface than we have been. I'm not just saying that we know the same thing, but the brothers that got the bald head in New York are the same people that got the bald head in Mississippi, the same brothers who got the bald head in Los Angeles. All over, we're starting to know the same thing, we're starting to say: Hey, we're trying not to identify with the slave master. Putting the contacts in, the jheri-curls[5] in, trying to be like somebody you shouldn't ever want to be like, ain't cool. Cut 'em off. Take 'em out.

AYD: Is that why you cut off your jheri-curl?

IC: Yes, that's why I cut off my jheri-curl. I was trying to identify with the slave master. I like it now. I'm nappy happy. You know what I'm saying? I'm nappy and happy.

AYD: So am I.

IC: You know that's the thing that we got to break down. We've got to break that down, and start teaching about ourselves, and stop teaching us about who they are. They learned civilization from us. Once you

---

4. See pp. 934 and 1103.
5. Processed hair style consisting of loose curls that required harsh and greasy chemicals to achieve and maintain; named for the white American hair product inventor and business owner Jheri Redding (1907–98), who created the perm product Jheri Curl; famously worn by Michael Jackson in the 1980s; for more debate on hair, see pp. 769–77 and 1084.

instill that in black kids and let them know who they are and who we are, all the problems will start [to] improve.

AYD: So what responsibilities do we have to Africa? South Africa for example?

IC: We can't help South Africa. That's just like the blind leading the blind. We can't help them because we can't even help ourselves.

AYD: If you were to talk to Nelson Mandela, he would say that the solidarity of African Americans has been extremely important. The work of anti-apartheid activists here was certainly not the primary factor that led to Mandela's release, because black people inside South Africa had been fighting for his freedom for twenty-five years. But Mandela himself has said that if it hadn't been for the fact that we organized a powerful anti-apartheid movement here in the United States, it would have taken them much longer to get to where they are now. If we don't do what we can— and I would say that African Americans have a special responsibility here—to continue to encourage a political consciousness in favor of an end to the white regime and for a free and democratic South Africa, it will probably take them a lot longer to achieve these goals. My position is that we need to stand up and say no.

IC: It's true, we do need to stand up and say no.

AYD: You were saying that nothing has been offered to us on a silver platter—we have always had to fight for what we have achieved.

IC: It's all about taking. They ain't never going to give us nothing. Nothing but heartaches and the blues. That's the only thing they are ever going to give to us.

AYD: We have already taken quite a bit. But it seems that the more we take, the more we lack.

IC: We've taken a whole lot, but more is ours. More is ours. We deserve more. We ain't taken enough.

AYD: So how do you think we can convince our young people to realize that instead of directing so much of their rage and violence against each other . . .

IC: They have to learn how to love themselves. They don't love themselves. If they don't love themselves, how are they going to love me and you? We need an organization that teaches them to love themselves.

AYD: How do we build this organization? Although I personally doubt that history can be repeated, there are people who say that we need another Black Panther Party. They point out that during the late sixties there was an abundance of gang violence between some of the same gangs that are around today in South Central Los Angeles—the Bloods, the Crips, etc.—and the Black Panther Party eliminated gang antagonisms. The more widespread the influence of the Black Panther became, the more the gang structure began to collapse. I can say from personal experience that it was empowering to witness young black people give up gang violence and begin to respect each other, regardless of their neighborhood allegiances.

IC: Did anybody in the Black Panther organization smoke?

AYD: I'm sure they did.

IC: Did anybody drink?

AYD: I'm sure they did.

IC: That ain't loving yourself.

AYD: Well, people didn't know that then.

IC: But now we do.

AYD: I'm not arguing that we need another Black Panther Party, because I think that would be a simplistic solution. History is far more complex. Each generation has to find its own way. You are standing on our shoulders and it is up to you to reach much higher.

IC: And somebody is going to end up standing on ours, and build something better than what we had. It's all about having a Black Panther Party, just making a more advanced Black Panther Party. Do you know what I mean? A more organized Black Panther Party. That's the key. More people in the party.

AYD: Would you say that your music calls upon young people to move from a state of knowing, a position of being educated, to a state of doing and a position of political activism, a position of transforming this society?

IC: Yes, of course. To me, the best organization around for black people is the Nation of Islam. It is the best organization: brothers don't drink, don't smoke, ain't chasing women. They have one job. They fear one person, though I wouldn't say it's a person—they fear Allah, that's it.

AYD: What about the women in the Nation?

IC: They fear Allah. Don't drink, don't smoke. Know who they are. Love themselves. Respect themselves. Love each other, respect each other. You know what I mean? That's what we need. But we don't need no Rodney Kings. I mean we won't have that incident. You pull your piece and try to take my brother's life, you going to have to take all of our lives. That's how it's got to go.

AYD: What is the difference, as you see it, between your role as an artist and your role as a political teacher—as a purveyor of political consciousness? You create and perform your music and at the same time you have a political agenda. How do you negotiate between the two positions?

IC: It is very delicate. I can't preach, so to speak, because I don't want to turn people off. I have to walk a thin line.

I have to sneak the message in there until they open up. When they open up is when I get to shove. You know how you open babies' mouths? Until they open up, you can just get a taste on their lips, but when they do open up, you just put it in there. It makes them feel good inside.

AYD: So what can we expect from you as an artist, as a musician?

IC: It's going to be raw. I'm starting to get that baby's mouth open. Now it's all about me learning and studying so I can know the right thing to put in it—and so I can know more as a person. I have to learn more as a person before I can pass it on to the kids who are buying my music.

BARBARA RANSBY AND TRACYE MATTHEWS

Black Popular Culture and the Transcendence
of Patriarchal Illusions [1993]

The scholars and activists Barbara Ransby and Tracye Matthews explore how characters in popular culture shape our conceptions of history and gender. Among the particular issues they discuss are the ways in which different media promote certain historical or political interpretations, such as how the typical focus in narrative film on one dominant hero can distort the role that groups have played in social history. They also explore the relationship between the revolutionary anti-racism of rap music and its reactionary misogyny and homophobia and how the use of symbols (such as Malcolm X's *X*) in popular media affects the revolutionary power of those symbols. Underlying these issues are two overarching questions. First, how does art shape social policies? Second, do black artists have a responsibility to avoid or confront problematic representations?

From *Race and Class* 35: No. 1 (1993): 57–68.

Over the past decade in African American communities throughout the United States, there has been a visible resurgence of various forms of black cultural nationalism. This has partly occurred in response to some of the crises currently facing African Americans, and partly reflects the sense of frustration and desperation many people, especially black youth, feel about the prospects for our collective future, and their hunger for some hopeful alternative.

There are three major components of this resurgence which have triggered heated debates within the halls of academia and on the streets of black America. They are: first, the cultural and intellectual movement known as Afrocentrism; second, a growing interest in and commercialization of the memory of Malcolm X;[1] and third, the provocative and popular lyrics of certain subgenres of rap music, which have emerged within the larger context of what is termed Hip Hop culture.

1. See p. 516. [Editor's note]

All three of these trends share two characteristics: they all contain an oppositional edge, which offers respite from the oppressive realities of daily life in a hostile dominant culture. At the same time, however, each trend represents a very male-centered definition of the problems confronting the black community and proposes pseudosolutions that further marginalize and denigrate black women. A masculinized vision of black empowerment and liberation resonates through the literature on Afrocentrism, the lyrics of male rappers, and the symbolic imagined homogeneous black community, the class biases in the rhetoric of the Afrocentric behaviorists is obvious. This racialized class discourse is painfully similar to the racist and sexist theory of the black matriarchy promoted by Daniel P. Moynihan in the 1960s to explain the reputed cultural inferiority, that is pathology, of "the matriarchal Negro family." The solution, of course, is to celebrate and re-create artificially the "greatness" and "authenticity" of a mythical and generic ancient African family.

An important corollary to discussions of the breakdown of the black family is the cry for black male role models. The underlying assumption here is that we need strong black patriarchs to give moral direction to the floundering female-headed households that have destabilized the black community. This dialogue has been framed even more specifically within a discussion of the crisis of the black male. Clearly, there is a legitimate cause for concern and action to address the specific ways in which black men are victimized in our society. The statistics on black male incarceration, homicide, and unemployment are both frightening and familiar. Yet, aside from some weak and ineffectual calls for an end to racism and creation of jobs for black youth, many cultural nationalists emphasize the recognition and visibility of more black male role models, whether historical or contemporary, as the key to black community empowerment. The struggle is defined as one to reclaim and redefine black manhood. Ironically, this is also the point at which the politics and positions of some cultural nationalists, liberals, and right-wing conservatives seem to converge. Consistent with the view that the problem with black people is culturally based, and centered around an alleged crisis in black manhood, their arguments are again framed by the use of certain race-, class- and gender-coded terms that blame

poor people for their own oppression. Personal characteristics such as low self-esteem, lack of self-awareness and pride and, most of all, lack of discipline are cited as the sources of many of the larger social problems confronting the black community, from drugs and gangs to teenage pregnancy.

In addition, the gendered nature of this discussion of the "problem with black people" becomes very obvious when one examines who is generally targeted, implicitly or explicitly, as its root cause. African American women, especially single mothers, are routinely vilified as the culprit. For example, regular attacks on our black women in the media, most often disguised as an attack on the admittedly inadequate welfare system, portray them as lazy, unfit mothers, members of a morally bankrupt underclass, who should be punished for their inability to sustain a middle-class family lifestyle on a subpoverty income. Programs are proposed and implemented that penalize black women and their children for the crime of being poor—for example, actions are being taken, at the local and national level, to make the surgical implant of the Norplant five-year contraceptive mandatory for women who receive welfare. In several states, funding restrictions have been imposed that will further impoverish women receiving public assistance by not affording women who have additional children any additional welfare benefits with which to feed and clothe the child. These women will have to stretch their meager allocations to accommodate the new family member or be forced to not have children. This type of anti-black woman victim blaming is echoed in the popular media—black and white—in some of the new black films being produced, such as on Malcolm X, in music lyrics, and in the theoretical debates about poverty.

Malcolm X and Popular Culture

Rap music and Malcolm X are two mainstays of popular black youth culture in the 1990s. Images of Malcolm are ubiquitous in African American communities from Harlem to South Central Los Angeles, and virtually every major city in between. In fact, the extensive commodification of Malcolm's profile and his quotes in the form of T-shirts, tennis shoes, posters, backpacks, baseball caps, and even underwear, is testimony to the ability of capitalism to exploit just about anything, including dead black revolutionaries. Similarly, the rap music industry, including rappers with explicitly political messages, has enjoyed considerable commercial success. But a careful scrutiny suggests that the more commercially successful artists are the ones whose music—like the pervasive images of Malcolm—has been sanitized and diluted, or at least sufficiently jumbled, as to be safe for mass consumption. (Even lyrical brews concocted with a distinctly militant flavor are frequently laced with enough counterproductive and counterrevolutionary messages, especially with regard to gender and the status of women, to dull their potentially radical edge.)

Just as rap artists have been labeled the "new black prophets," Malcolm has been crowned our "shining black prince," because both symbolize an uncompromising opposition to racism and cultural imperialism. Unfortunately, however, few critics have seriously interrogated the masculine imagery associated with these personas or the gender politics they represent. At a time when single black mothers are being ruthlessly maligned for contributing to the alleged moral decay of the larger black community, enter two types of black saviors, personified by Malcolm X, on the one hand, and rapper Ice Cube,[2] on the other. Malcolm is the strong, powerful, dignified black patriarch standing at the head of his family, acting as protector and provider. Ice Cube, conversely, is, as he proudly proclaims in his recent album, "the pimp," an angry macho, oversexed character, who, above all, is not soft. He doesn't take insults from his enemies or back talk from his women. Thus, Malcolm is the redemptive black patriarch, and Ice Cube is the warrior black pimp. In all cultures, the authority of patriarchs and the power of pimps rest squarely on the backs of the women whom they control or exploit.

Discussions about the alleged breakdown of the black family and the need for strong African American male role models serve as an important backdrop to the resurgent interest in and celebration of Malcolm X. Spike Lee's *X*, which has, unfortunately, become the

final word on Malcolm X for millions of Americans, is but an expensive Hollywood ending to a much longer period of reconstructing his memory. One of the many distortions and omissions surrounding the retrospective of Malcolm's life and times has been the conspicuous inattention to gender politics. Malcolm's own view of women, as well as the implications of a largely masculinized version of the black freedom movement, is uncritically accepted by many who invoke his memory.

In this revisionist reconstruction of the past, and especially in Lee's film, Malcolm has been amputated from the larger social and political context of the 1960s to stand on his own as representative of an entire movement and era. We rarely see the problematic dichotomy of Malcolm versus Martin[3] anymore—even that has been glossed over in an attempt to give an essentialist veneer of "race" as thicker than "politics." What we are also left with is an erasure of the grassroots component of the Black Power and Civil Rights movements, especially the role of grassroots women organizers, who were the very backbone of groups like SNCC (the Student Nonviolent Coordinating Committee), MFDP (Mississippi Freedom Democratic Party) and, in a different way, the Black Panther Party. Organizers like Fannie Lou Hamer and Ella Baker have been literally "X'd" out of the popular—and, unfortunately, most academic—histories, African American youth and others are left with the disempowering misperception that only larger-than-life great men can make or change history, and that this process is an individual rather than a collective venture. The struggle for black liberation is thus equated solely with the struggle to redeem black manhood, and with individual triumph over adversities and indignities. Moreover, black manhood is redeemed by militant posturing heroes, not by the arduous and often unrewarding task of daily organizing and struggle. The deified persona of Malcolm X, a strong black male who overcame a life of poverty, immorality, and crime to become a critic of American injustice, a steadfast and manly defender of black people and a paragon of puritanical morality, fits neatly into this scenario. Thus, the prescription for solving the

2. See p. 1015. [Editor's note]
3. See p. 559. [Editor's note]

problems and dilemmas facing the African American community today is—add strong black men and stir.

This Hollywood image of Malcolm X readily lends itself to the current political agendas of the various and disparate groups who seek opportunistically to lay claim to his legacy—from Nation of Islam leader and former Malcolm adversary, Louis Farrakhan, to ultraconservative Supreme Court Justice Clarence Thomas.[4] What has been created in popular culture, according to historian Robin D. G. Kelley, is a "Malcolm safe for democracy." While most portrayals of Malcolm, even twenty-second sound bites, display his incisive critique of racism, they systematically exclude any reference to his positions on other crucial issues such as imperialism, colonialism, capitalism, and, of course, gender. In one of the rare published critiques of Malcolm's gender politics, black feminist sociologist Patricia Hill Collins argues that "masculinist assumptions pervade Malcolm X's thinking, and these beliefs, in turn, impoverished his version of black nationalism . . . [his] views on women reflected dominant views of white manhood and womanhood applied uncritically to the situation of African Americans."[5] In most accounts, however, Malcolm's patriarchal and sexist ideas, which regrettably remained static through most of his life, are either ignored, downplayed, or reinforced. For example, in the movie *X*, Betty Shabazz is portrayed uncritically as "the strong woman behind the great man." No mention is made of the fact that she left Malcolm after the birth of each of their five children, or of her subordinate status within the context of their male-headed family. Furthermore, no mention is made of Malcolm's own effort to grapple with and challenge the sexism that characterized most of his adult life. In a correspondence to his cousin-in-law, Hakim Jamal, in January 1965, Malcolm himself confronts this issue:

> I taught brothers not only to deal unintelligently with the devil or the white woman, but I also taught many brothers to spit acid at the sisters. They were kept in their places—you probably didn't notice this in action, but it is a fact. I taught these brothers to spit acid at the sisters. If the sisters decided a thing was wrong, they had to suffer it out. If the sister wanted to have her husband at home with her for the evening, I taught the brothers that the sisters were standing in their way; in the way of the Messenger, in the way of progress, in the way of God Himself. I did these things brother. I must undo them.[6]

Although Paul Lee, one of the few researchers who has attempted to address Malcolm's gender politics, was a consultant to Spike Lee (no relation) during the making of the movie, Spike opted to ignore this aspect of Paul Lee's insightful work. It did not fit, apparently, with the type of Malcolm the filmmaker was attempting to fabricate. The hero worship of Malcolm as great black father and the uncritical acceptance of his retrograde views on gender, a weakness that he himself recognized, is quite consistent with the new culture of poverty theorists, who blame African American people—women, in particular—for perpetuating our own oppression, and who propose strong male-dominated families as the solution.

RAP MUSIC AND HIP HOP CULTURE

While the celebration of Malcolm as a cult hero offers us a stifled and restricted ideal of black womanhood safely relegated to the footnotes of a self-consciously masculine text, many male rappers project a different, although equally problematic, set of gender roles. The Nation of Islam's position on male-female relationships, and one that Malcolm endorsed most of his life, suggests that black women should be "respected and protected," confined to a domestic sphere, and serve a subordinate role relative to their husbands. In contrast, a significant amount of the gender imagery in rap, especially in the subgenre of gangsta rap, simultaneously celebrates and condemns the kind of black woman who is presumably undeserving of either respect or protection, the bad girl, Jezebel, whore, bitch. The oversexed black woman who is only relevant to the extent that

4. See p. 934; Farrakhan: see p. 861. [Editor's note]
5. Patricia Hill Collins, "Learning to Think for Ourselves," in *Malcolm X: In Our [Own] Image*, ed. J. Wood (New York, 1992), 74. [Unless otherwise indicated, all notes are those of the authors.]
6. Paul Lee, "Malcolm X's Evolved Views on the Role of Women in Society" (manuscript, 1991).

she serves as a source of male entertainment and pleasure. This prototype is described as a possession, a thing, like a car, jewelry, and clothes. And if she dares to overstep her bounds, assert her humanity, and demand something in return, she is characterized as a deserving recipient of violence. The imagery is graphically reinforced in the music videos and on stage, where back-up dancers gyrate, almost naked, and in some cases simulate sex acts. At the same time, they are taunted with insults and derogatory names by the male rappers. The women are usually smiling with welcoming approval at this abusive and degrading treatment. This is certainly not a liberatory vision, but one, sadly, quite consistent with the racist and sexist stereotypes we have endured for centuries. Moreover, it feeds directly into a public discourse in which the criminalization of poor black women is linked to their sexuality. For example, in the current debate about welfare reform, African American women have been scapegoated as the undeserving recipients of public aid because of their alleged sexual irresponsibility and immoral behavior.

The cultural and ideological assault upon black women not only helps to justify reactionary public policies that compromise the lives of poor black women and their children, it also helps to justify direct acts of physical violence. The real life case of Dee Barnes[7]—the New York City talk show host who was publicly beaten into submission by rapper Dr. Dre in a Manhattan nightclub for allegedly making critical comments about him on the air—is one clear example of the relationship between art and real life. This incident illustrates the extent to which some male rappers actually believe and internalize the misogynist messages they put forth in song. The believability of Dr. Dre's recent public service announcement against battering is undermined by the lyrics of his new single, "Nothin But a Thang," in which he once again advocates "puttin' the slap down"[8] on a ho that doesn't know her place.

At the same time, coexisting alongside these sexist lyrics are some that are very positive and progressive. Groups like Public Enemy and Arrested Development

call for "revolution" and for "poor whites and blacks [to] bum rush the system." Furthermore, an alternative to the antiwoman messages of other artists is offered by rap groups like Digable Planets, Disposable Heroes of Hiphoprisy, and Arrested Development. A few songs actually identify fighting sexism as a priority for the black freedom movement. Still, while some of these groups consciously reject the verbal slander and sexual objectification of black women, most do not advocate total gender equality or feminist/womanist empowerment. Rather, a number of these artists idealize traditional nuclear families with strong patriarchal father figures as the ultimate salvation of the race. But, in addition, female rappers from Queen Latifah to M. C. Lyte and Salt 'n Pepa also speak in a different and distinct voice with regard to gender politics. Although these women rappers have been reluctant to criticize fellow rappers in public for fear that such criticism might fuel racist biases against the genre as a whole, they have created a counterdiscourse through their own music. For example, in her song, "The Evil That Men Do,"[9] Queen Latifah challenges white male patriarchal power and outlines the ways in which it targets poor black women, especially those trapped by the welfare system. This type of lyrical content not only offers an alternative to the sexism of many male rappers, but is an indirect challenge to their authority to articulate the black experience in exclusive male terms.

Many critics have had a difficult time reconciling the positive and progressive messages of rap with the often sexist and misogynist references to African American women. For example, how do we reconcile the call for reparations, the freeing of political prisoners, and self-defense against police brutality with slanderous references to black women as bitches, hoes, freaks, and sack chasers? On one level, the ability of some (not all) rap artists to merge the call for black empowerment with the call for black female subjugation seems like a glaring inconsistency, yet, on another level, it is not incongruous at all. In fact, this issue reflects the ongoing

---

7. Denise "Dee" Barnes, a West Coast rapper and the host of the hip-hop television show, *Pump It Up!*, interviewed Ice Cube in 1990 during his feud with Dr. Dre and other N.W.A. members; when Dr. Dre encountered Barnes in January 1991 at a record release party in Hollywood, he beat her in retaliation for the interview; he pleaded no contest to assault charges, and as part of his sentence, he produced a public service announcement against violence. [Editor's note]

8. Reference to lyric "And if you bitches talk shit, I'll have to put the smack down" from *Nuthin But A 'G' Thang* (1993). [Editor's note]

9. "Evil That Men Do" on *All Hail the Queen* (1989). [Editor's note]

and long-standing contradictions of cultural nationalism with regard to gender and, by extension, the gender dilemma that the African American freedom movement has yet fully to address or resolve. As E. Frances White points out in her brilliant article on nationalism and gender, there is a precedent, in the cultural nationalist movements of the 1960s, for "an oppositional strategy that both counters racism and constructs conservative utopian images of African American life . . . [especially] utopian and repressive gender roles."[1] The reconciliation of sexism and antiracism is typical of a particular strain of cultural black nationalism. This vision of black struggle and empowerment equates black liberation with black male liberation only; uncritically accepts the dominant society's patriarchal model of gender and family relations; sees the sexual objectification and sexual manipulation of black women as a male prerogative; and defines political militancy as a part of some exclusive male domain.

These flawed and erroneous assumptions about gender and liberation provide a perfect rationale for the continued subjugation of black women, almost as a matter of principle. That is, if Black Power is defined as redeeming black manhood, and black manhood is defined uncritically as the right to be the patriarchal heads of black families, and the exclusive defenders of the black community, black women are by definition, relegated to a marginal status. The point here is to suggest that the type of political radicalism defined by some male rap artists is not antithetical to their promotion of antiwomanist messages, but, rather, is quite consistent, and goes to the core of the contradictions and limitations of the political framework itself.

To paraphrase the radical intellectual and activist Ella Baker, even dissidents are products of the societies we seek to transform. That is, it is part of the dialectical nature of popular protest that groups and individuals can and do oppose certain modes of oppression, while they simultaneously reinforce others. Therefore, while rap artists express a just and righteous rage against the myriad of forces poised to undermine the survival of black men, it is often an undirected rage and one in which black women get caught in the crossfire of a war to defend black manhood. In essence, some rappers embrace a political vision that uncritically accepts and internalizes the dominant society's narrow and patriarchal definition of manhood, and then defines liberation as the extent to which black men meet those criteria: the acquisition of money, violent military conquest, and the successful subjugation of women as domestic and sexual servants. This is, ultimately, not a revolutionary praxis, but an assimilationist one dressed up in black face.

Criticism of the negative, particularly sexist, tendencies within rap has often met with a defensive response. While, on the one hand, some observers have romanticized rap music as the authentic and uncensored voice of black protest, other scholars and activists have been reluctant to criticize certain rap artists for fear of being perceived as divisive, or of "airing the dirty laundry" of the black community to a mixed audience. These reservations are not without merit. It is true that part of the attack on black musicians by censors of various brands reflects a racial double standard, which exempts racist rock groups and sexually explicit performers like Madonna. Nevertheless, this fact alone does not explain away or excuse the negative and abusive verbal assaults made upon black women.

By and large, critics have either tried to dismiss or ignore the sexual politics of rap music, or, in a few cases, attempted to legitimize the macho and misogynist stance of black male rappers as an affirmation of their manhood: on occasion, this has even been elevated to the level of a distinct mode of resistance. For example, without mentioning black women, critic Jon Michael Spencer describes the sexism of male rappers as an "insurrection of subjugated sexualities," citing Foucault, Fanon,[2] and white fears of black male sexuality to underscore his point. He writes: "Male rappers, flaunting exaggerated perceptions of their sexual

1. E. Frances White, "Africa on My Mind: Gender Counter Discourse and African American Nationalism," *Journal of Women's History* (Spring 1990): 73.
2. Franz Fanon (1925–61), psychiatrist and philosopher from Martinique, specializing in issues of decolonization; Spenser: former professor of Music and American Studies at the University of Richmond who renamed himself Yahya Jongintaba and emigrated to East Africa; Foucault: Michel Foucault (1926–84), French philosopher known for his work on social institutions (including prisons), human sexuality, and power. [Editor's note]

capacities, tease white fears of alleged black illicit sexualities . . . rap's insurgence of subjugated sexualities is radical because there is no secret, no confession, no self-interrogation."[3] What this critic fails to recognize is that the aggressive assertion of male sexuality does not get expressed in a social vacuum, but that the aggression has a target, and that target is black women. And since when has black male hypersexuality been insurrectionary relative to racist stereotypes of black sexuality? And since when has sexual violence against and manipulation of black women been of any concern to the dominant society? Rappers who promote misogynist images of women are aiming those attacks point blank at black women.[4] This is not a militant assertion of black manhood; it is a militant debasement of black womanhood and, by extension, black personhood. Moreover, the black community has a right to, and should, expect something from its native sons that it does not expect—and certainly has never gotten—from white entertainers: a recognition of the humanity of all black people, men and women.

The popularity of rap music, commercialized Afrocentrism, and what David Maurrasse has termed Malcolmania are all testimony to the legitimate rage and disaffection from American society that millions of black youth feel. These trends also evidence the inability of traditional, or even ostensibly radical or revolutionary, black leaders to offer a serious political program that channels that rage into constructive political strategies. Political weaknesses notwithstanding, the appeal of Malcolm X and the popularity of militant rappers do represent a limited form of resistance to racial oppression. Wearing the symbolic "X" or blasting the lyrics to "Fight the Power," while not the most effective political strategy and not without contradictions, do represent defiant statements of opposition against a system that has deemed them powerless, subhuman, and expendable. The obvious problem, of course, is that such a male-centered definition of

oppression and liberation leaves out more than half of the African American population. The representation of those symbols in exclusively male form, the class bias and essentialism of Afrocentricity and, in the case of rap, the accompanying denigration of black women, dull the radical edge that these modes of cultural expression might otherwise represent. African American youth, male and female, are clearly searching for viable outlets for their pent-up, and potentially political, energy, anger, and creativity. This is, if nothing else, a hopeful sign and cause for optimism. Possibly the most profound political impact of both the celebration of Malcolm and the popularity of political rap has been to give legitimacy and international visibility to the rage and the humanity of a whole generation of disenfranchised black urban youth. Perhaps these searching young minds will find answers and political solutions, not on MTV or BET, or in the speeches of immortal prophets, but within themselves. It is a complex journey from consciousness to the concrete politics of empowerment, and one that is, by definition, full of contradictions and detours. It is perhaps most important, individually and collectively, simply to stay on the right road, and to resist the temptation to gloss over and silence our contradictions. The words of the radical Trinidadian intellectual, C. L. R. James, are inspiring in this regard. He writes:

> A revolution is first and foremost a movement from the old to the new, and needs, above all, new words, new verses, new passwords—all the symbols in which ideas and feelings are made tangible. The mass creation and appropriation of what is needed is a revealing picture of a whole people on their journey into the modern world, sometimes pathetic, sometimes vastly comic, ranging from the sublime to the ridiculous, but always vibrant with the life that only a mass of ordinary people can give.[5]

3. Jon Michael Spencer, "Rhapsody in Black: Utopian Aspirations," *Theology Today* 48, no. 4 (1992).
4. The whole argument is painfully reminiscent of Eldridge Cleaver's misogynist assertion, twenty years ago, that rape is a political act, and Norman Mailer's contention that black men were more in touch with their sexuality than whites.
5. C. L. R. James, in *Race Today* 6, no. 5 (1974): 144.

MICHAEL ERIC DYSON

Gangsta Rap and American Culture [1996]

Michael Eric Dyson (b. 1958), a professor of sociology at Georgetown University and an ordained Baptist minister, sees gangsta rap as an embodiment of representation, since it is an act of witnessing ("representin'"). His measured defense of gangsta rap explores the question: What makes a work of art admirable? Among the issues Dyson raises is whether a work of art is heroic if it gives voice to truths of disempowered people, or if it must also address the problems contained in those truths. In the case of gangsta rap, do its sexism and homophobia merely reflect social attitudes, or do they foster those attitudes? While Barbara Ransby and Tracye Matthews (p. 1027) argued that misogyny in rap promotes conservative social policies that do not serve the interests of most black people, Dyson suggests that repression (such as proposed censorship) has a greater role in reinforcing conservative policies.

Dyson also explores the role of the audience. Drawing an analogy to Nathan Huggins's famous reading of minstrel theater, gangsta rap can be seen as "the black face of white desire." Does this reading falsely minimize the role of black artists in developing rap? Moreover, should we judge rap based on how it affects white attitudes toward black people? In other words, do black artists represent the black community? If so, is there a place for transgressive art by black artists?

From Michael Eric Dyson, *Between God and Gangsta Rap: Bearing Witness to Black Culture* (New York: Oxford University Press, 1996), pp. 176–86.

The recent attacks on the entertainment industry, especially gangsta rap, by Senator Bob Dole, former Education Secretary William Bennett, and political activist C. Delores Tucker, reveal the fury that popular culture can evoke in a wide range of commentators. As a thirty-five-year-old father of a sixteen-year-old son and as a professor and ordained Baptist minister who grew up in Detroit's treacherous inner city, I too am disturbed by many elements of gangsta rap. But I'm equally anguished by the way many critics have used its artists as scapegoats. How can we avoid the pitfall of unfairly attacking black youth for problems that bewitched our culture long before they gained prominence? First, we should understand what forces drove the emergence of rap. Second, we should place the debate about gangsta rap in the context of a much older debate about "negative" and "positive" black images. Finally, we should acknowledge that gangsta rap crudely exposes harmful beliefs and practices that are often maintained with deceptive civility in much of mainstream society, including many black communities.

If the fifteen-year evolution of hip-hop teaches us anything, it's that history is made in unexpected ways by unexpected people with unexpected results. Rap is now safe from the perils of quick extinction predicted at its humble start. But its birth in the bitter belly of the '70s proved to be a Rosetta stone of black popular culture. Afros, "blunts,"[1] funk music, and carnal eruptions define a "back-in-the-day" hip-hop aesthetic. In reality, the severe '70s busted the economic boom of the '60s. The fallout was felt in restructured automobile industries and collapsed steel mills. It was extended in exported employment to foreign markets. Closer to home, there was the depletion of social services to reverse the material ruin of black life. Later, public spaces for black recreation were gutted by Reaganomics or violently transformed by lethal drug economies.

Hip-hop was born in these bleak conditions. Hip-hoppers joined pleasure and rage while turning the details of their difficult lives into craft and capital. This is the world hip-hop would come to "represent": privileged persons speaking for less visible or vocal peers. At their best, rappers shape the tortuous twists of urban fate into lyrical elegies. They represent lives swallowed by too little love or opportunity. They represent themselves and their peers with aggrandizing anthems that boast of their ingenuity and luck in surviving. The art of "representin'" that is much bally-

1. Cigars that are hollowed out and filled with marijuana.

hooed in hip-hop is the witness of those left to tell the afflicted's story.

As rap expands its vision and influence, its unfavorable origins and its relentless quest to represent black youth are both a consolation and challenge to hip-hoppers. They remind rappers that history is not merely the stuff of imperial dreams from above. It isn't just the sanitizing myths of those with political power. Representing history is within reach of those who seize the opportunity to speak for themselves, to represent their own interests at all costs. Even rap's largest controversies are about representation. Hip-hop's attitudes toward women and gays continually jolt in the unvarnished malevolence they reveal. The sharp responses to rap's misogyny and homophobia signify its central role in battles over the cultural representation of other beleaguered groups. This is particularly true of gangsta rap.

While gangsta rap takes the heat for a range of social maladies from urban violence to sexual misconduct, the roots of our racial misery remain buried beneath moralizing discourse that is confused and sometimes dishonest. There's no doubt that gangsta rap is often sexist and that it reflects a vicious misogyny that has seized our nation with frightening intensity. It is doubly wounding for black women who are already beset by attacks from outside their communities to feel the thrust of musical daggers to their dignity from within. How painful it is for black women, many of whom have fought valiantly for black pride, to hear the dissonant chord of disdain carried in the angry epithet "bitch."

The link between the vulgar rhetorical traditions expressed in gangsta rap and the economic exploitation that dominates the marketplace is real. The circulation of brutal images of black men as sexual outlaws and black females as "'ho's" in many gangsta rap narratives mirrors ancient stereotypes of black sexual identity. Male and female bodies are turned into commodities. Black sexual desire is stripped of redemptive uses in relationships of great affection or love.

gangsta rappers, however, don't merely respond to the values and visions of the marketplace; they help shape them as well. The ethic of consumption that pervades our culture certainly supports the rapacious materialism shot through the narratives of gangsta rap. Such an ethic, however, does not exhaust the literal or metaphoric purposes of material wealth in gangsta cul-

ture. The imagined and real uses of money to help one's friends, family, and neighborhood occupies a prominent spot in gangsta rap lyrics and lifestyles.

Equally troubling is the glamorization of violence and the romanticization of the culture of guns that pervades gangsta rap. The recent legal troubles of Tupac Shakur, Dr. Dre, Snoop Doggy Dogg, and other gangsta rappers chastens any defense of the genre based on simplistic claims that these artists are merely performing roles that are divorced from real life. Too often for gangsta rappers, life does indeed imitate and inform art.

But gangsta rappers aren't *simply* caving in to the pressure of racial stereotyping and its economic rewards in a music industry hungry to exploit their artistic imaginations. According to this view, gangsta rappers are easily manipulated pawns in a chess game of material dominance where their consciences are sold to the highest bidder. Or else gangsta rappers are viewed as the black face of white desire to distort the beauty of black life. Some critics even suggest that white record executives discourage the production of "positive rap" and reinforce the desire for lewd expressions packaged as cultural and racial authenticity.

But such views are flawed. The street between black artists and record companies runs both ways. Even though black artists are often ripe for the picking—and thus susceptible to exploitation by white and black record labels—many of them are quite sophisticated about the politics of cultural representation. Many gangsta rappers helped to create the genre's artistic rules. Further, they have figured out how to financially exploit sincere and sensational interest in "ghetto life." gangsta rap is no less legitimate because many "gangstas" turn out to be middle-class blacks faking home boy roots. This fact simply focuses attention on the genre's essential constructedness, its literal artifice. Much of gangsta rap makes voyeuristic whites and naive blacks think they're getting a slice of authentic ghetto life when in reality they're being served colorful exaggerations. That doesn't mean, however, that the best of gangsta rappers don't provide compelling portraits of real social and economic suffering.

Critics of gangsta rap often ignore how hip-hop has been developed without the assistance of a majority of black communities. Even "positive" or "nation-conscious" rap was initially spurned by those now calling for its revival in the face of gangsta rap's ascendancy. Long before white record executives sought to exploit transgressive sexual behavior among blacks, many of us failed to lend support to politically motivated rap. For instance, when political rap group Public Enemy was at its artistic and popular height, most of the critics of gangsta rap didn't insist on the group's prominence in black cultural politics. Instead, Public Enemy and other conscientious rappers were often viewed as controversial figures whose inflammatory racial rhetoric was cause for caution or alarm. In this light, the hue and cry directed against gangsta rap by the new defenders of "legitimate" hip-hop rings false.

Also, many critics of gangsta rap seek to curtail its artistic freedom to transgress boundaries defined by racial or sexual taboo. That's because the burden of representation falls heavily on what may be termed the race artist in a far different manner than the one I've described above. The race artist stands in for black communities. She represents millions of blacks by substituting or sacrificing her desires and visions for the perceived desires and visions of the masses. Even when the race artist manages to maintain relative independence of vision, his or her work is overlaid with, and interpreted within, the social and political aspirations of blacks as a whole. Why? Because of the appalling lack of redeeming or nonstereotypical representations of black life that are permitted expression in our culture.

This situation makes it difficult for blacks to affirm the value of nontraditional or transgressive artistic expressions. Instead of viewing such cultural products through critical eyes—seeing the good and the bad, the productive and destructive aspects of such art—many blacks tend to simply dismiss such work with hypercritical disdain. A suffocating standard of "legitimate" art is thus produced by the limited public availability of complex black art. Either art is seen as redemptive because it uplifts black culture and shatters stereotypical thinking about blacks, or it is seen as bad because it reinforces negative perceptions of black culture.

That is too narrow a measure for the brilliance and variety of black art and cultural imagination. Black folk should surely pay attention to how black art is perceived in our culture. We must be mindful of the social conditions that shape perceptions of our cultural expressions and that stimulate the flourishing of one kind of art versus another. (After all, die-hard hip-hop fans have long criticized how gangsta rap is eagerly embraced by white record companies while "roots" hip-hop is grossly underfinanced.)

But black culture is too broad and intricate—its artistic manifestations too unpredictable and challenging—for us to be *obsessed* with how white folk view our culture through the lens of our art. And black life is too differentiated by class, sexual identity, gender, region, and nationality to fixate on "negative" or "positive" representations of black culture. Black culture is good and bad, uplifting and depressing, edifying and stifling. All of these features should be represented in our art, should find resonant voicing in the diverse tongues of black cultural expressions.

gangsta rappers are not the first to face the grueling double standards imposed on black artists. Throughout African-American history, creative personalities have sought to escape or enliven the role of race artist with varying degrees of success. The sharp machismo with which many gangsta rappers reject this office grates on the nerves of many traditionalists. Many critics argue that since gangsta rap is often the only means by which many white Americans come into contact with black life, its pornographic representations and brutal stereotypes of black culture are especially harmful. The understandable but lamentable response of many critics is to condemn gangsta rap out of hand. They aim to suppress gangsta rap's troubling expressions rather than critically engage its artists and the provocative issues they address. Or the critics of gangsta rap use it for narrow political ends that fail to enlighten or better our common moral lives.

Tossing a moralizing *j'accuse*[2] at the entertainment industry may have boosted Bob Dole's standing in the polls over the short term. It did little, however, to clarify or correct the problems to which he has drawn dramatic attention. I'm in favor of changing the moral

2. I accuse [French], an outraged denunciation against a powerful person or institution; from an 1898 open letter to the president of France from French writer Émile Zola (1840–1902) accusing the government of anti-Semitism and the unjust imprisonment of Alfred Dreyfus (1859–1935), a Jewish French officer.

climate of our nation. I just don't believe that attacking movies, music, and their makers is very helpful. Besides, right-wing talk radio hosts wreak more havoc than a slew of violent films. They're the ones terrorist Timothy McVeigh was inspired by as he planned to bomb the Federal Building in Oklahoma City.

A far more crucial task lies in getting at what's wrong with our culture and what it needs to get right. Nailing the obvious is easy. That's why Dole, along with William Bennett and C. Delores Tucker, goes after popular culture, especially gangsta rap. And the recent attempts of figures like Tucker and Dionne Warwick, as well as national and local lawmakers, to censor gangsta rap or to outlaw its sale to minors are surely misguided. When I testified before the U.S. Senate's Subcommittee on Juvenile Justice, as well as the Pennsylvania House of Representatives, I tried to make this point while acknowledging the need to responsibly confront gangsta rap's problems. Censorship of gangsta rap cannot begin to solve the problems of poor black youth. Nor will it effectively curtail their consumption of music that is already circulated through dubbed tapes and without the benefit of significant airplay.

A crucial distinction needs to be made between censorship of gangsta rap and edifying expressions of civic responsibility and community conscientiousness. The former seeks to prevent the sale of vulgar music that offends mainstream moral sensibilities by suppressing the First Amendment. The latter, however, is a more difficult but rewarding task. It seeks to oppose the expression of misogynistic and sexist sentiments in hip-hop culture through protest and pamphleteering, through community activism, and through boycotts and consciousness raising.

What Dole, Bennett, and Tucker shrink from helping us understand—and what all effective public moralists must address—is why this issue now? Dole's answer is that the loss of family values is caused by the moral corruption of popular culture, and therefore we should hold rap artists, Hollywood moguls, and record executives responsible for our moral chaos. It's hard to argue with Dole on the surface, but a gentle scratch reveals that both his analysis and answer are flawed.

Too often, "family values" is a code for a narrow view of how families work, who gets to count as a legitimate domestic unit, and consequently, what values are crucial to their livelihood. Research has shown that nostalgia for the family of the past, when father knew best, ignores the widespread problems of those times, including child abuse and misogyny. Romantic portrayals of the family on television and the big screen, anchored by the myth of the Benevolent Patriarch, hindered our culture from coming to grips with its ugly domestic problems.

To be sure, there have been severe assaults on American families and their values, but they have not come mainly from Hollywood, but from Washington with the dismantling of the Great Society.[3] Cruel cuts in social programs for the neediest, an upward redistribution of wealth to the rich, and an unprincipled conservative political campaign to demonize poor black mothers and their children have left latter-day D. W. Griffiths[4] in the dust. Many of gangsta rap's most vocal black critics (such as Tucker) fail to see how the alliances they forge with conservative white politicians such as Bennett and Dole are plagued with problems. Bennett and Dole have put up roadblocks to many legislative and political measures that would enhance the fortunes of the black poor they now claim in part to speak for. Their outcry resounds as crocodile tears from the corridors of power paved by bad faith.

Moreover, many of the same conservative politicians who support the attack on gangsta rap also attack black women (from Lani Guinier[5] to welfare mothers), affirmative action, and the redrawing of voting districts to achieve parity for black voters. The war on gangsta

---

3. Programs initiated by President Johnson to combat poverty and racial injustice, including Head Start, the Elementary and Secondary Education Act, Medicare, Medicaid, the National Endowment for the Arts, the National Endowment for the Humanities, the Corporation for Public Broadcasting, and the Department of Transportation.

4. Reference to the white American filmmaker (1875–1948) whose 1915 film *The Birth of the Nation* promoted white supremacy and the Ku Klux Klan, and was the highest grossing silent film ever.

5. Lawyer, activist, and scholar (b. 1950); the first African American woman to be tenured at Harvard Law School, Guinier was nominated in April 1993 to be Assistant Attorney General for Civil Rights by President Clinton, but he withdrew the nomination under political pressure in June; factors contributing to the withdrawal included a critical op-ed in the *Wall Street Journal* titled "Clinton's Quota Queen" that misrepresented her views on racial quotas.

rap diverts attention away from the more substantive threat posed to women and blacks by many conservative politicians. gangsta rap's critics are keenly aware of the harmful effects that genre's misogyny can have on black teens. Ironically, such critics appear oblivious to how their rhetoric of absolute opposition to gangsta rap has been used to justify political attacks on poor black teens.

That doesn't mean that gratuitous violence and virulent misogyny should not be opposed. They must be identified and destroyed. I am wholly sympathetic, for instance, to sharp criticism of gangsta rap's ruinous sexism and homophobia, though neither Dole, Bennett, nor Tucker have made much of the latter plague. "Fags" and "dykes" are prominent in the genre's vocabulary of rage. Critics' failure to make this an issue only reinforces the inferior, invisible status of gay men and lesbians in mainstream and black cultural institutions. Homophobia is a vicious emotion and practice that links mainstream middle-class and black institutions to the vulgar expressions of gangsta rap. There seems to be an implicit agreement between gangsta rappers and political elites that gays, lesbians, and bisexuals basically deserve what they get.

But before we discard the genre, we should understand that gangsta rap often reaches higher than its ugliest, lowest common denominator. Misogyny, violence, materialism, and sexual transgression are not its exclusive domain. At its best, this music draws attention to complex dimensions of ghetto life ignored by many Americans. Of all the genres of hip-hop—from socially conscious rap to black nationalist expressions, from pop to hardcore—gangsta rap has most aggressively narrated the pains and possibilities, the fantasies and fears, of poor black urban youth. gangsta rap is situated in the violent climes of postindustrial Los Angeles and its bordering cities. It draws its metaphoric capital in part from the mix of myth and murder that gave the Western frontier a dangerous appeal a century ago.

gangsta rap is largely an indictment of mainstream and bourgeois black institutions by young people who do not find conventional methods of addressing personal and social calamity useful. The leaders of those institutions often castigate the excessive and romanticized violence of this music without trying to understand what precipitated its rise in the first place. In so doing, they drive a greater wedge between themselves and the youth they so desperately want to help.

If Americans really want to strike at the heart of sexism and misogyny in our communities, shouldn't we take a closer look at one crucial source of these blights: religious institutions, including the synagogue, the temple, and the church? For instance, the central institution of black culture, the black church, which has given hope and inspiration to millions of blacks, has also given us an embarrassing legacy of sexism and misogyny. Despite the great good it has achieved through a heroic tradition of emancipatory leadership, the black church continues to practice and justify *ecclesiastical apartheid*. More than 70 percent of black church members are female, yet they are generally excluded from the church's central station of power, the pulpit. And rarely are the few ordained female ministers elected pastors.

Yet black leaders, many of them ministers, excoriate rappers for their verbal sexual misconduct. It is difficult to listen to civil rights veterans deplore the hostile depiction of women in gangsta rap without mentioning the vicious sexism of the movements for racial liberation of the 1960s. And of course the problem persists in many civil rights organizations today.

Attacking figures like Snoop Doggy Dogg or Tupac Shakur—or the companies that record or distribute them—is an easy out. It allows scapegoating without sophisticated moral analysis and action. While these young black males become whipping boys for sexism and misogyny, the places in our culture where these ancient traditions are nurtured and rationalized—including religious and educational institutions and the nuclear family—remain immune to forceful and just criticism.

Corporate capitalism, mindless materialism, and pop culture have surely helped unravel the moral fabric of our society. But the moral condition of our nation is equally affected by political policies that harm the vulnerable and poor. It would behoove Senator Dole to examine the glass house of politics he abides in before he decides to throw stones again. If he really wants to do something about violence, he should change his mind about the ban on assault weapons he seeks to repeal. That may not be as sexy or self-serving as attacking pop culture, but it might help save lives.

gangsta rap's greatest "sin" may be that it tells the truth about practices and beliefs that rappers hold in common with the mainstream and with black elites. This music has embarrassed mainstream society and black bourgeois culture. It has forced us to confront the demands of racial representation that plague and provoke black artists. It has also exposed our polite sexism and our disregard for gay men and lesbians. We should not continue to blame gangsta rap for ills that existed long before hip-hop uttered its first syllable. Indeed, gangsta rap's in-your-face style may do more to force our nation to confront crucial social problems than countless sermons or political speeches.

LAURA B. RANDOLPH

What Can We Do about the Most Explosive Problem in Black America: The Widening Gap between Women Who Are Making It and Men Who Aren't [1990]

With this 1990 *Ebony* article, Laura B. Randolph, a journalist and lawyer, drew public attention to a growing class division between black men and black women. Scholars such as Walter Farrell, now a professor at the University of North Carolina, supported Randolph's assertion that black professional women are having an increasingly difficult time finding suitable partners because of what Farrell termed "the shrinking pool of economically stable or marriageable men."

Randolph suggests that black women are reaching higher socioeconomic levels than black men because black men face more racism on a daily basis, particularly from white men who perceive them as both an economic and a sexual threat. Randolph offers six ways to address the growing gap, which she calls "the most dangerous problem we have faced since slavery time." The ideas she develops in most detail ("Be political," "Be a mentor," "Monitor education authorities") are geared toward offering black men economic opportunities and showing black male professionals how to be role models. Randolph's other suggestions briefly touch on the need to organize communities in order to strengthen them while avoiding gender inequality and divisiveness.

From *Ebony,* August 1990, pp. 52–54, 56.

W e are losing them.
  Not just in small, isolated numbers but by the scores. Every day, every *hour,* more and more slip away until they are beyond reach and hope. They are young Black men in trouble—young Black men in crisis. They are our sons, our brothers, our lovers—our *future.*

"Not since slavery has so much calamity and ongoing catastrophe been visited on Black males," says U.S. Health and Human Services Secretary Louis Sullivan.

For young Black women, the Black male crisis in America is more than disquieting. It is deeply disturbing. The dearth of whole, healthy Black men is a constant topic of conversations and an ever-present source of pain. For the Black man's crisis is the Black woman's crisis too. Its consequences affect young Black women in ways other people can only imagine. It is our husbands who are being lost, our babies growing up fatherless, our beds, our arms that are empty.

"I'm 27 years old and I'm dateless," laments Janis Hazel, director of legislation for Detroit Congressman John Conyers. "What's so incredible is—because of my job—I'm constantly out there meeting people, but it's a rare day that I see a young, Black, serious-minded man. You want to know how bad it is? Now, if a friend introduces me to a man who *sounds* like he's got it together, I will, and have, hopped a plane to meet him."

Experts agree Janis' experience is quite common. Dr. Walter Farrell, professor of education at the University of Wisconsin, studied a cross-section of professional, single Black women to document the problems they face in establishing relationships with Black men. His conclusion underlined the most dangerous and explosive problem in Black America: "Large numbers of Black professional women are alone, unmarried and failing to procreate because of the shrinking pool of economically stable or marriageable men," says Farrell.

The Black male crisis is not new. But lately the pace of their decimation seems to have quickened in the new generation. Dozens of young Black women interviewed said the situation has reached the point where they now question their hopes of ever falling in love, marrying and having a family. "Our studies show that a Black woman would give her right arm to have a strong Black man to stand beside her, but she knows from observation and past experience that these are currently in short supply," says Dr. Julia Hare, executive director of The Black Think Tank and co-author of *The Endangered Black Family*.

National statistics confirm Dr. Hare's conclusion: A recent study stunned Black America when it disclosed that *one in every four Black men between 20–29 is either in prison, on probation or on parole.*

Worse, out of anger and frustration, young Black men are destroying themselves in record numbers, dying needless, violent deaths at each other's hands. (A Black man has one in 21 chance of being murdered before he is 25, and homicide is the leading cause of death for Black men 15–24. Not cancer. Not heart disease. *Murder.*) Dr. Conrad Worrill, national chairman of the National Black United Front, sums it up this way: "The potentiality of African-American men becoming extinct is staring us in the eyes."

If, as predicted, more and more Black women will end up alone, what are the implications for the future of the Black family? How wide is the educational and economic gap between young Black men and women going to be in the next 10 years? "If we don't turn things around, by the year 2000 the only place you will be able to find a sane, articulate, unincarcerated and unaddicted Black man is in the Smithsonian Institution," warns Dr. Hare.

Frightening and controversial as Dr. Hare's warning is, it is not, say her peers, far off the mark. Today, three out of five Blacks in college are women. There has been an average of 194,000 more Black women than men in college over each of the last ten years. In the last six years, the number of Black men in medical school declined by 12 percent while the number of Black women rose by almost one-third. The National Bar Association estimates seven of every ten Blacks entering law school are women. And 60 percent of all Black MBAs are women.

We must look beyond the numbers, however, to understand why so many young Black women are "making it" while their male counterparts aren't and, most importantly, what can be done about it. What the numbers don't say is that Black men, more than Black women, are forced to confront racism on a harrowing, daily basis.

"Historically, this society has been geared to see Black *men* as a threat," says Jewelle Taylor Gibbs of the University of California at Berkeley and author of *Young, Black and Male in America: An Endangered Species.* "It goes back to slavery and the myths of the Black man's overwhelming sexuality and aggressiveness." Dr. Hare puts it more bluntly: "White men have all kinds of ways to keep Black men down because they know a Black man can take their place in the bedroom as well as the boardroom."

What should Black America be doing to ensure the survival of our young men? Starting today, observers say, we must make them our No. 1 priority. As Dr. Wade Nobles, director of the Institute for the Advanced Study of Black Family Life and Culture, recently told Congress, "The functioning of Black families and . . . American society cannot be enhanced until the highest priority is assigned to ensuring that Black boys, Black male youths, Black adult men and Black fathers are able to fulfill their responsibilities as productive members of our society."

Here, according to national experts, are [six] things we can and must do to solve the most dangerous problem we have faced since slavery time:

- **Be political:** "We must force politicians to create policies and programs that strengthen the Black family," says Gibbs. "The United States has allocated billions of dollars for national defense and foreign aid yet it cannot find the funds to raise 2 million Black families above the poverty line, to feed 4 million poor Black children and to provide jobs for one million young Black men." There are many ways to become politically involved. In Washington, D.C., for example, a councilman is introducing a bill to create a Commission on Men to identify and change government policies that have proved destructive to the development of Black males in Washington. Similarly, Ohio Governor Richard Celeste has created a 40-person "Commission on Socially Disadvantaged Black Males" to recommend strategies to improve the quality of life for Ohio's Black men.

At the national level, Rep. Augustus F. Hawkins (D-Calif.) has introduced a bill that would create a '90s version of the Civilian Conservation Corps, the national program that provided federally funded jobs during the Depression. Hawkins' bill, the National Service Act of 1990, authorizes $93 million to establish a two-part version of the old CCC: the Youth Service Corps, which would offer jobs to unemployed urban youth in government agencies, nursing homes, day-care centers and other facilities, and the American Conservation Corps, which would provide jobs in parks, recreational areas and other such facilities. Write your Congressman to express your support.

On Capitol Hill, Morehouse alumni are lobbying for support for the establishment of a National Institute for the Study of Black Men whose mission would be the development of a new generation of Black leadership. Organize your neighbors to lobby local officials for action to improve the situation of Black men in your area.

- **Be a mentor:** We must all—each of us—reach back to help. Join a group dedicated to nurturing Black boys or start your own. In Washington, a group of young Black male lawyers, teachers, doctors and businessmen has joined to form "Concerned Black Men," an organization dedicated to providing role models for Black boys. Each week, the members take turns going to schools, community centers and playgrounds to talk with Black boys. The group has adopted an inner-city school. "Every concerned African-American man should ask himself if he is providing some positive direction to at least one male child," says Jawanza Kunjufu, author of *Countering the Conspiracy to Destroy Black Boys.*

- **Monitor education authorities:** "Black children live in neighborhoods with the worst schools where teachers expect little from Black boys,"

says Gibbs. Because of these low expectations, Black children are three times more likely than White children to be placed in classes for the educable mentally retarded. "We need to put a moratorium on placing Black boys in special education right now," says Kunjufu. "If it happens to your son, get up to the school and find out why."

The absence of role models in the classroom is another serious obstacle to the education of Black boys. "In order to *be* a Black man, you have to *see* a Black man," says Kunjufu, who estimates Black men make up less than 2 percent of all elementary school teachers. "Without Black men role models, our boys learn to see school as for girls and sissies."

To combat the problems, some educators have proposed segregating elementary school-age Black boys into separate classrooms, which would be taught by Black male teachers. Still in the debate stage, the controversial program has yet to be implemented. Until effective solutions are found, however, Kunjufu warns, "Black parents must monitor very closely the early education of their sons."

- **Be an equalizer:** Though it's hard for Black mothers to hear, many experts say Black women are unknowingly crippling their sons—teaching their daughters to be independent, self-sufficient members of society while neglecting to provide the same life skills to their male children. "Many Black mothers raise their daughters and spoil their sons," says Kunjufu. "Black mothers must commit to teaching their sons responsibility—cooking, cleaning and homework—just as they do their daughters."

- **Black family involvement:** "There is an old Southern saying, 'The good Lord helps those who first help themselves,'" says Gibbs. "Families must mobilize to form support networks for single-parent families, to set up child care and food cooperatives, to establish crime watch committees, to form car pools, to organize youth recreation and sports activities and to volunteer as aides in schools. With this kind of organization, the community will gradually be transformed from a disorganized ghetto to a liveable urban neighborhood."

- **Support each other:** "Black men and women have misplaced their rage and are directing it against each other instead of the system," says

Dr. Hare. "Black women need to love the man who is good to them, while Black men need to be proud, not intimidated, everytime a sister reaches for the top."

Let's all resolve to do something today. This is the zero hour.

DEBORAH K. KING

Unraveling Fabric, Missing the Beat: Class and Gender in Afro-American Social Issues [1992]

Deborah K. King (b. 1953), a sociologist at Dartmouth College, questions a basic premise of Laura B. Randolph's 1990 *Ebony* article (p. 1040)—namely, in King's words, "that African American males are *the* social issue." She argues that this widely held contention contributes to misperceptions and inappropriate solutions, particularly regarding the problems faced by black women. Specifically, King suggests that when black men are made to be "both definitive and representative of all African Americans," black women become falsely seen as "(1) invisible, (2) advantaged, or (3) victimizers."

By focusing on different statistics—such as domestic violence instead of murder and doctoral degrees instead of MBAs—King demonstrates how the contemporary period can be presented as a time of particular crisis for black women rather than black men. She also

calls into question any analysis that uses traditional social models, like "this theme of marriageable black males," used by scholars such as William Julius Wilson to explore both the causes of and solutions for black poverty. Such analyses, she says, assume that the best model for all African American families is a traditional nuclear family with a male provider, and they ignore the problems that this model can present for black women. In addition, using traditional social models makes it more difficult to see nontraditional solutions to the problems faced by African Americans, such as the need for all workers, regardless of gender, to earn a living wage. King emphasizes the need to understand the interplay among class, race, and gender and to recognize the full range of issues affecting African Americans instead of focusing only on certain issues to the exclusion of others.

From *The Black Scholar* 22 (Summer 1992): pp. 36–43.

The fortuitous videotaping of the savage beating of Rodney King by Los Angeles policemen documented the discriminatory nature of the criminal justice system and provided yet another example of the decimation of African American males. Regarding the unusual amount of media attention on other brutality cases, careful observation disclosed that most often the victims in those cases were black men. Police brutality has been added to the long litany of assaults, discriminations, and denigrations. The vanishing, diminishing, disappearing black man has become the penultimate social issue for African Americans. The media, both black and white, boldly announce and investigate the phenomenon. Headlines blare the impending demise

of African American men: "Lifespan of Black Males Is Declining," "Killing Spree Is Taking Our Children," "Do Black Males Need Special Schools?" and "What Can We Do about the Most Explosive Problem in Black America: The Widening Gap Between Women Who Are Making It and Men Who Aren't." Television journalists like Bill Moyers have interpreted the problems confronting black families as principally the problems of black men. News magazines of the dominant society have echoed this concern.

The problems that plague the African American males today—declining college enrollment, rising imprisonments, escalating death rates, increasing drug violence—have been well documented: "By almost every standard, young black men face very troubled futures. They are more likely to have lives that will be tinged by violence and run-ins with the law than either black girls or whites, . . ."

—*Newsweek*

Finally, we have the U.S. Secretary of Health and Human Services, Dr. Louis Sullivan declaring, "Not since slavery has so much calamity and ongoing catastrophe been visited on black males" (Randolph, 1990:52).

African American scholars have been in the forefront of recognizing and examining the dimension of this problem and in proposing solutions. Scholars have organized innumerable conferences to address this issue; including the "Summit on the African American Male: The Twenty-First Century" held in May 1991 at Brandeis University. A periodical, *Challenge: A Journal of Research on Black Men,* similarly observes the problems of the black male, citing "dismal reports on the status of African American men and boys; declining college enrollments; increasing joblessness, even among high school graduates; disproportionate numbers of black male perpetrators and victims of abuse, homicide, and suicide." Inaugurated in July 1990, *Challenge* attempts to facilitate the dissemination of ongoing research and program evaluations. Psychologist Wade Nobles, director of the Institute for the Advanced Study of Black Family Life and Culture, recently asserted that black Americans should and must make the survival of young black men our number one priority.

> "The functioning of black families and . . . American society cannot be enhanced until the highest priority is assigned to ensuring that black boys, black male youths, black adult men and black fathers are able to fulfill their responsibilities as productive members of our society." (*Ebony,* August 1990:54)

The African American community has taken the initiative in tackling this problem. For example, organizations of older black men, like the Concerned Black Men of Washington, D.C., have been formed to offer role models, support and guidance to black boys. There is a National African American Male Foundation in Washington, D.C.; the National Urban League

has established the African American Adolescent Male Development Center, and Morgan State University operates Project 2000. The black communities in Milwaukee and Baltimore have succeeded in establishing two experimental schools for black males, while several other communities are considering similar proposals. The governor of Ohio commissioned a 40-person Commission on Socially Disadvantaged Black Males. In April 1991, the United States Congress and the Twentieth Century Fund announced a jointly sponsored blue ribbon investigation into the number one social issue for African Americans—"the vanishing black male."

These headlines, studies, programs, and commissions are responding to conditions and circumstances that are detrimental to African American boys and men. I shall not and do not wish to dismiss concerns about their well being. There are grave matters involving black men's health, education, employment, self-determination—indeed their very lives—that demand and deserve our intellectual, political, economic, and emotional talents and commitment. Nevertheless, I do believe it is important that we carefully and critically consider the particular construction of African American social issues as being almost exclusively about the decimation of black males. I recognize that in raising this proposition, my intentions undoubtedly and regrettably will be misunderstood. But, as scholars of African American life in this country, we should ask ourselves a series of questions. What does this particular construction illuminate or obscure about African American life and social issues? Why are the myriad concerns facing African Americans reduced to a single issue? To what extent does this construction, implicitly or explicitly, place African American women and men in competition against and conflict with one another? In whose interest is it to define black men as the number one priority, (or, is it the number one problem)? What are its implications for the African American community?

This paper explores some of the answers. It begins with a discussion of how social problems are constructed and how such constructions are a product of cultural, sociohistorical, and political economic dynamics. In focusing on its construction, the paper treats the declaration of any social problem or issue as an instance where meaning is problematic. That is, it critically examines the widely held, and apparently unproblematic, assumption that African American males are *the* social issue. Second, the paper considers how theoretical works and empirical studies in the literature on African Americans and selected social conditions are part of and contributes to this construction. The third objective is to identify and examine the consequences of this construction for our understanding of the African American community.

CONSTRUCTING THE AFRICAN AMERICAN SOCIAL ISSUE OF THE TWENTY-FIRST CENTURY

The prevailing approach to social issues is premised on the idea that society is, in part, a product of human interactions and the dynamic creation of meanings that people attach to acts, values, social conditions and processes, institutions, and other people. Society is continually being made and remade (Berger and Luckman, 1966). Thus, social issues or problems achieve a certain "reality" when members of a community consider them as threatening some value, belief, standard, or expectation of life. This is not to argue, as many deconstructionists and post-moderns do, that there is no concrete political or economic reality aside from our imaginative texts and narratives. As a social scientist, I accept a certain reality of conditions such as hunger, unemployment, discrimination and other deprivations. In fact, it is the actuality of those conditions which make the nature of our construction of African American social issues so critical.

Our identification and explanation of the problem (i.e., its construction) means that that construction has import for future human interactions and will have real consequences for the lives of African Americans. Our acceptance of a particular construction makes it a potent force in our ability to recognize, understand, and address African Americans' actual circumstances. Herein lies the crux of my concerns with the current constructions.

The black male crisis has become reified, in the media and scholarly literature. In isolating and rein-

terpreting the actual conditions of black people's lives as "the crisis of black men," our social issues have been conceptualized and addressed outside the full and dynamic cultural, historical, political, and economic contexts of African Americans' lives. The crisis assumes what Lukacs called a "phantom objectivity, an autonomy that seems so strictly rational and all-embracing as to conceal every trace of its fundamental nature: the relation between people" (Lukacs, 1971:83–84). In uncritically accepting this as a valid construction, knowingly or not we have accepted a number of assumptions, inaccuracies, and biases. What has resulted is that the experiences of black men have become both definitive and representative of all African Americans. Black men become the focal point and the harms that disproportionately affect black men are highlighted. What are the implications of this construction? I want to answer by considering the lives of black women. In general, we learn that in the current conceptualization black women are either: (1) invisible, (2) advantaged, or (3) victimizers. I am not suggesting that we substitute this heuristic approach as the way of constructing African American social issues. Rather, it is useful in explicating how our current approach gives a distorted view of those issues: and how that view might serve purposes that are not in the interests of African Americans. Later in this discussion I will propose an approach for conceptualization that might enable us to capture the complexity of race, gender and class in our construction.

Black Women as Invisible

In the process of issue construction attention has been focused on several selected harms: school drop-out rates, imprisonment rates, homicide rates, college attendance. The statistics on black males in each of these areas are legitimate matters of concern. For example, in Milwaukee, it is reported that, 80% of black boys in high school earn less than a "C" average. In addition, they account for 50% of all suspensions, although they are only 27% of the school system's population. Black males' incarceration in the United States is four times that of South Africa, comprising approximately 45% of one million inmates. Finally, in 1988, firearm homicides became the greatest killer of young men, both black and white, in the United States, but a black male teenager is eleven times more likely to be murdered with a gun than a white male teenager. Black males have a 1 in 21 chance of being murdered before the age of 25, and homicide is the leading cause of death for black men 15–24 years of age. The crisis is confirmed.

How do we alter the construction of the problem when the following statistics were presented? The poverty rate for black single-parent heads of household is twice that of whites. Two significant factors in this higher poverty rate are an unemployment rate more than twice that of whites and black earnings from full-time employment only 60% of whites. By conservative estimate this group stands a 1 in 10 likelihood of being the victim of a violent sexual assault. Their lives are threatened by a diabetes death rate that is almost 300% higher than that of whites. But, most telling is that between 1980 and 1988, the AIDS death rate for blacks rose from 4.4 to 10.3 per 100,000, making it nine times more likely that a black will die from AIDS than a white. While among the five leading causes of death nationally, for blacks living in New York or New Jersey who are between the ages of 15 and 44, AIDS is the number 1 killer.

All of the African Americans referred to in the proceeding description are women. What I have done is to select a sample of social harms that dramatically and detrimentally affect their lives. Such a step might be the first in a process of creating a construction of African American social issues that illustrates the decimation of black women. With sufficient reiteration and elaboration, with media focus and popularization, with resources to organize scholarly conferences, commission studies, and implement programs and policies, we might be discussing the crisis of black women.[1]

Some might argue that I was biased in the conditions I selected, but I would respond no more so than

the construction of black men in crisis. Consider the matter of AIDS. Black women make up a larger proportion of the women with AIDS than do black men among men with AIDS. Of the 15,000 women with AIDS, 72% are African American or Latina.[2] A 1988 study reported that African American women do not live as long as other groups with AIDS (*MS*. Jan./Feb, 1991:24). The exact reasons are unclear. However, none of the major AIDS research, especially that funded by the National Institutes of Health or the Centers for Disease Control, have studied women. We know very little about the disease history in women. And, the findings of a recent Veterans Administration study indicate that early treatment with AZT may not benefit, and in fact may be counterindicated, for blacks and Latinos infected with the human immunodeficiency virus (*Valley News*, Feb. 15, 1991:8). Again, we don't know if gender matters. Furthermore, black women may be at greater risk because as women they are often excluded from experimental drug trials. Moreover, in addition to the suffering, humiliations, and discrimination that all AIDS patients face, women might experience insults and denials that are particular to being female. For example, more than 50% of those in New York who seek an abortion and have been identified as HIV positive, will be refused.

The AIDS example illustrates not only a grave problem, but one that differentially affects a portion of the African American community. So, why aren't black women and AIDS defined as comparable to black men and homicide? Although aspects of these problems are distinctive, both appear susceptible to various forms of human intervention. One of our points of examination should be to determine the criteria by which one specific condition or status is seen as threatening or harmful. Why do we focus only on certain ones to the exclusion of others? How do we assess the relative severity of various conditions? Why

1. For example, while reports decry black on black violence, the targets for much of this violence are black women but this is seldom discussed in this context (e.g., see Uzzell and Peebles-Wilkins, 1989, Robert L. Perry, 1989, "Re-examining the Black on Black Crime Issue: A Theoretical Essay," *Western Journal of Black Studies*, v13 n2:66–71). While the media continues to focus on the Central Park jogger case, another woman had been raped by two armed men on a roof top, then forced to jump naked from the roof. A television cable broke her fall, and neighbors finally rescued her (*New York Times*, May 7, 1989:27). The woman is black, the suspected offenders were black—we heard no more about it. [Unless otherwise indicated, all footnotes are those of the author.]

2. World Health Organization's limited data suggests that more than 80% of women of childbearing age who are infected with HIV are in sub-Saharan Africa (that's 2.5 million African women).

don't we acknowledge both conditions as requiring our attention?

Some might argue that I cited statistics without stipulating gender or without offering comparative statistics on other race-gender groups. I will concede that, but no more so that the current construction. For example, a recent report issued by the Department of Health and Human Services, found that while life expectancy generally has lengthened during the 1980s, the average lifespan of black males has dropped to 64.9 years in 1988 from 65.2 in 1987. This figure is the lowest since 1981, and rising homicide rates and AIDS are identified as the major contributory factors. This finding was reported in a headline that declared: "Lifespan of Black Males is Declining." Yet, in the second paragraph of that same article, those who read closely would learn that the lifespan of black women also declined from 73.6 years in 1987 to 73.4 years in 1988. Yes, it is .1 year less than the male decline and certainly black women, like women generally, have a longer life expectancy than black men, but they too are being negatively affected by their life circumstances. The current construction obscures our recognition of that fact.[3]

Many scholars also perpetuate the invisibility of black women through continual reference to African Americans as a monolithic, genderless population. This inclination appears evident across humanities and social science disciplines and within African American Studies, per se. Unfortunately, we encounter a sustained sensitivity to race-gender dynamics only in African American studies on the family or the history, literary criticism, sociology, politics, and psychology of African American women.

In *The Myth of Black Progress*, Pinkney (1984) vigorously challenges the extant notions of socio-economic mobility as characteristic of most blacks in the United States. Most of his discussion of health, educational, and economic statuses is phrased in terms of "blacks" as a generic category; and although he provides comparative information about black females and males at sev-

eral points, his aim is to demonstrate that blacks are oppressed. He raises what he perceives as a collective reservation about addressing the interplay of racism and sexism, because to do so would be divisive in the African American community.

Scholars often have failed to recognize how the construction of issues alienates and isolates the interdynamics of race, gender, and class discriminations. Consequently, black women become invisible as the subjects of social concerns. Scott and Black (1989) correctly observe that most of the current analyses of familial dynamics and problems in the United States have a nuclear family basis. In particular, specific kin structures of blood, legal, and fictive relations among African Americans that facilitate survival and role fulfillment are generally ignored in the current discussions of black family functioning. "These current analyses routinely omit consideration of female-centered, female-anchored and female-dominated kin networks which function in interaction with male-centered, male-anchored, and male-dominated kin networks (1989:17)." Although the authors raise an important point, even their discussion perpetuates certain other biases regarding African American family and social issues. Their examination of gendered kin network centers on the limited employment and wage earning capacity of black men as the catalyst for the social and economic necessity of kinship systems. While on the one hand acknowledging the competition and complementarity of these two networks, Scott and Black concluded their article with a statement on the scarcity of marriageable black males.

This theme of marriageable black males is repeated often as both a problem for black women (in terms of their scarcity) and the solution to black poverty. In the first instance, Dr. Walter Farrell of University of Wisconsin, has been quoted as saying that "Large numbers of black professional women are alone, unmarried, and failing to procreate because of the shrinking pool of economically stable or marriageable men (Randolph, 1990:53)." In the latter case, William J. Wilson in his book, *The Truly Disadvantaged* (1987), carefully

3. During the Persian Gulf war, much was made of the overrepresentation of blacks in the deployed military forces. While only 12% of the total United States population, they accounted for almost 30% of the 540,000 troops engaged in Desert Storm. But it is seldom noted that black women are even more disproportionally represented, comprising 40 percent of the Army's women soldiers (black men are only 30% of the men in the Army's forces).

detailed the economic hardships that black female householders, especially those with out-of-wedlock births or teenage pregnancy, find are particularly intractable, even when those women are employed full time. Later in discussing marital instability, family poverty (especially female-headed household), and family deterioration, Wilson argues that the major factors are black male joblessness and underemployment. "Evidence . . . makes a compelling case for once again placing the problem of black [read black male] joblessness as a top-priority item in public policy agendas designed to enhance the status of poor black families (1987:92)." In rightfully debunking the thesis that public assistance has caused these myriad black social conditions, Wilson unwittingly, or not uncritically, implies that the Eurocentric, traditional model of the nuclear family with men earning a family wage is the solution. First he doesn't nor do most other scholars on the black family (e.g., Staples, Billingsley, Murray) acknowledge as problematic assumptions which Collins aptly summarizes.

> The thesis underlying the two works (Moyer's "The Vanishing Family" and Moynihan's *The Negro Family*) is quite simple: appropriate values and their accompanying behavioral outcomes produce economic success, while deviant values shape behaviors that incur economic penalties (1989).

The question of whether this scheme is generally reliable, and particularly valid for African Americans remains uninvestigated. Yes, two-parent families are relatively better off than female-headed ones, but that fact does not necessarily support this explanation. Nor are the shadows of Moynihan's thesis of the detrimental impact of the alleged gender role reversal (i.e., deviant) in African American families avoided. The solution to family disorder and poverty is for black men to be real men (i.e., proper providers and household authority), and for black women to be proper wives and mothers.

Second, Wilson, again like other scholars, also posits the nuclear model without considering the dependencies, deprivations, and inequalities for women in such familial structures. Additionally, he totally ignores the dynamics of gender discrimination in wages, that, coupled with those of race, place black women at a dou-

ble disadvantage. Because women are marginal, if not quite invisible, as subjects in his study, patriarchy in familial and economic realms is unexamined. Consequently, Wilson totally misses the most obvious solution, that individuals regardless of their race, gender, or marital status should earn a meaningful wage.

Brewer (1988:338) described the impoverished black female-headed households as the product of a "whole series of social, political, and economic forces" that marginalized blacks in the urban economy, normatively devalued marriage, exacerbated the differential female obligations for child-rearing, and perpetuated sex discrimination in the labor force. To overlook these dynamics, or the biases in certain notions of family and well-being, contributes to some of the curious constructions of African American social issues that have been mentioned.

Black Women as Advantaged, Blaming Black Women

The perception that black women are educationally or economically advantaged in comparison to black men operates in tandem with the often understated perception that they also are accountable for black men's demise. One view of the black male crisis is constructed through implication of black women as not suffering as much as black men. This is most evident in the discussion of educational and economic concerns. Approximately 194,000 more black women than men have entered college in the last ten years. In the last seven years, studies report that the number of black men in medical school declined 12% while the number of black women rose by almost one-third. Similarly, the National Bar Association estimates that seven out of every ten blacks entering law school are women, while reportedly 60% of all black MBA's are women. Gibbs explains this apparent advantage for being black and female as a product of white males' historical efforts to subordinate black men, who are perceived as and known to be a threat to his dominance. Black women, less threatening, are given differential opportunities to attend school. There are various levels where this formulation might be challenged. First, we might ask what are the relevant male to female ratios for assessing an advantage. In 1987, in the 14–24 years range the ratio was 97.9, and it declines to 86.9 in the 24–44 range. Second, because the median level of educational attainment is roughly the same for both sexes, 12.4 years in 1987, then a similar proportion of black men must be in higher education, although not in law and business. For instance, black men are twice as likely to earn professional degrees and doctorates. Third, we also know that while representation may be increasing for black women or black men depending on the field, since 1976 there has been an overall downward trend in black undergraduate enrollment despite continuing increases in black high school completion rates (Sudarkasa, 1989; Wilson, 1990).

The Moynihan report and its aftermath in the 1960s, and its companion volume, Murray's *Losing Ground* (1984), have had a dual-edged impact. On the one hand, critics of Moynihan and of Murray have overromanticized the strengths of the black family. Yet, on the other hand, both works have fueled the identification of black woman as the culprit, if not the victimizer, in black social issues of that day. For example, Shahrazad Ali's infamous book *The Blackman's Guide to Understanding the Blackwoman,* makes explicit one of the underlying presumptions in constructing African American social problems as being principally those of the black male versus black women. The presumption is that black women offer minimal assistance or may be a direct hinderance to the development, mobility, and success of black boys and men. The threat to the well being of black men is presented in various guises, whether as teacher and sister students who preclude or subvert their learning, or as the mythical "twofers" who displace black men from colleges or employment.

The wide-spread notion that black women are advantaged discounts the myriad dimensions of oppression in their lives. The contradictions of the war against drugs and the inadequacy of treatment for black women illustrates this point. As of February 1990, there have been at least 35 attempts at prosecuting what is called "crack pregnancies", that is, expectant mothers with a record of drug use. Most of these women are African American. The so-called war on drugs has led to a criminalization of women's conduct during pregnancy. This persists despite the significant limited availability of insurance, treatment programs, and facilities for such women. For example, in New York, 87% of programs refuse pregnant crack addicts on Medicaid (Maher, 1989). As Maher correctly observed, the emergence of "crack pregnancies" as a public problem is a product of the interaction of political process, scholarly research, and the post-Reagan political culture. Under the guise of addressing health risks for the woman and preventing/halting those to the fetus, these prosecutions have sought to establish and legitimate a mechanism for further controlling the lives of African American and poor women.

> Every dollar spent on the cops, courts, corrections, and bureaucratic infrastructures required to sustain the drug-war machine is a dollar diverted from reversing the social policies that gave birth to the ghetto, nurtured sexism and racism, and spawned the crack culture (Maher, 1990:126).

Unfortunately, we who are African Americans and we who are scholars have often failed to recognize the dominant society's image-formation and manipulation of social issues confronting the black community and the larger society. Indeed, one tactic is for issues to be defined as "black", thus making them both the product and responsibility of black people.

AN AFROCENTRIC CONSTRUCTION OF AFRICAN AMERICAN SOCIAL ISSUES

Sociologist Patricia Hill Collins, in a review of two works on the black family, asserts that it is important for us to understand the broad question of "how race, class, and gender shape group status in general . . . (are) intertwined in maintaining relations of domination and subordination in general (1989:00)." Her critical evaluation demonstrates how the perception of any one factor, for example class in these works, fundamentally alters the analysis of how race and gender affect African American family life. She concludes that "removing any one piece of the triad of race, gender or class from the analysis seriously jeopardizes a full understanding of the experiences of any group of people (1989:00)."

In this essay, I have attempted to demonstrate how the removal, marginalization, or manipulation of gender dynamics have distinctly shaped the construction of African American social issues. In privileging African American men, we have defined their circumstances as definitive for the entire population; their problems as the social issue. Certainly, the lives and conditions of men are part of the status and conditions of the whole, they are important and require attention. But they alone do not constitute the whole, nor represent or substitute for all the concerns of African Americans. It is on that whole that identifying African American social issues toward the 21st century should be based, constructed, and remedied. What we require are the conceptual tools with which to address the whole, to handle the multiple dynamics of race, class, and gender.

Henry (1990) argues that the process of developing an understanding of African American political ideology must begin with its oral tradition and beliefs as expressed through folklore, music, proverbs, and religion. Historian Elsa Barkley Brown (1990) has described the task of historians as learning to listen to the gumbo ya ya (see Luisah Teish's discussion of "everyone talks at once") or jazz of history, that is the multiple rhythms of events and voices that are played simultaneously. The good historian, like the skilled jazz musician, should recognize the multiple rhythms of gender, class, ethnicity, sexuality and other differences.

I wish to argue that African American culture, its oral, expressive, and material manifestations, may inform our construction of social issues. In my own work, I have analyzed African American women's strip quilting, with its striking similarities in aesthetics to West African textiles known as kente cloth. Paralleling the distinctive qualities of African rhythms and jazz, their fabric is constructed through the asymmetric juxtaposition of strips in bold contrasting colors. The ability to discern and comprehend the experiences and circumstances of a variety of African Americans is critical for addressing the complexity of social issues for the community. In many ways, the current construction of those issues as primarily, if not exclusively, the decimation of African American males unfortunately suggests that we have lost a viable means for crafting social issues. In reviewing the literature, we see empha-

sis on the single rhythm of the black male, ignoring the counter-rhythmic and harmonizing voices of women; we must not focus on a single color of a particular socioeconomic class, blind to the brilliant interplay of varying class and race compositions. Have we as scholars, educators, and social activists lost the ability to appreciate and conceptualize the jazzy, asymmetrical polyrhythms of African American life?

As we look toward the 21st century, African American Studies pertaining to social issues will require of us greater skills in both listening to and playing jazz. As Elsa Barkley Brown observes, good jazz training might enable us to improvise, to respect the multiple, open-ended, and unexpected variations of human life. As scholars, we need to develop conceptual frameworks and conduct historical, literary, and social analyses that are inclusive of the experiences of African American women and men; that are inclusive in their consideration of the dynamics of class, race, gender and other oppressions, and that are inclusive in the recognition of the various mechanisms of self-determination, empowerment, and resistence that all African Americans have designed.

BIBLIOGRAPHY

Allen, Walter R. 1988. "Family Roles, Occupational Statuses, and Achievement Orientations among Black Women in the United States," in *Black Women in America: Social Science Perspectives*, edited by Micheline R. Malson, Elisabeth Mudimbe-Boyi, Jean F. O'Barr, and Mary Wyer. Chicago: University of Chicago Press:79–96.

Alliance Against Women's Oppression, 1991. "Poverty: Not for Women Only—A Critique of the 'Feminization of Poverty,'" in *The Black Family*, edited by Robert Staples. Belmont, CA: Wadsworth Publishing Co.:240–247.

Arnold, Regina A. 1990. "Processes of Victimization and Criminalization of Black Women," *Social Justice*, v17 n3, Fall:153–166.

Berger, Peter and Thomas Luckman. 1966. *The Social Construction of Reality*, Garden City, NY: Doubleday.

Bernstein, Blanche. 1991. "Since the Moynihan Report . . . ," in *The Black Family*, edited by Robert Staples. Belmont, CA: Wadsworth Publishing Co.

Blackwell, James E. 1985, 2nd edition, *The Black Community: Diversity and Unity,* New York: Harper and Row Publishers.

Bobo, Lawrence, 1991. "Social Responsibility, Individualism, and Redistributive Policies," *Sociological Forces,* v6 n1:71–92.

Brewer, Rose E. 1988. "Black Women in Poverty: Some Comments on Female-Headed Families," *Signs,* v13 n2.

Brown, Elsa Barkley. 1990. "Intersections and Collision Courses: Women, Blacks, and Workers Confront Gender, Race, and Class," Unpublished manuscript, presented at American Historical Association, December 28.

Center for the Study of Social Policy. 1991. "The 'Flip-Side' of Black Families Headed by Women: The Economic Status of Black Men," in *The Black Family,* edited by Robert Staples, Belmont, CA: Wadsworth Publishing Co.

Collins, Patricia Hill. 1990. *Black Feminist Thought: Knowledge, Consciousness, and the Politics of Empowerment.* Boston: Unwin Hyman.

Collins, Patricia Hill. 1989. "A Comparison of Two Works on Black Family Life," in *Signs,* v14 n4.

Geschwender, James A. and Rita Carroll-Sequin. 1988. "Exploding the Myth of African-American Progress," in *Black Women in America: Social Science Perspectives,* edited by Micheline R. Malson, Elisabeth Mudimbe-Boyi, Jean F. O'Barr, and Mary Wyer. Chicago: University of Chicago Press: 97–114.

Gibbs, Jewelle Taylor. 1988. *Young, Black and Male in America: An Endangered Species.*

Henry, Charles P. 1990. *Culture and African American Politics.* Bloomington, IN: Indiana University Press.

Johnson, Gloria Jones. 1989. "Underemployment, Underpayment, and Psychosocial Stress Among Working Black Men," *Western Journal of Black Studies,* v13 n2, Summer:57–65.

Jordan, June. 1987. "Don't You Talk About My Mama," *Essence,* December:53, 125–26.

Kunjufu, Jawaanza, *Countering the Conspiracy to Destroy Black Boys,* 1987, Chicago. African American Images.

Lemann, Nicholas. 1986b. "The Origins of the Underclass," *The Atlantic Monthly.* In two parts, June and July.

Maher, Lisa. 1990. "Criminalizing Pregnancy—The Downside of a Kinder, Gentler Nation?," *Social Justice,* v17 n3, Fall:111–135.

Mayfield, Lorraine P. 1991, 4th ed. "Early Parenthood among Low-Income Adolescent Girls," in *The Black Family: Essays and Studies.* Belmont, CA: Wadsworth Publishing Co.:227–239.

Murray, Charles. 1984. *Losing Ground: American Social Policy, 1950–1980.* New York: Basic Books.

National Urban League. 1986–1990. Annuals on *The State of Black America* edited by Janet Dewart. New York: National Urban League, Inc.

Perry, Robert L. 1989. "Re-examining the Black on Black Crime Issue: A Theoretical Essay." *Western Journal of Black Studies,* v13 n2, Summer:66–71.

Pinkney, Alphonso. 1984. *The Myth of Black Progress.* Cambridge: Cambridge University Press.

Ebony, Special Issue on the Black Male. August 1990.

Randolph, Laura B. 1990. "What Can We Do About the Most Explosive Problem in Black America: The Widening Gap Between Women who are Making It and Men Who Aren't." *Ebony,* v45 n10, August:52–58.

"Scapegoating the Black Family: Black Women Speak." 1989. Special issue of *The Nation.* July:24–31.

Scott, Joseph W. and Albert Black. 1989. "Deep Structures of African American Family Life: Female and Male Kin Networks. *Western Journal of Black Studies,* v13 n1. Spring:17–24.

Staples, Robert, ed. 1991, 4th ed. *The Black Family: Essays and Studies.* Belmont, CA: Wadsworth Publishing Co.

Staples, Robert. 1991. "The Political Economy of Black Family Life," in *The Black Family,* edited by Robert Staples. Belmont, CA: Wadsworth Publishing Co.:248–256.

Staples, Robert. 1991. "Substance Abuse and the Black Family Crisis: An Overview," in *The Black Family,* edited by Robert Staples. Belmont, CA: Wadsworth Publishing Co.:257–267.

Sudarkasa, Niara. 1988. "Black Enrollment in Higher Education: The Unfulfilled Promise of Equality," in National Urban League. 1988. Annuals on *The State of Black America* edited by Janet Dewart. New York: National Urban League, Inc.

Taylor, Ronald L. 1991, 4th ed. "Black Youth In Crisis," in *The Black Family: Essays and Studies,* Belmont, CA: Wadsworth Publishing Co.:211–226.

United States Department of Commerce. 1990. *Statistical Abstract of the United States—1989,* Washington, D.C., Government Printing Office.

Uzzell, Odell and Wilma Peebles-Wilkins. 1989. "Black Spouse Abuse: A Focus on Relational Factors and Intervention Strategies," *Western Journal of Black Studies*, v13 n1:10–16

White, Evelyn C., ed. 1990. *The Black Women's Health Book: Speaking for Ourselves*. Seattle, WA: The Seal Press.

Wilson, William J. 1984. *The Truly Disadvantaged*. Chicago: University of Chicago Press.

Zinn, Maxine Baca. 1988. "Family, Race, and Poverty in the Eighties," in *Black Women in America: Social Science Perspectives*, edited by Micheline R. Malson, Elisabeth Mudimbe-Boyi, Jean F. O'Barr, and Mary Wyer. Chicago: University of Chicago Press:245–264.

KEY DEBATE ∼ *Society and Individual Choice*

CHERYL CLARKE

The Failure to Transform: Homophobia in the Black Community [1983]

In her groundbreaking 1971 essay, "Toward a Black Feminist Criticism" (p. 723). Barbara Smith calls for new work to reflect the realities of black women and lesbians, while stressing the need to resist homophobia in the whole black community, "which is at least as homophobic" as white society. Critic and poet Cheryl Clarke (b. 1947) builds on these ideas in the essay reprinted here. "The more homophobic we are as a people the further removed we are from any kind of revolution," asserts Clarke, who self-identifies as a black lesbian feminist. Clarke connects black homophobia to class and gender issues, labeling it both "decidedly bourgeois" and "markedly male." But prominent black female intellectuals often avoid discussing homosexuality, she says; according to Clarke, some also exploit homophobia to maintain allegiances with men or to claim heterosexual privilege, one of the few hegemonic privileges available to black women. Clarke contrasts the homophobia of black artists and intellectuals with the general acceptance of diverse lifestyles within poor black communities and ends with a call for further study of the issues she raises.

From Barbara Smith, ed., *Home Girls: A Black Feminist Anthology* (Latham, N.Y.: Kitchen Table, Women of Color Press, 1983), pp. 197–208.

That there is homophobia among black people in America is largely reflective of the homophobic culture in which we live. The following passage from the proposed "Family Protection Act" (1981, S. 1378, H.R. 3955), a venomous bill before the U.S. Congress, vividly demonstrates the depth of the ruling class' fear and hatred of homosexuals, homosexuality, and the homosexual potential in everyone (themselves included).

> No federal funds may be made available under any provision of federal law to any public or private individual, group, foundation, commission, corporation, association, or other entity for the purpose of advocating, promoting, or suggesting homosexuality, male or female, as a lifestyle (p. 9, line 13, section 108)

Yet, we cannot rationalize the disease of homophobia among black people as the white man's fault, for to do so is to absolve ourselves of our responsibility to transform ourselves. When I took my black lesbian feminist self to the First National Plenary Conference on Self-Determination (December 4, 5, 6, 1981) in New York City, thinking surely that this proclaimed "historic meeting of the Black Liberation Movement" must include black lesbian feminists, I was struck by a passage from the printed flyer left on every seat:

> Revolutionary nationalists and genuine communists cannot uphold homosexuality in the leadership of the Black Liberation Movement nor uphold it as a correct practice. Homosexuality is a genocidal practice.... Homosexuality does not produce children.... Homosexuality does not birth new warriors for liberation ... homosexuality cannot be upheld as correct or revolutionary practice.... The practice of homosexuality is an accelerating threat to our survival as a people and as a nation.

Compare these two statements—the first from the ultra(white)-right and the second from self-proclaimed black "revolutionaries and genuine communists." Both reflect a decidedly similar pathology: homophobia. If I were a "revolutionary nationalist" or even a "genuine communist," I would be concerned if my political vision in any way supported the designs of my oppressors, the custodians of white male privilege. But it is these black macho intellectuals and politicos, these heirs of Malcolm X, who have never expanded

Malcolm's revolutionary ideals beyond the day of his death, who consciously or unwittingly have absorbed the homophobia of their patriarchal slavemasters. It is they who attempt to propagate homophobia throughout the entire black community. And it is they whom I will address in this writing.

Since 1965, the era which marked a resurgence of radical black consciousness in the United States, many black people of the post–World War II generation began an all-consuming process of rejecting the values of WASP America and embracing our African and Afro-American traditions and culture. In complete contrast to the conservative black bourgeoisie and to bourgeois reformist civil rights proponents, the advocates of Black Power demanded progressive remedies to the accumulated ills of black folk in America, viewed racism as international in scope, rescued Afro-American culture from anonymity, and elevated the black man to the pedestal of authority in the black liberation movement. In order to participate in this movement one had to be black (of course), be male-oriented, and embrace a spectrum of black nationalist, separatist, Pan Africanist sentiments, beliefs, and goals. Rejection of white people was essential as well as rejection of so-called white values, which included anything from reading Kenneth Clark's *Civilization*[1] to eating a t.v. dinner.

While the cult of Black Power spurned the assimilationist goals of the politically conservative black bourgeoisie, its devotees, nevertheless, held firmly to the value of heterosexual and male superiority. As Michele Wallace[2] states in her controversial essay, "Black Macho" (1979):

> . . . the contemporary black man no longer exists for his people or even for himself. . . . He has become a martyr. And he has arrived in this place, not because of the dependency inflicted upon him

in slavery, but because his black perspective, like the white perspective, supported the notion that manhood is more valuable than anything else. (p. 79)

It is ironic that the Black Power movement could transform the consciousness of an entire generation of black people regarding black self-determination and, at the same time, fail so miserably in understanding the sexual politics of the movement and of black people across the board.

Speaking of the "sexual-racial antagonisms" dividing the Student Non-violent Coordinating Committee during the 1960s, Manning Marable[3] assesses the dilemma of the black movement of that era:

> . . . . The prevailing popular culture of racism, the sexist stereotypes held by black men and women, and the psychological patterns of dependency which exploitation creates over several generations could not be uprooted easily. In the end the Movement may have failed to create a new interracial society in the South because its advocates had first failed to transform themselves. (1980, p. 125)

Like all Americans, black Americans live in a sexually repressive culture. And we have made all manner of compromise regarding our sexuality in order to live here. We have expended much energy trying to debunk the racist mythology which says our sexuality is depraved. Unfortunately, many of us have overcompensated and assimilated the Puritan value that sex is for procreation, occurs only between men and women, and is only valid within the confines of heterosexual marriage. And, of course, like everyone else in America who is ambivalent in these respects, black folk have to live with the contradictions of this limited sexual system by repressing or closeting any other sexual/ erotic urges, feelings, or desires.

1. *Civilization* (1969) is the book version of the widely viewed 1969 BBC television series of the same name, which ran on PBS in America; written, produced, and presented by the British art historian and museum director Sir Kenneth Clark (1903–83), *Civilization* presented the history of Western civilization as seen through Western art.
2. For debate about *Black Macho*, see pp. 817–34.
3. The M. Moran Weston and Black Alumni Council Professor of African-American Studies and professor of history and public affairs at Columbia University (b. 1950); Marable has been instrumental in developing African American and Africana studies departments at numerous American universities including Ohio State University, Colgate University, and Columbia, where he was founding director of African-American Studies from 1993 to 2003 and now directs the Center for Contemporary Black History.

Dennis Altman,[4] in his pivotal work, *Homosexuality: Oppression and Liberation* (1971), says the following of Western culture:

> The repression of polymorphous perversity in Western societies has two major components: the removal of the erotic from all areas of life other than the explicitly sexual and the denial of our inherent bisexuality. (p. 79)

That Western culture is limiting, few can deny. A tremendous amount of pressure is brought to bear on men, women, and children to be heterosexual to the exclusion of every other erotic impulse. I do not begrudge heterosexuals their right to express themselves, but rabid sexual preference is a stone drag on anybody's part. That the black community is homophobic and rabidly heterosexual is a reflection of the black movement's failure to "transform" its proponents with regard to the boundless potential of human sexuality. And this failure has prevented critical collaboration with politically motivated black lesbians and gay men. Time and again homophobia sabotages coalitions, divides would-be comrades, and retards the mental restructuring, essential to revolution, which black people need so desperately.

The concept of the black family has been exploited since the publication of the infamous Moynihan report, *The Negro Family: A Case for National Action* (1965).[5] Because the insular, privatized nuclear family is upheld as the model of Western family stability, all other forms—for example, the extended family, the female-headed family, the lesbian family—are devalued. Many black people, especially middle-class black people, have accepted the male-dominated nuclear family model, though we have had to modify it because black women usually must work outside the home. Though "revolutionary nationalists and genuine communists" have not accepted the nuclear family model per se, they have accepted African and Eastern patriarchal forms of the family, including polygamy (offering the specious rationalization that there are more black women than black

men). Homosexuality is viewed as a threat to the continued existence of the heterosexual family, because homosexual unions do not, in and of themselves, produce offspring—as if one's only function within a family, within a relationship, or in sex were to produce offspring. Black family lifestyles and homosexual lifestyles are not antithetical. Most black lesbians and gay men grew up in families and are still critically involved with their families. Many black lesbians and gay men are raising children. Why must the black family be so strictly viewed as the result of a heterosexual dyad?

And finally, why is the black male so-called left so vehement in its propagation of these destructive beliefs, and why have its proponents given such relentless expression to the homophobic potential in the mass of black people? Because the participation of open black lesbians and gay men in the black so-called liberation movement is a threat to the continued hegemony of dogmatic, doctrinaire black men who have failed to reject the Western institution of heterosexuality and the Christian fundamentalist notion of sex as "sin," no matter what doctrine or guru they subscribe to. Homophobic black intellectuals and politicos are so charged with messianic fervor that they seem like a perversion of the W. E. B. Du Bois concept of the "Talented Tenth,"[6] the hypothesis that "the Negro race . . . is going to be saved by its exceptional men." Indeed, this homophobic cult of black men seems to view itself as the "exceptional men" who will save the black liberation movement from homosexual "contamination." Furthermore, the black intellectual/political man, by dint of his knowledge, training, and male privilege—and in spite of racism—has access to numerous bourgeois resources (such as television, radio, the stage, the podium, publications, and schools) whereby he can advance his reactionary ideologies and make his opinions known to the public at large.

Let us examine the rhetoric and ravings of a few notable black heterosexuals.

Chairman Baraka, Imamu Baraka, LeRoi Jones[7]—whatever patriarchal designation he assumes—is a

---

4. Australian political scientist and gay rights activist who describes himself as an "international activist-academic" (b. 1943).
5. For debate about the Moynihan report, including an excerpt of the report, see pp. 638–57.
6. For more on Du Bois and debate about the "Talented Tenth," see p. 230.
7. See p. 694.

rabid homophobe. Wherever he makes his homophobic statements, his sexist invective is not far behind. From his early works on, this chameleon, the patriarch of the "new black poetry" of the 1960s, has viewed homosexuality as a symbol of a decadent establishment, as defectiveness, as weakness, as a strictly white male flaw.

In his first book of poems, *Preface to a Twenty Volume Suicide Note* (1961), in which he reveals himself as a versatile though imitative poet, Jones is homophobic and woman-hating. In a wildly imagistic poem, "To a Publisher ... cut out," he free-associates:

> ... Charlie Brown spent most of his time whacking his doodle, or having weird relations with that dopey hound of his (though that's a definite improvement over ... that filthy little lesbian he's hung up with). (p. 19)

In the same poem, Jones debunks the myth of the black woman's superior sexual prowess: "I have slept with almost every mediocre colored woman/On 23rd St ..." (p. 19).

In his notorious essay "American Sexual Reference: Black Male" (*Home*, 1965) Jones lays the ultimate disparagement on the American white man and white woman:

> Most American white men are trained to be fags. ... That red flush, those silk blue faggot eyes. So white women become men-things, a weird combination sucking male juices to build a navel orange, which is themselves. (p. 216)

But Jones is at his heterosexist best in the essay "Black Woman" (*Raise Race Rays Raze*, 1971), which should have been titled, "One Black Macho Man's Narcissistic Fantasy." He commands the black woman, with arrogant condescension, to "complement" her man, to "inspire" her man. He is laughable in his smugness, his heterosexist presumptions—to say nothing of his obvious contempt for women. It seems that his homophobic and misogynist attitudes have not abated since

he embraced Marxism. Leroi-Imamu-Chairman-Jones-Baraka is an irreversible homophobe. Methinks he protests too much.

In another classic example of sixties-style black woman-hatred, playwright Ed Bullins[8] attempts a portrayal of a lesbian relationship in *Clara's Ole Man* (1965). The action is set in the North Philadelphia flat of Clara and Big Girl, Clara's "ole man" who is stereotypically "butch." Clara and Big Girl are not disparaged by their "ghetto" community, symbolized by two older, alcoholic black women who stay upstairs and by three juvenile delinquents, Stoogie, Bama, and Hoss, who take refuge from a police chase in the couple's apartment, a familiar haunt. It is only Jack, an outsider and an ex-Marine in pursuit of upward mobility through "college prep courses," who is too narcissistic to understand the obvious bond between the two women. Jack, whose intention is to date Clara, "retches" when he realizes Clara and Big Girl are lovers. *Clara's Ole Man* is a substanceless rendering of the poor black community, a caricature of lesbianism, and a perpetuation of the stereotype of the pathological black community. But Ed Bullins gained a great deal of currency among black and white "avant-garde" intellectuals for his ability to replicate and create caricatures of black life.

In that same year (1965), a pivotal year in the political development of black people, Calvin Hernton[9] discusses the interrelationship of sex and racism in his popular book, *Sex and Racism in America*. Hernton does not address the issue of homosexuality in any of his four essays, "The White Woman," "The Negro Male," "The White Male," and "The Negro Woman." In several homophobic asides Hernton is alternately dismayed by, presumptuous about, and intrigued by his observations of homosexual behavior:

> The extent to which some white women are attracted to Negro lesbians is immensely revealing—even the Negro lesbian is a "man." It is not an uncommon sight (in Greenwich Village, for instance) to see these "men" exploiting this image of themselves to the zenith. (p. 113)

---

8. Playwright of the Black Arts Movement.
9. Sociologist, poet, and writer (1932–2001).

.... One man who seemed *effeminate* put coins into the jukebox, *swished* along side of me. (p. 114)

He had the appearance of a businessman or a politician—except for his eyes, which seemed to hold some dark secret, something in them that made me wonder...maybe this man was a homosexual. (p.89) [Ital.mine.]

We can see from the few passages cited above that homophobia in the black community has not only a decidedly bourgeois character but also a markedly male imprint. Which is not to say, however, that homophobia is limited to the psyche of the black intellectual male, but only that it is he who institutionalizes the illness within our political/intellectual community. And rest assured, we can find his homophobic counterpart in black women, who are, for the most part, afraid of risking the displeasure of their homophobic brothers were they to address, seriously and in a principled way, homosexuality. Black bourgeois female intellectuals practice homophobia by omission more often than rabid homophobia.

Michele Wallace's *Black Macho and the Myth of the Superwoman* is a most obvious example. This brave and scathing analysis of the sexual politics of the black political community after 1965 fails to treat the issues of gay liberation, black lesbianism, or homophobia vis-à-vis the black liberation or the women's liberation movement. In "Black Macho," the opening essay, Wallace addresses the homophobia of Eldridge Cleaver[1] and Amiri Baraka, but she neither calls it "homophobia" nor criticizes these attitudes as a failing of the black liberation movement. For the sake of her own argument re the black macho neurosis, Wallace exploits the popular conception of male homosexuality as passivity, the willingness to be fucked (preferably by a white man, according to Cleaver). It is then seen as antithetical to the concept of black macho, the object of which is to do the fucking. Wallace does not debunk this stereotype of male homosexuality. In her less effective essay, "The Myth of the Super-

woman," Wallace omits any mention of black lesbians. In 1979, when asked at a public lecture at Rutgers University in New Jersey why the book had not addressed the issues of homosexuality and homophobia, the author responded that she was not an "expert" on either issue. But Wallace, by her own admission, was also not an "expert" on the issues she *did* address in her book.

The black lesbian is not only absent from the pages of black political analysis, her image as a character in literature and her role as a writer are blotted out from or trivialized in literary criticism written by black women. Mary Helen Washington's[2] otherwise useful anthologies are a prime example of this omission of black lesbianism and black lesbian writers. In both *Black Eyed Susans* (1975) and *Midnight Birds* (1980), the editor examines the varied roles black women have played in the black community and how these roles are more authentically depicted in the fiction of black women than in the fiction of black men.

In her introduction to *Midnight Birds*, Washington speaks of the major themes of the material presented in this anthology: "women's reconciliation with one another," antagonisms with men, "areas of commonality among black and white women." Now, one would think with all the mention of these women-identified themes that there would be a lesbian story or two in the anthology. But, again, we are disappointed. There is no mention of lesbianism in the introduction, there are no open lesbian contributors to the anthology, and there is no lesbian story in the collection. And yet, we know there is certainly plenty of available work by black lesbian writers. For example, Audre Lorde's[3] lesbian fiction piece, "Tar Beach," which appeared in *Conditions: Five, The Black Women's Issue* in 1979—prior to the publication of *Midnight Birds*—would have powerfully enhanced the collection. Washington knows that black lesbian writers exist. In a footnote to the previously mentioned introduction (p. xxv), Washington credits Barbara Smith's essay, "Toward a Black Feminist Criticism"[4] (*Conditions: Two*, 1977), as one of

1. Activist and journalist (1935–98); one of the founders of the Black Panther Party in 1966 and their Minister of Information; his collection of autobiographical essays *Soul on Ice* (1968) was written while he was in jail for rape and assault with intent to murder; in the 1970s, he renounced the Black Panthers and became a born-again Christian and a conservative Republican.
2. Other major publications by Mary Helen Washington, professor of English at the University of Maryland at College Park, include *Invented Lives: Narratives of Black Women, 1860–1960* (1987) and *Memory of Kin: Stories About Family by Black Writers* (1991).
3. Reference to writer and activist (1934–92) who described herself as "Black, Lesbian, Mother, Warrior, Poet."
4. See p. 723.

two pieces of writing which has challenged and shaped her thinking. Smith is a lesbian and she writes about lesbianism. The other piece Washington refers to, Adrienne Rich's[5] "Disloyal to Civilization: Feminism, Racism, Gynephobia" (*On Lies, Secrets, and Silence*, 1979) is written by a lesbian as well.

One of the most recent books to appear in the name of feminism is Bell Hooks'[6] *Ain't I A Woman: Black Women and Feminism*. Hooks seems to purposely ignore the existence and central contributions of black lesbians to the feminist movement. Aside from a gross lack of depth in her analysis of the current women's movement in America, the most resounding short-coming of this work of modern feminism is its omission of any discussion of lesbian feminism, the radicalizing impact of which distinguishes this era of feminism from the previous eras. Hooks does not even mention the word *lesbian* in her book. This is unbearable. Ain't lesbians women, too? Homophobia in the black move-ment and in the women's movement is not treated, yet lesbians historically have been silenced and repressed in both. In her statement, "Attacking heterosexuality does little to strengthen the self-concept of the masses of women who desire to be with men" (p. 191), Hooks delivers a backhanded slap at lesbian feminists, a con-siderable number of whom are black. Hooks would have done well to attack the institution of heterosexu-ality, as it is a prime tool of black women's oppression in America. Like the previously discussed writers, Hooks fears alienating the black community cum the black bourgeois intellectual/political establishment. And there is the fear of transformation, the fear that the word will generate the deed. Like her black male counterpart, the black woman intellectual is afraid to relinquish heterosexual privilege. So little else is guar-anteed black people.

I must confess that, in spite of the undeniably homophobic pronouncements of black intellectuals, I sometimes become impatient with the accusations of homophobia hurled at the black community by many

gay men and lesbians, as if the whole black community were more homophobic than the heterosexist culture we live in. The entire black community gets blamed for the reactionary postures of a few petit-bourgeois intel-lectuals and politicos. Since no one has bothered to study the black community's attitudes on homosexuals, homosexuality, or homosexual lifestyles, it is not accu-rate to attribute homophobia to the mass of black people.

Prior to the growth of the contemporary black middle class, which has some access to the white world, the black community—due to segregation North and South—was even more diverse, encompassing a world of black folk of every persuasion, profession, status, and lifestyle. There have always been upwardly mobile blacks, but until the late 1950s and early sixties there had never been so many opportunities to reap the ten-uous fruits of affluence outside the traditional black community. The cordoning off of all types of black people into a single community because of race may be one influence on black attitudes toward difference.

The poor and working-class black community, historically more radical and realistic than the reform-ist and conservative black middle class and the atavis-tic, "blacker-than-thou" (bourgeois) nationalists, has often tolerated an individual's lifestyle prerogatives, even when that lifestyle was disparaged by the prevail-ing culture. Though lesbians and gay men were exotic subjects of curiosity, they were accepted as part of the community (neighborhood)—or at least, there were no manifestos calling for their exclusion from the community.

I can recall being about twelve years old when I first saw a black lesbian couple. I was walking down the street with my best friend, Kathy. I saw two young women walking together in the opposite direction. One wore a doo-rag, a Banlon button-down, and high-top sneakers. The other woman wore pink brush rollers, spit curls plastered with geech, an Oxford-tailored shirt, a mohair sweater, fitted skirt with a kick pleat, black stockings, and the famous I. Miller[7] flat, sling-back shoe, the most

---

5. Reference to the white American poet and activist (b. 1929) who, when awarded the National Book Award for Poetry in 1974, refused to accept it as an individual, instead accepting it with Audre Lorde and Alice Walker on behalf of all women.
6. Writer and activist bell hooks (née Gloria Watkins, b. 1952) is a distinguished professor in residence of Appalachian studies at Berea College; hooks critiques the "white-supremacist-capitalist-patriarchy," the interconnected political systems that she argues are the foundation of U.S. politics.
7. In the 1920s, Polish shoe designer and maker Israel Miller (d. 1929) established a national chain of stores selling the I. Miller line of shoes, a high-end brand produced through the 1960s.

prestigious pair of kicks any Dee Cee[8] black girl could own. I asked Kathy, "Who are they?" "Bulldaggers," she answered. "What's that?" I asked again. "You know, they go with each other," Kathy responded. "Why?" I continued. "Protection," Kathy said casually. "Protection?" I repeated. "Yeah, at least they won't get pregnant," Kathy explained.

It is my belief that poor black communities have often accepted those who would be outcast by the ruling culture—many times to spite the white man, but mainly because the conditions of our lives have made us empathic. And, as it stands now, the black political community seems bereft of that humanity which has always been a tradition among Afro-American freedom fighters, the most illustrious of whom have come from the grassroots.

As a group and as individuals, black lesbians and gay men—sometimes obvious and sometimes not—have been as diverse as the communities we've lived in. Like most other people, we have been workers, church-goers, parents, hustlers, and upwardly mobile. Since black gay men and lesbians have always been viable contributors to our communities, it is exceedingly painful for us to face public denunciation from black folk—the very group who should be championing our liberation. Because of the level of homophobia in the culture in general, many black gay men and lesbians remain in the closet, passing as heterosexuals. Thus, when public denunciations of our lifestyles are made by other black people, we remain silent in the face of their hostility and ignorance. The toll taken on us because we repress our rage and hurt makes us distrustful of all people whom we cannot identify as lesbian or gay. Also, for those of us who are isolated from the gay or lesbian community, the toll is greater self-hate, self-blame, and belief in the illness theory of homosexuality.

In the face of this, open and proud black gay men and lesbians must take an assertive stand against the blatant homophobia expressed by members of the black intellectual and political community, who consider themselves custodians of the revolution. For if we will not tolerate the homophobia of the culture in general, we cannot tolerate it from black people, no matter what their positions in the black liberation movement.

Homophobia is a measure of how far removed we are from the psychological transformation we so desperately need to engender. The expression of homophobic sentiments, the threatening political postures assumed by black radicals and progressives of the nationalist/communist ilk, and the seeming lack of any willingness to understand the politics of gay and lesbian liberation collude with the dominant white male culture to repress not only gay men and lesbians, but also to repress a natural part of all human beings, namely the bisexual potential in us all. Homophobia divides black people as political allies, it cuts off political growth, stifles revolution, and perpetuates patriarchal domination.

The arguments I have presented are not definitive. I hope that others may take some of the issues raised in this essay into consideration for further study. The sexual politics of the black liberation movement have yet to be addressed by its advocates. We will continue to fail to transform ourselves until we reconcile the unequal distribution of power in our political community accorded on the basis of gender and sexual choice. Visions of black liberation which exclude lesbians and gay men bore and repel me, for as a black lesbian I am obligated and dedicated to destroying heterosexual supremacy by "suggesting, promoting, and advocating" the rights of gay men and lesbians wherever we are. And we are everywhere. As political black people, we bear the twin responsibilities of transforming the social, political, and economic systems of oppression as they affect all our people—not just the heterosexuals—and of transforming the corresponding psychological structure that feeds into these oppressive systems. The more homophobic we are as a people the further removed we are from any kind of revolution. Not only must black lesbians and gay men be committed to destroying homophobia, but *all* black people must be committed to working out and rooting out homophobia in the black community. We begin to eliminate homophobia by engaging in dialogue with the advocates of gay and lesbian liberation, educating ourselves about gay and lesbian politics, confronting and correcting homophobic attitudes, and understanding how these attitudes prevent the liberation of the total being.

8. Reference to Washington, D.C., where Clarke grew up.

REFERENCES

[Altman, Dennis. *Homosexuality: Oppression and Liberation* New York: Outerbridge and Dienstfrey, 1971.]

Baldwin, James. *Another Country.* New York: Dial Press, 1968.

Baraka, Imamu Amiri. *Raise Race Rays Raze: Essays Since 1965.* New York: Random House, 1971.

Bullins, Ed. *Five Plays by Ed Bullins.* New York: Bobbs-Merrill Co., Inc., 1968.

Hernton, Calvin. *Sex and Racism in America.* New York: Grove Press, 1965.

[hooks, bell. *Ain't I A Woman: Black Women and Feminism.* Boston: South End Press, 1981.]

Jones, LeRoi. *Preface to a Twenty Volume Suicide Note.* New York: Totem/Corinth, 1961.

Jones, LeRoi. *The Dead Lecturer.* New York: Grove Press, 1964.

Jones, LeRoi. "American Sexual Reference: Black Male." *Home.* New York: William Morrow and Co., Inc., 1966.

Staples, Robert. "Mystique of Black Sexuality," in Staples (ed.) *The Black Family: Essays and Studies.* Belmont, California: Wadsworth Publishing Co., Inc., 1977.

Wallace, Michele. *Black Macho and the Myth of the Super-woman.* New York: Dial Press, 1979.

Washington, Mary Helen. "In Pursuit of Our Own History," in M.H. Washington (ed.) *Midnight Birds.* New York: Anchor Books, 1980.

BARBARA SMITH

Blacks and Gays: Healing the Great Divide [1993]

In June 1993, a group of black ministers from Cleveland published "The Black Church Position Statement on Homosexuality" in the city's African American newspaper, *Call and Post*. The ministers asserted that homosexuality is contrary to the teachings of the Bible. The ministers urged compassion for homosexuals but saw their "restoration" to heterosexuality as the ultimate goal. In this 1993 essay, black feminist activist and theorist Barbara Smith (b. 1946) details her challenge to the Cleveland ministers' campaign against homosexuality. She describes how her frustrated efforts at grassroots organization revealed a lack of cohesive leadership in both the black and white gay communities.

Smith's activist focus demonstrates that there are different ways to participate in a debate. Rather than engage each of the ministers' statements in a detailed argument and thereby imply that the statements have enough validity to make them worthy of a response, Smith's strategy is to reject their entire platform as homophobic. Thus, she is able to reframe the debate to focus on the challenges, and the necessity, of active resistance to such homophobic movements.

From *Gay Community News* (Boston, 1993); reprinted in Barbara Smith, *The Truth that Never Hurts: Writings in Race, Gender, and Freedom* (New Brunswick, N.J.: Rutgers University Press, 1998), pp. 125–31.

Perhaps the most maddening question anyone can ask me is "Which do you put first: being Black or being a woman, being Black or being gay?" The underlying assumption is that I should prioritize one of my identities because one of them is actually more important than the rest or that I must arbitrarily choose one of them over the others for the sake of acceptance in one particular community.

I always explain that I refuse to do political work and, more importantly, to live my life in this way. All of the aspects of who I am are crucial, indivisible, and pose no inherent conflict. They only seem to be in opposition in this particular time and place, living under U.S. capitalism, a system whose functioning has always required that large groups of people be economically, racially, and sexually oppressed and that these potentially dissident groups be kept divided from each other at all costs.

I've devoted many years to making the connections between issues and communities and to forging strong working coalitions. Although this work is far from finished, it has met with some success. In 1993, however, two aspects of my identity and two communities whose freedom I've always fought for are being publicly defined as being at war with one another.

For the first time, the relationship between the African American and lesbian and gay communities is being widely debated both within and outside of movement circles. One catalyst for this discussion has been gay leaders cavalierly comparing lifting the ban on homosexuals in the military with racially desegregating the armed forces following World War II. The National Association for the Advancement of Colored People (NAACP) and other Black civil rights organizations' decisions to speak out in favor of lesbian and gay rights and to support the April 1993 March on Washington have met with protests from some sectors of the Black community and have also spurred the debate.

Ironically, the group of people who are least often consulted about their perspectives on this great divide are those who are most deeply affected by it: Black lesbian and gay activists. Contradictions that we have been grappling with for years, namely homophobia in the Black community, racism in the lesbian and gay community, and the need for both communities to work together as allies to defeat our real enemies, are suddenly on other people's minds. Because Black lesbians and gays are not thought of as leaders in either movement, however, this debate has been largely framed by those who have frighteningly little and inaccurate information.

Thanks in part to the white lesbian and gay community's own public relations campaigns, Black Americans view the lesbian and gay community as uniformly wealthy, highly privileged, and politically powerful, a group that has suffered nothing like the centuries of degradation caused by U.S. racism. Rev. Dennis Kuby, a civil rights activist, states in a letter to *The New York Times:* "Gays are not subject to water hoses and police dogs, denied access to lunch counters, or prevented from voting." Most Blacks have no idea, however, that we are threatened with the loss of employment, of housing, and of custody of our children, and are subject to verbal abuse, gay bashing, and death at the hands of homophobes. Kuby's statement also does not acknowledge those lesbians and gays who have been subjected to all of the racist abuse he cites, because we are both Black and gay. Because we are rendered invisible in both Black and gay contexts, it is that much eas-

ier for the Black community to oppose gay rights and to express homophobia without recognizing that these attacks and the lack of legal protections affect its own members.

The racism that has pervaded the mainstream gay movement only fuels the perceived divisions between Blacks and gays. Single-issue politics, unlike lesbian and gay organizing that is consciously and strategically connected to the overall struggle for social and economic justice, do nothing to convince Blacks that lesbians and gays actually care about eradicating racial oppression. At the very same time that some gays make blanket comparisons between the gay movement and the Black Civil Rights movement, they also assume that Blacks and other people of color have won all our battles and are in terrific shape in comparison with lesbians and gays.

In an interview in the *Dallas Voice* (December 1992), lesbian publisher Barbara Grier states: "We are the last minority group unfairly legislated against in the U.S." Grier's perception is of course inaccurate. Legislation that negatively affects people of color, immigrants, disabled people, and women occurs every day, especially when court decisions that undermine existing legal protections are taken into account.

In 1991, well before the relationship between the gay community and the Black community was a hot topic, Andrew Sullivan, editor of the *New Republic* asserted the following in the *Advocate:*

> The truth is, our position is far worse than that of any ethnic minority or heterosexual women.
>
> Every fundamental civil right has already been granted to these groups: The issues that they discuss now involve nuances of affirmative action, comparable pay, and racial quotas. Gay people, however, still live constitutionally in the South of the '50s. . . .
>
> We are not allowed to marry—a right granted to American Blacks even under slavery and never denied to heterosexuals. We are not permitted to enroll in the armed services—a right granted decades ago to blacks and to heterosexual women.
>
> Our civil rights agenda, then, should have less to do with the often superfluous minority politics of the 1991 Civil Rights Act and more to do with

the vital moral fervor of the Civil Rights Act of 1964.

A better strategy to bring about a society more tolerant of gay men and women would involve dropping our alliance with the current Rainbow Coalition lobby and recapturing the clarity of the original civil rights movement. The point is to rekindle the cause of Martin Luther King Jr. and not to rescue the career of Jesse Jackson.

Sullivan's cynical distortions ignore that quality of life is determined by much more than legislation. Clearly, he also knows nothing about slavery. Slaves were frequently not permitted to marry and their marriages and family relationships were not legally recognized or protected. Until 1967 when the Supreme Court decided *Loving v. Virginia,* it was illegal for Blacks to marry whites in sixteen states. The armed services were rigidly segregated until after World War II. Racist abuse and denial of promotions and military honors typified the Black experience in the military. Sullivan also has not noticed that joblessness, poverty, racist and sexist violence, and the lack of decent housing, health care, and education make the lives of many "ethnic minorities" and "heterosexual women" a living hell. But Sullivan doesn't care about these folks. He just wants to make sure he gets what he thinks he deserves as an upper-class white male.

Lesbians and gay men of color have been trying to push the gay movement to grasp the necessity of antiracist practice for nigh on twenty years. Except in the context of organizing within the women's movement with progressive white lesbian feminists, we haven't made much progress.

I'm particularly struck by the fact that for the most part queer theory and queer politics, which are currently so popular, offer neither substantial antiracist analysis nor practice. Queer activists' understanding of how to deal with race is usually limited to their including a few lesbians or gay men of color in their ranks, who are expected to carry out the political agenda that the white majority has already determined.

In October 1993 Lesbian Avengers from New York City traveled to several states in the Northeast on what they called a "freedom ride."[1] Lesbians of color from Albany, New York, pointed out that the appropriation of this term was offensive because the organization had not demonstrated involvement in antiracist organizing and had made few links with people of color, including nonlesbians and nongays in the communities they planned to visit. Even when we explained that calling themselves "freedom riders" might negatively affect the coalitions we've been working to build with people of color in Albany, the group kept the name and simply made a few token changes in their press release.

These divisions are particularly dangerous at a time when the white right wing has actually targeted people of color with their homophobic message. As white lesbian activist Suzanne Pharr points out in an excellent article, "Racist Politics and Homophobia":

> Community by community, the religious Right works skillfully to divide us along fissures that already exist. It is as though they have a political seismograph to locate the racism and sexism in the lesbian and gay community, the sexism and homophobia in communities of color. While the Right is *united* by their racism, sexism, and homophobia in their goal to dominate all of us, we are *divided* by our own racism, sexism, and homophobia. (*Transformation*, July/August 1993; italics mine)

The right's divisive strategy of enlisting the Black community's support for their homophobic campaign literally hit home for me in June 1993. A Black lesbian who lives in Cleveland, Ohio, where I grew up, called to tell me that a group of Black ministers had placed a virulently homophobic article in the *Call and Post,* Cleveland's Black newspaper.

Entitled "The Black Church Position Statement on Homosexuality," the ministers condemn "HOMOSEXUALITY (including bisexual as well as gay or lesbian sexual activity) as a lifestyle that is contrary to the teachings of the Bible." Although they claim to have

---

1. Reference to the Freedom Riders, interracial groups of activists organized by CORE and SNCC, who, starting on May 4, 1961, rode through the South on interstate buses to test the December 5, 1960, Supreme Court ruling in *Boyton v. Virginia,* which had outlawed segregation in restaurants and waiting rooms of terminals serving interstate buses.

tolerance and compassion for homosexuals, their ultimate goal is to bring about "'restoration,'" that is, changing lesbians and gays back into heterosexuals in order "to restore such individuals back into harmony with God's will." One of the several sources they cite to prove that such "restoration" is possible is the *Traditional Values Foundation Talking Points, 1993,* a publication of the Traditional Values Coalition.

The ministers also held a meeting and announced their goal to gather one hundred thousand signatures in Cleveland in opposition to the federal civil rights bill, HB 431, and to take their campaign to Detroit and Pittsburgh. A major spokesperson for the ministers, Rev. Marvin McMichol, is the minister of Antioch Baptist Church, the church I was raised in and of which the women in my family were pillars. Antioch was on a number of levels one of the most progressive congregations in Cleveland, especially because of the political leadership it provided at a time when Black people were not allowed to participate in any aspect of Cleveland's civic life.

McMichol states, "It is our fundamental, reasoned belief that there is no comparison between the status of Blacks and women, and the status of gays and lesbians." He explains that being Black or being female is an "ontological reality . . . a fact that cannot be hidden," whereas "homosexuality is a chosen lifestyle . . . defined by behavior not ontological reality."

By coincidence, I met Rev. McMichol in May when Naomi Jaffe, an activist friend from Albany, and I did a presentation on Black and Jewish relations at the invitation of Cleveland's New Jewish Agenda. Antioch Baptist Church and a Jewish synagogue cosponsored the event. My cousin had informed me that McMichol was a very important person in Cleveland and that he had just stepped down as head of the NAACP. Naomi and I were struck by his coldness to us throughout the evening in sharp contrast to the kind reception we received from both the Black and Jewish participants who were mostly elder women. We guessed that it was because of his homophobia and sexism. Little did we know at the time how right we were.

When I first got news of what was going on in my hometown I was emotionally devastated. It would have been bad enough to find out about a major Black-led homophobic campaign in any city in this country,

but this place wasn't an abstraction, it was where I came from. It was while growing up in Cleveland that I first felt attraction toward women and it was also in Cleveland that I grasped the impossibility of ever acting upon those feelings. Cleveland is a huge city with a small-town mentality. I wanted to get out even before I dreamed of using the word *lesbian* to describe who I was. College provided my escape. Now I was being challenged to deal with homophobia, dead up, in the Black community at home.

I enlisted the help of the National Gay and Lesbian Task Force (NGLTF) and Scot Nakagawa who runs their Fight the Right office in Portland, Oregon, and of members of the Feminist Action Network (FAN), the multiracial political group to which I belong in Albany. Throughout the summer we were in constant contact with people in Cleveland. FAN drafted a counter petition for them to circulate and in early September several of us went there following NGLTF's and Stonewall Cincinnati's Fight the Right Midwest Summit. Unfortunately, by the time we arrived, the group that had been meeting in Cleveland had fallen apart.

We had several meetings, primarily with Black lesbians, but found very few people who were willing to confront through direct action the severe threat right in their midst. Remaining closeted, a reluctance to deal with Black people in Cleveland's inner city, and the fact that Cleveland's white lesbian and gay community had never proven particularly supportive of antiracist work were all factors that hampered Black lesbian and gay organizing. Ironically, racial segregation seemed to characterize the gay community, just as it did (and does) the city as a whole. The situation in Cleveland was very familiar to me, however, because I've faced many of the same roadblocks in attempts to do political work against racism and homophobia in my own community of Albany.

I cannot say that our effort to support a visible challenge to the ministers in Cleveland was particularly successful. The right wing's ability to speak to the concerns and play upon the fears of those it wishes to recruit; the lack of visionary political leadership among both Black and white lesbians and gays both nationally and locally; and the difficulty of countering homophobia in a Black context, especially when it is justified by religious pronouncements, makes this kind of organizing exceedingly hard. But we had better learn how to do it quickly and extremely well if we do not want the pseudo-Christian right wing to end up running this country.

Since returning from Cleveland we have been exploring the possibility of launching a nationwide petition campaign to gather at least one hundred thousand signatures from Black people who support lesbian and gay rights. One Black woman, Janet Perkins, a heterosexual Christian who works with the Women's Project in Little Rock, Arkansas, has already spoken out. In a courageous article entitled "The Religious Right: Dividing the African American Community" (*Transformation*, September/October 1993) Perkins takes on the ministers in Cleveland and the entire Black church. She calls for Black church members to practice love instead of condemnation. She writes:

> These African American ministers fail to understand they have been drawn into a plot that has as its mission to further separate, divide and place

additional pressure on African Americans so they are unable to come together to work on the problems of the community....

What is needed in our community is a unity and bond that can't be broken by anyone. We must see every aspect of our community as valuable and worth protecting, and yes we must give full membership to our sisters and brothers who are homosexual. For all these years we have seen them, now we must start to hear them and respect them for who they are.

This is the kind of risk taking and integrity that makes all the difference. Perkins publicly declares herself an ally who we can depend upon. I hope in the months to come the gay, lesbian, and Black movements in this country will likewise challenge themselves to close this great divide, which they can only do by working toward an unbreakable unity, a bond across races, nationalities, sexual orientations, and classes that up until now our movements have never achieved.

Us Helping Us
On the Down Low [2001]

The term "being on the down low" originated in the black community in the 1990s to mean secret sexual behavior. It then became a reference for a subculture of men who had sex with other men as well as women, but did not identify themselves as gay or bisexual. The HIV/AIDS awareness poster reprinted here is from "Us Helping Us," a Washington, D.C.-based group for black men. Although secret homosexual behavior exists among all ethnic groups and among women as well as men, black men "on the down low" became a widely discussed topic, fueled by national coverage on television and in print media (including the August 2003 *New York Times Magazine* cover story and reportage by the *Washington Post*, the *Advocate*, *USA Today*, *Essence*, and *The Oprah Winfrey Show*, among others). Press coverage typically was linked to the HIV epidemic, suggesting that secret bisexual behavior could explain the disproportionately high spread of HIV among black men and woman,

even though there was no concrete scientific evidence to support the idea. In his 2005 book, *Beyond the Down Low: Sex, Lies, and Denial in Black America*, writer and gay activist Keith Boykin (b. 1965) examined how media attention contributed to widespread misinformation about the prevalence and impact of a down low black male subculture, and argued for redefining down low as cheating on a partner, regardless of race, gender, or sexual orientation. At the same time, he traced how homophobia not only helped fuel the media coverage, but also served as a reason for some to be on the down low, concluding that "if we truly hope to break the cycle of the down low, we have to create an environment where men can be free to be who they are, and not just who we expect them to be." In October 2009, a report from the CDC's National Prevention Information Network confirmed that the assumed link between down low behavior and HIV transmission to black women is

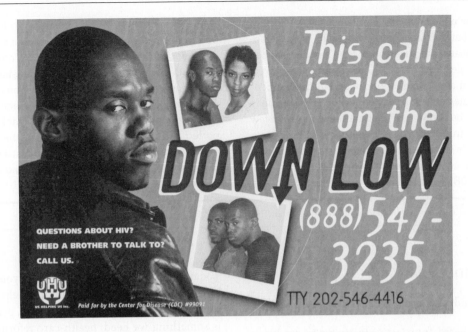

QUESTIONS ABOUT HIV?
NEED A BROTHER TO TALK TO?
CALL US.

This call is also on the DOWN LOW (888) 547-3235

TTY 202-546-4416

Paid for by the Center for Disease (CDC) #99091

not supported by scientific evidence. For black women, the high rate of infection (nearly 18 times higher that of white women) is linked mainly to heterosexual sex with black heterosexual men who have multiple sex partners or a history of drug use. However, this new evidence showing minimal impact of down low behavior on HIV transmission received modest media coverage, especially compared with the frenzy of reporting on down low subculture in the first years of the decade.

From Us Helping Us, Washington, D.C.

Tony Cox and Bishop Harry Jackson
Homosexuality in the Black Church [2007]

In the interview reprinted here with journalist Tony Cox, Bishop Harry Jackson (senior pastor of Hope Christian Church in the Washington, D.C. metropolitan area and regional bishop in the Fellowship of International Churches) argues that gay marriage would contribute to a "devaluation of the institution" of marriage. Black marriage is particularly at risk, Jackson suggests, since it was fractured by slavery (see E. Franklin Frazier, p. 385 and the Moynihan Report, p. 638), and further eroded by the cultural upheaval of the 1970s. Jackson focuses on the effects of gay marriage on heterosexuals and their children (i.e. arguing that legalizing homosexual marriage would further erode the value of marriage, so that heterosexual couples would get married later and not connect with their children). Jackson sees his position against homosexuality as a moral issue, grounded in the Bible.

In the second half of the interview focused on HIV and AIDS in the black community, Jackson subtly conveys his position on controversial topics through word choice and the juxtaposition of his statements. For example, he twice refers to "the gay lifestyle," suggesting that homosexuality is one option among many choices of behaviors available to all. Also, immediately after mentioning that "responsible sexual behavior of the gay community is a major issue," he states, "But it's got to be known that we are contracting AIDS from somewhere, and that is drug use and/or from sexual practices that aren't safe." Bishop does not say that the "sexual practices that aren't safe" are homosexual, but the context of his statement implies a connection, echoing ideas put forth in the "down low" debate that erupted a few years before (p. 1064).

Jackson's statement that many black people are against gay marriage proved to be modestly true in California in 2008. The high turnout of African American voters, inspired by Barack Obama's run for the presidency, was widely seen as a critical factor in the passing of Proposition 8 (named the California Marriage Protection Act), which amended the state constitution so that "only marriage between a man and a woman is valid or recognized in California." Analysis of precinct-level voting data suggests that 58 percent of black voters supported the measure, much less than the 70 percent originally estimated using exit polls, but still substantially higher that the 52 percent of all voters who voted for the proposition.

Transcript of "Homosexuality in the Black Church" interview, *News & Notes*, National Public Radio, April 2, 2007.

FARAI CHIDEYA[1], host:

I'm Farai Chideya and this is NEWS & NOTES.

Earlier, we heard from activists trying to get black churches invested in the fight against AIDS. But some pastors are reluctant to take a stand against AIDS, although it's not limited to the gay community because they've already taken a stand against homosexuality.

NPR's Tony Cox[2] spoke with one such pastor, Bishop Harry Jackson. He's senior pastor of Hope Christian Church in Washington, D.C., and founder of the High Impact Leadership Coalition.

TONY COX: Bishop Jackson, welcome.

Bishop HARRY JACKSON (Senior Pastor, Hope Christian Church): Thank you, Tony, for having me today.

COX: Tell us first of all about the High Impact Leadership Coalition. What is it and what is your thrust?

Bishop JACKSON: It is essentially an organization that has been designed to encourage Christians but primarily clergy to get involved in the political process of our day. We think that the civil rights movement was great for African-Americans but we need a resurgence of the kind of enthusiasm and power we had back then.

Today, we have a thrust of unifying, if you would, the black church and the white church to help us alleviate things like family breakdown, poverty, prison reform is something we need, health care reform and a few other items.

COX: The white church and the black church are both united, I suppose would be the correct word to use in terms of their being divided, if you follow my point, with regard to issues such as homosexuality.

Now, you have recently been quoted in *The New York Times* in regard to homosexuality as saying that it is one of several factors that are taking away the interest in traditional marriage in the African-American community. How do you mean that?

Bishop JACKSON: There's been a de facto don't ask, don't tell kind of policy in the black church. And although most African-Americans, if polled, would say they're against same-sex marriage, the fact is that we have many, many friends, brothers, cousins, who happened to be gay—we are attempting to minister to them.

But my point would be that if you have same-sex marriage openly condoned in all the nation, that the already faltering family structure of the black community can plummet even further. In the countries wherein there has been open acceptance of same-sex

---

1. From 2006–09, journalist and author Farai Chideya (b. 1969) was the host of the NPR program *News and Notes*, a daily national show about African American and African diaspora issues.

2. Cox has worked in television and radio broadcasting since 1969; his recent credits include hosting duties on *The Tavis Smiley Show*, *News and Notes*, and *Upfront with Tony Cox*.

marriage there has been a correlation with a devaluation of the institution. Therefore, people get married later and they don't connect with their kids.

COX: How do you, Bishop Jackson, minister to people that you don't feel belong in the church?

Bishop JACKSON: Well, I think everybody belongs in the church. The issue is that some folks—and this is not just gays—some folks want to live according to their own moral standard even though they want the excitement and the rhythm, the beat and the uplift of the black church.

And I think that there needs to be a raising of the bar morally in the black church, whether it be heterosexual or gay sexual practices. Because we're having too many babies out of wedlock, we're having dysfunctional disintegration of the black families we've already eluded to. And I think that has to do with the fact that we aren't preaching a moral standard and we are not encouraging people how to develop and prolong their relationships.

COX: Is it your opinion, your view, your belief that the devalued family values come from homosexuality or did it not occur before this instance of gay marriage?

Bishop JACKSON: Tony, you're very insightful. It happened before; we can't push off and foist upon the gay community the decline of African-American families. It starts really way back during the time of slavery and the breaking of tribal identity, which is family base, as we know. And then I think with the '70s and the free love movement what we had was a very, very stable unit called a black family who is under duress because of slavery, now gets twisted and turned with liberal concepts of anti-racism and anti-all these other things, somehow women's liberation, somehow feminism, all these things said to black people your foundational institution is not as valued as it once was.

So, this gay marriage issue and gays in the church is a secondary wind, not the primary wind that's helped bring destruction to our families.

COX: How difficult for you is this position, given the fact that HIV and AIDS as a disease is tearing apart literally the black community? And there is a connection obviously, between HIV and AIDS and drug use and homosexual behavior as well.

Bishop JACKSON: Absolutely.

COX: So how torn are you in terms of trying to say then help the community and at the same time separate yourself from part of it?

Bishop JACKSON: Well, It's interesting. I want to minister to folks who happen to be on a gay lifestyle. But I had to say at the recent conference that was referenced in *The New York Times*, as we were talking, I said, hey, responsible sexual behavior of the gay community is a major issue and the room iced over.

But it's got to be known that we are contracting AIDS from somewhere, and that is drug use and/or from sexual practices that aren't safe. Although some people say, well, you know, you're just the white man's toy, you're just standing up and saying what's some other group is telling you. That's not really true.

I believe that we need a restoration of fundamental Christianity. And if we'll get back to those things, it will bring healing to the church internally and then to the community externally as we become an ark of safety, if you will, for the entire black community.

COX: We have been talking with some other people who are involved as AIDS advocates, some who are a part of faith-based organizations and some who are not. And one of the things that I asked of this group was how do you convince those theologians who feel that the Bible supports their position with regard to not accepting homosexuality within the church and gay marriage, et cetera, et cetera.

And their answer was—and I like to get your response to it—was that we are educating these ministers about what is involved with HIV and AIDS, and we are bringing them around. So my question to you, Bishop Jackson, is can your mind be changed?

Bishop JACKSON: Wow. I don't see my mind being changed short-term. I feel as though the Bible is clear. What I think can be changed is how we minister to people in our community who are gay. I think that many, many people who are in the gay lifestyle feel trapped, they want out. I know that there are other folks who are advocates and they're passionately pursuing advancing gay causes.

But I want to say this is not something I have got this global mindset that it's the biggest deal that ever happened. But rather, it's part of me standing the ground and believing in what the [unintelligible] the scriptures, that's my take on that.

COX: Along that line, you're using the scriptures to sort of bolster your argument. Are you ever . . .

Bishop JACKSON: Yes, sir.

COX: Are you ever given pause that white Christians use those same scriptures in the Bible to defend their positions with regard to slavery and unequal treatment of people who looked like you?

Bishop JACKSON: Well. I am given pause by that. The thing that we have to look at, though, is a motive of heart, the issue of love. And when I say love—if I move from the idea that I'm attempting to serve someone into an idea that I want to harass or hurt someone, there's a problem. I think I'm operating within a Christian character and within a Christian kind of framework or theology, and therefore I don't have fear, I don't have concern. But I am concerned about the anger I sense on the other side about this issue specifically.

COX: Bishop Jackson. Thank you very much, sir.

Bishop JACKSON: Tony, thank you so much for the opportunity.

MICHAEL ERIC DYSON

from *Is Bill Cosby Right?* [2006]

What are the relative roles of social structures and individual agency on human behavior? This so-called "structure versus agency" debate is central to discussions about public policy. Those who emphasize the role of societal structures tend to call for large institutional changes but run the risk of contributing to a sense of individual powerlessness. Those who stress individual responsibility can inspire personal change but may fail to address structural issues or may promote blame of those who are not able to escape problems.

The 2004 NAACP speech by comedian Bill Cosby became a touchstone in the structure versus agency debate. In his talk commemorating the 50th Anniversary of *Brown v. Board of Education* (the Supreme Court decision that eliminated *de jure* racial segregation in public schools), Cosby called for more responsibility from parents whose children were not studying or were dropping out of school. "It's not what they're doing to us. It's what we're not doing," he told the receptive audience. "What the hell good is *Brown v. Board of Education* if nobody wants it?" Cosby asked. He urged his listeners to "hit the streets," to build up poor neighborhoods with new businesses, and to clean out the community by fostering a renewed respect for parents, the law, language, and education.

In his response to Cosby's speech, reprinted here, professor and Baptist minister Michael Eric Dyson links the problems Cosby cites to structural forces largely affecting poorer African Americans, including underfunded schools and a lack of economic opportunities. In contrast to Cosby's critique of individual behavior, Dyson focuses on the social context that fosters the development of people "snared in unhealthy and unproductive lifestyles" and "robbed of social standing and personal dignity by poverty and racial injustice." Dyson cites a variety of sources (most notably Cosby himself as a younger man) to support his position on a range of controversial issues, including Ebonics (p. 895), the link between class and justice, and the question of whether black culture is more anti-intellectual or materialistic than mainstream culture. Dyson also briefly touches on the idea of agency. "None of this is meant to dismiss black crime or serve as an apology for destructive behavior," he writes, but then adds, "but it is necessary to understand the social and personal forces that drive criminal activity, even as we fight against an unjust criminal justice system."

From Michael Eric Dyson, *Is Bill Cosby Right? Or Has the Black Middle Class Lost Its Mind?* (New York: Basic Civitas Books, 2005), pp. 60–103.

Bill Cosby, by his own admission, was a bad student, and "compiled a lackluster academic record from the moment he set foot in school."[1] His sixth-grade teacher noted on his report card that "William would rather clown than study."[2] He dropped out of high school after he flunked the tenth grade *three* times. He enlisted in the navy, where he. got his GED, and then enrolled at Temple University, where he dropped out to pursue a show business career. His unfinished bachelor's degree from Temple was eventually bestowed on him because of "life experience."[3] Cosby enrolled as a part-time doctoral student at the University of Massachusetts at Amherst, which awarded him the Ed.D. degree in 1977 for a dissertation on *Fat Albert and the Cosby Kids.* But not even that degree was unsullied by controversy: A professor who served on Cosby's dissertation committee, Reginald Damerell, said that Cosby hardly took a class—and that he got course credit for appearing on *Sesame Street* and *The Electric Company,* "and wrote a dissertation that analyzed the impact of his show."[4] Damerell concluded that degrees like Cosby's "do not attest to genuine academic achievement. They are empty credentials."[5] (While I think Damerell's conclusion is harsh and unfair, it does underscore the ironic route Cosby has traveled to become nearly as acclaimed for his educational pedigree as for his comedic genius.) Given his difficult educational background, it's a good thing Cosby didn't have Bill Cosby around to discourage him from achieving his goals by citing statistics about black high school dropouts that don't square with the facts. It's a shame that Cosby skewered the victims of educational neoapartheid, the very folk that *Brown v. Board* sought to help, instead of pointing to the social inequities and disparities in resources that continue to make American schools "separate and unequal." And for Cosby to overlook

how the criminal justice system mercilessly feeds on social inequality is just as tragic.

It may be partially accurate to describe the contemporary social and educational landscape for blacks in Dickensian terms: It is the best and worst of times, but only if we admit that one's perception of the times rests on rigid class divisions in black communities. For an expanded black middle class, which enjoys unprecedented success at work and in school, the times are much better than before *Brown,* though exorbitant optimism must be chastened by the racist barriers that remain. In 1954, the year of the *Brown* decision, the neonatal mortality rate for blacks per one thousand live births registered at 27 percent, compared to 17.8 percent for whites. The maternal mortality rates per one thousand live births were 14.4 percent for blacks and only 3.7 percent for whites. The average black household income was $2,890, 55 percent of the white average of $5,228. In 1952, black illiteracy for those age fourteen and above was 10.2 percent, five times the 1.8 percent level of white illiteracy. At the time, more than a quarter of black males had no more than four years of schooling, compared to less than 9 percent for white males.[6]

Today, the picture is dramatically different for the most well-to-do blacks. For instance, black households in the upper income bracket, those making $75,000 to $99,000, increased fourfold between 1967 and 2003, composing 7 percent of the black population.[7] And while the picture got far better for the bulk of the black middle class, they had a far less sure grasp of economic security. In 1960, for instance, there were only 385,586 blacks who were professionals, semiprofessionals, business owners, managers or officials, a number that swelled to 1,317,080 by 1980. By 1995, there were nearly seven million black folk employed in middle-class

1. Lawrence Linderman, "Playboy Interview: Bill Cosby—a Candid Conversation with the Kinetic Comedian-Actor-Singer-Entrepreneur," *Playboy*, May 1969, p. 73. [Unless otherwise indicated, all footnotes are those of the author.]

2. Ibid.

3. Richard Zoglin, "Cosby, Inc.: He Has a Hot TV Series, a New Book—and a Booming Comedy Empire," *Time*, September 28, 1987, p. 59.

4. Ibid.

5. Ibid. In the acknowledgments to his doctoral dissertation, Cosby thanks Damerell, who, he says, "guided me in the writing of the technical and creative components of my television research."

6. Howard Fuller, "The Struggle Continues," *Education Next*, Fall 2004, pp. 27–28.

7. Alec Klein, "A Tenuous Hold on the Middle Class," *Washington Post*, December 18, 2004, p. A1.

occupations, boosted by blacks joining the ranks of social workers, receptionists, insurance salespeople and government bureaucrats.[8] But signs of trouble persist. Despite the fact that the black median household income rose by 47 percent from 1967 to $29,026 in 2003, it still lagged by $16,000 the white median household income of $46,900.[9] Plus, the median household income for blacks fell by 3 percent in 2002 and fell by more than 6 percent between 2000 and 2003.[1] And the unemployment rate among blacks, at 10.1 percent, is twice the national rate of 5.6 percent. Between 1992 and 2002, the number of blacks with manufacturing jobs declined by 18 percent, forcing blacks into the service sector—including professions like data processing, advertising and housekeeping—which employs 43 percent of the black workforce, a larger percentage than for whites in the economy.[2] The problem with these jobs is that they have shown weak growth and provide fewer benefits. As a result, blacks, at 52 percent, lag far behind whites, at 71 percent, in employer-sponsored health care, and less than 40 percent of blacks have private pension plans, while more than 46 percent of whites are covered.[3] All in all, nearly two in five nonelderly black folk had no health insurance between 2002 and 2003. And since more than half of all black families live in major metropolitan areas, the steadily increasing cost of public transportation is a huge problem. More than 12 percent of the black population relies on public transportation to get to work—and many others must also get to school and other vital destinations—while only 3.1 percent of whites must do the same.[4] Finally, the poverty rate of black households is more than 24 percent, compared to 6.1 percent for white households.[5]

The educational prospects of black folk have suffered as well, but one may have never picked this up by listening to Cosby's comments. There is a direct link between the social and economic status of the most vulnerable and the quality of education they receive. As Stanford education professor Linda Darling-Hammond has eloquently argued, disparities in wealth and resources result in a significantly unequal education for the poorest members of society, especially minority students.

> [E]ducational outcomes for students of color are much more a function of their unequal access to key educational resources, including skilled teachers and quality curriculum, than they are a function of race. In fact, the United States educational system is one of the most unequal in the industrialized world, and students routinely receive dramatically different learning opportunities based on their social status. In contrast to European and Asian nations that fund schools centrally and equally, the wealthiest 10% of school districts in the United States spend nearly ten times more than the poorest 10%, and spending ratios of three to one are common within states. These disparities reinforce the wide inequalities in income among families, with the most resources being spent on children from the wealthiest communities, and the fewest on the children of the poor, especially in high-minority communities.[6]

The profound gulf between the wealthiest and poorest members of our society affects a huge portion of the black population and stretches between suburban schools and urban schools, where minorities account for between 95 and 99 percent of the student body.[7] As Jonathan Kozol showed in *Savage Inequalities*, there are telling differences between

8. Mary Pattillo-McCoy, "Black Picket Fences: Privilege and Peril among the Black Middle Class," in Dalton Conley, Editor, *Wealth and Poverty in America: A Reader* (Malden, Mass.: Blackwell Publishing, 2003), p. 106.

9. Klein, p. A1. "Vital Signs," *The Journal of Blacks in Higher Education*, Autumn 2003, p. 73.

1. "Black Middle Class: Getting Squeezed," *The Middle Class Squeeze*, Rep. George Miller, Committee on Education and the Workforce Democrats, July 15, 2004, Issue # 8, www.house.gov/georgemiller "Vital Signs," p. 73.

2. Klein, p. A1.

3. Ibid.

4. "Black Middle Class: Getting Squeezed" and "Vital Signs," p. 73.

5. "Vital Signs," p. 73.

6. Linda Darling-Hammond, "The Color Line in American Education: Race, Resources, and Student Achievement." *Du Bois Review* 1:2 (2004), p. 214.

7. Jonathan Kozol, *Savage Inequalities*, p. 3, cited in Darling-Hammond, p. 215.

how much money suburban and urban schools spend on each student: In 1989, Chicago public schools spent a little more than $5,000 per student, while Niles Township High School, in a nearby suburb, spent $9,371 per student; central city Camden, New Jersey, schools expended $3,500 per student, while each student in suburban Princeton enjoyed an expenditure of $7,725; and in 1990 New York City schools invested $7,300 in each student, while schools in suburban Manhasset and Great Neck spent over $15,000 per student, even though they didn't have nearly as many special needs.[8]

As a result of the wide disparity in wealth in school districts—since schools often get revenue from the local property tax, the wealthier the district and the higher its property values the more resources it has—and huge differences in expenditures on each student, there are corresponding differences between suburban and urban schools, especially in the quality of teachers (higher paid and more experienced in the suburbs), the courses presented (smaller class size and more offerings in the suburbs), curriculum materials (out of date in urban schools) and equipment and facilities (up to date in the suburbs). In most suburban schools, computer technology is cutting edge; in many urban schools, it is barebones. Textbooks are often in wretched condition in urban schools, offering outdated material—for example, in a Chicago elementary school, fifteen-year-old textbooks were used, which led to the impression that Richard Nixon was still in office—and in many cases can't be taken home by students because there are barely enough to go around. The infrastructures of urban schools are often in grave disrepair, featuring toilets that don't work, rooms without air conditioning and poor heating, and cracked or missing ceiling tiles in recreation rooms.

In the end, the huge wealth disparity not only enables white students to enjoy superior primary and secondary education but gives them an enormous advantage in the college sweepstakes.

In higher education, wealth confers stunning prerogatives and advantages. Affluent families can sidestep poor-quality education by sending their children to high-quality private schools. This gives them a major leg up for admission to our most prestigious universities. Judicial rulings that command an equalizing of expenditures on public schools have been consistently ignored.... These resource differences give students in the white districts a very big head start in the competition for places at quality colleges and universities. On top of this, it is students from affluent families who are able to afford $1,000 test-coaching seminars that typically improve a student's performance on the Scholastic Assessment Test by 100 points or more. Students from affluent families are more likely to have computers in the home and have broadband access to the Internet. These tools can give students very great advantages in preparing for the standardized tests that count so much in college applications.[9]

The wide resource gulf between suburban and urban schools is exacerbated by the profound resegregation of American schools.[1] Although *Brown* was to have destroyed the vicious segregation of American schools, patterns of disturbing neoapartheid have endured, bringing in their wake substantive inequalities. More than 70 percent of black students in the country attend schools that are composed largely of minority students. Even though the segregation of black students falls more than 25 points below its level in 1969, the existence of financially strapped, resource-starved, technologically underserved predominantly minority schools is a rebuke to the judicial mandate to integrate students, and, it was thought, resources, in schools attended by all races. But the mythology of either resource sharing or true integration lapses in the face of current trends. White students usually attend schools where less than 20 percent of the student body is drawn from races other than their own,

8. Kozol, pp. 236–237, cited in Darling-Hammond, p. 25.
9. "The Racial Wealth Gap Has Become a Huge Chasm That Severely Limits Black Access to Higher Education," *The Journal of Blacks in Higher Education*, 2005, pp. 23–25.
1. Gary Orfield, *Schools More Separate: Consequences of a Decade of Resegregation* (Cambridge, Mass.: The Civil Rights Project, Harvard University, 2001).

while black and brown students attend schools composed of 53 to 55 percent of their own race. In some cases, the percentage is much higher, as more than a third of them attend schools with a 90 to 100 percent minority population.[2] As black and brown students get concentrated in knots of ethnicity, and often poverty, in central city schools, their educational resources are, likewise, increasingly depleted, resulting in gross inequities between white students and their black and brown peers. If Cosby was aware of this disturbing trend, he gave little indication as he railed against the poor parents and their children who are victims of resegregation.

It wasn't always the case that Cosby blamed poor parents and students for their plight while ignoring the structural features of educational inequality. In his doctoral thesis, entitled, in the unwieldy fashion common to most dissertations, *An Integration of the Visual Media Via* Fat Albert and the Cosby Kids *into the Elementary School Curriculum as a Teaching Aid and Vehicle to Achieve Increased Learning*, Cosby got right to the heart of the matter as he argued that two fundamental issues had to be addressed if educators were to ensure equal education for all students: the development of a curriculum that would help students reach their full potential, but before that, "the need to eliminate institutional racism."[3] Cosby lucidly characterized his view of institutional racism when he elaborated on how schools instill harmful beliefs in black children.

> Schools are supposed to be the vehicle by which children are equipped with the skills and attitudes necessary to enter society. But a black child, because of the inherent racism in American schools will be ill prepared to meet the challenges of an adult future. The "American Dream" of upward mobility is just another myth.... Far from being prepared to move along an established career lattice, black children are trained to occupy those same positions held by their parents in a society economically dom-

inated and maintained by a white status quo. Through a series of subtly inflicted failures black children are taught early not to aspire to or compete with their white counterparts for those "esteemed" jobs.... It has become increasingly difficult to reconcile the urban child to his education.... Inner-city children not only dislike school but tend to be dissatisfied with themselves. They react negatively to the entire educational process for the simple reason that school does not provide them with successful and rewarding experiences. Further, school curricula lacks congruence with the realities of their world.[4]

It is evident from his dissertation that Cosby saw schools as hotbeds of ideology and politics that are transmitted through the curriculum, and more subtly through the attitudes of teachers as they interact with black students. Cosby also insisted on the link between systemic inequities and the diminished self-esteem of the student; he refused to unfairly blame black children for lacking the desire to succeed when the classroom passed along diseased ideas about black identity. Cosby argued that the "American Dream" is a myth—a myth, however, that he eagerly embraced a decade later, especially when he defended his *Cosby Show* family against critics who claimed that the Huxtables were insufficiently black. "To say they are not black enough is a denial of the American dream and the American way of life. My point is that this is an American family—an *American* family—and if you want to live like they do, and you're willing to work, the opportunity is there."[5] In his dissertation, however, Cosby acknowledged that such a dream was denied to black children taught to mark time by filling the jobs their parents filled before them, a way to preserve white privilege.

Cosby also spoke passionately in his dissertation about the reasons black students fail: because of the urban school's indifference to changing learning con-

2. Orfield, cited in Darling-Hammond, p. 217.
3. William Henry Cosby, Jr., *An Integration of the Visual Media Via* Fat Albert and the Cosby Kids *into the Elementary School Curriculum as a Teaching Aid and Vehicle to Achieve Increased Learning*, University of Massachusetts, September 1976, p. vi.
4. Ibid., pp. 3, 4, 5.
5. Cited in "Bill Cosby and the Politics of Race," in Michael Eric Dyson, *Reflecting Black: African-American Cultural Criticism* (Minneapolis: University of Minnesota Press, 1993), p. 85.

ditions; because they have had the right to fail removed; because they are bored, due to the unimaginative methods of teachers interested in controlling the student; and because little of what goes on in class makes sense. Cosby argued that the failure black children experienced would only reinforce "the debilitating sense of worthlessness whites convey in a variety of ways," feeding the self-hatred of the black student.[6] Cosby pleaded with urban schools to give urban children a sense of competence to ward off attitudes and behaviors that would destroy their character and intelligence. Thus, the urban schools had to develop a curriculum to fight institutional racism. Cosby concluded that blacks were not "the only victims" of racism, although they "bear the deepest scars of time-worn racial and intellectual inferiority myth preaching"; in his mind, "whites suffer in a more subtle way."[7] Cosby argued that the myth of black inferiority and white superiority was equally disastrous for black and white children. He said that whites

> are raised with a counter myth of white supremacy (power and domination) and intellectual superiority (by which to assert their power and domination).... Neither myth is healthy. Each breeds a negative ego position. On the one hand, there is a feeling of abject failure and pronounced inferiority, while on the other, there exists a super ego fed by continuous and demonstrated successes leading to an aggrandized sense of superiority. In combination they are combustible ingredients of a divided society.[8]

When Cosby raged against poor black parents and children in his recent comments, he forgot the lessons he had eloquently expressed nearly thirty years before. When he demanded, "What the hell good is *Brown v. the Board of Education* if nobody wants it?" he forgot what he had understood earlier: that desire is the child

of environment, that vision is the gift of context, and, as he said, black "children are taught early not to aspire to or compete with their white counterparts" for jobs, or, we might add, for education either.

Of course, on some matters, Cosby in his recent statements was plain misinformed. He said more than once that 50 percent of black students drop out of high school. That is simply not true. Cosby was nowhere near the facts on this one, since the dropout rate for blacks is 17 percent.[9] And while the white dropout rate is 9 percent, the dropout rate for black high school students has actually declined 44 percent since 1968, while the white dropout rate has slightly increased over the same period.[1] In 1960, only 20.1 percent of black adults had completed high school; today it is nearly 79 percent, compared to 89 percent for whites.[2] Despite the brutal obstacles blacks have faced, and which Cosby outlined in his dissertation, they have fought to become educated in far greater numbers than the generation he applauds, a fact that Cosby fails to recognize when he says that the black poor "don't want to accept that they have to study to get an education." Thus, contemporary blacks have not failed the civil rights generation; neither have they failed to extend the legacy of literacy we have created since our time here as slaves.[3]

Cosby also asserted that black youth—referring to them with the objectifying, abstracting, thing-like "it," not a new practice with Cosby, to be sure, but no less disconcerting in any case—"can't speak English," that "[i]t doesn't want to speak English," that Cosby can't speak like them (his speech, one supposes, notwithstanding), and that everyone knows "it's important to speak English except these knuckleheads." It is utterly remarkable that Cosby, after the mountain of scholarship on Ebonics (coined by Robert Williams in the '70s, Ebony + Phonics = Ebonics) and Black English, could with one wave of his Ebonics-indebted rhetorical wand

---

6. Cosby, p. 8.
7. Ibid., p. 11.
8. Ibid., pp. 11–12.
9. "Vital Signs," Autumn 2003, p. 73.
1. "The State of the Dream 2004," report by United for a Fair Economy, 2004, p. 16.
2. "Vital Signs," Autumn 2003, p. 73; "State of the Dream," p. 17.
3. See Janet Duitsman Cornelius, *When I Can Read My Title Clear: Literacy, Slavery, and Religion in the Antebellum South* (Columbia: University of South Carolina Press, 1991).

dismiss what he has so brilliantly deployed, and commercially exploited, over the years.[4] Black English captures the beautiful cadences, sensuous tones, kinetic rhythms, forensic articulations, and idiosyncrasies of expression that form the black vernacular voice. Bad grammar does not Black English make; it is a rhetorical practice laden with complex and technical rules—for instance, the use in Black English of zero copulas, or forms of the verb "to be." To say "I am going" is one thing, suggesting a present activity; but to say "I *be* going" in Black English is something else, suggesting a habitual practice, a repeated action.

Black English grows out of the fierce linguisticality of black existence, the insistence by blacks of carving a speech of their own from the remnants of African languages and piecing and stitching those remnants together in the New World with extant patterns of English for the purpose of communication and survival. Of course, much of that communication had to be masked through ranges and intensities of signifying, in terms of not only the content of black speech but its very form as well. Thus, complex linguistic rules emerged from the existential and political exigencies that shaped black destiny: speaking about white folk in their face without doing so in a way that resulted in punishment or perhaps death, leading to verbal hiccups, grammatical hesitations and linguistic lapses; articulating the moral certainties of black worldviews without compromising the ability to transmit them in the linguistic forms that best suited their expression, while adapting them to the religious passions of the white world; capturing in sound the seismic shifts in being and meaning of New World blacks that came in staccato phrases or elongated syllables; unleashing

through the palette a percussive sense of time peculiar to the negotiation of an ever-evolving identity with grace and humor (when I was in grad school, my German professor said about a certain phrase, "the tense can only be translated in the Black English terms, 'It bes like that'"); and situating the absurdity of modern blackness through the constantly modulating forms of diction that lent a protective veneer of spontaneous rationality to rapidly evolving patterns of speech.

And by their creative linguistic transformations, black slaves inflected, and infected, the speech of their masters. As one observer proclaimed, "It must be confessed, to the shame of the white population of the South, that they perpetuate many of these pronunciations in common with their Negro dependents."[5] For Cosby to dismiss *that*, the very kernel of black life in Black English, verges on self-denial; for him to ridicule its most vulnerable practitioners borders on racial disdain. As James Baldwin argued in his powerful essay "If Black English Isn't a Language, Then Tell Me, What Is?" black English

is the creation of the black diaspora.... *A language comes into existence by means of brutal necessity, and the rules of the language are dictated by what the language must convey....* There was a moment, in time, and in this place, when my brother, or my mother or my father, or my sister, had to convey to me, for example, the danger in which I was standing from the white man standing just behind me, and to convey this with a speed and in a language, that the white man could not possibly understand, and that, indeed, he cannot understand, until today. He cannot afford to understand it. This understanding

4. Among the voluminous research, see J. L. Dillard, *Black English: Its History and Usage in the United States* (New York: Random House, 1972); William Labov, *Language in the Inner City: Studies in the Black English Vernacular* (Philadelphia: University of Pennsylvania Press, 1972); Geneva Smitherman, *Talkin and Testifyin: The Language of Black America* [1977] (Detroit: Wayne State University Press, 1986); John Baugh, *Black Street Speech: Its History, Structure and Survival* (Austin: University of Texas Press, 1983); Geneva Smitherman, *Black Talk: Words and Phrases from the Hood to the Amen Corner* (Boston: Houghton Miflin, 1994); Salikoko S. Mufwene, John R. Rickdord, Guy Bailey and John Baugh, Editors, *African-American English: Structure, History and Use* (New York: Routledge, 1998); Theresa Perry and Lisa Delpit, Editors, *The Real Ebonics Debate: Power, Language, and the Education of African-American Children* (Boston: Beacon Press, 1998); John Rickford and Russell John Rickford, *Spoken Soul: The Story of Black English* (New York: John Wiley & Sons, Inc., 2000); Lisa J. Green, *African American English: A Linguistic Introduction* (Cambridge: Cambridge University Press, 2002); Marcyliena Morgan, *Language, Discourse and Power in African American Culture* (Cambridge: Cambridge University Press, 2002); and Sinfree Makoni, Geneva Smitherman, Ametha F. Ball, Arthur K. Spears, Editors, *Black Linguistics: Language, Society, and Politics in Africa and the Americas* (New York: Routledge, 2003).

5. James A. Harrison, "Negro English." *Anglia* 8 (1884), p. 232, cited in Shelley Fisher Fishkin, *Was Huck Black? Mark Twain and African-American Voices* (New York: Oxford University Press, 1993), p. 42.

would reveal to him too much about himself and smash that mirror before which he has been frozen for so long. . . . Now if this passion, this skill, this (to quote Toni Morrison) "sheer intelligence," this incredible music, the mighty achievement of having brought a people utterly unknown to, or despised by "history" . . . if this absolutely unprecedented journey does not indicate that black English is a language, I am curious to know what definition of language is to be trusted.[6]

Cosby has over the years, despite his rabid resistance to Black English, deployed its rhythms, tics and habits of speech. As linguist John McWhorter recently commented, "Bill Cosby speaks more ebonies than he knows . . . and people don't want to hear it. It's not their favorite flavor."[7] The theme song to *The Bill Cosby Show* included a string of nonsensical articulations, such as "flizzum flazzum," that owed their spirit of playful verbal invention, if not their content, to Ebonics. The speech Cosby gave damning poor black parents and their children is loaded with Ebonics, from its inflections, intonations, diction and stylistic flourishes to its grammatical eliminations (of syllables) and, simultaneously, its vernacular substitutions. That's also why it was especially troubling at the 2003 Emmys when comedienne Wanda Sykes, in all of her vernacular splendor and her animated shtick, asked an obviously peeved Cosby the secret of his and other early black comics' success, and he stared at her with menacing intensity and fatal scowl and said, icily, "We spoke English."[8]

Even earlier when *Fat Albert and the Cosby Kids*— not in the cleaned-up, linguistically correct language of the 2004 film but in the original cartoon series— appeared on the scene, they brought verbal resonances to Saturday morning television that were rooted in black community. A cartoon series set in the projects, with the intonations of black children ruling their roost through stories with moral meaning, it was *visual vernacular*; the aesthetic communicated a dialect of style. And when Mushmouth created a distinct pattern of speech, he created a linguistic rule of his own—by inserting the "B" sound into his speech, he asserted the rule of the ubiquitous "B" in syllabic construction. "Hey man" became "hey-ba man-ba," and his own name became "Mush-ba Mouth-ba." Cosby has reaped huge financial dividends, and cultural capital, off of that cartoon and its film; it seems disingenuous for him now to deprive real-life children of the very legitimacy of perspective and verbal creativity he allotted to cartoon and cinematic characters.

Cosby seemed not to notice his own Black English in 1997 when he penned an op-ed for the *Wall Street Journal*, "Elements of Igno-Ebonics Style."[9] Cosby was responding to the Oakland School Board's controversial, and widely misinterpreted, decision to use Ebonics in the classroom to help black children bridge the gulf between their native dialects and speech habits and "standard" English. Cosby lampooned Ebonics speakers in feigned dialects and then scolded the Oakland School Board: "Granted, if you don't teach Ebonics, the children will find it anyway. But legitimizing the street in the classroom is backwards. We should be working hard to legitimize the classroom—and English—in the street. On the other hand, we could jes letem do wha ever they wanna. Either way, Ima go over heanh an learn some maffa matics an then ge-sum 'n tee na' then I'll be witchya."[1] But Cosby, and many more besides, missed the point. The Oakland School Board made the decision to boost black children's literacy in "standard" English by meeting the students where they were rhetorically; like all good teachers, they began with the given and then used it to arrive at the goal. Between the given and the goal lay expanses of black linguistic practice that the Oakland teachers sought to use in their efforts to respect the speech of

6. James Baldwin, "If Black English Isn't a Language, Then Tell Me, What Is?" in *The Price of the Ticket: Collected Nonfiction 1948–1985* (New York: St. Martin's/Marek, 1985), p. 650.

7. Cited in Candace Murphy, "The Cosby Sweater Has Unraveled; Cosby has unraveled some woolly memories the past few months by lambasting African-American parents for their parental failures," *Oakland Tribune*, August 8, 2004.

8. Ta-Nehisi Coates, "Ebonics! Weird Names! $500 Shoes! Shrill Bill Cosby and the Speech That Shocked Black America," *Village Voice*, May 26–June 1, 2004.

9. Bill Cosby, "Elements of Igno-Ebonics Style," *Wall Street Journal*, January 10, 1997, p. A10.

1. Ibid.

their students while bringing them up to snuff on "standard English."

The Oakland teachers realized, as do most black folk, that we must code-switch, or, as Cosby phrased it, speak one variety of English on the streets and another in the home, on the job and the like. The recognition of Black English's legitimacy is not an argument against learning "standard" English; it is to recognize that discussions of language, especially involving poor and minority peoples, are discussions about the issues Cosby addressed in his dissertation: power, domination, black inferiority, white superiority and white supremacy. Who can, or should, determine what language is legitimate and useful, and when it can or cannot be spoken? Of course Cosby is right to stress the need for black youth, and their parents, to understand the contexts where some languages are more useful than others. But the sense of propriety is driven as much by power and the cultural normalizing of the taken-for-granted (and hence taken for standard and taken for true and right) linguistic styles of the white mainstream as by an innate sense of what is good or bad language. The more languages folk have at their disposal, the more easily they are able to negotiate with the hidden premises of power that underlie discussions about linguistic appropriateness. To ignore the cultural and racial contexts that deny access to such multilinguisticality, and to overlook the rigid racial and educational hierarchy that reinforces privilege and stigma, are intellectually dishonest.

Perhaps there is a deep element of shame that Cosby has not yet overcome in the use of black style and Black English. In a 1969 interview, Cosby movingly spoke of how he confronted the black embarrassment associated with black style. In his junior high school, at Christmastime, Cosby and his schoolmates had been allowed to bring in sound recordings to share with the class and celebrate the holiday season. Cosby didn't own any records, but a couple of black girls brought in Mahalia Jackson's version of *Silent Night*, while white kids brought in recordings like the Mormon Tabernacle Choir's version of the *Hallelujah Chorus* and Bing

Crosby's *White Christmas*. When the white kids listened to Mahalia Jackson, they snickered, "because of their own ignorance and, at the same time, we were embarrassed because it wasn't white. Mahalia just didn't sound like the Mormon Tabernacle Choir, and Clara Ward didn't sound like Bing Crosby." Cosby said at the time that "this no longer happens, because of the black-is-beautiful re-education, because of the fact that our culture, our music is something to be proud of."[2] Cosby admitted that it hadn't been easy to "throw out all the brainwashing," but black folk were making the effort. As an example, he told another, perhaps even more poignant, story from his life.

> Black people from the South have a common accent; it's almost a foreign language. I can't speak it, but I understand it, because my 85-year-old grandfather speaks it. I remember hearing him use the word "jimmin" and I had to go up to my grandmother to find out what he was saying. She told me he was saying "gentlemen." That was black; it's the way my grandfather talks, the way my Aunt Min talks, because she was down South picking cotton while I was in Philadelphia picking up white middle-class values and feeling embarrassed about hearing people talk like that and wanting to send them to school to straighten them out. I now accept this as black, the same way I accept an Italian whose father from the old country has a heavy accent. I accept it as black the same way chitlins and crab fingers and corn bread and collard greens and hush puppies and hog jaws and black-eyed peas and grits are black. This is what we were given to eat; this was our diet in the South, and we've done some groovy things with it. Now even white people are talking about Uncle So-and-So's sparerib place.[3]

If Cosby could only see Black English in this light, with this compassion and this discerning of the social and racial networks that sustain cultural expression, he might appreciate its power and beauty.

When Cosby claimed that black parents bought their kids $500 sneakers instead of spending $250 on

2. Lawrence Linderman, "Playboy Interview: Bill Cosby—a Candid Conversation with the Kinetic Comedian-Actor-Singer-Entrepreneur," *Playboy*, May 1969, p. 175.
3. Ibid.

Hooked on Phonics, I immediately had two thoughts. First, I recalled that in 1994 Hooked on Phonics had agreed to settle charges brought by the FTC that it lacked sufficient evidence to support its widely advertised claim that its products could rapidly teach children with learning disabilities to read, regardless of the problems they had. Educational experts countered the Hooked on Phonics advertising juggernaut by suggesting it only worked as an "after-school adjunct to comprehensive reading instruction that teaches children more than sounding out letters and words."[4] Hooked on Phonics has been the subject of very little academic research and, as a result, is not looked upon by many knowledgeable education specialists as an important means to help children to read. At best, it plays a supplementary role that helps with some of the skills necessary for children to read. Perhaps the black parents that Cosby blasted were more aware of the overstated claims of Hooked on Phonics than he appears to have been. If one has limited resources, spending $250 on a product that has not been proved to deliver what it promises is sound educational and consumer practice.

But I also thought of Elizabeth Chin's marvelous ethnographic study of the consumer behavior of poor black children, *Purchasing Power: Black Kids and American Consumer Culture*.[5] Although Cosby targeted poor black parents, a great deal of the consumption for youth in poor communities is done by youth themselves. The point of Chin's book is to dispel the sort of myths perpetuated by Cosby and many others, black and white, whose perceptions of black youth are strangled by stereotype. She thus chides those who make judgments about black youth based more on "guesswork" than "fieldwork."[6] Chin contends that black youth are not the "combat consumers" they are portrayed as being: either captives of a powerful fetish for brand names or predatory consumers willing to steal for Air Jordans or kill for a bike. Chin argues that "consumption is at its base a social process, and one that children use in

powerful ways to make connections between themselves and the people around them."[7] Chin also notices that, unlike their middle-class and upper-class peers, the children she studied were made profoundly conscious of what it costs to clothe, feed and take care of them; hence, they usually spent part of the money they had on necessary, not pleasurable, items. Chin explains her work in a powerful anecdote about the prejudice she confronted and, by extension, the black youth she studied, in examining the consumer behavior of black youth. She says she had developed, as do most researchers, a one-line response to questions at cocktail parties about the nature of her research in New Haven.

> I'm studying the role of consumption in the lives of poor and working-class black children." Here I would more often than not get a knowing look. "Ah," the response would be, "you must have seen a lot of Air Jordans." ... "Actually, no," I'd answer. "I only saw two pairs of Air Jordans on the kids I worked with." [T]his statement was nearly always met with incredulity. More than once people responded with something to the effect of "There must have been something wrong with your sample." ... [T]hese comments also disturb me because so many people seemed to prefer hanging on to ideas about poor black kids that had been gleaned from the pseudo experience provided by the kinds of news stories I have so extensively critiqued in the preceding pages. Like the terms *inner city* and *ghetto*, the "Air Jordans" response to thinking about poor and working-class black children and consumption obscures more about those children than it reveals.[8]

Cosby's gross generalizations about poor black parents and their consumptive behavior—based on his commonsense observations and likely not on a systematic examination of the buying habits of poor black parents or their children—reinforce the biases that

---

4. Jonathan D. Rockoff, "Phonics Called Helpful to a Point: Many Md. Educators Favor Comprehensive Approach," *Baltimore Sun*, January 14, 2005.

5. Elizabeth Chin, *Purchasing Power: Black Kids and American Consumer Culture* (Minneapolis: University of Minnesota Press, 2001).

6. Ibid., p. 9.

7. Ibid., p. 129.

8. Ibid., pp. 60–61.

Chin sought to challenge in her study. Cosby belongs to a group of critics who have, according to Chin, made black consumer behavior appear pathological.[9] And I couldn't help thinking when I read Cosby's "Igno-Ebonics" op-ed (which begins, "I remember one day 15 years ago, a friend of mine told me a racist joke. Question: Do you know what Toys 'R' Us is called in Harlem? Answer: We Be Toys,") of the touching story Chin tells of a shopping trip to Toys "R" Us with a black youth who had never heard of the store before, much less visited it, but who agonized greatly over the choice between two inexpensive toys that would enhance different social relationships.

Cosby's remark hints at the priorities of poor black parents and youth: are they educationally oriented or materially focused? It is interesting that Cosby expects poor parents, and youth, to be more fiscally responsible than those with far greater resources prove to be. Immediately, the defense of their consumer habits, however, rests on the assertion that wealthier parents and children have more latitude, while poor parents must be ever so careful about how they spend their money. There is a cruelty to such an observation, however; not only is the poor parent, or child, at a great disadvantage economically, but they are expected to be more judicious and responsible than their well-to-do counterparts, with far fewer resources. Moreover, the materialism that obviously can strike poor folk as well is, nevertheless, far less likely to do them or society as much harm as it does those with far greater wealth in our country. The perception that the meager resources of the poor are somehow atrociously misspent on expensive consumer items is far out of proportion to the facts of the case. And to begrudge poor parents the desire to provide their children some of the trinkets of capital in a profoundly rapacious consumer culture that endlessly promotes acquiring things as a mark of status and citizenship (didn't George Bush, in the aftermath of 9/11, direct Americans to prove they were uncowed by terrorists by returning to the stores?) is plain dishonest.

Perhaps Cosby has forgotten what it was like to be young, black and poor, or to be hungry for even more capital in the wake of a real first taste of money and the comforts it can bring. *Ebony* magazine reports that when Cosby was asked in 1965 why he entered the acting field, he had a one-word reply: "Money!"[1] He told the *Saturday Evening Post* that "I've got no great artistic ambitions. What show business mainly means to me is cash."[2] Neither should we forget that Cosby was once, and for a long while, one of the most recognized and successful pitchmen in American history, promoting products to the American public—from Jell-O to Ford automobiles, from Coca-Cola to E. F. Hutton—for our eager consumption. (It is not hard to imagine that Cosby, had he come along at the right time, might have pushed $250 sneakers [they don't cost $500, but we got his point], engaging in what cultural theorists term "the social construction of desire.") It even led to a brief, pungent, satirical editorial by Edward Sorel, "The Noble Cos," in *The Nation* in 1986 that assumes Cosby's voice: "So this buddy says, 'I didn't mind your commercials for Jello, Del Monte, Ford cars . . . Ideal Toys, or Cola-Cola, although Coke does do business in South Africa. . . . But, Bill, why do commercials for those crooks at E. F. Hutton?' My buddy didn't understand my commercials improve race relations. Y'see, by showing that a black man can be just as money-hungry as a white man . . . I'm proving that all men are brothers."[3]

Cosby's insistence, in his infamous May 2004 speech and on National Public Radio's *Talk of the Nation* in July 2004, that black youth are anti-intellectual because they chide high achievement as "acting white," repeats what is the academic equivalent of an urban legend.[4] Claiming that black youth are anti-intellectual is pretending somehow that *America* is not consumed with anti-intellectualism. Cosby's claim has the dubious virtue of being both true and uninformative. It is not that black anti-intellectualism doesn't exist, shouldn't be admitted, or doesn't reveal itself in ways that need to be vigorously opposed. But it is highly

9. Ibid., p. 60.
1. "I Spy: Comedian Bill Cosby Is First Negro Co-Star in TV Network Series," *Ebony*, September 1965, p. 68.
2. Stanley Karnow, "Bill Cosby: Variety Is the Life of Spies," *The Saturday Evening Post*, September 25, 1965, p. 88.
3. Edward Sorel, "The Noble Cos," *The Nation*, September 6, 1986, p. 243.
4. National Public Radio, *Talk of the Nation*, July 7, 2004.

misleading to tag black communities as any more anti-intellectual than the mainstream. Richard Hofstadter wrote a book in 1963 entitled *Anti-Intellectualism in American Life.*[5] He blamed McCarthyism's withering assault in the 1950s on "the critical mind" and the choice of Dwight D. Eisenhower—who, as Hofstadter says, was "conventional in mind [and] relatively inarticulate"—over Adlai Stevenson—whom Hofstadter termed "a politician of uncommon mind and style, whose appeal to intellectuals overshadowed anything in recent history"—as the defining moments of modern anti-intellectualism.[6] (One wonders if Hofstadter might today see parallels in the choice of George W. Bush over Al Gore, or even John Kerry, though Bush isn't Eisenhower and Gore and Kerry aren't Stevenson.)

But, according to Hofstadter, the plague of anti-intellectualism is even more ancient than the 1950s. Hofstadter says that "[o]ur anti-intellectualism is, in fact, older than our national identity."[7] And a recent National Endowment for the Arts report says that book reading has dramatically declined in the United States over the last ten years.[8] Neither is the anxiety especially American: There is hand-wringing over anti-intellectualism around the globe. There is the study that decries the effect of modernization on Russian youth, saying that anti-intellectualism might result if Russian intellectual life is ignored while Western education is celebrated.[9] And then there is the study, first done in the '60s and replicated in the '80s, of anti-intellectualism among Korean teachers because they favored athletic and nonstudious pupils over academically brilliant, studious and nonathletic pupils.[1] That certainly shreds the myth of the Asian model minority. And then there is the study of "Victorian Anti-Intellectualism."[2] The twist here is that it was the middle and upper classes who scorned intellectual engagement. Cosby should take note: They weren't worried about Puffy; they were putting down Puffendorf!

The notion that black youth who are smart and who study hard are accused by their black peers of "acting white" is rooted in a single 1986 study of a Washington, D.C., high school conducted by Signithia Fordham, a black anthropologist at Rutgers University, and John Ogbu, the late Nigerian professor of anthropology at the University of California at Berkeley.[3] According to Fordham and Ogbu, many black students at the school didn't study and deliberately got bad grades because their classmates thought they were "selling out" and "acting white." Fordham and Ogbu's study has gained iconic status in the anecdotage not only of Cosby but of figures like Henry Louis Gates, Jr., in the pages of *The New York Times* and Barack Obama in his thrilling keynote speech at the 2004 Democratic Convention.[4]

The trouble with such citations is that they help to circulate and give legitimacy to a theory that is in large part untrue. First, in 1997, Duke professor Philip J. Cook and Georgetown professor Jens Ludwig set out to determine, through field research, if the alleged grief visited upon those black students who study actually existed.[5] While Fordham and Ogbu studied one school, Cook and Ludwig studied 25,000 public and private school students, following them from eighth grade through high school. Cook and Ludwig concluded that black students were just as eager to excel in

5. Richard Hofstadter, *Anti-Intellectualism in American Life* (New York: Alfred A. Knopf, 1963).

6. Ibid., pp. 3–4.

7. Ibid., p. 6.

8. Les Christie, "Endangered: The American Reader," *CNNmoney*, July 12, 2004, http://money.cnn.com/2004/07/09/news/bookreading.

9. Vladimir I. Chuprov, "Youth in Social Reproduction." *Russian Social Science Review*, September–October 1999, vol. 40.

1. Seon-Young Lee, Bonnie Cramond, and Jongyeun Lee, "Korean Teachers' Attitudes Toward Academic Brilliance." *National Association for Gifted Children*, Winter 2004, vol. 48.

2. Walter E. Houghton, "Victorian Anti-Intellectualism." *Journal of the History of Ideas* 13:3 (June 1952), pp. 291–313.

3. Signithia Fordham and John Ogbu, "Black Students' School Success: Coping with the Burden of 'Acting White,'" *The Urban Review* 19:3, pp. 176–206.

4. Henry Louis Gates, Jr., "Breaking the Silence," *The New York Times*, Section 4, p. 11; "Transcript: Illinois Senate Candidate Barack Obama," http://www.washingtonpost.com/wedyn/articles/A1975-2004July27.html.

5. Philip J. Cook and Jens Ludwig, "Weighing the Burden of 'Acting White': Are There Race Differences in Attitudes Toward Education?" *Journal of Policy Analysis and Management*, Spring 1997, pp. 256–78.

school as whites and that black students dropped out of school only slightly more than white students, largely due to low family incomes or absent fathers.[6] Cook and Ludwig discovered that blacks and whites with similar family characteristics cut class, missed school and completed homework at nearly the same rate.[7]

Cook and Ludwig uncovered an intriguing fact: that the black students who were members of academic honor societies were *more* likely than other black students to view themselves as "popular." Further, they found that students who belonged to honor societies in predominantly black schools were more popular than their peers who had not received such an honor. Cook and Ludwig concluded that there was little evidence to support the notion of an oppositional peer culture to black academic achievement. In fact, other studies suggest that the parents of black students are more likely than white or Asian parents to have assisted their children with their homework or met with their children's teachers, and just as likely to encourage them to put forth their best effort in school. Black parents are more likely than white parents to place their children in educational camps, attend PTA meetings, check their children's homework and reward their children for academic success.[8] Moreover, while only 6 percent of white students in grades 6 through 12 reported discussing national news events with a parent on a daily basis, 26 percent of black students in comparable grades reported that they did so.[9] And there is evidence that high school black peer groups were more likely than comparable white peer groups to believe that it is important to study hard and get good grades, leading to the conclusion that white,

not black, academic peer culture opposes academic achievement.[1]

More recently, University of North Carolina professors Karolyn Tyson, a sociologist, and William Darity, Jr., an economist, coordinated an eighteen-month ethnographic study of eleven schools in North Carolina and concluded that black and white students are fundamentally the same when it comes to the desire to succeed, knowing that doing well in school can positively impact later life, and feeling good about themselves when they do well.[2] They also concluded that when anti-intellectual activity occurs in white culture, "it is seen as inevitable, but when the same dynamic is observed among black students, it is pathologized as racial neurosis."[3] The authors also argue that the single case where they found any evidence of the anxiety of "acting white" occurred at a school where there was an overrepresentation of whites in gifted-and-talented classes and a drastic underrepresentation of black students. But the anxiety occurred most frequently not among the students, but among the teachers and administrators, who accused the black students of being "averse to success" and placing a low value on education, underscoring how racial hierarchy and the social mythology of low black academic desire collude to deprive black students of an equal education.[4]

Finally, Cosby's remarks about black youth and the criminal justice system are incredibly naïve, mean-spirited or woefully uninformed. While it is true that most black men who are incarcerated are not "political prisoners," that doesn't mean that their imprisonment doesn't have political contexts and consequences. For instance, Ronald Reagan's "War on Drugs"—which, as both Lani Guinier and Tupac Shakur contended, is a

6. "'Acting White': Is It the Silent Killer of the Educational Aspirations of Inner-City Blacks?" *The Journal of Blacks in Higher Education,* Autumn 1997, p. 94.

7. Ibid.

8. Douglas Massey, Camille Z. Charles, Garvey Lundy and Mary J. Fischer, *The Source of the River,* cited in Tim Wise, *Affirmative Action: Racial Preference in Black and White* (New York: Routledge, 2005), p. 146; "Vital Signs," *Journal of Blacks in Higher Education,* Winter 2003/2004, p. 65.

9. "Vital Signs," *Journal of Blacks in Higher Education,* Winter 2003–2004, p. 65.

1. Massey et al., cited in Wise, p. 146.

2. Karolyn Tyson, William Darity & Domini Castellino. *Breeding Animosity: The "Burden of Acting White" and Other Problems of Status Group Hierarchies in Schools.* Paper # SAN04-03, September, 2004. Also see Paul Tough, "The 'Acting White' Myth," *New York Times Magazine,* December 12, 2004.

3. Ibid.

4. Ibid.

war on black and brown people—inaugurated changes in public policy and policing measures (leading eventually to racial profiling) that greatly increased the odds that blacks would do serious time for nonviolent, and often first-time, offenses. This political decision had grave, and foreseeable, consequences that disproportionately affected young blacks: They were more likely to become incarcerated. The increase of black incarceration was driven by political considerations, not a boost in, for instance, drug consumption. In fact, self-report surveys of students and adults suggest that black folk do not report greater rates of illegal drug consumption than do whites. In fact, it's often lower. For instance, in 2003, 26.5 percent of white students in the twelfth grade reported using illegal drugs within the past thirty days; for the same cohort among blacks, it was just 17.9 percent.[5] However, by a huge margin, black folk are much more likely to be arrested and to serve real prison time for drug-related offenses. This situation is unavoidably, unmistakably political, contrary to what Cosby contends.

It is also ironic that Cosby seems to justify the shooting by police of a black man who steals a piece of pound cake. Most black folk surely don't approve of stealing and certainly want criminals removed from the community, especially violent ones who menace neighborhoods. Yet, too many of us understand the nexus between poor schooling, severely limited life options and the subsequent self-destructive choices made by desperate young men. Moreover, despite a strong desire to see criminals arrested, black folk are justifiably wary of police who often seem incapable of distinguishing legitimate criminals from law-abiding citizens who call the police for protection—not for harassment or brutality. Years ago, Cosby understood the complex social arrangements that provided the backdrop for explaining certain forms of criminal behavior. He also understood how disparities in money offered differing brands of justice.

> Cats with dough don't commit armed robbery or most of the crimes poor people commit. Yet rich guys' crimes—like embezzling a bank or moving a million dollars' worth of heroin a year—hurt a hell

of a lot more people than some guy who sticks up a candy store and gets away with $12. So I think something's a little wrong there. When the rich man comes to court, he's got the best lawyers money can buy. But the poor man, the black man, gets a lawyer who's not necessarily interested in the case and may even consider it a pain in the ass. And then there's the whole thing about under-the-table payoffs to judges, which I won't attempt to document but which exist. What I'm saying is that there are two kinds of justice in this country: one for the rich and one for the poor—and blacks are poor. When the black people keep getting shafted by cops and courts, how can they have respect for people who are supposed to represent the law?

Cosby's blistering, brilliant analysis captures the harsh, excessive and unjust penalties imposed on poor blacks. It also situates in its historical and racial context the criminal justice system, and clarifies the link between class and justice. Of course, Cosby's powerful critique of the two-tiered justice system, one for the wealthy, the other for the poor, offers another jarring contrast between his past thought and his present practice. For instance, while condemning the black pound cake stealer, Cosby stood by Martha Stewart's side, and showed up in court to support her, even though she fit Cosby's description of a person with huge resources who buys justice and whose crime, perhaps, has a more harmful effect than the man robbing a candy store or stealing a piece of pound cake.

The disparity in the distribution of justice is painfully apparent in the case of black males. From 1974 to 2001, the percentage of black males who had been in state or federal prison increased from 8.7 percent to 16.6 percent, while the percentage for white males went from 1.4 percent to 2.6 percent during the same period. The percentage of black women who had been in state or federal prison rose from 0.6 percent to 1.7 percent, even as the rate for white women increased from 0.1 percent to 0.3 percent.[6] Blacks are six times as likely as whites to have gone to prison at some time in their lives. If the trends hold up, one out of three black males born in 2001 will be imprisoned at some point in his lifetime. In 1974,

---

5. "Vital Signs," Autumn 2004, p. 73.
6. "The State of the Dream 2004: Enduring Disparities in Black and White," *United for a Fair Economy*, January 2004, p. 20.

that number was one out of eleven. Only 5.9 percent of white males born in 2001 have a chance of imprisonment in their lifetimes. For black females, the number is 5.6 percent and for white females, a paltry 0.9 percent.[7]

And when one considers the relation between education and incarceration, things look even bleaker for black men. According to the Justice Policy Institute (JPI) report "Cellblocks or Classrooms? The Funding of Higher Education and Corrections and Its Impact on African American Men," we have a lethal public policy of prizing prisons over education.[8] There is a swelling prison industry that is sweeping ever larger numbers of blacks into local penitentiaries. The more black bodies fill the jails, the more cells are built and the more revenue is generated, particularly in the rural white communities where many prisons are located. The prison-industrial complex literally provides white economic opportunity across the class strata, from the lower- or working-class maintenance worker, the moderately middle-class guard and the solidly middle-class prison executive to the wealthy merchants of incarceration capital who manufacture and produce prison life. In 1995 alone, 150 new prisons were constructed and filled, while 171 more were expanded.[9]

Big money is at stake when it comes to making a crucial choice: to support blacks in the state university or the state penitentiary. As the report makes clear, we have chosen the latter. During the 1980s and 1990s, state spending on corrections grew at six times the rate of state spending on higher education. By the end of the last century, there were nearly a third more black men in prison and jail than in colleges and universities. The number of black men in jail or prison has increased fivefold in the last twenty years. In 1980, at the dawn of the prison construction boom, black men were three times more likely to be enrolled in college than incarcerated. In 1980, there were 143,000 black men in jail or prison and 463,700 enrolled in higher educational institutions. In 2000, there were 791,600 black men in jail or prison, while only 603,032 were enrolled in colleges or universities. It's not a matter of whether "Junior" stole the pound cake; it's a matter of whether he can get into a school

that will train him to cook rather than incarcerate him because he stole when he was hungry.

None of this is meant to dismiss black crime or serve as an apologia for destructive behavior, but it is necessary to underline the social and personal forces that drive criminal activity, even as we fight against an unjust criminal justice system that targets black men with vicious regularity. I speak as one who has been a victim of crime. As it is with most victims, I can remember the most recent event, though more than twenty-five years ago, with chilling accuracy.

"Give me yo' money, nigga," a voice icily demanded of me as I walked with a female companion on a hot summer night in Detroit in 1977.

I had barely glimpsed in my peripheral vision the approach of his grim, steely figure—young, black and male like me—before he pressed his demand on us, ominously backed by a coal black .357 Magnum. The threat evoked by his sudden appearance choked my vocal cords, and squashed any fantasies I may have had of heroic action under desperate circumstances. I hardly managed a reply, which, by tone and terseness, was calculated to inform him that we had no money (why else would we be walking near midnight in the ghetto neighborhood where the '67 riots began?) and to cushion the rebuke he would undoubtedly feel with my admission.

"Man, all I got in my pocket is a dollar and thirty-five cents," I uneasily pleaded, praying that my precision about my indigence would force him to acknowledge that we were poor targets for an armed robbery.

"I don't believe you," he angrily protested. "Now give me *all* yo' money."

My companion and I grew tenser, fearing that we were about to meet the fate of so many others who failed to have the goods when robbers came calling in Detroit, then known as the murder capital of the nation. By now, the hand that held our assailant's gun was visibly trembling, as much, I sensed, out of fear as out of frustration that we had no money. His quaking posture betrayed a vulnerability I desperately sought to exploit, hoping I might forge a bond of racial empa-

7. Ibid.
8. *Cellblocks or Classrooms? The Funding of Higher Education and Corrections and Its Impact on African American Men.* Justice Policy Institute, August 28, 2002.
9. Michael Eric Dyson, *Why I Love Black Women* (New York: Basic Civitas Books, 2003), p. 202.

thy with him beyond whatever forces drove him to assault us.

"Man, you don't look like the type of brother that would be doin' something like this," I hastily offered.

"I wouldn't be doin' this, man," he exclaimed, seemingly as surprised by his own willingness to explain his actions as by my desperation in provoking his response. "But I got a wife and three kids and we ain't got nothin' to eat."

Then came the cruel twist to his rationale for robbery, the partial cause of so-called black-on-black crime contained in his near-repentant revelation.

"And besides, last week, a brother did the same thing to me that I'm doin' to you."

Perhaps the irony lying awake in his own words burdened his conscience. Maybe it nudged him to reevaluate the laws of street survival that turn the victims of crime into its perpetrators. Or perhaps he took pity on our frightened but sympathetic faces. Whatever the case, he allowed us to flee from his potentially harmful grasp. We thanked God and our lucky stars, but only after we were at a safe enough distance to escape should he change his mind.

Too many others, particularly black men, are not as fortunate as I was that night. I know that's what angers Bill Cosby, in part: the sense that the carnage has become routine, perhaps acceptable. With chilling redundancy, black males are dying at the hands of other black males. The mutual harming of black males has furnished the themes of too many films to count, and too many rap narratives as well. The situation for black males, especially juvenile and young adult males, has darkened the outermost regions of hopelessness. Terms usually reserved for large-scale social catastrophes— terms like "genocide" and "endangered species"—are now applied to black men with troubling frequency.[1]

More foreboding is the common belief that relief appears nowhere in sight. There are over fifteen million black males in America, and despite the success and happiness that some enjoy, many others are snared in unhealthy and unproductive lifestyles. Matched in

extremity by the outsize cultural attainments of figures like LeBron James or, for many, Bill Cosby, millions of ordinary, anonymous black males are robbed of social standing and personal dignity by poverty and racial injustice. Often, these men are left to fend for themselves and their families with little more than mother wit and diligent labor that is poorly rewarded. Still others seek more satisfying and immediate material rewards in criminal lifestyles.

The social injuries to black male well-being are indexed in the mind-numbing statistical litany whose mere recitation testifies to the crisis at hand. Black males are more likely than any other group to be spontaneously aborted. Of all babies, black males have the lowest birth weights. Black males have the greatest chance of dying before they reach twenty. Although they are only 6 percent of the U.S. population, blacks make up half the male prisoners in local, state and federal jails. An overwhelming majority of the twenty thousand Americans killed in crime-related incidents each year are black males. Over 35 percent of all black males in American cities are drug and alcohol abusers. Twenty-five percent of the victims of AIDS are black men. Fifty percent of black men between sixteen and sixty-two are not active in the labor force. Thirty-two percent of black men have incomes below the poverty level.[2]

The situation is equally perilous for black youth, especially those trapped by the justice system. More than six in ten juvenile offenders in residential placement are minority youth. Minority youth accounted for seven in ten juveniles held in custody for a violent offense. Recently, I visited a detention center and jail for young people. Of course, most of the youth locked up—for petty thievery and, yes, for double murder— were black boys and girls. My wife and I spoke to them, and we were touched, even moved to tears, by their stories. They were young folk eager to make amends for what they had done wrong. But many of them were also hungry for love and affection. As I read Cosby's words, I thought about these young people often trapped by forces larger than their minds can explain.

1. For claims of genocide, see Robert Staples, "Black Male Genocide: A Final Solution to the Race Problem in America," *Black Scholar*, no. 3 (May–June 1987). For claims about young black males as an endangered species, see the essays in Jewelle Taylor Gibbs, editor, *Young, Black, and Male in America: An Endangered Species* (Dover, Massachusetts: Auburn House Publishing Company, 1988).

2. Gibbs, *Young, Black, and Male in America*.

[* * *]

If we could reach more, many, many, more, of our young people, and touch them, hold them and love them, then we might be able to change their lives and how they view themselves. But until we radically alter our educational system, and solve the problems of poverty and social deprivation, our children will continue to spiral down stairwells of suffering and oppression. While Bill Cosby's frustration is understandable, his mean-spirited attacks on the vulnerable and the poor will do nothing to lift them from the catastrophes they endure. Until we fight on the educational, political and social fronts—and change the way resources are drained from black schools, homes and neighborhoods, and redistribute them within our own black spaces—all of the raving and ranting in the world will only embolden the vicious enemies of black children to do even less, while it will dishearten those who want to see a better world for some of the most beautiful but buffeted children on the globe.

KATHY RUSSELL, MIDGE WILSON, AND RONALD HALL

Hair: The Straight and Nappy of It All [1992]

In this chapter from their book, *The Color Complex* (1992), Kathy Russell, Midge Wilson, and Ronald Hall assert that the "revolution in Blacks' attitudes about their hair" (evident in the 1966 *Ebony* article about the "natural look" on p. 769) was short-lived. The authors contend that since the 1960s, the choice of hairstyle—particularly for women—is seen as an indicator of everything from black consciousness to socioeconomic class. They explore the importance of hair but also caution against overemphasizing the issue, particularly when making gender distinctions. For example, they cite viewers of Spike Lee's film *School Daze* (1988) who found the characterization of black women as obsessed with issues of hair and skin color to be false and demeaning. In fact, say the authors, many women make choices about how to wear their hair for practical reasons. Social pressures, including class considerations, may push a woman to straighten her hair for a new job or when applying for a mortgage, even if she prefers a "natural" look. They note that straightened hair remains the norm, with over 75 percent of African American women either perming or relaxing their hair at the time the selection was written.

The authors suggest that, in contrast to the women in Lee's film, most African Americans are keenly aware of the politics of hair, and that this awareness contributes to a general understanding and acceptance of others' choices. On the other hand, the authors are concerned that long-standing social conventions, which reflect society's ideas about race, class, and gender, prevent individuals from freely choosing how they want to look. The authors' conclusion—that parents need to teach their children that there is no such thing as good or bad hair—can be seen as a direct rebuttal to the ad for Long Aid (p. 776), in which a mother passes down her appreciation of long straight hair to her daughter along with her beauty secrets. But the debate continues, as explored by the cartoonist Aaron McGruder in 2000 (p. 1096) and by comedian Chris Rock (b. 1965) in his 2009 documentary film *Good Hair*. In fact, it was Rock's young daughter's asking him why she did not have "good hair" that inspired him to make the film.

From Kathy Russell, Midge Wilson, and Ronald Hall, *The Color Complex: The Politics of Skin Color Among African Americans* (New York: Harcourt, Brace, Jovanovich, 1992), pp. 81–93.

As the twentieth century closes, I believe that Black women have come to better appreciate the array of beauty we portray, despite subtle, and not so subtle, pressure from the media, the workplace and the larger society to conform to their standards of attractiveness.

Yet I am sometimes troubled that too many of us still make snide and cruel comments about the politically, professionally or socially acceptable way to wear our hair. We would be a lot stronger as a people if we used that energy to support each other economically, emotionally and spiritually.

—A'Lelia Perry Bundles, Great-great-granddaughter of
Madam C. J. Walker, Black hair care industry pioneer

A half-dozen Black women vied for space in front of the restroom mirror, retouching their makeup and spraying their hair. One of them, whose hair was short and nappy, inquired of no one in particular, "What is this mass of sheep's wool that sits so prominently atop our heads? What did Black people do to deserve this bad-ass hair from hell?"

A light-skinned woman whose long hair was casually pulled up in a ponytail answered, "Oh, girl, stop taking your hair so damned seriously. It's just hair." And another dark-skinned sister with a short, kinky hairstyle interjected, "Sure, you can say that because you got 'good' hair, and ain't nobody ever called you no bald-headed bitch." During the shouting and name-calling that ensued no one bothered to ask, "Why does it matter so much?" Perhaps the answer is too obvious. As Susan Brownmiller[1] wrote, in *Femininity*, "Hair indeed may be trivial, but it is central to the feminine definition."

Embodying some Black women's worst fears, a working-class Black man named Darryl describes a far too popular formula for weighing the beauty of Black women in the following words:

> If a Black woman is light-skinned with good hair and good features, then she's the shit. Even if she has short hair, but good features, she'll be all right. But a dark-skinned girl with short hair can forget it. And if she has a big nose, then she should just be a nun. But if she has long hair and good features, then her skin color can be overlooked. Long hair really helps out those black ugly girls.

The politics of hair parallels the politics of skin color. Among Black women, straight hair and European hairstyles not only have been considered more feminine but have sent a message about one's standing in the social hierarchy. "Good hair" has long been associated with the light-skinned middle class, "bad hair" with Blacks who are less fortunate.

The sixties marked a revolution in Blacks' attitudes about their hair; for the first time young women in significant numbers stopped perming and processing, and members of both sexes let their hair grow wild and free in the style known as the Afro. But when the sixties ended, and the 'fro was no longer fashionable, the old attitudes about hair quickly resurfaced. The tradition of calling hair that was staight and wavy "good" and hair that was tightly curled and nappy "bad" had never really gone away. Men like Darryl continued to evaluate Black women according to what was on their heads instead of what was in them, and the self-confidence of many Black women continued to hinge on the freshness of their perms.

In this post-sixties era, hair remains a politically charged subject. To some, how an African American chooses to style his or her hair says everything there is to be said about that individual's Black consciousness, socioeconomic class, and probable life-style, particularly when the individual is a woman.

Clearly, hair is less an issue for men than for women. Beginning in childhood, boys conventionally wear short hair while girls grow their hair long. Adult Black males generally keep their hair cropped short, so its texture is usually not that important to them. But from an early age most Black girls, especially those with fuzzy edges and nappy "kitchens" (the hairline at the back of the neck), are taught to "fix" their hair—as if it were broken. Short hair is unfeminine but for many long hair is unmanageable. Still the hair of Black girls is braided and yanked, rubber-banded and barretted, into a presentable state. And when mothers grow weary of taming their daughters' hair, many opt to treat it with chemical relaxers. As one Black mother tired of fighting the comb declared, "I didn't have time to mess with that child's nappy head any longer, so I went and got it permed. It's been a lot easier on both of us since."

Some Black women come to regret what was done to their hair as children. A woman named Yvette longingly remembers what her hair was like when she was young. She says that many of her earliest

---

1. White American feminist and civil rights activist and writer (b. 1935), who came to prominence with her 1975 book *Against Our Will: Men, Women, and Rape*.

memories feature her Afro-puffs (hair that is parted in the middle, rubber-banded, and "picked out" into two small Afros, one on each side) or her thousand braids with bows at the end. She also remembers how fascinated the White children at school were by the natural softness of her hair and how they were always asking to touch it. "For me, my hair was a source of pride and uniqueness," she recalls. But as she neared adolescence her mother declared that she "was turning into a young lady" and it was time for her first permanent relaxer. Today, in her thirties, Yvette yearns for her natural hair, yet she continues to get permanents regularly. "In order to reverse the process now, it would mean a lot of hair breakage and hair loss," she sighs. "At this point in my life, it's a lot less effort just to deal with it the way it is." (The place where permed hair meets virgin hair is often weak and keeping the hair permed may actually prevent further breakage.)

For many other Black women, childhood memories of short, nappy locks bring forth feelings of shame, not sweet nostalgia. A dark-skinned woman named Caroline remembers other children's taunts of "Your hair's so short, you can smell yo' brains." Caroline was ecstatic when her mother marched her down to Sister Westbury's Beauty Nook for her first perm.

> I had it doubly hard when I was in grade school. Not only was I dark-skinned but I also had short beady hair. I always got teased by the boys and laughed at by the girls because my hair was so nappy and always stuck up in the air. I hated my hair and cried many nights. I was so glad when I got my hair straightened. It changed my whole life.

Many young Black girls view their first perm as a rite of passage, and sometimes it is their parents, particularly those who grew up in the sixties, who are sorry when a daughter stops going natural. In an article entitled "Life with Daughters or The Cakewalk with Shirley Temple," Gerald Early, a professor of English and African-American studies at Washington University, described his intense disappointment the day his two daughters, aged seven and ten, came home with their hair permed.

During that summer the girls abandoned their Afro hairstyles for good. When they burst through the door with their hair newly straightened, beaming, I was so taken aback in a kind of horror that I could only mutter in astonishment when they asked, "How do you like it?"

It was as if my children were no longer mine, as if a culture that had convinced them they were ugly had taken them from me. The look I gave my wife brought this response from her: "They wanted their hair straightened, and they thought they were old enough for it. Besides, there is no virtue in wearing an Afro. I don't believe in politically correct hair."

Yet for Black women hair *is* political, and those who are "happy nappy" consider perming "politically incorrect," just as others consider unstraightened hair a disgrace. No matter which choice a Black woman makes, someone may react negatively to it.

On a vacation trip to British Virgin Gorda, the Black poet, essayist, and writer Audre Lorde discovered just how easily her hairstyle could be interpreted politically. Wearing newly fashioned dreadlocks (a style in which the hair is either braided, twisted, or clumped together in separate strands all over the head), Lorde arrived at the Beef Island Airport and was told by the immigration officer—a Black woman with heavily processed hair—that her entry was being denied. Angry at the snag in her travel plans, Lorde demanded to speak to the woman's supervisor and was informed that her dreadlocks marked her as a dope-smoking Rastafarian revolutionary. Fortunately, the officer was eventually able to determine that Lorde was not a "dangerous" Rastafarian, and her passport was stamped "admit."

But unprocessed hair may also elicit political approval. Mary Morten, a former president of the Chicago chapter of the National Organization for Women, who keeps her hair in a short natural style, remembers the time a Black man came running up to her on the street holding a rolled-up poster. He said, "I've been waiting for a sister with natural hair so I can give her this poem." When Morten unfurled the poster, she found printed on it a Gwendolyn Brooks poem. She was so touched by the message and by the way it came to her that she hung the poster on the wall of the Chicago NOW office. The poem reads:

TO THOSE OF MY SISTERS
WHO KEPT THEIR NATURALS
         Never to look
         a hot comb in the teeth.

   Sisters!
   I love you
   Because you love you.

. . . .

You have not bought Blondine.
You have not hailed the hot-comb recently.
You never worshipped Marilyn Monroe.
You say: Farrah's hair is hers
You have not wanted to be white.
Nor have you testified to adoration of that state
with the advertisement of imitation,
(never successful because the hot comb is laughing
   too.)

But oh the rough dark Other music.
the Real,
the Right.
the natural Respect for self and seal.
    Sisters!
Your hair is Celebration in the world.

Nonetheless, Black women who wear their hair unprocessed are often squawked at, teased, and harassed. One sister with long brown dreadlocks says, "When my hair was going through the 'wile chile' stage [the first phase of growing dreadlocks, in which the hair looks completely untamed], a brother actually stopped me on the street demanding to know 'when in the hell' was I going to 'do somethin' with my nappy-headed ass hair.'" The award-winning actress Whoopi Goldberg often has members of her own community tell her that her dreadlocks are disgusting and that she should "take those nappy braids out." A generation earlier, the actress Cicely Tyson was told by members of the Black community that she might be a gifted actress but her short natural hairstyle was detrimental to the image of Black women.

Although political reasons for sporting European-looking hairstyles abound, some Black women relax their hair just because they like it that way. One of them, a woman named Catherine, who owns a small business, says that she loves her hair long and would never consider cutting it.

My long hair is my best feature. I realize it's high maintenance but I'd much rather get up an hour early and do my hair than to have short hair. There's something special about Black women with long hair.

A certain level of Black consciousness would seem to be necessary before a woman dares to go natural. The relationship between hairstyle and politics is far from clear, however. One African-American professional woman from Chicago has said that she could not imagine wearing her hair in any way but dreadlocks, or perhaps cornrows, since everything she does emanates from an Afrocentric perspective. Yet she admits to knowing women as strongly Afrocentric as she who routinely process their hair, and others with no interest at all in fostering Black culture or politics who wear natural styles like cornrows.

Dreadlocking perhaps carries a more radical political connotation than any other hairstyle. Yet all it entails is growing curly hair out to the point where it "locks," the stage at which dreadlocks become permanent and cannot be changed without cutting. Few Whites have hair curly enough to grow into "dreads"; with rare exceptions, the style is uniquely Black. Traditionally, dreadlocks have been associated with the Rastafarians of Jamaica, and American men with dreadlocks are usually musicians or members of the counterculture. However, an increasing number of American Black women are adopting the style. They are writers and performers, like Alice Walker and Whoopi Goldberg, or professors, journalists, and social workers—not exactly corporate types, but not members of a counterculture, either.

Dark-skinned Black women who grow dreadlocks appear to have reached a point in their lives at which they no longer feel the need to compensate for the color of their skin. Breaking free of all their past conditioning about hair may be part of a larger spiritual awakening. After being criticized by a "bro" for wearing her hair in dreads, one brown-skinned woman commented, "It's too bad Black men don't see the beauty and the spirituality of my hair." Sandra B., who manages an urban charity organization in Chicago, also describes her dreadlocks in spiritual terms.

> I love my hair like this. I wouldn't trade it for straight hair any day. There is something so spiritual and in-touch about my hair. I feel connected with my roots. My hair gives me a sense of oneness with nature. You know how beautiful nature is when it's just left alone to grow naturally the way God intended? Well, that's how I look at my hair. Just growing naturally the way God intended.

Freelance writer Naadu Blankson, in an article in *Essence*, has compared the unlocking of her inhibitions with the dreadlocking of her hair, and Alice Walker once wrote, in the same magazine, that the ability to "lock" may depend on the flow of one's natural energy not being blocked by "anger, hatred, or self-condemnation."

There are many misconceptions about dreadlocks, and those who wear them must answer a lot of questions, many of them from members of their own community. The most common include: "Can you wash your hair that way?" (yes); "Does it smell?" (no more than anyone else's); "If you want to change it, must you shave it off and begin anew?" (most likely); "How do you get your hair to do that?" (it just does it on its own). One woman who got tired of the constant inquiries tells how she turns the tables on the questioner.

> When Black people ask me what I did to my hair, I tell them, I haven't done anything to my hair. The question is, especially for those who have Jheri Curls, what have *you* done to *your* hair. Unlike you, I wash my hair all the time, and when I get up in the morning I don't have stains on my pillow.

Simone Hylton, an Afrocentric beautician, believes that most Black women are misinformed about what is good and bad for their hair. Many assume that dreadlocking is harmful, yet few know just how much damage constant processing can do. According to Hylton, Black hair is not as fragile as is commonly thought. Straightening, chemical relaxing, and frequent washing burn the scalp and cause hair breakage; dreadlocking does not. "Look at people who wear dreads; their hair is long.

If you wore dreads for ten years, your hair would grow past your butt, too."

When a Black woman comes to Hylton with hair damaged by years of perming, she sometimes has to cut off all the permed growth. If the woman still wants long hair, Hylton will braid extensions onto what remains, to give the hair a rest and help restore it to its natural state.

In the politically charged world of hairstyling, Hylton has even come under fire for weaving these extensions into hair—her own hair as well as that of her clients. Hylton, who wears a Senegalese twist (a style in which the hair is twisted into ringlets, sometimes with African linen intertwined), has this response to such criticism:

> Weaving extensions into the hair originated in Africa. Members of different tribes would take plants and weave them into their hair. Weaving or twisting isn't done just to get length. It's an art form and a part of African culture.

Black women with long hair, whether natural or processed, whether achieved by hair weaves or extensions, are acutely sensitive to accusations that they are trying to look White. Like Hylton, they often draw on ancient customs to defend their choices. When asked about the melange of long braids neatly twisted into a hair weave hanging down her back, Pamela, a Black graduate student in psychology, replied without missing a beat.

> I wear my hair like this for a reason. It's convenient and I feel very attractive. My ancestors from Egypt wore their hair long and straight or braided. Sometimes both. This is not about having long hair to try to be White; this is about being who I am as an African American. It has more to do with style and cosmetics than it has to do with being like some White woman. My hair is an accessory.

Black hairstylist Nantil Chardonnay, of Nantil for Egypt III Hair Salon, maintains that virtually all of today's popular hairstyles can be traced to early African cultures. But she laments that it has usually taken a White woman—like Bo Derek[2] with her braids in the 1980 hit film *10*—to popularize, even among Blacks,

---

2. White American actress (b. 1956) who became famous as a sex symbol for her cornrow-wearing character in the 1979 film *10*.

what has been a traditionally African hairstyle. Although some Black women in the sixties and seventies were wearing beaded braids and cornrows as an expression of their African heritage, this was not considered a mainstream thing to do within the Black community until after *10* came out. In Chardonnay's words, "I thought it was very shallow of them [African-American women] suddenly to want to copy someone else who was copying our culture to begin with."

Hair texture, like skin tone, carries much social and historical baggage for Blacks. All things being equal, a Black woman whose hair grows naturally straight is usually thought to be from a "better" family than a woman whose hair is very nappy. Black women who wear natural styles, like braids, cut across socioeconomic lines, but a politically defiant style like dreadlocks is generally a middle-class expression of Black consciousness. Inner-city girls and women are probably the least likely to wear dreadlocks. Poor Black women with very kinky hair strive instead for straighter-looking hair, but because they cannot afford constant professional relaxation treatments (which can cost up to $85 a session), their hair often looks stiff and overly processed, in what is derisively called a "ghetto 'do." Still, hair is so important to Black women that, regrettably, some would rather be late paying their rent than miss getting their hair permed.

But the split between Black women who process and those who do not is not as great or malevolent as Spike Lee's *School Daze*[3]—in which the men debate politics and the women fight about their skin color and hair—might lead one to think. In *School Daze* women with light skin and straight hair are derisively called "Wannabees," and dark-skinned women are "Jigaboos." Their big dance number takes place in Madam Re-Re's beauty parlor. There, among the hair dryers and chemical relaxers, the Black coeds sing a lively number called "Straight and Nappy." It opens with a spate of vicious name-calling between the two groups of women.

WANNABEES: Pick-a-ninny

JIGABOOS: Barbie Doll, High Yella Heffer

   W: Tarbaby

J: Wanna be White

W: Jig-a-boo

CHORUS: Talkin' 'bout good and bad hair
   whether you are dark or fair
   go on and swear
   see if I care
   good and bad hair. . . .

W: Your hair ain't no longer than (*finger snap*)
   so you'll never fling it all back
   and you 'fraid to walk in the rain
   oh, what a shame, who's to blame

J: Don't you ever worry 'bout that
   'cause I don't mind being BLACK
   go on with your mixed-up head
   I ain't gonna never be 'fraid

W: Well you got nappy hair

J: Nappy is all right with me

W: My hair is straight you see

J: But your soul's crooked as can be. . . .

Although many thought that *School Daze* was demeaning to Black women, Lee did inject some humor into the hair issue—doubtless a good thing in the long run.

While African Americans assign the hair issue various degrees of political weight, most Black women, whether they process or not, respect and understand the choices of others. There is, after all, a reality factor to contend with in White-dominated America. For example, a Black teacher from California who had been content with wearing her hair in a natural decided to straighten it when she and her husband began to look for a house to buy.

While more and more Black women today are daring to go natural, they remain a distinct minority. Straightened hair is the standard for "respectable" Black women—those with corporate careers as well as the wives of Black politicians and businessmen. An estimated 75 percent of American Black women continue to perm or relax their hair.

---

3. 1988 musical-drama film, directed and written by Lee (b. 1957), about fraternity and sorority members at a historically black college.

In all fairness, some Black women simply look better with their hair processed, and those who want to wear it that way have as much right to do so as Whites. As one Black sister puts it, "White people don't have a patent on long hair."

Meanwhile, in the nineties short styles are suddenly "in." From the boyish (but processed-looking) haircuts of the "Uh Huh" girls of the Diet Pepsi commercials to the closely cropped natural locks of Black actress Halle Berry (*Jungle Fever, Boomerang*), the traditional view that long hair is sexier seems to be changing. Berry says that she loves her short hair: "I feel people see me now. I will never grow my hair long again!"

Still, some Black women (and White women, too) say they continue to keep their hair long because that is what they think men prefer. A Black college student named Crystal says that when her boyfriend saw her getting her hair cut short, he walked out at the first snip and would not talk to her for two weeks. But it is hard to generalize: another Black man, an electrical engineer from the Chicago area, says that he is partial to Black women who wear their hair short and natural: "There's something so pure and genuine about these women," while another man counters, "Brothers like their women with long hair so they can grab hold of it during sex."

Sometimes the very men who like long hair tell their women not to "wear that arsenal [rollers] to bed," and then in the morning ask, "Why is your hair sticking up all over your head?" Fortunately, in this feminist era, a growing number of Black women are choosing to wear their hair in styles that please themselves first, not their men. At the same time, more African-American men are beginning to experiment with different hairstyles of their own. In the process, they may be becoming more tolerant and perhaps more sensitive to the difficulties of constant hair maintenance.

One currently popular Black men's hairstyle is the "high-top fade," popularized by the rapper Kid of *Kid N' Play* (who also starred in *House Party*). Short on the sides, long and flat on top, it goes by other names, including "wedge," "slant," "Philly fade," "gumbie," "low 'n' tight," or just "big hair." Like other inner-city trends, including ripped jeans and earrings on men, the fade appears to be making its way into mainstream culture. Modified versions of it are even cropping up on the heads of middle-class men, Black and White.

Another male street hairstyle, this one with roots in Africa, entails shaving a pattern through the hair so that the scalp shows through. Some Black youths have even taken to shaving their favorite logos, like Nike, onto the back of their heads. Like the Afro of the sixties, these radical razor designs are an artistic expression of Black culture. But these styles are also faddish and are already losing favor in some urban areas.

While hairstyle has never been a central part of the color complex in perceptions of Black men, certain 'dos are associated with certain life-styles. In the nineties, Black men who texturize their hair are usually entertainers—musicians, television celebrities, big-name athletes—although a few Black businessmen have experimented with hair relaxers to improve their corporate image. The more radical styles, like razor cuts, dreadlocks, and extreme high-top fades, are avoided by Black businessmen, just as very long hair and punk cuts are avoided by White businessmen who want the establishment to take them seriously.

In general, Black men seem to have a more positive attitude toward their hair than most Black women do. Even when they start to go bald, they can shave it all off, as the Chicago Bulls basketball star Michael Jordan does, and make a fashion statement.

Meanwhile, anguished concerns about hairstyles have hurt and held back Black women, and, as the quotation by A'Lelia Bundles implies, women must, together, begin to move beyond such concerns. Shameful attitudes about hair often begin at home. Within the family, Black parents need to teach their sons and daughters that though hair comes in a variety of textures, there is no such thing as good or bad hair. If you got hair, good!

DOROTHY ROBERTS
The Dark Side of Birth Control [1997]

"It is amazing how effective governments—especially our own—are at making sterilization and contraceptives available to women of color, despite their inability to reach these women with prenatal care, drug treatment and other health services," observes Dorothy Roberts (b. 1956), a professor of law and sociology at Northwestern University, in her book *Killing the Black Body* (1997). Earlier chapters in the book explore reproductive control during slavery and the effects on minority women of the eugenics movement, which sought to promote "desirable" human characteristics though selective breeding. In the selection reprinted here, Roberts traces the history of involuntary or coerced sterilization and birth control from World War II through the 1990s.

Asserting that government funding policies have encouraged the sterilization of poor women, Roberts calls for a middle ground between a blanket support of birth control programs and an outright rejection of such programs. She reinforces her support of that middle ground by exploring the gender split in black communities over birth control. Roberts doesn't associate birth control with "racial genocide," as do Dick Gregory (p. 792) and others, but she does argue that racially motivated birth control programs reinforce racism in society. Ultimately, for Roberts, the critical issue is whether birth control programs are controlled by and designed for members of the communities they serve.

From Dorothy Roberts, *Killing the Black Body: Race, Reproduction, and the Meaning of Liberty* (New York: Pantheon Books, 1997), pp. 56–57, 98–103, 325–26.

Race completely changes the significance of birth control to the story of women's reproductive freedom. For privileged white women in America, birth control has been an emblem of reproductive liberty. Organizations such as Planned Parenthood have long championed birth control as the key to women's liberation from compulsory motherhood and gender stereotypes. But the movement to expand women's reproductive options was marked by racism from its very inception in the early part of this century. The spread of contraceptives to American women hinged partly on its appeal to eugenicists bent on curtailing the birthrates of the "unfit," including Negroes. For several decades, peaking in the 1970s, government-sponsored family-planning programs not only encouraged Black women to use birth control but coerced them into being sterilized. While slave masters forced Black women to bear children for profit, more recent policies have sought to reduce Black women's fertility. Both share a common theme—that Black women's childbearing should be regulated to achieve social objectives.

This chapter explores how racism helped to create the view of birth control as a means of solving social problems. Birth control policy put into practice an explanation for racial inequality that was rooted in nature rather than power. At the same time, the connection between birth control and racial injustice split the Black community. While some community activists promoted birth control as a means of racial betterment, others denounced abortion and family planning as forms of racial "genocide." Black people's ambivalence about birth control adds an important dimension to the contemporary understanding of reproductive freedom as a woman's right to choose contraception and abortion. We must acknowledge the justice of ensuring equal access to birth control for poor and minority women without denying the injustice of imposing birth control as a means of reducing their fertility.

* * *

BIRTH CONTROL AS RACIAL GENOCIDE

The debate among Blacks over birth control, which began in the 1920s, persisted over the ensuing decades. In an article appearing in 1954 in the popular Black magazine *Jet*, Dr. Julian Lewis,[1] a former University of Chicago professor, criticized Planned Parenthood's work in the Black community and warned that the wide-scale practice of birth control would lead to "race suicide."[2] Nearly twenty years later, in a controversial cover story in *Ebony* magazine entitled "My Answer to Genocide," Dick Gregory[3] advocated large Black families as insurance against Black extermination. Gregory was especially wary of white people's motives underlying the promotion of family planning:

> For years they told us where to sit, where to eat, and where to live. Now they want to dictate our bedroom habits. First the white man tells me to sit in the back of the bus. Now it looks like he wants me to sleep under the bed. Back in the days of slavery, black folks couldn't grow kids fast enough for white folks to harvest. Now that we've got a little taste of power, white folks want us to call a moratorium on having children.[4]

Gregory's views were not an aberration. A number of articles in both the white and Black press raised the possibility of a plot to eliminate Blacks through birth control services. Two studies by William Darity and Castellano Turner, published in the *American Journal of Public Health* in 1972 and 1973, showed a widespread worry among Blacks that family-planning programs were a potential means of racial genocide, especially if the programs provided sterilization and abortion and were run by whites.[5] One reported that nearly 40 percent of Blacks surveyed believed that these programs were a scheme to exterminate Blacks. These fears were most prevalent among young, uneducated males in the North.

During the 1960s and 1970s, Black nationalists increasingly adopted the theory that birth control was a form of genocide. The Nation of Islam vehemently opposed birth control as a deliberate white strategy to deplete the Black population. A cartoon in *Muhammad Speaks* depicted a Black woman in an advanced state of pregnancy standing in a jail cell, with the caption: "My Only Crime Was Refusing to Take Birth Control Pills."[6] Another showed a bottle of birth control pills marked with a skull and crossbones. The Black Power conference held in Newark in 1967, organized by Amiri Baraka,[7] passed a resolution denouncing birth control.[8] The May 1969 issue of *The Liberator*[9] admonished readers that "[f]or us to speak in favor of birth control for Afro-Americans would be comparable to speaking in favor of genocide."

Even more mainstream organizations such as the NAACP and the Urban League reversed their earlier support for family planning as a means of racial progress. As head of Operation PUSH, Jesse Jackson[1] in

---

1. For Lewis's position on birth control in 1945, see p. 504. [Editor's note]

2. Julian Lewis, "Is Birth Control a Menace to Negroes?" *Jet*, Aug. 1954, pp. 52–55, quoted in [Robert G.] Weisbord, *Genocide? [Birth Control and the Black American* (Westport, Conn.: Greenwood and Two Continents, 1975),] p. 53. [Unless otherwise indicated, all footnotes are those of the author.]

3. See p. 792. [Editor's note]

4. Dick Gregory, "My Answer to Genocide," *Ebony*, Oct. 1971, p. 66, quoted in Weisbord, *Genocide?* p. 91.

5. William A. Darity and Castellano B. Turner, "Family Planning, Race Consciousness, and the Fear of Race Genocide," *American Journal of Public Health* 62 (1972), p. 1454; William A. Darity and Castellano B. Turner, "Fears of Genocide Among Black Americans as Related to Age, Sex, and Region," *American Journal of Public Health* 63 (1973), p. 1029.

6. *Muhammad Speaks*, Aug. 29, 1969, quoted in Weisbord, *Genocide?* p. 103.

7. See p. 694. [Editor's note]

8. Loretta J. Ross, "African-American Women and Abortion[: 1800–1970]," [in Stanlie M. James and Abena P. A. Busia, ed., *Theorizing Black Feminisms: The Visionary Pragmatism of Black Women* (London: Routledge, 1993),] pp. 153.

9. Called "the voice of the Black Protest Movement," *The Liberator*, published from 1961 to 1971, originated as the official magazine of the Liberation Committee for Africa (LCA), a New York–based group dedicated to a Pan-African vision and African independence; in 1963, the LCA changed its name to the Afro-American Research Institute, and the magazine shifted to focus on African American issues. [Editor's note]

1. Civil rights activist, Baptist minister, and candidate for the Democratic presidential nomination in 1984 and 1988 (b. 1941); after leaving SCLC in 1971, Jackson founded Operation PUSH (People United to Save Humanity), which merged in 1996 with the National Rainbow Coalition (established by Jackson in 1984) to form Rainbow/PUSH, a nonprofit organization devoted to social justice and civil rights. [Editor's note]

1972 questioned the timing of the government's interest in family planning for Blacks, noting that its growth "simultaneously with the emergence of blacks and other nonwhites as a meaningful force in the nation and the world appears more than coincidental."[2] Fannie Lou Hamer,[3] who had been sterilized without her consent, also viewed abortion and birth control as a form of racial genocide.[4] Some leaders went further to argue that increasing the Black population was essential for liberation. Marvin Dawes, leader of the Florida NAACP, asserted, "Our women need to produce more babies, not less . . . and until we comprise 30 to 35 percent of the population, we won't really be able to affect the power structure in this country."[5]

Numerous Black women challenged the characterization of birth control as a form of genocide, as well as the "strength in numbers" argument. By the 1940s, Blacks were visibly organizing to increase the availability of birth control in their communities. At its national meeting in 1941 the National Council of Negro Women created a standing committee on family planning and passed a resolution requesting every Black organization to include family planning in its agenda "to aid each family to have all the children it can afford and support but no more—in order to insure better health, security and happiness for all."[6] This was the first time a national women's organization officially endorsed birth control. Black women's groups were also asserting greater independence from the white-dominated mainstream organizations such as Planned Parenthood. In a speech addressed to Planned Parenthood in 1942, Dr. Dorothy Ferebee[7] admonished her audience, "It is well for this organization to realize that the Negro at his present advanced stage of development is increasingly interested more in programs that are worked out with and by him than in those worked out for him."[8]

Many women in the Black liberation movement rejected their brothers' charge to them to bear more children. In her anthology on Black women published in 1970, Toni Cade[9] took up the issue "The Pill: Genocide or Liberation?" "I've been made aware of the national call to Sisters to abandon birth control . . . to picket family-planning centers and abortion-referral groups and to raise revolutionaries," she wrote. "What plans do you have for the care of me and the child?"[1] As head of the Black Women's Liberation Committee of SNCC, Frances Beal[2] wrote, "Black women have the right and the responsibility to determine when it is in *the interest of the struggle to have children or not to have them and this right must not be relinquished to any . . . to determine when it is in her own best interests* to have children."[3]

The conflict escalated not only in journals but also in grassroots confrontations. One of the most heated disputes occurred in 1969 between women in the National Welfare Rights Organization and community leaders surrounding the opening of family-planning centers in Pittsburgh.[4] The city's antipoverty board became the first in the country to vote down federal

2. Quoted in Vanessa Northington Gamble, "Race, Class, and the Pill: A History," in Sarah E. Samuels and Mark D. Smith, eds., *The Pill: From Prescription to Over the Counter* (Menlo Park, Calif.: Kaiser Family Foundation, 1994), pp. 21, 30.

3. See discussion of Hamer and the Mississippi Freedom Democratic Party, p. 537. [Editor's note]

4. Kay Mills, *This Little Light of Mine: The Life of Fannie Lou Hamer* (New York: Plume, 1994), p. 274.

5. Quoted in Ross, "African-American Women and Abortion," p. 153.

6. Weisbord, *Genocide?* p. 47.

7. Physician and activist (1898–1980); helped establish Southeast Neighborhood House, a medical center for African Americans in Washington, D.C.; first medical director of the Mississippi Health Project, which brought health care to poor areas; while working as the director of health services at Howard University Medical School (from 1949 to 1968), she served as the second president (after Mary McLeod Bethune) of the National Council of Negro Women, from 1949 to 1953. [Editor's note]

8. [Jessie M.] Rodrique, "The Black Community and the Birth-Control Movement," [in Ellen Carol DuBois and Vicki L. Ruiz, eds., *Unequal Sisters: A Multicultural Reader in U.S. Women's History* (New York: Routeledge, 1990),] p. 341.

9. Toni Cade Bambara (née Miltona Mirkin Cade, 1939–1995), writer, activist, and educator; editor of foundational literature anthology *The Black Woman* (1970); her books of fiction include the short story collection *Gorilla, My Love* and the novels *The Salt Eaters* (1980) and *Those Bones Are Not My Child*, published posthumously in 1999 and edited by Toni Morrison. [Editor's note]

1. Toni Cade, "The Pall: Genocide of Liberation," in Toni Cade, ed., *The Black Woman: An Anthology* (New York: Signet, 1970), p. 163.

2. See p. 801. [Editor's note]

3. Quoted in Ross, "African-American Women and Abortion," p. 156.

4. Ibid., pp. 153–56; Weisbord, *Genocide?* pp. 120–21; Ralph Z. Hallow, "The Blacks Cry Genocide," *The Nation*, April 28, 1969, p. 535.

funds to continue Planned Parenthood clinics in six poor neighborhoods. The leader of the militant United Movement for Progress, William "Bouie" Haden, even threatened to firebomb a clinic. (It was discovered that Haden's organization received a $10,000 grant from the Catholic diocese of Pittsburgh.) One mother protested, "Who appointed him our leader anyhow? ... Why should I allow one loudmouth to tell me about having children?" Black women successfully organized to remove Haden as a delegate from the Homewood-Brushton Citizens Renewal Council and to restore funds to the clinics. In a Black neighborhood in Cleveland, a family-planning center was burned to the ground. The Black Panther Party (BPP)[5] was also split along gender lines on the subject of abortion and birth control. Despite opposition to birth control from some male members, however, the BPP offered contraceptives as part of its free health care program.

Shirley Chisholm,[6] a Black congresswoman from Brooklyn, worked tirelessly in the 1970s to increase the number of family-planning clinics in Black neighborhoods. She flatly rejected the argument equating birth control with genocide:

> To label family planning and legal abortion programs "genocide" is male rhetoric, for male ears. It falls flat to female listeners and to thoughtful male ones. Women know, and so do many men, that two or three children who are wanted, prepared for, reared amid love and stability, and educated to the limit of their ability will mean more for the future of the black and brown races from which they come

than any number of neglected, hungry, ill-housed and ill-clothed youngsters.[7]

In testimony before a Senate committee, Congresswoman Chisholm attested to her female constituents' pleas for family-planning services. One study published in 1970 found that 80 percent of the Black women in Chicago interviewed approved of birth control and 75 percent were practicing it.[8]

One reason Black women supported family planning was that they were disproportionately victims of unsafe abortions prior to the legalization of abortion in 1973. Half of the maternity-related deaths among Black women in New York City in the 1960s were attributed to illegal abortions. Black women were less likely than white women to be able to afford safe illegal abortions and were generally denied legal therapeutic abortions performed in hospitals. Of all therapeutic abortions performed in New York City at that time, for example, over 90 percent were performed on white women.[9] Black women knew that the *lack* of family planning services was a leading cause of death in their communities. In the 1950s, Dr. Dorothy Brown, the first Black female general surgeon in the United States and a Tennessee state representative, became the first state legislator to introduce a bill to legalize abortion.[1]

Today, with Black women having 24 percent of abortions in the United States, Black women's rights activist Loretta Ross[2] says, "The question is not *if* we support abortion, but *how*, and when, and why."[3] Black feminist critiques of the birth control movement, such as Angela Davis's[4] brilliant chapter "Racism, Birth

5. See p. 583. [Editor's note]

6. See p. 787. [Editor's note]

7. Quoted in Ross, "African-American Women and Abortion," p. 155.

8. Donald J. Bogue, "Family Planning in Negro Ghettos of Chicago," *Milbank Memorial Fund Quarterly*, April 1970, pt. 2, p. 283. An analysis of data from the 1965 National Fertility Study found "very little difference ... between large city blacks and whites in the proportions who have ever used contraception (78 per cent of the blacks and 80 per cent of the whites)." Charles F. Westoff and Norman B. Ryder, "Contraceptive Practice Among Urban Blacks in the United States, 1965," *Milbank Memorial Fund Quarterly*, April 1970, pt. 2, pp. 215, 218. Blacks, however, were less likely to be currently using contraceptives.

9. Weisbord, *Genocide?* p. 116.

1. Ross, "African-American Women and Abortion," p. 151.

2. Activist and writer (b. 1953); after being sterilized at the age of 23, became involved in anti-violence and reproductive rights activism, including serving as a director of the D.C. Rape Crisis Center in 1979; as director of Women of Color Programs for NOW in the 1980s, Ross organized the first national conference on Women of Color and Reproductive Rights in 1987; she helped found SisterSong (Women of Color Reproductive Justice Collective) in 1997 and became National Coordinator for the organization in 2005. [Editor's note]

3. Ross, "African American Women and Abortion," p. 141.

4. See p. 1015. [Editor's note]

Control, and Reproductive Rights" in her classic *Women, Race, and Class,* call for abortion rights along with an end to sterilization abuse. Contemporary grassroots organizations, such as the National Black Women's Health Project in Atlanta, take the position that Black women should empower themselves to take control of their reproductive health.

If family-planning programs are a covert attempt to extinguish the Black race, "genocide" is the right word to describe them. Created to describe the Nazi annihilation of the Jews, the term means "the use of deliberate systematic measures (as killing, bodily or mental injury, unlivable conditions, prevention of births) calculated to bring about the extermination of a racial, political, or cultural group or to destroy the language, religion, or culture of a group."[5] The United Nations Convention for the Prevention and Punishment of Genocide includes in its definition of genocide an effort to eradicate a portion of a group.[6] There is ample evidence that some family-planning clinics have been opened in Black communities for the purpose of reducing Black birthrates. But is this racial genocide?

The equation of birth control with racial genocide can also be dangerous. Opposition to all forms of family planning for Blacks leads to an unacceptable restriction of Black women's control over their own procreative decisions. Community activists who call for Black women to avoid birth control altogether in order to produce as many children as possible encroach on women's reproductive autonomy. They also buy into the eugenicist's misguided creed that reproduction determines a group's social status.

This is a minority position among those who oppose birth control as a form of racial domination, however. The predominant concern is not with contraception itself, but with contraception promoted by whites for the purpose of population control. Blacks, it turned out, had good cause to be suspicious of government-sponsored family-planning programs: subsequent investigation proved true nationalists' accusa-tion that these programs were coercing Black women to be sterilized. The critical issue is not whether a program is subsidized by public funds, however, but whether the program is controlled by the Black community it serves and designed to enhance its members' reproductive freedom.

Although some Blacks believe that white-controlled family planning literally threatens Black survival, I take the position that racist birth control policies serve primarily an ideological function. The chief danger of these programs is not the physical annihilation of a race or social class. Family planning policies never reduced the Black birthrate enough to accomplish this result. Rather, the chief danger of these policies is the legitimation of an oppressive social structure. Proposals to solve social problems by curbing Black reproduction make racial inequality appear to be the product of nature rather than power. By identifying procreation as the cause of Black people's condition, they divert attention away from the political, social, and economic forces that maintain America's racial order. This harm to the entire group compounds the harm to individual members who are denied the freedom to have children. Donald MacKenzie observed that eugenic social theory is "a way of reading the structure of social classes onto nature."[7] In the same way, the primary threat to the Black community posed by coercive birth control schemes is not the actual elimination of the Black race; it is the biological justification of white supremacy.

Claims that current government policies that penalize Black reproduction share this legitimating feature of the eugenic rationale are sometimes misinterpreted as an unwarranted fear of racial genocide. John Kramer, dean of Tulane Law School, criticized my argument that reproductive punishments for crime are similar to eugenic laws on the ground that "Black women need not fear that their right to bear children is under serious attack . . . nor do black birthrates suggest that they do."[8] Dean Kramer failed to understand my

5. *Webster's Third New International Dictionary,* p. 947.
6. Weisbord, *Genocide?* pp. 11–12.
7. Donald A. MacKenzie, *Statistics in Britain, 1865–1930: The Social Construction of Scientific Knowledge* (Edinburgh: Edinburgh University Press, 1981), p. 18.
8. John R. Kramer, "Introduction to Symposium: Criminal Law, Criminal Justice, and Race," *Tulane Law Review* 67 (1993), pp. 1725, 1733–34.

point about the dangerous message sent by both eugenic laws and policies that penalize Black child-bearing. It could as easily be argued that mandatory sterilization laws enforced during the first half of the twentieth century posed no serious danger since they resulted in the sterilization of only 70,000 people. But the impact of these laws went far beyond their reduction of victims' birthrates. They affected the way Amer-

icans valued each other and thought about social problems. Eugenic ideology may also facilitate truly genocidal actions. The Nazi compulsory sterilization law of 1933 foreshadowed the Holocaust.[9]

Condemnation of policies that devalue Black reproduction need not arise from a fear of Black extermination. This opposition can arise from the struggle to eradicate white supremacy.

Aaron McGruder

The Boondocks: Because I Know You Don't Read the Newspaper [2000]

In the following series of strips for his popular comic panels *The Boondocks*, cartoonist Aaron McGruder (b. 1974) explores black and biracial identity by presenting different perspectives on hair. The three main characters of the strip are members of the Freeman family: the radical Huey (named after Black Panther leader Huey Newton, p. 548), his brother Riley (a wanna-be "gangsta"), and Granddad (a grouchy skeptic and pragmatist). In a 2004 interview in *The New Yorker*, McGruder said that they represent "three different facets of the sort of angry-black-man archetype." One of the few developed female characters in the comic is their next-door neighbor Jazmine Dubois, the optimistic and innocent daughter of a white mother and black father. In the strips reprinted here, Jazmine and Huey's exchange continues the debate about "good hair" from 1966 (p. 769) and 1992 (p. 1084)

Critics frequently view the character of Huey as the alter ego of the comic strip's creator. However, McGruder has argued that the strip endorses multiple perspectives. "It would be inaccurate to say that Huey's opinions are my own," McGruder proclaimed in a 2001 interview with Philadelphia's *City Paper*. "I think there's a broad opinion being put out through the strip with a combination of all the characters' voices, and it's really up to the reader to figure out what that is." In this way, the strip functions as a format for debate, providing a platform for a variety of opinions. Underscoring his support for multiple perspectives, McGruder stated in the *City Paper* interview that

he is less interested in convincing others of a particular position than in encouraging them to "think differently" and to "question … what they're told on a daily basis."

The Boondocks first appeared in 1997 in *The Diamondback*, the college paper of the University of Maryland, College Park, where McGruder studied African American history. After publication in the hip hop magazine *The Source* increased the cartoon's popularity, Universal Press Syndicate adopted it for nationwide syndication. In April 1999, *The Boondocks* launched in over 150 newspapers, the second-largest debut ever for a syndicated comic strip. In the next few years, circulation increased to over 300 newspapers, but McGruder stopped writing the strip in 2006 to focus on other projects, including an animated television show based on the strip.

During its run, *The Boondocks* was often a source of controversy. It frequently lampooned black pop-culture figures, some of whom publicly went on the offensive against McGruder, such as the conservative commentator Larry Elders. Another frequent target of ridicule was Black Entertainment Television (BET), which Huey dubs "Black Exploitation Television" or "Butts Every Time." (Robert Johnson, the chief executive of BET, retorted by telling *The New Yorker* in 2004 that his station's employees do "more in one day to serve the interest of African-Americans than this young man has done in his entire life.") After September 11, 2001, McGruder decided not to self-censor his critiques of the government, and the

9. See Benno Muller-Hill, *Murderous Science: Elimination by Scientific Selection of Jews, Gypsies, and Others, Germany 1933–1945* (New York: Oxford University Press, 1988), pp. 28–38; Robert Proctor, *Racial Hygiene: Medicine Under the Nazis* (Cambridge: Harvard University Press, 1988), pp. 95–117. N.B. x-ref 1966 *Ebony* article/letters and p. 1092 article by Russel, Wilson and Hall.

strip took a markedly political turn. Particularly contentious responses followed the series of strips published beginning in October 2001, in which Huey calls the FBI's terrorism tip-line to report "Americans who helped train and finance" terrorists, starting with former President Ronald Reagan. In the following years, McGruder continued a sustained critique of President George W. Bush and his administration. Some newspapers responded by refusing to run cartoons they deemed inappropriate or by relegating the strip to the op-ed pages. For example, the *Washington Post* pulled a week's worth of strips (the longest suspension of a comic strip in the paper's history) in response to a storyline in which Huey and his friend write a personal ad for Secretary of State Condoleezza Rice.

From Aaron McGruder, *The Boondocks: Because I Know You Don't Read the Newspaper* (Kansas City, Mo.: Andrews McMeel Publishing, 2000), pp. 10, 23, 50.

BETH E. RICHIE
Battered Black Women: A Challenge for the Black Community [1985]

In the following essay, Beth E. Richie (b. 1957), a professor of women's studies and criminal justice at the University of Illinois, Chicago, recounts how her experiences working in a "multicultural, Third World–controlled agency with strong roots in the community" and her later work with Battered Minority Women (BMW) made her aware of the problem of domestic violence in the black community and helped her understand the complexities of fighting it. Social and political considerations both complicate the fight against black domestic violence. For example, the police's role as a key source of protection for battered women is hindered by its historically adversarial position in black communities. Richie's grappling with "the lonely, isolating experiences of a black feminist in the battered women's movement" led her to identify two key characteristics of black domestic violence and suggest specific directions for action. Her call to build coalitions, even between groups who disagree on some issues, underscores Richie's commitment to practical political activism.

From *The Black Scholar* 16 (March/April 1985): pp. 40–44.

Over the past decade, the question of domestic violence against women—including black women—has emerged as a major concern in the fight against women's oppression. This is a controversial subject because, unlike other aspects of the subjugation of black women that target racism and economic exploitation, the burgeoning problem of battered women at first appears as an individual problem: a man beating a woman.

Too many blacks still think this is a divisive issue that should not be aired in public. However, the problem of battered women is a social phenomenon, not an individual one, and combatting this expression of social malaise must be approached with as much vigor as those rooted in the vagaries of a racial and class society.

The purpose of this article is to trace some of the obstacles I have encountered as a young black woman who calls herself a feminist working in the battered women's movement. My experiences have led me to some conclusions, which I offer for consideration.

I was introduced to the battered women's movement while working in New York City. It is a rare privilege to be associated with a multicultural, Third World–controlled agency with strong roots in the community. I had such a privilege for two years as I joined with dedicated workers in service to a predominantly black and Hispanic population.

The goal of our multidimensional involvement with community families was empowerment to assist families in the development of skills and the accumulation of resources necessary to overcome the cultural, racial, economic, and political oppression that smothered the community. We saw the family as the only institution truly able to meet and nourish individual needs. The agency was designed to foster independence in the community and to support families fighting back against exploitation, while maintaining their cultural and racial identities. In sharp contrast, most educational, social-service, and health-care systems in the community discourage autonomy and self-determination. Being an enthusiast and sharing the commitment to community and individual empowerment, I joined in the work and began to call the community my home.

After a period of time, I gradually realized that some of these strong, culturally-identified families, which we had been supporting so vehemently, were dangerous places for some women to live in. Furthermore, the political machine at the forefront of the grassroots community movement was, in fact, subtly exploiting women by denying the reality of sexual oppression. As I began to look closely, the incidences of battering, I have since learned, may have been intentionally set for me. I can now recognize that this "trap" is analogous to the "trap" in which many battered women find themselves. It is the trap of silence. Because of the scarcity of agencies such as mine, I hesitated to disclose my observations. I was immobilized by denial and sadness. Fear of being cast out by the community silenced me in the beginning. Loyalty and devotion are enormous barriers to overcome.

The world is so hostile to Third World people that it seems much less painful to remain quietly ambivalent. I struggled with how to illuminate this dark secret about our homes and ourselves. Disclosure is so easily confused with treason!

After a few false starts, I found a way to break the silence. I began to hold regular meetings for women in the community to talk together about positive issues: community strength and survival techniques. Discussions ranged from cultural rituals, such as holidays, to practical skills, such as living on an inadequate income. As the passage of time built trust, so it certified alliances, and women began to talk about problems in the community and finally about incidents of violence in their homes. Survival techniques and community concerns were expanded to include violence against women. The acknowledgement of the problem brought great joy and many tears. Women freed themselves from the trap of silence.

These triumphant women developed a mighty support network, as all through history black women have done so well. They set out to create an arena in which battered women could meet the community in full voice. A great deal of progress was made in the eighteen months I knew these women. Certainly, there is a long way to go. My point is not to extol their virtues, but rather to relate the message about the trap.

Black women, be forewarned. It is a painful, unsettling task to call attention to violence in our community. You may find yourselves feeling caught by the trap called loyalty. There is already so much negative infor-

mation about our families that a need to protect ourselves keeps us quiet. Yet, we must not allow our voices to be silenced. Instead, we must strengthen and speak the truths about our families; we must support each other; but we must hear the cries of our battered sisters and let them be heard by others!

BATTERED MINORITY WOMEN

In an effort to verify my experience, I looked to other Third World communities. My quest led me to sixteen vivacious women who refer to themselves as "Battered Minority Women" (BMW). Despite the inaccessibility of mainstream educational systems to members of BMW, these women are extremely well-educated, particularly in terms of political strategies. Their life experiences have afforded them keen insight and expert technique. Their alliance is built upon: (1) a history of being physically battered by men in their homes; (2) the experience of having survived the trauma of a lifetime of poverty; and (3) a strong allegiance to various Third World community groups. Most significantly, however, BMW shares a common analysis of the causes of battering, and they agree about the most appropriate response.

BMW believes that domestic violence is not a problem in black communities. Its occurrence, like substance abuse, crime, and unwanted adolescent pregnancy, is a symptom of living systematically deprived in a society that is designed to dominate and control Third World people. (On this point, I concur with their analysis.)

They define battering as the "systematic deprivation inflicted upon Third World men by society, which, in turn, is inflicted upon Third World women." That is, black women are beaten solely because their men are deprived. The response they advocate lies herein.

According to the BMW, black women should involve themselves in the struggle for racial justice in order to end battering in their homes. They consider the only real issue to be racial liberation; the concept of sexual oppression does not exist for them. They assert that there is no inequality of power between men and women, and they reject the notion that they are being mistreated by the men who beat them. Complete responsibility lies with white society. (This summary of their analysis has been confirmed by BMW as accurate.)

BMW members do not consider themselves feminist and negate the need to be part of a larger movement for sexual equality. They provide temporary refuge for the battered women in their community through a safe-home model, demonstrating once again stalwart support for one another. Most of the women they protect return home after the violent episode. BMW proudly acknowledges a high return rate of women to the BMW safe-homes.

BMW is associated with groups in Boston, Los Angeles, Detroit, and Atlanta, who share a similar philosophy. I have heard their sentiments expressed frequently in quite convincing terms, and suspect that many women are lured by their analysis of racial oppression, just as I am.

I find this disturbing because if the argument is taken one step further, it approaches the theory of the black matriarch. This well-popularized myth suggests the notion of the "strong black woman," willing and able to accept beating in the support of her man. The implication is that the role of black women in our families is to receive regular whippings in order to alleviate black men's stress. Clearly, this is a dangerous betrayal.

Undoubtedly, the stress black men must endure is cruel and often overwhelming. The connection this has to black women's accepting beatings puzzles me. Who is responsible? And where is the strength in acceptance? It is true that black women have historically been able to secure employment at times when black men could not. Does this make us any less oppressed? Why are we arguing whose oppression is worse?

We must cease this senseless debate. To be black in this society is bad; it's bad for men, women, and children. While it remains critical that black people continue actively struggling against racism and discrimination, it must not be done at the physical and psychological expense of black women. We have paid our dues, and black men must be held responsible for every injury they cause. Yes, experience has taught black women to be strong and resilient. We must learn that on occasion we must use our strength for ourselves.

The position that BMW advocates concerning sexist oppression is problematic. To negate the notion of feminism in our lives is to deny a critical component of our personhood. There is no such thing as partial liberation. We must demand our share of equality, too-long denied.

CONFRONTING THE ISSUE

Thus, once we choose to speak out against the violence in our families, we may be confronted with serious challenges to our work based on differences in political understanding of women-battering. To meet these challenges we must take time to carefully talk, to construct and refine our analysis of violence against women, especially against black women. Even more, we must consider how to work side by side with those who disagree with our conclusions.

The Role of Police . . .

While we study and deliberate about women abuse, it is important for black women working in the battered women's movement to address the special problems associated with having to depend upon the criminal justice system as a vehicle for protection and problem resolution. The criminal justice and law enforcement systems have been the worst offenders in perpetuating violence against black people.

How can blacks in the domestic violence movement reconcile the reality of police brutality and blatant racism in the criminal justice system with the need for police and court intervention on behalf of battered women?

I cannot offer answers to these questions, but I suggest that black women confront these issues directly. As a movement, we must work within the system to assure that justice is available to our families. All the while, we must remain alert to the fact that the police may not necessarily respond consistently or responsibly. We must cultivate alternative methods of protecting black women in our communities.

. . . And the Issue of Homophobia

Black women also need to candidly confront the issue of homophobia in society, particularly within our communities. Hatred of homosexuals and fear of being associated with lesbian women are both commonly expressed reasons that black women do not identify with the feminist movement. We continue to negate the valuable contributions made by black lesbian women to our culture as well as our struggle for racial liberation. By doing so, we have alienated steadfast allies. Black women must assume a leadership role in challenging our communities to put in check institutional and individual homophobic behavior. Currently, it is a decided barrier in our struggle.

To learn of rampant homophobia and deep-seated hatred of homosexuals startled me. To realize that oppressed people sometimes oppress others curiously disturbed me. However, it has helped allay my confusion and guilt about holding black men responsible for their violent behavior. Black women must be held accountable for the homophobia within our ranks.

Women of Color Institute

The meaning of violence against women in our communities is different from that in white or other Third World communities. We need to create time and space for researching a new, more meaningful analysis that is relevant to our lives. This is work we must do alone with no apologies for not including others. (No one apologized for the long years we have been excluded.) Our community needs something that the white women's movement has not given us, and we should know better than to expect to be *given* anything. We must do our own work.

This concept was dramatically illustrated at the Women of Color Institute of the 1982 National Coalition Against Domestic Violence meeting and conference. The one-day Institute, "Building a Colorful Coalition," provided the occasion for assembling our vision and building our voice. By acknowledging our differences, we affirmed our union.

Nearly 100 Asian, Hispanic, Native American, black, and other Third World women gathered in Milwaukee, Wisconsin, to attend the Institute, a true celebration of sisterhood. Certainly, every participant considered it the highlight of the conference. For me it was the highlight of my work in the battered women's movement.

The brilliant organizers of the Institute created an arena where we could strength[en] our spirit as Third World women and clarify our dream for a violence-free world. The Institute and the Women of Color Caucus emerged in a leadership role of the conference, confirming my belief that Third World women will be catalysts in bringing about positive change in the struggle for the liberation of all people.

THE CHALLENGES AHEAD

Black women must also work on the direction for the struggle of the racial justice movement. Let us not be distracted by the progress we have made. Although we have won some critical battles, I have a troubling sense that some of the victories may be leading some of us astray. As we surround ourselves with objects rumored to bring happiness and success, we often forget that most black people do not have adequate resources with which to control their lives. It is tempting to push on for our individual advancement without regard for those we are leaving behind.

Black women must more critically analyze this system to which we have demanded access. We must reject those components that suggest exploitation. Too many individuals have been lost to an image of being free. The struggle against racial oppression must continue to be of utmost importance in our lives. The younger we are, the higher the risk of forgetting how far we have come and of limiting our vision of how far we will be able to go.

In conclusion, I have a sense that the lonely, isolating experiences of a black feminist in the battered women's movement can be over. I can soon recover from the exhaustion I feel at having to constantly make a place for myself in a society that negates my existence. It is clumsy and burdensome to live in constant defense against simultaneous racial and sexual oppression. I find it empowering to be sharing my journey with you.

The ideas I have discussed represent only a part of the agenda for our future. We must begin in our homes, our heads, and mostly our hearts to identify "traps" of loyalty. We must demand equality in our communities and in our relationships with black men. Homophobic behavior must become unacceptable in our lives. As black women we must rededicate ourselves to the struggle for racial equality and ending violence in the justice system. Finally, we must study together and plan our future in the battered women's and feminist movements in ways that are meaningful to our lives.

Clearly, we have a great task before us. Let's join together and use our spirit to move us towards our dream of peace.

I take full responsibility for the views expressed in this article, but I would like to acknowledge those who helped in their formation: The Committee to End Violence in the Lives of Women and Women of Color Caucus of the National Coalition Against Domestic Violence. I am most indebted to the Third World women of the communities I know, who taught me the meaning of survival and support.

IN THE HEADLINES:

The Hill/Thomas Hearings

CLARENCE THOMAS: *First Statement to the Senate Judiciary Committee* [1991]
ANITA F. HILL: *Statement to the Senate Judiciary Committee* [1991]
CLARENCE THOMAS: *Second Statement to the Senate Judiciary Committee* [1991]
ORLANDO PATTERSON: *Race, Gender, and Liberal Fallacies* [1991]
ELSA BARKLEY BROWN, DEBORAH KING, BARBARA RANSBY, ET AL.: *African American Women in Defense of Ourselves* [1991]

On July 1, 1991, President George H. W. Bush nominated Clarence Thomas to replace Supreme Court justice Thurgood Marshall. On October 5, law professor Anita Hill's allegations that Thomas sexually harassed her became public, and on October 11, hearings on the allegations before the Senate Judiciary Committee began. Less than a week later, on October 16, the Senate confirmed Clarence Thomas as an associate justice of the Supreme Court, by a 52–48 vote.

In his two statements before the Senate Judiciary Committee on October 11, 1991, Thomas (p. 934) presents himself as "a victim of this process." He catagorically denies the allegations of sexual harassment and expresses outrage that they were leaked to the media. He also reframes the debate, shifting the discussion from sexual harassment to racial discrimination: in his first statement, he declares that he "will not provide the rope for [his] own lynching, and in his second statement, he charges that he is being metaphorically lynched by the Senate Judiciary Committee.

In her October 11 statement to the Senate Judiciary Committee, Anita Hill (b. 1956), who had worked for Thomas on the U.S. Equal Employment Opportunities Commission, presents a history of sexual harassment that contrasts with Thomas's account in both substance and interpretation. While Thomas testifies that there were no statements at the time from Hill or their colleagues about inappropriate conduct, Hill says that her resistance to his overtures and harassment all took place in private conversations. While Thomas argues that Hill's continued professional association with him proves that her allegations are false, Hill relates that the jobs with Thomas were her best professional opportunities and that she had mistakenly judged, at the critical moments of decision, that the harassment was waning. Hill's alternate perspective provoked a national conversation about male-female relationships in the workplace.

In the massive media attention that accompanied the Senate Judiciary Committee hearings and Thomas's subsequent confirmation, public figures positioned themselves on both sides of the issue. Debates extended far beyond whether Thomas should be confirmed or whether Hill was telling the truth, covering topics that ranged from myths of black sexuality to gender relations. Four days after Thomas's confirmation, Harvard sociologist Orlando Patterson (b. 1940) published a controversial editorial in *The New York Times*. In it, he argues that the hearings not only did *not* reinforce racist stereotypes (as scholars such as Charles R. Lawrence III had argued), they actually represented a watershed moment for civil rights. For Patterson, the hearings both publicized the diversity of black life and opinion and publicly affirmed that African Americans had achieved a place of "unquestioned belonging" in American political life. Patterson also argues that the hearings suggest a new, positive direction for gender relations and proposes that gender inequality would be best addressed by accepting the reality of sexual tension between men and women in the workplace. His observation that "most of Professor Hill's supporters seem to be middle-class white women" echoes the 1970s criticism that white feminists were the primary supporters of Michele Wallace, author of *Black Macho and the Myth of the Superwoman* (see p. 817).

The influential statement "African American Women in Defense of Ourselves" was spearheaded by historian Elsa Barkley Brown (b. 1948), sociologist Deborah King (p. 1043), and historian Barbara Ransby (p. 1027). Signed by 1603 women, it was published a month after the hearings in *The New York Times*, as well as in seven African American newspapers. The statement moves the Thomas/Hill debate away from the formulation of "either gender or race," and promotes the creation of new allegiances based on shared interests and experiences, with black women at the core. In this way, it echoes key black feminist arguments: First, oppressions cannot be ranked or divided, since they are experienced simultaneously. Second, black women are central to the struggle for freedom, since the end of oppression for the most oppressed would mean the end of oppression for all.

CLARENCE THOMAS

First Statement to the Senate Judiciary Committee [1991]

Mr. Chairman, Senator Thurmond,[1] Members of the committee.

As excruciatingly difficult as the last two weeks have been, I welcome the opportunity to clear my name today. No one other than my wife and Senator Danforth,[2] to whom I read this statement at 6:30 A.M., has seen or heard the statement. No handlers, no advisers.

The first I learned of the allegations by Professor Anita Hill was on Sept. 25, 1991, when the F.B.I. came to my home to investigate her allegations. When informed by the F.B.I. agent of the nature of the allegations, and the person making them, I was shocked, surprised, hurt, and enormously saddened. I have not been the same since that day.

For almost a decade, my responsibilities included enforcing the rights of victims of sexual harassment. As a boss, as a friend, and as a human being I was proud that I have never had such an allegation leveled against me, even as I sought to promote women and minorities into nontraditional jobs.

In addition, several of my friends who are women have confided in me about the horror of harassment, on the job or elsewhere. I thought I really understood the anguish, the fears, the doubts, the seriousness of the matter. But since Sept. 25, I have suffered immensely as these very serious charges were leveled against me. I have been racking my brains and eating my insides out trying to think of what I could have said or done to Anita Hill to lead her to allege that I was interested in her in more than a professional way, and that I talked with her about pornographic or X-rated films.

Contrary to some press reports, I categorically denied all of the allegations, and denied that I ever attempted to date Anita Hill when first interviewed by the FBI. I strongly reaffirm that denial.

Let me describe my relationship with Anita Hill. In 1981, after I went to the Department of Education as an assistant secretary in the Office of Civil Rights, one of my closest friends from both college and law schools, Gil Hardy, brought Anita Hill to my attention. As I remember, he indicated that she was dissatisfied with her law firm, and wanted to work in government. Based primarily, if not solely, on Gil's recommendation, I hired Anita Hill.

During my tenure at the Department of Education, Anita Hill was an attorney-adviser who worked

---

1. Strom Thurmond (1902–2003), white American U.S. senator from South Carolina from 1954 to 2003, first as a Southern Democrat (and a vocal supporter of racial segregation), and then after 1964 as a conservative Republican.
2. John Danforth (b. 1936), white American Republican U.S. senator from Missouri from 1976 to 1995.

directly with me. She worked on special projects as well as day to day matters. As I recall, she was one of two professionals working directly with me at the time. As a result, we worked closely on numerous matters.

I recalled being pleased with her work product, and the professional but cordial relationship which we enjoyed at work. I also recall engaging in discussions about politics and current events.

Upon my nomination to become chairman of the Equal Employment Opportunity Commission, Anita Hill, to the best of my recollection, assisted me in the nomination and confirmation process. After my confirmation she and Diane Holt, then my secretary, joined me at E.E.O.C.

I do not recall that there was any question or doubt that she would become a special assistant to me at E.E.O.C., although as a career employee, she retained the option of remaining at the Department of Education.

At E.E.O.C. our relationship was more distant, and our contacts less frequent, as a result of the increased size of my personal staff, and the dramatic increase and diversity of my day-to-day responsibilities.

Upon reflection, I recall that she seemed to have had some difficulty adjusting to this change in her role. In any case, our relationship remained both cordial and professional. At no time did I become aware, either directly or indirectly, that she felt I had said or done anything to change the cordial nature of our relationship.

I detected nothing from her, or from my staff, or from Gil Hardy, our mutual friend, with whom I maintained regular contact.

I am certain that had any statement or conduct on my part been brought to my attention, I would remember it clearly because of the nature and seriousness of such conduct, as well as my adamant opposition to sex discrimination and sexual harassment.

But there were no such statements.

In the spring of 1983, Mr. Charles Coffey contacted me to speak at the law school at Oral Roberts University in Tulsa, Oklahoma. Anita Hill, who is from Oklahoma, accompanied me on that trip. It was not unusual that individuals on my staff would travel with me occasionally.

Anita Hill accompanied me on that trip, primarily because this was an opportunity to combine business and a visit to her home.

As I recall, during our visit at Oral Roberts University, Mr. Coffey mentioned to me the possibility of approaching Anita Hill to join the faculty at Oral Roberts University Law School.

I encouraged him to do so, and noted to him, as I recall, that Anita would do well in teaching. I recommended her highly, and she eventually was offered a teaching position.

Although I did not see Anita Hill often after she left E.E.O.C., I did see her on one or two subsequent visits to Tulsa, Okla., and on one visit, I believe she drove me to the airport.

I also occasionally received telephone calls from her. She would speak directly with me, or with my secretary, Diane Holt. Since Anita Hill and Diane Holt had been with me at the Department of Education, they were fairly close personally, and I believe they occasionally socialized together.

I would also hear about her through Linda Jackson, then Linda Lambert, whom both Anita Hill and I met at the Department of Education, and I would hear of her from my friend Gil.

Throughout the time that Anita Hill worked with me, I treated her as I treated my other special assistants. I tried to treat them all cordially, professionally and respectfully. And I tried to support them in their endeavors and be interested in and supportive of their success. I had no reason or basis to believe my relationship with Anita Hill was anything but this way until the FBI visited me a little more than two weeks ago.

I find it particularly troubling that she never raised any hint that she was uncomfortable with me. She did not raise or mention it when considering moving with me to E.E.O.C. from the Department of Education. And she never raised it with me when she left E.E.O.C. and was moving on in her life. And to my fullest knowledge, she did not speak to any other women working with or around me, who would feel comfortable enough to raise it with me, especially Diane Holt, to whom she seemed closest on my personal staff. Nor did she raise it with mutual friends such as Linda Jackson and Gil Hardy.

This is a person I have helped at every turn in the road since we met. She seemed to appreciate the continued cordial relationship we had since day one. She sought my advice and counsel, as did virtually all of he members of my personal staff.

During my tenure in the executive branch, as a manager, as a policy maker and as a person, I have adamantly condemned sex harassment. There is no member of this committee or this Senate who feels stronger about sex harassment than I do. As a manager, I made every effort to take swift and decisive action when sex harassment raised or reared its ugly head.

The fact that I feel so very strongly about sex harassment and spoke loudly about it at E.E.O.C has made these allegations doubly hard on me. I cannot imagine anything that I said or did to Anita Hill that could have been mistaken for sexual harassment. But with that said, if there is anything that I have said that has been misconstrued by Anita Hill or anyone else to be sexual harassment, then I can say that I am so very sorry and I wish I had known. If I did know, I would have stopped immediately and I would not, as I've done over the past two weeks, had to tear away at myself trying to think of what I could possibly have done.

But I have not said or done the things that Anita Hill has alleged. God has gotten me through the days since Sept. 25 and He is my judge.

Mr. Chairman, something has happened to me in the dark days that have followed since the F.B.I. agents informed me about these allegations. And the days have grown darker as this very serious, very explosive, and very sensitive allegation, or these sensitive allegations were selectively leaked in a distorted way to the media over the past weekend.

As if the confidential allegations themselves were not enough, this apparently calculated public disclosure has caused me, my family, and my friends enormous pain and great harm.

I have never, in all my life, felt such hurt, such pain, such agony.

My family and I have been done a grave and irreparable injustice. During the past two weeks, I lost the belief that if I did my best all would work out. I called

upon the strength that helped me get here from Pin Point.[3] And it was all sapped out of me.

It was sapped out of me because Anita Hill was a person I considered a friend, whom I admired and thought I had treated fairly and with the utmost respect.

Perhaps I could have been—better weathered this if it was from someone else. But here was someone I truly felt I had done my best with.

Though I am, by no means, a perfect—no means—I have not done what she has alleged. And I still don't know what I could possibly have done to cause her to make these allegations.

When I stood next to the President in Kennebunkport, being nominated to the Supreme Court of the United States, that was a high honor. But as I sit here before you, 103 days later, that honor has been crushed.

From the vary beginning, charges were levelled against me from the shadows—charges of drug abuse, anti-semitism, wife beating, drug use by family members, that I was a quota appointment, confirmation conversion, and much, much more. And now, this.

I have complied with the rules. I responded to a document request that produced over 30,000 pages of documents. And I have testified for five full days under oath.

I have endured this ordeal for 103 days. Reporters sneaking into my garage to examine books that I read. Reporters and interest groups swarming over divorce papers, looking for dirt. Unnamed people starting preposterous and damaging rumors. Calls all over the country specifically requesting dirt.

This is not American. This is Kafkaesque. It has got to stop. It must stop for the benefit of future nominees and our country. Enough is enough.

I am not going to allow myself to be further humiliated in order to be confirmed. I am here specifically to respond to allegations of sex harassment in the workplace. I am not here to be further humiliated by this committee or anyone else, or to put my private life on display for prurient interests or other reasons.

I will not allow this committee or anyone else to probe into my private life.

---

3. The small, predominantly African American community in Georgia where Thomas was born and lived until he was seven, when he went to live with his grandparents in Savannah.

This is not what America is all about. To ask me to do that would be to ask me to go beyond fundamental fairness.

Yesterday, I called my mother. She was confined to her bed, unable to work, and unable to stop crying. Enough is enough.

Mr. Chairman, in my 43 years on this earth, I have been able with the help of others and with help of God to defy poverty, avoid prison, overcome segregation, bigotry, racism, and obtain one of the finest educations available in this country.

But I have not been able to overcome this process. This is worse than any obstacle or anything that I have ever faced. Throughout my life I have been energized by the expectation and the hope that in this country I would be treated fairly in all endeavors. When there was segregation, I hoped there would be fairness one day, or someday. When there was bigotry and prejudice, I hoped that there would be tolerance and understanding—someday.

Mr. Chairman, I am proud of my life. Proud of what I have done, and what I've accomplished, proud of my family. And this process, this process, is trying to destroy it all.

No job is worth what I've been through—no job. No horror in my life has been so debilitating. Confirm me if you want. Don't confirm me if you are so led. But let this process end. Let me and my family regain our lives.

I never asked to be nominated. It was an honor. Little did I know the price, but it is too high.

I enjoy and appreciate my current position, and I am comfortable with the prospect of returning to my work as a judge on the U.S. Court of Appeals for the D.C. Circuit, and to my friends there. Each of these positions is public service, and I have given at the office.

I want my life and my family's life back, and I want them returned expeditiously.

I have experienced the exhilaration of new heights from the moment I was called to Kennebunkport by the President to have lunch and he nominated me. That was the high point. At that time I was told, eye to eye, that, Clarence, you made it this far on merit; the rest is going to be politics. And it surely has been.

There have been other highs. The outpouring of support from my friends of longstanding, a bonding like I have never experienced with my old boss, Senator Danforth. The wonderful support of those who have worked with me. There have been prayers said for my family and me by people I know and people I will never meet, prayers that were heard, and that sustained not only me but also my wife and my entire family.

Instead of understanding and appreciating the great honor bestowed upon me, I find myself here today defending my name, my integrity, because somehow select portions of confidential documents dealing with this matter were leaked to the public.

Mr. Chairman. I am a victim of this process. My name has been harmed. My integrity has been harmed. My character has been harmed. My family has been harmed. My friends have been harmed. There is nothing this committee, this body, or this country can do to give me my good name back. Nothing.

I will not provide the rope for my own lynching, or for further humiliation. I am not going to engage in discussions, nor will I submit to roving questions, of what goes on in the most intimate parts of my private life, or the sanctity of my bedroom. These are the most intimate parts of my privacy, and they will remain just that: private.

From *The Black Scholar* 22, 1992, no. 1–2 (Winter 1991–Spring 1992), 4–7.

ANITA F. HILL

Statement to the Senate Judiciary Committee [1991]

Mr. Chairman, Senator Thurmond, members of the committee.

My name is Anita F. Hill, and I am a professor of law at the University of Oklahoma. I was born on a farm in Okmulgee County, Okla., in 1956. I am the youngest of 13 children.

I had my early education in Okmulgee County. My mother's name is Irma Hill. She is also a farmer and a housewife.

My childhood was one of a lot of hard work and not much money, but it was one of solid family affection as represented by my parents. I was reared in a religious atmosphere in the Baptist faith, and I have been a member of the Antioch Baptist church in Tulsa, Okla., since 1983. It is a very warm part of my life at the present time.

For my undergraduate work, I went to Oklahoma State University and graduated from there in 1977. I am attaching to this statement a copy of my resume for further details of my education.

SENATOR JOSEPH R. BIDEN, JR.: It will be included in the record.

PROFESSOR HILL: Thank you.

I graduated from the university with academic honors, and proceeded to the Yale Law School, where I received my J.D. degree in 1980.

Upon graduation from law school, I became a practicing lawyer with the Washington, D.C., firm of Wald, Hardraker & Ross. In 1981 I was introduced to now Judge Thomas by a mutual friend.

Judge Thomas told me that he was anticipating a political appointment, and he asked if I would be interested in working with him.

He was in fact appointed as assistant secretary of education for civil rights. After he was—after he had taken that post, he asked if I would become his assistant, and I accepted that position.

In my early period there, I had two major projects. The first was an article I wrote for Judge Thomas's signature on the education of minority students. The second was the organization of a seminar on high-risk students, which was abandoned because Judge Thomas transferred to the E.E.O.C., where he became the chairman of that office.

During this period at the Department of Education my working relationship with Judge Thomas was positive. I had a good deal of responsibility and independence. I thought he respected my work, and that he trusted my judgment.

After approximately three months of working there, he asked me to go out socially with him. What happened next, and telling the world about it, are the two most difficult things—experiences of my life.

It is only after a great deal of agonizing consideration, and sleepless—number of—great number of sleepless nights, that I am able to talk of these unpleasant matters to anyone but my close friends.

I declined the invitation to go out socially with him, and explained to him that I thought it would jeopardize at—what at the time I considered to be a very good working relationship. I had a normal social life with other men outside the office. I believe then, as now, that having a social relationship with a person who was supervising my work would be ill advised. I was very uncomfortable with the idea and told him so.

I thought that by saying no and explaining my reasons, my employer would abandon his social suggestions. However, to my regret, in the following few weeks, he continued to ask me out on several occasions.

He pressed me to justify my reasons for saying no to him. These incidents took place in his office, or mine. They were in the form of private conversations, which not—would not have been overheard by anyone else.

My working relationship became even more strained when Judge Thomas began to use work situations to discuss sex. On these occasions he would call me into his office for a course on education issues and projects, or he might suggest that because of the time pressures of his schedule we go to lunch to a government cafeteria.

After a brief discussion of work, he would turn the conversation to a discussion of sexual matters. His conversations were very vivid. He spoke about acts that he had seen in pornographic films involving such matters as women having sex with animals, and films showing group sex or rape scenes.

He talked about pornographic materials depicting individuals with large penises or large breasts involving various sex acts.

---

1. White American politician (b. 1942); U.S. Senator from Delaware from 1973 until 2009, when he became Vice President of the United States, serving under President Barack Obama; during the Thomas-Hill Hearings, Biden was chair of the U.S. Senate Committee on the Judiciary (commonly known as the Senate Judiciary Committee), which is in charge of conducting hearings before the Senate votes on prospective judges nominated by the president.

On several occasions, Thomas told me graphically of his own sexual prowess.

Because I was extremely uncomfortable talking about sex with him at all, and particularly in such a graphic way, I told him that I did not want to talk about this subject. I would also try to change the subject to education matters or to nonsexual personal matters, such as his background or his beliefs.

My efforts to change the subject were rarely successful.

Throughout the period of these conversations, he also from time to time asked me for social engagements. My reaction to these conversations was to avoid them by eliminating opportunities for us to engage in extended conversations.

This was difficult because, at the time, I was his only assistant at the office of education—or office for civil rights. During the latter part of my time at the Department of Education, the social pressures, and any conversation of his offensive behavior, ended. I began both to believe and hope that our working relationship could be a proper, cordial and professional one.

When Judge Thomas was made chair of the E.E.O.C., I needed to face the question of whether to go with him. I was asked to do so, and I did.

The work itself was interesting, and at that time it appeared that the sexual overtures which had so troubled me had ended.

I also faced the realistic fact that I had no alternative job. While I might have gone back to private practice, perhaps in my old firm or at another, I was dedicated to civil rights work and my first choice was to be in that field. Moreover, at that time, the Department of Education itself was a dubious venture. President Reagan was seeking to abolish the entire department.

For my first months at the E.E.O.C. where I continued to be an assistant to Judge Thomas, there were no sexual conversations or overtures. However, during the fall and winter of 1982 these began again. The comments were random and ranged from pressing me about why I didn't go out with him to remarks about my personal appearance. I remember his saying that some day I would have to tell him the real reason that I wouldn't go out with him.

He began to show displeasure in his tone and voice and his demeanor and his continued pressure for an explanation. He commented on what I was wearing in terms of whether it made me more or less sexually attractive. The incidents occurred in his inner office at the E.E.O.C.

One of the oddest episodes I remember was an occasion in which Thomas was drinking a Coke in his office. He got up from the table at which we were working, went over to his desk to get the Coke, looked at the can and asked, "Who has put pubic hair on my Coke?"

On other occasions, he referred to the size of his own penis as being larger than normal and he also spoke on some occasions of the pleasures he had given to women with oral sex. At this point, late 1982, I began to be concerned that Clarence Thomas might take out his anger with me by degrading me or not giving me important assignments. I also thought that he might find an excuse for dismissing me.

In January of 1983, I began looking for another job. I was handicapped because I feared that if he found out, he might make it difficult for me to find other employment and I might be dismissed from the job I had. Another factor that made my search more difficult was that there was a period—this was during a period—of a hiring freeze in the government.

In February 1983 I was hospitalized for five days on an emergency basis for acute stomach pain, which I attributed to stress on the job. Once out of the hospital I became more committed to find other employment and sought further to minimize my contact with Thomas. This became easier when Allison Duncan became office director because most of my work was then funneled through her and I had contact with Clarence Thomas mostly in staff meetings.

In the spring of 1983, an opportunity to teach at Oral Roberts University opened up. I participated in a seminar, taught an afternoon session in a seminar at Oral Roberts University. The dean of the university saw me teaching and inquired as to whether I would be interested in further pursuing a career in teaching beginning at Oral Roberts University.

I agreed to take the job, in large part because of my desire to escape the pressures I felt at the E.E.O.C. due to Judge Thomas.

When I informed him that I was leaving in July, I recall that his response was that now I would no longer have an excuse for not going out with him. I told him that I still preferred not to do so. At some time after that meeting, he asked if he could take me to dinner at the end of the term. When I declined, he assured me that the dinner was a professional courtesy only and not a social invitation. I reluctantly agreed to accept that invitation but only if it was at the very end of a working day.

On, as I recall, the last day of my employment at the E.E.O.C. in the summer of 1983,

I may have used poor judgment early on in my relationship with this issue. I was aware, however, that telling at any point in my career could adversely affect my future career, and I did not want, early on, to burn all the bridges to the E.E.O.C.

As I said, I may have used poor judgment. Perhaps I should have taken angry or even militant steps, both when I was in the agency or after I left it. But I must confess to the world that the course that I took seemed the better as well as the easier approach.

I declined any comment to newspapers, but later, when Senate staff asked me about these matters, I felt I had a duty to report.

I have no personal vendetta against Clarence Thomas. I seek only to provide the committee with information which it may regard as relevant.

It would have been more comfortable to remain silent. It took no initiative to inform anyone. But when I was asked by a representative of this committee to report my experience, I felt that I had to tell the truth. I could not keep silent.

From *The Black Scholar* 22, 1992, no. 1–2 (Winter 1991–Spring 1992), 8–11.

CLARENCE THOMAS

Second Statement to the Senate Judiciary Committee [1991]

Senator, I would like to start by saying unequivocally, uncategorically, that I deny each and every single allegation against me today that suggested in any way that I had conversations of a sexual nature or about pornographic material with Anita Hill, that I ever attempted to date her, that I ever had any personal sexual interest in her, or that I in any way ever harassed her.

The second and I think more important point, I think that this today is a travesty. I think that it is disgusting. I think that this hearing should never occur in America. This is a case in which this sleaze, this dirt was searched for by staffers of members of this committee, was then leaked to the media, and this committee and this body validated it and displayed it at prime time, over our entire nation.

How would any member on this committee, any person in this room, or any person in this country would like sleaze said about him or her in this fashion? Or this dirt dredged up and this gossip and these lies displayed in this manner, how would any person like it?

The Supreme Court is not worth it. No job is worth it. I am not here for that. I am here for my name, my family, my life, and my integrity. I think something is dreadfully wrong with this country when any person, any person in this free country would be subjected to this.

This is not a closed room. There was an F.B.I. investigation. This is not an opportunity to talk about difficult matters privately or in a closed environment. This is a circus. It's a national disgrace.

And from my standpoint, as a black American, it is a high-tech lynching for uppity blacks who in any way deign to think for themselves, to do for themselves, to have different ideas, and it is a message that unless you kowtow to an old order, this is what will happen to you. You will be lynched, destroyed, caricatured by a committee of the U.S. Senate rather than hung from a tree.

From *The Black Scholar* 22, no. 1–2 (Winter 1991–Spring 1992), 12.

ORLANDO PATTERSON

Race, Gender, and Liberal Fallacies [1991]

Clarence Thomas's second round of confirmation hearings was one of the finest moments in the modern history of America's democratic culture, a riveting, civic drama that fully engaged the electorate in an exposure and examination of its most basic fears and contradictions concerning class, race, sex and gender.

But even as it urged us to question some of our basic values and position, it reconfirmed the strength and suppleness of our system of governance. It also revealed one of its greatest weaknesses: there are serious misperceptions of what is really going on in our society, and lamentable failure in our threadbare, predominantly liberal discourse on it.

Thanks to this drama, we have entered an important new phase in the nation's discourse on gender relations, and it goes well beyond the enhanced realization by men that the complaints of women must be taken seriously. Implicit in these hearings was an overdue questioning of the legalistic, neo-Puritan and elitist model of gender relations promoted by the dominant school of American feminists.

We must face certain stark sociological realities: in our increasingly female, work-centered world, most of our relationships, including intimate ones, are initiated in the workplace; gender relations especially new ones, are complex and invariably ambiguous; in our heterogeneous society, the perception of what constitutes proper and effective male-female relations varies across gender, class, ethnicity and region; and in keeping with our egalitarian ideals, we take pride in the fact that the WASP boss may legitimately desire or want to marry his or her Puerto Rican aide or chauffeur.

One revealing feature of these hearings is the startling realization that Judge Clarence Thomas might well have said what Prof. Anita Hill alleges and yet be the extraordinarily sensitive man his persuasive female defenders claimed. American feminists have no way of explaining this. They have correctly demanded a rigorously enforced protocol of gender relations in the workplace. But they have also demanded that same intimate bonding that men of power traditionally share, the exclusion from which has kept them below the glass ceiling. There is a serious lacuna in the discourse, for we have failed to ask one fundamental question: how is nonerotic intimacy between men and women possible?

Clarence Thomas emerged in the hearings as one of those rare men who, with one or two exceptions, has achieved both: in general, he rigorously enforced the formal rules of gender relations, and he had an admirable set of intimate, nonerotic relations with his female associates.

And yet, tragically, there is his alleged failing with Professor Hill. How is this possible? While middle-class neo-Puritans ponder this question, the mass of the white working class and nearly all African Americans except their intellectually exhausted leaders have already come up with the answer. He may well have said what he is alleged to have said, but he did so as a man not unreasonably attracted to an aloof woman who is esthetically and socially very similar to himself, who had made no secret of her own deep admiration for him.

With his mainstream cultural guard down, Judge Thomas on several misjudged occasions may have done something completely out of the cultural frame of his white, upper-middle-class work world, but immediately recognizable to Professor Hill and most women of Southern working-class backgrounds, white or black, especially the latter.

Now to most American feminists, and to politicians manipulating the nations' lingering Puritan ideals, an obscenity is always an obscenity, an absolute offense against God and the moral order; to everyone else, including all professional social linguists and qualitative sociologists, an obscene expression whether in Chaucerian Britain or the American South, has to be understood in context, I am convinced that Professor Hill perfectly understood the psycho-cultural context in which Judge Thomas allegedly regaled her with his Rabelaisian humor (possibly as a way of affirming their common origins), which is precisely why she never filed a complaint against him.

Raising the issue ten years later was unfair and disingenuous: unfair because, while she may well have been offended by his coarseness, there is no evidence that she suffered any emotional or career damage, and the punishment she belatedly sought was in no way commensurate with the offense; and disingenuous because she has lifted a verbal style that carries only minor sanction in one subcultural context and thrown it in the overheated cultural arena of mainstream, neo-Puritan America, where it incurs professional extinction.

If my interpretation is correct, Judge Thomas was justified in denying making the remarks, even if he had in fact made them, not only because the deliberate displacement of his remarks made them something else but on the utilitarian moral grounds that any admission would have immediately incurred a self-destructive and grossly unfair punishment.

The hearings also brought to light the fact that the American public is way ahead of its journalistic and social-science commentators with respect to race relations. The sociological truths are that America, while still flawed in its race relations and its stubborn refusal to institute a rational, universal welfare system, is now the least racist white-majority society in the world; has a better record of legal protection of minorities than any other society, white or black; offers more opportunities to a greater number of black persons than any other society, including all those of Africa; and has gone through a dramatic change in its attitude toward miscegenation over the past twenty-five years.

Increased reports of racial and gender conflicts are actually indicative of things getting better, not worse, as commentators seem to think, since they reflect the greatly increased number of contacts between blacks and whites, and males and females, in competitive, high-powered situations as the number of Thomases and the many capable, strong-willed women we saw during the hearings rapidly increase.

One great good to come out of the hearings was the revelation to the average white American that, superstar athletes, news anchors and politicians aside, not all African Americans are underclass cocaine junkies and criminals, which is an understandable delusion in any white person whose only knowledge of African Americans comes from the press and television.

Above all, they saw in Judge Thomas and Professor Hill two very complex, highly intelligent persons who knew how to get and use power in the mainstream society, and were role models for black and white people alike.

However, perhaps the most remarkable feature of the hearings is the response of the public. Here again, liberal expectations were at odds with realities. It was thought that racism would be reinforced by these hearings—which is one simple-minded reason given for criticizing them—but in fact what has emerged is not only the indifference of the white public to the

racial aspect of the proceedings but the degree to which white men and women have identified their own interests and deepest anxieties with the two African American antagonists. Indeed, the only aspect of these hearings likely to have increased racism was the journalists' shrill and self-fulfilling insistence that the nation is exploding with racism. This is one of those cases where the messengers deserved to be shot.

White men, especially those in power, are not tittering in locker rooms about black men, as the commentators all seem to think; instead, they are deeply worried about the implications for their relations with white women brought out by these hearings, as well they might. And women, white and black, are taking all kinds of positions on the issues raised. Indeed, most of Professor Hill's supporters seem to be middle-class white women.

My own daughter, Barbara, a post-feminist young woman brought up by two feminists who came of age in the 60's, believes along with her friends that Judge Thomas did say those raunchy things, should have been told at once what a "dog" he was and reported to the authorities by Professor Hill if his advances had continued to annoy her. But they cannot see the relevance of Judge Thomas's down-home style of courting to his qualifications for the Supreme Court.

African Americans must now realize that these hearings were perhaps the single most important cultural development for them since the great struggles of the civil rights years. Clarence Thomas and Anita Hill suffered inhuman, and undeserved pain, tragic pain, in their public ordeal, and they will never be quite the same again. Nor will we all, for what all African Americans won from their pain, "perfected by this deed," this ritual of inclusion, is the public cultural affirmation of what had already been politically achieved: unambiguous inclusion; unquestioned belonging. The culture of slavery is dead.

The great achievement of these hearings, then, has been, first, to bring us to a greater awareness of the progress in racial and gender relations already achieved by this country. Second, superficial liberal stereotypes of blacks as victims or bootstrap heroes are seen for what they are: a new form of racism that finds it hard to imagine African Americans not as a monolithic group but, as several of the African American panelists on TV correctly informed the nation, a diverse aggregate of perhaps 30 million individuals, with all the class differences, subcultural and regional resources, strength, flaws and ideologies we find in other large populations.

Finally, the hearings have also highlighted the need to go beyond mere legalistic protocol in gender relations at the workplace. If women are to break through the glass ceiling, they must escape the trap of neo-Puritan feminism with its reactionary sacralization of women's bodies, and along with men develop at the workplace something that America still conspicuously lacks: a civilized culture of intimate social intercourse between men and women that recognizes, and contains, the frailties of male and female passions. It's not going to be easy, but these extraordinary hearings have pushed us in the right direction.

The New York Times, October 20, 1991, E15.

ELSA BARKLEY BROWN, DEBORAH KING, BARBARA RANSBY, ET AL.

African American Women in Defense of Ourselves [1991]

As women of African descent, we are deeply troubled by the recent nomination, confirmation and seating of Clarence Thomas as an Associate Justice of the U.S. Supreme Court. We know that the presence of Clarence Thomas on the Court will be continually used to divert attention from historic struggles for social justice through suggestions that the presence of a Black man on the Supreme Court constitutes an assurance that the rights of African Americans will be protected. Clarence Thomas' public record is ample evidence this will not be true. Further, the consolidation of a conservative majority on the Supreme Court seriously endangers the rights of all women, poor and working class people and the elderly. The seating of Clarence Thomas is an affront not only to African American women and men, but to all people concerned with social justice.

We are particularly outraged by the racist and sexist treatment of Professor Anita Hill, an African American woman who was maligned and castigated for daring to speak publicly of her own experience of sexual abuse. The malicious defamation of Professor Hill insulted all women of African descent and sent a dangerous message to any woman who might contemplate a sexual harassment complaint.

We speak here because we recognize that the media are now portraying the Black community as prepared to tolerate both the dismantling of affirmative action and the evil of sexual harassment in order to have any Black man on the Supreme Court. We want to make clear that the media have ignored or distorted many African American voices. We will not be silenced.

Many have erroneously portrayed the allegations against Clarence Thomas as an issue of either gender or race. As women of African descent, we understand sexual harassment as both. We further understand that Clarence Thomas outrageously manipulated the legacy of lynching in order to shelter himself from Anita Hill's allegations. To deflect attention away from the reality of sexual abuse in African American women's lives, he trivialized and misrepresented this painful part of African American people's history. This country, which has a long legacy of racism and sexism, has never taken the sexual abuse of Black women seriously. Throughout U.S. history Black women have been sexually stereotyped as immoral, insatiable, perverse; the initiators in all sexual contacts—abusive or otherwise. The common assumption in legal proceedings as well as in the larger society has been that Black women cannot be raped or otherwise sexually abused. As Anita Hill's experience demonstrates, Black women who speak of these matters are not likely to be believed.

In 1991, we cannot tolerate this type of dismissal of any one Black woman's experience or this attack upon our collective character without protest, outrage, and resistance.

As women of African descent, we express our vehement opposition to the policies represented by the placement of Clarence Thomas on the Supreme Court. The Bush administration, having obstructed the passage of civil rights legislation, impeded the extension of unemployment compensation, cut student aid and dismantled social welfare programs, has continually demonstrated that it is not operating in our best interests. Nor is this appointee. We pledge ourselves to continue to speak out in defense of one another, in defense of the African American community and against those who are hostile to social justice

no matter what color they are. No one will speak for us but ourselves.

The New York Times, November 17, 1991, A19.

GLORIA STEINEM

Women Are Never Front-Runners [2008]

In this op-ed piece, white American feminist leader Gloria Steinem (b. 1934) looks at the presidential campaigns of Hillary Clinton and Barack Obama (p. 874) to explore the roles of race and gender in politics. While she presents race and gender as interconnected and stresses that they must be fought together, she argues that gender is "probably" more restrictive. Steinem's op-ed became a lightning rod for debate about the role of race and gender in the 2008 Democratic primary contest and beyond. In a later exchange with white progressive leader Sally Kohn on *AlterNet*, Steinem said that her intent in the op-ed had been misinterpreted and that she had meant that sexism affected the most people, of all racial

groups, not that it was the most serious type of discrimination. Since, in the original version reprinted here, it was the phrase "Gender is probably the most restricting force" that made people think she was ranking race and gender, rather than viewing them as interconnected, she announced that she was revising the op-ed for future printings, changing the phrase to "a restricting force." She also reinserted part of the last sentence that had been cut from the original for space reasons: "Just as it's possible to say, 'I support him because he'll be a great president and help us break down our racial barriers,' we have to be able to say: 'I'm supporting her because she'll be a great president and because she's a woman.'"

From *The New York Times*, January 8, 2008.

The woman in question became a lawyer after some years as a community organizer, married a corporate lawyer and is the mother of two little girls, ages 9 and 6. Herself the daughter of a white American mother and a black African father—in this race-conscious country, she is considered black—she served as a state legislator for eight years, and became an inspirational voice for national unity.

Be honest: Do you think this is the biography of someone who could be elected to the United States Senate? After less than one term there, do you believe she could be a viable candidate to head the most powerful nation on earth?

If you answered no to either question, you're not alone. Gender is probably the most restricting force in American life, whether the question is who must be in the kitchen or who could be in the White House. This country is way down the list of countries electing women and, according to one study, it polarizes gender roles more than the average democracy.

That's why the Iowa primary was following our historical pattern of making change. Black men were given the vote a half-century before women of any race were allowed to mark a ballot, and generally have ascended to positions of power, from the military to the boardroom, before any women (with the possible exception of obedient family members in the latter).

If the lawyer described above had been just as charismatic but named, say, Achola Obama instead of Barack Obama, her goose would have been cooked long ago. Indeed, neither she nor Hillary Clinton could have used Mr. Obama's public style—or Bill Clinton's either—without being considered too emotional by Washington pundits.

So why is the sex barrier not taken as seriously as the racial one? The reasons are as pervasive as the air we breathe: because sexism is still confused with nature as racism once was; because anything that affects males is seen as more serious than anything that affects "only" the female half of the human race;

because children are still raised mostly by women (to put it mildly) so men especially tend to feel they are regressing to childhood when dealing with a powerful woman; because racism stereotyped black men as more "masculine" for so long that some white men find their presence to be masculinity-affirming (as long as there aren't too many of them); and because there is still no "right" way to be a woman in public power without being considered a you-know-what.

I'm not advocating a competition for who has it toughest. The caste systems of sex and race are interdependent and can only be uprooted together. That's why Senators Clinton and Obama have to be careful not to let a healthy debate turn into the kind of hostility that the news media love. Both will need a coalition of outsiders to win a general election. The abolition and suffrage movements progressed when united and were damaged by division; we should remember that.

I'm supporting Senator Clinton because like Senator Obama she has community organizing experience, but she also has more years in the Senate, an unprecedented eight years of on-the-job training in the White House, no masculinity to prove, the potential to tap a huge reservoir of this country's talent by her example, and now even the courage to break the no-tears rule. I'm not opposing Mr. Obama; if he's the nominee, I'll volunteer. Indeed, if you look at votes during their two-year overlap in the Senate, they were the same more than 90 percent of the time. Besides, to clean up the mess left by President Bush, we may need two terms of President Clinton and two of President Obama.

But what worries me is that he is seen as unifying by his race while she is seen as divisive by her sex.

What worries me is that she is accused of "playing the gender card" when citing the old boys' club, while he is seen as unifying by citing civil rights confrontations.

What worries me is that male Iowa voters were seen as gender-free when supporting their own, while female voters were seen as biased if they did and disloyal if they didn't.

What worries me is that reporters ignore Mr. Obama's dependence on the old—for instance, the frequent campaign comparisons to John F. Kennedy—while not challenging the slander that her progressive policies are part of the Washington status quo.

What worries me is that some women, perhaps especially younger ones, hope to deny or escape the sexual caste system; thus Iowa women over 50 and 60, who disproportionately supported Senator Clinton, proved once again that women are the one group that grows more radical with age.

This country can no longer afford to choose our leaders from a talent pool limited by sex, race, money, powerful fathers and paper degrees. It's time to take equal pride in breaking all the barriers. We have to be able to say: "I'm supporting her because she'll be a great president and because she's a woman."

DeNeen L. Brown

A Vote of Allegiance [2008]

During her 1972 run for president, Shirley Chisholm (p. 787) compared how being a woman and being black each affected her campaign. The 2008 Democratic primary contest between Hillary Clinton and Barack Obama (p. 874) launched related debates about the roles of race and gender, but these discussions tended to be fraught and divisive, revealing fault lines in the hard-won allegiances between feminist and civil rights groups. In "A Vote of Allegiance," *Washington Post* staff writer DeNeen Brown gives a sampling of the debate. Most of the black women interviewed ultimately stress the impact of race, in contrast to Chisholm and Gloria Steinem (p. 1114). Still, the very form of Brown's article shows the complexity of the issue. By presenting a range of voices in debate (a variation of the straightforward debate format used by W. E. B. Du Bois in the 1920s, p. 199, and others), Brown recognizes a multiplicity of opinion. In this way, she presents an example of the dialogic method favored by Martin Luther King Jr. (p. 559), where the juxtaposition of different opinions enables the discovery of a more complex truth.

From the *Washington Post*, March 24, 2008.

Woman has an ocean of wrongs too deep for any plummet, and the Negro, too, has an ocean of wrongs that cannot be fathomed. There are two great oceans; in the one is the black man, and in the other is the woman. . . . I will be thankful in my soul if any body can get out of the terrible pit."
—Lucy Stone, nineteenth-century abolitionist and suffragist, after women were excluded from the Fifteenth Amendment, which gave black men the right to vote.

The "isms" have once again been pitted against each other. Sexism or racism—which ism is deepest? All things being equal, should a woman or a black man be lifted to the presidency? Which "first" is the imperative first?

The admonitions of white feminists urging black women to vote gender over race have cracked open a scab, a festering sore, that had crusted over the history of this country's competing isms. A scab that covered the lingering tension between some white feminists and some black women, with their dual historic burden of race and gender. It is black women, after all, who have faced both sexism and racism in their lives.

In the race for the Democratic presidential nomination, which ism goes first? Some women fear the question, say it is divisive, explosive, should never be asked. But it has been asked—in the recent writings of feminists including Gloria Steinem[1] and Robin Morgan.[2] The question is ripe, reeling under the surface, discussed with muffled outrage by black women grown weary of white feminists seeming to tell them what to do.

* * *

Alice Thomas, who is black, is thinking about the question, talking about the campaign, about Sens. Barack Obama and Hillary Clinton. About the recent comments by Geraldine Ferraro[3] and the exhortations of some feminist leaders.

A law professor at Howard University's School of Law, Thomas lives in northwest Washington, in an upper-middle-class, racially mixed neighborhood with grand houses and big trees that blow with the sway of affluence. Most of the prominent white feminists are affluent, too. But their language, their mission, says Thomas, do not resonate.

"I never felt a kinship with white feminists. There never was a time when I felt something familiar when I heard Gloria Steinem," she says. "I always thought these same women went home and slept with those men who were discriminating against me. I wanted to say, 'Could you talk to him on the pillow tonight?'"

"I felt they were women who had the luxury of taking on battles a little at a time. . . . With the presidential election, NOW[4] has taken a position against Barack Obama in favor of Hillary, making that a feminist stand. To take a position opposite Barack is to take a position opposite my family and our community."

She says her grade-school son looks at the Obama campaign with wide eyes and now believes he could grow up to be president. The white feminists, she says, have had the opportunity to have their boys dream that dream realistically for decades.

Seated at a restaurant, she looks out onto Connecticut Avenue. Black and white people walk by. The day is an awful shade of gray.

"I'm not going to stand against him simply because there is a woman on the other side. It means so much more for me if Barack wins than if Hillary wins. I don't pick Hillary because she is a woman and I

---

1. See p. 1114.
2. White American feminist activist, editor, and writer (b. 1941) whose February 3, 2008 essay "Goodbye To All That #2" (a sequel to her classic essay on sexism published in 1970) became a touchstone for discussion about gender politics and Hillary Clinton's campaign.
3. White American politician, attorney, member of the U.S. House of Representatives from New York from 1979 to 1985, and the first woman on a major party national ticket (in 1984); Ferraro resigned from Hillary Clinton's campaign finance committee after making controversial remarks about the roles of gender and race in the campaign; she told a reporter: "If Obama was a white man, he would not be in this position. And if he was a woman (of any color) he would not be in this position. He happens to be very lucky to be who he is. And the country is caught up in the concept"; she also criticized a "sexist media" for biased coverage of Clinton.
4. Acronym for the National Organization for Women, founded in 1966 as an organization committed to taking action to achieve equality for women.

am a woman. I don't pick Barack because he is black and I am black. I pick Barack because he is a man of substance."

* * *

Gender is probably the most restricting force in American life, whether the question is who must be in the kitchen or who could be in the White House.
—*Gloria Steinem*

Steinem's recent op-ed piece in *The New York Times* infuriated many black people. She argued that black men were given the right to vote before women, but failed to mention the lynchings that made it potentially fatal to take up that right.

"The thing that ends up being curious to me is what people like Gloria Steinem advocate," says Lisa Crooms, a black woman who is director of the Constitutional Law Center at Howard University School of Law.

"They should know better," she says of the white feminists. "That is the most disheartening thing for me: 'We white women do this and you black women don't get it.' I thought folks had learned those lessons in intro to women's studies courses. . . . I thought it was something white women got, but clearly they didn't. Something didn't translate."

Black women say the pangs they feel in this debate of the competing isms have been sharpened as the campaign rhetoric has intensified.

"White feminists reduce everything to their cultural experience," says Arica Coleman, 46, a professor of black American studies at the University of Delaware. "We had a different battle. We are fighting a war on two fronts, being both female and being black. I know when I walk into any office or anywhere, people see my skin color first and automatically make assumptions."

"I wish people would stick to the issues, and the ultra-feminists would stop crying wolf because their girl is not winning," Coleman says. "Obama is not crying racism."

NOW President Kim Gandy says the lines drawn between sexism and racism and white women and black women are not that clear. "I think people are still thinking about racism and sexism because they still exist," she says. "I wouldn't call it a dichotomy. The camps are quite diverse. There are African American women who support Hillary Clinton and white women who support Barack Obama. The campaigns crossed those racial and gender lines."

To the question of which ism has the greater burden to overcome, Gandy says, "I say that is unknowable. Having never experienced racism, I couldn't express an opinion about that." She says the greater burden depends on experience and perspective. "To suggest there is a competition between racism and sexism is delightful to people who would see us divided from each other," she says. "Until we as a country recognize the intersection of those isms and the terrible damage they do, we will not be as great as we could be as a nation."

* * *

Never has a campaign given voters who were not white men such power to participate in the "politics of identity." Blogs have exploded with people of all identities explaining why they favor one Democratic candidate over the other. Black women have been particular targets, with bloggers attacking them for deciding that voting for a black candidate was more important than voting for a woman.

And some black women have asked how they split their identities. Are they black first or women first? To which group do they pledge allegiance? Does the term *feminist* apply only to white women? Can a woman be black and feminist at the same time, even if she hardly understood Betty Friedan's[5] 1963 feminist classic, *The Feminine Mystique*, which asked the bored housewife's question: "Is this all?"

Avis Jones-DeWeever, director of research at the National Council of Negro Women, says the answer lies in perspective. "That was Betty Friedan's truth. That was her experience of feeling bound by the limitations of being a housewife. That was not the typical truth for the black woman."

Jones-DeWeever says many black women worked outside the home out of necessity, a fact that seemed to be ignored by arguments made at the height of the second wave of feminism in the 1960s and 1970s.

5. White American feminist activist and writer (1921–2006); a founder and the first president of NOW.

"You had a push by white women to get out in the workforce. That is fundamentally a different experience," Jones-DeWeever says. "Black women were always in the workforce. Even if part of that workforce was the work of raising white women's children. Our perspectives are different. There is the feeling that some second-wave feminists view life through a binary perspective; the male and female being the only line of division in their society."

The lines are more complex for women of color. "Personally, for me, I feel it cuts both ways," Jones-DeWeever continues. "In my experience, if I was to weigh the two, I would say race has had a greater impact on issues in my life. I am black. Both of my parents were educated in segregated schools in Virginia. . . . There was a lot of brouhaha about the Rev. [Jeremiah] Wright's statements in the news. He was saying Hillary was never called the N-word. I was first called the N-word in fourth grade and the last time I was called the N-word was in graduate school."

Race cuts even deeper now. Jones-DeWeever is raising two sons, 4 and 11. Her personal choice for president is Obama. "I worry about them as young black men driving a car," she says. "What will happen when they get pulled over by the police? I am realistic about what I need to teach them about how to conduct themselves in that situation. Those are issues most white women and white mothers don't have to be concerned about, life and death issues that will impact their children."

Latifa Lyles, vice president of membership of NOW, says sexism is a huge problem in the country, a learned behavior that doesn't seem to provoke as much outrage. "I am an African American woman," Lyles says. "There is not a day when I don't think of both."

Overt racism is less prominent, she says. "In my experience, I am more likely to see some kind of sexist incident than a racist incident. Because of the prevalence, people become more desensitized to it. If someone says something more overtly racist, I would have a much stronger reaction to it because I'm not used to hearing overtly racist comments."

Lani Guinier, a professor at Harvard's Law School, says white women and black women have had different relationships to power. White women, she says, have had a greater access to it: "They were sleeping with power. Even though they were disadvantaged in terms of access to conventional opportunities to their mates, they were also in an intimate relationship with power."

Guinier, who is black, was once nominated as assistant attorney general for civil rights in the Clinton administration, but her name was withdrawn after controversy erupted over her writings on affirmative action. "For black women, power was not represented by their mate or by their father or by their uncle, which is not to say—I am by no means excusing sexism within the black community or the fact there is violence against women," Guinier says. "It extends beyond any particular identity. I am trying to make this larger point that quote-unquote the man had a different footprint in the black community than in the white community."

* * *

In her book *Ain't I a Woman*, black feminist bell hooks[6] says there is a fragile bond between white and black women's rights advocates. And that bond has been broken again during this presidential campaign, some women say, as it was during the first women's rights movement in the late 1800s, during the second wave of women's rights in the 1960s and '70s, and then during the "mommy wars"[7] that still rage today.

"There are a fair number of women of color who would consider themselves to be feminists who have no time and interest in struggling with white women anymore," Crooms says. "Some people come from the view that if there is truly a difference between what is offered as mainstream white feminism and black feminism, black feminists are trying to figure out how we as black people can move forward as a community. We are not interested in fanning the flames between black women and black men. . . . Racism and sexism impact people differently. . . . You have race injuries. You have

---

6. The pen name of activist and writer Gloria Watkins who has published over thirty books, many of which explore the interconnectivity of gender, race, and class.

7. Highly publicized conflict between "stay-at-home mothers" and mothers who also work outside the home; focused on upper-middle-class women and predicated on the idea that one or the other "choice" is better for the well-being of the children.

sexism injuries. Pick between the two? No, it's not like that."

No one profits when oppressed people are split against each other, says Patricia J. Williams, author, columnist and professor of law at Columbia University. She argues there is often an ideological agenda involved when people claim that racism is no longer a major force in this country.

That is what Ferraro's recent comments seemed to imply, that race had become an advantage: "If Obama was a white man, he would not be in this position. And if he was a woman . . . he would not be in this position," Ferraro said.

Says Williams, who is black: "One ubiquitous subtext of the black-man-trumps-white-woman calculus is that it's easier to be a black man than it is to be a white woman or, even more reductively, that sexism is worse than racism. . . . That in turn fuels the not-so-coded diminishment asserting that Obama is getting 'preferential' treatment in the media; that he's simultaneously 'entitled' and 'elite' yet 'unqualified' and 'not ready.' A lot of this debate as it is currently framed is a product of a very segregated society."

* * *

Robin Morgan, an author and founder of the Women's Media Center, recently wrote an essay titled "Goodbye to All That (#2)," a reprise of her 1970 denunciation of sexism. In her latest manifesto, published online last month, she argued that she would vote for Clinton because of the historical importance of overcoming sexism.

"I was celebrating the pivotal power at last focused on African American women deciding on which of two candidates to bestow their vote—until a number of Hillary-supporting black feminists told me they're being called 'race traitors,'" she wrote. "So goodbye to conversations about this nation's deepest scar—slavery—which fail to acknowledge that labor- and sexual-slavery exist today in the U.S. and elsewhere on this planet, and the majority of those enslaved are women."

Morgan, who is white, received a flood of reaction, from women who thanked her for expressing what they needed to hear, from younger women saying they were tired of older feminists shoving the movement down their throats, from a black man who said he would be overjoyed to see a black family in the White House.

"I certainly won't begrudge a woman's desire to want to see a woman in the White House and basing, at least in some measure, her choice on such a possible milestone of achievement," he wrote in an online response. "What I take absolute exception to in this article by Mrs. Morgan however is the need to run down Obama for sake of supporting Hillary."

Morgan says she was not trying to run Obama down but trying to make a point about lingering sexism. She says she "cut her political eyeteeth in the civil rights movement." She agrees that racism is a major wound in this country's history and still is today. The society's consciousness about racism is nowhere near where it should be, but it is higher than it is about sexism, she asserts.

"Sexism is not as high as yet," Morgan says. "It is still there. It is still pervasive. It is so pervasive, sometimes you can't see it standing out from the background.

"Anything that can be interpreted as racist in the campaign is leapt upon and should be," Morgan says. "Stuff that is blatantly sexist is not leapt upon. It's often ignored, trivialized and laughed away."

Only now has it been highlighted after "women said, 'Excuse me!'" Morgan says the attacks on Clinton have ranged from trivialization to outright venom. "The Hillary Clinton nutcracker doll being sold in airports. They would not dare do that with a Stepin Fetchit[8] doll in the image of Senator Obama. And they shouldn't do that and there would be national outrage, and there should be national outrage."

Still, it is never a good idea to compare human suffering, Morgan says. "The only people in a position to say which bigotry they suffered worst from would be African American women. Some say they have suffered

---

8. Stage name of the actor Lincoln Perry (1902–85), who became famous in the 1930s playing an exaggerated comic character known as "The Laziest Man in the World," but lost popularity in the 1940s as the civil rights movement began to gain momentum; Perry's character has long been criticized for perpetuating negative racial stereotypes, although some now view his character as a trickster figure who effectively avoided work by feigning incompetence.

more from racism. And others, like Shirley Chisholm, said they have suffered more from sexism. That is not for me as a European American woman to say."

Mary Frances Berry[9] remembers those heated discussions of the 1970s, when Chisholm became the first black woman to run for president.

"Shirley Chisholm and I had long conversations about whether sexism or racism is a bigger barrier," says Berry, former chairwoman of the U.S. Commission on Civil Rights. "She said to me when she was running for president she found out how much sexism was a bar-

rier. The reaction of men to the fact she was going to run for president almost floored her. Other black politicians couldn't understand why she thought she could run for president. That campaign didn't go anywhere."

But Berry says it's dangerous to raise questions pitting sexism against racism. "I think anytime people who have been in subordinated groups start debating about whose discrimination is the worst is a problem," she says. "What they should do is reconcile the differences. Everybody has had something happen in their history. That's why it's called subordination."

---

9. Geraldine R. Segal, professor of American social thought and professor of history at the University of Pennsylvania (b. 1938); appointed to the U.S. Commission on Civil Rights in 1980 by President Carter, where she served until 2004.

PART SIX ～ *Works Cited*

Quotations and statistics in this section's headnotes and notes were drawn from the following sources:

Asante, Molefi Kete. *Afrocentricity*. Trenton: African World Press, 1988.

Barron, James. "Dueling Magazine Covers: A Police Photo vs. a 'Photo-Illustration.'" *The New York Times*. June 21, 1994: B8.

Boykin, Keith. *Beyond the Down Low: Sex, Lies, and Denial in Black America*. New York: Carroll & Graf Publishers, 2005.

Carbin, Jennifer A. "Boondocks Speaks: An Interview with Aaron McGruder." *City Paper* (Philadelphia). November 5, 2001. www.alternet.org.

Conyers, John. "Reparations: Statement from April 6, 2005 briefing: The Impact of Slavery on African Americans Today." http://conyers.house.gov.

Cosby, William. Address at the NAACP on the 50th Anniversary of *Brown v. Board of Education*. Constitutional Hall, Washington, DC, May 17, 2004. www.americanrhetoric .com/speeches/billcosbypoundcakespeech.htm.

Curry, George E. "Official Says 'Down Low' Men Not Responsible For High HIV Rates Among Black Women." National Prevention Information Network. 10/7/2009. www.cdcnpin.org.

DeNavas-Walt, Carmen, Bernadette D. Proctor, and Jessica C. Smith. *Income, Poverty, and Health Insurance Coerage in the United States: 2008*. U.S. Census Bureau, Current Population Reports, no. P60-236 (Washington, D.C.: U.S. Government Printing Office, 2009).

Denizet-Lewis, Benoit. "Double Lives On The Down Low." *The New York Times Magazine*. August 3, 2009: 28–33, 48, 52–3.

Farber, Jim. "Geraldine Ferraro Lets Her Emotions Do the Talking." *The Daily Breeze*. March 7, 2008. www.dailybreeze .com.

Farrakhan, Louis. "Minister Louis Farrakhan Calls for One Million Man March." *The Final Call*. December 14, 1994: 14, 4.

Forman, James. "Black Manifesto." Reprinted in *The New York Review of Books*. July 10, 1969. www.nybooks.com.

Horowitz, Jason. "Biden Unbound: Lays into Clinton, Obama, Edwards." *The New York Observer*. February 4, 2007. www.observer.com.

Huggins, Nathan. "White/Black Faces—Black Masks. *The Harlem Renaissance*. New York: Oxford University Press, 1971, 244–301.

Kennedy, John F. Address to the Greater Houston Ministerial Association. Rice Hotel, Houston, Texas. September 12, 1960.

Kohn, Sally and Gloria Steinem. "Gloria Steinem Debates Racism and Sexism in the '08 Election." *AlterNet*. Posted January 11, 2008. www.alternet.org.

Kraft, Marion. "Vorwort." *Die Quelle unserer Macht: Gedichte*. By Audre Lorde. Trans. Marion Kraft and Sigrid Markmann. Berlin: Orlanda, 1994, 9–14.

Lawrence, Charles R, III. "Cringing at Myths of Black Sexuality." *The Black Scholar*, 22, nos. 1/2. 1992: 65–66.

McGraph, Ben. "Profiles: The Radical: Why Do Editors Keep Throwing *The Boondocks* Off the Funnies Pages?" *New Yorker*. April 19, 2004. www.newyorker.com.

McGruder, Aaron. "The Boondocks." May 7, 2009.

Pager, Devah, and Bruce Western. "Discrimination in Low-Wage Labor Markets: Evidence from an Experimental Audit Study in New York City." Paper submitted to the annual meeting of the Population Association, 2005. http:// paa2005.priceton.edu.

Rock, Chris. *Good Hair*. 2009.

Terry, Don. "Black March Stirs Passion and Protests." *The New York Times*. October 8, 1995.

Thomas, Clarence. Concurrence. *Adarand Constructors, Inc. v. Pena 515 U. S. 200* (1995). Decided June 12, 1995.

Townes, Emilie M., ed. *A Troubling in My Soul: Womanist Perspectives On Evil and Suffering.* Maryknoll, N.Y.: Orbis Books, 1993.

U.S. Bureau of Justice Statistics, "Slower Growth in the Nation's Prison and Jail Populations." Press release. June 6, 2008. www.ojp.usdoj.gov.

U.S. Bureau of Justice Statistics. "Victim Characteristics." www.ojp.usdoj.gov.

Walker, Alice. *In Search of Our Mothers' Gardens: Womanist Prose.* Houghton Mifflin Harcourt, 1983.

Walker, Kara. "Out of Africa," Artist's page. *The New York Times Magazine.* September 19, 1999: 90–91.

Walraven, Jack. "The Simpson Trial Transcripts." http://walraven.org/simpson.

Wildermuth, John. "Black Support For Prop. 8 Called Exaggeration." *San Francisco Chronicle.* January 7, 2009. http://articles.sfgate.com.

Williams, Delores S. *Sisters in the Wilderness: The Challenge of Womanist God-Talk.* Maryknoll, N.Y.: Orbis Books, 1993.

Williams, Robert L. "The Ebonics Controversy." *The Journal of Black Psychology*, 23, 3 (August 1997): 208–14.

Index

≈ Credits

Text Credits

MARCUS GARVEY: "Editorial by Marcus Garvey in *The Black Man* (Sept.–Oct. 1936)," *The Marcus Garvey and Universal Negro Improvement Papers, Volume VII: November 1927-August 1940*, edited by Robert A. Hill, pp. 703–710, © 1990 Regents of the University of California. Published by the University of California Press. Reprinted by permission of the publisher. "Convention of Negro Peoples Meet at Edelweiss Park: Subject of Birth Control is Discussed" Published in the *Daily Gleaner* November 31, 1934. © The Gleaner Company Limited, 1934. Reprinted by permission.

HENRY LOUIS GATES, JR.: "Black Demagogues and Pseudo-Scholars," *The New York Times*, July 20, 1992, p. A15. Reprinted by permission of the author.
  "The Black Person in Art: How Should S/He Be Portrayed? (Part II)." Reprinted by permission from *Black American Literature Forum*, Volume 21, Number 3 (Autumn 1987). From *Thirteen Ways of Looking at a Black Man* by Henry Louis Gates, Jr., copyright © 1997 by Henry Louis Gates, Jr. Used by permission of Random House, Inc.

ADDISON GAYLE, JR.: "Introduction," *The Black Aesthetic* edited by Addison Gayle, Jr. (Doubleday, 1971). Copyright © 1971 by Addison Gayle, Jr. Reprinted by permission of Marie Brown Associates.

EUGENE D. GENOVESE: "Black Studies: Trouble Ahead," *Atlantic Monthly*, June 1969, pp. 37–41. Reprinted by permission of the author.

NIKKI GIOVANNI: "Black Poems, Poseurs, and Power," *Negro Digest* 18, June 1969, pp. 30–34. © Nikki Giovanni. Reprinted by permission of the author.

JACQUELYN GRANT: "Black Theology and the Black Woman" by Jacquelyn Grant. From James H. Cone & Gayraud S. Wilmore, Black Theology: A Documentary History, Vol. 1, (1993) pp. 323–338. Reprinted by permission of the publisher.

DICK GREGORY: "My Answer to Genocide," *Ebony*, October 1971, pp. 66–72. Reprinted by permission of the author.

MELVILLE J. HERSKOVITS: "On West African Influences," pp. 174–186 from *The Myth of the Negro Past* by Melville Herskovits. Copyright 1941 by Melville J. Herskovits, renewed © 1969 by Melville J. Herskovits. Reprinted by permission of HarperCollins Publishers.

A. LEON HIGGINBOTHAM, JR.: "Why I Didn't March," *The Washington Post*, October 17, 1995, p. A17. Reprinted by permission of Evelyn Brooks Higginbotham.

EVELYN BROOKS HIGGINBOTHAM: "The Black Church," reprinted by permission of the publisher from *Righteous Discontent: The Women's Movement in the Black Baptist Church, 1880–1920*, by Evelyn Brooks Higginbotham, pp. 1–18, 231–237, Cambridge, Mass.: Harvard University Press, Copyright © 1993 by the President and Fellows of Harvard College.

JACK HITT, ET AL.: "Making the Case for Racial Reparations," Copyright © 2000 by *Harper's Magazine*. All rights reserved. Reproduced from the November issue by special permission.

IRVING HOWE: Originally published in *Dissent*, "Black Boys and Native Sons," Autumn 1963, Vol. 10, No. 4. Reprinted with permission.

LANGSTON HUGHES: "The Negro Artist and the Racial Mountain" by Langston Hughes. Reprinted with permission from the June 23, 1926 issue of *The Nation*. "To the Editor of the Nation" by Langston Hughes. Reprinted with permission from the June 14, 1926 issue of *The Nation*. For subscription information, call 1-800-333-8536. Portions of each week's Nation magazine can be accessed at http://www.thenation.com.

ZORA NEALE HURSTON: "How It Feels to Be Colored Me," *The World Tomorrow* 11, May 1928, p. 215; "Stories of Conflict," *The Saturday Review of Literature*, April 2, 1938, p. 2; "The Emperor Effaces Himself," 1925. Used with the permission of the Zora Neale Hurston Trust.

MARGO JEFFERSON: "Labels Change, Carrying Different Emotional Baggage," *The New York Times*, 11/15/1999, © 1999 The New York Times. All rights reserved. Used by permission and protected by the Copyright Laws of the United States. The printing, copying, redistribution, or retransmission of the Material without express written permission is prohibited.

JAMES WELDON JOHNSON: "Preface to the Original Edition," from *The Book of American Negro Poetry*, Edited by James Weldon Johnson, copyright 1931, 1922 by Houghton Mifflin Harcourt Publishing Company and renewed 1959, 1950 by Mrs. Grace Nail Johnson, reprinted by permission of the publisher.

CLAUDIA JONES: "An End to the Neglect of the Problems of Negro Women," *Political Affairs*, June 1949. Reprinted by permission.

LEROI JONES: Excerpt from pp. 130–4 from *Blues People* by LeRoi Jones. Copyright © 1963 by LeRoi Jones. Reprinted by permission of HarperCollins Publishers (William Morrow).

WILLIAM N. JONES: "Self Determination: Black Belt Republic Plan" by William N. Jones, *The Baltimore Afro-American Newspapers*, September 24, 1932. Reprinted by permission of the *Afro-American* Newspapers Archives and Research Center.

WILLIAM R. JONES: "Divine Racism" and "James Cone: God, Champion of the Oppressed" from *Is God a White Racist?* (New York: Anchor Press/Doubleday, 1973), pp. 71–78,

WILLIAM L. PATTERSON AND GEORGE S. SCHUYLER: "Round Table: Have Communists Quit Fighting for Negro Rights?" *Negro Digest*, December 1945, pp. 57–70. Reprinted by permission of the Estates of William L. Patterson and George S. and Josephine Schuyler.

LAURA B. RANDOLPH: "What We Can Do About The Most Explosive Problem in Black America" by Laura B. Randolph, *Ebony* Magazine, August 1990. Courtesy *Ebony* Magazine. Reprinted by permission of the author.

BARBARA RANSBY AND TRACYE MATTHEWS: "Black Popular Culture and the Transcendence of Patriarchal Illusions," *Race and Class*, Vol. 35, No. 1 (1993): 57–68. Reprinted by permission of the Institute of Race Relations, London.

ADOLPH L. REED, JR.: "The Case Against Reparations" by Adolph L. Reed, Jr., *The Progressive* 64(12): 15–17. Reprinted by permission from *The Progressive*, 409 E Main St., Madison, WI 53703. www.progressive.org.

BETH E. RICHIE: "Battered Black Women: A Challenge for the Black Community," *The Black Scholar*, Vol. 16, March/April 1985, pp. 40–44. Reprinted by permission of The Black Scholar.

JOHN R. RICKFORD: "Letter to the Editor" by John R. Rickford, *Newsweek*, January 23, 1997. Reprinted by permission of the author, John R. Rickford, Professor of Linguistics, Stanford University. "Linguistics, Education, and the Ebonics Firestorm," from Georgetown University Round Table on Languages and Linguistics (GURT) 2000: Linguistics, Language, and the Professions: Education, Journalism, Law, Medicine, and Technology, James E. Alatis, Heidi E. Hamilton, and Ai-Hui Tan, Editors, pp. 25–30, 33–45. Copyright 2002 by Georgetown University Press. Reprinted with permission. www.press.georgetown.edu.

DOROTHY ROBERTS: From *Killing the Black Body* by Dorothy Roberts, pp. 98–103, copyright © 1997 by Dorothy Roberts. Used by permission of Pantheon Books, a division of Random House, Inc.

RANDALL ROBINSON: "Thoughts About Restitution," from *The Debt: What America Owes to Blacks* by Randall Robinson, copyright © 2000 by Randall Robinson. Used by permission of Dutton, a division of Penguin Group (USA) Inc.

J.A. ROGERS: "The Critic: Dean Miller Takes Fright at the Emancipation of the Negro Woman," *The Messenger*, April 1925. We have made diligent efforts to contact the copyright holder to obtain permission to reprint this selection. If you have information that would help us, please write to Permissions Department, W.W. Norton & Company, Inc., 500 Fifth Avenue, New York, NY 10110.

ELISE ROLLOCK: "A Negro Speaks to Jews" by Elise Rollock, *Jewish Currents* 22, No. 2, February 1968, pp. 13–15. Reprinted by permission.

KATHY Y. RUSSELL, MIDGE WILSON, AND RONALD E. HALL: "Hair: The Straight and Nappy of It All," from *The Color Complex*, copyright © 1992 by Kathy Y. Russell, Midge Wilson, and Ronald E. Hall, reprinted by permission of Houghton Mifflin Harcourt Publishing Company.

BAYARD RUSTIN: "From Protest to Politics: The Future of the Civil Rights Movement." Reprinted from *Commentary*, February 1965, by permission; copyright © 1965 by Commentary, Inc.

WILLIAM RYAN: "The New Genteel Racism," *The Crisis*, December 1965. The editors wish to thank the Crisis Publishing Co., Inc., the publisher of the magazine of the National Association for the Advancement of Colored People, for the use of Crisis Magazine materials.

GEORGE S. SCHUYLER: "The Negro-Art Hokum" by George Schuyler. Reprinted with permission from the June 16, 1926 issue of *The Nation*. "To the Editor of the Nation" by George Schuyler. Reprinted with permission from the June 21, 1926 issue of *The Nation*. For subscription information, call 1-800-333-8536. Portions of each week's Nation magazine can be accessed at http://www.thenation.com.

"Pan-Africanism: A Waste of Time," *The Pittsburgh Courier*, July 9, 1927 and "Pan-Africanism: A Wild Scheme," *The Pittsburgh Courier*, July 23, 1927. Reprinted by permission of Pittsburgh Courier Archives.

GEORGE S. AND JOSEPHINE SCHUYLER: "Does Interracial Marriage Succeed?" *Negro Digest*, June 1945, pp. 15–17. Reprinted by permission of the Estate of George S. and Josephine Schuyler.

NTOZAKE SHANGE: Reprinted with the permission of Scribner, a Division of Simon & Schuster Adult Publishing Group, from *For Colored Girls Who Have Considered Suicide When the Rainbow is Enuf* by Ntozake Shange. Copyright © 1975, 1976, 1977 by Ntozake Shange. All rights reserved.

ESTHER P. SHAW: Shaw, Esther P. (1955). Bourgeoisie Noire. *The Journal of Negro Education*, 25, 140–141. Reprinted with permission from *The Journal of Negro Education*, © 1955 Howard University. Web site: www.journalnegroed.org.

BARBARA SIZEMORE: "Sexism and the Black Male," *The Black Scholar*, March/April 1973, pp. 2–11. Reprinted by permission of The Black Scholar.

BARBARA SMITH: "Blacks and Gays: Healing the Great Divide" and "Toward a Black Feminist Criticism." From Smith, Barbara. *The Truth That Never Hurts: Writings on Race, Gender, and Freedom.* Copyright © 1998 by Barbara Smith. Reprinted by permission of Rutgers University Press.

BRENT STAPLES: "Editorial Observer; The Quota Bashers Come In From the Cold," *The New York Times*, 4/12/1998, © 1998 The New York Times. All rights reserved. Used by permission and protected by the Copyright Laws of the

"The Last Train From Oakland," *The New York Times*, 1/24/1997, © 1997 The New York Times. All rights reserved. Used by permission and protected by the Copyright Laws of the United States. The printing, copying, redistribution, or retransmission of the Material without express written permission is prohibited.

GLORIA STEINEM: "Women Are Never Front-Runners," *The New York Times*, January 8, 2008. © 2008, The New York Times. Reprinted by permission.

HARRIET BEECHER STOWE: "Letter to William Lloyd Garrison, December 19, 1853," *The Life and Writings of Frederick Douglass, Vol. II* by Philip S. Foner (1950). Reprinted by permission of International Publishers Co. / New York.

LELIA B. STRAYHORN, ET AL.: "Round Table: Should Negroes Attend Mixed or Negro Colleges?," *Negro Digest*, July 1945, pp. 71–77. We have made diligent efforts to contact the copyright holder to obtain permission to reprint this selection. If you have information that would help us, please write to Permissions Department, W.W. Norton & Company, Inc., 500 Fifth Avenue, New York, NY 10110.

CLARENCE THOMAS: "American Ideals, Policy Dilemmas," from Elliot (ed.), *Black Voices in American Politics*, 1E. © 1986 Wadsworth, a part of Cengage Learning, Inc. Reproduced by permission. www.cengage.com/permissions.

DARWIN T. TURNER: "The Teaching of Afro-American Literature," *College English*, Vol. 31, No. 7, April 1970, pp. 666–670. Reprinted by permission of the publisher, National Council of Teachers of English.

ROBERT L. VANN: "Back to the Farm," *The Pittsburgh Courier*, Sept. 24, 1932. Reprinted by permission of Pittsburgh Courier Archives.

MICHELE WALLACE: From *Black Macho and the Myth of the Superwoman* by Michele Wallace, pp. 13–33. © 1978 The Dial Press. Reprinted by permission of the author, Michele Wallace.

CORNEL WEST: "Affirmative Action in Context" from *The Affirmative Action Debate*, edited by George E. Curry, pp. 31–55. Copyright © 1996. Reprinted by permission of Basic Books, a member of Perseus Books Group. "Why I'm Marching On Washington," *The New York Times*, October 14, 1995. © 1995, The New York Times. Reprinted by permission.

WALTER WHITE: "Reply to Dr. Du Bois," *The Crisis*, April 1934. The editors wish to thank the Crisis Publishing Co., Inc., the publisher of the magazine of the National Association for the Advancement of Colored People, for the use of Crisis Magazine materials.

ROY WILKINS: "More Amos 'n Andy" by Roy Wilkins. Originally published in *Baltimore Afro-American*, March 22, 1930. Used with permission from the Afro-American Newspapers Archives and Research Center.

DELORES S. WILLIAMS: "Womanist Theology: Black Women's Voices," *Christianity and Crisis*, March 2, 1987. We have made diligent efforts to contact the copyright holder to obtain permission to reprint this selection. If you have information that would help us, please write to Permissions Department, W.W. Norton & Company, Inc., 500 Fifth Avenue, New York, NY 10110.

CHARLES V. WILLIE: "The Inclining Significance of Race" by Charles V. Willie, *Society*, Vol. 15, No. 5, July/August 1978, pp. 10–15. Copyright © 1978, Springer New York. Reprinted with permission of the author and Springer Science + Business Media.

WILLIAM JULIUS WILSON: "Race-Neutral Programs and The Democratic Coalition" by William Julius Wilson. Reprinted with permission from *The American Prospect*, Volume 1, Number 1: Spring 1990. The American Prospect, 5 Broad Street, Boston, MA 02109. All rights reserved.

Excerpts from "The Declining Significance of Race" as published in *Society*, Vol. 15, No. 2, January/February 1978. Copyright © 1978, the University of Chicago. Reprinted by permission of the University of Chicago Press.

"The Declining Significance of Race: Revisited But Not Revised," *Society*, Vol. 15, No. 5, July/August 1978. Copyright © 1978, Springer New York. Reprinted by permission of the author, William Julius Wilson, Lewis P. and Linda L. Geyser University Professor, Harvard University and Springer Science + Business Media.

CARTER G. WOODSON: "Preface and Chapters I and X" from *The Mis-Education of the Negro*, edited by Daryl Michael Scott with a Foreword by V.P. Franklin, pp. ixxx-xxxiv, 3-8, 100-110. Copyright © 2005 by the Association for the Study of African American Life and History. Originally published in 1933. Reprinted by permission of the Association for the Study of African American Life and History.

RICHARD WRIGHT: "Blueprint for Negro Writing," "Review of 'Their Eyes Were Watching God' by Zora Neale Hurston," Copyright © 1937, Richard Wright. Reprinted by permission of John Hawkins & Associates, Inc.

"Tradition and Industrialization: The Plight of the Tragic Elite in Africa," *Présence Africaine*, June-November 1956, pp. 357–360. Reprinted by permission of Présence Africaine.

MALCOLM X: "Message to the Grassroots," Speech delivered November 10, 1963, Detroit, Michigan. Reprinted by permission of the Family of Malcolm X. Malcolm X™ is a trademark of the Family of Malcolm X licensed by CMG Worldwide, Inc. / www.MalcolmX.com.

"Letters from Abroad," April 20, 1964 and May 10, 1964, pp. 74–77 from *Malcolm X Speaks: Selected Speeches and Statements*, ed. Breitman. Copyright © 1965, 1989 by Betty Shabazz and Pathfinder Press. Reprinted by permission.

MALCOLM X AND JAMES FARMER: "Separation or Integration: A Debate," *Dialogue Magazine* 3, May 1962, pp. 14–18. Reprinted by permission of the Estate of James Farmer and the Family of Malcolm X. Malcolm X™ is a trademark of the Family of Malcolm X licensed by CMG Worldwide, Inc. / www.MalcolmX.com.

MALCOLM X AND BAYARD RUSTIN: "Malcolm X Meets Bayard Rustin," Radio WRAI, New York, November 1960. Reprinted by permission of the Estate of Bayard Rustin and the Family of Malcolm X. Malcolm X™ is a trademark of the Family of Malcolm X licensed by CMG Worldwide, Inc. / www.MalcolmX.com.

HOWARD ZINN: "The Limits of Nonviolence," *Freedomways*, 4, First Quarter, 1964, pp. 143–148. Reprinted by permission of Howard Zinn, author, *A People's History of the United States.*

Illustration Credits

Part 1
Page 37: Wikipedia.

Part 2
Page 177: Library of Congress.

Part 3
Page 256: Schomberg Center for Research in Black Culture, The New York Public Library; p. 257: *Survey* May 1918; p. 297: *The Messenger* Sept. 1919; p. 298: *The Messenger* September 1919.

Part 4
Page 437: Library of Congress; p. 465: Douglas, Aaron (1899–1979) © Copyright *Aspects of Negro Life: An Idyll of the Deep South*. 1934. Oil on canvas, 5' × 11'7". Schomburg Center for Research in Black Culture, The New York Public Library, Art Resource, NY; p. 466: Sargent Johnson *Head of a Negro Woman*, ca. 1935; sculpture; terracotta, 7⅜ in. × 4½ in. × 5¼ in. (18.75 cm × 11.43 cm × 13.34 cm); Collection San Francisco Museum of Modern Art. Albert M. Bender Collection, Gift of Albert M. Bender. Photography credit: Don Myer; p. 467: Savage, Augusta (1900–1962) Gamin, c. 1929. Painted plaster, 9 × 5¾ × 4⅜ in. (22.9 × 14.7 × 11.2 cm). Gift of Benjamin and Olya Margolin. Smithsonian American Art Museum / Art Resource, NY; p. 468: *Self-Portrait* (1929) William Henry Johnson, National Museum of American Art, Smithsonian Institution; p. 469: *Midsummer Night in Harlem* (1936) Palmer Hayden, Harmon Collection, National Archives.

Part 5
Page 776: Courtesy of Keystone Labs; p. 777: Courtesy Spartan Brands, Inc.; p. 778: (c) Morrie Turner, 1969 Courtesy Morrie Turner.

Part 6
Page 858: Kara Walker "Untitled" 1999, Cut paper on paper, 18 × 12 inches, Courtesy of the artist and Sikkema Jenkins & Co; p. 1065: Us Helping Us, People Into Living, Inc. Funded by the Centers for Disease Control, PA 99091; p. 1097–1098 (all): The Boondocks © 1999 Aaron McGruder. Dist. by Universal Uclick. Reprinted with permission. All rights reserved.